FOURTH EDITION

ART HISTORY

MARILYN STOKSTAD
Judith Harris Murphy Distinguished Professor of Art History Emerita
The University of Kansas

MICHAEL W. COTHREN
Scheuer Family Professor of Humanities
Department of Art, Swarthmore College

CONTRIBUTORS

Frederick M. Asher, Douglass Bailey, David A. Binkley, Claudia L. Brittenham,

Claudia Brown, Patricia J. Darish, Patricia J. Graham,

Carol S. Ivory, D. Fairchild Ruggles, and Joy Sperling

Prentice Hall

Boston Columbus Indianapolis New York San Francisco Upper Saddle River
Amsterdam Cape Town Dubai London Madrid Milan Munich Paris Montréal Toronto
Delhi Mexico City São Paulo Sydney Hong Kong Seoul Singapore Taipei Tokyo

Editorial Director: Craig Campanella
Editor-in-Chief: Sarah Touborg
Senior Sponsoring Editor: Helen Ronan
Editorial Project Manager: David Nitti
Editorial Assistant: Carla Worner
Editor-in-Chief, Development: Rochelle Diogenes
Development Editors: Margaret Manos and Cynthia Ward
Media Director: Brian Hyland
Media Editor: Alison Lorber
Media Project Manager: Rich Barnes
Director of Marketing: Brandy Dawson
Senior Marketing Manager: Kate Mitchell
Marketing Assistant: Craig Deming
Senior Managing Editor: Ann Marie McCarthy
Assistant Managing Editor: Melissa Feimer
Production Project Managers: Barbara Cappuccio and Marlene Gassler
Senior Operations and Manufacturing Manager: Nick Sklitsis
Senior Operations Specialist: Brian Mackey
Manager of Design Development: John Christiana
Art Director and Interior Design: Kathy Mrozek
Cover Design: Kathy Mrozek
Site Supervisor, Pearson Imaging Center: Joe Conti
Pearson Imaging Center: Corin Skidds, Robert Uibelhoer, and Ron Walko
Cover Printer: Lehigh-Phoenix Color
Printer/Binder: Courier/Kendallville

This book was designed by
Laurence King Publishing Ltd, London
www.laurenceking.com

Commissioning Editor: Kara Hattersley-Smith
Senior Editors: Melissa Danny/Sophie Page
Production Manager: Simon Walsh
Page Design: Nick Newton/Randell Harris
Photo Researcher: Emma Brown
Copy Editors: Tessa Clark/Jenny Knight/Robert Shore/
Johanna Stephenson
Proofreader: Jennifer Speake
Indexer: Sue Farr

Cover photo: Gustave Caillebotte, *Paris Street, Rainy Day*. 1877. Oil on canvas, 83½ × 108¾″ (212.2 × 276.2 cm). Art Institute of Chicago. Part of the Charles H. and Mary F. S. Worcester Fund. Photograph © 2006 The Art Institute of Chicago. All Rights Reserved.

Library of Congress Cataloging-in-Publication Data
Stokstad, Marilyn
    Art History / Marilyn Stokstad, Michael W. Cothren; contributors, Frederick M. Asher ... [eg al.]. —4th ed.
      p. cm.
    Includes bibliographical references and index.
    ISBN-13: 978-0-205-74422-0 (hardcover : alk. paper)
    ISBN-10: 0205-74422-2 (hardcover : alk. paper)
    1. Art—History. I. Cothren, Michael Watt. II. Asher, Frederick M. III Title.
N5300.S923 2011
709—dc22   2010001489

10 9 8 7 6 5 4 3 2 1

Prentice Hall
is an imprint of

www.pearsonhighered.com

ISBN 10: 0-205-74422-2
ISBN 13: 978-0-205-74422-0
Exam Copy ISBN 10: 0-205-74423-0
ISBN 13: 978-0-205-74423-7

BRIEF CONTENTS

CONTENTS

CHAPTER 7
JEWISH, EARLY CHRISTIAN, AND BYZANTINE ART 216

JEWS, CHRISTIANS, AND MUSLIMS 218
  Early Jewish Art 218
  Early Christian Art 222
IMPERIAL CHRISTIAN ARCHITECTURE AND ART 226
  Architecture 226
  Sculpture 229
  Ravenna 230
EARLY BYZANTINE ART 233
  The Golden Age of Justinian 233
  Objects of Veneration and Devotion 242
  Icons and Iconoclasm 244
MIDDLE BYZANTINE ART 246
  Architecture and Mosaics 247
  Objects of Veneration and Devotion 252
LATE BYZANTINE ART 254
  Constantinople: The Chora Church 254
  Moscow: Rublyov 259

BOXES
■ ART AND ITS CONTEXTS
  Narrative and Iconic 224
  The Life of Jesus 231
  Naming Christian Churches: Designation + Dedication + Location 239
  Scroll and Codex 243
  Iconoclasm 246
■ THE OBJECT SPEAKS
  The Funerary Chapel of Theodore Metochites 256
■ A CLOSER LOOK
  The Mosaic Floor of the Beth Alpha Synagogue 221
■ ELEMENTS OF ARCHITECTURE
  Longitudinal-Plan and Central-Plan Churches 228
  Pendentives and Squinches 236
■ RECOVERING THE PAST
  Dura-Europos 223

CHAPTER 8
ISLAMIC ART 260

ISLAM AND EARLY ISLAMIC SOCIETY 262
ART AND ARCHITECTURE THROUGH THE FOURTEENTH CENTURY 265
  Early Architecture 265
THE LATER PERIOD 270
  Architecture of the Mediterranean 271
  Architecture of the East 275
  Portable Arts 276
  The Arts of the Book 279
  Manuscript Painting 280
ART AND ARCHITECTURE OF THE THREE EMPIRES 282
  The Ottoman Empire 282
  The Safavid Dynasty 285
  Mughal Dynasty 288
THE MODERN ERA 289

BOXES
■ ART AND ITS CONTEXTS
  The Five Pillars of Islam 267
■ THE OBJECT SPEAKS
  The Great Mosque of Cordoba 268
■ A CLOSER LOOK
  A Mamluk Glass Oil Lamp 273
■ ELEMENTS OF ARCHITECTURE
  Arches 271
■ TECHNIQUE
  Ornament 264
  Carpet Making 286

CHAPTER 9
ART OF SOUTH AND SOUTHEAST ASIA BEFORE 1200 290

THE INDIAN SUBCONTINENT 292
INDUS CIVILIZATION 292
THE VEDIC PERIOD 295
THE MAURYA PERIOD 295
THE PERIOD OF THE SHUNGAS AND EARLY ANDHRAS 298
  Stupas 298
  Buddhist Rock-Cut Halls 302
THE KUSHAN AND LATER ANDHRA PERIODS 302
  The Gandhara Style 303
  The Mathura Style 303
  The Southeast Indian Style 305
THE FOURTH THROUGH SEVENTH CENTURIES 306
  Buddhist Sculpture 306
  Painting 306
  The Early Northern Temple 308
  Monumental Narrative Reliefs 309
  The Early Southern Temple 312
THE EIGHTH THROUGH THE FOURTEENTH CENTURIES 312
  The Monumental Northern Temple 313
  The Monumental Southern Temple 317
  The Bhakti Movement in Art 318
ART OF SOUTHEAST ASIA 319

BOXES
■ ART AND ITS CONTEXTS
  Buddhism 297
  Hinduism 298
  Mudras 304
  Meaning and Ritual in Hindu Temples and Images 310
■ THE OBJECT SPEAKS
  Shiva Nataraja of the Chola Dynasty 314
■ A CLOSER LOOK
  Descent of the Ganges Relief, Mamallapuram 313
■ ELEMENTS OF ARCHITECTURE
  Stupas and Temples 301

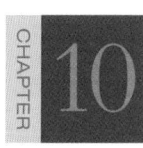

CHAPTER 10
CHINESE AND KOREAN ART BEFORE 1279 324

THE MIDDLE KINGDOM 326
NEOLITHIC CULTURES 326
  Painted Pottery Cultures 326
  Liangzhu Culture 326
BRONZE AGE CHINA 328
  Shang Dynasty 328
  Zhou Dynasty 329
THE CHINESE EMPIRE: QIN DYNASTY 332

32 THE INTERNATIONAL SCENE SINCE 1950   **1082**

PREFACE

This new edition of *Art History* is the result of a happy and productive collaboration between two scholar-teachers who share a common vision. In certain ways, we also share a common history. Neither of us expected to become professors of art history. Marilyn Stokstad took her first art history course as a requirement of her studio arts program. Michael Cothren discovered the discipline almost by chance during a semester abroad in Provence when a painting instructor sent him on a field trip to learn from the formal intricacies of Romanesque sculpture. Perhaps as a result of the unexpected delight we found in these revelatory formative experiences, we share a conviction that first courses in the history of art should be filled with as much enjoyment as erudition, that they should foster an enthusiastic, as well as an educated, public for the visual arts. With this end firmly in mind we will continue to create books intended to help students enjoy learning the essentials of a vast and complex field of study. For millennia human beings have embodied their most cherished ideas and values in visual and tangible form. We have learned that by engaging with these works from the past, we can all enrich our lives in the present, especially because we are living in a present when images have become an increasingly important aspect of how we communicate with each other.

Like its predecessors, this new edition seeks to balance formal and iconographic analysis with contextual art history in order to craft interpretations that will engage with a diverse student population. Throughout the text, the visual arts are treated as part of a larger world, in which geography, politics, religion, economics, philosophy, social life, and the other fine arts were related components of a vibrant cultural landscape. Art and architecture have played a central role in human history, and they continue to do so today. Our book will fulfill its purpose if it introduces a broad spectrum of students to some of the richest human achievements created through the centuries and across the globe, and if it inspires those students both to respect and to cherish their historical legacy in the visual arts. Perhaps it will convince some to dedicate themselves to assuring that our own age leaves a comparable artistic legacy, thereby continuing the ever evolving history of art.

So ... Why Use This New Edition?

We believe that even an established introductory art history text should continually respond to the changing needs of its audience—both students and educators. In this way it is more likely to make a greater difference in the role that art can and will assume in its readers' lives, both at the time of use and long into the future—indeed, long after the need for the next revision arises.

Our goal was to make this revised text an improvement over its earlier incarnations in sensitivity, readability, and accessibility without losing anything in comprehensiveness, in scholarly precision, or in its ability to engage the reader. Incorporating feedback from our many users and reviewers, we believe we have succeeded.

SOME HIGHLIGHTS OF THE NEW EDITION INCLUDE THE FOLLOWING:

- Every chapter now opens with a **Learn About It** feature (key learning objectives) and ends with a corresponding set of **Think About It** questions that probe back to the objectives and help students think through and apply what they have learned.
- The chapters are keyed to **MyArtsLab** resources that enrich and reinforce student learning (see p. xviii).
- **Newly colorized line art and 3D renderings** throughout the book provide the opportunity for students to better visualize architectural principles and key art processes.
- New **Recovering the Past boxes** document the discovery, restoration, or conservation of works of art. Some examples include discussions of the Rosetta stone, the Riace bronzes, and the Sutton Hoo find.
- There is **increased contextual emphasis** now visible with the linking of three key box categories by means of a "target" icon:
  - The new **Closer Look** feature, at the center of the target, pulls in for more specificity within the work of art itself, helping the student understand issues of usage, iconography, and style.
  - The **Object Speaks** box focuses on an in-depth contextual treatment of a work of art.
  - The **Art and Its Contexts** feature at the outer ring of the target represents discussions of ideas about art that are placed within the broad context of the chapter, or the history of art in general.
- **Global coverage has been deepened** with the addition of new works of art and revised discussions that incorporate new scholarship.
- A **new series of maps** has been created to enhance the clarity and accuracy of the relationship between the art discussed and its geographical location and political affiliation.
- Throughout, **images have been updated** whenever new and improved images were available. **New works have been added** to the discussion in many chapters to enhance and enrich what is said in the text.
- The **language used to characterize works of art**—especially those that attempt to capture the lifelike appearance of the natural world—has been **refined and clarified** to bring greater precision and nuance.
- In response to readers' requests, **discussion of many major monuments** has been expanded. For example, the Palette of

Narmer, Sainte Chapelle, Bosch's *Garden of Earthly Delights*, and the Contarelli Chapel.

- **Several chapters have been reorganized** for greater clarity and coherence. Prehistoric Art is now global in scope, the early nineteenth century has been incorporated into the chapter containing the eighteenth century to avoid breaking up the discussion of Neoclassicism and Romanticism, and the last two chapters now break at 1950.
- In keeping with this book's tradition of inclusivity, **an even broader spectrum of media is addressed** here, with expanded attention, for example, to Gothic stained glass, Renaissance tapestries, and Navajo textiles.

NEW SCHOLARSHIP

Over the many years we have taught undergraduate beginners, we have always enjoyed sharing—both with our students and our fellow educators—the new discoveries and fresh interpretive perspectives that are constantly enriching the history of art. We relished the opportunity here to incorporate some of the latest thinking and most recent discoveries—whether this involved revising the dating and interpretation of well-known Prehistoric monuments like Stonehenge (fig. 1–21), presenting fascinating new recreations of familiar masterworks such as the "colorized" Aegina archer from Ancient Greece (p.113), or including a new theory on the meaning of Jan van Eyck's masterful Double Portrait (fig. 18-1). Indeed, changes have been made on many levels—from the introduction to the bibliography, and from captions to chapter introductions. Every change aims to make the text more useful to the instructors and more vibrant for the students in today's art history classrooms.

WHAT'S NEW

Chapter by Chapter Revisions

Some of the key highlights of this new edition include the following:

Introduction

Completely rewritten, the introduction orients students to the process and nature of art historical investigation that underlies and, in essence, produced the historical narrative of the text itself.

Chapter 1: Prehistoric Art

Extensive revisions reflect the most current scholarship and broaden scope to global coverage. Key sections of the chapter rewritten to accommodate up-to-date interpretations, with new objects included. Thorough reworking of Stonehenge incorporates new thinking about the monument and landscape. Çatalhöyük and 'Ain Ghazal moved to this chapter.

Chapter 2: Art of the Ancient Near East

New chapter opener with *Stele of Naram-Sin* sets the stage for the chapter material. An historical photograph with a view of the guardian figures from the Citadel of Saragon II places the monument in context. New "Object Speaks" box on the "Great Lyre" includes a discussion of its archaeological discovery. Treatment of key monuments expanded.

Chapter 3: Art of Ancient Egypt

Historical and contextual material reduced to allow for richer discussions of the works of art. Sphinx moved from the Introduction to this chapter. Discussion of the Egyptian canon/grid system refined and updated. New images include stele of the sculptor Userwer and statue of Queen Karomama in the Louvre.

Chapter 4: Art of the Ancient Aegean

Completely revised discussion of Cycladic figures in light of recent research, including two new figures. Reworked Knossos complex text acknowledges its probable role as a ceremonial center. Treatment of *Harvester Rhyton* expanded. New box on Schliemann and the "Mask of Agamemnon" outlines reasons for suspicions about both. Discussion of Mycenaean tombs reorganized to include metalwork found in the shaft graves, with tholos tombs explanation now following.

Chapter 5: Art of Ancient Greece

Historical preludes reduced to focus on cultural and historical factors related to the history of art. Reorganized for greater clarity and coherence, including box placement. Expanded discussion of Aegina architecture and sculpture, and box on color in Greek sculpture focuses on Aegina, thus making it a model analysis for the basic points in architecture and architectural sculpture. Moved ceramic painting technique box to Archaic section in relation to the vessels where most relevant and added detailed views of use of each technique.

Chapter 6: Etruscan and Roman Art

Expanded treatment of the Etruscans with addition of a wall painting, a sarcophagus lid, and the *Ficoroni Cista*. Added clarity to discussions of representational modes—classicizing and veristic. Added box on portraiture using the Polybius text and the *Barberini Togatus*. Expanded treatment of tetrarchic sculpture, concentrating on introduction of a new ideal along with verism and classicism. Reorganized discussion of Constantinian art.

Chapter 7: Jewish, Early Christian, and Byzantine Art

New chapter opener introduces the eclecticism of Byzantine art and foregrounds the continuity of the classical heritage in the Byzantine world. Expanded treatment of Jewish art. Extensively revised Ravenna monuments, especially San Vitale. Reorganized Middle Byzantine discussion for clearer sense of chronology as well as geography. Much expanded section on the Chora church as a late Byzantine monument.

Chapter 8: Islamic Art

Revised to bring greater emphasis on art and society with simpler historical periodization. New chapter opener features *Maqamat* image of a preacher in a mosque, with many new images of art and architecture throughout. Expanded material on Mughal South Asia. Added new box on the topic of ornament with exemplary illustrations. New "Object Speaks" with in-depth explanation of the Mosque at Cordoba.

Chapter 9: Art of South and Southeast Asia before 1200

New coverage of sites, including Bamiyan whose Buddha images were destroyed in 2001. Period divisions updated for greater clarity and comprehension.

Chapter 10: Chinese and Korean Art before 1279

New illustrations of bronze-casting technique for improved understanding of process. New images include Neolithic cong, bronze *guang*, Tang equestrian pair, and detail of *Admonitions of the Imperial Instructress to Court Ladies*. "A Closer Look" examines in detail a section of stone relief in Wu family shrine.

Chapter 11: Japanese Art before 1333

New illustrations and discussion of art and architecture at the Great Buddha Hall (*Daibutsuden*) at Todaiji in "Recovering the Past" box. New discussion of Japan in the eighth century as the eastern terminus of the Silk Route. Increased emphasis on Japan's native religion of Shinto with addition of a Shinto painting. Expanded discussion of Chinese emigrant monks and their influence in section on Zen art.

Chapter 12: Art of the Americas before 1300

Substantially revised and updated sections on Mesoamerican and ancient Andean art. New images include Maya stela, Moche portrait vessel, Olmec sculptural offering, and cylinder vase with image of the Maya ballgame. Expanded discussion of Maya hieroglyphic writing.

Chapter 13: Early African Art

Revised and expanded discussion of Ife portraiture to emphasize idea that among earliest known examples of African sculpture, naturalistic representations of human body were not uncommon. Added treatment of the Ethiopian ancient sites of Lalibela, Gondar and Aksum. Fifteenth-century ivory hunting horn speaks to European contact and trade to west and central Africa that included the export of objects made in Africa for European aristocracy.

Chapter 14: Early Medieval Art in Europe

Added new "Recovering the Past" box on the Sutton Hoo find.

New "Object Speaks" box on the Lindisfarne Gospels allows comparison between the Matthew portrait and the Ezra from the Codex Amiatinus. Moved reduced discussion of Vikings before the Carolingians to permit continuity between Carolingians and Ottonians. Carolingian discussion enhanced with addition of bronze equestrian emperor, Corvey façade, new drawing of Aachen chapel, and expanded Saint Gall plan.

Chapter 15: Romanesque Art

Abbreviated and condensed historical discussions not directly related to the situation in the art. Added Canigou to flesh out and clarify the opening discussion of "First Romanesque." Discussion of painting and mosaics at San Clemente in Rome and Saint-Savin-sur-Gartempe moved from a media-based section to the discussion of the buildings themselves. Expanded discussion of Moissac to give sense of one ensemble in some detail.

Chapter 16: Gothic Art of the Twelfth and Thirteenth Centuries

Significant revisions in French Gothic discussion with removal of Amiens and expansion of Saint-Denis, Chartres, and Reims. Stained-glass technique box moved to coincide with the discussion of Saint-Denis and a full panel of glass from that church illustrated. Consolidated and expanded treatment of Assisi.

Chapter 17: Fourteenth-Century Art in Europe

Discussion of Giotto and Duccio reworked to include new focus work in each program, the *Kiss of Judas* for Giotto and the *Raising of Lazarus* for Duccio. Added Simone Martini with discussion of his *Annunciation*. Introduced Hedwig Codex for more variety in German section.

Chapter 18: Fifteenth-Century Art in Northern Europe

More developed discussion of *Hours of Mary of Burgundy* to elaborate on its evidence of new devotional practices. Expanded treatment of *Unicorn* tapestry to include technique and effect, as well as iconography. New box on the process of oil painting. Transformed discussion of Mérode Altarpiece based on new views about authorship. Revised discussion of Jan van Eyck's *Man in a Red Turban* as self-portrait. Reworked discussion of Fouquet's Melun Diptych.

Chapter 19: Renaissance Art in Fifteenth-Century Italy

New "Art and its Contexts" boxes on the Florentine Baptistery competition reliefs and *cassoni*. Expanded treatment of Orsanmichele including new image of building. Developed discussion of Donatello's David. Revised box on Renaissance perspective and moved to correspond with Masaccio. Expanded discussion of the Sistine mural project.

Chapter 20: Sixteenth-Century Art in Italy

Added Leonardo's *The Virgin of the Rocks*, Raphael portraits of Agnelo Doni and Maddalena Strozzi, and Michelangelo's Laurentian Library. Enhanced discussion of Palazzo del Tè with attention to social and political context. Reoriented treatment of Titian's "Venus" of Urbino in light of Rona Goffen's work. Discussion of

Mannerism and Council of Trent reversed to conform with chronology and history.

Chapter 21: Sixteenth-Century Art in Northern Europe and the Iberian Peninsula

Expanded discussion of *Garden of Earthly Delights* includes new interpretive ideas and incorporates exterior wing panels. New addition and discussion of Quentin Massys's *Money Changer and his Wife*. "Object Speaks" box explores two Bruegel paintings as part of a series of the months. Added "Closer Look" box for Holbein's *The French Ambassadors*.

Chapter 22: Seventeenth-Century Art in Europe

New images include Artemisia Gentileschi's *Susannah and the Elders*, a Murillo *Immaculate Conception*, Rubens's *Self-Portrait with Isabella Brandt*, Ruisdael's *View of Haarlem from the Dunes at Overveen* and Le Nain's *A Peasant Family in an Interior*. Added technique box on etchings and drypoint.

Chapter 23: Art of South and Southeast Asia after 1200

Expanded Southeast Asia coverage to include Islamic art. Incorporated discussion of European engagement with Mughal art. Added discussion of South Asian artists working in the Diaspora and Indian architect Charles Correa.

Chapter 24: Chinese and Korean Art after 1279

New image by Yun Shouping, *Amaranth*. New "Closer Look" feature for detail of section of *Spring Dawn in the Han Palace*.

Chapter 25: Japanese Art after 1333

Greater emphasis on importance of crafts with addition of porcelain plate, *kosode*, and contemporary lacquer box. New "Closer Look" highlights techniques used in creation of a *kosode* robe. Increased discussion of Japan's integration of foreign, particularly Western, influences in its art and culture. New emphasis on architecture and crafts in the postwar period. Tea Ceremony discussion consolidated into one section.

Chapter 26: Art of the Americas after 1300

New chapter opener focuses on Navajo textile woven by Julia Jumbo. Additional contemporary Native American art incorporated into chapter. Revised and updated sections on Aztec and Inca art.

Chapter 27: Art of Pacific Cultures

Revised and updated introduction to Australia. Reworked Melanesia section to broaden range of culture areas: added New Britain Tubuan mask, discussions of role of women and different uses of masks. Revamped Polynesia introduction to be Polynesian-centered, not European-centered. New "Object Speaks" for Maori meetinghouse with additional images to show regional difference and change over time (time depth) in Maori art. Contemporary art in Oceania included.

Chapter 28: Art of Africa in the Modern Era

Incorporated image of 1897 British punitive expedition to Benin with short discussion of development of major collections of African art in Europe and America. Collection development tied to European expansion, political and economic interests. New "Object Speaks" created for Kuba mask with additional photographs to help to integrate the mask within its performance and meaning contexts. Moved discussion of divination among the Chokwe closer to discussion of Yoruba divination.

Chapter 29: Eighteenth- and Early Nineteenth-Century Art in Europe and North America

Reorganized chapter now encompasses the early nineteenth century to avoid breaking up the discussion of Neoclassicism and Romanticism. Revised and expanded discussion of how courtly system of individual patronage transformed, first into a Salon system, and then into an academic system of training, exhibition, and sale of art. New images include Fragonard's *The Swing* and Boucher's *Girl Reclining: Louise O'Murphy*.

Chapter 30: Mid- to late Nineteenth-Century Art in Europe and the United States

Revised and updated to emphasize the varying ways the academy and avant-garde envisaged and expressed modernity. Expanded discussion also includes exploration of differing concepts of modernity in France, England, the United States, and elsewhere. Photography moved to early part of chapter. Works by Manet now discussed together and in relation to Realism.

Chapter 31: Modern Art in Europe and the Americas, 1900–1950

Reworked to extend to 1950 so chapter covers the years of Modernism more fully. Updated to reflect the early centrality of Paris in the first half of twentieth century as a center of innovation in the art-world and its subsequent displacement by New York.

Chapter 32: The International Scene Since 1950

Reorganized and revised according to a thematic structure. Emphasis placed on the 1960s as a turning point in the global understanding of art and the subsequent globalization of art in the fast-paced communications age. Fifty percent new images reflect themes outlined in the text.

PEARSON CHOICES AND RESOURCES

Ordering Options

Art History is offered in a variety of formats to suit any course need, whether your survey is Western, global, comprehensive or concise, online or on the ground. Please contact your local representative for ordering details or visit www.pearsonhighered.com/art. In addition to this combined hardcover edition, *Art History* may be ordered in the following formats:

Volume I, Chapters 1–17 (ISBN: 978-0-205-74420-6)
Volume II, Chapters 17–32 (ISBN: 978-0-205-74421-3)

Art History **Portable Edition** has all of the same content as the comprehensive text in six slim volumes. Available in value-package combinations (Books 1, 2, 4, and 6) to suit **Western-focused survey** courses or available individually for period or region specific courses.

Book 1: Ancient Art, Chapters 1–6
Book 2: Medieval Art, Chapters 7, 8, 14–17
Book 3: A View of the World: Part One, Chapters 8–13
Book 4: Fourteenth to Seventeenth Century Art, Chapters 17–22
Book 5: A View of the World: Part Two, Chapters 23–28
Book 6: Eighteenth to Twenty-first Century Art, Chapters 29–32

Books À La Carte Give your students flexibility and savings with the new Books à la Carte edition of *Art History*. This edition features exactly the same content as the traditional textbook in a convenient three-hole-punched, loose-leaf version—allowing students to take only what they need to class. The Books à la Carte edition costs less than a used text—which helps students save about 35% over the cost of a new book.
Volume I, Books à la Carte Edition, 4/e
(ISBN: 978-0-205-79557-4)
Volume II, Books à la Carte Edition, 4/e
(ISBN: 978-0-205-79558-1)

 CourseSmart Textbooks Online is an exciting new choice for students looking to save money. As an alternative to purchasing the print textbook, students can subscribe to the same content online and save up to 50% off the suggested list price of the print text. For more information, or to subscribe to the CourseSmart eTextbook, visit www.coursesmart.com.

Combined Volume (ISBN: 978-0-205-80032-2)
Volume I (ISBN: 978-0-205-00189-7)
Volume II (ISBN: 978-0-205-00190-3)

Digital Resources

 www.myartslab.com This dynamic website provides a wealth of resources geared to meet the diverse teaching and learning needs of today's instructors and students. Keyed specifically to the chapters of *Art History*, Fourth Edition, MyArtsLab's many tools will encourage students to experience and interact with works of art. Here are some of the key features:

- A complete **Pearson e-Text** of the book, enriched with multi-media, including: a unique human scale figure by all works of fine art, an audio version of the text read by the author, primary source documents, video demonstrations, and much more. Students can highlight, make notes and bookmark pages.
- 360 degree **Architectural Panoramas** for most of the major monuments in the book help students understand buildings from the inside and out.
- **Closer Look Tours** These interactive walkthroughs offer an in-depth look at key works of art, enabling the student to zoom in to see detail they could not otherwise see on the printed page or even in person. Enhanced with expert audio, they help students understand the meaning and message behind the work of art.
- A **Gradebook** that reports progress of students and the class as a whole.
- Instructors can also download the Instructor's Manual & Test Item File, PowerPoint questions for Classroom Response Systems, and obtain the PearsonMyTest assessment generation program.
- **MyArtsLab with e-Text** is available for no additional cost when packaged with any version of *Art History*, 4/e; it is also available standalone for less than the cost of a used text, and it is also available without e-Text for an even lower price.

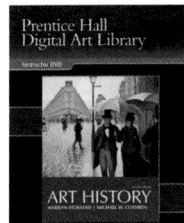 **The Prentice Hall Digital Art Library** Instructors who adopt *Art History* are eligible to receive this unparalleled resource containing all of the images in *Art History* at the highest resolution (over 300 dpi) and pixellation possible for optimal projection and easy download. This resource features over 1,600 illustrations in jpeg and in PowerPoint, an instant download function for easy import into any presentation software, along with a unique zoom and "Save Detail" feature. (ISBN: 978-0-205-80037-7)

ACKNOWLEDGMENTS AND GRATITUDE

Art History, which was first published in 1995 by Harry N. Abrams, Inc. and Prentice Hall, Inc., continues to rely, each time it is revised, on the work of many colleagues and friends who contributed to the original texts and subsequent editions. Their work is reflected here, and we extend to them our enduring gratitude.

In preparing this fourth edition, we worked closely with two gifted and dedicated editors at Pearson/Prentice Hall, Sarah Touborg and Helen Ronan, whose almost daily support in so many ways was at the center of our work and created the foundation of what we have done. At Pearson, Barbara Cappuccio, Marlene Gassler, Melissa Feimer, Cory Skidds, Brian Mackey, David Nitti, and Carla Worner also supported us in our work. For the design we thank Kathy Mrozek and John Christiana. At Laurence King Publishing, Melissa Danny, Sophie Page, Kara Hattersley-Smith, Julia Ruxton and Simon Walsh oversaw the production of this new edition. We are very grateful for the editing of Cynthia Ward, Margaret Manos, and Robert Shore. For layout design we thank Nick Newton and for photo research we thank Emma Brown. Much appreciation also goes to Brandy Dawson, Director of Marketing, and Kate Stewart Mitchell, Marketing Manager, as well as the entire Social Sciences and Arts team at Pearson.

From Marilyn Stokstad:

The fourth edition of *Art History* represents the cumulative efforts of a distinguished group of scholars and educators. The work done by Stephen Addiss, Chutsing Li, Marylin M. Rhie, and Christopher D. Roy for the original edition has been updated and expanded by David Binkley and Patricia Darish (Africa), Claudia Brown and Robert Mowry (China and Korea), Patricia Graham (Japan), and Rick Asher (South and Southeast Asia). Joy Sperling has reworked the modern material previously contributed by Patrick Frank, David Cateforis and Bradford R. Collins. Dede Ruggles (Islamic), Claudia Brittenham (Americas), and Carol Ivory (Pacific Cultures) also have contributed to the fourth edition.

In addition, I want to thank University of Kansas colleagues Sally Cornelison, Susan Craig, Susan Earle, Charles Eldredge, Kris Ercums, Valija Evalds, Sherry Fowler, Stephen Goddard, Saralyn Reece Hardy, Marsha Haufler, Marni Kessler, Amy McNair, John Pulz, Linda Stone Ferrier, and John Younger for their help and advice. My thanks also to my friends Katherine Giele and Katherine Stannard, David and Nancy Dinneen, William Crowe, David Bergeron, Geraldo de Sousa, and the entire Clement family for their sympathy and encouragement. Of course, my very special thanks go to my sister, Karen Leider, and my niece, Anna Leider.

From Michael Cothren:

Words are barely adequate to express my gratitude to Marilyn Stokstad for welcoming me with such trust, enthusiasm, and warmth into the collaborative adventure of revising this book. Working alongside her—and our extraordinary editors Sarah Touborg and Helen Ronan—has been delightful and rewarding, enriching and challenging. I look forward to continuing the partnership.

My work was greatly facilitated by two extraordinary research assistants, Fletcher Coleman and Andrew Finegold, who found materials and offered opinions just when I needed them. I also have been supported by a host of colleagues at Swarthmore College. Generations of students challenged me to hone my pedagogical skills and steady my focus on what is at stake in telling the history of art. My colleagues in the Art Department—especially Stacy Bomento, June Cianfrana, Randall Exon, Constance Cain Hungerford, Janine Mileaf, Patricia Reilly, and Tomoko Sakomura—have answered all sorts of questions, shared innumerable insights on works in their areas of expertise, and offered unending encouragement and support. I am so lucky to work with them. In Classics, Gil Rose and William Turpin generously shared their expertise in Latin.

Many art historians have provided assistance, often at a moment's notice, and I am especially grateful to Betina Bergman, Claudia Brown, Brigitte Buettner, Madeline Caviness, Cheri Falkenstien-Doyle, Ed Gyllenhaal, Julie Hochstrasser, Penny Jolly, Alison Kettering, Benton Kidd, Ann Kuttner, Cary Liu, Elizabeth Marlowe, Thomas Morton, Mary Shepard, David Simon, Donna Sadler, Jeffrey Chipps Smith, and Mark Tucker.

I was fortunate to have the support of many friends. John Brendler, David Eldridge, Tricia Kramer, Stephen Lehmann, Mary Marissen, Bianca O'Keefe, and Bruce and Carolyn Stephens, patiently listened and truly relished my enjoyment of this work.

My mother and my late father, Mildred and Wat Cothren believed in me and made significant sacrifices to support my education from pre-school to graduate school. My extraordinary daughters Emma and Nora are a constant inspiration. I am so grateful for their delight in my passion for art's history, and for their dedication to keeping me from taking myself too seriously. My deepest gratitude is reserved for Susan Lowry, my wife and soul-mate, who brings joy to every facet of my life. She was not only patient and supportive during the long distraction of my work on this book; she provided help in so very many ways. The greatest accomplishment of my life in art history occurred on the day I met her at Columbia in 1973.

If the arts are ultimately an expression of human faith and integrity as well as human thought and creativity, then writing and producing books that introduce new viewers to the wonders of art's history, and to the courage and visions of the artists and art historians that stand behind it—remains a noble undertaking. We feel honored to be a part of such a worthy project.

Marilyn Stokstad
Lawrence, KS

Michael W. Cothren
Swarthmore, PA

Winter 2010

In Gratitude:

As its predecessors did, this Fourth Edition of *Art History* benefited from the reflections and assessments of a distinguished team of scholars and educators. The authors and Pearson are grateful to the following academic reviewers for their numerous insights and suggestions for improvement:

Craig Adcock, University of Iowa
Kimberly Allen-Kattus, Northern Kentucky University
Susan Jane Baker, University of Houston
Stephen Caffey, Texas A & M University
Charlotte Lowry Collins, Southeastern Louisiana University
Cindy B. Damschroder, University of Cincinnati
Rachael Z. DeLue, Princeton University
Anne Derbes, Hood College
Caroline Downing, State University of New York at Potsdam
Suzanne Eberle, Kendall College of Art & Design of Ferris State University
April Eisman, Iowa State University
Allen Farber, State University of New York at Oneonta
Richard Gay, University of North Carolina - Pembroke
Regina Gee, Montana State University
Mimi Hellman, Skidmore College
Julie Hochstrasser, University of Iowa
Evelyn Kain, Ripon College
Nancy Kelker, Middle Tennessee State University
Patricia Kennedy, Ocean County College
Jennie Klein, Ohio University
Katie Kresser, Seattle Pacific University
Cynthia Kristan-Graham, Auburn University
Barbara Platten Lash, Northern Virginia Community College
Elisa C. Mandell, California State University, Fullerton
Elizabeth C. Mansfield, New York University
Pamela Margerm, Kean University
Elizabeth Marlowe, Colgate University
Marguerite Mayhall, Kean University
Katherine A. McIver, University of Alabama at Birmingham
Janine Mileaf, Swarthmore College
Johanna D. Movassat, San Jose State University
Jacqueline Marie Musacchio, Wellesley College
Lynn Ostling, Santa Rosa Junior College
Ariel Plotek, Clemson University
Patricia V. Podzorski, University of Memphis
Margaret Richardson, George Mason University
James Rubin, Stony Brook University
Donna Sandrock, Santa Ana College
Michael Schwartz, Augusta State University
Joshua A. Shannon, University of Maryland
Karen Shelby, Baruch College
Susan Sidlauskas, Rutgers University
Royce W. Smith, Wichita State University
Jeffrey Chipps Smith, University of Texas - Austin
Stephen Smithers, Indiana State University
Laurie Sylwester, Columbia College (Sonora)
Carolyn Tate, Texas Tech University
Rita Tekippe, University of West Georgia
Amelia Trevelyan, University of North Carolina at Pembroke
Julie Tysver, Greenville Technical College
Jeryn Woodard, University of Houston

This edition has continued to benefit from the assistance and advice of scores of other teachers and scholars who generously answered questions, gave recommendations on organization and priorities, and provided specialized critiques during the course of work on previous editions.

We are grateful for the detailed critiques that the following readers across the country who were of invaluable assistance during work on the third edition:

Charles M. Adelman, University of Northern Iowa; Fred C. Albertson, University of Memphis; Frances Altvater, College of William and Mary; Michael Amy, Rochester Institute of Technology; Jennifer L. Ball, Brooklyn College, CUNY; Samantha Baskind, Cleveland State University; Tracey Boswell, Johnson County Community College; Jane H. Brown, University of Arkansas at Little Rock; Roger J. Crum, University of Dayton; Brian A. Curran, Penn State University; Michael T. Davis,

Mount Holyoke College; Juilee Decker, Georgetown College; Laurinda Dixon, Syracuse University; Laura Dufresne, Winthrop University; Dan Ewing, Barry University; Arne Flaten, Coastal Carolina University; John Garton, Cleveland Institute of Art; Rosi Gilday, University of Wisconsin, Oshkosh; Eunice D. Howe, University of Southern California; Phillip Jacks, George Washington University; William R. Levin, Centre College; Susan Libby, Rollins College; Henry Luttikhuizen, Calvin College; Lynn Mackenzie, College of DuPage; Dennis McNamara, Triton College; Gustav Medicus, Kent State University; Lynn Metcalf, St. Cloud State University; Jo-Ann Morgan, Coastal Carolina University; Beth A. Mulvaney, Meredith College; Dorothy Munger, Delaware Community College; Bonnie Noble, University of North Carolina at Charlotte; Leisha O'Quinn, Oklahoma State University; Willow Partington, Hudson Valley Community College; Martin Patrick, Illinois State University; Albert Reischuck, Kent State University; Jeffrey Ruda, University of California, Davis; Diane Scillia, Kent State University; Stephanie Smith, Youngstown State University; Janet Snyder, West Virginia University; James Terry, Stephens College; Michael Tinkler, Hobart and William Smith Colleges; Reid Wood, Lorain County Community College. Our thanks also to additional expert readers including: Susan Cahan, Yale University; David Craven, University of New Mexico; Marian Feldman, University of California, Berkeley; Dorothy Johnson, University of Iowa; Genevra Kornbluth, University of Maryland; Patricia Mainardi, City University of New York; Clemente Marconi, Columbia University, Tod Marder, Rutgers University; Mary Miller, Yale University; Elizabeth Penton, Durham Technical Community College; Catherine B. Scallen, Case Western University; Kim Shelton, University of California, Berkeley.

Many people reviewed the original edition of *Art History* and have continued to assist with its revision. Every chapter was read by one or more specialists. For work on the original book and assistance with subsequent editions my thanks go to: Barbara Abou-el-Haj, SUNY Binghamton; Roger Aiken, Creighton University; Molly Aitken; Anthony Alofsin, University of Texas, Austin; Christiane Andersson, Bucknell University; Kathryn Arnold; Julie Aronson, Cincinnati Art Museum; Michael Auerbach, Vanderbilt University; Larry Beck; Evelyn Bell, San Jose State University; Janetta Rebold Benton, Pace University; Janet Berlo, University of Rochester; Sarah Blick, Kenyon College; Jonathan Bloom, Boston College; Suzaan Boettger; Judith Bookbinder, Boston College; Marta Braun, Ryerson University; Elizabeth Broun, Smithsonian American Art Museum; Glen R. Brown, Kansas State University; Maria Elena Buszek, Kansas City Art Institute; Robert G. Calkins; Annmarie Weyl Carr; April Clagget, Keene State College; William W. Clark, Queens College, CUNY; John Clarke, University of Texas, Austin; Jaqueline Clipsham; Ralph T. Coe; Robert Cohon, The Nelson-Atkins Museum of Art; Alessandra Comini; James D'Emilio, University of South Florida; Walter Denny, University of Massachusetts, Amherst; Jerrilyn Dodds, City College, CUNY; Lois Drewer, Index of Christian Art; Joseph Dye, Virginia Museum of Art; James Farmer, Virginia Commonwealth University; Grace Flam, Salt Lake City Community College; Mary D. Garrard; Paula Gerson, Florida State University; Walter S. Gibson; Dorothy Glass; Oleg Grabar; Randall Griffey, Amherst College; Cynthia Hahn, Florida State University; Sharon Hill, Virginia Commonwealth University; John Hoopes, University of Kansas; Reinhild Janzen, Washburn University; Wendy Kindred, University of Maine at Fort Kent; Alan T. Kohl, Minneapolis College of Art; Ruth Kolarik, Colorado College; Carol H. Krinsky, New York University; Aileen Laing, Sweet Briar College; Janet LeBlanc, Clemson University; Charles Little, The Metropolitan Museum of Art; Laureen Reu Liu, McHenry County College; Loretta Lorance; Brian Madigan, Wayne State University; Janice Mann, Bucknell University; Judith Mann, St. Louis Art Museum; Richard Mann, San Francisco State University; James Martin,; Elizabeth Parker McLachlan; Tamara Mikailova, St. Petersburg, Russia, and Macalester College; Anta Montet-White; Anne E. Morganstern, Ohio State University; Winslow Myers, Bancroft School; Lawrence Nees, University of Delaware; Amy Ogata, Cleveland Institute of Art; Judith Oliver, Colgate University; Edward Olszewski, Case Western Reserve University; Sara Jane Pearman; John G. Pedley, University of Michigan; Michael Plante, Tulane University; Eloise Quiñones-Keber, Baruch College and the Graduate Center, CUNY; Virginia Raguin, College of the Holy Cross; Nancy H. Ramage, Ithaca College; Ann M. Roberts, Lake Forest College; Lisa Robertson, The Cleveland Museum of Art; Barry Rubin; Charles Sack, Parsons, Kansas; Jan Schall, The Nelson-Atkins Museum of Art; Tom Shaw, Kean College; Pamela Sheingorn, Baruch College, CUNY; Raechell Smith, Kansas City Art Institute; Lauren Soth; Anne R. Stanton, University of Missouri, Columbia; Michael Stoughton; Thomas Sullivan, OSB, Benedictine College (Conception Abbey); Pamela Trimpe, University of Iowa; Richard Turnbull, Fashion Institute of Technology; Elizabeth Valdez del Alamo, Montclair State College; Lisa Vergara; Monica Visoná, University of Kentucky; Roger Ward, Norton Museum of Art; Mark Weil, St. Louis; David Wilkins; Marcilene Wittmer, University of Miami.

The various features of this book reinforce each other, helping the reader to become comfortable with terminology and concepts that are specific to art history.

Starter Kit and Introduction   The Starter Kit is a highly concise primer of basic concepts and tools. The Introduction explores the way they are used to come to an understanding of the history of art.

Captions   There are two kinds of captions in this book: short and long. Short captions identify information specific to the work of art or architecture illustrated:

> artist (when known)
> title or descriptive name of work date
> original location (if moved to a museum or other site)
> material or materials a work is made of
> size (height before width) in feet and inches, with meters
>   and centimeters in parentheses
> present location

The order of these elements varies, depending on the type of work illustrated. Dimensions are not given for architecture, for most wall paintings, or for most architectural sculpture. Some captions have one or more lines of small print below the identification section of the caption that gives museum or collection information. This is rarely required reading; its inclusion is often a requirement for gaining permission to reproduce the work.

Longer, discursive captions contain information that complements the narrative of the main text.

Definitions of Terms   You will encounter the basic terms of art history in three places:

> **In the Text**, where words appearing in boldface type are defined, or glossed, at their first use. Some terms are boldfaced and explained more than once, especially those that experience shows are hard to remember.
>
> **In Boxed Features**, on technique and other subjects, where labeled drawings and diagrams visually reinforce the use of terms.
>
> **In the Glossary**, at the end of the volume (p. 1137), which contains all the words in boldface type in the text and boxes.

Maps   At the beginning of each chapter you will find a map with all the places mentioned in the chapter.

Boxes   Special material that complements, enhances, explains, or extends the narrative text is set off in six types of tinted boxes.

Art and its Contexts and The Object Speaks boxes expand on selected works or issues related to the text. A Closer Look boxes use leader-line captions to focus attention on specific aspects of important works. Elements of Architecture boxes clarify specifically architectural features, often explaining engineering principles or building technology. Technique boxes outline the techniques and processes by which certain types of art are created. Recovering the Past boxes highlight the work of archaeologists who uncover and conservators who assure the preservation and clear presentation of art.

Bibliography   The bibliography at the end of this book beginning on page 1146 contains books in English, organized by general works and by chapter, that are basic to the study of art history today, as well as works cited in the text.

Learn About It   Placed at the beginning of each chapter, this feature captures in bulleted form the key learning objectives, or outcomes, of the chapter. They point to what will have been accomplished upon its completion.

Think About It   These critical thinking questions appear at the end of each chapter and help students assess their mastery of the learning objectives (Learn About It) by asking them to think through and apply what they have learned.

MyArtsLab prompts   These notations are found throughout the chapter and are keyed to MyArtsLab resources that enrich and reinforce student learning.

Dates, Abbreviations, and Other Conventions   This book uses the designations BCE and CE, abbreviations for "Before the Common Era" and "Common Era," instead of BC ("Before Christ") and AD ("Anno Domini," "the year of our Lord"). The first century BCE is the period from 99 BCE to 1 BCE; the first century CE is from the year 1 CE to 99 CE. Similarly, the second century CE is the period from 199 BCE to 100 BCE; the second century CE extends from 100 CE to 199 CE.

100's	**99–1**	**1–99**	**100's**
second	first	first	second
century BCE	century BCE	century CE	century CE

Circa ("about") is used with approximate dates, spelled out in the text and abbreviated to "c." in the captions. This indicates that an exact date is not yet verified.

An illustration is called a "figure," or "fig." Thus, figure 6–7 is the seventh numbered illustration in Chapter 6, and fig. Intro-3 is the third figure in the Introduction. There are two types of figures: photographs of artworks or of models, and line drawings. Drawings are used when a work cannot be photographed or when a diagram or simple drawing is the clearest way to illustrate an object or a place.

When introducing artists, we use the words *active* and *documented* with dates, in addition to "b." (for "born") and "d." (for "died"). "Active" means that an artist worked during the years given. "Documented" means that documents link the person to that date.

Accents are used for words in French, German, Italian, and Spanish only. With few exceptions, names of cultural institutions in Western European countries are given in the form used in that country.

Titles of Works of Art   It was only over the last 500 years that paintings and works of sculpture created in Europe and North America were given formal titles, either by the artist or by critics and art historians. Such formal titles are printed in italics. In other traditions and cultures, a single title is not important or even recognized.

In this book we use formal descriptive titles of artworks where titles are not established. If a work is best known by its non-English title, such as Manet's *Le Déjeuner sur l'Herbe (The Luncheon on the Grass)*, the original language precedes the translation.

Art history focuses on the visual arts—painting, drawing, sculpture, prints, photography, ceramics, metalwork, architecture, and more. This Starter Kit contains basic information and addresses concepts that underlie and support the study of art history. It provides a quick reference guide to the vocabulary used to classify and describe art objects. Understanding these terms is indispensable because you will encounter them again and again in reading, talking, and writing about art.

Let us begin with the basic properties of art. A work of art is a material object having both form and content. It is often described and categorized according to its *style* and *medium*.

FORM

Referring to purely visual aspects of art and architecture, the term *form* encompasses qualities of *line*, *shape*, *color*, *light*, *texture*, *space*, *mass*, *volume*, and *composition*. These qualities are known as *formal elements*. When art historians use the term *formal*, they mean "relating to form."

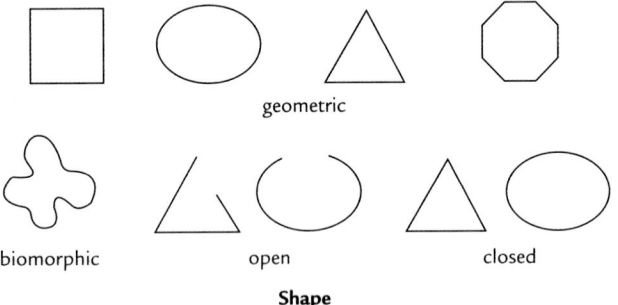

geometric

biomorphic   open   closed

Shape

Line and **shape** are attributes of form. Line is an element—usually drawn or painted—the length of which is so much greater than the width that we perceive it as having only length. Line can be actual, as when the line is visible, or it can be implied, as when the movement of the viewer's eyes over the surface of a work follows a path determined by the artist. Shape, on the other hand, is the two-dimensional, or flat, area defined by the borders of an enclosing *outline* or *contour*. Shape can be *geometric*, *biomorphic* (suggesting living things; sometimes called *organic*), *closed*, or *open*. The *outline* or *contour* of a three-dimensional object can also be perceived as line.

Color has several attributes. These include *hue*, *value*, and *saturation*.

Hue is what we think of when we hear the word *color*, and the terms are interchangeable. We perceive hues as the result of differing wavelengths of electromagnetic energy. The visible spectrum, which can be seen in a rainbow, runs from red through violet. When the ends of the spectrum are connected through the hue red-violet, the result may be diagrammed as a color wheel. The primary hues (numbered 1) are red, yellow, and blue. They are known as primaries because all other colors are made by combining these hues. Orange, green, and violet result from the mixture of two primaries and are known as secondary hues (numbered 2). Intermediate hues, or tertiaries (numbered 3), result from the mixture of a primary and a secondary. Complementary colors are the two colors directly opposite one another on the color wheel, such as red and green. Red, orange, and yellow are regarded as warm colors and appear to advance toward us. Blue, green, and violet, which seem to recede, are called cool colors. Black and white are not considered colors but neutrals; in terms of light, black is understood as the absence of color and white as the mixture of all colors.

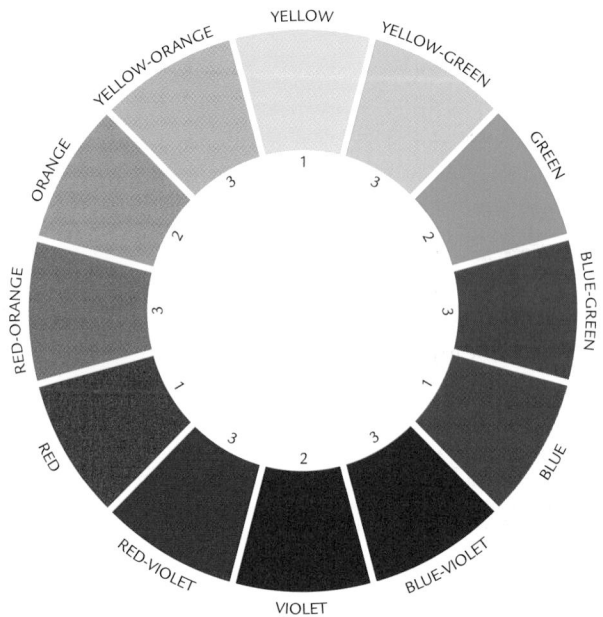

Value is the relative degree of lightness or darkness of a given color and is created by the amount of light reflected from an object's surface. A dark green has a deeper value than a light green, for example. In black-and-white reproductions of colored objects, you see only value, and some artworks—for example, a drawing made with black ink—possess only value, not hue or saturation.

Value scale from white to black.

+ WHITE   PURE HUE   + BLACK

Value variation in red.

Saturation, also sometimes referred to as *intensity*, is a color's quality of brightness or dullness. A color described as highly saturated looks vivid and pure; a hue of low saturation may or look a little muddy or greyed.

PURE HUE   DULLED   PURE HUE

Intensity scale from bright to dull.

Texture, another attribute of form, is the tactile (or touch-perceived) quality of a surface. It is described by words such as *smooth, polished, rough, prickly, grainy*, or *oily*. Texture takes two forms: the texture of the actual surface of the work of art and the implied (illusionistically described) surface of objects represented in the work of art.

Space is what contains forms. It may be actual and three-dimensional, as it is with sculpture and architecture, or it may be fictional, represented illusionistically in two dimensions, as when artists represent recession into the distance on a flat surface—such as a wall or a canvas--by using various systems of perspective.

Mass and volume are properties of three-dimensional things. Mass is solid matter—whether sculpture or architecture—that takes up space. Volume is enclosed or defined space, and may be either solid or hollow. Like space, mass and volume may be illusionistically represented on a two-dimensional surface, such as in a painting or a photograph.

Composition is the organization, or arrangement, of forms in a work of art. Shapes and colors may be repeated or varied, balanced symmetrically or asymmetrically; they may be stable or dynamic. The possibilities are nearly endless and artistic choice depends both on the time and place where the work was created as well as the objectives of individual artists. Pictorial depth (spatial recession) is a specialized aspect of composition in which the three-dimensional world is represented on a flat surface, or *picture plane*. The area "behind" the picture plane is called the *picture space* and conventionally contains three "zones": *foreground, middle ground*, and *background*.

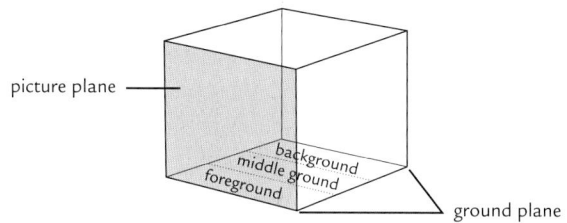

Various techniques for conveying a sense of pictorial depth have been devised by artists in different cultures and at different times. A number of them are diagrammed here. In some European art, the use of various systems of *perspective* has sought to create highly convincing illusions of recession into space. At other times and in other cultures, indications of recession are actually suppressed or avoided to emphasize surface rather than space.

TECHNIQUE | Pictorial devices for depicting recession in space

overlapping

In overlapping, partially covered elements are meant to be seen as located behind those covering them.

diminution

In diminution of scale, successively smaller elements are perceived as being progressively farther away than the largest ones.

vertical perspective

Vertical perspective stacks elements, with the higher ones intended to be perceived as deeper in space.

atmospheric perspective

Through atmospheric perspective, objects in the far distance (often in bluish-gray hues) have less clarity than nearer objects. The sky becomes paler as it approaches the horizon.

divergent perspective

In divergent or reverse perspective, forms widen slightly and imaginary lines called orthogonals diverge as they recede in space.

intuitive perspective

Intuitive perspective takes the opposite approach from divergent perspective. Forms become narrower and orthogonals converge the farther they are from the viewer, approximating the optical experience of spatial recession.

linear perspective

Linear perspective (also called scientific, mathematical, one-point and Renaissance perspective) is a rationalization or standardization of intuitive perspective that was developed in fifteenth-century Italy. It uses mathematical formulas to construct images in which all elements are shaped by, or arranged along, orthogonals that converge in one or more vanishing points on a horizon line.

CONTENT

Content includes *subject matter*, but not all works of art have subject matter. Many buildings, paintings, sculptures, and other art objects include no recognizable references to things in nature nor to any story or historical situation, focusing instead on lines, colors, masses, volumes, and other formal elements. However, all works of art—even those without recognizable subject matter—have content, or meaning, insofar as they seek to communicate ideas, convey feelings, or affirm the beliefs and values of their makers, their patrons, and usually the people who originally viewed or used them.

Content may derive from the social, political, religious, and economic *contexts* in which a work was created, the *intention* of the artist, and the *reception* of the work by beholders (the audience). Art historians, applying different methods of *interpretation*, often arrive at different conclusions regarding the content of a work of art, and single works of art can contain more than one meaning because they are occasionally directed at more than one audience.

The study of subject matter is called *iconography* (literally, "the writing of images") and includes the identification of *symbols*—images that take on meaning through association, resemblance, or convention.

STYLE

Expressed very broadly, *style* is the combination of form and composition that makes a work distinctive. *Stylistic analysis* is one of art history's most developed practices, because it is how art historians recognize the work of an individual artist or the characteristic manner of groups of artists working in a particular time or place. Some of the most commonly used terms to discuss *artistic styles* include *period style, regional style, representational style, abstract style, linear style,* and *painterly style.*

Period style refers to the common traits detectable in works of art and architecture from a particular historical era. It is good practice not to use the words "style" and "period" interchangeably. Style is the sum of many influences and characteristics, including the period of its creation. An example of proper usage is "an American house from the Colonial period built in the Georgian style."

Regional style refers to stylistic traits that persist in a geographic region. An art historian whose specialty is medieval art can recognize Spanish style through many successive medieval periods and can distinguish individual objects created in medieval Spain from other medieval objects that were created in, for example, Italy.

Representational styles are those that describe the appearance of recognizable subject matter in ways that make it seem lifelike.

  Realism and **Naturalism** are terms that some people used interchangeably to characterize artists' attempts to represent the observable world in a manner that appears to describe its visual appearance accurately. When capitalized, Realism refers to a specific period style discussed in Chapter 30.

  Idealization strives to create images of physical perfection according to the prevailing values or tastes of a culture. The artist may work in a representational style and idealize it to capture an underlying value or expressive effect.

Illusionism refers to a highly detailed style that seeks to create a convincing illusion of physical reality by describing its visual appearance meticulously.

Abstract styles depart from mimicking lifelike appearance to capture the essence of a form. An abstract artist may work from nature or from a memory image of nature's forms and colors, which are simplified, stylized, perfected, distorted, elaborated, or otherwise transformed to achieve a desired expressive effect.

  Nonrepresentational (or Nonobjective) Art is a term often used for works of art that do not aim to produce recognizable natural imagery.

  Expressionism refers to styles in which the artist exaggerates aspects of form to draw out the beholder's subjective response or to project the artist's own subjective feelings.

Linear describes both styles and techniques. In linear styles artists use line as the primary means of definition. But linear paintings can also incorporate *modeling*—creating an illusion of three-dimensional substance through shading, usually executed so that brushstrokes nearly disappear.

Painterly describes a style of representation in which vigorous, evident brushstrokes dominate, and outlines, shadows, and highlights are brushed in freely.

MEDIUM AND TECHNIQUE

Medium (plural, *media*) refers to the material or materials from which a work of art is made. Today, literally anything can be used to make a work of art, including not only traditional materials like paint, ink, and stone, but also rubbish, food, and the earth itself.

Technique is the process that transforms media into a work of art. Various techniques are explained throughout this book in Technique boxes. Two-dimensional media and techniques include painting, drawing, prints, and photography. Three-dimensional media and techniques are sculpture (for example, using stone, wood, clay or cast metal), architecture, and many small-scale arts (such as jewelry, containers, or vessels) in media such as ceramics, metal, or wood.

Painting includes wall painting and fresco, illumination (the decoration of books with paintings), panel painting (painting on wood panels), painting on canvas, and handscroll and hanging scroll painting. The paint in these examples is pigment mixed with a liquid vehicle, or binder. Some art historians also consider pictorial media such as mosaic and stained glass—where the pigment is arranged in solid form—as a type of painting.

Graphic arts are those that involve the application of lines and strokes to a two-dimensional surface or support, most often paper. Drawing is a graphic art, as are the various forms of printmaking. Drawings may be sketches (quick visual notes, often made in preparation for larger drawings or paintings); studies (more carefully drawn analyses of details or entire compositions); cartoons (full-scale drawings made in preparation for work in another medium, such as fresco, stained glass, or tapestry); or complete artworks in themselves. Drawings can be made with ink, charcoal, crayon, or pencil. Prints, unlike drawings, are made in multiple copies. The various forms of printmaking include woodcut, the intaglio processes (engraving, etching, drypoint), and lithography.

Photography (literally, "light writing") is a medium that involves the rendering of optical images on light-sensitive surfaces. Photographic images are typically recorded by a camera.

Sculpture is three-dimensional art that is *carved*, *modeled*, *cast*, or *assembled*. Carved sculpture is subtractive in the sense that the image is created by taking away material. Wood, stone, and ivory are common materials used to create carved sculptures. Modeled sculpture is considered additive, meaning that the object is built up from a material, such as clay, that is soft enough to be molded and shaped. Metal sculpture is usually cast or is assembled by welding or a similar means of permanent joining.

Sculpture is either free-standing (that is, surrounded by space) or in pictorial relief. Relief sculpture projects from the background surface of the same piece of material. High-relief sculpture projects far from its background; low-relief sculpture is only slightly raised; and sunken relief, found mainly in ancient Egyptian art, is carved into the surface, with the highest part of the relief being the flat surface.

Ephemeral arts include processions, ceremonies, or ritual dances (often with décor, costumes, or masks); performance art; earthworks; cinema and video art; and some forms of digital or computer art. All impose a temporal limitation—the artwork is viewable for a finite period of time and then disappears forever, is in a constant state of change, or must be replayed to be experienced again.

Architecture creates enclosures for human activity or habitation. It is three-dimensional, highly spatial, functional, and closely bound with developments in technology and materials. Since it is difficult to capture in a photograph, several types of schematic drawings are commonly used to enable the visualization of a building:

> **Plans** depict a structure's masses and voids, presenting a view from above of the building's footprint or as if it had been sliced horizontally at about waist height.

Plan: Philadelphia, Vanna Venturi House

Sections reveal the interior of a building as if it had been cut vertically from top to bottom.

Section: Rome, Sta. Costanza

Isometric Drawings show buildings from oblique angles either seen from above ("bird's-eye view") to reveal their basic three-dimensional forms (often cut away so we can peek inside) or from below ("worm's-eye view") to represent the arrangement of interior spaces and the upward projection of structural elements.

Isometric cutaway from above: Ravenna, San Vitale

Isometric projection from below: Istanbul, Hagia Sophia

INTRODUCTION

**INTRO-1 • Mark Rothko
NO. 3/NO. 13 (MAGENTA,
BLACK AND GREEN ON
ORANGE)**
1949. Oil on canvas, 7′1⅜″ × 5′5″
(2.165 × 1.648 m). Museum of
Modern Art, New York.

The title of this book seems clear. It defines a field of academic study and scholarly research that has achieved a secure place in college and university curricula across North America. But *Art History* couples two words—even two worlds—that are less well focused when separated. What is art? In what sense does it have a history? Students of art and its history should pause and engage, even if briefly, with these large questions before beginning the journey surveyed in the following chapters.

WHAT IS ART?

Artists, critics, art historians, and the general public all grapple with this thorny question. The *Random House Dictionary* defines "art" as "the quality, production, expression, or realm of what is beautiful, or of more than ordinary significance." Others have characterized "art" as something human-made that combines creative imagination and technical skill and satisfies an innate desire for order and harmony—perhaps a human hunger for the

LEARN ABOUT IT

I.1   Consider the criteria used to identify and characterize those cultural artifacts that are labeled as "art."

I.2   Survey the methods used by art historians to analyze works of art and interpret their meaning within their original cultural contexts.

I.3   Explore the methods and objectives of visual analysis.

I.4   Assess the way art historians identify conventional subject matter and symbols in a process called iconography.

I.5   Trace the process of art-historical interpretation in a case study.

HEAR MORE: Listen to an audio file of your chapter **www.myartslab.com**

beautiful. This seems relatively straightforward until we start to look at modern and contemporary art, where there has been a heated and extended debate concerning "What is Art?" The focus is often far from questions of transcendent beauty, ordered design, or technical skill, and centers instead on the meaning of a work for an elite target audience or the attempt to pose challenging questions or unsettle deep-seated cultural ideas.

The works of art discussed in this book represent a privileged subset of artifacts produced by past and present cultures. They were usually meant to be preserved, and they are currently considered worthy of conservation and display. The determination of which artifacts are exceptional—which are works of art— evolves through the actions, opinions, and selections of artists, patrons, governments, collectors, archaeologists, museums, art historians, and others. Labeling objects as art is usually meant to signal that they transcended or now transcend in some profound way their practical function, often embodying cherished cultural ideas or foundational values. Sometimes it can mean they are considered beautiful, well designed, and made with loving care, but this is not always the case, especially in the twentieth and twenty-first centuries when the complex notion of what is art has little to do with the idea of beauty. Some critics and historians argue that works of art are tendentious embodiments of power and privilege, hardly sublime expressions of beauty or truth. After all, art can be unsettling as well as soothing, challenging as well as reassuring, whether made in the present or surviving from the past.

Increasingly we are realizing that our judgments about what constitutes art—as well as what constitutes beauty—are conditioned by our own education and experience. Whether acquired at home, in classrooms, in museums, at the movies, or on the internet, our responses to art are learned behaviors, influenced by class, gender, race, geography, and economic status as well as education. Even art historians find that their definitions of what constitutes art—and what constitutes artistic quality—evolve with additional research and understanding. Exploring works by twentieth-century painter Mark Rothko and nineteenth-century quiltmakers Martha Knowles and Henrietta Thomas demonstrates how definitions of art and artistic value are subject to change over time.

Rothko's painting, **MAGENTA, BLACK AND GREEN ON ORANGE (FIG. INTRO–1)**, is a well-known example of the sort of abstract painting that was considered the epitome of artistic sophistication by the mid-twentieth-century New York art establishment. It was created by an artist who meant it to be a work of art. It was acquired by the Museum of Modern Art in New York, and its position on the walls of that museum is a sure sign that it was accepted as such by a powerful cultural institution. However, beyond the context of the American artists, dealers, critics, and collectors who made up Rothko's art world, such paintings were often received with skepticism. They were seen by many as incomprehensible—lacking both technical skill and recognizable subject matter, two criteria that were part of the general public's definition of art at the time. Abstract paintings

soon inspired a popular retort: "That's not art; my child could do it!" Interestingly enough, Rothko saw in the childlike character of his own paintings one of the qualities that made them works of art. Children, he said, "put forms, figures, and views into pictorial arrangements, employing out of necessity most of the rules of optical perspective and geometry but without the knowledge that they are employing them." He characterized his own art as childlike, as "an attempt to recapture the freshness and naiveté of childish vision." In part because they are carefully crafted by an established artist who provided these kinds of intellectual justifications for their character and appearance, Rothko's abstract paintings are broadly considered works of art and are treasured possessions of major museums across the globe.

Works of art, however, do not always have to be created by individuals who perceive themselves as artists. Nor are all works produced for an art market surrounded by critics and collectors ready to explain, exhibit, and disperse them, ideally to prestigious museums. Such is the case with this quilt **(FIG. INTRO–2)**, made by Martha Knowles and Henrietta Thomas a century before Rothko's painting. Their work is similarly composed of blocks of color, and like Rothko, they produced their visual effect by arranging these flat chromatic shapes carefully and regularly on a rectangular field. But this quilt was not meant to hang on the wall of an art museum. It is the social product of a friendship, intended as an intimate gift, presented to a loved one for use in her home. An inscription on the quilt itself makes this clear—"From M. A. Knowles to her Sweet Sister Emma, 1843." Thousands of such friendship quilts

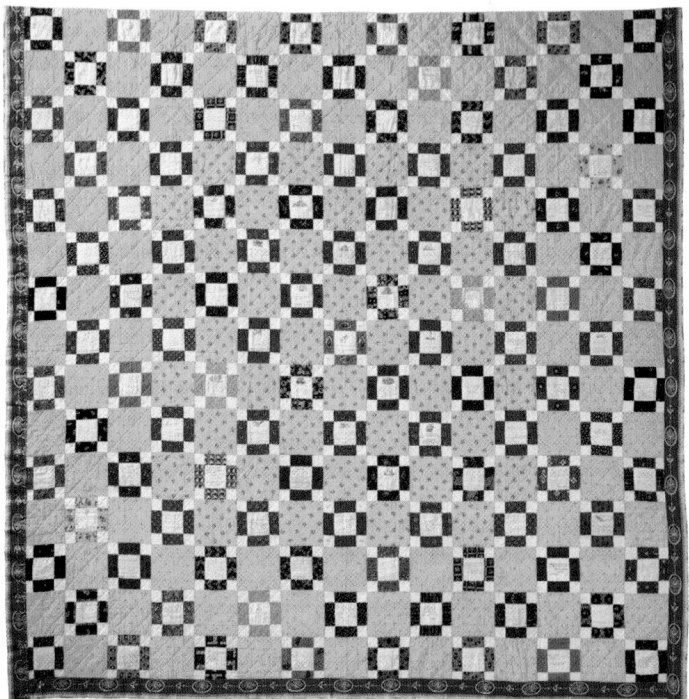

INTRO–2 • Martha Knowles and Henrietta Thomas
MY SWEET SISTER EMMA
1843. Cotton quilt, 8'11" × 9'1" (2.72 × 2.77 m). International Quilt Studies Center, University of Nebraska, Lincoln, Nebraska.

Art and Architecture

This book contains much more than paintings and textiles. Within these pages you will also encounter sculpture, vessels, books, jewelry, tombs, chairs, photographs, architecture, and more. But as with Rothko's *Magenta, Black, and Green on Orange* (SEE FIG. INTRO–1) and Knowles and Thomas's *My Sweet Sister Emma* (SEE FIG. INTRO–2), criteria have been used to determine which works are selected for inclusion in a book titled *Art History*. Architecture presents an interesting case.

Buildings meet functional human needs by enclosing human habitation or activity. Many works of architecture, however, are considered "exceptional" because they transcend functional demands by manifesting distinguished architectural design or because they embody in important ways the values and goals of the culture that built them. Such buildings are usually produced by architects influenced, like painters, by great works and traditions from the past. In some cases they harmonize with, or react to, their natural or urban surroundings. For such reasons, they are discussed in books on the history of art.

Typical of such buildings is the church of Nôtre-Dame-du-Haut in Ronchamp, France, designed and constructed between 1950 and 1955 by Swiss architect Charles-Edouard Jeanneret, better known by his pseudonym, Le Corbusier. This building is the product of a significant historical moment, rich in global cultural meaning. A pilgrimage church on this site had been destroyed during World War II, and the creation here of a new church symbolized the end of a devastating war, embodying hopes for a brighter global future. Le Corbusier's design—drawing on sources that ranged from Algerian mosques to imperial Roman villas, from crab shells to airplane wings—is sculptural as well as architectural. It soars at the crest of a hill toward the sky but at the same time seems solidly anchored in the earth. And its coordination with the curves of the natural landscape complement the creation of an outdoor setting for religious ceremonies (to the right in the figure) to supplement the church interior that Le Corbusier characterized as a "container for intense concentration." In fact, this building is so renowned today as a monument of modern architecture, that the bus-loads of pilgrims who arrive at the site are mainly architects and devotees of architectural history.

Le Corbusier **NÔTRE-DAME-DU-HAUT**
1950–1955. Ronchamp, France.

were made by women during the middle years of the nineteenth century for use on beds, either to provide warmth or as a covering spread. Whereas quilts were sometimes displayed to a broad and enthusiastic audience of producers and admirers at competitions held at state and county fairs, they were not collected by art museums or revered by artists until relatively recently.

In 1971, at the Whitney Museum in New York—an establishment bastion of the art world in which Rothko moved and worked—art historians Jonathan Holstein and Gail van der Hoof mounted an exhibition entitled "Abstract Design in American Quilts," demonstrating the artistic affiliation we have already noted in comparing the way Knowles and Thomas, like Rothko, create abstract patterns with fields of color. Quilts were later accepted—or should the word be "appropriated?"—as works of art and hung on the walls of a New York art museum because of their visual similarities with the avant-garde, abstract works of art created by establishment, New York artists.

Art historian Patricia Mainardi took the case for quilts one significant step further in a pioneering article of 1973 published in *The Feminist Art Journal*. Entitled, "Quilts: The Great American Art," her argument was rooted not only in the aesthetic affinity of quilts with the esteemed work of contemporary abstract painters, but also in a political conviction that the definition of art had to be broadened. What was at stake here was historical veracity. Mainardi began, "Women have always made art. But for most women, the arts highest valued by male society have been closed to them for just that reason. They have put their creativity instead into the needlework arts, which exist in fantastic variety wherever there are women, and which in fact are a universal female art, transcending race, class, and national borders." She argued for the inclusion of quilts within the history of art to give deserved attention to the work of women artists who had been excluded from discussion because they created textiles and because they worked outside the male-dominated professional structures of the art world—because they were women. Quilts now hang as works of art on the walls of museums and appear with regularity in books that survey the history of art.

As these two examples demonstrate, definitions of art are rooted in cultural systems of value that are subject to change. And as they change, the list of works considered by art historians is periodically revised. Determining what to study is a persistent part of the art historian's task.

WHAT IS ART HISTORY?

There are many ways to study or appreciate works of art. Art history represents one specific approach, with its own goals and its own methods of assessment and interpretation. Simply put, art historians seek to understand the meaning of art from the past within its original cultural contexts, both from the point of view of its producers—artists, architects, and patrons—as well as from the point of view of its consumers—those who formed its original audience. Coming to an understanding of the cultural meaning of a work of art requires detailed and patient investigation on many levels, especially with art that was produced long ago and in societies distinct from our own. This is a scholarly rather than an intuitive exercise. In art history, the work of art is seen as an embodiment of the values, goals, and aspirations of its time and place of origin. It is a part of culture.

Art historians use a variety of theoretical perspectives and a host of interpretive strategies to come to an understanding of works of art within their cultural contexts. But as a place to begin, the work of art historians can be divided into four types of investigation:

1. assessment of physical properties,
2. analysis of visual or formal structure,
3. identification of subject matter or conventional symbolism, and
4. integration within cultural context.

ASSESSING PHYSICAL PROPERTIES

Of the methods used by art historians to study works of art, this is the most objective, but it requires close access to the work itself. Physical properties include shape, size, materials, and technique. For instance, many pictures are rectangular (e.g., SEE FIG. INTRO–1), but some are round (see page xxxi, FIG. C). Paintings as large as Rothko's require us to stand back if we want to take in the whole image, whereas some paintings (see page xxx, FIG. A) are so small that we are drawn up close to examine their detail. Rothko's painting and Knowles and Thomas's quilt are both rectangles of similar size, but they are distinguished by the materials from which they are made—oil paint on canvas versus cotton fabric joined by stitching. In art history books, most physical properties can only be understood from descriptions in captions, but when we are in the presence of the work of art itself, size and shape may be the first thing we notice. To fully understand medium and technique, however, it may be necessary to employ methods of scientific analysis or documentary research to elucidate the practices of artists at the time when and place where the work was created.

ANALYZING FORMAL STRUCTURE

Art historians explore the visual character that artists bring to their works—using the materials and the techniques chosen to create them—in a process called **formal analysis**. On the most basic level, it is divided into two parts:

- assessing the individual visual elements or formal vocabulary that constitute pictorial or sculptural communication, and
- discovering the overall arrangement, organization, or structure of an image, a design system that art historians often refer to as **composition**.

THE ELEMENTS OF VISUAL EXPRESSION. Artists control and vary the visual character of works of art to give their subjects and ideas meaning and expression, vibrancy and persuasion, challenge or delight (see "A Closer Look," pages xxx–xxxi). For example, the motifs, objects, figures, and environments within paintings can be sharply defined by line (SEE FIGS. INTRO–2 and INTRO–3), or they can be suggested by a sketchier definition (SEE FIGS. **INTRO–1** and INTRO–4). Painters can simulate the appearance of three-dimensional form through **modeling** or shading (SEE FIG. INTRO–3 and page xxxi, FIG. C), that is by describing the way light from a single source will highlight one side of a solid while leaving the other side in shadow. Alternatively, artists can avoid any strong sense of three-dimensionality by emphasizing patterns on a surface rather than forms in space (SEE FIG. INTRO–1 and page xxx, FIG. A). In addition to revealing the solid substance of forms through modeling, dramatic lighting can guide viewers to specific areas of a

A CLOSER LOOK

Visual Elements of Pictorial Expression › Line, Light, Form, and Color.

LINE

A. *Carpet Page* **from the Lindisfarne Gospels**
From Lindisfarne, England.
c. 715–720. Ink and tempera on vellum, 13⅜ × 9⁷⁄₁₆″ (34 × 24 cm). British Library, London. Cotton MS Nero D.IV fol. 26v

Every element in this complicated painting is sharply outlined by abrupt barriers between light and dark or between one color and another; there are no gradual or shaded transitions. Since the picture was created in part with pen and ink, the linearity is a logical feature of medium and technique. And although line itself is a "flattening" or two-dimensionalizing element in pictures, a complex and consistent system of overlapping gives the linear animal forms a sense of shallow but carefully worked-out three-dimensional relationships to one another.

LIGHT

B. Georges de la Tour *The Education of the Virgin*
c. 1650. Oil on canvas, 33 × 39½″ (83.8 × 100.4 cm). The Frick Collection, New York.

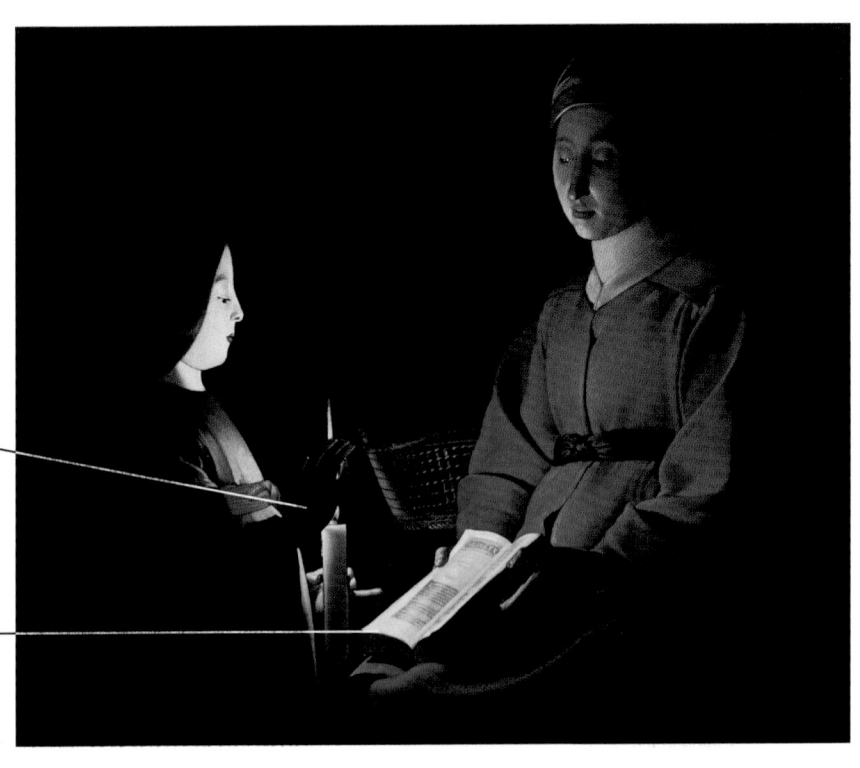

The source of illumination is a candle depicted within the painting. The young girl's upraised right hand shields its flame, allowing the artist to demonstrate his virtuosity in painting the translucency of human flesh.

Since the candle's flame is partially concealed, its luminous intensity is not allowed to distract from those aspects of the painting most brilliantly illuminated by it—the face of the girl and the book she is reading.

FORM

C. Michelangelo *The Holy Family* (*Doni Tondo*)
c. 1503. Oil and tempera on panel, diameter 3′11¼″ (1.2 m). Galleria degli Uffizi, Florence.

The complex overlapping of their highly three-dimensionalized bodies conveys the somewhat contorted spatial positioning and relationship of these three figures.

Through the use of modeling or shading—a gradual transition from lights to darks—Michelangelo imitates the way solid forms are illuminated from a single light source—the side closest to the light source is bright while the other side is cast in shadow—and gives a sense of three-dimensional form to his figures.

The actual three-dimensional projection of the sculpted heads in medallions around the frame—designed for this painting by Michelangelo himself—heightens the effect of fictive three-dimensionality in the figures painted on its flat surface.

In a technique called **foreshortening**, the carefully calculated angle of the Virgin's elbow makes it seem to project out toward the viewer.

COLOR

D. Junayd *Humay and Humayun*, **from a manuscript of the** *Divan* **of Kwaju Kirmani**
Made in Baghdad, Iraq. 1396. Color, ink, and gold on paper, 12⅝ × 9⁷⁄₁₆″ (32 × 24 cm). British Library, London. MS Add. 18113, fol. 31r

Junayd chose to flood every aspect of his painting with light, as if everything in it were illuminated from all sides at once. As a result, the emphasis here is on jewel-like color. The vibrant tonalities and dazzling detail of the dreamy landscape are not only more important than the simulation of three-dimensional forms distributed within a consistently described space; they actually upstage the human drama taking place against a patterned, tipped-up ground in the lower third of the picture.

picture (see page xxx, FIG. B), or it can be lavished on every aspect of a picture to reveal all its detail and highlight the vibrancy of its color (see page xxxi, FIG. D). Color itself can be muted or intensified, depending on the mood artists want to create or the tastes and expectations of their audiences.

Thus artists communicate with their viewers by making choices in the way they use and emphasize the elements of visual expression, and art historical analysis seeks to reveal how artists' decisions bring meaning to a work of art. For example in two paintings of women with children (SEE FIGS. INTRO–3 and INTRO–4), Raphael and Renoir work with the same visual elements of line, form, light, and color in the creation of their images, but they employ these shared elements to differing expressive ends. Raphael concentrates on line to clearly differentiate each element of his picture as a separate form. Careful modeling describes these outlined forms as substantial solids surrounded by space. This gives his subjects a sense of clarity, stability, and grandeur. Renoir, on the other hand, foregrounds the flickering of light and the play of color as he downplays the sense of three-dimensionality in individual forms. This gives his image a more ephemeral, casual sense. Art historians pay close attention to such variations in the use of visual elements—the building blocks of artistic expression—and use visual analysis to characterize the expressive effect of a particular work, a particular artist, or a general period defined by place and date.

COMPOSITION. When art historians analyze composition, they focus not on the individual elements of visual expression but on the overall arrangement and organizing design or structure of a work of art. In Raphael's **MADONNA OF THE GOLDFINCH (FIG. INTRO–3)**, for example, the group of figures has been arranged in a triangular shape and placed at the center of the picture. Raphael emphasized this central weighting by opening the clouds to reveal a patch of blue in the middle of the sky, and by flanking the figural group with lace-like trees. Since the Madonna is

at the center and since the two boys are divided between the two sides of the triangular shape, roughly—though not precisely—equidistant from the center of the painting, this is a bilaterally symmetrical composition: on either side of an implied vertical line at the center of the picture, there are equivalent forms on left and right, matched and balanced in a mirrored correspondence. Art historians refer to such an implied line—around which the elements of a picture are organized—as an **axis**. Raphael's painting has not only a vertical, but also a horizontal axis, indicated by a line of demarcation between light and dark—as well as between degrees of color saturation—in the terrain of the landscape. The belt of the Madonna's dress is aligned with this horizontal axis, and this correspondence, taken with the coordination of her head with the blue patch in the sky, relates her to the order of the natural world in which she sits, lending a sense of stability, order, and balance to the picture as a whole.

INTRO-3 • Raphael MADONNA OF THE GOLDFINCH (MADONNA DEL CARDELLINO)
1506. Oil on panel, 42 × 29½″ (106.7 × 74.9 cm). Galleria degli Uffizi, Florence.

The vibrant colors of this important work were revealed in the course of a careful, ten-year restoration, completed only in 2008.

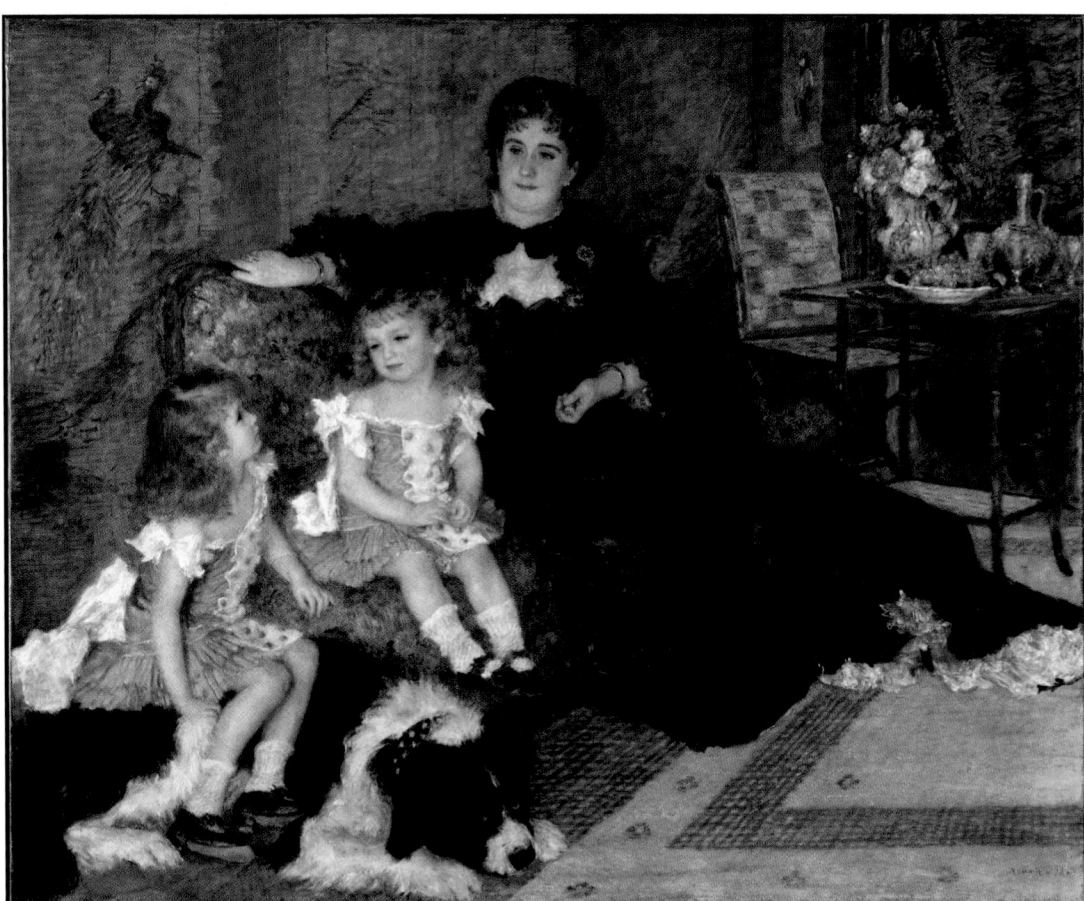

INTRO-4 •
Auguste Renoir
MME. CHARPENTIER
AND HER CHILDREN
1878. Oil on canvas,
60½ × 74⅞" (153.7 ×
190.2 cm). Metropolitan
Museum of Art, New York.

The main axis in Renoir's painting of **MME. CHARPENTIER AND HER CHILDREN (FIG. INTRO–4)** is neither vertical, nor horizontal, but diagonal, running from the upper right to the lower left corner of the painting. All major elements of the composition are aligned along this axis—dog, children, mother, and the table and chair that represent the most complex and detailed aspect of the setting. The upper left and lower right corners of the painting balance each other on either side of the diagonal axis as relatively simple fields of neutral tone, setting off and framing the main subjects between them. The resulting arrangement is not bilaterally symmetrical, but blatantly asymmetrical, with the large figural mass pushed into the left side of the picture. And unlike Raphael's composition, where the spatial relationship of the figures and their environment is mapped by the measured placement of elements that become increasingly smaller in scale and fuzzier in definition as they recede into the background, the relationship of Renoir's figures to their spatial environment is less clearly defined as they recede into the background along the dramatic diagonal axis. Nothing distracts us from the bold informality of this family gathering.

Both Raphael and Renoir arrange their figures carefully and purposefully, but they follow distinctive compositional systems that communicate different notions of the way these figures interact with each other and the world around them. Art historians pay special attention to how pictures are arranged because composition is one of the principal ways artists charge their paintings with expressive meaning.

IDENTIFYING SUBJECT MATTER

Art historians have traditionally sought subject matter and meaning in works of art with a system of analysis that was outlined by Irwin Panofsky (1892–1968), an influential German scholar who was expelled from his academic position by the Nazis in 1933 and spent the rest of his career of research and teaching in the United States. Panofsky proposed that when we seek to understand the subject of a work of art, we derive meaning initially in two ways:

- First we perceive what he called "natural subject matter" by recognizing forms and situations that we know from our own experience.
- Then we use what he called "**iconography**" to identify the conventional meanings associated with forms and figures as bearers of narrative or symbolic content, often specific to a particular time and place.

Some paintings, like Rothko's abstractions, do not contain subjects drawn from the world around us, from stories, or from conventional symbolism, but Panofsky's scheme remains a standard method of investigating meaning in works of art that present narrative subjects, portray specific people or places, or embody cultural values with iconic imagery or allegory.

A CLOSER LOOK

Iconography ⟩ The study and identification of conventional themes, motifs, and symbols to elucidate the subject matter of works of art.

These grapes sit on an imported, Italian silver *tazza*, a luxury object that may commemorate Northern European prosperity and trade. This particular object recurs in several of Peeters's other still lifes.

An image of the artist herself appears on the reflective surface of this pewter tankard, one of the ways that she signed her paintings and promoted her career.

Luscious fruits and flowers celebrate the abundance of nature, but because these fruits of the earth will eventually fade, even rot, they could be moralizing references to the transience of earthly existence.

Detailed renderings of insects showcased Peeters's virtuosity as a painter, but they also may have symbolized the vulnerability of the worldly beauty of flowers and fruit to destruction and decay.

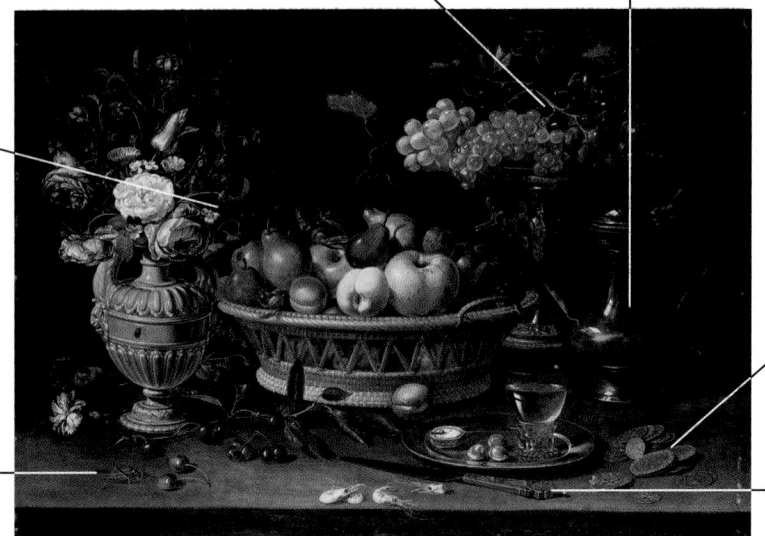

These coins, including one minted in 1608–1609, help focus the dating of this painting. The highlighting of money within a still life could reference the wealth of the owner—or it could subtly allude to the value the artist has crafted here in paint.

This knife—which appears in several of Peeters's still lifes—is of a type that is associated with wedding gifts.

A. Clara Peeters *Still Life with Fruit and Flowers*
c. 1612. Oil on copper, 25⅕ × 35″ (64 × 89 cm). Ashmolean Museum, Oxford.

Quince is an unusual subject in Chinese painting, but the fruit seems to have carried personal significance for Zhu Da. One of his friends was known as the Daoist of Quince Mountain, a site in Hunan province that was also the subject of a work by one of his favorite authors, Tang poet Li Bai.

The artist's signature reads "Bada Shanren painted this," using a familiar pseudonym in a formula and calligraphic style that the artist ceased using in 1695.

This red block is a seal with an inscription drawn from a Confucian text: "teaching is half of learning." This was imprinted on the work by the artist as an aspect of his signature, a symbol of his identity within the picture, just as the reflection and inscribed knife identify Clara Peeters as the painter of her still life.

B. Zhu Da (Bada Shanren) *Quince (Mugua)*
1690. Album leaf mounted as a hanging scroll; ink and colors on paper, 7⅞ × 5¾″ (20 × 14.6 cm). Princeton University Art Museum.

NATURAL SUBJECT MATTER. We recognize some things in works of visual art simply by virtue of living in a world similar to that represented by the artist. For example, in the two paintings by Raphael and Renoir just examined (SEE FIGS. INTRO–3 and **INTRO–**4), we immediately recognize the principal human figures in both as a woman and two children, boys in the case of Raphael's painting, girls in Renoir's. We can also make a general identification of the animals: a bird in the hand of Raphael's boys, and a pet dog under one of Renoir's girls. And natural subject matter can extend from an identification of figures to an understanding of the expressive significance of their postures and facial features. We might see in the boy who snuggles between the knees of the woman in Raphael's painting, placing his own foot on top of hers, an anxious child seeking the security of physical contact with a trusted caretaker—perhaps his mother—in response to fear of the bird he reaches out to touch. Many of us have seen insecure children take this very pose in response to potentially unsettling encounters.

The closer the work of art is in both time and place to our own situation temporally and geographically, the easier it sometimes is to identify what is represented. But although Renoir painted his picture over 125 years ago in France, the furniture in the background still looks familiar, as does the book in the hand of Raphael's Madonna, painted five centuries before our time. But the object hanging from the belt of the scantily clad boy at the left in this painting will require identification for most of us. Iconographic investigation is necessary to understand the function of this form.

ICONOGRAPHY. Some subjects are associated with conventional meanings established at a specific time or place; some of the human figures portrayed in works of art have specific identities; and some of the objects or forms have symbolic or allegorical meanings in addition to their natural subject matter. Discovering these conventional meanings of art's subject matter is called iconography. (See "A Closer Look," opposite.)

For example, the woman accompanied in the outdoors by two boys in Raphael's *Madonna of the Goldfinch* (SEE FIG. INTRO–3) would have been immediately recognized by members of its intended sixteenth-century Florentine audience as the Virgin Mary. Viewers would have identified the naked boy standing between her knees as her son Jesus, and the boy holding the bird as Jesus' cousin John the Baptist, sheathed in the animal skin garment that he would wear in the wilderness and equipped with a shallow cup attached to his belt, ready to be used in baptisms. Such attributes of clothing and equipment are often critical in making iconographic identifications. The goldfinch in the Baptist's hand was at this time and place a symbol of Christ's death on the cross, an allegorical implication that makes the Christ Child's retreat into secure contact with his mother—already noted on the level of natural subject matter—understandable in relation to a specific story. The comprehension of conventional meanings in this painting would have been almost automatic among those for whom it was painted, but for us,

separated by time and place, some research is necessary to recover associations that are no longer part of our everyday world.

Although it may not initially seem as unfamiliar, the subject matter of Renoir's 1878 portrait of *Mme. Charpentier and her Children* (SEE FIG. INTRO–4) is in fact even more obscure. Although there are those in twenty-first-century American culture for whom the figures and symbols in Raphael's painting are still recognizable and meaningful, Marguérite-Louise Charpentier died in 1904, and no one living today would be able to identify her based on the likeness Renoir presumably gave to her face in this family portrait commissioned by her husband, wealthy and influential publisher George Charpentier. We need the painting's title to make that identification. And Mme. Charpentier is outfitted here in a gown created by English designer Charles Frederick Worth, the dominant figure in late nineteenth-century Parisian high fashion. Her clothing was a clear attribute of her wealth for those who recognized its source; most of us need to investigate to uncover its meaning. But a greater surprise awaits the student who pursues further research on her children. Although they clearly seem to our eyes to represent two daughters, the child closest to Mme. Charpentier is actually her son Paul, who at age three, following standard Parisian bourgeois practice, has not yet had his first hair cut and still wears clothing comparable to that of his older sister Georgette, perched on the family dog. It is not unusual in art history to encounter situations where our initial conclusions on the level of natural subject matter will need to be revised after some iconographic research.

INTEGRATION WITHIN CULTURAL CONTEXT

Natural subject matter and iconography were only two of three steps proposed by Panofsky for coming to an understanding of the meaning of works of art. The third step he labeled "**iconology**," and its aim is to interpret the work of art as an embodiment of its cultural situation, to place it within broad social, political, religious, and intellectual contexts. Such integration into history requires more than identifying subject matter or conventional symbols; it requires a deep understanding of the beliefs and principles or goals and values that underlie a work of art's cultural situation as well as the position of an artist and patron within it.

In "A Closer Look" (opposite), the subject matter of two **still life** paintings (pictures of inanimate objects and fruits or flowers taken out of their natural contexts) is identified and elucidated, but to truly understand these two works as bearers of cultural meaning, more knowledge of the broader context and specific goals of artists and audiences is required. For example, the fact that Zhu Da (1626–1705) became a painter was rooted more in the political than the artistic history of China at the middle of the seventeenth century. As a member of the imperial family of the Ming dynasty, his life of privilege was disrupted when the Ming were overthrown during the Manchu conquest of China in 1644. Fleeing for his life, he sought refuge in a Buddhist monastery, where he wrote poetry and painted. Almost 40 years later, in the aftermath of a nervous breakdown (that could have been staged to avoid retribution for his family background), Zhu Da abandoned his monastic life and developed a career as a professional painter, adopting a series of descriptive pseudonyms—most notably Bada Shanren ("mountain man of eight greatnesses") by which he is most often known today. His paintings are at times saturated with veiled political commentary; at times they seek to accommodate the expectations of collectors to assure their marketability; and in paintings like the one illustrated here (see page xxxiv, FIG. B), the artist seems to hark back to the contemplative, abstract, and spontaneous paintings associated with great Zen masters such as Muqi (c. 1201–after 1269), whose calligraphic pictures of isolated fruits seem almost like acts of devotion or detached contemplations on natural forms, rather than the works of a professional painter.

Clara Peeters's still life (see page xxxiv, FIG. A), on the other hand, fits into a developing Northern European painting tradition within which she was an established and successful professional, specializing in portrayals of food and flowers, fruit and reflective objects. Still-life paintings in this tradition could be jubilant celebrations of the abundance of the natural world and the wealth of luxury objects available in the prosperous mercantile society of the Netherlands. Or they could be moralizing "*vanitas*" paintings, warning of the ephemeral meaning of those worldly possessions, even of life itself. But this painting has also been interpreted in a more personal way. Because the type of knife that sits in the foreground near the edge of the table was a popular wedding gift, and since it is inscribed with the artist's own name, some have suggested that this still life could have celebrated Peeters's marriage. Or it could simply be a witty way to sign her picture. It certainly could be both personal and participate in the broader cultural meaning of still-life paintings at the same time. Mixtures of private and public meanings have been proposed for Zhu Da's paintings as well. The picture of quince illustrated here (see page xxxiv, FIG. B) has been seen as one in a series of allegorical "self-portraits" that extend across his career as a painter. Art historians frequently reveal multiple meanings when interpreting single works of art. They usually represent complex cultural and personal situations.

A CASE STUDY: ROGIER VAN DER WEYDEN'S PHILADELPHIA CRUCIFIXION

The basic, four-part method of art historical investigation and interpretation just outlined and explored, becomes clearer when its extended use is traced in relation to one specific work of art. A particularly revealing subject for such a case study is a seminal and somewhat perplexing painting now in the Philadelphia Museum of Art—the **CRUCIFIXION WITH THE VIRGIN AND ST. JOHN THE EVANGELIST (FIG. INTRO–5)** by Rogier van der Weyden (c. 1400–1464), a Flemish artist who will be featured in Chapter 18. Each of the four levels of art historical inquiry reveals important information about this painting, information that has been used by art historians to reconstruct its relationship to its artist, its audience, and its broader cultural setting. The resulting interpretation is rich, but also complex. An investigation this extensive will not be possible for all the works of art in the following chapters, where the text will focus only on one or two facets of more expansive research. Because of the amount and complexity of information involved in a thorough art-historical interpretation, it is sometimes only in a second reading that we can follow the subtleties of its argument, after the first reading has provided a basic familiarity with the work of art, its conventional subjects, and its general context.

PHYSICAL PROPERTIES

Perhaps the most striking aspect of this painting's physical appearance is its division into two separate tall rectangular panels, joined by a frame to form a coherent, almost square composition. These are oak panels, prepared with chalk to form a smooth surface on which to paint with mineral pigments suspended in oil. A technical investigation of the painting in 1981 used infra-red reflectography to reveal a very sketchy underdrawing beneath the surface of the paint, proving to the investigators that this painting is almost entirely the work of Rogier van der Weyden himself. Famous and prosperous artists of this time and place employed many assistants to work in large production workshops, and they would render detailed underdrawings to assure that assistants replicated the style of the master. But in cases where the masters themselves intended to execute the work, only summary compositional outlines were needed. This modern technical investigation of Rogier's painting also used **dendrochronology** (the dating of wood based on the patterns of the growth rings) to date the oak panels and consequently the painting itself, now securely situated near the end of the artist's career, c. 1460.

The most recent restoration of the painting—during the early 1990s by Mark Tucker, Senior Conservator at the Philadelphia Museum of Art—returned it, as close as possible, to current views of its original fifteenth-century appearance (see "Recovering the Past," page xxxviii). This project included extensive technical analysis of almost every aspect of the picture, during which a critical clue emerged, one that may lead to a sharper understanding of its original use. X-rays revealed dowel holes and plugs running in a horizontal line about one-fourth of the way up from the bottom across the entire expanse of the two-panel painting. Tucker's convincing research suggests that the dowels would have attached these two panels to the backs of wooden boxes that contained sculptures in a complex work of art that hung over the altar in a fifteenth-century church.

FORMAL STRUCTURE

The visual organization of this two-part painting emphasizes both connection and separation. It is at the same time one painting and two. Continuing across both panels is the strip of midnight blue sky and the stone wall that constricts space within the picture to a shallow corridor, pushing the figures into the foreground and close

INTRO-5 • Rogier van der Weyden CRUCIFIXION WITH THE VIRGIN AND ST. JOHN THE EVANGELIST
c. 1460. Oil on oak panels, 71 × 73" (1.8 × 1.85 m). John G. Johnson Collection, Philadelphia Museum of Art.

to the viewer. The platform of mossy ground under the two-figure group in the left panel continues its sloping descent into the right panel, as does the hem of the Virgin's ice-blue garment. We look into this scene as if through a window with a mullion down the middle and assume that the world on the left continues behind this central strip of frame into the right side.

On the other hand, strong visual forces isolate the figures within their respective panels, setting up a system of "compare and contrast" that seems to be at the heart of the painting's design. The striking red cloths that hang over the wall are centered directly behind the figures on each side, forming internal frames that

highlight them as separate groups and focus our attention back and forth between them rather than on the pictorial elements that unite their environments. As we begin to compare the two sides, it becomes increasingly clear that the relationship between figures and environment is quite distinct on each side of the divide.

The dead figure of Christ on the cross, elevated to the very top of the picture, is strictly centered within his panel, as well as against the cloth that hangs directly behind him. The grid of masonry blocks and creases in the cloth emphasizes his rectilinear integration into a system of balanced, rigid regularity. His head is aligned with the cap of the wall, his flesh largely contained within

Ever since Rogier van der Weyden's strikingly asymmetrical, two-panel rendering of the *Crucifixion* (SEE FIG. INTRO–5) was purchased by Philadelphia lawyer John G. Johnson in 1906 for his spectacular collection of European paintings, it has been recognized not only as one of the greatest works by this master of fifteenth-century Flemish painting, but as one of the most important European paintings in North America. Soon after the Johnson Collection became part of the Philadelphia Museum of Art in 1933, however, this painting's visual character was significantly transformed. In 1941 the museum employed freelance restorer David Rosen to work on the painting. Deciding that Rogier's work was seriously marred by later overpainting and disfigured by the discoloration of old varnish, he subjected the painting to a thorough cleaning. He also removed the strip of dark blue paint forming the sky above the wall at the top—identifying it as an 18th-century restoration—and replaced it with gold leaf to conform with remnants of gold in this area that he assessed as surviving fragments of the original background. Rosen's restoration of Rogier's painting was uncritically accepted for almost half a century, and the gold background became a major factor in the interpretations of art historians as distinguished as Irwin Panofsky and Meyer Schapiro.

In 1990, in preparation for a new installation of the work, Rogier's painting received a thorough technical analysis by Mark Tucker, the museum's Senior Conservator. There were two startling discoveries:

- The dark blue strip that had run across the top of the picture before Rosen's intervention was actually original to the painting. Remnants of paint left behind in 1941 proved to be the same azurite blue that also appears in the clothing of the Virgin, and in no instance did the traces of gold discovered in 1941 run under aspects of the original paint surface. Rosen had removed Rogier's original midnight blue sky.

- What Rosen had interpreted as disfiguring varnish streaking the wall and darkening the brilliant cloths of honor hanging over it were actually Rogier's careful painting of lichens and water stains on the stone and his overpainting on the fabric that had originally transformed a vermillion undercoat into deep crimson cloth.

In meticulous work during 1992–1993, Tucker cautiously restored the painting based on the evidence he had uncovered. Neither the lost lichens and water stains nor the toning crimson overpainting of the hangings were replaced, but a coat of blue-black paint was laid over Rosen's gold leaf at the top of the panels, taking care to apply the new layer in such a way that should a later generation decide to return to the gold leaf sky, the midnight tonalities could be easily removed. That seems an unlikely prospect. The painting as exhibited today comes as close as possible to the original appearance of Rogier's *Crucifixion*. At least we think so.

---

the area defined by the cloth. His elbows mark the juncture of the wall with the edge of the hanging, and his feet extend just to the end of the cloth, where his toes substitute for the border of fringe they overlap. The environment is almost as balanced. The strip of dark sky at the top is equivalent in size to the strip of mossy earth at the bottom of the picture, and both are visually bisected by centered horizontals—the cross bar at the top and the alignment of bone and skull at the bottom. A few disruptions to this stable, rectilinear, symmetrical order draw the viewers' attention to the panel at the left: the downward fall of the head of Christ, the visual weight of the skull, the downturn of the fluttering loin cloth, and the tip of the Virgin's gown that transgresses over the barrier to move in from the other side.

John and Mary merge on the left into a single figural mass that could be inscribed into a half-circle. Although set against a rectilinear grid background comparable to that behind Jesus, they contrast with, rather than conform to, the regular sense of order. Their curving outlines offer unsettling unsteadiness, as if they are toppling to the ground, jutting into the other side of the frame. This instability is reinforced by their postures. The projection of Mary's knee in relation to the angle of her torso reveals that she is collapsing into a curve, and the crumpled mass of drapery circling underneath her only underlines her lack of support. John reaches out to catch her, but he has not yet made contact with her body. He strikes a stance of strident instability without even touching the ground, and he looks blankly out into space with an unfocused

expression, distracted from, rather than concentrating on, the task at hand. Perhaps he will come to his senses and grab her. But will he be able to catch her in time, and even then support her given his unstable posture? The moment is tense; the outcome is unclear. But we are moving into the realm of natural subject matter. The poignancy of this concentrated portrayal seems to demand it.

ICONOGRAPHY

The subject of this painting is among the most familiar themes in the history of European art. The dead Jesus has been crucified on the cross, and two of his closest associates—his mother and John, one of his disciples—mourn his loss. Although easily recognizable, the austere and asymmetrical presentation is unexpected. More usual is an earlier painting of this subject by the same artist, **CRUCIFIXION TRIPTYCH WITH DONORS AND SAINTS (FIG. INTRO–6)**, where he situates the crucified Christ at the center of a symmetrical arrangement, the undisputed axial focus of the composition. The scene unfolds here within an expansive landscape, populated with a wider cast of participants, each of whom takes a place with symmetrical decorum on either side of the cross. Because most crucifixions follow some variation on this pattern, Rogier's two-panel portrayal (SEE FIG. INTRO-5) in which the cross is asymmetrically displaced to one side, with a spare cast of attendants relegated to a separately framed space, severely restricted by a stark stone wall, requires some explanation. As does the mysterious dark world beyond the wall, and the artificial backdrop of the textile hangings.

INTRO–6 • Rogier van der Weyden CRUCIFIXION TRIPTYCH WITH DONORS AND SAINTS
c. 1440. Oil on wooden panels, 39¾ × 55″ (101 × 140 cm). Kunsthistorisches Museum, Vienna.

This scene is not only austere and subdued; it is sharply focused, and the focus relates it to the specific moment in the story that Rogier decided to represent. The Christian Bible contains four accounts of Jesus' crucifixion, one in each of the four Gospels. Rogier took two verses in John's account as his painting's text (John 19:26–27), cited here in the Douay-Rheims literal English translation of the Latin Vulgate Bible used by Western European Christians during the fifteenth century:

> When Jesus therefore had seen his mother and the disciple standing whom he loved, he saith to his mother: Woman, behold thy son. After that, he saith to the disciple: Behold thy mother. And from that hour, the disciple took her to his own.

Even the textual source uses conventions that need explanation, specifically the way the disciple John is consistently referred to in this Gospel as "the disciple whom Jesus loved." Rogier's painting, therefore, seems to focus on Jesus' call for a newly expanded relationship between his mother and a beloved follower. More specifically, he has projected us slightly forward in time to the moment when John needs to respond to that call—Jesus has died; John is now in charge.

There are, however, other conventional iconographic associations with the crucifixion that Rogier has folded into this spare portrayal. Fifteenth-century viewers would have understood the skull and femur that lie on the mound at the base of the cross as

the bones of Adam—the first man in the Hebrew Bible account of creation—on whose grave Jesus' crucifixion was believed to have taken place. This juxtaposition embodied the Christian belief that Christ's sacrifice on the cross redeemed believers from the death that Adam's original sin had brought to human existence.

Mary's swoon and presumed loss of consciousness would have evoked another theological idea, the *co-passio*, in which Mary's anguish while witnessing Jesus' suffering and death was seen as a parallel passion of mother with son, both critical for human salvation. Their connection in this painting is underlined visually by the similar bending of their knees, inclination of their heads, and closing of their eyes. They even seem to resemble each other in facial likeness, especially when compared to John.

CULTURAL CONTEXT

In 1981 art historian Penny Howell Jolly published an interpretation of Rogier's Philadelphia *Crucifixion* as a product of a broad personal and cultural context. In addition to building on the work of earlier art historians, she pursued two productive lines of investigation to explain the rationale for this unusually austere presentation:

- the prospect that Rogier was influenced by the work of another artist, and
- the possibility that the painting was produced for an institutional context that called for a special mode of visual presentation and a particular iconographic focus.

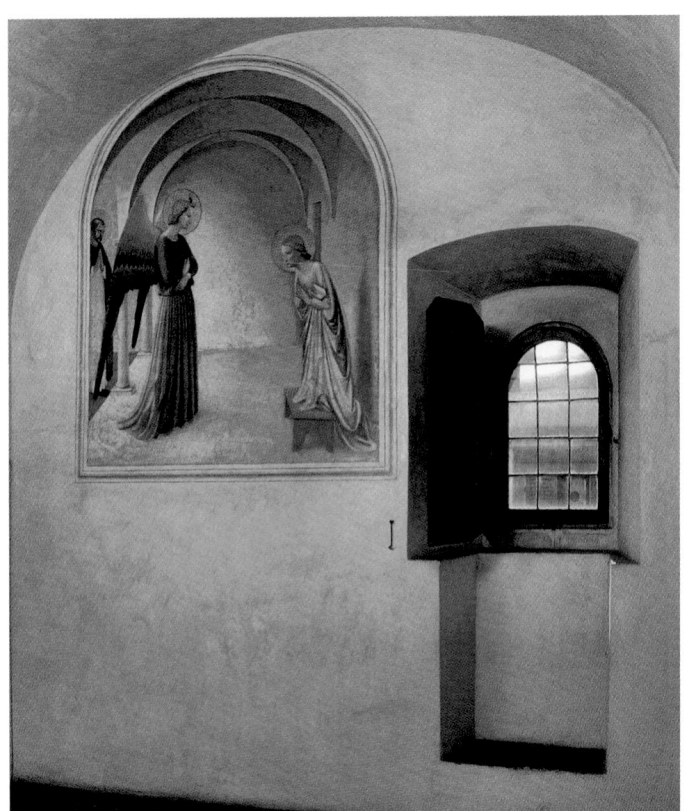

INTRO-7 • VIEW OF A MONK'S CELL IN THE MONASTERY OF SAN MARCO, FLORENCE
Including Fra Angelico's fresco of the *Annunciation*, c. 1438–1445.

FRA ANGELICO AT SAN MARCO. We know very little about the life of Rogier van der Weyden, but we do know that in 1450, when he was already established as one of the principal painters in northern Europe, he made a pilgrimage to Rome. Either on his way to Rome, or during his return journey home, he stopped off in Florence and saw the altarpiece, and presumably also the frescos, that Fra Angelico (c. 1400–1455) and his workshop had painted during the 1440s at the monastery of San Marco. The evidence of Rogier's contact with Fra Angelico's work is found in a work Rogier painted after he returned home, based on a panel of the San Marco altarpiece. For the Philadelphia *Crucifixion*, however, it was Fra Angelico's devotional frescos on the walls of the monks' individual rooms (or cells) that seem to have had the greatest impact (**FIG. INTRO–7**). Jolly compared the Philadelphia *Crucifixion* with a scene of

INTRO-8 • Fra Angelico MAN OF SORROWS FRESCO IN CELL 7
c. 1441–1445. Monastery of San Marco, Florence.

the Man of Sorrows at San Marco to demonstrate the connection (**FIG. INTRO–8**). Fra Angelico presented the sacred figures with a quiet austerity that recalls Rogier's unusual composition. More specific parallels are the use of an expansive stone wall to restrict narrative space to a shallow foreground corridor, the description of the world beyond that wall as a dark sky that contrasts with the brilliantly illuminated foreground, and the use of a draped cloth of honor to draw attention to a narrative vignette from the life of Jesus, to separate it out as an object of devotion.

THE CARTHUSIANS. Having established a possible connection between Rogier's unusual late painting of the crucifixion and frescos by Fra Angelico that he likely saw during his pilgrimage to Rome in 1450, Jolly reconstructed a specific context of patronage and meaning within Rogier's own world in Flanders that could explain why the paintings of Fra Angelico would have had such an impact on him at this particular moment in his career.

During the years around 1450, Rogier developed a personal and profession relationship with the monastic order of the Carthusians, and especially with the Belgian Charterhouse (or Carthusian monastery) of Hérrines, where his only son was invested as a monk in 1450. Rogier gave money to Hérrines, and a poignant moment in the life of St. John (**FIG INTRO-9**) could have been especially meaningful to the artist himself at the time this work was painted?

A CONTINUING PROJECT. The final word has not been spoken in the interpretation of this painting. Mark Tucker's recent work on the physical evidence revealed by x-ray analysis points toward seeing these two panels as part of a large sculptured altarpiece. Even if this did preclude the prospect that it is the panel painting Rogier donated to the chapel of St. Catherine at Hérinnes, it does not negate the relationship Jolly drew with Fra Angelico, nor the Carthusian context she outlined for the work's original situation. It simply reminds us that our historical understanding of works such as this will evolve when new evidence about them emerges.

As the history of art unfolds in the ensuing chapters of this book, it will be important to keep two things in mind as you read the characterizations of individual works of art and the larger story of their integration into the broader cultural contexts of those who made them and those for whom they were initially made. Art-historical interpretations are built on extended research comparable to that we have just summarily surveyed for Rogier van der Weyden's Philadelphia *Crucifixion*. But the work of interpretation is never complete. Art history is a continuing project, a work perpetually in progress.

texts document his donation of a painting to its chapel of Saint Catherine. Jolly suggested that the Philadelphia *Crucifixion* could be that painting. Its subdued colors and narrative austerity are consistent with Carthusian aesthetic attitudes, and the walled setting of the scene recalls the enclosed gardens that were attached to the individual dormitory rooms of Carthusian monks. The reference in this painting to the *co-passio* of the Virgin provides supporting evidence since this theological idea was central to Carthusian thought and devotion. The *co-passio* was even reflected in the monks' own initiation rites, during which they reenacted and sought identification with both Christ's sacrifice on the cross and the Virgin's parallel suffering.

In Jolly's interpretation, the religious framework of a Carthusian setting for the painting emerges as a personal framework for the artist himself, since this *Crucifixion* seems to be associated with important moments in his own life—his religious pilgrimage to Rome in 1450 and the initiation of his only son as a Carthusian monk at about the same time. Is it possible that the sense of loss and separation that Rogier evoked in his portrayal of

THINK ABOUT IT

I.1 How would you define a work of art?

I.2 What are the four separate steps proposed here for characterizing the methods used by art historians to interpret works of art?

I.3 Choose a painting illustrated in this chapter and analyze its composition.

I.4 Characterize the difference between natural subject matter and iconography, focusing your discussion on one work discussed in this chapter.

I.5 What aspect of the case study of Rogier van der Weyden's Philadelphia *Crucifixion* was especially interesting to you? Explain why. How did it broaden your understanding of what you will learn in this course?

PRACTICE MORE: Compose answers to these questions, get flashcards for images and terms, and review chapter material with quizzes
www.myartslab.com

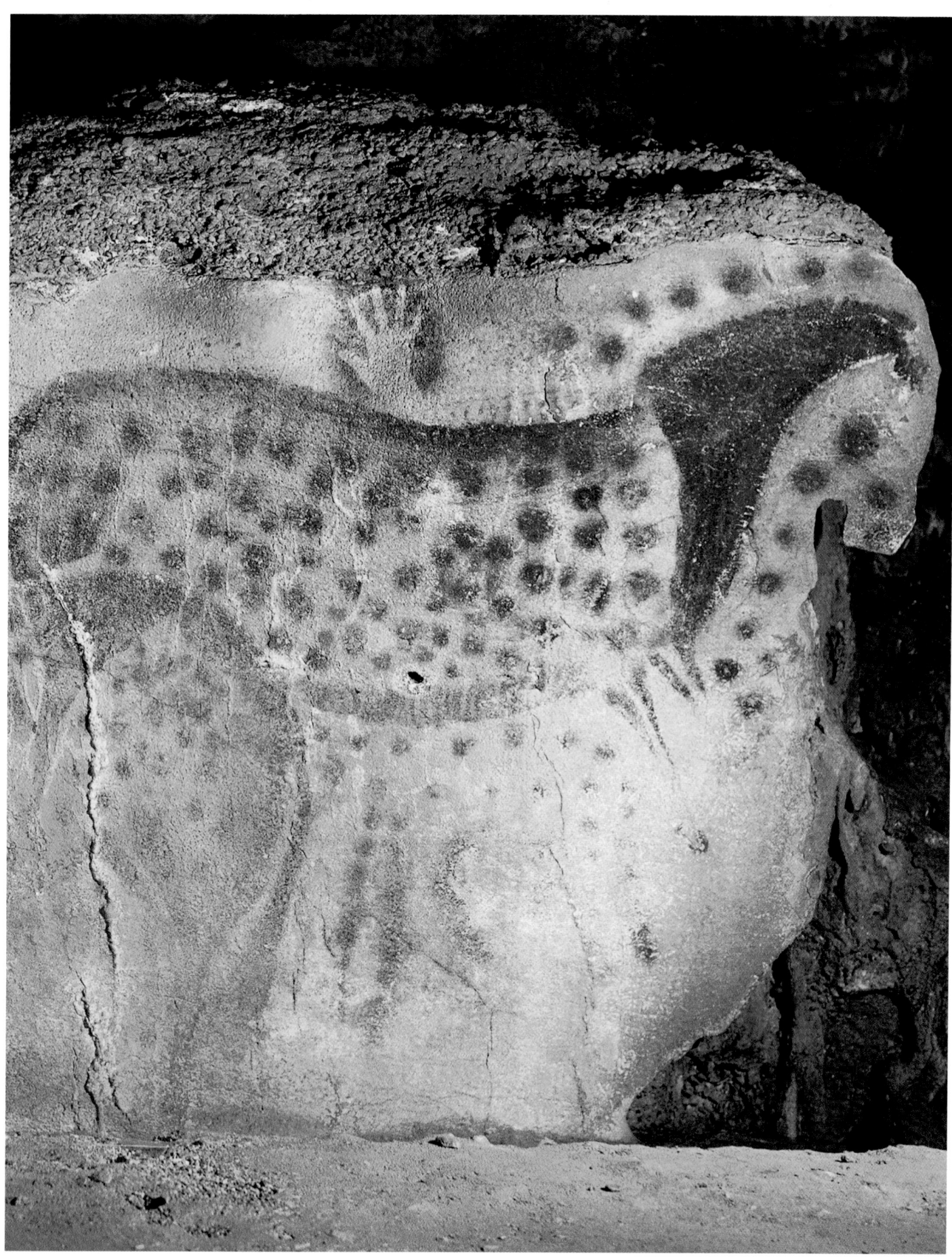

1-1 • SPOTTED HORSES AND HUMAN HANDS Pech-Merle Cave. Dordogne, France.
Horses 25,000–24,000 BCE; hands c. 15,000 BCE. Paint on limestone, individual horses over 5′ (1.5 m) in length.

PREHISTORIC ART

Two horses are positioned back to back on the wall of a chamber within the Pech-Merle Cave, located in France's Dordogne region; one of the horses is shown in the detail at left (FIG. 1–1). The head of the horse follows the natural shape of the rock. Black dots surround areas of both horses and cover their bodies. At a later date, a large fish (58 inches long and almost impossible to see) was painted in red on top of them. Yet the painters left more than images of animals, fish, and geometric shapes; they left their own handprints in various places around the animals. These images, and many others hidden in chambers at the ends of long, narrow passages within the cave, connect us to an almost unimaginably ancient world of 25,000 BCE.

Prehistory includes all of human existence before the emergence of writing, though long before that defining moment people were carving objects, painting images, and creating shelters and other structures. Thirty thousand years ago our ancestors were not making "works of art" and there were no "artists" as we understand the term today. They were flaking, chipping, and polishing flints into spear points, knives, and scrapers, not into sculptures, however pleasing these artifacts are to the eye and to the touch. Wall paintings, too, must have seemed vitally important to their makers in terms of everyday survival.

For art historians, archaeologists, and anthropologists, prehistoric art provides a significant clue—along with fossils, pollen, and artifacts—to understanding early human life and culture. Although specialists continue to discover more about when and how these works were created, they may never be able to tell us why they were made. In fact, there may be no single meaning or use for any one image on a cave wall; cave art probably meant different things to the different people who saw it, depending on their age, experience, and specific needs and desires. The sculpture, paintings, and structures that survive are only a tiny fraction of what must have been created over a very long time span. The conclusions and interpretations drawn from them are only hypotheses, making prehistoric art one of the most speculative, but exciting, areas of art history.

LEARN ABOUT IT

1.1   Examine the origins of art in the prehistoric past.

1.2   Discover the location and motifs of Paleolithic cave art and assess the range of scholarly interpretations for them.

1.3   Investigate the early use of architecture in domestic and sacred contexts, including megalithic monuments such as Stonehenge.

1.4   Explore the use and meaning of human figurines in the Paleolithic and Neolithic periods.

1.5   Trace the emergence of pottery making and metalworking and examine the earliest works made of fired clay and hammered gold.

HEAR MORE: Listen to an audio file of your chapter **www.myartslab.com**

THE STONE AGE

How and when modern humans evolved is the subject of ongoing debate, but anthropologists now agree that the species called *homo sapiens* appeared about 400,000 years ago, and that the subspecies to which we belong, *homo sapiens sapiens* (usually referred to as modern humans), evolved as early as 120,000 years ago. Based on archaeological evidence, it is now clear that modern humans spread from Africa across Asia, into Europe, and finally to Australia and the Americas. This vast movement of people took place between 100,000 and 35,000 years ago.

Scholars began the systematic study of prehistory only about 200 years ago. Nineteenth-century archaeologists, struck by the wealth of stone tools, weapons, and figures found at ancient sites, named the whole period of early human development the Stone Age. Today, researchers divide the Stone Age into the Paleolithic (from the Greek *paleo-*, "old," and *lithos*, "stone") and the Neolithic (from the Greek *neo-*, "new") periods. The Paleolithic period is divided into three phases reflecting the relative position of objects found in the layers of excavation: Lower (the oldest), Middle, and Upper (the most recent). In some places archaeologists can identify a transitional, or Mesolithic (from the Greek *meso-*, "middle") period.

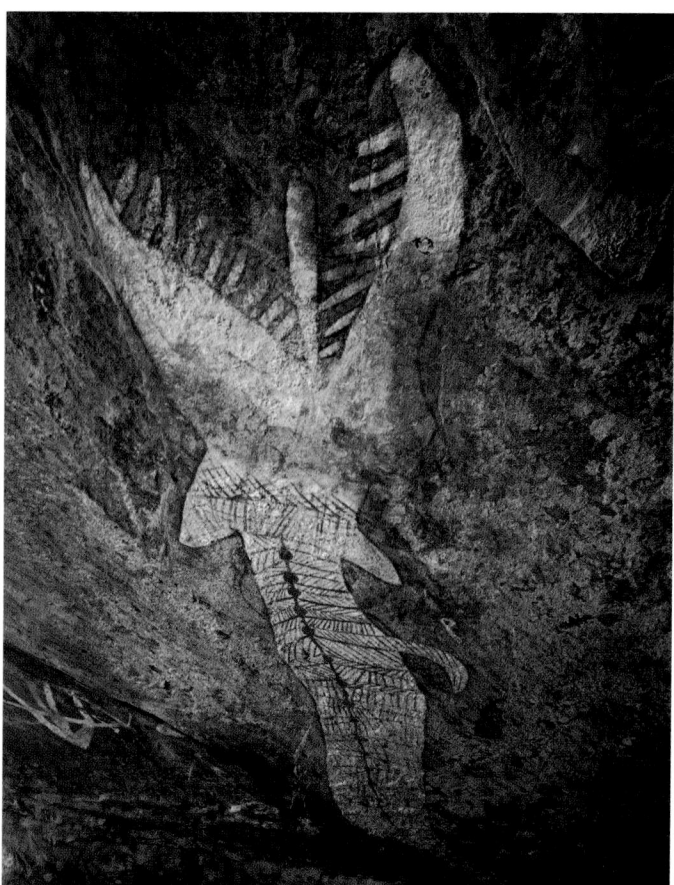

1-2 • RAINBOW SERPENT ROCK
Western Arnhem Land, Australia. Appearing in Australia as early as 6000 BCE, images of the Rainbow Serpent play a role in rituals and legends of the creation of human beings, the generation of rains, storms, and floods, and the reproductive power of nature and people.

The dates for the transition from Paleolithic to Neolithic vary with geography and with local environmental and social circumstances. For some of the places discussed in this chapter, such as Western Europe, the Neolithic way of living did not emerge until 3000 BCE; in others, such as the Near East, it appeared as early as 8000 BCE. Archaeologists mark time in so many years ago, or BP ("before present"). However, to ensure consistent style throughout the book, which reflects the usage of art historians, this chapter uses BCE (before the Common Era) and CE (the Common Era) to mark time.

Much is yet to be discovered about prehistoric art. In Australia, some of the world's very oldest images have been dated to between 50,000 and 40,000 years ago, and the tradition of transient communities who marked the land in complex, yet stunningly beautiful ways continues into historical time. In western Arnhem land **(FIG. 1–2)**, rock art images of the Rainbow Serpent have their origins in prehistory, and were perhaps first created during times of substantial changes in the environment. Africa, as well, is home to ancient rock art in both its northern and southern regions. In all cases, archaeologists associate the arrival of modern humans in these regions with the advent of image making.

Indeed, it is the cognitive capability to create and recognize symbols and imagery that sets us as modern humans apart from all of our predecessors and from all of our contemporary animal relatives. We are defined as a species by our abilities to make and understand art. This chapter focuses primarily on the rich traditions of prehistoric European art from the Paleolithic and Neolithic periods and into the Bronze Age **(MAP 1–1)**. Later chapters consider the prehistoric art of other continents and cultures, such as the Americas (Chapter 12), and sub-Saharan Africa (Chapter 13).

THE PALEOLITHIC PERIOD

Researchers found that human beings made tools long before they made what today we call "art." Art, in the sense of image making, is the hallmark of the Upper Paleolithic period and the emergence of our subspecies, *homo sapiens sapiens*. Representational images are seen in the archaeological record beginning about 38,000 BCE in Australia, Africa, and Europe. Before that time, during the Lower Paleolithic period in Africa, early humans made tools by flaking and chipping (knapping) flint pebbles into blades and scrapers with sharp edges. Dating to 2.5 million years ago, the earliest objects made by our human ancestors were simple stone tools, some with sharp edges, that were used to cut animal skin and meat and bash open bones to access marrow, and also to cut wood and soft plant materials. These first tools have been found at sites such as Olduvai Gorge in Tanzania. Although not art, they are important as they document a critical development in our evolution: humans' ability to transform the world around them into specific tools and objects that could be used to complete a task.

MAP 1–1 • PREHISTORIC EUROPE

As the Ice Age glaciers receded, Paleolithic, Neolithic, Bronze Age, and Iron Age settlements increased from south to north.

By 1.65 million years ago, significant changes in our ancestors' cognitive abilities and manual dexterity can be seen in sophisticated stone tools, such as the teardrop-shaped hand-axes **(FIG. 1–3)** that have been found at sites across Eurasia. These extraordinary objects, symmetrical in form and produced by a complex multistep process, were long thought of as nothing more than tools (or perhaps even as weapons), but the most recent analysis suggests that they had a social function as well. Some sites (as at Olorgesailie in Kenya) contain hundreds of hand-axes, far more than would have been needed in functional terms, suggesting that they served to announce an individual's skills, status, and standing in his or her community. Although these ancient hand-axes are clearly not art in the representational sense, it is important to see them in terms of performance and process, concepts that though central to modern Western art also have deep prehistoric roots.

Evolutionary changes took place over time and by 400,000 years ago, during the late Middle Paleolithic period, a *homo sapiens* subspecies called Neanderthal inhabited Europe. Its members used a wider range of stone tools and may have carefully buried their dead with funerary offerings. Neanderthals survived for thousands of years and overlapped with modern humans, though the two groups did not interbreed. *Homo sapiens sapiens*, who had evolved and spread out of Africa some 300,000 years after the Neanderthals, eventually replaced them, probably between 38,000 and 33,000 BCE.

The critical abilities that set modern humans apart from all of their predecessors were cognitive ones; indeed the fact that *homo sapiens sapiens*, as a species, outlasted Neanderthals was because they had the mental capacity to solve problems of human survival. The new cognitive abilities included improvements in recognizing and benefiting from variations in the natural environment, and in managing social networking and alliance making (skills that enabled organized hunting). The most important new ability, however, was the capacity to think symbolically: to create

1-3 • PALEOLITHIC HAND-AXE
From Isimila Korongo, Tanzania. 60,000 years ago. Stone, height 10″ (25.4 cm).

representational analogies between one person, animal, or object, and another, and to recognize and remember those analogies. This cognitive development marks the evolutionary origin of art.

The world's earliest pieces of art come from South Africa: two 77,000-year-old, engraved blocks of red ocher (probably used as crayons) found in the Blombos Cave (**FIG. 1–4**). Both the blocks are engraved in an identical way with cross-hatched lines on their sides. Archaeologists argue that the similarity of the engraved patterns means these two pieces were intentionally made and decorated following a common pattern. Thousands of fragments of ocher have been discovered at Blombos and there is little doubt that people were using it to draw patterns and images, the remains of which have long since disappeared. Although it is impossible to prove, it is highly likely that the ocher was used to decorate peoples' bodies as well as to color objects such as tools or shell ornaments. Indeed, in an earlier layer on the same site, archaeologists uncovered more than 36 shells, each of which had been perforated so that it could be hung from a string or thong, or attached to clothing or a person's hair; these shells would have been used to decorate the body. An ostrich eggshell bead came from the same site and would have served the same purpose. The importance of the Blombos finds cannot be overstated: Here we have our early ancestors, probably modern humans but possibly even their predecessors, using the earth's raw materials to decorate themselves with jewelry (with the shells) and body art (with the ocher).

SHELTER OR ARCHITECTURE?

The term architecture has been applied to the enclosure of spaces with at least some aesthetic intent. Some people object to its use in connection with prehistoric improvisations, but building even a simple shelter requires a degree of imagination and planning deserving of the name "architecture." In the Upper Paleolithic period, humans in some regions used great ingenuity to build shelters that were far from simple. In woodlands, evidence of floors indicates that circular or oval huts of light branches and hides were built. These measured as much as 15–20 feet in diameter. (Modern tents to accommodate six people vary from 10- by 11-foot ovals to 14- by 7-foot rooms.)

In the treeless grasslands of Upper Paleolithic Russia and Ukraine, builders created settlements of up to ten houses using the bones of the now extinct woolly mammoth, whose long, curving tusks made excellent roof supports and arched door openings (**FIG. 1–5**). This bone framework was probably covered with animal hides and turf. Most activities centered around the inside fire pit, or hearth, where food was prepared and tools were fashioned. Larger houses might have had more than one hearth and spaces were set aside for

1-4 • DECORATED OCHER
From Blombos Cave. Southern Cape coast, South Africa. 77,000 years ago.

1-5 • RECONSTRUCTION DRAWING OF MAMMOTH-BONE HOUSES
Ukraine. c. 16,000–10,000 BCE.

specific uses—working stone, making clothing, sleeping, and dumping refuse. Inside the largest dwelling on a site in Mezhirich, Ukraine, archaeologists found 15 small hearths that still contained ashes and charred bones left by the last occupants. Some people also colored their floors with powdered ocher in shades that ranged from yellow to red to brown. These Upper Paleolithic structures are important because of their early date: The widespread appearance of durable architecture concentrated in village communities did not occur until the beginning of the Neolithic period in the Near East and southeastern Europe.

ARTIFACTS OR WORKS OF ART?

As early as 30,000 BCE small figures, or figurines, of people and animals made of bone, ivory, stone, and clay appeared in Europe and Asia. Today we interpret such self-contained, three-dimensional pieces as examples of **sculpture in the round**. Prehistoric carvers also produced relief sculpture in stone, bone, and ivory. In **relief sculpture**, the surrounding material is carved away, forming a background that sets off the projecting figure.

THE LION-HUMAN.   An early and puzzling example of a sculpture in the round is a human figure—probably male—with a feline head **(FIG. 1–6)**, made about 30,000–26,000 BCE. Archaeologists excavating at Hohlenstein-Stadel, Germany, found broken pieces of ivory (from a mammoth tusk) that they realized were parts of an entire figure. Nearly a foot tall, this remarkable statue surpasses most early figurines in size and complexity. Instead of copying what he or she saw in nature, the carver created a unique creature, part human and part beast. Was the figure intended to represent a person wearing a ritual lion mask? Or has the man taken on the

1-6 • LION-HUMAN
From Hohlenstein-Stadel, Germany. c. 30,000–26,000 BCE. Mammoth ivory, height 11⅝″ (29.6 cm). Ulmer Museum, Ulm, Germany.

The Power of Naming

Words are only symbols for ideas, and it is no coincidence that the origins of language and of art are often linked in our evolutionary development. But the very words we invent—or our ancestors invented—reveal a certain view of the world and can shape our thinking. Today, we exert the power of naming when we select a name for a baby or call a friend by a nickname. Our ideas about art can also be affected by names, even the ones used for captions in a book. Before the twentieth century, artists usually did not name, or title, their works. Names were eventually supplied by the works' owners or by art historians writing about them, and thus often express the cultural prejudices of the labelers or of the times in which they lived.

An excellent example of such distortion is the names given to the hundreds of small prehistoric statues of women that have been found. Earlier scholars called them by the Roman name Venus. For example,

the sculpture in FIGURE 1–7 was once called the *Venus of Willendorf* after the place where it was found. Using the name of the Roman goddess of love and beauty sent a message that this figure was associated with religious belief, that it represented an ideal of womanhood, and that it was one of a long line of images of "classical" feminine beauty. In a short time, most similar works of sculpture from the Upper Paleolithic period came to be known as Venus figures. The name was repeated so often that even experts began to assume that the statues had to be fertility figures and Mother Goddesses, although there is no proof that this was so.

Our ability to understand and interpret works of art creatively is easily compromised by distracting labels. Calling a prehistoric figure a woman instead of Venus encourages us to think about the sculpture in new and different ways.

1-7 • WOMAN FROM WILLENDORF
From Austria. c. 24,000 BCE. Limestone, height 4⅜″ (11 cm).
Naturhistorisches Museum, Vienna.

appearance of an animal? Archaeologists now think that the people who lived at this time held very different ideas (from our twenty-first-century ones) about what it meant to be a human and how humans were distinct from animals; it is quite possible that they thought of animals and humans as parts of one common group of beings who shared the world. What is absolutely clear is that the Lion-Human shows highly complex thinking and creative imagination: the uniquely human ability to conceive and represent a creature never seen in nature.

FEMALE FIGURES. While a number of figurines representing men have been found recently, most human figures from the Upper Paleolithic period are female. The most famous of these, the **WOMAN FROM WILLENDORF (FIG. 1–7)**, from Austria, dates from about 24,000 BCE (see "The Power of Naming," above). Carved from limestone and originally colored with red ocher, the statuette's swelling, rounded forms make it seem much larger than its actual 4⅜-inch height. The sculptor exaggerated the figure's female attributes by giving it pendulous breasts, a big belly with a deep navel (a natural indentation in the stone), wide hips, dimpled knees and buttocks, and solid thighs. By carving a woman with a well-nourished body, the artist may have been expressing health and fertility, which could ensure the ability to produce strong children, thus guaranteeing the survival of the clan.

The most recent analysis of the Paleolithic female sculptures has replaced the traditional fertility interpretation with more nuanced understandings of how and why the human figure is represented in this way, and who may have had these kinds of objects made. According to archaeologist Clive Gamble, these little sculptures were subtle forms of nonverbal communication among

1-8 • WOMAN FROM DOLNÍ VEŠTONICE
From Moravia, Czech Republic. 23,000 BCE. Fired clay, 4¼ × 1⁷⁄₁₀"
(11 × 4.3 cm). Moravske Museum, Brno, Czech Republic.

these objects further still. The site of Dolní Veštonice is important because it marks a very early date (23,000 BCE) for humans to use fire to make durable objects out of mixtures of water and soil. What makes the figures from this site and those from other sites in the region (Pavlov and Předmosti) unusual is their method of manufacture. By mixing the soil with water—to a very particular recipe—and then placing the wet figures in a hot kiln to bake, the makers were not intending to create durable, well-fired statues. On the contrary, the recipe used and the firing procedure followed tell us that the intention was to make the figures explode in the kilns before the firing process was complete, and before a "successful" figure could be produced. Indeed, the finds at these sites support this interpretation: There are very few complete figures, but numerous fragments that bear the traces of explosions at high temperatures. The Dolní Veštonice fragments are records of performance and process art in their rawest and earliest forms.

Another remarkable female image, discovered in the Grotte du Pape in Brassempouy, France, is the tiny ivory head known as the **WOMAN FROM BRASSEMPOUY (FIG. 1–9)**. Though the finders did not record its archaeological context, recent studies prove it to

small isolated groups of Paleolithic people spread out across vast regions. Gamble noted the tremendous (and unusual) similarity in the shapes of figures, even those found in widely distant parts of Europe. He suggested that when groups of Paleolithic hunter-gatherers did occasionally meet up and interact, the female statues may have been among several signature objects that signaled whether a group was friendly and acceptable for interaction and, probably, for mating. As symbols, these figures would have provided reassurance of shared values about the body, and their size would have demanded engagement at a close personal level. It is not a coincidence, then, that the largest production of these types of Paleolithic figurine occurred during a period when climatic conditions were at their worst and the need for interaction and alliance building would have been at its greatest.

More provocative is art historian Leroy McDermott's suggestion that the body-shape of the female figures tell us a great deal about who made them. Noticing the bulbous shape of the figures and the fact that many do not have clearly defined feet, McDermott argued that the perspective was that of a pregnant woman looking down at her own body. McDermott 's theory that the figures were sculpted by pregnant women and were depictions of their own bodies offers an intriguing vision of women as artists, in control of how they were represented.

Another figure, found in the Czech Republic, the **WOMAN FROM DOLNÍ VEŠTONICE (FIG. 1–8)**, takes our understanding of

1-9 • WOMAN FROM BRASSEMPOUY
From Grotte du Pape, Brassempouy, Landes, France. Probably c. 30,000 BCE. Ivory, height 1¼" (3.6 cm). Musée des Antiquités Nationales, Saint-Germain-en-Laye, France.

be authentic and date it as early as 30,000 BCE. The carver captured the essence of a head, or what psychologists call the **memory image**—those generalized elements that reside in our standard memory of a human head. An egg shape rests atop a long neck, a wide nose and strongly defined browline suggest deep-set eyes, and an engraved square patterning may be hair or a headdress. The image is an abstraction (what has come to be known as **abstract** art): the reduction of shapes and appearances to basic yet recognizable forms that are not intended to be exact replications of nature. The result in this case looks uncannily modern to the contemporary viewer. Today, when such a piece is isolated in a museum case or as a book illustration we enjoy it as an aesthetic object, but we lose its original cultural context.

CAVE PAINTING

Art in Europe entered a rich and sophisticated phase after 30,000 BCE, when images were painted on the walls of caves in central and southern France and northern Spain. No one knew of the existence of prehistoric cave paintings until one day in 1879, when a young girl, exploring with her father in Altamira in northern Spain, crawled through a small opening in the ground and found herself in a chamber whose ceiling was covered with painted animals (SEE FIG. 1–13). Her father, a lawyer and amateur archaeologist, searched the rest of the cave, told authorities about the remarkable find, and published his discovery the following year. Few people believed that these amazing works could have been made by "primitive" people, and the scientific community declared the paintings a hoax. They were accepted as authentic only in 1902, after many other cave paintings, drawings, and engravings had been discovered at other places in northern Spain and in France.

THE MEANING OF CAVE PAINTINGS. What caused people to paint such dramatic imagery on the walls of caves? The idea that human beings have an inherent desire to decorate themselves and their surroundings—that an aesthetic sense is somehow innate to the human species—found ready acceptance in the nineteenth century. Many believed that people create art for the sheer love of beauty. Scientists now agree that human beings have an aesthetic impulse, but the effort required to accomplish the great cave paintings suggests their creators were motivated by more than simple pleasure (see "Prehistoric Wall Painting," page 10). Since the discovery at Altamira, anthropologists and art historians have devised several hypotheses to explain the existence of cave art. Like the search for the meaning of prehistoric female figurines, these explanations depend on the cultural views of those who advance them.

In the early twentieth century it was believed that art has a social function and that aesthetics are culturally relative. It was proposed that the cave paintings might be products both of rites to strengthen clan bonds and of ceremonies to enhance the fertility of animals used for food. In 1903, French archaeologist Salomon Reinach suggested that cave paintings were expressions of sympathetic magic (the idea, for instance, that a picture of a reclining bison would ensure that hunters found their prey asleep). Abbé Henri Breuil took these ideas further and concluded that caves were used as places of worship and were the settings for initiation rites. In the second half of the twentieth century, scholars rejected these ideas and based their interpretations on rigorous scientific methods and current social theory. André Leroi-Gourhan and Annette Laming-Emperaire, for example, dismissed the sympathetic magic theory because statistical analysis of debris from human settlements revealed that the animals used most frequently for food were not the ones traditionally portrayed in caves.

Researchers continue to discover new cave images and to correct earlier errors of fact or interpretation. A study of the Altamira Cave in the 1980s led anthropologist Leslie G. Freeman to conclude that the artists had faithfully represented a herd of bison during the mating season. Instead of being dead, asleep, or disabled—as earlier observers had thought—the animals were dust- wallowing, common behavior during the mating season. Similar thinking has led to a more recent interpretation of cave art by archaeologist Steve Mithen. In his detailed study of the motifs of the art and its placement within caves, Mithen argued that hoofprints, patterns of animal feces, and hide colorings were recorded and used as a text to teach novice hunters within a group about the seasonal appearance and behavior of the animals they hunted. The fact that so much cave art is hidden deep in almost inaccessible parts of caves (indeed, the fact that it is placed within caves at all), suggested to Mithen that this knowledge was intended for a privileged group and that certain individuals or groups were excluded from acquiring that knowledge.

South African rock-art expert David Lewis-Williams suggests a different interpretation. Using a deep comparative knowledge of art made by hunter-gatherer communities that are still in existence, Lewis-Williams has argued that Upper Paleolithic cave art is best understood in terms of shamanism: the belief that certain people (shamans) can travel outside of their bodies in order to mediate between the worlds of the living and the spirits. Traveling under the ground as a spirit, particularly within caves, or conceptually within the stone walls of the cave, Upper Paleolithic shamans would have participated in ceremonies that involved hallucinations. Images conceived during this trancelike state would likely combine recognizable (the animals) and abstract (the non-representational) symbols. In addition, Lewis-Williams interprets the stenciled human handprints found on the cave walls alongside the other marks as traces of the nonshaman participants in the ritual reaching towards and connecting with the shaman spirits traveling within the rock.

Although hypotheses that seek to explain cave art have changed and evolved over time, there has always been agreement that decorated caves must have had a special meaning because people returned to them time after time over many generations, in some cases over thousands of years. Perhaps Upper Paleolithic cave art was the product of rituals intended to gain the favor of the supernatural. Perhaps because much of the art was made deep inside the caves and nearly inaccessible, its significance may have had less to do with the finished painting than with the very act of creation. Artifacts and footprints (such as those found at Chauvet, below, and Le Tuc d'Audoubert, FIG. 1–14) suggest that the subterranean galleries, which were far from living quarters, had a religious or magical function. Perhaps the experience of exploring the cave may have been significant to the image-makers. Musical instruments, such as bone flutes, have been found in the caves, implying that even acoustical properties may have had a role to play.

CHAUVET.   The earliest known site of prehistoric cave paintings, discovered in December 1994, is the Chauvet Cave (called after one of the persons who found it) near Vallon-Pont-d'Arc in southeastern France—a tantalizing trove of hundreds of paintings **(FIG. 1–10)**. The most dramatic of the images depict grazing, running, or resting animals, including wild horses, bison, mammoths, bears, panthers, owls, deer, aurochs, woolly rhinoceroses, and wild goats (or ibex). Also included are occasional humans, both male and female, many handprints, and hundreds of geometric markings such as grids, circles, and dots. Footprints in the Chauvet Cave, left in soft clay by a child, go to a "room" containing bear skulls. The charcoal used to draw the rhinos has been radiocarbon-dated to 32,410 +/− 720 years before the present.

LASCAUX.   The best-known cave paintings are those found in 1940 at Lascaux, in the Dordogne region of southern France **(FIG. 1–11** and SEE FIG. 1–12**)**. They have been dated to about 15,000 BCE. Opened to the public after World War II, the prehistoric "museum" at Lascaux soon became one of the most popular tourist sites in France. Too popular, because the visitors brought heat, humidity, exhaled carbon dioxide, and other contaminants. The cave was closed to the public in 1963 so that conservators could battle an aggressive fungus. Eventually they won, but instead of reopening the site authorities created a facsimile of it. Visitors at what is called Lascaux II may now view copies of the paintings without harming the precious originals.

The scenes they view are truly remarkable. The Lascaux painters depicted cows, bulls, horses, and deer along the natural ledges of the rock, where the smooth white limestone of the ceiling and upper wall meets a rougher surface below. They also utilized the curving wall to suggest space. Lascaux has about 600 paintings and 1,500 engravings. Ibex, a bear, engraved felines, and a woolly rhinoceros have also been found. The animals appear singly, in rows, face to face, tail to tail, and even painted on top of one another. Their most characteristic features have been emphasized. Horns, eyes, and hooves are shown as seen from the front, yet heads and bodies are rendered in profile in a system known as **composite pose**. Even when their poses are exaggerated or

1–10 • WALL PAINTING WITH HORSES, RHINOCEROSES, AND AUROCHS
Chauvet Cave. Vallon-Pont-d'Arc, Ardèche Gorge, France. c. 32,000–30,000 BCE. Paint on limestone.

SEE MORE: View a video about cave painting **www.myartslab.com**

In a dark cave, working by the light of an animal-fat lamp, an artist chews a piece of charcoal to dilute it with saliva and water. Then he blows out the mixture on the surface of a wall, using his hand as a stencil. The drawing demonstrates how cave archaeologist Michel Lorblanchet and his assistant used the step-by-step process of the original makers of a cave painting at Pech-Merle (SEE FIG. 1–1) in France created a complex design of spotted horses.

By turning himself into a human spray can, Lorblanchet can produce clear lines on the rough stone surface much more easily than he could with a brush. To create the line of a horse's back, with its clean upper edge and blurry lower one, he blows pigment below his hand. To capture its angular rump, he places his hand vertically against the wall, holding it slightly curved. To produce the sharpest lines, such as those of the upper hind leg and tail, he places his hands side by side and blows between them. To create the forelegs and the hair on the horses' bellies, he fingerpaints. A hole punched in a piece of leather serves as a stencil for the horses' spots. It takes Lorblanchet only 32 hours to reproduce the Pech-Merle painting of spotted horses, his speed suggesting that a single artist created the

original (perhaps with the help of an assistant to mix pigments and tend the lamp).

Homo sapiens sapiens artists used three painting techniques: the spraying demonstrated by Lorblanchet, drawing with fingers or blocks of ocher, and daubing with a paintbrush made of hair or moss. In some places in prehistoric caves three stages of image creation can be seen: engraved lines using flakes of flint, followed by a color wash of ocher and manganese, and a final engraving to emphasize shapes and details.

distorted, the animals are full of life and energy, and the accuracy in the drawing of their silhouettes, or outlines, is remarkable.

Painters worked not only in large caverns, but also far back in the smallest chambers and recesses, many of which are almost inaccessible today. Small stone lamps found in such caves—over 100 lamps have been found at Lascaux—indicate that the artists worked in flickering light from burning animal fat (SEE FIG. 1–15). (Although 1 pound of fat would burn for 24 hours and produce no

1–11 • HALL OF BULLS
Lascaux Cave. Dordogne, France. c. 15,000 BCE. Paint on limestone, length of largest auroch (bull) 18′ (5.50 m).

1-12 • BIRD-HEADED MAN WITH BISON
Shaft scene in Lascaux Cave. c. 15,000 BCE. Paint on limestone, length approx. 9′ (2.75 m).

ALTAMIRA. The cave paintings at Altamira, near Santander in the Cantabrian Mountains in Spain—the first to be discovered and attributed to the Upper Paleolithic period—have been recently dated to about 12,500 BCE (see "How Early Art is Dated," page 12). The Altamira artists created sculptural effects by painting over and around natural irregularities in the cave walls and ceilings. To produce the herd of bison on the ceiling of the main cavern **(FIG. 1–13)**, they used rich, red and brown ocher to paint the large areas of the animals' shoulders, backs, and flanks, then sharpened the contours of the rocks and added the details of the legs, tails, heads, and horns in black and brown. They mixed yellow and brown from iron-based ocher to make the red tones, and they derived black from manganese or charcoal.

soot, the light would not have been as strong as that created by a candle.)

One scene at Lascaux was discovered in a remote setting on a wall at the bottom of a 16-foot shaft that contained a stone lamp and spears. The scene is unusual because it is the only painting in the cave complex that seems to tell a story **(FIG. 1–12)**, and it is stylistically different from the other paintings at Lascaux. A figure who could be a hunter, greatly simplified in form but recognizably male and with the head of a bird or wearing a bird's-head mask, appears to be lying on the ground. A great bison looms above him. Below him lie a staff, or baton, and a spear-thrower (*atlatl*)—a device that allowed hunters to throw farther and with greater force—the outer end of which has been carved in the shape of a bird. The long, diagonal line slanting across the bison's hindquarters may be a spear. The bison has been disemboweled and will soon die. To the left of the cleft in the wall a woolly rhinoceros seems to run off. Why did the artist portray the man as only a sticklike figure when the bison was rendered with such accurate detail? Does the painting illustrate a story or a myth regarding the death of a hero? Is it a record of an actual event? The painting may also depict the vision of a shaman.

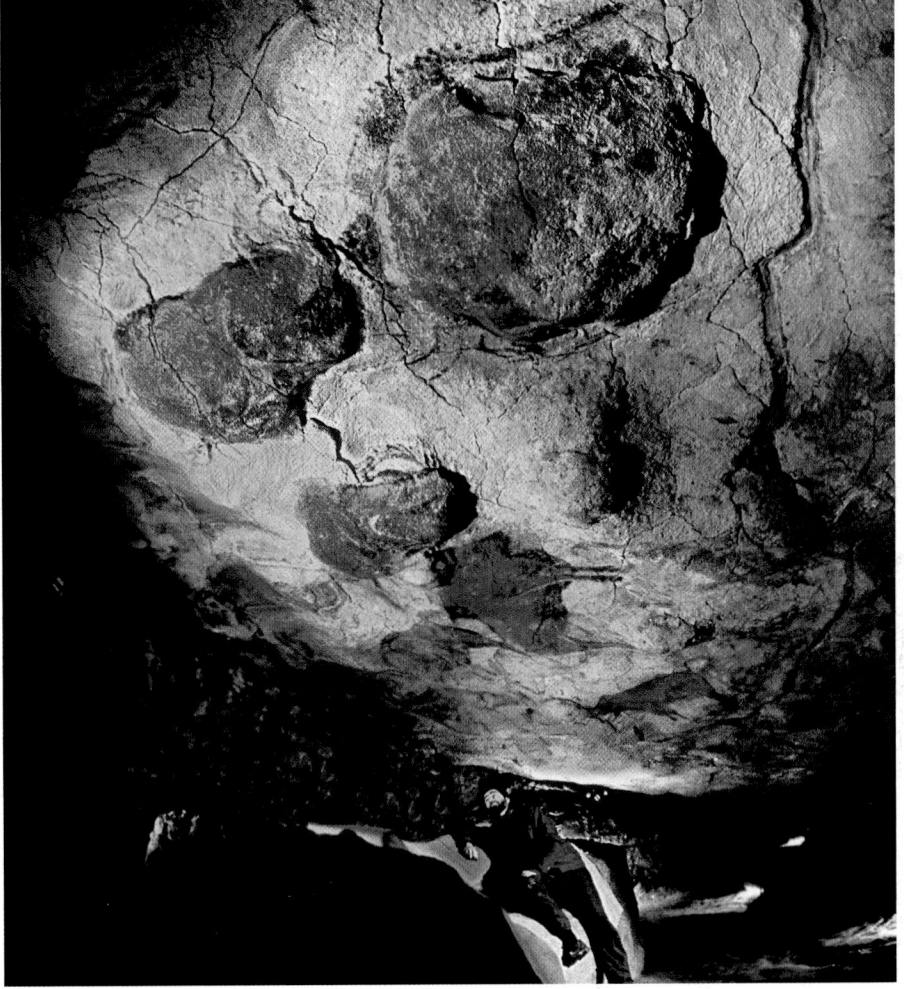

1-13 • BISON
Ceiling of a cave at Altamira, Spain. c. 12,500 BCE. Paint on limestone, length approx. 8′3″ (2.5 m).

Since the first discoveries at Altamira, archaeologists have developed increasingly sophisticated ways of dating cave paintings and other objects. Today, they primarily use two approaches to determine an artifact's age. **Relative dating** relies on the chronological relationships among objects in a single excavation or among several sites. If archaeologists have determined, for example, that pottery types A, B, and C follow each other chronologically at one site, they can apply that knowledge to another site. Even if type B is the only pottery present, it can still be assigned a relative date. **Absolute dating** aims to determine a precise span of calendar years in which an artifact was created.

The most accurate method of absolute dating is **radiometric dating**, which measures the degree to which radioactive materials have disintegrated over time. Used for dating organic (plant or animal) materials—including some pigments used in cave paintings—one radiometric method measures a carbon isotope called radiocarbon, or carbon-14, which is constantly replenished in a living organism. When an organism dies, it stops absorbing carbon-14 and starts to lose its store of the isotope at a predictable rate. Under the right circumstances, the amount of carbon-14 remaining in organic material can tell us how long ago an organism died.

This method has serious drawbacks for dating works of art. Using carbon-14 dating on a carved antler or wood sculpture shows only when the animal died or when the tree was cut down, not when the artist created the work using those materials. Also, some part of the object must be destroyed in order to conduct this kind of test—something that is never a desirable procedure to conduct on a work of art. For this reason, researchers frequently test organic materials found in the same context as the work of art rather than in the work itself.

Radiocarbon dating is most accurate for materials no more than 30,000 to 40,000 years old. **Potassium-argon dating**, which measures the decay of a radioactive potassium isotope into a stable isotope of argon, an inert gas, is most reliable with materials more than a million years old. Two newer techniques have been used since the mid 1980s. **Thermo-luminescence dating** measures the irradiation of the crystal structure of a material subjected to fire, such as pottery, and the soil in which it is found, determined by the luminescence produced when a sample is heated. **Electron spin resonance** techniques involve using a magnetic field and microwave irradiation to date a material such as tooth enamel and the soil surrounding it.

Recent experiments have helped to date cave paintings with increasing precision. Radiocarbon analysis has determined, for example, that the animal images at Lascaux are 17,000 years old—to be more precise, 17,070 years plus or minus 130 years.

CAVE SCULPTURES

Caves were sometimes adorned with relief sculpture as well as paintings. At Altamira, an artist simply heightened the resemblance of a natural projecting rock to a similar and familiar animal form. Other reliefs were created by **modeling**, or shaping, the damp clay of the cave's floor. An excellent example of such work in clay (dating to 13,000 BCE) is preserved at Le Tuc d'Audoubert, south of the Dordogne region of France. Here the sculptor created two bison leaning against a ridge of rock (**FIG. 1–14**). Although the beasts are modeled in very high relief (they extend well forward from the background), they display the same conventions as in earlier painted ones, with emphasis on the broad masses of the meat-bearing flanks and shoulders. To make the animals even more lifelike, their creator engraved short parallel lines below their necks to represent their shaggy coats. Numerous small footprints found in the clay floor of this cave suggest that important group rites took place here.

An aesthetic sense and the ability to express it in a variety of ways are among the characteristics unique to *homo sapiens sapiens*. Lamps found in caves provide an example of objects that were both functional and aesthetically pleasing. Some were carved in simple abstract shapes; others were adorned with engraved images, like one found at La Mouthe, France (**FIG. 1–15**). The maker decorated its underside with an

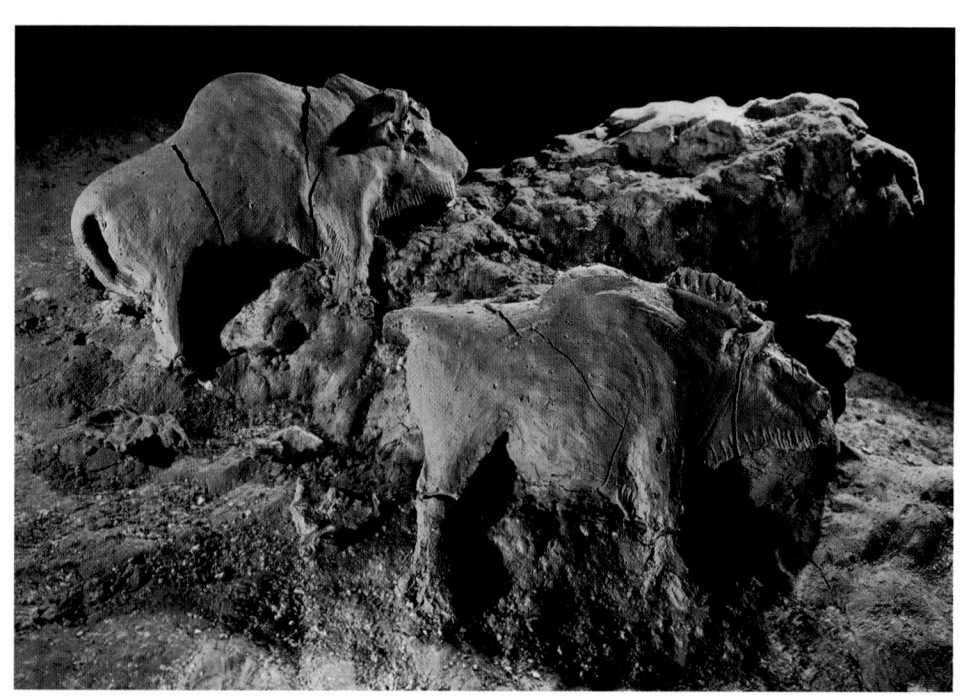

1-14 • BISON
Le Tuc d'Audoubert, France. c. 13,000 BCE. Unbaked clay, length 25″ (63.5 cm) and 24″ (60.9 cm).

1-15 • LAMP WITH IBEX DESIGN
From La Mouthe Cave. Dordogne, France. c. 15,000–13,000 BCE.
Engraved stone. Musée des Antiquités Nationales, Saint-Germain-en-
Laye, France.

ibex. The animal's distinctive head is shown in profile, its sweeping horns reflecting the curved outline of the lamp itself. Objects such as this were made by people whose survival depended upon their skill at hunting animals and gathering wild grains and other edible plants. But a change was already under way that would completely alter human existence.

THE NEOLITHIC PERIOD

Today, advances in technology, medicine, transportation, and electronic communication change human experience in a generation. Many thousands of years ago, change took place much more slowly. In the tenth millennium BCE the world had already entered the present interglacial period, and our modern climate was taking shape. The world was warming up, and this affected the distribution, density, and stability of plant and animal life and

marine and aquatic resources. However, the Ice Age ended so gradually and unevenly among regions that people could not have known what was happening.

One of the fundamental changes that took place in our prehistoric past was in the relationship people had with their environment. After millennia of established interactions between people and wild plants and animals (ranging from opportunistic foraging to well-scheduled gathering and collecting), people gradually started to exert increasing control over the land and its resources. Seen from the modern perspective, this change in economy (archaeologists use "economy" to refer to the ways people gather or produce food) seems abrupt and complete. Different communities adopted and adapted new sets of technologies, skills, and plant and animal species that allowed them to produce food: This is the origin of plant and animal domestication. Wheat and barley were cultivated; sheep, goats, cattle, and pigs were bred. This new economy appeared at different rates and to varying degrees of completeness in different parts of the Near East and Europe, and no community relied exclusively on the cultivation of plants or on breeding animals. Instead they balanced hunting, gathering, farming, and animal breeding in order to maintain a steady food supply.

ARCHITECTURE

At the same time as these new food technologies and species appeared, people began to establish stronger, more lasting connections to particular parts of the landscape. The beginnings of architecture in Europe are marked by people building their social environments by constructing simple but durable structures made of clay, mud, dung, and straw interwoven among wooden posts. While some of these buildings were simple huts, used for no more than a season at a time, others were much more substantial, with foundations made of stone, set into trenches, and supporting walls of large timbers. Some buildings were constructed from simple bricks made of clay, mud, and straw given shape by a rectangular mold and then dried in the sun. Regardless of the technique used, the result was the same: people developed a new attachment to the land, and with settlement came a new kind of social life.

At the site of Lepenski Vir, on the Serbian banks of the Danube River, rows of trapezoidal buildings made of wooden posts, branches, mud, and clay (but with stone foundations and stone-faced hearths) face the river from which the inhabitants took large river fish **(FIG. 1–16)**. Although this site dates to between 6300–5500 BCE, there is little evidence for the domesticated plants and animals one might expect at this time and in association with architecture. Archaeologists found human burials under the floors of these structures as well as in the spaces

1-16 • RECONSTRUCTION OF LEPENSKI VIR HOUSE/SHRINE
Serbia. 6000 BCE.

1-17 • HUMAN-FISH SCULPTURE
Lepenski Vir, Serbia. c. 6300–5500 BCE.

between individual buildings. In some houses extraordinary art was found, made of carefully pecked and shaped river boulders (FIG. 1–17). Some of the boulders appear to represent human forms. Others are more similar to fish. A few seem to consist of mixtures of human and fish features. Here we have a site with a confusing combination of architecture with a nondomesticated economy, very unusual art, and many burials. Archaeologists interpret sites like Lepenski Vir as temporary habitations where people carried out special rites and activities linked to death and to the natural and wild worlds. Art played a part in these.

In some places early architecture was dramatic and long-lasting, with the repeated building of house upon house in successive architectural generations (sometimes over 1,000 years or more) resulting in the gradual rise of great mounds of villages referred to as tells or mound settlements. A particularly spectacular example is Çatalhöyük (Chatal Huyuk) in the Konya Plain in central Turkey where the first traces of a village date to 7400 BCE in the early Neolithic. The oldest part of the site consists of many, densely clustered houses separated by areas of rubbish. They were made of rectangular mud bricks held together with mortar; walls, floors, and ceilings were covered with plaster and lime-based paint and were frequently replastered and repainted (see "A Closer Look," opposite). The site was large and was home to as many as 3,000 people at any one time. Beyond the early date of the site and its size and population, the settlement at Çatalhöyük is important to art history for two reasons: the picture it provides of the use of early architecture and the sensational art that has been found within its buildings.

It is often assumed by archaeologists and anthropologists that the decision to create buildings such as the houses at Neolithic sites was based on a universal need for shelter from the elements. However, as hinted at by the special nature of the activities at Lepenski Vir, recent work at Çatalhöyük shows clearly that while structures did provide shelter, early houses had much more significant functions for the communities of people who lived in them. For the Neolithic people of Çatalhöyük, their houses were the key component of their world-view. Most importantly, they became an emblem of the spirit and history of a community. The building of house upon house created a historical continuity that outlasted any human lifetime; indeed, some house rebuilding sequences lasted many hundreds of years. The seasonal replastering and repainting of walls and floors added to the long-term continuity of the buildings as history-makers. In fact, Ian Hodder, the current director of excavations at Çatalhöyük, and his colleagues call some of them "history houses" and have found no evidence to suggest that they were shrines or temples as earlier interpreters had mistakenly concluded.

The dead were buried under the floors of many of the buildings, so the site connected the community's past, present, and future. While there were no burials in some houses, a few contained between 30 and 60 bodies (the average is about six per house), and one had 62 burials, many of people who had lived their lives in other parts of the village. Periodically, perhaps to mark special community events and ceremonies, people dug down into the floors of their houses and removed the heads of the long-deceased, then buried the skulls in new graves under the floors. Skulls were also placed in the foundations of new houses as they were built (and rebuilt) and in other special deposits around the settlement. In one extraordinary burial, a deceased woman holds in her arms a man's skull that had been plastered and painted (perhaps it, too, had been removed from an earlier underfloor grave).

The houses of Çatalhöyük were powerful places not only because of the (literal) depths of their histories, but also because of the extraordinary art that decorated their interiors. Painted on the walls of some of the houses are violent and wild scenes. In some, humans are represented without heads as if they had been decapitated. Vultures or other birds of prey appear huge next to them. The narrative scenes are of dangerous interactions between people and animals. In one painting, a huge, horned wild animal (probably a deer) is surrounded by small humans who are jumping or running; one of them is pulling on something sticking out of the deer's mouth, perhaps its tongue. There is great reference to men and maleness: some of the human figures are bearded and the deer has an erect penis. The site's excavators see this painting as a depiction of a dangerous game or ritual of baiting and taunting a wild animal. In other paintings, people hunt or tease boars or bulls. Conservation of the wall paintings is highly complex and many of the most dramatic examples were excavated before modern preservation techniques existed, and thus we must rely on the archaeologist's narrative descriptions or quick field sketches.

Other representations of wild animals are modeled in relief on the interior walls, the most frequent are the heads and horns of bulls. In some houses, people placed boar tusks, vulture skulls, and fox and weasel teeth under the floors; in at least one case, they dug

Large wooden beams of juniper or oak supported the roof and the activities that took place above.

The walls were used to display special objects. Cattle skulls and horns (*bucrania*) were attached to the wall as relief art. Conical repositories in walls held special objects.

The only entrance to the house was through the roof (and down a ladder). Natural light was limited to what came through this opening because there were no windows in the house.

Domed ovens were placed both on the roof and in the house. The roof was utilized for cooking and other activities in the summer months.

Walls up to 1 foot 4 inches thick and 16 feet high were made of rows of mortared brick. The interior sides of the walls were replastered annually (up to 100 times).

Side rooms were used for storage, food preparation, and other domestic tasks.

Village residents were often buried under house floors.

Short walls and ridges created separate areas for different activities or social groups. Within some areas, raised platforms were coated with white plaster and covered with textile mats.

SEE MORE: View the Closer Look feature for the House in Çatalhöyük **www.myartslab.com**

into previous house generations to retrieve the plastered and painted heads of bulls.

The importance of sites such as Lepenski Vir and Çatalhöyük is that they have forced archaeologists to think in new ways about the role of architecture and art in prehistoric communities (see "Intentional House Burning," page 20). Critically, the mixture of shelter, architecture, art, spirit, ritual, and ceremony at these and many other Neolithic sites makes us realize that we cannot easily distinguish between "domestic" and "sacred" architecture. This point re-emerges from the recent work at Stonehenge in England (see page 18). In addition, the clear and repeated emphasis on death, violence, wild animals, and male body parts at Çatalhöyük has replaced previous interpretations that the Neolithic worldview was one in which representations of the female body, human fertility, and cults of the Mother Goddess were all-powerful.

Most early architectural sites in the Neolithic were not as visually sensational as Çatalhöyük. At the site of Sesklo in northern Greece, dated to 6500 BCE, people built stone-based, long-lasting structures **(FIG. 1–18)** in one part of a village and less substantial

1–18 • SESKLO STONE FOUNDATION HOUSE
Sesklo, Greece. 6500 BCE.

Of all the methods for spanning space, **post-and-lintel construction** is the simplest. At its most basic, two uprights (posts) support a horizontal element (**lintel**). There are countless variations, from the wood structures, dolmens, and other underground burial chambers of prehistory, to Egyptian and Greek stone construction, to medieval timber-frame buildings, and even to cast-iron and steel construction. Its limitation as a space spanner is the degree of tensile strength of the lintel material: the more flexible, the greater the span possible. Another early method for creating openings in walls and covering space is **corbeling**, in which rows or layers of stone are laid with the end of each row projecting beyond the row beneath, progressing until opposing layers almost meet and can then be capped with a stone that rests across the tops of both layers.

1. Post and lintel

2. Cross section of post-and-lintel underground burial chamber

3. Cross section of corbeled underground burial chamber

4. Wood-post framing of prehistoric structure

5. Granite post-and-lintel construction, Valley Temple of Khafre, Giza, Egypt, c. 2500 BCE

SEE MORE: View a simulation of post-and-lintel construction **www.myartslab.com**

mud, clay, and wood buildings in another part. The stone-based buildings may have had a special function within the community (whether ritual, crafts-based, or political is difficult to determine) as they were rebuilt again and again over a long period of time so that the part of the village where they were located "grew" vertically into a mound or tell. Some buildings had easily recognizable functions, such as a place for making ceramic vessels. The distinction between the area of the longer-lasting, often rebuilt buildings and the more temporary structures is clear in the style of architecture as well as in the quality of artifacts found (finer, decorated pottery is more abundant in the former).

In different parts of Europe, people created architecture in different ways, as the crowded buildings of Çatalhöyük differed from the structures at Sesklo, and as these differed from the trapezoidal huts at Lepenski Vir. To the northwest in Germany and central Europe, villages of this period typically consisted of three or four long timber buildings, each up to 150 feet long, housing 45 to 50 people. The structures were rectangular, with a row of posts down the center supporting a **ridgepole**, a long horizontal beam

1-19 • NEOLITHIC BUILDING METHODS
Thessaly, Greece. 6000 BCE.

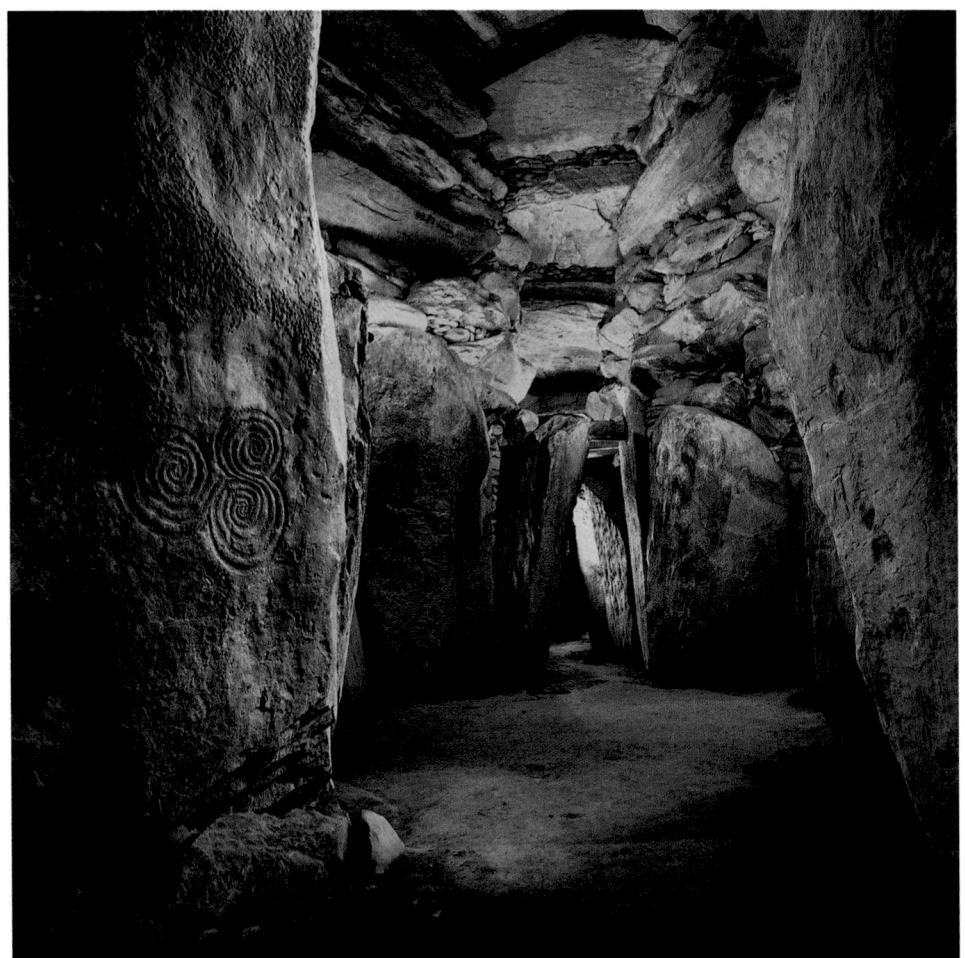

1-20 • TOMB INTERIOR WITH CORBELING AND ENGRAVED STONES
Newgrange, Ireland. c. 3000–2500 BCE.

societies in which powerful religious or political leaders dictated their design and inspired (and coerced) large numbers of people to contribute their labor to such engineering projects. Skilled "engineers" devised methods for shaping, transporting, and aligning the stones. Other interpreters argue that these massive monuments are clear evidence for equally shared collaboration within and between groups, with people working together on a common project, the successful completion of which fueled social cohesion in the absence of a powerful individual.

Many of these megalithic structures are associated with death. Most recent interpretations stress the role of death and burial as fundamental, public performances in which individual and group identity, cohesion, and dispute were played out. In this reasoning, death and its rituals are viewed as theater, with the deceased as well as grave goods perceived as props, the monument as a stage, the celebrants and mourners as actors, and the entire event proceeding in terms of an (unwritten) script with narrative and plot.

Elaborate megalithic tombs first appeared in the Neolithic period. Some were built for single burials; others consisted of multiple burial chambers. The simplest type of megalithic tomb was the **dolmen**, built on the post-and-lintel principle (see examples 1 and 2 in "Early Construction Methods," opposite). The tomb chamber was formed of huge upright stones supporting one or more tablelike rocks, or capstones. The structure was then mounded over with smaller rocks and dirt to form a **cairn** or artificial hill. A more imposing structure was the **passage grave**, which was entered by one or more narrow, stone-lined passageways into a large room at the center.

At Newgrange, in Ireland, the mound of an elaborate passage grave **(FIG. 1–20)** originally stood 44 feet tall and measured about 280 feet in diameter. The mound was built of sod and river pebbles and was set off by a circle of engraved standing stones around its perimeter. Its passageway, 62 feet long and lined with standing stones, leads into a three-part chamber with a corbel **vault** (an arched structure that spans an interior space) rising to a height of 19 feet (see example 3 in "Early Construction Methods," opposite). Some of the stones are engraved with linear designs, mainly rings, spirals, and diamond shapes. These patterns may have been marked out using strings or compasses, then carved by

against which the slanting roof poles were braced (see example 4 in "Early Construction Methods," opposite). The walls were probably made of what is known as **wattle and daub**, branches woven in a basketlike pattern, then covered with mud or clay **(FIG. 1–19)**. They were probably roofed with **thatch**, plant material such as reeds or straw tied over a framework of poles. These houses also included large granaries, or storage spaces for the harvest; some buildings contain sections for animals and for people. Around 4000 BCE, Neolithic settlers began to locate their communities at defensible sites—near rivers, on plateaus, or in swamps. For additional protection, they also frequently surrounded them with wooden walls, earth embankments, and ditches.

CEREMONIAL AND TOMB ARCHITECTURE.   In western and northern Europe, people erected megaliths to build ceremonial structures and tombs. In some cases, they had to transport these great stones over long distances. The monuments thus created are examples of what is known as **megalithic architecture**, the descriptive term derived from the Greek words for "large" (*mega-*) and "stone" (*lithos*).

Archaeologists disagree about the types of society that created these monuments. Some believe they reflect complex, stratified

1-21 • STONEHENGE
Salisbury Plain, Wiltshire, England. c. 2900–1500 BCE.

EXPLORE MORE:
Click the Google Earth link for Stonehenge
www.myartslab.com

1-22 • PLAN OF STONEHENGE AND ITS SURROUNDING SETTLEMENTS

the particularities of perception by the eye), and that we should understand them in terms of the neuropsychological effect they would have had on people visiting the tomb. These effects may have included hallucinations. Archaeologists argue that key entoptic motifs were positioned at entrances and other important thresholds inside the tomb, and that they played important roles in ritual or political ceremonies that centered around death, burial, and the commemoration and visitation of the deceased by the living.

STONEHENGE. Of all the megalithic monuments in Europe, the one that has stirred the imagination of the public most strongly is **STONEHENGE**, on Salisbury Plain in southern England (FIGS. 1–21, 1–22). A **henge** is a circle of stones or posts, often surrounded by a ditch with built-up embankments. Laying out such circles with accuracy would have posed no particular

picking at the rock surface with tools made of antlers. Recent detailed analysis of the art engraved on passage graves like Newgrange, but also at Knowth in Ireland, suggest that the images are entoptic (meaning that their significance and function relate to problem. Architects likely relied on the human compass, a simple but effective surveying method that persisted well into modern times. All that is required is a length of cord either cut or knotted to mark the desired radius of the circle. A person holding one end of the cord is stationed in the center; a co-worker, holding the other end and keeping the cord taut, steps off the circle's circumference. By the time of Stonehenge's construction, cords and ropes were readily available.

Stonehenge is not the largest such circle from the Neolithic period, but it is one of the most complex, with eight different phases of construction and activity starting in the Neolithic in 3000 BCE, and stretching over a millennium and a half through the Bronze Age. The site started as a cemetery of cremation burials marked by a circle of bluestones. Through numerous sequences of alterations and rebuildings, it continued to function as a place of the dead. Between 2900 and 2600 BCE, the bluestones were rearranged into an arc. Around 2500 BCE, a circle of sarsen stones was used to create the famous appearance of the site—sarsen is a gray sandstone—and the bluestones were rearranged within the sarsens. The center of the site was now dominated by a horseshoe-shaped arrangement of five sandstone trilithons, or pairs of upright stones topped by lintels. The one at the middle stood considerably taller than the rest, rising to a height of 24 feet, and its lintel was more than 15 feet long and 3 feet thick. This group was surrounded by the so-called sarsen circle, a ring of sandstone uprights weighing up to 26 tons each and averaging 13 feet 6 inches tall. This circle, 106 feet in diameter, was capped by a continuous lintel. The uprights were tapered slightly toward the top, and the gently curved lintel sections were secured by **mortise-and-tenon** joints, that is, joints made by a conical projection at the top of each upright that fits like a peg into a hole in the lintel. Over the next thousand years people continued to alter the arrangement of the bluestones and continued to make cremation burials in pits at the site.

The differences in the types of stone used in the different phases of construction are significant. The use of bluestone in the early phases (and maintained and rearranged through the sequence) is particularly important. Unlike the sarsen stone, bluestone was not locally available and would have been transported over 150 miles from the west, where it had been quarried in the mountains of west Wales. The means of transporting the bluestones such distances remains a source of great debate. Some argue that they were floated around the coast on great barges; others hold that they were brought over land on wooden rollers. Regardless of the means of transport, the use of this distant material tells us that the people who first transformed the Stonehenge landscape into a ceremonial one probably also had their ancestral origins in the west. By bringing the bluestones and using them in the early Stonehenge cemetery, these migrants made a powerful connection with their homelands.

Through the ages, many theories have been advanced to explain Stonehenge. In the Middle Ages, people thought that Merlin, the magician of the King Arthur legend, had built it. Later, the site was erroneously associated with the rituals of the Celtic druids (priests). Because its orientation is related to the movement of the sun, some people have argued that it may have been an observatory or that it had special importance as a calendar for regulating early agricultural schedules. Today none of these ideas is supported by archaeologists and the current evidence.

It is now believed that Stonehenge was the site of ceremonies linked to death and burial. This theory has been constructed from evidence that looks not only at the stone circles but also at the nearby sites dating from the periods when Stonehenge was in use. A new generation of archaeologists, led by Mike Parker Pearson, has pioneered this contextual approach to the puzzle of Stonehenge (SEE FIG. 1–22).

The settlements built near Stonehenge follow circular layouts, connecting them in plan to the ceremonial site (FIG. 1–23). Unlike the more famous monument, however, these habitations were built

1-23 • RECONSTRUCTION DRAWING OF DURRINGTON WALLS
The settlement at Durrington Walls, near Stonehenge in southern England, 2600 BCE.

Intentional House Burning

While much research has focused on the origins and technology of the earliest architecture as at Çatalhöyük, Lepenski Vir, and other sites, some of the most exciting new work has come from studies of how Neolithic houses were destroyed. Excavations of settlements dating to the end of the Neolithic in eastern and central Europe commonly reveal a level of ash and other evidence for great fires that burned down houses at these sites. The common interpretation had been that invaders, coming on horseback from Ukraine and Russia, had attacked these villages and burned the settlements.

In one of the most innovative recent studies, Mira Stevanović and Ruth Tringham exploited the methods of modern forensic science and meticulously reconstructed the patterns of Neolithic house conflagrations. The results proved that the fires were not part of village-wide destructions, but were individual events of firings, confined to particular houses. Most significantly, they showed that each fire had been deliberately set. In fact, in order to get the fires to consume the houses completely, buildings had been stuffed with combustibles before they were set alight. Repeated tests by experimental archaeologists have supported these conclusions. Each intentional, house-destroying fire was part of a ritual killing of the house and a rupture of the historical and social entity that the house had represented for the community. Critically, even in their destruction, prehistoric architecture played important and complex roles within the ways that individuals and community created (and destroyed) social identities and continuities.

of wood, in particular large posts and tree trunks. A mile from Stonehenge is one of these sites, Durrington Walls, which was a large settlement (almost 1,500 feet across) surrounded by a ditch. Inside the site are a number of circles made not from stone but from wood; there are also many circular houses also made with wooden posts. The rubbish left behind at this and similar sites has given archaeologists insights into the inhabitants. Chemical analysis of animal bone debris, for example, indicates that the animals consumed came from great distances before they were slaughtered, and therefore that the people who stayed here had come from regions very far from the site.

Significantly, both Stonehenge and Durrington Walls are connected to the Avon River by banked avenues. These connected the worlds of the living (the wood settlement) with the world of the dead (the stone circle). Neolithic people would have moved between these worlds as they walked the avenues, sometimes bringing the deceased to be buried or cremated, other times approaching the stone circle for ceremonies and rituals dedicated to the memories of the deceased and the very ancient ancestors. The meaning of Stonehenge therefore rests within an understanding of the larger landscape that contained not only other ritual sites but also the places of the living.

SCULPTURE AND CERAMICS

In addition to domestic and ceremonial architecture and a food-producing economy, the other critical component of the Neolithic way of life was the ability to make ceramic vessels (see "Pottery and Ceramics," page 22). This "pot revolution" marked a shift from a complete reliance on skin, textile, and wooden containers to the use of pots made by firing clay. Pottery provided a new medium of extraordinary potential for shaping and decorating durable objects. Ceramic technology emerged independently, at different times, across the globe, with the earliest examples being produced by the Jomon culture of hunter-gatherers in Japan in 12,000 BCE (FIG. 1–24). It is extremely difficult to determine with certainty why pottery was first invented or why subsequent cultures adopted it. The idea that pottery would only emerge out of farming settlements is confounded by the example of the Jomon. Rather, it seems that

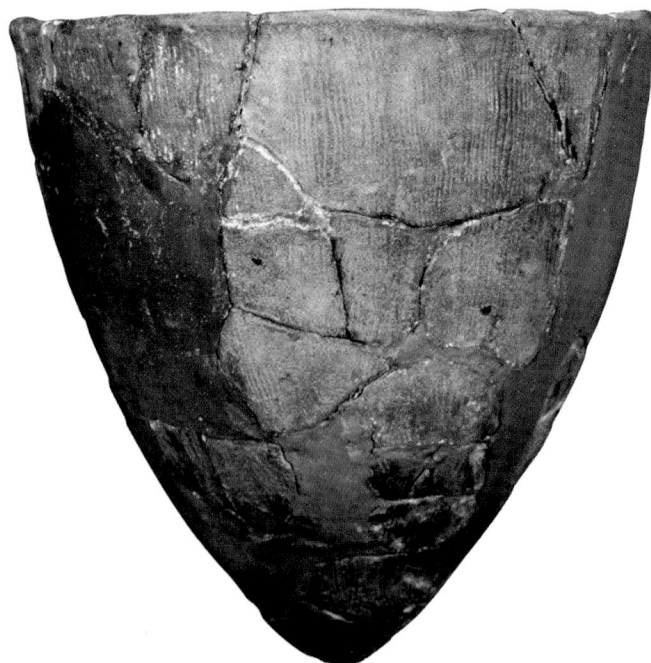

1-24 • EARLY POTTERY: FROM JAPAN'S JOMON CULTURE
12,000 BCE.

1-25 • EARLY POTTERY: FRANCHTHI CAVE, GREECE
6500 BCE.

pits: one assemblage consisted of 12 busts and 13 full figures; in the other were two full figures, two fragmental busts, and three figures which had two heads. The figures, each about 3 feet tall, are disturbing to look at (at least from a modern perspective): the eyes, made with cowrie shells painted with bitumen (a natural asphalt) to represent pupils and the edges of the eyes, are open and make the figures appear lifelike. Nostrils are clearly defined, but the mouths are tight-lipped. Clothes and other features were painted on the bodies. Though without arms, the legs and feet (with toes) are clearly modeled with plaster. The impression is of living, breathing individuals who are not able (or willing) to speak.

there was no one set of social, economic, or environmental circumstances that led to the invention of ceramics.

It is likely that the technology for producing ceramics evolved in stages. Archaeologist Karen Vitelli's detailed studies of the early Neolithic site at Franchthi Cave, Greece, have shown that pottery making at this site started with an experimental stage during which nonspecialist potters produced a small number of pots. These early pots were used in ceremonies, especially those where medicinal or narcotic plants were consumed (FIG. 1–25). Only later did specialist potters share manufacturing recipes to produce enough pots for standard activities such as cooking and eating. It is probable that a similar pattern occurred in other early potting communities.

In addition to firing clay to make pots, cups, pitchers, and large storage containers, Neolithic people made thousands of miniature figures of humans (see "Prehistoric Woman and Man," page 24). While it was once thought that these figurines refer to fertility cults and matriarchal societies, archaeologists now agree that they had many different functions (as toys, portraits, votives). More importantly, specialists have shown that there are great degrees of similarity in figurine shape and decoration within each distinct cultural region. This degree of similarity, and the huge numbers of figurines that would have been in circulation at any one (Neolithic) place and time, have convinced experts that the critical significance of these objects is that they mark the emergence of the human body as the core location of the human identity. Thus, the central role the body has played in the politics, philosophy and art of historical and modern times began in 6000 BCE with Neolithic figurines.

Prehistoric figures of the human form were most numerous and diverse in the Neolithic of central and eastern Europe. In Jordan in the Near East, at the site of 'Ain Ghazal, archaeologist Gary Rollefson found 32 extraordinary **HUMAN FIGURES (FIG. 1–26)**. Dated to 6500 BCE and constructed by covering bundled-twig figures with layers of plaster, the statues were found in two

1-26 • HUMAN FIGURE
From 'Ain Ghazal, Jordan. 6500 BCE. Fired lime plaster with cowrie shell, bitumen, and paint, height approx. 35″ (90 cm). National Museum, Amman, Jordan.

The terms pottery and ceramics may be used interchangeably—and often are. Because it covers all baked-clay wares, **ceramics** is technically a more inclusive term than pottery. Pottery includes all baked-clay wares except **porcelain**, which is the most refined product of ceramic technology.

Pottery vessels can be formed in several ways. It is possible, though difficult, to raise up the sides from a ball of raw clay. Another method is to coil long rolls of soft, raw clay, stack them on top of each other to form a container, and then smooth them by hand. A third possibility is to simply press the clay over an existing form, a dried gourd for example. By about 4000 BCE, Egyptian potters had developed the potter's wheel, a round, spinning platform on which a lump of clay is placed and then formed with the fingers, making it relatively simple to produce a uniformly shaped vessel in a very short time. The potter's wheel appeared in the ancient Near East about 3250 BCE and in China about 3000 BCE.

After a pot is formed, it is allowed to dry completely before it is fired. Special ovens for firing pottery, called **kilns**, have been discovered at prehistoric sites in Europe dating from as early as 26,000 BCE (as at Dolní Věstonice). For proper firing, the temperature must be maintained at a relatively uniform level. Raw clay becomes porous pottery when heated to at least 500° Centigrade. It then holds its shape permanently and will not disintegrate in water. Fired at 800° Centigrade, pottery is technically known as **earthenware**. When subjected to temperatures between 1,200° and 1,400° Centigrade, certain stone elements in the clay vitrify, or become glassy, and the result is a stronger type of ceramic called **stoneware**.

Pottery is relatively fragile, and new vessels were constantly in demand to replace broken ones, so fragments of low-fired ceramics—fired at the hearth, rather than the higher temperature kiln—are the most common artifacts found in excavations of prehistoric settlements. Pottery fragments, or **potsherds**, serve as a major key in dating sites and reconstructing human living and trading patterns.

Scholars have looked for clues about the function of these figures. The people who lived on the site built and rebuilt houses, replastered walls, and buried their dead under house floors—they even dug down through the floors to retrieve the skulls of long-deceased relatives—just like the inhabitants of Çatalhöyük. They used the same plaster to coat the walls of their houses that they used to make the figures. The site also contains buildings that may have served special, potentially ceremonial functions, and it has been suggested that the figures are linked to these rites. In addition to the figures' lifelike appearance, the similarity between the burial of bodies under house floors and the burial of the plaster figures in pits is striking. At the same time, however, there are differences in the burials: the figures are buried in groups while the humans are not; the figures are buried in pits and not in houses; the figures' eyes are open, as if they are alive and awake. At this point in the research it is difficult to get any closer to a clear understanding of how they were used and what they meant to the people of 'Ain Ghazal.

NEW METALLURGY, ENDURING STONE

The technology of metallurgy is closely allied to that of ceramics. Although Neolithic culture persisted in northern Europe until about 2000 BCE (and indeed all of its key contributions to human evolution—farming, architecture, and pottery—continue through present times), the age of metals made its appearance in much of Europe about 3000 BCE. In central and southern Europe, and in the Aegean region, copper, gold, and tin had been mined, worked, and traded even earlier. Smelted and cast copper beads and ornaments dated to 4000 BCE have been discovered in Poland.

Metals were first used for ornamentation. Toward the end of the Neolithic, people shaped simple beads by cold-hammering malachite, a green-colored carbonate mineral that can be found on the surface of the ground in many regions. Gold was also one of the first metals to be used in prehistory; it was used to make jewelry (ear, lip, and nose rings) or ornament clothing (appliqués sewn into fabric).

Over time, the objects made from copper and gold became more complicated and technologies of extraction (the mining of copper in Bulgaria) and of metalworking (casting copper) improved. Some of the most sensational (and earliest) gold and copper objects from prehistory were discovered by Ivan Ivanov in the late Neolithic cemetery at Varna on Bulgaria's Black Sea coast. While the cemetery consisted of several hundred burials of men, women and children, a few special burials contained gold and copper artifacts **(FIGS. 1–27, 1–28)**. Objects such as gold-covered scepters, bracelets, beads, armrings, lip-plugs, and copper axes and chisels mark out the graves of a few adult males. In a very few of these graves no skeleton was present: The body was represented by a clay mask richly decorated with gold adornments (SEE FIG. 1–27) and the grave contained extraordinary concentrations of metal and special marine-shell ornaments. As in other prehistoric contexts, death and its attendant ceremonies were the focus for large and visually expressive displays of status and authority.

THE BRONZE AGE

The period that followed the introduction of metalworking is commonly called the Bronze Age. Although copper is relatively abundant in central Europe and in Spain, objects fashioned from it are too soft to be functional and therefore usually have a ceremonial or metaphoric use and value. However, bronze—an **alloy**, or mixture, of tin and copper—is a stronger, harder substance with a wide variety of uses.

The introduction of bronze, especially for weapons such as daggers and short swords, changed the peoples of Europe in fundamental ways. Where copper ore was widely available across Europe, either as surface outcrops or to be mined, the tin that was required to make bronze had a much more limited natural distribution and often required extraction by mining. Power bases shifted within communities as the resources needed to make bronze were not widely available to all. Trade and intergroup contacts across the continent and into the Near East increased, and bronze objects circulated as prized goods.

ROCK CARVINGS

Bronze Age artistry is not limited to metalworking; indeed, some of the most exciting imagery of the period is found in the rock art of northern Europe. For a thousand years starting around 1500 BCE people scratched outlines of a design, then pecked and ground the surface of exposed rock faces using stone hammers and sometimes grains of sand as an abrasive. The Swedish region of northern Bohuslän is especially rich in rock carvings dating to this period; archaeologists have recorded over 40,000 individual images from more than 1,500 sites. The range of motifs is wide, including boats, animals (bulls, elk, horses, and a few snakes, birds, and fish), people (mostly sexless, some with horned helmets, but also men with erect penises), wheeled vehicles and ploughs (and unassociated

1-27 • GOLD FACE MASK
From Tomb 3, Varna I, Bulgaria. Neolithic, 3800 BCE. Terra cotta and gold. Archaeological Museum, Plovdiv, Bulgaria.

1-28 • GOLD SCEPTERS
From Varna, Bulgaria. 3800 BCE. National Museum of History, Sofia, Bulgaria.

Prehistoric Woman and Man

For all we know, the person who created these figurines at around 4500 BCE had nothing particular in mind—people had been modeling clay figures in southeastern Europe for a long time. Perhaps a woman who was making cooking and storage pots out of clay amused herself by fashioning images of the people she saw around her. But because these figures were found in a grave in Cernavodă, Romania, they suggest to us an otherworldly message.

The woman, spread-hipped and big-bellied, sits directly on the ground, expressive of the mundane world. She exudes stability and fecundity. Her ample hips and thighs seem to ensure the continuity of her family. But in a lively, even elegant, gesture, she joins her hands coquettishly on one raised knee, curls up her toes, and tilts her head upward. Though earthbound, is she a spiritual figure communing with heaven? Her upwardly tilted head could suggest that she is watching the smoke rising from the hearth, or worrying about holes in the roof, or admiring hanging containers of laboriously gathered drying berries, or gazing adoringly at her partner. The man is rather slim, with massive legs and shoulders. He rests his head on his hands in a brooding, pensive pose, evoking thoughtfulness, even weariness or sorrow.

We can interpret the Cernavodă woman and man in many ways, but we cannot know what they meant to their makers or owners. Depending on how they are displayed, we spin out different stories about them. When set facing each other, side by side as they are in the photograph, we tend to see them as a couple—a woman and man in a relationship. In fact, we do not know whether the artist conceived of them in this way, or even made them at the same time. For all their visual eloquence, their secrets remain hidden from us.

FIGURES OF A WOMAN AND A MAN
From Cernavodă, Romania. c. 4500 BCE. Ceramic, height 4½″ (11.5 cm). National Historical Museum, Bucharest.

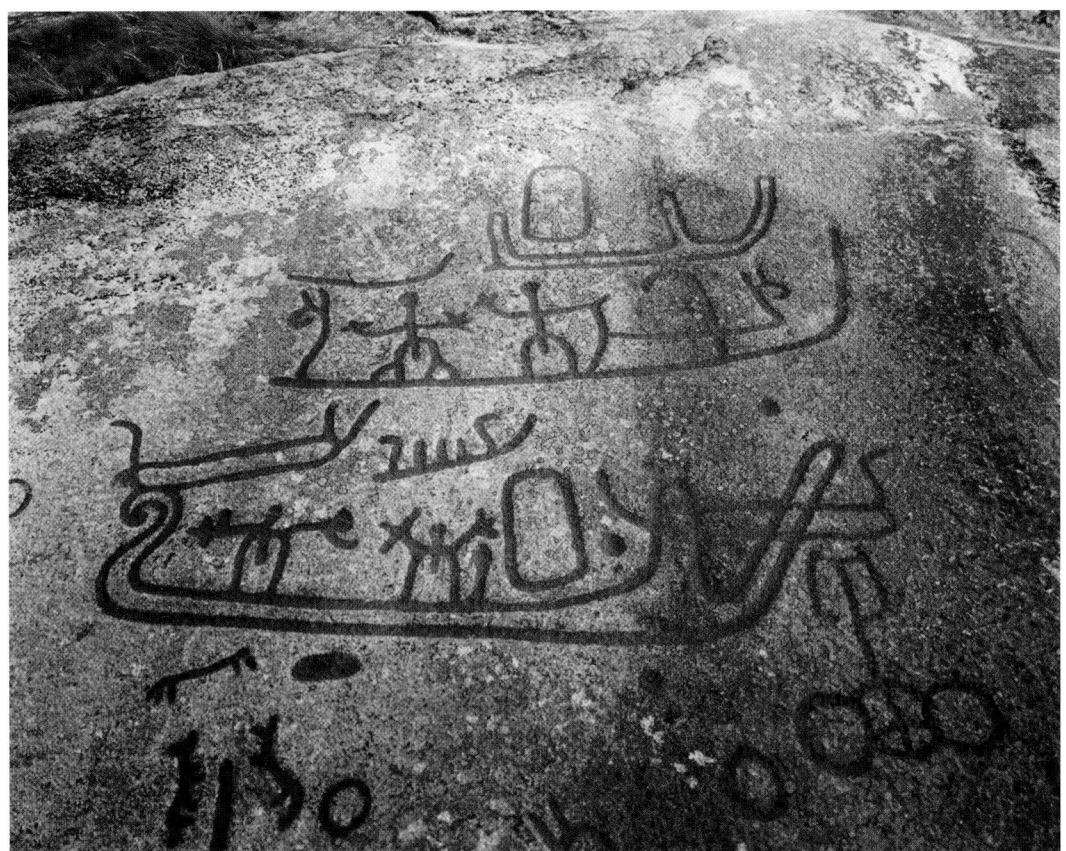

1-29 • ROCK ART: BOAT AND SEA BATTLE
Fossum, northern Bohuslän, Sweden. Bronze Age. c. 1500–500 BCE.

disks, circles, and wheels), and weapons (swords, shields, and helmets). Within this range, however, the majority of images are boats **(FIG. 1–29)**, not just in Sweden but across northern Europe. Interestingly, the boat images are unlike the boats that archaeologists have excavated. The rock-engraved images do not have masts nor are they the dugouts or log boats that are known from this period. Instead they represent boats made from wooden planks or with animal skins.

What is the meaning of these boat images? It is generally agreed that the location of the majority of the rock art (near current or past shorelines) is the critical clue to their meaning. Archaeologist Richard Bradley suggests that rock art connects sky, earth, and sea, perhaps reflecting the community's view of the three-part nature of the universe. Others suggest that the art is intentionally located between water and earth to mark a boundary between the living and the spirit worlds. In this view, the character of the rock (permanent and grounded deep in the earth) provided a means of communication and connection between distinct worlds.

For people of the prehistoric era, representational and abstract art had a symbolic importance that matched the labor required to paint in the deep recesses of caves, move enormous stones great distances, or create elaborately ornamented masks. This art and architecture connected the worlds of the living and the spirits, established social power hierarchies, and helped people learn and remember critical information about the natural world. It was not art for art's sake, but it was one of the fundamental elements of our development as a human species.

THINK ABOUT IT

1.1 Discuss the likely origins of art in its earliest days in the prehistoric past. What needs are the visual arts believed to have first fulfilled in human culture?

1.2 What are the common motifs found in cave paintings such as those at Lascaux and Altamira? Summarize the current theories about their original purpose.

1.3 Explain how Stonehenge was likely created and discuss its probable purpose, according to present interpretations.

1.4 Discuss what the use and meaning of figurines such as the Paleolithic *Woman from Willendorf* (SEE FIG. 1–7) and Neolithic *Figures of a Woman and a Man* (see "Prehistoric Woman and Man," opposite) might have been and contrast the forms of the two directly.

1.5 How did the emergence of ceramics and metallurgy transform art making in the Neolithic era? Select and analyze a work discussed in the chapter that was made in one of these new media and discuss the unique properties of the medium.

PRACTICE MORE: Compose answers to these questions, get flashcards for images and terms, and review chapter material with quizzes **www.myartslab.com**

2-1 • STELE OF NARAM-SIN
Sippar. Found at Susa.
Naram-Sin r. 2254–2218 BCE. Limestone,
height 6′6″ (1.98 m).
Musée du Louvre, Paris.

ART OF THE ANCIENT NEAR EAST

In public works such as this stone **stele** (upright stone slab), the artists of Mesopotamia developed a sophisticated symbolic visual language—a kind of conceptual art—that both celebrated and communicated the political stratification that gave order and security to their world. Akkadian ruler Naram-Sin (ruled 2254–2218 BCE) is pictured proudly here **(FIG. 2–1)**. His preeminence is signaled directly by size: he is by far the largest person in this scene of military triumph, conforming to an artistic practice we call **hieratic scale**, where relative size indicates relative importance. He is also elevated well above the other figures, boldly silhouetted against blank ground, striding toward a stylized peak that recalls his own shape, increasing his own sense of grandeur by association. He clasps a veritable arsenal of weaponry—spear, battle axe, bow and arrow—and the grand helmet that crowns his head sprouts horns, an attribute heretofore reserved for gods, here claiming divinity for this earthly ruler. Art historian Irene Winter has gone even further, pointing to the eroticized pose and presentation of Naram-Sin, to the conspicuous display of a well-formed male body. In ancient Mesopotamian culture, male potency and vigor were directly related to political power and dominance. Like the horns of his helmet, toned, muscular bodies were most frequently associated with gods. Thus every aspect of the representation of this ruler speaks to his religious and political authority as leader of the state.

This stele is more than an emblem of Naram-Sin's divine right to rule, however. It also tells the story of one of his important military victories. The ruler stands above a crowded scene enacted by smaller figures. Those to the left, dressed and posed in a fashion similar to their ruler, represent his army, marching in diagonal bands up the hillside into battle. The artist has included identifiable native trees along the mountain pathway to heighten the sense that this portrays an actual event rather than a generic battle scene. Before Naram-Sin, both along the right side of the stele and smashed under his forward striding leg, are representations of the enemy, in this case the Lullubi people from eastern Mesopotamia (modern Iran). One diminutive adversary has taken a fatal spear to the neck, while companions behind and below him beg for mercy.

Perhaps this ancient art, which combines symbols with stories, looks naïve or crude in relation to our own artistic standards, but we should avoid allowing such modern value judgments to block our appreciation of the artistic accomplishments of the ancient Near East—or, indeed, the art of any era or culture. For these ancient works of art maintain the power to communicate with us forcefully and directly, even across over four millennia of historical distance.

LEARN ABOUT IT

2.1 Explore the development of visual narrative conventions to tell stories of gods, heroes, and rulers in the sculpted reliefs of the ancient Near East.

2.2 Discover how artists of the ancient Near East used colorful and precious materials to create dazzling effects in art and architecture.

2.3 Survey the various ways rulers in the ancient Near East expressed their power in portraits, historical narrative, and great palace complexes.

2.4 Appreciate the distinctive form of architecture that evolved for worship.

HEAR MORE: Listen to an audio file of your chapter **www.myartslab.com**

THE FERTILE CRESCENT AND MESOPOTAMIA

Well before farming communities appeared in Europe, people in Asia Minor and the ancient Near East domesticated grains. This first occurred in an area known today as the Fertile Crescent (**MAP 2–1**). A little later, in the sixth or fifth millennium BCE, agriculture developed in the alluvial plains between the Tigris and Euphrates rivers, which the Greeks called *Mesopotamia*, meaning the "land between the rivers," now in present-day Iraq. Because of problems with periodic flooding as well as drought, there was a need for large-scale systems to control the water supply. Meeting this need may have contributed to the development of the first cities.

Between 4000 and 3000 BCE, a major cultural shift seems to have taken place. Agricultural villages evolved into cities simultaneously and independently in both northern and southern Mesopotamia. These prosperous cities joined with their surrounding territories to create what are known as city-states, each with its own gods and government. Social hierarchies—rulers and workers—emerged with the development of specialized skills beyond those needed for agricultural work. To grain mills and ovens were added brick and pottery kilns and textile and metal workshops. With extra goods and even modest affluence came increased trade and contact with other cultures.

Builders and artists labored to construct huge temples and government buildings. Organized religion played an important role, and the people who controlled rituals and the sacred sites eventually became priests. The people of the ancient Near East worshiped numerous gods and goddesses. Each city had a special protective deity, and people believed the fate of the city depended on the power of that deity. (The names of comparable deities varied over time and place—for example, Inanna, the Sumerian goddess of fertility, love, and war, was equivalent to the Babylonians' Ishtar.) Large architectural complexes—clusters of religious, administrative, and service buildings—developed in each city as centers of ritual and worship and also of government.

Although the stone-free alluvial plain of southern Mesopotamia was prone to floods and droughts, it was a fertile bed for agriculture and successive, interlinked societies. But its wealth and agricultural resources, as well as its few natural defenses, made Mesopotamia vulnerable to political upheaval. Over the centuries, the balance of power shifted between north and south and between local powers and outside invaders. First the Sumerians controlled the south, filling their independent city-states with the fruits of new technology, literacy, and impressive art and architecture. Then they were eclipsed by the Akkadians, their neighbors to the north. When invaders from farther north in turn conquered the Akkadians, the Sumerians regained power locally. During this period the city-states of Ur and Lagash thrived under strong leaders. The Amorites were next to dominate the south. Under them and their king, Hammurabi, a new, unified society arose with its capital in the city of Babylon.

SUMER

The cities and city-states that developed along the rivers of southern Mesopotamia between about 3500 and 2340 BCE are known collectively as Sumer. The Sumerians, who had migrated from the north but whose origins are otherwise obscure, are credited with important "firsts." They may have invented the wagon wheel and the plow. But perhaps their greatest contribution to later civilizations was the invention in about 3100 BCE of a form of writing on clay tablets.

WRITING. Sumerians pressed **cuneiform** ("wedge-shaped") symbols into clay tablets with a **stylus**, a pointed writing instrument, to keep business records (see "Cuneiform Writing," page 30). Thousands of surviving Sumerian tablets have allowed scholars to trace the gradual evolution of writing and arithmetic, another tool of commerce, as well as an organized system of justice. The world's first literary epic also has its origins in Sumer, although the fullest surviving version of this tale is written in Akkadian, the language of Sumer's neighbors to the north. The *Epic of Gilgamesh* records the adventures of a legendary Sumerian king of Uruk and his companion Enkidu. When Enkidu dies, a despondent King Gilgamesh sets out to find the secret of eternal life from the only man and woman who had survived a great flood sent by the gods to destroy the world, because the gods had granted them immortality. Gilgamesh ultimately accepts his own mortality, abandons his quest, and returns to Uruk, recognizing the majestic city as his lasting accomplishment.

THE ZIGGURAT. The Sumerians' most impressive surviving archaeological remains are their **ziggurats**, huge stepped structures with a temple or shrine on top. The first ziggurats may have developed from the practice of repeated rebuilding at a sacred site, with rubble from one structure serving as the foundation for the next. Elevating the buildings also protected the shrines from flooding.

Whatever the origin of their design, ziggurats towering above the flat plain proclaimed the wealth, prestige, and stability of a city's rulers and glorified its gods. Ziggurats functioned symbolically too, as lofty bridges between the earth and the heavens—a meeting place for humans and their gods. They were given names such as "House of the Mountain" and "Bond between Heaven and Earth."

URUK. Two large temple complexes in the 1,000-acre city at Uruk (present-day Warka, Iraq) mark the first independent Sumerian city-state. One was dedicated to Inanna, the goddess of love and war, while the other complex belonged to the sky god Anu. The temple platform of Anu, built up in stages over the centuries, ultimately rose to a height of about 40 feet. Around 3100 BCE, a whitewashed brick temple that modern archaeologists refer to as the White Temple was erected on top of the platform (**FIG. 2–2**). This now-ruined structure was a simple rectangle with an off-center doorway that led into a large chamber containing an altar, and smaller spaces opened to each side.

MAP 2-1 • THE ANCIENT NEAR EAST

The green areas represent fertile land that would support early agriculture, notably the area between the Tigris and Euphrates rivers and the strips of land on either side of the Nile in Egypt.

Anu District of Uruk

1. White Temple
2. altar
3. processional stairs
4. NW terrace

2-2 • RUINS AND PLAN OF THE ANU ZIGGURAT AND WHITE TEMPLE

Uruk (present-day Warka, Iraq). c. 3300–3000 BCE.

Many ancient Near Eastern cities still lie undiscovered. In most cases an archaeological site in a region is signaled by a large mound—known locally as a *tell*, *tepe*, or *huyuk*—that represents the accumulated debris of generations of human habitation. When properly excavated, such mounds yield evidence about the people who inhabited the site.

EXPLORE MORE: View a simulation about the White Temple www.myartslab.com

Sumerians invented writing around 3100 BCE, apparently as an accounting system for goods traded at Uruk. The symbols were pictographs, simple pictures cut into moist clay slabs with a pointed tool. Between 2900 and 2400 BCE, the symbols evolved from pictures into phonograms—representations of syllable sounds—thus becoming a writing system as we know it. During the same centuries, scribes adopted a stylus, or writing tool, with one triangular end and one pointed end that could be pressed easily and rapidly into a wet clay tablet to produce cuneiform writing.

These drawings demonstrate the shift from pictographs to cuneiform. The c. 3100 BCE drawing of a bowl (which means "bread" or "food") was reduced to a four-stroke sign by about 2400 BCE, and by about 700 BCE to a highly abstract arrangement of vertical marks. By combining the pictographs and, later, cuneiform signs, writers created composite signs; for example, a combination of the signs for "head" and "food" meant "to eat."

stylus

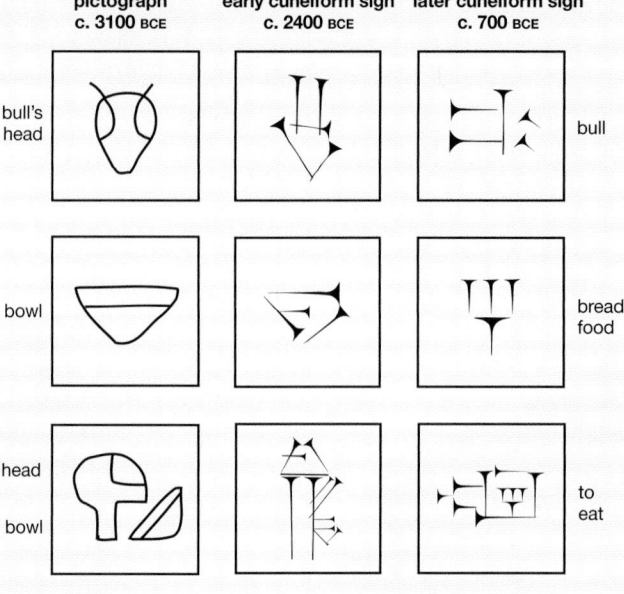

	pictograph c. 3100 BCE	early cuneiform sign c. 2400 BCE	later cuneiform sign c. 700 BCE	
bull's head				bull
bowl				bread, food
head bowl				to eat

symbols

Statues of gods and donors were placed in Sumerian temples. A striking life-size marble face from Uruk (see "Art as Spoils of War," page 32) may represent a goddess. It could have been attached to a wooden head on a full-size wooden body. Now stripped of its original paint, wig, and the **inlay** set in for brows and eyes, it appears as a stark white mask. Shells may have been used for the whites of the eyes and lapis lazuli for the pupils, and the hair may have been gold.

A tall vessel of carved alabaster (a fine, white stone) found near the temple complex of Inanna at Uruk **(FIG. 2–3)** shows how early Mesopotamian sculptors told stories in stone with great clarity and economy. The visual narrative here is organized into three **registers**, or horizontal bands, and the story condensed to its essential

2-3 • CARVED VESSEL
From Uruk (present-day Warka, Iraq).
c. 3300–3000 BCE. Alabaster, height 36"
(91 cm). Iraq Museum, Baghdad.

elements. The lowest register shows in a lower strip the sources of life in the natural world, beginning with water and plants (variously identified as date palm and barley, wheat and flax) and continuing in a superimposed upper strip, where alternating rams and ewes march single file along a solid ground line. In the middle register naked men carry baskets of foodstuffs, and in the top register, the goddess Inanna accepts an offering from two standing figures. Inanna stands in front of the gate to her richly filled shrine and storehouse, identified by two reed door poles hung with banners. The two men who face her are thought to be first a naked priest or acolyte presenting an offering-filled basket, followed by a partially preserved, ceremonially dressed figure of the priest-king (not visible in FIG. 2–3). The scene may represent a re-enactment of the ritual marriage between the goddess and Dumuzi, her consort—a role taken by the priest-king—that took place during the New Year's festival to ensure the fertility of crops, animals, and people, and thus the continued survival of Uruk.

VOTIVE FIGURES. Limestone statues dated to about 2900–2600 BCE from the Square Temple in Eshnunna (FIG. 2–4), excavated in 1932–1933, reveal another aspect of Sumerian religious art. These **votive figures** of men and women—images dedicated to the gods—are directly related to an ancient Near Eastern devotional practice in which individual worshipers could set up images of themselves in a shrine before a larger, more elaborate image of a god. A simple inscription might identify the figure as "One who offers prayers." Longer inscriptions might recount in detail all the things the donor had accomplished in the god's honor. Each sculpture served as a stand-in for the donor, locked in eye-contact with the god, caught perpetually in the act of worship.

The sculptors of these votive statues followed conventions that were important in Sumerian art. Figures are represented with stylized faces and bodies, dressed in clothing that emphasizes pure cylindrical shapes. They stand solemnly, hands clasped in respect, perhaps a posture expected in devotional contexts. The bold, glaring eyes may be related to statements in contemporary Sumerian texts that advise worshipers to approach their gods with an attentive gaze. As with the face of the woman from Uruk, arched brows were inlaid with dark shell, stone, or bitumen that once emphasized the huge, staring eyes. The male figures, bare-chested and dressed in what appear to be sheepskin skirts, are stocky and muscular, with heavy legs, large feet, big shoulders, and cylindrical bodies. The female figures are as massive as the men. Their long sheepskin skirts reveal sturdy legs and feet.

Sumerian artisans worked in various precious metals, and in bronze, often combining them with other materials. Many of these creations were decorated with—or were in the shape of—animals or composite animal-human-bird creatures. A superb example of their skill is a lyre—a kind of harp—from the city of Ur (present-day Muqaiyir, Iraq), to the south of Uruk. This combines wood, gold, lapis lazuli, and shell (see "A Lyre from a Royal Tomb in Ur," pages 34–35). Projecting from the base is a wood-sculpted head of a bearded bull overlaid with gold, intensely lifelike despite the decoratively patterned blue beard created from the semiprecious

2-4 • VOTIVE FIGURES
From the Square Temple, Eshnunna (present-day Tell Asmar, Iraq). c. 2900–2600 BCE. Limestone, alabaster, and gypsum, height of largest figure approx. 30″ (76.3 cm). Oriental Institute of the University of Chicago.

Art as Spoils of War—Protection or Theft?

Art has always been a casualty in times of social unrest. One of the most recent examples is the looting of the unguarded Iraq National Museum after the fall of Baghdad to U.S.-led coalition forces in April 2003. Among the many thousands of treasures that were stolen is a precious marble head of a woman from Warka, over 5,000 years old. Fortunately it was later recovered, but not without significant damage. Also looted was a carved Sumerian vessel (FIG. 2–3), eventually returned to the museum two months later, shattered into 14 pieces. The museum itself managed to reopen in 2009, but thousands of its antiquities are still missing.

Some of the most bitter resentment spawned by war has involved the taking by the victors of art objects that held great value for the conquered population. Two historically priceless objects unearthed in Elamite Susa, for example—the Akkadian Stele of Naram-Sin (SEE FIG. 2–1) and the Babylonian Stele of Hammurabi (see page 38)—were not Elamite at all, but Mesopotamian. Both had been brought there as military trophies by an Elamite king, who added an inscription to the Stele of Naram-Sin explaining that he had merely "protected" it. Uncovered in Susa during excavations organized by French archaeologist Jacques de Morgan, both works were taken back to Paris at the turn of the twentieth century and are now displayed in the Louvre. Museums around the world contain such works, either snatched by invading armies or acquired as a result of conquest.

The Rosetta Stone, the key to deciphering Egyptian hieroglyphs, was discovered in Egypt by French troops in 1799, fell into British hands when they forced the French from Egypt, and ultimately ended up in the British Museum in London (see page 77). In the early nineteenth century, the Briton Lord Elgin purchased and removed classical Greek sculpture from the Parthenon in Athens with the permission of the Ottoman authorities who governed Greece at the time (see page 135). Although his actions may indeed have protected these treasures from neglect and damage in later wars, they have remained installed in the British Museum, despite continuing protests from Greece. Many German collections include works that were similarly "protected" at the end of World War II and are surfacing now. In the United States, Native Americans are increasingly vocal in their demands that artifacts and human remains collected by anthropologists and archaeologists be returned to them.

"To the victor," it is said, "belong the spoils." But passionate and continuous debate surrounds the question of whether this notion remains valid in our own time, especially in the case of revered cultural artifacts.

FACE OF A WOMAN, KNOWN AS THE WARKA HEAD
Displayed by Iraqi authorities on its recovery in 2003 by the Iraq Museum in Baghdad. The head is from Uruk (present-day Warka, Iraq). c. 3300–3000 BCE. Marble, height approx. 8″ (20.3 cm).

---

gem stone, lapis lazuli. Since lapis lazuli had to be imported from Afghanistan, the work documents widespread trade in the region at this time.

CYLINDER SEALS. About the time written records appeared, Sumerians developed seals for identifying documents and establishing property ownership. By 3300–3100 BCE, record keepers redesigned the stamp seal as a cylinder. Rolled across documents on clay tablets or over the soft clay applied to a closure that needed sealing—a jar lid, the knot securing a bundle, or the door to a room—the cylinders left a raised mirror image of the design incised (cut) into their surface. Such sealing attested to the authenticity or accuracy of a text or assured that no unauthorized person could gain access to a room or container. Sumerian **cylinder seals**, usually less than 2 inches high, were generally made of a hard stone so that the tiny but elaborate incised scenes would not wear away during repeated use. Individuals often acquired seals as signs of status or on appointment to a high

2-5 • CYLINDER SEAL AND ITS MODERN IMPRESSION
Tomb of Queen Puabi (PG 800), Ur (present-day Muqaiyir, Iraq). c. 2600–2500 BCE. Lapis lazuli, height 1⁹⁄₁₆″ (4 cm), diameter ²⁵⁄₃₂″ (2 cm). University of Pennsylvania Museum of Archaeology and Anthropology, Philadelphia.

administrative position, and the seals were buried with them, along with other important possessions.

The lapis lazuli **CYLINDER SEAL** in **FIG. 2–5** is one of over 400 that were found in excavations of the royal burials at Ur. It comes from the tomb of a royal woman known as Puabi, and was found leaning against the right arm of her body. The modern clay impression of its incised design shows two registers of a convivial banquet at which all the guests are women, with fringed skirts and long hair gathered up in buns behind their necks. Two seated women in the upper register raise their glasses, accompanied by standing servants, one of whom, at far left, holds a fan. The single seated figure in the lower register sits in front of a table piled with food, while a figure behind her offers a cup of drink, presumably drawn from the jar she carries in her other hand, reminiscent of the container held by the lion on the lyre plaque (see page 35, FIG. C). Musical entertainment is provided by four women, standing to the far right.

AKKAD

During the Sumerian period, a people known as the Akkadians had settled north of Uruk. They adopted Sumerian culture, but unlike the Sumerians, the Akkadians spoke a Semitic language (the same family of languages that includes Arabic and Hebrew). Under the powerful military and political figure Sargon I (ruled c. 2332–2279 BCE), they conquered most of Mesopotamia. For more than half a century, Sargon, "King of the Four Quarters of the World," ruled this empire from his capital at Akkad, the actual site of which is yet to be discovered.

HEAD OF A RULER.   Few artifacts can be identified with Akkad, making a life-size bronze head—found in the northern city of Nineveh (present-day Kuyunjik, Iraq) and thought to date from the time of Sargon—especially precious **(FIG. 2–6)**. It is the earliest major work of hollow-cast copper sculpture known in the ancient Near East.

The facial features and hairstyle probably reflect a generalized ideal rather than the appearance of a specific individual, although

2-6 • HEAD OF A MAN (KNOWN AS AKKADIAN RULER)
From Nineveh (present-day Kuyunjik, Iraq). c. 2300–2200 BCE. Copper alloy, height 14⅜″ (36.5 cm). Iraq Museum, Baghdad.

THE OBJECT SPEAKS

A Lyre from a Royal Tomb in Ur

Sir Leonard Woolley's excavations at Ur during the 1920s initially garnered international attention because of the association of this ancient Mesopotamian city with the biblical patriarch Abraham. It was not long, however, before the exciting discoveries themselves moved to center stage, especially 16 royal burials that yielded spectacular objects crafted of gold and lurid evidence of the human sacrifices associated with Sumerian royal burial practices, when retainers were seemingly buried with the rulers they served.

Woolley's work at Ur was a joint venture of the University of Pennsylvania Museum in Philadelphia and the British Museum in London, and in conformance with Iraq's Antiquities Law of 1922, the uncovered artifacts were divided between the sponsoring

institutions and Iraq itself. Although Woolley worked with a large team of laborers and assistants over 12 seasons of digging at Ur, he and his wife Katherine reserved for themselves the painstakingly delicate process of uncovering the most important finds. Woolley's own account of work within one tomb outlines the practice—"Most of the workmen were sent away … so that the final work with knives and brushes could be done by my wife and myself in comparative peace. For ten days the two of us spent most of the time from sunrise to sunset lying on our tummies brushing and blowing and threading beads in their order as they lay…. You might suppose that to find three-score women all richly bedecked with jewelry could be a very thrilling experience, and so it

is, in retrospect, but I'm afraid that at the moment one is much more conscious of the toil than of the thrill" (quoted in Zettler and Horne, p. 31).

One of the most spectacular discoveries in the royal burials at Ur was an elaborate lyre, which rested over the body of the woman who had presumably played it during the funeral ceremony for the royal figure buried nearby. Like nine other lyres Woolley found at Ur, the wooden sound box of this one had long since deteriorated and disappeared, but an exquisitely crafted bull's head finial of gold and lapis lazuli survived, along with a plaque of carved shell inlaid with bitumen, depicting at the top a heroic image of a man interlocked with and in control of two bulls, and below them three scenes of animals personifying the activities of humans. On one register, a seated donkey plucks the strings of a bull lyre—similar to the instrument on which this set of images originally appeared—stabilized by a standing bear, while a fox accompanies him with a rattle. On the register above, upright animals bring food and drink for a feast. A hyena to the left—assuming the role of a butcher with a knife in his belt—carries a table piled high with meat. A lion follows, toting a large jar and pouring vessel.

The top and bottom registers are particularly intriguing in relation to the *Epic of Gilgamesh*, a 3,000-line poem that is Sumer's great contribution to world literature. Rich in descriptions of heroic feats and fabulous creatures, Gilgamesh's story probes the question of immortality and expresses the heroic aim to understand hostile surroundings and to find meaning in human existence. Gilgamesh encounters scorpion-men, like the one pictured in the lowest register, and it is easy to see the hero himself in the commanding but unprotected bearded figure centered in the top register, naked except for a wide belt, masterfully controlling in his grasp the two powerfully rearing human-headed bulls that flank him. Because the poem was first written down 700 years after this harp was created, this plaque may document a very long oral tradition.

On another level, because we know lyres were used in funeral rites, this imagery may

A. KATHERINE AND LEONARD WOOLLEY (ABOVE) EXCAVATING AT UR IN 1937, BESIDE TWO ARCHAEOLOGICAL ASSISTANTS IN ONE OF THE ROYAL BURIALS
Archives of the University of Pennsylvania Museum, Philadelphia.

depict a heroic image of the deceased in
the top register, and a funeral banquet in the
realm of the dead at the bottom. The
animals shown are the traditional guardians
of the gateway through which the deceased
had first to pass. Cuneiform tablets preserve
songs of mourning, perhaps chanted by
priests accompanied by lyres at funerals.
One begins, "Oh, lady, the harp of mourning
is placed on the ground," a particularly
poignant statement considering that the
lyres of Ur may have been buried on top of
the sacrificed bodies of the women who
originally played them.

B. THE GREAT LYRE WITH BULL'S HEAD
Royal Tomb (PG 789), Ur (present-day Muqaiyir, Iraq). c. 2600–2500 BCE.
Wood with gold, silver, lapis lazuli, bitumen, and shell, reassembled in
modern wood support; height of head 14″ (35.6 cm); height of front panel
13″ (33 cm); maximum length of lyre 55½″ (140 cm); height of upright
back arm 46½″ (117 cm). University of Pennsylvania Museum of
Archaeology and Anthropology, Philadelphia.

C. FRONT PANEL, THE SOUND BOX OF THE GREAT LYRE
Ur (present-day Muqaiyir, Iraq). Wood with shell inlaid in bitumen,
height 12¼ × 4½″ (31.1 × 11 cm). University of Pennsylvania Museum of
Archaeology and Anthropology, Philadelphia.

the sculpture was once identified as Sargon himself. The enormous curling beard and elaborately braided hair (circling the head and ending in a knot at the back) indicate both royalty and ideal male appearance. The deliberate damage to the left side of the face and eye suggests that the head was symbolically mutilated to destroy its power. Specifically, the ears and the inlaid eyes appear to have been removed to deprive the head of its ability to hear and see.

THE STELE OF NARAM-SIN.

The concept of imperial authority was literally carved in stone by Sargon's grandson Naram-Sin (SEE FIG. 2–1). This 6½-foot-high stele memorializes one of his military victories, and is one of the first works of art created to celebrate a specific achievement of an individual ruler. The inscription states that the stele commemorates the king's victory over the Lullubi people of the Zagros Mountains. Watched over by three solar deities (symbolized by the rayed suns at the top of the stele) and wearing a horned helmet-crown—heretofore associated only with gods—the hieratically scaled king stands proudly above his soldiers and his fallen foes, boldly silhouetted against the sky next to the smooth surface of a mountain. Even the shape of the stone slab is used as an active part of the composition. Its tapering top perfectly accommodates the carved mountain within it, and Naram-Sin is posed to reflect the profile of both.

UR AND LAGASH

The Akkadian Empire fell around 2180 BCE to the Guti, a mountain people from the northeast. For a brief time, the Guti controlled most of the Mesopotamian plain, but ultimately Sumerian people regained control of the region and expelled the Guti in 2112 BCE, under the leadership of King Urnammu of Ur. He reintroduced the Sumerian language and sponsored magnificent building campaigns, notably a ziggurat dedicated to the moon god Nanna, also called Sin (FIG. 2–7). Although located on the site of an earlier temple, this imposing mud-brick structure was not the accidental result of successive rebuilding. Its base is a rectangle 205 by 141 feet, with three sets of stairs converging at an imposing entrance gate atop the first of what were three platforms. Each platform's walls slope outward from top to base, probably to prevent rainwater from forming puddles and eroding the mud-brick pavement below. The first two levels of the ziggurat and their retaining walls are recent reconstructions.

One large Sumerian city-state remained independent throughout this period: Lagash, whose capital was Girsu (present-day Telloh, Iraq), on the Tigris River. Gudea, the ruler, built and restored many temples, and within them, following a venerable Mesopotamian tradition, he placed votive statues representing himself as governor and embodiment of just rule. The statues are made of diorite, a very hard stone, and the difficulty of carving it may have prompted sculptors to use compact, simplified forms for the portraits. Or perhaps it was the desire for powerful, stylized images that prompted the choice of this imported stone for this series of statues. Twenty of them survive, making Gudea a familiar figure in the study of ancient Near Eastern art.

Images of Gudea present him as a strong, peaceful, pious ruler worthy of divine favor (FIG. 2–8). Whether he is shown sitting or standing, he wears a long garment, which provides ample, smooth space for long cuneiform inscriptions. In this imposing statue, only 2½ feet tall, his right shoulder is bare, and he wears a cap with a wide brim carved with a pattern to represent fleece. He holds a vessel in front of him, from which life-giving water flows in two streams, each filled with leaping fish. The text on his garment states that he dedicated himself, the statue, and its temple to the goddess Geshtinanna, the divine poet and interpreter of dreams. The sculptor has emphasized the power centers of the human body: the eyes, head, and smoothly muscled chest and arms. Gudea's face is youthful and serene, and his eyes—oversized and

2-7 • NANNA ZIGGURAT
Ur (present-day Muqaiyir, Iraq). c. 2100–2050 BCE.

2-8 • VOTIVE STATUE OF GUDEA
Girsu (present-day Telloh, Iraq). c. 2090 BCE. Diorite, height 29″
(73.7 cm). Musée du Louvre, Paris.

EXPLORE MORE: Gain insight from a primary source related to
the statue of Gudea www.myartslab.com

wide open—perpetually confront the gaze of the
deity with intense concentration.

BABYLON

For more than 300 years, periods of political turmoil
alternated with periods of stable government in
Mesopotamia, until the Amorites (a Semitic-speaking
people from the Syrian Desert, to the west) reunited
the region under Hammurabi (ruled 1792–1750 BCE).
Hammurabi's capital city was Babylon and his subjects
were called Babylonians. Among Hammurabi's
achievements was a written legal code that detailed
the laws of his realm and the penalties for breaking
them (see "The Code of Hammurabi," page 38).

THE HITTITES OF ANATOLIA

Outside of Mesopotamia, other cultures developed
and flourished in the ancient Near East. Anatolia
(present-day Turkey) was home to several independent
cultures that had resisted Mesopotamian domination,
but the Hittites—whose founders had moved into the
mountains and plateaus of central Anatolia from the
east—were the most powerful among them.

The Hittites established their capital at Hattusha
(near present-day Boghazkoy, Turkey) about 1600
BCE, and the city thrived until its destruction about
1200 BCE. Through trade and conquest, the Hittites
created an empire that stretched along the coast of the
Mediterranean Sea in the area of present-day Syria
and Lebanon, bringing them into conflict with the
Egyptian Empire, which was expanding into the same
region (see Chapter 3). The Hittites also made
incursions into Mesopotamia, and their influence was
felt throughout the region.

The Hittites may have been the first people to
work in iron, which they used for war chariot fittings,
weapons, chisels, and hammers for sculptors and
masons. They are noted for the artistry of their fine
metalwork and for their imposing palace citadels with
double walls and fortified gateways, that survive today
only in the ruins of archaeological sites. One of the
most monumental of these sites consists of the
foundations and base walls of the Hittite stronghold
at Hattusha, which date to about 1400–1300 BCE. The
lower walls were constructed of stone supplied from
local quarries, and the upper walls, stairways, and
walkways were finished in brick.

The blocks of stone used to frame doorways at
Hattusha were decorated in high relief with a variety
of guardian figures—some of them 7 feet tall. Some
were half-human–half-animal creatures; others were

The Code of Hammurabi

Babylonian ruler Hammurabi's systematic codification of his people's rights, duties, and punishments for wrongdoing was engraved on a black diorite slab known as the Stele of Hammurabi. This imposing artifact, therefore, is both a work of art that depicts a legendary event and a precious historical document that records a conversation about justice between god and man.

At the top of the stele, we see Hammurabi standing in an attitude of prayer before Shamash, the sun god and god of justice. Rays rise from Shamash's shoulders as he sits, crowned by a conical horned cap, on a backless throne, holding additional symbols of his power—the measuring rod and the rope circle. Shamash gives the law to the king, his intermediary, and the codes of justice flow forth underneath them in horizontal bands of exquisitely engraved cuneiform signs. The idea of god-given laws engraved on stone tablets has a long tradition in the ancient Near East: Moses, the lawgiver of Israel, received two stone tablets containing the Ten Commandments from God on Mount Sinai (Exodus 32:19).

A prologue on the front of the stele lists the temples Hammurabi has restored, and an epilogue on the back glorifies him as a peacemaker, but most of the stele "publishes" the laws themselves, guaranteeing uniform treatment of people throughout his kingdom. Within the inscription, Hammurabi declares that he intends "to cause justice to prevail in the land and to destroy the wicked and the evil, that the strong might not oppress the weak nor the weak the strong." Most of the 300 or so entries that follow deal with commercial and property matters. Only 68 relate to domestic problems, and a mere 20 deal with physical assault.

Punishments are based on the wealth, class, and gender of the parties—the rights of the wealthy are favored over the poor, citizens over slaves, men over women. Most famous are instances when punishments are specifically tailored to fit crimes—an eye for an eye, a tooth for a tooth, a broken bone for a broken bone. The death penalty is decreed for crimes such as stealing from a temple or palace, helping a slave to escape, or insubordination in the army. Trial by water and fire could also be imposed, as when an adulterous woman and her lover were to be thrown into the water; if they did not drown, they were deemed innocent. Although some of the punishments may seem excessive today, Hammurabi was breaking new ground by regulating laws and punishments rather than leaving them to the whims of rulers or officials.

STELE OF HAMMURABI
Susa (present-day Shush, Iran). c. 1792–1750 BCE. Diorite, height of stele approx. 7′ (2.13 m); height of relief 28″ (71.1 cm). Musée du Louvre, Paris.

EXPLORE MORE: Gain insight from a primary source related to the Code of Hammurabi **www.myartslab.com**

2-9 • LION GATE
Hattusha (near present-day Boghazkoy, Turkey). c. 1400 BCE. Limestone.

more naturalistically rendered animals like the lions at the **LION GATE (FIG. 2–9)**. Carved from the building stones and consistent with the colossal scale of the wall itself, the lions seem to emerge from the gigantic boulders that form the gate. Despite extreme weathering, the lions have endured over the millennia and still possess a sense of both vigor and permanence.

ASSYRIA

After centuries of struggle among Sumer, Akkad, and Lagash in southern Mesopotamia, a people called the Assyrians rose to dominance in northern Mesopotamia. They began to extend their power by about 1400 BCE, and after about 1000 BCE started to conquer neighboring regions. By the end of the ninth century BCE, the Assyrians controlled most of Mesopotamia, and by the early seventh century BCE they had extended their influence as far west as Egypt. Soon afterward they succumbed to internal weakness and external enemies, and by 600 BCE their empire had collapsed.

Assyrian rulers built huge palaces atop high platforms inside the different fortified cities that served at one time or another as Assyrian capitals. They decorated these palaces with shallow stone reliefs of battle and hunting scenes, of Assyrian victories including presentations of tribute to the king, and of religious imagery.

KALHU

During his reign (883–859 BCE), Assurnasirpal II established his capital at Kalhu (present-day Nimrud, Iraq), on the east bank of the Tigris River, and undertook an ambitious building program. His architects fortified the city with mud-brick walls 5 miles long and 42 feet high, and his engineers constructed a canal that irrigated fields and provided water for the expanded population of the city. According to an inscription commemorating the event, Assurnasirpal gave a banquet for 69,574 people to celebrate the dedication of the new capital in 863 BCE.

Most of the buildings in Kalhu were made from mud bricks, but limestone and alabaster—more impressive and durable—were used to veneer walls with architectural decoration. Colossal guardian figures flanked the major **portals** (grand entrances, often decorated), and panels covered the walls with scenes in **low relief** (sculpted relief with figures that project only slightly from a recessed background) of the king participating in religious rituals, war campaigns, and hunting expeditions.

2–10 • ASSURNASIRPAL II KILLING LIONS

Palace complex of Assurnasirpal II, Kalhu (present-day Nimrud, Iraq). c. 875–860 BCE.
Alabaster, height approx. 39″ (99.1 cm). British Museum, London.

THE LION HUNT. In a vivid lion-hunting scene **(FIG. 2–10)**, Assurnasirpal II stands in a chariot pulled by galloping horses and draws his bow against an attacking lion, advancing from the rear with arrows already protruding from its body. Another expiring beast collapses on the ground under the horses. This was probably a ceremonial hunt, in which the king, protected by men with swords and shields, rode back and forth killing animals as they were released one by one into an enclosed area. The immediacy of this image marks a shift in Mesopotamian art, away from a sense of timeless solemnity, and toward a more dramatic, even emotional, involvement with the event portrayed.

ENEMIES CROSSING THE EUPHRATES TO ESCAPE ASSYRIAN ARCHERS. In another palace relief, the scene shifts from royal

citadel gate A   Nabu temple   ziggurat   palace   throne room

city wall

palace entrance

citadel gate B

citadel wall

2–11 • RECONSTRUCTION DRAWING OF THE CITADEL AND PALACE COMPLEX OF SARGON II
Dur Sharrukin (present-day Khorsabad, Iraq). c. 721–706 BCE. Courtesy the Oriental Institute of the University of Chicago.

A CLOSER LOOK

Enemies Crossing the Euphrates to Escape Assyrian Archers

Palace complex of Assurnasirpal II, Kalhu (present-day Nimrud, Iraq). c. 875–860 BCE. Alabaster, height approx. 39" (99.1 cm). British Museum, London.

These Assyrian archers are outfitted in typical fashion, with protective boots, short "kilts," pointed helmets, and swords, as well as bows and quivers of arrows. Their smaller scale conveys a sense of depth and spatial positioning in this relief, reinforced by the size and placement of the trees.

The detailed landscape setting documents the swirling water of the river, its rocky banks, and the airy environment of the trees, one of which is clearly described as a palm.

The oblique line of the river bank and the overlapping of the swimmers convey a sense of depth receding from the picture plane into pictorial space.

If this is the ruler of the enemy citadel, he seems shocked into powerlessness by the Assyrian invasion. Note the contrast between his lax weapon and those deployed by the archers of the Assyrian vanguard.

The long robes of the three enemy swimmers signal their high status. They are not ordinary foot soldiers.

The two lower swimmers were clearly taken by surprise. Already engaged in their watery retreat, they are still blowing through "tubes" to inflate their flotation devices, made from sewn animal skins.

This beardless swimmer is probably a eunuch, many of whom served as high officials in ancient Near Eastern courts.

Two figures react to the bleak fate of their arrow-riddled comrades attempting to swim to safety by raising their hands in despair.

SEE MORE: View the Closer Look feature for Enemies Crossing the Euphrates to Escape Assyrian Archers
www.myartslab.com

---

ceremony to the heat of battle set within a detailed landscape (see "A Closer Look," above). Three of the Assyrian's enemies—two using flotation devices made of inflated animal skins—swim across a raging river, retreating from a vanguard of Assyrian archers who kneel at its banks to launch their assault. The scene evokes a specific event from 878 BCE described in the annals of Assurnasirpal. As the Assyrian king overtook the army of an enemy leader named Kudurru near the modern town of Anu, both leader and soldiers escaped into the Euphrates River in an attempt to save their lives.

DUR SHARRUKIN

Sargon II (ruled 721–706 BCE) built a new Assyrian capital at Dur Sharrukin (present-day Khorsabad, Iraq). On the northwest side of the capital, a walled citadel, or fortress, straddled the city wall (**FIG. 2–11**). Within the citadel, Sargon's **palace complex** (the group of buildings where the ruler governed and resided) stood on a raised, fortified platform about 40 feet high and demonstrates the use of art as political propaganda.

Guarded by two towers, the palace complex was accessible only by a wide ramp leading up from an open square, around

2-12 • GUARDIAN FIGURES AT GATE A OF THE CITADEL OF SARGON II DURING ITS EXCAVATION
Dur Sharrukin (present-day Khorsabad, Iraq). c. 721–706 BCE.

which the residences of important government and religious officials were clustered. Beyond the ramp was the main courtyard, with service buildings on the right and temples on the left. The heart of the palace, protected by a reinforced wall with only two small, off-center doors, lay past the main courtyard. Within the inner compound was a second courtyard lined with narrative relief panels showing tribute bearers. Visitors would have waited to see the king in this courtyard that functioned as an audience hall; once granted access to the royal throne room, they would have passed

through a stone gate flanked, like the other gates of citadel and palace **(FIG. 2-12)**, by colossal guardian figures. These guardian figures, known as **lamassus**, combined the bearded head of a man, the powerful body of a lion or bull, the wings of an eagle, and the horned headdress of a god.

In an open space between the palace complex and temple complex at Dur Sharrukin rose a ziggurat declaring the might of Assyria's kings and symbolizing their claim to empire. It probably had seven levels, each about 18 feet high and painted a different

2-13 • ASSURBANIPAL AND HIS QUEEN IN THE GARDEN
The Palace at Nineveh (present-day Kuyunjik, Iraq). c. 647 BCE. Alabaster, height approx. 21″ (53.3 cm).
British Museum, London.

TECHNIQUE | Textiles

Textiles were usually a woman's art although men, as shepherds and farmers, often produced the raw materials (wool, flax, and other fibers). And as traveling merchants, men sold or bartered the extra fabrics not needed by the family. Early Assyrian cuneiform tablets preserve correspondence between merchants traveling by caravan and their wives. These astute businesswomen ran the production end of the business back home and often complained to their husbands about late payments and changed orders.

The woman shown spinning in the fragment from Susa is an imposing figure, wearing an elegant hairstyle, many ornaments, and a garment with a patterned border. She sits barefoot and cross-legged on a lion-footed stool covered with sheepskin, spinning thread with a large spindle. A servant stands behind the woman, fanning her, while a fish and six round objects (perhaps fruit) lie on an offering stand in front of her.

The production of textiles is complex. First, fibers gathered from plants (such as flax for linen cloth or hemp for rope) or from animals (wool from sheep, goats, and camels or hair from humans and horses) are cleaned, combed, and sorted. Only then can the fibers be twisted and drawn out under tension—that is, spun—into the long, strong, flexible thread needed for textiles. Weaving is done on a loom. Warp threads are laid out at right angles to weft threads, which are passed over and under the warp. In the earliest vertical looms, warp threads hung from a beam, their tension created either by wrapping them around a lower beam (a tapestry loom) or by tying them to heavy stones. Although weaving was usually a home industry, in palaces and temples slave women staffed large shops, and specialized as spinners, warpers, weavers, and finishers.

Early fiber artists depended on the natural colors of their materials and on natural dyes from the earth, plants, and animals. They combined color and techniques to create a great variety of fiber arts: Egyptians seem to have preferred white linen, elaborately folded and pleated, for their garments. The Minoans of Crete created multicolored patterned fabrics with fancy borders. Greeks excelled in the art of pictorial tapestries. The people of the ancient Near East used woven and dyed patterns and also developed knotted pile (the so-called Persian carpet) and felt (a cloth made of fibers bound by heat and pressure, not by spinning, weaving, or knitting).

WOMAN SPINNING
Susa (present-day Shush, Iran). c. 8th–7th century BCE. Bitumen compound, 3⅝ × 5⅛" (9.2 × 13 cm). Musée du Louvre, Paris.

color (SEE FIG. 2–11). The four levels still remaining were once white, black, blue, and red. Instead of separate flights of stairs between the levels, a single, squared-off spiral ramp rose continuously along the exterior from the base.

NINEVEH

Assurbanipal (ruled 669–c. 627 BCE), king of the Assyrians three generations after Sargon II, maintained his capital at Nineveh. Like that of Assurnasirpal II two centuries earlier, his palace was decorated with alabaster panels carved with pictorial narratives in low relief. Most show Assurbanipal and his subjects in battle or hunting, but there are occasional scenes of palace life.

An unusually peaceful example shows the king and queen relaxing in a pleasure garden (FIG. 2–13). The king reclines on a couch, and the queen sits in a chair at his feet, while a musician at far left plays diverting music. Three servants arrive from the left with trays of food, while others wave whisks to protect the royal couple from insects. The king has taken off his rich necklace and hung it on his couch, and he has laid aside his weapons—sword, bow, and quiver of arrows—on the table behind him, but this apparently tranquil domestic scene is actually a victory celebration. A grisly trophy, the severed head of his vanquished enemy, hangs upside down from a tree at the far left.

NEO-BABYLONIA

At the end of the seventh century BCE, Assyria was invaded by the Medes, a people from western Iran who were allied with the Babylonians and the Scythians, a nomadic people from northern Asia (present-day Russia and Ukraine). In 612 BCE, the Medes' army captured Nineveh. When the dust had settled, Assyria was no more and the Neo-Babylonians—so named because they recaptured the splendor that had marked Babylon 12 centuries earlier under Hammurabi—controlled a region that stretched from modern Turkey to northern Arabia and from Mesopotamia to the Mediterranean Sea.

The most famous Neo-Babylonian ruler was Nebuchadnezzar II (ruled 605–562 BCE), notorious today for his suppression of the Jews, as recorded in the book of Daniel in the Hebrew Bible, where he may have been confused with the final Neo-Babylonian ruler, Nabonidus. A great patron of architecture, Nebuchadnezzar II built temples dedicated to the Babylonian gods throughout his realm, and transformed Babylon—the cultural, political, and economic hub of his empire—into one of the most splendid cities of its day. Babylon straddled the Euphrates River, its two sections joined by a bridge.

The older, eastern sector of Babylon was traversed by the Processional Way, the route taken by religious processions honoring the city's patron god, Marduk **(FIG. 2–14)**. This street, paved with large stone slabs set in a bed of bitumen, was up to 66 feet wide at some points. It ran from the Euphrates bridge, through the temple district and palaces, and finally through the Ishtar Gate, the ceremonial entrance to the city. The Ishtar Gate's four **crenellated** towers (crenellations are notched walls for military defense) symbolized Babylonian power **(FIG. 2–15)**. Beyond the Ishtar Gate, walls on either side of the route—like the gate itself—were faced with dark blue glazed bricks. The glazed bricks consisted of a film of colored glass placed over the surface of the bricks and fired, a process used since about 1600 BCE. Against that blue background, specially molded turquoise, blue, and gold-colored bricks formed images of striding lions, symbols of the goddess Ishtar as well as the dragons that were associated with Marduk.

PERSIA

In the sixth century BCE, the Persians, a formerly nomadic, Indo-European-speaking people, began to seize power in Mesopotamia. From the region of Parsa, or Persis (present-day Fars, Iran), they established a vast empire. The rulers of this new empire traced their ancestry to a semilegendary Persian king named Achaemenes, and consequently they are known as the Achaemenids.

The dramatic expansion of the Achaemenids began in 559 BCE with the ascension of a remarkable leader, Cyrus II the Great (ruled 559–530 BCE). By the time of his death, the Persian Empire included Babylonia, Media (which stretched across present-day northern Iran through Anatolia), and some of the Aegean islands far to the west. Only the Greeks stood fast against them (see

2-14 • RECONSTRUCTION DRAWING OF BABYLON IN THE 6TH CENTURY BCE
Courtesy the Oriental Institute of the University of Chicago.

The palace of Nebuchadnezzar II, with its famous Hanging Gardens, can be seen just behind and to the right of the Ishtar Gate, west of the Processional Way. The Marduk Ziggurat looms in the far distance on the east bank of the Euphrates.

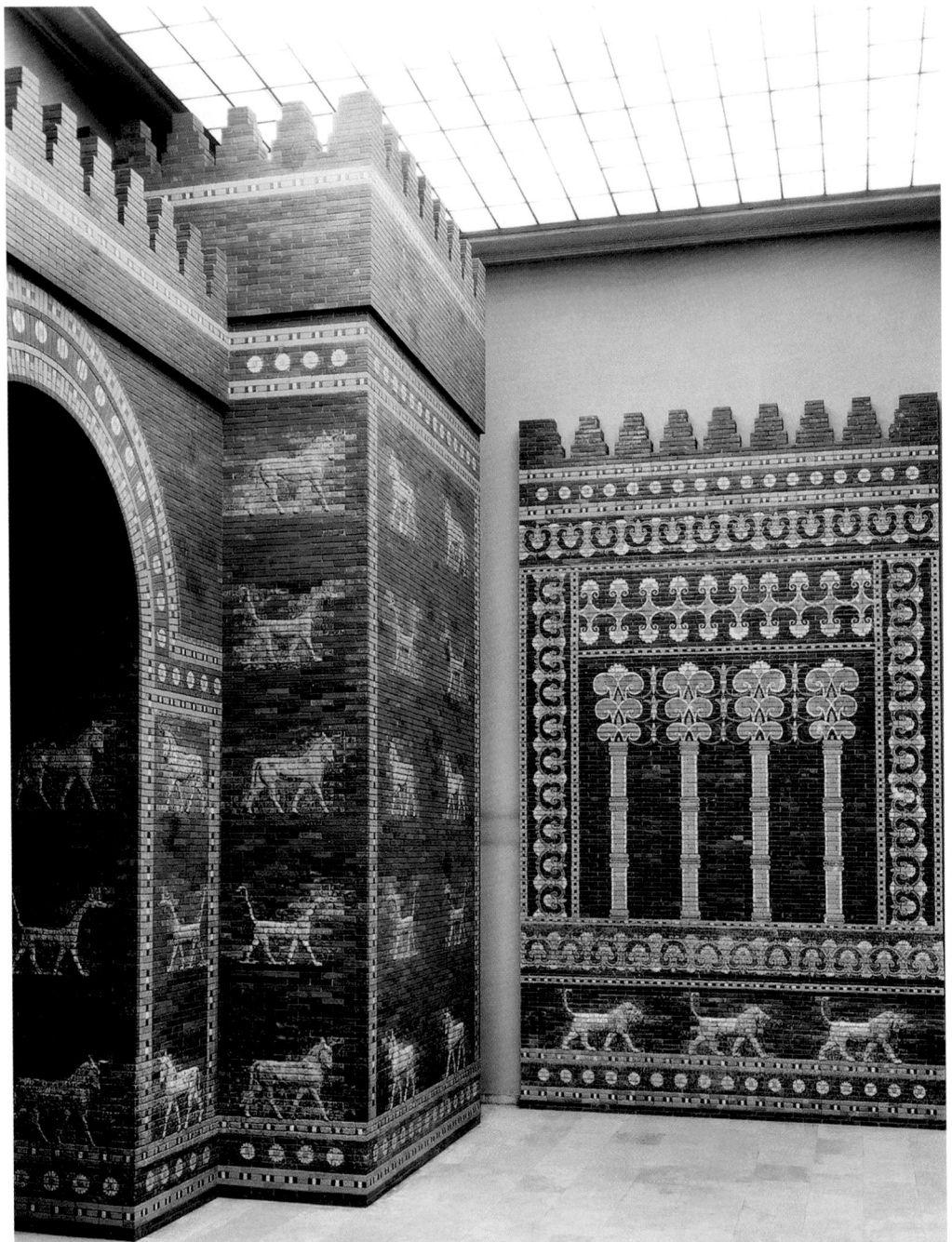

2-15 • ISHTAR GATE AND THRONE ROOM WALL
Reconstructed in a Berlin museum, originally from Babylon (present-day Iraq). c. 575 BCE. Glazed brick, height of gate originally 40′ (12.2 m) with towers rising 100′ (30.5 m). Vorderasiatisches Museum, Staatliche Museen zu Berlin, Preussischer Kulturbesitz.

The Ishtar Gate is decorated with tiers of dragons (with the head and body of a snake, the forelegs of a lion, and the hind legs of a bird of prey) that were sacred to Marduk, and with bulls with blue horns and tails that were associated with Adad, the storm god. Now reconstructed inside a Berlin Museum, it is installed next to a panel from the throne room in Nebuchadnezzar's nearby palace, in which lions walk beneath stylized palm trees.

Chapter 5). When Darius I (ruled 521–486 BCE) took the throne, he could proclaim: "I am Darius, great King, King of Kings, King of countries, King of this earth."

An able administrator, Darius organized the Persian lands into 20 tribute-paying areas under Persian governors. He often left local rulers in place beneath the governors. This practice, along with a tolerance for diverse native customs and religions, won the Persians the loyalty of many of their subjects. Like many powerful rulers, Darius created palaces and citadels as visible symbols of his authority. He made Susa his first capital and commissioned a 32-acre administrative compound to be built there.

In about 515 BCE, Darius began construction of Parsa, a new capital in the Persian homeland, today known by its Greek name:

Persepolis. It is one of the best-preserved and most impressive ancient sites in the Near East (FIG. 2–16). Darius imported materials, workers, and artists from all over his empire. He even ordered work to be executed in Egypt and transported to his capital. The result was a new multicultural style of art that combined many different traditions—Persian, Mede, Mesopotamian, Egyptian, and Greek.

In Assyrian fashion, the imperial complex at Persepolis was set on a raised platform, 40 feet high and measuring 1,500 by 900 feet, accessible only from a single approach made of wide, shallow steps that could be ascended on horseback. Like Egyptian and Greek cities, it was laid out on a rectangular grid. Darius lived to see the completion only of a treasury, the Apadana (audience hall), and a very small palace for himself. The **APADANA**, set above the rest of the

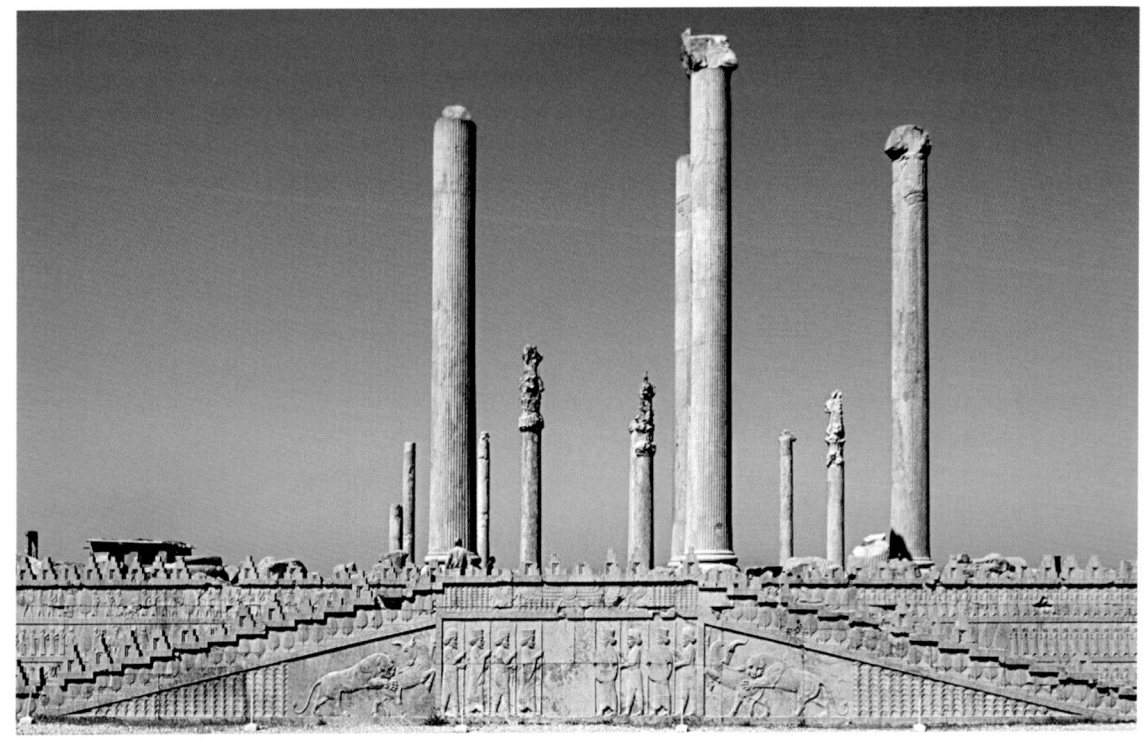

2-16 • AIR VIEW OF THE CEREMONIAL COMPLEX, PERSEPOLIS

Iran. 518–c. 460 BCE.

SEE MORE: View a video about Persepolis www.myartslab.com

2-17 • APADANA (AUDIENCE HALL) OF DARIUS AND XERXES

Ceremonial Complex, Persepolis, Iran. 518–c. 460 BCE.

2-18 • DARIUS AND XERXES RECEIVING TRIBUTE

Detail of a relief from the stairway leading to the Apadana (ceremonial complex), Persepolis, Iran. 491–486 BCE. Limestone, height 8′4″ (2.54 m). Courtesy the Oriental Institute of the University of Chicago.

SEE MORE: View a video about the process of sculpting in relief **www.myartslab.com**

complex on a second terrace **(FIG. 2–17)**, had open porches on three sides and a square hall large enough to hold several thousand people. Darius's son Xerxes I (ruled 485–465 BCE) added a sprawling palace complex for himself, enlarged the treasury building, and began a vast new public reception space, the Hall of 100 Columns.

The central stair of Darius's Apadana displays reliefs of animal combat, tiered ranks of royal guards (the "10,000 Immortals"), and delegations of tribute bearers. Here, lions attack bulls at each side of the Persian generals. Such animal combats (a theme found throughout the Near East) emphasize the ferocity of the leaders and their men. Ranks of warriors cover the walls with repeated patterns and seem ready to defend the palace. The elegant drawing, balanced composition, and sleek modeling of figures reflect the Persians' knowledge of Greek art and perhaps the use of Greek artists. Other reliefs throughout Persepolis depict displays of allegiance or economic prosperity. In one example, once the centerpiece, Darius holds an audience while his son and heir, Xerxes, listens from behind the throne **(FIG. 2–18)**. Such panels would have looked quite different when they were freshly painted in bright colors, with metal objects such as Darius's crown and necklace covered in **gold leaf** (sheets of hammered gold).

At its height, the Persian Empire extended from Africa to India. From Persepolis, Darius in 490 BCE and Xerxes in 480 BCE sent their armies west to conquer Greece, but mainland Greeks successfully resisted the armies of the Achaemenids, preventing them from advancing into Europe. Indeed, it was a Greek who ultimately put an end to their empire. In 334 BCE, Alexander the Great of Macedonia (d. 323 BCE) crossed into Anatolia and swept through Mesopotamia, defeating Darius III and nearly destroying

Persepolis in 330 BCE. Although the Achaemenid Empire was at an end, Persia eventually revived, and the Persian style in art continued to influence Greek artists (see Chapter 5) and ultimately became one of the foundations of Islamic art (see Chapter 8).

THINK ABOUT IT

2.1 Discuss the development of relief sculpture in the ancient Near East. Choose two specific examples, one from the Sumerian period and one from the Assyrian period, and explain how symbols and stories are combined to express ideas that were important to these two cultures.

2.2 Discuss how precious materials are used in "The Great Lyre with bull's head" (page 35, FIG. B). What are some likely motivations for employing these materials in this work?

2.3 Select two rulers discussed in this chapter and explain how each preserved his legacy through commissioned works of art and/or architecture.

2.4 What are the distinctive features of the Sumerian ziggurat and what led to its development?

PRACTICE MORE: Compose answers to these questions, get flashcards for images and terms, and review chapter material with quizzes **www.myartslab.com**

3–1 • FUNERARY MASK OF TUTANKHAMUN Eighteenth Dynasty (Tutankhamun, r. c. 1332–1322 BCE), c. 1327 BCE. Gold inlaid with glass and semiprecious stones, height 21¼″ (54.5 cm), weight 24 pounds (11 kg). Egyptian Museum, Cairo. JE 60672

ART OF ANCIENT EGYPT

On February 16, 1923, *The Times* of London cabled the *New York Times* with dramatic news of a discovery: "This has been, perhaps, the most extraordinary day in the whole history of Egyptian excavation…. The entrance today was made into the sealed chamber of [Tutankhamun's] tomb … and yet another door opened beyond that. No eyes have seen the King, but to practical certainty we know that he lies there close at hand in all his original state, undisturbed." And indeed he did. A collar of dried flowers and beads covered the chest, and a linen shroud was draped around the head. A gold **FUNERARY MASK** **(FIG. 3–1)** had been placed over the head and shoulders of his mummified body, which was enclosed in three nested coffins, the innermost made of gold (SEE FIG. 3–29, and page 73). The coffins were placed in a yellow quartzite **sarcophagus** (a stone coffin) that was itself encased within gilt wooden shrines nested inside one another.

The discoverer of this treasure, the English archaeologist Howard Carter, had worked in Egypt for more than 20 years before he undertook a last expedition, sponsored by the wealthy British amateur Egyptologist Lord Carnarvon. Carter was convinced that the tomb of Tutankhamun, one of the last Eighteenth-Dynasty royal burial places still unidentified, lay hidden in the Valley of the Kings. After 15 years of digging,

on November 4, 1922, he unearthed the entrance to Tutankhamun's tomb and found unbelievable treasures in the antechamber: jewelry, textiles, gold-covered furniture, a carved and inlaid throne, four gold chariots. In February 1923, Carter pierced the wall separating the anteroom from the actual burial chamber and found the greatest treasure of all, Tutankhamun himself.

Since ancient times, tombs have tempted looters; more recently, they also have attracted archaeologists and historians. The first large-scale "archaeological" expedition in history landed in Egypt with the armies of Napoleon in 1798. The French commander must have realized that he would find great wonders there, for he took French scholars with him to study ancient sites. The military adventure ended in failure, but the scholars eventually published richly illustrated volumes of their findings, unleashing a craze for all things Egyptian that has not dimmed since. In 1976, the first blockbuster museum exhibition was born when treasures from the tomb of Tutankhamun began a tour of the United States and attracted over 8 million visitors. Most recently, in 2006, Otto Schaden excavated a tomb containing seven coffins in the Valley of the Kings, the first tomb to be found there since Tutankhamun's in 1922.

LEARN ABOUT IT

3.1 Explore the pictorial conventions for representing the human figure in ancient Egyptian art, established early on and maintained for millennia.

3.2 Trace the evolution of royal portrait styles from the Old Kingdom through the New Kingdom and assess the differences between depictions of royalty and ordinary people.

3.3 Analyze how religious beliefs were reflected in the funerary art and architecture of ancient Egypt.

3.4 Appreciate the complexity of construction and decoration brought to New Kingdom temple architecture rooted in the same post-and-lintel architectural tradition that had been used since the Old Kingdom.

HEAR MORE: Listen to an audio file of your chapter **www.myartslab.com**

THE GIFT OF THE NILE

The Greek traveler and historian Herodotus, writing in the fifth century BCE, remarked, "Egypt is the gift of the Nile." This great river, the longest in the world, winds northward from equatorial Africa and flows through Egypt in a relatively straight line to the Mediterranean (MAP 3–1). There it forms a broad delta before emptying into the sea. Before it was dammed in 1970 by the Aswan High Dam, the lower (northern) Nile, swollen with the runoff of heavy seasonal rains in the south, overflowed its banks for several months each year. Every time the floodwaters receded, they left behind a new layer of rich silt, making the valley and delta a continually fertile and attractive habitat.

By about 8000 BCE, the valley's inhabitants had become relatively sedentary, living off the abundant fish, game, and wild plants. Not until about 5000 BCE did they adopt the agricultural village life associated with Neolithic culture (see Chapter 1). At that time, the climate of north Africa grew increasingly dry. To ensure adequate resources for agriculture, the farmers along the Nile began to manage flood waters in a system called basin irrigation.

The Predynastic period, from roughly 5000 to 2950 BCE, was a time of significant social and political transition that preceded the unification of Egypt under a single ruler. (After unification, Egypt was ruled by a series of family dynasties and is therefore characterized as "dynastic.") Rudimentary federations emerged and began conquering and absorbing weaker communities. By about 3500 BCE, there were several larger states, or chiefdoms, in the lower Nile Valley and a centralized form of leadership had emerged. Rulers were expected to protect their subjects, not only from outside aggression, but also from natural catastrophes such as droughts and insect plagues.

The surviving art of the Predynastic period consists chiefly of ceramic figurines, decorated pottery, and reliefs carved on stone plaques and pieces of ivory. A few examples of wall painting—lively scenes filled with small figures of people and animals—were found in a tomb at Hierakonpolis, in Upper Egypt, a Predynastic town of mud-brick houses that was once home to as many as 10,000 people.

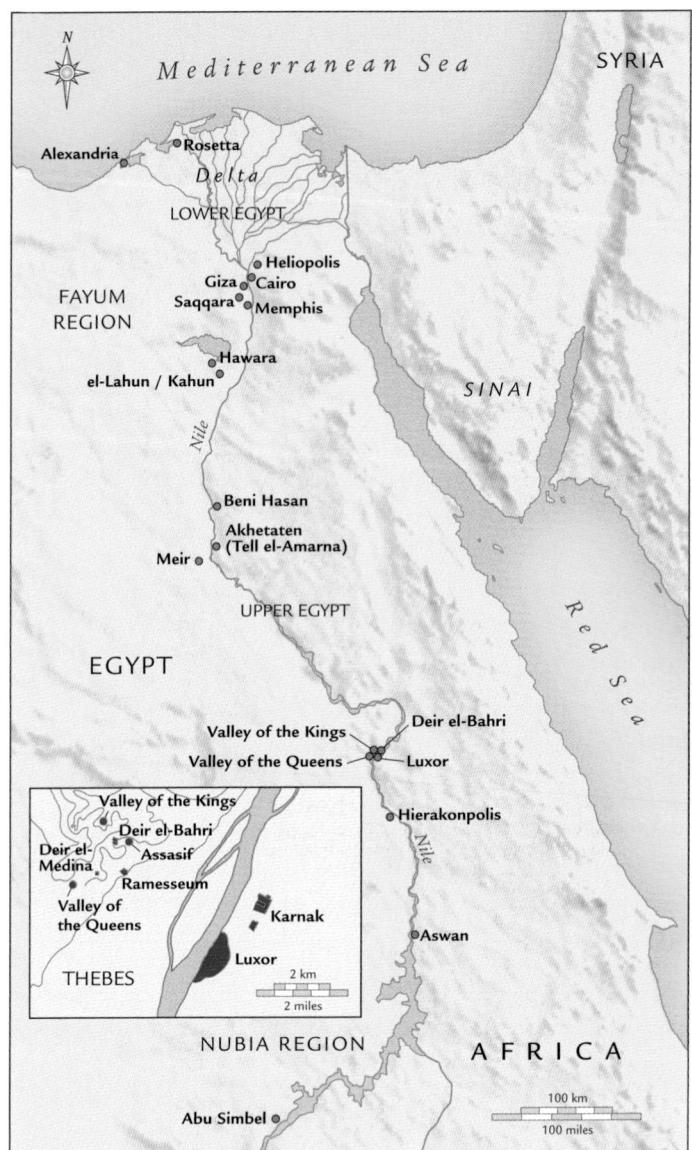

MAP 3–1 • ANCIENT EGYPT

Upper Egypt is below Lower Egypt on this map because the designations "upper" and "lower" refer to the directional flow of the Nile, not to our conventions for south and north in drawing maps. The two kingdoms were united c. 3000 BCE, just before the Early Dynastic period.

EARLY DYNASTIC EGYPT, C. 2950–2575 BCE

Around 3000 BCE, Egypt became a consolidated state. According to legend, the country had previously evolved into two major kingdoms—the Two Lands—Upper Egypt in the south (upstream on the Nile) and Lower Egypt in the north. But a powerful ruler from Upper Egypt conquered Lower Egypt and unified the two kingdoms. In the art of the subsequent Early Dynastic period we see the development of ideas about kingship and the cosmic order. Since the works of art and architecture that survive from ancient Egypt come mainly from tombs and temples—the majority of which were located in secure places and built with the most durable materials—most of what we now know about the ancient art of Egypt is rooted in religious beliefs and practices.

THE GOD-KINGS

The Greek historian Herodotus thought the Egyptians were the most religious people he had ever encountered. In their world-view, the movements of heavenly bodies, the workings of gods, and the humblest of human activities were all believed to be part of a balanced and harmonious grand design. Death was to be feared only by those who lived in such a way as to disrupt that harmony. Upright souls could be confident that their spirits would live on eternally.

Egyptian Symbols

Four crowns symbolize kingship: the tall, club-like white crown of Upper Egypt (sometimes adorned with two plumes); the flat or scooped red cap with projecting spiral of Lower Egypt; the double crown representing unified Egypt; and, in the New Kingdom, the blue oval crown, which evolved from a war helmet.

A striped gold and blue linen head cloth, known as the **nemes headdress**, having the cobra and vulture at the center front, was commonly used as royal headgear. The upright form of the cobra, known as the *uraeus*, represents the goddess Wadjet of Lower Egypt and is often included in king's crowns as well (SEE FIG. 3–1). The queen's crown included the feathered skin of the vulture goddess Nekhbet of Upper Egypt.

The god Horus, king of the earth and a force for good, is represented as a falcon or falcon-headed man. His eyes symbolize the sun and moon; the solar eye is called the *wedjat*. The looped cross, called the **ankh**, is symbolic of everlasting life. The **scarab** beetle (*khepri*, meaning "he who created himself") was associated with creation, resurrection, and the rising sun.

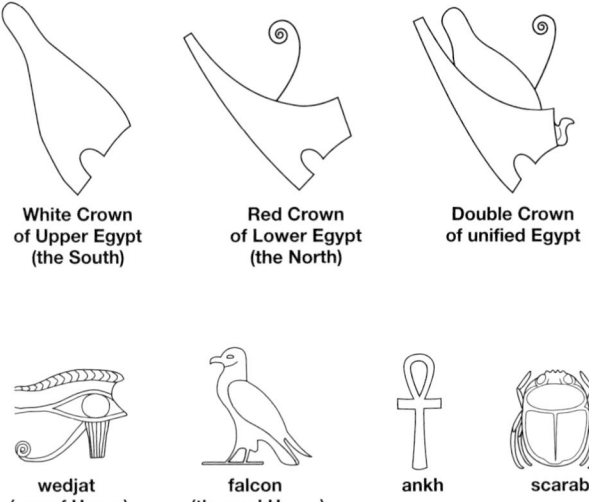

White Crown of Upper Egypt (the South) **Red Crown of Lower Egypt (the North)** **Double Crown of unified Egypt**

wedjat (eye of Horus) **falcon (the god Horus)** **ankh** **scarab**

scepter

ankh

Horus

By the Early Dynastic period, Egypt's kings were revered as gods in human form. A royal jubilee, the *heb sed* or *sed* festival, held in the thirtieth year of the living king's reign, renewed and re-affirmed his divine power, and when they died, kings rejoined their father, the sun god Ra, and rode with him in the solar boat as it made its daily journey across the sky.

In order to please the gods and ensure their continuing goodwill toward the state, kings built splendid temples and provided priests to maintain them. The priests saw to it that statues of the gods, placed deep in the innermost rooms of the temples, were never without fresh food and clothing. Egyptian gods and goddesses were depicted in various forms, some as human beings, others as animals, and still others as humans with animal heads. For example, Osiris, the overseer of the realm of the dead, regularly appears in human form wrapped in linen as a mummy. His son, the sky god Horus, is usually depicted as a falcon or falcon-headed man (see "Egyptian Symbols," above).

Over the course of ancient Egyptian history, Amun (chief god of Thebes, represented as blue and wearing a plumed crown), Ra (of Heliopolis), and Ptah (of Memphis) became the primary national gods. Other gods and their manifestations included Thoth (ibis), god of writing, science, and law; Ma'at (feather), goddess of truth, order, and justice; Anubis (jackal), god of embalming and cemeteries; and Bastet (cat), daughter of Ra.

ARTISTIC CONVENTIONS

Conventions in art are established ways of representing things, widely accepted by artists and patrons at a particular time and place. Egyptian artists followed a set of fairly strict conventions, often based on conceptual principles rather than on the observation of the natural world with an eye to rendering it in lifelike fashion. Eventually a system of mathematical formulas was developed to determine design and proportions (see "Egyptian Pictorial Relief," page 65). The underlying conventions that govern ancient Egyptian

The Palette of Narmer

> Hierakonpolis. Early Dynastic period, c. 2950 BCE.
> Green schist, height 25" (64 cm). Egyptian Museum, Cairo. JE 32169 = CG 14716

A sandal-bearer, named by hieroglyphic inscription, accompanies the king, standing on his own ground line. His presence emphasizes the fact that the king, being barefoot, is standing on sacred ground, performing sacred acts. The same individual, likewise labeled, follows Narmer on the other side of the palette.

Phonetic **hieroglyphs** at the center top of each side of the palette name the king: a horizontal fish (*nar*) above a vertical chisel (*mer*). A depiction of the royal palace—seen simultaneously from above, as a groundplan, and frontally, as a **façade** (front wall of a building)—surrounds Narmer's name to signify that he is king.

Narmer wears the Red Crown of Lower Egypt on this side of the palette and is identified by the hieroglyph label next to his head, as well by as his larger size in relation to the other figures (hieratic scale).

Two rows of decapitated enemies, their heads neatly tucked between their feet, are inspected by the royal procession.

Narmer is attacking a figure of comparable size who is also identified by a hieroglyphic label, indicating that he is an enemy of real importance, likely the ruler of Lower Egypt.

Next to the heads of these two defeated enemies are, on the left, an aerial depiction of a fortified city, and on the right, a gazelle trap, perhaps emblems of Narmer's control over both city and countryside.

A bull—symbolizing the might of the king, who is shown wearing a bull's tail on both sides of the palette—strikes down another enemy in front of a fortified city, seen both from above and in elevation.

Palettes were tablets with circular depressions on one side, in which eye makeup was ground and prepared. Although this example was undoubtedly ceremonial rather than functional, a mixing saucer is framed by the elongated, intertwined necks of lions, perhaps signifying the union of Upper and Lower Egypt.

SEE MORE: View the Closer Look feature for the Palette of Narmer **www.myartslab.com**

art appear early, however, and are maintained, with subtle but significant variations, over almost three millennia of its history.

THE NARMER PALETTE. This historically and artistically significant work of art (see "A Closer Look," opposite) dates from the Early Dynastic period and was found in the temple of Horus. It is commonly interpreted as representing the unification of Egypt and the beginning of the country's growth as a powerful nation-state. It employs many of the representational conventions that would dominate in royal Egyptian art from this point on.

On the reverse side of the palette, as in the Stele of Naram-Sin (SEE FIG. 2–1), hieratic scale signals the importance of Narmer by showing him overwhelmingly larger than the other human figures around him. He is also boldly silhouetted against a blank ground, just like Naram-Sin, distancing details of setting and story so they will not distract from his preeminence. He wears the white crown of Upper Egypt while striking the enemy who kneels before him with a mace. Above this foe, the god Horus—depicted as a falcon with a human hand—holds a rope tied around the neck of a man whose head is attached to a block sprouting stylized papyrus, a plant that grew in profusion along the Nile and symbolized Lower Egypt. This combination of symbols made the central message clear: Narmer, as ruler of Upper Egypt, is in firm control of Lower Egypt.

Many of the figures on the palette are shown in composite poses, so that each part of the body is portrayed from its most characteristic viewpoint. Heads are shown in profile, to capture most clearly the nose, forehead, and chin, while eyes are rendered frontally, from their most recognizable and expressive viewpoint. Hips, legs, and feet are drawn in profile, and the figure is usually striding, to reveal both legs. The torso, however, is fully frontal. This artistic convention for representing the human figure as a conceptualized composite of multiple viewpoints was to be followed for millennia in Egypt when depicting royalty and other dignitaries. Persons of lesser social rank engaged in active tasks (compare the figure of Narmer with those of his standard bearers) tend to be represented in ways that seem to us more lifelike.

FUNERARY ARCHITECTURE

Ancient Egyptians believed that an essential part of every human personality is its life force, or soul, called the *ka*, which lived on after the death of the body, forever engaged in the activities it had enjoyed in its former existence. But the *ka* needed a body to live in, either the mummified body of the deceased or, as a substitute, a sculpted likeness in the form of a statue. The Egyptians developed elaborate funerary practices to ensure that their deceased moved safely and effectively into the afterlife.

It was especially important to provide a comfortable home for the *ka* of a departed king, so that even in the afterlife he would continue to ensure the well-being of Egypt. Egyptians preserved the bodies of the royal dead with care and placed them in burial chambers filled with sculpted body substitutes and all the supplies

and furnishings the *ka* might require throughout eternity (see "Preserving the Dead," page 56).

MASTABA AND NECROPOLIS. In Early Dynastic Egypt, the most common tomb structure—used by the upper level of society, the king's family and relatives—was the **mastaba**, a flat-topped, one-story building with slanted walls erected above an underground burial chamber (see "Mastaba to Pyramid," page 55). Mastabas were at first constructed of mud brick, but toward the end of the Third Dynasty (c. 2650–2575 BCE), many incorporated cut stone, at least as an exterior facing.

In its simplest form, the mastaba contained a **serdab**, a small, sealed room housing the *ka* statue of the deceased, and a chapel designed to receive mourning relatives and offerings. A vertical shaft dropped from the top of the mastaba down to the actual burial chamber, where the remains of the deceased reposed in a coffin—at times placed within a larger stone sarcophagus—surrounded by appropriate grave goods. This chamber was sealed off after interment. Mastabas might have numerous underground burial chambers to accommodate whole families, and mastaba burial remained the standard for Egyptian elites for centuries.

Mastabas tended to be grouped together in a **necropolis**—literally, a "city of the dead"—at the edge of the desert on the west bank of the Nile, for the land of the dead was believed to be in the direction of the setting sun. Two of the most extensive of these early necropolises are at Saqqara and Giza, just outside modern Cairo.

DJOSER'S COMPLEX AT SAQQARA. For his tomb complex at Saqqara, the Third-Dynasty King Djoser (c. 2650–2631 BCE) commissioned the earliest known monumental architecture in Egypt (FIG. 3–2). The designer of the complex was Imhotep, who served as Djoser's prime minister. Imhotep is the first architect in history to be identified; his name is inscribed together with Djoser's on the base of a statue of the king found near the Step Pyramid.

It appears that Imhotep first planned Djoser's tomb as a single-story mastaba, only later deciding to enlarge upon the concept. The final structure is a step pyramid formed by six mastaba-like elements of decreasing size stacked on top of each other (FIG. 3–3). Although the step pyramid resembles the ziggurats of Mesopotamia, it differs in both meaning (signifying a stairway to the sun god Ra) and purpose (protecting a tomb). A 92-foot shaft descended from the original mastaba enclosed within the pyramid. A descending corridor at the base of the step pyramid provided an entrance from outside to a granite-lined burial vault.

The adjacent funerary temple, where priests performed rituals before placing the king's mummified body in its tomb, was used for continuing worship of the dead king. In the form of his *ka* statue, Djoser intended to observe these devotions through two peepholes in the wall between the serdab and the funerary chapel. To the east of the pyramid, buildings filled with debris represent actual structures in which the spirit of the dead king could continue to observe the *sed* rituals that had ensured his long reign.

3-2 • RECONSTRUCTION DRAWING OF DJOSER'S FUNERARY COMPLEX, SAQQARA
Third Dynasty, c. 2630–2575 BCE. Situated on a level terrace, this huge commemorative complex—some 1,800'
(544 m) long by 900' (277 m) wide—was designed as a replica in stone of the wood, brick, and reed buildings
used in rituals associated with kingship. Inside the wall, the step pyramid dominated the complex.

3-3 • THE STEP PYRAMID AND SHAM BUILDINGS, FUNERARY COMPLEX OF DJOSER, SAQQARA
Limestone, height of pyramid 204' (62 m).

EXPLORE MORE: Click the Google Earth link for the Pyramid of Djoser **www.myartslab.com**

As the gateway to the afterlife for Egyptian kings and members of the royal court, the Egyptian burial structure began as a low, solid, rectangular mastaba with an external niche that served as the focus of offerings. Later mastabas had either an internal serdab (the room where the *ka* statue was placed) and chapel (as in the drawing) or an attached chapel and serdab (not shown). Eventually, mastaba forms of decreasing size were stacked over an underground burial chamber to form the step pyramid. The culmination of this development is the pyramid, in which the actual burial site may be within the pyramid—not below ground—with false chambers, false doors, and confusing passageways to foil potential tomb robbers.

mastaba

chapel

offering table

serdab with statue of *ka*

shaft

underground burial chambers

blockage

stepped pyramid

original mastaba

shaft

burial chamber

blockage

Step Pyramid of Djoser, Saqqara, c. 2630–2575 BCE

pyramid

weight-relieving chamber

air shaft?

air shaft?

burial chamber

gallery to chambers

abandoned burial chamber

ascending corridor

air shaft?

escape route?

descending corridor

Pyramid of Khafre, Giza, c. 2600 BCE

SEE MORE: View a simulation about the pyramid **www.myartslab.com**

THE OLD KINGDOM, c. 2575–2150 BCE

The Old Kingdom was a time of social and political stability, despite increasingly common military excursions to defend the borders. The growing wealth of ruling families of the period is reflected in the enormous and elaborate tomb complexes they commissioned for themselves. Kings were not the only patrons of the arts, however. Upper-level government officials also could afford tombs decorated with elaborate carvings.

THE GREAT PYRAMIDS AT GIZA

The architectural form most closely identified with Egypt is the true pyramid with a square base and four sloping triangular faces,

Egyptians developed mummification techniques to ensure that the *ka*, soul or life force, could live on in the body in the afterlife. No recipes for preserving the dead have been found, but the basic process seems clear enough from images found in tombs, the descriptions of later Greek writers such as Herodotus and Plutarch, scientific analysis of mummies, and modern experiments.

By the time of the New Kingdom, the routine was roughly as follows: The body was taken to a mortuary, a special structure used exclusively for embalming. Under the supervision of a priest, workers removed the brains, generally through the nose, and emptied the body cavity—except for the heart—through an incision in the left side. They then covered the body with dry natron, a naturally occurring salt, and placed it on a sloping surface to allow liquids to drain. This preservative caused the skin to blacken, so workers often used paint or powdered makeup to restore some color, using red ocher for a man, yellow ocher for a woman. They then packed the body cavity with clean linen soaked in various herbs and ointments, provided by the family of the deceased. The major organs were wrapped in separate packets and stored in special containers called **canopic jars**, to be placed in the tomb chamber.

Workers next wound the trunk and each of the limbs separately with cloth strips, before wrapping the whole body in additional layers of cloth to produce the familiar mummy shape. The workers often inserted charms and other smaller objects among the wrappings.

first erected in the Fourth Dynasty (2575–2450 BCE). The angled sides may have been meant to represent the slanting rays of the sun, for inscriptions on the walls of pyramid tombs built in the Fifth and Sixth Dynasties tell of deceased kings climbing up the rays to join the sun god Ra.

Although not the first pyramids, the most famous are the three great pyramid tombs at Giza (**FIGS. 3–4, 3–5**). These were built by three successive Fourth-Dynasty kings: Khufu (r. c. 2551–2528 BCE), Khafre (r. 2520–2494 BCE), and Menkaure (r. c. 2490–2472 BCE). The oldest and largest pyramid at Giza is that of Khufu, which

3-4 • GREAT PYRAMIDS, GIZA
Fourth Dynasty (c. 2575–2450 BCE). Erected by (from the left) Menkaure, Khafre, and Khufu. Limestone and granite, height of pyramid of Khufu, 450′ (137 m).

EXPLORE MORE: Click the Google Earth link for the Pyramids of Giza **www.myartslab.com**

3-5 • MODEL OF THE GIZA PLATEAU
From left to right: the temples and pyramids of Menkaure, Khafre, and Khufu.

covers 13 acres at its base. It was originally finished with a thick veneer of polished limestone that lifted its apex to almost 481 feet, some 30 feet above the present summit. The pyramid of Khafre is slightly smaller than Khufu's, and Menkaure's is considerably smaller.

The site was carefully planned to follow the sun's east–west path. Next to each of the pyramids was a funerary temple connected by a causeway—an elevated and enclosed pathway or corridor—to a valley temple on the bank of the Nile (SEE FIG. 3–5). When a king died, his body was embalmed and ferried west across the Nile from the royal palace to his valley temple, where it was received with elaborate ceremonies. It was then carried up the causeway to his funerary temple and placed in its chapel, where family members presented offerings of food and drink, and priests performed rites in which the deceased's spirit consumed a meal. These rites were to be performed at the chapel in perpetuity. Finally, the body was entombed in a vault deep within the pyramid, at the end of a long, narrow, and steeply rising passageway. This tomb chamber was sealed off after the burial with a 50-ton stone block. To further protect the king from intruders, three false passageways obscured the location of the tomb.

CONSTRUCTING THE PYRAMIDS. Building a pyramid was a formidable undertaking. A large workers' burial ground discovered

at Giza attests to the huge labor force that had to be assembled, housed, and fed. Most of the cut stone blocks—each weighing an average of 2.5 tons—used in building the Giza complex were quarried either on the site or nearby. Teams of workers transported them by sheer muscle power, employing small logs as rollers or pouring water on mud to create a slippery surface over which they could drag the blocks on sleds.

Scholars and engineers have various theories about how the pyramids were raised. Some ideas have been tested in computerized projections and a few models on a small but representative scale have been constructed. The most efficient means of getting the stones into position might have been to build a temporary, gently sloping ramp around the body of the pyramid as it grew higher. The ramp could then be dismantled as the stones were smoothed out or slabs of veneer were laid.

The designers who oversaw the building of such massive structures were capable of the most sophisticated mathematical calculations. They oriented the pyramids to the points of the compass and may have incorporated other symbolic astronomical calculations as well. There was no room for trial and error. The huge foundation layer had to be absolutely level and the angle of each of the slanting sides had to remain constant so that the stones would meet precisely in the center at the top.

3-6 • GREAT SPHINX, FUNERARY COMPLEX OF KHAFRE
Giza. Old Kingdom, c. 2520–2494 BCE. Sandstone, height approx. 65′ (19.8 m).

EXPLORE MORE: Click the Google Earth link for The Great Sphinx
www.myartslab.com

KHAFRE'S COMPLEX. Khafre's funerary complex is the best preserved. Its pyramid is the only one of the three to have maintained some of its veneer facing at the top. But the complex is most famous for the Great Sphinx that sits just behind Khafre's valley temple. This colossal portrait of the king—65 feet tall—combines his head with the long body of a crouching lion, seemingly merging notions of human intelligence with animal strength (FIG. 3–6).

In the adjacent valley temple, massive blocks of red granite form walls and piers supporting a flat roof (FIG. 3–7). (See "Early Construction Methods," page 16.) A **clerestory** (a row of tall, narrow windows in the upper walls, not visible in the figure), lets in light that reflects off the polished Egyptian alabaster floor. Within the temple were a series of over-life-size statues, portraying **KHAFRE** as an enthroned king (FIG. 3–8). The falcon god Horus perches on the back of the throne, protectively enfolding the king's head with his wings. Lions—symbols of regal authority—form the throne's legs, and the intertwined lotus and papyrus plants beneath the seat symbolize the king's power over Upper (lotus) and Lower (papyrus) Egypt.

Khafre wears the traditional royal costume—a short, pleated kilt, a linen headdress, and a false beard symbolic of royalty. He exudes a strong sense of dignity, calm, and above all permanence. In his right hand, he holds a cylinder, probably a rolled piece of cloth. His arms are pressed tightly within the contours of his body, which is firmly anchored in the confines of the stone block from which it was carved. The statue was created from an unusual stone, a type of

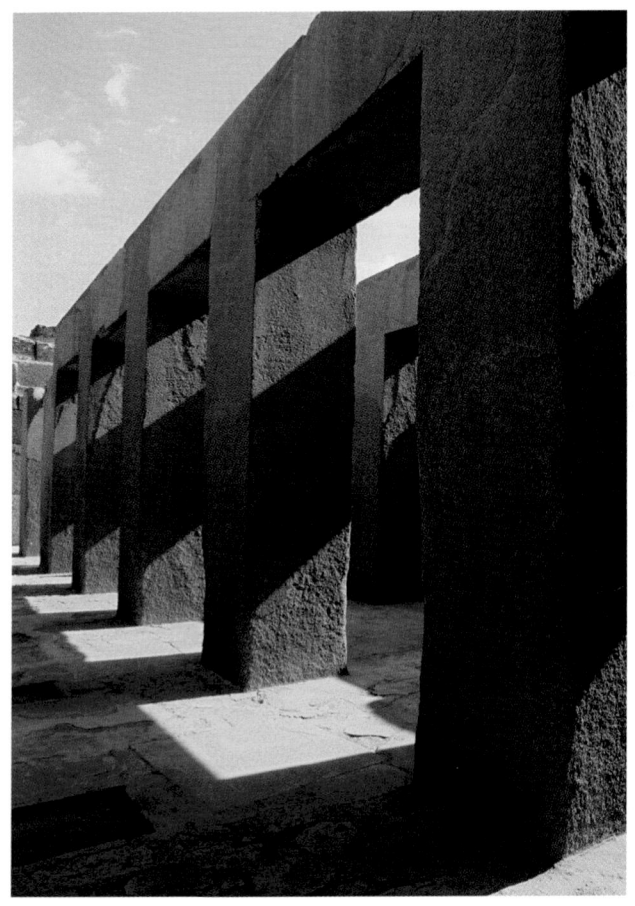

3-7 • VALLEY TEMPLE OF KHAFRE
Giza, Old Kingdom, c. 2520–2494 BCE. Limestone and red granite.

3-8 • KHAFRE
Giza, valley temple of Khafre. Fourth Dynasty, c. 2520–2494 BCE. Diorite-gabbro gneiss, height 5′6⅛″ (1.68 m). Egyptian Museum, Cairo. (JE 10062 = CG 14)

unit. They are further united by the queen's symbolic gesture of embrace. Her right hand comes from behind to clasp his torso, and her left hand rests gently, if stiffly, over his upper arm.

The king—depicted in accordance with Egyptian ideals as an athletic, youthful figure, nude to the waist and wearing the royal kilt and headcloth—stands in a conventional, balanced pose, striding with the left foot forward, his arms straight at his sides, and his fists clenched over cylindrical objects. His equally youthful queen, taking a smaller step forward, echoes his striding pose. Her sheer, close-fitting garment reveals the soft curves of her gently swelling body, a foil for the tight muscularity of the king. The time-consuming task of polishing this double statue was never completed, suggesting that the work may have been undertaken only a few years before Menkaure's death in about 2472 BCE. Traces of red paint remain on the king's face, ears, and neck (male figures were traditionally painted red), as do traces of black on the queen's hair.

3-9 • MENKAURE AND A QUEEN
Perhaps his wife Khamerernebty II, from Giza. Fourth Dynasty, 2490–2472 BCE. Graywacke with traces of red and black paint, height 54½″ (142.3 cm). Museum of Fine Arts, Boston. (11.1738) Harvard University–MFA Expedition

gneiss (related to diorite), imported from Nubia, that produces a rare optical effect. When illuminated by sunlight entering through the temple's clerestory, it glows a deep blue, the celestial color of Horus, filling the space with a blue radiance.

SCULPTURE

As the surviving statues of Khafre's valley temple demonstrate, Egyptian sculptors were adept at creating lifelike three-dimensional figures that also express a feeling of strength and permanence consistent with the unusually hard stones from which they were carved.

MENKAURE AND A QUEEN.   Dignity, calm, and permanence also characterize a sleek double portrait of Khafre's heir King Menkaure and a queen, probably Khamerernebty II, discovered in Menkaure's valley temple (FIG. 3–9). The couple's separate figures, close in size, are joined by the stone from which they emerge, forming a single

SEATED SCRIBE. Old Kingdom sculptors also produced statues of less prominent people, rendered in a more relaxed, lifelike fashion. A more lively and less formal mode is employed in the statue of a **SEATED SCRIBE** from early in the Fifth Dynasty **(FIG. 3–10)**—with round head, alert expression, and cap of close-cropped hair—that was discovered near the tomb of a government official named Kai. It could be a portrait of Kai himself. The irregular contours of his engaging face project a sense of individual likeness and human presence.

The scribe's sedentary vocation has made his sagging body slightly flabby, his condition advertising a life free from hard physical labor. An ancient Egyptian inscription emphasizes this point: "Become a scribe so that your limbs remain smooth and your hands soft and you can wear white and walk like a man of standing whom [even] courtiers will greet" (cited in Strouhal, p. 216). This scribe sits holding a papyrus scroll partially unrolled on his lap, his right hand clasping a now-lost reed brush used in writing. The alert expression on his face reveals more than a lively intelligence. Because the pupils are slightly off-center in the irises, the eyes give the illusion of being in motion, as if they were seeking contact, and the reflective quality of the polished crystal inlay reproduces with eerie fidelity the contrast between the moist surface of eyes and the surrounding soft flesh in a living human face.

3-11 • BUTCHER
Perhaps from the tomb of the official Ni-kau-inpu and his wife Hemet-re, Giza? Fifth Dynasty, c. 2450–2325 BCE. Painted limestone (knife restored), height 14⅝″ (37 cm). Oriental Institute of the University of Chicago. (10626)

Although statues such as this have been assumed to represent the deceased's servants, it has recently been proposed that instead they depict relatives and friends of the deceased in the role of servants, allowing these loved ones to accompany the deceased into the next life.

3-10 • SEATED SCRIBE
Found near the tomb of Kai, Saqqara. Fifth Dynasty, c. 2450–2325 BCE. Painted limestone with inlaid eyes of rock crystal, calcite, and magnesite mounted in copper, height 21″ (53 cm). Musée du Louvre, Paris. (N 2290 = E 3023)

High-ranking scribes could hope to be appointed to one of several "houses of life," where they would copy, compile, study, and repair valuable sacred and scientific texts.

STATUETTES OF SERVANTS. Even more lifelike than the scribe were smaller figures of servants at work that were made for inclusion in Old Kingdom tombs so that the deceased could be provided for in the next world. Poses are neither formal nor reflective, but rooted directly in the labor these figures were expected to perform throughout eternity. A painted limestone statuette from the Fifth Dynasty **(FIG. 3–11)** captures a butcher, raised up on the balls of his feet to bend down and lean forward, poised, knife in hand, over the throat of an ox that he has just slaughtered. Having accomplished his work, he looks up to acknowledge us, an action that only enhances his sense of lifelike presence. The emphasis on involved poses and engagement with the viewer may have been an attempt to underscore the ability of such figures to perform their assigned tasks, or perhaps it was meant to indicate their lower social status by showing them involved in physical labor. Both may be signified here. The contrast between the detached stylization of upper-class figures and the engaging lifelikeness of laborers can be seen in Old Kingdom pictorial relief works as well.

3-12 • TI WATCHING A HIPPOPOTAMUS HUNT
Tomb of Ti, Saqqara. Fifth Dynasty, c. 2450–2325 BCE. Painted limestone relief, height approx. 45″ (114.3 cm).

PICTORIAL RELIEF IN TOMBS

To provide the *ka* with the most pleasant possible living quarters for eternity, wealthy families often had the interior walls and ceilings of their tombs decorated with paintings and reliefs. This decoration carried religious meaning, but it could also evoke the deceased's everyday life or depict ceremonial events that proclaimed the deceased's importance. Tombs therefore provide a wealth of information about ancient Egyptian culture.

THE TOMB OF TI. On the walls of the large mastaba of a wealthy Fifth Dynasty government official named Ti, a painted relief shows him watching a hippopotamus hunt—an official duty of royal courtiers (**FIG. 3–12**). It was believed that Seth, the god of chaos, disguised himself as a hippo. Hippos were also destructive since they wandered into fields, damaging crops. Tomb depictions of such hunts therefore proclaimed the valor of the deceased and the triumph of good over evil, or at least order over destructiveness.

The artists who created this picture in painted limestone relief used a number of established Egyptian representational conventions. The river is conceived as if seen from above, rendered as a band of parallel wavy lines below the boats. The creatures in this river, however—fish, a crocodile, and hippopotami—are shown in profile for easy identification. The shallow boats carrying Ti and his men by skimming along the surface of the water are shown straight on in relation to the viewers' vantage point, and the papyrus stalks that choke the marshy edges of the river are disciplined into a regular pattern of projecting, linear, parallel, vertical forms that highlight the contrastingly crisp and smooth contour of Ti's stylized body. At the top of the papyrus grove, however, this patterning relaxes while enthusiastic animals of prey—perhaps foxes—stalk birds among the leaves and flowers. The hieratically scaled and sleekly stylized figure of Ti, rendered in the conventional composite pose, looms over all. In a separate boat ahead of him, the actual hunters, being of lesser rank and engaged in more strenuous activities, are rendered in a more lifelike and lively fashion than their master. They are captured at the charged moment of closing in on the hunted prey, spears positioned at the ready, legs extended for the critical lunge forward.

THE MIDDLE KINGDOM, c. 1975–c. 1640 BCE

The collapse of the Old Kingdom, with its long succession of powerful kings, was followed by roughly 150 years of political turmoil, fragmentation, and warfare traditionally referred to as the First Intermediate period (c. 2125–1975 BCE). About 2010 BCE, a series of kings named Mentuhotep (Eleventh Dynasty, c. 2010–c. 1938 BCE) gained power in Thebes, and the country was reunited under Nebhepetre Mentuhotep, who reasserted royal power and founded the Middle Kingdom.

The Middle Kingdom was another high point in Egyptian history. Arts and writing flourished in the Twelfth Dynasty (1938–1756 BCE), while reflecting a burgeoning awareness of the political upheaval from which the country had just emerged. Using a strengthened military, Middle Kingdom rulers expanded and patrolled the borders, especially in lower Nubia, south of present-day Aswan (SEE MAP 3–1, page 50). By the Thirteenth Dynasty (c. 1755–1630 BCE), however, central control by the government was weakened by a series of short-lived kings and an influx of foreigners, especially in the Delta.

PORTRAITS OF SENUSRET III

Some royal portraits from the Middle Kingdom appear to express an unexpected awareness of the hardship and fragility of human existence. Statues of Senusret III, a king of the Twelfth Dynasty, who ruled from c. 1836 to 1818 BCE, reflects this new sensibility. Old Kingdom rulers such as Khafre (SEE FIG. 3–8) gaze into eternity confident and serene, toned and unflinching, whereas the portrait of **SENUSRET III** seems to capture a monarch preoccupied and emotionally drained **(FIG. 3–13)**. Creases line his sagging cheeks, his eyes are sunken, his eyelids droop, his forehead is flexed, and his jaw is sternly set—a bold image of a resolute ruler, tested but unbowed.

Senusret was a dynamic king and successful general who led four military expeditions into Nubia, overhauled the Egyptian central administration, and was effective in regaining control over the country's increasingly independent nobles. To modern viewers, his portrait raises questions of interpretation. Are we looking at the face of a man wise in the ways of the world but lonely, saddened, and burdened by the weight of his responsibilities? Or are we looking at a reassuring statement that in spite of troubled times—that have clearly left their mark on the face of the ruler himself—royal rule endures in Egypt? Given what we know about Egyptian history at this time, it is difficult to be sure.

ROCK-CUT TOMBS

During the Eleventh and Twelfth Dynasties, members of the nobility and high-level officials commissioned tombs hollowed out of the face of a cliff. A typical rock-cut tomb included an entrance **portico** (projecting porch), a main hall, and a shrine with a burial chamber under the offering chapel. The chambers of these tombs, as well as their ornamental columns, lintels, false doors, and niches, were all carved into the solid rock. An impressive necropolis was created in the cliffs at **BENI HASAN** on the east bank of the Nile **(FIG. 3–14)**. Painted scenes cover the interior walls of many tombs. Among the best preserved are those in the Twelfth Dynasty tomb

3-13 • HEAD OF SENUSRET III
Twelfth Dynasty, c. 1836–1818 BCE. Yellow quartzite, height 17¾ × 13½ × 17" (45.1 × 34.3 × 43.2 cm). The Nelson-Atkins Museum of Art, Kansas City, Missouri. Purchase: Nelson Trust (62-11)

3-14 • ROCK-CUT TOMBS, BENI HASAN
Twelfth Dynasty (1938–1756 BCE). At the left is the entrance to the tomb of a provincial governor and the commander-in-chief Amenemhat.

3-15 • PICKING FIGS
Wall painting from the tomb of Khnumhotep, Beni Hasan. Twelfth Dynasty, c. 1890 BCE. Tempera facsimile by Nina de Garis.

of local noble Khnumhotep, some of which portray vivid vignettes of farm work on his estates. In one painting two men harvest figs, rushing to compete with three baboons who relish the ripe fruit

from their perches within the trees **(FIG. 3–15)**. One man reaches for a fig to add to the ordered stack in his basket, while his companion carefully arranges the harvest in a larger box for transport. Like the energetic hunters on the much earlier painted relief in the Tomb of Ti (SEE FIG. 3–12), the upper torsos of these farm workers take a more lifelike profile posture, deviating from the strict frontality of the royal composite pose.

FUNERARY STELAE

Only the wealthiest and noblest of ancient Egyptians could afford elaborately decorated mastabas or rock-cut tombs. Prosperous people, however, could still commission funerary stelae depicting themselves, their family, and offerings of food. These personal monuments—meant to preserve the memory of the deceased and inspire the living to make offerings to them—contain compelling works of ancient Egyptian pictorial art. An unfinished stele made for the tomb of the **SCULPTOR USERWER (FIG. 3–16)** presents three levels of decoration: one large upper block with five bands of hieroglyphs, beneath which are two registers with figures, each identified by inscription.

3-16 • STELE OF THE SCULPTOR USERWER
Twelfth Dynasty, c. 1850 BCE. Limestone, red and black ink, 20½ × 19″ (52 cm × 48 cm). British Museum London. (EA 579)

The text is addressed to the living, imploring them to make offerings to Userwer: "O living ones who are on the earth who pass by this tomb, as your deities love and favor you, may you say: 'A thousand of bread and beer, a thousand of cattle and birds, a thousand of alabaster [vessels] and clothes, a thousand of offerings and provisions that go forth before Osiris.'" (Robins, p. 103)

At left, on the register immediately below this inscription, Userwer sits before a table piled with offerings of food. Behind him is his wife Satdepetnetjer, and facing him on the other side of the offering table is Satameni, a standing woman also identified as his wife. Userwer could have had more than one wife, but one of these women might also be a deceased first wife of the sculptor. At the other side of the stele on this same register but facing in the opposite direction sits another couple before another table heaped with food. They are identified as Userwer's parents, and the figure on the other side of their offering table is his son, Sneferuweser. In the lowest register are representations of other family members (probably Userwer's children) and his grandparents.

One of the most striking features of the lowest register of this stele is its unfinished state. The two leftmost figures were left uncarved, but the stone surface still maintains the preparatory ink drawing meant to guide the sculptor, preserving striking evidence of a system of canonical figure proportions that was established in the Middle Kingdom (see "Egyptian Pictorial Relief," opposite). The unfinished state of this stele has led to the suggestion that Userwer might have been in the process of carving it for himself when his sudden death left it incomplete.

A more modest stele for a man named **AMENEMHAT** was brought to completion as a vibrantly painted relief (**FIG. 3–17**). Underneath an inscription, inviting food offerings for the deceased Amenemhat, is a portrait of his family. Amenemhat sits on a lion-legged bench between his wife Iyi and their son Antef, embraced by both. Next to the trio is an offering table, heaped with meat, topped with onions, and sheltering two loaves of bread standing under the table on the floor. On the far right is Anenemhat and Iyi's daughter, Hapy, completing this touching tableau of family unity, presumably projected into their life after death. The painter of this relief follows an established Egyptian convention of differentiating gender by skin tonality, dark red-brown for men and lighter yellow-ocher for women.

TOWN PLANNING

Although Egyptians used durable materials in the construction of tombs, they built their own dwellings with simple mud bricks, which have either disintegrated over time or been carried away for fertilizer by farmers. Only the foundations of these dwellings now remain.

Archaeologists have unearthed the remains of Kahun, a town built by Senusret II (ruled c. 1842–1837 BCE) for the many officials, priests, and workers who built and maintained his pyramid complex. Parallel streets were laid out on a **grid**, forming rectangular blocks divided into lots for homes and other buildings.

3-17 • STELE OF AMENEMHAT
Assasif. Late Eleventh Dynasty, c. 2000 BCE. Painted limestone, 11 × 15" (30 × 50 cm). Egyptian Museum, Cairo. (JE 45626)

The houses of priests, court officials, and their families were large and comfortable, with private living quarters and public rooms grouped around central courtyards. The largest had as many as 70 rooms spread out over half an acre. Workers and their families made do with small, five-room row-houses built back to back along narrow streets.

A New Kingdom workers' village, discovered at Deir el-Medina on the west bank of the Nile near the Valley of the Kings, has provided us with detailed information about the lives of the people who created the royal tombs. Workers lived together here under the rule of the king's chief minister. During a ten-day week, they worked for eight days and had two days off, and also participated in many religious festivals. They lived a good life with their families, were given clothing, sandals, grain, and firewood by the king, and had permission to raise livestock and birds and to tend a garden. The residents had a council, and the many written records that survive suggest a literate and litigious society that required many scribes. Because the men were away for most of the week working on the tombs, women had a prominent role in the town.

THE NEW KINGDOM, C. 1539–1075 BCE

During the Second Intermediate period (1630–1520 BCE)—another turbulent interruption in the succession of dynasties ruling a unified country—an eastern Mediterranean people called the Hyksos invaded Egypt's northernmost regions. Finally, the kings of the Eighteenth Dynasty (c. 1539–1292 BCE) regained control of the entire Nile region, extending from Nubia in the south to the Mediterranean Sea in the north, and restored political and economic strength. Roughly a century later, one of the same dynasty's most dynamic kings, Thutmose III (r. 1479–1425 BCE), extended Egypt's influence along the eastern Mediterranean coast as far as the region of present-day Syria. His accomplishment was the result of 15 or more military campaigns and his own skill at diplomacy. The heartland of ancient Egypt was now surrounded by a buffer of empire.

Painting usually relies on color and line for its effect, while relief sculpture usually depends on the play of light and shadow alone, but in Egypt, relief sculpture was also painted (SEE FIG. 3–17). The walls and closely spaced columns of Egyptian tombs and temples were almost completely covered with colorful scenes and hieroglyphic texts. Until the Eighteenth Dynasty (c. 1539–1292 BCE), the only colors used were black, white, red, yellow, blue, and green. Modeling might be indicated by overpainting lines in a contrasting color, although the sense of three-dimensionality was conveyed primarily by the carved forms and incised inscriptions underneath the paint. The crisp outlines created by such carving assured the primacy of line in Egyptian pictorial relief.

With very few exceptions, figures, scenes, and texts were composed in bands, or registers. The scenes were first laid out with inked lines, using a squared grid to guide the designer in proportioning the human figures. The sculptor who executed the carving followed these drawings, and it may have been another person who smoothed the carved surfaces of the relief and eventually covered them with paint.

The lower left corner of the unfinished Twelfth-Dynasty stele of Userwer shown here still maintains its preliminary underdrawings. In some figures there are also the tentative beginnings of the relief carving. The figures are delineated with black ink and the grid lines are rendered in red. Every body part had its designated place on the grid. For example, figures are designed 18 squares tall, measuring from the soles of their feet to their hairline; the tops of their knees conform with the sixth square up from the ground-line. Their shoulders align with the top of square 16 and are six squares wide. Slight deviations exist within this structured design format, but this **canon of proportions** represents an ideal system that was standard in pictorial relief throughout the Middle Kingdom.

DETAIL OF THE STELE OF THE SCULPTOR USERWER IN FIG. 3-16.

Thutmose III was the first ruler to refer to himself as "pharaoh," a term that literally meant "great house." Egyptians used it in the same way that Americans say "the White House" to mean the current U.S. president and his staff. The successors of Thutmose III continued to call themselves pharaohs, and the term ultimately found its way into the Hebrew Bible—and modern usage—as the title for the kings of Egypt.

THE GREAT TEMPLE COMPLEXES

At the height of the New Kingdom, rulers undertook extensive building programs along the entire length of the Nile. Their palaces, forts, and administrative centers disappeared long ago, but remnants of temples and tombs of this great age have endured. Thebes was Egypt's religious center throughout most of the New Kingdom, and worship of the Theban triad of deities—Amun, his wife Mut, and their son Khons—had spread throughout the country. Temples to these and other gods were a major focus of royal patronage, as were tombs and temples erected to glorify the kings themselves.

THE NEW KINGDOM TEMPLE PLAN. As the home of the god, an Egyptian temple originally took the form of a house—a simple, rectangular, flat-roofed building preceded by a courtyard and gateway. The builders of the New Kingdom enlarged and multiplied these elements. The gateway became a massive **pylon** with tapering walls; the semipublic courtyard was surrounded by columns (a **peristyle** court); the temple itself included an outer **hypostyle hall** (a vast hall filled with columns) and an inner offering hall and sanctuary. The design was symmetrical and axial—that is, all of its separate elements are symmetrically arranged along a dominant center line, creating a processional path from the outside straight into the sanctuary. The rooms became smaller, darker, and more exclusive as they neared the sanctuary, where the cult image of the god was housed. Only the pharaoh and the priests entered these inner rooms.

Two temple districts consecrated primarily to the worship of Amun, Mut, and Khons arose near Thebes—a huge complex at Karnak to the north and, joined to it by an avenue of sphinxes, a more compact temple at Luxor to the south.

KARNAK. Karnak was a longstanding sacred site, where temples were built and rebuilt for over 1,500 years. During the nearly 500 years of the New Kingdom, successive kings renovated and expanded the complex of the **GREAT TEMPLE OF AMUN** until it covered about 60 acres, an area as large as a dozen football fields (**FIG. 3–18**).

Access to the heart of the temple, a sanctuary containing the statue of Amun, was from the west (on the left side of the reconstruction drawing) through a principal courtyard, a hypostyle hall, and a number of smaller halls and courts. Pylons set off each of these separate elements. Between the reigns of Thutmose I (Eighteenth Dynasty, r. c. 1493–1482 BCE), and Ramses II (Nineteenth Dynasty, r. c. 1279–1213 BCE), this area of the complex underwent a great deal of construction and renewal. The greater part of the pylons leading to the sanctuary and the halls and courts behind them were renovated or newly built and embellished with colorful pictorial wall reliefs. A sacred lake was also added to the south of the complex, where the king and priests might undergo ritual purification before entering the temple. Thutmose III erected a court and festival temple to his own glory behind the sanctuary of Amun. His great-grandson Amenhotep III (r. 1390–1353 BCE) placed a large stone statue of the god Khepri, the scarab (beetle) symbolic of the rising sun, rebirth, and everlasting life, next to the sacred lake.

In the sanctuary of Amun, priests washed the god's statue every morning and clothed it in a new garment. Because the god was thought to derive nourishment from the spirit of food, his statue was provided with tempting meals twice a day, which the priests then removed and ate themselves. Ordinary people entered the temple precinct only as far as the forecourts of the hypostyle halls, where they found themselves surrounded by inscriptions and images of kings and the god on columns and walls. During religious festivals, they lined the waterways, along which statues of the gods were carried in ceremonial boats, and were permitted to submit petitions to the priests for requests they wished the gods to grant.

3-18 • RECONSTRUCTION DRAWING OF THE GREAT TEMPLE OF AMUN AT KARNAK
New Kingdom, c. 1579–1075 BCE.

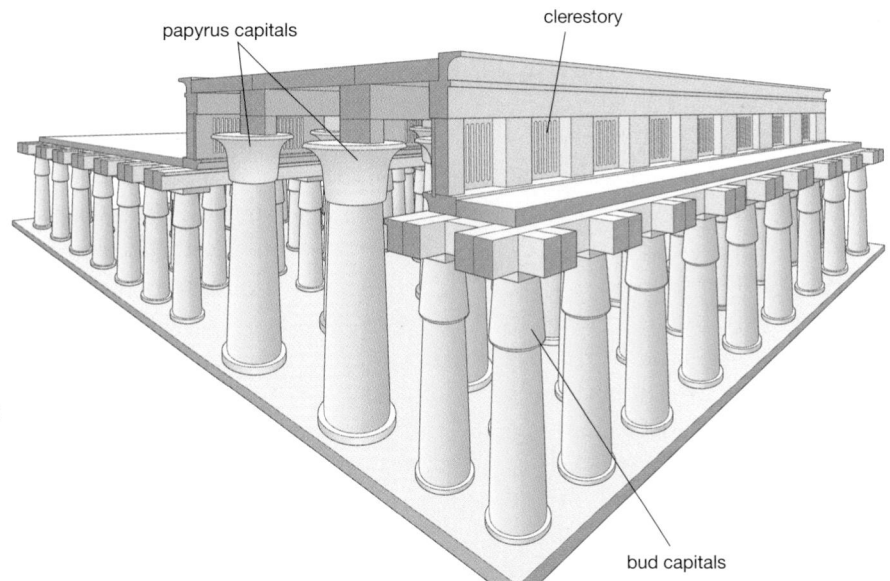

papyrus capitals — clerestory

bud capitals

3-19 • RECONSTRUCTION DRAWING OF THE HYPOSTYLE HALL, GREAT TEMPLE OF AMUN AT KARNAK
Nineteenth Dynasty (c. 1292–1190 BCE).

THE GREAT HALL AT KARNAK. One of the most prominent features of the complex at Karnak is the enormous hypostyle hall set between two pylons at the end of the main forecourt. Erected in the reigns of the Nineteenth-Dynasty rulers Sety I (r. c. 1290–1279 BCE) and his son Ramses II (r. c. 1279–1213 BCE), and called the "Temple of the Spirit of Sety, Beloved of Ptah in the House of Amun," it may have been used for royal coronation ceremonies. Ramses II referred to it as "the place where the common people extol the name of his majesty." The hall was 340 feet wide and 170 feet long. Its 134 closely spaced columns supported a roof of flat stones, the center section of which rose some 30 feet higher than the broad sides **(FIGS. 3–19, 3–20)**. The columns supporting this higher part of the roof are 69 feet tall and 12 feet in diameter, with massive papyrus capitals. On each side, smaller columns with bud capitals seem to march off forever into the darkness. In each of the side walls of the higher center section, a long row of window openings created a clerestory. These openings were filled with stone grillwork, so they cannot have provided much light, but they did permit a cooling flow of air through the hall. Despite the dimness of the interior, artists covered nearly every inch of the columns, walls, and cross-beams with painted pictorial reliefs and inscriptions.

HATSHEPSUT

Across the Nile from Karnak and Luxor lay Deir el-Bahri and the Valleys of the Kings and Queens. These valleys on the west bank of the Nile held the royal necropolis, including the tomb of the pharaoh Hatshepsut. The dynamic Hatshepsut (Eighteenth Dynasty, r. c. 1473–1458 BCE) is a notable figure in a period otherwise dominated by male warrior-kings. Besides Hatshepsut, very few women ruled Egypt—they included the little-known Sobekneferu, Tausret, and much later, the well-known Cleopatra VII.

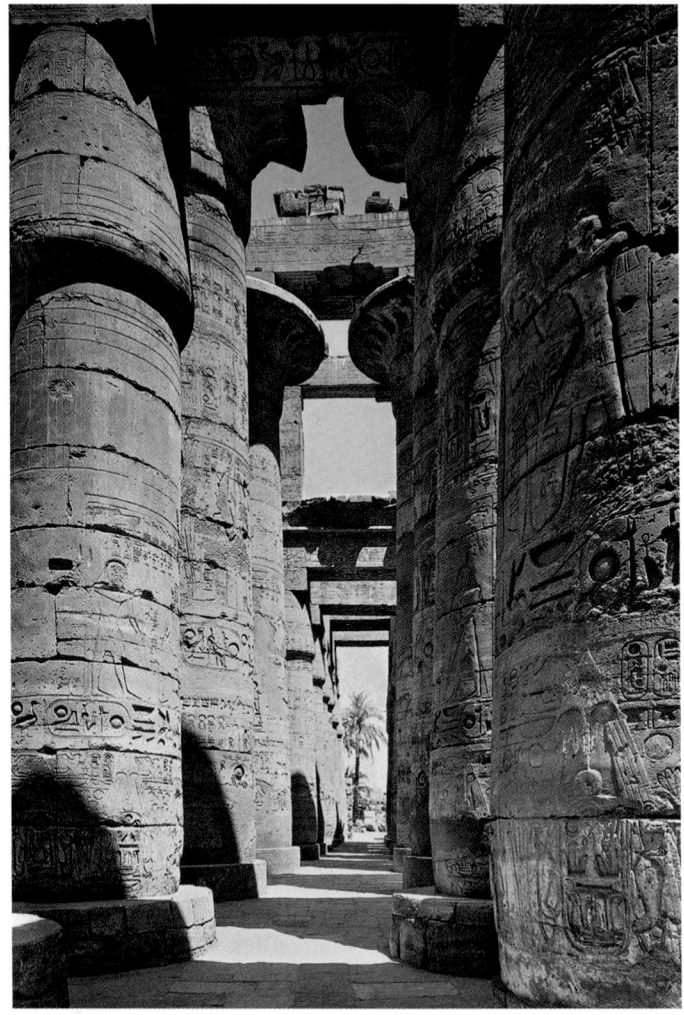

3-20 • COLUMNS WITH PAPYRIFORM AND BUD CAPITALS, HYPOSTYLE HALL, GREAT TEMPLE OF AMUN AT KARNAK

EXPLORE MORE: Click the Google Earth link for the Hypostyle Hall of Amun-Ra **www.myartslab.com**

3-21 • HATSHEPSUT KNEELING
Deir el-Bahri. Eighteenth Dynasty, c. 1473–1458 BCE. Red granite, height 8′6″ (2.59 m). Metropolitan Museum of Art, New York.

The daughter of Thutmose I, Hatshepsut married her half-brother, who then reigned for 14 years as Thutmose II. When he died in c. 1473, she became regent for his underage son—Thutmose III—born to one of his concubines. Within a few years, Hatshepsut had herself declared "king" by the priests of Amun, a maneuver that made her co-ruler with Thutmose III for 20 years. There was no artistic formula for a female pharaoh in Egyptian art, yet Hatshepsut had to be portrayed in her new role. What happened reveals something fundamentally important about the art of ancient Egypt. She was represented as a male king (**FIG. 3–21**), wearing a kilt and linen headdress, occasionally even a king's false beard. The formula for portraying kings was not adapted to suit one individual; she was adapted to conform to convention. There could hardly be a more powerful manifestation of the premium on tradition in Egyptian royal art.

At the height of the New Kingdom, rulers undertook extensive personal building programs, and Hatshepsut is responsible for one of the most spectacular: her funerary temple located at Deir el-Bahri, about a mile away from her actual tomb in the Valley of the Kings (**FIG. 3–22**). This imposing complex was designed for funeral rites and commemorative ceremonies and is much larger and more prominent than the tomb itself, reversing the scale relationship we saw in the Old Kingdom pyramid complexes.

Magnificently sited and sensitively reflecting the natural three-part layering in the rise of the landscape—from flat desert, through a sloping hillside, to the crescendo of sheer stone cliffs—Hatshepsut's temple was constructed on an axial plan (**FIG. 3–23**). A causeway lined with sphinxes once ran from a valley temple on the Nile to the huge open space of the first court, where rare myrrh trees were planted in the temple's garden terraces. From there, visitors ascended a long, straight ramp to a second court where shrines to Anubis and Hathor occupy the ends of the columned porticos. On the temple's uppermost court, colossal royal statues fronted another **colonnade**

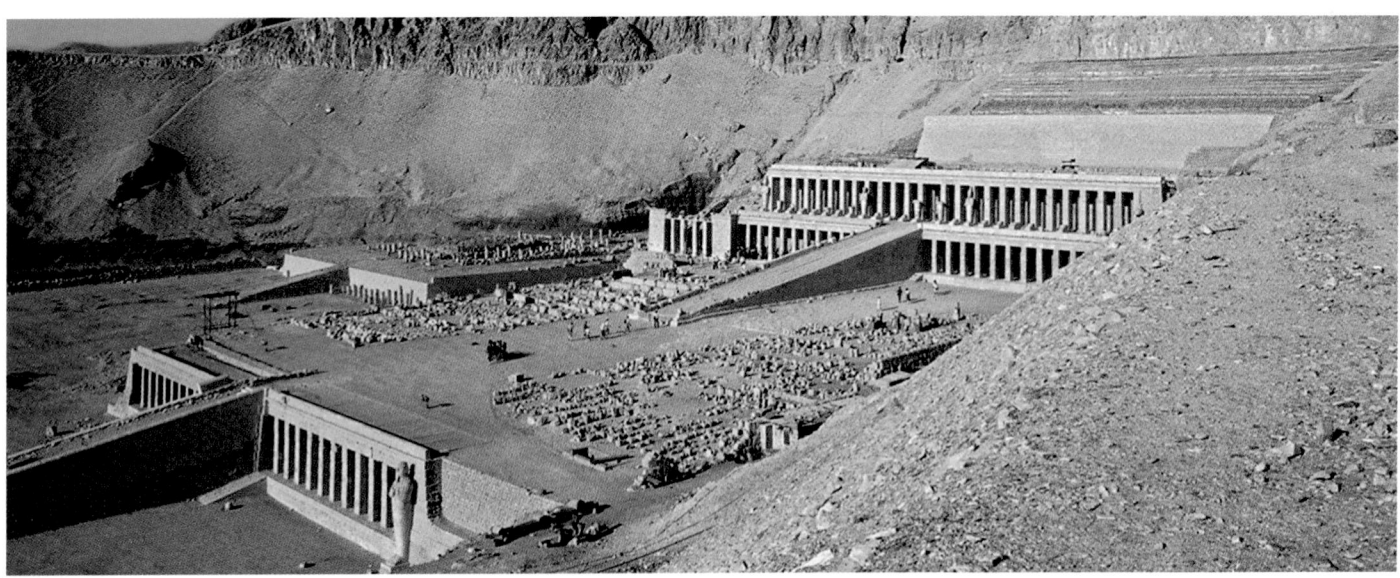

3-22 • FUNERARY TEMPLE OF HATSHEPSUT, DEIR EL-BAHRI
Eighteenth Dynasty, c. 1473–1458 BCE. (At the far left, ramp and base of the funerary temple of Mentuhotep III. Eleventh Dynasty, r. c. 2009–1997 BCE.)

3-23 • SCHEMATIC DRAWING OF THE FUNERARY TEMPLE OF HATSHEPSUT
Deir el-Bahri.

Temple of Thutmose III

Chapel of Hathor

Temple of Hatshepsut

Temple of Mentuhotep II

Avenue of Sphinxes leading to Karnak

(a row of columns supporting a lintel or a series of arches), and behind this lay a large hypostyle hall with chapels dedicated to Hatshepsut, her father, and the gods Amun and Ra-Horakhty—a powerful form of the sun god Ra combined with Horus. Centered in the hall's back wall was the entrance to the innermost sanctuary, a small chamber cut deep into the cliff.

THE TOMB OF RAMOSE

The traditional art of pictorial relief, employing a representational system that had dominated Egyptian figural art since the time of Narmer, reached a high degree of aesthetic refinement and technical sophistication during the Eighteenth-Dynasty reign of Amenhotep III (r. c. 1390–1353 BCE), especially in the reliefs carved for the unfinished tomb of Ramose near Thebes (FIG. 3–24).

As mayor of Thebes and vizier (principal royal advisor or minister) to both Amenhotep III and Amenhotep IV (r. 1353–c. 1336 BCE), Ramose was second only to the pharaoh in power and prestige. Soon after his ascent to political prominence, he began construction of an elaborate tomb comprised of four rooms, including an imposing hypostyle hall 82 feet wide. Walls were covered with paintings or with shallow pictorial relief carvings, celebrating the accomplishments, affiliations, and lineage of Ramose and his

wife Merytptah, or visualizing the funeral rites that would take place after their death. But the tomb was not used by Ramose. Work on it ceased in the fourth year of Amenhotep IV's reign, when, renamed Akhenaten, he relocated the court from Thebes to the new city of Akhetaten. Presumably Ramose moved with the court to the new capital, but neither his name nor a new tomb has been discovered there.

3-24 • RAMOSE'S BROTHER MAY AND HIS WIFE WERENER
Tomb of Ramose, Thebes. Eighteenth Dynasty, c. 1375–1365 BCE.

The tomb was abandoned in various stages of completion. The reliefs were never painted, and some walls preserve only the preliminary sketches that would have guided sculptors. But the works that were executed are among the most sophisticated relief carvings in the history of art. On one wall, Ramose and his wife Merytptah appear, hosting a banquet for their family. All are portrayed at the same moment of youthful perfection, even though they represent two successive generations. Sophisticated carvers lavished their considerable technical virtuosity on the portrayal of these untroubled and majestic couples, creating clear textural differentiation of skin, hair, clothes, and jewelry. The easy elegance of linear fluidity is not easy to obtain in this medium, and the convincing sense of three-dimensionality in forms and their placement is managed within an extraordinarily shallow depth of relief. In the detail of Ramose's brother May and sister-in-law Werener in FIG. 3–24, the traditional ancient Egyptian marital embrace (SEE FIGS. 3–9, 3–17) takes on a new tenderness, recalling—especially within the eternal stillness of a tomb—the words of a New Kingdom love poem:

> While unhurried days come and go,
> Let us turn to each other in quiet affection,
> Walk in peace to the edge of old age.
> And I shall be with you each unhurried day,
> A woman given her one wish: to see
> For a lifetime the face of her lord. (Foster, p. 18)

The conceptual conventions of Egyptian pharaonic art are rendered in these carvings with such warmth and refinement that they become almost believable. Our rational awareness of their artificiality is momentarily eclipsed by their sheer beauty. But within this refined world of stable convention, something very jarring took place during the reign of Amenhotep III's successor, Amenhotep IV.

AKHENATEN AND THE ART OF THE AMARNA PERIOD

Amenhotep IV was surely the most unusual ruler in the history of ancient Egypt. During his 17-year reign (c. 1353–1336 BCE), he radically transformed the political, spiritual, and cultural life of the country. He founded a new religion honoring a single supreme god, the life-giving sun deity Aten (represented by the sun's disk), and changed his own name in about 1348 BCE to Akhenaten ("One Who Is Effective on Behalf of Aten"). Abandoning Thebes, the capital of Egypt since the beginning of his dynasty and a city firmly in the grip of the priests of Amun, Akhenaten built a new capital much farther north, calling it Akhetaten ("Horizon of the Aten"). Using the modern name for this site, Tell el-Amarna, historians refer to Akhenaten's reign as the Amarna period.

THE NEW AMARNA STYLE.   Akhenaten's reign not only saw the creation of a new capital and the rise of a new religious focus; it also led to radical changes in royal artistic conventions. In portraits

3-25 • COLOSSAL FIGURE OF AKHENATEN
From the temple known as the Gempaaten, built early in Akhenaten's reign just southeast of the Temple of Karnak. Sandstone with traces of polychromy, height of remaining portion about 13′ (4 m). Egyptian Museum, Cairo. (JE 49528)

EXPLORE MORE: Gain insight from a primary source related to the Colossal Figure of Akhenaten
www.myartslab.com

of the king, artists subjected his representation to startling stylizations, even physical distortions. This new royal figure style can be seen in a colossal statue of Akhenaten, about 16 feet tall, created for a new temple to the Aten that he built near the temple complex of Karnak, openly challenging the state gods (FIG. 3–25). This portrait was placed in one of the porticos of a huge courtyard (c. 426 by 394 feet), oriented to the movement of the sun.

The sculpture's strange, softly swelling forms suggest androgyny. The sagging stomach and inflated thighs contrast with spindly arms, protruding clavicles, and an attenuated neck, on which sits a strikingly stylized head. Facial features are exaggerated, often distorted. Slit-like eyes turn slightly downward, and the bulbous, sensuous lips are flanked by dimples that evoke the expression of ephemeral human emotion. Such stark deviations from convention are disquieting, especially since Akhenaten holds the flail and shepherd's crook, traditional symbols of the pharoah's super-human sovereignty.

The new Amarna style characterizes not only official royal portraits, but also pictorial relief sculpture portraying the family life of Akhenaten and Queen Nefertiti. In one panel the king and queen sit on cushioned stools playing with their nude daughters (FIG. 3–26), whose elongated shaved heads conform to the newly minted figure type. The royal couple receive the blessings of the Aten, whose rays end in hands that penetrate the open pavilion to offer ankhs before their nostrils, giving them the "breath of life." The king holds one child and lovingly pats her head, while she pulls herself forward to kiss him. The youngest of the three perches on Nefertiti's shoulder, trying to attract her mother's attention by stroking her cheek, while the oldest sits on the queen's lap, tugging at her mother's hand and pointing to her father. What a striking contrast with the relief from Ramose's tomb! Rather than composed serenity, this artist has conveyed the fidgety behavior of children and the loving involvement of their parents in a manner not even hinted at in earlier royal portraiture.

3-26 • AKHENATEN AND HIS FAMILY
Akhetaten (present-day Tell el-Amarna). Eighteenth Dynasty, c. 1353–1336 BCE. Painted limestone relief, 12¼ × 15¼″ (31.1 × 38.7 cm). Staatliche Museen zu Berlin, Preussischer Kulturbesitz, Ägyptisches Museum. (14145)

Egyptian relief sculptors often employed the **sunken relief** technique seen here. In ordinary reliefs, the background is carved back so that the figures project out from the finished surface. In sunken relief, the original flat surface of the stone is reserved as background, and the outlines of the figures are deeply incised, permitting the development of three-dimensional forms within them.

EXPLORE MORE: Gain insight from a primary source about Akhenaten **www.myartslab.com**

THE PORTRAIT OF TIY. Akhenaten's goals were actively supported not only by Nefertiti but also by his mother, **QUEEN TIY (FIG. 3–27)**. She had been the chief wife of the king's father, Amenhotep III, and had played a significant role in affairs of state during his reign. Queen Tiy's personality seems to emerge from a miniature portrait head that reveals the exquisite bone structure of her dark-skinned face, with its arched brows, uptilted eyes, and slightly pouting lips. Originally, this portrait included a funerary silver headdress covered with gold cobras and gold jewelry. But after her son came to power and established his new religion, the portrait was altered. A brown cap covered with blue glass beads was placed over the original headdress.

THE HEAD OF NEFERTITI. The famous head of **NEFERTITI (FIG. 3–28)** was discovered in the studio of the sculptor Thutmose and may have served as a model for full-length sculptures or paintings of the queen. The proportions of Nefertiti's refined, regular features, long neck, and heavy-lidded eyes appear almost too ideal to be human, but are eerily consistent with standards of beauty in our own culture. Part of the appeal of this portrait bust, aside from its stunning beauty, may be the artist's dramatic use of color. The hues of the blue headdress and its striped band are repeated in the rich red, blue, green, and gold of the jeweled necklace. The queen's brows, eyelids, cheeks, and lips are heightened with color, as they no doubt were heightened with cosmetics in real life. Whether or not Nefertiti's beauty is exaggerated, phrases used by her subjects when referring to her—"Beautiful of Face," "Mistress

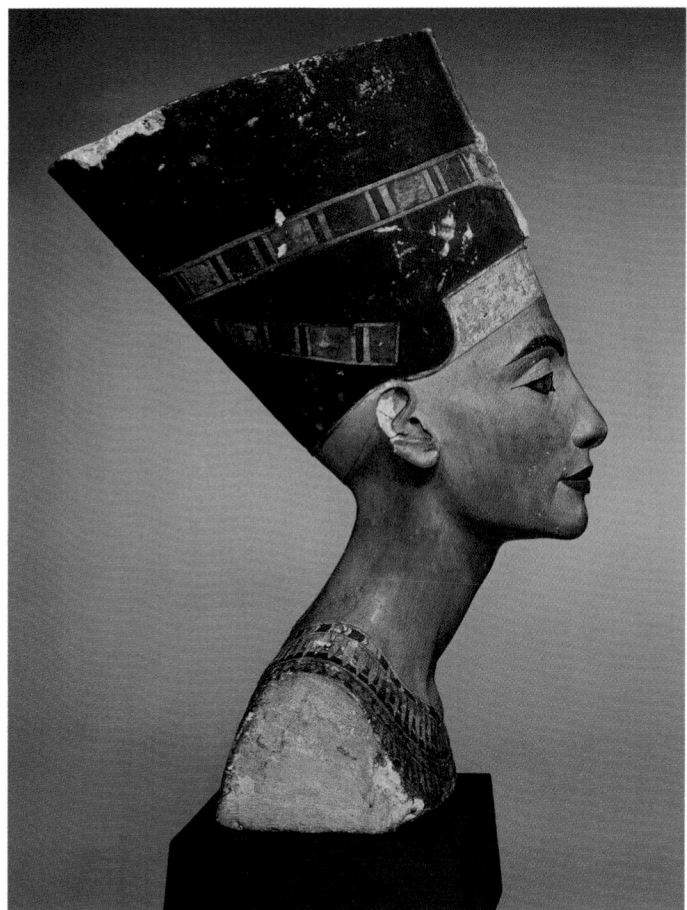

3-28 • NEFERTITI
Akhetaten (modern Tell el-Amarna). Eighteenth Dynasty, c. 1353–1336 BCE. Painted limestone, height 20″ (51 cm). Staatliche Museen zu Berlin, Preussischer Kulturbesitz, Ägyptisches Museum. (21300)

of Happiness," "Great of Love," or "Endowed with Favors"—tend to support the artist's vision.

GLASS. Glassmaking could only be practiced by artists working for the king, and Akhenaten's new capital had its own glassmaking workshops (see "Glassmaking," opposite). A bottle produced there and meant to hold scented oil was fashioned in the shape of a fish that has been identified as a bolti, a species that carries its eggs in its mouth and spits out its offspring when they hatch. The bolti was a common symbol for birth and regeneration, complementing the self-generation that Akhenaten attributed to the sun disk Aten.

THE RETURN TO TRADITION: TUTANKHAMUN AND RAMSES II

Akhenaten's new religion and revolutionary reconception of pharaonic art outlived him by only a few years. The priesthood of Amun quickly regained its former power, and his son Tutankhaten (Eighteenth Dynasty, r. c. 1332–1322 BCE) returned to traditional religious beliefs, changing his name to Tutankhamun—"Living Image of Amun"—and moving his court back to Thebes. He died young and was buried in the Valley of the Kings.

3-27 • QUEEN TIY
Kom Medinet el-Ghurab (near el-Lahun). Eighteenth Dynasty, c. 1352 BCE. Wood (perhaps yew and acacia), ebony, glass, silver, gold, lapis lazuli, cloth, clay, and wax, height 3¾″ (9.4 cm). Staatliche Museen zu Berlin, Preussischer Kulturbesitz, Ägyptisches Museum. (21834)

No one knows precisely when or where the technique of glassmaking first developed, but the basics of the process are quite clear. Heating a mixture of sand, lime, and sodium carbonate or sodium sulfate to a very high temperature produces glass. The addition of minerals can make the glass transparent, translucent, or opaque, as well as create a vast range of colors.

The first objects to be made entirely of glass in Egypt were produced with the technique known as core-formed glass. A lump of sandy clay molded into the desired shape was wrapped in strips of cloth, then skewered on a fireproof rod. It was then briefly dipped into a pot of molten glass. When the resulting coating of glass had cooled, the clay core was removed through the opening left by the skewer. To decorate the vessel, glassmakers frequently heated thin rods of colored glass and fused them on and flattened them against the surface in strips. In the fish-shaped bottle shown here—an example of core-formed glass from the New Kingdom's Amarna period—the body was created from glass tinted with cobalt, and the surface was then decorated with small rods of white and orange glass, achieving the wavy pattern that resembles fish scales by dragging a pointed tool along the surface. Then two slices of a rod of spiraled black and white glass were fused to the surface to create its eyes.

FISH-SHAPED PERFUME BOTTLE
Akhetaten (present-day Tell el-Amarna). Eighteenth Dynasty, reign of Akhenaten, c. 1353–1336 BCE. Core formed glass, length 5¾″ (14.5 cm). British Museum, London. (EA 55193)

TUTANKHAMUN'S TOMB. The sealed inner chamber of Tutankhamun's tomb was never plundered, and when it was found in 1922 its incredible riches were just as they had been left since his interment. His mummified body, crowned with a spectacular mask preserving his royal likeness (SEE FIG. 3–1), lay inside three nested coffins that identified him with Osiris, the god of the dead. The innermost coffin, in the shape of a mummy, is the richest of the three (FIG. 3–29). Made of over 240 pounds (110.4 kg) of gold, its surface is decorated with colored glass and semiprecious gemstones, as well as finely incised linear designs and hieroglyphic inscriptions. The king holds a crook and a flail, symbols that were associated with Osiris and had become a traditional part of the royal regalia. A *nemes* headcloth with projecting cobra and vulture covers his head, and a blue braided beard is attached to his chin. Nekhbet and Wadjet, vulture and cobra goddesses of Upper and Lower Egypt, spread their wings across his body. The king's features as reproduced on the coffin and masks are those of a very young man, and the unusually full lips, thin-bridged nose, and pierced earlobes suggest the continuing vitality of some Amarna stylizations.

3-29 • INNER COFFIN OF TUTANKHAMUN'S SARCOPHAGUS
Tomb of Tutankhamun, Valley of the Kings. Eighteenth Dynasty, c. 1332–1322 BCE. Gold inlaid with glass and semiprecious stones, height 6'⅞″ (1.85 m), weight nearly 243 pounds (110.4 kg). Egyptian Museum, Cairo. (JE 60671)

SEE MORE: View a video about Tutankhamen **www.myartslab.com**

The Temples of Ramses II at Abu Simbel

Many art objects speak to us subtly, through their enduring beauty or mysterious complexity. Monuments such as Ramses II's temples at Abu Simbel speak to us more directly across the ages with a sense of raw power born of sheer scale. This king-god of Egypt, ruler of a vast empire, a virile wonder who fathered nearly a hundred children, is self-described in an inscription he had carved into an obelisk (now standing in the heart of Paris): "Son of Ra: Ramses-Meryamun ['Beloved of Amun']. As long as the skies exist, your monuments shall exist, your name shall exist, firm as the skies."

Abu Simbel was an auspicious site for Ramses II's great temples. It is north of the second cataract of the Nile, in Nubia, the ancient land of Kush, which Ramses ruled and which was the source of his gold, ivory, and exotic animal skins. The monuments are carved directly into the living rock of the sacred hills. The larger temple is dedicated to Ramses and the Egyptian gods Amun, Ra-Horakhty, and Ptah. The dominant feature is a row of four colossal seated statues of the king himself, 65 feet high, flanked by relatively small statues of family members, including his principal wife Nefertari. Inside the temple, eight 23-foot statues of the god Osiris with the face of the god-king Ramses further proclaim his divinity. The corridor they form leads to seated figures of Ptah, Amun, Ramses II, and Ra. The corridor was oriented in such a way that twice a year the first rays of the rising sun shot through its entire depth to illuminate statues of the king and the three gods placed against the back wall.

About 500 feet away, Ramses ordered a smaller temple to be carved into a mountain sacred to Hathor, goddess of fertility, love, joy, and music, and to be dedicated to Hathor and to Nefertari. The two temples were oriented so that their axes crossed in the middle of the Nile, suggesting that they may have been associated with the annual life-giving flood.

Ironically, rising water nearly destroyed them both. Half-buried in the sand over the ages, the temples were only rediscovered early in the nineteenth century. But in the 1960s, construction of the Aswan High Dam flooded the Abu Simbel site. An international

TEMPLE OF RAMSES II
Abu Simbel. Nineteenth Dynasty, c. 1279–1213 BCE.

team of experts mobilized to find a way to safeguard Ramses II's temples, deciding in 1963 to cut them out of the rock in blocks and re-erect them on higher ground, secure from the rising waters of Lake Nasser. The projected cost of $32 million was financed by UNESCO, with Egypt and the United States each pledging contributions of $12 million. Work began in 1964 and was completed in 1968. Because of such international cooperation and a combination of modern technology and patient, hard labor, Ramses II's temples were saved from sure destruction so they can continue to speak to future generations.

REMOVAL OF THE FACE OF ONE OF THE COLOSSAL SCULPTURES OF RAMSES II AT ABU SIMBEL IN THE MID 1960S

a row of baboons greeting the rising sun

statue of Ra-Horakhty

inner sanctuary

vestibule with scenes of Ramses and Nefertari making offerings

statues of Osiris with the face of Ramses

storerooms

INTERIOR

entrance to temple

colossal statues of Ramses II

EXTERIOR

SCHEMATIC DRAWING OF THE TEMPLE OF RAMSES II
Abu Simbel.

EXPLORE MORE: Click the Google Earth link for the Temple of Ramses II at Abu Simbel **www.myartslab.com**

RAMSES II AND ABU SIMBEL. By Egyptian standards Tutankhamun was a rather minor king. Ramses II, on the other hand, was both powerful and long-lived. Under Ramses II (Nineteenth Dynasty, r. c. 1279–1213 BCE), Egypt was a mighty empire. Ramses was a bold leader and an effective political strategist. Although he did not win every battle, he was an effective master of royal propaganda, able to turn military defeats into glorious victories. He also triumphed diplomatically by securing a peace agreement with the Hittites, a rival power centered in Anatolia (see Chapter 2) that had tried to expand to the west and south at Egypt's expense. Ramses twice reaffirmed that agreement by marrying Hittite princesses.

In the course of a long and prosperous reign, Ramses II initiated building projects on a scale rivaling the Old Kingdom Pyramids at Giza. Today, the most awe-inspiring of his many architectural monuments are found at Karnak and Luxor, and at Abu Simbel in Egypt's southernmost region (see "The Temples of Ramses II at Abu Simbel," pages 74–75). At Abu Simbel, Ramses ordered two large temples to be carved into natural rock, one for himself and the other for his principal wife, Nefertari.

The temples at Abu Simbel were not funerary monuments. Ramses' and Nefertari's tombs are in the Valleys of the Kings and Queens. The walls of Nefertari's tomb are covered with exquisite paintings. In one mural, Nefertari offers jars of perfumed ointment to the goddess Isis (FIG. 3–30). The queen wears the vulture-skin headdress and jeweled collar indicating her royal position, and a long, semitransparent white linen gown. Isis, seated on her throne behind a table heaped with offerings, holds a long scepter in her left hand, the ankh in her right. She wears a headdress surmounted by the horns of Hathor framing a sun disk, clear indications of her divinity.

The artists responsible for decorating the tomb diverged very subtly but distinctively from earlier stylistic conventions. The outline drawing and use of pure colors within the lines reflect traditional practices, but quite new is the slight modeling of the body forms by small changes of hue to enhance the appearance of three-dimensionality. The skin color of these women is much darker than that conventionally used for females in earlier periods, and lightly brushed-in shading emphasizes their eyes and lips.

THE BOOKS OF THE DEAD

By the time of the New Kingdom, the Egyptians had come to believe that only a person free from wrongdoing could enjoy an afterlife. The dead were thought to undergo a last judgment consisting of two tests presided over by Osiris, the god of the underworld, and supervised by the jackal-headed god of embalming and cemeteries, Anubis. After the deceased were questioned about their behavior in life, their hearts—which the Egyptians believed to

3-30 • QUEEN NEFERTARI MAKING AN OFFERING TO ISIS
Wall painting in the tomb of Nefertari, Valley of the Queens. Nineteenth Dynasty, 1290–1224 BCE.

RECOVERING THE PAST | The Rosetta Stone

After centuries of foreign rule, beginning with the arrival of the Greeks in 332 BCE, the ancient Egyptian language gradually died out. Modern scholars were only able to recover this long-forgotten language through a fragment of a stone stele, dated 196 BCE. Known today as the Rosetta Stone—for the area of the Delta where one of Napoleon's officers discovered it in 1799—it contains a decree issued by the priests at Memphis honoring Ptolemy V (r. c. 205–180 BCE) carved in hieroglyphs, **demotic** (a simplified, cursive form of hieroglyphs), and Greek.

Even with the juxtaposed Greek translation, the two Egyptian texts remained incomprehensible until 1818, when Thomas Young, an English physician interested in ancient Egypt, linked some of the hieroglyphs to specific names in the Greek version. A short time later, French scholar Jean-François Champollion located the names Ptolemy and Cleopatra in both of the Egyptian scripts. With the phonetic symbols for P, T, O, and L in demotic, he was able to build up an "alphabet" of hieroglyphs, and by 1822 he had deciphered the two Egyptian texts.

ROSETTA STONE
196 BCE. British Museum, London.

p   t   o   l   m   y   s

Hieroglyphic signs for the letters P, T, O, and L, which were Champollion's clues to deciphering the Rosetta Stone.

be the seat of the soul—were weighed on a scale against an ostrich feather, the symbol of Ma'at, goddess of truth, order, and justice.

Family members commissioned papyrus scrolls containing magical texts or spells, which the embalmers sometimes placed among the wrappings of the mummified bodies. Early collectors of Egyptian artifacts referred to such scrolls, often beautifully illustrated, as "Books of the Dead." A scene in one that was created for a man named Hunefer (Nineteenth Dynasty) shows three successive stages in his induction into the afterlife **(FIG. 3–31)**. At the left, Anubis leads him by the hand to the spot where he will

3–31 • JUDGMENT OF HUNEFER BEFORE OSIRIS
Illustration from a Book of the Dead. Nineteenth Dynasty, c. 1285 BCE. Painted papyrus, height 15⅝" (39.8 cm). British Museum, London. (EA 9901)

ART OF ANCIENT EGYPT **CHAPTER 3** 77

weigh his heart against the "feather of Truth." Ma'at herself appears atop the balancing arm of the scales wearing the feather as a headdress. To the right of the scales, Ammit, the dreaded "Eater of the Dead"—part crocodile, part lion, and part hippopotamus—watches eagerly for a sign from the ibis-headed god Thoth, who prepares to record the result of the weighing

But the "Eater" goes hungry. Hunefer passes the test, and Horus, on the right, presents him to the enthroned Osiris, who floats on a lake of natron (see "Preserving the Dead," page 56). Behind the throne, the goddesses Nephthys and Isis support the god's left arm, while in front of him Horus's four sons, each entrusted with the care of one of the deceased's vital organs, stand atop a huge lotus blossom rising up out of the lake. In the top register, Hunefer, finally accepted into the afterlife, kneels before 14 gods of the underworld.

THE THIRD INTERMEDIATE PERIOD, C. 1075–715 BCE

After the end of the New Kingdom, Egypt was ruled by a series of new dynasties, whose leaders continued the traditional patterns of royal patronage and pushed figural conventions in new and interesting directions. One of the most extraordinary, and certainly one of the largest, surviving examples of ancient Egyptian bronze sculpture dates from this period (FIG. 3–32). An inscription on the base identifies the subject as Karomama, divine consort of Amun and member of a community of virgin priestesses selected from the pharaoh's family or retinue who were dedicated to him. Karomama herself was the granddaughter of king Osorkan I (Twenty-First Dynasty, r. c. 985–978 BCE). These priestesses amassed great power, held property, and maintained their own court, often passing on their position to one of their nieces. The *sistra* (ritual rattles) that Karomama once carried in her hands would have immediately identified her as a priestess rather than a princess.

The main body of this statue was cast in bronze and subsequently covered with a thin sheathing of bronze, which was then exquisitely engraved with patterns inlaid with gold, silver, and electrum (a natural alloy of gold and silver). Much of the inlay has disappeared, but we can still make out the elaborately incised drawing of the bird wings that surround Karomama and accentuate the fullness of her figure, conceived to embody a new female ideal. Her slender limbs, ample hips, and more prominent breasts contrast with the uniformly slender female figures of the late New Kingdom (SEE FIG. 3–30).

3-32 • KAROMAMA
Third Intermediate period, Twenty-Second Dynasty, c. 945–715 BCE.
Bronze inlaid with gold, silver, electrum, glass, and copper,
height 23½″ (59.5 cm). Musée du Louvre, Paris.

3-33 • MUMMY WRAPPING OF A YOUNG BOY
Hawara. Roman period, c. 100–120 CE. Linen wrappings with gilded stucco buttons and inserted portrait in encaustic on wood, height of mummy 53⅜″ (133 cm), portrait 9½ × 6½″ (24 × 16.5 cm). British Museum, London. (EA 13595)

LATE EGYPTIAN ART, C. 715–332 BCE

The Late period in Egypt saw the country and its art in the hands and service of foreigners. Nubians, Persians, Macedonians, Greeks, and Romans were all attracted to Egypt's riches and seduced by its art. The Nubians conquered Egypt and re-established capitals at Memphis and Thebes (712–657 BCE).

In 332 BCE the Macedonian Greeks led by Alexander the Great conquered Egypt, and after Alexander's death in 323 BCE, his generals divided up his empire. Ptolemy, a Greek, took Egypt, declaring himself king in 305 BCE. The Ptolemaic dynasty ended with the death of Cleopatra VII (r. 51–30 BCE), when the Romans succeeded as Egypt's rulers and made it the breadbasket of Rome.

Not surprisingly, works from this period combine the conventions of Greco-Roman and Egyptian art. For example, the tradition of mummifying the dead continued well into Egypt's Roman period. Thousands of mummies and hundreds of mummy portraits from that time have been found in the Fayum region of Lower Egypt. The mummy becomes a "soft sculpture" with a Roman-style portrait **(FIG. 3–33)** painted on a wood panel in **encaustic** (hot, colored wax), inserted over the face. Although great staring eyes invariably dominate the images—as they had in the funerary mask of Tutankhamun—these artists have seemingly recorded individual features of the deceased. Such Fayum portraits link Egyptian art with ancient Roman art (see Chapter 6).

THINK ABOUT IT

3.1 Discuss how the distinctive pictorial conventions for representing the human figure in ancient Egypt are used in the Palette of Narmer ("Closer Look," page 52) and the Tomb of Ramose (fig. 3–24).

3.2 Explain how depictions of royalty differ from those of ordinary people in ancient Egyptian art. Then compare and contrast Egyptian royal portraits from two different periods, making sure to explain the distinctive traits that characterize each.

3.3 Summarize the religious beliefs of ancient Egypt with regard to the afterlife, and explain how their beliefs inspired specific traditions in art and architecture.

3.4 Select a New Kingdom temple in this chapter that best represents the complexity of construction and decoration that New Kingdom builders brought to this traditional form of ancient Egyptian architecture. Support your choice with a discussion of its structural and decorative features.

PRACTICE MORE: Compose answers to these questions, get flashcards for images and terms, and review chapter material with quizzes
www.myartslab.com

4-1 • GIRL GATHERING SAFFRON CROCUS FLOWERS Detail of wall painting, Room 3 of House Xeste 3, Akrotiri, Thera, Cyclades. Before 1630 BCE. Thera Foundation, Petros M. Nomikos, Greece.

ART OF THE ANCIENT AEGEAN

This elegantly posed and sharply silhouetted girl, reaching to pluck the crocus flowers blooming on the hillside in front of her (FIG. 4–1), offers us a window into life in the ancient Aegean world. The image is from a fresco of c. 1650 BCE found in a house in Akrotiri, a town on the Aegean island of Thera that was famous for the saffron harvested from its crocuses. Saffron was valued in the Bronze Age Aegean mainly as a yellow dye in textile production, but it also had medicinal properties and was used to alleviate menstrual cramps. The latter use may be referenced in this image, since the fresco was part of the elaborate painted decoration of a room used for the coming of age ceremonies of young women at the onset of menses. The crocus gatherer's shaved head and looped long ponytail are attributes of childhood, but the light blue color of her scalp indicates that her hair is beginning to grow out, suggesting that she is entering adolescence.

The house that contained this painting disappeared suddenly more than 3,600 years ago, when the volcano that formed the island of Thera erupted, spewing pumice that filled and sealed every crevice of Akrotiri—fortunately, after the residents had fled. The rediscovery of the lost town in 1967 was among the most significant archaeological events of the second half of the twentieth century, and excavation of the city is still under way. The opportunity that Thera affords archaeologists to study works of art and architecture in context has allowed for a deeper understanding of the Bronze Age cultures of the Aegean. As the image of the girl gathering crocuses illustrates, wall paintings may reflect the ritual uses of a room or building, and the meanings of artifacts are better understood by considering both where they are found and how they are grouped with one another.

Before 3000 BCE until about 1100 BCE, several Bronze Age cultures flourished simultaneously across the Aegean: on a cluster of small islands (including Thera) called the Cyclades, on Crete and other islands in the eastern Mediterranean, and on mainland Greece (MAP 4–1). To learn about these cultures, archaeologists have studied shipwrecks, homes, and grave sites, as well as the ruins of architectural complexes. Archaeology—uncovering and interpreting material culture to reconstruct its original context—is our principal means of understanding the Bronze Age culture of the Aegean, since only one of its three written languages has been decoded. In recent years, archaeologists and art historians have collaborated with researchers in such areas of study as the history of trade and the history of climate change to provide an ever-clearer picture of ancient Aegean society. But many sites await excavation, or even discovery. The history of the Bronze Age Aegean is still being written.

LEARN ABOUT IT

4.1 Compare and contrast the art and architecture developed by three Aegean Bronze Age cultures.

4.2 Evaluate how archaeology has recovered, reconstructed, and interpreted ancient Aegean material culture despite the lack of written documents.

4.3 Assess differences in the designs and use of the large architectural complexes created by the Minoans and the Mycenaeans.

4.4 Investigate the relationship between art and social rituals or communal practices in the ancient Aegean cultures.

4.5 Discover the technical sophistication of Bronze Age artists working in metal, stone, and ceramics.

HEAR MORE: Listen to an audio file of your chapter **www.myartslab.com**

THE BRONZE AGE IN THE AEGEAN

Using metal ores imported from Europe, Arabia, and Anatolia, Aegean peoples created exquisite objects of bronze that were prized for export. This early period when the manufacture of bronze tools and weapons became widespread is known as the Aegean Bronze Age. (See Chapter 1 for the Bronze Age in northern Europe.)

For the ancient Aegean peoples, the sea provided an important link not only between the mainland and the islands, but also to the world beyond. In contrast to the landlocked civilizations of the Near East, and to the Egyptians, who used river transportation, the peoples of the Aegean were seafarers and their ports welcomed ships from other cultures around the Mediterranean. For this reason shipwrecks offer a rich source of information about the material culture of these ancient societies. For example, the wreck

4-2 • FIGURE OF A WOMAN WITH A DRAWING SHOWING EVIDENCE OF ORIGINAL PAINTING AND OUTLINING DESIGN SCHEME
Cyclades. c. 2600–2400 BCE. Marble, height 24¾″ (62.8 cm). Figure: Metropolitan Museum of Art, New York. Gift of Christos G. Bastis, 68.148. Drawing: Elizabeth Hendrix.

of a trading vessel (probably from the Levant, the Mediterranean coast of the Near East) thought to have sunk in or soon after 1306 BCE and discovered in the vicinity of Ulu Burun, off the southern coast of modern Turkey, carried an extremely varied cargo: metal ingots, bronze weapons and tools, aromatic resins, fruits and spices, jewelry and beads, African ebony, ivory tusks, ostrich eggs, disks of blue glass ready to be melted down for reuse, and ceramics from the Near East, mainland Greece, and Cyprus. Among the gold objects was a scarab associated with Nefertiti, wife of the Egyptian pharaoh Akhenaten. The cargo suggests that this vessel cruised from port to port along the Aegean and eastern Mediterranean seas, loading and unloading goods as it went. It also suggests that the peoples of Egypt and the ancient Near East were important trading partners.

Probably the thorniest problem in Aegean archaeology is that of dating the finds. In the case of the Ulu Burun wreck, the dating of a piece of freshly cut firewood on the ship to 1306 BCE—using a technique called dendrochronology that analyzes the spaces between growth rings—allowed unusual precision in pinpointing the moment this ship sunk. But archaeologists are not always able to find such easily datable materials. They usually rely on a relative dating system for the Aegean Bronze Age, based largely on pottery. But using it to assign specific dates to sites and objects is complicated and controversial. One cataclysmic event has helped: A huge volcanic explosion on the Cycladic island of Thera, as we have seen, devastated Minoan civilization there and on Crete, only 70 miles to the south. Evidence from tree rings from Ireland and California and traces of volcanic ash in ice cores from Greenland put the date of the eruption about 1650–1625 BCE. Sometimes in this book you will find periods cited without attached dates and in other books you may encounter different dates from those given for objects shown here. You should expect dating to change in the future as our knowledge grows and new techniques of dating emerge.

THE CYCLADIC ISLANDS

On the Cycladic Islands, late Neolithic and early Bronze Age people developed a thriving culture. They engaged in agriculture, herding, crafts, and trade, using local stone to build fortified towns and hillside burial chambers. Because they left no written records, their artifacts are our principal source of information about them. From about 6000 BCE, Cycladic artists used a coarse, poor-quality local clay to make a variety of ceramic objects, including engaging ceramic figurines of humans and animals, as well as domestic and ceremonial wares. Some 3,000 years later, they began to produce marble sculptures.

The Cyclades, especially the islands of Naxos and Paros, had ample supplies of a fine and durable white marble. Sculptors used this stone to create sleek, abstracted representations of human figures, ranging from a few inches to almost 5 feet tall. They were shaped—perhaps by women—with scrapers made of obsidian and

MAP 4–1 • THE ANCIENT AEGEAN WORLD

The three main cultures in the ancient Aegean were the Cycladic, in the Cyclades; the Minoan, on Thera and Crete; and the Helladic, including the Mycenaean, on mainland Greece but also encompassing the regions that had been the center of the two earlier cultures.

smoothed by polishing stones of emery, both materials easily available on the Cyclades.

These sculptures have been found almost exclusively in graves, and, although there are a few surviving male figures, the overwhelming majority represent nude women and conform to a consistent representational convention (**FIG. 4–2**). They are presented in extended poses of strict symmetry, with arms folded just under gently protruding breasts, as if they were clutching their abdomens. Necks are long, heads tilted back, and faces are featureless except for a prominent, elongated nose. All body parts are pared down to essentials, and some joints and junctures are indicated with incised lines. The sculptors carefully designed these figures, laying them out with a compass in conformity to three evenly spaced and equally

sized circles—the first delineated by the upper arch of the head and the waist, the second by the sloping shoulders and the line of the knees, and the third beginning with the curving limit of the paired feet and meeting the bottom of the upper circle at the waist.

For us, these elegant, pure stylizations recall the modern work of sculptors like Brancusi (SEE FIG. 31–28), but originally their smooth marble surfaces were enlivened by painted motifs in blue, red, and more rarely green paint, emphasizing their surfaces rather than their three-dimensional shapes. Today, evidence of such painting is extremely faint, but many patterns have been recovered using controlled lighting and microscopic investigation. Unlike the forms themselves, the painted features are often asymmetrical in organization. In the example illustrated here, wide-open eyes appear on forehead, cheeks, and thigh, as well as on either side of the nose.

Art historians have proposed a variety of explanations for the meaning of these painted motifs. The angled lines on some figures' bodies could bear witness to the way Cycladic peoples decorated their own bodies—whether permanently with tattoos or scarification, or temporarily with body paint, applied either during their lifetimes or to prepare their bodies for burial. The staring eyes, which seem to demand the viewer's return gaze, may have been a way of connecting these sculpted images to those who owned or used them. And eyes on locations other than faces may aim to draw viewers' attention—perhaps even healing powers—to a particular area of the body. Some have associated eyes on bellies with pregnancy.

4-3 • HEAD WITH REMAINS OF PAINTED DECORATION
Cyclades. c. 2500–2200 BCE. Marble and red pigment, height 9¹¹⁄₁₆″ (24.6 cm). National Museum, Copenhagen. (4697)

Art historian Gail Hoffman has argued that patterns of vertical red lines painted on the faces of some figures **(FIG. 4–3)** were related to Cycladic rituals of mourning their dead. Perhaps these sculptures were used in relation to a succession of key moments throughout their owners' lifetimes—such as puberty, marriage, and death—and were continually repainted with motifs associated with each ritual, before finally following their owners into their graves at death. Since there is no written evidence from Cycladic culture, it is difficult to be certain, but these sculptures were clearly important to Bronze Age Cycladic peoples and seem to have taken on meaning in relationship to their use.

Although some Cycladic islands retained their distinctive artistic traditions, by the Middle and Later Bronze Age, the art and culture of the Cyclades as a whole was subsumed by Minoan and, later, Mycenaean culture.

THE MINOAN CIVILIZATION ON CRETE

By 3000 BCE, Bronze Age people were living on Crete, the largest of the Aegean islands, 155 miles long and 36 miles wide. Crete was economically self-sufficient, producing its own grains, olives and other fruits, and cattle and sheep. With many safe harbors and a convenient location, Crete became a wealthy sea power, trading with mainland Greece, Egypt, the Near East, and Anatolia, thus acquiring the ores necessary for producing bronze.

Between about 1900 BCE and 1375 BCE, a distinctive culture flourished on Crete. The British archaeologist Sir Arthur Evans (see "Pioneers of Aegean Archaeology," page 91) named it Minoan after the legend of Minos, a king who had ruled from the capital, Knossos. According to this legend, a half-man, half-bull monster called the Minotaur—son of the wife of King Minos and a bull belonging to the sea god Poseidon—lived at Knossos in a maze called the Labyrinth. To satisfy the Minotaur's appetite for human flesh, King Minos ordered the mainland kingdom of Athens to send a yearly tribute of 14 young men and women, a practice that ended when the Athenian hero Theseus killed the beast.

Minoan chronology is divided into two main periods, the "Old Palace" Period, from about 1900 to 1700 BCE, and the "New Palace" Period, from around 1700 to 1450 BCE.

THE "OLD PALACE" PERIOD, c. 1900–1700 BCE

Minoan civilization remained very much a mystery until 1900 CE, when Sir Arthur Evans began uncovering the buried ruins of the architectural complex at Knossos, on Crete's north coast, that had been occupied in the Neolithic period, then built over with a succession of Bronze Age structures.

ARCHITECTURAL COMPLEXES. Like nineteenth-century excavators before him, Evans called these great architectural complexes "palaces." He believed they were occupied by a succession of kings. While some scholars continue to believe that

"Throne Room"

south propylaia

central court

north pillar hall

Hall of the "Double Axes"

south terrace

south porch

east entrance

4-4 • RECONSTRUCTION OF THE "PALACE" COMPLEX, KNOSSOS, CRETE
As it would have appeared during the "New Palace" Period. Site occupied 2000–1375 BCE; complex begun in "Old Palace" Period (c. 1900–1700 BCE); complex rebuilt after earthquakes and fires during "New Palace" Period (c. 1700–1450 BCE); final destruction c. 1375 BCE.

SEE MORE: View panoramas of the complex **www.myartslab.com**

Evans's "palaces" actually were the residences and administrative centers of hereditary rulers, the evidence has suggested to others that Minoan society was not ruled by kings drawn from a royal family, but by a confederation of aristocrats or aristocratic families who established a fluid and evolving power hierarchy. In this light, some scholars interpret these elaborate complexes not primarily as residences, but as sites of periodic religious ceremony or ritual, perhaps enacted by a community that gathered within the courtyards that are their core architectural feature.

The walls of early Minoan buildings were made of rubble and mud bricks faced with cut and finished local stone, our first evidence of **dressed stone** used as a building material in the Aegean. Columns and other interior elements were made of wood. Both in large complexes and in the surrounding towns, timber appears to have been used for framing and bracing walls. Its strength and flexibility would have minimized damage from the earthquakes common to the area. Nevertheless, an earthquake in c. 1700 BCE severely damaged several building sites, including Knossos and Phaistos. Damaged structures were repaired and enlarged, and the resulting new complexes shared a number of features. Multistoried, flat-roofed, and with many columns, they

were designed to maximize light and air, as well as to define access and circulation patterns. Daylight and fresh air entered through staggered levels, open stairwells, and strategically placed air shafts and light-wells (**FIG. 4–4**).

Courtyards—not audience halls or temples—were the central and most prominent components of these rectangular complexes. Suites of rooms were arranged around them. Corridors and staircases led from courtyard to courtyard, through apartments, ritual areas, and storerooms. Walls were coated with plaster, and some were painted with murals. Floors were plaster, or plaster mixed with pebbles, stone, wood, or beaten earth. The residential quarters had many luxuries: sunlit courtyards or light-wells, richly colored murals, and sophisticated plumbing systems.

Workshops clustered around the complexes formed commercial centers. Storeroom walls were lined with enormous clay jars for oil and wine, and in their floors stone-lined pits from earlier structures had been designed for the storage of grain. The huge scale of the centralized management of foodstuffs became apparent when excavators at Knossos found in a single (although more recent) storeroom enough ceramic jars to hold 20,000 gallons of olive oil.

CERAMIC ARTS. During the Old Palace Period, Minoans developed elegant new types of ceramics, spurred in part by the introduction of the potter's wheel early in the second millennium BCE. One type is called Kamares ware, after the cave on Mount Ida overlooking the architectural complex at Phaistos, in southern Crete, where it was first discovered. The hallmarks of this select ceramic ware—so sought-after that it was exported as far away as Egypt and Syria—were its extreme thinness, its use of color, and its graceful, stylized, painted decoration. An example from about 2000–1900 BCE has a globular body and a "beaked" pouring spout (FIG. 4–5). Created from brown, red, and creamy white pigments on a black body, the bold, curving forms—derived from plant life—that decorate this jug seem to swell with its bulging contours.

METALWORK. Matching Kamares ware in sophistication is early Minoan goldwork. By about 1700 BCE, Aegean metalworkers were producing objects rivaling those of Near Eastern and Egyptian jewelers, whose techniques they may have learned and adopted. For a pendant in gold found at Chryssolakkos (see "Aegean Metalwork,"

4-5 • KAMARES WARE JUG
Phaistos, Crete. "Old Palace" Period, c. 2000–1900 BCE. Ceramic, height 10⅝" (27 cm). Archaeological Museum, Iraklion, Crete.

page 87), the artist arched a pair of easily recognizable but geometrically stylized bees (or perhaps wasps) around a honeycomb of gold granules, providing their sleek bodies with a single pair of outspread wings. The pendant hangs from a spiderlike filigree form, with what appear to be long legs encircling a tiny gold ball. Small disks dangle from the ends of the wings and the point where the insects' bodies meet.

THE "NEW PALACE" PERIOD, c. 1700–1450 BCE

The early architectural complex at Knossos, erected about 1900 BCE, formed the core of an elaborate new one built after a terrible earthquake shook Crete in c. 1700 BCE. This rebuilding, at Knossos and elsewhere, belonged to the period termed "New Palace" by scholars, many of whom consider it the highest point of Minoan civilization. In its heyday, the Knossos complex covered six acres (SEE FIG. 4–4).

THE LABYRINTH AT KNOSSOS. Because double-axe motifs were used in its architectural decoration, the Knossos "palace" was referred to in later Greek legends as the Labyrinth, meaning the "House of the Double Axes" (Greek *labrys*, "double axe"). The organization of the complex seemed so complicated that the word labyrinth eventually came to mean "maze" and became part of the Minotaur legend.

This complicated layout provided the complex with its own internal security system: a baffling array of doors leading to unfamiliar rooms, stairs, yet more corridors, or even dead ends. Admittance could be denied by blocking corridors, and some rooms were accessible only from upper terraces. Close analysis, however, shows that the builders had laid out a square grid following predetermined principles, and that the apparently confusing layout may partially be the result of earthquake destruction and rebuilding over the centuries.

In typical Minoan fashion, the rebuilt Knossos complex was organized around a large central courtyard. A few steps led from the central courtyard down into the so-called Throne Room to the west, and a great staircase on the east side descended to the Hall of the Double Axes, an unusually grand example of a Minoan hall. (Evans gave the rooms their misleading but romantic names.) This hall and others were supported by the uniquely Minoan-type wooden columns that became standard in Aegean palace architecture. The tree trunks from which the columns were made were inverted so that they tapered toward the bottom. The top, supporting massive roof beams and a broad flattened capital, was wider than the bottom.

Rooms, following earlier tradition, were arranged around a central space rather than along an axis, as we have seen in Egypt and will see in mainland Greece. During the "New Palace" Period, suites functioned as archives, business centers, and residences. Some must also have had a religious function, though the temples, shrines, and elaborate tombs seen in Egypt are not found in Minoan architecture.

Aegean artists created exquisite luxury goods from imported gold. Their techniques included lost-wax casting (see "Lost-Wax Casting," page 413), inlay (see page 30), filigree, granulation, repoussé, niello, and gilding.

The early Minoan pendant with a pair of gold bees shown here exemplifies early sophistication in **filigree** (delicate decoration with fine wires) and **granulation** (minute granules or balls of precious metal fused to underlying forms), the latter used to enliven the surfaces and to outline or even create three-dimensional shapes

The *Vapheio Cup* (SEE FIG. 4–11) and the funerary mask (see "The 'Mask of Agamemnon," page 95) are examples of **repoussé**, in which artists gently pushed up relief forms (perhaps by hammering) from the back of a thin sheet of gold. Experienced goldsmiths may have formed simple designs freehand, or used standard wood forms or punches. For more elaborate decorations they would first have sculpted the entire design in wood or clay and then used this form as a mold for the gold sheet.

The artists who created the Mycenaean dagger blade (FIG. 4–16) not only inlaid one metal into another, but also employed a special technique called **niello**, still a common method of metal decoration. Powdered nigellum—a black alloy of lead, silver, and copper with sulfur—was rubbed into very fine engraved lines in a silver or gold surface, then fused to the surrounding metal with heat. The resulting lines appear as black drawings.

Gilding—the application of gold to an object made of some other material—was a technically demanding process by which paper-thin sheets of hammered gold called gold leaf (or, if very thin, **gold foil**) were meticulously affixed to the surface to be gilded. Gold sheets may once have covered the now-bare stone surface of the *Harvester Rhyton* (SEE FIG. 4–8) as well as the lost wooden horns of the *Bull's-head Rhyton* (SEE FIG. 4–9).

PENDANT OF GOLD BEES
Chryssolakkos, near Mallia, Crete. "Old Palace" Period, c. 1700–1550 BCE. Gold, height approx. 1¹³⁄₁₆″ (4.6 cm). Archaeological Museum, Iraklion, Crete.

SEE MORE: View a video about the process of lost-wax casting **www.myartslab.com**

BULL LEAPING AT KNOSSOS. Minoan painters worked on a large scale, covering entire walls of rooms with geometric borders, views of nature, and scenes of human activity. Murals can be painted on a still-wet plaster surface (**buon fresco**) or a dry one (**fresco secco**). The wet technique binds pigments to the wall, but forces the painter to work very quickly. On a dry wall, the painter need not hurry, but the pigments tend to flake off over time. Minoans used both techniques.

Minoan wall painting displays elegant drawing, and, like Egyptian painters, Minoan painters filled these linear contours with bright and unshaded fields of pure color. They preferred profile or full-faced views, and they turned natural forms into decorative patterns through stylization. One of the most famous and best-preserved paintings of Knossos depicts one of the most prominent subjects in Minoan art: **BULL LEAPING (FIG. 4–6)**. The restored panel is one of a group of paintings with bulls as subjects from a room in the east wing of the complex. The action—perhaps representing an initiation or fertility ritual—shows three scantily clad youths around a gigantic dappled bull, which is charging in

the **"flying-gallop"** pose. The pale-skinned person at the right—her paleness probably identifying her as a woman—is prepared to catch the dark-skinned man in the midst of his leap, and the pale-skinned woman at the left grasps the bull by its horns, perhaps to help steady it, or perhaps preparing to begin her own vault. Framing the action are strips of overlapping shapes, filled with ornament set within striped bands.

THE WOMAN WITH SNAKES. Surviving Minoan sculpture consists mainly of small, finely executed work in wood, ivory, precious metals, stone, and **faience** (colorfully glazed fine ceramic). Female figurines holding serpents are among the most characteristic images and may have been associated with water, regenerative power, and protection of the home.

The **WOMAN OR GODDESS WITH SNAKES** is intriguing both as a ritual object and as a work of art **(FIG. 4–7)**. This faience figurine was found with other ceremonial objects in a pit in one of Knossos's storerooms. Bare-breasted, arms extended, and brandishing a snake in each hand, the woman is a commanding

4-6 • BULL LEAPING
Wall painting with areas of modern reconstruction, from the palace complex, Knossos, Crete. Late Minoan period, c. 1550–1450 BCE. Height approx. 24½″ (62.3 cm). Archaeological Museum, Iraklion, Crete.

presence. Her shapely figure is dressed in a fitted, open bodice with an apron over a typically Minoan flounced skirt. A wide belt cinches the waist. The red, blue, and green geometric patterning on her clothing reflects the Minoan weavers' preference for bright colors, patterns, and fancy borders. Lifelike elements combine with formal stylization to create a figure that is both lively and dauntingly, almost hypnotically, powerful—a combination that has led scholars to disagree whether statues such as this one represent deities or their human attendants.

STONE RHYTONS. Almost certainly of ritual significance are a series of stone **rhytons**—vessels used for pouring liquids—that Minoans carved from steatite (a greenish or brown soapstone).

4-7 • WOMAN OR GODDESS WITH SNAKES
Knossos, Crete. "New Palace" Period, c. 1700–1550 BCE. Faience, height 11⅝″ (29.5 cm) as restored. Archaeological Museum, Iraklion, Crete.

This figure has been largely reconstructed from original fragments excavated at Knossos. The head, for instance, is a modern replacement, as is much of the left arm. Whereas the cat that sits on that modern head is authentic, it was not discovered in the same place as the figure. In fact, since there was no head on the "snake" in the figure's right hand, we are not even sure she was holding one.

4-8 • TWO VIEWS OF THE HARVESTER RHYTON
Hagia Triada, Crete. "New Palace" Period, c. 1650–1450 BCE. Steatite, diameter 4½" (11.3 cm). Archaeological Museum, Iraklion, Crete.

These have been found in fragments and reconstructed by archaeologists. **THE HARVESTER RHYTON** was a cone-shaped vessel (only the upper part is preserved) barely 4½ inches in diameter **(FIG. 4–8)**. It may have been covered with gold leaf, sheets of hammered gold (see "Aegean Metalwork," page 87).

A rowdy procession of 27 men has been crowded onto its curving surface. The piece is exceptional for the freedom with which the figures occupy three-dimensional space, overlapping and jostling one another instead of marching in orderly, patterned single file across the surface in the manner of some Near Eastern or Egyptian art. The exuberance of this scene is especially notable in the emotions expressed on the men's faces. They march and chant to the beat of a *sistrum*—a rattlelike percussion instrument—elevated in the hands of a man whose wide-open mouth seems to signal singing at the top of his lungs. The men have large, bold features and sinewy bodies so trim we can see their ribs. One man stands

out from the crowd because of his long hair, scale-covered ceremonial cloak, and commanding staff. Is he the leader of this enthusiastic band, or is he following along behind them? Archaeologists have proposed a variety of interpretations for the scene—a spring planting or fall harvest festival, a religious procession, a dance, a crowd of warriors, or a gang of forced laborers.

As we have seen, bulls are a recurrent theme in Minoan art, and rhytons were also made in the form of a bull's head **(FIG. 4–9)**. The sculptor carved this one from a block of greenish-black steatite to create an image that approaches animal portraiture. Lightly engraved lines, filled with white powder to make them visible, enliven the animal's coat: short, curly hair on top of the head; longer, shaggy strands on the sides; and circular patterns along the neck suggest its dappled coloring. White bands of shell outline the nostrils, and painted rock crystal and red jasper form the eyes. The horns (here restored) were made of wood covered with gold leaf. This rhyton was filled with liquid from a hole in the bull's neck, and during ritual libations, fluid flowed out from its mouth.

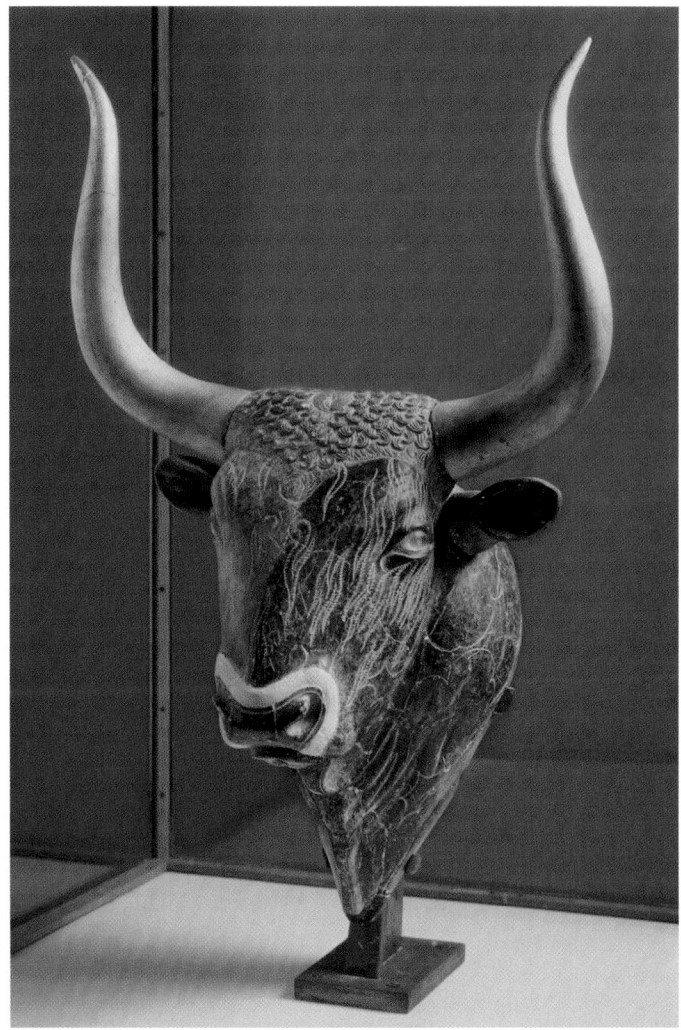

4-9 • BULL'S-HEAD RHYTON
Knossos, Crete. "New Palace" Period, c. 1550–1450 BCE. Steatite with shell, rock crystal, and red jasper; the gilt-wood horns are restorations, height 12" (30.5 cm). Archaeological Museum, Iraklion, Crete.

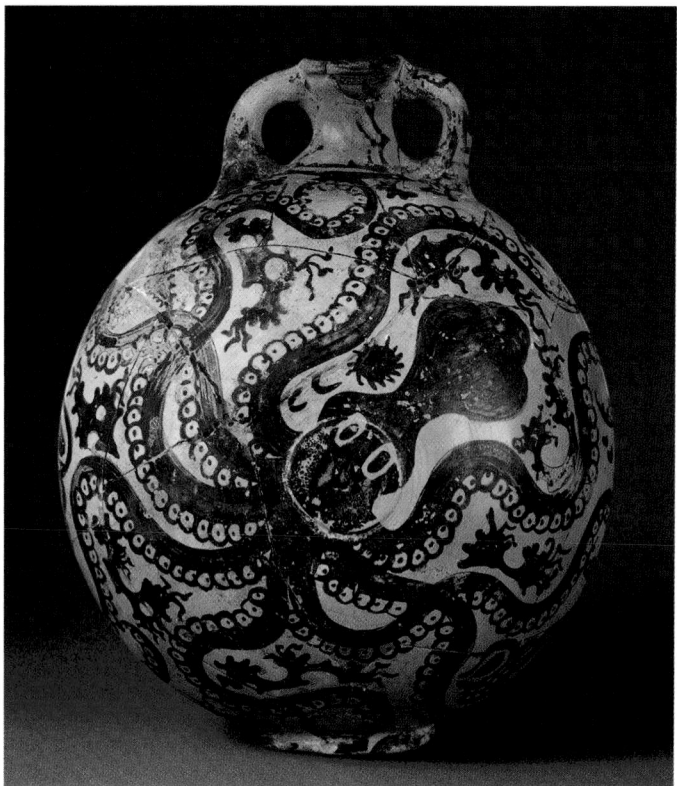

4-10 • OCTOPUS FLASK
Palaikastro, Crete. "New Palace" Period, c. 1500–1450 BCE. Marine style ceramic, height 11″ (28 cm). Archaeological Museum, Iraklion, Crete.

CERAMIC ARTS. The ceramic arts, so splendidly realized early on in Kamares ware, continued throughout the "New Palace" Period. Some of the most striking ceramics were done in what is called the "Marine style," because of the depictions of sea life on their surfaces. In a stoppered bottle of this style known as the **OCTOPUS FLASK**, made about 1500–1450 BCE **(FIG. 4–10)**, the painter

4-11 • VAPHEIO CUP
Found near Sparta, Greece. c. 1650–1450 BCE. Gold, height 4½″ (10.8 cm). Archaeological Museum, Iraklion, Crete.

created a dynamic arrangement of marine life, in seeming celebration of Minoan maritime prowess. Like microscopic life teeming in a drop of pond water, sea creatures float around an octopus's tangled tentacles. The decoration on the Kamares ware jug (SEE FIG. 4–5) had reinforced the solidity of its surface, but here the pottery skin seems to dissolve. The painter captured the grace and energy of natural forms while presenting them as a stylized design in calculated harmony with the vessel's bulging shape.

METALWORK. About 1450 BCE, a conquering people from mainland Greece, known as Mycenaeans, arrived in Crete. They occupied the buildings at Knossos and elsewhere until a final catastrophe and the destruction of Knossos about 1375 BCE caused them to abandon the site. But by 1400 BCE, the center of political and cultural power in the Aegean had shifted to mainland Greece.

The skills of Minoan artists, particularly metalsmiths, made them highly sought after on the mainland. A pair of magnificent gold cups found in a large tomb at Vapheio, on the Greek mainland south of Sparta, were made sometime between 1650 and 1450 BCE, either by Minoan artists or by locals trained in Minoan style and techniques. One side of one cup is shown here **(FIG. 4–11)**. The relief designs were executed in repoussé—the technique of pushing up the metal from the back of the sheet. The handles were attached with rivets, and the cup was then lined with sheet gold. In the scenes circling the cups, men are depicted trying to capture bulls in various ways. Here, a scantily clad man has roped a bull's hind leg. The figures dominate the landscape and bulge from the surface with a muscular vitality that belies the cup's small size—it is only 4½ inches tall. The depiction of olive trees could indicate that the scene is set in a sacred grove. Could the cups illustrate exploits in some long-lost heroic tale, or are they commonplace herding scenes?

WALL PAINTING AT AKROTIRI ON THERA. Minoan cultural influences seem to have spread to both the Cyclades and mainland Greece. Thera, for example, was so heavily under Crete's influence in the "New Palace" Period that it was a veritable outpost of Minoan culture. A girl picking crocuses in a fresco in a house at Akrotiri (SEE FIG. 4–1) wears the typically colorful Minoan flounced skirt with a short-sleeved, open-breasted bodice, large earrings, and bracelets (SEE FIG. 4–7). This wall painting demonstrates the sophisticated decorative sense found in Minoan art, both in color selection and in surface detail. The room in which this painting appears seems to have been dedicated to young women's coming-of-age ceremonies, and its frescos provide the visual context for ritual activity, just like the courtyard of the architectural complexes in Crete.

In another Akrotiri house, an artist has created an imaginative landscape of hills, rocks, and flowers **(FIG. 4–12)**, the first pure landscape painting we have encountered in ancient art. A viewer standing in the center of the room is surrounded by orange, rose, and

Some see Heinrich Schliemann (1822–1890) as the founder of the modern study of Aegean civilization. Schliemann was the son of an impoverished German minister and a largely self-educated polyglot. He worked hard, grew rich, and retired in 1863 to pursue his lifelong dream of becoming an archaeologist, inspired by the Greek poet Homer's epic tales, the *Iliad* and the *Odyssey*. In 1869, he began conducting fieldwork in Greece and Turkey. Scholars of that time considered Homer's stories pure fiction, but by studying the descriptions of geography in the *Iliad*, Schliemann located a multilayered site at Hissarlik, in present-day Turkey, whose sixth level up from the bedrock is now generally accepted as the closest chronological approximation of Homer's Troy. After his success in Anatolia, Schliemann pursued his hunch that the grave sites of Homer's Greek royal family would be found inside the citadel at Mycenae. But the graves he found were too early to contain the bodies of Atreus, Agamemnon, and their relatives—a fact only known through recent scholarship, after Schliemann's death.

The uncovering of what he considered the palace of the legendary King Minos fell to a British archaeologist, Sir Arthur Evans (1851–1941), who led the excavation at Knossos between 1900 and 1905. Evans gave the name Minoan—after legendary King Minos—to Bronze Age culture on Crete. He also made a first attempt to establish an absolute chronology for Minoan art, basing his conjectures on datable Egyptian artifacts found in the ruins on Crete and on Minoan artifacts found in Egypt. Later scholars have revised and refined both his dating and his interpretations of what he found at Knossos.

Evans was not the only pioneering archaeologist drawn to excavate on Crete. Boston-born Harriet Boyd Hawes (1871–1945), after graduating from Smith College in 1892 with a major in Classics and after a subsequent year of post-graduate study in Athens, traveled to Crete to find a site where she could begin a career in archaeology. She was in Knossos in 1900 to observe Evans's early work and was soon supervising her own excavations, first at Kavousi, and then at Gournia, where she directed work from 1901 until 1904. She is famous for the timely and thorough publication of her findings, accomplished while she was not only supervising these Bronze Age digs, but also pursuing her career as a beloved teacher of the liberal arts, first at Smith and later at Wellesley College.

4-12 • LANDSCAPE ("SPRING FRESCO")
Wall painting with areas of modern reconstruction, from Akrotiri, Thera, Cyclades. Before 1630 BCE. National Archaeological Museum, Athens.

The "Flotilla Fresco" from Akrotiri ›

from Room 5 of West House, Akrotiri, Thera. "New Palace" Period. c. 1650 BCE. National Archaeological Museum, Athens.

The depiction of lions chasing deer, signifying heroism, has a long history in Aegean art.

This smaller vessel, with five oarsmen and a helmsman, could depict a local dignitary, seated behind the helmsman, seeing off the fleet as it departs from port.

The important figure seated behind the helmsman on each vessel carries a long black spear. Since the red lines above the figures in the main cabins are also spears, the passengers are warriors, either departing for or returning from battle.

SEE MORE: View the Closer Look feature for the "Flotilla Fresco" from Akrotiri www.myartslab.com

blue rocky hillocks sprouting oversized deep red lilies. Swallows, sketched by a few deft lines, swoop above and around the flowers. The artist unifies the rhythmic flow of the undulating landscape, the stylized patterning imposed on the natural forms, and the decorative use of bright colors alternating with darker, neutral tones, which were perhaps meant to represent areas of shadow. The colors may seem fanciful to us, but sailors today who know the area well attest to their accuracy, suggesting that these artists recorded the actual colors of Thera's wet rocks in the sunshine, a zestful celebration of the natural world. How different this is from the cool, stable elegance of Egyptian wall painting!

The impact of Mycenaean culture is evident as well in Thera and is especially notable in the martial flavor of a long strip of wall painting known as the "Flotilla Fresco" (see "A Closer Look," above). The "Flotilla Fresco" appeared along the tops of the walls in the room of a house in Akrotiri comparable to that which contained the fresco of the girl gathering crocuses.

THE MYCENAEAN (HELLADIC) CULTURE

Archaeologists use the term *Helladic* (from *Hellas*, the Greek name for Greece) to designate the Aegean Bronze Age on mainland Greece. The Helladic period extends from about 3000 to 1000 BCE, concurrent with Cycladic and Minoan cultures. In the early part of the Aegean Bronze Age, Greek-speaking peoples, probably from the northwest, moved onto the mainland. They brought with them advanced techniques for metalworking, ceramics, and architectural design, and they displaced the local Neolithic culture. Later in the Aegean Bronze Age, the people of the mainland city of Mycenae rose to power and extended their influence into the Aegean islands as well.

HELLADIC ARCHITECTURE

Mycenaean architecture developed in distinct ways from that of the Minoans. Mycenaeans built fortified strongholds called citadels

Each of the seven vessels of the fleet on this fresco (only four can be seen in this partial view) is unique, differing in size, decoration (this one has lions painted on its side), and rigging.

Note the difference between the surviving fragments of the original fresco and the modern infill in this restored presentation of a dolphin swimming alongside the ships.

to protect the palaces of their rulers. These palaces contained a characteristic main or great room called a **megaron** that was axial in plan. The Mycenaeans also buried their dead in magnificent vaulted tombs, round in floor plan and crafted of cut stone.

MYCENAE. Later Greek writers called the walled complex of Mycenae **(FIGS. 4–13, 4–14)** the home of Agamemnon, legendary Greek king and leader of the Greek army that conquered the great city of Troy, as described in Homer's epic poem, the *Iliad*. The site was occupied from the Neolithic period to around 1050 BCE. Even today, the monumental gateway to the citadel at Mycenae is an impressive reminder of the importance of the city. The walls were rebuilt three times—c. 1340 BCE, c. 1250 BCE, and c. 1200 BCE—each time stronger than the last and enclosing more space. The second wall, of c. 1250 BCE, enclosed the grave circle and was pierced by two gates, the monumental "Lion Gate" (see pages 96–97) on the west and a smaller secondary, rear gate on the northeast side. The final

walls were extended about 1200 BCE to protect the water supply, an underground cistern. These walls were about 25 feet thick and nearly 30 feet high. The drywall masonry is known as **cyclopean**, because it was believed that only the enormous Cyclops (legendary one-eyed giants) could have moved such massive stones.

As in Near Eastern citadels, the Lion Gate was provided with guardian figures, which stand above the door rather than to the sides in the door jambs. From this gate, the Great Ramp led up the hillside, past the grave circle, to the courtyard for the building occupying the highest point in the center of the city, which may have been the residence of a ruler. From the courtyard one entered a porch, a vestibule, and finally the megaron, which seems to be the intended destination, in contrast to Minoan complexes where the courtyard itself seems to be the destination. A typical megaron had a central hearth surrounded by four large columns that supported the ceiling. The roof above the hearth was probably raised to admit light and air and permit smoke to escape (SEE FIG. 4–15). Some

4-13 • CITADEL AT MYCENAE
Greece. Aerial view. Site occupied c. 1600–1200 BCE; walls built c. 1340, 1250, 1200 BCE, creating a progressively larger enclosure.

House of Columns

megaron

great ramp

postern gate

"Palace" entrance

Warrior Vase House

Grave Circle A

Lion Gate

4-14 • RECONSTRUCTION OF THE CITADEL AT MYCENAE AT ITS MOST DEVELOPED STATE
Unlike at Knossos and Akrotiri, where we can understand multi-story structures because multiple levels survived and have been excavated, at Mycenae we have, for the most part, only foundations. To a certain extent, we can only conjecture concerning the upper portions of these buildings.

One of Heinrich Schliemann's most amazing and famous discoveries in the shaft graves in Mycenae was a solid gold mask placed over the face of a body he claimed was the legendary Agamemnon, uncovered on November 30, 1876. But Schliemann's identification of the mask with this king of Homeric legend has been disproven, and even the authenticity of the mask itself has been called into question over the last 30 years. Doubts are rooted in a series of stylistic features that separate this mask from the other four excavated by Schliemann in Grave Circle A—the treatment of the eyes and eyebrows, the cut-out separation of the ears from the flap of gold around the face, and most strikingly the beard and handlebar mustache that have suspicious parallels with nineteenth-century fashion in facial hair. Suspicions founded on such anomalies are reinforced by Schliemann's own history of deceit and embellishment when characterizing his life and discoveries, not to mention his freewheeling excavation practices, when judged against current archaeological standards. Some specialists have claimed a middle ground between genuine or fake for the mask, suggesting that the artifact itself may be authentic, but that Schliemann quickly subjected it to an overzealous restoration to make the face of "Agamemnon" seem more heroic and noble—at least to viewers in his own day—than the faces of the four other Mycenaean funerary masks. The resolution of this question awaits a full scientific study to determine the nature of the alloy (gold was regularly mixed with small amounts of other metals to make it stronger) from which this mask was made, as well as a microscopic analysis of its technique and the appearance of its surface.

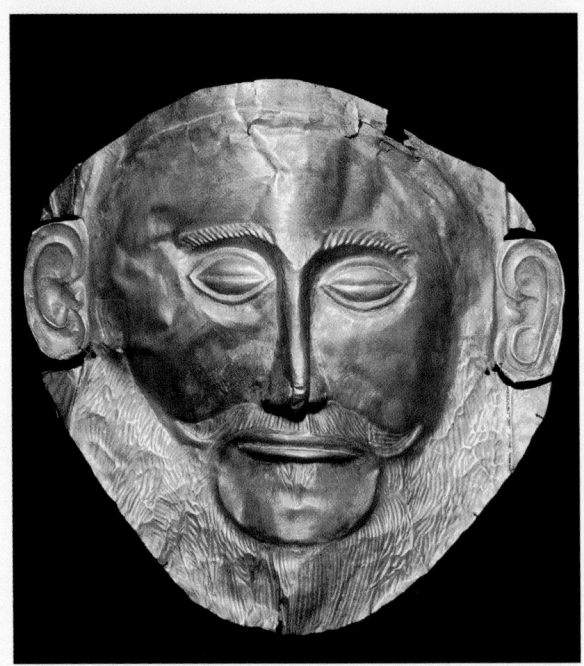

"MASK OF AGAMEMNON"
Funerary mask, from Shaft Grave v, Grave Circle A, Mycenae, Greece. c. 1600–1550 BCE. Gold, height approx. 12″ (35 cm). National Archaeological Museum, Athens.

4-15 • PYLOS PALACE: PLAN OF THE MEGARON
c. 1300–1200 BCE.

architectural historians think that the megaron eventually came to be associated with royalty. The later Greeks adapted its form when building temples, which they saw as earthly palaces for their gods.

PYLOS.   The rulers of Mycenae fortified their city, but the people of Pylos, in the extreme southwest of the Peloponnese, perhaps felt that their more remote and defensible location made them less vulnerable to attack. This seems not to have been the case, for within a century of its construction in c. 1340 BCE, the palace at Pylos was destroyed by fires, apparently set during the violent upheavals that brought about the collapse of Mycenae itself.

The architectural complex at Pylos was built on a raised site without fortifications, and it was organized around a special area that included an archive, storerooms, workshops, and a megaron for communal gatherings that focused on feasting (FIG. 4–15). Set behind a porch and vestibule facing the courtyard, the Pylos megaron was a magnificent display of architectural and decorative skill. Every inch was painted—floors, ceilings, beams, and door frames with brightly colored abstract designs, and walls with paintings of large mythical animals and highly stylized plant and landscape forms. The floor was finished with plaster painted with imitations of stone and tile patterns. There was a spot in the megaron where priests and priestesses poured libations to a deity from a ceremonial rhyton, fostering communication between the people of Pylos and their god(s).

Clay tablets found in the ruins of the palace include an inventory of its elegant furnishings. The listing on one tablet reads: "One ebony chair with golden back decorated with birds; and a footstool decorated with ivory pomegranates. One ebony chair with ivory back carved with a pair of finials and with a man's figure and heifers; one footstool, ebony inlaid with ivory and pomegranates."

MYCENAEAN TOMBS

SHAFT GRAVES.   Tombs were given much greater prominence in the Helladic culture of the mainland than they were by the Minoans, and ultimately they became the most architecturally sophisticated monuments of the entire Aegean Bronze Age. The

The Lion Gate

One of the most imposing survivals from the Helladic Age is the gate to the city of Mycenae. The gate is today a simple opening, but its importance is indicated by the very material of the flanking walls, a conglomerate stone that can be polished to glistening multicolors. A corbelled relieving arch above the lintel forms a triangle filled with a limestone panel bearing a grand heraldic composition—guardian beasts flanking a single Minoan column that swells upward to a large, bulbous capital.

The archival photograph (FIG. A) shows a group posing jauntily outside the gate. Visible is Heinrich Schliemann (standing at the left of the gate) and his wife and partner in archeology, Sophia (sitting at the right). Schliemann had already "discovered" Troy, and when he turned his attention to Mycenae in 1876, he unearthed graves containing rich treasures, including gold masks. The grave circle he excavated lay just inside the Lion Gate (SEE FIG. 4–14).

The Lion Gate has been the subject of much speculation in recent years. What are the animals? What does the architectural feature mean? How is the imagery to be interpreted? The beasts supporting and defending the column are magnificent, supple creatures rearing up on hind legs.

They once must have faced the visitor, but today only the attachment holes indicate the presence of their heads.

What were they—lions or lionesses? One scholar points out that since the beasts have neither teats nor penises, it is impossible to say. The beasts do not even have to be felines. They could have had eagle heads, which would make them griffins, in which case should they not also have wings? They could have had human heads, and that would turn them into sphinxes. Pausanias, a Greek traveler who visited Mycenae in the second century CE, described a gate guarded by lions. Did he see the now missing heads? Did the "object" not only speak, but roar?

Mixed-media sculpture—ivory and gold, marble and wood—was common. One could imagine that if the creatures had the heads of lions, the heads might have resembled the gold rhyton in the form of a lion that Schliemann excavated from a nearby shaft grave (FIG. C). Such heads would have gleamed and glowered out at the visitor. And if the stone sculpture was painted, as most was, the gold would not have seemed out of place.

A metaphor for power, the lions rest their feet on Mycenaean altars. Between them stands the mysterious column, also on an altar base. What does this composition mean? Scholars do not agree. Is it a temple? A palace? The entire city? Or the god of the place? The column and capital support a lintel or architrave, which in turn supports the butt ends of logs forming rafters of the horizontal roof, so the most likely theory is that the structure is the symbol of a palace or a temple. But some scholars suggest that by extension it becomes the symbol of a king or a deity. If so, the imagery of the Lion Gate, with its combination of guardian beasts and divine or royal palace, signifies the legitimate power of the ruler of Mycenae.

A. LION GATE, MYCENAE
c. 1250 BCE. Historic photo.

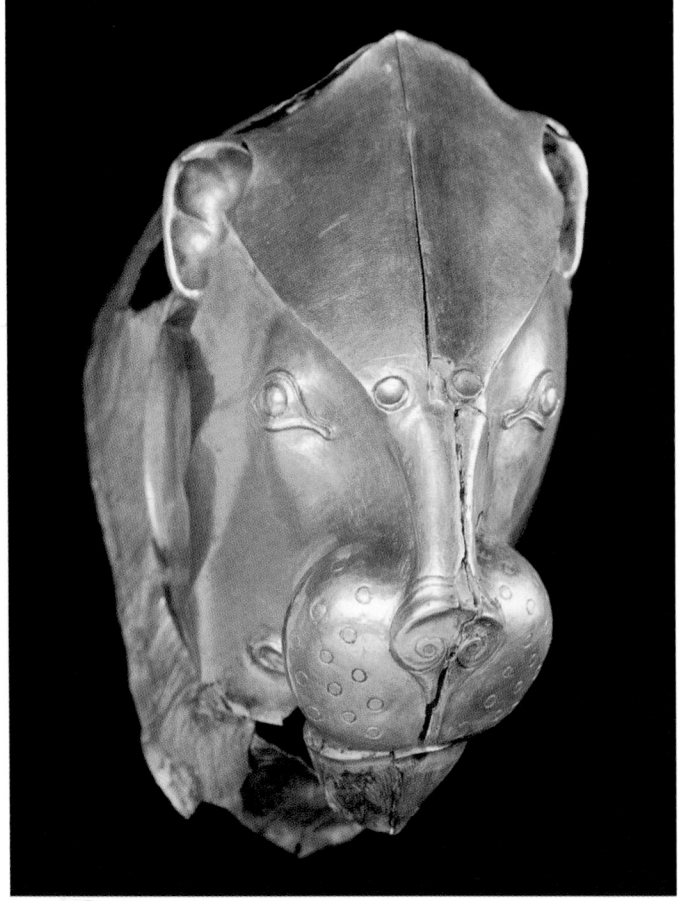

B. LION GATE, MYCENAE, AS IT APPEARS TODAY
c. 1250 BCE. Limestone relief, height of sculpture approx. 9'6" (2.9 m).

C. GOLDEN LION'S HEAD RHYTON
From Shaft Grave iv, Grave Circle A, south of Lion Gate, Mycenae. 16th century BCE. National Archaeological Museum, Athens.

4–16 • DAGGER BLADE WITH LION HUNT
Shaft Grave iv, Grave Circle A, Mycenae, Greece. c. 1550–1500 BCE. Bronze inlaid with gold, silver, and niello, length 9⅜″ (23.8 cm). National Archaeological Museum, Athens.

earliest burials were in **shaft graves**, vertical pits 20 to 25 feet deep. In Mycenae, the graves of important people were enclosed in a circle of standing stone slabs. In these graves, the ruling families laid out their dead in opulent dress and jewelry and surrounded them with ceremonial weapons (SEE FIG. 4–16), gold and silver wares, and other articles indicative of their status, wealth, and power.

Among the 30 pounds of gold objects archaeologist Heinrich Schliemann found in the shaft graves of Mycenae were five funerary masks, and he identified one of these golden treasures as the face of Agamemnon, commander-in-chief of the Greek forces in Homer's account of the Trojan War (see "the 'Mask of Agamemnon,'" page 95). We now know this mask has nothing to do with the heroes of the Trojan War since the Mycenae graves are about 300 years older than Schliemann believed, and the burial practices they display were different from those described by Homer.

Also found in these shaft graves were a gold lion's-head rhyton (see page 97, FIG. C) and a bronze **DAGGER BLADE** (FIG. 4–16) decorated with inlaid scenes, further attesting to the wealth of the Mycenaean ruling elite. To form the decoration of daggers like

this, Mycenaean artists cut shapes out of different-colored metals (copper, silver, and gold), inlaid them in the bronze blade, and then added fine details in niello (see "Aegean Metalwork," page 87). In Homer's *Iliad*, the poet describes similar decoration on Agamemnon's armor and Achilles' shield. The blade shown here depicts a lion attacking a deer, with four more terrified animals in full flight. Like the bull in the Minoan fresco (SEE FIG. 4–6), the animals spring forward in the "flying-gallop" pose to indicate speed and energy.

THOLOS TOMBS. By about 1600 BCE, members of the elite class on the mainland had begun building large above-ground burial places commonly referred to as **tholos tombs** (popularly known as **beehive tombs** because of their rounded, conical shape). More than a hundred such tombs have been found, nine of them in the vicinity of Mycenae. Possibly the most impressive is the so-called **TREASURY OF ATREUS** (FIGS. 4–17, 4–18), which dates from about 1300 to 1200 BCE.

A walled passageway through the earthen mound covering the tomb, about 114 feet long and 20 feet wide and open to the sky, led to the entrance, which was 34 feet high, with a door 16½ feet high, faced with bronze plaques. On either side of the entrance were upward-tapering columns carved from green serpentine porphyry, a kind of rock found near Sparta, and incised with decoration. The section above the lintel had smaller engaged

4–17 • CUTAWAY DRAWING OF THOLOS, THE SO-CALLED TREASURY OF ATREUS

4–18 • EXTERIOR VIEW OF THOLOS, THE SO-CALLED TREASURY OF ATREUS
Mycenae, Greece. c. 1300–1200 BCE.

SEE MORE: Click the Google Earth link for the Treasury of Atreus www.myartslab.com

columns on each side, and the relieving triangle was disguised behind a red-and-green engraved marble panel. The main tomb chamber (**FIG. 4–19**) is a circular room 47½ feet in diameter and 43 feet high. It is roofed with a **corbel vault** built up in regular **courses**, or layers, of **ashlar**—precisely cut blocks of stone—smoothly leaning inward and carefully calculated to meet in a single **capstone** (topmost stone that joins sides and completes structure) at the peak. Covered with earth, the tomb became a conical hill. It was a remarkable engineering feat.

CERAMIC ARTS

In the final phase of the Helladic Bronze Age, Mycenaean potters created highly refined ceramics. A large **krater**—a bowl for mixing water and wine, used both in feasts and as grave markers—is an example of the technically superior wares being produced on the Greek mainland between 1300 and 1100 BCE. Decorations could be highly stylized, like the scene of marching men on the **WARRIOR KRATER** (**FIG. 4–20**). On the side shown here, a woman at the far left bids farewell to a group of helmeted men marching off to the right, with lances and large shields. The vibrant energy of the *Harvester Rhyton* or the *Vapheio Cup* has changed to the regular rhythm inspired by the tramping feet of disciplined warriors. The only indication of the woman's emotions is the gesture of an arm raised to her head, a symbol of mourning. The men are seemingly interchangeable parts in a rigidly disciplined war machine.

4-20 • WARRIOR KRATER
Mycenae, Greece. c. 1300–1100 BCE. Ceramic, height 16″ (41 cm). National Archaelogical Museum, Athens.

The succeeding centuries, between about 1100 and 900 BCE, were a time of transformation in the Aegean, marked by less political, economic, and artistic complexity and control. A new culture was forming, one that looked back upon the exploits of the Helladic warrior-kings as the glories of a heroic age, while setting the stage for a new Greek civilization.

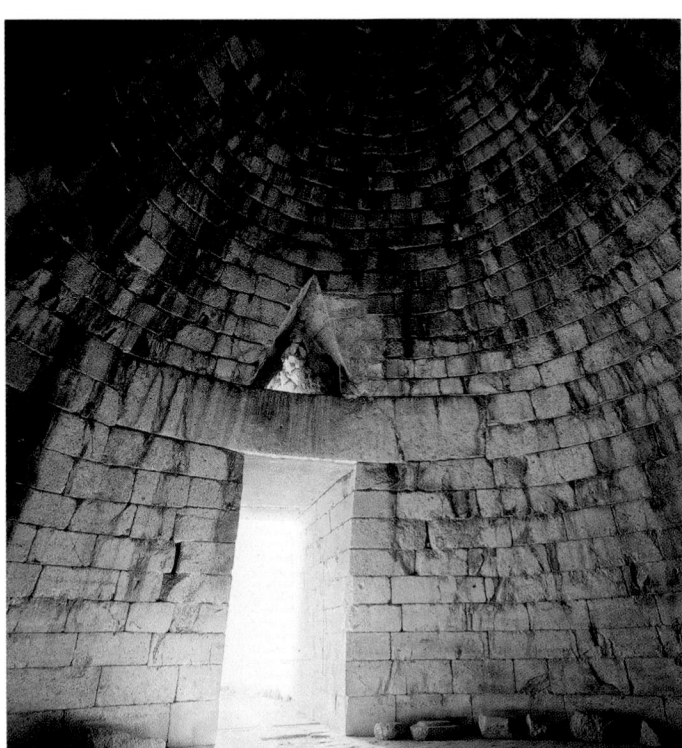

4-19 • CORBEL VAULT, INTERIOR OF THOLOS, THE SO-CALLED TREASURY OF ATREUS
Limestone vault, height approx. 43′ (13 m), diameter 47′6″ (14.48 m).

SEE MORE: View a simulation of the corbel vault
www.myartslab.com

THINK ABOUT IT

4.1 Choose a picture or sculpture of a human figure from two of the ancient Aegean cultures examined in this chapter. Characterize how the artist represents the human form and how that representation is related to the cultural significance of the works in their original context.

4.2 Assess the methods of two archaeologists whose work is discussed in this chapter. How have they recovered, reconstructed, and interpreted the material culture of the Bronze Age Aegean?

4.3 Compare the plans of the architectural complexes at Knossos and Mycenae. How have the arrangements of the buildings aided archaeologists in speculating on the way these complexes were used?

4.4 What explanations have art historians proposed for the use and cultural significance of the elegant figures of women that have been excavated in the Cyclades?

4.5 Select two metal objects from this chapter and explain how they were made. What aspects of the processes and details in the objects signal that these Bronze Age artists worked to a high level of technical sophistication?

PRACTICE MORE: Compose answers to these questions, get flashcards for images and terms, and review chapter material with quizzes
www.myartslab.com

5–1 • Exekias (potter and painter) AJAX AND ACHILLES PLAYING A GAME
c. 540–530 BCE. Black-figure painting on a ceramic amphora, height of amphora 2′ (61 cm). Vatican Museums, Rome.

ART OF ANCIENT GREECE

This elegantly contoured **amphora** was conceived and created to be more than the all-purpose storage jar signaled by its shape, substance, and size (FIG. 5–1). A strip around the belly of its bulging form was reserved by Exekias—the mid-sixth-century BCE Athenian artist who signed it proudly as both potter and painter—for the presentation of a narrative episode from the Trojan War, one of the signal stories of the ancient Greeks' mythical conception of their past. Two heroic warriors, Achilles and Ajax, sit across from each other, supporting themselves on their spears as they lean in toward the block between them that serves as a makeshift board for their game of dice. Ajax, to the right, calls out "three"—the spoken word written out diagonally on the surface as if issuing from his mouth. Achilles counters with "four," the winning number, his victory presaged by the visual prominence of the boldly silhouetted helmet perched on his head. (Ajax's headgear has been set casually aside on his shield, leaning behind him.) Ancient Greek viewers, however, would have perceived the tragic irony of Achilles' victory. When these two warriors returned from this playful diversion into the serious contest of battle, Achilles would be killed. Soon afterwards, the grieving Ajax would take his own life in despair.

The poignant narrative encounter portrayed on this amphora is also a masterful compositional design. Crisscrossing diagonals and compressed overlapping of spears, bodies, and table describe spatial complexity as well as surface pattern. The varying textures of hair, armor and clothing are dazzlingly evoked by the alternation between expanses of unarticulated surface and the finely incised lines of dense pattern. Careful contours convey a sense of three-dimensional human form. And the arrangement coordinates with the very shape of the vessel itself, its curving outline matched by the warriors' bending backs, the line of its handles continued in the tilt of the leaning shields.

There is no hint here of gods or kings. Focus rests on the private diversions of heroic warriors as well as on the identity and personal style of the artist who portrayed them. Supremely self-aware and self-confident, the ancient Greeks developed a concept of human supremacy and responsibility that required a new visual expression. Their art was centered in the material world, but it also conformed to strict ideals of beauty and mathematical concepts of design, paralleling the Greek philosophers' search for the human values of truth, virtue, and harmony, qualities that imbue both subject and style in this celebrated work.

LEARN ABOUT IT

5.1 Trace the emergence of a distinctive style and approach to art and architecture during the early centuries of Greek civilization.

5.2 Compare and contrast the black-figure and red-figure techniques of ceramic painting.

5.3 Assess the differences between the three order systems used in temple architecture.

5.4 Explore the nature and meaning of the High Classical style in ancient Greek art.

5.5 Discover the ways Hellenistic sculptors departed from the norms of High Classicism.

HEAR MORE: Listen to an audio file of your chapter www.myartslab.com

THE EMERGENCE OF GREEK CIVILIZATION

Ancient Greece was a mountainous land of spectacular natural beauty. Olive trees and grapevines grew on the steep hillsides, producing oil and wine, but there was little good farmland. In towns, skilled artisans produced metal and ceramic wares to trade abroad for grain and raw materials. Greek merchant ships carried pots, olive oil, and bronzes from Athens, Corinth, and Aegina around the Mediterranean Sea, extending the Greek cultural orbit from mainland Greece south to the Peloponnee, north to Macedonia, and east to the Aegean islands and the coast of Asia Minor (MAP 5–1). Greek colonies in Italy, Sicily, and Asia Minor rapidly became powerful independent commercial and cultural centers themselves, but they remained tied to the homeland by common language, heritage, religion, and art.

Within a remarkably brief time, Greek artists developed focused and distinctive ideals of human beauty and architectural design that continue to exert a profound influence today. From about 900 BCE until about 100 BCE, they concentrated on a new, rather narrow range of subjects and produced an impressive body of work with focused stylistic aspirations in a variety of media. Greek artists were restless. They continually sought to change and improve existing artistic trends and fashions, effecting striking stylistic change over the course of a few centuries. This is in stark contrast to the situation we discovered in ancient Egypt, where a desire for permanence and continuity maintained stable artistic conventions for nearly 3,000 years.

HISTORICAL BACKGROUND

In the ninth and eighth centuries BCE, long after Mycenaean dominance in the Aegean had come to an end, the Greeks began to form independently governed city-states. Each city-state was an autonomous region with a city—Athens, Corinth, Sparta—as its political, economic, religious, and cultural center. Each had its own form of government and economy, and each managed its own domestic and foreign affairs. The power of these city-states initially depended at least as much on their manufacturing and commercial skills as on their military might.

Among the emerging city-states, Corinth, located on major land and sea trade routes, was one of the oldest and most powerful. By the sixth century BCE, Athens rose to commercial and cultural preeminence. Soon it had also established a representative government in which every community had its own assembly and magistrates. All citizens participated in the assembly and all had an equal right to own private property, to exercise freedom of speech, to vote and hold public office, and to serve in the army or navy. Citizenship, however, was open only to Athenian men. The census of 309 BCE in Athens listed 21,000 citizens, 10,000 foreign residents, and 400,000 others—that is, women, children, and slaves.

RELIGIOUS BELIEFS AND SACRED PLACES

According to ancient Greek legend, the creation of the world involved a battle between the earth gods, called Titans, and the sky gods. The victors were the sky gods, whose home was believed to be atop Mount Olympos in the northeast corner of the Greek mainland. The Greeks saw their gods as immortal and endowed with supernatural powers, but more than peoples of the ancient Near East and the Egyptians, they also visualized them in human form and attributed to them human weaknesses and emotions. Among the most important deities were the supreme god and goddess, Zeus and Hera, and their offspring (see "Greek and Roman Deities," page 104).

Many sites throughout Greece, called **sanctuaries**, were thought to be sacred to one or more gods. The earliest sanctuaries included outdoor altars or shrines and a sacred natural element such as a tree, a rock, or a spring. As more buildings were added, a sanctuary might become a palatial home for the gods, with one or more temples, several treasuries for storing valuable offerings, various monuments and statues, housing for priests and visitors, an outdoor dance floor or permanent theater for ritual performances and literary competitions, and a stadium for athletic events. The Sanctuary of Zeus near Olympia, in the western Peloponnese, housed an extensive athletic facility with training rooms and arenas for track-and-field events. It was here that athletic competitions, prototypes of today's Olympic Games, were held.

Greek sanctuaries (SEE FIGS. 5–5, 5–6) are quite different from the religious complexes of the ancient Egyptians (see, for example, the Temple of Amun at Karnak, FIG. 3–18). Egyptian builders dramatized the power of gods or god-rulers by organizing their temples along straight, processional ways. The Greeks, in contrast, treated each building and monument as an independent element to be integrated with the natural features of the site, in an irregular arrangement that emphasized the exterior of each building as a discrete sculptural form on display.

GREEK ART c. 900–c. 600 BCE

Around the mid eleventh century BCE, a new culture began to form on the Greek mainland. Athens began to develop as a major center of ceramic production, creating both sculpture and vessels decorated with organized abstract designs. In this Geometric period, the Greeks, as we now call them, were beginning to create their own architectural forms and were trading actively with their neighbors to the east. By c. 700 BCE, in a phase called the Orientalizing period, they began to incorporate exotic foreign motifs into their native art.

THE GEOMETRIC PERIOD

What we call the Geometric period flourished in Greece between 900 and 700 BCE, especially in the decoration of ceramic vessels with linear motifs, such as spirals, diamonds, and cross-hatching. This abstract vocabulary is strikingly different from the stylized

MAP 5–1 • ANCIENT GREECE

The cultural heartland of ancient Greece consisted of the Greek mainland, the islands of the Aegean, and the west coast of Asian Minor, but colonies on the Italic peninsula and the island of Sicily extended Greek cultural influence further west into the Mediterranean.

plants, birds, and sea creatures that had characterized Minoan pots (SEE FIGS. 4–5, 4–10).

Large funerary vessels were developed at this time for use as grave markers, many of which have been uncovered at the ancient cemetery of Athens just outside the Dipylon Gate, once the main western entrance into the city. The krater illustrated here (FIG. 5–2) provides a detailed pictorial record of funerary rituals—including the relatively new Greek practice of cremation—associated with the important person whose death is commemorated by this work. On the top register, the body of the deceased is depicted laying on its side atop a funeral bier, about to be cremated. Male and female

5–2 • FUNERARY KRATER

From the Dipylon Cemetery, Athens. c. 750–700 BCE. Attributed to the Hirschfeld Workshop. Ceramic, height 42⅝″ (108 cm). Metropolitan Museum of Art, New York. Rogers Fund, 1914 (14.130.14)

ART AND ITS CONTEXTS

Greek and Roman Deities

(The Roman form of the name is given after the Greek name.)

THE FIVE CHILDREN OF EARTH AND SKY

Zeus (Jupiter), supreme Olympian deity. Mature, bearded man, often holding scepter or lightning bolt; sometimes represented as an eagle.
Hera (Juno), goddess of marriage. Sister/wife of Zeus. Mature woman; cow and peacock are sacred to her.
Hestia (Vesta), goddess of the hearth. Sister of Zeus. Her sacred flame burned in communal hearths.
Poseidon (Neptune), god of the sea. Holds a three-pronged spear.
Hades (Pluto), god of the underworld, the dead, and wealth.

THE SEVEN SKY GODS, OFFSPRING OF THE FIRST FIVE

Ares (Mars), god of war. Son of Zeus and Hera.
Hephaistos (Vulcan), god of the forge, fire, and metal handicrafts. Son of Hera (in some myths, also of Zeus); husband of Aphrodite.
Apollo (Phoebus), god of the sun, light, truth, music, archery, and healing. Sometimes identified with Helios (the Sun), who rides a chariot across the daytime sky. Son of Zeus and Leto (a descendant of Earth); brother of Artemis.
Artemis (Diana), goddess of the hunt, wild animals, and the moon. Sometimes identified with Selene (the Moon), who rides a chariot or oxcart across the night sky. Daughter of Zeus and Leto; sister of Apollo. Carries bow and arrows and is accompanied by hunting dogs.

Athena (Minerva), goddess of wisdom, war, victory, and the city. Also goddess of handcrafts and other artistic skills. Daughter of Zeus; sprang fully grown from his head. Wears helmet and carries shield and spear.
Aphrodite (Venus), goddess of love. Daughter of Zeus and the water nymph Dione; alternatively, born of sea foam; wife of Hephaistos.
Hermes (Mercury), messenger of the gods, god of fertility and luck, guide of the dead to the underworld, and god of thieves and commerce. Son of Zeus and Maia, the daughter of Atlas, a Titan who supports the sky on his shoulders. Wears winged sandals and hat; carries caduceus, a wand with two snakes entwined around it.

OTHER IMPORTANT DEITIES

Demeter (Ceres), goddess of grain and agriculture. Daughter of Kronos and Rhea, sister of Zeus and Hera.
Persephone (Proserpina), goddess of fertility and queen of the underworld. Wife of Hades; daughter of Demeter.
Dionysos (Bacchus), god of wine, the grape harvest, and inspiration. His female followers are called **maenads** (Bacchantes).
Eros (Cupid), god of love. In some myths, the son of Aphrodite. Shown as an infant or young boy, sometimes winged, carrying bow and arrows.
Pan (Faunus), protector of shepherds, god of the wilderness and of music. Half-man, half-goat, he carries panpipes.
Nike (Victory), goddess of victory. Often shown winged and flying.

---

figures stand on each side of the body, their arms raised and both hands placed on top of their heads in a gesture of anguish, as if these mourners were literally tearing their hair out with grief. In the register underneath, horse-drawn chariots and footsoldiers, who look like walking shields with tiny antlike heads and muscular legs, move in solemn procession.

The geometric shapes used to represent human figures on this pot—triangles for torsos; more triangles for the heads in profile; round dots for eyes; long, thin rectangles for arms; tiny waists; and long legs with bulging thigh and calf muscles—are what has given the Geometric style its name. Figures are shown in either full-frontal or full-profile views that emphasize flat patterns and crisp outlines. Any sense of the illusion of three-dimensional forms occupying real space has been avoided. But the artist has captured a deep sense of human loss by exploiting the stylized solemnity and strong rhythmic accents of the carefully arranged elements.

Egyptian funerary art reflected the strong belief that the dead, in the afterworld, could continue to engage in activities they enjoyed while alive. For the Greeks, the deceased entered a place of mystery and obscurity that living humans could not define

precisely, and their funerary art, in contrast, focused on the emotional reactions of the survivors. The scene of human mourning on this pot contains no supernatural beings, nor any identifiable reference to an afterlife, only poignant evocations of the sentiments and rituals of those left behind on earth.

Greek artists of the Geometric period also produced figurines of wood, ivory, clay, and cast bronze. These small statues of humans and animals are similar in appearance to those painted on pots. A tiny bronze of this type **(FIG. 5–3)**, depicting a **MAN AND CENTAUR**—a mythical creature, part man and part horse—dates to about the same time as the funerary krater. Although there were wise and good centaurs in Greek lore, this work takes up the theme of battling man and centaur, prominent throughout the history of Greek art (SEE FIG. 5–33). The two figures confront each other after the man—perhaps Herakles—has stabbed the centaur; the spearhead is visible on the centaur's left side. Like the painter of the contemporary funerary krater, the sculptor here has distilled the body parts of the figures to elemental geometric shapes, arranging them in a composition of solid forms and open, or negative, spaces that makes the piece pleasing from multiple

5-3 • MAN AND CENTAUR
Perhaps from Olympia. c. 750 BCE. Bronze, height 4⅝″ (11.1 cm).
Metropolitan Museum of Art, New York. Gift of J. Pierpont Morgan, 1917
(17.190.2072)

viewpoints. Most such sculptures have been found in sanctuaries, suggesting that they may have served as votive offerings to the gods.

THE ORIENTALIZING PERIOD

By the seventh century BCE, painters in major pottery centers in Greece had moved away from the dense linear decoration of the Geometric style. They now created more open compositions built around large motifs that included real and imaginary animals, abstract plant forms, and human figures. The source of these motifs can be traced to the arts of the Near East, Asia Minor, and Egypt. Greek painters did not simply copy the work of Eastern artists, however. Instead, they drew on work in a variety of media—including sculpture, metalwork, and textiles—to invent an entirely new approach to painting vessels.

The Orientalizing style (c. 700–600 BCE) began in Corinth, a port city where luxury wares from the Near East and Egypt inspired artists. The new style is evident in a Corinthian **olpe**, or wide-mouthed pitcher, dating to about 650–625 BCE **(FIG. 5–4)**. Silhouetted creatures—lions, panthers, goats, deer, bulls, boars, and

swans—stride in horizontal bands against a light background with stylized flower forms called **rosettes** filling the spaces around them. An example of the **black-figure** technique (see "Black-Figure and Red-Figure," page 120), dark shapes define the silhouettes of the animals against a background of very pale buff, the natural color of the Corinthian clay. The artist incised fine details inside the silhouetted shapes with a sharp tool and added touches of white and red slip to enliven the design.

5-4 • OLPE (PITCHER)
Corinth. c. 650–625 BCE. Ceramic with black-figure decoration, height 12⅞″ (32.8 cm). J. Paul Getty Museum, Malibu.

5-5 • SANCTUARY OF APOLLO, DELPHI
6th–3rd century BCE. View of archaeological site from the air.

5-6 • RECONSTRUCTION DRAWING OF THE SANCTUARY OF APOLLO, DELPHI

theater

Temple of Apollo

Treasury of the Athenians

Meeting Hall of the Knidians

Siphnian Treasury

Sikyonian Treasury

Arkadian monument

Stoa of Attalos

Altar of the Chians

Stoa of the Athenians

Sacred Way

THE ARCHAIC PERIOD, C. 600–480 BCE

The Archaic period does not deserve its name. "Archaic" means "antiquated" or "old-fashioned," even "primitive," and the term was chosen by art historians who wanted to stress what they perceived as a contrast between the undeveloped art of this time and the subsequent Classical period, once thought to be the most admirable and highly developed phase of Greek art. But the "Archaic" period was a time of great new achievement in Greece. In literature, Sappho wrote her inspired poetry on the island of Lesbos, while on another island the legendary storyteller, Aesop, crafted his animal fables. Artists and architects shared in the growing prosperity as city councils and wealthy individuals sponsored the creation of extraordinary sculpture and fine ceramics and commissioned elaborate civic and religious buildings in cities and sanctuaries.

THE SANCTUARY AT DELPHI

According to Greek myth, Zeus was said to have released two eagles from opposite ends of the earth and they met exactly at the rugged mountain site of Apollo's sanctuary (FIG. 5–5). From very early times, the sanctuary at Delphi was renowned as an oracle, a place where the god Apollo was believed to communicate with humans by means of cryptic messages delivered through a human intermediary, or medium (the Pythia). The Greeks and their leaders routinely sought advice at oracles, and attributed many twists of fate to misinterpretations of the Pythia's statements. Even foreign rulers journeyed to request help at Delphi.

Delphi was the site of the Pythian Games which, like the Olympian Games, attracted participants from all over Greece. The principal events were the athletic contests and the music, dance, and poetry competitions in honor of Apollo. As at Olympia, hundreds of statues dedicated to the victors of the competitions, as well as mythological figures, filled the sanctuary grounds. The sanctuary of Apollo was significantly developed during the Archaic period and included the main temple, performance and athletic areas, treasuries, and other buildings and monuments, which made full use of limited space on the hillside (FIG. 5–6).

After visitors climbed the steep path up the lower slopes of Mount Parnassos, they entered the sanctuary by a ceremonial gate in the southeast corner. From there they zigzagged up the Sacred Way, so named because it was the route of religious processions during festivals. Moving past the numerous treasuries and memorials built by the city-states, they arrived at the long colonnade of the Temple of Apollo, rebuilt in c. 530 BCE on the site of an earlier temple. Below the temple was a **stoa**, a columned pavilion open on three sides, built by the people of Athens. There visitors rested, talked, or watched ceremonial dancing. At the top of the sanctuary hill was a stadium area for athletic contests.

TREASURY OF THE SIPHNIANS. Sanctuaries also included treasuries built by the citizens of Greek city-states to house and protect their offerings. The small but luxurious **TREASURY OF THE SIPHNIANS (FIG. 5–7)** was built in the sanctuary of Apollo at Delphi by the residents of the island of Siphnos near the Cyclades, between about 530 and 525 BCE. It survives today only in fragments housed in the museum at Delphi. Instead of columns, the builders used two stately **caryatids**—columns carved in the form of clothed women with their finely pleated, flowing garments, raised on **pedestals** and balancing elaborately carved

5-7 • RECONSTRUCTION DRAWING OF THE TREASURY OF THE SIPHNIANS
Sanctuary of Apollo, Delphi. c. 530–525 BCE.

This small treasury building at Delphi was originally elegant and richly ornamented. The figure sculpture and decorative moldings were once painted in strong colors, mainly dark blue, bright red, and white, with touches of yellow to resemble gold.

5-8 • BATTLE BETWEEN THE GODS AND THE GIANTS (TITANS)
Fragments of the north frieze of the Treasury of the Siphnians, from the Sanctuary of Apollo, Delphi.
c. 530–525 BCE. Marble, height 26″ (66 cm). Archaeological Museum, Delphi.

capitals on their heads. The capitals support a tall **entablature** conforming to the **Ionic order**, which features a plain, or three-panel, **architrave** and a continuous carved **frieze**, set off by richly carved moldings (see "The Greek Orders," page 110).

Both the continuous frieze and the **pediments** of the Siphnian Treasury were originally filled with relief sculpture. A surviving section of the frieze from the building's north side, which shows a scene from the legendary **BATTLE BETWEEN THE GODS AND THE GIANTS (TITANS)**, is notable for its complex representation of space **(FIG. 5–8)**. To give a sense of three-dimensional recession, the sculptors placed some figures behind others, overlapping as many as three of them and varying the depth of the relief to allow viewers to grasp their placement within space. Originally such sculptures were painted with bright color that enhanced the lifelike effect.

TEMPLES

For centuries ancient Greeks had worshiped at sanctuaries where an outdoor altar stood near a temple that sheltered a statue of a god. As Greek temples grew steadily in size and complexity, stone and marble replaced the earlier mud-brick and wood construction. A number of standardized plans evolved, ranging from simple, one-room structures with columned **porches** (covered, open space in front of an entrance) to buildings with double porches (front and back), surrounded entirely by columns. Builders also experimented with the design of temple **elevations**—the arrangement, proportions, and appearance of the columns and the lintels, which now grew into elaborate entablatures. Two elevation designs emerged during the Archaic period: the **Doric order** and the Ionic order. The **Corinthian order**, a variant of the Ionic order, would develop later (see "The Greek Orders," page 110).

A particularly well-preserved Archaic temple, built around 550 BCE, still stands at the former Greek colony of Poseidonia (Roman Paestum) about 50 miles south of the modern city of Naples, Italy **(FIG. 5–9)**. Dedicated to Hera, the wife of Zeus, it is known today as Hera I to distinguish it from a second, adjacent temple to Hera built about a century later. The builders used the Doric order. A row of columns called the **peristyle** surrounded the main room, the **cella**. The columns of Hera I are especially robust—only about four times as high as their maximum diameter—and topped with a widely flaring capital and a broad, blocky **abacus**, creating an impression of great stability and permanence. As the column shafts rise, they swell in the middle and contract again toward the top, a refinement known as **entasis**. This adjustment gives a sense of energy and lift. Hera I has an uneven number of columns—nine—across the short ends of the peristyle, with a column instead of a space at the center of the two ends. The entrance to the **pronaos** (enclosed vestibule) has three columns in antis (between flanking wall piers), and a row of columns runs down the center of the wide cella to help support the ceiling and roof. The unusual two-aisle, two-door arrangement leading to the small room at the end of the cella proper suggests that the temple had two presiding deities: either Hera and Poseidon (patron of the city), or Hera and Zeus, or perhaps Hera in her two manifestations (as warrior and protector of the city and as mother and protector of children).

THE TEMPLE OF APHAIA ON AEGINA. A fully developed and somewhat sleeker Doric temple—part of a sanctuary dedicated to a local goddess named Aphaia—was built on the island of Aegina at the turn of the fifth century BCE **(FIG. 5–10)**. Spectacularly sited on the top of a hill overlooking the sea, the temple is reasonably well-preserved, in spite of the loss of pediments, roof, and sections

5-9 • PLAN AND EXTERIOR VIEW OF TEMPLE OF HERA I, POSEIDONIA (ROMAN PAESTUM)
Italy. c. 550–540 BCE.

EXPLORE MORE: Click the Google Earth link for The Temple of Hera I **www.myartslab.com**

5-10 • TEMPLE OF APHAIA, AEGINA
c. 500 BCE. View from the east. Column height about 17′ (5.18 m).

ELEMENTS OF ARCHITECTURE | The Greek Orders

Each of the three Classical Greek architectural **orders**—Doric, Ionic, and Corinthian—constitutes a system of interdependent parts whose proportions are based on mathematical ratios. No element of an order could be changed without producing a corresponding change in other elements.

The basic components are the **column** and the **entablature**, which function as post and lintel in the structural system. All three types of columns have a **shaft** and a **capital**; Ionic and Corinthian also have a **base**. The shafts are formed of stacked round sections, or **drums**, which are joined inside by metal pegs. In Greek temple architecture, columns stand on the **stylobate**, the "floor" of the temple, which rests on top of a set of steps that form the temple's base, known as the **stereobate**.

In the **Doric order**, shafts sit directly on the stylobate, without a base. They are **fluted**, or channeled, with sharp edges. The height of the substantial columns ranges from five-and-a-half to seven times the diameter of the base. A **necking** at the top of the shaft provides a

transition to the capital itself, composed of the rounded **echinus**, and the tabletlike **abacus**. The entablature includes the **architrave**, the distinctive frieze of alternating **triglyphs** and **metopes**, and the **cornice**, the topmost, projecting horizontal element. The roofline may have decorative waterspouts and terminal decorative elements called **acroteria**.

The **Ionic order** has more elongated proportions than the Doric, the height of a column being about nine times the diameter of its base. The flutes on the columns are deeper and are separated by flat surfaces called **fillets**. The capital has a distinctive spiral scrolled **volute**; the entablature has a three-panel architrave, continuous sculptured or decorated frieze, and richer decorative moldings.

The **Corinthian order**, a variant of the Ionic order originally developed by the Greeks for use in interiors, was eventually used on temple exteriors as well. Its elaborate capitals are sheathed with stylized **acanthus** leaves that rise from a convex band called the **astragal**.

Doric order — Ionic order — Corinthian order

5-11 • RECONSTRUCTION DRAWING OF THE TEMPLE OF APHAIA, AEGINA c. 500 BCE.

of its colonnade. Enough evidence remains to form a reliable reconstruction of its original appearance **(FIG. 5–11)**. The plan combines six columns on the façades with 12 on the sides, and the cella—whose roof was supported by superimposed colonnades—could be entered from porches on both short sides. The slight swelling of the columns (entasis) seen at Poseidonia is evident here as well, and the outside triglyphs are pushed to the ends of frieze, out of alignment with the column underneath them, to avoid the awkwardness of a half metope (rectangular panel with a relief or painting) at the corner.

Like most Greek temples, this building was neither isolated nor situated in open space, but set in relation to an outside altar where religious ceremonies were focused. By enclosing the temple within a walled precinct, the designer could control the viewer's initial experience of the temple. As the viewer entered the sacred space through a gatehouse—the Propylaia—the temple would be seen at an oblique angle **(FIG. 5–12)**. Unlike ancient Egyptian temples, where long processional approaches led visitors directly to the flat entrance façade of a building (SEE FIGS. 3–18, 3–22), the Greek architect revealed from the outset the full shape of a closed, compact, sculptural mass, inviting viewers not to enter seeking something within, but rather to walk around the exterior, exploring the rich sculptural embellishment on pediments and frieze. Cult ceremonies, after all, took place outside the temples.

Modern viewers, however, will not find exterior sculpture at Aegina. Nothing remains from the metopes, and substantial surviving portions of the two pediments were purchased in the early nineteenth century by the future Ludwig I of Bavaria and are now exhibited in Munich. They are precious documents in the development of Greek architectural sculpture. The triangular pediments in Greek temples created challenging compositional

enclosed precinct   temple

altar

propylaia

lodging for priests

N

5-12 • PLAN OF COMPLEX, TEMPLE OF APHAIA, AEGINA c. 500 BCE.

problems for sculptors intent on fitting figures into the tapering spaces at the outside corners, since the scale of figures could not change, only their poses. The earlier, west pediment of Aegina **(FIG. 5–13)**, dated about 500–490 BCE, represents a creative solution that became a design standard, appearing with variations throughout the fifth century BCE. The subject of the pediment, rendered in fully three-dimensional figures, is the participation of local warriors in the military expedition against Troy. Fallen warriors fill the angles at both ends of the pediment base, while others crouch and lunge, rising in height toward an image of Athena as warrior

5–13 • WEST PEDIMENT OF THE TEMPLE OF APHAIA, AEGINA
c. 500–490 BCE. Width about 49′ (15 m). Surviving fragments as assembled in the Staatliche Antikensammlungen und Glyptothek, Munich (early restorations removed).

5–14 • DYING WARRIOR
From the right corner of the west pediment of the Temple of Aphaia, Aegina. c. 500–490 BCE. Marble, length 5′6″ (1.68 m). Staatliche Antikensammlungen und Glyptothek, Munich.

5–15 • DYING WARRIOR
From the left corner of the east pediment of the Temple of Aphaia, Aegina. c. 490–480 BCE. Marble, length 6′ (1.83 m). Staatliche Antikensammlungen und Glyptothek, Munich.

TECHNIQUE | Color in Greek Sculpture

For many modern viewers, it comes as a real surprise, even a shock, that the stone sculptures of ancient Greece did not always have stark white, pure marble surfaces, comparable in appearance to—and consistent in taste with—the more recent, but still classicizing sculptures of Michelangelo or Canova (SEE FIGS. 20–9 and 29–14). But they were originally painted with brilliant colors. A close examination of Greek sculpture and architecture has long revealed evidence of polychromy, even to the unaided eye, but our understanding of the original appearance of these works has been greatly enhanced recently. Since the 1980s, German scholar Vinzenz Brinkmann has used extensive visual and scientific analysis to evaluate the traces of painting that remain on ancient Greek sculpture, employing tools such as ultraviolet and x-ray fluorescence, microscopy, and pigment analysis. Based on this research, he and his colleague Ulrike Koch-Brinkmann have fashioned reconstructions that allow us to imagine the exuberant effect these works would have had when they were new.

Illustrated here is their painted reconstruction of a kneeling archer from about 500 BCE that once formed part of the west pediment of the Temple of Aphaia at Aegina. To begin with they have replaced features of the sculpture—ringlet hair extensions, a bow, a quiver, and arrows—probably made of bronze or lead and attached to the stone after it was carved, using the holes still evident in the current state of the figure's hip and head. Most stunning, however, is the diamond-shaped patterns that were painted on his leggings and sleeves, using pigments derived from malachite, azurite, arsenic, cinnabar and charcoal. And the surfaces of such figures were not simply colored in. Artists created a sophisticated integration of three-dimensional form, color, and design. The patterning applied to this archer's leggings actually changes in size and shape in relation to the body beneath it, stretching out on expansive thighs and constricting on tapering ankles. Ancient authors indicate that sculpture was painted to make figures more lifelike, and these recent reconstructions certainly back them up.

A. Vinzenz Brinkmann and Ulrike Koch-Brinkmann
RECONSTRUCTION OF ARCHER
From the west pediment of the Temple of Aphaia, Aegina. 2004 CE.
Staatliche Antikensammlungen und Glyptothek, Munich.

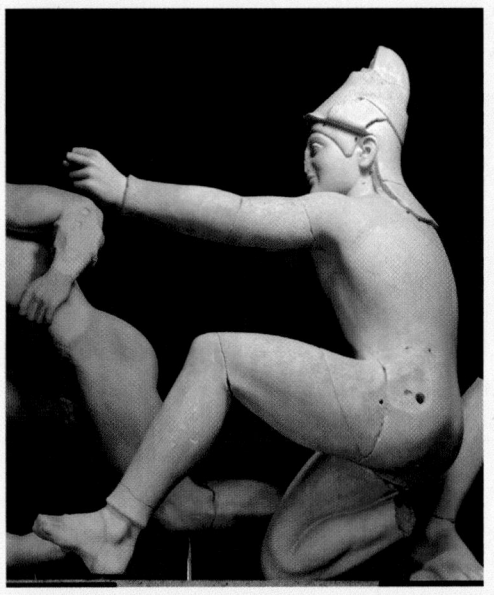

B. ARCHER ("PARIS")
From the west pediment of the Temple of Aphaia, Aegina.
c. 500–490 BCE. Marble. Staatliche Antikensammlungen und
Glyptothek, Munich.

goddess—who can fill the elevated pointed space at the center peak since she is allowed to be represented larger (hieratic scale) than the humans who flank her.

Among the best-preserved fragments from the west pediment is the **DYING WARRIOR** from the far right corner (**FIG. 5–14**). This tragic but noble figure struggles to rise up, supported on bent leg and elbow, in order to extract an arrow from his chest, even though his death seems certain. This figure originally would have been painted and fitted with authentic bronze accessories, heightening the sense of reality (see "Color in Greek Sculpture," above).

A similar figure appeared on the east pediment, created a decade or so after its counterpart on the west (**FIG. 5–15**). The sculptor of

this dying warrior also exploited the difficult framework of the pediment corner, only here, instead of an uplifted frontal form in profile, we see a twisted body capable of turning in space. The figure is more precariously balanced on his shield, clearly about to collapse. There is an increased sense of softness in the portrayal of human flesh and a greater sophistication in tailoring bodily posture not only to the tapering shape of the pediment, but also to the expression of the warrior's own emotional involvement in the agony and vulnerability of his predicament, which in turn inspires a sense of pathos or empathy in the viewer. Over the course of a decade, the sculptors of Aegina allow us to trace the transition from Archaic toward Early Classical art.

FREE-STANDING SCULPTURE

In addition to statues designed for temple exteriors, sculptors of the Archaic period created a new type of large, free-standing statue made of wood, **terra cotta** (clay fired over low heat, sometimes unglazed), limestone, or white marble from the islands of Paros and Naxos. These free-standing figures were brightly painted and sometimes bore inscriptions indicating that individual men or women had commissioned them for a commemorative purpose. They have been found marking graves and in sanctuaries, where they lined the sacred way from the entrance to the main temple.

A female statue of this type is called a **kore** (plural, *korai*), Greek for "young woman," and a male statue is called a **kouros** (plural, *kouroi*), Greek for "young man." Archaic *korai*, always clothed, probably represented deities, priestesses, and nymphs, young female immortals who served as attendants to gods. *Kouroi*, nearly always nude, have been variously identified as gods, warriors, and victorious athletes. Because the Greeks associated young, athletic males with fertility and family continuity, the *kouroi* figures may have symbolized ancestors.

METROPOLITAN KOUROS. A *kouros* dated about 600 BCE **(FIG. 5–16)** recalls the pose and proportions of Egyptian sculpture. As with Egyptian figures such as the statue of Menkaure (SEE FIG. 3–9), this young Greek stands rigidly upright, arms at his sides, fists clenched, and one leg slightly in front of the other. However, the Greek artist has cut away all stone from around the body to make the human form free-standing. Archaic *kouroi* are also much less lifelike than their Egyptian forebears. Anatomy is delineated with linear ridges and grooves that form regular, symmetrical patterns. The head is ovoid and schematized, and the wiglike hair evenly knotted into tufts and tied back with a narrow ribbon. The eyes are relatively large and wide open, and the mouth forms a conventional closed-lip expression known as the **Archaic smile**. In Egyptian sculpture, male figures usually wore clothing associated with their status, such as the headdresses, necklaces, and kilts that identified them as kings. The total nudity of the Greek *kouroi* is unusual in ancient Mediterranean cultures, but it is acceptable—even valued— in the case of young men. Not so with women.

BERLIN KORE. Early Archaic *korai* are as severe and stylized as the male figures. The **BERLIN KORE**, found in a cemetery at Keratea and dated about 570–560 BCE, stands more than 6 feet tall **(FIG. 5–17)**. The erect, immobile pose and full-bodied figure— accentuated by a crown and thick-soled clogs—seem appropriate to a goddess, although the statue may represent a priestess or an attendant. The thick robe and tasseled cloak over her shoulders fall in regularly spaced, symmetrically disposed, parallel folds like the

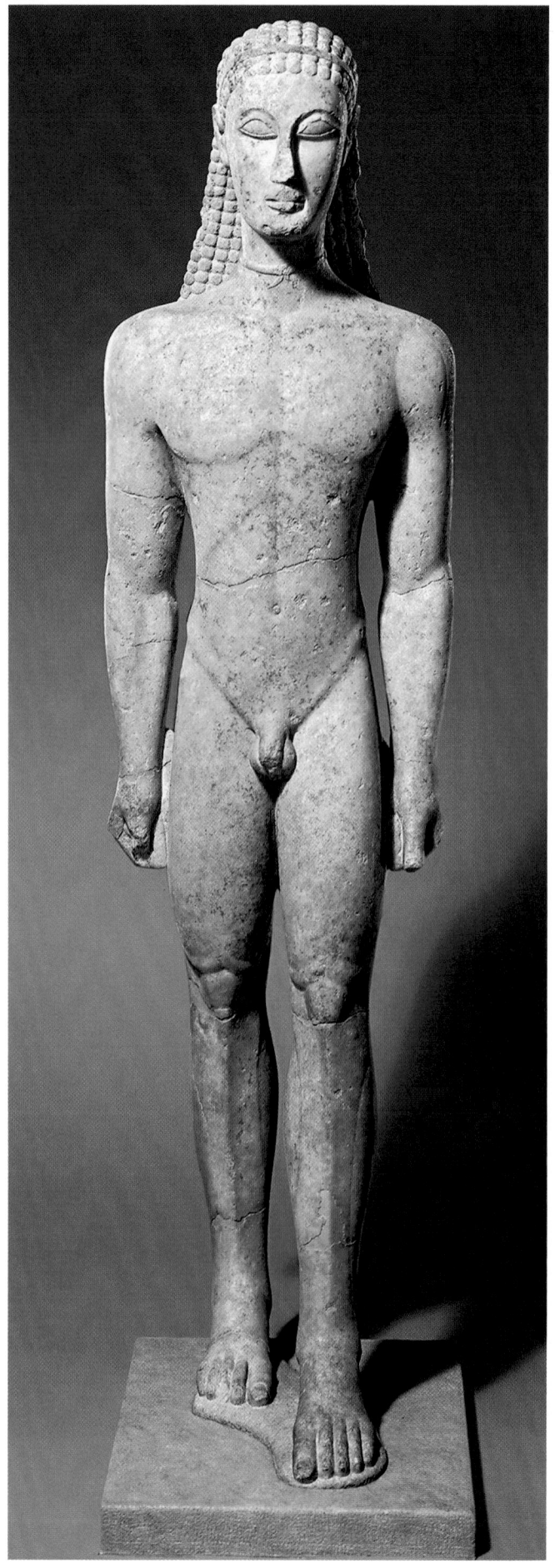

5-16 • METROPOLITAN KOUROS
Attica. c. 600 BCE. Marble, height 6′ (1.84 m). Metropolitan Museum of Art, New York. Fletcher Fund, 1932 (32.11.1)

fluting on a Greek column. This drapery masks her body but mimics its curving contours. Traces of red—perhaps the red clay used to make thin sheets of gold adhere—indicate that the robe was once painted or gilded. The figure holds a pomegranate in her right hand, a symbol of Persephone, who was abducted by Hades, the god of the underworld, and whose annual return brought the springtime.

ANAVYSOS KOUROS.   The powerful, rounded, athletic body of a *kouros* from Anavysos, dated about 530 BCE, documents the increasing interest of artists and their patrons in a more lifelike rendering of the human figure (**FIG. 5–18**). The pose, wiglike hair, and Archaic smile echo the earlier style, but the massive torso and limbs have carefully rendered, bulging muscularity, suggesting heroic strength. The statue, a grave monument to a fallen war hero, has been associated with a base inscribed: "Stop and grieve at the tomb of the dead Kroisos, slain by wild Ares [god of war] in the front rank of battle." However, there is no evidence that the figure was meant to preserve the likeness of Kroisos or anyone else. He is a symbolic type, not a specific individual.

"PEPLOS" KORE.   The kore in **FIG. 5–19** is dated about the same time as the *Anavysos Kouros*. Like the *kouros*, she has rounded body forms, but unlike him, she is clothed. She has the same motionless, vertical pose of the *Berlin Kore* (SEE FIG. 5–17), but her bare arms and head convey a sense of soft flesh covering a real bone structure, and her smile and hair are considerably less stylized. The original painted colors on both body and clothing must have made her seem even more lifelike, and she also once wore a metal crown and jewelry.

The name we use for this figure is based on an assessment of her clothing as a young girl's **peplos**—a draped rectangle of cloth pinned at the shoulders and belted to give a bloused effect—but it has recently been argued that this *kore* is actually wearing a sheath-like garment, originally painted with a frieze of animals, identifying her not as a young girl but a goddess, perhaps Athena or Artemis. Her missing left forearm—which was made of a separate piece of marble fitted into the still-visible socket—would have extended forward horizontally, and may have held an attribute that provided the key to her identity.

5–17 • BERLIN KORE
Cemetery at Keratea, near Athens. c. 570–560 BCE. Marble with remnants of red paint, height 6′3″ (1.9 m). Staatliche Museen zu Berlin, Antikensammlung, Preussischer Kulturbesitz, Berlin.

5–18 • ANAVYSOS KOUROS
Cemetery at Anavysos, near Athens. c. 530 BCE. Marble with remnants of paint, height 6′4″ (1.93 m). National Archaeological Museum, Athens.

5–19 • "PEPLOS" KORE
Acropolis, Athens. c. 530 BCE. Marble, height 4′ (1.21 m). Acropolis Museum, Athens.

PAINTED POTS

Greek potters created beautiful vessels whose standardized shapes were tailored to specific utilitarian functions (**FIG. 5–20**). Occasionally, these potters actually signed their work, as did the artists who painted scenes on the pots. Greek ceramic painters became highly accomplished at accommodating their pictures to the often awkward fields on utilitarian shapes, and they usually showcased not isolated figures but scenes of human interaction evoking a story.

BLACK-FIGURE VESSELS. During the Archaic period, Athens became the dominant center for pottery manufacture and trade in Greece, and Athenian painters adopted Corinthian black-figure techniques (SEE FIG. 5–4), which became the principal mode of decoration throughout Greece in the sixth century BCE. At first, Athenian vase painters retained the horizontal banded composition that was characteristic of the Geometric period. Over time, however, they decreased the number of bands and increased the size of figures until a single narrative scene dominates each side of the vessel.

THE AMASIS PAINTER. A mid-sixth-century BCE amphora—a large, all-purpose storage jar—with bands of decoration above and below a central figural composition illustrates this development (**FIG. 5–21**). The painting on this amphora has been attributed to an artist we call the Amasis Painter, since this distinctive style was first recognized on vessels signed by a prolific potter named Amasis.

5-21 • Amasis Painter DIONYSOS WITH MAENADS
c. 540 BCE. Black-figure decoration on an amphora. Ceramic, height of amphora 13″ (33.3 cm). Bibliothèque Nationale, Paris.

5-20 • SOME STANDARD SHAPES OF GREEK VESSELS

Two **maenads** (female worshippers of the wine god Dionysos), intertwined with arms around each other's shoulders, skip forward to present to Dionysos their offerings—a long-eared rabbit and a small deer. (Amasis signed his work just above the rabbit.) The maenad holding the deer wears the skin of a spotted panther (or leopard), its head still attached, draped over her shoulders and secured with a belt at her waist. The god, an imposing, richly dressed figure, clasps a large **kantharos** (wine cup). This encounter between humans and a god appears to be a joyful, celebratory occasion rather than one of reverence or fear. The Amasis Painter favored strong shapes and patterns over conventions for making figures appear to occupy real space. He emphasized fine details, such as the large, delicate petal and spiral designs below each handle, the figures' meticulously arranged hair, and the bold patterns on their clothing.

EXEKIAS. Perhaps the most famous of all Athenian black-figure painters, Exekias, signed many of his vessels as both potter and painter. He took his subjects from Greek mythology, which he and

5–22 • Exekias ACHILLES AND AJAX PLAYING A GAME
c. 540–530 BCE. Black-figure decoration on an amphora. Ceramic, height of amphora 2′ (61 cm).
Vatican Museums, Rome.

his patrons probably considered to be history. On the body of an amphora we have already seen at the beginning of this chapter, he portrayed Trojan War heroes Ajax and Achilles in a rare moment of relaxation playing dice (FIG. 5–22). This is an episode not included in any literary source, but for Greeks familiar with the story, this anecdotal portrayal of friendly play would have been a poignant reminder that before the end of the war, the heroes would be parted by death, Achilles in battle and Ajax by suicide. Knowing the story was critical to engaging with such paintings, and artists often included identifying labels beside the characters to guide viewers to the narrative source so they could delight in the painters' rich renderings of familiar narrative situations (SEE ALSO FIG. 5–1).

RED-FIGURE VESSELS. In the last third of the sixth century BCE, while many painters were still creating handsome black-figure wares, some turned away from this meticulous process to a new, more fluid technique called **red-figure** (see "Black-Figure and Red-Figure," page 120). In this mode of decoration, red figures stand out against a black background, the opposite of black-figure painting. The greater freedom and flexibility that resulted from

painting rather than engraving details led ceramic painters to adopt the red-figure technique widely in a relatively short time. It allowed them to create livelier human figures with a more developed sense of bodily form—qualities that were increasingly demanded of Greek artists in several media.

EUPHRONIOS. One of the best-known red-figure artists was Euphronios. His rendering of the *Death of Sarpedon*, about 515 BCE (see "A Closer Look," opposite), is painted on a krater—known as a **calyx krater** because its handles curve up like a flower's calyx. This vessel was used as a punchbowl during a **symposium**, a social gathering of rich and powerful men. According to Homer's *Iliad*, Sarpedon, a son of Zeus and a mortal woman, was killed by the Greek warrior Patroclus while fighting for the Trojans. Euphronios captures the scene in which the warrior is being carried off to the underworld, the land of the dead.

Euphronios has created a balanced composition of verticals and horizontals that take the shape of the vessel into account. The bands of decoration above and below the scene echo the long horizontal of the dead fighter's body, which seems to levitate in the

The Euphronios Krater ➤ by Euphronios (painter) and Euxitheos (potter). *Death of Sarpedon*. c. 515 BCE. Red-figure decoration on a calyx krater. Ceramic, height of krater 18″ (45.7 cm). Etruscan Museum, Villa Giulia, Rome.

Hypnos (Sleep) and Thanatos (Death), identified by inscriptions that seem to emerge from their mouths, face each other on either side of the fallen body of Sarpedon, gently raising the slain warrior.

The painting's field is framed by dense bands of detailed ornament, placed to highlight the contours of the krater.

The god Hermes is identified not only by inscription, but also by his caduceus (staff with coiled snakes) and winged headgear. The attention to contours, distribution of drapery folds, and overlapping of forms give the twisting figure three-dimensionality.

Sarpedon's body twists up to face the viewer, allowing Euphronios to outline every muscle and ligament of the torso, showing off both his knowledge of anatomy and his virtuosity in using the newly developed red-figure technique.

Euphronios makes it appear as if Sarpedon's left leg is projecting into the viewer's space through the technique of **foreshortening**.

Blood continues illogically to pour from the wounds in Sarpedon's corpse, not out of ignorance on the part of the artist but because of his determination to heighten the dramatic effect of the scene.

SEE MORE: View the Closer Look feature for the Euphronios Krater at **www.myartslab.com**

gentle grasp of its bearers, and the inward-curving lines of the handles mirror the arching backs and extended wings of Hypnos and Thanatos. The upright figures of the lance-bearers on each side and Hermes in the center counterbalance the horizontal and diagonal elements of the composition. While conveying a sense of the mass and energy of human subjects, Euphronios also portrayed the elaborate details of their clothing, musculature, and facial features with the fine tip of a brush. And he created the impression of real space around the figures by gently foreshortening Sarpedon's left leg that appears to be coming toward the viewer's own space. Such formal features, as well as a palpable sense of pathos in the face of Sarpedon's fate, seem to connect Euphronios' work with the dying warriors of the pediments at Aegina (SEE FIGS. 5–14, 5–15), which would be sculpted a little over a decade later.

THE EARLY CLASSICAL PERIOD, c. 480–450 BCE

Over the brief span of 160 years between c. 480 and 323 BCE, the Greeks established an ideal of beauty that has endured in the Western world to this day. Scholars have associated Greek Classical art with three general concepts: humanism, rationalism, and idealism (see "Classic and Classical," page 124). The ancient Greeks believed the words of their philosophers and followed these injunctions in their art: "Man is the measure of all things," that is, seek an ideal based on the human form; "Know thyself," seek the inner significance of forms; and "Nothing in excess," reproduce only essential forms. In their embrace of humanism, the Greeks even imagined their gods as perfect human beings. But the Greeks valued human

The two predominant techniques for painting on Greek ceramic vessels were black-figure (A) and red-figure (B). Both involved applying **slip** (a mixture of clay and water) to the surface of a pot and carefully manipulating the firing process in a kiln (a closed oven) to control the amount of oxygen reaching the ceramics. This firing process involved three stages. In the first stage, oxygen was allowed into the kiln, which "fixed" the whole vessel in one overall shade of red depending on the composition of the clay. Then, in the second (reduction) stage, the oxygen in the kiln was cut back (reduced) to a minimum, turning the vessel black, and the temperature was raised to the point at which the slip partially vitrified (became glasslike). Finally, in the third stage, oxygen was allowed back into the kiln, turning the unslipped areas back to a shade of red. The areas where slip had been applied, however, were sealed against the oxygen and remained black.

In the black-figure technique, artists silhouetted the forms—figures, objects, or abstract motifs—with slip against the unpainted clay of the background. Then, using a sharp tool (a **stylus**), they cut through the slip to the body of the vessel, incising linear details within the silhouetted shape by revealing the unpainted clay underneath. The characteristic color contrast only appeared in firing. Sometimes touches of white and reddish-purple gloss—made of metallic pigments mixed with slip—enhanced the decorative effect.

In the red-figure technique, the approach was reversed. Artists painted not the shapes of the forms themselves but the background around forms (**negative space**), reserving unpainted areas for silhouetted forms. Instead of engraving details, painters drew on the reserved areas with a fine brush dipped in liquid slip. The result was a lustrous black vessel with light-colored figures delineated in fluid black lines.

The contrasting effects obtained by these two techniques are illustrated in details of two sides of a single amphora of about 525 BCE, both portraying the same figural composition, one painted by an artist using black-figure, and the other painted by an innovative proponent of red-figure technique. The sharp precision and flattened decorative richness characterizing black-figure contrasts strikingly here with the increased fluidity and greater sense of three-dimensionality facilitated by the development of the red-figure technique.

A. Lysippides Painter **HERAKLES DRIVING A BULL TO SACRIFICE**
c. 525–520 BCE. Black-figure decoration on an amphora. Ceramic, height of amphora 20¹⁵⁄₁₆″ (53.2 cm). Museum of Fine Arts, Boston.

B. Andokides Painter **HERAKLES DRIVING A BULL TO SACRIFICE**
c. 525–520 BCE. Red-figure decoration on an amphora. Ceramic, height of amphora 20¹⁵⁄₁₆″ (53.2 cm). Museum of Fine Arts, Boston.

reason over human emotion. They saw all aspects of life, including the arts, as having meaning and pattern. Nothing happens by accident. It is not surprising that great Greek artists and architects were not only practitioners but theoreticians as well. In the fifth century BCE, the sculptor Polykleitos (see "The Canon of Polykleitos," page 134) and the architect Iktinos both wrote books on the theory underlying their practice.

Art historians usually divide the Classical into three phases, based on the formal qualities of the art: the Early Classical period (c. 480–450 BCE); the "High" Classical period (c. 450–400 BCE); and the Late Classical period (c. 400–323 BCE). The Early Classical period begins with the defeat of the Persians in 480 BCE by an alliance of city-states led by Athens and Sparta. The expanding Persian Empire had posed a formidable threat to the independence of the city-states, and the two sides had been locked in battle for decades until the Greek alliance was able to repulse a Persian invasion and score a decisive victory. Some scholars have argued that their success against the Persians gave the Greeks a self-confidence that accelerated artistic development, inspiring artists to seek new and more effective ways to express their cities' accomplishments. In any case, the period that followed the Persian Wars, extending to about 450 BCE, saw the emergence of a new stylistic direction, away from elegant stylizations and toward a sense of greater faithfulness to the natural appearance of human beings and their world.

MARBLE SCULPTURE

In the remarkably short time of only a few generations, Greek sculptors had moved far from the stiff frontality of the Archaic *kouroi* to more relaxed, lifelike figures such as the so-called **KRITIOS BOY** of about 480 BCE **(FIG. 5–23)**. The softly rounded body forms, broad facial features, and calm expression—there is not even a trace of an Archaic smile—give the figure an air of self-confident seriousness. He strikes an easy pose quite unlike the rigid bearing of Archaic *kouroi*. His weight rests on his left, engaged leg, while his right, relaxed leg bends slightly at the knee, and a noticeable curve in his spine counters the slight shifting of his hips and a subtle drop of one of his shoulders. We see here the beginnings of **contrapposto**, the convention of presenting standing figures with opposing alternations of tension and relaxation around a central axis that will dominate Classical art. The slight turn of the head invites the spectator to follow his gaze and move around the figure, admiring the small marble statue from every angle.

5-23 • KRITIOS BOY
From Acropolis, Athens.
c. 480 BCE. Marble, height
3'10" (1.17 m). Acropolis
Museum, Athens.

The damaged figure, excavated from the debris on the Athenian Acropolis, was thought by its finders to be by the Greek sculptor Kritios, whose work they knew only from Roman copies.

THE OBJECT SPEAKS

The Tomb of the Diver

Although ancient Greek commentators describe elaborate monumental wall paintings and discuss the output and careers of illustrious painters from the fifth and fourth centuries BCE, almost nothing of this art has survived. We rely heavily on ceramics to fill gaps in our knowledge of Greek painting, assuming that the decoration of these more modest utilitarian vessels reflects the glorious painting tradition documented in texts. There are also tantalizing survivals in provincial Greek sites. Principal among them are the well-preserved Early Classical wall paintings of c. 480–470 BCE in the Tomb of the Diver, discovered in 1968 just south of the Greek colony of Poseidonia (Roman Paestum) in southern Italy.

The paintings cover travertine slabs that formed the four walls and roof of a tomb submerged into the natural rock (FIG. A), approximately 7 feet long, 3½ feet wide, and 2½ feet deep. Painted in buon fresco (water-based pigments applied to wet plaster) on a white ground in earthy browns, yellows, and blacks, with accents of blue, the scenes on the walls surrounded the occupant of this tomb with a group of reclining men, assembled for a symposium—lively, elite male gatherings that focused on wine, music, games, and lovemaking. Many of the most distinguished of surviving Greek ceramic vessels were made for use in these playfully competitive drinking parties and they are highlighted in the tomb paintings. On one short side (visible in the reconstruction drawing), a striding nude youth has filled the oinochoe (wine jug) in his right hand with the mixture of wine and water that was served from large kraters (punch bowls, like that portrayed on the table behind him) as the featured beverage of the symposium. He extends his arm toward a group of revelers reclining along one of the long walls (FIG. B), each of whom has a kylix (wide, shallow, footed drinking cup), waiting to be filled. The man at the left reclines alone, raising his kylix to salute a couple just arriving— or perhaps toasting their departure—on the other short side. Behind him, the two couples on the long frieze—in each case a bearded, mature man paired with a youthful companion —are already engaged in the party. The young man in the middle pairing is slinging his upraised kylix, presumably to propel the dregs of his wine toward a target, a popular symposium game. His partner turns in the opposite direction to ogle at the amorous pair at the right, who have abandoned their cups on the table in front of them and turned to embrace, gazing into each other's eyes as the erotic action heats up.

The significance of these paintings in relationship to a young man's tomb is not absolutely clear. Perhaps they are indicative of the deceased's elevated social status, since only wealthy aristocrats participated in such gatherings. The symposium could also represent funerary feasting or a vision of the pleasures that awaits the deceased in a world beyond death.

The transition between this world and the next certainly seems to be the theme of the spare but energetic painting on the roof of the tomb, where a naked boy is caught in mid dive, poised to plunge into the water portrayed as a blue mound underneath him (FIG. C). Whereas the scene of the symposium accords with an ancient Greek pictorial tradition, especially prominent on ceramic vessels made for use by its male participants, this diver finds his closest parallels in Etruscan tomb painting (SEE FIG. 6–6), flourishing at this time further north in Italy. Since the scene was located directly over the body of the man entombed here, it is likely that it mirrors his own plunge from life into death. And since it combines Greek and Etruscan traditions, perhaps this tomb was made for an Etruscan citizen of Poseidonia, whose tomb was commissioned from a Greek artist working in this flourishing provincial center.

A. RECONSTRUCTION DRAWING OF THE TOMB OF THE DIVER
From Poseidonia (Roman Paestum). c. 480 BCE.

B. A SYMPOSIUM SCENE
From the Tomb of the Diver, Poseidonia (Roman Paestum). c. 480 BCE.
Fresco on travertine slab, height 31″ (78 cm). Paestum Museum.

C. A DIVER
From the Tomb of the Diver, Poseidonia (Roman Paestum). c. 480 BCE.
Fresco on travertine slab, height 3′4″ (1.02 m). Paestum Museum.

Classic and Classical

Our words "classic" and "classical" come from the Latin word *classis*, referring to the division of people into classes based on wealth. Consequently, "classic" has come to mean "first class," "the highest rank," "the standard of excellence." Greek artists in the fifth century BCE sought to create ideal images based on strict mathematical proportions. Since Roman artists were inspired by the Greeks, art historians often use the term Classical to refer to the culture of ancient Greece and Rome. By extension, the word may also mean "in the style of ancient Greece and Rome," whenever or wherever that style is used. In the most general usage, a "classic" is something—perhaps a literary work, an automobile, a film, even a soft drink—thought to be of lasting quality and universal esteem.

BRONZE SCULPTURE

The development of the technique of modeling and hollow-casting bronze in the lost-wax process gave Greek sculptors the potential to create more complex action poses with outstretched arms and legs. These were very difficult to create in marble, since unbalanced figures might topple over and extended appendages might break off due to their pendulous weight. Bronze figures were easier to balance, and the metal's greater tensile strength made complicated poses and gestures technically possible.

The painted underside of an Athenian **kylix** (broad, flat drinking cup) illustrates work in a late Archaic foundry for casting life-size figures (**FIG. 5–24**), providing clear evidence that the Greeks were creating large bronze statues in active poses as early as the first decades of the fifth century BCE. The walls of the workshop are filled with hanging tools and other foundry paraphernalia including several sketches—a horse, human heads, and human figures in different poses. One worker, wearing what looks like a modern-day construction helmet, squats to tend the

5-24 • Foundry Painter A BRONZE FOUNDRY
Red-figure decoration on a kylix from Vulci, Italy. 490–480 BCE. Ceramic, diameter of kylix 12″ (31 cm). Staatliche Museen zu Berlin, Preussischer Kulturbesitz, Antikensammlung, Berlin.

The Foundry Painter has masterfully organized this workshop scene within the flaring space that extends upward from the foot of the vessel and along its curving underside up to the lip, thereby using a circle as the groundline for his composition.

5-25 • CHARIOTEER

From the Sanctuary of Apollo, Delphi. c. 470 BCE. Bronze, copper (lips and lashes), silver (hand), onyx (eyes), height 5′11″ (1.8 m). Archaeological Museum, Delphi.

The setting of a work of art affects the impression it makes. Today, the *Charioteer* is exhibited on a low base in the peaceful surroundings of a museum, isolated from other works and spotlighted for close examination. Its effect would have been very different in its original outdoor location, standing in a horse-drawn chariot atop a tall monument. Viewers in ancient times, tired from the steep climb to the sanctuary and jostled by crowds of fellow pilgrims, could have absorbed only its overall effect, not the fine details of the face, robe, and body visible to today's viewers.

furnace on the left, perhaps aided by an assistant who peeks from behind. The man in the center, perhaps the supervisor, leans on a staff, while a third worker assembles a leaping figure that is braced against a molded support. The unattached head lies between his feet.

THE CHARIOTEER. A spectacular and rare life-size bronze, the **CHARIOTEER (FIG. 5–25)**, cast about 470 BCE, documents the skills of Early Classical bronze-casters. It was found in the sanctuary of Apollo at Delphi, together with fragments of a bronze chariot and horses, all buried after an earthquake in 373 BCE. (The earthquake may have saved them from the fate of most ancient bronzes, which were melted down so the material could be recycled and made into a new work.) According to its inscription, the sculptural group commemorated a victory by a driver in the Pythian Games of 478 or 474 BCE.

The face of this handsome youth is highly idealized, but it almost seems to preserve the likeness of a specific individual, calling to mind the report of the Roman historian and naturalist Pliny the Elder that three-time winners in Greek competitions had their features memorialized in stone. The charioteer's head turns slightly to one side, his intense, focused expression enhanced by glittering, onyx eyes and fine copper eyelashes. He stands at attention, sheathed in a long robe with folds falling naturally under their own weight, varying in width and depth, yet seemingly capable of swaying and rippling with the charioteer's movement. The feet, with their closely observed toes, toenails, and swelled veins over the instep, are so realistic that they seem to have been cast from molds made from the feet of a living person.

THE RIACE WARRIORS. The sea as well as the earth has protected ancient bronzes from recycling. As recently as 1972, divers recovered a pair of heavily corroded, larger-than-life-size bronze figures from the seabed off the coast of Riace, Italy. Known as the *Riace Warriors*, they date to about 460–450 BCE. Just what sent them to the bottom is not known, but conservators have restored them to their original condition (see "The Riace Warriors," page 127).

The **WARRIOR** in **FIG. 5–26** reveals a striking balance between the idealized smoothness of "perfected" anatomy conforming to Early Classical standards and the reproduction of details observed from nature, such as the swelling veins in the backs of the hands. Contrapposto is even more evident here than in the *Kritios Boy*, and the toned musculature suggests a youthfulness inconsistent with the maturity of the heavy beard and almost haggard face. The lifelike quality of this bronze is further heightened by inserted eyeballs of bone and colored glass, copper inlays on lips and nipples, silver plating on the teeth that show between parted lips, and attached eyelashes and eyebrows of separately cast strands of bronze. This accommodation of the intense study of the human figure to an idealism that belies the irregularity of nature will be continued by artists in the "High" Classical period.

5-26 • WARRIOR
Found in the sea off Riace, Italy. c. 460–450 BCE. Bronze with bone and glass eyes, silver teeth, and copper lips and nipples, height 6′9″ (2.05 m). National Archeological Museum, Reggio Calabria, Italy.

In 1972, a scuba diver in the Ionian Sea near the beach resort of Riace, Italy, found what appeared to be a human elbow and upper arm protruding from sand about 25 feet beneath the sea. Taking a closer look, he discovered that the arm was made of metal, not flesh, and was part of a large statue. He soon uncovered a second statue nearby.

Experienced underwater salvagers raised the statues: bronze warriors more than 6 feet tall, complete in every respect, except for swords, shields, and one helmet. But after centuries underwater, the *Warriors* were corroded and covered with accretions. The clay cores from the casting process were still inside the bronzes, adding to the deterioration by absorbing lime and sea salts. To restore the *Warriors*, conservators first removed all the exterior corrosion and lime encrustations using surgeon's scalpels, pneumatic drills, and high-technology equipment such as sonar (sound-wave) probes and micro-sanders. Then they painstakingly removed the clay core through existing holes in the heads and feet using hooks, scoops, jets of distilled water, and concentrated solutions of peroxide. Finally, they cleaned the figures thoroughly by soaking them in solvents, and they sealed them with a fixative specially designed for use on metals.

Since the *Warriors* were put on view in 1980, conservators have taken additional steps to ensure their preservation. In 1993, for example, a sonar probe mounted with two miniature video cameras found and blasted loose with sound waves the clay remaining inside the statues, which was then flushed out with water.

CERAMIC PAINTING

Greek potters and painters continued to work with the red-figure technique throughout the fifth century BCE, refining their ability to create supple, rounded figures, posed in ever more complicated and dynamic compositions. One of the most prolific Early Classical artists was Douris, whose signature appears on over 40 surviving pots, decorated with scenes from everyday life as well as from mythology. His conspicuous skill in composing complex figural scenes that respond to the complicated and irregular pictorial fields of a variety of vessel types is evident in a frieze of frisky satyrs that he painted c. 480 BCE around the perimeter of a **psykter** (**FIG. 5–27**). This strangely shaped pot was a wine cooler, made to float in a krater (see "A Closer Look," page 119) filled with chilled water, its extended bottom serving as a keel to keep it from tipping over.

Like the krater, the psykter was a vessel meant for use in exclusive male drinking parties—symposia—and the decoration was chosen with this context in mind. The acrobatic virtuosity of the satyrs is matched by the artist's own virtuosity in composing them as an interlocking set of diagonal gestures that alternately challenge and correspond with the bulging form around which they are

5-27 • Douris FROLICKING SATYRS
Red-figure decoration on a psykter. c. 480 BCE. Ceramic, height 11⁵⁄₁₆″ (28.7 cm).
British Museum, London.

5-28 • Douris A YOUTH POURING WINE INTO THE KYLIX OF A COMPANION
Red-figure decoration on a kylix. c. 480 BCE. Ceramic, height 12¾″ (32.4 cm). The Soprintendenza Speciale per i Beni Archeologici di Napoli e Pompei.

painted. The playful interaction of satyrs with their kylixes must have amused the tipsy revelers, especially when this pot was gently bobbing within the krater, making the satyrs seem to be walking around in circles on top of the wine. One satyr cups his kylix to his buttocks, juxtaposing convex and concave shapes. Another, balanced in a precarious handstand, seems to be observing his own reflection within the wine of his kylix.

But Douris was also capable of more lyrical compositions, as seen in the painting he placed within a kylix (**FIG. 5–28**), similar in shape to those used as props by the satyrs on the psykter. This **tondo** (circular painting) was an intimate picture. It became visible only to the user of the cup when he tilted up the kylix to drink from it; otherwise, sitting on a table, the painting would have been obscured by the dark wine pool within it. A languidly posed and elegantly draped youth stands behind an altar pouring wine from an **oinochoe** (wine jug) into the kylix of a more dignified, bearded older man. Euphronios' tentative essay in foreshortening Sarpedon's bent leg on his krater (see "A Closer Look," page 119) blossoms in the work of Douris to become full-scale formal projection as the graceful youth on this kylix bends his arm from the background to project his frontal oinochoe over the laterally held kylix of his seated companion.

For the well-educated reveler using this cup at a symposium, there were several possible readings for the scene he was observing. This could be the legendary Athenian king Kekrops, who appears, identified by inscription, in the scene Douris painted on the underside of the kylix. Also on the bottom of the cup are Zeus and the young Trojan prince Ganymede, whom the supreme god

abducted to Olympus to serve as his cup-bearer. Or, since the symposia themselves were the site of amorous conquests between older and younger men, the user of this cup might have found his own situation mirrored in what he was observing while he drank.

THE HIGH CLASSICAL PERIOD, C. 450–400 BCE

The "High" Classical period of Greek art lasted only a half-century, 450 to 400 BCE. The use of the word "high" to qualify the art of this time reflects the value judgments of art historians who have considered this period a pinnacle of artistic refinement, producing works that set a standard of unsurpassed excellence. Some have even referred to this half-century as Greece's "Golden Age," although these decades were also marked by turmoil and destruction. Without a common enemy, Sparta and Athens turned on each other in a series of conflicts known as the Peloponnesian War. Sparta dominated the Peloponnese peninsula and much of the rest of mainland Greece, while Athens controlled the Aegean and became the wealthy and influential center of a maritime empire. Today we remember Athens more for its cultural and intellectual brilliance and its experiments with democratic government, which reached its zenith in the fifth century BCE under the charismatic leader Perikles (c. 495–429 BCE), than for the imperialistic tendencies of its considerable commercial power.

Except for a few brief interludes, Perikles dominated Athenian politics and culture from 462 BCE until his death in 429 BCE.

Although comedy writers of the time sometimes mocked him, calling him "Zeus" and "The Olympian" because of his haughty personality, he was a dynamic, charismatic political and military leader. He was also a great patron of the arts, supporting the use of Athenian wealth for the adornment of the city, and encouraging artists to promote a public image of peace, prosperity, and power. Perikles said of his city and its accomplishments: "Future generations will marvel at us, as the present age marvels at us now." It was a prophecy he himself helped fulfill.

THE ACROPOLIS

Athens originated as a Neolithic **acropolis**, or "part of the city on top of a hill" (*akro* means "high" and *polis* means "city") that later served as a fortress and sanctuary. As the city grew, the Acropolis became the religious and ceremonial center devoted primarily to the goddess Athena, the city's patron and protector.

After Persian troops destroyed the Acropolis in 480 BCE, the Athenians vowed to keep it in ruins as a memorial, but Perikles convinced them to rebuild it, arguing that this project honored the

Erechtheion

Parthenon

Statue of Athena Promachos

Propylaia

Temple of Athena Nike

Picture gallery

5-29 • MODEL/RECONSTRUCTION OF THE ACROPOLIS, ATHENS
c. 447–432 BCE.

EXPLORE MORE: Click the Google Earth link for the Acropolis www.myartslab.com

5–30 • RECREATION OF PHEIDIAS' HUGE GOLD AND IVORY FIGURE
Royal Ontario Museum, Toronto.

gods, especially Athena, who had helped the Greeks defeat the Persians. Perikles intended to create a visual expression of Athenian values and civic pride that would bolster the city's status as the capital of the empire he was instrumental in building. He placed his close friend Pheidias, a renowned sculptor, in charge of the rebuilding and assembled under him the most talented artists in Athens.

The cost and labor involved in this undertaking were staggering. Large quantities of gold, ivory, and exotic woods had to be imported. Some 22,000 tons of marble had to be transported 10 miles from mountain quarries to city workshops. Perikles was severely criticized by his political opponents for this extravagance, but it never cost him popular support. In fact, many working-class Athenians—laborers, carpenters, masons, sculptors, and the farmers and merchants who kept them supplied and fed—benefited from his expenditures.

Work on the **ACROPOLIS** continued after Perikles' death and was completed by the end of the fifth century BCE **(FIG. 5–29)**. Visitors to the Acropolis in 400 BCE would have climbed a steep ramp on the west side of the hill (in the foreground of FIG. 5–29) to the sanctuary entrance, perhaps pausing to admire the small temple dedicated to Athena Nike (Athena as goddess of victory in war), poised on a projection of rock above the ramp. After passing

through an impressive porticoed gatehouse called the Propylaia, they would have seen a huge bronze figure of Athena Promachos (the Defender), designed and executed by Pheidias between about 465 and 455 BCE. Sailors entering the Athenian port of Piraeus, about 10 miles away, could see the sun reflected off her helmet and spear tip. Behind this statue was a walled precinct that enclosed the Erechtheion, a temple dedicated to several deities.

Religious buildings and votive statues filled the hilltop. On the right stood the largest building on the Acropolis—the Parthenon, a temple dedicated to Athena Parthenos (the Virgin). Visitors approached the temple from its northwest corner, seeing both its short and long side, instantly grasping the imposing size of this building, isolated like a work of sculpture elevated on a pedestal. With permission from the priests, they could have climbed the east steps to look into the cella, where they would have seen Pheidias' colossal gold and ivory statue of Athena— outfitted in armor and holding a shield in one hand and a winged Nike (Victory) in the other—which was installed in the temple and dedicated 438 BCE **(FIG. 5–30)**.

THE PARTHENON

Sometime around 490 BCE, Athenians had begun work on a temple to Athena Parthenos that was still unfinished when the Persians sacked the Acropolis a decade later. In 447 BCE Perikles commissioned the architects Kallikrates and Iktinos to design a larger temple using the existing foundation and stone elements. The finest white marble was used throughout—even on the roof, in place of the more usual terra-cotta tiles **(FIG. 5–31)**. The planning and execution of the Parthenon (dedicated in 438 BCE) required extraordinary mathematical and mechanical skills and would have been impossible without a large contingent of distinguished architects and builders, as well as talented sculptors and painters. The result is as much a testament to the administrative skills as to the artistic vision of Pheidias, who supervised the entire project.

One key to the Parthenon's sense of harmony and balance is an attention to proportions—especially the ratio of 4:9, expressing the relationship of breadth to length and also the relationship of column diameter to space between columns. Also important are subtle refinements of design, deviations from absolute regularity to create a harmonious effect when the building was actually viewed. For example, since long, straight horizontal lines seem to sag when seen from a distance, base and entablature curve slightly upward to correct this optical distortion. The columns have a subtle swelling (entasis) and tilt inward slightly from bottom to top; the corners are strengthened visually by reducing the space between columns at those points. These subtle refinements in the arrangement of seemingly regular elements give the Parthenon a buoyant organic appearance and assure that it will not look like a heavy, lifeless stone box. The significance of their achievement was clear to its builders— Iktinos even wrote a book on the proportions of this masterpiece.

The sculptural decoration of the Parthenon reflects Pheidias' unifying aesthetic vision. At the same time, it conveys a number of political and ideological themes: the triumph of the democratic Greek city-states over imperial Persia, the preeminence of Athens thanks to the favor of Athena, and the triumph of an enlightened Greek civilization over despotism and barbarism.

THE PEDIMENTS. As with most temples, sculpture in the round filled both pediments of the Parthenon, set on the deep shelf of the cornice and secured to the wall with metal pins. Unfortunately, much has been damaged or lost over the centuries (also see "Who Owns the Art?" page 135). Using the locations of the pinholes and weathering marks on the cornice, scholars have been able to determine the placement of surviving statues and infer the poses of missing ones. The west pediment sculpture, facing the entrance to the Acropolis, illustrated the contest Athena won over the sea god

5-31 • Kallikrates and Iktinos VIEW AND PLAN OF THE PARTHENON, ACROPOLIS
Athens. 447–432 BCE. Photograph: view from the northwest. Pantelic marble.

EXPLORE MORE: Click the Google Earth link for The Parthenon www.myartslab.com

5-32 • PHOTOGRAPHIC MOCK-UP OF THE EAST PEDIMENT OF THE PARTHENON (USING PHOTOGRAPHS OF THE EXTANT MARBLE SCULPTURE)

c. 447–432 BCE. The gap in the center represents the space that would have been occupied by the missing sculpture. The pediment is over 90 feet (27.45 m) long; the central space of about 40 feet (12.2 m) is missing.

Poseidon for rule over the Athenians. The east pediment figures, above the entrance to the cella, illustrated the birth of Athena, fully grown and clad in armor, from the brow of her father, Zeus.

The statues from the east pediment are the bestpreserved of the two groups (FIG. 5–32). Flanking the missing central figures—probably Zeus seated on a throne with the newborn adult Athena standing at his side—were groups of three goddesses followed by single reclining male figures. In the left corner was the sun god Helios in his horse-drawn chariot rising from the sea, while at the right the moon goddess Selene descends in her chariot to the sea, the head of her tired horse hanging over the cornice. The reclining male nude, who fits so easily into the left pediment, has been identified as either Herakles with his lion's skin or Dionysos (god of wine) lying on a panther skin. His easy pose conforms to the slope of the pediment without a hint of awkwardness. The two seated women may be the earth and grain goddesses Demeter and Persephone. The running female figure just to the left of center is Iris, messenger of the gods, already spreading the news of Athena's birth.

The three female figures on the right side, two sitting upright and one reclining, are probably Hestia (a sister of Zeus and the goddess of the hearth), Dione (one of Zeus's many consorts), and her daughter, Aphrodite. These monumental interlocked figures seem to be awakening from a deep sleep. The sculptor, whether Pheidias or someone working in his style, expertly rendered

5-33 • LAPITH FIGHTING A CENTAUR

Metope relief from the Doric frieze on the south side of the Parthenon. c. 447–432 BCE. Marble, height 56″ (1.42 m). British Museum, London.

the female form beneath the fall of draperies, which both cover and reveal their bodies. The clinging fabric also creates circular patterns rippling with a life of their own and uniting the three figures into a single mass.

THE DORIC FRIEZE. The all-marble Parthenon had two sculptured friezes, one above the outer peristyle and another atop the cella wall inside. The Doric frieze on the exterior had 92 metope reliefs depicting legendary battles, symbolized by combat between two representative figures: a centaur against a Lapith (a legendary people of pre-Hellenic times); a god against a Titan; a Greek against a Trojan; a Greek against an Amazon (members of the mythical tribe of female warriors sometimes said to be the daughters of the war god Ares). Each of these mythic struggles represented for the Greeks the triumph of reason over unbridled animal passion.

Among the best-preserved metope reliefs are several depicting the battle between Lapiths and centaurs from the south side of the Parthenon. The panel shown here (FIG. 5–33) presents a pause within the fluid struggle, a timeless image standing for an extended historical episode. Forms are reduced to their most characteristic essentials, and so dramatic is the chiasmic (X-shaped) composition that we easily accept its visual contradictions. The Lapith is caught at an instant of total equilibrium. What could be a grueling tug-of-war between a man and a man-beast has been transformed into an athletic ballet, choreographed to show off the Lapith warrior's flexed muscles and graceful movements against the implausible backdrop of his carefully draped cloak.

THE PROCESSIONAL FRIEZE. Enclosed within the Parthenon's Doric peristyle, a continuous, 525-foot-long Ionic frieze ran along the exterior wall of the cella. The subject is a procession celebrating the festival that took place in Athens every four years, when the women of the city wove a new wool *peplos* and carried it to the Acropolis to clothe an ancient wooden cult statue of Athena.

In Pheidias' portrayal of this major event, the figures—skilled riders managing powerful steeds, for example (FIG. 5–34), or graceful but physically sturdy young walkers (FIG. 5–35)—seem to be representative types, ideal inhabitants of a successful city-state.

5-34 • HORSEMEN
Detail of the Procession, from the Ionic frieze on the north side of the Parthenon. c. 447–432 BCE. Marble, height 41¾″ (106 cm). British Museum, London.

Just as Greek architects defined and followed a set of standards for ideal temple design, Greek sculptors sought an ideal for representing the human body. Studying actual human beings closely and selecting those human attributes they considered most desirable, such as regular facial features, smooth skin, and particular body proportions, sculptors combined them into a single ideal of physical perfection.

The best-known theorist of the High Classical period was the sculptor Polykleitos of Argos. About 450 BCE, balancing careful observation with generalizing idealization, he developed a set of rules for constructing what he considered the ideal human figure, which he set down in a treatise called "The Canon" (*kanon* is Greek for "measure," "rule," or "law"). To illustrate his theory, Polykleitos created a larger-than-lifesize bronze statue of a standing man carrying a spear—perhaps the hero Achilles. Neither the treatise nor the original statue has survived, but both were widely discussed in the writings of his contemporaries, and later Roman artists made marble copies of the *Spear Bearer* (*Doryphoros*). By studying these copies, scholars have tried to determine the set of measurements that defined ideal human proportions in Polykleitos' canon.

The canon included a system of ratios between a basic unit and the length of various body parts. Some studies suggest that this basic unit may have been the length of the figure's index finger or the width of its hand across the knuckles; others suggest that it was the height of the head from chin to hairline. The canon also included guidelines for *symmetria* ("commensurability"), by which Polykleitos meant the relationship of body parts to one another. In the *Spear Bearer*, he explored not only proportions, but also the relationships between weight-bearing and relaxed legs and arms in a perfectly balanced figure. The balancing of tense or supporting with relaxed or at ease elements in a figure is referred to as contrapposto.

The Roman marble copy of the *Spear Bearer* illustrated here shows a male athlete, perfectly balanced, with the whole weight of the upper body supported over the straight (engaged) right leg. The left leg is bent at the knee, with the left foot poised on the ball of the foot, suggesting preceding and succeeding movement. The pattern of tension and relaxation is reversed in the arrangement of the arms, with the right relaxed on the engaged side, and the left bent to support the weight of the (missing) spear. This dynamically balanced body pose—characteristic of High Classical standing figure sculpture—evolved out of the pose of the *Kritios Boy* (SEE FIG. 5–23) of a generation earlier. The tilt of the *Spear Bearer*'s hipline is a little more pronounced to accommodate the raising of the left foot onto its ball, and the head is turned toward the same side as the engaged leg.

Polykleitos **SPEAR BEARER (DORYPHOROS)**
Roman copy after the original bronze of c. 450–440 BCE.
Marble, height 6′11″ (2.12 m); tree trunk and brace strut are Roman additions. National Archeological Museum, Naples.

The underlying message of the frieze as a whole is that the Athenians are a healthy, vigorous people, united in a democratic civic body looked upon with favor by the gods. The people are inseparable from and symbolic of the city itself.

As with the metope relief of the *Lapith Fighting a Centaur* (SEE FIG. 5–33), viewers of the processional frieze easily accept its disproportions, spatial compression and incongruities, and such implausible compositional features as men and women standing as tall as rearing horses. Carefully planned rhythmic variations—indicating changes in the speed of the participants in the procession as it winds around the walls—contribute to the effectiveness of the frieze. Horses plunge ahead at full gallop; women proceed with a slow, stately step; parade marshals pause to look back at the progress of those behind them; and human-looking deities rest on conveniently placed benches as they await the arrival of the marchers.

In executing the frieze, the sculptors took into account the

ART AND ITS CONTEXTS

Who Owns the Art? The Elgin Marbles and the *Euphronios Krater*

At the beginning of the nineteenth century, Thomas Bruce, the British earl of Elgin and ambassador to Constantinople, acquired much of the surviving sculpture from the Parthenon, which was at that time being used for military purposes. He shipped it back to London in 1801 to decorate a lavish mansion for himself and his wife; but by the time he returned to England, his wife had left him and the ancient treasures were at the center of a financial dispute and had to be sold. Referred to as the Elgin Marbles, most of the sculpture is now in the British Museum, including all the elements seen in FIGURE 5–32. The Greek government has tried unsuccessfully to have the Elgin Marbles returned.

Recently, another Greek treasure has been in the news. In 1972, a krater, painted by Euphronios and depicting the death of the warrior Sarpedon during the Trojan War, had been purchased by the Metropolitan Museum of Art in New York (see "Closer Look," page 119). Museum officials were told that it had come from a private collection, and it became the centerpiece of the museum's galleries of Greek vessels. But in 1995, Italian and Swiss investigators raided a warehouse in Geneva, Switzerland, where they found documents showing that the krater had been stolen from an Etruscan tomb near Rome. The Italian government demanded its return. The controversy was only resolved in 2006. The krater, along with other objects known to have been stolen from other Italian sites, were returned, and the Metropolitan Museum will display pieces "of equal beauty" under long-term loan agreements with Italy.

spectators' low viewpoint and the dim lighting inside the peristyle. They carved the top of the frieze band in higher relief than the lower part, thus tilting the figures out to catch the reflected light from the pavement, permitting a clearer reading of the action. The subtleties in the sculpture may not have been as evident to Athenians in the fifth century BCE as they are now, because the frieze, seen at the top of a high wall and between columns, was originally completely painted. Figures in red and ocher, accented with glittering gold and real metal details, were set against a contrasting background of dark blue.

5-35 • MARSHALS AND YOUNG WOMEN
Detail of the procession, from the Ionic frieze on the east side of the Parthenon. c. 447–432 BCE.
Marble, height 3′6″ (1.08 m). Musée du Louvre, Paris.

THE PROPYLAIA AND THE ERECHTHEION

Upon completion of the Parthenon, Perikles commissioned an architect named Mnesikles to design a monumental gatehouse, the Propylaia **(FIG. 5–36)**. Work began in 437 and then stopped in 432 BCE, with the structure still incomplete. The Propylaia had no sculptural decoration, but its north wing was originally a dining hall that later became the earliest known museum (meaning "home of the Muses"), a gallery built specifically to house a collection of paintings for public view.

The designer of the **ERECHTHEION (FIG. 5–37)**, the second important temple erected on the Acropolis under Perikles' building program, is unknown. Work began on the building in 421 BCE and ended in 405 BCE, just before the fall of Athens to Sparta. The asymmetrical plan on several levels reflects the building's multiple functions in housing many different shrines, and it also conformed to the sharply sloping terrain on which it is located. The

Erechtheion stands on the site of the mythical contest between the sea god Poseidon and Athena for patronage over Athens. During this contest, Poseidon struck a rock with his trident (three-pronged harpoon), bringing forth a spout of water, but Athena gave an olive tree to Athens and won the contest. The Athenians enclosed what they believed to be this sacred rock, bearing the marks of the trident, in the Erechtheion's north porch. The Erechtheion also housed the venerable wooden cult statue of Athena that was the center of the Panathenic festival.

The north and east porches of the Erechtheion have come to epitomize the Ionic order, serving as an important model for European architects since the eighteenth century. Taller and more slender in proportion that the Doric, the Ionic order also has richer and more elaborately carved decoration (see "The Greek Orders," page 110). The columns rise from molded bases and end in volute (spiral) capitals; the frieze is continuous.

5-36 • THE MONUMENTAL ENTRANCE TO THE ACROPOLIS
The Propylaia (Mnesikles) with the Temple of Athena Nike (Kallikrates) on the bastion at the right. c. 437–423 BCE.

5-37 • ERECHTHEION
Acropolis, Athens. 421–406 BCE. View from the east. Porch of the Maidens at left; the north porch can be seen through the columns of the east wall.

EXPLORE MORE: Click the Google Earth link for Erechtheion **www.myartslab.com**

The **PORCH OF THE MAIDENS (FIG. 5–38)**, on the south side facing the Parthenon, is even more famous. Raised on a high base, its six stately caryatids support simple Doric capitals and an Ionic entablature made up of bands of carved molding. In a pose characteristic of Classical figures, each caryatid's weight is supported on one engaged leg, while the free leg, bent at the knee, rests on the ball of the foot. The three caryatids on the left have their right legs engaged, and the three on the right have their left legs engaged, creating a sense of closure, symmetry, and rhythm.

THE TEMPLE OF ATHENA NIKE

The Ionic Temple of Athena Nike (victory in war), located south of the Propylaia, was designed and built about 425 BCE, probably by Kallikrates (SEE FIG. 5–36). Reduced to rubble during the Turkish occupation of Greece in the seventeenth century CE, the temple has since been rebuilt. Its diminutive size—about 27 by 19

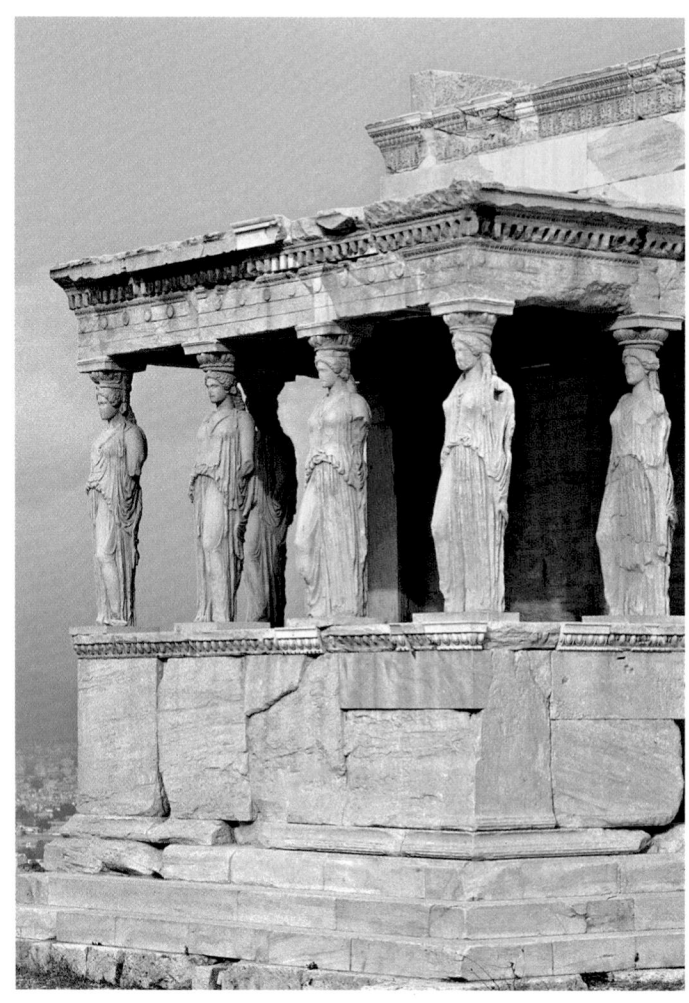

5-38 • PORCH OF THE MAIDENS (SOUTH PORCH), ERECHTHEION
Acropolis, Athens. Temple 430s–406 BCE; porch c. 420–410 BCE.

EXPLORE MORE: Click the Google Earth link for the Porch of the Maidens **www.myartslab.com**

5-39 • NIKE (VICTORY) ADJUSTING HER SANDAL
Fragment of relief decoration from the parapet (now destroyed),
Temple of Athena Nike, Acropolis, Athens. Last quarter of the 5th
century (perhaps 410–405) BCE. Marble, height 3'6" (1.06 m). Acropolis
Museum, Athens.

feet—and refined Ionic decoration are in marked contrast to the
weightier Doric Propylaia adjacent to it.

Between 410 and 405 BCE, this temple was surrounded by a
parapet or low wall, faced with sculptured panels depicting
Athena presiding over the preparation of a celebration by winged
Nikes (victory figures). The parapet no longer exists, but some panels have survived, including the greatly admired **NIKE (VICTORY)
ADJUSTING HER SANDAL** (FIG. 5–39). The figure bends forward
gracefully, allowing her *chiton* to slip off one shoulder. Her large
overlapping wings effectively balance her unstable pose. Unlike
the decorative swirls of heavy fabric covering the Parthenon
goddesses, or the weighty, pleated robes of the Erechtheion
caryatids, the textile covering this Nike appears delicate and light,
clinging to her body like wet silk, one of the most discreetly erotic
images in ancient art.

THE ATHENIAN AGORA

In Athens, as in most cities of ancient Greece, commercial, civic,
and social life revolved around the marketplace, or **agora**. The
Athenian Agora, at the foot of the Acropolis, began as an open
space where farmers and artisans displayed their wares. Over time,
public and private structures were erected on both sides of the
Panathenaic Way, a ceremonial road used during an important
festival in honor of Athena (FIG. 5–40). A stone drainage system
was installed to prevent flooding, and a large fountain house was
built to provide water for surrounding homes, administrative
buildings, and shops (see "Women at a Fountain House,"
opposite). By 400 BCE, the Agora contained several religious and
administrative structures and even a small racetrack. The Agora
also had the city mint, its military headquarters, and two buildings
devoted to court business.

In design, the stoa, a distinctively Greek structure found
nearly everywhere people gathered, ranged from a simple roof
held up by columns to a substantial, sometimes architecturally
impressive, building with two stories and shops along one side.
Stoas offered protection from the sun and rain, and provided a
place for strolling and talking business, politics, or philosophy.
While city business could be, and often was, conducted in the
stoas, agora districts also came to include buildings with specific
administrative functions.

In the Athenian Agora, the 500-member *boule*, or council, met
in a building called the *bouleuterion*. This structure, built before 450
BCE but probably after the Persian destruction of Athens in 480
BCE, was laid out on a simple rectangular plan with a vestibule and
large meeting room. Near the end of the fifth century BCE, a new
bouleuterion was constructed to the west of the old one. This too
had a rectangular plan. The interior, however, may have had
permanent tiered seating arranged in an ascending semicircle
around a ground-level **podium**, or raised platform.

Nearby was a small, round building with six columns
supporting a conical roof, a type of structure known as a **tholos**.
Built about 465 BCE, this tholos was the meeting place of the
50-member executive committee of the boule. The committee
members dined there at the city's expense, and a few of them
always spent the night there in order to be available for any
pressing business that might arise.

Private houses surrounded the Agora. Compared with the
often grand public buildings, houses of the fifth century BCE in
Athens were rarely more than simple rectangular structures of
stucco-faced mud brick with wooden posts and lintels supporting
roofs of terra-cotta tiles. Rooms were small and included a
dayroom in which women could sew, weave, and do other chores,
a dining room with couches for reclining around a table, a kitchen,
bedrooms, and occasionally an indoor bathroom. Where space was
not at a premium, houses sometimes opened onto small courtyards
or porches.

CITY PLANS

In older Greek cities such as Athens, buildings and streets
developed in conformance to the needs of their inhabitants and
the requirements of the terrain. As early as the eighth century BCE,

Women at a Fountain House

The Archaic period ceramic artist known as the Priam Painter has given us an insight into Greek city life in the agora by painting a Greek fountain house in use on a black-figure **hydria** (water jug). Since most women in ancient Greece were confined to their homes, their daily trip to the communal well or fountain house was an important event. At a fountain house, in the shade of a Doric-columned porch, three women fill hydriae just like the one on which they are painted. A fourth balances her empty jug on her head as she waits, while a fifth woman, without a jug, seems to be waving a greeting to someone. The building is designed like a stoa, open on one side, but having animal-head spigots on three walls. The Doric columns support a Doric entablature with an architrave above the colonnade and a colorful frieze—here black-and-white blocks replace carved metopes. The circular **palmettes** (fan-shaped petal designs) framing the main scenes suggest a rich and colorful civic center.

Priam Painter **WOMEN AT A FOUNTAIN HOUSE**
520–510 BCE. Black-figure decoration on a hydria. Ceramic, height of hydria 20⅞″ (53 cm). Museum of Fine Arts, Boston. William Francis Warden Fund (61.195)

5-40 • RECONSTRUCTION DRAWING OF THE AGORA (MARKETPLACE)
Athens. c. 400 BCE.

Temple of Hephaistos
new *bouleuterion*
Stoa of Zeus
Royal Stoa
Altar of the Twelve Gods
Painted Stoa
courtroom
old *bouleuterion*
tholos
racetrack
South Stoa
fountain house
mint
to the Acropolis
Panathenaic Way

however, builders in some western Greek settlements began to use a mathematical concept of urban development based on the **orthogonal** (or **grid**) **plan**. New cities or rebuilt sections of old cities were laid out on straight, evenly spaced parallel streets that intersected at right angles to create rectangular blocks. These blocks were then subdivided into identical building plots.

During the Classical period, Hippodamos of Miletos, a major urban planner of the fifth century BCE, held views on the reasoned perfectibility of urban design akin to those of the Athenian

philosophers (such as Socrates) and artists (such as Polykleitos). He believed the ideal city should be limited to 10,000 citizens divided into three classes—artists, farmers, and soldiers—and three zones—sacred, public, and private. The basic Hippodamian plot was a square 600 feet on each side, divided into quarters. Each quarter was subdivided into six rectangular building plots measuring 100 by 150 feet on a side, a scheme still widely used in American and European cities and suburbs.

Orthogonal plans obviously work best when laid out on relatively flat land. But the Greeks applied orthogonal planning even in less hospitable terrain, such as that of the Ionian city of Priene, which lies on a rugged hillside in Asia Minor. In this case, the city's planners made no attempt to accommodate their grid to the irregular mountainside, meaning that some streets are in fact stairs.

STELE SCULPTURE

Upright stone slabs called **stelae** (singular, stele) were used in Greek cemeteries as gravestones, carved in low relief with an image (actual or allegorical) of the person(s) to be remembered. Instead of the proud warriors or athletes used in the Archaic period, however, Classical stelae place figures in personal or domestic contexts that often feature women and children. A touching mid-fifth-century BCE example found on the island of Paros portrays a sweet young girl, seemingly bidding farewell to her pet birds, one of which she kisses on the beak **(FIG. 5–41)**. She wears a loose *peplos*, which parts at the side to disclose the tender flesh underneath and clings elsewhere over her body to reveal its three-dimensional form. The extraordinary carving recalls the contemporary reliefs of the Parthenon frieze, and like them, this stele would have been painted with color to provide details such as the straps of the girl's sandals or the feathers on her beloved birds.

Another, somewhat later, stele commemorates the relationship between a couple, identified by name across an upper frieze resting on two Doric pilasters **(FIG. 5–42)**. The husband Ktesilaos stands casually with crossed legs and joined hands, gazing at his wife Theano, who sits before him on a bench, pulling at her gauzy wrap with her right hand in a gesture that is often associated with Greek brides. Presumably this was a tombstone for a joint grave, since both names are inscribed on it, but we do not know which of the two might have died first, leaving behind a mate to mourn and memorialize by commissioning this stele. The air of introspective melancholy here, as well as the softness and delicacy of both flesh and fabric, seem to point forward, out of the High Classical period and into the increased sense of narrative and delicacy that was to characterize the fourth century BCE.

5-41 • GRAVE STELE OF A LITTLE GIRL
c. 450–440 BCE. Marble, height 31½″ (80 cm). Metropolitan Museum of Art, New York.

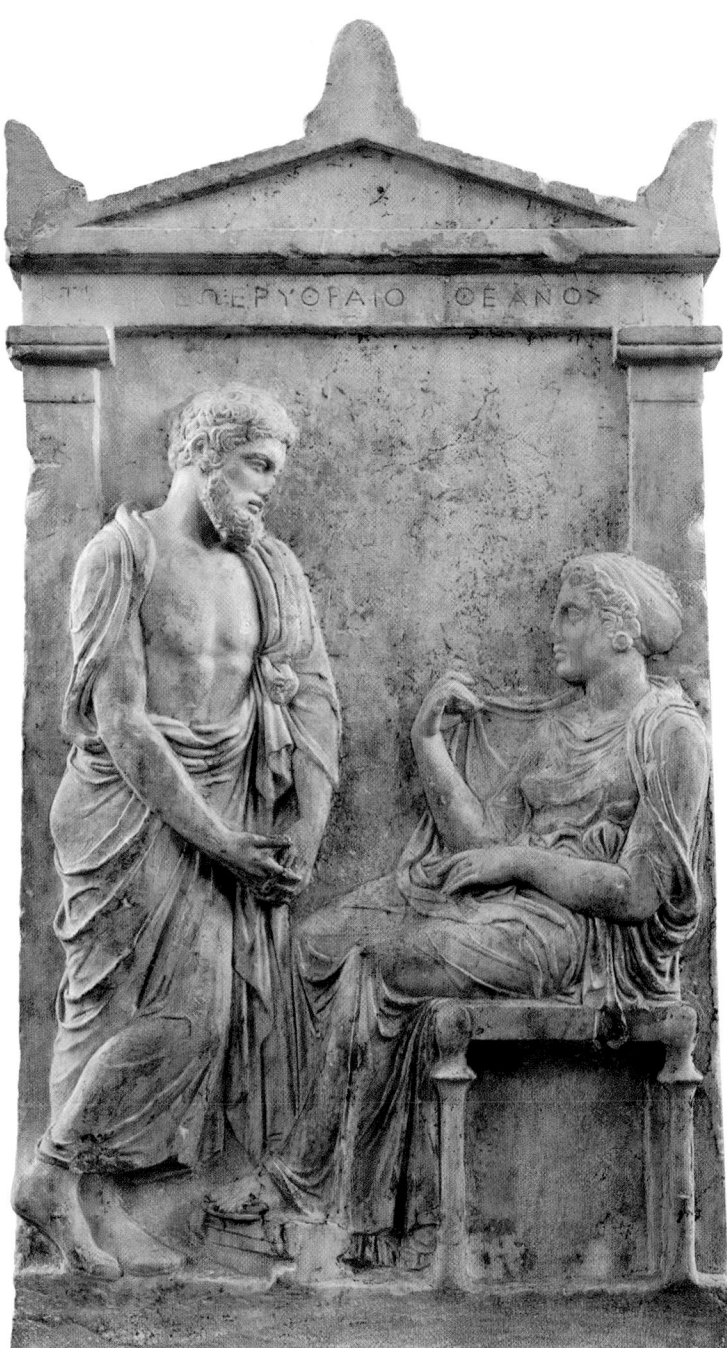

PAINTING

The Painted Stoa built on the north side of the Athenian Agora (SEE FIG. 5–40) about 460 BCE is known to have been decorated with paintings (hence its name) by the most famous artists of the time, including Polygnotos of Thasos (active c. 475–450 BCE). His contemporaries praised his talent for creating the illusion of spatial recession in landscapes, rendering female figures clothed in transparent draperies, and conveying through facial expressions the full range of human emotions. Ancient writers described his painting, as well as other famous works, enthusiastically, but nothing survives for us to see.

White-ground ceramic painting, however, may echo the style of lost contemporary wall and panel painting. The **white-ground** technique had been used as early as the seventh century BCE. Painters first applied refined white slip as the ground on which they painted designs with liquid slip. High Classical white-ground painting was far more complex than earlier efforts and became a specialty of Athenian potters. Artists enhanced the fired vessel with a full range of colors using paints made by mixing tints with white clay, and also using **tempera**, an opaque, water-based medium mixed with glue or egg white. This fragile decoration deteriorated easily, and for that reason seems to have been favored for funerary, votive, and other nonutilitarian vessels.

Tall, slender, one-handled white-ground **lekythoi** were used to pour libations during religious rituals. Some convey grief and loss, with scenes of departing figures bidding farewell. Others depict grave stelae draped with garlands. Still others envision the deceased returned to the prime of life and engaged in a seemingly everyday activity. A white-ground lekythos, dated about 450–440 BCE, shows a young servant girl carrying a stool for a small chest of valuables to a well-dressed woman of regal bearing, the dead person whom the vessel memorializes (FIG. 5–43). As on the *Stele of Ktesilaos and Theano* (SEE FIG. 5–42), the scene portrayed here contains no overt signs of grief, but a quiet sadness pervades it. The two figures seem to inhabit different worlds, their glances somehow failing to meet.

THE LATE CLASSICAL PERIOD, C. 400–323 BCE

After the Spartans defeated Athens in 404 BCE, they set up a pro-Spartan government so oppressive that within a year the Athenians rebelled against it, killed its leader, Kritias, and restored democracy. Athens recovered its independence and its economy revived, but it never regained its dominant political and military status. It did, however, retain its reputation as a center of artistic and intellectual life. In 387 BCE, the great philosopher-teacher Plato founded a school just outside Athens, as his student Aristotle did later. Among Aristotle's students was young Alexander of Macedon, known to history as Alexander the Great.

In 359 BCE, a crafty and energetic warrior, Philip II, had come to the throne of Macedon. In 338, he defeated Athens and rapidly conquered the other Greek cities. When he was assassinated two years later, his kingdom passed to his 20-year-old son, Alexander, who consolidated his power and led a united Greece in a war of revenge and conquest against the Persians. In 334 BCE, he crushed the Persian army and conquered Syria and Phoenicia. By 331, he had occupied Egypt and founded the seaport he named Alexandria. The Egyptian priests of Amun recognized him as the son of a god, an idea he readily adopted. That same year, he reached the Persian capital of Persepolis and continued east until reaching present-day Pakistan in 326 BCE; his troops then refused to go any farther (MAP 5–2). On the way home, Alexander died of a fever in 323 BCE. He was only 33 years old.

Changing political conditions never seriously dampened the Greeks' artistic creativity. Indeed, artists experimented widely with new subjects and styles. Although they maintained a Classical approach to composition and form, they relaxed its conventions, supported by a sophisticated new group of patrons drawn from the courts of Philip and Alexander, wealthy aristocrats in Asia Minor, and foreign aristocrats eager to import Greek works and, sometimes, Greek artists.

5-43 • Style of the Achilles Painter WOMAN AND MAID
c. 450–440 BCE. White-ground lekythos. Ceramic, with additional painting in tempera, height 15⅛″ (38.4 cm). Museum of Fine Arts, Boston. Francis Bartlett Donation of 1912 (13.201)

MAP 5-2 HELLENISTIC GREECE

Alexander the Great created a Greek empire that extended from the Greek mainland and Egypt across Asia Minor and as far east as India.

SCULPTURE

Throughout the fifth century BCE, sculptors accepted and worked within standards established by Pheidias and Polykleitos at mid century for the ideal proportions and idealized forms of the human figure. But fourth-century BCE artists began to challenge and modify those standards. On mainland Greece, in particular, a new canon of proportions emerged for male figures—now eight or more "heads" tall rather than the six-and-a-half or seven-head height of earlier works. The calm, noble detachment characteristic of High Classical figures gave way to more sensitively rendered images of men and women with expressions of wistful introspection, dreaminess, even fleeting anxiety or lightheartedness. This period also saw the earliest depictions of fully nude women in major works of art.

PRAXITELES.   According to the Greek traveler Pausanias, writing in the second century CE, the Late Classical sculptor Praxiteles (active in Athens from about 370 to 335 BCE or later) carved a "Hermes of stone who carries the infant Dionysos" for the Temple of Hera at Olympia. In 1875, just such a statue depicting the messenger god Hermes teasing the baby Dionysos with a bunch of grapes was

discovered in the ruins of this temple **(FIG. 5–44)**. Initially accepted as an original work of Praxiteles because of its high quality, recent studies hold that it is probably a very good Roman or Hellenistic copy.

The sculpture highlights the differences between the fourth- and fifth-century BCE Classical styles. Hermes has a smaller head and a more sensual and sinuous body than Polykleitos' *Spear Bearer* (see "The Canon of Polykleitos," page 134). His off-balance, S-curving pose, requires him to lean on a post—a clear contrast with the balanced posture of Polykleitos' work. Praxiteles also created a sensuous play of contrasting textures over the figure's surface, juxtaposing the gleam of smooth flesh with crumpled draperies and rough locks of hair. Praxiteles humanizes his subject with a hint of narrative—two gods, one a loving adult and the other a playful child, caught in a moment of absorbed companionship.

Around 350 BCE, Praxiteles created a daring statue of Aphrodite for the city of Knidos in Asia Minor. Although artists of the fifth century BCE had begun to hint boldly at the naked female body beneath tissue-thin drapery, as in *Nike Adjusting her Sandal* (SEE FIG. 5–39), this Aphrodite was apparently the first statue by a well-known Greek sculptor to depict a fully nude woman, and it set a

5-44 • Praxiteles or his followers HERMES AND THE INFANT DIONYSOS

Probably a Hellenistic or Roman copy after a Late Classical 4th-century BCE original. Marble, with remnants of red paint on the lips and hair, height 7′1″ (2.15 m). Archaeological Museum, Olympia.

5-45 • Praxiteles APHRODITE OF KNIDOS

Composite of two similar Roman copies after the original marble of c. 350 BCE. Marble, height 6′8″ (2.04 m). Vatican Museums, Museo Pio Clementino, Gabinetto delle Maschere, Rome.

The head of this figure is from one Roman copy, the body from another. Seventeenth- and eighteenth-century CE restorers added the nose, the neck, the right forearm and hand, most of the left arm, and the feet and parts of the legs. This kind of restoration would rarely be undertaken today, but it was frequently done and considered quite acceptable in the past, when archaeologists were trying to put together a body of work documenting the appearances of lost Greek statues.

EXPLORE MORE: Gain insight from a primary source related to Praxiteles' *Aphrodite of Knidos*
www.myartslab.com

new standard (FIG. 5–45). Although nudity among athletic young men was admired in Greek society, nudity among women was seen as a sign of low character. The eventual wide acceptance of female nudes in large statuary may be related to the gradual merging of the Greeks' concept of their goddess Aphrodite with some of the characteristics of the Phoenician goddess Astarte (the Babylonian Ishtar), who was nearly always shown nude in Near Eastern art.

In the version of Praxiteles' statue seen here (actually a composite of two Roman copies), the goddess is preparing to take a bath, with a water jug and her discarded clothing at her side. Her hand is caught in a gesture of modesty that only calls attention to her nudity. The bracelet on her upper left arm has a similar effect. Her strong and well-toned body leans forward slightly, with one projecting knee in a seductive pose that emphasizes the swelling forms of her thighs and abdomen. According to an old legend, the sculpture was so realistic that Aphrodite herself journeyed to Knidos to see it and cried out in shock, "Where did Praxiteles see me naked?" The Knidians were so proud of their Aphrodite that they placed it in an open shrine where people could view it from every side. Hellenistic and Roman copies probably numbered in the hundreds, and nearly 50 survive in various collections today.

LYSIPPOS. Compared to Praxiteles, more details of Lysippos' life are known, and, although none of his original works has survived, there are many copies of the sculpture he produced between c. 350 and 310 BCE. He claimed to be entirely self-taught and asserted that "nature" was his only model, but he must have received some technical training in the vicinity of his home, near Corinth. He expressed great admiration for Polykleitos, but his own figures reflect a different ideal and different proportions. For his famous portrayal of a man scraping himself (APOXYOMENOS), known today only from Roman copies (FIG. 5–46), he chose a typical Classical subject, a nude male athlete. But instead of a figure actively engaged in his sport, striding, or standing at ease, Lysippos depicted a young man after his workout, methodically removing oil and dirt from his body with a scraping tool called a *strigil*.

The *Man Scraping Himself*, tall and slender with a relatively small head, makes a telling comparison with Polykleitos' *Spear Bearer* (see "The Canon of Polykleitos," page 134). Not only does it reflect a different canon of proportions, but the legs are in a wider stance to counterbalance the outstretched arms, and there is a pronounced curve to his posture. The *Spear Bearer* is contained within fairly simple, compact contours and oriented toward a center front viewer. In contrast, the arms of the *Man Scraping Himself* break free into the surrounding space, inviting the viewer to move around the statue to absorb its full aspect. Roman authors, who may have been describing the bronze original rather than a marble copy, remarked on the subtle modeling of the statue's elongated body and the spatial extension of its pose.

Lysippos was widely admired for monumental bronze statues of Herakles (Hercules) and Zeus. Neither survives, but his statue of the weary Herakles, leaning on his club (resting after the last of

5–46 • Lysippos MAN SCRAPING HIMSELF (APOXYOMENOS)
Roman copy after the original bronze of c. 350–325 BCE. Marble, height 6′9″ (2.06 m). Vatican Museums, Museo Pio Clementino, Gabinetto dell'Apoxyomenos, Rome.

5-47 • Lysippos THE WEARY HERAKLES (FARNESE HERCULES)
A Roman copy by Glykon of the 4th-century BCE bronze original. Marble, height 10′6″ (3.17 m). National Archeological Museum, Naples.

Based on description and later copies, we know Lysippos idealized the ruler as a ruggedly handsome, heavy-featured young man with a large Adam's apple and short, tousled hair. According to the Roman historian Plutarch, Lysippos presented Alexander in a meditative pose, "with his face turned upward toward the sky, just as Alexander himself was accustomed to gaze, turning his neck gently to one side" (Pollitt, p. 20). Perhaps he was caught contemplating grave decisions, waiting to receive divine advice.

THE ART OF THE GOLDSMITH

The detailed, small-scale work of Greek goldsmiths followed the same stylistic trends and achieved the same high standards of technique and execution characterizing other arts. A specialty of Greek goldsmiths was the design of earrings in the form of tiny works of sculpture. They were often placed on the ears of marble statues of goddesses, but they adorned the ears of living women as well. Earrings dated about 330—300 BCE depict the youth Ganymede caught in the grasp of an eagle (Zeus) **(FIG. 5–48)**, a surprising subject for a decorative item (this is a scene of abduction) and a technical *tour-de-force*. Slightly more than 2 inches high, they were hollow-cast using the lost-wax process, no doubt to make them light on the ear. Despite their small size, the earrings convey some of the drama of their subject, evoking swift movement through space.

PAINTING AND MOSAICS

Roman observers such as Pliny the Elder praised Greek painters for their skill in capturing the appearance of the real world. Roman patrons also admired Greek murals, and they commissioned copies, in fresco or **mosaic**, to decorate their homes. (Mosaics—created from **tesserae**, small cubes of colored stone or marble—provide a permanent waterproof surface that the Romans used for floors in important rooms.) A first-century CE Roman mosaic, **ALEXANDER THE GREAT CONFRONTS DARIUS III AT THE BATTLE OF ISSOS (FIG. 5–49)**, for example, replicates a Greek painting of about 310 BCE. Pliny the Elder mentions a painting of this subject by Philoxenos of Eretria, but a new theory claims the original as a work of Helen of Egypt (see "Women Artists in Ancient Greece," page 148).

Such copies document a growing taste for dramatic narrative subjects in late fourth-century BCE Greek painting. Certainly the scene here is one of violent action, where diagonal disruption and radical foreshortening draw the viewer in and elicit an emotional response. Astride a rearing horse at the left, his hair blowing free and his neck bare, Alexander challenges the helmeted and armored Persian leader, who stretches out his arm in a gesture of defeat and apprehension as his charioteer whisks him back toward safety within the Persian ranks. The mosaicist has created an illusion of solid figures through modeling, mimicking the play of light on three-dimensional surfaces by highlights and shading.

The interest of fourth-century BCE artists in creating believable illusions of the real world was the subject of anecdotes repeated by later writers. One popular legend involved a floral

his Twelve Labors) and holding the apples of the Hesperides, is known from an early third-century CE Roman copy, signed by the Athenian sculptor Glykon **(FIG. 5–47)**. The Romans greatly admired Lysippos' heroic figure, and the marble copy was made for the Baths of Caracalla. In the Renaissance the sculpture was part of the Farnese collection in Rome, where it stood in the courtyard of the family's palace and was studied by artists from all over Europe. It has since been dubbed the *Farnese Hercules*.

When Lysippos was summoned to create a portrait of Alexander the Great, he portrayed Alexander as a full-length standing figure with an upraised arm holding a scepter, the same way he posed Zeus.

5-48 • EARRINGS
c. 330–300 BCE. Hollow-cast gold,
height 2⅜" (6 cm). The Metropolitan
Museum of Art, New York.
Harris Brisbane Dick Fund, 1937 (37.11.9–10)

5-49 • ALEXANDER THE GREAT CONFRONTS DARIUS III AT THE BATTLE OF ISSOS
Floor mosaic, Pompeii, Italy. 1st-century CE Roman copy of a Greek wall painting of c. 310 BCE, perhaps by Philoxenos
of Eretria or Helen of Egypt. Entire panel 8'10" × 17' (2.7 × 5.2 m). National Archeological Museum, Naples.

Women Artists in Ancient Greece

Although comparatively few artists in ancient Greece were women, there is evidence that women artists worked in many media. Ancient writers noted women painters—Pliny the Elder, for example, listed Aristarete, Eirene, Iaia, Kalypso, Olympias, and Timarete. Helen, a painter from Egypt who had been taught by her father, is known to have worked in the fourth century BCE and may have been responsible for the original Greek wall painting of c. 310 BCE of *Alexander the Great Confronts Darius III at the Battle of Issos* (SEE FIG. 5–49).

Greek women excelled in creating narrative or pictorial tapestries. They also worked in ceramic workshops. This hydria dating from about 450 BCE shows a woman artist in such a workshop, but her status is ambiguous. The composition focuses on the male painters, who are being approached by Nikes (Victories) bearing wreaths symbolizing victory in an artistic competition. A well-dressed woman sits on a raised dais, painting the largest vase in the workshop. She is isolated from the other artists as well as from the awards ceremony. Perhaps women were excluded from public artistic competitions, as they were from athletics. But could this woman be the head of this workshop? Secure in her own status, she may have encouraged her assistants to enter contests to further their careers and bring glory to her enterprise.

The Leningrad Painter **CERAMIC PAINTER AND ASSISTANTS CROWNED BY ATHENA AND VICTORIES** c. 450 BCE. Red-figure decoration on a hydria from Athens. Private collection, Milan.

designer named Glykera—widely praised for her artistry in weaving blossoms and greenery into wreaths, swags, and garlands for religious processions and festivals—and Pausias—the foremost painter of his day. Pausias challenged Glykera to a contest, claiming that he could paint a picture of one of her complex works that would appear as lifelike to the spectator as her real one. According to the legend, he succeeded. It is not surprising, although perhaps unfair, that the opulent floral borders so popular in later Greek painting and mosaics are described as "Pausian" rather than "Glykeran."

A Pausian design frames a mosaic floor from a palace at Pella (Macedonia), dated about 300 BCE **(FIG. 5–50)**. The floor features a series of hunting scenes, such as the *Stag Hunt* seen here, prominently signed by an artist named Gnosis. The blossoms, leaves, spiraling tendrils, and twisting, undulating stems that frame this scene, echo the linear patterns formed by the hunters, the dog, and the struggling stag. The human and animal figures are modeled in light and shade, and the dog's front legs are expertly foreshortened to create the illusion that the animal is turning at a sharp angle into the picture. The work is all the more impressive because it was not made with uniformly cut marble in different colors, but with a carefully selected assortment of natural pebbles.

5–50 • Gnosis STAG HUNT
Detail of mosaic floor decoration from Pella, Macedonia (in present-day Greece). 300 BCE. Pebbles, height 10′2″ (3.1 m). Archaeological Museum, Pella. Signed at top: "Gnosis made it."

THE HELLENISTIC PERIOD, 323–31/30 BCE

When Alexander died unexpectedly at age 33 in 323 BCE, he left a vast empire with no administrative structure and no accepted successor. Almost immediately his generals turned against one another, local leaders tried to regain their lost autonomy, and the empire began to break apart. By the early third century BCE, three of Alexander's generals—Antigonus, Ptolemy, and Seleucus—had carved out kingdoms. The Antigonids controlled Macedonia and mainland Greece; the Ptolemies ruled Egypt; and the Seleucids controlled Asia Minor, Mesopotamia, and Persia.

Over the course of the second and first centuries BCE, these kingdoms succumbed to the growing empire centered in Rome. Ptolemaic Egypt endured the longest, and its capital Alexandria, flourished as a prosperous seaport and great center of learning and the arts. Its library is estimated to have contained 700,000 papyrus and parchment scrolls. The Battle of Actium in 31 BCE and the death in 30 BCE of Egypt's last ruler, the remarkable Cleopatra, marks the end of the Hellenistic period.

Alexander's lasting legacy was the spread of Greek culture far beyond its original borders, but artists of the Hellenistic period developed visions discernibly distinct from those of their Classical Greek predecessors. Where earlier artists sought to codify a generalized artistic ideal, Hellenistic artists shifted focus to the individual and the specific. They turned increasingly away from the heroic to the everyday, from gods to mortals, from aloof serenity to individual emotion, and from decorous drama to emotional melodrama. Their works appeal to the senses through luscious or lustrous surface treatments and to our hearts as well as our intellects through expressive subjects and poses. Although such tendencies are already evident during the fourth century BCE, they become more pronounced in Hellenistic art.

THE CORINTHIAN ORDER IN HELLENISTIC ARCHITECTURE

Even the architecture of the Hellenistic period reflected the contemporary taste for high drama. A variant of the Ionic order featuring tall, slender columns with elaborate foliate capitals challenged the dominant Doric and Ionic orders (see "The Greek Orders," page 110). Invented in the late fifth century BCE and called Corinthian by the Romans, this highly decorative system had previously been reserved for interiors. In the Corinthian capital, curly acanthus leaves and coiled flower spikes surround a basket-shaped core. Above the capitals, the Corinthian entablature, like the Ionic, has a stepped-out architrave and a continuous frieze, but it includes additional bands of carved moldings. The Corinthian design became a symbol of elegance and refinement, and it is still used on banks, churches, and court buildings today.

The Corinthian **TEMPLE OF THE OLYMPIAN ZEUS**, located in the lower city of Athens at the foot of the Acropolis, was designed by the Roman architect Cossutius in the second century BCE **(FIG. 5–51)** on the foundations of an earlier Doric temple, but it was not completed until three centuries later, under the patronage of the Roman emperor Hadrian. The temple's great Corinthian columns, 55 feet 5 inches tall, may be the second-century BCE Greek originals or Roman replicas. Viewed through these columns, the Parthenon seems modest in comparison. But for all its height and luxurious decoration, the new temple followed long-established conventions. It was an enclosed rectangular building surrounded by a screen of columns standing on a three-stepped base. Its proportions and details followed traditional standards. It is, quite simply, a Greek temple grown very large.

5-51 • TEMPLE OF THE OLYMPIAN ZEUS, ATHENS, ACROPOLIS IN DISTANCE
Building and rebuilding phases: foundation c. 520–510 BCE, using the Doric order; temple designed by Cossutius, begun 175 BCE, left unfinished 164 BCE, completed 132 CE using Cossutius' design. Height of columns 55′5″ (16.89 m).

EXPLORE MORE: Click the Google Earth link for the Temple of the Olympian Zeus
www.myartslab.com

Greek Theaters

A. THEATER, EPIDAUROS
Fourth century BCE and later.

In ancient Greece, the theater was more than mere entertainment: it was a vehicle for the communal expression of religious beliefs through music, poetry, and dance. In very early times, theater performances took place on the hard-packed dirt or stone-surfaced pavement of an outdoor threshing floor—the same type of floor later incorporated into religious sanctuaries. Whenever feasible, dramas were also presented facing a steep hill that served as elevated seating for the audience. Eventually such sites were made into permanent open-air auditoriums. At first, tiers of seats were simply cut into the side of the hill. Later, builders improved them with stone.

During the fifth century BCE, the plays were usually tragedies in verse based on popular myths, and were performed at festivals dedicated to Dionysos; the three great Greek tragedians—Aeschylus, Sophocles, and Euripides—created works that would define tragedy for centuries. Because they were used continuously and frequently modified over many centuries, early theaters have not survived in their original form.

The theater at Epidauros, built in the second half of the fourth century BCE, is characteristic. A semicircle of tiered seats built into the hillside overlooked the circular performance area, called the orchestra, at the center of which was an altar to Dionysos. Rising behind the orchestra was a two-tiered stage structure made up of the vertical *skene* (scene)—an architectural backdrop for performances that also screened the backstage area from view—and the *proskenion* (**proscenium**), a raised platform in front of the *skene* that was increasingly used over time as an extension of the orchestra.

B. RECONSTRUCTION DRAWING OF THE THEATER AT EPIDAUROS

parodos
ramp
skene
proskenion
ramp
parodos
orchestra
aisles
tiered seating for audience
gangway

Ramps connecting the *proskenion* with lateral passageways provided access for performers. Steps gave the audience access to the 55 rows of seats and divided the seating area into uniform wedge-shaped sections. The tiers of seats above the wide corridor, or gangway, were added at a much later date. This design provided uninterrupted sight lines and good acoustics, and allowed for efficient entrance and exit of the 12,000 spectators. No better design has ever been created.

SCULPTURE

Hellenistic sculptors produced an enormous variety of work in a wide range of materials, techniques, and styles. The period was marked by two broad and conflicting trends. One (sometimes called anti-Classical) abandoned Classical strictures and experimented freely with new forms and subjects. The other trend emulated earlier Classical models; sculptors selected aspects of favored works of the fourth century BCE and incorporated them into their own work. The radical anti-Classical style was especially strong in Pergamon and other eastern centers of Greek culture.

PERGAMON. Pergamon—capital of a breakaway state within the Seleucid realm established in the early third century BCE—quickly became a leading center of the arts and the hub of an experimental sculptural style that had far-reaching influence throughout the Hellenistic period. This radical style characterizes a monument commemorating the victory in 230 BCE of Attalos I (ruled 241–197 BCE) over the Gauls, a Celtic people (see "The Celts," page 152). The monument extols the dignity and heroism of the defeated enemies and, by extension, the power and virtue of the Pergamenes.

The bronze figures of Gauls mounted on the pedestal of this monument are known today only from Roman copies in marble. One captures the slow demise of a wounded Celtic soldier-trumpeter (**FIG. 5–52**), whose lime-spiked hair, mustache, and twisted neck ring or **torc** (reputedly the only thing the Gauls wore into battle) identify him as a **barbarian** (a label the ancient Greeks used for all foreigners, whom they considered uncivilized). But the sculpture also depicts his dignity and heroism in defeat, inspiring in viewers both admiration and pity for this fallen warrior. Fatally injured, he struggles to rise, but the slight bowing of his supporting right arm and his unseeing, downcast gaze indicate that he is on the point of death. This kind of deliberate attempt to elicit a specific emotional response in the viewer is known as **expressionism**, and it was to become a characteristic of Hellenistic art.

Pliny the Elder described a work like the *Dying Gallic Trumpeter*, attributing it to an artist named Epigonos. Recent research indicates that Epigonos probably knew the early fifth-century BCE sculpture of the Temple of Aphaia at Aegina, which included the *Dying Warriors* (SEE FIGS. 5–14, 5–15), and could have had it in mind when he created his own works.

5-52 • Epigonos (?) DYING GALLIC TRUMPETER
Roman copy after the original bronze of c. 220 BCE. Marble, height, 36½″ (93 cm). Capitoline Museum, Rome.

The marble sculpture was found in Julius Caesar's garden in Rome. The bronze original was part of a victory monument made for the Sanctuary of Athena in Pergamon. Pliny wrote that Epigonos "surpassed others with his Trumpeter."

The Celts

During the first millennium BCE, Celtic peoples inhabited most of central and western Europe. The Celtic Gauls portrayed in the Hellenistic Pergamene victory monument (SEE FIG. 5–52) moved into Asia Minor from Thrace during the third century BCE. The ancient Greeks referred to these neighbors, like all outsiders, as barbarians. Pushed out by migrating people, attacked and defeated by challenged kingdoms like that at Pergamon, and then finally by the Roman armies of Julius Caesar, ultimately the Celts were pushed into the northwesternmost parts of the continent—Ireland, Cornwall, and Brittany. Their wooden sculpture and dwellings and their colorful woven textiles have disintegrated, but spectacular funerary goods such as jewelry, weapons, and tableware have survived.

This golden torc, dating sometime between the third and first centuries BCE, was excavated in 1866 from a Celtic tomb in northern France, but it is strikingly similar to the neck ring worn by the noble dying trumpeter illustrated in FIG. 5–52. Torcs were worn by noblemen and were sometimes awarded to warriors for heroic performance in combat. Like all Celtic jewelry, the decorative design of this work consists not of natural forms but of completely abstract ornament, in this case created by the careful twisting and wrapping of strands of pure gold, resolved securely by the definitive bulges of two knobs. In Celtic hands, pattern becomes an integral part of the object itself, not an applied decoration. In stark contrast to the culture of the ancient Greeks, where the human figure was at the heart of all artistic development, here it is abstract, non-representational form and its continual refinement that is the central artistic preoccupation.

TORC
Found at Soucy, France. Celtic Gaul, 3rd–1st century BCE. Gold, height 5″ × length 5⅝″ (12.7 × 14.5 cm). Musée Nationale du Moyen-Âge, Paris.

The sculptural style and approach seen in the monument to the defeated Gauls became more pronounced and dramatic in later works, culminating in the sculptured frieze wrapped around the base of a Great Altar on a mountainside at Pergamon (FIG. 5–53). Now reconstructed inside a Berlin museum, the original altar was enclosed within a single-story Ionic colonnade raised on a high podium reached by a monumental staircase 68 feet wide and nearly 30 feet deep. The over-7-feet high sculptural frieze, probably executed during the reign of Eumenes II (197–159 BCE), depicts the battle between the gods and the giants (Titans), a mythical struggle that the Greeks saw as a metaphor for their conflicts with outsiders, all of whom they labeled barbarians. In this case it evokes the Pergamenes' victory over the Gauls.

The Greek gods fight here not only with giants, but also with monsters with snakes for legs emerging from the bowels of the earth. In this detail (FIG. 5–54), the goddess Athena at the left has grabbed the hair of a winged male monster and forced him to his knees. Inscriptions along the base of the sculpture identify him as Alkyoneos, a son of the earth goddess Ge. Ge rises from the ground on the right in fear as she reaches toward Athena, pleading for her son's life. At the far right, a winged Nike rushes to crown Athena with a victor's wreath.

5-53 • RECONSTRUCTED WEST FRONT OF THE ALTAR FROM PERGAMON (IN MODERN TURKEY)

c. 175–150 BCE. Marble, height of figure 7'7" (2.3 m). Staatliche Museen zu Berlin, Pergamonmuseum, Preussischer Kulturbesitz, Berlin.

5-54 • ATHENA ATTACKING THE GIANTS

Detail of the frieze from the east front of the altar from Pergamon. c. 175–150 BCE. Marble, frieze height 7'7" (2.3 m). Staatliche Museen zu Berlin, Antikensammlung, Pergamonmuseum, Berlin.

The figures in the Pergamon frieze not only fill the space along the base of the altar, they also break out of their architectural boundaries and invade the spectators' space, crawling out onto the steps that visitors climbed on their way to the altar. Many consider this theatrical and complex interaction of space and form to be a benchmark of the Hellenistic style, just as they consider the balanced restraint of the Parthenon sculpture to be the epitome of the High Classical style. Where fifth-century BCE artists sought horizontal and vertical equilibrium and control, the Pergamene artists sought to balance opposing forces in three-dimensional space along dynamic diagonals. Classical preference for smooth, evenly illuminated surfaces has been replaced by dramatic contrasts of light and shade playing over complex forms carved with deeply undercut high relief. The composure and stability admired in the Classical style have given way to extreme expressions of pain, stress, wild anger, fear, and despair. Whereas the Classical artist asked only for an intellectual commitment, the Hellenistic artist demanded that the viewer also empathize.

THE LAOCOÖN. Pergamene artists may have inspired the work of Hagesandros, Polydoros, and Athenodoros, three sculptors on the island of Rhodes named by Pliny the Elder as the creators of the famed **LAOCOÖN AND HIS SONS (FIG. 5–55).** This work has been assumed by many art historians to be the original version from the second century BCE, although others argue that it is a brilliant copy commissioned by an admiring Roman patron in the first century CE.

This complex sculptural composition illustrates an episode from the Trojan War when the priest Laocoön warned the Trojans

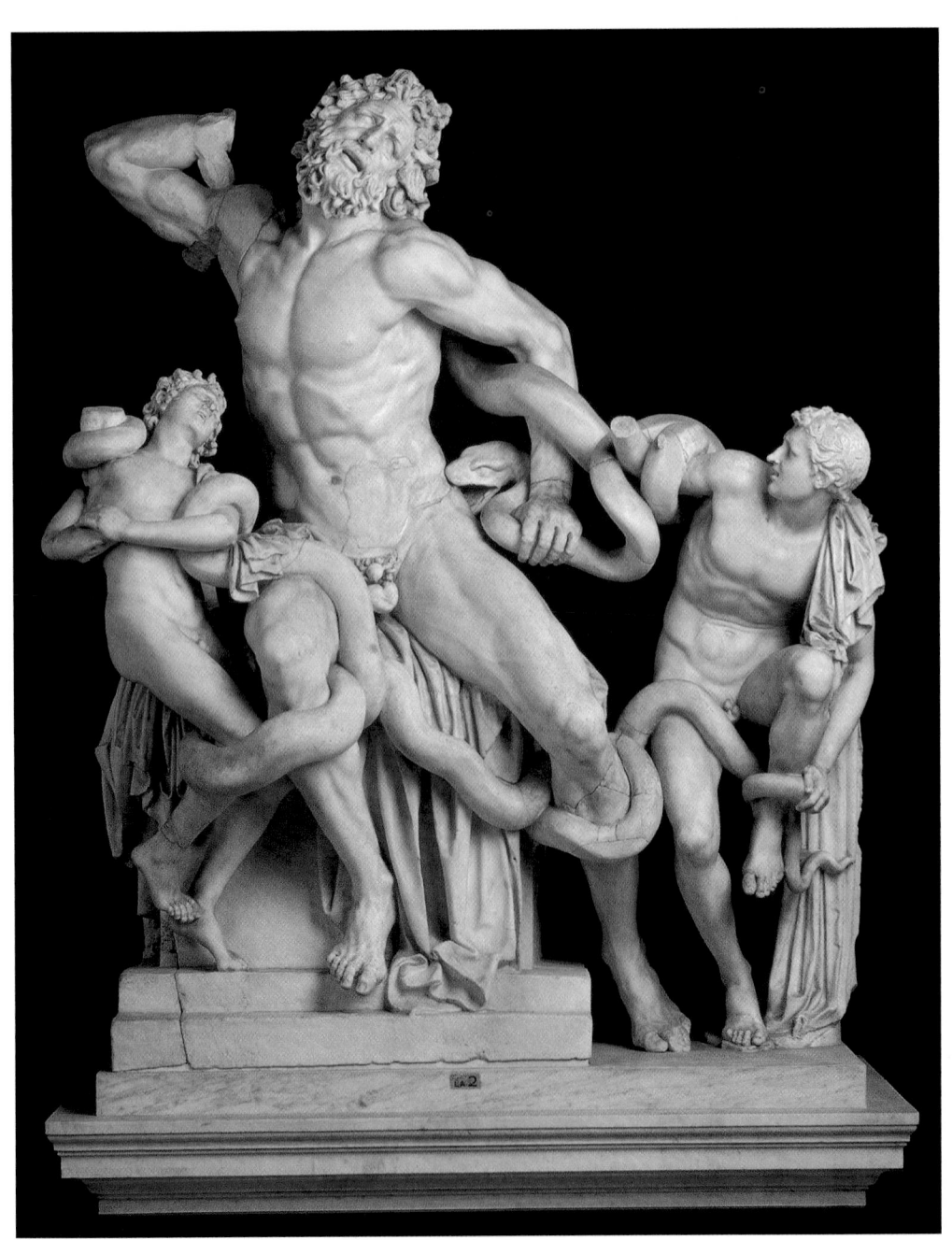

5-55 • Hagesandros, Polydoros, and Athenodoros of Rhodes LAOCOÖN AND HIS SONS
Probably the original of 1st century BCE or a Roman copy of the 1st century CE. Marble, height 8′ (2.44 m). Musei Vaticani, Museo Pio Clementino, Cortile Ottagono, Rome.

not to bring within their walls the giant wooden horse left behind by the Greeks. The gods who supported the Greeks retaliated by sending serpents from the sea to destroy Laocoön and his sons as they walked along the shore. The struggling figures, anguished faces, intricate diagonal movements, and skillful unification of diverse forces in a complex composition all suggest a strong relationship between Rhodian and Pergamene sculptors. Although

sculpted in the round, the Laocoön was composed to be seen frontally and from close range, and the three figures resemble the relief sculpture on the altar from Pergamon.

THE NIKE OF SAMOTHRACE. This winged figure of Victory (FIG. 5–56) is even more theatrical than the Laocoön. In its original setting—in a hillside niche high above the Sanctuary of the Great

OLD WOMAN. The Hellenistic world was varied and multicultural, and some artists turned from generalizing idealism to an attempt to portray the world as they saw it. Patrons were fascinated by representations of people from every level of society, of unusual physical types as well as of ordinary individuals. This aged woman, on her way to the agora with three chickens and a basket of vegetables, may seem an unlikely subject for sculpture (**FIG. 5–57**). Despite the bunched and untidy disposition of her dress, it appears to be of an elegant design and made of fine fabric, and her hair is not in total disarray. These characteristics, along with the woman's sagging lower jaw, unfocused stare, and lack of concern for her exposed breasts, have led some to speculate that she represents an aging, dissolute follower of the wine god Dionysos on her way to make an offering. Whether an elderly peasant or a Dionysian celebrant, the woman is the antithesis of the Nike of Samothrace. Yet in formal terms, both sculptures stretch out assertively into the space around them, both demand an emotional response from the viewer, and both display technical virtuosity in the rendering of forms and textures.

APHRODITE OF MELOS. Not all Hellenistic artists followed the descriptive and expressionist tendencies of the artists of Pergamon and Rhodes. Some turned to the past, creating an eclectic style by reexamining and borrowing elements from earlier Classical styles and combining them in new ways. Many looked back to Praxiteles and Lysippos for their models. This was the case with the sculptor of the *Aphrodite* (better known as the **VENUS DE MILO**) (**FIG. 5–58**) found on the island of Melos by French excavators in the early nineteenth century. The dreamy gaze recalls Praxiteles' work (SEE FIG. 5–45), and the figure has the heavier proportions of High Classical sculpture, but the twisting stance and the strong projection of the knee are typical of Hellenistic art, as is the rich three-dimensionality of the drapery. The juxtaposition of soft flesh and crisp drapery, seemingly in the process of slipping off the figure, adds a note of erotic tension.

5-57 • OLD WOMAN
Roman copy, 1st century CE. Marble, height 49½″ (1.25 m). Metropolitan Museum of Art, New York. Rogers Fund, 1909 (09.39)

gods at Samothrace, perhaps drenched with spray from a fountain—this huge goddess must have reminded visitors of the god in Greek plays who descends from heaven to determine the outcome of the drama. The forward momentum of the Nike's heavy body is balanced by the powerful backward thrust of her enormous wings. The large, open movements of the figure, the strong contrasts of light and dark on the deeply sculpted forms, and the contrasting textures of feathers, fabric, and skin, typify the finest Hellenistic art.

By the end of the first century BCE, the influence of Greek painting, sculpture, and architecture had spread to the artistic communities of the emerging Roman empire. Roman patrons and artists maintained their enthusiasm for Greek art into Early Christian and Byzantine times. Indeed, so strong was the urge to emulate the work of great Greek artists that, as we have seen throughout this chapter, much of our knowledge of Greek achievements comes from Roman replicas of Greek artworks and descriptions of Greek art by Roman writers.

5-58 • APHRODITE OF MELOS (ALSO CALLED VENUS DE MILO)

c. 150–100 BCE. Marble, height 6'8" (2.04 m). Musée du Louvre, Paris.

The original appearance of this famous statue's missing arms has been much debated. When it was dug up in a field in 1820, some broken pieces (now lost) found with it indicated that the figure was holding out an apple in its right hand. Many judged these fragments to be part of a later restoration, not part of the original statue. Another theory is that Aphrodite was admiring herself in the highly polished shield of the war god Ares, an image that was popular in the 2nd century BCE. This theoretical "restoration" would explain the pronounced S-curve of the pose and the otherwise unnatural forward projection of the knee.

THINK ABOUT IT

5.1 Discuss the emergence of a characteristically Greek approach to the representation of the male nude by comparing the *Anavysos Kouros* (FIG. 5–18) and the *Kritios Boy* (FIG. 5–23). What has changed and what remains constant?

5.2 How do the technical possibilities and limitations of black-figure and red-figure techniques affect the representation of the human form on ceramic vessels?

5.3 Distinguish the attributes of the three architectural orders of ancient Greece.

5.4 What ideals are embodied in the term "High Classicism" and what are the value judgments that underlie this art-historical category? Select one sculpture and one building discussed in the chapter, and explain why these works are regarded as High Classical.

5.5 In what ways do the Hellenistic sculptures of the *Dying Gallic Trumpeter* (FIG. 5–52) and *The Great Altar from Pergamon* (FIG. 5–54) depart from the norms of Classicism?

PRACTICE MORE: Compose answers to these questions, get flashcards for images and terms, and review chapter material with quizzes
www.myartslab.com

6–1 • A PAINTER AT WORK   From the House of the Surgeon, Pompeii. 1st century BCE–1st century CE. Fresco, 17⅞ × 17⅜″ (45.5 × 45.3 cm). Museo Archeologico Nazionale, Naples.

ETRUSCAN AND ROMAN ART

This fresco—portraying a painter absorbed in her art—once decorated the walls of a house in the ancient Roman city of Pompeii (FIG. 6–1). Like women in Egypt and Crete, Roman women were far freer and more worldly than their Greek counterparts. Many received a formal education and became physicians, writers, shopkeepers, even overseers in such male-dominated businesses as shipbuilding. But we have little information about the role women played in the visual arts, making the testimony of this picture all the more precious.

The painter sits within a room that opens behind her to the outdoors, holding her palette in her left hand, a sign of her profession. Dressed in a long robe, covered by an ample mantle, her hair is pulled back by a gold headband; but lighting and composition highlight two other aspects of her body: her centralized face, which focuses intently on the subject of her painting—a sculptured rendering of the bearded fertility god Priapus appearing in the shadows of the right background—and her right arm, which extends downward so she can dip her brush into a paintbox that rests precariously on a rounded column drum next to her folding stool. A small child steadies the panel on which she paints, and two elegantly posed and richly dressed women—perhaps her patrons—stand next to a pier behind her. The art she is practicing reflects well on her

social position. Pliny the Elder claimed that "Among artists, glory is given only to those who paint panel paintings" (cited in Mattusch, p. 159). Wall paintings, he claimed, are of lesser value because they cannot be removed in case of fire. In this fresco, however, fixed positioning facilitated survival. When Mount Vesuvius erupted in 79 CE, it was wall paintings like this one that were preserved for rediscovery by eighteenth-century archaeologists.

This painting of a female artist at work was actually conceived as a simulated panel painting, positioned on the yellow wall of a small room (as on the red wall in FIG. 6–25) that also included a fresco of a simulated panel portraying a male poet writing. Both paintings were revered so highly by the archaeologists who discovered them in 1771 that they were cut out of their walls to be exhibited as framed pictures in a museum, a practice that would be anathema today but was far from unusual in the eighteenth century. As we saw when examining the Aegean fresco painting of the crocus-gatherer that opened Chapter 4, only when such fascinating details drawn from wall-painting programs are situated within the larger pictorial and social context of the buildings in which they appeared can we grasp their significance for the people who brought them into being.

6.1 Examine the ways that Etruscan funerary art celebrates the vitality of human existence.

6.2 Trace the development of portraiture as a major form of artistic expression for the Romans.

6.3 Investigate the various ways Romans embellished the walls of their houses with illusionistic painting.

6.4 Explore the structural advances made by the Romans in the construction of large civic architecture.

6.5 Assess the ways Roman emperors used art and architecture as an arm of imperial propaganda.

HEAR MORE: Listen to an audio file of your chapter **www.myartslab.com**

THE ETRUSCANS

The boot-shaped Italian peninsula, shielded on the north by the Alps, juts into the Mediterranean Sea. At the end of the Bronze Age (about 1000 BCE), a central European people known as the Villanovans occupied the northern and western regions of the peninsula, while the central area was home to a variety of people who spoke a closely related group of Italic languages, Latin among them. Beginning in the eighth century BCE, Greeks established colonies on the mainland and in Sicily. From the seventh century BCE, people known as Etruscans, probably related to the Villanovans, gained control of the north and much of today's central Italy, an area known as Etruria. They reached the height of their power in the sixth century BCE, when they expanded into the Po River valley to the north and the Campania region to the south (MAP 6–1).

Etruscan wealth came from fertile soil and an abundance of metal ore. Both farmers and metalworkers, the Etruscans were also sailors and merchants, and they exploited their resources in trade with the Greeks and with other people of the eastern Mediterranean. Etruscan artists knew and drew inspiration from Greek and Near Eastern art, assimilating such influences to create a distinctive Etruscan style.

ETRUSCAN ARCHITECTURE

In architecture, the Etruscans established patterns of building that would be adopted later by the Romans. Cities were laid out on grid plans, like cities in Egypt and Greece, but with a difference: Two main streets—one usually running north–south and the other east–west—divided the city into quarters, with the town's business district centered at their intersection. We know something about Etruscan domestic architecture within these quarters, because they created house-shaped funerary urns and also decorated the interiors of tombs to resemble houses. Dwellings were designed around a central courtyard (or **atrium**) that was open to the sky, with a pool or cistern fed by rainwater.

Walls with protective gates and towers surrounded Etruscan cities. The third- to second-century BCE city gate of Perugia, called the **PORTA AUGUSTA**, is one of the few surviving examples of Etruscan monumental architecture (FIG. 6–2). A tunnel-like passageway between two huge towers, this gate is significant for anticipating the Roman use of the round arch, which is here extended to create a semicircular barrel vault over the passageway (see "The Roman Arch," page 172, and "Roman Vaulting," page 188). A square frame surmounted by a horizontal decorative element resembling an entablature sets off the entrance arch, which is accentuated by a molding. The decorative section is filled with a row of circular panels, or **roundels**, alternating with rectangular, columnlike upright strips called **pilasters** in an effect reminiscent of the Greek Doric frieze.

ETRUSCAN TEMPLES

The Etruscans incorporated Greek deities and heroes into their pantheon and, like the ancient Mesopotamians, used divination to predict future events. Beyond this and their burial practices (as

6-2 • PORTA AUGUSTA
Perugia, Italy. 3rd–2nd century BCE.

revealed by the findings in their tombs), we know little about their religious beliefs. Our knowledge of the appearance of Etruscan temples comes from the few remaining examples of foundations, from ceramic votive models, and from the later writings of the Roman architect Vitruvius.

Etruscans built their temples with mud-brick walls. The columns and entablatures were made of wood or a quarried volcanic rock called tufa, which hardens upon exposure to air. Sometime between 33 and 23 CE, Vitruvius compiled descriptions of the nature of Etruscan architecture (see "Roman Writers on Art," page 169). His account indicates that in certain ways Etruscan temples resembled Greek temples (FIG. 6–3). Etruscan builders also used

6-3 • RECONSTRUCTION OF AN ETRUSCAN TEMPLE
Based on archaeological evidence and descriptions by Vitruvius.
University of Rome, Istituto di Etruscologia e Antichità Italiche.

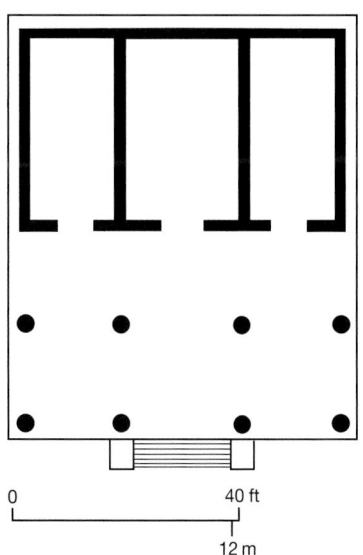

MAP 6-1 • THE ANCIENT ROMAN WORLD

This map shows the Roman Empire at its greatest extent, which was reached in 106 CE under the emperor Trajan.

6-4 • PLAN OF AN ETRUSCAN TEMPLE

Based on descriptions by Vitruvius.

post-and-lintel structure and gable roofs. The bases, column shafts, and capitals recall those of the earlier Doric or Ionic order, and the entablature resembles a Doric frieze. Vitruvius used the term "**Tuscan order**" to describe the characteristic Etruscan variation of the Doric order, with an unfluted shaft and simplified base, capital, and entablature (see "Roman Architectural Orders," page 163).

Like the Greeks, the Etruscans built their temples on a high platform positioned in a courtyard or a city square. However, they built a single flight of stairs leading to a columned porch on one short side of the rectangular temple rather than surrounding the temple uniformly on all sides with a stepped stereobate and peristyle colonnade, as was the practice in Greece (SEE FIGS. 5–9, 5–31). An approach to siting and orientation also constitutes an important difference from Greek temples, which were built toward the center of an enclosed, open precinct (SEE FIGS. 5–12, 5–29) rather than on the edge of a courtyard or public square. Also, there was an almost even division in Etruscan temples between porch and interior space (**FIG. 6–4**). Often this interior space was separated into three rooms that probably housed cult statues.

Although Etruscan temples were simple in form, they were embellished with dazzling displays of painting and terra-cotta sculpture. The temple roof, rather than the pediment, served as a base for large statue groups. Etruscan artists excelled at the imposing technical challenge of making huge terra-cotta figures for placement on temples. A splendid example is a life-size figure of **APOLLO (FIG. 6–5)**. To make such large clay sculptures, artists had to know how to construct figures so that they did not collapse under their own weight while the raw clay was still wet. They also had to regulate the kiln temperature during the long firing process. The names of some Etruscan terra-cotta artists have come down to us, including that of a sculptor from Veii (near Rome) called Vulca, in whose workshop this figure of Apollo may have been created.

Dating from about 510–500 BCE and originally part of a four-figure scene depicting one of the labors of Hercules, the Apollo comes from the temple dedicated to Minerva and other gods in the sanctuary of Portonaccio at Veii. Four figures on the temple's ridgepole (horizontal beam at the peak of the roof) depicted Apollo and Hercules fighting for possession of a deer sacred to Diana, while she and Mercury looked on. Apollo is shown striding forward boldly. To our eyes, he seems to have just stepped over the decorative scrolled element that helps support the sculpture.

Apollo's well-developed body and his "Archaic smile" clearly demonstrate that Etruscan sculptors were familiar with the kouroi of their Archaic Greek counterparts. But a comparison of the Apollo and a figure such as the Greek *Anavysos Kouros* (SEE FIG. 5–18) reveals telling differences. Unlike the Greek kouros, the body of the Etruscan Apollo is partially concealed by a rippling robe that cascades in knife-edged pleats to his knees. The forward-moving pose of the Etruscan statue also has a dynamic vigor that is avoided in the balanced, rigid stance of the Greek figure. This sense of energy expressed in purposeful movement is a defining characteristic of Etruscan sculpture and painting.

TOMB CHAMBERS

Like the Egyptians, the Etruscans seem to have conceived tombs as homes for the dead. The Etruscan cemetery of La Banditaccia at Cerveteri, in fact, was laid out like a small town, with "streets" running between the grave mounds. The tomb chambers were partially or entirely excavated below the ground, and some were hewn out of bedrock. They were roofed over, sometimes with corbel vaulting, and covered with dirt and stones.

Etruscan painters had a remarkable ability to suggest that their subjects inhabit a bright, tangible world just beyond the tomb walls. Brightly colored scenes of playing, feasting, dancing, hunting, fishing, and other leisure activities decorated the tomb walls. In a late sixth-century BCE tomb from Tarquinia, wall paintings show two boys spending a day in the country, surrounded by the graceful flights of brightly colored birds **(FIG. 6–6)**. The boy to the left is climbing a hillside up to the promontory of a cliff, soon to put aside his clothes and follow his naked companion, caught by the artist in mid-dive, plunging toward the water below. Such

6–5 • Master Sculptor Vulca (?) APOLLO
Temple of Minerva, Portonaccio, Veii. c. 510–500 BCE. Painted terra cotta, height 5′10″ (1.8 m). Museo Nazionale di Villa Giulia, Rome.

charming scenes of carefree diversions, removed from the routine demands of daily life, seem to promise a pleasurable post-mortem existence to the occupant of this tomb. But this diver could also symbolize the deceased's own plunge from life into death (see "The Tomb of the Diver," pages 122–123).

The Etruscans and Romans adapted Greek architectural orders (see "The Greek Orders," page 110) to their own tastes, often using them as applied decoration on walls. The Etruscans developed the **Tuscan order** by modifying the Doric order, adding a base under the shaft, which was often left unfluted. This system was subsequently adopted by the Romans. Later the Romans created the **Composite order** by combining the volutes of Greek Ionic capitals with the acanthus leaves from the Corinthian order. In this diagram, the two Roman orders are shown on pedestals, which consist of a **plinth**, a **dado**, and a cornice.

FAÇADE OF LIBRARY OF CELSUS, EPHESUS
Turkey, 135 CE. Detail showing capital, architrave, frieze, and cornice, conforming to the Composite order. Marble.

Tuscan order

Composite order

6-6 • BOYS CLIMBING ROCKS AND DIVING, TOMB OF HUNTING AND FISHING, TARQUINIA
Late 6th century BCE.

6-8 • BURIAL CHAMBER, TOMB OF THE RELIEFS

Cerveteri, Italy. 3rd century BCE.

6-9 • RECLINING COUPLE ON A SARCOPHAGUS FROM CERVETERI
c. 520 BCE. Terra cotta, length 6'7″ (2.06 m). Museo Nazionale di Villa Giulia, Rome.

Portrait sarcophagi like this one evolved from earlier terra-cotta cinerary urns with sculpted heads of the deceased whose ashes they held.

In a painted frieze in the **TOMB OF THE TRICLINIUM**, somewhat later but also from Tarquinia, the diversions are more mature in focus as young men and women frolic to the music of the lyre and 'double flute within a room whose ceiling is enlivened with colorful geometric decoration (**FIG. 6–7**). These dancers line the side walls, composed within a carefully arranged setting of stylized trees and birds, while at the end of the room couples recline on couches enjoying a banquet as cats prowl underneath the table looking for scraps. The immediacy of this wall painting is striking. Dancers and diners—women as well as men—are engaging in the joyful customs and diversions of human life as we know it.

Some tombs were carved out of the rock to resemble rooms in a house. The **TOMB OF THE RELIEFS**, for example, seems to have a flat ceiling supported by square stone posts (**FIG. 6–8**). Its walls were plastered and painted, and it was fully furnished. Couches were carved from stone, and other fittings were formed of stucco, a slow-drying type of plaster that can be easily molded and carved.

Simulated pots, jugs, robes, axes, and other items were molded and carved to look like real objects hanging on hooks. Could the animal rendered in low relief at the bottom of the post just left of center be the family pet?

The remains of the deceased were placed in urns or sarcophagi (coffins) made of clay or stone. On the terra-cotta **SARCOPHAGUS FROM CERVETERI**, dating from about 520 BCE (**FIG. 6–9**), a husband and wife are shown reclining comfortably on a dining couch. The smooth, lifelike forms of their upper bodies are vertical and square-shouldered, but their hips and extended legs seem to sink into the softness of the couch. Rather than a somber memorial to the dead, we encounter two lively individuals with alert eyes and warm smiles. The man once raised a drinking vessel, addressing the viewer with the lively and engaging gesture of a genial host, perhaps offering an invitation to dine with them for eternity or to join them in the sort of convivial festivities recorded in the paintings on the walls of Etruscan tombs.

6-10 • MARRIED COUPLE (LARTH TETNIES AND THANCHVIL TARNAI) EMBRACING
Lid of a sarcophagus. c. 350–300 BCE. Marble, length 7' (2.13 m). Museum of Fine Arts, Boston.

The lid of another Etruscan sarcophagus—slightly later in date and carved of marble rather than molded in clay—portrays another reclining Etruscan couple, but during a more private moment (FIG. 6–10). Dressed only in their jewelry and just partially sheathed by the light covering that clings to the forms of their bodies, this loving pair has been caught for eternity in a tender embrace, absorbed with each other rather than looking out to engage the viewer. The sculptor of this relief was clearly influenced by Greek Classicism in the rendering of human forms, but the human intimacy that is captured here is far removed from the cool, idealized detachment characterizing Greek funerary stelae (SEE FIG. 5–42).

WORKS IN BRONZE

The Etruscans developed special sophistication in casting and engraving on bronze. Some of the most extraordinary works were created for domestic use, including a group of surviving **cistae**—cylindrical containers used by wealthy women as cases for toiletry articles such as mirrors. Cistae were common wedding gifts for brides.

The richly decorated **FICORONI CISTA** (named after an eighteenth-century owner), dated to the second half of the fourth century BCE and found in Palestrina (FIG. 6–11), was made as a gift from a woman named Dindia Macolnia to her daughter. The artist Novios Plautios signed the precisely engraved drawings around the body of the container, accomplished while the bronze sheet was still flat, first by incising lines within the metal and then filling them with white material to make them stand out. The use of broad foliate and ornamental bands to frame the frieze of figural narrative recalls the practice of famous Greek ceramic painters like Euphronios (see "A Closer Look," page 119), and, like Greek pots, the most popular subjects for cistae were Greek myths. Here Novios has engraved sequential scenes drawn from an episode in the story of the Argonauts, sailors who sought water in the land of hostile King Amykos. The king would only give them water from his spring if they beat him in a boxing match. After the immortal Pollux defeated Amykos, the Argonauts tied the king to a tree, the episode highlighted on the side seen in FIG. 6–11.

The legs and handle of the cista were cast as separate pieces, attached during the assembly process. Figural groups attached to the top, such as the trio of Dionysus and two satyrs seen here, were common. The natural poses and individualization of these figures recalls the relaxed but lively naturalism we have already seen in Etruscan wall paintings.

Etruscan artists continued to be held in high regard by Roman patrons after the Etruscan cities fell to Rome. Since Etruscan bronze artists went to work for the Romans, distinguishing between Etruscan and early Roman art is often difficult. A head that was once part of a bronze statue of a man may be an example of an important Roman commission from an Etruscan artist (FIG. 6–12). Since it is over life size, this head may have been part of a commemorative work honoring a great man, and the downturned tilt of the head, as well as the flexing of the neck, have led many to propose that it was part of an equestrian figure. Traditionally dated to about 300 BCE, this rendering of a strong, broad face with heavy brows, hawk nose, firmly set lips, and clear-eyed expression is scrupulously detailed. The commanding, deep-set eyes are created with ivory inlay, within which float irises created of glass paste within a ring of bronze. The

6–11 • Novios Plautios THE FICORONI CISTA
350–300 BCE. Bronze, height 2′6¼″ (78.6 cm). Museo Nazionale di Villa Giulia, Rome.

It is possible that artist Novios Plautios' source for the scene he engraved on this cista was a monumental, mid-4th-century BCE Greek painting of the Argonauts by Kydias that seems to have been exhibited in Rome during this time. This may be why Novios tells us in his inscribed signature that he executed this work in Rome.

lifelike effect is further enhanced by added eyelashes of separately cut pieces of bronze. This work is often associated with a set of male virtues that would continue to be revered by the Romans: stern seriousness, strength of character, the age-worn appearance of a life well lived, and the wisdom and sense of purpose it confers.

Etruscan art and architectural forms left an indelible stamp on the art and architecture of early Rome that was rivaled only by the influence of Greece. By 88 BCE, when the Etruscans were granted Roman citizenship, their art had already been absorbed into that of Rome.

THE ROMANS

At the same time that the Etruscan civilization was flourishing, the Latin-speaking inhabitants of Rome began to develop into a formidable power. For a time, kings of Etruscan lineage ruled them, but in 509 BCE the Romans overthrew them and formed a republic centered in Rome. The Etruscans themselves were absorbed by the Roman Republic at the end of the third century BCE, by which time Rome had steadily expanded its territory in many directions. The Romans unified what is now Italy and, after defeating their rival, the North African city-state of Carthage, they established an empire that encompassed the entire Mediterranean region (SEE MAP 6–1).

At its greatest extent, in the early second century CE, the Roman Empire reached from the Euphrates River, in southwest Asia, to Scotland. It ringed the Mediterranean Sea—*mare nostrum*, or "our sea," the Romans called it. Those who were conquered by the Romans gradually assimilated Roman legal, administrative, and cultural structures that endured for some five centuries—and in the eastern Mediterranean until the fifteenth century CE—and left a lasting mark on the civilizations that emerged in Europe.

ORIGINS OF ROME

The Romans saw themselves as descendents of heroic ancestors. Two popular legends told the story of Rome's founding. One focused on Romulus and Remus, twin sons of the god Mars and a mortal woman, who were abandoned on the banks of the Tiber River and discovered by a she-wolf, who nursed them as her own pups. When they reached adulthood, the twins built a city near the place of their rescue. The other story of Rome's founding is part of Virgil's *Aeneid*, where the poet claims the Roman people to be descendants of Aeneas, a Trojan who was the mortal son of Venus. Aeneas and some companions escaped from Troy and made their way to the Italian peninsula. Their sons were the Romans, the people who in fulfillment of a promise by Jupiter to Venus were destined to rule the world.

Roman Writers on Art

Only one book devoted specifically to architecture and the arts survives from antiquity. All our other written sources consist of digressions and insertions in works on other subjects. That one book, the Ten Books on Architecture by Vitruvius (c. 80–c. 15 BCE), however, is invaluable. Written for Augustus in the first century BCE, it is a practical handbook for builders that discusses such things as laying out cities, siting buildings, and using the Greek architectural orders. Vitruvius argued for appropriateness and rationality in architecture, and he also made significant contributions to art theory, including studies on proportion.

Pliny the Elder (c. 23–79 CE) wrote a vast encyclopedia of "facts, histories, and observations" known as *Naturalis Historia* (*The Natural History*) that often included discussions of art and architecture. Pliny occasionally used works of art to make his points—for example, citing sculpture within his essays on stone and metals. Pliny's scientific turn of mind led to his death, for he was overcome while observing the eruption of Mount Vesuvius that buried Pompeii. His nephew, Pliny the Younger (c. 61–113 CE), a voluminous letter writer, added to our knowledge of Roman domestic architecture with his meticulous descriptions of villas and gardens.

Valuable bits of information can also be found in books by travelers and historians. Pausanias, a second-century CE Greek traveler, wrote descriptions that are basic sources on Greek art and artists. Flavius Josephus (c. 37–100 CE), a historian of the Flavians, wrote in his Jewish Wars a description of the triumph of Titus that includes the treasures looted from the Temple of Solomon in Jerusalem (SEE FIG. 6–33).

EXPLORE MORE: Gain insight from primary sources by Roman writers **www.myartslab.com**

Archaeologists and historians present a more mundane picture of Rome's origins. In Neolithic times, people settled in permanent villages on the plains of Latium, south of the Tiber River, and on the Palatine, one of the seven hills that would eventually become the city of Rome. By the sixth century BCE, these modest towns had become a major transportation hub and trading center.

ROMAN RELIGION

The Romans assimilated Greek gods, myths, religious beliefs and practices into their state religion. They also deified their emperors. Worship of ancient gods mingled with homage to past rulers, and oaths of allegiance to the living ruler made the official religion a political duty. Religious worship became increasingly ritualized, perfunctory, and distant from the everyday life of most people.

Many Romans adopted the so-called mystery religions of the people they had conquered. Worship of Isis and Osiris from Egypt, Cybele (the Great Mother) from Anatolia, the hero-god Mithras from Persia, and the single, all-powerful God of Judaism and Christianity from Palestine challenged the Roman establishment. These unauthorized religions flourished alongside the state religion, with its Olympian deities and deified emperors, despite occasional government efforts to suppress them.

THE REPUBLIC, 509–27 BCE

Early Rome was governed by kings and an advisory body of leading citizens called the Senate. The population was divided into two classes: a wealthy and powerful upper class, the patricians, and a lower class, the plebeians. In 509 BCE, Romans overthrew the last Etruscan king and established the Roman Republic as an oligarchy, a government by the aristocrats that would last about 450 years.

As a result of its stable form of government, and especially of its encouragement of military conquest, by 275 BCE Rome controlled the entire Italian peninsula. By 146 BCE, Rome had defeated its great rival, Carthage, on the north coast of Africa, and taken control of the western Mediterranean. By the mid second century BCE, Rome had taken Macedonia and Greece, and by 44 BCE, it had conquered most of Gaul (present-day France) as well as the eastern Mediterranean (SEE MAP 6–1). Egypt remained independent until Octavian defeated Mark Antony and Cleopatra at the Battle of Actium in 31 BCE.

During the Republic, Roman art was rooted in its Etruscan heritage, but territorial expansion brought wider exposure to the arts of other cultures. Like the Etruscans, the Romans admired Greek art. As Horace wrote (*Epistulae* II, 1): "Captive Greece conquered her savage conquerors and brought the arts to rustic Latium." The Romans used Greek designs and Greek orders in their architecture, imported Greek art, and employed Greek artists. In 146 BCE, for example, they stripped the Greek city of Corinth of its art treasures and shipped them back to Rome.

PORTRAIT SCULPTURE

Portrait sculptors of the Republican period sought to create lifelike images based on careful observation of their subjects, objectives that were related to the Romans' veneration of their ancestors and the making and public display of death masks of deceased relatives (see "Roman Portraiture," page 170).

Roman Portraiture

The strong emphasis on portraiture in Roman art may stem from the early practice of creating likenesses—in some cases actual wax death masks—of revered figures and distinguished ancestors for display on public occasions, most notably funerals. Contemporary historians have left colorful evocations of this distinctively Roman custom. Polybius, a Greek exiled to Rome in the middle of the second century BCE, wrote home with the following description:

> … after the interment [of the illustrious man] and the performance of the usual ceremonies, they place the image of the departed in the most conspicuous position in the house, enclosed in a wooden shrine. This image is a mask reproducing with remarkable fidelity both the features and the complexion of the deceased. On the occasion of public sacrifices, they display these images, and decorate them with much care, and when any distinguished member of the family dies they take them to the funeral, putting them on men who seem to bear the closest resemblance to the original in stature and carriage.… There could not easily be a more ennobling spectacle for a young man who aspires to fame and virtue. For who would not be inspired by the sight of the images of men renowned for their excellence, all together and as if alive and breathing?… By this means, by the constant renewal of the good report of brave men, the celebrity of those who performed noble deeds is rendered immortal, while at the same time the fame of those who did good services to their country becomes known to the people and a heritage for future generations. (The Histories, VII, 53, 54, trans. W. R. Paton, Loeb Library ed.)

Growing out of this heritage, Roman Republican portraiture is frequently associated with the notion of **verism**—an interest in the faithful reproduction of the immediate visual and tactile appearance of subjects. Since we find in these portrait busts the same sorts of individualizing physiognomic features that allow us to differentiate among the people we know in our own world, it is easy to assume that they are exact likenesses of their subjects as they appeared during their lifetime. Of course, this is impossible to verify, but our strong desire to believe it must realize the intentions of the artists who made these portraits and the patrons for whom they were made.

A life-size marble statue of a Roman patrician shown here, dating from the period of the Emperor Augustus, reflects the practices documented much earlier by Polybius and links the man portrayed with a revered tradition and its laudatory associations. The large marble format emulates a Greek notion of sculpture, and its use here signals not only this man's wealth but also his sophisticated artistic tastes, characteristics he shared with the emperor himself. His toga, however, is not Greek but indigenous and signifies his respectability as a Roman citizen of some standing. The busts of ancestors that he holds in his hands document his distinguished lineage in the privileged upper class—laws regulated which members of society could own such collections—and the statue as a whole proclaims his adherence to the family tradition by having his own portrait created.

PATRICIAN CARRYING PORTRAIT BUSTS OF TWO ANCESTORS (BARBERINI TOGATUS)
End of 1st century BCE or beginning of 1st century CE.
Marble, height 5′5″ (1.65 m). Palazzo de Conservatori, Rome.

The head of this standing figure, though ancient Roman in origin, is a later replacement and not original to this statue. The separation of head and body in this work is understandable since in many instances the bodies of full-length portraits were produced in advance, waiting in the sculptor's workshop for a patron to commission a head with his or her own likeness that could be attached to it. Presumably the busts carried by this patrician were likewise only blocked out until they could be carved with the faces of the commissioner's ancestors. These faces share a striking family resemblance, and the stylistic difference reproduced in the two distinct bust formats reveals that these men lived in successive generations. They could be the father and grandfather of the man who carries them.

6–13 • PORTRAIT HEAD OF AN ELDER
c. 80 BCE. Marble, life size. Metropolitan
Museum of Art, New York.

Perhaps growing out of this early tradition of maintaining images of ancestors as death masks, a new Roman artistic ideal emerged during the Republican period in relation to portrait sculpture, an ideal quite different from the one we encountered in Greek Classicism. Instead of generalizing a human face, smoothed of its imperfections and caught in a moment of detached abstraction, this new Roman idealization emphasized—rather than suppressed—the hallmarks of advanced age and the distinguishing aspects of individual likenesses. This mode is most prominent in bust portraits of Roman patricians (**FIG. 6–13**), whose time-worn faces embody the wisdom and experience that come with old age. Frequently we take these portraits of wrinkled elders at face value, as highly realistic and faithful descriptions of actual human beings—contrasting Roman realism with Greek idealism—but there is good reason to think that these portraits actually conform to a particularly Roman type of idealization that underscores the effects of aging on the human face.

THE ORATOR. The life-size bronze portrait of **AULUS METELLUS**—the Roman official's name is inscribed on the hem of his garment in Etruscan letters (**FIG. 6–14**)—dates to about 80

BCE. The statue, known from early times as *The Orator*, depicts a man addressing a gathering, his arm outstretched and slightly raised, a pose expressive of rhetorical persuasiveness. The orator wears sturdy laced leather boots and a folded and draped toga, the characteristic garment of a Roman senator. According to Pliny the Elder, large statues like this were often placed atop columns as memorials. It could also have been mounted on an inscribed base in a public space by officials grateful for Aulus' benefactions on behalf of their city.

6–14 • AULUS METELLUS (THE ORATOR)
Found near Perugia. c. 80 BCE. Bronze, height 5′11″ (1.8 m).
Museo Archeològico Nazionale, Florence.

The round arch was not an Etruscan or Roman invention, but the Etruscans and Romans were the first to make widespread use of it (SEE FIG. 6–2)—both as an effective structural idea and an elegant design motif.

Round arches displace most of their weight, or downward **thrust** (see arrows on diagram), along their curving sides, transmitting that weight to adjacent supporting uprights (door or window jambs, columns, or piers). From there, the thrust goes to, and is supported by, the ground. To create an arch, brick or cut stones are formed into a curve by fitting together wedge-shaped pieces, called **voussoirs**, until they meet and are locked together at the top center by the final piece, called the **keystone**. These voussoirs exert an outward as well as a downward thrust, so arches may require added support, called **buttressing**, from adjacent masonry elements.

Until the keystone is in place and the mortar between the bricks or stones dries, an arch is held in place by wooden scaffolding called **centering**. The points from which the curves of the arch rise, called **springings**, are often reinforced by masonry imposts. The wall areas adjacent to the curves of the arch are **spandrels**. In a succession of arches, called an **arcade**, the space encompassed by each arch and its supports is called a **bay**.

PONT DU GARD
Nîmes, France. Late 1st century BCE. Height above river 160′ (49 m), width of road bed on lower arcade 20′ (6 m).

A stunning example of the early Roman use of the round arch is a bridge known as the Pont du Gard, part of an aqueduct located near Nîmes, in southern France. An ample water supply was essential for a city, and the Roman invention to supply this water was the aqueduct, built with arcades—a linear series of arches. This aqueduct brought water from springs 30 miles to the north using a simple gravity flow, and it provided 100 gallons a day for every person in Nîmes. Each arch buttresses its neighbors and the huge arcade ends solidly in the hillsides. The structure conveys the balance, proportions, and rhythmic harmony of a great work of art, and although it harmonizes with its natural setting, it also makes a powerful statement about Rome's ability to control nature in order to provide for its cities. Both structure and function are marks of Roman civilization.

SEE MORE: View a simulation of the arch www.myartslab.com

THE DENARIUS OF JULIUS CAESAR. The propaganda value of portraits was not lost on Roman leaders. In 44 BCE, Julius Caesar issued a denarius (a widely circulated coin) bearing his portrait **(FIG. 6–15)** conforming to the Roman ideal of advanced age. He was the first Roman leader to place his own image on a coin, initiating a practice that would be adopted by his successors, but at the time when this coin was minted, it smacked of the sort of megalomaniacal behavior that would ultimately lead to his assassination. Perhaps it is for this reason that Caesar underscores his age, and thus his old-fashioned respectability, in this portrait, which reads as a mark of his traditionalism as a senator. But the inscription placed around his head—CAESAR DICT PERPETUE, or "Caesar, dictator forever"—certainly contradicts the ideal embodied in the portrait.

ROMAN TEMPLES

Architecture during the Roman Republic reflected both Etruscan and Greek practices. Like the Etruscans, the Romans built urban temples in commercial centers as well as in special sanctuaries. An early example is a small rectangular temple standing on a raised platform, or podium, beside the Tiber River in Rome **(FIG. 6–16)**, probably from the second century BCE and perhaps dedicated to Portunus, the god of harbors and ports. This temple uses the Etruscan system of a rectangular cella and a front porch at one end reached by a broad, inviting flight of steps, but the Roman architects have adopted the Greek Ionic order, with full columns on the porch and half-columns **engaged** (set into the wall) around

6–15 • DENARIUS WITH PORTRAIT OF JULIUS CAESAR
44 BCE. Silver, diameter approximately ¾″ (1.9 cm).
American Numismatic Society, New York.

the exterior walls of the cella **(FIG. 6–17)** and a continuous frieze in the entablature. The overall effect resembles a Greek temple, but there are two major differences. First, Roman architects liberated the form of the column from its post-and-lintel structural roots and engaged it onto the surface of the wall as a decorative feature. Second, while a Greek temple encourages viewers to walk around

6-16 • TEMPLE, PERHAPS DEDICATED TO PORTUNUS
Forum Boarium (Cattle Market), Rome. Late 2nd century BCE.

SEE MORE: Click the Google Earth link for the Temple of Portunus
www.myartslab.com

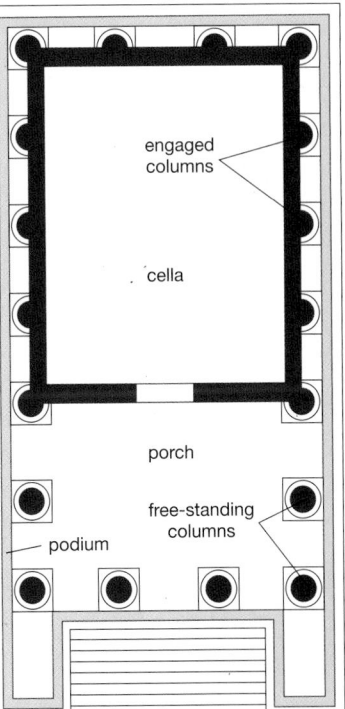

6-17 • PLAN OF TEMPLE
Forum Boarium (Cattle Market), Rome.

engaged columns

cella

porch

free-standing columns

podium

the building and explore its uniformly articulated sculptural mass, Roman temples are defined in relation to interior spaces, which visitors are invited to enter through one opening along the longitudinal axis of a symmetrical plan.

By the first century BCE, nearly a million people lived in Rome, which had evolved into the capital of a formidable commercial and political power with a growing overseas empire. As long as Republican Rome was essentially a large city-state, its form of government—an oligarchy under the control of a Senate— remained feasible. But as the empire around it grew larger and larger, a government of competing senators and military commanders could not enforce taxation and maintain order in what was becoming a vast and complicated territorial expanse. As governance of the Republic began to fail, power became concentrated in fewer and fewer leaders, until it was ruled by one man, an emperor, rather than by the Senate.

THE EARLY EMPIRE, 27 BCE–96 CE

The first Roman emperor was born Octavian in 63 BCE. When he was only 18 years old, his brilliant great-uncle, Julius Caesar, adopted him as son and heir, recognizing in him qualities that would make him a worthy successor. Shortly after Julius Caesar refused the Senate's offer of the imperial crown, early in 44 BCE, he was murdered by a group of conspirators, and the 19-year-old Octavian stepped up. Over the next 17 spectacular years, as general, politician, statesman, and public-relations genius, Octavian vanquished warring internal factions and brought peace to fractious provinces. By 27 BCE, the Senate had conferred on him the title of Augustus (meaning "exalted," "sacred"). Assisted by his astute and pragmatic second wife, Livia, Augustus led the state and the empire for 45 years. He established efficient rule and laid the foundation for an extended period of stability, domestic peace, and economic prosperity known as the *Pax Romana* ("Roman Peace"), which lasted over 200 years (27 BCE to 180 CE). In 12 CE, two years before his death, he was given the title Pontifex Maximus ("High Priest"), becoming the empire's highest religious official as well as its political leader.

Conquering and maintaining a vast empire required not only the inspired leadership and tactics of Augustus, but also careful planning, massive logistical support, and great administrative skill. Some of Rome's most enduring contributions to Western civilization reflect these qualities—its system of law, its governmental and administrative structures, and its sophisticated civil engineering and architecture.

To facilitate the development and administration of the empire, as well as to make city life comfortable and attractive to its citizens, the Roman state undertook building programs of unprecedented scale and complexity, mandating the construction of central administrative and legal centers (forums and basilicas), recreational facilities (racetracks, stadiums), temples, markets, theaters, public baths, aqueducts, middle-class housing, and even entire new towns. To accomplish these tasks without sacrificing

beauty, efficiency, and human well-being, Roman builders and architects developed rational plans using easily worked but durable materials and highly sophisticated engineering methods.

To move their armies about efficiently, to speed communications between Rome and the farthest reaches of the empire, and to promote commerce, the Romans built a vast and complex network of roads and bridges. Many modern European highways still follow the lines laid down by Roman engineers, some Roman bridges are still in use, and Roman-era foundations underlie the streets of many cities.

ART IN THE AGE OF AUGUSTUS

Roman artists of the Augustan age created a new style—a new Roman form of idealism that, though still grounded in the appearance of the everyday world, is heavily influenced by a revival of Greek Classical ideals. They enriched the art of portraiture in both official images and representations of private individuals, they recorded contemporary historical events on public monuments, and they contributed unabashedly to Roman imperial propaganda.

AUGUSTUS OF PRIMAPORTA.　In the sculpture known as **AUGUSTUS OF PRIMAPORTA** (FIG. 6–18)—because it was discovered in Livia's villa at Primaporta, near Rome—we see the emperor as he wanted to be seen and remembered. This work demonstrates the creative combination of earlier sculptural traditions that is a hallmark of Augustan art. In its idealization of a specific ruler and his prowess, the sculpture also illustrates the way Roman emperors would continue to use portraiture for propaganda.

The sculptor of this larger-than-life marble statue adapted the standard pose of a Roman orator (SEE FIG. 6–14) by melding it with the contrapposto and canonical proportions developed by the Greek High Classical sculptor Polykleitos, as exemplified by his *Spear Bearer* (see "The Canon of Polykleitos," page 134). Like the heroic Greek figure, Augustus' portrait captures him in the physical prime of youth, far removed from the image of advanced age idealized in the coin portrait of Julius Caesar. Although Augustus lived to age 70, in his portraits he is always a vigorous ruler, eternally young. But like Caesar, and unlike the *Spear Bearer*, Augustus' face is rendered with the kind of details that make this portrait an easily recognizable likeness.

To this combination of Greek and Roman traditions, the sculptor of the *Augustus of Primaporta* added mythological and historical imagery that exalts Augustus' family and celebrates his accomplishments. Cupid, son of the goddess Venus, rides a dolphin next to the emperor's right leg, a reference to the claim of the emperor's family, the Julians, to descent from the goddess Venus through her human son Aeneas. Augustus' anatomically conceived cuirass (torso armor) is also covered with figural imagery. Mid-torso is a scene representing Augustus' 20 BCE diplomatic victory over the Parthians; a Parthian (on the right) returns a Roman military standard to a figure variously identified as a Roman soldier or the goddess Roma. Looming above this scene at the top of the cuirass is a celestial deity who holds an arched canopy, implying that the peace signified by the scene below has cosmic implications. The personification of the earth at the bottom of the cuirass holds an overflowing cornucopia, representing the prosperity that peace brings.

Another Augustan monument that synthesizes Roman traditions and Greek Classical influence to express the peace and prosperity that Augustus brought to Rome is the **ARA PACIS AUGUSTAE** (see "The Ara Pacis Augustae," page 176– 177). The processional friezes on the exterior sides of the enclosure wall clearly reflect Classical Greek works like the Ionic frieze of the Parthenon (SEE FIG. 5–35), with their three-dimensional figures wrapped in revealing draperies that also create patterns of rippling folds. But unlike the Greek sculptors who created an unspecific, and thus timeless, procession for the Parthenon, the Roman sculptors of the Ara Pacis depicted actual individuals participating in a specific event at a known time. The Classical style may evoke the general notion of a Golden Age, but the historical references and identifiable figures in the Ara Pacis procession associate that Golden Age specifically with Augustus and his dynasty.

6-18 • AUGUSTUS OF PRIMAPORTA
Early 1st century CE. Perhaps a copy of a bronze statue of c. 20 BCE. Marble, originally colored, height 6′8″ (2.03 m). Musei Vaticani, Braccio Nuovo, Rome.

The Ara Pacis Augustae

A. ARA PACIS AUGUSTAE (ALTAR OF AUGUSTAN PEACE)
Rome. 13–9 BCE. Marble, approx. 34'5" × 38' (10.5 × 11.6 m). View of west side.

This monument was begun when Augustus was 50 (in 13 BCE) and was dedicated on Livia's 50th birthday (9 BCE).

One of the most extraordinary surviving Roman monuments from the time of Augustus is the Ara Pacis Augustae, or Altar of Augustan Peace (FIG. A), begun in 13 BCE and dedicated in 9 BCE, on the occasion of Augustus' triumphal return to the capital after three years spent establishing Roman rule in Gaul and Hispania. In its original location in the Campus Martius (Plain of Mars), the Ara Pacis was aligned with a giant sundial, marked out on the pavement with lines and bronze inscriptions, using as its pointer an Egyptian obelisk that Augustus had earlier brought from Heliopolis to signify Roman dominion over this ancient land.

The Ara Pacis itself consists of a walled rectangular enclosure surrounding an open-air altar, emulating Greek custom. Made entirely of marble panels carved with elaborate sculpture, the monument

presented powerful propaganda, uniting portraiture and allegory, religion and politics, the private and the public. On the inner walls, foliate garlands are suspended in swags from ox skulls. The skulls symbolize sacrificial offerings at the altar during annual commemorations, and the garlands— including fruits and flowers from every season—signify the continuing peace and prosperity that Augustus brought to the Roman world.

On the exterior, this theme of natural prosperity continues in lower reliefs of lavish, scrolling acanthus populated by animals. Above them, decorative allegory gives way to figural tableaux. On the front and back are framed allegorical scenes evoking the mythical history of Rome and the divine ancestry of Augustus. The longer sides portray two continuous processions,

seemingly representing actual historical events rather than myth or allegory. Perhaps they document Augustus' triumphal return, or they could memorialize the dedication and first sacrifice performed by Augustus on the completed altar itself. In any event, the arrangement of the participants is emblematic of the fundamental dualism characterizing Roman rule under Augustus. On one side march members of the Senate, a stately line of male elders. But on the other process Augustus' imperial family (FIG. B)— men, women, and notably children, who stand in the foreground as Augustus' hopes for dynastic succession. Whereas most of the adults maintain their focus on the ceremonial event, the imperial children are allowed to fidget, look at their cousins, or reach up to find comfort in holding the hands or tugging at the garments of the

B. IMPERIAL PROCESSION
Detail of a relief on the south side of the Ara Pacis. Height 5′2″ (1.6 m).

The figures in this frieze represent members of Augustus' extended family, and scholars have proposed some specific identifications. The middle-aged man with the shrouded head at the far left may be Marcus Agrippa, who would have been Augustus' successor had he not predeceased him in 12 CE. The bored but well-behaved youngster pulling at Agrippa's robe—and being restrained gently by the hand of the man behind him—is probably Agrippa's son Gaius Caesar. The heavily swathed woman next to Agrippa on the right may be Augustus' wife, Livia, followed by Tiberius, who would become the next emperor. Behind Tiberius could be Antonia, the niece of Augustus, looking back at her husband, Drusus, Livia's younger son. She may grasp the hand of Germanicus, one of her younger children. The depiction of children and real women in an official relief was new to the Augustan period and reflects Augustus' desire to promote private family life as well as to emphasize his potential heirs.

adults around them, one of whom puts her finger to her mouth in a shushing gesture, perhaps seeking to mitigate their distracting behavior. The lifelike aura brought by such anecdotal details underlines the earthborn reality of the ideology embodied here. Rome is now subject to the imperial rule of the family of Augustus, and this stable system will bring continuing peace and prosperity since his successors have already been born.

The Ara Pacis did not survive from antiquity in the form we see today. The monument eventually fell into disuse, ultimately into ruin. Remains were first discovered in 1568, but complete excavation took place only in 1937–1938, under the supervision of archaeologist Giuseppe Moretti, sponsored by dictator Benito Mussolini, who was fueled by his own ideological objectives. Once the monument had been unearthed, Mussolini had it reconstructed and commissioned a special building to house it, close to the **Mausoleum** of Augustus (a mausoleum is a monumental tomb), all in preparation for celebrating the 2,000th anniversary of the birth of Augustus and associating the Roman imperial past with Mussolini's fascist state. The dictator even planned his own burial within Augustus' mausoleum.

More recently, the City of Rome commissioned American architect Richard Meier to design a new setting for the Ara Pacis, this time within a sleek, white box with huge walls of glass that allow natural light to flood the exhibition space (seen in fig. A). Many Italian critics decried the Modernist design of Meier's building— completed in 2006—but this recent urban renewal project focused on the Ara Pacis has certainly revived interest in one of the most precious remains of Augustan Rome.

C. RECONSTRUCTION DRAWING OF THE ARA PACIS AUGUSTAE

THE JULIO-CLAUDIANS

After his death in 14 CE, Augustus was deified by decree of the Roman Senate. Augustus's successor was his stepson Tiberius (r. 14–37 CE), and in acknowledgment of the lineage of both—Augustus from Julius Caesar and Tiberius from his father, Tiberius Claudius Nero, Livia's first husband—the dynasty is known as the Julio-Claudian (14–68 CE). It ended with the death of Nero in 68 CE.

Exquisite skill characterizes the arts of the first century CE. A large onyx **cameo** (a gemstone carved in low relief) known as the **GEMMA AUGUSTEA** glorifies Augustus as triumphant over **barbarians** (a label for foreigners that the Romans adopted from the Greeks) and as the deified emperor (**FIG. 6–19**). The emperor, crowned with a victor's wreath, sits at the center right of the upper register. He has assumed the pose and identity of Jupiter, the king of the gods; an eagle, sacred to Jupiter, stands at his feet. Sitting next to him is a personification of Rome that seems to have Livia's features. The sea goat in the roundel between them may represent Capricorn, the emperor's zodiac sign.

Tiberius, as the adopted son of Augustus, steps out of a chariot at far left, returning victorious from the German front and prepared to assume the imperial throne as Augustus's chosen heir. Below this realm of godlike rulers, Roman soldiers are raising a post or standard on which armor captured from the defeated enemy is displayed as a trophy. The cowering, shackled barbarians on the bottom right wait to be tied to it. The artist of the *Gemma Augustea* brilliantly combines idealized, heroic figures based on Classical Greek art with recognizable Roman portraits, the dramatic action of Hellenistic art with Roman attention to descriptive detail and historical specificity.

ROMAN CITIES AND THE ROMAN HOME

In good times and bad, individual Romans—like people everywhere at any time—tried to live a decent or even comfortable life with adequate shelter, food, and clothing. The Romans loved to have contact with the natural world. The middle classes enjoyed their gardens, wealthy city dwellers maintained rural estates, and Roman emperors had country villas that were both functioning farms and places of recreation. Wealthy Romans even brought nature indoors by commissioning artists to paint landscapes on the interior walls of their homes. Through the efforts of the modern archaeologists who have excavated them, Roman cities and towns, houses, apartments, and country villas still evoke for us the ancient Roman way of life with amazing clarity.

ROMAN CITIES. Roman architects who designed new cities or who expanded and rebuilt existing ones based the urban plan on the layout of Roman army camps. Like Etruscan towns, they were laid out in a grid with two bisecting main streets crossed at right angles to divide the layout into quarters. The **forum** and other public buildings were located at this intersection, where the commander's headquarters was placed in a military camp.

Much of the housing in a Roman city consisted of brick apartment blocks called *insulae*. These apartment buildings had internal courtyards, multiple floors joined by narrow staircases, and occasionally overhanging balconies. City dwellers—then as now—were social creatures who spent much of their lives in public markets, squares, theaters, baths, and neighborhood bars. The city dweller returned to the *insulae* to sleep, perhaps to eat. Even women enjoyed a public life outside the home—a marked contrast to the circumscribed lives of Greek women.

The affluent southern Italian city of Pompeii, a thriving center of between 10,000 and 20,000 inhabitants, gives a vivid picture of Roman city life. In 79 CE Mount Vesuvius erupted, burying the city under more than 20 feet of volcanic ash and preserving it until its rediscovery and excavation, beginning in the eighteenth century (**FIGS. 6–20, 6–21**). Temples and government buildings surrounded a main square, or forum; shops and houses lined

6-19 • GEMMA AUGUSTEA
Early 1st century CE. Onyx, 7½ × 9″ (19 × 23 cm). Kunsthistorisches Museum, Vienna.

6-20 • AERIAL VIEW OF THE RUINS OF POMPEII
Destroyed 79 CE.

SEE MORE: See a video about Pompeii
www.myartslab.com

House of
the Vettii

baths

market

forum

sea gate

theater

6-21 • RECONSTRUCTION DRAWING OF POMPEII

6-22 • PLAN AND RECONSTRUCTION DRAWING, HOUSE OF THE SILVER WEDDING
Pompeii. 1st century CE.

cubicula
dining room
peristyle courtyard
cubicula
pool
vestibule
atrium

mostly straight, paved streets; and a protective wall enclosed the heart of the city. The forum was the center of civic life in Roman cities, as the agora was in Greek cities. Business was conducted in its basilicas and porticos, religious duties performed in its temples, and speeches delivered in its open square. For recreation, people went to the nearby baths or to events in the theater or amphitheater.

ROMAN HOUSES. City dwellers lived in houses, and even gracious private residences with gardens often had shops in front of them facing the street. The Romans emphasized the interior rather than the exterior in their domestic architecture.

A Roman house usually consisted of small rooms laid out around one or two open courts, the atrium and the peristyle (**FIG. 6–22**). People entered the house through a vestibule and stepped into the atrium, a large space with a pool or cistern for catching rainwater. The peristyle was a planted courtyard, further into the house, enclosed by columns. Off the peristyle was the formal reception room or office called the tablinum, and here the head of the household conferred with clients. Portrait busts of the family's ancestors might be displayed in the tablinum or in the atrium. The private areas—such as the family dining and sitting rooms, as well as bedrooms (cubicula)—and service areas—such as the kitchen and servants' quarters—could be arranged around the peristyle or the atrium. In Pompeii, where the mild southern climate permitted gardens to flourish year-round, the peristyle was often turned into an outdoor living room with painted walls, fountains, and

6-23 • PERISTYLE GARDEN, HOUSE OF THE VETTII
Pompeii. Rebuilt 62–79 CE.

sculpture, as in the mid first-century CE remodeling of the second-century BCE **HOUSE OF THE VETTII** (**FIG. 6–23**). Since Roman houses were designed in relation to a long axis that runs from the entrance straight through the atrium and into the peristyle, visitors were greeted at the door of the house with a deep vista, showcasing the lavish residence of their host and its beautifully designed and planted gardens extending into the distance.

Little was known about these gardens until archaeologist Wilhelmina Jashemski began the excavation of the peristyle in the House of G. Polybius in Pompeii in 1973. Earlier archaeologists had usually ignored, or unwittingly destroyed, evidence of gardens, but Jashemski developed a new way to find and analyze the layout and the plants cultivated in them. Workers first removed layers of debris and volcanic material to expose the level of the soil as it was before the eruption in 79 CE. They then collected samples of pollen, seeds, and other organic material and carefully injected plaster into underground root cavities. When the surrounding earth was removed, the roots, now in plaster, enabled botanists to identify the types of plants and trees cultivated in the garden and to estimate their size.

The garden in the house of Polybius was surrounded on three sides by a portico, which protected a large cistern on one side that supplied the house and garden with water. Young lemon trees in pots lined the fourth side of the garden, and nail holes in the wall above the pots indicated that the trees had been espaliered—pruned and trained to grow flat against a support—a practice still in use today. Fig, cherry, and pear trees filled the garden space, and traces of a fruit-picking ladder, wide at the bottom and narrow at the top to fit among the branches, was found on the site.

An aqueduct built during the reign of Augustus eliminated Pompeii's dependence on wells and rainwater basins and allowed residents to add pools, fountains, and flowering plants that needed heavy watering to their gardens. In contrast to earlier, unordered plantings, formal gardens with low, clipped borders and plantings of ivy, ornamental boxwood, laurel, myrtle, acanthus, and rosemary—all mentioned by writers of the time—became fashionable. There is also evidence of topiary work, the clipping of shrubs and hedges into fanciful shapes. Sculpture and purely decorative fountains became popular. The peristyle garden of the House of the Vettii, for example, had more than a dozen fountain statues jetting water into marble basins (SEE FIG. 6–23). In the most elegant peristyles, mosaic decorations covered the floors, walls, and even the fountains.

WALL PAINTING

The interior walls of Roman houses were plain, smooth plaster surfaces with few architectural moldings or projections. On these invitingly blank fields, artists painted decorations. Some used mosaic, but most employed pigment suspended in a water-based solution of lime and soap, sometimes with a little wax. After such paintings were finished, they were polished with a special metal, glass, or stone burnisher and then buffed with a cloth. Many fine wall paintings have come to light through excavations, first in Pompeii and other communities surrounding Mount Vesuvius, near Naples, and more recently in and around Rome.

HOUSE OF THE VETTII. Some of the finest surviving Roman wall paintings are found in the Pompeian House of the Vettii, whose peristyle garden we have already explored (SEE FIG. 6–23). The house was built in conformity to the axial house plan—with entrance leading through atrium to peristyle garden (**FIG. 6–24**)—by two brothers, wealthy freed slaves A. Vettius Conviva

6-24 • PLAN, HOUSE OF THE VETTII
Pompeii. Rebuilt 62–79 CE.

6-25 • WALL PAINTING IN THE "IXION ROOM," HOUSE OF THE VETTII
Pompeii. Rebuilt 62–79 CE.

and A. Vettius Restitutus. Between its damage during an earthquake in 62 CE and the eruption of Vesuvius in 79 CE, the walls of the house were repainted, and this spectacular decoration was uncovered in a splendid state of preservation during excavations at the end of the nineteenth century.

A complex combination of painted fantasies fills the walls of a reception room off the peristyle garden **(FIG. 6–25)**. At the base of the walls is a lavish frieze of simulated colored-marble revetment, imitating the actual stone veneers that are found in some Roman residences. Above this "marble" **dado** are broad areas of pure red or white, onto which are painted pictures resembling framed panel paintings (like that in FIG. 6–1), swags of floral garlands or unframed figural vignettes. The framed picture here illustrates a Greek mythological scene from the story of Ixion, who was bound by Zeus to a spinning wheel in punishment for attempting to seduce Hera. Between these pictorial fields, and along a long strip above them that runs around the entire room, are fantastic architectural vistas with multicolored columns and undulating entablatures that recede into fictive space through the use of fanciful linear perspective. The fact that this fictive architecture is occupied here and there by volumetric figures only enhances the sense of three-dimensional spatial definition. On the broad red fields covering the walls of another room of this house, energetic cupids play at industrious human pursuits such as pharmacy, goldsmithing, and making perfume **(FIG. 6–26)**.

6-26 • CUPIDS MAKING PERFUME, WALL PAINTING IN THE HOUSE OF THE VETTII
Pompeii. Rebuilt 62–79 CE.

VILLA OF THE MYSTERIES. The eruption of Vesuvius in 79 CE preserved not only the houses along the city streets within Pompeii, but also the so-called **VILLA OF THE MYSTERIES** just outside the city walls **(FIG. 6–27)**. Villas were the country houses of wealthy Romans, and their plans, though resembling town houses, were often more expansive and irregular. At the Villa of the Mysteries, for example, the entrance leads through the peristyle to the atrium, a reversal of the standard progression. Within this suburban villa a series of elaborate figural murals **(FIG. 6–28)** seem to portray the initiation rites of a mystery religion, probably the

6-27 • PLAN, VILLA OF THE MYSTERIES
Pompeii, early 2nd century BCE.
1 entrance foyer
2 peristyle
3 atrium
4 pool (water basin)
5 tablinum (office, official reception room)
6 room with paintings of mysteries
7 terrace
8 bedroom

6-28 • INITIATION RITES OF THE CULT OF BACCHUS (?), VILLA OF THE MYSTERIES
Pompeii. Wall painting. c. 60–50 BCE.

6-29 • CITYSCAPE, HOUSE OF PUBLIUS FANNIUS SYNISTOR
Boscoreale. Detail of a wall painting from a bedroom. c. 50–30 BCE. Metropolitan Museum of Art, New York. Rogers Fund, 1903 (03.14.13)

cult of Bacchus, which were often performed in private homes as well as in special buildings or temples. Perhaps this room in this villa was a shrine or meeting place for such a cult to this god of vegetation, fertility, and wine. Bacchus (or Dionysus) was one of the most important deities in Pompeii.

The entirely painted architectural setting consists of a simulated marble dado (similar to that which we saw in the House of the Vettii) and, around the top of the wall, an elegant frieze supported by pilaster strips. The figural scenes take place on a shallow "stage" along the top of the dado, with a background of a brilliant, deep red—now known as Pompeian red—that, as we have already seen, was very popular with Roman painters. The tableau unfolds around the entire room, perhaps depicting a succession of events that culminate in the acceptance of an initiate into the cult.

VILLA AT BOSCOREALE. The walls of a room from another villa, this one at Boscoreale, farther removed from Pompeii, open onto a fantastic urban panorama **(FIG. 6–29)**. Surfaces seem to dissolve behind an inner frame of columns and lintels, opening onto a maze of complicated architectural forms, like the painted scenic backdrops of a stage. Indeed, the theater may have inspired this kind of decoration, as the theatrical masks hanging from the lintels seem to suggest. By using a kind of **intuitive perspective**, the artists have created a general impression of real space. In intuitive perspective, the architectural details follow diagonal lines that the eye interprets as parallel lines receding into the distance, and objects meant to be perceived as far away from the surface plane of the wall are shown gradually smaller and smaller than those intended to appear in the foreground.

6–30 • STILL LIFE, HOUSE OF THE STAGS (CERVI)
Herculaneum. Detail of a wall painting. Before 79 CE. Approx. 1′2″ × 1′1½″ (35.5 × 31.7 cm). Museo Archeologico Nazionale, Naples.

ROMAN REALISM IN DETAILS: STILL LIFES AND PORTRAITS. In addition to city views and figural tableaux, other subjects that appeared in Roman art included delicately painted landscapes, exquisitely rendered **still lifes** (compositions of inanimate objects), and portraits. A still-life panel from Herculaneum, a community in the vicinity of Mount Vesuvius near Pompeii, depicts everyday domestic objects—still-green peaches just picked from the tree and a glass jar half-filled with water (**FIG. 6–30**). The items have been carefully arranged on two stepped shelves to give the composition clarity and balance. A strong, clear light floods the picture from left to right, casting shadows, picking up highlights, and enhancing the illusion of solid objects in real space.

Among the paintings discovered on the walls of Pompeian houses, few are as arresting as a double portrait of a young husband and wife (**FIG. 6–31**), who look out from their simulated spatial world through the wall into the viewers' space within the room. The swarthy, wispy-bearded man addresses us with a direct stare, holding a scroll in his left hand, a conventional attribute of educational achievement seen frequently in Roman portraits. Though his wife overlaps him to stake her claim to the

6–31 • PORTRAIT OF A MARRIED COUPLE
Wall painting from Pompeii. Mid 1st century CE. Height 25½″ (64.8 cm). Museo Archeologico Nazionale, Naples.

6–32 • THE ARCH OF TITUS

Rome. c. 81 CE (restored 1822–1824). Concrete and white marble, height 50′ (15 m).

The dedication inscribed across the tall attic story above the arch opening reads: "The Senate and the Roman people to the Deified Titus Vespasian Augustus, son of the Deified Vespasian." The perfectly sized and spaced Roman capital letters meant to be read from a distance and cut with sharp terminals (serifs) to catch the light established a standard that calligraphers and font designers still follow.

SEE MORE: Click the Google Earth link for the Arch of Titus **www.myartslab.com**

foreground, her gaze out at us is less direct. She also holds fashionable attributes of literacy—the stylus she elevates in front of her chin and the folding writing tablet on which she would have used the stylus to inscribe words into a wax infill. This picture is comparable to a modern studio portrait photograph—perhaps a wedding picture—with its careful lighting and retouching, conventional poses and accoutrements. But the attention to physiognomic detail—note the differences in the spacing of their eyes and the shapes of their noses, ears, and lips—makes it quite clear that we are in the presence of actual human likenesses.

THE FLAVIANS

The Julio-Claudian dynasty ended with the suicide of Nero in 68 CE, which led to a brief period of civil war. Eventually an astute general, Vespasian, seized control of the government in 69 CE, founding a new dynasty known as the Flavians. The new line of emperors were practical military men who inspired confidence and ruled for the rest of the first century. They restored the imperial finances and stabilized the frontiers. They also replaced the Julio-Claudian fashion for classicizing imperial portraiture with a return to the ideal of time-worn faces, enhancing the effects of old age.

THE ARCH OF TITUS.   Among the most impressive surviving official commissions from the Flavian dynasty is a distinctive Roman structure: the triumphal arch. Part architecture, part sculpture, the free-standing arch commemorates a triumph, or formal victory celebration, during which a victorious general or emperor paraded through Rome with his troops, captives, and booty. When Domitian assumed the throne in 81 CE, for example, he immediately commissioned a triumphal arch to honor the capture of Jerusalem in 70 CE by his brother and deified predecessor, Titus (FIG. 6–32). The ARCH OF TITUS, constructed of concrete and faced with marble, is essentially a free-standing gateway whose passage is covered by a barrel vault. The arch served as a giant base, 50 feet tall, for a lost bronze statue of the emperor in a four-horse chariot, a typical triumphal symbol. Applied to the faces of the arch are columns in the **Composite order** supporting an entablature. The inscription on the uppermost, or attic, story declares that the Senate and the Roman people erected the monument to honor Titus.

Titus' capture of Jerusalem ended a fierce campaign to crush a revolt of the Jews in Palestine. The Romans sacked and destroyed the Second Temple in Jerusalem, carried off its sacred treasures, then displayed them in a triumphal procession in Rome (FIG. 6–33). A relief on the inside walls of the arch, capturing the drama of the occasion, depicts Titus' soldiers flaunting this booty as they carry it through the streets of Rome. The soldiers are headed toward the right and through an arch, turned obliquely to project into the viewers' own space, thus allowing living spectators a sense

6-33 • SPOILS FROM THE TEMPLE OF SOLOMON
Relief in the passageway of the Arch of Titus. Marble, height 6′8″ (2.03 m).

The Romans became experts in devising methods of covering large, open architectural spaces with concrete and masonry, using barrel vaults, groin vaults, or domes.

A **barrel vault** is constructed in the same manner as the round arch (see "The Roman Arch," page 172). In a sense, it is a series of connected arches extended in sequence along a line. The outward pressure exerted by the curving sides of the barrel vault requires buttressing within or outside the supporting walls.

When two barrel-vaulted spaces intersect each other at the same level, the result is a **groin vault**. Both the weight and outward thrust of the groin vault are concentrated on four corner piers; only the piers require buttressing, so the walls on all four sides can be opened. The Romans used the groin vault to construct some of their grandest interior spaces.

A third type of vault brought to technical perfection by the Romans is the **dome**. The rim of the dome is supported on a circular wall, as in the Pantheon (SEE FIGS. 6–45, 6–46, 6–48). This wall is called a drum when it is raised on top of a main structure. Sometimes a circular opening, called an **oculus**, is left at the top.

barrel vault

groin vault

SEE MORE: View a simulation of the groin vault **www.myartslab.com**

---

of the press of a boisterous, disorderly crowd. They might expect at any moment to hear soldiers and onlookers shouting and chanting.

The mood of the procession depicted in this relief contrasts with the relaxed but formal solemnity of the procession portrayed on the Ara Pacis (see page 177, FIG. B). Like the sculptors of the Ara Pacis, the sculptors of the Arch of Titus showed the spatial relationships among figures, varying the depth of the relief by rendering nearer elements in higher relief than those more distant. A menorah, or seven-branched lampholder, from the Temple of Jerusalem, dominates the scene; the sculptors rendered it as if seen from the low point of view of a spectator at the event.

THE FLAVIAN AMPHITHEATER.   Romans were huge sports fans, and the Flavian emperors catered to their tastes by building splendid facilities. Construction of the **FLAVIAN AMPHITHEATER**, Rome's greatest arena **(FIG. 6–34)**, began under Vespasian in 70 CE and was completed under Titus, who dedicated it in 80 CE. The Flavian Amphitheater came to be known as the "Colosseum," because a gigantic statue of Nero called the *Colossus* stood next to it. "Colosseum" is a most appropriate description of this enormous entertainment center. Its outer wall stands 159 feet high. It is an oval, measuring 615 by 510 feet, with a floor 280 by 175 feet. This floor was laid over a foundation of service rooms and tunnels that provided an area for the athletes, performers, animals, and equipment. The floor was covered

by sand, *arena* in Latin, hence the English term "arena" for a building of this type.

Roman audiences watched a variety of athletic events, blood sports, and spectacles, including animal hunts, fights to the death

6-34 • RECONSTRUCTION DRAWING OF THE FLAVIAN AMPHITHEATER (COLOSSEUM)
Rome. 70–80 CE.

SEE MORE: View a video about the Flavian Amphitheater (Colosseum) **www.myartslab.com**

6-35 • FLAVIAN AMPHITHEATER, OUTER WALL
Rome. 70–80 CE.

between gladiators or between gladiators and wild animals, performances of trained animals and acrobats, and even mock sea battles, for which the arena would be flooded. The opening performances in 80 CE lasted 100 days, during which time it was claimed that 9,000 wild animals and 2,000 gladiators died for the amusement of the spectators.

The amphitheater is a remarkable piece of planning, with easy access, perfect sight lines for everyone, and effective crowd control. Stadiums today are still based on this efficient plan. Some 50,000 spectators could move easily through the 76 entrance doors to the three levels of seats and the standing area at the top. Each spectator had an uninterrupted view of the events below. Each level of seats was laid over barrel-vaulted access corridors and entrance tunnels (SEE FIG. 6–34). The intersection of the barrel-vaulted entrance tunnels and the ring corridors created groin vaults (see "Roman Vaulting," opposite). The walls on the top level of the arena supported a huge awning that could shade the seating areas. Sailors, who had experience in handling ropes, pulleys, and large expanses of canvas, worked the apparatus that extended the awning.

The curving, outer wall of the Colosseum consists of three levels of arcades surmounted by a wall-like attic (top) story. Each arch is framed by engaged columns. Entablature-like friezes mark the divisions between levels (FIG. 6–35). Each level also uses a different architectural order, increasing in complexity from bottom to top: the plain Tuscan order on the ground level, Ionic on the second level, Corinthian on the third, and Corinthian pilasters on the fourth. The attic story is broken by small, square windows, which originally alternated with gilded-bronze shield-shaped ornaments called **cartouches**, supported on brackets that are still in place.

All these elements are purely decorative. As we saw in the Etruscan Porta Augusta (SEE FIG. 6–2), the addition of post-and-lintel decoration to arched structures was an Etruscan innovation. The systematic use of the orders in a logical succession from sturdy Tuscan to lighter Ionic to decorative Corinthian follows a tradition inherited from Hellenistic architecture. This orderly, dignified, and visually satisfying way of organizing the façades of large buildings is still popular. Unfortunately, much of the Colosseum was dismantled in the Middle Ages as a source of marble, metal fittings, and materials for buildings such as churches.

6-36 • YOUNG FLAVIAN WOMAN
c. 90 CE. Marble, height 25″ (65.5 cm). Museo Capitolino, Rome.

PORTRAIT SCULPTURE. Roman patrons continued to expect recognizable likenesses in their portraits, but this did not preclude idealization. A portrait sculpture of a **YOUNG FLAVIAN WOMAN** **(FIG. 6–36)** is idealized in a manner similar to the *Augustus of Primaporta* (SEE FIG. 6–18). Her well-observed, recognizable features—a strong nose and jaw, heavy brows, deep-set eyes, and a long neck—contrast with the smoothly rendered flesh and soft, sensual lips. Her hair is piled high in an extraordinary mass of ringlets following the latest court fashion. Executing the head required skillful chiseling and **drillwork**, a technique for rapidly cutting deep grooves with straight sides, as was done here to render the holes in the center of the curls. The overall effect, especially from a distance, is quite lifelike. The play of natural light over the more subtly sculpted marble surfaces simulates the textures of real skin and hair.

A contemporary bust of an older woman **(FIG. 6–37)** presents a strikingly different image of its subject. Although she also wears her hair in the latest fashion, it is less elaborate and less painstakingly confected and carved than that of her younger counterpart. The work emphasizes not the fresh sheen of an unblemished face, but a visage clearly marked by the passage of

time during a life well lived. We may regard this portrait as less idealized and more naturalistic, but for a Roman viewer, it conformed to an ideal of age and accomplishment by showcasing signs of aging, facial features cherished since the Republican period as reflections of virtue and venerability.

THE HIGH IMPERIAL ART OF TRAJAN AND HADRIAN

Domitian, the last Flavian emperor, was assassinated in 96 CE and succeeded by a senator, Nerva (r. 96–98 CE), who designated as his successor Trajan, a general born in Spain who had commanded Roman troops in Germany. For nearly a century, the empire was under the control of brilliant administrators. Instead of depending on the vagaries of fate (or genetics) to produce intelligent heirs, the emperors Nerva (r. 96–98 CE), Trajan (r. 98–117 CE), Hadrian (r. 117–138 CE), and Antoninus Pius (r. 138–161 CE)—but not his successor, Marcus Aurelius (r. 161–180 CE)—each selected an able administrator to follow him, thus "adopting" his successor. Italy and the provinces flourished, and official and private patronage of the arts increased.

6-37 • MIDDLE-AGED FLAVIAN WOMAN
Late 1st century CE. Marble, height 9½″ (24.1 cm). Musei Vaticani, Museo Gregoriano Profano, ex-Lateranese, Rome.

Under Trajan, the empire reached its greatest territorial expanse. By 106 CE, he had conquered Dacia, roughly present-day Romania (SEE MAP 6–1), and his successor, Hadrian, consolidated the empire's borders and imposed far-reaching social, governmental, and military reforms. Hadrian was well educated and widely traveled, and his admiration for Greek culture spurred new building programs and classicizing works of art throughout the empire. Unfortunately, Marcus Aurelius broke the tradition of adoption and left his son, Commodus, to inherit the throne. Within 12 years, Commodus (r. 180–192 CE) had destroyed the stable government his predecessors had so carefully built.

IMPERIAL ARCHITECTURE

The Romans believed their rule extended to the ends of the Western world, but the city of Rome remained the nerve center of the empire. During his long and peaceful reign, Augustus had paved the city's old Republican Forum, restored its temples and basilicas, and followed Julius Caesar's example by building an Imperial Forum. These projects marked the beginning of a continuing effort to transform the capital itself into a magnificent monument to imperial rule. While Augustus' claim of having turned Rome into a

city of marble is exaggerated, he certainly began the process of creating a monumental civic center. Such grand structures as the Imperial Forums, the Colosseum, the Circus Maximus (a track for chariot races), the Pantheon, and aqueducts stood amid the temples, baths, warehouses, and homes in the city center as expressions of successive emperors' beneficence and their desire to leave their mark on, and preserve their memory in, the capital.

THE FORUM OF TRAJAN. A model of Rome's city center makes apparent the dense building plan (FIG. 6–38). The last and largest Imperial Forum was built by Trajan about 110–113 CE and finished under Hadrian about 117 CE on a large piece of property next to the earlier forums of Augustus and Julius Caesar (FIG. 6–39). For this major undertaking, Trajan chose a Greek architect, Apollodorus of Damascus, who was experienced as a military engineer. A straight, central axis leads from the Forum of Augustus through a triple-arched gate surmounted by a bronze chariot group into a large, colonnaded square with a statue of Trajan on horseback at its center. Closing off the courtyard at the north end was the **BASILICA ULPIA** (FIG. 6–40), dedicated in c. 112 CE, and named for the family to which Trajan belonged.

6–38 • MODEL OF IMPERIAL ROME
c. 324 CE.

Colosseum

Temple of Venus and Rome

Arch of Titus

Basilica of Maxentius and Constantine

Forum of Vespasian (Peace)

Forum of Augustus

Forum of Julius Caesar

Rostrum

Forum of Trajan

Markets of Trajan

Basilica Ulpia

Column of Trajan

Pantheon

A **basilica** was a large, rectangular building with an extensive interior space, adaptable for a variety of administrative governmental functions. The Basilica Ulpia was a court of law, but other basilicas served as imperial audience chambers, army drill halls, and schools. The Basilica Ulpia was a particularly grand interior space, 385 feet long (not including the apses) and 182 feet wide. A large central area (the **nave**) was flanked by double colonnaded aisles surmounted by open galleries or by a clerestory, an upper nave wall with windows. The timber truss roof had a span of about 80 feet. The two **apses**, rounded extensions at each end of the building, provided imposing settings for judges when the court was in session.

During the site preparation for Trajan's forum, part of a commercial district had to be razed and excavated. To make up for the loss, Trajan ordered the construction of a handsome public market (**FIGS. 6–41, 6–42**). The market, comparable in size to a

6–39 • PLAN OF TRAJAN'S FORUM AND MARKET
c. 110–113 CE.

N

Temple to
the Divine Trajan

Column of Trajan

Greek and
Latin libraries

market hall

Basilica Ulpia

Markets of
Trajan

Via Biberatica

Temple of Venus Genetrix
in the Forum of Julius Caesar

equestrian statue
of Trajan

0   50 m

0   100 ft

6–40 • RESTORED PERSPECTIVE VIEW OF THE CENTRAL HALL, BASILICA ULPIA

Rome. c. 112 CE. Drawn by Gilbert Gorski. Trajan's architect was Apollodorus of Damascus.

The building may have had clerestory windows instead of the gallery shown in this drawing. The Column of Trajan can be seen at the right.

6–41 • RECONSTRUCTION OF TRAJAN'S MARKET
Rome. 100–112 CE.

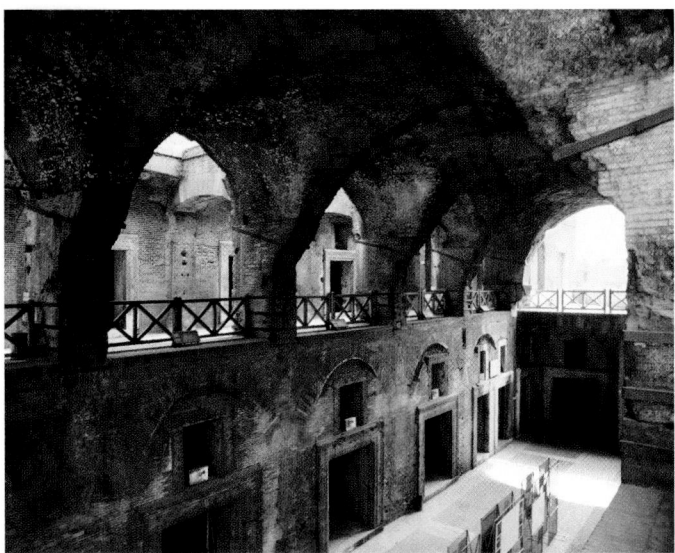

6-42 • MAIN HALL, TRAJAN'S MARKET
Rome. 100–112 CE.

large modern shopping mall, had more than 150 individual shops on several levels and included a large groin-vaulted main hall. In compliance with a building code that was put into effect after a disastrous fire in 64 CE, the market, like most Roman buildings of the time, was constructed of concrete (see "Concrete," page 196) faced with brick, with only occasional detailing in stone and wood.

Behind the Basilica Ulpia stood twin libraries built to house the emperor's collections of Latin and Greek manuscripts. These buildings flanked an open court, the location of the great spiral column that became Trajan's tomb when Hadrian placed a golden urn containing his predecessor's ashes in its base. The column commemorated Trajan's victory over the Dacians and was erected either c. 113 CE, at about the same time as the Basilica Ulpia, or by Hadrian after Trajan's death in 117 CE.

THE COLUMN OF TRAJAN. The relief decoration on the **COLUMN OF TRAJAN** spirals upward in a band that would stretch almost 625 feet if laid out straight. Like a giant, unfurled version of the scrolls housed in the libraries next to it, the column presents a continuous pictorial narrative of the Dacian campaigns of 102–103 and 105–106 CE **(FIG. 6–43)**. The remarkable sculpture includes more than 2,500 individual figures linked by landscape and

6-43 • COLUMN OF TRAJAN
Rome. 113–116 or after 117 CE. Marble, overall height with base 125' (38 m), column alone 97'8" (29.77 m); length of relief 625' (190.5 m).

The height of the column may have recorded the depth of the excavation required to build the Forum of Trajan. The column had been topped by a gilded bronze statue of Trajan that was replaced in 1588 CE with the statue of St. Peter seen today.

SEE MORE: Click the Google Earth link for the Column of Trajan www.myartslab.com

6-44 • ROMANS CROSSING THE DANUBE AND BUILDING A FORT
Detail of the lowest part of the Column of Trajan. 113–116 CE, or after 117 CE. Marble, height of the spiral band approx. 36″ (91 cm).

architecture, and punctuated by the recurring figure of Trajan. The narrative band slowly expands from about 3 feet in height at the bottom, near the viewer, to 4 feet at the top of the column, where it is farther from view. The natural and architectural elements in the scenes have been kept small so the important figures can occupy as much space as possible.

The scene at the beginning of the spiral, at the bottom of the column, shows Trajan's army crossing the Danube River on a pontoon bridge as the first Dacian campaign of 101 CE is launched (FIG. 6–44). Soldiers construct battlefield headquarters in Dacia from which the men on the frontiers will receive orders, food, and weapons. In this spectacular piece of imperial ideology or

The Romans were pragmatic builders, and their practicality extended from recognizing and exploiting undeveloped potential in construction methods and physical materials to organizing large-scale building works. Their exploitation of the arch and the vault is typical of their adapt-and-improve approach (see "The Roman Arch," page 172, and "Roman Vaulting," page 188). But their innovative use of concrete, beginning in the first century BCE, was a technological breakthrough of the greatest importance in the history of architecture.

In contrast to stone—which was expensive and difficult to quarry and transport—the components of concrete were cheap, relatively light, and easily transported. Building stone structures required highly skilled masons, but a large, semiskilled workforce directed by a few experienced supervisors could construct brick-faced concrete buildings.

Roman concrete consisted of powdered lime, a volcanic sand called pozzolana, and various types of rubble, such as small rocks and broken pottery. Mixing these materials in water caused a chemical reaction that blended them, and they hardened as they dried into a strong, solid mass. At first, concrete was used mainly for poured foundations, but with technical advances it became indispensable for the construction of walls, arches, and vaults for ever-larger buildings,

such as the Flavian Amphitheater (SEE FIG. 6–34) and the Markets of Trajan (SEE FIG. 6–42). In the earliest concrete wall construction, workers filled a framework of rough stones with concrete. Soon they developed a technique known as opus reticulatum, in which the framework is a diagonal web of smallish bricks set in a cross pattern. Concrete-based construction freed the Romans from the limits of right-angle forms and comparatively short spans. With this new freedom, Roman builders pushed the established limits of architecture, creating some very large and highly original spaces by pouring concrete over wooden frameworks to mold it into complex curving shapes.

Concrete's one weakness was that it absorbed moisture and would eventually deteriorate if unprotected, so builders covered exposed surfaces with a veneer, or facing, of finer materials—such as marble, stone, stucco, or painted plaster—to protect it. An essential difference between Greek and Roman architecture is that Greek builders reveal the building material itself and accept the design limitations of post-and-lintel construction, whereas Roman buildings expose only an externally applied surface covering. The sophisticated structural underpinnings that allow huge spaces molded by three-dimensional curves are set behind them, hidden from view.

SEE MORE: View a simulation of the Roman use of concrete www.myartslab.com

---

propaganda, Trajan is portrayed as a strong, stable, and efficient commander of a well-run army, and his barbarian enemies are shown as worthy opponents of Rome.

THE PANTHEON. Perhaps the most remarkable ancient building surviving in Rome—and one of the marvels of world architecture in any age—is a temple to the Olympian gods called the **PANTHEON** (literally, "all the gods") (FIG. 6–45). Although this magnificent monument was designed and constructed entirely during the reign of the emperor Hadrian, the long inscription on the architrave states that it was built by "Marcus Agrippa, son of Lucius, who was consul three times." Agrippa, the son-in-law and valued advisor of Augustus, was responsible for building on this site in 27–25 BCE. After a fire in 80 CE, Domitian built a new temple, which Hadrian then replaced in 118–128 CE with the Pantheon. Hadrian, who clearly had a strong sense of history, placed Agrippa's name on the façade in a grand gesture to the memory of the illustrious consul.

The current setting of the temple gives little suggestion of its original appearance. Centuries of dirt and street construction hide

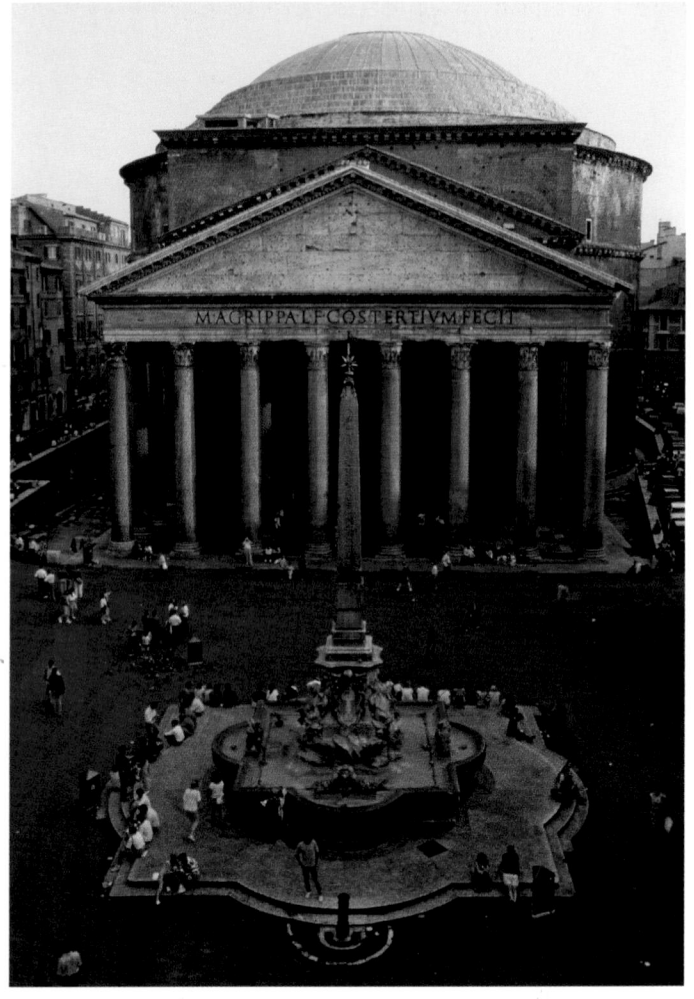

6-45 • PANTHEON
Rome. c. 118–128 CE.

Today a huge fountain dominates the square in front of the Pantheon. Built in 1578 by Giacomo della Porta, it now supports an Egyptian obelisk placed there in 1711 by Pope Clement XI.

6-46 • RECONSTRUCTION DRAWING OF THE PANTHEON

6-47 • PLAN OF THE PANTHEON

0   50m

0   100 ft

its podium and stairs. Attachment holes in the pediment indicate the placement of bronze sculpture, perhaps an eagle within a wreath, the imperial Jupiter. Today we can see the sides of the rotunda flanking the entrance porch, but when the Pantheon was constructed, the façade of this porch—resembling the façades of typical, rectangular temples—was literally all viewers could see of the building. Since their approach was controlled by an enclosed courtyard (SEE FIG. 6–38), the actual circular shape of the Pantheon was concealed. Viewers were therefore surprised to pass through the rectilinear and restricted aisles of the portico and the huge main door to encounter the gaping space of the giant **rotunda** (circular room) surmounted by a huge, bowl-shaped dome, 143 feet in diameter and 143 feet from the floor at its summit (**FIGS. 6–46, 6–47**). Even without the controlled courtyard approach, encountering this glorious space today is still an overwhelming experience—for many of us, one that is repeated even on successive visits to the rotunda.

Standing at the center of this hemispherical temple (**FIG. 6–48**), the visitor feels isolated from the outside world and intensely aware of the shape and tangibility of the space itself. Our eyes are drawn upward over the patterns made by the sunken panels, or **coffers**, in the dome's ceiling to the light entering the 29-foot-wide **oculus**, or central opening, which illuminates a brilliant circle against the surface of the dome. This disk of light

6-48 • DOME OF THE PANTHEON

With light from the oculus on its coffered ceiling. 125–128 CE. Brick, concrete, marble veneer, diameter of dome 143′ (43.5 m).

SEE MORE: View a panorama of the Pantheon
www.myartslab.com

moves around this microcosm throughout the day like a sun. Clouds can be seen traveling across the opening on some days; on others, rain falls through and then drains off through conduits planned by the original engineer. Occasionally a bird flies in. This open, luminous space gives the feeling that one could rise buoyantly upward and escape the spherical hollow of the building to commune with the cosmos.

The simple shape of the Pantheon's dome belies its sophisticated design and engineering (SEE FIG. 6–46). Marble veneer and two tiers of richly colored architectural detail conceal the internal brick arches and concrete structure of the 20-foot-thick walls of the rotunda. More than half of the original decoration—a wealth of columns, pilasters, and entablatures—survives. The

simple repetition of square against circle, established on a large scale by juxtaposing the rectilinear portico against the circular rotunda, is found throughout the building's ornamentation. The wall is punctuated by seven **exedrae** (niches)—rectangular alternating with semicircular—that originally held statues of gods. The square, boxlike coffers inside the dome, which help lighten the weight of the masonry, may once have contained gilded bronze rosettes or stars suggesting the heavens. In 609 CE, Pope Boniface IV dedicated the Pantheon as the Christian church of St. Mary of the Martyrs, thus ensuring its survival through the Middle Ages and down to our day.

HADRIAN'S VILLA AT TIVOLI. To imagine Roman life at its most luxurious, one must go to Tivoli, a little more than 20 miles from Rome. **HADRIAN'S VILLA**, or country residence, was not a single building but an architectural complex of many buildings, lakes, and gardens spread over half a square mile (**FIG. 6–49**). Each section had its own inner logic, and each took advantage of natural land formations and attractive views. Hadrian instructed his architects to re-create his favorite places throughout the empire. In his

6-49 • PLAN OF HADRIAN'S VILLA

Tivoli. c. 125–135 CE.

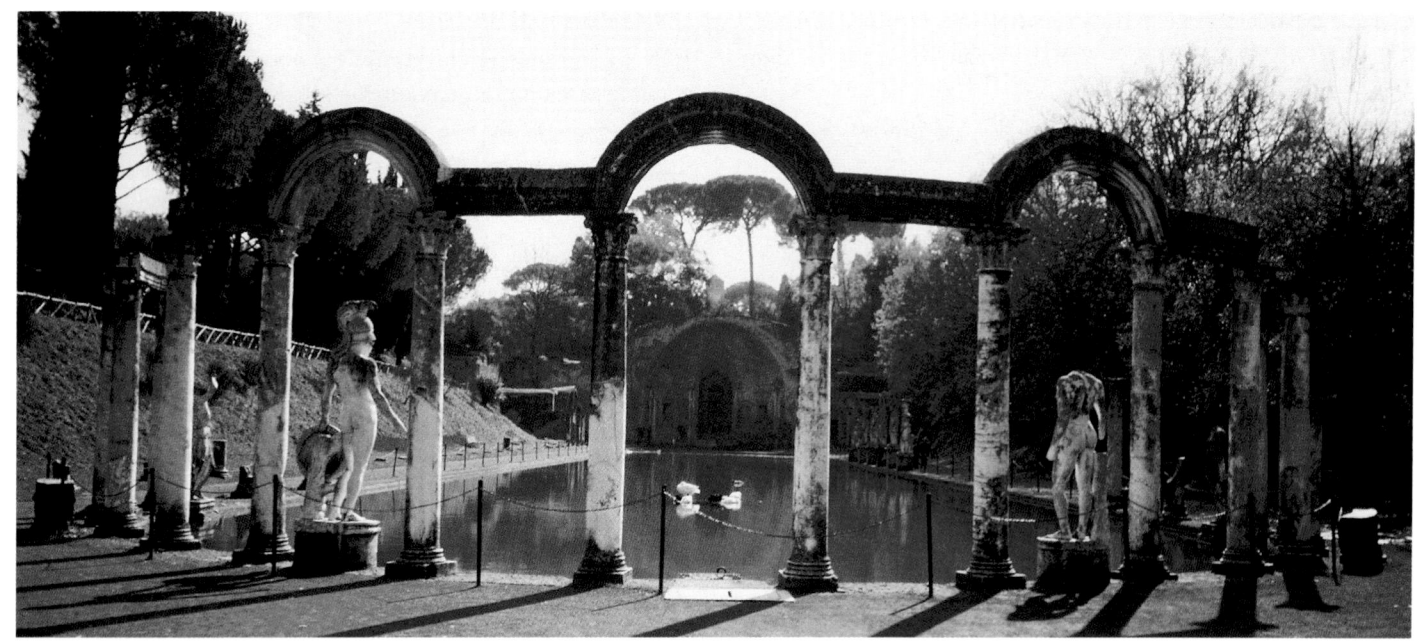

6–50 • THE CANAL (REFLECTING POOL), HADRIAN'S VILLA
Tivoli. c. 125–135 CE.

6–51 • BATTLE OF CENTAURS AND WILD BEASTS FROM HADRIAN'S VILLA
Tivoli. c. 125 CE. Mosaic, 23 × 36″ (58.4 × 91.4 cm). Staatliche Museen zu Berlin, Preussischer Kulturbesitz, Antikensammlung, Berlin.

This floor mosaic may be a copy of a much-admired painting of a fight between centaurs and wild animals done by the late 5th-century BCE Greek artist Zeuxis.

splendid villa, he could pretend to enjoy the Athenian Grove of Academe, the Painted Stoa from the Athenian Agora, and buildings of the Ptolemaic capital of Alexandria, Egypt.

Landscapes with pools, fountains, and gardens turned the villa into a place of sensuous delight. An area with a long reflecting pool, called the Canal, was framed by a colonnade with alternating semicircular and straight entablatures (**FIG. 6–50**). It led to an outdoor dining room with concrete couches facing the pool. Copies of famous Greek statues, and sometimes even the originals, filled the spaces between the columns. So great was Hadrian's love of Greek sculpture that he even had the caryatids of the Erechtheion (SEE FIG. 5–38) replicated for his pleasure palace.

The individual buildings were not large, but they were extremely complex and imaginatively designed. Roman builders and engineers exploited fully the flexibility offered by concrete vaulted construction. Walls and floors had veneers of marble and travertine or of exquisite mosaics and paintings. A panel from one of the floor mosaics (**FIG. 6–51**) demonstrates the extraordinary artistry of Hadrian's mosaicists (see "Roman Mosaics," page 202). In a rocky landscape with only a few bits of greenery, a desperate male centaur raises a large boulder over his head to crush a tiger that has attacked and severely wounded a female centaur. Two other felines apparently took part in the attack—the white leopard on the rocks to the left and the dead lion at the feet of the male centaur. The artist rendered the figures with three-dimensional shading, foreshortening, and a great sensitivity to a range of figure types, including human torsos and powerful animals in a variety of poses.

IMPERIAL PORTRAITS

Imperial portraits were objects of propaganda. Marcus Aurelius, like Hadrian, was a successful military commander who was equally proud of his intellectual attainments. In a lucky error—or twist of fortune—a gilded-bronze equestrian statue of the emperor, dressed as a military commander in a tunic and short, heavy cloak (**FIG. 6–52**), came mistakenly to be revered during the Middle Ages as a statue of Constantine, the first Christian emperor, and consequently the sculpture escaped being melted down. The raised foreleg of his horse once trampled a crouching barbarian.

Marcus Aurelius' head, with its thick, curly hair and full beard (a fashion that was begun by Hadrian), resembles the traditional "philosopher" portraits from the Greek world. The emperor wears

6-52 • EQUESTRIAN STATUE OF MARCUS AURELIUS

c. 176 CE. Bronze, originally gilded, height of statue 11′6″ (3.5 m). Museo Capitolino, Rome.

Between 1187 and 1538, this statue stood in the piazza fronting the palace and church of St. John Lateran in Rome. In January 1538, Pope Paul III had it moved to the Capitoline Hill, and Michelangelo made it the centerpiece of his newly redesigned Capitoline Piazza. After being removed from its base for cleaning and restoration in recent times, it was taken inside the Capitoline Museum to protect it from air pollution, and a copy has replaced it in the piazza.

Mosaics were used widely in Hellenistic times and became enormously popular for decorating homes in the Roman period. Mosaic designs were created with pebbles (SEE FIG. 5–50), or with small, regularly shaped pieces of colored stone and marble, called tesserae. The stones were pressed into a kind of soft cement called grout. When the stones were firmly set, the spaces between them were also filled with grout. After the surface dried, it was cleaned and polished. Since the natural stones produced only a narrow range of colors, glass tesserae were also used to extend the palette as early as the third century BCE.

Mosaic production was made more efficient by the use of **emblemata** (the plural of emblema, "central design"). These small, intricate mosaic compositions were created in the artist's workshop in square or rectangular trays. They could be made in advance, carried to a work site, and inserted into a floor decorated with an easily produced geometric pattern.

Some skilled mosaicists even copied well-known paintings, often by famous Greek artists. Employing a technique in which very small tesserae, in a wide range of colors, were laid down in irregular, curving lines, they effectively imitated painted brushstrokes. One example is The Unswept Floor. Herakleitos, a second-century CE Greek mosaicist living in Rome, made this copy of an original work by the renowned second-century BCE artist Sosos. Pliny the Elder, in his Natural History, mentions a mosaic of an unswept floor and another of doves that Sosos made in Pergamon.

A dining room would be a logical location for a floor mosaic of this theme, with table scraps re-created in meticulous detail, even to the shadows they cast, and a mouse foraging among them. The guests reclining on their banquet couches would certainly be amused by the pictures on the floor, but they could also have shown off their knowledge of the notable Greek precedents for the mosaic beneath their feet.

THE UNSWEPT FLOOR
Mosaic variant of a 2nd-century BCE painting by Sosos of Pergamon. 2nd century CE. Signed by Herakleitos. Musei Vaticani, Museo Gregoriano Profano, Rome.

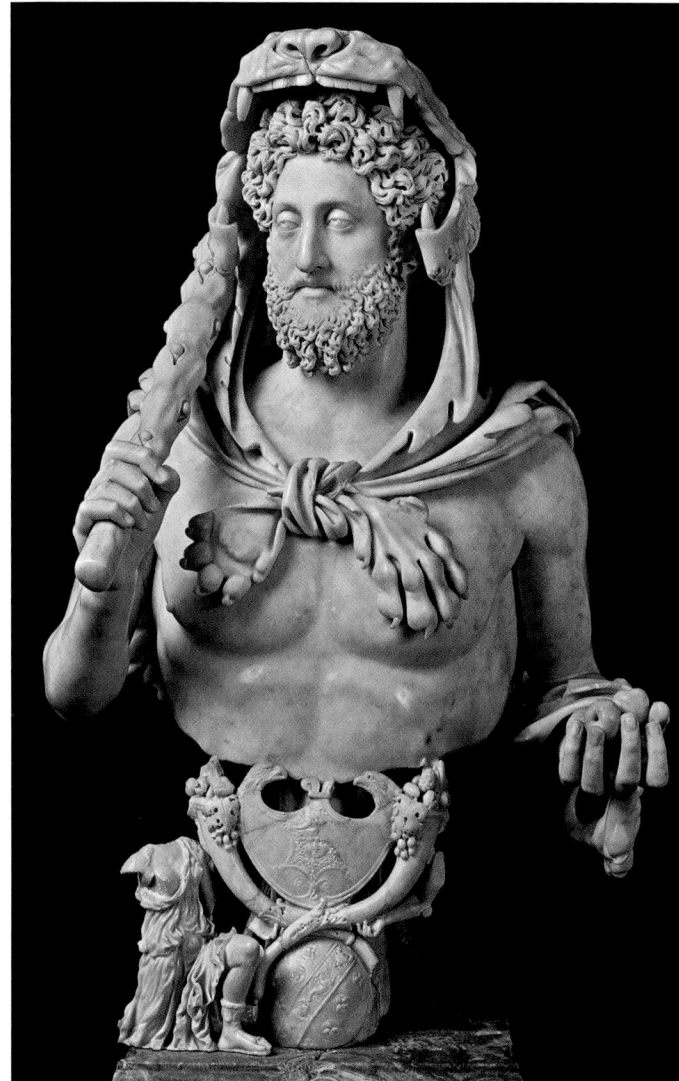

6-53 • COMMODUS AS HERCULES
Esquiline Hill, Rome. c. 191–192 CE. Marble, height 46½" (118 cm).
Palazzo dei Conservatori, Rome.

the finest artists of the day. In a spectacular marble bust, the emperor poses as **HERCULES (FIG. 6–53)**, adorned with references to the hero's legendary labors: Hercules' club, the skin and head of the Nemean lion, and the golden apples from the Garden of the Hesperides. Commodus' likeness emphasizes his family resemblance to his more illustrious and powerful father (SEE FIG. 6–52), but it also captures his vanity, through the grand pretensions of his costume and the Classical associations of his body type. The sculptor's sensitive modeling and expert drillwork exploit the play of light and shadow on the figure to bring out the textures of the hair, beard, facial features, and drapery, and to capture the illusion of life and movement.

FUNERARY SCULPTURE.   During the second and third centuries, a shift from cremation to inhumation created a growing demand for sarcophagi in which to bury the bodies of the deceased. Wealthy Romans commissioned thousands of massive and elaborate marble sarcophagi, encrusted with sculptural relief, created in large production workshops throughout the Roman empire.

In 1885, nine particularly impressive sarcophagi were discovered in private underground burial chambers built for use by a powerful, aristocratic Roman family—the Calpurnii Pisones. One of these sarcophagi, from c. 190 CE, portrays the **INDIAN TRIUMPH OF DIONYSUS** (see "A Closer Look," page 206). This is a popular theme in late second-century CE sarcophagi, but here the carved relief is of especially high quality—complex but highly legible at the same time. The mythological composition owes a debt to imperial ceremony. Dionysus, at far left in a chariot, receives from a personification of Victory standing behind him a laurel crown, identical to the headdress worn by Roman emperors during triumphal processions. Also derived from state ceremony is the display of booty and captives carried by the elephants at the center of the composition. But religion, rather than statecraft, is the real theme here. The set of sarcophagi to which this belongs indicates that the family who commissioned them adhered to a mystery cult of Dionysus that focused on themes of decay and renewal, death and rebirth. The triumph of the deceased over death is the central message here, not one particular episode in the life of Dionysus himself.

no armor and carries no weapons; like Egyptian kings, he conquers effortlessly by divine will. And like his illustrious predecessor Augustus, he reaches out to those around him in a rhetorical gesture of address. It is difficult to create an equestrian portrait in which the rider stands out as the dominant figure without making the horse look too small. The sculptor of this statue found a balance acceptable to viewers of the time and, in doing so, created a model for later artists.

Marcus Aurelius was succeeded as emperor by his son Commodus, a man without political skill, administrative competence, or intellectual distinction. During his unfortunate reign (180–192 CE), he devoted himself to luxury and frivolous pursuits. He claimed at various times to be the reincarnation of Hercules and the incarnation of the god Jupiter. When he proposed to assume the consulship dressed and armed as a gladiator, his associates, including his mistress, arranged to have him strangled in his bath by a wrestling partner. Commodus did, however, sponsor some of

THE LATE EMPIRE, THIRD AND FOURTH CENTURIES CE

The comfortable life suggested by the wall paintings in Roman houses and villas was, within a century, to be challenged by hard times. The reign of Commodus marked the beginning of a period of political and economic decline. Barbarian groups had already begun moving into the empire in the time of Marcus Aurelius. Now they pressed on Rome's frontiers. Many crossed the borders and settled within them, disrupting provincial governments. As perceived threats spread throughout the empire, imperial rule became increasingly authoritarian. Eventually the army controlled the government, and the Imperial Guards set up and deposed rulers almost at will, often selecting candidates from among poorly educated, power-hungry provincial leaders in their own ranks.

THE SEVERAN DYNASTY

Despite the pressures brought by political and economic change, the arts continued to flourish under the Severan emperors (193–235 CE) who succeeded Commodus. Septimius Severus (r. 193–211 CE), who was born in Africa, and his Syrian wife, Julia Domna, restored public buildings, commissioned official portraits, and revitalized the old cattle market in Rome into a well-planned center of bustling commerce. Their sons, Geta and Caracalla, succeeded Septimius Severus as co-emperors in 211 CE, but Caracalla murdered Geta in 212 CE and then ruled alone until he in turn was murdered in 217 CE.

PORTRAITS OF CARACALLA. The Emperor Caracalla appears in his portraits as a fierce and courageous ruler, capable of confronting Rome's enemies and safeguarding the security of the Roman Empire. In the example shown here **(FIG. 6–54)**, the sculptor has enhanced the intensity of the emperor's expression by producing strong contrasts of light and dark with careful chiseling and drillwork. Even the marble eyes have been drilled and engraved to catch the light in a way that makes them dominate his expression. The contrast between this style and that of the portraits of Augustus is a telling reflection of the changing character of imperial rule. Augustus envisioned himself as the suave initiator of a Golden Age of peace and prosperity; Caracalla presents himself as a no-nonsense ruler of iron-fisted determination, with a militaristic, close-cropped haircut and a glare of fierce intensity.

THE BATHS OF CARACALLA. The year before his death in 211 CE, Septimius Severus had begun a popular public-works project: the construction of magnificent new public baths on the southeast side of Rome as a new recreational and educational center. Caracalla completed and inaugurated the baths in 216–217 CE, today known by his name. The impressive brick and concrete structure was hidden under a sheath of colorful marble and mosaic. The builders used soaring groin and barrel vaults, which allow the maximum space with the fewest possible supports. The groin vaults also made possible large windows in every bay. Windows were important, since the baths depended on natural light and could only be open during daylight hours.

The **BATHS OF CARACALLA** (FIGS. **6–55, 6–56**) were laid out on a strictly symmetrical plan. The bathing facilities were grouped in the center of the main building to make efficient use of the below-ground furnaces that heated them and to allow bathers to move comfortably from hot to cold pools and then finish with a swim. Many other facilities—exercise rooms, shops, latrines, and dressing rooms—were housed on each side of the bathing block. The bath buildings alone covered 5 acres. The entire complex, which included gardens, a stadium, libraries, a painting

6-54 • CARACALLA
Early 3rd century CE. Marble, height 14½″ (36.2 cm). Metropolitan Museum of Art, New York. Samuel D. Lee Fund, 1940 (40.11.1A)

gallery, auditoriums, and huge water reservoirs, covered an area of 50 acres.

THE SOLDIER EMPERORS

Following the assassination of the last Severan emperor by one of his military commanders in 235 CE, Rome was plunged into a period of anarchy that lasted for 50 years. A series of soldier emperors attempted to rule the empire, but real order was only restored by Diocletian (r. 284–305 CE), also a military commander. This brilliant politician and general reversed the empire's declining fortunes, but he also began an increasingly autocratic form of rule, and the social structure of the empire became increasingly rigid.

To divide up the task of defending and administering the Roman world and to assure an orderly succession, in 286 CE Diocletian divided the empire in two parts. According to his plan, with the title of "Augustus" he would rule in the East, while another Augustus, Maximian, would rule in the West. Then, in 293 CE, he devised a form of government called a **tetrarchy**, or "rule of four," in which each Augustus designated a subordinate and heir, who held the title of "Caesar." And the Roman Empire, now divided into four quadrants, would be ruled by four individuals.

6-55 • BATHS OF CARACALLA
Rome. c. 211–217 CE.

SEE MORE: Click the Google Earth link for the Baths of Caracalla
www.myartslab.com

6-56 • PLAN OF THE BATHS OF CARACALLA

gymnasium

gymnasium

natatio (swimming pool)

caldarium (hot bath)

frigidarium (cold bath)

tepidarium (warm bath)

0   150 ft
40 m

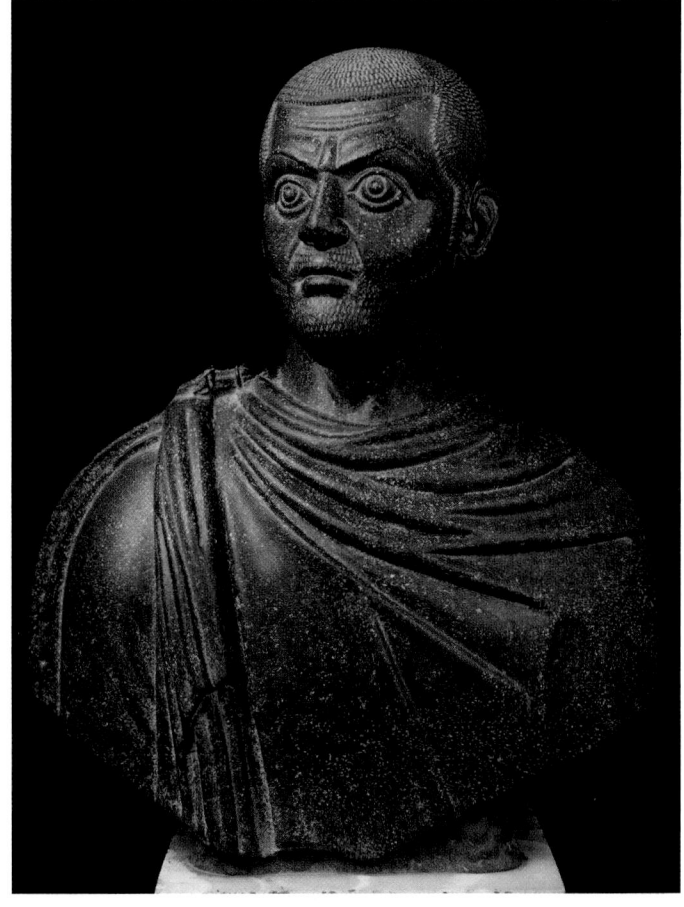

6-57 • PORTRAIT OF A TETRARCH (GALERIUS?)
Early 4th century CE. Porphyry, 2′5½″ (65 cm). Egyptian Museum, Cairo.

TETRARCHIC PORTRAITURE.   Diocletian's political restructuring is paralleled by the introduction of a radically new, hard style of geometricized abstraction, especially notable in portraits of the tetrarchs themselves. A powerful bust of a tetrarch, startlingly alert with searing eyes (FIG. 6–57), embodies this stylistic shift toward the antithesis of the suave Classicism seen in the portrait of Commodus as Hercules (SEE FIG. 6–53). There is no clear sense of likeness. Who this individual is seems to be less significant than the powerful position he holds. Some art historians have interpreted

Sarcophagus with the Indian Triumph of Dionysus

> c. 190 CE. Marble, 47½ × 92½ × 35¹³⁄₁₆″ (120.7 × 234.9 × 90.96 cm). Walters Art Museum, Baltimore.

Semele, mortal mother of the god Dionysus, gives birth prematurely and then dies. Once grown, Dionysus would travel to the underworld and bring his mother to paradise. Semele's death therefore suggests the promise of eternal life through her son.

These hooked sticks are identical to the ankusha still used by mahouts (elephant drivers) in India today.

As part of their worship, followers of Dionysiac mystery religions re-created the triumphant return of the god from India by parading in the streets after dark. A dancing maenad beats her tambourine here, suggesting the sounds and movements that would accompany such ritual re-enactments.

The presence of exotic animals such as elephants, a lion, a giraffe, and panthers, identifies this scene as Dionysus' triumphant return from India.

Snakes were not only used in the rites of Dionysiac mystery religions; they were powerful symbols of rebirth and phallic fertility, making them especially appropriate in the context of a sarcophagus. Three snakes appear along the groundline of the sculptural frieze.

The aged god Silenus leans on a thyrsos staff, composed of a giant fennel wound with ivy and topped with a pinecone, symbolizing fertility. Dionysus, with whom such staffs were associated, also carries one here as his triumphal scepter.

SEE MORE: View the Closer Look feature for the Sarcophagus with the Indian Triumph of Dionysus
www.myartslab.com

this change in style as a conscious embodiment of Diocletian's new concept of government, while others have pointed to parallels with the provincial art of Diocletian's Dalmatian homeland or with the Neoplatonic aesthetics of idealized abstraction promoted by Plotinus, a third-century CE philosopher who was widely read in the late Roman world. In any event, these riveting works represent not a degeneration of the Classical tradition but its conscious replacement by a different aesthetic viewpoint—militaristic, severe, and abstract rather than suave, slick, and classicizing.

This new mode is famously represented by an actual sculptural group of **THE TETRARCHS (FIG. 6–58)**. The four figures are nearly identical, except that the senior Augusti have beards while their

6-58 • THE TETRARCHS
c. 300 CE. Porphyry, height of figures 51″ (129 cm). Brought from Constantinople in 1204, installed at the corner of the façade of the Cathedral of St. Mark, Venice.

The sculpture is made of porphyry, an extremely hard, purple stone from Egypt that was reserved for imperial use (SEE FIG. 5–57). The most striking features of the tetrarchs—the simplification of natural forms to geometric shapes, flexibility with human proportions, and the emphasis on a message or idea—appear often in Roman art by the end of the third century. This particular sculpture may have been made in Egypt and moved to Constantinople after 330 CE. Christian crusaders who looted Constantinople in 1204 CE took the statue to Venice and installed it at the Cathedral of St. Mark, where it is today.

THE BASILICA AT TRIER. The tetrarchs ruled the empire from administrative headquarters in Milan (Italy), Trier (Germany), Thessaloniki (Greece), and Nicomedia (Turkey). Imposing architecture was used to house the government in these new capital cities. In Trier, for example, Constantius Chlorus (Caesar, 293–305; Augustus, 305–306 CE) and his son Constantine fortified the city with walls and a monumental gate that still stand. They built public amenities, such as baths, and a palace with a huge audience hall, later used as a Christian church **(FIGS. 6–59, 6–60)**. This early fourth-century basilica's large size and simple plan and structure exemplify the architecture of the tetrarchs: no-nonsense, imposing buildings that would impress their subjects.

The audience hall is a large rectangular building, 190 by 95 feet, with a strong directional focus given by a single apse opposite the door. Brick walls, originally stuccoed on the outside and covered with marble veneer inside, are pierced by two rows of arched windows. The flat roof, nearly 100 feet above the floor, covers both the nave and the apse. In a concession to the northern climate, the building was centrally heated with hot air flowing under the floor, a technique also used in Roman baths. The windows of the apse create an interesting optical effect. Slightly smaller than the windows in the hall, they create the illusion of greater distance, so that the tetrarch enthroned in the apse would appear larger than life and the hall would seem longer than it actually is.

juniors, the Caesars, are clean-shaven. Dressed in military garb and clasping swords at their sides, they embrace each other in a show of imperial unity, proclaiming an alliance rooted in strength and vigilance. As a piece of propaganda and a summary of the state of affairs at the time, it is unsurpassed.

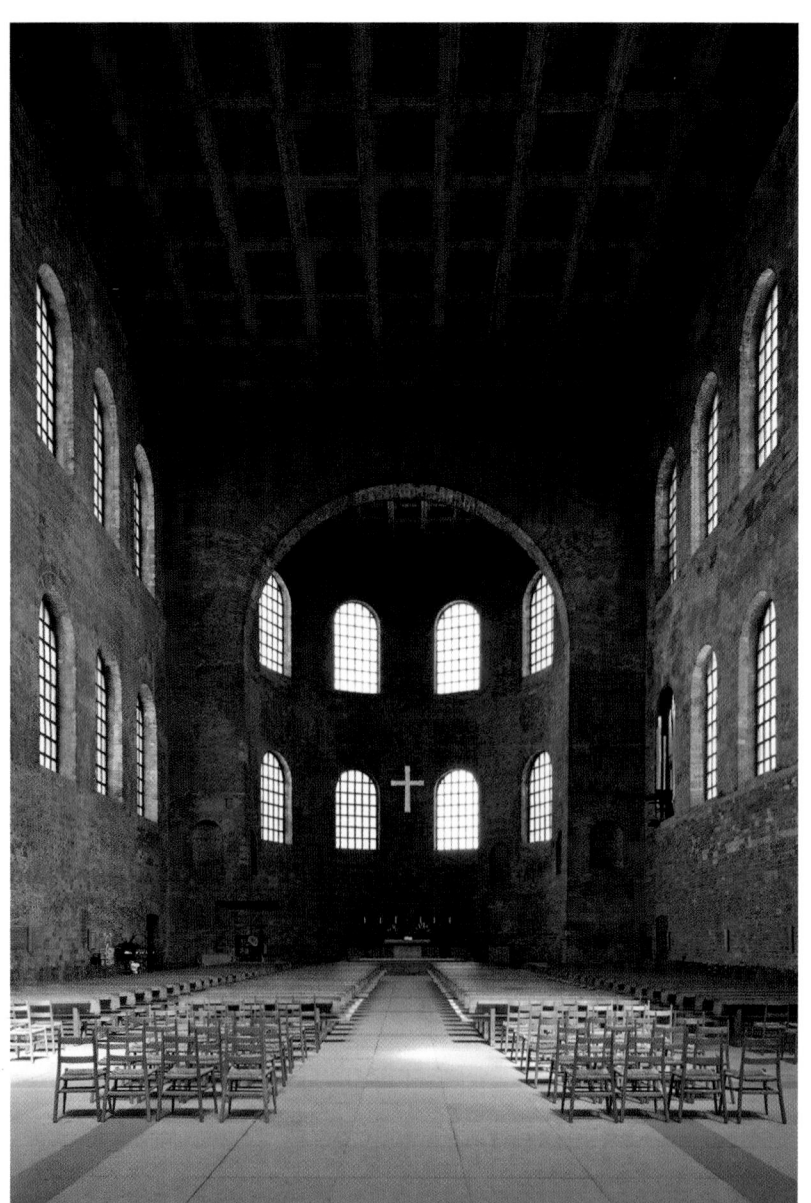

6-59 • AUDIENCE HALL OF CONSTANTIUS CHLORUS (NOW KNOWN AS THE BASILICA)
Trier, Germany. Early 4th century CE. View of the nave. Height of room 100′ (30.5 m).

Only the left wall and apse survive from the original Roman building. The hall became part of the bishop's palace during the medieval period.

CONSTANTINE THE GREAT

In 305 CE, Diocletian abdicated and forced his fellow Augustus, Maximian, to do so too. The orderly succession he had planned for failed to occur, and a struggle for position and advantage followed almost immediately. Two main contenders appeared in the Western Empire: Maximian's son Maxentius, and Constantine, son of Tetrarch Constantius Chlorus. Constantine emerged victorious in 312, defeating Maxentius at the Battle of the Milvian Bridge at the entrance to Rome.

According to Christian tradition, Constantine had a vision the night before the battle in which he saw a flaming cross in the sky and heard these words: "In this sign you shall conquer." The next morning he ordered that his army's shields and standards be inscribed with the monogram XP (the Greek letters *chi* and *rho*, standing for *Christos*). The victorious Constantine then showed his gratitude by ending the persecution of Christians and recognizing Christianity as a lawful religion. He may have been influenced in that decision by his mother, Helena, a devout Christian—later canonized. Whatever his motivation, in 313 CE, together with Licinius, who ruled the Eastern Empire, Constantine issued the Edict of Milan, a model of religious toleration.

6-60 • AUDIENCE HALL OF CONSTANTIUS CHLORUS (NOW KNOWN AS THE BASILICA)
Trier, Germany. Early 4th century CE.

6-61 • ARCH OF CONSTANTINE
Rome. 312–315 CE (dedicated July 25, 315).

This massive, triple-arched monument to Emperor Constantine's victory over Maxentius in 312 CE is a wonder of recycled sculpture. On the attic story, flanking the inscription over the central arch, are relief panels taken from a monument celebrating the victory of Marcus Aurelius over the Germans in 174 CE. On the attached piers framing these panels are large statues of prisoners made to celebrate Trajan's victory over the Dacians in the early second century CE. On the inner walls of the central arch and on the attic of the short sides (neither seen here) are reliefs also commemorating Trajan's conquest of Dacia. Over each of the side arches is a pair of large tondi taken from a monument to Hadrian (SEE FIG. 6–62). The rest of the decoration is early fourth century, contemporary with the arch.

SEE MORE: Click the Google Earth link for the Arch of Constantine **www.myartslab.com**

The Edict granted freedom to all religious groups, not just Christians. Constantine, however, remained the Pontifex Maximus of Rome's state religion and also reaffirmed his devotion to the military's favorite god, Mithras, and to the Invincible Sun, Sol Invictus, a manifestation of Helios Apollo, the sun god. In 324 CE, Constantine defeated Licinius, his last rival, and ruled as sole emperor until his death in 337. He made the port city of Byzantium the new capital of the Roman Empire after his last visit to Rome in 325, and renamed the city after himself—Constantinople (present-day Istanbul, in Turkey). Rome, which had already ceased to be the seat of government in the West, further declined in importance.

THE ARCH OF CONSTANTINE. In Rome, next to the Colosseum, the Senate erected a triumphal arch to commemorate Constantine's victory over Maxentius (FIG. 6–61), a huge, triple arch that dwarfs the nearby Arch of Titus (SEE FIG. 6–32). Its three barrel-vaulted passageways are flanked by columns on high pedestals and surmounted by a large attic story with elaborate sculptural decoration and a laudatory inscription: "To the Emperor

6-62 • HADRIAN/CONSTANTINE HUNTING BOAR AND SACRIFICING TO APOLLO; CONSTANTINE ADDRESSING THE ROMAN PEOPLE IN THE ROMAN FORUM

Tondi made for a monument to Hadrian and reused on the Arch of Constantine. c. 130–138 CE. Marble, diameter 40″ (102 cm). Frieze by Constantinian sculptors 312–315 CE.

The two tondi (circular compositions) were originally part of a lost monument erected by the emperor Hadrian (r. 117–138 CE). The boar hunt demonstrates his courage and physical prowess, and his sacrificial offering to Apollo shows his piety and gratitude to the gods for their support. The classicizing heads, form-enhancing drapery, and graceful poses of the figures betray a debt to the style of Late Classical Greek art. In the fourth century CE, Constantine appropriated these tondi, had Hadrian's head recarved with his own or his father's features, and incorporated them into his own triumphal arch (SEE FIG. 6–61) so that the power and piety of this predecessor could reflect on him and his reign. In a strip of relief underneath the tondi, sculptors from his own time portrayed a ceremony performed by Constantine during his celebration of the victory over his rival, Maxentius, at the Battle of the Milvian Bridge (312 CE). Rather than the Hellenizing mode popular during Hadrian's reign, the Constantinian sculptors employ the blocky and abstract stylizations that became fashionable during the tetrarchy.

Constantine from the Senate and the Roman People. Since through divine inspiration and great wisdom he has delivered the state from the tyrant and his party by his army and noble arms, [we] dedicate this arch, decorated with triumphal insignia." The "triumphal insignia" were in part appropriated from earlier monuments made for Constantine's illustrious predecessors—Trajan, Hadrian, and Marcus Aurelius. The reused items visually transferred the old Roman virtues of strength, courage, and piety associated with these earlier exemplary emperors to Constantine himself. New reliefs were made for the arch to recount the story

of Constantine's victory and to symbolize his own power and generosity. They run in strips underneath the reused Hadrianic tondi (a tondo is a circular composition) **(FIG. 6–62)**.

Although the new Constantinian reliefs reflect the long-standing Roman predilection for depicting important events with recognizable detail, they nevertheless represent a significant change in style, approach, and subject matter (see lower figural frieze in FIG. 6–62). In this scene of Constantine addressing the Roman people in the Roman Forum, the Constantinian reliefs are easily distinguished from the reused Hadrianic tondi mounted just above them because of the faithfulness of the new reliefs to the avant-garde tetrarchic style we have already encountered in portraiture. The forceful, blocky, mostly frontal figures are compressed into the foreground plane. The participants to the sides, below the enthroned Constantine (his head is missing), almost congeal into a uniformly patterned mass that isolates the new emperor and connects him visually with the seated statues of his illustrious predecessors flanking him on the dais. This two-dimensional, hierarchical approach with its emphasis on authority and power rather than on individualized outward form is far removed from the classicizing illusionism of earlier imperial reliefs. It is one of the Roman styles that will be adopted by the emerging Christian Church.

THE BASILICA NOVA. Constantine's rival Maxentius, who controlled Rome throughout his short reign (r. 306–312), ordered the repair of older buildings there and had new ones built. His most impressive undertaking was a huge new basilica, just southeast of the Imperial Forums, called the **BASILICA NOVA**, or New Basilica. Now known as the Basilica of Maxentius and Constantine, this was the last important imperial government building erected in Rome. Like all basilicas, it functioned as an administrative center and provided a magnificent setting for the emperor when he appeared as supreme judge.

Earlier basilicas, such as Trajan's Basilica Ulpia (SEE FIG. 6–40), had been columnar halls, but Maxentius ordered his engineers to create the kind of large, unbroken, vaulted space found in public baths. The central hall was covered with groin vaults, and the side aisles were covered with lower barrel vaults that acted as buttresses, or projecting supports, for the central vault and allowed generous window openings in the clerestory areas over the side walls.

Three of these brick-and-concrete barrel vaults still loom over the streets of present-day Rome **(FIG. 6–63)**. The basilica originally measured 300 by 215 feet and the vaults of the central nave rose to a height of 114 feet. A groin-vaulted porch extended across the short side and sheltered a triple entrance to the central hall. At the opposite end of the long axis of the hall was an apse of the same width, which acted as a focal point for the building

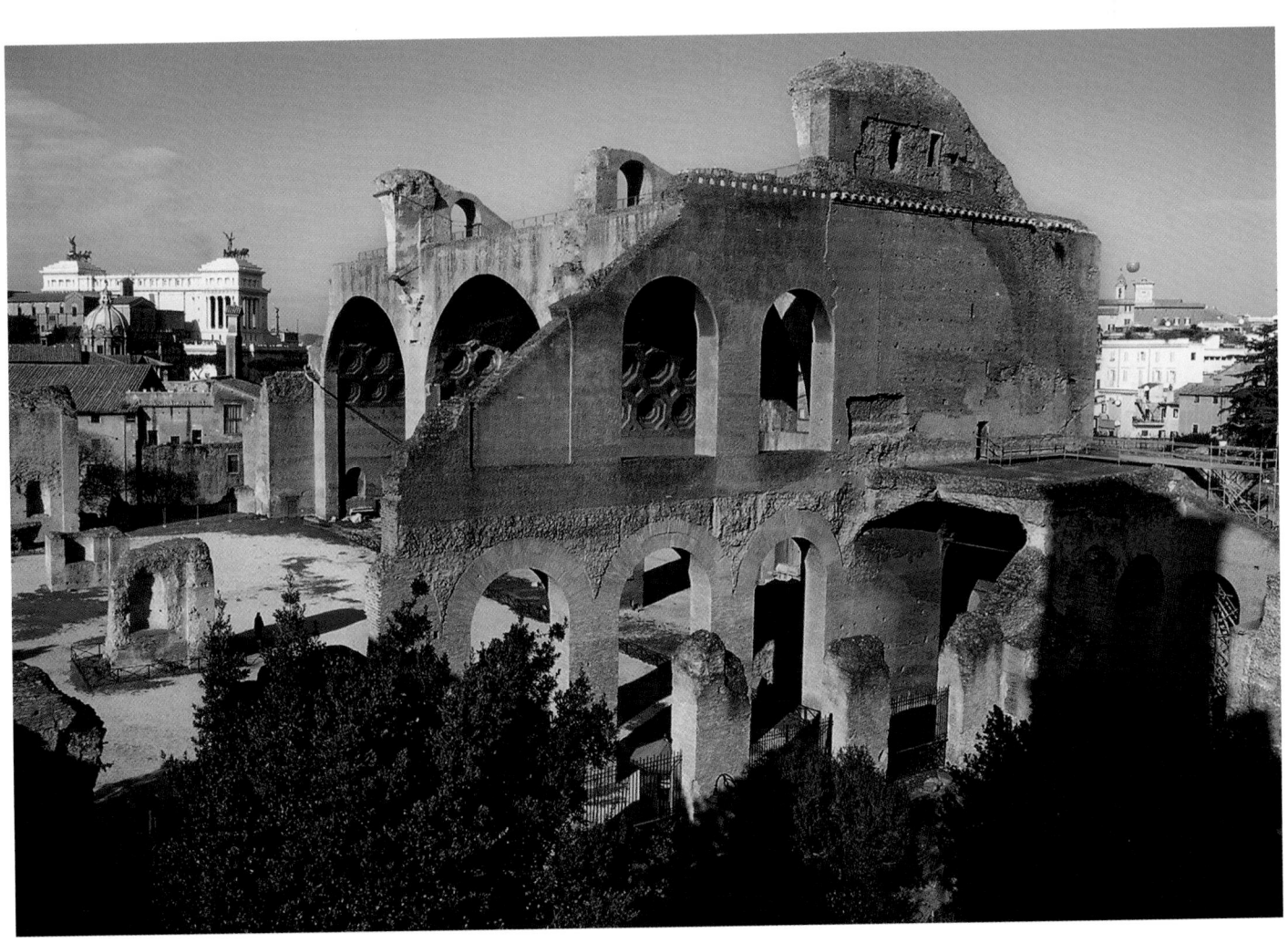

6-63 • BASILICA OF MAXENTIUS AND CONSTANTINE (BASILICA NOVA)
Rome. 306–313 CE.

apse added later

original
apse

barrel-vaulted
bay

groin-vaulted
nave

original
entrance

groin-
vaulted
porch

barrel-vaulted
bay

entrance added later

6-65 • RECONSTRUCTION OF THE BASILICA OF
MAXENTIUS AND CONSTANTINE (BASILICA NOVA)

(FIGS. 6–64, 6–65). The directional focus along a central axis from
entrance to apse was adopted by Christians for use in churches.

Constantine, seeking to impress the people of Rome with
visible symbols of his authority, put his own stamp on projects
Maxentius had started, including this one. He may have changed
the orientation of the Basilica Nova by adding an imposing new
entrance in the center of the long side facing the Via Sacra and a
giant apse facing it across the three aisles. He also commissioned a
colossal, 30-foot statue of himself to be placed inside within an
apse (FIG. 6–66). Sculptors used white marble for the head, chest,
arms, and legs, and sheets of bronze for the drapery, all supported

on a wooden frame. This statue became a permanent stand-in for
the emperor, representing him whenever the conduct of business
legally required his presence. The head combines features of
traditional Roman portraiture with some of the abstract qualities
evident in images of the tetrarchs (SEE FIG. 6–57). The defining
characteristics of Constantine's face—his heavy jaw, hooked nose,
and jutting chin—have been incorporated into a stylized, symmetrical pattern in which other features, such as his eyes, eyebrows, and
hair, have been simplified into repeated geometric arcs. The result
is a work that projects imperial power and dignity with no hint of
human frailty or imperfection.

6-66 • CONSTANTINE THE GREAT
Basilica of Maxentius and Constantine, Rome. 325–326 CE. Marble, height of head 8'6" (2.6 m). Palazzo dei Conservatori, Rome.

ROMAN ART AFTER CONSTANTINE

Although Constantine was baptized only on his deathbed in 337, Christianity had become the official religion of the empire by the end of the fourth century, and non-Christians had become targets of persecution. This religious shift, however, did not diminish Roman interest in the artistic traditions of their pagan Classical past. A large silver **PLATTER** dating from the mid-fourth century CE (**FIG. 6–67**) proves that artists working for Christian patrons continued to use themes involving Bacchus, allowing them the opportunity to create elaborate figural compositions displaying the

In 1942, a farmer plowing a field outside the town of Mildenhall in Suffolk, England, located near the site of an ancient Roman villa, accidentally discovered one of the greatest archaeological finds of the twentieth century. In total he unearthed 34 pieces of Roman silver dating from the fourth century CE. The find was not made public until four years later, since the farmer and his associates claimed they were unaware of how valuable it was, both materially and historically. When word of the discovery leaked out, however, the silver was confiscated by the government to determine if it was a "Treasure Trove"—gold or silver objects that have been intentionally hidden (rather than, for example, included in a burial) and that by law belong not to the finder, but to the Crown. The silver found at Mildenhall was deemed a "Treasure Trove" and is now one of the great glories of the British Museum in London.

This is the official story of the discovery at Mildenhall. But there are those who do not believe it. None of the silver in the hoard showed any sign of having been dented by a plough, and some believe that the quality and style of the objects are inconsistent with a provincial Roman context, especially so far in the hinterlands in England. Could the treasure have been looted from Italy during World War II, brought back to England (Mildenhall is not far from an American airfield), and buried to set up a staged discovery? The farmer who discovered the hoard and his associates, some argue, changed their story several times over the course of its history. Most scholars do believe the official story—that the silver was buried quickly for safekeeping by wealthy provincial Romans in Britain who felt threatened by a possible invasion or attack, and was forgotten (perhaps its owners were killed in the expected turmoil) until its accidental discovery in 1942. But when the history of art is founded on undocumented archaeological finds, there is usually room for doubt.

---

nude or lightly draped human body in complex, dynamic poses. The platter was found in a cache of silver tableware near Mildenhall, England, and although most of the objects are also decorated with pagan imagery, three of the spoons are engraved with Christian symbols. The original owner of the hoard was likely to have been a wealthy Roman Christian, living in the provinces. Such opulent items were often hidden or buried to protect them from theft and looting, a sign of the breakdown of the Roman peace, especially in provincial areas (see "The Mildenhall Treasure," above).

The Bacchic revelers on this platter whirl, leap, and sway in a dance to the piping of satyrs around a circular central medallion. In the centerpiece, the head of the sea god Oceanus is ringed by nude females frolicking in the waves with fantastic sea creatures. In the outer circle, the figure of Bacchus is the one stable element. With a bunch of grapes in his right hand, a krater at his feet, and one foot on the haunches of his panther, he listens to a male follower begging for another drink. Only a few figures away, the pitifully drunken hero Hercules has lost his lion-skin mantle and collapsed in a stupor into the supporting arms of two satyrs. The detail, clarity, and liveliness of this platter reflect the work of a virtuoso artist. Deeply engraved lines emphasize the contours of the subtly modeled bodies, echoing the technique of **undercutting** used to add depth to figures in stone and marble reliefs and suggesting a connection between silver-working and relief sculpture.

Not all Romans, however, converted to Christianity. Among the champions of paganism were the Roman patricians Quintus Aurelius Symmachus and Virius

6-67 • PLATTER
From Mildenhall, England. Mid 4th century CE. Silver, diameter approx. 24″ (61 cm). British Museum, London.

Nicomachus Flavianus. A famous ivory diptych (**FIG. 6–68**) attests to the close relationship between their families, perhaps through marriage, as well as to their firmly held beliefs. A **diptych** was a pair of panels attached with hinges, not unlike the modest object held by the woman in FIG. 6–31, but in this case made of a very precious material and carved with reliefs on the exterior sides. On the interior of a diptych there were shallow, traylike recessions filled with wax, into which messages could be written with a stylus and sent with a servant as a letter to a friend or acquaintance, who could then smooth out the wax surface, incise a reply with his or her own stylus, and send the diptych back to its owner with the servant. Here one family's name is inscribed at the top of each panel. On the panel inscribed "Symmachorum" (illustrated here), a stately, elegantly attired priestess burns incense at a beautifully decorated altar. On her head is a wreath of ivy, sacred to Bacchus. She is assisted by a small child, and the event takes place out of doors under an oak tree, sacred to Jupiter. Like the silversmiths, Roman ivory carvers of the fourth century CE were highly skillful, and their work was widely admired. For conservative patrons like the Nicomachus and Symmachus families, they imitated the Augustan style effortlessly. The exquisite rendering of the drapery and foliage recalls the reliefs of the Ara Pacis (see page 177, FIG. B).

Classical subject matter remained attractive to artists and patrons throughout the late Roman period. Even such great Christian thinkers as the fourth-century CE bishop Gregory of Nazianzus (a saint and Father of the Orthodox Church) spoke out in support of the right of the people to appreciate and enjoy their Classical heritage, so long as they were not seduced by it to return to pagan practices. As a result, stories of the ancient gods and heroes entered the secular realm as lively, visually delightful, even erotic decorative elements. As Roman authority gave way to local rule by powerful barbarian tribes in much of the West, many people continued to appreciate Classical learning and to treasure Greek and Roman art. In the East, Classical traditions and styles were cultivated to become an enduring element of Byzantine art.

6-68 • PRIESTESS OF BACCHUS (?)
Right panel of the diptych of Symmachus and Nicomachus.
c. 390–401 CE. Ivory, 11¾ × 4¾" (29.9 × 12 cm).
Victoria & Albert Museum, London.

THINK ABOUT IT

6.1 Compare the scenes celebrating the vitality of human life on the walls of Etruscan tombs with the scenes portrayed on the walls of the Egyptian tombs explored in Chapter 3.

6.2 Explain how the Roman interest in portraits grew out of early funeral rituals.

6.3 Describe three themes that are found in the murals of Roman houses in Pompeii, using specific examples from this chapter. Why do you think these themes were chosen for the decoration of homes?

6.4 Identify two key structural advances made by Roman builders and discuss their use in one large civic building in this chapter.

6.5 Discuss how Roman emperors used portraiture as imperial propaganda. Focus your discussion on a comparison of the busts of the emperor Commodus (FIG. 6–53) and a tetrarch (FIG. 6–57).

PRACTICE MORE: Compose answers to these questions, get flashcards for images and terms, and review chapter material with quizzes
www.myartslab.com

7-1 • DAVID BATTLING GOLIATH One of the "David Plates," made in Constantinople. 629–630 CE. Silver, diameter 19⅞" (49.4 cm). Metropolitan Museum of Art, New York.

JEWISH, EARLY CHRISTIAN, AND BYZANTINE ART

The robust figures on this huge silver plate (FIG. 7–1) enact three signature episodes in the youthful hero David's combat with the Philistine giant Goliath (I Samuel 17:41–51). In the upper register, David—easily identified not only by his youth but also by the prominent halo as the "good guy" in all three scenes—and Goliath challenge each other on either side of a seated Classical personification of the stream that will be the source of the stones David will use in the ensuing battle. The confrontation itself appears in the middle, in a broad figural frieze whose size signals its primary importance. Goliath is most notable here for his superior armaments—helmet, spear, sword, and an enormous protective shield. At the bottom, David, stones and slingshot flung behind him, consummates his victory by severing the head of his defeated foe, whose imposing weapons and armor are scattered uselessly behind him.

It may be surprising to see a Judeo–Christian subject portrayed in a style that was developed for the exploits of Classical heroes, but this mixture of traditions is typical of the eclecticism characterizing the visual arts as the Christianized Roman world became the Byzantine Empire. Patrons saw no conflict between the artistic principles of the pagan past and the Christian teaching undergirding their imperial present. To them, this Jewish subject, created for a Christian patron in a pagan style, would have attracted notice only because of its sumptuousness and its artistic virtuosity.

This was one of nine "David Plates" unearthed in Cyprus in 1902. Control stamps—guaranteeing the purity of the material, much like the stamps of "sterling" that appear on silver today—date them to the reign of the Byzantine emperor Heraclius (r. 613–641 CE). Displayed in the home of their owners, they were visual proclamations of wealth, but also of education and refined taste, just like collections of art and antiques in our own day. A constellation of iconographic and historical factors allows us to uncover a subtler message, however. For the original owners, the single combat of David and Goliath might have recalled a situation involving their own emperor and enemies.

The reign of Heraclius was marked by war with the Sassanian Persians. A decisive moment in the final campaign of 628–629 CE occurred when Heraclius himself stepped forward for single combat with the Persian general Razatis, and the emperor prevailed, presaging Byzantine victory. Some contemporaries referred to Heraclius as a new David. Is it possible that the set of David Plates was produced for the emperor to offer as a diplomatic gift to one of his aristocratic allies, who subsequently took them to Cyprus? Perhaps the owners later buried them for safekeeping—like the early silver platter from Mildenhall (SEE FIG. 6–67)—where they awaited discovery at the beginning of the twentieth century.

LEARN ABOUT IT

7.1 Investigate how aspects of Jewish and Early Christian art developed from the artistic traditions of the Roman world.

7.2 Interpret how Early Christian and Byzantine artists used narrative and iconic imagery to convey the foundations of the Christian faith for those already initiated into the life of the Church.

7.3 Analyze the connection between form and function in buildings created for worship.

7.4 Assess the central role of images in the devotional practices of the Byzantine world and explore the reasons for and impact of the brief interlude of iconoclasm.

7.5 Trace the growing Byzantine interest in conveying human emotions and representing human situations when visualizing sacred stories.

HEAR MORE: Listen to an audio file of your chapter **www.myartslab.com**

JEWS, CHRISTIANS, AND MUSLIMS

Three religions that arose in the Near East dominate the spiritual life of the Western world today: Judaism, Christianity, and Islam. All three are monotheistic—believing that the same God of Abraham created and rules the universe, and hears the prayers of the faithful. Jews believe that God made a covenant, or pact, with their ancestors, the Hebrews, and that they are God's chosen people. They await the coming of a savior, the Messiah, "the anointed one." Christians believe that Jesus of Nazareth was that Messiah (the name Christ is derived from the Greek term meaning "Messiah"). They believe that, in Jesus, God took human form, preached among men and women, suffered execution, then rose from the dead and ascended to heaven after establishing the Christian Church under the leadership of the apostles (his closest disciples). Muslims, while accepting the Hebrew prophets and Jesus as divinely inspired, believe Muhammad to be the last and greatest prophet of God (Allah), the Messenger of God through whom Islam was revealed some six centuries after Jesus' lifetime.

All three are "religions of the book," that is, they have written records of God's will and words: the Hebrew Bible; the Christian Bible, which includes the Hebrew Bible as its Old Testament as well as the Christian New Testament; and the Muslim Qur'an, believed to be the Word of God as revealed in Arabic directly to Muhammad through the archangel Gabriel.

Both Judaism and Christianity existed within the Roman Empire, along with various other religions devoted to the worship of many gods. The variety of religious buildings excavated in present-day Syria at the abandoned Roman outpost of Dura-Europos (see "Dura-Europos," page 223) represents the cosmopolitan religious character of Roman society in the second and third centuries. The settlement—destroyed in 256 CE— included a Jewish house-synagogue, a Christian house-church, shrines to the Persian cults of Mithras and Zoroaster, and temples to Greek and Roman gods, including Zeus and Artemis.

EARLY JEWISH ART

The Jewish people trace their origin to a Semitic people called the Hebrews, who lived in the land of Canaan. Canaan, known from the second century CE by the Roman name Palestine, was located along the eastern edge of the Mediterranean Sea (MAP 7–1). According to the Torah, the first five books of the Hebrew Bible, God promised the patriarch Abraham that Canaan would be a homeland for the Jewish people (Genesis 17:8), a belief that remains important for some Jews to this day.

Jewish settlement of Canaan probably began sometime in the second millennium BCE. According to Exodus, the second book of the Torah, the prophet Moses led the Hebrews out of slavery in Egypt to the promised land of Canaan. At one crucial point during the journey, Moses climbed alone to the top of Mount Sinai, where God gave him the Ten Commandments, the cornerstone of Jewish law. The commandments, inscribed on tablets, were kept in a gold-covered wooden box, the Ark of the Covenant.

Jewish law forbade the worship of idols, a prohibition that often made the representational arts—especially sculpture in the round—suspect. Nevertheless, artists working for Jewish patrons depicted both symbolic and narrative Jewish subjects, and they looked to both Near Eastern and Classical Greek and Roman art for inspiration.

THE FIRST TEMPLE IN JERUSALEM. In the tenth century BCE, the Jewish king Solomon built a temple in Jerusalem to house the Ark of the Covenant. According to the Hebrew Bible (2 Chronicles 2–7),

7-2 • MENORAHS AND ARK OF THE COVENANT

Wall painting in a Jewish catacomb, Villa Torlonia, Rome. 3rd century. 3'11" × 5'9" (1.19 × 1.8 m).

The menorah form probably derives from the ancient Near Eastern Tree of Life, symbolizing for the Jewish people both the end of exile and the paradise to come.

MAP 7-1 • THE LATE ROMAN AND BYZANTINE WORLD

The eastern shores of the Mediterranean, birthplace of Judaism and Christianity, were the focal point of the Byzantine Empire. It expanded further west under the Emperor Justinian, though by 1025 CE it had contracted again to the east.

he sent to nearby Phoenicia for cedar, cypress, and sandalwood, and for a superb construction supervisor. Later known as the First Temple, it was the spiritual center of Jewish life. Biblical texts describe courtyards, two bronze **pillars** (large, free-standing architectural forms), an entrance hall, a main hall, and the Holy of Holies, the innermost chamber that housed the Ark and its guardian cherubim, or attendant angels.

In 586 BCE, the Babylonians, under King Nebuchadnezzar II, conquered Jerusalem. They destroyed the Temple, exiled the Jews, and carried off the Ark of the Covenant. When Cyrus the Great of Persia conquered Babylonia in 539 BCE, he permitted the Jews to return to their homeland (Ezra 1:1–4) and rebuild the Temple, which became known as the Second Temple. When Canaan became part of the Roman Empire, Herod the Great (king of Judaea, 37–34 BCE) restored the Second Temple. In 70 CE, Roman forces led by the general and future emperor Titus

destroyed and looted the Second Temple and all of Jerusalem, a campaign the Romans commemorated on the Arch of Titus (SEE FIG. 6–33). The site of the Second Temple, the Temple Mount, is also an Islamic holy site, the Haram al-Sharif, and is now occupied by the shrine called the Dome of the Rock (SEE FIGS. 8–3, 8–4, 8–5).

JEWISH CATACOMB ART IN ROME.   Most of the earliest surviving examples of Jewish art date from the Hellenistic and Roman periods. Six Jewish **catacombs** (underground cemeteries), discovered on the outskirts of Rome and in use from the first to fourth centuries CE, display wall paintings with Jewish themes. In one example, from the third century CE, two **menorahs** (seven-branched lamps), flank the long-lost **ARK OF THE COVENANT (FIG. 7–2)**. The continuing representation of the menorah, one of the precious objects looted from the Second Temple, kept the memory of the lost Jewish treasures alive.

7-3 • WALL WITH TORAH NICHE
From a house-synagogue, Dura-Europos, Syria. 244–245 CE. Tempera on plaster, section approx.
40' (12.19 m) long. Reconstructed in the National Museum, Damascus, Syria.

SYNAGOGUES. Judaism has long emphasized religious learning. Jews gather in synagogues for study of the Torah—considered a form of worship. A synagogue can be any large room where the Torah scrolls are kept and read; it was also the site of communal social gatherings. Some synagogues were located in private homes or in buildings originally constructed like homes. The first Dura-Europos synagogue consisted of an assembly hall, a separate alcove for women, and a courtyard. After a remodeling of the building, completed in 244–245 CE, men and women shared the hall,

and residential rooms were added. Two architectural features distinguished the assembly hall: a bench along its walls and a niche for the Torah scrolls (**FIG. 7–3**).

Scenes from Jewish history and the story of Moses, as recorded in Exodus, unfold in a continuous visual narrative around the room, employing the Roman tradition of epic historical presentation (SEE FIG. 6–44). In the scene of **THE CROSSING OF THE RED SEA (FIG. 7–4)**, Moses appears twice to signal sequential moments in the dramatic narrative. To the left he leans toward the army of Pharaoh

7-4 • THE CROSSING OF THE RED SEA
Detail of a wall painting from a house-synagogue, Dura-Europos, Syria. 244–245 CE. National Museum, Damascus.

The Mosaic Floor of the Beth Alpha Synagogue

by Marianos and Hanina. Ritual Objects, Celestial Diagram, and Sacrifice of Isaac. Galilee, Israel. 6th century CE.

The shrine that holds the Torah is flanked by menorahs and growling lions, perhaps there as a security system to protect such sacred objects.

The figures in the four corners are winged personifications of the seasons; this figure holding a shepherd's crook and accompanied by a bird is Spring.

At the center of the zodiac wheel is a representation of the sun in a chariot set against a night sky studded with stars and a crescent moon.

The 12 signs of the zodiac appear in chronological order following a clockwise arrangement around the wheel of a year, implying perpetual continuity since the series has no set beginning and no end. This is Scorpio.

The peaceful coexistence of the lion and the ox (predator and prey) may represent a golden age or peaceable kingdom (Isaiah 11:6–9; 65:25).

Torah shrine and ritual objects.

The Metaphysical Realm

The sun, seasons, and signs of the zodiac.

The Celestial Realm

The Sacrifice of Isaac (Genesis 22:1–19).

The Terrestrial Realm

This ram (identified by inscription) will ultimately take Isaac's place as sacrificial offering. Throughout the mosaic, animals are shown consistently in profile, human beings frontally.

These two texts—one in Aramaic and one in Greek—identify the artists of the mosaic as Marianos and his son Hanina, and date their work to the reign of Emperor Justin I or II (518–578).

Abraham, preparing to sacrifice Isaac, is interrupted by the hand of God rather than by the angel specified in the Bible. Both Abraham and Isaac are identified by inscription, but Abraham's advanced age is signaled pictorially by the streaks of gray in his beard.

SEE MORE: View the Closer Look feature for the Mosaic Floor of the Beth Alpha Synagogue **www.myartslab.com**

marching along the path that had been created for the Hebrews by God's miraculous parting of the waters, but at the right, wielding his authoritative staff, he returns the waters over the Egyptian soldiers to prevent them from pursuing his followers. Over both scenes hovers a large hand, representing God's presence in both miracles—the parting and the unparting—using a symbol that will also be frequent in Christian art. Hieratic scale makes it clear who is the hero in this two-part narrative, but the clue to his identity is provided only by the context of the story, which observers would have already known.

In addition to house-synagogues, Jews built meeting places designed on the model of the ancient Roman basilica. A typical basilica synagogue had a central nave; an aisle on both sides, separated from the nave by a line of columns; a semicircular apse with Torah shrine in the wall facing Jerusalem; and perhaps an atrium and porch, or **narthex** (vestibule). The small, fifth-century CE synagogue at Beth Alpha—discovered between the Gilboa mountains and the River Jordan by farmers in 1928—fits well into this pattern, with a three-nave interior, vestibule, and courtyard. Like some other very grand synagogues, it also has a mosaic floor, in this case a later addition from the sixth century. Most of the floor decoration is geometric in design, but in the central nave there are three complex panels full of figural compositions and symbols (see "A Closer Look," page 221) created using 21 separate colors of stone and glass tesserae. The images of ritual objects, a celestial diagram of the zodiac, and a scene of Abraham's near-sacrifice of Isaac, bordered by strips of foliate and geometric ornament, draw on both Classical and Near Eastern pictorial traditions.

EARLY CHRISTIAN ART

Christians believe in one God manifest in three persons—the Trinity of Creator-Father (God), Son (Jesus Christ), and Holy Spirit—and that Jesus was the Son of God by a human mother, the Virgin Mary. At the age of 30, Jesus gathered a group of followers, male and female; he performed miracles of healing and preached love of God and neighbor, the sanctity of social justice, the forgiveness of sins, and the promise of life after death. Christian belief holds that, after his ministry on Earth, Jesus was executed by crucifixion, and after three days rose from the dead.

THE CHRISTIAN BIBLE. The Christian Bible is divided into two parts: the Old Testament (the Hebrew Bible) and the New Testament. The life and teachings of Jesus of Nazareth were recorded between about 70 and 100 CE in New Testament Gospels attributed to the four evangelists (from the Greek *evangelion*, meaning "good news"): Matthew, Mark, Luke, and John. The order was set by St. Jerome, an early Church Father who made a translation of the books from Greek into Latin.

In addition to the four Gospels, the New Testament includes the Acts of the Apostles and the Epistles, 21 letters of advice and encouragement written to Christian communities in Greece, Asia Minor, and other parts of the Roman Empire. The final book is Revelation (Apocalypse), a series of enigmatic visions and prophecies concerning the eventual triumph of God at the end of the world, written about 95 CE.

THE EARLY CHURCH. Jesus limited his ministry primarily to Jews; it was his apostles, as well as later followers such as Paul, who took his teachings to gentiles (non-Jews). Despite sporadic persecutions, Christianity persisted and spread throughout the Roman Empire. The government formally recognized the religion in 313, and Christianity grew rapidly during the fourth century. As well-educated, upper-class Romans joined the Christian Church, they established an increasingly elaborate organizational structure along with ever-more complicated rituals and doctrine.

Christian communities became organized by geographic units, called dioceses, along the lines of Roman provincial governments. Senior church officials called bishops served as governors of dioceses made up of smaller units, parishes, headed by priests. A bishop's church is a **cathedral**, a word derived from the Latin *cathedra*, which means "chair" but took on the meaning of "bishop's throne."

Communal Christian worship focused on the central "mystery," or miracle, of the Incarnation of God in Jesus Christ and the promise of salvation. At its core was the ritual consumption of bread and wine, identified as the Body and Blood of Christ, which Jesus had inaugurated at the Last Supper, a Passover seder meal with his disciples just before his crucifixion. Around these acts developed an elaborate religious ceremony, or liturgy, called the **Eucharist** (also known as Holy Communion or the Mass).

The earliest Christians gathered to worship in private apartments or houses, or in buildings constructed after domestic models such as the third-century church-house excavated at Dura-Europos (see "Dura-Europos," opposite). As their rites became more ritualized and complicated, however, Christians developed special buildings—churches and baptisteries—as well as specialized ritual equipment. They also began to use art to visualize their most important stories and ideas (see "Narrative and Iconic," page 224). The earliest surviving Christian art dates to the early third century and derives its styles and its imagery from Jewish and Roman visual traditions. In this process, known as **syncretism**, artists assimilate images from other traditions and give them new meanings. The borrowings can be unconscious or quite deliberate. For example, **orant** figures—worshipers with arms outstretched in prayer—can be pagan, Jewish, or Christian, depending on the context in which they occur. Perhaps the best-known syncretic image is the Good Shepherd. In pagan art, he was Apollo, or Hermes the shepherd, or Orpheus among the animals, or a personification of philanthropy. For Early Christians, he became the Good Shepherd of the Psalms (Psalm 23) and the Gospels (Matthew 18:12–14, John 10:11–16). Such images, therefore, do not have a stable meaning, but are associated with the meaning(s) that a particular viewer brings to them. They remind rather than instruct.

Our understanding of buildings used for worship by third-century Jews and Christians was greatly enhanced—even revolutionized—by the spectacular discoveries made in the 1930s while excavating the Roman military garrison and border town of Dura-Europos (in modern Syria). In 256, threatened by the Parthians attacking from the east, residents of Dura built a huge earthwork mound around their town in an attempt to protect themselves from the invading armies. In the process—since they were located on the city's margins right against its defensive stone wall—the houses used by Jews and Christians as places of worship were buried under the earthwork perimeter. In spite of this enhanced fortification, the Parthians conquered Dura-Europos. But since the victors never unearthed the submerged margins of the city, an intact Jewish house-synagogue and Christian house-church remained underground awaiting the explorations of modern archaeologists.

We have already seen the extensive strip narratives flanking the Torah shrine in the house-synagogue (SEE FIG. 7–3). The discovery of this expansive pictorial decoration contradicted a long-held scholarly belief that Jews of this period avoided figural decoration of any sort, in conformity to Mosaic law (Exodus 20:4). And a few blocks down the street that ran along the city wall, a typical Roman house built around a central courtyard held another surprise. Only a discreet red cross above the door distinguished it from the other houses on its block, but the arrangement of the interior clearly documents its use as a Christian place of worship. A large assembly hall that could seat 60–70 people sits on one side of the courtyard, and across from it is a smaller but extensively decorated room with a water tank set aside for baptism, the central rite of Christian initiation (FIG. A). Along the walls were scenes from Christ's miracles and a monumental portrayal of women visiting his tomb about to discover his resurrection (below). Above the baptismal basin is a **lunette** (semicircular wall section) featuring the Good Shepherd with his flock, but also including at lower left diminutive figures of Adam and Eve covering themselves in shame after their sinful disobedience (FIG. B). Even this early in Christian art, sacred spaces were decorated with pictures proclaiming the theological meaning of the rituals they housed. In this painting, Adam and Eve's fall from grace is juxtaposed with a larger image of the Good Shepherd (representing Jesus) who came to Earth to care for and guide his sheep (Christian believers) toward redemption and eternal life—a message that was especially appropriate juxtaposed with the rite of Christian baptism, which signaled the converts' passage from sin to salvation.

A. MODEL OF WALLS AND BAPTISMAL FONT
Baptistery of a Christian house-church, Dura-Europos, Syria. Before 256. Fresco. Yale University Art Gallery, New Haven, Connecticut.

B. THE GOOD SHEPHERD WITH ADAM AND EVE AFTER THE FALL
Detail of lunette painting above.

Narrative and Iconic

In this Roman catacomb painting (scene at left), Peter, like Moses before him, strikes a rock and water flows from it. Imprisoned in Rome after the arrest of Jesus, Peter converted his fellow prisoners and jailers to Christianity, but he needed water with which to baptize them. Miraculously a spring gushed forth at the touch of his staff.

In the star-studded heavens painted on the vault of this chamber floats the face of Christ, flanked by the first and last letters of the Greek alphabet, alpha and omega. Here Christ takes on the guise not of the youthful teacher or miracle-worker seen so often in Early Christian art, but of a Greek philosopher, with long beard and hair. The halo of light around his head indicates his importance and his divinity, a symbol appropriated from the conventions of Roman imperial art, where haloes often appear around the heads of emperors.

These two catacomb paintings represent two major directions of Christian art—the narrative and the iconic. The **narrative image** recounts an event drawn from St. Peter's life—striking the rock for water—which in turn evokes the establishment of the Church as well as the essential Christian rite of baptism. The **iconic image**—Christ's face flanked by alpha and omega—offers a tangible expression of an intangible concept. The letters signify the beginning and end of time, and, combined with the image of Christ, symbolically represent not a story, but an idea—the everlasting dominion of the heavenly Christ.

Throughout the history of Christian art these two tendencies will be apparent—the narrative urge to tell a good story, whose moral or theological implications often have instructional or theological value, and the desire to create iconic images that symbolize the core concepts and values of the developing religious tradition. In both cases, the works of art take on meaning only in relation to viewers' stored knowledge of Christian stories and beliefs.

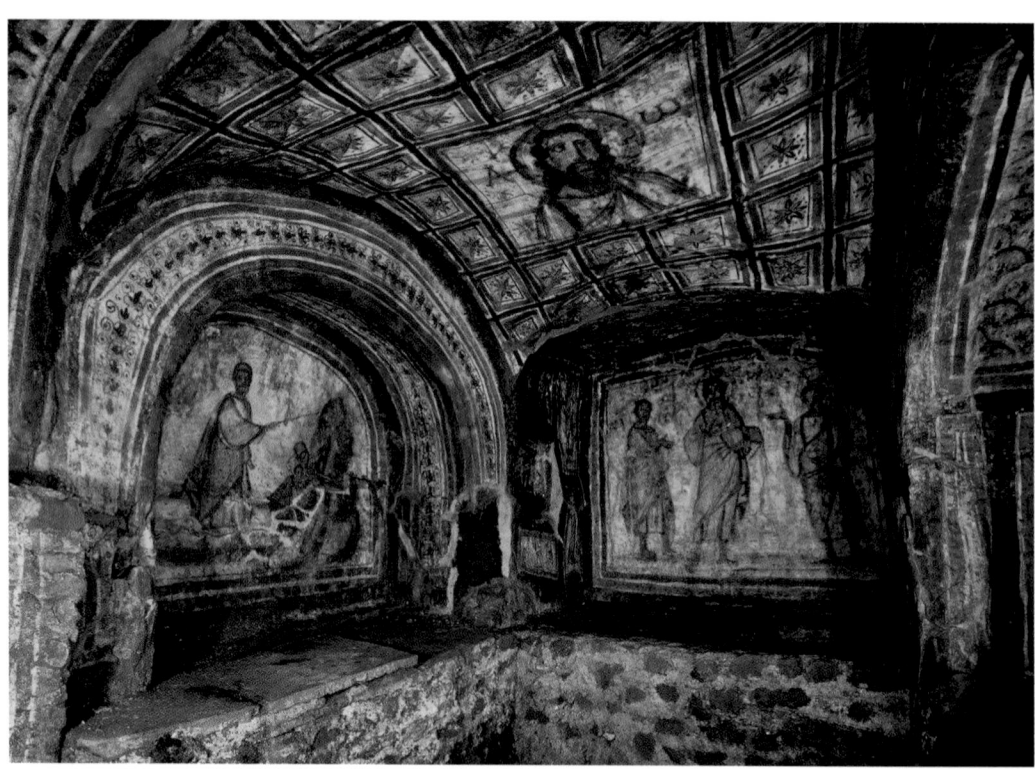

CUBICULUM OF LEONIS, CATACOMB OF COMMODILLA
Near Rome. Late 4th century.

In the niche seen on the right, two early Roman Christian martyrs, Felix (d. 274) and Adauctus (d. 303) flank a youthful, beardless Jesus, who holds a book emphasizing his role as teacher. By including Peter and Roman martyrs in the chamber's decoration, the early Christians, who dug this catacomb as a place to bury their dead, emphasized the importance of their city in Christian history.

CATACOMB PAINTINGS. Christians, like Jews, used catacombs for burials and funeral ceremonies, not as places of worship. In the Christian Catacomb of Commodilla, dating from the fourth century, long rectangular niches in the walls, called *loculi*, each held two or three bodies. Affluent families created small rooms, or **cubicula** (singular, *cubiculum*), off the main passages to house sarcophagi (see "Narrative and Iconic," above). The *cubicula* were hewn out of tufa, soft volcanic rock, then plastered and painted with imagery related to their owners' religious beliefs. The finest Early Christian catacomb paintings resemble murals in houses such as those preserved at Rome and Pompeii.

One fourth-century Roman catacomb contained remains, or relics, of SS. Peter and Marcellinus, two third-century Christians martyred for their faith. Here, the ceiling of a *cubiculum* is

7-5 • THE GOOD SHEPHERD, ORANTS, AND THE STORY OF JONAH
Painted ceiling of the Catacomb of SS. Peter and Marcellinus, Rome. Late 3rd–early 4th century.

partitioned by a central **medallion**, or round compartment, and four **lunettes**, semicircular framed by arches **(FIG. 7–5)**. At the center is a Good Shepherd, whose pose has roots in Classical sculpture. In its new context, the image was a reminder of Jesus' promise "I am the good shepherd. A good shepherd lays down his life for the sheep" (John 10:11).

The semicircular compartments surrounding the Good Shepherd tell the story of Jonah and the sea monster from the Hebrew Bible (Jonah 1–2), in which God caused Jonah to be thrown overboard, swallowed by the monster, and released, repentant and unscathed, three days later. Christians reinterpreted this story as a parable of Christ's death and resurrection—and hence of the everlasting life awaiting true believers—and it was a popular subject in Christian catacombs. On the left, Jonah is thrown from the boat; on the right, the monster spits him up; and at the center, Jonah reclines in the shade of a vine, a symbol of paradise. Orant figures stand between the lunettes, presumably images of the faithful Christians who were buried here.

SCULPTURE. Early Christian sculpture before the fourth century is even rarer than painting. What survives is mainly sarcophagi and small statues and reliefs. A remarkable set of small marble figures, discovered in the 1960s and probably made in third-century Asia Minor, features a gracious **GOOD SHEPHERD (FIG. 7–6)**. Because it was found with sculptures depicting Jonah—as we have already seen, a popular Early Christian theme—it is probably from a Christian home.

7-6 • THE GOOD SHEPHERD
Eastern Mediterranean, probably Anatolia (Turkey). Second half of the 3rd century. Marble, height 19¾" (50.2 cm), width 16" (15.9 cm). Cleveland Museum of Art. John L. Severance Fund, 1965.241

IMPERIAL CHRISTIAN ARCHITECTURE AND ART

When Constantine issued the Edict of Milan in 313, granting all people in the Roman Empire freedom to worship whatever god they wished, Christianity and Christian art and architecture entered a new phase. Sophisticated philosophical and ethical systems developed, incorporating many ideas from Greek and Roman pagan thought. Church scholars edited and commented on the Bible, and the papal secretary who would become St. Jerome (c. 347–420) undertook a new translation from Hebrew and Greek versions into Latin, the language of the Western Church. The so-called Vulgate (from the same root as the word "vulgar," the Latin *vulgaris*, meaning "common" or "popular") became the official version of the Bible.

ARCHITECTURE

The developing Christian community had special architectural needs. Greek temples had served as the house and treasury of the gods, forming a backdrop for ceremonies that took place at altars in the open air. In Christianity, an entire community gathered inside a building to worship. Christians also needed places or buildings for activities such as the initiation of new members, private prayer, and burials. From the age of Constantine, pagan basilicas provided the model for congregational churches, and tombs provided a model for baptisteries and martyrs' shrines (see "Longitudinal-Plan and Central-Plan Churches," page 228).

OLD ST. PETER'S CHURCH.   Constantine also ordered the construction of a large new basilica to mark the place where Christians believed St. Peter was buried (see "Longitudinal-Plan and Central-Plan Churches," page 228, FIG. A). Our knowledge of what is now called Old St. Peter's (it was destroyed and replaced

7-7 • Jacopo Grimaldi INTERIOR OF OLD ST. PETER'S
1619 copy of an earlier drawing. Vatican Library, Rome. MS Barberini Lat. 2733, fols. 104v–105r

EXPLORE MORE: Gain insight from a primary source related to Old St. Peter's **www.myartslab.com**

by a new building in the sixteenth century) is based on written descriptions, drawings made before and while it was being dismantled (FIG. 7–7), the study of other churches inspired by it, and modern archaeological excavations at the site.

Old St. Peter's included architectural elements in an arrangement that has characterized Christian basilica churches ever since. A narthex across the width of the building provided a place for people who had not yet been baptized. Five doorways—a large, central portal into the nave and two portals on each side—gave access to the church. Columns supporting an entablature lined the nave, forming what is called a nave colonnade. Running parallel to the nave colonnade on each side was another row of columns that

7-8 • CHURCH OF SANTA SABINA
Rome. Exterior view from the southeast. c. 422–432.

SEE MORE: Click the Google Earth link for Santa Sabina **www.myartslab.com**

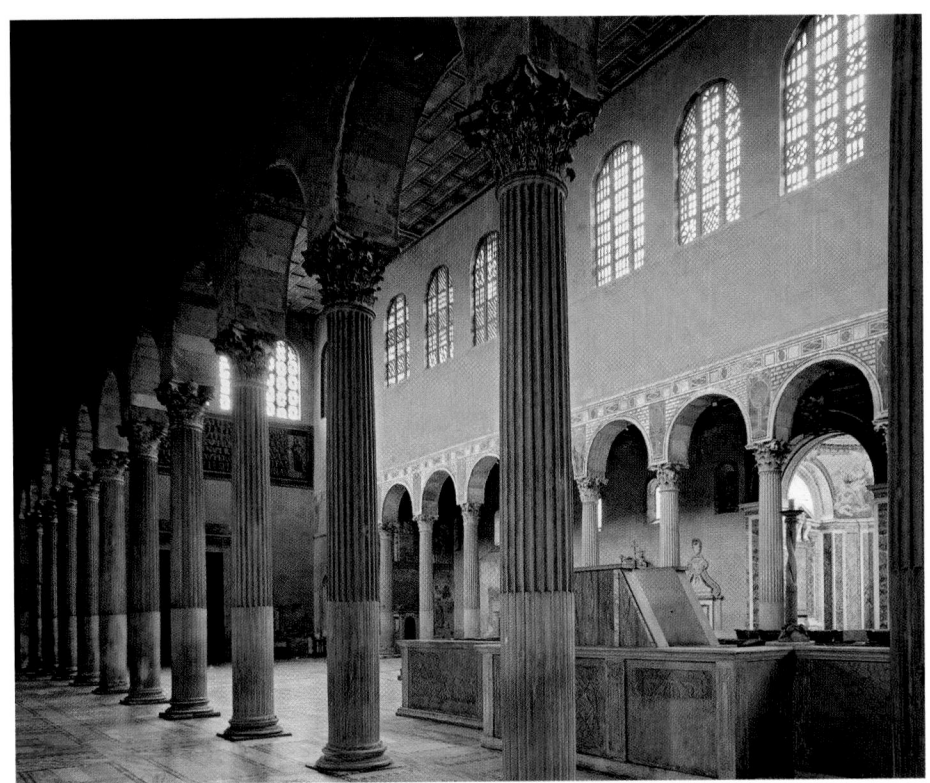

7-9 • INTERIOR, CHURCH OF SANTA SABINA
Rome. View from the south aisle near the sanctuary toward the entrance. c. 422–432.

created double side aisles; these columns supported round arches rather than an entablature. The roofs of both nave and aisles were supported by wooden rafters. Sarcophagi and tombs lined the side aisles. At the apse end of the nave, Constantine's architects added an innovative transept—a perpendicular hall crossing in front of the apse. This area provided additional space for the large number of clergy serving the church, and it also accommodated pilgrims visiting the tomb of St. Peter. Old St. Peter's could hold at least 14,000 worshipers, and it remained the largest church in Christendom until the eleventh century.

SANTA SABINA. Old St. Peter's is gone, but the church of Santa Sabina in Rome, constructed by Bishop Peter of Illyria (a region in the Balkan peninsula) a century later, between about 422 and 432, appears much as it did in the fifth century (FIGS. 7–8, 7–9). The basic elements of the Early Christian basilica church are clearly visible here, inside and out: a nave lit by clerestory windows, flanked by single side aisles, and ending in a rounded apse.

Santa Sabina's exterior is simple brickwork. In contrast, the church's interior displays a wealth of marble veneer and 24 fluted marble columns with Corinthian capitals reused from a second-century pagan building. (Material reused from earlier buildings is known as *spolia*, Latin for "spoils.") The columns support round arches, creating a nave arcade, in contrast to the straight rather than arching nave colonnade in Old St. Peter's. The spandrels—above the columns and between the arches—are inlaid with marble images of the chalice (wine cup) and paten (bread plate)—essential equipment for the Eucharistic rite that took place at the altar. In such basilicas, the blind wall between the arcade and the clerestory

typically had paintings or mosaics with biblical scenes, but here the decoration of the upper walls is lost.

SANTA COSTANZA. Central-plan Roman buildings, with vertical (rather than longitudinal) axes, served as models for Christian tombs, martyrs' churches, and baptisteries (see "Longitudinal-Plan and Central-Plan Churches," page 228). One of the earliest surviving central-plan Christian buildings is the mausoleum of Constantina, daughter of Constantine. Her tomb was built outside the walls of Rome just before 350 (FIG. 7–10), and it was consecrated as a church

7-10 • CHURCH OF SANTA COSTANZA
Rome. c. 350. View from ambulatory into rotunda.

The forms of Early Christian buildings were based on two Roman prototypes: rectangular basilicas (SEE FIGS. 6–40, 6–59, 6–65) and circular or squared structures—including rotundas like the Pantheon (SEE FIGS. 6–46, 6–47). As in the basilica of Old St. Peter's in Rome (FIG. A), **longitudinal-plan** churches are characterized by a forecourt, the atrium, leading to an entrance porch, the **narthex**, which spans one of the building's short ends. Doorways—known collectively as the church's portals—lead from the narthex into a long, congregational area called a nave. Rows of columns separate the high-ceilinged nave from one or two lower **aisles** on either side. The nave can be lit by windows along its upper level just under the ceiling, called a **clerestory**, that rises above the side aisles' roofs. At the opposite end of the nave from the narthex is a semicircular projection, the **apse**. The apse functions as the building's focal point where the altar, raised on a platform, is located. Sometimes there is also a **transept**, a wing that crosses the nave in front of the apse, making the building T-shape. When additional space (a liturgical choir) comes between the transept and the apse, the plan is known as a Latin cross.

Central-plan buildings were first used by Christians, like their pagan Roman forebears, as tombs. Central planning was also employed for baptisteries (where Christians "died"—giving up their old life—and were reborn as believers), and churches dedicated to martyrs (e.g. San Vitale, SEE FIG. 7–20), often built directly over their tombs. Like basilicas, central-plan churches can have an atrium, a narthex, and an apse. But instead of the longitudinal axis of basilican churches, which draws worshipers forward along a line from the entrance toward the apse, central-plan buildings, such as the Mausoleum of Constantina—rededicated in 1256 as the church of Santa Costanza (FIG. B)—have a more vertical axis, from the center up through the dome, which may have functioned as a symbolic "vault of heaven."

A. PLAN AND RECONSTRUCTION DRAWING, OLD ST. PETER'S BASILICA
Rome. c. 320–327; atrium added in later 4th century.
Approx. 394′ (120 m) long and 210′ (64 m) wide.

B. PLAN AND SECTION, CHURCH OF SANTA COSTANZA
Rome. c. 350.

in 1256, dedicated to Santa Costanza (the Italian form of Constantina, who was sanctified after her death). The building is a tall rotunda with an encircling barrel-vaulted passageway called an **ambulatory**. Paired columns with Composite capitals and richly molded entablature blocks support the arcade and dome. Originally, the interior was entirely sheathed in mosaics and veneers of fine marble.

Mosaics still surviving in the ambulatory vault recall the syncretic images in the catacombs. In one section, for example, a bust portrait of Constantina at the crest of the vault is surrounded by a tangle of grapevines filled with **putti**—naked cherubs, derived from pagan art—who vie with the birds to harvest the grapes (FIG. 7–11). Along the bottom edges on each side, other *putti* drive wagonloads of grapes toward pavilions housing large vats in which more *putti* trample the grapes into juice for the making of wine.

The technique, subject, and style are Roman and traditionally associated with Bacchus and his cult, but the meaning here is new. In a Christian context, the wine references the Eucharist and the trampling of grapes to transform them into wine becomes an image of death and resurrection. Constantina's pagan husband, however, may have appreciated the double allusion.

SCULPTURE

In sculpture, as in architecture, Christians adapted Roman forms for their own needs, especially monumental stone sarcophagi. For instance, within her mausoleum, Constantina (d. 354) was buried within a spectacularly huge porphyry sarcophagus (FIG. 7–12) that was installed across from the entrance on the other side of the ambulatory in a rectangular niche (visible on the plan on page 228, FIG. B; an in-place replica peeks over the altar in FIG. 7–10). The motifs are familiar. The same theme of *putti* making wine that we saw highlighted in the mosaics of the ambulatory vaults appears here as well, focused within areas framed by a huge, undulating grapevine, whose subsidiary shoots curl above and below over the flat sides of the box. Striding along its

7-12 • SARCOPHAGUS OF CONSTANTINA
c. 350. Porphyry, height 7'5" (2.26 m). Musei Vaticani, Vatican, Rome.

base, peacocks symbolize eternal life in paradise, while a lone sheep could represent a member of Jesus' flock, presumably Constantina herself.

The contemporary marble **SARCOPHAGUS OF JUNIUS BASSUS (FIG. 7–13)** is packed with elaborate figural scenes like the second-century CE Dionysiac Sarcophagus (see "A Closer Look," page 206), only here they are separated into two registers, where columns, entablatures, and gables divide the space into fields for individual scenes. Junius Bassus was a Roman official who, as the inscription here tells us, was "newly baptized" and died on August 25, 359, at the age of 42.

In the center of both registers is a triumphant Christ. Above, he appears as a Roman emperor, distributing legal authority in the form of scrolls to flanking figures of SS. Peter and Paul, and resting his feet on the head of Coelus, the pagan god of the heavens, here representing the cosmos to identify Christ as Cosmocrator (ruler of the cosmos). In the bottom register, the earthly Jesus makes his triumphal entry into Jerusalem, like a Roman emperor entering a conquered city. Jesus, however, rides on a humble ass rather than a powerful steed.

Even in the earliest Christian art, such as that in catacomb paintings and here on the *Sarcophagus of Junius Bassus*, artists employed episodes from the Hebrew Bible allegorically since Christians saw them as prefigurations of important events in the New Testament. At the top left, Abraham passes the test of faith and need not sacrifice his son Isaac. Christians saw in this story an allegory that foreshadowed God's sacrifice of his own son, Jesus, which culminates not in Jesus' death, but his resurrection. Under the triangular gable, second from the end at bottom right, the

Hebrew Bible story of Daniel saved by God from the lions prefigures Christ's emergence alive from his tomb. At bottom far left, God tests the faith of Job, who provides a model for the sufferings of Christian martyrs. Next to Job, Adam and Eve have sinned to set in motion the entire Christian redemption story. Lured by the serpent, they have eaten the forbidden fruit and, conscious of their nakedness, are trying to hide their genitals with leaves.

On the upper right side, spread over two compartments, Jesus appears before Pontius Pilate, who is about to wash his hands, symbolizing that he denies responsibility for Jesus' death. Jesus' position here, held captive between two soldiers, recalls (and perhaps could also be read as) his arrest in Gethsemane, especially since the composition of this panel is reflected in the arrests of the apostles Peter (top, second frame from the left) and Paul (bottom, far right).

RAVENNA

As Rome's political importance dwindled, that of the northern Italian city of Ravenna grew. In 395, Emperor Theodosius I split the Roman Empire into Eastern and Western divisions, each ruled by one of his sons. Heading the West, Honorius (r. 395–423) first established his capital at Milan, but in 402, to escape the siege of Germanic settlers, he moved his government to Ravenna on the east coast. Its naval base, Classis (present-day Classe), had been important since the early days of the empire. In addition to military security, Ravenna offered direct access by sea to Constantinople. When Italy fell in 476 to the Ostrogoths, Ravenna became one of their headquarters, but the beauty and richness of Early Christian buildings can still be experienced there in a remarkable group of well-preserved fifth- and sixth-century buildings.

The Life of Jesus

Episodes from the life of Jesus as recounted in the Gospels form the principal subject matter of Christian visual art. What follows is a list of main events in his life with parenthetical references citing their location in the Gospel texts.

INCARNATION AND CHILDHOOD OF JESUS

The Annunciation: The archangel Gabriel informs the Virgin Mary that God has chosen her to bear his Son. A dove often represents the **Incarnation**, her miraculous conception of Jesus through the Holy Spirit. (Lk 1:26–28)

The Visitation: The pregnant Mary visits her older cousin Elizabeth, pregnant with the future St. John the Baptist. (Lk 1:29–45)

The Nativity: Jesus is born in Bethlehem. The Holy Family—Jesus, Mary, and her husband, Joseph—is usually portrayed in a stable, or, in Byzantine art, a cave. (Lk 2:4–7)

Annunciation to and Adoration of the Shepherds: Angels announce Jesus's birth to shepherds, who hurry to Bethlehem to honor him. (Lk 2:8–20)

Adoration of the Magi: Wise men from the east follow a bright star to Bethlehem to honor Jesus as king of the Jews, presenting him with precious gifts. Eventually these Magi became identified as three kings, often differentiated through facial type as young, middle-aged, and old. (Mat 2:1–12)

Presentation in the Temple: Mary and Joseph bring the Infant Jesus to the Temple in Jerusalem, where he is presented to the high priest. (Lk 2:25–35)

Massacre of the Innocents and Flight into Egypt: An angel warns Joseph that King Herod—to eliminate the threat of a newborn rival king—plans to murder all male babies in Bethlehem. The Holy Family flees to Egypt. (Mat 2:13–16)

JESUS' MINISTRY

The Baptism: At age 30, Jesus is baptized by John the Baptist in the River Jordan. The Holy Spirit appears in the form of a dove and a heavenly voice proclaims Jesus as God's Son. (Mat 3:13–17, Mk 1:9–11, Lk 3:21–22)

Marriage at Cana: At his mother's request Jesus turns water into wine at a wedding feast, his first public miracle. (Jn 2:1–10)

Miracles of Healing: Throughout the Gospels, Jesus performs miracles of healing the blind, possessed (mentally ill), paralytic, and lepers; he also resurrects the dead.

Calling of Levi/Matthew: Jesus calls to Levi, a tax collector, "Follow me." Levi complies, becoming the disciple Matthew. (Mat 9:9, Mk 2:14)

Raising of Lazarus: Jesus brings his friend Lazarus back to life four days after his death. (Jn 11:1–44)

The Transfiguration: Jesus reveals his divinity in a dazzling vision on Mount Tabor as his closest disciples—Peter, James, and John—look on. (Mat 17:1–5, Mk 9:2–6, Lk 9:28–35)

Tribute Money: Challenged to pay the temple tax, Jesus sends Peter to catch a fish, which turns out to have the required coin in its mouth. (Mat 17:24–27, Lk 20:20–25)

JESUS' PASSION, DEATH, AND RESURRECTION

Entry into Jerusalem: Jesus, riding an ass and accompanied by his disciples, enters Jerusalem, while crowds honor him, spreading clothes and palm fronds in his path. (Mat 21:1–11, Mk 11:1–11, Lk 19:30–44, Jn 12:12–15)

The Last Supper: During the Jewish Passover seder, Jesus reveals his impending death to his disciples. Instructing them to drink wine (his blood) and eat bread (his body) in remembrance of him, he lays the foundation for the Christian Eucharist (Mass). (Mat 26:26–30, Mk 14:22–25, Lk 22:14–20)

Jesus Washing the Disciples' Feet: At the Last Supper, Jesus washes the disciples' feet, modeling humility. (Jn 13: 4–12)

The Agony in the Garden: In the Garden of Gethsemane on the Mount of Olives, Jesus struggles between his human fear of pain and death and his divine strength to overcome them. The apostles sleep nearby, oblivious. (Lk 22:40–45)

Betrayal (the Arrest): Judas Iscariot (a disciple) has accepted a bribe to indicate Jesus to an armed band of his enemies by kissing him. (Mat 26:46–49, Mk 14:43–46, Lk 22:47–48, Jn 18:3–5)

Jesus before Pilate: Jesus is taken to Pontius Pilate, Roman governor of Judaea, and charged with treason for calling himself king of the Jews. Pilate proposes freeing Jesus but is shouted down by the mob, which demands Jesus be crucified. (Mat 27:11–25, Mk 15:4–14, Lk 23:1–24, Jn 18:28–40)

The Crucifixion: Jesus is executed on a cross, often shown between two crucified criminals and accompanied by the Virgin Mary, John the Evangelist, Mary Magdalen, and other followers at the foot of the cross; Roman soldiers sometimes torment Jesus—one extending a sponge on a pole with vinegar instead of water for him to drink, another stabbing him in the side with a spear. A skull can identify the execution ground as **Golgotha**, "the place of the skull." (Mat 27:35–50, Mk 15:23–37, Lk 23:38–49, Jn 19:18–30)

Descent from the Cross (the Deposition): Jesus' followers take his body down from the cross. (Mat 27:55–59, Mk 15:40–46, Lk 23:50–56, Jn 19:38–40)

The Lamentation/Pietà and Entombment: Jesus' sorrowful followers gather around his body to mourn and then place his body in a tomb. An image of the grieving Virgin alone with Jesus across her lap is known as a **pietà** (from Latin *pietas*, "pity"). (Mat 27:60–61, Jn 19:41–42)

The Resurrection/Holy Women at the Tomb: Three days after his entombment, Christ rises from the dead, and his female followers—usually including Mary Magdalen—discover his empty tomb. An angel announces Christ's resurrection. (Mat 28, Mk 16, Lk 24:1–35, Jn 20)

Descent into Limbo (Harrowing of Hell or Anastasis): The resurrected Jesus descends into limbo, or hell, to free deserving predecessors, among them Adam, Eve, David, and Moses. (Not in the Gospels)

Noli Me Tangere ("Do Not Touch Me"): Christ appears to Mary Magdalen as she weeps at his tomb. When she reaches out to him, he warns her not to touch him. (Lk 24:34–53, Jn 20:11–31)

The Ascension: Christ ascends to heaven from the Mount of Olives, disappearing in a cloud, while his mother and apostles watch. (Acts 1)

7-14 • ORATORY OF GALLA PLACIDIA
Ravenna. c. 425–426.

THE ORATORY OF GALLA PLACIDIA.   One of the earliest surviving Christian structures in Ravenna is an **oratory** (small chapel), attached about 425–426 to the narthex of the church of the imperial palace **(FIG. 7–14)**. It is named after Honorius' remarkable half-sister, Galla Placidia—daughter of the Western Roman emperor, wife of a Gothic king, and mother of Emperor Valentinian. As regent for her son after 425, she ruled the West until about 440. The oratory came to be called the Mausoleum of Galla Placidia because she and her family were once believed to be buried there.

This small building is **cruciform**, or cross-shape. A barrel vault covers each of its arms, and a pendentive dome—a dome continuous with its pendentives—covers the square space at the center (see "Pendentives and Squinches," page 236). The interior of the chapel contrasts markedly with the unadorned exterior, a transition seemingly designed to simulate the passage from the real world into the supernatural realm **(FIG. 7–15)**. The worshiper looking from the western entrance across to the eastern bay of the chapel sees brilliant mosaics in the vaults and panels of veined marble sheathing the walls below. Bands of luxuriant floral designs and geometric patterns cover the arches and barrel vaults. The upper walls of the central space are filled with the figures of standing

7-15 • ORATORY OF GALLA PLACIDIA
Ravenna. View from entrance, barrel-vaulted arms housing sarchophagi, lunette mosaic of the martyrdom of St. Lawrence. c. 425–426.

7-16 • THE GOOD SHEPHERD
Lunette over the entrance, Oratory of Galla Placidia. c. 425–426. Mosaic.

apostles, gesturing like orators. Doves flanking a small fountain between the apostles symbolize eternal life in heaven.

In the lunette at the end of the barrel vault opposite the entrance, a mosaic depicts the third-century St. Lawrence, to whom the building may have been dedicated. The triumphant martyr carries a cross over his shoulder like a trophy and gestures toward the fire-engulfed metal grill on which he was literally roasted in martyrdom. At the left stands a tall cabinet containing the Gospels, signifying the faith for which he gave his life. Opposite St. Lawrence, in a lunette over the entrance portal, is a mosaic of **THE GOOD SHEPHERD** (**FIG. 7–16**). A comparison of this version with a fourth-century depiction of the same subject (SEE FIG. 7–5) reveals significant changes in content and design.

Jesus is no longer a boy in a simple tunic, but an adult emperor wearing purple and gold royal robes, his imperial majesty signaled by the golden halo surrounding his head and by a long golden staff that ends in a cross instead of a shepherd's crook. At the time this mosaic was made, Christianity had been the official state religion for 45 years, and nearly a century had past since the last official persecution of Christians. The artists and patrons of this mosaic chose to assert the glory of Jesus Christ in mosaic, the richest known medium of wall decoration, in an imperial image still imbued with pagan spirit but now signaling the triumph of a new faith.

EARLY BYZANTINE ART

Byzantine art can be thought of broadly as the art of Constantinople (whose ancient name, before Constantine renamed it after himself, was Byzantium) and the regions under its influence. In this chapter, we focus on Byzantine art's three "golden ages." The Early Byzantine period, most closely associated with the reign of Emperor Justinian I (527–565), began in the fifth century and ended in 726, at the onset of the iconoclast controversy that led to the destruction of religious images. The Middle Byzantine period began in 843, when Empress Theodora (c. 810–867) reinstated the veneration of icons. It lasted until 1204, when Christian crusaders from the west occupied Constantinople. The Late Byzantine period began with the restoration of Byzantine rule in 1261 and ended with the empire's fall to the Ottoman Turks in 1453, at which point Russia succeeded Constantinople as the "Third Rome" and the center of the Eastern Orthodox Church. Late Byzantine art continued to flourish into the eighteenth century in Ukraine, Russia, and much of southeastern Europe.

THE GOLDEN AGE OF JUSTINIAN

During the fifth and sixth centuries, while invasions and religious controversy wracked the Italian peninsula, the Eastern Empire prospered. Byzantium became the "New Rome." Constantine had chosen the site of his new capital city well. Constantinople lay at the crossroads of the overland trade routes between Asia and Europe and the sea route connecting the Black Sea and the Mediterranean. It was during the sixth century under Emperor Justinian I and his wife, Theodora, that Byzantine political power, wealth, and culture were at their peak. Imperial forces held northern Africa, Sicily, much of Italy, and part of Spain. Ravenna became the Eastern Empire's administrative capital in the west, and Rome remained under nominal Byzantine control until the eighth century.

7-17 • Anthemius of Tralles and Isidorus of Miletus
CHURCH OF HAGIA SOPHIA
Istanbul. 532–537. View from the southwest.

The body of the original church is now surrounded by later
additions, including the minarets built after 1453 by the
Ottoman Turks. Today the building is a museum.

SEE MORE: Click the Google Earth link for Hagia
Sophia **www.myartslab.com**

**7-18 • PLAN AND ISOMETRIC DRAWING OF THE
CHURCH OF HAGIA SOPHIA**

HAGIA SOPHIA. In Constantinople, Justinian and Theodora
embarked on a spectacular campaign of building and renovation,
but little now remains of their architectural projects or of the old
imperial capital itself. The church of Hagia Sophia, meaning "Holy
Wisdom," is a spectacular exception (FIG. 7–17). It replaced a
fourth-century church destroyed when crowds, spurred on by Justinian's foes during the devastating urban Nika Revolt in 532, set
the old church on fire and cornered the emperor within his palace.
Empress Theodora, a brilliant, politically shrewd woman, is said to
have goaded Justinian, who was plotting an escape, not to flee the
city, saying "Purple makes a fine shroud"—meaning that she would
rather remain and die an empress (purple was the royal color) than
retreat and preserve her life. Taking up her words as a battle cry, Justinian led the imperial forces in crushing the rebels and restoring
order, reputedly slaughtering 30,000 of his subjects in the process.

To design a new church that embodied imperial power and
Christian glory, Justinian chose two scholar-theoreticians,
Anthemius of Tralles and Isidorus of Miletus. Anthemius was a specialist in geometry and optics, and Isidorus a specialist in physics
who had also studied vaulting. They developed an audacious and
awe-inspiring design, executed by builders who had refined their
masonry techniques building the towers and domed rooms that
were part of the city's defenses. So when Justinian ordered the construction of domed churches, and especially Hagia Sophia, master
masons with a trained and experienced workforce stood ready
to give permanent form to his architects' dreams.

The new Hagia Sophia was not constructed by the
miraculous intervention of angels, as was rumored, but by
mortal builders in only five years (532–537). Procopius of
Caesarea, who chronicled Justinian's reign, claimed poetically
that Hagia Sophia's gigantic dome seemed to hang suspended
on a "golden chain from heaven." Legend has it that Justinian
himself, aware that architecture can be a potent symbol of
earthly power, compared his accomplishment with that of the
legendary builder of the First Temple in Jerusalem, saying
"Solomon, I have outdone you."

Hagia Sophia is an innovative hybrid of longitudinal and
central architectural planning (FIG. 7–18). The building is clearly
dominated by the hovering form of its gigantic dome (FIG. 7–19).
But flanking **conches**—semidomes—extend the central space
into a longitudinal nave that expands outward from the central
dome to connect with the narthex on one end and the halfdome
of the sanctuary apse on the other. This processional core, called

7–19 • INTERIOR OF THE CHURCH OF HAGIA SOPHIA

EXPLORE MORE: Gain insight from a primary source related to Hagia Sophia www.myartslab.com

Pendentives and squinches are two methods of supporting a round dome or its drum over a square space. **Pendentives** are concave, spherical triangles between arches that rise upward and inward to form a circular opening on which a dome rests. **Squinches** are diagonal lintels placed across the upper corner of the wall and supported by an arch or a series of corbeled arches that give it a nichelike shape. Because squinches create an octagon, which is close in shape to a circle, they provide a solid base around the perimeter of a dome, usually elevated on a drum (a circular wall), whereas pendentives project the dome slightly inside the square space it covers, making it seem to float. Byzantine builders preferred pendentives (as at Hagia Sophia, SEE FIG. 7–19), but elaborate, squinch-supported domes became a hallmark of Islamic architecture.

dome on pendentives

dome on squinches

SEE MORE: View a simulation of pendentives and squinches **www.myartslab.com**

the **naos** in Byzantine architecture, is flanked by side aisles and **galleries** above them overlooking the naos.

Since its idiosyncratic mixture of basilica and rotunda precludes a ring of masonry underneath the dome to provide support around its circumference (as in the Pantheon, SEE FIGS. 6–46, 6–47), the main dome of Hagia Sophia rests instead on four **pendentives** (triangular curving vault sections) that connect the base of the dome with the huge supporting piers at the four corners of the square area beneath it (see "Pendentives and Squinches," above). And since these piers are essentially submerged back into the darkness of the aisles, rather than expressed within the main space itself (SEE FIG. 7–18), the dome seems to float mysteriously over a void. The miraculous, weightless effect was reinforced by the light-reflecting gold mosaic that covered the surfaces of dome and pendentives alike, as well as the band of 40 windows that perforate the base of the dome right where it meets its support. This daring move challenges architectural logic by seeming to weaken the integrity of the masonry at the very place where it needs to be strong, but the windows created the circle of light that helps the dome appear to hover, and a reinforcement of buttressing on the exterior made the solution sound as well as shimmering. The origin of the dome on pendentives is obscure, but its large-scale use at Hagia Sophia was totally unprecedented and represents one of the boldest experiments in the history of architecture. It was to become the preferred method of supporting domes in Byzantine architecture.

The architects and builders of Hagia Sophia clearly stretched building materials to their physical limits, denying the physicality of the building in order to emphasize its spirituality. In fact, when the first dome fell in 558, it did so because a pier and pendentive shifted and because the dome was too shallow and exerted too much outward force at its base, not because the windows weakened the support. Confident of their revised technical methods, the architects designed a steeper dome that raised the summit 20 feet higher. They also added exterior buttressing. Although repairs had to be made in 869, 989, and 1346, the church has since withstood numerous earthquakes.

The liturgy used in Hagia Sophia in the sixth century has been lost, but it presumably resembled the rites described in detail for the church in the Middle Byzantine period. The celebration of the Mass took place behind a screen—at Hagia Sophia a crimson curtain embroidered in gold, in later churches an iconostasis, a wall hung with devotional paintings called **icons** (from the Greek *eikon*, meaning "image"). The emperor was the only layperson permitted to enter the sanctuary; men stood in the aisles and women in the galleries. Processions of clergy moved in a circular path from the sanctuary into the nave and back five or six times during the ritual. The focus of the congregation was on the iconostasis and the dome rather than the altar and apse. This upward focus reflects the interests of Byzantine philosophers, who viewed meditation as a way to rise from the material world to a spiritual state. Worshipers standing on the church floor must have felt just such a spiritual uplift as they gazed at the mosaics of saints, angels, and, in the golden central dome, heaven itself.

SAN VITALE. In 540, Byzantine forces captured Ravenna from the Arian Christian Ostrogoths who had themselves taken it from the Romans in 476. Much of our knowledge of the art of this turbulent period comes from the well-preserved monuments at Ravenna. In 526, Ecclesius, bishop of Ravenna, commissioned two new churches, one for the city and one for its port, Classis. Construction began on a central-plan church, a **martyrium** (church built over the grave of a martyr) dedicated to the fourth-century Roman martyr St. Vitalis (Vitale in Italian) in the 520s, but it was not finished until after Justinian had conquered Ravenna and established it as the administrative capital of Byzantine Italy (FIG. 7–20).

The design of San Vitale is basically a central-domed octagon surrounded by eight radiating exedrae (wall niches), surrounded in turn by an ambulatory and gallery, all covered by vaults. A rectangular sanctuary and semicircular apse project from one of the sides of the octagon, and circular rooms flank the apse. A separate oval narthex, set off-axis, joined church and palace and also led to cylindrical stair towers that gave access to the second-floor gallery.

The floor plan of San Vitale only hints at the effect of the complex, interpenetrating interior spaces of the church, an effect that was enhanced by the offset narthex, with its double sets of doors leading into the church. People entering from the right saw only arched openings, whereas those entering from the left approached on an axis with the sanctuary, which they saw straight

7-20 • PLAN AND CUTAWAY DRAWING, CHURCH OF SAN VITALE
Ravenna. Under construction from c. 520; consecrated 547; mosaics, c. 546–548.

7–21 • CHURCH OF SAN VITALE

Ravenna. View into the sanctuary toward the northeast. Consecrated 547.

SEE MORE: View a panorama of San Vitale **www.myartslab.com**

Naming Christian Churches: Designation + Dedication + Location

Christian churches are identified by a three-part descriptive title combining (1) designation (or type), with (2) dedication (usually to a saint), and finally (3) geographic location, cited in that order.

DESIGNATION: There are various types of churches, fulfilling a variety of liturgical and administrative objectives, and the identification of a specific church often begins with an indication of its function within the system. For example, an **abbey church** is the place of worship within a monastery or convent; a **pilgrimage church** is a site that attracts visitors wishing to venerate **relics** (material remains or objects associated with a saint) as well as attend services. A cathedral is a bishop's primary church (the word derives from the Latin *cathedra*, meaning chair, since the chair or throne of a bishop is contained within his cathedral). A bishop's domain is called a diocese, and there can be only one church in the diocese designated as its bishop's cathedral, but the diocese is full of **parish churches** where local residents attend regular services.

DEDICATION: Christian churches are always dedicated to a saint or a sacred concept, for example St. Peter's Basilica or the Church of Hagia Sophia ("Holy Wisdom"). In short-hand identification, when we omit the church designation at the beginning, we always add an apostrophe and an *s* to the saint's name, as when using "St. Peter's" to refer to the Vatican Basilica of St. Peter in Rome

LOCATION: The final piece of information that clearly pinpoints the specific church referred to in a title is its geographic location, as in the Church of San Vitale in Ravenna or the Cathedral of Notre-Dame (French for "Our Lady," referring to the Virgin Mary) in Paris. "Notre-Dame" alone usually refers to this Parisian cathedral, in spite of the fact that many contemporary cathedrals elsewhere (e.g. at Chartres and Reims) were also dedicated to "Notre-Dame." Similarly, "St. Peter's" usually means the Vatican church of the pope in Rome.

---

ahead of them. The dome rests on eight large piers that frame the exedrae and the sanctuary. The undulating, two-story exedrae open through superimposed arcades into the outer aisles on the ground floor and into galleries on the second floor. They push out the circular central space and create an airy, floating sensation, reinforced by the liberal use of veined marble veneer and colored glass and gold mosaics in the surface decoration. The structure seems to dissolve into shimmering light and color.

In the halfdome of the sanctuary apse (**FIGS. 7–21, 7–22**), an image of **CHRIST ENTHRONED** is flanked by St. Vitalis and Bishop Ecclesius. The other sanctuary images relate to its use for the celebration of the Eucharist. The lunette on the north wall shows an altar table set for a meal that Abraham offers to three holy visitors, and next to it a portrayal of his near-sacrifice of Isaac. In the spandrels and other framed wall spaces appear prophets and evangelists, and the program is bristling with symbolic references to Jesus, but the focus of the sanctuary program is the courtly tableau in the semidome of the apse.

A youthful, classicizing Christ appears on axis, dressed in imperial purple and enthroned on a cosmic orb in paradise, the setting indicated by the four rivers that flow from the ground underneath him. Two winged angels flank him, like imperial bodyguards or attendants. In his left hand Christ holds a scroll with seven seals that he will open at his Second Coming at the end of time, proclaiming his authority not only over this age, but over the age to come. He extends his right hand to offer a crown of martyrdom to a figure on his right (our left) labeled as St. Vitalis, the saint to whom this church is dedicated. On

7-22 • CHRIST ENTHRONED, FLANKED BY ANGELS, ST. VITALIS AND BISHOP ECCLESIUS
Church of San Vitale, Ravenna. Consecrated 547. Mosaic.

7-23 • EMPEROR JUSTINIAN AND HIS ATTENDANTS, NORTH WALL OF THE APSE

Church of San Vitale, Ravenna. Consecrated 547. Mosaic, 8'8" × 12' (2.64 × 3.65 m).

As head of state, the haloed Justinian wears a huge jeweled crown and a purple cloak; he carries a large golden paten (plate for Eucharistic bread) that he is donating to San Vitale for the celebration of the Eucharist. Bishop Maximianus at his left holds a jeweled cross and another churchman holds a jewel-covered book. Government officials stand at Justinian's right, followed by barbarian mercenary soldiers, one of whom wears a neck torc, another a Classical cameo cloak clasp.

7-24 • EMPRESS THEODORA AND HER ATTENDANTS, SOUTH WALL OF THE APSE
Church of San Vitale, Ravenna. Consecrated 547. Mosaic 8'8" × 12' (2.64 × 3.65 m).

Theodora and her ladies wear the rich textiles and jewelry of the Byzantine court. Both men and women are dressed in linen or silk tunics and cloaks. The men's cloaks are fastened on the right shoulder with a fibula (brooch) and are decorated with a rectangular embroidered panel (tablion). Women wore a second full, long-sleeved garment over their tunics and a large rectangular shawl. Like Justinian, Theodora has a halo and wears imperial purple. Her elaborate jewelry includes a wide collar of embroidered and jeweled cloth. A crown, hung with long strands of pearls (thought to protect the wearer from disease), frames her face.

the other side is the only un-nimbed figure in the tableau, labeled as Bishop Ecclesius, the founder of San Vitale, who holds forward a model of the church itself, offering it to Christ. The artist has imagined a scene of courtly protocol in paradise, where Christ, as emperor, gives a gift to, and receives a gift from, visiting luminaries.

Further visitors appear in separate, flanking rectangular compositions, along the curving wall of the apse underneath the scene in the semidome—Justinian and Theodora and their retinues (the former can be seen in FIG. 7–21). The royal couple did not attend the dedication ceremonies for the church of San Vitale, conducted by Archbishop Maximianus in 547. They may never actually have set foot in Ravenna, but these two large mosaic panels that face each other across its sanctuary picture their presence here in perpetuity. Justinian (FIG. 7–23), on the north wall, carries a large golden paten that will be used to hold the Eucharistic Host and

stands next to Maximianus, who holds a golden, jewel-encrusted cross. The priestly celebrants at the right carry the Gospels, encased in a golden, jeweled book cover, symbolizing the coming of the Word, and a censer containing burning incense to purify the altar prior to the Eucharist.

On the south wall, Theodora, standing beneath a fluted shell canopy and singled out by a golden halo and elaborate crown, carries a huge golden chalice studded with jewels (FIG. 7–24). The rulers present these gifts as precious offerings to Christ— emulating most immediately Bishop Ecclesius, who offers a model of the church to Christ in the apse, but also the three Magi who brought valuable gifts to the infant Jesus, depicted in "embroidery" at the bottom of Theodora's purple cloak. In fact, the paten and chalice offered by the royal couple will be used by this church to offer Eucharistic bread and wine to the local Christian community during the liturgy. In this way the entire program of mosaic decoration revolves around themes of offering, extended into the theme of the Eucharist itself.

Theodora's group stands beside a fountain, presumably at the entrance to the women's gallery. The open doorway and curtain are Classical space-creating devices, but here the mosaicists have deliberately avoided allowing their illusionistic power to overwhelm their ability also to create flat surface patterns. Notice, too, that the figures cast no shadows, and, though modeled, their outlines as silhouetted shapes are more prominent than their sense of three-dimensionality. Still, especially in Justinian's panel, a complex and carefully controlled system of overlapping allows us to see these figures clearly and logically situated within a shallow space, moving in a stately procession from left to right toward the entrance to the church and the beginning of the liturgy. So the scenes portrayed in these mosaic paintings are both flattened and three-dimensional, abstract and representational, patterned and individualized. Like Justinian and Theodora, their images are both there and not there at the same time.

7-25 • THE TRANSFIGURATION OF CHRIST WITH SANT'APOLLINARE, FIRST BISHOP OF RAVENNA

Church of Sant'Apollinare in Classe. Consecrated 549. Mosaics: apse, 6th century; wall above apse, 7th and 9th centuries; side panels, 7th century.

SANT'APOLLINARE IN CLASSE. At the same time that he was building the church of San Vitale, Bishop Ecclesius ordered a basilica church in the port of Classis dedicated to St. Apollinaris (Sant'Apollinare), the first bishop of Ravenna. The apse mosaic (FIG. 7–25) is a symbolic depiction of the Transfiguration (Matthew 17:1–5)—Jesus' revelation of his divinity. A narrative episode from the life of Christ has been transformed into an iconic embodiment of its underlying idea. One man and 15 sheep stand in a stylized, verdant landscape below a jeweled cross with the face of Christ at its center. The hand of God and the figures of Moses and Elijah from the Hebrew Bible appear in the heavens to authenticate the divinity of Christ. The apostles Peter, James, and John, who witness the event, are represented here by the three sheep with raised heads. Below the cross, Bishop Apollinaris raises his hands in an orant posture of prayer, flanked by 12 lambs who seem to represent the apostles.

This highly complicated work of symbolic narrative, like the mosaics of San Vitale, must have been aimed at a sophisticated population, prepared to appreciate its theological speculations and diagrammatic outlines of Christian doctrine. At this moment in its history, the Church is directing its message to an inside audience of faithful believers, who encounter its visualization within churches in their own community. Such an art could not have been conceived to educate an uninitiated public; rather it was developed to celebrate the values that hold Christian society together by representing them in a refined and urbane visual language.

OBJECTS OF VENERATION AND DEVOTION

The court workshops of Constantinople excelled in the production of luxurious, small-scale works in gold, ivory, and textiles. The Byzantine elite also sponsored vital **scriptoria** (writing centers for **scribes**—professional document writers) for the production of **manuscripts** (handwritten books).

THE ARCHANGEL MICHAEL DIPTYCH. Commemorative ivory diptychs—two carved panels hinged together—originated with Roman politicians elected to the post of consul. New consuls would send notices of their election to friends and colleagues by inscribing them in wax that filled a recessed rectangular area on the inner sides of a pair of ivory panels carved with elaborate decoration on the reverse. Christians adapted the practice for religious use, inscribing a diptych with the names of people to be remembered with prayers during the liturgy.

This large panel depicting the **ARCHANGEL MICHAEL**—the largest surviving Byzantine ivory—was half of such a diptych (**FIG. 7–26**). In his classicizing beauty, imposing physical presence, and elegant architectural setting, the archangel is comparable to the (supposed) priestess of Bacchus in the fourth-century pagan Symmachus diptych panel (SEE FIG. 6–68). His relationship to the architectural space and the frame around him, however, is more complex. His heels rest on the top step of a stair that clearly lies behind the columns and pedestals, but the rest of his body projects in front of them—since it overlaps the architectural setting— creating a striking tension between this celestial figure and his terrestrial backdrop.

The angel is outfitted here as a divine messenger, holding a staff of authority in his left hand and a sphere symbolizing worldly power in his right. Within the arch is a similar cross-topped orb, framed by a wreath bound by a ribbon with long, rippling extensions, that is set against the background of a scallop shell. The lost half of this diptych would have completed the Greek inscription across the top, which reads: "Receive these gifts, and having learned the cause…." Perhaps the other panel contained a

7-26 • ARCHANGEL MICHAEL
Panel of a diptych, probably from the court workshop at Constantinople. Early 6th century. Ivory, 17 × 15½" (43.3 × 14 cm). British Museum, London.

Scroll and Codex

Since people began to write some 5,000 years ago, they have kept records on a variety of materials, including clay or wax tablets, pieces of broken pottery, papyrus, animal skins, and paper. Books have taken two forms: scroll and codex.

Scribes made **scrolls** from sheets of papyrus glued end to end or from thin sheets of cleaned, scraped, and trimmed sheepskin or calfskin, a material known as **parchment** or, when softer and lighter, **vellum**. Each end of the scroll was attached to a rod; the reader slowly unfurled the scroll from one rod to the other. Scrolls could be written to be read either horizontally or vertically.

At the end of the first century CE, the more practical and manageable **codex** (plural, codices)—sheets bound together like the modern book—replaced the scroll as the primary form of recording texts. The basic unit of the codex was the eight-leaf quire, made by folding a large sheet of parchment twice, cutting the edges free, then sewing the sheets together up the center. Heavy covers kept the sheets of a codex flat. The thickness and weight of parchment and vellum made it impractical to produce a very large manuscript, such as an entire Bible, in a single volume. As a result, individual sections were made into separate books.

Until the invention of printing in the fifteenth century, all books were **manuscripts**—that is, they were written by hand. Manuscripts often included illustrations, called **miniatures** (from *minium*, the Latin word for a reddish lead pigment). Manuscripts decorated with gold and colors were said to be illuminated.

---

portrait of the emperor—many think he would be Justinian—or of another high official who presented the panels as a gift to an important colleague, acquaintance, or family member. Nonetheless, the emphasis here is on the powerful celestial messenger who does not need to obey the laws of earthly scale or human perspective.

THE VIENNA GENESIS.   Byzantine manuscripts were often made with very costly materials. For example, sheets of purple-dyed **vellum** (a fine writing surface made from calfskin) and gold and silver inks were used to produce a codex now known as the Vienna Genesis. It was probably made in Syria or Palestine, and the purple vellum indicates that it may have been created for an imperial patron (costly purple dye, made from the secretions of murex mollusks, was usually restricted to imperial use). The Vienna Genesis is written in Greek and illustrated with pictures that appear below the text at the bottom of the pages.

The story of **REBECCA AT THE WELL** (FIG. 7–27) (Genesis 24) appears here in a single composition, but the painter—clinging to the continuous narrative tradition that had characterized the illustration of scrolls—combines events that take place at different times in the story within a single narrative space. Rebecca, the heroine, appears at the left walking away from the walled city of Nahor with a large jug on her shoulder, going to fetch water. A colonnaded road leads toward a spring, personified by a reclining pagan water nymph who holds a flowing jar. In the foreground, Rebecca appears again. Her jug now full, she encounters a thirsty camel driver and offers him water to drink. Since he is Abraham's servant, Eliezer, in search of a bride for Abraham's son Isaac, Rebecca's generosity results in her marriage to Isaac. The lifelike poses and rounded, full-bodied figures of this narrative scene

7-27 • REBECCA AT THE WELL
Page from a codex featuring the book of Genesis (known as the Vienna Genesis). Syria or Palestine. Early 6th century. Tempera, gold, and silver paint on purple-dyed vellum, 13½ × 9⅞" (33.7 × 25 cm). Österreichische Nationalbibliothek, Vienna.

7–28 • DAVID BATTLING GOLIATH
Detail of silver plate in FIG. 7–1.
Made in Constantinople,
629–630. Metropolitan Museum
of Art, New York.

conform to the conventions of traditional Roman painting. The sumptuous purple of the background and the glittering metallic letters of the text situate the book within the world of the privileged and powerful in Byzantine society.

LUXURY WORKS IN SILVER. The imperial court at Constantinople had a monopoly on the production of some luxury goods, especially those made of precious metals. It seems to have been the origin of a spectacular set of nine silver plates portraying events in the early life of the biblical King David, including the plate that we examined at the beginning of the chapter (SEE FIG. 7–1).

The plates would have been made by hammering a large silver ingot (the plate in FIG. 7–1 weighs 12 pounds 10 ounces) into a round shape and raising on it the rough semblance of the human figures and their environment. With finer chisels, silversmiths then refined these shapes, and at the end of their work, they punched ornamental motifs and incised fine details. The careful modeling,

lifelike postures, and intricate engraving characterizing the detail reproduced in **FIG. 7–28** document the highly refined artistry and stunning technical virtuosity of these cosmopolitan artists at the imperial court who still practiced a classicizing art that can be traced back to the traditions of ancient Greece.

ICONS AND ICONOCLASM

Christians in the Byzantine world prayed to Christ, Mary, and the saints while looking at images of them on independent painted panels known as icons. Church doctrine toward the veneration of icons was ambivalent. Christianity, like Judaism and Islam, has always been uneasy with the power of religious images. But key figures of the Eastern Church, such as Basil the Great of Cappadocia (c. 329–379) and John of Damascus (c. 675–749), distinguished between idolatry—the worship of images—and the veneration of an idea or holy person depicted in a work of art. Icons were thus accepted as aids to meditation and prayer, as intermediaries between worshipers and the holy personages they depicted. Honor showed to the image was believed to transfer directly to its spiritual prototype. Icons were often displayed in Byzantine churches on a screen separating the congregation from the sanctuary called the **iconostasis**.

Surviving early icons are rare, but a few precious examples were preserved in the Monastery of St. Catherine on Mount Sinai, among them the **VIRGIN AND CHILD WITH SAINTS AND ANGELS (FIG. 7–29)**. As Theotokos (Greek for "bearer of God"), Jesus' earthly mother was viewed as the powerful, ever-forgiving intercessor, appealing to her divine son for mercy on behalf of repentant worshipers. She was also called the Seat of Wisdom, and many images of the Virgin and Child, like this one, show her holding Jesus on her lap in a way that suggests that she represents the throne of Solomon. Virgin and Child are flanked here by Christian warrior-saints Theodore (left) and George (right)—both legendary figures said to have slain dragons, representing the triumph of the Church over the "evil serpent" of paganism. Angels behind them twist upward to look heavenward. The artist has painted the Christ Child, the Virgin, and the angels in an illusionistic Roman manner that renders them lifelike and three-dimensional in appearance. But the warrior-saints are more stylized. The artist barely hints at bodily form beneath the richly patterned textiles of their cloaks, and their tense faces are frozen in frontal stares of gripping intensity.

In the eighth century, the veneration of icons sparked a major controversy in the Eastern Church, and in 726 Emperor Leo III launched a campaign of **iconoclasm** ("image breaking"), banning the use of icons in Christian worship and ordering the destruction of devotional pictures (see "Iconoclasm," page 246). Only a few early icons survived in isolated places like Mount Sinai, which was no longer a part of the Byzantine Empire at this time. But the iconoclasm did not last. In 843, Empress Theodora, widow of Theophilus, last of the iconoclastic emperors, reversed her husband's policy, and icons would play an increasingly important role as the history of Byzantine art developed.

7-29 • VIRGIN AND CHILD WITH SAINTS AND ANGELS
Icon. Second half of the 6th century. Encaustic on wood, 27 × 18⅞" (69 × 48 cm). Monastery of St. Catherine, Mount Sinai, Egypt.

EXPLORE MORE: Gain insight from a primary source about painting icons www.myartslab.com

Iconoclasm

Iconoclasm (literally "image breaking," from the Greek words *eikon* for "image" and *klao* meaning "break" or "destroy") is the prohibition and destruction of works of visual art, usually because they are considered inappropriate in religious contexts.

During the eighth century, mounting discomfort with the place of icons in Christian devotion grew into a major controversy in the Byzantine world and, in 726, Emperor Leo III (r. 717–741) imposed iconoclasm, initiating the systematic destruction of images of saints and sacred stories on icons and in churches, as well as the persecution of those who made them and defended their use. His successor, Constantine V (r. 741–775), enforced these policies and practices with even greater fervor. Iconoclasm endured as imperial policy until 843, when the widowed Empress Theodora reversed her husband Theophilus' policy and reinstated the central place of images in Byzantine devotional practice.

A number of explanations have been proposed for this interlude of Byzantine iconoclasm. Some church leaders feared that the use of images in worship could lead to idolatry or at least distract worshipers from their spiritual exercises. Specifically there were questions surrounding the relationship between images and the Eucharist, the latter considered by iconoclasts as sufficient representation of the presence of Christ in the church. But there was also anxiety in Byzantium about the weakening state of the empire, especially in relation to the advances of Arab armies into Byzantine territory. It was easy to pin these hard times on God's displeasure with the idolatrous use of images. Coincidentally, Leo III's success fighting the Arabs could be interpreted as divine sanction of his iconoclastic position, and its very adoption might appease the iconoclastic Islamic enemy itself. Finally, since the production and promotion of icons was centered in monasteries—at that time rivaling the state in strength and wealth—attacking the use of images might check their growing power. Perhaps all these factors played a part, but at the triumph of the **iconophiles** (literally "lovers of images") in 843, the place of images in worship was again secure: Icons proclaimed Christ as God incarnate and facilitated Christian worship by acting as intermediaries between humans and saints. Those who had suppressed icons became heretics.

But iconoclasm is not restricted to Byzantine history. It reappears from time to time throughout the history of art. Protestant reformers in sixteenth-century Europe adopted what they saw as the iconoclastic position of the Hebrew Bible (Exodus 20:4), and many works of Catholic art were destroyed by zealous reformers and their followers.

Even more recently, in 2001, the Taliban rulers of Afghanistan dynamited two gigantic fifth-century CE statues of the Buddha carved into the rock cliffs of the Bamiyan Valley, specifically because they believed such "idols" violated Islamic law.

CRUCIFIXION AND ICONOCLASTS
From the Chludov Psalter. Mid 9th century. Tempera on vellum, 7¾ × 6" (19.5 × 15 cm). State Historical Museum, Moscow. MS D.29, fol. 67v

This page and its illustration of Psalm 21—made soon after the end of the iconoclastic controversy in 843—records the iconophiles' harsh judgment of the iconoclasts. Painted in the margin at the right, a scene of the Crucifixion shows a soldier tormenting Christ with a vinegar-soaked sponge. In a striking visual parallel, two named iconoclasts—identified by inscription—in the adjacent picture along the bottom margin employ a whitewash-soaked sponge to obliterate an icon portrait of Christ, thus linking their actions with those who had crucified him.

MIDDLE BYZANTINE ART

After the defeat of the iconoclasts, Byzantine art flourished once again, beginning in 867 under the leadership of an imperial dynasty from Macedonia. This support for the arts continued until Christian crusaders from the west, setting out on a holy war against Islam, diverted their efforts to conquering the wealthy Christian Byzantine Empire. The western crusaders who took Constantinople in 1204 looted the capital and set up a Latin dynasty of rulers to replace the Byzantine emperors.

Early Byzantine civilization had been centered in lands along

7-30 • MONASTERY CHURCHES AT HOSIOS LOUKAS

Greece. View from the east: Katholikon (left), early 11th century, and church of the Theotokos, late 10th century.

7-31 • PLAN OF MONASTERY CHURCHES AT HOSIOS LOUKAS

Katholikon at left, church of the Theotokos at right.

the rim of the Mediterranean Sea that had been within the Roman Empire. During the Middle Byzantine period, Constantinople's scope was reduced to present-day Turkey and other areas by the Black Sea, as well as the Balkan peninsula, including Greece, and southern Italy. The influence of Byzantine culture also extended into Russia and Ukraine, and to Venice, Constantinople's trading partner in northeastern Italy, at the head of the Adriatic Sea.

Under the Macedonian dynasty (867–1056) initiated by Basil I, the empire prospered and enjoyed a cultural rebirth. Middle Byzantine art and architecture, visually powerful and stylistically coherent, reflect the strongly spiritual focus of the period's autocratic, wealthy leadership. From the mid eleventh century, however, other powers entered Byzantine territory. The empire stabilized temporarily under the Comnenian dynasty (1081–1185), extending the Middle Byzantine period well into the time of the western Middle Ages.

ARCHITECTURE AND MOSAICS

Comparatively few Middle Byzantine churches in Constantinople have survived intact, but many central-plan domed churches, favored by Byzantine architects, survive in Greece to the southwest and Ukraine to the northeast, and are reflected in Venice within the Western medieval world. These structures reveal the Byzantine taste for a multiplicity of geometric forms, verticality, and rich decorative effects both inside and out.

HOSIOS LOUKAS.   Although an outpost, Greece still lay within the Byzantine Empire, and the eleventh-century Katholikon of the Monastery of Hosios Loukas, built a few miles from the village of Stiris, Greece, is an excellent example of Middle Byzantine architecture. It stands next to the earlier church of the Theotokos (FIGS. 7–30, 7–31, 7–32). The church has a compact central plan with a dome, supported on squinches, rising over an octagonal core (see "Pendentives and Squinches," page 236). On the exterior, the rising forms of apses, walls, and roofs disguise the vaulting roofs of the interior. The Greek builders created a decorative effect

7-32 • CENTRAL DOMED SPACE AND APSE (THE NAOS), KATHOLIKON
Monastery of Hosios Loukas. Near Stiris, Greece. Early 11th century and later.

on the exterior, alternating stones with bricks set both vertically and horizontally and using diagonally set bricks to form saw-toothed moldings. Inside the churches, the high central space carries the eyes of worshipers upward into the main dome, which soars above a ring of tall arched openings.

Unlike Hagia Sophia, with its clear, sweeping geometric forms, the Katholikon has a complex variety of forms, including domes, groin vaults, barrel vaults, pendentives, and squinches, all built on a relatively small scale. The barrel vaults and tall sanctuary apse with flanking rooms further complicate the space. Single, double, and triple windows create intricate and unusual patterns of light that illuminated a mosaic of Christ Pantokrator (now lost) in the center of the main dome. The secondary, sanctuary dome is decorated with a mosaic of the Lamb of God surrounded by the Twelve Apostles at Pentecost, and the apse semi-dome has a mosaic of the Virgin and Child Enthroned. Biblical scenes (the Nativity appears on the squinch visible in FIG. 7–32) and figures of saints fill the interior with brilliant color and dramatic images. As at Hagia Sophia, the lower walls are faced with a multicolored stone veneer. An iconostasis separates the congregation from the sanctuary.

SANTA SOPHIA IN KIEV.   During the ninth century, the rulers of Kievan Rus—Ukraine, Belarus, and Russia—adopted Orthodox Christianity and Byzantine culture. These lands had been settled by eastern Slavs in the fifth and sixth centuries, but later were ruled by Scandinavian Vikings who had sailed down the rivers from the Baltic to the Black Sea. In Constantinople, the Byzantine emperor hired the Vikings as his personal bodyguards, and Viking traders established a headquarters in the upper Volga region and in the city of Kiev, which became the capital of the area under their control.

The first Christian member of the Kievan ruling family was Princess Olga (c. 890–969), who was baptized in Constantinople by the patriarch himself, with the Byzantine emperor as her godfather. Her grandson Grand Prince Vladimir (r. 980–1015) established Orthodox Christianity as the state religion in 988. Vladimir sealed the pact with the Byzantines by accepting baptism and marrying Anna, the sister of the powerful Emperor Basil II (r. 976–1025).

Vladimir's son Grand Prince Yaroslav (r. 1036–1054) founded the **CATHEDRAL OF SANTA SOPHIA** in Kiev **(FIG. 7–33)**. The church originally had a typical Byzantine multiple-domed cross design, but the building was expanded with double side aisles, leading to five apses. It culminated in a large central dome surrounded by 12 smaller domes. The small

domes were said to stand for the 12 apostles gathered around the central dome, representing Christ Pantokrator, ruler of the universe. The central domed space of the crossing focuses attention on the nave and the main apse. Nonetheless, the many individual bays create a complicated and compartmentalized interior. The walls glow with lavish decoration: Mosaics glitter from the central dome, the apse, and the arches of the crossing. The remaining surfaces are frescoed with scenes from the lives of Christ, the Virgin, the apostles Peter and Paul, and the archangels.

The Kievan mosaics established a standard system of iconography used in Russian Orthodox churches. The Pantokrator fills the curving surface at the crest of the main dome (not visible above the window-pierced drum in FIG. 7–33). At a lower level, the apostles stand between the windows of the drum, with the four

7-33 • INTERIOR, CATHEDRAL OF SANTA SOPHIA
Kiev. 1037–1046. Apse mosaics: Orant Virgin and Communion of the Apostles.

7-34 • CHRIST PANTOKRATOR AT CREST OF CENTRAL DOME, WITH SCENES FROM THE LIFE OF CHRIST IN THE PENDENTIVES
Church of the Dormition, Daphni, Greece. Late 11th century. Mosaic.

evangelists occupying the pendentives. An orant figure of the Virgin Mary seems to float in a golden heaven on the semidome and upper wall of the apse. In the mosaic on the wall below the Virgin is the Communion of the Apostles. Christ appears not once, but twice, in this scene, offering the Eucharistic bread and wine to the apostles, six on each side of the altar. With such extravagant use of costly mosaic, Prince Yaroslav made a powerful political declaration of his own power and wealth—and that of the Kievan Church as well.

CHURCH OF THE DORMITION AT DAPHNI. The refined mosaicists who worked at the church of the Dormition at Daphni, near Athens, conceived their compositions in relation to an intellectual ideal. They eliminated all "unnecessary" detail to focus on the essential elements of a narrative scene, conveying its mood and message in a moving but elegant style. The main dome of this church has maintained its riveting image of the Pantokrator, centered at the crest of the dome like a seal of divine sanction and surveillance (FIG. 7–34). This imposing figure manages to be elegant and awesome at the same time. Christ blesses or addresses the assembled congregation with one hand, while the slender, attenuated fingers of the other spread to clutch a massive book securely. In the squinches of the corner piers are four signal episodes from his life: Annunciation, Nativity, Baptism, and Transfiguration.

A mosaic of the **CRUCIFIXION** from the lower part of the church (FIG. 7–35) exemplifies the focus on emotional appeal to individuals that characterizes late eleventh-century Byzantine art. The figures inhabit an otherworldly space, a golden universe anchored to the material world by a few flowers, which suggest the promise of new life. A nearly nude Jesus is shown with bowed head and gently sagging body, his eyes closed in death. The witnesses have been reduced to two isolated mourning figures, Mary and the young apostle John, to whom Jesus had just entrusted the care of his mother. The elegant cut of the contours and the eloquent restraint of the gestures only intensify the emotional power of the

7-35 • CRUCIFIXION
Church of the Dormition, Daphni, Greece. East wall of the north arm. Late 11th century. Mosaic.

image. The nobility and suffering of these figures was meant to move worshipers toward a deeper involvement with their own meditation and worship.

This depiction of the Crucifixion has symbolic as well as emotional power. The mound of rocks and the skull at the bottom of the cross represent Golgotha, the "place of the skull," the hill outside ancient Jerusalem where Adam was thought to be buried and where the Crucifixion was said to have taken place. The faithful saw Jesus Christ as the new Adam, whose sacrifice on the cross saved humanity from the sins brought into the world by Adam and Eve. The arc of blood and water springing from Jesus' side refers to Eucharistic and baptismal rites. As Paul wrote in his First Letter to the Corinthians: "For just as in Adam all die, so too in Christ shall all be brought to life" (1 Corinthians 15:22). The timelessness and simplicity of this image were meant to aid the Christian worshiper seeking to achieve a mystical union with the divine through prayer and meditation, both intellectually and emotionally.

THE CATHEDRAL OF ST. MARK IN VENICE. The northeastern Italian city of Venice, set on the Adriatic at the crossroads of Europe and Asia Minor, was a major center of Byzantine art in Italy. Venice had been subject to Byzantine rule in the sixth and seventh centuries, and up to the tenth century, the city's ruler, the doge ("duke" in Venetian dialect), had to be ratified by the Byzantine emperor. At the end of the tenth century, Constantinople granted Venice a special trade status that allowed its merchants to control much of the commerce between east and west, and the city grew enormously wealthy.

Venetian architects looked to Byzantine domed churches for inspiration in 1063, when the doge commissioned a church to replace the palace chapel that had housed the relics of St. Mark the Apostle since they were brought to Venice from Alexandria in 828/29 **(FIG. 7–36)**. The Cathedral of St. Mark has a Greek-cross plan, each square unit of which is covered by a dome, that is, five great domes in all, separated by barrel vaults and supported by pendentives. Unlike Hagia Sophia in Constantinople, where the space seems to flow from the narthex up into the dome and through the nave to the apse, St. Mark's domed compartments produce a complex space in which each dome maintains its own separate vertical axis. As we have seen elsewhere, marble veneer covers the lower walls, and golden mosaics glimmer above on the vaults, pendentives, and domes. The dome visible in FIG. 7–36 depicts Pentecost, the descent of the Holy Spirit on the apostles. A view of the exterior of St. Mark's as it would have appeared in early modern times can be seen in a painting by the fifteenth-century Venetian artist Gentile Bellini (SEE FIG. 19–36).

7-36 • INTERIOR AND PLAN OF THE CATHEDRAL OF ST. MARK
Venice. Begun 1063. View looking toward apse.

This church is the third one built on the site. It was both the palace chapel of the doge and the burial place for the bones of the patron of Venice, St. Mark. The church was consecrated as a cathedral in 1807. Mosaics have been reworked continually to the present day.

OBJECTS OF VENERATION AND DEVOTION

As in the Early Byzantine period, artists of great talent and high aesthetic sensibility produced small luxury items for members of the court as well as for the Church. Many of these items were commissioned by rulers and secular and Church functionaries as official gifts for one another. They had to be portable, sturdy, and exquisitely refined. These works often combined exceptional beauty and technical virtuosity with religious meaning. Icons, ivory carving, gold and enamel work, and fine books were especially prized.

THE VIRGIN OF VLADIMIR. The revered icon of Mary and Jesus known as the **VIRGIN OF VLADIMIR** (FIG. 7–37) was probably created in Constantinople but brought to Kiev. This distinctively humanized image suggests the growing desire for a more immediate and personal religion that we have already seen in the Crucifixion mosaic at Daphni, dating from about the same period. This exquisite icon employs an established iconographic type, known as the "Virgin of Compassion," showing Mary and the Christ Child pressing their cheeks together and gazing at each other with tender affection. It was widely believed that St. Luke had been the first to paint such a portrait of the Virgin and Child as they appeared to him in a vision.

Almost from its creation, the *Virgin of Vladimir* was thought to protect the people of the city where it resided. It arrived in Kiev sometime between 1131 and 1136 and was taken to the city of Suzdal and then to Vladimir in 1155. In 1480, it was moved to the Cathedral of the Dormition in the Moscow Kremlin. Today, even in a museum, it inspires prayer.

THE HARBAVILLE TRIPTYCH. Dating from the mid eleventh century, the small devotional ivory known as the **HARBAVILLE TRIPTYCH** features a tableau of Christ flanked by Mary and St. John the Baptist, a group known as the "Deësis" (FIG. 7–38). Deësis means "entreaty" in Greek, and here Mary and John intercede, presumably for the owner of this work, pleading with Christ for forgiveness and salvation. The emergence of the Deësis as an important theme is in keeping with an increasing personalization in Byzantine religious art. St. Peter stands directly under Christ, gesturing upward toward him. Inscriptions identify SS. James, John, Paul, and Andrew. The figures in the outer panels are military saints and martyrs. All these figures stand in a neutral space given definition only by the small bases under their feet, effectively removing them from the physical world. They are, however, fully realized human forms with rounded shoulders, thighs, and knees that suggest physical substance beneath their linear, decorative drapery.

THE PARIS PSALTER. The painters of luxuriously illustrated manuscripts matched the combination of intense religious expression, aristocratic elegance, and a heightened appreciation of rich decoration that we have experienced in monumental architectural painting.

7-37 • VIRGIN OF VLADIMIR
Icon, probably from Constantinople. Faces, 11th–12th century; the figures have been retouched. Tempera on panel, height approx. 31″ (78 cm). Tretyakov Gallery, Moscow.

7-38 • HARBAVILLE TRIPTYCH
Mid 11th century. Ivory, closed 11 × 9½″ (28 × 24.1 cm);
open 11 × 19″ (28 × 48.2 cm). Musée du Louvre, Paris.

The luxurious Paris Psalter (named after its current library location), with 14 full-page paintings, was created for a Byzantine aristocrat during the second half of the tenth century. According to ancient tradition, the author of the Psalms was Israel's King David, who as a young shepherd and musician had saved the people of God by killing the giant Goliath (SEE FIG. 7–1). In Christian times, the Psalms were often extracted from the Bible and copied into a separate book called a **psalter**, used by wealthy Christians for private prayer and meditation.

The painters who worked on the Paris Psalter framed their scenes on full pages without text. The first of these depicts a seated David playing his harp (**FIG. 7–39**). The monumental, idealized figures occupy a spacious landscape filled with lush foliage, a meandering stream, and a distant city. The image seems to have been transported directly from an ancient Roman wall painting. The ribbon-tied memorial column is a convention in Greek and Roman funerary art and, in the ancient manner, the illustrator has personified abstract ideas and landscape features: Melody, a female figure, leans casually on David's shoulder, while another woman, perhaps the nymph Echo, peeks out from behind the column. The swarthy reclining youth in

7-39 • DAVID THE PSALMIST
Page from the Paris Psalter. Second half of 10th century. Paint and gold on vellum, sheet size 14 × 10½″ (35.6 × 26 cm). Bibliothèque Nationale, Paris.

7-40 • PLAN OF THE MONASTERY CHURCH OF CHRIST IN CHORA
Constantinople. (Present-day Kariye Müzesi, Istanbul, Turkey.) 1077–1081, c. 1310–1321.

7-41 • MOSAICS IN THE VAULTING OF THE INNER NARTHEX
Church of Christ in Chora, Constantinople. (Present-day Kariye Müzesi, Istanbul, Turkey.) c. 1315–1321.

the lower foreground is a personification of Mount Bethlehem, as we learn from his inscription. The image of the dog watching over the sheep and goats while his master strums the harp suggests the Classical subject of Orpheus charming wild animals with music. The subtle modeling of forms, the integration of the figures into a three-dimensional space, and the use of atmospheric perspective all enhance the Classical flavor of the painting, in yet another example of the enduring vitality of pagan artistic traditions at the Christian court in Constantinople.

LATE BYZANTINE ART

The third great age of Byzantine art began in 1261, after the Byzantines expelled the Christian crusaders who had occupied Constantinople for nearly 60 years. Although the empire had been weakened and its realm decreased to small areas of the Balkans and Greece, its arts underwent a resurgence known as the Palaeologue Renaissance after the dynasty of emperors who ruled from Constantinople. The patronage of emperors, wealthy courtiers, and the Church stimulated renewed church building as well as the production of icons, books, and precious objects.

CONSTANTINOPLE: THE CHORA CHURCH

In Constantinople, many existing churches were renovated, redecorated, and expanded during the Palaeologue Renaissance. Among these is the church of the Monastery of Christ in Chora. The expansion of this church was one of several projects that Theodore Metochites (1270–1332), a humanist poet and scientist, and the administrator of the Imperial Treasury at Constantinople, sponsored between c. 1315 and 1321. He added a two-story annex

7-42 • THE INFANT
VIRGIN MARY
CARESSED BY HER
PARENTS (JOACHIM
AND ANNA)
Inner narthex, church
of Christ in Chora,
Constantinople. (Present-day
Kariye Müzesi, Istanbul,
Turkey.) c. 1315–1321.
Mosaic.

The Greek inscription
placed over the family group
identifies this scene as the
fondling of the Theotokos
(bearer of God).

on the north side, two narthexes on the west, and a parekklesion (side chapel) used as a funerary chapel on the south (FIG. 7–40). These structures contain the most impressive interior decorations remaining in Constantinople from the Late Byzantine period, rivaling in splendor and technical sophistication the works of the age of Justinian, but on a more intimate scale. The walls and vaults of the parekklesion are covered with frescos (see "The Funerary Chapel of Theodore Metochites," pages 256–257), and the vaults of the narthexes are encrusted with mosaics.

In the new narthexes of the Chora church, above an expanse of traditional marble revetment on the lower walls, mosaics cover every surface—the domical groin vaults, the wall lunettes, even the undersides of arches—with narrative scenes and their ornamental framework (FIG. 7–41). The small-scale figures of these mosaics seem to dance with relentless enthusiasm through the narrative episodes they enact from the lives of Christ and his mother. Unlike the stripped-down narrative scenes of Daphni (SEE FIG. 7–35), here the artists have lavished special attention on the settings, composing their stories against backdrops of architectural fantasies and stylized plants. The architecture of the background is presented in an innovative system of perspective, charting its three-dimensionality not in relation to a point of convergence in the background—as will be the case in the linear, one-point perspective of fifteenth-century Florentine art (see "Renaissance Perspective," page 608)—but projecting forward in relationship to a point in the foreground, thereby drawing attention to the figural scenes themselves.

The Chora mosaics build on the growing Byzantine interest in the expression of emotions within religious narrative, but they broach a level of human tenderness that surpasses anything we have seen in Byzantine art thus far. The artists invite viewers to see the participants in these venerable sacred stories as human beings just like themselves, only wealthier and holier. For example, an entire narrative field in one vault is devoted to a scene where the infant Mary is cuddled between her adoring parents, Joachim and Anna (FIG. 7–42; part of the scene is visible lit up in FIG. 7–41). Servants on either side of the family look on with gestures and expressions of admiration and approval, perhaps modeling the response that is expected from viewers within the narthex itself. The human inter-action even extends to details, such as the nuzzling of Mary's head into the beard of her father as she leans back to look into his eyes, and her tentative reach toward her mother's face at the same time. In another scene, the young Jesus rides on the shoulders of Joseph, in a pose still familiar to fathers and children in our own time. The informality and believability that these anecdotal details bring to this sacred narrative recalls developments as far away as Italy, where at this same time Giotto and Duccio were using similar devices to bring their stories to life (see Chapter 17).

The Funerary Chapel of Theodore Metochites

Theodore Metochites (1270–1332) was one of the most fascinating personalities of the Late Byzantine world. Son of a disgraced intellectual cleric—condemned and exiled for championing the union of the Roman and Byzantine Churches—Metochites became a powerful intellectual figure in Constantinople. As a poet, philosopher, and astronomer who wrote scores of convoluted commentaries in an intentionally cultivated, arcane, and mannered literary style, he ridiculed a rival for his prose style of "excess clarity." In 1290, Emperor Andronicus II Palaeologus (r. 1282–1328) called Metochites to court service, where the prolific young scholar became an influential senior statesman, ascending to the highest levels of the government and amassing power and wealth second only to that of the emperor himself. Metochites' political and financial status fell when the emperor was overthrown by his grandson in 1328. Stripped of his wealth and sent into exile, he was allowed to return to the capital two years later, retiring to house arrest at the Chora monastery, where he died and was buried in 1332.

It is his association with this monastery that has become Theodore Metochites' greatest claim to enduring fame. Beginning in about 1315, at the peak of his power and wealth, he funded an expansion and restoration of the church of Christ in Chora (meaning "in the country"), part of an influential monastery on the outskirts of Constantinople. The mosaic decoration he commissioned for the church's expansive narthexes (SEE FIGS. 7–41, 7–42) may be the most sumptuous product of his beneficence, but the project probably revolved around a funerary chapel (or parekklesion) that he built adjacent to the main church (FIG. B), potentially motivated by a desire to create a location for his own funeral and tomb.

The extensive and highly integrative program of frescos covering every square inch of the walls and vaults of this jewel-box space focuses on funerary themes and expectations of salvation and its rewards. Above a dado of imitation marble stand a frieze of 34 stately saints ready to fulfill their roles as intercessors for the faithful. Above them, on the side walls of the main space, are stories from the Hebrew Bible interpreted as prefigurations of the Virgin Mary's own intercessory powers. A portrayal of Jacob's ladder (Genesis 28:11–19), for example, evokes her position between heaven and earth as a bridge from death to life. In the pendentives of the dome over the main space (two of which are seen in the foreground) sit famous Byzantine hymn writers, with quotations from their work. These carefully chosen passages highlight texts associated with funerals, including one that references the story of Jacob's ladder.

The climax of the decorative program, however, is the powerful rendering of the Anastasis that occupies the halfdome of the apse (FIG. A). In this popular Byzantine representation of the Resurrection—drawn not from the Bible but from the apocryphal Gospel of Nicodemus—Jesus demonstrates his powers of salvation by descending into hell after his death on the cross to save his righteous Hebrew forebears from Satan's grasp. Here a boldly striding Christ—brilliantly outfitted in a pure white that makes him shine to prominence within the fresco program—lunges to rescue Adam and Eve from their tombs, pulling them upward with such force that they seem to float airborne under the spell of his power. Satan lies tied into a useless bundle at his feet, and patriarchs, kings, and prophets to either side look on in admiration, perhaps waiting for their own turn to be rescued. During a funeral in this chapel, the head of the deceased would have been directed toward this engrossing tableau, closed eyes facing upward toward a painting of the Last Judgment, strategically positioned on the vault over the bier. In 1332, this was the location of Metochites' own dead body since this parekklesion was indeed the site of his funeral. He was buried in one of the niche tombs cut into the walls of the chapel itself.

A. ANASTASIS
Apse of the funerary chapel, church of the Monastery of Christ in Chora. Fresco. Getty Research Library, Los Angeles. Wim Swaan Photograph Collection, 96.P.21

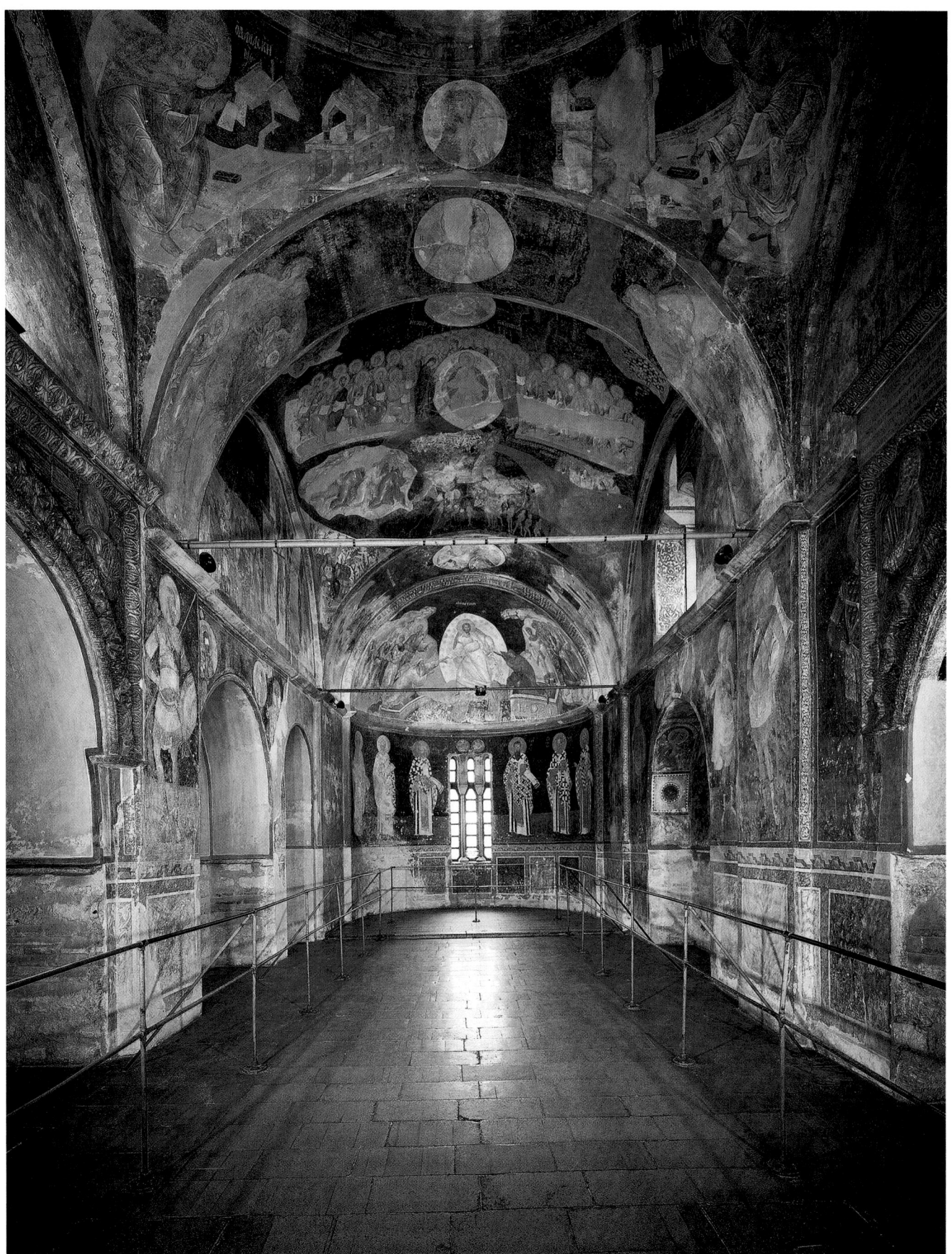

**B. FUNERARY CHAPEL (PAREKKLESION), CHURCH OF THE MONASTERY OF
CHRIST IN CHORA**
Constantinople. (Present-day Kariye Müzesi, Istanbul, Turkey.) c. 1310–1321.

7-43 • Andrey Rublyov **THE OLD TESTAMENT TRINITY (THREE ANGELS VISITING ABRAHAM)**
Icon. c. 1410–1425. Tempera on panel, 55½ × 44½" (141 × 113 cm).

MOSCOW: RUBLYOV

In the fifteenth and sixteenth centuries, architecture of the Late Byzantine style flourished outside the borders of the empire in regions that had adopted Eastern Orthodox Christianity. After Constantinople's fall to the Ottoman Turks in 1453, leadership of the Orthodox Church shifted to Russia, whose rulers declared Moscow to be the "Third Rome" and themselves the heirs of Caesar (the tsar).

The practice of venerating icons continued—perhaps even intensified—in Russia, where regional schools of icon painting flourished, fostering the work of remarkable artists. A magnificent icon from this time is THE OLD TESTAMENT TRINITY (THREE ANGELS VISITING ABRAHAM), a large panel created sometime between about 1410 and 1425 by the renowned artist-monk Andrey Rublyov (FIG. 7–43). It was commissioned in honor of Abbot Sergius of the Trinity-Sergius Monastery, near Moscow. The theme is the Trinity, always a challenge for artists. One late medieval solution was to show three identical divine individuals—here three angels—to suggest the idea of the Trinity. Rublyov's composition was inspired by a story in the Hebrew Bible of the patriarch Abraham and his wife Sarah, who entertained three strangers who were in fact God represented by three divine beings in human form (Genesis 18). Tiny images of Abraham and Sarah's home and the oak of Mamre can be seen above the angels. On the table, the food the couple offered to the strangers becomes a chalice on an altarlike table.

Rublyov's icon clearly illustrates how Late Byzantine artists relied on mathematical conventions to create ideal figures, as did the ancient Greeks, giving their works remarkable consistency. But unlike the Greeks, who based their formulas on close observation of nature, Byzantine artists invented an ideal geometry to evoke a spiritual realm and conformed their representations of human forms and features to it. Here, as is often the case, the circle—most apparent in the haloes—forms the basic underlying structure for the composition. Despite the formulaic approach, talented artists like Rublyov created a personal, expressive style working within it. Rublyov relied on typical Byzantine conventions—salient contours, elongation of the body, and a focus on a limited number of figures—to capture the sense of the spiritual in his work, yet he distinguished his art by imbuing it with a sweet, poetic ambience. In this master's hands, the Byzantine style took on a graceful and eloquent new life.

The Byzantine tradition would continue in the art of the Eastern Orthodox Church and is carried on to this day in Greek and Russian icon painting. In Constantinople, however, the three golden ages of Byzantine art—and the empire itself—came to an end in 1453. When the forces of the Ottoman sultan Mehmed II overran the capital, the Eastern Empire became part of the Islamic world. But the Turkish conquerors were so impressed with the splendor of the Byzantine art and architecture in the capital that they adopted its traditions and melded them with their own rich aesthetic heritage into a new, and now Islamic, artistic efflorescence.

THINK ABOUT IT

7.1 Discuss the Roman foundations of Early Christian sculpture, focusing your answer on the *Sarcophagus of Junius Bassus* (FIG. 7–13). Look back to Chapter 6 to help form your ideas.

7.2 Distinguish the "iconic" from the "narrative" in Early Christian and Byzantine art, locating one example of each in this chapter. How are these two traditions used by the Church and its members?

7.3 Distinguish the identifying features of basilicas and central-plan churches, and discuss how the forms of these early churches were geared toward specific types of Christian worship and devotional practice.

7.4 How were images used in Byzantine worship? Why were images suppressed during Iconoclasm?

7.5 Compare and contrast the mosaics of San Vitale in Ravenna with those in the Chora church in Constantinople. Consider, in particular, how figures are represented, what kinds of stories are told, and in what way.

PRACTICE MORE: Compose answers to these questions, get flashcards for images and terms, and review chapter material with quizzes
www.myartslab.com

8-1 • Yahya Ibn al-Wasiti **THE *MAQAMAT* OF AL-HARIRI** From Baghdad, Iraq. 1237. Paper.
Bibliothèque Nationale, Paris. (Arabic MS. 5847, f. 18v)

ISLAMIC ART

The *Maqamat* ("*Assemblies*"), by al-Hariri (1054–1122), belongs to a popular literary genre of cautionary tales dating from the tenth century. The manuscript's vividly detailed scenes provide windows into ordinary Muslim life, here prayer in the congregational **mosque**, a religious and social institution central to Islam. Al-Hariri's stories revolve around a silver-tongued scoundrel named Abu Zayd, whose cunning inevitably triumphs over other people's naivety. His adventures take place in a world of colorful settings—desert camps, ships, pilgrim caravans, apothecary shops, mosques, gardens, libraries, cemeteries, and courts of law. Humans activate the scenes, pointing fingers, arguing, riding horses, stirring pots, and strumming musical instruments. These comic stories of trickery and theft would seem perfectly suited for illustration, but of the hundreds of surviving manuscript copies, only 13 have pictures.

This illustration (**FIG. 8–1**) shows a mosque with the congregation gathered to hear a sermon preached by the deceitful Abu Zayd, who plans to steal the alms collected from the congregation. The men sit directly on the ground, as is customary in mosques (and traditional dwellings). They look generally forward, but the listener in the front row tilts his chin upward to focus his gaze directly upon the speaker. He is framed and centered by the arch of the niche (**mihrab**) on the rear wall, his white turban contrasting noticeably with the darker background. To the extent that he represents any specific individual, he seems to stand in for the manuscript's reader who, perusing the illustrations of these captivating stories, pauses and perhaps projects himself or herself into the scene.

The columns of the arcades have ornamental capitals from which spring half-round arches. Glass mosque lamps filled with oil hang from the center of each arch. All the figures wear turbans and flowing, loose-sleeved robes with epigraphic borders (*tiraz*) embroidered in gold.

The sermon is delivered from a pulpit (**minbar**) of steps with an arched opening at the lowest level. This *minbar* and the arcades that form the backdrop to the scene and define the mosque's interior are unnaturally reduced in scale. The painter has manipulated the sizes so as to fit the maximum amount of detail into the scene, sacrificing natural space in order to make the painting more communicative. Likewise, although in an actual mosque the *minbar* would share the same wall as the niche in the center, here they have been separated to keep the niche from being hidden by the *minbar*. There is little modeling to represent volume: Instead depth of field is suggested by the overlapping of forms.

LEARN ABOUT IT

8.1 Discover Islamic art's eclecticism and embrace of other cultures.

8.2 Compare and contrast the variety of art and architecture in the disparate areas of the Islamic world.

8.3 Interpret art as a reflection of both religion and secular society.

8.4 Explore the use of ornament and inscription in Islamic art.

8.5 Recognize the role of trade routes and political ties in the creation of Islamic artistic unity.

HEAR MORE: Listen to an audio file of your chapter **www.myartslab.com**

ISLAM AND EARLY ISLAMIC SOCIETY

Islam arose in seventh-century Arabia, a land of desert oases with no cities of great size, sparsely inhabited by tribal nomads. Yet, under the leadership of its founder, the Prophet Muhammad (c. 570–632 CE), and his successors, Islam spread rapidly throughout northern Africa, southern and eastern Europe, and much of Asia, gaining territory and converts with astonishing speed. Because Islam encompassed geographical areas with a variety of long-established cultural traditions, and because it admitted diverse peoples among its converts, it absorbed and combined many different techniques and ideas about art and architecture. The result was a remarkable eclecticism and artistic sophistication.

In the desert outside of Mecca in 610, Muhammad received revelations that led him to found the religion called Islam ("submission to God's will"), whose adherents are Muslims ("those who have submitted to God"). Many powerful Meccans were hostile to the message of the young visionary, and in 622 he and his companions were forced to flee to Medina. There Muhammad built a house that became a gathering place for the converted and thus the first Islamic mosque. Muslims date their history as beginning with this *hijira* ("emigration").

In 630, Muhammad returned to Mecca with an army of 10,000, routed his enemies, and established the city as the spiritual capital of Islam. After his triumph, he went to the Kaaba **(FIG. 8–2)**, a cubical, textile-draped shrine said to have been built for God by Ibrahim (Abraham) and Isma'il (Ishmael) and long the focus of pilgrimage and polytheistic worship. He emptied the shrine, repudiating its accumulated pagan idols, while preserving the enigmatic cubical structure itself and dedicating it to God.

The Kaaba is the symbolic center of the Islamic world, the place to which all Muslim prayer is directed and the ultimate destination of Islam's obligatory pilgrimage, the *hajj*. Each year, huge numbers of Muslims from all over the world travel to Mecca to circumambulate the Kaaba during the month of pilgrimage. The exchange of ideas that occurs during the intermingling of these diverse groups of pilgrims has contributed to Islam's cultural eclecticism.

Muhammad's act of emptying the Kaaba of its pagan idols instituted the fundamental concept of **aniconism** (avoidance of

8-2 • THE KAABA, MECCA
The Kaaba represents the center of the Islamic world. Its cubical form is draped with a black textile that is embroidered with a few Qur'anic verses in gold.

MAP 8-1 • THE ISLAMIC WORLD

Within 200 years after 622 CE, the Islamic world expanded from Mecca to India in the east, and to Morocco and Spain in the west.

figural imagery) in Islamic art. Following his example, the Muslim faith discourages the representation of figures in religious contexts (although such images abound in palaces and illustrated manuscripts). Instead, Islamic artists elaborated a rich vocabulary of nonfigural ornament, including complex geometric designs and scrolling vines sometimes known as **arabesques**. Islamic art revels in surface decoration, in manipulating line, color, and especially pattern, often highlighting the interplay of pure abstraction, organic form, and script.

According to tradition, the Qur'an assumed its final form during the time of the third caliph (successor to the Prophet), Uthman (r. 644–56). As the language of the Qur'an, the Arabic language and script have been a powerful unifying force within Islam. From the eighth through the eleventh centuries, it was the universal language among scholars in the Islamic world and in some Christian lands as well. Inscriptions frequently ornament works of art, sometimes written clearly to provide a readable message, but in other cases written as complex patterns simply to delight the eye.

The Prophet was succeeded by a series of caliphs. The accession of Ali as the fourth caliph (r. 656–61) provoked a power struggle that led to his assassination and resulted in enduring divisions within Islam. Followers of Ali, known as Shi'ites (referring to the party or *shi'a* of Ali), regard him alone as the Prophet's rightful successor. Sunni Muslims, in contrast, recognize all of the first four caliphs as "rightly guided." Ali was succeeded by his rival Muawiya (r. 661–80), a close relative of Uthman and the founder of the first Muslim dynasty, the Umayyad dynasty (661–750).

Islam expanded dramatically. In just two decades, seemingly unstoppable Muslim armies conquered the Sasanian Persian Empire, Egypt, and the Byzantine provinces of Syria and Palestine. By the early eighth century, under the Umayyads, they had reached India, conquered northern Africa and Spain, and penetrated France before being turned back **(MAP 8–1)**. In these newly conquered lands, the treatment of Christians and Jews who did not convert to Islam was not consistent, but in general, as "People of the Book"— followers of a monotheistic religion based on a revealed scripture —they enjoyed a protected status. However, they were also subject to a special tax and restrictions on dress and employment.

Muslims participate in congregational worship at a mosque (*masjid*, "place of prostration"). The Prophet Muhammad himself lived simply and instructed his followers in prayer at his house, now known as the Mosque of the Prophet, where he resided in Medina. This was a square enclosure that framed a large courtyard with rooms along the east wall where he and his family lived. Along the

Islamic art delights in complex ornament that sheathes surfaces, distracting the eye from the underlying structure or physical form.

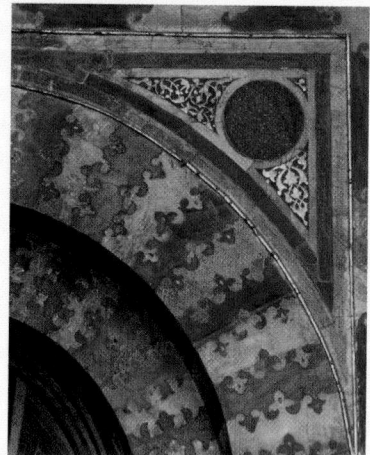

ablaq masonry (*Madrasa*-Mausoleum-Mosque of Sultan Hasan, Cairo) juxtaposes stone of contrasting colors. The ornamental effect is enhanced here by the interlocking jigsaw shape of the blocks, called **joggled voussoirs**.

cut tile (Shah-i Zinda, Samarkand), made up of dozens of individually cut ceramic tile pieces fitted precisely together, emphasizes the clarity of the colored shapes.

muqarnas (Court of the Lions, Alhambra, Granada) consists of small nichelike components, usually stacked in multiples as successive, nonload-bearing units in arches, cornices, and domes, hiding the transition from the vertical to the horizontal plane.

wooden strapwork (Kutubiya *Minbar*, Marrakesh) assembles finely cut wooden pieces to create the appearance of geometrically interlacing ribbons, often framing smaller panels of carved wood and inlaid ivory or mother-of-pearl (shell).

mosaic (Dome of the Rock, Jerusalem) is comprised of thousands of small glass or glazed ceramic tesserae set on a plaster ground. The luminous white circular shapes are mother-of-pearl.

water (Court of the Myrtles, Alhambra, Granada) is a fluid architectural element that reflects surrounding architecture, adds visual dynamism and sound, and, running in channels between halls, unites disparate spaces.

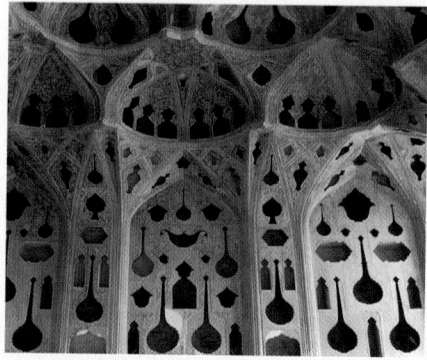

chini khana (Ali Qapu Pavilion, Isfahan)—literally "china cabinet"—is a panel of niches, sometimes providing actual shelving, but used here for its contrast of material and void which reverses the typical figure-ground relationship.

south wall, a thatched portico supported by palm-tree trunks sheltered both the faithful as they prayed and Muhammad as he spoke from a low platform. This simple arrangement inspired the design of later mosques. Lacking an architectural focus such as an altar, nave, or dome, the space of this prototypical **hypostyle** (multicolumned) mosque reflected the founding spirit of Islam in which the faithful pray as equals directly to God, led by an imam, but without the intermediary of a priesthood.

ART AND ARCHITECTURE THROUGH THE FOURTEENTH CENTURY

The caliphs of the Umayyad dynasty (661–750) ruled from Damascus in Syria, and throughout the Islamic Empire they built mosques and palaces that projected the authority of the new rulers and reflected the growing acceptance of Islam. In 750 the Abbasid clan replaced the Umayyads in a coup d'état, ruling as caliphs until 1258 from Baghdad, in Iraq, in the grand manner of the ancient Persian emperors. Their long and cosmopolitan reign saw achievements in medicine, mathematics, the natural sciences, philosophy, literature, music, and art. They were generally tolerant of the ethnically diverse populations in the territories they subjugated, and they admired the past achievements of Roman civilization and the living traditions of Byzantium, Persia, India, and China, freely borrowing artistic techniques and styles from all of them.

In the tenth century, the Islamic world split into separate kingdoms ruled by independent caliphs. In addition to the Abbasids of Iraq, there was a Fatimid Shi'ite caliph ruling Tunisia and Egypt, and a descendant of the Umayyads ruling Spain and Portugal (together then known as al-Andalus). The Islamic world did not reunite under the myriad dynasties who thereafter ruled from northern Africa to Asia, but the loss to unity was a gain to artistic diversity.

EARLY ARCHITECTURE

While Mecca and Medina remained the holiest Muslim cities, the political center shifted to the Syrian city of Damascus in 656. In the eastern Mediterranean, inspired by Roman and Byzantine architecture, the early Muslims became enthusiastic builders of shrines, mosques, and palaces. Although tombs were officially discouraged in Islam, they proliferated from the eleventh century onward, in part due to funerary practices imported from the Turkic northeast, and in part due to the rise of Shi'ism with its emphasis on genealogy and particularly ancestry through Muhammad's daughter, Fatima.

THE DOME OF THE ROCK. The Dome of the Rock is the first great monument of Islamic art. Built in Jerusalem, it is the third most holy site in Islam. In the center of the city rises the Haram al-Sharif ("Noble Sanctuary") (FIG. 8–3), a rocky outcrop from which Muslims believe Muhammad ascended to the presence of God on the "Night Journey" described in the Qur'an. It is the site of the First and Second Jewish Temples, and Jews and Christians variously associate it with Solomon, the site of the creation of Adam, and the place where the patriarch Abraham prepared to sacrifice his son Isaac at the command of God. In 691–92, a shrine was built over the rock using artisans trained in the Byzantine tradition. By appropriating a site holy to the Jewish and Christian

8-3 • AERIAL VIEW OF HARAM AL-SHARIF, JERUSALEM
The Dome of the Rock occupies a place of visual height and prominence in Jerusalem and, when first built, strikingly emphasized the arrival of Islam and its community of adherents in that ancient city.

8-4 • CUTAWAY DRAWING OF THE DOME OF THE ROCK

faiths, the Dome of the Rock is the first architectural manifestation of Islam's view of itself as completing the prophecies of those faiths and superseding them.

Structurally, the Dome of the Rock imitates the centrally planned form of Early Christian and Byzantine martyria (SEE FIG. 7-20). However, unlike its models, with their plain exteriors, it is crowned by a golden dome that dominates the Jerusalem skyline. The ceramic tiles on the lower portion of the exterior were added later, but the opulent marble veneer and mosaics of the interior are original (see "Ornament," page 264). The dome, surmounting a circular drum pierced with windows and supported by arcades of alternating **piers** and **columns**, covers the central space containing the rock (**FIG. 8–4**). These arcades create concentric **aisles** (**ambulatories**) that permit devout visitors to circumambulate the rock. Inscriptions from the Qur'an interspersed with passages from other texts, including information about the building itself, form a frieze around the inner and outer arcades. As the pilgrim walks around the central space to read the inscriptions in brilliant gold mosaic on turquoise green ground, the building communicates both as a text and as a dazzling visual display (**FIG. 8–5**). These passages of text are especially notable because they are the oldest surviving written Qur'an verses and the first use of monumental Qur'anic inscriptions in architecture. Below are walls covered with pale marble, the veining of which creates abstract symmetrical patterns, and columns with shafts of gray marble and gilded capitals. Above the calligraphic frieze is another mosaic frieze depicting thick, symmetrical vine scrolls and trees in turquoise, blue, and green, embellished with imitation jewels, over a gold ground. The mosaics are variously

thought to represent the gardens of Paradise and trophies of Muslim victories offered to God. The decorative program is extraordinarily rich but, remarkably enough, the focus of the building is neither art nor architecture but the plain rock within it.

THE GREAT MOSQUE OF KAIROUAN. Muslim congregations gather on Fridays for regular worship in a mosque. The earliest mosque type was the hypostyle, following the model of the Prophet's own house. The Great Mosque of Kairouan, Tunisia (**FIG. 8–6**), built in the ninth century, reflects the early form of the mosque but is elaborated with later additions. The large rectangular space is divided between a courtyard and a flat-roofed hypostyle prayer hall oriented toward Mecca. The system of repeated bays and aisles can easily be extended as the congregation grows in size—

8-5 • DOME OF THE ROCK, JERUSALEM
691. Interior. The arches of the inner and outer face of the central arcade are encrusted with golden mosaics, a Byzantine technique adapted for Islamic use. The carpets and ceilings are modern but probably reflect the original patron's intention.

EXPLORE MORE: Click the Google Earth link for the Dome of the Rock www.myartslab.com

The Five Pillars of Islam

Islam emphasizes a direct, personal relationship with God. The Pillars of Islam, sometimes symbolized by an open hand with the five fingers extended, enumerate the duties required of Muslims by their faith.

- The first pillar (*shahadah*) is to proclaim that there is only one God and that Muhammad is his messenger. While monotheism is common to Judaism, Christianity, and Islam, and Muslims worship the god of Abraham, and also acknowledge Hebrew and Christian prophets such as Musa (Moses) and Isa (Jesus), Muslims deem the Christian Trinity polytheistic and assert that God was not born and did not give birth.
- The second pillar requires prayer (*salat*) to be performed by turning to face the Kaaba in Mecca five times daily: at dawn, noon, late afternoon, sunset, and nightfall. Prayer can occur almost anywhere, although the prayer on Fridays takes place in the congregational mosque. Because ritual ablutions are required for purity, mosque courtyards usually have fountains.
- The third pillar is the voluntary payment of annual tax or alms (*zakah*), equivalent to one-fortieth of one's assets. *Zakah* is used for charities such as feeding the poor, housing travelers, and paying the dowries of orphan girls. Among Shi'ites, an additional tithe is required to support the Shi'ite community specifically.

- The fourth pillar is the dawn-to-dusk fast (*sawm*) during Ramadan, the month when Muhammad received the revelations set down in the Qur'an. The fast of Ramadan is a communally shared sacrifice that imparts purification, self-control, and kinship with others. The end of Ramadan is celebrated with the feast day 'Id al-Fitr (Festival of the Breaking of the Fast).
- For those physically and financially able to do so, the fifth pillar is the pilgrimage to Mecca (*hajj*), which ideally is undertaken at least once in the life of each Muslim. Among the extensive pilgrimage rites are donning simple garments to remove distinctions of class and culture; collective circumambulations of the Kaaba; kissing the Black Stone inside the Kaaba (probably a meteorite that fell in pre-Islamic times); and the sacrificing of an animal, usually a sheep, in memory of Abraham's readiness to sacrifice his son at God's command. The end of the *hajj* is celebrated by the festival 'Id al-Adha (Festival of Sacrifice).

The directness and simplicity of Islam have made the Muslim religion readily adaptable to numerous varied cultural contexts throughout history. The Five Pillars instill not only faith and a sense of belonging, but also a commitment to Islam in the form of actual practice.

---

one of the hallmarks of the hypostyle plan. New is the large tower (the **minaret**, from which the faithful are called to prayer) that rises from one end of the courtyard and that stands as a powerful sign of Islam's presence in the city.

The **qibla** wall, marked by a centrally positioned *mihrab* niche, is the wall of the prayer hall that is closest to Mecca. Prayer is oriented towards this wall. In the Great Mosque of Kairouan, the *qibla* wall is given heightened importance by a raised roof, a dome over the *mihrab*, and a central aisle that marks the axis that extends from the minaret to the *mihrab* (for a fourteenth-century example of a *mihrab*, SEE FIG. 8–12). The *mihrab* belongs to the historical tradition of niches that signify a holy place—the shrine for the Torah scrolls in a synagogue, the frame for the sculpture of a god or ancestor in Roman architecture, the apse in a church.

8-6 • THE GREAT MOSQUE, KAIROUAN, TUNISIA
836–875.

EXPLORE MORE: Click the Google Earth link for the Great Mosque of Kairouan **www.myartslab.com**

The Great Mosque of Cordoba

When the Umayyads were toppled in 750, a survivor of the dynasty, Abd al-Rahman I (r. 756–788), fled across north Africa into southern Spain (al-Andalus) where, with the support of Muslim settlers, he established himself as the provincial ruler, or emir. This newly transplanted Umayyad dynasty ruled in Spain from their capital in Cordoba (756–1031). The Hispano-Umayyads were noted patrons of the arts, and one of the finest surviving examples of Umayyad architecture is the Great Mosque of Cordoba.

In 785, the Umayyad conquerors began building the Cordoba mosque on the site of a Christian church built by the Visigoths, the pre-Islamic rulers of Spain. The choice of site was both practical—for the Muslims had already been renting space within the church—and symbolic, an appropriation of place (similar to the Dome of the Rock) that affirmed their presence. Later rulers expanded the building three times, and today the walls enclose an area of about 620 by 460 feet, about a third of which is the courtyard. This patio was planted with fruit trees, beginning in the early ninth century; today orange trees seasonally fill the space with color and sweet scent. Inside, the proliferation of pattern in the repeated columns and double flying arches is colorful and dramatic. The marble columns and capitals in the hypostyle prayer hall were recycled from the Christian church that had formerly occupied the site, as well as from classical buildings in the region, which had been a wealthy Roman province. The mosque's interior incorporates *spolia* (reused) columns of slightly varying heights. Two tiers of arches, one over the other, surmount these columns; the upper tier springs from rectangular posts that rise from the columns. This double-tiered design dramatically increases the height of the interior space, inspiring a sense of

monumentality and awe. The distinctively shaped **horseshoe arches**—a form known from Roman times and favored by the Visigoths—came to be closely associated with Islamic architecture in the West (see "Arches," page 271). Another distinctive feature of these arches, adopted from Roman and Byzantine precedents, is the alternation of white stone and red brick voussoirs forming the curved arch. This mixture of materials may have helped the building withstand earthquakes.

In the final century of Umayyad rule, Cordoba emerged as a major commercial and intellectual hub and a flourishing center for the arts, surpassing Christian European cities in science, literature, and philosophy. As a sign of this new wealth, prestige, and power, Abd al-Rahman III (r. 912–961) boldly reclaimed the title of caliph in 929. He and his son al-Hakam II (r. 961–976) made the Great Mosque a focus of patronage, commissioning costly and luxurious renovations such as a new *mihrab* with three bays in front of it. These capped the **maqsura**, an enclosure in front of the *mihrab* reserved for the ruler and other dignitaries, which became a feature of congregational

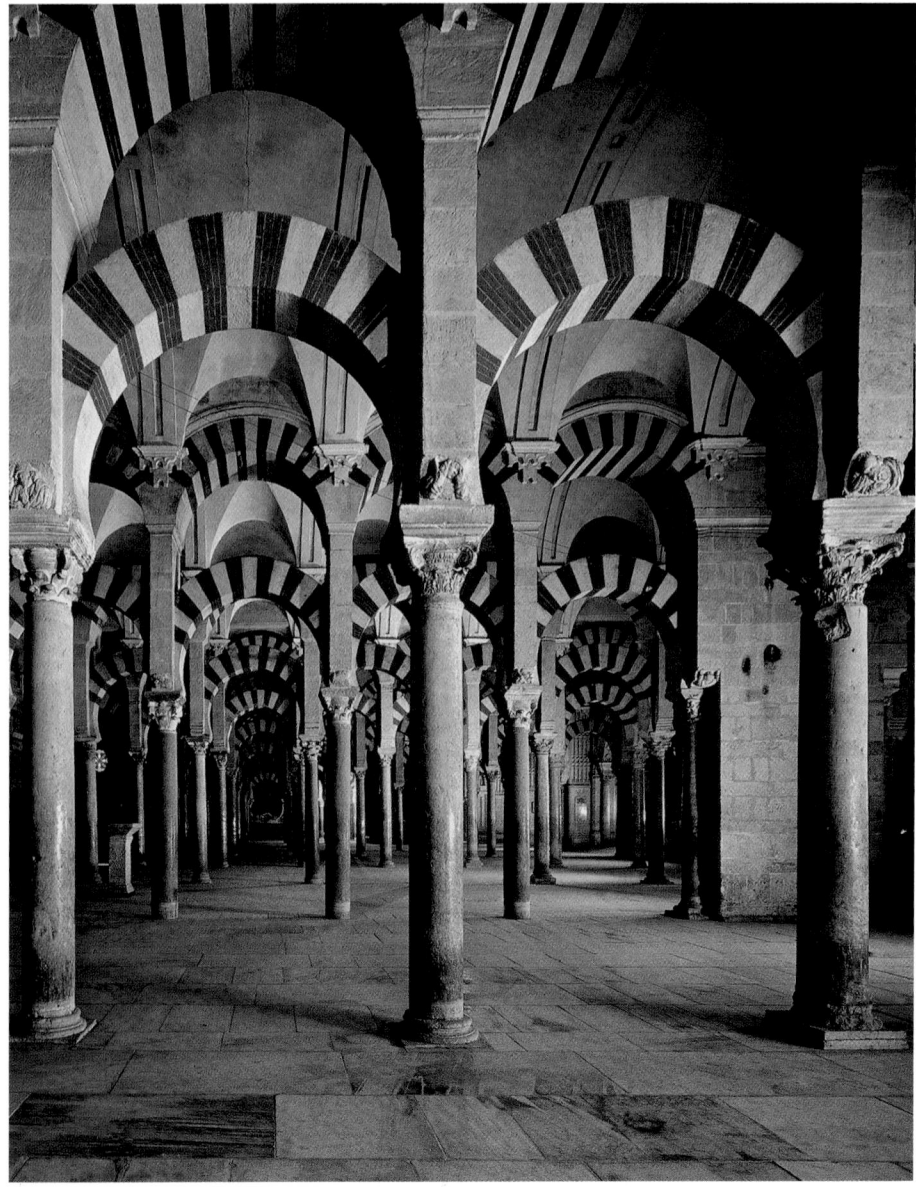

PRAYER HALL, GREAT MOSQUE, CORDOBA, SPAIN
Begun 785/786.

mosques after an assassination attempt on one of the Umayyad rulers. A *minbar* formerly stood by the *mihrab* as the place for the prayer leader and as a symbol of authority. The melon-shaped, ribbed dome over the central bay may be a metaphor for the celestial canopy. It seems to float upon a web of crisscrossing arches, the complexity of the design reflecting the Islamic interest in mathematics and geometry, not purely as abstract concepts but as sources for artistic inspiration. Lushly patterned mosaics with inscriptions, geometric motifs, and stylized vegetation clothe both this dome and the *mihrab* below in brilliant color and gold. These were installed by a Byzantine master who was sent by the emperor in Constantinople, bearing boxes of small glazed ceramic and glass pieces (*tesserae*). Such artistic exchange is emblematic of the interconnectedness of the medieval Mediterranean—through trade, diplomacy, and competition.

DOME IN FRONT OF THE MIHRAB, GREAT MOSQUE, CORDOBA
965.

mihrab

al-Hakam II addition (961–976 CE)

al-Mansur addition (987 CE)

Abd al-Rahman II addition (822–852 CE)

original mosque (786 CE)

Abd al-Rahman III addition (912–961 CE)

minaret

0   50 meters
0   150 feet

PLAN, GREAT MOSQUE, CORDOBA

EXPLORE MORE: Click the Google Earth link for the Great Mosque at Cordoba **www.myartslab.com**

THE KUTUBIYA MOSQUE. In the Kutubiya Mosque, the principal mosque of Marrakesh, Morocco, an exceptionally exquisite wooden *minbar* survives from the twelfth century **(FIG. 8–7)**. It consists of a staircase from which the weekly sermon was delivered to the congregation (for example, SEE FIG. 8–1). The sides are paneled in wooden marquetry with strapwork in a geometric pattern of eight-pointed stars and elongated hexagons inlaid with ivory (see "Ornament," page 264). The body of each figure is filled with wood carved in swirling vines. The risers of the stairs represent **horseshoe arches** resting on columns with ivory capitals and bases: Thus the pulpit (which had been made originally for the Booksellers' Mosque in Marrakesh) reflected the arcades of its surrounding architectural context. This *minbar* resembled others across the Islamic world, but those at the Kutubiya Mosque and the Great Mosque of Cordoba were the finest, according to Ibn Marzuq (1311–1379), a distinguished preacher who had given sermons from 48 such *minbars*.

THE LATER PERIOD

The Abbasid caliphate began a slow disintegration in the ninth century, and thereafter power in the Islamic world became fragmented among more or less independent regional rulers. During the eleventh century, the Saljuqs, a Turkic people, swept from north of the Caspian Sea into Khurasan and took Baghdad in

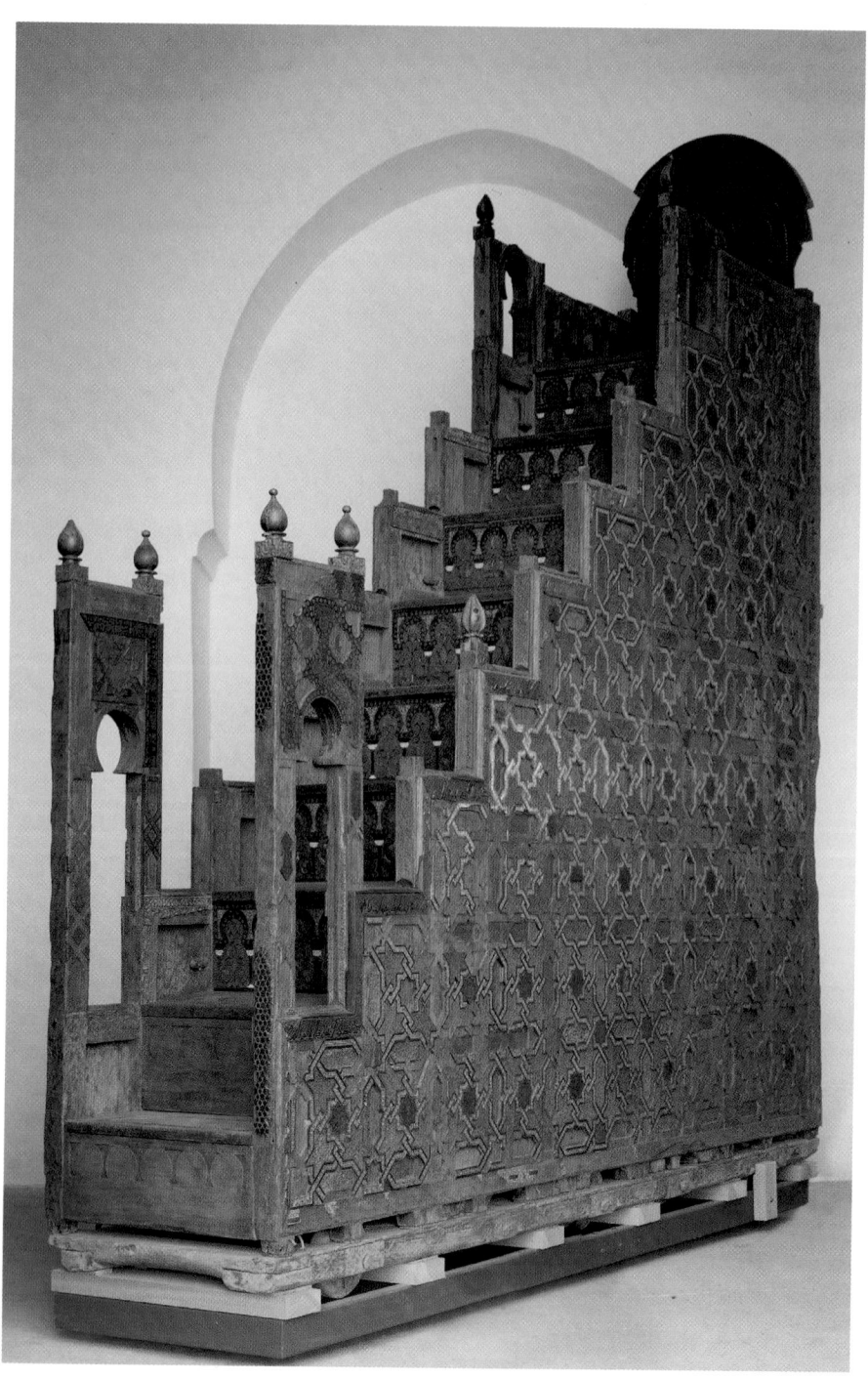

8-7 • *MINBAR*
From the Kutubiya Mosque, Marrakesh, Morocco. 1125–1130. Wood and ivory, 12'8" × 11'4" × 2'10" (3.86 × 3.46 × 0.87 m). Badi Palace Museum, Marrakesh.

Islamic builders explored structure in innovative ways, using a variety of different arch types. The earliest is the simple semicircular arch, inherited from the Romans and Byzantines. It has a single center point that is level with the points from which the arch springs.

The horseshoe arch is a second type, which predates Islam but became the prevalent arch form in the Maghreb (see "The Great Mosque of Cordoba," page 268). The center point of this kind of arch is above the level of the arch's springing point, so that it pinches inward above the capital.

The pointed arch, introduced after the beginning of Islam, has two (sometimes four) center points, the points generating different circles that overlap (for a very slightly pointed arch, SEE FIG. 8–24).

A keel arch has flat sides, and slopes where other arches are curved. It culminates at a pointed apex (see "Ornament," cut tile, page 264).

round arch   horseshoe arch   pointed arch   keel arch

SEE MORE: View a simulation about arches www.myartslab.com

1055, becoming the virtual rulers of the Abbasid Empire. The Saljuqs united most of Iran and Iraq, establishing a dynasty that endured from 1037/38 to 1194. A branch of the dynasty, the Saljuqs of Rum, ruled much of Anatolia (Turkey) from the late eleventh to the beginning of the fourteenth century. The central and eastern Islamic world suffered a dramatic rift in the early thirteenth century when the nomadic Mongols—non-Muslims led by Genghiz Khan (r. 1206–1227) and his successors—attacked northern China, Central Asia, and ultimately Iran. The Mongols captured Baghdad in 1258, encountering weak resistance until they reached Egypt, where they were firmly defeated by the new **Mamluk** ruler. The Maghreb (Morocco, Spain, and Portugal) was ruled by various Arab and Berber dynasties. In Spain the borders of Islamic territory were gradually pushed southward by Christian forces until the rule of the last Muslim dynasty, the Nasrids (1230–1492), was ended. Morocco was ruled by the Berber Marinids (from the mid thirteenth century until 1465).

Although the religion of Islam remained a dominant and unifying force throughout these developments, the history of later Islamic society and culture reflects largely regional phenomena. Only a few works have been selected here and in Chapter 23 to characterize the art of Islam, and they by no means provide a comprehensive history of Islamic art.

ARCHITECTURE OF THE MEDITERRANEAN

The new dynasties built on a grand scale, expanding their patronage from mosques and palaces to include new functional buildings, such as tombs, **madrasas** (colleges for religious and legal studies), public fountains, urban hostels, and remote caravanserais (inns) for traveling merchants in order to encourage long-distance trade. A distinguishing characteristic of architecture in the later period is its complexity. Multiple building types were now combined in large and diverse complexes, supported by perpetual endowments (called *waqf*) that funded not only the building, but its administration and maintenance. Increasingly, these complexes included the patron's own tomb, thus giving visual prominence to the act of individual patronage and the expression of personal identity through commemoration. A new plan emerged, organized around a central courtyard framed by four large **iwans** (large vaulted halls with rectangular plans and monumental arched openings); this **four-iwan** plan was used for schools, palaces, and especially mosques.

THE *MADRASA*-MAUSOLEUM-MOSQUE IN CAIRO. Beginning in the eleventh century, Muslim rulers and wealthy individuals endowed hundreds of charitable complexes that displayed piety as well as personal wealth and status. The combined *madrasa*-mausoleum-mosque complex established in mid-fourteenth-century Cairo by

8-8 • *QIBLA* WALL WITH *MIHRAB* AND *MINBAR*, SULTAN HASAN *MADRASA*-MAUSOLEUM-MOSQUE COMPLEX
Main *iwan* (vaulted chamber) in the mosque, Cairo. 1356–1363.

EXPLORE MORE: Click the Google Earth link for the *Qibla* wall with *mihrab* and *minbar*,
Sultan Hasan *Madrasa*-Mausoleum-Mosque **www.myartslab.com**

the Mamluk Sultan Hasan **(FIGS. 8–8 and 8–9)** is such an example.
A dark corridor—a deflected entrance that is askew from the
building's orientation—leads from the street into a central, well-lit
courtyard of majestic proportions. The complex has a classic four-
iwan plan, each *iwan* serving as a classroom for a different branch of
study, the students housed in a multi-storied cluster of tiny rooms
around each one. The sumptuous *qibla iwan* served as the prayer
hall for the complex. Its walls are ornamented with typically
Mamluk panels of sharply contrasting marbles (*ablaq* masonry, see
"Ornament," page 264) that culminate in a doubly recessed *mihrab*
framed by slightly pointed arches on columns. The marble blocks
of the arches are ingeniously joined in interlocking pieces called
joggled voussoirs. The paneling is surmounted by a wide band of
Kufic (an angular Arabic script) inscription in stucco set against a
background of scrolling vines, both the text and the ornament

**8-9 • THE SULTAN HASAN *MADRASA*-
MAUSOLEUM-MOSQUE COMPLEX**
The *qibla iwan* is visible in the top left face of the courtyard, and the
domed tomb looms behind it.

A CLOSER LOOK

A Mamluk Glass Oil Lamp › from Cairo, Egypt. c. 1350–1355. Glass, polychrome enamel, and gold. Diameter of the top 10⅜″ (26 cm), height 13⅝″ (35 cm). British Museum, London.

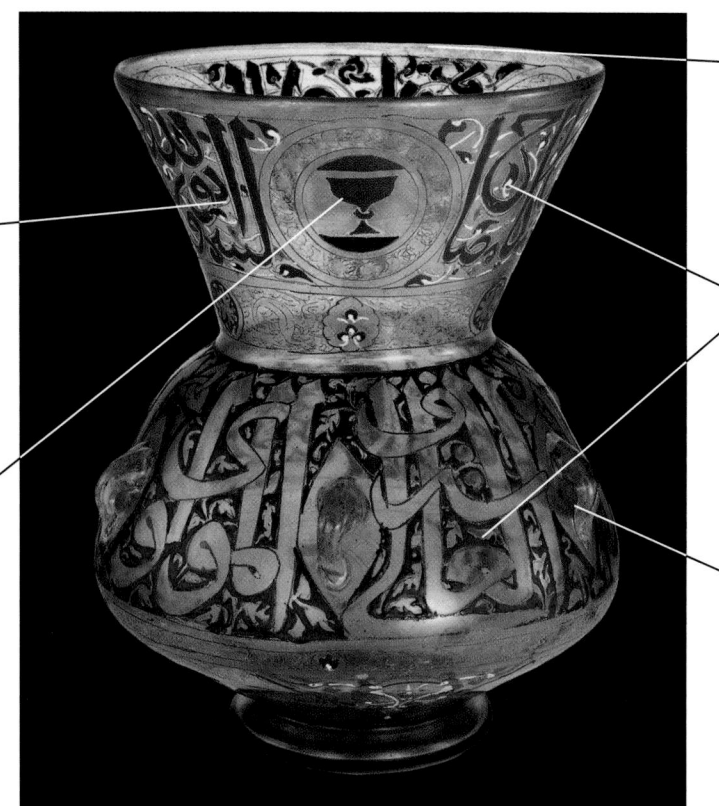

The inscription on the vessel's flared neck is a Qur'anic quotation (Surah 24:35): "God is the light of the heavens and the earth. His light is as a niche wherein is a lamp, the lamp in a glass, the glass as a glittering star."

The roundel's emblem, called a blazon, identifies the patron; on this cup, it is the sign of Sayf al-Din Shaykhu al-Umari, who built a mosque in Cairo in 1349. The blazon passed to Western Europe during the crusades, where it evolved into the system we know as heraldry.

During the thirteenth and fourteenth centuries, glassmakers derived a new elegant thinness through blowing and molding techniques.

Blue, red, and white enamel and gilding cover the surface of the lamp in vertical bands that include vegetal designs and inscriptions interrupted by roundels containing emblems. Mamluk glassmakers excelled in the application of enameled surface decoration in gold and various colors.

This mosque lamp was suspended from chains attached to its handles, although it could also stand on its footed base.

SEE MORE: View the Closer Look feature for the Mamluk Glass Oil Lamp www.myartslab.com

referring to the paradise that is promised to the faithful. Next to the *mihrab* stands an elaborate, thronelike *minbar*. A platform for reading the Qur'an is in the foreground. Standing just beyond the *qibla iwan*, the patron's monumental domed tomb attached his identity ostentatiously to the architectural complex. The Sultan Hasan complex is excessive in its vast scale and opulent decoration, but money was not an object: The project was financed by the estates of victims of the bubonic plague that had raged in Cairo from 1348 to 1350.

The mosque in the Sultan Hasan complex—and many smaller establishments—required hundreds of lamps, and glassmaking was a booming industry in Egypt and Syria. Made of ordinary sand and ash, glass is the most ethereal of materials. The Egyptians produced the first glassware during the second millennium BCE, yet the tools and techniques for making it have changed little since then.

Exquisite glass was also used for beakers and vases, but lamps, lit from within by oil and wick, glowed with special brilliance (see "A Closer Look," above).

THE ALHAMBRA. Muslim patrons also spent lavishly on luxurious palaces set in gardens. The Alhambra in Granada, in southeastern Spain, is an outstanding example of beautiful and refined Islamic palace architecture. Built on the hilltop site of an early Islamic fortress, this palace complex was the seat of the Nasrids (1232–1492), the last Spanish Muslim dynasty, by which time Islamic territory had shrunk from covering most of the Iberian Peninsula to the region around Granada. To the conquering Christians at the end of the fifteenth century, the Alhambra represented the epitome of luxury. Thereafter, they preserved the complex as much to commemorate the defeat of Islam as for its beauty. Essentially a

8-10 • COURT OF THE LIONS, ALHAMBRA, GRANADA, SPAIN
1354–1391.

EXPLORE MORE: Click the Google Earth link for the Court of the Lions, Alhambra **www.myartslab.com**

small town extending for about half a mile along the crest of a high hill overlooking Granada, it included government buildings, royal residences, gates, mosques, baths, servants' quarters, barracks, stables, a mint, workshops, and gardens. Much of what one sees at the site today was built in the fourteenth century or by Christian patrons in later centuries.

8-11 • *MUQARNAS* DOME, HALL OF THE ABENCERRAJES, PALACE OF THE LIONS, ALHAMBRA
1354–1391.

The stucco *muqarnas* (stalactite) ornament does not support the dome but is actually suspended from it, composed of some 5,000 individual plaster pieces. Of mesmerizing complexity, the vault's effect can be perceived but its structure cannot be fully comprehended.

SEE MORE: View a video about the Alhambra **www.myartslab.com**

The Alhambra offered dramatic views to the settled valley and snow-capped mountains around it, while enclosing gardens within its courtyards. One of these is the Court of the Lions which stood at the heart of the so-called Palace of the Lions, the private retreat of Sultan Muhammad V (r. 1354–1359 and 1362–1391). The Court of the Lions is divided into quadrants by cross-axial walkways—a garden form called a *chahar bagh*. The walkways carry channels that meet at a central marble fountain held aloft on the backs of 12 stone lions **(FIG. 8–10)**. Water animates the fountain, filling the courtyard with the sound of its life-giving abundance. In an adjacent courtyard, the Court of the Myrtles, a basin's round shape responds to the naturally concentric ripples of the water that spouts from a central jet (see "Ornament," page 264). Water has a practical role in the irrigation of gardens, but here it is raised to the level of an art form.

The Court of the Lions is encircled by an arcade of stucco arches embellished with **muqarnas** (see "Ornament," page 264) and supported on single columns or clusters of two and three. Second-floor **miradors**—windows that frame specifically intentioned views—look over the courtyard, which was originally either gardened or more likely paved, with aromatic citrus confined to corner plantings. From these windows, protected by latticework screens, the women of the court, who did not appear in public, would watch the activities of the men below. At one end of the Palace of the Lions, a particularly magnificent *mirador* looks out onto a large, lower garden and the plain below. From here, the sultan literally oversaw the fertile valley that was his kingdom.

On the south side of the Court of the Lions, the lofty Hall of the Abencerrajes was designed as a winter reception hall and music room. In addition to having excellent acoustics, its ceiling exhibits dazzling geometrical complexity and exquisitely carved stucco **(FIG. 8–11)**. The star-shaped vault is formed by a honeycomb of clustered *muqarnas* arches that alternate with corner **squinches** that are filled with more *muqarnas*. The square room thus rises to an eight-pointed star, pierced by 16 windows, that culminates in a burst of *muqarnas* floating high overhead, perceived and yet ultimately unknowable, like the heavens themselves.

ARCHITECTURE OF THE EAST

The Mongol invasions brought devastation and political instability but also renewal and artistic exchange that provided the foundation for successor dynasties with a decidedly eastern identity. One of the empires to emerge after the Mongols was the vast Timurid Empire (1370–1506), which conquered Iran, Central Asia, and the northern part of South Asia. Its founder, Timur (known in the West as Tamerlane), was a Mongol descendant, a lineage strengthened through marriage to a descendant of Genghiz Khan. Timur made his capital at Samarkand, which he embellished by means of the forcible relocation of expert artisans from the areas he subdued. Because the empire's compass was vast, Timurid art could integrate Chinese, Persian, Turkic, and Mediterranean artistic ideas into a Mongol base. Its architecture is characterized by axial symmetry, tall double-shelled domes (an inner dome capped by an outer shell of much larger proportions), modular planning with rhythmically repeated elements, and brilliant cobalt blue, turquoise, and white glazed ceramics. Although the empire itself lasted only 100 years after the death of Timur, its legacy endured in the art of the later Safavid dynasty in Iran and the Mughals of South Asia.

A TILE MIHRAB. Made during a period of uncertainty as Iran shifted from Mongol to Timurid rule, this *mihrab* (1354), originally from a *madrasa* in Isfahan, is one of the finest examples of architectural ceramic decoration from this era **(FIG. 8–12)**. More than 11 feet tall, it was made by painstakingly cutting each individual piece of tile, including the pieces making up the letters on the curving

8-12 • TILE MOSAIC *MIHRAB*
From the Madrasa Imami, Isfahan, Iran. Founded 1354. Glazed and cut tiles, 11'3" × 7'6" (3.43 × 2.29 m). Metropolitan Museum of Art, New York. Harris Brisbane Dick Fund (39.20)

This *mihrab* has three inscriptions: the outer inscription, in cursive, contains Qur'anic verses (Surah 9) that describe the duties of believers and the Five Pillars of Islam. Framing the niche's pointed arch, a Kufic inscription contains sayings of the Prophet. In the center, a panel with a line in Kufic and another in cursive states: "The mosque is the house of every pious person."

8-13 • SHAH-I ZINDA FUNERARY COMPLEX, SAMARKAND
Late 14th–15th century.

Timurid princesses were buried here and built many of the tombs. The lively experimentation in varied artistic motifs indicates that women were well versed in the arts and empowered to exercise personal taste.

(a cousin of the Prophet and a saint). The women sought burial in the vicinity of the holy man in order to gain *baraka* (blessing) from his presence. Like all Timurid architecture, the tombs reflect modular planning—noticeable in the repeated dome-on-square unit—and a preference for blue glazed tiles. The domes of the individual structures were double-shelled and, for exaggerated effect, stood on high drums inscribed with Qur'anic verses. The ornament adorning the exterior façades consists of an unusually exuberant array of patterns and techniques, from geometry to chinoiserie, and both painted and cut tiles (see "Ornament," page 264). The tombs reflect a range of individual taste and artistic experimentation that was possible precisely because they were private commissions that served the patrons themselves, rather than the city or state (as in a congregational mosque).

PORTABLE ARTS

Islamic society was cosmopolitan, with pilgrimage, trade, and a well-defined road network fostering the circulation of marketable goods. In addition to the import and export of basic foodstuffs and goods, luxury arts brought particular pleasure and status to their owners and were visible signs of cultural refinement. On objects made of ceramics, ivory, and metal, as well as textiles, calligraphy was prominently displayed. These art objects were eagerly exchanged and collected from one end of the Islamic world to the other, and despite their Arabic lettering—or perhaps precisely because of its artistic cachet—they were sought by European patrons as well.

surface of the keel-profiled niche. The color scheme—white against turquoise and cobalt blue with accents of dark yellow and green— was typical of this type of decoration, as were the harmonious, dense, contrasting patterns of organic and geometric forms. The cursive inscription of the outer frame is rendered in elegant white lettering on a blue ground, while the Kufic inscription bordering the pointed arch reverses these colors for a pleasing contrast.

THE SHAH-I ZINDA.   Near Samarkand, the preexisting Shah-i Zinda (Living King) funerary complex was adopted for the tombs of Timurid family members, especially princesses, in the late fourteenth and fifteenth centuries **(FIG. 8–13)**. The mausolea are arrayed along a central avenue that descends from the tomb of Qutham b. Abbas

CERAMICS.   Script was the sole decoration on a type of white pottery made from the tenth century onward in and around the region of Nishapur (in Khurasan, in present-day Iran) and Samarkand (in present-day Uzbekistan). These elegant pieces are characterized by the use of a clear lead glaze applied over a black inscription on a white slip-painted ground. In **FIGURE 8–14** the script's horizontals and verticals have been elongated to fill the bowl's rim. The fine quality of the lettering indicates that a calligrapher furnished the model. The inscription translates: "Knowledge [or magnanimity]: the beginning of it is bitter to taste, but the end is sweeter than honey," an apt choice for tableware and appealing to an educated patron. The inscriptions on Islamic ceramics provide a storehouse of such popular sayings.

8-14 • BOWL WITH KUFIC BORDER

Khurasan, 11th–12th century. Earthenware with slip, pigment, and lead glaze, diameter 14½″ (33.8 cm). Musée du Louvre, Paris.

The white ground of this piece imitated prized Chinese porcelains made of fine white kaolin clay. Khurasan was connected to the Silk Road, the great caravan route to China (Chapter 10), and was influenced by Chinese culture.

8-15 • THE MACY JUG

Iran. 1215/1216. Composite body glazed, painted fritware and incised (glaze partially stained with cobalt), with pierced outer shell, 6⅝ × 7¾″ (16.8 × 19.7 cm). Metropolitan Museum of Art, New York. Fletcher Fund, 1932 (32.52.1)

Fritware was used to make beads in ancient Egypt and may have been rediscovered there by Islamic potters searching for a substitute for Chinese porcelain. Its components were one part white clay, ten parts quartz, and one part quartz fused with soda, which produced a brittle white ware when fired. The colors on this double-walled ewer and others like it were produced by applying mineral glazes over black painted detailing. The deep blue comes from cobalt and the turquoise from copper. Luster—a thin, transparent glaze with a metallic sheen—was applied over the colored glazes.

In the ninth century, potters developed a technique to produce a lustrous metallic surface on their ceramics. They may have learned the technique from Islamic glassmakers who had produced luster-painted vessels a century earlier. First the potters applied a paint laced with silver, copper, or gold oxides to the surface of already fired and glazed tiles or vessels. In a second firing with relatively low heat and less oxygen, these oxides burned away to produce a reflective sheen. The finished **lusterware** resembled precious metal. At first the potters covered the entire surface with luster, but soon they began to use luster to paint dense, elaborate patterns using geometric design, foliage, and animals in golden brown, red, purple, and green. Lusterware tiles, dated 862/863, decorated the *mihrab* of the Great Mosque at Kairouan.

The most spectacular lusterware pieces are the double-shell fritware, in which an inner solid body is hidden beneath a densely decorated and perforated outer shell. A jar in the Metropolitan Museum known as the *Macy Jug* (after a previous owner) exemplifies this style **(FIG. 8–15)**. The black underglaze-painted decoration represents animals and pairs of harpies and sphinxes set into an elaborate "water-weed" pattern. The outer shell is covered with a turquoise glaze, enhanced by a deep cobalt-blue glaze on parts of the floral decoration and finally an overglaze that gives the entire surface its metallic luster. An inscription includes the date AH 612 (1215/1216 CE).

METAL. Islamic metalsmiths enlivened the surface of vessels with scrolls, interlacing designs, human and animal figures, and calligraphic inscriptions. A shortage of silver in the mid twelfth century prompted the development of inlaid brasswork that used the more precious metal sparingly, as in **FIGURE 8–16**. This basin, made in Mamluk Egypt in the late thirteenth or early fourteenth century, may be the finest work of metal produced by a Muslim artisan. Its dynamic surface is adorned with three bands, the upper and lower depicting running animals, and the center showing chivalric scenes of horsemen flanked by attendants, soldiers, and falcons. The surface is crowded with overlapping figures, in vigorous poses, that nevertheless remain distinct by means of hatching, modeling, and the framing device of the four roundels. The piece was made and signed (six times) by Muhammad Ibn al-Zain. The narrative band displays scenes of the princely art of

This beautifully crafted basin, with its princely themes of hunting and horsemanship, was made for an unknown Mamluk patron, judging by its emblems and coats of arms. However, it became known as the *Baptistery of St. Louis*, because it was acquired by the French sometime before the end of the fourteenth century (long after the era of St. Louis) and used for royal baptisms.

horsemanship and hunting, but in later metalwork such pictorial cycles were replaced by large-scale inscriptions.

TEXTILES.   A Kufic inscription appears on a tenth-century piece of silk from Khurasan **(FIG. 8–17)**: "Glory and happiness to the Commander Abu Mansur Bukhtakin. May God prolong his prosperity." Such good wishes were common in Islamic art, appearing as generic blessings on ordinary goods sold in the marketplace or, as here, personalized for the patron. The woven bands of script are known as *tiraz* ("embroidered"), and they appear in textiles as well as illustrated manuscripts, such as the *Maqamat*, where the robes of figures have *tiraz* on their sleeves (SEE FIG. 8.1). Texts can sometimes help determine where and when a work was made, but they can be frustratingly uninformative when

little is known about the patron, and they are not always truthful. Stylistic comparisons—in this case with other textiles, with the way similar subjects appear in other media, and with other inscriptions—sometimes reveal more than the inscription alone.

This silk must have been brought from the Near East to France by knights at the time of the First Crusade. Known as the Shroud of St. Josse, it was preserved in the church of Saint-Josse-sur-Mer, near Caen in Normandy. Rich Islamic textiles of brilliantly hued silk, gold thread, brocade, and especially *tiraz* were prized by Christians and were often preserved in Christian burial chambers and church treasuries. Textiles were one of the most actively traded commodities in the medieval Mediterranean region and formed a significant portion of dowries and inheritances. For these reasons, they were an important means of disseminating

8–17 • TEXTILE WITH ELEPHANTS AND CAMELS
Known today as the Shroud of St. Josse. From Khurasan or Central Asia. Before 961. Dyed silk, largest fragment 20½ × 37″ (52 × 94 cm). Musée du Louvre, Paris.

Silk textiles were both sought-after luxury items and a medium of economic exchange. Government-controlled factories, known as *dar al-tiraz*, produced cloth for the court as well as for official gifts and payments. A number of Islamic fabrics have been preserved in the treasuries of medieval European churches, where they were used for priests' ceremonial robes and as altar cloths, and to wrap the relics of Christian saints.

artistic styles and techniques. This fragment shows two elephants, themselves bearing highly ornamental coverings with Sasanian straps, facing each other on a dark red ground, each with a mythical griffin (a Chinese motif) between its feet. A caravan of two-humped Bactrian camels linked with rope moves up the elaborately patterned border along the left side. The inscription at the bottom is upside down, suggesting that the missing portion of the textile was a fragment from a larger and more complex composition. The technique and design derive from the sumptuous pattern-woven silks of Sasanian Iran (Persia). The Persian weavers had, in turn, adapted Chinese silk technology to the Sasanian taste for paired heraldic beasts and other Near Eastern imagery. The eclecticism of Islamic culture is demonstrated by the blending of Sasanian and Chinese sources in a textile made for a Turkic patron.

THE ARTS OF THE BOOK

The art of book production flourished from the first century of Islam because Islam's emphasis on the study of the Qur'an promoted a high level of literacy among both men and women. With the availability of paper, books on a wide range of religious as well as secular subjects were available, although hand-copied books always remained fairly costly. (Muslims did not adopt the printing press until the eighteenth and nineteenth centuries.) Libraries, often associated with *madrasas*, were endowed by members of the educated elite. Books made for royal patrons had luxurious bindings and highly embellished pages, the result of workshop collaboration between noted calligraphers and illustrators.

CALLIGRAPHY. Muslim society holds **calligraphy** (the art of fine hand lettering) in the highest esteem. Since the Qur'an is believed to reveal the word of God, its words must be written accurately, with devotion and embellishment. Writing was not limited to books and documents but—as we have seen—was displayed on the walls of buildings and on artwork. Since pictorial imagery developed relatively late in Islamic art (and there was no figural imagery at all in the religious context), text became a principal vehicle for visual communication. The written word thus played two roles: It could convey information about a building or object, describing its beauty or naming its patron, and it could delight the eye in an entirely aesthetic sense. Arabic script is written from right to left, and a letter's form varies depending on its position in a word. With its rhythmic interplay between verticals and horizontals, Arabic lends itself to many variations. Formal Kufic script (after Kufa, a city in Iraq) is blocky and angular, with strong upright strokes and long horizontals. It may have developed first for carved or woven inscriptions where clarity and practicality of execution were important.

Most early Qur'ans had large Kufic letters and only three to five lines per page, which had a horizontal orientation. The visual clarity was necessary because one book was often shared by multiple readers simultaneously. A page from a ninth-century Syrian Qur'an exemplifies the style common from the eighth to the tenth century (FIG. 8–18). Red diacritical marks (pronunciation guides) accent the dark brown ink; the *surah* ("chapter") title is embedded in the burnished ornament at the bottom of the sheet. Instead of

8-18 • PAGE FROM THE QUR'AN
Surah 2:286 and title of Surah 3 in Kufic script. Syria. 9th century. Black ink pigments, and gold on vellum, 8⅜ × 11⅛" (21.8 × 29.2 cm). Metropolitan Museum of Art, New York. Rogers Fund, 1937 (37.99.2)

EXPLORE MORE: Gain insight from a primary source, the Qur'an
www.myartslab.com

8-19 • Attributed to Galinus ARABIC MANUSCRIPT PAGE
Iraq. 1199. Bibliothèque Nationale, Paris.

Headings are in ornamental Kufic script with a background of scrolling vines, while the text—a medical treatise—is written horizontally and vertically in *naskhi* script.

page numbers, the brilliant gold of the framed words and the knoblike projection in the left-hand margin are a distinctive means of marking chapter breaks.

Calligraphers enjoyed the highest status of all artists in Islamic society. Included in their number were princes and women. Apprentice scribes had to learn secret formulas for inks and paints; become skilled in the proper ways to sit, breathe, and manipulate their tools; and develop their individual specialties. They also had to absorb the complex literary traditions and number symbolism that had developed in Islamic culture. Their training was long and arduous, but unlike other artisans who were generally anonymous in the early centuries of Islam, outstanding calligraphers received public recognition.

By the tenth century, more than 20 cursive scripts had come into use. They were standardized by Ibn Muqla (d. 940), an Abbasid official who fixed the proportions of the letters in each script and devised a method for teaching calligraphy that is still in use today. The Qur'an was usually written on **parchment** (treated animal

skin) and **vellum** (calfskin or a fine parchment). Paper was first manufactured in Central Asia during the mid eighth century, having been introduced earlier by Buddhist monks. Muslims learned how to make high-quality, rag-based paper, and eventually established their own paper mills. By about 1000, paper had largely replaced the more costly parchment for everything but Qur'an manuscripts, which adopted the new medium much later. It was a change as momentous as that brought about by movable type or the internet, affecting not only the appearance of manuscripts but also their content. The inexpensive new medium sparked a surge in book production and the proliferation of increasingly elaborate and decorative cursive scripts which generally superseded Kufic by the thirteenth century. Of the major styles, one extraordinarily beautiful form, known as *naskhi*, was said to have been revealed and taught to scribes in a vision. In **FIGURE 8–19**, its beautifully flowing lines alternate with an eastern variety of Kufic set against a field of swirling vine scrolls.

MANUSCRIPT PAINTING

The manuscript illustrators of Mamluk Egypt (1250–1517) executed intricate nonfigural geometric designs for the Qur'ans they

8-20 • QUR'AN FRONTISPIECE (RIGHT HALF OF TWO-PAGE SPREAD)
Cairo. c. 1368. Ink, pigments, and gold on paper, 24 × 18″ (61 × 45.7 cm). National Library, Cairo. MS. 7

The Qur'an to which this page belonged was donated in 1369 by Sultan Shaban to the *madrasa* established by his mother. A close collaboration between illuminator and scribe can be seen here and throughout the manuscript.

produced. Geometric and botanical ornamentation contributed to unprecedented sumptuousness and complexity. As in architectural decoration, the exuberant ornament was underlaid by strict geometric organization. In an impressive frontispiece originally paired with its mirror image on the facing left page, the design radiates from a 16-pointed starburst, filling the central square (FIG. 8–20). The surrounding frames are filled with interlacing foliage and stylized flowers that embellish the holy scripture. The page's resemblance to court carpets was not coincidental. Designers worked in more than one medium, leaving the execution of their efforts to specialized artisans. In addition to religious works, scribes copied and recopied famous secular texts—scientific treatises, manuals of all kinds, stories, and especially poetry. Painters supplied illustrations for these books and also created individual small-scale paintings—miniatures—that were collected by the wealthy and placed in albums.

THE HERAT SCHOOL. One of the great royal centers of miniature painting was at Herat in western Afghanistan. A **school** of painting and calligraphy was founded there in the early fifteenth century under the highly cultured patronage of the Timurid dynasty (1370–1507). In the second half of the fifteenth century, the leader of the Herat School was Kamal al-Din Bihzad (c. 1450–1514). When the Safavids supplanted the Timurids in 1506/07 and established their capital at Tabriz in northwestern Iran, Bihzad moved to Tabriz and briefly resumed his career there. Bihzad's paintings, done around 1494 to illustrate the *Khamsa* (*Five Poems*), written by Nizami, demonstrate his ability to render human activity convincingly. He set his scenes within complex, stagelike architectural spaces that are stylized according to Timurid conventions, creating a visual balance between activity and architecture. In a scene depicting the caliph Harun al-Rashid's visit to a bath (FIG. 8–21), the bathhouse, its tiled entrance leading to a high-ceiling dressing room with brick walls, provides the structuring element. Attendants wash long, blue towels and hang them to dry on overhead clotheslines. A worker reaches for one of the towels with a long pole, and a client prepares to wrap himself discreetly in a towel before removing his outer garments. The blue door on the left leads to a room where a barber grooms the caliph while attendants bring water for his bath. The asymmetrical composition depends on a balanced placement of colors and architectural ornaments within each section.

8-21 • Attributed to Kamal al-Din Bihzad **THE CALIPH HARUN AL-RASHID VISITS THE TURKISH BATH**
From a copy of the 12th-century *Khamsa* (*Five Poems*) of Nizami. From Herat, Afghanistan. c. 1494. Ink and pigments on paper, approx. 7 × 6″ (17.8 × 15.3 cm). The British Library, London. Oriental and India Office Collections MS. Or. 6810, fol. 27v

Despite early warnings against it as a place for the dangerous indulgence of the pleasures of the flesh, the bathhouse (*hammam*), adapted from Roman and Hellenistic predecessors, became an important social center in much of the Islamic world. The remains of an eighth-century *hammam* still stand in Jordan, and a twelfth-century *hammam* is still in use in Damascus. *Hammam*s had a small entrance to keep in the heat, which was supplied by steam ducts running under the floors. The main room had pipes in the wall with steam vents. Unlike the Romans, who bathed and swam in pools of water, Muslims preferred to splash themselves from basins, and the floors were slanted for drainage. A *hammam* was frequently located near a mosque, part of the commercial complex provided by the patron to generate income for the mosque's upkeep.

ART AND ARCHITECTURE OF THE THREE EMPIRES

In the pre-modern era, three great powers emerged in the Islamic world. The introduction of gunpowder for use in cannons and guns caused a shift in military strategy because isolated lords in lone castles could not withstand gunpowder sieges. Power lay not in thick walls but in strong centralized governments that had the wherewithal to invest in fire power and train armies in its use. To the west was the Ottoman Empire (1342–1918), which grew from a small principality in Asia Minor. In spite of setbacks inflicted by the Mongols, the Ottomans ultimately created an empire that extended over Anatolia, western Iran, Iraq, Syria, Palestine, western Arabia (including Mecca and Medina), northern Africa (excepting Morocco), and part of eastern Europe. In 1453, their stunning capture of Constantinople (ultimately renamed Istanbul) brought the Byzantine Empire to an end. To the east of the Ottomans, Iran was ruled by the Safavid dynasty (1501–1732), distinguished for their Shi'ite branch of Islam. Their patronage of art and architecture favored the refinement of artistic ideas and techniques drawn from the Timurid period. The other heirs to the Timurids were the Mughals of South Asia (1526–1858). The first Mughal emperor, Babur, invaded Hindustan (India and Pakistan) from Afghanistan, bringing with him a taste for Timurid gardens, architectural symmetry, and modular planning.

THE OTTOMAN EMPIRE

Imperial Ottoman mosques were strongly influenced by Byzantine church plans and reflect a drive toward ever larger domes. The prayer hall interiors are dominated by a large domed space uninterrupted by structural supports. Worship is directed, as in other mosques, toward a *qibla* wall and *mihrab* opposite the entrance.

Upon conquering Constantinople, the rulers of the Ottoman Empire converted the great Byzantine church of Hagia Sophia into a mosque, framing it with two graceful Turkish-style minarets in the fifteenth century and two more in the sixteenth century (SEE FIG. 7–17). In conformance with Islamic aniconism, the church's mosaics were destroyed or whitewashed. Huge calligraphic disks with the names of God (Allah), Muhammad, and the early caliphs were added to the interior in the mid nineteenth century (SEE FIG. 7–19). At present, Hagia Sophia is neither a church nor a mosque but a state museum.

THE ARCHITECT SINAN. Ottoman architects had already developed the domed, centrally planned mosque, but the vast open interior and structural clarity of Hagia Sophia inspired them to strive for a more ambitious scale. For the architect Sinan (c. 1489–1588) the development of a monumental centrally planned mosque was a personal quest. Sinan began his career in the army and served as engineer in the Ottoman campaigns at Belgrade, Vienna, and Baghdad. He rose through the ranks to become, in 1528, chief architect for Suleyman "the Magnificent," the tenth Ottoman sultan (r. 1520–1566). Suleyman's reign marked the height of Ottoman power, and the sultan sponsored an ambitious building program on a scale not seen since the days of the Roman Empire. Serving Suleyman and his successor, Sinan is credited with more than 300 imperial commissions, including palaces, *madrasas* and Qur'an schools, tombs, public kitchens, hospitals, caravanserais, treasure houses, baths, bridges, viaducts, and 124 large and small mosques.

8-22 • Sinan MOSQUE OF SULTAN SELIM
Edirne, Turkey. 1568–1575.

The minarets that pierce the sky around the prayer hall of this mosque, their sleek, fluted walls and needle-nosed spires soaring to more than 295 feet, are only 12½ feet in diameter at the base, an impressive feat of engineering. Only royal Ottoman mosques were permitted multiple minarets, and having more than two was unusual.

EXPLORE MORE: Click the Google Earth link for the Mosque of Sultan Selim **www.myartslab.com**

8-23 • PLAN OF MOSQUE OF SULTAN SELIM

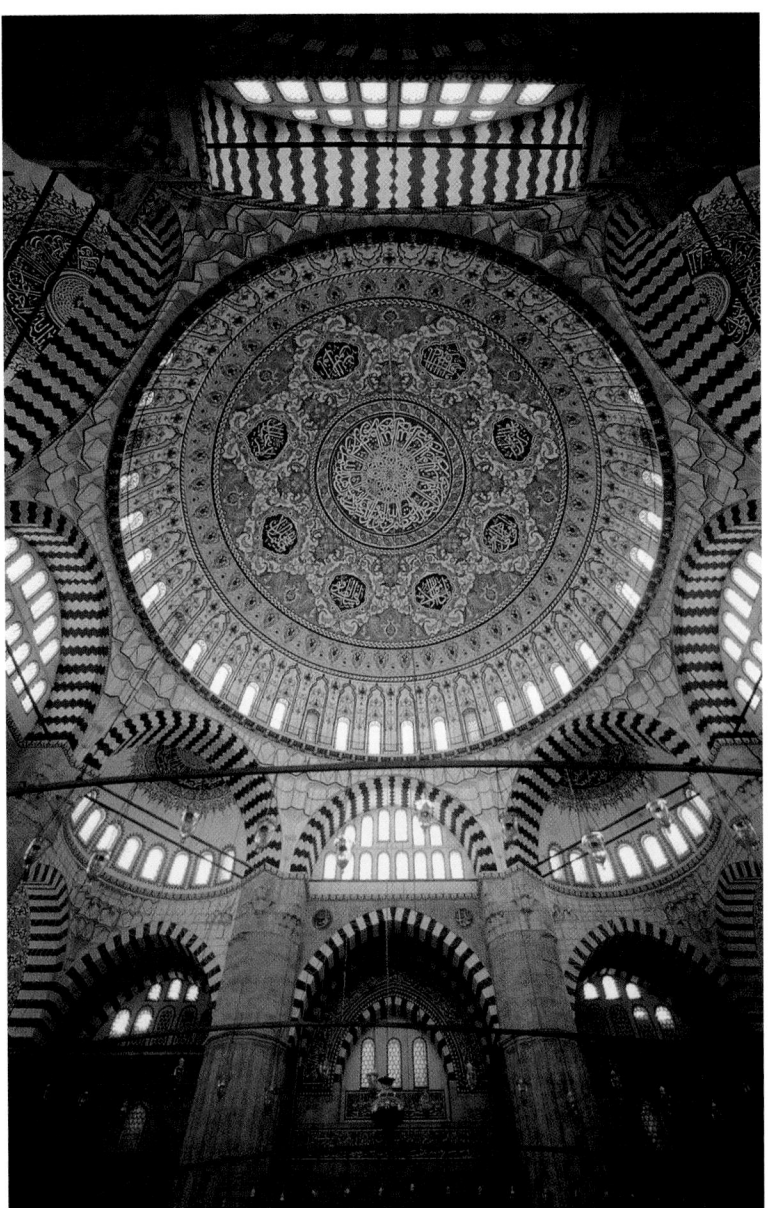

8-24 • INTERIOR, MOSQUE OF SULTAN SELIM

Sinan's crowning accomplishment, completed about 1579, when he was over 80, was a mosque he designed in the provincial capital of Edirne for Suleyman's son Selim II (r. 1566–1574) (FIGS. 8–22, 8–23). The gigantic hemispheric dome that tops this structure is more than 102 feet in diameter, larger than the dome of Hagia Sophia, as Sinan proudly pointed out. It crowns a building of extraordinary architectural coherence. The transition from square base to the central dome is accomplished by corner half-domes that enhance the spatial plasticity and openness of the prayer hall's airy interior (FIG. 8–24). The eight massive piers that bear the dome's weight are visible both within and without—on the exterior they resolve in pointed towers that encircle the main dome—revealing the structural logic of the building and clarifying its form. In the arches that support the dome and span from one pier to the next—and indeed at every level—light pours from windows into the interior, a space at once soaring and serene.

The interior was clearly influenced by Hagia Sophia—an open expanse under a vast dome floating on a ring of light—but it rejects Hagia Sophia's longitudinal pull from entrance to sanctuary. The Selimiye Mosque is truly a centrally planned structure. In addition to the mosque, the complex housed a *madrasa* and other educational buildings, a cemetery, a hospital, and charity kitchens, as well as the income-producing covered market and baths. Framed by the vertical lines of four minarets and raised on a platform at the city's edge, the Selimiye Mosque dominates the skyline.

The Topkapi, the Ottomans' enormous palace in Istanbul, was a city unto itself. Built and inhabited from 1473 to 1853, it consisted of enclosures within walled enclosures that mirrored the immense political bureaucracy of the state. Inside, the sultan was removed from virtually all contact with the public. At the end of the inner palace, a free-standing pavilion, the Baghdad Kiosk (1638), provided him with a sumptuous retreat (FIG. 8–25). The kiosk consists of a low dome set above a cruciform hall with four alcoves. Each recess contains a low sofa (a Turkish word) laid with cushions and flanked by cabinets of wood inlaid with ivory and shell. Alternating with the cabinets are niches with ornate profiles: When stacked in profusion such niches—called *chini khana*— form decorative panels. On the walls, the blue and turquoise glazed tiles contain an inscription of the Throne Verse (2:255) which proclaims God's dominion "over the heavens and the earth," a reference to divine power that appears in many throne rooms and places associated with Muslim sovereigns. Light sparkles through the stained glass above.

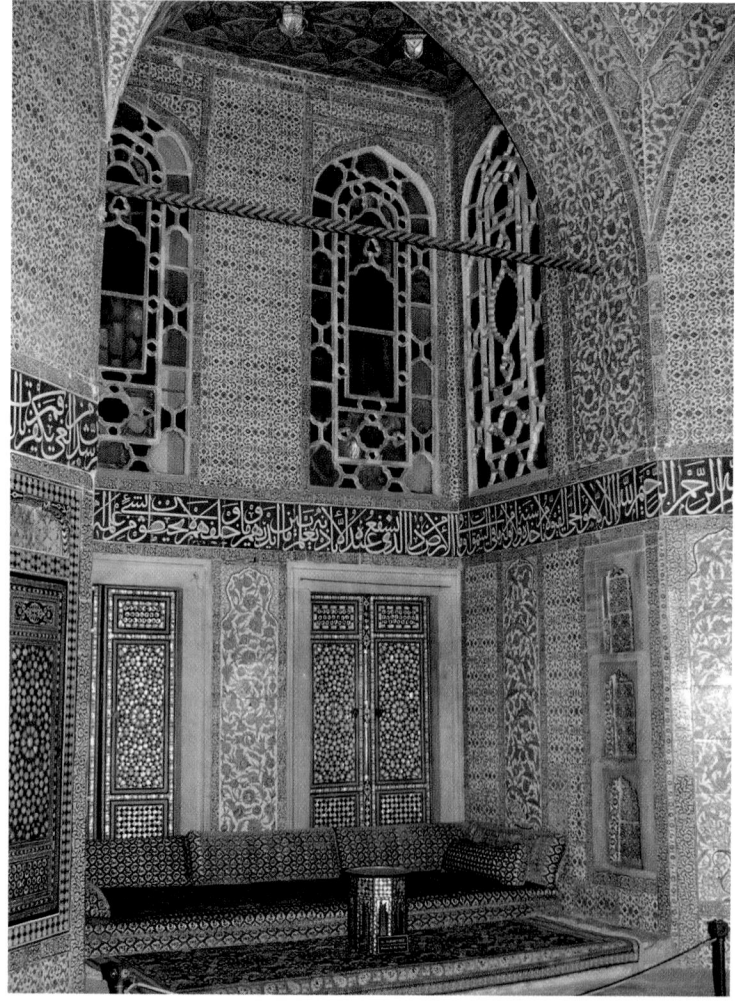

8-25 • BAGHDAD KIOSK
Topkapi Palace, Istanbul. 1638.

ILLUMINATED MANUSCRIPTS AND *TUGRAS*. A combination of abstract setting with realism in figures and details characterizes Ottoman painting. Ottoman painters adopted the style of the Herat School (influenced by Timurid conventions) for their miniatures, enhancing its decorative aspects with an intensity of religious feeling. At the Ottoman court of Sultan Suleyman in Istanbul, the imperial workshops produced remarkable illuminated manuscripts.

Following a practice begun by the Saljuqs and Mamluks, the Ottomans put calligraphy to political use, developing the design of imperial ciphers—**tugras**—into a specialized art form. Ottoman *tugras* combined the ruler's name and title with the motto "Eternally Victorious" into a monogram denoting the authority of the sultan and of those select officials who were also granted an emblem. *Tugras* appeared on seals, coins, and buildings, as well as on official documents called *firmans*, imperial edicts supplementing Muslim law. Suleyman issued hundreds of edicts, and a high court official supervised specialist calligraphers and illuminators who produced the documents with fancy *tugras* (FIG. 8–26).

Tugras were drawn in black or blue with three long, vertical strokes to the right of two concentric horizontal teardrops. Decorative foliage patterns fill the space. Fill decoration became more naturalistic by the 1550s and in later centuries spilled outside the emblems' boundary lines. The rare, oversized *tugra* below has a sweeping, fluid line drawn with perfect control according to set proportions. The color scheme of delicate floral interlace enclosed in the body of the *tugra* may have been inspired by Chinese blue-and-white ceramics; similar designs appear on Ottoman ceramics and textiles.

8-26 • ILLUMINATED *TUGRA* OF SULTAN SULEYMAN
From Istanbul, Turkey. c. 1555–1560. Ink, paint, and gold on paper, removed from a *firman* and trimmed to 20½ × 25⅜" (52 × 64.5 cm). Metropolitan Museum of Art, New York. Rogers Fund, 1938 (38.149.1)

The *tugra* shown here is from a document endowing an institution in Jerusalem that had been established by Suleyman's powerful wife, Hurrem.

THE SAFAVID DYNASTY

Whereas the Ottomans took their inspiration from regional cultures such as that of the Byzantine Empire, the Safavids looked to the Timurid architecture of tall, double-shell domes, sheathed in blue tiles. In the Safavid capital of Isfahan, the typically Timurid taste for modular construction re-emerged on a grand scale that extended well beyond works of architecture to include avenues, bridges, public spaces, and gardens. To the preexisting city of Isfahan, the Safavid Shah Abbas I (1588–1629) added an entirely new extension, planned around an immense central plaza (*maydan*) and a broad avenue, called the Chahar Bagh, that ran through a zone of imperial palace pavilions and gardens down to the river. The city's prosperity and beauty so amazed visitors who flocked from around the world to conduct trade and diplomacy that it led to the popular saying, "Isfahan is half the world."

With the Masjid-i Shah (1611–1638) in Isfahan, the four-*iwan* plan mosque reached its apogee **(FIGS. 8–27, 8–28)**. Stately and huge, it anchors the south end of the city's *maydan*. Its 90-foot portal is aligned with the *maydan*, which is oriented astrologically,

maydan

8-27 • PLAN OF THE MASJID-I SHAH

8-28 • MASJID-I SHAH, ISFAHAN
1611–1638.

Four *iwan*s with *pishtaq* frames face onto the courtyard, and a fifth faces the *maydan*. The tall bulbous dome behind the *qibla iwan* and the large *pishtaq*s are pronounced vertical elements that made royal patronage visible not only from the far end of the *maydan* but throughout the city and beyond.

SEE MORE: View a video about Masjid-i Shah **www.myartslab.com**

Because textiles are made of organic materials that are destroyed through use, very few carpets from before the sixteenth century have survived. There are two basic types of carpet: flat-weave carpets and pile, or knotted, carpets. Both can be made on either vertical or horizontal looms.

The best-known flat-weaves today are kilims, which are typically woven in wool with bold, geometric patterns and sometimes with brocaded details. Kilim weaving is done with a **tapestry** technique called slit tapestry (see a).

Knotted carpets are an ancient invention. The oldest known example, excavated in Siberia and dating to the fourth or fifth century BCE, has designs evocative of Achaemenid art, suggesting that the technique may have originated in Central Asia. In knotted carpets, the pile—the plush, thickly tufted surface—is made by tying colored strands of yarn, usually wool but occasionally silk for deluxe carpets, onto the vertical elements (the **warp**) of a yarn grid (see b and c).

These knotted loops are later trimmed and sheared to form the plush pile surface of the carpet. The **weft** strands (crosswise threads) are shot horizontally, usually twice, after each row of knots is tied, to hold the knots in place and to form the horizontal element common to all woven structures. The weft is usually an undyed yarn and is hidden by the colored knots of the warp. Two common knot tying techniques are the asymmetrical knot, used in many carpets from Iran, Egypt, and Central Asia (formerly termed the Sehna knot), and the symmetrical knot (formerly called the Gördes knot) more commonly used in Anatolian Turkish carpet weaving. The greater the number of knots, the shorter the pile. The finest carpets can have as many as 2,400 knots per square inch, each one tied separately by hand.

Although royal workshops produced luxurious carpets (SEE FIG. 8–29), most knotted rugs have traditionally been made in tents and homes. Depending on local custom, either women or men wove carpets.

a. Kilim weaving pattern used in flat-weaving

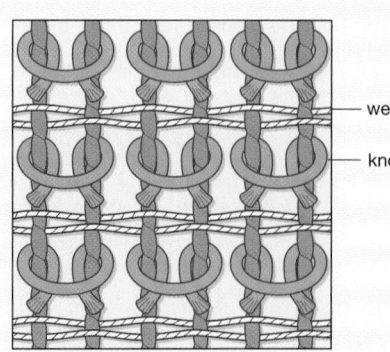

b. Symmetrical knot, used extensively in Turkey

c. Asymmetrical knot, used extensively in Iran

but then turns to conform to the prayer hall, which is oriented to Mecca. The portal's great *iwan* is framed by a *pishtaq* (a rectangular panel framing an *iwan*) that rises above the surrounding walls, slender minarets enhancing its soaring verticality. The hood is filled with *muqarnas* and covered with glazed tiles with vine and flower motifs. The *iwan*'s profile is imitated and repeated by the double-tiered *iwan*s that parade across the façade of the mosque courtyard and the *maydan* as a whole. Achieving unity through the regular replication of a single element—the arch—is a hallmark of Safavid architecture. The Masjid-i Shah represents the culmination of Timurid aesthetics, but achieved on an unprecedented scale and integrated within a well-planned urban setting.

The Safavid period was also a golden age of carpet making (see "Carpet Making," above). Shah Abbas built workshops in Isfahan and Kashan that produced large, costly carpets that were often signed—indicating the weaver's growing prestige. Among the types produced were the medallion, centered around a sun or star, and the garden carpet, which represents Paradise as a shady garden with four rivers. Laid out on the floor of an open-air hall, and per-

haps set with bowls of ripe fruit and other delicacies, such carpets brought the beauty of nature indoors. Written accounts indicate that elaborate patterns appeared on Persian carpets as early as the seventh century. In one fabled royal carpet, garden paths were rendered in real gold, leaves were modeled with emeralds, and highlights on flowers, fruits, and birds were created from pearls and jewels. There were close parallels between carpet making and other arts: Many works of Islamic art represent flowers to evoke both garden and paradisiac associations.

The seventeenth-century *Wagner Carpet* is an extraordinarily sumptuous garden carpet made of wool pile (**FIG. 8–29**). It represents a dense field of trees (including cypresses) and flowers, populated with birds, animals, and even fish, and traversed by three large water channels that form an H with a central pool at the center. The carpet fascinates not only for the fact that so simple a technique as a knotted yarn can produce such complex, layered designs, but also for the combination of perspectives: From above, the carpet resembles a plan, but the trees are shown in profile, as if from ground level.

8-29 • WAGNER CARPET
From Iran. 17th century. Wool pile, cotton warp, cotton and wool weft, 17′5″ × 13′11″ (5.31 × 4.25 m). Burrell Collection, Glasgow.

When this extraordinarily detailed large carpet was laid on the floor of a palace or wealthy home, it gave the illusion of a garden underfoot. Natural motifs in carpets, textiles, and tiled walls, together with large windows and porches offering delightful vistas, invited the outdoors inside and blurred any distinction between them.

Rugs have long been used for Muslim prayer, which involves repeatedly kneeling and touching the forehead to the floor before God. While individuals often had their own small prayer rugs, with representations of niches to orient the faithful in prayer, many mosques were furnished with wool-pile rugs received as pious donations (the floor of the Selimiye Mosque would have had such rugs). In Islamic houses, people sat and slept on cushions, carpets, and thick mats laid directly on the floor, so cushions took the place of the fixed furnishings of Western domestic environments. From the late Middle Ages to today, carpets and textiles are one of the predominant Islamic arts and the Islamic art form best known in the West. Historically, rugs from Iran, Turkey, and elsewhere were highly valued by Westerners, who often displayed them on tables rather than floors.

MUGHAL DYNASTY

Like the Safavids in Iran, the Mughals brought Timurid models with them from Central Asia into Hindustan. Although Islam had flourished in the Delhi region from the early thirteenth century onward, the Mughals unified the Muslim- and Hindu-ruled states of north India into an empire (see Chapter 23). The illustrations of the emperor Babur's memoirs, the *Baburnama*, show his active patronage of forms such as the *chahar bagh* four-part garden plan. In FIGURE 8–30, Babur—in an orange robe and turban—oversees the construction of a walled garden in Kabul, teeming with fruit trees and flowers. Babur had been raised in an environment thoroughly saturated with the Timurid artistic legacy of *iwan*s with *pishtaq* frames, tall bulbous domes, modular planning, axial symmetry, and the *chahar bagh*. His introduction of such forms into South Asia culminated several generations later in the Taj Mahal (SEE FIG. 23–1).

8–30 • Bishnadas "BABUR BUILDS THE BAGH-I WAFA," FROM THE *BABURNAMA*
India. c. 1590. Gouache and gold on paper, 8⅝ × 5⅝" (21.9 × 14.4 cm). Victoria & Albert Museum, London. IM.276-1913, f. 276

The Mughal emperor Babur, on the right, gestures to his architect who holds a red board with grid lines—reflecting the legacy of Timurid modular planning—while workmen measure and shovel, their leggings rolled up to their knees.

8-31 • Paolo Portoghesi, Vittorio Gigliotti, and Sami Mousawi **ISLAMIC MOSQUE AND CULTURAL CENTRE, ROME** 1984–1992.

The prayer hall (197 × 13 feet/ 60 × 40 meters), which has an ablution area on the floor below, can accommodate a congregation of 2,500 on its main floor and balconies. The large central dome (65½ feet/ 20 meters in diameter) is surrounded by 16 smaller domes, all similarly articulated with concrete ribs.

THE MODERN ERA

The twentieth century saw the dissolution of the great Islamic empires and the formation of smaller nation-states in their place. The question of identity and its expression in art changed significantly as Muslim artists and architects sought training abroad and participated in an international movement that swept away many of the visible signs that formerly expressed their cultural character and difference. The abstract work of the architect Zaha Hadid (SEE FIG. 32–55), who was born in Baghdad and studied and practiced in London, is exemplary of the new internationalism. Other architects sought to reconcile modernity with an Islamic cultural identity that was distinct from the West. Thus the Iraqi architect Sami Mousawi and the Italian firm of Portoghesi-Gigliotti designed the Islamic Centre in Rome (completed 1992) with clean modern lines, exposing the structure while at the same time taking full advantage of opportunities for ornament (**FIG. 8–31**). The structural logic appears in the prayer hall's columns, made of concrete with an aggregate of crushed Carrara marble. These rise to meet abstract capitals in the form of plain rings, then spring upward to make a geometrically dazzling eight-pointed star supporting a dome of concentric circles. There are references here to the interlacing ribs of the *mihrab* dome in the Great Mosque of Cordoba, to the great domed spans of Sinan's prayer halls, and to the simple palm-tree trunks that supported the roof of the Mosque of the Prophet in Medina.

THINK ABOUT IT

8.1 The Islamic Empire rapidly spread east to India and west to Spain. Explain how the form of the mosque varies among the far-flung lands of the empire with reference to three examples. Despite the contrasts, what features do mosques typically have in common?

8.2 Select an Islamic structure discussed in this chapter that is influenced by Rome and/or Byzantium, and note which forms are borrowed and how, in their new Islamic context, they are transformed.

8.3 What is a *tugra*? Although it is a secular art form, how is it linked to Islamic religious art traditions?

8.4 Islamic art has no images of people in religious contexts. Instead, what decorative motifs and techniques are used?

8.5 Discuss the spread of carpet making within the rapidly growing Islamic Empire. Can you discern any geographical features that would have expedited the sharing of carpet-making techniques and specific styles? Use the map on page 263.

PRACTICE MORE: Compose answers to these questions, get flashcards for images and terms, and review chapter material with quizzes www.myartslab.com

9-1 • ASHOKAN PILLAR
Lauriya Nandangarh, Bihar, India. Maurya period, c. 246 BCE.

ART OF SOUTH AND SOUTHEAST ASIA BEFORE 1200

According to legend, the ruler Ashoka (r. 273–232 BCE) was stunned by grief and remorse as he looked across the battlefield. As was the custom of his dynasty, he had gone to war, expanding his empire until he had conquered many of the kingdoms that had comprised the Indian subcontinent. Now, about 265 BCE, after the final battle in his conquest of the northern kingdoms, he was suddenly—unexpectedly—shocked by the horror of the suffering he had caused. In the traditional account, it is said that only one form on the battlefield moved: The stooped figure of a Buddhist monk slowly making his way through the carnage. Watching this spectral figure, Ashoka abruptly turned the moment of triumph into one of renunciation. Decrying violence and warfare, he vowed to become a *chakravartin* ("world-conquering ruler"), not through the force of arms but through spreading the teachings of the Buddha and establishing Buddhism as the major religion of his realm.

Although there is no proof that Ashoka himself converted to Buddhism, he erected and dedicated monuments to the Buddha throughout his empire—shrines, monasteries, and the columns commonly called **Ashokan pillars (FIG. 9–1)**. With missionary ardor, he dispatched delegates throughout the Indian subcontinent and to countries as distant as Syria, Egypt, and Greece. In his impassioned propagation of Buddhism, perhaps as a means of securing his enormous empire, Ashoka stimulated an intensely rich period of art.

Despite the emissaries he sent and his widespread placement of inscriptions on the face of large rocks, his pillars are few in number and quite concentrated in location. Only eight can be attributed to Ashoka's time by the inscriptions they bear, although several other pillars are commonly assigned to this period. Most were placed at the site of Buddhist monasteries along a route leading from Punjab in the northwest to Ashoka's capital, Pataliputra, in the northeast. One pillar some distance from this route, at Sanchi, suggests that others, perhaps not yet discovered, may have been placed along a more southerly path.

Not only are the pillars the first sculptural remains in India after a hiatus of some 1,600 years, but their inscriptions are the first preserved Indian writing that we can read and interpret. The script, known as Brahmi, was deciphered in 1837 by James Prinsep, a brilliant amateur scholar who served the East India Company as assay master of the Calcutta mint. He discovered that the inscriptions were written in Prakrit, a language closely related to classical Sanskrit, and that they set down laws of righteous behavior for the monks and nuns resident in the monasteries where the pillars were erected, as well as for passing travelers. Like so many aspects of Indian art, these pillars raise intriguing questions that have yet to be answered, most notably: How could such pillars be made in the absence of any known precedent?

LEARN ABOUT IT

9.1   Recognize the characteristic differences between a Hindu temple and a Buddhist stupa.

9.2   Appreciate the diffusion of religion in Southeast Asia.

9.3   Understand the correlation between religious worldviews and architectural form.

9.4   Assess the variety of ways in which storytelling can be accomplished in pictorial art.

9.5   Identify the distinguishing features of a Buddha image.

HEAR MORE: Listen to an audio file of your chapter **www.myartslab.com**

THE INDIAN SUBCONTINENT

The South Asian subcontinent, or Indian subcontinent, as it is commonly called, is a peninsular region that includes the present-day countries of India, Afghanistan, Pakistan, Nepal, Bhutan, Bangladesh, and Sri Lanka (MAP 9–1). From the beginning, these areas have been home to societies whose cultures are closely linked and which have maintained remarkable continuity over time. (South Asia is distinct from Southeast Asia, which includes Brunei, Myanmar, Cambodia, East Timor, Indonesia, Laos, Malaysia, the Philippines, Singapore, Thailand, and Vietnam.) Although the modern Republic of India is about a third the size of the United States, South Asia as a whole is about two-thirds its size. A low mountain range, the Vindhya Hills, acts as a natural division that separates north India from south India. On the northern border rises the protective barrier of the Himalayas, the world's highest mountains. To the northwest are other mountains through whose passes came invasions and immigrations that profoundly affected the civilization of the subcontinent. Over these passes, too, wound the major trade routes that linked the Indian subcontinent by land to the rest of Asia and to Europe. Surrounded on its remaining sides by oceans since ancient times, the subcontinent has also been connected to the world by maritime trade, and during much of the period under discussion here it formed part of a coastal trading network that extended from eastern Africa to China.

Differences in language, climate, and terrain within India have fostered distinct regional and cultural characteristics and artistic traditions. However, despite such diversity, several overarching traits tend to unite Indian art. Most evident is a distinctive sense of beauty, with voluptuous forms and a profusion of ornament, texture, and color. Visual abundance is considered auspicious, and it reflects a belief in the generosity and favor of the gods. Another characteristic is the pervasive symbolism that enriches all Indian arts with intellectual and emotional layers. Third, and perhaps most important, is an emphasis on capturing the vibrant quality of a world seen as infused with the dynamics of the divine. Gods and humans, ideas and abstractions, are given tactile, sensuous forms, radiant with inner spirit.

INDUS CIVILIZATION

The earliest civilization of South Asia was nurtured in the lower reaches of the Indus River, in present-day Pakistan and in northwestern India. Known as the Indus or Harappan civilization (after Harappa, the first-discovered site), it flourished from approximately 2600 to 1900 BCE, or during roughly the same time as the Old Kingdom period of Egypt, the Minoan civilization of the Aegean, and the dynasties of Ur and Babylon in Mesopotamia. Indeed, it is considered, along with Egypt and Mesopotamia, to be one of the world's earliest urban river-valley civilizations.

It was the chance discovery in the late nineteenth century of some small seals, such as those in FIGURE 9–2, that provided the

9-2 • SEAL IMPRESSIONS
a., d. horned animal; b. buffalo; c. sacrificial rite to a goddess (?); e. yogi; f. three-headed animal. Indus Valley civilization, c. 2500–1500 BCE. Steatite, each seal approx. 1¼ × 1¼" (3.2 × 3.2 cm).

The more than 2,000 small seals and impressions that have been found offer an intriguing window on the Indus Valley civilization. Usually carved from steatite stone, the seals were coated with alkali and then fired to produce a lustrous, white surface. A perforated knob on the back of each may have been for suspending them. The most popular subjects are animals, most commonly a one-horned bovine standing before an altarlike object (a, d). Animals on Indus Valley seals are often portrayed with remarkable naturalism, their taut, well-modeled surfaces implying their underlying skeletons. The function of the seals remains enigmatic, and the script that is so prominent in the impressions has yet to be deciphered.

first clue that an ancient civilization had existed in this region. The seals appeared to be related to, but not the same as, seals known from ancient Mesopotamia (SEE FIG. 2–5). Excavations begun in the 1920s and continuing into the present subsequently uncovered a number of major urban areas at points along the lower Indus River, including Harappa, Mohenjo-Daro, and Chanhu-Daro.

MOHENJO-DARO. The ancient cities of the Indus Valley resemble each other in design and construction, suggesting a coherent culture. At Mohenjo-Daro, the best preserved of the sites, archaeologists discovered an elevated citadel area about 50 feet high, presumably containing important government structures, surrounded by a wall. Among the buildings is a remarkable water tank, a large watertight pool that may have been a public bath but could also have had a ritual use (FIG. 9–3). Stretching out below the elevated area was the city, arranged in a gridlike plan with wide avenues and narrow side streets. Its houses, often two stories high, were generally built

MAP 9-1 • SOUTH AND SOUTHEAST ASIA

The borders of India are created by natural features, with the Himalayas to the north and the Indian Ocean on the remaining borders. Nearly all the rivers in the region flow east–west and are an important conduit for trade and new ideas.

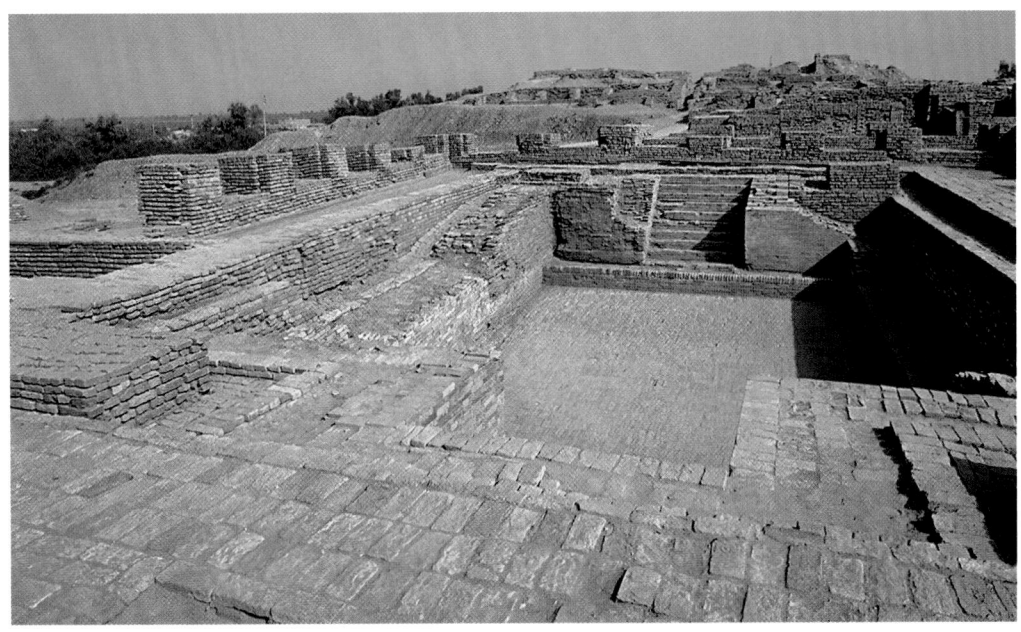

9-3 • LARGE WATER TANK, MOHENJO-DARO
Indus Valley civilization (Harappan), c. 2600–1900 BCE.

Possibly a public or ritual bathing area.

around a central courtyard. Like other Indus Valley cities, Mohenjo-Daro was constructed of fired brick, in contrast to the less durable sun-dried brick used in other cultures of the time. The city included a network of covered drainage systems that channeled away waste and rainwater. Clearly the technical and engineering skills of this civilization were highly advanced. At its peak, about 2500 to 2000 BCE, Mohenjo-Daro was approximately 6–7 square miles in size and had a population of about 20,000–50,000.

INDUS VALLEY SEALS. Although our knowledge of the Indus civilization is limited by the fact that we cannot read its writing, motifs on seals as well as the few artworks that have been discovered

9-4 • TORSO OF A "PRIEST-KING"
From Mohenjo-Daro. Indus Valley civilization, c. 2600–1900 BCE.
Steatite, height 6⅞″ (17.5 cm). National Museum of Pakistan, Karachi.

strongly suggest continuities with later South Asian cultures. The seal in FIGURE 9–2e, for example, depicts a man in the meditative posture associated in Indian culture with a yogi, one who seeks mental and physical purification and self-control, usually for spiritual purposes. In FIGURE 9–2c, the persons with elaborate headgear in a row or procession observe a figure standing in a tree—possibly a goddess—and a kneeling worshiper. This scene may offer some insight into the religious or ritual customs of Indus people, whose deities may have been ancient prototypes of later Indian gods and goddesses.

Numerous terra-cotta figurines and a few stone and bronze statuettes have been found at Indus sites. They reveal a confident maturity of artistic conception and technique. The terra cottas resemble Mesopotamian art in their motifs and rather abstract rendering. On the other hand, the stone figures foreshadow the later Indian artistic tradition in their sensuous naturalism.

"PRIEST-KING" FROM MOHENJO-DARO. The identity of the male torso in FIGURE 9–4, sometimes called the "priest-king," is uncertain, suggesting a structure of society—where priests functioned as kings—for which we have no evidence at all. Several features of this figure, including a low forehead, a broad nose, thick lips, and long slit eyes, are seen on other works from Mohenjo-Daro. The man's garment is patterned with a **trefoil** (three-lobed) motif. The depressions of the trefoil pattern were originally filled with red paint, and the eyes were inlaid with colored shell or stone. A narrow band with a circular ornament encircles the upper arm and the head. It falls in back into two long strands and may be an indication of rank. Certainly, with its formal pose and simplified, geometric form, the statue conveys a commanding human presence.

NUDE TORSO FROM HARAPPA. Although its date is disputed by some, a nude male torso found at Harappa is an example of a contrasting naturalistic style (FIG. 9–5) of ancient Indus origins. Less than 4 inches tall, it is one of the most extraordinary portrayals of the human form to survive from any early civilization. In contrast to the more athletic male ideal developed much later in ancient Greece, this sculpture emphasizes the soft texture of the human body and the subtle nuances of muscular form. The abdomen is relaxed in the manner of a yogi able to control his breath. With these characteristics the Harappa torso forecasts the essential aesthetic attributes of later Indian sculpture.

The reasons for the demise of this flourishing civilization are not yet understood. All we know is

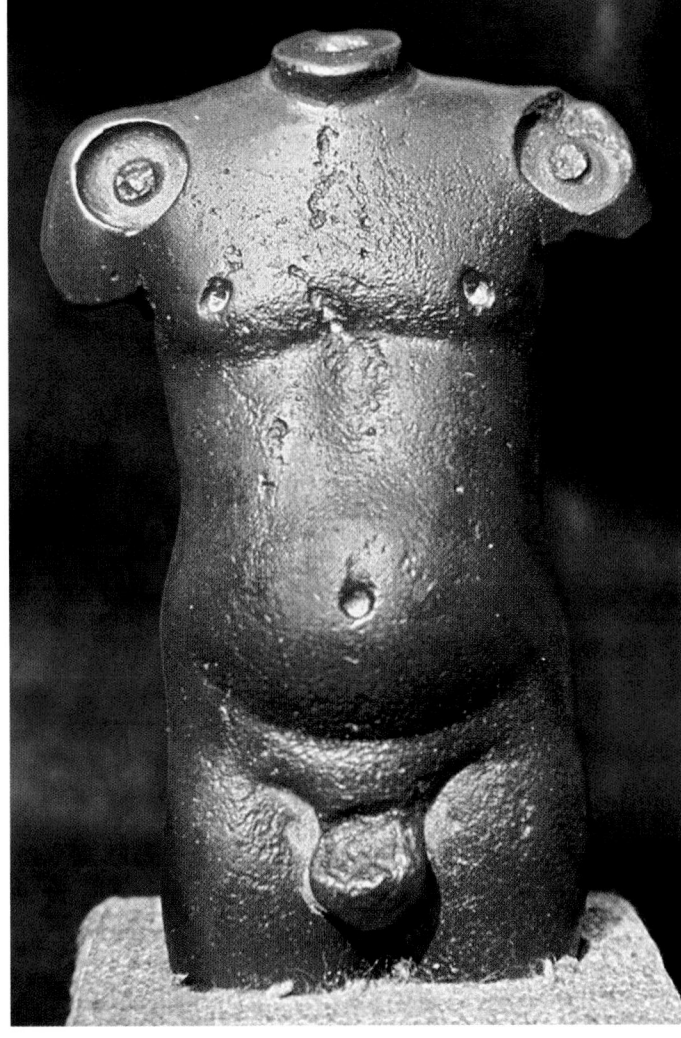

9-5 • TORSO

From Harappa. Indus Valley civilization, c. 2600–1900 BCE. Red sandstone, height 3¾″ (9.5 cm). National Museum, New Delhi.

that between 2000 and 1750—possibly because of climate change, a series of natural disasters, and invasions—the cities of the Indus civilization declined, and predominantly rural societies evolved.

THE VEDIC PERIOD

About 2000 BCE nomadic shepherds, the Aryans, entered India from central Asia and the Russian steppes. Gradually they supplanted the indigenous populations and introduced the horse and chariot, the Sanskrit language, a hierarchical social order, and religious practices that centered on the propitiation of gods through fire sacrifice. Their sacred writings known as the Vedas, gave the period its name. The earliest Veda consists of hymns to various Aryan gods including the divine king Indra. The importance of the fire sacrifice, overseen by a powerful priesthood—the Brahmins—and religiously sanctioned social classes, persisted through the Vedic period. At some point, the class structure became hereditary and immutable, with lasting consequences for Indian society.

During the latter part of this period, from about 800 BCE, the Upanishads were composed. These metaphysical texts examine the meanings of the earlier, more cryptic Vedic hymns. They focus on the relationship between the individual soul, or *atman*, and the universal soul, or Brahman, as well as on other concepts central to subsequent Indian philosophy. One is the assertion that the material world is illusory and that only Brahman is real and eternal. Another holds that our existence is cyclical and that beings are caught in *samsara*, a relentless cycle of birth, life, death, and rebirth. Believers aspire to attain liberation from *samsara* and to unite the individual *atman* with the eternal, universal Brahman.

The latter portion of the Vedic period also saw the flowering of India's epic literature, written in the melodious and complex Sanskrit language. By around 400 BCE, the 18-volume *Mahabharata*, the longest epic in world literature, and the *Ramayana*, the most popular and enduring religious epic in India and Southeast Asia, were taking shape. These texts, the cornerstones of Indian literature, relate histories of gods and humans that bring the philosophical ideas of the Vedas to a more accessible and popular level.

In this stimulating religious, philosophical, and literary climate numerous religious communities arose. The most influential teachers of these times were Shakyamuni Buddha and Mahavira. The Buddha, or "enlightened one," lived and taught in India around 500 BCE; his teachings form the basis of the Buddhist religion (see "Buddhism," page 297). Mahavira (c. 599–527 BCE), regarded as the last of 24 highly purified superbeings called pathfinders *(tirthankaras)*, was the founder of the Jain religion. Both Shakyamuni Buddha and Mahavira espoused some basic Upanishadic tenets, such as the cyclical nature of existence and the need for liberation from the material world. However, they rejected the authority of the Vedas, and with it the legitimacy of the fire sacrifice and the hereditary class structure of Vedic society, with its powerful, exclusive priesthood. In contrast, Buddhism and Jainism were open to all, regardless of social position.

Buddhism became a vigorous force in South Asia and provided the impetus for much of the major surviving art created between the third century BCE and the fifth century CE. The Vedic tradition, meanwhile, continued to evolve, emerging later as Hinduism, a loose term that encompasses the many religious forms that resulted from the mingling of Vedic culture with indigenous beliefs (see "Hinduism," page 298).

THE MAURYA PERIOD

After about 700 BCE, cities again began to reappear on the subcontinent, especially in the north, where numerous kingdoms arose. For most of its subsequent history, India was a shifting mosaic of regional kingdoms. From time to time, however, a particularly powerful dynasty formed an empire. The first of these was the Maurya dynasty (c. 322–185 BCE), which extended its rule over all but the southernmost portion of the subcontinent.

9-6 • FEMALE FIGURE HOLDING A FLY-WHISK
From Didarganj, Patna, Bihar, India. Probably Maurya period, c. 250 BCE. Polished sandstone, height 5'4¼" (1.63 m). Patna Museum, Patna.

Commonly identified as a *yakshi*, this sculpture has become one of the most famous works of Indian art. Holding a fly-whisk in her raised right hand, the figure wears only a long shawl and a skirtlike cloth. The cloth rests low on her hips, held in place by a girdle. Subtly sculpted parallel creases indicate that it is gathered closely about her legs. The ends, drawn back up over the girdle, cascade down to her feet in a broad, central loop of flowing folds ending in a zigzag of hems. Draped low over her back, the shawl passes through the crook of her arm and then flows to the ground. (The missing left side of the shawl probably mirrored this motion.) The figure's jewelry is prominent. A double strand of pearls hangs between her breasts, its shape echoing and emphasizing the voluptuous curves of her body. Another strand of pearls encircles her neck. She wears a simple tiara, plug earrings, and rows of bangles. The nubbled tubes about her ankles probably represent anklets made of beaten gold. Her hair is bound behind in a large bun, and a small bun sits on her forehead. This hairstyle appears again in Indian sculpture of the later Kushan period (c. second century CE).

FEMALE FIGURE FROM DIDARGANJ. The art of the Maurya period reflects an age of heroes. At this time emerged the ideal of upholding *dharma*, the divinely ordained moral law believed to keep the universe from falling into chaos. This heroic ideal seems fully embodied in a life-size statue found at Didarganj, near the Maurya capital of Pataliputra (FIG. 9–6). The statue, dated by most scholars to the Maurya period, probably represents a **yakshi**, a spirit associated with the productive forces of nature. With its large breasts and pelvis, the figure embodies the association of female beauty with procreative abundance, bounty, and auspiciousness—qualities that in turn reflect the generosity of the gods and the workings of *dharma* in the world.

Sculpted from fine-grained sandstone, the statue conveys the *yakshi's* authority through the frontal rigor of her pose, the massive volumes of her form, and the strong, linear patterning of her

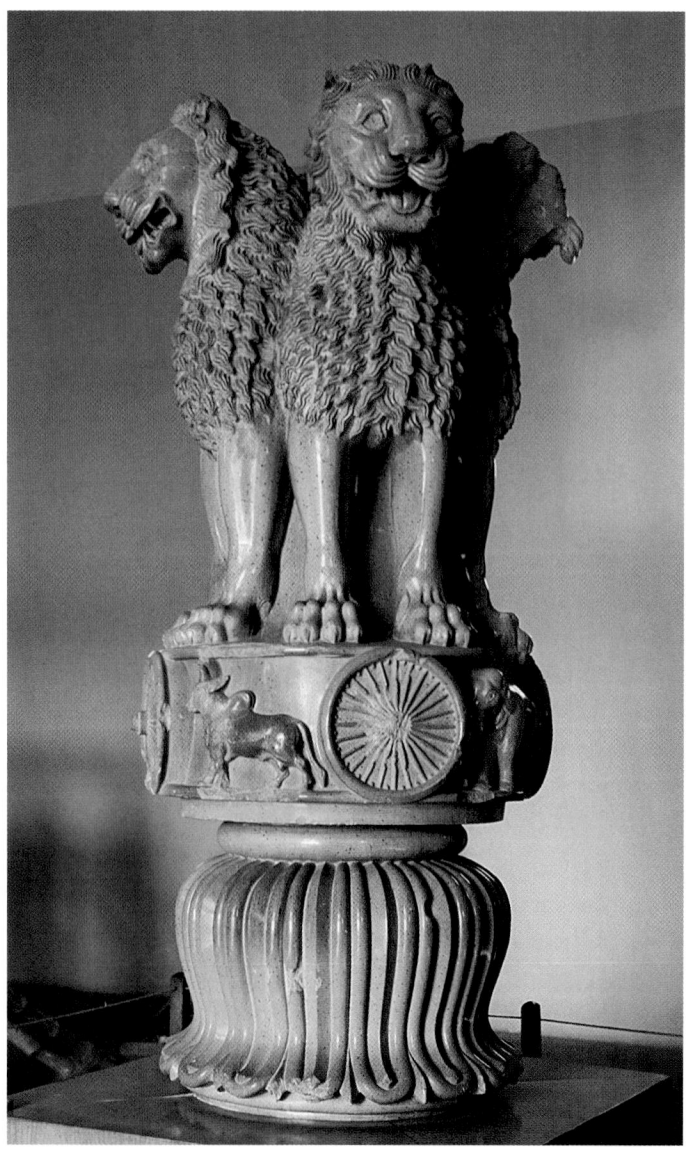

9-7 • LION CAPITAL
From Ashokan pillar at Sarnath, Uttar Pradesh, India. Maurya period, c. 250 BCE. Polished sandstone, height 7' (2.13 m). Archaeological Museum, Sarnath.

Buddhism

The Buddhist religion developed from the teachings of Shakyamuni Buddha, who lived from about 563 to 483 BCE in the present-day regions of Nepal and northern India. At his birth, it is believed, seers foretold that the infant prince, named Siddhartha Gautama, would become either a *chakravartin* ("world-conquering ruler") or a *buddha* ("fully enlightened being"). Hoping for a ruler like himself, Siddhartha's father tried to surround his son with pleasure and shield him from pain. Yet the prince was eventually exposed to the sufferings of old age, sickness, and death—the inevitable fate of all mortal beings. Deeply troubled by the human condition, Siddhartha at age 29 left the palace, his family, and his inheritance to live as an ascetic in the wilderness. After six years of meditation, he attained complete enlightenment at a site in India now called Bodh Gaya.

Following his enlightenment, the Buddha ("Enlightened One") gave his first teaching in the Deer Park at Sarnath. Here he expounded the Four Noble Truths that are the foundation of Buddhism: (1) life is suffering; (2) this suffering has a cause, which is ignorance; (3) this ignorance can be overcome and extinguished; (4) the way to overcome this ignorance is by following the eightfold path of right view, right resolve, right speech, right action, right livelihood, right effort, right mindfulness, and right concentration. After the Buddha's death at age 80, his many disciples developed his teachings and established the world's oldest monastic institutions.

A buddha is not a god but rather one who sees the ultimate nature of the world and is therefore no longer subject to *samsara*, the cycle of birth, death, and rebirth that otherwise holds us in its grip, whether we are born into the world of the gods, humans, animals, demons, tortured spirits, or hellish beings.

The early form of Buddhism, known as Theravada or Hinayana, stresses self-cultivation for the purpose of attaining *nirvana*, which is the extinction of *samsara* for oneself. Theravada Buddhism has continued mainly in Sri Lanka and Southeast Asia. Within 500 years of the Buddha's death, another form of Buddhism, known as Mahayana, became popular mainly in northern India; it eventually flourished in China, Korea, Japan, and in Tibet (as Vajrayana). Compassion for all beings is the foundation of Mahayana Buddhism, whose goal is not *nirvana* for oneself but buddhahood (enlightenment) for every being throughout the universe. Mahayana Buddhism recognizes buddhas other than Shakyamuni from the past, present, and future. One such is Maitreya, the next buddha to appear on earth. Another is Amitabha Buddha, the Buddha of Infinite Light and Infinite Life (that is, incorporating all space and time), who dwells in a paradise known as the Western Pure Land. Amitabha Buddha became particularly popular in east Asia. Mahayana Buddhism also developed the category of **bodhisattvas** ("those whose essence is wisdom"), saintly beings who are on the brink of achieving buddhahood but have vowed to help others achieve buddhahood before crossing over themselves. In art, bodhisattvas and buddhas are most clearly distinguished by their clothing and adornments: bodhisattvas wear the princely garb of India, while buddhas wear monks' robes.

EXPLORE MORE: Gain insight from a primary source of words spoken by the Buddha **www.myartslab.com**

ornaments and dress. Alleviating and counterbalancing this hierarchical formality are her soft, youthful face, the precise definition of prominent features such as the stomach muscles, and the polished sheen of her exposed flesh. This lustrous polish is a special feature of Maurya sculpture.

THE RISE OF BUDDHISM. During the reign of the third Maurya emperor Ashoka (ruled c. 273–232 BCE), Buddhism was expanded from a religion largely localized in the Maurya heartland, a region known as Magadha, to one extending across the entire empire. Among the monuments he erected were monolithic pillars set up primarily at the sites of Buddhist monasteries.

Pillars may have been used as flag-bearing standards in India since earliest times. Thus the creators of the pillars erected during Ashoka's reign may have adapted this already ancient form to the symbolism of Indian creation myths and the new religion of Buddhism. The fully developed Ashokan pillar—a slightly tapered sandstone shaft that usually rested on a stone foundation slab sunk more than 10 feet into the ground—rose to a height of around 50 feet (SEE FIG. 9–1). On it were carved inscriptions relating to rules of *dharma* that ideal kings were enjoined to uphold, and that many later Buddhists interpreted as also referring to Buddhist teachings or exhorting the Buddhist community to unity. At the top, carved from a separate block of sandstone, an elaborate capital bore animal sculpture. Both shaft and capital were given the characteristic Maurya polish. Scholars believe that the pillars symbolized the **axis mundi** ("axis of the world"), joining earth with the cosmos. It represented the vital link between the human and celestial realms, and through it the cosmic order was impressed onto the terrestrial.

LION CAPITAL FROM SARNATH. The capital in **FIGURE 9–7** originally crowned the pillar erected at Sarnath in north central India, the site of the Buddha's first sermon. The lowest portion represents the down-turned petals of a lotus blossom. Because the lotus flower emerges from murky waters without any mud sticking to its petals, it symbolizes the presence of divine purity in the imperfect world. Above the lotus is an **abacus** (the slab forming the top of a capital) embellished with low-relief carvings

ART AND ITS CONTEXTS

Hinduism

Hinduism is not one religion but many related beliefs and innumerable sects. It results from the mingling of Vedic beliefs with indigenous, local beliefs and practices. All three major Hindu sects draw upon the texts of the Vedas, which are believed to be sacred revelations set down about 1200–800 BCE. The gods lie outside the finite world, but they can appear in visible form to believers. Each Hindu sect takes its particular deity as supreme. By worshiping gods with rituals, meditation, and intense love, individuals may be reborn into increasingly higher positions until they escape the cycle of life, death, and rebirth, which is called *samsara*. The most popular deities are Vishnu, Shiva, and the Great Goddess, Devi. Deities are revealed and depicted in multiple aspects.

Vishnu: Vishnu is a benevolent god who works for the order and well-being of the world. He is often represented lying in a trance or asleep on the Cosmic Waters, where he dreams the world into existence. His symbols are the wheel and a conch shell, the mace and lotus. He usually has four arms and wears a crown and lavish jewelry. He rides a man-bird, Garuda. Vishnu appears in ten different incarnations, including Rama and Krishna, who have their own sects. Rama embodies virtue, and, assisted by the monkey king, he fights the demon Ravana. As Krishna, Vishnu is a supremely beautiful, blue-skinned youth who lives with the cowherds, loves the maiden Radha, and battles the demon Kansa.

Shiva: Shiva is both creative and destructive, light and dark, male and female. His symbol is the *linga*, an upright phallus, which is represented as a low pillar. As an expression of his power and creative energy, he is often represented as Lord of the Dance, dancing the Cosmic Dance, the endless cycle of death and rebirth,

destruction and creation (see "Shiva Nataraja of the Chola Dynasty," page 314). He dances within a ring of fire, his four hands holding fire, a drum, and gesturing to the worshipers. Shiva's animal vehicle is the bull. His consort is Parvati; their sons are the elephant-headed Ganesha, the overcomer of obstacles, and Karttikeya, often associated with war.

Devi: Devi, the Great Goddess, controls material riches and fertility. She has forms indicative of beauty, wealth, and auspiciousness, but also forms of wrath, pestilence, and power. As the embodiment of cosmic energy, she provides the vital force to all the male gods. Her symbol is an abstract depiction of female genitals, often associated with the *linga* of Shiva. When armed and riding a lion (as the goddess Durga), she personifies righteous fury. As the goddess Lakshmi, she is the goddess of wealth and beauty. She is often represented by the basic geometric forms: squares, circles, triangles.

Brahma: Brahma, who once had his own cult, embodies spiritual wisdom. His four heads symbolize the four cosmic cycles, four earthly directions, and four classes of society: priests (brahmins), warriors, merchants, and laborers.

There are countless other deities, but central to Hindu practice are *puja* (forms of worship) and *darshan* (beholding a deity), generally performed to obtain a deity's favor and in the hope that this favor will lead to liberation from *samsara*. Because desire for the fruits of our actions traps us, the ideal is to consider all earthly endeavors as sacrificial offerings to a god. Pleased with our devotion, he or she may grant us an eternal state of pure being, pure consciousness, and pure bliss.

---

of wheels, called in Sanskrit *chakra*s, alternating with four different animals: lion, horse, bull, and elephant. The animals may symbolize the four great rivers of the world, which are mentioned in Indian creation myths. Standing on this abacus are four back-to-back lions. Facing the four cardinal directions, the lions may be emblematic of the universal nature of Buddhism and the universal currency of Ashoka's law inscribed on the pillar. Their roar might be compared with the speech of the Buddha that spreads far and wide. The lions may also refer to the Buddha himself, who is known as "the lion of the Shakya clan" (the clan into which the Buddha was born as prince). The lions originally supported a great wheel, now lost. A universal Buddhist symbol, the wheel refers to Buddhist teaching, for with his sermon at Sarnath the Buddha "set the wheel of the law [*dharma*] in motion." The wheel is also a symbol of the *chakravartin*, the ideal universal monarch, and so refers to Ashoka as well as the Buddha.

Their formal, heraldic pose imbues the lions with something of the monumental quality evident in the statue of the *yakshi* of the same period. We also find the same strong patterning of realistic

elements: Veins and tendons stand out on the legs; the claws are large and powerful; the mane is richly textured; and the jaws have a loose and fluttering edge.

THE PERIOD OF THE SHUNGAS AND EARLY ANDHRAS

With the demise of the Maurya Empire, India returned to rule by regional dynasties. Between the second century BCE and the early first century CE, two of the most important of these dynasties were the Shunga dynasty (185–72 BCE) in central India and the Andhra dynasty (72 BCE–third century CE) who initially ruled in central India and after the first century in the south. During this period, some of the most magnificent early Buddhist structures were created.

STUPAS

Religious monuments called **stupas**, solid mounds enclosing a reliquary, are fundamental to Buddhism (see "Stupas and Temples," page 301). A stupa may be small and plain or large and elaborate. Its

9-8 • GREAT STUPA, SANCHI
Madhya Pradesh, India. Founded 3rd century BCE, enlarged c. 150–50 BCE.

SEE MORE: View a video about the Great Stupa, Sanchi **www.myartslab.com**

form may vary from region to region, but its symbolic meaning remains virtually the same, and its plan is a carefully calculated **mandala**, or diagram of the cosmos as it is envisioned in Buddhism. Stupas are open to all for private worship.

The first stupas were constructed to house the Buddha's remains after his cremation. According to tradition, the relics were divided into eight portions and placed in eight **reliquaries**. Each reliquary was then encased in its own burial mound, called a stupa. Since the early stupas held actual remains of the Buddha, they were venerated as his body and, by extension, his enlightenment and attainment of *nirvana* (liberation from rebirth). The method of veneration was, and still is, to circumambulate, or walk around, the stupa in a clockwise direction. In the mid third century BCE, King Ashoka is said to have opened the original eight stupas and divided their relics among many more stupas, probably including the Great Stupa at Sanchi.

THE GREAT STUPA AT SANCHI. Probably no early Buddhist structure is more famous than the **GREAT STUPA** at Sanchi in central India **(FIG. 9–8)**. In its original form probably dating to the

time of Ashoka, the Great Stupa was part of a large monastery complex crowning a hill. During the mid second century BCE, it was enlarged to its present size, and the surrounding stone railing was constructed. About 100 years later, elaborately carved stone gateways were added to the railing.

The Great Stupa at Sanchi is a representative of the early central Indian type. Its solid, hemispherical dome was built up from rubble and dirt, faced with dressed stone, then covered with a shining white plaster made from lime and powdered seashells. The dome—echoing the arc of the sky—sits on a raised base. Around the perimeter is a walkway enclosed by a railing; an elevated walkway is approached by a staircase on the south side. As is often true in religious architecture, the railing provides a physical and symbolic boundary between an inner, sacred area and the outer, profane world. On top of the dome, another stone railing, square in shape, defines the abode of the gods atop the cosmic mountain. It encloses the top of a mast bearing three stone disks, or "umbrellas," of decreasing size. These disks have been interpreted in various ways. They may correspond to the "Three Jewels of Buddhism"—the Buddha, the Law, and the Monastic inscription, also on the south gateway, specifies a gift during the reign of King Satakarni of the Andhra dynasty, providing the first-century BCE date for the gateways. The only elements of the Great Stupa at Sanchi to be ornamented with sculpture, the gateways rise to a height of 35 feet. Their square posts and horizontal members are carved with symbols and scenes drawn mostly from the Buddha's life and the **jataka tales**, stories of the Buddha's past lives. A relief from the east gateway is illustrated in **FIGURE 9–9**. Typical of Indian narrative relief of the second and first centuries BCE, the scenes are organized not in a time sequence, but according to where they take place. Thus, at the top of this relief is a scene of Queen Maya's dream anticipating the birth of the Buddha, while below is a scene showing the Buddha's father in a chariot, riding out to greet his return, and at the bottom the Buddha, symbolized by a plank, levitates above the crowd gathered to witness the gift of a garden for the Buddha and his followers. All three of these scenes take place at Kapilavastu, the city of his birth.

9-9 • RELIEF FROM EAST GATEWAY OF THE GREAT STUPA, SANCHI
Early Andhra period, mid 1st century BCE. Stone.

This relief illustrates the birth of the Buddha at the top and the return of the Buddha to the city of his birth in the panels below.

Order—and they may also refer to the Buddhist concept of the three realms of existence: desire, form, and formlessness. The mast itself symbolizes an *axis mundi*, connecting the Cosmic Waters below the earth with the celestial realm above it and anchoring everything in its proper place.

A 10-foot-tall stone railing demarcates a circumambulatory path at ground level. Carved with octagonal uprights and lens-shaped crossbars, it probably simulates the wooden railings of the time. This design pervaded early Indian art, appearing in relief sculpture and as architectural ornament. Four stone gateways, or **toranas**, punctuate the railing. Aligned with the four cardinal directions, the gateways symbolize the Buddhist cosmos. An inscription on the south gateway indicates that it was provided by ivory carvers from the nearby town of Vidisha, while another

9-10 • *YAKSHI* BRACKET FIGURE
East *torana* of the Great Stupa at Sanchi. Stone, height approx. 60″ (152.4 cm).

Buddhist architecture in South Asia consists mainly of stupas and temples, often at monastic complexes containing **viharas** (monks' cells and common areas). These monuments may be either structural—built up from the ground—or rock-cut—hewn out of a mountainside. Stupas derive from burial mounds and contain relics beneath a solid, dome-shaped core. A major stupa is surrounded by a railing that creates a sacred path for ritual circumambulation at ground level. This railing is punctuated by gateways, called **toranas** in Sanskrit, aligned with the cardinal points. The stupa sits on a round or square terrace; stairs lead to an upper circumambulatory path around the platform's edge. On top of the stupa's dome a railing defines a square, from the center of which rises a mast supporting tiers of disk-shaped "umbrellas."

Hindu architecture in South Asia consists mainly of temples, either structural or rock-cut, executed in a number of styles and dedicated to diverse deities. The two general Hindu temple types are the northern

and southern styles prevalent in northern India and southern India respectively. Within these broad categories is great stylistic diversity, though all are raised on plinths and dominated by their superstructures. In north India, the term **shikhara** is used to refer to the entire superstructure, while in the south it refers only to the finial, that is, the uppermost member of the superstructure. North Indian *shikhara*s are crowned by **amalakas**. Inside, a series of **mandapas** (halls) leads to an inner sanctuary, the **garbhagriha**, which contains a sacred image. An *axis mundi* is imagined to run vertically up from the Cosmic Waters below the earth, through the *garbhagriha*'s image, and out through the top of the tower.

Jain architecture consists mainly of structural and rock-cut monasteries and temples that have much in common with their Buddhist and Hindu counterparts. Buddhist, Hindu, and Jain temples may share a site, as may the structures of still other religions.

stupa

northern-style temple

southern-style temple

SEE MORE: View a simulation of stupas and temples **www.myartslab.com**

The capitals above the posts consist of four back-to-back elephants on the north and east gates, dwarfs on the west gate, and lions on the south gate. The capitals in turn support a three-tiered superstructure in which posts and crossbars are elaborately carved with still more symbols and scenes, and studded with free-standing sculptures depicting such subjects as *yakshi*s and *yaksha*s, riders on real and mythical animals, and the Buddhist wheel. As in other early Buddhist art before the late first century BCE, the Buddha himself is not shown in human form. Instead, he is represented by symbols such as his footprints, an empty "enlightenment" seat, or a plank.

Forming a bracket between each capital and the lowest cross-bar is a sculpture of a *yakshi* (**FIG. 9–10**). These *yakshi*s are some of the finest female figures in Indian art, and they make an instructive comparison with the *yakshi* of the Maurya period (SEE FIG. 9–6).

The earlier figure was distinguished by a formal, somewhat rigid pose, an emphasis on realistic details, and a clear distinction between clothed and nude parts of the body. In contrast, the Sanchi *yakshi* leans daringly into space with casual abandon, supported by one leg as the other charmingly crosses behind. Her thin, diaphanous garment is noticeable only by its hems, and so she appears almost nude, which emphasizes her form. The band pulling gently at her abdomen accentuates the suppleness of her flesh. The swelling, arching curves of her body evoke this deity's procreative and bountiful essence. As the personification of the waters, she is the source of life. Here she symbolizes the sap of the tree, which flowers at her touch.

The profusion of designs, symbols, scenes, and figures carved on all sides of the gateways to the Great Stupa not only relates the history and lore of Buddhism, but also represents the teeming life of the world and the gods.

BUDDHIST ROCK-CUT HALLS

From ancient times, caves have been considered hallowed places in India, for they were frequently the abode of holy men and ascetics. Around the second century BCE, cavelike sanctuaries were hewn out of the stone plateaus in the region of south central India known as the Deccan. Made for the use of Buddhist monks, the sanctuaries were carved from top to bottom like great pieces of sculpture, with all details completely finished in stone. To enter one of these remarkable halls is to feel transported to an otherworldly, sacred space. The atmosphere created by the dark recess and the echo that magnifies the smallest sound combine to promote a state of heightened awareness.

THE CHAITYA HALL AT KARLE.   The monastic community made two types of rock-cut halls. One was the **vihara**, used for the monks' living quarters, and the other was the **chaitya** ("sanctuary"), which usually enshrined a stupa. A *chaitya* hall at Karle, dating from the first century BCE to the first century CE, is one of the largest and most fully developed examples of these early Buddhist works **(FIG. 9–11)**. At the entrance, columns once supported a balcony, in front of which a pair of Ashokan-type

9-11 • CHAITYA HALL, KARLE
Maharashtra, India. 1st century BCE–1st century CE.

pillars stood. The walls of the vestibule are carved in relief with rows of small balcony railings and arched windows, simulating the façade of a great multi-storied palace. At the base of the side walls, enormous statues of elephants seem to be supporting the entire structure on their backs. Dominating the upper portion of the main façade is a large horseshoe-shaped opening, which provides the hall's main source of light. The window was originally fitted with a carved wood screen, some of which remains, that filtered the light streaming inside.

Three entrances pierce the main façade. Flanking the entrances are sculpted panels of **mithuna** couples, amorous male and female figures that evoke the harmony and fertility of life and suggest the devotion with which the worshiper should confront the Buddha represented by the stupa inside. The interior hall, 123 feet long, has a 46-foot-high ceiling carved in the form of a barrel vault ornamented with arching wooden ribs. Both the interior and exterior of the hall were once brightly painted. Pillars demarcate a pathway for circumambulation around the stupa in the apse at the far end.

The side aisles are separated from the main aisle by closely spaced columns whose bases resemble a large pot set on a stepped pyramid of planks. From this potlike form rises a massive octagonal shaft. Crowning the shaft, a bell-shaped lotus capital supports an inverted pyramid of planks, which serves in turn as a platform for sculpture. The statues depict pairs of kneeling elephants, each bearing a *mithuna* couple. These figures, the only sculpture within this austere hall, may represent the nobility coming to pay homage at the temple. The pillars around the apse are plain, and the stupa is simple. A railing motif ornaments the base; the dome was once topped with wooden "umbrella" disks, only one of which remains. As with nearly everything in the cave, the stupa is carved from the cliff's rock. Like the stupa at Sanchi, the sculptural decoration is restricted to the entranceway. This stupa, however, could not contain the Buddha's relics because it is solid rock; likely it was worshiped as if it did.

THE KUSHAN AND LATER ANDHRA PERIODS

Around the first century CE, the regions of present-day Afghanistan, Pakistan, and north India came under the control of the Kushans, originally a nomadic people forced out of northwest China by the Han. Exact dates are uncertain, but they ruled from the first to the third century CE. The beginning of the long reign of their most illustrious king, Kanishka, is variously dated from 78 to 143 CE.

Buddhism during this period underwent a profound evolution that resulted in the form known as Mahayana, or Great Vehicle (see "Buddhism," page 297). This vital new movement, which was to sweep most of northern India and eastern Asia, probably inspired the first depictions of the Buddha himself in art. (Previously, as in the Great Stupa at Sanchi, the Buddha had been indicated solely by symbols.) Distinctive styles arose in the Gandhara region in the northwest (present-day Pakistan and Afghanistan) and in the famous religious center of Mathura in central India. Both of these areas were ruled by the Kushans. About the same time, a third style evolved in southeast India under the Andhra dynasty, whose rule continued in this region through the third century CE.

9–12 • STANDING BUDDHA
From Gandhara, Pakistan. Kushan period, c. 2nd–3rd century CE. Schist, height 7′6″ (2.28 m). Lahore Museum, Lahore.

While all three styles are quite distinct, they shared a basic visual language, or iconography, in which the Buddha is readily recognized by certain characteristics. He wears a monk's robe, a long length of cloth draped over the left shoulder and around the body. The Buddha is said to have had 32 major distinguishing marks, called **lakshanas**, some of which are reflected in the iconography (see "Buddhist Symbols," page 362). These include a golden-colored body, long arms that reached to his knees, the impression of a wheel *(chakra)* on the palms of his hands and the soles of his feet, and the **urna**—a tuft of white hair between his eyebrows. Because he had been a prince in his youth and had worn the customary heavy earrings, his earlobes are usually shown elongated. The top of his head is said to have had a protuberance called an **ushnisha**, which in images often resembles a bun or top-knot and symbolizes his enlightenment.

THE GANDHARA STYLE

Gandhara art combines elements of Hellenistic, Persian, and Indian styles. A typical image from Gandhara portrays the Buddha as a superhuman figure, more powerful and heroic than an ordinary human (**FIG. 9–12**). Although it is difficult to determine the dates of Gandhara images, this over-life-size Buddha may date to the fully developed stage of the Gandhara style, possibly around the third century CE. It is carved from schist, a fine-grained dark stone. The Buddha's body, revealed through the folds of the garment, is broad and massive, with heavy shoulders and limbs and a well-defined torso. His left knee bends gently, suggesting a slightly relaxed posture.

The treatment of the robe is especially characteristic of the Gandhara manner. Tight, riblike folds alternate with delicate creases, setting up a clear, rhythmic pattern of heavy and shallow lines. On the upper part of the figure, the folds break asymmetrically along the left arm; on the lower part, they drape in a symmetric U shape. The strong tension of the folds suggests life and power within the image. This complex fold pattern resembles the treatment of togas on certain Roman statues (SEE PAGE 177, FIG. A), and it exerted a strong influence on portrayals of the Buddha in central and east Asia. The Gandhara region's relations with the Hellenistic world may have led to this strongly Western style in its art. Pockets of Hellenistic culture had thrived in neighboring Bactria (present-day northern Afghanistan and southern Uzbekistan) since the fourth century BCE, when the Greeks under Alexander the Great reached the borders of India. Also, Gandhara's position near the east–west trade routes appears to have stimulated contact with Roman culture in the Near East during the early centuries of the first millennium CE.

THE MATHURA STYLE

The second major style of Buddhist art in the Kushan period—that found at Mathura—was not allied with the Hellenistic-Roman tradition. Instead, the Mathura style evolved from representations of *yaksha*s, the indigenous male nature deities. Images produced at

ART AND ITS CONTEXTS

Mudras

*Mudra*s (the Sanskrit word for "signs") are ancient symbolic hand gestures that are regarded as physical expressions of different states of being. In Buddhist art, they function iconographically. *Mudra*s are also used during meditation to release these energies. The following are the most common *mudras* in Asian art.

Dharmachakra Mudra

The gesture of teaching, setting the *chakra* (wheel) of the *dharma* (law or doctrine) in motion. Hands are at chest level.

Dhyana Mudra

A gesture of meditation and balance, symbolizing the path toward enlightenment. Hands are in the lap, the lower representing *maya*, the physical world of illusion, the upper representing *nirvana*, enlightenment and release from the world.

Vitarka Mudra

This variant of *dharmachakra mudra* stands for intellectual debate. The right and/or left hand is held at shoulder level with thumb and forefinger touching.

Abhaya Mudra

The gesture of reassurance, blessing, and protection, this *mudra* means "have no fear." The right hand is at shoulder level, palm outward.

Bhumisparsha Mudra

This gesture calls upon the earth to witness Shakyamuni Buddha's enlightenment at Bodh Gaya. A seated figure's right hand reaches toward the ground, palm inward.

Varada Mudra

The gesture of charity, symbolizing the fulfillment of all wishes. Alone, this *mudra* is made with the right hand; but when combined with *abhaya mudra* in standing Buddha figures (as is most common), the left hand is shown in *varada mudra*.

Mudras

Mathura during the early days of the Kushan period may be the first representations of the Buddha to appear in art.

The stele in **FIGURE 9–13** is one of the finest of the early Mathura images. The sculptors worked in a distinctive red sandstone flecked with cream-colored spots. Carved in **high relief** (forms projecting strongly from the background), it depicts a seated Buddha with two attendants. The Buddha sits in a yogic posture on a pedestal supported by lions. His right hand is raised in a symbolic gesture meaning "have no fear." Images of the Buddha rely on a repertoire of such gestures, called **mudras**, to communicate certain ideas, such as teaching, meditation, or the attaining of enlightenment (see "Mudras," above). The Buddha's *urna*, his *ushnisha*, and the impressions of wheels on his palms and soles are all clearly visible in this figure. Behind his head is a large, circular halo; the scallop points of its border represent radiating light. Behind the halo are branches of the pipal tree, the tree under which the Buddha was seated when he achieved enlightenment. Two celestial beings hover above.

As in Gandhara sculptures, the Mathura work gives a powerful impression of the Buddha. Yet this Buddha's riveting outward gaze and alert posture impart a more intense, concentrated energy. The robe is pulled tightly over the body, allowing the fleshy form to be seen as almost nude. Where the pleats of the robe appear, such as over the left arm and fanning out between the legs, they are depicted abstractly through compact parallel formations of ridges with an incised line in the center of each ridge. This characteristic

Mathura tendency to abstraction also appears in the face, whose features take on geometric shapes, as in the rounded forms of the widely opened eyes. Nevertheless, the torso with its subtle and soft modeling is strongly naturalistic.

9-13 • BUDDHA AND ATTENDANTS
From Katra Keshavdev, Mathura, Madhya Pradesh, India. Kushan period, c. late 1st–early 2nd century CE. Red sandstone, height 27¼″ (69.2 cm). Government Museum, Mathura.

THE SOUTHEAST INDIAN STYLE

Events from the Buddha's life were popular subjects in the reliefs decorating stupas and Buddhist temples. One example from Nagarjunakonda depicts a scene when he was Prince Siddhartha, before his renunciation of his princely status and his subsequent quest for enlightenment **(FIG. 9–14)**. Carved in low relief, the panel reveals a scene of pleasure around a pool of water. Gathered around Siddhartha, the largest figure and the only male, are some of the palace women. One holds his foot, entreating him to come into the water; another sits with legs drawn up on the nearby rock; others lean over his shoulder or fix their hair; one comes into the scene with a box of jewels on her head. The panel is framed by decorated columns, crouching lions, and amorous *mithuna* couples. (One of these couples is visible at the right of the illustration.) The scene is skillfully orchestrated to revolve around the prince as the main focus of all eyes. Typical of the southeast Indian style, the figures are slighter than those of Gandhara and Mathura. They are sinuous and mobile, even while at rest. The rhythmic nuances of the limbs and varied postures not only create interest in the activity of each individual but also engender a light and joyous effect.

During the first to third century CE, each of the three major styles of Buddhist art developed its own distinct idiom for expressing the complex imagery of Buddhism and depicting the image of the Buddha. The production of art in Gandhara and the region around Nagarjunakonda declined over the ensuing centuries. However, the artists of central India continued to work productively, and from them came the next major development in Indian Buddhist art.

9-14 • SIDDHARTHA IN THE PALACE
Detail of a relief from Nagarjunakonda, Andhra Pradesh, India. Later Andhra period, c. 3rd century CE. Limestone. National Museum, New Delhi.

EXPLORE MORE: Gain insight from a primary source about the life of the Buddha
www.myartslab.com

THE FOURTH THROUGH SEVENTH CENTURIES

The Guptas, who founded a dynasty in the eastern region of central India known as Magadha, expanded their territories during the fourth century CE to form an empire that encompassed northern and much of central India. Although Gupta power ended in 550, the influence of Gupta culture was felt long after that.

The period of the Guptas and their contemporaries is renowned for the flourishing artistic and literary culture that brought forth some of India's most widely admired sculpture and painting. While Buddhism continued to be a major religion, the earliest surviving Hindu temples also date from this time.

BUDDHIST SCULPTURE

Two distinctive styles of Gupta Buddhist sculpture prevailed during the second and third quarters of the fifth century and dominated in northern India: one was based at Mathura, the major center of north Indian sculpture during the Kushan period, and the other at Sarnath, whose style is reflected in Buddhist sculpture over much of northern India.

The **STANDING BUDDHA** in FIGURE **9–15** embodies the fully developed Sarnath Gupta style. Carved from fine-grained sandstone, the figure stands in a mildly relaxed pose, the body clearly visible through a clinging robe. This plain robe, portrayed with none of the creases and folds so prominent in the Kushan period images, is distinctive of the Sarnath style. Its effect is to concentrate attention on the form of the body, which emerges in high relief. The body is graceful and slight, with broad shoulders and a well-proportioned torso. Only a few lines of the garment at the neck, waist, and hems interrupt the purity of its subtly shaped surfaces; the face, smooth and ovoid, has the same refined elegance. The downcast eyes suggest otherworldly introspection, yet the gentle, open posture maintains a human link. Behind the head are the remains of a large, circular halo. Carved in concentric circles of pearls and foliage, the ornate halo contrasted with the plain surfaces of the figure. Details also may have been indicated by paint.

At the site of Bamiyan, about 155 miles northwest of Kabul, Afghanistan, were two enormous Buddhas carved from the rock of a cliff, one some 115 feet in height (FIG. **9–16**), the other about 165 feet. They were seen by a Chinese pilgrim who came to Bamiyan in the fifth century, so they clearly date before his visit, probably to the early fifth century. Pilgrims could walk within the cliff up a staircase on the right side of the smaller figure that ended at the Buddha's shoulder. There they could look into the vault of the niche and see a painted image of the sun god, suggesting a metaphoric pilgrimage to the heavens. They then could circumambulate the figure at the level of the head and return to ground level on a staircase on the figure's left side. These huge figures likely served as the model for those at rock-cut sanctuaries in China, for example, at Yungang. Despite the historical and religious importance of these figures, and

9-15 • STANDING BUDDHA
From Sarnath, Uttar Pradesh, India. Gupta period, 474 CE. Chunar sandstone, height 6′4″ (1.93 m). Archaeological Museum, Sarnath.

ignoring the pleas of world leaders, the Taliban demolished the Bamiyan Buddhas in 2001.

PAINTING

The Gupta aesthetic also found expression in painting, though in a region of India just beyond the Gupta realm. Some of the finest surviving works are murals from the Buddhist rock-cut halls of Ajanta, in the western Deccan region of India (FIG. **9–17**). Under a ruling house known as the Vakataka dynasty, many caves were carved around 475 CE, including Cave I, a large *vihara* hall with monks' chambers around the sides and a Buddha shrine chamber in the back. The walls of the central court were covered with murals painted in mineral pigments on a prepared plaster surface. Some of these paintings depict episodes from the Buddha's past lives. Flanking the entrance to the shrine chamber are two large **bodhisattvas**, one of which is seen in FIGURE 9–17.

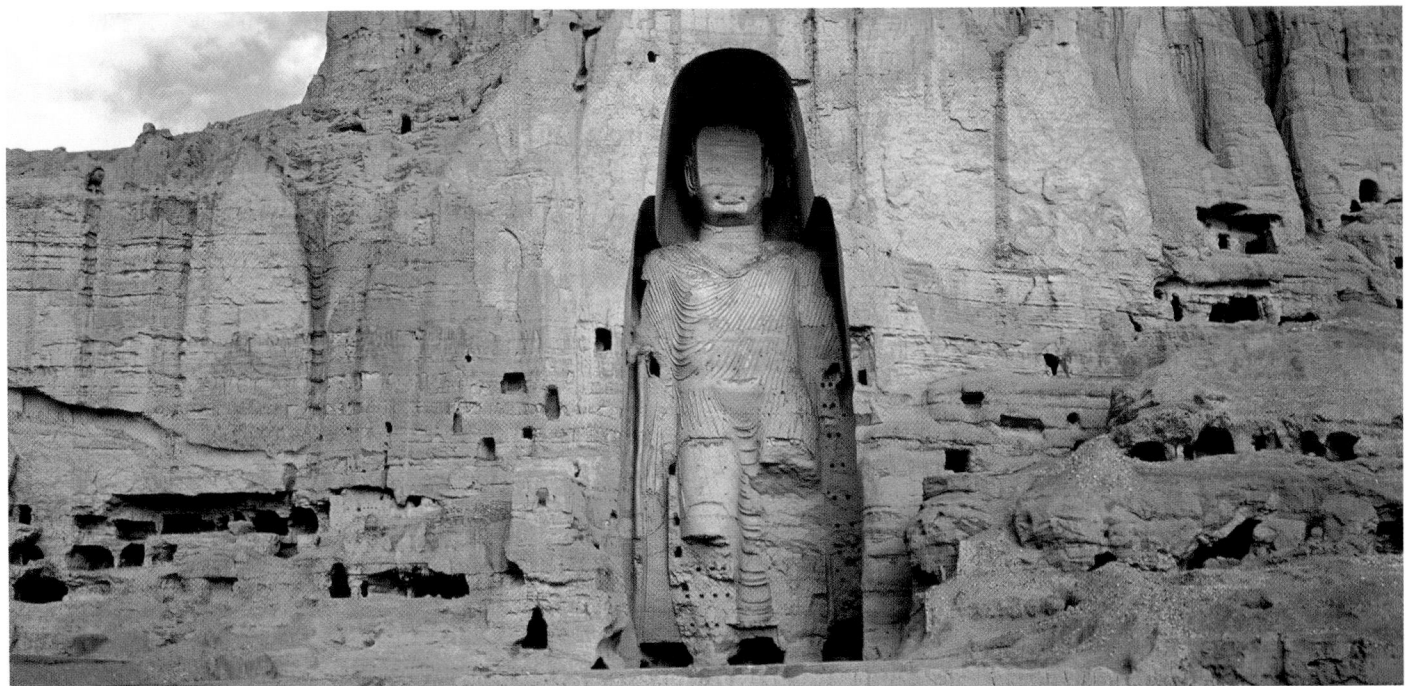

9–16 • STANDING BUDDHA
Bamiyan, Afghanistan. c. 5th century CE.

Bodhisattvas are enlightened beings who postpone *nirvana* and buddhahood to help others achieve enlightenment. They are distinguished from Buddhas in art by their princely garments. The bodhisattva here is lavishly adorned with delicate ornaments. He wears a bejeweled crown, large earrings, a pearl necklace, armbands, and bracelets. A striped cloth covers his lower body. The graceful bending posture and serene gaze impart a sympathetic attitude. His spiritual power is suggested by his large size in comparison to the surrounding figures, and his identity as the compassionate bodhisattva Avalokiteshvara is indicated by the lotus flower he holds in his right hand.

The naturalistic style balances outline and softly graded color tones. Outline drawing, always a major ingredient of Indian painting, clearly defines shapes; tonal gradations impart the illusion of three-dimensional form, with lighter tones used for protruding parts such as the nose, brows, shoulders, and chest muscles. Together with the details of the jewels, these highlighted areas resonate against the subdued tonality of the figure. Sophisticated, realistic detail is balanced by the languorous human form. In no other known examples of Indian painting do bodhisattvas appear so graciously divine yet, so palpably human. This particular synthesis is evident also in the Sarnath statue (SEE FIG. 9–15), which shares much in common as well with the sculpture of Ajanta.

Although Buddhism had flourished in India during the fifth century, some of the most important Buddhist monasteries, attracting pilgrims from as far away as China, prospered especially after the Gupta period. Hindu temples, generally small and relatively simple structures during the fifth century, subsequently became increasingly complex and elaborately adorned with sculptured images.

9–17 • BODHISATTVA
Detail of a wall painting in Cave I, Ajanta, Maharashtra, India. Vakataka dynasty, c. 475 CE.

9–18 • VISHNU TEMPLE, DEOGARH
Uttar Pradesh, India. Gupta dynasty, c. 530 CE.

THE EARLY NORTHERN TEMPLE

The Hindu temple developed many different forms throughout India, but it can be classified broadly into two types: northern and southern. The northern type is chiefly distinguished by a superstructure called a **shikhara** (see "Stupas and Temples," page 301). The *shikhara* rises as a solid mass above the flat stone ceiling and windowless walls of the sanctum, or **garbhagriha**, which houses an image of the temple's deity. As it rises, it curves inward in a mathematically determined ratio. (In geometric terms, the *shikhara* is a paraboloid.) Crowning the top is a circular, cushion-like element called an **amalaka**, a fruit. From the *amalaka*, a **finial** (a knoblike decoration at the top point of a spire) takes the eye to a point where the earthly world is thought to join the cosmic world. An imaginary *axis mundi* penetrates the entire temple, running from the point of the finial, through the exact center of the *amalaka* and *shikhara*, down through the center of the *garbhagriha* and its image, finally passing through the base of the temple and into the earth below. In this way the temple becomes a conduit between the celestial realms and the earth. This theme, familiar from Ashokan pillars and Buddhist stupas, is carried out with elaborate exactitude in Hindu temples, and it is one of the most important elements underlying their form and function (see "Meaning and Ritual in Hindu Temples and Images," page 310).

TEMPLE OF VISHNU AT DEOGARH. One of the earliest northern-style temples is the temple of Vishnu at Deogarh in north central India, which dates from around 530 CE **(FIG. 9–18)**. Much of the *shikhara* has crumbled away, so we cannot determine its original shape with precision. Nevertheless, it was clearly a massive, solid structure built of large cut stones. It would have given the impression of a mountain, which is one of several metaphoric meanings of a Hindu temple. This early temple has only one chamber, the *garbhagriha*, which corresponds to the center of a sacred diagram called a *mandala* on which the entire temple site is patterned. As the deity's residence, the *garbhagriha* is likened to a sacred cavern within the "cosmic mountain" of the temple.

Large panels sculpted in relief with images of Vishnu appear as "windows" on the temple's exterior. These elaborately framed panels do not function literally to let light *into* the temple; they function symbolically to let the light of the deity *out* of the temple to be seen by those outside.

One panel depicts Vishnu lying on the Cosmic Waters at the beginning of creation **(FIG. 9–19)**. He sleeps on the serpent of infinity, Ananta, whose body coils endlessly into space. Stirred by his female aspect (*shakti*, or female energy), personified here by the goddess Lakshmi, seen holding his foot, Vishnu dreams the universe into existence. From his navel springs a lotus (shown in this relief behind Vishnu), and the unfolding of space-time begins.

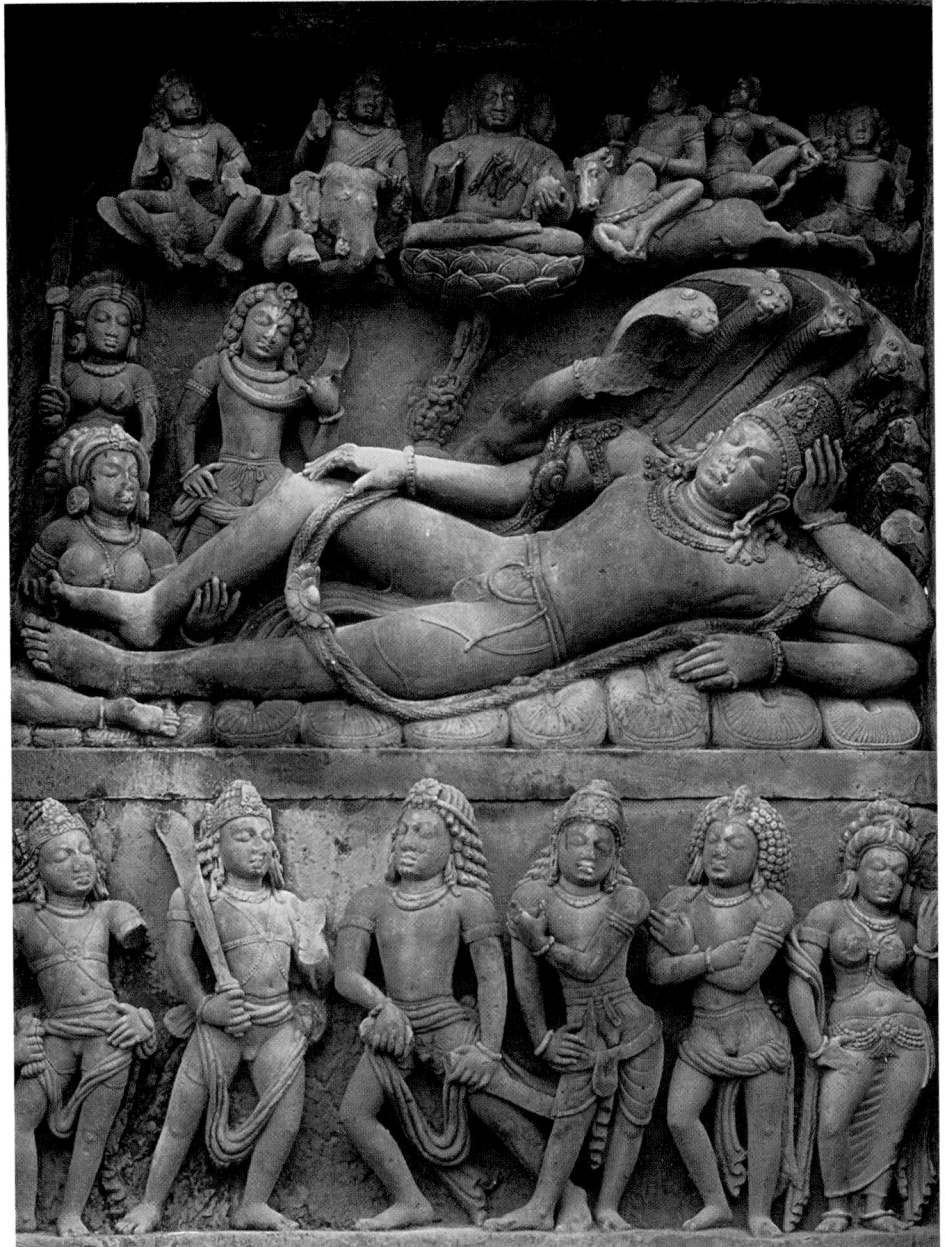

9-19 • VISHNU ON THE COSMIC WATERS
Relief panel in the Vishnu Temple, Deogarh. c. 530 CE. Stone, height approx. 5′ (1.5 m).

SEE MORE: View a video about the process of sculpting in relief
www.myartslab.com

frieze below personify Vishnu's four attributes. They stand ready to fight the appearance of evil, represented at the left of the frieze by two demons who threaten to kill Brahma and jeopardize all creation.

The birth of the universe and the appearance of evil are thus portrayed here in three clearly organized registers. Typical of Indian religious and artistic expression, these momentous events are set before our eyes not in terms of abstract symbols, but as a drama acted out by gods in super-human form.

MONUMENTAL NARRATIVE RELIEFS
The Hindu god Shiva exhibits a wide range of aspects or forms, both gentle and wild: He is the Great Yogi who dwells for vast periods of time in meditation in the Himalayas; he is also the husband par excellence who makes love to the goddess Parvati for eons at a time; he is the Slayer of Demons; and he is the Cosmic Dancer who dances the destruction and re-creation of the world.

TEMPLE OF SHIVA AT ELEPHANTA. Many of these forms of Shiva appear in the monumental relief panels adorning the cave-temple of Shiva carved in the mid sixth century on the island of Elephanta off the coast of Mumbai in western India. The cave-temple is complex in layout and conception, perhaps to reflect the nature of Shiva. While most temples have one entrance, this temple offers three—one facing north, one east, and one west. The interior, impressive in its size and grandeur, is designed along two main axes, one running north–south, the other east–west. The three entrances provide the only source of light, and the resulting cross and backlighting effects add to the sense of the cave as a place of mysterious, almost confusing complexity.

Along the east–west axis, large pillars cut from the rock appear to support the low ceiling and its beams, although, as with all architectural elements in a cave-temple, they are not structural (FIG. 9–20). The pillars form orderly rows, but the rows are hard to discern within the framework of the cave shape, which is neither square nor longitudinal, but formed of overlapping *mandalas* that create a symmetric yet irregular space. The pillars are an important aesthetic component of the cave. Each has an

The first being to be created is Brahma (not to be confused with Brahman), who appears here as the central, four-headed figure in the row of gods portrayed above the reclining Vishnu. Brahma turns himself into the universe of space and time by thinking, "May I become Many."

The sculptor has depicted Vishnu as a large, resplendent figure with four arms. His size and his multiple arms denote his omni-potence. He is lightly garbed but richly ornamented. The ideal of the Gupta style is evident in the smooth, perfected shape of the body and in the lavishly detailed jewelry, including Vishnu's characteristic cylindrical crown. The four figures on the right in the

Meaning and Ritual in Hindu Temples and Images

The Hindu temple is one of the most complex and meaningful architectural forms in Asian art. Age-old symbols and ritual functions are embedded not only in a structure's many parts, but also in the process of construction itself. Patron, priest, and architect worked as a team to ensure the sanctity of the structure from start to finish. No artist or artisan was more highly revered in ancient Indian society than the architect, who could oversee the construction of an abode in which a deity would dwell.

For a god to take up residence, however, everything had to be done properly in exacting detail. By the end of the first millennium, the necessary procedures had been recorded in texts called the *Silpa Shastra*. First, an auspicious site was chosen; a site near water was especially favored, for water makes the earth fruitful. Next, the ground was prepared in an elaborate process that took several years: Spirits already inhabiting the site were invited to leave; the ground was planted and harvested through two seasons; then cows—sacred beasts since the Indus civilization—were pastured there to lend their potency to the site. When construction began, each phase was accompanied by ritual to ensure its purity and sanctity.

All Hindu temples are built on a plan known as a **mandala**, a schematic design of a sacred realm or space—specifically, Vastupurusha *mandala*, the *mandala* of the Cosmic Man, the primordial progenitor of the human species. His body, fallen on earth, is imagined as superimposed on the *mandala* design; together, they form the base on which the temple rises. The Vastupurusha *mandala* always takes the form of a square subdivided into a number of equal squares (usually 64) surrounding a central square. The central square represents Brahman, the primordial, unmanifest Formless One. This square corresponds to the temple's sanctum, the windowless *garbhagriha* ("womb chamber"). The nature of Brahman is clear, pure light; that we perceive the *garbhagriha* as dark is considered a testament to our deluded nature. The surrounding squares belong to lesser deities, while the outermost compartments hold protector gods. These compartments are usually represented by the enclosing wall of a temple compound.

The *garbhagriha* houses the temple's main image—most commonly a stone, bronze, or wood statue of Vishnu, Shiva, or Devi. In the case of Shiva, the image is often symbolic rather than anthropomorphic. To ensure perfection, the proportions of the image follow a set canon, and rituals surround its making. When the image is completed, a priest recites *mantras* (mystic syllables), that bring the deity into the image. The belief that a deity is literally present is not taken lightly. Even in India today, any image "under worship"—whether it be in a temple or a field, an ancient work or a modern piece—will be respected and not taken from the people who worship it.

A Hindu temple is a place for individual devotion, not congregational worship. It is the place where a devotee can make offerings to one or more deities and be in the presence of the god who is embodied in the image in the *garbhagriha*. Worship generally consists of prayers and offerings such as food and flowers or water and oil for the image, but it can also be much more elaborate, including dancing and ritual sacrifices.

---

unadorned, square base rising to nearly half its total height. Above is a circular column, which has a curved contour and a billowing "cushion" capital. Both column and capital are delicately fluted, adding a surprising refinement to these otherwise sturdy forms. The focus of the east–west axis is a square **linga shrine**, shown here at the center of illustration 9–20. Each of its four entrances is flanked by a pair of colossal standing guardian figures. In the center of the shrine is the *linga*, the phallic symbol of Shiva. The *linga* represents the presence of Shiva as the unmanifest Formless One, or Brahman. It symbolizes both his erotic nature and his aspect as the Great Yogi who controls his seed. The *linga* is synonymous with Shiva and is seen in nearly every Shiva temple and shrine.

The focus of the north–south axis, in contrast, is a relief on the south wall with a huge bust of Shiva representing his Sadashiva, or **ETERNAL SHIVA**, aspect **(FIG. 9–21)**. Three heads are shown resting upon the broad shoulders of the upper body, but five heads are implied: the fourth behind and the fifth, never depicted, on top. The heads summarize Shiva's fivefold nature as creator (back), protector (left), destroyer (right), obscurer (front), and releaser (top). The head in the front depicts Shiva deep in introspection. The massiveness of the broad head, the large eyes barely delineated, and the mouth with its heavy lower lip suggest the god's serious depths. Lordly and majestic, he easily supports his huge crown, intricately carved with designs and jewels, and the matted, piled-up hair of a yogi. On his left shoulder, his protector nature is depicted as female, with curled hair and a pearl-festooned crown. On his right shoulder, his wrathful, destroyer nature wears a fierce expression, and snakes encircle his neck.

Like the relief panels at the temple to Vishnu in Deogarh (SEE FIG. 9–19), the reliefs at Elephanta are early examples of the Hindu monumental narrative tradition. Measuring 11 feet in height, they are set in recessed niches. The panels portray the range of Shiva's powers and some of his different aspects, presented in the context of narratives that help devotees understand his nature. Taken as a whole, the reliefs represent the manifestation of Shiva in our world. Indian artists often convey the many aspects or essential nature of a deity through multiple heads or arms—which they

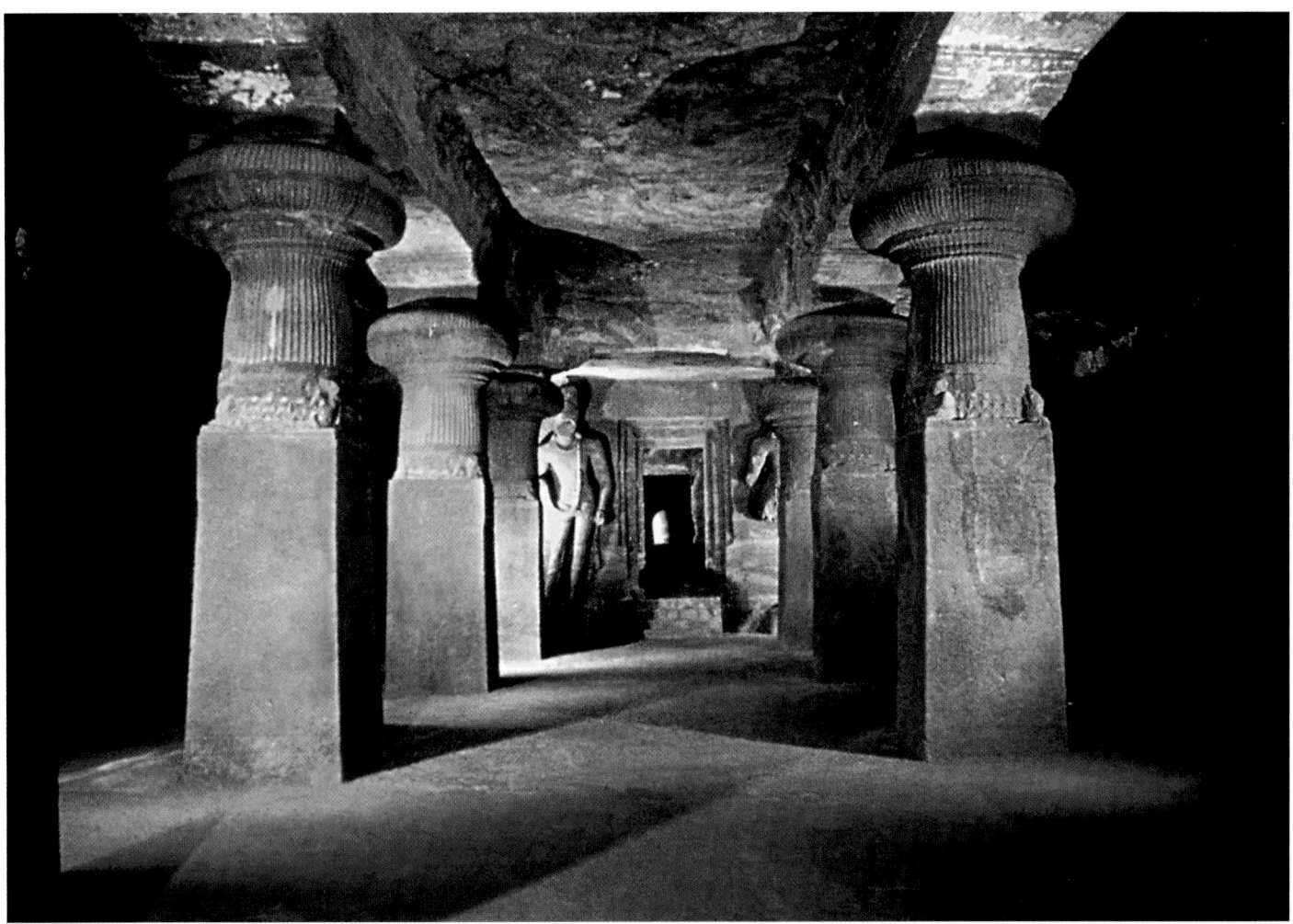

9-20 • CAVE-TEMPLE OF SHIVA, ELEPHANTA
Maharashtra, India. Post-Gupta period, mid 6th century CE. View along
the east–west axis to the *linga* shrine.

do with such convincing naturalism that we readily accept the
additions. Here, for example, the artist has united three heads onto
a single body so skillfully that we still relate to the statue as an
essentially human presence.

"DESCENT OF THE GANGES" RELIEF AT MAMALLAPURAM. An
enormous relief at Mamallapuram, near Chennai, in southeastern
India, depicts the penance of a king, Bhagiratha, who sought to
save his people from drought by subjecting himself to terrible
austerities. In response, the god Shiva sent the Ganges River,
represented by the natural cleft in the rock, to earth, thereby
ending the drought (see "A Closer Look," page 313). Bhagiratha is
shown standing in frigid waters while staring directly at the sun
through his parted fingers, standing for interminable periods on

9-21 • ETERNAL SHIVA
Rock-cut relief in the cave-temple of Shiva, Elephanta.
Mid 6th century CE. Height approx. 11′ (3.4 m).

one foot, and in deep prayer before a temple. In the upper left part of the relief, Shiva, shown four-armed, appears before Bhagiratha to grant his wish. Elsewhere in the relief, animal families are depicted, generally in mutually protective roles.

This richly carved relief was executed under the Pallava dynasty, which flourished in southeastern India from the seventh to ninth century CE. It very likely serves as a visual allegory for the benevolent king, who protects his people, perhaps specifically by providing canals to control water, a notion reinforced by the relief carved in a cave-temple on the same boulder, to the left of the Descent relief. It shows the god Krishna protecting his people from a deluge by raising a mountain to serve as a sort of natural umbrella. Themes relating to water are particularly appropriate to Mamallapuram, situated on the Bay of Bengal and possibly serving as a port for the Pallavas.

THE EARLY SOUTHERN TEMPLE

The coastal city of Mamallapuram was also a major temple site under the Pallavas. Along the shore are many large granite boulders and cliffs, and from these the Pallava-period stonecutters carved entire temples as well as reliefs such as the one discussed in "A Closer Look," opposite. Among the most interesting of these rock-cut temples is a group known as the Five Rathas, which preserve diverse early architectural styles that probably reflect the forms of contemporary wood or brick structures that have long since disappeared.

DHARMARAJA RATHA AT MAMALLAPURAM. One of this group, called today the Dharmaraja Ratha, epitomizes the early southern-style temple (FIG. 9–22). Although strikingly different in appearance from the northern style, it uses the same symbolism to link the heavens and earth and it, too, is based on a *mandala*. The temple, square in plan, remains unfinished, and the *garbhagriha* usually found inside was never hollowed out, suggesting that, like cave-temples, Dharmaraja Ratha was executed from the top downward. On the lower portion, only the columns and niches have been carved. The use of a single deity in each niche forecasts the main trend in temple sculpture in the centuries ahead: The tradition of narrative reliefs declined, and the stories they told became concentrated in statues of individual deities, which conjure up entire mythological episodes through characteristic poses and a few symbolic objects.

Southern- and northern-style temples are most clearly distinguished by their superstructures. The Dharmaraja Ratha does not culminate in the paraboloid of the northern *shikhara* but in a pyramidal tower. Each story of the superstructure is articulated by a cornice and carries a row of miniature shrines. Both shrines and cornices are decorated with a window motif from which faces peer. The shrines not only demarcate each story, but also provide loftiness for this palace intended to enshrine a god. Crowning the superstructure is a dome-shaped octagonal capstone quite different from the *amalaka* of the northern style.

During the centuries that followed, both northern- and southern-style temples developed into complex, monumental forms, but their basic structure and symbolism remained the same as those we have seen in these simple, early examples at Deogarh and Mamallapuram.

THE EIGHTH THROUGH THE FOURTEENTH CENTURIES

During the eighth through the fourteenth centuries, regional styles developed in the realms of the dynasties ruling kingdoms that were generally smaller than the Maurya and Kushan empires. Some dynasties were relatively long-lived, such as the Pallavas and Cholas in the south and the Palas in the northeast. Although Buddhism remained strong in a few areas—notably under the Palas—it generally declined, while the Hindu gods Vishnu, Shiva, and the Great Goddess (mainly Durga) grew increasingly popular. Monarchs rivaled each other in the building of temples to their favored deity, and many complicated and subtle variations of the Hindu temple emerged with astounding rapidity in different regions. By around 1000 the Hindu temple reached unparalleled heights of grandeur and engineering.

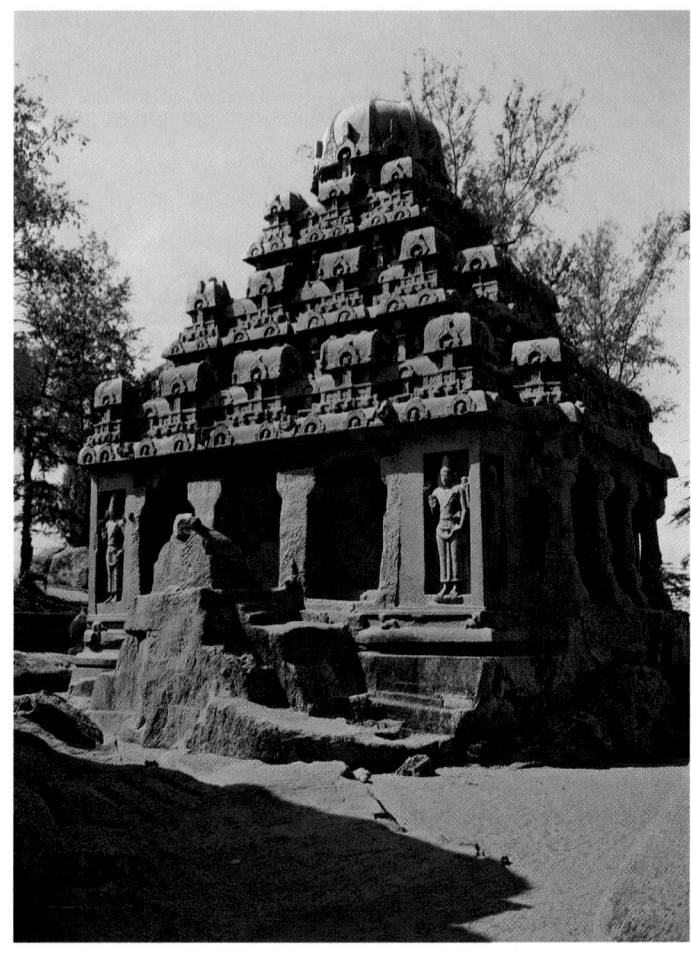

9-22 • DHARMARAJA RATHA, MAMALLAPURAM
Tamil Nadu, India. Pallava period, c. mid 7th century CE.

"Descent of the Ganges" Relief ›

Rock-cut relief, Mamallapuram, Tamil Nadu, India.
Pallava period, c. mid 7th century CE. Granite, height approx. 20′ (6 m).

Unfinished cave. Beyond it, on the same rock formation, is the Krishna Cave.

Unfinished portion of the relief suggesting work from the top downward, as at other Mamallapuram monuments.

Shiva offering boon to Bhagiratha.

Bhagiratha meditating in front of a temple.

Bhagiratha gazing directly at the sun.

A cat imitating the penance of Bhagiratha, a whimsical touch by the artist.

A family of elephants, the bull elephant in front protecting his young elephant, probably a metaphor for the king's protection of his people.

SEE MORE: View the Closer Look feature for the "Descent of the Ganges" relief at Mamallapuram
www.myartslab.com

THE MONUMENTAL NORTHERN TEMPLE

The Kandariya Mahadeva, a temple dedicated to Shiva at Khajuraho, in central India, was probably built by a ruler of the Chandella dynasty in the late tenth or early eleventh century **(FIG. 9–23)**. Khajuraho was the capital and main temple site for the Chandellas, who constructed more than 80 temples there, about 25 of which are well preserved. The Kandariya Mahadeva Temple is in the northern style, with a curvilinear *shikhara* rising over its *garbhagriha*. Larger, more extensively ornamented, and expanded through the addition of halls on the front and porches to the sides and back, the temple seems at first glance to have little in common with its precursor at Deogarh (SEE FIG. 9–18). Actually, however, the basic elements and their symbolism remain unchanged.

Shiva Nataraja of the Chola Dynasty

Perhaps no sculpture is more representative of Hinduism than the statues of Shiva Nataraja, or Dancing Shiva, a form perfected by sculptors under the royal patronage of the south Indian Chola dynasty in the late tenth to eleventh century. (For the architecture and painting of the period, SEE FIGS. 9–25, 9–26.) The dance of Shiva is a dance of cosmic proportions, signifying the universe's cycle of death and rebirth; it is also a dance for each individual, signifying the liberation of the believer through Shiva's compassion. In the iconography of the Nataraja, this sculpture shows Shiva with four arms dancing on the prostrate body of Apasmara, a dwarf figure who symbolizes "becoming" and whom Shiva controls. Shiva's extended left hand holds a ball of fire; a circle of fire rings the god. The fire is emblematic of the destruction of *samsara* and the physical universe as well as the destruction of *maya* (illusion) and our ego-centered perceptions. Shiva's back right hand holds a drum; its beat represents the irrevocable rhythms of creation and destruction, birth and death. His front right arm gestures the "have no fear" *mudra* (see "Mudras," page 304). The front left arm, gracefully stretched across his body with the hand pointing to his raised foot, signifies the promise of liberation.

The artist has rendered the complex pose with great clarity. The central axis, which aligns the nose, navel, and insole of the weight-bearing foot, maintains the figure's equilibrium while the remaining limbs asymmetrically extend far to each side. Shiva wears a short loincloth, a ribbon tied above his waist, and delicately tooled ornaments. The scant clothing reveals his perfected form with its broad shoulders tapering to a supple waist. The jewelry is restrained and the detail does not detract from the beauty of the body.

The deity does not appear self-absorbed and introspective as he did in the Eternal Shiva relief at Elephanta (SEE FIG. 9–21). He turns to face the viewer, appearing lordly and aloof yet fully aware of his benevolent role as he generously displays himself for the devotee. Like the Sarnath Gupta Buddha (SEE FIG. 9–15), the Chola Shiva Nataraja presents a characteristically Indian synthesis

of the godly and the human, this time expressing the *bhakti* belief in the importance of an intimate relationship with a lordly god through whose compassion one is saved. The earlier Hindu emphasis on ritual and the depiction of the heroic feats of the gods is subsumed into the all-encompassing, humanizing factor of grace.

The fervent religious devotion of the *bhakti* movement was fueled by the sublime writings of a series of poet-saints who lived in the south of India. One of them, Appar, who lived from the late sixth to mid seventh century CE, wrote this vision of the Shiva Nataraja. The ash the poem refers to is one of many symbols associated with the deity.

In penance for having lopped off one of the five heads of Brahma, the first created being, Shiva smeared his body with ashes and went about as a beggar.

> If you could see
> the arch of his brow,
> the budding smile
> on lips red as the kovvai fruit,
> cool matted hair,
> the milk-white ash on coral skin,
> and the sweet golden foot
> raised up in dance,
> then even human birth on this wide earth
> would become a thing worth having.

(Translated by Indira Vishvanathan Peterson)

SHIVA NATARAJA
From Thanjavur, Tamil Nadu. Chola dynasty, 12th century CE. Bronze, height 32″ (81.25 cm). National Museum of India, New Delhi.

9-23 • KANDARIYA MAHADEVA TEMPLE, KHAJURAHO
Madhya Pradesh, India. Chandella dynasty, c. 1000 CE.

As at Deogarh, the temple rests on a stone terrace that sets off a sacred space from the mundane world. A steep flight of stairs at the front (to the right in the illustration) leads to a series of three halls, called **mandapas** (distinguished on the outside by pyramidal roofs), preceding the *garbhagriha*. The *mandapa*s serve as spaces for ritual, such as dances performed for the deity, and for the presentation of offerings. The temple is built of stone blocks using only post-and-lintel construction. Because vault and arch techniques are not used, the interior spaces are not large.

The exterior has a strong sculptural presence, its massiveness suggesting a "cosmic mountain" composed of ornately carved stone. The *shikhara* rises more than 100 feet over the *garbhagriha* and is crowned by a small *amalaka*. The *shikhara* is bolstered by the many smaller *shikhara* motifs bundled around it. This decorative scheme adds a complex richness to the surface, but it also obscures the shape of the main *shikhara*, which is slender, with a swift and impetuous upward movement. The roofs of the *mandapa*s contribute to the impression of rapid ascent by growing progressively taller as they near the *shikhara*.

Despite its apparent complexity, the temple has a clear structure and unified composition. The towers of the superstructure are separated from the lower portion by strong horizontal moldings and by the open spaces over the *mandapa*s and porches. The **moldings** (shaped or sculpted strips) and rows of sculpture adorning the lower part of the temple create a horizontal emphasis that stabilizes the vertical thrust of the superstructure. Three rows of sculpture—some 600 figures—are integrated into the exterior walls. Approximately 3 feet tall and carved in high relief, the sculptures depict gods and goddesses, as well as figures in erotic postures. They are thought to express Shiva's divine bliss, the manifestation of his presence within, and the transformation of one into many.

In addition to its horizontal emphasis, the lower portion of the temple is characterized by a verticality that is created by protruding and receding elements. Their visual impact is similar to that of engaged columns and buttresses, and they account for much of the rich texture of the exterior. The porches, two on each side and one in the back, contribute to the complexity by outwardly expanding the ground plan, yet their bases also

9-24 • EROTIC COUPLES ON WALL OF KANDARIYA MAHADEVA TEMPLE, KHAJURAHO
Height of sculptures approx. 3′3″ (1 m).

reinforce the sweeping vertical movements that unify the entire structure.

The Khajuraho temples are especially well known for their numerous erotic sculptures such as those illustrated in **FIGURE 9–24**. These carvings are not placed haphazardly, but rather in a single vertical line at the juncture of the walls enclosing the *garbhagriha* and the last *mandapa*. Their significance is uncertain; perhaps they derive from the amorous couples that adorn temple doorways leading to the *garbhagriha*. Such couples are found on some early temples such as the Deogarh temple as well as on Buddhist rock-cut sanctuaries such as the one at Karle, serving as reminders that devotion to god resembles the passion of love.

THE MONUMENTAL SOUTHERN TEMPLE

The Cholas, who succeeded the Pallavas in the mid ninth century, founded a dynasty that governed most of the far south well into the late thirteenth century. The Chola dynasty reached its peak during the reign of Rajaraja I (r. 985–1014). As an expression of gratitude for his many victories in battle, Rajaraja built the Rajarajeshvara Temple to Shiva in his capital, Thanjavur (formerly known as Tanjore). The name Rajarajeshvara means the temple of Rajaraja's Lord, that is, Shiva. Commonly called the Brihadeshvara (the temple of the Great Lord), this temple is a remarkable achievement of the southern style of Hindu architecture **(FIG. 9–25)**. It stands within a huge, walled compound near the banks of the Kaveri River. Although smaller shrines dot the compound, the Rajarajeshvara dominates the area.

Clarity of design, a formal balance of parts, and refined décor contribute to the Rajarajeshvara's majesty. Rising to an astonishing height of 216 feet, this temple was probably the tallest structure in India in its time. Like the contemporaneous Kandariya Mahadeva Temple at Khajuraho, the Rajarajeshvara has a longitudinal axis and greatly expanded dimensions, especially with regard to its superstructure. Typical of the southern style, the *mandapa* at the front of the Rajarajeshvara has a flat roof, as opposed to the pyramidal roofs of the northern style. The walls of the sanctum rise for two

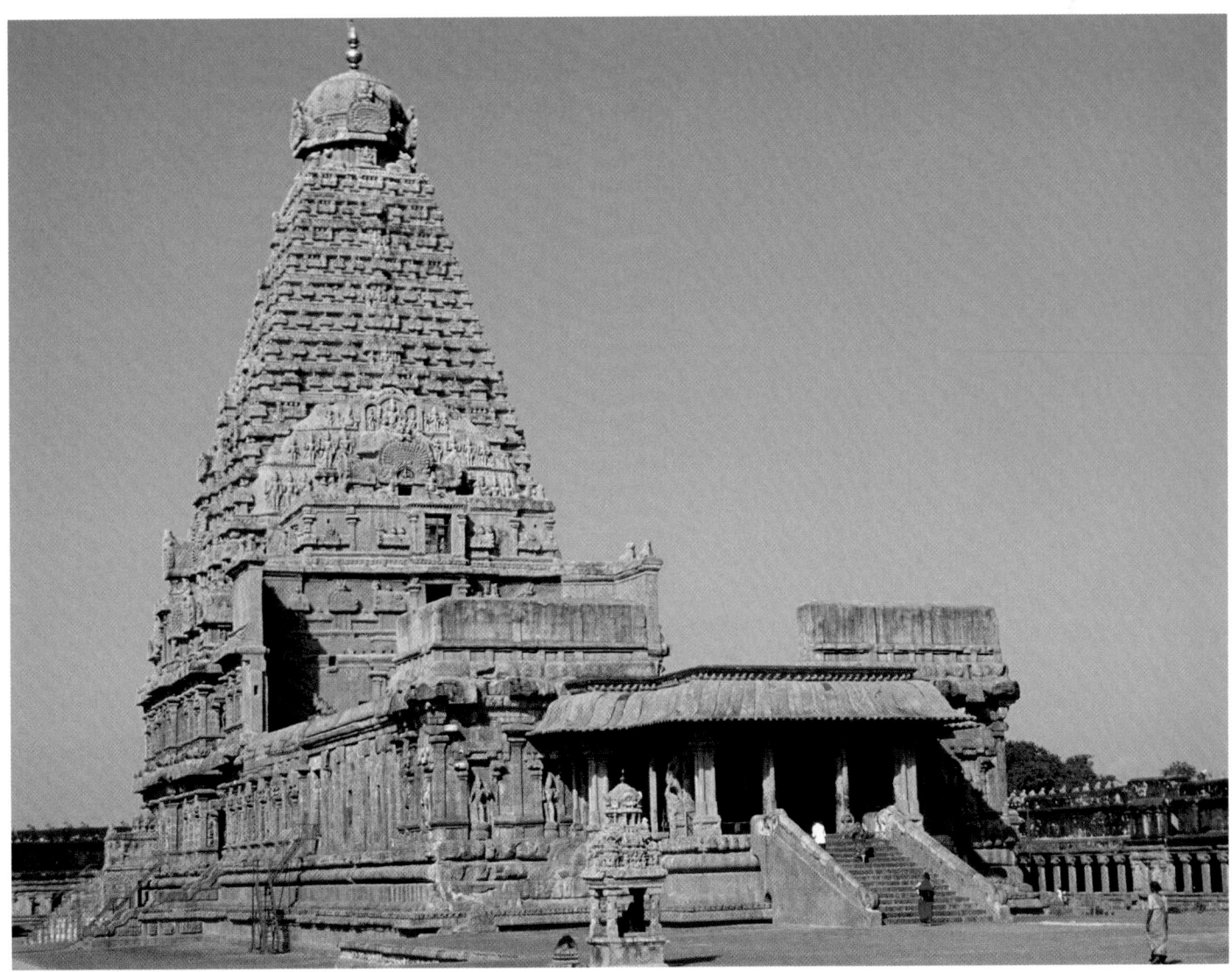

9-25 • RAJARAJESHVARA TEMPLE OF SHIVA, THANJAVUR
Tamil Nadu, India. Chola Dynasty, 1003–1010 CE.

stories, with each story emphatically articulated by a large cornice. The exterior walls are ornamented with niches, each of which holds a single statue, usually depicting a form of Shiva. The clear, regular, and wide spacing of the niches imparts a calm balance and formality to the lower portion of the temple, in marked contrast to the irregular, concave-convex rhythms of the northern style.

The superstructure of the Rajarajeshvara is a four-sided, hollow pyramid that rises for 13 stories. Each story is decorated with miniature shrines, window motifs, and robust dwarf figures who seem to be holding up the next story. Because these sculptural elements are not large in the overall scale of the superstructure, they appear well integrated into the surface and do not obscure the thrusting shape. This is quite different from the effect of the small *shikhara* motifs on the superstructure of the Kandariya Mahadeva Temple (SEE FIG. 9–23). Notice also that in the earlier southern style, as embodied in the Dharmaraja Ratha (SEE FIG. 9–22), the shrines on the temple superstructure were much larger in proportion to the whole and thus each appeared to be nearly as prominent as the superstructure's overall shape.

Because the Rajarajeshvara superstructure is not obscured by its decorative motifs, it forcefully ascends skyward. At the top is an octagonal dome-shaped capstone similar to the one that crowned the earlier southern-style temple. This huge capstone is exactly the same size as the *garbhagriha* housed 13 stories directly below. It thus evokes the shrine a final time before the eye ascends to the point separating the worldly from the cosmic sphere above.

THE BHAKTI MOVEMENT IN ART

Throughout this period, two major religious movements were developing that affected Hindu practice and its art: the Tantric, or Esoteric, and the *bhakti*, or devotional. Although both movements evolved throughout India, the influence of Tantric sects appeared during this period primarily in the art of the north (see Chapter 23 for a discussion of their continued development), while the *bhakti* movements found artistic expression in the south as well as the north.

The *bhakti* devotional movement was based on ideas expressed in ancient texts, especially the *Bhagavad-Gita*. *Bhakti* revolves around the ideal relationship between humans and deities. According to *bhakti*, it is the gods who create *maya* (illusion), in which we are all trapped. They also reveal truth to those who truly love them and whose minds are open to them. Rather than focusing on ritual and the performance of *dharma* according to the Vedas, *bhakti* stresses an intimate, personal, and loving relation with the god, and complete devotion and surrender to the deity. Inspired and influenced by *bhakti*, Indian artists produced some of South Asia's most interesting works, among them the few remaining mural paintings and the famous bronze works of sculpture (see "Shiva Nataraja of the Chola Dynasty," page 314).

WALLPAINTING AT RAJARAJESHVARA TEMPLE. Rajaraja's building of the Rajarajeshvara was in part a reflection of the fervent Shiva *bhakti* movement which had reached its peak by that time. The corridors of the circumambulatory passages around the *garbhagriha* were originally adorned with wall paintings. Overpainted later, they were only recently rediscovered. One painting apparently depicts the ruler Rajaraja himself, not as a warrior or majestic king on his throne, but as a simple mendicant humbly standing behind his religious teacher (FIG. 9–26). With his white beard and dark

9-26 • RAJARAJA I AND HIS TEACHER
Detail of a wall painting in the Rajarajeshvara Temple to Shiva. Chola dynasty, c. 1010 CE.

skin, the aged teacher contrasts with the youthful, bronze-skinned king. The position of the two suggests that the king treats the saintly teacher, who in the devotee's or *bhakta's* view is equated with god, with intimacy and respect. Both figures allude to their devotion to Shiva by holding a small flower as an offering, and both emulate Shiva in their appearance by wearing their hair in the "ascetic locks" of Shiva in his Great Yogi aspect.

The portrayal does not represent individuals so much as a contrast of types: the old and the youthful, the teacher and the devotee, the saint and the king—the highest religious and worldly models, respectively—united as followers of Shiva. Line is the essence of the painting. With strength and grace, the even, skillfully executed line defines the boldly simple forms and features. With less shading and fewer details, these figures are flattened, more linear versions of those in the earlier paintings at Ajanta (SEE FIG. 9–17). A cool, sedate calm infuses the monumental figures, but the power of line also invigorates them with a sense of strength and inner life.

The *bhakti* movement spread during the ensuing centuries into northern India. However, during this period a new religious culture penetrated the subcontinent: Turkic peoples, Persians, and Afghans had been crossing the northwest passes into India since the tenth century, bringing with them Islam and its artistic tradition. New religious forms eventually evolved from Islam's long and complex interaction with the peoples of the subcontinent, and so too arose uniquely Indian forms of Islamic art, adding yet another dimension to India's artistic heritage.

ART OF SOUTHEAST ASIA

Trade and cultural exchange, notably by the sea routes linking China and India, brought Buddhism, Hinduism, and other aspects of India's civilization to the various regions of Southeast Asia and the Asian archipelago. Although Theravada Buddhism (see "Buddhism," page 297) had the most lasting impact in the region, other trends in Buddhism, including Mahayana and esoteric (tantric) traditions, also played a role. Elements of Hinduism, including its epic literature, were also adopted.

THAILAND—PRAKHON CHAI STYLE. Even the earliest major flowering of Buddhist art in eighth- and ninth-century Southeast Asia was characterized by distinctly local interpretations of the inheritance from India. For example, a strikingly beautiful style of Buddhist sculpture in Thailand, one with distinct iconographic elements, has been identified based on the 1964 discovery of a hoard of images in an underground burial chamber in the vicinity of Prakhon Chai, Buriram Province, near the present-day border with Cambodia. Distinguished by exquisite craftsmanship and a charming naturalism, enhanced by inlaid materials for the eyes, a standing figure of the bodhisattva Maitreya (FIG. 9–27) exemplifies the lithe and youthful proportions typical of the Prakhon Chai style. The iconography departs from the princely interpretation of

9–27 • BUDDHA MAITREYA
From Buriram Province, Thailand. 8th century CE. Copper alloy with inlaid black glass eyes, 38″ (96.5 cm). Asia Society, New York.
Mr. and Mrs. John D. Rockefeller 3rd Collection, 1979.063

the Buddha, presenting instead ascetic elements—abbreviated clothing and a loose arrangement of long hair. The esoteric (tantric) associations of these features are further emphasized by the multiple forearms, an element that was highly developed in Hindu sculpture and which came to be common in Esoteric Buddhist art.

9-28 • BUDDHA SHAKYAMUNI
From Thailand. Mon Dvaravati period, 9th century CE. Sandstone.
Norton Simon Museum, Los Angeles.

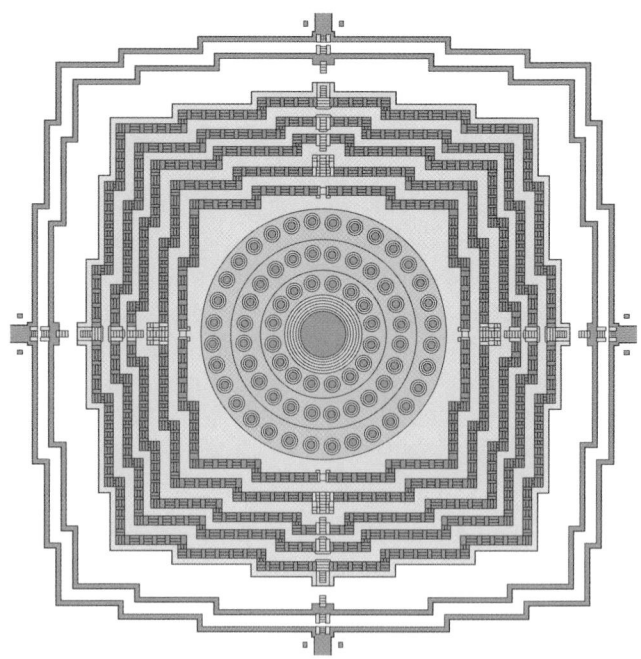

9-29 • PLAN OF BOROBUDUR

THAILAND—DVARAVATI STYLE. The Dvaravati kingdom, of Mon people, flourished in central Thailand from at least the sixth to the eleventh century. This kingdom embraced Theravada Buddhism and produced some of the earliest Buddhist images in Southeast Asia, perhaps based on Gupta-period Indian models. During the later centuries, Dvaravati sculptors restated elements of the Gupta style (SEE FIG. 9–15), and introduced Mon characteristics into classical forms inherited from India (FIG. 9–28).

JAVA—BOROBUDUR. The most monumental of Buddhist sites in Southeast Asia is **BOROBUDUR** (FIGS. **9–29, 9–30**) in central Java, an island of Indonesia. Built about 800 CE and rising more than 100 feet from ground level, this stepped pyramid of volcanic-stone blocks is surmounted by a large stupa, itself ringed by 72 smaller openwork stupas. Probably commissioned to celebrate the Buddhist merit of the Shailendra dynasty rulers, the monument expresses a complex range of Mahayana symbolism, incorporating earthly and cosmic realms. Jataka tales and scenes from the Buddha's life are elaborately narrated in the reliefs of the lower galleries (FIG. **9–31**), and more than 500 sculptures of transcendental buddhas on the balustrades and upper terraces complete the monument, conceived as a *mandala* in three dimensions.

CAMBODIA—ANGKOR VAT. In Cambodia, Khmer kings ruled at Angkor for more than 400 years, from the ninth to the thirteenth century. Among the state temples, Buddhist as well as Hindu, they built **ANGKOR VAT** (FIG. **9–32**), the crowning achievement of Khmer architecture. Angkor had already been the site of royal capitals of the Khmer, who had for centuries vested temporal as well as spiritual authority in their kings, long before King Suryavarman II (r. 1113–1150) began to build the royal complex known today as Angkor Vat. Dedicated to the worship of Vishnu, the vast array of structures is both a temple and a symbolic cosmic mountain. The complex incorporates a stepped pyramid with five towers set within four enclosures of increasing perimeter. Suryavarman's predecessors had associated themselves with Hindu and Buddhist deities at Angkor by building sacred structures. His

9-30 • BOROBUDUR
Central Java, Indonesia. c. 800 CE.

SEE MORE: View a video about Borobudur **www.myartslab.com**

9-31 • MAYA RIDING TO LUMBINI
Detail of a narrative relief sculpture, Borobudur.

9-32 • ANGKOR VAT
Angkor, Cambodia. 12th century CE.

SEE MORE: View a video about Angkor Vat **www.myartslab.com**

9-33 • VISHNU CHURNING THE OCEAN OF MILK
Detail of relief sculpture, Angkor Vat.

9-34 • PARINIRVANA OF THE BUDDHA
Gal Vihara, near Polonnaruwa, Sri Lanka. 11th–12th century CE. Stone.

construction pairs him with Vishnu to affirm his royal status as well as his ultimate destiny of union with the Hindu god. Low-relief sculptures illustrate scenes from the *Ramayana*, the *Mahabharata*, and other Hindu texts **(FIG. 9–33)**, and also depict Suryavarman with his armies.

SRI LANKA.   Often considered a link to Southeast Asia, the island of Sri Lanka is so close to India's southeastern coast that Ashoka's son is said to have brought Buddhism there within his father's lifetime. Sri Lanka played a major role in the strengthening of Theravada traditions, especially by preserving scriptures and relics, and it became a focal point for the Theravada Buddhist world. Sri Lankan sculptors further refined Indian styles and iconography in colossal Buddhist sculptures. The rock-cut Parinirvana of the Buddha at Gal Vihara **(FIG. 9–34)** is one of three colossal Buddhas at the site. This serene and dignified image restates one of the early themes of Buddhist art, that of the Buddha's final transcendence, with a sophistication of modeling and proportion that updates and localizes the classical Buddhist tradition.

THINK ABOUT IT

9.1   Describe the typical form of Indian temples. Contrast the stupa and the temple directly, paying attention to specific building features, such as the superstructure.

9.2   Angkor Vat in Cambodia draws both religious and architectural influence from the Indian subcontinent. Explain what the Khmer architects in Cambodia took from India, with reference to specific religious architectural forms borrowed.

9.3   How does architecture in India and Southeast Asia express a view of the world, even the cosmos?

9.4   Select one architectural work from the chapter, and explain how either Buddhist or Hindu stories are told through its decoration.

9.5   What are some distinguishing features of representations of Buddha?

PRACTICE MORE: Compose answers to these questions, get flashcards for images and terms, and review chapter material with quizzes
www.myartslab.com

10-1 • SOLDIERS From the mausoleum of Emperor Shihuangdi, Lintong, Shaanxi. Qin dynasty, c. 210 BCE. Earthenware, life-size.

CHINESE AND KOREAN ART BEFORE 1279

As long as anyone could remember, the huge mound in China's Shaanxi Province in northern China had been part of the landscape. No one dreamed that an astonishing treasure lay beneath the surface until one day in 1974 peasants digging a well accidentally brought to light the first hint of riches. When archaeologists began to excavate, they were stunned by what they found: a vast underground army of some 8,000 life-size terra-cotta soldiers with 100 life-size ceramic horses standing in military formation, facing east, supplied with weapons, and ready for battle (FIG. 10–1). For more than 2,000 years, while the tumultuous history of China unfolded overhead, they had guarded the tomb of Emperor Shihuangdi, the ruthless ruler who first united the states of China into an empire, the Qin.

In ongoing excavations at the site, additional bronze carriages and horses were found, further evidence of the technology and naturalism achieved by artisans during Qin Shihuangdi's reign. The tomb mound itself has not been excavated.

China has had a long-standing fascination with antiquity, but archaeology is a relatively young discipline there. Only since the 1920s have scholars methodically dug into the layers of history at thousands of sites across the country, yet so much has been unearthed that ancient Chinese history has been rewritten many times.

The archaeological record shows that Chinese civilization arose several millennia ago, and was distinctive for its early advances in ceramics and metalwork, as well as for the elaborate working of jade. Early use of the potter's wheel, mastery of reduction firing, and the early invention of high-fired stoneware and porcelain distinguish the technological advancement of Chinese ceramics. Highly imaginative bronze castings and proficient techniques of mold making characterize early Chinese metalworking. Early attainments in jade reflect a technological competence with rotary tools and abrasive techniques, and a passion for the subtleties of shape, proportion, and surface texture.

Archaeology has supplemented our understanding of historically appreciated Chinese art forms. These explored human relationships and heroic ideals, exemplifying Confucian values and teaching the standards of conduct that underlie social order. Later, China also came to embrace the Buddhist tradition from India. In princely representations of Buddhist divinities and in sublime and powerful, but often meditative, figures of the Buddha, China's artists presented the divine potential of the human condition. Perhaps the most distinguished Chinese tradition is the presentation of philosophical ideals through the theme of landscape. Paintings simply in black ink, depictions of mountains and water, became the ultimate artistic medium for expressing the vastness, abundance, and endurance of the universe.

Chinese civilization radiated its influence throughout east Asia. Chinese learning repeatedly stimulated the growth of culture in Korea, which in turn transmitted influence to Japan.

LEARN ABOUT IT

10.1 Examine the interaction of art and ritual in early periods of Chinese and Korean history.

10.2 Discuss the development of Confucian philosophy and its impact on the pictorial art of China.

10.3 Analyze the Daoist elements in early landscape motifs of China.

10.4 Assess the introduction and spread of Buddhism, and its adherents as patrons (including the court) in both China and Korea.

10.5 Discuss the development of naturalistic depiction and the achievement of verisimilitude in both landscapes and figures in the painting and sculpture of China before 1279.

HEAR MORE: Listen to an audio file of your chapter **www.myartslab.com**

THE MIDDLE KINGDOM

Among the cultures of the world, China is distinguished by its long, uninterrupted development, now traced back some 8,000 years. From Qin, pronounced "chin," comes our name for the country that the Chinese call the Middle Kingdom, the country in the center of the world. Present-day China occupies a large landmass in the center of Asia, covering an area slightly larger than the continental United States. Within its borders lives one-fifth of the human race.

The historical and cultural heart of China is the land watered by its three great rivers, the Yellow, the Yangzi, and the Xi (MAP 10–1). The Qinling Mountains divide Inner China into north and south, regions with strikingly different climates, cultures, and historical fates. In the south, the Yangzi River flows through lush green hills to the fertile plains of the delta. Along the southern coastline, rich with natural harbors, arose China's port cities, the focus of a vast maritime trading network. The Yellow River, nicknamed "China's Sorrow" because of its disastrous floods, winds through the north. The north country is a dry land of steppe and desert, hot in the summer and lashed by cold winds in the winter. Over its vast and vulnerable frontier have come the nomadic invaders that are a recurring theme in Chinese history, but caravans and emissaries from Central Asia, India, Persia, and, eventually, Europe also crossed this border.

10-2 • BOWL
From Banpo, near Xi'an, Shaanxi. Neolithic period, Yangshao culture, 5000–4000 BCE. Painted pottery, height 7″ (17.8 cm). Banpo Museum.

NEOLITHIC CULTURES

Early archaeological evidence had led scholars to believe that agriculture, the cornerstone technology of the Neolithic period, made its way to China from the ancient Near East. More recent findings, however, suggest that agriculture based on rice and millet arose independently in east Asia before 5000 BCE and that knowledge of Near Eastern grains followed some 2,000 years later. One of the clearest archaeological signs of Neolithic culture in China is evidence of the vigorous emergence of towns and cities. At Jiangzhai, near modern Xi'an, for example, the foundations of more than 100 dwellings have been discovered surrounding the remains of a community center, a cemetery, and a kiln. Dated to about 4000 BCE, the ruins point to the existence of a highly developed early society. Elsewhere in China, the foundations of the earliest known palace have been uncovered and dated to about 2000 BCE.

PAINTED POTTERY CULTURES

In China, as in other places, distinctive forms of Neolithic pottery identify different cultures. One of the most interesting objects thus far recovered is a shallow red bowl with a turned-out rim (FIG. 10–2). Found in the village of Banpo near the Yellow River, it was crafted sometime between 5000 and 4000 BCE. The bowl is an artifact of the Yangshao culture, one of the most important of the so-called Painted Pottery cultures of Neolithic China. Although the potter's wheel had not yet been developed, the bowl is perfectly round and its surfaces are highly polished, bearing witness

to a distinctly advanced technology. The decorations are especially intriguing. The marks on the rim may be evidence of the beginnings of writing in China, which was fully developed by the time the first definitive examples appear during the second millennium BCE, in the later Bronze Age.

Inside the bowl, a pair of stylized fish suggests that fishing was an important activity for the villagers. The image between the two fish represents a human face with four more fish, one on each side. Although there is no certain interpretation of the image, it may be a depiction of an ancestral figure who could assure an abundant catch, for the worship of ancestors and nature spirits was a fundamental element of later Chinese beliefs.

LIANGZHU CULTURE

Banpo lies near the great bend in the Yellow River, in the area traditionally regarded as the cradle of Chinese civilization, but archaeological finds have revealed that Neolithic cultures arose over a far broader area. Recent excavations in sites more than 800 miles away, near Hangzhou Bay, in the southeastern coastal region, have turned up human and animal images—often masks or faces— more than 5,000 years old (FIG. 10–3). Large, round eyes, a flat nose, and a rectangular mouth protrude slightly from the background pattern of wirelike lines. Above the forehead, a second, smaller face grimaces from under a huge headdress. The upper face may be human, perhaps riding the animal figure below. The image is one of eight that were carved in low relief on the outside of a large jade **cong**, an object resembling a cylindrical tube encased in

MAP 10-1 • CHINA AND KOREA

The map shows the borders of contemporary China and Korea. Bright-colored areas indicate the extent of China's Han dynasty (206 BCE–221 CE).

10-3 • DETAIL OF MASK DECORATION ON A JADE *CONG*

Neolithic period, Liangzhu culture, 3200–2200 BCE.

10-4 • CONG
Neolithic period, Liangzhu culture, 3200–2200 BCE. Jade, height 1⅞ × width 2⅝″ (5 × 6.6 cm). Shanghai Museum.

The *cong* is one of the most prevalent and mysterious of early Chinese jade shapes. Originating in the Neolithic period, it continued to play a prominent role in burials through the Shang and Zhou dynasties. Many experts believe the *cong* was connected with the practice of contacting the spirit world. They suggest that the circle symbolized heaven; the square, earth; and the hollow, the axis connecting these two realms.

a rectangular block. Another *cong* (FIG. 10–4) also from Liangzhu bears a beautiful finish and similar delineated mask motifs. These were found near the remains of persons buried with what appear to be sets of numerous jade objects.

The intricacy of the carving shows the technical sophistication of this jade-working culture, named the Liangzhu, which seems to have emerged around 3300 BCE. Jade, a stone cherished by the Chinese throughout their history, is extremely hard and is difficult to carve. Liangzhu artists must have used sand as an abrasive to slowly grind the stone down; modern artisans marvel at how they produced such fine work.

The meaning of the masklike image in FIGURE 10–3 is open to interpretation. Its combination of human and animal features seems to show how the ancient Chinese imagined supernatural beings, either deities or dead ancestors. Similar masks later formed the primary decorative motif of Bronze Age ritual objects. Still later, Chinese historians began referring to the ancient mask motif as **taotie**, but the motif's original meaning had already been lost. The jade carving here seems to be a forerunner of this most central and mysterious image.

BRONZE AGE CHINA

China entered its Bronze Age in the second millennium BCE. As with agriculture, scholars at first theorized that the technology had been imported from the Near East. Archaeological evidence now makes clear, however, that bronze casting using the **piece-mold casting** technique arose independently in China, where it attained an unparalleled level of excellence (see "Piece-Mold Casting," opposite).

SHANG DYNASTY

Traditional Chinese histories tell of three Bronze Age dynasties: the Xia, the Shang, and the Zhou. Experts at one time tended to dismiss the Xia and Shang as legendary, but twentieth-century archaeological discoveries fully established the historical existence of the Shang (c. 1700–1100 BCE) and point strongly to the historical existence of the Xia as well.

Shang kings ruled from a succession of capitals in the Yellow River Valley, where archaeologists have found walled cities, palaces, and vast royal tombs. Their state was surrounded by numerous other states—some rivals, others clients—and their culture spread widely. Society seems to have been highly stratified, with a ruling group that had the bronze technology needed to make weapons. They maintained their authority in part by claiming power as intermediaries between the supernatural and human realms. The chief Shang deity, Shangdi, may have been a sort of "Great Ancestor." It is thought that nature and fertility spirits were also honored, and that regular sacrifices were thought necessary to keep the spirits of dead ancestors vital so that they might help the living.

Shang priests communicated with the supernatural world through oracle bones. An animal bone or piece of tortoiseshell was inscribed with a question and heated until it cracked, then the crack was interpreted as an answer. Oracle bones, many of which have been recovered and deciphered, contain the earliest known form of Chinese writing, a script fully recognizable as the ancestor of the system still in use today (see "Chinese Characters," page 331).

RITUAL BRONZES.   Shang tombs reveal a warrior culture of great splendor and violence. Many humans and animals were sacrificed to accompany the deceased. In one tomb, for example, chariots were found with the skeletons of their horses and drivers; in another, dozens of human skeletons lined the approaches to the central burial chamber. The tombs contain hundreds of jade, ivory, and lacquer objects, gold and silver ornaments, and bronze vessels. The enormous scale of Shang burials illustrates the great wealth of the civilization and the power of a ruling class able to consign such great quantities of treasure to the earth, and also suggests this culture's reverence for the dead.

Bronze vessels are the most admired and studied of Shang artifacts. Like oracle bones and jade objects, they were connected with ritual practices, serving as containers for offerings of food and wine. A basic repertoire of about 30 shapes evolved. Some shapes derive from earlier pottery forms, while others seem to reproduce wooden containers. Still others are highly sculptural and take the form of fantastic composite animals.

One functional shape, the **fang ding**, a rectangular vessel with four legs, was used for food offerings. Early examples (see "Piece-Mold Casting," oppposite) featured decoration of raised bosses and mask-like (*taotie*) motifs in horizontal registers on the sides and the legs. A late Shang example, one of hundreds of vesesels recovered from the royal tombs near the last of the Shang capitals, Yin

TECHNIQUE | Piece-mold Casting

The early piece-mold technique for bronze casting is different from the lost-wax process developed in the ancient Mediterranean and Near East. Although we do not know the exact steps ancient Chinese artists followed, we can deduce the general procedure for casting a vessel.

First, a model of the bronze-to-be was made of clay and dried. Then, to create a mold, damp clay was pressed onto the model; after the clay mold dried, it was cut away in pieces, which were keyed for later reassembly and then fired. The original model itself was shaved down to serve as the core for the mold. After this, the pieces of the mold were reassembled around the core and held in place by bronze spacers, which locked the core in position and ensured an even casting space around the core. The reassembled mold was then

covered with another layer of clay, and a sprue, or pouring duct, was cut into the clay to receive the molten metal. A riser duct may also have been cut to allow the hot gases to escape. Molten bronze was then poured into the mold. When the metal cooled, the mold was broken apart to reveal a bronze copy of the original clay model. Finely cast relief decoration could be worked into the model or carved into the sectional molds, or both. Finally, the vessel could be burnished—a long process that involved scouring the surface with increasingly fine abrasives.

The vessel shown here is a *fang ding*. A *ding* is a ceremonial cooking vessel used in Shang rituals and buried in Shang tombs. The Zhou people also made, used, and buried *ding* vessels.

Sectional clay molds for casting bronze vessels. This sketch is based on a vessel in the Zhengzhou Institute of Cultural Relics and Archaeology.

(present-day Anyang), is extraordinary for its size. Weighing nearly 2,000 pounds, it is the largest Shang *ding* vessel thus far recovered. In typical Shang style, its surface is decorated with a complex array of images based on animal forms, including *taotie* masks, confronting horned animals (dragons?) and composite beaked animals (birds?). A ritual pouring vessel, called a *guang* (**FIG. 10–5**), shows a highly sculptural rendition of animal forms. The pouring spout and cover are modeled as the head and body of a tiger, while the rear portion of the vessel and cover is conceived as an owl. Overall geometric decoration combines with suggestive zoomorphic forms. Such images seem to be related to the hunting life of the Shang, but their deeper significance is unknown. Sometimes strange, sometimes fearsome, Shang creatures seem always to have a sense of mystery, evoking the Shang attitude toward the supernatural world.

ZHOU DYNASTY

Around 1100 BCE, the Shang were conquered by the Zhou from western China. During the Zhou dynasty (1100–221 BCE) a feudal society developed, with nobles related to the king ruling over numerous small states. (Zhou nobility are customarily ranked in English by such titles as duke and marquis.) The supreme deity became known as Tian, or Heaven, and the king ruled as the Son of Heaven. Later Chinese ruling dynasties continued to follow the belief that imperial rule emanated from a mandate from Heaven.

The first 300 years of this longest-lasting Chinese dynasty were generally stable and peaceful. In 771 BCE, however, the Zhou suffered defeat in the west at the hands of a nomadic tribe. Although they quickly established a new capital to the east, their authority had been crippled, and the later Eastern Zhou period was a troubled one. States grew increasingly independent, giving

10-5 • COVERED RITUAL WINE-POURING VESSEL (*GUANG*) WITH TIGER AND OWL DÉCOR

Shang dynasty, 13th century BCE. Cast bronze, height with cover 9¾″ (25 cm), width including handle 12⅜″ (31.5 cm). Arthur M. Sackler Museum, Harvard Art Museum, Cambridge, Massachusetts. Bequest of Grenville L. Winthrop 1943.52.103

the Zhou kings merely nominal allegiance. Smaller states were swallowed up by their larger neighbors. During the time historians call the Spring and Autumn period (722–481 BCE), 10 or 12 states, later reduced to seven, emerged as powers. During the ensuing Warring States period (481–221 BCE) intrigue, treachery, and increasingly ruthless warfare became routine.

Against this background of social turmoil, China's great philosophers arose—such thinkers as Confucius, Laozi, and Mozi. Traditional histories speak of China's "one hundred schools" of philosophy, indicating a shift of focus from the supernatural to the human world. Nevertheless, elaborate burials on an even larger scale than before reflected the continuation of traditional beliefs.

BRONZE BELLS. Ritual bronze objects continued to play an important role during the Zhou dynasty, and new forms developed. One of the most spectacular recent discoveries is a carillon of 65 bronze components, mostly bells arranged in a formation 25 feet long **(FIG. 10–6)**, found in the tomb of Marquis Yi of the state of Zeng. Each bell is precisely calibrated to sound two tones—one when struck at the center, another when struck at a corner. The bells are arranged in scale patterns in a variety of registers, and several musicians would have moved around the carillon, striking the bells in the appointed order.

Music may well have played a part in rituals for communicating with the supernatural, for the *taotie* typically appears on the front and back of each bell. The image is now much more intricate and stylized, partly in response to the refinement available with the lost-wax casting process (see "Lost-Wax Casting," page 413), which had replaced the older piece-mold technique. On the coffin of the marquis are painted guardian warriors with half-human, half-animal attributes. The marquis, who died in 433 BCE, must have considered music important, for among the more than 15,000 objects recovered from his tomb were many musical instruments. Zeng was one of the smallest and shortest-lived states of the Eastern Zhou, but the contents of this tomb, in quantity and quality, attest to the high level of its culture.

Chinese Characters

Each word in Chinese is represented by its own unique symbol, called a character. Some characters originated as **pictographs**, images that mean what they depict. Writing reforms over the centuries have often disguised the resemblance, but if we place modern characters next to their ancestors, the picture comes back into focus:

	water	horse	moon	child	tree	mountain
Ancient	川	馬	月	子	木	山
Modern	水	馬	月	子	木	山

Other characters are **ideographs**, pictures that represent abstract concepts or ideas:

sun	+	moon	=	bright
日		月		明

woman	+	child	=	good
女		子		好

Most characters were formed by combining a radical, which gives the field of meaning, with a phonetic, which originally hinted at pronunciation. For example, words that have to do with water have the character for "water" 水 abbreviated to three strokes 氵 as their radical. Thus "to bathe," 沐 pronounced *mu*, consists of the water radical and the phonetic 木 , which by itself means "tree" and is also pronounced *mu*. Here are other "water" characters. Notice that the connection to water is not always literal.

river	sea	weep	pure, clear	extinguish, destroy
河	海	泣	清	滅

These phonetic borrowings took place centuries ago. Many words have shifted in pronunciation, and for this and other reasons there is no way to tell how a character is pronounced or what it means just by looking at it. While at first this may seem like a disadvantage, in the case of Chinese it is advantageous. Spoken Chinese has many dialects. Some are so far apart in sound as to be virtually different languages. But while speakers of different dialects cannot understand each other, they can still communicate through writing, for no matter how they say a word, they write it with the same character. Writing has thus played an important role in maintaining the unity of Chinese civilization through the centuries.

10-6 • SET OF BELLS
From the tomb of Marquis Yi of Zeng, Suixian, Hubei. Zhou dynasty, 433 BCE. Bronze, with bronze and timber frame, frame height 9′ (2.74 m), length 25′ (7.62 m). Hubei Provincial Museum, Wuhan.

THE CHINESE EMPIRE: QIN DYNASTY

Toward the middle of the third century BCE, the state of Qin launched military campaigns that led to its triumph over the other states by 221 BCE. For the first time in its history, China was united under a single ruler. This first emperor of Qin, Shihuangdi, a man of exceptional ability, power, and ruthlessness, was fearful of both assassination and rebellion. Throughout his life, he sought ways to attain immortality. Even before uniting China, he began his own mausoleum at Lintong, in Shaanxi Province. This project continued throughout his life and after his death, until rebellion abruptly ended the dynasty in 206 BCE. Since that time, the mound over the mausoleum has always been visible, but not until an accidental discovery in 1974 was its army of terra-cotta soldiers and horses even imagined (SEE FIG. 10–1). Modeled from clay and then fired, the figures claim a prominent place in the great tradition of Chinese ceramic art. Individualized faces and meticulously rendered uniforms and armor demonstrate the sculptors' skill. Literary sources suggest that the tomb itself, which has not yet been opened, reproduces the world as it was known to the Qin, with stars overhead and rivers and mountains below. Thus did the tomb's architects try literally to ensure that the underworld—the world of souls and spirits—would match the human world.

Qin rule was harsh and repressive. Laws were based on a totalitarian philosophy called legalism, and all other philosophies were banned, their scholars executed, and their books burned. Yet the Qin also established the mechanisms of centralized bureaucracy that molded China both politically and culturally into a single entity. Under the Qin, the country was divided into provinces and prefectures, the writing system and coinage were standardized, roads were built to link different parts of the country with the capital, and battlements on the northern frontier were connected to form the Great Wall. To the present day, China's rulers have followed the administrative framework first laid down by the Qin.

HAN DYNASTY

The commander who overthrew the Qin became the next emperor and founded the Han dynasty (206 BCE–220 CE). During this period the Chinese enjoyed peace, prosperity, and stability. Borders were extended and secured, and Chinese control over strategic stretches of Central Asia led to the opening of the Silk Road, a land route that linked China by trade all the way to Rome. One of the precious goods traded, along with spices, was silk, which had been cultivated and woven in China since at least the third millennium BCE. From as early as the third century BCE, Chinese silk cloth was treasured in Greece and Rome (for more on this topic, see "The Silk Road during the Tang Period," page 342).

PAINTED BANNER FROM CHANGSHA. The early Han dynasty marks the twilight of China's so-called mythocentric age, when people believed in a close relationship between the human and supernatural

10-7 • PAINTED BANNER
From the tomb of the Marquess of Dai, Mawangdui, Changsha, Hunan. Han dynasty, c. 160 BCE. Colors on silk, height 6′8½″ (2.05 m). Hunan Provincial Museum.

worlds. The most elaborate and most intact painting that survives from this time is a T-shaped silk banner, which summarizes this early worldview (FIG. 10–7). Found in the tomb of a noblewoman on the outskirts of present-day Changsha, the banner dates from the second century BCE and is painted with scenes representing three levels of the universe: heaven, earth, and underworld. The pictorial motifs include a portrait of the deceased.

The heavenly realm is shown at the top, in the crossbar of the T. In the upper-right corner is the sun, inhabited by a mythical crow; in the upper left, a mythical toad stands on a crescent moon. Between them is a primordial deity shown as a man with a long serpent's tail—a Han image of the Great Ancestor. Dragons and other celestial creatures swarm below.

A gate guarded by two seated figures stands where the horizontal of heaven meets the banner's long, vertical stem. Two intertwined dragons loop through a circular jade piece known as a **bi**, itself usually a symbol of heaven, dividing this vertical segment into two areas. The portion above the *bi* represents the earthly realm. Here, the deceased woman and three attendants stand on a platform while two kneeling figures offer gifts. The portion beneath the *bi* represents the underworld. Silk draperies and a stone chime hanging from the *bi* form a canopy for the platform below. Like the bronze bells we saw earlier, stone chimes were ceremonial instruments dating from Zhou times. On the platform, ritual bronze vessels contain food and wine for the deceased, just as they did in Shang tombs. The squat, muscular man holding up the platform stands in turn on a pair of fish whose bodies form another *bi*. The fish and the other strange creatures in this section are inhabitants of the underworld.

PHILOSOPHY AND ART

The Han dynasty marked the beginning of a new age. During this dynasty, the philosophical ideals of Daoism and Confucianism, formulated during the troubled times of the Eastern Zhou, became central to Chinese thought. Their influence since then has been continuous and fundamental.

DAOISM AND NATURE.   Daoism emphasizes the close relationship between humans and nature. It is concerned with bringing the individual life into harmony with the Dao, or the Way, of the universe (see "Daoism," page 334). For some a secular, philosophical path, Daoism on a popular level developed into an organized religion, absorbing many traditional folk practices and the search for immortality.

Immortality was as intriguing to Han rulers as it had been to the first emperor of Qin. Daoist adepts experimented with diet, physical exercise, and other techniques in the belief that immortal life could be achieved on earth. Popular Daoist legend told of the Land of Immortals in the Eastern Sea, depicted on a bronze **INCENSE BURNER** from the tomb of Prince Liu Sheng, who died in 113 BCE **(FIG. 10–8)**. Around the bowl, gold inlay outlines the stylized waves of the sea. Above them rises the mountainous island, busy with birds, animals, and the immortals themselves, all cast in bronze with highlights of inlaid gold. Technically, this exquisite piece represents the ultimate development of the long tradition of bronze casting in China.

10-8 • INCENSE BURNER
From the tomb of Prince Liu Sheng, Mancheng, Hebei. Han dynasty, 113 BCE. Bronze with gold inlay, height 10½″ (26 cm). Hebei Provincial Museum, Shijiazhuang.

CONFUCIANISM AND THE STATE.   In contrast to the metaphysical focus of Daoism, Confucianism is concerned with the human world, and its goal is the attainment of equity. To this end, it proposes a system of ethics based on reverence for ancestors and the correct relationships among people. Beginning with self-discipline in the individual, Confucianism teaches how to rectify relationships within the family, and then, in ever-widening circles, with friends and others, all the way up to the level of the emperor and the state (see "Confucius and Confucianism," page 337).

Emphasis on social order and respect for authority made Confucianism especially attractive to Han rulers, who were eager to distance themselves from the disastrous legalism of the Qin. The Han emperor Wudi (r. 141–87 BCE) made Confucianism the official imperial philosophy, and it remained the state ideology of China for more than 2,000 years, until the end of imperial rule in the twentieth century. Once institutionalized, Confucianism took on so many rituals that it too eventually assumed the form and force of a religion. Han philosophers contributed to this process by

Daoism

Daoism is an outlook on life that brings together many ancient ideas regarding humankind and the universe. Its primary text, a slim volume called the *Daodejing* (*The Way and Its Power*), is ascribed to the Chinese philosopher Laozi, who is said to have been a contemporary of Confucius (551–479 BCE). Later, a philosopher named Zhuangzi (369–286 BCE) took up many of the same ideas in a book that is known simply by his name: *Zhuangzi*. Together the two texts formed a body of ideas that crystallized into a school of thought during the Han period.

A *dao* is a way or path. The Dao is the Ultimate Way, the Way of the universe. The Way cannot be named or described, but it can be hinted at. It is like water. Nothing is more flexible and yielding, yet water can wear down the hardest stone. Water flows downward, seeking the lowest ground. Similarly, a Daoist sage seeks a quiet life, humble and hidden, unconcerned with worldly success. The Way is great precisely because it is small. The Way may be nothing, yet nothing turns out to be essential.

To recover the Way, we must unlearn. We must return to a state of nature. To follow the Way, we must practice *wu wei* (nondoing). "Strive for nonstriving," advises the *Daodejing*.

All our attempts at asserting ourselves, at making things happen, are like swimming against a current and are thus ultimately futile, even harmful. If we let the current carry us, however, we will travel far. Similarly, a life that follows the Way will be a life of pure effectiveness, accomplishing much with little effort.

It is often said that the Chinese are Confucians in public and Daoists in private, and the two approaches do seem to balance each other. Confucianism is a rational political philosophy that emphasizes propriety, deference, duty, and self-discipline. Daoism is an intuitive philosophy that emphasizes individualism, nonconformity, and a return to nature. If a Confucian education molded scholars outwardly into responsible, ethical officials, Daoism provided some breathing room for the artist and poet inside.

---

infusing Confucianism with traditional Chinese cosmology. They emphasized the Zhou idea, taken up by Confucius, that the emperor ruled by the mandate of Heaven. Heaven itself was reconceived more abstractly as the moral force underlying the universe. Thus the moral system of Confucian society became a reflection of universal order (see "Confucius and Confucianism," page 337).

Confucian subjects turn up frequently in Han art. Among the most famous examples are the reliefs from the Wu family shrines built in 151 CE in Jiaxiang. Carved and engraved in low relief on stone slabs, the scenes were meant to teach Confucian themes such as respect for the emperor, filial piety, and wifely devotion. Daoist motifs also appear, as do figures from traditional myths and legends. Such mixed iconography is characteristic of Han art (see "A Closer Look," opposite).

When compared with the Han-dynasty banner (SEE FIG. 10–7), this late Han relief clearly shows the change that took place in the Chinese worldview in the span of 300 years. The banner places equal emphasis on heaven, earth, and the underworld; human beings are dwarfed by a great swarming of supernatural creatures and divine beings. In the relief in the Wu shrine, the focus is clearly on the human realm. The composition conveys the importance of the emperor as the holder of the

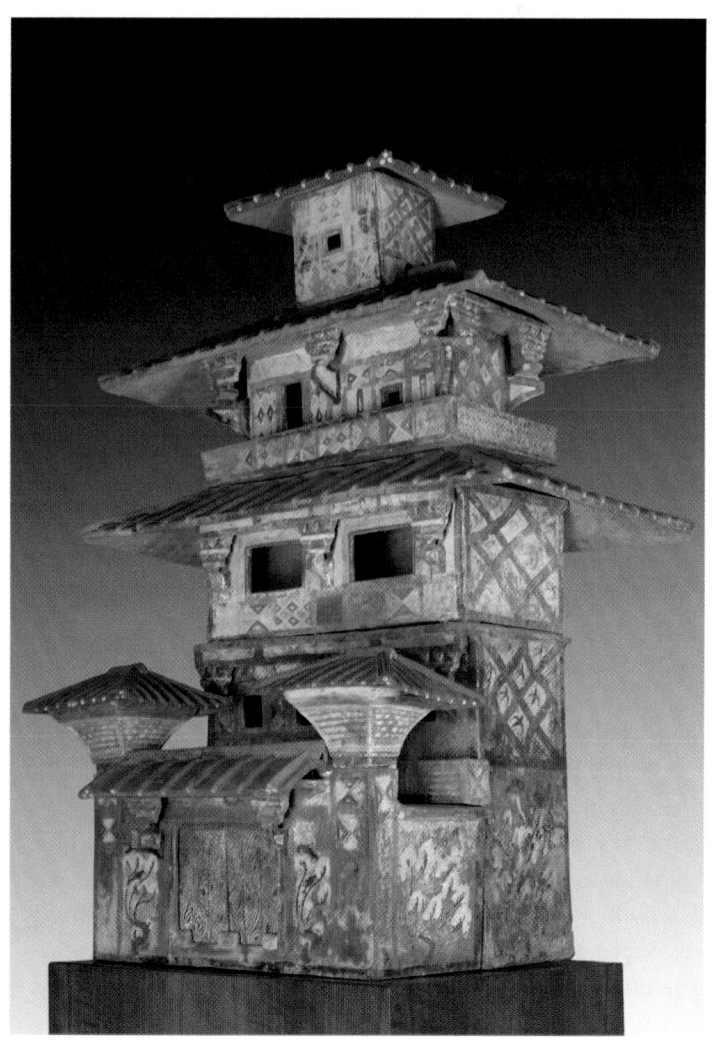

10-9 • TOMB MODEL OF A HOUSE
Eastern Han dynasty, 1st–mid 2nd century CE. Painted earthenware, 52 × 33½ × 27" (132.1 × 85.1 × 68.6 cm). The Nelson-Atkins Museum of Art, Kansas City, Missouri. Purchase, Nelson Trust (33-521)

Rubbing of a Stone Relief

Detail from a rubbing of a stone relief in the Wu family shrine (Wuliangci). Jiaxiang, Shandong. Han dynasty, 151 CE. 27½ × 66½″ (70 × 169 cm).

Birds and small figures, possibly alluding to mythical creatures or immortals.

Women—and an empress?—receiving visitors on the upper floor.

The archer Yi saves the world by shooting the extra sun-crows that were threatening it.

More visitors arriving in horse-drawn chariots.

Men—and the emperor?—receiving visitors on the lower floor.

SEE MORE: View the Closer Look feature for the Rubbing of a Stone Relief in the Wu Family Shrine (Wuliangci) www.myartslab.com

mandate of Heaven and illustrates fundamental Confucian themes of social order and decorum.

ARCHITECTURE

Contemporary literary sources are eloquent on the wonders of the Han capital. Unfortunately, nothing of Han architecture remains except ceramic models. One model of a house found in a tomb, where it was provided for the dead to use in the afterlife, represents a Han dwelling (FIG. 10–9). Its four stories are crowned with a watchtower and face a small walled courtyard. Pigs and oxen probably occupied the ground floor, while the family lived in the upper stories.

Aside from the multi-level construction, the most interesting feature of the house is the **bracketing** system (architectural elements projecting from the wall) that supports the rather broad eaves of its tiled roofs. Bracketing became a standard element of east Asian architecture, not only in private homes but more typically in palaces and temples (SEE, FOR EXAMPLE, FIG. 10–15). Another interesting aspect of the model is the elaborate painting on the exterior walls. Much of the painting is purely decorative, though some of it illustrates structural features such as posts and lintels. Still other images evoke the world outdoors, for example, the trees flanking the gateway with crows perched in their branches. Literary sources describe the walls of Han palaces as decorated with paint and lacquer, and also inlaid with precious metals and stones.

SIX DYNASTIES

With the fall of the Han in 220 CE, China splintered into three warring kingdoms. In 280 CE the empire was briefly reunited, but invasions by nomadic peoples from central Asia, a source of disruption throughout Chinese history, soon forced the court to flee south. For the next three centuries, northern and southern China developed separately. In the north, 16 kingdoms carved out by invaders rose and fell before giving way to a succession of largely foreign dynasties. Warfare was commonplace. Tens of thousands of Chinese fled south, where six short-lived dynasties succeeded each other in an age of almost constant turmoil broadly known as the Six Dynasties period or the period of the Southern and Northern dynasties (265–589 CE).

In such chaos, the Confucian system lost influence. In the south especially, many intellectuals—the creators and custodians of China's high culture—turned to Daoism, which contained a strong escapist element. Educated to serve the government, they increasingly withdrew from public life. They wandered the landscape, drank, wrote poems, practiced calligraphy, and expressed their disdain for the world through willfully eccentric behavior.

The rarefied intellectual escape route of Daoism was available only to the educated elite. Far more people sought answers in the magic and superstitions of Daoism in its religious form. Though weak and disorganized, the southern courts continued to patronize traditional Chinese culture, and Confucianism remained the official doctrine. Yet ultimately it was a newly arrived religion, Buddhism, that flourished in the troubled China of the Six Dynasties.

PAINTING

Although few paintings survive from the Six Dynasties, abundant descriptions in literary sources make clear that the period was an important one for painting. Landscape, later a major theme of Chinese art, first appeared as a subject during this era. For Daoists, wandering through China's countryside was a source of spiritual refreshment. Painters and scholars of the Six Dynasties found that wandering in the mind's eye through a painted landscape could serve the same purpose. This new emphasis on the spiritual value

of painting contrasted with the Confucian view, which had emphasized art's moral and didactic uses.

Reflections on the tradition of painting also inspired the first works on theory and aesthetics. Some of the earliest and most succinct formulations of the ideals of Chinese painting are the six principles set out by the scholar Xie He (fl. c. 500–535 CE). The first two principles in particular offer valuable insight into the spirit in which China's painters worked.

The first principle announces that "spirit consonance" imbues a painting with "life's movement." This "spirit" is the Daoist *qi*, the breath that animates all creation, the energy that flows through all things. When a painting has *qi*, it will be alive with inner essence, not merely outward resemblance. Artists must cultivate their own spirit so that this universal energy flows through them and infuses their work. The second principle recognizes that brushstrokes are the "bones" of a picture, its primary structural element. Traditional Chinese judge a painting above all by the quality of its brushwork. Each brushstroke is a vehicle of expression; it is through the vitality of a painter's brushwork that "spirit consonance" makes itself felt. We can sense this attitude already in the rapid, confident brushstrokes that outline the figures of the Han banner (SEE FIG. 10–7) and again in the more controlled, rhythmical lines of one of the most important works associated with this period, a painted scroll known as *Admonitions of the Imperial Instructress to Court Ladies*. Attributed to the painter Gu Kaizhi (344–407 CE), it alternates illustrations and text to relate seven Confucian stories of wifely virtue from Chinese history.

The first illustration depicts the courage of Lady Feng (**FIG. 10–10**). An escaped circus bear rushes toward her husband, a Han emperor, who is filled with fear. Behind his throne, two female servants have turned to run away. Before him, two male attendants, themselves on the verge of panic, try to fend off the bear with

10-10 • After Gu Kaizhi DETAIL OF *ADMONITIONS OF THE IMPERIAL INSTRUCTRESS TO COURT LADIES*
Six Dynasties period. Handscroll, ink and colors on silk, 9¾″ × 11′6″ (24.8 × 348.2 cm). British Museum, London.

Confucius and Confucianism

Confucius was born in 551 BCE in the state of Lu, roughly present-day Shandong Province, into a declining aristocratic family. While still in his teens he set his heart on becoming a scholar; by his early twenties he had begun to teach.

By this time, wars for supremacy had begun among the various states of China, and the traditional social fabric seemed to be breaking down. Looking back to the early Zhou dynasty as a sort of golden age, Confucius thought about how a just and harmonious society could again emerge. For many years he sought a ruler who would put his ideas into effect, but to no avail. Frustrated, he spent his final years teaching. After his death in 479 BCE, his conversations with his students were collected by his disciples and their followers into a book known in English as the *Analects*, which is the only record of his words.

At the heart of Confucian thought is the concept of *ren* (human-heartedness). *Ren* emphasizes morality and empathy as the basic standards for all human interaction. The virtue of *ren* is most fully realized in the Confucian ideal of the *junzi* (gentleman). Originally indicating noble birth, the term was redefined to mean one who through education and self-cultivation had become a superior person, right-thinking and right-acting in all situations. A *junzi* is the opposite of a petty or small-minded person. His characteristics include moderation, integrity, self-control, loyalty, reciprocity, and altruism. His primary concern is justice.

Together with human-heartedness and justice, Confucius emphasized *li* (etiquette). *Li* includes everyday manners as well as ritual, ceremony, and protocol—the formalities of all social conduct and interaction. Such forms, Confucius felt, choreographed life so that an entire society moved in harmony. *Ren* and *li* operate in the realm of the Five Constant Relationships that define Confucian society: parent and child, husband and wife, elder sibling and younger sibling, elder friend and younger friend, ruler and subject. Deference to age is clearly built into this view, as is the deference to authority that made Confucianism attractive to emperors. Yet responsibilities flow the other way as well: The duty of a ruler is to earn the loyalty of subjects, of a husband to earn the respect of his wife, of age to guide youth wisely.

During the early years of the People's Republic of China, and especially during the Great Proletarian Cultural Revolution (1966–1976), Confucius and Confucian thought were denigrated. Recently, however, Confucian temples in Beijing and elsewhere have been restored. Notably, the Chinese government has used the philosopher's name officially in establishing hundreds of Confucius Institutes in more than 80 countries, to promote the learning of the Chinese language abroad.

---

spears. Only Lady Feng is calm as she rushes forward to place herself between the beast and the emperor.

The figures are drawn with a brush in a thin, even-width line, and a few outlined areas are filled with color. Facial features, especially those of the men, are quite well depicted. Movement and emotion are shown through conventions such as the scarves flowing from Lady Feng's dress, indicating that she is rushing forward, and the upturned strings on both sides of the emperor's head, suggesting his fear. There is no hint of a setting; instead, the artist relies on careful placement of the figures to create a sense of depth.

The painting is on silk, which was typically woven in bands about 12 inches wide and up to 20 or 30 feet long. Early Chinese painters thus developed the format used here, the **handscroll**—a long, narrow, horizontal composition, compact enough to be held in the hand when rolled up. Handscrolls are intimate works, meant to be viewed by only two or three people at a time. They were not displayed completely unrolled as we commonly see them today in museums. Rather, viewers would open a scroll and savor it slowly from right to left, displaying only an arm's length at a time.

CALLIGRAPHY

The emphasis on the expressive quality and structural importance of brushstrokes finds its purest embodiment in calligraphy. The same brushes are used for both painting and calligraphy, and a relationship between them was recognized as early as Han times. In his teachings, Confucius had extolled the importance of the pursuit of knowledge and the arts. Among the visual arts, painting was felt to reflect moral concerns, while calligraphy was believed to reveal the character of the writer.

Calligraphy is regarded as one of the highest forms of expression in China. For more than 2,000 years, China's **literati**, Confucian scholars and literary men who also served the government as officials, have enjoyed being connoisseurs and practitioners of this abstract art. During the fourth century CE, calligraphy came to full maturity. The most important practitioner of the day was Wang Xizhi (c. 307–365), whose works have served as models of excellence for all subsequent generations. The example here comes from a letter, now somewhat damaged and mounted as part of an album, known as *Feng Ju* (FIG. 10–11).

Feng Ju is an example of "walking" or semicursive style, which is neither too formal nor too free but is done in a relaxed, easy-going manner. Brushstrokes vary in width and length, creating rhythmic vitality. Individual characters remain distinct, yet within each character the strokes are run together and simplified as the brush moves from one to the other without lifting off the page. The effect is fluid and graceful, yet still strong and dynamic. The

10-11 • Wang Xizhi PORTION OF A LETTER FROM THE FENG JU ALBUM

Six Dynasties period, mid-4th century CE. Ink on paper, 9¾ × 18½″ (24.7 × 46.8 cm). National Palace Museum, Taibei, Taiwan, Republic of China.

The stamped characters that appear on Chinese artworks are **seals**—personal emblems. The use of seals dates from the Zhou dynasty, and to this day seals traditionally employ the archaic characters, known appropriately as "seal script," of the Zhou or Qin. Cut in stone, a seal may state a formal, given name, or it may state any of the numerous personal names that China's painters and writers adopted throughout their lives. A treasured work of art often bears not only the seal of its maker, but also those of collectors and admirers through the centuries. In the Chinese view, these do not disfigure the work but add another layer of interest. This sample of Wang Xizhi's calligraphy, for example, bears the seals of two Song-dynasty emperors, a Song official, a famous collector of the sixteenth century, and two Qing-dynasty emperors of the eighteenth and nineteenth centuries.

walking style as developed by Wang Xizhi came to be officially accepted and learned along with other script styles.

BUDDHIST ART AND ARCHITECTURE

Buddhism originated in India during the fifth century BCE (see Chapter 9), then gradually spread north into central Asia. With the opening of the Silk Road during the Han dynasty, its influence reached China. To the Chinese of the Six Dynasties, beset by constant warfare and social devastation, Buddhism offered consolation in life and the promise of salvation after death. The faith spread throughout the country to all social levels, first in the north, where many of the invaders promoted it as the official religion, then

slightly later in the south, where it found its first great patron in the emperor Liang Wu Di (r. 502–549 CE). Thousands of temples and monasteries were built, and many people became monks and nuns.

Almost nothing remains in China of the Buddhist architecture of the Six Dynasties, but we can see what it must have looked like in the Japanese temple Horyuji (SEE FIG. 11–4), which was based on Chinese models of this period. The slender forms and linear grace of Horyuji might be compared to the figures in Gu Kaizhi's handscroll (SEE FIG. 10–10), and they indicate the delicate, almost weightless style cultivated in southern China.

ROCK-CUT CAVES OF THE SILK ROAD. The most impressive works of Buddhist art surviving from the Six Dynasties are the hundreds of northern rock-cut caves along the trade routes between Xinjiang in central Asia and the Yellow River Valley. Both the caves and the sculptures that fill them were carved from the solid rock of the cliffs. Small caves high above the ground were retreats for monks and pilgrims, while larger caves at the base of the cliffs were wayside shrines and temples.

The caves at Yungang, in Shanxi Province in central China, contain many examples of the earliest phase of Buddhist sculpture in China, including the monumental seated Buddha in Cave 20 **(FIG. 10–12)**. The figure was carved in the latter part of the fifth century by the imperial decree of a ruler of the Northern Wei dynasty (386–534 CE), the longest-lived and most stable of the northern kingdoms. Most Wei rulers were avid patrons of Buddhism, and under their rule the religion made its greatest advances in the north.

The front part of the cave has crumbled away, and the 45-foot statue, now exposed to the open air, is clearly visible from a distance. The elongated ears, protuberance on the head (*ushnisha*), and monk's robe are traditional attributes of the Buddha. The masklike face, full torso, massive shoulders, and shallow, stylized drapery indicate strong central Asian influence. The overall effect of this colossus is remote and austere, less human than the more sensuous expression of the early Buddhist traditions in India.

SUI AND TANG DYNASTIES

In 581 CE, a general from the last of the northern dynasties replaced a child emperor and established a dynasty of his own, the Sui. Defeating all opposition, he molded China into a centralized empire as it had been in Han times. The short-lived Sui dynasty fell in 618, but, in reunifying the empire, paved the way for one of the greatest dynasties in Chinese history: the Tang (618–907). Even today many Chinese living abroad still call themselves "Tang people." To them, Tang implies that part of the Chinese character that is strong and vigorous (especially in military power), noble and idealistic, but also realistic and pragmatic.

10-12 • SEATED BUDDHA, CAVE 20, YUNGANG
Datong, Shanxi. Northern Wei dynasty, c. 460. Stone, height 45′ (13.7 m).

BUDDHIST ART AND ARCHITECTURE

The new Sui emperor was a devout Buddhist, and his reunification of China coincided with a fusion of the several styles of Buddhist sculpture that had developed. This new style is seen in a bronze altar to Amitabha Buddha **(FIG. 10–13)**, one of the many Buddhas of Mahayana Buddhism. Amitabha dwelled in the Western Pure Land, a paradise into which his faithful followers were promised rebirth. With its comparatively simple message of salvation, the Pure Land sect eventually became the most popular form of Buddhism in China and one of the most popular in Japan (see Chapter 11).

The altar depicts Amitabha in his paradise, seated on a lotus throne beneath a canopy of trees. Each leaf cluster is set with jewels. Seven celestial figures sit on the topmost clusters, and ropes of "pearls" hang from the tree trunks. Behind Amitabha's head is a halo of flames. To his left, the bodhisattva Guanyin holds a pomegranate; to his right, another bodhisattva clasps his hands in prayer. Behind are four disciples who first preached the teachings of the Buddha. On the lower level, an incense burner is flanked by

10-13 • ALTAR TO AMITABHA BUDDHA
Sui dynasty, 593. Bronze, height 30⅛″ (76.5 cm). Museum of Fine Arts, Boston. Gift of Mrs. W. Scott Fitz (22.407) and Gift of Edward Holmes Jackson in memory of his mother, Mrs. W. Scott Fitz (47.1407–1412)

10-14 • THE WESTERN PARADISE OF AMITABHA BUDDHA
Detail of a wall painting in Cave 217, Dunhuang, Gansu. Tang dynasty, c. 750. 10′2″ × 16′ (3.1 × 4.86 m).

seated lions and two smaller bodhisattvas. Focusing on Amitabha's benign expression and filled with objects symbolizing his power, the altar combines the sensuality of Indian styles, the schematic abstraction of central Asian art, and the Chinese emphasis on linear grace and rhythm into a harmonious new style.

Buddhism reached its greatest development in China during the subsequent Tang Dynasty, which for nearly three centuries ruled China and controlled much of Central Asia. From emperors and empresses to common peasants, virtually the entire country adopted the Buddhist faith. A Tang vision of the most popular sect, Pure Land, was expressed in a wall painting from a cave in Dunhuang **(FIG. 10–14)**. A major stop along the Silk Road, Dunhuang has nearly 500 caves carved out of its sandy cliffs, all filled with painted clay sculpture and decorated with wall paintings from floor to ceiling. The site was worked on continuously from the fourth to the fourteenth century, a period of almost 1,000 years. In the detail shown here, Amitabha Buddha is seated in the center, surrounded by four bodhisattvas, who serve as his messengers to the

world. Two other groups of bodhisattvas are clustered at the right and left. In the foreground, musicians and dancers create a heavenly atmosphere. In the background, great halls and towers rise. The artist has imagined the Western Paradise in terms of the grandeur of Tang palaces. Indeed, the lavish entertainment depicted could just as easily be taking place at the imperial court. This worldly vision of paradise, recorded with great attention to naturalism in the architectural setting, gives us our best visualization of the splendor of Tang civilization at a time when Chang'an (present-day Xi'an) was probably the greatest city in the world.

The early Tang emperors proclaimed a policy of religious tolerance, but during the ninth century a conservative reaction set in. Confucianism was reasserted and Buddhism was briefly persecuted as a "foreign" religion. Thousands of temples, shrines, and monasteries were destroyed and innumerable bronze statues melted down. Nevertheless, several Buddhist structures survive from the Tang dynasty. One of them, the Nanchan Temple, is the earliest important example of surviving Chinese architecture.

NANCHAN TEMPLE. Of the few structures earlier than 1400 CE to have survived, the Nanchan Temple is the most significant, for it shows characteristics of both temples and palaces of the Tang Dynasty (FIG. 10–15). Located on Mount Wutai (Wutaishan) in the eastern part of Shanxi Province, this small hall was constructed in 782. The tiled roof, seen earlier in the Han tomb model (SEE FIG. 10–9), has taken on a curved silhouette. Quite subtle here, this curve became increasingly pronounced in later centuries. The very broad overhanging eaves are supported by a correspondingly elaborate bracketing system.

Also typical is the bay system of construction, in which a cubic unit of space, a bay, is formed by four posts and their lintels. The bay functioned in Chinese architecture as a **module**, a basic unit of construction. To create larger structures, an architect multiplied the number of bays. Thus the Nanchan Temple—modest in scope with three bays—gives an idea of the vast, multi-storied palaces of the Tang depicted in such paintings as FIGURE 10–14.

GREAT WILD GOOSE PAGODA. Another important monument of Tang architecture is the Great Wild Goose Pagoda at the Ci'en Temple in Chang'an, the Tang capital (FIG. 10–16). The temple was constructed in 645 for the famous monk Xuanzang (600–664) on his return from a 16-year pilgrimage to India. At the Ci'en Temple, Xuanzang taught and translated the materials he had brought back with him.

The **pagoda**, a typical east Asian Buddhist structure, originated in the Indian Buddhist stupa, the elaborate burial mound that housed relics of the Buddha (see "Pagodas," page 345). In India the stupa had developed a multi-storied form in the Gandhara region under the Kushan dynasty (c. 50–250 CE). In China this form blended with a traditional Han watchtower to produce the pagoda. Built entirely in masonry, the Great Wild Goose Pagoda nevertheless imitates the wooden architecture of the time. The walls are decorated in low relief to resemble bays,

and bracket systems are reproduced under the projecting roofs of each story. Although modified and repaired in later times (its seven stories were originally five, and a new finial has been added), the pagoda still preserves the essence of Tang architecture in its simplicity, symmetry, proportions, and grace.

10-16 • GREAT WILD GOOSE PAGODA AT CI'EN TEMPLE, CHANG'AN
Shanxi. Tang dynasty, first erected 645; rebuilt mid 8th century CE.

The Silk Road during the Tang Period

Under a series of ambitious and forceful Tang emperors, Chinese control once again extended over central Asia. Goods, ideas, and influence flowed along the Silk Road. In the South China Sea, Arab and Persian ships carried on a lively trade with coastal cities. Chinese cultural influence in east Asia was so important that Japan and Korea sent thousands of students to study Chinese civilization.

Cosmopolitan and tolerant, Tang China was confident and curious about the world. Many foreigners came to the splendid new capital Chang'an (present-day Xi'an), and they are often depicted in the art of the period. A ceramic statue of a camel carrying a troupe of musicians reflects the Tang fascination with the "exotic" Turkic cultures of central Asia. The three bearded musicians (one with his back to us) are central Asian, while the two smooth-shaven ones are Han Chinese. Bactrian, or two-humped, camels, themselves exotic central Asian "visitors," were beasts of burden in the caravans that traversed the Silk Road. The stringed lute (which the Chinese called the *pipa*) came from central Asia to become a lasting part of Chinese music.

Stylistically, the statue reveals a new interest in naturalism, an important trend in both painting and sculpture. Compared with the rigid, staring ceramic soldiers of the first emperor of Qin, this Tang band is alive with gesture and expression. The majestic camel throws its head back; the musicians are vividly captured in mid-performance. Ceramic figurines such as this, produced by the thousands for Tang tombs, offer glimpses into the gorgeous variety of Tang life. The statue's three-color glaze technique was a specialty of Tang ceramicists. The glazes—usually chosen from a restricted palette of amber-yellow, green, and blue— were splashed freely and allowed to run over the surface during firing to convey a feeling of spontaneity. The technique is emblematic of Tang culture itself in its robust, colorful, and cosmopolitan expressiveness.

The Silk Road had first flourished in the second century CE. A 5,000-mile network of caravan routes from the Han capital (near present-day Luoyang, Henan, on the Yellow River) to Rome, it brought Chinese luxury goods to Western markets.

The journey began at the Jade Gate (Yumen) at the westernmost end of the Great Wall, where Chinese merchants turned their goods over to central Asian traders. Goods would change hands many more times before reaching the Mediterranean. Caravans headed first for the nearby desert oasis of Dunhuang. Here northern and southern routes diverged to skirt the vast Taklamakan Desert. At Khotan, in western China, farther west than the area shown in MAP 10–1, travelers on the southern route could turn off toward a mountain pass into Kashmir, in northern India. Or they could continue on, meeting up with the northern route at Kashgar, on the western border of the Taklamakan, before proceeding over the Pamir Mountains into present-day Afghanistan. There, travelers could turn off into present-day Pakistan and India, or travel west through present-day Uzbekistan, Iran, and Iraq, arriving finally at Antioch, in Syria, on the coast of the Mediterranean. From there, land and sea routes led to Rome.

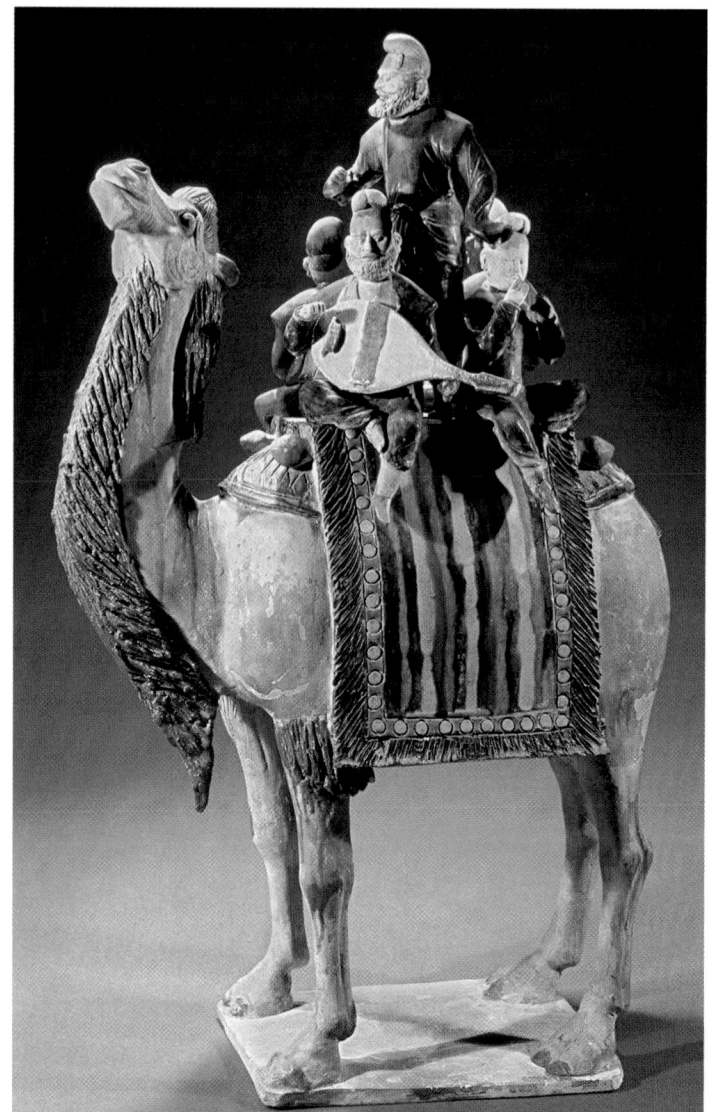

CAMEL CARRYING A GROUP OF MUSICIANS
From a tomb near Xi'an, Shanxi. Tang dynasty, c. mid 8th century CE. Earthenware with three-color glazes, height 26⅛" (66.5 cm). National Museum, Beijing.

10–17 • Attributed to Emperor Huizong DETAIL OF LADIES PREPARING NEWLY WOVEN SILK
Copy after a lost Tang dynasty painting by Zhang Xuan. Northern Song dynasty, early 12th century CE. Handscroll, ink and colors on silk, 14½ × 57½″ (36 × 145.3 cm). Museum of Fine Arts, Boston. Chinese and Japanese Special Fund (12.886)

Confucius said of himself, "I merely transmit, I do not create; I love and revere the ancients." In this spirit, Chinese painters regularly copied paintings of earlier masters. Painters made copies both to absorb the lessons of their great predecessors and to perpetuate the achievements of the past. In later centuries, they took up the practice of regularly executing a work "in the manner of" some particularly revered ancient master. This was at once an act of homage, a declaration of artistic allegiance, and a way of reinforcing a personal connection with the past.

FIGURE PAINTING

Later artists looking back on their heritage recognized the Tang dynasty as China's great age of figure painting. Unfortunately, very few scroll paintings that can be definitely identified as Tang still exist. We can get some idea of the character of Tang figure painting from the wall paintings of Dunhuang (SEE FIG. 10–14). Another way to savor the particular flavor of Tang painting is to look at copies made by later, Song-dynasty artists. An outstanding example can be seen in *Ladies Preparing Newly Woven Silk*, attributed to Huizong (r. 1101–1126 CE), the last emperor of the Northern Song dynasty **(FIG. 10–17)**. A long handscroll, it depicts the activities of court women as they weave and iron silk. An inscription on the scroll informs us that the painting is a copy of a famous work by Zhang Xuan, an eighth-century painter known for his depictions of women at the Tang court. The original no longer exists, so we cannot know how faithful the copy is. Still, its refined lines and bright colors seem to share the grace and dignity of Tang sculpture and architecture. Two horses and riders **(FIG. 10–18)**, a man and a woman, made for use as tomb furnishings, reveal more of the robust naturalism and exuberance achieved during the Tang period. Accurate in proportion and lively in demeanor, the figures are not glazed (as is the tomb figure in "The Silk Road during the Tang Period," opposite) but are "cold-painted" using pigments after firing to render details of costume and facial features. The pair are indicative of the lively participation of women as well as men in sport and riding.

10–18 • TWO EQUESTRIAN FIGURES
Tang dynasty, first half 8th century CE. Molded, reddish-buff earthenware with cold-painted pigments over white ground, height (male figure) 14½″ (37 cm). Arthur M. Sackler Museum, Harvard Art Museum, Cambridge, Massachusetts. Gift of Anthony M. Solomon (2003.207.1-2)

The figures, one male, one female, each have pointed boots and are mounted on a standing, saddled and bridled horse; their hands are positioned to hold the reins. The male figure wears a tall, elaborately embellished hat, and the female figure has her hair arranged in a topknot.

SONG DYNASTY

A brief period of disintegration followed the fall of the Tang before China was again united, this time under the Song dynasty (960–1279), which established a new capital at Bianjing (present-day Kaifeng), near the Yellow River. In contrast to the outgoing confidence of the Tang, the mood during the Song was more introspective, a reflection of China's weakened military situation. In 1126 the Jurchen tribes of Manchuria invaded China, sacked the capital, and took possession of much of the northern part of the country. Song forces withdrew south and established a new capital at Hangzhou. From this point on, the dynasty is known as the Southern Song (1127–1179), with the first portion called in retrospect the Northern Song (960–1126).

Although China's territory had diminished, its wealth had increased because of advances in agriculture, commerce, and technology begun under the Tang. Patronage was plentiful, and the arts flourished.

SEATED GUANYIN BODHISATTVA.   In spite of changing political fortunes in the eleventh and twelfth centuries, artists continued to create splendid works. No hint of political disruption or religious questioning intrudes on the sublime grace and beauty of this seated Guanyin bodhisattva (FIG. 10–19). Bodhisattvas, beings who are close to enlightenment but who voluntarily remain on earth to help others achieve enlightenment, are represented as young princes wearing royal garments and jewelry, their finery indicative of their worldly but virtuous lives. Guanyin is the Bodhisattva of Infinite Compassion, who appears in many guises, in this case as the Water and Moon Guanyin. He sits on rocks by the sea, in the position known as royal ease. His right arm rests on his raised and

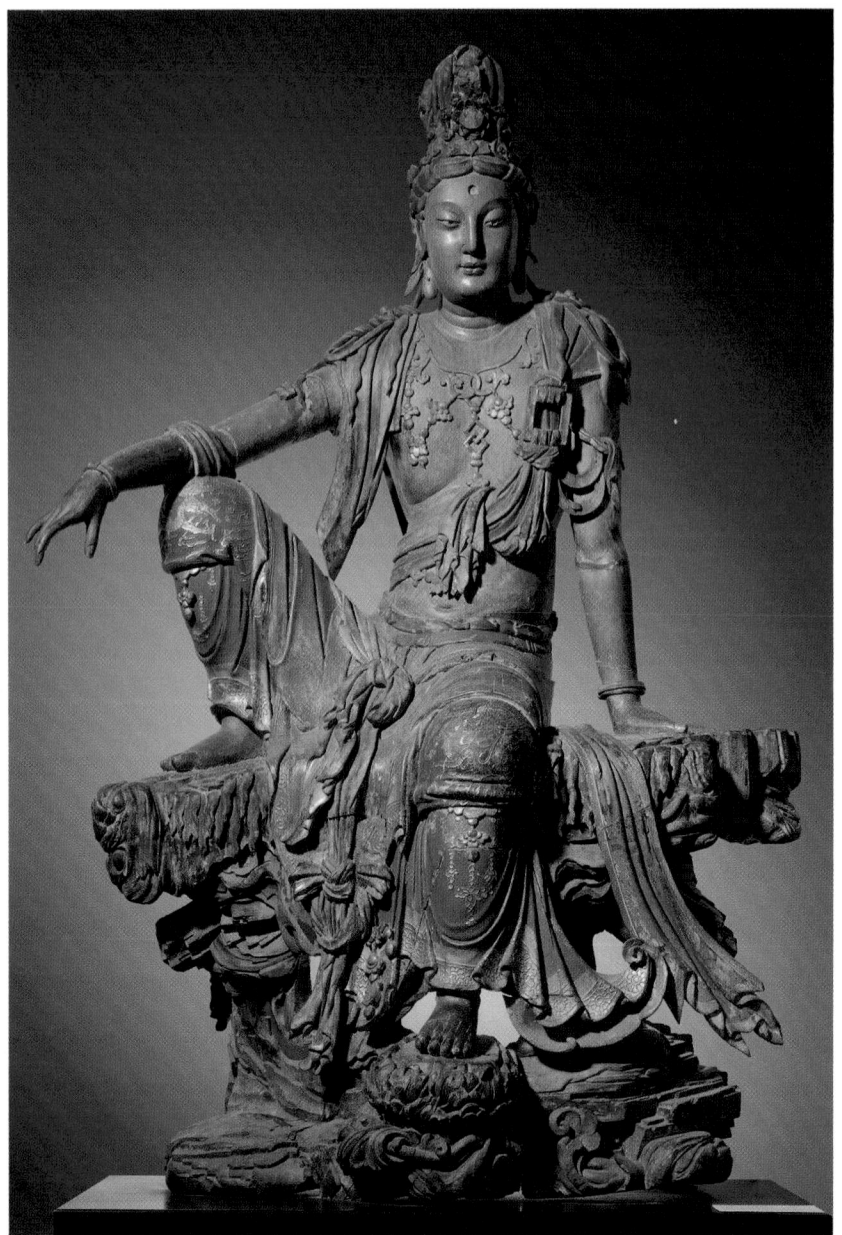

10-19 • SEATED GUANYIN BODHISATTVA
Liao dynasty, 10th–12th century CE. Wood with paint and gold, 95 × 65″ (241.3 × 165.1 cm). The Nelson-Atkins Museum of Art, Kansas City, Missouri. Purchase, Nelson Trust (34–10)

ELEMENTS OF ARCHITECTURE | Pagodas

Pagodas developed from Indian stupas as Buddhism spread northeast along the Silk Road. Stupas merged with the watchtowers of Han-dynasty China in multi-storied stone or wood structures with projecting tiled roofs. This transformation culminated in wooden pagodas with upward-curving roofs supported by elaborate bracketing in China, Korea, and Japan. Buddhist pagodas retain the *axis mundi* masts of stupas. Like their south Asian prototypes, early east Asian pagodas were symbolic rather than enclosing structures. Later examples often provided access to the ground floor and sometimes to upper levels.

early stupa
India, 2nd century BCE

later stupa
Central Asia,
5th–6th century CE

watchtower
China, Han dynasty,
c. 206 BCE–220 CE

stone pagoda
northwestern China,
c. 5th century CE

wooden pagoda
Japan, 7th century CE

SEE MORE: View a simulation about pagodas www.myartslab.com

bent right knee and his left arm and foot hang down, the foot touching a lotus blossom. The wooden figure was carved in the eleventh or twelfth century in a territory on the northern border of Song China, a region ruled by the Liao dynasty (907–1125); the painting and gilding were restored in the sixteenth century.

Song culture is noted for its refined taste and intellectual grandeur. Where the Tang had reveled in exoticism, eagerly absorbing influences from Persia, India, and Central Asia, Song culture was more self-consciously Chinese. Philosophy experienced its most creative era since the "one hundred schools" of the Zhou. Song scholarship was brilliant, especially in history, and its poetry is noted for its depth. Perhaps the finest expressions of the Song are in art, especially painting and ceramics.

PHILOSOPHY: NEO-CONFUCIANISM

Song philosophers continued the process, begun during the Tang, of restoring Confucianism to dominance. In strengthening Confucian thought, they drew on Daoist and especially Buddhist ideas, even as they openly rejected Buddhism itself as foreign. These innovations provided Confucianism with a metaphysical aspect it had previously lacked, allowing it to propose a more satisfying, all-embracing explanation of the universe. This new synthesis of China's three main paths of thought is called Neo-Confucianism.

Neo-Confucianism teaches that the universe consists of two interacting forces known as *li* (principle or idea) and *qi* (matter). All pine trees, for example, consist of an underlying *li* we might call "Pine Tree Idea" brought into the material world through *qi*. All the *li* of the universe, including humans, are but aspects of an eternal first principle known as the Great Ultimate (*taiji*), which is completely present in every object. Our task as human beings is to rid our *qi* of impurities through education and self-cultivation so that our *li* may realize its oneness with the Great Ultimate. This lifelong process resembles the striving to attain buddhahood, and if we persist in our attempts, one day we will be enlightened—the term itself comes directly from Buddhism.

NORTHERN SONG PAINTING

The Neo-Confucian ideas found visual expression in art, especially in landscape, which became the most highly esteemed subject for painting. Northern Song artists studied nature closely to master its many appearances—the way each species of tree grew, the distinctive character of each rock formation, the changes of the seasons, the myriad birds, blossoms, and insects. This passion for realistic detail was the artist's form of self-cultivation: Mastering outward forms showed an understanding of the principles behind them.

Yet despite the convincing accumulation of detail, the paintings

10-20 • Fan Kuan TRAVELERS AMONG MOUNTAINS AND STREAMS
Northern Song dynasty, early 11th century CE. Hanging scroll, ink and colors on silk, height 6′9½″ (2.06 m). National Palace Museum, Taibei, Taiwan, Republic of China.

the desire for the spiritual communion with nature that was the key to enlightenment. As the tradition progressed, landscape also became a vehicle for conveying human emotions, even for speaking indirectly of one's own deepest feelings.

In the earliest times, art reflected the mythocentric worldview of the ancient Chinese. Later, as religion came to dominate people's lives, the focus of art shifted, and religious images and human actions became important subjects. Subsequently, during the Song dynasty, artists developed landscape as the chief means of expression, preferring to avoid direct depiction of the human condition and to show ideals in a symbolic manner. The major form of Chinese artistic expression thus moved from the mythical, through the religious and ethical, and finally to the philosophical and aesthetic.

FAN KUAN.   One of the first great masters of Song landscape was the eleventh-century painter Fan Kuan (active c. 990–1030 CE), whose surviving major work, **TRAVELERS AMONG MOUNTAINS AND STREAMS**, is regarded as one of the great monuments of Chinese art (**FIG. 10–20**). The work is physically large—almost 7 feet high—but the sense of monumentality also radiates from the composition itself, which makes its impression even when much reduced.

The composition unfolds in three stages, comparable to three acts of a drama. At the bottom a large, low-lying group of rocks, taking up about one-eighth of the picture surface, establishes the extreme foreground. The rest of the landscape pushes back from this point. In anticipating the shape and substance of the mountains to come, the rocks introduce the main theme of the work, much as the first act of a drama introduces the principal characters. In the middle ground, travelers and their mules are coming from the right. Their size confirms our human scale—how small we are, how vast is nature. This middle ground takes up twice as much picture surface as the foreground, and, like the second act of a play, shows variation and development. Instead of a solid mass, the rocks here are separated into two groups by a waterfall that is spanned by a bridge. In the hills to the right, the rooftops of a temple stand out above the trees.

Mist veils the transition to the background, with the result that the mountain looms suddenly. This background area, almost twice as large as the foreground and middle ground combined, is the climactic third act of the drama. As our eyes begin their ascent, the mountain solidifies. Its ponderous weight increases as it billows upward, finally bursting into the sprays of energetic brushstrokes that describe the scrubby growth on top. To the right, a slender waterfall plummets, not to balance the powerful upward thrust of the mountain but simply to enhance it by contrast. The whole painting, then, conveys the feeling of climbing a high mountain, leaving the human world behind to come face to face with the Great Ultimate in a spiritual communion.

All the elements are depicted with precise detail and in proper scale. Jagged brushstrokes describe the contours of rocks and trees and express their rugged character. Layers of short, staccato strokes

do not record a specific site. The artist's goal was to paint the eternal essence of "mountain-ness," for example, not to reproduce the appearance of a particular mountain. Painting a landscape required an artist to orchestrate his cumulative understanding of *li* in all its aspects—mountains and rocks, streams and waterfalls, trees and grasses, clouds and mist. A landscape painting thus expressed

10-21 • Xu Daoning SECTION OF FISHING IN A MOUNTAIN STREAM
Northern Song dynasty, mid 11th century CE. Handscroll, ink on silk, 19″ × 6′10″ (48.9 cm × 2.09 m).
The Nelson-Atkins Museum of Art, Kansas City, Missouri. Purchase, Nelson Trust (33–1559)

(translated as "raindrop texture" from the Chinese) accurately mimic the texture of the rock surface. Spatial recession from foreground through middle ground to background is logically and convincingly handled, if not quite continuous.

Although it contains realistic details, the landscape represents no specific place. In its forms, the artist expresses the ideal forms behind appearances; in the rational, ordered composition, he expresses the intelligence of the universe. The arrangement of the mountains, with the central peak flanked by lesser peaks on each side, seems to reflect both the ancient Confucian notion of social hierarchy, with the emperor flanked by his ministers, and the Buddhist motif of the Buddha with bodhisattvas at his side. The landscape, a view of nature uncorrupted by human habitation, expresses a kind of Daoist ideal. Thus we find the three strains of Chinese thought united, much as they are in Neo-Confucianism itself.

The ability of Chinese landscape painters to take us out of ourselves and to let us wander freely through their sites is closely linked to the avoidance of perspective as it is understood in the West. Fifteenth-century European painters, searching for fidelity to appearances, developed a scientific system for recording exactly the view that could be seen from a single, fixed vantage point. The goal of Chinese painting is precisely to avoid such limits and show a totality beyond what we are normally given to see. If the ideal for centuries of Western painters was to render what can be seen from a fixed viewpoint, that of Chinese artists was to reveal nature through a distant, all-seeing, and mobile viewpoint.

XU DAONING. The sense of shifting perspective is clearest in the handscroll, where our vantage point changes constantly as we move through the painting. One of the finest handscrolls to survive from the Northern Song is **FISHING IN A MOUNTAIN STREAM (FIG. 10–21)**, a painting executed in the middle of the eleventh century by Xu Daoning (c. 970–c. 1052). Starting from a thatched hut in the right foreground, we follow a path that leads to a broad, open view of a deep vista dissolving into distant mists and mountain peaks. (Remember that viewers observed only a small section of the scroll at a time. To mimic this effect, use two pieces of paper to frame a small viewing area, then move them slowly leftward.) Crossing over

a small footbridge, we are brought back to the foreground with the beginning of a central group of high mountains that show extraordinary shapes. Again our path winds back along the bank, and we have a spectacular view of the highest peaks from another small footbridge the artist has placed for us. At the far side of the bridge, we find ourselves looking up into a deep valley, where a stream lures our eyes far into the distance. We can imagine ourselves resting for a moment in the small pavilion halfway up the valley on the right. Or perhaps we may spend some time with the fishers in their boats as the valley gives way to a second, smaller group of mountains, serving both as an echo of the spectacular central group and as a transition to the painting's finale, a broad, open vista. As we cross the bridge here, we meet travelers coming toward us who will have our experience in reverse. Gazing out into the distance and reflecting on our journey, we again feel that sense of communion with nature that is the goal of Chinese artistic expression.

Such handscrolls have no counterpart in the Western visual arts and are often compared instead to the tradition of Western music, especially symphonic compositions. Both are generated from opening motifs that are developed and varied, both are revealed over time, and in both our sense of the overall structure relies on memory, for we do not see the scroll or hear the composition all at once.

ZHANG ZEDUAN. The Northern Song fascination with precision extended to details within landscape. The emperor Huizong, whose copy of *Ladies Preparing Newly Woven Silk* was seen in FIGURE 10–17, gathered around himself a group of court painters who shared his passion for quiet, exquisitely detailed, delicately colored paintings of birds and flowers. Other painters specialized in domestic and wild animals, still others in palaces and buildings. One of the most spectacular products of this passion for observation is **SPRING FESTIVAL ON THE RIVER**, a long handscroll painted in the late eleventh or early twelfth century by Zhang Zeduan, an artist connected to the court **(FIG. 10–22)**. Beyond its considerable visual delights, the painting is also a valuable record of daily life in the Song capital.

The painting depicts a festival day when local inhabitants and visitors from the countryside thronged the streets. One high

10-22 • Zhang Zeduan SECTION OF SPRING FESTIVAL ON THE RIVER
Northern Song dynasty, late 11th–early 12th century CE. Handscroll, ink and colors on silk, 9½″ ×
7′4″ (24.8 × 2.28 m). The Palace Museum, Beijing.

point is the scene reproduced here, which takes place at the
Rainbow Bridge. The large boat to the right is probably bringing
goods from the southern part of China up the Grand Canal that
ran through the city at that time. The sailors are preparing to pass
beneath the bridge by lowering the sail and taking down the
mast. Excited figures on ship and shore gesture wildly, shouting
orders and advice, while a noisy crowd gathers at the bridge
railing to watch. Stalls on the bridge are selling food and other
merchandise; wine shops and eating places line the banks of the
canal. Everyone is on the move. Some people are busy carrying
goods, some are shopping, some are simply enjoying themselves.
Each figure is splendidly animated and full of purpose; the
depiction of buildings and boats is highly detailed, almost
encyclopedic.

Little is known about the painter Zhang Zeduan other than
that he was a member of the scholar-official class, the highly
educated elite of imperial China. His painting demonstrates skill in
the fine-line architectural drawing called *jiehua* ("ruled-line")
painting. Interestingly, some of Zhang Zeduan's peers were already

beginning to cultivate quite a different attitude toward painting as
a form of artistic expression, one that placed overt display of
technical skill at the lowest end of the scale of values. This
emerging scholarly aesthetic, developed by China's literati, later
came to dominate Chinese thinking about art.

SOUTHERN SONG PAINTING AND CERAMICS

Landscape painting took a very different course after the fall of the
north to the Jurchen in 1127, and the removal of the court to its
new capital in the south, Hangzhou.

XIA GUI.   A new sensibility is reflected in the extant portion of
TWELVE VIEWS OF LANDSCAPE (FIG. 10–23) by Xia Gui (fl. c.
1195–1235), a member of the newly established Academy of
Painters. In general, academy members continued to favor such
subjects as birds and flowers in the highly refined, elegantly colored
court style patronized earlier by Huizong (SEE FIG. 10–17). Xia
Gui, however, was interested in landscape and cultivated his own
style. Only the last four of the 12 views that originally made up

10-23 • Xia Gui SECTION OF TWELVE VIEWS OF LANDSCAPE
Southern Song dynasty, early 13th century CE. Handscroll, ink on silk, height 11″ (28 cm); length of extant portion 7′7½″
(2.31 m). The Nelson-Atkins Museum of Art, Kansas City, Missouri. Purchase, Nelson Trust (32-159/2)

this long handscroll have survived, but they are enough to illustrate the unique quality of his approach.

In contrast to the majestic, austere landscapes of the Northern Song painters, Xia Gui presents an intimate and lyrical view of nature. Subtly modulated, perfectly controlled ink washes evoke a landscape veiled in mist, while a few deft brushstrokes suffice to indicate the details showing through the mist—the grasses growing by the bank, the fishers at their work, the trees laden with moisture, the two bent-backed figures carrying their heavy loads along the path that skirts the hill. Simplified forms, stark contrasts of light and dark, asymmetrical composition, and great expanses of blank space suggest a fleeting world that can be captured only in glimpses. The intangible has more presence than the tangible. By limiting himself to a few essential details, the painter evokes a deep feeling for what lies beyond.

This development in Song painting from the rational and intellectual to the emotional and intuitive, from the tangible to the intangible, had a parallel in philosophy. During the late twelfth century a new school of Neo-Confucianism called School of the Mind insisted that self-cultivation could be achieved through contemplation, which might lead to sudden enlightenment. The idea of sudden enlightenment may have come from Chan Buddhism, better known in the West by its Japanese name, Zen. Chan Buddhists rejected formal paths to enlightenment such as scripture, knowledge, and ritual, in favor of meditation and techniques designed to "short-circuit" the rational mind. Xia Gui's painting seems also to suggest this intuitive approach.

The subtle and sophisticated paintings of the Song were created for a highly cultivated audience who were equally discerning in other arts such as ceramics. Building on the considerable accomplishments of the Tang, Song potters achieved a technical and aesthetic perfection that has made their wares models of excellence throughout the world. Like their painter contemporaries, Song potters turned away from the exuberance of Tang styles to create more quietly beautiful pieces.

GUAN WARE.   Among the most prized of the many types of Song ceramics is Guan ware, made mainly for imperial use **(FIG. 10–24)**. The everted lip, high neck, and rounded body of this simple vase show a strong sense of harmony. Enhanced by a

10-24 • GUAN WARE VASE
Southern Song dynasty, 13th century CE. Gray stoneware with crackled grayish-blue glaze, height 6⅝″ (16.8 cm). Percival David Foundation of Chinese Art, British Museum, London.

SEE MORE: View a video about the process of ceramic making **www.myartslab.com**

lustrous grayish-blue glaze, the form flows without break from base to lip. The piece has an introspective quality as eloquent as the blank spaces in Xia Gui's painting. The aesthetic of the Song is most evident in the crackle pattern on the glazed surface. The crackle technique was probably discovered accidentally, but came to be used deliberately in some of the most refined Song wares. In the play of irregular, spontaneous crackles over a perfectly regular, perfectly planned form we can sense the same spirit that hovers behind the self-effacing virtuosity and freely intuitive insights of Xia Gui's landscape.

In 1279 the Southern Song dynasty fell to the conquering forces of the Mongol leader Kublai Khan (1215–1294). China was subsumed into the vast Mongol Empire. Mongol rulers founded the Yuan dynasty (1279–1368), setting up their capital in the northeast in what is now Beijing. Yet the cultural center of China remained in the south, in the cities that rose to prominence during the Song, especially Hangzhou. This separation of political and cultural centers, coupled with a lasting resentment toward "barbarian" rule, created the climate for later developments in the arts.

THE ARTS OF KOREA

Set between China and Japan, Korea occupies a peninsula in northeast Asia. Inhabited for millennia, the peninsula gave rise to a distinctively Korean culture during the Three Kingdoms period.

THE THREE KINGDOMS PERIOD

Traditionally dated 57 BCE to 668 CE, the Three Kingdoms period saw the establishment of three independent nation-states: Silla in the southeast, Baekje in the southwest, and Goguryeo in the north. Large tomb mounds built during the fifth and sixth centuries are enduring monuments of this period.

A GOLD HEADDRESS. The most spectacular items recovered from these tombs are trappings of royal authority (FIG. 10–25). Made expressly for burial, this elaborate crown was assembled from cut pieces of thin gold sheet, held together by gold wire. Spangles of gold embellish the crown, as do comma-shaped ornaments of green and white jadeite—a form of jade mineralogically distinct from the nephrite prized by the early Chinese. The tall, branching forms rising from the crown's periphery resemble trees and antlers. Within the crown is a conical cap woven of narrow strips of sheet gold and ornamented with appendages that suggest wings or feathers.

HIGH-FIRED CERAMICS. The tombs have also yielded ceramics in abundance. Most are containers for offerings of food placed in the tomb to nourish the spirit of the deceased. These items generally are of unglazed **stoneware**, a high-fired ceramic ware that is impervious to liquids, even without glaze.

The most imposing ceramic shapes are the tall stands that were used to support round-bottomed jars (FIG. 10–26). Such stands typically have a long, cylindrical shaft set on a bulbous base. Cut into the moist clay before firing, their openwork apertures lighten what otherwise would be rather ponderous forms. Although few examples of Three Kingdoms ceramics exhibit surface ornamentation, other than an occasional combed wave pattern or an incised configuration of circles and **chevrons** (v-shapes), here snakes inch their way up the shaft of the stand.

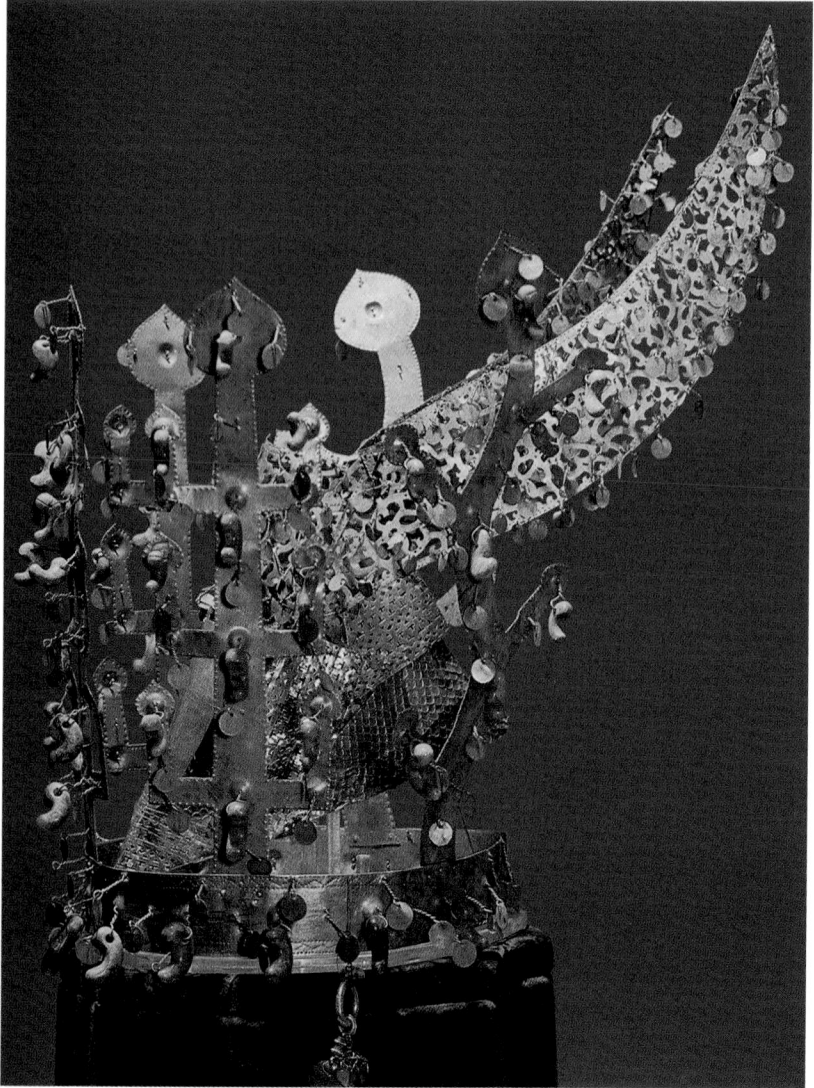

10-25 • CROWN
Korea. Three Kingdoms period, Silla kingdom, probably 6th century CE. From the Gold Crown Tomb, Gyeongju, North Gyeongsang Province. Gold with jadeite ornaments, height 17½″ (44.5 cm). National Museum of Korea, Seoul, Republic of Korea.

10-26 • CEREMONIAL STAND WITH SNAKE, ABSTRACT, AND OPENWORK DECORATION
Korean. Three Kingdoms period, Silla kingdom, 5th–6th century CE. Gray stoneware with combed, stamped, applied, and openwork decoration and with traces of natural ash glaze, height 23⅛″ (58.7 cm). Reportedly recovered in Andong, North Gyeongsang Province. Arthur M. Sackler Museum, Harvard University, Cambridge, Massachusetts. Partial gift of Maria C. Henderson and partial purchase through the Ernest B. and Helen Pratt Dane Fund for the Acquisition of Oriental Art (1991.501)

A BODHISATTVA SEATED IN MEDITATION. Buddhism was introduced into the Goguryeo kingdom from China in 372 CE and into Baekje by 384. Although it probably reached Silla in the second half of the fifth century, Buddhism gained recognition as the official religion of the Silla state only in 527.

At first, Buddhist art in Korea was a mere imitation of Chinese art. However, by the late sixth century, Korean sculptors had created a style of their own, as illustrated by a magnificent gilt bronze image of a bodhisattva (probably the bodhisattva Maitreya) seated in meditation that likely dates to the early seventh century **(FIG. 10–27)**. Although the pose links it to Chinese sculpture of the late sixth century, the slender body, elliptical face, elegant drapery folds, and trilobed crown distinguish it as Korean.

Buddhism was introduced to Japan from Korea—from the Baekje kingdom, according to literary accounts. In fact, historical sources indicate that numerous Korean sculptors were active in

10-27 • BODHISATTVA SEATED IN MEDITATION
Korean. Three Kingdoms period, probably Silla kingdom, early 7th century CE. Gilt bronze, height 35⅞″ (91 cm). National Museum of Korea, Seoul, Republic of Korea (formerly in the collection of the Toksu Palace Museum of Fine Arts, Seoul).

Japan in the sixth and seventh centuries; several early masterpieces of Buddhist art in Japan show pronounced Korean influence (SEE FIG. 11–6).

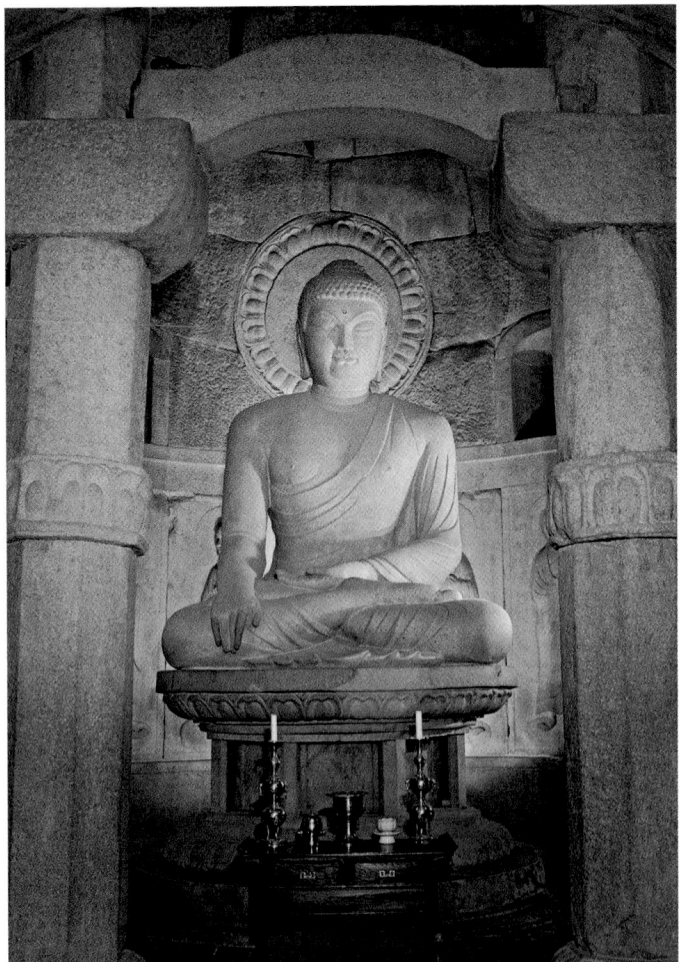

10-28 • SEATED SHAKYAMUNI BUDDHA
Seokguram Grotto, near Gyeongju, North Gyeongsang Province, Korea. Unified Silla period, c. 751 CE. Granite, height of Buddha 11′2½″ (342 cm).

The Buddha's hands are in the *bhumisparsha mudra*, the earth-touching gesture symbolizing his enlightenment.

THE UNIFIED SILLA PERIOD

In 660, the Silla kingdom conquered Baekje, and, in 668, through an alliance with Tang-dynasty China, it vanquished Goguryeo, uniting the peninsula under the rule of the Unified Silla dynasty, which lasted until 935. Buddhism prospered under Unified Silla, and many large, important temples were erected in and around Gyeongju, the Silla capital.

SEOKGURAM.   The greatest monument of the Unified Silla period is Seokguram, an artificial cave-temple constructed under royal patronage atop Mount Toham, near Gyeongju. The temple is modeled after Chinese cave-temples of the fifth, sixth, and seventh centuries, which were in turn inspired by the Buddhist cave-temples of India.

Built in the mid eighth century of cut blocks of granite, Seokguram consists of a small rectangular antechamber joined by a narrow vestibule to a circular main hall with a domed ceiling. More than 11 feet in height, a huge seated Buddha dominates the

main hall **(FIG. 10–28)**. Seated on a lotus pedestal, the image represents the historical Buddha Shakyamuni at the moment of his enlightenment, as indicated by his earth-touching gesture, or *bhumisparsha mudra*. The full, taut forms, diaphanous drapery, and anatomical details of his chest relate this image to eighth-century Chinese sculptures. Exquisitely carved low-relief images of bodhisattvas and lesser deities grace the walls of the antechamber, vestibule, and main hall.

GORYEO DYNASTY

Established in 918, the Goryeo dynasty eliminated the last vestiges of Unified Silla rule in 935; it would continue until 1392, ruling from its capital at Gaeseong—to the northwest of present-day Seoul and now in North Korea. A period of courtly refinement, the Goryeo dynasty is best known for its celadon-glazed ceramics.

CELADON-GLAZED CERAMICS.   The term **celadon** refers to a high-fired, transparent glaze of pale bluish-green hue, typically applied over a pale gray stoneware body. Chinese potters invented celadon glazes

10-29 • MAEBYEONG BOTTLE WITH DECORATION OF BAMBOO AND BLOSSOMING PLUM TREE
Korea. Goryeo dynasty, late 12th–early 13th century CE. Inlaid celadon ware: light gray stoneware with decoration inlaid with black and white slips under celadon glaze, height 13¼″ (33.7 cm). Tokyo National Museum, Tokyo, Japan. (TG-2171)

techniques of decoration. Most notable among their inventions was inlaid decoration, in which black and white slips, or finely ground clays, were inlaid into the intaglio lines of decorative elements incised or stamped in the body, creating underglaze designs in contrasting colors. The bottle in FIGURE 10–29 displays three different pictorial scenes inlaid in black and white slips. The scene featured here depicts a clump of bamboo growing at the edge of a lake, the stalks intertwined with the branches of a blossoming plum tree (which flowers in late winter, before donning its leaves). Geese swim in the lake and butterflies flutter above, linking the several scenes around the bottle. Called *maebyeong* ("plum bottle"), such broad-shouldered vessels were used as storage jars for wine, vinegar, and other liquids. A small, bell-shaped cover originally capped the bottle, protecting its contents and complementing its curves.

BUDDHIST PAINTING.   Buddhism, the state religion of Goryeo, enjoyed royal patronage; many temples were thus able to commission the very finest architects, sculptors, and painters. The most sumptuous Buddhist works produced during the Goryeo period were paintings. Wrought in ink and colors on silk, the fourteenth-century hanging scroll illustrated in FIGURE 10–30 depicts Gwanse'eum Bosal (whom the Chinese called Guanyin), the bodhisattva of compassion. The flesh tones used for the bodhisattva's face and hands, along with the rich colors and gold pigment used for the deity's clothing, reflect the luxurious taste of the period. Numerous paintings of this type were exported to Japan, where they influenced the course of Buddhist painting.

10–30 • SEATED WILLOW-BRANCH GWANSE'EUM BOSAL (THE BODHISATTVA AVALOKITESHVARA)
Korea. Goryeo dynasty, late 14th century CE. Hanging scroll, ink, colors, and gold pigment on silk, height 62½″ (159.6 cm). Arthur M. Sackler Museum, Harvard University, Cambridge, Massachusetts. Bequest of Grenville L. Winthrop (1943.57.12)

and had initiated the continuous production of celadon-glazed wares as early as the first century CE. Korean potters began to experiment with such glazes in the eighth and ninth centuries; their earliest celadons reflect the strong imprint of Chinese ware. Soon, the finest Goryeo celadons rivaled the best Chinese court ceramics. These wares were used by people of various socioeconomic classes during the Goryeo dynasty, with the finest examples going to the palace, nobles, or the powerful Buddhist clergy.

Prized for their classic simplicity, Korean celadons of the eleventh century often have little decoration, while those of the twelfth century frequently sport incised, carved, or molded decoration, thus generally mimicking the style and ornamentation of contemporaneous Chinese ceramics. By the mid twelfth century, Korean potters began to explore new styles and

THINK ABOUT IT

10.1 Examine the *guang* (fig. 10–5) and consider how its iconography may have related to a ritual-oriented culture in Bronze Age China.

10.2 Summarize the main tenets of Confucianism. Then select a work from the chapter that gives visual form to Confucian philosophy and explain how it does so.

10.3 Select one of the Song-era Chinese landscape paintings included in the chapter and explain how it may embody Daoist ideals.

10.4 Compare and contrast the Chinese seated Guanyin bodhisattva (FIG. 10–19) and the Korean bodhisattva seated in meditation (FIG. 10–27). Define the meaning of bodhisattva, and examine how the artists gave visual expression to the deity's attributes.

10.5 Based on examples illustrated in the chapter, identify parallel developments in painting and sculpture from the Han through the Song dynasty.

PRACTICE MORE: Compose answers to these questions, get flashcards for images and terms, and review chapter material with quizzes
www.myartslab.com

11–1 • KASUGA SHRINE MANDALA Kamakura period, early 14th century CE. Hanging scroll, ink, color, and gold on silk, 39½ × 15⅝″ (100.3 × 39.8 cm). Mary and Jackson Burke Collection.

JAPANESE ART BEFORE 1333

A group of Buddhist deities hovers in the sky across the top of this painting (FIG. 11–1), above verdant hills and meadows filled with blossoming cherry and plum trees, and a diagrammatic, bird's-eye view of a religious compound. The sacred site depicted in recognizable, but partially idealized, form is the Kasuga Shrine in Nara, dedicated to deities, known as *kami*, of Japan's native Shinto religion. It served as the family shrine for the most powerful aristocratic clan in ancient Japan, the Fujiwara, who chose the site because of its proximity to their home as well as for its natural beauty. As life in Japan revolved around natural seasonal rhythms, so too did conceptions of *kami*, who give and protect life and embody the life-sustaining forces of nature. The Japanese believe that *kami* descend from mysterious heavens at supremely beautiful places such as majestic mountains, towering waterfalls, old and gnarled trees, or unusual rock formations, thus rendering such locations holy. They consider them as places where they can go to commune with *kami*. The deer glimpsed scampering about the grounds are sacred messengers of *kami*, and freely roam the area even today.

That foreign deities associated with Buddhism preside over a native Shinto shrine presents no anomaly to the Japanese. By the Heian period (794–1185 CE), the interaction of Buddhist and Shinto doctrines resulted in the belief that *kami* were emanations of Buddhist deities who were their original forms. When Buddhism first entered Japan in the sixth century, efforts began to integrate that new faith with the indigenous Japanese religious belief system centered around *kami*, which only later came to be called Shinto. Until the government forcibly separated the two religions in the latter part of the nineteenth century, and elevated Shinto to bolster worship of the emperor, the two religions were intimately intertwined and evolved in a co-mingled manner. The two faiths could exist side by side because of their complementary values. Shinto explains the origins of the Japanese people and its deities protect them, while Buddhism offers salvation after death.

This painting encapsulates various aspects of the essential character of Japanese art and culture in the ancient and early medieval eras. Like all religious art from early Japan, it was created to aid religious teachings and beliefs. In its own time it was not considered a work of art. It testifies to the importance of nature in the Japanese worldview and how reverence for the natural world informed religious practice and visual vocabulary. Additionally, it shows how the Japanese integrated the foreign religion of Buddhism with indigenous belief systems without sacrificing either one. Finally, it reveals the existence at this early date of a sophisticated and uniquely Japanese courtly style aesthetic.

LEARN ABOUT IT

11.1 Recognize the native elements in early Japanese art.

11.2 Understand Japan's cultural relationship with China and Korea.

11.3 Summarize the transformation of Japanese Buddhist sculpture.

11.4 Discuss the ways Shinto influences Japanese aesthetic perceptions.

11.5 Distinguish different uses of Buddhist paintings in connection with the different sects of Buddhism for which they were made.

HEAR MORE: Listen to an audio file of your chapter www.myartslab.com

PREHISTORIC JAPAN

Human habitation in Japan dates to around 30,000 years ago (MAP 11–1). Sometime after 15,000 years ago Paleolithic peoples gave way to Neolithic hunter-gatherers, who gradually developed the ability to make and use ceramics. Recent scientific dating methods have shown that some works of Japanese pottery date to earlier than 10,000 BCE, making them the oldest now known.

JOMON PERIOD

The early potters lived during the Jomon period (c. 11,000–400 BCE), named for the patterns on much of the pottery they produced. They made functional earthenware vessels, probably originally imitating reed baskets, by building them up with coils of clay, then firing them in bonfires at relatively low temperatures. They also created small humanoid figures known as **dogu**, which were probably effigies that manifested a kind of sympathetic magic. Around 5000 BCE agriculture emerged with the planting and harvesting of beans and gourds.

YAYOI PERIOD

During the succeeding Yayoi era (c. 400 BCE–300 CE), the introduction of rice cultivation by immigrants from Korea helped transform Japan into an agricultural nation. As it did elsewhere in the world, this shift to agriculture brought larger permanent settlements, class structure with the division of labor into agricultural and nonagricultural tasks, more hierarchical forms of social organization, and a more centralized government. Korean settlers also brought metal technology. Bronze was used to create weapons as well as ceremonial objects such as bells. Iron metallurgy developed later in this period, eventually replacing stone tools in everyday life.

KOFUN PERIOD

Centralized government developed further during the ensuing Kofun ("old tombs") period (c. 300–552 CE), named for the large royal tombs that were built then. With the emergence of a more complex social order, the veneration of leaders grew into the beginnings of an imperial system. Still in existence today in Japan, this system eventually explained that the emperor (or, very rarely, empress) descended directly from Shinto deities. When an emperor died, chamber tombs were constructed following Korean examples. Various grave goods were placed inside the tomb chambers, including large amounts of pottery, presumably to pacify the spirits of the dead and to serve them in their next life. As part of a general cultural transfer from China through Korea, fifth-century potters in Japan gained knowledge of finishing techniques and improved kilns, and began to produce high-fired ceramic ware.

The Japanese government has never allowed the major sacred tombs to be excavated, but much is known about the mortuary practices of Kofun-era Japan. Some of the huge tombs of the fifth and sixth centuries were constructed in a shape resembling a large

MAP 11-1 • JAPAN

Melting glaciers at the end of the Ice Age in Japan 15,000 years ago raised the sea level and formed the four main islands of Japan: Hokkaido, Honshu, Shikoku, and Kyushu.

keyhole and surrounded by moats dug to protect the sacred precincts. Tomb sites might extend over more than 400 acres, with artificial hills built over the tombs themselves. On the top of the hills were placed ceramic works of sculpture called **haniwa**.

HANIWA. The first *haniwa* were simple cylinders that may have held jars with ceremonial offerings. By the fifth century, these cylinders came to be made in the shapes of ceremonial objects, houses, and boats. Gradually, living creatures were added to the repertoire of *haniwa* subjects, including birds, deer, dogs, monkeys, cows, and horses. By the sixth century, **HANIWA** in human shapes were crafted, including males and females of various types, professions, and classes (FIG. 11–2).

Haniwa illustrate several enduring characteristics of Japanese aesthetic taste. Unlike Chinese tomb ceramics, which were often

ART AND ITS CONTEXTS

Writing, Language, and Culture

Chinese culture enjoyed great prestige in east Asia. Written Chinese served as an international language of scholarship and cultivation, much as Latin did in medieval Europe. Educated Koreans, for example, wrote almost exclusively in Chinese until the fifteenth century. In Japan, Chinese continued to be used for certain kinds of writing, such as Buddhist *sutras*, philosophical and legal texts, and Chinese poetry (by Japanese writers), into the nineteenth century.

When it came to writing their own language, the Japanese initially borrowed Chinese characters, or *kanji*. Differences between the Chinese and Japanese languages made this system extremely unwieldy, so during the ninth century they developed two syllabaries, or *kana*, from simplified Chinese characters. (A syllabary is a system of lettering in which each symbol stands for a syllable.) *Katakana*, consisting of angular symbols, was developed to aid pronunciation of Chinese Buddhist texts and now is generally used for foreign words. *Hiragana*, comprised of graceful, cursive symbols, was the written language the Japanese first used to write native poetry and prose. Eventually it came to be used to represent only the grammatical portions of the written Japanese language in conjunction with Chinese characters that convey meaning. Japanese written in *hiragana* was once called "women's hand" because its rounded forms looked feminine. During the Heian period *hiragana* were used to create a large body of literature, written either by women or sometimes for women by men.

A charming poem originated in Heian times to teach the new writing system. In two stanzas of four lines each, it uses almost all of the syllable sounds of spoken Japanese and thus almost every *kana* symbol. It was memorized as we would recite our ABCs. The first stanza translates as:

> Although flowers glow with color
> They are quickly fallen,
> And who in this world of ours
> Is free from change?
> (Translation by Earl Miner)

Like Chinese, Japanese is written in columns from top to bottom and across the page from right to left. (Following this logic, Chinese and Japanese narrative paintings also read from right to left.) Below is the stanza written three ways. At the right, it appears in *katakana* glossed with the original phonetic value of each symbol. (Modern pronunciation has shifted slightly.) In the center, the stanza appears in flowing *hiragana*. To the left is the mixture of *kanji* and *hiragana* that eventually became standard.

kanji hiragana mixed

常ならむ
我世誰ぞ
散りぬるを
色は匂へど

hiragana

つねならむ
わかよたれそ
ちりぬるを
いろはにほへと

katakana

ツネナラム Tsu-ne-na-ra-mu
ワカヨタレソ Wa-ka-yo-ta-re-so
チリヌルヲ Chi-ri-nu-ru-wo
イロハニホヘト I-ro-ha-ni-he-to

11–2 • HANIWA
Kyoto. Kofun period, 6th century CE. Earthenware, height 27″ (68.5 cm). Collection of the Tokyo National Museum. Important Cultural Property.

There have been many theories as to the function of *haniwa*. The figures seem to have served as some kind of link between the world of the dead, over which they were placed, and the world of the living, from which they could be viewed. This figure has been identified as a seated female shaman, wearing a robe, belt, and necklace and carrying a mirror at her waist. In early Japan, shamans acted as agents between the natural and the supernatural worlds, just as *haniwa* figures were links between the living and the dead.

glazed, *haniwa* were left with their clay bodies unglazed. Nor do *haniwa* show a preoccupation with technical skill seen in Chinese ceramics. Instead, their makers explored the expressive potentials of simple and bold form. *Haniwa* are never perfectly symmetrical; their slightly off-center eye slits, irregular cylindrical bodies, and unequal arms impart the idiosyncrasy of life and individuality.

SHINTO. As described at the outset of this chapter, Shinto is Japan's indigenous religious belief system. It encompasses a variety of ritual practices that center around family, village, and national devotion to *kami* (Shinto deities). The term Shinto was not coined until after the arrival of Buddhism in the sixth century CE, and as *kami* worship was influenced by and incorporated into Buddhism it became more systematized, with shrines, a hierarchy of deities, and more strictly regulated ceremonies.

THE ISE SHRINE. One of the great Shinto monuments is the Grand Shrine of Ise, on the coast southwest of Tokyo **(FIG. 11–3)**, where the main deity worshiped is the sun goddess Amaterasu-o-mi-*kami*, the legendary progenitor of Japan's imperial family. Japan's earliest written historical texts recorded by the imperial

court in the eighth century state that the Ise Shrine dates to the first century CE. Although we do not know for certain if this is true, it is known that it has been ritually rebuilt, alternately on two adjoining sites at 20-year intervals with few breaks since the year 690, a time when the imperial family was solidifying its hegemony. Its most recent rebuilding took place in 1993, by carpenters who train for the task from childhood. After the *kami* is ceremonially escorted to the freshly copied shrine, the old shrine is dismantled. Thus—like Japanese culture itself—this exquisite shrine is both ancient and constantly renewed. In this sense it embodies one of the most important characteristics of Shinto faith—ritual purification—derived from respect for the cycle of the seasons in which pure new life emerges in springtime and gives way to death in winter, yet is reborn again in the following year.

Although Ise is visited by millions of pilgrims each year, only members of the imperial family and a few Shinto priests are allowed within the enclosure that surrounds its inner shrine. Although detailed documents on its appearance date back to the tenth century, shrine authorities never allowed photographers access to its inner compound until 1953, when the iconic photograph of it reproduced in FIGURE 11–3 was taken by a photographer officially

11-3 • MAIN HALL, INNER SHRINE, ISE
Mie Prefecture. Last rebuilt 1993. Photograph by Watanabe Yoshio (1907–2000), 1953. National Treasure.

SEE MORE: View a video about the re-building of the Ise Shrine
www.myartslab.com

engaged by a quasi-governmental cultural relations agency. The reluctance of shrine officials to permit photography even then may stem from beliefs that such intimate pictures would violate the privacy of the shrine's most sacred spaces.

The Ise Shrine has many aspects that are typical of Shinto architecture, including wooden piles raising the building off the ground, a thatched roof held in place by horizontal logs, the use of unpainted cypress wood, and the overall feeling of natural simplicity rather than overwhelming size or elaborate decoration. The building's shape is indebted to raised granaries used by the Yayoi people, which are known from drawings on bronze artifacts of the Yayoi period. The sensitive use of wood and thatch in the Ise Shrine suggests an early origin for the Japanese appreciation of natural materials that persists to the present day.

ASUKA PERIOD

During the Asuka period's single century (552–645 CE), new forms of philosophy, medicine, music, food, clothing, agriculture, city planning, religion, visual art, and architecture entered Japan from Korea and China at an astonishing pace. Most significant among these were the Buddhist religion, a centralized governmental structure, and a system of writing. Each was adopted and gradually modified to suit Japanese conditions, and each has had an enduring legacy.

Buddhism reached Japan in Mahayana form, with its many buddhas and bodhisattvas (see "Buddhism," page 297). After being accepted by the imperial family, it was soon adopted as a state religion. Buddhism represented not only different gods from Shinto but an entirely new concept of religion. Worship of Buddhist deities took place inside worship halls of temples situated in close proximity to imperial cities. The temples looked like nothing constructed in Japan before, with Chinese-influenced buildings housing anthropomorphic Buddhist icons possessing an elaborate iconography (see "Buddhist Symbols," page 362). At that time, *kami* were not portrayed in human form. Yet Buddhism attracted followers because it offered a rich cosmology with profound teachings of meditation and enlightenment, and the protective powers of its deities enabled the ruling elites to justify their own power, through association with Buddhism. They called upon Buddhist deities to nurture and protect the populace over whom they ruled. Many highly developed aspects of continental Asian art accompanied the new religion, including new methods of painting and sculpture.

11-4 • AERIAL VIEW OF
HORYUJI COMPOUND
Pagoda to the west (left), golden hall
(kondo) to the east (right). Nara
Prefecture. Asuka period, 7th century CE.
UNESCO World Heritage Site, National
Treasure.

HORYUJI

The most significant surviving early Japanese temple is Horyuji,
located on Japan's central plains not far from Nara. The temple was
founded in 607 by Prince Shotoku (574–622), who ruled Japan as
a regent and became the most influential early proponent of
Buddhism. Rebuilt after a fire in 670, Horyuji is the oldest wooden
temple in the world. It is so famous that visitors are often surprised
at its modest size. Yet its just proportions and human scale, together
with the artistic treasures it contains, make Horyuji an enduringly
beautiful monument to Buddhist faith in early Japan.

The main compound of Horyuji consists of a rectangular
courtyard surrounded by covered corridors, one of which contains
a gateway. Within the compound are only two buildings, the
kondo (golden hall), and a five-story pagoda. Within a simple
asymmetrical layout, the large *kondo* perfectly balances the tall,
slender pagoda (**FIG. 11–4**). The *kondo* is filled with Buddhist
images and is used for worship and ceremonies. The pagoda serves
as a reliquary and is not entered. Other monastery buildings lie
outside the main compound, including an outer gate, a lecture hall,
a repository for sacred texts, a belfry, and dormitories for monks.

Among the many treasures still preserved in Horyuji is a
shrine decorated with paintings in lacquer. It is known as the
Tamamushi Shrine after the *tamamushi* beetle, whose iridescent
wings were originally affixed to the shrine to make it glitter, much

11-5 • HUNGRY TIGRESS JATAKA
Panel of the Tamamushi Shrine, Horyuji. Asuka period, c. 650 CE.
Lacquer on wood, height of shrine 7'7½" (2.33 m). Horyuji Treasure
House, Nara. National Treasure.

11-6 • Tori Busshi **BUDDHA SHAKA AND ATTENDANT BODHISATTVAS IN THE HORYUJI** *KONDO*
Asuka period, c. 623 CE. Gilt bronze, height of seated figure 34½"
(87.5 cm). Horyuji, Nara. National Treasure.

like mother-of-pearl. Its architectural form replicates an ancient palace-form building type that predates Horyuji itself.

HUNGRY TIGRESS JATAKA. Paintings on the sides of the Tamamushi Shrine are among the few two-dimensional works of art to survive from the Asuka period. Most celebrated among them are two that illustrate Jataka tales, stories about former lives of the Buddha. One depicts the future Buddha nobly sacrificing his life in order to feed his body to a starving tigress and her cubs **(FIG. 11–5)**. The tigers are at first too weak to eat him, so he must jump off a cliff to break open his flesh. The anonymous artist has created a full narrative within a single frame. The graceful form of the Buddha appears three times, harmonized by the curves of the rocky cliff and tall sprigs of bamboo. First, he hangs his shirt on a tree, then he dives downward onto the rocks, and finally starving animals devour his body. The elegantly slender renditions of the figure and the somewhat abstract treatment of the cliff, trees, and bamboo represent an international Buddhist style that was

transmitted to Japan via China and Korea. These illustrations of Jataka tales helped popularize Buddhism in Japan.

SHAKA TRIAD. Another example of the international style of early Buddhist art at Horyuji is the sculpture called the Shaka Triad, traditionally identified as being made by Tori Busshi **(FIG. 11–6)**. (Shaka is the Japanese name for Shakyamuni, the historical Buddha.) Tori Busshi (Busshi means Buddhist image-maker) may have been a descendant of Korean craftsmen who emigrated to Japan as part of an influx of Buddhists and artisans from Korea. The Shaka Triad reflects the strong influence of Chinese art of the Northern Wei dynasty (SEE FIG. 10–12). The frontal pose, the outsized face and hands, and the linear treatment of the drapery all suggest that the maker of this statue was well aware of earlier continental models, while the fine bronze casting of the figures shows his advanced technical skill. The Shaka Triad and the Tamamushi Shrine reveal the importance of Buddhist imagery to the transmission of the faith.

NARA PERIOD

The Nara period (645–794) is named for Japan's first permanent imperial capital, founded in 710. Previously, an emperor's death was thought to taint his entire capital city, so for reasons of purification (and perhaps also of politics), his successor usually selected a new site. As the government adopted ever more complex aspects of the Chinese political system, necessitating construction of huge administrative complexes, it abandoned this custom in the eighth century when Nara was founded. During this period, divisions of the imperial bureaucracy grew exponentially and hastened the swelling of the city's population to perhaps 200,000 people.

One result of the strong central authority was the construction in Nara of magnificent Buddhist temples and Shinto shrines that dwarfed those built previously. The expansive park in the center of Nara today is the site of the largest and most important of these, including the Shinto Kasuga Shrine illustrated in FIGURE 11–1. The grandest of the Buddhist temples in Nara Park is Todaiji, which Emperor Shomu (r. 724–749) conceived as the headquarters of a vast network of branch temples throughout the nation. He had it constructed because of his deep faith in Buddhism. Todaiji served as both a state-supported central monastic training center and as the setting for public religious ceremonies. The most spectacular of these took place in 752 and celebrated the consecration of the main Buddhist statue of the temple in a traditional "eye-opening" ceremony, in its newly constructed Great Buddha Hall (*Daibutsuden*; see "The Great Buddha Hall," page 364). The statue, a giant gilt bronze image of the Buddha Birushana (Vairochana in Sanskrit), was inspired by the Chinese tradition of erecting monumental stone Buddhist statues in cave-temples (SEE, FOR EXAMPLE, FIG. 10–12).

The ceremony, which took place in the vast courtyard in front of the Great Buddha Hall, was presided over by an illustrious

Buddhist Symbols

A few of the most important Buddhist symbols, which have myriad variations, are described here in their most generalized forms.

Lotus flower: Usually shown as a white waterlily, the lotus (Sanskrit, *padma*) symbolizes spiritual purity, the wholeness of creation, and cosmic harmony. The flower's stem is an *axis mundi* ("axis of the world").

Lotus throne: Buddhas are frequently shown seated on an open lotus, either single or double, a representation of *nirvana* (SEE FIG. 11–10).

Chakra: An ancient sun symbol, the *chakra* (wheel) symbolizes both the various states of existence (the Wheel of Life) and the Buddhist doctrine (the Wheel of the Law). A *chakra*'s exact meaning depends on how many spokes it has (SEE FIG. 9–7).

Marks of a buddha: A buddha is distinguished by 32 physical attributes (*lakshana*s). Among them are a bulge on top of the head (*ushnisha*), a tuft of hair between the eyebrows (*urna*), elongated earlobes, and 1,000-spoked *chakra*s on the soles of the feet.

Mandala: *Mandala*s are diagrams of cosmic realms, representing order and meaning within the spiritual universe. They may be simple or complex, three- or two-dimensional, and in a wide array of forms—such as an Indian stupa (SEE FIG. 9–8) or a Womb World *mandala* (SEE FIG. 11–8), an early Japanese type.

lotus flower

double lotus flower

chakra

ushnisha

urna

elongated earlobes

chakra

marks of a buddha

Indian monk and included *sutra* chanting by over 10,000 Japanese Buddhist monks and sacred performances by 4,000 court musicians and dancers. Vast numbers of Japanese courtiers and emissaries from the Asian continent comprised the audience. Numerous ritual objects used in the ceremony came from exotic Asian and Near Eastern lands. The resulting cosmopolitan atmosphere reflected the position Nara then held as the eastern terminus of the Central Asian Silk Road.

Many of these treasures have been preserved in the Shosoin Imperial Repository at Todaiji, which today contains some 9,000

11-7 • FIVE-STRINGED LUTE (*BIWA*) WITH DESIGN OF A CENTRAL ASIAN MAN PLAYING A *BIWA* ATOP A CAMEL
Chinese. Tang dynasty, 8th century CE. Red sandalwood and chestnut inlaid with mother-of-pearl, amber, and tortoiseshell. Length 42½" (108.1 cm), width 12" (30.9 cm), depth 3½" (9 cm). Shosoin, Todaiji, Nara.

objects. The Shosoin came into being in the year 756, when Emperor Shomu died and his widow donated some 600 of his possessions to the temple, including a number of objects used during the Great Buddha's consecration ceremony. Many years later, objects used in Buddhist rituals and previously stored elsewhere at Todaiji were added to these. The objects formerly owned by Emperor Shomu consisted mainly of his personal possessions, such as documents, furniture, musical instruments, games, clothing, medicine, weapons, food and beverage vessels of metal, glass, and lacquer, and some Buddhist ritual objects. Some of these were made in Japan while others were clearly not and came from as far away as China, India, Iran, Greece, Rome, and Egypt. They reflect the vast international trade network that existed at this early date.

One of the items Emperor Shomu's widow donated in 756 is a magnificently crafted five-stringed lute (*biwa*) made of lacquered red sandalwood and chestnut, and inlaid with mother-of-pearl, amber, and tortoiseshell. Its plectrum guard features a design of a man of central Asian origin (apparent from his clothing and physical features) sitting atop a camel and playing a lute (**FIG. 11–7**). This instrument is the only existing example of an ancient five-stringed lute. Its form was invented in India and transmitted to China and Japan via the Silk Road. The Shosoin piece is generally identified as Chinese. However, as with many of the objects preserved in the Shosoin, the location of its manufacture is not absolutely certain. While it was most likely crafted in China and imported to Japan for use in the consecration ceremony (researchers have recently conclusively determined that it was indeed played), it is also plausible that Chinese (or Japanese) craftsmen made it in Japan using imported materials. Its meticulous workmanship reveals the high level of crafts production that artists of this era achieved. Such consummate skill has been a hallmark of Japanese crafts since then.

Influenced by Emperor Shomu, the Buddhist faith permeated all aspects of court society of the Nara period. Indeed, in 749 Shomu abdicated the throne to retire as a monk. His daughter, who succeeded him as empress, was also a devout Buddhist and wanted to cede her throne to a Buddhist monk. This dismayed her advisors and prompted them to move the capital city away from Nara, where they felt Buddhist influence had become overpowering, and establish a new one, Kyoto, within whose bounds, at first, only a few Buddhist temples would be allowed. The move of the capital to Kyoto marked the end of the Nara period.

HEIAN PERIOD

The Japanese fully absorbed and transformed their cultural borrowings from China and Korea during the Heian period (794–1185). Generally peaceful conditions contributed to a new air of self-reliance. The imperial government severed ties to China in the ninth century, a time when the power of related aristocratic families increased. An efficient method of writing the Japanese language was developed, and the rise of vernacular literature generated such prose masterpieces as Lady Murasaki's *The Tale of Genji*. During these four centuries of splendor and refinement, two major streams of Buddhism emerged—first, esoteric sects and, later, those espousing salvation in the Pure Land Western Paradise of the Buddha Amida.

ESOTERIC BUDDHIST ART

With the removal of the capital to Kyoto, the older Nara temples lost their influence. Soon two new Esoteric sects of Buddhism, Tendai and Shingon, grew to dominate Japanese religious life. Strongly influenced by polytheistic religions such as Hinduism,

The Great Buddha Hall (*Daibutsuden*) is distinguished today as the largest wooden structure in the world. To give a sense of its unprecedented scale, it was so large that the area surrounding only one of the two pagodas that flanked it, within its own cloistered compound, could accommodate the entire main compound of Horyuji. Yet the present Great Buddha Hall, dating to a reconstruction of 1707, is 30 percent smaller than the original, which towered nearly 90 feet in height. Since it was first erected in 752 CE natural disasters and intentional destruction by foes of the imperial family necessitated its reconstruction four times. It was first destroyed during civil wars in the twelfth century and rebuilt in 1203, then destroyed in yet another civil war in 1567. Reconstruction did not occur until the late seventeenth century under the direction of a charismatic monk who solicited funds not from the government, which was then impoverished, but through popular subscription. This building, completed in 1707, is essentially the structure that stands on the site today. However, by the late nineteenth century its condition had deteriorated so profoundly that restoration finally undertaken between 1906 and 1913 entailed completely dismantling it and putting it back together, this time utilizing steel (imported from England) and concrete to provide invisible support to the roof, which had nearly collapsed. Architects adapted this nontraditional solution mainly because no trees of sufficiently large dimensions could be found, and no traditional carpenters then living possessed knowledge of ancient construction techniques. This project occurred only after laws were enacted in 1897 to preserve ancient architecture. Since then, another major restoration on the building took place between 1973 and 1980.

Like the building, the Great Buddha Daibutsu statue has not survived intact. Its head was completely destroyed in the late sixteenth century and replaced as part of the hall's reconstruction in the late seventeenth century, when its torso and lotus petal throne also required extensive restoration. The present statue, though impressive in scale, appears stiff and rigid. Its more lyrical original appearance can be approximated from that of engraved images of seated Buddhist deities found on a massive cast-bronze lotus petal from the original statue that has survived in fragmentary form. The petal features a buddha with a narrow waist, broad shoulders, and elegantly flowing robes that characterize the style of contemporaneous buddha images of the Tang dynasty (see, for example, the central buddha in FIG. 10–14).

THE BUDDHA SHAKA, DETAIL OF A PARADISE SCENE
Engraved bronze lotus petal from the original Great Buddha (Daibutsu) statue of the Buddha Birushana. 8th century CE. Height of petal 79″ (200 cm). *Daibutsuden*, Todaiji. National Treasure.

GREAT BUDDHA HALL (*DAIBUTSUDEN*), TODAIJI, NARA
Original structure completed in 752 CE. Destroyed and rebuilt in 1707. Extensively restored 1906–13. UNESCO World Heritage Site, National Treasure.

11-8 • WOMB WORLD *MANDALA*
Heian period, late 9th century CE. Hanging scroll, colors on silk, 6' × 5'1½"
(1.83 × 1.54 m). Toji, Kyoto. National Treasure.

*Mandala*s are used not only in teaching, but also as vehicles for practice. A monk, initiated into secret teachings, may meditate upon and assume the gestures of each deity depicted in the *mandala*, gradually working out from the center, so that he absorbs some of each deity's powers. The monk may also recite magical phrases, called *mantra*s, as an aid to meditation. The goal is to achieve enlightenment through the powers of the different forms of the Buddha. *Mandala*s are created in sculptural and architectural forms as well as in paintings (SEE FIG. 9–29). Their integration of the two most basic shapes, the circle and the square, is an expression of the principles of ancient geomancy (divining by means of lines and figures) as well as Buddhist cosmology.

art, especially *mandalas*, cosmic diagrams of the universe that portray the deities in schematic order. The Womb World *mandala* from Toji, for example, is entirely filled with depictions of gods. Dainichi is at the center, surrounded by buddhas of the four directions (**FIG. 11–8**). Other deities, including some with multiple heads and limbs, branch out in diagrammatical order, each with a specific symbol of power. To believers, the *mandala* represents an ultimate reality beyond the visible world.

Perhaps the most striking attribute of many Esoteric Buddhist images is their sense of spiritual force and potency, especially in depictions of the wrathful deities, which are often surrounded by flames, like those visible in the Womb World *mandala* just below the main circle of Buddhas. Esoteric Buddhism, with its intricate theology and complex doctrines, was a religion for the educated aristocracy, not for the masses. Its intricate network of deities, hierarchy, and ritual found a parallel in the elaborate social divisions of the Heian court.

PURE LAND BUDDHIST ART

Rising militarism, political turbulence, and the excesses of the imperial court marked the beginning of the eleventh century in Japan. To many Japanese of this century, the unsettled times seemed to confirm the coming of *Mappo*, a long-prophesied dark age of spiritual degeneration. Japanese of all classes reacted by increasingly turning to the promise of salvation after death through simple faith in the existence of a Buddhist realm known as the Western

Esoteric Buddhism (known as Tantric Buddhism in Nepal and Tibet) included a daunting number of deities, each with magical powers. The historical Buddha was no longer very important. Instead, most revered was the universal Buddha, called Dainichi ("Great Sun") in Japanese, who was believed to preside over the universe. He was accompanied by buddhas and bodhisattvas, as well as guardian deities who formed fierce counterparts to the more benign gods.

Esoteric Buddhism is hierarchical, and its deities have complex relationships to one another. Learning all the different gods and their interrelationships was assisted greatly by works of

Paradise of the Pure Land, a resplendent place filled with divine flowers and music. Amida (Amithaba in Sanskrit) and his attendant bodhisattvas preside there as divine protectors who compassionately accept into their land of bliss all who submit wholeheartedly to their benevolent powers. Pure Land beliefs had spread to Japan from China by way of Korea, where they also enjoyed great popularity. They offered a more immediate and easy means to achieve salvation than the elaborate rituals of the Esoteric sects. The religion held that merely by chanting *Namu Amida Butsu* ("Hail to Amida Buddha"), the faithful would be reborn into the Western Paradise.

Wood is a temperamental material because fluctuations in moisture content cause it to swell and shrink. Cut from a living, sap-filled tree, it takes many years to dry to a state of stability. While the outside of a piece of wood dries fairly rapidly, the inside yields its moisture only gradually, causing a difference in the rates of shrinkage between the inside and the outside, which induces the wood to crack. Consequently, a large statue carved from a single log must inevitably crack as it ages. Natural irregularities in wood, such as knots, further accentuate this problem. Thus, wood with a thinner cross section and fewer irregularities is less susceptible to cracking because it can dry more evenly. (This is the logic behind sawing logs into boards before drying.)

Japanese sculptors developed an ingenious and unique method, the joined-block technique, to reduce cracking in heavy wooden statues. This allowed them to create larger statues in wood than ever before, enabled standardization of body proportions, and encouraged division of labor among teams of carvers, some of whom became specialists in certain parts, such as hands or crossed legs or lotus thrones. To create large statues seated in the lotus pose, sculptors first put four blocks together vertically two by two in front and back, to form the main body, then added several blocks horizontally at what would become the front of the statue for the lap and knees. After carving each part, they assembled the figure and hollowed out the interior. This cooperative approach also had the added benefit of enabling workshops to produce large statues more quickly to meet a growing demand. Jocho is credited as the master sculptor who perfected this technique. The diagram shows how he assembled the Amida Buddha at the Byodoin (SEE FIG. 11–10).

Diagram of the joined-block wood sculpture technique used on the Amida statue by Jocho (SEE FIG. 11–10).

SEE MORE: View a simulation about the joined-block technique **www.myartslab.com**

11-9 • PHOENIX HALL, BYODOIN, UJI
Kyoto Prefecture. Heian period, c. 1053 CE. Unesco World Heritage Site, National Treasure.

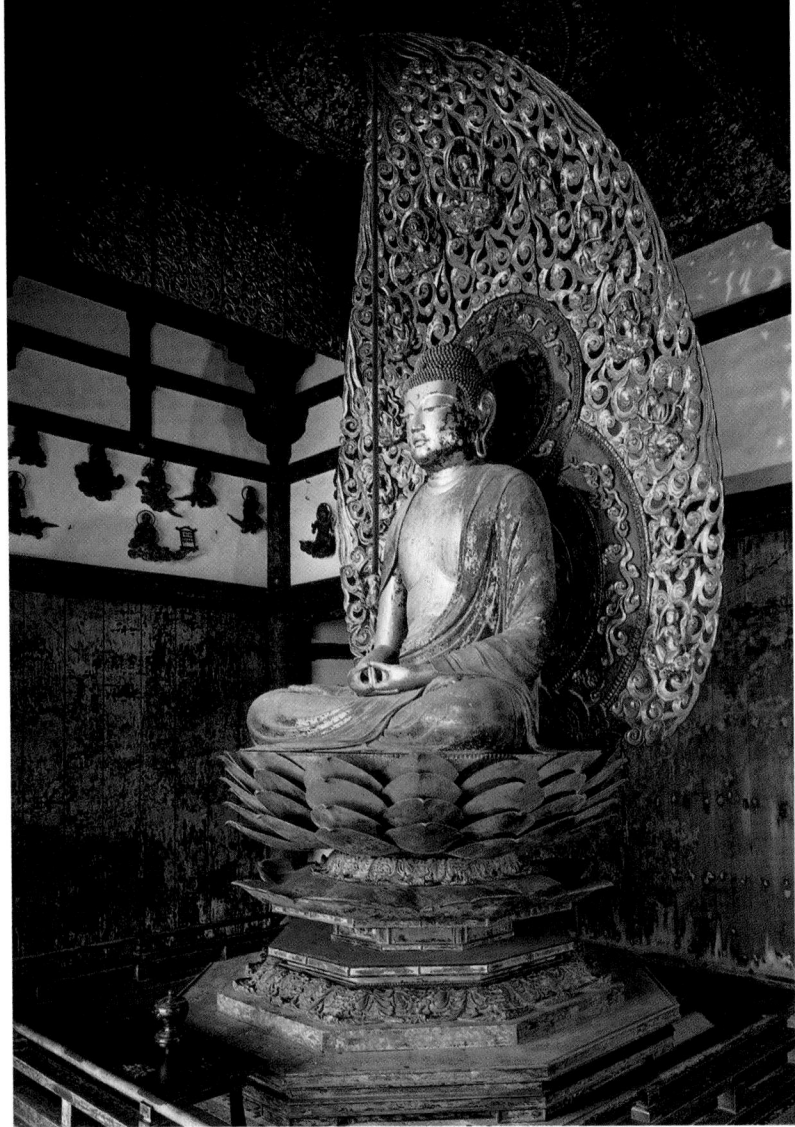

11–10 • Jocho AMIDA BUDDHA
Phoenix Hall, Byodoin. Heian period, c. 1053 CE. Gold leaf and lacquer on wood, height 9′8″ (2.95 m). National Treasure.

The Byodoin's central image of Amida, carved by the master sculptor Jocho (d. 1057), exemplifies the serenity and compassion of this Buddha (FIG. 11–10). When reflected in the water of the pond before it, the Amida image seems to shimmer in its private mountain retreat. The figure was not carved from a single block of wood like earlier sculpture, but from several blocks in Jocho's new **joined-block** method of construction (see "Joined-Block Wood Sculpture," opposite). This technique allowed sculptors to create larger and lighter statuary. It also reflects the growing importance of wood as the medium of choice for Buddhist sculpture, reflecting the Japanese love for this natural material.

Surrounding the Amida on the walls of the Byodoin are smaller wooden figures of bodhisattvas and angels, some playing musical instruments. Everything about the Byodoin was designed to simulate the appearance of the paradise that awaits the believer after death. Its remarkable state of preservation after more than 900 years allows visitors to experience the late Heian religious ideal at its most splendid.

SECULAR PAINTING AND CALLIGRAPHY

Alongside the permeation of Buddhism during the Heian era (794–1185), a refined secular culture also arose at court. Gradually, over the course of these four centuries, the pervasive influence of Chinese culture in aristocratic society gave rise to new, uniquely Japanese developments. Above all, Heian court culture greatly valued refinement: Pity any man or woman at court who was not accomplished in several forms of art. A woman would be admired merely for the way she arranged the 12 layers of her robes by color, or a man for knowing which kind of incense was being burned. Concurrently, court life became preoccupied by the poetical expression of human love. In this climate, women became a vital force in Heian society. Although the status of women was to decline in later periods, they contributed greatly to art at the Heian court and became famous for their prose and poetry.

Although male couriers continued to be required to read and write Chinese, both men and women of court society wrote prose and poetry in their native Japanese language using the newly devised *kana* script (see "Writing, Language, and Culture," page 357). They also used *kana* on text portions of new types of small-scale secular paintings—handscrolls or folding albums designed to be appreciated in private settings.

At the beginning of the eleventh century, the lady-in-waiting Lady Murasaki transposed the lifestyle of Heian aristocrats into fiction for the amusement of her fellow court ladies, in *The Tale of Genji*, which some experts consider the world's first novel. The Japanese today admire this book as the pinnacle of their culture's

BYODOIN. One of the most beautiful temples of Pure Land Buddhism is the Byodoin, located in the Uji Mountains not far from Kyoto (FIG. 11–9). The temple itself was originally a secular palace whose form was intended to suggest the appearance of the palatial residence of Amida in his Western Paradise (SEE FIG. 10–14). It was built for a member of the powerful Fujiwara family who served as the leading counselor to the emperor. After the counselor's death in the year 1052, his descendants converted the palace into a memorial temple to honor his spirit. The Byodoin is often called the Phoenix Hall, not only for the pair of phoenix images on its roof, but also because the shape of the building itself suggests the mythical bird. Its thin columns give the Byodoin a sense of airiness, as though the entire temple could easily rise up through the sky to Amida's Western Paradise. The hall rests gently in front of an artificial pond created in the shape of the Sanskrit letter A, the sacred symbol for Amida.

The Tale of Genji ▶

Scene from *The Tale of Genji*, Kashiwagi chapter.
Heian period, 12th century CE. Handscroll, ink and colors on paper, 8⅝ × 18⅞″
(21.9 × 47.9 cm). Tokugawa Art Museum, Nagoya. National Treasure.

Only 19 illustrated scenes from this earliest known example of an illustrated hand-scroll of *The Tale of Genji*, created about 100 years after the novel was written, have been preserved. Scholars assume that it once contained illustrations from the entire novel of 54 chapters, approximately 100 pictures in all. Each scroll seems to have been produced by a team of artists. One was the calligrapher, most likely a member of the nobility. Another was the master painter, who outlined two or three illustrations per chapter in fine brushstrokes and indicated the color scheme. Next, colorists went to work, applying layer after layer of color to build up patterns and textures. After they had finished, the master painter returned to reinforce outlines and apply the finishing touches, among them the details of the faces.

Thickly applied mineral colors are now cracking and flaking.

A "line for an eye, hook for a nose" style is used for facial features.

The building interior is seen from a bird's-eye perspective via a "blown-away roof".

A court lady beneath 12 layers of robes holds a fan to shield her face.

Court ladies have long, flowing hair.

A free-standing curtain screen creates privacy.

Wooden verandas surround Japanese houses, merging interior and exterior.

SEE MORE: View the Closer Look feature for the Scene from *The Tale of Genji* www.myartslab.com

literary achievements (in 2009, the official 1,000-year anniversary of its completion, numerous exhibitions and celebrations took place throughout Japan). Underlying the story of the love affairs of Prince Genji and his companions is the Japanese conception of fleeting pleasures and ultimate sadness in life, an echo of the Buddhist view of the vanity of earthly pleasures.

YAMATO-E HANDSCROLLS—*THE TALE OF GENJI*. One of the earliest extant secular paintings from Japan in a new native style is a series of scenes from an illustrated handscroll that depicts *The Tale of Genji*, which unknown artists painted in the twelfth century. The painting of Japanese native subjects in Japanese rather than Chinese styles is known as *yamato-e* (native Japanese-style pictures; Yamato is the old Japanese word for Japan). The type of *yamato-e* painting in the handscroll alternated sections of text with illustrations of scenes from the story and featured delicate lines, strong (but sometimes muted) mineral colors, and asymmetrical compositions. The *Genji* paintings have a refined, subtle emotional impact. They generally show court figures in architectural settings, with the frequent addition of natural elements, such as sections of gardens, that help to convey the mood of the scene. Thus a blossoming cherry tree appears in a scene of happiness, while unkempt weeds appear in a depiction of loneliness. Such correspondence between nature and human emotion is an enduring feature of Japanese poetry and art. The figures in *The Tale of Genji* paintings do not show their emotions directly on their faces, which are rendered with a few simple lines. Instead, their feelings are conveyed by colors, poses, and the total composition of the scenes.

One scene evokes the seemingly happy Prince Genji holding a baby boy borne by his wife, Nyosan. In fact, the baby was fathered by another court noble. Since Genji himself has not been faithful to Nyosan, who appears in profile below him, he cannot complain; meanwhile the true father of the child has died, unable to acknowledge his only son (see "A Closer Look," opposite). Thus, what should be a joyful scene has undercurrents of irony and sorrow. The irony is even greater because Genji himself is the illegitimate son of an emperor.

11–11 • ALBUM LEAF FROM THE *ISHIYAMA-GIRE* (DISPERSED VOLUMES, ONCE OWNED BY THE ISHIYAMA TEMPLE, OF THE ANTHOLOGY OF THE THIRTY-SIX IMMORTAL POETS)
Heian period, early 12th century CE. Ink with gold and silver on decorated and collaged paper, 52 × 17⅓″ (131.8 × 44 cm). Freer Gallery of Art, Smithsonian Institution, Washington, D.C. (F1969.4)

One might expect a painting of such an emotional scene to focus on the people involved. Instead, they are rendered in rather small size, and the scene is dominated by a screen that effectively squeezes Genji and his wife into a corner. This composition deliberately represents how their positions in courtly society have forced them into this unfortunate situation.

CALLIGRAPHY IN JAPANESE. The text portions of the *The Tale of Genji* handscroll were written in *kana* script, which was also used to write poetry in Japanese. In the Heian period, the most popular form of native poetry was a 31-syllable format known as *waka*,

which had first been composed in the eighth century. During the Heian era, the finest *waka* by various writers were collected together and hand-copied in albums, the most popular of which, compiled in the eleventh century, featured writers collectively known as the Thirty-Six Immortal Poets, which is still appreciated by educated Japanese today. The earliest of many surviving examples of this iconic collection originally contained 39 volumes of poems. Two volumes were taken apart and sold in 1929, and now survive in single page sections (FIG. 11–11). Collectively these separated volumes are known as the *Ishiyama-gire* (Ishiyama fragments, named after Ishiyamadera, the temple that originally owned the volumes).

11–12 • Attributed to Toba Sojo DETAIL OF FROLICKING ANIMALS
Heian period, 12th century CE. Handscroll, ink on paper, height 12″ (30.5 cm). Kozanji, Kyoto. National Treasure.

With its simple, flowing symbols interspersed occasionally with more complex Chinese characters, this style of writing created a distinctive asymmetrical balance to the appearance of the written words, entirely different from the formal symmetry of Chinese calligraphy. In these album leaves, the poems seem to float elegantly on fine colored papers decorated with painting, block printing, scattered gold and silver, and sometimes paper collage. Often, as in FIGURE 11–11, the irregular pattern of torn paper edges adds a serendipitous element. The page shown here reproduces two verses by the eighth-century courtier Ki no Tsurayuki that express melancholy emotions. One reads:

> Until yesterday
> I could meet her,
> But today she is gone—
> Like clouds over the mountain
> She has been wafted away.

The spiky, flowing calligraphy and the patterning of the papers, the rich use of gold, and the suggestions of natural imagery match the elegance of the poetry, epitomizing courtly Japanese taste.

YAMATO-E HANDSCROLLS—FROLICKING ANIMALS. In its sedate portrayal of courtly life, *The Tale of Genji* scroll represents one side of *yamato-e*. But another style of native painting emerged contemporaneously. Characterized by bold, rapid strokes of the brush, and little or no use of color, it most often depicted subjects outside the court, in playful and irreverent activities. One of the early masterpieces of this style is *Frolicking Animals*, a set of handscrolls satirizing the life of many different levels of society. Painted entirely in ink,

the scrolls are attributed to Toba Sojo, the abbot of a Buddhist temple, and they represent the humor of Japanese art to the full.

In one scene, a frog buddha sits upon an altar while a monkey dressed as a monk prays proudly to him; in other scenes frogs, donkeys, foxes, and rabbits play, swim, and wrestle, with one frog boasting of his prowess when he flings a rabbit to the ground (FIG. 11–12). Unlike the *Genji* scroll, there is no text to *Frolicking Animals*, so it is hard to know exactly what was being satirized. Nevertheless, the universality of the humorous antics portrayed in this scroll highlights an important aspect of Japanese art that makes it instantly engaging to viewers everywhere.

KAMAKURA PERIOD

The courtiers of the Heian era became so engrossed in their own refinement that they neglected their responsibilities for governing the country. Clans of warriors—samurai—from outside the capital grew increasingly strong. Two of these, the Taira and Minamoto, wielded the most power and took opposing sides in the factional conflicts of the imperial court, in order to control the weakened emperor and take charge of running the country.

The Kamakura era (1185–1333) began when the head of the Minamoto clan, Yoritomo (1147–1199), defeated the Taira family and ordered the emperor to appoint him as shogun (general-in-chief). To resist the softening effects of courtly life in Kyoto, he established his military capital in Kamakura, while the emperor continued to reside in Kyoto. Although Yoritomo's newly invented title of shogun nominally respected the authority of the emperor, at the same time it assured him of supreme military and political

Arms and Armor

Battles such as the one depicted in *Night Attack on the Sanjo Palace* (SEE FIG. 11–13) were fought largely by archers on horseback. Samurai archers charged the enemy at full gallop and loosed their arrows just before they wheeled away. The scroll clearly shows their distinctive bow, with its asymmetrically placed handgrip. The lower portion of the bow is shorter than the upper so it can clear the horse's neck. The samurai wear a long, curved sword at the waist.

By the tenth century, Japanese swordsmiths had perfected techniques for crafting their legendarily sharp swords. Sword-makers face a fundamental difficulty: steel hard enough to hold a razor-sharp edge is brittle and breaks easily, but steel resilient enough to withstand rough use is too soft to hold a keen edge. The Japanese ingeniously forged a blade which laminated a hard cutting edge within less brittle support layers.

The earliest form of samurai armor, illustrated here, known as *yoroi*, was intended for use by warriors on horseback, as seen in FIGURE 11–13. It was made of overlapping iron and lacquered leather scales, punched with holes and laced together with leather thongs and brightly colored silk braids. The principal piece wrapped around the chest, left side, and back. Padded shoulder straps hooked it together back to front. A separate piece of armor was tied to the body to protect the right side. The upper legs were protected by a four-sided skirt that attached to the body armor, while two large rectangular panels tied on with cords guarded the arms. The helmet was made of iron plates riveted together. From it hung a neckguard flared sharply outward to protect the face from arrows shot at close range as the samurai wheeled away from an attack.

helmet

detail of scales

body armor

power. This tradition of rule by shogun that Yoritomo initiated lasted in various forms until 1868.

A BATTLE HANDSCROLL. The battles for domination between the Minamoto and the Taira became famous not only in medieval Japanese history but also in literature and art. One of the great painted handscrolls depicting these battles is **NIGHT ATTACK ON THE SANJO PALACE (FIG. 11–13)**. Painted perhaps 100 years after the actual event, the scroll conveys a sense of eye-witness reporting even though the anonymous artist had to imagine the scene from verbal (and at best semifactual) descriptions. The style of the painting includes some of the brisk and lively linework of *Frolicking Animals* and also traces of the more refined brushwork, use of color, and bird's-eye viewpoint of *The Tale of Genji* scroll. The main element, however, is the savage depiction of warfare (see "Arms and Armor," above). Unlike the *Genji* scroll, *Night Attack* is full of action: flames engulf the palace, horses charge, warriors behead their enemies, court ladies try to hide, and a sense of

energy and violence is conveyed with great sweep and power. The era of poetic refinement was now over in Japan, and the new world of the samurai began to dominate the secular arts.

PURE LAND BUDDHIST ART

By the beginning of the Kamakura period, Pure Land Buddhist beliefs had swept throughout Japan, and several charismatic priests founded new sects to preach this ideology. They traveled all around the country spreading the new gospel, which appealed to people of all levels of education and sophistication. They were so successful that since the Kamakura period, Pure Land Buddhist sects have remained the most popular form of Buddhism in Japan.

A PORTRAIT SCULPTURE. The itinerant monk Kuya (903–972), famous for urging country folk to join him in singing chants in praise of the Buddha Amida, was one of the early proponents of Pure Land practices. Kamakura-period Pure Land Buddhist followers regarded him as a founder of their religious tradition.

11-13 • SECTION OF *NIGHT ATTACK ON THE SANJO PALACE*

Kamakura period, late 13th century CE. Handscroll, ink and colors on paper, 16¼ × 275½" (41.3 × 699.7 cm). Museum of Fine Arts, Boston.

Fenollosa-Weld Collection (11.4000)

The battles between the Minamoto and Taira clans were fought primarily by mounted and armored warriors, who used both bows and arrows, and the finest swords. In the year 1160, some 500 Minamoto rebels opposed to the retired emperor Go-Shirakawa carried out a daring raid on the Sanjo Palace. In a surprise attack in the middle of the night, they abducted the emperor. The scene was one of great carnage, much of it caused by the burning of the wooden palace. Despite the drama of the scene, this was not the decisive moment in the war. The Minamoto rebels would eventually lose more important battles to their Taira enemies. Yet Minamoto forces, heirs to those who carried out this raid, would eventually prove victorious, destroying the Taira clan in 1185.

Believers would have immediately recognized Kuya in this thirteenth-century portrait statue by Kosho **(FIG. 11–14)**: The traveling clothes, the small gong, the staff topped by deer horns (symbolic of his slaying a deer, whose death converted him to Buddhism), clearly identify the monk, whose sweetly intense expression gives this sculpture a radiant sense of faith. As for Kuya's chant, Kosho's solution to the challenge of putting words into sculptural form was simple but brilliant: He carved six small buddhas emerging from Kuya's mouth, one for each of the six syllables of *Na-mu-A-mi-da-Buts(u)* (the final u is not articulated). Believers would have understood that these six small buddhas embodied the Pure Land chant.

RAIGO PAINTINGS.   Pure Land Buddhism taught that even one sincere invocation of the sacred chant could lead the most wicked sinner to the Western Paradise. Paintings called **raigo** ("welcoming approach") were created depicting the Amida Buddha, accompanied by bodhisattvas, coming down to earth to welcome the soul of the dying believer. Golden cords were often attached to these paintings, which were taken to the homes of the dying. A person near death held onto these cords, hoping that Amida would escort the soul directly to paradise.

Raigo paintings differ significantly in style from the complex *mandala*s and fierce guardian deities of esoteric Buddhism. The

11-14 • Kosho KUYA PREACHING

Kamakura period, before 1207 CE. Painted wood with inlaid eyes, height 46½" (117.5 cm). Rokuhara Mitsuji, Kyoto. Important Cultural Property.

11–15 • DESCENT OF AMIDA AND THE TWENTY-FIVE BODHISATTVAS
Kamakura period, 13th century CE. Hanging scroll, colors and gold on silk, 57¼ × 61½″ (145 × 155.5 cm).
Chionin, Kyoto. National Treasure.

earliest known example of this subject is found on the walls and
doors of the Phoenix Hall, surrounding Jocho's sculpture of Amida
(SEE FIG. 11–10). Like that statue, they radiate warmth and
compassion. In the Kamakura period, *raigo* paintings were made in
great numbers, reflecting the popularity of Pure Land Buddhism at
that time. One magnificent example portrays Amida Buddha and
25 bodhisattvas swiftly descending over mountains. The artist used
gold paint and thin slivers of gold leaf cut in elaborate patterning
to suggest the divine radiance of the deities (FIG. 11–15). This

painstaking cut-gold leaf technique, known as *kirikane*, is one
of the great achievements of early Japanese Buddhist artists. It
originated in China, but Japanese artists refined and perfected it. In
this painting, the darkened silk behind the figures heightens the
sparkle of their golden aura. In the flickering light of oil lamps and
torches, *raigo* paintings would have appeared magical in a temple or
a dying person's home.

One of the most remarkable aspects of this painting is its
sensitive rendering of the landscape, full of rugged peaks and

Daruma, Founder of Zen

Zen monks modeled their behavior on that of the patriarch or founder of their lineage, the mythical Indian Buddhist sage Daruma (Bodhidharma in Sanskrit), who emigrated to China in the sixth century CE, and famously transmitted his teachings to a Chinese disciple, who became the second Chan patriarch. This portrait of *Daruma* (FIG. A) is one of the earliest surviving examples of a Japanese Zen painting. Using fine ink outlines and a touch of color for the robe and the figure's sandals, the artist portrays the Zen master seated meditating atop a rock, with an unwavering focused gaze that is intended to convey his inner strength and serenity. At the top of the scroll is an inscription in Chinese by Yishan Yining (1247–1317), one of several influential early Chinese Chan masters to emigrate to Japan. He had actually planned only to visit in his role as head of an official diplomatic delegation from China in 1299, but he wound up staying for the duration of his life. Although wary of him at first, his sincere intentions to teach Zen and his erudite abilities quickly attracted influential supporters, to whom he taught Chinese religious practices and cultural traditions. Thus soon after arrival, Yishan was appointed as the tenth head abbot of the large Zen temple of Kenchoji in Kamakura, a post he held briefly, before moving on to head several other Zen temples.

Kenchoji had been founded in 1253 by another emigrant Chan master, Lanxi Daolong (1213–1278). Lanxi had been the first Chan master to travel to Japan. There, he was warmly received by the fifth Minamoto shogun who helped him plan construction of Kenchoji where, for the first time, authentic Chinese Chan Buddhism was to be taught in Japan. Kenchoji remains one of the most important Zen monasteries in Japan today. The temple owns many formal portraits of its founder, including this one (FIG. B), considered by many to be the best, in that it seems to capture Daolong's inner spirit as well as his outer form. This type of painting is peculiar to Chan and Zen sects and is known as *chinso*. These paintings were often gifts given by a master to disciples when they completed their formal training and departed his presence to officiate at their own temples. They served as personal reminders of their master's teachings and tangible evidence of their right to transmit Zen teachings to their own pupils (like a diploma). Lanxi Daolong dedicated the inscription of this painting to an important regent (samurai official), a confidant of the shogun, and not an ordained Zen monk. This shows that Zen, from its early days in Japan, also strove to attract followers from among those in power who could not abandon their secular life for the rigorous, cloistered existence required of Zen monks who lived in temples.

A. DARUMA
Artist unknown, inscription by Chinese Chan (Zen) master Yishan Yining (1247–1317). Kamakura period, early 14th century CE. Hanging scroll, ink and colors on silk, 39⅝ × 20″ (100.8 × 50.8 cm). Tokyo National Museum. Important Cultural Property.

B. PORTRAIT OF THE CHINESE ZEN MASTER LANXI DAOLONG
Inscription by Lanxi Daolong. Kamakura period, dated 1271 CE. Hanging scroll, colors on silk, 41⅓ × 18″ (105 × 46.1 cm). Kenchoji, Kamakura. National Treasure.

flowering trees. These natural elements reveal that the Japanese possessed great appreciation for the beautiful land in which they dwelled, an appreciation that stems from Shinto beliefs. Coincidence cannot account for the fact that Shinto pictures portraying the landscape of Japan as divine first appeared in the Kamakura period, just when Pure Land Buddhism grew popular. One of these paintings is the Kasuga Shrine *mandala* of FIGURE 11–1. It illustrates how artists contributed to the merging of the two faiths of Buddhism and Shinto at that time. The artist of this work intentionally made the shrine buildings resemble those of the palatial abode of Amida in his Western Paradise and rendered the landscape details with the radiant charm of Amida's heaven.

ZEN BUDDHIST ART

Toward the latter part of the Kamakura period, Zen Buddhism was introduced to Japan from China where it was already highly developed and known as Chan. Zen had been slow to reach Japan because of the interruption of relations between the two countries during the Heian period. But during the Kamakura era, both emigrant Chinese (see "Daruma, Founder of Zen," opposite) and Japanese monks who went to China to study Buddhism, and returned home enthused about the new teachings they learned there, brought Zen to Japan. The monk Kuya, represented in the statue by Kosho (SEE FIG. 11–14), epitomized the itinerant life of a Pure Land Buddhist monk who wandered the countryside and relied on the generosity of believers to support him. Zen monks lived very differently. They secluded themselves in monasteries, leading an austere life of simplicity and self-responsibility.

In some ways, Zen resembles the original teachings of the historical Buddha in that it emphasizes individual enlightenment through meditation, without the help of deities or magical chants. It especially appealed to the self-disciplined spirit of samurai warriors, who were not satisfied with the older forms of Buddhism connected with the Japanese court. Zen was the last major form of Buddhism to reach Japan from the Asian mainland and it had a profound and lasting impact on Japanese arts and culture.

Just as the *Night Attack* (SEE FIG. 11–13) reveals a propensity for recording the consequences of political turbulence through representation of gruesome battle scenes in vivid colors, Kamakura-era Buddhist sculpture and painting also emphasized realism. Various factors account for this new taste. Society was dominated by samurai warriors, who possessed a more pragmatic outlook on the world than the Heian-period courtiers who lived a dreamlike existence at court. In addition, renewed contacts with China introduced new styles for Buddhist art that also emphasized realism. Finally, forging personal connections with heroic exploits and individuals, both past and present, political and religious, greatly concerned the people of the Kamakura period. Representing these figures in arresting pictorial and sculpted images helped reinforce legends and perpetuate their influence, which accounts for the predominance of these subjects in the period's art.

As the Kamakura era ended, the seeds of the future were planted both politically and culturally: The coming age witnessed the nation's continued dominance by the warrior class and the establishment of Zen as the religion of choice among those warriors who wielded power at the highest levels. As before, the later history of Japanese art continued to be marked by an intriguing interplay between native traditions and imported foreign culture.

THINK ABOUT IT

11.1 Discuss Japan's relationship with China during the Kamakura period with respect to patterns of influence. Include specific examples related to society, as well as art techniques learned, referring to Chapter 10 as necessary.

11.2 Discuss the development of Japanese native-style arts during the Heian period. Define the main characteristics of native traditions of writing and secular painting. Describe how the innovations in new forms of Buddhist sculpture then differed from older forms in appearance, technique, and materials used.

11.3 Discuss the development of Buddhist practice and Buddhist sculpture over the course of time in Japan by selecting an image or object from three of the following four periods: Asuka, Nara, Heian, Kamakura. Explain each work in the context of its respective culture, including its relation to particular practices of Buddhism, for example Zen.

11.4 Summarize the beliefs of the Shinto religion and discuss the integration of Shinto and Buddhist traditions in Japanese culture.

11.5 Distinguish the defining characteristics of esoteric and Pure Land Buddhist painting and explain these differences with reference to one work of each from the chapter.

PRACTICE MORE: Compose answers to these questions, get flashcards for images and terms, and review chapter material with quizzes **www.myartslab.com**

12-1 • OFFERING 4, LA VENTA   Mexico. Olmec culture, c. 900–400 BCE. Jade, greenstone, and sandstone, height of figures 6¼–7″ (16–18 cm). Museo Nacional de Antropología, Mexico City.

ART OF THE AMERICAS BEFORE 1300

The scene hints at a story in progress. Fifteen figures of precious greenstone converge on a single figure made of a baser, more porous stone. The tall oblong stones (**celts**) in the background evoke an architectural space, perhaps a location within the Olmec center of La Venta, where this tableau was created sometime between 900 and 400 BCE. The figures have the slouching bodies, elongated heads, almond-shaped eyes, and downturned mouths characteristic of Olmec art. Holes for earrings and the simple lines of the bodies suggest that these sculptures may originally have been dressed and adorned with perishable materials. The poses of the figures, with their knees slightly bent and their arms flexed at their sides, lend a sense of arrested movement to this enigmatic scene. Is it a council? a trial? an initiation? Are the greenstone figures marching in front of the reddish granite figure as he reviews them, or moving to confront him? With no texts to explain the scene, the specific tale it narrates may never be known, but it is clear that this offering commemorates an important event.

And it was remembered. This tableau (FIG. 12–1) was set up in the earth and buried underneath a plaza at La Venta, one of a number of offerings of works of art and precious materials beneath the surface of the city. Colored sand and floors covered the offerings, each colored floor signifying a successive renovation of the plaza. Over a century after these sculptures were buried, a hole was dug directly over the offering and it was viewed once more. Pieces of the later floors fell into the hole, but the figures themselves were not disturbed. After this, the scene was buried once again. The precision of this later excavation suggests that the exact location of the tableau was remembered. The archaeological record makes clear that this work of art, although hidden, still exerted tremendous power.

This extraordinary find demonstrates the importance of scientific archaeological excavations for understanding ancient art. Had these objects been torn out of the ground by looters and sold piecemeal on the black market, we would never have known how Olmec sculptures were used to create narrative installations or imagined that buried art could be remembered for so long. Instead, this discovery provides a context for isolated greenstone figures that have been found throughout Mesoamerica (modern Mexico, Guatemala, and Honduras). It provides evidence that these sculptures were made by the Olmec, Mesoamerica's first great civilization, and suggests that these objects, scattered today, might have once been assembled in meaningful ways like the offering at La Venta.

LEARN ABOUT IT

12.1 Recognize how differences in environmental conditions affected the artistic output of Mesoamerica, South America, and North America.

12.2 Explore how the role or function of an object is critical to understanding its meaning in ancient American visual arts.

12.3 Compare and contrast the use of urban planning in ancient American cultures.

12.4 Examine how Maya writing functions, and how it relates to Maya images.

HEAR MORE: Listen to an audio file of your chapter www.myartslab.com

CHAPTER 12

377

THE NEW WORLD

In recent years the question of the original settlement of the Americas has become an area of debate. The traditional view has been that human beings arrived in North and South America from Asia during the last Ice Age, when glaciers trapped enough of the world's water to lower the level of the oceans and expose a land bridge across the Bering Strait. Although most of present-day Alaska and Canada was covered by glaciers at that time, an ice-free corridor along the Pacific coast would have provided access from Asia to the south and east. Thus, this theory holds that sometime before 12,000 years ago, perhaps as early as 20,000 to 30,000 years ago, Paleolithic hunter-gatherers emerged through this corridor and began to spread out into two vast, uninhabited continents. This view is now challenged by the early dates of some new archaeological finds and by evidence suggesting the possibility of early connections with Europe as well, perhaps along the Arctic coast of the North Atlantic. In any event, by between 10,000 and 12,000 years ago, bands of hunters roamed throughout the Americas, and after the ice had retreated, the peoples of the Western Hemisphere were essentially cut off from the rest of the world until they were overrun by European invaders, beginning at the end of the fifteenth century CE.

In this isolation the peoples of the Americas experienced cultural transformations similar to those seen elsewhere around the world following the end of the Paleolithic era. In most regions they developed an agricultural way of life. A trio of native plants—corn, beans, and squash—was especially important, but people also cultivated potatoes, tobacco, cacao, tomatoes, and avocados. New World peoples also domesticated many animals: dogs, turkeys, guinea pigs, llamas, and their camelid cousins—alpacas, guanacos, and vicuñas.

As elsewhere, the shift to agriculture in the Americas was accompanied by population growth and, in some places, the rise of hierarchical societies, the appearance of ceremonial centers and towns with monumental architecture, and the development of sculpture, ceramics, and other arts. The people of Mesoamerica—the region that extends from central Mexico well into Central America—developed writing, astronomy, a complex and accurate calendar, and a sophisticated system of mathematics. Central and South American peoples had advanced metallurgy and produced exquisite gold, silver, and copper objects. The metalworkers of the Andes, the mountain range along the western coast of South America, began to produce metal jewelry, weapons, and agricultural implements in the first millennium CE, and people elsewhere in the Americas made tools, weapons, and art from other materials such as bone, ivory, stone, wood, and, where it was available, obsidian, a volcanic glass capable of a cutting edge 500 times finer than surgical steel. Basketry and weaving became major art forms. In the American Southwest, Native American people built multi-storied, apartmentlike village and cliff dwellings, as well as elaborate irrigation systems with canals. Evidence of weaving in the American Southwest dates to about 7400 BCE.

Extraordinary artistic traditions flourished in many regions in the Americas before 1300 CE. This chapter explores the accomplishments of some of the cultures in five of those areas: Mesoamerica, Central America, the central Andes of South America, the Southeastern Woodlands and great river valleys of North America, and the North American Southwest.

MESOAMERICA

Ancient Mesoamerica encompasses the area from north of the Valley of Mexico (the location of Mexico City) to present-day Belize, Honduras, and western Nicaragua in Central America (MAP 12–1). The region is one of great contrasts, ranging from tropical rainforest to semiarid mountains. The civilizations that arose in Mesoamerica varied, but they were linked by cultural similarities and trade. Among their shared features were a ballgame with religious and political significance (see "The Cosmic Ballgame," page 389), aspects of monumental building construction, and a complex system of multiple calendars including a 260-day divinatory cycle and a 365-day ritual and agricultural cycle. Many Mesoamerican societies were sharply divided into elite and commoner classes.

The transition to farming began in Mesoamerica between 7000 and 6000 BCE, and by 3000 to 2000 BCE settled villages were widespread. Customarily the region's subsequent history is divided into three broad periods: Formative or Preclassic (1500 BCE–250 CE), Classic (250–900 CE), and Postclassic (900–1521 CE). This chronology derives primarily from the archaeology of the Maya—the people of Guatemala, southern Mexico, and the Yucatan Peninsula—with the Classic period bracketing the era during which the Maya erected dated stone monuments. The term reflects the view of early scholars that the Classic period was a kind of golden age. Although this view is no longer current—and the periods are only roughly applicable to other cultures of Mesoamerica—the terminology has endured.

THE OLMEC

The first major Mesoamerican art style, that of the Olmec, emerged during the Formative/Preclassic period, beginning around 1500 BCE. Many of the key elements of Mesoamerican art, including monumental stone sculpture commemorating individual rulers, finely carved jades, elegant ceramics, and architectural elements such as pyramids, plazas, and ballcourts, were first developed by the Olmec. In the fertile, swampy coastal areas of the present-day Mexican states of Veracruz and Tabasco, the Olmec raised massive earth mounds on which they constructed ceremonial centers. These centers probably housed an elite group of rulers and priests supported by a larger population of farmers who lived in villages of pole-and-thatch houses. The presence at Olmec sites of goods such as obsidian, iron ore, and jade that are not found in the Gulf of Mexico region but come from throughout Mesoamerica indicates that the Olmec participated in extensive long-distance trade. They went to especially great lengths

MAP 12-1 • THE AMERICAS BEFORE 1300

People moved across North America, then southward through Central America until they reached the Tierra del Fuego region of South America.

to acquire jade, which was one of the most precious materials in ancient Mesoamerica.

The earliest Olmec ceremonial center (c. 1200–900 BCE), at San Lorenzo, was built atop a giant earthwork, nearly three-quarters of a mile long, with an elaborate stone drainage system running throughout the mound. Other architectural features included a palace with basalt columns, a possible ballcourt, and a stone-carving workshop. Another center, at La Venta, thriving from about 900 to 400 BCE, was built on high ground between rivers. Its most prominent feature, an earth mound known as the Great Pyramid, still rises to a height of over 100 feet (FIG. 12–2). The pyramid stands at the south end of a large, open plaza arranged on a north–south axis and defined by long, low earth mounds. Many of the physical features of La Venta—including the symmetrical arrangement of earth mounds, platforms, and central open spaces along an axis that was probably determined by

astronomical observations—are characteristic of later monumental and ceremonial architecture throughout Mesoamerica. What was buried beneath the surface of La Venta—massive stone mosaics, layers of colored clay, and greenstone figures like those in FIGURE 12–1, discussed at the beginning of the chapter—may have been as important as what was visible on the surface.

The Olmec produced an abundance of monumental basalt sculpture, including **COLOSSAL HEADS** (FIG. 12–3), altars, and seated figures. The huge basalt blocks for the large works of sculpture were quarried at distant sites and transported to San Lorenzo, La Venta, and other centers. Colossal heads ranged in height from 5 to 12 feet and weighed from 5 to more than 20 tons. The heads portray adult males wearing close-fitting caps with chin straps and large, round earspools (cylindrical earrings that pierce the earlobe). The fleshy faces have almond-shaped eyes, flat broad noses, thick protruding lips, and downturned mouths. Each face is different, suggesting that they may represent specific individuals. Ten colossal heads were found at San Lorenzo. Many had been mutilated and buried by about 900 BCE, when the site went into decline. At La Venta, 102 basalt monuments have been found, including four more colossal heads, massive thrones or altars, tall stone **stelae**, and other kinds of figural sculpture. The colossal heads and the subjects depicted on other monumental sculpture suggest that the Olmec elite were interested in commemorating rulers and historic events.

In addition to these heavy basalt monuments, Olmec artists also made smaller, more portable jade and ceramic objects (SEE FIG. 12–1). Jade, available only from the Motagua River valley in present-day Guatemala, was prized for its brilliant blue-green color and the smooth, shiny surfaces it could achieve with careful polishing. Jade is one of the hardest materials in Mesoamerica, and with only stone tools available, Olmec craftsmen used jade tools and powdered jade dust as an abrasive to carve and polish these sculptures. Other figurines were made out of softer and more malleable greenstones, like serpentine, which occur in many parts of Mesoamerica. Olmec ceramics, including decorated vessels and

12-3 • COLOSSAL HEAD, SAN LORENZO
Mexico. Olmec culture, c. 1200–900 BCE. Basalt, height 7′5″ (2.26 m).

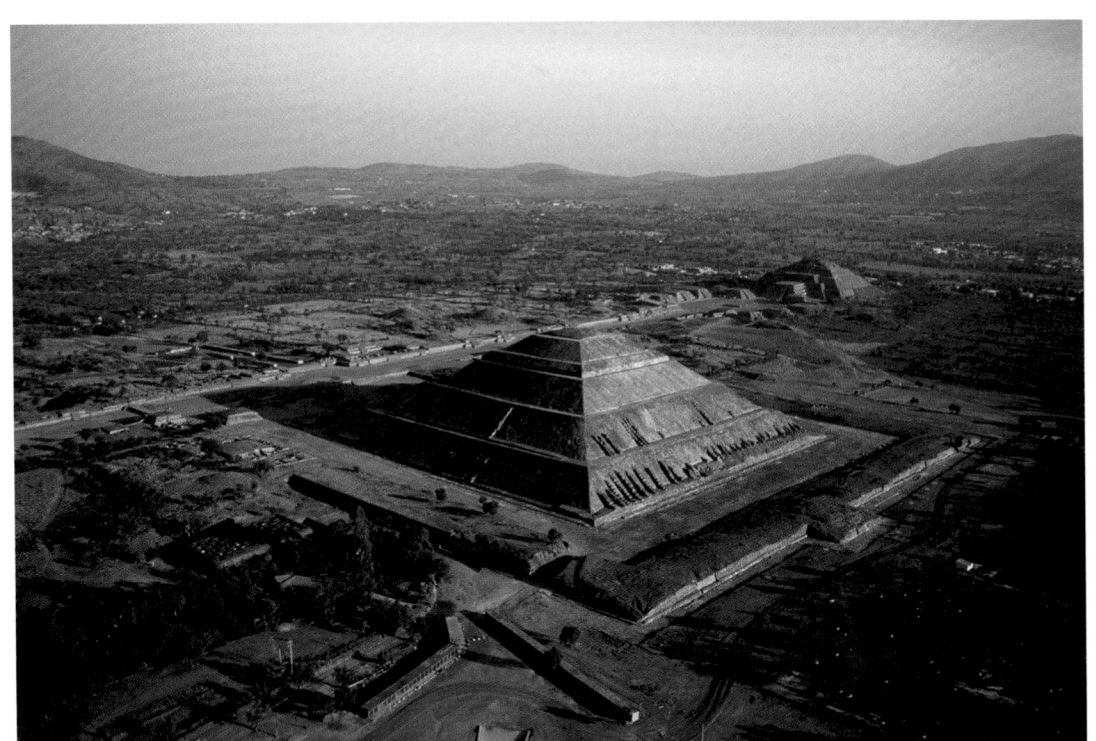

12-4 • CEREMONIAL CENTER OF THE CITY OF TEOTIHUACAN

Mexico. Teotihuacan culture, c. 100–650 CE. View from the southeast. The Pyramid of the Sun is in the foreground, and the Pyramid of the Moon is visible in the distance. The Avenue of the Dead, the north–south axis of the city, which connects the two pyramids, continues for over a mile.

SEE MORE: View a simulation about the Ceremonial Center of Teotihuacan
www.myartslab.com

remarkably lifelike clay babies, also appear to have been prized far beyond the Olmec heartland. Olmec greenstone and ceramic objects have been found throughout Mesoamerica, evidence of the extensive reach and influence of Olmec art and culture.

By 200 CE, forests and swamps had begun to reclaim Olmec sites, but Olmec civilization had spread widely throughout Mesoamerica and was to have an enduring influence on its successors. As the Olmec centers of the Gulf Coast faded, the great Classic period centers in the Maya region and Teotihuacan area in the Valley of Mexico were beginning their ascendancy.

TEOTIHUACAN

Located some 30 miles northeast of present-day Mexico City, the city of Teotihuacan experienced a period of rapid growth early in the first millennium CE. By 200 CE, it had emerged as Mesoamerica's first truly urban settlement, a significant center of commerce and manufacturing. At its height, between 300 and 650, Teotihuacan covered nearly nine square miles and had a population of at least 125,000, making it the largest city in the Americas and one of the largest in the world at that time (FIG. 12–4). Its residents lived in walled "apartment compounds," and the entire city was organized on a grid (FIG. 12–5), its orientation chosen both for its calendrical significance and to respond to the surrounding landscape.

Although Teotihuacan declined in power after 650, it was never forgotten. Centuries later, it remained a legendary pilgrimage center. The much later Aztec people (c. 1300–1525) revered the site, believing it to be the place where the gods created the sun and the moon. In fact, Teotihuacan, a word indicating a place of divinity, is the Aztec name for the city. The names we use for its principal monuments are also Aztec names. We do not know what

12-5 • PLAN OF THE CEREMONIAL CENTER OF TEOTIHUACAN

12-6 • PYRAMID OF THE FEATHERED SERPENT

The Ciudadela, Teotihuacan, Mexico. Teotihuacan culture, c. 200 CE.

the original inhabitants of Teotihuacan called these buildings or what they called their own city.

The center of the city is bisected by a broad thoroughfare laid out on a north–south axis, extending for more than a mile and in places as much as 150 feet wide, which the Aztecs called the Avenue of the Dead. At the center of the Teotihuacan grid, a series of canals forced the San Juan River to run perpendicular to the avenue. At the north end of this central axis stands the Pyramid of the Moon, facing a large plaza flanked by smaller, symmetrically placed platforms. It seems to echo the shape of the mountain behind it, and as one walks towards the pyramid, it looms above, eclipsing the mountain completely. The Pyramid of the Moon was enlarged several times, as were many Mesoamerican pyramids; each enlargement completely enclosed the previous structure and was accompanied by rich sacrificial offerings.

The largest of Teotihuacan's architectural monuments, the Pyramid of the Sun, located just to the east of the Avenue of the Dead, is slightly over 200 feet high and measures about 720 feet on each side at its base, similar in size to, but not as tall as, the largest Egyptian pyramid at Giza. It is built over a multi-chambered cave

with a spring that may have been the original focus of worship at the site and its source of prestige. The pyramid rises in a series of sloping steps to a flat platform, where a small temple once stood. A monumental stone stairway led from level to level up the side of the pyramid to the temple platform. The exterior was faced with stone, which was then stuccoed and painted.

At the southern end of the ceremonial center, and at the heart of the city, is the Ciudadela (Spanish for a fortified city center), a vast sunken plaza surrounded by temple platforms. One of the city's principal religious and political centers, the plaza could accommodate an assembly of more than 60,000 people. Early in Teotihuacan's history, its focal point was the **PYRAMID OF THE FEATHERED SERPENT (FIG. 12–6)**. This seven-tiered structure exhibits the *talud-tablero* (slope-and-panel) construction that is a hallmark of the Teotihuacan architectural style. The *talud* (sloping base) of each platform supports a *tablero* (entablature), that rises vertically and is surrounded by a frame.

Archaeological excavations of the temple's early phase have revealed undulating feathered serpents floating in a watery space punctuated by reliefs of aquatic shells. Their flat, angular, abstract

12-7 • BLOODLETTING RITUAL
Fragment of a fresco from Teotihuacan, Mexico. Teotihuacan culture, c. 550–650 CE. Pigment on lime plaster, 32¼ × 45¼″ (82 × 116.1 cm). The Cleveland Museum of Art. Purchase from the J. H. Wade Fund (63.252)

The maguey plant supplied the people of Teotihuacan with food, with fiber for making clothing, rope, and paper, and with the precious drink pulque. As this painting indicates, priestly officials used its spikes in rituals to draw their own blood as a sacrifice.

style, typical of Teotihuacan art, is in marked contrast to the curvilinear forms of Olmec art. While the bodies of the feathered serpents are rendered in low relief, three-dimensional fanged serpent heads emerge from aureoles of stylized feathers. In the vertical *tablero* sections, each serpent carries on its body a squarish headdress with a protruding upper jaw, huge, round eyes originally inlaid with obsidian, and a pair of round goggles on its forehead between the eyes. These mosaic headdresses seem to represent an aspect of the Teotihuacan Storm God associated with warfare—other works of art at Teotihuacan and elsewhere in Mesoamerica show armed warriors wearing the same headdress. Inside the pyramid, this militaristic message was reinforced by the burials of dozens of sacrificial victims, some of them wearing necklaces made of human maxillae and jawbones (or shell imitations thereof), their arms tied behind their backs. In the fourth century, the elaborate sculptural façade of the Pyramid of the Feathered Serpent was concealed behind a plainer *talud-tablero* structure tacked onto the front of the pyramid.

The residential sections of Teotihuacan fanned out from the city's center. The large and spacious palaces of the elite, with as many as 45 rooms and seven patios, stood nearest the ceremonial center. Artisans, foreign traders, and peasants lived farther away, in more crowded compounds, all aligned to the Teotihuacan grid. Palaces and more humble homes alike were rectangular one-story structures with high walls and suites of rooms arranged around open courtyards. Walls were plastered and covered with paintings.

Teotihuacan's artists worked in a fresco technique, applying pigments directly on damp lime plaster. Once the paint was applied, the walls were polished to give a smooth, shiny, and durable surface. The style, like that of the sculpture, was flat, angular, and abstract, often featuring processions of similarly dressed figures, rows of mythological animals, or other kinds of repeating images. Teotihuacan painters worked in several different coloristic modes, including a bright polychrome and a more restricted palette emphasizing tones of red. A detached fragment of a wall painting, now in the Cleveland Museum of Art, depicts a **BLOODLETTING RITUAL** in which an elaborately dressed man enriches and revitalizes the earth with his own blood **(FIG. 12–7)**. The man's large animal headdress, decorated with precious feathers from the quetzal bird, indicates his high rank. He stands between rectangular plots of earth or bundles of grass pierced with bloody maguey spines (used in bloodletting), and he scatters seeds or drops of blood from his right hand, as indicated by the stream of conventionalized symbols for blood, seeds, and flowers falling from his hand. The sound scroll emerging from his open mouth symbolizes his ritual chant. The visual weight accorded the headdress and the sound scroll suggests that the man's priestly office and chanted words were essential elements of the ceremony. Such bloodletting rituals were widespread in Mesoamerica.

Teotihuacan was a wealthy and cosmopolitan city, home to people from all over Mesoamerica. One reason for its wealth was its control of a source of high-quality obsidian. Goods made at Teotihuacan, including obsidian tools and pottery, were distributed widely throughout Mesoamerica in exchange for luxury items such as the brilliant green feathers of the quetzal bird. Yet not all interactions between Teotihuacan and other Mesoamerican centers were peaceful—the threat of Teotihuacan military force, so clearly expressed at the Pyramid of the Feathered Serpent, was always present.

Sometime in the early seventh century disaster struck Teotihuacan. The ceremonial center was sacked and burned, and the city went into a permanent decline. Nevertheless, its influence continued as other centers throughout Mesoamerica, as far south as the highlands of Guatemala, borrowed and transformed its imagery over the next several centuries.

THE MAYA

The ancient Maya are noted for a number of achievements. In densely populated cities they built imposing pyramids, temples, palaces, and administrative structures. They developed the most advanced hieroglyphic writing in Mesoamerica and perfected a sophisticated version of the Mesoamerican calendrical system (see "Maya Writing," opposite). Using these, they recorded the accomplishments of their rulers on sculpture, ceramic vessels, wall paintings, and in books. They studied astronomy and the natural cycles of plants and animals, and used sophisticated mathematical concepts such as zero and place value.

An increasingly detailed picture of the Maya has been emerging from recent archaeological research and from advances in deciphering their writing. That picture shows a society divided into competing city-states, each with a hereditary ruler and an elite class of nobles and priests supported by a large group of farmer-commoners. Rulers established their legitimacy, maintained links with their divine ancestors, commemorated important calendrical dates, and sustained the gods through elaborate rituals, including ballgames, bloodletting ceremonies, and human sacrifice. Rulers commemorated such events and their military exploits on carved stelae. A complex pantheon of deities presided over the Maya universe.

12-8 • BASE OF NORTH ACROPOLIS (LEFT) AND TEMPLE I
Tikal, Guatemala. Maya culture. North Acropolis, 4th century BCE–5th century CE; Temple I (Tomb of Ruler A), c. 734 CE.

ART AND ITS CONTEXTS

Maya Writing

Maya writing is **logosyllabic**—it consists of ideographs or logographs that represent entire words as well as a set of symbols that stand for the sound of each syllable in the Maya language. Thus, a word like *balam* (jaguar) could be written in many different ways: with the logograph "BALAM", a picture of the head of a jaguar (top right); with three syllables, "ba-la-ma", for the sounds of the word *balam* (bottom right); or a combination of the two systems—the logograph "BALAM" complemented with one or more phonetic syllables, to make it clear which logograph was represented (to avoid the possibility of confusing this logograph with the symbol for *hix*, another kind of feline, for example) (middle right). The combination of these two systems allowed Maya scribes extraordinary flexibility, and some calligraphers seem to have delighted in finding as many different ways as possible to write the same word. Many Maya logographs remained very pictorial, like the glyph for jaguar illustrated here, which meant that Maya writing was never too distant from other kinds of image making. In fact, the same word, *ts'ib*, signified both writing and painting in the Classic Mayan language.

With major advances in the decipherment of Maya hieroglyphic writing—beginning in the 1950s and continuing to this day—it has become clear that the inscriptions on Maya architecture and stelae appear almost entirely devoted to historical events. They record the dates of royal marriages, births of heirs, alliances between cities, and great military victories, and they tie these events to astronomical events and propitious dates in the Maya calendar. We know that the Maya also wrote books, but only four of these fragile manuscripts—called codices—have survived, all of them from the Postclassic period.

BALAM

ba-BALAM

BALAM-ma

ba-BALAM-ma

ba-la-ma

Maya civilization emerged during the late Preclassic period (400 BCE–250 CE), reached its peak in the southern lowlands of Mexico and Guatemala during the Classic period (250–900 CE), and shifted to the northern Yucatan Peninsula during the Postclassic period (900–1521 CE). Throughout this time, the Maya had strong ties with other regions of Mesoamerica: They inherited many ideas and technologies from the Olmec, had trade and military interactions with Teotihuacan, and, centuries later, were in contact with the Aztec Empire.

TIKAL. The monumental buildings of Maya cities were masterly examples of the use of architecture for public display. Tikal (in present-day Guatemala) was one of the largest Maya cities, with a population of as many as 70,000 at its height. Like other Maya cities—yet unlike Teotihuacan, with its grid plan—Tikal conformed to the uneven terrain of the rainforest. Plazas, pyramid-temples, ballcourts, and other structures stood on high ground connected by wide elevated roads, or causeways.

Tikal was settled in the Late Preclassic period, in the fourth century BCE, and continued to flourish through the Early Classic period. The kings of Tikal were buried in funerary pyramids in the North Acropolis, visible on the left in **FIGURE 12–8**, which was separated by a wide plaza from the royal palace to the south.

Tikal suffered a major upheaval in 378 CE, recorded in texts from the city and surrounding centers, when the arrival of strangers from Teotihuacan precipitated the death of Tikal's king and the installation of a new ruler with ties to Central Mexico. Art from this period shows strong Teotihuacan influence in ceramic and architectural forms, though both were soon adapted to suit local Maya aesthetics. The city enjoyed a period of wealth and regional dominance until a military defeat led to a century of decline.

In the eighth century CE, the city of Tikal again flourished during the reign of Jasaw Chan K'awiil (nicknamed Ruler A before his name could be fully read, r. 682–734), who initiated an ambitious construction program and commissioned many stelae decorated with his own portrait. One of these, Stela 16, was dedicated on the period-ending date of 9.14.0.0.0 in the Maya calendar (December 5, 711; see "A Closer Look," page 387). His portrait fills nearly the entire space of this nearly 6-foot-tall stone. He stands with his head in profile, his body frontal, and his legs splayed out with the heels together. His elaborate costume—embellished with quetzal feathers, jade, and other precious materials—almost completely conceals his body. Ruler A's program culminated in the construction of Temple I (SEE FIG. 12–8), a tall pyramid that faces a companion pyramid, Temple II, across a large central plaza. Containing Ruler A's tomb in the limestone bedrock

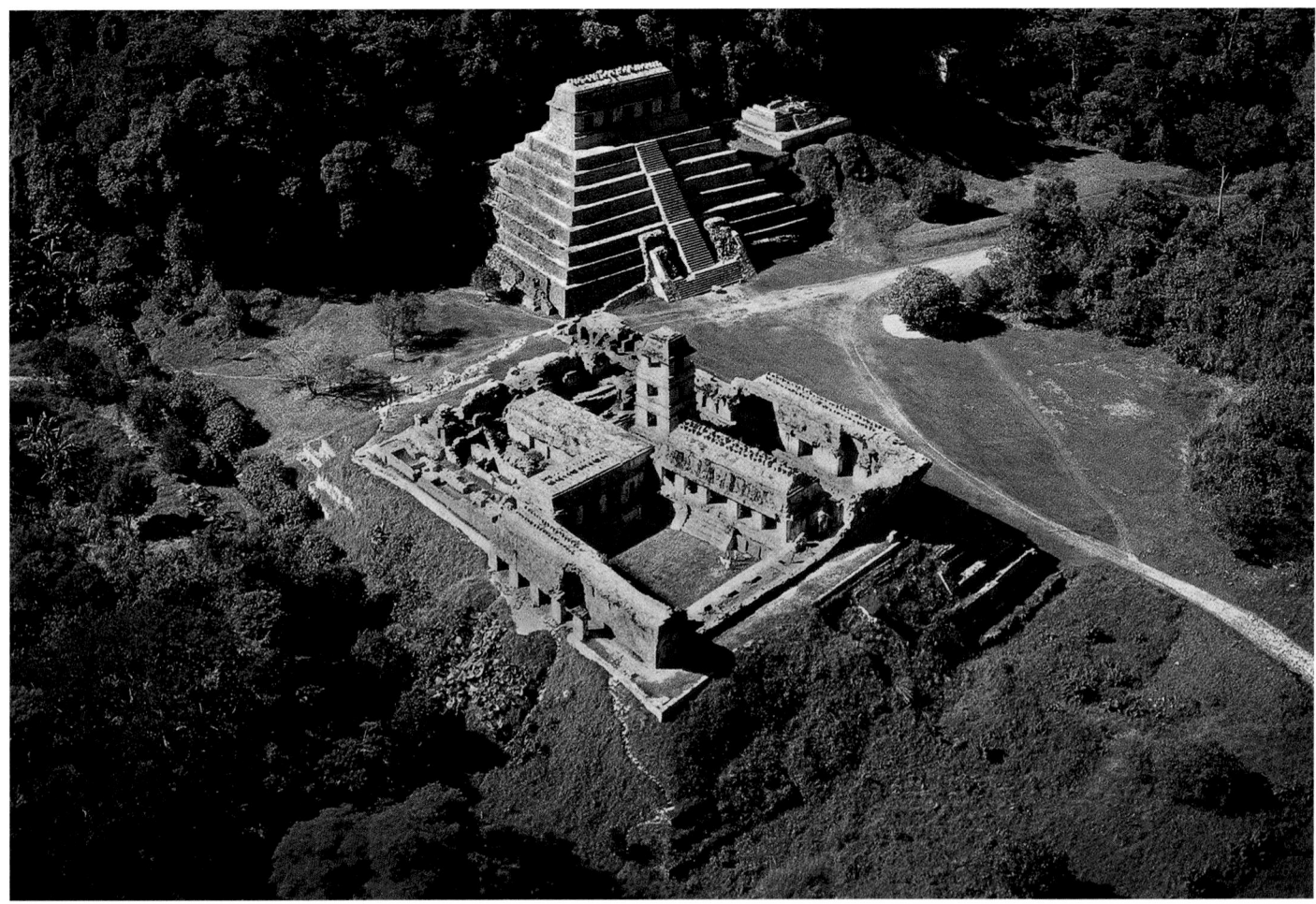

12-9 • PALACE (FOREGROUND) AND TEMPLE OF THE INSCRIPTIONS
Palenque, Mexico. Maya culture. Palace, 5th–8th century CE; Temple of the Inscriptions
(Tomb of Pakal the Great), c. 683 CE.

below, Temple I rises above the forest canopy to a height of more than 140 feet. Its base has nine layers, probably reflecting the belief that the underworld had nine levels. Priests climbed the steep stone staircase on the exterior to the temple on top, which consists of two narrow, parallel rooms covered with a steep roof supported by corbel vaults. The crest that rises over the roof of the temple, known as a **roof comb**, was originally covered with brightly painted sculpture. Ritual performances on the narrow platform at the top of the pyramid would have been visible throughout the plaza. Inspired by Ruler A's building program, later kings of Tikal also built tall funerary pyramids that still tower above the rainforest canopy.

PALENQUE.   The small city-state of Palenque (in the present-day Mexican state of Chiapas) rose to prominence later than Tikal, during the Classic period. Hieroglyphic inscriptions record the beginning of its royal dynasty in 431 CE, but the city had only limited regional importance until the ascension of a powerful ruler, K'inich Janahb Pakal (*pakal* is Mayan for "shield"), who ruled from 615 to 683. Known as Pakal the Great, he and his sons, who succeeded him, commissioned most of the structures visible at Palenque today. As at Tikal, urban planning responds to the

landscape. Perched on a ridge over 300 feet above the swampy lowland plains, the buildings of Palenque are terraced into the mountains with a series of aqueducts channeling rivers through the urban core. The center of the city houses the palace, the Temple of the Inscriptions, and other temples **(FIG. 12–9)**. Still other temples, elite palaces, and a ballcourt surround this central group.

The palace was an administrative center as well as a royal residence. At its core was the throne room of Pakal the Great, a spacious structure whose stone roof imitated the thatched roofs of more humble dwellings. Over time, the palace grew into a complex series of buildings organized around four courtyards, where the private business of the court was transacted. From the outside, the palace presented an inviting façade of wide staircases and open colonnades decorated with stucco sculptures, but access to the interior spaces was tightly limited.

Next to the palace stands the Temple of the Inscriptions, Pakal the Great's funerary pyramid. Rising 75 feet above the plaza, it has nine levels like Temple I at Tikal (SEE FIG. 12–8). The shrine on the summit consists of a portico with five entrances and a vaulted inner chamber originally surmounted by a tall roof comb. Its façade still retains much of its stucco sculpture. The inscriptions that give the

Maya Stela

Stela 16
Tikal, Guatemala. Maya culture, 711 CE.

The text in this cartouche records the dedication date for this stela, 6 Ahaw 13 Muwaan (9.14.0.0.0, or December 5, 711 CE), an important period-ending date that was celebrated throughout the Maya region.

Ruler A's face peers out from all his finery. He wears large jade earspools and a long bar or nose ornament reaches out in front of his face.

Pectoral necklaces, made of jade and bone, lie above a collar of round jade beads. Jade and feathers were among the most precious materials in ancient Mesoamerica, so this costume is a stunning display of wealth.

The text in these two cartouches names Jasaw Chan K'awiil (Ruler A) as Holy Lord of Tikal and lists other of his titles.

Elaborate feathered headdress decorated with a skull mask, perhaps representing a deity that Ruler A impersonated in the dedication ceremony for this monument. Note how some of the plumes break the borders of the stela.

This feathered backrack, like the feathered headdress, may have been made out of quetzal feathers or other precious tropical plumes. These brightly colored, iridescent feathers would have shimmered as Ruler A moved.

In his hands Ruler A holds a ceremonial bar of rulership, the traditional emblem of authority of Maya kings.

Ruler A also wears a belt decorated with three jade masks, one shown frontally at the center and two shown in profile at the hips. Jade masks like these have been found at several Maya sites.

SEE MORE: View the Closer Look feature for the Maya Stela **www.myartslab.com**

building its name consist of three large panels of text that line the back wall of the outer chamber at the top of the temple, linking Pakal's accomplishments to the mythical history of the city. A corbel-vaulted stairway beneath the summit shrine zigzags down 80 feet to a small subterranean chamber that contained the undisturbed tomb of Pakal, which was discovered in the 1950s.

Pakal the Great lay in a monolithic carved sarcophagus that represented him balanced between the underworld and the earth.

12-10 • PORTRAIT OF PAKAL THE GREAT
From Pakal's tomb, Temple of the Inscriptions, Palenque, Mexico. Maya culture, mid 7th century CE. Stucco and red paint, height 16⅞″ (43 cm). Museo Nacional de Antropología, Mexico City.

His ancestors, carved on the sides of the sarcophagus, witness his death and apotheosis. The stucco portrait of Pakal found with his sarcophagus shows him as a young man wearing a diadem of jade and flowers **(FIG. 12–10)**. His features—sloping forehead and elongated skull (babies' heads were bound to produce this shape), large curved nose (enhanced by an ornamental bridge), full lips, and open mouth—are characteristic of the Maya ideal of beauty, that of the youthful Maize God whose stepped and upswept hairstyle this portrait adopts. His long, narrow face and jaw are individual characteristics. Traces of pigment indicate that this portrait, like much Maya sculpture, was colorfully painted.

SCULPTURE FOR LADY XOK. Elite men and women, rather than gods, were the usual subjects of Maya sculpture, and most works show rulers performing religious rituals in elaborate costumes and headdresses. Although they excelled at three-dimensional clay and stucco sculpture (SEE FIG. 12–10), the Maya favored low relief for carving stelae and buildings. One outstanding example is a carved

lintel from a temple in the city of Yaxchilan, dedicated in 726 by Lady Xok, the principal wife and queen of the ruler nicknamed "Shield Jaguar the Great." In this retrospective image of a rite conducted when Shield Jaguar became the ruler of Yaxchilan in 681, Lady Xok conjures up a serpent vision that spews forth a warrior in Teotihuacan costume who aims his spear at the kneeling queen **(FIG. 12–11)**. The relief is unusually high, giving the sculptor ample opportunity to display a virtuoso carving technique, for example, in Lady Xok's garments and jewelry. The lintels were originally brightly painted as well. The calm idealized face of the queen recalls the portrait of Pakal the Great. That the queen commissioned her depictions on the lintels of this temple is an indication of her importance at court, and of the power that elite Maya women could attain.

12-11 • LADY XOK'S VISION (ACCESSION CEREMONY)
Lintel 25 of a temple (Structure 23), Yaxchilan, Mexico. Maya culture. Dedicated in 726 CE. Limestone, 46½ × 29⅛″ (118 × 74 cm). British Museum. Acquired by the British Museum in 1883

The Cosmic Ballgame

The ritual ballgame was one of the defining characteristics of Mesoamerican society. It was generally played on a long, rectangular court with a large, solid, heavy rubber ball. Using their elbows, knees, or hips—but not their hands—heavily padded players directed the ball toward a goal or marker. The rules, size and shape of the court, the number of players on a team, and the nature of the goal varied. The largest surviving ballcourt at Chichen Itza was about the size of a modern football field. Large stone rings set in the walls of the court about 25 feet above the field served as goals.

The game was a common subject in Mesoamerican art (SEE FIG. 12–12). Players, complete with equipment, appear as ceramic figurines and on stone sculptures and painted vases. The game may have had religious and political significance: It features in creation stories, and was sometimes associated with warfare. Captive warriors might have been made to play the game, and players might have been sacrificed when the stakes were high.

PAINTING.   Artists had high status in Maya society: Vase painters and scribes were sometimes members of the ruling elite, perhaps even members of the royal family. Some of our most vivid impressions of Maya courtly life and painting style come from cylindrical vessels. The example illustrated in **FIGURE 12–12** shows four lords playing the ballgame, the architectural space of the ballcourt suggested by a few horizontal lines (see "The Cosmic Ballgame," above). The men wear elaborate headdresses and padded protective gear to protect them from the heavy rubber ball. The painter has chosen a moment of arrested movement: One player

kneels to hit the ball—or has just hit it—while the others gesture and lean toward him. The roll-out photograph here shows the entire scene, but a person holding the vase would have to turn the vessel to see what was happening. The text running around the rim of the vase is a standard dedicatory inscription, naming it as a vessel for drinking chocolate, and tests of residues inside such vases have confirmed this use. Without sugar or milk, Maya chocolate was a very different drink from the one we are used to, a frothy and bitter beverage consumed on courtly and ritual occasions.

12–12 • CYLINDRICAL VESSEL WITH BALLGAME SCENE
(Roll-out photograph) Maya culture, 600–800 CE. Painted ceramic, diameter 6⅜″ (15.9 cm), height 8⅛″ (20.5 cm). Dallas Museum of Art. 1983.148. Gift of Mr. and Mrs. Raymond Nasher

EXPLORE MORE: Gain insight from a primary source on the Maya civilization **www.myartslab.com**

POSTCLASSIC PERIOD. After warfare and environmental crisis led to the abandonment of the lowland Maya city-states around 800, the focus of Maya civilization shifted north to the Yucatan Peninsula. One of the principal cities of the Postclassic period was Chichen Itza, which means "at the mouth of the well of the Itza," and may refer to the deep *cenote* (sinkhole) at the site that was sacred to the Maya. The city flourished from the ninth to the thirteenth century, and at its height covered about 6 square miles.

One of Chichen Itza's most conspicuous structures is a massive nine-level pyramid in the center of a large plaza, nicknamed El Castillo ("the castle" in Spanish) **(FIG. 12–13)**. A stairway on each side of the radial pyramid leads to a square temple on the summit. At the spring and fall equinoxes, the setting sun casts undulating shadows on the stairway, forming bodies for the serpent heads carved at the base of the north balustrades, pointing towards the Sacred Cenote. Many prominent features of Chichen Itza are markedly different from earlier Maya sites and hint at ties to Central Mexico, including long, colonnaded halls and inventive columns in the form of inverted, descending serpents. Brilliantly colored relief sculpture and painting covered the buildings of Chichen Itza. Many of the surviving works show narrative scenes that emphasize military conquests. Sculpture at Chichen Itza, including the serpent columns and balustrades, and the half-reclining figures known as **chacmools**, has the sturdy forms, proportions, and angularity of architecture, rather than the curving subtlety of Classic Maya sculpture. The *chacmools* may represent fallen warriors and were used to receive sacrificial offerings.

After Chichen Itza's decline, Mayapan, in the center of the Yucatan Peninsula, became the principal Maya center. But by the time the Spanish arrived in the early sixteenth century, Mayapan, too, had declined (destroyed in the mid fifteenth century), and smaller cities like Tulum, located on the Caribbean coast, were all that remained. The Maya people and much of their culture would survive the devastation of the conquest, adapting to the imposition of Hispanic customs and beliefs. Many Maya continue to speak their own languages, to venerate traditional sacred places, and to follow traditional ways.

CENTRAL AMERICA

Unlike their neighbors in Mesoamerica, who lived in complex hierarchical societies, the people of Central America lived in extended family groups, in towns led by chiefs. A notable example of these small chiefdoms was the Diquis culture (located in present-day Costa Rica), which lasted from about 700 to 1500 CE. The Diquis occupied fortified villages and seem to have engaged in constant warfare with one another. Although they did not produce monumental architecture or sculpture, they created fine featherwork, ceramics, textiles, and objects of gold and jade.

Metallurgy and the use of gold and copper-gold alloys were widespread in Central America. The technique of lost-wax casting probably first appeared in present-day Colombia between 500 and 300 BCE. From there it spread north to the Diquis. A small, exquisite pendant **(FIG. 12–14)** illustrates the style and technique of Diquis goldwork. The pendant depicts a male figure wearing bracelets, anklets, and a belt with a snake-headed penis sheath. He plays a drum while holding the tail of a snake in his teeth and its head in his left hand. The wavy forms with serpent heads emerging from his scalp suggest an elaborate headdress, and the creatures emerging from his legs suggest some kind of reptile costume. The inverted triangles on the headdress probably represent birds' tails.

In Diquis mythology, serpents and crocodiles inhabited a lower world, humans and birds a higher one. Diquis art depicts animals and insects as fierce and dangerous. Perhaps the man in the pendant is a shaman transforming himself into a composite serpent-bird or performing a ritual snake dance surrounded by serpents or crocodiles. The scrolls on the sides of his head may represent the shaman's power to hear and understand the speech of

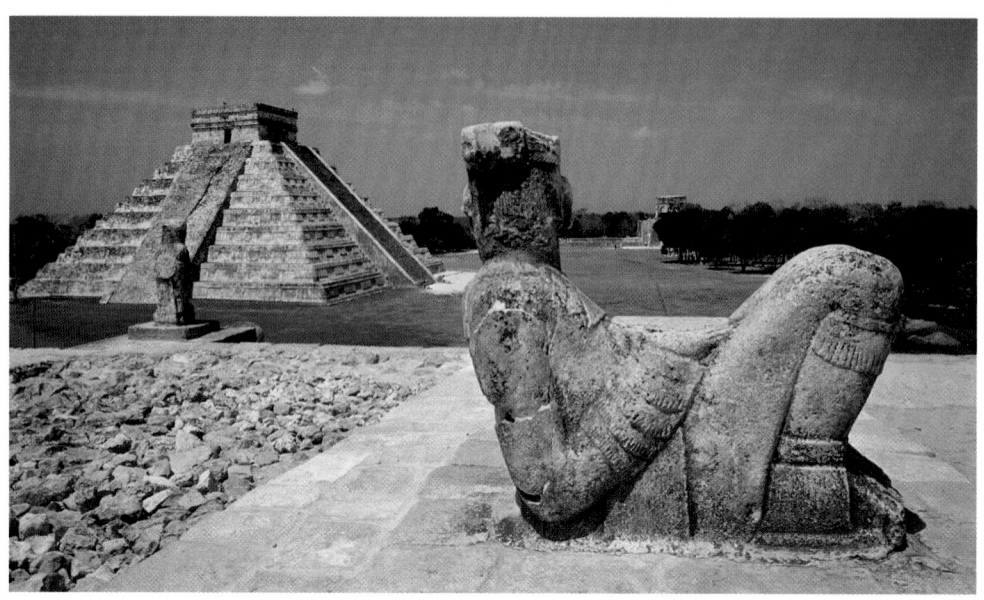

12–13 • PYRAMID ("EL CASTILLO") WITH CHACMOOL IN FOREGROUND
Chichen Itza, Yucatan, Mexico. Maya culture, 9th–12th century CE. Library, Getty Research Institute, Los Angeles.

From the top of the Temple of the Warriors, where a reclining *chacmool* sculpture graces the platform, there is a clear view of the radial pyramid nicknamed "El Castillo."

12-14 • SHAMAN WITH DRUM AND SNAKE
Costa Rica. Diquis culture, c. 13–16th century CE. Gold, 4¼ × 3¼″
(10.8 × 8.2 cm). Museos del Banco Central de Costa Rica, San José,
Costa Rica.

animals. Whatever its specific meaning, the pendant evokes a ritual
of mediation between earthly and cosmic powers involving music,
dance, and costume.

Whether gold figures of this kind were protective amulets
or signs of high status, they were certainly more than personal
adornment. Shamans and warriors wore gold to inspire fear,
perhaps because gold was thought to capture the energy and
power of the sun. This energy was also thought to allow shamans to
leave their bodies and travel into cosmic realms.

SOUTH AMERICA: THE CENTRAL ANDES

Like Mesoamerica, the central Andes of South America—
primarily present-day Peru and Bolivia—saw the development of
complex hierarchical societies with rich and varied artistic
traditions. The area is one of dramatic contrasts. The narrow coastal
plain, bordered by the Pacific Ocean on the west and the abruptly
soaring Andes mountains on the east, is one of the driest deserts in
the world. Life here depends on the rich marine resources of the
Pacific Ocean and the rivers that descend from the Andes, forming
a series of valley oases. The Andes themselves are a region of lofty

snowcapped peaks, high grasslands, steep slopes, and deep, fe
river valleys. The high grasslands are home to the Andean camel.
that have served for thousands of years as beasts of burden and a
source of wool and meat. The lush eastern slopes of the Andes
descend to the tropical rainforest of the Amazon basin.

In contrast to developments in other parts of the world,
Andean peoples developed monumental architecture and textiles
long before ceramics and intensive agriculture, usually the two hallmarks of early civilization. Thus, the earliest period of monumental
architecture, beginning around 3000 BCE, is called the Preceramic
period. On the coast, sites with ceremonial mounds and plazas were
located near the sea, while in the highlands early centers consisted
of multi-roomed stone-walled structures with sunken central fire
pits for burning ritual offerings. In the second millennium BCE (the
Initial Period), as agriculture became more important both in the
highlands and on the coast, the scale and pace of construction
increased dramatically. Communities in the coastal valleys built
massive U-shaped ceremonial complexes, while highland religious
centers focused on sunken circular courtyards. By adding to these
constructions bit by bit over generations, and using older constructions as the nucleus of new buildings, relatively small communities
could generate mountain-size pyramids.

CHAVIN DE HUANTAR

Located on a trade route between the coast and the Amazon basin,
the highland site of Chavin de Huantar was an important religious
center between 900 and 200 BCE, home to an art style that spread
through much of the Andes. In Andean chronology, this era is
known as the Early Horizon, the first of three so-called Horizon
periods. The period was one of artistic and technical innovation in
ceramics, metallurgy, and textiles.

The architecture of Chavin synthesizes coastal and highland
traditions, combining the U-shaped pyramid typical of the coast
with a sunken circular plaza lined with carved reliefs, a form
common in the highlands. The often fantastical animals that adorn
Chavin sculpture have features of jaguars, hawks, caimans, and
other tropical Amazonian beasts.

Within the U-shaped Old Temple at Chavin is a mazelike system of narrow galleries, at the very center of which lies a sculpture
called the Lanzón **(FIG. 12–15)**. Wrapped around a 15-foot-tall
blade-shaped stone with a narrow projection at the top—a form
that may echo the shape of traditional Andean planting sticks—
this complex carving depicts a powerful creature with a humanoid
body, clawed hands and feet, and enormous fangs. Its eyebrows and
strands of hair terminate in snakes—a kind of composite and
transformational imagery shared by many Chavin images. The
image is bilaterally symmetrical, except that the creature has one
hand raised and the other lowered. Compact frontality, flat relief,
curvilinear design, and the combination of human, animal, bird,
and reptile parts characterize this early art.

It has been suggested that the Lanzón was an oracle (a chamber
directly above the statue would allow priests' disembodied voices to

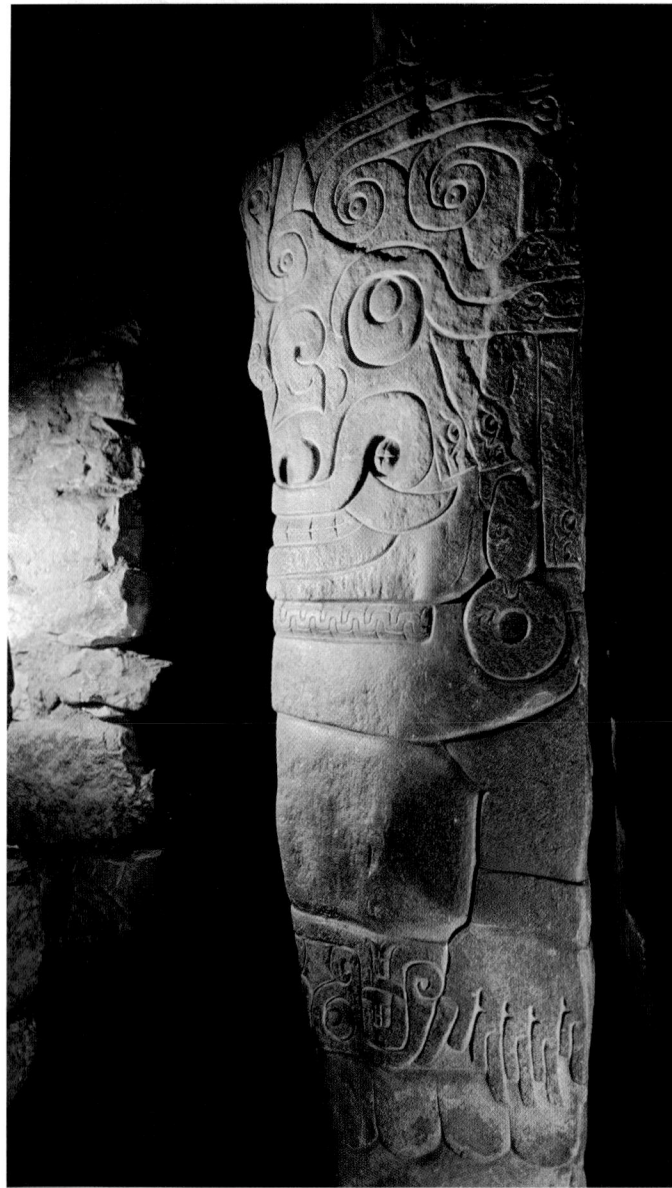

12-15 • LANZÓN, CHAVIN DE HUANTAR
Peru. Chavin culture, c. 900 BCE. Height, 15' (4.5 m). Granite.

filter into the chamber below), which would explain why people from all over the Andes made pilgrimages to Chavin, bringing exotic goods to the highland site and spreading its art style throughout the Andean region as they returned home.

THE PARACAS AND NAZCA CULTURES

While Chavin de Huantar was flourishing as a highland center whose art was enormously influential throughout the Andes, different valleys on the Pacific coast developed distinctive art styles and cultures.

PARACAS. The Paracas culture of the Peruvian south coast flourished from about 600 BCE to 200 CE, overlapping the Chavin period. It is best known for its stunning textiles, which were found in cemeteries as wrappings, in many layers, around the

bodies of the dead. Some bodies were wrapped in as many as 200 pieces of cloth.

Weaving is of great antiquity in the central Andes and continues to be among the most prized arts in the region (see "Andean Textiles," page 394). Fine textiles were a source of prestige and wealth. The designs on Paracas textiles include repeated embroidered figures of warriors, dancers, and composite creatures such as bird-people (FIG. 12–16). Embroiderers used tiny overlapping stitches to create colorful, curvilinear patterns, sometimes using as many as 22 different colors within a single figure, but only one simple stitch. The effect of the clashing and contrasting colors and tumbling figures is dazzling.

NAZCA. The Nazca culture, which dominated portions of the south coast of Peru from about the year 0 to 700 CE, overlapped the Paracas culture to the north. Nazca artisans wove fine fabrics, and also produced multicolored pottery with painted and modeled images reminiscent of those on Paracas textiles.

The Nazca are best known for their colossal earthworks, or **geoglyphs**, which dwarf even the most ambitious twentieth-century environmental sculpture. On great stretches of desert they literally drew in the earth. By removing dark, oxidized stones, they exposed the light underlying stones. In this way they created gigantic images—including a hummingbird with a beak 120 feet long (FIG. 12–17), a killer whale, a monkey, a spider, a duck, and other birds—similar to those with which they decorated their pottery. They also made abstract patterns and groups of straight, parallel lines that extend for up to 12 miles. The purpose and meaning of the glyphs remain a mystery, but the "lines" of stone are wide enough to have been ceremonial pathways.

12-16 • MANTLE WITH BIRD IMPERSONATORS
Paracas Peninsula, Peru. Paracas culture, c. 200 BCE–200 CE. Camelid fiber, plain weave with stem-stitch embroidery (detail), approx. 40″ × 7′11″ (1.01 × 2.41 m). Museum of Fine Arts, Boston. Denman Waldo Ross Collection (16.34a)

THE MOCHE CULTURE

The Moche culture dominated the north coast of Peru from the Piura Valley to the Huarmey Valley—a distance of some 370 miles—between about 100 and 700 CE. Moche lords ruled each valley in this region from a ceremonial-administrative center. The largest of these, in the Moche Valley (from which the culture takes its name), contained the so-called Huaca del Sol (Pyramid of the Sun) and Huaca de la Luna (Pyramid of the Moon), both built of **adobe** brick (sun-baked blocks of clay mixed with straw). The Huaca del Sol, one of the largest ancient structures in South America, was originally 1,100 feet long by 500 feet wide, rising in a series of terraces to a height of 59 feet. Much of this pyramid was destroyed in the seventeenth century, when a Spanish mining company diverted a river through it to wash out the gold contained in its many burials. Recent excavations at the Huaca de la Luna have revealed brightly painted reliefs of deities, captives, and warriors, remade during successive renovations of the pyramid. This site had been thought to be the capital of the entire Moche realm, but evidence is accumulating that indicates that the Moche maintained a decentralized social network.

The Moche were exceptional potters and metalsmiths. Vessels were made in the shape of naturalistically modeled human beings, animals, and architectural structures. They developed ceramic molds, which allowed them to mass-produce some forms. They also created realistic **PORTRAIT VESSELS** (**FIG. 12–18**) and recorded mythological narratives and ritual scenes in intricate fine-line painting. Similar scenes were painted on the walls of

12-18 • MOCHE PORTRAIT VESSEL
Moche culture, Peru. c. 100–700 CE. Clay, height 11" (28 cm). Ethnologisches Museum, Staatliche Museen zu Berlin.

This is one of several portrait vessels, made from the same mold, that seems to show a particular individual.

12-17 • EARTH DRAWING (GEOGLYPH) OF A HUMMINGBIRD, NAZCA PLAIN
Southwest Peru. Nazca culture, c. 0–700 CE. Length approx. 450′ (137 m); wingspan approx. 220′ (60.9 m).

Textiles were one of the most important forms of art and technology in Andean society. Specialized fabrics were developed for everything from ritual burial shrouds and shamans' costumes to rope bridges and knotted cords for record keeping. Clothing indicated ethnic group and social status and was customized for certain functions, the most rarefied being royal ceremonial garments made for specific occasions and worn only once. The creation of textiles, among the most technically complex cloths ever made, consumed a major portion of ancient Andean societies' resources.

Andean textile artists used two principal materials: cotton and camelid fiber. (Camelid fiber—llama, alpaca, guanaco, or vicuña hair—is the Andean equivalent of wool.) Cotton grows on the coast, while llamas, alpacas, and other camelids thrive in the highlands. The presence of cotton fibers in the highlands and camelid fibers on the coast demonstrates trade between the two regions from very early times. The production of textiles was an important factor in the domestication of both plants (cotton) and animals (llamas).

The earliest Peruvian textiles were made by twining, knotting, wrapping, braiding, and looping fibers. Those techniques continued to be used even after the invention of weaving looms in the early second millennium BCE. Most Andean textiles were woven on a simple, portable backstrap loom in which the undyed cotton warp (the lengthwise threads) was looped and stretched between two bars. One bar was tied to a stationary object and the other strapped to the waist of the weaver. The weaver controlled the tension of the warp threads by leaning back and forth while threading a shuttle from side to side to insert the weft (crosswise threads). Changing the arrangement of the warp threads between each passage of the weft created a stable interlace of warp and weft: a textile.

Andean artists used a variety of different techniques to decorate their textiles, creating special effects that were prized for their labor-intensiveness and difficulty of manufacture as well as their beauty. In tapestry weaving, a technique especially suited to representational textiles, the weft does not run the full width of the fabric; each colored section is woven as an independent unit. Embroidery with needle and thread on an already woven textile allows even greater freedom from the rigid warp-and-weft structure of the loom, allowing the artist to create curvilinear forms with thousands of tiny stitches. As even more complex techniques developed, the production of a single textile might involve a dozen processes requiring highly skilled workers. Dyeing technology, too, was an advanced art form in the ancient Andes, with some textiles containing dozens of colors.

Because of their complexity, deciphering how these textiles were made can be a challenge, and scholars rely on contemporary Andean weavers—inheritors of this tradition—for guidance. Now, as then, fiber and textile arts are primarily in the hands of women.

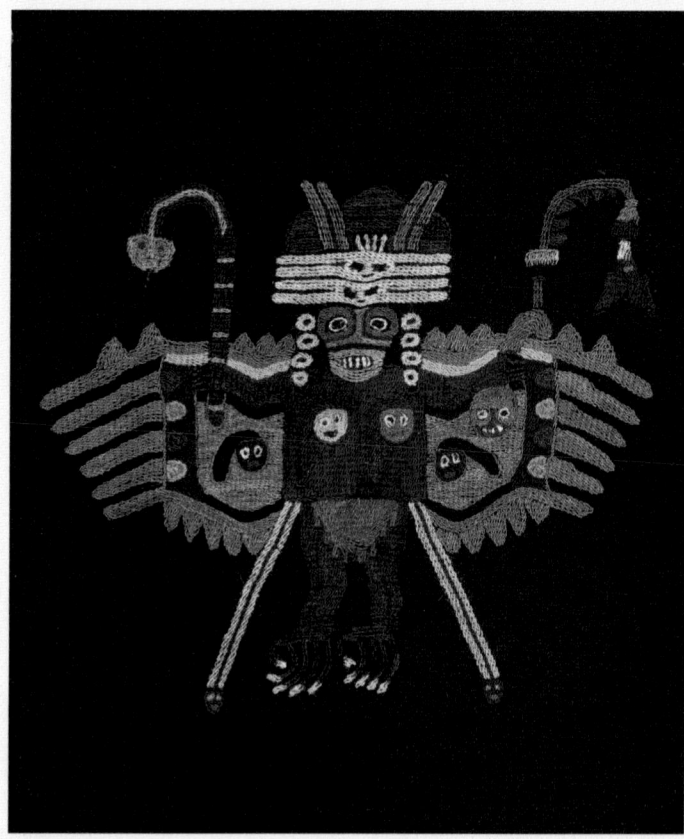

MANTLE WITH BIRD IMPERSONATORS (DETAIL)
From the Paracas Peninsula, Peru. Paracas culture, c. 200 BCE–200 CE. Camelid fiber, plain weave with stem-stitch embroidery. Museum of Fine Arts, Boston. Denman Waldo Ross Collection (16.34a)

---

temples and administrative buildings. Moche metalsmiths, the most sophisticated in the central Andes, developed several innovative metal alloys.

THE TOMB OF THE WARRIOR PRIEST.   A central theme in Moche iconography is the sacrifice ceremony, in which prisoners captured in battle are sacrificed and several elaborately dressed figures then drink their blood. Archaeologists have labeled the principal figure in the ceremony as the Warrior Priest and other important figures as the Bird Priest and the Priestess. The recent discovery of a number of spectacularly rich Moche tombs indicates that the sacrifice ceremony was an actual Moche ritual and that Moche lords and ladies assumed the roles of the principal figures. The occupant of a tomb at Sipán, in the Lambayeque Valley on the northwest coast, was buried with the regalia of the Warrior Priest. In tombs at the site of San José de Moro, just south of Sipán, several women were buried with the regalia of the Priestess.

Among the riches accompanying the Warrior Priest at Sipán was a pair of exquisite gold-and-turquoise **EARSPOOLS**, each of which depicts three Moche warriors (**FIG. 12–19**). The central figure bursts into three dimensions, while his companions are shown in profile, in a flat inlay technique. All three are adorned

12–19 • EARSPOOL
Sipán, Peru. Moche culture, c. 300 CE. Gold, turquoise, quartz, and shell, diameter approx. 3″ (9.4 cm). Bruning Archaeological Museum, Lambayeque, Peru.

with tiny gold-and-turquoise earspools, simpler versions of the object they themselves adorn. They wear gold-and-turquoise headdresses topped with delicate sheets of gold that resemble the crescent-shaped knives used in sacrifices. The central figure has a crescent-shaped nose ornament and carries a removable gold club and shield. A necklace of owl's-head beads strung with gold thread hangs around his shoulders; similar objects have been found in other tombs at Sipán. These earspools illustrate some of the most notable features of Moche art: its capacity for naturalism and its close attention to detail.

NORTH AMERICA

Compared to the densely inhabited agricultural regions of Mesoamerica and South America, most of North America remained sparsely populated. Early people lived primarily by hunting, fishing, and gathering edible plants. Agriculture was developed on a limited scale: People cultivated squash, sunflowers, and other plants to supplement their diet of game, fish, and berries.

THE EAST

The culture of eastern North America is only beginning to be understood. Archaeologists have shown that people lived in communities that included both burial and ceremonial earthworks—mounds of earth-formed platforms that probably supported a chief's house and served as the shrines of ancestors and places for a sacred fire, tended by special guardians. One of the

largest, though not the earliest of the ceremonial centers (this distinction goes to Watson Brake, Louisiana, dating to 3400–3000 BCE), is Poverty Point, Louisiana. Between 1800 and 500 BCE people constructed huge, concentric earthen arcs three-quarters of a mile wide. Scholars have noted that these earthworks are contemporary with Stonehenge in England (SEE FIG. 1–21) and with Olmec constructions in Mexico (SEE FIG. 12–2).

THE WOODLAND PERIOD. The Woodland period (300 BCE–1000 CE) saw the creation of impressive earthworks along the great river valleys of the Ohio and Mississippi. People built monumental mounds and buried individuals with valuable grave goods. Objects discovered in these burials indicate that the people of the Mississippi, Illinois, and Ohio river valleys traded widely with other regions of North and Central America. For example, the burial sites of the Adena (c. 1100 BCE–200 CE) and the Hopewell (c. 100 BCE–550 CE) cultures contained objects made with copper from present-day Michigan's Upper Peninsula, and cut sheets of mica from the Appalachian Mountains, turtle shells and sharks' teeth from Florida, and obsidian from Wyoming and Idaho. The pipes the Hopewell people created from fine-grained pipestone have been found from Lake Superior to the Gulf of Mexico.

The Hopewell carved their pipes with representations of forest animals and birds, sometimes with inlaid eyes and teeth of freshwater pearls and bone. Combining realism and elegant simplification, a beaver crouching on a platform forms the bowl of a pipe found in present-day Illinois (FIG. 12–20). As in a modern pipe, the bowl—a hole in the beaver's back—could be filled with tobacco or other dried leaves, the leaves lighted, and smoke drawn through the hole in the stem. Using the pipe in this way, the

12–20 • BEAVER EFFIGY PLATFORM PIPE
Bedford Mound, Pike County, Illinois. Hopewell culture, c. 100–400 CE. Pipestone, river pearls, and bone, 4⁹⁄₁₆ × 1⁷⁄₈ × 2″. Gilcrease Museum, Tulsa, Oklahoma.

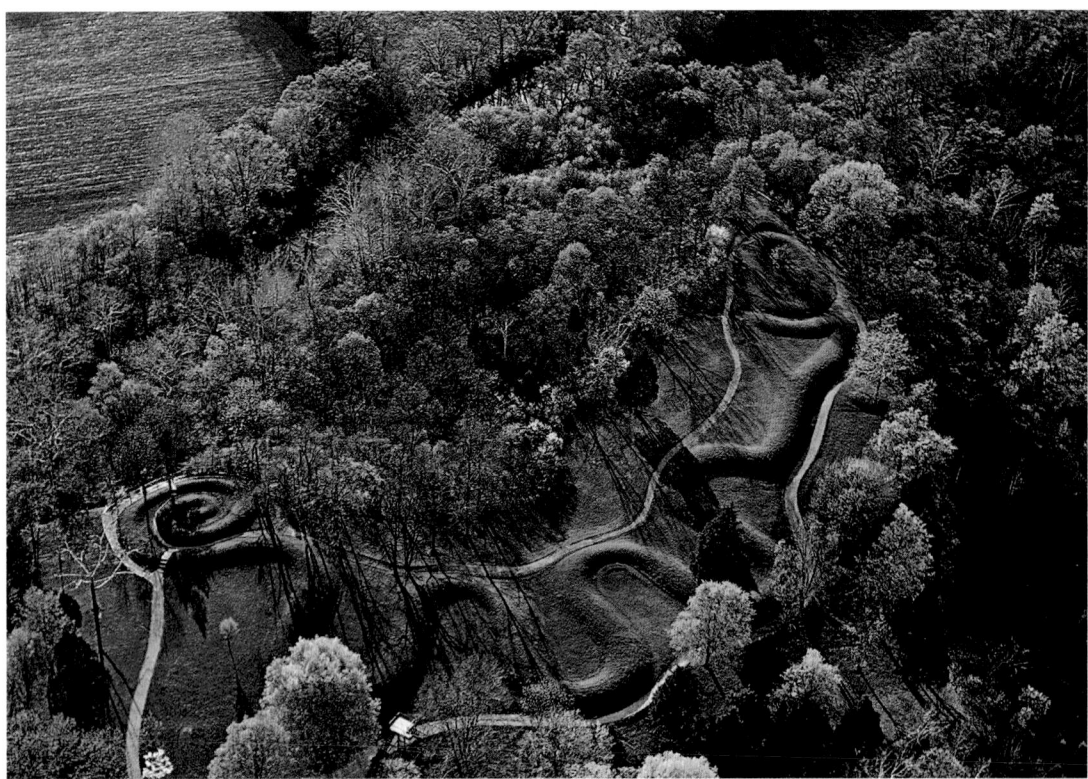

12-21 • GREAT SERPENT MOUND
Adams County, Ohio.
c. 1070 CE. Length approx.
1,254' (328.2 m).

smoker would be face to face with the beaver, whose shining pearl eyes may suggest an association with the spirit world.

THE MISSISSIPPIAN PERIOD. The Mississippian period (c. 700–1550 CE) is characterized by the widespread distribution of complex chiefdoms, both large and small, that proliferated throughout the region. The people of the Mississippian culture continued the mound-building tradition begun by the Adena, Hopewell, and others. From 1539 to 1543 Hernando de Soto explored the region and encountered Mississippian societies. However, contact between native North American people and Europeans resulted in catastrophe. The Europeans introduced the germs of diseases, especially smallpox, to which native populations had had no previous exposure and hence no immunity. In short order, 80 percent of the native population perished, an extraordinary disruption of society, far worse than the Black Death in fourteenth-century Europe. By the time other Europeans reached the area, the great earthworks of the Mississippian culture were long abandoned.

One of the most impressive Mississippian period earthworks is the **GREAT SERPENT MOUND** in present-day Adams County, Ohio (FIG. 12–21). Researchers using carbon-14 dating have recently proposed dating the mound at about 1070 CE. There have been many interpretations of the twisting snake form, especially the "head" at the highest point, a Y-shape and an oval enclosure that some see as the

12-22 • RECONSTRUCTION OF CENTRAL CAHOKIA, AS IT WOULD HAVE APPEARED ABOUT 1150 CE
East St. Louis, Illinois. Mississippian culture, c. 1000–1300 CE. East–west length approx. 3 miles (4.5 km), north–south length approx. 2¼ miles (3.6 km); base of great mound, 1,037 × 790' (316 × 241 m), height approx. 100' (30 m). Monk's Mound is the large platform in the center of the image. Painting by William R. Iseminger. Courtesy of Cahokia Mounds Historic site.

12-23 • PELICAN FIGUREHEAD
Florida Glades culture, Key Marco, Florida. c. 1000 CE. Wood and paint, 4⅜ × 2⅜ × 3⅛" (11.2 × 6 × 8 cm). The University Museum of Archaeology and Anthropology, Philadelphia. (T4.303)

Postholes indicate that woodhenges (circles of wooden columns) were a significant feature of Cahokia. The largest (seen to the extreme left in FIGURE 12–22) had 48 posts forming a circle with a diameter of about 420 feet. Sight lines between a 49th post set east of the center of the enclosure and points on the perimeter enabled native astronomers to determine solstices and equinoxes.

FLORIDA GLADES CULTURE. In 1895, excavators working in submerged mud and shell mounds off Key Marco on the west coast of Florida made a remarkable discovery. Posts carved with birds and animals were found preserved in the swamps. The large mound called Fort Center, in Glades Country, Florida, gives the culture its name: Florida Glades.

In Key Marco painted wooden animal and bird heads, a human mask, and the figure of a kneeling cat-human were found in circumstances that suggested a ruined shrine. Recently carbon-14 dating of these items has confirmed a date of about 1000 CE. Although the heads are spare in details, the artists show a remarkable power of observation in reproducing the creatures they saw around them, such as the **PELICAN** in **FIGURE 12–23**. The surviving head, neck, and breast of the pelican are made of carved wood, painted black, white, and gray (other images also had traces of pink and blue paint). The bird's outstretched wings were found nearby, but the wood shrank and disintegrated as it dried. Carved wooden wolf and deer heads were also found. Archaeologists think the heads might have been attached to ceremonial furniture or posts. Such images suggest the existence of a bird and animal cult or perhaps the use of birds and animals as clan symbols.

THE NORTH AMERICAN SOUTHWEST

Farming cultures were slower to arise in the arid American Southwest, which became home to three major early cultures. The Mimbres/Mogollon culture, located in the mountains of west-central New Mexico and east-central Arizona, flourished from about 200 to about 1250 CE. Potters made deep bowls with lively scenes of humans and animals inside. The Hohokam culture, centered in the central and southern parts of present-day Arizona, emerged around 200 BCE and endured until sometime around 1300 CE. The Hohokam built large-scale irrigation systems, multi-story residences, and ballcourts that demonstrate ties with Mesoamerica.

The third southwestern culture, the Ancestral Puebloans (formerly called Anasazi), emerged around 500 CE in the Four Corners region, where present-day Colorado, Utah, Arizona, and New Mexico meet. The Puebloans adopted the irrigation technology of the Hohokam and began building elaborate, multi-storied, apartmentlike "great houses" with many rooms for specialized purposes, including communal food storage and ritual.

Ancestral Puebloan people found aesthetic expression in their pottery, an ancient craft refined over generations. Women were the potters in ancient Pueblo society. They developed a functional, aesthetically pleasing, coil-built earthenware, or low-fired ceramic. Ceramic traditions continue to be important today among the

serpent opening its jaws to swallow a huge egg. Perhaps the people who built it were responding to the spectacular astronomical display of Halley's Comet in 1066.

Mississippian peoples built a major urban center known as Cahokia, near the juncture of the Illinois, Missouri, and Mississippi rivers (now East St. Louis, Illinois). Although the site may have been inhabited as early as about 3000 BCE, most monumental construction at Cahokia took place between about 1000 and 1300 CE. At its height the city had a population of as many as 15,000 people, with another 10,000 in the surrounding countryside **(FIG. 12–22)**.

The most prominent feature of Cahokia is an enormous earth mound called Monk's Mound, covering 15 acres and originally 100 feet high. A small, rounded platform on its summit initially supported a wooden fence and a rectangular building. The mound is aligned with the sun at the equinox and may have had a special use during planting or harvest festivals. Smaller rectangular and rounded mounds in front of the principal mound surrounded a large, roughly rectangular plaza. The city's entire ceremonial center was protected by a stockade, or fence, of upright wooden posts. In all, the walled enclosure contained more than 100 mounds, platforms, wooden enclosures, and houses. The various earthworks functioned as tombs and bases for palaces and temples, and also served to make astronomical observations.

12-24 • SEED JAR
Ancestral Puebloan culture, c. 1150 CE. Earthenware and black-and-white pigment, diameter 14½" (36.9 cm). The St. Louis Art Museum, St. Louis, Missouri. Purchase: Funds given by the Children's Art Bazaar, St. Louis

Pueblo peoples of the Southwest. One type of vessel, a wide-mouthed **SEED JAR** with a globular body and holes near the rim (**FIG. 12–24**), would have been suspended from roof poles by thongs attached to the jar's holes, out of reach of voracious rodents. The example shown here is decorated with black-and-white dotted squares and zigzag patterns. The patterns conform to the body of the jar, and in spite of their angularity they enhance its curved shape.

CHACO CANYON. Chaco Canyon, a New Mexico canyon of about 30 square miles with nine great houses, or pueblos, was an important center of Ancestral Puebloan civilization. The largest known "great house" is **PUEBLO BONITO** (**FIG. 12–25**), which was built in stages between the tenth and mid thirteenth centuries. Eventually it comprised over 800 rooms in four or five stories, arranged in a D shape. Within the crescent part of the D, 32 **kivas** recall the round, semisubmerged pit houses of earlier Southwestern cultures. Here men performed religious rituals and instructed youths in their responsibilities. Interlocking pine logs formed a shallow, domelike roof with a hole in the center through which the men entered by climbing down a ladder. Inside the kiva, in the

12-25 • PUEBLO BONITO
Chaco Canyon, New Mexico. 830–1250 CE.

12-26 • SUN DAGGER SOLAR MARKER AT EQUINOX
Fajada Butte, Chaco Canyon, New Mexico. 850–1250 CE.

floor directly under the entrance and behind the fire pit, a small indentation—the "navel of the earth"—may have symbolized the place where the Ancestral Pueblo ancestors had emerged from the earth in the mythic "first times," based on analogies with later Pueblo beliefs. The top of the kivas formed the floor of the communal plaza.

Pueblo Bonito stood at the hub of a network of wide, straight roads that radiated out to some 70 other communities. Almost invisible today, the roads were discovered through aerial photography. They make no detour to avoid topographic obstacles; when they encounter cliffs, they become stairs. Their undeviating course

suggests that they were more than practical thoroughfares: They may have served as processional ways. Was Pueblo Bonito a gathering place for people in the entire region at specific times of year?

On the morning of the summer solstice a streak of light strikes a high cliff in Chaco Canyon. Slowly this "Sun Dagger" descends, and by noontime it pierces the heart of a large spiral engraved into the rock (**FIG. 12–26**; see also "Rock Art," page 400). The Ancestral Puebloans pecked out this spiral, along with a smaller one, on the face of the bluff. The shaft of light forming the dagger is created by openings between huge slabs of rock, which admit streaks of light that project on the wall. The light moves with

Rock Art

Rock art consists of pictographs, which are painted, and petroglyphs, which are pecked or engraved. While occurring in numerous distinctive styles, rock art images include humans, animals, and geometric figures, represented singly and in multi-figured compositions. Petroglyphs are often found in places where the dark brown bacterial growths and staining known as "**desert varnish**" streak down canyon walls (FIG. B). To create an image, the artist scrapes or pecks through the layer of varnish, exposing the lighter sandstone beneath.

In the Great Gallery of Horseshoe Canyon, Utah, the painted human figures have long, decorated rectangular bodies and knoblike heads (FIG. A). One large, wide-eyed figure (popularly known as the "Holy Ghost") is nearly 8 feet tall. Archaeologists have dated these paintings to as early as 1900 BCE and as recently as 300 CE; rock art is very difficult to date precisely.

In Nine Mile Canyon in central Utah, a large human hunter draws his bow and arrow on a flock of bighorn sheep. Other hunters and a large, rectangular armless figure wearing a horned headdress—perhaps a shaman—mingle with the animals. The scene gives rise to the same questions and arguments we have noted with regard to the prehistoric art discussed in Chapter 1: Is this a record of a successful hunt or is it part of some ritual activity to ensure success? The petroglyphs are attributed to the Fremont people (800–1300 CE), who were agriculturists as well as hunters.

A. ANTHROPOMORPHS, THE GREAT GALLERY, HORSESHOE (BARRIER) CANYON

Utah. c. 1900 BCE–300 CE. Largest figure about 8′ (2.44 m) tall.

The figures may represent shamans and are often associated with snakes, dogs, and other small energetic creatures. Big-eyed anthropomorphs may be rain gods. Painters used their fingers and yucca-fiber brushes to apply the reddish pigment made from hematite (iron oxide).

B. HUNTER'S MURAL
Nine Mile Canyon, Utah. Fremont people, 800–1300 CE.

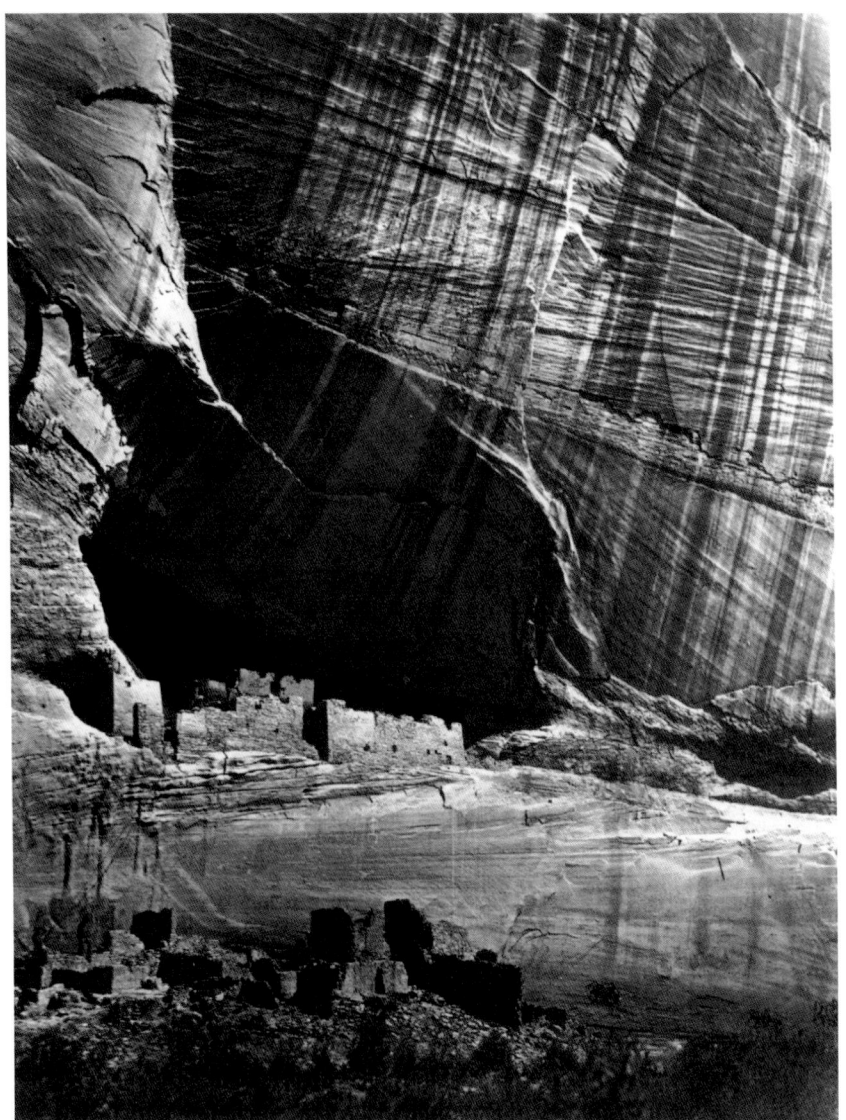

12–27 • Timothy O'Sullivan ANCIENT RUINS IN THE CANON DE CHELLEY
Arizona, 1873. Albumen print. National Archives, Washington, D.C.

While ostensibly a documentary photograph, Timothy O'Sullivan's depiction of "The White House," built by 12th-century Ancestral Puebloans, is both a valuable document for the study of architecture and an evocative photograph, filled with the Romantic sense of sublime melancholy.

River valleys. They built their new apartmentlike dwellings on ledges under sheltering cliffs (**FIG. 12–27**). Difficult as it must have been to live high on canyon walls and farm the valley below, the cliff communities had the advantage of being relatively secure. The rock shelters in the cliffs also acted as insulation, protecting the dwellings from extremes of heat and cold. Like a modern apartment complex, the many rooms housed an entire community comfortably. Communal solidarity and responsibility became part of the heritage of the Pueblo peoples.

Throughout the Americas, for the next several hundred years, artistic traditions would continue to emerge, develop, and be transformed as the indigenous peoples of various regions interacted. The sudden incursions of Europeans, beginning in the late fifteenth century, would have a dramatic and lasting impact on these civilizations and their art.

the seasonal motion of the sun. Only at the summer solstice in June does the great dagger appear. At the winter solstice two streaks frame the spiral petroglyph, and at both spring and fall equinoxes a small spike of light hits the center of the small spiral, and a large shaft cuts through the large spiral but misses its center. The rock formation that, together with the moving sun, creates the daggers of light is natural, but the two spirals were deliberately placed. Nature and art combine, as they do in the work of a modern environmental artist. Among Ancestral Puebloans spirals were signs for journeys, as well as for wind and water, serpents and snails. The later Zuni call the spiral a "journey in search of the Center." The clocklike workings of the spiral petroglyphs, together with their location on a high point distant from living areas in the canyon, have led to the speculation that the Sun Dagger was once a shrine.

Though no one knows for certain why the people of Chaco Canyon abandoned the site, the population declined during a severe drought in the twelfth century, and building at Pueblo Bonito ceased around 1250. The Pueblo population of Chaco Canyon may have moved to the Rio Grande and Mogollon

THINK ABOUT IT

12.1 Discuss the environmental challenges posed to the ancient peoples of the American Southwest and explain how they responded to them. Contrast this set of circumstances with that of another ancient people from Mesoamerica or South America, and explain how the respective circumstances impacted their art and culture.

12.2 Explain the original function of two ancient American objects from two different cultures. Discuss these objects within their larger sociocultural context.

12.3 Compare and contrast urban planning at Tikal and Teotihuacan. In your answer, make sure to give consideration to the issue of natural topography.

12.4 Explain how the Maya writing system functions, and discuss the impact this system had on the visual arts.

PRACTICE MORE: Compose answers to these questions, get flashcards for images and terms, and review chapter material with quizzes www.myartslab.com

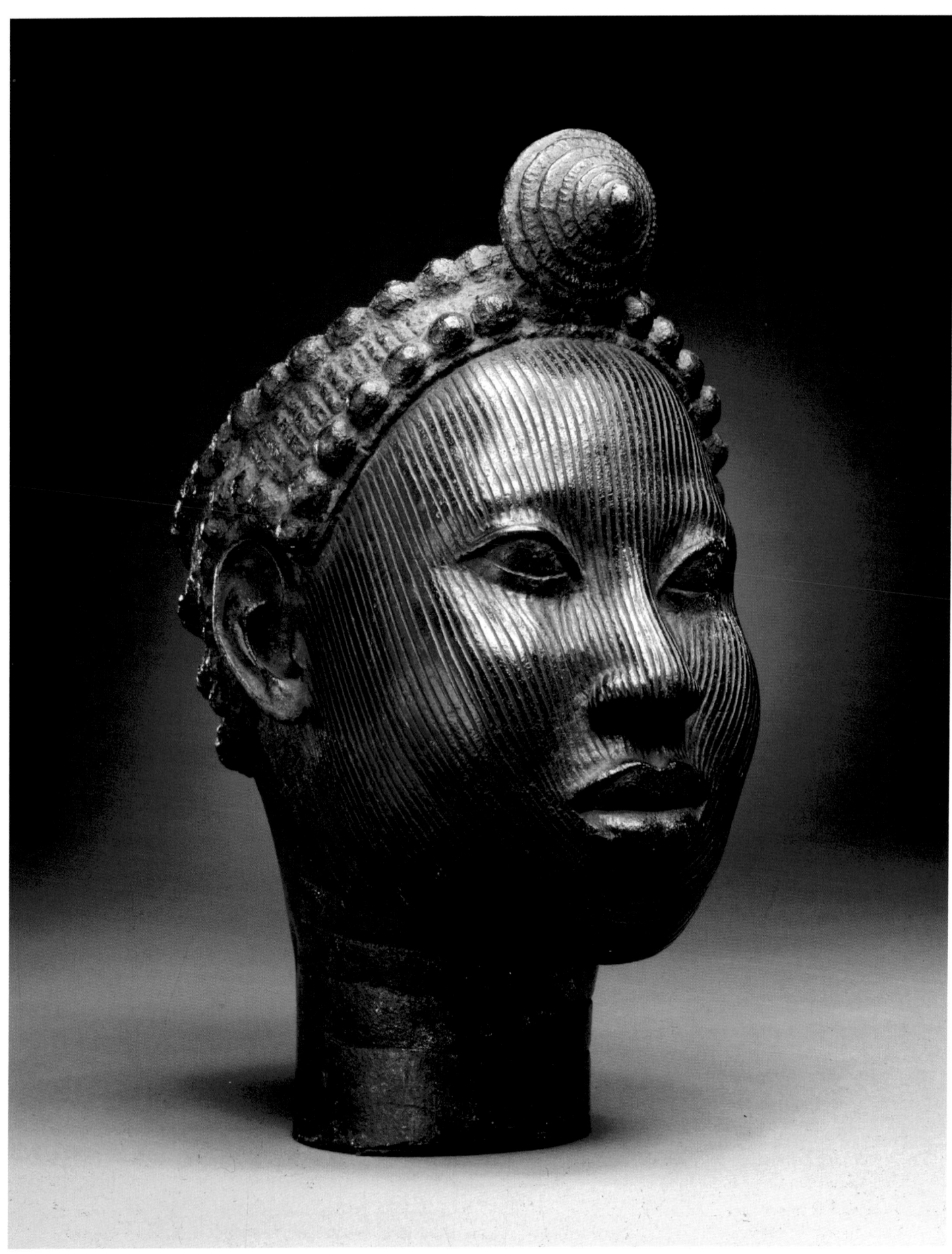

13-1 • CROWNED HEAD OF A KING   Ife, Yoruba. 12th–15th century CE.
Zinc brass, height 9⁷⁄₁₆″ (24 cm). Museum of Ife Antiquities, Ife, Nigeria.

EARLY AFRICAN ART

The Yoruba people of southwestern Nigeria regard the city of Ife (also known as Ile-Ife) as the "navel of the world," the site of creation, the place where Ife's first ruler—the *oni* Oduduwa— came down from heaven to create earth and then to populate it. By the eleventh century CE, Ife was a lively metropolis. Today, every Yoruba city claims "descent" from Ife.

Ife was, and remains, the sacred city of the Yoruba people. A tradition of naturalistic sculpture began there about 1050 CE and flourished for some four centuries. Although the ancestral line of the Ife *oni* (king) has continued unbroken, knowledge of the precise purpose of these works has been lost.

A cast-bronze head (FIG. 13–1) shows the extraordinary artistry of ancient Ife. The modeling of the flesh is remarkably sensitive, especially the subtle transitions around the nose and mouth. The lips are full and delicate, and the eyes are strikingly similar in shape to those of some modern Yoruba. The face is covered with thin, parallel **scarification** patterns (decorations made by scarring). The head was cast of zinc brass using the lost-wax method.

The head was cast with a crown; its size and delicate features suggest it may represent a female *oni*. Although its precise use is not known, similar life-size heads have large holes in the neck, suggesting they may have been attached to wooden figures. Mannequins with naturalistic facial features have been documented at memorial services for deceased individuals among contemporary Yoruba peoples. The Ife mannequin was probably dressed in the *oni*'s robes; the head probably bore his crown. The head could also have been used to display a crown during annual purification and renewal rites.

There is debate as to whether the Ife heads are true portraits. Their realism gives an impression that they could be. The heads, however, all seem to represent individuals of the same age and embody a similar concept of physical perfection, suggesting they are idealized images representing both physical beauty and moral character. Idealized images of titled individuals are a common feature of sub-Saharan African sculpture, as they are among many cultures throughout the world.

The superb naturalism of Ife sculpture contradicted everything Europeans thought they knew about African art. The German scholar, Leo Frobenius, who "discovered" Ife sculpture in 1910 suggested that it was created not by Africans but by survivors from the legendary lost island of Atlantis. Later, there was speculation that influence from ancient Greece or Renaissance Europe must have reached Ife. Scientific study, however, finally put such prejudiced ideas to rest.

LEARN ABOUT IT

13.1 Identify and summarize the key roles that the visual arts play in sub-Saharan Africa.

13.2 Explore how African arts mediate and support communication between the temporal and the supernatural worlds of various spirit forces.

13.3 Specify how African visual arts are only fully realized in their context of use.

13.4 Contrast the role of African arts related to leadership as compared to the role of leadership arts in Western cultural traditions.

HEAR MORE: Listen to an audio file of your chapter **www.myartslab.com**

THE LURE OF ANCIENT AFRICA

"I descended [the Nile] with three hundred asses laden with incense, ebony, grain, panthers, ivory, and every good product." Thus the Egyptian envoy Harkhuf described his return from Nubia, the African land to the south of Egypt, in 2300 BCE. The riches of Africa attracted merchants and envoys in ancient times, and trade brought the continent in contact with the rest of the world. Egyptian relations with the rest of the African continent continued through the Hellenistic era and beyond. Phoenicians and Greeks founded dozens of settlements along the Mediterranean coast of North Africa between 1000 and 300 BCE to extend trade routes across the Sahara to the peoples of Lake Chad and the bend of the Niger River (MAP 13–1). When the Romans took control of North Africa, they continued this lucrative trans-Saharan trade. In the seventh and eighth centuries CE, the expanding empire of Islam swept across North Africa, and thereafter Islamic merchants were regular visitors to Bilad al-Sudan (the Land of the Blacks—sub-Saharan Africa). Islamic scholars chronicled the great West African empires of Ghana, Mali, and Songhay, and West African gold financed the flowering of Islamic culture.

East Africa, meanwhile, had been drawn since at least the beginning of the Common Era into the maritime trade that ringed the Indian Ocean and extended east to Indonesia and the South China Sea. Arab, Indian, and Persian ships plied the coastline. A new language, Swahili, evolved from centuries of contact between Arabic-speaking merchants and Bantu-speaking Africans, and great port cities such as Kilwa, Mombasa, and Mogadishu arose.

In the fifteenth century, Europeans ventured by ship into the Atlantic Ocean and down the coast of Africa. Finally rediscovering the continent firsthand, they were often astonished by what they found (see "The Myth of 'Primitive' Art," page 406). "Dear King My Brother," wrote a fifteenth-century Portuguese king to his new trading partner, the king of Benin in west Africa. The Portuguese king's respect was well founded—Benin was vastly more powerful and wealthier than the small European country that had just stumbled upon it.

As we saw in Chapter 3, Africa was home to one of the world's earliest great civilizations, that of ancient Egypt, and as we saw in Chapter 8, Egypt and the rest of North Africa contributed prominently to the development of Islamic art and culture. This chapter examines the artistic legacy of the rest of ancient Africa.

AFRICA—THE CRADLE OF ART AND CIVILIZATION

During the twentieth century, the sculpture of traditional African societies—wood carvings of astonishing formal inventiveness and power—found admirers the world over. While avidly collected, these works were much misunderstood. For the past 75 years, art historians and cultural anthropologists have studied African art firsthand, which has added to our overall understanding of art

making in many African cultures. However, except for a few isolated examples (such as in Nigeria and Mali), the historical depth of our understanding is still limited by the continuing lack of systematic archaeological research. Our understanding of traditions that are more than 100 years old is especially hampered by the fact that most African art was made from wood, which decays rapidly in sub-Saharan Africa. Consequently, few examples of African masks and sculpture remain from before the nineteenth century, and for the most part it is necessary to rely on contemporary traditions and oral histories to help extrapolate backward in time to determine what may have been the types, styles, and meaning of art made in the past. Nevertheless, the few ancient African artworks we have in such durable materials as terra cotta, stone, and bronze, and from an extensive record in rock art that has been preserved in sheltered places, bear eloquent witness to the skill of ancient African artists and the splendor of the civilizations in which they worked.

Twentieth-century archaeology has made it popular to speak of Africa as the cradle of human civilization. Certainly the earliest evidence for our human ancestors comes from southern Africa (see "Southern African Rock Art," page 408). Now evidence of the initial stirrings of artistic activity also comes from the southern tip of Africa. Recently, quantities of ocher pigment thought to have been used for ceremonial or decorative purposes, and perforated shells thought to have been fashioned into beads and worn as personal adornment, have been found in Blombos Cave on the Indian Ocean coast of South Africa, dating to approximately 77,000 years ago. Also discovered together with these were two small, ocher blocks that had been smoothed and then decorated with geometric arrays of carved lines (SEE FIG. 1.4 for an illustration of the decorated ocher). These incised abstract patterns predate any other findings of ancient art by more than 30,000 years, and they suggest a far earlier development of modern human behavior than had been previously recognized.

The earliest known figurative art works from the African continent are animal figures dating to about 25,000 BCE, painted in red and black pigment on flat stones found in a cave designated as Apollo 11, located in the desert mountains of Namibia. These figures are comparable to the better-known European cave drawings such as those from the Chauvet Cave (c. 32,000–30,000 BCE) and Lascaux Cave (c. 15,000–13,000 BCE) discussed in Chapter 1.

AFRICAN ROCK ART

Like the Paleolithic inhabitants of Europe, early Africans painted and inscribed images on the walls of caves and rock shelters. Rock art is found throughout the African continent in places where the environment has been conducive to preservation—areas ranging from small, isolated shelters to great cavernous formations. Distinct geographic zones of rock art can be identified broadly encompassing the northern, central, southern, and eastern regions of the continent. These rock paintings and engravings range in

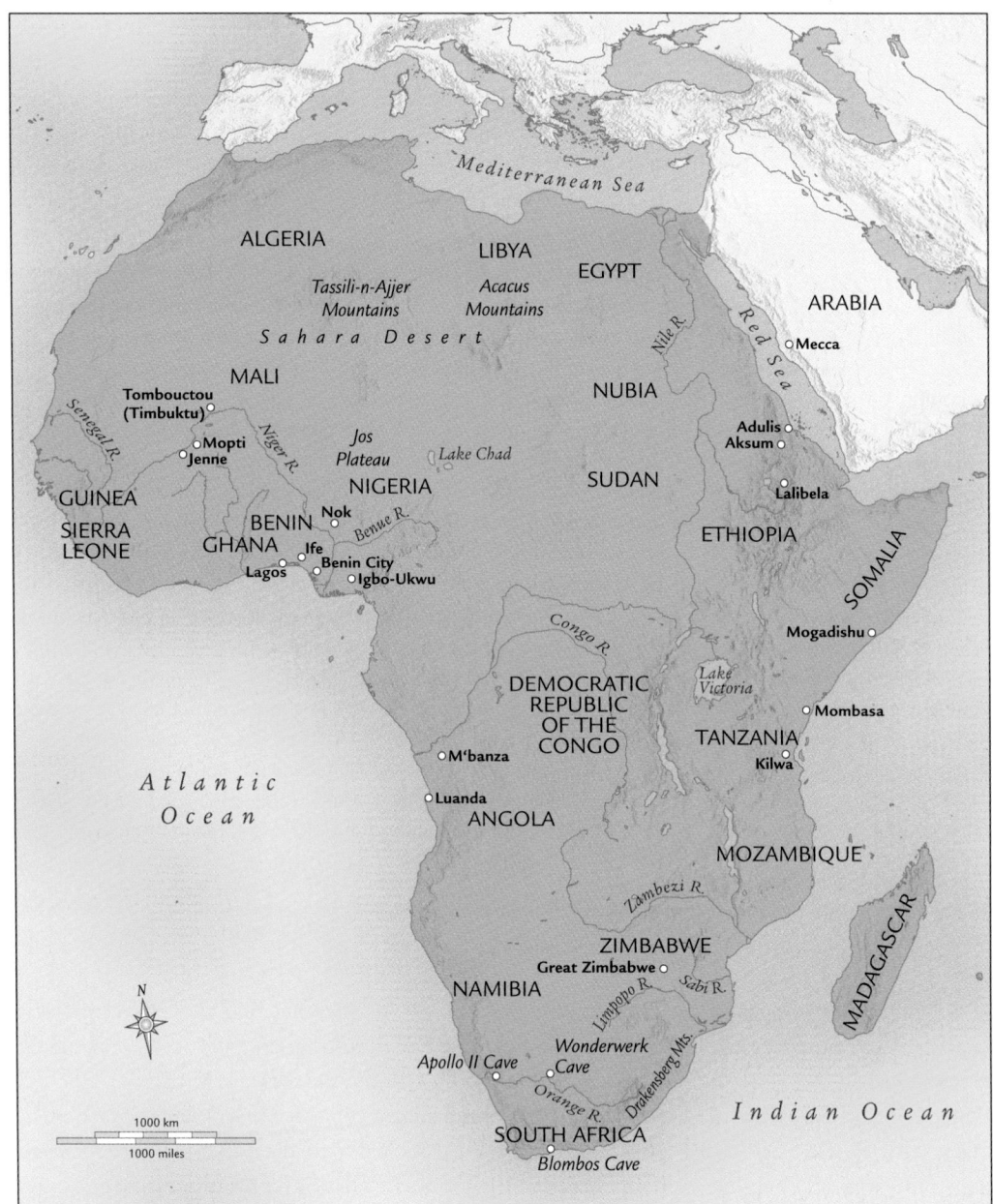

MAP 13-1 • ANCIENT AFRICA

Nearly 5,000 miles from north to south, Africa is the second-largest continent and was the home of some of the earliest and most advanced cultures of the ancient world.

form from highly abstract geometric designs to abstract and naturalistic representations of human and animal forms, including hunting scenes, scenes of domestic life, and costumed figures that appear to be dancing. The long record of rock art, extending over thousands of years in numerous places, charts dramatic environmental and social change in the deserts of Africa. Images depicting human subjects are also important evidence that the African artistic traditions of body decoration, mask-making and performance spring from ancient African roots.

SAHARAN ROCK ART

The mountains of the central Sahara—principally the Tassili-n-Ajjer range in the south of present-day Algeria and the Acacus Mountains in present-day Libya—contain images that span a period of thousands of years. They record not only the artistic and

cultural development of the peoples who lived in the region, but also the transformation of the Sahara from a fertile grassland to the vast desert we know today.

The earliest images of Saharan rock art are thought to date from at least 8000 BCE, during the transition into a geological period known as the Makalian Wet Phase. At that time the Sahara was a grassy plain, perhaps much like the game-park reserves of modern east Africa. Vivid images of hippopotamus, elephant, giraffe, antelope, and other animals incised on rock surfaces attest to the abundant wildlife that roamed the region.

A variety of scenes found on rock walls in both southern Algeria and Libya depict men and women dancing or performing various ceremonial activities. The artists who created these works paid close attention to details of clothing, body decoration, and headdresses; in some examples the figures are depicted wearing

The Myth of "Primitive" Art

The word "primitive" was once used by Western art historians to categorize the art of Africa, the art of the Pacific islands, and the indigenous art of the Americas. The term itself means "early" or "first of its kind," but its use was meant to imply that these cultures were crude, simple, backward, and stuck in an early stage of development.

This attitude was accepted by Christian missionaries and explorers, who often described the peoples among whom they worked as "heathen," "barbaric," "ignorant," "tribal," "primitive," and other terms rooted in racism and colonialism. Such usages were extended to these peoples' creations, and "primitive art" became the conventional label for their cultural products.

Criteria that have been used to label a people "primitive" include the use of so-called Stone Age technology, the absence of written histories, and the failure to build great cities. Based on these criteria, however, the accomplishments of the peoples of Africa, to take just one example, contradict such prejudiced condescension: Africans south of the Sahara have smelted and forged iron since at least 500 BCE. Africans in many areas made and used high-quality steel for weapons and tools. Many African peoples have recorded their histories in Arabic since at least the tenth century CE. The first European visitors to Africa admired the style and sophistication of urban centers such as

Benin and Luanda, to name only two of the continent's great cities. Clearly, neither the cultures of ancient Africa nor the artworks they produced were "primitive" at all.

Until quite recently, Westerners tended to see Africa as a single country and not as an immense continent of vastly diverse cultures. Moreover, they perceived artists working in Africa as craftworkers bound to styles and images dictated by village elders and producing art that was anonymous and interchangeable. Over the past several decades, however, these misconceptions have crumbled. Art historians and anthropologists have now identified numerous African cultures and artists and compiled catalogs of their work. For example, the well-known Yoruba artist Olowe of Ise (see Chapter 28) was commissioned by rulers throughout the Yoruba region in the early twentieth century to create prestige objects such as palace veranda posts and palace doors or *tour-de-force* carvings such as magnificent lidded bowls supported by kneeling figures. Certainly we will never know the names of the vast majority of African artists of the past, just as we do not know the names of the sculptors responsible for the portrait busts of ancient Rome or the monumental reliefs of the Hindu temples of South Asia. But, as elsewhere, the greatest artists in Africa were famous and sought after, while innumerable others labored honorably and not at all anonymously.

---

masks that cover their faces. It is suggested that they are engaged in rituals intended to ensure adequate rainfall or success in hunting, or to honor their dead. These images, produced in a variety of styles, document the development of the complex ceremonial and ritual lives of the people who created them (FIG. 13–2).

By 4000 BCE the climate had become more arid, and hunting had given way to herding as the primary life-sustaining activity of the Sahara's inhabitants. Among the most beautiful and complex examples of Saharan rock art created in this period are scenes of sheep, goats, and cattle and of the daily lives of the people who tended them. Some scenes found at Tassili-n-Ajjer date from late in the herding period, about 5000–2000 BCE, and illustrate men and women gathered in front of round, thatched houses. As the men tend cattle, the women prepare a meal and care for children. Some scenes attempt to create a sense of depth and distance with overlapping forms, and the placement of near figures lower and distant figures higher in the picture plane.

By 2500–2000 BCE the Sahara was drying and the great game had disappeared, but other animals were introduced that appear in the rock art. The horse was brought from Egypt by about 1500 BCE and is seen regularly in rock art over the ensuing millennia. The fifth-century BCE Greek historian Herodotus described a chariot-driving people called the Garamante, whose kingdom corresponds roughly to present-day Libya. Rock-art images of horse-drawn

chariots bear out his account. Around 600 BCE the camel was introduced into the region from the east, and images of camels were painted on and incised into the rock.

The drying of the Sahara coincided with the rise of Egyptian civilization along the Nile Valley to the east. Similarities can be noted between Egyptian and Saharan motifs, among them images of rams with what appear to be disks between their horns. These similarities have been interpreted as evidence of Egyptian influence on the less-developed regions of the Sahara. Yet in light of the great age of Saharan rock art, it seems just as plausible that the influence flowed the other way, carried by people who had migrated into the Nile Valley when the grasslands of the Sahara disappeared.

SUB-SAHARAN CIVILIZATIONS

Saharan peoples presumably migrated southward as well, into the Sudan, the broad belt of grassland that stretches across Africa south of the Sahara Desert. They brought with them knowledge of settled agriculture and animal husbandry. The earliest evidence of settled agriculture in the Sudan dates from about 3000 BCE. Toward the middle of the first millennium BCE, at the same time that iron technology was being developed elsewhere in Africa, knowledge of ironworking spread across the Sudan as well,

13-2 • DANCERS IN CEREMONIAL ATTIRE
Section of rock-wall painting, Tassili-n-Ajjer, Algeria. c. 5000–2000 BCE.

Nok sculpture was discovered in modern times by tin miners digging in alluvial deposits on the Jos plateau north of the confluence of the Niger and Benue rivers. Presumably, floods from centuries past had removed the sculptures from their original contexts, dragged and rolled them along, and then deposited them, scratched and broken, often leaving only the heads from what must have been complete human figures. Following archaeological convention, the name of a nearby village, Nok, was given to the culture that created these works. Nok-style works of sculpture have since been found in numerous sites over a wide area.

The Nok head shown (**FIG. 13–3**), slightly larger than life-size, probably formed part of a complete figure. The triangular or D-shaped eyes are characteristic of Nok style and appear also on sculptures of animals. Holes in the pupils, nostrils, and mouth allowed air to pass freely as the figure was fired. Each of the large buns of its elaborate hairstyle is pierced with a hole that may have held ornamental feathers. Other Nok figures were created displaying beaded necklaces,

enabling its inhabitants to create more effective weapons and farming tools. In the wake of these developments, larger and more complex societies emerged, especially in the fertile basins of Lake Chad in the central Sudan and the Niger and Senegal rivers to the west.

NOK

Some of the earliest evidence of iron technology in sub-Saharan Africa comes from the so-called Nok culture, which arose in the western Sudan, in present-day Nigeria, as early as 500 BCE. The Nok people were farmers who grew grain and oil-bearing seeds, but they were also smelters with the technology for refining ore. Slag and the remains of furnaces have been discovered, along with clay nozzles from the bellows used to fan the fires. The Nok people created the earliest known sculpture of sub-Saharan Africa, producing accomplished terra-cotta figures of human and animal subjects between about 500 BCE and 200 CE.

13-3 • HEAD
From Nok. c. 500 BCE–200 CE. Terra cotta, height 14 3/16″ (36 cm).
National Museum, Lagos, Nigeria.

Southern African Rock Art

Rock painting and engraving from sites in southern Africa differ in terms of style and age from those discussed for the Sahara region. Some works of art predate those found in the Sahara, while others continued to be produced into the modern era. Early works include an engraved fragment found in dateable debris in Wonderwerk Cave, South Africa, which dates back to 10,000 years ago. Painted stone flakes found at a site in Zimbabwe suggest dates between 13,000 and 8000 BCE.

Numerous examples of rock painting are also found in South Africa in the region of the Drakensberg Mountains. Almost 600 sites have been located in rock shelters and caves, with approximately 35,000 individual images catalogued. It is believed the paintings were produced, beginning approximately 2,400 years ago, by the predecessors of San peoples who still reside in the region. Ethnographic research among the San and related peoples in southern Africa suggest possible interpretations for some of the paintings. For example, rock paintings depicting groups of dancing figures may relate to certain forms of San rituals that are still performed today to heal individuals or to cleanse communities. These may have been created by San ritual specialists or shamans to record their curing dances or trance experiences of the spirit world. San rock artists continued to create rock paintings into the late nineteenth century. These latter works depict the arrival of Afrikaner pioneers in the region as well as British soldiers brandishing guns used to hunt eland.

SECTION OF SAN ROCK-WALL PAINTING San peoples, n.d. Drakensberg Mountains, South Africa. Pigment and eland blood on rock.

armlets, bracelets, anklets, and other prestige ornaments. Nok sculpture may represent ordinary people dressed for special occasions or it may portray people of high status, thus reflecting social stratification in this early farming culture. In either case, the sculpture provides evidence of considerable technical accomplishment, which has led to speculation that Nok culture was built on the achievements of an earlier culture still to be discovered.

IGBO-UKWU

A number of significant sites were excavated in Nigeria in the mid twentieth century that increase our understanding of the development of art and culture in west Africa. This includes the archaeological site of Igbo-Ukwu in eastern Nigeria where Igbo peoples reside, numerically one of Nigeria's largest populations. The earliest-known evidence for copper alloy or bronze casting in sub-Saharan Africa is found at Igbo-Ukwu. This evidence dates to the ninth and tenth centuries CE. Igbo-Ukwu is also the earliest-known site containing an elite burial and shrine complex yet found in sub-Saharan Africa. Three distinct archaeological sites have been excavated at Igbo-Ukwu—one containing a burial chamber, another resembling a shrine or storehouse containing ceremonial objects, and the third an ancient pit containing ceremonial and prestige objects.

The **BURIAL CHAMBER (FIG. 13–4)** contained an individual dressed in elaborate regalia, placed in a seated position, and surrounded by emblems of his power and authority. These

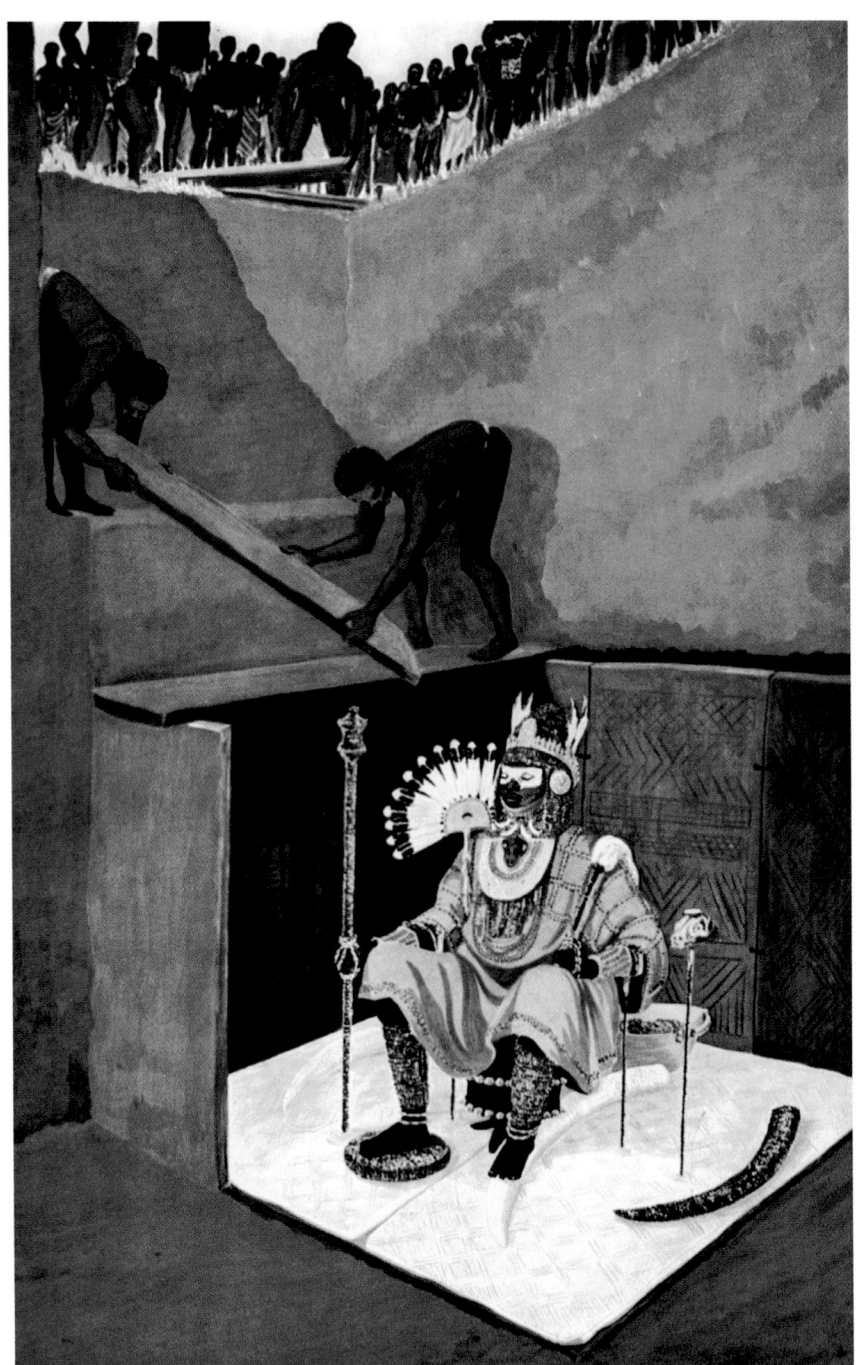

ornaments. Igbo-Ukwu's unique style consists of the representation in bronze of natural objects such as gourd bowls and snail shells whose entire outer surface is covered with elaborate raised and banded decorations. These decorations include linear, spiral, circular, and granular designs, sometimes with the addition of small animals or insects such as snakes, frogs, crickets, or flies applied to the decorated surface. Some castings are further enlivened with the addition of brightly colored beads.

A cast fly-whisk handle is topped with the representation of an equestrian figure whose face, like that of a pendant head also found during excavation, is represented scarified in a style similar to the patterning found on some of the terra-cotta and cast heads of rulers at Ife. These markings are similar to markings called *ichi*, which are still used by Igbo men as a symbol of high achievement.

A roped pot is among the most technically sophisticated castings found at Igbo-Ukwu (see "A Closer Look," page 411). It has been suggested that the vessel resembles a form of water-pot drum still used in this region of Nigeria. The vessel is filled with water and a flat mallet is struck across the surface of the water at the rim to create a percussive sound.

IFE

The naturalistic works of sculpture created by the artists of the city of Ife are among the most remarkable in art history. Ancient Ife, which arose in the southwestern forested part of Nigeria about 800 CE, was essentially circular in plan, with

included three ivory tusks, thousands of imported beads that originally formed part of an elaborate necklace, other adornments, and a cast-bronze representation of a leopard skull. Elephants and leopards are still symbols of temporal and spiritual leadership in Africa today. Ethnographic research among the Nri, an Igbo-related people currently residing in the region, suggests that the burial site is that of an important Nri king or ritual leader (*eze*).

The second excavation uncovered a shrine or storehouse complex containing ceremonial and prestige objects. These copper alloy castings were made by the lost-wax technique (see "Lost-Wax Casting," page 413) in the form of elaborately decorated small bowls, fly-whisk handles, altar stands, staff finials (decorative tops), and

the *oni*'s palace at the center. Ringed by protective stone walls and moats, it was connected to other Yoruba cities by roads that radiated from the center, passing through the city walls at fortified gateways decorated with mosaics created from stones and pottery shards. From these elaborately patterned pavement mosaics, which covered much of Ife's open spaces, comes the name for Ife's most artistically cohesive historical period (c. 1000–1400), the Pavement period.

Just as the *oni*'s palace was located in a large courtyard in the center of Ife, so too were ritual spaces elsewhere in Ife located in paved courtyards with altars. In the center of such a sacred courtyard, outlined by rings of pavement mosaic, archaeologists

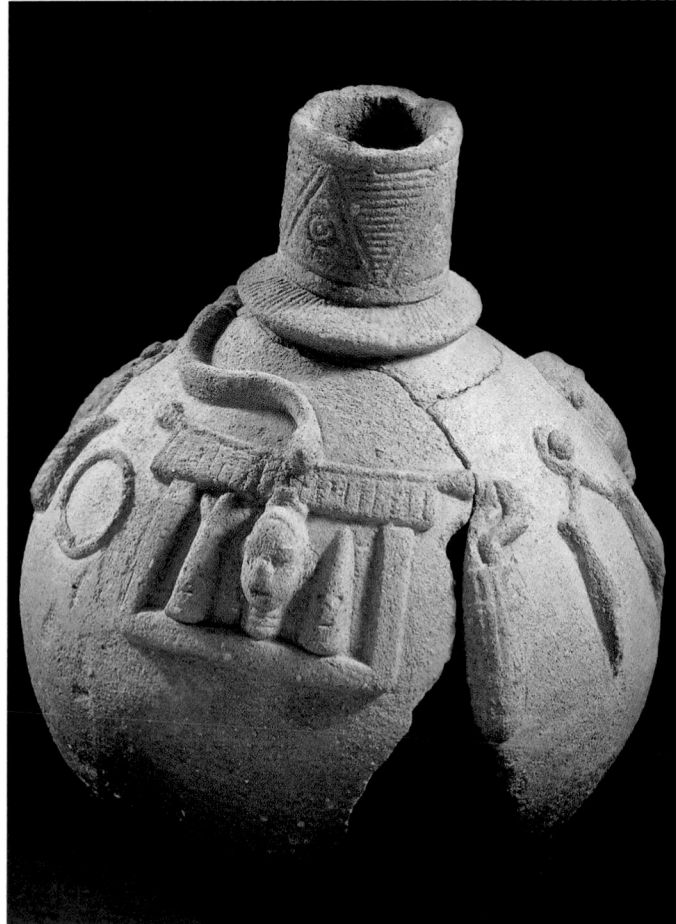

13-5 • RITUAL VESSEL
From Ife, Yoruba. 13th–14th century CE. Terra cotta, height 9¹³⁄₁₆″ (24.9 cm). University Art Museum, Obafemi, Awolowo University, Ife, Nigeria.

to Ife for a master metalcaster named Iguegha. The tradition of casting memorial heads for the shrines of royal ancestors endures among the successors of Oranmiyan to this day **(FIG. 13–6)**.

Benin came into contact with Portugal in the late fifteenth century. The two kingdoms established cordial relations in 1485 and carried on an active trade, at first in ivory and forest products, but eventually in slaves. Benin flourished until 1897, when, in reprisal for the massacre of a party of trade negotiators, British troops sacked and burned the royal palace, sending the *oba* into an exile from which he did not return until 1914 (see Chapter 28, pages 880–881). The palace was later rebuilt, and the present-day *oba* continues the dynasty started by Oranmiyan.

The British invaders discovered shrines to deceased *oba*s covered with brass heads, bells, and figures. They also found

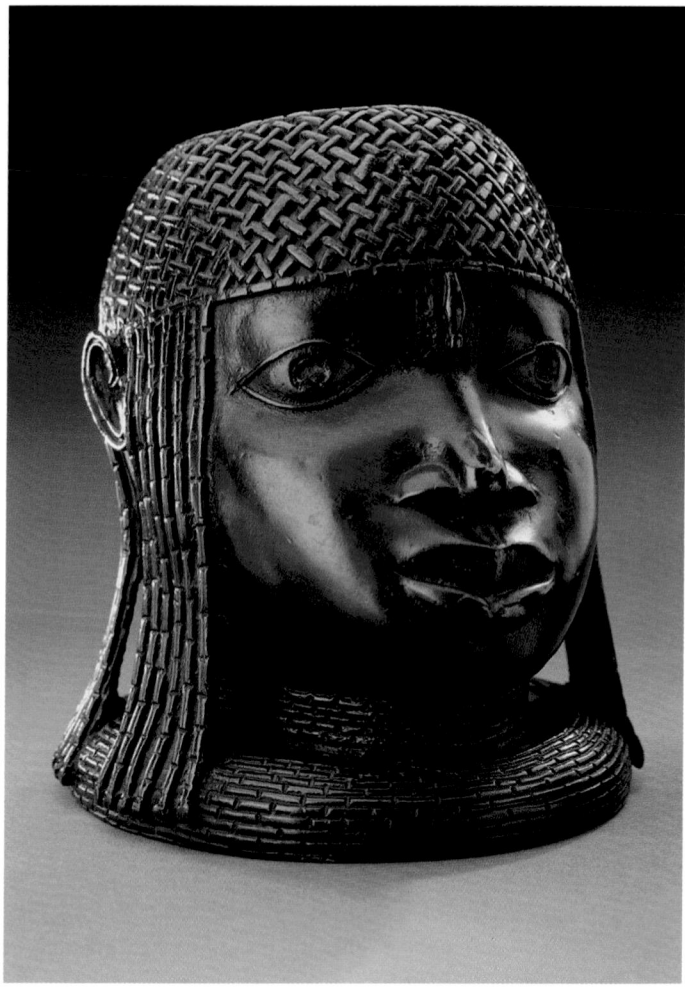

13-6 • MEMORIAL HEAD OF AN *OBA*
From Benin. Early Period, c. 16th century CE. Brass, height 9″ (23 cm). The Nelson-Atkins Museum of Art, Kansas City, Missouri. Purchase: Nelson Trust through the generosity of Donald J. and Adele C. Hall, Mr. and Mrs. Herman Robert Sutherland, an anonymous donor, and the exchange of Nelson Gallery Foundation properties (87-7)

This belongs to a small group of rare Early Period sculptures called "rolled-collar" heads that are distinguished by the rolled collar that serves as a firm base for the exquisitely rendered head.

excavated an exceptional terra-cotta vessel **(FIG. 13–5)**. The jar's bottom had been ritually broken before it was buried, so that liquid offerings (libations) poured into the neck opening would flow into the earth. The objects depicted in relief on the surface of the vessel include what looks like an altar platform with three heads under it, the outer two quite abstract and the middle one almost naturalistic in the tradition of free-standing Yoruba portrait heads. The abstraction of the two outside heads may have been a way of honoring or blessing the central portrait, a practice that survives among Yoruba royalty today.

BENIN

Ife was probably the artistic parent of the great city-state of Benin, which arose some 150 miles to the southeast. According to oral histories, the earliest kings of Benin belonged to the Ogiso, or Skyking, dynasty. After a long period of misrule, however, the people of Benin asked the *oni* of Ife for a new ruler. The *oni* sent Prince Oranmiyan, who founded a new dynasty in 1170. Some two centuries later, the fourth king, or *oba*, of Benin decided to start a tradition of memorial sculpture like that of Ife, and he sent

Roped Pot on a Stand ›
From Igbo-Ukwu. 9th–10th century CE.
Leaded bronze, height 12¹¹⁄₁₆″ (32.3 cm). National Museum, Lagos.

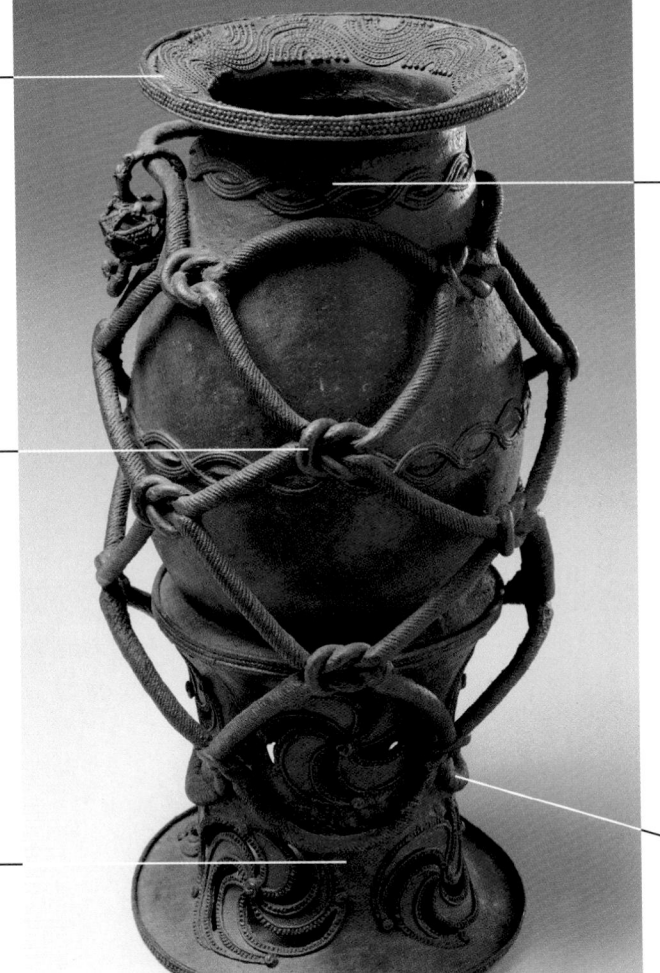

Like a number of other objects excavated at Igbo-Ukwu, this vessel is a skeuomorph—an object created in a different material from the original but made to resemble the original form.

The flaring neck of the vessel just below the rim and the lower half of the pot stand were cast separately. Molten metal was then applied to the edges of the separate castings to join them together.

The knotted rope cage appears to be made from one continuous piece of "rope." Even the individual strands of the "rope" are replicated in leaded bronze.

Pot stands are used to support containers placed on sacred altars so that the water contained in the vessels should never touch the ground before its use in ritual ceremony.

The rope cage surrounding the pot and stand was cast separately and then positioned around the pot and upper part of the stand. The lower part of the knotted rope was then bent inward to grip the pot stand.

wooden rattles and enormous ivory tusks carved with images of kings, court attendants, and sixteenth-century Portuguese soldiers. The British appropriated the treasure as war booty, making no effort to note which head came from which shrine, thus destroying evidence that would have helped establish the relative age of the heads and determine a chronology for the evolution of Benin style. Nevertheless, it has been possible to piece together a chronology from other evidence.

The Benin heads, together with other objects, were originally placed on a semicircular platform or **ALTAR** and surmounted by large elephant tusks, another symbol of power (**FIG. 13–7**). Benin brass heads range from small, thinly cast, and naturalistic to large,

thickly cast, and highly stylized. Many scholars have concluded that the smallest, most naturalistic heads with only a few strands of beads around the neck were created during a so-called Early Period (1400–1550), when Benin artists were still heavily influenced by Ife. Heads grew heavier and increasingly stylized, and the strands of beads increased in number until they concealed the chin during the Middle Period (1550–1700). Heads from the ensuing Late Period (1700–1897) are very large and heavy, with angular, stylized features and an elaborate beaded crown. During the Late Period, the necklaces form a tall, cylindrical mass. In addition, broad, horizontal flanges, or projecting edges, bearing small images cast in low relief ring the base of the Late Period

13-7 • ALTAR
Edo Culture, Nigeria.
c. 1959. The National
Museum of African
Art, Smithsonian
Institution, Washington,
D.C. Eliot Elisofon
Photographic Archives
(7584)

heads. The increase in size and weight of Benin memorial heads over time may reflect the growing power and wealth flowing to the *oba* from Benin's expanding trade with Europe.

At Benin, as in many other African cultures, the head is the symbolic center of a person's intelligence, wisdom, and ability to succeed in this world or to communicate with spiritual forces in the ancestral world. One of the honorifics used for the king is "Great Head": The head leads the body as the king leads the people. All of the memorial heads include representations of coral-beaded caps and necklaces and royal costume. Coral, enclosing the head and displayed on the body, is still the ultimate symbol of the *oba*'s power and authority.

The art of Benin is a royal art, for only the *oba* could commission works in brass (see "A Warrior Chief Pledging Loyalty," pages 414–415). Artisans who served the court were organized into guilds and lived in a separate quarter of the city. *Obas* also commissioned important works in ivory. One example is a beautiful ornamental mask (FIG. 13–8). It represents an *iyoba* (queen mother—the *oba*'s mother), the senior female member of

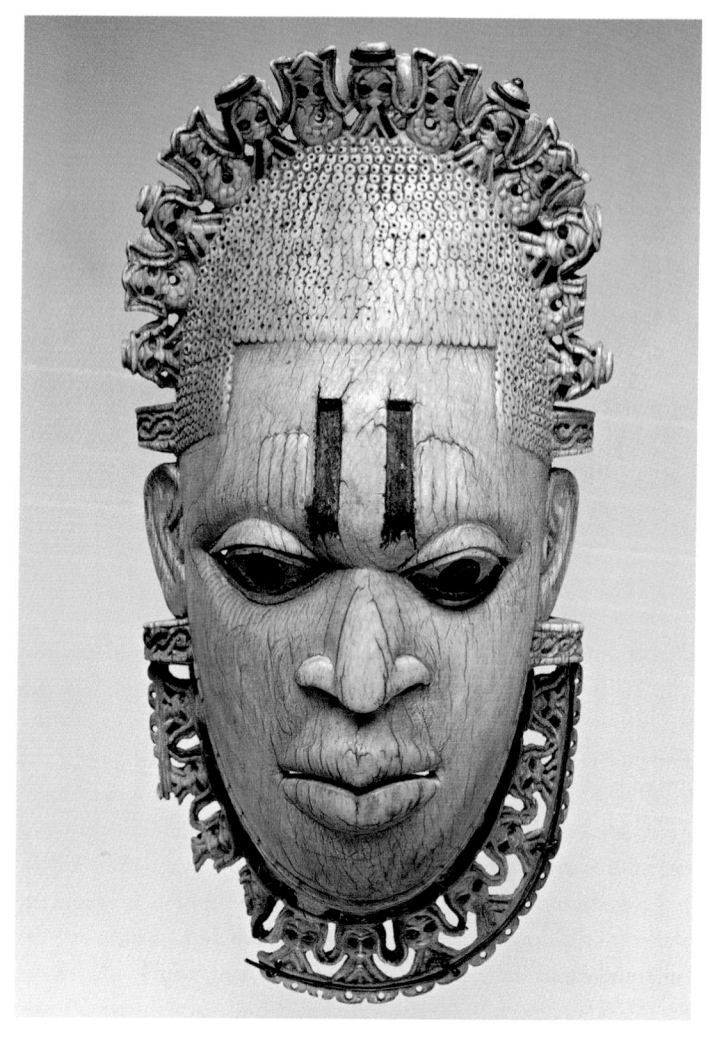

**13-8 • HIP MASK REPRESENTING AN *IYOBA*
("QUEEN MOTHER")**
From Benin. Middle Period, c. 1550 CE. Ivory, iron, and copper, height
9⅜" (23.4 cm). Metropolitan Museum of Art, New York. The Michael C.
Rockefeller Memorial Collection, Gift of Nelson A. Rockefeller, 1972
(1978.412.323)

In the **lost-wax casting** process a metal copy is produced from an original image made of wax. The usual metals for this casting process are bronze, an alloy of copper and tin, and brass, an alloy of copper and zinc. First, the sculptor models a wax original. Then the wax is invested in a heat-resistant mold. Next, the wax is melted, leaving an empty cavity into which molten metal is poured. After the metal cools and solidifies, the mold is broken away and the metal copy is chased and polished.

The progression of drawings here shows the steps used by the Benin sculptors of Africa. A heat-resistant "core" of clay (a) approximating the shape of the sculpture-to-be (and eventually becoming the hollow inside the sculpture) was covered by a layer of wax that had the thickness of the final sculpture. The sculptor carved or modeled (b) the details in the wax. Rods and a pouring cup made of wax were attached (c) to the model. A thin layer of fine, damp sand was pressed very firmly into the surface of the wax model, and then model, rods, and cup were encased (d) in thick layers of clay. When the clay was completely dry, the mold was heated (e) to melt out the wax. The mold was then placed upside down in the ground to receive (f) the molten metal, heated to the point of liquefication. When the metal was completely cool, the outside clay cast and the inside core were broken up and removed (g), leaving the cast-brass sculpture. Details were polished to finish the piece, which could not be duplicated because the mold had been destroyed.

clay core
a

wax
tool
b

layer of clay
layer of fine sand
wax rods (drains) and wax cup
c

d

molten metal
f

draining wax
e

finished cast
g

SEE MORE: View a video about the process of lost-wax casting **www.myartslab.com**

the royal court. The mask was carved as a belt ornament and was worn at the *oba*'s hip. Its pupils were originally inlaid with iron, as were the scarification patterns on the forehead. This particular belt ornament may represent Idia, who was the mother of Esigie, a powerful *oba* who ruled from 1504 to 1550. Idia is particularly remembered for raising an army and using magical powers to help her son defeat his enemies. Like Idia, the Portuguese helped Esigie expand his kingdom. The necklace represents heads of Portuguese soldiers with beards and flowing hair. In the crown, more Portuguese heads alternate with figures of mudfish, which symbolize Olokun, the Lord of the Great Waters. Mudfish live near riverbanks, mediating between water and land, just as the *oba*, who is viewed as semidivine, mediates between the human world and the supernatural world of Olokun.

A Warrior Chief Pledging Loyalty

Produced during the sixteenth and seventeenth centuries, approximately 900 brass plaques, each averaging about 16 to 18 inches in height, once decorated the walls and pillars of the royal palace of the kingdom of Benin. Like the brass memorial heads and figure sculpture, the plaques were made following the lost-wax casting process. They illustrate a variety of subjects including ceremonial scenes at court, showing the *oba*, other court functionaries, and (at times) Portuguese soldiers. Modeled

in relief, the plaques depict one or more figures, with precise details of costume and regalia. Some figures are modeled in such high relief that they appear almost free-standing as they emerge from a textured surface background that often includes foliate patterning representing the leaves employed in certain healing rituals.

This plaque features a warrior chief in ceremonial attire. His rank is indicated by a necklace of leopard's teeth, and coral-decorated cap and collar. He also wears

an elaborately decorated skirt with a leopard mask on his hip. The chief is depicted holding a spear in one hand and an *eben* sword held above his head in the other hand. The *eben* sword, with its distinctive leaf-shaped blade made of iron with openwork surface decoration is a major symbol of high rank in Benin even today.

The plaque is organized in a hierarchal order with the warrior chief larger in size and in the center of the composition. The chief is

PLAQUE: WARRIOR CHIEF FLANKED BY WARRIORS AND ATTENDANTS
From Benin, Nigeria. Middle Period, c. 1550–1650 CE. Brass, height 14¾ × 15½″ (37.5 × 39.4 cm).
The Nelson-Atkins Museum of Art, Kansas City, Missouri. (58-3)

Senior town chief supported by two attendants, one of them carries his *eben* sword.

flanked by two warriors holding shields and spears, and two smaller figures representing court attendants. One attendant is depicted playing a side-blown horn that announces the warrior chief's presence, while the other attendant carries a ceremonial box for conveying gifts to the *oba*. The scene is a ceremony of obeisance to the *oba*. The warrior chief's gesture of raising the *eben* sword is still performed at annual ceremonies in which chiefs declare their allegiance and loyalty to the *oba* by raising the sword and spinning it in the air. The kinetic movement of the sword spinning as it is held aloft certainly adds a degree of conviction and authority to the ceremony.

Oba Erediauwa wearing coral-beaded regalia and seated on a dais.

OTHER URBAN CENTERS

Ife and Benin were but two of the many cities that arose in ancient Africa. The first European visitors to the west African coast at the end of the fifteenth century were impressed not only by Benin, but also by the city of Mbanza Kongo, south of the mouth of the Congo River. Along the east African coastline, Europeans also happened upon cosmopolitan cities that had been busily carrying on long-distance trade across the Indian Ocean and as far away as China and Indonesia for hundreds of years.

Important centers also existed in the interior, especially across the central and western Sudan. There, cities and the states that developed around them grew wealthy from the trans-Saharan trade that had linked west Africa to the Mediterranean from at least the first millennium BCE. Indeed, the routes across the desert were probably as old as the desert itself. Among the most significant goods exchanged in this trade were salt from the north and gold from west Africa. Such fabled cities as Mopti, Timbuktu, and Jenné arose in the vast area of grasslands along the Niger River in the region known as the Niger Bend (present-day Mali), a trading crossroads as early as the first century BCE. They were great centers of commerce, where merchants from all over west Africa met caravans arriving from the Mediterranean. Eventually the trading networks extended across Africa from the Sudan in the east to the Atlantic coast in the west. In the twelfth century CE a Mande-speaking people formed the kingdom of Mali (Manden). The rulers adopted Islam, and by the fourteenth century they controlled the oases on which the traders' caravans depended. Mali prospered, and wealthy cities like Timbuktu and Jenné became famed as centers of Islamic learning.

At a site near Jenné known as Jenné-Jeno or Old Jenné, excavations (by both archaeologists and looters) have uncovered hundreds of terra-cotta figures dating from the thirteenth to the sixteenth centuries. The figures were polished, covered with a red clay slip, and fired at a low temperature. A **HORSEMAN**, armed with quiver, arrows, and a dagger, is a good example of the technique **(FIG. 13–9)**. Man and horse are formed of rolls of clay on which details of the face, clothing, and harness are carved, engraved, and painted. The rider has a long oval head and jutting chin, pointed oval eyes set in multiple framing lids, and a long straight nose. He wears short pants and a helmet with a chin strap, and his horse has an ornate bridle. Such elaborate trappings suggest that the horseman could be a guardian figure, hero, or even a deified ancestor. Similar figures have been found in sanctuaries. But, as urban life declined, so did the arts. The long tradition of ceramic sculpture came to an end in the fifteenth and sixteenth centuries, when rivals began to raid the Manden cities.

JENNÉ

In 1655, the Islamic writer al-Sadi wrote this description of Jenné:

> This city is large, flourishing, and prosperous; it is rich, blessed, and favoured by the Almighty.... Jenne [Jenné] is one of the great markets of the Muslim world. There one meets the salt merchants from the mines of Teghaza and merchants carrying gold from the mines of Bitou.... Because of this blessed city, caravans flock to Timbuktu from all points of the horizon.... The area around Jenne is fertile and well populated; with numerous markets held there on all the days of the week. It is certain that it contains 7,077 villages very near to one another.
>
> (Translated by Graham Connah in *Connah*, page 97)

By the time al-Sadi wrote his account, Jenné already had a long history. Archaeologists have determined that the city was established by the third century CE, and that by the middle of the ninth century it had become a major urban center. Also by the ninth century, Islam was becoming an economic and religious force in west and north Africa, and the northern terminals of the trans-Saharan trade routes had already been incorporated into the Islamic empire.

When Koi Konboro, the 26th king of Jenné, converted to Islam in the thirteenth century, he transformed his palace into the first of three successive mosques in the city. Like the two that followed, the first mosque was built of adobe brick, a sun-dried

13-9 • HORSEMAN
From Old Jenné, Mali. 13th–15th century CE. Terra cotta, height 27¾″ (70.5 cm). National Museum of African Art, Smithsonian Institution, Washington, D.C. Museum Purchase (86-12-2)

mixture of clay and straw. With its great surrounding wall and tall towers, it was said to have been more beautiful and more lavishly decorated than the Kaaba, the central shrine of Islam, at Mecca. The mosque eventually attracted the attention of austere Muslim rulers who objected to its sumptuous furnishings. Among these was the early nineteenth-century ruler Sekou Amadou, who had it razed and a far more humble structure erected on a new site. This second mosque was in turn replaced by the current grand mosque, constructed between 1906 and 1907 on the ancient site in the style of the original. The reconstruction was supervised by the architect Ismaila Traoré, the head of the Jenné guild of masons.

The mosque's eastern, or "marketplace," façade boasts three tall towers, the center of which contains the *mihrab* (**FIG. 13–10**). The finials, or crowning ornaments, at the top of each tower bear ostrich eggs, symbols of fertility and purity. The façade and sides of the mosque are distinguished by tall, narrow, engaged columns, which act as buttresses. These columns are characteristic of west African mosque architecture, and their cumulative rhythmic effect is one of great verticality and grandeur. The most unusual features of west African mosques are the **torons**, wooden beams projecting from the walls. Torons provide permanent supports for the scaffolding erected each year so that the exterior of the mosque can be replastered.

Traditional houses resemble the mosque on a small scale. Adobe walls, reinforced by buttresses, rise above the roofline in conical turrets, emphasizing the entrance. Rooms open inward onto a courtyard. Extended upper walls mask a flat roof terrace that gives more private space for work and living.

GREAT ZIMBABWE

Thousands of miles from Jenné, in southeastern Africa, an extensive trade network developed along the Zambezi, Limpopo, and Sabi rivers. Its purpose was to funnel gold, ivory, and exotic skins to the coastal trading towns that had been built by Arabs and Swahili-speaking Africans. There, the gold and ivory were exchanged for prestige goods, including porcelain, beads, and other manufactured items. Between 1000 and 1500 CE, this trade was largely controlled from a site that was called Great Zimbabwe, home of the Shona people.

The word *zimbabwe* derives from the Shona term *dzimba dza mabwe* ("venerated houses" or "houses of stone"). The stone buildings at Great Zimbabwe were constructed by the ancestors of

13-10 • GREAT FRIDAY MOSQUE
Jenné, Mali, showing the eastern and northern façades. Rebuilding of 1907, in the style of 13th-century original.

The plan of the mosque is not quite rectangular. Inside, nine rows of heavy adobe columns, 33 feet (10 meters) tall and linked by pointed arches, support a flat ceiling of palm logs. An open courtyard on the west side (not seen here) is enclosed by a great double wall only slightly lower than the walls of the mosque itself. The main entrances to the prayer hall are in the north wall (to the right in the photograph).

the present-day people of this region. The earliest construction at the site took advantage of the enormous boulders abundant in the vicinity. Masons incorporated the boulders and used the uniform granite blocks that split naturally from them to build a series of tall enclosing walls high on a hilltop. Each enclosure defined a family's living space and housed dwellings made of adobe with conical, thatched roofs.

The largest building complex at Great Zimbabwe is located in a broad valley below the hilltop enclosures. Known as Imba Huru (the Great Enclosure), the complex is ringed by a masonry wall more than 800 feet long, up to 32 feet tall, and 17 feet thick at the base. Inside the great outer wall are numerous smaller stone enclosures and adobe platforms **(FIG. 13–11)**. The buildings at Great Zimbabwe were built without mortar; for stability the walls are **battered**, or built so that they slope inward toward the top. Although some of the enclosures at Great Zimbabwe were built on hilltops, there is no evidence that they were constructed as fortresses. There are neither openings for weapons to be thrust through nor battlements for warriors to stand on. Instead, the walls and structures seem intended to reflect the wealth and power of the city's rulers. The Imba Huru was probably a royal residence, or palace complex, and other structures housed members of the ruler's family and court. The complex formed the nucleus of a city that radiated for almost a mile in all directions. Over the centuries, the builders grew more skillful, and the later additions are distinguished by dressed stones, or smoothly finished stones, laid in fine, even, level courses. One of these later additions is a structure known simply as the **CONICAL TOWER (FIG. 13–12)**. Some 18 feet in diameter and 30 feet tall, the tower was originally capped with three courses of ornamental stonework. Constructed between the two walls and resembling a granary, it may have represented the good harvest and prosperity believed to result from allegiance to the ruler of Great Zimbabwe.

It is estimated that at the height of its power, in the fourteenth century, Great Zimbabwe and its surrounding city housed a population of more than 10,000 people. A large cache of goods containing items of such far-flung origin as Portuguese medallions, Persian pottery, and Chinese porcelain testify to the extent of its trade. Yet beginning in the mid fifteenth century Great Zimbabwe was gradually abandoned as control of the lucrative southeast African trade network passed to the Mwene Mutapa and Kami empires a short distance away.

13–11 • DRAWING OF GREAT ZIMBABWE

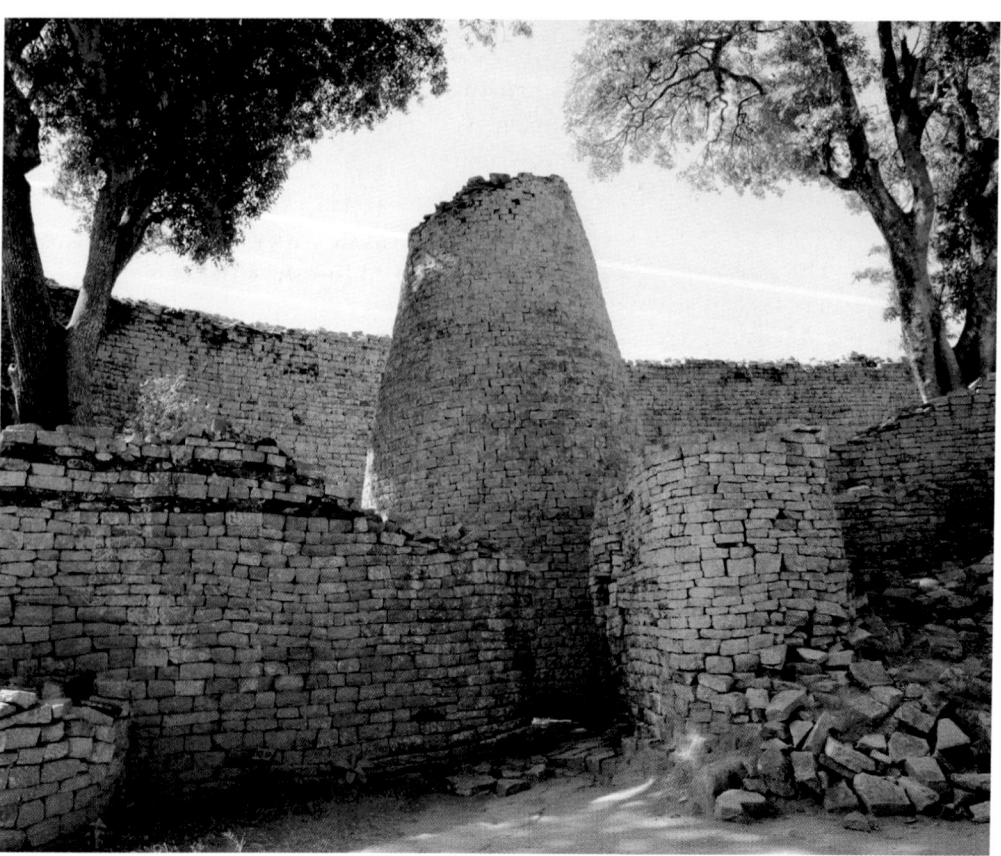

13–12 • CONICAL TOWER
Great Zimbabwe. c. 1200–1400 CE.
Height of tower 30' (9.1 m).

AKSUM AND LALIBELA

In the second century BCE Aksumite civilization increased in importance in the Ethiopian highlands through the control of trade routes from the African interior to the Red Sea port of Adulis. Its exports included ivory, gold, slaves, frankincense, myrrh, and salt. In the mid fourth century CE the Aksumite king Ezana converted to Christianity, and soon gold and silver coinage minted at Aksum bore the Christian cross.

The archaeological remains at Aksum and Gondar speak of the splendor of the ancient kingdom. By the third century CE a series of stone palaces were built at Aksum. The elites also erected a number of monolithic granite stelae which date from the third and fourth centuries, the largest over 95 feet in height. Their outer surfaces were decorated with such carved architectural details as false doors, inset windows, and timber beams. The stelae served as commemorative markers among the tombs and burial sites of the elite.

The power and influence of the Aksumite state was diminished by the displacement of the Red Sea trade routes after the Persian conquest of south Arabia, and Aksum was conquered by the Zagwe from Ethiopia's western highlands. After its demise and abandonment, a new capital arose, the influence and prestige of which lasted until near the end of the thirteenth century.

The Zagwe king Lalibela, wishing to create a "new" Jerusalem (the holy city revered by Christians, Jews, and Muslims) in Ethiopia, founded a holy site named after himself in the highlands south of Aksum. The cultural embrace of Christianity by the populace during the thirteenth century is evidenced by the numerous rock-hewn sanctuaries that were created in Lalibela at this time. Rather than being built from the ground up, the churches and other structures were hewn from the living rock. A wide trench was first cut around the four sides of a block of volcanic tuff that would become the church. Stonemasons then carved out the exterior and interior of the sanctuaries with hammers and chisels. Each aspect of the structure had to be planned with precision before work could begin. The interior of the church was created with a hemispherical domed ceiling in the style of Byzantine churches: Ethiopian priests must have seen this form of architecture during their pilgrimages to Jerusalem.

The largest of the 11 churches is **BET GIORGIS** (Church of St. George) which was cut 40 feet down in the form of a modified cross **(FIG. 13–13)**. Most rock-cut sanctuaries have architectural details that appear to have been modeled in part from earlier Aksum palaces. However, Bet Giorgis has window details that are

13-13 • BET GIORGIS (THE CHURCH OF ST. GEORGE), LALIBELA, ETHIOPIA

similar to the organic tendril forms found in later Ethiopian painted manuscripts. The origins of the rock-cut church are unknown. The churches at Lalibela may have been modeled on earlier Aksumite cave sanctuaries, but it has also been suggested that they have their origins in central and southern India where Buddhist and Hindu temples, shrines, and monasteries have been excavated from the living rock for over 2,000 years.

KONGO KINGDOM

As in other parts of sub-Saharan Africa, art-making traditions in the Kongo cultural region developed over thousands of years. However, as elsewhere on the African continent, the climate here is often not conducive to the survival of objects made from wood. Among the earliest known wooden artworks from central Africa is a wood

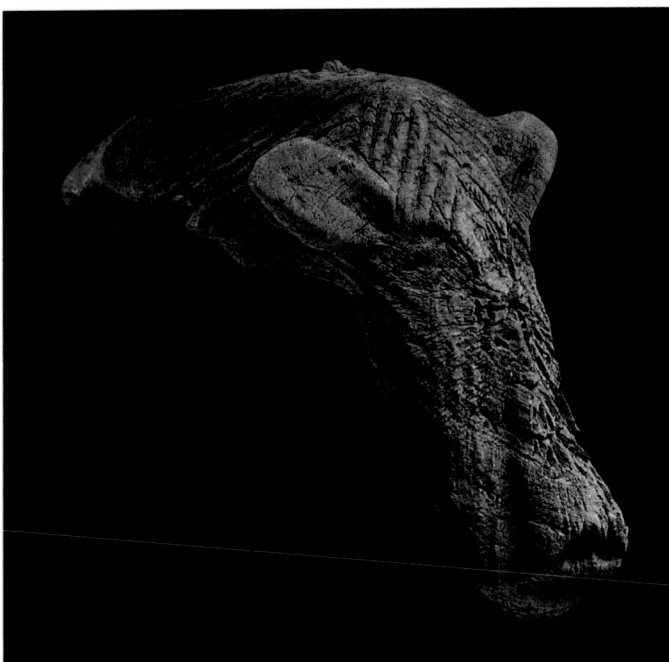

13-14 • ZOOMORPHIC HEAD
From Angola. c. 750 CE. Wood, 19⅞ × 6⅛″ (50.5 × 15.5 cm).
Royal Museum of Central Africa, Tervuren, Belgium.

13-15 • DECORATED TEXTILE
From Kongo. Early 17th century CE. Raffia, 9½ × 18½″ (24 × 47 cm).
Pitt Rivers Museum, University of Oxford, England.

carving unearthed in Angola in 1928 (**FIG. 13–14**). This **ZOOMORPHIC HEAD** may have been created for use as a headdress or mask. Its elongated snout, pointed ears and geometric surface patterning resemble some masking traditions and sculptural practices that endured in the region well into the twentieth century.

The Portuguese first encountered Kongo culture in 1482 at approximately the same time contact was made with the royal court of Benin in present-day western Nigeria. They visited the capital of Mbanza Kongo (present-day M'banza Congo) and met the *manikongo* ("king"), who ruled over a kingdom that was remarkable in terms of its complex political organization and artistic sophistication. The kingdom, divided into six provinces, encompassed over 100,000 square miles of present-day northwestern Angola and the western part of the Democratic Republic of the Congo. In 1491, King Nzinga aNkuwa converted to Christianity, as did his son and successor Afonso I, who established it as the state religion. The conversions helped to solidify trade relations with the Portuguese, and trade in copper, salt, ivory, cloth, and, later, slaves brought increased prosperity to the kingdom. Kongo's influence expanded until the mid seventeenth century when its trading routes were taken over by neighboring peoples, including the Lunda and Chokwe.

The increase in wealth brought a corresponding increase in the production of specialty textiles, baskets, and regalia for the nobility. Textiles in central Africa, as elsewhere in Africa, are of extreme importance in terms of their value as wealth. Textiles were used as forms of currency before European contact and figure prominently in funerary rituals even to the present day. Kongo decorated textiles were lauded by the Portuguese from first contact and were accepted as gifts or collected and found their way into European museum collections (**FIG. 13–15**).

Following Portuguese contact in the fifteenth century and Nzinga aNkuwa's conversion, Kongolese art increasingly absorbed Western influences. With the arrival of Catholic missionaries, who brought with them various religious objects—including the monstrance (a highly decorated vessel used to display the consecrated bread or "body" of Christ), figures of the Virgin Mary and various saints, and the **CRUCIFIX**—the crucifix became a potent symbol of both conversion and political authority. Cast in brass and copper alloy (**FIG. 13–16**) the forms mirror their European prototypes, but are often restated in African terms. The features of the crucified Christ, as well as his hands and feet and those of the supporting figures, suggest an African aesthetic, as does the placement of supporting figures above and below the central figure. Although the supporting figures appear to be praying, in Kongo iconography, as elsewhere in central Africa, the clapping of hands is a common gesture of respect for another person.

13–16 • CRUCIFIX
From Kongo. Early 17th century CE. Bronze, height 10½″ (26.7 cm). Metropolitan Museum of Art. Collection of Ernst Anspach (1999.295.7)

13–17 • SAPI-PORTUGUESE STYLE HUNTING HORN
From Sierra Leone. Late 15th century CE, ivory, length 25″ (63.5 cm). National Museum of African Art, Smithsonian Institution. Walt Disney-Tishman African Art Collection (2005-6-9)

EXPORTING TO THE WEST

Shortly after initial contact with European explorers, merchants, and traders African artisans not only continued to fashion objects for their own consumption but also began to produce them for export to Europe. For example, by the late fifteenth century, artisans residing in present-day Sierra Leone (called Sapi by the Portuguese) and Nigeria (Bini) began to make objects such as ivory saltcellars, powder flasks, spoons and forks, as well as exquisitely carved oliphants, or horns **(FIG. 13–17)** for European patrons.

The form of the Sapi-Portuguese oliphant and virtually all its decorative motifs are European-inspired. The mouthpiece is at the narrow end rather than on the side as is typical for African horns. The various carvings on the horns, including the coat of arms of Portugal and Spain, the motto of Spain's Ferdinand V, and heraldic emblems and hunting scenes, were derived from illustrations found in European prayer books and other publications that were given to the artists as source material. However, not all of the designs found on some export ivories are derived from European sources. For example, some saltcellars depicting human subjects were carved in a style that resembles stone figures found locally that predate Portuguese contact with the west African coast. As Chapter 28 will show, the synthesis of Western and traditional influences continued to affect African art in both subtle and overt ways.

THINK ABOUT IT

13.1 Select one three-dimensional artwork and one two-dimensional artwork discussed in the chapter, and identify and summarize the original purpose of each. What role did these works play in society?

13.2 What is the spiritual role of the *oba* in Benin? What is his relationship to the spirit world, and how is that relationship represented in one work discussed in the chapter?

13.3 Explain the original purpose of the Benin royal plaque (see "A Warrior Chief Pledging Loyalty," pages 410–411), and how the identity of the individuals on the plaque and their posture relate to hierarchy at the royal court and the glorification of Benin kingship.

13.4 Consider a representation of African royalty, such as FIGURE 13–1. How was this artwork used in the context of its culture? Explain differences between African portrayals of royalty and those of the West, such as the imperial portraits of ancient Rome studied in Chapter 6. Are the African heads *portraits*?

PRACTICE MORE: Compose answers to these questions, get flashcards for images and terms, and review chapter material with quizzes
www.myartslab.com

14–1 • CHI RHO IOTA PAGE FROM THE BOOK OF KELLS   Probably made at Iona, Scotland.
Late 8th or early 9th century. Oxgall inks and pigments on vellum, 12¾ × 9½″ (32.5 × 24 cm).
The Board of Trinity College, Dublin. MS. 58, fol. 34r

EARLY MEDIEVAL ART IN EUROPE

The explosion of ornament surrounding—almost suffocating— the words on this page from an early medieval manuscript clearly indicates the importance of what is being expressed **(FIG. 14–1)**. The large Greek letters *chi rho iota* (*XPI*) abbreviate the word *Christi* that starts the Latin phrase *Christi autem generatio*. The last word is written out fully and legibly at bottom right, clear of the decorative expanse. These words begin Matthew 1:18: "Now the birth of Jesus the Messiah took place in this way." So what is signaled here—not with a picture of the event but with an ornamental celebration of its initial mention in the text—is Christ's first appearance within this Gospel book. The book itself not only contains the four biblical accounts of Christ's life; it would also evoke Christ's presence on the altar of the monastery church where this lavish book was once housed. It is precisely the sort of ceremonial book that we have already seen carried in the hands of a deacon in Justinian's procession into San Vitale in Ravenna to begin the Mass (SEE FIG. 7–23).

There is nothing explicitly Christian about the ornamental motifs celebrating the first mention of the birth of Christ in this manuscript—the Book of Kells, produced in Ireland or Scotland sometime around the year 800. The swirling spirals and interlaced tangles of stylized animal forms have their roots in jewelry created by the migrating "barbarian" tribes that formed the "other" of the Greco-Roman world. But by this time, this ornamental repertory had been subsumed into the flourishing art of Irish monasteries. Irish monks became as famous for writing and copying books as for their intense spirituality and missionary fervor.

Wealthy, isolated, and undefended, Irish monasteries were easy victims to Viking attacks. In 806, fleeing Viking raids on the island of Iona (off the coast of modern Scotland), its monks established a refuge at Kells on the Irish mainland. They probably brought the Book of Kells with them. It was precious. Producing this illustrated version of the Gospels entailed lavish expenditure: Four scribes and three major painters worked on it (modern scribes take about a month to complete such a page), 185 calves were slaughtered to make the vellum, and colors for some of its paintings came from as far away as Afghanistan.

Throughout the Middle Ages and across Europe, monasteries were principal centers of art and learning. While prayer and acts of mercy represented their primary vocation, some talented monks and nuns also worked as painters, jewelers, carvers, weavers, and embroiderers. Few, however, could claim a work of art as splendid as this one.

LEARN ABOUT IT

14.1 Investigate how barbarian ornamental styles became the basis for illustrating Christian manuscripts in Ireland and Northumbria, and learn how these manuscripts were made and used.

14.2 Assess the Carolingian revival of Roman artistic traditions in relation to the political position of the rulers as emperors sanctioned by the pope.

14.3 Appreciate and understand the variety of styles used to illustrate early medieval sacred books.

14.4 Discover the distinctive style of manuscript painting developed by Christian artists in Spain.

14.5 Analyze the planning and function of monasteries in the early Middle Ages.

HEAR MORE: Listen to an audio file of your chapter **www.myartslab.com**

THE EARLY MIDDLE AGES

As Roman authority crumbled at the dissolution of the Western Empire in the fifth century, it was replaced by "barbarians," people from outside the Roman empire and cultural orbit who could only "barble" Greek or Latin (MAP 14–1). Thus far we have seen these "barbarians" as adversaries viewed through Greek and Roman eyes—the defeated Gauls at Pergamon (SEE FIG. 5–52), the captives on the *Gemma Augustea* (SEE FIG. 6–19), or the enemy beyond the Danube River on Trajan's Column (SEE FIG. 6–43). But by the fourth century many Germanic tribes were allies of Rome. In fact, most of Constantine's troops in the decisive battle with Maxentius at the Milvian Bridge were Germanic.

A century later the situation was entirely different. The adventures of the Roman princess Galla Placidia, whom we have already met as a patron of the arts (SEE FIG. 7–14), bring the situation vividly to life. She had the misfortune to be in Rome when Alaric and the Visigoths sacked the city in 410 (the emperor and pope were living safely in Ravenna). Carried off as a prize of war by the Goths, Galla Placidia had to join their migrations through France and Spain and eventually married the Gothic king, who was soon murdered. Back in Italy, married and widowed yet again, Galla Placidia ruled the Western Empire as regent for her son from 425 to 437/38. She died in 450, thus escaping yet another sack of Rome, this time by the Vandals, in 455. The fall of Rome shocked the Christian world, although the wounds were more psychological than physical. Bishop Augustine of Hippo (St. Augustine, d. 430) was inspired to write *The City of God*, a cornerstone of Christian philosophy, as an answer to people who claimed that the Goths represented the vengeance of the pagan gods on people who had abandoned them for Christianity.

Who were these people living outside the Mediterranean orbit? Their wooden architecture is lost to fire and decay, but their metalwork and its animal and geometric ornament has survived.

MAP 14–1 • EUROPE OF THE EARLY MIDDLE AGES

This map shows the routes taken by the groups of people who migrated into and through the western Roman world at the dawn of the Middle Ages. Modern country names have been used here for convenience, but at this time, these countries, as we know them, did not yet exist.

Defining the Middle Ages

The roughly 1,000 years of European history between the dissolution of the Western Roman Empire during the fifth century and the Florentine Renaissance in the fifteenth century are generally referred to as the Middle Ages, or the medieval period. These terms reflect the view of Renaissance humanists who regarded the period that preceded theirs as a "dark age" of ignorance, decline, and barbarism, standing in the middle and separating their own "golden age" from the golden ages of ancient Greece and Rome. Although scholars now acknowledge the ridiculousness of this self-serving formulation and recognize the millennium of the "Middle Ages" as a period of great richness, complexity, creativity, and innovation, the term has endured.

Art historians commonly divide the Middle Ages into three periods: early medieval (ending c. 1000), Romanesque (eleventh and twelfth centuries), and Gothic (beginning in the mid-twelfth and extending into the fifteenth century). In this chapter we can look at only a few of the many cultures that flourished during the early medieval period. For convenience, we will use modern geographic names as familiar points of reference (SEE MAP 14–1), but, in fact, European nations as we know them today did not yet exist.

They were hunters and fishermen, shepherds and farmers living in villages with a social organization based on extended families and tribal loyalties. They engaged in the practical crafts—pottery, weaving, woodwork—and they fashioned metals into weapons, tools, and jewelry.

The Celts controlled most of western Europe (see "The Celts," page 152), and the Germanic people—Goths and others—lived around the Baltic Sea. Increasing population evidently forced the Goths to begin to move south, into better lands and climate around the Mediterranean and Black Seas, but the Romans had extended the borders of their empire across the Rhine and Danube rivers. Seeking the relative security and higher standard of living they saw in the Roman Empire, the Germanic people crossed the borders and settled within the Roman world.

The tempo of migration speeded up in the fifth century when the Huns from Central Asia swept down on western Europe; the Ostrogoths (Eastern Goths) moved into Italy and deposed the last Western Roman emperor in 476; the Visigoths (Western Goths) ended their wanderings in Spain; the Burgundians settled in Switzerland and eastern France; the Franks in Germany, France, and Belgium; and the Vandals crossed over into Africa, making Carthage their headquarters before circling back to Italy, sacking Rome in 455.

As these barbarian groups gradually converted to Christianity, the Church served to unify Europe's heterogeneous population. As early as 345, the Goths adopted Arian Christianity, beliefs considered heretical by the Church in Rome. (Arian Christians did not believe that Christ was divine or co-equal with God the Father.) Not until 589 did they accept Roman Christianity. But the Franks under Clovis (r. 481–511), influenced by his Burgundian wife Clotilda, converted to Roman Christianity in 496, beginning a fruitful alliance between French rulers and the popes. Kings and nobles defended the claims of the Roman Church, and the pope, in turn, validated their authority. As its wealth and influence increased throughout Europe, the Church emerged as the principal patron of the arts to fulfill growing needs for buildings and liturgical equipment, including altars, altar vessels, crosses, candlesticks, containers for the remains of saints (reliquaries), vestments (ritual garments), images of Christian figures and stories, and copies of sacred texts such as the Gospels. (See "Defining the Middle Ages," above.)

THE ART OF THE "BARBARIANS" IN EUROPE

Out of a tangled web of themes and styles originating from inside and out of the empire, from pagan and Christian beliefs, from urban and rural settlements, brilliant new artistic styles were born across Europe as barbarian people settled within the former Western Roman Empire. Many of the migratory groups were superb metalworkers and created magnificent colorful jewelry, both with precious metals and with inlays of gems. Most of the motifs were geometric or highly abstracted from natural forms.

THE MEROVINGIANS

One of the barbarian groups that moved into the Western Roman world during the fifth century was the Franks, who migrated westward from what is now Belgium and settled in the northern part of Roman Gaul (modern France). There they were soon ruled by a succession of leaders from a dynasty named "Merovingian" after its legendary founder, Merovech. The Merovingians established a powerful kingdom during the reigns of Childeric I (c. 457–481) and his son Clovis I (481–511), whose conversion to Christianity in 496 connected the Franks to the larger European world through an ecclesiastical network of communication and affiliation.

Though some early **illuminated** books (books that include not only text but pictures and decoration in color and gold) have

14–2 • JEWELRY OF QUEEN ARNEGUNDE
Discovered in her tomb, excavated at the Abbey of Saint-Denis, Paris. Burial c. 580–590. Gold, silver, garnets, and glass beads; length of pin $10^3/_8''$ (26.4 cm). Musée des Antiquités Nationales, Saint-Germain-en-Laye, France.

been associated with the dynasty, our knowledge of Merovingian art is based primarily on the jewelry that has been uncovered in the graves of kings, queens, and aristocrats, indicating that both men and women expressed their wealth (in death, as presumably in life) by wearing earrings, necklaces, finger rings, bracelets, and weighty leather belts, from which they suspended even more ornamental metalwork. One of the most spectacular royal tombs was that of Queen Arnegunde, unearthed during excavations in 1959 at the Abbey of Saint-Denis, near Paris, which was a significant center of Merovingian patronage.

Arnegunde was discovered within a stone sarcophagus—undisturbed since her burial in c. 580–590. From her bodily remains, archaeologists determined that she was slight and blond, 5 feet tall, and about 70 years old at the time of her death. The inscription of her name on a gold ring on her left thumb provided

the first clue to her identity, and her royal pedigree was confirmed by the sumptuousness of her clothing. She was outfitted in a short, purple silk tunic, cinched at the waist by a substantial leather belt from which was suspended ornamental metalwork. The stockings that covered her legs were supported by leather garters with silver strap tongues and dangling ornaments. Over this ensemble was a dark red gown embroidered in gold thread. This overgarment was opened up the front, but clasped at neck and waist by round brooches and a massive buckle (**FIG. 14–2**). These impressive objects were made by casting their general shape in two-piece molds, refining and chasing them with tools, and inlaying within reserved and framed areas carefully cut garnets to provide color and sparkle. Not long after Arnegunde's interment, Merovingian royalty ceased the practice of burying such precious items with the dead—encouraged by the Church to donate them instead to religious institutions in honor of the saints—but we are fortunate to have a few early examples that presumably document the way these royal figures presented themselves on state occasions.

THE NORSE

In Scandinavia (present-day Denmark, Norway, and Sweden), which was never part of the Roman Empire, people spoke variants of the Norse language and shared a rich mythology with other Germanic peoples. Scandinavian artists had exhibited a fondness for abstract patterning from early prehistoric times. During the first millennium BCE, trade, warfare, and migration had brought a variety of jewelry, coins, textiles, and other portable objects into northern Europe. The artists incorporated the solar disks and stylized animals on these objects into their already rich artistic vocabulary.

By the fifth century CE, the so-called **animal style** dominated the arts, displaying an impressive array of serpents, four-legged beasts, and squat human figures, as can be seen in their metalwork. The **GUMMERSMARK BROOCH (FIG. 14–3)**, for example, is a large silver-gilt pin dating from the sixth century in Denmark. This elegant ornament consists of a large, rectangular panel and a medallionlike plate covering the safety pin's catch connected by an arched bow. The surface of the pin seethes with human, animal, and geometric forms. An eye-and-beak motif frames the rectangular panel, a man is compressed between dragons just below the bow, and a pair of monster heads and crouching dogs with spiraling tongues frame the covering of the catch.

Certain underlying principles govern works with animal style design: The compositions are generally symmetrical, and artists depict animals in their entirety either in profile or from above. Ribs and spinal columns are exposed as if they had been x-rayed; hip and shoulder joints are pear-shape; tongues and jaws extend and curl; and legs end in large claws.

The northern jewelers carefully crafted their molds to produce a glittering surface on the cast metal, turning a process intended to speed production into an art form of great refinement.

14-3 • GUMMERSMARK BROOCH
Denmark. 6th century. Silver gilt, height 5¾" (14.6 cm).
Nationalmuseet, Copenhagen.

THE CELTS AND ANGLO-SAXONS IN BRITAIN

After the Romans departed Britain at the beginning of the fifth century, Angles and Saxons from Germany and the Low Lands, and Jutes from Denmark, crossed the sea to occupy southeastern Britain. Gradually they extended their control northwest across the island. Over the next 200 years, the arts experienced a spectacular efflorescence. A fusion of Celtic, Roman, Germanic, and Norse cultures generated a new style of art, sometimes known as Hiberno-Saxon (from the Roman name for Ireland, Hibernia). Anglo-Saxon literature is filled with references to sumptuous jewelry and weapons made of or decorated with gold and silver, and fortunately, some of it has survived to this day.

The Anglo-Saxon epic *Beowulf*, composed perhaps as early as the seventh century, describes its hero's burial with a hoard of treasure in a grave mound near the sea. Such a burial site was discovered near the North Sea coast in Suffolk at a site called Sutton Hoo (*hoo* means "hill"). The grave's occupant had been buried in a ship—90 feet long and designed for rowing, not sailing—whose traces in the earth were recovered by careful excavators. The wood—and the hero's body—had disintegrated, and no inscriptions record his name. He has sometimes been identified with the ruler Raedwald, who died about 625. Whoever he was, the treasures buried with him prove that he was a wealthy and powerful man. They include weapons, armor, other equipment to provide for the ruler's afterlife, and many luxury items. The objects from Sutton Hoo represent the broad multicultural heritage characterizing Britain, Ireland, and Scotland at this time—Celtic, Scandinavian, and classical Roman, as well as Anglo-Saxon. There was even a Byzantine silver bowl at Sutton Hoo.

The story of the discovery of Sutton Hoo—unquestionably one of the most important archaeological discoveries in Britain—begins with Edith May Pretty, who decided late in her life to explore the burial mounds that were located on her estate in southeast Suffolk, securing the services of a local amateur archaeologist, Basil Brown. Excavations began in 1938 as a collaborative effort between the two of them, and in the following year they encountered the famous ship burial. As rumors spread of the importance of the find, its excavation was gradually taken over by renowned experts and archaeologists who moved from the remains of the ship to the treasures of the burial chamber for which Sutton Hoo is most famous. Police officers were posted to guard the site, and the treasures were sent for safekeeping to the British Museum in London, although, since Sutton Hoo was determined not to be "Treasure Trove" (buried objects meant to be retrieved by their original owners and now considered property of the Crown—see "The Mildenhall Treasure," page 214), it was the legal property of Mrs. Pretty. She, however, decided to donate the entire contents of the burial mound to the British Museum.

Excavation of Sutton Hoo was interrupted by World War II, but in 1945 Rupert Bruce-Mitford of the British Museum began a scholarly study of its treasures that would become his life work. He not only subjected each piece to detailed scrutiny; he proposed reconstructions of objects that were only partially preserved, such at the harp, helmet, and drinking horns. Using the evidence that had been gathered in a famous murder case, he proposed that Sutton Hoo was actually a burial, even though no evidence of human remains were ever found, since they could have disappeared completely in the notably acidic soil of the mound. Other scholars used radiocarbon dating of timber fragments and close analysis of coins to focus the dating of the burial to c. 625, which happened to coincide with the death date of King Raedwald of East Anglia, the most popular candidate for the identity of the person buried at Sutton Hoo.

After heated discussions and considerable controversy, new excavations were carried out in the area of Sutton Hoo during the 1980s and 1990s. These revealed a series of other discoveries in what emerged as an important early medieval burial ground and proved that the area had been inhabited since the Neolithic period, but they uncovered nothing to rival the collection of treasures that were preserved at Sutton Hoo.

One of the most exquisite finds was a clasp of pure gold that once secured over his shoulder the leather body armor of its distinguished owner (**FIG. 14–4**). The two sides of the clasp—essentially identical in design—were connected when a long gold pin, attached to one half by a delicate but strong gold chain, was inserted through a series of aligned channels on the back side of the inner edge of each. The superb decoration of this work is created by thin pieces of garnet and blue-checkered glass (known as **millefiori**, from the Italian for "a thousand flowers") cut into precisely stepped geometric shapes or to follow the sinuous contours of stylized animal forms. The cut shapes were then inserted into channels and supplemented by granulation (the use of minute granules of gold fused to the surface; see also "Aegean Metalwork," page 87). Under the stepped geometric pieces that form a rectangular patterned field on each side, jewelers placed gold foil stamped with incised motifs that reflect light back up through the transparent garnet to spectacular effect. Around these carpetlike rectangles are borders of interlacing snakes, and in the curving compartments to the outside stand pairs of semi-transparent, overlapping boars stylized in ways that reflect the traditions of Scandinavian jewelry. Their curly pig's tails overlap their strong rumps at the outer edges on each side of the clasp, and following the visible vertebrae along the arched forms of their backs, we arrive at their heads, with floppy ears and extended tusks. Boars represented strength and bravery, important virtues in warlike Anglo-Saxon society.

14-4 • HINGED CLASP, FROM THE SUTTON HOO BURIAL SHIP
Suffolk, England. First half of 7th century. Gold plaques with granulation and inlays of garnet and checked millefiori glass, length 5″ (12.7 cm). British Museum, London.

THE EARLY CHRISTIAN ART OF THE BRITISH ISLES

Although the Anglo-Saxons who settled in Britain had their own gods and myths, Christianity survived. Monasteries flourished in the Celtic north and west, and Christians from Ireland founded influential missions in Scotland and northern England. Cut off from Rome, these Celtic Christians developed their own liturgical practices, church calendar, and distinctive artistic traditions. Then, in 597, Pope Gregory the Great (pontificate 590–604) dispatched missionaries from Rome to the Anglo-Saxon king Ethelbert of Kent, whose Christian wife, Bertha, was sympathetic to their cause. The head of this successful mission, the monk Augustine (St. Augustine of Canterbury, d. 604), became the first archbishop of Canterbury in 601. The Roman Christian authorities and the Irish monasteries, although allied in the effort to Christianize Britain, came into conflict over their divergent practices. The Roman Church eventually triumphed and brought British Christians under its authority. Local traditions, however, continued to influence their art.

ILLUSTRATED BOOKS

Among the richest surviving artworks of the period are the lavishly decorated Gospel books, not only essential for spiritual and liturgical life within established monasteries, but also critical for the missionary activities of the Church, since a Gospel book was required in each new foundation. Often bound in gold and jeweled covers, they were placed on the altars of churches, carried in processions, and even thought to protect parishioners from enemies, predators, diseases, and all kinds of misfortune. Such sumptuous books were produced by monks in local monastic workshops called **scriptoria** (see "The Medieval Scriptorium," page 432).

THE BOOK OF DURROW.   One of the earliest surviving decorated Gospels of the period is the **BOOK OF DURROW**, dating to the second half of the seventh century (**FIG. 14–5**). The book's format reflects Roman Christian models, but its paintings are an encyclopedia of Hiberno-Saxon design. Each of the four Gospels is introduced by a three-part decorative sequence: a page with the symbol of its evangelist author, followed by a page of pure ornament, and finally elaborate decoration highlighting the initial words of the text (the *incipit*).

The Gospel of Matthew is preceded by his symbol, the man, but what a difference there is from the way humans were represented in the Greco-Roman tradition. The armless body is formed by a colorful checkered pattern recalling the rectangular panels of the Sutton Hoo clasp (SEE FIG. 14–4). Set on the body's rounded shoulders, a schematic, symmetrical, frontal face stares directly out at the viewer, and the tiny feet that emerge at its other end are seen from a contrasting profile view, as if to deny any hint of lifelike form or earth-based spatial placement. Equally prominent is the bold band of complicated but coherent interlacing ornament that borders the figure's field.

14–5 • PAGE WITH MAN, GOSPEL BOOK OF DURROW
Gospel of Matthew. Probably made at Iona, Scotland, or in northern England. Second half of 7th century. Ink and tempera on parchment, 9⅝ × 6⅛″ (24.4 × 15.5 cm). The Board of Trinity College, Dublin. MS. 57 fol. 21v

THE BOOK OF KELLS.   The monastic scribes and artists of England, Scotland, and Ireland developed and expanded this artistic tradition in works of breathtaking virtuosity like the Lindisfarne Gospels (see "The Lindisfarne Gospels," pages 430–431) and the Book of Kells. This chapter began with a close look at the most celebrated page in the Book of Kells—the page introducing Matthew's account of Jesus' birth (SEE FIG. 14–1). At first this appears to be a dense thicket of spiral and interlace patterns derived from metalworking traditions embellishing—in fact practically overwhelming—the Chi Rho monogram of Christ. The illuminators outlined each letter in the Chi Rho monogram, and then they subdivided the letters into panels filled with interlaced animals and snakes, as well as extraordinary spiral and knot motifs. The spaces between the letters form a whirling ornamental field, dominated by spirals.

In the midst of these abstractions, the painters inserted numerous pictorial and symbolic references to Christ—a fish (the

The Lindisfarne Gospels

The Lindisfarne Gospels is one of the most extraordinary books ever created, admired for the astonishing beauty of its words and pictures (SEE FIGS. A, B, and the first Closer Look in the Introduction, FIG. A), but also notable for the wealth of information we have about its history. Two and a half centuries after it was made, a priest named Aldred added a colophon to the book, outlining with rare precision the book's history, as he knew it—that it was written by Eadfrith, bishop of Lindisfarne (698–721), and bound by Ethelwald, his successor. Producing this stupendous example of book art was an expensive and laborious proposition—requiring 300 calfskins to make the vellum and using pigments imported from as far away as the Himalayas for the decoration. Preliminary outlines were made for each of the pictures, using compasses, dividers, and straight edges to produce precise underdrawings with a sharp point of silver or lead, forerunner to our pencils.

The full pages of ornament set within cross-shape frameworks (see example in the Introduction) are breathtakingly complex, like visual puzzles that require patient and extended viewing. Hybrid animal forms tangle in acrobatic interlacing, disciplined by strict symmetry and sharp framing. Some have speculated that members of the religious community at Lindisfarne might have deciphered the patterns as a spiritual exercise. But principally the book was carried in processions and displayed on the altar, not shelved in the library to be consulted as a part of intellectual life. The text is heavily ornamented and abbreviated, difficult to read. The words that begin the Gospel of Matthew (FIG. A)—*Liber generationis ihu xpi filii david filii abraham* (The book of the generation of Jesus Christ, son of David, son of Abraham)—are jammed together, even stacked on top of each other. They are also framed, subsumed, and surrounded by a proliferation of the decorative forms, ultimately deriving from barbarian visual traditions, that we have already seen moving from jewelry into books in the Durrow Gospels (SEE FIG. 14–5) and the Book of Kells (SEE FIG. 14–1).

But the paintings in the Lindisfarne Gospels document more than the developing sophistication of an abstract artistic tradition. Roman influence is evident here as well. Instead of beginning each Gospel with a symbol of its author, the designer of this book introduced portraits of the evangelists writing their texts, drawing on a Roman tradition (FIG. B). The monastic library at Wearmouth-Jarrow, not far from Lindisfarne, is known to have had a collection of Roman books, and an author portrait in one of them seems to have provided the model for an artist there, who portrayed *Ezra Restoring the Sacred Scriptures* within a huge Bible (FIG. C).

A. PAGE WITH THE BEGINNING OF THE TEXT OF MATTHEW'S GOSPEL, LINDISFARNE GOSPEL BOOK

Lindisfarne, c. 715–720. Ink and tempera on vellum, 13⅜ × 9⁷⁄₁₆″ (34 × 24 cm). The British Library, London. Cotton MS. Nero D.IV fol. 27r

The words written in the right margin, just beside the frame, are an Old English gloss translating the Latin text, added here in the middle of the tenth century by the same Aldred who added the colophon. They represent the earliest surviving English text of the Gospels.

B. MATTHEW WRITING HIS GOSPEL, LINDISFARNE GOSPEL BOOK

Lindisfarne. c. 715–720. Ink and tempera on vellum, 13⅜ × 9⁷⁄₁₆″ (34 × 24 cm). The British Library, London. Cotton MS. Nero D.IV fol. 25v

The identity of the haloed figure peeking from behind the curtain is still a topic of debate. Some see him as Christ confronting us directly around the veil that separated the holy of holies from worshipers in the Jewish Temple; others think he is Moses, holding the closed book of the law that was meant to be seen in contrast to the open book into which Matthew writes his Gospel. Also curious here is the Greek form of "saint" in Matthew's title ("O Agios" or "the holy"), written, however, with letters from the Latin alphabet.

C. EZRA RESTORING THE SACRED SCRIPTURES, IN THE BIBLE KNOWN AS THE CODEX AMIATINUS

Wearmouth-Jarrow. c. 700–715. Ink and tempera on vellum, 20 × 13½″ (50.5 × 34.3 cm). Biblioteca Medicea Laurenziana, Florence. Cod. Amiat. I, fol. 5r

This huge manuscript (at over 2,000 pages, it weighs more than 75 pounds) is the earliest surviving complete text of the Bible in the Latin Vulgate translation of St. Jerome.

This painter worked to emulate the illusionistic traditions of the Greco-Roman world. Ezra is a modeled, three-dimensional form, sitting on a foreshortened bench and stool, both drawn in perspective to make them appear to recede into the distance. In the background, the obliquely placed books on the shelves of a cabinet seem to occupy the depth of its interior space.

Interestingly, the artist of the Matthew portrait in the Lindisfarne Gospels worked with the same Roman prototype, judging from the number of details these two portraits share, especially the figures' poses. But instead of striving to capture the lifelike features of his Roman model, the Lindisfarne artist sought to undermine them. Matthew appears against a blank background. All indications of modeling have been stripped from his clothing to foreground the decorative pattern and contrasting color created by the drapery "folds." By carefully arranging the ornament on the legs of Matthew's bench, the three-dimensional shading and perspective evident in the portrait of Ezra have been successfully suppressed. The footstool has been liberated from its support to float freely on the surface, while still resting under the evangelist's silhouetted feet. Playing freely with an acknowledged and clearly understood alien tradition, the painter situates an enigmatic figure in the "background" at upper right behind a gathered drape—suspended from a curtain rod hanging from a screw eye sunk into the upper frame—that is not long enough to conceal the rest of his figure. Clearly there were important cultural reasons for such divergent reactions to a Mediterranean model—Wearmouth-Jarrow seeking to emphasize its Roman connections and Lindisfarne its indigenous roots. We are extremely fortunate to have two surviving works of art that visualize the contrast so clearly.

The Medieval Scriptorium

Today books are made with the aid of computer software that can lay out pages, set type, and insert and prepare illustrations. Modern presses can produce hundreds of thousands of identical copies in full color. In medieval Europe, however, before the invention of printing from movable type in the mid 1400s, books were made by hand, one at a time, with ink, pen, brush, and paint. Each one was a time-consuming and expensive undertaking. No two were exactly the same.

At first, medieval books were usually made by monks and nuns in a workshop called a **scriptorium** (plural, scriptoria) within the monastery. As the demand for books increased, rulers set up palace workshops employing both religious and lay scribes and artists, supervised by scholars. Books were written on carefully prepared animal skin—either **vellum**, which was fine and soft, or **parchment**, which was heavier

and shinier. Ink and water-based paints also required time and experience to prepare, and many pigments—particularly blues and greens—were prepared from costly semiprecious stones. In very rich books, artists also used gold leaf or gold paint.

Work on a book was often divided between scribes, who copied the text, and artists, who painted or drew illustrations, large initials, and other decorations. Occasionally, scribes and artists signed and dated their work on the last page, in what was called the **colophon**. One scribe even took the opportunity to warn: "O reader, turn the leaves gently, and keep your fingers away from the letters, for, as the hailstorm ruins the harvest of the land, so does the injurious reader destroy the book and the writing" (cited in Dodwell, p. 247).

Greek word for "fish," *ichthus*, comprises in its spelling the first letters of Jesus Christ, Son of God, Savior), moths (symbols of rebirth), the cross-inscribed wafer of the Eucharist, and numerous chalices and goblets. In a particularly intriguing image at bottom left, two cats pounce on a pair of mice nibbling the Eucharistic wafer, and two more mice torment the vigilant cats. Is this a metaphor for the struggle between good (cats) and evil (mice), or an acknowledgment of the perennial problem of keeping the sacred Host safe from rodents? Perhaps it is both.

IRISH HIGH CROSSES. Metalworking traditions influenced not only manuscript decoration, but also the monumental stone crosses erected in Ireland during the eighth century. The **SOUTH CROSS** of Ahenny, in County Tipperary, is an especially well-preserved example (**FIG. 14–6**). It seems to have been modeled on metal ceremonial or reliquary crosses, that is, cross-shape containers for holy relics. It is outlined with ropelike, convex moldings and covered with spirals and interlace. The large bosses (broochlike projections), which form a cross within this cross, resemble the jewels that were similarly placed on metal crosses. The circle enclosing the arms of such Irish high crosses—so called because of their size—has been interpreted as a ring of heavenly light or as a purely practical means of supporting the projecting arms.

MOZARABIC ART IN SPAIN

In 711, Islamic invaders conquered Spain, ending Visigothic rule. Bypassing the small Christian kingdom of Asturias on the north coast, they crossed the Pyrenees Mountains into France, but in 732 Charles Martel and the Frankish army stopped them before they

14-6 • SOUTH CROSS, AHENNY
County Tipperary, Ireland. 8th century. Stone.

reached Paris. The Moors, as they were known in Spain, remained in the Iberian peninsula (Spain and Portugal) for nearly 800 years, until the fall of Granada to the Christians in 1492.

With some exceptions, Christians and Jews who acknowledged the authority of the Islamic rulers and paid the taxes required of non-Muslims were left free to follow their own religious practices. The Iberian peninsula became a melting pot of cultures in which Muslims, Christians, and Jews lived and worked together, all the while officially and firmly separated. Christians in the Muslim territories were called Mozarabs (from the Arabic *mustarib*, meaning "would-be Arab"). In a rich exchange of artistic influences, Christian artists incorporated some features of Islamic art into a colorful new style known as **Mozarabic**. When the Mozarabic communities migrated to northern Spain, which returned to Christian rule not long after the initial Islamic invasion, they took this Mozarabic style with them.

BEATUS MANUSCRIPTS

One of the most influential books of the eighth century was the Commentary on the Apocalypse, compiled by Beatus, abbot of the Monastery of San Martín at Liébana in the northern kingdom of Asturias. Beatus described the end of the world and the Last Judgment of the Apocalypse, rooted in the Revelation to John at the end of the New Testament, which vividly describes Christ's final, fiery triumph.

A lavishly illustrated copy of Beatus' Commentary called the Morgan Beatus was produced c. 940–945, probably at the Monastery of San Salvator at Tábara, by an artist named Maius (d. 968), who both wrote the text and painted the illustrations. His gripping portrayal of the *Woman Clothed with the Sun*, based on the biblical text of Apocalypse (Revelation) 12:1–18, extends over two pages to cover an entire opening of the book **(FIG. 14–7)**. Maius has stayed close to the text in composing his tableau, which is

14-7 • Maius WOMAN CLOTHED WITH THE SUN, THE MORGAN BEATUS
Monastery of San Salvador at Tábara, León, Spain. 940–945. Tempera on vellum, 15⅛ × 22⅙" (38.5 × 56 cm).
The Pierpont Morgan Library, New York. MS. M644, fols. 152v–153r

When the modern abstract French painter Fernand Léger (1881–1955; SEE FIG. 31–21) was visiting the great art historian Meyer Schapiro (1904–1996) in New York during World War II, the artist asked the scholar to suggest the single work of art that was most important for him to see while there. Schapiro took him to the Morgan Library to leaf through this manuscript, and the strong impact it had on Léger can be clearly seen in the boldness of his later paintings.

dominated by the long, seven-headed, red dragon that slithers across practically the entire width of the picture to threaten at top left the "woman clothed with the sun, with the moon under her feet, and on her head a crown of twelve stars" (12:1). With his tail, at upper right, he sweeps a third of heaven's stars toward Earth while the woman's male child appears before the throne of God. Maius presents this complex allegory of the triumph of the Church over its enemies with a forceful, abstract, ornamental style that accentuates the dramatic, nightmarish qualities of the events outlined in the text. The background has been distilled into horizontal strips of color; the figures become striped bundles of drapery capped with faces dominated by staring eyes and silhouetted, framing haloes. Momentous apocalyptic events have been transformed by Maius into exotic abstractions that still maintain their power to captivate our attention.

Another copy of Beatus' Commentary was produced about 30 years later for Abbot Dominicus of San Salvator at Tábara. A colophon identifies Senior as the scribe for this project. Emeterius and a woman named Ende (or simply En), who signed herself "painter and servant of God," shared the task of illustration. For the first time in the West, a woman artist is identified by name with a specific surviving work of art. In an allegory of the triumph of Christ over Satan (FIG. 14–8), the painters show a peacock grasping a red-and-orange snake in its beak. The text explains that a bird with a powerful beak and beautiful plumage (Christ) covers itself with mud to trick the snake (Satan). Just when the snake decides the bird is harmless, the bird swiftly attacks and kills it. "So Christ in his Incarnation clothed himself in the impurity of our [human] flesh that through a pious trick he might fool the evil deceiver.... [W]ith the word of his mouth [he] slew the venomous killer, the devil" (cited in Williams, page 95).

14–8 • Emeterius and Ende, with the scribe Senior **BATTLE OF THE BIRD AND THE SERPENT, COMMENTARY ON THE APOCALYPSE BY BEATUS AND COMMENTARY ON DANIEL BY JEROME (DETAIL)**
Made for Abbot Dominicus, probably at the Monastery of San Salvador at Tábara, León, Spain. Completed July 6, 975. Tempera on parchment, 15¾ × 10¼" (40 × 26 cm). Cathedral Library, Gerona, Spain. MS. 7[11], fol. 18v

THE VIKING ERA

In the eighth century, seafaring bands of Norse seamen known as Vikings (*viken*, "people from the coves") descended on the rest of Europe. Setting off in flotillas of as many as 350 ships, they explored, plundered, traded with, and colonized a vast area during the ninth and tenth centuries. The earliest recorded Viking incursions were two devastating attacks on wealthy isolated Christian monasteries: one in 793, on the religious community on Lindisfarne, an island off the northeast coast of England; and another in 795, at Iona, off Scotland's west coast.

Norwegian and Danish Vikings raided a vast territory stretching from Iceland and Greenland, where they settled in 870 and 985, respectively, to Ireland, England, Scotland, and France. The Viking Leif Eriksson reached North America in 1000. In good weather a Viking ship could sail 200 miles in a day. In the early tenth century, the rulers of France bought off Scandinavian raiders (the Normans, or "northmen") with a large grant of land that became the duchy of Normandy. Swedish Vikings turned eastward and traveled down the Russian rivers to the Black Sea and Constantinople, where the Byzantine emperor recruitedthem to form an elite personal guard. Others, known as Rus, established settlements around Novgorod, one of the earliest cities in what would become Russia. They settled in Kiev in the tenth century and by 988 had become became Orthodox Christians (see Chapter 7).

THE OSEBERG SHIP

Since prehistoric times Northerners had represented their ships as sleek sea serpents, and, as we saw at Sutton Hoo, they used them for burials as well as sea journeys. The ship of a dead warrior symbolized his passage to Valhalla (a legendary great hall that welcomed fallen warriors), and Viking chiefs were sometimes cremated in a ship in the belief that this hastened their journey. Women as well as men were honored by ship burials. A 75-foot-long ship, discovered in Oseberg, Norway, and dated 815–820, served as the vessel for two women on their journey to eternity in 834, a queen and her companion or servant. Although the burial chamber was long ago looted of jewelry and precious objects, the ship itself and its equipment attest to the wealth and prominence of the ship's owner. A cart and four sleds, all made of wood with beautifully carved decorations, were stored on board. At least 12 horses, several dogs, and an ox had been sacrificed to accompany these women on their last journey.

This Oseberg ship itself, propelled by both sail and oars, was designed for travel in the relatively calm waters of fjords (narrow coastal inlets), not for voyages in the open sea. The rising prow spirals into a tiny serpent's head, and bands of interlaced animals carved in low relief run along the edges (**FIG. 14–9**). Viking beasts are grotesque, broad-bodied creatures with bulging eyes, short muzzles, snarling mouths, and large teeth who clutch each other with sharp claws. Images of these strange beasts adorned all sorts of

14-9 • GRIPPING BEASTS, DETAIL OF OSEBERG SHIP
c. 815–820. Wood. Vikingskiphuset, Universitets Oldsaksamling, Oslo, Norway.

Viking belongings—jewelry, houses, tent poles, beds, wagons, and sleds. Traces of color—black, white, red, brown, and yellow—indicate that the carved wood was originally painted.

All women, including the most elite, worked in the fiber arts. The Oseberg queen took her spindles, a frame for sprang (braiding), and tablets for tablet-weaving, as well as two upright looms, with her to the grave. Her cabin walls had been hung with tapestries, fragments of which survive. Women not only produced clothing and embroidered garments and wall hangings, but also wove the huge sails of waterproof unwashed wool that gave the ships a long-distance capability. The entire community—men and women—worked to create these ships, which represent the Vikings' most important surviving contribution to world architecture.

14–10 • ROYAL RUNE STONES, RIGHT-HAND STONE ORDERED BY KING HARALD BLUETOOTH
Jelling, Denmark. 983–985. Granite, 3-sided, height about 8′ (2.44 m).

PICTURE STONES AT JELLING

Both at home and abroad, the Vikings erected large memorial stones. Those covered mostly with inscriptions are called **rune stones** (runes are twiglike letters of an early Germanic alphabet). Those with figural decoration are called **picture stones**. Traces of pigments suggest that the memorial stones were originally painted in bright colors.

About 980, the Danish king Harald Bluetooth (c. 940–987) ordered a picture stone to be placed near an old, smaller rune stone and the family burial mounds at Jelling (FIG. 14–10). Carved in runes on a boulder 8 feet high is the inscription "King Harald had this memorial made for Gorm his father and Thyra his mother: that Harald who won for himself all Denmark and Norway and made the Danes Christians." Harald and the Danes had accepted Christianity in c. 960, but Norway did not become Christian until 1015.

During the tenth century, a new style emerged in Scandinavia and the British Isles, one that combined interlacing foliage and ribbons with animals that are more recognizable than the gripping beasts of the Oseberg ship. On one face of the larger Jelling stone the sculptor carved the image of Christ robed in the Byzantine manner, with arms outstretched as if crucified. He is entangled in a double-ribbon interlace instead of nailed to a cross. A second side holds runic inscriptions, and a third, a striding creature resembling a lion fighting a snake. The loosely twisting double-ribbon interlace covering the surface of the stone could have been inspired by Hiberno-Saxon art.

TIMBER ARCHITECTURE

The vast forests of Scandinavia provided the materials for timber buildings of many kinds. Two forms of timber construction evolved: one that stacked horizontal logs, notched at the ends, to form a rectangular building (the still-popular log cabin); and the other that stood the wood on end to form a palisade or vertical plank wall, with timbers set directly in the ground or into a sill (a horizontal beam). More modest buildings consisted of wooden frames filled with wattle-and-daub (woven branches covered with mud or other substances). Typical buildings had a turf or thatched roof supported on interior posts. The same basic structure was used for almost all building types—feasting and assembly halls, family homes (which were usually shared with domestic animals), workshops, barns, and sheds. The great hall had a central open hearth (smoke escaped through a louver in the roof) and an off-center door designed to reduce drafts. People secured their residences and trading centers by building massive circular earthworks topped with wooden palisades.

THE BORGUND STAVE CHURCH. Subject to decay and fire, early timber buildings have largely disappeared, leaving only postholes and other traces in the soil. In rural Norway, however, a few timber **stave churches** survive—named for the four huge timbers (staves) that form their structural core. Borgund church, from about 1125–1150 (FIG. 14–11), has four corner staves supporting the central roof, with additional interior posts that create the effect of

14–11 • EXTERIOR AND CUTAWAY DRAWING OF STAVE CHURCH, BORGUND, NORWAY
c. 1125–1150.

SEE MORE: View a simulation of stave church construction
www.myartslab.com

a nave and side aisles, narthex, and choir. A rounded apse covered with a timber tower is attached to the choir. Steeply pitched roofs covered with wooden shingles protect the walls—planks slotted into the sills—from the rain and snow. Openwork timber stages set on the roof ridge create a tower and give the church a steep pyramidal shape. On all the gables either crosses or dragon heads protect the church and its congregation from trolls and demons.

The Vikings were not always victorious. Their colonies in Iceland and the Faeroe Islands survived, but in North America their trading posts eventually had to be abandoned. In Europe, south of the Baltic Sea, a new German dynasty challenged and then defeated the Vikings. By the end of the eleventh century the Viking era came to an end.

THE CAROLINGIAN EMPIRE

During the second half of the eighth century, while Christians and Muslims were creating a rich multicultural art in Spain and the Vikings were surging through Europe, a new force emerged on the Continent. Charlemagne (the French form of *Carolus Magnus*, Latin for "Charles the Great") established a dynasty and an empire known today as the Carolingian. He descended from a family that had succeeded the Merovingians in the late seventh century as rulers of the Franks in northern Gaul (parts of present-day France and Germany). Under Charlemagne (r. 768–814), the Carolingian realm reached its greatest extent, encompassing western Germany, France, the Lombard kingdom in Italy, and the Low Countries (present-day Belgium and Holland). Charlemagne imposed Christianity throughout this territory, and in 800, Pope Leo III (pontificate 795–816) crowned Charlemagne emperor in a ceremony in St. Peter's Basilica in Rome, declaring him the rightful successor to Constantine, the first Christian emperor. This endorsement reinforced Charlemagne's authority and strengthened the bonds between the papacy and secular government in the West.

The Carolingian rulers' ascent to the Roman imperium, and the political pretensions it implied, are clearly signaled in a small bronze equestrian statue—once thought to be a portrait of Charlemagne himself but now usually identified with his grandson **CHARLES THE BALD (FIG. 14–12)**. The idea of representing an emperor as a proud equestrian figure recalls the much larger image of Marcus Aurelius (SEE FIG. 6–52) that was believed during the Middle Ages to portray Constantine, the first Christian emperor and an ideal prototype for the ruler of the Franks, newly legitimized by the pope. But unlike the bearded Roman, this Carolingian king sports a mustache, a Frankish sign of nobility that had also been common among the Celts (SEE FIG. 5–52). Works of art such as this are not the result of a slavish mimicking of Roman prototypes, but of a creative appropriation of Roman imperial typology to glorify manifestly Carolingian rulers.

Charlemagne sought to restore the Western Empire as a Christian state and to revive the arts and learning. As inscribed on his official seal, Charlemagne's ambition was "the Renewal of the Roman Empire." To lead this revival, Charlemagne turned to Benedictine monks and nuns. By the early Middle Ages, monastic communities had spread across Europe. In the early sixth century, Benedict of Nursia (c. 480–547) wrote his *Rule for Monasteries*, and this set of guidelines for a secluded life of monastic work and prayer became the model for Benedictine monasticism, soon the dominant form throughout Europe. The Benedictines became Charlemagne's "cultural army," and the imperial court at Aachen, Germany, one of the leading intellectual centers of western Europe.

CAROLINGIAN ARCHITECTURE

To proclaim the glory of the new empire in monumental form, Charlemagne's architects turned to the two former Western imperial capitals, Rome and Ravenna, for inspiration. Charlemagne's biographer Einhard reported that the ruler, "beyond all sacred and venerable places… loved the church of the holy apostle Peter in Rome." Not surprisingly, Constantine's basilica of St. Peter, with its long nave and side aisles ending in a transept and projecting apse (see page 228, FIG. A), served as a model for many important churches in Charlemagne's empire. The basilican plan, which had fallen out of favor since the Early Christian period, emerged again as the principal arrangement of large congregational churches and would remain so throughout the Middle Ages and beyond.

14–12 • EQUESTRIAN PORTRAIT OF CHARLES THE BALD (?)
9th century. Bronze, height 9¹⁄₂″ (24.4 cm). Musée du Louvre, Paris.

14–13 • PALACE CHAPEL OF CHARLEMAGNE

Interior view, Aachen (Aix-la-Chapelle), Germany. 792–805.

Extensive renovations took place in the nineteenth century, when the chapel was reconsecrated as the Cathedral of Aachen, and in the twentieth century, after it was damaged in World War II.

SEE MORE: View a video about the Palace Chapel of Charlemagne www.myartslab.com

clerestory

tribune

aisle

14–14 • SECTION DRAWING OF THE PALACE CHAPEL OF CHARLEMAGNE

CHARLEMAGNE'S PALACE AT AACHEN. Charlemagne's palace complex provides an example of the Carolingian synthesis of Roman, Early Christian, and northern styles. Charlemagne, who enjoyed hunting and swimming, built a headquarters and palace complex amid the forests and natural hot springs of Aachen in the northern part of his empire and installed his court there about 794. The palace complex included a large masonry audience hall and chapel facing each other across a large square (reminiscent of a Roman forum), and a monumental gateway supporting a hall of judgment. Other administrative buildings, a palace school, homes for his circle of advisors and his large family, and workshops supplying all the needs of Church and state, were mostly constructed using the wooden building traditions indigenous to this part of Europe.

The **PALACE CHAPEL** (FIGS. 14–13, 14–14) functioned as Charlemagne's private place of worship, the church of his imperial court, a place for precious relics, and, after the emperor's death, the imperial mausoleum. The central, octagonal plan recalls the church of San Vitale in Ravenna (SEE FIG. 7–20), but the Carolingian architects have added a monumental western entrance block. Known as a **westwork**, this structure combined a ground-floor narthex (vestibule) and an upper-story throne room which opened onto the chapel interior, allowing the emperor an unobstructed view of the liturgy at the high altar, and at the same time assuring his privacy and safety. The room also opened outside into a large walled forecourt where the emperor could make public appearances and speak to the assembled crowd.

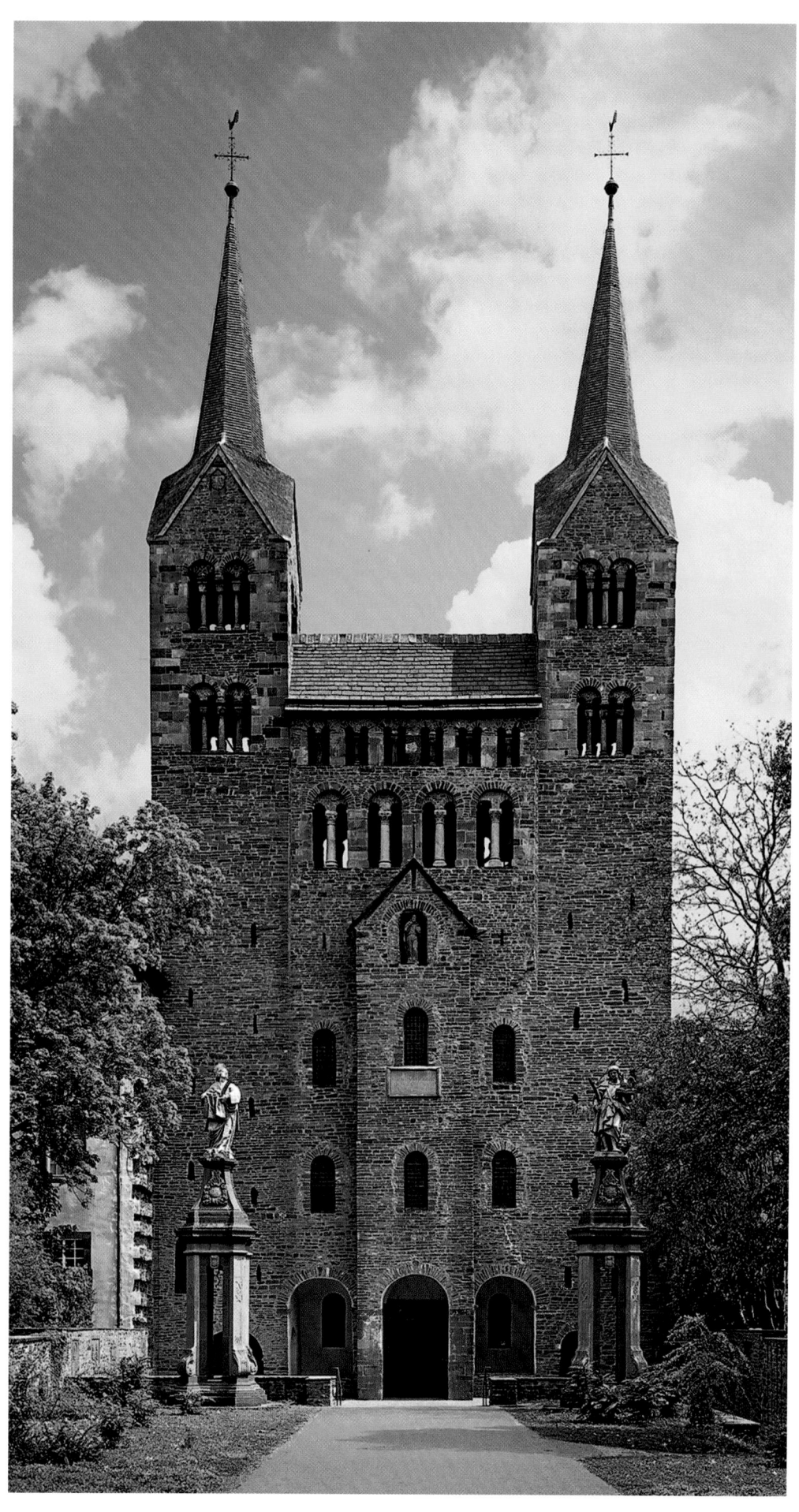

14–15 • WESTWORK, ABBEY CHURCH OF CORVEY
Germany. Late 9th century
(upper stories mid 12th century).

The soaring core of the chapel is an octagon, surrounded at the ground level by an ambulatory (curving aisle passageway) and on the second floor by a gallery (upper-story passageway overlooking the main space), and rising to a clerestory above the gallery level and under the octagonal dome. Two tiers of paired Corinthian columns and railings at the gallery level form a screen that re-emphasizes the flat, pierced walls of the octagon and enhances the clarity and planar geometry of its design. The effect is quite different from the dynamic spatial play and undulating exedrae of San Vitale, but the veneer of richly patterned and multicolored stone—some imported from Italy—on the walls and the mosaics covering the dome at Aachen were clearly inspired by Byzantine architecture.

THE WESTWORK AT CORVEY.

Originally designed to answer practical requirements of protection and display in buildings such as Charlemagne's palace chapel, the soaring multitowered westwork came to function symbolically as the outward and very visible sign of an important building and is one of the hallmarks of Carolingian architecture. A particularly well-preserved example is the late ninth-century westwork at the **ABBEY CHURCH OF CORVEY** (**FIG. 14–15**). Even discounting the pierced upper story and towers that were added in the middle of the twelfth century, this is a broad and imposing block of masonry construction. The strong, austere exterior is a symmetrical arrangement of towers flanking a central core punched with a regular pattern of windows and doors, devoid of elaborate carving or decoration. In addition to providing private spaces for local or visiting dignitaries, the interiors of westworks may have been used for choirs—medieval musical graffiti have been discovered in the interior of this westwork—and they were the starting point for important liturgical processions.

THE SAINT GALL PLAN.

Monastic life centered on prayer and work, and since it also demanded seclusion, it required a special type of architectural planning. While contemplating how best to house a monastic community, Abbot Haito of Reichenau developed, at the request of his colleague Abbot Gozbert of Saint Gall, a conceptual plan for the layout of monasteries. This extraordinary ninth-century drawing survives in the library of the Abbey of Saint Gall in modern Switzerland and is known as the

14-16 • SAINT GALL PLAN (ORIGINAL AND REDRAWN WITH CAPTIONS)
c. 817. Original in red ink on parchment, 28 × 44⅛″ (71.1 × 112.1 cm). Stiftsbibliothek, Saint Gall, Switzerland. Cod. Sang. 1092

SAINT GALL PLAN (FIG. **14–16**). This is not a "blueprint" in the modern sense, prepared to guide the construction of an actual monastery, but an intellectual record of Carolingian meditations on the nature of monastic life. It does, however, reflect the basic design used in the layout of medieval monasteries, an efficient and functional arrangement that continues to be used by Benedictine monasteries to this day.

At the center of the Saint Gall plan is the **cloister**, an enclosed courtyard around which open all the buildings that are most central to the lives of monks. Most prominent is a large basilican church north of the cloister, with towers and multiple altars in nave and aisles as well as in the sanctuary at the east end, where monks would gather for communal prayer throughout the day and night. On the north side of the church were public buildings such as the abbot's house, the school, and the guesthouse. The monks' living quarters lie off the southern and eastern sides of the cloister, with dormitory, refectory (dining room), and work rooms. For night services the monks could enter the church directly from their dormitory. The kitchen, brewery, and bakery were attached to the refectory, and a huge cellar (indicated on the plan by giant barrels) was on the west side. Along the east edge of the plan are the cemetery, hospital, and an educational center for novices (monks in training).

The Saint Gall plan indicates beds for 77 monks in the dormitory. Practical considerations for group living include latrines attached to every unit—dormitory, guesthouse, and abbot's house. Six beds and places in the refectory were reserved for visiting monks. In the surrounding buildings were special spaces for scribes and painters, who spent much of their day in the scriptorium studying and copying books, and teachers who staffed the monastery's schools and library. St. Benedict had directed that monks extend hospitality to all visitors, and the plan includes a hospice for the poor. South and west of the central core were the workshops, farm buildings, and housing for the lay community of support staff.

ILLUSTRATED BOOKS

Books played a central role in the efforts of Carolingian rulers to promote learning, propagate Christianity, and standardize church law and practice. Imperial workshops produced authoritative copies of key religious texts, weeding out the errors that had inevitably crept into books over centuries of copying them by hand. The scrupulously edited versions of ancient and biblical texts that emerged are among the lasting achievements of the Carolingian period. For example, the Anglo-Saxon scholar Alcuin of York, whom Charlemagne called to his court, spent the last eight years of his life producing a corrected copy of the Latin Vulgate Bible. His revision served as the standard text of the Bible for the remainder of the medieval period and is still in use.

Carolingian scribes also worked on standardizing script. Capitals (majuscules) based on ancient Roman inscriptions continued to be used for very formal writing, titles and headings, and luxury manuscripts. But they also developed a new, clear script called Carolingian minuscule, based on Roman forms but with a

14-17 • PAGE WITH ST. MATTHEW THE EVANGELIST, CORONATION GOSPELS
Gospel of Matthew. Early 9th century. 12¾ × 9⅞" (36.3 × 25 cm). Kunsthistorische Museum, Vienna.

Tradition holds that this Gospel book was buried with Charlemagne in 814, and that in the year 1000 Emperor Otto III removed it from his tomb. Its title derives from its use in the coronation ceremonies of later German emperors.

uniform lowercase alphabet that increased legibility and streamlined production. So like those who transformed revived Roman types—such as basilicas, central-plan churches, or equestrian Roman portraits—into creative new works, scribes and illuminators revived, reformed, and revitalized established traditions of book production. Notably, they returned the representation of lifelike human figures to a central position. For example, portraits of the evangelists (the authors of the Gospels)—as opposed to the symbols used to represent them in the Book of Durrow (SEE FIG. 14–5)—began to look like pictures of Roman authors.

THE CORONATION GOSPELS. The portait of Matthew **(FIG. 14–17)** in the early ninth-century Coronation Gospels of Charlemagne conforms to principles of idealized, lifelike representation quite consistent with the Greco-Roman Classical tradition.

14-18 • PAGE WITH ST. MATTHEW THE EVANGELIST, EBBO GOSPELS
Gospel of Matthew. Second quarter of 9th century. Ink, gold, and colors on vellum, 10¼ × 8¾″ (26 × 22.2 cm). Bibliothèque Municipale, Épernay, France. MS. 1, fol. 18v

The full-bodied, white-robed figure is modeled in brilliant white and subtle shading and seated on the cushion of a folding chair set within a freely painted landscape. The way his foot lifts up to rest on the solid base of his writing desk emphasizes his three-dimensional placement within an outdoor setting, and the frame enhances the Classical effect of a view seen through a window. Conventions for creating the illusion of solid figures in space may have been learned from Byzantine manuscripts in a monastic library, or from artists fleeing Byzantium as a result of the iconoclastic controversy (see "Iconoclasm," page 246).

THE EBBO GOSPELS. The incorporation of the Roman tradition in manuscript painting was not an exercise in blind copying. It became the basis for a series of creative Carolingian variations. One of the most innovative and engaging is a Gospel book made for Archbishop Ebbo of Reims (archbishop 816–835, 840–841) at the nearby Abbey of Hautevillers **(FIG. 14–18)**. The calm, carefully painted grandeur characterizing Matthew's portrait in the Coronation Gospels (SEE FIG. 14–17) has given way here to spontaneous, calligraphic painting suffused with energetic abandon. The passion may be most immediately apparent in the intensity of Matthew's gaze, but the whole composition is charged with energy, from the evangelist's wiry hairdo and rippling drapery, to the rapidly sketched landscape, and even extending into the windblown acanthus leaves of the frame. These forms are related to content since the marked expressionism evokes the evangelist's spiritual excitement as he hastens to transcribe the Word of God delivered by the angel (also serving as Matthew's symbol), who is almost lost in the upper right corner. As if swept up in the saint's turbulent emotions, the footstool tilts precariously, and the top of the desk seems about to detach itself from the pedestal.

THE UTRECHT PSALTER. One of the most famous Carolingian manuscripts, the Utrecht Psalter, is illustrated with ink drawings that match the nervous linear vitality encountered in Ebbo's Gospel book. Psalms do not tell straightforward stories but use metaphor and allegory in poems of prayer; they are exceptionally difficult to illustrate. Some psalters bypass this situation by illustrating scenes from the life of the presumed author (SEE FIG. 7–39), but the artists of the Utrecht Psalter decided to interpret the words and images of individual psalms literally (see "A Closer Look," page 444). Sometimes the words are acted out, as in a game of charades.

Psalm 23 in the Utrecht Psalter

Second quarter of 9th century. Ink on vellum or parchment, 13 × 9⅞″ (33 × 25 cm). Universiteitsbibliotheek, Utrecht, Holland. MS. 32, fol. 13r

The basilica curtains are drawn back to reveal an altar and hanging votive crown: "I will dwell in the house of the Lord forever" (verse 6).

The artist has situated the psalmist in a pasture filled with sheep, goats, and cattle, "beside the still water" (verse 2) of a gently flowing stream.

The text of Psalm 23 (22 in the Latin Vulgate) begins here with the words *Dominus regit me* ("The Lord ruleth me"). This is the Latin translator's rewording of the Hebrew text of the opening, which is more familiar to us as: "The Lord is my shepherd."

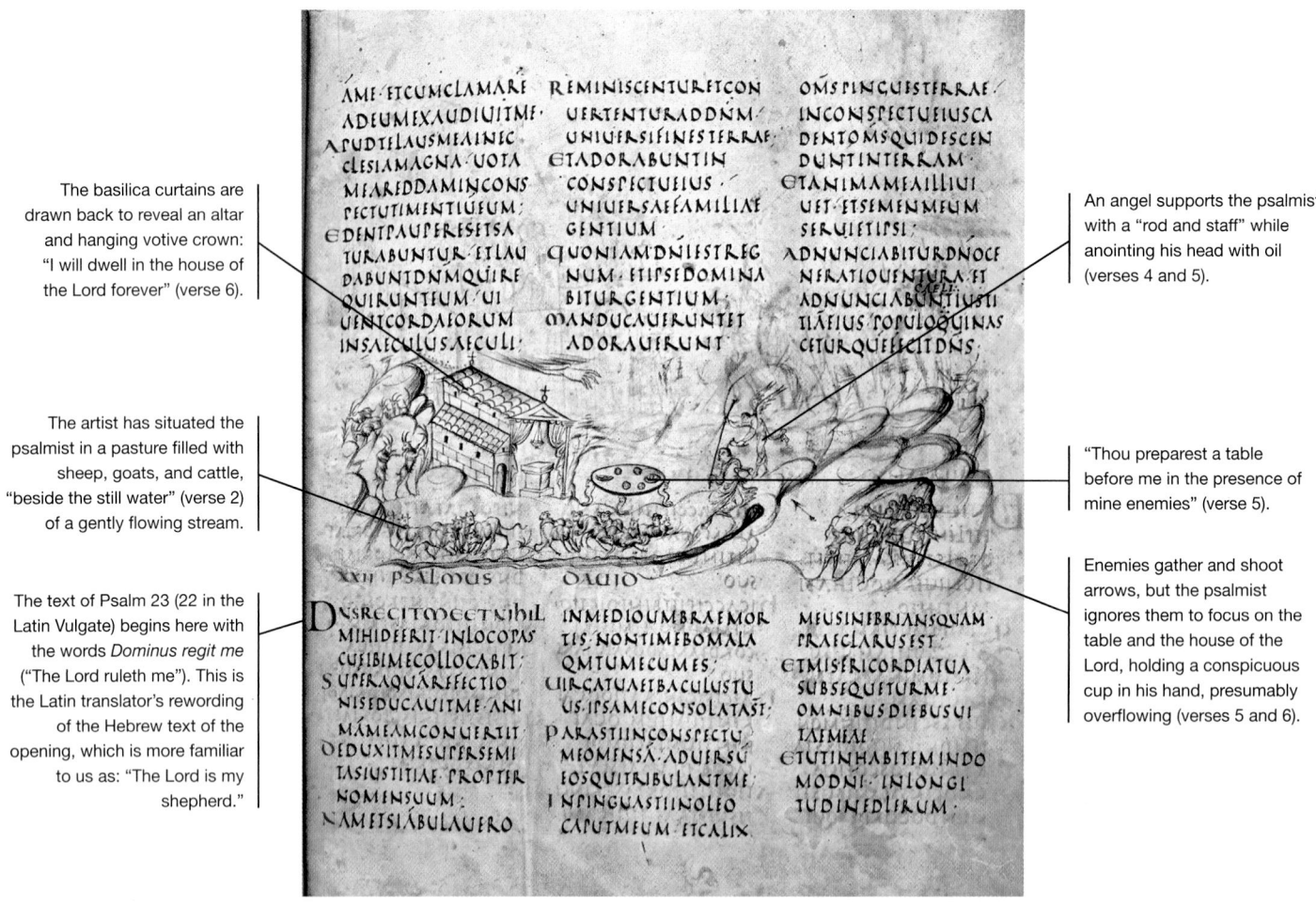

An angel supports the psalmist with a "rod and staff" while anointing his head with oil (verses 4 and 5).

"Thou preparest a table before me in the presence of mine enemies" (verse 5).

Enemies gather and shoot arrows, but the psalmist ignores them to focus on the table and the house of the Lord, holding a conspicuous cup in his hand, presumably overflowing (verses 5 and 6).

SEE MORE: View the Closer Look feature for Psalm 23 in the Utrecht Psalter **www.myartslab.com**

CAROLINGIAN METALWORK

The sumptuously illustrated manuscripts of the medieval period represented an enormous investment of time, talent, and materials, so it is not surprising that they were often protected with equally sumptuous covers. But because these covers were themselves made of valuable materials—ivory, enamelwork, precious metals, and jewels—they were frequently recycled or stolen. The elaborate book cover of gold and jewels, now on the Carolingian manuscript known as the **LINDAU GOSPELS (FIG. 14–19)**, was probably made between 870 and 880 at one of the monastic workshops of Charlemagne's grandson, Charles the Bald (r. 840–877), but not for this book. Sometime before the sixteenth century it was reused on a late ninth-century manuscript from the Monastery of Saint Gall.

The cross and the Crucifixion were common themes for medieval book covers. This one is crafted in pure gold with figures in repoussé (low relief produced by pushing or hammering up from the back of a panel of metal to produce raised forms on the front) surrounded by heavily jeweled frames. The jewels are raised on miniature arcades to allow reflected light to pass through them from beneath, imparting a lustrous glow, and also to allow light traveling in the other direction to reflect from the shiny surface of the gold.

14–19 • CRUCIFIXION WITH ANGELS AND MOURNING FIGURES, LINDAU GOSPELS
Outer cover. c. 870–880. Gold, pearls, sapphires, garnets, and emeralds, 13¾ × 10⅜" (36.9 × 26.7 cm).
The Pierpont Morgan Library, New York. MS. 1

14-20 • OTTO I PRESENTING MAGDEBURG CATHEDRAL TO CHRIST

One of a series of 17 ivory plaques known as the Magdeburg Ivories, possibly carved in Milan. c. 962–968. Ivory, 5 × 4½″ (12.7 × 11.4 cm). Metropolitan Museum of Art, New York. Bequest of George Blumenthal, 1941 (41.100.157)

Grieving angels hover above the arms of the cross, and earthbound mourners twist in agony below. Over Jesus' head personifications of the sun and the moon hide their faces in anguish. The gracefully animated poses of these figures, who seem to float around the jeweled bosses in the compartments framed by the arms of the cross, extend the expressive style of the Utrecht Psalter illustrations into another medium and a later moment. Jesus, on the other hand, has been modeled in a more rounded and calmer Classical style. He seems almost to be standing in front of the cross—straight, wide-eyed, with outstretched arms, as if to prefigure his ultimate triumph over death. The flourishes of blood that emerge from his wounds are almost decorative. There is little, if any, sense of his suffering.

OTTONIAN EUROPE

In 843, the Carolingian Empire was divided into three parts, ruled by three grandsons of Charlemagne. One of them was Charles the Bald, whom we have already encountered (SEE FIG. 14–12). Another, Louis the German, took the eastern portion, and when his family died out at the beginning of the tenth century, a new

Saxon dynasty came to power in lands corresponding roughly to present-day Germany and Austria. We call this dynasty Ottonian after its three principal rulers—Otto I (r. 936–973), Otto II (r. 973–983), and Otto III (r. 994–1002; queens Adelaide and Theophanu had ruled as regents for him, 983–994). After the Ottonian armies defeated the Vikings in the north and the Magyars (Hungarians) on the eastern frontiers, the resulting peace permitted increased trade and the growth of towns, making the tenth century a period of economic recovery. Then, in 951, Otto I added northern Italy to his domain by marrying the widowed Lombard Queen Adelaide. He also re-established Charlemagne's Christian Roman Empire by being crowned emperor by the pope in 962. The Ottonians and their successors so dominated the papacy and appointments to other high church offices that in the twelfth century this union of Germany and Italy under a German ruler came to be known as the Holy Roman Empire. The empire survived in modified form as the Habsburg Empire into the early twentieth century.

The Ottonian ideology, rooted in unity of Church and state, takes visual form on an ivory plaque, one of several that may once have been part of the decoration of an altar or pulpit presented to Magdeburg Cathedral at the time of its dedication in 968 (FIG. 14–20). Otto I presents a model of the cathedral to Christ and St. Peter. Hieratic scale demands that the mighty emperor be represented as a tiny, doll-like figure, and that the saints and angels, in turn, be taller than Otto but smaller than Christ. Otto is embraced by the patron saint of this church, St. Maurice, who was a third-century military commander martyred for refusing to worship pagan gods. The cathedral Otto holds is a basilica with prominent clerestory windows and a rounded apse that, like the character of the Carolingian basilicas before it, was intended to recall the churches of Rome.

OTTONIAN ARCHITECTURE

As we have just seen, Ottonian rulers, in keeping with their imperial status, sought to replicate the splendors both of the Christian architecture of Rome and of the Christian empire of their Carolingian predecessors. German officials knew Roman basilicas well, since the German court in Rome was located near the Early Christian church of Santa Sabina (SEE FIGS. 7–8, 7–9). The buildings of Byzantium were another important influence, especially after Otto II married a Byzantine princess, cementing a tie with the East. But large timber-roofed basilicas were terribly vulnerable to fire. Magdeburg Cathedral burned down in 1008, only 40 years after its dedication; it was rebuilt in 1049, burned down again in 1207, and was rebuilt yet again. In 1009, the Cathedral of Mainz burned down on the day of its consecration. The church of St. Michael at Hildesheim was destroyed in World War II. Luckily the convent church of St. Cyriakus at Gernrode, Germany, still survives.

THE CONVENT CHURCH OF ST. CYRIAKUS IN GERNRODE. During the Ottonian Empire, aristocratic women often held positions of authority, especially as leaders of religious communities. When, in 961, the provincial military governor Gero founded the convent and church of St. Cyriakus, he made his widowed daughter-in-law the convent's first abbess. The church was designed as a basilica with a westwork flanked by circular towers (FIG. 14–21). At the eastern end of the church a transept with chapels led to a choir with an apse built over a crypt.

Like an Early Christian or Carolingian basilica, the interior of St. Cyriakus (FIG. 14–22) has a nave flanked by side aisles. But the design of the three-level wall elevation—nave arcade, gallery, and clerestory—creates a rhythmic effect distinct from the uniformity that had characterized earlier basilicas. Rectangular piers alternate with round columns in the two levels of arcades, and at gallery level, pairs of openings are framed by larger arches and then grouped in threes. The central rectangular piers, aligned on the two levels, bisect the walls vertically into two units, each composed of two broad arches of the nave arcade surmounted by three pairs of arches at the gallery level. This seemingly simple design, with its rhythmic alternation of heavy and light supports, its balance of rectangular and rounded forms, and its combination of horizontal and vertical movements, seems to prefigure the aesthetic exploration of wall design that will characterize the Romanesque architecture of the next two centuries.

14-21 • PLAN OF THE CHURCH OF ST. CYRIAKUS, GERNRODE
Germany. Begun 961; consecrated 973.

14-22 • NAVE, CHURCH OF ST. CYRIAKUS, GERNRODE

OTTONIAN SCULPTURE

Ottonian sculptors worked in ivory, bronze, wood, and other materials rather than stone. Like their Early Christian and Byzantine predecessors, they and their patrons focused on church furnishings and portable art rather than architectural sculpture. Drawing on Roman, Early Christian, Byzantine, and Carolingian models, they created large works in wood and bronze that would have a significant influence on later medieval art.

14-23 • GERO CRUCIFIX
Cologne Cathedral, Germany. c. 970. Painted and gilded wood, height of figure 6′2″ (1.88 m).

This life-size sculpture is both a crucifix to be suspended over an altar and a special kind of reliquary. A cavity in the back of the head was made to hold a piece of the Host, or communion bread, already consecrated by the priest. Consequently, the figure not only represents the body of the dying Jesus but also contains a "relic" of the Eucharistic body of Christ. In fact, the Ottonian chronicle of Thietmar of Meresburg (written 1012–1018) claims that Gero himself placed a consecrated Host, as well as a fragment of the true cross, in a crack that formed within the head of this crucifix and prayed that it be closed, which it was.

THE GERO CRUCIFIX. The **GERO CRUCIFIX** is one of the few large works of carved wood to survive from the early Middle Ages **(FIG. 14–23)**. Archbishop Gero of Cologne (archbishop 969–976) commissioned the sculpture for his cathedral about 970. The figure of Christ is life-size and made of painted and gilded oak. The focus here is on Jesus' human suffering. He is shown as a tortured martyr, not as the triumphant hero of the Lindau Gospels cover (SEE FIG. 14–19). Jesus' broken body sags on the cross and his head falls forward, eyes closed. The straight, linear fall of his golden drapery heightens the impact of his drawn face, emaciated arms and legs, sagging torso, and limp, bloodied hands. This is a poignant image of distilled anguish, meant to inspire pity and awe in the empathetic responses of its viewers.

THE HILDESHEIM DOORS. Under the last of the Ottonian rulers, Henry II and Queen Kunigunde (r. 1002–1024), Bishop Bernward of Hildesheim emerged as an important patron. His biographer, the monk Thangmar, described Bernward as a skillful goldsmith who closely supervised the artisans working for him. Bronze doors made under his direction for the abbey church of St. Michael in Hildesheim—and installed by him, according to the doors' inscription, in 1015—represented the most ambitious and complex bronze-casting project undertaken since antiquity **(FIG. 14–24)**. Each door, including the impressive lion heads holding the ring handle, was cast as a single piece in the lost-wax process (see page 413) and later detailed and reworked with chisels and fine tools. Rounded and animated figures populate spacious backgrounds. Architectural elements and features of the landscape are depicted in lower relief, so that the figures stand out prominently, with their heads fully modeled in three dimensions. The result is lively, visually stimulating, and remarkably spontaneous for so monumental an undertaking.

The doors, standing more than 16 feet tall, portray scenes from the Hebrew Bible on the left (reading down from the creation of Eve at the top to Cain's murder of Abel at the bottom) and New Testament scenes on the right (reading upward from the Annunciation at the bottom to the *Noli me tangere* at the top). In each pair of scenes across from each other, the Hebrew Bible event is meant to present a prefiguration of or complement to the adjacent

Life in Paradise
- Formation of Eve
- Eve presented to Adam

The Fall
- Temptation and Fall of Adam and Eve
- Accusation and Judgment of Adam and Eve

Life in the World
- Expulsion of Adam and Eve from Paradise
- Adam and Eve Laboring

Eve's Children
- Offerings by Cain (grain) and Abel (lamb)
- Cain Murders Abel

Promise of Return to Paradise
- *Noli me tangere*
- Three Marys at the Tomb

The Passion
- Crucifixion
- Judgment of Jesus by Pilate

Infancy of Jesus
- Presentation of Jesus in the Temple
- Adoration of the Magi

Mary's Child
- Nativity
- Annunciation

14–24 • DOORS OF BISHOP BERNWARD
Abbey church of St. Michael, Hildesheim, Germany. 1015. Bronze, height 16′6″ (5 m).

New Testament event. For instance, the third panel down on the left shows Adam and Eve picking the forbidden fruit of knowledge in the Garden of Eden, believed by Christians to be the source of human sin, suffering, and death. This paired scene on the right shows the Crucifixion of Jesus, whose sacrifice was believed to have atoned for Adam and Eve's original sin, bringing the promise of eternal life. At the center of the doors, six panels down—between the door pulls—Eve (left) and Mary (right) sit side by side, holding their sons. Cain (who murdered his brother) and Jesus (who was unjustly executed) signify the opposition of evil and good, damnation and salvation. Other telling pairs are the murder of Abel (the first sin) with the Annunciation (the advent of salvation) at the bottom, and, fourth from the top, the passing of blame from Adam and Eve to the serpent paired with Pilate washing his hands of any responsibility in the execution of Jesus.

ILLUSTRATED BOOKS

Like their Carolingian predecessors, Ottonian monks and nuns created richly illuminated manuscripts, often funded by secular rulers. Styles varied from place to place, depending on the traditions of the particular scriptorium and the models available in its library.

THE HITDA GOSPELS. The presentation page of a Gospel book made in the early eleventh century for Abbess Hitda (d. 1041) of Meschede, near Cologne (FIG. 14–25) represents one of the most distinctive local styles. The abbess herself appears here, offering the book to St. Walpurga, her convent's patron saint. The artist has angled the buildings of the sprawling convent in the background to frame the figures and draw attention to their interaction. The size of the architectural complex underscores the abbess's position of authority. The foreground setting—a rocky, undulating strip of landscape—is meant to be understood as holy ground, separated from the rest of the world by golden trees and the huge

arch-shape aura that silhouettes St. Walpurga. The energetic spontaneity of the painting style suffuses the scene with a sense of religious fervor appropriate to the visionary saintly encounter.

THE GOSPELS OF OTTO III. This Gospel book, made in a German monastery near Reichenau about 1000, shows another Ottonian painting style, in this case inspired by Byzantine art in the use of sharply outlined drawing and lavish fields of gold (FIG. 14–26). Backed by a more controlled and balanced architectural canopy than that sheltering Hitda and St. Walpurga, these tall, slender men gesture dramatically with long, thin fingers. The scene captures the moment when Jesus washes the feet of his disciples during their final meal together (John 13:1–17). Peter, who had tried to stop his Savior from performing this ancient ritual of hospitality, appears at left, one leg reluctantly poised over the basin,

14-25 • PRESENTATION PAGE WITH ABBESS HITDA AND ST. WALPURGA, HITDA GOSPELS
Early 11th century. Ink and colors on vellum, 11⅜ × 5⅝″ (29 × 14.2 cm). Hessische Lanesund Hochschulbibliothek, Darmstadt, Germany.

14-26 • PAGE WITH CHRIST WASHING THE FEET OF HIS DISCIPLES, AACHEN GOSPELS OF OTTO III

c. 1000. Ink, gold, and colors on vellum, approx. 8 × 6″ (20.5 × 14.5 cm). Staatsbibliothek, Munich. Nr. 15131, Clm 4453, fol. 237r

while a centrally silhouetted and slightly overscale Jesus gestures emphatically to underscore the necessity and significance of the act. Another disciple, at far right, enthusiastically lifts his leg to untie his sandals so he can be next in line. Selective stylization has allowed the artist of this picture to transform the received Classical tradition into a style of stunning expressiveness and narrative power, features that will also characterize the figural styles associated with the Romanesque.

THINK ABOUT IT

14.1 Briefly outline how illuminated manuscripts were made and used in the early medieval period. Then trace the source of two motifs in the Chi Rho page of the Book of Kells (FIG. 14–1) in pre-Christian ornamental styles.

14.2 Explain the reference to ancient Roman tradition in the small bronze portrait of a Carolingian emperor in FIG. 14–12.

14.3 Compare and contrast representations of the Gospel author Matthew in two books covered in this chapter.

14.4 Characterize the style of painting that developed in Spain for the illustration of commentaries on the Apocalypse. Focus your answer on a specific example discussed in this chapter.

14.5 How does the Saint Gall Plan represent the organization of the medieval monastery in relation to its function as a retreat from the secular world as well as in relationship to the secular world?

PRACTICE MORE: Compose answers to these questions, get flashcards for images and terms, and review chapter material with quizzes www.myartslab.com

15–1 • CHRIST AND DISCIPLES ON THE ROAD TO EMMAUS
Cloister of the Abbey of Santo Domingo, Silos, Castile, Spain. Pier relief, figures nearly life-size. c. 1100.

ROMANESQUE ART

These three men seem to glide forward on tiptoe as their leader turns back, reversing their forward movement (FIG. 15–1). Their bodies are sleek; legs cross in languid curves rather than vigorous strides; their shoulders, elbows, and finger joints seem to melt; draperies delicately delineate curving contours; bearded faces stare out with large, wide eyes under strong, arched brows. The figures interrelate and interlock, pushing against the limits of the architectural frame.

Medieval viewers would have quickly identified the leader as Christ, not only by his commanding size, but specifically by his cruciform halo. The sanctity of his companions is signified by their own haloes. The scene recalls to faithful Christians the story of the resurrected Christ and two of his disciples on the road from Jerusalem to Emmaus (Luke 24:13–35). Christ has the distinctive attributes of a medieval pilgrim—a hat, a satchel, and a walking stick. Even the scallop shell on his satchel is the badge worn by pilgrims to a specific site: the shrine of St. James at Santiago de Compostela. Early pilgrims reaching this destination in the far northwestern corner of the Iberian peninsula continued to the coast to pick up a shell as evidence of their journey. Soon shells were gathered (or fabricated from metal as brooches) and sold to the pilgrims—a lucrative business for both the sellers and the church. On the return journey home, the shell became the pilgrims' passport, a badge attesting to their piety and accomplishment. Other distinctive badges were adopted at other pilgrimage sites.

This relief was carved on a corner pier in the cloister of the Monastery of Santo Domingo in Silos, a major eleventh- and twelfth-century center of religious and artistic life south of the pilgrimage road across Spain (see "The Pilgrim's Journey," page 458). It engaged an audience of monks and religious pilgrims—who were well versed in the meaning of Christian images—through a new sculptural style that we call Romanesque. Not since the art of ancient Rome half a millennium earlier had sculptors carved monumental figures in stone within an architectural fabric. During the early Middle Ages, sculpture was small-scale, independent, and created from precious materials—a highlighted object within a sacred space rather than a part of its architectural envelope. But during the Romanesque period, narrative and iconic figural imagery in deeply carved ornamental frameworks would collect around the entrances to churches, focusing attention on their compelling portal complexes. These public displays of Christian doctrine and moral teaching would have been part of the cultural landscape surveyed by pilgrims journeying along the road to Santiago. Travel as a pilgrim opened the mind to a world beyond the familiar towns and agricultural villages of home, signaling a new era in the social, economic, and artistic life of Europe.

LEARN ABOUT IT

15.1 Explore the emergence of Romanesque architecture—with its emphasis on the aesthetic qualities of a sculptural wall—out of early masonry construction techniques.

15.2 Assess the impact of pilgrimage as a cultural phenomenon on the design and embellishment of church architecture.

15.3 Compare and contrast Romanesque architectural styles in different regions of Europe.

15.4 Investigate the integration of painting and sculpture within the Romanesque building, and consider the implications of placing art on the church exterior and what theological themes were emphasized.

15.5 Explore the eleventh- and twelfth-century interest in telling stories of human frailty and sanctity in sculpture, textiles, and manuscript painting—stories that were meant to appeal to the feelings as well as to the minds of the viewers.

HEAR MORE: Listen to an audio file of your chapter **www.myartslab.com**

EUROPE IN THE ROMANESQUE PERIOD

At the beginning of the eleventh century, Europe was still divided into many small political and economic units ruled by powerful families, such as the Ottonians in Germany (MAP 15–1). The nations we know today did not exist, although for convenience we shall use present-day names of countries. The king of France ruled only a small area around Paris known as the Île-de-France. The southern part of modern France had close linguistic and cultural ties to northern Spain; in the north the duke of Normandy (heir of the Vikings) and in the east the duke of Burgundy paid the French king only token homage.

When in 1066 Duke William II of Normandy (r. 1035–1087) invaded England and, as William the Conqueror, became that country's new king, Norman nobles replaced the Anglo-Saxon nobility there, and England became politically and culturally allied with Normandy. As astute and skillful administrators, the Normans formed a close alliance with the Church, supporting it with grants of land and gaining in return the allegiance of abbots and bishops. Normandy became one of Europe's most powerful feudal domains. During this period, the Holy Roman Empire, re-established by the Ottonians, encompassed much of Germany and northern Italy, while the Iberian peninsula remained divided between Muslim rulers in the south and Christian rulers in the north. By 1085, Alfonso VI of Castile and León (r. 1065–1109) had conquered the Muslim stronghold of Toledo, a center of Islamic and Jewish culture in the kingdom of Castile. Catalunya (Catalonia) emerged as a power along the Mediterranean coast.

By the end of the twelfth century, however, a few exceptionally intelligent and aggressive rulers had begun to create national states. The Capetians in France and the Plantagenets in England were especially successful. In Germany and northern Italy, the power of local rulers and towns prevailed, and Germany and Italy remained politically fragmented until the nineteenth century.

POLITICAL AND ECONOMIC LIFE

Although towns and cities with artisans and merchants grew in importance, Europe remained an agricultural society, with land the primary source of wealth and power for a hereditary aristocracy. In France and England in particular, social, economic, and political relations were governed by a system commonly referred to as "feudalism." Arrangements varied considerably from place to place, but typically a landowning lord granted property and protection to a subordinate, called a vassal. In return, the vassal pledged allegiance and military service to the lord. Peasants worked the land in exchange for a place to live, military protection, and other services from the lord. Allegiances and obligations among lords, vassals, and peasants were largely inherited but constantly shifting.

THE CHURCH

In the early Middle Ages, Church and state had forged some fruitful alliances. Christian rulers helped ensure the spread of Christianity throughout Europe and supported monastic communities with grants of land. Bishops and abbots were often royal relatives, younger brothers and cousins, who supplied crucial social and spiritual support and a cadre of educated administrators. As a result, secular and religious authority became tightly intertwined, and this continued through the Romanesque period. Monasteries continued to sit at the center of European culture, but there were two new cultural forces fostered by the Church: pilgrimages and crusades.

MONASTICISM.   Although the first universities were established in the eleventh and twelfth centuries in the growing cities of Bologna, Paris, Oxford, and Cambridge, monastic communities continued to play a major role in intellectual life. Monks and nuns also provided valuable social services, including caring for the sick and destitute, housing travelers, and educating the elite. Because monasteries were major landholders, abbots and priors were part of the feudal power structure. The children of aristocratic families joined religious orders, helping forge links between monastic communities and the ruling elite.

As life in Benedictine communities grew increasingly comfortable and intertwined with the secular world, reform movements arose. Reformers sought a return to earlier monastic austerity and spirituality. The most important groups of reformers for the arts were the Burgundian congregation of Cluny, established in the tenth century, and later the Cistercians, who sought reform of what they saw as Cluniac decadence and corruption of monastic values.

PILGRIMAGES.   Pilgrimages to the holy places of Christendom—Jerusalem, Rome, and Santiago de Compostela—increased, despite the great physical hardships they entailed (see "The Pilgrim's Journey," page 458). As difficult and dangerous as these journeys were, rewards awaited courageous travelers along the routes. Pilgrims could venerate the relics of local saints during the journey, and artists and architects were commissioned to create spectacular and enticing new buildings and works of art to capture their attention.

CRUSADES.   In the eleventh and twelfth centuries, Christian Europe, previously on the defensive against the expanding forces of Islam, became the aggressor. In Spain, Christian armies of the north were increasingly successful against the Islamic south. At the same time, the Byzantine emperor asked the pope for help in his war with the Muslims surrounding his domain. The Western Church responded in 1095 by launching a series of holy wars, military offensives against Islamic powers known collectively as the crusades (from the Latin *crux*, referring to the cross crusaders wore).

This First Crusade was preached by Pope Urban II (pontificate 1088–1099) and fought by the lesser nobility of France, who had economic and political as well as spiritual objectives. The crusaders

MAP 15–1 • EUROPE IN THE ROMANESQUE PERIOD

Although a few large political entities began to emerge in places like England and Normandy, Burgundy, and León/Castile, Europe remained a land of small economic entities. Pilgrimages and crusades acted as unifying international forces.

captured Jerusalem in 1099 and established a short-lived kingdom. The Second Crusade in 1147, preached by St. Bernard and led by France and Germany, accomplished nothing. The Muslim leader Saladin united the Muslim forces and captured Jerusalem in 1187, inspiring the Third Crusade, led by German, French, and English kings. The Christians recaptured some territory, but not Jerusalem, and in 1192 they concluded a truce with the Muslims, permitting the Christians access to the shrines in Jerusalem. Although the crusades were brutal military failures, the movement had far-reaching cultural and economic consequences, providing western Europeans with direct encounters with the more sophisticated material culture of the Islamic world and the Byzantine Empire. This in turn helped stimulate trade, and with trade came the development of an increasingly urban society during the eleventh and twelfth centuries.

ROMANESQUE ART

The word "Romanesque," meaning "in the Roman manner," was coined in the early nineteenth century to describe early medieval European church architecture, which often displayed the solid masonry walls and rounded arches and vaults characteristic of imperial Roman buildings. Soon the term was applied to all the arts of the period from roughly the mid-eleventh century to the second half of the twelfth century, even though that art derives from a variety of sources and reflects a multitude of influences, not just Roman.

This was a period of great building activity in Europe. New castles, manor houses, churches, and monasteries arose everywhere. As one eleventh-century monk put it, the Christian faithful were so relieved to have passed through the apocalyptic anxiety that had gripped their world at the millennial change around the year 1000, that, in gratitude, "Each people of Christendom rivaled with the other, to see which should worship in the finest buildings. The world shook herself, clothed everywhere in a white garment of churches" (Radulphus Glaber, cited in Holt, vol. I, p. 18) (SEE FIG. 15–2). The desire to glorify the house of the Lord and his saints (whose earthly remains in the form of relics kept their presence alive in the minds of the people) increased throughout Christendom. There was a veritable building boom.

ARCHITECTURE

Romanesque architecture and art is a trans-European phenomenon, but it is inflected regionally, and the style varies in character from place to place. Although timber remained common in construction, Romanesque builders used stone masonry whenever possible. Masonry vaults were stronger and more durable, and they enhanced the acoustical effect of the Gregorian chants (plainsong, named after

15-2 • SAINT-MARTIN-DU-CANIGOU
French Pyrenees. 1001–1026.

Pope Gregory the Great, pontificate 590–604) sung inside. Tall stone towers, at times flanking the main entrance portal, marked the church as the most important building in the community. The portals themselves were often encrusted with sculpture that broadcast the moral and theological messages of the Church to a wide public audience.

"FIRST ROMANESQUE"

Soon after the year 1000—while Radulphus Glaber was commenting on the rise of church building across the land—patrons and builders in Catalunya (northeast Spain), southern France, and northern Italy were already constructing all-masonry churches, employing the methods of late Roman builders. The picturesque Benedictine monastery of **SAINT-MARTIN-DU-CANIGOU**, nestled into the Pyrenees on a building platform stabilized by strongly buttressed retaining walls, is a typical example **(FIG. 15–2)**. Patronized by the local Count Guifred, who took refuge in the monastery and died here in 1049, the complex is capped by a massive stone tower sitting next to the sanctuary of the two-story church. Art historians call such early stone-vaulted buildings "First Romanesque," employing the term that Catalan architect and theorist Josep Puig I Cadafalch first associated with them in 1928.

THE CHURCH OF SANT VINCENC, CARDONA. One of the finest examples of "First Romanesque" is the **CHURCH OF SANT VINCENC** (St. Vincent) in the Catalan castle of Cardona **(FIG. 15–3)**. Begun in the 1020s, it was consecrated in 1040. Castle residents entered the church through a two-story narthex into a nave with low narrow side aisles that permitted clerestory windows in the nave wall. The sanctuary was raised dramatically over an aisled crypt. The Catalan masons used local materials—small split stones, bricks, even river pebbles, and very strong mortar—to raise plain walls and round barrel or groin vaults. Today we can admire their skillful stonework both inside and out, but the builders originally covered their masonry with a facing of stucco.

To strengthen the walls and vaults, the masons added vertical bands of masonry (called strip buttresses) joined by arches and additional courses of masonry to counter the outward thrust of the vault and to enrich the sculptural quality of the wall. On the interior these masonry strips project from the piers and continue up and over the vault, creating a **transverse arch**. Additional projecting bands line the underside of the arches of the nave arcade. The result is a compound pier that works in concert with the transverse arches to divide the nave into a series of bays. This system of bay division became standard in Romanesque architecture. It is a marked contrast to the flat-wall continuity and undivided space within a pre-Romanesque church like Gernrode (SEE FIG. 14–22).

PILGRIMAGE CHURCHES

The growth of a cult of relics and the desire to visit shrines such as St. Peter's in Rome or St. James's in Spain increasingly inspired the Christians of western Europe to travel on pilgrimages (see

15-3 • INTERIOR, CHURCH OF SANT VINCENC, CARDONA
1020s–1030s.

"The Pilgrim's Journey," page 458). To accommodate the faithful and proclaim church doctrine, many monasteries on the major pilgrimage routes built large new churches, filled them with sumptuous altars and reliquaries, and encrusted them with elaborate stone sculpture on the exterior around entrances.

The Pilgrim's Journey

Western Europe in the eleventh and twelfth centuries saw an explosive growth in the popularity of religious pilgrimage. The rough roads that led to the most popular destinations—the tomb of St. Peter and other martyrs in Rome, the church of the Holy Sepulcher in Jerusalem, and the Cathedral of St. James in Santiago de Compostela in the northwest corner of Spain—were often crowded with pilgrims. Their journeys could last a year or more; church officials going to Compostela were given 16 weeks' leave of absence. Along the way the pilgrims had to contend with bad food and poisoned water, as well as bandits and dishonest innkeepers and merchants.

In the twelfth century, the priest Aymery Picaud wrote a guidebook for pilgrims on their way to Santiago through what is now France. Like travel guides today, Picaud's book provided advice on local customs, comments on food and the safety of drinking water, and a list of useful words in the Basque language. In Picaud's time, four main pilgrimage routes crossed France, merging into a single road in Spain at Puente la Reina and leading on from there through Burgos and León to Compostela. Conveniently spaced monasteries and churches offered food and lodging, as well as relics to venerate. Roads and bridges were maintained by a guild of bridge builders and guarded by the Knights of Santiago.

Picaud described the best-traveled routes and most important shrines to visit along the way. Chartres, for example, housed the tunic that the Virgin was said to have worn when she gave birth to Jesus. The monks of Vézelay had the bones of St. Mary Magdalen, and at Conques, the skull of Sainte Foy was to be found. Churches associated with miraculous cures—Autun, for example, which claimed to house the relics of Lazarus, raised by Jesus from the dead—were filled with the sick and injured praying to be healed.

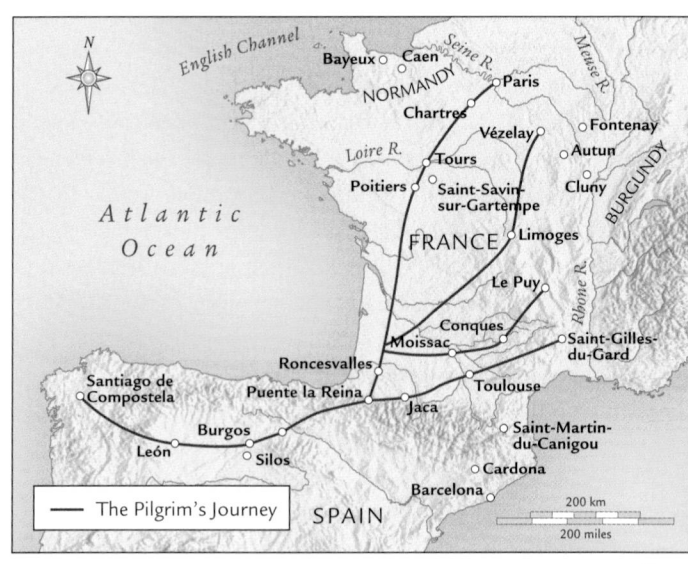

MAP 15–2 • THE PILGRIMAGE ROUTES TO SANTIAGO DE COMPOSTELA

THE CATHEDRAL OF ST. JAMES IN SANTIAGO DE COMPOSTELA. One major goal of pilgrimage was the **CATHEDRAL OF ST. JAMES IN SANTIAGO DE COMPOSTELA** (FIG. 15–4), which held the body of St. James, the apostle to the Iberian peninsula. Builders of this and other major churches along the roads leading through France to the shrine developed a distinctive plan designed to accommodate the crowds of pilgrims and allow them to move easily from chapel to chapel in their desire to venerate relics (see "Relics and Reliquaries," page 462). This "pilgrimage plan" is a model of functional planning and traffic control. To the aisled nave the builders added aisled transepts with eastern chapels leading to an ambulatory (curving walkway) with additional radiating chapels around the apse (FIGS. 15–5, 15–6). This expansion of the basilican plan allowed worshipers to circulate freely around the church's perimeter, visiting chapels and venerating relics without disrupting services within the main space.

At Santiago, pilgrims entered the church through the large double doors at the ends of the transepts rather than through the western portal, which served ceremonial processions. Pilgrims from France entered the north transept portal; the approach from the town was through the south portal. All found themselves in a transept in which the design exactly mirrored the nave in height and structure. Both nave and transept have two stories—an arcade and a gallery. Compound piers with attached half-columns on all four sides support the immense barrel vault and are projected over it vertically through a rhythmic series of transverse arches. They give sculptural form to the interior walls and also mark off individual vaulted bays in which the sequence is as clear and regular as the ambulatory chapels of the choir. Three different kinds of vaults are used here: barrel vaults with transverse arches cover the nave, groin vaults span the side aisles, and halfbarrel or quadrant vaults cover the galleries and strengthen the building by countering the outward thrust of the high nave vaults and transferring it to the outer walls and buttresses. Without a clerestory, light enters the nave only indirectly, through windows in the outer walls of the aisles and upper-level galleries that overlook the nave. Light from the choir clerestory and the large windows of an octagonal **lantern** tower (a structure built above the height of the main ceiling with windows that illuminate the space below) over the crossing would therefore spotlight the

15-4 • TRANSEPT, CATHEDRAL OF ST. JAMES, SANTIAGO DE COMPOSTELA
Galicia, Spain. 1078–1122. View toward the crossing.

SEE MORE: Click the Google Earth link for the Cathedral of Saint James, Santiago de Compostela **www.myartslab.com**

15-5 • PLAN OF CATHEDRAL OF ST. JAMES, SANTIAGO DE COMPOSTELA

SEE MORE: View a video about the Cathedral of Saint James, Santiago de Compostela **www.myartslab.com**

15-6 • RECONSTRUCTION DRAWING (AFTER CONANT) OF CATHEDRAL OF ST. JAMES, SANTIAGO DE COMPOSTELA
1078–1122; western portions later. View from the east.

EXPLORE MORE: Gain insight from primary sources related to the Cathedral of Saint James, Santiago de Compostela **www.myartslab.com**

15-7 • RECONSTRUCTION DRAWING OF THE ABBEY AT CLUNY
Burgundy, France. 1088–1130. View from the east.

EXPLORE MORE: Gain insight from a primary source related to the abbey at Cluny **www.myartslab.com**

glittering gold and jeweled shrine of the principal relic at the high altar.

In its own time, Santiago was admired for the excellence of its construction—"not a single crack is to be found," according to the twelfth-century pilgrims' guide—"admirable and beautiful in execution…large, spacious, well-lighted, of fitting size, harmonious in width, length, and height…." Pilgrims arrived at Santiago de Compostela weary after weeks of difficult travel through dense woods and mountains. Grateful to St. James for his protection along the way, they entered a church that welcomed them with open portals, encrusted with the dynamic moralizing sculpture that characterized Romanesque churches. The cathedral had no doors to close—it was open day and night.

CLUNY

In 909, the duke of Burgundy gave land for a monastery to Benedictine monks intent on strict adherence to the original rules of St. Benedict. They established the reformed congregation of Cluny. From its foundation, Cluny had a special independent status; its abbot answered directly to the pope in Rome rather than to the local bishop or feudal lord. This unique freedom, jealously safeguarded by a series of long-lived and astute abbots, enabled Cluny to keep the profits from extensive gifts of land and treasure. Independent, wealthy, and a center of culture and learning, Cluny and its affiliates became important patrons of architecture and art.

The monastery of Cluny was a city unto itself. By the second half of the eleventh century, there were some 200 monks in residence, supplemented by troops of laymen on whom they depended for material support. As we have seen in the Saint Gall plan of the Carolingian period (SEE FIG. 14–16), the cloister lay at the center of the monastic community, joining the church with domestic buildings and workshops (FIG. 15–7). In wealthy monasteries like this, the arcaded galleries of the cloister had elaborate carved capitals as well as relief sculpture on piers (SEE FIG. 15–1). The capitals may have served as memory devices or visualized theology to direct and inspire the monks' thoughts and prayers.

Cluniac monks observed the traditional eight Hours of the Divine Office (including prayers, scripture readings, psalms, and hymns) spread over the course of each day and night. Mass was celebrated after the third hour (terce), and the Cluniac liturgy was especially elaborate. During the height of its power, plainsong (or Gregorian chant) filled the church with music 24 hours a day.

The hallmark of Cluny—and the Cluniac churches of its host of dependent monasteries—was careful and elegant design that combined the needs of the monks with the desires of pilgrims to visit shrines and relics. They were also notable for their fine stone masonry with rich sculptured and painted decoration. In their homeland of Burgundy, the churches were distinguished by their use of classicizing elements from Roman art, such as fluted pilasters and Corinthian capitals. Cluniac monasteries elsewhere, however, were free—and perhaps even encouraged—to follow regional traditions and styles.

THE THIRD CHURCH AT CLUNY. The original church at Cluny, a small barnlike building, was soon replaced by a basilica with two towers and narthex at the west and a choir with tower and chapels at the east. Hugh de Semur, abbot of Cluny for 60 years (1049–1109), began rebuilding the abbey church for the third time in 1088 (FIGS. 15–7, 15–8). Money paid in tribute by Muslims to victorious Christians in Spain financed the building. When King Alfonso VI of León and Castile captured Toledo in 1085, he sent 10,000 pieces of gold to Cluny. The church (known to art historians as Cluny III because it was the third building at the site) was the largest in Europe when it was completed in 1130: 550 feet long, with five aisles like Old St. Peter's in Rome. Built with superbly cut masonry, and richly carved, painted, and furnished, Cluny III was a worthy home for the relics of St. Peter and St. Paul, which the monks had acquired from the church of St. Paul's Outside the Walls in Rome. It was also a fitting headquarters for a monastic order that had become so powerful within Europe that popes were chosen from its ranks.

In simple terms, the church was a basilica with five aisles, double transepts with chapels, and an ambulatory and radiating chapels around the high altar. The large number of chapels was necessary so that each monk-priest had an altar at which to perform the services of daily Mass. Octagonal towers over the two crossings and additional towers over the transept arms created a dramatic pyramidal design at the east end. The nave had a three-part elevation. A nave arcade with tall compound piers, faced by pilasters to the inside and engaged columns at the sides, supported pointed arches lined by Classical ornament. At the next level a blind arcade and pilasters created a continuous sculptural strip that could have been modeled on an imperial Roman triumphal monument. Finally, triple clerestory windows in each bay let sunlight directly into the church around its perimeter. The pointed barrel vault with transverse arches rose to a daring height of 98 feet with a span of about 40 feet, made possible by giving the vaults a steep profile, rather than the weaker round profile used at Santiago de Compostela.

The church was consecrated in 1130, but it no longer exists. The monastery was suppressed during the French Revolution, and this grandest of French Romanesque churches was sold stone by stone, transformed into a quarry for building materials. Today the site is an archaeological park, with only one transept arm from the original church still standing.

15-8 • RECONSTRUCTION DRAWING OF THE THIRD ABBEY CHURCH AT CLUNY LOOKING EAST
1088–1130.

ART AND ITS CONTEXTS

Relics and Reliquaries

Christians turned to the heroes of the Church, the martyrs who had died for their faith, to answer their prayers and to intercede with Christ on their behalf. In the Byzantine Church, the faithful venerated icons, that is, pictures of the saints, but Western Christians wanted to be close to the saints' actual earthly remains. Scholars in the Church assured the people that the veneration of icons or relics was not idol worship. Bodies of saints, parts of bodies, and things associated with the Holy Family or the saints were kept in richly decorated containers called reliquaries. Reliquaries could be simple boxes, but they might also be given the shape of the relic—the arm of St. John the Baptist, the rib of St. Peter, the sandal of St. Andrew. By the eleventh century, many different arrangements of crypts, chapels, and passageways gave people access to the relics kept in churches. When the Church decided that every altar required a relic, the saints' bodies and possessions were subdivided. In this way relics were multiplied; for example, hundreds of churches held relics of the true cross.

Owning and displaying these relics so enhanced the prestige and wealth of a community that people went to great lengths to acquire them, not only by purchase but also by theft. In the ninth century, for example, the monks of Conques stole the relics of the child martyr Sainte Foy (St. Faith) from her shrine at Agen. Such a theft was called "holy robbery," for the new owners insisted that it had been sanctioned by the saint who had communicated to them her desire to move. In the late ninth or tenth century, the monks of Conques encased their new relic—the skull of Sainte Foy—in a gold and jewel statue whose unusually large head was made from a reused late Roman work. During the eleventh century, they added the crown and more jeweled banding, and, over subsequent centuries, jewels, cameos, and other gifts added by pilgrims continued to enhance the splendor of the statue.

This type of reliquary—taking the form of a statue of the saint—was quite popular in the region around Conques, but not everyone was comfortable with the way these works functioned as cult images. Early in the eleventh century, the learned Bernard of Angers prefaces his tendentious account of miracles associated with the cult of Sainte Foy by confessing his initial misgivings about such reliquaries, specifically the way simple folks adored them. Bernard thought it smacked of idolatry: "To learned people this may seem to be full of superstition, if not unlawful, for it seems as if the rites of the gods of ancient cultures, or that the rites of demons, are being observed" (*Book of Sainte Foy*, p. 77). But when he witnessed firsthand the interaction of the reliquary statue with the faithful, he altered his position: "For the holy image is consulted not as an idol that requires sacrifices, but because it commemorates a martyr. Since reverence to her honors God on high, it was despicable of me to compare her statue to statues of Venus or Diana. Afterwards I was very sorry that I had acted so foolishly toward God's saint." (ibid., p. 78)

RELIQUARY STATUE OF SAINTE FOY (ST. FAITH)
Abbey church of Conques, Conques, France. Late 9th or 10th century with later additions. Silver gilt over a wood core, with added gems and cameos of various dates. Height 33″ (85 cm). Church Treasury, Conques.

THE CISTERCIANS

New religious orders devoted to an austere spirituality arose in the late eleventh and early twelfth centuries. Among these were the Cistercians, who spurned Cluny's elaborate liturgical practices and emphasis on the arts, especially sculpture in cloisters (see "St. Bernard and Theophilus: The Monastic Controversy over the Visual Arts," page 464). The Cistercian reform began in 1098 with the founding of the abbey of Cîteaux (Cistercium in Latin, hence the order's name). Led in the twelfth century by the commanding figure of Abbot Bernard of Clairvaux, the Cistercians advocated strict mental and physical discipline and a life devoted to prayer and intellectual pursuits combined with shared manual labor. Like the Cluniacs, however, they did depend on the work of laypeople. To seclude themselves as much as possible from the outside world, the Cistercians settled and reclaimed swamps and forests in the wilderness, where they then farmed and raised sheep. In time, their monasteries could be found from Russia to Ireland.

FONTENAY. Cistercian architecture embodies the ideals of the order—simplicity, austerity, and purity. Always practical, the Cistercians made a significant change to the already very efficient monastery plan. They placed key buildings such as the refectory at right angles to the cloister walk so that the building could easily be extended should the community grow. The cloister fountain was relocated from the center of the cloister to the side, conveniently in front of the refectory, where the monks could wash when coming from their work in the fields for communal meals. For easy access to the sanctuary during their prayers at night, monks entered the church directly from the cloister into the south transept or from the dormitory by way of the "night stairs."

The **ABBEY OF FONTENAY** in Burgundy is among the best-preserved early Cistercian monasteries. The abbey church, begun in 1139, has a simple geometric plan (FIGS. 15–9, 15–10) with a long bay-divided nave, rectangular chapels off the square-ended transept arms, and a shallow choir with a straight east wall. One of its characteristic features is the use of pointed barrel vaults over the nave and pointed arches in the nave arcade and side-aisle bays. Although pointed arches are usually associated with Gothic architecture, they are actually common in the Romanesque buildings of some regions, including Burgundy (we have already seen them at Cluny). Pointed arches are structurally more stable than round ones, directing more weight down into the floor instead of outward to the walls. Consequently, they can span greater distances at greater heights without collapsing.

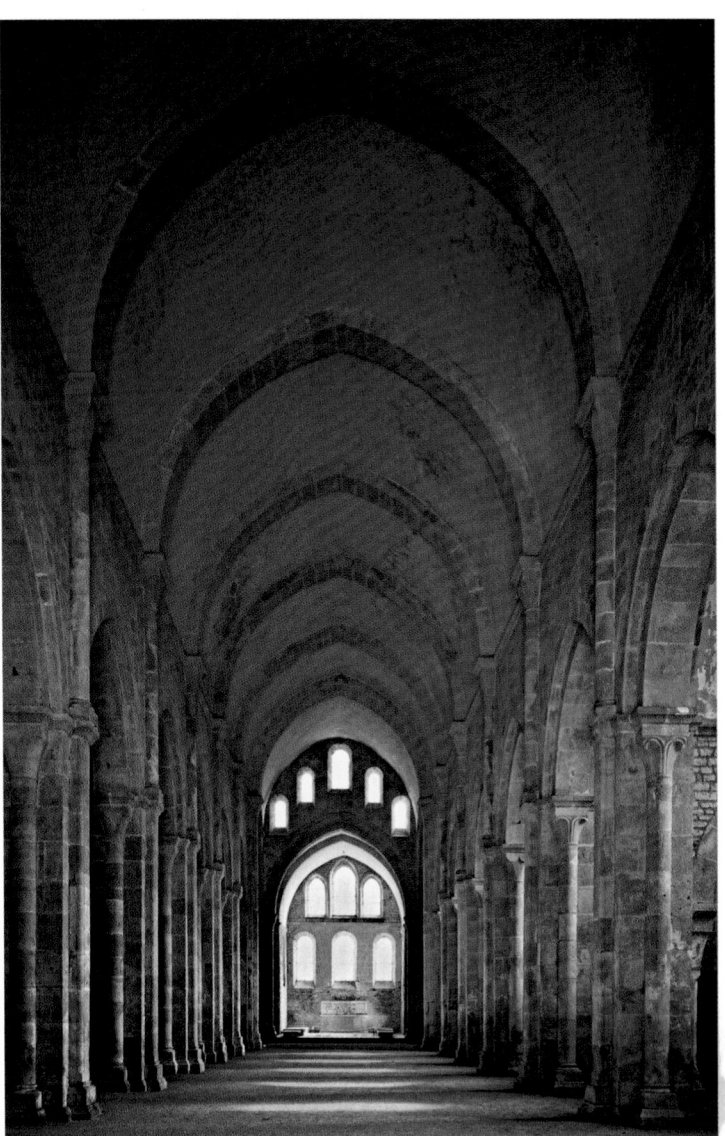

15-9 • NAVE, ABBEY CHURCH OF NOTRE-DAME, FONTENAY
1139–1147.

15-10 • PLAN OF THE ABBEY OF NOTRE-DAME, FONTENAY
Burgundy, France. 1139–1147.

ART AND ITS CONTEXTS

St. Bernard and Theophilus: The Monastic Controversy over the Visual Arts

The twelfth century saw a heated controversy over the place and appropriateness of lavish art in monasteries. In a letter to William of Saint-Thierry, Bernard of Clairvaux wrote:

> What excuse can there be for these ridiculous monstrosities in the cloisters where the monks do their reading, extraordinary things at once beautiful and ugly? Here we find filthy monkeys and fierce lions, fearful centaurs, harpies, and striped tigers, soldiers at war, and hunters blowing their horns. Here is one head with many bodies, there is one body with many heads. Over there is a beast with a serpent for its tail, a fish with an animal's head, and a creature that is horse in front and goat behind, and a second beast with horns and the rear of a horse. All round there is such an amazing variety of shapes that one could easily prefer to take one's reading from the walls instead of a book. One could spend the whole day gazing fascinated at these things, one by one, instead of meditating on the law of God. Good Lord, even if the foolishness of it all occasion no shame, a least one might balk at the expense.
>
> (Bernard, "Apologia to Abbot William," p. 66)

"Theophilus" is the pseudonym used by a monk who wrote a book during the first half of the twelfth century on the practice of artistic craft, voiced as a defense of the place of the visual arts within the monastic traditions of work and prayer. The book gives detailed instructions for panel painting, **stained glass** (colored glass assembled into ornamental or pictorial windows), and goldsmithing. In contrast to the stern warnings of Bernard, perhaps even in response to them, "Theophilus" assured artists that "God delights in embellishments" and that artists worked "under the direction and authority of the Holy Spirit."

He wrote:

> Therefore, most beloved son, you should not doubt but should believe in full faith that the Spirit of God has filled your heart when you have embellished His house with such great beauty and variety of workmanship …
>
> … do not hide away the talent given to you by God, but, working and teaching openly and with humility, you faithfully reveal it to those who desire to learn.
>
> … if a faithful soul should see a representation of the Lord's crucifixion expressed in the strokes of an artist, it is itself pierced; if it sees how great are the tortures that the saints have endured in their bodies and how great the rewards of eternal life that they have received, it grasps at the observance of a better life; if it contemplates how great are the joys in heaven and how great are the torments in the flames of hell, it is inspired with hope because of its good deeds and shaken with fear on considering its sins.
>
> (Theophilus, *On Divers Arts*, pp. 78–79)

As we will see in the next chapter, Abbot Suger of Saint-Denis shared the position of Theophilus, rather than that of Bernard, and from this standpoint would sponsor a reconstruction of his abbey church that gave birth to the Gothic style.

Although Fontenay and other early Cistercian monasteries fully reflect the architectural developments of their time in masonry construction, vaulting, and planning, the Cistercians relied on harmonious proportions and superbly refined stonework, not elaborately carved and painted figural decoration, to achieve beauty in their architecture. Church furnishings included little other than altars with crosses and candles. The large windows in the end wall, rather than a clerestory, provided light, concentrated here as at Santiago, on the sanctuary. The sets of triple windows may have reminded the monks of the Trinity. Some scholars have suggested that the numerical and proportional systems guiding the design of such seemingly simple buildings are saturated with the sacred numerical systems outlined by such eminent early theologians as St. Augustine of Hippo. The streamlined but sophisticated architecture favored by the Cistercians spread from their homeland in Burgundy to become an international style. From Scotland and Poland to Spain and Italy, Cistercian designs and building techniques varied only slightly in relation to local building traditions. Cistercian experiments with masonry vaulting and harmonious proportions influenced the development of the French Gothic style in the middle of the twelfth century.

REGIONAL STYLES IN ROMANESQUE ARCHITECTURE

The Cathedral of Santiago de Compostela and the abbey church at Cluny reflect the cultural exchanges along the pilgrimage roads and the international connections fostered by powerful monastic orders, but Europe remained a land divided by competing kingdoms, regions, and factions. Romanesque architecture reflects this regionalism in the wide variety of its styles, traditions, and building techniques. Only a few examples can be examined here.

THE CATHEDRAL OF ST. MARY OF THE ASSUMPTION IN PISA. Throughout Italy artists looked to the still-standing remains of imperial Rome and Early Christianity. The influence remained especially strong in Pisa, on the west coast of Tuscany. Pisa became a maritime power, competing with Barcelona and Genoa as well as the Muslims for control of trade in the western Mediterranean. In 1063, after a decisive victory over the Muslims, the jubilant

15–11 • CATHEDRAL COMPLEX, PISA

Tuscany, Italy. Cathedral, begun 1063; baptistery, begun 1153; campanile, begun 1174; Campo Santo, 13th century.

When finished in 1350, the Leaning Tower of Pisa stood 179 feet high. The campanile had begun to tilt while still under construction, and today it leans about 13 feet off the perpendicular. In the latest effort to keep it from toppling, engineers filled the base with tons of lead.

SEE MORE: Click the Google Earth link for the Cathedral complex, Pisa
www.myartslab.com

Pisans began an imposing new cathedral dedicated to the Virgin Mary **(FIG. 15–11)**. The cathedral was designed as a cruciform basilica by the master builder Busketos. A long nave with double side aisles (usually an homage to Old St. Peter's) is crossed by projecting transepts, designed like basilicas with their own aisles and apses. The builders added galleries above the side aisles, and a dome covers the crossing. Unlike Early Christian basilicas, the exteriors of Tuscan churches were richly decorated with marble— either panels of green and white marble or arcades. At Pisa, pilasters, applied arcades, and narrow galleries in white marble adorn the five-story façade.

In addition to the cathedral itself, the complex eventually included a baptistery, a campanile, and the later Gothic Campo Santo, a walled burial ground. The baptistery, begun in 1153, has arcading and galleries on the lower levels of its exterior that match those on the cathedral (the baptistery's present exterior dome and ornate upper levels were built later). The campanile (a free-standing bell tower—now known for obvious reasons as "the Leaning Tower of Pisa") was begun in 1174 by master builder Bonanno Pisano. Built on inadequate foundations, it began to lean almost immediately. The cylindrical tower is encased in tier upon tier of marble columns. This creative reuse of the Classical theme of

the colonnade, turning it into a decorative arcade, is characteristic of Tuscan Romanesque art.

THE BENEDICTINE CHURCH OF SAN CLEMENTE IN ROME. The Benedictine church of San Clemente in Rome was rebuilt beginning in the eleventh century (it was consecrated in 1128) on top of the previous church (which had itself been built over a Roman sanctuary of Mithras). The architecture and decoration reflect a conscious effort to reclaim the artistic and spiritual legacy of the early church **(FIG. 15–12)**. As with the columns of Santa Sabina (SEE FIG. 7–9), the columns in San Clemente are **spolia**: that is, they were reused from ancient Roman buildings. The church originally had a timber roof (now disguised by an ornate eighteenth-century ceiling). Even given the Romanesque emphasis on stone vaulting, the construction of timber-roofed buildings continued throughout the Middle Ages.

At San Clemente, the nave ends in a semicircular apse opening directly off the rectangular hall without a sanctuary extension or transept crossing. To accommodate the increased number of participants in the twelfth-century liturgy, the liturgical choir for the monks was extended into the nave itself, defined by a low barrier made up of ninth-century relief panels reused from the earlier

15–12 • NAVE, CHURCH OF SAN CLEMENTE, ROME
Consecrated 1128.

San Clemente contains one of the finest surviving collections of early church furniture: choir stalls, pulpit, lectern, candlestick, and also the twelfth-century inlaid floor pavement. Ninth-century choir screen panels were reused from the earlier church on the site. The upper wall and ceiling decoration date from the eighteenth century.

church. In Early Christian basilicas, the area in front of the altar had been similarly enclosed by a low stone parapet (SEE FIG. 7–9), and the Romanesque builders may have wanted to revive what they considered a glorious Early Christian tradition. A **baldachin** (a canopy suspended over a sacred space, also called a ciborium), symbolizing the Holy Sepulcher, covers the main altar in the apse.

The apse of San Clemente is richly decorated with marble revetment on the curving walls and mosaic in the semidome, in a system familiar from the Early Christian and Byzantine world (SEE FIGS. 7–15, 7–21, 7–25). The mosaics attempt to recapture this past glory, portraying the trees and rivers of paradise, a lavish vine scroll inhabited by figures, in the midst of which emerges the crucified Christ flanked by Mary and St. John. Twelve doves on the cross and the 12 sheep that march in single file below represent the apostles. Stags drink from streams flowing from the base of the cross, evocation of the tree of life in paradise **(FIG. 15–13)**. An inscription running along the base of the apse explains, "We liken the Church of Christ to this vine that the law causes to wither and the Cross causes to bloom," a statement that recalls Jesus' reference to himself as the true vine and his followers as the branches (John 15:1–11), The learned monks of San Clemente would have been prepared to derive these and other meanings from the evocative symbols within this elaborate and arresting composition.

Although the subject of the mosaic recalls Early Christian art, the style and technique are clearly Romanesque. The artists have suppressed the sense of lifelike illusionism that characterized earlier mosaics in favor of ornamental patterns and schemas typical of the twelfth century. The doves silhouetted on the dark blue cross, the symmetrical repetition of circular vine scrolls, even the animals, birds, and humans among their leaves conform to an overriding formal design. By an irregular setting of mosaic tesserae in visibly rough plaster, the artists are able to heighten color and increase the glitter of the pervasive gold field, allowing the mosaic to sparkle.

15–13 • STAGS DRINKING FROM STREAMS FLOWING UNDER THE CRUCIFIED CHRIST
Detail of mosaics in the apse of the church of San Clemente, Rome. Consecrated 1128.

The Paintings of San Climent in Taull: Mozarabic Meets Byzantine

As we see at San Clemente in Rome and at Saint-Savin-sur-Gartempe (SEE FIGS. 15–12, 15–14), Romanesque church interiors were not bare expanses of stone, but were often covered with images that glowed in flickering candlelight amid clouds of incense. Outside Rome during the Romanesque period, murals largely replaced mosaics on the walls of churches. Wall painting was subject to the same influences as the other visual arts: that is, the mural painters could be inspired by illuminated manuscripts, or ivories, or enamels in their treasuries or libraries. Some artists must have seen examples of Byzantine art; others had Carolingian or even Early Christian models.

Artists in Catalunya brilliantly combined the Byzantine style with their own Mozarabic and Classical heritage in the apse paintings of the church of San Climent in the mountain village of Taull (Tahull), consecrated in 1123, just a few years before the church of San Clemente in Rome. The curve of the semi-dome of the apse contains a magnificently expressive Christ in Majesty holding an open book inscribed *Ego sum lux mundi* ("I am the light of the world," John 8:12)—recalling in his commanding presence the imposing Byzantine depictions of Christ Pantocrator, ruler and judge of the world, in Middle Byzantine churches (SEE FIG. 7–34). The San Climent artist was one of the finest painters of the Romanesque period, but where he came from and where he learned his art is unknown. His use of elongated oval faces, large staring eyes, and long noses, as well as the placement of figures against flat bands of color and his use of heavy outlines, reflect the Mozarabic past (SEE FIG. 14–7). At the same time his work betrays the influence of Byzantine art in his painting technique of modeling from light to dark through repeated colored lines of varying width in three shades—dark, medium, and light. Instead of blending the colors, he delights in the striped effect, as he also does in the patterning potential in details of faces, hair, hands, and muscles.

CHRIST IN MAJESTY
Detail of apse, church of San Climent, Taull, Catalunya, Spain.
Consecrated 1123. Museu Nacional d'Art de Catalunya, Barcelona.

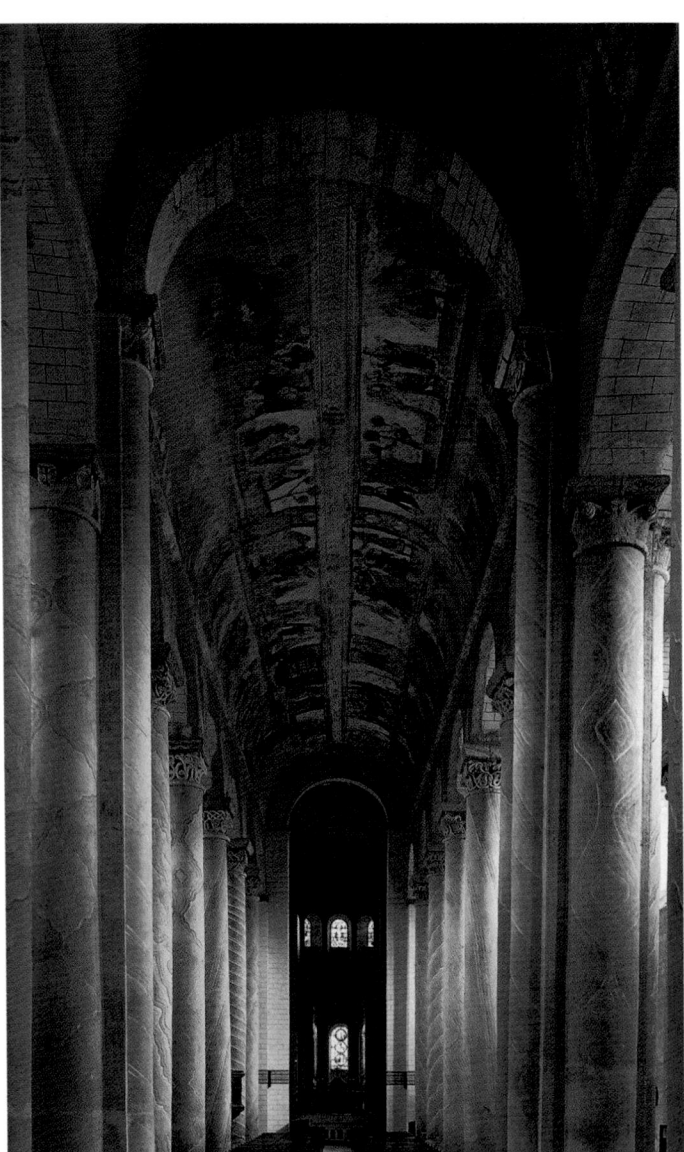

15–14 • ABBEY CHURCH OF SAINT-SAVIN-SUR-GARTEMPE, POITOU
France. Choir c. 1060–1075; nave c. 1095–1115.

THE ABBEY CHURCH OF SAINT-SAVIN-SUR-GARTEMPE. At the Benedictine abbey church in Saint-Savin-sur-Gartempe in western France, a tunnel-like barrel vault runs the length of the nave and choir (FIG. 15–14). Without galleries or clerestory windows, the nave at Saint-Savin approaches the form of a "hall church," where the nave and aisles rise to an equal height. And unlike other churches we have seen (SEE, FOR EXAMPLE, FIG. 15–4), at Saint-Savin the barrel vault is unbroken by projecting transverse arches, making it ideally suited for paintings.

The paintings on the high vaults of Saint-Savin survive almost intact, presenting scenes from the Hebrew Bible and New Testament. The nave was built c. 1095–1115, and the painters seem to have followed the masons immediately, probably using the same scaffolding. Perhaps their intimate involvement with the building process accounts for the vividness with which they portrayed the biblical story of the TOWER OF BABEL (FIG. 15–15).

According to the account in Genesis (11:1–9), God (represented here by a striding figure of Christ on the left) punished the prideful people who had tried to reach heaven by means of their own architectural ingenuity by scattering them and making their languages mutually unintelligible. The tower in the painting is a medieval structure, reflecting the medieval practice of visualizing all stories in contemporary settings, thereby underlining their relevance for the contemporary audience. Workers haul heavy stone blocks toward the tower, presumably intending to lift them to masons on the top with the same hoist that has been used to haul up a bucket of mortar. The giant Nimrod, on the far right, simply hands over the blocks. These paintings embody the energy

15–15 • TOWER OF BABEL
Detail of painting in nave vault, abbey church of Saint-Savin-sur-Gartempe, Poitou, France. c. 1115.

15-16 • INTERIOR, SPEYER CATHEDRAL
Germany. As remodeled c. 1080–1106.

with smaller piers supporting the vaults of the aisle bays. This rhythmic, alternating pattern of heavy and light elements, first suggested for aesthetic reasons in Ottonian wooden-roofed architecture (SEE FIG. 14–22), became an important design element in Speyer. Since groin vaults concentrate the weight and thrust of the vault on the four corners of the bay, they relieve the stress on the side walls of the building. Windows can be safely inserted in each bay to flood the building with light.

The exterior of Speyer Cathedral emphasizes its Ottonian and Carolingian background. Soaring towers and wide transepts mark both ends of the building, although a narthex, not an apse, stands at the west. A large apse housing the high altar abuts the flat wall of the choir; transept arms project at each side; a large octagonal tower rises over the crossing; and a pair of tall slender towers flanks the choir **(FIG. 15–17)**. A horizontal arcade forms an exterior gallery at the top of the apse and transept wall, recalling the Italian practice we saw at Pisa (SEE FIG. 15–11).

and narrative vigor that characterizes Romanesque art. A dynamic figure of God confronts the wayward people, stepping away from them even as he turns back, presumably to scold them. The dramatic movement, monumental figures, bold outlines, broad areas of color, and patterned drapery all promote the legibility of these pictures to viewers looking up in the dim light from far below. The team of painters working here did not use the *buon fresco* technique favored in Italy for its durability, but they did moisten the walls before painting, which allowed some absorption of pigments into the plaster, making them more permanent than paint applied to a dry surface.

THE CATHEDRAL OF THE VIRGIN AND ST. STEPHEN AT SPEYER. The imperial cathedral at Speyer in the Rhine River Valley was a colossal structure rivaled only by Cluny III. An Ottonian, wooden-roofed church built between 1030 and 1060 was given a masonry vault c. 1080–1106 **(FIG. 15–16)**. Massive compound piers mark each nave bay and support the transverse ribs of a groin vault that rises to a height of over 100 feet. These compound piers alternate

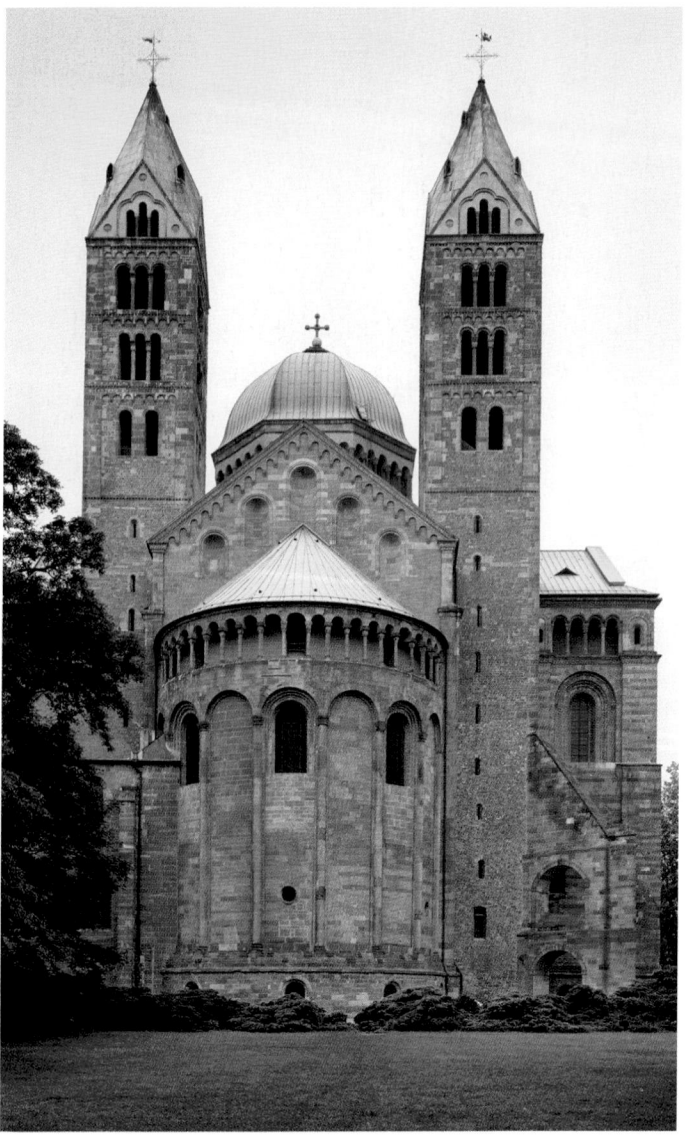

15-17 • EXTERIOR, SPEYER CATHEDRAL
c. 1080–1106 and second half of the 12th century.

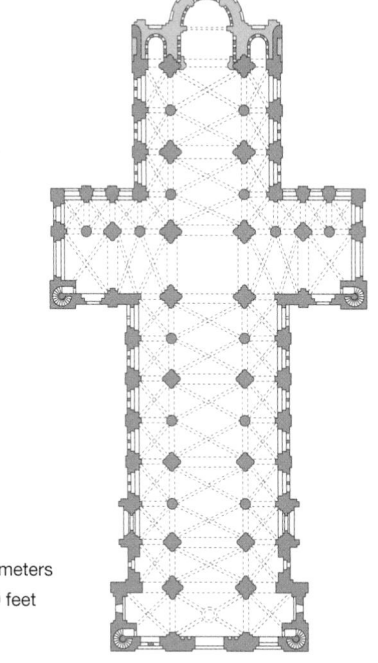

15-18 • DURHAM CATHEDRAL
England. 1087–1133. Original east
end replaced by a Gothic choir,
1242–c. 1280. Vault height about 73′
(22.2 m).

SEE MORE: View a panorama
of Durham Cathedral
www.myartslab.com

DURHAM CATHEDRAL.   In Durham, an English military outpost
near the Scottish border, a prince-bishop held both secular and
religious authority. For his headquarters he chose a natural defensive
site where the bend in the River Wear formed a natural moat.
Durham grew into a powerful fortified complex including a castle, a
monastery, and a cathedral. The great tower of the castle defended
against attack from the land, and an open space between buildings
served as the courtyard of the castle and the cathedral green.

   DURHAM CATHEDRAL, begun in 1087 and vaulting
constructed from 1093, is an impressive example of Norman
Romanesque, but like most buildings that have been in continuous
use, it has been altered several times **(FIGS. 15–18, 15–19)**. The

0   30 meters
0   100 feet

15-19 • PLAN OF DURHAM CATHEDRAL
Showing original east end.

nave retains its Norman character, but the huge circular window lighting the choir is a later Gothic addition. The cathedral's size and décor are ambitious. Enormous compound piers and robust columnar piers form the nave arcade and establish a rhythmic alternation. The columnar piers are carved with chevrons, spiral fluting, and diamond patterns, and some have scalloped, cushion-shape capitals. The richly carved arches that sit on them have multiple round moldings and chevron ornaments. All this carved ornamentation was originally painted.

Above the cathedral's massive piers and walls rises a new system of ribbed groin vaults. Romanesque masons in Santiago de Compostela, Cluny, Fontenay, Speyer, and Durham were all experimenting with stone vaulting—and reaching different conclusions. The Durham builders divided each bay with two pairs of diagonal crisscrossing rounded ribs and so kept the crowns of the vaults close in height to the keystones of the pointed transverse arches (SEE FIG. 15–18). Although this allows the eye to run smoothly down the length of the vault, and from vault to vault down the expanse of the nave, the richly carved zigzagging moldings on the ribs themselves invite us to linger over each bay, acknowledging traditional Romanesque bay division. This new system of ribbed groin vaulting will become a hallmark of Gothic architecture, though there it will create a very different aesthetic effect.

SECULAR ARCHITECTURE: DOVER CASTLE, ENGLAND

The need to provide for personal security in a time of periodic local warfare and political upheaval, as well as the desire to glorify the house of Christ and his saints, meant that communities used much of their resources to build castles and churches. Fully garrisoned, castles were sometimes as large as cities. In the twelfth century, **DOVER CASTLE**, safeguarding the coast of England from invasion, was a bold manifestation of military power (**FIG. 15–20**). It illustrates the way in which a key defensive position developed over the centuries.

The Romans had built a lighthouse on the point where the English Channel separating England and France narrows. The Anglo-Saxons added a church (both lighthouse and church can be seen in FIG. 15–20 behind the tower, surrounded by the remains of

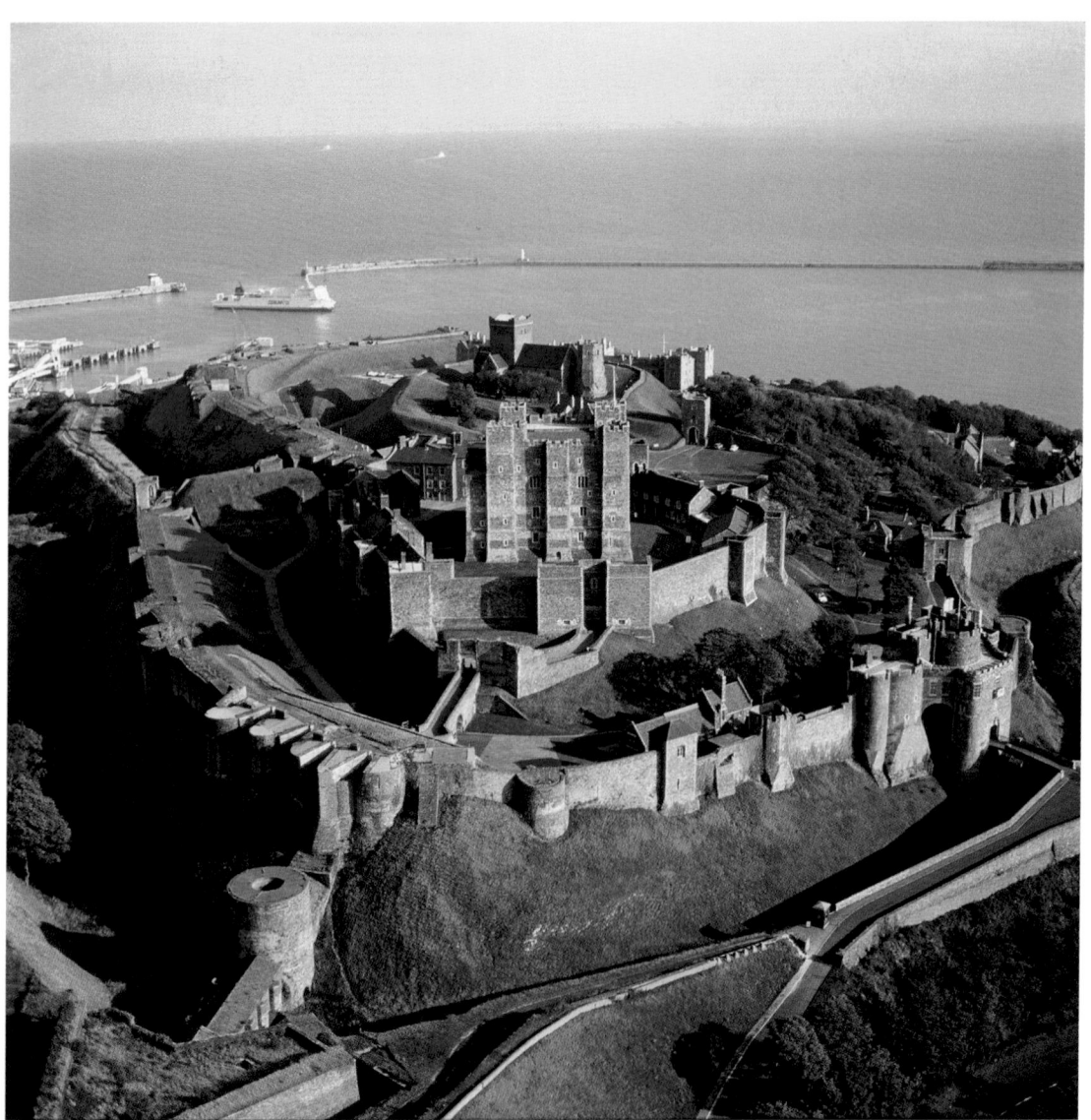

15-20 • DOVER CASTLE
England

Aerial view overlooking the harbor and the English Channel. Center distance: Roman lighthouse tower, rebuilt Anglo-Saxon church, earthworks. Center: Norman Great Tower, surrounding earthworks and wall, twelfth century. Outer walls, thirteenth century. Modern buildings have red tile roofs. The castle was used in World War II and is now a museum.

The most important imagery on a Romanesque portal appears on the semicircular **tympanum** directly over the door—often a hieratically scaled image of abstract grandeur such as Christ in Majesty or Christ presiding over the Last Judgment—as well as on the **lintel** beneath it. **Archivolts**—curved moldings composed of the wedge-shape stone voussoirs of the arch—frame the tympanum. On both sides of the doors, the **jambs** (vertical elements) and occasionally a central pier (called the **trumeau**), support the lintel and archivolts, providing further fields for figures, columns, or narrative friezes. The jambs can extend forward to form a porch.

SEE MORE: View a simulation of a Romanesque church portal **www.myartslab.com**

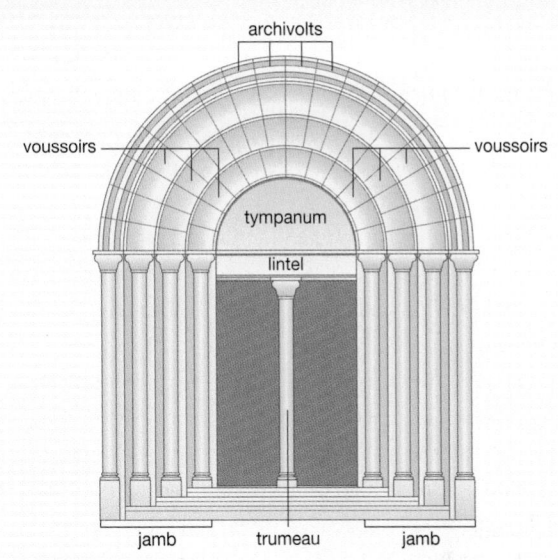

ARCHITECTURAL SCULPTURE

Architecture dominated the arts in the Romanesque period—not only because it required the material and human resources of entire communities, but because it provided the physical context for a revival of the art of monumental stone sculpture, an art that had been dormant in European art for 500 years. The "mute" façades used in early medieval buildings (SEE FIG. 14–15) were transformed by Romanesque sculptors into "speaking" façades with richly carved portals projecting bold symbolic and didactic programs to the outside world (SEE FIG. 15–22). Christ Enthroned in Majesty might be carved over the entrance, and increasing importance is accorded to the Virgin Mary. The prophets, kings, and queens of the Hebrew Bible were seen by medieval Christians as precursors of people and events in the New Testament, so these were depicted, and we can also find representations of contemporary bishops, abbots, other noble patrons, and even ordinary folk. A profusion of monsters, animals, plants, geometric ornament, allegorical figures such as Lust and Greed, and depictions of real and imagined buildings surround the sculpture within its architectural setting. The elect rejoice in heaven with the angels; the damned suffer in hell, tormented by demons; biblical and historical tales come alive. All these events seem to take place in a contemporary medieval setting, and they are juxtaposed with scenes drawn from the viewer's everyday life.

These innovative portals are among the greatest artistic achievements of Romanesque art, taking the central messages of the Christian Church out of the sanctuary (SEE FIGS. 7–21, 7–25) and into the public spaces of medieval towns. And figural sculpture appeared not only at entrances, but on the capitals of interior as well as exterior piers and columns, and occasionally spread all over

earthen walls). In the early Middle Ages, earthworks topped by wooden walls provided a measure of security, and a wooden tower signified an important administrative building and residence. The advantage of fire-resistant walls was obvious, and in the twelfth and thirteenth centuries, military engineers replaced the timber tower and palisades with stone walls. They added the massive stone towers we see today.

The Great Tower, as it was called in the Middle Ages (but later known as a **keep** in England, and donjon in France), stood in a courtyard (called the **bailey**) surrounded by additional walls. Ditches outside the walls added to the height of the walls. In some castles, ditches were filled with water to form moats. A gate-house—perhaps with a drawbridge—controlled the entrance. In all castles, the bailey was filled with buildings, the most important of which was the lord's hall; it was used to hold court and for feasts and ceremonial occasions. Timber buildings housed troops, servants, and animals. Barns and workshops, ovens and wells were also needed since the castle had to be self-sufficient.

If enemies broke through the outer walls, the castle's defenders retreated to the Great Tower. In the thirteenth century, the builders at Dover doubled the walls and strengthened them with towers, even though the castle's position on cliffs overlooking the sea made scaling the walls nearly impossible. The garrison could be forced to surrender only by starving its occupants.

During Dover Castle's heyday, improvements in farming and growing prosperity provided the resources for increased building activity across Europe. Churches, castles, halls, houses, barns, and monasteries proliferated. The buildings that still stand—despite the ravages of weather, vandalism, neglect, and war—testify to the technical skills and creative ingenuity of the builders and the power, local pride, and faith of the patrons.

15-21 • Wiligelmo CREATION AND FALL, WEST FAÇADE, MODENA CATHEDRAL
Emilia, Italy. Building begun 1099; sculpture c. 1099. Height approx. 3′ (92 cm).

the building in friezes, on corbels, even peeking around cornices or from behind moldings. There was plenty of work for stone sculptors on Romanesque building sites.

WILIGELMO AT THE CATHEDRAL OF MODENA

The spirit of ancient Rome pervades the sculpture of Romanesque Italy, and the sculptor Wiligelmo may have been inspired by Roman sarcophagi still visible in cemeteries when he carved horizontal reliefs across the west façade of Modena Cathedral, c. 1099. Wiligelmo took his subjects here from Genesis, focusing on events from the **CREATION AND FALL OF ADAM AND EVE (FIG. 15–21)**. On the far left, God, in a **mandorla** (body halo) supported by angels, appears in two persons as both Creator and Christ, identified by a cruciform halo. Following this iconic image, the narrative of creation unfolds in three scenes, from left to right: God brings Adam to life, then brings forth Eve from Adam's side, and finally Adam and Eve cover their genitals in shame as they greedily eat fruit from the forbidden tree, around which the wily serpent twists.

Wiligelmo's deft carving gives these figures a strong three-dimensionality. The framing arcade establishes a stagelike setting, with the rocks on which Adam lies and the tempting tree of paradise serving as stage props. Wiligelmo's figures exude life and personality. They convey an emotional connection with the narrative they enact, and bright paint, now almost all lost, must have increased their lifelike impact still further. An inscription at Modena proclaims, "Among sculptors, your work shines forth, Wiligelmo." This self-confidence turned out to be justified.

Wiligelmo's influence can be traced throughout Italy and as far away as Lincoln Cathedral in England.

THE PRIORY CHURCH OF SAINT-PIERRE AT MOISSAC

The Cluniac priory of Saint-Pierre at Moissac was a major stop on the pilgrimage route to Santiago de Compostela. The shrine at the site dates back to the Carolingian period, and after affiliating with Cluny in 1047, the monastery prospered from the donations of pilgrims and local nobility, as well as from its control of shipping on the nearby Garonne River. During the twelfth century, Moissac's monks launched an ambitious building campaign, and much of the sculpture from the cloister (c. 1100, under Abbot Ansquetil) and the church portal and porch (1100–1130, under Abbot Roger) has survived. The quantity and quality of the carving here are outstanding.

A flattened figure of **CHRIST IN MAJESTY** dominates the huge tympanum (**FIG. 15–22**), visualizing a description of the Second Coming in Chapters 4 and 5 of Revelation. This gigantic Christ is an imposing, iconic image of enduring grandeur. He is enclosed by a mandorla; a cruciform halo rings his head. Although Christ is stable, even static, in this apocalyptic appearance, the four winged creatures symbolizing the evangelists—Matthew the man (upper left), Mark the lion (lower left), Luke the ox (lower right), and John the eagle (upper right)—who frame him on either side move with dynamic force, as if activated by the power of his unchanging majesty. Rippling bands extending across the tympanum at Christ's sides and under him—perhaps representing waves in the "sea of glass like crystal" (Revelation 4:6)—delineate three registers in which 24 elders with "gold crowns on their heads" and either a harp or a gold bowl of incense (Revelation 4:4 and 5:8) twist nervously to catch a glimpse of Christ's majestic arrival. Each of them takes an individually conceived pose and gesture, as if the sculptors were demonstrating their ability to represent three-dimensional human figures turning in space in a variety of postures, some quite challengingly contorted. Foliate and geometric ornament covers every surface surrounding this tableau. Monstrous heads in the lower corners of the tympanum spew ribbon scrolls, and other creatures appear at each end of the lintel, their tongues growing into ropes encircling acanthus rosettes.

Two side jambs and a trumeau (central portal pier) support the weight of the lintel and tympanum. These elements have scalloped profiles that playfully undermine the ability of the colonettes on the door jambs to perform their architectural function and give a sense of instability to the lower part of the portal, as if to underline the ability of the stable figure of Christ in Majesty to provide his own means of support. St. Peter and the prophet Isaiah flank the doorway on the jambs. Peter, a tall, thin saint, steps away from the door but twists back to look through it.

The **TRUMEAU** (**FIG. 15–23**) is faced by a crisscrossing pair of lions. On the side visible here, a prophet, usually identified as

15-22 • SOUTH PORTAL AND PORCH, SHOWING CHRIST IN MAJESTY, PRIORY CHURCH OF SAINT-PIERRE, MOISSAC
France. c. 1115.

Jeremiah, twists toward the viewer, with legs crossed in a pose that would challenge his ability to stand, much less move. The sculptors placed him in skillful conformity with the constraints of the scalloped trumeau; his head, pelvis, knees, and feet moving into the pointed cusps. This decorative scalloping, as well as the trumeau lions and lintel rosettes, may reveal influence from Islamic art. Moissac was under construction shortly after the First Crusade, when many Europeans first encountered the Islamic art and architecture of the Holy Land. People from the region around Moissac participated in the crusade; perhaps they brought Islamic objects and ideas home with them.

15-23 • TRUMEAU, SOUTH PORTAL, PRIORY CHURCH OF SAINT-PIERRE, MOISSAC
France. c. 1115.

A porch covering the area in front of the portal at Moissac provided a sheltered space for pilgrims to congregate and view the sculpture during their stopover along the way to Santiago. The side walls are filled with yet more figural sculptural (FIG. 15–24), but the style of presentation changes here with the nature of the subject matter and the response that was sought from the audience. Instead of the stylized and agitated figures on the tympanum and its supports, here sculptors have substituted more lifelike and approachable human beings. Rather than embodying unchanging theological notions or awe-inspiring apocalyptic appearances, these figures convey human frailties and torments in order to persuade viewers to follow the Church's moral teachings.

Behind the double arcade framework of the lower part of the wall are hair-raising portrayals of the torments of those who fall prey to the two sins that particularly preoccupied twelfth-century moralists: avarice (greed and the hoarding of money) and lust (sexual misconduct). At bottom left, a greedy man is attacked by demons while the money bags around his neck weigh him down, strangling him. On the other side of the column, his counterpart, the female personification of lust (*luxuria*), is confronted by a pot-bellied devil while snakes bite at her breasts and another predator attacks her pubic area. In the scene that extends behind the column and across the wall above them, *luxuria* reappears, kneeling beside the deathbed of the miser, as devils make off with his money and conspire to make his final moments miserable. These scenes are made as graphic as possible so that medieval viewers could identify with these situations, perhaps even feel the pain in their own bodies as a warning to avoid the behaviors that lead to such gruesome consequences.

In the strip of relief running across the top of the wall, the mood is calmer, but the moral message remains strong and clear, at least for those who know the story. The sculpture recounts the tale of Lazarus and Dives (Luke 16:19–31), the most popular parable of Jesus in Romanesque art. The broad scene to the right shows the greedy, rich Dives, relishing the feast that is being laid before him by his servants and refusing even to give his table scraps to the leprous beggar Lazarus, spread out at lower left. Under the table, dogs—unsatisfied by leftovers from Dives' feast—turn to lick the pus from Lazarus' sores as the poor man draws his last breath. The angel above Lazarus, however, transfers his soul (represented as a naked baby, now missing) to the lap of Abraham (a common image of paradise), where he is cuddled by the patriarch, the eternal reward for a pious life. The fate of Dives is not portrayed here, but it is certainly evoked on the lower section of this very wall in the torments of the greedy man, whom we can now identify with Dives himself. Clearly some knowledge is necessary to recognize the characters and story of this sculpture, and a "guide" may have been present to aid those viewers who did not readily understand. Nonetheless, the moral of sin and its consequences can be read easily and directly from the narrative presentation. This is not scripture for an ignorant illiterate population. It is a sermon sculpted in stone.

The parable of Lazarus and Dives that runs across the top of this wall retains its moral power to our own day. This was the text of Martin Luther King's last Sunday sermon, preached only a few days before his assassination in Memphis, where he was supporting a strike by sanitation workers. Perhaps he saw the parable's image of the table scraps of the rich and greedy as particularly appropriate to his context. Just as in this portal, in Dr. King's sermon the story is juxtaposed with other stories and ideas to craft its interpretive message in a way that is clear and compelling for the audience addressed.

THE CHURCH OF SAINT-LAZARE AT AUTUN

A different sculptural style and another subject appear at Autun on the main portal of the abbey church (now cathedral) of Saint-Lazare (see "A Closer Look," page 478). This is the Last Judgment, in which Christ—enclosed in a mandorla held by two svelte angels—has returned at the end of time to judge the cowering, naked humans whose bodies rise from their sarcophagi along the lintel at his feet. The damned writhe in torment at Christ's left (our right), while on the opposite side the saved savor serene bliss. The inscribed message on the side of the damned reads: "Here let fear strike those whom earthly error binds, for their fate is shown by the horror of these figures," and under the blessed: "Thus shall rise again everyone who does not lead an impious life, and endless light of day shall shine for him" (translations from Grivot and Zarnecki).

Another text, right under the feet of Christ, ascribes the Autun tympanum to a man named Gislebertus—*Gislebertus hoc fecit* ("Gislebertus made this"). Traditionally art historians have interpreted this inscription as a rare instance of a twelfth-century artist's signature, assigning this façade and related sculpture to an

The Last Judgment Tympanum at Autun

by Gislebertus (?), west portal, Cathedral (originally abbey church) of Saint-Lazare. Autun, Burgundy, France. c. 1120–1130 or 1130–1145.

In one of the most endearing vignettes, an angel pushes one of the saved up through an open archway and into the glorious architectural vision of heaven. Another figure at the angel's side reaches up, impatient for his turn to be hoisted up into paradise.

Christ's mother, Mary, is enthroned as queen of heaven. Below, St. Peter—identified by the large keys slung over his shoulder—performs his duties as heavenly gatekeeper, clasping the hands of someone waiting to gain entrance.

This inscription proclaims "I alone dispose of all things and crown the just. Those who follow crime I judge and punish." Clearly, some of the viewers could read Latin.

The cross (a badge of Jerusalem) and scallop shell (a badge of Santiago de Compostela) identify these two figures as former pilgrims. The clear message is that participation in pilgrimage will be a factor in their favor at the Last Judgment.

The incised ornament on these sarcophagi is quite similar to that on ancient Roman sarcophagi, one of many indications that the Autun sculptors and masons knew the ancient art created when Autun was a Roman city.

Interestingly, hell is represented here as a basilica, with a devil emerging from the toothy maw that serves as a side entrance, capturing sinners for eternal torment. The devil uses a sharp hook to grab *luxuria*, the female personification of lust.

SEE MORE: View the Closer Look feature for the Last Judgment Tympanum at Autun **www.myartslab.com**

individual named Gislebertus, who was at the head of a large workshop of sculptors. Recently, however, art historian Linda Seidel has challenged this reading, arguing that Gislebertus was actually a late Carolingian count who had made significant donations to local churches. Like the names inscribed on many academic buildings of American universities, this legendary donor's name would have been evoked here as a reminder of the long and rich history of secular financial support in Autun, and perhaps also as a challenge to those currently in power to respect and continue that venerable tradition of patronage themselves.

Thinner and taller than their counterparts at Moissac, stretched out and bent at sharp angles, the stylized figures at Autun are powerfully expressive and hauntingly beautiful. As at Moissac, a huge, hieratic figure of Christ dominates the composition at the center of the tympanum, but the surrounding figures are not arranged here in regular compartmentalized tiers. Their posture and placement conform to their involvement in the story they enact. Since that story is filled with human interest and anecdotal narrative detail, viewers can easily project themselves into what is going on. On the lintel, angels physically assist the resurrected bodies rising from their tombs, guiding them to line up and await their turn at being judged. Ominously, a pair of giant, pincer-like hands descends aggressively to snatch one of the damned on the right side of the lintel. Above these hands, the archangel Michael competes with devils over the fate of someone whose judgment is being weighed on the scales of good and evil. The man himself perches on the top of the scale, hands cupped to his mouth to project his pleas for help toward the Savior. Another man hides nervously in the folds of Michael's robe, perhaps hoping to escape judgment or cowering from the loathsome prospect of possible damnation.

By far the most riveting players in this drama are the frenzied, grotesque, screaming demons who grab and torment the damned and even try, in vain, to cheat by yanking the scales to favor damnation. The fear they inspire, as well as the poignant portrayal of the psychological state of those whom they torment, would have been moving reminders to medieval viewers to examine the way they were leading their own lives, or perhaps to seek the benefits of entering the doors in front of them to participate in the community of the Church.

The creation of lively narrative scenes within the geometric confines of capitals (called **historiated capitals**) was an important Romanesque innovation in architectural sculpture. The same sculptors who worked on the Autun tympanum carved historiated capitals for pier pilasters inside the church. Two capitals (FIG. 15–25) depict scenes from the childhood of Jesus drawn from Matthew 2:1–18. In one capital, the Magi—who have previously adored and offered gifts to the child Jesus—are interrupted in their sleep by an angel who warns them not to inform King Herod of the location of the newborn king of the Jews. In an ingenious compositional device, the sculptor has shown the reclining Magi and the head of their bed as if viewed from above, whereas the angel and the foot of the bed are viewed from the side. This allows us to see clearly the angel—who is appearing to them in a dream—as he touches the hand of the upper Magus, whose eyes have suddenly popped open. As on the façade, the sculptor has conceived this scene in ways that emphasize the human qualities of its story, not its deep theological significance. With its charming, doll-like figures, the other capital shows an event that occurred just after the Magi's dream: Joseph, Mary, and Jesus are journeying toward Egypt to escape King Herod's order to murder all young boys so as to eliminate the newborn royal rival the Magi had journeyed to venerate.

15-25 • THE MAGI ASLEEP AND THE FLIGHT INTO EGYPT
Capitals from the choir, Cathedral of Saint-Lazare, Autun, Burgundy, France. c. 1125.

CHRIST ON THE CROSS (MAJESTAT BATLLÓ)

This mid-twelfth-century painted wooden crucifix from Catalunya, known as the **MAJESTAT BATLLÓ** (**FIG. 15–26**), presents a clothed, triumphant Christ, rather than the seminude figure we have seen at Byzantine Daphni (SEE FIG. 7–35) or on the Ottonian Gero Crucifix (SEE FIG. 14–23). This Christ's royal robes emphasize his kingship, although his bowed head, downturned mouth, and heavy-lidded eyes convey a quiet sense of sadness or introspection. The hem of his long, medallion-patterned tunic has pseudo-kufic inscriptions—designs meant to resemble Arabic script—a reminder that silks from Islamic Spain were highly prized in Europe at this time. Islamic textiles were widely used as cloths of honor hung behind thrones and around altars to designate royal and sacred places. They were used to wrap relics and to cover altars with apparently no concern for their Muslim source.

MARY AS THE THRONE OF WISDOM

Any Romanesque image of Mary seated on a throne and holding the Christ Child on her lap is known as "The Throne of Wisdom." In a well-preserved example in painted wood dating from the second half of the twelfth century (**FIG. 15–27**), Mother and Child are frontal and regal. Mary's thronelike bench symbolized the lion-throne of Solomon, the Hebrew Bible king who represented earthly wisdom in the Middle Ages. Mary, as Mother and "God-bearer" (the Byzantine *Theotokos*), gave Jesus his human nature. She forms a throne on which he sits in majesty, but she also represents the Church. Although the Child's hands are missing, we can assume that the young Jesus held a book—the Word of God—in his left hand and raised his right hand in blessing.

15-26 • CRUCIFIX (MAJESTAT BATLLÓ)
Catalunya, Spain. Mid-12th century. Polychromed wood, height approx. 37¾" (96 cm). Museu Nacional d'Art de Catalunya, Barcelona.

SCULPTURE IN WOOD AND BRONZE

Painted wood was commonly used when abbey and parish churches of limited means commissioned statues. Wood was not only cheap; it was lightweight, a significant consideration since these devotional images were frequently carried in processions. Whereas wood seems to have been a sculptural medium that spread across Europe, three geographic areas—the Rhineland, the Meuse River Valley, and German Saxony—were the principal metalworking centers. Bronze sculpture was produced only for wealthy aristocratic and ecclesiastical patrons. It drew on a variety of stylistic sources, including the work of contemporary Byzantine and Italian artists, as well as Classical precedents as reinterpreted by the sculptors' Carolingian and Ottonian forebears.

Such statues of the Virgin and Child served as cult objects on the altars of many churches during the twelfth century. They also sometimes took part in the liturgical dramas being added to church services at that time. At the feast of the Epiphany, celebrating the arrival of the Magi to pay homage to the young Jesus, townspeople representing the Magi acted out their journey by searching through the church for the newborn king. The roles of Mary and Jesus were "acted" by the sculpture, which the Magi discovered on the altar. On one of the capitals from Autun in FIG. 15–25, the Virgin and Child who sit on the donkey in the Flight to Egypt may record the theatrical use of a wooden statue, strapped to the back of a wooden donkey that would have been rolled into the church on wheels, possibly referenced by the round forms at the base of the capital.

15-27 • VIRGIN AND CHILD
Auvergne region, France. Late 12th century. Oak with polychromy, height 31″ (78.7 cm). Metropolitan Museum of Art, New York.
Gift of J. Pierpont Morgan, 1916 (16.32.194)

TOMB OF RUDOLF OF SWABIA

The oldest known bronze tomb effigy (recumbent portraits of the deceased) is that of **KING RUDOLF OF SWABIA (FIG. 15–28)**, who died in battle in 1080. The spurs on his oversized feet identify him as a heroic warrior, and he holds a scepter and cross-surmounted orb, emblems of Christian kingship. Although the tomb is in the Cathedral of Merseburg, in Saxony, the effigy has been attributed to an artist originally from the Rhine Valley. Nearly life-size, it was cast in one piece and gilt, though few traces of the gilding survive. The inscription around the frame was incised after casting, and glass paste or semiprecious stones may have originally been set into the eyes and crown. We know that during the battle that ultimately led to Rudolph's death he lost a hand—which was mummified separately and kept in a leather case—but the sculptor of his effigy presents him idealized and whole.

15-28 • TOMB COVER WITH EFFIGY OF KING RUDOLF OF SWABIA
Saxony, Germany. c. 1080. Bronze with niello, approx. 6′5½″ × 2′2½″ (1.97 × 0.68 m). Cathedral of Merseburg, Germany.

RENIER OF HUY

Bronze sculptor Renier of Huy (Huy is near Liège in present-day Belgium) worked in the Mosan region under the profound influence of classicizing early medieval works of art, as well as the humanistic learning of church scholars. Hellinus of Notre-Dame-aux-Fonts in Liège (abbot 1107–1118) commissioned a bronze baptismal font from Renier (FIG. 15–29) that was inspired by the basin carried by 12 oxen in Solomon's Temple in Jerusalem (I Kings 7:23–24). Christian commentators identified the 12 oxen as the 12 apostles and the basin as the baptismal font, and their interpretive thought is given visual form in Renier's work. On the sides of the font are images of St. John the Baptist preaching and baptizing Christ, St. Peter baptizing Cornelius, and St. John the Evangelist baptizing the philosopher Crato. Renier models sturdy but idealized bodies—nude or with clinging drapery—that move and gesture with lifelike conviction, infused with dignity, simplicity, and harmony. His understanding of human anatomy and movement must derive from his close observation of the people around him. He placed these figures within defined landscape settings, standing on an undulating ground line, and separated into scenes by miniature trees. Water rises in a mound of rippling waves (in Byzantine fashion) to cover nude figures discreetly.

TEXTILES AND BOOKS

Among the most admired arts during the Middle Ages are those that later critics patronized as the "minor" or "decorative" arts. Although small in scale, these works are often produced with very precious materials, and they were vital to the Christian mission and devotion of the institutions that housed them.

Artists in the eleventh and twelfth centuries were still often monks and nuns. They labored within monasteries as calligraphers and painters in the scriptorium to produce books and as metalworkers to craft the enamel- and jewel-encrusted works used in liturgical services. They also embroidered the vestments, altar coverings, and wall hangings that clothed both celebrants and settings in the Mass. Increasingly, however, secular urban workshops supplied the aristocratic and royal courts with textiles, tableware, books, and weapons, as well as occasional donations to religious institutions.

CHRONICLING HISTORY

Romanesque artists were commissioned not only to illllustrate engaging stories and embody important theological ideas within the context of sacred buildings and sacred books. They also created visual accounts of secular history, although here as well moralizing was one of the principal objectives of pictorial narrative.

THE BAYEUX EMBROIDERY. Elaborate textiles, including embroideries and tapestries, enhanced a noble's status and were thus necessary features in castles and palaces. The Bayeux Embroidery (see pages 484–485) is one of the earliest examples to have survived. This long narrative strip chronicles the events leading to Duke William of Normandy's conquest of England in 1066. The images depicted on this long embroidered band may have been drawn by a Norman designer since there is a clear Norman bias in the telling of the story, but style suggests that it may have been Anglo-Saxons who did the actual needlework. This represents the kind of secular art that must once have been part of most royal courts. It could be rolled up and transported from residence to residence as the noble Norman owner traveled throughout his domain, and some have speculated that it may have been the backdrop at banquets for stories sung by professional performers who could have received their cues from the identifying descriptions that accompany most scenes. Eventually the embroidery was given to Bayeux Cathedral, perhaps by Bishop Odo, William's brother; we know it was displayed around the walls of the cathedral on the feast of the relics.

THE WORCESTER CHRONICLE. Another Romanesque chronicle is the earliest known illustrated history book: the **WORCESTER CHRONICLE** (FIG. 15–30), written in the twelfth century by a monk named John. The pages shown here concern Henry I (r. 1100–1135), the second of William the Conqueror's sons to sit on the English throne. The text relates a series of nightmares the

15–30 • John of Worcester **THOSE WHO WORK; THOSE WHO FIGHT; THOSE WHO PRAY— THE DREAM OF HENRY I, WORCESTER CHRONICLE**
Worcester, England. c. 1140. Ink and tempera on vellum, each page 12¾ × 9⅜″ (32.5 × 23.7 cm).
Corpus Christi College, Oxford. CCC MS. 157, pages 382–383

The Bayeux Embroidery

Rarely has art spoken more vividly than in the Bayeux Embroidery, a strip of embroidered linen that recounts the history of the Norman Conquest of England. Its designer was a skillful storyteller who used a staggering number of images to chronicle this history. In the 50 surviving scenes there are more than 600 human figures; 700 horses, dogs, and other creatures; and 2,000 inch-high letters.

On October 14, 1066, William, Duke of Normandy, after a hard day of fighting, became William the Conqueror, king of England. The story told in embroidery seeks to justify his action, with the intensity of an eyewitness account: The Anglo-Saxon nobleman Harold initially swears his feudal allegiance to William, but later betrays his feudal vows, accepting the crown of England for himself. Unworthy to be king, he dies in battle at the hands of William and the Normans.

Harold is a heroic figure at the beginning of the story, but then events overtake him. After his coronation, cheering crowds celebrate—until Halley's Comet crosses the sky (FIG. A). The Anglo-Saxons, seeing the comet as a portent of disaster, cringe and point at this brilliant ball of fire with a flaming

A. MESSENGERS SIGNAL THE APPEARANCE OF A COMET (HALLEY'S COMET), THE BAYEUX EMBROIDERY

tail, and a man rushes to inform the new king. Harold slumps on his throne in the Palace of Westminster. He foresees what is to come: Below his feet is his vision of a ghostly fleet of Norman ships already riding the waves.

Duke William has assembled the last great Viking flotilla on the Normandy coast.

The tragedy of this drama has spoken movingly to audiences over the centuries. It is the story of a good man who, like

B. BISHOP ODO BLESSING THE FEAST, THE BAYEUX EMBROIDERY
Norman–Anglo-Saxon embroidery from Canterbury, Kent, England, or Bayeux, Normandy, France. c. 1066–1082. Linen with wool, height 20" (50.8 cm). Centre Guillaume le Conquérant, Bayeux, France.

Odo and William are feasting before the battle. Attendants bring in roasted birds on skewers, placing them on a makeshift table made of the knights' shields set on trestles. The diners, summoned by the blowing of a horn, gather at a curved table laden with food and drink. Bishop Odo— seated at the center, head and shoulders above William to his right—blesses the meal while others eat. The kneeling servant in the middle proffers a basin and towel so that the diners may wash their hands. The man on Odo's left points impatiently to the next event, a council of war between William (now the central and tallest figure), Odo, and a third man labeled "Rotbert," probably Robert of Mortain, another of William's halfbrothers. Translation of text: "and here the servants (*ministra*) perform their duty. / Here they prepare the meal (*prandium*) / and here the bishop blesses the food and drink (*cibu et potu*). Bishop Odo. William. Robert."

— stem stitching

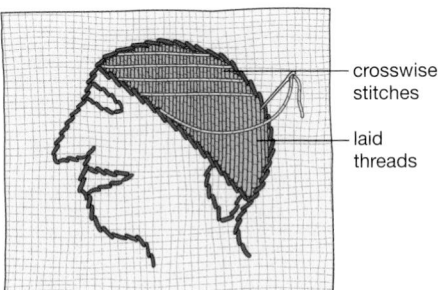

— crosswise stitches

— laid threads

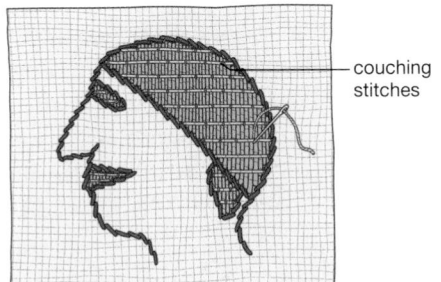

— couching stitches

Shakespeare's Macbeth, is overcome by his lust for power and so betrays his lord. The images of this Norman invasion also spoke to people during the darkest days of World War II. When the Allies invaded Nazi-occupied Europe in June 1944, they took the same route in reverse from England to beaches on the coast of Normandy. The Bayeux Embroidery still speaks to us of the folly of human greed and ambition and of two battles that changed the course of history.

Although traditionally referred to as the "Bayeux Tapestry," this work is really an embroidery. In tapestry, colored threads that form the images or patterns are woven in during the process of making the fabric itself; **embroidery** consists of stitches applied on top of an already woven fabric ground. The embroiderers, probably Anglo-Saxon women, worked in tightly twisted wool that was dyed in eight colors. They used only two stitches: the quick, overlapping stem stitch that produced a slightly jagged line or outline, and the time-consuming laid-and-couched work used to form blocks of color. For the latter, the embroiderer first "laid" a series of long, parallel covering threads; then anchored them with a second layer of regularly spaced crosswise stitches; and finally tacked all the strands down with tiny "couching" stitches. Some of the laid-and-couched work was done in contrasting colors to achieve particular effects. The creative coloring is often fanciful: for example, some horses have legs in four different colors. Skin and other light-toned areas are represented by the bare linen cloth that formed the ground of the work.

C. DETAIL OF BISHOP ODO BLESSING THE FEAST, THE BAYEUX EMBROIDERY

king had in 1130, in which his subjects demanded tax relief. The artist depicts the dreams with energetic directness. On the first night, angry farmers confront the sleeping king; on the second, armed knights surround his bed; and on the third, monks, abbots, and bishops present their case. In the fourth illustration, the king travels in a storm-tossed ship and saves himself by promising God that he will rescind the tax increase for seven years. The author of the Worcester Chronicle assured his readers that this story came from a reliable source, the royal physician Grimbald, who appears in the margins next to three of the scenes. The angry farmers capture our attention today because we seldom see working men with their equipment and simple clothing depicted in painting from this time.

SACRED BOOKS

Illustrated books played a key role in the transmission of artistic styles from one region to another. Monastic scriptoria continued to be the centers of production, which increased dramatically during the twelfth century. But the scriptoria sometimes employed lay scribes and artists who traveled from place to place. In addition to the books needed for the church services, scribes produced copies of sacred texts, scholarly commentaries, visionary devotional works, lives of saints, and collections of letters and sermons.

THE CODEX COLBERTINUS.   The portrait of **ST. MATTHEW FROM THE CODEX COLBERTINUS (FIG. 15–31)** is an entirely Romanesque conception, quite different from Hiberno-Saxon and Carolingian author portraits. Like the sculptured pier figures of Silos (SEE FIG. 15–1), he stands within an architectural frame that completely surrounds him. He blesses and holds his book—rather than writing it—within the compact silhouette of his body. His dangling feet bear no weight, and his body has little sense of three-dimensionality, with solid blocks of color filling its strong outlines. The evangelist is almost part of the text—the opening lines of *Liber generationis*.

The text of Matthew's Gospel begins with a complementary block of ornament left of the evangelist. The "L" of *Liber generationis* ("The book of the generation") is a framed picture formed of plants and animals—called a historiated initial. Dogs or catlike creatures and long-necked birds twist, claw, and bite each other and themselves while, in the center, two humans—one dressed and one nude—

15-31 • ST. MATTHEW, FROM THE CODEX COLBERTINUS
c. 1100. Tempera on vellum, 7½ × 4″ (19 × 10.16 cm). Bibliothèque Nationale, Paris.

clamber up the letter. This manuscript was made in the region of Moissac at about the same time that sculptors were working on the abbey church, and the stacking of intertwined animals here recalls the outer face of the Moissac trumeau (SEE FIG. 15–23).

Hildegard of Bingen

We might expect women to have a subordinate position in the hierarchical and militaristic society of the twelfth century. On the contrary, aristocratic women took responsibility for managing estates during their male relatives' frequent absences in wars or while serving at court. And women also achieved positions of authority and influence as the heads of religious communities. Notable among them was Hildegard of Bingen (1098–1179).

Born into an aristocratic German family, Hildegard transcended the barriers that limited most medieval women. She began serving as leader of her convent in 1136, and about 1147 she founded a new convent near Bingen. Hildegard also wrote important treatises on medicine and natural science, invented an alternate alphabet, and was one of the most gifted and innovative composers of her age, writing not only motets and liturgical settings, but also a musical drama that is considered by many to be the first opera. Clearly a major, multitalented figure in the intellectual and artistic life of her time—comparison with the later Leonardo da Vinci comes to mind—she also corresponded with emperors, popes, and the powerful abbots Bernard of Clairvaux and Suger of Saint-Denis.

Following a command she claimed to have received from God in 1141, and with the assistance of her nuns and the monk Volmar, Hildegard began to record the mystical visions she had been experiencing since she was 5 years old. The resulting book, called the *Scivias* (from the Latin *scite vias lucis*, "know the ways of the light"), is filled not only with words but with striking images of the strange and wonderful visions themselves (FIG. A). The opening page (FIG. B) shows Hildegard receiving a flash of divine insight, represented by the tongues of flame encircling her head—she said, "a fiery light, flashing intensely, came from the open vault of heaven and poured through my whole brain"—while her scribe Volmar writes to her dictation. But was she also responsible for the arresting pictures that accompany the text in this book? Art historian Madeline Caviness thinks so, both because of their unconventional

A. Hildegard of Bingen
THE UNIVERSE
1927–1933 facsimile of Part I, Vision 3 of the *Liber Scivias* of Hildegard of Bingen. Original, 1150–1175.

Hildegard begins her description of this vision with these words: "After this I saw a vast instrument, round and shadowed, in the shape of an egg, small at the top, large in the middle, and narrowed at the bottom; outside it, surrounding its circumference, there was a bright fire with, as it were, a shadowy zone under it. And in that fire there was a globe of sparkling flame so great that the whole instrument was illuminated by it."

nature and because they conform in several ways to the "visionary" effects experienced by many people during migraines, which plagued Hildegard throughout her life but especially during her forties while she was composing the *Scivias*. She said of her visions, "My outward eyes are open. So I have never fallen prey to ecstacy in the visions, but I see them wide awake, day and night. And I am constantly fettered by sickness, and often in the grip of pain so intense that it threatens to kill me." (Translated in Newman, p. 16.)

Perhaps in this miniature Hildegard is using the large stylus to sketch on the wax tablets in her lap the pictures of her visions that were meant to accompany the verbal descriptions she dictates to Volmar, who sits at the right with a book in his hand, ready to write them down.

B. HILDEGARD AND VOLMAR
From a 1927–1933 facsimile of the frontispiece of the *Liber Scivias* of Hildegard of Bingen. Original, 1150–1175.

This author portrait was once part of a manuscript of Hildegard's *Scivias* that many believe was made in her own lifetime, but it was lost in World War II. Today we can study its images only from prewar black-and-white photographs or from a full-color facsimile that was lovingly hand-painted by the nuns of the Abbey of St. Hildegard in Eigingen under the direction of Joesepha Krips between 1927 and 1933, the source of both pictures reproduced here.

15-32 • The Nun Guda
BOOK OF HOMILIES
Westphalia, Germany.
Early 12th century. Ink
on parchment. Stadtund
Universitäts-Bibliothek,
Frankfurt, Germany. MS.
Barth. 42, fol. 110v

THE GERMAN NUN GUDA. In another historiated initial, this one from Westphalia in Germany, the nun Guda has a more modest presentation. In a **BOOK OF HOMILIES** (sermons), she inserted her self-portrait into the letter *D* and signed it as scribe and painter, "Guda, the sinful woman, wrote and illuminated this book" (**FIG. 15–32**). This is a simple colored drawing with darker blocks of color in the background, but Guda and her monastic sisters played an important role in the production of books in the twelfth century, and not all of them remain anonymous. Guda's image is the earliest signed self-portrait by a woman in western Europe. Throughout the Middle Ages, women were involved in the production of books as authors, scribes, painters, and patrons (see "Hildegard of Bingen," page 487).

A CISTERCIAN TREE OF JESSE. The Cistercians were particularly devoted to the Virgin Mary and are also credited with popularizing themes such as the Tree of Jesse as a device for showing her position as the last link in the genealogy connecting Jesus to King David. (Jesse, the father of King David, was an ancestor of Mary and, through her, of Jesus.) A manuscript of St. Jerome's Commentary on Isaiah, made in the scriptorium of the Cistercian mother house of Cîteaux in Burgundy about 1125, contains an image of an abbreviated **TREE OF JESSE** (**FIG. 15–33**).

A monumental Mary, with the Christ Child sitting on her veiled arm, stands over the forking branches of the tree, dwarfing the sleeping patriarch, Jesse, from whose body a small tree trunk grows. The long, vertical folds of Mary's voluminous drapery—especially the flourish at lower right, where a piece of her garment billows up, as if caught in an updraft—recall the treatment of drapery in the portal at Autun (see "A Closer Look," page 478), also from Burgundy. The manuscript artist has drawn, rather than painted, with soft colors, using subtle tints that seem somehow in keeping with Cistercian restraint. Christ embraces his mother's neck, pressing his cheek against hers in a display of tender affection that recalls Byzantine icons of the period, like the Virgin of Vladimir (SEE FIG. 7–37). The foliate form Mary holds in her hands could be a flowering sprig from the Jesse Tree, or it could be a lily symbolizing her purity.

The building held by the angel on the left equates Mary with the Church, and the crown held by the angel on the right is hers as queen of heaven. The dove above her halo represents the Holy Spirit; Jesse Trees often have doves sitting in the uppermost branches. In the early decades of the twelfth century, church doctrine came increasingly to stress the role of the Virgin Mary and the saints as intercessors who could plead for mercy on behalf of repentant sinners, and devotional images of Mary became increasingly popular during the later Romanesque period. As we will see, this popularity would continue into the Gothic period.

THINK ABOUT IT

15.1 Discuss what is meant by the term "Romanesque" and distinguish some of the key stylistic features associated with architecture in this style.

15.2 What is a pilgrimage site? How did pilgrimage sites function for medieval Christians? Ground your answer in a discussion of Santiago de Compostela (FIGS. 15–4, 15–5, 15–6), focusing on specific features that were geared towards pilgrims.

15.3 Compare and contrast two Romanesque churches from different regions of Europe. Explain the key aspects of each regional style.

15.4 Discuss the sculpture that was integrated into the exteriors of Romanesque churches. Why was it there? Whom did it address? What were the prominent messages? Make reference to at least one church discussed in this chapter.

15.5 Analyze one example of a Romanesque work of art in this chapter that tells a story of human frailty and a second work that focuses on an exemplary, holy life. Compare and contrast their styles and messages.

PRACTICE MORE: Compose answers to these questions, get flashcards for images and terms, and review chapter material with quizzes **www.myartslab.com**

15-33 • PAGE WITH THE TREE OF JESSE, EXPLANATIO IN ISAIAM (ST. JEROME'S COMMENTARY ON ISAIAH)

Abbey of Cîteaux, Burgundy, France. c. 1125. Ink and tempera on vellum, 15 × 4¾" (38 × 12 cm). Bibliothèque Municipale, Dijon, France. MS. 129, fol. 4v

16–1 • SCENES FROM GENESIS   From the Good Samaritan Window, nave aisle, Cathedral of Notre-Dame, Chartres, France. Stained and painted glass. c. 1200–1210.

GOTHIC ART OF THE TWELFTH AND THIRTEENTH CENTURIES

The Gothic style—originating in the powerful monasteries of the Paris region—dominated much of European art and architecture for 400 years. By the mid 12th century, advances in building technology, increasing financial resources, and new intellectual and spiritual aspirations led to the development of a new art and architecture that expressed the religious and political values of cloistered Christian communities. Soon bishops and rulers, as well as abbots, vied to build the largest and most elaborate churches. Just as residents of twentieth-century American cities raced to erect higher and higher skyscrapers, so too the patrons of western Europe competed during the Middle Ages in the building of cathedrals and churches with ever-taller naves and towers, diaphanous walls of glowing glass, and breathtakingly airy interiors that seemed to open in all directions.

The light captured in stained-glass windows created luminous pictures that must have captivated a faithful population whose everyday existence included little color, outside the glories of the natural world. And the light that passed through these windows transformed interior spaces into a many-colored haze. Walls, objects, and even people seemed to dissolve—dematerializing into color. Truly, Gothic churches became the glorious jeweled houses of God, evocations of the heavenly Jerusalem. They were also glowing manifestations of Christian doctrine, and invitations to faithful living, encouraging worshipers to follow in the footsteps of the saints whose lives were frequently featured in the windows of Gothic churches. Stained glass soon became the major medium of monumental painting.

This detail from the **GOOD SAMARITAN WINDOW** at Chartres Cathedral **(FIG. 16–1)**, created in the early years of the thirteenth century, well into the development of French Gothic architecture, includes scenes from Genesis, the first book of the Bible. The window portrays God's creation of Adam and Eve, and continues with their subsequent temptation, fall into sin, and expulsion from the paradise of the Garden of Eden to lead a life of work and woe. Adam and Eve's story is used here to interpret the meaning of the parable of the Good Samaritan for medieval viewers, reminding them that Christ saves them from the original sin of Adam and Eve just as the Good Samaritan saves the injured and abused traveler (SEE FIG. 16–12). The stained-glass windows of Gothic cathedrals were more than glowing walls activated by color and light; they were also luminous sermons, preached with pictures rather than with words. These radiant pictures were directed at a diverse audience of worshipers, drawn from a broad spectrum of medieval society, who derived multiple meanings from gloriously complicated works of art.

LEARN ABOUT IT

16.1 Investigate the ideas, events, and technical innovations that led to the development of Gothic architecture.

16.2 Contrast English and German styles of Gothic with their French prototypes.

16.3 Trace the development of stained glass as the major medium of monumental Gothic painting.

16.4 Appreciate how artists were able to communicate complex theological ideas in stained glass, sculpture, and illustrated books.

16.5 Analyze the relationship between the Franciscan ideals of empathy and the emotional appeals of sacred narrative painting and sculpture in Italy.

HEAR MORE: Listen to an audio file of your chapter **www.myartslab.com**

THE EMERGENCE OF THE GOTHIC STYLE

In the middle of the twelfth century, a distinctive new architecture known today as Gothic emerged in the Île-de-France, the French royal domain around Paris **(MAP 16–1)**. The appearance there of a new style and technique of building coincided with the emergence of the monarchy as a powerful centralizing force. Within 100 years, an estimated 2,700 Gothic churches, shimmering with stained glass and encrusted with sculpture, were built in the Île-de-France region alone.

Advances in building technology allowed progressively larger windows and even loftier vaults supported by more and more streamlined skeletal exterior buttressing. Soon, the Gothic style spread throughout western Europe, gradually displacing Romanesque forms while taking on regional characteristics inspired by them. Gothic prevailed until about 1400, lingering even longer in some regions. It was adapted to all types of structures, including town halls and residences, as well as Christian churches and synagogues.

The term "Gothic" was popularized by the sixteenth-century Italian artist and historian Giorgio Vasari, who disparagingly attributed the by-then-old-fashioned style to the Goths, Germanic invaders who had "destroyed" the Classical civilization of the Roman Empire that Vasari preferred. In its own day the Gothic style was simply called "modern art" or the "French style."

THE RISE OF URBAN AND INTELLECTUAL LIFE

The Gothic period was an era of both communal achievement and social change. Although Europe remained rural, towns gained increasing prominence. They became important centers of artistic patronage, fostering strong communal identity by public projects and ceremonies. Intellectual life was also stimulated by the inter-action of so many people living side by side. Universities in Bologna, Padua, Paris, Cambridge, and Oxford supplanted monastic

MAP 16–1 • EUROPE IN THE GOTHIC ERA

The color changes on this map chart the gradual expansion of territory ruled by the king of France during the period when Gothic was developing as a modern French style.

Abbot Suger on the Value of Art in Monasteries

Suger, who masterminded the reconstruction of the abbey church at Saint-Denis while he was its abbot (1122–1151), weighed in on the twelfth-century monastic debate concerning the appropriateness of elaborate art in monasteries (see "St. Bernard and Theophilus," page 464) both through the magnificence of the new church he built and by the way he described and discussed the project in the account he wrote of his administration of the abbey.

These are his comments on the bronze doors (destroyed in 1794):

Bronze casters having been summoned and sculptors chosen, we set up the main doors on which are represented the Passion of the Saviour and His Resurrection, or rather Ascension, with great cost and much expenditure for their gilding as was fitting for the noble porch…

The verses on the door are these:

Whoever thou art, if thou seekest to extol the glory of these doors,
Marvel not at the gold and the expense but at the craftsmanship of the work,
Bright is the noble work; but being nobly bright, the work
Should lighten the minds, so that they may travel, through the true lights,
To the True Light where Christ is the true door,
In what manner it be inherent in this world the golden door defines:
The dull mind rises to truth through that which is material
And, in seeing this light, is resurrected from its former subversion.

On the lintel, just under the large figure of Christ at the Last Judgment on the tympanum, Suger had inscribed:

Receive, O stern Judge, the prayers of Thy Suger; grant that I be mercifully numbered among Thy own sheep.

(Translations from Panofsky, pp. 47, 49)

EXPLORE MORE: Gain insight from another primary source by Abbot Suger **www.myartslab.com**

and cathedral schools as centers of learning. Brilliant teachers like Peter Abelard (1079–1142) drew crowds of students, and in the thirteenth century an Italian theologian, Thomas Aquinas (1225–1274), made Paris the intellectual center of Europe.

A system of reasoned analysis known as scholasticism emerged from these universities, intent on reconciling Christian theology with Classical philosophy. Scholastic thinkers used a question-and-answer method of argument and arranged their ideas into logical outlines. Thomas Aquinas, the foremost Scholastic, applied Aristotelian logic to comprehend religion's supernatural aspects, setting up the foundation on which Catholic thought rests to this day. Some have seen a relationship between the development of these new ways of thinking and the geometrical order that permeates the design of Gothic cathedrals, as well as with the new interest in describing the appearance of the natural world in sculpture and painting.

THE AGE OF CATHEDRALS

Urban cathedrals, the seats of the ruling bishops, superseded rural monasteries as centers of religious culture and patronage. So many cathedrals were rebuilt between 1150 and 1400—often to replace earlier churches destroyed in the fires that were an unfortunate byproduct of population growth and housing density within cities—that some have dubbed the period the "Age of Cathedrals." Cathedral precincts functioned almost as towns within towns—containing a palace for the bishop, housing for the clergy, and workshops for the multitude of artists and laborers necessary to support building campaigns. These gigantic churches certainly dominated their urban surroundings. But even if their grandeur inspired admiration, their enormous expense and some bishops' intrusive displays of power inspired resentment, even urban rioting.

GOTHIC ART IN FRANCE

The invention and initial flowering of the Gothic style in France took place against the backdrop of the growing power of the Capetian monarchy. Louis VII (r. 1137–1180) and Philip Augustus (r. 1180–1223) consolidated royal authority in the Île-de-France and began to exert more control over powerful nobles in other regions. Louis VII's queen, Eleanor of Aquitaine, brought southwestern France into the royal domain, but when their marriage was annulled, Eleanor reclaimed her lands and married Henry Plantagenet—count of Anjou, duke of Normandy—who became King Henry II of England. The resulting tangle of conflicting claims kept France and England at odds for centuries.

As French kings continued to consolidate royal authority and to increase their domains and privileges, they also sparked a building boom with the growing centralization of their government in Paris, which developed from a small provincial town into a thriving urban center beginning in the middle of the twelfth century. Concentrated architectural activity in the capital may have provided the impetus—or perhaps simply the opportunity—for the developments in architectural technology and the new ways of planning and thinking about buildings that ultimately led to the birth of a new style.

THE BIRTH OF GOTHIC
AT THE ABBEY CHURCH OF SAINT-DENIS

The first Gothic building was the church of the Benedictine abbey of Saint-Denis, just north of Paris. This monastery had been founded in the fifth century over the tomb of St. Denis, the Early Christian martyr who had been sent from Rome to convert the local pagan population and was considered the first bishop of Paris. Early on, the abbey developed special royal significance. It housed tombs of the kings of France, the regalia of the French crown, and the relics of St. Denis, patron saint of France.

Construction began in the 1130s of a new church that was to replace the early medieval church at the abbey, under the supervision of Abbot Suger (abbot 1122–1151). In a written account of his administration of the abbey, Suger discusses the building of the church, a rare first-hand chronicle and justification of a medieval building program. Suger prized magnificence, precious materials, and especially fine workmanship (see "Abbot Suger on the Value of Art in Monasteries," page 493). He invited an international team of masons, sculptors, metalworkers, and glass painters, making this building site a major center of artistic exchange. Such a massive undertaking was extraordinarily expensive. The abbey received substantial annual revenues from the town's inhabitants, and Suger was not above forging documents to increase the abbey's landholdings, which constituted its principal source of income.

Suger began building c. 1135, with a new west façade and narthex attached to the old church, but it was in the new choir—completed in three years and three months between July 13, 1140, and June 14, 1144—where the fully formed Gothic architectural style first appeared. In his account of the reconstruction, Suger argues that that older building was inadequate to accommodate the crowds of pilgrims who arrived on feast days to venerate the body of St. Denis, and too modest to express the importance of the saint himself. In working with builders to conceive a radically new church design, he turned for inspiration to texts that were attributed erroneously to a follower of St. Paul named Dionysius (the Greek form of Denis), who considered radiant light a physical manifestation of God. Through the centuries, this Pseudo-Dionysius

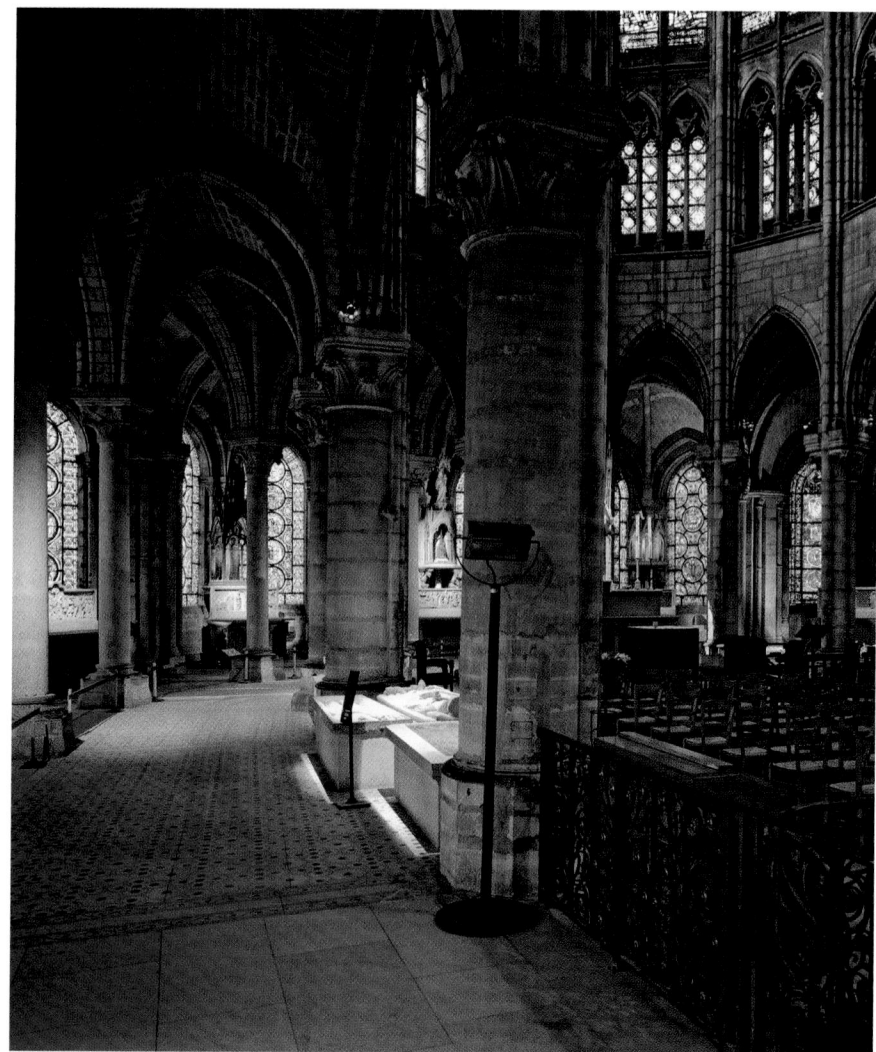

16-3 • AMBULATORY AND APSE CHAPELS OF THE ABBEY CHURCH OF SAINT-DENIS
France. 1140–1144.

Envisioning the completion of the abbey church with a transept, and presumably also a nave, Abbot Suger had the following inscription placed in the church to commemorate the 1144 dedication of the choir: "Once the new rear part is joined to the part in front, the church shines with its middle part brightened. For bright is that which is brightly coupled with the bright, and bright is the noble edifice which is pervaded by the new light." (Panofsky, p. 51).

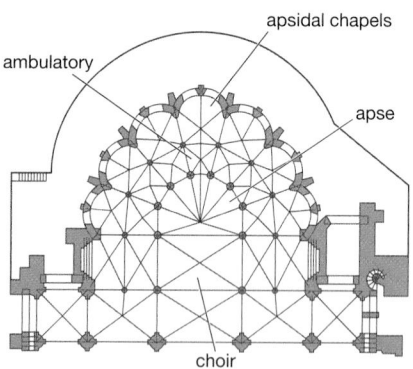

16-2 • PLAN OF THE CHOIR OF THE ABBEY CHURCH OF SAINT-DENIS
France. 1140–1144.

An important innovation of Romanesque and Gothic builders was **rib vaulting**. Rib vaults are a form of groin vault (see "Roman Vaulting," page 188), in which the diagonal ridges (groins) rest on and are covered by curved moldings called ribs. After the walls and piers of the building reached the desired height, timber scaffolding to support these masonry ribs was constructed. When the mortar of the ribs was set, the web of the vault was then laid on forms built on the ribs themselves. After all the temporary forms were removed, the ribs may have provided strength at the intersections of the webbing to channel the vaults' thrust outward and downward to the foundations; they certainly add decorative interest. In short, ribs formed the "skeleton" of the vault; the webbing, a lighter masonry "skin." In Late Gothic buildings, additional, decorative ribs give vaults a lacelike appearance.

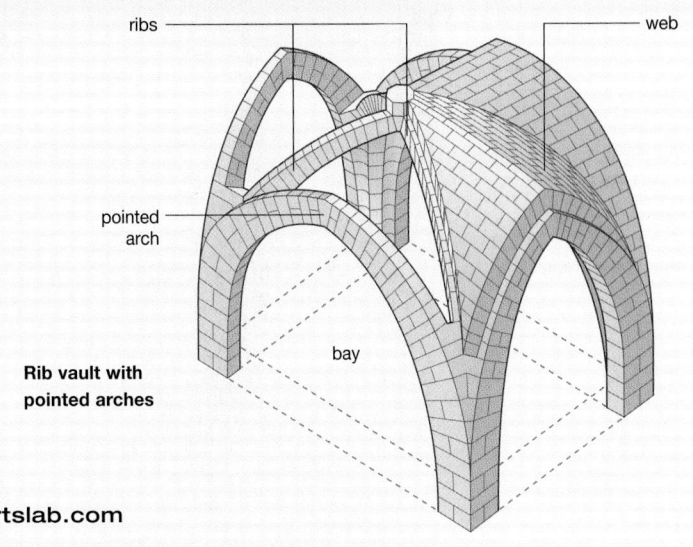

Rib vault with pointed arches

SEE MORE: View a simulation about rib vaulting **www.myartslab.com**

also became identified with the martyred Denis whose body was venerated at the abbey, so Suger was adapting what he believed was the patron saint's concept of divine luminosity in designing the new abbey church with walls composed essentially of stained-glass windows. In inscriptions he composed for the bronze doors (now lost), he was specific about the motivations for the church's new architectural style: "being nobly bright, the work should lighten the minds, so that they may travel, through the true lights, to the True Light where Christ is the true door" (Panofsky, p. 49).

The **PLAN OF THE CHOIR (FIG. 16–2)** retains key features of the Romanesque pilgrimage church (SEE FIG. 15–6), with a semi-circular apse surrounded by an ambulatory, around which radiate seven chapels of uniform size. And the structural elements of the choir had already appeared in Romanesque buildings, including pointed arches, ribbed groin vaults, and external buttressing that relieves stress on the walls. The most dramatic achievement of Suger's builders was the coordinated use of these features to create an architectural whole that emphasized open, flowing space, enclosed by non-load-bearing walls of colorful, glowing stained glass **(FIG. 16–3)**. As Suger himself put it, the church becomes "a circular string of chapels by virtue of which the whole would shine with the wonderful and uninterrupted light of most luminous windows, pervading the interior beauty" (Panofsky, p. 101). And since Suger saw the contemplation of light as a means of illuminating the soul and uniting it with God, he was providing his monks with an environment especially conducive to their primary vocation of prayer and meditation.

The revolutionary stained-glass windows of Suger's Saint-Denis were almost lost in the wake of the French Revolution, when this royal abbey represented everything the new leaders were intent on suppressing. Thanks to an enterprising antiquarian named Alexandre Lenoir, however, the twelfth-century windows,

though removed from their architectural setting, were saved from destruction. During the nineteenth century, parts of them returned to the abbey, but many panels are now in museums. One of the best-preserved panels—from a window that narrated Jesus' childhood—portrays **THE FLIGHT INTO EGYPT (FIG. 16–4)**. The crisp elegance of the delineation of faces, foliage, and drapery—painted with vitreous enamel on the vibrantly colored pieces of glass that make up the panel (see "Stained-Glass Windows," page 497)—is almost as clear today as it was when the windows were new. One unusual detail—the Virgin reaching to pick a date from a palm tree that has bent down at the infant Jesus' command to accommodate her hungry grasp—is based on an apocryphal Gospel that was not included in the canonical Christian scriptures but that was a very popular source for twelfth-century artists.

Louis VII and Eleanor of Aquitaine attended the consecration of the new choir in June 1144, along with a constellation of secular and sacred dignitaries. Since the bishops and archbishops of France were assembled at the consecration—celebrating Mass simultaneously at altars throughout the choir and crypt—they had the opportunity to experience firsthand this new Gothic style of building. The history of French architecture over the next few centuries indicates that they were quite impressed.

GOTHIC CATHEDRALS

The abbey church of Saint-Denis became the prototype for a new architecture of space and light based on a highly adaptable skeletal framework that supported rib vaulting on the points of slender piers—rather than massive Romanesque walls—reinforced by external buttress systems. It initiated a period of competitive experimentation in France that resulted in ever-larger churches—principally cathedrals—enclosing increasingly taller interior spaces, walled with ever-greater expanses of stained glass.

16-4 • THE FLIGHT INTO EGYPT
From the Incarnation (Infancy of Christ) Window, axial choir chapel, abbey church of Saint-Denis, c. 1140–1144.
The Glencairn Museum, Bryn Athyn, Pennsylvania.

THE CATHEDRAL OF NOTRE-DAME IN PARIS. The **CATHEDRAL OF NOTRE-DAME** ("Our Lady," the Virgin Mary) in Paris—known today simply as Notre-Dame—bridges the period between Abbot Suger's rebuilding of his abbey church and the High Gothic cathedrals of the thirteenth century (FIG. 16–5). The building was begun in the 1160s with the choir, and it was essentially complete by the middle of the thirteenth century with the achievement of the façade. To increase the window size and secure the soaring 115-foot-high vault, builders here employed the first true flying buttresses, probably during the 1180s. The **flying buttress**, a gracefully arched, skeletal exterior support, counters the lateral thrust of the nave vault and transfers its weight outward, over the side aisles, where it is resolved into and supported by a vertical external buttress, rising from the ground. During the thirteenth century, builders modernized Notre-Dame by reworking the two upper levels into the large clerestory windows we see today. The huge, spiderlike flying buttress system visible to modern visitors is

the result of even later remodeling. The original flying buttresses were more modest quadrant arches, but they represented a structural innovation that would become central to the future development of Gothic architecture.

THE CATHEDRAL OF NOTRE-DAME IN CHARTRES. The new conceptions of space and wall, and the structural techniques that made them possible, initiated at Saint-Denis and expanded at Notre-Dame in Paris, were developed further at Chartres. The great cathedral dominates this town southwest of Paris and, for many people, is a near-perfect embodiment of the Gothic style in stone and glass. Constructed in several stages beginning in the mid twelfth century and extending into the mid thirteenth, with additions such as the north spire as late as the sixteenth century, Chartres Cathedral reflects the transition from an experimental twelfth-century architecture to a mature thirteenth-century style.

TECHNIQUE | Stained-Glass Windows

The "wonderful and uninterrupted light" that Suger sought in the reconstruction of the choir of Saint-Denis in the 1140s was provided by stained-glass artists that—as he tells us—he called in from many nations to create glowing walls for the radiating chapels, perhaps the clerestory as well. As a result of their exquisite work, this influential building program not only constituted a new architectural style; it catapulted what had been a minor curiosity among pictorial techniques into the major medium of monumental European painting. For several centuries, stained glass would be integral to architectural design, not decoration added subsequently to a completed building. Windows were produced at the same time as masons were building walls and carving capitals and moldings.

Our knowledge about the medieval art of stained glass is based on a precious twelfth-century text—*De Diversis Artibus (On the Various Arts)*—written by a German monk who called himself Theophilus Presbyter (see "St. Bernard and Theophilus," page 464). In fact, the basic procedures of producing a stained-glass window have changed little since the Middle Ages. It is not a lost art, but it is a complex and costly process. The glass itself was made by bringing sand and ash to the molten state under intense heat, and "staining" it with color through the addition of metallic oxides. This molten material was then blown and flattened into sheets. Using a **cartoon** (full-scale drawing) painted on a whitewashed board as a guide, the glass painter would cut from these sheets the individual shapes of color that would make up a figural scene or ornamental passage. This was done with a hot iron that would crack the glass into a rough approximation that could be refined by chipping away at the edges carefully with an iron tool—a process called **grozing**—to achieve the precise shape needed in the composition.

The artists used a vitreous paint (made, Theophilus tells us, of iron filings and ground glass suspended in wine or urine) at full strength to block light and delineate features such as facial expressions or drapery folds. It could also be diluted to create modeling washes. Once painted, the pieces of glass would be fired in a kiln to fuse the painting with the glass surface. Only then did the artists assemble these shapes of color—like pieces of a complex compositional puzzle—with strips of lead (called **cames**), and subsequently mount a series of these individual panels on an iron framework within the architectural opening to form an ensemble we call a stained-glass window. Lead was used in the assembly process because it was strong enough to hold the glass pieces together but flexible enough to bend around their complex shapes and—perhaps more critically—to absorb the impact from gusts of wind and prevent the glass itself from cracking under pressure.

16–5 • CATHEDRAL OF NOTRE-DAME, PARIS
Begun 1163; choir chapels, 1270s; crossing spire, 19th-century. View from the south.

For all its spiritual and technological glory, Notre-Dame barely survived the French Revolution. The revolutionaries decapitated the statues associated with deposed nobility and their "superstitious" religion, and transformed the cathedral into a secular "Temple of Reason" (1793–1795). But it would not be long until Notre-Dame was returned to religious use. Napoleon crowned himself emperor at its altar in 1804, and Parisians gathered there to celebrate the liberation of Paris from the Nazis in August 1944. Today, boats filled with tourists glide under bridges that link the island where the cathedral stands with the Left Bank, the traditional students' and artists' quarter. Notre-Dame so resonates with the life and history of the city that it has become more than a house of worship and work of art; it is a symbol of Paris itself.

SEE MORE: View panoramas of the Cathedral of Notre-Dame, Paris **www.myartslab.com**

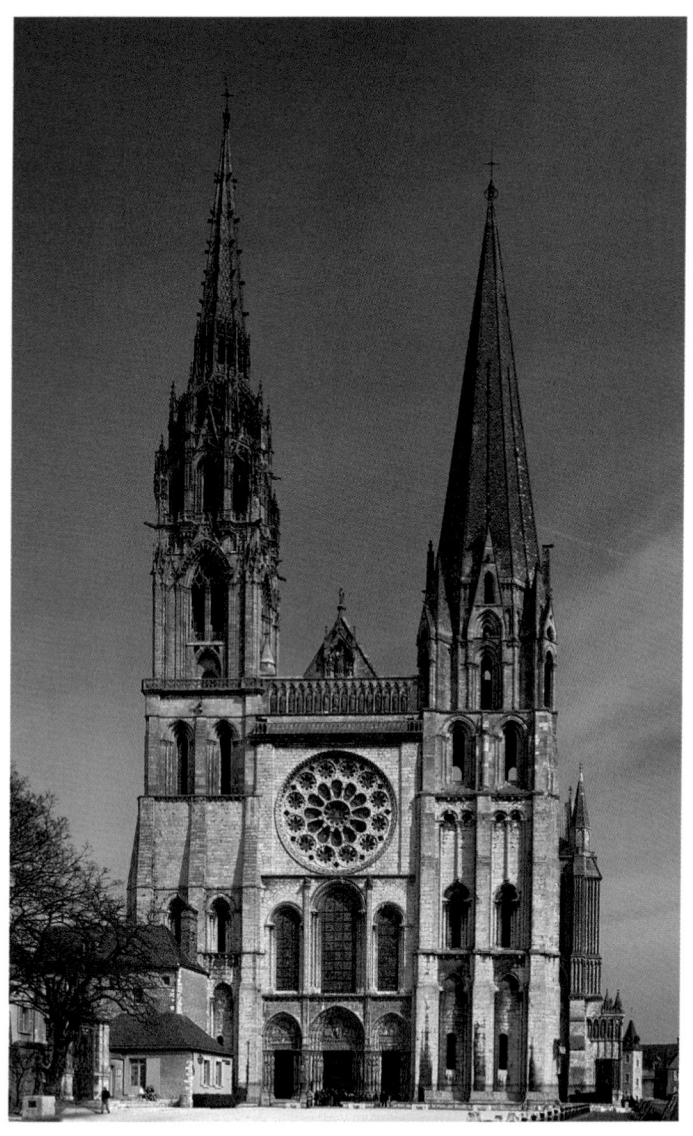

16-6 • WEST FAÇADE, CHARTRES CATHEDRAL
(THE CATHEDRAL OF NOTRE-DAME)
France. West façade begun c. 1134; cathedral rebuilt after
a fire in 1194; building continued to 1260; north spire 1507–1513.

SEE MORE: View panoramas of Chartres Cathedral
www.myartslab.com

Chartres was the site of a pre-Christian virgin-goddess cult, and later, dedicated to the Virgin Mary, it became one of the oldest and most important Christian shrines in France. Its main treasure was a piece of linen believed to have been worn by the Virgin Mary when she gave birth to Jesus. This relic was a gift from the Byzantine empress Irene to Charlemagne, whose grandson Charles the Bald donated it to Chartres in 876. It was kept below the high altar in a huge basement crypt. The healing powers attributed to the cloth made Chartres a major pilgrimage destination, especially as the cult of the Virgin grew in popularity in the twelfth and thirteenth centuries. Its association with important market fairs—especially cloth markets—held at Chartres on the feast days of the Virgin put the textile relic at the intersection of local prestige and the local economy, increasing the income of the cathedral not only through pilgrimage but also through tax revenue it received from the markets.

The west façade of Chartres preserves an early sculptural program created within a decade of the reconstruction of Saint-Denis (FIG. 16–6). Surrounding these three doors—the so-called Royal Portal, used not by the general public but only for important ceremonial entrances of the bishop and his retinue—sculpted figures calmly and comfortably fill their architectural settings. On the central tympanum, Christ is enthroned in majesty, returning at the end of time surrounded by the four evangelists (FIG. 16–7).

16-7 • ROYAL PORTAL, WEST FAÇADE, CHARTRES CATHEDRAL
c. 1145–1155.

EXPLORE MORE:
Gain insight from a primary source related to the building of Chartres Cathedral
www.myartslab.com

Most large Gothic churches in western Europe were built on the Latin cross plan, with a projecting transept marking the transition from nave to choir, an arrangement that derives ultimately from the fourth-century, Constantinian basilica of Old St. Peter's (see page 228, FIG. A). The main entrance portal was generally on the west, with the choir and its apse on the east. A western narthex could precede the entrance to the nave and side aisles. An ambulatory with radiating chapels circled the apse and facilitated the movement of worshipers through the church. Many Gothic churches have a three-story elevation, with a triforium sandwiched between the nave arcade and a glazed clerestory. Rib vaulting usually covered all spaces. **Flying buttresses** helped support the soaring nave vaults by transferring their outward thrust over the

aisles to massive, free-standing, upright external buttresses. Church walls were decorated inside and out with arcades of round or pointed arches, engaged columns and colonnettes, an applied filigree of tracery, and horizontal moldings called **stringcourses**. The pitched roofs above the vaults—necessary to evacuate rainwater from the building—were supported by wooden frameworks. A spire or crossing tower above the junction of the transept and nave was usually planned, though often never finished. Portal façades were also customarily marked by high, flanking towers or gabled porches ornamented with **pinnacles** and finials. Architectural sculpture proliferated on each portal's tympanum, archivolts, and jambs, and in France a magnificent rose window typically formed the centerpiece of the flat portal façades.

Schematic drawing of Chartres Cathedral

Although imposing, he seems more serene and more human than in the hieratic and stylized portrayal of the same subject at Moissac (SEE FIG. 15–22). The apostles, organized into four groups of three fill the lintel, and the 24 Elders of the Apocalypse line the archivolts.

The right portal is dedicated to the Incarnation (God's first earthly appearance), highlighting the role of Mary in the early life of Christ, from the Annunciation to the Presentation in the Temple. On the left portal is the Ascension (the Incarnate God's return from earth to heaven). Jesus floats heavenward in a cloud, supported by angels. Running across all three portals, historiated capitals, on the top of the jambs just underneath the level of the lintels, depict Jesus' life on Earth in a series of small, lively narrative scenes.

Flanking all three openings on the jambs are serenely calm column statues (FIG. 16–8)—kings, queens, and prophets from the Hebrew Bible, evocations of Christ's royal and spiritual ancestry, as well as a reminder of the close ties between the Church and the French royal house. The prominence of kings and queens here is what has given the Royal Portal its name. The elegantly elongated proportions and linear, but lifelike, drapery of these column statues echo the cylindrical shafts behind them. Their meticulously carved, idealized heads radiate a sense of beatified calm. In fact, tranquility and order prevail in the overall design as well as in the individual components of this portal, a striking contrast to the dynamic configurations and energized figures on the portals of Romanesque churches.

The bulk of Chartres Cathedral was constructed after a fire in 1194 destroyed an earlier Romanesque church but spared the Royal Portal, the windows above it, and the crypt with its precious relics. A papal representative convinced reluctant local church officials to rebuild. He argued that the Virgin had permitted the fire because she wanted a new and more beautiful church to be built in her honor. Between 1194 and about 1260 that new cathedral was built (see "The Gothic Church," page 499).

Such a project required vast resources—money, raw materials, and skilled labor (see "Master Masons," opposite). A contemporary painting shows a building site with the masons at work (FIG. 16–9). Carpenters have built scaffolds, platforms, and a lifting machine. Master stonecutters measure and cut the stones; workers carry and hoist the blocks by hand or with a lifting wheel. Thousands of stone had to be accurately cut and placed. In the illustration a laborer carries mortar up a ladder to men working on the top of the wall, where the lifting wheel delivers cut stones. To support this work, the bishop and cathedral officials usually pledged all

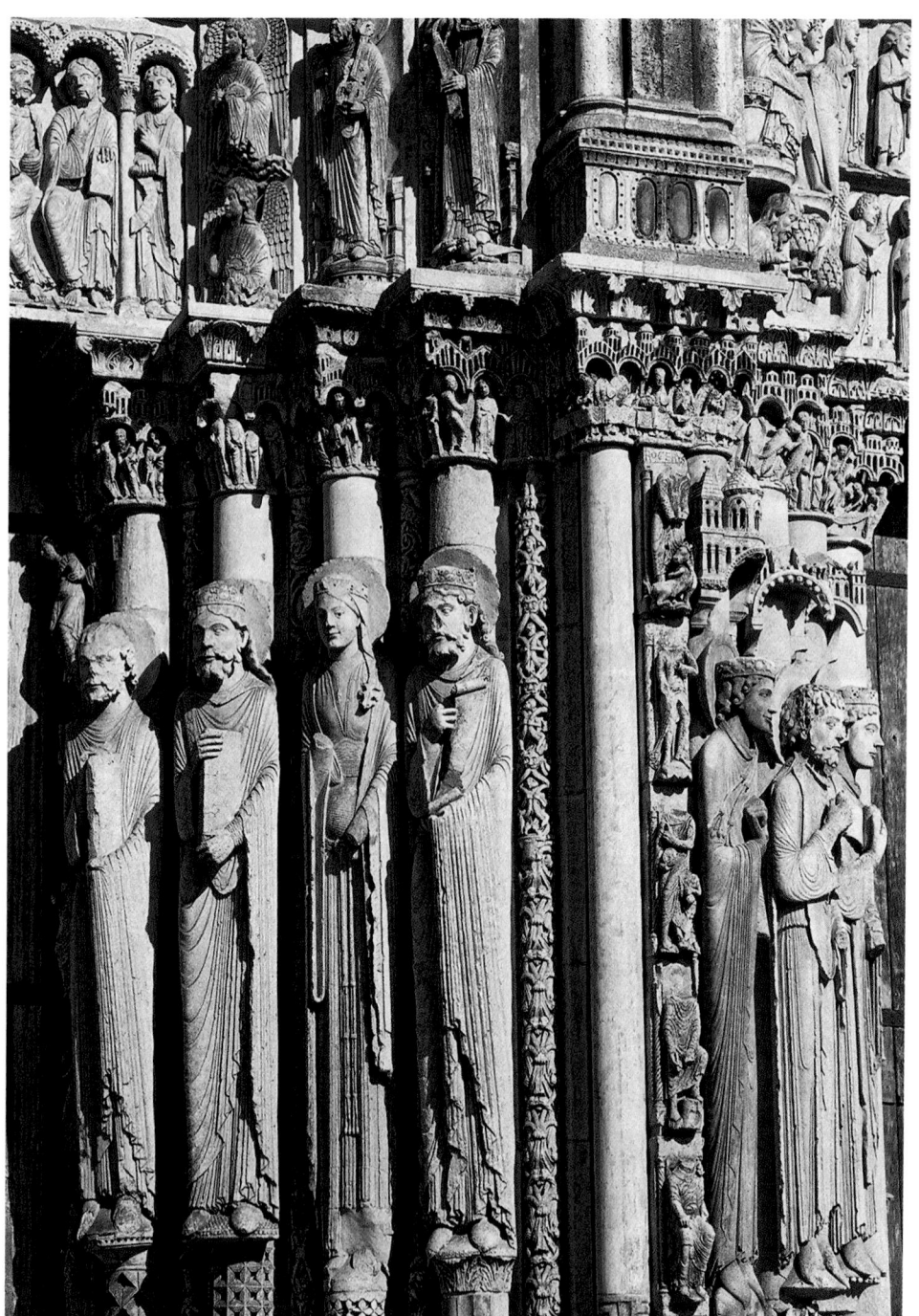

16-8 • ROYAL PORTAL, WEST FAÇADE, CHARTRES CATHEDRAL

Detail: prophets and ancestors of Christ (kings and queens of Judea). Right side, Central Portal. c. 1145–1155.

Master Masons

Master masons oversaw all aspects of church construction in the Middle Ages, from design and structural engineering to construction and decoration. The master mason at Chartres coordinated the work of roughly 400 people scattered, with their equipment and supplies, across many locations, from distant stone quarries to high scaffolding. It has been estimated that this workforce set in place some 200 blocks of stone each day.

Funding shortages and technical delays, such as the need to let mortar harden for three to six months, made construction sporadic, so master masons and their crews moved constantly from job to job, with several masters and many teams of masons often contributing to the construction of a single building. Fewer than 100 master builders are estimated to have been responsible for all the major architectural projects around Paris during the century-long building boom there, some of them working on parts of as many as 40 churches. This was dangerous work. Masons were always at risk of injury, which could cut short a career in its prime. King Louis IX of France actually provided sick pay to a mason injured in the construction of Royaumont Abbey in 1234, but not all workers were this lucky. Master mason William of Sens, who supervised construction at Canterbury Cathedral, fell from a scaffold. His grave injuries forced him to return to France in 1178 because of his inability to work. Evidence suggests that some medieval contracts had pension arrangements or provisions that took potential injury or illness into account, but some did not.

Today the names of more than 3,000 master masons are known to us, and the close study of differences in construction techniques often discloses the participation of specific masters. Master masons gained in prestige during the thirteenth century as they increasingly differentiated themselves from the laborers they supervised. In some cases their names were prominently inscribed in the labyrinths on cathedral floors. From the thirteenth century on, in what was then an exceptional honor, masters were buried, along with patrons and bishops, in the cathedrals they built.

or part of their incomes for three to five, even ten years. Royal and aristocratic patrons joined in the effort. In an ingenious scheme that seems very modern, the churchmen at Chartres solicited contributions by sending the cathedral relics, including the Virgin's tunic, on tour as far away as England.

As the new structure rose higher during the 1220s, the work grew more costly and funds dwindled. But when the bishop and the cathedral clergy tried to make up the deficit by raising feudal and commercial taxes, the townspeople drove them into exile for four years. This action in Chartres was not unique; people often opposed the building of cathedrals because of the burden of new taxes. The economic privileges claimed by the Church for the cathedral sparked intermittent uprisings by townspeople and the local nobility throughout the thirteenth century.

Building on the principles pioneered at Saint-Denis—a glass-filled masonry skeleton enclosing a large open space—the masons at Chartres erected a church over 45 feet wide with vaults that soar approximately 120 feet above the floor. As at Saint-Denis, the plan is rooted in the Romanesque

16-9 • MASONS AT WORK
Detail of a miniature from a Picture Bible made in Paris during the 1240s. Pierpont Morgan Library, New York. Ms. M638, fol. 3r

chapels

ambulatory

apse

choir

porch — transept — crossing — transept — porch

side aisle — nave — side aisle

narthex

west portal

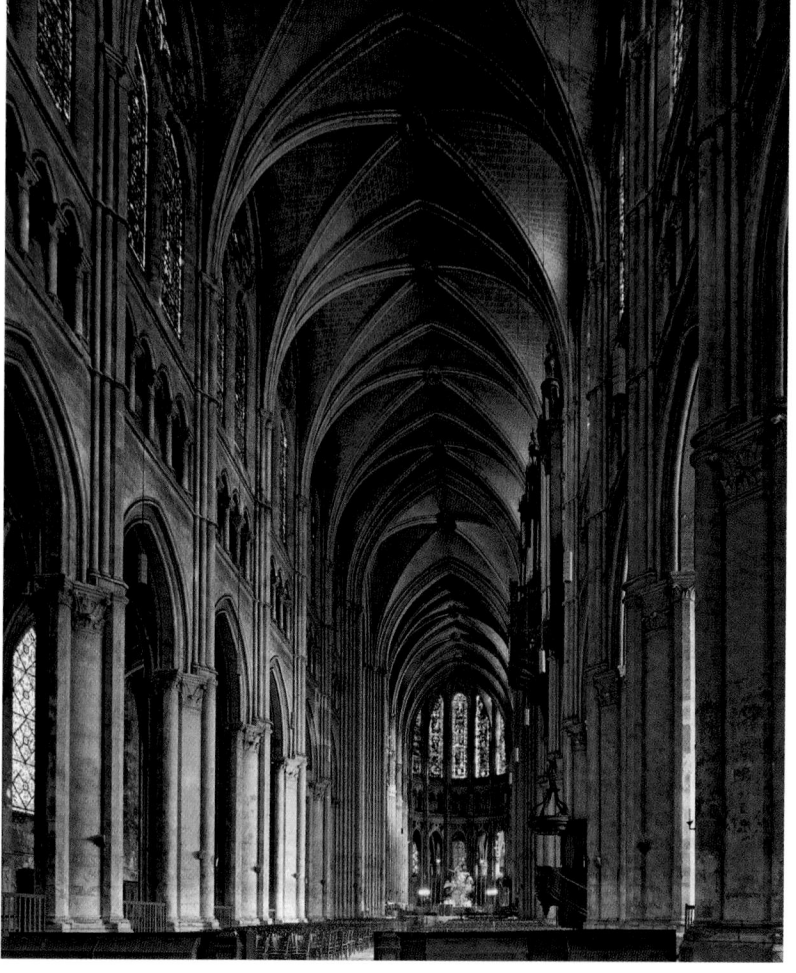

pilgrimage plan, but with a significantly enlarged sanctuary occupying a full third of the building (**FIG. 16–10**). The Chartres builders codified what were to become the typical Gothic structural devices: pointed arches and ribbed groin vaults rising from compound piers over rectangular bays, supported by exterior flying buttresses (**FIG. 16–11**). The skillful use of the newly discovered flying buttress system permitted much larger clerestory windows, nearly equal in height to the nave arcade; the band between upper and lower stories was now occupied by a **triforium** (arcaded wall passageway) rather than a tall gallery. The alternating heavy and light piers typical of Romanesque naves such as those at Speyer and Durham cathedrals (SEE FIGS. 15–16, 15–18) become a very subtle alternation at Chartres between round and octagonal compound pier cores.

In Romanesque churches, worshipers are mainly drawn forward toward the apse, which is often more brilliantly illuminated than the nave. But at Chartres, visitors are drawn upward as well, to the glowing clerestory windows flanking the soaring vaults. The large and luminous clerestory is formed by paired **lancets** (tall openings with pointed tops), surmounted by small circular rose windows. The technique used is known as **plate tracery**—holes are cut into the stone wall and nearly half the wall surface is filled with stained glass.

Chartres is unusual among French Gothic buildings in that most of its stained-glass windows have survived. Stained glass is an enormously expensive and complicated medium of painting, but its effect on the senses and emotions made the effort worthwhile for medieval patrons and builders. By 1260, glass painters had installed about 22,000 square feet of stained glass in 176 windows (see "Stained-Glass Windows," page 497). Most of the glass dates from between about 1200 and 1250, but a few earlier windows, from the 1150s—comparable in style to the windows of Suger's Saint-Denis—survived the fire of 1194 and were maintained in the west wall above the Royal Portal.

In the aisles and chapels, where the windows were low enough to be easily seen, were elaborate multiscene narratives, with small figures composed into individual episodes within the irregularly shaped compartments of windows designed as stacked medallions set against dense, multicolored fields of ornament. Art historians refer to these as cluster medallion windows. The **GOOD SAMARITAN WINDOW**

16–11 • NAVE, CHARTRES CATHEDRAL
c. 1194–1220.

of c. 1200–1210 in the nave aisle is a typical example of the design **(FIG. 16–12)**. Its learned allegory on sin and salvation also typifies the complexity of Gothic narrative art.

The principal subject is a parable Jesus told his followers to teach a moral truth (Luke 10:25–37). The protagonist is a traveling Samaritan who cares for a stranger, beaten, robbed, and left for dead by thieves on the side of a road. Jesus' parable is an allegory for his imminent redemption of humanity's sins, and within this window a story from Genesis is juxtaposed with the parable to underscore that association (SEE FIG. 16–1). Adam and Eve's fall introduced sin into the world, but Christ (the Good Samaritan) rescues humanity (the traveler) from sin (the thieves) and ministers to them within the Church, just as the Good Samaritan takes the wounded traveler for refuge and healing to an inn (bottom scene, FIG. 16–1). Stylistically, these willowy, expressive figures avoid the classicizing stockiness in Wiligelmo's folksy Romanesque rendering of the Genesis narrative at Modena (SEE FIG. 15–21). Instead they take the dancelike postures that will come to characterize Gothic figures as the style spreads across Europe in ensuing centuries.

In the clerestory windows, the Chartres glaziers mainly used not multiscene narratives, but large-scale single figures that could be seen at a distance because of their size, bold drawing, and strong colors. Iconic ensembles were easier to "read" in lofty openings more removed from viewers, such as the huge north transept rose window (over 42 feet in diameter) with five lancets beneath it **(FIG. 16–13)**, which proclaims the royal and priestly heritage of Mary and Jesus, and through them of the Church itself. In the central lancet, St. Anne holds her daughter, the baby Mary, flanked left to right by statuesque figures of Hebrew Bible leaders Melchizedek, David, Solomon, and Aaron. Above, in the very center of the rose window itself, Mary and Jesus are enthroned, surrounded by a radiating array of doves, angels, and kings and prophets from the Hebrew Bible.

This vast wall of glass was a gift from the young King Louis IX (r. 1226–1270), perhaps arranged by his powerful mother, Queen Blanche of Castile (1188–1252), who ruled as regent 1226–1234 during Louis's minority. Royal heraldic emblems secure the window's association with the king. The arms of France—golden *fleurs-de-lis* on a blue ground—fill a prominent shield under St. Anne at the bottom of the central lancet. *Fleurs-de-lis* also appear in the graduated lancets bracketing the base of the rose window and in a series of **quatrefoils** (four-lobed designs) within the rose itself. But also prominent is the Castilian device of golden castles on a red ground, a reference to the royal lineage of Louis' powerful

16–12 • GOOD SAMARITAN WINDOW
South nave aisle, Chartres Cathedral. Stained and painted glass.
c. 1200–1210.

SEE MORE: View a video about the stained glass at
Chartres Cathedral **www.myartslab.com**

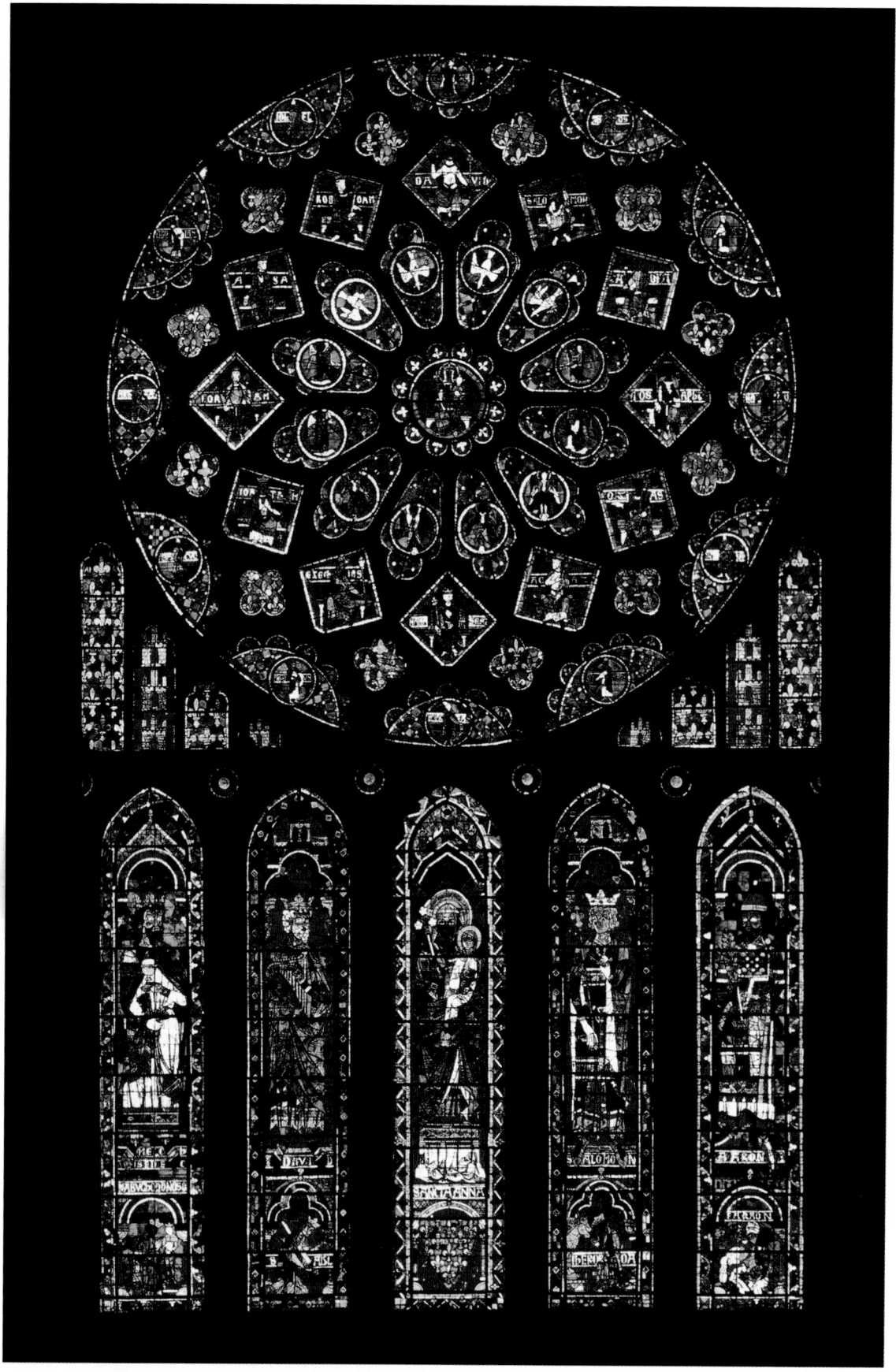

16-13 • ROSE WINDOW AND LANCETS, NORTH TRANSEPT, CHARTRES CATHEDRAL
France. Stained and painted glass. c. 1230–1235.

EXPLORE MORE: Gain insight from a primary source related to the stained glass at Chartres Cathedral www.myartslab.com

mother. Light radiating from the deep blues and reds creates a hazy purple atmosphere in the soft light of the north side of the building. On a sunny day the masonry may seem to dissolve in color, but the bold theological and political messages of the rose window remain clear.

THE CATHEDRAL OF NOTRE-DAME IN REIMS.   Reims Cathedral, northeast of Paris in the region of Champagne, was the coronation church of the kings of France and, like Saint-Denis, had been a cultural and educational center since Carolingian times. When, in 1210, fire destroyed this historic building, the community at Reims began to erect a new Gothic structure, planned as a large basilica **(FIG. 16–14)** similar to the model set earlier at the Cathedral of Chartres (SEE FIG. 16–10), only at Reims priority is given to an extended nave rather than an expanded choir, perhaps a reference to the processional emphasis of the coronation ceremony. The cornerstone of the cathedral was laid in 1211, and work continued throughout the century. The expense of the project sparked such local opposition that twice in the 1230s revolts drove the archbishop and canons into exile. At Reims, five master masons directed the work on the cathedral over the course of a century— Jean d'Orbais, Jean le Loup, Gaucher de Reims, Bernard de Soissons, and Robert de Coucy.

The west front of the Cathedral of Reims is a magnificent ensemble, in which almost every square inch of stone surface seems encrusted with sculptural decoration **(FIG. 16–15)**. Its tall gabled portals form a broad horizontal base and project forward to display an expanse of sculpture, while the tympana they enclose

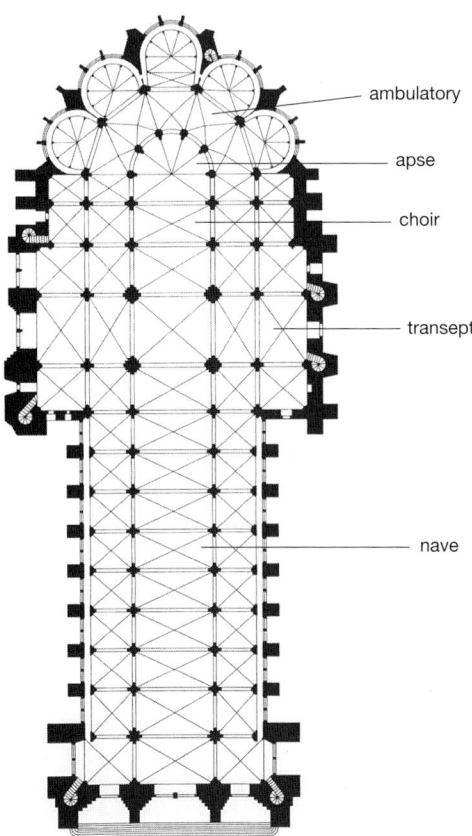

16-14 • PLAN, CATHEDRAL OF
NOTRE-DAME, REIMS
France. Begun in 1211.

16-15 • WEST FAÇADE, CATHEDRAL
OF NOTRE-DAME, REIMS
France. Rebuilding begun 1211; façade begun
c. 1225; to the height of rose window by 1260;
finished for the coronation of Philip the Fair in
1286; towers left unfinished 1311; additional work
1406–1428.

SEE MORE: View panoramas of Reims
Cathedral **www.myartslab.com**

are filled with stained-glass windows rather than stone carvings. Their soaring peaks—the middle one reaching to the center of the dominating rose window—unify the façade vertically. In a departure from tradition, Mary rather than Christ is featured in the central portal, a reflection of the growing popularity of her cult. Christ crowns her as queen of heaven in the central gable. The towers were later additions, as was the row of carved figures that runs from the base of one tower to the other above the rose window. This "gallery of kings" is the only strictly horizontal element of the façade.

The sheer magnitude of sculpture envisioned for this elaborate cathedral front required the skills of many sculptors, working in an impressive variety of styles over several decades. Four figures from the right jamb of the central portal illustrate the rich stylistic diversity **(FIG. 16–16)**. The pair on the right portrays the Visitation, in which Mary (left), pregnant with Jesus, visits her older cousin, Elizabeth (right), pregnant with St. John the Baptist. The sculptor of these figures, active in Reims about 1230–1235, drew heavily on ancient sources. Reims had been a major Roman city, and there were remaining Roman works at the disposal of medieval sculptors. The bulky bodies show the same solidity seen in Roman sculpture (see "Roman Portraiture," page 170), and the women's full faces, wavy hair, and heavy mantles recall imperial portrait statuary, even in their use of the two imperial facial ideals of unblemished youth (Mary) and aged accomplishment (Elizabeth) (compare FIGS. 6–36, 6–37). The figures shift their weight to one leg in contrapposto as they turn toward each other in conversation.

The pair to the left of the Visitation enacts the Annunciation, in which the archangel Gabriel announces to Mary that she will bear Jesus. This Mary's slight body, broad planes of simple drapery, restrained gesture, inward focus, and delicate features contrast markedly with the bold tangibility of the Mary in the Visitation next to her. She is clearly the work of a second sculptor. The archangel Gabriel (at the far left) represents a third artist, active at the middle of the century. This sculptor created tall, gracefully swaying figures with small, fine-featured heads, whose

16–16 • WEST FAÇADE, CENTRAL PORTAL, RIGHT SIDE, REIMS CATHEDRAL
Annunciation (left pair: Mary [right] c. 1240, angel [left] c. 1250) and Visitation (right pair: Mary [left] and Elizabeth [right] c. 1230).

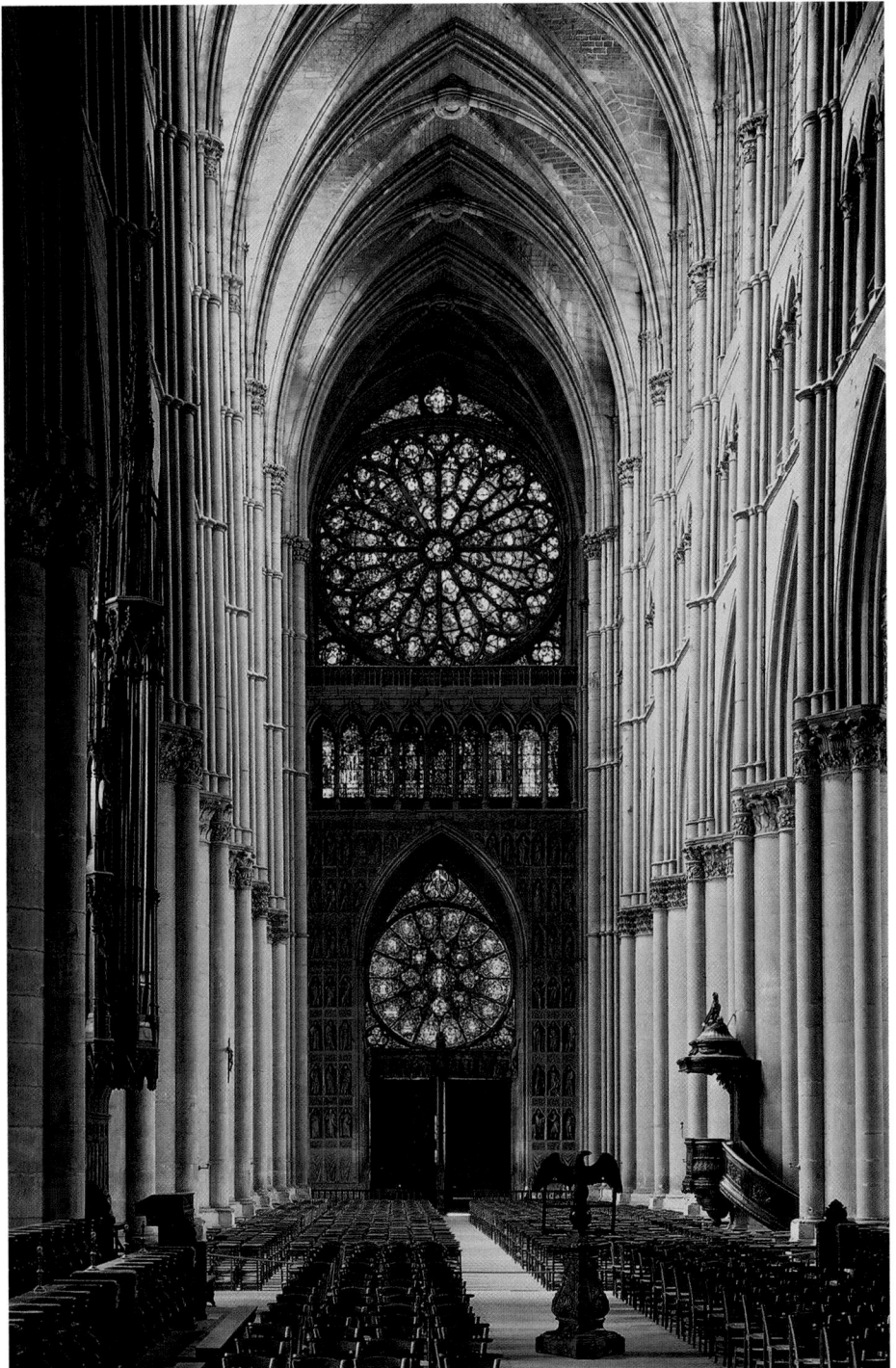

enlarged colonnette at the middle of the triforium. This design feature was certainly noticed by one contemporary viewer, since it is (over)emphasized in the drawings Villard de Honnecourt made during a visit to Reims Cathedral c. 1230 (see "Villard de Honnecourt," page 510). Villard also highlighted one of the principal innovations at Reims: the development of **bar tracery**, in which thin stone bars, called **mullions**, are inserted into an expansive opening in the wall to form a lacy framework for the stained glass (see rose window in FIG. 16–17). Bar tracery replaced the older plate tracery—still used at Chartres—and made possible even larger areas of stained glass in relation to wall surface.

A remarkable ensemble of sculpture and stained glass fills the interior west wall at Reims, which visually "dissolves" in the glow of colored light within delicate mullions of bar tracery. A great rose window fills the clerestory level; a row of lancets illuminates the triforium; and a smaller rose window replaces the stone of the portal tympanum. The lower level is anchored visually by an expanse of sculpture covering the inner wall of the façade. Here ranks of carved prophets and royal ancestors represent moral guides for the newly crowned monarchs who faced them while processing down the elongated nave and out of the cathedral following the coronation ceremony as they began the job of ruling France.

precious expressions, carefully crafted hairdos, and mannered poses of aristocratic refinement grew increasingly to characterize the figural arts in later Gothic sculpture and painting. These characteristics became the basis for what is called the International Gothic Style, fashionable across Europe well into the fifteenth century.

Inside the church (FIG. 16–17), the wall is designed, as at Chartres, as a three-story elevation with nave arcade and clerestory of equal height divided by the continuous arcade of a narrow triforium passageway. The designer at Reims gives a subtle emphasis to the center of each bay in the wall elevation, coordinating the central division of the clerestory into two lancets with a slightly

ART IN THE AGE OF ST. LOUIS

During the time of Louis IX (r. 1226–1270; canonized as St. Louis in 1297), Paris became the artistic center of Europe. Artists from all over France were lured to the capital, responding to the growing local demand for new and remodeled buildings, as well as to the international demand for the extraordinary works of art that were the specialty of Parisian commercial workshops. Especially valued were small-scale objects in precious materials and richly illuminated manuscripts. The Parisian style of this period is often called the "Court Style," since its association with the court of St. Louis was one reason it spread beyond the capital to the courts of

The Sainte-Chapelle in Paris

In 1237, Baldwin II, Latin ruler of Constantinople—descendant of the crusaders who had snatched the Byzantine capital from Emperor Alexius III Angelus in 1204—was in Paris, offering to sell the relic of Christ's crown of thorns to his cousin, King Louis IX of France. The relic was at that time hocked in Venice, securing a loan to the cash-poor Baldwin, who had decided, rather than redeeming it, to sell it to the highest bidder. Louis purchased the relic in 1239, and on August 18, when the newly acquired treasure arrived at the edge of Paris, the humble, barefoot king carried it through the streets of his capital to the royal palace. Soon after its arrival, plans were under way to construct a glorious new palace building to house it—the Sainte-Chapelle, completed for its ceremonial consecration on April 26, 1248. In the 1244 charter establishing services in the Sainte-Chapelle, Pope Innocent IV claimed that Christ had crowned Louis with his own crown, strong confirmation for Louis's own sense of the sacred underpinnings of his kingship.

The Sainte-Chapelle is an extraordinary manifestation of the Gothic style. The two-story building (FIG. A)—there is both a lower and an upper liturgical space—is large for a chapel, and though it is now swallowed up into modern Paris, when it was built it was one of the tallest and most elaborately decorated buildings in the capital. The upper chapel is a completely open interior space surrounded by walls composed almost entirely of stained glass (FIG. B), presenting viewers with a glittering, multicolored expanse. Not only the king and his court experienced this chapel; members of the public came to venerate

and celebrate the relic, as well as to receive the indulgences offered to pious visitors. The Sainte-Chapelle resembles a reliquary made of painted stone and glass instead of gold and gems, turned inside out so that we experience it from within. But this arresting visual impression is only part of the story.

The stained-glass windows present extensive narrative cycles related to the special function of this chapel. Since they are painted in a bold, energetic style, the stories are easily legible, in spite of their breadth and complexity. Around the sanctuary's **hemicycle** (apse or semicircular interior space) are standard themes relating to the celebration of the Mass. But along

the straight side walls are broader, four-lancet windows whose narrative expanse is dominated by the exploits of the sacred kings and queens of the Hebrew Bible, heroes Louis claimed as his own royal ancestors. Above the recessed niche where Louis himself sat at Mass was a window filled with biblical kings, whereas in the corresponding niche on the other side of the chapel, his mother, Queen Blanche of Castile, and his wife, Queen Marguerite of Provence, sat under windows devoted to the lives of Judith and Esther, alternatively appropriate role models for medieval queens. Everywhere we look we see kings being crowned, leading soldiers into holy warfare, or performing royal duties, all framed with heraldic

A. SCHEMATIC DRAWING OF THE SAINTE-CHAPELLE
Paris. 1239–1248.

references to Louis and the French royal house. There is even a window that includes scenes from the life of Louis IX himself.

After the French Revolution, the Sainte-Chapelle was transformed into an archive, and some stained glass was removed to allow more light into the building. Deleted panels made their way onto the art market, and, in 1803, wealthy Philadelphia merchant William Powell bought three medallions from the Judith Window during a European tour, returning home to add them to his collection, the first in America to concentrate on medieval art. One portrays the armies of Holofernes crossing the Euphrates River (FIG. C). A compact crowd of equestrian warriors to the right conforms to a traditional system of representing crowds as a measured, overlapping mass of essentially identical figures, but the warrior at the rear of the battalion breaks the pattern, turning to acknowledge a knight behind him. The foreshortened rump of this soldier's horse projects out into our space, as if he were marching from our real world into the fictive world of the window—an avant-garde touch from a major artist working in the progressive climate of the mid-thirteenth-century Parisian art world.

B. UPPER CHAPEL, THE SAINTE-CHAPELLE
Paris. 1239–1248.

C. HOLOFERNES' ARMY CROSSING THE EUPHRATES RIVER
From the Judith Window, the Sainte-Chapelle, Paris. c. 1245. Stained, painted, and leaded glass, diameter 23⁵/₁₆″ (59.2 cm). Philadelphia Museum of Art.

Villard de Honnecourt

One of the most fascinating and enigmatic works surviving from Gothic France is a set of 33 sheets of parchment covered with about 250 drawings in leadpoint and ink, signed by a man named Villard from the Picardy town of Honnecourt, and now bound into a book housed in the French National Library. Villard seems to have made these drawings in the 1220s and 1230s judging from the identifiable buildings that he recorded, during what seem to have been extensive travels, made for unknown reasons, mainly in France—where he recorded plans or individual details of the cathedrals of Cambrai, Chartres, Laon, and especially Reims—but also in Switzerland and Poland.

Villard seems simply to have drawn those things that interested him—animals, insects, human beings, church furnishings, buildings, and construction devices. Although the majority of his drawings have nothing to do with architecture, his renderings of aspects of Gothic buildings have received the most attention since the book was rediscovered in the mid nineteenth century, and led to a widespread belief that he was an architect or master mason. There is no evidence for this. In fact, the evidence we have argues against it, since the architectural drawings actually suggest the work of someone passionately interested in, but without a great deal of knowledge of, the structural systems and design priorities of Gothic builders. This in no way diminishes the value of this amazing document, which allows us rare access into the mind of a curious, well-traveled thirteenth-century amateur, who drew the things that caught his fancy in the extraordinary world around him.

A. Villard de Honnecourt **SHEET OF DRAWINGS WITH GEOMETRIC FIGURES**

c. 1230. Ink on vellum, 9¼ × 6″ (23.5 × 15.2 cm). Bibliothèque Nationale, Paris. MS. fr. 19093

This page, labeled "help in drawing figures according to the lessons taught by the art of geometry," demonstrates how geometric configurations underlie the shapes of natural forms and the designs of architectural features. They seem to give insight into the design process of Gothic artists, but could they also represent the fertile doodlings of a passionate amateur?

B. Villard de Honnecourt **DRAWINGS OF THE INTERIOR AND EXTERIOR ELEVATION OF THE NAVE OF REIMS CATHEDRAL**

c. 1230. Ink on vellum, 9¼ × 6″ (23.5 × 15.2 cm). Bibliothèque Nationale, Paris. MS. fr. 19093

Scholars still debate whether Villard's drawings of Reims Cathedral—the church he documented most extensively, with five leaves showing views and two containing details—were made from observing the building itself, during construction, or copied from construction drawings that had been prepared to guide the work of the masons. But in either case, what Villard documents here are those aspects of Reims that distinguish it from other works of Gothic architecture, such as the use of bar tracery, the enlarged central colonettes of the triforium, the broad bands of foliate carving on the pier capitals, or the statues of angels that perch on exterior buttresses. He seems to have grasped what it was that separated this building from the other cathedrals rising across France at this time.

EXPLORE MORE: Gain insight from a primary source related to Villard de Honnecourt **www.myartslab.com**

other European rulers. Parisian works became trans-European benchmarks of artistic quality and sophistication.

THE SAINTE-CHAPELLE IN PARIS. The masterpiece of the mid-thirteenth-century Parisian style is the Sainte-Chapelle (Holy Chapel) of the royal palace, commissioned by Louis IX to house his collection of relics of Christ's Passion, especially the crown of thorns (see "The Sainte-Chapelle in Paris," pages 508–509). In many ways this huge chapel can be seen as the culmination of the Gothic style that emerged from Suger's pioneering choir at Saint-Denis. The interior walls have been reduced to a series of slender piers and mullions that act as skeletal support for a vast skin of stained glass. The structure itself is stabilized by external buttressing that projects from the piers around the exterior of the building. Interlocking iron bars between the piers and concealed within the windows themselves run around the entire building, adding further stabilization. The viewer inside is unaware of these systems of support, being focused instead on the kaleidoscopic nature of this jewelbox reliquary and the themes of sacred kingship that dominate the program of stained-glass windows.

ILLUMINATED MANUSCRIPTS. Paris gained renown in the thirteenth century not only for its new architecture and sculpture but also for the production of books. Manuscript painters flocked to Paris from other regions to join workshops supervised by university officials who controlled the production and distribution of books. These works ranged from small Bibles used as textbooks by university students to extravagant devotional and theological works filled with exquisite miniatures for the use of wealthy patrons.

A particularly sumptuous Parisian book from the time of St. Louis is a three-volume Moralized Bible from c. 1230, in which selected scriptural passages are paired with allegorical or moralized interpretations, using pictures as well as words to convey the message. The dedication page **(FIG. 16–18)** shows the teenage King Louis IX and his mother, Queen Blanche of Castile, who served as regent of France (1226–1234) until he came of age. The royal pair—emphasized by their elaborate thrones and slightly oversized heads—appear against a solid gold background under a multicolored architectural framework. Below them, a clerical scholar (left) dictates to a scribe, who seems to be working on a page from this very manuscript, with a column of roundels already outlined for paintings.

This design of stacked medallions—forming the layout for most of this monumental manuscript **(FIG. 16–19)**—clearly derives from stained-glass lancets with their columns of superimposed images **(SEE FIG. 16–12)**. In the book, however, the schema combines pictures with words. Each page has two vertical strips of painted scenes set against a mosaiclike repeated pattern and filled out by half-quatrefoils in the interstices—the standard format of mid-thirteenth-century windows. Adjacent to each

16-18 • QUEEN BLANCHE OF CASTILE AND KING LOUIS IX
From a Moralized Bible made in Paris. 1226–1234. Ink, tempera, and gold leaf on vellum, 15 × 10½″ (38 × 26.6 cm). The Pierpont Morgan Library, New York. MS. M. 240, fol. 8r

16-19 • MORALIZATIONS FROM THE APOCALYPSE
From a Moralized Bible made in Paris. 1226–1234. Ink, tempera, and gold leaf on vellum, each page 15 × 10½" (38 × 26.6 cm). The Pierpont Morgan Library, New York. MS. M. 240, fol. 6r

people continued to live in rural villages and bustling market towns. Textile production dominated manufacture and trade, and fine embroidery continued to be an English specialty. The French Gothic style influenced English architecture and manuscript illumination, but these influences were tempered by local materials and methods, traditions and tastes. Notable is a continuing interest in using expressive line to enliven surface decoration.

MANUSCRIPT ILLUMINATION

The universities of Oxford and Cambridge dominated intellectual life, but monasteries continued to house active scriptoria, in contrast to France, where book production became centralized in the professional workshops of Paris. By the end of the thirteenth century, secular workshops became increasingly active in England, meeting demands for books from students as well as from royal and noble patrons.

MATTHEW PARIS. The monastic tradition of history writing that we saw in the Romanesque Worcester Chronicle (SEE FIG. 15–30) flourished into the Gothic period at the Benedictine monastery of St. Albans, where monk Matthew Paris (d. 1259) compiled a series of historical works. Paris wrote the texts of his chronicles, and he also added hundreds of marginal pictures that were integral to his history writing. The tinted drawings have a freshness that reveals the artist as someone working outside the rigid strictures of compositional conventions—or at least pushing against them. In one of his books, Paris included an almost full-page, framed image of the Virgin and Child in a tender embrace (FIG. 16–20). Under this picture, outside the sacred space of Mary and Jesus, Paris drew a picture of himself—identified not by likeness but by a label with his name, strung out in alternating red and blue capital letters behind him. He looks not at the holy couple, but at the words in front of him. These offer his commentary on the image, pointing to the affection shown in the playful Christ Child's movement toward his earthly mother, but emphasizing the authority he has as the divine incarnation of his godly father. Matthew Paris seems almost to hold his words in his hands, pushing them upward toward the object of his devotion.

medallion is an excerpt of text, either a summary of a scriptural passage or a terse contemporary interpretation or allegory. Both painted miniatures and texts alternate between scriptural summaries and their moralizing explications, outlined in words and visualized with pictures. This adds up to a very learned and complicated compilation, perhaps devised by clerical scholars at the University of Paris, but certainly painted by some of the most important professional artists in the cosmopolitan French capital.

GOTHIC ART IN ENGLAND

Plantagenet kings ruled England from the time of Henry II and Eleanor of Aquitaine until 1485. Many were great patrons of the arts. During this period, London grew into a large city, but most

THE WINDMILL PSALTER. The dazzling artistry and delight in ambiguity and contradiction that had marked early medieval manuscripts in the British Isles (SEE FIG. 14–1) also survived into the Gothic period in the Windmill Psalter of c. 1270–1280 (see "A Closer Look," page 514). The letter *B*—the first letter of

16–20 • Matthew Paris
SELF-PORTRAIT KNEELING BEFORE THE VIRGIN AND CHILD
From the *Historia Anglorum*, made in St. Albans, England. 1250–1259. Ink and color on parchment, 14 × 9¾″ (35.8 × 25 cm). The British Library, London. Royal MS. 14.c.vii, fol. 6r

Psalm 1, which begins with the words *Beatus vir qui non abit in consilio impiorum* ("Happy are those who do not follow the advice of the wicked")—fills an entire left-hand page and outlines a densely interlaced thicket of tendrils and figures. This is a Tree of Jesse, a genealogical diagram of Jesus' royal and spiritual ancestors in the Hebrew Bible based on a prophesy in Isaiah 11:1–3. An oversized, semi-reclining figure of Jesse, father of King David, appears sheathed in a red mantle, with the blue trunk of a vinelike tree emerging from his side. Above him is his majestically enthroned royal son, who, as an ancestor of Mary (shown just above him), is also an ancestor of Jesus, who appears at the top of the sequence. In the circling foliage flanking this sacred royal family tree are a series of prophets, representing Jesus' spiritual heritage.

E, the second letter of the psalm's first word, appears at the top of the right-hand page and is formed from large tendrils emerging from delicate background vegetation to support characters in the story of the Judgment of Solomon portrayed within it (I Kings 3:16–27). Two women (one above the other at the right) claiming the same baby appear before King Solomon (enthroned on the crossbar) to settle their dispute. The king orders a guard to slice the baby in half with his sword and give each woman her share. This trick exposed the real mother, who hastened to give up her claim in order to save the baby's life. It has been suggested that the positioning of this story within the letter *E* may have made a subtle association between Solomon and the reigning King Edward I. The rest of the psalm's five opening words appear on a banner carried by an angel who swoops down at the bottom of the *E*.

The Opening of Psalm 1 in the Windmill Psalter

> Psalm 1 (Beatus Vir). London, c. 1270–1280. Ink, pigments, and gold on vellum, each page 12¾ × 8¾" (32.3 × 22.2 cm). The Pierpont Morgan Library, New York. MS. 102, fols. lv–2r

Although this page initially seems to have been trimmed at left, the flattened outside edge of the roundels marks the original end of the page. What might have started as an independent Jesse Tree may later have been expanded into the initial *B*, widening the pictorial composition farther than originally planned.

The four evangelists appear in the corner roundels as personified symbols writing at desks.

The windmill that has given this psalter its name seems to be a religious symbol based on the fourth verse of this Psalm: "Not so the wicked, not so: but like the dust, which the wind driveth from the face of the earth."

Tucked within the surrounds of the letter *B* are scenes from God's creation of the world, culminating in the forming of Adam and Eve. Medieval viewers would meditate on how the new Adam (Christ) and Eve (Mary)—featured in the Jesse Tree—had redeemed humankind from the sin of the first man and woman. Similarly, Solomon's choice of the true mother would recall Christ's choice of the true Church. Medieval manuscripts are full of cross-references and multiple meanings, intended to stimulate extended reflection and meditation, not embody a single truth or tell a single story.

Participants in this scene of the Judgment of Solomon here have been creatively distributed within the unusual narrative setting of the letter *E*. Solomon sits on the crossbar; the two mothers are stacked one above the other; and the knight balancing the baby has to hook his toe under the curling extension of the crossbar to maintain his balance.

SEE MORE: View the Closer Look feature for The Opening of Psalm I in the Windmill Psalter **www.myartslab.com**

ARCHITECTURE

The Gothic style in architecture appeared early in England, introduced by Cistercian and Norman builders and by traveling master masons. But in England there was less emphasis on height than in France. English churches have long, broad naves and screenlike façades.

SALISBURY CATHEDRAL. The thirteenth-century cathedral in Salisbury is an excellent example of English Gothic. It has unusual origins. The first cathedral in this diocese had been built within the castle complex of the local lord. In 1217, Bishop Richard Poore petitioned the pope to relocate the church, claiming the wind on the hilltop howled so loudly that the clergy could not hear themselves sing the Mass. A more pressing concern was pro... his desire to escape the lord's control. As soon as he moved, ... bishop established a new town, called Salisbury. Material from the old church was carted down the hill and used in the new cathedral, along with dark, fossil-filled Purbeck stone from quarries in southern England and limestone imported from Caen. Building began in 1220, and most of the cathedral was finished by 1258, an unusually short period for such an undertaking **(FIG. 16–21)**.

The west façade, however, was not completed until 1265. The small flanking towers project beyond the side walls and buttresses, giving the façade an increased width, underscored by tier upon tier of blind tracery and arcaded niches. Instead of a western rose window floating over triple portals (as seen in France), the English

16-21 • SALISBURY CATHEDRAL
England. Church building 1220–1258; west façade finished 1265; spire c. 1320–1330; cloister and chapter house 1263–1284.

SEE MORE: Click the Google Earth link for Salisbury Cathedral **www.myartslab.com**

16–22 • PLAN OF SALISBURY CATHEDRAL

Trinity chapel

chapter house

cloister

entrance porch

16–23 • NAVE OF SALISBURY CATHEDRAL

In the eighteenth century, the English architect James Wyatt subjected the building to radical renovations, during which the remaining stained glass and figure sculpture were removed or rearranged. Similar campaigns to refurbish medieval churches were common at the time. The motives of the restorers were complex and their results far from our notions of historical authenticity today.

master masons placed tall lancet windows above rather insignificant doorways. A mighty crossing tower (the French preferred a slender spire) became the focal point of the building. (The huge crossing tower and its 400-foot spire are a fourteenth-century addition at Salisbury, as are the flying buttresses, which were added to stabilize the tower.) The slightly later cloister and chapter house provided for the cathedral's clergy.

Salisbury has an equally distinctive plan **(FIG. 16–22)**, with wide projecting double transepts, a square east end with a single chapel, and a spacious sanctuary—more like a monastic church. The nave interior reflects the Norman building tradition of heavy walls and a tall nave arcade surmounted by a gallery and a clerestory with simple lancet windows **(FIG. 16–23)**. The walls alone are substantial enough to buttress the four-part ribbed vault. The emphasis on the horizontal movement of the arcades, unbroken by continuous vertical colonnettes extending from the compound piers, directs worshipers' attention forward toward the altar behind the choir screen, rather than upward into the vaults, as preferred in France (SEE FIG. 16–17). The use of color in the stonework is reminiscent of the decorative effects in Romanesque interiors. The shafts supporting the four-part rib vaults are made of dark Purbeck stone that contrasts with the lighter limestone of the rest of the interior. The original painting and gilding of the stonework would have enhanced the effect.

MILITARY AND DOMESTIC ARCHITECTURE. Cathedrals were not the only buildings constructed during the Early and High Gothic periods. Western European knights who traveled east during the crusades were inspired by the architectural forms they saw in Muslim castles and Byzantine fortifications. When they returned home, Europeans built their own versions of these fortifications. Castle gateways now became complex, nearly independent fortifications, often guarded by twin towers rather than just one. New D-shape and round towers eliminated the corners that had

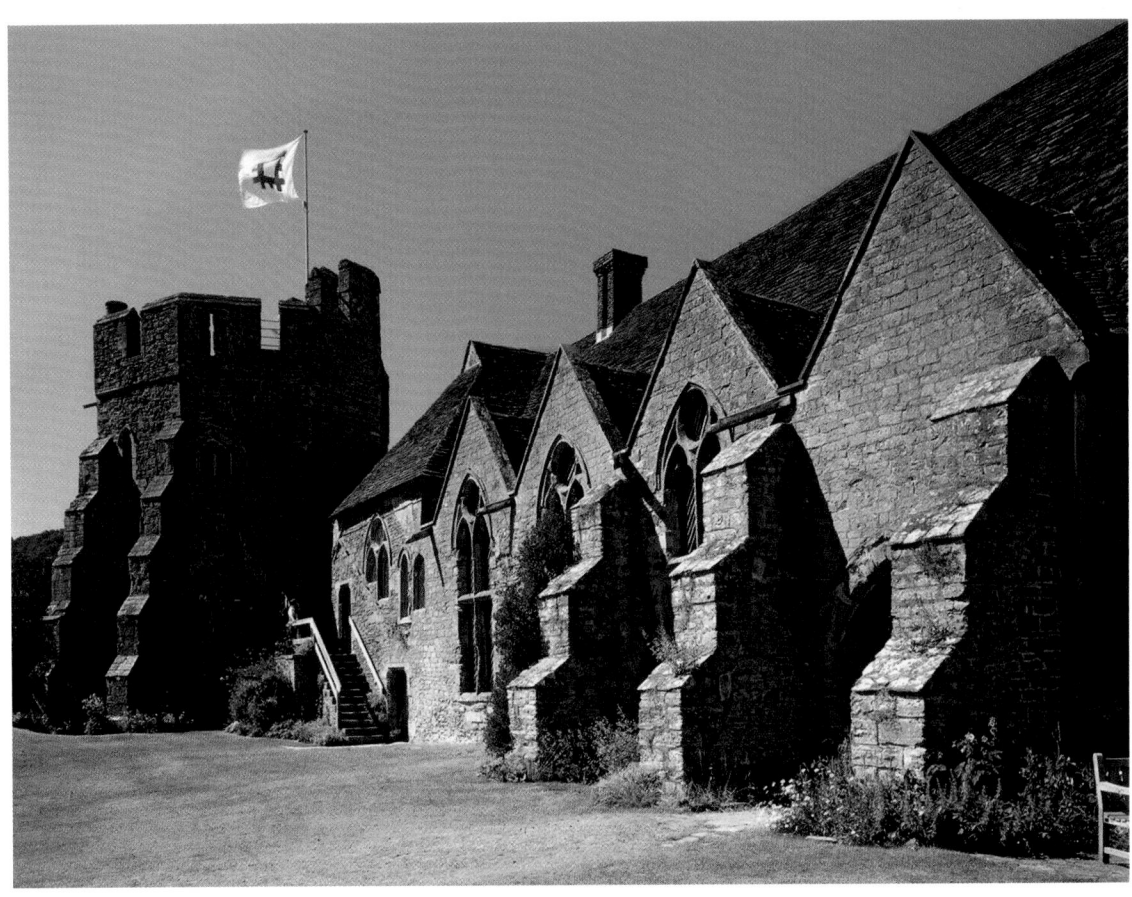

made earlier square towers vulnerable to battering rams, and crenellations (notches) were added to tower tops in order to provide stone shields for more effective defense. The outer, enclosing walls of the castles were strengthened. The open, interior space was enlarged and filled with more comfortable living quarters for the lord and wooden buildings to house the garrison and the staff necessary to repair armor and other equipment. Barns and stables for animals, including the extremely valuable war horses, were also erected within the enclosure.

STOKESAY CASTLE.   Military structures were not the only secular buildings outfitted for defense. In uncertain times, the manor (a landed estate), which continued to be an important economic unit in the thirteenth century, also had to fortify its buildings. A country house that was equipped with a tower and crenellated rooflines became a status symbol as well as a necessity. Stokesay Castle, a remarkable fortified manor house, survives in England near the Welsh border. In 1291, a wool merchant, Lawrence of Ludlow, acquired the property of Stokesay and secured permission from King Edward I to fortify his dwelling—officially known as a "license to crenellate" **(FIG. 16–24)**. He built two towers, including a massive crenellated south tower and a great hall that still survive.

Life in the Middle Ages revolved around the hall. Windows on each side of Stokesay's hall open both toward the courtyard and out across a moat toward the countryside. By the thirteenth century, people began to expect some privacy as well as security;

therefore at both ends of the hall are two-story additions that provided retiring rooms for the family and workrooms where women could spin and weave. Rooms on the north end could be reached from the hall, but the upper chamber at the south was accessible only by means of an exterior stairway. A tiny window— a peephole—let women and members of the household observe the often rowdy activities in the hall below. In layout, there was essentially no difference between this manor far from the London court and the mansions built by the nobility in the city. A palace followed the same pattern of hall and retiring rooms; it was simply larger than a manor.

GOTHIC ART IN GERMANY AND THE HOLY ROMAN EMPIRE

The Holy Roman Empire, weakened by internal strife and a prolonged struggle with the papacy, ceased to be a significant power in the thirteenth century. England and France were becoming strong nation-states, and the empire's hold on southern Italy and Sicily ended at mid century with the death of Emperor Frederick II. Subsequent emperors—who were elected—had only nominal authority over a loose conglomeration of independent principalities, bishoprics, and free cities. As in England, the French Gothic style, avidly embraced in the western Germanic territories, shows regional adaptations and innovations.

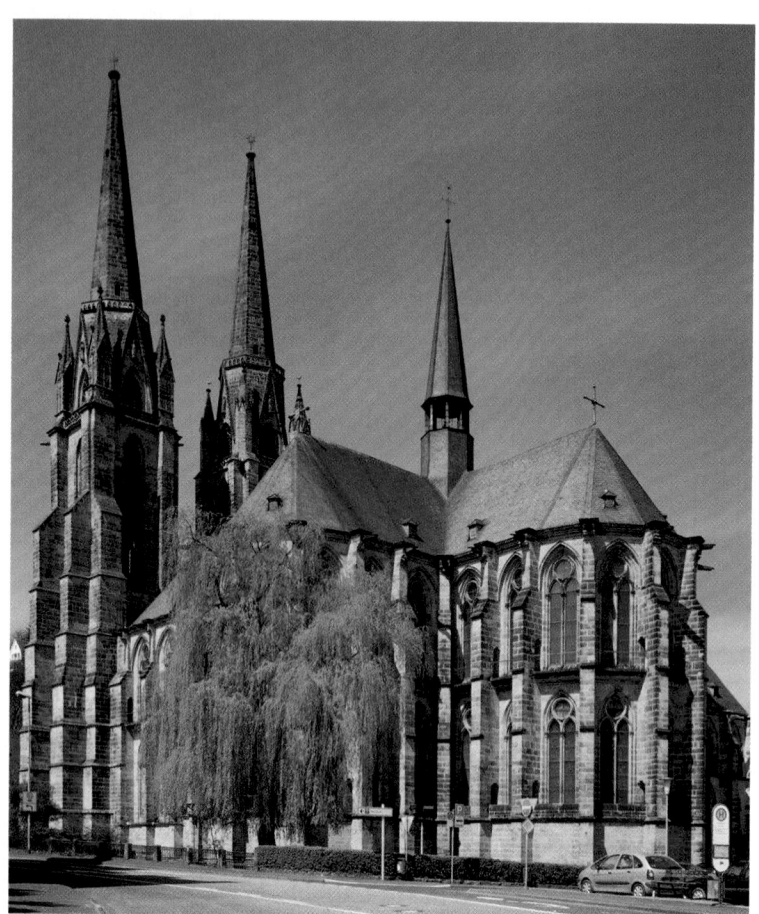

of windows suggest a two-story building, which is not the case. Inside, the closely spaced piers of the nave support the ribbed vault and, as with the buttresses, give the building a vertical, linear quality (FIG. 16–26). Light from the two stories of tall windows fills the interior, unimpeded by walls, galleries, or triforia (plural of triforium, arcaded wall passageways). The hall-church design was adopted widely for civic and residential buildings in Germanic lands and also for Jewish architecture.

THE ALTNEUSCHUL. Built in the third quarter of the thirteenth century, Prague's ALTNEUSCHUL ("Old-New Synagogue") is the oldest functioning synagogue in Europe and one of two principal synagogues serving the Jews of Prague (FIG. 16–27). The Altneuschul demonstrates the adaptability of the Gothic hall-church design for non-Christian use. Like a hall church, the vaults of the synagogue are all the same height. Unlike a basilican church, however, with its division into nave and side aisles, the Altneuschul has only two aisles, each with three bays supported by the

ARCHITECTURE

In the thirteenth century, the increasing importance of the sermon in church services led architects in Germany to develop the **hall church**, a type of open, light-filled interior space that appeared in Europe in the early Middle Ages, characterized by a nave and side aisles of equal height. The spacious and well-lit design of the hall church provided accommodation for the large crowds drawn by charismatic preachers.

CHURCH OF ST. ELIZABETH OF HUNGARY IN MARBURG. Perhaps the first true Gothic hall church, and one of the earliest Gothic buildings in Germany, was the **CHURCH OF ST. ELIZABETH OF HUNGARY** in Marburg (FIG. 16–25). The Hungarian princess Elizabeth (1207–1231) had been sent to Germany at age 4 to marry the ruler of Thuringia. He soon died of the plague, and she devoted herself to caring for people with incurable diseases. It was said that she died at age 24 from exhaustion, and she was canonized in 1235. Between 1235 and 1283, the knights of the Teutonic Order (who had moved to Germany from Jerusalem) built a church to serve as her mausoleum and a center of pilgrimage.

The plan of the church is an early German form, a **trefoil** (three-lobed design) with choir and transepts of equal size. The elevation of the building, however, is new—the nave and aisles are of equal height. On the exterior wall, buttresses run the full height of the building and emphasize its verticality. The two rows

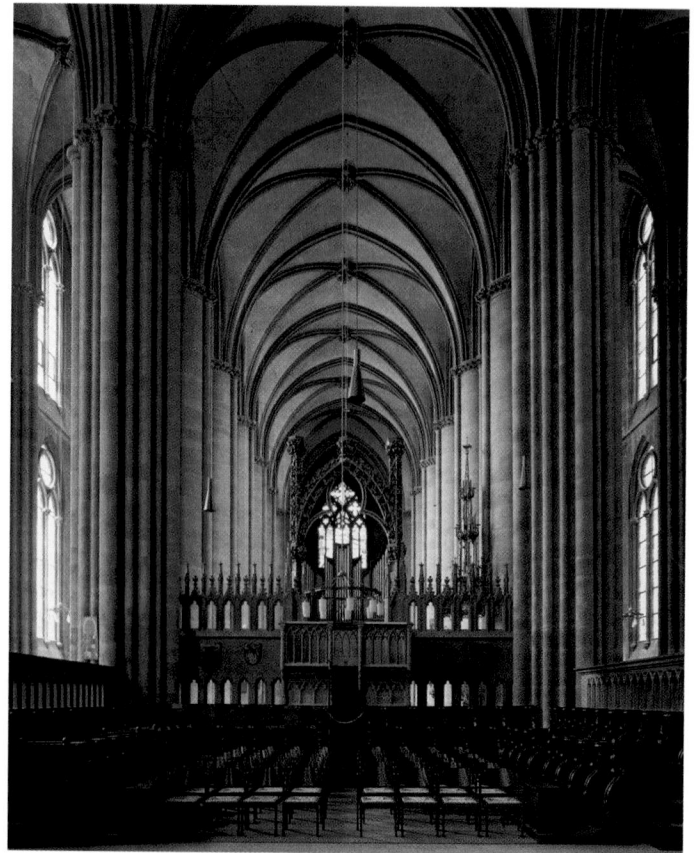

16-26 • INTERIOR, CHURCH OF ST. ELIZABETH OF HUNGARY Marburg, Germany. 1235–1283.

16–27 • INTERIOR, ALTNEUSCHUL
Prague, Bohemia (Czech Republic). c. late 13th century; *bimah* after 1483.

walls and two octagonal piers. The bays have Gothic four-part ribbed vaulting to which a nonfunctional fifth rib has been added. Some say that this fifth rib was added to undermine the cross form made by the intersecting diagonal ribs.

The medieval synagogue was both a place of prayer and a communal center of learning and inspiration where men gathered to read and discuss the Torah. The synagogue had two focal points, the *aron*, or shrine for the Torah scrolls, and a raised reading platform called the *bimah*. The congregation faced the *aron*, which was located on the east wall, in the direction of Jerusalem. The *bimah* stood in the center of the hall, straddling the two center bays, and in Prague it was surrounded by an ironwork open screen. The single entrance was placed off-center in a corner bay at the west end. Men worshiped and studied in the main space; women had to worship in annexes on the north and west sides.

SCULPTURE

One of the most creative centers of European sculpture since the eleventh century had been the Rhine River Valley and the region known as the Mosan (from the Meuse River, in present-day Belgium), with centers in Liège and Verdun. Ancient Romans had built camps and cities in this area, and Classical influence lingered on through the Middle Ages. Nicholas of Verdun and his fellow goldsmiths inspired a new classicizing style in the arts.

SHRINE OF THE THREE KINGS. For the archbishop of Cologne, Nicholas created the magnificent **SHRINE OF THE THREE KINGS** (c. 1190–c. 1205/10), a reliquary for what were believed to be relics of the three Magi. Shaped in the form of a basilican church **(FIG. 16–28)**, it is made of gilded bronze and silver, set with gemstones and dark blue enamel plaques that accentuate its architectural details. Like his fellow Mosan artists, Nicholas was inspired by ancient Roman art still found in the region, as well as classicizing Byzantine works. The figures are lifelike, fully modeled, and swathed in voluminous but revealing drapery. The three Magi and the Virgin fill the front gable end, and prophets and apostles sit in the niches in the two levels of arcading on the sides. The work combines robust, expressively mobile sculptural forms with a jeweler's exquisitely ornamental detailing to create an opulent, monumental setting for its precious contents.

ST. MAURICE. A powerful current of realism runs through German Gothic sculpture. Some works seem to be carved after a living model. Among them is an arresting mid-thirteenth-century statue of **ST. MAURICE** in Magdeburg Cathedral **(FIG. 16–29)**, the location of his relics since 968. The Egyptian Maurice, a commander in the Roman army, was martyred in 286 together with his Christian battalion while they were stationed in Germany. As patron saint of Magdeburg, he was revered by Ottonian

16–28 • Nicholas of Verdun and workshop SHRINE OF THE THREE KINGS
Cologne (Köln) Cathedral, Germany. c. 1190–c. 1205/10. Silver and gilded bronze with enamel and gemstones, 5′8″ × 6′ × 3′8″ (1.73 × 1.83 × 1.12 m).

16-29 • ST. MAURICE
Magdeburg Cathedral, Magdeburg, Germany. c. 1240–1250.
Dark sandstone with traces of polychromy.

16-30 • EKKEHARD AND UTA
West chapel, Naumburg Cathedral, Germany. c. 1245–1260.
Stone with polychromy, height approx. 6′2″ (1.88 m).

emperors, who were anointed in St. Peter's in Rome at the altar of St. Maurice. He remained a favorite saint of military aristocrats. This is the first surviving representation of Maurice as a black African, an acknowledgment of his Egyptian origins and an aspect of the growing German interest in realism, which extends here to the detailed rendering of his costume of chain mail and riveted leather.

EKKEHARD AND UTA.   Equally portraitlike is the depiction of this couple, commissioned about 1245 by Dietrich II, bishop of Wettin, for the family funeral chapel, built at the west end of Naumburg Cathedral. Bishop Dietrich ordered life-size statues of 12 of his ancestors, who had been patrons of the church, to be placed on pedestals mounted at window level around the chapel.

In the representations of Margrave Ekkehard of Meissen (a margrave—count of the march or border—was a territorial governor whose duty it was to defend the frontier) and his Polish-born wife, Uta **(FIG. 16–30)**, the sculptor created highly individualized figures and faces. Since these are eleventh-century people, sculpted in the thirteenth century, we are not looking at portrait likenesses of Ekkehard and Uta themselves, but it is still possible that live models were used to heighten the sense of a living presence in their portraits. But more than their faces contribute to this liveliness. The margrave nervously fingers the strap of the shield that is looped over his arm, and the coolly elegant Uta pulls her cloak around her neck as if to protect herself from the cold, while the extraordinary spread of her left hand is necessary to control the voluminous, thick cloth. The survival of original **polychromy** (multicolored painting on the surface of sculpture or architecture) indicates that color added to the impact of the figures. The impetus toward descriptive realism and psychological presence, initiated in the thirteenth century, will expand in the art of northern Europe into the fifteenth century and beyond.

GOTHIC ART IN ITALY

The thirteenth century was a period of political division and economic expansion for the Italian peninsula. Part of southern Italy and Sicily was controlled by Frederick II von Hohenstaufen (1194–1250), Holy Roman emperor from 1220. Frederick was a politically unsettling force. He fought with a league of north Italian cities and briefly controlled the Papal States. On his death, however, Germany and the Holy Roman Empire ceased to be an important factor in Italian politics and culture.

In northern Italy, in particular, organizations of successful merchants created communal governments in their prosperous and independent city-states and struggled against powerful families for political control. Artists began to emerge as independent agents, working directly with wealthy clients and with civic and religious institutions.

It was during this time that new religious orders known as the mendicants (begging monks) arose to meet the needs of the growing urban population. They espoused an ideal of poverty, charity, and love, and they dedicated themselves to teaching and preaching, while living among the urban poor. Most notable in the beginning were the Franciscans, founded by St. Francis of Assisi (1182–1226; canonized in 1228). This son of a wealthy merchant gave away his possessions and devoted his life to God and the poor. As others began to join him, he wrote a simple rule for his followers, who were called brothers, or friars (from the Latin *frater*, meaning "brother"), and the pope approved the new order in 1209–1210.

16-31 • Nicola Pisano **PULPIT**
Baptistery, Pisa, Italy. 1260. Marble, height approx. 15′ (4.6 m).

SCULPTURE: THE PISANO FAMILY

During his lifetime, the culturally enlightened Frederick II had fostered a Classical revival. He was a talented poet, artist, and naturalist, and an active patron of the arts and sciences. In the Romanesque period, artists in southern Italy had already turned to ancient sculpture for inspiration, but Frederick, mindful of his imperial status as Holy Roman emperor, encouraged this tendency to help communicate a message of power. He also encouraged artists to emulate the natural world around them. Nicola Pisano (active in Tuscany c. 1258–1278), who moved from the southern region of Apulia to Tuscany at mid century, became the leading exponent of this classicizing and naturalistic style.

NICOLA PISANO'S PULPIT AT PISA. In an inscription on a free-standing marble pulpit in the Pisa Baptistery (FIG. 16–31), Nicola identifies himself as a supremely self-confident sculptor: "In the year 1260 Nicola Pisano carved this noble work. May so gifted a hand be praised as it deserves." Columns topped with leafy Corinthian capitals support standing figures and Gothic trefoil arches, which in turn provide a platform for the six-sided pulpit. The columns rest on high bases carved with crouching figures, domestic

On the morning of September 27, 1997, tragedy struck. An earthquake convulsed the small town of Assisi, shaking the church of St. Francis and damaging architecture and frescos. Where the vault collapsed, priceless frescos crumbled and plunged to the floor. The photographer Ghigo Roli had just finished recording every painted surface of the interior when the sound of the first earthquake was heard in the basilica. As the building shook and the paintings fell, "I wanted to cry," he later wrote.

When such disasters happen, the whole world seems to respond. Volunteers immediately raised money to restore the frescos, with the hope and intention of paying the costs of repairing and strengthening the basilica, reassembling the paintings from millions of tiny pieces, and finally reinstalling the restored treasures. So successful was the effort that visitors today would not guess that an earthquake had brought down the vault shown here scarcely more than a decade ago. But in other parts of the church the remains are insufficient to reconstruct entire paintings, and computers work to match the fragments and bring together at least sections of them.

CHURCH OF ST. FRANCIS, ASSISI, ITALY: RESTORED
Painting dating 1228–1253.

CHURCH OF ST. FRANCIS, ASSISI, ITALY: DURING THE 1997 EARTHQUAKE
Caught by a television camera during the quake, some of the vaults and archivolts in the upper church plunged to the floor, killing four people. The camera operator eventually emerged, covered with the fine dust of the shattered brickwork and plaster, as a "white, dumbfounded phantom."

animals, and shaggy-maned lions. Panels forming the pulpit enclosure illustrate New Testament subjects, each framed as an independent composition.

Each panel illustrates several scenes in a continuous narrative; FIG. **16–32** depicts the Annunciation, Nativity, and Adoration of the Shepherds. The Virgin reclines in the middle of the composition after having given birth to Jesus, who below receives his first bath from midwives. The upper left-hand corner holds the Annunciation—the moment of Christ's conception, as announced by the archangel Gabriel. The scene in the upper right combines the Annunciation to the Shepherds with their Adoration of the Child. The viewer's attention moves from group to group within the shallow space, always returning to the regally detached mother of God. The format, style, and technique of Roman sarcophagus reliefs—readily accessible in the burial ground near the baptistery—may have provided Nicola's models for this carving. The sculptural treatment of the deeply cut, full-bodied forms is certainly Classical in inspiration, as are the heavy, placid faces.

16-33 • Giovanni Pisano
NATIVITY
Detail of pulpit, Cathedral, Pisa. 1302–1310. Marble, 34⅜ × 43" (87.2 × 109.2 cm).

16–34 • Coppo di Marcovaldo
CRUCIFIX
From the Franciscan convent of Santa Chiara in
San Gimignano, Italy. c. 1250–1270. Tempera and
gold on wood panel, 9′7⅜″ × 8′1¼″ (2.93 × 2.47 m).
Pinacoteca, San Gimignano, Italy.

GIOVANNI PISANO'S PULPIT AT PISA. Nicola's son Giovanni (active c. 1265–1314) assisted his father while learning from him, and he may also have worked or studied in France. By the end of the thirteenth century, he had emerged as a versatile artist in his own right. Between 1302 and 1310, he and his workshop carved a huge pulpit for Pisa Cathedral that is similar to his father's in conception but significantly different in style and execution. In his rendering of the **NATIVITY**, Giovanni places graceful, animated figures in an uptilted, deeply carved setting **(FIG. 16–33)**. He replaces Nicola's imperious Roman matron with a lithe, younger Mary who, sheltered by a shell-like cave, gazes delightedly at her baby. Below her, a midwife who had doubted the virgin birth has her withered hand restored while preparing the baby's bath water. Sheep, shepherds, and angels spiral up through the trees at the right and more angelic onlookers replace the Annunciation. Giovanni's sculpture is as dynamic as Nicola's is static.

PAINTING

The capture of Constantinople by crusaders in 1204 brought an influx of Byzantine art and artists to Italy. The imported style of painting, the *maniera greca* ("the Greek manner"), influenced thirteenth- and fourteenth-century Italian painting in style and technique and introduced a new emphasis on pathos and emotion.

PAINTED CRUCIFIXES. One example, a large wooden crucifix attributed to the thirteenth-century Florentine painter Coppo di Marcovaldo **(FIG. 16–34)**, represents an image of a suffering Christ on the cross, a Byzantine type with closed eyes and bleeding, sagging body that encourages viewers to respond emotionally and empathetically to the image (SEE FIGS. 7–35, 14–23). This is a "historiated crucifix," meaning that narrative scenes flank Christ's body, in this case episodes from the story of his Passion. Such monumental crosses—this one is almost 10 feet

16-35 • SCHEMATIC DRAWING OF THE CHURCH OF ST. FRANCIS
Assisi, Italy. 1228–1253.

high—were mounted on the choir screens that separated the clergy in the sanctuary from the lay people in the nave, especially in the churches of the Italian mendicants. One such cross can be seen from behind with its wooden bracing in FIG. 16–36, tilted out to lean toward the worshiper's line of vision and increase the emotional impact.

THE CHURCH OF ST. FRANCIS AT ASSISI. Two years after St. Francis's death in 1226, the church in his birthplace, Assisi, was begun. It was nearly finished in 1239 but was not dedicated until 1253. This building was unusually elaborate in its design, with upper and lower churches on two stories and a crypt at the choir end underneath both (FIG. 16–35). Both upper and lower churches have a single nave of four square vaulted bays, and both end in a transept and a single apse. The lower church has massive walls and a narrow nave flanked by side chapels. The upper church is a spacious, well-lit hall with excellent visibility and acoustics, designed to accommodate the crowds of pilgrims who came to see and hear the friars preach as well as to participate in church rituals and venerate the tomb of the saint. The church walls

presented expanses of uninterrupted wall surface where sacred stories could unfold in murals. In the wall paintings of the upper church, the focus was on the story of Francis himself, presented as a model Christian life to which pilgrims as well as resident friars might aspire.

Scholars differ over whether the murals of the upper church were painted as early as 1290, but they agree on their striking narrative effectiveness. Like most Franciscan paintings, these scenes were designed to engage with viewers by appealing to their memories of their own life experiences, evoked by the inclusion of recognizable anecdotal details and emotionally expressive figures. A good example is **THE MIRACLE OF THE CRIB AT GRECCIO** (FIG. 16–36), portraying St. Francis making the first Christmas manger scene in the church at Greccio.

The scene—like all Gothic visual narratives, set in the pres-ent even though the event portrayed took place in the past—unfolds within a Gothic church that would have looked very familiar to late thirteenth-century viewers. A large wooden crucifix, similar to the one by Coppo di Marcovaldo (SEE FIG. 16–34), has been suspended from a stand on top of a screen

16-36 • THE MIRACLE OF THE CI
AT GRECCIO
From a cycle of the Life of St. Francis, church o.
St. Francis, Assisi, Italy. Late 13th or early 14th
century. Fresco.

separating the sanctuary from the nave. The cross has been reinforced on the back and tilted forward to hover over people in the nave, whom we see crowding behind an open door in the choir screen. A pulpit, with stairs leading up to its entrance and candlesticks at its corners, rises above the screen at the left. An elaborate carved baldacchino (canopy) surmounts the altar at the right, and an adjustable wooden lectern stands in front of the altar. Other small but telling touches include a seasonal liturgical calendar posted on the lectern, foliage swags decorating the baldacchino, and an embroidered altar cloth. And sound as well as sight is referenced here in the figures of the friars who throw their heads back, mouths wide open, to provide the liturgical soundtrack to this cinematic tableau.

The focus on the sacred narrative is confined to a small area at lower right, where St. Francis reverently holds the Holy Infant above a plain, boxlike crib next to miniature representations of various animals that might have been present at the Nativity, capturing the miraculous moment when, it was said, the Christ Child himself appeared in the manger. But even if the story is about a miracle, it takes place in a setting rich in worldly references that allowed contemporary viewers to imagine themselves as part of the scene, either as worshipers kneeling in front of the altar or as spectators pushing toward the doorway to get a better view.

THINK ABOUT IT

16.1 What are the most important technological innovations and sociocultural formations that made the "Age of the Cathedrals" possible?

16.2 Analyze Salisbury Cathedral in England and the German church of St. Elizabeth of Hungary in Marburg. How does each reflect characteristics of French Gothic style, and how does each depart from that style and express architectural features characteristic of its region?

16.3 Explain the process for making medieval stained glass, and trace its development as the key pictorial medium in France during the Gothic period from the abbey church of Saint-Denis to the Parisian Sainte-Chapelle. What are the similarities and differences when comparing windows from these two sites?

16.4 Explain how manuscript illumination was used to convey complex theological ideas during the Gothic period. Analyze the iconography of one manuscript discussed in the chapter.

16.5 How was St. Francis of Assisi's message of empathy conveyed in the church of St. Francis?

PRACTICE MORE: Compose answers to these questions, get flashcards for images and terms, and review chapter material with quizzes
www.myartslab.com

17–1 • Ambrogio Lorenzetti FRESCOS OF THE SALA DEI NOVE (OR SALA DELLA PACE)
Palazzo Pubblico, Siena, Italy. 1338–1339. Length of long wall about 46′ (14 m).

EXPLORE MORE: Gain insight from a primary source related to the frescos in the Palazzo Pubblico
www.myartslab.com

FOURTEENTH-CENTURY
ART IN EUROPE

In 1338, the Nine—a council of merchants and bankers that governed Siena as an oligarchy—commissioned frescos from renowned Sienese painter Ambrogio Lorenzetti (c. 1295–c. 1348) for three walls in the chamber within the Palazzo Pubblico where they met to conduct city business. This commission came at the moment of greatest prosperity and security since the establishment of their government in 1287.

Lorenzetti's frescos combine allegory with panoramic landscapes and cityscapes, communicating ideology to visualize the justification for and positive effects of Sienese government. The moral foundation of the rule of the Nine is outlined in a complicated allegory in which seated personifications (far left in **FIG. 17–1**) of Concord, Justice, Peace, Strength, Prudence, Temperance, and Magnanimity not only diagram good governance but actually reference the Last Judgment in a bold assertion of the relationship between secular rule and divine authority. This tableau contrasts with a similar presentation of bad government, where Tyranny is flanked by the personified forces that keep tyrants in power—Cruelty, Treason, Fraud, Fury, Division, and War. A group of scholars would have devised this complex program of symbols and meanings; it is unlikely that Lorenzetti would have known the philosophical works that underlie them.

Lorenzetti's fame, however, and the wall paintings' secure position among the most remarkable surviving mural programs of the period, rests on the other part of this ensemble—the effects of good and bad government in city and country life (SEE FIG. 17–15).

Unlike the tableau showing the perils of life under tyrannical rule, the panoramic view of life under good government—which in this work of propaganda means life under the rule of the Nine—is well preserved. A vista of fourteenth-century Siena—identifiable by the cathedral dome and tower peeking over the rooftops in the background—details carefree life within shops, schools, taverns, and worksites, as the city streets bustle with human activity. Outside, an expansive landscape highlights agricultural productivity.

Unfortunately, within a decade of the frescos' completion, life in Siena was no longer as stable and carefree. The devastating bubonic plague visited in 1348—Ambrogio Lorenzetti himself was probably one of the victims—and the rule of the Nine collapsed in 1355. But this glorious vision of joyful prosperity preserves the dreams and aspirations of a stable government, using some of the most progressive and creative ideas in fourteenth-century Italian art, ideas whose development we will trace over the next two centuries.

LEARN ABOUT IT

17.1 Assess the close connections between works of art and their patrons in fourteenth-century Europe.

17.2 Compare and contrast the Florentine and Sienese narrative painting traditions as exemplified by Giotto and Duccio.

17.3 Discover the rich references to everyday life and human emotions that begin to permeate figural art in this period.

17.4 Explore the production of small-scale works, often made of precious materials and highlighting extraordinary technical virtuosity, that continues from the earlier Gothic period.

17.5 Evaluate the regional manifestations of the fourteenth-century Gothic architectural style.

HEAR MORE: Listen to an audio file of your chapter **www.myartslab.com**

MAP 17-1 • EUROPE IN THE FOURTEENTH CENTURY

From its outbreak in the Mediterranean the Black Death in 1347 swept across the European mainland over the next four years.

The Spread of the Black Death
- 1347
- mid-1348
- early 1349
- late 1349
- 1350
- 1351
- after 1351
- minor outbreak

FOURTEENTH-CENTURY EUROPE

Literary luminaries Dante, Petrarch, Boccaccio, Chaucer, and Christine de Pizan (see "A New Spirit in Fourteenth-Century Literature," opposite) and the visionary painters Cimabue, Duccio, Jean Pucelle, and Giotto participated in a cultural explosion that swept through fourteenth-century Europe, and especially Italy. The poet Petrarch (1304–1374) was a towering figure in this change, writing his love lyrics in Italian, the language of everyday life, rather than Latin, the language of ceremony and high art. Similarly the deeply moving murals of Florentine painter Giotto di Bondone (c. 1277–1337) were rooted in his observation of the people around him, giving the participants in sacred narratives both great dignity and striking humanity, thus making them familiar, yet new, to the audiences that originally experienced them. Even in Paris—still the artistic center of Europe as far as refined taste and technical

A New Spirit in Fourteenth-Century Literature

For Petrarch and his contemporaries, the essential qualifications for a writer were an appreciation of Greek and Roman authors and an ability to observe the people living around them. Although fluent in Latin, they chose to write in the language of their own time and place—Italian, English, French. Leading the way was Dante Alighieri (1265–1321), who wrote *The Divine Comedy*, his great summation of human virtue and vice, and ultimately human destiny, in Italian, establishing his daily vernacular as worthy to express great literary themes.

Francesco Petrarca, called simply Petrarch (1304–1374), raised the status of secular literature with his sonnets to his unobtainable beloved, Laura, his histories and biographies, and his writings on the joys of country life in the Roman manner. Petrarch's imaginative updating of Classical themes in a work called *The Triumphs*—which examines the themes of Chastity triumphant over Love, Death over Chastity, Fame over Death, Time over Fame, and Eternity over Time— provided later Renaissance poets and painters with a wealth of allegorical subject matter.

More earthy, Giovanni Boccaccio (1313–1375) perfected the art of the short story in *The Decameron*, a collection of amusing and moralizing tales told by a group of young Florentines who moved to the countryside to escape the Black Death. With wit and sympathy, Boccaccio presents the full spectrum of daily life in Italy. Such secular literature, written in Italian as it was then spoken in Tuscany, provided a foundation for fifteenth-century Renaissance writers.

In England, Geoffrey Chaucer (c. 1342–1400) was inspired by Boccaccio to write his own series of stories, *The Canterbury Tales*, told by pilgrims traveling to the shrine of St. Thomas à Becket (1118?–1170) in Canterbury. Observant and witty, Chaucer depicted the pretensions and foibles, as well as the virtues, of humanity.

Christine de Pizan (1364–c. 1431), born in Venice but living and writing at the French court, became an author out of necessity when she was left a widow with three young children and an aged mother to support. Among her many works are a poem in praise of Joan of Arc and a history of famous women—including artists—from antiquity to her own time. In *The Book of the City of Ladies*, she defended women's abilities and argued for women's rights and status.

These writers, as surely as Giotto, Duccio, Peter Parler, and Master Theodoric, led the way into a new era.

---

sophistication were concerned—the painter Jean Pucelle began to show an interest in experimenting with established conventions.

Changes in the way that society was organized were also under way, and an expanding class of wealthy merchants supported the arts as patrons. Artisan guilds—organized by occupation— exerted quality control among members and supervised education through an apprenticeship system. Admission to the guild came after examination and the creation of a "masterpiece"—literally, a piece fine enough to achieve master status. The major guilds included cloth finishers, wool merchants, and silk manufacturers, as well as pharmacists and doctors. Painters belonged to the pharmacy guild, perhaps because they used mortars and pestles to grind their colors. Their patron saint, Luke, who was believed to have painted the first image of the Virgin Mary, was also a physician—or so they thought. Sculptors who worked in wood and stone had their own guild, while those who worked in metals belonged to another. Guilds provided social services for their members, including care of the sick and funerals for the deceased. Each guild had its patron saint, maintained a chapel, and participated in religious and civic festivals.

Despite the cultural flourishing and economic growth of the early decades, by the middle of the fourteenth century much of Europe was in crisis. Prosperity had fostered population growth, which began to exceed food production. A series of bad harvests compounded this problem with famine. To make matters worse, a prolonged conflict known as the Hundred Years' War (1337–1453) erupted between France and England. Then, in mid century, a lethal plague known as the Black Death swept across Europe (**MAP 17–1**), wiping out as much as 40 percent of the population. In spite of these catastrophic events, however, the strong current of cultural change still managed to persist through to the end of the century and beyond.

ITALY

As great wealth promoted patronage of art in fourteenth-century Italy, artists began to emerge as individuals, in the modern sense, both in their own eyes and in the eyes of patrons. Although their methods and working conditions remained largely unchanged from the Middle Ages, artists in Italy contracted freely with wealthy townspeople and nobles as well as with civic and religious bodies. Perhaps it was their economic and social freedom that encouraged ambition and self-confidence, individuality and innovation.

FLORENTINE ARCHITECTURE AND METALWORK

The typical medieval Italian city was a walled citadel on a hilltop. Houses clustered around the church and an open city square. Powerful families added towers to their houses, both for defense

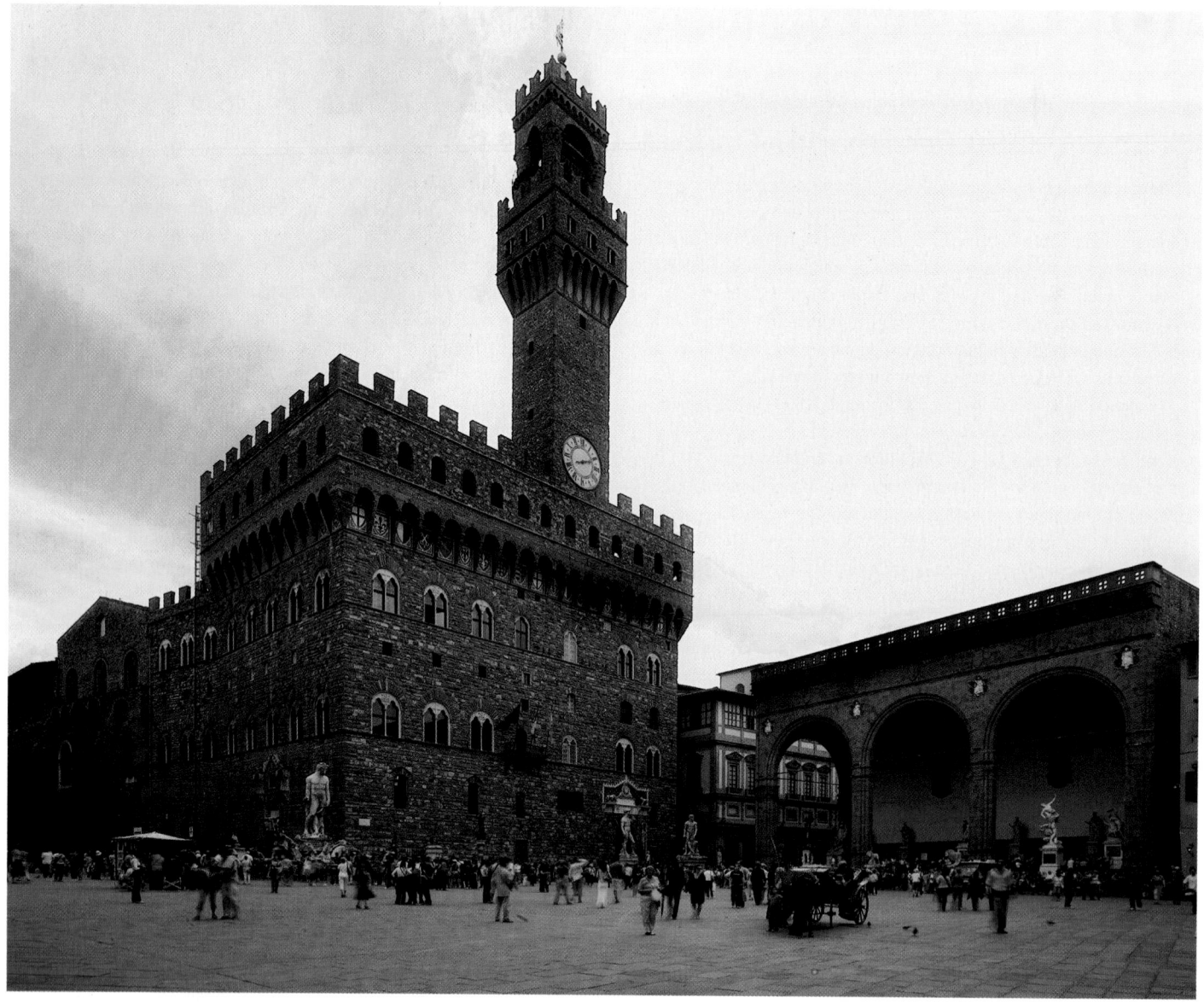

17-2 • PIAZZA DELLA SIGNORIA WITH PALAZZO DELLA SIGNORIA (TOWN HALL) 1299–1310, AND LOGGIA DEI LANZI (LOGGIA OF THE LANCERS), 1376–1382
Florence.

SEE MORE: Click the Google Earth link for the Palazzo della Signoria www.myartslab.com

and as expressions of family pride. In Florence, by contrast, the ancient Roman city—with its axial rectangular plan and open city squares—formed the basis for civic layout. The cathedral stood northeast of the ancient forum and a street following the Roman plan connected it with the Piazza della Signoria, the seat of the government.

THE PALAZZO DELLA SIGNORIA. The Signoria (ruling body, from *signore*, meaning "Lord") that governed Florence met in the **PALAZZO DELLA SIGNORIA**, a massive fortified building with a tall bell tower 300 feet high (**FIG. 17–2**). The building faces a large square, or piazza, which became the true center of Florence. The town houses around the piazza often had benches along their walls to provide convenient public seating. Between 1376 and 1382,

master builders Benci di Cione and Simone Talenti constructed a huge **loggia** or covered open-air corridor at one side—now known as the Loggi dei Lanzi (Loggia of the Lancers)—to provide a sheltered locale for ceremonies and speeches.

THE BAPTISTERY DOORS. In 1330, Andrea Pisano (c. 1290–1348) was awarded the prestigious commission for a pair of gilded bronze doors for the Florentine Baptistery of San Giovanni, situated directly in front of the cathedral. (Andrea's "last" name means "from Pisa;" he was not related to Nicola and Giovanni Pisano.) The doors were completed within six years and display 20 scenes from the **LIFE OF JOHN THE BAPTIST** (the San Giovanni to whom the baptistery is dedicated) set above eight personifications of the Virtues (**FIG. 17–3**). The overall effect is two-dimensional and

17-3 • Andrea Pisano **LIFE OF JOHN THE BAPTIST**
South doors, Baptistery of San Giovanni, Florence. 1330–1336. Gilded bronze, each panel 19¼ × 17″
(48 × 43 cm). Frame, Ghiberti workshop, mid-15th century.

The bronze vine scrolls filled with flowers, fruits, and birds on the lintel and jambs framing the door
were added in the mid fifteenth century.

17-4 • Andrea Pisano
**THE BAPTISM OF THE
MULTITUDE**
From the south doors, Baptistery
of San Giovanni, Florence.
1330–1336. Gilded bronze,
19¼ × 17″ (48 × 43 cm).

decorative: a grid of 28 rectangles with repeated quatrefoils filled by the graceful, patterned poses of delicate human figures. Within the quatrefoil frames, however, the figural compositions create the illusion of three-dimensional forms moving within the described spaces of natural and architectural worlds.

The scene of John baptizing a multitude (FIG. 17–4) takes place on a shelflike stage created by a forward extension of the rocky natural setting, which also expands back behind the figures into a corner of the quatrefoil frame. Composed as a rectangular group, the gilded figures present an independent mass of modeled forms. The illusion of three-dimensionality is enhanced by the way the curving folds of their clothing wrap around their bodies. At the same time, their graceful gestures and the elegant fall of their drapery reflect the soft curves and courtly postures of French Gothic art. Their quiet dignity, however, seems particular to the work of Andrea himself.

FLORENTINE PAINTING

Florence and Siena, rivals in so many ways, each supported a flourishing school of painting in the fourteenth century. Both grew out of thirteenth-century painting traditions and engendered individual artists who became famous in their own time. The Byzantine influence—the *maniera greca* ("Greek style")—continued to provide models of dramatic pathos and narrative iconography, as well as stylized features including the use of gold for drapery folds and striking contrasts of highlights and shadows in the modeling of individual forms. By the end of the fourteenth century, the painter and commentator Cennino Cennini (see "Cennino Cennini on Panel Painting," page 544) would be struck by the accessibility and modernity of Giotto's art, which, though it retained traces of the *maniera greca*, was moving toward the depiction of a lifelike, contemporary world anchored in three-dimensional forms.

CIMABUE. In Florence, this transformation to a more modern style began a little earlier than in Siena. About 1280, a painter named Cenni di Pepi (active c. 1272–1302), better known by his nickname "Cimabue," painted a panel portraying the **VIRGIN AND CHILD ENTHRONED (FIG. 17–5)**, perhaps for the main altar of the church of Santa Trinità in Florence. At over 12 feet tall, this enormous painting set a new precedent for monumental altarpieces. Cimabue surrounds the Virgin and Child with angels and places a row of Hebrew Bible prophets beneath them. The hieratically scaled figure of Mary holds the infant Jesus in her lap. Looking out at the viewer while gesturing toward her son as the path to salvation, she adopts a formula popular in Byzantine iconography since at least the seventh century (SEE FIG. 7–29).

Mary's huge throne, painted to resemble gilded bronze with inset enamels and gems, provides an architectural framework for the figures. Cimabue creates highlights on the drapery of Mary, Jesus, and the angels with thin lines of gold, as if to capture their divine radiance. The viewer seems suspended in space in front of the image, simultaneously looking down on the projecting elements of the throne and Mary's lap, while looking straight ahead at the prophets at the base of the throne and the angels at each side. These spatial ambiguities, the subtle asymmetries within the

17-5 • Cimabue VIRGIN AND CHILD ENTHRONED
Most likely painted for the high altar of the church of Santa Trinità, Florence. c. 1280. Tempera and gold on wood panel, 12'7" × 7'4" (3.53 × 2.2 m). Galleria degli Uffizi, Florence.

SEE MORE: See a video about the egg tempera process
www.myartslab.com

centralized composition, the Virgin's engaging gaze, and the individually conceived faces of the old men give the picture a sense of life and the figures a sense of presence. Cimabue's ambitious attention to spatial volumes, his use of delicate modeling in light and shade to simulate three-dimensional form, and his efforts to give naturalistic warmth to human figures had an impact on the future development of Italian painting.

GIOTTO DI BONDONE. According to the sixteenth-century chronicler Giorgio Vasari, Cimabue discovered a talented shepherd boy, Giotto di Bondone, and taught him to paint—and "not only did the young boy equal the style of his master, but he became such an excellent imitator of nature that he completely banished that crude Greek [i.e., Byzantine] style and revived the modern and excellent art of painting, introducing good drawing from live natural models, something which had not been done for more than two hundred years" (Vasari, translated by Bondanella and Bondanella, p. 16). After his training, Giotto may have collaborated on murals at the prestigious church of St. Francis in Assisi. We know he worked for the Franciscans in Florence and absorbed facets of their teaching. St. Francis's message of simple, humble devotion, direct experience of God, and love for all creatures was

17-6 • Giotto di Bondone VIRGIN AND CHILD ENTHRONED
Most likely painted for the high altar of the church of the Ognissanti (All Saints), Florence. 1305–1310. Tempera and gold on wood panel, 10′8″ × 6′8¼″ (3.53 × 2.05 m). Galleria degli Uffizi, Florence.

EXPLORE MORE: Gain insight from a primary source by Dante Alighieri that references Giotto di Bondone
www.myartslab.com

TECHNIQUE | *Buon Fresco*

The two techniques used in mural painting are *buon* ("true") *fresco* ("fresh"), in which paint is applied with water-based paints on wet plaster, and *fresco secco* ("dry"), in which paint is applied to a dry plastered wall. The two methods can be used on the same wall painting.

The advantage of *buon fresco* is its durability. A chemical reaction occurs as the painted plaster dries, which bonds the pigments into the wall surface. In *fresco secco*, by contrast, the color does not become part of the wall and tends to flake off over time. The chief disadvantage of *buon fresco* is that it must be done quickly without mistakes. The painter plasters and paints only as much as can be completed in a day, which explains the Italian term for each of these sections: **giornata**, or a day's work. The size of a *giornata* varies according to the complexity of the painting within it. A face, for instance, might take an entire day, whereas large areas of sky can be painted quite rapidly. In Giotto's Scrovegni Chapel, scholars have identified 852 separate *giornate*, some worked on concurrently within a single day by assistants in Giotto's workshop.

In medieval and Renaissance Italy, a wall to be frescoed was first prepared with a rough, thick undercoat of plaster known as the *arriccio*. When this was dry, assistants copied the master painter's composition onto it with reddish-brown pigment or charcoal. The artist made any necessary adjustments. These underdrawings, known as **sinopia**, have an immediacy and freshness lost in the finished painting. Work proceeded in irregularly shaped *giornate* conforming to the contours of major figures and objects. Assistants covered one section at a time with a fresh, thin coat of very fine plaster—the *intonaco*—

over the *sinopia*, and when this was "set" but not dry, the artist worked with pigments mixed with water, painting from the top down so that drips fell on unfinished portions. Some areas requiring pigments such as ultramarine blue (which was unstable in *buon fresco*), as well as areas requiring gilding, would be added after the wall was dry using the *fresco secco* technique.

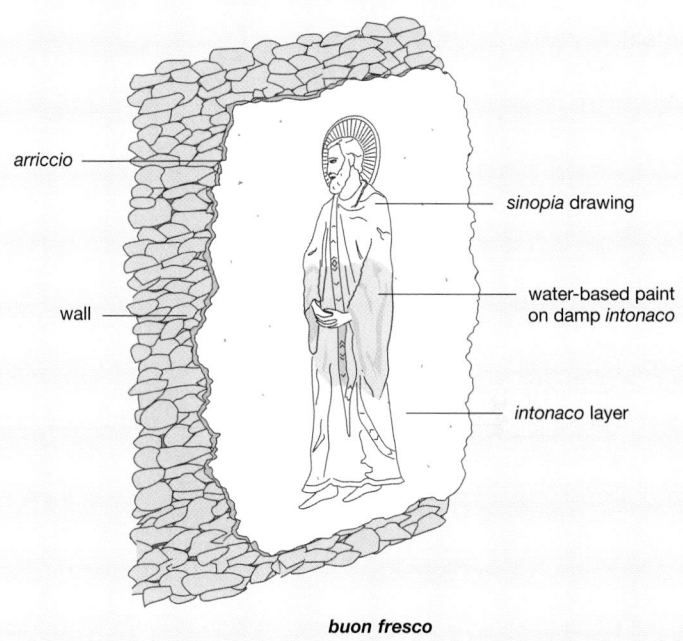

arriccio

sinopia drawing

wall

water-based paint on damp *intonaco*

intonaco layer

buon fresco

gaining followers throughout western Europe, and it had a powerful impact on thirteenth- and fourteenth-century Italian literature and art.

Compared to Cimabue's *Virgin and Child Enthroned*, Giotto's panel of the same subject **(FIG. 17–6)**, painted about 30 years later for the church of the Ognissanti (All Saints) in Florence, exhibits greater spatial consistency and sculptural solidity while retaining some of Cimabue's conventions. The position of the figures within a symmetrical composition reflects Cimabue's influence. Gone, however, are Mary's modestly inclined head and the delicate gold folds in her drapery. Instead, light and shadow play gently across her stocky form, and her action—holding her child's leg instead of pointing him out to us—seems less contrived. This colossal Mary overwhelms her slender Gothic tabernacle of a throne, where figures peer through openings and haloes overlap faces. In spite of the hieratic scale and the formal, enthroned image and flat, gold background, Giotto has created the sense that these are fully three-dimensional beings, whose plainly draped, bulky bodies inhabit real space. The Virgin's solid torso is revealed by her thin tunic, and Giotto's angels are substantial solids whose foreshortened postures project from the foreground toward us, unlike those of Cimabue, which stay on the surface along lateral strips composed of overlapping screens of color.

Although he was trained in the Florentine tradition, many of Giotto's principal works were produced elsewhere. After a sojourn in Rome during the last years of the thirteenth century, he was called to Padua in northern Italy soon after 1300 to paint frescos (see "Buon Fresco," above) for a new chapel being constructed at the site of an ancient Roman arena—explaining why it is usually referred to as the Arena Chapel. The chapel was commissioned by Enrico Scrovegni, whose family fortune was made through the practice of usury—which at this time meant charging interest when loaning money, a sin so grave that it resulted in exclusion from the Christian sacraments. Enrico's father, Regibaldo, was a particularly egregious case (he appears in Dante's *Inferno* as the prototypical usurer), but evidence suggests that Enrico followed in his father's footsteps, and the building of the Arena Chapel next to his new palatial residence seems to have been conceived at least in part as a penitential act, part of Enrico's campaign not only to atone for his father's sins, but also to seek absolution for his own. He was pardoned by Pope Benedict XI (pontificate 1303–1304).

That Scrovegni called two of the most famous artists of the time—Giotto and Giovanni Pisano (SEE FIG. 16–33)—to decorate his chapel indicates that his goals were to express his power, sophistication, and prestige, as well as to atone for his sins. The building itself has little architectural distinction. It is a simple,

17-7 • Giotto di Bondone **SCROVEGNI (ARENA) CHAPEL**
Padua. 1305–1306. Frescos. View toward east wall.

barrel-vaulted room that provides broad walls, a boxlike space to showcase Giotto's paintings **(FIG. 17–7)**. Giotto covered the entrance wall with the *Last Judgment* (not visible here), and the sanctuary wall with three highlighted scenes from the life of Christ. The Annunciation spreads over the two painted architectural frameworks on either side of the high arched opening into the sanctuary itself. Below this are, to the left, the scene of Judas receiving payment for betraying Jesus, and, to the right, the scene of the Visitation, where the Virgin, pregnant with God incarnate, embraces her cousin Elizabeth, pregnant with John the Baptist. The compositions and color arrangement of these two scenes create a symmetrical pairing that encourages viewers to relate them, comparing the ill-gotten financial gains of Judas (a rather clear reference to Scrovegni usury) to the miraculous pregnancy that brought the promise of salvation.

Giotto subdivided the side walls of the chapel into framed pictures. A dado of faux-marble and allegorical **grisaille** (monochrome paintings in shades of gray) paintings of the Virtues and Vices support vertical bands painted to resemble marble inlay into which are inserted painted imitations of carved medallions. The central band of medallions spans the vault, crossing a brilliant, lapis-blue, star-spangled sky in which large portrait disks float like glowing moons. Set into this framework are three horizontal bands of rectangular narrative scenes from the life of the Virgin and her parents at the top, and Jesus along the middle and lower registers, constituting together the primary religious program of the chapel.

Both the individual scenes and the overall program display Giotto's genius for distilling complex stories into a series of compelling moments. He concentrates on the human dimensions of the unfolding drama—from touches of anecdotal humor to expressions of profound anguish—rather than on its symbolic or theological weight. His prodigious narrative skills are apparent in a set of scenes from Christ's life on the north wall **(FIG. 17–8)**. At top left Jesus performs his first miracle, changing water into wine at the wedding feast at Cana. The wine steward—looking very much like the jars of new wine himself—sips the results. To the right is the

17-8 • Giotto di Bondone MARRIAGE AT CANA, RAISING OF LAZARUS, LAMENTATION, AND RESURRECTION / NOLI ME TANGERE
North wall of Scrovegni (Arena) Chapel, Padua. 1305–1306. Fresco, each scene approx. 6′5″ × 6′ (2 × 1.85 m).

Raising of Lazarus, where boldly modeled and individualized figures twist in space. Through their postures and gestures they react to the human drama by pleading for Jesus' help, or by expressing either astonishment at the miracle or revulsion at the smell of death. Jesus is separated from the crowd. His transforming gesture is highlighted against the dark blue of the background, his profile face locked in communication with the similarly isolated Lazarus, whose eyes—still fixed in death—let us know that the miracle is just about to happen.

On the lower register, where Jesus' grief-stricken followers lament over his dead body, Giotto conveys palpable human suffering, drawing viewers into a circle of personal grief. The stricken Virgin pulls close to her dead son, communing with mute intensity, while John the Evangelist flings his arms back in convulsive despair and others hunch over the corpse. Giotto has

linked this somber scene—much as he linked the scene of Judas' pact and the Visitation across the sanctuary arch—to the mourning of Lazarus on the register above through the seemingly continuous diagonal implied by the sharply angled hillside behind both scenes and by the rhyming repetition of mourners in each scene—facing in opposite directions—who throw back their arms to express their emotional state. Viewers would know that the mourning in both scenes is resolved by resurrection, portrayed in the last picture in this set.

Following traditional medieval practice, the fresco program is full of scenes and symbols like these that are intended to be contemplated as coordinated or contrasting juxtapositions. What is new here is the way Giotto draws us into the experience of these events. This direct emotional appeal not only allows viewers to imagine these scenes in relation to their own life experiences; it

17-9 • Giotto di
Bondone **KISS
OF JUDAS**
South wall of Scrovegni
(Arena) Chapel, Padua.
1305–1306. Fresco,
6'6¾" × 6'⅞"
(2 × 1.85 m).

also embodies the new Franciscan emphasis on personal devotion rooted in empathetic responses to sacred stories.

One of the most gripping paintings in the chapel is Giotto's portrayal of the **KISS OF JUDAS**, the moment of betrayal that represents the first step on Jesus' road to the Crucifixion **(FIG. 17–9)**. Savior and traitor are slightly off-center in the near foreground. The expansive sweep of Judas' strident yellow cloak—the same outfit he wore at the scene of his payment for the betrayal on the strip of wall to the left of the sanctuary arch—almost completely swallows Christ's body. Surrounding them, faces glare from all directions. A bristling array of weapons radiating from the confrontation draws attention to the encounter between Christ and Judas and documents the militarism of the arresting battalion. Jesus stands solid, a model of calm resolve that recalls his visual characterization in the Resurrection of Lazarus, and forms a striking foil to the noisy and chaotic aggression that engulfs him. Judas, in simian profile, purses his lips for the treacherous kiss that will betray Jesus to his captors, setting up a mythic confrontation of good and evil. In a subplot to the left, Peter lunges forward to sever the ear of a member of the arresting retinue. They are behind another broad sweep of fabric, this one extended by an ominous figure seen from behind and completely concealed except for the clenched hand that pulls at Peter's mantle. Indeed, a broad expanse of cloth and lateral gestures creates a barrier along the picture plane—as if to protect viewers from the compressed chaos of the scene itself. Rarely has this poignant event been visualized with such riveting power.

SIENESE PAINTING

Like their Florentine rivals, Sienese painters were rooted in thirteenth-century pictorial traditions, especially those of Byzantine art. Sienese painting emphasized the decorative potential of narrative painting, with brilliant, jewel-like colors and elegantly posed figures. For this reason, some art historians consider Sienese art more conservative than Florentine art, but we will see that it has its own charm, and its own narrative strategy.

DUCCIO DI BUONINSEGNA. Siena's foremost painter was Duccio di Buoninsegna (active 1278–1318), whose creative synthesis of Byzantine and French Gothic sources transformed the tradition in which he worked. The format of a large altarpiece he painted for the church of Santa Maria Novella in Florence after 1285 **(FIG. 17–10)** is already familiar from the Florentine altarpieces of Cimabue and Giotto (SEE FIGS. 17-5 and 17-6). A monumental Virgin and Child sit on an elaborate throne, set against a gold ground and seemingly supported by flanking angels. But in striking contrast both with Cimabue's Byzantine drapery stylizations and sense of three-dimensional form and space, and with Giotto's matter-of-fact emphasis on weightiness and references to an earthly setting, Duccio's figural composition foregrounds gracefulness of pose and gesture and a color scheme rich in luminous pastels. Drapery not only models his figures into convincing forms; it also falls into graceful lines and patterns, especially apparent in the sinuous golden edge of the Virgin's deep blue mantle and the ornamental extravagance of the brocade hangings on her throne.

17–10 • Duccio di Buoninsegna
VIRGIN AND CHILD ENTHRONED (RUCELLAI MADONNA)
Commissioned in 1285. Tempera and gold on wood panel, 14′9⅛″ × 9′6⅛″ (4.5 × 2.9 m). Galleria degli Uffizi, Florence.

This altarpiece, commissioned in 1285 for the church of Santa Maria Novella in Florence by the Society of the Virgin Mary, is now known as the *Rucellai Madonna* because it was installed at one time in the Rucellai family's chapel within the church.

17–11a • Duccio di Buoninsegna
CONJECTURAL RECONSTRUCTION OF THE FRONT OF THE MAESTÀ ALTARPIECE
Made for Siena Cathedral. 1308–1311. Tempera and gold on wood, main front panel 7 × 13′ (2.13 × 4.12 m).

EXPLORE MORE: Gain insight from a primary source related to Duccio's *Maestà*
www.myartslab.com

17–11b • Duccio di Buoninsegna
CONJECTURAL RECONSTRUCTION OF THE BACK OF THE MAESTÀ ALTARPIECE

Between 1308 and 1311, Duccio and his workshop painted a huge altarpiece commissioned by Siena Cathedral and known as the *Maestà* ("Majesty") **(FIG. 17–11)**. Creating this altarpiece—assembled from many wood panels bonded together before painting—was an arduous undertaking. The work was not only large—the central panel alone was 7 by 13 feet—but it had to be painted on both sides since it could be seen from all directions when installed on the main altar at the center of the sanctuary.

Because the *Maestà* was dismantled in 1771, its power and beauty can only be imagined from scattered parts, some still in Siena but others elsewhere. **FIG. 17–11a** is a reconstruction of how the front of the original altarpiece might have looked. It is dominated by a large representation of the Virgin and Child in Majesty (thus its title of *Maestà*), flanked by 20 angels and ten saints, including the four patron saints of Siena kneeling in the foreground. Above and below this lateral tableau were small narrative scenes from the last days of the life of the Virgin (above) and the infancy of Christ (spread across the predella). An inscription running around the base of Mary's majestic throne places the artist's signature within an optimistic framework: "Holy Mother of God, be thou the cause of peace for Siena and life to Duccio because he painted thee thus." This was not Duccio's first work for the cathedral. In 1288 he had designed a stunning stained-glass window portraying the Death, Assumption, and Coronation of the Virgin for the huge circular opening in the east wall of the sanctuary. It would have hovered over the installed *Maestà* when it was placed on the altar in 1311.

On the back of the *Maestà* **(FIG. 17–11b)** were episodes from the life of Christ, focusing on his Passion. Sacred narrative unfolds in elegant episodes enacted by graceful figures who seem to dance their way through these stories while still conveying emotional content. Characteristic of Duccio's narrative style is the scene of the **RAISING OF LAZARUS (FIG. 17–12)**. Lyrical figures enact the event with graceful decorum, but their highly charged glances and expressive gestures—especially the bold reach of Christ—convey a strong sense of dramatic urgency that contrasts with the tense stillness that we saw in Giotto's rendering of this same moment of confrontation (SEE FIG. 17–8). Duccio's shading of drapery, like his modeling of faces, faithfully describes the figures' three-dimensionality, but the crisp outlines of the jewel-colored shapes created by their drapery, as well as the sinuous continuity of folds and gestures, generate rhythmic patterns across the surface. Experimentation with the portrayal of space extends from the receding rocks of the mountainous landscape to carefully studied interiors, here the tomb of Lazarus whose heavy door was removed by the straining hug of a bystander to reveal the shrouded figure of Jesus' resurrected friend, propped up against the door jamb.

The enthusiasm with which citizens greeted a great painting or altarpiece like the *Maestà* demonstrates the power of images as

17-12 • Duccio di Buoninsegna RAISING OF LAZARUS
From the back of the *Maestà* altarpiece (lower right corner of FIG. 17–9b), made for Siena Cathedral. 1308–1311. Tempera and gold on wood, 17⅛ × 18¼" (43.5 × 46.4 cm). Kimbell Art Museum, Fort Worth, Texas.

Il Libro dell' Arte (*The Book of Art*) of Cennino Cennini (c. 1370–1440) is a compendium of Florentine painting techniques from about 1400 that includes step-by-step instructions for making panel paintings, a process also used in Sienese paintings of the same period.

The wood for the panels, he explains, should be fine-grained, free of blemishes, and thoroughly seasoned by slow drying. The first step in preparing such a panel for painting was to cover its surface with clean white linen strips soaked in a **gesso** made from gypsum, a task, he tells us, best done on a dry, windy day. Gesso provided a ground, or surface, on which to paint, and Cennini specified that at least nine layers should be applied. The gessoed surface should then be burnished until it resembles ivory. Only then could the artist sketch the composition of the work with charcoal made from burned willow twigs. At this point, advised Cennini, "When you have finished drawing your figure, especially if it is in a very valuable [altarpiece], so that you are counting on profit and reputation from it, leave alone for a few days, going back to it now and then to look it over and improve it wherever it still needs something. When it seems to you about right (and bear in mind that you may copy and examine things done by other good masters; that it is no shame to you) when the figure is satisfactory, take the feather and rub it over the drawing very lightly, until the drawing is practically effaced" (Cennini, trans. Thompson, p. 75). At this point, the final design would be inked in with a fine squirrel-hair brush. Gold leaf, he advises, should be affixed on a humid day, the tissue-thin sheets carefully glued down with a mixture of fine powdered clay and egg white on the reddish clay ground called bole. Then the gold is burnished with a gemstone or the tooth of a carnivorous animal. Punched and incised patterning should be added to the gold leaf later.

Fourteenth- and fifteenth-century Italian painters worked principally in tempera paint, powdered pigments mixed with egg yolk, a little water, and an occasional touch of glue. Apprentices were kept busy grinding pigments and mixing paints, setting them out for more senior painters in wooden bowls or shell dishes.

Cennini outlined a detailed and highly formulaic painting process. Faces, for example, were always to be done last, with flesh tones applied over two coats of a light greenish pigment and highlighted with touches of red and white. The finished painting was to be given a layer of varnish to protect it and intensify its colors.

EXPLORE MORE: Gain insight from a primary source by Cennino Cennini **www.myartslab.com**

17-13 • Simone Martini and Lippo Memmi **ANNUNCIATION** Made for Siena Cathedral. 1333. Tempera and gold on wood, 10′ × 8′9″ (3 × 2.67 m). Galleria degli Uffizi, Florence.

17-14 • AERIAL VIEW OF THE CAMPO IN SIENA WITH THE PALAZZO PUBBLICO (CITY HALL INCLUDING ITS TOWER) FACING ITS STRAIGHT SIDE
Siena. Palazzo Pubblico 1297–c. 1315; tower 1320s–1340s.

well as the association of such magnificent works with the glory of the city itself. According to a contemporary account, on December 20, 1311, the day that Duccio's altarpiece was carried from his workshop to the cathedral, all the shops were shut, and everyone in the city participated in the procession, with "bells ringing joyously, out of reverence for so noble a picture as is this" (Holt, p. 69).

SIMONE MARTINI. The generation of painters who followed Duccio continued to paint in the elegant style he established, combining the evocation of three-dimensional form with a graceful continuity of linear pattern. One of Duccio's most successful and innovative followers was Simone Martini (c. 1284–1344), whose paintings were in high demand throughout Italy, including in Assisi where he covered the walls of the St. Martin Chapel with frescos between 1312 and 1319. His most famous work, however, was commissioned in 1333 for the cathedral of his native Siena, an altarpiece of the **ANNUNCIATION** flanked by two saints **(FIG. 17–13)** that he painted in collaboration with his brother-in-law, Lippo Memmi.

The smartly dressed figure of Gabriel—the extended flourish of his drapery behind him suggesting he has just arrived, and with some speed—raises his hand to address the Virgin. The words of his message are actually incised into the gold-leafed gesso of the background, running from his opened mouth toward the Virgin's ear: *Ave gratia plena dominus tecum* (Luke 1:28: "Hail, full of grace, the Lord is with thee"). Seemingly frightened—at the very least startled—by this forceful and unexpected celestial messenger, Mary recoils into her lavish throne, her thumb inserted into the book she had been reading to safeguard her place, while her other hand pulls at her clothing in an elegant gesture of nobility ultimately deriving from the courtly art of thirteenth-century Paris (see Solomon, second lancet from the right in FIG. 16–13).

AMBROGIO LORENZETTI. The most important civic structure in Siena was the **PALAZZO PUBBLICO (FIG. 17–14)**, the town hall which served as the seat of government, just as the Palazzo della Signoria did in rival Florence. There are similarities between these two buildings. Both are designed as strong, fortified structures sitting on the edge of a public piazza; both have a tall tower, making them visible signs of the city from a considerable distance. The Palazzo Pubblico was constructed from 1297 to 1310, but the tower was not completed until 1348, when the bronze bell, which rang to signal meetings of the ruling council, was installed.

The interior of the Palazzo Pubblico was the site of important commissions by some of Siena's most famous artists. In c. 1315, Simone Martini painted a large mural of the Virgin in Majesty surrounded by saints—clearly based on Duccio's recently installed *Maestà*. Then, in 1338, the Siena city council commissioned Ambrogio Lorenzetti to paint frescos for the council room of the Palazzo known as the Sala della Pace (Chamber of Peace) on the theme of the contrast between good and bad government (SEE FIG. 17–1).

Ambrogio painted the results of both good and bad government on the two long walls. For the expansive scene of the **EFFECTS OF GOOD GOVERNMENT IN THE CITY AND IN THE COUNTRY**, and in tribute to his patrons, Ambrogio created an idealized but recognizable portrait of the city of Siena and its immediate environs **(FIG. 17–15)**. The cathedral dome and the distinctive striped campanile are visible in the upper left-hand corner; the streets are filled with the bustling activity of productive citi-zens who also have time for leisurely diversions. Ambrogio shows the city from shifting viewpoints so we can see as much as possible, and renders its inhabitants larger in scale than the buildings around them so as to highlight their activity. Featured in the foreground is a circle of dancers—probably a professional troupe of male entertainers masquerading as women as part of a spring festival—and above them, at the top of the painting, a band of masons stand on exterior scaffolding constructing the wall of a new building.

The Porta Romana, Siena's gateway leading to Rome, divides the thriving city from its surrounding countryside. In this panoramic landscape painting, Ambrogio describes a natural world marked by agricultural productivity, showing activities of all seasons simultaneously—sowing, hoeing, and harvesting. Hovering above the gate that separates city life and country life is a woman clad in a wisp of transparent drapery, a scroll in one hand and a miniature gallows complete with a hanged man in the other. She represents Security, and her scroll bids those coming to the city to enter without fear because she has taken away the power of the guilty who would harm them.

The world of the Italian city-states—which had seemed so full of promise in Ambrogio Lorenzetti's *Good Government* fresco—was transformed as the middle of the century approached into uncertainty and desolation by a series of natural and societal disasters—in 1333, a flood devastated Florence, followed by banking failures in the 1340s, famine in 1346–1347, and epidemics of the bubonic plague, especially virulent in the summer of 1348, just a few years after Ambrogio's frescos were completed. Some art historians have traced the influence of these calamities on the visual arts at the middle of the fourteenth century (see "The Black Death," page 548). Yet as dark as those days must have seemed to the men and women living through them, the strong currents of cultural and artistic change initiated earlier in the century would persist. In a relatively short span of time, the European Middle Ages gave way in Florence to a new movement that would blossom in the Italian Renaissance.

17-15 • Ambrogio Lorenzetti THE EFFECTS OF GOOD GOVERNMENT IN THE CITY AND IN THE COUNTRY
Sala dei Nove (also known as Sala della Pace), Palazzo Pubblico, Siena, Italy. 1338–1339. Fresco, total length about 46' (14 m).

FRANCE

At the beginning of the fourteenth century, the royal court in Paris was still the arbiter of taste in western Europe, as it had been in the days of King Louis IX (St. Louis). During the Hundred Years' War, however, the French countryside was ravaged by armed struggles and civil strife. The power of the old feudal nobility, weakened significantly by warfare, was challenged by townsmen, who took advantage of new economic opportunities that opened up in the wake of the conflict. As centers of art and architecture, the duchy of Burgundy, England, and, for a brief golden moment, the court of Prague began to rival Paris.

French sculptors found lucrative new outlets for their work—not only in stone, but in wood, ivory, and precious metals, often decorated with enamel and gemstones—in the growing demand among wealthy patrons for religious art intended for homes as well as churches. Manuscript painters likewise created lavishly illustrated books for the personal devotions of the wealthy and powerful. And architectural commissions focused on smaller, exquisitely detailed chapels or small churches, often under private patronage, rather than on the building of cathedrals funded by church institutions.

MANUSCRIPT ILLUMINATION

By the late thirteenth century, private prayer books became popular among wealthy patrons. Because they contained special prayers to be recited at the eight canonical devotional "hours" between morning and night, an individual copy of one of these books came to be called a **Book of Hours**. Such a book included everything the lay person needed for pious practice—psalms, prayers to and offices of the Virgin and other saints (like the owner's patron or the patron of their home church), a calendar of feast days, and sometimes prayers for the dead. During the fourteenth century, a richly decorated Book of Hours was worn or carried like jewelry, counting among a noble person's most important portable possessions.

THE BOOK OF HOURS OF JEANNE D'ÉVREUX. Perhaps at their marriage in 1324, King Charles IV gave his 14-year-old queen, Jeanne d'Évreux, a tiny Book of Hours—it fits easily when open within one hand—illuminated by Parisian painter Jean Pucelle (see "A Closer Look," page 550). This book was so precious to the queen that she mentioned it and its illuminator specifically in her will, leaving this royal treasure to King Charles V. Pucelle painted the book's pictures in *grisaille*—monochromatic painting in shades of gray with only delicate touches of color. His style clearly derives from the courtly mode established in Paris at the time of St. Louis, with its softly modeled, voluminous draperies gathered loosely and falling in projecting diagonal folds around tall, elegantly posed figures with carefully coiffed curly hair, broad foreheads, and delicate features. But his conception of space, with figures placed within coherent, discrete architectural settings, suggests a firsthand knowledge of contemporary Sienese art.

Jeanne appears in the initial *D* below the Annunciation, kneeling in prayer before a lectern, perhaps using this Book of Hours to guide her meditations, beginning with the words written

The Black Death

A deadly outbreak of the bubonic plague, known as the Black Death after the dark sores that developed on the bodies of its victims, spread to Europe from Asia, both by land and by sea, in the middle of the fourteenth century. At least half the urban population of Florence and Siena—some estimate 80 percent—died during the summer of 1348, probably including the artists Andrea Pisano and Ambrogio Lorenzetti. Death was so quick and widespread that basic social structures crumbled in the resulting chaos; people did not know where the disease came from, what caused it, or how long the pandemic would last.

Mid-twentieth-century art historian Millard Meiss proposed that the Black Death had a significant impact on the development of Italian art in the middle of the fourteenth century. Pointing to what he saw as a reactionary return to hieratic linearity in religious art, Meiss theorized that artists had retreated from the rounded forms that had characterized the work of Giotto to old-fashioned styles, and that this artistic change reflected a growing reliance on traditional religious values in the wake of a disaster that some interpreted as God's punishment of a world in moral decline.

An altarpiece painted in 1354–1357 by Andrea di Cione, nicknamed Orcagna ("Archangel"), under the patronage of Tommasso Strozzi—the so-called *Strozzi Altarpiece*—is an example of the sort of paintings that led Meiss to his interpretation. The painting's otherworldly vision is dominated by a central figure of Christ, presumably enthroned, but without any hint of an actual seat, evoking the image of the judge at the Last Judgment, outside time and space. The silhouetted outlines of the standing and kneeling saints emphasize surface over depth; the gold expanse of floor beneath them does not offer any reassuring sense of spatial recession to contain them and their activity. Throughout, line and color are more prominent than form.

Recent art historians have stepped back from Meiss's theory of stylistic change in mid-fourteenth-century Italy. Some have pointed out logical relationships between style and subject in the works Meiss cites; others have seen in them a mannered outgrowth of current style rather than a reversion to an earlier style; still others have discounted the underlying notion that stylistic change is connected with social situations. But there is no denying the relationship of works such as the *Strozzi Altarpiece* with death and judgment, sanctity and the promise of salvation. These themes are suggested in the narrative scenes on the **predella** (the lower zone of the altarpiece): Thomas Aquinas's ecstasy during Mass, Christ's miraculous walk on water to rescue Peter, and the salvation of Emperor Henry II because of his donation of a chalice to a religious institution. While these are not uncommon scenes in sacred art, it is difficult not see a relationship between their choice as subject matter here and the specter cast by the Black Death over a world that had just imagined its prosperity in path-breaking works of visual art firmly rooted in references to everyday life.

Andrea di Cione (nicknamed Orcagna) **ENTHRONED CHRIST WITH SAINTS, FROM THE STROZZI ALTARPIECE** Strozzi Chapel, Santa Maria Novella, Florence. 1354–1357. Tempera and gold on wood, 9' × 9'8" (2.74 × 2.95 m).

EXPLORE MORE: Gain insight from a primary source related to the Black Death www.myartslab.com

on this page: *Domine labia mea aperies* (Psalm 51:15: "O Lord, open thou my lips"). The juxtaposition of the praying Jeanne's portrait with a scene from the life of the Virgin Mary suggests that the sacred scene is actually a vision inspired by Jeanne's meditations. The young queen might have identified with and sought to feel within herself Mary's joy at Gabriel's message. Given what we know of Jeanne's own life story and her royal husband's predicament, it might also have directed the queen's prayers toward the fulfillment of his wish for a male heir.

In the Annunciation, Mary is shown receiving the archangel Gabriel in a Gothic building that seems to project outward from the page toward the viewer, while rejoicing angels look on from windows under the eaves. The group of romping children at the bottom of the page at first glance seems to echo the angelic jubilation. Folklorists have suggested, however, that the children are playing "froggy in the middle" or "hot cockles," games in which one child was tagged by the others. To the medieval viewer, if the game symbolized the mocking of Christ or the betrayal of Judas, who "tags" his friend, it would have evoked a darker mood by referring to the picture on the other page of this opening, foreshadowing Jesus' imminent death even as his life is beginning.

METALWORK AND IVORY

Fourteenth-century French sculpture is intimate in character. Religious subjects became more emotionally expressive; objects became smaller and demanded closer scrutiny from the viewer. In the secular realm, tales of love and valor were carved on luxury items to delight the rich (see "An Ivory Chest with Scenes of Romance," pages 552–553). Precious materials—gold, silver, and ivory—were preferred.

THE VIRGIN AND CHILD FROM SAINT-DENIS. A silver-gilt image of a standing **VIRGIN AND CHILD** (FIG. **17–16**) is a rare survivor that verifies the acclaim that was accorded Parisian fourteenth-century goldsmiths. An inscription on the base documents the statue's donation to the abbey church of Saint-Denis in 1339 and the donor's name, the same Queen Jeanne d'Évreux whose Book of Hours we have just examined. In a style that recalls the work of artist Jean Pucelle in that Book of Hours, the Virgin holds Jesus in her left arm with her weight on her left leg, standing in a graceful, characteristically Gothic S-curve pose. Mary originally wore a crown, and she still holds a large enameled and jeweled *fleur-de-lis*—the heraldic symbol of royal France—which served as a reliquary container for strands of Mary's hair. The Christ Child, reaching out tenderly to caress his mother's face, is babylike in both form and posture. On the base, minuscule statues of prophets stand on projecting piers to separate 14 enameled scenes from Christ's Infancy and Passion, reminding us of the suffering to come. The apple in the baby's hand carries the theme further with its reference to Christ's role as the new Adam, whose sacrifice on the cross—medieval Christians believed—redeemed humanity from the first couple's fall into sin when Eve bit into the forbidden fruit.

17-16 • VIRGIN AND CHILD
c. 1324–1339. Silver gilt and enamel, height 27⅛" (69 cm).
Musée du Louvre, Paris.

The Hours of Jeanne d'Évreux

> by Jean Pucelle, Two-Page Opening with the Kiss of Judas and the Annunciation. Paris. c. 1325–1328. *Grisaille* and color on vellum, each page 3½ × 2¼" (8.9 × 6.2 cm). Metropolitan Museum of Art, New York. The Cloisters Collection (54.1.2), fols. 15v–16r

In this opening Pucelle juxtaposes complementary scenes drawn from the Infancy and Passion of Christ, placed on opposing pages, in a scheme known as the Joys and Sorrows of the Virgin. The "joy" of the Annunciation on the right is paired with the "sorrow" of the betrayal and arrest of Christ on the left.

Christ sways back gracefully as Judas betrays him with a kiss. The S-curve of his body mirrors the Virgin's pose on the opposite page, as both accept their fate with courtly decorum.

The prominent lamp held aloft by a member of the arresting battalion informs the viewer that this scene takes place at night, in the dark.

The angel who holds up the boxlike enclosure where the Annunciation takes place is an allusion to the legend of the miraculous transportation of this building from Nazareth to Loreto in 1294.

Christ reaches casually down to heal Malchus, the assistant of the high priest whose ear Peter had just cut off in angry retaliation for his participation in the arrest of Jesus.

Scenes of secular amusements from everyday life, visual puns, and off-color jokes appear at the bottom of many pages of this book. Sometimes they relate to the themes of the sacred scenes above them. These comic knights riding goats may be a commentary on the lack of valor shown by the soldiers assaulting Jesus, especially if this wine barrel conjured up for Jeanne an association with the Eucharist.

The candle held by the cleric who guards the "door" to Jeanne's devotional retreat, as well as the rabbit emerging from its burrow in the marginal scene, are sexually charged symbols of fertility that seem directly related to the focused prayers of a child bride required to produce a male heir.

SEE MORE: View the Closer Look feature for The Hours of Jeanne d'Évreux **www.myartslab.com**

ENGLAND

Fourteenth-century England prospered in spite of the ravages of the Black Death and the Hundred Years' War with France. English life at this time is described in the brilliant social commentary of Geoffrey Chaucer in the *Canterbury Tales* (see "A New Spirit in Fourteenth-Century Literature," page 531). The royal family, especially Edward I (r. 1272–1307)—the castle builder—and many of the nobles and bishops were generous patrons of the arts.

EMBROIDERY: OPUS ANGLICANUM

Since the thirteenth century, the English had been renowned for pictorial needlework, using colored silk and gold thread to create images as detailed as contemporary painters produced in manuscripts. Popular throughout Europe, the art came to be called *opus anglicanum* ("English work"). The popes had more than 100 pieces in the Vatican treasury. The names of several prominent embroiderers are known, but in the thirteenth century no one surpassed Mabel of Bury St. Edmunds, who created both religious and secular articles for King Henry III (r. 1216–1272).

THE CHICHESTER-CONSTABLE CHASUBLE. This *opus angicanum* liturgical vestment worn by a priest during Mass **(FIG. 17–17)** was embroidered c. 1330–1350 with images formed by subtle gradations of colored silk. Where gold threads were laid and couched (tacked down with colored silk), the effect resembles the burnished gold-leaf backgrounds of manuscript illuminations. The Annunciation, the Adoration of the Magi, and the Coronation of the Virgin are set in cusped, crocketed **ogee** (S-shape) arches, supported on animal-head corbels and twisting branches sprouting oak leaves with seed-pearl acorns. Because the star and crescent moon in the Coronation of the Virgin scene are heraldic emblems of Edward III (r. 1327–1377), perhaps he or a family member commissioned this luxurious vestment.

During the celebration of the Mass, especially as the priest moved, *opus anglicanum* would have glinted in the candlelight amid treasures on the altar. Court dress was just as rich and colorful, and at court such embroidered garments proclaimed the rank and status of the wearer. So heavy did such gold and bejeweled garments become that their wearers often needed help to move.

17-17 • LIFE OF THE VIRGIN, BACK OF THE CHICHESTER-CONSTABLE CHASUBLE

From a set of vestments embroidered in *opus anglicanum* from southern England. c. 1330–1350. Red velvet with silk and metallic thread and seed pearls, length 4′3″ (129.5 cm), width 30″ (76 cm). Metropolitan Museum of Art, New York.

Fletcher Fund, 1927 (27 162.1)

An Ivory Chest with Scenes of Romance

Fourteenth-century Paris was renowned for more than its goldsmiths (SEE FIG. 17–16). Among the most sumptuous and sought-after Parisian luxury products were small chests assembled from carved ivory plaques that were used by wealthy women to store jewelry or other personal treasures. The entirely secular subject matter of these chests was romantic love. Indeed, they seem to have been courtship gifts from smitten men to desired women, or wedding presents offered by grooms to their brides.

A chest from around 1330–1350, now in the Walters Museum (SEE FIG. A), is one of seven that have survived intact; there are fragments of a dozen more. It is a delightful and typical example. Figural relief covers five exterior sides of the box: around the perimeter and on the hinged top. The assembled panels were joined by metal

hardware—strips, brackets, hinges, handles, and locks—originally wrought in silver. Although some chests tell a single romantic story in sequential episodes, most, like this one, anthologize scenes drawn from a group of stories, combining courtly romance, secular allegory, and ancient fables.

On the lid of the Walters casket (SEE FIG. B), jousting is the theme. Spread over the central two panels, a single scene catches two charging knights in the heat of a tournament, while trumpeting heralds call the attention of spectators, lined up above in a gallery to observe this public display of virility. The panel at right mocks the very ritual showcased in the middle panels by pitting a woman against a knight, battling not with lances but with a long-stemmed rose (symbolizing sexual surrender) and an oak bough (symbolizing fertility). Instead of

observing these silly goings-on, however, the spectators tucked into the upper architecture pursue their own amorous flirtations. Finally, in the scene on the left, knights use crossbows and a catapult to hurl roses at the Castle of Love, while Cupid returns fire with his seductive arrows.

On the front of the chest (SEE FIG. A), generalized romantic allegory gives way to vignettes from a specific story. At left, the long-bearded Aristotle teaches the young Alexander the Great, using exaggerated gestures and an authoritative text to emphasize his point. Today's lesson is a stern warning not to allow the seductive power of women to distract the young prince from his studies. The subsequent scene, however, pokes fun at his eminent teacher, who has become so smitten by the wiles of a young beauty named Phyllis that he lets

A. SMALL IVORY CHEST WITH SCENES FROM COURTLY ROMANCES
Made in Paris. c. 1330–1350. Elephant ivory with modern iron mounts, height 4½″ (11.5 cm), width 9¹¹⁄₁₆″ (24.6 cm), depth 4⅞″ (12.4 cm). The Walters Art Museum, Baltimore.

her ride him around like a horse, while his student observes this farce, peering out of the castle in the background. The two scenes at right relate to an eastern legend of the fountain of youth, popular in medieval Europe. A line of bearded elders approaches the fountain from the left, steadied by their canes. But after having partaken of its transforming effects, two newly rejuvenated couples, now nude, bathe and flirt within the fountain's basin. The man first in line for treatment, stepping up to climb into the fountain, looks suspiciously like the figure of the aging Aristotle, forming a link between the two stories on the casket front.

Unlike royal marriages of the time, which were essentially business contracts based on political or financial exigencies, the romantic love of the aristocratic wealthy involved passionate devotion. Images of gallant knights and their coy paramours, who could bring intoxicating bliss or cruelly withhold their love on a whim, captured the popular Gothic imagination. They formed the principal subject matter on personal luxury objects, not only chests like this, but mirror backs, combs, writing tablets, even ceremonial saddles. And these stories evoke themes that still captivate us since they reflect notions of desire and betrayal, cruel rejection and blissful folly, at play in our own romantic conquests and relationships to this day. In this way they allow us some access to the lives of the people who commissioned and owned these precious objects, even if we ourselves are unable to afford them.

B. ATTACK ON THE CASTLE OF LOVE
Top of the chest.

C. TRISTAN AND ISEULT AT THE FOUNTAIN; CAPTURE OF THE UNICORN
Left short side of the chest.

Two other well-known medieval themes are juxtaposed on this plaque from the short side of the ivory chest. At left, Tristan and Iseult have met secretly for an illicit romantic tryst, while Iseult's husband, King Mark, tipped off by an informant, observes them from a tree. But when they see his reflection in a fountain between them, they alter their behavior accordingly, and the king believes them innocent of the adultery he had (rightly) suspected. The medieval bestiary ("book of beasts") claimed that only a virgin could capture the mythical unicorn, which at right lays his head, with its aggressively phallic horn, into the lap of just such a pure maiden so that the hunter can take advantage of her alluring powers over the animal to kill it with his phallic counterpart of its horn, a large spear.

ARCHITECTURE

In the later years of the thirteenth century and early years of the fourteenth, a distinctive and influential Gothic architectural style, popularly known as the "Decorated style," developed in England. This change in taste has been credited to Henry III's ambition to surpass St. Louis, who was his brother-in-law, as a royal patron of the arts.

THE DECORATED STYLE AT EXETER. One of the most complete Decorated-style buildings is **EXETER CATHEDRAL**. Thomas of Witney began construction in 1313 and remained master mason from 1316 to 1342. He supervised construction of the nave and redesigned upper parts of the choir. He left the towers of the original Norman cathedral but turned the interior into a dazzling stone forest of colonnettes, moldings, and vault ribs **(FIG. 17–18)**. From piers formed by a cluster of colonnettes rise multiple moldings that make the arcade seem to ripple. Bundled colonnettes spring from sculptured foliate **corbels** (brackets that project from a wall) between the arches and rise up the wall to support conical clusters of 13 ribs that meet at the summit of the vault, a modest 69 feet above the floor. The basic structure here is the four-part vault with intersecting cross-ribs, but the designer added additional ribs, called **tiercerons**, to create a richer linear pattern. Elaborately carved **bosses** (decorative knoblike elements) signal the point where ribs meet along the ridge of the vault. Large bar-tracery clerestory windows illuminate the 300-foot-long nave. Unpolished gray marble shafts, yellow sandstone arches, and a white French stone, shipped from Caen, add subtle gradations of color to the upper wall.

Detailed records survive for the building of Exeter Cathedral, documenting work over the period from 1279 to 1514, with only two short breaks. They record where masons and carpenters were housed (in a hostel near the cathedral) and how they were paid (some by the day with extra for drinks, some by the week, some for each finished piece); how materials were acquired and transported (payments for horseshoes and fodder for the horses); and, of course, payments for the building materials (not only stone and wood but rope for measuring and parchment on which to draw forms for the masons). The bishops contributed generously to the building funds. This was not a labor only of love.

Thomas of Witney also designed the intricate, 57-foot-high bishop's throne (at right in FIG. 17–18), constructed by Richard de Galmeton and Walter of Memburg, who led a team of a dozen carpenters. The canopy resembles embroidery translated into wood, with its maze of pinnacles, bursting with leafy crockets and tiny carved animals and

17-18 • EXETER CATHEDRAL
Devon, England. Thomas of Witney, choir, 14th century and bishop's throne, 1313–1317; Robert Lesyngham, east window, 1389–1390.

heads. To finish the throne in splendor, Master Nicolas painted and gilded the wood. When the bishop was seated on his throne wearing embroidered vestments like the Chichester-Constable Chasuble (SEE FIG. 17–17), he must have resembled a golden image in a shrine—more a symbol of the power and authority of the Church than a specific human being.

THE PERPENDICULAR STYLE AT EXETER.   During years following the Black Death, work at Exeter Cathedral came to a standstill. The nave had been roofed but not vaulted, and the windows had no glass. When work could be resumed, tastes had changed. The exuberance of the Decorated style gave way to an austere style in which rectilinear patterns and sharp angular shapes replaced intricate curves, and luxuriant foliage gave way to simple stripped-down patterns. This phase is known as the Perpendicular style.

In 1389–1390, well-paid master mason Robert Lesyngham rebuilt the great east window (SEE FIG. 17–18), and he designed the window tracery in the new Perpendicular style. The window fills the east wall of the choir like a glowing altarpiece. A single figure in each light stands under a tall painted canopy that flows into and blends with the stone tracery. The Virgin with the Christ Child stands in the center over the high altar, with four female saints at the left and four male saints on the right, including St. Peter, to whom the church is dedicated. At a distance the colorful figures silhouetted against the silver *grisaille* glass become a band of color, conforming to and thus reinforcing the rectangular pattern of the mullions and transoms. The combination of *grisaille*, silver-oxide stain (staining clear glass with shades of yellow or gold), and colored glass produces a glowing wall, and casts a cool, silvery light over the nearby stonework.

Perpendicular architecture heralds the Renaissance style in its regularity, its balanced horizontal and vertical lines, and its plain wall or window surfaces. When Tudor monarchs introduced Renaissance art into the British Isles, builders were not forced to rethink the form and structure of their buildings; they simply changed the ornament from the pointed cusps and crocketed arches of the Gothic style to the round arches and columns and capitals of Roman Classicism. The Perpendicular style itself became an English architectural vernacular. It remains popular today in the United States for churches and college buildings.

THE HOLY ROMAN EMPIRE

By the fourteenth century, the Holy Roman Empire existed more as an ideal fiction than a fact. The Italian territories had established their independence, and in contrast to England and France, Germany had become further divided into multiple states with powerful regional associations and princes. The Holy Roman emperors, now elected by Germans, concentrated on securing the fortunes of their families. They continued to be patrons of the arts, promoting local styles.

MYSTICISM AND SUFFERING

The by-now-familiar ordeals of the fourteenth century—famines, wars, and plagues—helped inspire a mystical religiosity in Germany that emphasized both ecstatic joy and extreme suffering. Devotional images, known as *Andachtsbilder* in German, inspired worshipers to contemplate Jesus' first and last hours, especially during evening prayers, or vespers, giving rise to the term *Vesperbild* for the image of Mary mourning her son. Through such religious exercises, worshipers hoped to achieve understanding of the divine and union with God.

VESPERBILD.   In this well-known example **(FIG. 17–19)**, blood gushes from the hideous **rosettes** that form the wounds of an emaciated and lifeless Jesus who teeters improbably on the lap of his hunched-over mother. The Virgin's face conveys the intensity

17-19 • VESPERBILD (PIETÀ)
From the Middle Rhine region, Germany. c. 1330. Wood and polychromy, height 34½″ (88.4 cm). Landesmuseum, Bonn.

of her ordeal, mingling horror, shock, pity, and grief. Such images took on greater poignancy since they would have been compared, in the worshiper's mind, to the familiar, almost ubiquitous images of the young Virgin mother holding her innocent and loving baby Jesus.

THE HEDWIG CODEX.   The extreme physicality and emotionalism of the *Vesperbild* finds parallels in the actual lives of some medieval saints in northern Europe. St. Hedwig (1174–1243), married at age 12 to Duke Henry I of Silesia and mother of his seven children, entered the Cistercian convent of Trebniz (in modern Poland) on her husband's death in 1238. She devoted the rest of her life to caring for the poor and seeking to emulate the suffering of Christ by walking barefoot in the snow. As described in her *vita*, she had a

particular affection for a small ivory statue of the Virgin and Child, which she carried with her at all times, and which "she often took up in her hands to envelop it in love, so that out of passion she could see it more often and through the seeing could prove herself more devout, inciting her to even greater love of the glorious Virgin. When she once blessed the sick with this image they were cured immediately" (translation from Schleif, p. 22). Hedwig was buried clutching the statue, and when her tomb was opened after her canonization in 1267, it was said that although most of her body had deteriorated, the fingers that still gripped the beloved object had miraculously not decayed.

A picture of Hedwig serves as the frontispiece **(FIG. 17–20)** of a manuscript of her *vita* (biography) known as the Hedwig Codex, commissioned in 1353 by one her descendants, Ludwig I of

17–20 • ST. HEDWIG OF SILESIA WITH DUKE LUDWIG I OF LIEGNITZ-BRIEG AND DUCHESS AGNES
Dedication page of the Hedwig Codex. 1353. Ink and paint on parchment. 13⁷⁄₁₆ × 9¾″ (115 × 94 cm). J. Paul Getty Museum, Los Angeles. MS. Ludwig XI 7, fol. 12v

Liegnitz-Brieg. Duke Ludwig and his wife, Agnes, are shown here kneeling on either side of St. Hedwig, dwarfed by the saint's architectural throne and her own imposing scale. With her prominent, spidery hands, she clutches the famous ivory statue, as well as a rosary and a prayer book, inserting her fingers within it to maintain her place as if our arrival had interrupted her devotions. She has draped her leather boots over her right wrist in a reference to her practice of removing them to walk in the snow. Hedwig's highly volumetric figure stands in a swaying pose of courtly elegance derived from French Gothic, but the fierce intensity of her gaze and posture are far removed from the mannered graciousness of the smiling angel of Reims (see statue at far left in FIG. 16–16), whose similar gesture and extended finger are employed simply to grasp his drapery and assure its elegant display.

THE SUPREMACY OF PRAGUE

Charles IV of Bohemia (r. 1346–1375) was raised in France, and his admiration for the French king Charles IV was such that he changed his own name from Wenceslas to Charles. He was officially crowned king of Bohemia in 1347 and Holy Roman Emperor in 1355. He established his capital in Prague, which, in the view of its contemporaries, replaced Constantinople as the "New Rome." Prague had a great university, a castle, and a cathedral overlooking a town that spread on both sides of a river joined by a stone bridge, a remarkable structure itself.

When Pope Clement VI made Prague an archbishopric in 1344, construction began on a new cathedral in the Gothic style—to be named for St. Vitus. It would also serve as the coronation church and royal pantheon. But the choir was not finished for Charles's first coronation, so he brought Peter Parler from Swabia to complete it.

THE PARLER FAMILY. In 1317, Heinrich Parler, a former master of works on Cologne Cathedral, designed and began building the church of the Holy Cross in Schwäbisch Gmünd, in southwest Germany. In 1351, his son Peter (c. 1330–1399), the most brilliant architect of this talented family, joined the workshop. Peter designed the choir (FIG. 17–21) in the manner of a hall church whose triple-aisled form was enlarged by a ring of deep

choir

nave

17-21 • Heinrich and Peter Parler **PLAN AND INTERIOR OF CHURCH OF THE HOLY CROSS**
Schwäbisch Gmünd, Germany. Begun in 1317 by Henrich Parler; choir by Peter Parler begun in 1351; vaulting completed 16th century.

17-22 • Master Theodoric ST. LUKE
Holy Cross Chapel, Karlstejn Castle, near Prague. 1360–1364. Paint and gold on panel. 45¼ × 37″ (115 × 94 cm).

chapels between the buttresses. The contrast between Heinrich's nave and Peter's choir (seen clearly in the plan of FIG. 17–21) illustrates the increasing complexity of rib patterns covering the vaults, which emphasizes the unity of interior space rather than its division into bays.

Called by Charles IV to Prague in 1353, Peter turned the unfinished St. Vitus Cathedral into a "glass house," adding a vast clerestory and glazed triforium supported by double flying buttresses, all covered by net vaults that created a continuous canopy over the space. Because of the success of projects such as this, Peter and his family became the most successful architects in the Holy Roman Empire. Their concept of space, luxurious decoration, and intricate vaulting dominated central European architecture for three generations.

MASTER THEODORIC. At Karlstejn Castle, a day's ride from Prague, Charles IV built another chapel, covering the walls with gold and precious stones as well as with paintings. There were 130 paintings of the saints serving as reliquaries, with relics inserted into their frames. Master Theodoric, the court painter, provided drawings on the wood panels, and he painted about 30 images himself. Figures are crowded into—even extend over—their frames, emphasizing their size and power. Master Theodoric was head of the Brotherhood of St. Luke, and the way that his painting of **ST. LUKE (FIG. 17–22)**, patron saint of painters, looks out at the viewer has suggested to scholars that this may be a self-portrait. His personal style combined a preference for substantial bodies, oversized heads and hands, dour and haunted faces, and soft, deeply modeled drapery, with a touch of grace derived from the French Gothic style. The chapel, consecrated in 1365, so pleased the emperor that in 1367 he gave the artist a farm in appreciation of his work.

Prague and the Holy Roman Empire under Charles IV had become a multicultural empire where people of different religions (Christians and Jews) and ethnic heritages (German and Slav) lived side by side. Charles died in 1378, and without his strong central government, political and religious dissent overtook the empire. Jan Hus, dean of the philosophy faculty at Prague University and a powerful reforming preacher, denounced the immorality he saw in the Church. He was burned at the stake, becoming a martyr and Czech national hero. The Hussite Revolution in the fifteenth century ended Prague's—and Bohemia's—leadership in the arts.

THINK ABOUT IT

17.1 Discuss the circumstances surrounding the construction and decoration of the Scrovegni (Arena) Chapel, with special attention to its relationship to the life and aspirations of its patron.

17.2 Compare and contrast Giotto's and Duccio's renderings of the biblical story of Christ's Raising of Lazarus (FIGS. 17–8, 17–12).

17.3 Discuss Ambrogio Lorenzetti's engagement with secular subject matter in his frescos for Siena's Palazzo Pubblico (FIG. 17–15). How did these paintings relate to their sociopolitical context?

17.4 Choose one small work of art in this chapter that is crafted from precious materials with exceptional technical skill. Explain how it was made and how it was used. How does the work of art relate to its cultural and social context?

17.5 Analyze how the Decorated Gothic style of Exeter Cathedral (FIG. 17–18) preserves certain traditions from the thirteenth-century Gothic that you learned about in Chapter 16, and assess how it departs from the traditional Gothic style.

PRACTICE MORE: Compose answers to these questions, get flashcards for images and terms, and review chapter material with quizzes
www.myartslab.com

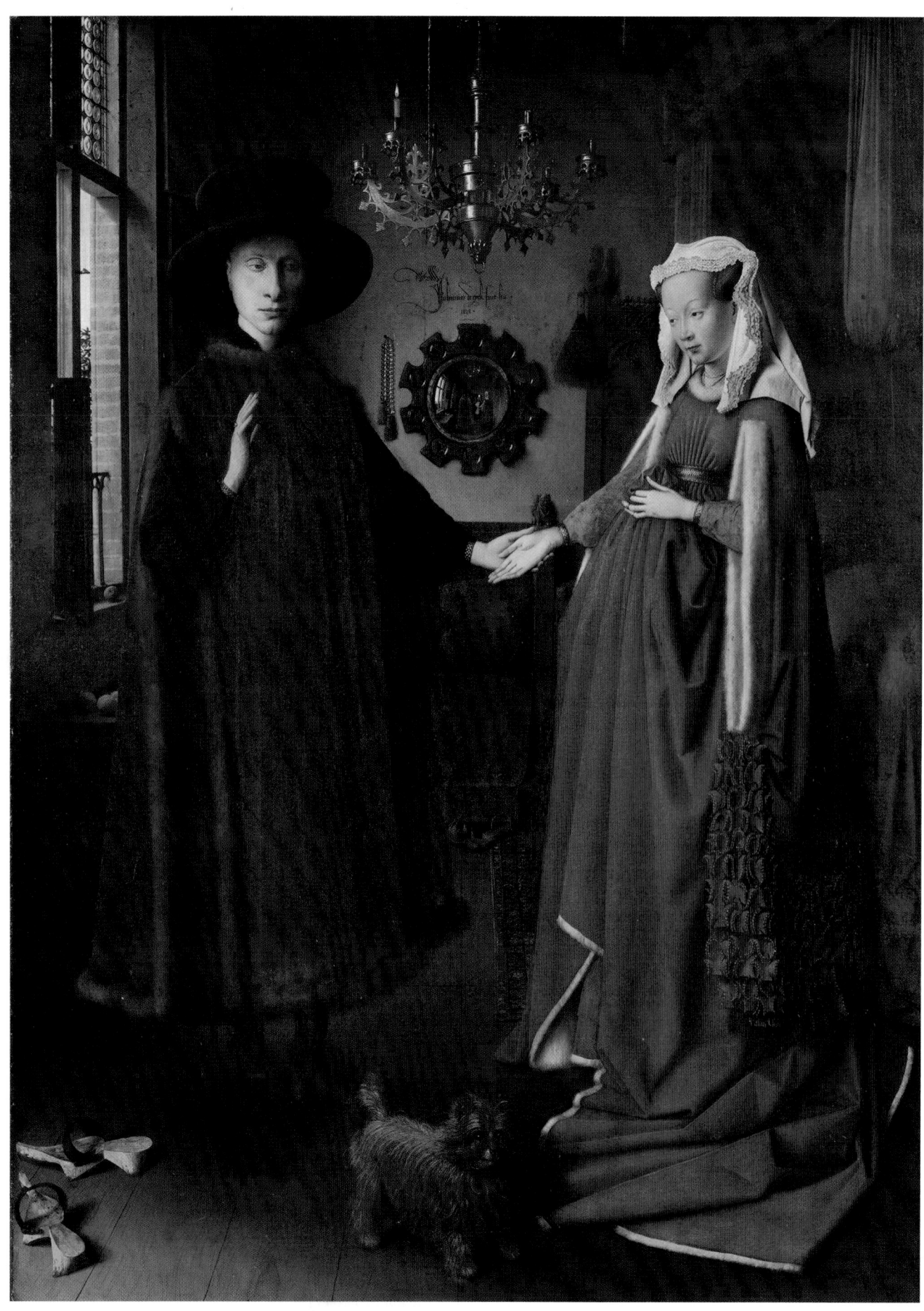

18–1 • Jan van Eyck DOUBLE PORTRAIT OF A GIOVANNI ARNOLFINI AND HIS WIFE
1434. Oil on wood panel, 33 × 22½″ (83.8 × 57.2 cm). The National Gallery, London.

FIFTEENTH-CENTURY ART
IN NORTHERN EUROPE

Fifteenth-century Europe saw the emergence of wealthy merchants whose rise to power was fueled by individual accomplishment, rather than hereditary succession within noble families. Certainly Giovanni Arnolfini—the pasty gentleman with the extravagant hat in this double portrait (FIG. 18–1)—earned, rather than inherited, the right to have himself and his wife recorded by renowned artist Jan van Eyck. It was the wealth and connections he made as an Italian cloth merchant providing luxury fabrics to the Burgundian court that put him in the position to commission such a precious picture, in which both patron and painter are identified with conspicuous clarity. Giovanni's face looks more like a personal likeness than anything we have seen since ancient Rome, and not only did Jan van Eyck inscribe his name above the convex mirror ("Jan van Eyck was here, 1434") but his personal painting style carries an equally sure stamp of authorship. The doll-like face of the woman standing next to Giovanni is less individualized. Has she lifted her skirt over her belly so she can follow Giovanni, who has taken her by the hand? Or are most modern observers correct in assuming that she is pregnant? This painting is full of mysteries.

The precise identity of the couple is still open to scholarly debate. And is this a wedding, a betrothal, or perhaps security for a shady financial deal? Recently it has been interpreted as a memorial to a beloved wife lost to death. Only the wealth of the couple is beyond dispute. They are surrounded by luxury objects: lavish bed hangings, sumptuous chandelier, precious oriental carpet, rare oranges, not to mention their extravagant clothing. The man wears a fur-lined, silk velvet *heuque* (sleeveless overgarment). The woman's gown not only employs more costly wool fabric than necessary to cover her slight body; the elaborate cutwork decoration and white fur lining of her sleeves is an ostentatious indicator of cost. In fact, the painting itself—probably hung in the couple's home—was an object of considerable value.

Even within its secular setting, however, the picture resonated with sacred meaning. The Church still provided spiritual grounding for men and women of the Renaissance. The crystal prayer beads hanging next to the convex mirror imply the couple's piety, and the mirror itself—a symbol of the all-seeing eye of God—is framed with a circular cycle of scenes from Christ's Passion. A figure of St. Margaret—protector of women in childbirth—is carved at the top of a post in the high-backed chair beside the bed, and the perky *Affenpinscher* in the foreground may be more than a pet. Dogs served as symbols of fidelity and also have funerary associations, but choosing a rare, ornamental breed for inclusion here may have been yet another opportunity to express wealth.

LEARN ABOUT IT

18.1 Analyze how Flemish painters gave scrupulous attention to describing the textures and luminosity of objects in the natural world and in domestic interiors.

18.2 Trace the development of an extraordinary interest in evoking human likeness in portraits, unlike anything seen since ancient Rome.

18.3 Explore how paintings in northern Europe of the fifteenth century captured in concrete form visions of their meditating donors.

18.4 Uncover the complex symbolic meanings that saturated the settings of Flemish paintings.

18.5 Investigate how prints developed into a major pictorial medium.

HEAR MORE: Listen to an audio file of your chapter **www.myartslab.com**

THE NORTHERN RENAISSANCE

Revitalized civic life and economic growth in the late fourteenth century gave rise to a prosperous middle class that supported scholarship, literature, and the arts. Their patronage resulted in the explosion of learning and creativity we call the Renaissance (French for "rebirth")—a term that was assigned to this period by later historians.

A major manifestation of the Renaissance in northern Europe was a growing and newly intense interest in the natural world manifested in the close observation and detailed recording of nature. Artists depicted birds, plants, and animals with breathtaking descriptive accuracy. They applied the same scrutiny to people and objects, modeling forms with light and shadow to give them the semblance of three-dimensionality. These carefully described subjects were situated into spatial settings, applying an **intuitive perspective** system by diminishing their scale as they receded into the distance. In the portrayal of landscapes—which became a northern specialty—artists used **atmospheric** or **aerial perspective** in which distant elements appear increasingly indistinct and less colorful as they approach the background. The sky, for instance, becomes paler near the horizon and the distant landscape turns bluish-gray.

One aspect of the desire for accurate visual depictions of the natural world was a new interest in individual personalities. Fifteenth-century portraits have an astonishingly lifelike quality, combining careful—sometimes seemingly unflattering—surface description with an uncanny sense of vitality. Indeed, the individual becomes important in every sphere. More names of artists survive from the fifteenth century, for example, than in the entire span from the beginning of the Common Era to the year 1400, and some artists begin regularly to sign their work.

The new power of cities in Flanders and the greater Netherlands (present-day Belgium, Luxembourg, and the Netherlands; SEE MAP 18.1) provided a critical tension and balance with the traditional powers of royalty and the Church. Increasingly, the urban lay public sought to express personal and civic pride by sponsoring secular architecture, sculptured monuments, or paintings directed toward the community. The commonsense values of the merchants formed a solid underpinning for the Northern Renaissance, but their influence remained intertwined with the continuing power of the Church and the royal and noble courts. Giovanni Arnolfini's success at commerce and negotiation provided the funding for his extraordinary double portrait, but he was able to secure the services of Jan van Eyck only with the cooperation of the duke of Burgundy.

ART FOR THE FRENCH DUCAL COURTS

The dukes of Burgundy were the most powerful rulers in northern Europe for most of the fifteenth century. They controlled not only Burgundy itself but also the Flemish and Netherlandish centers of finance and trade, including the thriving cities of Ghent, Bruges, Tournai, and Brussels. The major seaport, Bruges, was the commercial center of northern Europe, rivaling the Italian city-states of Florence, Milan, and Venice as an economic hub. In the late fourteenth century, Burgundian Duke Philip the Bold (r. 1363–1404) had acquired territory in the Netherlands—including the politically desirable region of Flanders—by marrying the daughter of the Flemish count. Though dukes Philip the Bold of Burgundy, Jean of Berry, and Louis of Anjou were brothers of King Charles V of France, their interests rarely coincided. Even the threat of a common enemy, England, during the Hundred Years' War was not a strong unifying factor, since Burgundy and England were often allied because of common financial interests in Flanders.

While the French king held court in Paris, the dukes held even more splendid courts in their own cities. The dukes of Burgundy (including present-day east-central France, Belgium, Luxembourg, and the Netherlands) and Berry (central France), not the king in Paris, were the real arbiters of taste. Especially influential was Jean, duke of Berry, who commissioned many works from Flemish and Netherlandish painters in the fashionable International Gothic style.

This new, composite style emerged in the late fourteenth century from the multicultural papal court in Avignon in southern France, where artists from Italy, France, and Flanders worked side by side. The International Gothic style became the prevailing manner of late fourteenth-century Europe. It is characterized by slender, gracefully posed figures whose delicate features are framed by masses of curling hair and extraordinarily complex headdresses. Noble men and women wear rich brocaded and embroidered fabrics and elaborate jewelry. Landscape and architectural settings are miniaturized; however, details of nature—leaves, flowers, insects, birds—are rendered with nearly microscopic detail. Spatial recession is represented by rising tiled floors in rooms that are open to view like stage sets, by fanciful mountains and meadows with high horizon lines, and by progressive diminution in the size of receding objects and by atmospheric perspective. Artists and patrons preferred light, bright colors and a liberal use of gold in manuscript and panel paintings, tapestries, and polychromed sculpture. The International Gothic was so appealing that it endured well into the fifteenth century.

PAINTING AND SCULPTURE FOR THE CHARTREUSE DE CHAMPMOL

One of Philip the Bold's most lavish projects was the Carthusian monastery, or *chartreuse* ("charterhouse"), at Champmol, near Dijon, his Burgundian capital city. Land was acquired in 1377 and 1383, and construction began in 1385. The monastic church was intended to house the family's tombs, and the monks were expected to pray continuously for the souls of Philip and his family. Carthusian monasteries were particularly expensive to maintain because Carthusian monks did not provide for themselves by farming or other physical work but were dedicated exclusively to prayer and solitary meditation.

MAP 18–1 •
FIFTEENTH-CENTURY
NORTHERN EUROPE

The dukes of Burgundy—
whose territory included
much of present-day
Belgium and Luxembourg,
the Netherlands, and
eastern France—became
the cultural and political
leaders of western Europe.
Their major cities of
Bruges (Belgium) and
Dijon (France) were
centers of art and
industry as well as
politics.

Extent of Burgundy at the
death of Philip the Good, 1467

Border between the Kingdom of
France and the German Empire

North Sea

Haarlem

HOLLAND

BRABANT

Limbourg

Bruges   Antwerp
Ghent

FLANDERS   Brussels

ARTOIS   Tournai

Arras

HAINAUT

LUXEMBOURG

Cologne

Rhine R.

Mainz

GERMAN
EMPIRE

Nuremberg

Rouen

Seine R.

Reims

Paris

Buxheim

Melun

KINGDOM OF
FRANCE

Loire R.

Champmol
Dijon

FRANCHE-
COMTÉ OF
BURGUNDY

BERRY

Bourges

BURGUNDY

Moulins

100 km

100 miles

MELCHIOR BROEDERLAM. The duke ordered a magnificent carved and painted altarpiece (see "Altars and Altarpieces," page 564) for the Chartreuse de Champmol. The interior of the altarpiece, carved and gilded by Jacques de Baerze, depicts scenes of the Crucifixion flanked by the Adoration of the Magi and the Entombment. The exteriors of the protective shutters of this triptych were covered not by carvings but by two paintings by Melchior Broederlam (active 1381–1410) showing scenes from the life of the Virgin and the infancy of Christ **(FIG. 18–2)**. Broederlam situates his closely observed, International Style figures within

fanciful miniature architectural and landscape settings. His lavish use of brilliantly seductive colors foregrounds one of the features that made International Gothic so popular.

The archangel Gabriel greets Mary while she is at prayer. She sits in a Gothic room with a back door leading into the dark interior of a Romanesque rotunda that symbolizes the Temple of Jerusalem as a repository of the Old Law. According to legend, Mary was an attendant in the Temple prior to her marriage to Joseph. The tiny enclosed garden and conspicuous pot of lilies are symbols of Mary's virginity. In International Gothic fashion, both

Altars and Altarpieces

The altar in a Christian church symbolizes both the table of Jesus' Last Supper and the tombs of Christ and the saints. As a table, the altar is the site where priests celebrate Mass. And as a tomb, it traditionally contained a relic before the Reformation, placed in a reliquary on the altar, beneath the floor on which the altar rests, or even enclosed within the altar itself.

Altarpieces are painted or carved constructions placed at the back of or behind the altar so that altar and altarpiece appear visually to be joined. By the fifteenth century, important altarpieces had evolved into large and elaborate architectural structures filled with images and protected by movable wings that function like shutters. An altarpiece can sit on a base, called a predella. A winged altarpiece can be a **diptych**, in which two panels are hinged together; a **triptych**, in which two wings fold over a center section, forming a diptych when closed; or a **polyptych**, consisting of many panels.

diptych	**triptych**	**altar and polyptych altarpiece**

the interior and exterior of the building are shown, and the floors are tilted up at the back to give clear views of the action. Next, in the Visitation, just outside the temple walls, the now-pregnant Mary greets her older cousin Elizabeth, who will soon give birth to John the Baptist.

On the right shutter is the Presentation in the Temple. Mary and Joseph have brought the newborn Jesus to the Temple for his redemption as a first-born son and for Mary's purification, where Simeon takes the baby in his arms to bless him (Luke 2:25–32). At the far right, the Holy Family flees to Egypt to escape King Herod's order that all Jewish male infants be killed. The family travels along treacherous terrain similar to that in the Visitation scene, where a path leads the viewers' eyes up from the foreground and into the distance along a rising ground plane. Broederlam has created a sense of light and air around his solid figures. Anecdotal details drawn from the real world are scattered throughout the pictures—a hawk flies through the golden sky, the presented baby looks anxiously back at his mother, and Joseph drinks from a flask and carries the family belongings in a satchel over his shoulder on the journey to Egypt. The statue of a pagan god, visible at the upper right, breaks and tumbles from its pedestal as the Christ Child approaches. A new era dawns and the New Law replaces the Old, among both Jews and gentiles.

CLAUS SLUTER. Flemish sculptor Jean de Marville (active 1366–1389) initially directed the decoration of the Chartreuse, and when he died in 1389, he was succeeded by his talented assistant Claus Sluter (c. 1360–1406), from Haarlem, in Holland. Sluter's distinctive work survives in a monumental **WELL OF MOSES** carved for the main cloister (**FIG. 18–3**), begun in 1395 and left unfinished at Sluter's death.

The design of this work is complex. A pier rose from the water to support a large free-standing figure of Christ on the cross, mourned by the Virgin Mary, Mary Magdalen, and John the Evangelist. Forming a pedestal for this Crucifixion group at the viewers' eye level are life-size stone figures from the Hebrew Bible who Christians believe foretold the coming of Christ: Moses, David, and the prophets Jeremiah, Zachariah, Daniel, and Isaiah. This concept may have been inspired by contemporary mystery plays, in which prophets foretell and explain events of Christ's Passion. Sluter's patriarchs and prophets are distinct individuals, physically and psychologically. Moses' sad old eyes blaze out from a memorable face entirely covered with a fine web of wrinkles. Even his horns are wrinkled. (These horns are traditional attributes based on a mistranslation of Exodus 34:29–35 in the Latin Vulgate Bible, where the rays of light radiating from Moses's face become horns.) A mane of curling hair and beard cascades over his heavy

18-2 • Melchior Broederlam ANNUNCIATION, VISITATION, PRESENTATION IN THE TEMPLE, AND FLIGHT INTO EGYPT
Exterior of the wings of the altarpiece of the Chartreuse de Champmol. 1393–1399. Oil on wood panel, 5′5¾″ × 4′1¼″ (1.67 × 1.25 m). Musée des Beaux-Arts, Dijon.

shoulders and chest, and an enormous cloak envelops his body. Beside him stands David, in the voluminous robes of a medieval king, the very personification of nobility.

Sluter looked at human figures in new ways—as a weighty mass defined by voluminous drapery that lies in deep folds and falls in horizontal arcs and cascading lines—both concealing and revealing the body, creating strong highlights and shadows. With these vigorous, imposing, and highly individualized figures of the Well of Moses, Sluter abandoned the idealized faces, elongated figures, and vertical drapery of International Gothic for surface realism and the broad horizontal movement of forms. He retained, however, the detailed naturalism and rich colors (now almost lost but revealed in recent cleaning) and surfaces still preferred by his patrons.

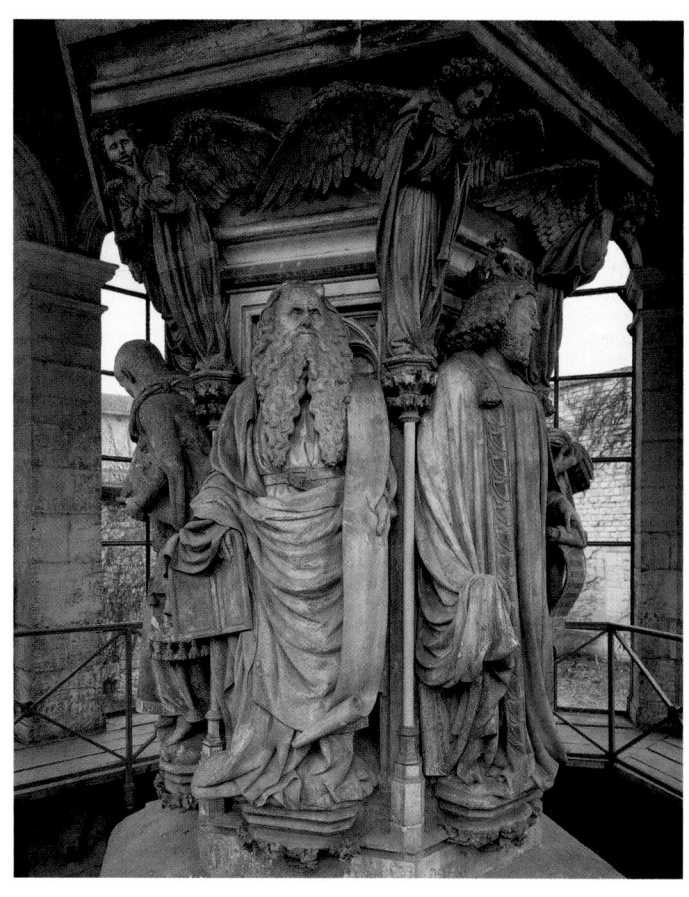

18-3 • Claus Sluter WELL OF MOSES, DETAIL OF MOSES AND DAVID
The Chartreuse de Champmol, Dijon, France. 1395–1406. Limestone with traces of paint, height of figures about 5′8″ (1.69 m).

The sculpture's original details included metal used for buckles and even eyeglasses. It was also painted: Moses wore a gold mantle with a blue lining over a red tunic; David's gold mantle had a painted lining of ermine, and his blue tunic was covered with gold stars and wide bands of ornament.

Women Artists in the Middle Ages and the Renaissance

Since most formal apprenticeships were not open to them, medieval and Renaissance women artists typically learned to paint from their husbands and fathers. Noblewomen, who were often educated in convents, also learned to draw, paint, and embroider. One of the earliest examples of a signed work by a woman is in a tenth-century Spanish manuscript of the Apocalypse illustrated by an artist named Ende (SEE FIG. 14–8), who describes herself as "painter and servant of God." In the twelfth century, a German nun named Guda not only signed her work but also included a self-portrait (SEE FIG. 15–32).

Examples proliferate during the later Middle Ages. In the fourteenth century, Jeanne de Montbaston and her husband, Richart, worked together as book illuminators under the auspices of the University of Paris. After Richart's death, Jeanne maintained the workshop and, following the custom of the time, was sworn in as a *libraire* (publisher) by the university in 1353. Bourgot, the daughter of the miniaturist Jean le Noir, illuminated books for King Charles V of France and Duke Jean of Berry. In the fifteenth century, women could be admitted to guilds in the Flemish towns of Ghent, Bruges, and Antwerp. By the 1480s, one-quarter of the membership in the painters' guild of Bruges was female.

In a French edition of a book by the Italian author Boccaccio entitled *Concerning Famous Women*, there is a picture of Thamyris, an artist of antiquity, at work in her studio. She appears in fifteenth-century dress, painting an image of the Virgin and Child. At the right, an assistant grinds and mixes her colors. In the foreground, her brushes and paints are laid out neatly and conveniently on a table.

PAGE WITH THAMYRIS
From Giovanni Boccaccio's *De Claris Mulieribus (Concerning Famous Women)*. 1402. Ink and tempera on vellum, 14 × 9½" (35.5 × 24 cm). Bibliothèque Nationale, Paris.

MANUSCRIPT ILLUMINATION

Besides religious texts, wealthy patrons treasured richly illuminated secular writings such as herbals (encyclopedias of plants), health manuals, and works of history and literature. A typical manuscript page might have leafy tendrils framing the text, decorated opening initials, and perhaps a small inset picture (see the illustration in "Women Artists in the Middle Ages and the Renaissance," above). Only the most lavish books would have full-page miniature paintings, set off with frames. These inset pictures are like windows looking into rooms or out onto landscapes with distant horizons.

THE LIMBOURG BROTHERS. Among the finest Netherlandish painters at the beginning of the century were three brothers—Paul, Herman, and Jean Limbourg—their "last" name referring to

their home region. At this time people generally did not have family names in the modern sense, but were known instead by their first names, often followed by a reference to their place of origin, parentage, or occupation.

About 1404 the Limbourg brothers entered the service of avid bibliophile Duke Jean of Berry (1340–1416), for whom they produced their most impressive surviving work, the so-called **TRÈS RICHES HEURES** (Very Sumptuous Book of Hours), between 1413 and 1416 (**FIGS. 18–4, 18–5**). A Book of Hours, in addition to containing prayers and readings used in daily devotion, also included a calendar of holy days. The Limbourgs created full-page illustrations for the calendar in the *Très Riches Heures*, with subjects including both peasant labors and aristocratic pleasures in a framed lower field while elaborate calendar devices, with the chariot of

18-4 • Paul, Herman, and Jean Limbourg FEBRUARY, LIFE IN THE COUNTRY. TRÈS RICHES HEURES
1411–1416. Colors and ink on parchment, 11⅜ × 8¼" (29 × 21 cm). Musée Condé, Chantilly, France.

18-5 • Paul, Herman, and Jean Limbourg JANUARY, THE DUKE OF BERRY AT TABLE. TRÈS RICHES HEURES
1411–1416. Colors and ink on parchment, 11⅜ × 8¼" (29 × 21 cm). Musée Condé, Chantilly, France.

the sun and the zodiac symbols, fill the upper part of the page. Like most European artists of the time, the Limbourgs showed the laboring classes in a light acceptable to aristocrats—that is, happily working for the nobles' benefit or displaying an uncouth lifestyle for aristocratic amusement. At times they also seem to be depicting peasants enjoying the pleasures of their leisure moments.

In the February page (SEE FIG. 18–4), farm folks relax cozily before a blazing fire. Although many country people at this time lived in hovels, this farm looks comfortable and well maintained, with timber-framed buildings, a row of beehives, a sheepfold, and tidy woven wattle fences. In the distance are a village and church. Within this scene, although all are much lower in social standing than the duke himself, there is a hierarchy of class. Largest in scale and most elegantly dressed is the woman closest to us, perhaps the owner of the farm, who carefully lifts her overgarment, balancing it daintily with both hands as she warms herself. She shares her fire with a couple, smaller because farther in the background, who

wear more modest clothing and are considerably less well behaved, especially the uncouth man, who exposes himself as he lifts his clothing to take advantage of the fire's warmth.

One of the most remarkable aspects of this painting is the way it conveys the feeling of cold winter weather: the leaden sky and bare trees, the soft snow and huddled sheep, the steamy breath of the bundled-up worker blowing on his hands, and the comforting smoke curling from the farmhouse chimney. The artists employ several International Gothic conventions: the high placement of the horizon line, the small size of trees and buildings in relation to people, and the cutaway view of the house showing both interior and exterior. The muted palette is sparked with touches of yellowish-orange, blue, and patches of bright red, including the man's turban at the lower left. Scale relationships seem consistent with our experience in the natural world since as the landscape recedes, the size of figures and buildings diminishes progressively in stages from foreground to middle ground to background.

18-6 • Mary of Burgundy Painter **MARY AT HER DEVOTIONS, HOURS OF MARY OF BURGUNDY**
Before 1482. Colors and ink on parchment, size of image 7½ × 5¼"
(19.1 × 13.3 cm). Österreichische Nationalbibliothek, Vienna.

In contrast, the illustration for the other winter month—January—depicts an aristocratic household (SEE FIG. 18–5). The duke of Berry sits behind a table laden with food and rich tableware, presiding over his new year's feast and surrounded by servants and allies. His chamberlain invites smartly dressed courtiers to greet the duke (the words written overhead say "approach"), who is himself singled out visually by the red cloth of honor with his heraldic arms—swans and the lilies of France—hanging over him and by a large fire screen that circles his head like a secular halo. Tapestries with battle scenes cover the walls. Such luxury objects attest to the wealth and lavish lifestyle of this great patron of the arts, a striking contrast to the farm life that will be revealed in February when turning the book to its next page.

THE MARY OF BURGUNDY PAINTER. One of the finest painters of Books of Hours later in the century was an artist known as the Mary of Burgundy Painter—so called because he painted a Book of Hours for Mary of Burgundy (1457–1482), only child of Charles the Bold. Within a full-page miniature in a book only 7½

by 5¼ inches, earthly reality and a religious vision have been rendered equally tangible (**FIG. 18–6**). The painter conjures up a complex pictorial space. We look not only through the "window" of the illustration's frame but through another window in the wall of the room depicted in the foreground of the painting. The artist shows real virtuosity in representing these worlds. Spatial recession leads the viewer into the far reaches of the church interior, past the Virgin and the gilded altarpiece in the sanctuary to two people conversing in the far distance. The filmy veil covering Mary's steeple headdress is exquisitely described, as is the transparency of the glass vase, and the distinctive bull's eye glass (circular panes whose center "lump" was formed by the glassblower's pontil) filling the foreshortened, open window.

Mary of Burgundy appears twice. She is seated in the foreground by a window, reading from, or contemplating a picture within, her Book of Hours, held carefully and protected by a lush green cloth, perhaps from the diminutive dog cuddled into her lap. She appears again in the background, within the representation of the personal vision inspired by her private meditations. For a glorious Gothic church may form the setting for her vision, but it results not from attendance at Mass nor from the direction of a priestly advisor. She experiences it in private, a reward of her personal faith. Christians were encouraged in this period to imagine themselves participating in biblical stories and sacred events so as to feel within bodies and souls the experiences of the protagonists. Secluded into her private space, and surrounded by devotional aids on the window ledge—book, rosary, and symbolic flowers (carnations symbolized the nails of the Crucifixion, the irises Mary's sorrow)—it seems that Mary of Burgundy is doing just that. In her vision, she kneels with attendants and angels in front of a gracefully human Virgin and Child.

TEXTILES

In the fifteenth and sixteenth centuries, the best European tapestries came from Flanders. Major weaving centers at Brussels, Tournai, and Arras produced intricately woven wall hangings for royal and aristocratic patrons across Europe, important church officials including the pope, and even town councils. Among the most common subjects were foliage and flower patterns, scenes from the lives of the saints, and themes from classical mythology and history, such as the Battle of Troy seen hanging on the walls of Duke Jean of Berry's reception room (SEE FIG. 18–5). Tapestries provided both insulation and luxurious decoration for the stone walls of castle halls, churches, and municipal buildings, and because they were much more expensive than wall or panel paintings, they also showed off the owners' wealth. Since they were portable, many were included among aristocratic baggage as courts moved from residence to residence.

The price of a tapestry depended on the artists involved, the work required, and the materials used. Rarely was a fine, commissioned series woven only with wool; instead, tapestry producers enhanced the weaving with silk, and with silver and

18-7 • UNICORN IS FOUND AT THE FOUNTAIN
From the Hunt of the Unicorn tapestry series. c. 1495–1505. Wool, silk, and silver- and gilt-wrapped thread
(13–21 warp threads per inch), 12′1″ × 12′5″ (3.68 × 3.78 m). Metropolitan Museum of Art, New York.
Gift of John D. Rockefeller Jr., The Cloisters Collection, 1937 (37.80.2)

gold threads that must have glittered on the walls of princely residences, especially at night, illuminated by flickering lamps or candles. Because silver and gold threads were made of silk wrapped with real silver and gold, people later burned many tapestries to retrieve the precious materials. As a result, few royal tapestries in France survived the French Revolution. If a greater percentage had survived, these luxurious and monumental textile wall paintings would surely figure more prominently in the history of art.

THE UNICORN TAPESTRY. Tapestries were often produced in series. One of the best known is the Hunt of the Unicorn series from c. 1500. Four of the seven surviving hangings present scenes of people and animals set against a dense field of trees and flowers, with a distant view of a castle, as in the **UNICORN IS FOUND AT THE FOUNTAIN (FIG. 18–7)**. The unusually fine condition of the tapestry allows us to appreciate its rich colors and the subtlety in modeling the faces, the tonal variations in the animals' fur, and

18-8 • COPE OF THE ORDER OF THE GOLDEN FLEECE
Flemish. Mid 15th century. Cloth with gold and colored silk embroidery, 5'4⁹⁄₁₆" × 10'9⁵⁄₁₆" (1.64 × 3.3 m). Imperial Treasury, Vienna.

even the depiction of reflections in the water. The technical skill of its weavers is astonishing.

In tapestry, designs are woven directly into the fabric. The Unicorn tapestries seem to have been woven on huge, horizontal looms, where weavers interwove fine weft yarn of wool and silk—dyed in a multitude of colors from the creative combination of three vegetal dyes—onto the parallel strands of the coarser wool warp. Weavers worked from behind what would be the front surface of the finished tapestry, following the design on a full-scale cartoon laid on the floor under the loom. They could only see the actual effect of their work by checking the front with mirrors. Making a tapestry panel this large was a collaborative effort that required the organizational skills of a talented production manager and five or six weavers working side by side on a single loom. What is so extraordinary about their work is the skillful way they created curving lines—since the tapestry process is based on a rectilinear network of threads, curves have be simulated—and the lighting effects of shading and reflections, which require using yarn in the same hue with a multitude of values.

The subject of this series concerns the unicorn, a mythical horselike animal with a single long twisted horn, said to be supernaturally swift; it could only be captured by a virgin, to whom it came willingly. Thus, the unicorn became both a symbol of the Incarnation (Christ is the unicorn captured by the Virgin Mary) and also a metaphor for romantic love (see page 553, FIG. C). The capture and killing of the unicorn was also equated with Christ's death on the cross to save humanity.

The natural world represented so splendidly in this tapestry also has potential symbolic meaning. For instance, lions represented valor, faith, courage, and mercy, and even—because they were thought to breathe life into their cubs—the Resurrection of Christ. The stag is another Resurrection symbol (it sheds and grows its antlers) and a protector against poisonous serpents and evil in general. Even today we see rabbits as symbols of fertility, and dogs of fidelity. Many of the easily identifiable flowers and trees also carry both religious and secular meaning. There is a strong theme of marriage: the strawberry is a common symbol of sexual love; the pansy means remembrance; and the periwinkle, a cure for spiteful feelings and jealousy. The trees include oak for fidelity, beech for nobility, holly for protection against evil, hawthorn for the power of love, and pomegranate and orange for fertility.

COPE OF THE ORDER OF THE GOLDEN FLEECE. Surviving vestments of the Order of the Golden Fleece are remarkable examples of Flemish textiles. The Order of the Golden Fleece was an honorary fraternity founded by Duke Philip the Good of Burgundy in 1430 with 23 knights chosen for their moral character and bravery. Religious services were an integral part of the order's meetings, and opulent liturgical and clerical objects were created for the purpose.

The surface of the sumptuous cope (cloak) in FIG. 18–8 is divided into compartments filled with the standing figures of saints. At the top of the neck edge, as if presiding over the company, is an enthroned figure of Christ, flanked along the front edge by

Whereas Italian artists favored tempera, using it almost exclusively for panel painting until the end of the fifteenth century (see "Cennino Cennini on Panel Painting," page 544), Flemish artists preferred oil paints, in which powdered pigments are suspended in linseed—and occasionally walnut—oil. They exploited the potential of this medium during the fifteenth century with a virtuosity that has never been surpassed.

Tempera had to be applied in a very precise manner because it dried almost as quickly as it was laid down. Shading was restricted to careful overlying strokes in graded tones ranging from white and gray to dark brown and black. Because tempera is opaque—light striking its surface does not penetrate to lower layers of color and reflect back—the resulting surface is **matte**, or dull, taking on a sheen only with burnishing or an overlay of varnish.

On the other hand, oil paint is a viscous medium which takes much longer to dry, and while it is still wet changes can be made easily.

Once applied, the paint has time to smooth out during the drying process, erasing traces of individual brushstrokes on the surface of the finished panel. Perhaps even more importantly, oil paint is translucent when applied in very thin layers, called glazes. Light striking a surface built up of glazes penetrates to the lower layers and is reflected back, creating the appearance of an interior glow. These luminous effects enabled artists to capture jewel-like colors and the varying effects of light on changing textures, enhancing the illusion that viewers are looking at real objects rather than their painted imitation.

So brilliant was Jan van Eyck's use of oil paint that he was credited by Giorgio Vasari with inventing the medium. Actually, it had been in use at least since the twelfth century, when it is described in Theophilus Presbyter's *De diversis artibus* (see "Stained Glass Windows," page 497).

SEE MORE: View videos about the processes of oil painting and grinding oil paint **www.myartslab.com**

scholar-saints in their studies. The embroiderers worked with great precision to match the illusionistic effects of contemporary Flemish painting. The particular stitch used here is known as couching. Gold threads are tacked down using unevenly spaced colored silk threads to create images and an iridescent effect.

PAINTING IN FLANDERS

A strong economy based on the textile industry and international trade provided stability and money for a Flemish efflorescence in the arts. Civic groups, town councils, and wealthy merchants were important patrons in the Netherlands, where the cities were self-governing and largely independent of landed nobility. Guilds oversaw nearly every aspect of their members' lives, and high-ranking guild members served on town councils and helped run city governments. Even experienced artists who moved from one city to another usually had to work as assistants in a local workshop until they met the requirements for guild membership.

Throughout most of the fifteenth century, Flemish art and artists were greatly admired across Europe. Artists from abroad studied Flemish works, and their influence spread even to Italy. Only at the end of the fifteenth century did a pervasive preference for Netherlandish painting give way to a taste for the new styles of art and architecture developing in Italy.

THE FOUNDERS OF THE FLEMISH SCHOOL

Flemish panel painters preferred using an oil medium rather than the tempera paint that was standard in the works of Italian artists. Since it was slow to dry, oil paint provided flexibility, and it had a luminous quality (see "Oil Painting," above). Like manuscript illuminations, Flemish panel paintings provided a window onto a scene rendered with keen attention to describing individual features—people, objects, or aspects of the natural world—with consummate skill.

THE MASTER OF FLÉMALLE. Some of the earliest and most outstanding exponents of the new Flemish style were painters in the workshop of an artist known as the Master of Flémalle, identified by some art historians as Robert Campin (active 1406–1444). About 1425–1430, these artists painted the triptych now known as the **MÉRODE ALTARPIECE**, after its later owners **(FIG. 18–9)**. Its relatively small size—slightly over 2 feet tall and about 4 feet wide with the wings open—suggests that it was probably made for a small private chapel.

The Annunciation of the central panel is set in a Flemish home and incorporates common household objects, many invested with symbolic religious meaning. The lilies in the **majolica** (glazed earthenware) pitcher on the table, for example, often appear in Annunciations to symbolize Mary's virginity. The hanging water pot in the background niche refers to Mary's purity and her role as the vessel for the Incarnation of God. What seems at first to be a towel hung over the prominent, hinged rack next to the niche may be a tallis (Jewish prayer shawl). Some art historians have referred to these as "hidden" or "disguised" symbols because they are treated as a normal part of the setting, but their routine religious meanings would have been obvious to the intended audience.

Some have interpreted the narrative episode captured in the central panel as the moment immediately following Mary's acceptance of her destiny. A rush of wind riffles the book pages and snuffs the candle (the flame, symbolic of God's divinity, extinguished at the moment he takes human form) as a tiny figure of Christ carrying a cross descends on a ray of light. Having accepted the miracle of the Incarnation (God assuming human

18-9 • Workshop of the Master of Flémalle
MÉRODE ALTARPIECE (TRIPTYCH OF THE
ANNUNCIATION) (OPEN)
c. 1425–1430s. Oil on wood panel, center 25¼ × 24⅞″ (64.1 × 63.2 cm);
each wing approx. 25⅜ × 10¾″ (64.5 × 27.6 cm). Metropolitan
Museum of Art, New York. The Cloisters Collection, 1956 (56.70)

In the late nineteenth century, this triptych was associated with a
group of stylistically related works and assigned to an artist called the
Master of Flémalle, who was subsequently identified by some art
historians as a documented artist named Robert Campin. Recently,
however, experts have questioned this association and proposed that
the triptych we now see was the work of several artists working within
the workshop that created the stylistic cluster. Current opinion holds
that the Annunciation was initially created as an independent panel,
and a short time later expanded into a triptych with the addition of the
side panels under the patronage of the donor in the foreground at left.
Finally, some time later in the 1430s, the figure of his wife was added
behind him, presumably on the occasion of his marriage.

form), Mary reads her Bible while sitting humbly on the footrest
of the long bench. Her position becomes a symbol of her submission
to God's will. Other art historians have proposed that the scene
represents the moment just prior to the Annunciation. In this view,
Mary is not yet aware of Gabriel's presence, and the rushing wind
is the result of the angel's rapid entry into the room, where he
appears before her, half kneeling and raising his hand in salutation.

In the left wing of the triptych, the donors—presumably a
married couple—kneel in an enclosed garden, another symbol of
Mary's virginity, before the open door of the house where the
Annunciation is taking place, implying that the scene is a vision
brought on by their faithful meditations, comparable to the vision
we have already seen in the Hours of Mary of Burgundy (SEE FIG.
18–6). Such presentations, very popular with Flemish patrons,
allowed those who commissioned a religious work to appear in the
same space and time, and often on the same scale, as religious
figures. The donors' eyes, which seem oddly unfocused, are
directed not outward but inward, intent on the spiritual exercise of
imagining their own presence within this sacred narrative.

18–10 • Workshop of the Master of Flémalle **A FLEMISH CITY**
Detail of the right wing of the Mérode Altarpiece in FIG. 18–9.

On the right wing, Joseph is working in his carpentry workshop. A prosperous Flemish city is exquisitely detailed in the view through the shop window, with people going about their daily business **(FIG. 18–10)**. Even here there is religious symbolism. On the windowsill of Joseph's shop is a mousetrap (another sits on the workbench next to him), which fifteenth-century viewers would understand as a reference to Christ as the bait in a trap set by God to catch Satan. Joseph is drilling holes in a small board used as a drainboard for making wine, calling to mind the Eucharist and Christ's Passion.

The complex and consistent treatment of light in the Mérode Altarpiece represents a major preoccupation of Flemish painters. The strongest illumination comes from an unseen source at the upper left in front of the **picture plane** (the picture's front surface) as if sunlight were entering through the opened front of the room. More light comes from the rear windows, and a few painted, linear rays come from the round window at left, a symbolic vehicle for the Christ Child's descent. Jesus seems to slide down the rays of light linking God with Mary, carrying the cross of human salvation

over his shoulder. The light falling on the Virgin's lap emphasizes this connection, and the transmission of the symbolic light through a transparent panel of glass (which remains intact) recalls the virginal nature of Jesus' conception.

JAN VAN EYCK. In 1425 Jan van Eyck (active 1420s–1441) became court painter to Duke Philip the Good of Burgundy (r. 1419–1467), who was the uncle of the king of France and one of the most sophisticated men in Europe. He made Jan one of his confidential employees and even sent him on a diplomatic mission to Portugal, charged with painting a portrait of a prospective bride for Philip. The duke alluded to Jan's remarkable technical skills in a letter of 1434–1435, saying that he could find no other painter equal to his taste or so excellent in art and science. So brilliant was Jan's use of oil glazes that he was mistakenly credited with the invention of oil painting (see "Oil Painting," page 571).

Jan's 1433 portrait of a **MAN IN A RED TURBAN** (FIG. **18–11**) projects a particularly strong sense of personality, and the signed and dated frame also bears Jan's personal motto—"As I can, [but

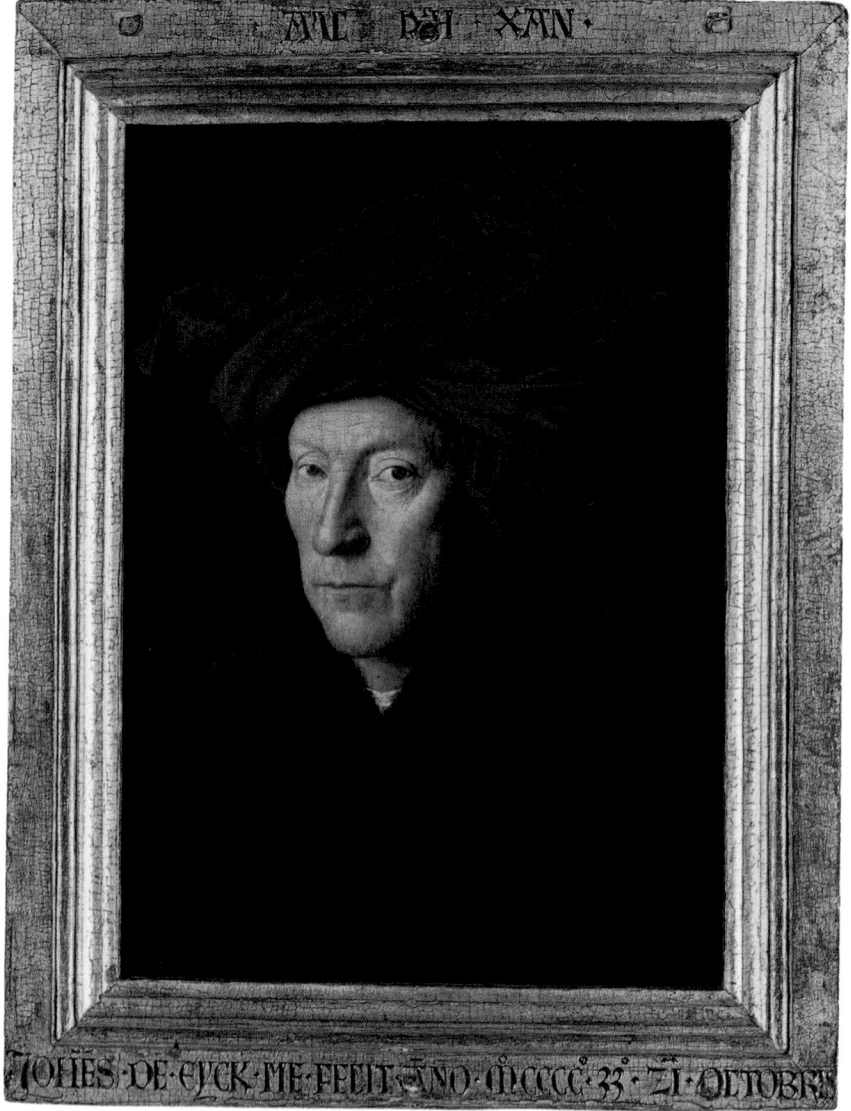

18-11 • Jan van Eyck MAN IN A RED TURBAN
1433. Oil on wood panel, 13⅛ × 10¼″ (33.3 × 25.8 cm). National Gallery, London.

as well as their remarkable surface realism, and the scrupulous attention to the luminous details of textures as variable as jewels and human flesh, are magnificent examples of Jan's artistic wizardry. He has carefully controlled the lighting within this multi-panel ensemble to make it appear that the objects represented are illuminated by sunlight coming through the window of the very chapel where it was meant to be installed. Jan's painting is firmly grounded in the terrestrial world even when he is rendering a visionary subject.

The Ghent altarpiece may have been Jan's most famous painting during his lifetime, but his best-known painting today is a distinctive double portrait of a couple identified as a Giovanni Arnolfini and his wife (SEE FIG. 18–1). Early interpreters saw this fascinating work as a wedding or betrothal. Above the mirror on the back wall **(FIG. 18–12)**, the artist inscribed the words: *Johannes de eyck fuit hic 1434* ("Jan van Eyck was here 1434"). More normal on a signature would have been, "Jan van Eyck made this," so the words "was here" might suggest that Jan served as a witness to a matrimonial episode portrayed in the painting. Jan is not the only witness recorded in the painting. The convex mirror between the figures reflects not only the back of the couple but a front view of two visitors standing in the doorway, entering the room. Perhaps one of them is the artist himself.

New research has complicated the developing interpretation of this painting by revealing that the Giovanni Arnolfini traditionally identified as the man in this painting married his wife Giovanna Cenami only in 1447, long after the date on the wall and Jan van Eyck's own death. One scholar has proposed that the picture is actually a prospective portrait of Giovanni and Giovanna's marriage in the future, painted in 1434 to secure the early transfer of the dowry from her father to her future husband. Others have more recently suggested the man portrayed here is a different Giovanni Arnolfini, accompanied either by his putative second wife or a memorial portrait of his first wife, Costanza Trenta, who died the year before this picture was painted, perhaps in childbirth. The true meaning of this fascinating masterpiece may remain a mystery, but it is doubtful that scholars will stop trying to solve it.

ROGIER VAN DER WEYDEN. Little as we know about Jan van Eyck, we know even less about the life of Rogier van der Weyden (c. 1400–1464). Not a single existing work of art bears his name. He may have studied under the Master of Flémalle, but the relationship is not altogether clear. First establishing himself in

not as I would]"—in Greek letters at the top. Since these letters also form an anagram of his own name, most scholars see this painting as a self-portrait in which physical appearance seems recorded in a magnifying mirror. We see the stubble of a day's growth of beard on his chin and cheeks, and every carefully described wrinkle around the artist's eyes, reddened from the strain of his work, and reflecting light that seems to emanate from our own space. That same light source gives the inscriptions the *trompe l'oeil* sense of having been engraved into the frame, heightening the illusionistic wizardry of Jan's painting. Is Jan looking out directly at us, or are we seeing his reflection in a mirror?

In his lifetime, one of the most famous works of Jan van Eyck was a huge polyptych with a very complicated and learned theological program that he (perhaps in collaboration with his brother Hubert) painted for a chapel in what is now the Cathedral of St. Bavo in Ghent (see "The Ghent Altarpiece," pages 576–577). The three-dimensional mass of the figures, the voluminous draperies

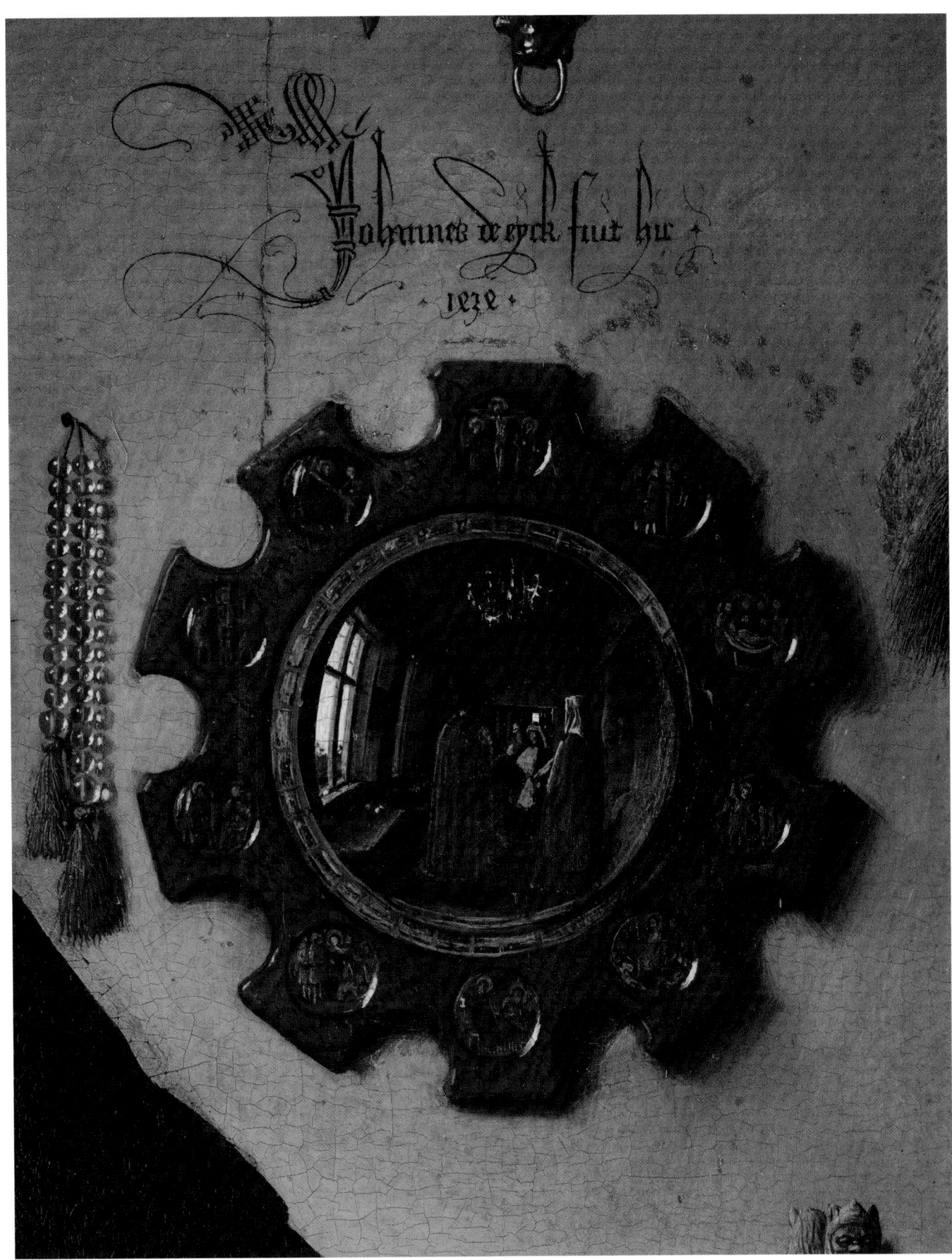

18–12 • Jan van Eyck DETAIL OF MIRROR AND SIGNATURE IN A DOUBLE PORTRAIT OF A GIOVANNI ARNOLFINI AND HIS WIFE (FIG. 18-1)
1434. Oil on wood panel. The National Gallery, London.

THE OBJECT SPEAKS

The Ghent Altarpiece

An inscription on the frame of the Ghent Altarpiece seems to identify both Jan and Hubert van Eyck as its artists: "The painter Hubert van Eyck, greater than whom no one was found, began [this work]; and Jan, his brother, second in art, having carried through the task at the expense of Jodocus Vyd, invites you by this verse, on the sixth of May [1432], to look at what has been done."

Many art historians believe Hubert began this altarpiece, and after his death in 1426, Jan completed it, when free of ducal responsibilities in 1430–1432. Others believe the entire painting was produced by Jan and his workshop, Hubert perhaps being responsible for the frame. At least commission and situation are clear. Jodocus Vijd, who appears with his wife Isabella Borluut on the outside of the polyptych's shutters—both visible only when the altarpiece is closed—commanded the work. Part of a wealthy family of financiers, Jodocus was a city official in Ghent—holding an office comparable to mayor in 1433–1434—and the altarpiece was part of a renovation he funded in the family chapel at the parish church of St. John (now the Cathedral of St. Bavo). He also endowed daily Masses in the chapel for the couple's salvation, and that of their ancestors.

When the altarpiece was closed, the exterior of the shutters displayed the striking likenesses of the donor couple kneeling to face painted statues of SS. John the Baptist (patron of Ghent) and John the Evangelist (patron of this church) that recall those on Sluter's Well of Moses (SEE FIG. 18–3). Above this row is an expansive rendering of the Annunciation—whose somber color scheme coordinates with the *grisaille* statues painted below—situated in an upstairs room that looks out over a panoramic cityscape. As in Simone Martini's Annunciation altarpiece (SEE FIG. 17–13), the words that issue from Gabriel's mouth ("Hail, full of grace, the Lord is with thee") appear on the painting's surface, and here there is Mary's response as well ("Behold the handmaid of the Lord"), only it is painted upside down since it is

directed to God, who hovers above her head as the dove of the Holy Spirit. Prophets and sibyls perch in the irregular compartments at the top, unfurling scrolls recording their predictions of Christ's coming.

When the shutters were opened on Sundays and feast days, the mood changed. The effect is no longer muted, but rich in

both color and implied sound. Dominating the altarpiece by size, central location, and brilliant color is the enthroned figure of God, wearing the triple papal crown, with an earthly crown at his feet, and flanked by the Virgin Mary and John the Baptist, each holding an open book. To either side are first angel musicians and then Adam and Eve,

A. Jan and Hubert (?) van Eyck **GHENT ALTARPIECE (CLOSED), ANNUNCIATION WITH DONORS**
Completed 1432. Oil on panel, height 11′5¾″ (3.5 m). Cathedral of St. Bavo, Ghent.

represented as lifelike nudes. Adam seems to have been painted from a model, from whom Jan reproduced even the "farmer's tan" of his hands and face. Eve displays clear features of the female anatomy; the pigmented line running downward from her navel appears frequently during pregnancy. Each of the three themes of the upper register—God with Mary and John, musical angels, and Adam and Eve—is set in a distinct space: the holy trio in a golden shrine, angels against a blue sky, Adam and Eve in shallow stone niches.

The five lower panels present a unified field. A vast landscape with meadows, woods, and distant cities is set against a continuous horizon. A diverse array of saints—apostles, martyrs, confessors, virgins, hermits, pilgrims, warriors, judges—assemble to adore the Lamb of God as described in the book of Revelation. The Lamb stands on an altar, blood flowing into a chalice, ultimately leading to the fountain of life.

The Ghent altarpiece became a famous work of art almost as soon as it was completed. To celebrate Duke Philip the Good's visit to the city in 1458, citizens of Ghent welcomed him with *tableaux vivants* (living pictures) of its scenes. German artist Albrecht Dürer traveled to Ghent to see the altarpiece in 1521. During the French occupation of Flanders in 1794 it was transferred to Paris (returned in 1815), and during World War II it was confiscated by the Nazis. It is now displayed within a secure glass case in the baptismal chapel of the church for which it was made.

B. Jan and Hubert (?) van Eyck **GHENT ALTARPIECE (OPEN), ADORATION OF THE MYSTIC LAMB**
Completed 1432. Oil on panel, 11′5¾″ × 15′1½″ (3.5 × 4.6 m). Cathedral of St. Bavo, Ghent.

18–13 • Rogier van der Weyden DEPOSITION
From an altarpiece commissioned by the crossbowmen's guild, Louvain, Belgium. Before 1443, possibly c. 1435–1438. Oil on wood panel, 7'2⅝" × 8'7⅛" (2.2 × 2.62 m). Museo del Prado, Madrid.

EXPLORE MORE: Gain insight from a primary source regarding Rogier van der Weyden
www.myartslab.com

1432 as an independent master in Tournai, at the peak of his career, Rogier maintained a large workshop in Brussels, where he was the official city painter, attracting apprentices and shop assistants from as far away as Italy. To establish the stylistic characteristics of Rogier's art, scholars have turned to a painting of the **DEPOSITION** (**FIG. 18–13**), an altarpiece commissioned by the Louvain crossbowmen's guild (crossbows can be seen in the tracery painted in the upper corners) sometime before 1443, the date of the earliest known copy of it by another artist.

The Deposition was a popular theme in the fifteenth century because of its potential for dramatic, personally engaging portrayal. Rogier sets the act of removing Jesus' body from the cross on the shallow stage of a gilt wooden box, just like the case of a carved and painted altarpiece. The ten solid, three-dimensional figures, however, are not simulations of polychromed wood carving, but near life-size renderings of actual human figures who seem to press forward into the viewer's space, allowing them no escape from the forceful expressions of heartrending grief. Jesus' friends seem palpably real, with their portraitlike faces and scrupulously described contemporary dress, as they tenderly and sorrowfully remove his body from the cross for burial. Jesus' corpse dominates the center of the composition, drooping in a languid curve, framed by jarringly thin, angular arms. His pose is echoed by the rhyming form of the swooning Virgin. It is as if mother and son share in the redemptive passion of his death on the cross, encouraging viewers to identify with them both, or join their assembled companions in mourning their fate. Although united by their sorrow, the mourning figures react in personal ways, from the intensity of Mary Magdalen at far right, wringing her hands in anguish, to John the Evangelist's blank stare at left, lost in grief as he reaches to support the collapsing Virgin. The anguish of the woman behind him, mopping her tear-soaked eyes with the edge of her veil, is almost unbearably poignant.

Rogier's choice of color and pattern balances and enhances his composition. The complexity of the gold brocade worn by Joseph of Arimathea, who offered his new tomb for the burial, and the contorted pose and vivid dress of Mary Magdalen increase the visual impact of the right side of the panel to counter the pictorial weight of the larger number of figures at the left. The palette contrasts subtle, slightly muted colors with brilliant expanses of blue and red, while white accents focus the viewers' attention on the main subjects. The whites of the winding cloth and the tunic of the youth on the ladder set off Jesus' pale body, as the white turban and shawl emphasize the ashen face of Mary.

Another work by Rogier, painted at about the same time as the Deposition, is both quieter and more personal. It represents the evangelist St. Luke executing a preparatory drawing in silverpoint for a painting of the Virgin and Child who seem to have materialized to pose for him (FIG. 18–14). The painting is based on a legend with origins in sixth-century Byzantium of a miraculous appearance of the Virgin and Child to Luke so he could record their appearance and pass on his authentic witness to his Christian followers. Rogier's version takes place in a carefully defined interior

18-14 • Rogier van der Weyden ST. LUKE DRAWING THE VIRGIN AND CHILD
c. 1435–1440. Oil and tempera on wood panel, 54¼ × 43⅝" (137.7 × 110.8 cm).
Museum of Fine Arts, Boston.

space that opens onto a garden, and from there into a distant vista of urban life before dissolving into the countryside through which a winding river guides our exploration all the way to the horizon. The Virgin is preoccupied with a routine maternal activity. Her baby has pulled away from her breast, producing a smile and flexing his hand—familiar gestures of actual babies during nursing. The good mother and happy baby are observed by Luke, who perches on his knees and captures the scene in a silverpoint sketch, a common preliminary step used by fifteenth-century Flemish painters in the planning of their paintings, especially portraits. And the portraitlike quality of Luke's face here has led scholars to propose that this image of a saint is a self-portrait of its artist.

Art historians have traditionally interpreted this painting in two ways. Some see it—especially if it is a self-portrait—as a

document of Rogier's sense of his own profession. They see him distancing himself and his fifteenth-century Flemish colleagues from identification with the laboring artisans of the Middle Ages, and staking a claim for his special role as an inspired creator who recorded sacred visions in valuable, individualistic works of art. The notion of Rogier's own identification with Luke in this painting is supported by the fact that later artists emulated his composition in creating their own self-portraits as the century progressed. But other art historians, proposing that this painting was created for the chapel of the guildhall of the painters in Brussels (the evidence is suggestive but unclear), have interpreted it as a claim for the importance of the painters' profession because it is rooted in saintly legend. Perhaps this extraordinary picture was both self-fashioning and professional propaganda. But it was also a devotional image.

Luke's tenuous, half-kneeling perch, and his dreamy, introspective gaze certainly remind us that one of the tasks of painters in this period was to create inspiring pictures of religious visions that are also materialized by meticulous references to the real world. This most certainly is that.

PAINTING AT MID CENTURY: THE SECOND GENERATION

The extraordinary accomplishments of the Master of Flémalle, Jan van Eyck, and Rogier van der Weyden attracted many followers in Flanders. The work of this second generation of Flemish painters may have been simpler, more direct, often easier to understand than that of their predecessors, but they produced extraordinary works of great emotional power. They were in large part responsible for the rapid spread of the Flemish style throughout Europe.

PETRUS CHRISTUS. Among the most interesting of these painters was Petrus Christus (active 1444–c. 1475/1476), who became a citizen of Bruges in 1444 and signed and dated six paintings in a career that extended over three decades.

In 1449, Christus painted a portrait of a goldsmith, serving two well-dressed customers in his shop (see "A Closer Look," opposite). A halo around the head of the seated figure—not originally a part of the painting—was removed by restorers in 1993. This coincided with a reevaluation of the subject matter of the work, now seen as a vocational portrait of an actual goldsmith, rather than an image of St. Eloi, patron saint of goldsmiths, set in the present. Both finished products and raw materials of the jeweler's trade sit on the shelves behind the goldsmith: containers, rings, brooches, a belt buckle, a string of beads, pearls, gemstones, coral, and crystal cylinders. A betrothal belt curls across the counter. Such a combination of objects suggests that the painting expresses the hope for health and well-being for the couple who may be in the process of procuring rings for their upcoming marriage.

As in Jan van Eyck's double portrait, a convex mirror extends the viewer's field of vision, in this instance to the street outside, where two men appear. One is stylishly dressed in red and black, and the other holds a falcon, another indication of high status. Whether or not the reflected image has symbolic meaning, the mirror would have had practical value in a goldsmith's shop, allowing him to observe the approach of potential customers to the counter outside his shop window.

DIRCK BOUTS. Dirck Bouts (active c. 1444–1475) is best known among Flemish painters as a storyteller, and he exercised those skills in a series of large altarpieces, with narrative scenes drawn from the life of Christ and the lives of the saints. But he also created more intimate pictures, such as this tender rendering of the **VIRGIN AND CHILD**, just 8½ inches tall **(FIG. 18–15)**. Even it evokes a story. Mary holds her baby securely, using both of her plain, strong hands to surround completely the lower part of his body. The baby reaches across his mother's chest and around her neck, pulling himself closer to press his face next to hers, cheek to cheek,

18-15 • Dieric Bouts **VIRGIN AND CHILD**
c. 1455–1460. Oil on wood panel, 8½ × 6½″ (21.6 × 16.5 cm). Metropolitan Museum of Art, New York.

nose to nose, mouth to mouth, eyes locked together, forming a symmetrical system that links them in pattern and almost melds them into a single mirrored form. It is as if a fifteenth-century St. Luke had captured a private moment between the Virgin and Child—a dimpled mother and baby looking very much like the actual people in the artist's world—during their miraculous appearance to sit as his model (compare FIG. 18–14). The concept is actually not so far fetched. Bouts's painting is modeled after a fourteenth-century Italian image in the cathedral of Cambrai that in the fifteenth century was believed to have been painted by St. Luke himself.

HUGO VAN DER GOES. Hugo van der Goes (c. 1440–1482), dean of the painters' guild in Ghent (1468–1475), united the intellectual prowess of Jan van Eyck with the emotional sensitivity of Rogier van der Weyden to create an entirely new personal style. Hugo's major work was an exceptionally large altarpiece, more than 8 feet tall, of the Nativity **(FIG. 18–16)**, commissioned by Tommaso Portinari, head of the Medici bank in Bruges. Painted probably

A Goldsmith in his Shop ▶ by Petrus Christus. 1449. Oil on oak panel, 38⅝ × 33½″ (98 × 85 cm). Metropolitan Museum of Art, New York, Robert Lehman Collection, 1975. 1975.1.110

The coat of arms of the dukes of Guelders hangs from a chain around this man's neck, leading some to speculate that the woman, who is the more active of the pair, is Mary of Guelders, niece of Duke Philip the Good, who married King James II of the Scots the same year this picture was painted.

Goldsmiths were expected to perform all their transactions, including the weighing of gold, in public view to safeguard against dishonesty. Here the scales tip toward the couple, perhaps an allusion to the scales of the Last Judgment, which always tip to the side of the righteous.

Three types of coins rest on the shop counter: "florins" from Mainz, "angels" from English King Henry VI's French territories, and "riders" minted under Philip the Good. Such diversity of currency could show the goldsmith's cosmopolitanism, or they could indicate his participation in money changing, since members of that profession belonged to the same guild as goldsmiths.

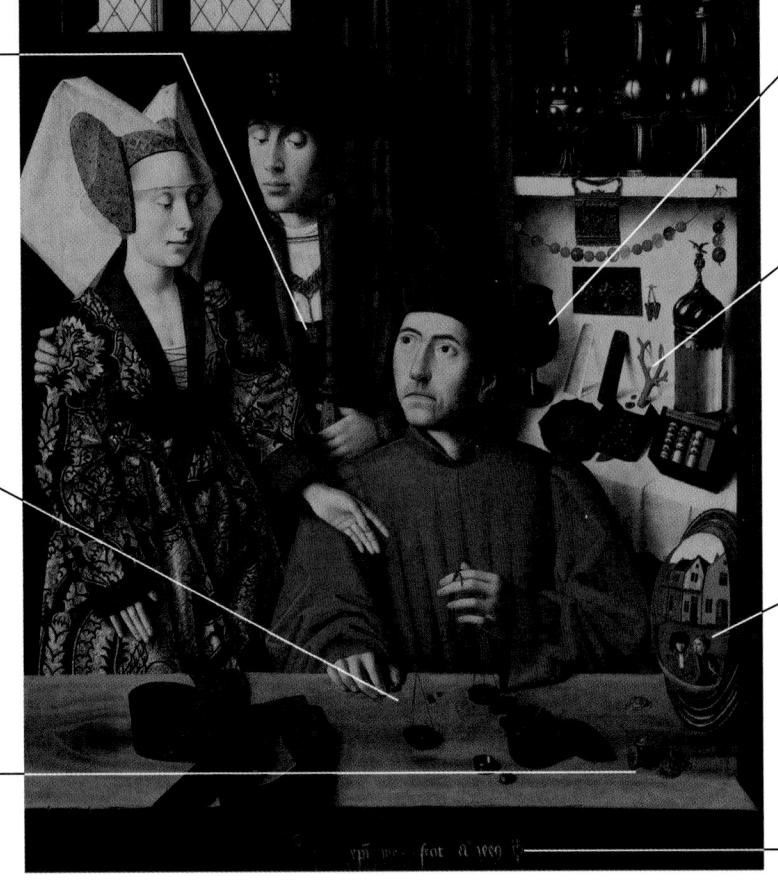

This coconut cup was supposed to neutralize poison. The slabs of porphyry and rock crystal were "touchstones," used to test gold and precious stones.

The red coral and serpents' tongues (actually fossilized sharks' teeth) were intended to ward off the evil eye.

Two men, one with a falcon on his arm, are reflected in the obliquely placed mirror as they stand in front of the shop. The edges of the reflection catch the red sleeve of the goldsmith and the door frame, uniting the interior and exterior spaces and drawing the viewer into the painting.

The artist signed and dated his work in a bold inscription that appears just under the tabletop at the bottom of the painting: "Master Petrus Christus made me in the year 1449."

SEE MORE: View the Closer Look feature for *A Goldsmith in his Shop* **www.myartslab.com**

---

between 1474 and 1476, the triptych was sent to Florence and installed in 1483 in the Portinari family chapel, where it had a noticeable impact on Florentine painters.

Tommaso, his wife Maria Baroncelli, and their three oldest children are portrayed kneeling in prayer on the side panels of the wing interiors. On the left wing, looming larger than life behind Tommaso and his son Antonio, are the saints for whom they are named, St. Thomas and St. Antony. Since the younger son, Pigello, born in 1474, was apparently added after the original composition was set, his name saint is lacking. On the right wing, Maria and her daughter Margherita are presented by SS. Mary Magdalen and Margaret.

The theme of the altarpiece is the Nativity as told by Luke (2:10–19). The central panel represents the Adoration of the newborn Christ Child by Mary and Joseph, a host of angels, and the shepherds who have rushed in from the fields. In the middle ground of the wings are additional scenes. Winding their way through the winter landscape are two groups headed for Bethlehem. On the left wing, Mary and Joseph travel there to take part in a census. Near term in her pregnancy, Mary has dismounted from her donkey and staggers, supported by Joseph. On the right wing, a servant of the three Magi, who are coming to honor the awaited Savior, asks directions from a peasant.

Hugo paints meadows and woods meticulously, and he used atmospheric perspective to approximate distance in the landscape. He shifts figure size for emphasis: The huge figures of Joseph, Mary, and the shepherds are the same size as the patron saints on the wings, in contrast to the much smaller Portinari family and still

18–16 • Hugo van der Goes **PORTINARI ALTARPIECE (OPEN)**
c. 1474–1476. Tempera and oil on wood panel; center 8′3½″ × 10′ (2.53 × 3.01 m), wings each 8′3½″ × 4′7½″ (2.53 × 1.41 m). Galleria degli Uffizi, Florence.

smaller angels. Hugo also uses light, as well as the gestures and gazes of the figures, to focus our eyes on the center panel where the mystery of the Incarnation takes place. Instead of lying swaddled in a manger or in his mother's arms, Jesus rests naked and vulnerable on the barren ground. Rays of light emanate from his body. This image was based on the visionary writing of the medieval Swedish mystic St. Bridget (who composed her work c. 1360–1370), which describes Mary kneeling to adore the Christ Child immediately after giving birth.

As in the work of Jan van Eyck, aspects of the setting of this painting are infused with symbolic meaning. In the foreground, the wheatsheaf refers both to the location of the event at Bethlehem, which in Hebrew means "house of bread," and to the Eucharistic Host, which represents the body of Christ. The majolica albarello is decorated with vines and grapes, alluding to the Eucharistic wine, which represents the blood of Christ. It holds a red lily for Christ's blood and three irises—white for purity and purple for Christ's royal ancestry. The seven blue columbines in the glass vessel remind the viewer of the Virgin's future sorrows, and scattered on the ground are violets, symbolizing humility. But Hugo's artistic vision transcends such formal religious symbolism. For example, the shepherds, who stand in unaffected awe before the miraculous event, are among the most sympathetically rendered images of common people to be found in the art of any period, and the portraits of the Portinari children are unusually sensitive renderings of the delicate features of youthful faces.

HANS MEMLING. The artist who seems to summarize and epitomize painting in Flanders during the second half of the fifteenth century is German-born Hans Memling (c. 1435–1494). Memling combines the intellectual depth and virtuoso rendering of his predecessors with a delicacy of feeling and exquisite grace, a "prettiness" that made his work exceptionally popular. Memling may have worked in Rogier van der Weyden's Brussels workshop in the 1460s, but soon after Rogier's death in 1464, Memling moved to Bruges, where he developed an international clientele that supported a thriving workshop. He also worked for local patrons.

In 1487, the 24-year-old Maarten van Nieuwenhove (1463–1500), member of a powerful political family in Bruges (he would himself become mayor of Bruges in 1497), commissioned from Memling a diptych that combined a meticulously detailed portrait with a visionary apparition of the Virgin and Child, presented as a powerful fiction of their physical encounter in Maarten's own home (FIG. 18–17). This type of devotional diptych was a specialty of Rogier van der Weyden, but Memling transforms the type into something more intimate by placing it in a domestic setting. An expensively outfitted figure of Maarten appears in the right wing of the diptych, seen from an oblique angle, hands folded in prayer. He seems caught in a moment of introspection inspired by personal devotions—his Book of Hours lies still open on the table in front of him. The window just over his shoulder holds a stained-glass rendering of his name saint, Martin, in the top pane, while a recognizable landmark in Bruges can be seen through the pane below. The Virgin and Child on the adjacent panel are presented frontally, and the strong sense of specific likeness characterizing Maarten's portrait has given way to an idealized delicacy and grace in the visage of the Virgin that complements the extravagance of her clothing. Although she does not seem to be focusing on him, a completely nude Jesus stretches out on the silk pillow in front of her; she stabilizes him with one hand and offers him an apple with the other. This seems a clear reference to their roles as the new Adam and Eve, ready to redeem the sin brought into the world by the first couple. The stained glass behind them is filled with heraldry, devices, and a motto associated with Maarten's family.

Memling's construction of a coherent interior space for these figures is both impressive and meaningful. We are looking through two windows into a rectangular room containing this devotional group. The pillow under the Christ Child casts a shadow, painted on the lower frame of the left panel, to intensify the illusion, and the Virgin's scarlet mantle extends under the division between the two wings of the diptych to reappear on Maarten's side of the painting underneath his Book of Hours. This mantle not only connects the two sides of the painting spatially but also relates Maarten's devotional exercise and the apparition of the Virgin and Child. This relationship is also documented with a device already familiar to us in paintings by Jan van Eyck (SEE FIG. 18–12) and Petrus Christus (see "A Closer Look," page 581). On the shadowy back wall, over the Virgin's right shoulder and set against the closed shutters of a window, is a convex mirror that reflects the backs of both Maarten and Mary, bearing visual witness to their presence together within his domestic space and undoing the division between them that is endemic to the diptych format. Maarten's introspective gaze signals that for him the encounter is internal and spiritual, but Memling transforms Maarten's private devotion into a public statement that promotes an image of his piety and freezes him in perpetual prayer. We bear witness to his vision as an actual event.

EUROPE BEYOND FLANDERS

Flemish art—its complex symbolism, its coherent configurations of atmospheric space, its luminous colors and sensuous surface textures—delighted wealthy patrons and well-educated courtiers both inside and outside Flanders. At first, Flemish artists worked in foreign courts or their works were commissioned and exported abroad. Flemish manuscripts, tapestries, altarpieces, and portraits

18–17 • Hans Memling DIPTYCH OF MAARTEN VAN NIEUWENHOVE
1487. Oil on wood panel, each panel (including frames) 20½ × 16¼″ (52 × 41.5 cm). Hans Memling Museum, Musea Brugge, Sint-Jans Hospital, Bruges.

appeared in palaces and chapels throughout Europe. Soon regional artists traveled to Flanders to learn oil-painting techniques and practice emulating the Flemish style. By the end of the fifteenth century, distinctive regional variations of Flemish art could be found throughout Europe, from the Atlantic Ocean to the Danube.

FRANCE

The centuries-long struggle for power and territory between France and England continued well into the fifteenth century. When King Charles VI of France died in 1422, England claimed the throne for the king's 9-month-old grandson, Henry VI of England. The plight of Charles VII, the late French king's son, inspired Joan of Arc to lead a crusade to return him to the throne. Thanks to Joan's efforts, Charles was crowned at Reims in 1429. Although Joan was burned at the stake in 1431, the revitalized French forces drove the English from French lands. In 1461, Louis XI succeeded his father, Charles VII, as king of France. Under his rule the French royal court again became a major source of patronage for the arts.

JEAN FOUQUET. The leading court artist of fifteenth-century France, Jean Fouquet (c. 1425–1481), was born in Tours and may have trained in Paris as an illuminator and in Bourges in the workshop of Jacob de Littemont, Flemish court painter to Charles VII. He was part of a French delegation to Rome in 1446–1448, but by mid century he had established a workshop in Tours and was a renowned painter. Fouquet drew from contemporary Italian Classicism, especially in rendering architecture, and he was also strongly influenced by Flemish illusionism. He painted pictures of Charles VII, the royal family, and courtiers, and he illustrated manuscripts and designed tombs.

Among the court officials who commissioned paintings from Fouquet was Étienne Chevalier, treasurer of France under Charles VII. Fouquet painted a diptych for him that was installed over the tomb of Chevallier's wife Catherine Budé (d. 1452) in the church of Notre-Dame in Melun (FIG. 18–18). Chevalier appears in the left panel, kneeling in prayer with clasped hands and an introspective, meditative gaze within an Italianate palace, accompanied by his name saint Stephen (Étienne in French). Fouquet describes the courtier's ruddy features with a mirrorlike precision that is reminiscent of Flemish art. He is expensively dressed in a heavy red wool garment lined with fur, and his "bowl cut" represents the latest Parisian fashion in hair styling. St. Stephen's features convey a comparable sense of likeness and sophistication. A deacon in the Early Christian church in Jerusalem, Stephen was the first Christian martyr, stoned to death for defending his beliefs. Here he wears the fifteenth-century liturgical, or ritual, vestments of a deacon and carries a large stone on a closed Gospel book as evidence of his martyrdom. A trickle of blood can be seen on his tonsured head (male members of religious orders shaved the tops of their heads as a sign of humility). Placing his arm around Étienne Chevalier's back, the saint seems to be introducing the treasurer to the Virgin and Child in the adjacent panel.

18–18 • Jean Fouquet ÉTIENNE CHEVALIER AND ST. STEPHEN, VIRGIN AND CHILD
The Melun Diptych. c. 1452–1455. Oil on oak panel. Left wing: 36½ × 33½″ (92.7 × 85.5 cm), Staatliche Museen zu Berlin, Preussischer Kulturbesitz, Gemäldegalerie; right wing: 37¼ × 33½″ (94.5 × 85.5 cm). Koninklijk Museum voor Schone Kunsten, Antwerp, Belgium.

The Virgin and Child, however, exist in another world. A supernatural vision unfolds here as the queen of heaven is enthroned surrounded by red and blue seraphim and cherubim, who form a tapestrylike background. Even the Virgin seems a celestial being, conceived by Fouquet as a hybrid of careful description and powerful abstraction. Her fashionable, tightly waisted bodice has been unlaced so she can present her spherical breast to a substantial, seated baby, who points across the juncture between the two wings of the diptych to acknowledge Chevalier. According to tradition, Fouquet gave this image of the Virgin the features of the king's much loved and respected mistress, Agnès Sorel, who died in 1450. The original frame that united these two panels—now divided between two museums—into a diptych is lost, but among the fragments that remain is a stunning medallion self-portrait that served as the artist's signature.

JEAN HEY, THE MASTER OF MOULINS. Perhaps the greatest French follower of Jean Fouquet is an artist who for many years was known as the Master of Moulins after a large triptych he painted at the end of the fifteenth century under the patronage of Duke Jean II of Bourbon, for the Burgundian Cathedral of Moulins. This triptych combines the exuberance of Flemish attention to brilliant color and the differentiation of surface texture with a characteristically French air of reserved detachment. Recently the work of this artist has been associated with the name Jean Hey, a painter of Flemish origin, who seems to have been trained in the workshop of Hugo van der Goes, but who pursued his career at the French court.

This charming portrait (FIG. 18–19)—which may have been one half of a devotional diptych comparable to that painted by Memling for Maarten van Nieuwenhove (SEE FIG. 18–17)—portrays Margaret of Austria (1480–1530), daughter of Emperor Maximilian I, who had been betrothed to the future French king Charles VIII (r. 1483–1498) at age 2 or 3 and was being brought up at the French court. She would return home to her father in 1493 after Charles decided to pursue another, more politically expedient marriage (after two political marriages of her own, the widowed Margaret would eventually become governor of the Habsburg Netherlands), but Hey captures her at a tender moment a few years before those troubled times. She kneels in front of a strip of wall between two windows that open onto a lush country landscape, fingering the pearl beads of her rosary. Details of her lavish velvet and ermine outfit not only proclaim her wealth but provide the clues to her identity—the *Cs* and *Ms* embroidered on her collar signal her betrothal to Charles and the ostentatious *fleur-de-lis* pendant set with large rubies and pearls proclaims her affiliation with the French court. But it is the delicacy and sweet vulnerability of this 10-year-old girl that are most arresting. They recall Hugo van der Goes's sensitivity to the childlike qualities of the young members of donor families (SEE FIG. 18–16) and provide one strong piece of evidence for ascribing Hey's training to the workshop of this Flemish master.

18–19 • Jean Hey (The Master of Moulins)
PORTRAIT OF MARGARET OF AUSTRIA
c. 1490. Oil on wood panel, 12⅞ × 9⅛" (32.7 × 23 cm). Metropolitan Museum of Art, New York, Robert Lehman Collection.

FLAMBOYANT ARCHITECTURE. The great age of cathedral building that had begun in the mid twelfth century was essentially over by the end of the fourteenth century, but growing urban populations needed houses, city halls, guildhalls, and more parish churches. It was in buildings such as these that late Gothic architecture took form in a style we call "Flamboyant" because of its repeated, twisted, flamelike tracery patterns. Late Gothic masons covered their buildings with increasingly elaborate, complex, and at times playful architectural decoration. Like painters, sculptors also turned to describing the specific nature of the world around them, and they covered capitals and moldings with ivy, hawthorn leaves, and other vegetation, not just the conventional acanthus motifs rooted in the Classical world.

The church of Saint-Maclou in Rouen, which was begun after a fund-raising campaign in 1432 and dedicated in 1521, is an outstanding and well-preserved example of Flamboyant Gothic (FIG. 18–20) probably designed by the Paris architect Pierre Robin. A projecting porch bends to enfold the façade of the church in a screen of tracery. Sunlight on the flame-shape openings casts ever-changing shadows across the intentionally complex surface. **Crockets**—small, knobby leaflike ornaments that line the steep gables and slender buttresses—break every defining line. In

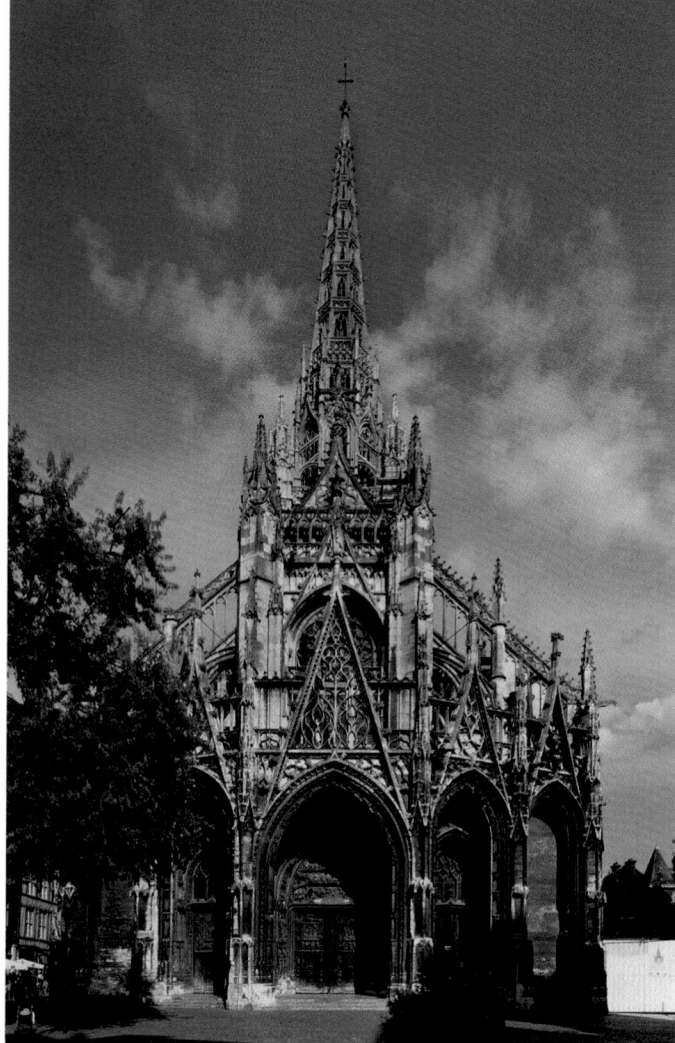

18-20 • Pierre Robin (?) **CHURCH OF SAINT-MACLOU, ROUEN**

Normandy, France. West façade, 1432–1521; façade c. 1500–1514.

SEE MORE: Click the Google Earth link for Saint-Maclou
www.myartslab.com

SEE MORE: Click the Google Earth link for Saint-Maclou www.myartslab.com

the Flamboyant style, decoration sometimes disguises structural elements with an overlay of tracery and ornament in geometric and natural shapes, all to dizzying effect.

The house of Jacques Coeur, a fabulously wealthy merchant in Bourges, reflects the popularity of the Flamboyant style for secular architecture **(FIGS. 18–21, 18–22)**. Built at great expense between 1443 and 1451, it survives almost intact, although it has been stripped of its rich furnishings. The rambling, palatial house is built around an irregular open courtyard, with spiral stairs in octagonal towers giving access to the upper-floor rooms. Tympana over doors indicate the function of the rooms within; for example, over the door to the kitchen a cook stirs the contents of a large bowl. Among the carved decorations are puns on the patron's surname, Coeur (meaning "heart" in French). The house was also Jacques Coeur's place of business, so it had large storerooms for goods and a strongroom for treasure.

GERMANY AND SWITZERLAND

Present-day Germany and Switzerland were situated within the Holy Roman Empire, a loose confederation of primarily German-speaking states. Artisan guilds grew powerful and trade flourished under the auspices of the Hanseatic League, an association of cities and trading outposts, stimulating a strengthening of the merchant class. The Fugger family, for example, began their spectacular rise

courtyard

18-21 • PLAN OF JACQUES COEUR HOUSE
Bourges, France. 1443–1451.

18-22 • INTERIOR COURTYARD OF JACQUES COEUR HOUSE
Bourges, France. 1443–1451.

18-23 • Konrad Witz **MIRACULOUS DRAFT OF FISHES**
From an altarpiece for the Cathedral of St. Peter, Geneva, Switzerland. 1444. Oil on wood panel,
4′3″ × 5′1″ (1.29 × 1.55 m). Musée d'Art et d'Histoire, Geneva.

from simple textile workers and linen merchants to bankers for the Habsburgs and the popes.

KONRAD WITZ. Germanic fifteenth-century artists worked in two very different styles. Some, clustered around Cologne, continued the International Gothic style with increased prettiness, softness, and sweetness of expression. Other artists began an intense investigation and detailed description of the physical world. The major exponent of the latter style was Konrad Witz (active 1434–1446). A native of Swabia in southern Germany, Witz moved to Basel (in present-day Switzerland), where he found a rich source of patronage in the Church.

Witz's last large commission before his early death in 1446 was an altarpiece dedicated to St. Peter for the Cathedral of Geneva, signed and dated to 1444. In one of its scenes—the **MIRACULOUS DRAFT OF FISHES** (FIG. **18–23**)—Jesus appears posthumously to his disciples as they fish on the Sea of Galilee and Peter leaps from the boat to greet him. But Witz sets the scene on the Lake of Geneva, with the distinctive dark mountain (the Mole) rising on the north

shore and the snow-covered Alps shining in the distance. Witz records every nuance of light and water—the rippling surface, the reflections of boats, figures, and buildings, even the lake bottom. Peter's body and legs, visible through the water, are distorted by the refraction. For one of the earliest times in European art, an artist captures both the appearance and the spirit of nature.

MICHAEL PACHER. In Germanic lands, patrons preferred altarpieces that featured polychromed wood carvings rather than the large ensembles of panel paintings that we saw in Flanders (see, for example, "The Ghent Altarpiece," pages 576–577). One of the greatest artists working in this tradition was painter and sculptor Michael Pacher (1435–1498), based in Bruneck, now in the Italian Alps. In 1471, Benedict Eck, abbot of Mondsee, commissioned from Pacher for the pilgrimage church of St. Wolfgang a grand high altarpiece that is still installed in its original church setting (FIG. **18–24**). The surviving contract specifies materials and subject matter and even documents the cost—1,200 Hungarian florins—but sets no time limit for its completion. Pacher and his shop worked on it for ten years.

18-24 • Michael Pacher ST. WOLFGANG ALTARPIECE
St. Wolfgang, Austria, 1471–1481. Carved, painted, and gilt wood; wings are oil on wood panel.

When it is open (as in FIG. 18–24), a dizzyingly complicated sculptural ensemble aligns up the middle, flanked by four large panel paintings portraying scenes from the life of the Virgin on the opened shutters. Both the design and execution were supervised by Pacher, but many other artists collaborated with him on the actual carving and painting. In the main scene, the wood carvings create a vision in Paradise where Christ crowns his mother as the queen of heaven flanked by imposing images of local saints. The use of soft wood facilitated deep undercutting and amazing detail in the rendering of these figures, and the elaborate polychromy and gold leaf sheathed them in a shimmering finish that glitters in the changing patterns of natural light or the flickering glow of candles. It must have been an otherworldly sight.

THE GRAPHIC ARTS

Printmaking emerged in Europe at the end of the fourteenth century with the development of printing presses and the increased local manufacture and wider availability of paper. The techniques used by printmakers during the fifteenth century were woodcut and engraving (see "Woodcuts and Engravings on Metal," page 590). **Woodblocks** cut in relief had long been used to print designs on cloth, but only in the fifteenth century did the printing of images and texts on paper and the production of books in multiple copies of a single edition, or version, begin to replace the copying of each book by hand. Both hand-written and printed books were often illustrated, and printed images were sometimes hand-colored.

SINGLE SHEETS

Large quantities of single-sheet prints were made using woodcut and engraving techniques in the early decades of the fifteenth century. Often artists drew the images for professional woodworkers to cut from the block.

THE BUXHEIM ST. CHRISTOPHER.   Devotional images were sold as souvenirs to pilgrims at holy sites. The **BUXHEIM ST. CHRISTOPHER** was found in the Carthusian Monastery of Buxheim, in southern Germany, glued to the inside of the back cover of a manuscript **(FIG. 18–25)**. St. Christopher, patron saint of travelers and protector from the plague, carries the Christ Child across the river. His efforts are witnessed by a monk holding out a light to guide him to the monastery door, but ignored by the hardworking millers on the opposite bank. Both the cutting of the block and the quality of the printing are very high. Lines vary in width to strengthen major forms. Delicate lines are used for inner modeling (facial features) and short parallel lines to indicate shadows (the inner side of draperies). The date 1423, which is cut into the block, was once thought to identify this print as among the earliest to survive. Recent studies have determined that the date refers to some event, and the print is now dated at mid century.

MARTIN SCHONGAUER.   Engraving may have originated with goldsmiths and armorers, who recorded their work by rubbing

18-25 • THE BUXHEIM ST. CHRISTOPHER
Mid 15th century. Hand-colored woodcut, 11⅜ × 8⅛" (28.85 × 20.7 cm). Courtesy of the Director and Librarian, the John Rylands University Library, the University of Manchester, England

The Latin text reads, "Whenever you look at the face of St. Christopher, you will not die a terrible death that day."

lampblack into the engraved lines and pressing paper over the plate. German artist Martin Schongauer (c. 1435–1491), who learned engraving from his goldsmith father, was an immensely skillful printmaker who excelled both in drawing and in the difficult technique of shading from deep blacks to faintest grays using only line. In **DEMONS TORMENTING ST. ANTHONY**, engraved about 1470–1475 **(FIG. 18–26)**, Schongauer illustrated the original biblical meaning of temptation as a physical assault rather than a subtle inducement. Wildly acrobatic, slithery, spiky demons lift Anthony up off the ground to torment and terrify him in midair. The engraver intensified the horror of the moment by condensing the action into a swirling vortex of figures beating, scratching, poking, tugging, and no doubt shrieking at the stoical saint, who remains impervious to all, perhaps because of his power to focus inwardly on his private meditations.

PRINTED BOOKS

The explosion of learning in Europe in the fifteenth century encouraged experiments in faster and cheaper ways of producing books than by hand-copying them. The earliest printed books were block books, for which each page of text, with or without

Woodcuts are made by drawing on the smooth surface of a block of fine-grained wood, then cutting away all the areas around the lines with a sharp tool called a gouge, leaving the lines in high relief. When the block's surface is inked and a piece of paper pressed down hard on it, the ink on the relief areas transfers to the paper to create a reverse image. The effects can be varied by making thicker and thinner lines, and shading can be achieved by placing the lines closer or farther apart. Sometimes the resulting black-and-white images were then painted by hand.

Engraving on metal requires a technique called **intaglio**, in which the lines are cut into the plate with tools called gravers or **burins**. The engraver then carefully burnishes the plate to ensure a clean, sharp image. Ink is applied over the whole plate and forced down into the lines, then the plate's surface is carefully wiped clean of the excess ink. When paper and plate are held tightly together by a press, the ink in the recessed lines transfers to the paper.

Woodblocks and metal plates could be used repeatedly to make nearly identical images. If the lines of the block or plate wore down, the artists could repair them. Printing large numbers of identical prints of a single version, called an edition, was usually a team effort in a busy workshop. One artist would make the drawing. Sometimes it was drawn directly on the block or plate with ink, in reverse of its printed direction, sometimes on paper to be transferred in reverse onto the plate or block by another person, who then cut the lines. Others would ink and print the images.

In the illustration of books, the plates or blocks would be reused to print later editions and even adapted for use in other books. A set of blocks or plates for illustrations was a valuable commodity and might be sold by one workshop to another. Early in publishing, there were no copyright laws, and many entrepreneurs simply had their workers copy book illustrations onto woodblocks and cut them for their own publications.

illustrations, was cut in relief on a single block of wood. Movable-type printing, in which individual letters could be arranged and locked together, inked, and then printed onto paper, was first achieved in Europe in the workshop of Johann Gutenberg in Mainz, Germany. More than 40 copies of Gutenberg's Bible, printed around 1455, still exist. As early as 1465, two German printers were working in Italy, and by the 1470s there were presses in France, Flanders, Holland, and Spain. With the invention of this fast way to make a number of identical books, the intellectual and spiritual life of Europe—and with it the arts—changed forever.

THE NUREMBERG CHRONICLE. The publication of the *Nuremberg Chronicle* by prosperous Nuremberg printer Anton Koburger was the culmination of his complicated collaboration with scholars, artists, and investors, in an early capitalist enterprise that is a landmark in the history of printed books. The text of this history of the world was compiled by physician and scholar Hartmann Schedel, drawing from the work of colleagues and the extensive holdings of his private library. When Koburger set out to publish Schedel's compilation, he sought financial support from Sebald Schregel and his brother-in-law Sebastian Kammermaister,

18-26 • Martin Schongauer DEMONS TORMENTING ST. ANTHONY
c. 1480–1490. Engraving, 12¼ × 9″ (31.1 × 22.9 cm). Metropolitan Museum of Art, New York. Rogers Fund, 1920 (20.5.2)

§NVREMBERGA§

S. Laurentii.

S. Sebaldus.

18-27 • Michael Wolgemut, Wilhelm Pleydenwurff and workshop **THE CITY OF NUREMBERG**
Nuremberg Chronicle, published by Anton Koberger in 1493. Woodcut within a printed book, hand-colored after printing, each page 18½ × 12¾″ (47 × 32.4 cm). Bibliothèque Mazarine, Paris.

who had a proven record of patronage in book publishing. He also contracted in the 1480s with artists Michael Wolgemut and Wilhelm Pleydenwurff to produce the woodcut illustrations and in 1491 to work on the layout.

The *Nuremberg Chronicle* was published in 1493 in an edition of 2,500. Woodcut illustrations—1,809 in total—were dispersed throughout the book, spreading across the width of whole pages or tucked into the text along either margin. Those interested in purchasing the book could obtain it in Latin or German, on parchment or on paper, bound or unbound, as it came from the press or tinted with color. It seems fitting that the only instance of a double-page picture—filling the entire expanse of an opening with text restricted to headings and labels—is a panoramic view of the city of Nuremberg where this collaborative enterprise was centered **(FIG. 18–27)**. Illustrated here is a view of this expansive cityscape in a copy of the book that was originally owned by a bibliophile who could afford to have the woodcuts painted by hand with color to enhance the appearance of this proud Renaissance city's portrait. As we will see, it was the site of significant artistic developments in the sixteenth century as well.

THINK ABOUT IT

18.1 Explain how oil-painting technique allowed fifteenth-century Flemish painters to achieve unprecedented descriptive effects in their work. Support your answer by discussing one specific work in this chapter.

18.2 Discuss the development of portraiture in northern Europe during the fifteenth century. Choose one example in this chapter and elucidate the portrait's social purpose for the patron.

18.3 How have fifteenth-century northern paintings been characterized as devotional visions of the patrons who are portrayed within them? Use a specific work discussed in this chapter as the focus of your answer.

18.4 Discuss the symbolic meanings that fifteenth-century viewers would have comprehended in the objects contained in the domestic environment of either the Merode Altarpiece (FIG. 18–9) or the Arnolfini double portrait (FIG. 18–1).

18.5 Why did printmaking become a major pictorial medium in northern Europe during the fifteenth century? Choose a work discussed in this chapter and explain how it supports your answer.

PRACTICE MORE: Compose answers to these questions, get flashcards for images and terms, and review chapter material with quizzes **www.myartslab.com**

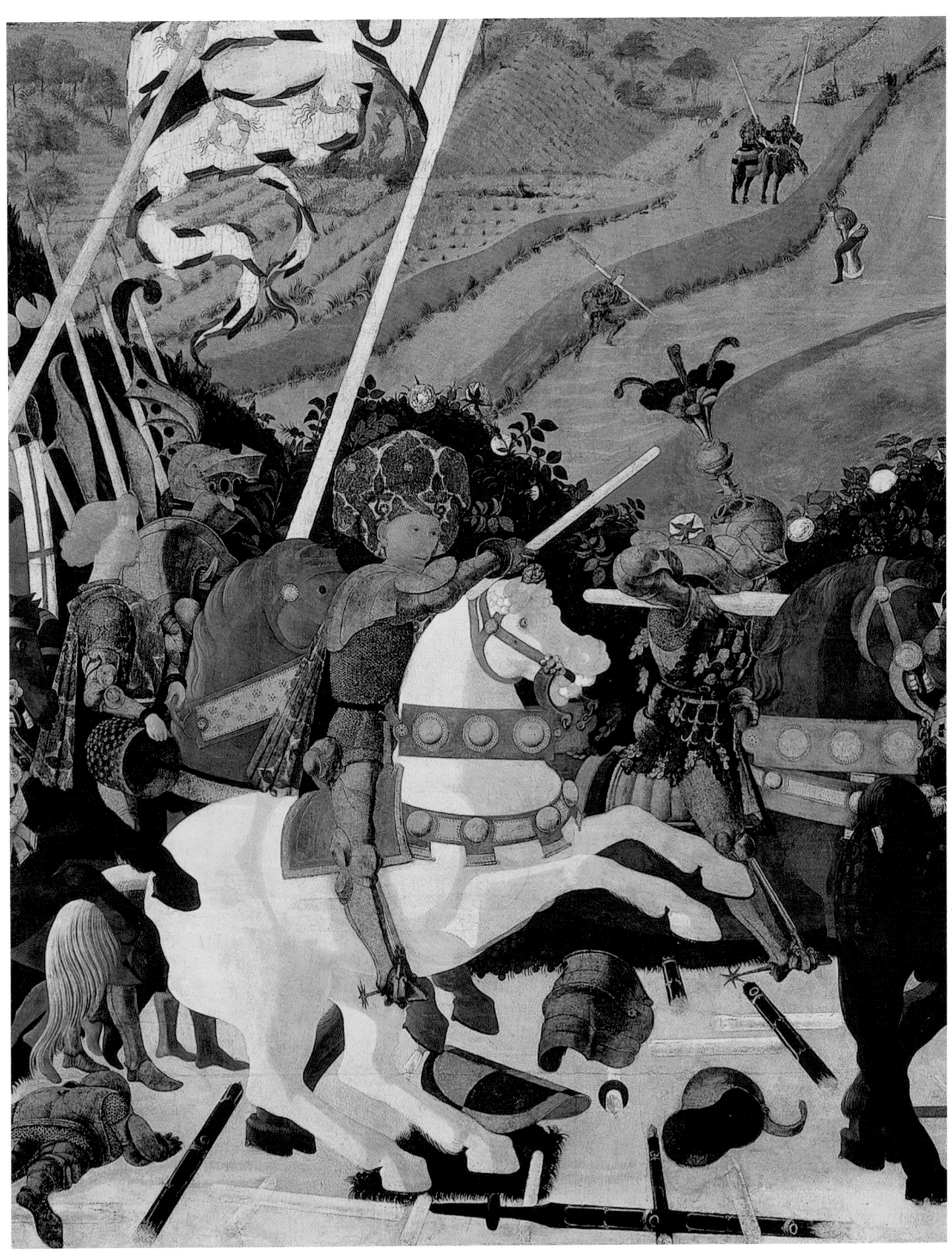

19-1 • Paolo Uccello **NICCOLÒ DA TOLENTINO LEADING THE CHARGE**
Detail from *The Battle of San Romano* (FIG. 19–21), 1438–1440. Tempera on wood panel. National Gallery, London.

RENAISSANCE ART IN FIFTEENTH-CENTURY ITALY

This ferocious but bloodless battle seems to take place only in a dream (FIG. 19–1). Under an elegantly fluttering banner, the Florentine general Niccolò da Tolentino leads his men against the Sienese at the Battle of San Romano, which took place on June 1, 1432. The battle rages across a shallow stage defined by the debris of warfare arranged in a neat pattern on a pink ground and backed by blooming hedges. In the center foreground, Niccolò holds aloft a baton of command, the sign of his authority. His bold gesture—together with his white horse and outlandish, though quite fashionable, crimson and gold damask hat—ensures that he dominates the scene. His knights charge into the fray, and when they fall, like the soldier at the lower left, they join the many broken lances on the ground—all arranged in conformity with the new mathematical depiction of receding space called **linear perspective**, posed to align with the implied lines that would converge at a single point on the horizon.

An eccentric Florentine painter nicknamed Paolo Uccello ("Paul Bird") created the panel painting (SEE FIG. 19–21) from which the detail in FIG. 19–1 is taken. It is one of three related panels now separated, hanging in major museums in Florence, London, and Paris. The complete history of these paintings has only recently come to light.

Lionardo Bartolini Salimbeni (1404–1479), who led the Florentine governing Council of Ten during the war against Lucca and Siena, probably commissioned the paintings. Uccello's remarkable accuracy when depicting armor from the 1430s, heraldic banners, and even fashionable fabrics and crests surely would have appealed to Lionardo's civic pride. The hedges of oranges, roses, and pomegranates—all ancient fertility symbols—suggest that Lionardo might have commissioned the paintings at the time of his wedding in 1438. Lionardo and his wife, Maddalena, had six sons, two of whom inherited the paintings. According to a complaint brought by Damiano, one of the heirs, Lorenzo de' Medici, the powerful *de facto* ruler of Florence, "forcibly removed" the paintings from Damiano's house. They were never returned, and Uccello's masterpieces are recorded in a 1492 inventory as hanging in the Medici palace. Perhaps Lorenzo, who was called "the Magnificent," saw Uccello's heroic pageant as a trophy more worthy of a Medici merchant prince. We will certainly discover that princely patronage was a major factor in the genesis of the Italian Renaissance as it developed in Florence during the early years of the fifteenth century.

LEARN ABOUT IT

19.1 Explore the development and use of linear perspective in fifteenth-century Florentine painting.

19.2 Examine how sculptors were instrumental in the early development of the Italian Renaissance by increasing the lifelike qualities of human figures and drawing inspiration from ancient Roman sculpture.

19.3 Assess the role of wealthy merchants and *condottieri* in driving the development of Renaissance art and architecture.

19.4 Consider how the new focus on artistic competition and individual achievement created a climate for innovative and ambitious works.

19.5 Evaluate the importance of the Classical past to the development of early Renaissance architecture.

HEAR MORE: Listen to an audio file of your chapter **www.myartslab.com**

HUMANISM AND THE ITALIAN RENAISSANCE

By the end of the Middle Ages, the most important Italian cultural centers lay north of Rome in the cities of Florence, Milan, and Venice, and in the smaller duchies of Mantua, Ferrara, and Urbino. Much of the power and influential art patronage was in the hands of wealthy families: the Medici in Florence, the Montefeltro in Urbino, the Gonzaga in Mantua, the Visconti and Sforza in Milan, and the Este in Ferrara (MAP 19–1). Cities grew in wealth and independence as people moved to them from the countryside in unprecedented numbers. As in northern Europe, commerce became increasingly important. Money conferred status, and a shrewd business or political leader could become very powerful. The period saw the rise of mercenary armies led by entrepreneurial (and sometimes brilliant) military commanders called *condottieri*. Unlike the knights of the Middle Ages, they owed allegiance only to those who paid them well; their employer might be a city-state, a lord, or even the pope. Some *condottieri*, like Niccolò da Tolentino (SEE FIG. 19–1), became rich and famous. Others, like Federico da Montefeltro (SEE FIG. 19–27), were lords or dukes themselves, with their own territories in need of protection. Patronage of the arts was an important public activity with political overtones. As one Florentine merchant, Giovanni Rucellai, succinctly noted, he supported the arts "because they serve the glory of God, the honour of the city, and the commemoration of myself" (cited in Baxandall, p. 2).

The term Renaissance (French for "rebirth") was only applied to this period by later historians. However, its origins lie in the thought of Petrarch and other fourteenth-century Italian writers, who emphasized the power and potential of human beings for great individual accomplishment. These Italian humanists also looked back at the thousand years extending from the disintegration of the Western Roman Empire to their own day and determined that the achievements of the Classical world were followed by what they perceived as a period of decline—a "middle" or "dark" age. They proudly saw their own era as a third age characterized by a revival, rebirth, or renaissance, when humanity began to emerge from what they erroneously saw as intellectual and cultural stagnation to appreciate once more the achievement of the ancients and the value of rational, scientific investigation. They looked to the accomplishments of the Classical past for inspiration and instruction, and in Italy this centered on the heritage of ancient Rome. They sought the physical and literary records of the ancient world—assembling libraries, collecting sculpture and fragments of architecture, and beginning archaeological investigations. Their aim was to live a rich, noble, and productive life—usually within the framework of Christianity, but always adhering to a school of philosophy as a moral basis.

Artists, like the humanists, turned to Classical antiquity for inspiration, emulating what they saw in ancient Roman sculpture and architecture, even as they continued to fulfill commissions for predominantly Christian subjects and buildings. But from the secular world a number of home furnishings such as birth trays and marriage chests have survived, richly painted with allegorical and mythological themes (see "The Morelli-Nerli Wedding Chests," page 616). Patrons began to collect art for their personal enjoyment.

Like the Flemish artists, Italian painters and sculptors increasingly focused their attention on rendering the illusion of physical reality. They did so in a more analytical way than the northerners. Rather than seeking to describe the detailed visual appearance of nature through luminosity and textural differentiation, Italian artists aimed at achieving lifelike but idealized weighty figures set within a rationally configured space organized through strict adherence to a mathematical system called linear perspective, which achieved the illusion of a measured and continuously receding space (see "Renaissance Perspective," page 608).

FLORENCE

In seizing Uccello's battle painting (SEE FIG. 19–1), Lorenzo de' Medici was asserting the role his family had come to expect to play in the history of Florence. The fifteenth century witnessed the rise of the Medici from among the most successful of a newly rich middle class (comprising primarily merchants and bankers) to become the city's virtual rulers. Unlike the hereditary aristocracy, the Medici emerged from obscure roots to make their fortune in banking. And from their money came their power.

The competitive Florentine atmosphere that had fostered mercantile success and civic pride also cultivated competition in the arts and encouraged an interest in ancient literary texts. This has led many to consider Florence the cradle of the Italian Renaissance. Under Cosimo the Elder (1389–1464), the Medici became leaders in intellectual and artistic patronage. They sponsored philosophers and other scholars who wanted to study the Classics, especially the works of Plato and his followers, the Neoplatonists. Neoplatonism distinguished between the spiritual (the ideal or Idea) and the physical (Matter) and encouraged artists to represent ideal figures. But it was writers, philosophers, and musicians—and not artists—who dominated the Medici Neoplatonic circle. Architects, sculptors, and painters learned their craft in apprenticeships and were therefore considered manual laborers. Nevertheless, interest in the ancient world rapidly spread from the Medici circle to visual artists, who gradually began to see themselves as more than laborers. Florentine society soon recognized their best works as achievements of a very high order.

Although the Medici were the *de facto* rulers, Florence was considered to be a republic. The Council of Ten (headed for a time by Salimbeni, who commissioned Uccello's *Battle of San Romano*) was a kind of constitutional oligarchy where wealthy men formed the government. At the same time, the various guilds wielded tremendous power; evidence of this is provided by the fact that guild membership was a prerequisite for holding government office. Consequently, artists could look to the Church and the

MAP 19–1 • FIFTEENTH-CENTURY ITALY

Powerful families divided the Italian peninsula into city-states—the Medici in Florence, the Visconti and Sforza in Milan, the Montefeltro in Urbino, the Gonzaga in Mantua, and the Este in Ferrara. After 1420, the popes ruled Rome, while in the south Naples and Sicily were French and then Spanish (Aragonese) territories. Venice maintained its independence as a republic.

state—the city government and the guilds—as well as private individuals for patronage, and these patrons expected the artists to re-affirm and glorify their achievements with works that were not only beautiful but intellectually powerful.

ARCHITECTURE

The defining civic project of the early years of the fifteenth century was the completion of Florence Cathedral with a magnificent dome over the high altar. The construction of the cathedral had begun in the late thirteenth century and had continued intermittently during the fourteenth century. As early as 1367, builders had envisioned a very tall dome to span the huge interior space of the crossing, but they lacked the engineering know-how to construct it. When interest in completing the cathedral revived, around 1407, the technical solution was proposed by a young sculptor-turned-architect, Filippo Brunelleschi.

19-2 • Filippo Brunelleschi DOME OF FLORENCE CATHEDRAL (SANTA MARIA DEL FIORE)
1420–1436; lantern completed 1471.

SEE MORE: View a simulation about doming
www.myartslab.com

19-3 • SCHEMATIC DRAWING OF THE CATHEDRAL OF FLORENCE
The separate, central-plan building in front of the façade is the Baptistery. Adjacent to the façade is a tall tower designed by Giotto in 1334.

FILIPPO BRUNELLESCHI. Filippo Brunelleschi (1377–1446), whose father had been involved in the original plans for the cathedral dome in 1367, achieved what many considered impossible: He solved the problem of the dome. Brunelleschi had originally trained as a goldsmith (see "The Competition Reliefs," page 601). To further his education, he traveled to Rome to study ancient Roman sculpture and architecture, and it was on his return to Florence that he tackled the dome. After the completion of a tall octagonal drum in 1412, Brunelleschi designed the dome itself in 1417, and it was built between 1420 and 1436 (FIGS. 19–2, 19–3). A revolutionary feat of engineering, the dome is a double shell of masonry 138 feet across. The octagonal outer shell is supported on eight large and 16 lighter ribs. Instead of using a costly and even dangerous scaffold and centering, Brunelleschi devised a system in which temporary wooden supports were cantilevered out from the drum. He moved these supports up as building progressed. As the dome was built up course by course, each portion of the structure reinforced the next one. Vertical marble ribs interlocked with horizontal sandstone rings, connected and reinforced with iron rods and oak beams. The inner and outer shells were linked internally by a system of arches. When completed, this self-buttressed unit required no external support to keep it standing.

An oculus (round opening) in the center of the dome was surmounted by a lantern designed in 1436. After Brunelleschi's death, this crowning structure, made up of Roman architectural forms, was completed by another Florentine architect, Michelozzo di Bartolomeo (1396–1472). The final touch—a gilt bronzed ball—was added in 1468–1471.

Other commissions came quickly after the cathedral dome project established Brunelleschi's fame. From about 1418 until his death in 1446, Brunelleschi was involved in a series of influential projects. In 1419, he designed a foundling hospital for the city (see "The Foundling Hospital," pages 598–599). Between 1419 and 1423, he built the elegant Capponi Chapel in the church of Santa Felicità (SEE FIG. 20–25). For the Medicis' parish church of San Lorenzo, he designed and built a centrally planned sacristy (a room where ritual attire and vessels are kept), from 1421 to 1428, and also conceived plans for a new church.

Brunelleschi's **SAN LORENZO** has a basilican plan with a long nave flanked by side aisles that open into shallow lateral chapels **(FIG. 19–4)**. A short transept and square crossing lead to a square sanctuary flanked by additional chapels opening off the transept. Projecting from the left transept, as one faces the altar, are Brunelleschi's sacristy and the older Medici tomb. Brunelleschi based his mathematically regular plan on a square **module**—a basic unit of measure that could be multiplied or divided and

19-4 • Filippo Brunelleschi; continued by Michelozzo di Bartolomeo **INTERIOR AND PLAN OF CHURCH OF SAN LORENZO, FLORENCE**
c. 1421–1428; nave (designed 1434?) 1442–1470.

The Foundling Hospital

In 1419, the guild of silk manufacturers and goldsmiths (Arte della Seta) in Florence undertook a significant public service: It established a large public orphanage and commissioned the brilliant young architect Filippo Brunelleschi to build it next to the church of the Santissima Annunziata (Most Holy Annunciation), which housed a miracle-working painting of the Annunciation, making it a popular pilgrimage site. Completed in 1444, the Foundling Hospital—*Ospedale degli Innocenti*—was unprecedented in terms of scale and design (FIG. A).

Brunelleschi created a building that paid homage to traditional forms while introducing features that we associate with the Italian Renaissance style. Traditionally, a charitable foundation's building had a portico open to the street to provide shelter, and Brunelleschi built an arcade of unprecedented lightness and elegance, using smooth round columns and richly carved capitals—his own interpretation of the Classical Corinthian order. Although we might initially assume that the sources for this arcade lay in the Roman architecture of Classical antiquity, columns were not actually used in antiquity to support free-standing arcades, only to support straight architraves. In fact, it was local Romanesque architecture that was the source for Brunelleschi's graceful design. It is the details of capitals and moldings that bring an air of the antique to this influential building.

The underlying mathematical basis for Brunelleschi's design—traced to the same Pythagorean proportional systems that were believed to create musical harmony—creates a distinct sense of harmony in this graceful arcade. Each bay encloses a cube of space defined by the 10-*braccia* (20-foot) height of the columns and the diameter of the arches. Hemispherical pendentive domes, half again as high as the columns, cover the cubes. The bays at the end of the arcade are slightly larger than the rest, creating a subtle frame for the composition. Brunelleschi defined the perfect squares and semicircles of his building with dark gray stone (*pietra serena*) against plain white walls. His training as a goldsmith and sculptor (see "The

Competition Reliefs," page 601) served him well as he led his artisans to carve crisp, elegantly detailed capitals and moldings for the covered gallery.

A later addition to the building seems eminently suitable: About 1487, Andrea della Robbia, who had inherited the family firm and its secret glazing formulas from his uncle Luca, created for the interstices between the arches glazed terra-cotta medallions (FIG. B) that signified the building's function. Molds were used in the ceramic workshop to facilitate the production of the series of identical babies in swaddling clothes that float at the center of each medallion. The molded terra-cotta forms were covered with a tin glaze to make the sculptures both weatherproof and decorative, and the baby-blue ceramic backgrounds—a signature color for the della Robbia family workshop—makes

them seem to float as celestial apparitions. This is not altogether inappropriate: They are meant to evoke the "innocent" baby boys martyred by King Herod in his attempt to rid his realm of the potential rival the Magi had journeyed to venerate (Matthew 2:16).

Andrea della Robbia's adorable ceramic babies—which remain among the most beloved images of the city of Florence—seem to lay claim to the human side of Renaissance humanism, reminding viewers that the city's wealthiest guild cared for the most helpless members of society. Perhaps the Foundling Hospital spoke to fifteenth-century Florentines of an increased sense of social responsibility. Or perhaps, by so publicly demonstrating social concerns, the wealthy guild that sponsored it solicited the approval and support of the lower classes in the cut-throat power politics of the day.

B. Andrea della Robbia **INFANT IN SWADDLING CLOTHES (ONE OF THE HOLY INNOCENTS MASSACRED BY HEROD)**
Ospedale degli Innocenti (Foundling Hospital), Florence. 1487. Glazed terra cotta.

A. Filippo Brunelleschi **OSPEDALE DEGLI INNOCENTI (FOUNDLING HOSPITAL), FLORENCE**
Designed 1419; built 1421–1444.

19-5 • Attributed to Michelozzo di Bartolomeo FAÇADE, PALAZZO MEDICI-RICCARDI, FLORENCE
Begun 1446.

For the palace site, Cosimo de' Medici the Elder chose the Via de' Gori at the corner of the Via Larga, the widest city street at that time. Despite his practical reasons for constructing a large residence and the fact that he chose simplicity and austerity over grandeur in the exterior design, his detractors commented and gossiped. As one exaggerated: "[Cosimo] has begun a palace which throws even the Colosseum at Rome into the shade."

SEE MORE: Click the Google Earth link for the Palazzo Medici-Riccardi **www.myartslab.com**

THE MEDICI PALACE. Brunelleschi may have been involved in designing the nearby Medici Palace (now known as the Palazzo Medici-Riccardi) in 1446. According to Giorgio Vasari, the sixteenth-century artist and theorist who wrote what some consider the first history of art, Cosimo de' Medici the Elder rejected Brunelleschi's model for the **palazzo** as too grand (any large house was called a *palazzo*—"palace"). Many now attribute the design of the building to Michelozzo. The austere exterior **(FIG. 19–5)** was in keeping with the Florentine political climate and concurrent religious attitudes, imbued with the Franciscan ideals of poverty and charity. Like many other European cities, Florence had sumptuary laws, which forbade ostentatious displays of wealth—but they were often ignored. For example, private homes were supposed to be limited to a dozen rooms, but Cosimo acquired and demolished 20 small houses to provide the site for his new residence. His house was more than a dwelling place; it was his place of business, his company headquarters. The palazzo symbolized the family and established its proper place in the Florentine social hierarchy.

Huge in scale—each story is more than 20 feet high—the building is marked by harmonious proportions and elegant, Classically inspired details. On one side, the ground floor originally opened through large, round arches onto the street, creating in effect a loggia that provided space for the family business. These arches were walled up in the sixteenth century and given windows designed by Michelangelo. The large, **rusticated** stone blocks—that is, blocks with their outer faces left rough—facing the lower story clearly set it off from the upper two levels. In fact, all three stories are distinguished by stone surfaces that vary from sculptural at the ground level to almost smooth on the third floor.

The builders followed the time-honored tradition of placing rooms around a central courtyard. Unlike the plan of the house of Jacques Coeur (SEE FIG. 18–22), however, the **PALAZZO MEDICI-RICCARDI COURTYARD** is square in plan with rooms arranged symmetrically **(FIG. 19–6)**. Round arches on slender columns form a continuous arcade under an enclosed second story. Tall windows

applied to every element of the design, creating a series of clear, harmonious spaces. Architectural details, all in a Classical style, were carved in **pietra serena**, a gray Tuscan sandstone that became synonymous with Brunelleschi's interiors. Below the plain clerestory with its unobtrusive openings, the arches of the nave arcade are carried on tall, slender Corinthian columns made even taller by the insertion of an **impost block** between the column capital and the springing of the round arches—one of Brunelleschi's favorite details. Flattened architectural moldings in *pietra serena* repeat the arcade in the outer walls of the side aisles, and each bay is covered by its own shallow domical vault. Brunelleschi's rational approach, clear sense of order, and innovative incorporation of Classical motifs inspired later Renaissance architects, many of whom learned from his work firsthand by completing his unfinished projects.

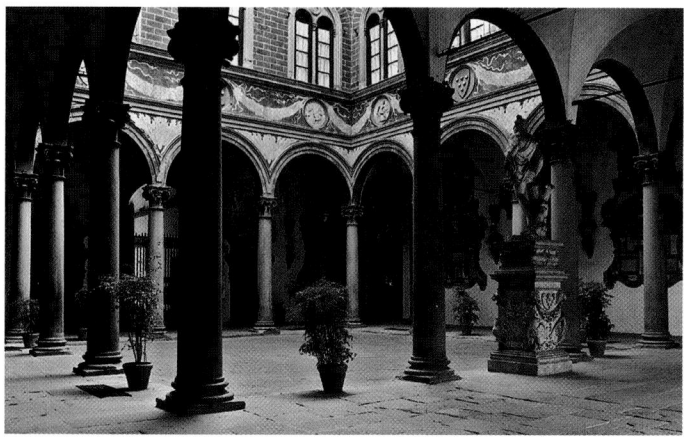

19-6 • COURTYARD WITH SGRAFFITO DECORATION, PALAZZO MEDICI-RICCARDI, FLORENCE
Begun 1446.

The Competition Reliefs

In 1401, the building supervisors of the Baptistery of Florence Cathedral decided to commission a new pair of bronze doors, funded by the powerful wool merchants' guild. Instead of choosing a well-established sculptor with a strong reputation, a competition was announced for the commission. This prestigious project would be awarded to the artist who demonstrated the greatest talent and skill in executing a trial piece: a bronze relief representing Abraham's sacrifice of Isaac (Genesis 22:1–13) composed within the same Gothic quatrefoil framework used in Andrea Pisano's first set of bronze doors for the Baptistery, made in the 1330s (SEE FIG. 17–3). The narrative subject was full of dramatic potential. Abraham, commanded by God to slay his beloved son Isaac as a burnt offering, has traveled to the mountains for the sacrifice. Just as he is about to slaughter Isaac, an angel appears, commanding him to save his son and substitute a ram tangled in the bushes behind him.

Two competition panels have survived, those submitted by the presumed finalists—Filippo Brunelleschi and Lorenzo Ghiberti, both young artists in their early twenties. Brunelleschi's composition (FIG. A) is rugged and explosive, marked by raw dramatic intensity. Abraham lunges in from the left, grabbing his son by the neck, while the angel swoops energetically to stay his hand just as the knife is about to

strike. Isaac's awkward pose embodies his fear and struggle. Ghiberti's version (FIG. B) is quite different, suave and graceful rather than powerful and dramatic. Poses are controlled and choreographed; the harmonious pairing of son and father contrasts sharply with the wrenching struggle in Brunelleschi's rendering. And Ghiberti's Isaac is not a stretched, scrawny youth, but a fully idealized Classical figure exuding calm composure.

The cloth merchants chose Ghiberti to make the doors. Perhaps they preferred the suave elegance of his figural composition. Perhaps they liked the prominence of elegantly disposed swags of cloth, reminders of the source of their patronage and prosperity. But they also may have been swayed by the technical superiority of Ghiberti's relief. Unlike Brunelleschi, Ghiberti cast background and figures mostly as a single piece, making his bronze stronger, lighter, and less expensive to produce. The finished doors—installed in the Baptistery in 1424—were so successful that Ghiberti was commissioned to create another set (SEE FIG. 19–12), his most famous work, hailed by Michelangelo as the "Gates of Paradise." Brunelleschi would refocus his career on buildings rather than bronzes, becoming one of the most important architects of the Italian Renaissance (SEE FIGS. 19–2 TO 19–4).

A. Filippo Brunelleschi **SACRIFICE OF ISAAC**
1401–1402. Bronze with gilding, 21 × 17½″ (53 × 44 cm) inside molding. Museo Nazionale del Bargello, Florence.

B. Lorenzo Ghiberti **SACRIFICE OF ISAAC**
1401–1402. Bronze with gilding, 21 × 17½″ (53 × 44 cm) inside molding. Museo Nazionale del Bargello, Florence.

in the second story match the exterior windows on this same level. Disks bearing the Medici arms surmount each arch in a frieze decorated with swags in **sgraffito** work (decoration produced by scratching through a darker layer of plaster or glaze). Such classicizing elements, inspired by the study of Roman ruins, gave the great house an aura of dignity and stability that enhanced the status of its owners. The Medici Palace inaugurated a new fashion for monumentality and regularity in residential Florentine architecture. Wealthy Florentine families soon emulated it in their own houses.

SCULPTURE

The new architectural language inspired by ancient Classical forms was accompanied by a similar impetus in sculpture. By 1400, Florence had enjoyed internal stability and economic prosperity for over two decades. However, until 1428, the city and its independence were challenged by two great antirepublican powers: the duchy of Milan and the kingdom of Naples. In an atmosphere of wealth and civic patriotism, Florentines turned to commissions that would express their self-esteem and magnify the importance of their city. A new attitude toward realism, space, and the Classical past set the stage for more than a century of creativity. Sculptors led the way.

ORSANMICHELE. In 1339, 14 of Florence's most powerful guilds had been assigned to fill the ground-floor niches that decorated the exterior of **ORSANMICHELE**—a newly completed loggia that served as a grain market—with sculpted images of their patron saints (FIG. 19–7). By 1400, only three had fulfilled this responsibility. In the new climate of republicanism and civic pride, the government pressured the guilds to furnish their niches with statuary. In the wake of this directive, Florence witnessed a dazzling display of sculpture produced by the most impressive local practitioners, including Nanni di Banco, Lorenzo Ghiberti, and Donatello, each of whom took responsibility for filling three niches.

In about 1409, Nanni di Banco (c. 1385–1421), son of a sculptor in the Florence Cathedral workshop, was commissioned by the stonecarvers and woodworkers' guild (to which he himself belonged) to produce **THE FOUR CROWNED MARTYRS** (FIG. 19–8). According to tradition, these third-century Christian martyrs were sculptors, executed for refusing to make an image of a pagan Roman god for Emperor Diocletian. Although the architectural setting is Gothic in style, Nanni's figures—with their solid bodies, heavy, form-revealing togas, noble hair and beards, and portraitlike features—reveal his interest in ancient Roman sculpture, particularly portraiture. They stand as a testimony to this sculptor's role in the Florentine revival of interest in antiquity.

19-7 • EXTERIOR VIEW OF ORSANMICHELE SHOWING SCULPTURE IN NICHES
Florence, begun in 1337.

At street level, Orsanmichele was constructed originally as an open loggia (similar to the Loggia dei Lanzi in FIG. 17–2); in 1380 the spaces under the arches were filled in. In this view of the southeast corner, appearing on the receding wall to the left is first (in the foreground on the corner pier) Donatello's *St. George*, then, Nanni di Banco's *Four Crowned Martyrs*. However, the sculptures seen in this photograph are modern replicas; the originals have been removed to museums for safekeeping.

SEE MORE: Click the Google Earth link for Orsanmichele
www.myartslab.com

The saints convey a new spatial relationship to the building and to the viewer. They stand in a semicircle, with feet and drapery protruding beyond the floor of the niche and into the viewer's space. The saints appear to be four individuals interacting within their own world, but a world that opens to engage with pedestrians (SEE FIG. 19–7). The relief panel below the niche shows the four sculptors at work, embodied with a similar solid vigor. Nanni deeply undercut both figures and objects to cast shadows that enhance the illusion of three-dimensionality.

Donatello (Donato di Niccolò di Betto Bardi, c. 1386/1387–1466) also received three commissions for the niches at Orsanmichele during the first quarter of the century. A member of

19–8 • Nanni di Banco THE FOUR CROWNED MARTYRS
c. 1409–1417. Marble, height of figures 6′ (1.83 m). Orsanmichele, Florence (photographed before removal of figures to a museum).

19–9 • Donatello ST. GEORGE
1417–1420. Marble, height 6′5″ (1.95 m). Bargello, Florence. Formerly Orsanmichele, Florence.

the guild of stonecarvers and woodworkers, he worked in both media, as well as in bronze. During a long and productive career, he developed into one of the most influential and distinguished figures in the history of Italian sculpture, approaching each commission as if it were the opportunity for a new experiment. One of Florence's lesser guilds—the armorers and sword-makers—called on Donatello to carve a majestic and self-assured St. George for their niche **(FIG. 19–9)**. As originally conceived, the saint would have been a standing advertisement for their trade, carrying a metal

19–10 • Donatello DAVID

c. 1446–1460(?). Bronze, height 5'2¼" (1.58 m). Museo Nazionale del Bargello, Florence.

This sculpture is first recorded as being in the courtyard of the Medici Palace in 1469, where it stood on a base inscribed with these lines:

The victor is whoever defends the fatherland.
All-powerful God crushes the angry enemy.
Behold, a boy overcomes the great tyrant.
Conquer, O citizens!

sword in his right hand and probably wearing a metal helmet and sporting a scabbard, all now lost. The figure has remarkable presence, even without his accessories. St. George stands in solid contrapposto, legs braced to support his armor-heavy torso, the embodiment of alertness and determination. He seems to be staring out into our world, perhaps surveying his most famous adversary—a dragon that was holding a princess captive—lurking unsettlingly in the space behind us. With his wrinkled brow and fierce expression, he is tense, alert, focused, if perhaps also somewhat worried. Donatello's complex psychological characterization of this warrior-saint particularly impressed Donatello's contemporaries, not least among them his potential patrons.

For the base of the niche, Donatello carved a remarkable shallow relief showing St. George slaying the dragon and saving the princess, the next scene in his story. The contours of the foreground figures are slightly undercut to emphasize their mass, while the landscape and architecture are in progressively lower relief until they are barely incised rather than carved, an ingenious emulation of the painters' technique of atmospheric perspective. This is also a pioneering example of linear perspective (see "Renaissance Perspective," page 608), in which the orthogonals converge on the figure of the saint himself, using this burgeoning representational system not only to simulate spatial recession but also to provide narrative focus.

DONATELLO. Donatello's long career as a sculptor in a broad variety of media established him as one of the most successful and admired sculptors of the Italian Renaissance. He excelled in part because of his attentive exploration of human emotions and expression, as well as his ability to solve the technical problems posed by various media—from lost-wax casting in bronze and carved marble to polychromed wood. In a bronze **DAVID**, he produced the first life-size male nude since antiquity (**FIG. 19–10**), and in his portrait of the soldier Erasmo da Narni, one of the first life-size bronze equestrian portraits of the Renaissance (SEE FIG. 19–11).

Since nothing is known about the circumstances of its creation, the *David* has been the subject of continuing inquiry and speculation. Although the statue clearly draws on the Classical tradition of heroic nudity, the meaning of this sensuous, adolescent boy in a jaunty laurel-trimmed shepherd's hat and boots has long piqued interest. Some art historians have stressed an overt homoeroticism, especially in the openly effeminate conception of David and the way a wing from the helmet on Goliath's severed head caresses the young hero's inner thigh. Others have seen in David's angular pose and boyish torso a sense that he is poised between childish interests and adult responsibility, an image of improbable heroism. David was a potent political image in Florence, a symbol of the citizens' resolve to oppose tyrants regardless of their superior power, since virtue brings divine support and preternatural strength. Indeed, an inscription engraved into the base where the sculpture once stood suggests that it could have celebrated the

Florentine triumph over the Milanese in 1425, a victory that brought resolution to a quarter-century struggle with despots and helped give Florence a vision of itself as a strong, virtuous republic.

In 1443, Donatello was probably called to Padua to execute an **EQUESTRIAN STATUE (FIG. 19–11)** to commemorate the Paduan general of the Venetian army, Erasmo da Narni, nicknamed "Gattamelata" (meaning "Honeyed Cat"—a reference to his mother, Melania Gattelli). If any image could be said to characterize the self-made men of the Italian Renaissance, surely it would be those of the *condottieri*—the brilliant generals such as Gattamelata and Niccolò da Tolentino (SEE FIG. 19–1) who organized the armies and fought for any city-state willing to pay for their services. As guardians for hire, they were tough, opportunistic mercenaries. But they also subscribed to an ideal of military and civic virtue. Horsemanship was more than a necessary skill for the *condottieri*.

The horse, a beast of enormous brute strength, symbolized animal passions, and skilled horsemanship demonstrated physical and intellectual control—self-control, as well as control of the animal—the triumph of the intellect, of "mind over matter."

Donatello's sources for this statue were surviving Roman bronze equestrian portraits, notably the famous image of Marcus Aurelius (SEE FIG. 6–52), which the sculptor certainly knew from his stay in Rome. Viewed from a distance, Donatello's man–animal juggernaut, installed on a high marble base in front of the church of Sant'Antonio in Padua, seems capable of thrusting forward at the first threat. Seen up close, however, the man's sunken cheeks, sagging jaw, ropy neck, and stern but sad expression suggest a warrior grown old and tired from the constant need for military vigilance and rapid response.

THE GATES OF PARADISE. The bronze doors that Lorenzo Ghiberti (1381?–1455) produced for the Florentine Baptistery after winning his famous competition with Brunelleschi in 1401 (see "The Competition Reliefs," page 601) were such a success that in 1425 he was awarded the commission for yet another set of bronze doors for the east side of the Baptistery, and his first set was moved to the north side. The new door panels, funded by the wool manufacturers' guild, were a significant conceptual leap from the older schemes of 28 small scenes employed for Ghiberti's earlier doors and those of Andrea Pisano in the fourteenth century (SEE FIG. 17–3). Ghiberti departed entirely from the old arrangement, producing a set of ten scenes from the Hebrew Bible—from the Creation to the reign of Solomon—composed in rectangular fields, like a set of framed paintings. Michelangelo reportedly said that the results, installed in 1452, were worthy of the **"GATES OF PARADISE"**—the name by which they are now commonly known **(FIG. 19–12)**.

Ghiberti organized the space in the ten square reliefs either by a system of linear perspective with obvious orthogonal lines (see "Renaissance Perspective," page 608)

19-11 • Donatello EQUESTRIAN STATUE OF ERASMO DA NARNI (GATTAMELATA)
Piazza del Santo, Padua. 1443–1453. Bronze, height approx. 12′2″ (3.71 m).

19-12 • Lorenzo Ghiberti "GATES OF PARADISE" (EAST DOORS), BAPTISTERY OF SAN GIOVANNI, FLORENCE

1425–1452. Gilt bronze, height 15′ (4.57 m). Museo dell'Opera del Duomo, Florence.

The door panels, commissioned by the wool manufacturers' guild, depict ten scenes from the Hebrew Bible beginning with the Creation in the upper left panel. The murder of Abel by his brother, Cain, follows in the upper right panel, succeeded in the same left–right paired order by the Flood and the drunkenness of Noah, Abraham sacrificing Isaac, the story of Jacob and Esau, Joseph sold into slavery by his brothers, Moses receiving the Tablets of the Law, Joshua and the fall of Jericho, David and Goliath, and finally Solomon and the queen of Sheba. Ghiberti placed his own portrait as a signature in the frame at the lower right corner of the Jacob and Esau panel. He wrote in his *Commentaries* (c. 1450–1455): "I strove to imitate nature as clearly as I could, and with all the perspective I could produce, to have excellent compositions with many figures."

19-13 • Lorenzo Ghiberti JACOB AND ESAU, PANEL OF THE "GATES OF PARADISE" (EAST DOORS)
Formerly on the Baptistery of San Giovanni, Florence. c. 1435. Gilded bronze, 31¼" (79 cm) square. Museo dell'Opera del Duomo, Florence.

POLLAIUOLO. Sculptors in the fifteenth century not only worked on a monumental scale in the public sphere; they also created small works, each designed to inspire the mind and delight the eye of its private owner. The ambitious and multi-talented Antonio del Pollaiuolo—goldsmith, embroiderer, printmaker, sculptor, and painter—who came to work for the Medici family in Florence about 1460, mostly created small bronze sculptures. His **HERCULES AND ANTAEUS** of about 1475 is one of the largest **(FIG. 19–14)**. This study of complex interlocking figures has an explosive energy that can best be appreciated by viewing it from every angle.

Statuettes of religious subjects were still popular, but humanist patrons began to collect bronzes of Classical subjects. Many sculptors, especially those trained as goldsmiths, started to cast small copies after well-known ancient works. Some artists also executed

or more intuitively by a series of arches or rocks or trees charting the path into the distance. Foreground figures are grouped in the lower third of each panel, while the other figures decrease gradually in size to map their positioning in deep space. The use of a system of perspective, with clearly differentiated background and foreground, also helped Ghiberti combine a series of related events, separated by narrative time, within a single pictorial frame.

The story of Jacob and Esau (Genesis 25 and 27) fills the center panel of the left door. Ghiberti creates a coherent and measurable space peopled by graceful, idealized figures **(FIG. 19–13)**. He pays careful attention to one-point perspective in laying out the architectural setting. Squares in the pavement establish the receding lines of the orthogonals that converge to a central vanishing point under the loggia, while towering arches overlap and gradually diminish in size from foreground to background to define the receding space above the figures. The story unfolds in a series of individual episodes and begins in the background. On the rooftop (upper right) Rebecca stands, listening as God warns of her unborn sons' future conflict; under the left-hand arch she gives birth to the twins. The adult Esau sells his rights as oldest son to his brother Jacob, and when he goes hunting (center right), Rebecca and Jacob plot against him. Finally, in the right foreground, Jacob receives Isaac's blessing, while in the center, Esau faces his father. Ghiberti's portrayal of the scene relates more closely to developments in painting than to contemporary sculpture. Ghiberti not only signed his work, but also included his self-portrait in the medallion beside the lower right-hand corner of this panel.

19-14 • Antonio del Pollaiuolo HERCULES AND ANTAEUS
c. 1475. Bronze, height with base 18" (45.7 cm). Museo Nazionale del Bargello, Florence.

Fifteenth-century Italian artists developed a system known as linear, or mathematical perspective that enabled them to represent three dimensions on a two-dimensional surface, simulating the recession of space in the visible world pictorially in a way they found convincing. The sculptor and architect Filippo Brunelleschi first demonstrated the system about 1420, and the theorist and architect Leon Battista Alberti codified it in 1436 in his treatise *Della Pittura* (*On Painting*).

For Alberti, in one-point linear perspective a picture's surface was conceived as a flat plane that intersected the viewer's field of vision at right angles. This highly artificial concept presumed a viewer standing dead center at a prescribed distance from a work of art. From this single fixed vantage point, everything would appear to recede into the distance at the same rate, following imaginary lines called **orthogonals** that met at a single **vanishing point** on the horizon. By using orthogonals in concert with controlled diminution of scale as forms move back toward the vanishing point, artists could replicate the optical illusion that things appear to grow smaller, rise higher, and come closer together as they get farther away from us. Linear perspective makes pictorial spaces seem almost like extensions of the viewer's real space, creating a compelling, even exaggerated sense of depth.

Linear perspective is not the only way to simulate spatial recession in two-dimensional painting. In atmospheric perspective, variations in color and clarity convey the feeling of distance when objects and landscape are portrayed less clearly, and colors become grayer, in the background, imitating the natural effects of a loss of clarity and color when viewing things in the distance through an atmospheric haze.

Perugino **THE DELIVERY OF THE KEYS TO ST. PETER, WITH A SCHEMATIC DRAWING SHOWING THE ORTHOGONALS AND VANISHING POINT**
Fresco on the right wall of the Sistine Chapel, Vatican, Rome. 1481. 11′5½″ × 18′8½″ (3.48 × 5.70 m).

The Delivery of the Keys to St. Peter is a remarkable study in linear perspective. The clear demarcation of the paving stones of the piazza provides a network of orthogonal and horizontal lines for the measured placement of the figures. People and buildings become increasingly, and logically, smaller as the space recedes. Horizontally, the composition is divided between the foreground frieze of figures and the widely spaced background buildings, vertically by the open space at the center between Christ and Peter and by the symmetrical architectural forms on either side of this central axis. Perugino's painting is, among other things, a representation of Alberti's ideal city, described in *De re aedificatoria* as having a "temple" (that is, a church) at the very center of a great open space raised on a dais and separate from any other buildings that might obstruct its view.

original designs *all'antica* ("in the antique style") to appeal to a cultivated humanist taste. Hercules was always a popular figure; as a patron of Florence, he was on the city seal. Among the many courageous acts by which Hercules gained immortality was the slaying of the evil Antaeus in a wrestling match by lifting him off the earth, the source of the giant's great physical power.

An engraving by Pollaiuolo, **THE BATTLE OF THE NUDES** (**FIG. 19–15**), reflects two interests of Renaissance scholars—the study of Classical sculpture and anatomical research. Pollaiuolo may have intended this, his only known—but highly influential—print, as a study in composition involving the human figure in action. The naked men, fighting each other ferociously against a tapestrylike

19–15 • Antonio del Pollaiuolo THE BATTLE OF THE NUDES
c. 1465–1470. Engraving, 15⅛ × 23¼″ (38.3 × 59 cm). Cincinnati Art Museum, Ohio. Bequest of Herbert Greer French. 1943.118

background of foliage, seem to have been drawn from a single model in a variety of poses, many of which were taken from Classical sources. Like the artist's *Hercules and Antaeus*, much of the engraving's fascination lies in how it depicts muscles of the male body reacting under tension.

PAINTING

Italian patrons commissioned murals and large altarpieces for their local churches and smaller panel paintings for their houses and private chapels. Artists experienced in fresco were in great demand and traveled widely to execute wall and ceiling decorations. At first the Italians showed little interest in oil painting, for the most part using tempera even for their largest works. But, in the last decades of the century, oil painting became popular in Venice.

MASACCIO.   Even though his brief career lasted less than a decade, Tommaso di Ser Giovanni di Mone Cassai (1401–1428/1429?), nicknamed "Masaccio" (meaning "Big Tom"), established a new direction in Florentine painting, much as Giotto had a

century earlier. He did this by integrating monumental and consistently scaled figures into rational architectural and natural settings using linear perspective. The chronology of Massaccio's works is uncertain, but his fresco of the **TRINITY** in the church of Santa Maria Novella in Florence must have been painted around 1426, the date on the Lenzi family tombstone that once stood in front of it (**FIGS. 19–16, 19–17**).

Masaccio's fresco was meant to give the illusion of a stone funerary monument and altar table set below a deep **aedicula** (framed niche) in the wall. The effect of looking up into a barrel-vaulted niche was made plausible through precisely rendered linear perspective. The eye level of an adult viewer standing within the church determined the horizon line on which the vanishing point was centered, just below the kneeling figures above the altar. And the painting demonstrates not only Masaccio's intimate knowledge of Brunelleschi's perspective experiments (see "Renaissance Perspective," opposite), but also his architectural style (SEE FIG. 19–4). The painted architecture is an unusual combination of Classical orders. On the wall surface, Corinthian pilasters support a plain architrave below a cornice, while inside the niche Renaissance variations on Ionic columns support arches on all four sides. The "source" of the consistent illumination of the architecture lies in front of the picture, casting reflections on the coffers, or sunken panels, of the ceiling.

The figures are organized in a measured progression through space. At the near end of the recessed, barrel-vaulted space is the Trinity—Jesus on the cross, the dove of the Holy Spirit poised in downward flight above his tilted halo, and God the Father, who stands behind to support the cross from his elevated perch on a high platform, apparently supported on the rear columns. As in many scenes of the Crucifixion, Jesus is flanked by the Virgin Mary and John the Evangelist, who contemplate the scene on either side of the cross. Mary gazes calmly out at us, her raised hand drawing our attention to the Trinity. Members of the Lenzi family kneel in front of the pilasters—thus closer to us than the Crucifixion; the red robes of the male donor signify that he was a member of the governing council of Florence. Below these donors, in an open sarcophagus, is a skeleton, a grim reminder of the Christian belief that since death awaits us all, our only hope is redemption and the promise of life in the hereafter, rooted in Christ's sacrifice on the cross. The inscription above the skeleton reads: "I was once that which you are, and what I am you also will be."

19-16 • Masaccio TRINITY WITH THE VIRGIN, ST. JOHN THE EVANGELIST, AND DONORS
Church of Santa Maria Novella, Florence. c. 1425–1427/1428.
Fresco, 21′ × 10′5″ (6.4 × 3.2 m).

19-17 • SECTION DIAGRAM OF THE ILLUSIONISTIC SPATIAL WORLD PORTRAYED IN MASACCIO'S TRINITY
After Gene Brucker, *Florence: The Golden Age*, Berkeley, 1998.

horizon

picture plane

viewing point

THE BRANCACCI CHAPEL. Masaccio's brief career culminated in the frescos he painted on the walls of the Brancacci Chapel in the church of Santa Maria del Carmine in Florence. Reproduced here are two of the best-known scenes: **THE EXPULSION OF ADAM AND EVE FROM PARADISE** (FIG. 19–18) and **THE TRIBUTE MONEY** (FIG. 19–19). In *The Expulsion*, he presented Adam and Eve as monumental nude figures, combining his studies of the human figure with an intimate knowledge of ancient Roman sculpture. In contrast to Flemish painters, who sought to record every visible detail of a figure's surface (compare Adam and Eve from the Ghent Altarpiece, page 577, FIG. B), Masaccio focused on the mass of bodies formed by the underlying bone and muscle structure, and a single light source emphasizes their tangibility with modeled forms and cast shadows. Departing from earlier interpretations of the event that emphasized wrongdoing and the fall from grace, Masaccio concerns himself with the psychological impact of shame on these first humans, who have been cast out of paradise mourning and protesting, thrown naked into the world.

In *The Tribute Money* (SEE FIG. 19–19), Masaccio portrays an incident from the life of Jesus that highlights St. Peter (Matthew 17: 24–27), to whom this chapel was dedicated. In the central scene a tax collector (dressed in a short red tunic and seen from behind) asks Peter (in the left foreground with the short gray beard) if Jesus pays the Jewish temple tax (the "tribute money" of the title). Set against the stable backdrop of a semicircular block of apostolic observers, a masterful series of dynamic diagonals in the postures and gestures of the three main figures interlocks them in a compositional system that imbues their interaction with a sense of tension calling out for resolution. Jesus instructs Peter to "go to the sea, drop in a hook, and take the first fish that comes up," which Peter does at the far left. In the fish's mouth is a coin worth twice the tax demanded, which Peter gives to the tax collector at the far right. The tribute story was especially significant for Florentines because in 1427, to raise money for defense against military aggression, the city enacted a graduated tax, based on the value of people's personal property.

The Tribute Money is particularly remarkable for its early use of both linear and atmospheric perspective to integrate figures, architecture, and landscape into a consistent whole. The group of disciples around Jesus and his disciples forms a clear central focus, from which the landscape seems to recede naturally into the far distance. To foster this illusion, Masaccio used linear perspective in the depiction of the house, and then reinforced it by diminishing the sizes of the barren trees and reducing the size of the crouching Peter at far left. At the central vanishing point established by the orthogonals of the house is the head of Jesus. A second vanishing point determines the position of the steps and stone rail at the right.

The cleaning of the painting in the 1980s revealed that it was painted in 32 *giornate* (a *giornata* is a section of fresh plaster that could be prepared and painted in a single day; see "Buon Fresco," page 537). The cleaning also uncovered Masaccio's subtle use of

19-18 • Masaccio THE EXPULSION OF ADAM AND EVE FROM PARADISE

Brancacci Chapel, church of Santa Maria del Carmine, Florence. c. 1427. Fresco, 7′ × 2′11″ (214 × 90 cm).

Cleaning and restoration of the Brancacci Chapel paintings revealed the remarkable speed and skill with which Masaccio worked. He painted Adam and Eve in four *giornate* (each *giornata* of fresh plaster representing a day's work). Working from the top down and left to right, he painted the angel on the first day; on the second day, the portal; Adam on the third day; and Eve on the fourth.

19–19 • Masaccio THE TRIBUTE MONEY
Brancacci Chapel, church of Santa Maria del Carmine, Florence. c. 1427. Fresco, 8′1″ × 19′7″ (2.46 × 6 m).

color to create atmospheric perspective in the distant landscape, where mountains fade from grayish-green to grayish-white and the houses and trees on their slopes are loosely sketched to simulate the lack of clear definition when viewing things in the distance through a haze. Green leaves were painted on the branches *al secco* (meaning "on the dry plastered wall").

As in *The Expulsion*, Masaccio modeled the foreground figures here with bold highlights and long shadows on the ground toward the left, giving a strong sense of volumetric solidity and implying a light source at the far right, as if the scene were lit by the actual window in the rear wall of the Brancacci Chapel. Not only does the lighting give the forms sculptural definition, but the colors vary in tone according to the strength of the illumination. Masaccio used a wide range of hues—pale pink, mauve, gold, blue-green, seafoam-green, apple-green, peach—and a sophisticated shading technique using contrasting colors, as in Andrew's green robe which is shaded with red instead of darker green. The figures of Jesus and the apostles originally had gold-leaf haloes, several of which have flaked off. Rather than silhouette the heads against consistently flat gold circles in the medieval manner, however, Masaccio conceived of haloes as gold disks hovering in space above each head that moved with the heads as they moved, and he foreshortened them depending on the angle from which each head is seen.

Some stylistic innovations take time to be fully accepted, and Masaccio's innovative depictions of volumetric solidity, consistent lighting, and spatial integration were best appreciated by a later generation of painters. Many important sixteenth-century Italian artists, including Michelangelo, studied and sketched Masaccio's Brancacci Chapel frescos, as they did Giotto's work in the Scrovegni Chapel. In the meantime, painting in Florence after Masaccio's death developed along somewhat different lines.

PAINTING IN FLORENCE AFTER MASACCIO

The tradition of covering walls with paintings in fresco continued uninterrupted through the fifteenth century. Between 1438 and 1445, the decoration of the Dominican monastery of San Marco in Florence, where Fra Angelico lived, was one of the most extensive projects.

FRA ANGELICO. Guido di Piero da Mugello (c. 1395/1400–1455), earned his nickname "Fra Angelico" ("Angelic Brother") through his piety as well as his painting: in 1984, he was beatified, the first step toward sainthood. Fra Angelico is first documented painting in Florence in 1417–1418, and he remained an active painter after taking vows as a Dominican monk in nearby Fiesole between 1418 and 1421.

Between 1438 and 1445, in the monastery of San Marco, Fra Angelico and his assistants—probably working under the patronage of Cosimo de' Medici—created paintings to inspire meditation in each monk's cell (44 in all; SEE FIGS INTRO-7, INTRO-8), in the chapter house (meeting room), and even in the corridors (hallways). At the top of the stairs in the north corridor, where the monks would pass frequently on their way to their individual cells, Fra Angelico painted a serene picture of the **ANNUNCIATION (FIG. 19–20)**. To describe the quiet, measured space where the demure archangel greets the unassuming, youthful Mary, Fra Angelico used linear perspective with unusual skill, extending the monks' stairway and corridor outward into an imagined portico and garden beside the Virgin's home. The slender, graceful figures, wearing quietly flowing draperies, assume modest poses. Natural light falling from the left models their forms gently, casting an almost supernatural radiance over their faces and hands. The scene is a sacred vision rendered in a contemporary setting, welcoming the monks to the most intimate areas of the monastery and preparing them for their private meditations.

UCCELLO. At mid century, when Fra Angelico was still painting his radiant visions of Mary and Jesus in the monastery of San Marco, a new generation of artists began to emerge. Thoroughly conversant with the theories of Brunelleschi and Alberti, they had mastered the techniques (and tricks) of depicting figures in a constructed architectural space. Some artists became specialists, among them Paolo Uccello, who devoted his life to the study of linear perspective (FIG. 19–21; SEE ALSO FIG. 19–1). Vasari devoted a chapter in his biographies of Italian artists to Uccello, whom he described as a man so obsessed with the science of perspective that he neglected his painting, his family, and even his pet birds (his *uccelli*). According to Vasari, Uccello's wife complained that he sat up drawing all night and when she called to him to come to bed he would say, "Oh, what a sweet thing this perspective is!" (Vasari, trans. Bondanella and Bondanella, p. 83).

19-21 • Paolo Uccello **THE BATTLE OF SAN ROMANO**
1438–1440. Tempera on wood panel, approx. 6' × 10'7" (1.83 × 3.23 m). National Gallery, London.

19-22 • Andrea del Castagno THE LAST SUPPER
Refectory, convent of Sant'Apollonia, Florence. 1447. Fresco, width approx. 16 × 32′ (4.6 × 9.8 m).

CASTAGNO. Notable Florentine painter Andrea del Castagno (c. 1417/19–1457) painted a fresco of **THE LAST SUPPER** for a convent of Benedictine nuns in 1447 **(FIG. 19–22)**. The Last Supper was often painted in monastic refectories (dining halls) to remind the monks or nuns of Christ's Last Supper with his first followers and encourage them to see their daily gatherings for meals almost as a sacramental act rooted in this biblical tradition. Here Castagno has not portrayed the scene in the biblical setting of an "upper room." Rather, the humble house of the original account has become a great palace with sumptuous marble revetment. The most brilliantly colored and wildly patterned marble panel frames the heads of Christ and Judas to focus viewers on the most important part of the picture. Judas sits on the viewer's side of the table, separated from the other apostles, and St. John sleeps, head collapsed onto the tabletop. The strong perspective lines of floor tiles, ceiling rafters, and paneled walls draw viewers into the scene, especially the nuns

19-23 • Fra Filippo Lippi PORTRAIT OF A WOMAN AND MAN (ANGIOLA DI BERNARDO SAPITI AND LORENZO DI RANIERI SCOLARI?)
c. 1435–1445. Tempera on wood panel, 25¼ × 16½″ (64.1 × 41.9 cm). Metropolitan Museum of Art, New York

Some art historians have seen in the sumptuousness of this woman's costume an indication that she is a newlywed, especially since the pearls sewn with gold threads into the embroidery on her sleeve spell out the word *lealtà*, meaning "loyalty." But since technical evidence shows that the face of the man was added after the portrait of the woman, and since he is unable to meet her gaze, others speculate that this was transformed into a memorial portrait after her death.

who would have seen the painting as an extension of their own dining hall. At first, the lines of the orthogonals seem perfectly logical, but close examination reveals that only the lines of the ceiling converge to a single point, below the hands of St. John. Two windows light the painting's room from the direction of the actual refectory windows, further unifying the two spaces. Castagno worked quickly, completing this huge mural in at most 32 days.

FRA FILIPPO LIPPI. Not all Florentine paintings of the mid fifteenth century were sacred scenes on the walls of religious buildings. It is during this period that portraiture comes into its own as a major artistic form in Italy, and among the most extraordinary—if enigmatic—examples is this **PORTRAIT OF A WOMAN AND MAN (FIG. 19–23)**, an early work of Fra Filippo Lippi (c. 1406–1469). This painting is also the earliest surviving double portrait of the Italian Renaissance. Lippi grew up as an orphan in the Carmelite church where Masaccio had painted frescos in the Brancacci Chapel, and art historians have stressed the impact this work had on Lippi's development as an artist. But although he may have absorbed Massacio's predilection for softly rounded forms situated in carefully mapped spaces, in Lippi's hands these artistic tools became the basis for pictures that often ask more questions than they answer, by stressing outline at the same time as form, and by creating complex and often confusing spatial systems.

The emphasis in this double portrait is squarely on the woman. She is spotlighted in the foreground, sharply profiled against a window that serves as an unsettling internal frame, not big enough to contain her. This window opens onto a vista, clearly a fragment of a larger world, but one that highlights an orthogonal to emphasize a spatial recession only partially revealed. The woman blocks most of this vista with her shining visage and sumptuous costume—notably its embroidered velvet, fur lining, and luminous pearls. There is no engagement with the viewer and little sense of likeness. And it is not at all clear where or to what she directs her attention, especially since the gaze of the man in the background does not meet hers. He is even more of a mystery. We see only a masklike sliver of his profile, although the substantiality of his face is reinforced by the strong shadow it casts against the window casement through which he looks. Unlike the woman, who clasps her inert hands in front of her as if to highlight her rings, this man fidgets with his fingers, perhaps to draw our attention to the heraldic device below him that may identify him as a member of the Scolari family. This could be a double portrait of Lorenzo di Ranieri Scolari and Angiola di Bernardo Sapiti, who married in 1436. But what does the painting say about them? Does it commemorate their marriage, celebrate the birth of their child, or memorialize one of their deaths? All have been proposed by art historians as an explanation for this innovative double portrait, but it remains a puzzle to be pondered. Could that pondering be the point of the picture?

ITALIAN ART IN THE SECOND HALF OF THE FIFTEENTH CENTURY

In the second half of the fifteenth century, the ideas and ideals of artists like Brunelleschi, Donatello, and Masaccio began to spread from Florence to the rest of Italy, as artists who had trained or worked in Florence traveled to other cities to work, carrying the style with them. Northern Italy embraced the new Classical ideas swiftly, especially in the ducal courts at Urbino and Mantua. Venice and Rome also emerged as innovative art centers in the last quarter of the century.

URBINO

Under Federico da Montefeltro, Urbino developed into a thriving artistic center. A new palace was under construction, and prominent architects and artists were brought into the court to make the new princely residence a showcase of ducal splendor.

THE PALACE AT URBINO. Construction of the palace had been under way for about 20 years in 1468 when Federico hired Luciano Laurana (c. 1420/1425– 1479) to direct the work. Among Laurana's major contributions to the palace were closing the courtyard with a fourth wing and redesigning the courtyard façades **(FIG. 19–24)**. The result is a superbly rational solution to the problems

19-24 • Luciano Laurana COURTYARD, DUCAL PALACE, URBINO
Courtyard c. 1467–1472; palace begun c. 1450.

The Morelli–Nerli Wedding Chests

The palazzos of wealthy Florentine families housed not only panels painted with portraits or Madonnas; they were also appointed with massive pieces of elaborate furniture. Constructed of richly carved wood that was gilded and often covered with paintings, these household objects were not a minor sideline, but a central feature of the fifteenth-century Florentine art world. Some of the most impressive surviving examples of Renaissance furniture are a series of great chests—called **cassoni**—that were used to store clothing and other precious personal objects in a couple's bedroom. They were frequently commissioned in pairs on the occasion of a wedding.

Marriages between members of wealthy Florentine families were not the result of romantic connections between two young people. They were political alliances and economic transactions that involved the transfer of capital and the exchange of gifts as a display of wealth. In preparation for such high-class marriages, husbands refurbished their living quarters in the family palazzo in preparation for bringing a bride into the household. We have a detailed accounting of the extent of work, as well as the required expenditure, when 30-year-old Lorenzo di Matteo Morelli prepared his apartments for the arrival of his young bride, Vaggia di Tanai Nerli, after their marriage in 1472. His commissioning of a pair of *cassoni*—one for him and one for Vaggia—represented almost two-thirds of the entire cost of redecoration. Fortunately, the two chests still survive. They are among the most important and best-preserved Renaissance *cassoni* that have come down to us, especially since they still maintain the original backboard—called a *spalliera*—that was produced concurrent with and hung on the wall directly behind the chests when they were placed in Lorenzo's bedroom. The lion's feet on which the chests now stand are modern additions, and the *spalliera* was originally a long, continuous painting hung over both *cassoni*, not a separate panel mounted behind the lid, but otherwise these chests give a strong sense of their original appearance.

Like most Renaissance *cassoni*, Lorenzo's chest is painted with pictures drawn from stories that extol moral virtues, and intended to reflect some of their values and glories on Lorenzo himself. The long painted scene on the front tells the story of ancient Roman hero Marcus Furius Camillus' defeat of the Gauls as he chases them out of Rome. On the *spalliera*, *trompe-l'oeil* curtains part to reveal the scene of another

Roman hero defending a bridge against insurmountable odds. Presumably Lorenzo wanted to be seen as a heroic descendant of such illustrious Romans—strong, brave, and triumphant. The scenes portrayed on Vaggia's chest (like Lorenzo's, identified by her coat of arms) challenge her to care for the children she is expected to produce and practice the virtues of temperance, prudence, and patience that were valued in Florentine patrician brides.

The Morelli–Nerli *cassoni* passed from Lorenzo to his son, and they remained in the Morelli family at least until 1680, maybe into the nineteenth century, when they first appeared together in the art market. Elaborate Renaissance furniture became coveted items in the homes of wealthy art collectors in late nineteenth-century Europe and America, where the new owners doubtless saw themselves as worthy successors to the wealthy and powerful merchants who had commissioned them at the height of the Italian Renaissance.

Jacabo del Sellaio, Biagio d'Antonio (painters), and Zanobi di Domenico (woodworker) **CASSONE MADE FOR THE MARRIAGE OF LORENZO DI MATTEO MORELLI AND VAGGIA DI TANAI NERLI**
1472. Tempera and gold on wood, chest 83½ × 75 × 30″ (212 × 193 × 76.2 cm). Courtauld Gallery, London.

19-25 • Giuliano da
Maiano (?) **STUDIOLO
OF FEDERICO DA
MONTEFELTRO**
Ducal Palace, Urbino. 1476.
Intarsia, height 7'3" (2.21 m).

created in courtyard design by the awkward juncture of the arcades at the four corners. The ground-level portico on each side has arches supported by columns, but piers embellished with pilasters bridge the corner angles. This arrangement avoided the awkward visual effect of two arches springing from a single column and gave the corner a greater sense of stability. A variation of the composite capital (a Corinthian capital with added Ionic volutes) was used, perhaps for the first time, on the ground level. Corinthian pilasters flank the windows in the story above, forming divisions that repeat the bays of the portico. (The two low upper stories were added later.) The plain architrave was engraved with inscriptions lauding Federico's many virtues, added when the count became duke of Urbino in 1476.

The interior of the Urbino palace likewise reflected its patron's embrace of new Renaissance ideas and interest in Classical antiquity, seen in carved marble fireplaces and window and door surrounds. In creating luxurious home furnishings and interior decorations for sophisticated clients such as Federico, Italian artists found freedom to experiment with new subjects, treatments, and techniques. Among these was the creation of remarkable **trompe-l'oeil** ("fool-the-eye") effects using scrupulously applied linear perspective and foreshortening in **intarsia** (wood inlay) decoration. An extraordinary example is on the walls of Federico da Montefeltro's **studiolo**, or study, a room for private conversation and the owner's collection of fine books and art objects **(FIG. 19–25)**. The work was probably done by the architect and woodworker Giuliano da Maiano (1432–1490) and carries the date 1476.

The elaborate scenes in the small room are created entirely of wood inlaid on flat surfaces. Each detail is rendered with convincing illusionism: pilasters, carved cupboards with latticed doors, niches with statues, paintings, and built-in tables. Prominent in the decorative scheme is the prudent and industrious squirrel, a Renaissance symbol of the ideal ruler: in other words, of Federico da Montefeltro. A large window looks out onto an elegant marble loggia with a distant view of the countryside through its arches; and the shelves, cupboards, and tables are filled with all manner of fascinating things—scientific instruments, books, even the duke's armor hanging like a suit in a closet.

PIERO DELLA FRANCESCA. Federico brought the artist Piero della Francesca (c. 1415–1492) to Urbino. Piero had worked in Florence in the 1430s before settling in his native Borgo San Sepolcro, a Tuscan hill town under papal control. He knew current art theory and art practice—including Brunelleschi's system of spatial illusion and linear perspective, Masaccio's powerful modeling of forms and atmospheric perspective, and Alberti's theoretical treatises. Piero was one of the few practicing artists who also wrote his own books of theory. Not surprisingly, in his treatise on perspective he emphasized the geometry and the volumetric construction of forms and spaces that were so apparent in his own work.

19-26 • Piero della Francesca BAPTISM OF CHRIST
c. 1450. Tempera on wood panel, 66 × 45¾" (1.67 × 1.16 m).
National Gallery, London.

The three angels standing in a cluster at left, partially overlapped by the foreground tree, have been interpreted as an emblem of concord—representing the rapprochement reached between the Roman and Byzantine Christian churches in 1439 at the Council of Florence. Another reference to this council has been seen in the exotic costumes of the figures in the far background. Since the accord reached at the council was very short-lived, this interpretation would place the date of the painting in the early 1440s rather than the 1450s.

These characteristic features of Piero's painting are marvelously apparent in a serene image of the **BAPTISM OF CHRIST** that has become one of Piero's signature works (**FIG. 19–26**). It was commissioned by the Graziani family, probably during the 1450s, for the priory of San Giovanni Battista in Borgo San Sepolchro. The central figure of Christ dominates the painting, standing in a shallow stream of glassy water under a tree of manicured regularity. Christ's legs and the sleek tree trunk set up a series of emphatically

upright forms, one of many formal relationships that reverberate both across the picture's surface and into its carefully measured space. Feet and ankles rotate across the lower quarter of the painting, providing a clear and well-distributed sense of grounding for the figural composition, while the radically foreshortened dove (Holy Spirit), John's baptismal dish, and the clouds create a rhythmic line of horizontals that adds stability above and creates a staccato rhythm that merges foreground and background on the painting's surface. The mirrored profiles and gestures of the outside angel and the baptizing John provide an internal frame for the central action. Such carefully crafted formal correspondences infuse this picture with an air of beatific calm and peaceful stasis—a stillness suggesting that nothing will ever change, no one will ever move in this frozen moment within a story that for Christian believers actually changed everything.

Piero traveled widely—to Rome, to the Este court in Ferrara, and especially to Urbino. In about 1474, he painted the portraits of Federico da Montefeltro and his recently deceased wife, Battista Sforza (**FIG. 19–27**). The small panels resemble Flemish painting in their detail and luminosity, their record of surfaces and textures, and their vast landscapes. But in traditional Italian fashion, figures are portrayed in strict profile, disengaged psychologically from the viewer. The profile format also allowed for an accurate recording of Federico's likeness without emphasizing two disfiguring scars—the loss of his right eye from a sword blow and his broken nose. His good left eye is shown, and the angular profile of his nose might easily be merely a distinctive family trait. Typically, Piero emphasized the underlying geometry of the forms. Dressed in the most elegant fashion (Federico wears his red ducal robe and Battista's jewels are meticulously recorded), they are silhouetted against a panoramic landscape. These are the hills around Urbino, seemingly dissolving into infinity through an atmospheric perspective as subtle and luminous as in any Flemish panel painting. Piero used another northern European device in the harbor view just in front of Federico, where the water narrows into a river that leads us into the distant landscape (SEE FIG. 18–14). He would have had contact in Urbino with the Flemings who were also working there.

The painting on the reverse of the portraits reflects the humanist interests of the Urbino court (**FIG. 19–28**). "Engraved" on the fictive parapets in letters inspired by ancient Roman inscriptions are stanzas praising the couple—the fame of Federico's virtue and Battista's restraint, shining in the reflected glory of her

19-27 • Piero della Francesca **BATTISTA SFORZA AND FEDERICO DA MONTEFELTRO**
c. 1474. Oil on wood panel, each 18½ × 13″ (47 × 33 cm). Galleria degli Uffizi, Florence.

19-28 • Piero della Francesca **TRIUMPH OF FEDERICO AND BATTISTA**
Reverse of FIG. 19–27.

Federico's inscription can be translated: "He that the perennial fame of virtues rightly celebrates holding the scepter, equal to the highest dukes, the illustrious, is borne in outstanding triumph." Battista had been dead two years when hers was written: "She that kept her modesty in favorable circumstances, flies on the mouths of all men, adorned with the praise of the acts of her great husband."

husband. Behind these laudatory inscriptions a wide landscape of hills and valleys runs nearly continuously across the two panels. In the foreground, triumphal carts roll, and we catch a glimpse of the kind of pageantry and spectacle that must have been enacted at court. The *Triumphs* of Petrarch—poetic allegories of love, chastity, fame, time, eternity (Christianized as divinity), and death—inspired many of these extravaganzas. White horses pull Federico's wagon. The duke is crowned by a winged figure—either Victory or Fortune—and accompanied by personifications of Justice, Prudence, Fortitude, and Temperance. Battista's cart is controlled by a winged putto (nude little boy) driving a team of unicorns. The virtues standing behind her may be personifications of Chastity and Modesty. Seated in front of her are Faith and Charity, who holds a pelican. This bird, believed to feed its young from its own blood, may symbolize the recently deceased Battista's maternal sacrifices. She died in 1472 at age 26, shortly after the birth of her ninth child, a son who would one day be duke. We are told that Federico was disconsolate. Some arranged aristocratic marriage alliances blossomed into loving partnerships.

MANTUA

Lodovico Gonzaga, the marquis of Mantua, ruled a territory that lies on the north Italian plain between Venice and Milan. Like Federico, he made his fortune as a *condottiere*. Lodovico was schooled by humanist teachers and created a court where humanist ideas flourished in art as well as in literature.

MANTEGNA. Working at Lodovico's court was Andrea Mantegna (1431–1506), a painter trained in Padua and profoundly influenced by the sculptor Donatello, who arrived in Padua in 1443 and worked there for a decade. Mantegna learned the Florentine system of linear perspective and pushed to their limits experiments in radically foreshortened forms and dramatic spatial recessions. He went to work for Ludovico Gonzaga in 1460, and he continued to work for the Gonzaga family for the rest of his life.

Perhaps his finest works are the frescos of the **CAMERA PICTA** ("Painted Room"), a tower chamber in Ludovico's palace, which Mantegna decorated between 1465 and 1474 (**FIG. 19–29**). Around the walls the family—each member seemingly identified by a portrait likeness—receives in landscapes and in loggias the return of Ludovico's son, Cardinal Francesco Gonzaga. On the domed ceiling, the artist painted a *tour de force* of radical perspective in a technique called *di sotto in sù* ("from below upwards"). The room appears to be open to a cloud-filled sky through a large oculus in a simulated marble- and mosaic-covered vault. On each side of a precariously balanced planter, three young women and an exotically turbaned African man peer over a marble balustrade into the room below. A fourth young woman in a veil looks dreamily upward. Joined by a large peacock, several putti play around the balustrade, three standing on the interior ledge of a cornice, unprotected by the balustrade, toes projecting into space but seemingly oblivious to the danger of their perch. This ceiling began a long tradition of illusionistic ceiling painting that

19-29 • Andrea Mantegna TWO VIEWS OF THE CAMERA PICTA, DUCAL PALACE, MANTUA
1465–1474. Fresco, diameter of false oculus 8′9″ (2.7 m); room 26′6″ square (8 m square).

culminated in the extravagant and explosive ceilings of Baroque churches (see Chapter 22).

ROME

Rome's development into a Renaissance center of the arts was greatly enhanced when Pope Sixtus IV called to the city in the early 1480s a group of young Florentine and Umbrian artists to decorate the walls of his newly built chapel (1479–1481), now named the **SISTINE CHAPEL** after him (FIG. 19–30). Botticelli and Ghirlandaio were among the most famous artists summoned to the chapel to paint, but many art historians believe that Perugino was the supervising artist in charge of the project.

PERUGINO.   Pietro Vannucci, called "Perugino" (c. 1445–1523), was originally from near the town of Perugia in Umbria (thus the nickname), and he worked for a while in Florence, but by 1479 he was in Rome. Two years later, he was working on the Sistine murals. One of his contributions, *The Delivery of the Keys to St. Peter* (foreground painting at lower right in FIG. 19–30; see also "Renaissance Perspective," page 608), portrayed the event that provided biblical support for the supremacy of papal authority (Matthew 16:19). In a light-filled piazza in which banded paving stones provide a geometric grid for perspectival recession, the figures stand like chess pieces on the squares, scaled to size according to their distance from the picture plane and modeled by a consistent light source from the

19–31 • Perugino CRUCIFIXION WITH SAINTS
1480s. Tempera on wood panel (now transferred to canvas) center panel 40 × 22¼″ (101 × 56 cm),
side panels 37½ × 12″ (95 × 30 cm). National Gallery of Art, Washington, D.C.

upper left. Triumphal arches inspired by ancient Rome frame the church and focus the attention on the center of the composition, where the vital key is being transferred. The carefully calibrated scene is softened by the subdued colors, the distant idealized landscape and cloudy skies, and the variety of the figures' positions.

Just as carefully organized is Perugino's transcendent portrayal of the **CRUCIFIXION (FIG. 19–31)** as a measured tableau, where a line of decorous saints, and the Crucifixion itself, are aligned on a narrow, flat shelf of land in the foreground, close to the picture plane. Behind them a craggy but verdant landscape plunges into the background, clearly rooted in the influence of Flemish painters, matching their attention to fine detail—especially in the flowers growing along the front edge of the painting—and their sensitive use of atmospheric perspective. Unlike in most Italian

Crucifixions, Perugino's figures are eerily calm. Christ's composure suppresses any sign of suffering; his mourning companions convey much more elegance than grief. Jesus is uniquely disconnected from the landscape setting, which dips at the center to frame him. His elevation into the upper half of the paining, isolated against the shaded expanse of an ethereal blue sky, separates him from his grounded mother and disciple, so that he appears almost like an elevated crucifix rather than the protagonist in a tragic narrative.

THE LATER FIFTEENTH CENTURY IN FLORENCE

In the final decades of the fifteenth century, Florentine painting was characterized on one hand by a love of material opulence and an interest in describing the natural world, and on the other by a poetic, mystical spirit. The first trend was encouraged by the influence of Netherlandish art and the patronage of citizens who sought to advertise their wealth and prestige, the second by intellectual circles surrounding the Medici and the religious fervor that arose at the very end of the century.

GHIRLANDAIO. In Florence, the most prolific painting workshop of the later fifteenth century was that of the painter Domenico di Tommaso Bigordi (1449–1494), known as Domenico "Ghirlandaio" ("Garland-Maker"), a nickname first adopted by his father, who was a goldsmith noted for his floral wreaths. A skilled storyteller, the younger Ghirlandaio reinterpreted the art of earlier fifteenth-century painters into a visual language of descriptive immediacy.

Among Ghirlandaio's most effective narrative programs were the frescos of the **LIFE OF ST. FRANCIS** created between 1483 and 1486 for the Sassetti family burial chapel in the church of Santa Trinità, Florence (**FIG. 19–32**). In the uppermost tier of the paintings, Pope Honorius confirms the Franciscan order, with the Loggia dei Lanzi and the Palazzo della Signoria (SEE FIG. 17–2) in the background. All the figures, including those coming up the stairs, are portrait likenesses of well-known Florentines. In the middle register, a small boy who has fallen from an upper window is resurrected by St. Francis. The miracle is witnessed by contemporary Florentines, including members of the Sassetti family, and the scene takes place in the piazza outside the actual church. Ghirlandaio has transferred the events of the traditional story from thirteenth-century Rome to contemporary Florence, painting views of the city and portraits of living Florentines, delighting in local color and anecdotal detail. Perhaps Renaissance painters, like Gothic painters, represented sacred narratives in contemporary settings to emphasize their current relevance, or perhaps they and their patrons simply enjoyed seeing themselves in their fine clothes acting out the dramas in the cities of which they were justifiably proud.

19–32 • Domenico Ghirlandaio **SCENES FROM THE LIFE OF ST. FRANCIS; ALTARPIECE WITH NATIVITY AND ADORATION OF THE SHEPHERDS**
Sassetti Chapel, Church of Santa Trinità. 1483–1486. Fresco, chapel 12'2" deep × 17'2" wide (3.7 × 5.25 m).

The altarpiece Ghirlandaio painted for the Sassetti Chapel portrays the **NATIVITY AND ADORATION OF THE SHEPHERDS (FIG. 19–33)**. It is still in its original frame, still in the place for which it was painted (SEE FIG. 19–32). The influence of Hugo's Portinari Altarpiece (SEE FIG. 18–16), which had been placed on the high altar of the church of Sant'Egidio two years earlier, in 1483, is strong. Ghirlandaio's Christ Child also lies on the ground, adored by the Virgin while rugged shepherds kneel at the right. Ghirlandaio even copies some of Hugo's flowers—although here the iris, a symbol of the Passion, springs not from a vase, but from the earth in the lower right corner. But Ghirlandaio highlights references to Classical Rome. First to catch the eye are the two

Classical pilasters with Corinthian capitals, one of which has the date 1485 on it. The manger is an ancient sarcophagus with an inscription that promises resurrection (as in the fresco directly above the altarpiece where St. Francis is reviving a child); and in the distance a Classical arch inscribed with a reference to the Roman general Pompey the Great frames the road along which the Magi travel. Weighty, restrained actors replace the psychologically intense figures of Hugo's painting. Ghirlandaio joins a clear foreground, middle ground, and background in part by the road and in part by aerial perspective, which creates a seamless transition of color, from the sharp details and primary hues of the Adoration to the soft gray mountains in the distance.

19-33 • Domenico Ghirlandaio NATIVITY AND ADORATION OF THE SHEPHERDS
Altarpiece in the Sassetti Chapel, Santa Trinità, Florence, 1485. Panel, 65¾″ square (1.67 m square).

BOTTICELLI. Like most artists in the second half of the fifteenth century, Sandro Botticelli (1445–1510) learned to draw and paint sculptural figures that were modeled by light from a consistent source and placed in a setting rendered illusionistic by linear perspective. An outstanding portraitist, he, like Ghirlandaio, often included recognizable contemporary figures among the saints and angels in religious paintings. He worked in Florence, often for the Medici, then was called to Rome in 1481 by Pope Sixtus IV to help decorate the new Sistine Chapel along with Ghirlandaio, Perugino, and other artists.

Botticelli returned to Florence that same year and entered a new phase of his career. Like other artists working for patrons steeped in Classical scholarship and humanistic thought, he was exposed to philosophical speculations on beauty—as well as to the examples of ancient art in his employers' collections. For the Medici, Botticelli produced secular paintings of mythological subjects inspired by ancient works and by contemporary Neoplatonic thought. Art historian Michael Baxandall has shown that these works were also patterned on the slow movements of fifteenth-century Florentine dance, in which figures acted out their relationships to one another in public performances that would have influenced the thinking and viewing habits of both painters and their audience.

The overall appearance of Botticelli's *Primavera*, or *Spring* (see "A Closer Look," page 626), recalls Flemish tapestries (SEE FIG. 18–7), which were very popular in Italy at the time. And its subject—like the subjects of many tapestries—is a highly complex **allegory** (a symbolic illustration of a concept or principle), interweaving Neoplatonic ideas with esoteric references to Classical sources. In simple terms, Neoplatonic philosophers and poets conceived Venus, the goddess of love, as having two natures.

The first ruled over earthly, human love and the second over universal, divine love. In this way the philosophers could argue that Venus was a Classical equivalent of the Virgin Mary. *Primavera* was painted at the time of the wedding of Lorenzo di Pierfrancesco de' Medici and Semiramide d'Appiano in 1482. The theme suggests love and fertility in marriage, and the painting can be read as a lyrical wish for a similar fecundity in the union of Lorenzo and Semiramide—a sort of highly refined fertility dance.

Several years later, some of the same mythological figures reappeared in Botticelli's **BIRTH OF VENUS (FIG. 19–34)**, in which the central image represents the Neoplatonic idea of divine love in the form of a nude Venus based on an antique statue type known as the "modest Venus" that ultimately derives from Praxiteles' *Aphrodite of Knidos* (SEE FIG. 5–45). Botticelli's Classical goddess of love and beauty, born of sea foam, averts her eyes from our gaze as she floats ashore on a scallop shell, gracefully arranging her hands and hair to hide—but actually drawing attention to—her sexuality. Indeed, she is an arrestingly alluring figure, with voluminous hair highlighted with gold. Blown by the wind—Zephyr (with his love, the nymph Chloris)—Venus arrives at her earthly home. She is welcomed by a devotee who offers Venus a garment embroidered with flowers. The circumstances of this commission are uncertain. It is painted on canvas, which suggests that it may have been a banner or a painted tapestrylike wall hanging.

Botticelli's later career was affected by a profound spiritual crisis. While the artist was creating his mythologies for the Medici, a Dominican monk, Fra Girolamo Savonarola (active in Florence 1490–1498), had begun to preach impassioned sermons denouncing the worldliness of Florence. Many Florentines reacted with orgies of self-recrimination, and processions of weeping penitents wound through the streets. Botticelli, too, fell into a state of religious fervor.

19-34 • Sandro Botticelli
BIRTH OF VENUS
c. 1484–1486. Tempera and gold on canvas, 5'8⅞" × 9'1⅞" (1.8 × 2.8 m). Galleria degli Uffizi, Florence.

A CLOSER LOOK

Primavera ▶ **by Sandro Botticelli, c. 1482. Tempera on wood panel.** 6′8″ × 10′4″ (2.03 × 3.15 m). Galleria degli Uffizi, Florence.

Mercury, the sign for the month of May, disperses the winter clouds with his caduceus. This staff wound with serpents became a symbol for the medical profession. The name Medici means "doctors."

Venus, clothed in contemporary costume and crowned with a marriage wreath, appears in her role as the goddess of wedded love. The presence of both Venus and Mercury may be an astrological reference; prominent Neoplatonist Marsilio Ficino told Lorenzo de Pierfrancesco de' Medici that these planets were aligned in his horoscope.

The setting of the painting is a grove of orange trees. These hold a double meaning—both suggestive of Venus's Garden of the Hesperides, with its golden fruit, and perhaps an allusion to the Medici, whose coat of arms featured golden orbs.

This three-figure grouping tells a story. Zephyrus, the west wind, is accosting the virgin nymph Chloris, identifiable from the roses pouring out of her mouth. Once Zephyrus makes her his bride, Chloris is transformed into the goddess Flora, the elaborately dressed personification of spring at the front of the group.

These gold flames are also an attribute of St. Lawrence, the namesake of Lorenzo di Pierfrancesco de' Medici, for whom this painting was made. The laurel tree (*laurus* in Latin) behind Zephyrus also alludes to Lorenzo's name.

The Three Graces symbolize ideal female virtues—Chastity, Beauty, Love. Venus' son Cupid—the embodiment of romantic desire—playfully aims his arrow at them.

So accurate is their representation, 138 of the 190 flowering plants depicted in the painting have been identified. Almost all grow in the neighborhood of Florence between the months of March and April, and most carry symbolic associations with love and marriage.

Flora scatters flowers held in a fold of her dress at the level of her womb, equating the fecundity brought about by changing seasons with female procreative fertility.

SEE MORE: View the Closer Look feature for *Primavera* **www.myartslab.com**

In a dramatic gesture of repentance, he burned many of his earlier paintings and began to produce highly emotional pictures pervaded by an intense religiosity.

VENICE

In the last quarter of the fifteenth century, Venice emerged as a major Renaissance art center. Ruled as an oligarchy (government by a select few) with an elected duke (*doge* in the Venetian dialect), the city government was founded at the end of the Roman Empire and survived until the Napoleonic era. In building their city, the Venetians had turned marshes into a commercial seaport, and they saw the sea as a resource, not a threat. They depended on naval power and on the natural defense of their lagoons rather than city walls. Venice turned toward the east, especially after the crusaders' conquest of 1204, designing the church of St. Mark as a great Byzantine building sheathed in mosaics (SEE FIG. 7–36). Venice excelled in the arts of textiles, gold and enamel, glass and mosaic, and fine printing as well as bookbinding.

VENETIAN PALACES. Venice was a city of waterways with few large public spaces. Even palaces had only small interior courtyards and tiny gardens, and were separated by narrow alleys. Their façades overlooked the canals, whose waters gave protection and permitted the owners to project on these major thoroughfares the large portals, windows, and loggias that proclaimed their importance through the lavishness of their residences—a sharp contrast to the fortresslike character of most Florentine town houses (SEE FIG. 19–5). But, as with the Florentine great houses, Venician owners combined in these structures a place of business with a dwelling.

The Ca d'Oro (House of Gold), home of the wealthy nobleman Marino Contarini, has a splendid front with three super-imposed loggias facing the Grand Canal (FIG. 19–35). The house was constructed between 1421 and 1437, and its asymmetrical elevation is based on a traditional Byzantine plan. A wide central hall ran from front to back all the way through the building to a small inner courtyard with a well and garden. An outside stair led to the main floor on the second level. The entrance on the canal permitted goods to be delivered directly into the warehouse that constituted the ground floor. The principal floor, on the second level, had a salon and reception room opening on the richly decorated loggia. It was filled with light from large windows, and more light reflected off the polished terrazzo floor. Private family rooms filled the upper stories. Contarini's instructions to his contractors and workers specified that the façade was to be painted with white enamel and ultramarine blue and that the red stones in the patterned wall should be oiled to make them even brighter. Details of carving, such as coats of arms and balls on the crest at the roofline, were to be gilded. Beautiful as the palace is today, in the fifteenth and sixteenth centuries it must have been truly spectacular.

19-35 • CA D'ORO (CONTARINI PALACE), VENICE
1421–1437.

SEE MORE: Click the Google Earth link for the Ca d'Oro www.myartslab.com

THE BELLINI BROTHERS. The domes of the church of St. Mark dominated the city center, and the rich colors of its glowing mosaics captured painters' imaginations. Perhaps it was their love of color that encouraged the Venetian painters to embrace the oil medium for both panel and canvas painting.

The most important Venetian artists of this period were two brothers: Gentile (c. 1429–1507) and Giovanni (c. 1430–1516) Bellini, whose father, Jacopo (c. 1400–1470), had also been a central figure in Venetian art. Andrea Mantegna was also part of this circle, for he had married Jacopo's daughter in 1453.

**19-36 • Gentile Bellini
PROCESSION OF
THE RELIC OF THE
TRUE CROSS
BEFORE THE
CHURCH OF
ST. MARK**
1496. Oil on canvas,
12′ × 24′5″ (3.67 × 7.45 m).
Galleria dell'Accademia,
Venice.

Gentile Bellini celebrated the daily life of the city in large, lively narratives, such as the **PROCESSION OF THE RELIC OF THE TRUE CROSS BEFORE THE CHURCH OF ST. MARK** (FIG. **19–36**). Every year on the feast of St. Mark (April 25), the Confraternity of St. John the Evangelist carried the miracle-working relic of the true cross in a procession through the square in front of the church. Bellini's painting of 1496 depicts an event that had occurred in 1444: the miraculous recovery of a sick child whose father (the man in red kneeling to the right of the relic) prayed for help as the relic passed by. Gentile has rendered the cityscape with great attention to detail. The mosaic-encrusted Byzantine Cathedral of St. Mark (SEE FIG. 7–36) forms a backdrop for the procession, and the doge's palace and base of the bell tower can be seen at the right. The gold reliquary is carried under a canopy, surrounded by marchers with giant candles, led by a choir and followed at the far right by the doge and other officials. Gentile's procession serves as a reminder that fifteenth-century piazzas and buildings were sites of ritual ceremony, and it was in moments such as this that they were brought to life.

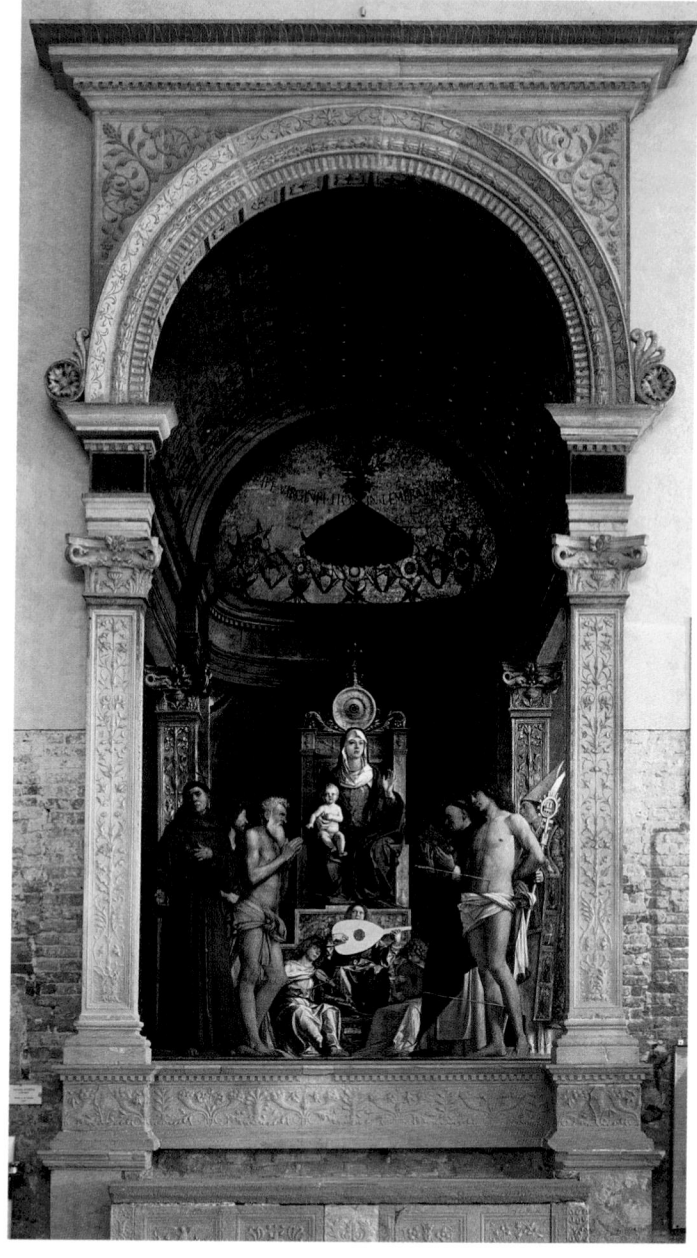

19-37 • Giovanni Bellini VIRGIN AND CHILD ENTHRONED WITH SS. FRANCIS, JOHN THE BAPTIST, JOB, DOMINIC, SEBASTIAN, AND LOUIS OF TOULOUSE
(Computer reconstruction). Originally commissioned for the chapel of the Hospital of San Giobbe, Venice. c. 1478. Oil on wood panel, 15′4″ × 8′4″ (4.67 × 2.54 m). Galleria dell'Accademia, Venice. The original frame is in the chapel of the Hospital of San Giobbe, Venice.

Art historians have given the special name *sacra conversazione* ("holy conversation") to this type of composition that shows saints, angels, and sometimes even the painting's donors in the same pictorial space with the enthroned Virgin and Child. Despite the name, no "conversation" or spoken interaction takes place in a literal sense. Instead, the individuals portrayed are joined in a mystical and eternal communion that occurs outside human time and space.

19-38 • Giovanni Bellini
ST. FRANCIS IN ECSTASY
c. 1470s. Oil and tempera on wood
panel, 49 × 55⅞″ (125 × 142 cm).
The Frick Collection, New York.

sylvan delight. Like most of the fifteenth-century religious art we have seen, however, Bellini presents viewers with a natural world saturated in symbolism. Here a relationship between St. Francis and Moses is outlined. The tree symbolizes the burning bush; the stream, the miraculous spring brought forth by Moses. The crane and donkey represent the monastic virtue of patience. The detailed description, luminous palette, and symbolic surroundings suggest Flemish art, but the golden light suffusing the painting is unmistakably Venetian.

Gentile's brother Giovanni amazed and attracted patrons with his artistic virtuosity for almost 60 years. The **VIRGIN AND CHILD ENTHRONED WITH SS. FRANCIS, JOHN THE BAPTIST, JOB, DOMINIC, SEBASTIAN, AND LOUIS OF TOULOUSE** (FIG. 19–37), painted about 1478 for the chapel of the Hospital of San Giobbe (St. Job), exhibits a dramatic perspectival view up into a tunnel vault that leads to an apse. Giovanni may have known his brother-in-law Mantegna's early experiments in radical foreshortening and in the use of a low vanishing point. Here Giovanni positions the vanishing point for the rapidly converging lines of the architecture at bottom center, on the feet of the lute-playing angel. His figures stand in a Classical architectural interior with a coffered barrel vault reminiscent of Masaccio's *Trinity* (SEE FIG. 19–16). The gold mosaic, with its identifying inscription and stylized seraphim (angels of the highest rank), recalls Byzantine art and the long tradition of Byzantine-inspired painting and mosaics produced in Venice.

Giovanni Bellini's early painting of **ST. FRANCIS IN ECSTASY** (FIG. 19–38), painted in the 1470s, recalls Flemish painting in the fine detail with which he rendered the natural world. The saint stands bathed in early morning sunlight, his outspread hands showing his stigmata. Francis had moved to a cave in the barren wilderness in his search for communion with God, but in the world Giovanni creates for him, the fields blossom and flocks of animals graze. The grape arbor over his desk adds to the atmosphere of

THINK ABOUT IT

19.1 Discuss Masaccio's use of linear perspective in either *The Tribute Money* or *Trinity with the Virgin, St. John the Evangelist, and Donors*. How does he use this technique? Illustrate your points with a comparative reference to a work discussed earlier in this chapter or in a previous chapter.

19.2 Explain how one Florentine sculptor discussed in this chapter helped establish the increasing naturalism and growing emulation of Classical models that would be central to the early Italian Renaissance.

19.3 Choose a wealthy merchant or *condottiere* and discuss how his patronage fostered the emergence of the Renaissance in fifteenth-century Italy. Make reference to specific works in forming your answer.

19.4 Discuss the 1401 competition to choose an artist to create the bronze doors of the Florence Baptistery. How did the competition affect the careers of the two finalists, Ghiberti and Brunelleschi?

19.5 Discuss the role of the Classical past in Brunelleschi's architecture, focusing on one of the buildings he designed in Florence.

PRACTICE MORE: Compose answers to these questions, get flashcards for images and terms, and review chapter material with quizzes
www.myartslab.com

20–1 • Raphael **STANZA DELLA SEGNATURA**   Vatican, Rome. Fresco in the left lunette, *Parnassus*;
in the right lunette, *The School of Athens*. 1510–1511.

SIXTEENTH-CENTURY ART IN ITALY

Two young artists—Raphael and Michelangelo—although rivals in almost every sense, were linked in service to Pope Julius II (pontificate 1503–1513) in the early years of the sixteenth century. Raphael was painting the pope's private library (1509–1511) while, nearby, Michelangelo painted the ceiling of his Sistine Chapel (1508–1512). The pope demanded an art that reflected his imperial vision of a new, worldwide Church based on humanistic ideas, which he would lead as a new St. Peter, founding a second great age of papal dominion. In fulfilling this proud demand, Raphael and Michelangelo united Renaissance principles of harmony and balance with a new monumentality based on Classical ideals, and they knit these elements into a dynamic and synthetic whole, rich in color and controlled by cohesive design. Working alongside the architect Donato Bramante and the multifaceted genius Leonardo da Vinci, they created a style we call the High Renaissance.

Julius II intended the **STANZA DELLA SEGNATURA**, or Room of the Signature, to be his personal study (FIG. 20–1). Raphael sought to create an ideal setting for papal activities, with murals proclaiming that all human knowledge exists under the power of divine wisdom. He organized the mural program itself like a library, separated into divisions of theology, philosophy, the arts, and justice. He created pictorial allegories to illustrate each theme. On one wall, churchmen discussing the sacraments represent theology, while across the room ancient philosophers led by Plato and Aristotle debate in the School of Athens. Plato holds his book *Timaeus*, in which creation is seen in terms of geometry, and in which humanity encompasses and explains the universe. Aristotle holds his *Nicomachean Ethics*, a decidedly human-centered book concerned with relations among people. Ancient representatives of the academic curriculum—Grammar, Rhetoric, Dialectic, Arithmetic, Music, Geometry, and Astronomy—surround them. On a window wall, Justice, holding a sword and scales, assigns each his due. Across the room, Poetry and the Arts are represented by Apollo and the Muses, and the poet Sappho reclines against the fictive frame of an actual window. Raphael included his own portrait among the onlookers on the extreme lower right in the *School of Athens* fresco and signed the painting with his initials—a signal that both artists and patrons were becoming increasingly aware of their individual significance.

Raphael achieved a lofty style in keeping with papal ambition—using ideals of Classical grandeur, professing faith in human rationality and perfectibility, and celebrating the power of the pope as God's earthly administrator. But when Raphael died at age 37 on April 6, 1520, the grand moment was already passing: Luther and the Protestant Reformation were challenging papal authority, and the world would never be the same again.

LEARN ABOUT IT

20.1 Trace the shift in the artistic center of Italy from Florence to Rome, and recognize the efforts of Pope Julius II to create a new "golden age."

20.2 Understand the Vatican as a site for the creative energies of the most important artists of the Italian Renaissance.

20.3 Explore the intentional subversion of Classical style and decorum in the work of Mannerist artists.

20.4 Compare and contrast the emphasis on drawing and clearly structured compositions in the work of Roman and Florentine painters with the expressive potential of color that characterizes the work of their Venetian counterparts.

20.5 Examine the architectural creativity lavished on the design of both grand churches and pleasurable retreats for the wealthy in sixteenth-century Italy.

HEAR MORE: Listen to an audio file of your chapter **www.myartslab.com**

EUROPE IN THE SIXTEENTH CENTURY

The sixteenth century was an age of social, intellectual, and religious ferment that transformed European culture. It was marked by continual warfare triggered by the expansionist ambitions of warring rulers. The humanism of the fourteenth and fifteenth centuries, with its medieval roots and its often uncritical acceptance of the authority of Classical texts, slowly developed into a critical exploration of new ideas, the natural world, and distant lands. Cartographers began to acknowledge the Earth's curvature and the degrees of distance, giving Europeans a more accurate understanding of their place within the world. The printing press sparked an explosion in book production, spreading new ideas through the translation and publication of ancient and contemporary texts, broadening the horizons of educated Europeans and encouraging the development of literacy. Since travel was growing more common, artists and their work became mobile, and the world of art was transformed into a more international community.

At the start of the sixteenth century, England, France, and Portugal were nation-states under strong monarchs. German-speaking central Europe was divided into dozens of principalities, counties, free cities, and small territories. But even states as powerful as Saxony and Bavaria acknowledged the supremacy of the Habsburg Holy Roman Empire—in theory the greatest power in Europe. Charles V, elected emperor in 1519, also inherited Spain, the Netherlands, and vast territories in the Americas. Italy, which was divided into numerous small states, was a diplomatic and military battlefield where, for much of the century, the Italian city-states, Habsburg Spain, France, and the papacy fought each other in shifting alliances. Popes behaved like secular princes, using diplomacy and military force to regain control over central Italy and in some cases to establish family members as hereditary rulers.

The popes' incessant demands for money, to finance the rebuilding of St. Peter's as well as their self-aggrandizing art projects and luxurious lifestyles, aggravated the religious dissent that had long been developing, especially north of the Alps. Early in the century, religious reformers within the established Church challenged beliefs and practices, especially Julius II's sale of indulgences promising forgiveness of sins and assurance of salvation in exchange for a financial contribution to the Church. Because they protested, these northern European reformers came to be called Protestants; their demand for reform gave rise to a movement called the Reformation.

The political maneuvering of Pope Clement VII (pontificate 1523–1534) led to a direct clash with Holy Roman Emperor Charles V. In May 1527, Charles's German mercenary troops attacked Rome, beginning a six-month orgy of killing, looting, and burning. The Sack of Rome, as it is called, shook the sense of stability and humanistic confidence that until then had characterized the Renaissance, and it sent many artists fleeing from the ruined city. Nevertheless, Charles saw himself as the leader of the Catholic forces—and he was the sole Catholic ally Clement had at the time. In 1530, Clement VII crowned Charles emperor in Bologna.

Sixteenth-century patrons valued artists highly and rewarded them well, not only with generous commissions but sometimes even with high social status. Charles V, for example, knighted the painter Titian. Some painters and sculptors became entrepreneurs and celebrities, selling prints of their works on the side and creating international reputations for themselves. Many artists recorded their activities—professional and private—in diaries, notebooks, and letters that have come down to us. In addition, contemporary writers began to report on the lives of artists, documenting their physical appearance and assessing their individual reputations. In 1550, Giorgio Vasari wrote the first survey of Italian art history—*Lives of the Best Architects, Painters, and Sculptors*—organized as a series of critical biographies but at its core a work of critical judgment. Vasari also commented on the role of patrons, and argued that art had become more realistic and more beautiful over time, reaching its apex of perfection in his own age. From his characterization developed our notion of this period as the High Renaissance—that is, as a high point in art since the early experiments of Cimabue and Giotto, marked by a balanced synthesis of Classical ideals and a lifelike rendering of the natural world.

During this period, the fifteenth-century humanists' notion of painting, sculpture, and architecture not as manual arts but as liberal (intellectual) arts, requiring education in the Classics and mathematics as well as in the techniques of the craft, became a topic of intense interest. And from these discussions arose the Renaissance formulation—still with us today—of artists as divinely inspired creative geniuses, a step above most of us in their gifts of hand and mind. This idea weaves its way through Vasari's work like an organizing principle. And this newly elevated status to which artists aspired favored men. Although few artists of either sex had access to the humanist education required by the sophisticated, often esoteric, subject matter used in paintings (usually devised by someone other than the artist), women were denied even the studio practice necessary to draw lifelike nude figures in foreshortened poses. Furthermore, it was almost impossible for an artist to achieve international status without traveling extensively and frequently relocating to follow commissions—something most women could not do. Still, some European women managed to follow their gifts and establish careers as artists during this period despite the obstacles that blocked their entrance into the profession.

ITALY IN THE EARLY SIXTEENTH CENTURY: THE HIGH RENAISSANCE

Italian art from the 1490s to about the time of the Sack of Rome in 1527 has been called the "High Renaissance." As we have already seen with the "High Classical" period in ancient Athens, the term "High Renaissance" encapsulates an art-historical

MAP 20-1 • RENAISSANCE AND EARLIER MONUMENTS IN ROME

In addition to situating the principal works of the Roman Renaissance that emerged from Julius II's campaign to revitalize the papal city, this map also locates the surviving works of Roman antiquity that would have been available to the Renaissance artists and architects who masterminded the Classical revival.

judgment, claiming that what happened in Rome at this time represents a pinnacle of achievement within a longer artistic movement, and that it set standards for the future (MAP 20–1). High Renaissance art is characterized by a sense of gravity and decorum, a complex but ordered relationship of individual parts to the whole, and an emulation of the principles artists saw in ancient Classical art. Art historian Sydney Freedberg has stressed the way High Renaissance art fuses the real and the ideal, characterizing Leonardo's *Mona Lisa*, for example, as "a rare perfection between art and reality; an image in which a breathing instant and a composure for all time are held in suspension" (Freedberg, p. 28).

Two important practical developments at the turn of the sixteenth century affected the arts in Italy. Technically, the use of tempera gave way to the more flexible oil painting medium; and economically, commissions from private sources increased so that artists no longer depended so exclusively on the patronage of the Church, the court, or civic associations.

THREE GREAT ARTISTS OF THE EARLY SIXTEENTH CENTURY

Florence's renowned artistic tradition attracted a stream of young artists to that city, traveling there to study Masaccio's solid, monumental figures, with their eloquent facial features, poses, and gestures, in the Brancacci Chapel paintings. The young Michelangelo's sketches of the chapel frescos document the importance of Masaccio to his developing style. In fact, Michelangelo, Leonardo, and Raphael—the three leading artists of the High Renaissance—all began their careers in Florence, although they soon moved to other centers of patronage and their influence spread well beyond that city, even beyond Italy.

LEONARDO DA VINCI. Leonardo da Vinci (1452–1519) was 12 or 13 when his family moved to Florence from the Tuscan village of Vinci. After an apprenticeship in the shop of the Florentine painter and sculptor Verrocchio, and a few years on his own, Leonardo traveled to Milan in 1481 or 1482 to work for the ruling Sforza family.

Leonardo spent much of his time in Milan on military and civil engineering projects, including both urban-renewal and fortification plans for the city, but he also created a few key monuments of Renaissance painting. In April 1483, Leonardo contracted with the Confraternity of the Immaculate Conception to paint an altarpiece for their chapel in the church of San Francesco Grande in Milan, a painting now known as *The Virgin of the Rocks* (FIG. 20–2). The contract stipulates a painting of the Virgin and Child with angels, but Leonardo added a figure of the young John the Baptist, who balances the composition at the left, pulled into dialogue with his younger cousin Jesus by the long, protective arm of the Virgin. She draws attention to her child by extending her other hand over his head, while the enigmatic figure of the angel—who looks out without actually making eye contact with the viewer—points to the center of interaction. The stable, balanced, pyramidal figural group—a compositional formula that will become a standard feature of High Renaissance Classicism—is set against an exquisitely detailed landscape that dissolves mysteriously into the misty distance.

To assure their dominance in the picture, Leonardo picks out the four figures with spotlights, creating a strong **chiaroscuro** (from the Italian words *chiaro*, meaning "light," and *oscuro*, meaning "dark") that enhances their modeling as three-dimensional forms. This painting is an excellent early example of a specific variant of this technique, called **sfumato** ("smoky"), in which there are subtle, almost imperceptible, transitions between light and dark in shading, as if the picture were seen through smoke or fog. *Sfumato* becomes a hallmark of Leonardo's style, and the effect is artificially enhanced in this painting by the yellowing of its thick varnish, which masks the original vibrancy of its color.

At Duke Ludovico Sforza's request, Leonardo painted **THE LAST SUPPER** (FIGS. 20–3, 20–4) in the refectory, or dining hall, of the monastery of Santa Maria delle Grazie in Milan between 1495 and 1498. In fictive space defined by a coffered ceiling and four pairs of tapestries that seem to extend the refectory itself into another room, Jesus and his disciples are seated at a long table placed parallel to the picture plane and to the monastic diners who would have been seated in the hall below. In a sense, Jesus' meal with his disciples prefigures the daily gathering of this local monastic community at mealtimes. The stagelike space recedes from the table to three windows on the back wall, where the vanishing point of the one-point linear perspective lies behind Jesus' head. A stable, pyramidal Jesus at the center is

20-2 • Leonardo da Vinci THE VIRGIN OF THE ROCKS
c. 1485. Oil on wood panel (now transferred to canvas), 6'6" × 4' (1.9 × 1.2 m). Musée du Louvre, Paris.

20-3 • Leonardo da Vinci THE LAST SUPPER
Refectory of the monastery of Santa Maria delle Grazie, Milan, Italy. 1495–1498. Tempera and oil on plaster, 15′2″ × 28′10″ (4.6 × 8.8 m).

SEE MORE: View a video about Leonardo da Vinci's *The Last Supper* **www.myartslab.com**

20-4 • REFECTORY OF THE MONASTERY OF SANTA MARIA DELLE GRAZIE, SHOWING LEONARDO'S LAST SUPPER
Milan, Italy.

Instead of painting in fresco, Leonardo devised an experimental technique for this mural. Hoping to achieve the freedom and flexibility of painting on wood panel, he worked directly on dry *intonaco*— a thin layer of smooth plaster—with an oil-and-tempera paint for which the formula is unknown. The result was disastrous. Within a short time, the painting began to deteriorate, and by the middle of the sixteenth century its figures could be seen only with difficulty. In the seventeenth century, the monks saw no harm in cutting a doorway through the lower center of the composition. The work has barely survived the intervening period, despite many attempts to halt its deterioration and restore its original appearance. The painting narrowly escaped complete destruction in World War II, when the refectory was bombed to rubble. The coats of arms at the top are those of patron Ludovico Sforza, the duke of Milan (r. 1494–1499), and his wife, Beatrice.

20-5 • Leonardo da Vinci MONA LISA
c. 1503–1506. Oil on wood panel, 30¼ × 21″ (77 × 53 cm).
Musée du Louvre, Paris. (INV. 779)

EXPLORE MORE: Gain insight from a primary source by
Leonardo **www.myartslab.com**

flanked by his 12 disciples, grouped in four interlocking sets of three.

On one level, Leonardo has painted a scene from a story—one that captures the individual reactions of the apostles to Jesus' announcement that one of them will betray him. Leonardo was an acute observer of human behavior, and his art captures human emotions with compelling immediacy. On another level, *The Last Supper* is a symbolic evocation of Jesus' coming sacrifice for the salvation of humankind, the foundation of the institution of the Mass. Breaking with traditional representations of the subject (SEE FIG. 19–22), Leonardo placed the traitor Judas—clutching his money bags in the shadows—within the first triad to the left of Jesus, along with the young John the Evangelist and the elderly Peter, rather than isolating him on the opposite side of the table. Judas, Peter, and John were each to play an essential role in Jesus' mission: Judas set in motion the events leading to Jesus' sacrifice; Peter led the Church after Jesus' death; and John, the visionary, foretold the Second Coming and the Last Judgment in the book of Revelation.

The painting's careful geometry, the convergence of its perspective lines, the stability of its pyramidal forms, and Jesus' calm demeanor at the mathematical center of all the commotion together reinforce the sense of gravity, balance, and order. The clarity and stability of this painting epitomize High Renaissance style.

Leonardo returned to Florence in 1500, after the French, who had invaded Italy in 1494, claimed Milan by defeating Leonardo's Milanese patron, Ludovico Sforza. Perhaps the most famous of his Florentine works is the portrait he painted between about 1503 and 1506 known as the **MONA LISA (FIG. 20–5)**. The subject may have been 24-year-old Lisa Gherardini del Giocondo, the wife of a prominent Florentine merchant. Leonardo never delivered the painting and kept it with him for the rest of his life. In a departure from tradition, the young woman is portrayed without jewelry, not even a ring. The solid pyramidal form of her halflength figure—another departure from traditional portraiture, which was limited to the upper torso—is silhouetted against distant hazy mountains, giving the painting a sense of mystery reminiscent of *The Virgin of the Rocks* (SEE FIG. 20–2). Mona Lisa's facial expression has been called "enigmatic" because her gentle smile is not accompanied by the warmth one would expect to see in her eyes, which have boldly—perhaps flirtatiously—shifted to the side to look straight out at the viewer. It is this expressive complexity, and the sense of psychological presence it gives the human face—especially in the context of the masklike detachment that was more characteristic of Renaissance portraiture (compare FIG. 19–27, or even FIG. 20–8)—that makes the innovative *Mona Lisa* so arresting and haunting, even today.

A fiercely debated topic in Renaissance Italy was the question of the relative merits of painting and sculpture. Leonardo insisted on the supremacy of painting as the best and most complete means of creating an illusion of the natural world, while Michelangelo argued for sculpture. Yet in creating a painted illusion, Leonardo considered color to be secondary to the depiction of sculptural volume, which he achieved through his virtuosity in *sfumato*. He also unified his compositions by covering them with a thin, lightly tinted varnish, which enhanced the overall smoky haze. Because early evening light tends to produce a similar effect naturally, Leonardo considered dusk the finest time of day and recommended that painters set up their studios in a courtyard with black walls and a linen sheet stretched overhead to reproduce twilight.

Leonardo's fame as an artist is based on only a few works, for his many interests took him away from painting. Unlike his humanist contemporaries, he was not particularly interested in Classical literature or archaeology. Instead, his passions were mathematics, engineering, and the natural world. He compiled volumes of detailed drawings and notes on anatomy, botany, geology, meteorology, architectural design, and mechanics. In his drawings of human figures, he sought not only the precise details of anatomy but also the geometric basis of perfect proportions (see "The Vitruvian Man," opposite). Leonardo's searching mind is

The Vitruvian Man

Artists throughout history have turned to geometric shapes and mathematical proportions to seek the ideal representation of the human form. Leonardo, and before him the first-century BCE Roman architect and engineer Vitruvius, equated the ideal man with both circle and square. Ancient Egyptian artists laid out square grids as aids to design (see "Egyptian Pictorial Relief," page 65). Medieval artists adapted a variety of figures, from triangles to pentagrams (see "Villard de Honnecourt," page 510).

Vitruvius, in his ten-volume *De architectura* (*On Architecture*), wrote: "For if a man be placed flat on his back, with his hands and feet extended, and a pair of compasses centered at his navel, the fingers and toes of his two hands and feet will touch the circumference of a circle described therefrom. And just as the human body yields a circular outline, so too a square figure may be found from it. For if we measure the distance from the soles of the feet to the top of the head, and then apply that measure to the outstretched arms, the breadth will be found to be the same as the height" (Book III, Chapter 1, Section 3). Vitruvius determined that the ideal body should be eight heads high. Leonardo added his own observations in the reversed writing he always used in his notebooks when he created his well-known diagram for the ideal male figure, called the Vitruvian Man.

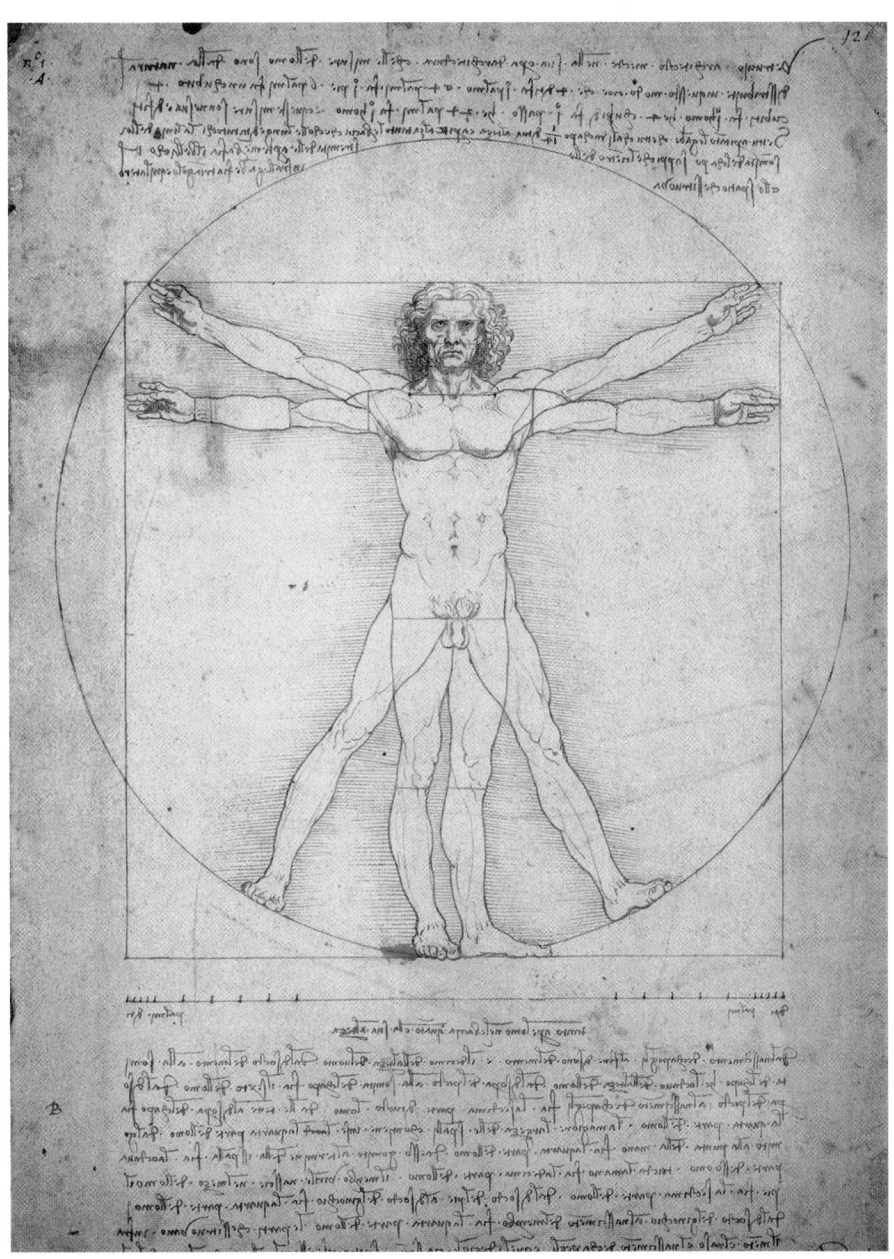

Leonardo da Vinci
VITRUVIAN MAN
c. 1490. Ink, 13½ × 9⅝"
(34.3 × 24.5 cm).
Galleria dell'Accademia, Venice.

20–6 • Raphael THE SMALL COWPER MADONNA
c. 1505. Oil on wood panel, 23⅜ × 17⅜" (59.5 × 44.1 cm).
National Gallery of Art, Washington, D.C.
Widener Collection (1942.9.57)

In the distance on a hilltop, Raphael has painted a scene he knew
well from his childhood, the domed church of San Bernardino, two
miles outside Urbino. The church contains the tombs of dukes of
Urbino, Federico and Guidobaldo da Montefeltro, and their wives
(SEE FIG. 19–27). Donato Bramante, whose architecture was key in
establishing the High Renaissance style, may have designed the
church.

evident in his drawings, not only of natural objects and human
beings, but also of machines, so clearly and completely worked
out that modern engineers have used them to construct working
models. He designed flying machines, a kind of automobile, a
parachute, and all sorts of military equipment, including a mobile
fortress. His imagination outran his means to bring his creations
into being. For one thing, he lacked a source of power other than
men and horses. For another, he may have lacked focus and
follow-through. His contemporaries complained that he never
finished anything and that his inventions distracted him from his
painting.

Leonardo returned to Milan in 1508 and lived there until
1513. He also lived for a time in the Vatican at the invitation of
Pope Leo X, but there is no evidence that he produced any works
of art during his stay. In 1516, he accepted the French king Francis

I's invitation to relocate to France as an advisor on architecture,
taking the *Mona Lisa* with him. He remained at Francis's court
until his death in 1519.

RAPHAEL. About 1505—while Leonardo was working on the
Mona Lisa—Raphael (Raffaello Santi or Sanzio, 1483–1520)
arrived in Florence from his native Urbino after studying in
Perugia with the city's leading artist, Perugino (SEE FIG. 19–31).
Raphael quickly became successful in Florence, especially with
small, polished paintings of the Virgin and Child, such as **THE
SMALL COWPER MADONNA** (named for a modern owner) of about
1505 **(FIG. 20–6)**. Already a superb painter technically, the youthful
Raphael shows his indebtedness to his teacher in the delicate tilt of
the figures' heads, the brilliant tonalities, and the pervasive sense of
serenity. But Leonardo's impact is also evident here in the simple
grandeur of these monumental shapes, the pyramidal composition
activated by the spiraling movement of the child, and the draperies
that cling to the Virgin's substantial form. In other Madonnas from
this period, Raphael included the young John the Baptist (SEE FIG.
INTRO–3), experimenting with the multiple figure interactions
pioneered by Leonardo in *The Virgin of the Rocks* (SEE FIG. 20–2).

At the same time as he was producing engaging images
of elegant Madonnas, Raphael was also painting portraits of
prosperous Florentine patrons. To commemorate the marriage in
1504 of 30-year-old cloth merchant Agnelo Doni to Maddalena
Strozzi, the 15-year-old daughter of a powerful banking family,
Doni commissioned from Raphael pendent portraits of the newly-
weds **(FIGS. 20–7, 20–8)**. They are flawlessly executed by the
mature painter at the peak of his illusionistic virtuosity. Like Piero
della Francesca in his portraits of Battista Sforza and Federico da
Montefeltro (SEE FIG. 19–27), Raphael silhouettes Maddalena and
Agnelo against a meticulously described panoramic landscape. But
unlike their predecessors, they turn to address the viewer. Agnelo is
commanding but casual, leaning his arm on a balustrade to add
three-dimensionality to his posture. Maddalena's pose imitates
Leonardo's innovative presentation of his subject in the *Mona Lisa*
(SEE FIG. 20–5), which Raphael had obviously seen in progress,
but with Maddalena there is no sense of mystery, indeed little
psychological presence, and Raphael follows tradition in
emphasizing the sumptuousness of her clothing and making
ostentatious display of her jewelry. Only the wisps of hair
that escape from her sculpted coiffure offer a hint of human
vulnerability in her haughty demeanor.

Raphael left Florence about 1508 for Rome, where Pope
Julius II put him to work almost immediately decorating rooms
(*stanze*, singular *stanza*) in the papal apartments. In the Stanza della
Segnatura (SEE FIG. 20–1)—the papal library—Raphael painted the
four branches of knowledge as conceived in the sixteenth century:
Religion (the *Disputà*, depicting discussions concerning the true
presence of Christ in the Eucharistic Host), Philosophy (the
School of Athens), Poetry (Parnassus, home of the Muses), and Law
(the Cardinal Virtues under Justice).

20-7 • Raphael AGNELO DONI
c. 1506. Oil on wood panel, 24½ × 17¼" (63 × 45 cm). Palazzo Pitti, Florence.

These portraits were not the only paintings commissioned by Agnelo Doni to commemorate his upwardly mobile marriage alliance with Maddalena Strozzi. He ordered a *tondo* portraying the holy family from rival artist Michelangelo (see Introduction, "A Closer Look"). Tradition holds that Doni tried to haggle with Michelangelo over the cost of the painting, but ultimately had to pay the price demanded by the artist.

20-8 • Raphael MADDALENA STROZZI
c. 1506. Oil on wood panel, 24½ × 17¼" (63 × 45 cm). Palazzo Pitti, Florence.

Raphael's most influential achievement in the papal rooms was *The School of Athens*, painted about 1510–1511 (see "A Closer Look," page 640). Here, the painter seems to summarize the ideals of the Renaissance papacy in a grand conception of harmoniously arranged forms in a rational space, as well as in the calm dignity of the figures that occupy it. If the learned Julius II did not actually devise the subjects, he certainly must have approved them. Greek philosophers Plato and Aristotle take center stage—placed to the right and left of the vanishing point—silhouetted against the sky and framed under three successive barrel vaults. Surrounding Plato and Aristotle are mathematicians, naturalists, astronomers, geographers, and other philosophers, debating and demonstrating their theories with and to onlookers and each other. The scene takes place in an immense barrel-vaulted interior, flooded with a clear, even light from a single source, and seemingly inspired by the

new design for St. Peter's, under construction at the time. The grandeur of the building is matched by the monumental dignity of the philosophers themselves, each of whom has a distinct physical and intellectual presence. The sweeping arcs of the composition are activated by the variety and energy of their poses and gestures, creating a dynamic unity that is a prime characteristic of High Renaissance art.

In 1515, Raphael was commissioned by Pope Leo X (pontificate 1513–1521) to provide designs on themes from the Acts of the Apostles to be woven into tapestries for the strip of blank wall below the fifteenth-century wall paintings of the Sistine Chapel (SEE FIG. 19–30). For the production of the tapestries, woven in Brussels, Raphael and his large workshop of assistants made full-scale charcoal drawings, then painted over them with color for the weavers to match (see "Raphael's Cartoons for Tapestries in the Sistine Ceiling," pages 646–647). Pictorial weaving was the most prestigious and expensive kind of wall decoration. With murals by the leading painters of the fifteenth century above and Michelangelo's work circling over all, Raphael must have felt both honored and challenged. The pope had given him the place of honor among the artists in the papal chapel.

The School of Athens ▸ by Raphael, fresco in the Stanza della Segnatura, Vatican, Rome.
c. 1510–1511. 19 × 27′ (5.79 × 8.24 m).

Looking down from niches in the walls are sculptures of Apollo, the god of sunlight, rationality, poetry, music, and the fine arts; and of Minerva, the goddess of wisdom and the mechanical arts.

Plato points upward to the realm of ideas and pure forms that were at the center of his philosophy. His pupil Aristotle gestures toward his surroundings, signifying the empirical world that for him served as the basis for understanding.

The figure bent over a slate with a compass is Euclid, the father of geometry. Vasari claimed that Raphael gave this mathematician the portrait likeness of Bramante, the architect whose redesigned St. Peter's was under construction not far from this room.

Raphael placed his own portrait in a group that includes the geographer Ptolemy, who holds a terrestrial globe, and the astronomer Zoroaster, who holds a celestial globe.

The brooding figure of Heraclitus, a late addition to the composition, is a portrait of Michelangelo, who was working next door on the ceiling of the Sistine Chapel, and whose monumental figural style is here appropriated (or is it mimicked?) by Raphael. The stonecutter's boots on his feet refer to Michelangelo's self-identification—or Raphael's insistence that he be seen—as a sculptor rather than a painter.

This figure is usually identified as Diogenes the Cynic following Vasari's account of the painting. It is more likely that he is Socrates, however. The cup next to him could refer to his deadly draught of hemlock, and his recumbent position recalls his teaching from his prison bed.

The group of figures gathered around Euclid illustrate the various stages of understanding: literal learning, dawning comprehension, anticipation of the outcome, and assisting the teacher. Raphael received acclaim for his ability to communicate so clearly through the poses and expressions of his figures.

SEE MORE: View the Closer Look feature for *The School of Athens* **www.myartslab.com**

MICHELANGELO'S EARLY WORK. Michelangelo Buonarroti (1475–1564) was born in the Tuscan town of Caprese into an impoverished Florentine family that laid a claim to nobility—a claim the artist carefully advanced throughout his life. He grew up in Florence, where at age 13 he was apprenticed to Ghirlandaio (SEE FIG. 19–32), in whose workshop he learned the technique of fresco painting and studied drawings of Classical monuments. Soon the talented youth joined the household of Lorenzo the Magnificent, head of the ruling Medici family, where he came into contact with Neoplatonic philosophy and studied sculpture with Bertoldo di Giovanni, a pupil of Donatello. After Lorenzo died in 1492, Michelangelo traveled to Venice and Bologna, then returned to Florence.

Michelangelo's major early work at the turn of the century was a marble sculpture of the **PIETÀ**, commissioned by a French cardinal and installed as a tomb monument in Old St. Peter's **(FIG. 20–9)**. The theme of the *pietà* (in which the Virgin supports and mourns the dead Jesus in her lap), long popular in northern Europe (SEE FIG. 17–19), was an unusual theme in Italy at the time. Michelangelo traveled to the marble quarries at Carrara in central Italy to select the block from which to make this large work, a practice he was to continue for nearly all of his sculpture. The choice of stone was important to him because he envisioned his sculpture as already existing within the marble, needing only his tools to set it free. Michelangelo was a poet as well as an artist, and later wrote in his Sonnet 15: "The greatest artist has no conception which a single block of marble does not potentially contain within its mass, but only a hand obedient to the mind can penetrate to this image."

20-9 • Michelangelo
PIETÀ
c. 1500. Marble, height 5′8½″ (1.74 m). St. Peter's, Vatican, Rome.

EXPLORE MORE:
Gain insight from a primary source by Michelangelo on his *Pietà*
www.myartslab.com

Michelangelo's Virgin is a young woman of heroic stature holding the unnaturally smaller, lifeless body of her grown son. Inconsistencies of scale and age are forgotten, however, when contemplating the sweetness of expression, technical virtuosity of the carving, and smooth modeling of the luscious forms. Michelangelo's compelling vision of beauty was meant to be seen up close so that the viewer can look directly into Jesus' face. The 25-year-old artist is said to have slipped into the church at night to sign the statue on a strap across the Virgin's breast after it was finished, answering directly questions that had come up about the identity of its creator.

In 1501, Michelangelo accepted a Florentine commission for a statue of the biblical hero **DAVID** (**FIG. 20–10**), to be placed high atop a buttress of the cathedral. But when it was finished in 1504, the *David* was so admired that the city council instead placed it in the principal city square, next to the Palazzo della Signoria (SEE FIG. 17–2), the seat of Florence's government. There it stood as a reminder of Florence's republican status, which was briefly reinstated after the expulsion of the powerful Medici oligarchy in 1494. Although in its muscular nudity Michelangelo's *David* embodies the antique ideal of the athletic male nude, the emotional power of its expression and its concentrated gaze are entirely new. Unlike Donatello's bronze *David* (SEE FIG. 19–10), this is not a triumphant hero with the trophy head of the giant Goliath already under his feet. Slingshot over his shoulder and a rock in his right hand, Michelangelo's *David* knits his brow and stares into space, seemingly preparing himself psychologically for the danger ahead, a mere youth confronting a gigantic experienced warrior. No match for his opponent in experience, weaponry, or physical strength, Michelangelo's powerful *David* stands for the supremacy of right over might—a perfect emblem for the Florentines, who had recently fought the forces of Milan, Siena, and Pisa, and still faced political and military pressure.

THE SISTINE CHAPEL. Despite Michelangelo's contractual commitment to Florence Cathedral for additional statues, in 1505, Pope Julius II, who saw Michelangelo as an ideal collaborator in

20-10 • Michelangelo **DAVID**
1501–1504. Marble, height 17′ (5.18 m) without pedestal. Galleria dell'Accademia, Florence.

Michelangelo's most famous sculpture was cut from an 18-foot-tall marble block. The sculptor began with a small model in wax, then sketched the contours of the figure as they would appear from the front on one face of the marble. Then, according to his friend and biographer Vasari, he chiseled in from the drawn-on surface, as if making a figure in very high relief. The completed statue took four days to move on tree-trunk rollers down the narrow streets of Florence from the premises of the cathedral shop where he worked to its location outside the Palazzo della Signoria (SEE FIG. 17–2). In 1504, the Florentines gilded the tree stump and added a gilded wreath to the head and a belt of 28 gilt-bronze leaves, since removed. In 1873, the statue was replaced by a copy, and the original was moved into the museum of the Florence Academy.

20-11 • INTERIOR, SISTINE CHAPEL
Vatican, Rome. Built 1475–1481; ceiling painted 1508–1512; end wall, 1536–1541. The ceiling measures 45 × 128′ (13.75 × 39 m).

the artistic aggrandizement of the papacy, arranged for him to come to Rome to work on the spectacular tomb Julius planned for himself. Michelangelo began the tomb project, but two years later the pope ordered him to begin painting the ceiling of the **SISTINE CHAPEL** instead (**FIG. 20–11**).

Michelangelo considered himself a sculptor, but the strong-minded pope wanted paintings; work began in 1508. Michelangelo complained bitterly in a sonnet to a friend: "This miserable job has given me a goiter….The force of it has jammed my belly up beneath my chin. Beard to the sky….Brush splatterings make a pavement of my face…. I'm not a painter." Despite his physical misery as he stood on a scaffold, painting the ceiling just above him, the results were extraordinary, and Michelangelo established a new and remarkably powerful style in Renaissance painting.

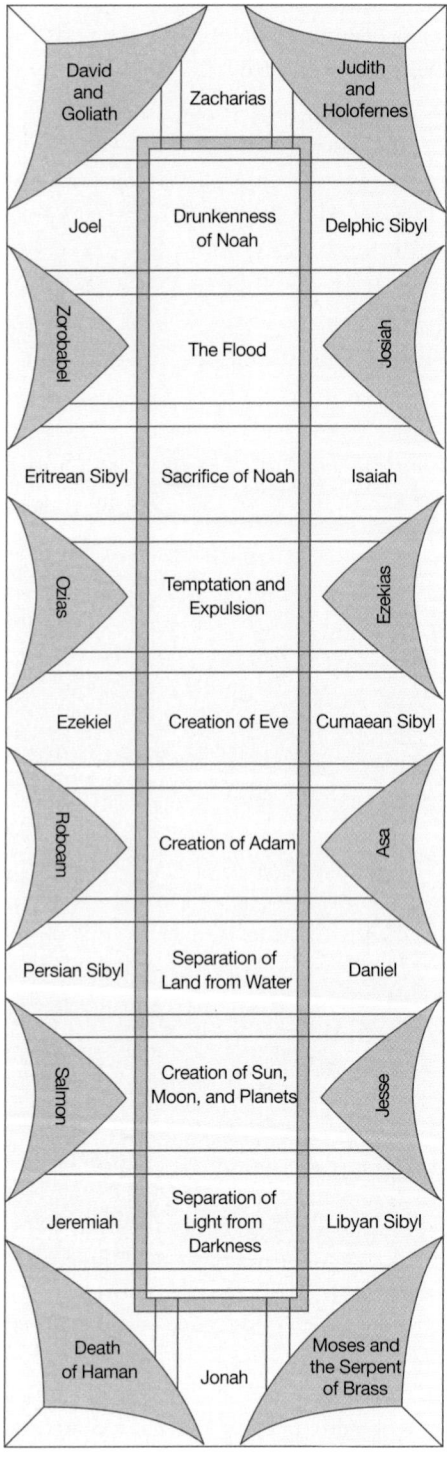

David and Goliath	Zacharias	Judith and Holofernes
Joel	Drunkenness of Noah	Delphic Sibyl
Zorobabel	The Flood	Josiah
Eritrean Sibyl	Sacrifice of Noah	Isaiah
Ozias	Temptation and Expulsion	Ezekias
Ezekiel	Creation of Eve	Cumaean Sibyl
Roboam	Creation of Adam	Asa
Persian Sibyl	Separation of Land from Water	Daniel
Salmon	Creation of Sun, Moon, and Planets	Jesse
Jeremiah	Separation of Light from Darkness	Libyan Sibyl
Death of Haman	Jonah	Moses and the Serpent of Brass

ALTAR

20–12 • Michelangelo SISTINE CHAPEL CEILING WITH DIAGRAM IDENTIFYING SCENES
1508–1512. Fresco.

Julius's initial order for the ceiling was simple: *trompe-l'oeil* coffers to replace the original star-spangled blue decoration. Later he wanted the 12 apostles seated on thrones on the triangular spandrels between the lunettes framing the windows. According to Michelangelo, when he objected to the limitations of Julius's plan, the pope told him to paint whatever he liked. This Michelangelo presumably did, although he was certainly guided by a theological advisor and his plan no doubt required the pope's approval. Then, as master painter, Michelangelo assembled a team of expert assistants to work with him.

In Michelangelo's design, an illusionistic marble architecture establishes a framework for the figures and narrative scenes on the vault of the chapel (FIG. 20–12). Running completely around the ceiling is a painted cornice with projections supported by pilasters decorated with "sculptured" *putti*. Between the pilasters are figures of prophets and sibyls (female seers from the Classical world) who were believed to have foretold Jesus' birth. Seated on the fictive cornice are heroic figures of nude young men (called **ignudi**, singular, *ignudo*), holding sashes attached to large gold medallions. Rising behind the *ignudi*, shallow bands of fictive stone span the center of the ceiling and divide it into nine compartments containing successive scenes from Genesis—the Creation, the Fall, and the Flood—beginning over the altar and ending near the chapel entrance. God's earliest acts of creation are therefore closest to the altar, the Creation of Eve at the center of the ceiling, followed by the imperfect actions of humanity: Temptation, Fall, Expulsion from Paradise, and God's eventual destruction of all people except Noah and his family by the Flood. The eight triangular spandrels over the windows contain paintings of the ancestors of Jesus.

Perhaps the most familiar scene on the ceiling is the **CREATION OF ADAM** (FIG. 20–13), where Michelangelo captures the moment when God charges the languorous Adam with the spark of life. As if to echo the biblical text, Adam's heroic body, outstretched arm, and profile almost mirror those of God, in whose image he has been created. Emerging under God's other arm, and looking across him in the direction of her future mate, is the robust and energetic figure of Eve before her creation. Directly below Adam, an *ignudo* grasps a bundle of oak leaves and giant acorns, which refer to Pope Julius's family name (della Rovere, or "of the oak") and possibly also to a passage in the prophecy of Isaiah (61:3): "They will be called oaks of justice, planted by the Lord to show his glory."

20–13 • Michelangelo **CREATION OF ADAM, SISTINE CHAPEL CEILING**
1511–1512. Fresco. 9'2" × 18'8" (2.8 × 5.7 m).

Raphael's Cartoons for Tapestries in the Sistine Chapel

The Sistine Chapel was a major focus of papal patronage during the Renaissance. The building was constructed in 1475–1481 by Sixtus IV, who also began its painted embellishment by calling a constellation of illustrious artists to Rome in the early 1480s to create a band of framed frescos recounting the life of Moses on one wall and the life of Christ on the other (SEE FIG. 19–30). Between 1508 and 1512, Michelangelo painted the chapel's ceiling at the behest of Julius II. And soon after he became pope in 1513, Leo X commissioned Raphael to produce ten cartoons (full-size preparatory designs for a work of art executed in another medium) for a lavish set of tapestries portraying scenes from the lives of SS. Peter and Paul that would complete the decorative program on the chapel's lower level. At the time, these would have been considered its most prestigious and expensive works of art. The tapestry program cost Leo X more than five times what Julius II had paid Michelangelo to paint the ceiling. For designing the program and producing the cartoons, however, Raphael only received a sixteenth of the total cost of the tapestries; the expense here involved production more than design.

The cartoons were created in Raphael's workshop between 1515 and 1516. Raphael was clearly the intellect behind the compositions, and he participated in the actual preparation and execution. This was a prestigious commission that would reflect directly on the reputation of the master. But he could not have accomplished this imposing task in a little over a year without the collaboration of numerous assistants working in his thriving workshop. The completed cartoons—first drawn with charcoal on paper (160–170 separate sheets were glued together to form the expanse of a single tapestry) and then

overpainted with color—were sent to Brussels, where they were woven into tapestries in the workshop of Pieter van Aelst. The first was complete in 1517, seven were hanging in the chapel for Christmas 1519, and the entire cycle was installed by Leo X's death in 1521.

The process of creation, from design through production, can be charted by examining the tapestry portraying *Christ's Charge to Peter* (John 21:15–17; Matthew 16:17–19) at three stages in its development. We have Raphael's preliminary drawing (FIG. A), where models—it is tempting to see these as Raphael's assistants, stripped to their drawers to help the master work out his composition—are posed to enact the moment when Jesus addresses his apostles. This is a preliminary idea for the pose of Christ. In the final cartoon (FIG. B), Raphael changes Christ's gesture so that he addresses the kneeling Peter specifically rather than the whole apostolic group; for the patron, this would be an important detail since papal power rested in the belief that Christ had transferred authority to Peter, who was considered the first pope, with subsequent popes inheriting this authority in unbroken succession. Comparison of drawing and cartoon also reveals an important aspect of the design process.

The cartoon reverses the figural arrangement of the drawing because in the production process the tapestry would be woven from the back, and if the weavers followed the reversed version of the composition on the cartoon, the resulting tapestry (FIG. C) would show the scene in its intended orientation. Comparison of cartoon and tapestry also indicates that the weavers were not required to follow their models slavishly. They have embellished the costume of Christ, perhaps in an attempt to assure that the viewers' attention will be immediately directed to this most important figure in the scene.

After they had been used to create the tapestries hung in the Sistine Chapel, Raphael's cartoons remained in Brussels, where several additional sets of tapestries were made from them—one for Henry VIII of England, another for Francis I of France—before seven surviving cartoons were acquired in 1623 by the future Charles I of England. They remain in the British Royal Collection. The tapestries themselves, although still in the Vatican, are displayed in the museum rather than on the walls of the chapel for which they were originally conceived, as one of the most prestigious artistic projects from the peak of the Roman High Renaissance.

A. Raphael STUDY FOR CHRIST'S CHARGE TO PETER c. 1515. Red chalk. Royal Library, Windsor Castle.

B. Raphael
CARTOON FOR TAPESTRY PORTRAYING CHRIST'S CHARGE TO PETER
c. 1515–1516. Distemper on paper (now transferred to canvas), 11′1″ × 17′4″ (3.4 × 5.3 m). Lent by Her Majesty the Queen to the Victoria & Albert Museum, London

C. Shop of Pieter van Aelst, Brussels, after cartoons by Raphael and assistants **CHRIST'S CHARGE TO PETER**
Woven 1517, installed 1519 in the Sistine Chapel. Wool and silk with silver-gilt wrapped threads. Musei Vaticani, Pinacoteca, Rome.

MICHELANGELO AT SAN LORENZO. After the Medici regained power in Florence in 1512, and Leo X succeeded Julius in 1513, Michelangelo became chief architect for Medici family projects at the church of San Lorenzo in Florence—including a new chapel for the tombs of Lorenzo the Magnificent, his brother Giuliano, and two younger dukes, also named Lorenzo and Giuliano, ordered in 1519 for the so-called New Sacristy (SEE FIG. 19–4). The older men's tombs were never built to Michelangelo's designs, but the unfinished tombs for the younger relatives were placed on opposite side walls (FIG. 20–14).

Each of the two monuments consists of an idealized portrait of the deceased, who turns to face the family's unfinished ancestral tomb. The men are dressed in a sixteenth-century interpretation of Classical armor and seated in wall niches above pseudo-Classical sarcophagi. Balanced precariously atop the sarcophagi are male and female figures representing the times of day. Their positions would not seem so unsettling had reclining figures of river gods been installed below them, as originally planned, but even so there is a conspicuous tension here between the substantiality of the figures and the limitations imposed on them by their architectural surrounds. In the tomb illustrated here, Michelangelo represents Giuliano as the Active Life, and his sarcophagus figures are allegories of Night and Day. Night at left is accompanied by her symbols: a star and crescent moon on her tiara; poppies, which induce sleep; and an owl under the arch of her leg. The huge mask at her back may allude to Death, since Sleep and Death were said to be the children of Night. Some have seen in this mask that glares out at viewers in the chapel a self-portrait of the artist, serving both as signature and as a way of proclaiming his right to be here because of his long relationship with the family. On the other tomb, Lorenzo, representing the Contemplative Life, is supported by Dawn and Evening.

Concurrent with work on the Medici tombs was the construction of a new library at San Lorenzo. The idea for the library belongs to Cardinal Giulio de' Medici and dates to 1519, but it was only after he was elected Pope Clement VII in 1523 that the money became available to realize it. Michelangelo was commissioned to design and also supervise construction of the new **VESTIBULE** (FIG. 20–15) and reading room and to spare no expense in making them both grand and ambitious. The pope paid keen attention to the library's progress—not, he said, to verify the quality of the design, but because the project had a special interest for him.

20–14 • Michelangelo TOMB OF GIULIANO DE' MEDICI WITH ALLEGORICAL FIGURES OF NIGHT AND DAY
New Sacristy (Medici Chapel), church of San Lorenzo, Florence. 1519–1534. Marble, height of seated figure approx. 5'10" (1.8 m).

Michelangelo coordinated his work within a decorative tradition established at San Lorenzo when Brunelleschi designed the church itself a century earlier (SEE FIG. 19–4), using stylized architectural elements carved in dark gray *pietra serena*, set against and within a contrasting white wall. However, Michelangelo plays with the Classical architectural etiquette that Brunelleschi had used to create such clarity, harmony, and balance in the nave. In Michelangelo's vestibule, chunky columns are recessed into rectangular wall niches that can barely contain them. They are crowded and overlapped by the aggressive lateral extension of the pediment over the door. The door itself is broken into parts, sides jutting forward as fluted pilasters that are then partially obscured by the frame around the opening. The three flights of stairs leading up to the reading room almost fill the vestibule, and the central stairs cascade forward forcefully toward visitors, hardly encouraging them to go against the flow and step up. Through their playfulness, these creative combinations of architectural forms draw attention to themselves and their design rather than the function of the building or the comfortable accommodation of its users.

Fearing for his life when ongoing political struggles flared up in Florence, Michelango returned to Rome in 1534 and settled permanently. He had left both the Medici chapel and the library unfinished. In 1557, he sent a plaster model of the library staircase to Florence to assure that its completion conformed to his design. In 1545, his students had assembled the tomb sculptures, including unfinished figures of the times of day, into the composition we see today.

The figures of the dukes are finely finished, but the times of day are notable for their contrasting areas of rough unfinished and polished marble. These are the only unfinished sculptures Michelangelo apparently permitted to be put in place, and we do not know what his reasons were. Michelangelo specialists, characterizing these works with the word *nonfinito* ("unfinished"), propose that Michelangelo had begun to view his artistic creations as symbols of human imperfection. Indeed, Michelangelo's poetry often expressed his belief that humans could achieve perfection only in death.

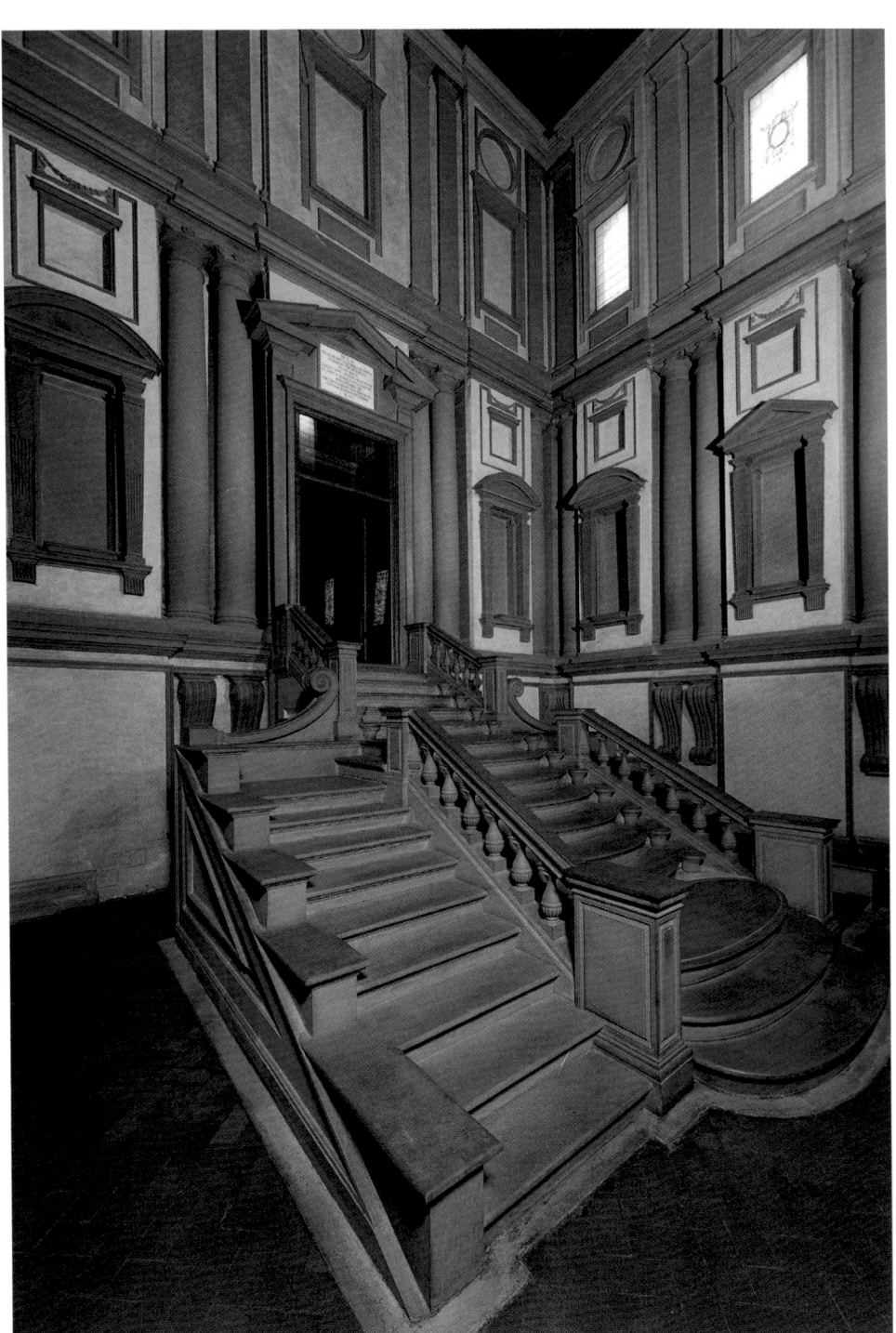

20–15 • Michelangelo
VESTIBULE OF THE LAURENTIAN LIBRARY
Church of San Lorenzo, Florence. Begun 1524; stairway designed 1550s.

ARCHITECTURE IN ROME AND THE VATICAN

The election of Julius II as pope in 1503 crystallized a resurgence of papal power, but France, Spain, and the Holy Roman Empire all had designs on Italy. During his ten-year papacy, Julius fought wars and formed alliances to consolidate his power. He also enlisted Bramante, Raphael, and Michelangelo as architects to carry out his vision of a revitalized Rome as the center of a new Christian architecture, inspired by the achievements of their fifteenth-century predecessors as well as the monuments of antiquity. Although most commissions were for churches, opportunities also arose to build urban palaces and country villas.

BRAMANTE.   Donato Bramante (1444–1514) was born near Urbino and trained as a painter, but turned to architectural design early in his career. About 1481, he became attached to the Sforza

court in Milan, where he would have known Leonardo da Vinci. In 1499, Bramante settled in Rome, but work came slowly. The architect was nearing 60 when Julius II asked him to redesign St. Peter's (see "St. Peter's Basilica," opposite) and the Spanish rulers Queen Isabella and King Ferdinand commissioned a small shrine over the spot in Rome where the apostle Peter was believed to have been crucified **(FIG. 20–16)**. In this tiny building, known as *Il Tempietto* ("Little Temple"), Bramante combined his interpretation of the principles of Vitruvius and Alberti from the stepped base, to the Doric columns and frieze (Vitruvius had advised that the Doric order be used for temples to gods of particularly forceful character), to the elegant balustrade. The centralized plan and the tall drum (circular wall) supporting a hemispheric dome recall Early Christian shrines built over martyrs' relics, as well as ancient Roman circular temples. Especially notable is the sculptural effect of the building's exterior, with its deep wall niches and sharp contrasts of light and shadow. Bramante's design called for a circular cloister around the church, but the cloister was never built.

ARCHITECTURE, PAINTING, AND SCULPTURE IN NORTHERN ITALY

While Rome was Italy's preeminent arts center at the beginning of the sixteenth century, wealthy and powerful families elsewhere also patronized the arts and letters just as the Montefeltro and Gonzaga had in Urbino and Mantua during the fifteenth century. The architects and painters working for these sixteenth-century patrons created fanciful structures and developed a new colorful, illusionistic painting style. The result was witty, elegant, and finely executed art designed to appeal to the jaded taste of the intellectual elite in cities such as Mantua, Parma, and Venice.

GIULIO ROMANO.   In Mantua, Federigo II Gonzaga (r. 1519–1540) continued the family tradition of patronage when, in 1524, he lured a Roman follower of Raphael, Giulio Romano (c. 1499–1546), to Mantua to build him a pleasure palace. Indeed, the Palazzo del

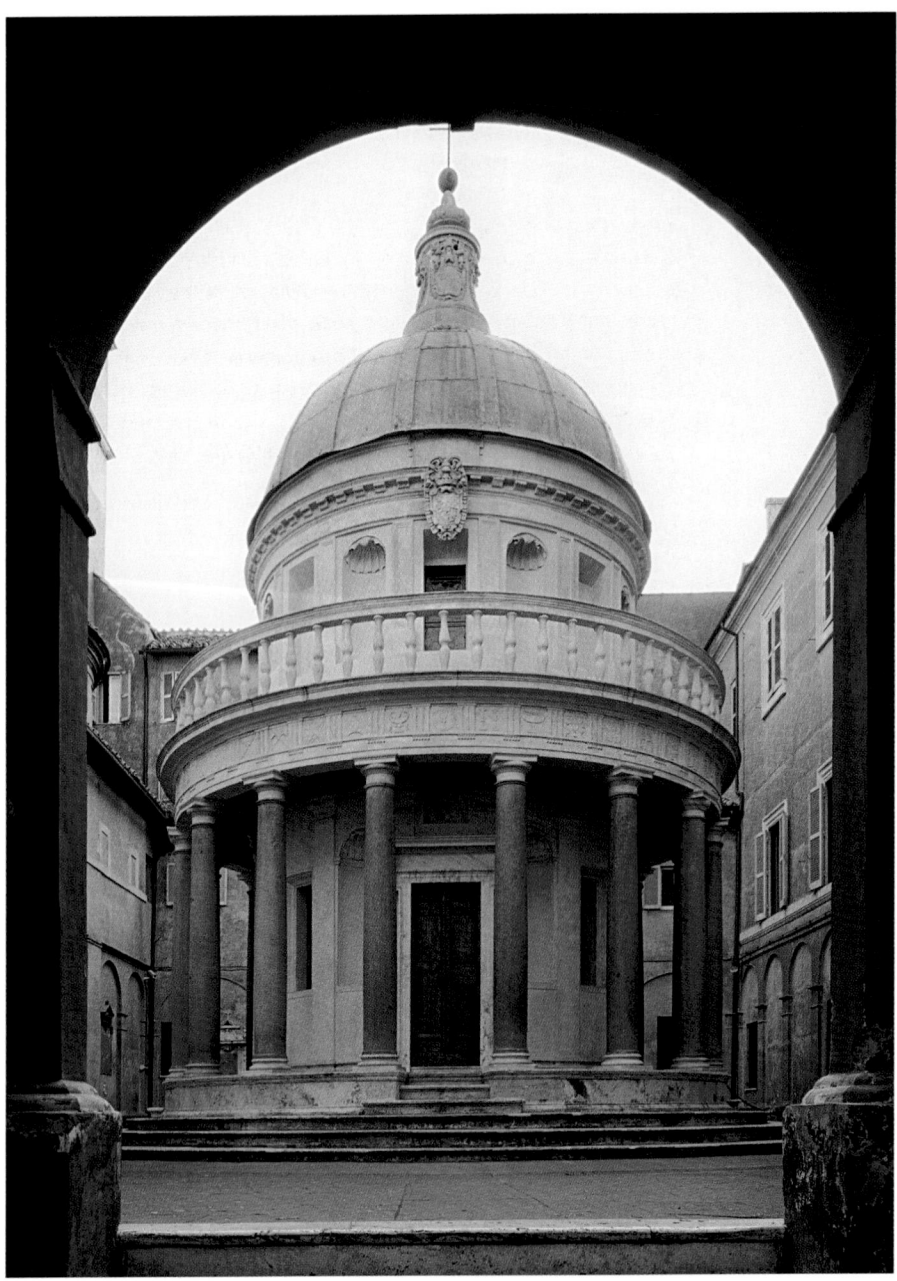

20-16 • Donato Bramante
IL TEMPIETTO, CHURCH OF SAN PIETRO IN MONTORIO
Rome. 1502–1510; dome and lantern were restored in the 17th century.

ART AND ITS CONTEXTS

St. Peter's Basilica

The history of St. Peter's in Rome is an interesting case of the effects of individual and institutional demands on a religious building of major sacred significance. The original church, now referred to as Old St. Peter's, was built in the fourth century by Constantine, the first Christian Roman emperor, to mark the grave of the apostle Peter, the first bishop of Rome and therefore considered the first pope. Because the site was so holy, Constantine's architect had to build a structure large enough to hold the crowds of pilgrims who came to visit St. Peter's tomb. To provide a platform for the church, a huge terrace was cut into the side of the Vatican Hill, across the Tiber River from the city. Here Constantine's architect erected a basilica with a new feature, a transept, to allow large numbers of visitors to approach the shrine at the front of the apse. The rest of the church was, in effect, a covered cemetery, carpeted with the tombs of believers who wanted to be buried near the apostle's grave. When it was built, Constantine's basilica, as befitted an imperial commission, was one of the largest buildings in the Roman world (interior length 368 feet, width 190 feet). For more than a thousand years it was the most important pilgrimage site in Europe.

In 1506, Pope Julius II made the astonishing decision to demolish the Constantinian basilica, which had fallen into disrepair, and to replace it with a new building. That anyone, even a pope, should have had the nerve to pull down such a venerated building is an indication of the extraordinary self-assurance of the Renaissance—and of Julius himself. To design and build the new church, the pope appointed Donato Bramante, who envisioned the new St. Peter's as a central-plan building, in this case a Greek cross (with four arms of equal length) crowned by an enormous dome. This design was intended to emulate the Early Christian tradition of constructing domed and round buildings over the tombs of martyrs (SEE FIG. 7–20), itself derived from the Roman practice of building centrally planned tombs (see "Central-Plan Churches," page 228). In Renaissance thinking, the central plan and dome symbolized the perfection of God.

The deaths of pope and architect in 1513–1514 put a temporary halt to the project. Successive plans by Raphael, Antonio da Sangallo, and others changed the Greek cross into a Latin cross (with three shorter arms and one long one) to provide the church with an extended nave. However, when Michelangelo was appointed architect in 1546, he returned to the Greek-cross plan and simplified Bramante's design to create a single, unified space covered with a hemispherical dome. The dome was finally completed some years after Michelangelo's death by Giacomo della Porta, who retained Michelangelo's basic design but gave the dome a taller profile (SEE FIG. 20–35).

During the Counter-Reformation, the Catholic Church emphasized congregational worship; as a result, more space was needed to house the congregation and allow for processions. To expand the church—and to make it more closely resemble Old St. Peter's—Pope Paul V in 1606 commissioned the architect Carlo Maderno to change Michelangelo's Greek-cross plan back once again into a Latin-cross plan. Maderno extended the nave to its final length of slightly more than 636 feet and added a new façade, thus completing St. Peter's as we see it today. Later in the seventeenth century, the sculptor and architect Gianlorenzo Bernini changed the approach to the basilica by surrounding it with a great colonnade, like a huge set of arms extended to embrace the faithful as they approach the principal church of Western Christendom.

Old St. Peter's
4th century

Bramante, Plan for New
St. Peter's
1506

Michelangelo, Plan for New
St. Peter's
1546–1564

Maderno, Plan of St. Peter's
Basilica
1607–1612

SEE MORE: View a simulation about plans for St. Peter's Basilica **www.myartslab.com**

20-17 • Giulio Romano COURTYARD FAÇADE, PALAZZO DEL TÈ, MANTUA
1527–1534.

SEE MORE: Click the Google Earth link for the Palazzo del Tè **www.myartslab.com**

Tè **(FIG. 20–17)** devoted more space to gardens, pools, and stables than to rooms for residential living. Since Federigo and his erudite friends would have known Classical orders and proportions, they could appreciate the playfulness with which they are used here. The building is full of visual jokes, such as lintels masquerading as arches and triglyphs that slip sloppily out of place. Like the similar, if more sober, subversions of Classical architectural decorum in Michelangelo's contemporary Laurentian Library (SEE FIG. 20–15), its sophisticated humor and exquisite craft have been seen as a precursor to Mannerism or as a manifestation of Mannerism itself.

Giulio Romano continued his witty play in the decoration of the two principal rooms. One, dedicated to the loves of the gods, depicted the marriage of Cupid and Psyche. The other room is a remarkable feat of *trompe-l'oeil* painting in which the entire building seems to be collapsing about the viewer as the gods defeat the giants **(FIG. 20–18)**. Here, Giulio Romano accepted the challenge Andrea Mantegna had laid down in the Camera Picta of the Gonzaga Palace (SEE FIG. 19–29), painted for Federigo's grandfather: to dissolve architectural barriers and fantasize a world of playful delight beyond the walls and ceilings. But the Palazzo del Tè was not just fun and games. The unifying

20-18 • Giulio Romano FALL OF THE GIANTS
Sala dei Giganti, Palazzo del Tè. 1530–1532. Fresco.

themes were love and politics, the former focused on the separate apartments built to house Federigo's mistress, Isabella Boschetti. The palace was constructed in part as a place where they could meet beyond the watchful gaze of her husband. But the decoration also seems to reflect Federigo's dicey alliance with Charles V, who stayed in the palace in 1530 and again in 1532, when the scaffolding was removed from the Sala dei Giganti so the emperor could see the paintings in progress. He must have been impressed with his host's lavish new residence, and doubtless he saw a connection between these reeling paintings and his own military successes.

CORREGGIO. At about the same time that Giulio Romano was building and decorating the Palazzo del Tè, in nearby Parma an equally skillful master, Correggio (Antonio Allegri da Correggio, c. 1489–1534), was creating similarly theatrical effects with dramatic foreshortening in Parma Cathedral. Correggio's great work, the **ASSUMPTION OF THE VIRGIN** (FIG. 20–19), a fresco painted between about 1526 and 1530 in the cathedral's dome, distantly recalls the illusionism of Mantegna's ceiling in the Gonzaga Palace, but Correggio has also assimilated Leonardo da Vinci's use of *sfumato* and Raphael's idealism into his personal style. Correggio's

20–19 • Correggio ASSUMPTION OF THE VIRGIN
Main dome, interior, Parma Cathedral, Italy. c. 1526–1530. Fresco, diameter of base of dome approx. 36′ (11 m).

Assumption is a dazzling illusion—the architecture of the dome seems to dissolve and the forms seem to explode through the building, drawing viewers into the swirling vortex of saints and angels who rush upward amid billowing clouds to accompany the Virgin as she soars into heaven. Correggio's sensual rendering of the figures' flesh and clinging draperies contrasts with the spirituality of the theme (the miraculous transporting of the Virgin to heaven at the moment of her death). The viewer's strongest impression is of a powerful, upward-spiraling motion of alternating cool clouds and warm, alluring figures.

PROPERZIA DE' ROSSI. Very few women had the opportunity or inclination to become sculptors. Properzia de' Rossi (c. 1490–1529/30), who lived in Bologna, was an exception. She mastered many arts, including engraving, and was famous for her miniature sculptures, including an entire *Last Supper* carved on a peach pit! She carved several pieces in marble—two sibyls, two angels, and this relief of **JOSEPH AND POTIPHAR'S WIFE**—for the Cathedral of San Petronio in Bologna (**FIG. 20–20**). Vasari wrote that a rival male sculptor prevented her from being paid fairly and from securing additional commissions. This particular relief, according to Vasari, was inspired by her own love for a young man, which she got over by carving this panel. Joseph escapes, running, as the partially clad seductress snatches at his cloak. Properzia is the only woman Vasari included in the 1550 edition of *Lives of the Artists*.

VENICE AND THE VENETO

In the sixteenth century the Venetians did not see themselves as rivals of Florence and Rome, but rather as their superiors. Their city was the greatest commercial sea power in the Mediterranean; they had challenged Byzantium and now they confronted the Muslim Turks. Favored by their unique geographical situation—protected by water and controlling sea routes in the Adriatic Sea and the eastern Mediterranean—the Venetians became wealthy and secure patrons of the arts. Their Byzantine heritage, preserved by their conservative tendencies, encouraged an art of rich patterned surfaces emphasizing light and color.

The idealized style and oil-painting technique initiated by the Bellini family in the late fifteenth century (see Chapter 19) were developed further by sixteenth-century Venetian painters. Venetians were the first in Italy to use oils for painting on both wood panel and canvas. Possibly because they were a seafaring people accustomed to working with large sheets of canvas, and possibly because humidity made their walls crack and mildew, the Venetians were also the first to cover walls with large canvas paintings instead of frescos. Because oils dried slowly, errors could be corrected and changes made easily during the work. The flexibility of the canvas support, coupled with the radiance and depth of oil-suspended pigments, eventually made oil on canvas the preferred medium, especially since it was particularly well suited to the rich color and lighting effects favored by Giorgione and Titian, two of the city's major painters of the sixteenth century.

GIORGIONE. The career of Giorgione (Giorgio da Castelfranco, c. 1475–1510) was brief—he died from the plague—and most scholars accept only four or five paintings as entirely by his hand. But his importance to Venetian painting is critical. He introduced new, enigmatic pastoral themes, known as *poesie* (or "painted poems"), that were inspired by the contemporary literary revival of ancient pastoral verse. He is significant for his sensuous nude figures, and, above all, for his appreciation of nature in his landscape painting. His early life and training are undocumented, but his work suggests that he studied with Giovanni Bellini. Perhaps Leonardo da Vinci's subtle lighting system and mysterious, intensely observed landscapes also inspired him.

Giorgione's most famous work, called today **THE TEMPEST** (**FIG. 20–21**), was painted shortly before his death, potentially in response to personal, private impulses—as with many modern artists—rather than to fulfill an external commission. Simply trying to understand what is happening in the picture piques our interest. At the right, a woman is seated on the ground, nude except for the end of a long white cloth thrown over her shoulders. Her nudity seems maternal rather than erotic as she nurses the baby at her side. Across the dark, rock-edged spring stands a man wearing the uniform of a German mercenary soldier. His head is turned in the direction of the woman, but he only appears to have paused for a moment before continuing to turn toward the viewer. X-rays of

the painting show that Giorgione altered his composition while he was still at work on it—the soldier replaces a second woman. Inexplicably, a spring gushes forth between the figures to feed a lake surrounded by substantial houses, and in the far distance a bolt of lightning splits the darkening sky. Indeed, the artist's attention seems more focused on the landscape and the unruly elements of nature than on the figures.

TITIAN. In 1507, Giorgione took on a new assistant, Tiziano Vecellio, better known today as Titian (c. 1488–1576). For the next

20-21 • Giorgione THE TEMPEST
c. 1506. Oil on canvas, 32 × 28¾″ (82 × 73 cm). Galleria dell'Accademia, Venice.

20-22 • Titian THE PASTORAL CONCERT OR ALLEGORY ON THE INVENTION OF PASTORAL POETRY
c. 1510. Oil on canvas, 41¼ × 54¾″ (105 × 136.5 cm). Musée du Louvre, Paris.

three years, before Giorgione's untimely death, the two artists' careers were closely bound together. The painting known as **THE PASTORAL CONCERT (FIG. 20–22)** has been attributed to both of them, although today scholarly opinion favors Titian. As in Giorgione's *The Tempest*, the idyllic, fertile landscape, here bathed in golden, hazy late-afternoon sunlight, seems to be one of the main subjects of the painting. In this mythic world, two men—an aristocratic musician in rich red silks and a barefoot, singing peasant in homespun cloth—turn toward each other, seemingly unaware of the two naked women in front of them. One woman plays a pipe and the other pours water into a well; their swaths of white drapery sliding to the ground enhance rather than hide their nudity. Are they the musicians' muses? Behind the figures the sunlight illuminates another shepherd and his animals near lush woodland. The painting evokes a golden age of love and innocence recalled in

ancient Roman pastoral poetry. In fact, the painting is now interpreted as an allegory on the invention of poetry. Titian displays here his renowned talent for painting sensuous female nudes whose bodies seem to glow with an incandescent light, inspired by flesh and blood beauty as much as any source from poetry or art.

Titian's early life is obscure. He supposedly began an apprenticeship as a mosaicist, then studied painting under Gentile and Giovanni Bellini. He was about 20 when he began work with Giorgione, and whatever Titian's early work had been, he had completely absorbed Giorgione's style by the time Giorgione died two years later. Titian completed paintings that they had worked on together, and when Giovanni Bellini died in 1516, Titian became the official painter to the republic of Venice.

In 1519, Jacopo Pesaro, commander of the papal fleet that had defeated the Turks in 1502, commissioned Titian to commemorate the victory in a votive altarpiece for a side-aisle chapel in the Franciscan church of Santa Maria Gloriosa dei Frari in Venice. Titian worked on the painting for seven years and changed the concept three times before he finally came up with a revolutionary composition—one that complemented the viewer's approach from the left. He created an asymmetrical setting of huge columns on high bases soaring right out of the frame (FIG. 20–23). Into this architectural setting, he placed the Virgin and Child on a high throne at one side and arranged saints and the Pesaro family below on a diagonal axis, crossing at the central figure of St. Peter (a reminder of Jacopo's role as head of the papal forces in 1502). The red of Francesco Pesaro's brocade garment and of the banner diagonally across sets up a contrast of primary colors against St. Peter's blue tunic and yellow mantle and the red and blue draperies of the Virgin. St. Maurice (behind the kneeling Jacopo at the left) holds the banner with the papal arms, and a cowering

20-23 • Titian
PESARO MADONNA
1519–1526. Oil on canvas,
16′ × 8′10″ (4.9 × 2.7 m).
Side-aisle altarpiece, Santa Maria
Gloriosa dei Frari, Venice.

Women Patrons of the Arts

In the sixteenth century, many wealthy women, from both the aristocracy and the merchant class, were enthusiastic patrons of the arts. The Habsburg princesses Margaret of Austria and Mary of Hungary presided over brilliant humanist courts. The marchesa of Mantua, Isabella d'Este (1474–1539), became a patron of painters, musicians, composers, writers, and literary scholars. Married to Francesco II Gonzaga at age 15, she had great beauty, great wealth, and a brilliant mind that made her a successful diplomat and administrator. A true Renaissance woman, her motto was the epitome of rational thinking—"Neither through Hope nor Fear." An avid collector of manuscripts and books, she sponsored the publication of an edition of Virgil while still in her twenties. She also collected ancient art and objects, as well as works by contemporary Italian artists such as Mantegna, Leonardo, Perugino, Correggio, and Titian. Her study in her Mantuan palace was a veritable museum. The walls above the storage and display cabinets were painted in fresco by Mantegna, and the carved wood ceiling was covered with mottoes and visual references to Isabella's impressive literary interests.

Titian ISABELLA D'ESTE
1534–1536. Oil on canvas, 40⅛ × 25³⁄₁₆″ (102 × 64.1 cm).
Kunsthistorisches Museum, Vienna.

Turkish captive reminds the viewer of the Christian victory. The arresting image of the youth who turns to meet our gaze at lower right guarantees our engagement, and light floods in from above, illuminating not only this and other faces, but also the great columns, where *putti* in the clouds carry a cross. Titian was famous for his mastery of light and color even in his own day, but this altarpiece demonstrates that he also could draw and model as solidly as any Florentine. The perfectly balanced composition, built on diagonals instead of a vertical and horizontal grid, looks forward to the art of the seventeenth century.

In 1529, Titian, who was well known outside Venice, began a long professional relationship with Emperor Charles V, who vowed to let no one else paint his portrait and ennobled Titian in 1533. The next year Titian was commissioned to paint a portrait of Isabella d'Este (see "Women Patrons of the Arts," above). Isabella was past 60 when Titian portrayed her in 1534–1536, but she asked to appear as she had in her twenties. Titian was able to satisfy her wish by referring to an early portrait by another

artist, but he also conveyed the mature Isabella's strength, self-confidence, and energy.

No photograph can convey the vibrancy of Titian's paint surfaces, which he built up in layers of pure colors, chiefly red, white, yellow, and black. A recent scientific study of Titian's paintings revealed that he ground his pigments much finer than had earlier wood-panel painters. The complicated process by which he produced many of his works began with a charcoal drawing on the prime coat of lead white that was used to seal the pores and smooth the surface of the rather coarse Venetian canvas. The artist then built up the forms with fine glazes of different colors, sometimes in as many as 10 to 15 layers. Titian and others had the advantage of working in Venice, the first place to have professional retail "color sellers." These merchants produced a wide range of specially prepared pigments, even mixing their oil paints with ground glass to increase their glowing transparency. Not until the second half of the sixteenth century did color sellers open their shops in other cities.

20-24 • Titian "VENUS" OF URBINO
c. 1538. Oil on canvas, 3'11" × 5'5" (1.19 × 1.65 m). Galleria degli Uffizi, Florence.

Paintings of nude reclining women became especially popular in sophisticated court circles, where male patrons could enjoy and appreciate the "Venuses" under the cloak of respectable Classical mythology. Seemingly typical of such paintings is the **"VENUS"** Titian delivered to Guidobaldo della Rovere, duke of Urbino, in spring 1538 **(FIG. 20–24)**. Here, we seem to see a beautiful Venetian courtesan, with deliberately provocative gestures, stretching languidly on her couch in a spacious palace, her glowing flesh and golden hair set off by white sheets and pillows. But for its original audience, art historian Rona Goffen has argued, the painting was more about marriage than mythology or seductiveness. The multiple matrimonial references in this work include the pair of *cassoni* (see "The Morelli–Nerli Wedding Chests," page 616) where servants are removing or storing the woman's clothing in the background, the bridal symbolism of the myrtle and roses she holds in her hand, and even the spaniel snoozing at her feet—a traditional symbol of fidelity and domesticity, especially when sleeping so peacefully. Titian's picture might be associated with Duke Guidobaldo's marriage in 1534 to the 10-year-old Giulia Verano. Four years later, when this painting arrived, she would have been considered an adult rather

than a child bride. It seems to represent not a Roman goddess nor a Venetian courtesan, but a physically and emotionally mature bride welcoming her husband into their lavish bedroom.

In his late work from a very lengthy career, Titian sought the essence of form and idea, not the surface perfection of his youthful paintings, in part because he was beset by failing eyesight and a trembling hand. Like Michelangelo, Titian outlived the Classical phase of the Renaissance and his late style profoundly influenced Italian art of the later years of the sixteenth century.

MANNERISM

A new style developed in Florence and Rome in the 1520s that art historians have associated with the death of Raphael and labeled "Mannerism," a word deriving from the Italian *maniera* (meaning "style"). Mannerism was an anti-Classical movement in which artificiality, grace, and elegance took priority over the ordered balance and lifelike references that were hallmarks of High Renaissance art. Patrons favored esoteric subjects, displays of extraordinary technical virtuosity, and the pursuit of beauty for its own sake. Painters and sculptors quoted from ancient and modern works of art in the same self-conscious manner that contemporary poets and authors were quoting from ancient and modern literary classics. Architects working in the Mannerist style designed buildings that defied uniformity and balance and used Classical orders in unconventional ways.

PAINTING

Painters working in the Mannerist style fearlessly manipulated and distorted accepted formal conventions, creating contrived compositions and irrational spatial environments. Figures take on elongated proportions, complicated artificial poses, enigmatic gestures, and dreamy expressions. The pictures are full of quoted references to the works of illustrious predecessors.

PONTORMO. The frescos and altarpieces painted between 1525 and 1528 by Jacopo da Pontormo (1494–1557) for the 100-year-old **CAPPONI CHAPEL** in the church of Santa Felicità in Florence **(FIG. 20–25)** bear the hallmarks of early Mannerist painting. Open on two sides, Brunelleschi's chapel forms an interior loggia in which frescos on the right-hand wall depict the Annunciation and **tondi** (circular paintings) under the cupola represent the four evangelists. In the *Annunciation* the Virgin accepts the angel's message but also seems moved by the adjacent vision of her future sorrow, as she sees her son's body lowered from the cross in the **ENTOMBMENT**, portrayed in the altarpiece on the adjoining wall **(FIG. 20–26)**.

Pontormo's ambiguous composition in the *Entombment* enhances the visionary quality of the altarpiece. Shadowy ground

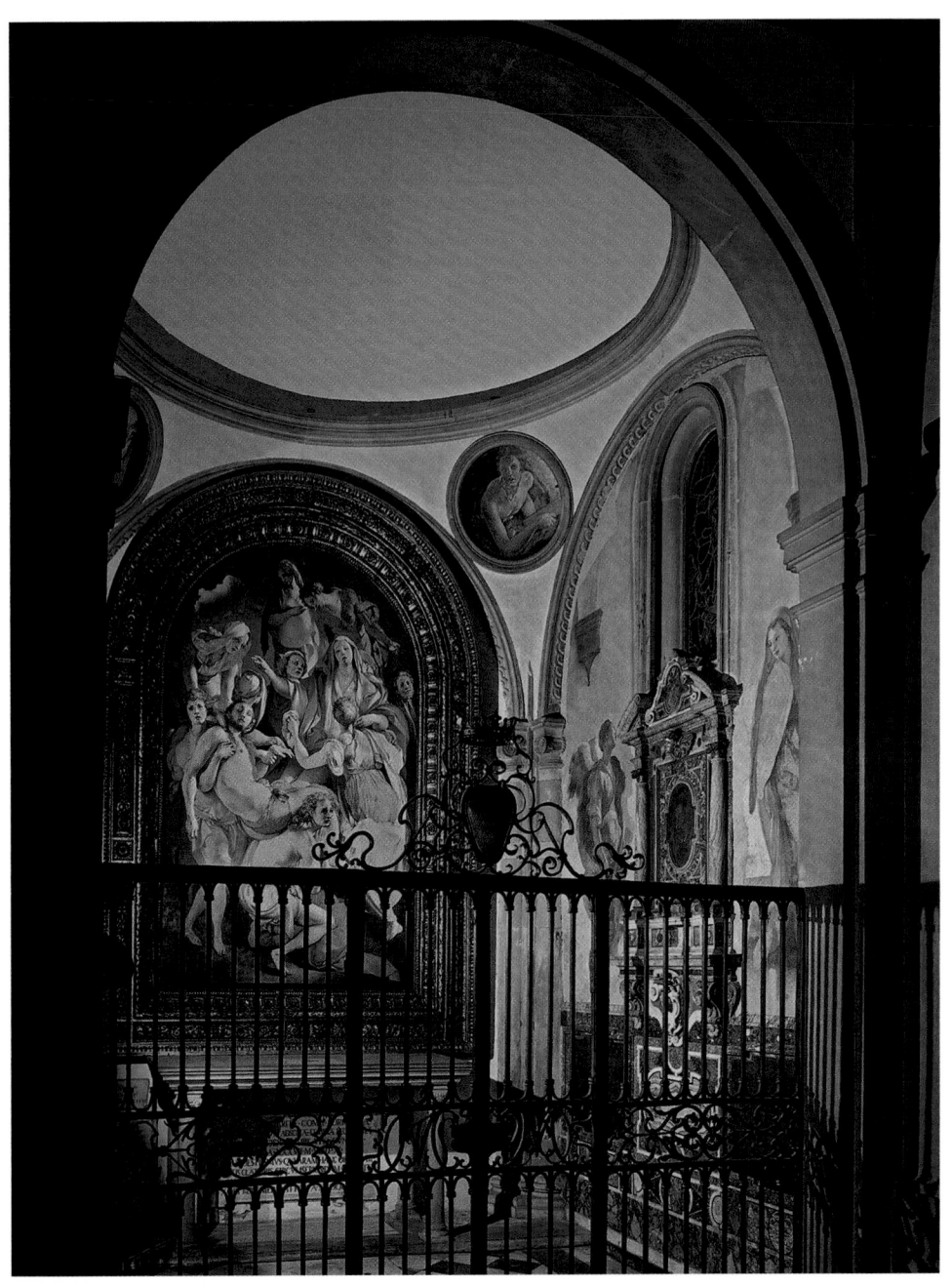

20-25 • CAPPONI CHAPEL, CHURCH OF SANTA FELICITÀ, FLORENCE
Chapel by Filippo Brunelleschi for the Barbadori family, 1419–1423; acquired by the Capponi family, who ordered paintings by Pontormo, 1525–1528.

20-26 • Pontormo ENTOMBMENT

Altarpiece in Capponi Chapel, church of Santa Felicità, Florence. 1525–1528. Oil and tempera on wood panel, 10′3″ × 6′4″ (3.1 × 1.9 m).

and cloudy sky give no sense of a specific location, and little sense of grounding for the figures. Some press forward into the viewer's space, while others seem to levitate or stand precariously on tiptoe. Pontormo chose a moment just after Jesus' removal from the cross, when the youths who have lowered him pause to regain their hold on the corpse, which recalls Michelangelo's Vatican *Pietà* (SEE FIG. 20–9). Odd poses and drastic shifts in scale charge the scene emotionally, but perhaps most striking is the use of weird colors in odd juxtapositions—baby blue and pink with accents of olive-green, yellow, and scarlet. The overall tone of the picture is set by the unstable youth crouching in the foreground, whose skintight bright pink shirt is shaded in iridescent, pale gray-green, and whose anxious expression is projected out of the painting, directly at the viewer.

PARMIGIANINO. When Parmigianino (Francesco Mazzola, 1503–1540) left his native Parma in 1524 for Rome, the strongest influence on his work was Correggio. In Rome, however, Parmigianino met

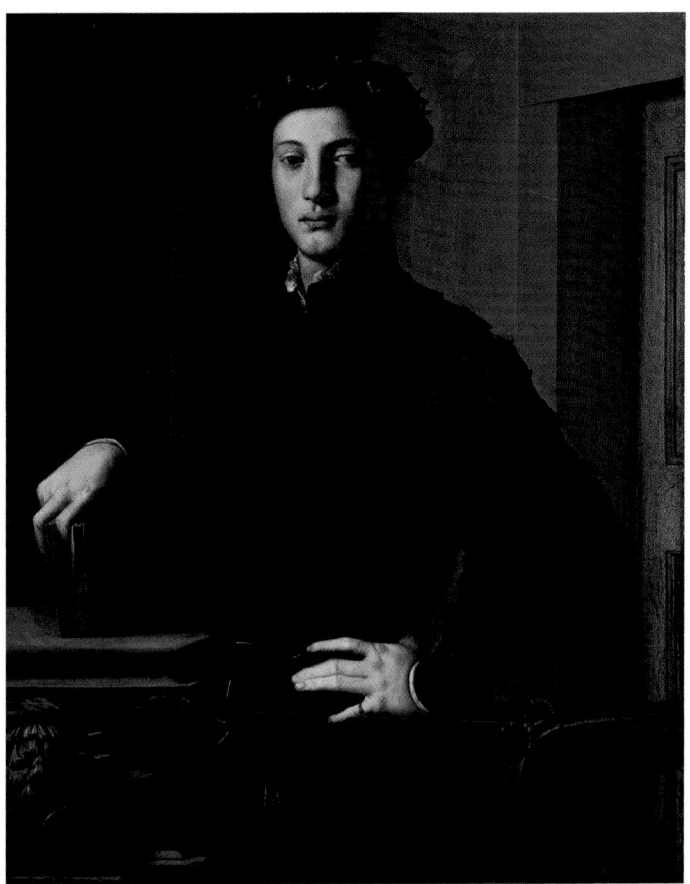

20-28 • Bronzino PORTRAIT OF A YOUNG MAN
c. 1540–1545. Oil on wood panel, 37½ × 29½″ (95.5 × 74.9 cm). Metropolitan Museum of Art, New York. The H. O. Havemayer Collection 29.100.16

Giulio Romano; he also studied the work of Raphael and Michelangelo. What he assimilated developed into a distinctive Mannerist style, calm but strangely unsettling. After the Sack of Rome in 1527, he moved to Bologna and then back to Parma.

Left unfinished at the time of his early death is a disconcerting painting known as the **MADONNA WITH THE LONG NECK (FIG. 20–27)**. The unnaturally proportioned figure of Mary, whose massive legs and lower torso contrast with her narrow shoulders and long neck and fingers, is presumably seated on a throne, but there is no seat in sight. The languid expanse of the sleeping child recalls the pose of the ashen Christ in a *pietà*. The plunge into a deep background to the right reveals a startlingly small St. Jerome, who unrolls a scroll in front of huge white columns that support absolutely nothing, whereas at the left a crowded mass of blushing boys blocks any view into the background. Like Pontormo, Parmigianino presents a well-known image in a challenging manner calculated to unsettle viewers.

20-27 • Parmigianino MADONNA WITH THE LONG NECK
1534–1540. Oil on wood panel, 7′1″ × 4′4″ (2.16 × 1.32 m). Galleria degli Uffizi, Florence.

BRONZINO. About 1522, Agnolo di Cosimo (1503–1572), whose nickname of "Bronzino" means "copper-colored" (just as we might call someone "Red"), became Pontormo's assistant, probably helping with the tondi in the corners of the Capponi Chapel (SEE FIG. 20–25). In 1530, he established his own workshop, though he continued to work with Pontormo on occasional large projects. In 1540, Bronzino became court painter to the Medici. Although he was a versatile artist who produced altarpieces, fresco decorations, and tapestry designs over his long career, he is best known today for his elegant portraits. Bronzino's virtuosity in rendering costumes and settings creates a rather cold and formal effect, but the self-contained demeanor of his subjects admirably conveys their haughtiness. **PORTRAIT OF A YOUNG MAN (FIG. 20–28)** demonstrates Bronzino's characteristic portrayal of his subjects as intelligent, aloof, elegant, and self-assured. The youth's spidery fingers toy with a book, suggesting his scholarly interests, but his wall-eyed stare creates a slightly unsettling, artificial effect, associating his face with the carved masks on the furniture. His costume seems more present than his personality.

Bronzino's **ALLEGORY WITH VENUS AND CUPID** is one of the strangest paintings of the sixteenth century **(FIG. 20–29)**. It contains all the formal, iconographical, and psychological characteristics of Mannerist art and could almost stand alone as a summary of the movement. Seven figures, two masks, and a dove interweave in an intricate, claustrophobic formal composition pressed breathlessly into the foreground plane. Taken as individual images, they display the exaggerated poses, graceful forms, polished surfaces, and delicate colors that characterize Mannerist art. But a closer look into this composition uncovers disturbing erotic attachments and bizarre irregularities. The painting's complex allegory and relentless ambiguity probably delighted mid-sixteenth-century courtiers who enjoyed equally sophisticated wordplay and esoteric Classical references, but for us it defies easy explanation. Nothing is quite what it seems.

Venus and her son Cupid engage in an unsettlingly lascivious dalliance, encouraged by a *putto* sauntering in from the right—representing Folly, Jest, or Playfulness—who is about to throw pink roses at them while stepping on a thorny branch that draws blood from his foot. Cupid gently kisses his mother and pinches her erect nipple while Venus snatches an arrow from his quiver, leading some scholars to suggest that the painting's title should be *Venus Disarming Cupid*. Venus holds the golden apple of discord given to her by Paris; her dove conforms to the shape of Cupid's foot without actually touching it, while a pair of masks lying at her feet reiterates the theme of duplicity. An old man, Time or Chronos, assisted by an outraged Truth or Night, pulls back a curtain to expose the couple. Lurking just behind Venus a monstrous serpent—which has the upper body and head of a beautiful young girl and the legs and claws of a lion—crosses her hands to hold a honeycomb and the stinger at the end of her tail. This strange hybrid has been identified both as Fraud and Pleasure.

20-29 • Bronzino ALLEGORY WITH VENUS AND CUPID
Mid 1540s. Oil on panel, 57½ × 46″ (1.46 × 1.16 m). National Gallery, London.
Reproduced by courtesy of the Trustees of the National Gallery, London

In the shadows to the left, a pale and screaming man tearing at his hair has recently been identified as a victim of syphilis, which raged as an epidemic during this period. This interpretation suggests that the painting could be a warning of the dangers of this disease, believed in the sixteenth century to be spread principally by coitus, kissing, and breast feeding, all of which are alluded to in the intertwined Cupid and Venus. But the complexity of the painting makes room for multiple meanings, and deciphering them would be typical of the sorts of games enjoyed by sixteenth-century intellectuals. Perhaps the allegory tells of the impossibility of constant love and the folly of lovers, which becomes apparent across time. Or perhaps it is an allegorical warning of the dangers of illicit sexual liaisons, including the pain, hair loss, and disfiguration of venereal disease. Maybe it is both, and even more. Duke Cosimo ordered the painting himself, and presented it as a diplomatic gift to King Francis I of France, who would doubtless have relished its overt eroticism and flawless execution.

SOFONISBA ANGUISSOLA. Northern Italy, more than any other part of the peninsula, produced a number of gifted women artists. In the latter half of the sixteenth century, Bologna, for example, boasted some two dozen women painters and sculptors, as well as a number of learned women who lectured at the university. Sofonisba Anguissola (c. 1532–1625), born into a noble family in Cremona (between Bologna and Milan), was unusual in that she was not the daughter of an artist. Her father gave all his children a humanistic education and encouraged them to pursue careers in literature, music, and especially painting. He consulted Michelangelo about Sofonisba's artistic talents in 1557, asking for a drawing that she might copy and return to be critiqued. Michelangelo evidently obliged because Sofonisba Anguissola's father wrote an enthusiastic letter of thanks.

Anguissola was a gifted portrait painter who also created miniatures, an important aspect of portraiture in the sixteenth century, when people had few means of recording the features of a lover, friend, or family member. Anguissola painted a miniature **SELF-PORTRAIT** holding a medallion, the border of which spells out her name and home town, Cremona (**FIG. 20–30**). The interlaced letters at the center of the medallion pose a riddle; they seem to form a monogram with the first letters of her sisters' names: Minerva, Europa, Elena. Such names are further evidence of the Anguissola family's enthusiasm for the Classics.

In 1560, Anguissola accepted the invitation of the queen of Spain to become a lady-in-waiting and court painter, a post she held for 20 years. Unfortunately, most of her Spanish works were lost in a seventeenth-century palace fire, but a 1582 Spanish inventory described her as "an excellent painter of portraits above all the painters of this time"—extraordinary praise in a court that patronized Titian. After her years at court, she returned to Sicily (a Spanish territory), where she died at age 92. Anthony Van Dyck met her in Palermo in 1624, where he sketched her and claimed that she was then 96 years old. He wrote that she

20-30 • Sofonisba Anguissola SELF-PORTRAIT
c. 1552. Oil on parchment on cardboard, 2½ × 3¼" (6.4 × 8.3 cm). Museum of Fine Arts, Boston. Emma F. Munroe Fund 60.155

advised him on positioning the light for her portrait, asking that it not be placed too high because the strong shadows would bring out her wrinkles.

LAVINIA FONTANA. Bolognese artist Lavinia Fontana (1552–1614) learned to paint from her father. By the 1570s, her success was so well rewarded that her husband, the painter Gian Paolo Zappi, gave up his own painting career to care for their large family and help his wife with the technical aspects of her work, such as framing. In 1603, Fontana moved to Rome as an official painter to the papal court. She also soon came to the attention of the Habsburgs, who became major patrons.

While still in her twenties, Fontana painted a **NOLI ME TANGERE** (**FIG. 20–31**), where Christ reveals himself for the first time to Mary Magdalen following his Resurrection, warning her not to touch him (John 20:17). Christ's broad-brimmed hat and spade refer to the passage in the Gospel of John that tells us that Mary Magdalen at first thought Christ was the gardener. In the middle distance Fontana portrays a second version of the Resurrection, where women followers of Christ discover an angel in his empty tomb. This secondary scene's dizzying diagonal plunge into depth is a typical feature of late Mannerist painting in Italy.

20-31 • Lavinia Fontana NOLI ME TANGERE
1581. Oil on canvas, 47⅜ × 36⅝″ (120.3 × 93 cm).
Galleria degli Uffizi, Florence.

SCULPTURE

Mannerist sculpture—often small in size and made from precious metals—stylizes body forms and foregrounds displays of technical skill in ways that are reminiscent of Mannerist painting.

CELLINI. The Florentine goldsmith and sculptor Benvenuto Cellini (1500–1571), who wrote a dramatic—and scandalous—autobiography and a practical handbook for artists, worked in the French court at Fontainebleau. There he made the famous **SALTCELLAR OF KING FRANCIS I (FIG. 20–32)**, a table accessory transformed into an elegant sculptural ornament by fanciful imagery and superb execution. In gold and enamel, the Roman sea god Neptune, representing the source of salt, sits next to a tiny boat-shape container that carries the seasoning, while a personification of Earth guards the plant-derived pepper, contained in the triumphal arch to her right. Representations of the seasons and the times of day on the base refer to both daily meal schedules and festive seasonal celebrations. The two main figures lean away from each other at impossible angles yet are connected and visually balanced by glance, gestures, and coordinated poses—they mirror each other with one bent and one straight leg. Their supple, elongated bodies and small heads reflect the Mannerist conventions of artists like Parmigianino. Cellini wrote, "I represented the Sea and the Land, both seated, with their legs intertwined just as some branches of the sea run into the land and the land juts into the sea…" (Cellini, *Autobiography*, trans G. Bull, p. 291).

20-32 • Benvenuto Cellini SALTCELLAR OF KING FRANCIS I OF FRANCE
1540–1543. Gold and enamel, 10½ × 13⅛″ (26.67 × 33.34 cm). Kunsthistorisches Museum, Vienna.

EXPLORE MORE: Gain insight from a primary source about Benvenuto Cellini
www.myartslab.com

GIAMBOLOGNA. In the second half of the sixteenth century, probably the most influential sculptor in Italy was Jean de Boulogne, better known by his Italian name, Giovanni da Bologna or Giambologna (1529–1608). Born in Flanders, he had settled by 1557 in Florence, where both the Medici family and the sizable Netherlandish community were his patrons. He not only influenced a later generation of Italian sculptors, he also spread the Mannerist style to the north through artists who came to study his work. Although inspired by Michelangelo, Giovanni favored graceful forms and poses, as in his gilded-bronze **ASTRONOMY, OR VENUS URANIA** (FIG. 20–33) of about 1573. The figure's identity is suggested by the astronomical device on the base of the plinth. Although she is based on a Classical prototype, Giambologna has twisted Venus' upper torso and arms to one side

20-33 • Giovanni da Bologna (Giambologna)
ASTRONOMY, OR VENUS URANIA
c. 1573. Bronze gilt, height 15¼″ (38.8 cm). Kunsthistorisches Museum, Vienna.

and bent her neck back in the opposite direction so that her chin is over her right shoulder, straining the torsion of the human body to its limits. Consequently, viewers are encouraged to walk around this figure to explore it fully; it cannot be understood from any single viewpoint. The elaborate coiffure and the detailed engraving of drapery texture contrast strikingly with the smooth, gleaming flesh of Venus' body. Following standard practice for cast-metal sculpture, Giambologna replicated this statuette several times for different patrons.

ART AND THE COUNTER-REFORMATION

Pope Clement VII, whose miscalculations had spurred Emperor Charles V to attack and destroy Rome in 1527, also misjudged the threat to the Church and to papal authority posed by the Protestant Reformation. His failure to address the issues raised by the reformers enabled the movement to spread. His successor, Paul III (pontificate 1534–1549), the rich and worldly Roman noble Alessandro Farnese, was the first pope to pursue church reform in response to the rise of Protestantism. In 1536, he appointed a commission to investigate charges of church corruption and convened the Council of Trent (1545–1563) to define Catholic dogma, initiate disciplinary reforms, and regulate the training of clerics.

Pope Paul III also addressed Protestantism through repression and censorship. In 1542, he instituted the Inquisition, a papal office that sought out heretics for interrogation, trial, and sentencing. The enforcement of religious unity extended to the arts. Traditional images of Christ and the saints were sanctioned, but art was scrutinized for traces of heresy and profanity. Guidelines issued by the Council of Trent limited what could be represented in Christian art and led to the destruction of some works. At the same time, art became a powerful weapon of propaganda, especially in the hands of members of the Society of Jesus, a new religious order founded by the Spanish nobleman Ignatius of Loyola (1491–1556) and confirmed by Paul III in 1540. Dedicated to piety, education, and missionary work, the Jesuits, as they are known, spread worldwide and became important leaders of the Counter-Reformation movement and the revival of the Catholic Church.

ART AND ARCHITECTURE IN ROME AND THE VATICAN

To restore the heart of the city of Rome, Paul III began rebuilding the Capitoline Hill as well as continuing work on St. Peter's. His commissions include some of the finest art and architecture of the late Italian Renaissance. His first major commission brought Michelangelo, after a quarter of a century, back to the Sistine Chapel.

MICHELANGELO'S LATE WORK. In his early sixties, Michelangelo complained bitterly of feeling old, but he nonetheless undertook the important and demanding task of painting the **LAST JUDGMENT** on the 48-foot-high end wall above the Sistine Chapel altar between 1536 and 1541 (FIG. 20–34).

20-34 • Michelangelo LAST JUDGMENT, SISTINE CHAPEL
1536–1541. Fresco, 48 × 44′ (14.6 × 13.4 m).

Dark, rectangular patches left by recent restorers (visible, for example, in the upper left and right corners) contrast with the vibrant colors of the chapel's frescos. These dark areas show just how dirty the walls had become over the centuries before their recent cleaning.

EXPLORE MORE: Gain insight from a primary source of Michelangelo's poetry **www.myartslab.com**

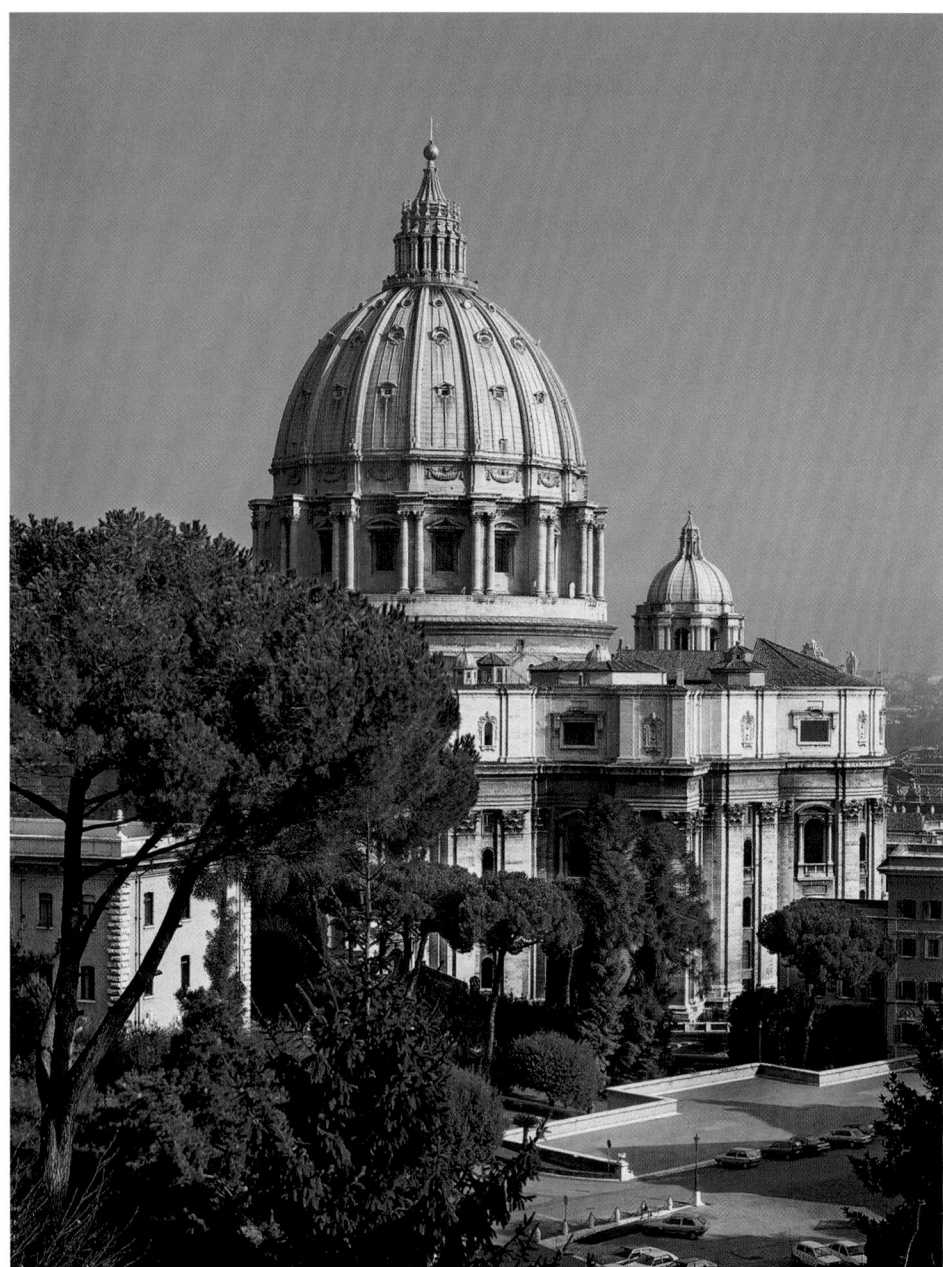

20-35 • Michelangelo **ST.
PETER'S BASILICA, VATICAN**
c. 1546–1564; dome completed 1590 by
Giacomo della Porta; lantern 1590–1593.
View from the west.

Abandoning the clearly organized medieval conception of the Last Judgment, in which the saved are neatly separated from the damned, Michelangelo painted a writhing swarm of resurrected humanity. At left (on Christ's right side), the dead are dragged from their graves and pushed up into a vortex of figures around Christ, who wields his arm like a sword of justice. The shrinking Virgin under Christ's raised right arm represents a change from Gothic tradition, where she had sat enthroned beside, and equal in size to, her son. To the right of Christ's feet is St. Bartholomew, who in legend was martyred by being skinned alive. He holds his flayed skin, and Michelangelo seems to have painted his own distorted features on the skin's face. Despite the efforts of several saints to save them at the last minute, the damned are plunged toward hell on the right, leaving the elect and still-unjudged in a dazed, almost uncomprehending state. On the lowest level of the mural, right above the altar, is the gaping, fiery entrance to hell, toward which Charon, the ferryman of the dead to the underworld, propels his craft. The painting was long interpreted as a grim and constant reminder to celebrants of the Mass—the pope and his cardinals—that ultimately they too would face stern judgment at the end of time. Conservative clergy criticized the painting for its frank nudity, and after Michelangelo's death they ordered bits of drapery to be added by artist Daniele da Volterra to conceal the offending areas, earning Daniele the unfortunate nickname *Il Braghettone* ("breeches painter").

Another of Paul III's ambitions was to complete the new St. Peter's, a project that had been under way for 40 years (see "St. Peter's Basilica," page 651). Michelangelo was well aware of the work done by his predecessors—from Bramante to Raphael to Antonio da Sangallo the Younger. The 71-year-old sculptor, confident of his

20-36 • Giacomo della Porta and Vignola
FAÇADE AND PLAN OF THE CHURCH OF IL GESÙ, ROME
c. 1573–1584.

architectural expertise, demanded the right to deal directly with the pope, rather than through a committee of construction deputies. Michelangelo further shocked the deputies—but not the pope—by tearing down or canceling parts of Sangallo's design and returning to Bramante's central plan, long associated with shrines of Christian martyrs. Although seventeenth-century additions and renovations dramatically changed the original plan of the church and the appearance of its interior, Michelangelo's **ST. PETER'S** (FIG. 20–35) still can be seen in the contrasting forms of the flat and angled exterior walls and the three surviving hemicycles (semicircular structures). Colossal pilasters, blind windows (frames without openings), and niches surround the sanctuary of the church. The current dome, erected by Giacomo della Porta in 1588–1590, retains Michelangelo's basic design: segmented with regularly spaced ribs, seated on a high drum with pedimented windows between paired columns, and surmounted by a tall lantern reminiscent of Bramante's *Il Tempietto* (SEE FIG. 20–16).

Michelangelo—often described by his contemporaries as difficult and even arrogant—alternated between periods of depression and frenzied activity. Yet he was devoted to his friends and helpful to young artists. He believed that his art was divinely inspired; later in life, he became deeply absorbed in religion and

dedicated himself to religious works—many left unfinished—that subverted Renaissance ideals of human perfectibility and denied his own youthful idealism. In the process he pioneered new stylistic directions that would inspire succeeding generations of artists.

VIGNOLA.   A young artist who worked to meet the need for new Roman churches was Giacomo Barozzi (1507–1573), known as Vignola after his native town. He worked in Rome during the late 1530s, surveying ancient Roman monuments and providing illustrations for an edition of Vitruvius. From 1541 to 1543, he was in France with Francesco Primaticcio at the château of Fontainebleau. After returning to Rome, he secured the patronage of the Farnese family and profited from the Counter-Reformation program of church building.

Catholicism's new emphasis on individual, emotional participation brought a focus on sermons and music, requiring churches with wide naves and unobstructed views of the altar, instead of the complex interiors of medieval and earlier Renaissance churches. Ignatius of Loyola was determined to build **IL GESÙ**, the Jesuit headquarters church in Rome, according to these precepts, although he did not live to see it finished (FIG. 20–36). The cornerstone was laid in 1540, but construction of *Il Gesù* did not begin until 1568; the Jesuits had considerable funds to raise first. Cardinal Alessandro Farnese (Paul III's namesake and grandson) donated to the project in 1561 and selected Vignola as architect. After Vignola died in 1573, Giacomo della Porta finished the dome and façade.

Il Gesù was admirably suited for congregational worship. Vignola designed a wide, barrel-vaulted nave with shallow connected side chapels; there are no aisles and only truncated transepts contained within the line of the outer walls—enabling all worshipers to gather in the central space. A single huge apse and dome over the crossing directed attention to the altar. The design also allows the building to fit compactly into a city block—a requirement that now often overrode the desire to orient a church along an east–west axis. The symmetrical façade emphasized the central portal with Classical pilasters, engaged columns and pediments, and volutes scrolling out laterally to hide the buttresses of the central vault and to link the tall central section with the lower sides.

As finally built by Giacomo della Porta, the façade design would have significant influence well into the next century. The early Renaissance grid of Classical pilasters and entablatures is abandoned for a two-story design that coordinates paired columns or pilasters, aligned vertically to tie together the two stories of the central block which corresponds with the nave elevation. The main entrance, with its central portal aligned with a tall upper-story window, became the focus of the composition. Centrally aligned pediments break into the level above, leading the eye upward to the cartouches with coats of arms—here of both Cardinal Farnese, the patron, and the Jesuits (whose arms display the initials IHS, the monogram of Christ).

LATER SIXTEENTH-CENTURY ART IN VENICE AND THE VENETO

By the second half of the sixteenth century, Venice ruled supreme as "queen of the Adriatic." Her power was not, however, unchallenged, and the Turks were a constant threat. In 1571, allied with Spain and the pope, the Christian fleet with Venetian ships defeated the Turkish fleet at the Battle of Lepanto, establishing Christian preeminence for future generations. Victorious and wealthy, Venetians built palaces and villas to contain their lavish lifestyle, filling them with lush oil paintings.

OIL PAINTING

Rather than the cool, formal, technical perfection sought by Mannerist painters, Venetian artists expanded upon the manner initiated by Giorgione and Titian, concerning themselves above all with color, light, and expressively loose brushwork.

VERONESE. Paolo Caliari (1528–1588) took his nickname "Veronese" from his hometown, Verona, but he worked mainly in Venice. His paintings are nearly synonymous today with the popular image of Venice as a splendid city of pleasure and pageantry sustained by a nominally republican government and great mercantile wealth. Veronese's elaborate architectural settings and costumes, still lifes, anecdotal vignettes, and other everyday details—often unconnected with the main subject—proved immensely appealing to Venetian patrons.

Veronese's most famous work is a Last Supper that he renamed *Feast in the House of Levi* (see "Veronese is Called before the Inquisition," opposite), painted in 1573 for the Dominican Monastery of Santi Giovanni e Paolo. At first glance, the subject of the painting seems to be primarily its architectural setting and only secondarily Christ seated at the table. Levi's house is an enormous loggia framed by colossal arches and reached by balustraded stairs. Beyond the loggia gleams an imaginary city of white marble. Within this grand setting, lifelike figures in lavish costumes strike theatrical poses, and Veronese has included the sort of anecdotal details loved by the Venetians—like parrots and monkeys—but detested by the Church's Inquisitors, who saw them as profane distractions.

TINTORETTO. Jacopo Robusti (1518–1594), called Tintoretto ("Little Dyer," because his father was a dyer), carried Venetian painting in another direction. Tintoretto's goal, declared on a sign in his studio, was to combine Titian's color with the drawing of Michelangelo. His large painting of **THE LAST SUPPER** (FIG. 20–37) for the choir of Palladio's church of San Giorgio Maggiore (SEE FIG. 20–38) is quite different from Leonardo da Vinci's painting of the same subject almost a century earlier (SEE FIG. 20–3). Instead of Leonardo's frontal view of a closed and logical space with massive figures reacting in individual ways to Jesus' statement, Tintoretto views the scene from a corner, with the vanishing point on a high horizon line at far right. The table, coffered ceiling, and inlaid floor all seem to plunge dramatically into the distance. The figures, although still large bodies modeled by flowing draperies, turn and move in a continuous serpentine line that unites apostles, servants, and angels. Tintoretto used two light sources: one real, the other supernatural. Over the near end of the table, light streams from the oil lamp flaring exuberantly, with angels swirling out from the flame and smoke. A second light emanates from Jesus himself and is repeated in the glow of the apostles' halos. The intensely spiritual, otherworldly mood is enhanced by deep colors flashed with dazzling highlights, recalling Byzantine art. The elongated figures, however, are consistent with Mannerist tendencies. The still lifes on the tables and homey details like the cat that peers in the foreground basket connect with viewers' own experiences. And the narrative emphasis has shifted from Leonardo's more worldly study of personal betrayal to Tintoretto's reference to the institution of the Eucharist. Jesus offers bread and wine to a disciple in the manner of a priest administering the sacrament at the altar next to the painting.

The speed with which Tintoretto drew and painted was the subject of comment in his own time, and the brilliance and

Veronese is Called before the Inquisition

According to the New Testament, Jesus revealed his impending death to his disciples during a seder, a meal celebrating the Jewish festival of Passover. This occasion, known to Christians as the Last Supper, and situated in the Gospels on the evening before the Crucifixion, was a popular subject in sixteenth-century European art. But in 1573, when the painter Veronese delivered an enormous canvas of this subject to fulfill a commission, the patrons were shocked. Some were offended by the grandiose pageantry of the scene. Others protested the impiety of surrounding Jesus with a man picking his teeth, scruffy dogs, and foreign soldiers. As a result of the furor, Veronese was called before the Inquisition to explain his painting. There he justified himself first by asserting that the picture actually depicted not the Last Supper, but rather the feast in the house of Simon, a small dinner held shortly before Jesus' final entry into Jerusalem. He also noted that artists customarily invent details in their pictures and that he had received a commission to paint the piece "as I saw fit." His argument fell on unsympathetic ears, and he was ordered to change the painting. Later he sidestepped the issue by changing its title to that of another banquet, one given by the tax collector Levi, whom Jesus had called to follow him (Luke 5:27–32). Perhaps with this change of subject, Veronese took a modest revenge on the Inquisitors: When Jesus himself was criticized for associating with such unsavory people at this meal, he replied, "I have not come to call the righteous to repentance but sinners" (Luke 5:32).

Veronese FEAST IN THE HOUSE OF LEVI
From the refectory of the monastery of Santi Giovanni e Paolo, Venice. 1573. Oil on canvas, 18'3" × 42' (5.56 × 12.8 m). Galleria dell'Accademia, Venice.

EXPLORE MORE: Gain insight from a primary source about Paolo Veronese **www.myartslab.com**

immediacy so admired in his work today—his slashing brushwork was much appreciated by twentieth-century gestural painters—were derided as evidence of carelessness in his own time. Rapid production may have been a byproduct of his working methods. Tintoretto had a large workshop of assistants and he usually provided only the original conception, the beginning drawings, and the final brilliant touches on the finished paintings. Tintoretto's workshop included members of his family—of his eight children, four became artists. His oldest daughter, Marietta Robusti, worked with him as a portrait painter, and two or perhaps three of his sons

20–37 • Tintoretto THE LAST SUPPER
1592–1594. Oil on canvas, 12′ × 18′8″ (3.7 × 5.7 m). Church of San Giorgio Maggiore, Venice.

Tintoretto, who had a large workshop, often developed a composition by creating a small-scale model like a miniature stage set, which he populated with wax figures. He then adjusted the positions of the figures and the lighting until he was satisfied with the entire scene. Using a grid of horizontal and vertical threads placed in front of this model, he could easily sketch the composition onto squared paper for his assistants to copy onto a large canvas. His assistants also primed the canvas, blocking in the areas of dark and light, before the artist himself, free to concentrate on the most difficult passages, finished the painting. This efficient working method allowed Tintoretto to produce a large number of paintings in all sizes.

also joined the shop. So skillfully did Marietta capture her father's style and technique that today art historians cannot identify her work in the shop.

ARCHITECTURE: PALLADIO

Just as Veronese and Tintoretto expanded upon the rich Venetian tradition of oil painting initiated by Giorgione and Titian, Andrea Palladio dominated architecture during the second half of the century by expanding upon the principles of Alberti and ancient Roman architecture. His buildings—whether villas, palaces, or churches—were characterized by harmonious symmetry and controlled ornamentation. Born Andrea di Pietro della Gondola (1508–1580), probably in Padua, Palladio began his career as a stonecutter. After moving to Vicenza, he was hired by the nobleman, humanist scholar, and amateur architect Giangiorgio Trissino, who gave him the nickname "Palladio" for the Greek goddess of wisdom, Pallas Athena, and the fourth-century Roman

writer Palladius. Palladio learned Latin at Trissino's small academy and accompanied his benefactor on three trips to Rome, where he made drawings of Roman monuments.

Over the years, Palladio became involved in several publishing ventures, including a guide to Roman antiquities and an illustrated edition of Vitruvius. He also published his own books on architecture—including ideal plans for country estates, using proportions derived from ancient Roman buildings—that for centuries would be valuable resources for architectural design. Despite their theoretical bent, his writings were often more practical than earlier treatises. Perhaps his early experience as a stonemason provided him with the knowledge and self-confidence to approach technical problems and discuss them as clearly as he did theories of ideal proportion and uses of the Classical orders. By the eighteenth century, Palladio's *Four Books of Architecture* had been included in the libraries of most educated people. Thomas Jefferson had one of the first copies in America.

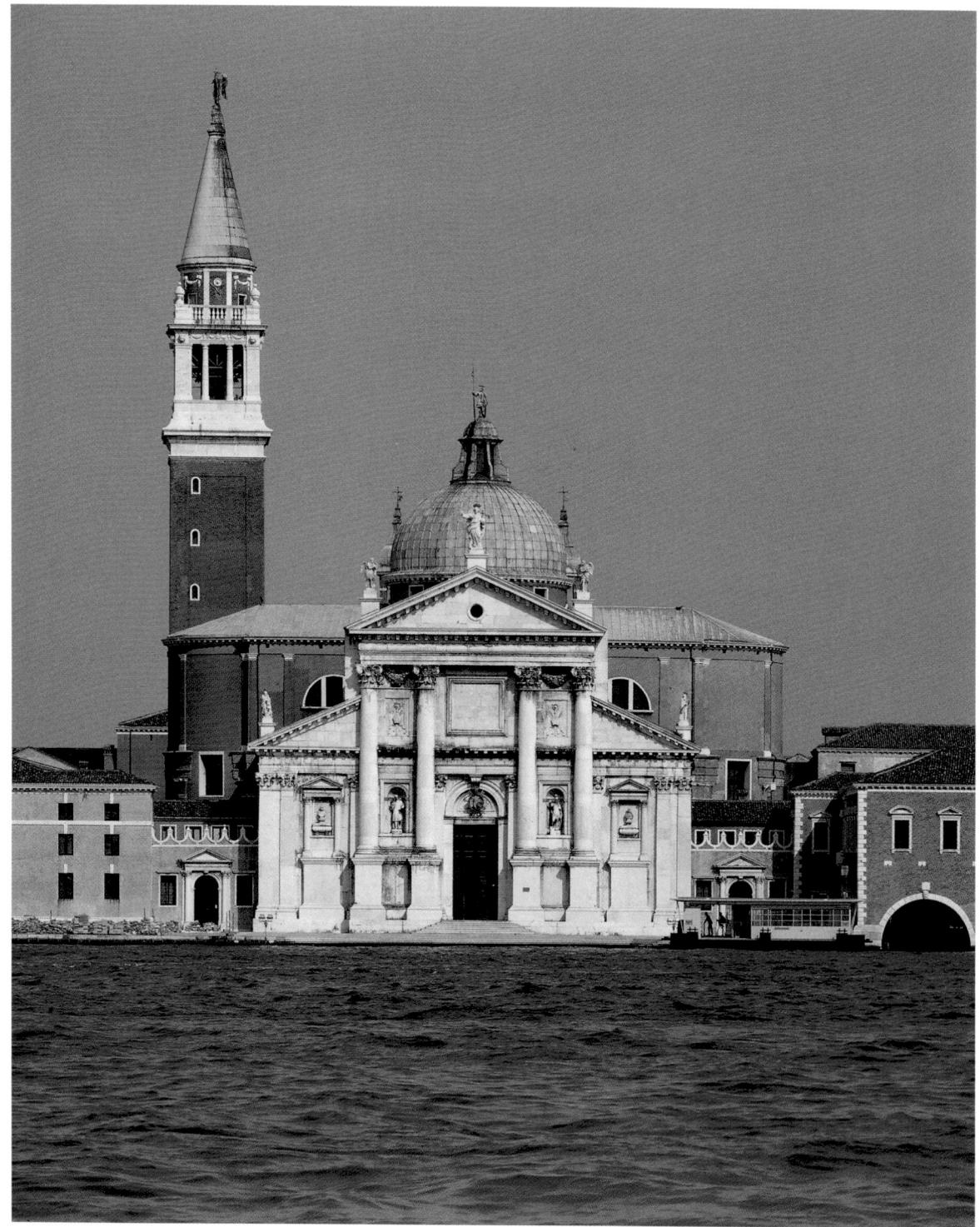

20-38 • Palladio CHURCH OF SAN GIORGIO MAGGIORE, VENICE
Plan 1565; construction 1565–1580; façade 1597–1610; campanile 1791.
Finished by Vincenzo Scamozzi following Palladio's design.

SEE MORE: Click the Google Earth link for San Giorgio Maggiore **www.myartslab.com**

SAN GIORGIO MAGGIORE. By 1559, when he settled in Venice, Palladio was one of the foremost architects in Italy. In 1565, he undertook a major architectural commission: the monastery **CHURCH OF SAN GIORGIO MAGGIORE** (FIG. 20–38). His variation on the traditional Renaissance façade for a basilica— a wide lower level fronting the nave and side aisles, surmounted by a narrower front for the nave clerestory—creates the illusion of two temple fronts of different heights and widths, one set inside the other. At the center, colossal columns on high pedestals support an entablature and pediment; these columns correspond to

20-39 • NAVE, CHURCH OF SAN GIORGIO MAGGIORE, VENICE
Begun 1566. Tintoretto's *Last Supper* (not visible) hangs to the left of the altar.

the width of the nave within. Behind the taller temple front, a second front consists of pilasters supporting another entablature and pediment; this wider front spans the entire width of the church, including the triple aisle. Although the façade was not built until after the architect's death, his original design was followed.

The interior of **SAN GIORGIO (FIG. 20–39)** is a fine example of Palladio's harmoniously balanced geometry, expressed here in strong verticals and powerfully opened arches. The tall engaged columns and shorter pilasters of the nave arcade piers echo the two levels of orders on the façade, thus unifying the building's exterior and interior.

THE VILLA ROTONDA. Palladio's versatility was already apparent in numerous villas built early in his career. In the 1560s, he started his most famous and influential villa just outside Vicenza. Although

villas were traditionally working farms, Palladio designed this one as a retreat, literally a party house. To maximize vistas of the countryside, he placed a porch elevated at the top of a wide staircase on each face of the building. The main living quarters are on this second level, and the lower level is reserved for the kitchen, storage, and other utility rooms. Upon its completion in 1569, the building was dubbed the **VILLA ROTONDA (FIG. 20–40)** because it had been inspired by another round building, the Roman Pantheon. The plan **(FIG. 20–41)** shows the geometric clarity of Palladio's conception: a circle inscribed in a small square inside a larger square, with symmetrical rectangular compartments and identical rectangular projections from each of its faces. The use of a central dome on a domestic building was a daring innovation that effectively secularized the dome and initiated what was to become a long tradition of domed country houses, particularly in England and the United States.

20-40 • Palladio EXTERIOR VIEW OF VILLA ROTONDA, VICENZA
Italy. Begun 1560s.

After its purchase in 1591 by the Capra family, the Villa Rotonda became known as the Villa Capra.

SEE MORE: Click the Google Earth link for the Villa Rotonda, Vicenza **www.myartslab.com**

20-41 • Palladio PLAN OF VILLA ROTONDA, VICENZA
Italy. Begun 1560s.

EXPLORE MORE: Gain insight from a primary source by Andrea Palladio **www.myartslab.com**

THINK ABOUT IT

20.1 Discuss Julius II's efforts to aggrandize the city of Rome and create a new golden age of papal art. Focus your answer on at least two specific works he commissioned.

20.2 Write about either Michelangelo's or Raphael's extensive work in the Sistine Chapel. How did papal commissions push these two established artists in new creative directions?

20.3 Select either Pontormo's *Entombment* (FIG. 20–26) or Parmigianino's *Madonna with the Long Neck* (FIG. 20–27), and explain why the painting characterizes Mannerist style. How does your chosen work depart from the Classical norms of the High Renaissance?

20.4 Elaborate on the idea that whereas Rome and Florence were oriented toward drawing, Venice was oriented toward color. Compare and contrast a specific work from each tradition in forming your answer.

20.5 Analyze either the Palazzo del Tè (FIG. 20–17) or the Villa Rotonda (FIG. 20–40). Explain how the design of the building differs from the design of grand churches during this same period, even though architects clearly used Classical motifs in both sacred and secular contexts.

PRACTICE MORE: Compose answers to these questions, get flashcards for images and terms, and review chapter material with quizzes **www.myartslab.com**

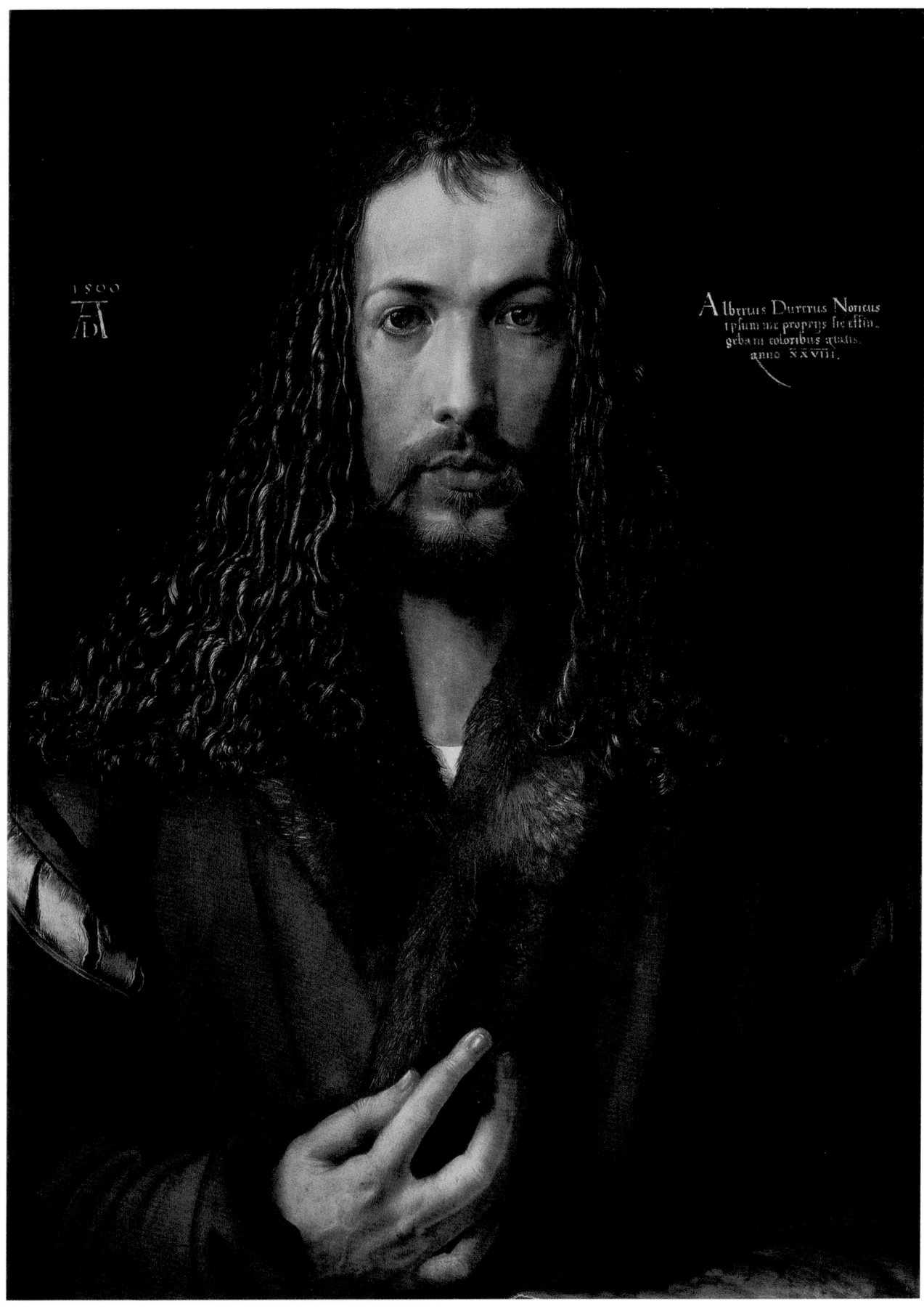

1500. Signed "Albrecht Dürer of Nuremberg…age 28."

21–1 • Albrecht Dürer SELF-PORTRAIT
Oil on wood panel, 26¼ × 19¼″ (66.3 × 49 cm). Alte Pinakothek, Munich.

EXPLORE MORE: Gain insight from a primary source by Albrecht Dürer **www.myartslab.com**

SIXTEENTH-CENTURY ART IN NORTHERN EUROPE AND THE IBERIAN PENINSULA

This striking image (**FIG. 21–1**), dated 1500, seems to depict a blessing Christ, meant to rivet our attention and focus our devotion. But an inscription to the right of the iconic visage identifies this as a **SELF-PORTRAIT** by Albrecht Dürer, painted when he was 28 years old. We are already familiar with the practice of artists painting their own image. Self-portraits appear with some frequency during the Middle Ages (SEE FIGS. 15–32, 16–20); they truly blossom during the Renaissance (SEE FIGS. 18–11, 20–30). But this image is still peculiar, marked by an artistic hubris that may embarrass us. The picture becomes less puzzling, however, seen in context.

Dürer strikes an odd pose for a self-portrait—frontal and hieratic, intentionally recalling iconic images of Christ as *salvator mundi* (savior of the world) that were very popular in northern Europe. Dürer even alters the natural color of his own hair to align the image more closely with contemporary notions of Christ's physical appearance. But there is no reason to see this as blasphemous. Since a principal component of contemporary Christian devotion was the attempt to imitate Christ in the believer's own life, Dürer could be visualizing a popular spiritual practice. He could also be literalizing the biblical statement that humans are created in the image of God. But he is also claiming that artists are learned and creative geniuses—perhaps God-like—not laboring craftsmen. He wrote, "The more we know, the more we resemble the likeness of Christ who truly knows all things" (Snyder, p. 314).

Dürer had traveled to Italy in 1494–1495, where he encountered a new conception of artists as noble intellectuals, participants in humanistic discourse, purveyors of ideas as well as pictures. In 1498, back in Nuremberg, he published a wood-cut series on the Apocalypse (SEE FIG. 21–6) that brought him a kind of international notice that was new to the German art world. He certainly had reason to feel pride. This stable, triangular composition—so consistent with High Renaissance norms of harmony and balance—could reflect Dürer's Italian adventure. But at its core, this picture fits into a long-standing northern European interest in the meticulous description of surface texture—the soft sheen of human flesh, the reflective wetness of eyes, the matte softness of cloth, and the tactile quality of hair, emphasized here by the way Dürer's hand fingers the fur collar of his outfit, encouraging viewers also to feel it as they see it. Ultimately what is showcased here are Dürer's awesome artistic gifts of hand as much as his intellectual gifts of mind, two aspects perhaps emblemized by the brightly illuminated body parts that align on a vertical axis to dominate this arresting self-portrait.

LEARN ABOUT IT

21.1 Investigate the broadening of regional interaction in the art of European courts as artists traveled across Europe to work for wealthy patrons and study with acclaimed masters.

21.2 Evaluate the impact of Italian ideas on the traditions of northern art and architecture, including the developing notion of artists as uniquely gifted individuals.

21.3 Analyze the developments that led to the creation of an art market in the Netherlands.

21.4 Assess the relationship between the religious conflicts in northern Europe and the growing interest in new secular subjects in works of art.

21.5 Recognize the continuing interest among northern European artists and patrons in the virtuosity of works in media such as wood and gold.

HEAR MORE: Listen to an audio file of your chapter **www.myartslab.com**

MAP 21-1 • WESTERN EUROPE DURING THE REFORMATION, C. 1560

Sixteenth-century Europe remained largely Roman Catholic, except in Switzerland and the far north, where the impact of the Protestant Reformation was strongest.

THE REFORMATION AND THE ARTS

In spite of the dissident movements and heresies that had challenged the Roman Catholic Church through the centuries, its authority and that of the pope always prevailed—until the sixteenth century (**MAP 21–1**). Then, against a backdrop of broad dissatisfaction with financial abuses and decadent lifestyles among the clergy, religious reformers from within the Church itself challenged first its practices and then its beliefs.

Two of the most important reformers in the early sixteenth century were themselves Catholic priests and trained theologians: Desiderius Erasmus (1466?–1536) of Rotterdam in Holland, who worked to reform the Roman Catholic Church from within, and Martin Luther (1483–1546) in Germany, who eventually broke with it. Indeed, many locate the beginning of the Reformation in 1517, when Luther issued his "95 Theses" calling for church reform. Among Luther's concerns were the practice of selling indulgences

(guarantees of relief from the punishment required after death for forgiven sins) and the excessive veneration of saints and their relics, which he considered superstitious. Luther and others emphasized individual faith and regarded the Bible as the ultimate religious authority. As they challenged the pope's supremacy, it became clear that the Protestants had to break away from Rome. The Roman Catholic Church condemned Luther in 1521.

Increased literacy and the widespread use of the printing press aided the reformers and allowed scholars throughout Europe to enter the religious debate. In Germany, the wide circulation of Luther's writings—especially his German translation of the Bible and his works maintaining that salvation comes through faith alone—eventually led to the establishment of the Protestant (Lutheran) Church there. In Switzerland, John Calvin (1509–1564) led an even more austere Protestant revolt; and in England, King Henry VIII (r. 1509–1547) also broke with Rome in

1534, for reasons of his own. By the end of the sixteenth century, Protestantism in some form prevailed throughout northern Europe.

Leading the Catholic cause was Holy Roman Emperor Charles V. Europe was wracked by religious war from 1546 to 1555 as Charles battled Protestant forces in Germany, until a meeting of the provincial legislature of Augsburg in 1555 determined that the emperor must accommodate the Protestant Reformation in his lands. By the terms of the peace, local rulers could select the religion of their subjects—Catholic or Protestant. Tired of the strain of government and prematurely aged, Charles abdicated in 1556 and retired to a monastery in Spain, where he died in 1558. His son Philip II inherited Habsburg Spain and the Spanish colonies, while his brother Ferdinand led the Austrian branch of the dynasty.

The years of political and religious strife had a grave impact on artists and art. Some artists found their careers at an end because of their reformist religious sympathies. Then as Protestantism gained ascendancy, Catholic artists had to leave their homes to seek patronage abroad. There was also widespread destruction of religious art. In some places, Protestant zealots smashed sculpture and stained-glass windows and destroyed or whitewashed religious paintings to rid the churches of what they considered idols—though Luther himself never directly supported **iconoclasm** (the smashing of religious images). With the sudden loss of patronage for religious art in the newly Protestant lands, many artists turned to portraiture and other secular subjects, including moralizing depictions of human folly and weaknesses, still lifes (paintings of inanimate objects), and landscapes. The popularity of these themes stimulated the burgeoning of a free art market, centered in Antwerp.

GERMANY

In German-speaking regions, the arts flourished until religious upheavals and iconoclastic purges took their toll at mid century. German cities had strong business and trade interests, and their merchants and bankers accumulated self-made, rather than inherited, wealth. They ordered portraits of themselves and fine furnishings for their large, comfortable houses. Entrepreneurial artists, like Albrecht Dürer, became major commercial successes.

SCULPTURE

Although, like the Italians, German Renaissance sculptors worked in stone and bronze, they produced their most original work in wood, especially fine-grained limewood. Most of these wooded images were gilded and painted, continuing an interest in heightening naturalism, until Tilman Riemenschneider began to favor natural wood finishes.

TILMAN RIEMENSCHNEIDER. Tilman Riemenschneider (c. 1460–1531) became a master in 1485 and soon had the largest workshop in Würzburg, which included specialists in both wood and stone sculpture. Riemenschneider attracted patrons from other cities, and

in 1501 he signed a contract with the church of St. James in Rothenburg, where a relic said to be a drop of Jesus' blood was preserved. The **ALTARPIECE OF THE HOLY BLOOD** (FIG. 21–2) is a spectacular limewood construction standing nearly 30 feet high.

21-2 • Tilman Riemenschneider ALTARPIECE OF THE HOLY BLOOD (WINGS OPEN)
Center, *Last Supper*. c. 1499–1505. Limewood, glass, height of tallest figure 39″ (99.1 cm), height of altar 29′6″ (9 m). Sankt Jakobskirche (Church of St. James), Rothenburg ob der Tauber, Germany.

In Nuremberg, a city known for its master metalworkers, Hans Krug (d. 1519) and his sons Hans the Younger and Ludwig were among the finest. They created marvelous display pieces for the wealthy, such as this silver-gilt apple cup. Made about 1510, a gleaming apple, in which the stem forms the handle of the lid, balances on a leafy branch that forms its base.

The Krug family was responsible for the highly refined casting and finishing of the final product, but several artists worked together to produce such pieces—one drawing designs, another making the models, and others creating the final piece in metal. A drawing by Dürer may have been the basis for the apple cup. Though we know of no piece of goldwork by the artist himself, Dürer was a major catalyst in the growth of Nuremberg as a key center of German goldsmithing. He accomplished this by producing designs for metalwork throughout his career. Designers played an essential role in the metalwork process. With design in hand, the modelmaker created a wooden form for the goldsmith to follow. The result of this artistic collaboration was a technical *tour de force*, an intellectual conceit, and an exquisite object.

Workshop of Hans Krug (?) APPLE CUP
c. 1510–1515. Gilt silver, height 8½″ (21.5 cm). Germanisches Nationalmuseum, Nuremberg.

Erhart Harschner, a specialist in architectural shrines, had begun work on the elaborate Gothic frame in 1499, and was paid 50 florins for his work. Riemenschneider was commissioned to provide the figures and scenes to be placed within this frame. He was paid 60 florins for the sculpture, giving us a sense of the relative value patrons placed on their contributions.

The main panel of the altarpiece portrays the moment at the Last Supper when Christ revealed that one of his followers would betray him. Unlike Leonardo da Vinci, who chose the same moment (SEE FIG. 20–3), Riemenschneider puts Judas at center stage and Jesus off-center at the left. The disciples sit around the table. As the event is described in the Gospel of John (13:21–30), Jesus extends a morsel of food to Judas, signifying that he will be the traitor who sets in motion the events leading to the Crucifixion. One apostle points down, a strange gesture until we realize that he is pointing to the crucifix in the predella, to the relic of Christ's blood, and to the altar table, the symbolic representation of the table of the Last Supper and the tomb of Christ.

Rather than creating individual portraits of the apostles, Riemenschneider repeated a limited number of facial types. His figures have large heads, prominent features, sharp cheekbones, sagging jowls, baggy eyes, and elaborate hair with thick wavy locks and deeply drilled curls. The muscles, tendons, and raised veins of hands and feet are also especially lifelike. His assistants and apprentices copied these faces and figures, either from drawings or from three-dimensional models made by the master. In the altarpiece, deeply hollowed folds create active patterns in the voluminous draperies whose strong highlights and dark shadows harmonize the figural composition with the intricate carving of the framework. The Last Supper is set in a "real" room containing actual benches for the figures. Windows in the back wall are glazed with bull's-eye glass so that natural light shines in from two directions to illuminate the scene, producing changing effects depending on the time of day and the weather. Although earlier sculpture had been painted and gilded, Riemenschneider introduced the use of a natural wood finish toned with varnish. This meant that details of both figures and environment had to be carved into the wood itself, not quickly added later with paint. Since this required more skillful carvers and more time for them to carve, this new look was a matter of aesthetics, not cost-saving.

In addition to producing an enormous number of religious images for churches, Riemenschneider was politically active in the city's government, and he even served as mayor in 1520. His career ended during the Peasants' War (1524–1526), an early manifestation of the Protestant movement. His support for the peasants led to a fine and imprisonment in 1525, and although he survived, Riemenschneider produced no more sculpture and died in 1531.

NIKOLAUS HAGENAUER. Prayer was the principal source of solace and relief to the ill before the advent of modern medicine. About 1505, the Strasbourg sculptor Nikolaus Hagenauer (active

21–3 • Nikolaus Hagenauer ST. ANTHONY ENTHRONED BETWEEN SS. AUGUSTINE AND JEROME, SHRINE OF THE ISENHEIM ALTARPIECE (OPEN, SHOWING GRÜNEWALD WINGS)
From the Community of St. Anthony, Isenheim, Alsace, France. c. 1500. Painted and gilt limewood, center panel 9′9½″ × 10′9″ (2.98 × 3.28 m), predella 2′5½″ × 11′2″ (0.75 × 3.4 m), wings 8′2½″ × 3′½″ (2.49 × 0.93 m). Predella: *Christ and the Apostles*. Wings: *SS. Anthony and Paul the Hermit* (left); *The Temptation of St. Anthony* (right). 1510–1515. Musée d'Unterlinden, Colmar, France.

1493–1530s) carved an altarpiece for the abbey of St. Anthony in Isenheim near Colmar **(FIG. 21–3)** where a hospital specialized in the care of patients with skin diseases, including the plague, leprosy, and St. Anthony's Fire (caused by eating rye and other grains infected with the ergot fungus). The shrine includes images of SS. Anthony, Jerome, and Augustine. Three tiny men—their size befitting their subordinate status—kneel at the feet of the saints: the donor, Jean d'Orliac, and two men offering a rooster and a piglet.

In the predella below, Jesus and the apostles bless the altar, Host, and assembled patients in the hospital. This limewood sculpture was painted in lifelike colors, and the shrine itself was gilded to enhance its resemblance to a precious reliquary. A decade later, Matthias Grünewald painted wooden shutters to cover the shrine (SEE FIGS. 21–4, 21–5).

PAINTING

The work of two very different German artists has come down to us from the first decades of the sixteenth century. Matthias

Grünewald continued currents of medieval mysticism and emotional spirituality to create extraordinarily moving paintings. Albrecht Dürer, on the other hand, used intense observation of the world to render lifelike representations of nature, mathematical perspective to create convincing illusions of space, and a reasoned canon of proportions to standardize depictions of the human figure.

MATTHIAS GRÜNEWALD. As a court artist to the archbishop of Mainz, Matthias Grünewald (Matthias Gothart Neithart, c. 1470/ 1475–1528) was a man of many talents, who worked as an architect and hydraulic engineer as well as a painter. He is best known today for painting the shutters or wings attached to Nikolaus Hagenauer's carved Isenheim Altarpiece (SEE FIG. 21–3). The completed altarpiece is impressive in size and complexity. Grünewald painted one set of fixed wings and two sets of movable ones, plus one set of sliding panels to cover the predella. The altarpiece could be exhibited in different configurations depending upon the church calendar. The wings and carved wooden shrine

21-4 • Matthias Grünewald ISENHEIM ALTARPIECE (CLOSED)
From the Community of St. Anthony, Isenheim, Alsace, France. Center panels: *Crucifixion*; predella: *Lamentation*; side panels: *SS. Sebastian* (left) and Anthony Abbot (right). c. 1510–1515. Date 1515 on ointment jar. Oil on wood panel, center panels 9′9½″ × 10′9″ (2.97 × 3.28 m) overall; each wing 8′2½″ × 3′½″ (2.49 × 0.93 m); predella 2′5½″ × 11′2″ (0.75 × 3.4 m). Musée d'Unterlinden, Colmar, France.

21-5 • Matthias Grünewald ISENHEIM ALTARPIECE (FIRST OPENING)
Left to right: *Annunciation, Virgin and Child with Angels, Resurrection*. c. 1510–1515. Oil on wood panel, center panel 9′9½″ × 10′9″ (2.97 × 3.28 m), each wing 8′2½″ × 3′½″ (2.49 × 0.92 m). Musée d'Unterlinden, Colmar, France.

complemented one another, the inner sculpture seeming to bring the surrounding paintings to life, and the painted wings protecting the precious carvings.

On weekdays, when the altarpiece was closed, viewers saw a grisly image of the Crucifixion in a darkened landscape, a *Lamentation* below it on the predella, and life-size figures of SS. Sebastian and Anthony Abbot—both associated with the plague—standing on *trompe l'oeil* pedestals on the fixed wings (FIG. 21–4). The intensity of feeling here has suggested that Grünewald may have been inspired by the visions of St. Bridget of Sweden, a fourteenth-century mystic whose works—including morbidly detailed descriptions of the Crucifixion—were published in Germany beginning in 1492. Grünewald has scrupulously described the horrific character of the tortured body of Jesus, covered with gashes from his beating and pierced by the thorns used to form a crown for his head. His ashen body, clotted blood, open mouth, and blue lips signal his death. In fact, he appears already to be decaying, an effect enhanced by the palette of putrescent green, yellow, and purplish-red—all described by St. Bridget. She wrote, "The color of death spread through his flesh…." An immaculately garbed Virgin Mary has collapsed in the arms of a ghostlike John the Evangelist, and Mary Magdalen has fallen in anguish to her knees; her clasped hands with outstretched fingers seem to echo Jesus' fingers, cramped in rigor mortis. At the right, John the Baptist points to Jesus and repeats his prophecy, "He shall increase." The Baptist and the lamb, holding a cross and bleeding from its breast into a golden chalice, allude to baptism, the Eucharist, and to Christ as the sacrificial Lamb of God. In the predella below, Jesus' bereaved mother and friends prepare his racked body for burial—an activity that must have been a common sight in the abbey's hospital.

In contrast to these grim scenes, the first opening displays events of great joy—the Annunciation, the Nativity, and the Resurrection—appropriate for Sundays and feast days (FIG. 21–5). Praying in front of these pictures, the patients must have hoped for miraculous recovery and taken comfort in these visions of divine rapture and orgiastic color. Unlike the awful darkness of the Crucifixion, the inner scenes are brilliantly illuminated, in part by phosphorescent auras and haloes, and stars glitter in the night sky of the Resurrection. The technical virtuosity of Grünewald's painting alone is enough to inspire euphoria.

The *Annunciation* on the left wing may be related to a special liturgy called the Golden Mass, which celebrated the divine motherhood of the Virgin. The Mass included a staged reenactment of the angel's visit to Mary, as well as readings from the story of the Annunciation (Luke 1:26–38) and the Hebrew Bible prophecy of the Savior's birth (Isaiah 7:14–15), which is inscribed in Latin on the pages of the Virgin's open book.

The central panels show the heavenly and earthly realms joined in one space. In a variation on the northern European visionary tradition, the new mother adores her miraculous Christ Child while envisioning her own future as queen of heaven amid angels and cherubims. Grünewald portrayed three distinct types of angels in the foreground—young, mature, and a feathered hybrid with a birdlike crest on its human head. The range of ethnic types in the heavenly realm may have emphasized the global dominion of the Church, whose missionary efforts were expanding as a result of European exploration. St. Bridget describes the jubilation of the angels as "the glowing flame of love."

The second opening of the altarpiece (SEE FIG. 21–3) reveals Hagenauer's sculpture and was reserved for the special festivals of St. Anthony. The wings in this second opening show to the left the meeting of St. Anthony with the hermit St. Paul, and to the right St. Anthony attacked by horrible demons, perhaps inspired by the horrors of the diseased patients, but also modeled in part on Schongauer's well-known print of the same subject (SEE FIG. 18–26). The meeting of the two hermits in the desert glorifies the monastic life, and in the wilderness Grünewald depicts medicinal plants used in the hospital's therapy. Grünewald painted the face of St. Paul with his own self-portrait, while St. Anthony is a portrait of the donor and administrator of the hospital, the Italian Guido Guersi, whose coat of arms Grünewald painted on the rock next to him.

Like Riemenschneider, Grünewald's involvement with the Peasants' War may have damaged his artistic career. He left Mainz and spent his last years in Halle, whose ruler was the chief protector of Martin Luther and a long-time patron of Grünewald's contemporary Albrecht Dürer.

ALBRECHT DÜRER. Studious, analytical, observant, and meticulous —and as self-confident as Michelangelo—Albrecht Dürer (1471–1528) was the foremost artist of the German Renaissance. He made his home in Nuremberg, where he became a prominent citizen. Nuremberg was a center of culture as well as of business, with an active group of humanists and internationally renowned artists. It was also a leading publishing center. Dürer's father was a goldsmith and must have expected his son to follow in his trade (see "German Metalwork: A Collaborative Venture," page 680). Dürer did complete an apprenticeship in gold-working, as well as in stained-glass design, painting, and the making of woodcuts—which he learned from Michael Wolgemut, illustrator of the *Nuremberg Chronicle* (SEE FIG. 18–27). But ultimately it was as a painter and graphic artist that he built his artistic fame.

In 1490, Dürer began traveling to extend his education. He went to Basel, Switzerland, hoping to meet Martin Schongauer, but arrived after the master's death. By 1494, Dürer had moved from Basel to Strasbourg. His first trip to Italy (1494–1495) introduced him to Italian Renaissance ideas and attitudes and, as we considered at the beginning of this chapter, to the concept of the artist as an independent creative genius. In his self-portrait of 1500 (SEE FIG. 21–1), Dürer represents himself as an idealized, Christ-like figure in a severely frontal pose, staring directly at the viewer.

On his return to Nuremberg, Dürer began to publish his own prints to bolster his income, and ultimately it was prints, not

21-6 • Albrecht Dürer THE FOUR HORSEMEN OF THE APOCALYPSE
From *The Apocalypse*. 1497–1498. Woodcut, 15½ × 11⅛"
(39.4 × 28.3 cm). Metropolitan Museum of Art, New York.
Gift of Junius S. Morgan, 1919 (19.73.209)

as a goldsmith is evident in his meticulous attention to detail, and in his decorative cloud and drapery patterns. Following the tradition established by his late fifteenth-century predecessors, he fills the foreground with large, active figures.

Perhaps as early as the summer of 1494, Dürer began to experiment with engravings, cutting the metal plates himself with an artistry rivaling Schongauer's. His growing interest in Italian art and his theoretical investigations are reflected in his 1504 engraving **ADAM AND EVE** (FIG. **21–7**), which represents his first documented use of ideal human proportions based on Roman copies of ancient Greek sculpture. He may have seen figures of Apollo and Venus in Italy, and he would have known ancient sculpture from contemporary prints and drawings. But around these idealized human figures he represents plants and animals with typically northern attention to descriptive detail.

Dürer filled the landscape with symbolic content reflecting the medieval theory that after Adam and Eve disobeyed God, they and their descendants became vulnerable to imbalances in the body fluids that controlled human temperament. An excess of black bile from the liver would produce melancholy, despair, and greed. Yellow bile caused anger, pride, and impatience; phlegm in the lungs resulted in lethargy and disinterest; and an excess of

paintings, that made his fortune. His first major publication, *The Apocalypse*, appeared simultaneously in German and Latin editions in 1497–1498. It consisted of a woodcut title page and 14 full-page illustrations with the text printed on the back of each. Perhaps best known is **THE FOUR HORSEMEN OF THE APOCALYPSE** (FIG. **21–6**), based on figures described in Revelation 6:1–8: a crowned rider, armed with a bow, on a white horse (Conquest); a rider with a sword, on a red horse (War); a rider with a set of scales, on a black horse (Plague and Famine); and a rider on a sickly pale horse (Death). Earlier artists had simply lined up the horsemen in the landscape, but Dürer created a compact, overlapping group of wild riders charging across the world and trampling its cowering inhabitants, men and women, clerical and lay.

Dürer probably did not cut his own woodblocks but employed a skilled carver who followed his drawings faithfully. Dürer's dynamic figures show affinities with Schongauer's *Temptation of St. Anthony* (SEE FIG. 18–26). He adapted Schongauer's metal-engraving technique to the woodcut medium, using a complex pattern of lines to model the forms. Dürer's early training

21-7 • Albrecht Dürer ADAM AND EVE
1504. Engraving, 9⅞ × 7⅝" (25.1 × 19.4 cm).
Philadelphia Museum of Art.
Purchased: Lisa Nora Elkins Fund

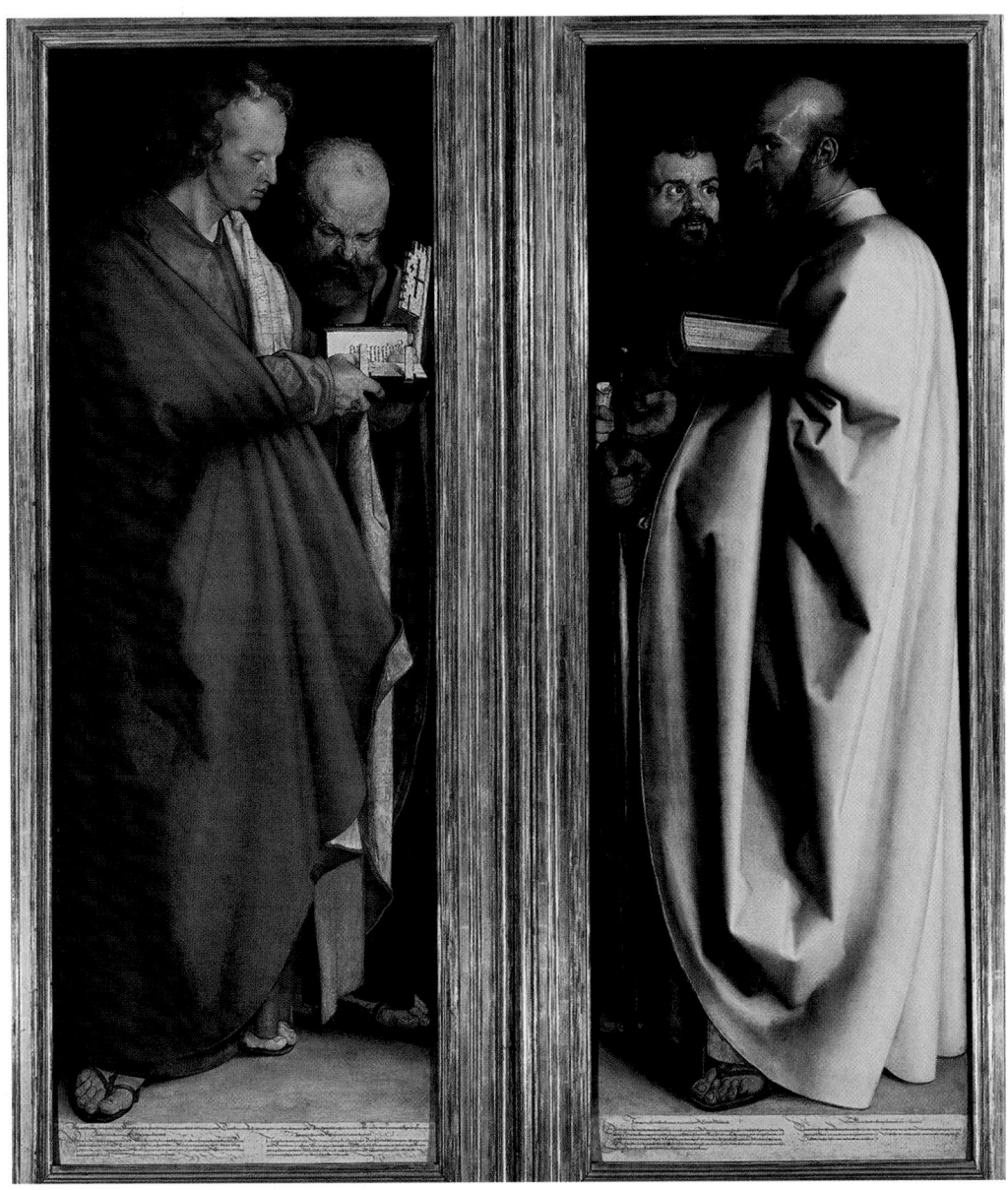

21-8 • Albrecht Dürer
FOUR APOSTLES
1526. Oil on wood panel,
each panel 7'½" × 2'6"
(2.15 × 0.76 m).
Alte Pinakothek, Munich.

blood made a person unusually optimistic but also compulsively interested in the pleasures of the flesh. These four human temperaments, or personalities, are symbolized here by the melancholy elk, the choleric cat, the phlegmatic ox, and the sanguine (or sensual) rabbit. The mouse is a symbol of Satan (see the mousetrap in FIG. 18–10), whose earthly power, already manifest in the Garden of Eden, was capable of bringing human beings to a life of woe through their own bad choices. Adam seems to be releasing the mouse into the world of his paradise as he contemplates eating the forbidden fruit that Eve receives from the snake. Dürer placed his signature prominently on a placard hung on a tree branch in Adam's grasp and on which perches a parrot—possibly symbolizing false wisdom, since it can only repeat mindlessly what it hears.

Dürer's familiarity with Italian art was greatly enhanced by a second, leisurely trip over the Alps in 1505–1506. Thereafter, he seems to have resolved to reform the art of his own country by publishing theoretical writings and manuals that discussed Renaissance problems of perspective, ideal human proportions, and the techniques of painting.

Dürer admired Martin Luther, but they never met. In 1526, the artist openly professed his Lutheranism in a pair of inscribed panels, the **FOUR APOSTLES** (FIG. **21–8**). On the left panel, the elderly Peter, who normally has a central position as the first pope, has been displaced with his keys to the background by Luther's favorite evangelist, John, who holds an open Gospel that reads "In the beginning was the Word," reinforcing the Protestant emphasis on the Bible. On the right panel, Mark stands behind Paul, whose epistles were particularly admired by the Protestants. A long inscription on the frame warns the viewer not to be led astray by "false prophets" but to heed the words of the New Testament as recorded by these "four excellent men." Below each figure are excerpts from their letters and from the Gospel of Mark—drawn from Luther's German translation of the New Testament—warning

FONTIS NYMPHA SACRI SOM NVM NE RVMPE QVIESCO·

21-9 • Lucas Cranach the Elder NYMPH OF THE SPRING
c. 1537. Oil on panel, 19 × 28½″ (48.5 × 72.9 cm). National Gallery of Art, Washington, D.C.

against those who do not understand the true Word of God. These paintings were surely meant to chart the possibility of a Protestant visual art.

Dürer presented the panels to the city of Nuremberg, which had already adopted Lutheranism as its official religion. Dürer wrote, "For a Christian would no more be led to superstition by a picture or effigy than an honest man to commit murder because he carries a weapon by his side. He must indeed be an unthinking man who would worship picture, wood, or stone. A picture therefore brings more good than harm, when it is honourably, artistically, and well made" (Snyder, p. 333).

LUCAS CRANACH THE ELDER. Martin Luther's favorite painter, Lucas Cranach the Elder (1472–1553), moved his workshop to Wittenberg in 1504, after a number of years in Vienna. In addition to the humanist milieu of its university and library, Wittenberg offered the patronage of the Saxon court. Appointed court painter to Elector Frederick the Wise, Cranach created woodcuts, altarpieces, and many portraits.

Just how far German artists' style and conception of the figure could differ from Italian Renaissance idealism is easily seen in

Cranach's **NYMPH OF THE SPRING (FIG. 21–9)**, especially when compared with Titian's *"Venus" of Urbino* (SEE FIG. 20–24). The sleeping nymph was a Renaissance theme, not an ancient one. Cranach was inspired by a fifteenth-century inscription on a fountain beside the Danube, cited in the upper left corner of the painting: "I am the nymph of the sacred font. Do not interrupt my sleep for I am at peace." Cranach records the Danube landscape with characteristic northern attention to detail and turns his nymph into a rather provocative young woman, who glances slyly out at the viewer through half-closed eyes. She has cast aside a fashionable red velvet gown, but still wears her jewelry, which together with her transparent veil enhances rather than conceals her nudity—especially those coral beads that fall between her breasts, outlining their contours. Unlike other artists working for Protestant patrons, many of whom looked on earthly beauty as a sinful vanity, Cranach seems delighted by earthly things—the lush foliage that provides the nymph's couch, the pair of partridges (symbols of Venus and married love), and Cupid's bow and quiver of arrows hanging on the tree. Could this nymph be a living beauty from the Wittenburg court? She is certainly not an embodiment of an idealized, Classical Venus.

21–10 • Hans Baldung Grien DEATH AND THE MATRON

c. 1520–1525. Oil on wood panel, 12⅜ × 7⅜″ (31.3 × 18.7 cm). Öffentliche Kunstsammlung, Basel.

Although more erotically charged and certainly more dramatic than Dürer's Eve in FIG. 21–7, Baldung's woman is based in certain ways on this famous image, which was engraved while he was assisting in Dürer's workshop. In many respects, the similarities in pose (especially the feet) and form (wide hips with narrowing waist and torso) only point up the differences in expressive content.

HANS BALDUNG GRIEN. Cranach's slightly younger contemporary Hans Baldung (1484/1485–1545)—his nickname tag "Grien" ("green," apparently a favorite color) dates from his apprenticeship days and was used to distinguish him from the numerous other apprentices named Hans—is known for very different visualizations of women. Born into an affluent and well-educated family, Baldung was working in Strasbourg by 1500, before moving to Nuremberg in 1503 and eventually joining Dürer's workshop in 1505–1507. Over the course of his long career, he also worked in Halle and Freiburg, but his principal artistic home was Strasbourg, where he lived out a prosperous professional life as a painter, printmaker, and stained-glass designer.

During the first half of his career, Baldung created a series of paintings on the theme of **DEATH AND THE MATRON** that juxtapose sensuality with mortality, voluptuousness with decay, attraction with repulsion. The example in **FIG. 21–10**—painted in about 1520–1525 for a private collector in Basel—uses brilliant illumination and expansive posture to draw our attention first to the voluptuous nude, fleshier and considerably more sensual than Cranach's nymph (SEE FIG. 21–9) or Dürer's Eve (SEE FIG. 21–7). But this focus is soon overtaken by a sense of surprise that mirrors her own, as she turns her head to discover that the figure stroking her hair and clutching at her breast is not her lover but Death himself. The putrid decay of his yellowing flesh contrasts sharply

21-11 • Albrecht Altdorfer
DANUBE LANDSCAPE
c. 1525. Oil on vellum on wood
panel, 12 × 8½″
(30.5 × 22.2 cm).
Alte Pinakothek, Munich.

with her soft contours, and his bony molting head is the antithesis of her full pink cheeks, flowing tresses, and soft traces of body hair. That the encounter takes place in a cemetery, on top of a tombstone, serves to underline the warning against the transitory pleasures of the flesh, but Baldung also seems to depend on the viewers' own erotic engagement to make the message not only moral but personal.

ALBRECHT ALTDORFER. Landscape, with or without figures, became a popular theme in the sixteenth century. In the fifteenth century, northern artists had examined and recorded nature with the care and enthusiasm of biologists, but painted landscapes were reserved for the backgrounds of figural compositions, usually sacred subjects. In the 1520s, however, religious art found little favor among Protestants. Landscape painting, on the other hand, had no overt religious content, although it could be seen as a reflection or even glorification of God's works on Earth. The most accomplished German landscape painter of the period was Albrecht Altdorfer (c. 1480–1538).

Altdorfer probably received his early training in Bavaria from his father, but he became a citizen of Regensburg in 1505 and remained there painting the Danube River Valley for the rest of his life. **DANUBE LANDSCAPE** of about 1525 **(FIG. 21–11)** is an early example of pure landscape painting, without a narrative subject, human figures, or overt religious significance. A small work on vellum laid down on a wood panel, it shows a landscape that seems to be a minutely detailed reproduction of the natural terrain, but the forest seems far more poetic and mysterious than Dürer's or Cranach's carefully observed views of nature. The low mountains, gigantic lacy pines, neatly contoured shrubberies, and fairyland castle with red-roofed towers at the end of a winding path announce a new sensibility. The eerily glowing yellow–white horizon below moving gray and blue clouds in a sky that takes up more than half the composition prefigures the Romanticism of German landscape painting in later centuries.

FRANCE

Renaissance France followed a different path from that taken in Germany. In 1519, Pope Leo X came to an agreement with French King Francis I (r. 1515–1547) that spared the country the turmoil suffered in Germany. Furthermore, whereas Martin Luther had devoted followers in France, French reformer John Calvin (1509–1564) fled to Switzerland in 1534, where he led a theocratic state in Geneva.

During the second half of the century, however, warring political factions favoring either Catholics or Huguenots (Protestants) competed to exert power over the French crown, with devastating consequences. In 1560, the devoutly Catholic Catherine de' Medici, widow of Henry II (r. 1547–1559), became regent for her young son, Charles IX, and tried, but failed, to balance the warring factions. Her machinations ended in religious polarization and a bloody conflict that began in 1562. When her third son, Henry III (r. 1574–1589), was murdered by a fanatical Dominican friar, a Protestant cousin, Henry, king of Navarre, the first Bourbon king, inherited the throne. Henry converted to Catholicism and ruled as Henry IV. Backed by a country sick of bloodshed, he quickly settled the religious question by proclaiming tolerance of Protestants in the Edict of Nantes in 1598.

A FRENCH RENAISSANCE UNDER FRANCIS I

Immediately after his ascent to the throne, Francis I sought to "modernize" the French court by acquiring the versatile talents of Leonardo da Vinci, who moved to France in 1516. Officially, Leonardo was there to advise the king on royal architectural projects and, the king said, for the pleasure of his conversation. Francis supported an Italian-inspired Renaissance in French art and architecture throughout his long reign.

JEAN CLOUET. Not all the artists working at the court of Francis I, however, were Italian. Flemish artist Jean Clouet (c. 1485–c. 1540) found great favor at the royal court, especially as a portrait painter. About the same time that he became principal court painter in 1527, he produced an official portrait of the king **(FIG. 21–12)**. Clouet created a flattering image of Francis by modulating the king's distinctive features with soft shading and highlighting the nervous activity of his fingers. At the same time he conceived an image of pure power. Elaborate, puffy sleeves broaden the king's

21-12 • Jean Clouet FRANCIS I
1525–1530. Oil and tempera on wood panel, 37¾ × 29⅛" (95.9 × 74 cm). Musée du Louvre, Paris.

The Castle of the Ladies

Women played an important role in the patronage of the arts during the Renaissance. Nowhere is their influence stronger than in the châteaux of the Loire River Valley. At Chenonceau, built beside and literally over the River Cher, a tributary of the Loire, women built, saved, and restored the château. Catherine Briconnet and her husband, Thomas Bohier, originally acquired the property, including a fortified mill, on which they built their country residence. Catherine supervised the construction, which included such modern conveniences as a straight staircase (an Italian and Spanish feature) instead of traditional medieval spiral stairs, and a kitchen inside the château instead of in a distant outbuilding. After Thomas died in 1524 and Catherine in 1526, their son gave Chenonceau to King Francis I.

King Henry II, Francis's son, gave Chenonceau to his mistress Diane de Poitiers in 1547. She managed the estate astutely, increased its revenue, developed the vineyards, added intricately planted gardens in the Italian style, and built a bridge across the Cher. When Henry died in a tournament, his queen, Catherine de' Medici (1519–1589), appropriated the château for herself.

Catherine, like so many in her family a great patron of the arts, added the two-story gallery to the bridge at Chenonceau, as well as outbuildings and additional formal gardens. Her parties were famous: mock naval battles on the river, fireworks, banquets, dances, and on one occasion two choruses of young women dressed as mermaids in the moat and nymphs in the shrubbery—who were then chased about by young men costumed as satyrs!

When Catherine's third son became king as Henry III in 1574, she gave the château to his wife, Louise of Lorraine, who lived in mourning at Chenonceau after Henry III was assassinated in 1589. She wore only white and covered the walls, windows, and furniture in her room with black velvet and damask. She gave Chenonceau to her niece when she died.

In the eighteenth and nineteenth centuries, the ladies continued to determine the fate of Chenonceau. During the French Revolution (1789–1793), the owner, Madame Dupin, was so beloved by the villagers that they protected her and saved her home. Then, in 1864, Madame Pelouze bought Chenonceau and restored it by removing Catherine de' Medici's Italian "improvements."

Chenonceau continued to play a role in the twentieth century. During World War I, it was used as a hospital. During the German occupation in World War II (1940–1942), when the River Cher formed the border with Vichy "Free" France, the gallery bridge at Chenonceau became an escape route.

CHÂTEAU OF CHENONCEAU
Touraine, France. Original building (at right) 1513–1521; gallery on bridge at left by Philibert de l'Orme, finished c. 1581.

shoulders to fill the entire width of the panel, much as Renaissance parade armor turned scrawny men into giants. The detailed rendering of the delicately worked costume of silk, satin, velvet, jewels, and gold embroidery could be painted separately from the portrait itself. Royal clothing was often loaned to the artist or modeled by a servant to spare the "sitter" the boredom of posing. In creating such official portraits, the artist sketched the subject, then painted a prototype that, upon approval, became the model for numerous replicas made for diplomatic and family purposes.

THE CHÂTEAU OF CHENONCEAU. With the enthusiasm of Francis for things Italian and the widening distribution of Italian books on architecture, the Italian Renaissance style soon infiltrated French architecture. Builders of elegant rural palaces, called **châteaux**, were quick to introduce Italianate decoration to otherwise Gothic buildings, but French architects soon adapted Classical principles of building design as well.

One of the most beautiful châteaux was not built as a royal residence, although it soon became one. In 1512, Thomas Bohier, a royal tax collector, bought the castle of Chenonceau on the River Cher, a tributary of the Loire (see "The Castle of the Ladies," opposite). He demolished the old castle, leaving only a tower. Using the piers of a water mill on the river bank as part of the foundations, he and his wife erected a new Renaissance home. The plan reflects the Classical principles of geometric regularity and symmetry—a rectangular building with rooms arranged on each side of a wide central hall. Only the library and chapel, which are corbelled out over the water, break the line of the walls. In the upper story, the builders used traditional features of medieval castles—

battlements, corner turrets, steep roofs, and dormer windows. The owners died soon after the château was finished in 1521, and their son gave it to Francis I, who turned it into a hunting lodge.

Later, Roman-trained French Renaissance architect Philibert de l'Orme (d. 1570) designed a gallery on a bridge across the river for Catherine de' Medici, completed about 1581 and incorporating contemporary Italianate window treatments, wall molding, and cornices that harmonized almost perfectly with the forms of the original turreted building.

FONTAINEBLEAU. Having chosen as his primary residence the medieval hunting lodge at Fontainebleau, Francis I began transforming it into a grand country palace. In 1530, he imported a Florentine artist, the Mannerist painter Rosso Fiorentino (1495–1540), to direct the project. After Rosso died, he was succeeded by his Italian colleague Francesco Primaticcio (1504–1570), who had earlier worked with Giulio Romano in Mantua (SEE FIG. 20–18), then joined Rosso in 1532, and would spend the rest of his career working on the decoration of Fontainebleau. During that time, he also commissioned and imported a large number of copies and casts of original Roman sculpture, from the newly discovered Laocoön (SEE FIG. 5–55) to the relief decoration on the Column of Trajan (SEE FIG. 6–44). These works provided an invaluable visual resource of figures and techniques for the northern European artists employed on the Fontainebleau project.

Among Primaticcio's first projects at Fontainebleau was the redecoration, in the 1540s, of the rooms of the king's official mistress, Anne, duchess of Étampes (FIG. 21–13). The artist

21-13 • Primaticcio **STUCCO AND WALL PAINTING, CHAMBER OF THE DUCHESS OF ÉTAMPES, CHÂTEAU OF FONTAINEBLEAU**
France. 1540s.

21-14 • Pierre Lescot and Jean Goujon WEST WING OF THE COUR CARRÉE, PALAIS DU LOUVRE
Paris. Begun 1546.

combined woodwork, stucco relief, and fresco painting in his complex but whimsical and graceful interior design. The lithe figures of stucco nymphs, with their elongated bodies and small heads, recall Parmigianino's paintings (SEE FIG. 20–27). Their spiraling postures and teasing bits of clinging drapery are playfully erotic. Garlands, mythological figures, and Roman architectural ornament almost overwhelm the walls with visual enrichment, yet the whole remains ordered and lighthearted. The first School of Fontainebleau, as this Italian phase of the palace decoration is called, established an Italianate tradition of Mannerism in painting and interior design that spread to other centers in France and into the Netherlands.

THE LOUVRE.   Before the defeat of Francis I at Pavia by Holy Roman Emperor Charles V, and the king's subsequent imprisonment in Spain in 1525, the French court had been a mobile unit, and the locus of French art resided outside Paris in the Loire Valley. After his release in 1526, Francis made Paris his bureaucratic seat, and the Île-de-France—Paris and its region—took the artistic lead. The move to the capital gave birth to a style of French Classicism when Francis I and Henry II decided to modernize the medieval castle of the Louvre. Work began in 1546, with the replacement of the west wing of the square court, or **COUR CARRÉE (FIG. 21–14)**, by architect Pierre Lescot (c. 1510–1578) working with sculptor

Jean Goujon (1510–1568). They designed a building that incorporated Renaissance ideals of balance and regularity with Classical architectural details and rich sculptural decoration. The irregular rooflines seen in a château such as the one at Chenonceau (see "The Castle of the Ladies," page 690, right side of the photograph) gave way to discreetly rounded arches and horizontal balustrades. Classical pilasters and entablatures replaced Gothic buttresses and stringcourses. A round-arched arcade on the ground floor suggests an Italian loggia. On the other hand, the sumptuousness of the decoration recalls the French Flamboyant style (see Chapter 18), only with Classical pilasters and acanthus replacing Gothic colonnettes and cusps.

SPAIN AND PORTUGAL

The sixteenth century saw the high point of Spanish political power. The country had been united in the fifteenth century by the marriage of Isabella of Castile and Ferdinand of Aragon. Only Navarre (in the Pyrenees) and Portugal remained outside the union of the crowns. (See "Sculpture for the Knights of Christ at Tomar," opposite.) When Isabella and Ferdinand's grandson Charles V abdicated in 1556, his son Philip II (r. 1556–1598) became the king of Spain, the Netherlands, and the Americas, as well as ruler of Milan, Burgundy, and Naples, but Spain was

Sculpture for the Knights of Christ at Tomar

One of the most beautiful, if also one of the strangest, sixteenth-century sculptures in Portugal seems to float over the cloisters of the Convent of Christ in Tomar. Unexpectedly, in the heart of the castle-monastery complex, one comes face to face with the Old Man of the Sea. He supports on his powerful shoulders an extraordinary growth—part roots and trunk of a gnarled tree; part tangled mass of seaweed, algae, ropes, and anchor chains. Barnacle- and coral-encrusted piers lead the eye upward, revealing a large lattice-covered window, the great west window of the church of the Knights of Christ.

When, in 1314, Pope Clement V disbanded the Templars (a monastic order of knights founded in Jerusalem after the First Crusade), King Dinis of Portugal offered them a renewed existence as the Knights of Christ. As a result, in 1356, they made the former Templar castle and monastery in Tomar their headquarters. When Prince Henry the Navigator (1394–1460) became the grand master of the order, he invested their funds in the exploration of the African coast and the Atlantic Ocean. The Templar insignia, the squared cross, became the emblem used on the sails of Portuguese ships.

King Manuel I of Portugal (r. 1495–1521) commissioned the present church, with its amazing sculpture by Diogo de Arruda, in 1510. So distinctive is the style developed under King Manuel by artists like the Arruda brothers, Diogo (active 1508–1531) and Francisco (active 1510–1547), that Renaissance art in Portugal is called "Manueline." In the window of Tomar, every surface is carved with architectural and natural detail associated with the sea. Twisted ropes form the corners of the window; the coral pillars support great swathes of seaweed. Chains and cables drop through the watery depths to the place where the head of a man—could this Old Man of the Sea be a self-portrait of Diogo de Arruda?—emerges from the roots of a tree. Above the window, more ropes, cables, and seaweed support the emblems of the patron—armillary spheres at the upper outside corners (topped by pinnacles) and at dead center, the coat of arms of Manuel I with its Portuguese castles framing the five wounds of Christ. Topping the composition is the square cross of the Order of Christ—clearly delineated against the wall of the chapel.

The armillary sphere became a symbol of the era. This complex form of a celestial globe, with the sun at the center surrounded by rings marking the paths of the planets, was a teaching device that acknowledged the new scientific theory that the sun, not the Earth, is the center of the solar system. (Copernicus, teaching in Germany at this time, only published his theories in 1531 and 1543.) King Manuel's use of the armillary sphere as his emblem signals his determination to make Portugal the leader in the exploration of the sea. Indeed, in Manuel's reign the Portuguese reached India and Brazil.

Diogo de Arruda **WEST WINDOW, CHURCH IN THE CONVENT OF CHRIST**
Tomar, Portugal. c. 1510. Commissioned by King Manuel I of Portugal.

Philip's permanent residence. For more than half a century, he supported artists in Spain, Italy, and the Netherlands. His navy, the famous Spanish Armada, halted the advance of Islam in the Mediterranean and secured control of most American territories. Despite enormous effort, however, Philip could not suppress the revolt of the northern provinces of the Netherlands, nor could he prevail in his war against the English, who destroyed his navy in 1588. He was able to gain control of the entire Iberian peninsula, however, by claiming Portugal in 1580, and it remained part of Spain until 1640.

ARCHITECTURE

Philip built **THE ESCORIAL** (**FIG. 21–15**), the great monastery-palace complex outside Madrid, partly to comply with his father's direction to construct a "pantheon" in which all Spanish kings might be buried and partly to house his court and government. In 1559, Philip summoned from Italy Juan Bautista de Toledo (d. 1567), who had been Michelangelo's supervisor of work at St. Peter's from 1546 to 1548. Juan Bautista's design for the monastery-palace reflected his indoctrination in Bramante's Classical principles in Rome, but the king himself dictated the severity and size of the structure. The Escorial's grandeur comes from its overwhelming size, fine proportions, and excellent masonry. The complex includes not only the royal residence but also the Royal Monastery of San Lorenzo, a school, a library, and a church, its crypt serving as the royal burial chamber. The plan was said to resemble a gridiron, the instrument of martyrdom of its patron saint, Lawrence, who was roasted alive.

In 1572, Juan Bautista's assistant, Juan de Herrera, was appointed architect, and he immediately changed the design, adding second stories on all wings and breaking the horizontality of the main façade with a central frontispiece that resembled the superimposed temple fronts that were fashionable on Italian churches at this time (SEE FIGS. 20–36, 20–38). Before beginning the church in the center of the complex, Philip solicited the advice of Italian architects—including Vignola and Palladio. The final design combined ideas that Philip approved and Herrera carried out, and it embodies Italian Classicism in its geometric clarity, symmetry, and superimposed temple-front façade. In its austerity, it embodies the deep religiosity of Philip II.

PAINTING

Although Philip II was a great patron of the Venetian painter Titian, and he collected Netherlandish artists such as Bosch, the most famous painter working in Spain during the last quarter of the sixteenth century is Domenikos Theotokopoulos (1541–1614), who arrived in Spain in 1577 after working for ten years in Italy. "El Greco" ("The Greek"), as he is called, was trained as an icon painter in the Byzantine manner in his native Crete, then under Venetian rule. In about 1566, he went to Venice and entered Titian's studio, where he also studied the paintings of Tintoretto and Veronese. From about 1570 to 1577, he worked in Rome, apparently without finding sufficient patronage, although he lived for a time in the Farnese Palace. Probably encouraged by Spanish church officials whom he met in Rome, El Greco settled in Toledo, seat of the Spanish archbishop. He had hoped for a court appointment, but Philip II disliked the painting he had commissioned from El Greco for The Escorial and never again gave him work.

In Toledo, El Greco joined the circle of humanist scholars. He wrote that the artist's goal should be to copy nature, that Raphael relied too heavily on the ancients, and that the Italians' use of mathematics to achieve ideal proportions hindered their painting of nature. At this same time an intense religious revival was under way in Spain, expressed in the impassioned preaching of Ignatius of Loyola, as well as in the poetry of two great Spanish mystics: St. Teresa of Ávila (1515–1582) and her follower St. John of the Cross (1542–1591). El Greco's style—rooted in Byzantine icon painting and strongly reflecting the rich colors and loose brushwork of Venetian painting—was well equipped to express the intense spirituality of these mystics.

In 1586, the Orgaz family commissioned El Greco to paint a large altarpiece honoring an illustrious fourteenth-century ancestor. Count Orgaz had been a great benefactor of the Church, and at his funeral in 1323, SS. Augustine and Stephen were said to have appeared to lower his body into his tomb as his soul was seen ascending to heaven. El Greco's painting the **BURIAL OF COUNT ORGAZ** (**FIG. 21–16**) captures these miracles. An angel lifts Orgaz's

21-15 • Juan Bautista de Toledo and Juan de Herrera THE ESCORIAL
Madrid. 1563–1584. Detail from an anonymous 18th-century painting.

SEE MORE: Click the Google Earth link for The Escorial
www.myartslab.com

21–16 • El Greco BURIAL OF COUNT ORGAZ
1586. Oil on canvas, 16′ × 11′10″ (4.88 × 3.61 m). Church of Santo Tomé, Toledo, Spain.

ghostly soul along the central axis of the painting toward the enthroned Christ at the apex of the canvas. El Greco filled the space around the burial scene with portraits of the local aristocracy and religious notables. He placed his own 8-year-old son at the lower left next to St. Stephen and signed the painting on the boy's white kerchief. El Greco may also have put his own features on the man just above the saint's head, the only other

figure who, like the child, looks straight out at the viewer.

In composing the painting, El Greco used Mannerist devices reminiscent of Pontormo (SEE FIG. 20–26), packing the pictorial field with figures and eliminating specific reference to the spatial setting. Yet he has distinguished between heaven and earth by the light emanating from Christ, whose otherworldly luminescence is quite unlike the natural light below.

THE NETHERLANDS

In the Netherlands, the sixteenth century was an age of bitter religious and political conflict. Despite the opposition of the Spanish Habsburg rulers, the Protestant Reformation took hold in the northern provinces. Seeds of unrest were sown still deeper over the course of the century by continued religious persecution, economic hardship, and inept governors. Widespread iconoclasm characterized 1566–1567, and a long battle for independence began with a revolt in 1568 that lasted until Spain relinquished all claims to the region 80 years later. As early as 1579, when the seven northern Protestant provinces declared themselves the United Provinces, the discord split the Netherlands, eventually dividing it along religious lines into the United Provinces (the present-day Netherlands) and Catholic Flanders (present-day Belgium).

Even with the turmoil, the Netherlanders found the resources to pay for art, and Antwerp and other cities developed into thriving art centers. The Reformation led artists to seek patrons outside the Church. While courtiers and burghers alike continued to commission portraits, the demand arose for small paintings with interesting secular subjects appropriate for homes. For example, some artists became specialists known for their landscapes or satires. In addition to painting, textiles, ceramics, printmaking, and sculpture in wood and metal flourished in the Netherlands. Flemish tapestries were sought after and highly prized across Europe, as they had been in the fifteenth century, and leading Italian artists made cartoons to be woven into tapestries in Flemish workshops (see "Raphael's Cartoons for Tapestries in the Sistine Chapel," pages 646–647). The graphic arts emerged as an important medium, providing many artists with another source of income. Pieter Bruegel the Elder began his career drawing amusing and moralizing images to be printed and published by At the Four Winds, an Antwerp publishing house. Artists such as Hendrick Goltzius, who traveled with sketchbook in hand, turned their experiences to profit when they returned home.

Like Vasari in Italy, Carel van Mander (1548–1606) recorded the lives of his Netherlandish contemporaries in engaging biographies that mix fact and gossip. He, too, intended his 1604 book *Het Schilder-boeck* (*The Painter's Book*) to be a survey of the history of art, and he included material from the ancient Roman writers Pliny and Vitruvius as well as from Vasari's revised and expanded *Lives*, published in 1568.

ART FOR ARISTOCRATIC AND NOBLE PATRONS

Artistic taste among the wealthy bourgeoisie and noble classes in the early sixteenth-century Netherlands was characterized by a striking diversity, encompassing the imaginative and difficult visions of Hieronymus Bosch, as well as the more Italianate compositions of Jan Gossaert. In the later years of his life, Bosch's membership in a local but prestigious confraternity called the Brotherhood of Our Lady seems to have opened doors to noble patrons such as Count Hendrick III of Nassau and Duke Philip the Fair. His younger contemporary Gossaert left the city of Antwerp as a young man to spend the majority of his active years as the court painter for the natural son of Duke Philip the Good. His art also attracted members of the Habsburgs, including Charles V, who were seduced by Gossaert's combination of northern European and Italian styles.

HIERONYMUS BOSCH.   Among the most fascinating Netherlandish painters to modern viewers is Hieronymus Bosch (1450–

21-17 • Hieronymus Bosch GARDEN OF EARTHLY DELIGHTS (OPEN)
c. 1505–1515. Oil on wood panel, center panel 7′2½″ × 6′4¾″ (2.20 × 1.95 m), each wing 7′2½″ × 3′2″ (2.20 × 0.97 m). Museo del Prado, Madrid.

Despite—or perhaps because of—its bizarre subject matter, this triptych was woven in 1566 into tapestries, and at least one painted copy was made as well. Bosch's original triptych was sold at the onset of the Netherlands Revolt and sent in 1568 to Spain, where it entered the collection of Philip II.

EXPLORE MORE: Gain insight from a primary source on Hieronymus Bosch
www.myartslab.com

1516), who depicted the sort of imaginative fantasies more often associated with medieval than Renaissance art. A superb colorist and virtuoso technician, Bosch spent his career in the town whose name he adopted, 's-Hertogenbosch. Bosch's religious devotion is certain, and his range of subjects shows that he was well educated. Challenging and unsettling paintings such as his **GARDEN OF EARTHLY DELIGHTS** (FIG. 21–17) have led modern scholars to label Bosch both a mystic and a social critic. The subject of the triptych seems to be founded on Christian belief in the natural state of human sinfulness, but it was not painted for a church.

In the left wing, God introduces doll-like figures of Adam and Eve, under the watchful eye of the owl of perverted wisdom. The owl symbolizes both wisdom and folly. Folly had become an important concept to the northern European humanists, who believed in the power of education. They believed that people would choose to follow the right way once they knew it. Here the owl peers out from an opening in the spherical base of a fantastic

pink fountain in a lake from which vicious creatures creep out into the world.

In the central panel, the Earth teems with such monsters, but also with vivacious human revelers and luscious huge fruits, symbolic of fertility and sexual abandon. In hell, at the right, sensual pleasures—eating, drinking, music, and dancing—become instruments of torture in a dark world of fire and ice. The emphasis in the right wing on the torments of hell, with no hint of the rewards of heaven, seems to caution that damnation is the natural outcome of a life lived in ignorance and folly, that humans ensure their damnation through their self-centered pursuit of pleasures of the flesh—the sins of gluttony, lust, greed, and sloth—outlined with such fantastic and graphic abandon in the central panel.

One scholar has proposed that the central panel is a parable on human salvation in which the practice of alchemy—the process that sought to turn common metals into gold—parallels Christ's power to convert human dross into spiritual gold. In this theory, the bizarre fountain at the center of the lake in the middle distance can

21-18 • Hieronymus Bosch **GARDEN OF EARTHLY DELIGHTS (CLOSED)**

be seen as an alchemical "marrying chamber," complete with the glass vessels for collecting the vapors of distillation. Others see the theme known as "the power of women." In this interpretation, the central pool is the setting for a display of seductive women and sex-obsessed men. Women frolic alluringly in the pool while men dance and ride in a mad circle trying to attract them. In this strange garden, men are slaves to their own lust. An early seventeenth-century critic focused on the fruit, writing that the triptych was known as *The Strawberry Plant* because it represented the "vanity and glory and the passing taste of strawberries or the strawberry plant and its pleasant odor that is hardly remembered once it has passed." Luscious fruits of obvious sexual symbolism—straw-berries, cherries, grapes, and pomegranates—appear every-where in the garden, serving as food, as shelter, and even as a boat. Is human life as fleeting and insubstantial as the taste of a straw-berry? Yet another modern reading sees the central tableau imagin-ing the course of life in paradise, assuming that Adam and Even had not consigned humanity to sin by eating the forbidden fruit.

Conforming to a long tradition of triptych altarpieces made for churches, Bosch painted a more sober, *grisaille* picture on the reverse of the side wings. When the triptych is closed, a less enigmatic, but equally fascinating, scene is displayed (**FIG. 21–18**). A transparent, illusionistic rendering of a receding sphere floating within a void encloses the flat circular shelf of Earth on its third day of creation. Fragments of the fantastic fruit that will appear fully formed in the interior pictures float here in the primordial sea, while ominous dark clouds promise the rain that will nurture them into their full seductive ripeness. A tiny crowned figure of God the Creator hovers in a bubble within dark clouds at upper left, displaying a book, perhaps a Bible opened to the words from Psalm 33:9 that are inscribed across the top: "For he spoke, and it came to be; he commanded, and it stood firm."

The *Garden of Earthly Delights* was commissioned by an aristocrat (probably Count Hendrick III of Nassau) for his Brussels town house, and the artist's choice of a triptych format, which suggests an altarpiece, may have been an understated irony. In a private home the painting surely inspired lively discussion, even ribald commentary, much as it does today in the Prado Museum. Perhaps that, rather than a single meaning or interpretation, is the true intention behind this dazzling display of artistic imagination.

JAN GOSSAERT. In contrast to the private visions of Bosch, Jan Gossaert (c. 1478–c. 1533) maintained traditional subject matter and embraced the new Classical art of Italy. Gossaert (who later called himself Mabuse after his native city Maubeuge) entered the service of Philip, the illegitimate son of the duke of Burgundy, accompanying him to Italy in 1508, and remaining in his service after Philip became archbishop of Utrecht in 1517.

Gossaert's "Romanizing" style—inspired by Italian Mannerist paintings and decorative details drawn from ancient Roman art—is evident in his painting of **ST. LUKE DRAWING THE VIRGIN MARY** (**FIG. 21–19**), a traditional subject we already know from a painting

21-19 • Jan Gossaert
ST. LUKE DRAWING THE VIRGIN MARY
1520. Oil on panel,
43⅜ × 32¼″
(110.2 × 81.9 cm).
Kunsthistorisches
Museum, Vienna.

by Rogier van der Weyden (SEE FIG. 18–14). In Gossaert's version, the artist's studio is an extraordinary structure of Classical piers and arches, carved with a dense ornament of foliage and medallions. Mary and the Christ Child appear in a blaze of golden light and clouds before the saint, who kneels at a desk, his hand guided by an angel as he records the vision in a drawing. Luke's crumpled red robe replicates fifteenth-century drapery conventions in a seeming reference to Rogier's famous picture. Seated above and behind Luke on a round, columnar structure, Moses holds the Tablets of the Law, referencing his own visions of God on Mount Sinai. Just

as Moses had removed his shoes in God's presence, so has Luke in the presence of his vision. Gossaert, like Dürer before him, seems to be staking a claim for the divine inspiration of the artist.

ANTWERP

During the sixteenth century, Antwerp was the commercial and artistic center of the southern Netherlands. Its deep port made it an international center of trade (it was one of the European centers for trade in spices), and it was the financial center of Europe. Painting, printmaking, and book production flourished in this

21-20 • Quentin Massys MONEY CHANGER AND HIS WIFE
1514. Oil on panel, 28 × 26¾″ (71.2 × 68 cm). Kunsthistorisches Museum, Vienna.

environment, attracting artists and craftsmen from all over Europe. The demand for luxury goods fostered the birth of the art market, in which art was transformed into a commodity for both local and international consumption. In responding to this market system, many artists became specialists in one area, such as portraiture or landscape, working with art dealers, who emerged as middlemen, further shaping the commodification of art, its production, and its producers.

QUENTIN MASSYS. Early accounts of the prosperous Antwerp artist Quentin Massys (1466–1530) claim that he began working in his native Louvain as a blacksmith (his father's profession) but changed to painting to compete with a rival for the affections of a young woman; Carel van Mander claims he was a self-trained artist. We know he entered the Antwerp painters' guild in 1491, and at his death in 1530 he was among its most prosperous and renowned members, supervising a large workshop to meet the market in this burgeoning art center.

One of his most fascinating paintings—**MONEY CHANGER AND HIS WIFE (FIG. 21–20)**—recalls, like Gossaert's *St. Luke*, a famous fifteenth-century work, in this case the picture of a goldsmith painted for the Antwerp goldsmiths' guild by Petrus Christus (see "A Closer Look," page 581). Here, however, a couple is in charge of business, and they present us with two different profiles of engagement. The soberly dressed proprietor himself focuses intently on weighing coins in a suspended balance. His brightly outfitted wife —dressed in an archaic fifteenth-century costume that harks back to a golden age of Flemish painting—looks to the side, distracted by her husband's activity from the attention she was giving to the meticulously described Book of Hours spread out on the table in front of her. It would be easy to jump to the conclusion that this is a moral fable, warning of the danger of losing "sight" of religious obligations because of a preoccupation with affairs of business. But the painting is not that simple. An inscription that ran around the original frame quoted Leviticus 19:36—"You shall have honest balances and honest weights"—claiming just business practices as a form of righteous living. Is it possible the moral here juxtaposes not worldliness and spirituality, but attentive and distracted devotional practice? The sidetracked wife seems to have been idly flipping through her prayer book before turning to observe what her husband is doing, whereas a man in a red turban reflected in the convex mirror next to her Book of Hours is caught in rapt attention to the book in front of him, and the nature of his reading is suggested by

21-21 • Caterina van Hemessen SELF-PORTRAIT
1548. Oil on wood panel, 12¼ × 9¼″ (31.1 × 23.5 cm). Öffentliche Kunstsammlung, Basel, Switzerland.

the church steeple through the window behind him. The sermon here concerns the challenge of godly living in a worldly society, but wealth itself is not necessarily the root of the problem.

CATERINA VAN HEMESSEN. Antwerp painter Caterina van Hemessen (1528–1587) developed an illustrious reputation as a portraitist. She had learned to paint from her father, the Flemish Mannerist Jan Sanders van Hemessen, who was dean of the Antwerp painters' guild in 1548, but the quiet realism and skilled rendering of her subjects is distinctively her own. To maintain focus on her foreground subjects, van Hemessen painted them against even, dark-colored backgrounds, on which she identified the sitter by name and age, signing and dating each work. The inscription in her **SELF-PORTRAIT (FIG. 21–21)** reads: "I Caterina van Hemessen painted myself in 1548. Her age 20." In delineating

Bruegel's Cycle of the Months

Cycles, or series, of paintings unified by a developing theme or allegorical subject—for instance, the Times of the Day, the Four Seasons, or the Five Senses—became popular wall decorations in prosperous Flemish homes during the sixteenth century. In 1565, Pieter Bruegel the Elder was commissioned to paint a series of six large paintings, each over 5 feet wide, surveying the months of the year, two months to a picture. They were made to be hung together in a room—probably the dining room since food figures prominently in these pictures—in the suburban villa of wealthy merchant Niclaes Jonghelinck, just outside Antwerp.

Return of the Hunters (FIG. A) represents December and January. The bleak landscape is gripped by winter as hunters return home at dusk with meager results: a single rabbit slung over the largest man's shoulder. But the landscape, rather than the figures, seems to be the principal subject here. A row of trees forms a receding set, consistently diminishing in scale, to draw our attention into the space of the painting along the orthogonal descent on the hillside of houses on the left. Like the calendar illustrations of medieval Books of Hours, the landscape is filled with behavior emblematic of the time of year: the singeing of the pig outside the farmhouse at left, the playful movement of ice skaters across frozen fields. We see it all from an omnipotent elevated viewpoint, like one of the birds that perch in the trees or glide across the snow-covered fantasy of an alpine background.

The mood is very different in the painting representing the hazy late summer days of August and September (FIG. B). Birds still perch and glide, and a silhouetted tree still dominates the foreground—as if Bruegel wanted to set up obvious relationships between the scenes so that viewers would assess them comparatively— but the setting here is more rural than residential. Architecture keeps its distance or is screened by foliage. Agricultural workers trudge through their labor, harvesting grain, and gathering stalks into tidy sheaves, ready for transport. The figural focus, however, is in the foreground, on a

A. Pieter Bruegel the Elder **RETURN OF THE HUNTERS**
1565. Oil on wood panel, 3'10½" × 5'3¾" (1.18 × 1.61 m). Kunsthistorisches Museum, Vienna.

B. Pieter Bruegel the Elder **THE HARVESTERS**
1565. Oil on wood panel, 46⅞ × 63¾″ (1.17 × 1.6 m). Metropolitan Museum of Art, New York.

shift of workers on their lunch break—serving themselves from baskets, gnawing on hard pieces of bread, spooning milk from bowls, or gulping from an uplifted jug. One man takes the opportunity of this break for a quick nap. Some have seen in this lounging figure an emblem of sloth, or a wanton display of uncouth behavior, reminiscent of the embarrassing exposure of the peasant couple invited in to warm themselves before the fire in the farmhouse of the February page of Duke Jean de Berry's *Très Riches Heures* (SEE FIG. 18–4), painted by the Netherlandish Limbourg brothers a century and a half earlier.

Indeed, Bruegel's series of the months invites comparison with this venerable tradition—dating to the early Middle Ages—of showing peasant activity within the calendar cycles of prayer books made for wealthy patrons. Were they amused by peasant behavior? Did they enjoy representations of the productivity of their land and the availability of willing laborers to work it? Or do these vignettes embody their own longings for a simpler life, idealized for them as a harmony between the natural world and the people who live on it, and off it? But the peasants enjoying the good life in this sunny scene of harvesting are only on a lunch break. Another shift is already hard at work in the fields, and the wealth of the patrons who supported the growth of an art market was dependent on the labor of countless folks like them.

EXPLORE MORE: Gain insight from a primary source on Pieter Bruegel **www.myartslab.com**

The French Ambassadors
by Hans Holbein the Younger. 1533. Oil on wood panel. 81⅛ × 82⅝" (2.07 × 2.1 m). National Gallery, London.

Embossing on the sheath of the dagger tells us that de Dinteville is 28, while an inscription on the edge of the book (Bible?) under de Selve's arm records that he is 24.

This globe has Polisy, the de Dinteville family estate, marked at the center. It was here that this painting was hung when the ambassador returned to France at the end of 1533.

These objects on the top shelf were used to observe natural heavenly phenomena and chart the passage of time. The items displayed on the lower shelf relate more to terrestrial concerns.

Music is a common symbol of harmony in this period, and the broken string on this lute has been understood as an allusion to the discord created by the sweep of Protestant reform across Europe.

This bizarre, but prominently placed skull—as well as the skull badge that appears on de Dinteville's cap—reminded viewers of their own mortality. The foreground skull is distorted by anamorphosis, in which images are stretched horizontally with the use of a trapezoidal grid so that they must be viewed from the side to appear correctly proportioned.

This pavement—known as "Cosmati work" after the thirteenth-century Italian family that specialized in it—is copied from the floor in Westminster Abbey and may proclaim the ambassadors' involvement in a holy enterprise of reconciliation. The artist signed the painting on the left edge of the floor: "Johannes Holbein pingebat, 1533."

This is a Lutheran hymnal published in 1527, open at one of Luther's best-known compositions: "Come, Holy Ghost, our souls inspire." Neither man was a Protestant, but some of de Selve's contemporaries saw him as sympathetic to the cause of the reformers.

SEE MORE: View the Closer Look feature for *The French Ambassadors* **www.myartslab.com**

her own features, van Hemessen presented a serious young person who looks up to acknowledge us, interrupting her work on a portrait of a woman client. Between the date of this self-portrait and 1552, she painted ten signed and dated portraits of women, which seems to have been a specialty. She became a favored court artist to Mary of Hungary, sister of Emperor Charles V and regent of the Netherlands, for whom she painted not only portraits but also religious works, and whom she followed back to Spain when Mary ceased to be regent in 1556.

PIETER BRUEGEL THE ELDER. So popular did the works of Hieronymus Bosch remain that, nearly half a century after his death, Pieter Bruegel (c. 1525–1569) began his career by imitating them. Like Bosch, he often painted large narrative works crowded with figures, and he chose moralizing or satirical subject matter. He traveled throughout Italy, but, unlike many Renaissance artists, he did not record the ruins of ancient Rome or the wonders of the Italian cities. Instead, he seems to have been fascinated by the landscape, particularly the formidable jagged rocks and sweeping panoramic views of Alpine valleys, which he recorded in detailed drawings. Back home in his studio, he made an impressive leap of the imagination as he painted the flat and rolling lands of Flanders as broad panoramas, even adding imaginary mountains on the horizon. He also visited country fairs to sketch the farmers and townspeople who became the focus of his paintings, presenting humans not as unique individuals but as well-observed types, whose universality makes them familiar even today.

Bruegel depicted nature in all seasons and in all moods. *Return of the Hunters* (see "Bruegel's Cycle of the Months," pages 702–703, FIG. A) captures the bleak atmosphere of early nightfall during a damp, cold winter, with a freshness that recalls the much earlier paintings of his compatriots the Limbourgs (SEE FIG. 18–4). The hunters are foregrounded before a sharp plunge into space; the juxtaposition of near and far without middle ground is a typically sixteenth-century device. But this is clearly not an accidental image; it is a slice of everyday life faithfully reproduced within a carefully calculated composition. The same can be said of Breugel's portrayal of late summer harvest (SEE "Bruegel's Cycle of the Months," pages 702–703, FIG. B), where the light is warmer, the landscape lush and verdant, the human activity rooted in agricultural labor or a momentary respite from it. As a depiction of Netherlandish life, these peasant scenes focusing on landscape represent a relative calm before the storm. Three years after they were painted, the anguished struggle of the northern provinces for independence from Spain began.

Pieter the Elder died in 1569, leaving two children, Pieter the Younger (1564/1565–1637/1638) and Jan (1568–1625), both of whom became successful painters. And the dynasty continued with Jan's son, Jan the Younger (1601–1678), who changed the family name from Bruegel to Brueghel.

ENGLAND

Tudor England, in spite of the disruption caused by the Reformation, was economically and politically stable enough to provide sustained support for the arts, as Henry VIII strived to compete with the wealthy, sophisticated court of Francis I. Music, literature, and architecture flourished, but painting was principally left to foreigners.

As a young man, Henry VIII (r. 1509–1547) was loyal to the Church, defending it against Luther's attacks. He was rewarded by the pope in 1521 by being granted the title "Defender of the Faith." But when the pope refused to annul his marriage to Catherine of Aragon, Henry broke with Rome. By action of Parliament in 1534 he became the "Supreme Head on Earth of the Church and Clergy of England." He mandated an English translation of the Bible in every church, and in 1536 and 1539, he dissolved the monasteries, confiscating their great wealth and rewarding his followers with monastic lands and buildings. Shrines and altars were stripped of their jewels and precious metals to bolster the royal purse, and in 1548, during the reign of Henry's son, Edward VI, religious images were officially prohibited.

During the brief reign of Mary (r. 1553–1558), England officially returned to Catholicism, but the accession of Elizabeth in 1558 confirmed England as a Protestant country. So effective was Elizabeth, who ruled until 1603, that the last decades of the sixteenth century in England are called the Elizabethan Age.

ARTISTS IN THE TUDOR COURT

A remarkable record of the appearance of Tudor notables survives in portraiture. Since the Tudors had long favored Netherlandish and German artists, it is hardly surprising that it was a German-born painter, Hans Holbein the Younger (c. 1497–1543), who shaped the taste of the English court and upper classes.

HANS HOLBEIN. Holbein first visited London from 1526 to 1528 and was introduced by the Dutch scholar Erasmus to the humanist circle around the English statesman Thomas More. He returned to England in 1532 and was appointed court painter to Henry VIII about four years later. During the 1530s, he created a spectacular series of portraits of nobles and diplomats associated with the Tudor court. The court's climate of international interaction is embodied in a double portrait that Holbein painted in 1533 (see "A Closer Look," opposite)—a German painter's rendering in England of two French diplomats, one of them representing the court of Francis I in the Vatican. *The French Ambassadors* foregrounds Holbein's virtuosity as a painter and constructs a rich characterization of Jean de Dinteville, French ambassador to England, and his friend Georges de Selve, bishop of Lavaur and ambassador to the Holy See. With a loving detail that recalls the work of Jan van Eyck, the artist describes the surface textures and luminosity of the many objects placed in the painting to reflect the intellectual gifts and symbolize the political accomplishments of these two men. References in these objects to the conflicts

21-22 • Marcus Gheeraerts the Younger QUEEN ELIZABETH I (THE DITCHLEY PORTRAIT)
c. 1592. Oil on canvas, 95 × 60″ (2.4 × 1.5 m). National Portrait Gallery, London.

(FIG. 21–22). Called the *Ditchley Portrait* because it seems to have been commissioned for Ditchley, the estate of her courtier Sir Henry Lee, to commemorate the Queen's visit in 1592, the full-length figure of Elizabeth—more costume than body—stands supreme on a map of her realm with her feet in Oxfordshire, near Ditchley. The stark whiteness of her elaborate dress and the pale abstraction of her severe face assert the virginal purity that she cultivated as a part of her image. A storm passes out of the picture on the right while the sun breaks through on the left. It is as if the queen is in control not only of England but of nature itself.

NICHOLAS HILLIARD. In 1570, Nicholas Hilliard (1547–1619) arrived in London from southwest England to pursue a career as a jeweler, goldsmith, and painter of miniatures. Hilliard never received a court appointment, but he created miniature portraits of the queen and court notables, including George Clifford, third earl of Cumberland **(FIG. 21–23)**. Cumberland was a regular participant in the annual tilts and festivals celebrating the anniversary of Elizabeth's ascent to the throne. In Hilliard's miniature, Cumberland, a

between European states, and within the Catholic Church itself, imply that these bright and confident young ambassadors will apply their considerable diplomatic skills to finding a resolution.

PORTRAITS OF ELIZABETH. Queen Elizabeth I carefully controlled the way artists represented her in official portraits and was known to have imprisoned artists whose unofficial images did not meet with her approval. A stark and hieratic regal image by Flemish artist Marcus Gheeraerts typifies the look she was after

21-23 • Nicholas Hilliard GEORGE CLIFFORD, THIRD EARL OF CUMBERLAND (1558-1605)
c. 1595. Watercolor on vellum on card, oval 2¾ × 2³⁄₁₆″ (7.1 × 5.8 cm). The Nelson-Atkins Museum of Art, Kansas City, Missouri. Gift of Mr. and Mrs. John W. Starr through the Starr Foundation. F58-60/188

Armor for Royal Games

The medieval tradition of holding tilting, or jousting, competitions at English festivals and public celebrations continued during Renaissance times. Perhaps most famous were the Accession Day Tilts, held annually to celebrate the anniversary of Elizabeth I's coming to the throne. The gentlemen of the court, dressed in armor made especially for the occasion, held mock battles in the queen's honor. They rode their horses from opposite directions, trying to strike each other with long lances during six passes, as judges rated their performances.

The elegant armor worn by George Clifford, third Earl of Cumberland, at the Accession Day Tilts has been preserved in the collection of the Metropolitan Museum of Art in New York. Tudor roses and back-to-back capital *E*s in honor of the queen decorate the armor's surface. As the queen's champion, beginning in 1590, Clifford also wore her jeweled glove attached to his helmet as he met all comers in the tiltyard of Whitehall Palace in London.

Made by Jacob Halder in the royal armories at Greenwich, the 60-pound suit of armor is recorded in the sixteenth-century Almain Armourers' Album along with its "exchange pieces." These allowed the owner to vary his appearance by changing mitts, side pieces, or leg protectors, and also provided backup pieces if one were damaged.

Jacob Halder **ARMOR OF GEORGE CLIFFORD, THIRD EARL OF CUMBERLAND**
Made in the royal workshop at Greenwich, England. c. 1580–1585. Steel and gold, height 5′9½″ (1.77 m). Metropolitan Museum of Art, New York. Munsey Fund, 1932 (32.130.6)

man of about 30, wears a richly engraved and gold-inlaid suit of armor, forged for his first appearance in 1583 (see "Armor for Royal Games," page 707). Hilliard gives him a marked air of courtly jauntiness, with a stylish beard, mustache, and curled hair, but Cumberland is also humanized by his direct gaze and receding hairline. Cumberland's motto—"I bear lightning and water"—is inscribed on a stormy sky, with a lightning bolt in the form of a caduceus, one of his emblems. After all, he was that remarkable Elizabethan type—a naval commander and a gentleman pirate.

ARCHITECTURE

To increase support for the Tudor dynasty, Henry and his successors granted titles to rich landowners. To display their wealth and status, many of these newly created aristocrats embarked on extensive building projects, constructing lavish country residences, which sometimes surpassed the French châteaux in size and grandeur. Rooted in the Perpendicular Gothic style (SEE FIG. 17–18), Elizabethan architecture's severe walls and broad expanses of glass were modernized by replacing medieval ornament with Classical motifs copied from architectural handbooks and pattern books. The first architectural manual in English, published in 1563, was written by John Shute, one of the few builders who had spent time in Italy. Most influential were the treatises on architectural design by the Italian architect Sebastiano Serlio.

HARDWICK HALL. One of the grandest of all the Elizabethan houses was Hardwick Hall, the home of Elizabeth, Countess of Shrewsbury, known as "Bess of Hardwick" (FIG. 21–24). When she was in her seventies, the redoubtable countess—who inherited riches from all four of her deceased husbands—employed Robert Smythson (c. 1535–1614), England's first Renaissance architect, to build Hardwick Hall (1591–1597).

The medieval great hall was transformed into a two-story entrance hall, with rooms arranged symmetrically around it— a nod to Classical balance. A sequence of rooms leads to a grand stair up to the long gallery and high great chamber on the second floor that featured an ornately carved fireplace (FIG. 21–25). It was here the countess received guests, entertained, and sometimes dined. The room seems designed to showcase a precious set of six Brussels tapestries featuring the story of Ulysses and is illuminated by its enormous windows. They serve as yet another reminder of the international character of the lavish decoration of residences created for wealthy patrons across Europe during this Renaissance century.

21-24 • Robert Smythson HARDWICK HALL
Derbyshire, England. 1591–1597.

21–25 • Robert Smythson **HIGH GREAT CHAMBER, HARDWICK HALL**
Derbyshire, England. 1591–1597. Brussels tapestries 1550s; painted plaster sculpture by Abraham Smith.

THINK ABOUT IT

21.1 Choose one European court that patronized artists working in a "foreign" tradition from another part of Europe and assess how this internationalism fostered breaking down regional and national boundaries in European art. Be sure to ground your discussion in the work of specific artists.

21.2 Explore the impact of Italian art and ideas on the work and persona of German artist Albrecht Dürer. Choose one of his works from the chapter, and discuss its Italianate features and the ways in which it departs from and draws on earlier northern European traditions.

21.3 Summarize the factors that led to a burgeoning art market in the Netherlands in the sixteenth century. Who are some of the artists who benefited from this more fluid system of patronage? How and why were they successful within it?

21.4 Discuss the impact of the Protestant Reformation on the visual arts in northern Europe, focusing your discussion on types of subject matter that patrons sought.

21.5 Choose a work of art discussed in this chapter that displays extraordinary technical skill in more than one medium. How was its virtuosity achieved, and how is it highlighted as an important factor in the work's significance?

PRACTICE MORE: Compose answers to these questions, get flashcards for images and terms, and review chapter material with quizzes
www.myartslab.com

22-1 • Gianlorenzo Bernini ST. TERESA OF ÁVILA IN ECSTASY
1645–1652. Marble, height of the group 11′6″ (3.5 m). Cornaro Chapel, church of Santa Maria della Vittoria, Rome.

SEVENTEENTH-CENTURY
ART IN EUROPE

In the Church of Santa Maria della Vittoria in Rome, the sixteenth-century Spanish mystic St. Teresa of Ávila (1515–1582, canonized 1622) swoons in ecstasy on a bank of billowing marble clouds (FIG. 22–1). A puckish angel tugs open her robe, aiming a gilded arrow at her breast. Gilded bronze rays of supernatural light descend, even as actual light illuminates the figures from a hidden window above. This dramatic scene, created by Gianlorenzo Bernini (1598–1680) between 1645 and 1652, represents a famous vision described with startling physical clarity by Teresa, in which an angel pierced her body repeatedly with an arrow, transporting her to a state of ecstatic oneness with God, charged with erotic associations.

The sculpture is an exquisite example of the emotional, theatrical style perfected by Bernini in response to the religious and political climate in Rome during the period of spiritual renewal known as the Counter-Reformation. Many had seen the Protestant Reformation of the previous century as an outgrowth of Renaissance Humanism with its emphasis on rationality and independent thinking. In response, the Catholic Church took a reactionary, authoritarian position, supported by the new Society of Jesus founded by Ignatius Loyola (d. 1556, canonized 1622). In the "spiritual exercises"

(1522–1523) initiated by St. Ignatius, Christians were enjoined to use all their senses to transport themselves emotionally as they imagined the events on which they were meditating. They were to feel the burning fires of hell or the bliss of heaven, the lashing of the whips and the flesh-piercing crown of thorns. Art became an instrument of propaganda and also a means of leading the spectator to a reinvigorated Christian practice and belief.

Of course, the arts had long been used to convince or inspire, but nowhere more effectively than by the Catholic Church in the seventeenth century. To serve the educational and evangelical mission of the revitalized and conservative Church, paintings and sculpture had to depict events and people accurately and clearly, following guidelines established by religious leaders. Throughout Catholic Europe, painters such as Rubens and Caravaggio created brilliant religious art under official Church sponsorship. And although today some viewers find this sculpture of St. Teresa uncomfortably charged with sexuality, the Church approved of the depictions of such sensational and supernatural mystical visions. They helped worshipers achieve the emotional state of religious ecstasy that was a goal of the Counter-Reformation.

LEARN ABOUT IT

22.1 Assess the impact of the Council of Trent's guidelines for the Counter-Reformation art of the Roman Catholic Church.

22.2 Explore how the work of Bernini and Caravaggio established a new dramatic intensity, technical virtuosity, and unvarnished naturalism that blossomed into the Baroque.

22.3 Trace the broad influence of Caravaggio's style on art across Europe during the seventeenth century.

22.4 Assess the resurgence of Classicism, especially in the work of seventeenth-century French artists and architects.

22.5 Analyze the way that seventeenth-century artists created works that embodied the power and prestige of the monarchy.

22.6 Examine the development of portraiture, still life, landscape, and genre scenes as major subjects for painting, especially within the prosperous art market of the Netherlands.

HEAR MORE: Listen to an audio file of your chapter **www.myartslab.com**

"BAROQUE"

The intellectual and political forces set in motion by the Renaissance and Reformation of the fifteenth and sixteenth centuries intensified during the seventeenth century. Religious wars continued, although gradually the Protestant forces gained control in the north, where Spain recognized the independence of the Dutch Republic in 1648. Catholicism maintained its primacy in southern Europe, the Holy Roman Empire, and France through the efforts of an energized papacy, aided by the new Society of Jesus, also known as the Jesuit Order **(MAP 22–1)**. At the same time, scientific advances compelled people to question their worldview. Of great importance was the growing understanding that the Earth was not the center of the universe but rather was a planet revolving around the sun. As rulers' economic strength began to slip away, artists found patrons in the Church and the secular state, as well as in the newly confident and prosperous urban middle class. What evolved was a style that art historians have called "the Baroque." The label may be related to the Italian word *barocco*, a jeweler's term for an irregularly shaped pearl—something beautiful, fascinating, and strange.

Baroque art deliberately evokes intense emotional responses from viewers. Dramatically lit, theatrical compositions often combine several media within a single work as artists highlight their technical virtuosity. But the seventeenth century also saw its own version of Classicism, a more moving and dramatic variant of Renaissance ideals and principles featuring idealization based on observation of the material world; balanced (though often asymmetrical) compositions; diagonal movement in space; rich, harmonious colors; and the inclusion of visual references to ancient Greece and Rome. Many seventeenth-century artists sought lifelike depiction of their world in portraiture, **genre paintings** (scenes from everyday life), still life (paintings of inanimate objects such as food, fruit, or flowers), and religious scenes enacted by ordinary people in ordinary settings. Intense emotional involvement, lifelike renderings, and Classical references may exist in the same work, and are all part of the stylistic complexion of the seventeenth century.

The role of viewers also changed. Italian Renaissance painters and patrons had been fascinated with the visual possibilities of perspective and treasured idealism of form and subject which kept viewers at a distance, reflecting intellectually on what they were seeing. Seventeenth-century masters, on the other hand, sought to engage viewers as participants in the work of art, and often reached out to incorporate or activate the world beyond the frame into the nature and meaning of the work itself. In Catholic countries, representations of horrifying scenes of martyrdom or the passionate spiritual life of a mystic in religious ecstasy were intended to inspire viewers to a renewed faith by making them feel what was going on, not simply by causing them to think about it. In Protestant countries, images of communal parades and city views sought to inspire pride in civic accomplishments. Viewers participated in works of art like audiences in a theater—vicariously but completely—as the work of art drew them visually and emotionally

into its orbit. The seventeenth-century French critic Roger de Piles (1635–1709) described this exchange when he wrote: "True painting … calls to us; and has so powerful an effect, that we cannot help coming near it, as if it had something to tell us" (Puttfarken, p. 55).

ITALY

Italy in the seventeenth century remained a divided land in spite of a common history, language, and geography, with borders defined by the seas. The Kingdom of Naples and Sicily was Spanish; the Papal States crossed the center; Venice maintained its independence as a republic; and the north remained divided among small principalities. Churchmen and their families remained powerful patrons of the arts, especially as they recognized the visual arts' role in revitalizing the Roman Catholic Church. The Council of Trent (1563) had set guidelines for Church art that went against the arcane, worldly, and often lascivious trends exploited by Mannerism. The clergy's call for clarity, simplicity, chaste subject matter, and the ability to rouse a very Catholic piety in the face of Protestant revolt found a response in the fresh approaches to subject matter and style offered by a new generation of artists.

ARCHITECTURE AND SCULPTURE IN ROME

A major goal of the Counter-Reformation was to embellish churches properly, and Pope Sixtus V (pontificate 1585–1590) had begun the renewal in Rome by cutting long, straight avenues through the city to link the major pilgrimage churches with one another and with the main gates of Rome. Sixtus also ordered open spaces—piazzas—to be cleared in front of major churches, marking each site with an Egyptian obelisk. In a practical vein, he also reopened one of the ancient aqueducts to stabilize the city's water supply. Unchallengeable power and vast financial resources were required to carry out such an extensive plan of urban renewal and to refashion Rome—parts of which had been the victim of rapacity and neglect since the Middle Ages—once more into the center of spiritual and worldly power.

The Counter-Reformation popes had great wealth, although they eventually nearly bankrupted the Church with their building programs. Sixtus began to renovate the Vatican and its library; he completed the dome of St. Peter's and built splendid palaces. The Renaissance ideal of the central-plan church continued to be used for the shrines of saints, but Counter-Reformation thinking called for churches with long, wide naves to accommodate large congregations assembled to hear inspiring sermons as well as to participate in the Mass. In the sixteenth century, the decoration of new churches had been relatively austere, but seventeenth- and eighteenth-century Catholic taste favored opulent and spectacular visual effects to heighten the emotional involvement of worshipers.

ST. PETER'S BASILICA IN THE VATICAN. Half a century after Michelangelo had returned St. Peter's Basilica to Bramante's original

MAP 22-1 • SEVENTEENTH-CENTURY EUROPE

Protestantism still dominated northern Europe, while in the south Roman Catholicism remained strong after the
Counter-Reformation. The Habsburg Empire was now divided into two parts, under separate rulers.

vision of a central-plan building, Pope Paul V Borghese (pontificate
1605–21) commissioned Carlo Maderno (1556–1629) to provide
the church with a longer nave and a new façade **(FIG. 22–2)**.
Construction began in 1607, and everything but the façade bell
towers was completed by 1615 (see "St. Peter's Basilica," page 651).
In essence, Maderno took the concept of *Il Gesù*'s façade (SEE FIG.
20–36) and enlarged it for the most important church of the
Catholic world. Maderno's façade for St. Peter's "steps out" in three
progressively projecting planes: from the corners to the doorways
flanking the central entrance area, then the entrance area, then the
central doorway itself. Similarly, the colossal orders connecting the
first and second stories are flat pilasters at the corners but fully
round columns where they flank the doorways. These columns
support a continuous entablature that also steps out—following
the columns—as it moves toward the central door.

When Maderno died in 1629, he was succeeded as Vatican
architect by his collaborator of five years, Gianlorenzo Bernini
(1598–1680). The latter was taught by his father, and part of
his training involved sketching the Vatican collection of ancient
sculpture, such as *Laocoön and His Sons* (SEE FIG. 5–55) and the *Farnese
Hercules* (SEE FIG. 5–47), as well as the many examples of Renaissance
painting in the papal palace. Throughout his life, Bernini admired
antique art and, like other artists of this period, considered himself a
Classicist. Today, we not only appreciate his strong debt to the
Renaissance tradition but also acknowledge the way he broke
through that tradition to take us into a new, Baroque style.

When Urban VIII was elected pope in 1623, he unhesitatingly
gave the young Bernini the daunting task of designing an
enormous bronze baldachin, or canopy, over the high altar of St.
Peter's. The church was so large that a dramatic focus on the altar

22-2 • ST. PETER'S BASILICA AND PIAZZA, VATICAN, ROME
Carlo Maderno, façade, 1607–1626; Gianlorenzo Bernini, piazza design, c. 1656–1657.

Perhaps only a Baroque artist of Bernini's talents could have unified the many artistic periods and styles that come together in St. Peter's Basilica (starting with Bramante's original design for the building in the sixteenth century). The basilica in no way suggests a piecing together of parts made by different builders at different times but rather presents itself as a triumphal unity of all the parts in one coherent whole.

SEE MORE: Click the Google Earth link for an aerial view of St. Peter's, Vatican City
www.myartslab.com

was essential. The resulting *baldacchino* (**FIG. 22–3**), completed in 1633, stands almost 100 feet high and exemplifies the Baroque objective to create multimedia works, combining architecture and sculpture—and sometimes painting as well—that defy simple categorization. The gigantic corner columns symbolize the union of Christianity and its Jewish tradition—the vine of the Eucharist climbing the twisted columns associated with the Temple of Solomon. They support an entablature with a crowning element topped with an orb (a sphere representing the universe) and a cross (symbolizing the reign of Christ). Figures of angels and *putti* decorate the entablature, which is hung with tasseled panels in imitation of a cloth canopy. This imposing work not only marks the site of the tomb of St. Peter, but also serves as a tribute to Urban VIII and his family, the Barberini, whose emblems—honeybees and suns on the tasseled panels, and laurel leaves on the climbing vines—are prominently displayed.

Between 1627 and 1641, Bernini and several other sculptors, again in multimedia extravaganzas, rebuilt Bramante's crossing piers as giant reliquaries. Statues of SS. Helena, Veronica, Andrew, and Longinus stand in niches below alcoves containing their relics, to the left and right of the *baldacchino*. Visible through the *baldacchino*'s columns in the apse of the church is another reliquary: the gilded-stone, bronze, and stucco shrine made by Bernini between 1657 and 1666 for the ancient wooden throne thought to have belonged to St. Peter as the first bishop of Rome. The Chair of Peter symbolized the direct descent of Christian authority from Peter to the current pope, a belief rejected by Protestants and therefore deliberately emphasized in Counter-Reformation Catholicism. Above the shrine, a brilliant stained-glass window portrays the Holy Spirit as a dove surrounded by an oval of golden rays. Adoring gilded angels and gilt-bronze rays fan out around the window and seem to extend the penetration of the natural light—

made the basilica and its setting an even more awe-inspiring vision. The approach today—along the grand avenue of the Via della Conciliazione running from the Tiber to the Basilica—was conceived by Mussolini in 1936 as part of his masterplan to transform Rome into a grand fascist capital.

BERNINI AS SCULPTOR. Even after Bernini's appointment as Vatican architect in 1629, he was still able to accept outside commissions by virtue of his large workshop. In fact, he first became famous as a sculptor, and he continued to work as one throughout his career, for both the papacy and private clients. A man of many talents, he was also a painter and even a playwright—an interest that dovetailed with his genius for theatrical and dramatic presentation.

Bernini's *David* (FIG. 22–4), made for a nephew of Pope Paul V in 1623, introduced a new type of three-dimensional composition that intrudes forcefully into the viewer's space. The young hero bends at the waist and twists far to one side, ready to launch the lethal rock at Goliath. Unlike Donatello's already victorious sassy

22-3 • Gianlorenzo Bernini BALDACCHINO
1624–1633. Gilt bronze, height approx. 100′ (30.48 m). Chair of Peter shrine, 1657–1666. Gilt bronze, marble, stucco, and glass. Pier decorations, 1627–1641. Gilt bronze and marble. Crossing, St. Peter's Basilica, Vatican, Rome.

and the Holy Spirit—into the apse of the church. The gilding also reflects the light back to the window, creating a dazzling, ethereal effect that the seventeenth century, with its interest in mystics and visions, would equate with the activation of divinity.

At approximately the same time that he was at work on the Chair of Peter, Bernini designed and supervised the building of a colonnade to form a huge double piazza in front of the entrance to St. Peter's (SEE FIG. 22–2). The open space that he had to work with was irregular, and an Egyptian obelisk and a fountain previously installed by Sixtus V had to be incorporated into the overall plan. Bernini's remarkable design frames the oval piazza with two enormous curved porticos, or covered walkways, supported by Doric columns. These curved porticos are connected to two straight porticos, which lead up a slight incline to the two ends of the church façade. Bernini characterized his design as the "motherly arms of the Church" reaching out to the world. He had intended to build a third section of the colonnade closing the side of the piazza facing the church so that only after pilgrims had crossed the Tiber River bridge and made their way through narrow streets, would they encounter the enormous open space before the imposing church. This element of surprise would have

22-4 • Gianlorenzo Bernini DAVID
1623. Marble, height 5′7″ (1.7 m). Galleria Borghese, Rome.

22-5 • Gianlorenzo Bernini
CORNARO CHAPEL, CHURCH OF SANTA MARIA DELLA VITTORIA, ROME
1642–1652.

EXPLORE MORE: Gain insight from a primary source on Gianlorenzo Bernini www.myartslab.com

SEE MORE: View a simulation related to the Cornaro Chapel www.myartslab.com

was dedicated to the Spanish saint Teresa of Ávila, canonized only 20 years earlier. Bernini designed it as a rich and theatrical setting for the portrayal of a central event in Teresa's life. He covered the walls with multicolored marble panels and crowned them with a projecting cornice supported by marble pilasters.

In the center of the chapel and framed by columns in the huge oval niche above the altar, Bernini's marble group *St. Teresa of Ávila in Ecstasy* (SEE FIG. 22–1) represents a vision described by the Spanish mystic in which an angel pierced her body repeatedly with an arrow, transporting her to a state of indescribable pain, religious ecstasy, and a sense of oneness with God. St. Teresa and the angel, who seem to float upward on clouds of stucco (a moistened mixture of lime and marble dust that can be molded), are cut from a heavy mass of solid marble supported on a seemingly drifting pedestal that was fastened by hidden metal bars to the chapel wall. Bernini's skill at capturing the movements and emotions of these figures is matched by his virtuosity in simulating different textures and colors in the pure white medium of marble; the angel's gauzy, clinging draperies seem silken in contrast with Teresa's heavy woolen monastic robe. Bernini effectively used the configuration of the garment's folds to convey the saint's swooning, sensuous body beneath, even though only Teresa's face, hands, and bare feet are actually visible.

Kneeling against what appear to be balconies on both sides of the chapel are marble portrait sculptures of Federigo, his deceased father (a Venetian doge), and six cardinals of the Cornaro family.

adolescent (SEE FIG. 19–10), or Michelangelo's pensive young man contemplating the task ahead (SEE FIG. 20–10), Bernini's more mature David, with his lean, sinewy body, tightly clenched mouth, and straining muscles, is all tension, action and determination. By creating a twisting figure caught in movement, Bernini incorporates the surrounding space within his composition, implying the presence of an unseen adversary somewhere behind the viewer. Thus, the viewer becomes part of the action, rather than its displaced and dispassionate observer.

From 1642 until 1652, Bernini worked on the decoration of the funerary chapel of Venetian cardinal Federigo Cornaro **(FIG. 22–5)** in the Church of Santa Maria della Vittoria, designed by Carlo Maderno earlier in the century. The Cornaro family chapel

The figures are informally posed and naturalistically portrayed. Two read from their prayer books, others exclaim at the miracle taking place in the light-infused realm above the altar, and one leans out from his seat, apparently to look at someone entering the chapel—perhaps the viewer, whose space these figures share. Bernini's intent was not to produce a spectacle for its own sake, but to capture a critical, dramatic moment at its emotional and sensual height, and by doing so guide viewers to identify totally with the event—and perhaps be transformed in the process.

BORROMINI'S CHURCH OF SAN CARLO. The intersection of two of the wide, straight avenues created by Pope Sixtus V inspired city planners to add a special emphasis, with fountains marking each of the four corners of the crossing. In 1634, Trinitarian monks decided to build a new church at the site and awarded the commission for **SAN CARLO ALLE QUATTRO FONTANE** (St. Charles at the Four Fountains) to Francesco Borromini (1599–1667). Borromini, a nephew of architect Carlo Maderno, had arrived in Rome in 1619 from northern Italy to enter his uncle's workshop. Later, he worked under Bernini's supervision on the decoration of St. Peter's, and some details of the Baldacchino, as well as its structural engineering, are now attributed to him, but San Carlo was his first independent commission. Unfinished at Borromini's death, the church was nevertheless completed according to his design.

San Carlo stands on a narrow piece of land, with one corner cut off to accommodate one of the four fountains that give the church its name (**FIG. 22–6**). To fit the irregular site, Borromini created an elongated central-plan interior space with undulating walls (**FIG. 22–7**). Robust pairs of columns support a massive entablature, over which an oval dome, supported on pendentives, seems to float (**FIG. 22–8**). The coffers (inset panels in geometric shapes) filling the interior of the oval-shaped dome form an eccentric honeycomb of crosses, elongated hexagons, and octagons. These coffers decrease sharply in size as they approach the apex, or highest point, where the dove of the Holy Spirit hovers in a climax that brings together the geometry used in the chapel: oval, octagon, circle, and—very important—a triangle, symbol of the Trinity as well as of the church's patrons. The dome appears to be shimmering and inflating—almost floating up and away—thanks to light sources placed in the lower coffers and the lantern.

It is difficult today to appreciate how audacious Borromini's design for this small church was. In it he abandoned the modular,

22-6 • Francesco Borromini FAÇADE, CHURCH OF SAN CARLO ALLE QUATTRO FONTANE, ROME 1638–1667.

22-7 • Francesco Borromini PLAN OF THE CHURCH OF SAN CARLO ALLE QUATTRO FONTANE, ROME 1638–1667.

additive system of planning taken for granted by every architect since Brunelleschi. He worked instead from an overriding geometrical scheme, as a Gothic architect might, subdividing modular units to obtain more complex, rational shapes. For example, the elongated, octagonal plan of San Carlo is composed of two triangles set base to base along the short axis of the plan (SEE FIG. 22–7). This diamond shape is then subdivided into secondary triangular units made by calculating the distances between what will become the concave centers of the four major and five minor niches. Yet Borromini's conception of the whole is not medieval. The chapel is dominated horizontally by a Classical entablature that breaks any surge upward toward the dome. Borromini's treatment of the architectural elements as if they were malleable was also unprecedented. His contemporaries understood immediately what an extraordinary innovation the church represented; the Trinitarian monks who had commissioned it received requests for plans from visitors from all over Europe. Although Borromini's innovative work had little impact on the architecture of Classically minded Rome, it was widely imitated in northern Italy and beyond the Alps.

22-8 • Francesco Borromini VIEW INTO THE DOME OF THE CHURCH OF SAN CARLO ALLE QUATTRO FONTANE, ROME
1638–1667.

Borromini's design for San Carlo's façade (SEE FIG. 22–6), executed more than two decades later, was as innovative as his planning of the interior. He turned the building's front into an undulating, sculpture-filled screen punctuated with large columns and deep concave and convex niches that create dramatic effects of light and shadow. Borromini also gave his façade a strong vertical thrust in the center by placing over the tall doorway a statue-filled niche, then a windowed niche covered with a canopy, then a giant, forward-leaning cartouche held up by angels carved in such high relief that they appear to hover in front of the wall. The entire composition is crowned with a balustrade broken by the sharply pointed frame of the cartouche. As with the design of the building itself, Borromini's façade was enthusiastically imitated in northern Italy and especially in northern and eastern Europe.

PAINTING

Painting in seventeenth-century Italy followed one of two principal paths: the ordered Classicism of the Carracci or the dramatic naturalism of Caravaggio. Although the leading exponents of these paths were northern Italians—the Carracci family was from Bologna, and Caravaggio was born in or near Milan—they were all eventually drawn to Rome, the center of power and patronage. The Carracci family, like Caravaggio, were schooled in northern Italian Renaissance traditions, with its emphasis on *chiaroscuro*, as well as in Venetian color and *sfumato*. The Carracci quite consciously rejected the artifice of the Mannerist style and fused their northern roots with the central Italian Renaissance insistence on line (*disegno*), compositional structure, and figural solidity. They looked to Raphael, Michelangelo, and antique Classical sculpture for their ideal figural types and their expressive but decorous compositions. Caravaggio, on the other hand, satisfied the Baroque demand for drama and clarity by developing realism in a powerful new direction. He painted people he saw in the world around him—even the lowlife of Rome—and worked directly from models without elaborate drawings and compositional notes. Unlike the Carracci, he claimed to ignore the influence of the great masters so as to focus steadfastly on a sense of immediacy and invention.

THE CARRACCI. The brothers Agostino (1557–1602) and Annibale Carracci (1560–1609) and their cousin Ludovico (1555–1619) shared a studio in Bologna. As their re-evaluation of the High Renaissance masters attracted interest among their peers, they opened their doors to friends and students and then, in 1582, founded an art academy, where students drew from live models and studied art theory, Renaissance painting, and antique Classical sculpture. The Carracci placed a high value on accurate drawing, complex figure compositions, complicated narratives, and technical expertise in both oil and fresco painting. During its short life, the academy had an impact on

22-9 • Annibale Carracci **CEILING OF GALLERY, PALAZZO FARNESE, ROME** 1597–1601. Fresco, approx. 68 × 21′ (20.7 × 6.4 m).

the development of the arts—and art education—through its insistence on both life drawing (to achieve naturalism) and aesthetic theory (to achieve artistic harmony).

In 1595, Annibale was hired by Cardinal Odoardo Farnese to decorate the principal rooms of his family's immense Roman palace. In the long *galleria* (gallery), to celebrate the wedding of Duke Ranuccio Farnese of Parma to the niece of the pope, the artist was requested to paint scenes of love based on Ovid's *Metamorphoses* **(FIG. 22–9)**. Undoubtedly, Annibale and Agostino, who assisted him, felt both inspiration and competition from the important Farnese collection of antique sculpture exhibited throughout the palace.

The primary image, set in the center of the vault, is *The Triumph of Bacchus and Ariadne*, a joyous procession celebrating the wine god Bacchus's love for Ariadne, whom he rescued after her lover, Theseus, abandoned her on the island of Naxos. Annibale combines the great northern Italian tradition of ceiling painting—seen in the work of Mantegna and Correggio (FIGS. 19–29, 20–19)—with his study of central Italian Renaissance painters and the Classical heritage of Rome. Annibale organized his complex theme by using illusionistic devices to create multiple levels of reality. Painted imitations of gold-framed easel paintings called *quadri riportati* ("transported paintings") appear to "rest" on

22–10 • Annibale Carracci LANDSCAPE WITH THE FLIGHT INTO EGYPT
1603–1604. Oil on canvas, 48 × 90½″ (1.22 × 2.29 m). Galleria Doria Pamphili, Rome.

the actual cornice of the vault and overlap "bronze" medallions that are flanked, in turn, by realistically colored *ignudi*, dramatically lit from below. The viewer is invited to compare the warm flesh tones of these youths, and their lifelike poses, with the more idealized "painted" bodies in the framed scenes next to them. Above, paintings of stucco-colored sculptures of herms (plain shafts topped by human torsos) twist and turn as they support the painted framework of the vault, exposing a variety of feelings with their expressions and seemingly communicating with one another. Many of Annibale's ideas are inspired by motifs in Michelangelo's Sistine Chapel ceiling (FIG. 20–12). The figure types, true to their source, are heroic, muscular, and drawn with precise anatomical accuracy. But instead of Michelangelo's cool illumination and intellectual detachment, the Carracci ceiling glows with a warm light that recalls the work of the Venetian painters Titian and Veronese, and seems buoyant with optimism and lively engagement.

The ceiling was highly admired, famous from the moment it was finished. The proud Farnese family generously allowed young artists to sketch the figures there, so that Carracci's masterpiece influenced Italian art well into the following century. Among those impressed at the initial viewing of the *galleria* was the nephew of Pope Clement VIII, Pietro Aldobrandini, who subsequently commissioned the artist to decorate the six lunettes of his private chapel with scenes from the life of the Virgin, sometime between 1603 and 1604. **LANDSCAPE WITH THE FLIGHT INTO EGYPT (FIG. 22–10)**, the largest of the six—one of only two that show painting

from Annibale's own hand—was probably above the altar. In contrast to the dramatic figural compositions in the Farnese gallery, the escape of the Holy Family is conceived within a contemplative pastoral landscape filled with golden light in the Venetian tradition of Giorgione (SEE FIG. 20–21). The design of the work and its affective spirit of melancholy derive, however, from a fundamental aspect of Baroque Classicism that would influence artists for generations to come. Here nature is ordered by humans. Trees in the left foreground and right middle ground gracefully frame the scene; and the collection of ancient buildings in the center of the composition forms a stable and protective canopy for the flight of the Holy Family. Space progresses gradually from foreground to background in diagonal movements that are indicated by people, animals, and architecture. Nothing is accidental, yet the whole appears unforced and entirely natural.

CARAVAGGIO. Michelangelo Merisi (1571–1610), known as "Caravaggio" after his family's home town in Lombardy, introduced a powerfully frank realism and dramatic, theatrical lighting and gesture to Italian Baroque art. The young painter brought an interest, perhaps a specialization, in still-life painting with him when he arrived in Rome from Milan late in 1592 and found studio work as a specialist painter of fruit and vegetables. When he began to work on his own, he continued to paint still lifes but also began to include half-length figures with them. By this time, his reputation had grown to the extent that an agent offered to market his pictures.

22–11 • Caravaggio **BACCHUS**
1595–1596. Oil on canvas, 37 × 33½″
(94 × 85.1 cm). Galleria degli Uffizi,
Florence.

image about the transitory nature of sensual pleasure, either admonishing viewers to avoid sins of the flesh or encouraging them to enjoy life's pleasures while they can? The ambiguity seems to make the painting even more provocative.

Most of Caravaggio's commissions after 1600 were religious, and reactions to them were mixed. On occasion, patrons rejected his powerful, sometimes brutal, naturalism as unsuitable to the subject's dignity. Critics differed as well. An early critic, the Spaniard Vincente Carducho, wrote in his *Dialogue on Painting* (Madrid, 1633) that Caravaggio was an "omen of the ruin and demise of painting" because he painted "with nothing but nature before him, which he simply copied in his amazing way" (Enggass and Brown, pp. 173–174). Others recognized him as a great innovator who reintroduced realism into art and developed new, dramatic lighting effects. The art historian Giovanni Bellori, in his *Lives of the Painters* (1672), described Caravaggio's painting as

Caravaggio painted for a small, sophisticated circle associated with the household of art patron Cardinal del Monte, where the artist was invited to reside. His subjects from this early period of the 1590s include not only still lifes but also genre scenes featuring fortune-tellers, cardsharps, and glamorous young men dressed as musicians or mythological figures. The **BACCHUS** of 1595–1596 **(FIG. 22–11)** is among the most polished of these early works. Caravaggio seems to have painted exactly what he saw, reproducing the "farmer's tan" of those parts of this partially dressed youth's skin—hand and face—that have been exposed to the sun, as well as the dirt under his fingernails. The figure himself is strikingly androgynous. Made up with painted lips and smoothly arching eyebrows, he seems to offer the viewer the gorgeous goblet of wine held delicately in his left hand, while fingering the black bow that holds his loose clothing together at the waist. Is this a provocative invitation to an erotic encounter or a young actor outfitted for the role of Bacchus, god of wine? Does the juxtaposition of the youth's invitation with a still life of rotting fruit transform this into an

... reinforced throughout with bold shadows and a great deal of black to give relief to the forms. He went so far in this manner of working that he never brought his figures out into the daylight, but placed them in the dark brown atmosphere of a closed room, using a high light that descended vertically over the principal parts of the bodies while leaving the remainder in shadow in order to give force through a strong contrast of light and dark.... (Bellori, *Lives of the Painters*, Rome, 1672, in Enggass and Brown, p. 79)

Caravaggio's approach has been likened to the preaching of Filippo Neri (1515–1595), the Counter-Reformation priest and mystic who founded a Roman religious group called the Congregation of the Oratory. Neri, called the Apostle of Rome and later canonized, focused his missionary efforts on ordinary people for whom he strove to make Christian history and doctrine understandable and meaningful. Caravaggio, too, interpreted his

Caravaggio in the Contarelli Chapel

As soon as he had established himself as an up-and-coming artist during the 1590s, Caravaggio turned to a series of important commissions for religious paintings in the chapels of Roman churches. Unlike in the Renaissance, where frescos were applied directly to the walls, Caravaggio produced large oil paintings on canvas in his studio, only later installing them within the chapels to form coordinated ensembles. Several such installations survive, giving us the precious opportunity to experience the paintings as Caravaggio and his patrons intended. One of these intact programs, in the Contarelli Chapel of San Luigi dei Francesi, was Caravaggio's earliest religious commission in Rome, perhaps obtained through the efforts of Cardinal del Monte, who had supported the artist through the 1590s.

This church served the French community in Rome, and the building itself was constructed between 1518 and 1589, begun under the patronage of Catherine de' Medici, Queen of France. The chapel Caravaggio decorated was founded in 1565 by Mathieu Cointrel—Matteo Contarelli—a French noble at the papal court who would serve as a financial administrator under Gregory XIII (pontificate 1572–1585). Although earlier artists had been called on to provide paintings for the chapel, it was only after Contarelli's death in 1585 that the executors of his will brought the decoration to completion, hiring Giuseppe Cesare in

1591 to paint the ceiling frescos, and Caravaggio in 1599 to provide paintings of scenes from the life of the patron's patron saint: *The Calling of St. Matthew* on the left wall and *The Martyrdom of St. Matthew* on the right (not visible in FIG. A), both installed in July 1600.

The commissioning document was explicit, requiring the artist to show, in *The Calling of St. Matthew* (fig. B), the saint rising from his seat to follow Christ in ministry. But Caravaggio was never very good at following the rules. Among the group of smartly dressed Romans who form Matthew's circle of cohorts seated at the left, no one rises to leave. Art historians have not even been able to agree on which figure is Matthew. Most identify him with a bearded man in the center, interpreting his pointing gesture as a self-referential, questioning response to Jesus' call. But some see Matthew in the figure hunched over the scattered coins at far left, seemingly unmoved by Jesus' presence. In this case, the bearded figure's pointing would question whether this bent-over colleague was the one Jesus

A. CONTARELLI CHAPEL, SAN LUIGI DEI FRANCESI
Rome. Paintings by Caravaggio 1599–1602.

sought. The painting is marked by mystery, not by the clarity sought by Counter-Reformation guidelines.

In February 1602, Caravaggio received a second commission for the Contarelli Chapel, this time for a painting over the altar showing St. Matthew, accompanied by his angelic symbol and writing his Gospel. It was to be completed within three months, but Caravaggio did not receive payment for the picture until September of that year, and the painting he delivered was rejected. The clergy considered Caravaggio's rendering of the saint unacceptably crude and common, his cross-legged pose uncouth and unnecessarily revealing. The fleshiness of the angel, who sidles cozily up to Matthew, was judged inappropriately risqué. In short, the painting was inconsistent with guidelines for saintly decorum set for artists by the Council of Trent. Caravaggio had to paint a second, more decorous altarpiece for the chapel (seen in FIG. A), with a nobler Matthew and a more distant angel. The rejected version was snapped up by Roman collector Vincenzo Giustiniani, who actually paid for the replacement in order to acquire the more sensational original. Unfortunately, this first painting was destroyed in the 1945 bombing of Berlin during World War II.

B. Caravaggio **THE CALLING OF ST. MATTHEW**
Contarelli Chapel, Church of San Luigi dei Francesi, Rome. 1599–1600.
Oil on canvas, 10′7½″ × 11′2″ (3.24 × 3.4 m).

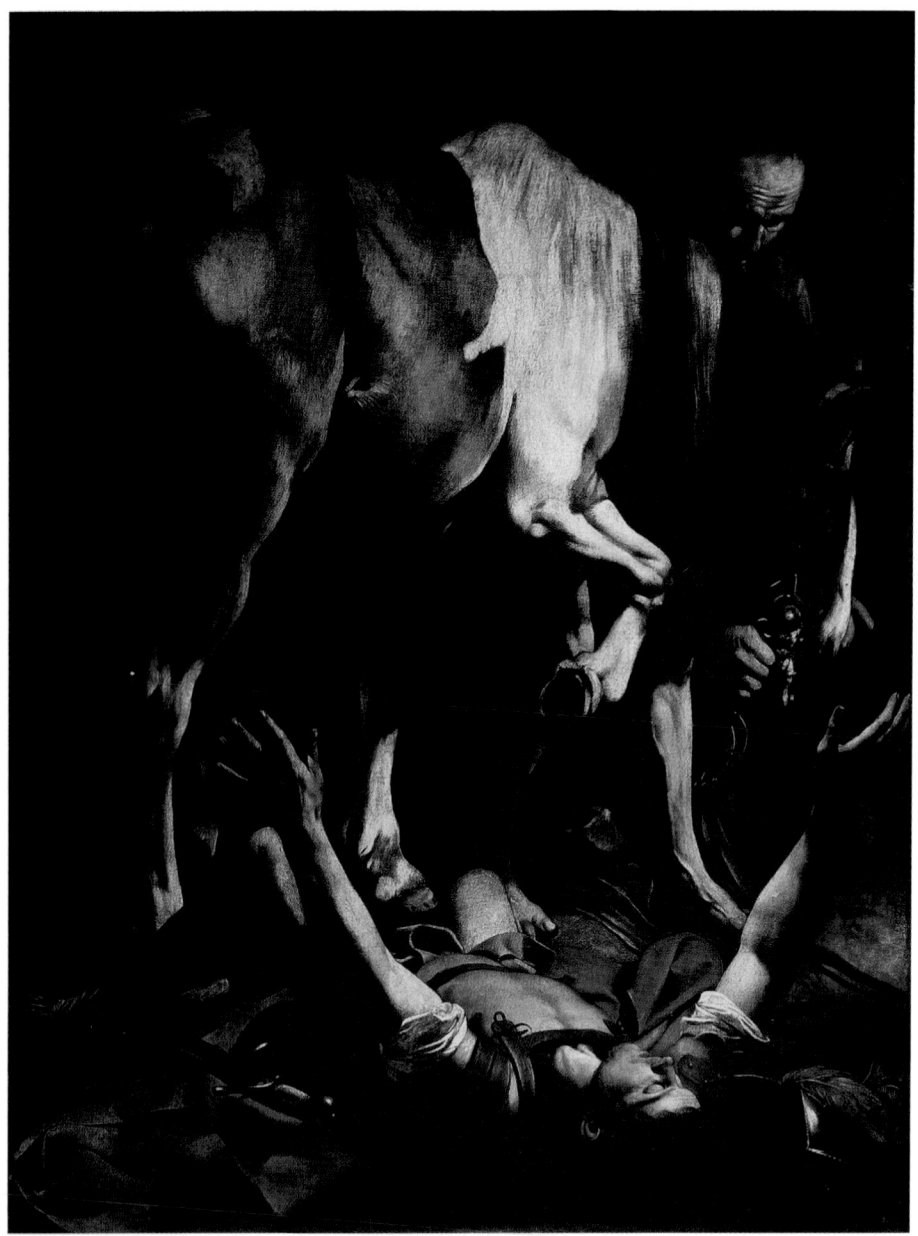

22-12 • Caravaggio **THE CONVERSION OF ST. PAUL**
Cerasi Chapel, Santa Maria del Popolo, Rome. c. 1601. Oil on canvas, 7′6″ × 5′8″ (2.3 × 1.75 m).

EXPLORE MORE: Gain insight from a primary source on Caravaggio
www.myartslab.com

religious subjects directly and dramatically, combining intensely observed figures, poses, and expressions with strongly contrasting effects of light and color. His knowledge of Lombard painting, where the influence of Leonardo was strong, must have aided him in his development of the technique now known as **tenebrism**, in which forms emerge from a dark background into a strong light that often falls from a single source outside the painting. The effect is that of a theatrical spotlight.

One of Caravaggio's first religious commissions, paintings for the Contarelli Chapel in the French community's church of St. Louis (San Luigi dei Francesi), included *The Calling of St. Matthew*, painted about 1599–1600 (see "Caravaggio in the Contarelli Chapel," pages 722–723). The subject is conversion, a common Counter-Reformation theme. Jesus calls Levi, the tax collector, to join his apostles (Matthew 9:9; Mark 2:14). Levi—who will become St. Matthew—sits at a table, counting or collecting money,

surrounded by elegant young men in plumed hats, velvet doublets, and satin shirts. Nearly hidden behind the back of the beckoning apostle—probably St. Peter—at the right, the gaunt-faced Jesus points dramatically at Levi with a gesture that is repeated in the presumed (other than Jesus, identities are not certain here) tax collector's own surprised response of pointing to himself, as if to say, "Who, me?" An intense raking light enters the painting from upper right, as if it were coming from the chapel's actual window above the altar to spotlight the important features of this darkened scene. Viewers encountering the painting obliquely across the empty space of the chapel interior seem to be witnessing the scene as it is occurring, elevated on a recessed stage opening through the wall before them.

The emotional power of Caravaggio's theatrical approach to sacred narrative is nowhere more evident than in his rendering of **THE CONVERSION OF ST. PAUL** for the Cerasi Chapel of Santa

Maria del Popolo (**FIG. 22–12**). This is one of two paintings commissioned for this chapel in 1600; the other portrayed the Crucifixion of St. Peter. The first pair was rejected when Caravaggio delivered them, and they were acquired by a private collector (see also "Caravaggio in the Contarelli Chapel," pages 722–723). This second version of Paul's conversion is direct and simple. Caravaggio focuses on Paul's internal involvement with a pivotal moment, not its external cause. There is no indication of a heavenly apparition, only Paul's response to it. There is no clear physical setting, only mysterious darkness. And Paul's experience is personal. Whereas he has been flung from his horse and threatens to tumble into the viewers' own space—arms outstretched and legs akimbo, bathed in a strong spotlight—the horse and groom behind him seem oblivious to Paul's experience. The horse actually takes up more space in the painting than the saint, and the unsettling position of its lifted foreleg, precariously poised over the sprawled body of Paul, adds further tension to an already charged presentation.

Despite the great esteem in which Caravaggio was held by some, especially the younger generation of artists, his violent temper repeatedly got him into trouble. During the last decade of his life, he was frequently arrested, initially for minor offenses such as carrying arms illegally or street brawling. But in May of 1606 he killed a man in a duel fought over a disputed tennis match and had to flee Rome as a fugitive under a death sentence. He supported himself on the run by painting in Naples, Malta, and Sicily. The Knights of Malta awarded him the cross of their religious and military order in July 1608, but in October he was imprisoned for insulting one of their number, and again he escaped and fled. Caravaggio died on July 18, 1610, just short of his 39th birthday, of a fever contracted during a journey back to Rome where he expected to be pardoned of his capital offense. Caravaggio's unvarnished realism and tenebrism influenced nearly every important European artist of the seventeenth century.

ARTEMISIA GENTILESCHI. One of Caravaggio's most brilliant Italian followers was Artemisia Gentileschi (1593–c. 1652/1653), whose international reputation helped spread the Caravaggesque style beyond Rome. Artemisia first studied and worked under her father, Orazio, one of the earliest followers of Caravaggio. In 1616, she moved from Rome to Florence, where she worked for the grand duke of Tuscany and was elected, at the age of 23, to

the Florentine Academy of Design. But like many great artists, her promise as a painter was already evident in her early work. At the age of 17, while she was still part of her father's studio, she painted a stunning rendering of the popular subject of *Susannah and the Elders* (**FIG. 22–13**), perhaps an intentional "masterpiece," meant to showcase her talent and secure her reputation as one of the preeminent painters of the age.

The subject is biblical, drawn from a part of the Book of Daniel that was excluded from the Protestant Bible, but—perhaps consequently—especially popular as a subject in Roman Catholic art. While bathing alone in her garden, the beautiful young Susannah is observed by two lecherous elders—Peeping Toms—who threaten to claim they saw her engaged in a lovers' tryst unless

22–13 • Artemisia Gentileschi **SUSANNAH AND THE ELDERS**
1610. Oil on canvas, 67 × 47⅝″ (1.7 × 1.21 m). Count Schönborn Kunstsammlungen, Pommersfelden.

22-14 • Artemisia Gentileschi SELF-PORTRAIT AS THE ALLEGORY OF PAINTING
1630. Oil on canvas, 38 × 29″ (96.5 × 73.7 cm). The Royal Collection, Windsor Castle, England.

EXPLORE MORE: Gain insight from a primary source on Artemisia Gentileschi **www.myartslab.com**

figures up against the picture plane. But Artemisia has blended her sources and influences into a personal rendering of a traditional subject that moves viewers to empathize with the heroine's condition, and will perhaps inspire them to emulate her righteousness in a world still dominated by overpowering men.

Twenty years after this painting, Artemisia painted a **SELF-PORTRAIT AS THE ALLEGORY OF PAINTING (FIG. 22–14)**. A richly dressed woman, with palette and brushes in hand, is totally immersed in her work. Aspects of the image are derived from Cesare Ripa's sourcebook *Iconologia* (1593), which became an essential tool for creating and deciphering seventeenth- and eighteenth-century art. For instance, *Iconologia* is the source for the woman's gold necklace with its mask pendant: Ripa writes that the mask imitates the human face, as painting imitates nature, and the gold chain symbolizes "the continuity and interlocking nature of painting, each man [*sic*] learning from his master and continuing his master's achievements in the next generation" (Maser, trans. no. 197). By painting her own features on a personification of Painting, Artemisia not only commemorates her profession but also claims her own place within it.

22-15 • BARBERINI PALACE AND SQUARE
1628–1636. Drawing by Lieven Cruyl, 1665. Ink and chalk on paper, 15 × 19¾″ (38.2 × 49.4 cm). Cleveland Museum of Art, Cleveland, Ohio. Dudley P. Allen Fund 1943.265

Maderno, Bernini, and Borromini collaborated on the Barberini Palace between 1628 and 1636, and in the 1670s the structure underwent considerable remodeling. The original plan is unique, having no precedents or imitators in the history of Roman palaces. The structure appears as a single massive pile, but in fact it consists of a central reception block flanked by two residential wings and two magnificent staircases. Designed to house two sides of the family, the rooms are arranged in suites allowing visitors to move through them, achieving increasing intimacy and privacy. Since Cruyl visited the city during Carnival, a float with musicians and actors takes center stage among the strollers. Carnival floats are among the ephemera of art. (Today we might call them "performance art.") Cruyl, who includes his own image at the left, published his drawings as engravings, a set of 15 plates called *Views of Rome*, in 1665.

she agrees to have sex with them. Susannah refuses to surrender her chastity, and they make good on their threat. Initially sentenced to death for her supposed sexual transgression, through the intervention of Daniel, she is proven innocent, and the two dishonest voyeurs are executed instead.

Most male artists who painted this scene emphasized Susannah's sexual allure and the elders' lustful stares, but Artemesia shifts the narrative focus to the powerless young woman's vulnerability—and this Susannah actually looks like a woman. Although female artists were excluded from using male models, Artemesia has clearly studied the appearance and anatomy of unclothed women, creating one of the first truly lifelike female nudes in the European tradition. Her interest in unvarnished naturalism is probably derived from Caravaggio. His revolutionary art is also behind the theatricality of the heroine's rhetorical gesture (recalling that of Adam when expelled from paradise in the Sistine Ceiling), the complex interlocking of the figures' postures (note the patterned relationship between the hands), and the crowding of

BAROQUE CEILINGS: CORTONA AND GAULLI. Theatricality, intricacy, and the opening of space reached an apogee in Baroque ceiling decoration—complex constructions combining architecture, painting, and stucco sculpture. These grand illusionistic projects were carried out on the domes and vaults of churches, civic buildings, palaces, and villas, and went far beyond even Michelangelo's Sistine Chapel ceiling (SEE FIG. 20–11) or Correggio's dome (SEE FIG. 20–19). Baroque ceiling painters sought the drama of an immeasurable heaven that extended into vertiginous zones far beyond the limits of High Renaissance taste. To achieve this, they employed the system of *quadratura* (literally, "squaring" or "gridwork"): an architectural setting painted in meticulous perspective and usually requiring that it be viewed from a specific spot to achieve the desired effect of soaring space. The resulting viewpoint is called *di sotto in su* ("from below to above"), which we first saw, in a limited fashion, in Mantegna's ceiling in Mantua (FIG. 19–29). Because it required such careful calculation, figure painters usually had specialists in *quadratura* paint the architectural frame for them.

Pietro Berrettini (1596–1669), called "Pietro da Cortona" after his hometown, carried the development of the Baroque ceiling away from Classicism into a more strongly unified and illusionistic direction. Trained in Florence and inspired by Veronese's ceiling in the Doge's Palace, which he saw on a trip to Venice in 1637, the artist was commissioned in the early 1630s by the Barberini family of Pope Urban VIII to decorate the ceiling of the audience hall of their Roman palace. A drawing by a Flemish artist visiting Rome, Lieven Cruyl (1640–c. 1720), gives us a view of the Barberinis' huge palace, piazza, and the surrounding city. Bernini's Trident Fountain stands in the center of the piazza, and his scallop-shell fountain can be seen at the right (FIG. 22–15).

Pietro da Cortona's great fresco *The Glorification of the Papacy of Urban VIII* became a model for a succession of Baroque illusionistic palace ceilings throughout Europe (FIG. 22–16). He structured his mythological scenes around a vaultlike skeleton of architecture, painted in *quadratura*, that appears to be attached to the actual cornice of the room. But in contrast to Annibale Carracci's neat separations and careful *quadro riportato* framing (SEE FIG. 22–9), Pietro's figures weave in and out of their setting in active and complex profusion; some rest on the actual cornice, while others float weightlessly against the sky. Instead of Annibale's warm, nearly even light, Pietro's dramatic illumination, with its bursts of brilliance alternating with deep shadows, fuses the ceiling into a dense but unified whole.

The subject is an elaborate allegory of the virtues of the pope. Just below the center of the vault, seated at the top of a pyramid of clouds and figures personifying Time and the Fates, Divine Providence (in gold against an open sky) gestures toward three giant bees surrounded by a huge laurel wreath (both Barberini emblems) carried by Faith, Hope, and Charity. Immortality offers a crown of stars, while other figures present the crossed keys and the triple-tiered crown of the papacy. Around these figures are scenes of Roman gods and goddesses, who demonstrate the pope's wisdom and virtue by triumphing over the vices. So complex was the imagery that a guide gave visitors an explanation, and one member of the household published a pamphlet, still in use today, explaining the painting.

22-16 • Pietro da Cortona THE GLORIFICATION OF THE PAPACY OF URBAN VIII
Ceiling in the Gran Salone, Palazzo Barberini, Rome. 1632–1639. Fresco.

22–17 • Giovanni Battista Gaulli **THE TRIUMPH OF THE NAME OF JESUS AND FALL OF THE DAMNED**

Vault of the church of *Il Gesù*, Rome. 1672–1685. Fresco with stucco figures.

The most spectacular of all illusionistic Baroque ceilings is Giovanni Battista Gaulli's **THE TRIUMPH OF THE NAME OF JESUS AND FALL OF THE DAMNED (FIG. 22–17)**, which fills the vault of the Jesuit church *Il Gesù*. In the 1560s, Giacomo da Vignola had designed an austere interior for *Il Gesù*, but when the Jesuits renovated their church a century later, they commissioned a religious allegory to cover the nave's plain ceiling. Gaulli (1639–1709) designed and executed the spectacular illusion between 1672 and 1685, fusing sculpture and painting to eliminate any appearance of architectural division. It is difficult to sort carved three-dimensional figures from the painted imitations, and some paintings are on real panels that extend over the actual architectural frame. Gaulli, who arrived in Rome from Genoa in 1657, had worked in his youth for Bernini, from whom he absorbed a taste for drama and multimedia effects. The elderly Bernini, who worshiped daily at *Il Gesù*, may well have offered his personal advice to his former assistant, and Gaulli was certainly familiar with other illusionistic paintings in Rome as well, including Pietro da Cortona's Barberini ceiling.

Gaulli's astonishing creation went beyond anything that had preceded it in unifying architecture, sculpture, and painting. Every element is dedicated to creating the illusion that clouds and angels have floated down through an opening in the top of the church into the upper reaches of the nave. The extremely foreshortened figures are projected as if seen from below, and the whole composition is focused off-center on the golden aura around the letters IHS, the monogram of Jesus and the insignia of the Jesuits. The subject is, in fact, the Last Judgment, with the elect rising joyfully toward the name of God and the damned plummeting through the ceiling toward the nave floor. The sweeping extension of the work into the nave space, the powerful appeal to the viewer's emotions, and the near-total unity of the multimedia visual effect—all hallmarks of Italian Baroque—were never surpassed.

SPAIN

When the Holy Roman Emperor Charles V abdicated in 1556, he left Spain and its American colonies, the Netherlands, Burgundy, Milan, and the Kingdom of Naples and Sicily to his son Philip II and the Holy Roman Empire (Germany and Austria) to his brother Ferdinand. Ferdinand and the Habsburg emperors who succeeded him ruled their territories from Vienna in Austria, but much of German-speaking Europe remained divided into small units in which local rulers decided on the religion of their territory. Catholicism prevailed in southern and western Germany and in Austria, while the north was Lutheran.

The Spanish Habsburg kings Philip III (r. 1598–1621), Philip IV (r. 1621–1665), and Charles II (r. 1665–1700) reigned over a weakening empire. After repeated local rebellions, Portugal re-established its independence in 1640. The Kingdom of Naples remained in a constant state of unrest. After 80 years of war, the Protestant northern Netherlands—which had formed the United Provinces—gained independence in 1648. Amsterdam grew into one of the wealthiest cities in Europe, and the Dutch Republic became an increasingly serious threat to Spanish trade and colonial possessions. The Catholic southern Netherlands (Flanders) remained under Spanish and then Austrian Habsburg rule.

What had seemed an endless flow of gold and silver from the Americas to Spain diminished, as precious-metal production in Bolivia and Mexico lessened. Agriculture, industry, and trade at home also suffered. As they tried to defend the Roman Catholic Church and their empire on all fronts, the Spanish kings squandered their resources and finally went bankrupt in 1692. Nevertheless, despite the decline of the Habsburgs' Spanish empire, seventeenth-century writers and artists produced some of the greatest Spanish literature and art, and the century is often called the Spanish Golden Age.

PAINTING IN SPAIN'S GOLDEN AGE

The primary influence on Spanish painting in the fifteenth century had been the art of Flanders; in the sixteenth, it had been the art of Florence and Rome. Seventeenth-century Spanish painting, profoundly influenced by Caravaggio's powerful art, was characterized by an ecstatic religiosity combined with realistic surface detail that emerges from the deep shadows of tenebrism.

JUAN SÁNCHEZ COTÁN. Late in the sixteenth century, Spanish artists developed a significant interest in paintings of artfully arranged objects rendered with intense attention to detail. Juan Sánchez Cotán (1561–1627) was one of the earliest painters of these pure still lifes in Spain. In **STILL LIFE WITH QUINCE, CABBAGE, MELON, AND CUCUMBER (FIG. 22–18)**, of about 1602, he plays off the irregular, curved shapes of the fruits and vegetables against the angular geometry of their setting. His precisely ordered subjects—

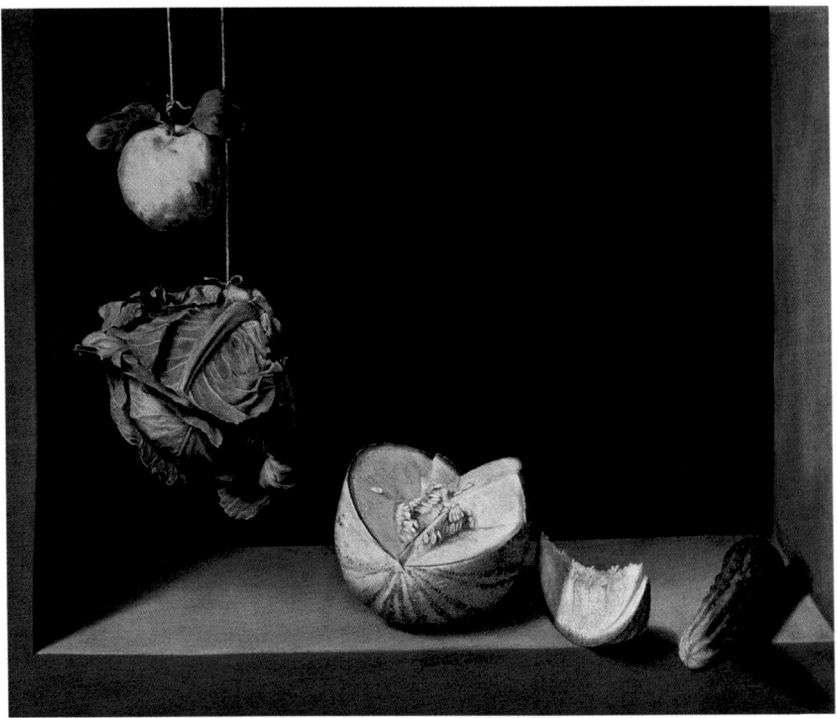

22-18 • Juan Sánchez Cotán STILL LIFE WITH QUINCE, CABBAGE, MELON, AND CUCUMBER
c. 1602. Oil on canvas, 27⅛ × 33¼″ (68.8 × 84.4 cm). San Diego Museum of Art. Gift of Anne R. and Amy Putnam

22-19 • Jusepe de Ribera MARTYRDOM OF ST. BARTHOLOMEW
1634. Oil on canvas, 41¼ × 44⅞" (1.05 × 1.14 m). National Gallery of Art, Washington, D.C.

two of which are suspended from strings—form a long arc from the upper left to the lower right. The fruits and vegetables appear within a *cantarero* (primitive larder), but it is unclear why they have been arranged in this way. Set in a strong light against impenetrable darkness, this highly artificial arrangement of strikingly lifelike forms suggests not only a fascination with spatial ambiguity, but also a contemplative sensibility and interest in the qualities of objects that look forward to the work of Zurbarán and Velázquez.

JUSEPE DE RIBERA. Jusepe (or José) de Ribera (c. 1591–1652) was born in Seville but studied in Rome and settled in Spanish-ruled Naples; in Italy, he was known as "Lo Spagnoletto" ("the

22-20 • Francisco de Zurbarán
ST. SERAPION
1628. Oil on canvas, 47½ × 40¾" (120.7 × 103.5 cm). Wadsworth Atheneum, Hartford, Connecticut.
Ella Gallup Sumner and Mary Catlin Sumner Collection Fund

Little Spaniard"). He combined the Classical and Caravaggesque styles he had learned in Rome to create a new Neapolitan—and eventually Spanish—style. Ribera became the link extending from Caravaggio in Italy to the Spanish masters Zurbarán and Velázquez.

During this period, the Church—aiming to draw people back to Catholicism—commissioned portrayals of heroic martyrs who had endured shocking torments as witness to their faith. Ribera's painting of the **MARTYRDOM OF ST. BARTHOLOMEW**, an apostle who was martyred by being skinned alive, captures the horror of the violence to come while emphasizing the saint's spirituality and acceptance **(FIG. 22–19)**. The bound Bartholomew looks heavenward as his executioner tests the sharpness of the knife that he will soon use on his still-living victim. Ribera has learned the lessons of Caravaggio well, as he highlights the intensely realistic faces with the dramatic light of tenebrism and describes the aging wrinkled flesh in great detail. The compression of the figures into the foreground space heightens our sense of being witness to this scene.

FRANCISCO DE ZURBARÁN. Francisco de Zurbarán (1598–1664) represents another martyrdom, but with understated control, in his 1628 painting of **ST. SERAPION (FIG. 22–20)**. Little is known of his early years before 1625, but Zurbarán too came under the influence of the Caravaggesque taste prevalent in Seville, the major city in southwestern Spain. His own distinctive style incorporated an interest in abstract design, which some have traced to the heritage of Islamic art in Spain.

Zurbarán primarily worked for the monastic orders. In this painting, he portrays the martyrdom of Serapion, member of the thirteenth-century Mercedarians, a Spanish order founded to rescue the Christian prisoners of the Moors. Following the vows of his order, Serapion sacrificed himself in exchange for Christian captives. The dead man's pallor, his rough hands, and the coarse ropes contrast with the off-white of his creased Mercedarian habit, its folds carefully arranged in a pattern of highlights and varying depths of shadow. The only colors are the red and gold of the insignia. This timelessly immobile composition is like a tragic still life, a study of fabric and flesh become inanimate, silent, and at rest.

DIEGO VELÁZQUEZ. Diego Rodríguez de Silva y Velázquez (1599–1660), the greatest painter to emerge from the Caravaggesque school of Seville, shared Zurbarán's fascination with objects. He entered Seville's painters' guild in 1617. Like Ribera, he began his career as a tenebrist and naturalist. During his early years, he painted scenes set in taverns, markets, and kitchens, and emphasized still lifes of various foods and kitchen utensils. His early **WATER CARRIER OF SEVILLE (FIG. 22–21)** is a study of surfaces and textures of the splendid ceramic pots that characterized folk art through the centuries. Velázquez was devoted to studying and sketching from life: The man in the painting was a well-known Sevillian waterseller. Like Sánchez Cotán, Velázquez arranged the elements of his paintings with almost mathematical rigor. The objects and figures allow the artist to exhibit his virtuosity in rendering sculptural volumes and describing contrasting textures illuminated by dramatic natural light. Light reflects in different ways off the glazed waterpot at the left and the coarser clay jug in the foreground; it is absorbed by the rough wool and dense velvet of the costumes; it

22-21 • Diego Velázquez WATER CARRIER OF SEVILLE
c. 1619. Oil on canvas, 41½ × 31½″ (105.3 × 80 cm). Victoria & Albert Museum, London.

is refracted as it passes through the clear glass held by the man and the waterdrops on the jug's surface.

In 1623, Velázquez moved to Madrid, where he became court painter to the young King Philip IV, a prestigious position that he held until his death in 1660. The opportunity to study paintings in the royal collection, as well as to travel, enabled the development of his distinctive personal style. The Flemish painter Peter Paul Rubens, during a 1628–1629 diplomatic visit to the Spanish court, convinced the king that Velázquez should visit Italy. Velázquez made two trips, the first in 1629–1631 and the second in 1649–1651. He was profoundly influenced by contemporary Italian painting, and on the first trip seems to have taken a special interest in narrative paintings with complex figure compositions.

Velázquez's Italian studies and his growing skill in composition are apparent in both figure and landscape paintings. In **THE SURRENDER AT BREDA** (FIG. 22–22), painted in 1634–1635, Velázquez treats the theme of triumph and conquest in an entirely new way—far removed from traditional gloating military propaganda. Years earlier, in 1625, Ambrosio Spinola, the Duke of Alba and the Spanish governor, had defeated the Dutch at Breda. In Velázquez's imagination, the opposing armies stand on a hilltop overlooking a vast valley where the city of Breda burns and soldiers are still deployed. The Dutch commander, Justin of Nassau, hands over the keys of Breda to the victorious Spanish commander. The entire exchange seems extraordinarily gracious, an emblem of a courtly ideal of gentlemanly conduct. The victors stand at attention, holding their densely packed lances upright in a vertical pattern—giving the painting its popular name, "The Lances"—while the defeated Dutch, a motley group, stand out of order, with pikes and banners drooping. In fact, according to reports, no keys were involved and the Dutch were more presentable in appearance than the Spaniards. Velázquez has taken liberties with historical fact to create a work of art that embodied an idealized rendering of the meaning of the surrender to his Spanish patron.

Velázquez displays here his ability to arrange a large number of figures and tell a story effectively. A strong diagonal, starting in the sword of the Dutch soldier in the lower left foreground and ending in the checked banner on the upper right, unites the composition and moves the viewer from the defeated to the victorious soldiers in the direction of the surrender itself. Portrait-like faces, meaningful gestures, and controlled color and texture convince us of the reality of the scene. The landscape painting is almost startling. Across the huge canvas, Velázquez painted an entirely imaginary Netherlands in greens and blues worked with flowing, liquid brushstrokes. Luminosity is achieved by laying down a thick layer of lead white and then flowing the layers of color over it. The silvery light forms a background for dramatically silhouetted figures and weapons. Velázquez revealed a breadth and intensity unsurpassed in his century, and became an inspiration to modern artists such as Manet and Picasso.

Perhaps Velázquez's most striking, certainly his most enigmatic work is the enormous multiple portrait, nearly 10½ feet tall and over 9 feet wide, known as **LAS MENINAS (THE MAIDS OF HONOR)**

**22-22 • Diego Velázquez
THE SURRENDER AT BREDA
(THE LANCES)**
1634–1635. Oil on canvas,
10'⅞" × 12'½" (3.07 × 3.67 m).
Museo del Prado, Madrid.

22–23 • Diego Velázquez LAS MENINAS (THE MAIDS OF HONOR)
1656. Oil on canvas, 10′5″ × 9′1½″ (3.18 × 2.76 m). Museo del Prado, Madrid.

EXPLORE MORE: Gain insight from a primary source on Diego Velázquez **www.myartslab.com**

(FIG. 22–23), painted in 1656, near the end of his life. This painting continues to challenge the viewer and stimulate debate among art historians. Velázquez draws viewers directly into the scene. In one interpretation, the viewer stands in the very space occupied by King Philip and his queen, whose reflections can be seen in the large mirror on the back wall, perhaps a clever reference to Jan van Eyck's *Double Portrait of a Giovanni Arnolfini and his Wife* (SEE FIG. 18–1), which was a part of the Spanish royal collection at this time. Echoing pictorially the claim made in Jan's signature, Velázquez himself is also present, brushes in hand, beside a huge canvas. The central focus, however, is neither the artist nor the royal couple but their brilliantly illuminated 5-year-old daughter, the Infanta (princess) Margarita, who is surrounded by her attendants, most of whom are identifiable portraits.

The cleaning of *Las Meninas* in 1984 revealed much about Velázquez's methods. He used a minimum of underdrawing, building up his forms with layers of loosely applied paint and finishing off the surfaces with dashing highlights in white, lemon yellow, and pale orange. Rather than using light to model volumes in the time-honored manner, Velázquez tried to depict the optical properties of light reflecting from surfaces. On close inspection his forms dissolve into a maze of individual strokes of paint.

No consensus exists today on the meaning of this monumental painting. It is a royal portrait; it is also a self-portrait of Velázquez standing at his easel. But fundamentally, *Las Meninas* is a personal statement. Throughout his life, Velázquez had sought respect and acclaim for himself and for the art of painting. Here, dressed as a courtier, the Order of Santiago on his chest (added later) and the keys of the palace tucked into in his sash, Velázquez proclaims the dignity and importance of painting itself.

BARTOLOMÉ ESTEBAN MURILLO.   The Madrid of Velázquez was the center of Spanish art. Seville declined after an outbreak of plague in 1649, but it remained a center for trade with the Spanish

colonies, where the work of Bartolomé Esteban Murillo (1617–1682) had a profound influence on art and religious iconography. Many patrons wanted images of the Virgin Mary and especially of the Immaculate Conception, the controversial idea that Mary was born free from original sin. Although the Immaculate Conception became Catholic dogma only in 1854, the concept, as well as devotion to Mary, grew during the seventeenth and eighteenth centuries.

Counter-Reformation authorities had provided specific instructions for artists painting the Virgin: Mary was to be dressed in blue and white, her hands folded in prayer, as she is carried upward by angels, sometimes in large flocks. She may be surrounded by an unearthly light ("clothed in the sun") and may stand on a crescent moon in reference to the woman of the Apocalypse (SEE FIG. 14–7). Angels often carry palms and symbols of the Virgin, such as a mirror, a fountain, roses, and lilies, and they may vanquish the serpent, Satan. The Church exported to the New World many paintings faithful to these orthodox guidelines by Murillo, Zurbarán, and others. When the indigenous population began to visualize the Christian story (SEE FIG. 29–45), paintings such as Murillo's **THE IMMACULATE CONCEPTION** provided prompts for their imaginings (**FIG. 22–24**).

ARCHITECTURE IN SPAIN

Turning away from the severity displayed in the sixteenth-century El Escorial monastery-palace (SEE FIG. 21–15), seventeenth-century Spanish architects again embraced the lavish decoration that had characterized their art since the fourteenth century. Profusions of ornament swept back into fashion, first in huge *retablos* (altarpieces), then in portals (main doors often embellished with sculpture), and finally in entire buildings.

THE CATHEDRAL OF SANTIAGO DE COMPOSTELA.   In the seventeenth century, the role of St. James as patron saint of Spain was challenged by the supporters of St. Teresa of Ávila and then by supporters of St. Michael, St. Joseph, and other popular saints. It became important to the archbishop and other leaders in Santiago de Compostela, where the Cathedral of St. James was located, to establish their primacy. They reinforced their efforts to revitalize the yearly pilgrimage to the city, undertaken by Spaniards since the ninth century, and used architecture as part of their campaign.

22–24 • Bartolomé Esteban Murillo
THE IMMACULATE CONCEPTION
c. 1660–1665. Oil on canvas, 81⅛ × 56⅝″
(2.06 × 1.44 m). Prado, Madrid.

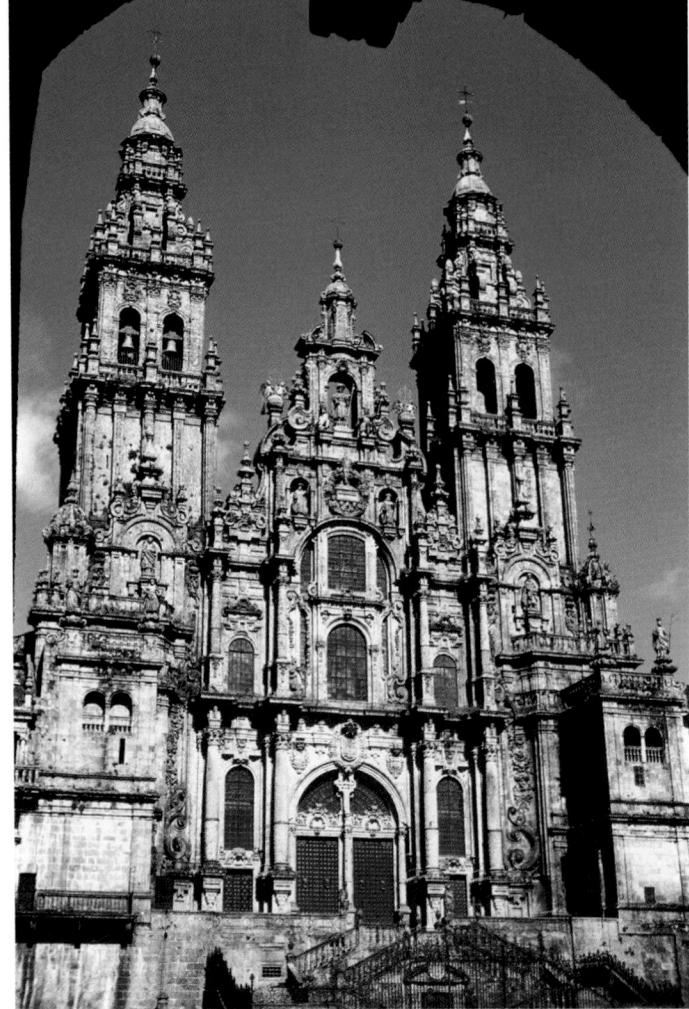

22-25 • WEST FAÇADE, CATHEDRAL OF ST. JAMES, SANTIAGO DE COMPOSTELA, SPAIN
South tower 1667–1680; north tower and central block finished mid-18th century by Fernando de Casas y Nóvoas.

Renewed interest in pilgrimages to the shrines of saints in the seventeenth century brought an influx of pilgrims, and consequently financial security, to the city and the Church. The cathedral chapter ordered a façade of almost unparalleled splendor to be added to the twelfth-century pilgrimage church (**FIG. 22–25**). The twelfth-century portal had already been closed with doors in the sixteenth century. A south tower was built in 1667–1680 and then later copied as the north tower.

The last man to serve as architect and director of works at the cathedral, Fernando de Casas y Nóvoas (active 1711–1749), tied the disparate elements together at the west end—towers, portal, stairs—in a grand design focused on a veritable wall of glass, popularly called "The Mirror." His design culminates in a free-standing gable soaring above the roof, visually linking the towers, and framing a statue of St. James. The extreme simplicity of the cloister walls and the archbishop's palace at each side of the portal heightens the dazzling effect of this enormous expanse of glass windows, glittering, jewel-like, in their intricately carved granite frame.

FLANDERS AND THE NETHERLANDS

Led by the nobleman Prince William of Orange, the Netherlands' Protestant northern provinces (present-day Holland) rebelled against Spain in 1568. The seven provinces joined together as the United Provinces in 1579 and began the long struggle for independence, achieved only in the seventeenth century. The king of Spain considered the Dutch heretical rebels, but finally the Dutch prevailed. In 1648, the United Provinces joined emissaries from Spain, the Vatican, the Holy Roman Empire, and France on equal footing in peace negotiations. The resulting Peace of Westphalia recognized the independence of the northern Netherlands.

FLANDERS

After a period of relative autonomy from 1598 to 1621 under Habsburg regents, Flanders, the southern—and predominantly Catholic—part of the Netherlands, returned to direct Spanish rule. Catholic churches were restored and important commissions went to religious subject matter. As Antwerp, the capital city and major arts center of the southern Netherlands, gradually recovered from the turmoil of the religious wars, artists of great talent flourished there. Painters like Peter Paul Rubens and Anthony van Dyck established international reputations that brought them important commissions from foreign as well as local patrons.

RUBENS. Peter Paul Rubens (1577–1640), whose painting has become synonymous with Flemish Baroque art, was born in Germany, where his father, a Protestant, had fled from his native Antwerp to escape religious persecution. In 1587, after her husband's death, Rubens's mother and her children returned to Antwerp and to Catholicism. Rubens decided in his late teens to become an artist and at age 21 was accepted into the Antwerp painters' guild, a testament to his energy, intelligence, and skill. Shortly thereafter, in 1600, he left for Italy. In Venice, his work came to the attention of the duke of Mantua, who offered him a court post. His activities on behalf of the duke over the next eight years did much to prepare him for the rest of his long and successful career. The duke had him copy famous paintings in collections all over Italy to add to the ducal collection.

Rubens visited every major Italian city, went to Madrid as the duke's emissary, and spent two extended periods in Rome, where he studied the great works of Roman antiquity and the Italian Renaissance. While in Italy, Rubens studied the paintings of two contemporaries, Caravaggio and Annibale Carracci. Hearing of Caravaggio's death in 1610, Rubens encouraged the duke of Mantua to buy the artist's *Death of the Virgin*, which the patron had rejected because of its shocking realism. The duke eventually bought the painting.

In 1608, Rubens returned to Antwerp, where in 1609 he accepted a position as court painter to the Habsburg regents of Flanders, Archduke Albert and Princess Isabella Clara Eugenia, the daughter of Philip II. Ten days after that appointment, he married the 18-year-old Isabella Brandt (1596–1626), an alliance that was

22–26 • Peter Paul Rubens SELF-PORTRAIT WITH ISABELLA BRANDT
1609–1610. Oil on canvas, 5'9" × 4'5" (1.78 × 1.36 m). Alte Pinakothek, Munich.

financially beneficial to the artist, then almost twice the age of his bride. He commemorated the marriage with a spectacular double portrait of himself and his bride seated together in front of a honeysuckle bower that evokes a state of marital bliss **(FIG. 22–26)**. The self-confident couple look out to engage viewers directly, and the rich detail of their lavish costumes is described with meticulous precision, foregrounding both the artist's virtuosity and the couple's wealth and sophistication. They join right hands in a traditional gesture of marriage, and the artist slips his foot into the

folds of Isabella's flowing red skirt, suggesting a more intimate connection between them. They would have three children before Isabella's untimely death in 1626.

In 1611, Rubens purchased a residence in Antwerp. The original house was large and typically Flemish, but Rubens added a studio in the Italian manner across a courtyard, joining the two buildings by a second-floor gallery over the entrance portal **(FIG. 22–27)**. Beyond the courtyard lay the large formal garden, laid out in symmetrical beds. The living room permitted access to a gallery overlooking Rubens's huge studio, a room designed to accommodate large paintings and to house what became virtually a painting factory. The tall, arched windows provided ample light for the single, two-story room, and a large door permitted the assistants to move finished paintings out to their designated owners. Through the gates at one side of the courtyard, one can see the architectural features of the garden, which inspired the architectural setting of *The Garden of Love* (SEE FIG. 22–30).

Rubens's first major commission in Antwerp was a large canvas triptych for the main altar of the church of St. Walpurga, **THE RAISING OF THE CROSS** (FIG. 22–28), painted in 1610–1611.

22–28 • Peter Paul Rubens THE RAISING OF THE CROSS
Church of St. Walpurga, Antwerp, Belgium. 1610–1611. Oil on canvas, center panel 15′1⅞″ × 11′1½″ (4.62 × 3.39 m), each wing 15′1⅞″ × 4′11″ (4.62 × 1.52 m). Cathedral of Our Lady, Antwerp.

22-29 • Peter Paul Rubens
HENRY IV RECEIVING THE PORTRAIT OF MARIE DE' MEDICI
1621–1625. Oil on canvas,
12'11⅛" × 9'8⅛" (3.94 × 2.95 m).
Musée du Louvre, Paris.

EXPLORE MORE: Gain insight from a primary source on Peter Paul Rubens
www.myartslab.com

He extended the central action and the landscape through all three panels. At the center, Herculean figures strain to haul upright the wooden cross with Jesus already stretched upon it. At the left, the followers of Jesus join in mourning, and at the right, soldiers supervise the execution. The drama and intense emotion of Caravaggio is merged here with the virtuoso technique of Annibale Carracci, but transformed and reinterpreted according to Rubens's own unique ideal of thematic and formal unity. The heroic nude figures, dramatic lighting effects, dynamic diagonal composition, and intense emotions show his debt to Italian art, but the rich colors and careful description of surface textures reflect his native Flemish tradition.

Rubens's expressive visual language was deemed as appropriate for representing secular rulers as it was for dramatic religious subjects. Moreover, his intelligence, courtly manners, and personal charm made him a valuable and trusted courtier to his royal patrons, who included Philip IV of Spain, Queen Marie de' Medici of France, and Charles I of England. In 1621, Marie de' Medici, who had been regent for her son Louis XIII, asked Rubens to paint the story of her life, to glorify her role in ruling France, and also to commemorate the founding of the new Bourbon royal dynasty. In 24 paintings, Rubens portrayed Marie's life and political career as one continuous triumph overseen by the ancient gods of Greece and Rome.

In the painting depicting the royal engagement (FIG. 22–29), Henry IV falls in love at once with Marie as he gazes at her portrait, shown to him—at the exact center of the composition—by Cupid and Hymen, the god of marriage. The supreme Roman god Jupiter and his wife Juno look down approvingly from the clouds. A personification of France encourages Henry, outfitted with steel breastplate and silhouetted against a landscape in which the smoke of a battle lingers in the distance, to abandon war for love, as *putti* play below with the rest of his armor. The ripe colors, lavish textures, and dramatic diagonals give sustained visual excitement to these enormous canvases, making them not only important works of art but also political propaganda of the highest order.

In **THE GARDEN OF LOVE**—a garden reminiscent of his own—Rubens may have portrayed his second wife, Helene Fourment, as the leading lady among a crowd of beauties (FIG. 22–30). *Putti* encourage the lovers, and one pushes a hesitant young woman into the garden so she and her partner can join the ladies and gentlemen who are already enjoying the pleasures of nature, and of each other. The sculpture and architectural setting recall Italian Mannerism—a stone nymph presses water from her breasts to create the fountain,

herms and columns banded with rough-hewn rings flank the entrance to the pavilion that forms the approach to the grotto of Venus. All is lush color, shimmering satin, falling water, and sunset sky—rich in the visual and tactile effects so appreciated by seventeenth-century viewers.

To satisfy his clients all over Europe, Rubens employed dozens of assistants, many of whom were, or became, important painters in their own right. Using workshop assistants was standard practice for a major artist, but Rubens was particularly methodical, training or hiring specialists in costumes, still lifes, landscapes, portraiture, and animal painting who together could complete works from his detailed sketches. Among his friends and collaborators were Anthony van Dyck and his friend and neighbor Jan Brueghel.

PORTRAITS AND STILL LIFES. One of Rubens's collaborators, Anthony van Dyck (1599–1641), had an illustrious independent career as a portraitist. Son of an Antwerp silk merchant, he was listed as a pupil of the dean of Antwerp's Guild of St. Luke at age 10. He had his own studio and roster of pupils at age 16 but was not made a member of the guild until 1618, the year after he began

22–30 • Peter Paul Rubens THE GARDEN OF LOVE
1630–1632. Oil on canvas, 6′6″ × 9′3½″ (1.98 × 2.83 m). Museo del Prado, Madrid.

Allegory of Sight ▶ by Jan Brueghel and Peter Paul Rubens, from the Allegories of the Five Senses series. c. 1617–1618. Oil on wood panel, 25⅝ × 43" (65 × 109 cm). Museo del Prado, Madrid.

Coudenberg, the Brussels residence of the patrons, appears in the background.

The double-headed eagle crowning the brass chandelier is the symbol of the Habsburg Dynasty.

On the top shelf are small-scale reproductions of sculptures by Michelangelo—slaves from the tomb of Julius II and personifications of the times of the day from the Medici tombs—and on the lower shelves are portraits of Roman emperors.

The Tiger Hunt seen on the back wall was a recent painting by Rubens. Along with his *Daniel in the Lions' Den* in the upper left and his and Brueghel's *Madonna and Child in a Garland of Flowers* at right, this seems to have been included to showcase the artists' latest work.

A double portrait of the patrons Albert and Isabella sits on the table, while an equestrian portrait of Albert is seen on the floor at the center of the room. Both copy actual paintings by Rubens.

Personifying sight, Juno Optica—identified by her bird, the peacock, seen in the doorway next to her head—contemplates a painting of *Christ Healing the Blind* that invokes Sight through its opposite, while linking the senses to the doctrine of salvation.

Instruments such as the telescope and magnifying glass, as well as the spectacles worn by the monkey in the immediate foreground, all refer to the sense of sight and its limitations.

This painting—the Madonna and Child is by Rubens and the framing floral wreath by Brueghel—is identical to one now in the Louvre, except it is shown larger here in proportion to the other objects in the room.

SEE MORE: View the Closer Look feature for *Allegory of Sight* **www.myartslab.com**

his association with Rubens as a specialist in painting heads. The need to blend his work seamlessly with that of Rubens enhanced Van Dyck's technical skill. After a trip to the English court of James I (r. 1603–1625) in 1620, Van Dyck traveled to Italy and worked as a portrait painter for seven years before returning to Antwerp. In 1632, he returned to England as the court painter to Charles I (r. 1625–1649), by whom he was knighted and given a studio, a summer home, and a large salary.

Van Dyck's many portraits of the royal family provide a sympathetic record of their features and demeanor. In **CHARLES I AT THE HUNT** (FIG. 22–31), of 1635, Van Dyck was able, by clever manipulation of the setting, to portray the king truthfully and still present him as an imposing figure. Dressed casually for the hunt and standing on a bluff overlooking a distant view (a device used by Rubens to enhance the stature of Henry IV; SEE FIG. 22–29), Charles, who was in fact very short, appears here taller than his pages and even than his horse, since its head is down and its heavy body is partly off the canvas. The viewer's gaze is diverted from the king's delicate and rather short frame to his pleasant features, framed by his jauntily cocked cavalier's hat and the graceful cascade

of his hair. As if in decorous homage, the tree branches bow gracefully toward him, echoing the circular lines of the hat.

Yet another painter working with Rubens, Jan Brueghel (1568–1625), specialized in settings rather than portraits. Jan was the son of Pieter Bruegel the Elder (see "Breugel's Cycle of the Months," pages 702–703), and it was Jan who added the "h" to the family name. Brueghel's and Rubens's series of allegories of the five senses—five paintings, made for Habsburg regents Princess Isabella Clara Eugenia and Archduke Albert, and illustrating sight, hearing, touch, taste, and smell—in effect invited the viewer to wander in an imaginary space enjoying an amazing collection of works of art and scientific equipment (see "A Closer Look," opposite). Their allegory of sight is a display, a virtual inventory, and a summary of the wealth, scholarship, and **connoisseurship** (the study of style to assess quality and determine authorship) that was made possible through the patronage of the Habsburg rulers of the Spanish Netherlands.

Our term, "still life," for paintings of artfully arranged objects on a table, comes from the Dutch *stilleven*, a word coined about 1650. The Antwerp artist Clara Peeters (1594–c. 1657) specialized

22-31 • Anthony van Dyck
CHARLES I AT THE HUNT
1635. Oil on canvas, 8'11" × 6'11"
(2.75 × 2.14 m). Musée du Louvre, Paris.

22-32 • Clara Peeters STILL LIFE WITH FLOWERS, GOBLET, DRIED FRUIT, AND PRETZELS
1611. Oil on panel, 20½ × 28¾″ (52 × 73 cm). Museo del Prado, Madrid.

Like many "breakfast pieces," this painting features a pile of pretzels among the elegant tableware. The salty, twisted bread was called *pretzel* (from the Latin *pretiola*, meaning "small reward") because it was invented by German monks to reward children who had learned their prayers. The twisted shapes represented the crossed arms of a child praying.

in still-life tabletop arrangements (see Iconography box in the Introduction, FIG. A). She was a precocious young woman whose career seems to have begun before she was 14. Of some 50 paintings now attributed to her (of which more than 30 are signed), many are of the type called "breakfast pieces," showing a table set for a meal of bread and fruit. Peeters was one of the first artists to combine flowers and food in a single painting, as in her **STILL LIFE WITH FLOWERS, GOBLET, DRIED FRUIT, AND PRETZELS** **(FIG. 22–32)**, of 1611. Peeters arranged rich tableware and food against neutral, almost black backgrounds, the better to emphasize the fall of light over the contrasting surface textures. In a display of precious objects that must have appealed to her clients, the luxurious goblet and bowl contrast with simple stoneware and pewter, as do the delicate flowers with the homey pretzels. The pretzels, piled on the pewter tray, are a particularly interesting Baroque element, with their complex multiple curves.

THE DUTCH REPUBLIC

The House of Orange was not notable for its patronage of the arts, but patronage improved significantly under Prince Frederick Henry (r. 1625–1647), and Dutch artists found many other eager patrons among the prosperous middle class in Amsterdam, Leiden, Haarlem, Delft, and Utrecht. The Hague was the capital city and the preferred residence of the House of Orange, but Amsterdam was the true center of power, because of its sea trade and the enterprise of its merchants, who made the city an international commercial center. The Dutch delighted in depictions of themselves and their country—the landscape, cities, and domestic life—not to mention beautiful and interesting objects to be seen in still-life paintings and interior scenes. A well-educated people, the Dutch were also fascinated by history, mythology, the Bible, new scientific discoveries, commercial expansion abroad, and colonial exploration.

22-33 • Hendrick ter Brugghen
ST. SEBASTIAN TENDED BY ST. IRENE
1625. Oil on canvas, 58¹⁵⁄₁₆ × 47½″
(149.6 × 120 cm). Allen Memorial Art
Museum, Oberlin College, Ohio.

Visitors to the Netherlands in the seventeenth century noted the popularity of art among merchants and working people. Peter Mundy, an English traveler, wrote in 1640 that even butchers, bakers, shoemakers, and blacksmiths had pictures in their houses and shops. This taste for art stimulated a free market for paintings that functioned like other commodity markets. Artists had to compete to capture the interest of the public by painting on speculation. Specialists in particularly popular types of images were most likely to be financially successful, and what most Dutch patrons wanted were paintings of themselves, their country, their homes, their possessions, and the life around them. The demand for art also gave rise to an active market for the graphic arts, both for original compositions and for copies of paintings, since one copperplate could produce hundreds of impressions, and worn-out plates could be reworked and used again.

THE INFLUENCE OF ITALY. Hendrick ter Brugghen (1588–1629) had spent time in Rome, perhaps between 1608 and 1614, where he must have seen Caravaggio's works and became an enthusiastic follower. On his return home, in 1616, he entered the Utrecht painters' guild, bringing Caravaggio's style into the Netherlands. Ter Brugghen's **ST. SEBASTIAN TENDED BY ST. IRENE** introduced the Netherlandish painters to the new art of Baroque Italy (FIG. 22–33). The sickly gray-green flesh of the nearly dead St. Sebastian, painted in an almost monochromatic palette, contrasts with the brilliant red and gold brocade of what seems to be his crumpled garment. Actually this is the cope of the bishop of Utrecht, which had survived destruction by Protestants and become a symbol of Catholicism in Utrecht. The saint is cast as a heroic figure, his strong, youthful body still bound to the tree. But St. Irene (the patron saint of nurses) delicately removes one of the

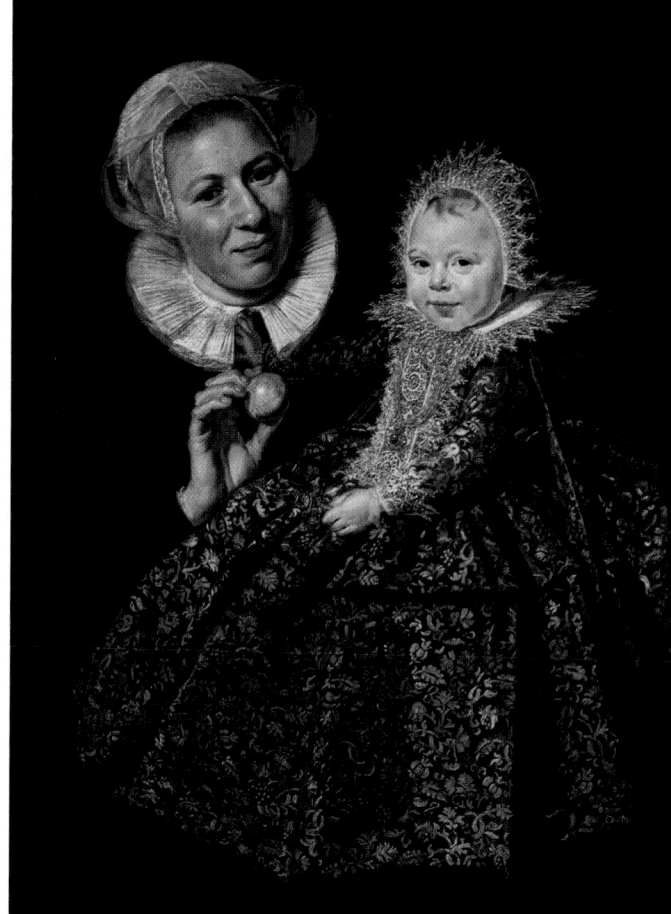

22-34 • Frans Hals CATHARINA HOOFT AND HER NURSE
c. 1620. Oil on canvas, 33¾ × 25½″ (85.7 × 64.8 cm). Staatliche Museen zu Berlin, Preussischer Kulturbesitz, Gemäldegalerie.

of identity rooted in recognizable faces. Group portraiture documenting the membership of corporate organizations was a Dutch specialty. These large canvases, filled with many individuals who shared the cost of the commission, challenged painters to present a coherent, interesting composition that nevertheless gave equal attention to each individual portrait.

Frans Hals (c. 1581/1585–1666), the leading painter of Haarlem, developed a style grounded in the Netherlandish love of description and inspired by the Caravaggesque style introduced by artists such as Ter Brugghen. Like Velázquez, he tried to recreate the optical effects of light on the shapes and textures of objects. He painted boldly, with slashing strokes and angular patches of paint. Only when seen at a distance do the colors merge into solid forms over which a flickering light seems to move. In Hals's hands, this seemingly effortless, loose technique suggests the spontaneity of an infectious joy in life.

In his portrait of **CATHARINA HOOFT AND HER NURSE (FIG. 22–34)**, painted about 1620, Hals captured the vitality of a gesture caught within a fleeting moment in time. The portrait records for posterity the great pride of the parents in their child, but it also records their wealth in its study of rich fabrics, elaborate laces, and expensive toys (a golden rattle). Hals's depiction highlights the heartwarming delight of the child, who seems to be acknowledging the viewer as a loving family member, while her doting nurse attempts to distract her with an apple and at the same time looks out admiringly at the attention the viewer is directing to her charge.

In contrast to this intimate individual portrait are Hals's official group portraits, such as his **OFFICERS OF THE HAARLEM MILITIA COMPANY OF ST. ADRIAN (FIG. 22–35)**, of about 1627. Most artists arranged their sitters in neat rows to depict every face clearly, but Hals's dynamic composition has turned the group portrait into a lively social event. The composition is based on a strong underlying geometry of diagonal lines—gestures, banners, and sashes—balanced by the stabilizing perpendiculars of table, window, and tall glass. The black suits and hats make the white ruffs and sashes of rose, white, and baby blue even more brilliant.

The company, made up of several guard units, was charged with the military protection of Haarlem. Officers came from the upper middle class and held their commissions for three years, whereas the ordinary guards were tradespeople and craftworkers. Each company was organized like a guild, traditionally under the patronage of a saint. The company functioned mainly as a fraternal order, holding archery competitions, taking part in city processions, and originally maintaining an altar in the local church (SEE ALSO FIG. 22–38).

A painting that had long been praised as one of Hals's finest works is actually by Judith Leyster (c. 1609–1660), Hals's contemporary. A cleaning uncovered her distinctive signature, the monogram "JL" with a star, which refers to her surname, meaning "pole star." Leyster's work shows clear echoes of her exposure to the Utrecht painters who had enthusiastically adopted the

arrows that pierce him, and her maid reaches to untie his wrists. In a typically Baroque manner, the powerful diagonal created by St. Sebastian's left arm dislodges him from the triangular stability of the group. The immediacy and emotional engagement of the work are enhanced by crowding all the figures into the foreground plane, an effect strengthened by the low horizon line, another aspect of this painting that recalls the work of Caravaggio. The tenebrism and dramatic lighting effects are likewise Caravaggesque, as is the frank realism of the women's faces, with reddened noses and rosy cheeks. Rembrandt, Vermeer, and Rubens all admired Ter Brugghen's painting.

PORTRAITS. Seventeenth-century Dutch portraiture took many forms, ranging from single figures in sparsely furnished settings to allegorical depictions of groups in elaborate costumes surrounded by symbols and attributes. Although the faithful description of facial features and costumes was the most important gauge of a portrait's success, some painters went beyond likeness to convey a sense of mood or emotion in the sitter. Fundamentally, portraits functioned as social statements of the sitters' status coupled with a clear sense

22-35 • Frans Hals **OFFICERS OF THE HAARLEM MILITIA COMPANY OF ST. ADRIAN**
c. 1627. Oil on canvas, 6′ × 8′8″ (1.83 × 2.67 m). Frans Halsmuseum, Haarlem.

principal features of Caravaggio's style. Since in 1631 Leyster signed as a witness at the baptism in Haarlem of one of Hals's children, it is assumed they were close; she may also have worked in his shop. She entered Haarlem's Guild of St. Luke in 1633, which allowed her to take pupils into her studio, and her competitive relationship with Frans Hals around that time is made clear by the complaint she lodged against him in 1635 for luring away one of her apprentices.

Leyster is known primarily for informal scenes of daily life, which often carry an underlying moralistic theme. In her lively **SELF-PORTRAIT** of 1635 (**FIG. 22–36**), the artist has interrupted her work to lean back and look at viewers, as if they had just entered the room. Her elegant dress and the fine chair in which she sits are symbols of her success as an artist whose popularity was based on the very type of painting in progress on her easel. One critic has suggested that her subject—a man playing a violin—may be a visual pun on the painter with palette and brush. Leyster's understanding of light and texture is truly remarkable. The brushwork she used to depict her own flesh and delicate ruff is more controlled than Hals's loose technique, and forms an interesting contrast to the broad strokes of thick paint she used to create her full, stiff skirt. She further emphasized

the difference between her portrait and her painting by executing the image on her easel in lighter tones and softer, looser brushwork. The narrow range of colors sensitively dispersed in the composition and the warm spotlighting are typical of Leyster's mature style.

22-36 • Judith Leyster **SELF-PORTRAIT**
1635. Oil on canvas, 29⅜ × 25⅝″ (72.3 × 65.3 cm).
National Gallery of Art, Washington, D.C.
Gift of Mr. and Mrs. Robert Woods Bliss

22-37 • Rembrandt van Rijn THE ANATOMY LESSON OF DR. NICOLAES TULP
1632. Oil on canvas, 5'3¾" × 7'1¼" (1.6 × 2.1 m). Mauritshuis, The Hague.

REMBRANDT VAN RIJN.   The most important painter working in Amsterdam in the seventeenth century was Rembrandt van Rijn (1606–1669). One of nine children born in Leiden to a miller and his wife, Rembrandt studied under Pieter Lastman (1583–1633), the principal painter in Amsterdam at the time. From Lastman, a history painter who had worked in Rome, Rembrandt absorbed an interest in the naturalism, drama, and tenebrism championed by Caravaggio. By the 1630s, Rembrandt was established in Amsterdam primarily as a portrait painter, although he also painted a wide range of narrative themes and landscapes.

In his first group portrait, **THE ANATOMY LESSON OF DR. NICOLAES TULP (FIG. 22–37)** of 1632, Rembrandt combined his scientific and humanistic interests. Frans Hals had activated the group portrait rather than conceiving it as a simple reproduction of posed figures and faces; Rembrandt transformed it into a charged moment from a life story. Dr. Tulp, head of the surgeons' guild from 1628 to 1653, sits right of center, while a group of fellow physicians gathers around to observe the cadaver and learn from the famed anatomist. Rembrandt built his composition on a sharp

diagonal that pierces space from right to left, uniting the cadaver on the table, the calculated arrangement of speaker and listeners, and the open book into a dramatic narrative event. Rembrandt makes effective use of Caravaggio's tenebrist technique, as the figures emerge from a dark and undefined ambience, their attentive faces framed by brilliant white ruffs. Radiant light streams down to spotlight the ghostly flesh of the cadaver, drawing our attention to the extended arms of Dr. Tulp, who flexes his own left hand to demonstrate the action of the cadaver's arm muscles that he lifts up with silver forceps. Unseen by the viewers are the illustrations of the huge book, presumably an edition of Andreas Vesalius's study of human anatomy, published in Basel in 1543, which was the first attempt at accurate anatomical illustrations in print. Rembrandt's painting has been seen as an homage to Vesalius and to science, as well as a portrait of the members of the Amsterdam surgeons' guild.

Prolific and popular with his Amsterdam clientele, Rembrandt ran a busy studio, producing works that sold for high prices. The prodigious output of his large workshop and of the many followers who imitated his manner has made it difficult for scholars to define his body of work, and many paintings formerly attributed to Rembrandt have recently been assigned to other artists. Rembrandt's mature work reflected his cosmopolitan city environment, his study of science and nature, and the broadening of his artistic vocabulary by the study of Italian Renaissance art, chiefly from engravings and paintings imported by the busy Amsterdam art market.

In 1642, Rembrandt was one of several artists commissioned by a wealthy civic-guard company to create large group portraits of its members for its new meeting hall. The result, **THE COMPANY OF CAPTAIN FRANS BANNING COCQ (FIG. 22–38)**, carries the idea of a group portrait as a dramatic event even further. Because a dense layer of grime had darkened and obscured its colors, this painting was once thought to be a nocturnal scene and was therefore called *The Night Watch*. After cleaning and restoration in 1975–1976, it now exhibits a natural golden light that sets afire the palette of rich colors—browns, blues, olive-green, orange, and red—around a central core of lemon yellow in the costume of a lieutenant. To the dramatic group composition, showing a company forming for a parade in an Amsterdam street, Rembrandt added several colorful but seemingly unnecessary figures. While the officers stride purposefully forward, the rest of the men and several mischievous children mill about. The radiant young girl in the left middle ground, carrying a chicken with prominent claws (*klauw* in Dutch), may be a pun on the kind of guns (*klover*) that gave the name (the *Kloveniers*) to the company. Chicken legs with claws also are part of its coat of arms. The complex interactions of the figures and the vivid, individualized likenesses of the militiamen make this one of the greatest group portraits in the Dutch tradition.

22-38 • Rembrandt van Rijn **THE COMPANY OF CAPTAIN FRANS BANNING COCQ (THE NIGHT WATCH)**
1642. Oil on canvas, 11′11″ × 14′4″ (3.63 × 4.37 m) (cut down from the original size). Rijksmuseum, Amsterdam.

Rembrandt was the first artist to popularize etching as a major form of artistic expression. In the **etching** process, a metal plate is coated on both sides with an acid-resistant resin that dries hard without being brittle. Then, instead of laboriously cutting the lines of the desired image directly into the plate as in an engraving (see "Woodcuts and Engravings on Metal," page 590) the artist draws through the resin with a sharp needle to expose the metal. The plate is then immersed in acid, which eats into the metal exposed by the drawn lines. By controlling the time the acid stays on different parts of the plate, the artist can make shallow, fine lines or deep, heavy ones. After the resin coating is removed from the surface of the plate, an impression is taken. If changes need to be made, lines can be "erased" with a sharp metal scraper. Not surprisingly, a complex image with a wide range of tones requires many steps.

Another intaglio technique for registering images with incised lines on a metal plate is called drypoint, in which a sharp needle is used to scratch lines directly into the metal. In drypoint, however, the burr (metal pushed up by the drypoint needle) is left in place. Unlike engraving, in which the burr is scraped off, here both the burr and the groove hold the ink. This creates a printed line with a rich black appearance that is impossible to achieve with engraving or etching alone. Unfortunately, drypoint burr is fragile, and no more than a dozen prints can be made before it flattens and loses its character. Rembrandt's earliest prints were entirely etched, but later he added drypoint to develop tonal richness.

SEE MORE: View a video about the process of intaglio www.myartslab.com

In his enthusiasm for printmaking as an important art form with its own aesthetic qualities, Rembrandt was remarkably like Albrecht Dürer (SEE FIGS. 21–6, 21–7). Beginning in 1627, he focused on etching, which uses acid to inscribe a design on metal plates. About a decade later, he began to experiment with making additions to his compositions in the **drypoint** technique, in which the artist uses a sharp needle to scratch shallow lines in a plate. Because etching and drypoint allow the artist to work directly on the plate, the style of the finished print can have the relatively free and spontaneous character of a drawing (see "Etching and Drypoint," above). In these works Rembrandt alone took charge of the creative process, from the preparation of the plate to its inking and printing, and he constantly experimented with the technique, with methods of inking, and with papers for printing.

22-39 • Rembrandt van Rijn THREE CROSSES (FIRST STATE)
1653. Drypoint and etching, 15⅛ × 17¾″ (38.5 × 45 cm). Rijksmuseum, Amsterdam.

Rembrandt's prints were sought after, widely collected, and attracted high prices, even in his lifetime.

Rembrandt's deep speculations on the meaning of the life of Christ evolve in a series of prints, **THREE CROSSES**, that comes down to us in five states, or stages, of the creative and printing process. (Only the first is reproduced here.) Rembrandt tried to capture the moment described in the Gospels when, during the Crucifixion, darkness covered the Earth and Jesus cried out, "Father, into thy hands I commend my spirit." In the first state **(FIG. 22–39)**, the centurion kneels in front of the cross while other terrified people run from the scene. The Virgin Mary and St. John share the light flooding down from heaven. By the fourth and fifth states, Rembrandt had completely reworked and reinterpreted the theme. The scene is considerably darker, and some of the people in the first state, including even Mary and Jesus' friends, have almost disappeared. The composition becomes more compact, the individual elements are simplified, and the emotions are intensified. The first state is a detailed rendering of the scene in realistic terms; by the fourth and fifth, the event has been reduced to its mysterious essence. The eternal battles of dark and light, doom and salvation, evil and good—all seem to be waged anew.

As he aged, Rembrandt painted ever more brilliantly, varying textures and paint from the thinnest glazes to thick **impasto** (heavily applied pigments), creating a rich, luminous *chiaroscuro*, ranging from deepest shadow to brilliant highlights in a dazzling display of gold, red, and chestnut-brown. His sensitivity to the human condition is perhaps nowhere more powerfully expressed than in his late self-portraits, which became more searching as he aged. Distilling a lifetime of study and contemplation, he expressed an internalized spirituality new in the history of art. In a **SELF-PORTRAIT** of 1658 **(FIG. 22–40)**, the artist assumes a regal pose, at ease, with arms and legs spread and holding a staff as if it were a baton of command. Yet we know that fortune no longer smiled on him (he had to declare bankruptcy that same year). A few well-placed brushstrokes suggest the physical tension in the

22-40 • Rembrandt van Rijn **SELF-PORTRAIT**
1658. Oil on canvas, 52⅝ × 40⅞″ (133.6 × 103.8 cm).
The Frick Collection, New York.

fingers and the weariness of the deep-set eyes. Mercilessly analytical, the portrait depicts the furrowed brow, sagging flesh, and aging face of one who has suffered pitfalls but managed to survive, retaining his dignity.

JOHANNES VERMEER.   One of the most intriguing Dutch artists of this period is Johannes Vermeer (1632–1675), who was also an innkeeper and art dealer. He entered the Delft artists' guild in 1653 and painted only for local patrons. Meticulous in his technique, with a unique compositional approach and painting style, Vermeer produced fewer than 40 canvases that can be securely attributed to him, and the more these paintings are studied, the more questions arise about the artist's life and his methods. Vermeer's **VIEW OF DELFT** (**FIG. 22–41**), for example, is no simple cityscape. Although the artist convinces the viewer of its authenticity, he does not paint a photographic reproduction of the scene; Vermeer moves buildings around to create an ideal composition. He endows the city with a timeless stability by a stress on horizontal lines, the careful placement of buildings, the quiet atmosphere, and the clear, even light that seems to emerge from beneath low-lying clouds. Vermeer

22-41 • Johannes Vermeer **VIEW OF DELFT**
c. 1662. Oil on canvas, 38½ × 46¼″ (97.8 × 117.5 cm).
Mauritshuis, The Hague.
The Johan Maurits van Nassau Foundation

may have experimented with the mechanical device known as the **camera obscura** (see Chapter 30), not as a method of reproducing the image but as another tool in the visual analysis of the composition. The camera obscura would have enhanced optical distortions that led to the "beading" of highlights (seen here on the harbored ships and dark gray architecture), which creates the illusion of brilliant light but does not dissolve the underlying form.

Most of Vermeer's paintings portray enigmatic scenes of women in their homes, alone or with a servant, occupied with some cultivated activity, such as writing, reading letters, or playing a musical instrument. These are quiet interior scenes, low-key in color, asymmetrical but strongly geometric in organization. By creating a contained and consistent architectonic world in which each object adds to the clarity and balance of the composition, Vermeer transports everyday scenes to a level of unearthly perfection. An even, pearly light from a window often gives solidity to the figures and objects in a room. All emotion is subdued, as Vermeer evokes a mood of quiet meditation. The brushwork is so controlled that it becomes invisible, except when he paints his characteristic pools of reflected light as tiny, pearl-like droplets of color.

In **WOMAN HOLDING A BALANCE** (FIG. **22–42**), perfect equilibrium creates a monumental composition and a moment of

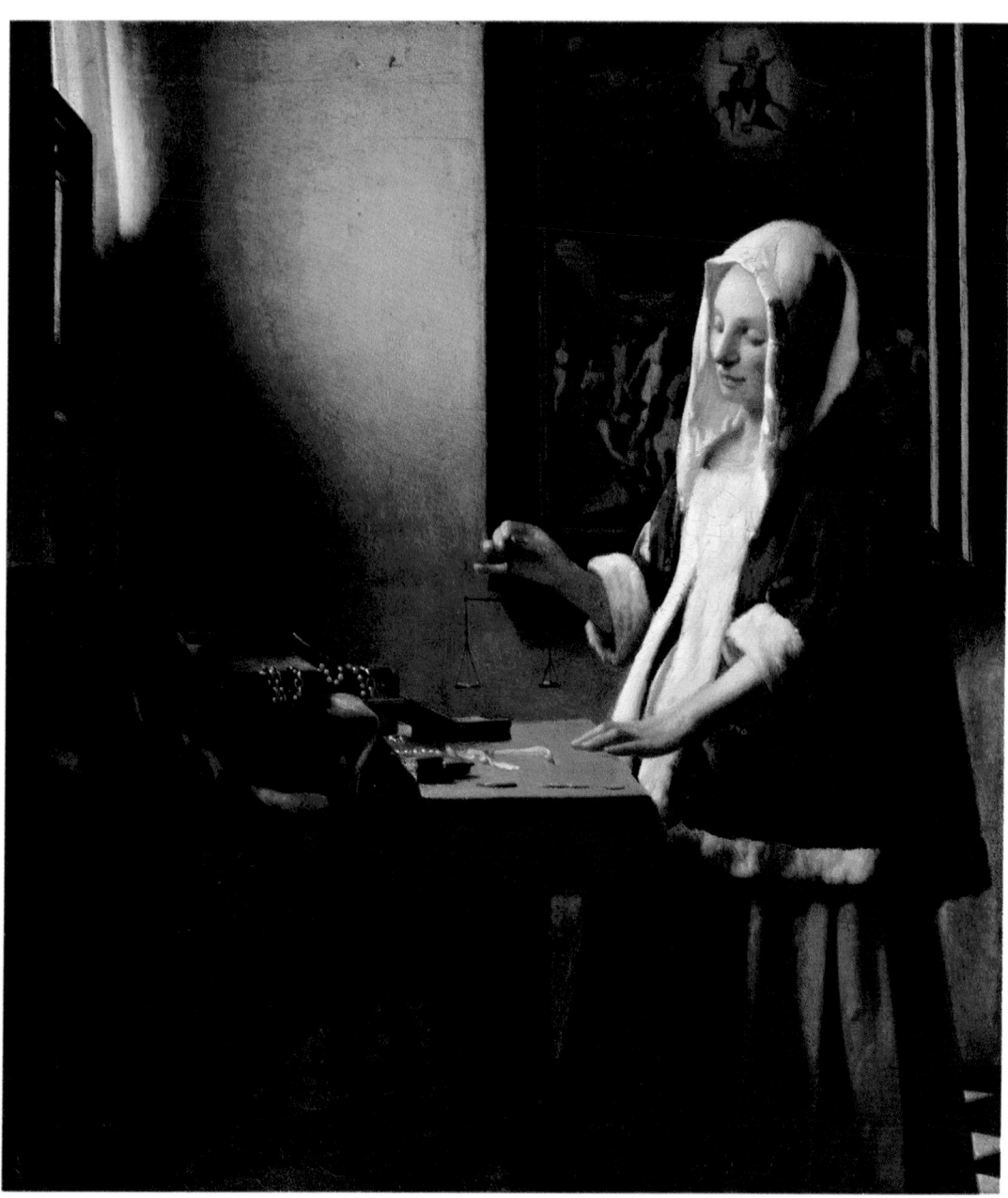

22-42 • Johannes Vermeer WOMAN HOLDING A BALANCE
c. 1664. Oil on canvas, 15⅞ × 14″ (39 × 35 cm). National Gallery of Art, Washington, D.C.
Widener Collection 1942.9.97

SEE MORE: View a video about Vermeer's *Woman Holding a Balance* **www.myartslab.com**

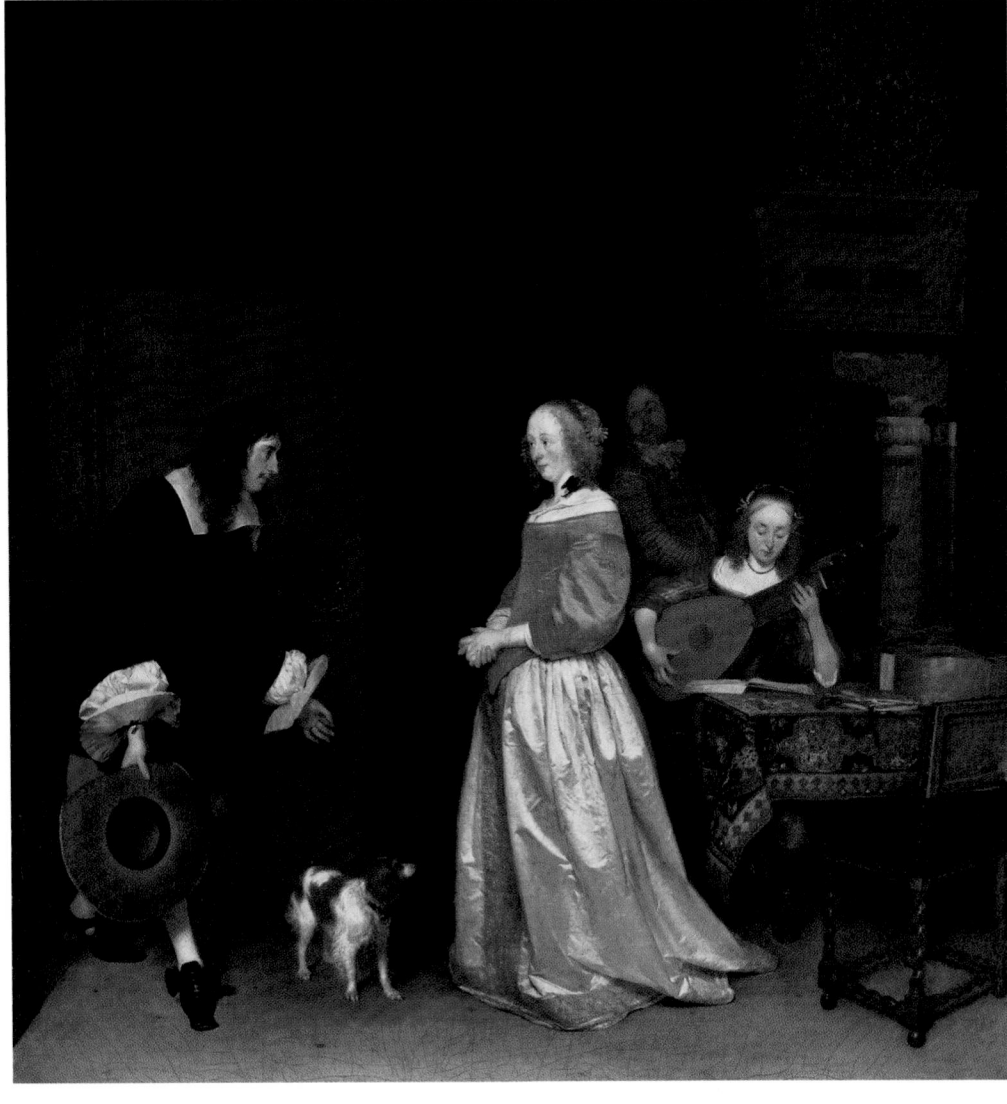

22–43 • Gerard ter Borch
THE SUITOR'S VISIT
c. 1658. Oil on canvas, 32½ × 29⅝″
(82.6 × 75.3 cm). National Gallery
of Art, Washington, D.C.

supreme stillness. The woman contemplates the balance in her right hand, drawing our attention to the act of weighing and judging. Her hand and the scale are central, but directly behind her head, on the wall of the room, is a painting of the Last Judgment, highlighting the figure of Christ the Judge in a gold aureole above her head. The juxtaposition seems to turn Vermeer's genre scene into a metaphor for eternal judgment, a sobering religious reference that may reflect the artist's own position as a Catholic living in a Protestant country. The woman's moment of quiet introspection in front of the gold and pearls displayed on the table before her, shimmering with reflected light from the window, also evokes the **vanitas** theme of the transience of earthly life, allowing the painter to comment on the ephemeral quality of material things.

GENRE SCENES. Continuing a long Netherlandish tradition, seventeenth-century genre paintings—generally made for private patrons and depicting scenes of contemporary daily life—were often laden with symbolic references, although their meaning is not always clear to us now. A clean house might indicate a virtuous

housewife and mother, while a messy household suggested laziness and the sin of sloth. Ladies dressing in front of mirrors certainly could be succumbing to vanity, and drinking parties led to overindulgence and lust.

One of the most refined of the genre painters was Gerard ter Borch (1617–1681). In his painting traditionally known as **THE SUITOR'S VISIT** (FIG. 22–43), from about 1658, a well-dressed man bows gracefully to an elegant woman arrayed in white satin, who stands in a sumptuously furnished room in which another woman plays a lute. Another man, in front of a fireplace, turns to observe the newcomer. The painting appears to represent a prosperous gentleman paying a call on a lady of equal social status, possibly a courtship scene. The spaniel and the musician seem to be simply part of the scene, but we are already familiar with the dog as a symbol of fidelity, and stringed instruments were said to symbolize, through their tuning, the harmony of souls and thus, possibly, a loving relationship. On the other hand, it has been suggested that the theme is not so innocent: that the gestures here suggest a liaison. The dog could be interpreted sexually, as sniffing around, and the music making could be associated with sensory pleasure

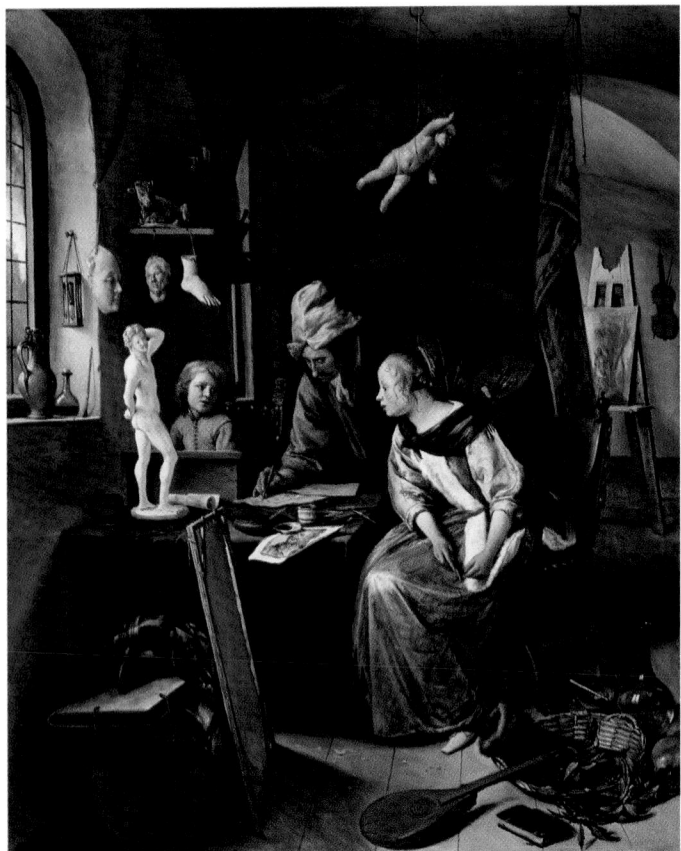

22–44 • Jan Steen THE DRAWING LESSON
1665. Oil on wood panel, 19⅜ × 16¼″ (49.3 × 41 cm).
The J. Paul Getty Museum, Los Angeles.

still-life objects such as a lute, wine jug, book, and skull may remind the viewer of the transitory nature of life in spite of the permanence art may seem to offer.

Emanuel de Witte (1617–1692) of Rotterdam specialized in architectural interiors, first in Delft in 1640 and then in Amsterdam after settling there permanently in 1652. Although many of his interiors were composites of features from several locations combined in one idealized architectural view, De Witte also painted faithful "portraits" of actual buildings. One of these is his **PORTUGUESE SYNAGOGUE, AMSTERDAM (FIG. 22–45)** of 1680. The synagogue, which still stands and is one of the most impressive buildings in Amsterdam, is shown here as a rectangular hall divided into one wide central aisle with narrow side aisles, each covered with a wooden barrel vault resting on lintels supported by columns. De Witte's shift of the viewpoint slightly to one side has created an interesting spatial composition, and strong contrasts of light and shade add dramatic movement to the simple interior. The elegant couple and the dogs in the foreground provide a sense of scale for the architecture and add human interest.

Today, this painting is interesting not only as a work of art, but also as a record of seventeenth-century synagogue architecture. It also reflects Dutch religious tolerance in an age when Jews were often persecuted. Expelled from Spain and Portugal from the late

evoked by touch. Ter Borch was renowned for his exquisite rendition of lace, velvet, and especially satin, and such wealth could be seen as a symbol of excess. One critic has even suggested that the white satin is a metaphor for the women's skin. If there is a moral lesson, it is presented discreetly and ambiguously.

Another important genre painter is Jan Steen (1626–1679), whose larger brushstrokes contrast with the meticulous treatment of Ter Borch. Steen painted over 800 works but never achieved financial success. Most of his scenes used everyday life to portray moral tales, illustrate proverbs and folk sayings, or make puns to amuse the spectator. Steen moved about the country for most of his life, and from 1670 until his death he kept a tavern in Leiden. He probably found inspiration and models all about him. Early in his career Steen was influenced by Frans Hals, but his work could be either very summary or extremely detailed.

Jan Steen's paintings of children are especially remarkable, for he captured not only their childish physiques but also their fleeting moods and expressions with rapid and fluid brushstrokes. His ability to capture such transitory dispositions was well expressed in his painting **THE DRAWING LESSON (FIG. 22–44)**. Here, youthful apprentices—a boy and a well-dressed young woman—observe the master artist correct an example of drawing, a skill widely believed to be the foundation of art. The studio is cluttered with all the supplies the artists need. On the floor at the lower right,

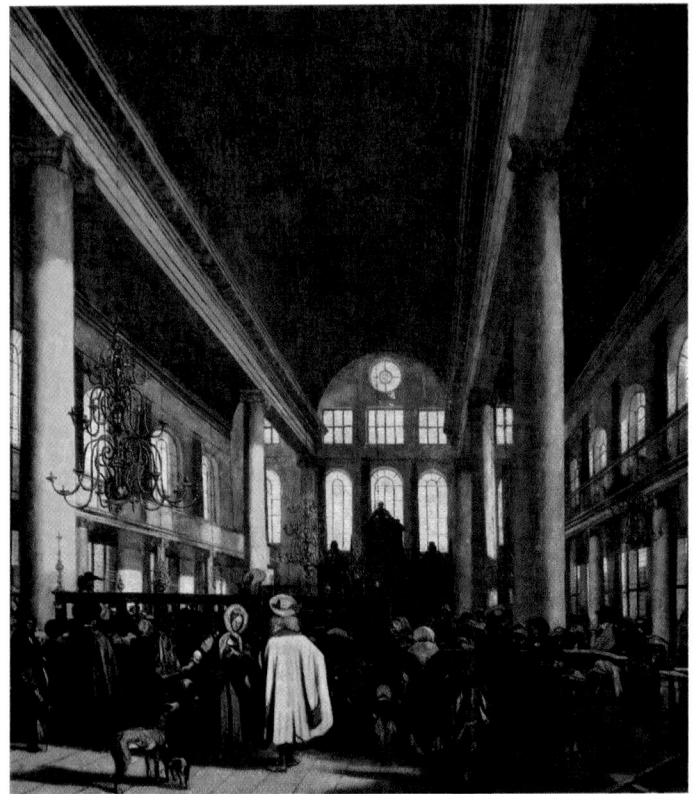

22–45 • Emanuel de Witte PORTUGUESE SYNAGOGUE, AMSTERDAM
1680. Oil on canvas, 43½ × 39″ (110.5 × 99.1 cm). Rijksmuseum, Amsterdam. Architects Daniel Stalpaert and Elias Bouman built the synagogue in 1671–1675.

22–46 • Jacob van Ruisdael VIEW OF HAARLEM FROM THE DUNES AT OVERVEEN
c. 1670. Oil on canvas, 22″ × 24¼″ (55.8 × 62.8 cm). Mauritshuis, The Hague.

fifteenth century on, many Jews had settled in Amsterdam, and their community numbered about 2,300 people, most of whom were well-to-do merchants. Fund-raising for a new synagogue began in 1670, and in 1671 Elias Bouman and Daniel Stalpaert began work on the building. With its classical architecture, Brazilian jacaranda-wood furniture, and 26 brass chandeliers, this synagogue was considered one of the most impressive buildings in Amsterdam.

LANDSCAPE. The Dutch loved the landscapes and vast skies of their own country, but landscape painters worked in their studios rather than in nature, and they were never afraid to rearrange, add to, or subtract from a scene in order to give their compositions formal organization or a desired mood. Starting in the 1620s,

landscape painters generally adhered to a convention in which little color was used beyond browns, grays, and beiges. After 1650, they tended to be more individualistic in their styles, but nearly all brought a broader range of colors into play. One continuing motif was the emphasis on cloud-filled expanses of sky dominating a relatively narrow horizontal band of earth below.

The Haarlem landscape specialist Jacob van Ruisdael (1628/29–1682), whose popularity drew many pupils to his workshop, was especially adept at both the invention of dramatic compositions and the projection of moods in his canvases. His **VIEW OF HAARLEM FROM THE DUNES AT OVERVEEN (FIG. 22–46)**, painted about 1670, celebrates the flatlands outside Haarlem that had been reclaimed from the sea as part of a massive landfill project. The Dutch compared it with God's restoration of the Earth after Noah's Flood. Such a religious interpretation may be referenced here in the prominent Gothic church of St. Bavo, looming on the horizon. There may be other messages as well. While almost three-quarters of this painting is devoted to a rendering of the powerfully cloudy sky, tiny humans can be seen laboring below. They are caught in the process of spreading white linen across the broad fields to bleach in the sun. This glorification of the industriousness of citizens engaged in one of Haarlem's principal industries must have made the painting particularly appealing to the patriotic local market.

STILL LIFES AND FLOWER PIECES.   The Dutch were so proud of their still-life painting tradition that they presented a flower painting by Rachel Ruysch to the French queen Marie de' Medici when she made a state visit to Amsterdam. Like genre paintings, a still-life painting might carry moralizing connotations and commonly had a *vanitas* theme, reminding viewers of the transience of life and material possessions, even art. Yet it can also document and showcase the wealth of its owner.

One of the first Dutch still-life painters was Pieter Claesz (1596/97–1660) of Haarlem, who, like Antwerp artist Clara Peeters, painted "breakfast pieces," that is, a meal of bread, fruits, and nuts. In subtle, nearly monochromatic paintings, such as **STILL LIFE WITH TAZZA** (FIG. **22–47**), Claesz seems to give life to inanimate objects. He organizes dishes in diagonal positions to give a strong sense of space—here reinforced by the spiraling strip of lemon peel, foreshortened with the plate into the foreground and reaching toward the viewer's own space—and he renders the maximum contrast of textures within a subtle palette of yellows, browns, greens, and silvery whites. The tilted silver *tazza* contrasts with the half-filled glass that becomes a towering monumental presence and permits Claesz to display his skill at transparencies and reflections. Such paintings suggest the prosperity of Claesz's patrons. The food might be simple, but the silver ornamental cup graced the tables of only the wealthy. The meticulously painted timepiece could suggest deeper meanings—it alludes to human technological achievement, but also to the inexorable passage of time and the fleeting nature of human life, thoughts also suggested by the interrupted breakfast, casually placed knife, and toppled tableware.

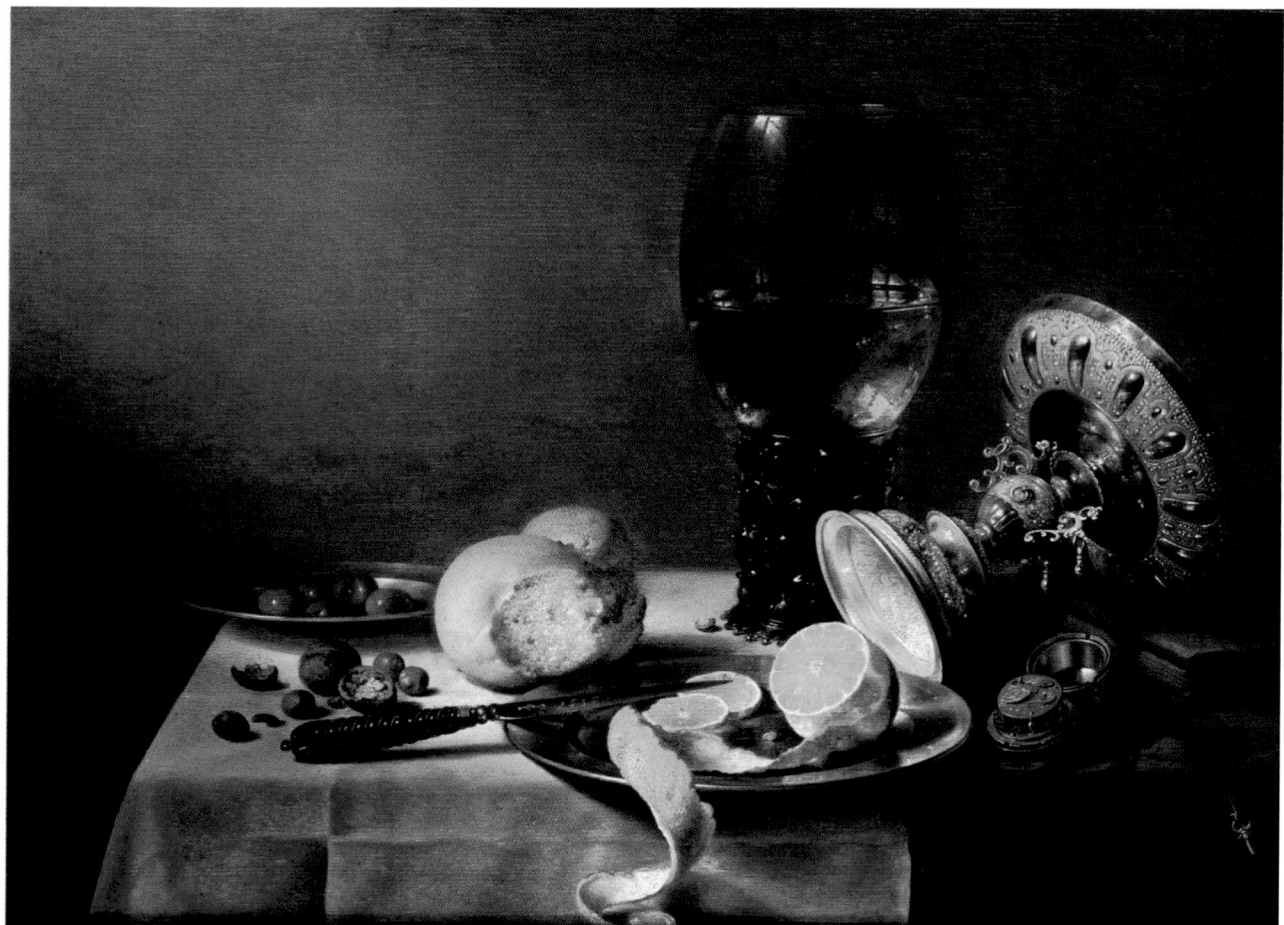

22-47 • Pieter Claesz **STILL LIFE WITH TAZZA**
1636. Oil on panel, 17⅜ × 24″ (44 × 61 cm). Royal Cabinet of Paintings Mauritshuis, The Hague.

The heavy round glass is a Roemer, a relatively inexpensive, everyday item, as are the pewter plates. The gilt cup (*tazza*) was a typical ornamental piece. Painters owned and shared such valuable props, and this and other showpieces appear in many paintings.

22-48 • Rachel Ruysch **FLOWER STILL LIFE**
After 1700. Oil on canvas, 30 × 24″ (76.2 × 61 cm). The Toledo Museum of Art, Ohio.
Purchased with funds from the Libbey Endowment. Gift of Edward Drummond Libbey 1956.57

offset by the strong diagonal of the tabletop. To further balance the painting, she placed highlighted blossoms and leaves against the dark left half of the canvas and silhouetted them against the light wall area on the right. Ruysch often emphasized the beauty of curving flower stems and enlivened her compositions with interesting additions, such as casually placed pieces of fruit or insects, in this case a large gray moth (lower left) and two snail shells.

Flower painting was almost never a straightforward depiction of actual fresh flowers. Instead, artists made color sketches of fresh examples of each type of flower and studied scientifically accurate color illustrations in botanical publications. Using their sketches and notebooks, in the studio, they would compose bouquets of perfect specimens of a variety of flowers that could never be found blooming at the same time. The short life of blooming flowers was a poignant reminder of the fleeting nature of beauty and of human life.

Still-life paintings in which cut-flower arrangements predominate were referred to simply as "flower pieces." Significant advances were made in botany during the seventeenth century through the application of orderly scientific methods and objective observation (see "Science and the Changing Worldview," page 756). Then, as now, the Dutch were major growers and exporters of flowers, especially tulips, which appear in nearly every flower piece in dozens of exquisite variations. The Dutch tradition of flower painting peaked in the long career of Rachel Ruysch (1664–1750) of Amsterdam. Her flower pieces were highly prized for their sensitive, free-form arrangements and their unusual and beautiful color harmonies. During her 70-year career, she became one of the most sought-after and highest-paid still-life painters in Europe—her paintings brought in twice what Rembrandt's did.

In her **FLOWER STILL LIFE (FIG. 22–48)**, painted after 1700, Ruysch placed the container at the center of the canvas's width, then created an asymmetrical floral arrangement of pale oranges, pinks, and yellows rising from lower left to top right of the picture,

FRANCE

Early seventeenth-century France was marked by almost continuous foreign and civil wars. The assassination of King Henry IV in 1610 left France in the hands of the queen, Marie de' Medici (regency 1610–1617; SEE FIG. 22–29), as regent for her 9-year-old son, Louis XIII (r. 1610–1643). When Louis came of age, the brilliant and unscrupulous Cardinal Richelieu became chief minister and set about increasing the power of the Crown at the expense of the French nobility. The death of Louis XIII again left France with a child king, the 5-year-old Louis XIV (r. 1643–1715). His mother, Anne of Austria, became regent, with the assistance of another powerful minister, Cardinal Mazarin. At Mazarin's death in 1661, Louis XIV began his long personal reign, assisted by yet another able minister, Jean-Baptiste Colbert.

An absolute monarch whose reign was the longest in European history, Louis XIV made the French court the envy of every ruler in Europe. He became known as *le Roi Soleil* ("the Sun King") and was sometimes glorified in art through identification

Science and the Changing Worldview

From the mid-sixteenth through the seventeenth centuries, new discoveries about the natural world brought a sense of both the grand scale and the microscopic detail of the universe. To publish their theories and research, early scientists learned to draw or depended on artists to draw what they discovered in the world around them. This practice would continue until the invention of photography in the nineteenth century.

Artist and scientist were seldom the same person, but Anna Maria Sibylla Merian (1647–1717) contributed to botany and entomology both as a researcher and as an artist. German by birth and Dutch by training, Merian was once described by a Dutch contemporary as a painter of worms, flies, mosquitoes, spiders, "and other filth." In 1699, the city of Amsterdam subsidized Merian's research on plants and insects in the Dutch colony of Surinam in South America, where she spent two years exploring the jungle and recording insects. On her return to the Dutch Republic, she published the results of her research as *The Metamorphosis of the Insects of Surinam*, illustrated with 72 large plates engraved after her watercolors. For all her meticulous scientific accuracy, Merian carefully arranged her depictions of exotic insects and elegant fruits and flowers into skillful and harmonious compositions.

But interest in scientific exploration was not limited to the Netherlands. The writings of philosophers Francis Bacon (1561–1626) in England and René Descartes (1596–1650) in France helped establish a new scientific method of studying the world by insisting on scrupulous objectivity and logical reasoning. Bacon argued that the facts be established from observation and tested by controlled experiments. Descartes, who was also a mathematician, argued for the deductive method of reasoning, in which conclusions were arrived at logically from basic premises.

In 1543, the Polish scholar Nicolaus Copernicus (1473–1543) published *On the Revolutions of the Heavenly Spheres*, which contradicted the long-held view that the Earth is the center of the universe (the Ptolemaic theory) by arguing instead that it and the other planets revolve around the sun. The Church put Copernicus's work on its *Index of Prohibited Books* in 1616, but Johannes Kepler (1571–1630) continued demonstrating that the planets revolve around the sun in elliptical orbits. Galileo Galilei (1564–1642), an astronomer, mathematician, and physicist, developed the telescope as a tool for observing the heavens and provided further confirmation of Copernican theory but since the Church prohibited its teaching, Galileo was tried for heresy by the Inquisition and forced to recant his views.

The new seventeenth-century science turned to the study of the very small as well as to the vast reaches of space. This included the development of the microscope by the Dutch lens-maker and amateur scientist Anton van Leeuwenhoek (1632–1723). Leeuwenhoek perfected grinding techniques and increased the power of his lenses far beyond what was required for a simple magnifying glass. Ultimately, he was able to study the inner workings of plants and animals and even see micro-organisms.

Anna Maria Sibylla Merian **PLATE 9 FROM THE METAMORPHOSIS OF THE INSECTS OF SURINAM** 1719. Hand-colored engraving, 18⅞ × 13″ (47.9 × 33 cm). National Museum of Women in the Arts, Washington, D.C. Gift of Wallace and Wilhelmina Holladay Collection, funds contributed by Mr. and Mrs. George G. Anderman and an anonymous donor 1976.56

---

with the Classical sun god, Apollo. In a 1701 portrait by court painter Hyacinthe Rigaud (1659–1743), the richly costumed **LOUIS XIV** is framed by a lavish, billowing curtain (**FIG. 22–49**).

Proudly showing off his elegant legs, the 63-year-old monarch poses in a blue robe of state, trimmed with gold *fleurs-de-lis* and lined with white ermine. He wears the high-heeled shoes

22-49 • Hyacinthe Rigaud
LOUIS XIV
1701. Oil on canvas,
9′2″ × 7′10¾″ (2.19 × 2.4 m).
Musée du Louvre, Paris.

Louis XIV had ordered this portrait as a gift for his grandson, the future Philip V of Spain (r. 1700–1746), but when Rigaud finished the painting, Louis liked it too much to give it away and only three years later ordered a copy from Rigaud to give to his grandson. The request for copies of royal portraits was not unusual since the aristocratic families of Europe were linked through marriage. Paintings made appropriate gifts and at the same time memorialized important political alliances by recording them in visual form.

he devised to compensate for his shortness. Despite his pompous pose and magnificent surroundings, the directness of the king's gaze and the frankness of his aging face make him appear surprisingly human.

The arts, like everything else, came under royal control. In 1635, Cardinal Richelieu had founded the French Royal Academy, directing the members to compile a definitive dictionary and grammar of the French language. In 1648, the Royal Academy of Painting and Sculpture was founded, which, as reorganized by Colbert in 1663, maintained strict control over the arts (see "Grading the Old Masters," page 764). Although it was not the first European arts academy, none before it had exerted such dictatorial authority—an authority that lasted in France until the late nineteenth century. Membership of the academy assured an artist of royal and civic commissions and financial success, but many talented artists did well outside it.

ARCHITECTURE AND ITS DECORATION AT VERSAILLES

French architecture developed along Classical lines in the second half of the seventeenth century under the influence of François Mansart (1598–1666) and Louis Le Vau (1612–1670). When the Royal Academy of Architecture was founded in 1671, its members developed guidelines for architectural design based on the belief that mathematics was the true basis of beauty. Their chief sources for ideal models were the books of Vitruvius and Palladio.

In 1668, Louis XIV began to enlarge the small château built by Louis XIII at Versailles, not far from Paris. Louis moved to the palace in 1682 and eventually required his court to live in Versailles; 5,000 aristocrats lived in the palace itself, together with 14,000 servants and military staff members. The town had another 30,000 residents, most of whom were employed by the palace. The designers of the palace and park complex at Versailles were Le Vau, Charles Le Brun (1619–1690), who oversaw the interior decoration, and André Le Nôtre (1613–1700), who planned the gardens (see "Garden Design," page 760). For both political and sentimental reasons, the old château was left standing, and the new building went up around it. This project consisted of two phases: the first additions by Le Vau, begun in 1668; and an enlargement completed after Le Vau's death by his successor, Jules Hardouin-Mansart (1646–1708), from 1670 to 1685.

Hardouin-Mansart was responsible for the addition of the long lateral wings and the renovation of Le Vau's central block on the garden side to match these wings **(FIG. 22–50)**. The three-story façade has a lightly rusticated ground floor, a main floor lined with enormous arched windows separated by Ionic columns or pilasters, an attic level whose rectangular windows are also flanked by pilasters, and a flat, terraced roof. The overall design is a sensitive balance of horizontals and verticals relieved by a restrained overlay of regularly spaced projecting blocks with open, colonnaded porches.

In his renovation of Le Vau's center-block façade, Hardouin-Mansart enclosed the previously open gallery on the main level, creating the famed **HALL OF MIRRORS (FIG. 22–51)**, which is about 240 feet (73 meters) long and 47 feet (13 meters) high. He achieved architectural symmetry and extraordinary effects by lining the interior wall opposite the windows with Venetian glass mirrors the same size and shape as the arched windows. Mirrors were small and extremely expensive in the seventeenth century, and these huge walls of reflective glass were created by fitting 18-inch panels together. The mirrors reflect the natural light from

22-50 • Louis Le Vau and Jules Hardouin-Mansart **GARDEN FAÇADE OF THE PALACE OF VERSAILLES** with (foreground) Jean-Baptiste Tuby **NEPTUNE.** 1678–1685.

SEE MORE: View a video about Versailles **www.myartslab.com**

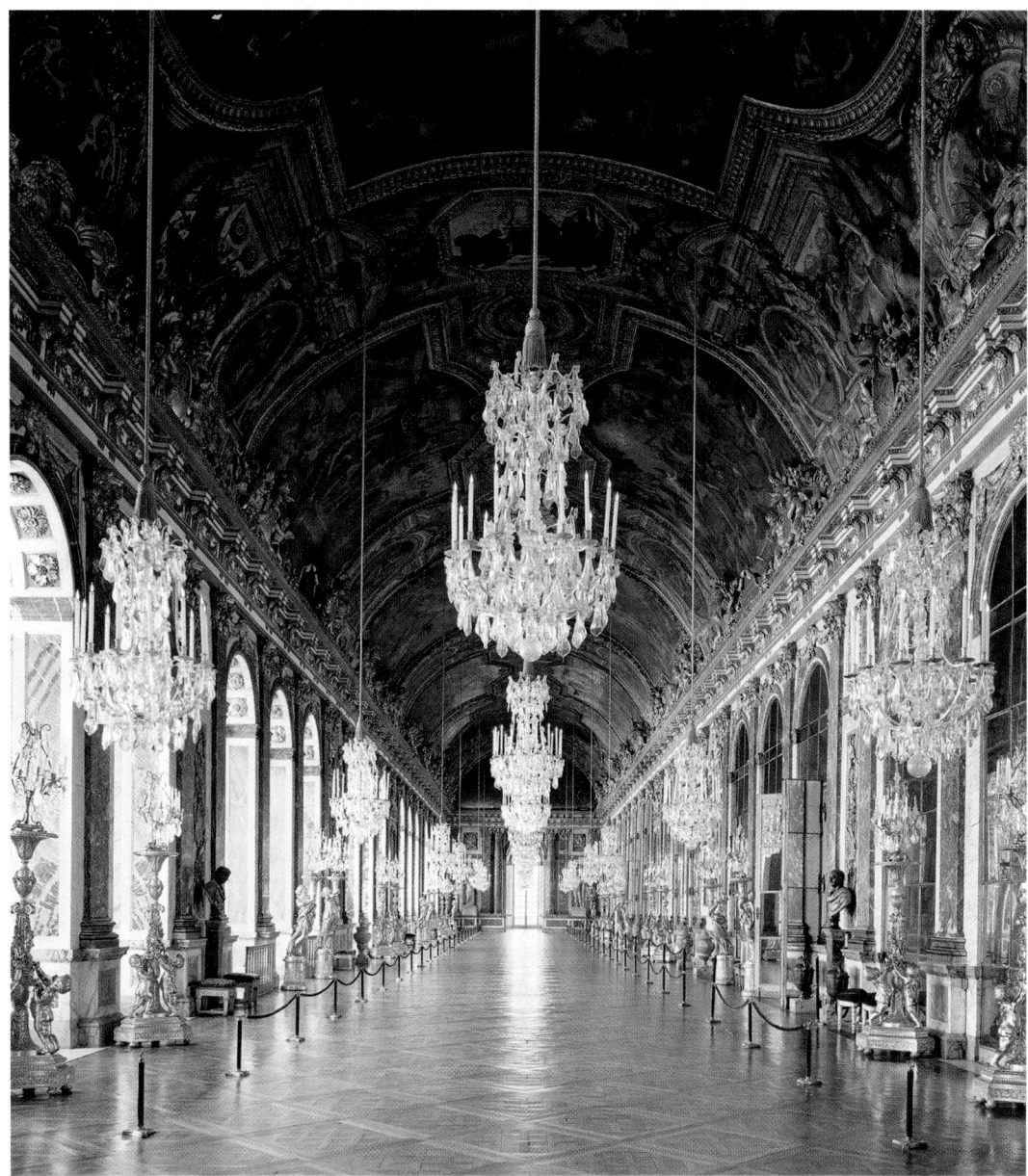

22-51 • Jules Hardouin-Mansart and Charles Le Brun **HALL OF MIRRORS, PALACE OF VERSAILLES**
Begun 1678. Length approx. 240′ (73 cm).

In the seventeenth century, mirrors and clear window glass were enormously expensive. To furnish the Hall of Mirrors, hundreds of glass panels of manageable size had to be assembled into the proper shape and attached to one another with glazing bars, which became part of the decorative pattern of the vast room.

the windows and give the impression of an even larger space; at night, the reflections of flickering candles must have turned the mirrored gallery into a veritable painting in which the king and courtiers saw themselves as they promenaded.

Inspired by Carracci's Farnese ceiling (SEE FIG. 22–9), Le Brun decorated the vaulted ceiling with paintings (on canvas, which is more stable in the damp northern climate) glorifying the reign of Louis XIV and Louis's military triumphs, assisted by the Classical gods. In 1642, Le Brun had studied in Italy, where he came under the influence of the Classical style of his compatriot Nicolas Poussin. As "first painter to the king" and director of the Royal Academy of Painting and Sculpture, Le Brun controlled art education and patronage from 1661/63 until his death in 1690. He tempered the warmly exuberant Baroque ceilings he had seen in Rome with Poussin's cool Classicism to produce spectacular decorations for the king. The underlying theme for the design and decoration of the palace was the glorification of the king as Apollo the sun god, with whom Louis identified. Louis XIV thought of the duties of kingship, including its pageantry, as a solemn performance, so it is most appropriate that Rigaud's portrait presents him on a raised, stagelike platform, with a theatrical curtain (SEE FIG. 22–49). Versailles was the splendid stage on which the king played the principal role in the grandiose drama of state.

PAINTING

The lingering Mannerism of the sixteenth century in France gave way as early as the 1620s to Classicism and Caravaggism (tenebrism and the compression of large-scale figures into the foreground). Later in the century, under the control of the Royal Academy and inspired by studies of the Classics and the surviving antiquities in Rome, French painting was dominated by the Classical influences propounded by Le Brun.

Wealthy and aristocratic French landowners commissioned garden designers to transform their large properties into gardens extending over many acres. The challenge for garden designers was to unify diverse elements—buildings, pools, monuments, plantings, natural land formations—into a coherent whole. At Versailles, André Le Nôtre imposed order upon the vast expanses of palace gardens and park by using broad, straight avenues radiating from a series of round focal points. He succeeded so thoroughly that his plan inspired generations of urban designers as well as landscape architects.

In Le Nôtre's hands, the palace terrain became an extraordinary work of art and a visual delight for its inhabitants. Neatly contained expanses of lawn and broad, straight vistas seemed to stretch to the horizon, while the formal gardens became an exercise in precise geometry. The gardens at Versailles are classically harmonious in their symmetrical, geometric design but Baroque in their vast size and extension into the surrounding countryside, where the gardens thickened into woods cut by straight avenues.

The most formal gardens lay nearest the palace, and plantings became progressively less elaborate and larger in scale as their distance from the palace increased. Broad, intersecting paths separated reflecting pools and planting beds, which are called embroidered **parterres** for their colorful patterns of flowers outlined with trimmed hedges. After the formal zone of *parterres* came lawns, large fountains on terraces, and trees planted in thickets to conceal features such as an open-air ballroom and a colonnade. Statues carved by at least 70 sculptors also adorned the park. A mile-long canal, crossed by a second canal nearly as large, marked the main axis of the garden. Fourteen waterwheels brought the water from the river to supply the canals and the park's 1,400 fountains. Only the fountains near the palace played all day; the others were turned on only when the king approached.

At the north of the secondary canal, a smaller pavilion-palace, the Trianon, was built in 1669. To satisfy the king's love of flowers year-round, the gardens of the Trianon were bedded out with blooming plants from the south, shipped in by the French navy. Even in midwinter, the king and his guests could stroll through a summer garden. The head gardener is said to have had nearly 2 million flowerpots at his disposal. In the eighteenth century, Louis XV added greenhouses and a botanical garden. The facilities of the fruit and vegetable garden that supplied the palace in 1677–1683 today house the National School of Horticulture.

Louis Le Vau and André Le Nôtre **PLAN OF THE GARDENS OF THE PALACE OF VERSAILLES**
Versailles, France. c. 1661–1785.

CARAVAGGIO'S INFLUENCE: GEORGES DE LA TOUR AND THE LE NAIN BROTHERS. One of Caravaggio's most important followers in France, Georges de La Tour (1593–1652) received major royal and ducal commissions and became court painter to Louis XIII in 1639. La Tour may have traveled to Italy in 1614–1616, and in the 1620s he almost certainly visited the Netherlands, where Caravaggio's style was being enthusiastically emulated. Like Caravaggio, La Tour filled the foreground of his canvases with imposing figures, but in place of Caravaggio's focus on descriptive detail, his work revels in the effects of lighting. Often, it seems, light is his real subject (see Introduction, "A Closer Look").

La Tour painted many images of Mary Magdalen. In **MARY MAGDALEN WITH THE SMOKING FLAME (FIG. 22–52)**, as in many of his other paintings, the light emanates from a source within the picture itself, in this case the flame from a lamp. It gently brushes over hand and skull—symbol of mortality—to establish the foreground. The compression of the figure into the front of the pictorial space lends a sense of intimacy to the saint's relationship with viewers, although the Magdalen is completely unaware of our presence. Light not only unifies the painting; it creates its somber mood. Mary Magdalen has put aside her rich clothing and jewels and meditates on the frailty and vanity of human life. Even the flickering light that rivets our attention on her meditative face and gesture is of limited duration.

This same feeling of timelessness, and a comparable interest in effects of light, characterize the paintings of the Le Nain brothers, Antoine (c. 1588–1648), Louis (c. 1593–1648), and Mathieu (1607–1677). Although the three were working in Paris by about 1630 and were founding members of the Royal Academy of Painting and Sculpture in 1648, little else is known about their lives and careers. Because they collaborated closely with each other, art historians have only recently begun to sort out their

22-52 • Georges de La Tour
MARY MAGDALEN WITH THE SMOKING FLAME
c. 1640. Oil on canvas, 46¼ × 36⅛″ (117 × 91.8 cm). Los Angeles County Museum of Art. Gift of the Ahmanson Foundation (M. 77.73)

22-53 • Louis or Antoine Le Nain **A PEASANT FAMILY IN AN INTERIOR**
c. 1640. Oil on canvas, 44½ × 62½″ (1.13 × 1.59 m). Musée du Louvre, Paris.

22-54 • Nicolas Poussin **LANDSCAPE WITH ST. MATTHEW AND THE ANGEL**
1639–1640. Oil on canvas, 39 × 53⅛″ (99 × 135 cm). Staatliche Museen, Berlin.

individual styles. They are best known for their painting of genre scenes in which French peasants pause from their honest labor for quiet family diversions. **A PEASANT FAMILY IN AN INTERIOR (FIG. 22–53)** of about 1640, probably by Louis Le Nain, is the largest, and one of the most lyrical, of these noble scenes of peasant life. Three generations of this family are gathered around a table. The adults acknowledge our presence—a spotlighted woman at left even seems to offer us some wine—whereas the children remain lost in their dreams or focused on their play. The casualness of costume and deportment is underlined by the foreground clutter of pets and kitchen equipment. It is only after we survey the frieze of figures illuminated around the table that the painting reveals one of its most extraordinary passages—a boy in the left background, warming himself in front of a fireplace and represented only as a dark silhouette from behind, edged by the soft golden firelight. Why the brothers chose to paint these peasant families, and who bought their paintings, are questions still unresolved.

THE CLASSICAL LANDSCAPE: POUSSIN AND CLAUDE LORRAIN. Painters Nicolas Poussin (1594–1665) and Claude Gellée (called "Claude Lorrain" or simply "Claude," 1600–1682) pursued their careers in Italy although they usually worked for French patrons. They perfected the French ideal of the "Classical" landscape and profoundly influenced painters for the next two centuries. We refer to Poussin and Claude as Classicists because they organized natural elements and figures into gently illuminated, idealized compositions. Both were influenced by Annibale Carracci and to some extent by Venetian painting, yet each evolved an unmistakably personal style that conveyed an entirely different mood from that of their sources and from each other.

Nicolas Poussin was born in Normandy but settled in Paris, where his initial career as a painter was unremarkable. Determined to go to Rome, he arrived there in 1624, and the Barberini became his foremost patrons. Bernini considered Poussin one of the greatest painters in Rome, and others clearly agreed. In 1639, Giovanni Maria Roscioli, secretary to Pope Urban VIII, commissioned from Poussin two large paintings showing the evangelists John and Matthew writing their gospels within expansive landscapes dotted with Classical buildings and antique ruins **(FIGS. 22–54, 22–55)**. The paintings were completed by

22-55 • Nicolas Poussin LANDSCAPE WITH ST. JOHN ON PATMOS
1640. Oil on canvas, 40 × 53½″ (101.8 × 136.3 cm). The Art Institute of Chicago. A. A. Munger Collection, 1930.500

EXPLORE MORE: Gain insight from a primary source by Nicolas Poussin **www.myartslab.com**

ART AND ITS CONTEXTS

Grading the Old Masters

The members of the French Royal Academy of Painting and Sculpture considered ancient Classical art to be the standard by which contemporary art should be judged. By the 1680s, however, younger artists of the academy began to argue that modern art might equal, or might even surpass, the art of the ancients—a radical thought that sparked controversy.

A debate arose over the relative merits of drawing and color in painting. The conservatives argued that drawing was superior to color because drawing appealed to the mind while color appealed to the senses. They saw Nicolas Poussin as embodying perfectly the Classical principles of subject and design. But the young artists who admired the vivid colors of Titian, Veronese, and Rubens claimed that painting should deceive the eye, and since color achieves this deception more convincingly than drawing, application of color should be valued over drawing. Adherents of the two positions were called *poussinistes* (in honor of Poussin) and *rubénistes* (for Rubens).

The portrait painter and critic Roger de Piles (1635–1709) took up the cause of the *rubénistes* in a series of pamphlets. In *The Principles of Painting*, de Piles evaluated the most important painters on a scale of 0 to 20 in four categories. He gave no score higher than 72 (18 in each category), since no mortal artist could achieve perfection. Caravaggio received a 0 in expression and a 6 in drawing, while Michelangelo and Leonardo both got a 4 in color and Rembrandt a 6 in drawing.

Most of the painters examined here do not do very well. Raphael and Rubens get 65 points (A on our grading scale), Van Dyck comes close with 55 (C+). Poussin and Titian earn 53 and 51 (solid Cs), while Rembrandt slips by with 50 (C–). Leonardo da Vinci gets 49 (D), and Michelangelo and Dürer with 37 and Caravaggio with 28 are resounding failures in de Piles's view. Tastes change. Someday our own ideas may seem just as misguided as those of the academicians.

October 1640, just before Poussin left for two years in Paris to work for Louis XIII. Perhaps they were the first installment of a set of four evangelists within landscapes, but these were the only two painted by the time of the patron's death in 1644.

These two paintings epitomize and are among the earliest examples of the new style of rigorously ordered and highly idealized Classical landscapes with figures. This artistic theme and format, created by Poussin while working in Rome, would have a long history in European painting. Although each painting was individually composed to create an ordered whole on its own, they were designed as a pair. The large clumps of trees at the outside edges form "bookends" that bring lateral closure to the broad panorama that stretches across both canvases. Their unity is signaled by the evangelists' postures, turned inward toward each other, and solidified at the lower inside corners where huge blocks of Classical masonry converge from both pictures as coordinated remains of the same ruined monument. There is a consistent perspective progression in both pictures from the picture plane back into the distance through a clearly defined foreground, middle ground, and background, illuminated by an even light with gentle shadows and highlights. In the middle distance behind St. John are a ruined temple and an obelisk, and the round building in the distant city is Hadrian's Tomb, which Poussin knew from Rome. Precisely placed trees, hills, mountains, water, and even clouds take on a solidity of form that seems almost as structural as this architecture. The subject of Poussin's paintings is not the writing evangelists but the balance and order of nature.

When Claude Lorrain went to Rome in 1613, he first studied with Agostino Tassi, an assistant of Guercino and a

specialist in architectural painting. Claude, however, preferred landscape. He sketched outdoors for days at a time, then returned to his studio to compose his paintings. Claude was fascinated with light, and his works are often studies of the effect of the rising or setting sun on colors and the atmosphere. A favorite and much-imitated device was to place one or two large objects in the foreground—a tree, building, a figural group, or hill—past which the viewer's eye enters the scene and proceeds, often by diagonal paths, into the distance.

Claude used this compositional device to great effect in paintings such as **A PASTORAL LANDSCAPE** of the late 1640s **(FIG. 22–56)**. Instead of balancing symmetrically placed elements in a statement of stable order, Claude leads his viewers actively into the painting in a continuing, zigzagging fashion. A conversing couple frames the composition at the right; their gestures and the ambling of the cows they are tending lead our attention toward the left on a slightly rising diagonal, where a bridge and the traveler moving across it establish a middle ground. Across the bridge into the distance is a city, setting up a contrast between the warm, soft contours of the pastoral right foreground and the misty angularity of the fortified walls and blocks composing the distant city. More distant still are the hazy outlines of hills that seem to take this space into infinity. The picture evokes a city dweller's nostalgia and longing for the simpler and more sensuous life of the country, and it is easy to imagine the foreground shepherd extolling to his companion the superior virtues of their own life in contrast to that in the city, toward which he gestures to underline his point.

22-56 • Claude Lorrain A PASTORAL LANDSCAPE
c. 1648. Oil on copper, 15½ × 21" (39.3 × 53.3 cm). Yale University Art Gallery, New Haven, Connecticut.

ENGLAND

England and Scotland were joined in 1603 with the ascent to the English throne of James VI of Scotland, who reigned over Great Britain as James I (r. 1603–1625). James increased royal patronage of British artists, especially in literature and architecture. William Shakespeare wrote *Macbeth*, featuring the king's legendary ancestor Banquo, in tribute to the new royal family, and the play was performed at court in December 1606.

Although James's son Charles I was an important collector and patron of painting, religious and political tensions that erupted into civil war cost Charles his throne and his life in 1649. A succession of republican and monarchical rulers who alternately supported Protestantism or Catholicism followed, until the Catholic king James II was deposed in the Glorious Revolution of 1689 by his Protestant son-in-law and daughter, William and Mary. After Mary's death in 1694, William (the Dutch great-grandson of William of Orange, who had led the Netherlands' independence

movement) ruled on his own until his death in 1702. He was succeeded by Mary's sister, Anne (r. 1702–1714).

ARCHITECTURE

In sculpture and painting, the English court patronized foreign artists. The field of architecture, however, was dominated in the seventeenth century by the Englishmen Inigo Jones, Christopher Wren, and Nicholas Hawksmoor. They replaced the country's long-lived Gothic style with Classicism.

INIGO JONES. In the early seventeenth century, Inigo Jones (1573–1652) introduced his version of Renaissance Classicism—based on the style of the architect Andrea Palladio—into England. Jones had studied Palladio's work in Venice, and he filled his copy of Palladio's *Four Books of Architecture*—still preserved—with notes. Appointed surveyor-general in 1615, Jones was commissioned to design the Queen's House in Greenwich and the Banqueting House for the royal palace of Whitehall.

22-57 • Inigo Jones **BANQUETING HOUSE, WHITEHALL PALACE**
London. 1619–1622.

The **BANQUETING HOUSE (FIG. 22–57)**, built in 1619–1622 to replace an earlier hall destroyed by fire, was used for court ceremonies and entertainments such as the popular masques—stylized dramas combining theater, music, and dance in spectacles performed by professional actors, courtiers, and even members of the royal family itself. The west front, shown here, consisting of what appears to be two upper stories with superimposed Ionic and Composite orders raised over a plain basement level, exemplifies the understated elegance of Jones's interpretation of Palladian design. Pilasters flank the end bays, and engaged columns subtly emphasize the three bays at the center. These vertical elements are repeated in the balustrade along the roofline. A rhythmic effect results from varying window treatments—triangular and segmental (semicircular) pediments on the first level, cornices with volute (scroll-form) brackets on the second. The sculpted garlands just below the roofline add an unexpected decorative touch, as does the use of different stone colors—pale golden, light brown, and white—for each story (no longer visible after the building was refaced in uniformly white Portland stone).

Although the exterior suggests two stories, the interior of the Banqueting House **(FIG. 22–58)** is actually one large hall divided by a balcony, with antechambers at each end. Ionic pilasters suggest a colonnade but do not impinge on the ideal, double-cube space, which measures 55 feet in width by 110 feet in length by 55 feet in height. In 1630, Charles I commissioned Peter Paul Rubens—who was in England on a peace mission—to decorate the ceiling. Jones had divided the flat ceiling into nine compartments, for which Rubens painted canvases glorifying the reign of James I. Installed in 1635, the paintings show the triumph of the Stuart dynasty with the king carried to heaven on clouds of glory. The large rectangular panel beyond it depicts the birth of the new nation, flanked by allegorical paintings of heroic strength and virtue overcoming vice. In the long paintings on each side, *putti* holding the fruits of the earth symbolize the peace and prosperity of England and Scotland under Stuart rule. So proud was Charles of the result that, rather than allow the smoke of candles and torches to harm the ceiling decoration, he moved evening entertainments to an adjacent pavilion.

CHRISTOPHER WREN.   After Jones's death, English architecture was dominated by Christopher Wren (1632–1723). Wren began his professional career in 1659 as a professor of astronomy; for him architecture was a sideline until 1665, when he traveled to France to further his education. While there, he met with French architects and with Bernini, who was in Paris to consult on designs for the Louvre. Wren returned to England with architecture books,

22-58 • INTERIOR, BANQUETING HOUSE, WHITEHALL PALACE
Ceiling paintings of the apotheosis of King James and the glorification of the Stuart monarchy by Peter Paul Rubens. 1630–1635.

22-59 • Christopher Wren FAÇADE OF ST. PAUL'S CATHEDRAL
London. Designed 1673, built 1675–1710.

EXPLORE MORE: Gain insight from a primary source on Christopher Wren
www.myartslab.com

engravings, and a greatly increased admiration for French Classical Baroque design. In 1669, he was made surveyor-general, the position once held by Inigo Jones, and in 1673, he was knighted.

After the Great Fire of 1666 destroyed large parts of central London, Wren was continuously involved in rebuilding the city.

He built more than 50 churches. His major project from 1675 to 1710, however, was the rebuilding of **ST. PAUL'S CATHEDRAL** (**FIGS. 22–59, 22–60**). Attempts to salvage the burned-out Gothic church on the site failed, and a new cathedral was needed. Wren's famous second design for St. Paul's (which survives in the so-called masonry vault with an oculus and an exterior sheathing of lead-covered wood, but also has a brick cone rising from the inner oculus to support a tall lantern. The ingenuity of the design and engineering remind us that Wren had been a mathematician and professor of astronomy at Oxford. The columns surrounding the drum on the exterior recall Bramante's *Tempietto* in Rome (SEE FIG. 20–16), although Wren never went to Italy and knew Italian architecture only from books.

On the façade of St. Paul's (SEE FIG. 22–59), two levels of paired Corinthian columns support a carved pediment. The deep-set porticos and columned pavilions atop the towers create dramatic areas of light and shadow. Not only the huge size of the cathedral, but also its triumphant verticality, complexity of form, and *chiaroscuro* effects, make it a major monument of English architecture. Wren recognized the importance of the building. On the simple marble slab that forms his tomb in the crypt of the cathedral, he had engraved: "If you want to see his memorial, look around you."

22-60 • SCHEMATIC DRAWING OF ST. PAUL'S CATHEDRAL

"Great Model" of 1672–1673) was for a centrally planned building with a great dome in the manner of Bramante's original plan for St. Peter's. This was rejected, but Wren ultimately succeeded both in satisfying Reformation tastes for a basilica and in retaining the unity inherent in the dome. St. Paul's has a long nave and equally long sanctuary articulated by small, domed bays. Semicircular, colonnaded porticos open into short transepts that compress themselves against the crossing, where the dome rises 633 feet from ground level. Wren's dome for St. Paul's has an interior

THINK ABOUT IT

22.1 Summarize the goals and interests of the Counter-Reformation, and explain the impact of the Council of Trent on Italian artists working in its wake. It may be helpful to look back to Chapters 20 and 21 in forming your answer.

22.2 Discuss how Bernini and Caravaggio established the Baroque style in sculpture and painting respectively. Locate the defining traits of the period style in at least one work from the chapter by each of these artists.

22.3 Trace the influence of Caravaggio's painting style by demonstrating how specific stylistic features that he pioneered were adopted by artists in other parts of Europe. Discuss at least one Spanish artist and at least one Northern European artist in your answer.

22.4 Determine how Poussin's landscapes depart from other stylistic currents at the time. What is meant by the term "Classicism" in relation to Poussin's style? Comment on its importance for the future of French art.

22.5 Choose two paintings of monarchs in this chapter and explain how the artists who painted them embodied the ruler's prestige and power. Are the strategies of these painters different from those employed by painters of powerful people in the sixteenth century?

22.6 Discuss the development of portraiture, still life, and genre painting in the Dutch Republic during the seventeenth century. What accounts for the increased importance of these subjects at this time?

PRACTICE MORE: Compose answers to these questions, get flashcards for images and terms, and review chapter material with quizzes **www.myartslab.com**

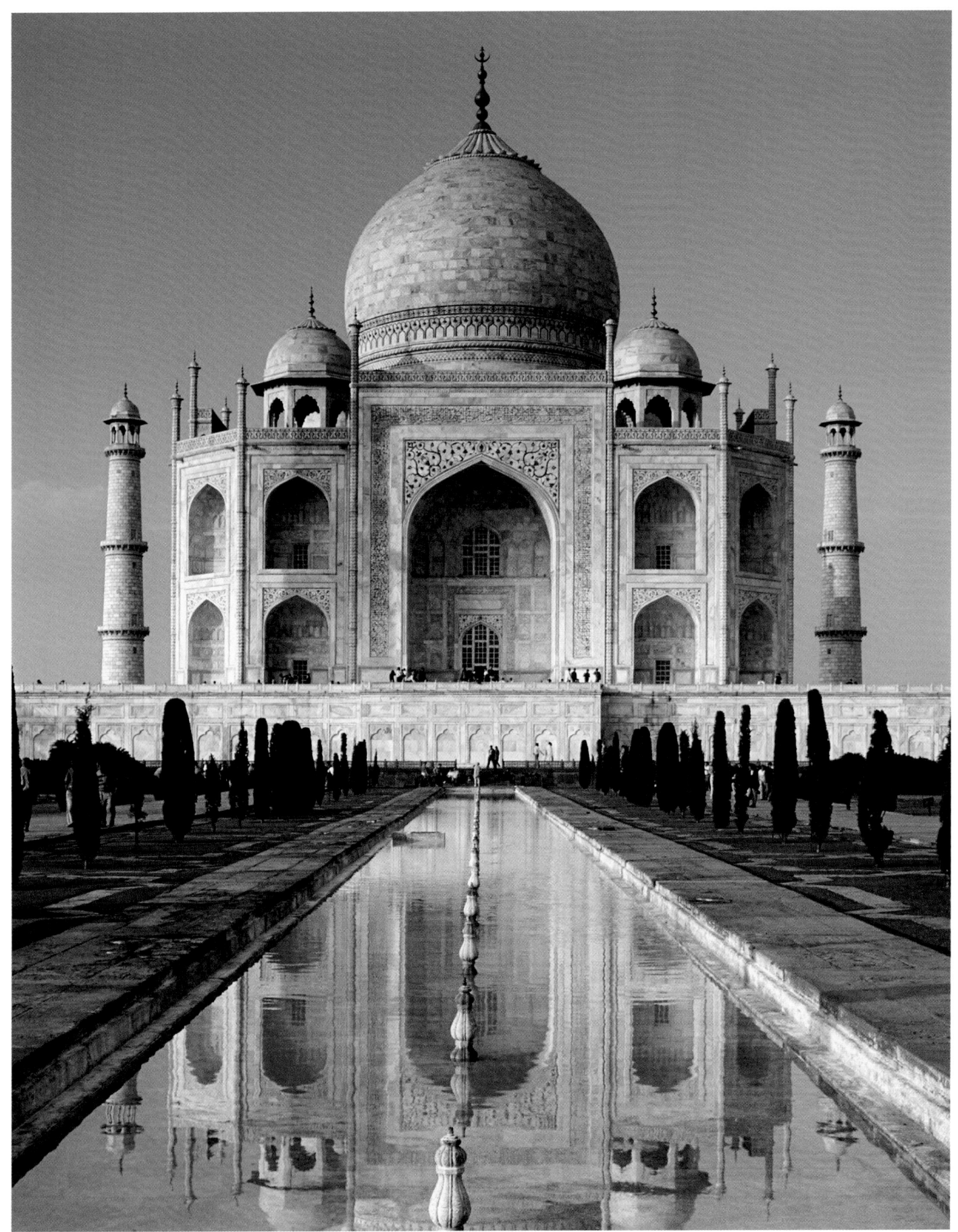

23-1 • TAJ MAHAL   Agra, India. Mughal period, reign of Shah Jahan, c. 1631–1648.

SEE MORE: View a simulation about the Taj Mahal **www.myartslab.com**

ART OF SOUTH AND SOUTHEAST ASIA AFTER 1200

Upon entering the gateway that today serves as the entrance to the great Taj Mahal complex, the visitor beholds the majestic white marble structure that is one of the world's best-known monuments. Its reflection shimmers in the pools of the garden meant to evoke a vision of paradise as described in the Qur'an, the holy book of Islam. The building's façades are delicately inlaid with inscriptions designed by India's foremost calligrapher of the time, Amanat Khan, and floral arabesques in semiprecious stones—carnelian, agate, coral, turquoise, garnet, lapis, and jasper. Above, its luminous, white marble dome reflects each shift in light, flushing rose at dawn, dissolving in its own brilliance in the noonday sun. This extraordinary building, originally and appropriately called the Illuminated Tomb and only from the nineteenth century known as the TAJ MAHAL (FIG. 23–1), was built between 1632 and 1648 by the Mughal ruler Shah Jahan as a mausoleum for his favorite wife, Mumtaz Mahal, who died in childbirth, and likely as a tomb for himself.

Inside, the Taj Mahal invokes the *hasht behisht* ("eight paradises"), a plan named for the eight small chambers that ring the interior—one at each corner and one behind each *iwan*, a vaulted opening with an arched portal, that is a typical feature of eastern Islamic architecture. In two stories (for a total of 16 chambers), the rooms ring the octagonal central area, which rises the full two stories to a domed ceiling that is lower than the outer dome. In this central chamber, surrounded by a finely carved octagonal openwork marble screen, are the exquisite inlaid **cenotaphs** (funerary monuments) of Shah Jahan and his wife, whose actual tombs lie in the crypt below.

The Taj Mahal includes much more than the white marble tomb. On one side is a mosque, while opposite and very similar in appearance is a building that may have served as a rest house. The enormous garden, both in front of the building and in its continuation on the opposite side of the Jamuna River, lends a lush setting consistent with Islamic notions of paradise. Both the side buildings and the two parts of the garden provide a sense of perfect symmetry to the entire complex.

A dynasty of central Asian origin, the Mughals were the most successful of the many Islamic groups that established themselves in India beginning in the twelfth century. Under their patronage, Persian and central Asian influences mingled with older traditions of the South Asian subcontinent, adding yet another dimension to the already ancient and complex artistic heritage of India.

LEARN ABOUT IT

23.1 Understand the impact of Islam on the art of India and Southeast Asia.

23.2 Understand how exogenous influences affect the form of a nation's arts.

23.3 Recognize how nationalism can be expressed in art.

23.4 Understand the way global styles can address indigenous themes.

23.5 Recognize the ways in which art of diverse religions is produced simultaneously in the same nation.

HEAR MORE: Listen to an audio file of your chapter **www.myartslab.com**

MAP 23-1 • SOUTH AND SOUTHEAST ASIA

Throughout its history, the kingdoms comprising the Indian subcontinent engaged—sometimes peacefully, sometimes militarily—with neighboring and more distant people, contributing significantly to the development of its art.

INDIA AFTER 1200

By 1200 India was already among the world's oldest civilizations (see "Foundations of Indian Culture," page 774). The art that survives from its earlier periods is almost exclusively sacred, most of it inspired by the three principal religions: Buddhism, Hinduism, and Jainism. These three religions remained a primary focus for Indian art, even as dynasties arriving from the northwest began to establish the new religious culture of Islam.

BUDDHIST ART

After many centuries of prominence, Buddhism had been in decline as a cultural force in India since the seventh or eighth century. By 1200, the principal Buddhist centers were concentrated in the northeast, in the region that had been ruled by the Pala dynasty (c. 750–1199). There, in great monastic universities that attracted monks from as far away as China, Korea, and Japan, was cultivated a form of Buddhism known as Tantric (Vajrayana) Mahayana.

ICONOGRAPHY OF A TANTRIC BODHISATTVA. The practices of Tantric Buddhism, which include techniques for visualizing deities, encourage the development of images with precise iconographic details such as the twelfth-century gilt-bronze sculpture of **THE BODHISATTVA AVALOKITESHVARA** in FIGURE 23–2 from the site of Kurkihar in eastern India. Bodhisattvas are beings who are well advanced on the path to buddhahood (enlightenment), the goal of Mahayana Buddhists, and who have vowed out of compassion to help others achieve enlightenment. Avalokiteshvara, the bodhisattva of greatest compassion, whose vow is to forgo buddhahood until all others become buddhas, became the most popular of these saintly beings in India and in East Asia.

Characteristic of bodhisattvas, Avalokiteshvara is distinguished in art by his princely garments, unlike a buddha, who wears a monk's robes. Avalokiteshvara is specifically recognized by the lotus flower he holds and by the presence in his crown of his "parent" Buddha, in this case Amitabha, the Buddha of the Western Pure

Land (the Buddhist paradise). Other marks of Avalokiteshvara's extraordinary status are the third eye (symbolizing the ability to see in miraculous ways) and the wheel on his palm (signifying the ability to teach the Buddhist truth).

Avalokiteshvara is shown here in the relaxed pose known as the posture of royal ease. One leg angles down; the other is drawn up onto the lotus seat, itself considered an emblem of spiritual purity. His body bends gracefully, if a bit stiffly, to one side. The chest scarf and lower garment cling to his body, fully revealing its shape. Delicate floral patterns enliven the textiles, and closely set parallel folds provide a wiry, linear tension that contrasts with the hard but silken surfaces of the body. Linear energy continues in the sweep of the tightly pleated hem emerging from under the right thigh, in the sinuous lotus stalks on each side, and in the fluttering ribbons of the elaborate crown. A profusion of details and varied textures creates an ornate effect—the lavish jewelry, the looped hair piled high and cascading over the shoulders, the ripe blossoms, the rich layers of the lotus seat. Though still friendly and human, the image is somewhat formalized. The features of the face, where we instinctively look for a human echo, are treated abstractly, and despite its reassuring smile the statue's expression remains remote. Through richness of ornament and tension of line, this style expresses the heightened power of a perfected being.

With the fall of the Pala dynasty in the late twelfth century, the last centers of Buddhism in northern India collapsed, and most

23-3 • DETAIL OF A LEAF WITH THE BIRTH OF MAHAVIRA
Kalpa Sutra, western Indian school (probably Gujarat). c. 1375–1400. Gouache on paper, 3⅜ × 3″ (8.5 × 7.6 cm). Prince of Wales Museum, Bombay.

of the monks dispersed, mainly into Nepal and Tibet **(SEE MAP 23–1)**. From that time, Tibet has remained the principal stronghold of Tantric Buddhist practice and its arts (see "Tantric Influence in the Art of Nepal and Tibet," page 776). The artistic style perfected under the Palas, however, became an influential international style throughout East and Southeast Asia.

JAIN ART

The Jain religion traces its roots to a spiritual leader called Mahavira (c. 599–527 BCE), whom it regards as the final in a series of 24 saviors known as pathfinders (*tirthankaras*). Devotees seek through purification to become worthy of rebirth in the heaven of the pathfinders, a zone of pure existence at the zenith of the universe. Jain monks live a life of austerity, and even laypersons avoid killing any living creature.

A MANUSCRIPT LEAF FROM THE *KALPA SUTRA*. Muslim dynasties brought with them a rich tradition of book illustration, and non-Islamic religions began to write and illustrate their own sacred books, previously intended largely for memorization. The Jains of western India, primarily in the region of Gujarat, created many illustrated manuscripts, such as this *Kalpa Sutra*, which explicates the lives of the pathfinders **(FIG. 23–3)**. Produced during the late fourteenth century, it is one of the first Jain manuscripts on

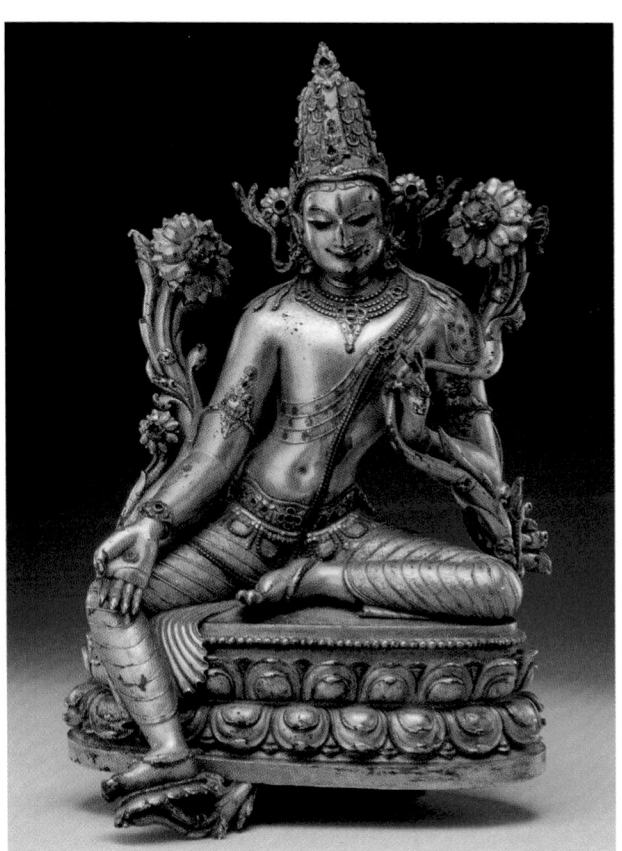

23-2 • THE BODHISATTVA AVALOKITESHVARA
From Kurkihar, Bihar. Pala dynasty, 12th century. Gilt-bronze, height 10″ (25.5 cm). Patna Museum, Patna.

ART AND ITS CONTEXTS

Foundations of Indian Culture

The earliest civilization on the Indian subcontinent flourished toward the end of the third millennium BCE along the Indus River in present-day Pakistan. Remains of its expertly engineered brick cities have been uncovered, together with works of art that intriguingly suggest spiritual practices and reveal artistic traits known in later Indian culture.

The decline of the Indus civilization during the mid second millennium BCE coincides with (and may be related to) the arrival from the northwest of a seminomadic people who spoke an Indo-European language and referred to themselves as Aryans. Over the next millennium they were influential in formulating the new civilization that gradually emerged. The most important Aryan contributions to this new civilization included the Sanskrit language and the sacred texts called the Vedas. The evolution of Vedic thought under the influence of indigenous Indian beliefs culminated in the mystical, philosophical texts called the Upanishads, which took shape sometime after 800 BCE.

The Upanishads teach that the material world is illusory; only Brahman, the universal soul, is real and eternal. We—that is, our individual souls—are trapped in this illusion in a relentless cycle of birth, death, and rebirth. The ultimate goal of religious life is to liberate ourselves from this cycle and to unite our individual soul with Brahman.

Buddhism and Jainism are two of the many religions that developed in the climate of Upanishadic thought. Buddhism (see "Buddhism" page 297) is based on the teachings of Shakyamuni Buddha, who lived in central India about 500 BCE; Jainism was shaped about the same time by the followers of the spiritual leader Mahavira. Both religions acknowledged the cyclical nature of existence and taught a means of liberation from it, but they rejected the authority,

rituals, and social strictures of Vedic religion. Whereas the Vedic religion was in the hands of a hereditary priestly class, Buddhist and Jain communities welcomed all members of society, which gave them great appeal. The Vedic tradition eventually evolved into the many sects now collectively known as Hinduism (see "Hinduism" page 298).

Through most of its history India was a mosaic of regional dynastic kingdoms, but from time to time empires emerged that unified large parts of the subcontinent. The first was that of the Maurya dynasty (c. 322–185 BCE), whose great king Ashoka patronized Buddhism. From this time Buddhist doctrines spread widely and its artistic traditions were established.

In the first century CE the Kushans, a central Asian people, created an empire extending from present-day Afghanistan down into central India. Buddhism prospered under Kanishka, the most powerful Kushan king, and spread into central Asia and to east Asia. At this time, under the evolving thought of Mahayana Buddhism, traditions first evolved for depicting the image of the Buddha in art.

Later, under the Gupta dynasty (c. 320–550 CE) in northern India, Buddhist art and culture reached their high point. However, Gupta monarchs also patronized Hindu art, and from this time Hinduism grew to become the dominant Indian religious tradition, with its emphasis on the great gods Vishnu, Shiva, and the Goddess—all with multiple forms.

After the tenth century, numerous regional dynasties prevailed, some quite powerful and long-lasting. Hindu temples, in particular, developed monumental and complex forms that were rich in symbolism and ritual function, with each region of India producing its own variation.

---

paper rather than palm leaf, the material that had previously been used for written documents.

With great economy, the illustration, inserted between blocks of Sanskrit text, depicts the birth of Mahavira. He is shown cradled in his mother's arms as she reclines in her bed under a canopy |connoting royalty, attended by three ladies-in-waiting. Decorative pavilions and a shrine with peacocks on the roof suggest a luxurious palace setting. Everything appears two-dimensional against the brilliant red or blue ground. Vibrant colors and crisp outlines impart an energy to the painting that suggests the arrival of the divine in the mundane world. Transparent garments with variegated designs reveal the swelling curves of the figures, whose alert postures and gestures convey a sense of the importance and excitement of the event. Strangely exaggerated features, such as the protruding eyes, contribute to the air of the extraordinary. With its angles and tense curves, the drawing is closely linked to the aesthetics of Sanskrit calligraphy, and the effect is as if the words themselves had suddenly flared into color and image.

HINDU ART

With the increasing popularity of Hindu sects came the rapid development of Hindu temples. Spurred by the ambitious building programs of wealthy rulers, well-formulated regional styles had evolved by about 900 CE. The most spectacular structures of the era were monumental, with a complexity and grandeur of proportion rarely equaled even in later Indian art.

Emphasis on monumental individual temples gave way to the building of vast temple complexes and more moderately scaled, yet more richly ornamented, individual temples. These developments took place largely in the south of India, although some of the largest temples are in the north, for example, the Sun Temple at Konarak, built in the thirteenth century, and the Govind Deva Temple in Brindavan, built in the sixteenth century under the patronage of the Mughal emperor Akbar. The mightiest of the southern Indian kingdoms was Vijayanagar (c. 1336–1565), whose rulers successfully countered the potential incursions of neighboring dynasties, both Hindu and Muslim, for more than 200 years. Under the patronage of the Vijayanagar kings and their successors, the Nayaks, some of India's most spectacular Hindu architecture was created.

TEMPLE AT MADURAI. The enormous temple complex at Madurai, one of the capitals of the Nayaks, is an example of this fervent expression of Hindu faith. Founded around the thirteenth century, it is dedicated to the goddess Minakshi (the local name for Parvati, the consort of the god Shiva) and to Sundareshvara (the local name for Shiva himself). The temple complex stands in the center of the city and is the focus of Madurai life. At its heart are the two oldest shrines, one to Minakshi and the other to Sundareshvara. Successive additions over the centuries gradually expanded the complex around these small shrines and came to dominate the visual landscape of the city. The most dramatic features of this and similar "temple cities" of the south were the thousand-pillar halls, large ritual-bathing pools, and especially the entrance gateways, **gopuras** in Sanskrit, that tower above the temple site and the surrounding city like modern skyscrapers (**FIG. 23–4**).

Gopuras proliferated as a temple city grew, necessitating new and bigger enclosing walls, and thus new gateways. Successive rulers, often seeking to outdo their predecessors, donated taller and taller *gopuras*. As a result, the tallest structures in temple cities are often at the periphery, rather than at the central temples, which are sometimes totally overwhelmed by the height of the surrounding structures. The temple complex at Madurai has 11 *gopuras*, the largest over 160 feet tall.

Formally, the *gopura* has its roots in the pyramidal tower characteristic of the seventh-century southern temple style. As the *gopura* evolved, it took on the graceful concave silhouette shown here. The exterior is embellished with thousands of sculpted figures, evoking a teeming world of gods and goddesses. Inside, stairs lead to the top for an extraordinary view.

23-4 • OUTER GOPURA OF THE MINAKSHI-SUNDARESHVARA TEMPLE
Madurai, Tamil Nadu, south India. Nayak dynasty, mostly 13th to mid 17th century, with modern renovations.

ART AND ITS CONTEXTS

Tantric Influence in the Art of Nepal and Tibet

The legacy of India's Tantric Buddhist art can be traced in the regions of Nepal and Tibet. Artistic expression of Esoteric Buddhist ideals reached a high point in the seventeenth and eighteenth centuries. Indeed, even today, artists worldwide continue to explore aspects of this tradition.

Inlaid Devotional Sculpture. In Nepal, where Hinduism intermingled with Buddhism, sculptors developed a metalwork style in which a traditional artistic use of polished stones became prevalent in devotional sculptures as well. Inlaid gems and semiprecious stones often enlivened their copper or bronze sculptures, which were almost always brightly gilded. Complex representations of deities, often multiarmed and adorned with celestial attributes, predominated, but some themes from early Buddhism were revived. In one particularly fine eighteenth-century example (FIG. A), Maya, the Mother of the Buddha, holds the legendary tree branch while the Buddha emerges from her side. The cast and **chased** (ornamented by hammering or incising the metal surface) details of the regal costume of Queen Maya, including fluttering scarves, elaborate jewelry, and a large crown, are studded with real jewels, pearls, and semiprecious stones. The tree, also, is richly inlaid, symbolizing the auspicious nature of the event. Both the tree and the figure rise from a pedestal shaped to

suggest the blossoming lotus, a reference to the appearance of the Buddha's purity in the muddy pond of the material world.

***Tangka* Painting.** Buddhism was established relatively late in Tibet, but the region has since become almost wholly identified with the religion. With the rule of a lineage of Dalai Lamas established in the seventeenth century and continuing through to the twentieth century, and a related expansion of monasteries, the arts associated with Tantric Buddhism flourished. Wrathful manifestations of powerful deities were evoked in sculpted and painted forms, with the scroll-like *tangka* emerging as a major format. A nineteenth-century painting of Achala (FIG. B), one of a group of wrathful deities associated with truth, resolve, and the overcoming of obstacles, exemplifies this major aspect of Tibetan art. The deity exudes brilliant red flames while brandishing a sword and posing as if to strike. Following traditional practice, the artist—or artists, as such paintings may have employed highly specialized craftsmen—positions the terrifying figure on a lotus pedestal, establishing his ethereal nature. The background suggests the green hills and blue sky of the material world as well as the cosmic geometry envisioned in Tantric Buddhism. Repeated representations of the deity emphasize the efficacious function and conspicuous power of the image.

A. MAYA, MOTHER OF BUDDHA, HOLDING A TREE BRANCH
From Nepal. 18th century. Gilt bronze with inlaid precious stones, height 22″ (56 cm). Musée Guimet, Paris.

B. ACHALA
From Tibet. 19th century. Gouache on cotton, 33½ × 23⅔″ (85 × 60 cm). Musée Guimet, Paris.

continues to be a center of Theravada devotion amid symbolic ornamentation—especially lotus elements symbolic of the Buddha's purity—and splendid decoration in gilding and precious stones supplied by pious contributions. Images of the Buddha, and sometimes his footprints alone, provide focal points for devotion.

In Thailand, the Sukhothai kingdom (mid thirteenth to late fourteenth century) also embraced Theravada Buddhism, although Hindu shrines were constructed as well in its capital city, Sukhothai (ancient name Sukhodaya). Artisans working under royal patrons developed a classic statement of Theravada ideals in bronze sculptures of the Buddha. Notable was their development of a free-standing walking Buddha. Especially evocative of the ascetic simplicity of Theravada Buddhism, however, are their many renditions of the Buddha Calling the Earth to Witness (FIG. 23–6). Inspired by devotional texts and poetry, and further refined through reference to models from Sri Lanka, the iconographic and stylistic elements became notably formalized. The Buddha's cranial protuberance is interpreted as a flame of divine knowledge, as it was in southern India and Sri Lanka, and details of his ecclesiastical garb are reduced to a few elegant lines. The *mudras* (see page 304), or hand gestures, are quietly eloquent.

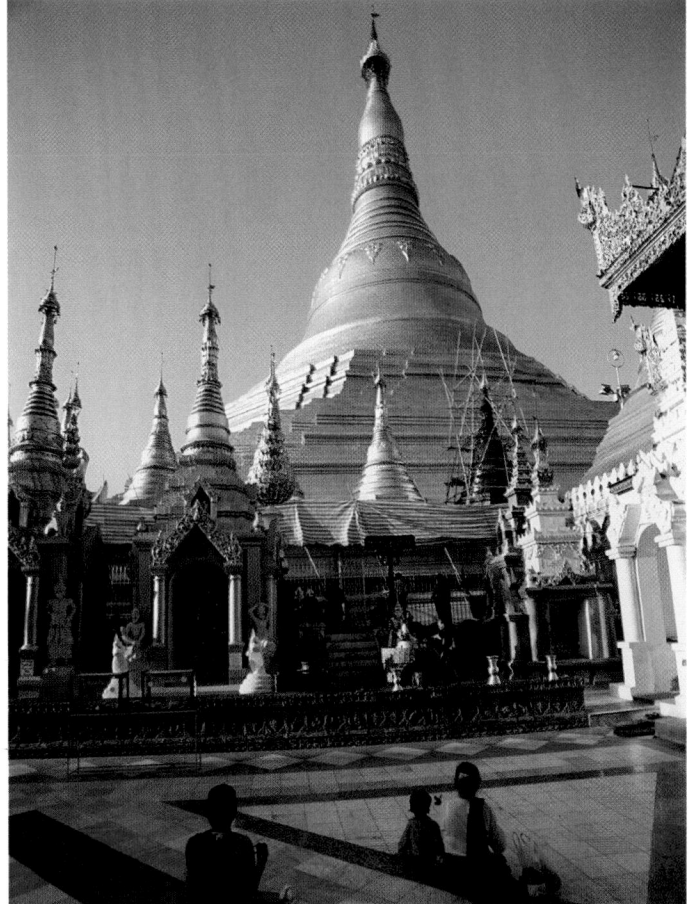

23-5 • SHWE-DAGON STUPA (PAGODA)
Yangon.15th century. Construction at the site dates from at least the 14th century, with continuous replastering and redecoration to the present.

THE BUDDHIST AND HINDU INHERITANCE IN SOUTHEAST ASIA

India's Buddhist and Hindu traditions influenced Southeast Asia (discussed in Chapter 9), where they were absorbed by newly rising kingdoms in the regions now comprising Burma (Myanmar), Thailand, Cambodia, Vietnam, and Indonesia.

THERAVADA BUDDHISM IN BURMA AND THAILAND

In northern Burma, from the eleventh to the thirteenth century, rulers raised innumerable religious monuments—temples, monasteries, and stupas—in the Pagan Plain, following the Scriptures of Theravada Buddhism (also called Hinayana Buddhism, see Chapter 9). To the south arose the port city of Yangon (formerly known as Rangoon, called Dagon in antiquity), the nation's present-day capital. Established by Mon rulers (SEE FIG. 9–29) at least by the eleventh century, Yangon is site of the **SHWE-DAGON STUPA** (FIG. 23–5), which enshrines relics of the Buddha. The modern structures of Shwe-dagon ("Golden Dagon") rise from an ancient core—fourteenth century or earlier—and reflect centuries of continual restoration and enhancement. The site

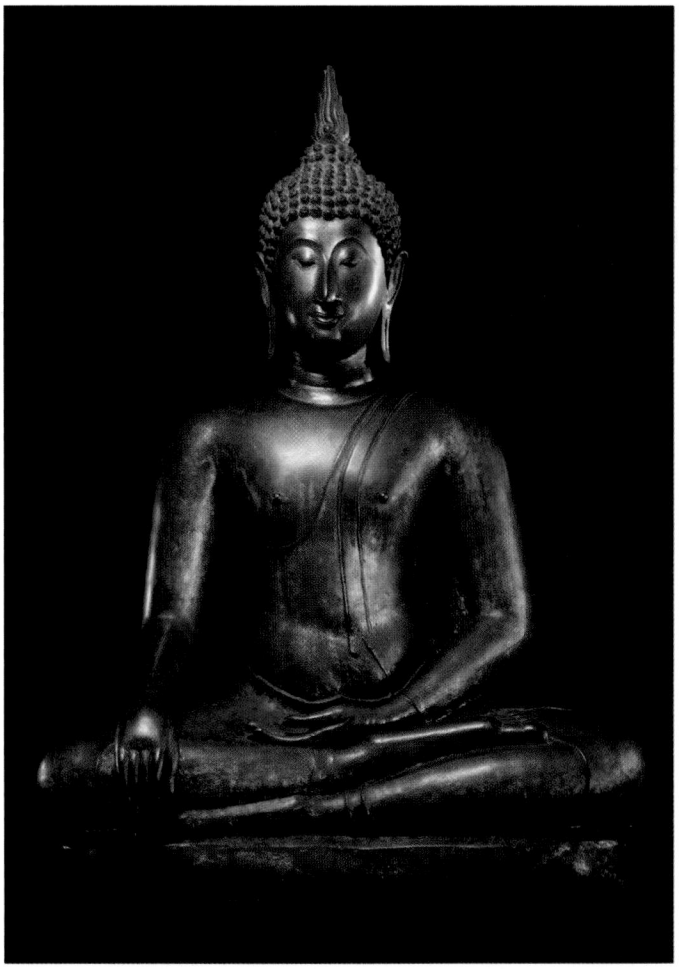

23-6 • SEATED SUKHOTAI BRONZE BUDDHA
Leaded bronze, height 35⅜" (90 cm). The Walters Art Museum, Baltimore. Bequest of A.B. Griswold, 1992. 54.2775

23-7 • GROUP OF VIETNAMESE CERAMICS FROM THE HOI AN HOARD
Late 15th to early 16th century, porcelain with underglaze blue decoration; barbed-rim dishes: (left) diameter 14″ (35.1 cm); (right) diameter 13¼″ (34.7 cm). Phoenix Art Museum. (2000.105–109)

More than 150,000 blue-and-white ceramic items were found in the hold of a sunken ship excavated in the late 1990s under commission from the Vietnamese government, which later sent many of the retrieved items for public auction. The 23 small cups among the works shown here were found packed inside the jar.

VIETNAMESE CERAMICS

Both the Burmese and Thai kingdoms produced ceramics, often inspired by stonewares and porcelains from China. Sukhothai potters, for example, made green-glazed and brown-glazed wares, called Sawankhalok wares. Even more widespread were the wares of Vietnamese potters. For example, excavation of the Hoi An "hoard" (FIG. 23–7), actually the contents of a sunken ship laden with ceramics for export, brought to light an impressive variety of ceramic forms made by Vietnamese potters of the late fifteenth to early sixteenth century. Painted in underglaze cobalt blue and further embellished with overglaze enamels, these wares were shipped throughout Southeast Asia and beyond, as far east as Japan and as far west as England and the Netherlands.

INDONESIAN TRADITIONS

Indonesia, now the world's most populous Muslim country, experienced a Hindu revival in the centuries following its Buddhist period, which came to a close in the eighth or ninth century (see Chapter 9). As a consequence, it has maintained unique traditions that build upon the Hindu epics, especially the *Ramayana*. Islamic monuments in Indonesia, like the Hindu and Buddhist ones, draw from a rich and diverse repertoire of styles and motifs. The **MINARET MOSQUE** of Kudus in central Java (FIG. 23–8) was built in 1549. The minaret serves as the tower from which Muslims are called to worship five times daily, but the minaret's red brick, general shape, and the niches that adorn its façade all recall Hindu temples built in east Java about two centuries earlier. As in India, Javanese artists worked in a consistent style, independent of the religion of the patron. Their architecture did, of course, accommodate the specific ritual functions of the building.

MUGHAL PERIOD

Islam first touched the South Asian subcontinent in the eighth century, when Arab armies captured a small territory near the Indus River. Later, beginning around 1000, Turkic factions from central Asia, relatively recent converts to Islam, began military campaigns into north India, at first purely for plunder, then seeking territorial control. From 1193, various Turkic and Afghan dynasties ruled portions of the subcontinent from the northern city of Delhi. These sultanates, as they are known, constructed forts, mausoleums, monuments, and mosques. Although these early dynasties left their mark, it was the Mughal dynasty that made the most inspired and lasting contribution to the art of India.

The Mughals, too, came from central Asia. Muhammad Zahir-ud-Din, known as Babur ("Lion" or "Panther"), was the first Mughal emperor of India (r. 1526–30). He emphasized his Turkic

23-8 • MINARET MOSQUE
1549. Kudus, Java.

heritage, though he had equally impressive Mongol ancestry. After some initial conquests in central Asia, he amassed an empire stretching from Afghanistan to Delhi, which he conquered in 1526. Akbar (r. 1556–1605), the third ruler, extended Mughal control over most of north India, and under his two successors, Jahangir and Shah Jahan, northern India was generally unified by 1658. The Mughal Empire lasted until 1858, when the last Mughal emperor was deposed and exiled to Burma by the British.

MUGHAL ARCHITECTURE

Mughal architects were heir to a 300-year-old tradition of Islamic building in India. The Delhi sultans who preceded them had great forts housing government and court buildings. Their architects had introduced two fundamental Islamic structures, the mosque and the tomb, along with construction based on the arch and the dome. (Earlier Indian architecture had been based primarily on post-and-lintel construction.) They had also drawn freely on Indian architecture, borrowing both decorative and structural elements to create a variety of hybrid styles, and had especially benefited from the centuries-old Indian virtuosity in stonecarving and masonry. The Mughals followed in this tradition, synthesizing Indian, Persian, and central Asian elements for their forts, palaces, mosques, tombs, and cenotaphs (tombs or monuments to someone whose remains are actually somewhere else).

Akbar, an ambitious patron of architecture and city planning, constructed a new capital at a place he named Fatehpur Sikri ("City of Victory at Sikri"), celebrating his military conquests and the birth of his son Salim, who subsequently took on the throne name of Jahangir. The palatial and civic buildings, built primarily during Akbar's residence there from about 1572 to 1585, have drawn much admiration. There are two major components to Fatehpur Sikri: a religious section including the Jami Mosque and the administrative and residential section. Among the most extraordinary buildings in the administrative and residential section is the private audience hall (Diwan-i Khas) (see "A Closer Look," page 780). In the center of the hall is a tall pillar supporting a circular platform on which Akbar could sit as he received his nobles and dispensed justice. The structure recalls, perhaps consciously, the pillars erected by Ashoka (see Chapter 9) to promulgate his law.

THE TAJ MAHAL. Perhaps the most famous of all Indian Islamic structures, the Taj Mahal is sited on the bank of the Jamuna River at Agra, in northern India. Built between 1631 and 1648, it was commissioned as a mausoleum for his wife by the emperor Shah Jahan (r. 1628–58), who is believed to have taken a major part in overseeing its design and construction.

Visually, the Taj Mahal never fails to impress (SEE FIG. 23–1). As visitors enter through a monumental, hall-like gate, the tomb rises before them across a spacious garden set with long reflecting pools. Measuring some 1,000 by 1,900 feet, the enclosure is unobtrusively divided into quadrants planted with trees and flowers, and framed by broad walkways and stone inlaid in geometric patterns. In Shah Jahan's time, fruit trees and cypresses—symbolic of life and death, respectively—lined the walkways, and fountains played in the shallow pools. Truly, the senses were beguiled in this earthly evocation of paradise.

The garden in which the mausoleum is set is comprised of two parts divided by the Jamuna River. Thus while the structure appears to visitors to be set at the end of a garden, it is in fact in the center of a four-part garden, a traditional Mughal tomb setting used for earlier Mughal tombs. The tomb is flanked by two smaller structures not visible here, one a mosque and the other a hall designed in mirror image. They share a broad base with the tomb and serve visually as stabilizing elements. Like the entrance hall, they are made mostly of red sandstone, rendering even more startling the full glory of the tomb's white marble, a material previously reserved for the tombs of saints and so here implying an elevated religious stature for Shah Jahan and Mumtaz Mahal. The tomb is raised higher than these structures on its own marble platform. At each corner of the platform, a minaret defines the surrounding space. The minarets' three levels correspond to those of the tomb, creating a bond between them. Crowning each minaret is a **chattri** (pavilion). Traditional embellishments of Indian palaces, *chattris* quickly passed into the vocabulary of Indian Islamic architecture, where they appear prominently. Minarets occur in architecture throughout the Islamic world; from their heights, the faithful are called to prayer.

Private Audience Hall, Fatehpur Sikri ≫ c.1570, north-central India.

The circular throne. Here Akbar sat, probably on a large cushion, able to look down on those petitioning for justice.

Ramps to the four directions. These gave Akbar access to his throne. They were also probably intended to recall the rivers that flowed to the four corners of the world, conveying Akbar's justice.

Closely spaced brackets serve as the capital for the pillar and structural base for the throne

This pillar, reminiscent of Ashoka's pillars, supported the throne from which Akbar dispensed justice.

One of the four doorways providing access to the private audience hall.

SEE MORE: View the Closer Look feature for the Private Audience Hall at Fatehpur Sikri **www.myartslab.com**

A lucid geometric symmetry pervades the tomb. It is basically square, but its **chamfered** (sliced-off) corners create a subtle octagon. Measured to the base of the **finial** (the spire at the top), the tomb is almost exactly as tall as it is wide. Each façade is identical, with a central *iwan* flanked by two stories of smaller *iwans*. By creating voids in the façades, these *iwans* contribute markedly to the building's sense of weightlessness. On the roof, four octagonal *chattris*, one at each corner, create a visual transition to the lofty, bulbous dome, the crowning element that lends special power to this structure. Framed but not obscured by the *chattris*, the dome rises more gracefully and is lifted higher by its drum than in

earlier Mughal tombs, allowing the swelling curves and elegant lines of its beautifully proportioned, surprisingly large form to emerge with perfect clarity.

By the seventeenth century, India was well known for exquisite craftsmanship and luxurious decorative arts (see "Luxury Arts," page 782). The pristine surfaces of the Taj Mahal are embellished with utmost subtlety (FIG. 23–9). Even the sides of the platform on which the Taj Mahal stands are carved in relief with a **blind arcade** (decorative arches set into a wall) motif and carved relief panels of flowers. The portals are framed with verses from the Qur'an and inlaid in black marble, while the spandrels are

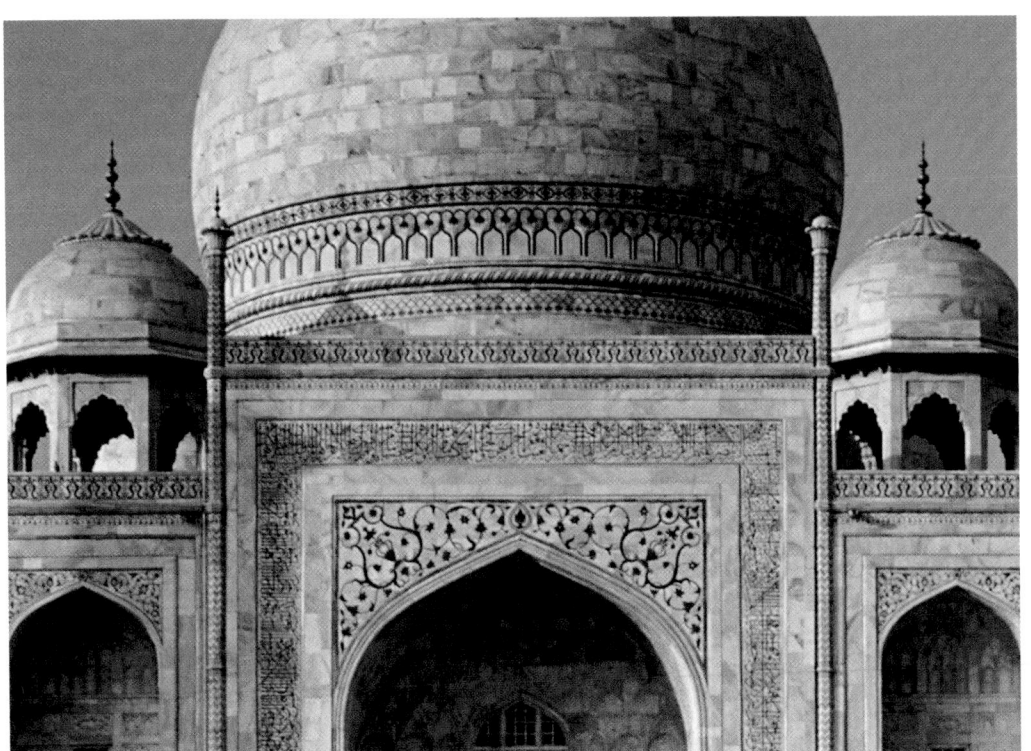

23-10 • AKBAR INSPECTING THE CONSTRUCTION OF FATEHPUR SIKRI
Akbarnama. c. 1590. Opaque watercolor on paper, 14¾ × 10″ (37.5 × 25 cm). Victoria & Albert Museum, London. (I.S.2-1896 91/117)

Many of the painters in the Mughal imperial workshops are recorded in texts of the period. Based on those records and on signatures that occur on some paintings, the design of this work has been attributed to Tulsi Kalan (Tulsi the Elder), the painting to Bandi, and the portraits to Madhu Kalan (Madhu the Elder) or Madhu Khurd (Madhu the Younger).

decorated with floral arabesques inlaid in colored semiprecious stones, a technique known by its Italian name **pietra dura**. Not strong enough to detract from the overall purity of the white marble, the embellishments enliven the surfaces of this impressive yet delicate masterpiece.

MUGHAL PAINTING

Probably no one had more control over the solidification of the Mughal Empire and the creation of Mughal art than the emperor Akbar. A dynamic, humane, and just leader, Akbar enjoyed religious discourse and loved the arts, especially painting. He created an imperial atelier (workshop) of painters, which he placed under the direction of two artists from the Persian court. Learning from these two masters, the Indian painters of the atelier soon transformed Persian styles into the more vigorous, naturalistic styles that mark Mughal painting (see "Indian Painting on Paper," page 784). At Akbar's cosmopolitan court, pictorial sources from Europe also became inspiration for Mughal artists.

PAINTING AT THE COURT OF AKBAR. Akbar's court artists also produced paintings documenting Akbar's own life and accomplishments recorded in the *Akbarnama*, a text written by Akbar's court biographer, Abul Fazl. Among the most fascinating in this imperial manuscript are those that record Akbar's supervision of the construction of Fatehpur Sikri. One painting (FIG. 23–10) documents his inspection of the stonemasons and other craftsmen.

PAINTING IN THE COURTS OF JAHANGIR AND SHAH JAHAN. Jahangir (r. 1605–1627), Akbar's son and successor, was a connoisseur of painting; he had his own workshop, which he

Luxury Arts

The decorative arts of India have been widely appreciated since the first century CE. An Indian ivory carving was found at Pompeii, while other Indian works of the time have been found along the Silk Route connecting China with Rome. For centuries Indian textiles have been made for export and copied in Europe for domestic consumption. Technically superb and crafted from precious materials, tableware, jewelry, furniture, and containers enhance the prestige of their owners and give visual pleasure as well. Metalwork and work in rock crystal, agate, and jade, carving in ivory, and intricate jewelry are all characteristic Indian arts. Because of the intrinsic value of their materials, however, pieces have been disassembled, melted down, and reworked, making the study of Indian luxury arts very difficult. Many pieces, like the carved ivory panel illustrated here, have no date or records of manufacture or ownership. And, like it, many such panels have been removed from a larger container or piece of furniture.

Carved in ivory against a golden ground, where openwork, stylized vines with spiky leaves weave an elegant arabesque, loving couples dally under the arcades of a palace courtyard, whose thin columns and cusped arches resemble the arcades of the palace of Tirumala Nayak (r. 1623–1659) in Madurai (present-day Tamil Nadu). Their huge eyes under heavy brows suggest the intensity of their gaze, and the artist's choice of the profile view shows off their long noses and sensuously thick lips. Their hair is tightly controlled; the men have huge buns, and the women long braids hanging down their backs. Are they divine lovers? After all, Krishna lived and loved on earth among the cowherd maidens. Or are we observing scenes of courtly romance?

The rich jewelry and well-fed look of the couples indicate a high station in life. Men as well as women have voluptuous figures—rounded buttocks and thighs, abdomens hanging over jeweled belts, and sharply indented slim waists that emphasize seductive breasts. Their smooth flesh contrasts with the diaphanous fabrics that swath their plump legs, and their long arms and elegant gestures seem designed to show off their rich jewelry—bracelets, armbands, necklaces, huge earrings, and ribbons. Such amorous couples symbolize harmony as well as fertility.

The erotic imagery suggests that the panel illustrated here might have adorned a container for personal belongings such as jewelry, perfume, or cosmetics. In any event, the ivory relief is a brilliant example of south Indian secular arts.

PANEL FROM A BOX
From Tamil Nadu, south India. Nayak dynasty, late 17th–18th century. Ivory backed with gilded paper, 6 × 12⅜ × ⅛″ (15.2 × 31.4 × 0.3 cm). Virginia Museum of Fine Arts.
The Arthur and Margaret Glasgow Fund. 80.171

established even before he became emperor. His focus on detail was much greater than that of his father. In his memoirs, he claimed:

> My liking for painting and my practice in judging it have arrived at such a point that when any work is brought before me, either of deceased artists or of those of the present day, without their names being told me I say on the spur of the moment that it is the work of such and such a man, and if there be a picture containing many portraits, and each face be the work of a different master, I can discover which face is the work of each of them. And if any other person has put in the eye and eyebrow of a face, I can perceive whose work the original face is and who has painted the eye and eyebrows.

Portraits become a major art under Jahangir. The portrait Jahangir commissioned of himself with the Safavid-dynasty Persian emperor Shah Abbas (FIG. 23–11) demonstrates his sense of his superiority: Jahangir is depicted much larger than Shah Abbas, who appears to bow deferentially to the Mughal emperor; Jahangir's head is centered in the halo; and he stands on the lion, whose body

23–11 • Nadir al-Zaman (Abu'l Hasan) **JAHANGIR AND SHAH ABBAS**
From the St. Petersburg Album. Mughal period, c. 1618. Opaque watercolor, gold and ink on paper, 9⅜ × 6″ (23.8 × 15.4 cm). Freer Museum of Art, Smithsonian Institution, Washington, DC. Purchase, F1945.9. Freer Gallery, Washington

23–12 • Nadir al-Zaman (Abu'l Hasan) **PRINCE KHURRAM, THE FUTURE SHAH JAHAN AT AGE 25**
From the Minto Album. Mughal period, c. 1616–1617. Opaque watercolor, gold and ink on paper, 18⅛ × 4½″ (20.6 × 11.5 cm); page 15¼ × 10½″ (39 × 26.7 cm). Victoria & Albert Museum, London

spans a vast territory, including Shah Abbas's own Persia. We can only speculate on the target audience for this painting. Because it is small, it certainly would not be intended for Jahangir's subjects; a painting of this size could not be publicly displayed. But because we know that paintings were commonly sent by embassies from one kingdom to another, it may have been intended as a gift for Shah Abbas, one with a message of clear strength and superiority cloaked in the diplomatic language of cordiality.

Jahangir was succeeded by his son, Prince Khurram, who took the title Shah Jahan. Although Shah Jahan's greatest artistic achievements were in architecture, painting continued to flourish during his reign. A portrait of Prince Khurram bears an inscription indicating that he considered it "a very good likeness of me at age 25" (FIG. 23–12). Like all portraits of Shah Jahan, this one depicts him in profile, the view that has least likelihood of distortion. Holding an exquisite turban ornament, the prince stands quite

Before the fourteenth century most painting in India had been on walls or palm leaves. With the introduction of paper, about the same time in India as in Europe, Indian artists adapted painting techniques from Persia and over the ensuing centuries produced jewel-toned works on paper.

Painters usually began their training early. As young apprentices, they learned to make brushes and grind pigments. Brushes were made from the curved hairs of a squirrel's tail, arranged to taper from a thick base to a single hair at the tip. Paint came from pigments of vegetables and minerals—lapis lazuli to make blue, malachite for pale green—that were ground to a paste with water, then bound with a solution of gum from the acacia plant. Paper was made by crushing fibers of cotton and jute to a pulp, pouring the mixture onto a woven mat, drying it, and then burnishing with a smooth piece of agate, often achieving a glossy finish.

Artists frequently worked from a collection of sketches belonging to a master painter's atelier. Sometimes, to transfer the drawing to a blank sheet beneath, sketches were pricked with small, closely spaced holes that were then daubed with wet color. The resulting dots were connected into outlines, and the process of painting began.

First, the painter applied a thin wash of a chalk-based white, which sealed the surface of the paper while allowing the underlying sketch to show through. Next, outlines were filled with thick washes of brilliant, opaque, unmodulated color. When the colors were dry, the painting was laid face down on a smooth marble surface and burnished with a rounded agate stone, rubbing first up and down, then side to side. The indirect pressure against the marble polished the pigments to a high luster. Then outlines, details, and modeling—depending on the style—were added with a fine brush.

Sometimes certain details were purposely left for last, such as the eyes, which were said to bring the painting to life. Gold and raised details were applied when the painting was nearly finished. Gold paint, made from pulverized, 24-carat gold leaf bound with acacia gum, was applied with a brush and burnished to a high shine. Raised details such as the pearls of a necklace were made with thick, white, chalk-based paint, with each pearl a single droplet hardened into a tiny raised mound.

---

formally against a dark background, allowing nothing in the painting to compete for the viewer's attention.

RAJPUT PAINTING

Outside of the Mughal strongholds at Delhi and Agra, much of northern India was governed regionally by local Hindu princes, descendants of the so-called Rajput warrior clans, who were allowed to keep their lands in return for allegiance to the Mughals. Like the Mughals, Rajput princes frequently supported painters at their courts, and in these settings a variety of strong, indigenous Indian painting styles were perpetuated. Rajput painting, more abstract than the Mughal style, included subjects like those treated by Mughal painters, royal portraits and court scenes, as well as indigenous subjects such as Hindu myths, love poetry, and Ragamala illustrations (illustrations of musical modes).

The Hindu devotional movement known as *bhakti*, which had done much to spread the faith in the south from around the seventh century, now experienced a revival in the north. As it had earlier in the south, *bhakti* inspired an outpouring of poetic literature, this time devoted especially to Krishna, the popular human incarnation of the god Vishnu. Most renowned is the *Gita Govinda*, a cycle of rhapsodic poems about the love between God and humans expressed metaphorically through the love between the young Krishna and the cowherd Radha.

The illustration here (FIG. 23–13) is from a manuscript of the *Gita Govinda* probably produced in present-day Rajasthan about 1525–50. The blue god Krishna sits in dalliance with a group of cowherd women. Standing with her maid and consumed with love for Krishna, Radha peers through the trees, overcome by jealousy. Her feelings are indicated by the cool blue color behind her, while the crimson red behind the Krishna grouping suggests passion. The curving stalks and bold patterns of the flowering vines and trees express not only the exuberance of springtime, when the story unfolds, but also the heightened emotional tensions of the scene. Birds, trees, and flowers are as brilliant as fireworks against the black, hilly landscape edged in an undulating white line. As in the Jain manuscript earlier (SEE FIG. 23–3), all the figures are of a single type, with plump faces in profile and oversized eyes. Yet the resilient line of the drawing gives them life, and the variety of textile patterns provides some individuality. The intensity and resolute flatness of the scene seem to thrust all of its energy outward, irrevocably engaging the viewer in the drama.

Quite a different mood pervades **HOUR OF COWDUST**, a work from the Kangra School in the Punjab Hills, foothills of the Himalayas north of Delhi (FIG. 23–14). Painted around 1790, some 250 years later than the *Gita Govinda* illustration, it shows the influence of Mughal naturalism on the later schools of Indian painting. The theme is again Krishna. Wearing his peacock crown, garland of flowers, and yellow garment—all traditional iconography of Krishna-Vishnu—he returns to the village with his fellow cowherds and their cattle. All eyes are upon him as he plays his flute, said to enchant all who hear it. Women with water jugs on their heads turn to look; others lean from windows to watch and call out to him. We are drawn into this charming village scene by the diagonal movements of the cows as they surge through the gate and into the courtyard beyond. Pastel houses and walls create a sense of space, and in the distance we glimpse other villagers going about their work or peacefully sitting in their houses. A rim of dark trees softens the horizon, and an atmospheric sky completes the aura of enchanted naturalism. Again, all the figures are similar in

23-13 • KRISHNA AND THE *GOPIS*
From the *Gita Govinda*, Rajasthan, India. Mughal period,
c. 1525–1550. Gouache on paper, 4⅞ × 7½″ (12.3 × 19 cm). Prince of
Wales Museum, Bombay.

The lyrical poem *Gita Govinda*, by the poet-saint Jayadeva, was
probably written in eastern India during the latter half of the twelfth
century. The episode illustrated here occurs early in the relationship
of Radha and Krishna, which in the poem is a metaphor for the
connection between humans and God. The poem traces the progress
of their love through separation, reconciliation, and fulfillment.
Intensely sensuous imagery characterizes the entire poem, as in the
final song, when Krishna welcomes Radha to his bed. (Narayana is the
name of Vishnu in his role as cosmic creator.)

> Leave lotus footprints on my bed of tender shoots, loving Radha!
> Let my place be ravaged by your tender feet!
> Narayana is faithful now. Love me Radhika!
> I stroke your feet with my lotus hand—you have come far.
> Set your golden anklet on my bed like the sun.
> Narayana is faithful now. Love me Radhika!
> Consent to my love. Let elixir pour from your face!
> To end our separation I bare my chest of the silk that bars your breast.
> Narayana is faithful now. Love me Radhika!

(Translated by Barbara Stoler Miller)

23-14 • HOUR OF COWDUST
From Punjab Hills, India. Mughal period, Kangra School,
c. 1790. Gouache on paper, 14¹⁵⁄₁₆ × 12⁹⁄₁₆″ (36 × 31.9 cm). Museum
of Fine Arts, Boston. Denman W. Ross Collection (22.683)

type, this time with a perfection of proportion and a gentle, lyrical movement that complement the idealism of the setting. The scene embodies the sublime purity and grace of the divine, which, as in so much Indian art, is evoked into our human world to coexist with us as one.

INDIA'S ENGAGEMENT WITH THE WEST

By the time *Hour of Cowdust* was painted, India's regional rulers, both Hindu and Muslim, had reasserted themselves, and the vast Mughal Empire had shrunk to a small area around Delhi. At the same time, however, a new power, Britain, was making itself felt, inaugurating a markedly different period in Indian history.

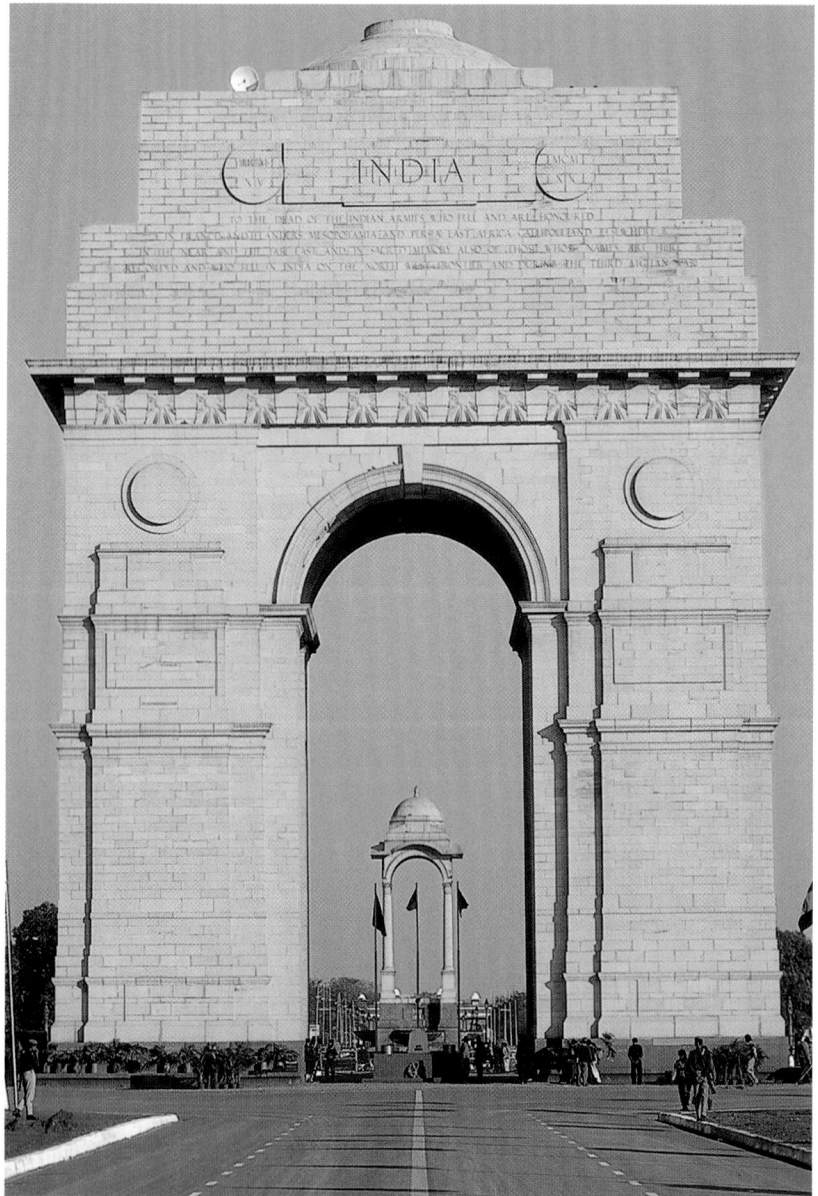

23-15 • Sir Edwin Lutyens INDIA GATE
Originally the All India War Memorial. New Delhi. British colonial period, 20th century.

BRITISH COLONIAL PERIOD

First under the mercantile interests of the British East India Company in the seventeenth and eighteenth centuries, and then under the direct control of the British government as a part of the British Empire in the nineteenth century, India was brought forcefully into contact with the West and its culture, a very different situation from its long-standing role in a world system that had included trade in both commodities and culture. The political concerns of the British Empire extended even to the arts, especially architecture. Over the course of the nineteenth century, the great cities of India, such as Calcutta (present-day Kolkata), Madras (Chennai), and Bombay (Mumbai), took on a European aspect as British architects built in the revivalist styles favored in England.

NEW DELHI. In 1911, the British announced its intention to move the seat of government from Calcutta to a newly constructed Western-style capital city to be built at New Delhi, a move intended to capitalize on the long-standing association of Delhi with powerful rulers such as the Mughals. Two years later, Sir Edwin Lutyens (1869–1944) was appointed joint architect for New Delhi (with Herbert Baker), and was charged with laying out the new city and designing the Viceroy's House, the present-day Rashtrapati Bhavan (President's House). Drawing inspiration from Classical antiquity—as well as from more recent urban models, such as Paris and Washington, D.C.—Lutyens sited the Viceroy's House as a focal point along with the triumphal arch that he designed as the All India War Memorial, now called the **INDIA GATE** (FIG. **23–15**). In these works Lutyens sought to maintain the tradition of Classical architecture—he developed a "Delhi order" based on the Roman Doric—while incorporating massing, detail, and ornamentation derived from Indian architecture as well. The new capital was inaugurated in 1931.

MOTHER INDIA. Far prior to Britain's consolidation of imperial power in New Delhi a new spirit asserting Indian independence and pan-Asiatic solidarity was awakening. For example, working near Calcutta, the painter Abanindranath Tagore (1871–1951)—nephew of the poet Rabindranath Tagore (1861–1941), who went on to win the Nobel Prize for Literature in 1913—deliberately rejected the medium of oil painting and the academic realism of Western art. Like the Nihonga artists of Japan (SEE FIG. 25–15) with whom he was in contact, Tagore strove to create a style that reflected his ethnic origins. In **BHARAT MATA** (Mother India) he invents a nationalistic icon by using Hindu symbols while

23-16 • Abanindranath Tagore
BHARAT MATA (MOTHER INDIA)
1905. Watercolor on paper, 10½ × 6″
(26.7 × 15.3 cm). Rabindra Bharati Society,
Calcutta.

also drawing upon the format and techniques of Mughal and Rajput painting **(FIG. 23–16)**.

THE MODERN PERIOD

In the wake of World War II, the imperial powers of Europe began to shed their colonial domains. The attainment of self-rule had been five long decades in the making, when finally—chastened by the nonviolent example of Mahatma Gandhi (1869–1948)—the British Empire relinquished its "Jewel in the Crown," which was partitioned to form two modern nations: India and Pakistan. After independence in 1947, the exuberant young nation welcomed a modern, internationalist approach to art and architecture.

JAWAHAR KALA KENDRA. Architect Charles Correa often draws on traditional Indian architectural forms. One example is his impressive **JAWAHAR KALA KENDRA**, a center for the visual and performing arts in Jaipur that was completed in 1992 **(FIG. 23–17)**. Like the original design of Jaipur, the building's design is based on a nine-square plan, and its elevation makes visual reference to the city's historic buildings. Correa's work is not confined to India, but

23-17 • Charles Correa JAWAHAR KALA KENDRA
1992. Jaipur. Like many of Correa's buildings, this arts center draws upon traditional Indian motifs and forms. Its many open spaces provide a feeling of connected space rather than individual rooms.

includes buildings in Europe and the United States, for example the Cognitive Sciences Complex at MIT completed in 2005.

Two Modern Artists. Artists working after Indian independence have continued to study and work abroad, but often draw upon India's distinctive literary and religious traditions as well as regional and folk art traditions. One example is Manjit Bawa (b. 1941), who worked in Britain as a silkscreen artist before returning to India to settle in New Delhi. His distinctive canvases, painted meticulously in oil, juxtapose illusionistically modeled figures and animals against brilliantly colored backgrounds of flat, unmodulated color. The composite result, for example in **DHARMA AND THE GOD** (**FIG. 23–18**), brings a strikingly new interpretation to the heroic figures of Indian tradition.

With Anish Kapoor (b. 1954), as with so many artists living abroad, we must consider issues of identity. Although some of his work draws inspiration from his Indian origins, for example, his 1981 composition **AS IF TO CELEBRATE, I DISCOVERED A MOUNTAIN BLOOMING WITH RED FLOWERS (23–19)**, whose red and ocher mounds recall the vermilion and other pigments beautifully piled for sale outside Indian temples, other works make no reference to India. Kapoor represented Britain, where he now lives and works, at the Venice Biennale in 1990, further complicating the issue of his identity.

23-18 • Manjit Bawa DHARMA AND THE GOD
1984. Oil on canvas, 85 × 72¹⁵⁄₁₆″ (216 × 185.4 cm). Peabody Essex Museum, Salem, Massachusetts. The Davida and Chester Herwitz Collection

23-19 • Anish Kapoor **AS IF TO CELEBRATE, I DISCOVERED A MOUNTAIN BLOOMING WITH RED FLOWERS**
1981. Wood, cement, polystyrene and pigment, 3 elements, 38¼ (highest point) × 30 (widest point) × 63″ (97 × 76.2 × 160 cm); 13 × 28 × 32″ (33 × 71.1 × 81.3 cm); 8¼ × 6 × 18½″ (21 × 15.3 × 47 cm), overall dimensions variable. Arts Council Collection, South Bank Centre, London.

THINK ABOUT IT

23.1 Explain some of the ways that Islamic art and culture impacted that of the Indian subcontinent. Explain how the Taj Mahal demonstrates influence from building styles studied in Chapter 8, and indicate how it departs from prior styles on the Indian subcontinent.

23.2 Analyze the Shwe-Dagon Stupa (Pagoda) in Yangon, and determine how the structure incorporates influence from Indian buildings. In your answer, compare the stupa to at least one Indian building.

23.3 Analyze the form of the India Gate (SEE FIG. 23–15) and explain how the ancient Roman form of the triumphal arch (see, for example, the Arch of Titus (SEE FIG. 6–32) is used within a new Indian context.

23.4 Explain how the artist Anish Kapoor utilizes Indian themes in his work *As if to Celebrate, I Discovered a Mountain Blooming with Red Flowers* (SEE FIG. 23–19). What other ideas can you infer from this work?

23.5 From the works discussed in this chapter, select a two-dimensional religious artwork from each of two religions practiced in India. Compare and contrast both directly, determining similarities in regional style and technique as well as differences due to their varying religious contexts.

PRACTICE MORE: Compose answers to these questions, get flashcards for images and terms, and review chapter material with quizzes **www.myartslab.com**

石上苔荄水上桐蕭蕭琴上觀門
荷千歲石膚分流去天引飛光
入洞天

癸丑臘月既望寫此仿董太史畫法
烏目山中人石谷王翬

日照層峯翠
翠相桂神人
在搞園翠堂
林阿閟永遂
靜倚是四窿
天上天
下此馬麗

**24-1 • Wang Hui A THOUSAND
PEAKS AND MYRIAD RAVINES**
Qing dynasty, 1693. Hanging scroll, ink on
paper, 8′2½″ × 3′4½″ (2.54 × 1.03 m).
National Palace Museum, Taibei, Taiwan,
Republic of China.

EXPLORE MORE: Gain insight
from a primary source related to
*A Thousand Peaks and Myriad
Ravines* www.myartslab.com

CHINESE AND
KOREAN ART AFTER 1279

A THOUSAND PEAKS AND MYRIAD RAVINES (FIG. 24–1), painted by Wang Hui (1632–1717) in 1693, exemplifies the subjects of Chinese landscape painting: mountains, rivers, waterfalls, trees, rocks, temples, pavilions, houses, bridges, boats, wandering scholars, fishers—familiar motifs from a tradition now many centuries old. On it, the artist has written:

> Moss and weeds cover the rocks and mist hovers over the water.
> The sound of dripping water is heard in front of the temple gate.
> Through a thousand peaks and myriad ravines the spring flows,
> And brings the flying flowers into the sacred caves.

> In the fourth month of the year 1693, in an inn in the capital, I painted this based on a Tang-dynasty poem in the manner of [the painters] Dong [Yuan] and Ju[ran].

> (Translation by Chu-tsing Li)

The inscription refers to the artist's inspiration found in the lines of a Tang-dynasty poem, which offered the subject, and in the paintings of tenth-century painters Dong Yuan and Juran, on which he based his style. Wang Hui's art reflects ideals of the scholar in imperial China.

China's scholar class was unique, the product of an examination system designed to recruit the finest minds in the country for government service. Instituted during the Tang dynasty (618–907) and based on even earlier traditions, the civil service examinations were excruciatingly difficult, but for the tiny percentage who passed at the highest level, the rewards were prestige, position, power, and wealth. Steeped in philosophy, literature, and history, China's scholars—often called *wenren* (literati)—shared a common outlook. Following Confucianism, they became officials to fulfill their obligation to the world; pulled by Daoism, they retreated from society in order to come to terms with nature and the universe: to create a garden, to write poetry, to paint.

During the Song dynasty (960–1279) the examinations were expanded and regularized. More than half of all government positions came to be filled by scholars. In the subsequent Yuan and Ming periods, the tradition of **literati painting** (a style that reflected the taste of the educated class) further developed. When the Yuan period of foreign rule came to an end, the new Ming ruling house revived the court traditions of the Song. The Ming became the model for the rulers of Korea's Joseon dynasty, under whose patronage these styles achieved a distinctive and austere beauty.

In the Qing era, China was again ruled by an outside group, this time the Manchus. While maintaining their traditional connections to Tibet and inner Asia through their patronage of Tibetan Buddhism, the Manchu rulers also embraced Chinese ideals, especially those of the literati. Practicing painting and calligraphy, composing poetry in Chinese, and collecting esteemed Chinese works of art, these rulers amassed the great palace collections that can now be seen in Beijing and Taibei.

LEARN ABOUT IT

24.1 Analyze the continued importance of the three ways of thought (Daoism, Confucianism, and Buddhism) in Chinese art of the thirteenth century to the present.

24.2 Assess the influence of court life and patronage on art in China and Korea.

24.3 Examine the continuing relationship of calligraphy and painting in Chinese art.

24.4 Discuss literati values and the scholarly life in art in later China and Korea.

24.5 Assess the emergence of expression as a value of importance beyond representation in China and Korea, from the thirteenth century to the present.

HEAR MORE: Listen to an audio file of your chapter **www.myartslab.com**

THE MONGOL INVASIONS

At the beginning of the thirteenth century the Mongols, a nomadic people from the steppes north of China, began to amass an empire. Led first by Genghiz Khan (c. 1162–1227), then by his sons and grandsons, they swept westward into central Europe and overran Islamic lands from Central Asia through present-day Iraq. To the east, they quickly captured northern China, and in 1279, led by Kublai Khan, they conquered southern China as well. Grandson of the mighty Genghiz, Kublai proclaimed himself emperor of China and founder of the Yuan dynasty (1279–1368).

The Mongol invasions were traumatic, and their effect on China was long-lasting. During the Song dynasty, China had grown increasingly introspective. Rejecting foreign ideas and influences, intellectuals had focused on defining the qualities that constituted true "Chinese-ness." They drew a clear distinction between their own people, whom they characterized as gentle, erudite, and sophisticated, and the "barbarians" outside China's borders, whom they regarded as crude, wild, and uncivilized. Now, faced with the reality of barbarian occupation, China's inward gaze intensified in spiritual resistance. For centuries to come, long after the Mongols had gone, leading scholars continued to seek intellectually more challenging, philosophically more profound, and artistically more subtle expressions of all that could be identified as authentically Chinese (see "Foundations of Chinese Culture," opposite).

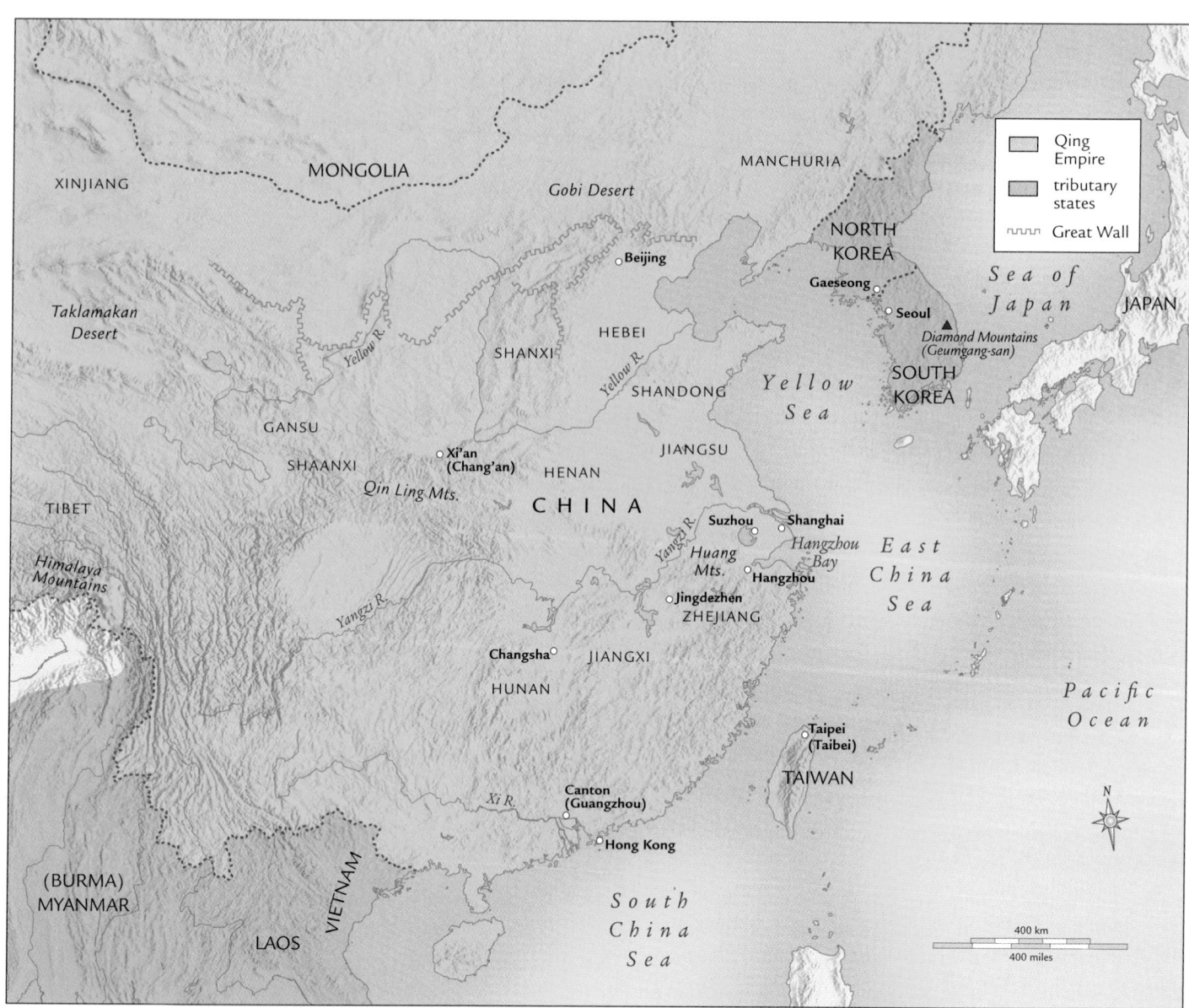

MAP 24–1 • CHINA AND KOREA

The map shows the borders of both contemporary China and Korea. The colored areas indicate the historical extent of the Qing dynasty empire (1644–1911) including its tributary states.

Foundations of Chinese Culture

Chinese culture is distinguished by its long and continuous development. Between 6000 and 2000 BCE a variety of Neolithic cultures flourished across China. Through long interaction these cultures became increasingly similar and they eventually gave rise to the three Bronze Age dynastic states with which Chinese history traditionally begins: the Xia, the Shang (c. 1700–1100 BCE), and the Zhou (1100–221 BCE).

The Shang developed traditions of casting ritual vessels in bronze, working jade in ceremonial shapes, and writing consistently in scripts that directly evolved into the modern Chinese written language. Society was stratified, and the ruling group maintained its authority in part by claiming power as intermediaries between the human and spirit worlds. Under the Zhou a feudal society developed, with nobles related to the king ruling over numerous small states.

During the latter part of the Zhou dynasty, states began to vie for supremacy through intrigue and increasingly ruthless warfare. The collapse of social order profoundly influenced China's first philosophers, who largely concerned themselves with the pragmatic question of how to bring about a stable society.

In 221 BCE, rulers of the state of Qin triumphed over the remaining states, unifying China as an empire for the first time. The Qin created the mechanisms of China's centralized bureaucracy, but their rule was harsh and the dynasty was quickly overthrown. During the ensuing Han dynasty (206 BCE–220 CE), China at last knew peace and prosperity. Confucianism was made the official state ideology, in the process assuming the form and force of a religion. Developed from the thought of Confucius (551–479 BCE), one of the many philosophers of the Zhou, Confucianism is an ethical system for the management of society based on establishing correct relationships among people. Providing a counterweight was Daoism, which also came into its own during the Han dynasty. Based on the thought of Laozi, a possibly legendary contemporary of Confucius, and the philosopher Zhuangzi (369–286 BCE), Daoism is a view of life that seeks to harmonize the individual with the Dao, or Way, the process of the universe. Confucianism and Daoism have remained central to Chinese thought—the one addressing the public realm of duty and conformity, the other the private world of individualism and creativity.

Following the collapse of the Han dynasty, China experienced a centuries-long period of disunity (220–589 CE). Invaders from the north and west established numerous kingdoms and dynasties, while a series of six precarious Chinese dynasties held sway in the south. Buddhism, which had begun to spread over trade routes from India during the Han era, now flourished. The period also witnessed the economic and cultural development of the south (previous dynasties had ruled from the north).

China was reunited under the Sui dynasty (581–618 CE), which quickly fell to the Tang (618–907), one of the most successful dynasties in Chinese history. Strong and confident, Tang China fascinated and, in turn, was fascinated by the cultures around it. Caravans streamed across central Asia to the capital, Chang'an, then the largest city in the world. Japan and Korea sent thousands of students to study Chinese culture, and Buddhism reached the height of its influence before a period of persecution signaled the start of its decline.

The mood of the Song dynasty (960–1279) was quite different. The martial vigor of the Tang gave way to a culture of increasing refinement and sophistication, and Tang openness to foreign influences was replaced by a conscious cultivation of China's own traditions. In art, landscape painting emerged as the most esteemed genre, capable of expressing both philosophical and personal concerns. With the fall of the north to invaders in 1126, the Song court set up a new capital in the south, which became the cultural and economic center of the country.

YUAN DYNASTY

The Mongols established their capital in the northern city now known as Beijing (MAP 24–1). The cultural centers of China, however, remained the great cities of the south, where the Song court had been located for the previous 150 years. Combined with the tensions of Yuan rule, this separation of China's political and cultural centers created a new dynamic in the arts.

Throughout most of Chinese history, the imperial court had set the tone for artistic taste: Artisans attached to the court produced architecture, paintings, gardens, and objects of jade, lacquer, ceramics, and silk especially for imperial use. Over the centuries, painters and calligraphers gradually moved higher up the social scale, for these "arts of the brush" were often practiced by scholars and even emperors, whose high status reflected positively on whatever interested them. With the establishment of an imperial painting academy during the Song dynasty, painters finally achieved a status equal to that of court officials. For the literati, painting came to be grouped with calligraphy and poetry as the trio of accomplishments suited to members of the cultural elite.

But while the literati elevated the status of painting by virtue of practicing it, they also began to develop their own ideas of what painting should be. Not needing to earn an income from their art, they cultivated an amateur ideal in which personal expression counted for more than "mere" professional skill. They created for themselves a status as artists totally separate from and superior to professional painters, whose art they felt was inherently compromised, since it was done to please others, and impure, since it was tainted by money.

The conditions of Yuan rule now encouraged a clear distinction between court taste, ministered to by professional

Marco Polo

China under Kublai Khan was one of four Mongol khanates that together extended west into present-day Iraq and through Russia to the borders of Poland and Hungary. For roughly a century, travelers moved freely across this vast expanse, making the era one of unprecedented cross-cultural exchange. Diplomats, missionaries, merchants, and adventurers flocked to the Yuan court, and Chinese envoys were dispatched to the West. The most celebrated European traveler of the time was a Venetian named Marco Polo (c. 1254–1324), whose descriptions of his travels were for several centuries the only firsthand account of China available in Europe.

Marco Polo was still in his teens when he set out for China in 1271. He traveled with his uncle and father, both merchants, bearing letters for Kublai Khan from Pope Gregory X. After a four-year journey the

Polos arrived at last in Beijing. Marco became a favorite of the emperor and spent the next 17 years in his service, during which time he traveled extensively throughout China. He eventually returned home in 1295.

Imprisoned later during a war between Venice and Genoa, rival Italian city-states, Marco Polo passed the time by dictating an account of his experiences to a fellow prisoner. The resulting book, *A Description of the World*, has fascinated generations of readers with its depiction of prosperous and sophisticated lands in the East. Translated into many European languages, it was an important influence in stimulating further exploration. When Columbus set sail across the Atlantic in 1492, one of the places he hoped to find was a country Marco Polo called Zipangu—Japan.

artists and artisans, and literati taste. The Yuan dynasty continued the imperial role as patron of the arts, commissioning buildings, murals, gardens, paintings, and decorative arts. Western visitors such as the Italian Marco Polo were impressed by the magnificence of the Yuan court (see "Marco Polo," above). But scholars, profoundly alienated from the new government, took little notice of these accomplishments. Nor did Yuan rulers have much use for scholars, especially those from the south. The civil service examinations were abolished, and the highest government positions were bestowed, instead, on Mongols and their foreign allies. Scholars now tended to turn inward, to search for solutions of their own and to try to express themselves in personal and symbolic terms.

ZHAO MENGFU. Zhao Mengfu (1254–1322) was a descendant of the imperial line of Song. Unlike many scholars of his time, he eventually chose to serve the Yuan government and was made a high official. A painter, calligrapher, and poet, all of the first rank,

Zhao was especially known for his carefully rendered paintings of horses. But he also cultivated another manner, most famous in his landmark painting **AUTUMN COLORS ON THE QIAO AND HUA MOUNTAINS** (FIG. 24–2).

Zhao painted this work for a friend whose ancestors came from Jinan, the present-day capital of Shandong Province, and the painting supposedly depicts the landscape there. Yet the mountains and trees are not painted in the accomplished naturalism of Zhao's own time but rather in the archaic yet oddly elegant manner of the earlier Tang dynasty (618–907). The Tang dynasty was a great era in Chinese history, when the country was both militarily strong and culturally vibrant. Through his painting Zhao evoked a nostalgia not only for his friend's distant homeland but also for China's past.

This educated taste for the "spirit of antiquity" became an important aspect of literati painting in later periods. Also typical of literati taste are the unassuming brushwork, the subtle colors sparingly used (many literati paintings forgo color altogether), the use of landscape to convey personal meaning, and even the

24-2 • Zhao Mengfu AUTUMN COLORS ON THE QIAO AND HUA MOUNTAINS
Yuan dynasty, 1296. Handscroll, ink and color on paper, 11¼ × 36¾″ (28.6 × 9.3 cm). National Palace Museum, Taibei, Taiwan, Republic of China.

intended audience—a close friend. The literati did not paint for public display but for each other. They favored small formats such as **handscrolls**, **hanging scrolls**, or **album leaves** (book pages), which could easily be shown to friends or shared at small gatherings (see "Formats of Chinese Painting," page 797).

NI ZAN.   Of the considerable number of Yuan painters who took up Zhao's ideas, several became models for later generations. One such was Ni Zan (1301–74), whose most famous surviving painting is **THE RONGXI STUDIO** (FIG. 24–3). Done entirely in ink, the painting depicts the lake region in Ni's home district. Mountains, rocks, trees, and a pavilion are sketched with a minimum of detail using a dry brush technique—a technique in which the brush is not fully loaded with ink but rather is about to run out, so that white paper "breathes" through the ragged strokes. The result is a painting with a light touch and a sense of simplicity and purity. Literati styles were believed to reflect the painter's personality. Ni's spare, dry style became associated with a noble spirit, and many later painters adopted it or paid homage to it.

Ni Zan was one of those eccentrics whose behavior has become legendary in the history of Chinese art. In his early years he was one of the richest men in the region, the owner of a large estate. His pride and his aloofness from daily affairs often got him into trouble with the authorities. His cleanliness was notorious. In addition to washing himself several times daily, he also ordered his servants to wash the trees in his garden and to clean the furniture after his guests had left. He was said to be so unworldly that late in life he gave away most of his possessions and lived as a hermit in a boat, wandering on rivers and lakes.

Whether these stories are true or not, they were important elements of Ni's legacy to later painters, for Ni's life as well as his art served as a model. The painting of the literati was bound up with certain views about what constituted an appropriate life. The ideal, as embodied by Ni Zan and others, was of a brilliantly gifted scholar whose spirit was too refined for the dusty world of government service and who thus preferred to live as a recluse, or as one who had retired after having become frustrated by a brief stint as an official.

MING DYNASTY

The founder of the next dynasty, the Ming (1368–1644), came from a family of poor uneducated peasants. As he rose through the ranks in the army, he enlisted the help of scholars to gain power and solidify his following. Once he had driven the Mongols from Beijing and firmly established himself as emperor, however, he grew to distrust intellectuals. His rule was despotic, even ruthless. Throughout the nearly 300 years of Ming rule most emperors shared his attitude, so although the civil service examinations were reinstated, scholars remained alienated from the government they were trained to serve.

24-3 • Ni Zan THE RONGXI STUDIO
Yuan dynasty, 1372. Hanging scroll, ink on paper, height 29⅜" (74.6 cm). National Palace Museum, Taibei, Taiwan, Republic of China.

The idea that a painting is not done to capture a likeness or to satisfy others but is executed freely and carelessly for the artist's own amusement is at the heart of the literati aesthetic. Ni Zan once wrote this comment on a painting: "What I call painting does not exceed the joy of careless sketching with a brush. I do not seek formal likeness but do it simply for my own amusement. Recently I was rambling about and came to a town. The people asked for my pictures, but wanted them exactly according to their own desires and to represent a specific occasion. [When I could not satisfy them,] they went away insulting, scolding, and cursing in every possible way. What a shame! But how can one scold a eunuch for not growing a beard?" (translated in Bush and Shih, p. 266).

24-4 • Yin Hong HUNDREDS OF BIRDS ADMIRING THE PEACOCKS
Ming dynasty, late 15th–early 16th century. Hanging scroll, ink and color on silk, 7′10½″ × 6′5″ (2.4 × 1.96 m). Cleveland Museum of Art. Purchase from the J. H. Wade Fund, 74.31

24-5 • Dai Jin RETURNING HOME LATE FROM A SPRING OUTING
Ming dynasty. Hanging scroll, ink on silk, 5½′ × 2′8¾″ (1.68 × 0.83 m). National Palace Museum, Taibei, Taiwan, Republic of China.

COURT AND PROFESSIONAL PAINTING

The contrast between the luxurious world of the court and the austere ideals of the literati continued through the Ming dynasty.

A typical example of Ming court taste is **HUNDREDS OF BIRDS ADMIRING THE PEACOCKS**, a large painting on silk by Yin Hong, an artist active during the late fifteenth and early sixteenth centuries (**FIG. 24-4**). A pupil of well-known courtiers, Yin most probably served in the court at Beijing. The painting is an example of the birds-and-flowers genre, which had been popular with artists

of the Song academy. Here the subject takes on symbolic meaning, with the homage of the birds to the peacocks representing the homage of court officials to the imperial state. The style goes back to Song academy models, although the large format and multiplication of details are traits of the Ming.

A related, yet bolder and less constrained, landscape style was also popular during this period. Sometimes called the Zhe style since its roots were in Hangzhou, Zhejiang Province, where the Southern Song court had been located, this manner especially influenced

24-6 • Qiu Ying SECTION OF SPRING DAWN IN THE HAN PALACE
Ming dynasty, 1500–1550. Handscroll, ink and color on silk, 1′ × 18′13⁄16″ (0.30 × 5.7 m). National Palace Museum, Taibei, Taiwan, Republic of China.

With the exception of large wall paintings that typically decorated palaces, temples, and tombs, most Chinese paintings were done in ink and water-based colors on silk or paper. Finished works were generally mounted as **handscrolls**, **hanging scrolls**, or leaves in an album.

An album comprises a set of paintings of identical size mounted in a book. (A single painting from an album is called an **album leaf**.) The paintings in an album are usually related in subject, such as various views of a famous site or a series of scenes glimpsed on one trip.

Album-sized paintings might also be mounted as a handscroll, a horizontal format generally about 12 inches high and anywhere from a few feet to dozens of feet long. More typically, however, a handscroll would be a single continuous painting. Handscrolls were not meant to be displayed all at once, the way they are commonly presented today in museums. Rather, they were unrolled only occasionally, to be savored in much the same spirit as we might view a favorite film. Placing the scroll on a flat surface such as a table, a viewer would unroll it a foot or two at a time, moving gradually through the entire scroll from right to left, lingering over favorite details. The scroll was then rolled up and returned to its box until the next viewing.

Like handscrolls, hanging scrolls were not displayed permanently but were taken out for a limited time: a day, a week, a season. Unlike a handscroll, however, the painting on a hanging scroll was viewed as a whole—unrolled and put up on a wall, with the roller at the lower end

acting as a weight to help the scroll hang flat. Although some hanging scrolls are quite large, they are still fundamentally intimate works, not intended for display in a public place.

Creating a scroll was a time-consuming and exacting process accomplished by a professional mounter. The painting was first backed with paper to strengthen it. Next, strips of paper-backed silk were pasted to the top, bottom, and sides, framing the painting on all four sides. Additional silk pieces were added to extend the scroll horizontally or vertically, depending on the format. The assembled scroll was then backed again with paper and fitted with a half-round dowel, or wooden rod, at the top of a hanging scroll or on the right end of a handscroll, with ribbons for hanging and tying, and with a wooden roller at the other end. Hanging scrolls were often fashioned from several patterns of silk, and a variety of piecing formats were developed and codified. On a handscroll, a painting was generally preceded by a panel giving the work's title and often followed by a long panel bearing **colophons**—inscriptions related to the work, such as poems in its praise or comments by its owners over the centuries. A scroll would be remounted periodically to better preserve it, and colophons and inscriptions would be preserved in each remounting. **Seals** added another layer of interest. A treasured scroll often bears not only the seal of its maker but also those of collectors and admirers through the centuries.

colophon panel

frontispiece

label

handscroll rolled for storage

handscroll

front   back

hanging scroll

painters in Korea and Japan. A major example is **RETURNING HOME LATE FROM A SPRING OUTING (FIG. 24–5)**, unsigned but attributed to Dai Jin (1388–1462). This work reflects the Chinese sources for such artists as An Gyeon (SEE FIG. 24–17) and Sesshu (SEE FIG. 25–3).

QIU YING. A preeminent professional painter in the Ming period was Qiu Ying (1494–1552), who lived in Suzhou, a prosperous

southern city. He inspired generations of imitators with exceptional works, such as a long handscroll known as **SPRING DAWN IN THE HAN PALACE (FIG. 24–6)**. The painting is based on Tang-dynasty depictions of women in the court of the Han dynasty (206 BCE–220 CE). While in the service of a well-known collector, Qiu Ying had the opportunity to study many Tang paintings, whose artists usually concentrated on the figures, leaving out the

Spring Dawn in the Han Palace ›

Ming dynasty, 1500–1550. Section of a handscroll, ink and color on silk, 1′ × 18′13⁄16″ (0.30 × 5.7 m). National Palace Museum, Taibei, Taiwan, Republic of China.

Two ladies unwrap a *qin*, the zither or lute that was the most respected of musical instruments.

A seated lady plays the *pipa*, an instrument introduced from Central Asia during the Tang dynasty.

Antique vessels of bronze, lacquer, and porcelain adorn the room and suggest the ladies' refined taste.

A tray landscape featuring an eroded rock provides a sculptural counterpart to landscape (mountain-and-water) painting and suggests a place where immortals might dwell.

Two ladies dance together letting their sleeves and sashes swirl.

SEE MORE: View the Closer Look feature for the detail of *Spring Dawn in the Han Palace* **www.myartslab.com**

background entirely. Qiu's graceful and elegant figures—although modeled after those in Tang works—are portrayed in a setting of palace buildings, engaging in such pastimes as chess, music, calligraphy, and painting. With its antique subject matter, refined technique, and flawless taste in color and composition, *Spring Dawn in the Han Palace* brought professional painting to a new high point (see "A Closer Look," above).

DECORATIVE ARTS

Qiu Ying painted to satisfy his patrons in Suzhou. The cities of the south were becoming wealthy, and newly rich merchants collected

paintings, antiques, and art objects. The court, too, was prosperous and patronized the arts on a lavish scale. In such a setting, the decorative arts thrived.

MING BLUE-AND-WHITE WARES. The Ming became famous the world over for its exquisite ceramics, especially **porcelain** (see "The Secret of Porcelain," opposite). The imperial kilns in Jingdezhen, in Jiangxi Province, became the most renowned center for porcelain not only in all of China, but in all the world. Particularly noteworthy are the blue-and-white wares produced there during the ten-year reign of the ruler known as the Xuande

Marco Polo, it is said, was the one who named a new type of ceramic he found in China. Its translucent purity reminded him of the smooth whiteness of the cowry shell, *porcellana* in Italian. **Porcelain** is made from kaolin, an extremely refined white clay, and petuntse, a variety of the mineral feldspar. When properly combined and fired at a sufficiently high temperature, the two materials fuse into a glasslike, translucent ceramic that is far stronger than it looks.

Porcelaneous stoneware, fired at lower temperatures, was known in China by the seventh century, but true porcelain was perfected during the Song dynasty. To create blue-and-white porcelain such as the flask in FIGURE 24–7, blue pigment was made from cobalt oxide, finely

ground and mixed with water. The decoration was painted directly onto the unfired porcelain vessel, then a layer of clear glaze was applied over it. (In this technique, known as **underglaze** painting, the pattern is painted beneath the glaze.) After firing, the piece emerged from the kiln with a clear blue design set sharply against a snowy white background.

Entranced with the exquisite properties of porcelain, European potters tried for centuries to duplicate it. The technique was finally discovered in 1709 by Johann Friedrich Böttger in Dresden, Germany, who tried—but failed—to keep it a secret.

24-7 • FLASK

Ming dynasty, 1426–1435. Porcelain with decoration painted in underglaze cobalt blue. Collection of the Palace Museum, Beijing.

Dragons have featured prominently in Chinese folklore from earliest times—Neolithic examples have been found painted on pottery and carved in jade. In Bronze Age China, dragons came to be associated with powerful and sudden manifestations of nature, such as wind, thunder, and lightning. At the same time, dragons became associated with superior beings such as virtuous rulers and sages. With the emergence of China's first firmly established empire during the Han dynasty, the dragon was appropriated as an imperial symbol, and it remained so throughout Chinese history. Dragon sightings were duly recorded and considered auspicious. Yet even the Son of Heaven could not monopolize the dragon. During the Tang and Song dynasties the practice arose of painting pictures of dragons to pray for rain, and for Chan (Zen) Buddhists, the dragon was a symbol of sudden enlightenment.

Emperor (ruled 1426–1435), such as the **FLASK** in FIGURE 24–7. The subtle shape, the refined yet vigorous decoration of dragons posturing above the sea, and the flawless glazing embody the high achievement of Ming artisans.

ARCHITECTURE AND CITY PLANNING

Centuries of warfare and destruction have left very few Chinese architectural monuments intact. The most important remaining example of traditional Chinese architecture is **THE FORBIDDEN CITY**, the imperial palace compound in Beijing, whose principal buildings were constructed during the Ming dynasty **(FIG. 24–8)**.

THE FORBIDDEN CITY.   The basic plan of Beijing was the work of the Mongols, who laid out their capital city according to traditional Chinese principles. City planning began early in China—in the seventh century, in the case of Chang'an (present-day Xi'an), the capital of the Sui and Tang emperors. The walled city of Chang'an was laid out on a rectangular grid, with evenly spaced streets that ran north–south and east–west. At the northern end stood a walled imperial complex.

Beijing, too, was developed as a walled, rectangular city with streets laid out in a grid. The palace enclosure occupied the center of the northern part of the city, which was reserved for the Mongols. Chinese lived in the southern third of the city. Later, Ming and Qing emperors preserved this division, with officials living in the northern or Inner City and commoners living in the southern or Outer City. Under the third Ming emperor, Yongle (ruled 1403–1424), the Forbidden City was rebuilt as we see it today.

The approach to the Forbidden City was impressive. Visitors entered through the Meridian Gate, a monumental gate with side wings (SEE FIG. 24–8). Inside the Meridian Gate a broad courtyard is crossed by a bow-shaped waterway that is spanned by five arched marble bridges. At the opposite end of the courtyard is the Gate of Supreme Harmony, opening onto an even larger courtyard that houses three ceremonial halls raised on a broad platform. First is the Hall of Supreme Harmony, where, on the most important state occasions, the emperor was seated on his throne,

24-8 • THE FORBIDDEN CITY
Now the Palace Museum, Beijing. Mostly Ming dynasty.
View from the southwest.

SEE MORE: View a simulation about the Forbidden City
www.myartslab.com

facing south. Beyond is the smaller Hall of Central Harmony, then the Hall of Protecting Harmony. Behind these vast ceremonial spaces, still on the central axis, is the inner court, again with a progression of three buildings, this time more intimate in scale. In its balance and symmetry the plan of the Forbidden City reflects ancient Chinese beliefs about the harmony of the universe, and it emphasizes the emperor's role as the Son of Heaven, whose duty was to maintain the cosmic order from his throne in the middle of the world.

THE LITERATI AESTHETIC

In the south, particularly in the district of Suzhou, literati painting, associated with the educated men who served the court as government officials, remained the dominant trend. One of the major literati figures from the Ming period is Shen Zhou (1427–1509), who had no desire to enter government service and spent most of his life in Suzhou. He studied the Yuan painters avidly and tried to recapture their spirit in such works as *Poet on a Mountaintop* (see "*Poet on a Mountaintop*," page 802). Although the style of the painting recalls the freedom and simplicity of Ni Zan (SEE FIG. 24–3), the motif of a poet surveying the landscape from a mountain plateau is Shen's creation.

24-9 • ARMCHAIR
Ming dynasty, 16th–17th century. Huanghuali wood (hardwood), 39⅜ × 27¼ × 20″ (100 × 69.2 × 50.8 cm). The Nelson-Atkins Museum of Art, Kansas City, Missouri. Purchase, Nelson Trust (46-78/1)

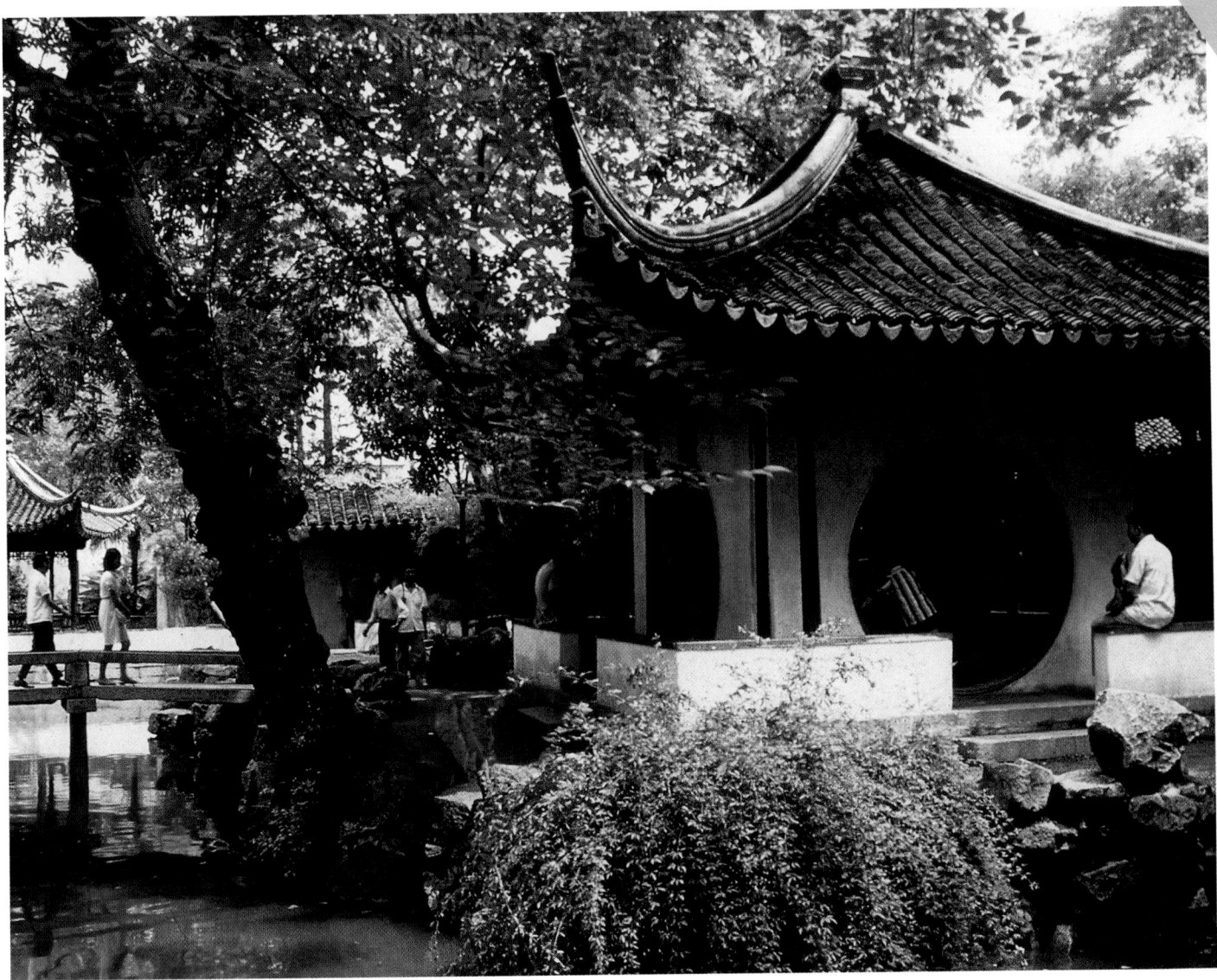

24-10 • GARDEN OF THE CESSATION OF OFFICIAL LIFE (ALSO KNOWN AS THE HUMBLE ADMINISTRATOR'S GARDEN)
Suzhou, Jiangsu. Ming dynasty, early 16th century.

Early in the sixteenth century, an official in Beijing, frustrated after serving in the capital for many years without promotion, returned home. Taking an ancient poem, "The Song of Leisurely Living," for his model, he began to build a garden. He called his retreat the Garden of the Cessation of Official Life to indicate that he had exchanged his career as a bureaucrat for a life of leisure. By leisure, he meant that he could now dedicate himself to calligraphy, poetry, and painting, the three arts dear to scholars in China.

LITERATI INFLUENCE ON FURNITURE, ARCHITECTURE, AND GARDEN DESIGN. The taste of the literati came to influence furniture and architecture, and especially the design of gardens. Chinese furniture made for domestic use reached the height of its development in the sixteenth and seventeenth centuries. Characteristic of Chinese furniture, the chair in FIGURE 24–9 is constructed without the use of glue or nails. Instead, pieces fit together based on the principle of the **mortise-and-tenon** joint, in which a projecting element (tenon) on one piece fits snugly into a cavity (mortise) on another. Each piece of the chair is carved, as opposed to being bent or twisted, and the joints are crafted with great precision. The patterns of the wood grain provide subtle interest unmarred by any

painting or other embellishment. The style, like that of Chinese architecture, is one of simplicity, clarity, symmetry, and balance. The effect is formal and dignified but natural and simple—virtues central to the Chinese view of proper human conduct as well.

The art of landscape gardening also reached a high point during the Ming dynasty, as many literati surrounded their homes with gardens. The most famous gardens were created in the southern cities of the Yangzi Delta, especially in Suzhou. The largest surviving garden of the era is the **GARDEN OF THE CESSATION OF OFFICIAL LIFE (FIG. 24–10)**. Although modified and reconstructed many times through the centuries, it still reflects many of the basic ideas of the original Ming owner. About a third of the garden is

THE OBJECT SPEAKS

Poet on a Mountaintop

In earlier landscape paintings, human figures were typically shown dwarfed by the grandeur of nature. Travelers might be seen scuttling along a narrow path by a stream, while overhead towered mountains whose peaks conversed with the clouds and whose heights were inaccessible. Here, the poet has climbed the mountain and dominates the landscape. Even the clouds are beneath him. Before his gaze, a poem hangs in the air, as though he were projecting his thoughts.

The poem, composed by Shen Zhou himself, and written in his distinctive hand, reads:

White clouds like a scarf enfold the mountain's waist;
Stone steps hang in space—a long, narrow path.
Alone, leaning on my cane, I gaze intently at the scene,
And feel like answering the murmuring brook with the music of my flute.

(Translation by Jonathan Chaves, *The Chinese Painter as Poet*, New York, 2000, p. 46.)

Shen Zhou composed the poem and wrote the inscription at the time he painted the album. The style of the calligraphy, like the style of the painting, is informal, relaxed, and straightforward—qualities that were believed to reflect the artist's character and personality.

The painting reflects Ming philosophy, which held that the mind, not the physical world, was the basis for reality. With its perfect synthesis of poetry, calligraphy, and painting, and with its harmony of mind and landscape, *Poet on a Mountaintop* represents the essence of Ming literati painting.

Shen Zhou **POET ON A MOUNTAINTOP**
Leaf from an album of landscapes; painting mounted as part of a handscroll. Ming dynasty, c. 1500.
Ink and color on paper, 15¼ × 23¾″ (40 × 60.2 cm). Nelson-Atkins Museum of Art, Kansas City, Missouri.
Purchase, Nelson Trust (46-51/2)

devoted to water through artificially created brooks and ponds. The landscape is dotted with pavilions, kiosks, libraries, studios, and corridors. Many of the buildings have poetic names, such as Rain Listening Pavilion and Bridge of the Small Flying Rainbow.

DONG QICHANG, LITERATI THEORIST. The ideas underlying literati painting found their most influential expression in the writings of Dong Qichang (1555–1636). A high official in the late Ming period, Dong Qichang embodied the literati tradition as poet, calligrapher, and painter. He developed a view of Chinese art history that divided painters into two opposing schools, northern and southern. The names have nothing to do with geography— a painter from the south might well be classed as northern—but reflect a parallel Dong drew with the northern and southern schools of Chan (Zen) Buddhism in China. The southern school of Chan, founded by the eccentric monk Huineng (638–713), was unorthodox, radical, and innovative; the northern school was traditional and conservative. Similarly, Dong's two schools of painters represented progressive and conservative traditions. In Dong's view the conservative northern school was dominated by professional painters whose academic, often decorative, style emphasized technical skill. In contrast, the progressive southern school preferred ink to color and free brushwork to meticulous detail. Its painters aimed for poetry and personal expression. In promoting this theory, Dong gave his unlimited sanction to literati painting, which he positioned as the culmination of the southern school, and he fundamentally influenced the way the Chinese viewed their own tradition.

Dong Qichang summarized his views on the proper training for literati painters in the famous statement "Read ten thousand books and walk ten thousand miles." By this he meant that one must first study the works of the great masters, then follow "heaven and earth," the world of nature. These studies prepared the way for greater self-expression through brush and ink, the goal of literati painting. Dong's views rested on an awareness that a painting of scenery and the actual scenery are two very different things. The excellence of a painting does not lie in its degree of resemblance to reality—that gap can never be bridged—but in its expressive power. The expressive language of painting is inherently abstract and lies in its nature as a construction of brushstrokes. For example, in a painting of a rock, the rock itself is not expressive; rather, the brushstrokes that suggest a rock are expressive.

With such thinking Dong brought painting close to the realm of calligraphy, which had long been considered the highest form of artistic expression in China. More than a thousand years before Dong's time, a body of critical terms and theories had evolved to discuss calligraphy in light of the formal and expressive properties of brushwork and composition. Dong introduced some of these terms—ideas such as opening and closing, rising and falling, and void and solid—to the criticism of painting.

Dong's theories are fully embodied in his painting **THE QING-BIAN MOUNTAINS** (FIG. 24–11). According to his own inscription,

24-11 • Dong Qichang **THE QINGBIAN MOUNTAINS**
Ming dynasty, 1617. Hanging scroll, ink on paper, 21'8″ × 7'4⅜″
(6.72 × 2.25 m). Cleveland Museum of Art. Leonard C. Hanna, Jr., Fund

the painting was based on a work by the tenth-century artist Dong Yuan. Dong Qichang's style, however, is quite different from the styles of the masters he admired. Although there is some indication of foreground, middle ground, and distant mountains, the space is ambiguous, as if all the elements were compressed to the surface of the picture. With this flattening of space, the trees, rocks, and mountains become more readily legible in a second way, as semi-abstract forms made of brushstrokes.

Six trees arranged diagonally define the extreme foreground and announce themes that the rest of the painting repeats, varies, and develops. The tree on the left, with its outstretched branches and full foliage, is echoed first in the shape of another tree just across the river and again in a tree farther up and toward the left. The tallest tree of the foreground grouping anticipates the high peak that towers in the distance almost directly above it. The forms of the smaller foreground trees, especially the one with dark leaves,

are repeated in numerous variations across the painting. At the same time, the simple and ordinary-looking boulder in the foreground is transformed in the conglomeration of rocks, ridges, hills, and mountains above. This double reading, both abstract and representational, parallels the work's double nature as a painting of a landscape and an interpretation of a traditional landscape painting.

The influence of Dong Qichang on the development of Chinese painting of later periods cannot be overstated. Indeed, nearly all Chinese painters since the early seventeenth century have reflected his ideas in one way or another.

QING DYNASTY

In 1644, when the armies of the Manchu people to the northeast of China marched into Beijing, many Chinese reacted as though their civilization had come to an end. Yet, the Manchus had already

24-12 • Yun Shouping AMARANTH
Leaf from an album of flowers, bamboo, fruits, and vegetables. 1633–1690. Album of 10 leaves; ink and color on paper; each leaf 10 × 13″ (25.3 × 33.5 cm). Collection of Phoenix Art Museum. Gift of Marilyn and Roy Papp

The leaf is inscribed by the artist: "Autumn garden abounds in beauty, playfully painted by Ouxiangguan (Yun Shouping)." Translation by Momoko Soma Welch.

24–13 • Shitao
LANDSCAPE
Leaf from *An Album of Landscapes*. Qing dynasty, c. 1700. Ink and color on paper, 9½ × 11″ (24.1 × 28 cm). Collection C. C. Wang family

adopted many Chinese customs and institutions before their conquest. After gaining control of all of China, a process that took decades, they showed great respect for Chinese tradition. In art, all the major trends of the late Ming dynasty eventually continued into the Manchu, or Qing, dynasty (1644–1911).

ORTHODOX PAINTING

Literati painting had been established as the dominant tradition; it now became orthodox. Scholars followed Dong Qichang's recommendation and based their approach on the study of past masters, and they painted large numbers of works in the manner of Song and Yuan artists as a way of expressing their learning, technique, and taste.

The Qing emperors of the late seventeenth and eighteenth centuries were painters themselves. They collected literati painting, and their taste was shaped mainly by artists such as Wang Hui (SEE FIG. 24–1). Thus literati painting, long associated with reclusive scholars, ultimately became an academic style practiced at court. Imbued with values associated with scholarship and virtue, these paintings constituted the highest art form of the Qing court. The emperors also esteemed a style of bird-and-flower painting developed by Yun Shouping (1633–1690). Like the orthodox style of landscape painting, it was embraced by literati painters—many of them court officials themselves. The style, most often seen in

albums or fans, recalled aspects of Song- and Yuan-dynasty bird-and-flower painting, and artists cited their ancient models as a way to enrich both the meaning and the beauty of these small-format works. In a leaf from an album of flowers, bamboo, fruits and vegetables, which employs a variety of brush techniques (**FIG. 24–12**), Yun Shouping represents flowers of the autumn season.

INDIVIDUALIST PAINTING

The first few decades of Qing rule had been both traumatic and dangerous for those who were loyal—or worse, related—to the Ming. Some committed suicide, while others sought refuge in monasteries or wandered the countryside. Among them were several painters who expressed their anger, defiance, frustration, and melancholy in their art. They took Dong Qichang's idea of painting as an expression of the artist's personal feelings very seriously and cultivated highly original styles. These painters have become known as the individualists.

SHITAO.   One of the individualists was Shitao (1642–1707), who was descended from the first Ming emperor and who took refuge in Buddhist temples when the dynasty fell. In his later life he brought his painting to the brink of abstraction in such works as **LANDSCAPE** (**FIG. 24–13**). A monk sits in a small hut, looking out onto mountains that seem to be in turmoil. Dots, used for centuries to indicate vegetation on rocks, here seem to have taken on a life of their own. The rocks also seem alive—about to swallow up the monk and his hut. Throughout his life Shitao continued to identify himself with the fallen Ming, and he felt that his secure world had turned to chaos with the Manchu conquest.

THE MODERN PERIOD

In the mid and late nineteenth century, China was shaken from centuries of complacency by a series of humiliating military defeats at the hands of Western powers and Japan. Only then did the government finally realize that these new rivals were not like the Mongols of the thirteenth century. China was no longer at the center of the world, a civilized country surrounded by "barbarians." Spiritual resistance was no longer sufficient to solve the problems brought on by change. New ideas from Japan and the West began to filter in, and the demand arose for political and cultural reforms. In 1911 the Qing dynasty was overthrown, ending 2,000 years of imperial rule, and China was reconceived as a republic.

During the first decades of the twentieth century Chinese artists traveled to Japan and Europe to study Western art. Returning to China, many sought to introduce the ideas and techniques they had learned, and they explored ways to synthesize the Chinese and the Western traditions. After the establishment of the present-day Communist government in 1949, individual artistic freedom was curtailed as the arts were pressed into the service of the state and its vision of a new social order. After 1979, however, cultural attitudes began to relax, and Chinese painters again pursued their own paths.

WU GUANZHONG. One artist who emerged during the 1980s as a leader in Chinese painting is Wu Guanzhong (b. 1919). Combining his French artistic training and Chinese background, Wu Guanzhong developed a semiabstract style to depict scenes from the Chinese landscape. He made preliminary sketches on site, then, back in his studio, he developed these sketches into free interpretations based on his feeling and vision. An example of his work, **PINE SPIRIT**, depicts a scene in the Huang (Yellow) Mountains (**FIG. 24–14**). The technique, with its sweeping gestures of paint, is clearly linked to Abstract Expressionism, an influential Western movement of the post–World War II years (Chapter 32); yet the painting also claims a place in the long tradition of Chinese landscape as exemplified by such masters as Shitao.

Like all aspects of Chinese society, Chinese art has felt the strong impact of Western influence, and the question remains whether Chinese artists will absorb Western ideas without losing their traditional identity. Interestingly, landscape remains an important subject, as it has been for more than a thousand years, and calligraphy continues to play a vital role. Using the techniques and methods of the West, some of China's artists have joined an international avant-garde (see, for example, Wenda Gu in Chapter 32), while other painters still seek communion with nature through their ink brushstrokes as a means to come to terms with human life and the world.

24-14 • Wu Guanzhong PINE SPIRIT
1984. Ink and color on paper, 2′3⅝″ × 5′3½″ (0.70 × 1.61 m). Spencer Museum of Art, The University of Kansas, Lawrence. Gift of the E. Rhodes and Leonard B. Carpenter Foundation

ARTS OF KOREA: THE JOSEON DYNASTY TO THE MODERN ERA

In 1392, General Yi Seonggye (1335–1408) overthrew the Goryeo dynasty (918–1392), establishing the Joseon dynasty (1392–1910), sometimes called the Yi dynasty. He first maintained his capital at Gaeseong, the old Goryeo capital, but moved it to Seoul in 1394, where it remained through the end of the dynasty. The Joseon regime rejected Buddhism, espousing Neo-Confucianism as the state philosophy. Taking Ming-dynasty China as its model, the new government patterned its bureaucracy on that of the Ming emperors, even adopting as its own such outward symbols of Ming imperial authority as blue-and-white porcelain. The early Joseon era was a period of cultural refinement and scientific achievement, during which Koreans invented Han'geul (the Korean alphabet) and movable type, not to mention the rain gauge, astrolabe, celestial globe, sundial, and water clock.

JOSEON CERAMICS

Like their Silla and Goryeo forebears (see Chapter 10), Joseon potters excelled in the manufacture of ceramics, taking their cue from contemporaneous Chinese wares, but seldom copying them directly.

BUNCHEONG CERAMICS. Descended from Goryeo celadons, Joseon-dynasty stonewares, known as *buncheong* wares, enjoyed widespread usage throughout the peninsula. Their decorative effect relies on the use of white slip that makes the humble stoneware resemble more expensive white porcelain. In fifteenth-century examples, the slip is often seen inlaid into repeating design elements stamped into the body.

Sixteenth-century *buncheong* wares are characteristically embellished with wonderfully fluid, calligraphic brushwork painted in iron-brown slip on a white slip ground. Most painted *buncheong* wares have stylized floral décor, but rare pieces, such as the charming wine bottle in **FIGURE 24–15**, feature pictorial decoration. In fresh, lively brushstrokes, a bird with outstretched wings grasps a fish that it has just caught in its talons; waves roll below, while two giant lotus blossoms frame the scene.

Japanese armies repeatedly invaded the Korean peninsula between 1592 and 1597, destroying many of the *buncheong* kilns, and essentially bringing the ware's production to a halt. Tradition holds that the Japanese took many *buncheong* potters home with them to produce *buncheong*-style wares, which were greatly admired by connoisseurs of the tea ceremony. In fact, the spontaneity of Korean *buncheong* pottery has inspired Japanese ceramics to this day.

PAINTED PORCELAIN. Korean potters produced porcelains with designs painted in underglaze cobalt blue as early as the fifteenth century, inspired by Chinese porcelains of the early Ming period (SEE FIG. 24–7). The Korean court dispatched artists from the royal painting academy to the porcelain kilns—located some 30 miles southeast of Seoul—to train porcelain decorators. As a result, from the fifteenth century onward, the painting on the best Korean porcelains closely approximated that on paper and silk, unlike in China, where ceramic decoration followed a path of its own with but scant reference to painting traditions.

In another unique development, Korean porcelains from the sixteenth and seventeenth centuries often feature designs painted in underglaze iron-brown rather than the cobalt blue customary in Ming porcelain. Also uniquely Korean are porcelain jars with bulging shoulders, slender bases, and short, vertical necks, which

24-15 • HORIZONTAL WINE BOTTLE WITH DECORATION OF A BIRD CARRYING A NEWLY CAUGHT FISH
Korea. Joseon dynasty, 16th century. *Buncheong* ware: light gray stoneware with decoration painted in iron-brown slip on a white slip ground, 6¹⁄₁₀ × 9½″ (15.5 × 24.1 cm). Museum of Oriental Ceramics, Osaka, Japan. Gift of the Sumitomo Group (20773)

24-16 • BROAD-SHOULDERED JAR WITH DECORATION OF A FRUITING GRAPEVINE
Korea. Joseon dynasty, 17th century. Porcelain with decoration painted in underglaze iron-brown slip, height 22⅛″ (53.8 cm). Ewha Women's University Museum, Seoul, Republic of Korea.

Chinese potters invented porcelain during the Tang dynasty, probably in the eighth century. Generally fired in the range of 1300° to 1400° C, porcelain is a high-fired, white-bodied ceramic ware. Its unique feature is its translucency. Korean potters learned to make porcelain during the Goryeo dynasty, probably as early as the eleventh or twelfth century, though few Goryeo examples remain today. For many centuries, only the Chinese and Koreans were able to produce porcelains.

appeared by the seventeenth century and came to be the most characteristic ceramic shapes in the later Joseon period. Painted in underglaze iron-brown, the seventeenth-century jar shown in **FIGURE 24–16** depicts a fruiting grape branch around its shoulder. In typical Korean fashion, the design spreads over a surface unconstrained by borders, resulting in a balanced but asymmetrical design that incorporates the Korean taste for unornamented spaces.

JOSEON PAINTING

Korean secular painting came into its own during the Joseon dynasty. Continuing Goryeo traditions, early Joseon examples employ Chinese styles and formats, their range of subjects expanding from botanical motifs to include landscapes, figures, and a variety of animals.

Painted in 1447 by An Gyeon (b. 1418), **DREAM JOURNEY TO THE PEACH BLOSSOM LAND** (**FIG. 24–17**) is the earliest extant and dated Joseon secular painting. It illustrates a fanciful tale by China's revered nature poet Tao Qian (365–427), and recounts a dream about chancing upon a utopia secluded from the world for centuries while meandering among the peach blossoms of spring.

As with their Goryeo forebears, the monumental mountains and vast, panoramic vistas of such fifteenth-century Korean paintings, echo Northern Song painting styles. Chinese paintings of the Southern Song (1127–1279) and Ming periods (1368–1644) also influenced Korean painting of the fifteenth, sixteenth, and seventeenth centuries, though these styles never completely supplanted the imprint of the Northern Song masters.

THE SILHAK MOVEMENT. In the eighteenth century, a truly Korean style emerged, inspired by the *silhak* ("practical learning") movement, which emphasized the study of things Korean in addition to the Chinese classics. The impact of the movement is

24-17 • An Gyeon DREAM JOURNEY TO THE PEACH BLOSSOM LAND
Korea. Joseon dynasty, 1447. Handscroll, ink and light colors on silk, 15¼ × 41¾″ (38.7 × 106.1 cm). Central Library, Tenri University, Tenri (near Nara), Japan.

金剛全圖
謙齋

萬二千峯皆骨山何人用
意貌真顏衆香浮
勃扶尔外
積氣雄鎊
世界
问
或团
芙蓉乎素
或车林松
柏保玄闹很今脚
楮顶今通事似枕邊者不憷
甲寅
冬題

24-18 • Jeong Seon
PANORAMIC VIEW OF THE
DIAMOND MOUNTAINS
(GEUMGANG-SAN)
Korean. Joseon Dynasty, 1734. Hanging
scroll, ink and colors on paper,
40⅝ × 37″ (130.1 × 94 cm). Lee'um,
Samsung Museum, Seoul, Republic
of Korea.

exemplified by the painter Jeong Seon (1676–1759), who chose well-known Korean vistas as the subjects of his paintings, rather than the Chinese themes favored by earlier artists. Among Jeong Seon's paintings are numerous representations of the Diamond Mountains (Geumgang-san), a celebrated range of craggy peaks along Korea's east coast. Painted in 1734, the scroll reproduced in **FIGURE 24–18** aptly captures the Diamond Mountains' needlelike peaks. The subject is Korean, and so is the energetic spirit and the intensely personal style, with its crystalline mountains, distant clouds of delicate ink wash, and individualistic brushwork.

Among figure painters, Sin Yunbok (b. 1758) is an important exemplar of the *silhak* attitude. Active in the late eighteenth and early nineteenth centuries, Sin typically depicted aristocratic figures in native Korean garb. The album leaf entitled **PICNIC AT THE LOTUS POND (FIG. 24–19)** represents a group of Korean gentlemen enjoying themselves in the countryside on an autumn day in the company of several *gisaeng* (female entertainers). The figures are recognizably Korean—the women with their full coiffures, short jackets, and generous skirts, and the men with their beards, white robes, and wide-brimmed hats woven of horsehair and coated with black lacquer. The stringed instrument played by

24–19 • Sin Yunbok PICNIC AT THE LOTUS POND
Leaf from an album of genre scenes. Korea. Joseon dynasty, late 18th century. Album of 30 leaves;
ink and colors on paper, 11⅛ × 13⅞″ (28.3 × 35.2 cm). Kansong Museum of Art, Seoul, Republic of Korea.

the gentleman seated at lower right is a *gayageum* (Korean zither), the most hallowed of all Korean musical instruments.

MODERN KOREA

Long known as "the Hermit Kingdom," the Joseon dynasty pursued a policy of isolationism, closing its borders to most of the world, except China, until 1876. Japan's annexation of Korea in 1910 brought the Joseon dynasty to a close, but effectively prolonged the country's seclusion from the outside world. The legacy of self-imposed isolation compounded by colonial occupation (1910–1945)—not to mention the harsh circumstances imposed by World War II (1939–1945), followed by the even worse conditions of the Korean War (1950–1953)—impeded Korea's artistic and cultural development during the first half of the twentieth century.

A MODERNIST PAINTER FROM KOREA. Despite these privations, some modern influences did reach Korea indirectly via China and Japan, and beginning in the 1920s and 1930s a few Korean artists experimented with contemporary Western styles, typically painting in the manner of Cézanne or Gauguin, but sometimes trying abstract, nonrepresentational styles. Among these, Gim Hwangi (1913–1974) was influenced by Constructivism and geometric abstraction and would become one of twentieth-century Korea's influential painters. Like many Korean artists after the Korean War, Gim wanted to examine Western modernism at its source. He visited Paris in 1956 and then, from 1964 to 1974, lived and worked in New York, where he produced his best-known works. His painting **5-IV-71** presents a large pair of circular radiating patterns composed of small dots and squares in tones of blue, black, and gray **(FIG. 24–20)**. While appearing wholly Western in style, medium, concept, and even title—Gim Hwangi typically adopted the date of a work's creation as its title—*5-IV-71* also seems related to Asia's venerable tradition of monochrome **ink painting**, while suggesting a transcendence that seems Daoist or

24-20 • Gim Hwangi 5-IV-71 Korea. 1971. Oil on canvas, 39½ × 39½″ (100 × 100 cm). Whanki Museum, Seoul, Republic of Korea.

Buddhist in feeling. Given that the artist was Korean, that he learned the Chinese classics in his youth, that he studied art in Paris, and that he then worked in New York, it is possible that his painting embodies all of the above. Gim's painting illustrates the paradox that the modern artist faces while finding a distinctive, personal style: whether to paint in an updated version of a traditional style, in a wholly international style, in an international style with a distinctive local twist, or in an eclectic, hybrid style that incorporates both native and naturalized elements from diverse traditions. By addressing these questions, Gim Hwangi blazed a trail for subsequent Korean-born artists, such as the renowned video artist Nam June Paik (1932–2006), whose work can be seen in FIGURE 32–57.

THINK ABOUT IT

24.1 Explain the role played by one of the following three ways of thought prevalent in Chinese society—Daoism, Confucianism, and Buddhism—and discuss the implications that it had for the visual arts. Make specific reference to works from this chapter.

24.2 Examine a work commissioned by the court at Beijing and distinguish which of its features are typical of court art.

24.3 Discuss the place that calligraphy held within Chinese society and in relation to other arts. Then, explain why Dong Qichang's *The Qingbian Mountains* (SEE FIG. 24–11) has elicited comparison with the art of calligraphy.

24.4 Discuss the culture of the literati, including their values and their system of art patronage, and distinguish the formats of painting that they used.

24.5 Theorize reasons for the emergence of individualist painting in China, using works such as Shitao's *Landscape* (SEE FIG. 24–13) to support your argument.

PRACTICE MORE: Compose answers to these questions, get flashcards for images and terms, and review chapter material with quizzes **www.myartslab.com**

**25-1 • Suzuki Harunobu THE FLOWERS OF BEAUTY IN THE FLOATING WORLD:
MOTOURA AND YAEZAKURA OF THE MINAMI YAMASAKIYA**   Edo period, 1769.
Polychrome woodblock print on paper, 11⅜ × 8½″ (28.9 × 21.8 cm). Chicago Art Institute.
Clarence Buckingham Collection (1925.2116)

JAPANESE ART
AFTER 1333

Lounging at a window seat, a young woman pauses from smoking her pipe while the young girl at her side peers intently through a telescope at boats in a bay below (FIG. 25–1). The scene takes place in the city of Edo (now Tokyo) in the 1760s, during an era of peace and prosperity that started some 150 years earlier when the Tokugawa shoguns unified the nation. Edo was then the largest city in the world, with over 1 million inhabitants: samurai-bureaucrats and working-class townspeople. The commoners possessed a vibrant culture centered in urban entertainment districts, where geisha and courtesans (licenced prostitutes), such as the lady and her young trainee portrayed in this woodblock print, worked.

In the 1630s, the Tokugawa shogunate banned Japanese citizens from traveling abroad and restricted foreign access to the country. Nagasaki became Japan's sole international port, which only Koreans, Chinese, and Dutch could enter (and they could not travel freely around the country). The government did this to deter Christian missionaries and to assert authority over foreign powers. Not until 1853, when Commodore Matthew Perry of the United States forced Japan to open additional ports, did these policies change. Even so, foreign influences could not be prevented, as the tobacco pipe and telescope in this print testify.

The Japanese had first encountered Westerners—Portuguese traders—in the mid sixteenth century. The Dutch reached Japan by 1600 and brought tobacco and, soon after that, the telescope and other exotic optical devices, including spectacles, microscopes, other curious objects, and books, many illustrated. The Japanese people eagerly welcomed these foreign goods and imitated foreign customs, which conferred an air of sophistication on the user. Looking through the telescopes like the one in this print was a popular amusement of prostitutes and their customers. It also conveyed sexual overtones, because of its phallic shape, and suggests the ribald humor then in vogue. Novel optical devices, all readily available by the mid eighteenth century, offered a new way of seeing, and impacted the appearance of Japanese pictorial art. Yet Chinese influences in the arts still remained strong and spread throughout the population as never before, due to new efforts to educate the broader populace in Chinese studies. In varying degrees, the intermingling of diverse native and foreign artistic traditions has continued to shape the arts of Japan up to the present.

LEARN ABOUT IT

25.1 Evaluate the importance of Zen Buddhism to Japan's visual arts.

25.2 Compare art created in Kyoto to art made in the city of Edo during the Edo period.

25.3 Appraise the role and significance of crafts in Japanese artistic culture.

25.4 Recognize foreign influences on Japanese art in the Muromachi and Edo periods.

25.5 Understand the changing role of patronage in the development of Japanese art.

HEAR MORE: Listen to an audio file of your chapter **www.myartslab.com**

MUROMACHI PERIOD

By the year 1333, Japanese art had already developed a long and rich history (see "Foundations of Japanese Culture," page 817). Very early, a particularly Japanese sensitivity to artistic production had emerged, including a love of natural materials, fondness for representing elements of the natural world, and an overriding attention to fine craftsmanship. Aesthetically, Japanese arts had come to feature a taste for asymmetry, abstraction, brevity or boldness of expression, and humor—characteristics that continue to distinguish Japanese art, appearing and reappearing in ever-changing guises.

Late in the twelfth century, the authority of the emperor had been supplanted by rule by powerful and ambitious warriors (samurai) under the leadership of the shogun, the general-in-chief. But in 1333, Emperor Go-Daigo attempted to retake power. He failed and was forced into hiding in the mountains south of Kyoto where he set up a "southern court." Meanwhile, the shogunal family then in power, the Minamoto, was overthrown by warriors of the Ashikaga clan, who placed a rival to the upstart emperor on the throne in Kyoto, in a "northern court," and had him declare their clan head as shogun. They ruled the country from the Muromachi district in Kyoto, and finally vanquished the southern court emperors in 1392. The Muromachi period, also known as the Ashikaga era (1392–1573), formally began with this event.

The Muromachi period is marked by the ascendance of Zen Buddhism, introduced into Japan in the late twelfth century, whose austere ideals particularly appealed to the highly disciplined samurai. While Pure Land Buddhism, which had spread widely during the latter part of the Heian period (794–1185), remained popular, Zen (which means meditation) became the dominant cultural force in Japan among the ruling elite.

ZEN INK PAINTING

During the Muromachi period, brightly colored narrative handscrolls depicting native themes continued to be produced, but monochrome ink painting in black ink and its diluted grays—which had just been introduced to Japan from the continent at the end of the Kamakura period (1185–1333)—reigned supreme. Muromachi ink painting was heavily influenced by the aesthetics of Zen, but unlike earlier Zen paintings that had concentrated on depictions of important individuals associated with the Zen monastic tradition, many artists also began painting Chinese-style ink landscapes. Traditionally, the monk-artist Shubun (active c. 1418–1463) is regarded as Japan's first great master of the ink landscape. Unfortunately, no works survive that can be proven to be his. Two landscapes by Shubun's pupil Bunsei (active c. 1450–1460) have survived, however. The one shown in **FIGURE 25–2** is closely modeled on Korean ink landscape paintings that themselves copied Chinese Ming period models (such as FIG. 24–5). It contains a foreground consisting of a spit of rocky land with an overlapping series of motifs—a spiky pine tree, a craggy rock, a poet seated in a hermitage, and a brushwood fence

MAP 25–1 • JAPAN

Japan's wholehearted emulation of myriad aspects of Chinese culture began in the fifth century and was challenged by new influences from the West only in the mid nineteenth century after Western powers forced Japan to open its treaty ports to international trade.

surrounding a small garden of trees and bamboo. In the middle ground is space—emptiness, the void. We are expected to "read" the empty paper as representing water. Beyond the blank space, subtle tones of gray ink delineate a distant shore where fishing boats, a small hut, and two people stand. The two parts of the painting seem to echo each other across a vast expanse. The painting illustrates well the pure, lonely, and ultimately serene spirit of the Zen-influenced poetic landscape tradition.

SESSHU. Another of Shubun's pupils, Sesshu (1420–1506), outshone his master, and has come to be regarded as one of the greatest Japanese painters of all time. Although they completed training to become Zen monks, at the monastery, Shubun and his followers specialized in art rather than in religious ritual or teaching, unlike earlier Zen monk-painters for whom art production was just one facet of their lives. By Shubun's day, temples had formed their own to head a small provincial Zen temple in western Japan, in his quest to concentrate on painting unencumbered by monastic duties and entanglements with the political elite. His new temple was patronized by a private and wealthy warrior clan that was engaged in trade with China. With funding from them, he had the opportunity to visit China in 1467 on a diplomatic mission. He traveled extensively there for three years, viewing the scenery, stopping at Zen (Chan in Chinese) monasteries, and studying Chinese paintings by professional artists rather than those by contemporary literati masters. When he returned from China, he remained in the provinces to avoid the turmoil in Kyoto, which was being devastated by civil warfare that would last for the next hundred years. Only a few paintings from Sesshu's years prior to his sojourn in China have recently come to light. These he painted in a style closer to Shubun and he signed them with another name. His paintings after his return demonstrate he consciously broke artistically with the refined landscape style of his teacher. These masterful paintings by Sesshu exhibit a bold, new spirit, evident in his **WINTER LANDSCAPE** (**FIG. 25–3**). A cliff descending from the mist seems to cut the composition in two. Sharp, jagged brushstrokes delineate a series of

25-2 • Bunsei LANDSCAPE
Muromachi period, mid 15th century. Hanging scroll, ink and light colors on paper, 28¾ × 13″ (73.2 × 33 cm). Museum of Fine Arts, Boston. Special Chinese and Japanese Fund (05.203)

25-3 • Sesshu WINTER LANDSCAPE
Muromachi period, c. 1470s. Hanging scroll, ink on paper, 18¼ × 11½″ (46.3 × 29.3 cm). Collection of the Tokyo National Museum. National Treasure.

professional painting ateliers in order to meet demands for large numbers of paintings from warrior patrons. Sesshu trained as a Zen monk at Shokokuji, where Shubun had his studio. There, he worked in the painting atelier under Shubun for 20 years, but then left Kyoto rocky hills, where a lone figure makes his way to a Zen monastery. Instead of a gradual recession into space, flat overlapping planes fracture the composition into crystalline facets. The white of the paper is left to indicate snow, while the sky is suggested by tones of gray. A few trees cling desperately to the rocky land, and the harsh chill of winter is boldly expressed.

THE ZEN DRY GARDEN

Zen monks led austere monastic lives in their quest for the attainment of enlightenment. In addition to daily meditation, they engaged in manual labor to provide for themselves and maintain their temple properties. Many Zen temples constructed dry landscape courtyard gardens, not for strolling in but for contemplative viewing. Cleaning and maintaining these gardens—pulling weeds, tweaking unruly shoots, and raking the gravel—was a kind of active meditation. It helped to keep their minds grounded.

The dry landscape gardens of Japan, *karesansui* ("dried-up mountains and water"), exist in perfect harmony with Zen Buddhism. The dry garden in front of the abbot's quarters in the Zen temple at Ryoanji is one of the most renowned Zen creations in Japan (**FIG. 25–4**). A flat rectangle of raked gravel, about 29 by 70 feet, surrounds 15 stones of different sizes in islands of moss. The stones are set in asymmetrical groups of two, three, and five. Low, plaster-covered walls establish the garden's boundaries, but beyond the perimeter wall maple, pine, and cherry trees add color and texture to the scene. Called "borrowed scenery," these elements are a considered part of the design even though they grow outside the garden. The garden is celebrated for its severity and emptiness.

Dry gardens began to be built in the fifteenth and sixteenth centuries in Japan. By the sixteenth century, Chinese landscape painting influenced the gardens' composition, and miniature clipped plants and beautiful stones were arranged to resemble famous paintings. Especially fine and unusual stones were coveted and even carried off as war booty, such was the cultural value of these seemingly mundane objects.

The Ryoanji garden's design, as we see it today, probably dates from the mid seventeenth century. By the time the garden was created, such stone and gravel gardens had become highly intellectualized, abstract reflections of nature. This garden has been interpreted as representing islands in the sea, or mountain peaks rising above the clouds, perhaps even a swimming tigress with her cubs, or constellations of stars and planets. All or none of these interpretations may be equally satisfying—or irrelevant—to a monk seeking clarity of mind through contemplation.

25-4 • ROCK GARDEN, RYOANJI, KYOTO
Muromachi period, c. 1480. Photographed spring 1993. Photograph by Michael S. Yamashita. UNESCO World Heritage Site, National Treasure.

The American composer John Cage once exclaimed that every stone at Ryoanji was in just the right place. He then said, "And every other place would also be just right." His remark is thoroughly Zen in spirit. There are many ways to experience Ryoanji. For example, we can imagine the rocks as having different visual "pulls" that relate them to one another. Yet there is also enough space between them to give each one a sense of self-sufficiency and permanence.

ART AND ITS CONTEXTS

Foundations of Japanese Culture

With the end of the last Ice Age roughly 15,000 years ago, rising sea levels submerged the lowlands connecting Japan to the Asian landmass, creating the chain of islands we know today as Japan (MAP 25–1). Not long afterward, early Paleolithic cultures gave way to a Neolithic culture known as Jomon (c. 11,000–400 BCE) after its characteristic cord-marked pottery. During the Jomon period, a sophisticated hunter-gatherer culture developed. Agriculture supplemented hunting and gathering by around 5000 BCE, and rice cultivation began some 4,000 years later.

A fully settled agricultural society emerged during the Yayoi period (c. 400 BCE–300 CE), accompanied by hierarchical social organization and more centralized forms of government. As people learned to manufacture bronze and iron, use of those metals became widespread. Yayoi architecture, with its unpainted wood and thatched roofs, already showed the Japanese affinity for natural materials and clean lines, and the style of Yayoi granaries in particular persisted in the design of shrines in later centuries. The trend toward centralization continued during the Kofun period (c. 300–552 CE), an era characterized by the construction of large royal tombs, following the Korean practice. Veneration of leaders grew into the beginnings of the imperial system that has lasted to the present day.

The Asuka era (552–645 CE) began with a century of profound change as elements of Chinese civilization flooded into Japan, initially through the intermediary of Korea. The three most significant Chinese contributions to the developing Japanese culture were Buddhism (with its attendant art and architecture), a system of writing, and the structures of a centralized bureaucracy. The earliest extant Buddhist temple compound in Japan, Horyuji, which contains the oldest currently existing wooden buildings in the world, dates from this period.

The arrival of Buddhism also prompted some formalization of Shinto, the loose collection of indigenous Japanese beliefs and practices. Shinto is a religion that connects people to nature. Its rites are shamanistic and emphasize ceremonial purification. These include the invocation and appeasement of spirits, including those of the recently dead. Many Shinto deities are thought to inhabit various aspects of nature, such as particularly magnificent trees, rocks, and waterfalls, and living creatures such as deer. Shinto and Buddhism have in common an intense awareness of the transience of life, and as their goals are complementary—purification in the case of Shinto, enlightenment in the case of Buddhism—they have generally existed comfortably alongside each other to the present day.

The Nara period (645–794) takes its name from Japan's first permanently established imperial capital. During this time the founding works of Japanese literature were compiled and Buddhism became the most important force in Japanese culture. Its influence at court grew so great that in 794 the emperor moved the capital from Nara to Heian-kyo (present-day Kyoto), far from powerful monasteries.

During the Heian period (794–1185) an extremely refined court culture thrived, embodied today in an exquisite legacy of poetry, calligraphy, and painting. An efficient method for writing the Japanese language was developed, and with it a woman at the court wrote Japan's most celebrated fictional story, which some describe as the world's first novel: *The Tale of Genji*. Esoteric Buddhism, as hierarchical and intricate as the aristocratic world of the court, became popular.

The end of the Heian period was marked by civil warfare as regional warrior (samurai) clans were drawn into the factional conflicts at court. Pure Land Buddhism, with its simple message of salvation, offered consolation to many in troubled times. In 1185 the Minamoto clan defeated their arch rivals, the Taira, and their leader, Minamoto Yoritomo, assumed the position of shogun (general-in-chief). While paying respects to the emperor, Minamoto Yoritomo kept actual military and political power to himself, setting up his own capital in Kamakura. The Kamakura era (1185–1333) began a tradition of rule by shogun that lasted in various forms until 1868. It was also the time in which renewed contacts with China created the opportunity for Zen Buddhism, which was then flourishing in China (known there as Chan), to be introduced to Japan. By the end of the Kamakura period, numerous Zen monasteries had been founded in Kyoto and Kamakura, and Chinese and Japanese Chan/Zen monks were regularly visiting each others' countries.

MOMOYAMA PERIOD

The civil wars sweeping Japan laid bare the basic flaw in the Ashikaga system, which was that samurai were primarily loyal to their own feudal lord (*daimyo*), rather than to the central government. Battles between feudal clans grew more frequent, and it became clear that only a warrior powerful and bold enough to unite the entire country could control Japan. As the Muromachi period drew to a close, three leaders emerged who would change the course of Japanese history.

The first of these leaders was Oda Nobunaga (1534–1582), who marched his army into Kyoto in 1568 and overthrew the reigning Ashikaga shogun in 1573, initiating a new age of Japanese politics. A ruthless warrior, Nobunaga went so far as to destroy a Buddhist monastery because the monks refused to join his forces. Yet he was also a patron of the most rarefied and refined arts. Assassinated in the midst of one of his military campaigns, Nobunaga was succeeded by one of his generals, Toyotomi Hideyoshi (1537–1598), who soon gained complete power in Japan. He, too, patronized the arts when not leading his army, and he considered culture a vital adjunct to his rule. Hideyoshi, however, was overly ambitious. He believed that he could conquer both Korea and China, and he wasted much of his resources on two ill-fated invasions. A stable and long-lasting military regime

25-5 • HIMEJI CASTLE, HYOGO, NEAR OSAKA
Momoyama period, 1601–1609. Unesco World Heritage Site, National Treasure.

finally emerged soon after 1600 with the triumph of a third leader, Tokugawa Ieyasu (1543–1616), a former ally of Nobunaga who served as a senior retainer to Hideyoshi, and only asserted his power after Hideyoshi's death. But despite its turbulence, the era of Nobunaga and Hideyoshi, known as the Momoyama period (1573–1615), was one of the most creative eras in Japanese history.

Today the very word Momoyama conjures up images of bold warriors, luxurious palaces, screens shimmering with gold leaf, and, in contrast, rustic tea-ceremony ceramics. Europeans first made an impact in Japan at this time. After the arrival of a few wayward Portuguese explorers in 1543, traders and missionaries soon followed. It was only with the rise of Nobunaga, however, that Westerners were able to extend their activities beyond the ports of Kyushu, Japan's southernmost island. Nobunaga welcomed foreign traders, who brought him various products, the most influential of which were firearms.

ARCHITECTURE

European muskets and cannons quickly changed the nature of Japanese warfare and Japanese castle architecture. To protect castles from these new weapons, in the late sixteenth century they became heavily fortified garrisons. Some were eventually lost to warfare or torn down by victorious enemies, and others have been extensively altered over the years. One of the most beautiful of the few that have survived intact is Himeji, not far from the city of Osaka (**FIG. 25–5**). Rising high on a hill above the plains, Himeji has been given the name White Heron. To reach the upper fortress, visitors must follow angular paths beneath steep walls, climbing from one area to the next past stone ramparts and through narrow fortified gates, all the while feeling as though lost in a maze, with no sense of direction or progress. At the main building, a further climb up a series of narrow ladders leads to the uppermost chamber. There, the footsore visitor is rewarded with a stunning 360-degree view of the surrounding countryside.

DECORATIVE PAINTINGS FOR *SHOIN* ROOMS

Castles such as Himeji were sumptuously decorated, offering artists unprecedented opportunities to work on a grand scale. Interiors were divided into rooms by paper-covered sliding doors (**fusuma**), perfect canvases for large-scale murals. Free-standing folding screens (*byobu*) were also popular. Some had gold-leaf backgrounds, whose glistening surfaces not only conveyed light within the castle rooms but also displayed the wealth of the warrior leaders. Temples, too, commissioned large-scale paintings in these formats for grand reception rooms where the monks met with their wealthy warrior patrons (see "*Shoin* Design," opposite).

The Japanese tea ceremony and *shoin*-style interior residential architecture are undoubtedly the most significant and most enduring expressions of Japanese taste to emerge during the Momoyama period. **Shoin** combine a number of interior features in more-or-less standard ways, though no two rooms are ever the same. These features include wide verandas, walls divided by wood posts, floors covered with woven straw *tatami* mats, recessed panels in ceilings, sometimes painted and sometimes covered with reed matting, several shallow alcoves for prescribed purposes, *fusuma* (paper-covered sliding doors), and **shoji** screens—wood frames covered with translucent rice paper. The *shoin* illustrated here was built in 1601 as a guest hall, called Kojoin, at the Buddhist temple of Onjoji near Kyoto.

The *shoin* is a formal room for receiving important upper-class guests. With some variations due to differences in status, these rooms were designed for buildings used by samurai, aristocrats, and even well-to-do commoners. They are found in various types of buildings including private residences, living quarters at religious complexes (both Shinto shrines and Buddhist temples) and guesthouses or reception rooms at these places for use by high-ranking patrons, and at the finest houses of entertainment (such as seen in fig. 25–1) where geisha and courtesans entertained important guests. The owner of the building or the most important guest would be seated in front of the main alcove (*tokonoma*), which would contain a hanging scroll, an arrangement of flowers, or a large painted screen. Alongside that alcove was another that featured staggered shelves, often for displaying writing instruments. The veranda side of the room also contained a writing space fitted with a low writing desk.

The architectural harmony of a *shoin* is derived from standardization of its basic units, or modules. In Japanese carpentry, the common module of design and construction is the **bay**, reckoned as the distance from the center of one post to the center of another, which is governed in turn by the standard size of **tatami** floor mats. Although varying slightly from region to region, the size of a single *tatami* is about 3 by 6 feet. Room area in Japan is still expressed in terms of the number of *tatami* mats; for example, a room may be described as an eight-mat room.

shoji

veranda   writing alcove   *tokonoma*   *tatami*   staggered shelves   *fusuma*

ARTIST'S RENDERING OF THE KOJOIN GUEST HOUSE AT ONJOJI
Otsu, Shiga prefecture. Momoyama period, 1601. National Treasure.

SEE MORE: View a simulation of *Shoin* Design **www.myartslab.com**

Daitokuji, a celebrated Zen monastery in Kyoto, has a number of subtemples for which Momoyama artists painted magnificent *fusuma*. One, the Jukoin, possesses *fusuma* by Kano Eitoku (1543–1590), one of the most brilliant painters from the hereditary lineage of professional artists known as the Kano school. Eitoku headed this school, which was founded by his grandfather. The Kano school painted for the highest ranking warriors from the sixteenth century through 1868. They perfected a new style that combined the Muromachi ink-painting tradition with brightly colored decorative subjects. **FIGURE 25–6** shows two of the three walls of **FUSUMA** panels at Jukoin painted by Eitoku when was in his mid twenties. To the left, the subject is the familiar Kano school theme of cranes and pines, both symbols of long life; to the right is a great gnarled plum tree, symbol of spring. The trees are so massive they seem to extend far beyond the panels. An island rounding both walls of the far corner provides a focus for the outreaching trees. Ingeniously, it

25-6 • Kano Eitoku FUSUMA
Depicting pine and cranes (left) and plum tree (right) from the central room of the Jukoin, Daitokuji, Kyoto. Momoyama period, c. 1563–1573. *Fusuma* (sliding door panels), ink and gold on paper, height 5′9⅛″ (1.76 m). National Treasure.

belongs to both compositions at the same time, thus uniting them into an organic whole. Eitoku's vigorous use of brush and ink, his powerfully jagged outlines, and his dramatic compositions recall the style of Sesshu, but the bold new sense of scale in his works is a defining characteristic of the Momoyama period.

THE TEA CEREMONY

Japanese art is never one-sided. Along with castles and their opulent interior decoration, there was an equal interest during the Momoyama period in the quiet, the restrained, and the natural. This was expressed primarily through the tea ceremony.

The term "tea ceremony," a phrase now in common use, does not convey the full meaning of *chanoyu*, the Japanese ritual drinking of tea, which has no counterpart in Western culture. Tea had been introduced to Japan in the ninth century. Then, it was molded into cakes and boiled. However, the advent of Zen brought to Japan a different way of preparing tea, with the leaves crushed into powder and then whisked in bowls with hot water. Zen monks used such tea as a mild stimulant to aid meditation. Others found it had medicinal properties.

SEN NO RIKYU.   The most famous tea master in Japanese history was Sen no Rikyu (1522–1591). He conceived of the tea ceremony as an intimate gathering in which a few people would enter a small rustic room, drink tea carefully prepared in front of them by their host, and quietly discuss the tea utensils or a Zen scroll hanging on the wall. He largely established the aesthetic of modesty, refinement, and rusticity that permitted the tearoom to serve as a respite from the busy and sometimes violent world outside. A traditional tearoom combines simple elegance and rusticity. It is made of natural materials such as bamboo and wood,

with mud walls, paper windows, and a floor covered with *tatami*. One tearoom that preserves Rikyu's design is named Taian **(FIG. 25–7)**. Built in 1582, it has a tiny door (guests must crawl to enter)

25-7 • Sen no Rikyu TAIAN TEAROOM
Myokian Temple, Kyoto. Momoyama period, 1582. National Treasure.

and miniature *tokonoma* for displaying a Zen scroll or a simple flower arrangement. At first glance, the room seems symmetrical. But a longer look reveals the disposition of the *tatami* does not match the spacing of the *tokonoma*, providing a subtle undercurrent of irregularity. The walls seem scratched and worn with age, but the *tatami* are replaced frequently to keep them clean and fresh. The mood is quiet; the light is muted and diffused through three small paper windows. Above all, there is a sense of spatial clarity. Nonessentials have been eliminated, so there is nothing to distract from focused attention. This tearoom aesthetic became an important element in Japanese culture.

THE TEA BOWL. Every utensil connected with tea, including the water pot, the kettle, the bamboo spoon, the whisk, the tea caddy, and, above all, the tea bowl, came to be appreciated for its aesthetic quality, and many works of art were created for use in *chanoyu*.

The age-old Japanese admiration for the natural and the asymmetrical found full expression in tea ceramics. Korean-style rice bowls made for peasants were suddenly considered the epitome of refined taste, and tea masters urged potters to mimic their imperfect shapes. But not every misshapen bowl would be admired. A rarified appreciation of beauty developed that took into consideration such factors as how well a tea bowl fitted into the hands, how subtly the shape and texture of the bowl appealed to the eye, and who had previously used and admired it. For this purpose, the inscribed storage box became almost as important as the ceramic that fitted within it, and if a bowl had been given a name by a leading tea master, it was especially treasured by later generations.

One of the finest tea bowls extant is named Mount Fuji after Japan's most sacred peak (FIG. 25–8). (Mount Fuji is depicted in FIGURE 25–12.) An example of **raku** ware—a hand-built, low-fired ceramic developed for use in the tea ceremony—the bowl was crafted by Hon'ami Koetsu (1558–1637), a leading cultural figure of his day. Koetsu was most famous as a calligrapher, but he was also a painter, poet, lacquer designer, sword connoisseur, and potter. With its small foot, straight sides, irregular shape, and crackled texture, this bowl exemplifies tea taste.

EDO PERIOD

When Tokugawa Ieyasu gained control of Japan, he forced the emperor to proclaim him shogun, a title neither Nobunaga nor Hideyoshi had held. His reign initiated the Edo period (1615–1868), named after the city that he founded (present-day Tokyo) as his capital. This period is alternatively known as the Tokugawa era. Under the rule of the Tokugawa family, peace and prosperity came at the price of a rigid and repressive bureaucracy. The problem of a potentially rebellious *daimyo* was solved by ordering all feudal lords to spend either half of each year, or every other year, in Edo, where their families were required to live. Zen Buddhism was supplanted as the prevailing intellectual force by a

25-8 • Hon'ami Koetsu TEA BOWL, CALLED MOUNT FUJI
Momoyama-Edo period, early 17th century. *Raku* ware, height 3⅜″ (8.5 cm). Sakai Collection, Tokyo. National Treasure.

Connoisseurs developed a subtle vocabulary to discuss the aesthetics of tea. A favorite term was *sabi* ("loneliness"), which refers to the tranquility found when feeling alone. Other virtues were *wabi* ("poverty"), which suggests the artlessness of humble simplicity, and *shibui* ("bitter" or "astringent"), meaning elegant restraint. Tea bowls, such as this example, embody these aesthetics.

form of Neo-Confucianism, a philosophy formulated in Song-dynasty China that emphasized loyalty to the state, although the popularity of Buddhism among the commoner population surged at this time.

The shogunate officially divided Edo society into four classes. Samurai officials constituted the highest class, followed by farmers, artisans, and finally merchants. As time went on, however, merchants began to control the money supply, and in Japan's increasingly mercantile economy their accumulation of wealth soon exceeded that of the samurai, which helped, unofficially, to elevate their status. Reading and writing became widespread at all levels of society, and with literacy came intellectual curiosity and interest in the arts. All segments of the population—including samurai, merchants, townspeople, and rural peasants—were able to patronize artists. A rich cultural atmosphere developed unlike anything Japan had experienced before, in which artists worked in a wide variety of styles that appealed to these different groups of consumers.

RINPA SCHOOL PAINTING

During the Edo period, Edo was the shogun's city while life in Kyoto took its cues from the emperor and his court who resided there. Kyoto was also home to wealthy merchants, artists, and craftsmakers who served the needs of the courtiers and shared their interest in refined pursuits, such as the tea ceremony, and also their appreciation of art styles that recalled those perfected by aristocratic

THE OBJECT SPEAKS

Lacquer Box for Writing Implements

This lacquer box reflects the collaborative nature of Japanese artistic production and the fluidity with which artists worked in various media. It was designed by the Rinpa school painter Ogata Korin (1658–1716), who oversaw its execution, although he left the actual work to trained crafts specialists. He also frequently collaborated with his brother Kenzan, a celebrated potter. The upper tray housed writing implements, the larger bottom section stored paper (see "Inside a Writing Box," page 824). Korin's design sets a motif of irises and a plank bridge in a dramatic asymmetrical combination of mother-of-pearl, silver, lead, and gold lacquer. The subject was one he frequently also represented in painting because it was immensely popular with the educated Japanese of his day. They immediately recognized the imagery as an allusion to a famous passage from the tenth-century *Tales of Ise*, a classic of Japanese literature. A nobleman poet, having left his wife in the capital, pauses at a place called Eight Bridges, where a river branches into eight streams, each covered

with a plank bridge. Irises are in full bloom, and his traveling companions urge the poet to write a *waka*—a five-line, 31-syllable poem—beginning each line with a syllable from the word for "iris": *Kakitsubata* (*ka-ki-tsu-ba-ta*). The poet responds (substituting *ha* for *ba*):

Karagoromo
kitsutsu narenishi
tsuma shi areba
harubaru kinuru
tabi o shi zo omou.
When I remember
my wife, fond and familiar
as my courtly robe,
I feel how far and distant
my travels have taken me.
(Translated by Stephen Addiss)

The poem in association with the scene became so famous that any image of a group of irises, with or without a plank bridge, immediately calls the episode to mind.

Lacquer is derived in Asia from the sap of the lacquer tree, *Rhus verniciflua*,

indigenous to China but very early in history also grown commercially throughout east Asia. It is gathered by tapping into a tree and letting the sap flow into a container. It can be colored with vegetable or mineral dyes. Applied in thin coats to a surface of wood or leather, lacquer hardens into a glasslike protective coating that is waterproof, heat- and acid-resistant, and airtight. Its practical qualities made it ideal for storage containers, and vessels for food and drink. The creation of a piece of lacquer can take several years. First, the item is fashioned of wood and sanded smooth. Next, up to 30 layers of lacquer are thinly applied, each dried and polished before the next is brushed on.

Japanese craftsmakers exploited the decorative potential of lacquer to create expensive luxury items, such as this box, which was created when lacquer arts had been perfected. It features inlays of mother-of-pearl and precious metals in a style known as *makie* ("sprinkled design"), in which flaked or powdered gold or silver was embedded in a still-damp coat of lacquer.

Ogata Korin **LACQUER BOX FOR WRITING IMPLEMENTS**
Edo period, late 17th–early 18th century. Lacquer, lead, silver, and mother-of-pearl, 5⅝ × 10¾ × 7¾" (14.2 × 27.4 × 19.7 cm). Tokyo National Museum, Tokyo. National Treasure.

DETAILS OF BOX INTERIOR AND LID
Left: interior of lid;
center: top tray with ink stone and waterpot;
right: exterior view of box lid.

25–9 • Tawaraya Sotatsu WAVES AT MATSUSHIMA
Edo period, 17th century. Pair of six-panel folding screens, ink, mineral colors, and gold leaf on paper; each screen 4′9⅞″ × 11′8½″ (1.52 × 3.56 m). Freer Gallery of Art, Smithsonian Institution, Washington, D.C. Gift of Charles Lang Freer (F1906.231 & 232)

The six-panel screen format was a triumph of scale and practicality. Each panel consisted of a light wood frame surrounding a latticework interior covered with several layers of paper. Over this foundation was pasted a high-quality paper, silk, or gold-leaf ground, ready to be painted by the finest artists. Held together with ingenious paper hinges, a screen could be folded for storage or transportation, resulting in a mural-size painting light enough to be carried by a single person, ready to be displayed as needed.

artists in the Heian period. The most famous and original Kyoto painter who worked for this group of patrons was Tawaraya Sotatsu (active c. 1600–40), who occasionally collaborated with the potter Koetsu (SEE FIG. 25–8). Sotatsu is considered the first great painter of the Rinpa school, the modern name given to a group of artists whose art reinterpreted ancient courtly-style arts. These artists are grouped together because of their shared interests and art styles,

and did not constitute a formal school, such as the Kano. Rinpa masters were not just painters, however: They sometimes collaborated with craftsmakers (see "Lacquer Box for Writing Implements," opposite).

One of Sotatsu's most famous pairs of screens depict the islands of Matsushima near the northern city of Sendai (FIG. 25–9). On the right screen (shown here on top), mountainous islands echo

Writing boxes hold tools basic for both writing and painting: ink stick, ink stone, brushes, and paper, which are beautiful objects in their own right.

Ink sticks are basically soot from burning wood or oil that is bound into a paste with resin, and pressed into small stick-shaped or cake-shaped molds to harden.

Fresh ink is made for each writing or painting session by grinding the hard, dry ink stick in water against a fine-grained stone. A typical ink stone has a shallow well at one end sloping up to a grinding surface at the other. The artist fills the well with water from a waterpot. The ink stick, held vertically, is dipped into the well to pick up a small amount of water, then is rubbed in a circular motion firmly on the grinding surface. Grinding ink is viewed as a meditative task, time for collecting one's thoughts and concentrating on the painting or calligraphy ahead.

Brushes are made from animal hair set in simple bamboo or hollow-reed handles. Brushes taper to a fine point that responds sensitively to any shift in pressure. Although great painters and calligraphers do eventually develop their own styles of holding and using the brush, all begin by learning the basic position for writing. The brush is held vertically, grasped firmly between the thumb and first two fingers, with the fourth and fifth fingers often resting against the handle for more subtle control.

well

ink stone

ink stick

writing implements

brushes

the swing and sweep of the waves, with stylized gold clouds in the upper left. The left screen continues the gold clouds until they become a sand spit from which twisted pines grow. Their branches seem to lean toward a strange island in the lower left, composed of an organic, amoebalike form in gold surrounded by mottled ink. This mottled effect was a specialty of Rinpa school painters.

As one of the "three famous beautiful views of Japan," Matsushima was often depicted in art. Most painters showed the pine-covered islands that make the area famous from above. Sotatsu's genius was to portray them in an abbreviated manner and from a fresh vantage point, as though the viewer were passing the islands in a boat on the roiling waters. The artist's asymmetrical composition and use of thick mineral colors in combination with soft, playful brushwork and sparkling gold leaf create the boldly decorative effect that is the hallmark of the Rinpa tradition.

NATURALISTIC PAINTING

NAGASAWA ROSETSU. By the middle of the eighteenth century, the taste of wealthy Kyoto merchants had shifted, influencing the styles of artists who competed for their patronage. The public was enthralled with novel imagery captured in magnifying glasses, telescopes, and an optical device that enhanced the three-

25–10 • Nagasawa Rosetsu BULL AND PUPPY
Edo period, late 18th century. Left of a pair of six-panel screens, ink and gold wash on paper, 5′7¼″ × 12′3″ (1.70 × 3.75 m). Los Angeles County Museum of Art, California. Joe and Etsuko Price Collection (L.83.45.3a)

dimensional effects of Western-style perspective pictures. Schools of independent artists emerged in Kyoto to satisfy demands for naturalistic-style paintings that reflected this fascination. The most influential was founded by Maruyama Okyo, who had perfected methods to incorporate Western shading and perspective into a more native Japanese decorative style, creating a sense of volume new to east Asian painting, while still retaining a sense of familiarity.

Okyo's most famous pupil was Nagasawa Rosetsu (1754–1799), a painter of great natural talent who added his own boldness and humor to his master's tradition. Rosetsu delighted in surprising his viewers with odd juxtapositions and unusual compositions. One of his finest works is a pair of screens, the left one depicting a bull and a puppy (FIG. 25–10). The bull is so immense that his mammoth body exceeds the borders of the screen, undoubtedly influenced by new optical devices. The puppy, white against the dark gray of the bull, helps to emphasize the huge size of the bull by its own smallness. The puppy's relaxed and informal pose, looking happily right out at the viewer, gives this powerful painting a humorous touch that increases its charm. In the hands of a master such as Rosetsu, plebeian subject matter became simultaneously delightful and monumental.

LITERATI PAINTING

Because the city of Kyoto was far from the watchful eyes of the government in Edo, and the emperor resided there with his court, it enjoyed a degree of privilege and independence not found in any other Japanese city. These conditions allowed for the creation of art in the new Rinpa and naturalistic styles. They also encouraged the emergence of new schools of philosophy based on interpretations of Chinese Confucianism that disagreed with those taught at schools sponsored by Tokugawa shoguns. These new interpretations incorporated ideas from Chinese Daoism, which promoted cultivation of a person's uniqueness, thus encouraging artistic creativity. Kyoto's intellectuals, who admired Chinese culture, even created a new, more informal tea ceremony of their own, featuring steeped tea called *sencha* because it was the tea drunk by Ming-dynasty Chinese literati. They did this as political protest—by then *chanoyu* had become encumbered by rules and was closely associated with the repressive shogunate. Influenced by the new ideas, a Chinese manner of painting arose in the mid eighteenth century in emulation of Chinese literati painting. Artists who embraced this style, both professionals who painted for paying clients and amateurs who painted for their own enjoyment, quickly grew to number hundreds as its popularity spread throughout Japan alongside increased interest in drinking *sencha*, as well as in other aspects of Chinese culture. They learned about Chinese literati painting from paintings and woodblock-printed painting manuals imported from China, and also from Chinese emigrant monks and merchants who lived in Japan.

The best and most successful of these artists took Chinese literati painting models as starting points for their original interpretations of literati themes. One of them was Ike Taiga (1723–1776),

admired as much for his magnetic personality as for his art. He was born into a poor farming family near Kyoto and showed innate talent for painting at a young age. Moving to Kyoto in his teens, he became friends with Chinese scholars there, including those who promoted drinking *sencha*. Taiga became a leader in this group, attracting admirers who were enamored of both his quasi-amateurish painting style and his quest for spiritual self-cultivation. His character and personal style are seen in the scintillating, rhythmic layering of strokes used to define the mountains in his **TRUE VIEW OF KOJIMA BAY (FIG. 25–11)** which blends Chinese

25–11 • Ike Taiga TRUE VIEW OF KOJIMA BAY
Edo period, third quarter of 18th century. Hanging scroll, ink and color on silk. 39¼ × 14⅝″ (99.7 × 37.6 cm). Hosomi Museum, Kyoto.

The production of woodblock prints combined the expertise of three people: the artist, the carver, and the printer. Coordinating and funding the endeavor was a publisher, who commissioned the project and distributed the prints to stores or itinerant peddlers, who would sell them.

The artist supplied the master drawing for the print, executing its outlines with brush and ink on tissue paper. Colors might be indicated, but more often they were understood or decided on later. The drawing was passed on to the carver, who pasted it face down on a hardwood block, preferably cherrywood, so that the outlines showed through the paper in reverse. A light coating of oil might be brushed on to make

Toshusai Sharaku ONOE MATSUSUKE AS MATSUSHITA MIKINOSHIN
Edo period, 1794–95. Polychrome woodblock print, ink and colors on mica ground paper, 14³⁄₁₆ × 9¹¹⁄₁₆″ (36.1 × 24.6 cm). British Museum, London. (1909,0618,0.42)

the paper more transparent, allowing the drawing to stand out clearly. The carver then cut around the lines of the drawing with a sharp knife, always working in the same direction as the original brushstrokes. The rest of the block was chiseled away, leaving the outlines in relief. This block, which reproduced the master drawing, was called the **key block**. If the print was to be **polychrome**, having multiple colors, prints made from the key block were in turn pasted face down on blocks that would be used as guides for the carver of the color blocks. Each color generally required a separate block, although both sides of a block might be used for economy.

Once the blocks were completed, the printer took over. Paper for printing was covered lightly with animal glue (gelatin). Before printing, the paper was lightly moistened so that it would take ink and color well. Water-based ink or color was brushed over the block, and the paper placed on top and rubbed with a smooth, padded device called a *baren*, until the design was completely transferred. The key block was printed first, then the colors one by one. Each block was carved with two small marks called **registration marks**, in exactly the same place in the margins, outside of the image area—an L in one corner, and a straight line in another. By aligning the paper with these marks before letting it fall over the block, the printer ensured that the colors would be placed correctly within the outlines. One of the most characteristic effects of later Japanese prints is a grading of color from dark to pale. This was achieved by wiping some of the color from the block before printing, or by moistening the block and then applying the color gradually with an unevenly loaded brush—a brush loaded on one side with full-strength color and on the other with diluted color.

Much as people today buy posters of their favorite sports, music, or movie stars, so, too, in the Edo period people clamored for images of their idols, actors of the popular form of drama known as Kabuki. The artist of this print was renowned for capturing the personality of his subjects. The actor has his eyes crossed, in what was a frozen, tension-filled moment in an action-packed play. The print has a shiny mica background, made of crushed shells, painstakingly applied by printers.

SEE MORE: View a video about the printmaking process of woodcut **www.myartslab.com**

models, Japanese aesthetics, and personal brushwork. The gentle rounded forms of the mountains intentionally recall the work of famous Chinese literati painters, and Taiga utilizes a stock landscape composition that separates foreground and background mountains with a watery expanse (SEE FIG. 25–2). However, he did not paint an imaginary Chinese scene but a personal vision of an actual Japanese place that he had visited—Kojima Bay—as a document accompanying the painting explains. Still, in deference to his admiration for Chinese literati, Taiga places two figures clad in Chinese robes on the right, midway up the mountain.

UKIYO-E: PICTURES OF THE FLOATING WORLD

Edo served as the shogun's capital as well as the center of a flourishing popular culture associated with tradespeople. Deeply Buddhist, commoners were acutely aware of the transience of life, symbolized, for example, by the cherry tree which blossoms so briefly. Putting a positive spin on this harsh realization, they sought to live by the mantra: Let's enjoy it to the full as long as it lasts. This they did to excess in the restaurants, theaters, bathhouses, and brothels of the city's pleasure quarters, named after the Buddhist phrase *ukiyo* ("floating world"). Every major city in Japan had these

25-12 • Katsushika Hokusai THE GREAT WAVE
From *Thirty-Six Views of Mt. Fuji*. Edo period, c. 1831. Polychrome woodblock print on paper, 9⅞ × 14⅝″
(25 × 37.1 cm). Honolulu Academy of Arts, Honolulu, Hawaii. James A. Michener Collection (HAA 13, 695)

EXPLORE MORE: Gain insight from a primary source related to *The Great Wave* **www.myartslab.com**

quarters, and most were licensed by the government. But those of Edo were the largest and most famous. The heroes of the floating world were not famous samurai or aristocratic poets. Instead, swashbuckling Kabuki actors and beautiful courtesans were admired. These paragons of pleasure soon became immortalized in paintings and—because paintings were too expensive for common people—in woodblock prints known as *ukiyo-e* ("pictures of the floating world"; see "Japanese Woodblock Prints," opposite). Most prints were inexpensively produced by the hundreds and not considered serious fine art. Yet when first imported to Europe and America, they were immediately acclaimed and strongly influenced late nineteenth- and early twentieth-century Western art (see Chapter 30).

HARUNOBU. The first woodblock prints had no color, only black outlines. Soon artists added colors by hand to make them more resemble paintings. But to produce colored prints more rapidly they gradually devised a system to print colors using multiple blocks. The first artist to design prints that took advantage of this new technique,

known as **nishiki-e** ("brocade pictures"), was Suzuki Harunobu (1724–1770), famous for his images of courtesans (SEE FIG. 25–1).

HOKUSAI. During the first half of the nineteenth century, the heyday of popular travel, pictures of famous sights of Japan grew immensely popular. The two most famous *ukiyo-e* printmakers, Utagawa Hiroshige (1797–1858) and Katsushika Hokusai (1760–1849), specialized in this genre. Hiroshige's *Fifty-Three Stations of the Tokaido* and Hokusai's *Thirty-Six Views of Mt. Fuji* became the most successful sets of graphic art the world has known. The woodblocks were printed, and printed again, until they wore out. They were then recarved, and still more copies were printed. This process continued for decades, and thousands of prints from the two series are still extant.

THE GREAT WAVE (FIG. 25–12) is the most famous of the scenes from *Thirty-Six Views of Mt. Fuji*. The great wave rears up like a dragon with claws of foam, ready to crash down on the figures huddled in the boats below. Exactly at the point of imminent disaster, but far in the distance, rises Japan's most sacred peak, Mount Fuji, whose slopes, we suddenly realize, swing up like waves and whose snowy crown is like foam—comparisons the artist makes clear in the wave nearest us, caught just at the moment of greatest resemblance. In the late nineteenth century when Japonisme, or *japonism*, became the vogue in the West, Hokusai's art was greatly appreciated, even more so than it had been in Japan: The first book on the artist was published in France.

ZEN PAINTING: BUDDHIST ART FOR RURAL COMMONERS

Outside Japan's urban centers, art for commoners also flourished, much of it tied to their devotion to Buddhism. Deprived of the support of the samurai officials who now favored Confucianism, Buddhism nevertheless thrived during the Edo period through patronage from private individuals, many of them rural peasants. In the early eighteenth century, one of the great monks who preached in the countryside was the Zen master Hakuin Ekaku (1685–1769), born in a small village near Mount Fuji. After hearing a fire-and-brimstone sermon in his youth he resolved to become a monk and for years he traveled around Japan seeking out the strictest Zen teachers. He became the most important Zen master of the last 500 years, and invented many *koan* (questions posed to novices by Zen masters to guide their progression towards enlightenment during meditation), including the famous "What is the sound of one hand clapping?" He was also, in his later years, a self-taught painter and calligrapher, who freely gave away his scrolls to admirers (who included not only farmers but also artisans, merchants, and even samurai) as a way of spreading his religious message.

Hakuin's art differed from that of Muromachi period monk-painters like Bunsei and Sesshu (SEE FIGS. 25–2, 25–3). His work featured everyday Japanese subjects or Zen themes that conveyed his ideas in ways his humble followers could easily understand. He often painted Daruma (Bodhidharma in Sanskrit) **(FIG. 25–13)**, the semilegendary Indian monk who founded Zen (see Chapter 11). Hundreds of Zen monks of the Edo period and later created simply brushed Zen ink paintings. Hakuin largely set the standards that subsequent Zen artists followed.

CRAFTS

The ingenuity and technical proficiency that contributed to the development of *ukiyo*-prints came about because of Japan's long history of fine crafts production. Textiles, ceramics, lacquer, woodwork, and metalwork were among the many crafts in which Japanese artisans excelled. In pre-modern Japan, unlike the West, no separate words distinguished fine arts (painting and sculpture) from crafts. (The Japanese word for fine art and corresponding modern Japanese language words for various types of craft were not coined until 1872.) This was largely because professional Japanese artist and crafts studios basically followed the same hereditary, hierarchical structure. A master artist directed all

activity in a workshop of trainees, who gradually gained seniority through years of apprenticeship and innate talent. Sometimes, such as when a pupil was not chosen to succeed the master, he would go off and start his own studio. This teamwork approach to artistic production is characteristic of the way most traditional Japanese arts were created.

25-13 • Hakuin Ekaku GIANT DARUMA
Edo period, mid 18th century. Hanging scroll, ink on paper 4′3½″ × 1′9¾″ (130.8 × 55.2 cm). Manyo'an Collection, New Orleans 1973.2

As a self-taught amateur painter, Hakuin's painting style is the very antithesis of that of consummate professionals, such as painters of the Kano or Rinpa schools. The appeal of his art lies in its artless charm, humor, and astonishing force. Here Hakuin has portrayed the wide-eyed Daruma during his nine years of meditation in front of a temple wall in China. Intensity, concentration, and spiritual depth are conveyed by a minimal number of broad, forceful brushstrokes. The inscription is the ultimate Zen message, attributed to Daruma himself: "Pointing directly to the human heart, see your own nature and become Buddha."

Kosode Robe ›

With design of waves and floral bouquets. Edo period, second half of 18th century to early 19th century.
White figured satin ground with silk and metallic thread embroidery, stencil tie-dyeing, brush painting; indigo blue dyed silk lining, height 64¾″ (163 cm), width 24½″ (61.5 cm) below sleeve, 50″ (127 cm) sleeve top. The Nelson-Atkins Museum of Art, Kansas City, Missouri. Gift of Mrs. Harold J. Owens (57-45)

The white silk background is woven with a key-fret textured pattern.

Ink drawing was used to define the vines, leaves, ribbons, and flower petals.

Embroidery with gold and brightly colored thread embellishes the flowers and leaves.

Stencil dyeing makes up some of the leaf, flower, and wave patterns.

SEE MORE: View the Closer Look feature for *Kosode* Robe **www.myartslab.com**

KOSODE ROBES. The kimono is as much a symbol of Japanese culture as is the tea ceremony. Before the late nineteenth century, it was known as *kosode*. These loose, unstructured garments that wrap around the body and are cinched with a sash were the principal outer article of clothing of both men and women, beginning in the Muromachi period. *Kosode* ("small sleeves") refers to the vertical length of the sleeves (in contrast, young, unmarried women wore robes with long, flowing sleeves). Because of their fragility, few *kosode* prior to the Edo period

survive. But those from the eighteenth century reveal the opulent tastes of affluent merchant-class women of the day (see "A Closer Look," page 830). In the example shown, ribbons and flower bouquets float above abstract waves and scalloped-edged clouds in a playful, asymmetrical composition. Artisans used many techniques to create the rich interplay of textures and designs on this gorgeous robe, made in the country's premier textile center of Kyoto. Its design elements resemble those found in paintings of the period.

THE MODERN PERIOD

The tensions that resulted from Commodore Matthew Perry's forced opening of trade ports in Japan in 1853 precipitated the downfall of the Tokugawa shogunate. In 1868 the emperor was formally restored to power, an event known as the Meiji Restoration. The court soon moved from Kyoto to Edo, which was renamed Tokyo ("Eastern Capital"). After a period of intense industrialization in the first two decades after the Meiji Restoration, influential private individuals and government officials, sometimes working cooperatively, created new arts institutions including juried exhibitions, artists' associations, arts universities, and cultural heritage laws. These rekindled appreciation for the art of the past, encouraged

25-14 • LARGE PLATE WITH LEAF DESIGN
Edo period, early 18th century. Arita ware, *Ko*-Imari type. Porcelain with underglaze blue decoration, diameter 15⅜" (39.1 cm). Nelson-Atkins Museum of Art, Kansas City. Purchase: Nelson Trust (63-4)

JAPANESE PORCELAIN.   While the history of ceramic production dates to the earliest days of Japanese civilization, production of glazed, high-fired stoneware ceramics proliferated in Japan only from the sixteenth century, encouraged largely by the tea ceremony. The industry thrived in southern Japan, where, around 1600, influxes of more highly skilled Korean potters helped native artisans to learn new continental technologies that allowed them to manufacture porcelain for the first time. One town, Arita, became the center for the production of porcelain, created for export to the West and for domestic use. While tea ceremony aesthetics still favored rustic wares such as Koetsu's tea bowl (SEE FIG. 25–8), porcelain was more widely adopted for everyday use in response to a growing fashion for Chinese arts. Porcelains made in Arita are known by various names according to their dating and decorative schemes. Those ornamented exclusively with underglaze cobalt blue, the first porcelains made in Japan, are generally known as Imari, the name for the port city from which some of them were exported to Europe. However, the piece shown in **FIGURE 25–14** must have been made for domestic use, as the audaciously abstracted design would not have appealed to Europeans, who preferred more recognizable natural forms. Complementing the strong, vertical stylized leaves are small, half-round forms resembling chestnuts.

25-15 • Yokoyama Taikan FLOATING LIGHTS
Meiji period, 1909. One of a pair of hanging scrolls, ink, colors, and gold on silk, 56½ × 20½" (143 × 52 cm). The Museum of Modern Art, Ibaraki.

perpetuation of artistic techniques threatened by adoption of Western ways, and stimulated new artistic production. Many of these arts institutions still exist today.

MEIJI-PERIOD NATIONALIST PAINTING

The Meiji period (1868–1912) marked a major change for Japan. Japanese society adapted various aspects of Western education, governmental systems, clothing, medicine, industrialization, and technology in efforts to modernize the nation. Teachers of sculpture and oil painting came from Italy, while adventurous Japanese artists traveled to Europe and America to study.

A MEIJI PAINTER. Ernest Fenollosa (1853–1908), an American who had recently graduated from Harvard, traveled to Japan in 1878 to teach philosophy and political economy at Tokyo University. Within a few years, he and a former student, Okakura Kakuzo (1862–1913), began urging artists to study traditional Japanese arts rather than to focus exclusively on Western art styles and media, but infuse them with a modern sensibility. Yokoyama Taikan (1868–1958) subsequently developed his personal style within the Nihonga (modern Japanese painting) genre promoted by Okakura. Encouraged by Okakura, who had gone there before him, Taikan visited India in 1903. He embraced Okakura's ideals of pan-Asian cultural nationalism, expressed in the first line of Okakura's book, *Ideals of the East* (1903), with the words "Asia is One." This outlook later contributed to fueling Japan's imperialist ambitions. Taikan's **FLOATING LIGHTS (FIG. 25–15)** was inspired by a visit to Calcutta, where he observed women engaged in divination on the banks of the Ganges. The naturalism of their semitransparent robes and the flowing water reveal his indebtedness to Western art. In contrast, the lightly applied colors, and graceful branches with delicate, mottled brushwork defining the leaves, recall techniques of Rinpa-school artists.

JAPAN AFTER WORLD WAR II

In the aftermath of World War II (1941–1945), Japan was a shambles, her great cities ruined. Nevertheless, under the U.S.-led Allied Occupation (1946–1952), the Japanese people immediately began rebuilding, unified by a sense of national purpose. Within ten years, Japan established nascent automobile, electronics, and consumer goods industries. Rail travel, begun in 1872, expanded and improved significantly after the war and by the time of the Tokyo Olympics in 1964 the capital had an extensive commuter rail system, and Japan was the world leader in city-to-city high-speed rail transit with its new Shinkansen (bullet train). As the rest of the world came to know Japan, foreign interest in its arts focused especially on the country's still thriving crafts traditions. Not only were these a source of national pride and identity, the skills and attitudes they fostered also served as the basis for Japan's national revival.

POSTWAR ARCHITECTURE. The Hiroshima Peace Memorial Museum and Park **(FIG. 25–16)** was one of the first monuments constructed after World War II. A memorial to those who perished on August 6, 1945, and an expression of prayers for world peace, it attests to the spirit of the Japanese people at this difficult juncture in history. Tange Kenzo (1913–2005), who would eventually become one of the masters of Modernist architecture, designed the complex after winning an open competition as a young, up-and-coming architect.

The building's design befits the solemnity of its function. Concrete piers raise its stripped concrete form 20 feet off the ground. The wood formwork of the concrete recalls the wooden forms of traditional Japanese architecture. But the use of concrete is also inspired by Le Corbusier's 1920s Modernist villas. Evenly spaced vertical concrete fins lining the façade afford light shade. They suggest both the regular spacing of elements present in modular *shoin* architecture (see "*Shoin* Design," page 819) and the values of Modernist architects who advocated that structure should

25-16 • Tange Kenzo HIROSHIMA PEACE MEMORIAL MUSEUM
Showa period, 1955. Main building (center) repaired in Heisei period, 1991. East building (right), the former Peace Memorial Hall, which first opened in 1955, was rebuilt in June 1994 and attached to the main building. Designated UNESCO World Heritage site in 1996.

This exquisite wooden box was crafted by Eri Sayoko (1945–2007). In 2002, the government designated her a Living National Treasure for her accomplishment in the art of cut-gold leaf (*kirikane*), traditionally used to decorate Buddhist sculpture and paintings (as in FIG. 11–15). The National Treasure designation originated in Japanese laws of 1897 that were intended to safeguard the nation's artistic heritage at a time when art was being bought by Western collectors but suffering neglect at home. In 1955 the government added provisions to honor living individuals who excel in traditional craft techniques with the title Living National Treasure. This historic preservation system is the most complex of its type in the world.

Eri was the third person awarded the title for cut-gold-leaf decoration and the first woman. In its encouragement of traditional crafts, the Living National Treasure system has greatly assisted women in gaining much-deserved recognition. In pre-modern Japan (encompassing the prehistoric era up to the start of the Meiji period in 1868), women mostly operated in the private sphere of the home where they created crafts for their own enjoyment or for devotional purposes. By the eighteenth century, this situation had begun to change, so that women could be poets, calligraphers, and painters;

the wives or daughters of famous male artists gained the most recognition. Among the most famous was Gyokuran, wife of the literati painter Ike Taiga (SEE FIG. 25–11). However, the conservative nature of traditional Japanese crafts workshops meant women could not hold leadership positions in them, and until the postwar period they were seldom recognized for their achievements in crafts. Eri Sayoko flourished in the new climate, as one of the first women to work in the medium of cut-gold, which she took up via an unorthodox route.

Eri specialized in Japanese painting in high school and in design-dyeing in junior college. After marriage to a traditional Buddhist sculptor she started producing Buddhist paintings and began an apprenticeship with a master *kirikane* craftsman. She was so talented that after only three years she was able to exhibit her work professionally. Her art is informed by her deep study of the history of the technique, and her marvelous sensitivity for color betrays her training in dyeing. Eri's elegant, functional objects, typified by this box, are infused with modern sensibilities, although her designs have a basis in traditional *kirikane* patterns. Her art reveals that adherence to a craft tradition can still result in artistic originality.

Eri Sayoko ORNAMENTAL BOX: DANCING IN THE COSMOS
Heisei period, 2006. Wood with polychrome and cut gold, height 33⅞" (86 cm), width 6½" (16.5 cm), depth 6½" (16.5 cm). Collection of Eri Kokei.

dictate form. In this commission Tange infuses Modernist tendencies and materials with a Japanese sense of interval and refinement, characteristics also seen in the work of most younger contemporary Japanese architects active today.

POSTWAR CRAFTS. Throughout their history, the Japanese have displayed a heightened sensitivity toward the surface quality of things, for polish, for line, for exquisiteness and stylishness. Their appreciation of craft has continued to the present (see "Craftsmakers as Living National Treasures," above). Some crafts are made for use

in the tea ceremony, which remains popular today. Others are produced as functional objects for use in the home, as high-fashion apparel, or simply as decoration. Many combine diverse influences, native and foreign, that the maker integrates uniquely, often using novel techniques invented to achieve the desired results. In this way, the traditions of fine crafts in Japan, among the signature achievements of Japanese culture, continue to be enriched.

A MODERN CERAMICIST. Perhaps because the arts of tea ceremony and flower arrangement both require ceramic vessels,

25-17 • Fukami Sueharu SKY II
Heisei period, c. 1990. Celadon-glazed porcelain with wood base 3 × 44⅛ × 9½″ (7.7 × 112.1 × 24.2 cm).
Helen Foresman Spencer Museum of Art, University of Kansas, Lawrence, Kansas.
Museum purchase: R. Charles and Mary Margaret Clevenger Fund (1992.0072)

the Japanese have a particular love for pottery. While some ceramicists continue to create *raku* tea bowls and other traditional wares, others experiment with new styles and innovative techniques.

Fukami Sueharu (b. 1947) is among the most innovative clay artists in Japan today. Yet his art has roots in the past—in his case, in Chinese porcelains with pale bluish-green glazes (*seihakuji*). Even so, his forms and fabrication methods, typified by his **SKY II**, are ultramodern **(FIG. 25–17)**. He created the piece using a slip casting technique, in which he injected liquid clay into a mold using a high-pressure compressor. Although he sometimes makes functional pieces, mainly cylinders that could hold flower arrangements, *Sky II* shows his mastery of pure form. The title suggests sources of his abstract sculptural form: a wing or a blade of an aircraft slicing through the heavens. The pale blue sky-colored glaze enhances this allusion.

A plurality of artistic styles and media reflects Japan's long history and idiosyncratic worldview. While maintaining a strong sense of national identity, it has been able to absorb techniques and ideas from other lands, improve them, polish and refine them, and paradoxically make them its own. Deeply influenced by the Shinto and Buddhist religions, benefiting from a rich topography and mild climate, with citizens' lives revolving around a complex and hierarchical social structure, and reflecting a well-educated population curious about the rest of the world yet self-consciously different from it, the arts of Japan share common aesthetic principles that make them distinctively Japanese.

THINK ABOUT IT

25.1 Discuss the unique characteristics of Japanese Zen gardens, and explain how the rock garden at Ryoanji embodies the ideals of Zen Buddhism.

25.2 Explain how differences between pictorial styles of artists from the cities of Kyoto and Edo reflect the variations in the social status, and cultural and intellectual interests of the residents. Build your discussion upon a comparison of a painting or lacquer box by a Rinpa-school artist from Kyoto with a woodblock print that was made in Edo.

25.3 Discuss how the Japanese tea ceremony works and observe the role that craft arts play within it. Explore the unique aesthetics of the tearoom and craft arts associated with the ceremony, making reference to at least one work from this chapter.

25.4 Discuss Chinese influences on Japanese art styles and techniques in the Muromachi and Edo periods; for your answer, look back to Chapter 24 and draw specific comparisons between two works from each chapter.

25.5 Distinguish at least three different patron groups for Japanese arts and architecture in the Muromachi, Momoyama, and Edo periods. Discuss the kinds of arts and architecture each group preferred and how they were used by these patrons.

PRACTICE MORE: Compose answers to these questions, get flashcards for images and terms, and review chapter material with quizzes
www.myartslab.com

26-1 • Julia Jumbo TWO GREY HILLS TAPESTRY WEAVING Navajo, 2003.
Handspun wool, 36 × 24½″ (91.2 × 62.1 cm). Wheelwright Museum of the American Indian,
Santa Fe, New Mexico.

ART OF THE AMERICAS
AFTER 1300

According to Navajo mythology, the universe itself is a weaving, its fibers spun by Spider Woman out of sacred cosmic materials. Spider Woman taught the art of weaving to Changing Woman (a Mother Earth figure), and she in turn taught it to Navajo women, who continue to keep this art vital, seeing its continuation as a sacred responsibility. Early Navajo blankets were composed of simple horizontal stripes, but over time weavers have introduced more intricate patterns, and today Navajo rugs are woven in numerous distinctive styles.

The tapestry weaving in FIGURE 26–1 is designed in the Two Grey Hills style that developed during the early twentieth century around a trading post of that name in northwest New Mexico. Weavers who work in this style use the natural colors of undyed sheep's wool (only the black wool is sometimes dyed) to create dazzling geometric patterns. The artist Julia Jumbo (1928–2007), who learned to weave as a child, used her weavings to support her family. She raised her own sheep, and carded and spun her wool by hand before incorporating it into painstakingly made textiles. Jumbo is renowned for the clarity of her designs and the technical perfection of her fine weave. This outstanding work, created in 2003, attests to the vital and dynamic nature of Native American arts today.

When the first Europeans arrived, the Western Hemisphere was already inhabited from the Arctic Circle to Tierra del Fuego by peoples with long histories and rich cultural traditions (MAP 26–1). After 1492, when Christopher Columbus and his companions first sailed to the New World, the arrival of Europeans completely altered the destiny of the Americas. In Mesoamerica and South America the break with the past was sudden and violent: two great empires—the Aztec in Mexico and the Inca in South America—that had risen to prominence in the fifteenth century were rapidly destroyed. In North America the change took place more gradually, but the outcome was much the same. In both North and South America, natives succumbed to European diseases to which they had no immunity, especially smallpox, leading to massive population loss and social disruption. Over the next 400 years, many Native Americans were displaced from their ancestral homelands, and many present-day Native American ethnic groupings were formed by combinations of various survivor groups.

Despite all the disruption, during the past century the indigenous arts of the Americas have undergone a re-evaluation that has renewed the conception of what constitutes "American art." Native artists like Julia Jumbo continue to revive and reimagine indigenous traditions, revisit traditional outlooks, and restate their ancient customs and ideas in new ways. After being pushed to the brink of extinction, Native American cultures are experiencing a revival in both North and South America, as Native Americans assert themselves politically and insist on the connections between their history and the land.

LEARN ABOUT IT

26.1 Distinguish the styles, symbols, and techniques characteristic of Native American arts and crafts.

26.2 Explore the cultural developments and achievements of the Aztec and Inca empires.

26.3 Assess the role of portable and ephemeral media in the arts of the Americas.

26.4 Observe how indigenous arts have changed in the centuries since contact with Europe.

26.5 Explore the gender divisions in the production of the arts of the Americas.

HEAR MORE: Listen to an audio file of your chapter **www.myartslab.com**

THE AZTEC EMPIRE

In November 1519, the army of the Spanish soldier Hernán Cortés beheld for the first time the great Aztec capital of Tenochtitlan. The shimmering city, which seemed to be floating on the water, was built on an island in the middle of Lake Texcoco in the Valley of Mexico, and linked by broad causeways to the mainland. One of Cortés's companions later recalled the wonder the Spanish felt at that moment: "When we saw so many cities and villages built on the water and other great towns on dry land and that straight and level causeway going towards [Tenochtitlan], we were amazed … on account of the great towers and temples and buildings rising from the water, and all built of masonry. And some of our soldiers even asked whether the things that we saw were not a dream." (Bernal Díaz del Castillo, cited in Coe and Koontz 2005, p. 190.)

The Mexica people who lived in the remarkable city that Cortés found were then rulers of much of the land that later took their name, Mexico. Their rise to power had been recent and swift. Only 400 years earlier, according to their own legends, they had been a nomadic people living far north of the Valley of Mexico in a distant place called Aztlan. The term Aztec derives from the word Aztlan, and refers to all those living in Central Mexico who came from this mythical homeland, not just to the Mexica of Tenochtitlan.

The Mexica arrived in the Valley of Mexico in the thirteenth century. They eventually settled on an island in Lake Texcoco where they had seen an eagle perching on a prickly pear cactus (*nochtli*) growing out of a stone (*tetl*), a sign that their god Huitzilopochtli told them would mark the end of their wandering. They called the place Tenochtitlan. The city on the island was gradually expanded by reclaiming land from the lake, and serviced by a grid of artificial canals. In the fifteenth century, the Mexica—joined by allies in a triple alliance—began an aggressive campaign of expansion. The tribute they exacted from all over Mexico transformed Tenochtitlan into a glittering capital.

Aztec religion was based on a complex pantheon that combined Aztec deities with more ancient ones that had long been worshiped in central Mexico. According to Aztec belief, the gods had created the current era, or sun, at the ancient city of Teotihuacan in the Valley of Mexico (see Chapter 12). The continued existence of the world depended on human actions, including rituals of bloodletting and human sacrifice. Many Mesoamerican peoples believed that the world had been created multiple times before the present era. But while most Mesoamericans believed that they were living in the fourth era, or sun, the Mexica asserted that they lived in the fifth sun, a new era that coincided with the Aztec Empire. The Calendar Stone (see "A Closer Look," page 839) boldly makes this claim, using the dates of the destructions of the four previous eras to form the glyph that names the fifth sun, 4 Motion. The end of each period of 52 years in the Mesoamerican calendar was a particularly dangerous time that required a special fire-lighting ritual.

TENOCHTITLAN

An Aztec scribe drew an idealized representation of the city of Tenochtitlan and its sacred ceremonial precinct (**FIG. 26–2**) for the Spanish viceroy in 1545. It forms the first page of the *Codex Mendoza*. An eagle perched on a prickly pear cactus growing out of a stone—the symbol of the city—fills the center of the page. Waterways divide the city into four quarters, and indicate the lake surrounding the city. Early leaders of Tenochtitlan are shown sitting in the four quadrants. The victorious warriors at the bottom of the page represent Aztec conquests, and a count of years surrounds the entire scene. This image combines historical narration with idealized cartography, showing the city in the middle of the lake at the moment of its founding.

At the center of Tenochtitlan was the sacred precinct, a walled enclosure that contained dozens of temples and other buildings. The focal point of the sacred precinct was the Great Pyramid, a twin pyramid with paired temples on top: the one on the north dedicated to Tlaloc, an ancient rain god with a history extending

26-2 • THE FOUNDING OF TENOCHTITLAN
Page from *Codex Mendoza*. Mexico. Aztec, 1545. Ink and color on paper, 12⅜ × 8⁷⁄₁₆″ (21.5 × 31.5 cm). Bodleian Library, University of Oxford, England. MS. Arch Selden. A.1.fol. 2r

MAP 26–1 • THE AMERICAS AFTER 1300

Diverse cultures inhabited the Americas, each shaping a distinct artistic tradition.

back to Teotihuacan, and the one on the south dedicated to Huitzilopochtli, the solar god of the newly arrived Mexica tribe. Two steep staircases led up the west face of the pyramid from the plaza in front. Sacrificial victims climbed these stairs to the Temple of Huitzilopochtli, where priests threw them over a stone, quickly cut open their chests, and pulled out their still-throbbing hearts, a sacrifice that ensured the survival of the sun, the gods, and the Aztecs. The bodies were then rolled down the stairs and dismembered. Thousands of severed heads were said to have been kept on a skull rack in the plaza, represented in FIGURE 26–2 by the rack with a single skull to the right of the eagle.

During the winter rainy season the sun rose behind the Temple of Tlaloc, and during the dry season it rose behind the Temple of Huitzilopochtli. The double temple thus united two natural forces, sun and rain, or fire and water. During the spring and autumn equinoxes, the sun rose between the two temples.

SCULPTURE

Aztec sculpture was monumental, powerful, and often unsettling (see "A Closer Look," page 839). A particularly striking example is an imposing statue of Coatlicue, mother of the Mexica god Huitzilopochtli (FIG. 26–3). Coatlicue means "she of the serpent skirt," and this broad-shouldered figure with clawed feet has a skirt of twisted snakes. The statue may allude to the moment of Huitzilopochtli's birth: when Coatlicue conceived Huitzilopochtli from a ball of down, her other children—the stars and the moon—jealously conspired to kill her. As they attacked, Huitzilopochtli emerged from his mother's body fully grown and armed, drove off his half-brothers, and destroyed his half-sister, the moon goddess Coyolxauhqui. Coatlicue, however, did not survive the encounter. In this sculpture, she has been decapitated and a pair of serpents, symbols of gushing blood, rise from her neck to form her head. Their eyes are her eyes; their fangs, her tusks. Around her stump of

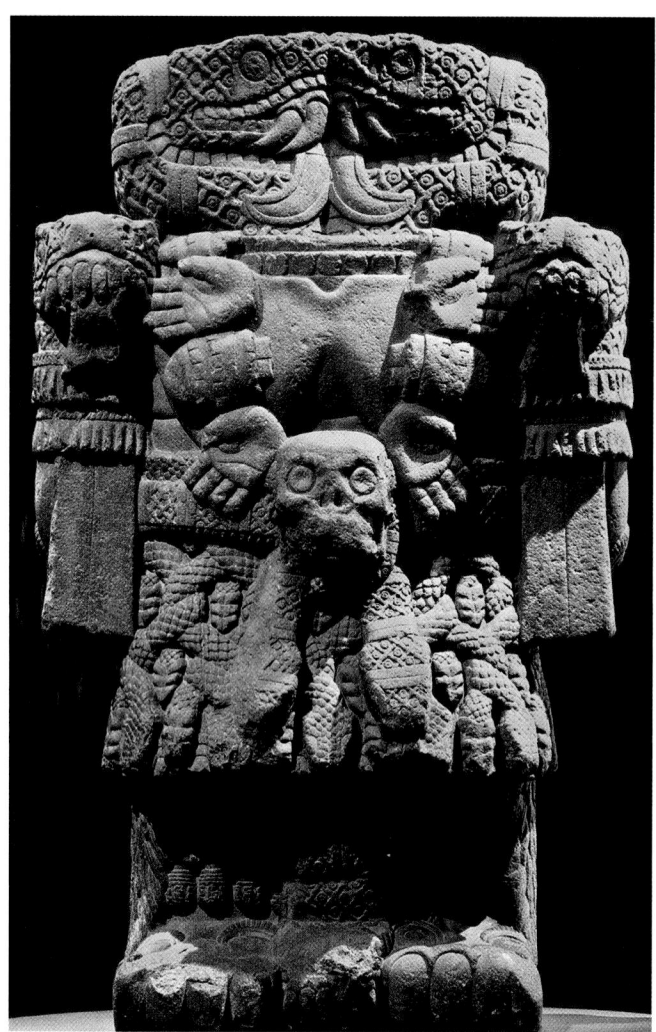

26-3 • THE GODDESS COATLICUE
Mexico. Aztec, c. 1500. Basalt, height 8′6″ (2.65 m).
Museo Nacional de Antropología, Mexico City.

a neck hangs a necklace of human hands, hearts, and a dangling skull. Despite the surface intricacy, the statue's massive form creates an impression of solidity, and the entire sculpture leans forward, looming over the viewer. The colors with which it was originally painted would have heightened its dramatic impact.

FEATHERWORK

Indeed Aztec art was colorful. An idea of its iridescent splendor is captured in the feather headdress **(FIG. 26–4)** said to have been given by the Aztec emperor Moctezuma to Cortés, and thought to be the one listed in the inventory of treasures Cortés shipped to Charles V, the Habsburg emperor in Spain, in 1519. Featherwork was one of the glories of Mesoamerican art but very few of these extremely fragile artworks survive. The tropical feathers in this headdress exemplify the exotic tribute paid to the Aztecs; the long iridescent green feathers that make up most of the headdress are the exceedingly rare tail feathers of the quetzal bird—each male quetzal has only two such plumes. The feathers were gathered in small bunches, their quills reinforced with reed tubes, and then

26-4 • FEATHER HEADDRESS OF MOCTEZUMA
Mexico. Aztec, before 1519.
Quetzal, blue cotinga, and other feathers and gold on a fiber frame, 45⅝ × 68⅞″ (116 × 175 cm). Museum für Völkerkunde, Vienna.

26-5 • A VIEW OF THE WORLD
Page from *Codex Fejervary-Mayer*. Mexico. Aztec or Mixtec, c. 1400–1519. Paint on animal hide, each page 6⅞ × 6⅞" (17.5 × 17.5 cm), total length 13'3" (4.04 m). The National Museums and Galleries on Merseyside, Liverpool, England.

sewn to the frame in overlapping layers, the joins concealed by small gold plaques. Featherworkers were esteemed craftspeople. After the Spanish invasion, they turned their exacting skills to "feather paintings" of Christian subjects.

MANUSCRIPTS

Aztec scribes also created brilliantly colored books: histories, maps, and divinatory almanacs. Instead of being bound on one side like European books, Mesoamerican books took the form of a screenfold, accordion-pleated so that each page was connected only to the two adjacent pages. This format allowed great flexibility: a book could be opened to show two pages, or unfolded to show six or eight pages simultaneously; different sections of the book could also be juxtaposed. A rare manuscript that survived the Spanish conquest provides a concise summary of Mesoamerican cosmology **(FIG. 26–5)**. Mesoamerican peoples recognized five key directions: north, south, east, west, and center. At the center of the image is Xiuhtecutli, god of fire, time, and the calendar. Radiating from him are the four cardinal directions—each associated with a specific color, a deity, and a tree with a bird in its branches. Two hundred and sixty dots trace the eight-lobed path around the

central figure, referring to the 260-day Mesoamerican divinatory calendar; the 20 day signs of this calendar are also distributed throughout the image. By linking the 260-day calendar to the four directions, this image speaks eloquently of the unity of space and time in the Mesoamerican worldview.

The Aztec Empire was short-lived. Within two years of their arrival in Mexico, the Spanish conquistadors and their indigenous allies overran Tenochtitlan. They built their own capital, Mexico City, over its ruins and established their own cathedral on the site of Tenochtitlan's sacred precinct.

THE INCA EMPIRE

At the beginning of the sixteenth century the Inca Empire was one of the largest states in the world. It extended more than 2,600 miles along western South America, encompassing most of modern Peru, Ecuador, Bolivia, and northern Chile and reaching into present-day Argentina. Like the Aztec Empire, its rise was rapid and its destruction sudden.

The Incas called their empire the "Land of the Four Quarters." At its center was their capital, Cuzco, "the navel of

Calendar Stone ▶ **Mexico. Aztec, c. 1500. Diameter 11'6¾" (3.6 m).**
Museo Nacional de Antropología, Mexico City.

According to Mexica belief, the gods created the world four times before the present era. These cartouches name the days on which the four previous suns were destroyed: 4 Jaguar, 4 Wind, 4 Rain, and 4 Water.

Together, these four calendrical glyphs and the face and claws of the central god combine to form the glyph for 4 Motion, the day on which the fifth sun will be destroyed by a giant earthquake.

This central face combines elements of the sun god as the night sun in the underworld with the clawed hands and flint tongue of earth gods, symbolizing the night sun and the hungry earth.

This band forms the Aztec symbol for the sun, a round disk with triangular projections denoting the sun's rays.

This band contains the 20 day signs of the 260-day divinatory calendar.

Two fire serpents encircle the outer part of the disk. Stylized flames rise off their backs. Their heads meet at the bottom, and human faces emerge from the mouths of the serpents.

SEE MORE: View the Closer Look feature for the Calendar Stone www.myartslab.com

the world," located high in the Andes Mountains. The Inca state began as one of many small competing kingdoms that emerged in the highlands. In the fifteenth century the Incas began to expand, suddenly and rapidly, and had subdued most of their vast domain—through conquest, alliance, and intimidation—by 1500.

To hold this linguistically and ethnically diverse empire together, the Inca ("Inca" refers to both the ruler and the people) relied on religion, an efficient bureaucracy, and various forms of labor taxation, in which the payment was a set amount of time spent performing tasks for the state. In return the state provided gifts through local leaders and sponsored lavish ritual entertainments. Men might cultivate state lands, serve in the army, or work periodically on public works projects—building roads and terracing hillsides, for example—while women wove cloth as

tribute. No Andean civilization ever developed writing, but the Inca kept detailed accounts and historical records on knotted and colored cords (*quipu*).

To move their armies and speed transport and communication within the empire, the Incas built more than 23,000 miles of roads. These varied from 50-foot-wide thoroughfares to 3-foot-wide paths. Two main north–south roads, one along the coast and the other through the highlands, were linked by east–west roads. Travelers journeyed on foot, using llamas as pack animals. Stairways helped them negotiate steep mountain slopes, and rope suspension bridges allowed river gorge crossings. All along the roads, storehouses and lodgings—more than a thousand have been found—were spaced a day's journey apart. A relay system of runners could carry messages between Cuzco and the farthest reaches of the empire in about a week.

CUZCO

Cuzco, a capital of great splendor, was home to the Inca, ruler of the empire. Its urban plan was said to have been designed by the Inca Pachacuti (r. 1438–1471) in the shape of a puma, its head the fortress of Sacsahuaman, and its belly the giant plaza at the center of town. The city was divided into upper and lower parts, reflecting the dual organization of Inca society. Cuzco was the symbolic as well as the political center of the Inca Empire: everyone had to carry a burden when entering the city, and gold, silver, or textiles brought into the city could not afterward be removed from it.

Cuzco was a showcase of the finest Inca masonry, some of which can still be seen in the present-day city (see "Inca Masonry," page 842). Architecture was a major expressive form for the Inca, the very shape of individually worked stones conveying a powerful aesthetic impact **(FIG. 26–6)**. In contrast to the massive walls, Inca buildings had gabled, thatched roofs. Doors, windows, and niches were trapezoid-shaped, narrower at the top than the bottom.

MACHU PICCHU

MACHU PICCHU, one of the most spectacular archaeological sites in the world, provides an excellent example of Inca architectural planning **(FIG. 26–7)**. At 9,000 feet above sea level, it straddles a

26-6 • INCA MASONRY, DETAIL OF A WALL AT MACHU PICCHU
Peru. Inca, 1450–1530.

26-7 • MACHU PICCHU
Peru. Inca, 1450–1530.

SEE MORE: View a video about Machu Picchu
www.myartslab.com

Working with the simplest of tools—mainly heavy stone hammers—and using no mortar, Inca builders created stonework of great refinement and durability: roads and bridges that linked the entire empire, terraces for growing crops, and structures both simple and elaborate. The effort expended on stone construction by the Inca was prodigious. Fine Inca masonry consisted of either rectangular blocks or irregular polygonal blocks (SEE FIG. 26–6). In both types, adjoining blocks were painstakingly shaped to fit tightly together without mortar. Their stone faces might be slightly beveled along their edges so that each block presented a "pillowed" shape expressing its identity, or walls might be smoothed into a continuous flowing surface in which the individual

blocks form a seamless whole. At a few Inca sites, the stones used in construction were boulder-size: up to 27 feet tall. In Cuzco, and elsewhere in the Inca empire, Inca masonry has survived earthquakes that have destroyed later structures.

At Machu Picchu (SEE FIGS. 26–6, 26–7), all buildings and terraces within its 3-square-mile extent were made of granite, the hard stone occurring at the site. Commoners' houses and some walls were constructed of irregular stones that were carefully fitted together, while fine polygonal or smoothed masonry distinguished palaces and temples.

polygonal-stone wall   smooth-surfaced wall

SEE MORE: View a simulation about Inca masonry www.myartslab.com

---

ridge between two high peaks in the eastern slopes of the Andes and looks down on the Urubamba River. Stone buildings, today lacking only their thatched roofs, occupy terraces around central plazas, and narrow agricultural terraces descend into the valley. The site, near the eastern limits of the empire, was the royal estate of the Inca ruler Pachacuti. The court might retire to this warmer, lower-altitude palace when the Cuzco winter became too harsh to enjoy. Important diplomatic negotiations and ceremonial feasts may also have taken place at this country retreat. The entire complex is designed with great sensitivity to its surroundings, with walls and plazas framing stupendous vistas of the surrounding landscape, and carefully selected stones echoing the shapes of the mountains beyond.

TEXTILES

The production of fine textiles was already an important art in the Andes by the third millennium BCE (see Chapter 12). Among the

26-8 • TUNIC
Peru. Inca, c. 1500. Camelid fiber and cotton, 35⅞ × 30″
(91 × 76.5 cm). Dumbarton Oaks Research Library and Collections,
Pre-Columbian Collection, Washington, D.C.

Incas, textiles of cotton and camelid fibers (from llama, vicuña, and alpaca) were a primary form of wealth. One form of labor taxation required the manufacture of fibers and cloth, and textiles as well as agricultural products filled Inca storehouses. Cloth was deemed a fitting gift for the gods, so fine garments were draped around statues, and even burned as sacrificial offerings.

The patterns and designs on garments were not simply decorative but also carried symbolic messages, including indications of a person's ethnic identity and social rank. In the elaborate **TUNIC** in **FIGURE 26–8**, each square represents a miniature tunic. For example, tunics with checkerboard patterns were worn by military officers and royal escorts, and the four-part motifs may refer to the empire as the Land of the Four Quarters. The diagonal key motif is often found on tunics with horizontal border stripes but its meaning is not known. While we may not be sure what was meant in every case, patterns and colors appear to have been standardized like uniforms in order to convey information at a glance. Encompassing all these patterns associated with different ranks and statuses, this exquisitely woven tunic may have been a royal garment.

METALWORK

When they arrived in Peru in 1532, the Spanish were far less interested in Inca cloth than in their vast quantities of gold and silver. The Inca valued objects made of gold and silver not for their precious metal, but because they saw in them symbols of the sun and the moon. They are said to have called gold the "sweat of the sun" and silver the "tears of the moon." On the other hand, the Spanish exploration of the New World was propelled by feverish tales of native treasure. Whatever gold and silver objects the Spanish could obtain were melted down to enrich their royal coffers. Only a few small figures buried as offerings, like the little **LLAMA** shown in **FIGURE 26–9**, escaped the conquerors. The llama was thought to have a special connection with the sun, with rain, and with fertility, and a llama was sacrificed to the sun every morning in Cuzco. In this small silver figurine, the essential character of a llama is rendered with a few well-chosen details, but in keeping with the value that Andeans placed on textiles the blanket on its back is carefully described.

THE AFTERMATH OF THE SPANISH CONQUEST

Native American populations in Mexico and Peru declined sharply after the conquest because of the exploitative policies of the conquerors and the ravages of smallpox and other diseases that spread from Europe and against which the indigenous people had no immunity. This demographic collapse meant that the population of the Americas declined by as much as 90 percent in the century after contact with Europe. European missionaries suppressed local beliefs and practices and worked to spread Christianity throughout the Americas. Although increasing numbers of Europeans began to settle and dominate the land, native arts did not end with the Spanish conquest. Traditional arts,

26-9 • LLAMA
From Bolivia or Peru, found near Lake Titicaca, Bolivia. Inca, 15th century. Cast silver with gold and cinnabar, 9 × 8½ × 1¾" (22.9 × 21.6 × 4.4 cm). American Museum of Natural History, New York.

including fine weaving, continue to this day, transforming and remaining vital as indigenous peoples adjust to a changing world.

NORTH AMERICA

In America north of Mexico, from the upper reaches of Canada and Alaska to the southern tip of Florida, many different peoples with widely varying cultures coexisted. Here, the Europeans came less as military men seeking riches to plunder than as families seeking land to farm. Unlike the Spaniards, they found no large cities with urban populations to resist them. However, although they imagined that the lands they settled were an untended wilderness, in fact nearly all of North America was populated and possessed by indigenous peoples. Over the next 400 years, by means of violence, bribery, and treaties, the English colonies and, in turn, the United States displaced nearly all Native Americans from their ancestral homelands. What indigenous art Euro-Americans encountered they viewed as a curiosity, not art.

Much Native American artwork was small, portable, fragile, and impermanent. In previous times these artworks were not

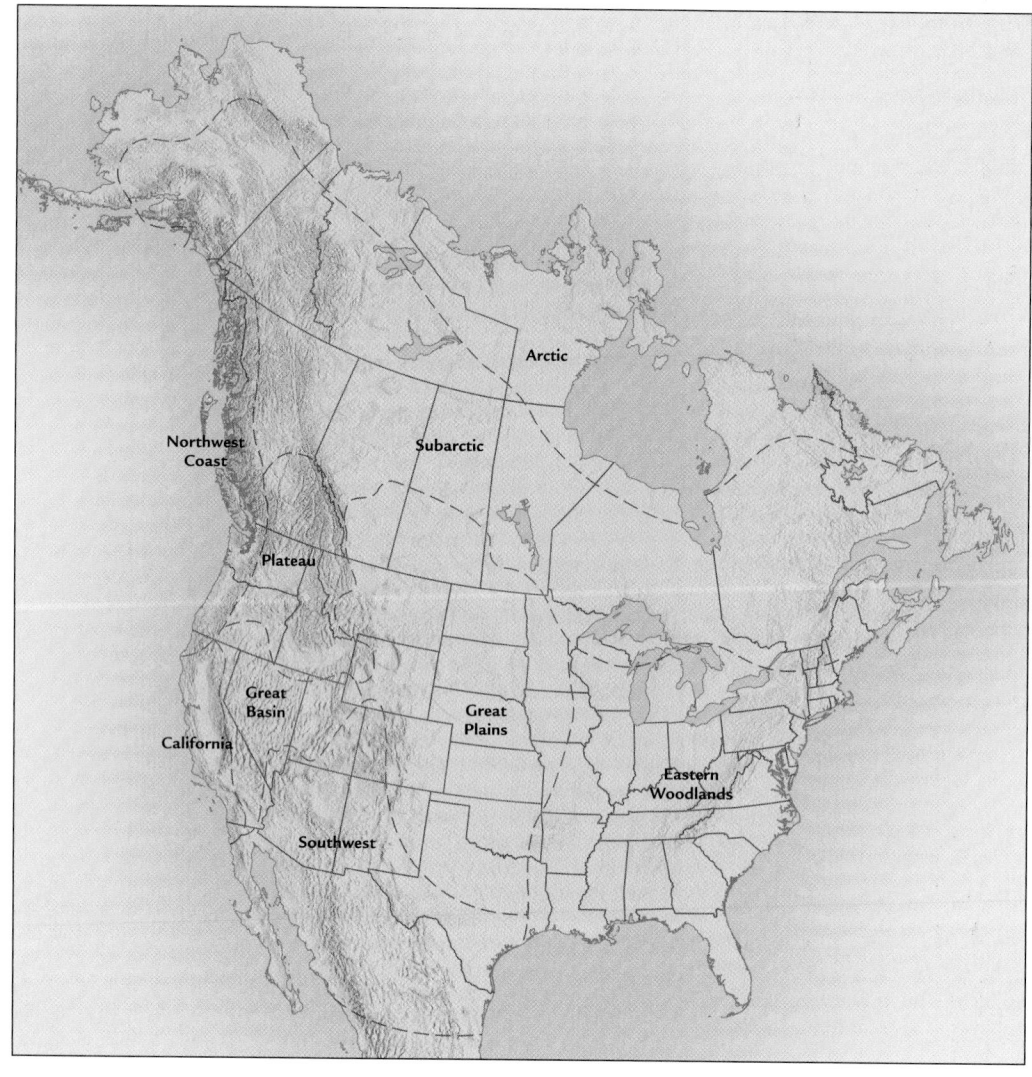

MAP 26-2 • NORTH AMERICAN CULTURAL AREAS

The varied geographic regions of North America supported diverse cultures adapted to their distinct environments.

appreciated for their aesthetic qualities, but were collected as anthropological artifacts or souvenirs, often under coercive conditions. Today, many Native peoples have begun to reclaim sacred objects and human remains that were forcibly taken from them, and museums are beginning to work with Native communities to present their art in respectful and culturally sensitive ways. We will look at art from only four North American cultural areas: the Eastern Woodlands, the Great Plains, the Northwest Coast, and the Southwest (MAP 26–2).

THE EASTERN WOODLANDS

In the Eastern Woodlands, after the decline of the great Mississippian centers (see Chapter 12), most tribes lived in stable villages, and they combined hunting, gathering, and agriculture for their livelihood. In the sixteenth century, the Iroquois formed a powerful confederation of five northeastern Native American nations, which played a prominent military and political role until after the American Revolution. The Huron and Illinois also formed sizable confederacies.

The arrival in the seventeenth century on the Atlantic coast of a few boatloads of Europeans seeking religious freedom, land

to farm, and a new life for themselves brought major changes. Trade with these settlers gave the Woodlands peoples access to things they valued, while on their part the colonists learned native forms of agriculture, hunting, and fishing—skills they needed in order to survive. In turn, Native Americans traded furs for such useful items as metal tools, cookware, needles, and cloth, and they especially prized European glass beads and silver. These trade items largely replaced older materials, such as crystal, copper, and shell.

WAMPUM. Woodlands peoples made belts and strings of cylindrical purple and white shell beads called wampum. The Iroquois and Delaware peoples used wampum to keep records (the purple and white patterns served as memory devices) and exchanged belts of wampum to conclude treaties (FIG. 26–10). Few actual wampum treaty belts have survived, so this one, said to commemorate an unwritten treaty when the land now comprising the state of Pennsylvania was ceded by the Delawares in 1682, is especially prized. The belt, with two figures of equal size holding hands, suggests the mutual respect enjoyed by the Delaware and

TECHNIQUE | Basketry

Basketry is the weaving of reeds, grasses, and other plant materials to form containers. In North America the earliest evidence of basketwork, found in Danger Cave, Utah, dates to as early as 8400 BCE. Over the subsequent centuries, Native American women, notably in California and the American Southwest, developed basketry into an art form that combined utility with great beauty.

There are three principal basket-making techniques: coiling, twining, and plaiting. **Coiling** involves sewing together a spiraling foundation of rods with some other material. **Twining** twists multiple elements around a vertical warp of rods. Plaiting weaves strips over and under each other.

The coiled basket shown here was made by a Pomo woman in California. According to Pomo legend, the Earth was dark until their ancestral hero stole the sun and brought it to Earth in a basket. He hung the basket first just over the horizon, but, dissatisfied with the light it gave, he kept suspending it in different places across the dome of the sky. He repeats this process every day, which is why the sun moves across the sky from east to west. In the Pomo basket, the structure of coiled willow and bracken fern root produces a spiral surface into which the artist worked sparkling pieces of clam shell, trade beads, and soft tufts of woodpecker and quail feathers. The underlying basket, the glittering shells, and the soft, moving feathers make this an exquisite container. Such baskets were treasured possessions, cremated with their owners at death.

FEATHERED BOWL
c. 1877. Willow, bulrush, fern, feather, shells, glass beads. Height 5½″ (14 cm), diameter 12″ (36.5 cm). Philbrook Museum, Tulsa, Oklahoma. Gift of Clark Field (1948.39.37)

Penn's Society of Friends (Quakers), a respect that later collapsed into land fraud and violence. In general, wampum strings and belts had the authority of legal agreement and also symbolized a moral and political order.

QUILLWORK. Woodlands art focused on personal adornment—tattoos, body paint, elaborate dress—and fragile arts such as **quillwork**. Quillwork involved dyeing porcupine and bird quills with a variety of natural dyes, soaking the quills to soften them,

26-10 • WAMPUM BELT, TRADITIONALLY CALLED WILLIAM PENN'S TREATY WITH THE DELAWARE
1680s. Shell beads, 17⅜ × 6⅛″ (44 × 15.5 cm). Royal Ontario Museum, Canada. HD6364

26-11 • BABY CARRIER
Upper Missouri River area. Eastern Sioux, 19th century. Wooden board, buckskin, porcupine quill, length 31″ (78.8 cm). Department of Anthropology, Smithsonian Institution Libraries, Washington, D.C. Catalogue No. 7311

and then working them into rectilinear, ornamental surface patterns on deerskin clothing and on birch-bark items like baskets and boxes. A Sioux legend recounts how a mythical ancestor, Doublewoman ("double" because she was both beautiful and ugly, benign and dangerous), appeared to a woman in a dream and taught her the art of quillwork. As the legend suggests, quillwork was a woman's art form, as was basketry (see "Basketry," page 845). The Sioux **BABY CARRIER** in **FIGURE 26–11** is richly decorated with symbols of protection and well-being, including bands of antelopes in profile and thunderbirds flying with their heads turned and tails outspread. The thunderbird was an especially beneficent symbol, thought to be capable of protecting against both human and supernatural adversaries.

BEADWORK. In spite of the use of shell beads in wampum, decorative beadwork did not become commonplace until after European contact. In the late eighteenth century, Native American artists began to acquire European colored-glass beads, and in the nineteenth century they favored the tiny seed beads from Venice

and Bohemia. Early beadwork mimicked the patterns and colors of quillwork. In the nineteenth century it largely replaced quillwork and incorporated European designs. Among other sources of inspiration, Canadian nuns introduced the young women in their schools to embroidered European floral motifs, and Native embroiderers began to adapt these designs, as well as European needlework techniques and patterns from European garments, into their own work. Functional aspects of garments might be transformed into purely decorative motifs; for example, a pocket would be replaced by an area of beadwork shaped like a pocket. A **SHOULDER BAG** from Kansas, made by a Delaware woman (**FIG. 26–12**), is covered with curvilinear plant motifs in contrast to the rectilinear patterns of traditional quillwork. White lines outline brilliant pink and blue leaf-shaped forms, heightening the intensity of the colors, which alternate within repeated patterns. This Delaware bag exemplifies the evolution of beadwork design and its adaptation to a changing world. The very shape of this bandolier bag is adapted from European military uniforms.

THE GREAT PLAINS

Between the Eastern Woodlands region and the Rocky Mountains to the west lay an area of prairie grasslands called the Great Plains. On the Great Plains, two differing ways of life developed, one a relatively recent and short-lived (1700–1870) nomadic lifestyle—dependent on the region's great migrating herds of buffalo for food, clothing, and shelter—and the other, a much older sedentary and agricultural lifestyle. Horses, from wild herds descended from feral horses brought to America by Spanish explorers in the sixteenth and seventeenth centuries, made travel and a nomadic life easier for the dispossessed eastern groups that moved to the plains.

European settlers on the eastern seaboard put increasing pressure on the Eastern Woodlands peoples, seizing their farmlands and forcing them westward. Both Native Americans and back-country settlers were living in loosely village-based, farming societies and thus were competing for the same resources. The resulting interaction of Eastern Woodlands artists with one another and with Plains artists led in some cases to the emergence of a new hybrid style, while other artists consciously fought to maintain their own cultures.

PORTABLE ARCHITECTURE. The nomadic Plains peoples hunted buffalo for food and hides from which they created clothing and a light, portable dwelling known as a tipi (formerly spelled teepee) (**FIG. 26–13**). The tipi was well adapted to withstand the strong and constant wind, the dust, and the violent storms of the prairies. The framework of a tipi consisted of a stable pyramidal frame of three or four long poles, filled out with about 20 additional poles, in a roughly oval plan. The framework was covered with hides (or, later, with canvas) to form a conical structure. The hides were specially prepared to make them flexible and waterproof. Between 20 and 40 hides were used to make a tipi, depending on its size. An opening at the top served as the smoke hole for a central hearth.

26-12 • SHOULDER BAG
Kansas. Delaware people, c. 1860. Wool fabric, cotton fabric and thread, silk ribbon, and glass beads, 23 × 7¾" (58.5 × 19.8 cm). The Detroit Institute of Arts. Founders Society Purchase (81.216)

26-13 • BLACKFOOT WOMEN RAISING A TIPI
Photographed c. 1900. Montana Historical Society, Helena, Montana.

26-14 • BATTLE SCENE, HIDE PAINTING
North Dakota. Mandan, 1797–1800. Tanned buffalo hide, dyed
porcupine quills, and black, red, green, yellow, and brown pigment,
7'10" × 8'6" (2.44 × 2.65 m). Peabody Museum of Archaeology,
Harvard University, Cambridge, Massachusetts. 99-12-10/53121

This robe, collected in 1804 by Meriwether Lewis and William Clark on
their expedition into western lands acquired by the United States in
the Louisiana Purchase, is the earliest documented example of Plains
painting. It was one of a number of Native American artworks that Lewis
and Clark sent to President Thomas Jefferson. Jefferson displayed the
robe in the entrance hall of his home at Monticello, Virginia.

The tipi leaned slightly into the prevailing west wind while the
flap-covered door and smoke hole faced east, away from the wind.
An inner lining covered the lower part of the walls and the
perimeter of the floor to protect the occupants from drafts.

Tipis were the property and responsibility of women, who set
them up at new encampments and lowered them when the group
moved on. Blackfoot women could set up their huge tipis in less

than an hour. Women quilled, beaded, and embroidered tipi
linings, as well as backrests, clothing, and equipment. The patterns
with which tipis were decorated, like their proportions and colors,
varied from nation to nation, family to family, and individual to
individual. In general, the bottom was covered with traditional
motifs and the center section held personal images. When
disassembled and packed to be dragged by a horse to another
location, the tipi served as a platform for transporting other
possessions. The Sioux arranged their tipis in two half-circles—one
for the sky people and one for the earth people—divided along an
east–west axis. When the Blackfoot people gathered in the summer
for their ceremonial Sun Dance, their encampment contained
hundreds of tipis in a circle a mile in circumference.

PLAINS INDIAN PAINTING.   Plains men recorded their exploits in
paintings on tipis and on buffalo-hide robes. The earliest
documented painted buffalo-hide robe, presented to Lewis and

Clark during their transcontinental expedition, illustrates a battle fought in 1797 by the Mandan (of what is now North Dakota) and their allies against the Sioux (FIG. 26–14). The painter, trying to capture the full extent of a conflict in which five nations took part, shows a party of warriors in 22 separate episodes. The party is led by a man with a pipe and an elaborate eagle-feather headdress, and the warriors are armed with bows and arrows, lances, clubs, and flintlock rifles. Details of equipment and emblems of rank—headdresses, sashes, shields, feathered lances, powder horns for the rifles—are depicted carefully. Horses are shown in profile with stick legs, C-shaped hooves, and either clipped or flowing manes.

The figures stand out clearly against the light-colored background of the buffalo hide. The painter pressed lines into the hide, then filled in the forms with black, red, green, yellow, and brown pigments. A strip of colored porcupine quills runs down the spine of the buffalo hide. The robe would have been worn draped over the shoulders of the powerful warrior whose deeds it commemorates. As the wearer moved, the painted horses and warriors would seem to come alive, transforming the warrior into a living representation of his exploits.

Life on the Great Plains changed abruptly in 1869, when the transcontinental railway linking the east and west coasts of the United States was completed, providing easy access to Native American lands. Between 1871 and 1890, Euro-American hunters killed off most of the buffalo, and soon ranchers and then farmers moved into the Great Plains. The U.S. government forcibly moved the outnumbered and outgunned Native Americans to reservations, land considered worthless until the later discovery of oil and, in the case of the Black Hills, gold.

THE NORTHWEST COAST

From southern Alaska to northern California, the Pacific coast of North America is a region of unusually abundant resources. Its many rivers fill each year with salmon returning to spawn. Harvested and dried, the fish could sustain large populations throughout the year. The peoples of the Northwest Coast—among them the Tlingit, the Haida, and the Kwakwaka'wakw (formerly spelled Kwakiutl)—exploited this abundance to develop a complex and distinctive way of life in which the arts played a central role.

ANIMAL IMAGERY. Animals feature prominently in Northwest Coast art because each extended family group (clan) claimed descent from a mythic animal or animal-human ancestor, from whom the family derived its name and the right to use certain animals and spirits as totemic emblems, or crests. These emblems appear frequently in Northwest Coast art, notably in carved cedar house poles and the tall, free-standing poles (mortuary poles) erected to memorialize dead chiefs. Chiefs, who were males in the most direct line of

descent from the mythic ancestor, validated their status and garnered prestige for themselves and their families by holding ritual feasts known as potlatches, during which they gave valuable gifts to the invited guests. Shamans, who were sometimes also chiefs, mediated between the human and spirit worlds. Some shamans were female, giving them unique access to certain aspects of the spiritual world.

Northwest Coast peoples lived in large, elaborately decorated communal houses made of massive timbers and thick planks. Carved and painted partition screens separated the chief's quarters from the rest of the house. The Tlingit screen illustrated in FIGURE 26–15 came from the house of Chief Shakes of Wrangell (d. 1916), whose family crest was the grizzly bear. The image of a rearing

26–15 • GRIZZLY BEAR HOUSE-PARTITION SCREEN
The house of Chief Shakes of Wrangell, Canada. Tlingit people, c. 1840. Cedar, paint, and human hair, 15 × 8′ (4.57 × 2.74 m). Denver Art Museum, Denver, Colorado.

Hamatsa Masks

During the harsh winter season, when spirits are thought to be most powerful, many Northwest Coast peoples seek spiritual renewal through their ancient rituals—including the potlatch, or ceremonial gift giving, and the initiation of new members into the prestigious Hamatsa society. With snapping beaks and cries of "Hap! Hap! Hap!" ("Eat! Eat! Eat!"), Hamatsa, the people-eating spirit of the north, and his three assistants—horrible masked monster birds—begin their wild, ritual dance. The dancing birds threaten and even attack the Kwakwaka'wakw people who gather for the Winter Ceremony.

In the Winter Ceremony, youths are captured, taught the Hamatsa lore and rituals, and then in a spectacular theater-dance performance are "tamed" and brought back into civilized life. All the members of the community, including singers, gather in the main room of the great house, which is divided by a painted screen (SEE FIG. 26–15). The audience members fully participate in the performance; in early times, they brought containers of blood so that when

the bird-dancers attacked them, they could appear to bleed and have flesh torn away.

Whistles from behind the screen announce the arrival of the Hamatsa (danced by an initiate), who enters through the central hole in the screen in a flesh-craving frenzy. Wearing hemlock, a symbol of the spirit world, he crouches and dances wildly with outstretched arms as attendants try to control him. He disappears but returns again, now wearing red cedar and dancing upright. Finally tamed, a full member of society, he even dances with the women.

Then the masked bird-dancers appear—first Raven-of-the-North-End-of-the-World, then Crooked-Beak-of-the-End-of-the-World, and finally the untranslatable Huxshukw, who cracks open skulls with his beak and eats the brains of his victims. Snapping their beaks, these masters of illusion enter the room backward, their masks pointed up as though the birds are looking skyward. They move slowly counterclockwise around the floor. At each change in the music they crouch, snap their beaks, and let out their wild cries of "Hap!

Hap! Hap!" Essential to the ritual dances are the huge carved and painted wooden masks, articulated and operated by strings worked by the dancers. Among the finest masks are those by Willie Seaweed (1873–1967), a Kwakwaka'wakw chief, whose brilliant colors and exuberantly decorative carving style determined the direction of twentieth-century Kwakwaka'wakw sculpture.

The Canadian government, abetted by missionaries, outlawed the Winter Ceremony and potlatches in 1885, claiming the event was injurious to health, encouraged prostitution, endangered children's education, damaged the economy, and was cannibalistic. But the Kwakwaka'wakw refused to give up their "oldest and best" festival—one that spoke powerfully to them in many ways, establishing social rank and playing an important role in arranging marriages. By 1936, the government and the missionaries, who called the Kwakwaka'wakw "incorrigible," gave up. But not until 1951 could the Kwakwaka'wakw people gather openly for winter ceremonies, including the initiation rites of the Hamatsa society.

Edward S. Curtis HAMATSA DANCERS, KWAKWAKA'WAKW

Canada. Photographed 1914. Smithsonian Institution Libraries, Washington, D.C.

The photographer Edward S. Curtis (1868–1952) devoted 30 years to documenting the lives of Native Americans. This photograph shows participants in a film he made about the Kwakwaka'wakw. For the film, his Native American assistant, Richard Hunt, borrowed family heirlooms and commissioned many new pieces from the finest Kwakwaka'wakw artists. Most of the pieces are now in museum collections. The photograph shows carved and painted posts, masked dancers (including those representing people-eating birds), a chief at the left (holding a speaker's staff and wearing a cedar neck ring), and spectators at the right.

Attributed to Willie Seaweed KWAKWAKA'WAKW BIRD MASK

Alert Bay, Vancouver Island, Canada. Prior to 1951. Cedar wood, cedar bark, feathers, and fiber, 10 × 72 × 15″ (25.4 × 183 × 38.1 cm). Collection of the Museum of Anthropology, Vancouver, Canada. (A6120)

The name "Seaweed" is an anglicization of the Kwakwaka'wakw name *Siwid*, meaning "Paddling Canoe," "Recipient of Paddling," or "Paddled To"—referring to a great chief to whose potlatches guests paddled from afar. Willie Seaweed was not only the chief of his clan, but a great orator, singer, and tribal historian who kept the tradition of the potlatch alive during years of government repression.

grizzly painted on the screen is itself made up of smaller bears and bear heads that appear in its ears, eyes, nostrils, joints, paws, and body. The oval door opening is a symbolic vagina; passing through it re-enacts the birth of the family from its ancestral spirit.

TEXTILES.   Blankets and other textiles produced by the Chilkat Tlingit had great prestige among Northwest Coast peoples **(FIG. 26–16)**. Both men and women worked on the blankets. Men drew the patterns on boards, and women wove the patterns into the blankets, using shredded cedar bark and mountain-goat wool. The weavers did not use looms; instead, they hung cedar warp threads from a rod and twined colored goat wool back and forth through them to make the pattern. The ends of the warp form the fringe at the bottom of the blanket.

The small face in the center of the blanket shown here represents the body of a large stylized creature, perhaps a sea bear (a fur seal) or a standing eagle. Above the body are the creature's large eyes; below it and to the sides are its legs and claws. Characteristic of Northwest painting and weaving, the images are composed of two basic elements: the ovoid, a slightly bent rectangle with rounded corners, and the formline, a continuous, shape-defining line. Here, subtly swelling black formlines define shapes with gentle curves, ovoids, and rectangular C shapes. When the blanket was worn, its two-dimensional shapes would have become three-dimensional, with the dramatic central figure curving over the wearer's back and the intricate side panels crossing over his shoulders and chest.

MASKS.   Many Native American cultures stage ritual dance ceremonies to call upon guardian spirits. The participants in Northwest Coast dance ceremonies wore elaborate costumes and striking carved and painted wooden masks. Among the most elaborate masks were those used by the Kwakwaka'wakw in their Winter Ceremony, in which they initiated members into the shamanistic Hamatsa society (see "Hamatsa Masks," opposite). The dance re-enacted the taming of Hamatsa, a cannibal spirit, and his three attendant bird spirits. Magnificent carved and painted masks transformed the dancers into Hamatsa and the bird attendants, who searched for victims to eat. Strings allowed the dancers to manipulate the masks so that the beaks opened and snapped shut with spectacular effect. Isolated in museums as "art," the masks doubtless lose some of the shocking vivacity they have in performance; nevertheless their bold forms and color schemes retain power and meaning that can be activated by the viewer's imagination.

26–16 • CHILKAT BLANKET
Tlingit people, before 1928. Mountain-goat wool and shredded cedar bark, 55⅛ × 63¾″ (140 × 162 cm).
American Museum of Natural History, New York.

THE SOUTHWEST

The Native American peoples of the southwestern United States include, among others, the Pueblo (sedentary village-dwelling groups) and the Navajo. The Pueblo groups are heirs of the Ancestral Puebloans (Anasazi) and Hohokam cultures (see Chapter 12). The Ancestral Puebloans built apartmentlike villages and cliff dwellings whose ruins are found throughout the Four Corners region of New Mexico, Colorado, Arizona, and Utah in the American Southwest. The Navajo, who arrived in the region sometime between 1100 and 1500 CE, developed a semisedentary way of life based on agriculture and (after the introduction of sheep by the Spaniards) shepherding. Being among the very few Native American tribal groups whose reservations are located on their actual ancestral homelands, both groups have succeeded in maintaining the continuity of their traditions despite Euro-American pressure. Today, their arts reflect the adaptation of traditional forms to new technologies, new mediums, and the influences of the dominant American culture that surrounds them.

THE PUEBLOS.   Some Pueblo villages, like those of their ancient ancestors, consist of multi-storied dwellings made of adobe. One of these, **TAOS PUEBLO**, shown in FIGURE **26–17** in a photograph taken in 1947 by the American photographer of the Southwest, Laura Gilpin (1891–1979), is located in north-central New Mexico. Continually occupied and modified for over 500 years, the up to five-story house blocks of Taos Pueblo provide flexible, communal dwellings. Ladders provide access to the upper stories and to insulated inner rooms, entered through holes in the ceiling. Two large house blocks are arrayed around a central plaza that opens toward the neighboring mountains, rising in a stepped fashion to provide a series of roof terraces that can serve as viewing platforms. The plaza and roof terraces are centers of communal life and ceremony, as can be seen in Pablita Velarde's painting of the winter solstice celebrations (SEE FIG. 26–19).

CERAMICS.   Pottery traditionally was a woman's art among Pueblo peoples. Wares were made by coiling and other hand-building techniques, and then fired at low temperature in wood bonfires. The best-known twentieth-century Pueblo potter was

26-17 • Laura Gilpin TAOS PUEBLO
Taos, New Mexico. Photographed 1947. Amon Carter Museum, Fort Worth, Texas.

Laura Gilpin, photographer of the landscape, architecture, and people of the American Southwest, began her series on the Pueblos and Navajos in the 1930s. She published her work in four volumes of photographs between 1941 and 1968.

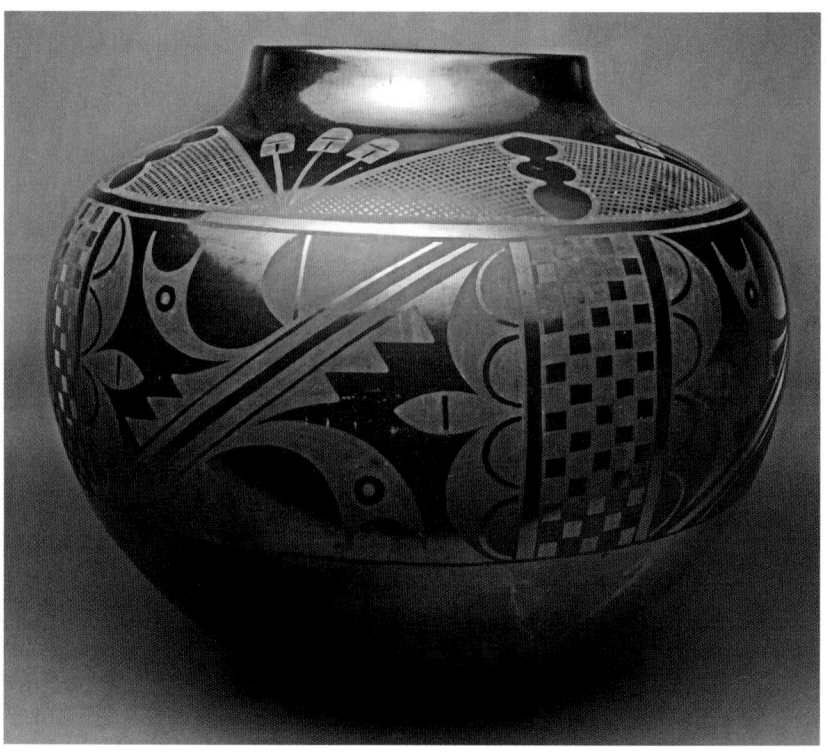

26-18 • Maria Montoya Martinez and Julian Martinez BLACKWARE STORAGE JAR
New Mexico. c. 1942. Ceramic, height 18¾″ (47.6 cm), diameter 22½″ (57.1 cm). Museum of Indian Arts and Culture/Laboratory of Anthropology, Museum of New Mexico, Santa Fe.

Maria Montoya Martinez (1887–1980) of San Ildefonso Pueblo in New Mexico. Inspired by prehistoric pottery that was unearthed at nearby archaeological excavations and by the then fashionable Art Deco style, she and her husband, Julian Martinez (1885–1943), developed a distinctive **blackware** ceramic style notable for its elegant forms and subtle textures (FIG. 26–18). Maria Martinez made pots covered with a slip that was then burnished. Using additional slip, Julian Martinez painted the pots with designs that interpreted traditional Pueblo and Ancestral Puebloan imagery. After firing, the burnished ground became a lustrous black and the slip painting retained a matte surface. By the 1930s, production of blackware in San Ildefonso had become a communal enterprise. Family members and friends all worked making pots, and Maria Martinez signed all the pieces so that, in typical Pueblo communal solidarity, everyone profited from the art market.

THE SANTA FE INDIAN SCHOOL.   In the 1930s Anglo-American art teachers and dealers worked with Native Americans of the Southwest to create a distinctive, stereotypical "Indian" style in several mediums—including jewelry, pottery, weaving, and painting—to appeal to tourists and collectors. A leader in this effort was Dorothy Dunn (1903–1991), who taught painting in the Santa Fe Indian School, an off-reservation government boarding school in New Mexico, from 1932 to 1937. Dunn inspired her

students to create a painting style that combined the outline drawing and flat colors of folk art, the decorative qualities of Art Deco, and "Indian" subject matter. She and her students formed the Studio School. Restrictive as the school was, Dunn's success made painting a viable occupation for young Native American artists.

Pablita Velarde (1918–2006), from Santa Clara Pueblo in New Mexico and a 1936 graduate of Dorothy Dunn's school, was only a teenager when one of her paintings was selected for exhibition at the Chicago World's Fair in 1933. Thereafter, Velarde documented Pueblo ways of life in a large series of murals for Bandelier National Monument, launching a long and successful career. In smaller works on paper, such as the one illustrated here, she continued this focus on Pueblo life. **KOSHARES OF TAOS** (FIG. 26–19) illustrates a moment during a ceremony celebrating the winter solstice when koshares, or clowns, take over the plaza from the Katsinas. Katsinas—the supernatural counterparts of animals, natural phenomena like clouds, and geological features like mountains—are central to traditional Pueblo religion. They manifest themselves in the human dancers who impersonate them during the winter solstice ceremony, as well as in the small figures known as Katsina dolls that are given to children as educational aids in learning to identify the masks. Velarde's painting combines bold, flat colors and a simplified decorative line with European perspective. Her paintings, with their Art Deco abstraction, influenced the popular idea of the "Indian" style in art.

26–19 • Pablita Velarde KOSHARES OF TAOS
New Mexico. 1940s. Watercolor on paper, 13⅞ × 22⅜″ (35.3 × 56.9 cm). Philbrook Museum of Art, Tulsa, Oklahoma.
Museum Purchase (1947.37)

Navajo Night Chant

This chant accompanies the creation of a sand painting during a Navajo curing ceremony. It is sung toward the end of the ceremony and indicates the restoration of inner harmony and balance.

In beauty (happily) I walk.
With beauty before me I walk.
With beauty behind me I walk.
With beauty below me I walk.
With beauty above me I walk.
With beauty all around me I walk.
It is finished (again) in beauty.
It is finished in beauty.

(Cited in Washington Matthews, "The Night Chant: A Navaho Ceremony," in *Memoirs of the American Museum of Natural History*, Vol. 6. New York, 1902, p. 145.)

THE NAVAJOS. While some Navajo arts, like sand painting, have deep traditional roots, others have developed over the centuries of European contact. Navajo weaving (SEE FIG. 26–1) depends on the wool of sheep introduced by the Spaniards, and the designs and colors of Navajo blankets continue to evolve today in response to tourism and changing aesthetics. Similarly, jewelry made of turquoise and silver did not become an important Navajo art form until the mid nineteenth century. Traditionally, Navajo arts had strict gender divisions: women wove cloth, and men worked metal.

Sand painting, a traditional Navajo art, is the exclusive province of men. Sand paintings are made to the accompaniment of chants by shaman-singers in the course of healing and blessing ceremonies, and they have great sacred significance (see "Navajo Night Chant," above). The paintings depict mythic heroes and events; and as ritual art, they follow prescribed rules and patterns that ensure their power. To make them, the singer dribbles pulverized colored stones, pollen, flowers, and other natural colors over a hide or sand ground. The rituals are intended to cure by restoring harmony to the world. The paintings are not meant to be seen by the public and certainly not to be displayed in museums. They are meant to be destroyed by nightfall of the day on which they are made.

In 1919 a respected shaman-singer named Hosteen Klah (1867–1937) began to incorporate sand-painting images into weaving, breaking with the traditional prohibitions. Many Navajos took offense at Klah both for recording the sacred images and for doing so in what was traditionally a woman's art form. Klah had learned to weave from his mother and sister. The Navajo traditionally recognize at least three genders; Hosteen Klah was a *nadle*, or Navajo third-gender. Hence, he could learn both female and male arts; that is, he was trained both to weave and to heal. Hosteen Klah was not breaking artistic barriers in a conventional sense, but rather exemplifying the complexities of the traditional

Navajo gender system. Klah's work was ultimately accepted because of his great skill and prestige.

The **WHIRLING LOG CEREMONY** sand painting, woven into tapestry **(FIG. 26–20)**, depicts part of the Navajo creation myth. The Holy People create the earth's surface and divide it into four parts. They create humans, and bring forth corn, beans, squash, and tobacco—the four sacred plants. A male-female pair of humans and

26-20 • Hosteen Klah WHIRLING LOG CEREMONY
Sand painting; tapestry by Mrs. Sam Manuelito. Navajo, c. 1925. Wool, 5′5″ × 5′10″ (1.69 × 1.82 m). Heard Museum, Phoenix, Arizona.

A NEW BEGINNING

While Native American art has long been displayed in anthropology and natural history museums, today the art of indigenous peoples is finally achieving full recognition by the art establishment (see "Craft or Art?," page 856). The Institute of American Indian Arts (IAIA), founded in 1962 in Santa Fe and attended by Native American students from all over North America, supports Native American aspirations in the arts today just as Dorothy Dunn's Studio School did in the 1930s. Staffed by Native American artists, the school encourages the incorporation of indigenous ideals in the arts without creating an official "style." As alumni achieved distinction and the IAIA museum in Santa Fe established a reputation for excellence, the institute has led Native American art into the mainstream of contemporary art (see Chapter 31).

To cite just one example, contemporary Native American artist Jaune Quick-to-See Smith (b. 1940) borrowed a well-known image by Leonardo da Vinci for her **THE RED MEAN** (**FIG. 26–21**). She describes the work as a self-portrait, and indeed the center of the work has a bumper sticker that reads "Made in the U.S.A." above an identification number. The central figure quotes Leonardo's Vitruvian Man (see "The Vitruvian Man," page 637), but the message here is autobiographical. Leonardo inscribed the human form within perfect geometric shapes to emphasize the perfection of the human body, while Smith put her silhouette inside the red X that signifies nuclear radiation. This image alludes both to the uranium mines found on some Indian reservations and to the fact that many have become temporary repositories for nuclear waste. The image's background is a collage of Native American tribal newspapers. Her self-portrait thus includes her ethnic identity and life on the reservation as well as the history of Western art.

26–21 • Jaune Quick-to-See Smith **THE RED MEAN: SELF PORTRAIT** 1992. Acrylic, newspaper collage, and mixed media on canvas, 90 × 60″ (228.6 × 154.4 cm). Smith College Museum of Art, Northampton, Massachusetts. Part gift from Janet Wright Ketcham, class of 1953, and part purchase from the Janet Wright Ketcham, class of 1953, Fund © Jaune Quick-to-See Smith

one of the sacred plants stand in each of the four quarters, defined by the central cross. The four Holy People (the elongated figures) surround the image, and the guardian figure of Rainbow Maiden frames the scene on three sides. Like all Navajo artists, Hosteen Klah hoped that the excellence of the work would make it pleasing to the spirits. Recently, shaman-singers have made permanent sand paintings on boards for sale, but they usually introduce slight errors in them to render the paintings ceremonially harmless.

Other artists, such as the Canadian Haida artist Bill Reid (1920–1998), have sought to sustain and revitalize traditional art in their work. Trained as a woodcarver, painter, and jeweler, Reid revived the art of carving totem poles and dugout canoes in the Haida homeland of Haida Gwaii—"Islands of the People"—known on maps today as the Queen Charlotte Islands. Late in life he began to create large-scale sculptures in bronze. With their

ART AND ITS CONTEXTS

Craft or Art?

In many world cultures, the distinction between "fine art" and "craft" does not exist. The traditional Western academic hierarchy of materials —in which marble, bronze, oil, and fresco are valued more than terra cotta and watercolor—and the equally artificial hierarchy of subjects— in which history painting, including religious history, stands supreme— are irrelevant to non-Western art, and to much art produced in the West before the modern era.

The indigenous peoples of the Americas did not produce objects as works of art to be displayed in museums. In their eyes all pieces were utilitarian objects, adorned in ways necessary for their intended purposes. A work was valued for its effectiveness and for the role it played in society. Some, like a Sioux baby carrier (SEE FIG. 26–11), enrich mundane life with their aesthetic qualities. Others, such as Pomo baskets (see "Basketry," page 845), commemorate important events. The function of an Inca tunic may have been to identify or confer status on its owner or user through its material value or symbolic associations. And as with art in all cultures, many pieces had great spiritual or magical power. Such works of art cannot be fully comprehended or appreciated when they are seen only on pedestals

or encased in glass boxes in museums or galleries. They must be imagined, or better yet seen, as acting in their societies. How powerfully might our minds and emotions be engaged if we saw Kwakwaka'wakw masks functioning in religious drama, changing not only the outward appearance, but also the very essence of the individual.

At the beginning of the twentieth century, European and American artists broke away from the academic bias that extolled the Classical heritage of Greece and Rome. They found new inspiration in the art— or craft, if you will—of many different non-European cultures. Artists explored a new freedom to use absolutely any material or technique that effectively challenged outmoded assumptions and opened the way for a free and unfettered delight in, and an interest in understanding, Native American art as well as the art of other non-Western cultures. The more recent twentieth- and twenty-first-century conception of art as a multimedia adventure has helped validate works of art once seen only in ethnographic collections. Today objects once called "primitive" are recognized as great works of art and acknowledged to be an essential dimension of a twenty-first-century worldview. The line between "art" and "craft" seems more artificial and less relevant than ever before.

26-22 • Bill Reid THE SPIRIT OF HAIDA GWAII
Haida, 1991. Bronze, approx. 13 × 20′ (4 × 6 m). Canadian Embassy, Washington, D.C.

black patina, these works recall traditional Haida carvings in shiny black argillite.

Reid's imposing **THE SPIRIT OF HAIDA GWAII** now stands outside the Canadian Embassy in Washington, D.C. (**FIG. 26–22**). This sculpture, which Reid viewed as a metaphor for modern Canada's multicultural society, depicts a boatload of figures from the natural and mythic worlds struggling to paddle forward. The dominant figure is a shaman in a spruce-root basket hat and Chilkat blanket holding a speaker's pole. On the prow, the place reserved for the chief in a war canoe, sits the Bear. He faces backward rather than forward, and is bitten by an Eagle, with formline-patterned wings. The Eagle, in turn, is bitten by the Seawolf. The Eagle and the Seawolf, together with the man behind them, nevertheless continue paddling. At the stern, steering the canoe, is the Raven, the trickster in Haida mythology. The Raven is assisted by Mousewoman, the traditional guide and escort of humans in the spirit realms. According to Reid, the work represents a "mythological and environmen-

26-23 • NATIONAL MUSEUM OF THE AMERICAN INDIAN
The Smithsonian Institution, Washington, D.C. Opened September, 2004. Architectural design: GBQC in association with
Douglas Cardinal (Blackfoot). Architectural consultants: Johnpaul Jones (Cherokee-Choctaw) and Ramona Sakiestewa (Hopi).
Landscape consultant: Donna House (Navajo-Oneida), ethno-botanist.

tal lifeboat," where "the entire family of living things ... whatever their differences, ... are paddling together in one boat, headed in one direction." (Bringhurst, 1991.)

THE NATIONAL MUSEUM OF THE AMERICAN INDIAN. In September 2004 the National Museum of the American Indian finally opened on the Mall in Washington, D.C., directly below Capitol Hill and across from the National Gallery of Art. Inspired by the colors, textures, and forms of the American Southwest, the museum building establishes a new presence for Native Americans on the Mall (FIG. 26–23). Symbolizing the Native relationship to the environment, the museum is surrounded by boulders ("Grandfather Rocks"), water, and plantings that recall the varied landscapes of North America, including wetlands, meadows, forest, and traditional cropland with corn, squash, and tomatoes. The entrance to the museum on the east side faces the morning sun and recalls the orientation of prairie tipis. Inside the building a Sun Marker of stained glass in the south wall throws its dagger of light across the vast atrium as the day progresses. Once again the great spirits of earth and sky take form in a creation of the art of the Americas.

THINK ABOUT IT

26.1 Distinguish characteristic styles and techniques developed by three Native American cultures, and discuss their application in one work from each of these three cultures considered in the chapter.

26.2 Discuss Aztec and Inca achievements in the area of architecture and urbanism. Identify and analyze the function of one achievement of each culture and explain its importance.

26.3 Explain the idea of portable architecture, citing at least one specific example discussed in the chapter. Discuss the unique advantages of portable architecture.

26.4 Explore two examples of work from the chapter that exhibit influence from other cultures.

26.5 Discuss the gender system in Navajo society, and explain the roles for making art assigned to different genders.

PRACTICE MORE: Compose answers to these questions, get flashcards for images and terms, and review chapter material with quizzes
www.myartslab.com

THE BARUNGA STATEMENT

We the indigenous owners and occupiers of Australia call on the Australian Government and people to recognise our rights

— to self determination and self management including the freedom to pursue our own economic, social religious and cultural development;

— to permanent control and enjoyment of our ancestral lands;

— to compensation for the loss of use of lands, there having been no extinction of original title;

— to protection and control of access to our sacred sites, sacred objects, artifacts, designs, knowledge and works of art;

— to the return of the remains of our ancestors for burial in accordance with our traditions;

— to respect for and promotion of our Aboriginal identity, including the cultural, linguistic, religious and historical aspects, including the right to be educated in our own languages, and in our own culture and history;

— in accordance with the Universal Declaration of Human Rights, the International Covenant on Economic, Social and Cultural Rights, the International Covenant on Civil and Political Rights, and the International Convention on the Elimination of All Forms of Racial Discrimination, including rights to life, liberty, security of person, food, clothing, housing, medical care, education and employment opportunities, necessary social services and other basic human rights.

We call on the Commonwealth Parliament to pass laws providing:

— a national elected Aboriginal and Islander organisation to oversee Aboriginal and Islander affairs;

— a national system of land rights;

— a police and justice system which recognises our customary laws and frees us from discrimination and any activity which may threaten our identity or security, interfere with our freedom of expression or association, or otherwise prevent our full enjoyment and exercise of universally recognised human rights and fundamental freedoms.

We call on the Australian Government to support Aborigines in the development of an International Declaration of Principles for Indigenous Rights, leading to an International Covenant.

And we call on the Commonwealth Parliament to negotiate with us a Treaty or Compact recognising our prior ownership, continued occupation and sovereignty and affirming our human rights and freedoms.

27-1 • THE BARUNGA STATEMENT   Various artists from Arnhem Land and central Australia. 1988.
Ochers on composition board with collage of printed text on paper, 48 × 47¼″ (122 × 120 cm). Parliament House Art Collection, Parliament House, Canberra.

ART OF PACIFIC CULTURES

In 1788, when Captain James Cook arrived in Australia, at least 300,000 Indigenous Australians, whose ancestors had arrived 50,000 years earlier, and who spoke over 250 languages, were living there. For 40,000 years these Aboriginal Australians had been creating rock art—the oldest continuous culture in the world. Nevertheless, Cook claimed Australia for Britain as a *terra nullius*, a land that belonged to no one. Within a few decades, European diseases had killed 50 percent of Indigenous Australians. Colonization and the advent of missionaries would change their lives forever.

Two hundred years later, Indigenous Australians presented what is now known as **THE BARUNGA STATEMENT (FIG. 27–1)** to the then prime minister Bob Hawke. It was inspired by the Yirrkala Bark Petitions, which 25 years earlier had gained national attention when indigenous land rights claims were presented to the government on traditional bark paintings from Arnhem Land in the Northern Territory. The Barunga Statement placed its call for broader Aboriginal rights in text on paper collaged onto composition board decorated with two different styles of indigenous painting: one from Arnhem Land (on the left; SEE ALSO FIG. 27–3) and the other from Australia's central desert area (on the right; see also "A Closer Look," page 876).

Painted in natural ochers, the cross hatching (*rarrk*) and zigzag patterns from the north contrast with the more fluid curved lines and dots that fill the central desert painting. In both, the artists use symbols to retell stories about the adventures of ancestral beings while dazzling the eye.

In 1992, the Australian High Court rejected Cook's *terra nullius* argument and granted land rights to Indigenous Australians. When no treaty between the national government and Indigenous Australians followed, Galarrwuy Yunupingu, an indigenous leader, asked for the Barunga Statement back so that he could bury it. Today, however, it still hangs in Parliament and the struggle for full rights for Indigenous Australians continues.

Throughout the Pacific, indigenous cultures have been impacted by contact with the West, though to different degrees. In New Zealand, for example, the Treaty of Waitangi (1840) recognized Maori ownership of land and gave Maori the rights of British subjects, establishing a different political dynamic. Nonetheless, numerous issues remain there, as in other parts of the region. Pacific islanders today use the arts to express and preserve their own rich and distinctive cultural identities.

LEARN ABOUT IT

27.1 Recognize how the availability of raw materials affects artistic choices and styles throughout the Pacific.

27.2 Investigate ways that ancestor rituals influence the art in different Pacific cultures.

27.3 Examine the role the human body plays as a subject in Pacific art.

27.4 Compare the differences between ephemeral and enduring materials in different societies across the Pacific.

27.5 Assess the impact of Western contact on art in the Pacific.

HEAR MORE: Listen to an audio file of your chapter **www.myartslab.com**

THE PEOPLING OF THE PACIFIC

On a map with the Pacific Ocean as its center, only the peripheries of the great landmasses of Asia and the Americas appear. Nearly one-third of the earth's surface is taken up by this vast expanse. Europeans arriving in Oceania in the late eighteenth and early nineteenth centuries noted four distinct but connected cultural-geographic areas: Australia, Melanesia, Micronesia, and Polynesia (MAP 27–1). Australia includes the continent, as well as the island of Tasmania to the southeast. Melanesia ("black islands," a reference to the dark skin color of its inhabitants) includes New Guinea and the string of islands that extend eastward from it as far as Fiji and New Caledonia. Micronesia ("small islands"), to the north of Melanesia, is a region of small islands and coral atolls. Polynesia ("many islands") is scattered over a huge, triangular region defined by New Zealand in the south, Rapa Nui (Easter Island) in the east, and the Hawaiian Islands to the north. The last region on earth to be inhabited by humans, Polynesia covers some 7.7 million square miles, of which fewer than 130,000 square miles are dry land—and most of that is New Zealand. With the exception of temperate New Zealand, with its marked seasons and snowcapped mountains, Oceania is in the tropics, that is, between the tropic of Cancer in the north and the tropic of Capricorn to the south.

Australia, Tasmania, and New Guinea formed a single continent during the last Ice Age, which began some 2.5 million years ago. About 50,000 years ago, when the sea level was some 330 feet lower than it is today, people moved to this continent from Southeast Asia, making at least part of the journey over open water.

27-2 • FRAGMENTS OF A LARGE LAPITA JAR
Venumbo Reef, Santa Cruz Island, Solomon Islands. c. 1200–1100 BCE. Clay, height of human face motif approx. 1½″ (4 cm).

Some 27,000 years ago humans were settled on the large islands north and east of New Guinea as far south as San Cristobal, but they ventured no farther for another 25,000 years. By about 4000 BCE—possibly as early as 7000 BCE—the people of Melanesia were raising pigs and cultivating taro, a plant with edible rootstocks. As the glaciers melted, the sea level rose, flooding low-lying coastal land. By around 4000 BCE a 70-mile-wide waterway, now called the Torres Strait, separated New Guinea from Australia, whose indigenous people continued their hunting and gathering way of life into the twentieth century.

The settling of the rest of the islands of Melanesia and the westernmost islands of Polynesia—Samoa and Tonga—coincided with the spread of the Lapita culture, named for a site in New Caledonia. The Lapita people were Austronesian speakers who probably migrated from Taiwan to Melanesia about 6,000 years ago. They spread throughout the islands of Melanesia beginning around 1500 BCE. They were farmers and fisherfolk who cultivated taro and yams, and brought with them dogs, pigs, and chickens, animals that these colonizers needed for food. They also carried with them the distinctive ceramics whose remnants today enable us to trace the extent of their travels. Lapita potters produced dishes, platters, bowls, and jars. Sometimes they covered their wares with a red slip, and they often decorated them with bands of incised and stamped patterns—dots, lines, and hatching—that may also have been used to decorate bark cloth and for tattooing. Most of the decoration was geometric, but some was figurative. The human face that appears in the example in FIGURE 27–2 is among the earliest representations of a human being, one of the most important subjects in Oceanic art. The Lapita people were skilled shipbuilders and navigators and engaged in inter-island trade. Over time the Lapita culture lost its widespread cohesion and evolved into various local forms. Its end is generally dated to the early centuries of the Common Era.

Polynesian culture emerged in the eastern Lapita region on the islands forming Tonga and Samoa. Just prior to the beginning of the first millennium CE, daring Polynesian seafarers, probably in double-hulled sailing canoes, began settling the scattered islands of Far Oceania and eastern Micronesia. Voyaging over open water, sometimes for thousands of miles, they reached Hawaii and Rapa Nui after about 500 CE and settled New Zealand around 800/900–1200 CE.

While this history of migrations across Melanesia to Polynesia and Micronesia allowed for cross-cultural borrowings, there are distinctions between these areas and within the regions as well. The islands that make up Micronesia, Melanesia, and Polynesia include both low-lying coral atolls and the tall tops of volcanic mountains that rise from the ocean floor. Raw materials available to residents of these islands vary greatly, and islander art and architecture utilize these materials in different ways. The soil of volcanic islands can be very rich and thus can support densely populated settlements with a local diversity of plants and animals. On the other hand, coral atolls do not generally have very good soil and thus cannot support

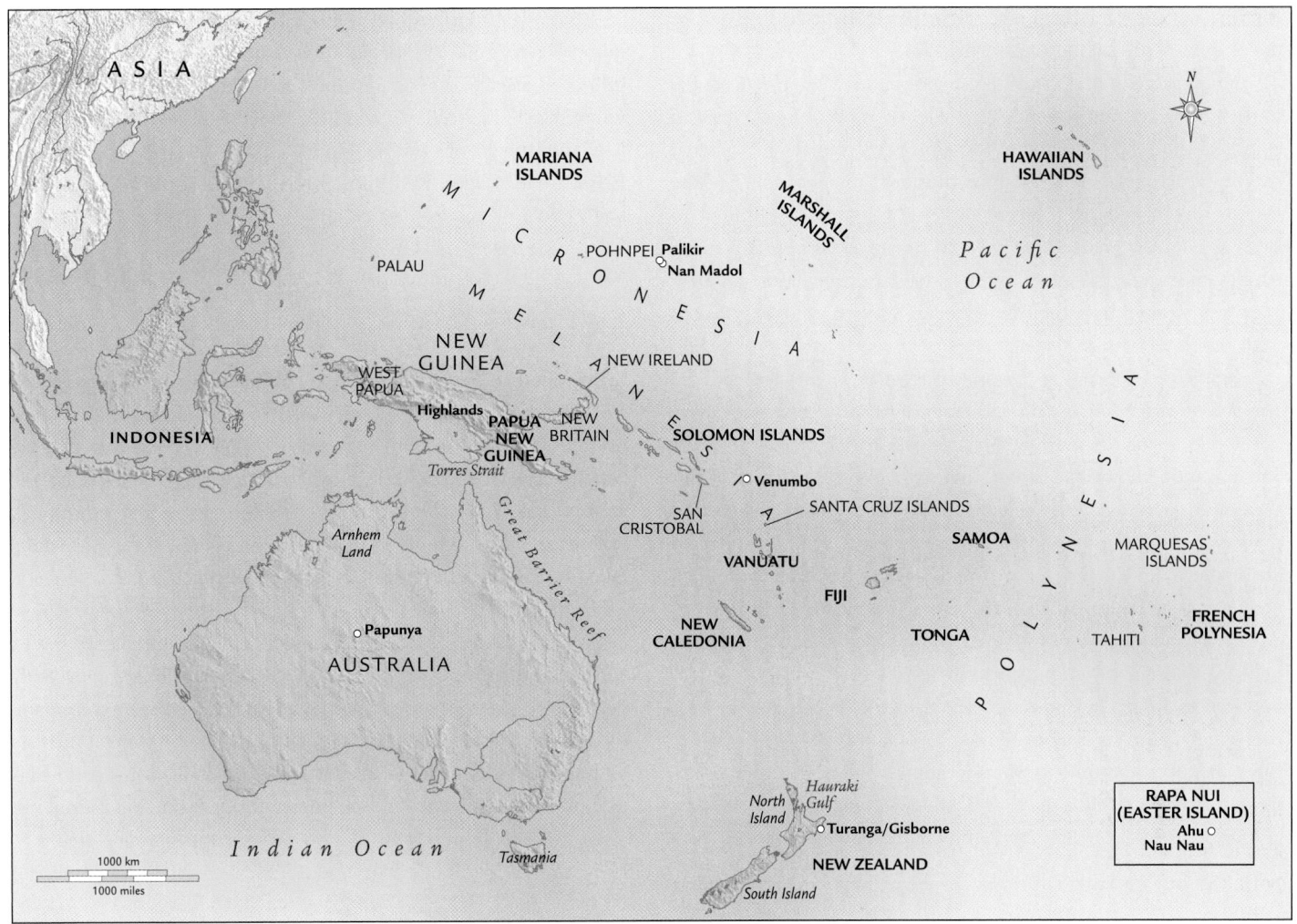

MAP 27-1 • PACIFIC CULTURAL-GEOGRAPHIC REGIONS

The Pacific cultures are found in four vast areas: Australia, Melanesia, Micronesia, and Polynesia.

large populations. In a like manner, volcanic islands can provide good stone for tools and building (as at Nan Madol, SEE FIG. 27–10), while coral is sharp but not particularly hard, and the strongest tools on a coral atoll are often those made from giant clam shells. Generally, the diversity of both plants and animals decreases from west to east among the Pacific islands.

The arts of this vast and diverse region display an enormous variety that is closely linked to each community's ritual and religious life. In this context, the visual arts were often just one strand in a rich weave that also included music, dance, and oral literature.

AUSTRALIA

The hunter-gatherers of Australia were closely attuned to the environments in which they lived until European settlers disrupted their way of life. Their only modification of the landscape was regular controlled burning of the underbrush, which encouraged new plant life and attracted animals. Their intimate knowledge of plants, animals, and water sources enabled them to survive and thrive in a wide range of challenging environments.

Indigenous Australian life is intimately connected with the concept of the Dreamtime, or the Dreaming. Not to be confused with our notions of sleep and dreams, the Dreaming refers to the period before humans existed. (The term, a translation from Arrente, one of the more than 250 languages spoken in Australia when Europeans arrived, was first used in the late nineteenth century to try to understand the indigenous worldview.) According to this complex belief system, the world began as a flat, featureless place. Ancestral Spirit Beings emerged from the earth or arrived from the sea, taking many different forms. The Spirit Beings had many adventures, and in crossing the continent they created all of its physical features: mountains, sand hills, creeks, and water holes. They also brought about the existence of animals, plants, and humans and created the ceremonies and sacred objects needed to ensure that they themselves were remembered, a system sometimes referred to as Aboriginal Laws. The Spirit Beings eventually returned to the earth or became literally one of its features. Thus, they are identified with specific places, which are honored as sacred sites. Indigenous Australians who practice this traditional religion believe that they are descended from the Spirit

Beings and associate themselves with particular places related to the ancestors' stories and transformations.

Knowledge of the Dreaming stories, and of the objects related to them, is sacred and secret. Multiple levels of meaning are learned over a lifetime and restricted to those properly trained and initiated to know each level. As a result, an outsider's understanding of the stories and related art (objects and motifs) is strictly limited to what is allowed to be public. Some stories are shared by many tribes across great distances, while others are specific to an area. Men and women have their own stories, women's often associated with food and food gathering.

Since the Dreaming has never ceased, the power of the ancestral Spirit Beings still exists. Indigenous Australians have developed a rich artistic life to relive the stories of the ancestors and transmit knowledge about them to subsequent generations. Ceremonial art forms include paintings on rock and bark, sand drawings, and ground sculptures. Sacred objects, songs, and dances are used to renew the supernatural powers of the ancestors in ceremonial meetings, called corroborees. In **FIGURE 27–3**, Western Arnhem Land artist Jimmy Midjaw Midjaw depicts such a meeting held by a group of Mimi, spirits who live in the narrow spaces between rocks by day and come out at night. Specific to this area, they taught humans how to hunt and cook animals, and to dance, sing, and play instruments in ceremonies. Tall, thin, human-like figures, often in motion, they were painted in ancient rock shelters, and since at least the late nineteenth century, on eucalyptus bark.

Bark paintings are found throughout northern Australia, where numerous regional styles exist. In Western Arnhem Land, the background is usually a monochromatic red ocher wash, with figures in white, black, and red pigments. In the 1950s and 1960s, Midjaw Midjaw was part of a prolific group of artists on Minjilang (Croker Island) that became well known through the anthropologists and collectors working in the area.

MELANESIA

In Melanesia the people usually rely at least partially on agriculture, and as a result they live in permanent settlements, many of which feature spaces set aside for ritual use. Position and status in society are not inherited or determined by birth, but are achieved by the accumulation of wealth (often in the form of pigs), prestige through leadership, and, often, participation in men's societies. Much ceremony is related to rituals associated with these societies, such as initiation into different levels or grades. Other important rituals facilitate relationships with the deceased and with supernatural forces. Melanesian art is often bold and dazzling. Masking and body decoration, often as part of ceremonial performances, are important, though often ephemeral, aspects of Melanesian art. Although men are prominent in the sculptural and masking traditions, women play significant roles as audience and are known for their skill in making bark cloth, woven baskets, pottery, and other aesthetically pleasing objects.

27-3 • Jimmy Midjaw Midjaw THREE DANCERS AND TWO MUSICIANS: CORROBOREE OF MIMI, SPIRITS OF THE ROCKS
Minjilang (Croker Island), West Arnhem Land, Australia. Mid 20th century. Natural pigments on eucalyptus bark, 23 × 35″ (59 × 89 cm). Musée du Quai Branly, Paris, France. MNAO 64.9.103

NEW GUINEA

New Guinea, the largest island in the Pacific (and, at 1,500 miles long and 1,000 miles wide, the second-largest island in the world), is today divided between two countries. Its eastern half is part of the modern nation of Papua New Guinea; the western half is West Papua, a province of present-day Indonesia. Located near the equator and with mountains that rise to 16,000 feet, the island inhabitants utilize a variety of environments, from coastal mangrove marshes to grasslands, from dense rainforests to swampy river valleys. The population is equally diverse, with coastal fishermen, riverine hunters, slash-and-burn agriculturalists, and more stable farmers in the highlands. Between New Guinea itself and the smaller neighboring islands more than 700 languages have been identified.

THE *KORAMBO* OR CEREMONIAL HOUSE OF THE ABELAM OF PAPUA NEW GUINEA.

The Abelam, who live in the foothills of

27-4 • EXTERIOR OF *KORAMBO* (*HAUS TAMBARAN*)
Kinbangwa village, Sepik River, Papua New Guinea. Abelam,
20th century.

the mountains on the north side of the Sepik River in Papua New Guinea, raise pigs and cultivate yams, taro, bananas, and sago palms. In traditional Abelam society, people live in extended families or clans in hamlets. Wealth among the Abelam is measured in pigs, but men gain status from participation in a yam cult that has a central place in Abelam society. The yams that are the focus of this cult—some of which reach an extraordinary 12 feet in length—are associated with clan ancestors and the potency of their growers. Village leaders renew their relationship with the forces of nature that yams represent during the Long Yam Festival, which is held at harvest time and involves processions, masked figures, singing, and the ritual exchange of the finest yams.

An Abelam hamlet includes sleeping houses, cooking houses, storehouses for yams, a central space for rituals, and a ceremonial or spirit house, the **korambo** (*haus tambaran* in Pidgin). In this ceremonial structure reserved for the men of the village, the objects associated with the yam cult and with clan identity are kept hidden from women and uninitiated boys. Men of the clan gather in the *korambo* to organize rituals, especially initiation rites, and conduct community business. The prestige of a hamlet is linked to the quality of its *korambo* and the size of its yams. Constructed on a frame of poles and rafters and roofed with split cane and thatch, *korambo* are built with a triangular floor plan, the side walls meeting at the back of the building. The elaborately decorated façade consists of three parts, beginning at the bottom: a woven mat, a painted and carved wooden lintel, and painted sago bark panels (**FIG. 27–4**). In this example, built about 1961, red, white, and black faces of spirits (*nggwal*) appear on the façade's bark panels, and the figure at the top is said to represent a female flying witch. This last figure is associated with the feminine power of the house itself. The projecting pole at the top of the *korambo* is the only male element of the architecture, and is said to be the penis of the house. The small door at the lower right is a female element, a womb; entering and exiting the house is the symbolic equivalent to death and rebirth. The Abelam believe the paint itself has magical qualities. Regular, ritual repainting revitalizes the images and ensures their continued potency.

Every stage in the construction of a *korambo* is accompanied by ceremonies, which are held in the early morning while women and boys are still asleep. The completion of the façade of a house is celebrated with a ceremony called *mindja*, which includes all-night dancing, and which may continue for six months, until the roof is completely thatched. Women participate in these inaugural ceremonies and are allowed to enter the new house, which afterward is ritually cleansed and closed to them.

BILUM—CONTEMPORARY NET BAGS OF HIGHLAND NEW GUINEA.

Women's arts in Papua New Guinea tend to be less spectacular and more subtle than men's, but nonetheless significant. Both functionally and symbolically, they contribute to a balance between male and female roles in society. **Bilum**, for example, are netted bags made mainly by women throughout the central

27-5 • WOMEN WEARING NET BAGS (*BILUM*)
Wahgi valley, Western Highlands Province, Papua New Guinea. 1990.

highlands of New Guinea **(FIG. 27–5)**. Looped from a single long thread spun on the thigh, *bilum* are very strong and, as loosely woven work bags, are used to carry items from vegetables to beer. The bones of a deceased man may be stored in a special *bilum* in a village's men's house (which is similar in function to the Abelam *korambo* in FIGURE 27–4), while his widow wears his personal bag as a sign of mourning. Women wear decorative *bilum*, into which marsupial fur is often incorporated, as adornment, exchange them as gifts, and use them to carry babies.

Bilum are rich metaphorical symbols. Among the women of the Wahgi tribe, who live in the Wahgi valley of the central highlands, seen in FIGURE 27–5, the term *bilum* may be used as a synonym for womb and bride, and they are also associated with ideas of female attractiveness; depending on how they are worn, they can indicate whether a girl is eligible for marriage.

In the past, *bilum* were made from natural fibers, most commonly the inner bark of a ficus plant. Today, while the technique for making them remains unchanged, a wide array of colorful, contemporary fibers, including nylon and acrylic yarn, are used, and new designs incorporating complicated patterns and

words are constantly appearing. *Bilum* are now made by women throughout Papua New Guinea, not just in the highlands. They are sold commercially in markets and towns, and have become one of the country's national symbols.

SPIRIT POLES OF THE ASMAT OF WEST PAPUA. The Asmat, who live along rivers in the coastal swamp forests on the southwest coast, were known in the past as warriors and headhunters (head-hunting was generally believed to maintain balance between hostile groups). In their culture, they identified trees with human beings, their fruit with human heads. Fruit-eating birds were thus the equivalent of headhunters, and were often represented in war and mortuary arts, along with the praying mantis, whose female bites off the head of the male during mating. In the past, the Asmat believed that death was always caused by an enemy, either by direct killing or through magic, and that it required revenge, usually in the form of taking an enemy's head, to appease the spirit of the person who had died.

Believing that the spirit of the dead person remained in the village, the Asmat erected elaborately sculpted memorial poles

(FIG. 27–6), known as *bisj* (pronounced bish), which embodied the spirits of the ancestors and paid tribute to them. *Bisj* poles are generally carved from mangrove trees, although some in a museum in Leiden recently have been found to be from the wild nutmeg. The felling of a tree is a ritual act in which a group of men attack the tree as if it were an enemy. The figures on the poles represent the dead individuals who are to be avenged; small figures represent dead children. The bent pose of the figures associates them with the praying mantis. The large, lacy phalluses emerging from the figures at the top of the poles are carved from the projecting roots of the tree and symbolize male fertility, while the surface decoration suggests body ornamentation. The *bisj* were placed in front of special houses belonging to the village's men's society. The poles faced the river to ensure that the spirits of the dead would travel to the realm of the ancestors (*safan*), which lay beyond the sea. The *bisj* pole also served symbolically as the dugout canoe that would take the spirit of the deceased down the river to *safan*.

By carving *bisj* poles (usually for several deceased at the same time) and organizing a *bisj* feast, relatives publicly indicated their responsibility to avenge their dead in a headhunting raid. As part of the ceremonies, mock battles were held, the men boasting of their bravery, the women cheering them on. After the ceremonies, the poles were left in the swamp to deteriorate and transfer their supernatural power back to nature. Today, Asmat continue to carve *bisj* poles and use them in funerary ceremonies, although they stopped headhunting in the 1970s. Poles are also made to sell to outsiders.

NEW IRELAND

MALAGAN DISPLAY OF NEW IRELAND. New Ireland is one of the large eastern islands of the nation of Papua New Guinea. The northern people on the island still practice a complex set of death and commemorative rites known as *malagan* (pronounced malang-gan), which could take place as much as two years after a person's death. In the past, clan leaders rose to prominence primarily through *malagan* ceremonies that honored their wives' recently deceased family members. The greater the *malagan* ceremony, the greater prominence the clan leader had achieved.

27-6 • ASMAT ANCESTRAL SPIRIT POLES (*BISJ*)
Buepis village, Fajit River, West Papua Province, Indonesia. c. 1960. Wood, paint, palm leaves, and fiber, height approx. 18′ (5.48 m).

Malagan also included rites to initiate young men and women into adulthood. After several months' training in seclusion in a ritual enclosure, they were presented to the public and carved and painted figures were given to them. The combined funerary and initiation ceremonies included feasts, masked dances, and the creation of a special house to display elaborately carved and painted sculptures **(FIG. 27–7)** that honored the dead. The display house illustrated, which dates to the early 1930s, is more than 14 feet wide and 12 deceased individuals are being honored. The carvings are large (the first on the left is nearly 6 feet in height) and take the form of horizontal friezes, standing figures, and poles containing several figures. They are visually complex, with tensions created between solid and pierced void, and between the two-dimensional painted patterns on three-dimensional sculptural forms. Kept secret until the final phase of the ceremonies, their unveiling was the climax of the festivities. After the ceremonies they were no longer considered ritually "active" and were destroyed or, since the late nineteenth century, sold to outsiders. *Malagan* figures are still being carved and ceremonies are held today.

NEW BRITAIN

TUBUAN MASK OF NEW BRITAIN. In the Papua New Guinea province of New Britain, which includes the Duke of York Islands, Tubuan masks represent the Tolai male secret society. This has different levels or grades of increasing knowledge and power, and wields both spiritual and social control, especially during the three months of ceremonies known as the "Time of the Tubuan."

Though initiation to the society is the main purpose of the ceremonies, the men of the village, who have achieved power through the accumulation of wealth, and in the past through bravery in war, use this period to call up the spirits represented by the masks, who have the authority to settle disputes, stop fights, punish lawbreakers, and force the payment of debts. Political power and authority are underscored and enhanced by their appearance, and in the past they had the power of life and death.

The masks represent both female and male spirits, though all the masks are danced by men. Local stories say women originally owned the masks and that they were stolen from them by men. The **TUBUAN MASK (FIG. 27–8)** represents the Mother, who gives birth to her children, the Duk Duk masks, which represent the new initiates into the society. With the appearance, first of the Mother masks, then of the Duk Duk masks, the initiates return to the village from the bush, where they have undergone intensive preparation to enter the society. The Tubuan mask has a distinctive, tall conical shape and prominent eyes formed by concentric white circles. The green leaf skirt is a very sacred part of the mask, which is made from painted bark cloth, various fibers, and feathers: Black feathers on top indicate a more powerful spirit than white feathers.

MICRONESIA

The majority of Micronesia's islands are small, low-lying coral atolls, but in the western region several are volcanic in origin. The eastern islands are more closely related culturally to Polynesia,

27-7 • *MALAGAN* DISPLAY
Medina village, New Ireland, Papua New Guinea. c. 1930. Height 82⅝" (210 cm), width 137¾" (350 cm).
Museum für Völkerkunde, Basel, Switzerland.

while those in the west show connections to Melanesia, especially in the men's houses found on Palau and Yap. The atolls—circular coral reefs surrounding lagoons where islands once stood—have a limited range of materials for creating objects of any kind. Micronesians are known especially for their navigational skills and their fine canoes. They also create textiles from banana and coconut fibers, bowls from turtle shells, and abstract human figures from wood, which is scarce. As in other parts of the Pacific, tattooing and the performative arts remain central to life.

WAPEPE NAVIGATION CHART. Sailors from the Marshall Islands relied on celestial navigation (navigating by the sun and moon and stars) as well as a detailed understanding of the ocean currents and trade winds to travel from one island to another. To teach navigation to younger generations, elders traditionally used stick charts (*wapepe* or *mattang*)—maps that showed land, but also the path from one island to the next, the water a sailor would cross during his voyage.

In common use until the 1950s, the stick chart (**FIG. 27–9**) was a schematic diagram of the prevailing ocean currents and the characteristic wave patterns encountered between islands. The currents are represented by sticks held together by coconut fibers; the shells mark islands on the route. The arrangement of sticks around a shell indicates a zone of distinctive waves shaped by the effect of an island deflecting the prevailing wind. Such refracted waves enable a

27-9 • *WAPEPE* NAVIGATION CHART
Marshall Islands. 19th century. Sticks, coconut fiber, shells, 29½ × 29½″ (75 × 75 cm). Peabody Essex Museum, Salem.

navigator to sense the proximity of land without being able to see it, and to discern the least difficult course for making landfall. Although the *wapepe* is primarily functional, its combination of clarity, simplicity, and abstraction has an aesthetic impact.

NAN MADOL. The basalt cliffs of the island of Pohnpei provided the building material for one of the largest and most remarkable stone architectural complexes in Oceania. Nan Madol, on its southeast coast, consists of 92 artificial islands set within a network of canals covering about 170 acres (**MAP 27–2**). Seawalls and breakwaters 15 feet high and 35 feet thick protect the area from the ocean. When it was populated, openings in the breakwaters gave canoes access to the ocean and allowed seawater to flow in and out with the tides, flushing clean the canals. While other similar complexes have been identified in Micronesia, Nan Madol is the largest and most impressive, reflecting the importance of the kings who ruled from the site. The artificial islands and the buildings atop them were built between the early thirteenth and seventeenth centuries, until the dynasty's political decline. The site had been abandoned by the time Europeans discovered it in the nineteenth century.

Nan Madol was an administrative and ceremonial center as well as, at one time, a home for as many as 1,000 people. The powerful kings drew upon this labor force to construct a monumental city. Both the buildings and the underlying islands are built of massive pieces of stone set in alternating layers of log-shaped stones and boulders of prismatic basalt. The largest of the

27-8 • TUBUAN MASK BEING DANCED
Tolai people, Duke of York Islands, New Britain, Papua New Guinea. c. 1990. Cloth, paint, fiber, feathers.

MAP 27-2 • THE COMPLEX OF NAN MADOL

Pohnpei, Federated States of Micronesia. c. 1200/1300– c. 1500/1600.

artificial islets is more than 100 yards long, and one basalt corner-stone alone is estimated to weigh about 50 tons. The stone logs were split from the cliffs by alternately heating the stone and dousing it with water. Most of the islands are oriented northeast–southwest, receiving the benefit of the cooling prevailing winds.

The royal mortuary compound, which once dominated the southeast side of Nan Madol (**FIG. 27–10**), has walls rising in subtle upward and outward curves to a height of 25 feet. To achieve the sweeping, rising lines, the builders increased the number of stones in the header courses (those with the ends of the stones laid facing out along the wall) relative to the stretcher courses (those with the lengths of the stones laid parallel to the wall) as they came to the corners and entryways. The plan of the structure consists simply of progressively higher rectangles within rectangles—the outer walls leading by steps up to interior walls that lead up to a central courtyard with a small, cubical tomb.

POLYNESIA

The settlers of the far-flung islands of Polynesia developed distinctive cultural traditions but also retained linguistic and cultural affinities that reflect their common origin. Traditional Polynesian

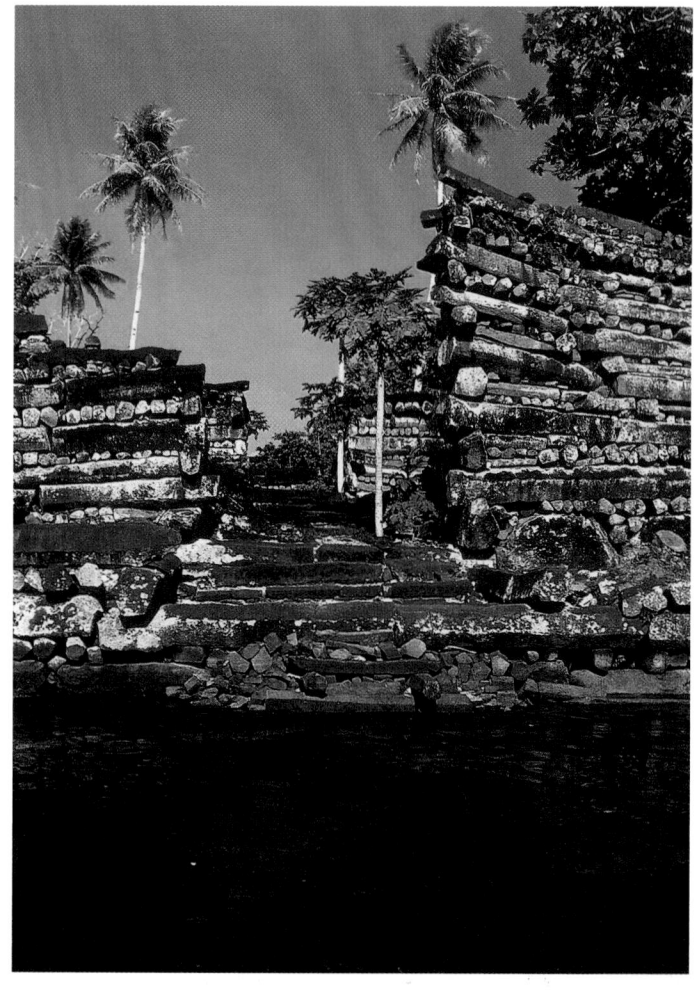

27-10 • ROYAL MORTUARY COMPOUND, NAN MADOL
Pohnpei, Federated States of Micronesia. Basalt blocks, wall height up to 25′ (7.62 m).

society was generally far more stratified than Melanesian society: A person's genealogy, tracing his or her descent from an ancestral god, determined his or her place in society. First-born children of the hereditary elite were considered the most sacred because they inherited more spiritual power (*mana*) at their birth. *Mana* could be gained through leadership, courage, or skill or lost due to failure in warfare. It was protected by strict laws of conduct called *tapu*, a word that came into the English language as taboo.

All of the arts in Polynesia were sacred, and their creation was a sacred act: Master artists were also ritual specialists. Objects were crafted from a variety of materials, some of which, like jadite in New Zealand, were considered spiritually powerful. Some objects were useful ones, such as canoes, fishhooks, and weapons; others indicated the status and rank of the society's elite. The objects had their own *mana* that could increase or decrease depending on how successful they were in performing their functions. Their quality and beauty were important: Objects were made to endure and many were handed down as heirlooms from generation to generation. In addition, the human body itself was the canvas for the art of tattoo (*tatau* in several Polynesian languages).

Polynesian religions included many levels of gods, from creator gods and semidivine hero-gods (such as Maui, who appears in the stories of many of the Polynesian cultures) to natural forces, but the most important were one's ancestors, who became gods at their death. They remained influential in daily life, so needed to be honored and placated, and their help was sought for important projects and in times of trouble. Throughout much of Polynesia, figures in human form, often generically called *tiki*, were carved in stone, wood, and in some places, such as the Marquesas Islands, human bone. These statues represented the ancestors and were often placed on sacred ritual sites attended by ritual specialists (SEE FIG. 27–13) or, as in New Zealand, incorporated into meeting houses (see "Te-Hau-ki-Turanga," pages 870–871).

MARQUESAS ISLANDS

TATTOO IN THE MARQUESAS ISLANDS. The art of tattoo was widespread and ancient in Oceania. Tattoo chisels made of bone have been found in Lapita sites. They are quite similar to the tools used to create the decorated Lapita pottery, suggesting some symbolic connection between the marking of the pottery and of human skin. The Polynesians, descendants of the Lapita people, brought tattooing with them as they migrated throughout the Pacific. As they became isolated from each other over time, distinctive styles evolved: Spirals became a hallmark of the Maori facial tattoo (*moko*), and rows of triangles became prominent in Hawaiian designs.

The people of the Marquesas Islands, an archipelago about 900 miles northeast of Tahiti, were the most extensively tattooed of all Polynesians. The process of tattooing involves shedding blood, the most *tapu* (sacred), substance in Polynesia. In the Marquesas, the process for a young man of high social rank began around age 18; by age 30 he would be fully tattooed. Because of the sacredness

and prestige of the process, some men continued to be tattooed until their skin was completely covered and the designs disappeared. Marquesan women were also tattooed, usually on the hands, ankles, lips, and behind the ears.

The process was painful and expensive. Though women could be tattooed with little ceremony in their own homes, in the case of both high-ranking men and women, special houses were built for the occasion. The master tattooer and his assistants had to be fed and paid. At the end of the session a special feast was held to display the new tattoos. Each design had a name and a meaning: Tattooing was done to mark passages in people's lives and their social positions, and to commemorate special events or accomplishments. Some tattoos denoted particular men's societies or eating groups. Especially for men, tattoos showed their courage and were essential to their sexual attractiveness to women.

Tattooing was forbidden in the nineteenth century by French colonial administrators and Catholic missionaries, and died out in the Marquesas. Beginning in the 1970s, tattooing underwent a resurgence throughout the Pacific and in 1980 **TEVE TUPUHIA** became the first Marquesan in modern times to be fully tattooed (**FIG. 27–11**). He went to Samoa, the only place in Polynesia where the traditional art form continued, to be tattooed by master

27-11 • TEVE TUPUHIA
Marquesan man tattooed in 1980 by Samoan Lese Ii'o.

Te-Hau-ki-Turanga

New Zealand was settled sometime after 800 CE by intrepid seafaring Polynesians now known as the Maori. As part of the process of adapting their Polynesian culture to the temperate New Zealand environment, they began to build wooden-frame homes, the largest of which, the chief's house, evolved after Western contact into the meeting house (*whare nui*). The meeting house stands on an open plaza (*marae*) a sacred place where a Maori tribe (*iwi*) or subtribe (*hapu*) still today greets visitors, discusses important issues, and mourns the dead. In it, tribal history and genealogy are recorded and preserved. Carved by the master carver Raharuhi Rukupo in the early

1840s, Te-Hau-ki-Turanga is the oldest existing, fully decorated meeting house in New Zealand (FIG. A). Built by Rukupo as a memorial to his elder brother, its name refers to the region of New Zealand where it was made—Turanga, today Gisborne, on the northeast coast of North Island—and can be translated as the Breezes of Turanga.

In this area of New Zealand, the meeting house symbolizes the tribe's founding ancestor, for whom it is often named. The ridgepole is the backbone, the rafters are the ribs, and the slanting **bargeboards**—the boards attached to the projecting end of the gable—are the outstretched enfolding arms. The face appears in the gable mask. Relief

figures of ancestors cover the support poles, wall planks, and the lower ends of the rafters. The ancestors, in effect, support the house. They were thought to take an active interest in community affairs and to participate in the discussions held in the meeting house. Rukupo, an important political and religious leader as well as a master carver, included an unusual naturalistic portrait of himself among them.

Painted curvilinear patterns (**kowhaiwhai**) decorate the rafters in red and black on a white background. The **koru** pattern, a curling stalk with a bulb at the end that resembles the young tree fern, dominates the design system. Lattice panels

A. Raharuhi Rukupo, master carver **TE-HAU-KI-TURANGA (MAORI MEETING HOUSE)**
Gisborne/Turanga, New Zealand; built and owned by the Rongowhakaata people of Turanga. 1842–1843, restored in 1935.
Wood, shell, grass, flax, and pigments. Museum of New Zealand/Te Papa Tongarewa, Wellington. Neg. B18358

(tukutuku) made by women fill the spaces between the wall planks. Because ritual prohibitions, or taboos, prevented women from entering the meeting house, they worked from the outside and wove the panels from the back. They created the black, white, and orange patterns from grass, flax, and flat slats. Each pattern has a symbolic meaning: chevrons represent the teeth of the sea monster Taniwha; steps represent the stairs of heaven climbed by the hero-god Tawhaki; and diamonds represent the flounder.

When Captain Cook arrived in New Zealand in the second half of the eighteenth century, each tribe and geographical region had its own style. A storehouse doorway from the Ngati Paoa tribe (FIG. B), who lived in the Hauraki Gulf area to the west of Turanga, dates to this period of time (or earlier) and shows the soft, shallow surface carving resulting from the use of stone tools. In comparison, a house panel (poupou) from Te-Hau-ki-Turanga, carved with steel tools, is much more fully three-dimensional, with the deeply cut, very precisely detailed surface carving characteristic of that time.

As is typical throughout Polynesia (SEE FIG. 27–13), the figures face frontally and have large heads with open eyes. Their hands are placed on the stomach and their tongues stick out in defiance from their figure-eight-shaped mouths. The Hauraki Gulf figure represents a male ancestor, while the Te-Hau-ki-Turanga figure (FIG. C) is a female ancestor nursing a child. Both have a small figure, representing their descendants, between their legs.

Considered a national treasure by the Maori, this meeting house was restored in 1935 by Maori artists who knew the old, traditional methods; it is now preserved at the Museum of New Zealand/Te Papa Tongarewa in Wellington and considered *taonga* (cultural treasure).

B. CARVED FIGURE FROM STOREHOUSE DOORWAY
Ngäti Päoa, Hauraki Gulf, New Zealand. 1500–1800. Wood, height 33⅞″ (86 cm). Museum of New Zealand/Te Papa Tongarewa, Wellington.

C. POUPOU
(panel) from Te-Hau-ki-Turanga. Wood and red pigment, height 4′7″ (140 cm). Museum of New Zealand/Te Papa Tongarewa, Wellington.

Interior side wall

Parts of the meeting house

Front

Interior rear wall

27-12 • FEATHER CLOAK, KNOWN AS THE KEARNY CLOAK
Hawaii. c. 1843. Red, yellow, and black feathers, olona cordage, and netting, length 55¾" (143 cm). Bishop Museum, Honolulu.

King Kamehameha III (r. 1825–1854) presented this cloak to Commodore Lawrence Kearny, commander of the frigate USS *Constellation*.

Samoan artist Lese I'io. The process took six weeks and cost $35,000. Teve based his tattoo designs on drawings made by George Langsdorff, a German naturalist who visited the Marquesas in 1804 as part of a Russian scientific expedition. Today, Marquesan-style tattoo designs are seen throughout French Polynesia.

HAWAII

FEATHER CLOAK FROM HAWAII.   The Hawaiian islanders had one of the most highly stratified of all Polynesian societies, with valleys and whole islands ruled by high chiefs. Soon after contact with the West, the entire archipelago was unified for the first time under the rule of Kamehameha I (r. 1810–1819), who assumed the title of king in the European manner.

Among the members of the Hawaiian elite, feathered capes and cloaks were emblems of their high social status. The most valuable were full-length and made with thousands of red and yellow feathers. A full-length cloak, like the one in FIGURE 27–12, was reserved for the highest ranks of the elite men. It was called an *'ahu 'ula* ("red cloak"); the color red is associated with high status and rank throughout Polynesia. Often given as gifts to important visitors to Hawaii, this particular cloak was presented in 1843 to Commodore Lawrence Kearny, commander of the USS *Constellation*, by King Kamehameha III (r. 1825–1854).

Draped over the wearer's shoulders, such a cloak creates a sensuously textured and colored abstract design, which in this example joins to create matching patterns of paired crescents on front and back. The cloak's foundation consisted of coconut fiber netting onto which bundles of feathers were tied. The feathers were part of an annual tribute paid to the king by his subjects. The red, and especially the yellow feathers, were highly prized and came from several species of birds including the *i'iwi, apapane, 'o'o,* and *mamo* (which is now extinct). In some cases, each bird yielded only seven or eight feathers, making the collecting of feathers very labor-intensive and increasing the value of the cloaks.

The cloaks were so closely associated with the spiritual power (*mana*) of the elite person that they could be made only by specialists trained in both the complicated technique of manufacture and the rituals attending their fabrication. Surrounded by protective objects, they created the cloak while reciting the chief's genealogy and imbuing it with the power of his ancestors. As a result, the cloaks were seen as protective of the wearer, while also proclaiming his elite status, and political and economic power.

Feathers were used for decorating not just cloaks, but also helmets, capes, blankets, and garlands (*leis*), all of which conferred status and prestige. The annual tribute paid to the king by his subjects included feathers, and tall feather pompons (*kahili*) mounted on long slender sticks were symbols of royalty. Even the effigies of gods that Hawaiian warriors carried into battle were made of light, basketlike structures covered with feathers.

MONUMENTAL MOAI ON RAPA NUI

Rapa Nui (Easter Island) is the most isolated inhabited locale in Oceania, some 2,300 miles west of the coast of South America and 1,200 miles from Pitcairn Island, the nearest Polynesian outpost. Three volcanoes, one at each corner, make up the small triangular island. Originally known to its native inhabitants as Te Pito o te Henúa (Navel of the World) and now known as Rapa Nui, it was named Easter Island by Captain Jacob Roggeveen, the Dutch explorer who first landed there on Easter Sunday in 1722. Rapa Nui became part of Chile in 1888.

MONUMENTAL MOAI.   Rapa Nui is the site of Polynesia's most impressive stone sculpture. Though many imaginative theories have been posited regarding the origins of its statues, from space aliens to Native Americans, they are most definitely part of an established Polynesian tradition. Sacred religious sites (*marae*) with stone altar platforms (*ahu*) are common throughout Polynesia. On Rapa Nui, most of the *ahu* are near the coast, parallel to the shore. About 900 CE, the islanders began to erect stone figures on the *ahu*, perhaps as memorials to deceased chiefs. Nearly 1,000 of the figures, called **moai**, have been found on the island, including some 400 unfinished ones in the quarry at Rano Raraku where they were being carved. The statues themselves are made from tufa, a yellowish-brown volcanic stone. On their heads, *pukao* (topknots of hair) were rendered in red scoria. When the statues were in place, the insertion of white coral and stone "opened" the eyes. In 1978 several figures on Ahu Nau Nau (**FIG. 27–13**) were restored to their original condition. They are about 36 feet tall, but *moai* range in size from much smaller to a 65-foot statue that is still in the quarry. Like other Polynesian statues, the figures here face frontally. Their large heads have deep-set eyes under a prominent brow ridge; a long, concave, pointed nose; a small mouth with pursed lips; and an angular chin. The extremely elongated earlobes have parallel engraved lines that suggest ear ornaments. The figures have schematically indicated breastbones and pectorals, and small arms with hands pressed close to the sides. Their bodies emerge from the site at just below waist level, so they have no legs.

The islanders stopped erecting *moai* around 1500 and entered a period of warfare among themselves, apparently because overpopulation was straining the island's available resources. Most of the *moai* were knocked down and destroyed during this period, which marked the emergence of a new religious focus on what is usually termed the bird-man cult. The island's indigenous population, which may at one time have consisted of as many as 10,000 people, was

27-13 • *MOAI* ANCESTOR FIGURES
Ahu Nau Nau, Rapa Nui (Easter Island).
c. ?1000–1500 CE, restored 1978.
Volcanic stone (tufa), average height
approx. 36′ (11 m).

SEE MORE: View the podcast on
the *Moai* Ancestor Figures
www.myartslab.com

nearly eradicated in 1877 when Peruvian slave traders precipitated an epidemic of smallpox and tuberculosis that left only 110 inhabitants alive. Today, a vibrant population of some 4,000 people is known especially for its energetic and athletic dance performances.

SAMOA

TAPA (SIAPO) IN SAMOA. As they migrated across the Pacific, Polynesians brought with them the production of bark cloth. Known by various names throughout the Pacific, most commonly as **tapa**, in Samoa it is called **siapo**. Bark cloth is usually made by women, although sometimes men help to obtain the bark or decorate the completed cloth. In Samoa, *siapo* is made by stripping the inner bark from branches of the paper mulberry tree, although banyan and breadfruit are sometimes used in other archipelagoes. The bark is beaten with a wooden mallet, then folded over and beaten again, to various degrees of softness. Larger pieces can be made by building up the cloth in a process of felting or using natural pastes as glue. The heavy wooden mallets used for beating the cloth are often incised with complex patterns, which leave impressions like watermarks in the cloth, viewable when the cloth is held up to the light.

Plain and decorated *tapa* of various thicknesses and qualities was used throughout Polynesia for clothing, sails, mats, and ceremonial purposes, including wrapping the dead. *Tapa* was also used to wrap wooden or wicker frames to make human effigies in the Marquesas and Rapa Nui, serving a purpose we still do not completely understand. In western Polynesia (Samoa and Tonga) very large pieces, 7–10 feet across and hundreds of feet long, were traditionally given in ceremonial exchanges of valuables and as gifts. Along with fine mats, *siapo* is still sometimes given as gifts on important ceremonial occasions.

A widespread use of *tapa* was for clothing. For example, Samoan men and women wore large pieces of *siapo* as wraparound skirts (*lavalava*) (SEE FIG. 27–16). Special chiefs, called talking chiefs, who spoke on behalf of the highest-ranking chief in the village council, wore special *tapa* skirts called *siapo vala* (FIG. 27–14).

Distinctive design styles for *tapa* cloth evolved across the Pacific, even when the material used was essentially the same from one island to the next. It could be dyed bright yellow with turmeric or brown with dyes made from nuts. It could also be exposed to smoke to turn it black or darker brown. Today, contemporary fabric paint is often used. Decorative designs were made through a variety of means from freehand painting to impressing on the coloring with tiny bamboo stamps, or using stencils, as is done in Fiji. This Samoan *siapo vala* has designs that are produced by first placing the cloth over a wooden design tablet, an **upeti**, and then rubbing pigment over the cloth to pick up the carved pattern. The second stage is to overpaint this lighter rubbed pattern by hand. The result is a boldly patterned, symmetrical design.

RECENT ART IN OCEANIA

In the late 1960s and early 1970s, a cultural resurgence swept across the Pacific. Growing independence and autonomy throughout the region, the model of civil rights and other movements in the United States, and dramatic increases in tourism, among other factors, brought a new awareness of the importance of indigenous cultures. Many of them had been fundamentally changed, if not nearly destroyed, by colonial rule and missionary efforts to eradicate local customs and beliefs.

PACIFIC ARTS FESTIVAL

In the early 1970s, the South Pacific Commission conceived the idea of an arts festival that would promote traditional song and dance. The first Festival of Pacific Arts was held in 1972 in Fiji; subsequent festivals, held every four years, have been hosted by New Zealand, Papua New Guinea, Tahiti, Australia, Cook Islands, Samoa, New Caledonia, Palau, and American Samoa.

Musicians from the highlands of Papua New Guinea (FIG. 27–15) were among the more than 2,000 participants from 27 countries at the tenth festival at Pago Pago, American Samoa, in 2008. Carrying traditional drums, they wore elaborate headdresses topped with bird of paradise feathers, and neck ornaments made from kina shells, a once valuable medium of exchange in New Guinea.

In the 36 years since their founding, the festivals have had an enormous impact on the arts. Many Pacific cultures now have their own festivals, such as in the Marquesas Islands where they are held every four years. In an age of globalization and the Internet, festivals are one of the main ways in which young people become involved in, and learn about, their cultures. However, the festivals

27-14 • TAPA (SIAPO VALA)
Samoa. 20th century. 58⅝ × 57″ (149 × 145 cm).
Auckland Museum, New Zealand. AM 46892

27-15 • MUSICIANS FROM PAPUA NEW GUINEA AT THE PACIFIC ARTS FESTIVAL
Pago Pago, American Samoa, 2008.

are not without controversy: Some people are critical of an increasing level of professionalism and commercialism.

CENTRAL DESERT PAINTING. In Australia, indigenous artists have adopted canvas and acrylic paint for rendering imagery traditionally associated with more ephemeral media like body and sand drawing. Sand drawing is an ancient ritual art form that involves creating large colored designs on bare earth. Made with red and yellow ochers, seeds, and feathers arranged on the ground in symbolic patterns, they are used to convey tribal knowledge to initiates. In 1971, several indigenous Pintubi men who were trained and initaated to know the sacred knowledge, and were living in government-controlled Papunya Tula in the central desert of Australia, were encouraged by nonindigenous art teacher Geoffrey Bardon to transform their ephemeral art into a painted mural on the school wall. The success of the public mural encouraged community elders to allow others to try their hand at painting. In Utopia, a neighboring community, it was the women who began painting in 1988 after success in tie-dyeing with fabrics. Art galleries, originally located in Alice Springs, spread the art form, and "dot paintings" were a worldwide phenomenon by the late 1980s. Paintings also became an economic mainstay for many Aboriginal groups in the central and western Australia desert.

Although they are creating work for sale, the artists can paint only stories to which they have rights, and must be careful to depict only what a noninitiated person is allowed to know.

Clifford Possum Tjapaltjarri (c. 1932–2002), a founder of the Papunya Tula Artists Cooperative (1972), gained an international reputation after an exhibition of his paintings in 1988. He worked with his canvases on the floor, as in traditional sand painting, using ancient patterns and colors, principally red and yellow, as well as touches of blue. The superimposed layers of concentric circles and undulating lines and dots in a painting like *Man's Love Story* (see "A Closer Look," page 876) create an effect of shifting colors and lights.

The painting seems entirely abstract, but it actually conveys a narrative involving two mythical ancestors: one of these ancestors came to Papunya in search of honey ants; the white U shape on the left represents him seated in front of a water hole with an ants' nest, represented by the concentric circles. His digging stick lies to his right, and white sugary leaves lie to his left. The straight white "journey line" represents his trek from the west. The second ancestor, represented by the brown-and-white U-shaped form, came from the east, leaving footprints, and sat down by another water hole nearby. He began to spin a hair string on a spindle (the form leaning toward the upper right of the painting) but was

A CLOSER LOOK

Man's Love Story ▶ by Clifford Possum Tjapaltjarri, 1978. Synthetic polymer paint on canvas. 6'11¾" × 8'4¼" (2.15 × 2.57 m). Art Gallery of South Australia, Adelaide. Visual Arts Board of the Australia Council Contemporary Art Purchase Grant, 1980

Designs may have multiple meanings. A circle can represent a water hole or ant hole, as here, but also a hole where the ancestral spirit beings exited and entered the earth, a person as viewed from above, or a campfire.

Honey ants are sweet and are a delicacy. A digging stick is used to open up the nest, exposing the ant colony so that the ants can be removed and eaten.

Hair is spun into string using a spindle that is rotated across the thigh. The string is surprisingly strong and was used for utilitarian and ceremonial purposes, depending on the region.

Synthetic polymer, or acrylic, paint replaces the earth-toned ochers used in the original sand paintings that provide the model for these.

Women are important figures in the Dreaming stories and are represented in several places in this painting. Indigenous women are artists and paint their own stories, too, which usually center on food and food gathering.

The dots are made using a stick with a round, flat end that is dipped into the paint. Several people can work at the same time to fill in dotted areas.

SEE MORE View the Closer Look feature for Clifford Possum Tjapaltjarri's *Man's Love Story* **www.myartslab.com**

distracted by thoughts of the woman he loved, who belonged to a kinship group into which he could not marry. When she approached, he let his hair string blow away (represented by the brown flecks below him) and lost all his work. Four women (the dotted U shapes) came at night and surrounded the camp to guard the lovers. Rich symbolism also fills other areas of the painting: the white footprints are those of another ancestral figure following a woman, and the wavy line at the top is the path of yet another ancestor. The black, dotted oval area indicates the site where young men were taught this story. The long horizontal bars are mirages, while the wiggly shapes represent caterpillars, a source of food. Possum Tjapaltjarri painted numerous variations of this Dreaming story.

The painting is effectively a map showing the ancestors' journeys. To begin the work Possum Tjapaltjarri first painted the landscape features and the impressions left on the earth by the figures—their tracks, direction lines, and the U-shaped marks they left when sitting. Then, working carefully, dot by dot, he captured the vast expanse and shimmering light of the arid landscape. The painting's resemblance to modern Western painting styles such as Abstract Expressionism, gestural painting, pointillism, or color field painting (see Chapter 32) is accidental. Possum Tjapaltjarri's work is rooted in the mythic, narratives of the Dreaming. He and other contemporary artists working in both age-old and new media continue to create arts that express the deepest meanings of their culture.

ULUGALI'I SAMOA: SAMOAN COUPLE. Many contemporary Pacific artists live in urban settings, were trained at colleges and universities, and create artworks in modern media that deal with a range of political issues. These include the colonial legacy, discrimination, misappropriation, cultural identity, land rights, and many others. Shigeyuki Kihara is a multimedia and performance artist of Samoan and Japanese descent who lives in New Zealand. In **ULUGALI'I SAMOA: SAMOAN COUPLE** (FIG. 27–16), she explores issues of culture, identity, stereotypes, authenticity, representation, and gender roles through a reappropriation of nineteenth- and early twentieth-century colonial photographs. Made in studio settings, those photographs were often turned into postcards depicting Pacific Island men and women, both alone and in couples, the women as bare-breasted and sexualized "dusky maidens" and the men as emasculated "noble savages." Kihara confronts these stereotyped images of the South Seas in carefully restaged, sepia-toned photographs that, through ironic twists, also directly challenge the viewer's understanding of gender and gender roles.

In this photograph of a male and female couple both figures are clothed as they might have been in the nineteenth century, wearing large pieces of Samoan bark cloth (SEE FIG. 27–14), and holding traditional Samoan status objects, a plaited fan and a flywhisk. Kihara herself poses as the native woman, but has also superimposed her own face, with wig and mustache, onto the body of the male figure. *Ulugali'i Samoa: Samoan Couple* is part of a series of photographs called "Fa'a fafine: In a Manner of a Woman." *Fa'a fafine* is the Samoan word for a biological male who lives as a woman, the "third gender" socially accepted historically throughout much of Polynesia (and also in the Americas, SEE FIG. 26–20). Kihara is, herself, *fa'a fafine*, a transgender woman who lives and identifies in that gender role. In this photograph and the others in the series, she blurs stereotyped notions of who or what is male or female, original or copy, reality or perception. This work was part of the exhibition "Shigeyuki Kihara: Living Photographs," the first solo exhibition by a Samoan in the Metropolitan Museum of Art in New York. Her work and that of other urban artists draws on the richness of Pacific cultures while addressing the issues of the twenty-first century.

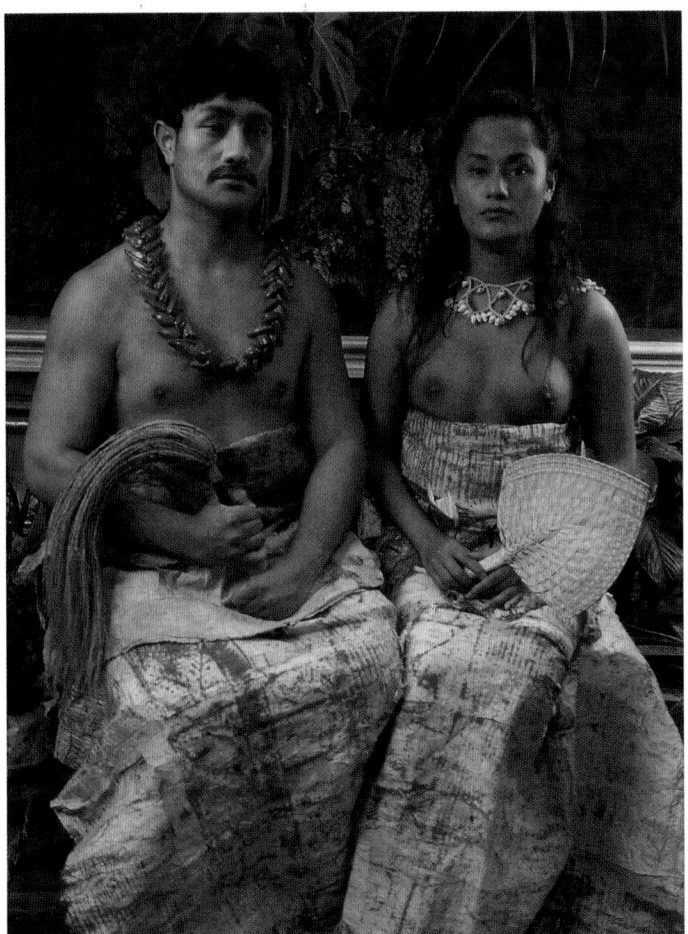

27–16 • Shigeyuki Kihara ULUGALI'I SAMOA: SAMOAN COUPLE
2004–2005. C-type photograph, edition 5, 31½ × 23⅜″ (80 × 60 cm). Metropolitan Museum of Art, New York. Gift of Shigeyuki Kihara, 2009

THINK ABOUT IT

27.1 Discuss how differences in environment, affecting available resources, impact the visual arts, including architectural forms and body adornment.

27.2 Assess the importance of ancestors in Pacific art and the different ways in which ancestors are engaged, honored, or invoked through various art forms.

27.3 Discuss the ways in which the human body is adorned and/or depicted in art across the Pacific, and how these define or enhance status, authority, and gender roles.

27.4 Discuss the variety of materials used in ceremonies and adornment throughout the Pacific and explain how their permanence or impermanence reflects cultural difference.

27.5 Examine the impact of contact with Western society on the arts and cultures of the peoples of the Pacific. Discuss the different ways in which contemporary indigenous artists throughout the Pacific are addressing issues that remain today.

PRACTICE MORE: Compose answers to these questions, get flashcards for images and terms, and review chapter material with quizzes
www.myartslab.com

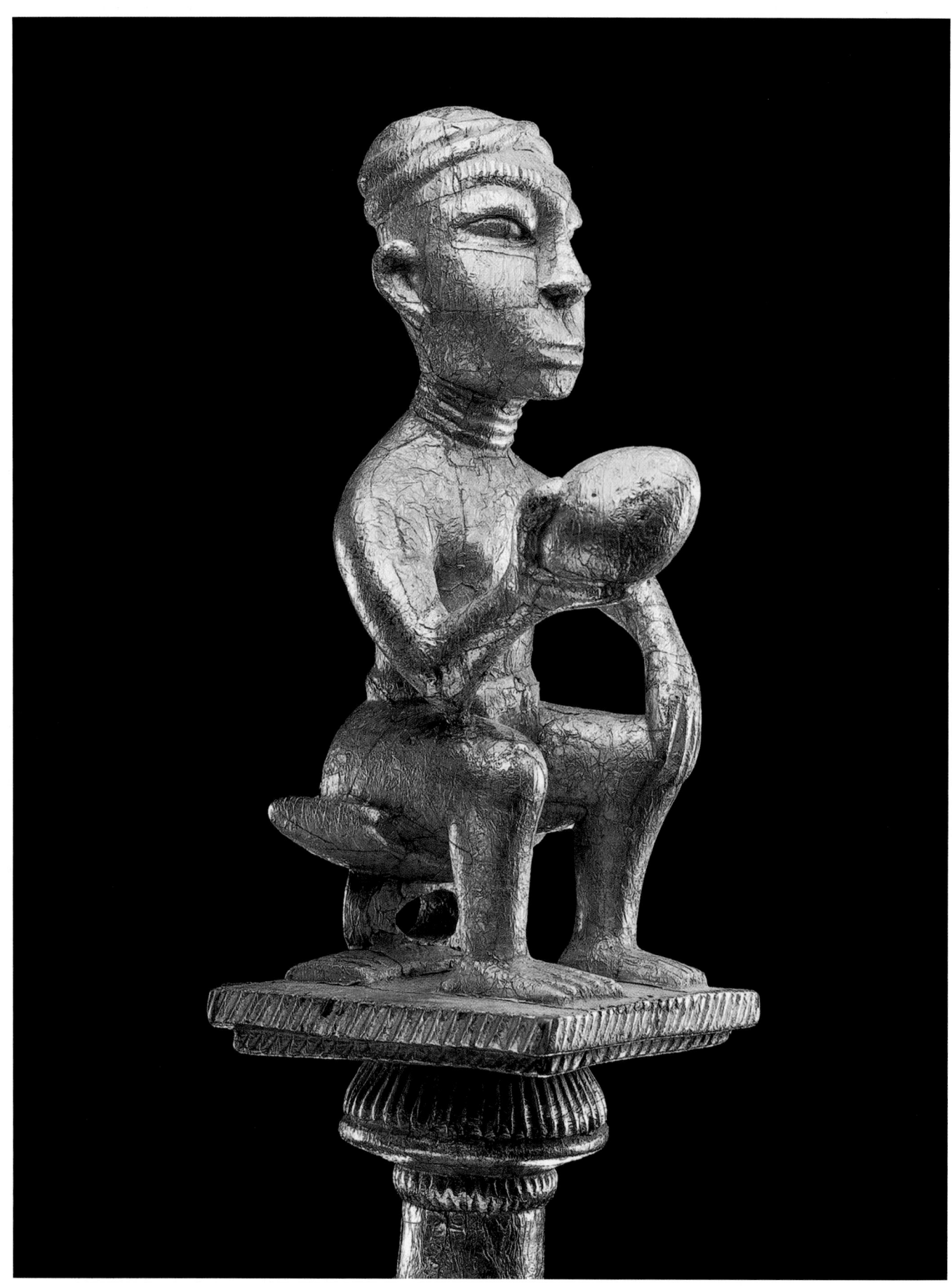

28-1 • Attributed to Kojo Bonsu FINIAL OF A SPOKESPERSON'S STAFF (*OKYEAME POMA*)
From Ghana. Ashanti culture, 1960s–1970s. Wood and gold, height 11¼″ (28.57 cm).
Sarah Da Vanzo Collection, Johannesburg, South Africa.

ART OF AFRICA IN THE MODERN ERA

Political power is like an egg, says an Ashanti proverb. Grasp it too tightly and it will shatter in your hand; hold it too loosely and it will slip from your fingers. Whenever the *okyeame* (spokesman) for one twentieth-century Ashanti ruler was conferring with that ruler or communicating the ruler's words to others, he held a staff with this symbolic caution on the use and abuse of power prominently displayed on the gold-leaf-covered finial (FIG. 28–1). Since about 1900 these advisors have carried staffs of office such as the one pictured here. The carved figure at the top illustrates a story that may have multiple meanings when told by a witty owner. This staff was probably carved in the 1960s or 1970s by Kojo Bonsu. The son of Osei Bonsu (1900–1976), a famous carver, Kojo Bonsu lives in the Ashanti city of Kumasi and continues to carve prolifically.

A staff or scepter is a nearly universal symbol of authority and leadership. Today in many colleges and universities a ceremonial mace is still carried by the leader of an academic procession, and it is often placed in front of the speaker's lectern, as a symbol of the speaker's authority. The Ashanti spokesmen who carry their image-topped staffs are part of this widespread tradition.

Since the fifteenth century, when the first Europeans explored Africa, objects such as this staff have been shipped back to Western museums of natural history or ethnography, where they were catalogued as curious artifacts of "primitive cultures." Toward the end of the nineteenth century, however, changes in Western thinking about African culture gradually led more and more people to appreciate the inherent aesthetic qualities of these unfamiliar objects and at last to embrace them fully as art. In recent years the appreciation of traditional African arts have been further enhanced through the exploration of their meaning from the point of view of the people who made them.

If we are to understand African art such as this staff on its own terms, we must take it out of the glass case of the museum where we usually encounter it and imagine the artwork playing its vital role in a human community. Indeed, this is true of any work of art produced anywhere in the world. When we recognize in an artwork the true expression of values and beliefs, our imaginations cross a bridge to understanding.

LEARN ABOUT IT

28.1 Examine the role of the visual arts in the expression of power and authority by modern African leaders.

28.2 Summarize the role of the arts in divination to disclose the cause of misfortune in several African cultures.

28.3 Examine the role of African arts in its reaction to the colonial experience.

28.4 Contrast the ways in which African contemporary artists explore their search for an identity through their art.

28.5 Evaluate the role of masquerade in African rites of passage such as initiation and funeral rituals.

HEAR MORE: Listen to an audio file of your chapter **www.myartslab.com**

TRADITIONAL AND CONTEMPORARY AFRICA

The second-largest continent in the world, Africa is a land of enormous diversity (MAP 28–1). Geographically, it ranges from vast deserts to tropical rainforest, from flat grasslands to spectacular mountains and dramatic rift valleys. Cultural diversity in Africa is equally impressive. More than 1,000 African languages have been identified and grouped into five major linguistic families. Various languages represent unique cultures, with their own history, customs, and art forms.

Before the nineteenth century, the most important outside influence to pervade Africa had been the religious culture of Islam, which spread gradually and largely peacefully through much of west Africa and along the east African coast (see "Foundations of African Cultures," page 883). The modern era, in contrast, begins with the European exploration during the nineteenth century and subsequent colonization of the African continent, developments that brought traditional African societies into sudden and traumatic contact with the "modern" world that Europe had largely created.

European ships first visited sub-Saharan Africa in the fifteenth century. For the next several hundred years, however, European contact with Africa was almost entirely limited to coastal areas, where trade, including the tragic slave trade, was carried out. Between the sixteenth and nineteenth centuries, over 10 million slaves were taken from Africa to colonies in North and South America and the Caribbean islands. Countries that participated in the Atlantic slave trade included Great Britain, Portugal, France, Spain, Denmark, Holland, and the United States.

During the nineteenth century, as the slave trade was gradually eliminated, European explorers began to investigate the unmapped African interior in earnest. They were soon followed by Christian missionaries, whose reports excited popular interest in the continent. Drawn by the potential wealth of Africa's natural resources, European governments began to seek territorial concessions from African rulers. Diplomacy soon gave way to force, and toward the end of the century competition among rival European powers fueled the so-called Scramble for Africa, during which England, France, Germany, Belgium, Italy, Spain, and Portugal raced to lay claim to whatever part of the continent they could. By 1914 virtually all of Africa had fallen under colonial rule.

Public and private collections of African art grew rapidly in size during this period. This was due not only to geographic exploration and colonial expansion, but also to the development of anthropology as a field of study. Artifacts from various African cultures became instruments through which university professors and museum curators could explain human development in purely evolutionary terms. Museums and collectors competed with one another to collect everywhere and as quickly as possible, believing that "traditional" African cultures were being quickly altered by the colonial experience. As territory was subsumed under European control, vast quantities of art objects flowed into European city, state, and national collections.

Objects also entered Western collections through conflict. For example, when a British expedition headed by the newly appointed Acting Council-General, James Phillips, embarked on a mission to discuss the trade agreement with the *oba* of Benin, he was told he could not meet with the king because he was engaged in an important annual ceremony honoring his ancestors. Phillips refused to postpone his visit and the expedition was

28-2 • MEMBERS OF THE BRITISH PUNITIVE EXPEDITION IN THE BENIN PALACE IN 1897 WITH OBJECTS FROM THE ROYAL TREASURY

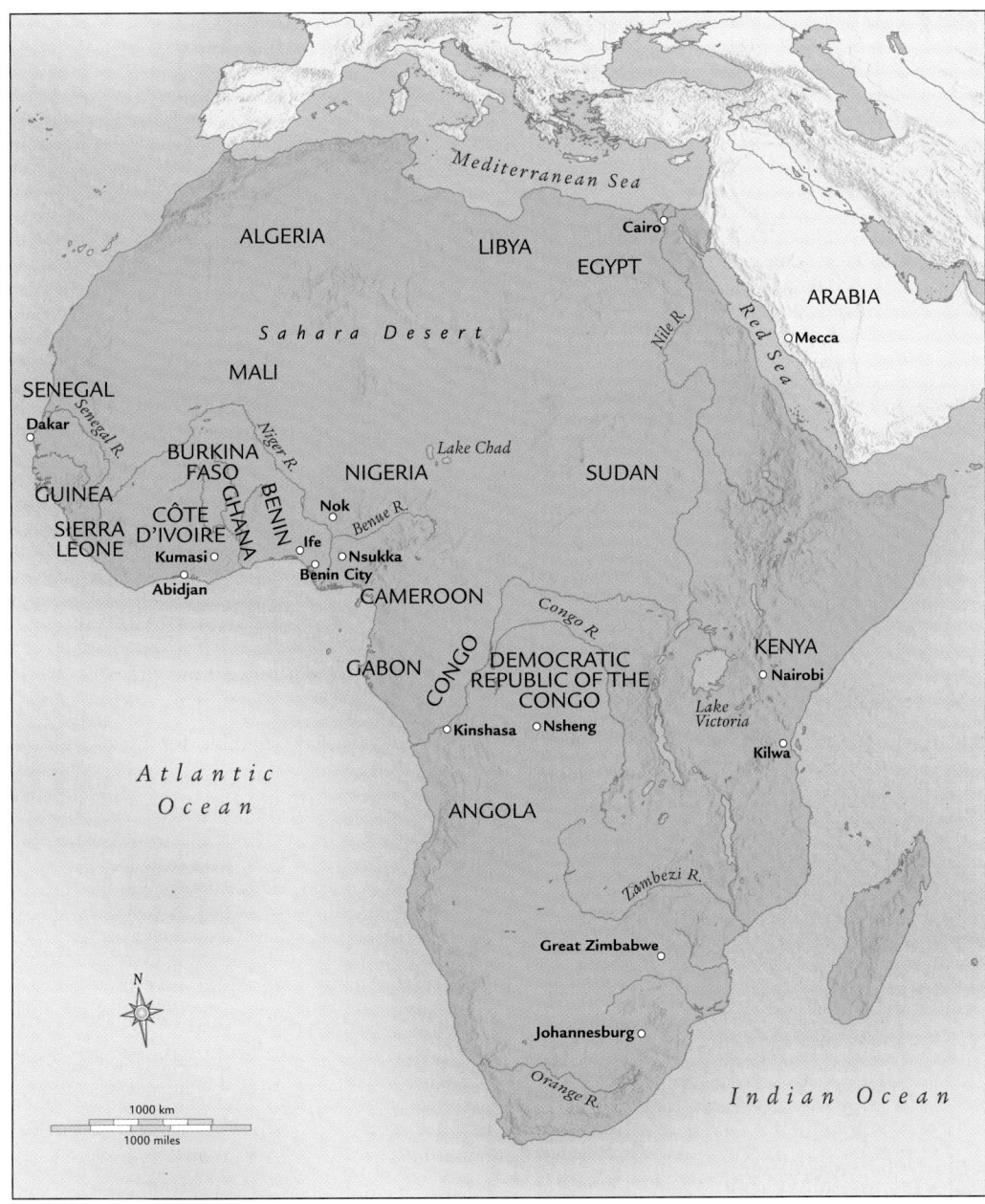

MAP 28–1 •
PRESENT-DAY AFRICA

The vast continent of Africa is home to over fifty countries and innumerable cultures.

attacked by a group headed by two chiefs, without the king's knowledge, killing all but two expedition members. A punitive expedition was launched in 1897 by the British (FIG. 28–2) which resulted in much of the town, including the palace, being destroyed and over 2,000 antiquities—nearly the entire store of artifacts from the royal palace—being seized. The king was deposed and sent into exile. His successor assumed the throne in 1914. The antiquities were taken to Europe and auctioned to defray the costs of the expedition and provide pensions for those who had been ambushed or their survivors. These objects are now dispersed in museums and private collections throughout the world.

Changes in Western thinking about art gradually led people to appreciate the aesthetic qualities of tradition-based African "artifacts" and finally to embrace them fully as art. As noted earlier, the earliest collections of African art were, for the most part, acquired by museums of natural history or ethnography, which exhibited the works as curious artifacts of "primitive" cultures. By the latter half of the twentieth century, art museums, both in Africa and in the West, began to collect African art seriously and methodically. Today, these collections afford us a rich sampling of African art created for the most part in the nineteenth and twentieth centuries.

In the years following World War I, nationalistic movements resisting European incursion arose across Africa. Their leaders generally did not advocate a return to earlier forms of political organization but rather demanded the transformation of colonial divisions into modern nation-states governed by Africans. From the 1950s through the mid 1970s, one colony after another gained its independence, and the present-day map of Africa took shape. Today, the continent is composed of over 50 independent countries.

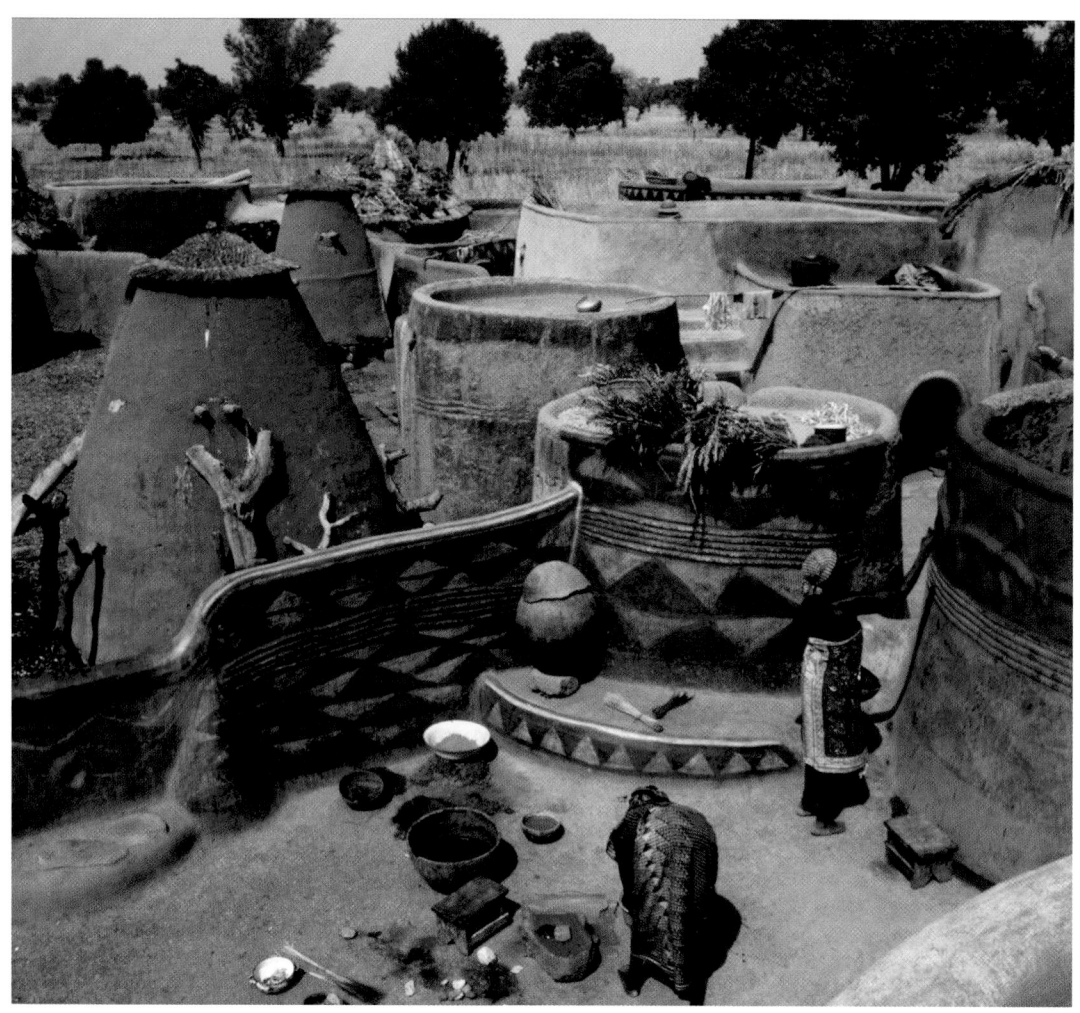

28-3 • NANKANI COMPOUND
Sirigu, Ghana. 1972.

Among the Nankani people, creating living areas is a cooperative but gender-specific project. Men build the structures, women decorate the surfaces. The structures are also gendered. The round dwellings shown here are women's houses located in an interior courtyard; men occupy rectangular flat-roofed houses. The bisected lozenge design on the dwelling to the left is called *zalanga*, the name for the braided sling that holds a woman's gourds and most treasured possessions.

While African societies were profoundly disrupted during the colonial period, numerous tradition-based societies persist, both within and across contemporary political borders, and art continues to play a vital role in the spiritual and social life of the community. This chapter explores African art in light of how it addresses some of the fundamental concerns of human existence. Works of art are often directly related to the commemoration of significant rites of passage such as procreation and birth, initiation to adulthood, socialization in adult life, and death. While political leaders throughout the world use art to express their authority and status, in Africa community leaders are thought to connect the living community with the spirit world. In this regard, African art often especially idealizes the spirits of community leaders and deceased persons, who are expected to mediate between the temporal and supernatural worlds to help achieve well-being both for themselves and for the entire community. In these contexts, art is often intended to help mediate aid and support from a supernatural world of ancestors and other spirit forces. These concerns—rather than geographical region or time frame—form the backdrop against which we look at artworks in this chapter, as African art can be more fully understood within contexts of production and use.

Generally, the full meaning of a tradition-based work of art can only be realized in the context of its use. For instance, when masked dancers perform within a specific ceremonial event, the mask itself (which we may later see as an artwork in a museum) is only a part of a process that most fully reveals its meaning in performance.

DOMESTIC ARCHITECTURE

Shelter is a basic human concern, yet each culture approaches it in a unique way that helps define that culture. The farming communities of the Nankani people in the border area between Burkina Faso and Ghana, in west Africa, have developed a distinctive painted architecture. The earthen buildings of their walled compounds are low and single-storied with either flat roofs that form terraces or conical roofs. Each compound is surrounded by a defensive wall with a single entrance on the west side. Each building inside the enclosure is arranged so that it has a direct view of the entrance. Some buildings are used only by men, others only by women. For example, Nankani men are in charge of the ancestral shrine near the entrance of the compound, the corral for cattle, and the granary; they have rectangular houses. The inner courtyards, outdoor kitchen, and round houses are

Foundations of African Cultures

Africa was the site of one of the great civilizations of the ancient world—that of Egypt, which arose along the fertile banks of the Nile River over the course of the fourth millennium BCE and lasted for some 3,000 years. Egypt's rise coincided with the emergence of the Sahara—now the largest desert in the world—from the formerly lush grasslands of northern Africa. Some of the oldest-known African art, images inscribed and painted in the mountains of the central Sahara beginning around 8000 BCE, bear witness to this gradual transformation as well as to the lives of the pastoral peoples who once lived in the region.

As the grassland dried, its populations migrated in search of pasture and arable land. Many probably made their way to the Sudan, the broad band of savanna south of the Sahara. During the sixth century BCE, knowledge of iron smelting spread across the Sudan, enabling larger and more complex societies to emerge. One such society was the ironworking Nok culture, which arose in present-day Nigeria around 500 BCE and lasted until about 200 CE. Terra-cotta figures created by Nok artists are the earliest known sculpture from sub-Saharan Africa.

Farther south in present-day Nigeria, a remarkable culture developed in the city of Ife, which rose to prominence around 800 CE. There, from roughly 1000 to 1400, a tradition of naturalistic sculpture in bronze and terra cotta flourished. Ife was, and remains, the sacred city of the Yoruba people. According to legend, Ife artists brought the techniques of bronze casting to the kingdom of Benin to the west. From 1170 to the present century, Benin artists in the service of the court created numerous works in bronze, at first in the naturalistic style of Ife, then in an increasingly stylized and elaborate manner.

With the Arab conquest of North Africa during the seventh and eighth centuries, Islamic travelers and merchants became regular visitors to the Sudan. Largely through their writings, we know of the powerful west African empires of Ghana and Mali, which flourished successively from the fourth through the sixteenth centuries along the great bend in the Niger River. Both grew wealthy by controlling the flow of African gold and forest products into the lucrative trans-Sahara trade. The city of Jenné, in Mali, served not only as a commercial hub but also as a prominent center of Islam.

Meanwhile, since before the Common Era, peoples along the coast of east Africa had participated in a maritime trade network that ringed the Indian Ocean and extended east to the islands of Indonesia. Over time, trading settlements arose along the coastline, peopled by Arab, Persian, and Indian merchants as well as Africans. By the thirteenth century these settlements were important port cities, and a new language, Swahili, had developed from the longtime mingling of Arabic with local African languages. Peoples of the interior organized extensive trade networks to funnel goods to these ports. From 1000 to 1500 many of these interior routes were controlled by the Shona people from the site called Great Zimbabwe. The extensive stone palace compound there stood in the center of a city of some 10,000 people at its height. Numerous cities and kingdoms, often of great wealth and opulence, greeted the astonished eyes of the first European visitors to Africa at the end of the fifteenth century.

---

women's areas (FIG. 28–3). Men build the compound; women paint the buildings inside and out.

The women decorate the walls with horizontal molded ridges called *yidoor* ("rows in a cultivated field") and long eye ("long life"), to express good wishes for the family. They paint the walls with rectangles and squares divided diagonally to create triangular patterns that contrast with the curvature of the walls. The painted patterns are called braided sling, broken pottery, broken gourd, and sometimes, since the triangular motifs can be seen as pointing up or down, they are sometimes called filed teeth. The same geometric motifs are used on pottery and baskets, and for scarification of the skin. When people decorate themselves, their homes, and their possessions with the same patterns, art serves to enhance cultural identity.

CHILDREN AND THE CONTINUITY OF LIFE

Among the most fundamental of human concerns is the continuation of life from one generation to the next. In tradition-based societies children are especially important: Not only do they represent the future of the family and the community, but they also provide a form of "social security," guaranteeing that parents will have someone to care for them when they are old.

In the often harsh and unpredictable climates of Africa, human life can be fragile. In some areas half of all infants die before the age of 5, and the average life expectancy may be as low as 40 years. In these areas women bear many children in hopes that at least a few will survive into adulthood, and failure to have children is a disaster for a wife, her husband, and her husband's lineage. Women who have had difficulty bearing children appeal for help with special offerings or prayers, often involving the use of art.

YORUBA TWIN FIGURES. The Yoruba people of Nigeria have one of the highest rates of twin births in the world. The birth of twins is a joyful occasion, yet it is troubling as well, for twins are more delicate than single babies, and one or both may well die. Many African peoples believe that a dead child continues its life in a spirit world and that the parents' care and affection may reach it there, often through the medium of art. When a Yoruba twin dies, the parents often consult a diviner, a specialist in ritual and spiritual practices, who may tell them that an image of a twin (*ere ibeji*) must

28-4 • TWIN FIGURES (ERE IBEJI)
From Nigeria. Yoruba culture, 20th century. Wood, height 7⅞" (20 cm).
The University of Iowa Museum of Art, Iowa City.
The Stanley Collection (x1986.489 and x1986.488)

As with other African sculpture, patterns of use result in particular signs of wear. The facial features of *ere ibeji* are often worn down or even obliterated by repeated feedings and washings. Camwood powder applied as a cosmetic builds to a thick crust in areas that are rarely handled, and the blue indigo dye regularly applied to the hair eventually builds to a thin layer of color.

CHILDREN, ART, AND PERFORMANCE. In sub-Saharan Africa, as elsewhere, children from an early age are intensely interested in adult roles and activities including art making and the performative arts. In many societies a child's link to a particular artistic or craft activity is fixed. For example, in Africa, wood carving is universally a male-dominated activity, while women are most often involved in pottery production, and individual children may be apprenticed to a wood carver or potter according to their gender. But, even beyond such formal apprenticeships, children are especially interested in the festive activities of community life, such as masquerade. While mask making and masquerade performance are usually controlled by adult associations, children are given space at the edges of events to experiment with their homemade masks and costumes. Yoruba masquerades such as Gelede or Egungun are often organized so that children perform first (FIG. 28–5). Some families even purchase or make elaborate costuming for their children in a similar style to that worn by adults. Adults view these early forays into masquerade as a

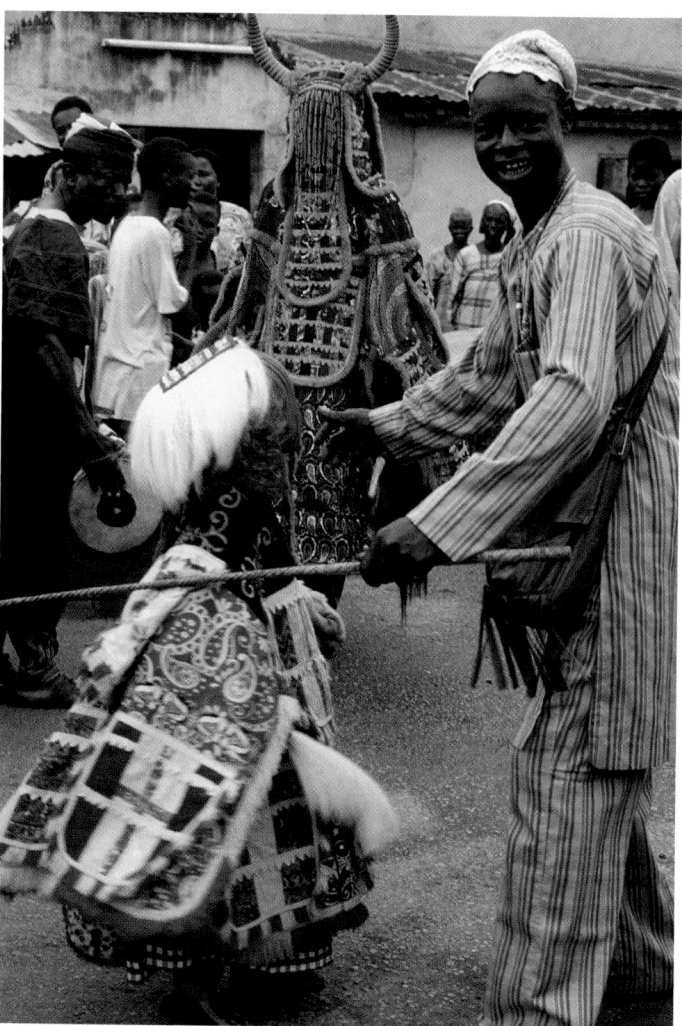

28-5 • ELDER GUIDING SMALL BOY IN EGUNGUN PERFORMANCE WHILE ADULT EGUNGUN PERFORMER LOOKS ON
Nigeria. Yoruba culture. National Museum of African Art, Smithsonian Institution, Washington, D.C. Eliot Elisofon Photographic Archive (EEPA 1992-028-02691)

be carved to serve as a dwelling place for the deceased twin's spirit (FIG. 28–4).

When the image is finished, the mother brings the artist gifts. Then, carrying the figure as she would a living child, she dances home accompanied by the singing of neighborhood women. She places the figure in a shrine in her bedroom and lavishes care upon it, feeding it, dressing it with beautiful textiles and jewelry, anointing it with cosmetic oils. The Yoruba believe that the spirit of a dead twin, thus honored, is appeased and will look with favor on the surviving family members.

The twins here are female. They may be the work of the Yoruba artist Akiode, who died in 1936. Like most objects that Africans produce to encourage the birth and growth of children, the figures emphasize health and well-being. They have beautiful, glossy surfaces to suggest that they are well fed, as well as marks of adulthood, such as elaborate hairstyles and scarification patterns, that will one day be achieved. They represent hope for the future, for survival, and for prosperity.

training ground. As children perform, they are encouraged and gently corrected from the sidelines by family members. The Yoruba of Nigeria, especially, place a significant value on the training of children in adult performance and aesthetic forms, and children are encouraged to perform from an early age.

INITIATION

In contemporary Western societies, initiation into the adult world is extended over several years and punctuated by numerous rites, such as being confirmed in a religion, earning a driver's license, graduating from high school, and reaching the age of majority. All of these steps involve acquiring the knowledge society deems appropriate and accepting the corresponding responsibilities. In other societies, initiation can take other forms, and the acquisition of knowledge is usually supplemented by trials of endurance to prove that the candidate is equal to the responsibilities of adult life.

MASKS OF BWA INITIATION.   The Bwa people of central Burkina Faso initiate young men and women into adulthood following the onset of puberty. The initiates are first separated from younger playmates by being "kidnapped" by older relatives, though their disappearance is explained in the community by saying that they have been devoured by wild beasts. The initiates remove their clothing and sleep on the ground without blankets. Isolated from the community, they are instructed about the world of nature spirits and about the masks that represent them. They learn of the spirit each mask represents, and they memorize the story of each spirit's encounter with the founding ancestors of the clan. They learn how to construct costumes from hemp to be worn with the masks, and they learn the songs and instruments that accompany the masks in performance. Only boys wear each mask in turn and learn the dance steps that express the character and personality each mask represents. Returning to the community, the initiates display their new knowledge in a public ceremony. Each boy performs with one of the masks, while the girls sing the accompanying songs. At the end of the mask ceremony the young men and young women rejoin their families as adults, ready to marry, to start farms, and to begin families of their own.

Most Bwa masks depict spirits that have taken an animal form, such as crocodile, hyena, hawk, or serpent. Others represent spirits in human form. Among the most spectacular masks, however, are those that represent spirits that have taken neither human nor animal form. Crowned with tall, narrow planks (FIG. 28–6), these masks are covered in abstract patterns that are easily recognized by

28-6 • FIVE MASKS IN PERFORMANCE
Dossi, Burkina Faso. Bwa culture, 1984. Wood, mineral pigments, and fiber, height approx. 7' (2.13 m).

The Bwa have been making and using such masks since well before Burkina Faso achieved its independence in 1960. We might assume their use is centuries old, but in this case, the masks are a comparatively recent innovation. The elders of the Bwa family who own these masks state that they, like all Bwa, once followed the cult of the spirit of Do, who is represented by masks made of leaves. In the last quarter of the nineteenth century, the Bwa were the targets of slave raiders from the north and east. Their response to this new danger was to acquire wooden masks from their neighbors, for such masks seemed a more effective and powerful way of communicating with spirits who could help them. Thus, faced with a new form of adversity, the Bwa sought a new tradition to cope with it.

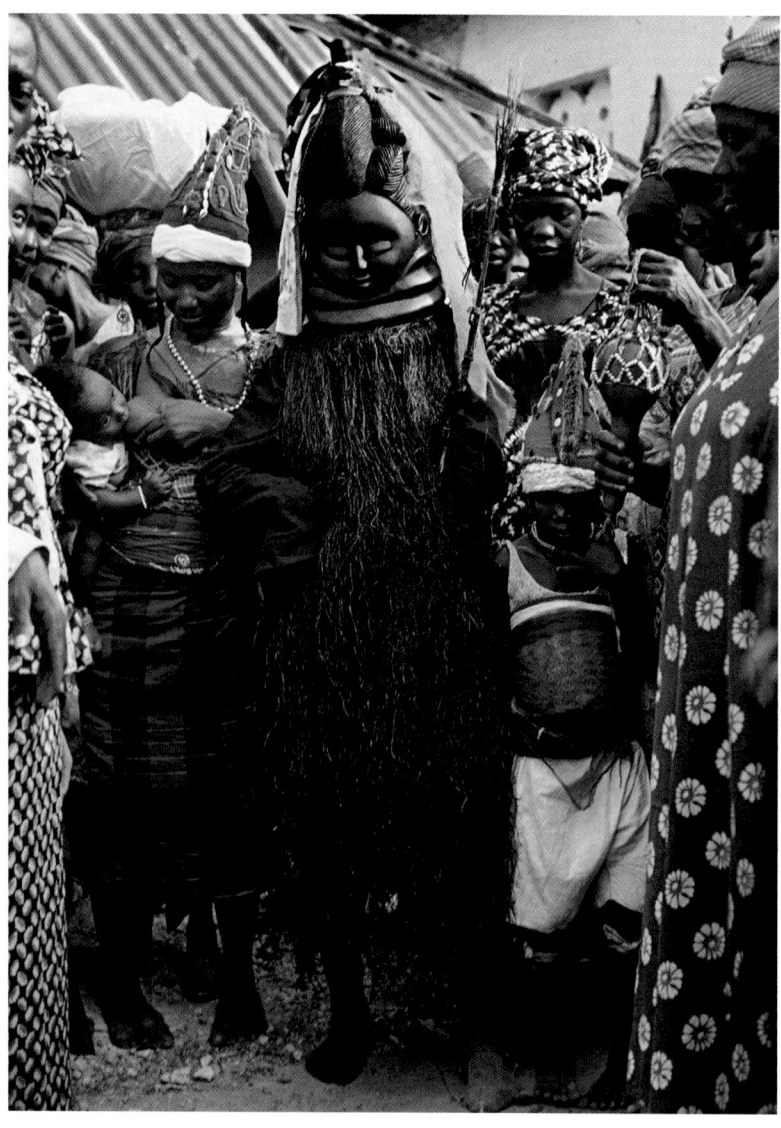

28-7 • TEMNE *NOWO* MASQUERADE WITH ATTENDANTS
Sierra Leone. 1980.

the initiated. The white crescent at the top represents the quarter moon, under which the initiation is held. The white triangles below represent bull roarers—sacred sound-makers that are swung around the head on a long cord to recreate spirit voices. The large central X represents the scar that every initiated Bwa bears as a mark of devotion. The horizontal zigzags at the bottom represent the path of the ancestors and symbolize adherence to ancestral ways. That the path is difficult to follow is clearly conveyed. The curving red hook that projects in front of the face is said to represent the beak of the hornbill, a bird associated with the supernatural world and believed to be an intermediary between the living and the dead. The mask thus proudly announces the initiate's passage to adulthood while encoding secrets of initiation in abstract symbols of proper moral conduct.

INITIATION TO WOMANHOOD IN WEST AFRICA. Among the Mende, Temne, Vai, and Kpelle peoples of Sierra Leone, the initiation of girls into adulthood is organized by a society of older women called Sande or Bondo. The initiation culminates with a ritual bath in a river, after which the initiated return to the village.

At the ceremony, the Sande women wear black gloves and stockings, black costumes of shredded raffia fibers that cover the entire body, and black masks called *nowo* or *sowei* **(FIG. 28–7)**.

With its glossy black surface, high forehead, elaborately plaited hairstyle decorated with combs, and refined facial features, the mask represents ideal female beauty. The mask is worn by a senior member of the women's Sande society whose responsibility it is to prepare Sande girls for their adult roles in society, including marriage and child rearing. The meanings of the mask are complex. It has been shown that the mask can be compared with the chrysalis of a certain African butterfly, with the creases at the base of the mask representing the segments of the chrysalis. Thus, the young woman entering adulthood is like a butterfly emerging from its cocoon. The comparison extends even further, for just as the butterfly feeds on the toxic sap of the milkweed to make itself poisonous to predatory birds, so the medicinal powers of the Sande society is believed to protect the young women from danger. The creases may additionally refer to the concentric waves that radiate outward as the initiate emerges from the river to take her place as a member of the adult community.

Bwami Association among the Lega. A ceremony of initiation may also accompany the achievement of other types of membership. Among the Lega people, who live in the dense forests between the headwaters of the Congo River and the great lakes of east Africa, the political system is based on a voluntary association called *bwami*, which comprises six levels or grades. Some 80 percent of all male Lega belong to *bwami*, and all aspire to the highest grade. Women can belong to *bwami* as well, although not at a higher grade than their husbands.

Promotion from one grade of *bwami* to the next takes many years. It is based not only on a candidate's character but also on his or her ability to pay the initiation fees, which increase dramatically with each grade. No candidate for any level of *bwami* can pay the fees without assistance: All must enlist the help of relatives to provide the necessary payment, which may include cowrie shells, goats, wild game, palm oil, clothing, and trade goods. Thus, the ambition to move from one level of *bwami* to the next encourages a harmonious community, for all must stay on good terms with other members of the community if they are to advance **(FIG. 28–8)**.

Bwami initiations into advanced grades are held in the plaza at the center of the community in the presence of all members.

28-9 • BWAMI MASK (LUKWAKONGO)
From Democratic Republic of Congo. 20th century. Wood, plant fiber, and pigment, height 22¾″ (57.5 cm). UCLA Fowler Museum of Cultural History, Los Angeles.

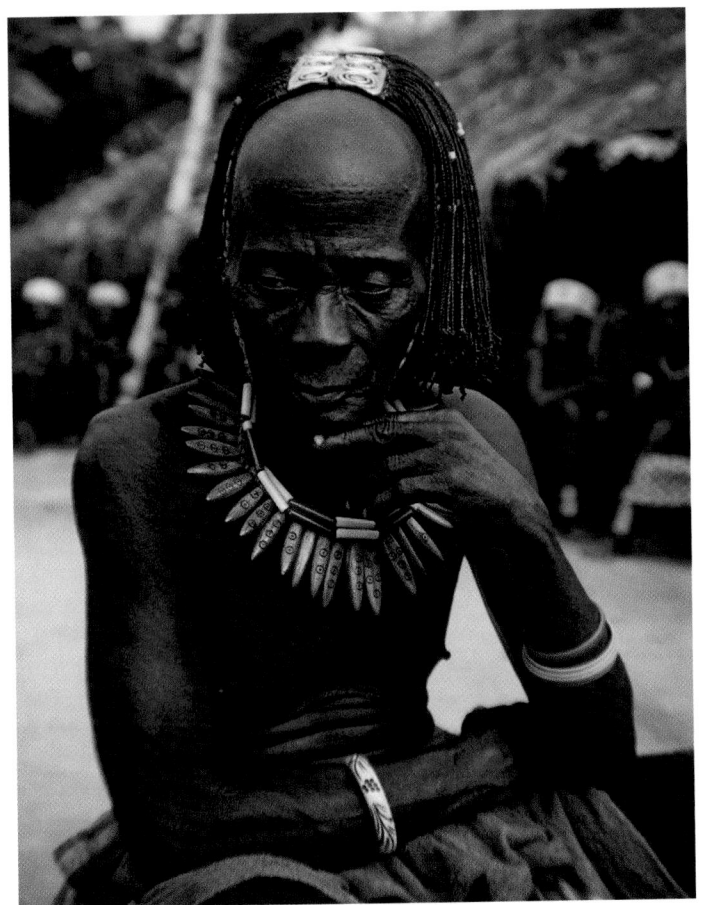

28-8 • LEGA TITLED-ELDER WEARING PRESTIGE HAT
From Democratic Republic of Congo, 1967. National Museum of African Art, Smithsonian Institution, Washington, D.C.
Eliot Elisofon Photographic Archive (EEPA EECL 2238)

Dances and songs are performed, and the values and ideals of the appropriate grade are explained through proverbs and sayings. These standards are illustrated by natural or crafted objects, which are presented to the initiate as signs of membership. At the highest two levels of *bwami*, such objects include exquisitely made small masks and sculpted figures.

The mask in **FIGURE 28–9** is associated with *yananio*, the second-highest grade of *bwami*. Typical of Lega masks, the head is fashioned as an oval into which is carved a concave, heart-shaped face with narrow, raised features. The masks are often colored white with clay and fitted with a long beard made of plant fibers. Too small to cover the face, they are displayed in other ways—held in the palm of a hand, for example, or attached to a thigh. Each means of display recalls a different value or saying, so that one mask may convey a variety of meanings. Generally, the masks symbolize continuity between the ancestors and the living community and are thought to be direct links to deceased relatives and past members of *bwami*.

AFRICAN ART CONFRONTING THE WEST. During the late nineteenth and early twentieth century, Nkanu peoples residing in the Democratic Republic of the Congo and Angola created brightly painted figurative sculpture and decorated wall panels adorned with human and animal figures to celebrate the completion of initiation rites (*nkanda*). These artworks were displayed in a three-sided roofed enclosure, a *kikaku*, which was built at a crossroads near the initiation campground. These displays were made to reinforce the values taught during *nkanda* and to announce to the community that initiation was coming to a close and that their children would soon be home.

The *kikaku* resembled a stage. Wall panels were carved, painted, and attached to its back and sides, and sculpted figures were placed in front of the wall panels on the floor of the structure. The *kikaku* wall panels were accentuated with brightly colored and symbolically charged patterns that conveyed specific meanings associated with the coming-of-age ritual. European colonial officials were a favorite subject in *kikaku* (FIG. 28–10). Their depictions were considered "portraits" of specific individuals, and included distinguishing characteristics such as costume and hairstyle. Nkanu artists seem to have singled out specific colonial officials whom they especially despised for their cruelty or whom they wanted to ridicule because of their dalliances with Nkanu women. These caricatures became a means of confronting colonial domination without openly attacking colonial officials, which would have undoubtedly led to severe repercussions.

In the wall panels here, the central figure represents a colonial administrator. He is flanked by two figures representing Congolese men who are members of the Force Publique, the Belgian colonial military force. One soldier is depicted wearing an ammunition belt, while the other assumes the awkward stance of an initiate who must balance on one leg. Both the stance and the painted patterns on the panels symbolically relate to the virility and procreative capacity of the initiate upon the successful completion of *nkanda*. After the initiation sequence, the *kikaku* and its contents were left to decay. Only a few individual pieces have been acquired by Western museums—there is no extant example of an entire *kikaku* in any museum collection.

28–10 • INITIATION WALL PANELS
From Democratic Republic of the Congo. Nkanu, early 20th century. Wood, pigment, height 33⅜" (84.8 cm).
National Museum of African Art, Smithsonian Institution, Washington, D.C. Museum purchase (99-2-1)

THE SPIRIT WORLD

While African religious beliefs have been influenced by Christianity and Islam for hundreds of years, many African peoples still rely on traditional customs and belief systems to find the answers to universal human problems. Why does one child fall ill and die while another remains healthy? Why does one year bring rain and a bountiful crop, while the next brings drought and famine? People everywhere confront these fundamental and troubling questions. In many African belief systems it is usually thought that a supreme creator god is not fundamentally involved in the daily lives of humans. Instead, numerous subordinate spirit forces are said to be ever-present and involved in human affairs. For instance, such spirits may inhabit agricultural fields, the river that provides fish, the forest that is home to game, or the land that must be cleared in order to build a new village. Families, too, may acknowledge the existence of ancestral spirits. These spirits control success and failure in life, and if a proper relationship is not maintained with them, harm in the form of illness or misfortune can befall an individual, his family, or the entire community.

To communicate with these all-important spirits, many African societies rely on a specialist, such as a diviner who serves as a link between the supernatural and human worlds, opening the lines of communication through such techniques as prayer, sacrifice, offerings, ritual performance, and divination. Sometimes art plays a role in the diviner's dealings with the spirit world, giving visible identity and personality to what is imaginary and intangible (see "Divination Among the Chokwe," page 892). *Nkisi* are objects that harness spirit forces or powers and are made by the Kongo and Songye peoples of the Democratic Republic of Congo to alleviate illness, protect vulnerable individuals such as children, provide success in hunting, trade, and other endeavors, and serve a divinatory function to seek out wrongdoers and punish them for their misdeeds (see "A Closer Look," page 890). A *nkisi nkonde* is a specific type of *nkisi* and begins its life as an unadorned wooden figure, often in human form, that is purchased from a carver at a market or commissioned by a diviner on behalf of a client who has encountered some adversity. The diviner prescribes medicinal ingredients (*bilongo*), which are taken from the plant, animal, and mineral worlds, and are specific to a client's problem. Each ingredient has a unique role. When *bilongo* are added to the *nkonde* they infuse it with a spirit force and focus the power in a particular direction. The word *nkonde* shares a stem with *konda* ("to hunt") for the figure is quick to hunt down a client's enemies and destroy them. A *nkisi nkonde* may serve many private and public functions. Two warring communities might agree to end their conflict by swearing an oath of peace and then driving a nail into the *nkonde* to seal the agreement, or a mother might invoke the power of the *nkonde* to heal her sick child.

SPIRIT SPOUSE OF THE BAULE. Some African peoples conceive of the spirit world as a parallel realm in which spirits may have families, live in villages, attend markets, and possess personalities complete with faults and virtues. The Baule people in Côte d'Ivoire believe that each of us lived in the spirit world before we were born. While there, we had a spirit spouse, whom we left behind when we entered this life. A person who has difficulty assuming his or her gender-specific role as an adult Baule—a man who has not married or achieved his expected status in life, for example, or a woman who has not borne children—may dream of his or her spirit spouse.

For such a person, the diviner may prescribe the carving of an image of the **SPIRIT SPOUSE** (FIG. 28–11). A man has a *blolo bla* (otherworld wife) and a woman has a *blolo bian* (otherworld husband) carved. The figures display the most admired and

28-11 • SPIRIT SPOUSE (*BLOLO BLA*)
From Côte d'Ivoire. Baule culture, early–mid 20th century. Wood, glass beads, gold hollow beads, plant fiber, white pigment, encrustation, height 19¼″ (48.9 cm). National Museum of African Art, Smithsonian Institution Washington, D.C. (85-15-2)

Kongo *Nkisi Nkonde*

Power Figure (*Nkisi Nkonde*).
From the Democratic Republic of Congo. Kongo culture, 19th century. Wood, nails, pins, blades, and other materials, height 44″ (111.7 cm). The Field Museum, Chicago.

The *bilongo* may be placed on the head of the figure, thought to be an especially appropriate site to communicate with spirit forces.

Clients drive a nail, blade, or other pointed object into the figure to get the *nkonde*'s attention and prick it into action. The large number of objects driven into this *nkonde* suggests that its powers were both formidable and efficacious.

This *nkonde* stands in a pose called *pakalala*, a stance of alertness like that of a wrestler challenging an opponent. Other *nkonde* figures hold a knife or spear in an upraised hand, ready to strike or attack.

Bilongo may also be suspended in a packet from the figure's neck or waist or even placed into the figure's beard. The beard is associated with the powers that come with age and seniority.

Additonal *bilongo* are inserted into a body cavity such as the figure's belly, as this is thought to be the seat of a person's life or soul. The term *mooyo* means both "belly" and "life."

SEE MORE: View the Closer Look feature for Kongo *Nkisi Nkonde* **www.myartslab.com**

desirable marks of beauty so that the spirit spouses may be encouraged to enter and inhabit them. Spirit spouse figures are broadly naturalistic, with swelling, fully rounded musculature and careful attention to details of hairstyle, jewelry, and scarification patterns. They may be carved standing in a quiet, dignified pose or seated on a stool. The owner keeps the figure in his or her room, dressing it in beautiful textiles and jewelry, washing it, anointing it with oil, feeding it, and caressing it. Over time, the surface of the figure softens as it takes on a glossy sheen indicating the attention it has been given. The Baule hope that by caring for and pleasing his or her spirit spouse a balance may be restored that will free the individual's human life to unfold smoothly.

YORUBA DIVINATION.   While spirit beings are often portrayed in African art, major deities are generally considered to be far removed from the everyday lives of humans and are thus rarely depicted. Such is the case with Olodumare, the creator god of the Yoruba people of southwestern Nigeria.

The Yoruba have a sizable pantheon of lesser, but still important, gods (*orisha*). Two *orisha* are principal mediators: Orunmila who represents certainty, fate, order, and equilibrium; and his counterpart Eshu who represents uncertainty, disorder, and chance. Commonly represented in art, Eshu is a capricious and mischievous trickster who loves nothing better than to disrupt things that appear to be going well. The opposing forces of order and disorder are mediated through the agency of a diviner (*babalawo*) who employs a divination board (*opon ifa*) and its paraphernalia to reveal the causes of a client's problems (FIG. 28–12). The divination board is sprinkled with a white wood dust

28-12 • *IFA* DIVINATION SESSION
Yoruba culture, Nigeria. National Museum of African Art, Smithsonian Institution, Washington, D.C. Eliot Elisofon Photographic Archives (EEPA 1992-028-02016)

and the *orisha* Orunmila and Eshu are called to the divination by tapping the board with a special tapper. The *babalawo* throws 16 palm nuts and after each toss records the way the palm nuts have landed in the white wood dust on the divination board. Each configuration of the palm nuts relates to particular verses from a complex oral tradition also known as Ifa. As the selected verses are recited by the diviner, the client relates the verses to his or her own particular problems or concerns.

Eshu's image often appears on divination objects and in shrines employed by his worshipers. His image always appears at the top of the divination board, while other images along the edge of the board relate symbolically to the world of Ifa divination. Eshu is associated with two eternal sources of human conflict—sex and money—and is usually portrayed with a long hairstyle: The Yoruba consider long hair to represent excess libidinous energy and unrestrained sexuality. Figures of Eshu are usually adorned with long strands of cowrie shells, a traditional African currency. Shrines to him are erected wherever there is the potential for encounters that lead to conflict, especially at crossroads, in markets, or in front of banks. Eshu's followers hope that their offerings will persuade the god to spare them the pitfalls he places in front of others.

LEADERSHIP

As in societies throughout the world, art in Africa is used to identify those who hold power, to validate their right to their authority as representatives of the family or community, and to communicate the rules for moral behavior that must be obeyed by all members of the society. The gold-and-wood spokesman's staff shown in FIGURE 28–1 with which this chapter opened is an example of the art of leadership. It belongs to the culture of the Ashanti peoples of Ghana, in west Africa. The Ashanti greatly admire fine language—one of their adages is, "We speak to the wise man in proverbs, not in plain speech"— and consequently their governing system includes the special post of spokesman to the ruler.

The Ashanti use gold not only for objects, such as the staff, that are reserved for the use of rulers, but also for jewelry, as do other peoples of the region. But for the Ashanti, who live in the middle of the richest goldfields of west Africa, gold was long a major source of power; for centuries they traded it, first via intermediaries across the Sahara to the Mediterranean world, then later directly to Europeans on the west African coast.

ART AND ITS CONTEXTS

Divination among the Chokwe

Chokwe peoples of the Democratic Republic of the Congo and Angola consult diviners (*nganga*) about problems such as death, illness, impotence, sterility, and theft. As the mediator between this world and the supernatural, the diviner's role is to ascertain the true meaning and underlying cause of an affliction or misfortune, and whether it is due to a conflict with human protagonists or with spirit forces. The diviner's ability to uncover the cause of a client's problems comes through the agency of powerful spirit forces and the efficacy of divinatory paraphernalia. A Chokwe *nganga*, utilizing a rattle to call the spirits to the divination, begins to shake a shallow covered basket (*ngombo ya kusekula*) containing a variety of natural objects including small antelope horns, seeds, and minerals. The basket also contains a number of carved wooden objects representing humans (in various symbolic poses), animals, and other objects such as small models of masks and masked figures. The objects in the basket are tossed about as the basket is shaken and when finished the cover is removed to reveal the arrangement of the objects as they came to rest inside. The *nganga* interprets the results of multiple tosses to disclose the underlying cause of the client's problem and suggests what steps need to be taken to remedy the situation.

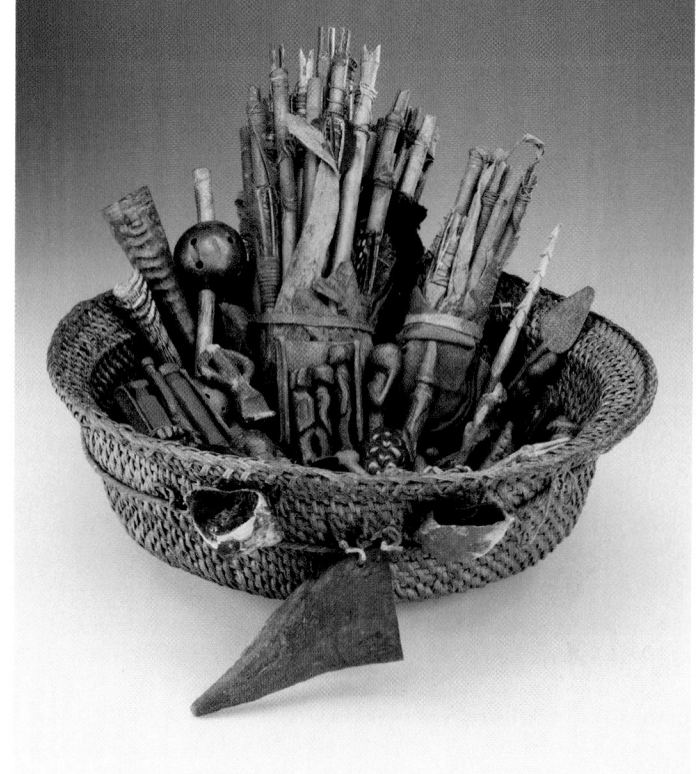

DIVINATION BASKET (*NGOMBO*)
Democratic Republic of the Congo and Angola. Chokwe peoples, mid 19th–early 20th century. Plant fiber, seed, stone, horn, shell, bone, metal, feather, camwood, depth 12¹⁄₁₆″ (30.7 cm). National Museum of African Art, Smithsonian Institution, Washington, D.C. (86-12-17.1)

KENTE CLOTH. The Ashanti are also renowned for the beauty of their woven textiles (**kente**) (FIG. 28–13). Weaving was introduced in Ghana sometime during the seventeenth century from neighboring regions of west Africa. The weavers were, traditionally, men. Ashanti weavers work on small, light, horizontal looms that produce long, narrow strips of cloth. They begin by laying out the long warp threads in brightly colored stripes. Today the threads are likely to be rayon. Formerly, however, they were cotton and later silk, which the Ashanti first procured in the seventeenth century by unraveling silk cloth obtained through European trade. Weft threads are woven through the warp to produce complex patterns that are named after the warp-faced patterns or weft designs. The long strips produced by the loom are then cut to size and sewn together to form large rectangles of finished *kente* cloth.

Kente cloth was originally reserved for state regalia. A man wore a single piece, about 6–7 feet by 12–13 feet, wrapped like a toga, with no belt and the right shoulder bare. Women wore two pieces—a skirt and a shawl. The *kente* cloth shown here began with a warp pattern that alternates red, green, and yellow. The pattern is known as *oyokoman ogya da mu* ("there is a fire between two factions of the Oyoko clan") and refers to the civil war that followed the death of the Ashanti king Osei Tutu in about 1730. Traditionally, only the king of the Ashanti was allowed to wear this pattern. Other complex patterns were reserved for the royal family or members of the court.

THE KUBA *NYIM*. The Kuba people of the Democratic Republic of Congo produce elaborate and sophisticated arts tied to leadership. At the pinnacle of the hierarchy sits the Kuba paramount ruler (*nyim*) whose residence was located approximately in the center of the Kuba region. The current *nyim* can trace his predecessors back to the founding of the kingdom in the seventeenth century. At the installation of a new monarch, a new capital city (*Nsheng*) is built that includes the residence of the *nyim*, his wives, and children, as well as areas for other governmental functions, all surrounded by a high palisade.

28-13 • *KENTE* CLOTH
From Ghana. Ashanti culture, 20th century. Silk, 6'10⁹⁄₁₆" × 4'3⁹⁄₁₆" (2.09 × 130 m). National Museum of African Art and National Museum of Natural History, Smithsonian Institution, Washington, D.C. Purchased with funds provided by the Smithsonian Collections Acquisition Program, 1983–85 (EJ 10583)

Titled individuals will often lavish elaborate surface decoration on objects that belong to them to indicate their rank and prestige within the political and social hierarchy. This is exemplified in the geometric woven decoration on the walls of royal buildings **(FIG. 28–14)** and decorated mats, and on the intricate carved decoration of wooden drums, boxes, and other objects. It is also seen on the variety of embroidered textiles for men and women and on regalia such as headdresses and jewelry that serve as prestige and festive attire for celebratory occasions. An eagle feather chief (*kum*

28-14 • DECORATED BUILDING (SLEEPING ROOM FOR *NYIM*) IN THE ROYAL COMPOUND OF THE KUBA *NYIM*
Nsheng, Democratic Republic of the Congo. 1980.

SEE MORE: View a simulation of woven decoration on walls **www.myartslab.com**

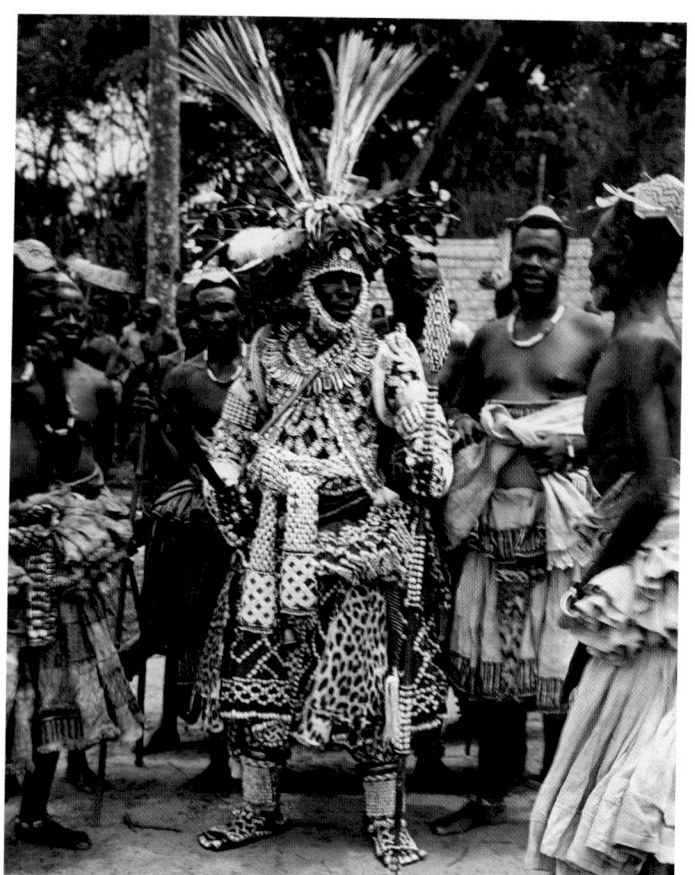

apoong) displays sumptuous adornment at his investiture. Each element of regalia signifies a prerogative of an individual's titled position relative to the position of others within a complicated system of titleholding. Naturally the most extravagant adornment is worn by the paramount ruler, as can be seen in the photograph taken by Eliot Elisofon of the Kuba *nyim* in 1971 (FIG. 28–15). Textile display is also an essential aspect of funeral rituals where textiles are worn at celebratory dances and displayed on the body of the deceased. The textiles are subsequently buried with the deceased, where the Kuba believe an individual remains for a period of time before being reborn.

YORUBA PALACE ART. The kings of the Yoruba people of Nigeria also manifested their authority and power through the large palaces in which they lived. In a typical palace plan, the principal rooms opened onto a veranda with elaborately carved posts facing a courtyard (FIG. 28–16). Elaborate carving also covered the palace doors. Among the most important Yoruba artists of the early twentieth century was Olowe of Ise (d. 1938), who

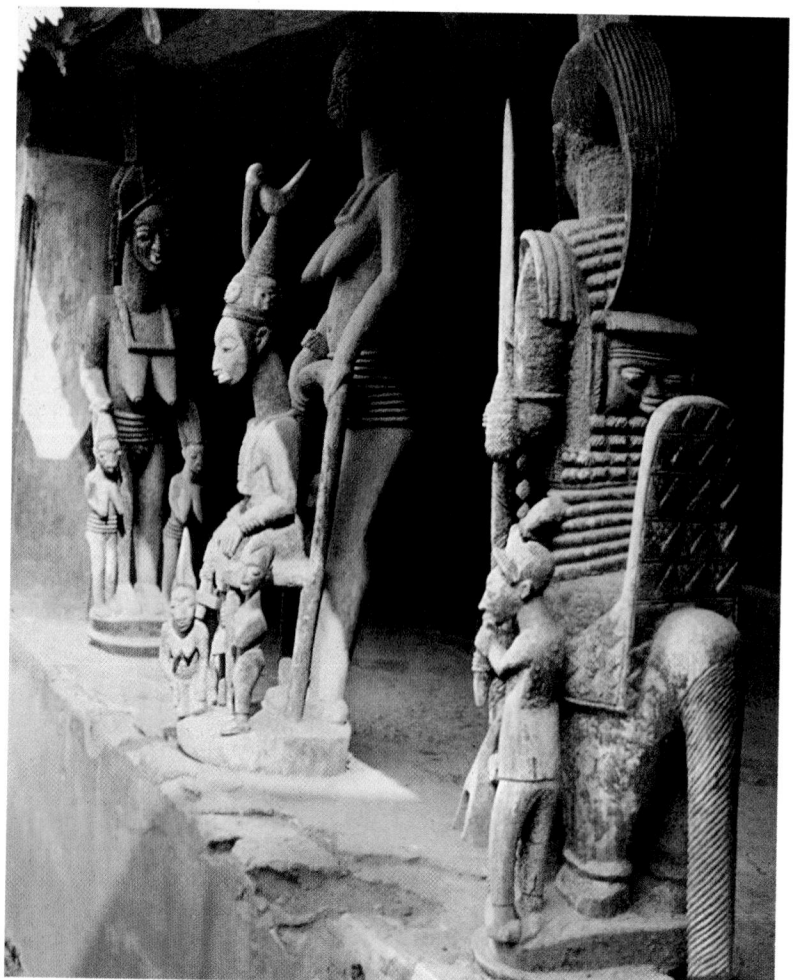

28-16 • VERANDA POSTS BY OLOWE OF ISE INSTALLED IN THE COURTYARD OF THE PALACE OF THE *OGAGA* OF IKERE
Nigeria, c. 1910–1914. Wood and pigment. Photograph taken in 1964.

EXPLORE MORE: Gain insight from a primary source related to Olowe of Ise's veranda posts www.myartslab.com

28–17 • PALACE DOOR BY OLOWE OF ISE
From Ise Palace, Nigeria, Yoruba peoples. c. 1904–1910. Wood, pigment, height 81½″ × width 34⅝″ × depth 6¼″ (207 × 88 × 15.9 cm). National Museum of African Art, Smithsonian Institution, Washington, D.C. (88-13-1)

viewer. Their long necks and elaborate hairstyles make them appear even taller, unlike typical Yoruba sculpture which uses short, static figures. The figures are in such high relief that the upper portions are actually carved in the round. The figures move energetically against an underlying decorative pattern, and the entire surface of the doors was painted; only traces of the original colors remain.

This door panel commemorates the *arinjale* (king) of Ise receiving Major W.R. Reeve-Tucker, the first British traveling commissioner for the province, and his entourage. A separate door panel, in a private collection, presents the European entourage. In the second register of this panel, the *arinjale* is portrayed on horseback wearing a conical crown and accompanied by court messengers. A variety of other members of the court, including royal wives who are lifting their breasts (a gesture of generosity and affection performed by elder women), bearers carrying kegs of gunpowder, royal guards, and priests appear in other registers. The bottom register portrays a human sacrifice, with birds pecking at the corpse. Human sacrifice occurred rarely and was usually undertaken to ensure community survival. The two rows of heads on the left side of the panel may represent either ancestors of the *arinjale* or enemies taken in battle.

Olowe seems to have worked from the early 1900s until his death in 1938. Although he was famous throughout Yorubaland and called upon by patrons as distant as 60 miles from his home, few records of his activities remain, and only one European, Philip Allison, wrote of meeting him and watching him work. Allison described Olowe carving the iron-hard African oak "as easily as [he would] a calabash [gourd]."

DEATH AND ANCESTORS

In the view of many African peoples, death is not an end but a transition—the leaving behind of one phase of life and the beginning of another. Just as ceremonies mark the initiation of young men and women into the community of adults, so too they mark the initiation of the newly dead into the community of spirits. Like the rites of initiation into adulthood, death begins with a separation from the community, in this case the community of the living. A period of isolation and trial follows, during which the newly dead spirit may, for example, journey to the land of ancestors. Finally, the deceased is reintegrated into a community, this time the community of ancestral spirits. The living who preserve the memory of the deceased may appeal to his or her spirit to intercede on their behalf with nature spirits or to prevent the spirits of the dead from using their powers to harm (see "Kuba Funerary Mask," pages 896–897).

carved doors and veranda posts for the rulers of the Ekiti-Yoruba kingdoms in southwestern Nigeria.

The door panel from the royal palace at Ise **(FIG. 28–17)** illustrates Olowe's artistry. Its asymmetrical composition combines narrative and symbolic scenes in horizontal rectangular panels. Tall figures carved in profile end in heads facing out to confront the

Kuba Funerary Mask

The Kuba people of the Democratic Republic of Congo perform funerary masquerades to honor deceased members of the men's initiation society and high-ranking individuals who belonged to the community council of elders.

In the southern Kuba region, funeral rites for initiated men are often accompanied by the appearance of one or more masquerade figures on the day of interment of the deceased. On these occasions initiation society members, family, and friends of the deceased celebrate the departed's life while mourning his death. In part, funeral rites are elaborate because of the belief that the spirit of the recently deceased (*mwendu*) may bring harm to his family or community if his achievements and status in life are not acknowledged at the funeral. The *mwendu* may be angered for a variety of reasons. Perhaps outstanding debts were not paid and the money or other goods were kept by a family member. Or the deceased had asked for something to be buried with him and this request was not honored. Disrespect is most often shown if the deceased is not given a proper burial, one equal to his rank in life. For an initiated man, a funeral masquerade is mandatory in this region, and members of the community-based men's initiation society show their solidarity with the deceased and his spirit by performing a masquerade at his funeral.

Among the most spectacular masquerades performed in the Kuba region is that of *Ngady mwaash*—the name means literally "female mask." The mask is carved from wood, and attached to a framework covered with cloth and decorated with beads and shells that forms the top, sides, and back of the head. Wooden ears, carved separately, are attached to the sides of the head. The face of the mask presents an exuberant blend of bold geometric patterns composed of contrasting areas of triangles and parallel lines. A triangular-shaped hat, identical to that worn by female diviners, is attached to the mask. The hat signifies that *Ngady mwaash* is invested with the power of nature spirits (*ngesh*) to whom Kuba diviners attribute their extraordinary powers.

The costume for *Ngady mwaash* is composed of a shirt and leggings made from animal hide or cloth, often extensively decorated with painted black-and-white triangles. Small wooden dowels attached to the front of the shirt represent breasts. Although wearing a woman's long embroidered skirt under a short decorated skirt affixed with a belt, *Ngady mwaash* is always performed by a man. Costume accessories include strands of beaded and shell-laden bandoliers that crisscross the

Ngady mwaash mask. Democratic Republic of Congo, Kuba peoples. Late 19th–mid 20th century. Wood, pigment glass beads, cowrie shells, fabric, thread, height 12½" (31.8 cm). The Art Institute of Chicago. (1982.1505)

Bwoom masked dancer at the funeral of an initiated man. Democratic Republic of the Congo, Southern Kuba peoples. 1982.

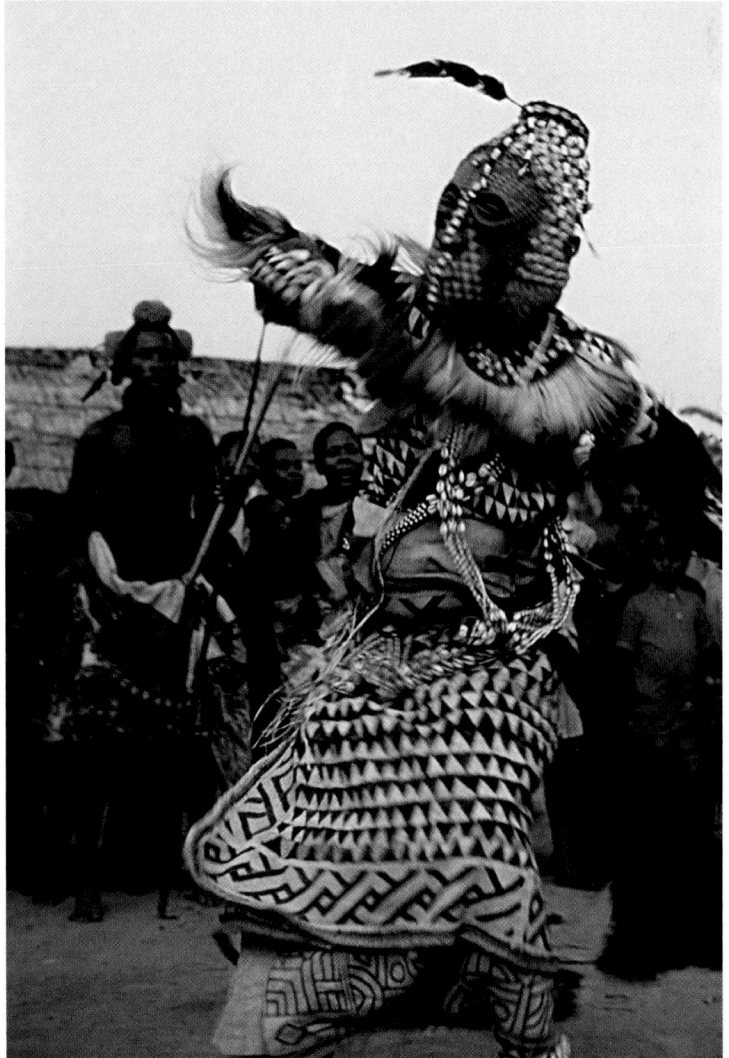

chest and decorated arm- and legbands. The mask, costume, and accessories, as well as the fly whisk that *Ngady mwaash* carries, represent wealth and high status.

The funeral masquerade performance is held near the residence of the man who has died, just prior to burial. The perimeter of the dance ground is lined with family, friends, and onlookers who have come to bid a final farewell to the deceased and witness the performance. *Ngady mwaash* takes turns performing with another masked figure designated as male, such as the masked figure *Bwoom*.

The individual character or persona of male and female masked figures is fully realized during performance. *Bwoom*, who carries a short sword, exudes power and restrained aggression. The dancer employs lunging movements and quick short jabs with his sword, causing onlookers to suspect that he may suddenly lose control and harm someone. This feeling of apprehension is a constituent part of the performance style of *Bwoom*, and is a principal reason why community members look forward to masquerade with such anticipation. In contrast, the performance style of *Ngady mwaash* is decidedly nonthreatening, with graceful movements as the dancer's body, legs, arms, and hands move in fluid gestures. The differences in the performance styles of male and female masquerade figures parallel the difference in the dance styles of men and women in Kuba culture. The men's initiation society, which organizes funeral masquerades, expresses its control and dominance of ritual affairs in part through the contrasting performance styles of *Bwoom* and *Ngady mwaash*.

Ngady mwaash masked dancer at the funeral of an initiated man. Democratic Republic of the Congo, Southern Kuba peoples. 1982.

DOGON FUNERARY *DAMA*. Among the Dogon people of Mali, in west Africa, a collective funeral rite called *dama*, is held every 12 to 13 years (**FIG. 28–18**). During *dama*, a variety of different masks perform to the sound of gunfire to drive the souls of the deceased from the village. Among the most common masks to perform is the *kanaga*, whose rectangular face supports a superstructure of planks that depict a woman, bird, or lizard with splayed legs.

For a deceased man, men from the community later engage in a mock battle on the roof of his home and participate in ritual hunts; for a deceased woman, the women of the community smash her cooking vessels on the threshold of her home. These portions of *dama* are reminders of human activities the deceased will no longer engage in. The *dama* may last as long as six days and include the performance of hundreds of masks. Because a *dama* is so costly, it is performed for several deceased elders at the same time. However, in certain Dogon communities frequented by tourists, *dama* performances have become more frequent as new masked characters are invented, including masks representing tourists holding wooden cameras or anthropologists holding notebooks in their hands. In response to tourists, Dogon mask-makers produce additional masks that are offered for sale at the conclusion of the performance.

FANG ANCESTOR GUARDIAN. The Fang, along with other peoples who live near the Atlantic coast from southern Cameroon through Rio Muni and into Gabon, shared a number of similar institutions and beliefs in which the skulls, bones, and relics of ancestors who had performed great deeds during their lifetimes were collected after burial and placed in a cylindrical bark container (*nsek-bieri*), which was preserved by the family. Deeds thus honored included being victorious in warfare, killing an elephant, being the first to trade with Europeans, bearing an especially large number of children, or founding a particular lineage or community. The bones and relics of deceased family members were thought to have special powers that could be drawn upon to aid the living with problems that confronted or threatened the family. Before colonial officials banned many ritual practices, ancestral spirits represented by the reliquaries were regularly consulted on problems with fertility—failure in conceiving and bringing to term children—or with hunting and farming, or before embarking on a commercial venture.

As a point of focus for mediation between the ancestors and the living, the Fang placed a wooden sculpture called a *bieri* on top of the container holding the relics. These sculptures functioned as

28–18 • *KANAGA* AND RABBIT MASQUERADE FIGURES AT *DAMA*
Mali. Dogon culture, 1959. National Museum of African Art, Smithsonian Institution, Washington, D.C. Eliot
Elisofon Photographic Archives (EEPA 3502)

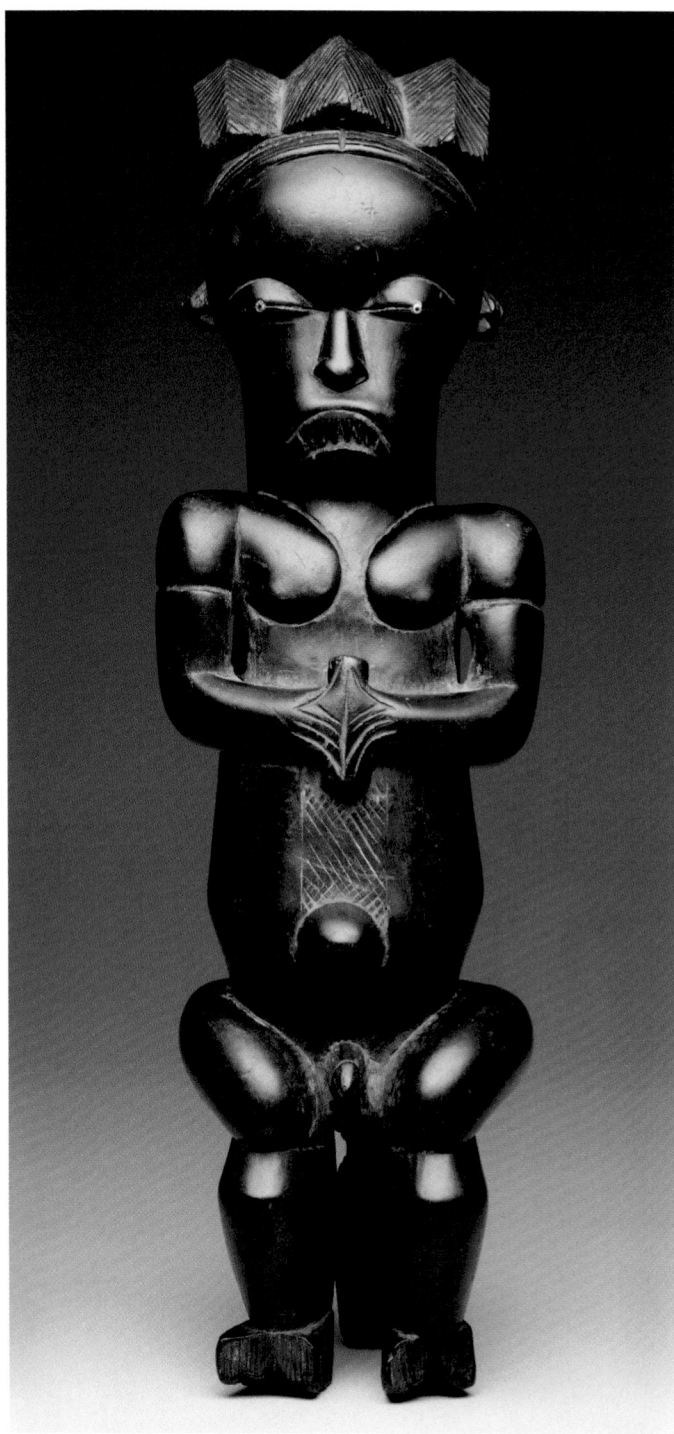

naturalistic style, with carefully arranged hairstyles, fully rounded torsos, and heavily muscled legs and arms. Both forms are today considered among the great masterpieces of African sculpture. Here, the figure's firmly set jaw and powerfully built, muscular body exudes a sense of authority and confidence. These powerfully realized sculptures were often enhanced by the frequent application of cleansing and purifying palm oil over an extended period of time. This has produced a rich, glossy black surface that may literally excrete oil.

An authority on Fang culture suggests that the Fang strive to achieve a balance between the opposing forces of chaos and order, male and female, pure and impure, powerful and weak. They value an attitude of quiet composure, of reflection and tranquility. These qualities are embodied in the symmetry of the *bieri*, which communicates the calm and wisdom of the ancestor while also instilling awe and fear in those not initiated into the Fang religion.

CONTEMPORARY ART

The photographs of rituals and ceremonies in this chapter show ways in which African traditional arts have continued during the modern era. All of the photographs are somewhat dated, yet even today performances are staged in which the traditional types of masks appear. Many African communities continue to recreate art forms according to their traditions. But Africa is ever-changing and, as new experiences pose new challenges and offer new opportunities, African art changes over time.

Perhaps the most obvious development in African art has been the adaptation of modern materials to traditional forms. Some Yoruba, for example, have used photographs and children's brightly colored, imported plastic dolls in place of the traditional *ere ibeji*, images of twins, shown in FIGURE 28–4. The Guro people of Côte d'Ivoire continue to commission delicate masks dressed with costly textiles and other materials, but they paint them with brilliantly colored oil-based enamel paints. The Baule create brightly painted versions of spirit-spouse figures dressed as businessmen or soccer players.

Throughout the colonial period and especially during the years following World War II, many African artists trained in the techniques of European art. In the postcolonial era, numerous African artists have studied in Europe and the United States, and many have become known internationally through exhibitions of their work in galleries and museums. Yet the diversity of influences on contemporary Africa makes it impossible to render a homogeneous view of what constitutes contemporary African art. As the art historian and curator Salah Hassan writes: "The development of a modern idiom in African art is closely linked to modern Africa's search for identity. Most contemporary works have apparent ties to traditional African folklore, belief systems and imagery. The only way to interpret or understand these works is in the light of the dual experience of colonialism and assimilation into Western culture in Africa. They reflect the search for a new identity."

28–19 • RELIQUARY GUARDIAN (*EYEMA BIERI*)
From Gabon. Fang people, Mvai group, mid–late 19th century. Wood, metal, and shell, height 21¼″ (53.97 cm). Dallas Museum of Art. The Eugene and Margaret McDermott Art Fund, Inc. (2000.3.MCD)

points of contact for ancestral support and veneration and also as guardians to protect the relics from malevolent spirit forces **(FIG. 28–19)**.

Bieri were carved in a number of different forms and styles, including large heads with long necks which were secured into the lid of the container; the container thus represents the body of the ancestors. Other *bieri* were created as full figures in a relatively

EL ANATSUI OF GHANA. This search for identity inspired a desire to affirm Africa's rich legacy of tradition-based art in the work of El Anatsui. Born in Ghana in 1944, Anatsui studied art in Kumasi where he took course work he describes as predominantly Western in orientation. He found the emphasis on Western traditions irrelevant, while Ghana's own rich legacy was ignored and, following his own inclinations, he began to study Ghanaian surface design traditions as produced by Ewe and Asante textile artists. In 1975, Anatsui took a position in the Fine Arts Department of the University of Nigeria at Nsukka. There he found a like-minded spirit in Uche Okeke, who was intensely interested in revitalizing *uli*, an important Igbo surface design system. Anatsui began to create what would become a large body of work inspired by *uli* and other graphic systems using tools such as chain saws and blowtorches. More recently, while still concerned with the survival and transmission of inherited traditions, Anatsui began to appropriate cast-off objects he found in and around Nsukka, including broken and discarded mortars, large coconut graters, and liquor-bottle caps, to create revelatory art forms in a variety of media. These include visually stunning, immense wall sculptures that fold and undulate like textiles but are made from metal bottle caps sewn together with copper wire **(FIG. 28–20)**.

Although he lives in Nigeria, El Anatsui, like many contemporary African artists, also participates in international art events—including workshops, symposia, biennial exhibitions, and art festivals that dramatically invigorate our global visual culture. On the other hand, many other African artists have moved permanently to major European and American cities, which offer them increased opportunities for exposure to art dealers, museum curators, art critics, and the expanding base of public and private collectors of African contemporary art.

AFRICAN ARTISTS IN DIASPORA. While many African artists are primarily influenced by their own culture and traditions, others—especially some who no longer live on the continent—seem entirely removed from African stylistic influences and yet still express the search for a new African identity in revelatory ways. Their experiences of movement, accommodation, and change often become important elements in their art making and form an additional basis for the interpretation of their work.

Julie Mehretu **(FIG. 28–21)** is an eminent example of this kind of artist. Born in Ethiopia in 1970, but having lived as well in Senegal and the United States, and now in New York City, Mehretu makes large-scale paintings and wall drawings that exude intense

28-20 • El Anatsui
FLAG FOR A NEW WORLD POWER
2004. Aluminum bottle tops, copper wire, 196 × 177″ (500 × 450 cm). October Gallery, London.

28-21 • Julie Mehretu DISPERSION
2002. Ink and acrylic on canvas, 90 × 144″ (228.6 × 365.8 cm). Collection of Nicolas and Jeanne Greenberg Rohatyn, New York

EXPLORE MORE: Gain insight from a primary source related to *Dispersion* **www.myartslab.com**

energy. Her works speak not only to her own history of movement and change, but also to the transnational movement of myriad others uprooted by choice or by force as they create new identities in this increasingly turbulent period of globalization and change.

The underpinnings of her intricately layered canvases are architectural plans of airports, passenger terminals, and other places where people congregate and pass through during their lives. Layered and at times obscuring these architectural elements is an immense inventory of signs and markings influenced by cartography, weather maps, Japanese and Chinese calligraphy, tattooing, graffiti, and various stylized forms suggesting smoke and explosions borrowed from cartoons, comic books, and anime. Occasionally architectural details such as arches, stairways, and columns reminiscent of Dürer or Piranesi can also be discerned. The ambiguous reading of the paintings as either implosion and chaos or explosion and regeneration gives the works visual and conceptual complexity. Mehretu explains that she is not interested in describing or mapping specific locations but "in the multi-faceted layers of place, space, and time that impact the formation of personal and communal identity." Mehretu's concerns echo those of other contemporary African artists whose identification with the continent becomes increasingly complex as they move from Africa and enter a global arena.

THINK ABOUT IT

28.1 Compare and contrast the ways two African leaders express their power and authority through the visual arts.

28.2 Explain the use of art during divination rituals and discuss one artwork from the chapter that is used in the practice.

28.3 Analyze the initiation wall panels shown in FIGURE 28–10 and discuss how the artist addresses the experience of colonialism in the work.

28.4 Compare and contrast the works of two African-born contemporary artists, El Anatsui's *Flag for a New World Power* and Julie Mehretu's *Dispersion*. Assess what, if anything, about these works ties them to long-standing African traditions, and what, if anything, about them demonstrates influence from external sources, particularly Western sources, including works treated in Chapters 31 and 32.

28.5 Explain the role of masquerade in African art by analyzing a rite-of-passage ceremony such as the Bwa culture's performance in Burkina Faso or the Kuba funeral ceremony in the Democratic Republic of Congo.

PRACTICE MORE: Compose answers to these questions, get flashcards for images and terms, and review chapter material with quizzes **www.myartslab.com**

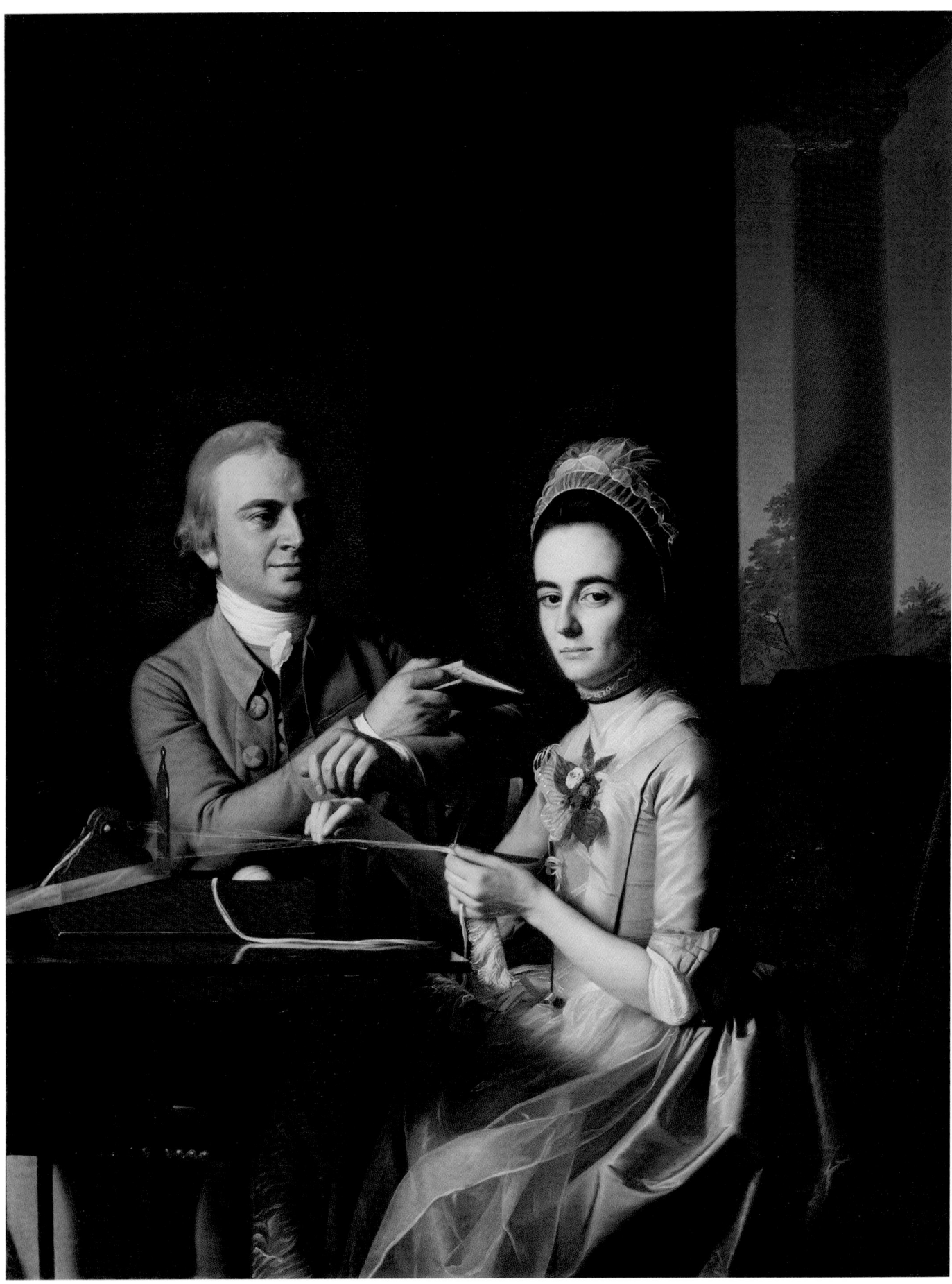

29-1 • John Singleton Copley **THOMAS MIFFLIN AND SARAH MORRIS (MR. AND MRS. MIFFLIN)**
1773. Oil on canvas, 61⅝ × 48″ (156.5 × 121.9 cm). Philadelphia Museum of Art.

EIGHTEENTH- AND EARLY NINETEENTH-CENTURY ART IN EUROPE AND NORTH AMERICA

The portrait by John Singleton Copley (1738–1815) of Thomas Mifflin and his wife, Sarah Morris (FIG. 29–1), was painted in 1773, the same year that American colonists protested against the British tax on tea by staging the Boston Tea Party—seizing British tea and tossing it into Boston harbor. The painting must have hung in the couple's Philadelphia home when Thomas Mifflin, a prominent merchant and politician, and other leading representatives of the colonies negotiated a strategy for the impending break with Britain at the First Continental Congress. Indeed, the painting reflects the couple's identity as American patriots, committed to the cause of independence.

Sarah, and not her famous husband, is the center of attention in this painting. She sits in the foreground dressed in a stylish silk dress decorated with expensive laces, a finely wrought lace cap atop her smoothly coiffed head. She is rich and elegant, but wears no jewelry except for a decorated choker. In fact, rather uncharacteristically for a woman of her social status, she is shown with her sleeves rolled up, working silk threads on the large wooden frame that sits on her polished table. Her work is domestic work, not the kind of activity normally chosen as the subject of a large and expensive portrait, but it was included here for important political reasons. She is weaving a type of decorative silk fringe that would have been imported from England in the past. By including this frame, Copley demonstrates her commitment both to her home as a good and industrious wife, and also to the revolutionary cause as a woman without pretension who can manage well without British imported goods. Meeting the viewer's gaze with confidence and intelligence, she is clearly partner to her husband in the important work of resisting British colonial power.

John Singleton Copley was, by 1773, Boston's preeminent portrait painter and a wealthy man. (The Philadelphia Mifflins were in Boston the summer that Copley painted them.) His reputation stood on his remarkable ability to represent the upper strata of society in a clear, sharp, precise painting style that seemed to reveal not only every minute detail of his sitter's physical appearance and personality, but also the gorgeous satins, silks and laces of the women's dresses and the expensive polished furniture that were the signs of his patrons' wealth and status. Although his father-in-law was the Boston representative of the East India Company (whose tea was dumped into the harbor), Copley was nonetheless sympathetic to the revolutionary cause and, in fact, tried unsuccessfully to mediate the crisis in Boston. This portrait of Sarah and Thomas Mifflin was painted when Copley himself was ambivalent about the political future of the colonies, but his sitters reveal only their own sober commitment to the cause.

LEARN ABOUT IT

29.1 Discover how the ornate style of the Rococo era was a reflection of salon life among the aristocracy in eighteenth-century France.

29.2 Investigate Neoclassicism as a reflection of Enlightenment values with roots in the study of Classical antiquity in Rome.

29.3 Explore the many subjects of Romanticism, from the sublime in nature to the cruelty of the slave trade with a common interest in emotion and feeling.

29.4 Examine the Grand Manner in history painting and portraiture and the role of art academies.

29.5 Trace the complex political climate of the times through the work of Francisco Goya.

HEAR MORE: Listen to an audio file of your chapter **www.myartslab.com**

INDUSTRIAL, INTELLECTUAL, AND POLITICAL REVOLUTIONS

The American War of Independence was just one of many revolutions to shake the established order during the eighteenth and early nineteenth centuries. This was an age of radical change in society, thought, and politics, and while these transformations were felt especially in England, France and the United States, they had consequences throughout the West and, eventually, the world.

The transformations of this period were informed by a new way of thinking that had its roots in the scientific revolution of the previous century (see "Science and the Changing Worldview," page 756). In England, John Locke (1632–1704) argued that reasonable and rational thought should supplant superstition, and Isaac Newton (1643–1727) insisted upon empirical observation, rational evaluation, and logical consideration in mathematics and science. In 1702, Bernard de Fontenelle (1657–1757), a French popularizer of scientific innovation, wrote that he anticipated "a century which will become more enlightened day by day, so that all previous centuries will be lost in darkness by comparison." Over the course of the eighteenth century, this emphasis on thought "enlightened" by reason was applied to political and moral philosophy. Enlightenment thinking is marked by a conviction that humans are not superstitious beings ruled by God or the aristocracy, and that all men (some thinkers also included women) should have equal rights and opportunities for the pursuit of freedom, happiness, and fulfillment. Most Enlightenment philosophers believed that, when freed of past religious and political shackles, men and women could and would act rationally and morally. The role of the state was to protect and facilitate these rights, and when the state failed, the moral solution was to change it. Both the American Revolution of 1776 and the French Revolution of 1789 were justified on this basis.

The eighteenth century was also a period of economic and social transformation, set into motion by the Industrial Revolution. In 1700, Europe was still semi-feudal. Wealth and power belonged to the aristocracy, who owned the land and controlled the lives of poor tenant farmers. The Industrial Revolution replaced the land-based power of the aristocracy with the financial power of capitalists, who were able to use new sources of energy to mechanize manufacturing and greatly increase the quantity and profitability of saleable goods. Factory work lured the poor away from the countryside to the cities with the promise of wages and greater independence. The conditions that urban workers endured, however, were dreadful, both at their grueling factory jobs and in their overcrowded and unsanitary neighborhoods. These conditions would sow the seeds of dissent and revolution in several European countries in the mid nineteenth century. Industrialization also produced a large middle class that both bought and sold the new goods made in factories.

By the early nineteenth century, the aristocracy was weak and ineffectual in many nations, and virtually eliminated in France.

Upper-middle-class industrialists and merchants dominated European commerce, industry, and politics, and their beliefs and mores defined social norms. At the same time, the idealism of the Enlightenment had eroded, particularly in France in the wake of the Revolution, when the new republican form of government "by the people" brought chaos and bloodshed rather than order and stability. A new intellectual trend, known as Romanticism, started as a literary movement in the 1790s and served as a counterpoint to Enlightenment idealism. It critiqued the idea that the world was knowable and ruled by reason alone. The central premise of Romanticism was that an exploration of emotions, the imagination, and intuition—areas of the mind not addressed by Enlightenment philosophy—could lead to a more nuanced understanding of the world. Rather than one supplanting the other, Romanticism and Enlightenment thought co-existed as different parts of a complex whole.

THE ROCOCO STYLE

In the modern age, the shift from art produced at the behest of individual patrons—usually the monarchy, aristocracy, or Church—to art produced for sale to the industrial rich and even

29-2 • Germain Boffrand SALON DE LA PRINCESSE, HÔTEL DE SOUBISE
Paris. Begun 1732. Library, Getty Research Institute, Los Angeles. Wim Swaan Photograph Collection (96, p. 21)

MAP 29–1 • EUROPE AND NORTH AMERICA IN THE EIGHTEENTH CENTURY

During the 18th century, three major artistic styles—Rococo, Neoclassicism, and Romanticism—flourished in Europe and North America.

the emerging middle classes had its roots in the Rococo when the court culture of Versailles changed to salon culture in Paris. The term *Rococo* combines the Italian word *barocco* (an irregularly shaped pearl, possibly the source of the word "baroque") and the French *rocaille* (a popular form of garden or interior ornamentation using shells and pebbles) to describe the refined and fanciful style that became fashionable in parts of Europe during the eighteenth century. The Rococo developed in France around 1715, when the duc d'Orléans, regent for the boy-king Louis XV (r. 1715–1774), moved his home and the French court from Versailles to Paris. The movement spread quickly across Europe (**MAP 29–1**).

ROCOCO SALONS

The French court was happy to escape its confinement in the rural palace of Versailles and relocate to Paris. There courtiers built elegant town houses (in French, *hôtels*), whose social rooms may have been smaller than at Versailles, but were no less lavishly decorated. These became the center of social life for aristocrats who cultivated witty exchanges, elegant manners, and a luxurious life specifically dedicated to pleasure, leisure, and sensuality that frequently masked social insecurity and ambivalence. **Salons**, as

the rooms and the events held in them were known, were intimate, fashionable, and intellectual gatherings, often including splendid entertainments that mimicked in miniature the rituals of the Versailles court. The salons were hosted on a daily basis by accomplished, educated women of the upper class including Mesdames de Staël, de La Fayette, de Sévigné, and du Châtelet.

The Rococo style cannot be fully appreciated through single objects, but is evident everywhere in the salons, with their profusely decorated walls and ceilings bursting with exquisite three-dimensional embellishments in gold, silver, and brilliant white paint; their intimate, sensual paintings hung among the rich ornament; and their elaborate crystal chandeliers, mirrored walls, and delicate decorated furniture and tabletop sculptures. When these Parisian salons were lit by candles, they must have glittered with light reflected and refracted by the gorgeous surfaces. The rooms were no doubt also enlivened by the energy of aristocrats, fancifully dressed in a profusion of pastel blues, yellows, greens, and pinks to complement the light, bright details of the Rococo architecture, paintings, and sculptures around them.

The **SALON DE LA PRINCESSE** in the Hôtel de Soubise (**FIG. 29–2**), designed by Germain Boffrand (1667–1754), was the

29-3 • Jean-Antoine Watteau THE SIGNBOARD OF GERSAINT
c. 1721. Oil on canvas, 5′4″ × 10′1″ (1.62 × 3.06 m). Stiftung Preussische Schlössen und Gärten Berlin-Brandenburg, Schloss Charlottenburg.

Watteau's signboard painting was designed for the Paris art gallery of Edmé-François Gersaint, a dealer who introduced to France the English idea of selling paintings by catalog. The systematic listing of works for sale gave the name of the artist and the title, the medium, and the dimensions of each work of art. The shop depicted on the signboard is not Gersaint's but an ideal gallery visited by elegant and cultivated patrons. The sign was so admired that Gersaint sold it only 15 days after it was installed. Later it was cut down the middle and each half was framed separately, which resulted in the loss of some canvas along the sides of each section. The painting was restored and its two halves reunited in the twentieth century.

EXPLORE MORE: Gain insight from a primary source on Jean-Antoine Watteau **www.myartslab.com**

setting for intimate gatherings of the Parisian aristocracy in the years prior to the French Revolution. Its delicacy and lightness are typical of French Rococo salon design of the 1730s, with architectural elements, rendered in sculpted stucco, including arabesques (characterized by flowing lines and swirling shapes), S-shapes, C-shapes, reverse C-shapes, volutes, and naturalistic plant forms. Intricate polished surfaces included carved wood panels called *boiseries* and inlaid wood designs on furniture and floors. The glitter of silver and gold against white and pastel shades and the visual confusion of mirror reflections all added to this Rococo interior.

ROCOCO PAINTING AND SCULPTURE

The paintings and sculpture that decorated Rococo salons and other elegant spaces contributed to their atmosphere of sensuality and luxury. Pictorial themes were often taken from Classical love stories, and sculpted ornaments were typically filled with *putti*, cupids, and clouds. The paintings of Jean-Antoine Watteau,

François Boucher, and John-Honoré Fragonard and the tabletop sculpture of Claude Michel, known as Clodion, were highly coveted in salon culture.

WATTEAU. Jean-Antoine Watteau (1684–1721) was the originator and greatest proponent of the French Rococo style in painting. Born in the provincial town of Valenciennes, Watteau came to Paris around 1702, where he studied Rubens's paintings for Marie de' Medici (SEE FIG. 22–29), then displayed in the Luxembourg Palace, and the paintings and drawings of sixteenth-century Venetians such as Giorgione (SEE FIG. 20–21), which he saw in a Parisian private collection. Watteau perfected a graceful personal style informed by the fluent brushwork and rich colors of Rubens and the Venetians.

Watteau painted for the new urban aristocrats who frequently purchased paintings for their homes through art dealers in the city. His **SIGNBOARD OF GERSAINT** (FIG. 29–3) shows the interior of one of these shops. Painted for the art dealer Edmé-François Gersaint, the painting shows an art gallery filled with paintings from the Venetian and Netherlandish schools that Watteau admired. Indeed, the glowing satins and silks of the women's gowns pay homage to artists such as Gerard ter Borch (SEE FIG. 22–43). The visitors to the gallery are elegant ladies and gentlemen, at ease in these surroundings and apparently knowledgeable about painting, who create an atmosphere of aristocratic sophistication. At the left, a woman in shimmering pink satin steps across the threshold, ignoring her companion's outstretched hand, to watch the two porters packing. While one porter holds a mirror, the other carefully lowers into the wooden case a portrait of Louis XIV, which may be a reference to the name of Gersaint's shop, *Au Grand Monarque* ("At the Sign of the Great King"). It also suggests the passage of time, for Louis had died six years earlier.

Other elements in the work also suggest transience. On the left, the clock directly above the king's portrait, surmounted by an allegorical figure of Fame and sheltering a pair of lovers, is a **memento mori**, a reminder of mortality, suggesting that both love and fame are subject to the ravages of time. Well-established *vanitas* emblems are the easily destroyed straw (in the foreground) and the young woman gazing into the mirror (set next to a vanity case on

the counter)—mirrors and images of young women looking at their reflections had been familiar symbols of the fragility of human life since the Baroque period. Notably, the two gentlemen at the end of the counter also appear to gaze at the mirror, and are thus also implicated in the *vanitas* theme. Watteau, who died from tuberculosis before he was 40, produced this painting during his last illness. Gersaint later wrote that he had completed the painting in eight days, working only in the mornings because of his failing health. When *The Signboard* was installed, it was greeted with almost universal admiration; Gersaint sold it within a month.

In his **PILGRIMAGE TO THE ISLAND OF CYTHERA (FIG. 29–4)**, painted four years earlier, Watteau portrayed an imaginary idyllic and sensual life of Rococo aristocrats but with the same melancholic undertone that hints at the fleeting quality of human happiness. The painting depicts a dream world in which beautifully dressed couples, accompanied by *putti*, conclude their day's romantic trysts on Cythera, the island sacred to Venus, the goddess of love, whose garlanded statue appears at the extreme right. The lovers, dressed in exquisite satins, silks, and velvets, gather in the verdant landscape. This kind of idyllic and wistfully melancholic vision charmed both early eighteenth-century Paris and most of Europe. Watteau painted *Pilgrimage to the Island of Cythera* in 1717

29-4 • Jean-Antoine Watteau PILGRIMAGE TO THE ISLAND OF CYTHERA
1717. Oil on canvas, 4′3″ × 6′4½″ (1.3 × 1.9 m). Musée du Louvre, Paris.

**29-5 • François Boucher
GIRL RECLINING:
LOUISE O'MURPHY**
1751. Oil on canvas,
28³/₄ × 23¹/₄″ (73 × 59 cm).
Wallfaf-Richartz Museum,
Cologne.

as his official examination canvas for admission to membership in the Royal Academy of Painting and Sculpture (see "Academies and Academy Exhibitions," page 924). Although there was no academic category to cover the painting, the academicians were so impressed by the canvas that they created a new category, the **fête galante**, or elegant outdoor entertainment, to describe this genre of painting.

BOUCHER. The artist most closely associated with Parisian Rococo painting after Watteau's death is François Boucher (1703–1770). The son of a minor painter, Boucher in 1723 entered the workshop of an engraver where he was hired to reproduce Watteau's paintings for a collector, firmly establishing the future direction of his career.

After studying at the French Academy in Rome from 1727 to 1731, he settled in Paris and became an academician. Soon his life and career were intimately bound up with two women. The first was his artistically talented wife, Marie-Jeanne Buseau, who was a frequent model as well as a studio assistant to her husband. The other was Louis XV's mistress, Madame de Pompadour, who became his major patron and supporter. Pompadour was an amateur artist herself and took lessons in printmaking from Boucher. After he received his first royal commission in 1735, Boucher worked almost continuously on the decorations for the royal residences at Versailles and Fontainebleau. In 1755, he was made chief inspector at the Gobelins tapestry manufactory, and provided designs for them as well as for the Sèvres porcelain and Beauvais tapestry manufactories. All these workshops produced both furnishings for the king and wares for sale on the open market by merchants such as Gersaint. Indeed, Boucher operated in a much more commercial market than artists in the previous century.

In 1765, Boucher became First Painter to the King. In this role he painted several portraits of Louis XV, scenes of daily life and mythological pictures, and a series of erotic works for private enjoyment often depicting the adventures of Venus. One such painting is **GIRL RECLINING: LOUISE O'MURPHY (FIG. 29–5)**. In this painting, the 18-year old Louise O'Murphy (whose identity is still debated by scholars), provocatively pink and completely nude, lies on her stomach on a couch. Her satiny pink and white clothing is strewn about beneath her, and pillows are scattered at her feet and on the floor; her hair is decorated with braids and a blue ribbon and a fallen pink rose lies on the floor. Louise's plump buttocks are displayed enticingly at the very center of the painting. There is little doubt about the subject of the painting; Boucher intended it to be overtly sensual. In contrast to Watteau's *fête galante*, in which nude gods, goddesses, and *putti* frolic around in unreal settings, the woman shown here is clearly human, contemporary, and lying in a very real Rococo room. Boucher's robust world of sensual pleasure recalls the style of Rubens (SEE FIG. 22–29), but Boucher has a lighter touch.

FRAGONARD. Another noteworthy master of French Rococo painting, Jean-Honoré Fragonard (1732–1806), studied with Boucher, who encouraged him to enter the competition for the Prix de Rome, the three- to five-year scholarship awarded to the top students in painting and sculpture graduating from the French Academy's art school. Fragonard won the prize in 1752 and spent the years 1756 to 1761 in Italy; however, it was not until 1765 that he was finally accepted as a member of the Royal Academy. He catered to the tastes of an aristocratic clientele, and, as a decorator of interiors, began to fill the vacuum left by Boucher's death in 1770.

Fragonard's **THE SWING** (**FIG. 29–6**) of 1767 was not part of an interior scheme. It was originally commissioned from painter Gabriel-François Doyen. Although the patron is unknown, Doyen's description reveals that the painting was clearly intended to be sensually explicit. He refused the commission, and gave it to

29–6 • Jean-Honoré Fragonard THE SWING
1766. Oil on canvas, 2′8⅝″ × 2′2″ (82.9 × 66 cm). The Wallace Collection, London.

Fragonard, who created a small jewel of a painting. The subject is a pretty young girl on a swing, being pushed by an elderly bishop obscured by the shadow of the bushes on the right. On the left, however, the girl's lover swoons, flushed with anticipation. As the swing approaches, he is rewarded with an unobstructed view of the girl's pretty legs. The young man reaches out to her with his hat as

if to make a mockingly useless attempt to cover the view, while she glances down and seductively tosses one shoe at him. The abandon of the lovers, the complicity of the sculpture of Cupid on the left, gesturing that he will not tell, the *putti* with a dolphin beneath the swing who seem to urge her on, and the poor bishop to the right, all work together to create an image that bursts with anticipation and desire, but also maintains a sense of humor.

CLODION. In the last quarter of the eighteenth century, the Rococo largely fell out of favor in France, its style and subject matter attacked for being frivolous at best and immoral at worst. One sculptor who clung onto the Rococo almost until the French Revolution, however, was Claude Michel, known as Clodion (1738–1814). Most of his work consisted of playful, erotic tabletop sculpture, mainly in unpainted terra cotta. Typical of his Rococo designs is the terra-cotta model he submitted to win a 1784 royal commission for a large monument to the invention of the hot-air balloon (FIG. 29–7). Hot-air balloons then were elaborately decorated with painted Rococo scenes, gold braid, and tassels. Clodion's balloon, decorated with bands of ornament, rises from a columnar launching pad in billowing clouds of smoke, assisted at the left by a puffing wind god with butterfly wings and heralded at the right by a trumpeting Victory. *Putti* stoke the fire basket, providing the hot air to make the balloon ascend, while others gather reeds for fuel and fly up toward them.

ROCOCO CHURCH DECORATION

The beginning of the Rococo signaled an end to the Church as a major patron of art in northern Europe. Although churches continued to be built and decorated, the dominance of the Church and hereditary aristocracy as patrons diminished significantly. The Rococo proved, however, to be a powerful vehicle for spiritual experience and there were several important churches built in the style, showing how one visual style can have many meanings in society. One of the most opulent Rococo churches still standing in German-speaking Europe is that of the church of the Vierzehnheiligen (the "Fourteen Auxiliary Saints" or "Holy Helpers") designed by Johann Balthasar Neumann (1687–1753) and constructed between 1743 and 1772. The plan (FIG. 29–8), which is based on six interpenetrating oval spaces of varying sizes around a vaulted ovoid center, recalls that of Borromini's Baroque church of San Carlo alle Quattro Fontane in Rome (SEE FIG. 22–7). But the effect here is airy lightness. In the nave (FIG. 29–9), the Rococo love of undulating surfaces with overlays of decoration creates a visionary world where flat wall surfaces scarcely exist. Instead, the viewer is surrounded by clusters of pilasters and engaged columns interspersed with two levels of arched openings to the side aisles, and large clerestory windows illuminating the gold and white of the interior. The foliage of the fanciful capitals is repeated in arabesques, wreaths, and the ornamented frames of irregular panels lining the vault. An ebullient sense of spiritual uplift is achieved by the complete integration of architecture and decoration.

29-7 • Clodion THE INVENTION OF THE BALLOON
1784. Terra-cotta model for a monument, height 43½″ (110.5 cm). The Metropolitan Museum of Art, New York. Rogers Fund and Frederick R. Harris Gift, 1944 (44.21a b)

Clodion had a long career as a sculptor in the exuberant, Rococo manner seen in this work commemorating the 1783 invention of the hot-air balloon. During the austere revolutionary period of the First Republic (1792–1795), he became one of the few Rococo artists to adopt successfully the more acceptable Neoclassical manner. In 1806, he was commissioned by Napoleon to provide the relief sculpture for two Paris monuments, the Vendôme Column and the Carrousel Arch near the Louvre.

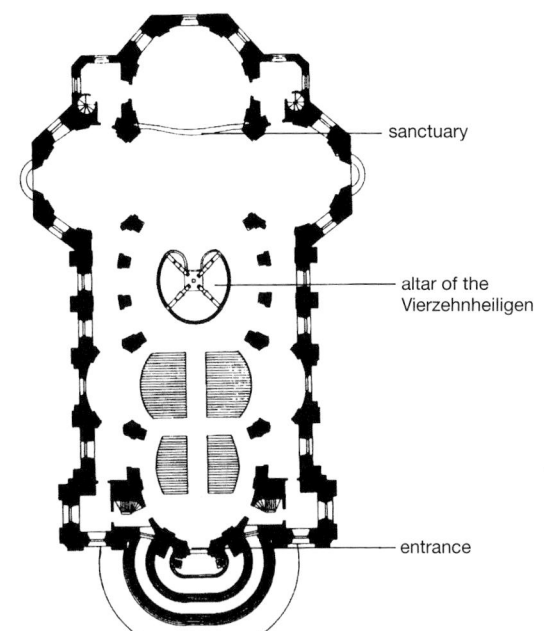

29-8 • PLAN OF THE CHURCH OF THE VIERZEHNHEILIGEN
c. 1743. Near Bamberg, Bavaria, Germany.

sanctuary

altar of the Vierzehnheiligen

entrance

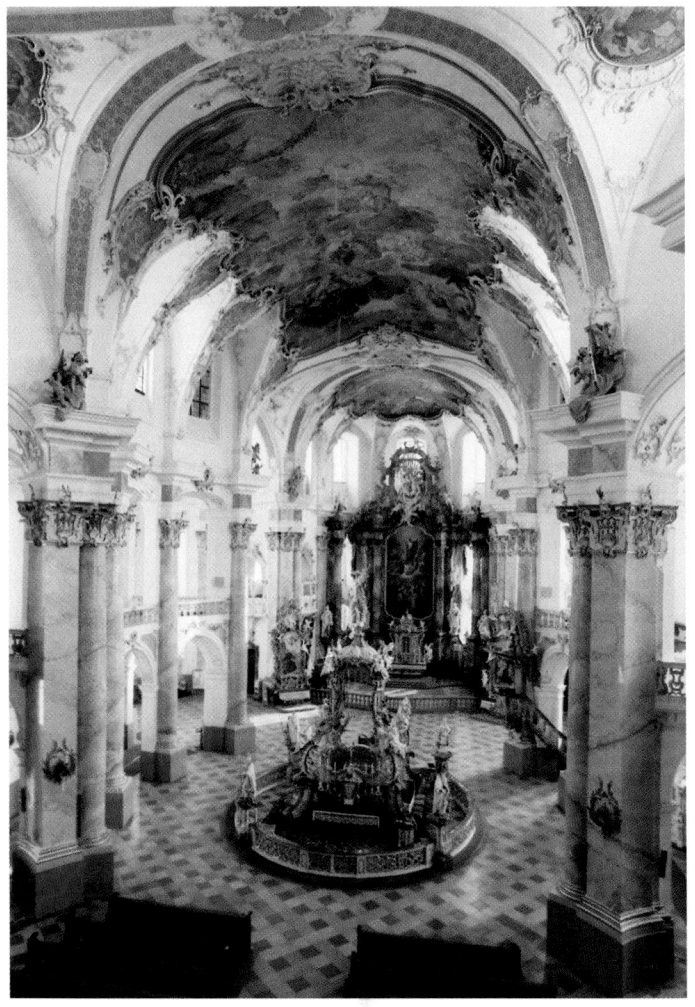

29-9 • Johann Balthasar Neumann INTERIOR, CHURCH OF THE VIERZEHNHEILIGEN
1743–1772. Near Bamberg, Bavaria, Germany.

ITALY: THE GRAND TOUR AND NEOCLASSICISM

From the late 1600s until well into the nineteenth century, the education of a wealthy young northern European or American gentleman—few women were considered worthy of such education—was completed on the **Grand Tour**, an extended visit to the major cultural sites of southern Europe. Accompanied by a tutor and an entourage of servants, the Grand Tourist began in Paris, moved on to southern France to visit a number of well-preserved Roman buildings and monuments there, then headed to Venice, Florence, Naples, and Rome. As the repository of the Classical and Renaissance pasts, Italy was the focus of the Grand Tour.

Italy, and Rome in particular, was also the primary destination for artists and scholars interested in the Classical past. In addition to the ancient architecture and sculpture to be found in collections throughout Rome, the nearby sites of Pompeii and Herculaneum offered sensational new material for study and speculation (see Chapter 6). These two prosperous Roman towns, buried by a sudden volcanic eruption in 79 CE, were discovered by archaeologists in the mid eighteenth century.

The artists and intellectuals who were inspired by the Classical past contributed to early Neoclassicism, which was both a way of viewing the world and a visual style. Neoclassicism (*neo* means "new") sought to present Classical ideals and subject matter in a style derived from Classical Greek and Roman sources. Neoclassical paintings reflect the frozen forms, tight compositions, and shallow space of ancient relief sculpture. Because the ancient world was considered the font from which British and European democracy, secular government, and civilized thought and action flowed, its art was viewed as the embodiment of timeless civic and moral lessons. Neoclassical paintings and sculptures were frequently painted for and displayed in public places in order to inspire patriotism, nationalism, and courage in defense of the state. Neoclassicism was frequently used in Britain, America, and especially France as a visual expression of the state or government.

GRAND TOUR PORTRAITS AND VIEWS

Artists in Italy benefitted not only from their access to authentic works of antiquity, but also from the steady stream of wealthy art collectors on the Grand Tour. Tourists visited the studios of important Italian artists in order to view and purchase works that could be brought home and displayed as evidence of their cultural travels.

CARRIERA. Wealthy European visitors to Italy frequently sat for portraits by Italian artists. Rosalba Carriera (1675–1757), the leading portraitist in Venice in the first half of the eighteenth century, worked mainly in pastel, a medium better suited than slow-drying oil to accommodate sitters whose time in the city was limited.

Pastel is a fast and versatile medium: Pastel crayons, made of pulverized pigment bound to a chalk base by weak gum water, can be used to sketch quickly and spontaneously, or they can be rubbed and blended on the surface of paper to produce a shiny and highly finished surface.

Carriera began her career designing lace patterns and painting miniature portraits on the ivory lids of snuffboxes before she graduated to pastel portraits. Her portraits were so widely admired that she was awarded honorary membership of Rome's Academy of Saint Luke in 1705, and was later admitted to the academies in Bologna and Florence. In 1720, she traveled to Paris, where she made a pastel portrait of the young Louis XV and was elected to the Royal Academy of Painting and Sculpture, despite the 1706 rule forbidding the further admission of women. Returning to Italy in 1721, she established herself in Venice as a portraitist of handsome young men such as the British aristocrat **CHARLES SACKVILLE, 2ND DUKE OF DORSET** (FIG. 29–10).

CANALETTO. A painted city view was by far the most prized souvenir of a stay in Venice. Two kinds of views were produced in Venice: the **capriccio** ("caprice," plural *capricci*), an imaginary

29-11 • Canaletto THE DOGE'S PALACE AND THE RIVA DEGLI SCHIAVONI
Late 1730s. Oil on canvas, 24⅛ × 39¼″ (61.3 × 99.8 cm). National Gallery,
London. Wynn Ellis Bequest 1876 (NG 940)

29-12 • Giovanni Battista Piranesi **VIEW OF THE PANTHEON, ROME**
From the Views of Rome series, first printed in 1756. Etching, 18⁹⁄₁₆ × 27⅛" (47.2 × 69.7 cm). Kupferstich-kabinett, Staatliche Museen, Berlin.

landscape or cityscape in which the artist mixed actual structures, such as famous ruins, with imaginary ones to create attractive compositions; and the **veduta** ("view;" plural *vedute*), a more naturalistic rendering of famous views and buildings, well-known tourist attractions, and local color in the form of tiny figures of the Venetian people and visiting tourists. *Vedute* often encompassed panoramic views of famous landmarks, such as **THE DOGE'S PALACE AND THE RIVA DEGLI SCHIAVONI (FIG. 29–11)** by the Venetian artist Giovanni Antonio Canal, called Canaletto (1697–1768). It was thought that Canaletto used the camera obscura (see page 967) to render his *vedute* with exact topographical accuracy, but his drawings show that he seems to have worked freehand. In fact, his views are rarely topographically accurate and more often than not are composite images: It is a mark of his skill that Canaletto makes us want to believe that his *vedute* are "real." He painted and sold so many to British visitors that his dealer sent him to London from 1746 to 1755 to paint views of the English capital city for his British clients, who included several important aristocrats as well as King George III.

PIRANESI. The city of Rome was also captured in *vedute* for the pleasure of tourists and armchair travelers, most notably by Giovanni Battista Piranesi (1720–1778). Trained in Venice as an architect, he moved to Rome and studied etching, eventually establishing a publishing house and becoming one of the century's most successful printmakers. Piranesi produced a large series of *vedute* of ancient Roman monuments and ruins. His **VIEW OF THE PANTHEON (FIG. 29–12)** is informed by a careful study of ancient Roman architecture. Piranesi succeeds in breathing life into his images by creating grand, monumental scenes.

NEOCLASSICISM IN ROME

The intellectuals and artists who came to study and work in Rome often formed communities with a shared interest in Neoclassical ideals. A British coterie, for example, included Angelica Kauffmann (SEE FIG. 29–26), Benjamin West (SEE FIG. 29–27), and Gavin Hamilton, all of whom contributed to early Neoclassicism. Communities of artists from France and Germany were also established. One of the most influential communities of the period formed at the Villa Albani on the outskirts of Rome, under the sponsorship of Cardinal Alessandro Albani (1692–1779).

Cardinal Albani built his villa in 1760–1761 specifically to house and display his vast collection of antique sculpture, sarcophagi, intaglios (objects in which the design is carved out of the surface), cameos, and vases, and it became one of the most important stops on the Grand Tour. The villa was more than a museum: It was also a place to buy art and artifacts. Albani sold items to artists and tourists alike, to help satisfy the growing craze for antiquities; unfortunately, many were faked or heavily restored by artisans in the cardinal's employ.

In 1758 Albani hired Johann Joachim Winckelmann (1717–1768), the leading theoretician of Neoclassicism, as his secretary and librarian. The Prussian-born Winckelmann became an expert on Classical art while working in Dresden, where the French Rococo style that he deplored was still fashionable. In 1755, he published a pamphlet, *Thoughts on the Imitation of Greek*

29-13 • Anton Raphael Mengs PARNASSUS
Ceiling fresco in the Villa Albani, Rome. 1761.

Works in Painting and Sculpture, in which he attacked the Rococo as decadent, arguing that modern artists could only claim their status as legitimate artists by imitating Greek art. Shortly afterward he went to work for Albani in Rome. In 1764, he published a second influential treatise, *The History of Ancient Art*, often considered one of the earliest art-historical studies. Here Winckelmann analyzed the history of art for the first time as a succession of period styles, an approach which later became the norm for art history books (including this one).

MENGS. Winckelmann's closest friend and colleague in Rome was a fellow German, Anton Raphael Mengs (1728–1779). In 1761 Cardinal Albani commissioned Mengs to create a painting for the ceiling of the great gallery in his new villa **(FIG. 29–13)**. To our eyes Mengs's **PARNASSUS** ceiling may seem stilted, but it is nevertheless significant as the first full expression of Neoclassicism in painting. The scene is taken from Classical mythology. Mount Parnassus in central Greece was where the ancients believed Apollo (god of poetry, music, and the arts) and the nine Muses (female personifications of artistic inspiration) resided. Mengs depicted Apollo standing at the center, almost nude and in the pose of the famous *Apollo Belvedere* in the Vatican collection; he holds a lyre and olive branch to represent artistic accomplishment. Around him are the Muses and their mother, Mnemosyne (Memory, leaning on a Doric column). Mengs arranged his figures in a roughly symmetrical, pyramidal

composition parallel to the picture plane, like the relief sculpture he had studied at Herculaneum. Winckelmann praised this work, claiming that it captured the "noble simplicity and calm grandeur" of ancient Greek sculpture. Shortly after completing this work Mengs left for Spain, where he served as court painter until 1777. Similarly, other artists from Rome moved around Europe, bringing Neoclassical ideas with them.

CANOVA. The theories of the Albani–Winckelmann circle were applied most vigorously by sculptors in Rome, who remained committed to Neoclassicism for almost 100 years. The leading Neoclassical sculptor of the late eighteenth and early nineteenth centuries was Antonio Canova (1757–1822). Born near Venice into a family of stonemasons, he settled in Rome in 1781, where he adopted the Neoclassical style under the guidance of the Scottish painter Gavin Hamilton and quickly became the most sought-after European sculptor of the period.

Canova specialized in two types of sculpture: grand public monuments for Europe's leaders, and erotic mythological subjects for the pleasure of private collectors. His **PAULINE BORGHESE AS VENUS (FIG. 29–14)** falls into the latter category, although it was commissioned by one of the most powerful rulers of Europe in the later eighteenth century, Emperor Napoleon of France (1769–1821). The subject is Napoleon's sister, Pauline, whom the emperor had arranged to marry Prince Camillo Borghese, a member of the

29-14 • Antonio Canova PAULINE BORGHESE AS VENUS
1808. Marble, length 6′7″ (218.4 cm). Galleria Borghese, Rome.

famous Roman Borghese family. Pauline wished to be portrayed as Venus. She is shown semi-nude, reclining on a divan with the golden apple given to Venus by Paris, prince of Troy, as a sign that she was the fairest of the three major goddesses. The cushions and drapery seem impossibly real. The glistening white marble evokes the sensuality of Hellenistic sculpture, and the grey, white, and gold marble base brings a materiality to the sculpture above. Pauline's husband was displeased with the sculpture, which seemed to confirm rumors about his wife's questionable behavior, and installed the sculpture in a private room in the Villa Borghese, where it remains today.

NEOCLASSICISM AND EARLY ROMANTICISM IN BRITAIN

British tourists and artists in Italy were the leading supporters of early Neoclassicism, partly because of the burgeoning taste for revival styles at home. Nonetheless, the British interest in Classical revival styles was inflected slightly differently from Roman Neoclassicism. While Roman Neoclassicism looked to the past in order to revive a sense of moral and civic virtue, many later eighteenth-century British artists harnessed the concept of civic

virtue to patriotism to create more Romantic works of art dedicated specifically to the British nation. It is in British art and literature that we find the beginnings of Romanticism.

Like Neoclassicism, Romanticism describes not only a style but also an attitude: It celebrates the individual and the subjective, while Neoclassicism celebrates the universal and the high-minded. Romanticism takes its name and many of its themes from the "romances"—novellas, stories, and poems written in Romance (Latin-derived) languages. The term "Romantic" suggests something fantastic or novelistic, perhaps set in a remote time or place, infused by a poetic, melancholic, or even terrifying spirit. One of the best examples of early Romanticism in literature is *The Sorrows of Young Werther* (1774) by Johann Wolfgang von Goethe (1749–1832), in which a sensitive, outcast young man fails at love and kills himself. This is a story about a troubled individual who loses his way; it does not recall ancient virtues or civic responsibility.

Neoclassicism and Romanticism existed side by side in the later eighteenth and early nineteenth centuries, the two ways of looking at the world each serving a purpose in society. Neoclassicism tended to be a more public art form, and Romanticism more individual and private. Sometimes Neoclassicism even functioned within Romanticism.

THE CLASSICAL REVIVAL IN ARCHITECTURE AND DESIGN

The vogue for the Classical spread throughout the arts in late eighteenth-century England. Ancient Greece and Rome provided impeccable pedigrees for British buildings, utensils, poetry, and even clothing fashions. Women donned white muslin gowns and men curled their hair forward in imitation of Classical statues. In the 1720s, a group of professional architects and wealthy amateurs in Britain, led by the Scot Colen Campbell (1676–1729), stood against what they viewed as the immoral extravagance of the Italian Baroque. They advocated a return to the austerity and simplicity of the Classically inspired architecture of Andrea Palladio, and his country houses in particular.

CHISWICK HOUSE.   Designed in 1724 by its owner, Richard Boyle, the third Earl of Burlington (1695–1753), **CHISWICK HOUSE** **(FIG. 29–15)** is a fine example of British Neo-Palladianism. Burlington visited several of Palladio's country houses in Italy and was particularly struck by the Villa Rotonda (SEE FIG. 20–40), which inspired his plan for Chiswick House. The building plan **(FIG. 29–16)** shares the bilateral symmetry of Palladio's villa, although its central core is octagonal rather than round and there are only two entrances. The main entrance, flanked now by matching

29–16 • PLAN OF CHISWICK HOUSE
1724.

29–15 • Richard Boyle (Lord Burlington) CHISWICK HOUSE
West London, England. 1724–1729. Interior decoration (1726–1729) and new gardens (1730–1740) by William Kent.

SEE MORE: Click the Google Earth link for Chiswick House **www.myartslab.com**

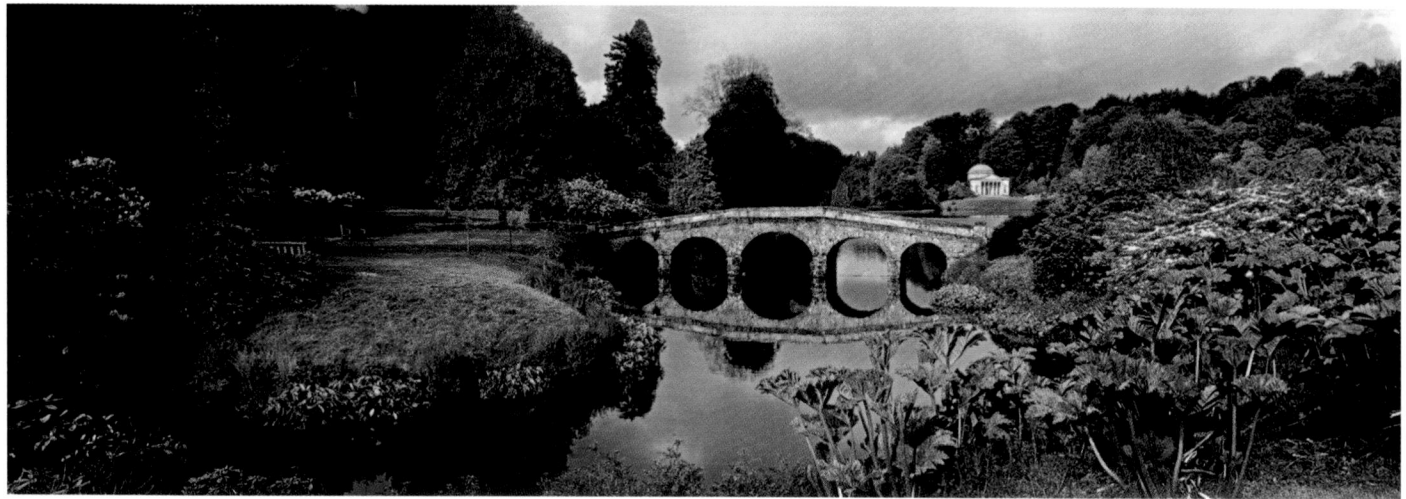

29-17 • Henry Flitcroft and Henry Hoare THE PARK AT STOURHEAD
Wiltshire, England. Laid out 1743, executed 1744–1765, with continuing additions.

staircases, is a Roman temple front, an imposing entrance for the earl. Chiswick's elevation is characteristically Palladian, with a main floor resting on a basement, and tall, rectangular windows with triangular pediments. The few, crisp details seem perfectly suited to the refined proportions of the whole. The result is a lucid evocation of Palladio's design.

When in Rome, Burlington persuaded the English expatriate William Kent (1685–1748) to return to London as his collaborator. Kent designed Chiswick's surprisingly ornate interior as well as its grounds, the latter in a style that became known throughout Europe as the English landscape garden. Kent's garden abandoned the regularity and rigid formality of Baroque gardens (see "Garden Design," page 760). It featured winding paths, a lake with a cascade, irregular plantings of shrubs, and other effects that imitated the appearance of a natural rural landscape—while it was, in fact, carefully designed and manicured.

STOURHEAD. Following Kent's lead at Chiswick, landscape architecture flourished in England in the hands of such designers as Lancelot ("Capability") Brown (1716–1783) and Henry Flitcroft (1697–1769). In the 1740s, the banker Henry Hoare began redesigning the grounds of his estate at Stourhead in Wiltshire (FIG. 29–17) with the assistance of Flitcroft, a protégé of Burlington. The resulting gardens at Stourhead carried Kent's ideas for the English garden much further. Stourhead is a perfect example of the English **picturesque** garden: Its conception and views intentionally mimic the compositional devices of "pictures" by French landscape painter Claude Lorrain (SEE FIG. 22–56), whose paintings were popular in England. The picturesque view illustrated here shows a garden designed with "counterfeit neglect": It is carefully designed to look natural and unkempt. The small lake is crossed by a rustic bridge, while in the background we see a "folly," a miniature version of the Pantheon in Rome. The park is punctuated by other Classically inspired temples, copies of antique statues, artificial grottoes, a rural

cottage, a Chinese bridge, a Gothic spire, and even a Turkish tent: The result is a delightful mixture of styles and cultures that successfully combines the Neoclassical and the Romantic. Inside the house, Hoare commissioned Mengs to paint *The Meeting of Antony and Cleopatra*, a work that similarly combines Classical history with a Romantic subject.

WEDGWOOD. The interiors of country houses like Chiswick and Stourhead were designed partly as settings for the art collections of British aristocrats, which included antiquities as well as a range of Neoclassical paintings, sculpture, and decorative wares (see "A Closer Look," page 919). The most successful producer of Neoclassical decorative art was Josiah Wedgwood (1730–1795). In 1769, near his native village of Burslem, he opened a pottery factory called Etruria after the ancient Etruscan civilization in central Italy known for its pottery. His production-line shop had several divisions, each with its own **kilns** (firing ovens) and workers trained in individual specialties. A talented chemist, in the mid 1770s Wedgwood perfected a fine-grained, unglazed, colored pottery which he called **jasperware**. His most popular jasperware featured white figures against a blue ground, as in **THE APOTHEOSIS OF HOMER** vase (FIG. 29–18). The low-relief decoration was designed by the sculptor John Flaxman, Jr. (1755–1826), who worked for Wedgwood from 1775 to 1787. Flaxman based this scene on a book illustration portraying a particular Greek vase in the collection of William Hamilton (1730–1803), a leading collector of antiquities and one of Wedgwood's major patrons. Flaxman simplified the original design to accommodate both the popular and idealized notion of ancient Greek art and the demands of mass production.

The socially conscious Wedgwood, informed by Enlightenment thinking, established a village for his employees and showed concern for their well-being. He was active in the international effort to halt the African slave trade and abolish slavery. In an

29-19 • William Hackwood for Josiah Wedgwood "AM I NOT A MAN AND A BROTHER?"
1787. Black-and-white jasperware, 1⅜ × 1⅜″ (3.5 × 3.5 cm).
Trustees of the Wedgwood Museum, Barlaston, Staffordshire, England

29-18 • Josiah Wedgwood THE APOTHEOSIS OF HOMER
Made at the Wedgwood Etruria factory, Staffordshire, England.
1790–1795. White jasperware body with a mid-blue dip and white
relief, height 18″ (45.7 cm). Relief of *The Apotheosis of Homer* adapted
from a plaque by John Flaxman, Jr., 1778. Trustees of the Wedgwood
Museum, Barlaston, Staffordshire, England

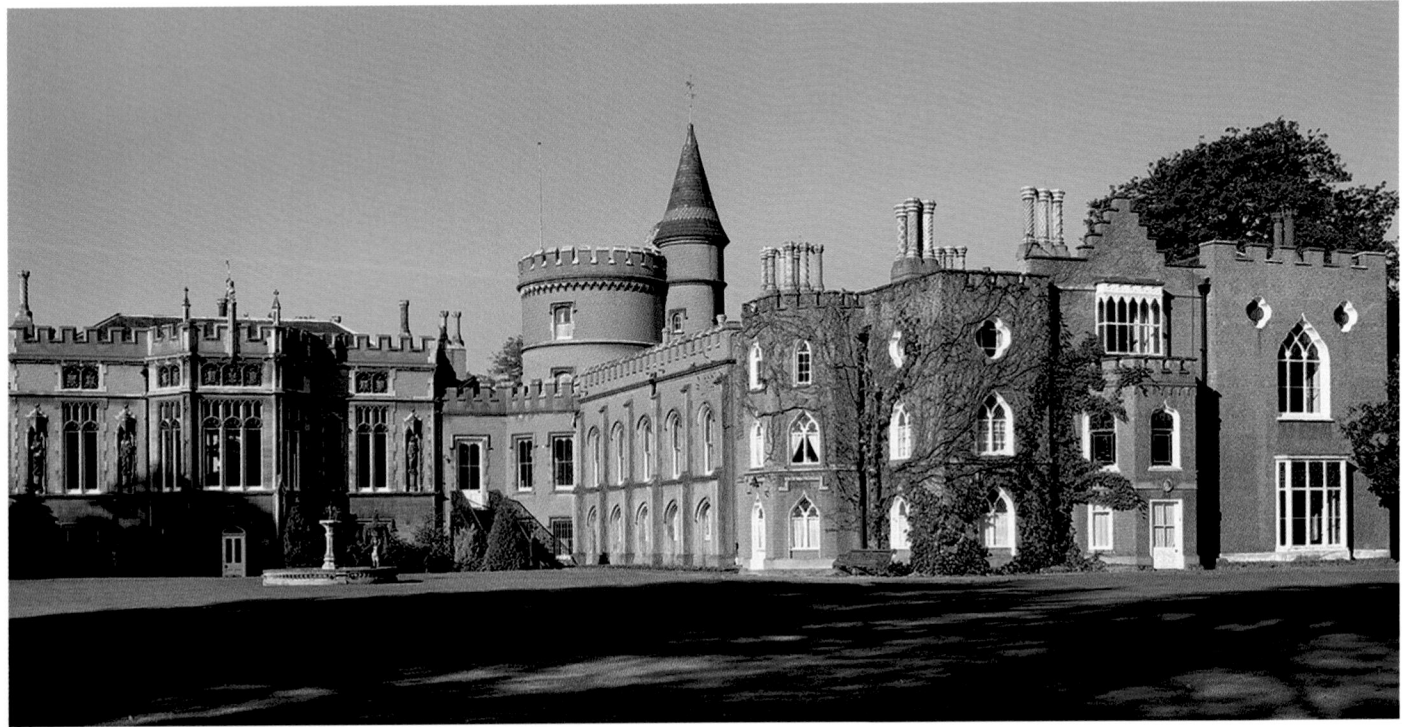

29-20 • Horace Walpole and others STRAWBERRY HILL
Twickenham, England. 1749–1776.

Georgian Silver

Elizabeth Morley **GEORGE III TODDY LADLE, 1802**; Alice and George Burrows
GEORGE III SNUFFBOX, 1802; Elizabeth Cooke **GEORGE III SALVER, 1767**; Ann and Peter Bateman
GEORGE III GOBLET, 1797; Hester Bateman **GEORGE III DOUBLE BEAKER, 1790**
National Museum of Women in the Arts, Washington, D.C. Silver Collection assembled by Nancy Valentine.
Purchased with funds donated by Mr. and Mrs. Oliver Grace and family

All of the objects shown here bear the marks of silver shops run either wholly or partly by women, who played a significant role in the production of silver during the Georgian period—the years from 1714 to 1830, when Great Britain was ruled by four successive kings named George.

This goblet was used for drinking punch, a potent alcoholic beverage enjoyed by British high society. The gilded interior protected the silver from the acid in alcoholic drinks.

The filled goblets would have been served on a flat salver.

This box contained snuff, a pulverized tobacco inhaled by both men and women of the upper class. This snuffbox has curved sides for easy insertion into the pocket of a gentleman's tight-fitting trousers.

These "double beaker" cups are also for drinking punch. The smaller size made them convenient for use when traveling.

This ladle was used to pour punch from a bowl into a goblet. Its twisted whalebone handle floats, making it easy to retrieve from the bowl.

SEE MORE: View the Closer Look feature for Georgian Silver **www.myartslab.com**

attempt to publicize the abolitionist cause, he commissioned the sculptor William Hackwood (c. 1757–1839) to design an emblem for the British Committee to Abolish the Slave Trade, formed in 1787. Hackwood created a small medallion of black-and-white jasperware, with a cameo likeness of an African man kneeling in chains, and the legend **"AM I NOT A MAN AND A BROTHER?" (FIG. 29–19)**. Wedgwood sent copies of the medallion to Benjamin Franklin, the president of the Philadelphia Abolition Society, and to others in the abolitionist movement. The image was so compelling that the women's suffrage movement in the United States later used it to represent a woman in chains with the motto "Am I Not a Woman and a Sister?"

THE GOTHIC REVIVAL IN ARCHITECTURE AND DESIGN

The Gothic Revival style emerged alongside the Neoclassical in Britain in the mid eighteenth century and spread to several other nations after 1800. An early advocate of the Gothic Revival was the conservative politician and author Horace Walpole (1717– 1797). In 1764, Walpole published *The Castle of Otranto*, widely regarded as the first Gothic novel. This tale of mysterious and supernatural happenings, set in the Middle Ages, almost single-handedly launched a fashion for the Gothic. In 1749, Walpole began to remodel his country house, **STRAWBERRY HILL**, transforming it into the kind of Gothic castle that he described in his fiction **(FIG. 29–20)**. Working with several friends and architects, over the next

29-21 • Horace Walpole, John Chute, and Richard Bentley **PICTURE GALLERY SHOWING FAN-VAULTED CEILING, STRAWBERRY HILL** After 1754.

30 years he added decorative **crenellations** (alternating higher and lower sections along the top of a wall), tracery windows, and turrets, to create an imaginary Gothic castle. The interior, too, was redesigned according to Walpole's interpretation of the British historical past. In the **PICTURE GALLERY (FIG. 29–21)**, he drew on engravings of medieval architecture from antiquarian books in his library. The gallery ceiling is designed after that of the Chapel of Henry VII at Westminster, but transformed to suit Walpole's taste: For example, there is a very unmedieval strawberry design on the fan vaults.

TRENDS IN BRITISH PAINTING

In the mid nineteenth century, portraiture remained a popular genre in British painting among those with the means to purchase art. But a taste was also developing for other subjects, such as moralizing satire and caricature, ancient and modern history, scenes from British literature, and British landscape and people. Whatever their subject matter, many of the paintings and prints created in Britain reflected Romantic sensibilities and Enlightenment values, including an interest in social change, an embrace of natural beauty, and an enthusiasm for science and technology.

THE SATIRIC SPIRIT. The industrialization of Britain created a large and affluent middle class with the disposable income to purchase smaller and less formal paintings such as landscapes and genre scenes, as well as prints. Relatively inexpensive printed versions of paintings could also be sold to large numbers of people. William Hogarth (1697–1764) capitalized on this new market for art and was largely responsible for reviving the British print industry in the eighteenth century.

Trained as a portrait painter, Hogarth believed art should contribute to the improvement of society. He worked within the flourishing culture of satire in Britain directed at a variety of political and social targets. He illustrated works by John Gay, a writer whose 1728 play *The Beggar's Opera* portrayed all classes as corrupt, but caricatured aristocrats in particular as feckless. In about 1730, Hogarth began illustrating moralizing tales of his own invention in sequences of four to six paintings, which he then produced in sets of mass-produced prints, enabling him to both maximize his profits and reach as many people as possible.

Between 1743 and 1745, Hogarth produced his *Marriage à la Mode* suite, inspired by Joseph Addison's 1712 essay in the *Spectator* promoting the concept of marriage based on love rather than on aristocratic machinations. In his series of paintings and later prints, Hogarth portrays the sordid story and sad end of an arranged marriage between the children of an impoverished aristocrat and a social-climbing member of the newly wealthy merchant class. In the opening scene of the series, **THE MARRIAGE CONTRACT (FIG. 29–22)**, the cast of characters is assembled to legalize the union. At the right of the painting sits Lord Squanderfield, raising his gouty right foot on a footstool as he points to his lengthy family tree (with a few wilted branches), which goes all the way back to medieval knights, as if to say that the pile of money in front of him on the table is not payment enough for the marriage contract he is being asked to sign. Young Squanderfield, a fop and a simpleton, sits on the far left, admiring himself in the mirror and ignoring his

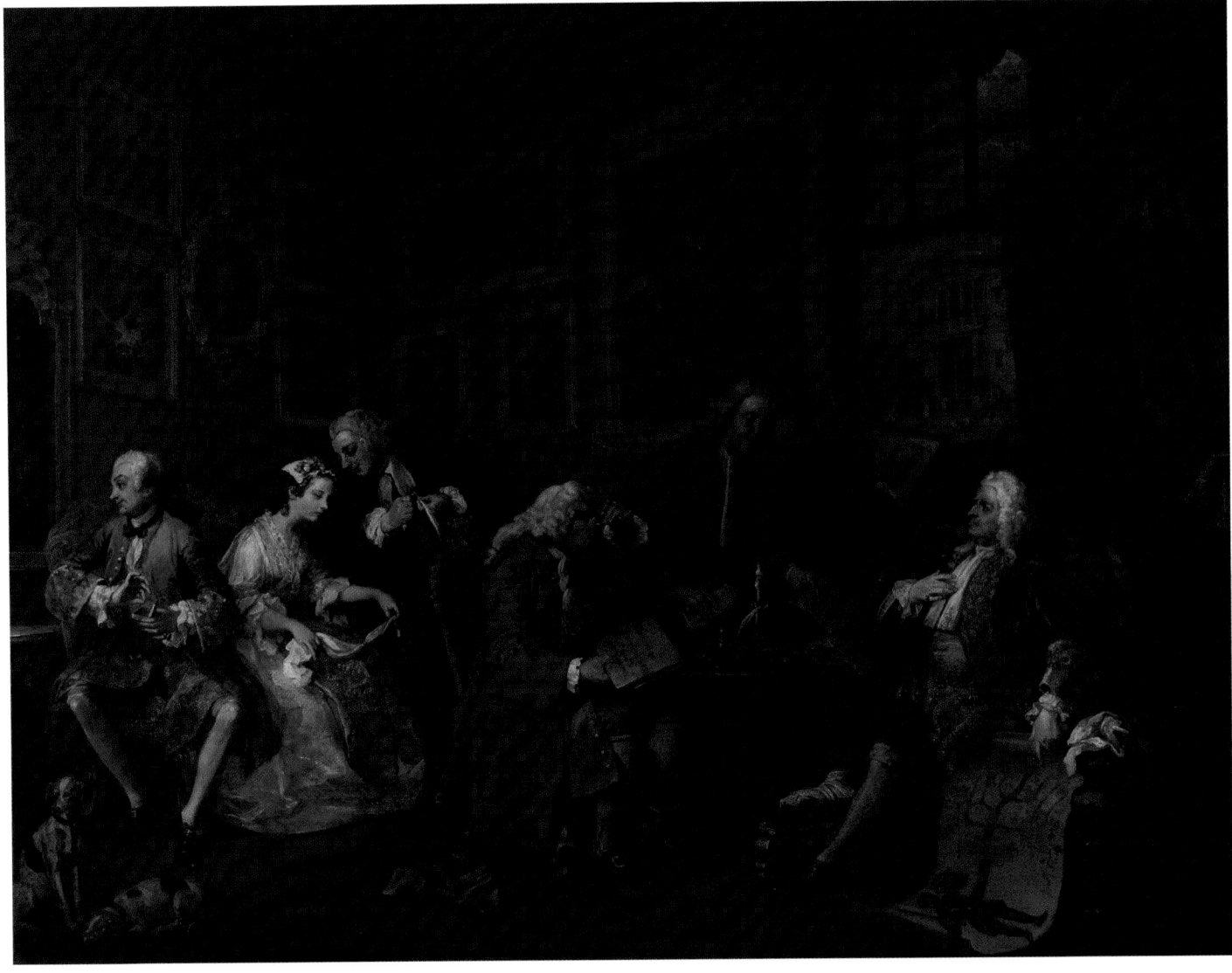

29-22 • William Hogarth THE MARRIAGE CONTRACT
From *Marriage à la Mode*, 1743–1745. Oil on canvas, 27½ × 35¾" (69.9 × 90.8 cm). National Gallery, London.

future wife as he takes a pinch of snuff. His neck is already showing signs of syphilis. The unhappy bride-to-be is extravagantly dressed but rather plain, and her wedding ring is threaded through a handkerchief to wipe away her tears. In the center, her father, the uncultured but wealthy merchant in the brash red coat, leans forward to study Lord Squanderfield's pedigree, an empty sack of money at his feet. The other men are lawyers, including the slippery Silvertongue, who is sharpening the quill that will seal the young couple's fate. The next five scenes of this sad tale describe the progressively disastrous results of such a union.

Hogarth hoped to create a distinctively British style of art, free of obscure mythological references and encouraging the self-improvement in viewers that would lead to social progress. His contempt for the decadent tastes of the aristocracy can be seen in the comic detail of the paintings hanging on Lord Squanderfield's walls. Hogarth wanted to entertain and amuse his audiences, but at the same time his acerbic wit lays open the tensions of class and wealth so prevalent in the Britain of his day. Hogarth's work

became so popular that in 1745 he was able to give up portraiture, which he considered a deplorable form of vanity.

PORTRAITURE. Sir Joshua Reynolds (1723–1792) was a generation younger than Hogarth, and represented the mainstream of British art at the end of the century. After studying Renaissance art in Italy, Reynolds settled in London in 1753, where he worked vigorously to educate artists and patrons to appreciate Classically inspired history painting. In 1768, he was appointed the first president of the Royal Academy (see "Academies and Academy Exhibitions," page 924). His *Fifteen Discourses to the Royal Academy* (1769–1790) set out his theories on art in great detail. He argued that artists should follow rules derived from studying the great masters of the past, especially those who worked in the Classical tradition; he claimed that the ideal image communicated universal truths, and that artists should avoid representations based solely on observation, as these paintings merely communicated base reality.

29–23 • Joshua Reynolds LADY SARAH BUNBURY SACRIFICING TO THE GRACES

1765. Oil on canvas, 7'10" × 5' (2.42 × 1.53 m). The Art Institute of Chicago. Mr. and Mrs. W. W. Kimball Collection, 1922.4468

Lady Sarah Bunbury was one of the great beauties of her era. A few years before this portrait was painted, she turned down a proposal of marriage from George III.

EXPLORE MORE: Gain insight from a primary source on Joshua Reynolds **www.myartslab.com**

Reynolds was able to combine his own taste for history painting with his patrons' desire for images of themselves by developing a type of historical or mythological portraiture that he called the **Grand Manner**. **LADY SARAH BUNBURY SACRIFICING TO THE GRACES** (FIG. 29–23) is just such a portrait. The large scale

of the canvas suggests that it is a history painting, and its details evoke a Classical setting. Framed by a monumental Classical pier and arch, and dressed in a classicizing costume, Lady Sarah plays the part of a Roman priestess making a sacrifice to the Three Graces, personifications of female beauty. Portraits such as this were intended for the public rooms, halls, and stairways of aristocratic residences. Reynolds's Grand Manner portraits were widely celebrated, and his London studio was abuzz with sitters, patrons, and assistants. But Reynolds experimented with his paints, so many of his canvases have faded badly.

A counterpoint to Reynolds's style of portraiture is found in the art of Thomas Gainsborough (1727–1788). Gainsborough later set up a studio in Bath, a resort frequented by the rich and fashionable, and catered to his clients' tastes for the informal poses and natural landscapes introduced to England by Van Dyck in the 1620s. Gainsborough's earlier unfinished **ROBERT ANDREWS AND FRANCES CARTER (FIG. 29–24)**, painted soon after their wedding in 1748, shows the wealthy young rural landowner and his wife posed on the grounds of their estate, with the Sudbury River and the hills of Suffolk in the background. The youthful Frances Carter sits stiffly on a decorative seat, her fine dress arranged around her (the pheasant on her lap is unfinished), while her husband appears more relaxed, his gun in hand and his favorite dog at his side. The couple's good care of the land is revealed as well: The neat rows of corn stocks and stubble in the foreground show Robert Andrews's use of the seed drill and plant husbandry. Sheep and horses graze in separate fields. The significance of this painting lies in the natural pose of the couple, the depictions of their land and the pride they take in it, and the artist's emphasis on nature as the source of bounty and beauty. The painting prefigures the English landscapes of Constable half a century later.

THE ROMANCE OF SCIENCE. In the English Midlands, artist Joseph Wright of Derby (1734–1797) shows a similar admixture of Enlightenment aspirations, industrial innovation, and Romantic sensibility in his depiction of **AN EXPERIMENT ON A BIRD IN THE AIR-PUMP (FIG. 29–25)**. Wright set up his studio during the first wave of the Industrial Revolution, and many of his patrons were self-made wealthy industrial entrepreneurs. Wright belonged to the Lunar Society, a group of industrialists (including Wedgwood), merchants, traders, and progressive aristocrats who met monthly in or near Birmingham

29-24 • Thomas Gainsborough **ROBERT ANDREWS AND FRANCES CARTER (MR. AND MRS. ANDREWS)**
c. 1748–1750. Oil on canvas, 27½ × 47″ (69.7 × 119.3 cm). National Gallery, London.

29-25 • Joseph Wright of Derby **AN EXPERIMENT ON A BIRD IN THE AIR-PUMP**
1768. Oil on canvas, 6 × 8′ (1.82 × 2.43 m). National Gallery, London.

Academies and Academy Exhibitions

During the seventeenth century, the French government founded a number of **academies** for the support and instruction of students in literature, painting and sculpture, music and dance, and architecture. In 1664, the Royal Academy of Painting and Sculpture in Paris began to mount occasional exhibitions of members' recent work. This exhibition came to be known as the Salon because it was held in the Salon Carré in the Palace of the Louvre. As of 1737, the Salon was held every other year, with a jury of members selecting the works to be shown.

History paintings (based on historical, mythological, or biblical narratives and generally conveying a high moral or intellectual idea) were accorded highest place in the Academy's hierarchy of genres, followed by historical portraiture, landscape painting, various other forms of portraiture, genre painting, and still life. The Salon shows were the only public art exhibitions of importance in Paris, so they were highly influential in establishing officially approved styles and in molding public taste; they also consolidated the Academy's control over the production of art.

In recognition of Rome's importance as a training ground for aspiring history painters, the Royal Academy of Painting and Sculpture opened a French Academy in Rome in 1666. A competitive "Prix de Rome," or Rome Prize, enabled the winners to study in Rome for three to five years. A similar prize was established by the French Royal Academy of Architecture in 1720. Many Western cultural capitals emulated the French academic model: Academies were established in Berlin in 1696, Dresden in 1705, London in 1768, Boston in 1780, Mexico City in 1785, and New York in 1802. Members of London's Royal Academy of Arts are depicted in Johann Zoffany's portrait of 1771–1772.

Although there were several women members of the European academies of art before the eighteenth century, their inclusion amounted to little more than an honorary recognition of their achievements. In France, Louis XIV proclaimed in his founding address to the Royal Academy that its purpose was to reward all worthy artists "without regard to the difference of sex," but this resolve was not put into practice. Only seven women gained the title of "Academician" between 1648 and 1706, after which the Royal Academy was closed to women. Nevertheless, four more women were admitted by 1770; however, the men, worried that women would become "too numerous," limited the total number of female members to four. Young women were neither admitted to the Academy School nor allowed to compete for Academy prizes, both of which were required for professional success. They fared even worse at London's Royal Academy. The Swiss painters Mary Moser and Angelica Kauffmann were both founding members in 1768, but no other women were elected until 1922, and then only as associates.

Johann Zoffany **ACADEMICIANS OF THE ROYAL ACADEMY**
1771–1772. Oil on canvas, 47½ × 59½" (120.6 × 151.2 cm). The Royal Collection, Windsor Castle, England.

Zoffany's group portrait of members of the London Royal Academy reveals how mainstream artists were taught in the 1770s. The painting shows artists, all men, setting up a life-drawing class and engaging in lively conversation. The studio is decorated with the Academy's study collection of Classical statues and plaster copies. Propriety prohibited the presence of women in life-drawing studios, so Zoffany includes Royal Academicians Mary Moser and Angelica Kauffmann in portraits on the wall on the right.

---

to exchange ideas about science and technology. As part of the society's attempts to popularize science, Wright painted a series of "entertaining" scenes of scientific experiments.

The second half of the eighteenth century was an age of rapid technological change (see "Iron as a Building Material," page 926), and the development of the air-pump was among the many scientific innovations of the time. Although primarily used to study the properties of gas, it was also widely used in dramatic public demonstrations of scientific principles. In the experiment shown here, air was pumped out of the large glass vessel above the scientist's head until the bird inside collapsed from lack of oxygen. Before it died, air was reintroduced by a simple mechanism at the top. Wright depicts the moment before air is reintroduced, engaging the viewer with the excitement of the moment: Dramatically lit from below by a single light source on the table, the scientist peers out of the picture and gestures like a magician about to perform a trick. By delaying the reintroduction of air, the scientist has created considerable suspense. The three men on the left watch the experiment with great interest, while the young girls on the right have a more emotional response to

29-26 • Angelica Kauffmann CORNELIA POINTING TO HER CHILDREN AS HER TREASURES
c. 1785. Oil on canvas, 40 × 50″ (101.6 × 127 cm). Virginia Museum of Fine Arts, Richmond, Virginia. The Adolph D. and
Wilkins C. Williams Fund

the proceedings. One man is lost in thought, perhaps contemplating the meaning of life, as he stares at a skull suspended in fluid. The moon shines in through the window, a reference to the name of the Lunar Society. Science, the painting suggests, holds the potential for wonder, excitement, and discovery about matters of life and death.

HISTORY PAINTING.   By the time it was adapted to Neoclassicism, history painting had long been considered the highest form of art. The Swiss history painter Angelica Kauffmann (1741–1807), trained in Italy and one of the greatest exponents of early Neoclassicism, arrived in London in 1766 to great acclaim, inspiring British artists to paint Classical history paintings and British patrons to buy them. She was welcomed immediately into Joshua Reynolds's inner circle; in 1768 she was

one of only two women artists named among the founding members of the Royal Academy (see "Academies and Academy Exhibitions," opposite).

Already accepting portrait commissions at age 15, Kauffmann painted Winckelmann's portrait in Rome, became an ardent practitioner of Neoclassicism, and was elected to the Academy of Saint Luke, also in Rome. Most eighteenth-century women artists specialized in the "lower" painting genres of portraiture or still life, but Kauffmann boldly embarked on an independent career as a history painter. In London, where she lived from 1766 to 1781, she produced numerous history paintings, many of them with subjects drawn from Classical antiquity. After her return to Italy, Kauffmann painted **CORNELIA POINTING TO HER CHILDREN AS HER TREASURES** (FIG. 29–26) for an English patron. The scene in the painting took place in the second century BCE, during the

In 1779, Abraham Darby III built a bridge over the Severn River at Coalbrookdale in Shropshire, England, a town typical of industrial England, with factories and workers' housing filling the valley. Built primarily for function, the bridge demonstrated a need for newer, better transportation routes for moving industrial goods. Its importance lies in the fact that it is probably the first large-scale example of the use of structural metal in bridge building, in which iron struts replace the heavy, hand-cut stone voussoirs of earlier bridges. Five pairs of cast-iron, semicircular arches form a strong, economical 100-foot span. In functional architecture such as this, the available technology, the properties of the material, and the requirements of engineering in large part determine form, often producing an unintended new aesthetic. Here, the use of metal made possible the light, open, skeletal structure sought by builders since the twelfth century. Cast iron was quickly adopted for the construction of such engineering wonders as the soaring train stations of the nineteenth century, leading ultimately to such marvels as the Eiffel Tower (FIG. 30–1).

Abraham Darby III
SEVERN RIVER BRIDGE
Coalbrookdale, England. 1779.

SEE MORE: View a simulation on cast-iron structures **www.myartslab.com**

---

republican era of Rome. A woman visitor shows Cornelia her jewels and then asks to see those of her hostess. In response, Cornelia shows her daughter and two sons, saying: "These are my most precious jewels." Cornelia exemplifies the "good mother," a popular theme among some later eighteenth-century patrons who preferred Classical subjects that taught metaphorical lessons of civic virtue. The value of her maternal dedication is emphasized by the fact that her sons, Tiberius and Gaius Gracchus, grew up to be political reformers. Kauffmann's composition is severe and Classical, but she softens the image with warm, subdued lighting and with the tranquil grace of her figures.

Kauffmann's devotion to Neoclassical history painting emerged during her friendship with American-born Benjamin West (1738–1820) in Rome. West studied in Philadelphia before he left for Rome in 1759, where he met Winckelmann and became a student of Mengs. In 1763, he moved permanently to London, where he specialized in Neoclassical history painting. In 1768, along with Kauffmann and Reynolds, he became a founding member of the Royal Academy.

Two years later, West shocked Reynolds and his other academic friends with his painting **THE DEATH OF GENERAL WOLFE (FIG. 29–27)**, which seemed to break completely with Neoclassicism and academic history painting. West argued that history painting was not dependent on dressing figures in Classical costume; in fact, it could represent a contemporary subject as long as the grand themes and elevated message remained intact. Thus, West's painting, and the genre it spawned, came to be known as "modern history" painting. At first, George III and Joshua Reynolds were appalled, but modern history pieces had too strong an attraction for both British collectors and the British public. The king eventually commissioned one of the four replicas of the painting.

West's painting glorifies the British general James Wolfe, who died in 1759 in a British victory over the French for the control of Quebec during the Seven Years War (1756–1763). West depicted Wolfe in his red uniform expiring in the arms of his comrades under a cloud-swept sky. In fact, Wolfe actually died at the base of a tree, surrounded by two or three attendants, but the laws of artistic decorum demanded a much nobler scene. Thus, though West's

29-27 • Benjamin West THE DEATH OF GENERAL WOLFE
1770. Oil on canvas, 4'11½" × 7' (1.51 × 2.14 m). National Gallery of Canada, Ottawa. Transfer from the
Canadian War Memorials, 1921. Gift of the 2nd Duke of Westminster, Eaton Hall, Cheshire, 1918

The famous actor David Garrick was so moved by this painting that he enacted an impromptu interpretation of the dying
Wolfe in front of the work when it was exhibited at the Royal Academy.

painting seems naturalistic, it is not an objective document, nor was it intended to be. West employs the Grand Manner that Reynolds proposed in his *Discourses*, celebrating the valor of the fallen hero, the loyalty of the British soldiers, and the justice of their cause. To indicate the North American setting, West also included at the left a Native American warrior who contemplates the fallen Wolfe. This was another fiction, since the Native Americans in this battle fought on the side of the French, but his presence here establishes the North American site of the event. The dramatic illumination increases the emotional intensity of the scene, as do the poses of Wolfe's attendants, arranged to suggest a Lamentation over the dead Christ. Extending the analogy, the British flag above Wolfe replaces the Christian cross. Just as Christ died for humanity, Wolfe sacrificed himself for the good of the nation. The brilliant color, emotional intensity, and moralizing message made this image extremely popular with the British public. It was translated into a print and received the widest circulation of any image in Britain up to that time.

ROMANTIC PAINTING.   The emotional drama of West's painting helped launch Romanticism in Britain. Among its early practitioners was John Henry Fuseli (1741–1825), who arrived in London from his native Switzerland in 1764. Trained in theology, philosophy, and the Neoclassical aesthetics of Winckelmann (whose writings he translated into English), Fuseli quickly became a member of London's intellectual elite. Joshua Reynolds encouraged Fuseli to become an artist, and in 1770 he left England to study in Rome, where he spent most of the next eight years. His encounter with the sometimes tortured and expressive aspects of both Roman sculpture and Michelangelo's painting led him not to Neoclassicism but to develop his own powerfully expressive style. In his work, Fuseli drew more heavily on the passion of some Roman art, and later that of Michelangelo, than on the ancient Greek art admired by Winckelmann.

Back in London, Fuseli established himself as a history painter, but he specialized in dramatic subjects drawn from Homer, Dante,

29-28 • John Henry Fuseli THE NIGHTMARE
1781. Oil on canvas, 39¾ × 49½″ (101 × 127 cm). The Detroit Institute of Arts. Gift of Mr. and Mrs. Bert Smokler and Mr. and Mrs. Lawrence A. Fleischmann

Fuseli was not popular with the English critics. One writer said that his 1780 entry in the London Royal Academy exhibition "ought to be destroyed," and Horace Walpole called another painting in 1785 "shockingly mad, mad, mad, madder than ever." Even after achieving the highest official acknowledgment of his talents, Fuseli was called "the Wild Swiss" and "Painter to the Devil." But the public appreciated his work, and *The Nightmare*, exhibited at the Royal Academy in 1782, was repeated in at least three more versions and its imagery was disseminated through prints published by commercial engravers. One of these prints would later hang in the office of the Austrian psychoanalyst Sigmund Freud, who believed that dreams were manifestations of the dreamer's repressed desires.

Shakespeare, and Milton. His interest in the dark recesses of the human mind led him to paint supernatural and irrational subjects. In **THE NIGHTMARE (FIG. 29–28)**, he depicts a woman sprawled across a divan with her head thrown back. She is oppressed by a gruesome incubus (or *mara*, an evil spirit) crouching on her pelvis. According to legend, the incubus was believed to feed by stealing women and having sex with them; in her erotic dream the woman dreams that the incubus is about to feed upon her. In the background a horse with wild, phosphorescent eyes thrusts its head into the room through a curtain. The image communicates fear of

the unknown and unknowable, and sexuality without restraint. The painting was exhibited at the Royal Academy in 1782, and although not well received by Fuseli's peers, it clearly struck a chord with the public. He painted at least four versions of this subject and prints of it had a wide circulation.

Fuseli's friend William Blake (1757–1827), a highly original poet, painter, and printmaker, was also inspired by the dramatic aspect of Michelangelo's art. Trained as an engraver, he enrolled briefly at the Royal Academy, where he quickly rejected the teachings of Reynolds, believing that rules hinder rather than aid

29-29 • William Blake **NEWTON**
1795–c. 1805. Color print finished in ink and watercolor, 18⅛ × 23⅝″ (46 × 60 cm). Tate, London.

creativity. He became a lifelong advocate of probing the unfettered imagination. For Blake, the imagination provided access to the higher realm of the spirit and reason was confined to the lower world of matter.

Blake was interested in probing the nature of good and evil, developing an idiosyncratic form of Christian belief, drawing on elements from the Bible, Greek mythology, and British legend. His "prophetic books," designed and printed in the mid 1790s, brought together painting and poetry to explore themes of spiritual crisis and redemption. Thematically related to the prophetic books are an independent series of 12 large color prints that he executed mostly in 1795, which may have some overarching theme; it is not obvious, however, what it is. These include the large print of **NEWTON** (FIG. 29–29), the epitome of eighteenth-century rationalism, naked in a cave and obsessed with reducing the universe to a mathematical drawing with his compasses.

John Singleton Copley, whose portrait of the Mifflins is described above (SEE FIG. 29–1), moved from Boston to London after the Revolutionary War, never to return to his native country. In London, he established himself as a portraitist and painter of modern history in the vein of fellow American expatriate Benjamin West. Copley's most successful modern history painting

was **WATSON AND THE SHARK** (FIG. 29–30), commissioned by Brook Watson, a wealthy London merchant and Tory politician, in 1778. Copley's painting dramatizes an episode of 1749, in which the 14-year-old Watson was attacked by a shark while swimming in Havana Harbor, and lost part of his right leg before being rescued by his comrades. Copley's pyramidal composition is made up of figures in a boat and the hapless Watson in the water with a highly imaginary shark set against the backdrop of the harbor. Several of the figures were inspired by Classical sources, but the scene portrayed is anything but Classical. In the foreground, the ferocious shark rushes on the helpless, naked Watson, while at the prow of the rescue boat a man raises his harpoon to attack the shark. At the left, two of Watson's shipmates strain to reach him while others in the boat look on in alarm. An African man, standing at the apex of the painting, holds a rope that curls over Watson's extended right arm, connecting him to the boat.

Some scholars have read the African figure as a servant waiting to hand the rope to his white master, but his inclusion has also been interpreted in more overtly political terms. The shark attack on Watson in Havana Harbor occurred while he was working in the transatlantic shipping trade, one aspect of which involved the shipment of slaves from Africa to the West Indies. At the time when

29–30 • John Singleton Copley **WATSON AND THE SHARK**
1778. Oil on canvas, 5′10¾″ × 7′6½″ (1.82 × 2.29 m). National Gallery of Art, Washington, D.C. Ferdinand Lammot Belin Fund

Watson commissioned this painting, debate was raging in the British Parliament over the interconnected issues of the Americans' recent Declaration of Independence and the slave trade. Several Tories, including Watson, opposed American independence, highlighting the hypocrisy of American calls for freedom from the British Crown while the colonists continued to deny freedom to African slaves. Indeed, during the Revolutionary War the British offered freedom to every runaway American slave who joined the British army or navy.

Copley's painting, its subject doubtless dictated by Watson, may therefore indicate Watson's sympathy for American slaves; or the figure may be included simply to indicate that the event took place in Havana. Copley was one of the first artists in the capital to exhibit his modern history paintings in public places around London, making money by charging admission fees and advertising his large paintings for sale. His sensational images and exhibitions took advantage of the spectacular displays of the *Phantasmagoria* (a sensational magic lantern display with smoke, mirrors, lights, and gauze "ghosts"), panoramas, dioramas, and the Eidophusikon (a miniature theater with special effects) of London in the early nineteenth century.

LATER EIGHTEENTH-CENTURY ART IN FRANCE

In late eighteenth-century France, the Rococo was replaced by Enlightenment ideas and by the gathering storm clouds of revolution. French art moved increasingly toward Neoclassicism. French architects held closer to Roman proportions and sensibility, while painters and sculptors increasingly embraced didactic Classicism and a plain Classical style.

ARCHITECTURE

French architects of the late eighteenth century generally considered Classicism not one of many alternative artistic styles but as the single, true style. Winckelmann's argument that "imitation of the ancients" was the key to good taste was taken to heart in France. The leading French Neoclassical architect was Jacques-Germain Soufflot (1713–1780), whose Church of Sainte-Geneviève **(FIG. 29–31)**, known today as the **PANTHÉON**, is the most typical Neoclassical building in Paris. In it, Soufflot attempted to integrate three traditions: the Roman architecture he had seen on two trips to Italy; French and English Baroque Classicism; and the Palladian style

29-31 • Jacques-Germain Soufflot PANTHÉON (CHURCH OF SAINTE-GENEVIÈVE)
Paris. 1755–1792.

This building has an interesting history. Before it was completed, the Revolutionary government in control of Paris confiscated all religious properties to raise desperately needed public funds. Instead of selling Sainte-Geneviève, however, they voted in 1791 to make it the Temple of Fame for the burial of Heroes of Liberty. Under Napoleon I (r. 1799–1814), the building was resanctified as a Catholic church and was again used as such under King Louis-Philippe (r. 1830–1848) and Napoleon III (r. 1852–1870). Then it was permanently designated a nondenominational lay temple. In 1851, the building was used as a physics laboratory. Here the French physicist Jean-Bernard Foucault suspended his now-famous pendulum in the interior of the high crossing dome, and by measuring the path of the pendulum's swing proved his theory that the Earth rotated on its axis in a counterclockwise motion. In 1995, the ashes of Marie Curie, who had won the Nobel Prize in chemistry in 1911, were moved into this "memorial to the great men of France," making her the first woman to be enshrined there.

being revived at the time in England. The façade of the Panthéon, with its huge portico, is modeled on the proportions of ancient Roman temples. The dome, on the other hand, was inspired by seventeenth-century architecture, including Sir Christopher Wren's St. Paul's Cathedral in London (SEE FIG. 22–60), while the radical geometry of its central-plan Greek cross (FIG. 29–32)

29-32 • PANTHÉON (CHURCH OF SAINTE-GENEVIÈVE), CUTAWAY ILLUSTRATION

SEE MORE: Click the Google Earth link for the Panthéon (Church of Sainte-Geneviève)
www.myartslab.com

owes as much to Burlington's Neo-Palladian Chiswick House (SEE FIG. 29–16) as it does to Christian tradition. The Panthéon, however, is not simply the sum of its parts. Its rational, ordered plan is constructed with rectangles, squares, and circles, while its relatively plain surfaces communicate severity and powerful simplicity.

PAINTING AND SCULPTURE

While French painters such as Boucher, Fragonard, and their followers continued to work in the Rococo style in the later decades of the eighteenth century, a strong reaction against the Rococo had set in by the 1760s. A leading detractor of the Rococo was Denis Diderot (1713–1784), whose 32-volume compendium of knowledge and skill, the *Encyclopédie* (produced in collaboration with Jean le Rond d'Alembert, 1717–1783) served as an archive of Enlightenment thought in France. In 1759, Diderot began to write reviews of the official Salon for a periodic newsletter for wealthy subscribers, and he is generally considered to be the founder of modern art criticism. Diderot believed that it was art's proper function to "inspire virtue and purify manners," a function that the Rococo was not designed to fulfill.

CHARDIN.   Diderot greatly admired Jean-Siméon Chardin (1699–1779), an artist who as early as the 1730s began to create moralizing pictures in the tradition of seventeenth-century Dutch

genre painting by focusing on carefully structured but touching scenes of everyday middle-class life. **THE GOVERNESS (FIG. 29–33)**, for instance, shows a finely dressed boy with books under his arm, being addressed by his governess as she prepares to brush his tricorn (three-cornered) hat. Scattered on the floor are a racquet, a shuttlecock, and playing cards, the childish pleasures that the boy leaves behind as he prepares to go to his studies and, ultimately, to a life of responsible adulthood. The work suggests the benevolent exercise of authority and willing submission to it.

GREUZE.   Diderot reserved his highest praise for Jean-Baptiste Greuze (1725–1805), and his own plays of the late 1750s served as a source of inspiration for Greuze's painting. Diderot expanded the traditional range of theatrical works in Paris from mostly tragedy and comedy to include the *drame bourgeois*, the middle-class drama, and "middle tragedy," later called the "melodrama," both moralizing plays that communicated moral and civic lessons through simple, clear stories of ordinary life. Greuze's domestic genre paintings, such as **THE VILLAGE BRIDE (FIG. 29–34)**, were visual counterparts to Diderot's *drame bourgeois* and 'middle tragedy'. In this painting, Greuze presents the action on a shallow, stagelike space under a dramatic spotlight. An elderly father reaches out to his affectionate family as he hands the dowry for his daughter to his new son-in-law; a notary records the event. The young couple link arms but are not overly familiar with one another; the bride is held by her mother and sister. In contrast to Hogarth's marriage contract (SEE FIG. 29–22), Greuze's painting demonstrates that virtue and poverty can coexist. This kind of highly emotional, theatrical, and moralizing genre scene was widely praised in Greuze's time, offering a counterpoint to early Neoclassical history painting in France.

VIGÉE-LEBRUN.   While Greuze painted scenes of the poor and middle class, Marie-Louise-Élisabeth Vigée-Lebrun (1755–1842) became famous as Queen Marie Antoinette's favorite portrait painter. Vigée-Lebrun was also notable for her election into the French Royal Academy of Painting and Sculpture, which then made only four places available to women. In 1787, she painted **MARIE ANTOINETTE WITH HER**

29-33 • Jean-Siméon Chardin THE GOVERNESS
1739. Oil on canvas, 18⅛ × 14¾" (46 × 37.5 cm). National Gallery of Canada, Ottawa. Purchase, 1956

Chardin was one of the first French artists to treat the lives of women and children with sympathy and to portray the dignity of women's work in his images of young mothers, governesses, and kitchen maids. Shown at the Salon of 1739, *The Governess* was praised by contemporary critics, one of whom noted "the graciousness, sweetness, and restraint that the governess maintains in her discipline of the young man about his dirtiness, disorder, and neglect; his attention, shame, and remorse; all are expressed with great simplicity."

CHILDREN (FIG. 29–35). Drawing on the theme of the "good mother" seen earlier in Angelica Kauffmann's Neoclassical painting of Cornelia (SEE FIG. 29–26), Vigée-Lebrun portrays the queen as a kindly, stabilizing mother to try to counter public perceptions of her as selfish, extravagant, and immoral. The queen maintains her regal pose, as is appropriate, but her children are depicted more sympathetically: The princess leans affectionately against her mother's arm and the little dauphin, the heir to a throne he would never inherit, points to the empty cradle of a recently deceased sibling. The image alludes to the allegory of Abundance and is intended to assure peace and prosperity for France under the reign of her husband, Louis XVI, who came to the throne in 1774 but was executed, as was she, in 1792 during the Reign of Terror.

29-35 • Marie-Louise-Élisabeth Vigée-Lebrun
PORTRAIT OF MARIE ANTOINETTE WITH HER CHILDREN
1787. Oil on canvas, 9′1½″ × 7′5⅝″ (2.75 × 2.15 m). Musée National du Château de Versailles.

As the favorite painter to the queen, Vigée-Lebrun escaped from Paris with her daughter on the eve of the Revolution of 1789 and fled to Rome. After a very successful self-exile working in Italy, Austria, Russia, and England, the artist finally resettled in Paris in 1805 and again became popular with Parisian art patrons. Over her long career, she painted about 800 portraits in a vibrant style that changed very little over the decades.

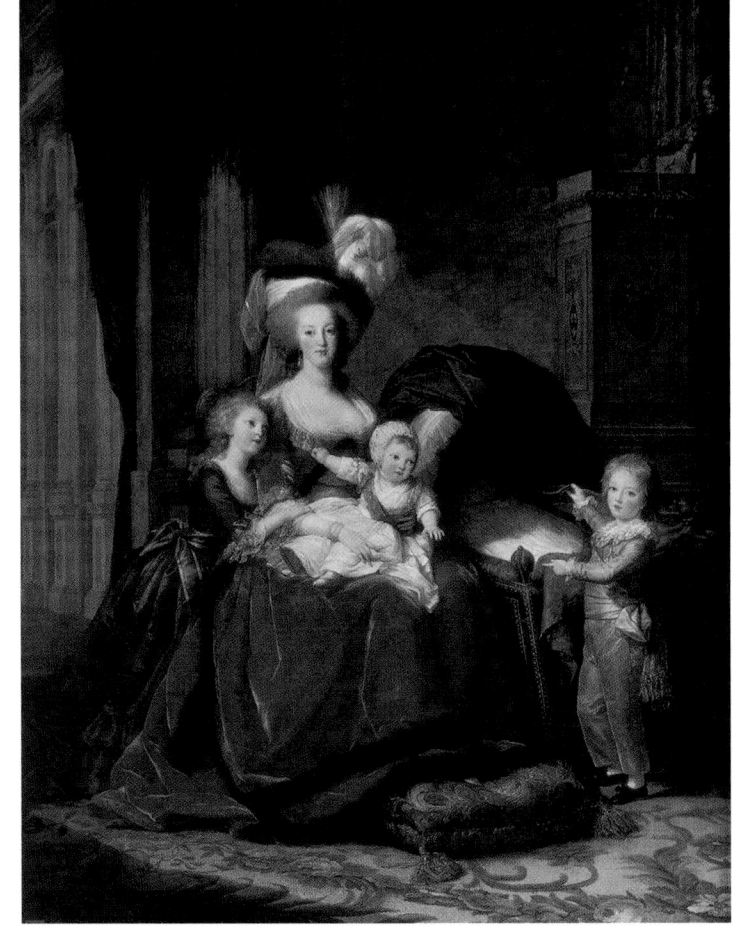

DAVID. The most important French Neoclassical painter of the era was Jacques-Louis David (1748–1825), who dominated French art for over 20 years during the French Revolution and the subsequent reign of Napoleon. In 1774, he won the Prix de Rome and spent six years there, studying antique sculpture and learning the principles of Neoclassicism. After his return to Paris, he produced a series of severely plain Neoclassical paintings extolling the antique virtues of stoicism, masculinity, and patriotism.

Perhaps the most significant of these works was the **OATH OF THE HORATII** (FIG. 29–36) of 1784–1785. A royal commission, the work reflects the taste and values of Louis XVI, who along with his minister of the arts, Count d'Angiviller, was sympathetic to the Enlightenment. Like Diderot, d'Angiviller and the king believed that art should improve public morals. One of d'Angiviller's first official acts was to ban indecent nudity from the Salon of 1775 and commission a series of didactic history paintings. David's

commission for the *Oath of the Horatii* in 1784 was part of that general program.

The subject of the painting was inspired by the drama *Horace,* written by the great French playwright Pierre Corneille (1606–1684), which was in turn based on ancient Roman historical texts; the patriotic oath-taking incident depicted by David here, however, is not taken directly from these sources and seems to have been the artist's own invention. The scene is set in the seventh century BCE, at a time when Rome and its rival, Alba, a neighboring city-state, agreed to settle a border dispute and avert a war by holding a battle to the death between the three sons of Horace (the Horatii), representing Rome, and the three Curatii, representing Alba. In David's painting, the Horatii stand with arms outstretched toward their father, who reaches to them with the swords on which they pledge to fight and die for Rome. The power running through the outstretched fingers of young men to their father almost makes him

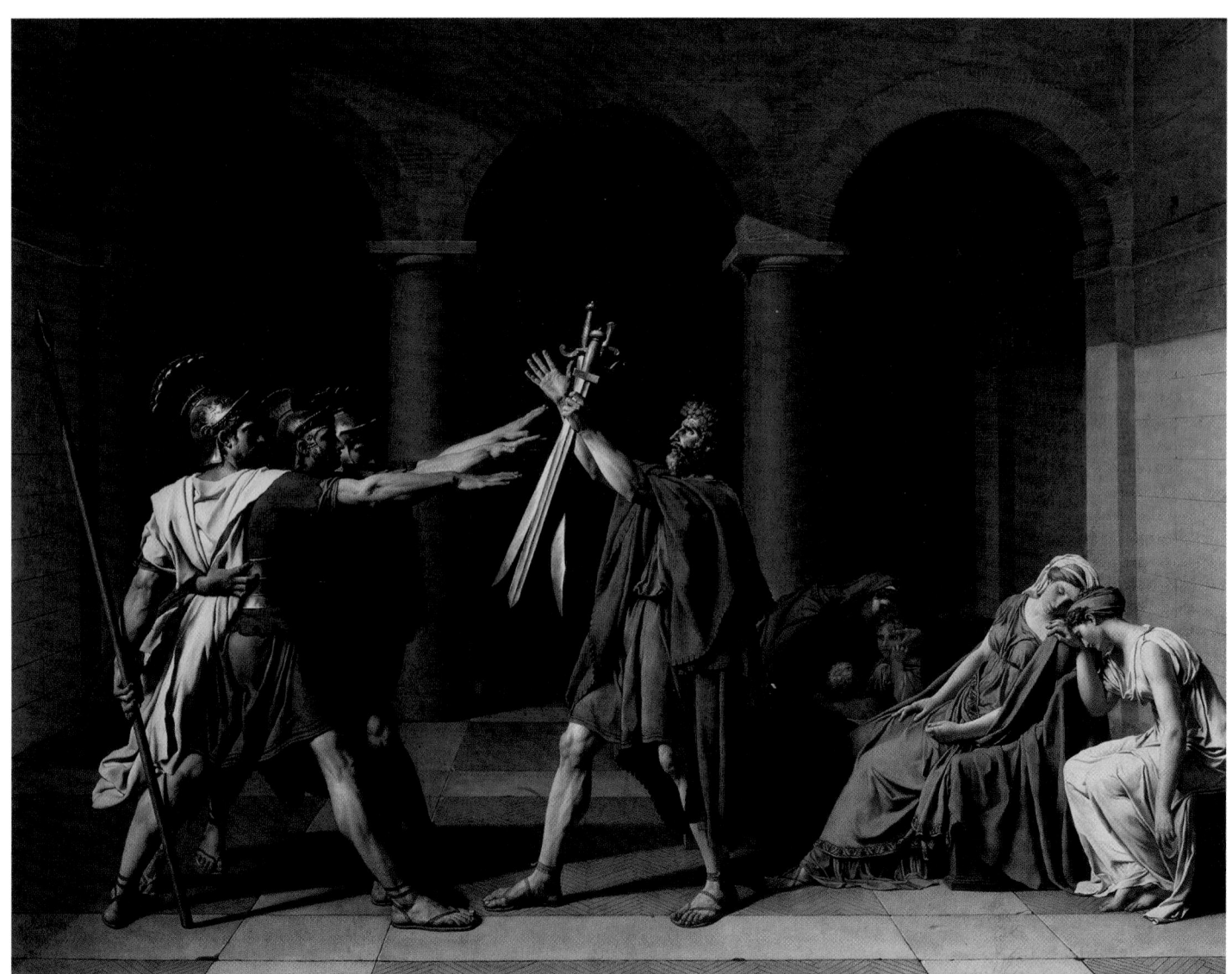

29–36 • Jacques-Louis David OATH OF THE HORATII
1784–1785. Oil on canvas, 10'8¼" × 14' (3.26 × 4.27 m). Musée du Louvre, Paris.

EXPLORE MORE: Gain insight from a primary source on Jacques-Louis David **www.myartslab.com**

step back. In contrast to the upright, muscular angularity of the men, the group of weeping women and frightened children are limp. They weep for the lives of both the Horatii and the Curatii. Sabina (in the center) is a sister of the Curatii, and also married to one of the Horatii; Camilla (at the far right) is sister to the Horatii and engaged to one of the Curatii. David's composition, which separates the men from the women and children spatially using framing background arches, dramatically contrasts the young men's stoic and willing self-sacrifice with the women's emotional collapse.

The emotional intensity of this history painting pushed French academy rules on decorum to the limit. Originally commissioned by the monarchy, it quickly and ironically became an emblem of the 1789 French Revolution. Its message of patriotism and sacrifice for the greater good effectively captured the mood of the leaders of the new French Republic established in 1792. As the revolutionaries abolished the monarchy and titles of nobility, took education out of the hands of the Church, and wrote a declaration of human rights, David joined the leftist Jacobin party and served very briefly as President of the National Convention in 1792 and as President of the Jacobin Club.

In 1793, David painted the death of the Jacobin leader, Jean-Paul Marat (FIG. 29–37). A radical journalist, Marat lived simply among the packing cases that he used as furniture, writing pamphlets urging the abolition of aristocratic privilege. Because he suffered from a painful skin ailment, he would often write while sitting in a medicinal bath. Charlotte Corday, a supporter of an opposition party, held Marat partly responsible for the 1792 riots in which hundreds of political prisoners judged sympathetic to the king were killed, and in retribution she stabbed Marat as he sat in his bath. David avoids the potential for sensationalism in the

29-37 • Jacques-Louis David
DEATH OF MARAT
1793. Oil on canvas, 5′5″ × 4′2½″ (1.65 × 1.28 m). Musées Royaux des Beaux-Arts de Belgique, Brussels.

In 1793, David was elected a deputy to the National Convention and was named propaganda minister and director of public festivals. Because he supported Robespierre and the Reign of Terror, he was twice imprisoned after its demise in 1794, albeit under lenient conditions that allowed him to continue painting.

subject by portraying the tragic aftermath: the dead Marat slumped in his bathtub, his right hand still holding a quill pen, while his left hand grasps the letter that Corday used to gain access to his home. The simple wooden block beside the bath, which Marat used as a desk, is inscribed with Marat's name and the painter's dedication, and becomes his tombstone. David's painting is a tightly composed, powerfully stark image. The background is blank and undifferentiated, adding to the quiet mood of the piece in the way that the background of the *Oath of the Horatii* added to its drama. The color of Marat's pale body is echoed by the bloodstained sheets on which he lies; he is framed by the dark background and green blanket draped over the bath. David has transformed an ugly, brutal scene into one of somber eloquence. Marat's pose, which echoes Michelangelo's Sistine *Pietà* (SEE FIG. 20–9), implies that, like Christ, Marat was a martyr for the people.

The French Revolution eventually degenerated into mob rule in 1793–1794 as various political parties ruthlessly executed thousands of their opponents in what became known as the Reign of Terror. David, as a Jacobin, served a two-week term as president, during which time he signed several arrest warrants. When the Jacobins lost power in 1794, he was twice imprisoned, but he later emerged as a supporter of Napoleon and reestablished his career at the height of Napoleon's ascendancy to power.

GIRODET-TRIOSON. David was a charismatic and influential teacher who trained most of the major French painters of the 1790s and early 1800s. His teaching is evident, for example, in the **PORTRAIT OF JEAN-BAPTISTE BELLEY (FIG. 29–38)** by Anne-Louis Girodet-Trioson (1767–1824). The painting combines the restrained color and composition of early David with a relaxed new elegance. In addition, this portrait has a significant political aspect. The Senegal-born Belley (1747?–1805) was a former slave who was sent to Paris as a representative to the French Convention by the colony of Saint-Domingue (now Haiti). The Haitian Revolution of 1791, in which African slaves overturned the French colonial power, resulted in the first republic to be ruled by freed African slaves. In 1794, Belley led the successful legislative campaign to abolish slavery in the colonies and to grant full citizenship to people of African descent. In the portrait, Belley leans casually on the pedestal of a bust of the abbot Guillaume Raynal (1711–1796), the French philosopher whose 1770 book condemned slavery and paved the way for such legislation, making the portrait a tribute to both Belley and Raynal. Napoleon reestablished slavery in the Caribbean islands in 1801, but the revolt continued until 1804, when Haiti finally achieved full independence.

29-38 • Anne-Louis Girodet-Trioson **PORTRAIT OF JEAN-BAPTISTE BELLEY**
1797. Oil on canvas, 5′2½″ × 3′8½″ (1.59 × 1.13 m).
Musée National du Château de Versailles.

LABILLE-GUIARD. Also reflecting the revolutionary spirit of the age, the painter Adélaïde Labille-Guiard (1749–1803) championed the rights of women artists. Elected to the French Royal Academy of Painting and Sculpture in the same year as Vigée-Lebrun, Labille-Guiard asserted her worthiness for this honor in a **SELF-PORTRAIT WITH TWO PUPILS** that she submitted to the Salon of 1785 **(FIG. 29–39)**. The painting was a response to sexist rumors that her work, and that of Vigée-Lebrun, had actually been painted by men. In a witty role reversal, the only male in this monumental painting of the artist at her easel is her father, shown in a bust behind her canvas, as her muse, a role usually played by women. While the self-portrait flatters the painter, it also portrays Labille-Guiard as a force to be reckoned with, a woman who engages the gaze of the viewer uncompromisingly, and whose students are serious and intent on their study. In the year following the French Revolution, Labille-Guiard successfully petitioned the Royal Academy of Painting and Sculpture to end the restriction that limited its membership to four women. The reform was later reversed by the revolutionary government as it became more authoritarian.

HOUDON. The French Neoclassical sculptor Jean-Antoine Houdon (1741–1828), who studied in Italy between 1764 and 1768 after winning the Prix de Rome, imbued the Classical style with a new realism. His commitment to Neoclassicism began during his stay in Rome through his contact with the leading artists and theorists of the movement. He carved busts and full-length statues of a number of important figures of his era, including Diderot, Voltaire, Jean-Jacques Rousseau, Catherine the Great, Thomas Jefferson, Benjamin Franklin, Lafayette (a Revolutionary hero), and Napoleon. On the basis of his bust of Benjamin Franklin, Houdon was commissioned by the Virginia State Legislature to make a portrait of its native son **GEORGE WASHINGTON** to be installed in the Neoclassical Virginia state capitol building designed by Jefferson. In 1785, Houdon traveled to the United States to

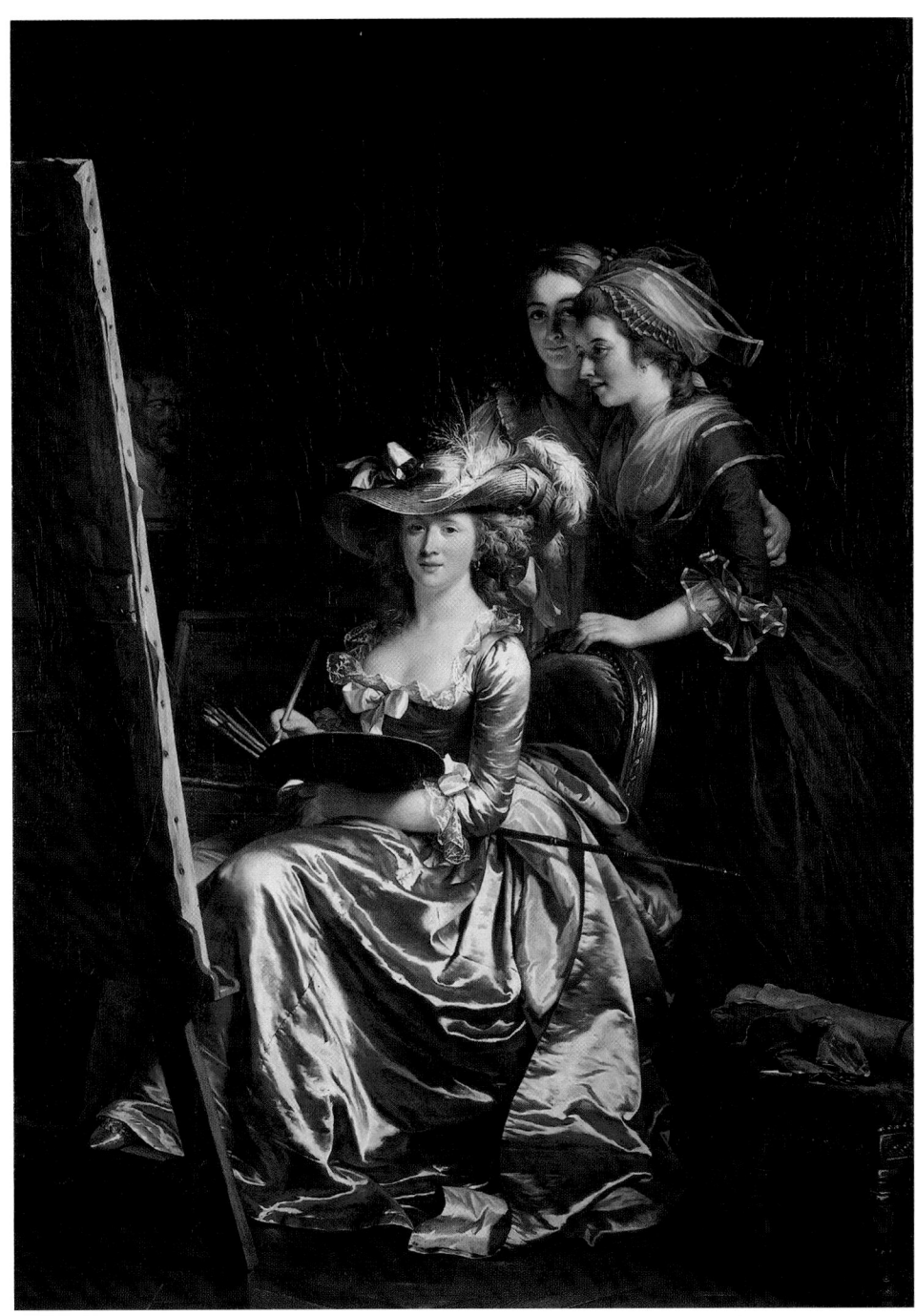

29–39 • Adélaïde Labille-Guiard **SELF-PORTRAIT WITH TWO PUPILS**
1785. Oil on canvas, 6′11″ × 4′11½″ (2.11 × 1.51 m). Metropolitan Museum of Art, New York.
Gift of Julia A. Berwind, 1953 (53.225.5)

The plow blade behind Washington alludes to Cincinnatus, a Roman soldier of the fifth century BCE who was appointed dictator and dispatched to defeat the Aequi, who had besieged a Roman army. After the victory, Cincinnatus resigned the dictatorship and returned to his farm. Washington's contemporaries compared him with Cincinnatus because, after leading the Americans to victory over the British, he resigned his commission and went back to farming rather than seeking political power. Just below Washington's waistcoat hangs the badge of the Society of the Cincinnati, founded in 1783 by the officers of the disbanding Continental Army who were returning to their peacetime occupations. Washington lived in retirement at his Mount Vernon, Virginia, plantation for five years before his 1789 election as the first president of the United States.

ART IN SPAIN AND SPANISH AMERICA

In the first half of the eighteenth century, the Spanish art world was marginalized by Philip V, who awarded most royal commissions to foreign artists. Mengs's art for Charles III brought Neoclassicism to Spain, but Neoclassicism was not embraced by Spanish artists in the way that the Baroque had been in the previous century. In the late eighteenth century, however, the Spanish court appointed as court painter one of the greatest artists of the period, Francisco Goya y Lucientes (1746–1828), whose work defies easy categorization.

The Spanish commissioned art in their American colonies as well. The art and architecture of these distant lands tended to reflect both the continuing influence of the Spanish Baroque and the artistic traditions of native peoples. Both the symbolism and the artistic vocabulary of the two cultures were joined in the new art of Mexico and the American Southwest.

PORTRAITURE AND PROTEST IN SPAIN: GOYA

Goya was introduced to the Spanish royal workshop in 1774, when he produced tapestry cartoons under the direction of Mengs. He painted for Charles III and served as court painter to Charles IV, but he also belonged to an intellectual circle that embraced the ideals of the French Revolution, and his work began to criticize subtly the court in which he served.

King Charles IV, threatened by the possibility of similar social upheaval in Spain, reinstituted the Inquisition soon after the French Revolution, halted reform, and even prohibited the entry of French books into Spain. Goya responded to this new situation by creating a series of prints aimed at the ordinary people, with whom he identified. *Los Caprichos* (*The Caprices*) is a folio of 80 etchings produced between 1796 and 1798. The overall theme of the series is that reason ignored is a sleeping monster. In the print entitled **THE SLEEP OF REASON PRODUCES MONSTERS (FIG. 29–41)**, the slumbering personification of Reason is haunted by a menagerie of demonic-looking owls, bats, and a cat that are let loose when Reason sleeps. Other *Caprichos* enumerate the follies

make a cast of Washington's features and a bust in plaster, returning to Paris to execute the life-size marble figure (FIG. 29–40). The sculpture represents Washington in the Classical manner but with contemporary clothes, much as Benjamin West had represented General Wolfe (SEE FIG. 29–27). Houdon draws on the Classical ideals of dignity, honor, and civic responsibility. Washington wears the uniform of a general, the rank he held in the Revolutionary War, but he also rests his left hand on a Roman *fasces*, a bundle of 13 rods (representing the 13 colonies) tied together with an axe face, that served as a Roman symbol of authority. Attached to the *fasces* are both a sword of war and a plowshare of peace. Significantly, Houdon's Washington does not touch the sword.

Houdon's studio produced a steady supply of replicas of his sculptures as part of a cult of great men promoted by Enlightenment thinkers as models of virtue and patriotism.

29-41 • Francisco Goya THE SLEEP OF REASON PRODUCES MONSTERS
No. 43 from *Los Caprichos* (*The Caprices*). 1796–1798; published 1799. Etching and aquatint, 8½ × 6″ (21.6 × 15.2 cm). Courtesy of the Hispanic Society of America, New York.

After printing about 300 sets of this series, Goya offered them for sale in 1799. He withdrew them two days later without explanation. Historians believe that he was probably warned by the Church that if he did not do so he might have to appear before the Inquisition because of the unflattering portrayal of the Church in some of the etchings. In 1803, Goya donated the plates to the Royal Printing Office.

of Spanish society that Goya and his circle considered equally monstrous. His implicit goal with this series was to incite action: He tried to market his etchings as Hogarth had done in England, but his work aroused controversy and was brought to the attention of his royal patrons. To deflect additional controversy, Goya presented the metal plates of the series to the king, suggesting that the images were not intentionally critical of the monarchy. He was torn between his position as a court painter who owed allegiance to the king and his passionate desire for a more open Spain.

His large portrait of the **FAMILY OF CHARLES IV (FIG. 29–42)** reveals some of Goya's ambivalence. He clearly wanted his patron to connect the portrait to an earlier Spanish royal portrait, *Las Meninas* by Velázquez (SEE FIG. 22–23), thereby raising his own status as well as that of the king. Like Velázquez, Goya includes

29-42 • Francisco Goya FAMILY OF CHARLES IV
1800. Oil on canvas, 9′12″ × 11′ (2.79 × 3.36 m). Museo del Prado, Madrid.

29-43 • Francisco Goya THIRD OF MAY, 1808
1814–1815. Oil on canvas, 8'9" × 13'4" (2.67 × 4.06 m). Museo del Prado, Madrid.

himself in the painting, to the left behind the easel. The king and queen appear at the center of this large family portrait, surrounded by their immediate family. The figures are formal and stiff. Much has been written about how Goya seems to show his patrons as faintly ridiculous here: Some of the subjects seem bored; the some-what dazed king, chest full of medals, stands before a relative who looks distractedly out of the painting (perhaps the face was added at the last minute); the double-chinned queen gazes obliquely out of the canvas (at that time she was having an open affair with the prime minister); their eldest daughter, to the left, stares into space; and another, older relative behind seems almost surprised to be there. One French art critic even described the painting as resembling "The corner baker and his family after they have won the lottery." Yet the royal family was apparently satisfied with Goya's depiction. At a time when the authority of the Spanish aristocracy was crumbling, this complex representation of conflicted emotions, aspirations, and responsibilities may have struck a chord with them.

In 1808, Napoleon conquered Spain and placed his brother, Joseph Bonaparte (1768–1844), on the Spanish throne. At first many Spanish citizens, Goya included, welcomed the French, who brought political reform, including a new, more liberal constitution. But on May 2, 1808, a rumor spread through Madrid that the French planned to kill the royal family. The people rose up against the French and a day of bloody street fighting ensued, followed by mass arrests. Hundreds were herded into a convent and then executed by a French firing squad before dawn on May 3. Goya's impassioned memorial to that slaughter **(FIG. 29–43)** portrays the victims as defenseless and frightened. The French are shown as a row of faceless executioners, the pose of the victim in white seems almost Christlike. This painting is not a cool, didactic representation of civic sacrifice like David's *Oath of the Horatii* (SEE FIG. 29–36), it is an image of blind terror and desperate fear. There is no moral here, only hopeless rage. Everything about this work is Romantic: the sensational current event, the loose brushwork, the poses based on reality, the off-balance composition, and the dramatic lighting. When asked why he painted such a brutal scene, Goya responded: "To warn men never to do it again." Thus, his painting moves from the relative restraint of the court to impassioned Romanticism.

Soon after, the Spanish monarchy was restored. Ferdinand VII (r. 1808; 1814–1833) once again reinstated the Inquisition and abolished the new constitution. In 1815, Goya was called before the Inquisition and charged with obscenity for an earlier painting of a female nude. He was acquitted and retired to his home outside Madrid, where he vented his anger at the world in a series of nightmarish "black paintings" rendered directly on the walls, and then spent the last four years of his life in France.

THE ART OF THE AMERICAS UNDER SPAIN

In the wake of the Spanish conquest of Central and South America, indigenous religions and their practice were suppressed. Temples were torn down and replaced with Roman Catholic churches, and Franciscan, Dominican, and Augustinian friars worked to convert the indigenous populations. Some missionaries were so appalled by the conquerors' brutal treatment of the native peoples that they petitioned the Spanish king to help improve conditions.

In the course of the Mesoamericans' forced conversion to Roman Catholicism, Christian symbolism became inextricably mixed with the symbolism of their own long-held religious beliefs. An example of this admixture can be seen in early colonial **atrial crosses**, carved by indigenous sculptors. Missionaries placed these crosses in church atriums, where converts gathered for education in Christianity. The sixteenth-century **ATRIAL CROSS** now in the Basilica of Guadalupe near Mexico City (**FIG. 29–44**) is richly carved in low relief, reflecting native sculptural traditions. The images show a complex interweaving of Christian and native religions. The Christian symbols were probably taken from the illustrated books and Bibles of the missionaries, and represent the Arms of Christ, or the "weapons" that Christ used to defeat the devil: the holy face, placed where his head would appear on a crucifix; the crown of thorns, draped around the cross bar; and the holy shroud, wrapped around the cross's arms. (The image of the holy face is believed to have been miraculously impressed on a cloth used by Veronica to wipe the face of the suffering Christ before his death.) Winged angel heads and pomegranates surround the inscription at the top as symbols of regeneration. While the cross represents Christ's redemption of humanity in Christianity, it is also symbolic of the tree of life in Mesoamerican religions. The blood that sprays out where the nails pierce the hands of Christ are a reference to his sacrifice; the representation of sacrificial blood may also refer to native religions.

Images of the Virgin Mary also took on a Mesoamerican inflection after she was believed to have appeared in Mexico. In one such case, in 1531, a Mexican named Juan Diego claimed that the Virgin Mary visited him and told him to build a church on a hill

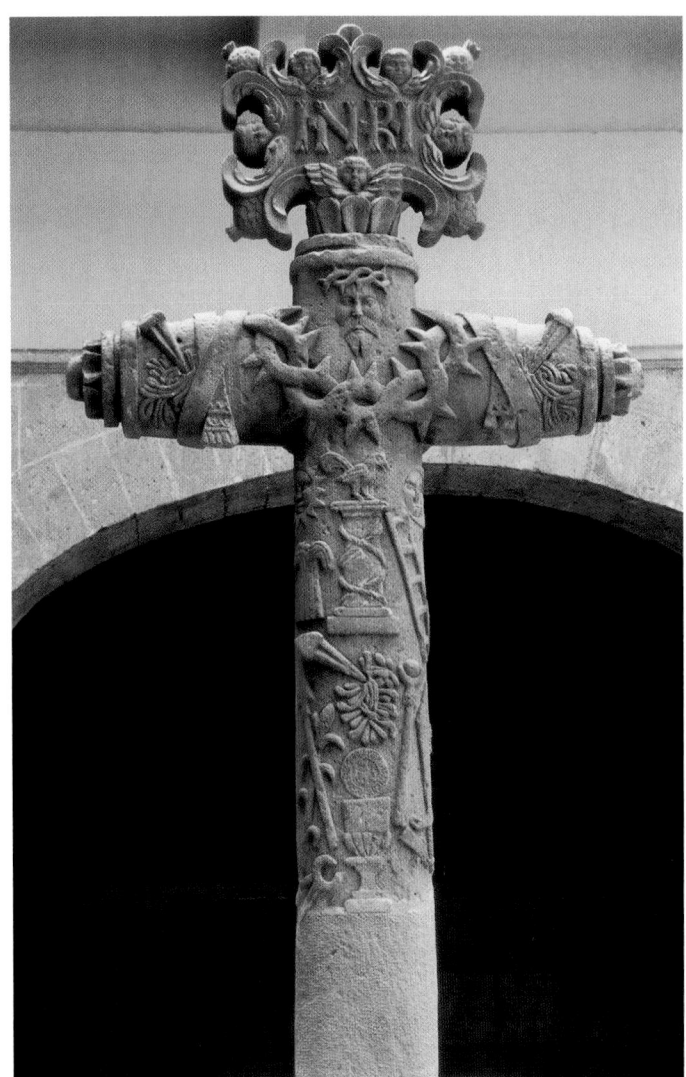

29-44 • ATRIAL CROSS
Before 1556. Stone, height 11′3″ (3.45 m). Chapel of the Indians, Basilica of Guadalupe, Mexico City.

where an Aztec goddess had once been worshiped. She also apparently caused flowers to bloom so that Juan Diego could show them to the archbishop as proof of his vision. When Juan Diego opened his bundle of flowers, the cloak he had used to wrap them is said to have borne the image of a Mexican Mary. A European version of this image, known as the Virgin of the Immaculate Conception, also became popular in Spain. The site of the vision was renamed Guadalupe after Our Lady of Guadalupe in Spain, and it became a venerated pilgrimage center. In 1754, the pope declared the Virgin of Guadalupe, as depicted here in a 1779 work by Sebastian Salcedo, the patron saint of the Americas (**FIG. 29–45**).

Spanish colonial builders tried to replicate the architecture of their native country in the Americas. One of the finest examples of Spanish-influenced architecture is the **MISSION SAN XAVIER DEL BAC**, in the American Southwest near Tucson, Arizona (**FIG. 29–46**). In 1700, the Jesuit priest Eusebio Kino (1644–1711) began laying the foundations for San Xavier del Bac using stone quarried

29–45 • Sebastian Salcedo VIRGIN OF GUADALUPE
1779. Oil on panel and copper, 25 × 19″ (63.5 × 48.3 cm). Denver Art Museum.

At the bottom right is the female personification of New Spain (Mexico) and at the left is Pope Benedict XIV (pontificate 1740–1758), who in 1754 declared the Virgin of Guadalupe to be the patroness of the Americas. Between the figures, the sanctuary of Guadalupe in Mexico can be seen in the distance. The four small scenes circling the Virgin represent the story of Juan Diego, and at the top three scenes depict Mary's miracles. The six figures above the Virgin represent Hebrew Bible prophets and patriarchs and New Testament apostles and saints.

29-48 • Antoine-Jean Gros NAPOLEON IN THE PLAGUE HOUSE AT JAFFA
1804. Oil on canvas, 17'5" × 23'7" (5.32 × 7.2 m). Musée du Louvre, Paris.

converted mosque in the town of Jaffa (then part of the Ottoman Empire, and now in Israel). The format of Gros's painting—a shallow stage and a series of arcades behind the main protagonists—seems to have been inspired by David's *Oath of the Horatii*. But Gros's painting is quite different from David's: His color is more vibrant and his brushwork more spontaneous. The overall effect is Romantic, not simply because of the dramatic lighting and the wealth of details, both exotic and horrific, but also because the main action is meant to incite veneration of Napoleon the man more than republican virtue. At the center of the painting, surrounded by a small group of soldiers and a doctor, Napoleon reaches toward the sores of one of the victims in a pose that was meant to evoke Christ healing the sick with his touch. The huddled figures to the left remind us of the mouth of hell in Michelangelo's *Last Judgment* (SEE FIG. 20–34). At that time there was a rumor that shortly after Napoleon's visit to Jaffa, he ordered the remaining sick to be poisoned. Gros may have been aware of this rumor when he painted Napoleon as small and tentative compared to the Arab doctors and even the sick.

GÉRICAULT.   Théodore Géricault (1791–1824) was a major early Romantic painter in Paris, although his career was cut short by his untimely death at age 32. After a brief stay in Rome in 1816–1817, where he discovered the art of Michelangelo, Géricault returned to Paris determined to paint a great modern history painting. He chose for his subject the scandalous and sensational shipwreck of the *Medusa* (see "*The Raft of the 'Medusa,*'" pages 946–947). In 1816, the *Medusa*, a ship carrying around 400 French colonists bound for Senegal, ran aground close to its destination. Its captain, an incompetent aristocrat commissioned by the newly restored monarchy of Louis XVIII, reserved all six lifeboats for himself, his officers, and several government representatives. The remaining 152 people were set adrift on a makeshift raft. When those on the raft were rescued 13 days later, only 15 had survived, some by living on human flesh. Since the captain had been a political appointee, the press used the horrific story to indict the monarchy for this and other atrocities in French-ruled Senegal. The moment in the story that Géricault chose to depict is one fraught with emotion, as the survivors on the raft experience both the fear that

The Raft of the "Medusa"

Théodore Géricault's monumental *The Raft of the "Medusa"* (FIG. A) fits the definition of a history painting in that it is a large (16 by 23 feet), multi-figured composition that represents an event in history. It may not qualify, however, on the basis of its function— to expose incompetence and a willful disregard for human life rather than to ennoble, educate, or remind viewers of their civic responsibility. The hero of this painting is also an unusual choice for a history painting; he is not an emperor or a king, or even an intellectual, but Jean Charles, a black man from French Senegal who showed endurance and emotional fortitude in the face of extreme peril.

The painting speaks powerfully through a composition that is arranged in a pyramid of bodies. The diagonal that begins in the lower left extends upwards to the waving figure of Jean Charles; the diagonal beginning with the dead man in the lower right extends through the mast and billowing sail, directs our attention to a huge wave. The painting captures the moment between hope of rescue and despair that the distant ship has not seen the survivors. The figures are emotionally suspended between hope of salvation and fear of imminent death. Significantly, the "hopeful" diagonal in Géricault's painting terminates in the vigorous figure of Jean Charles. By placing him at the top of the pyramid of survivors and giving him the power to save his comrades by signaling to the rescue ship, Géricault suggests metaphorically that freedom is often dependent on the most oppressed members of society.

Géricault prepared his painting carefully, using each of the prescribed steps for history painting in the French academic system. The work was the culmination of extensive study and experimentation. An early pen drawing (*The Sighting of the "Argus,"* FIG. B) depicts the survivors' hopeful response to the appearance of the rescue ship on the horizon at the extreme left. Their excitement is in contrast to the mournful scene of a man grieving over a dead youth on the right side of the raft. The drawing is quick, spontaneous and bursting with energy, like the *esquisse*. A later pen-and-wash drawing (FIG. C) reverses the composition, creates greater unity among the figures, and establishes the modeling of their bodies through light and shade. This is primarily a study of light and shade. Other

A. Théodore Géricault THE RAFT OF THE "MEDUSA"
1818–1819. Oil on canvas, 16′1″ × 23′6″ (4.9 × 7.16 m). Musée du Louvre, Paris.

studies would have focused on further analyses of the composition, arrangement of figures, and overall color scheme. The drawings look ahead to the final composition of the *The Raft of the "Medusa,"* but both still lack the figure of Jean Charles at the apex of the painting and the dead and dying figures at the extreme left and lower right, which fill out the composition's base.

Géricault also made separate studies of many of the figures, as well as of actual corpses, severed heads, and dissected limbs (FIG. D) supplied to him by friends who worked at a nearby hospital. For several months, according to Géricault's biographer, "his studio was a kind of morgue. He kept cadavers there until they were half-decomposed, and insisted on working in this charnel-house atmosphere…" However, he did not use cadavers for any specific figures in *The Raft of the "Medusa."* Rather, he traced the outline of his final composition onto its large canvas, and then painted each body directly from a living model, gradually building up his composition figure by figure. He drew from corpses and body parts in his studio to make sure that he understood the nature of death and its impact on the human form.

Indeed, Géricault did not describe the actual physical condition of the survivors on the raft: exhausted, emaciated, sunburned, and close to death. Instead, following the dictates of the Grand Manner, he gave his men athletic bodies and vigorous poses, evoking the work of Michelangelo and Rubens (Chapters 20 and 22). He did this to generalize and ennoble his subject, elevating it above the particulars of a specific shipwreck in the hope that it would speak to more fundamental human conflicts: humanity against nature, hope against despair, and life against death.

B. Théodore Géricault **THE SIGHTING OF THE "ARGUS"** (top)
1818. Pen and ink on paper, 13¾ × 16⅛″ (34.9 × 41 cm). Musée des Beaux-Arts, Lille.

C. Théodore Géricault **THE SIGHTING OF THE "ARGUS"** (middle)
1818. Pen and ink, sepia wash on paper, 8⅛ × 11¼″ (20.6 × 28.6 cm). Musée des Beaux-Arts, Rouen.

D. Théodore Géricault **STUDY OF HANDS AND FEET** (bottom)
1818–1819. Oil on canvas, 20½ × 25⅜″ (52 × 64 cm). Musée Fabre, Montpellier.

the distant ship might pass them by and the hope that they will be rescued.

Géricault exhibited *The Raft of the "Medusa"* at the 1819 Salon, where it caused a great deal of controversy. Most contemporary French critics and royalists interpreted the painting as a political jibe at the king, on whose good grace many academicians depended, while independent liberals praised Géricault's attempt to expose corruption. This debate raises the larger question of the point at which a painting crosses the line between art and political advocacy. If David's and Gros's paintings of Napoleon still fall under the definition of contemporary history painting for supporting the state, does Géricault's painting fall outside it because it criticizes the state or because the intention of the painting was to shock and horrify rather than to edify and ennoble? Admittedly, Géricault's painting is sensationalist and topical, but it also conforms to academy rules in every other way (see "*The Raft of the 'Medusa,'*"

pages 946–947). The crown refused to buy the canvas, so Géricault exhibited it commercially on a two-year tour of Ireland and England; the London exhibition alone attracted more than 50,000 paying visitors.

DELACROIX. The French novelist Stendhal characterized the Romantic spirit when he wrote, "Romanticism in all the arts is what represents the men of today and not the men of those remote, heroic times which probably never existed anyway." Eugène Delacroix (1798–1863), the most important Romantic painter in Paris after Géricault's early death, depicted contemporary heroes and victims engaged in the violent struggles of the times. In 1830, he created his masterpiece, **LIBERTY LEADING THE PEOPLE: JULY 28, 1830** (FIG. 29–49), a painting that encapsulated the history of France after the fall of Napoleon. When Napoleon was defeated in 1815, the victorious neighboring nations reimposed a monarchy

29–49 • Eugène Delacroix **LIBERTY LEADING THE PEOPLE: JULY 28, 1830**
1830. Oil on canvas, 8′6½″ × 10′8″ (260 × 325 cm). Musée du Louvre, Paris.

on France under Louis XVIII, brother of the last pre-revolutionary monarch. The king's power was limited by a constitution and a parliament, but the government became more conservative as years passed, undoing many revolutionary reforms. Louis's successor, Charles X, reinstated press censorship, returned education to the control of the Catholic Church, and limited voting rights. These actions triggered a large-scale uprising in the streets of Paris. Over the course of three days in July 1830, the Bourbon monarchical line was overthrown and Charles X was replaced by a more moderate king from the Orleanist line, who promised to abide by a new constitution. This period in French history is known as the "July Monarchy."

Delacroix memorialized the July 1830 revolution just a few months after it took place. His large modern history painting reports significant events, but it also departs from facts in ways appropriate to the intended message. His revolutionaries are a motley crew of students, craftworkers, day laborers, and even children and top-hatted intellectuals. They stumble forward through the smoke of battle, crossing a barricade of refuse and dead bodies. The towers of Notre-Dame are visible through the smoke and haze of the background. This much of the work is plausibly accurate. Their leader, however, is an energetic, allegorical figure of Liberty, personified by a gigantic, muscular, half-naked woman charging across the barricade with the revolutionary flag in one hand and a bayoneted rifle in the other. Delacroix has literally placed a Classical allegorical figure in the thick of battle, replete with a contemporary weapon and Phrygian cap (the ancient symbol for a freed slave and the cap used by the insurgents). He presents the event as an emotionally charged moment, full of passion, turmoil and danger. He chooses to show the moment just before the ultimate sacrifice, as the revolutionaries charge the barricades to near-certain death, making this a dramatic example of Romanticism.

29-50 • François Rude DEPARTURE OF THE VOLUNTEERS OF 1792 (THE MARSEILLAISE)
1833–1836. Limestone, height approx. 42′ (12.8 m). Arc de Triomphe, Place de l'Étoile, Paris.

RUDE. Artists working for the July Monarchy increasingly used the more dramatic subjects and styles of Romanticism to represent the 1830 revolution, just as Neoclassical principles had been used to represent the previous revolution. Early in the July Monarchy, the minister of the interior decided, as an act of national reconciliation, to complete the triumphal arch on the Champs-Élysées in Paris begun by Napoleon in 1806. François Rude (1784–1855) received the commission for a sculpture to decorate the main arcade with a scene that commemorated the volunteer army that had halted a Prussian invasion in 1792–1793. Beneath the urgent exhortations of the winged figure of Liberty, the volunteers surge forward, some nude, some in Classical armor (FIG. 29–50). Despite these Classical details, the overall impact of this sculpture is Romantic. The crowded, excited group stirred patriotism in Paris, and the

29-51 • Jean-Auguste-Dominique Ingres **LARGE ODALISQUE**
1814. Oil on canvas, approx. 35 × 64″ (88.9 × 162.5 m). Musée du Louvre, Paris.

During Napoleon's campaigns against the British in North Africa, the French discovered the exotic Near East.
Upper-middle-class European men were particularly attracted to the institution of the harem, partly as a reaction
against the egalitarian demands of women of their own class that had been unleashed by the French Revolution.

sculpture quickly became known simply as **THE MARSEILLAISE**, the name of the French national anthem written in 1792, the same year as the action depicted.

INGRES. Jean-Auguste-Dominique Ingres (1780–1867) served as director of the French Academy in Rome between 1835 and 1841. As a teacher and theorist, Ingres became one of the most influential artists of his time. His paintings offer another variant on the Romantic and Neoclassical, combining the precise drawing, formal idealization, Classical composition, and graceful lyricism of Raphael (SEE FIG. 20–6) with an interest in creating sensual and erotically charged images.

Although Ingres fervently desired to be accepted as a history painter, it was his paintings of female nudes and his portraits of women that made him famous. He painted numerous versions of the **odalisque**, an exoticized version of a female slave or concubine in a sultan's harem. In his **LARGE ODALISQUE (FIG. 29–51)**, the cool gaze of the odalisque is leveled at her master, while she twists her naked body in a sinuous, snakelike reclining pose, revealing a calculated eroticism. The cool blues of the divan and the curtain at the right heighten the effect of her cool, white skin and blue eyes; she is Ingres's and his patrons' fantasy of a "white" slave. The exotic details of her headdress, fan, and the

jeweled object in the foreground add to her languid sensuality. Ingres's commitment to academic line and formal structure was grounded in his Neoclassical training, but his fluid, attenuated female nudes are much more in the Romantic tradition.

Although Ingres complained that making portraits was a "considerable waste of time," his skill in rendering a physical likeness in a scintillating way and in mimicking the material qualities of clothing, hairstyles, and jewelry in paint was unparalleled. He painted many life-size and highly polished portraits, but he also produced—usually in just a day—exquisite, small portrait drawings that are extraordinarily fresh and lively. The charming **PORTRAIT OF MADAME DÉSIRÉ RAOUL-ROCHETTE (FIG. 29–52)** is a flattering yet credible interpretation of the relaxed and elegant sitter. With her gloved right hand, Madame Raoul-Rochette has removed her left-hand glove, drawing attention to her social status (traditionally, fine kid gloves were worn by members of the European upper class, who did not work with their hands) and her marital status (a wedding band is on her left hand). Her shiny taffeta dress, with its fashionably high waist and puffed sleeves, is rendered with deft yet light strokes that suggest rather than describe the fabric. Greater emphasis is given to her refined face and elaborate coiffure, which Ingres has drawn precisely and modeled with subtle handling of light and shade.

29-52 • Jean-Auguste-Dominique Ingres **PORTRAIT OF MADAME DÉSIRÉ RAOUL-ROCHETTE**

1830. Graphite on paper, 12⅝ × 9½″ (32.2 × 24.1 cm). Cleveland Museum of Art, Ohio.
Purchase from the J. H. Wade Fund (1927.437)

Madame Raoul-Rochette (1790–1878), née Antoinette-Claude Houdon, was the youngest daughter of the famous Neoclassical sculptor Jean-Antoine Houdon (SEE FIG. 29–40). In 1810, at age 20, she married Désiré Raoul-Rochette, a noted archaeologist, who later became the secretary of the Académie des Beaux-Arts (Academy of Fine Arts, founded in 1816 to replace the French Royal Academy of Painting and Sculpture) and a close friend of Ingres. Ingres's drawing of Madame Raoul-Rochette is inscribed to her husband, whose portrait Ingres also drew around the same time.

EXPLORE MORE: Gain insight from a primary source about Jean-Auguste-Dominique Ingres **www.myartslab.com**

DAUMIER. Honoré Daumier (1808–1879) came to Paris from Marseille in 1816. He studied drawing at the Académie Suisse, but he learned the technique of **lithography** (see page 952) as assistant to the lithographer Bélaird. He published his first lithograph in 1829, at age 21, in the weekly satirical magazine *La Silhouette*. In the wake of the 1830 revolution in Paris, Daumier began supplying pictures to *La Caricature*, an anti-monarchist, pro-republican magazine, and the equally partisan *Le Charivari*, the first daily newspaper illustrated with lithographs. In 1834, Daumier made a lithographic print of the atrocities on **RUE TRANSNONAIN** (**FIG. 29–53**). A government guard was shot and killed on this street during a demonstration by workers, and in response the guards

Lithography, invented in the mid 1790s, is based on the natural antagonism between oil and water. The artist draws on a flat surface—traditionally, fine-grained stone (*lithos* is Greek for stone)—with a greasy, crayonlike instrument. The stone's surface is first wiped with water and then with an oil-based ink. The ink adheres to the greasy areas but not to the damp ones. After a series of such steps, a sheet of paper is laid face down on the inked stone, pressed together with a scraper, and then rolled through a flatbed press. This transfers ink from stone to paper, thus making lithography (like relief and intaglio) a direct method of creating a printed image. Unlike earlier processes, however, grease-based lithography enables the artist to capture the subtleties of drawing with crayon and a liquid mixture called *tusche*. Francisco Goya, Théodore Géricault, Eugène Delacroix, Honoré Daumier, and Henri de Toulouse-Lautrec used the medium to great effect.

Daumier is probably the greatest exponent of lithography in the nineteenth century. The technique was widely used in France for fine-art prints and to illustrate popular magazines and even newspapers. By the 1830s, the print trade in France had exploded. Artists could use lithography to produce their own prints without the cumbersome, expensive, and time-consuming intermediary of the engraver. Daumier's lithograph of *The Print Lovers* shows three men who have fixed their attention on the folio of prints in front of them, despite being surrounded by works of art packed tightly on the wall behind them. By the end of the nineteenth century, inexpensive prints were in every house and owned by people at every level of society.

Honoré Daumier THE PRINT LOVERS
Watercolor, black pencil, black ink, gray wash, 10⅛ × 12⅛″ (25.8 × 30.7 cm). Musée du Louvre, Paris.

scraper   paper   inked   moving
                         stone   base

Diagram of the lithographic process

SEE MORE: View a video about the process of lithography **www.myartslab.com**

killed everyone in the building where they believed the marksman was hiding. The moment shown by Daumier is the bloody aftermath of the event, a family disturbed from their sleep and then murdered. The wife lies in the shadows to the left, her husband in the center of the room, and an elderly man to the right. It takes a few minutes for the viewer to realize that under the central figure's back there are also the bloody head and arms of a murdered child. Daumier was known for his biting caricatures and social commentary in print form, but this image is one of his most powerful.

29-53 • Honoré Daumier RUE TRANSNONAIN, LE 15 AVRIL 1834
Lithograph, 11 × 17⅜″ (28 × 44 cm). Bibliothèque Nationale, Paris.

ROMANTIC LANDSCAPE PAINTING

The Romantics saw nature as ever-changing, unpredictable, and uncontrollable, and they interpreted its many aspects as analogous to equally unpredictable and changeable human moods and emotions. They found nature awesome, fascinating, powerful, domestic, and delightful. The landscape became perhaps the most important visual vehicle for Romantic thought.

CONSTABLE.   John Constable (1776–1837), the son of a successful miller, claimed that the quiet domestic landscape of his youth in southern England had made him a painter before he ever picked up a paintbrush. Although he was trained at the Royal Academy, he was equally influenced by the British topographic watercolor tradition of the late eighteenth century and by seventeenth-century Dutch landscape painting (SEE FIG. 22–46). After moving to London in 1816, he dedicated himself to painting monumental views of the agricultural landscape (known as "six-footers"), which he considered as important as history painting. Constable's commitment to contemporary English subjects was so strong that he opposed the establishment of the English National Gallery of Art in

1832 on the grounds that it might distract painters by enticing them to paint foreign or ancient themes in unnatural styles.

THE HAY WAIN (FIG. 29–54) of 1821 shows a quiet, slow-moving scene from Constable's England. It has the fresh color and sense of visual exactitude that persuades viewers to believe that it must have been painted directly from nature. Constable made numerous drawings and small-scale color studies for his open-air paintings, but the final works were carefully constructed images produced in the studio. The paintings are very large even for landscape themes of historic importance, never mind views derived from the local landscape. *The Hay Wain* represents England as Constable imagined it had been for centuries—comfortable, rural and idyllic. Even the carefully rendered and meteorologically correct details of the sky seem natural. The painting is, however, deeply nostalgic, harking back to an agrarian past that was fast disappearing in industrializing England.

TURNER.   Joseph Mallord William Turner (1775–1851) is often paired with Constable. Both were landscape painters of roughly the same period, but Turner's career followed a different path. He

29-54 • John Constable THE HAY WAIN
1821. Oil on canvas, 51¼ × 73″ (130.2 × 185.4 cm). National Gallery, London. Gift of Henry Vaughan, 1886

EXPLORE MORE: Gain insight from a primary source by John Constable **www.myartslab.com**

29-55 • Joseph Mallord William Turner SLAVERS THROWING OVERBOARD THE DEAD AND DYING—TYPHOON COMING ON ("THE SLAVE SHIP")
1840. Oil on canvas, 35¾ × 48¼″ (90.8 × 122.6 cm). Museum of Fine Arts, Boston.

SEE MORE: View a video on Joseph Mallord William Turner **www.myartslab.com**

29-56 • Joseph Mallord William Turner THE BURNING OF THE HOUSES OF LORDS AND COMMONS, 16TH OCTOBER 1834
Oil on canvas, 36¼ × 48½″ (92.1 × 123.2 cm). Philadelphia Museum of Art. The John Howard McFadden Collection, 1928

entered the Royal Academy in 1789, was elected a full academician at the unusually young age of 27, and later became a professor at the Royal Academy Schools. During the 1790s, Turner helped revolutionize the British watercolor tradition by rejecting careful underdrawing and topographic accuracy in favor of a freer application of paint and more generalized atmospheric effects. By the late 1790s, he was also exhibiting large-scale oil paintings of grand natural scenes and historical subjects. In his later work he sought to capture the **sublime**, a concept defined by philosopher Edmund Burke (1729–1797) as something that strikes awe and terror into the heart of the viewer. There is no real threat, however; the sublime is experienced vicariously and it is therefore thrilling and exciting.

Turner engages with contemporary social and political issues in his art on a sublime and cataclysmic scale. One of his later works, **SLAVERS THROWING OVERBOARD THE DEAD AND DYING —TYPHOON COMING ON ("THE SLAVE SHIP") (FIG. 29–55)**, depicts an event of genuine horror, based on an account in Thomas Clarkson's *The History of the Abolition of the Slave Trade* (1783), which was reprinted in 1840. Clarkson described the captain of a slave ship caught in the path of a typhoon. It was widely believed that insurance companies reimbursed for slaves lost at sea but not for those who died from sickness on board ship. In the foreground of Turner's painting, not readily recognizable and never quite legible, are the writhing bodies of slaves thrown overboard but still shackled together, fighting in vain for their lives. The fiery swirl of the sun, storm, and waves overwhelms these doomed souls.

Blazing color and light also dominate Turner's portrayal of **THE BURNING OF THE HOUSES OF LORDS AND COMMONS, 16TH OCTOBER 1834 (FIG. 29–56)**, which thrills with a sense of drama. We are not the only ones transfixed by the sight of a magnificent conflagration here: The foreground of the painting shows the south bank of the Thames packed with spectators. The fire was a national tragedy. London's ancient Houses of Parliament in Westminster Palace had witnessed some of the most important events in English history. The fire completely destroyed the House of Lords and left the House of Commons without a roof. Turner himself was witness to the scene and hurriedly made watercolor sketches; within a few months he had the large painting ready for exhibition. The brilliant light and color is the true theme of this painting, explaining why Turner was called "the painter of light."

COLE. Thomas Cole (1801–1848) was one of the first great professional landscape painters in the United States. Cole emigrated from England at age 17 and by 1820 was working as an itinerant portrait painter. With the help of a patron, he traveled in Europe between 1829 and 1832; upon his return to the United States he settled in New York and became a successful landscape painter. He frequently worked from observation when making sketches for his paintings, but, like most landscape painters of his generation, he produced his large finished works in the studio during the winter months.

In the mid 1830s, Cole painted **THE OXBOW (FIG. 29–57)** for exhibition at the National Academy of Design in New York. He

29-57 •
Thomas Cole
THE OXBOW
1836. Oil on canvas, 51½ × 76″ (1.31 × 1.94 m). Metropolitan Museum of Art, New York. Gift of Mrs. Russell Sage, 1908 (08.228)

considered this one of his "view" paintings because it represents a specific place and time. Although most of his other view paintings were small, this one was for exhibition at the National Academy, so it is monumentally large. Its scale allows for a sweeping view of a spectacular oxbow bend in the Connecticut River from the top of Mount Holyoke in western Massachusetts. Cole wrote that the American landscape lacked the historic monuments that made European landscape interesting; there were no castles on the Hudson River of the kind found on the Rhine, and there were no ancient monuments in America of the kind found in Rome. On the other hand, he argued, America's natural wonders, such as this oxbow, should be viewed as America's natural "antiquities." The painting's title tells us that Cole depicts an actual spot, but, like other landscape painters who wished to impart a larger message about the course of history in their work, he composed the scene to convey the landscape's grandeur and significance, exaggerating the steepness of the mountain and setting the scene below a dramatic sky. Along a great sweeping arc produced by the dark clouds and the edge of the mountain, he contrasts the two sides of the American landscape: its dense, stormy wilderness and its congenial, pastoral valleys with settlements. The fading storm seems to suggest that the land is bountiful and ready to yield its fruits to civilization.

FRIEDRICH. In Germany, the Romantic landscape painter Caspar David Friedrich (1774–1840) considered landscape as a vehicle through which to achieve spiritual revelation. As a young man, he was influenced by the writings and teachings of Gotthard Kosegarten, a local Lutheran pastor and poet who taught that the divine was visible through a deep personal connection with nature. Kosegarten argued that just as God's book was the Bible, the landscape was God's "Book of Nature." Friedrich studied at the Copenhagen Academy before settling in Dresden, where the poet Johann Wolfgang von Goethe encouraged him to make landscape the principal subject of his art. He sketched from nature but painted in the studio, synthesizing his sketches with his memories of and feelings about nature. In **MONK BY THE SEA (FIG. 29–58)**, a long expanse of dark, moody beach is differentiated from the sky by no more than a vague horizon. The tiny figure of a monk contemplates the vastness and sublimity of the landscape from the edge of the water. The coastline is mysteriously quiet and fog has drawn a veil over most of the details of the landscape, creating a mood that is hushed and solemn.

Friedrich's landscape paintings were popular among members of the emerging nationalist movement in Germany after Napoleon's invasion in 1806. Interestingly, his work became less popular after Napoleon's defeat in 1815.

GOTHIC AND NEOCLASSICAL STYLES IN ARCHITECTURE

A mixture of Neoclassicism and Romanticism motivated architects in the early nineteenth century, many of whom worked in either mode, depending on the task at hand. Neoclassicism in architecture often imbued secular public buildings with a sense of grandeur and timelessness, while Romanticism evoked, for instance, the Gothic past with its associations of spirituality and community.

GOTHIC ARCHITECTURE. The British claimed the Gothic as part of their patrimony and erected a plethora of Gothic Revival buildings in the nineteenth century, among them the **HOUSES OF**

Pugin published two influential books in 1836 and 1841, in which he argued that the Gothic style of Westminster Abbey was the embodiment of true English genius. In his view, the Greek and Roman Classical orders were stone replications of earlier wooden forms and therefore fell short of the true principles of stone construction.

PARLIAMENT (FIG. 29–59). After Westminster Palace had burned down in 1834, in the fire so memorably painted by Turner (SEE FIG. 29–56), the British government announced a competition for a new building to be designed in the English Perpendicular Gothic style, and to harmonize with the neighboring Westminster Abbey, the thirteenth-century church where English monarchs are crowned.

Charles Barry (1795–1860) and Augustus Welby Northmore Pugin (1812–1852) won the commission. Barry was responsible for the basic plan of the new building, whose symmetry suggests the balance of powers within the British parliamentary system; Pugin provided the intricate Gothic decoration laid over Barry's essentially Classical plan. The leading advocate of Gothic architecture in his era, Pugin published *Contrasts* in 1836, in which he compared the troubled modern era of materialism and mechanization unfavorably with the Middle Ages, which he represented as an idyllic epoch of deep spirituality and satisfying handcraft. For Pugin, Gothic was not a style but a principle, like Classicism. The Gothic, he insisted, embodied two "great rules" of architecture: "first, that there should be no features about a building which are not necessary for convenience, construction or propriety; second, that all ornament should consist of enrichment of the essential structure of the building."

In the nineteenth century, architects used the Gothic primarily for Roman Catholic and Anglican (Episcopalian in the United States) churches. The British-born American architect Richard Upjohn (1802–1878) designed many of the most important Gothic Revival churches in the United States, including **TRINITY CHURCH** in New York (**FIG. 29–60**). With its tall spire, long nave, and squared-off chancel, Trinity church quotes the early fourteenth-century British Gothic style particularly admired by Anglicans and Episcopalians. Every detail is rendered with historical accuracy, but the vaults are plaster, not masonry. The stained-glass windows above the altar were among the earliest of their kind in the United States.

29-60 • Richard Upjohn **TRINITY CHURCH, NEW YORK CITY**

1839–1846.

NEOCLASSICAL ARCHITECTURE. In several European capitals in the early nineteenth century, national museums were designed in the Neoclassical style, which positioned the new buildings as both temples of culture and displays of nationalism. Perhaps the most significant of these was the **ALTES MUSEUM** in Berlin, designed in 1822 by Karl Friedrich Schinkel (1781–1841) and built between 1824 and 1830 **(FIG. 29–61)**. The Altes Museum (Old Museum) was commissioned to display the royal art collection, and was thus built directly across from the Baroque royal palace on an island on the Spree River in the heart of Berlin. The museum's imposing façade consists of a screen of 18 Ionic columns raised on a platform with a central staircase. Attentive to the problem of lighting artworks on both the ground and the upper floors, Schinkel created interior courtyards on either side of a central rotunda.

Tall windows on the museum's outer walls provide natural illumination, and partition walls perpendicular to the windows eliminate glare on the varnished surfaces of the paintings on display.

Large public works in the Neoclassical style were also constructed in the United States. The most significant and symbolic Neoclassical building in Washington, D.C. is the **U.S. CAPITOL**, initially designed in 1792 by William Thornton (1759–1828), an amateur architect. His monumental plan featured a large dome over a temple front flanked by two wings to accommodate the House of Representatives and the Senate. In 1803, President Thomas Jefferson (1743–1826), also an amateur architect, hired a British-trained professional, Benjamin Henry Latrobe (1764–1820), to oversee the actual construction of the Capitol. Latrobe modified Thornton's design by adding a grand staircase and Corinthian colonnade on the

29-62 • Benjamin Henry Latrobe **U.S. CAPITOL, WASHINGTON, D.C.**
c. 1808. Engraving by T. Sutherland, 1825. New York Public Library. I. N. Phelps Stokes Collection, Myriam and Ira Wallach Division of Art, Prints, and Photographs

29-63 • Thomas Jefferson **MONTICELLO**
Charlottesville, Virginia. 1769–1782, 1796–1809.

SEE MORE: View multimedia features on Monticello **www.myartslab.com**

east front **(FIG. 29–62)**. After the British gutted the building in the war of 1812, Latrobe repaired the wings and designed a higher dome. Seeking new symbolic forms for the nation within the traditional Classical vocabulary, he also created a variation on the Corinthian order for the interior by substituting indigenous crops such as corn and tobacco for the Corinthian order's acanthus leaves. In 1817, he resigned his post. The reconstruction was completed under Charles Bulfinch (1763–1844), and another major renovation, resulting in a much larger dome, began in 1850.

Jefferson's designs for the mountaintop home he called **MONTICELLO** (Italian for "little mountain") near Charlottesville, Virginia, is an example of Neoclassical architecture in a private setting **(FIG. 29–63)**. Jefferson began the first phase of construction (1769–1782) when Virginia was still a British colony, and he based his design on the English Palladian style (see Chiswick House, FIG. 29–15). By 1796, however, he had become disenchanted with both the English and their architecture, and had come to admire French architecture while serving as the American minister in Paris. He then embarked upon a second building campaign at Monticello (1796–1809), enlarging the house and redesigning its brick and wood exterior so that its two stories appeared from the outside as one large story, in the manner then fashionable in Paris. The modern worlds of England, France, and America, as well as the ancient worlds of Greece and Rome, come together in this residence. In the second half of the nineteenth century, cultural borrowings would take on an even broader global scope.

THINK ABOUT IT

29.1 Summarize some of the key stylistic traits of French Rococo art and architecture, and explain how these traits relate to the social context of salon life. Then analyze one Rococo work from the chapter and explain how it is typical of the period style.

29.2 Write about how the Enlightenment interest in archaeology propelled the new movement of Neoclassicism in the eighteenth century.

29.3 Explain why artists as visually diverse as Delacroix and Friedrich can be classified under the category of Romanticism. Then evaluate the merits and pitfalls of "Romanticism" as a classifying term.

29.4 Discuss attitudes toward subject matter in the academies of Europe, particularly France and England. Explain what was included and excluded in the academic Grand Manner and why.

29.5 Write about the political climate during Francisco Goya's life, and then, through an analysis of his *Third of May, 1808* (FIG. 29–43), demonstrate how politics affected his art.

PRACTICE MORE: Compose answers to these questions, get flashcards for images and terms, and review chapter material with quizzes **www.myartslab.com**

30-1 • Gustave Eiffel **EIFFEL TOWER**   Paris. 1887–1889.

SEE MORE: View a video about Eiffel Tower **www.myartslab.com**

MID- TO LATE NINETEENTH-CENTURY ART IN EUROPE AND THE UNITED STATES

THE EIFFEL TOWER (FIG. 30–1) was designed and built by Gustave Eiffel (1832–1923) for the 1889 Universal Exposition in Paris. When completed, it stood 984 feet tall and was the tallest structure in the world, taller than the Egyptian pyramids or Gothic cathedrals. The Eiffel Tower served as the entrance to and was the main attraction of the Universal Exposition, one of more than 20 such international fairs staged throughout Europe and the United States in the second half of the nineteenth century. These events showcased and compared international industry, science, and the applied, decorative, and fine arts. An object of pride for the French nation, the Eiffel Tower was intended to demonstrate France's superior engineering, technological and industrial knowledge, and power. Although originally conceived as a temporary structure, it still stands today.

The initial response to the Eiffel Tower was mixed. In 1887, a group of 47 writers, musicians, and artists wrote to *Le Temps* protesting "the erection ... of the useless and monstrous Eiffel Tower," which they described as "a black and gigantic factory chimney." Gustave Eiffel, however, said, "I believe the tower will have its own beauty," and that it "will show that we [the French] are not simply an amusing people, but also the country of engineers." Indeed, when completed, the Eiffel Tower quickly became an international symbol of advanced thought and modernity among artists, and was admired by the public as a wondrous spectacle. The great French theorist Roland Barthes described it in 1979 as the "universal symbol of Paris."

The tower was one of the city's most photographed structures in 1889, its immensity dwarfing the tiny buildings below. Copies of photographs taken by professional and commercial photographers were sold to thousands of tourists visiting the Universal Exposition. This photograph, from late March 1889, shows the tower still under construction but almost complete; the bottom two tiers with the fairgrounds below show evidence of rapid last-minute construction.

LEARN ABOUT IT

30.1 Evaluate the role played by academic art and architecture in the art world of the late nineteenth century.

30.2 Examine the early experiments that led to the emergence of photography as a new art form.

30.3 Analyze the ways in which the movement toward realism in art reflected the social and political concerns of the nineteenth century.

30.4 Investigate the origins of Impressionism and describe its form and content.

30.5 Compare and contrast the several manifestations of Post-Impressionism.

HEAR MORE: Listen to an audio file of your chapter **www.myartslab.com**

EUROPE AND THE UNITED STATES IN THE MID TO LATE NINETEENTH CENTURY

The technological, economic, and social transformations set in motion by the Industrial Revolution intensified in the nineteenth century. Increasing demands for coal and iron necessitated improvements in mining, metallurgy, and transportation. Likewise, the development of the locomotive and steamship facilitated the shipment of raw materials and merchandise, made passenger travel easier, and encouraged the growth of cities (SEE MAP 30–1). These changes also set in motion a vast population migration, as the rural poor moved to cities to find work in factories, mines, and mechanical manufacturing. Industrialists and entrepreneurs enjoyed new levels of wealth and prosperity in this system, but conditions for workers—many of them women and children—were often abysmal. Although new government regulations led to some improvements, socialist movements condemned the exploitation of workers by capitalist factory owners and advocated communal or state ownership of the means of production and distribution.

In 1848, workers' revolts broke out in several European capitals. In that year also, Karl Marx and Friedrich Engels published the *Communist Manifesto*, which predicted the violent overthrow of the bourgeoisie (middle class) by the proletariat (working class), the abolition of private property, and the creation of a classless society. At the same time, the Americans Lucretia Mott and Elizabeth Cady Stanton organized the country's first women's rights convention, in Seneca Falls, New York. They called for the equality of women and men before the law, property rights for married women, the acceptance of women into institutions of higher education, the admission of women to all trades and professions, equal pay for equal work, and women's suffrage.

The nineteenth century also witnessed the rise of imperialism. In order to create new markets for their products and to secure access to cheap raw materials and cheap labor, European nations established numerous new colonies by dividing up most of Africa and nearly a third of Asia. Colonial rule frequently suppressed indigenous cultures while exploiting the economic development of colonized areas.

Scientific discoveries led to the telegraph, telephone, and radio. By the end of the nineteenth century, electricity powered lighting, motors, trams, and railways in most European and American cities. Developments in chemistry created many new products, such as aspirin, disinfectants, photographic chemicals, and more effective explosives. The new material of steel, an alloy of iron and carbon, was lighter, harder, and more malleable than iron, and replaced it in heavy construction and transportation. In medicine and public health, Louis Pasteur's purification of beverages through heat (pasteurization) and the development of vaccines, sterilization, and antiseptics led to a dramatic decline in mortality rates all over the Western world.

Some scientific discoveries challenged traditional religious beliefs and affected social philosophy. Geologists concluded that the Earth was far older than the estimated 6,000 years sometimes claimed by biblical literalists. In 1859, Charles Darwin proposed that life evolved through natural selection. Religious conservatives attacked Darwin's account, which seemed to deny divine creation and even the existence of God. Some of his more extreme supporters, however, suggested that the "survival of the fittest" had advanced the human race, with certain types of people—particularly the Anglo-Saxon upper classes—achieving the pinnacle of social evolution. "Social Darwinism" provided a rationalization for the poor conditions of the working class and a justification for colonizing the "underdeveloped" parts of the world.

In the arts, industrialists, merchants, professionals, the middle classes, some governments, and national academies of art became new sources of patronage. Large annual exhibitions in European and American cultural centers took on increasing importance as a means for artists to show their work, win prizes, attract buyers, and gain commissions. Cheap illustrated newspapers and magazines published art criticism that influenced the reception and production of art, both making and breaking artistic careers, and commercial art dealers emerged as important brokers of art and taste.

The second half of the nineteenth century saw vast changes in how art was conceptualized and created. Some artists became committed political or social activists as industrialization and social unrest continued, while others retreated into their own imagination. Some responded to the ways in which photography transformed vision and perception, many setting themselves up as photographers, while other artists emulated the new medium's clarity in their own work. Still others investigated the difference between photography's detailed but superficial description of visual reality and a deeper, more human reality as a source of inspiration, and others explored the artistic potential of photography's sometimes visually unbalanced compositions, its tendency to compress the illusion of depth and assert its flatness, its lack of an even focus across the picture plane or sometimes the reverse, or even the inability of early photography to "see" red and green equally, causing blank areas of white and black in a photograph. Thus, by the late nineteenth century, while many artists were exploring the reliability of observed reality, others were venturing into the realm of abstraction.

FRENCH ACADEMIC ARCHITECTURE AND ART

The Académie des Beaux-Arts (founded in 1816 to replace the disbanded Royal Academy of Painting and Sculpture) and its official art school, the École des Beaux-Arts, continued to exert a powerful influence over the visual arts in France during the nineteenth century. Academic artists controlled the Salon juries, and major public commissions routinely went to academic architects, painters,

MAP 30-1 • EUROPE AND THE UNITED STATES IN THE NINETEENTH CENTURY

In the nineteenth century, Europe and the United States became increasingly industrialized and many European nations established colonial possessions around the world. Paris was firmly established as the center of the Western art world.

and sculptors. Artists and architects from Europe and the United States came to Paris to study the conventions of academic art.

Academic art and architecture frequently depended upon motifs drawn from historic models—a practice called **historicism**. Elaborating on earlier Neoclassical and Romantic revivals, historicist art and architecture encompassed the sweep of history. Historicists often combined allusions to several different historical periods in a single work. Some academic artists catered to the public taste for exotic sights with Orientalist paintings (see "Orientalism," page 966). These works also combined disparate elements, borrowing from Egyptian, Turkish and Indian cultures to create an imaginary Middle Eastern world.

ACADEMIC ARCHITECTURE

In 1848, after rioting over living conditions erupted in French cities, Napoleon III launched sweeping new reforms. The riots devastated Paris's central neighborhoods, and Georges-Eugène Haussmann (1809–1891) was engaged to redraw the street grid and rebuild the city. Haussmann's ideal was to impose a new rational plan of broad avenues, parks, and open public places upon the medieval heart of Paris. He demolished entire neighborhoods of narrow, winding, medieval streets, summarily evicting the poor from their slums, and replaced them with grand new buildings erected along wide, straight, tree-lined avenues that were suitable for horse-drawn carriages and strolling pedestrians.

The **OPÉRA** (**FIG. 30–2**), a new city opera house designed by Charles Garnier (1825–1898) and now one of the major Parisian landmarks, was built at an intersection of Haussmann's grand avenues. Accessible from all directions, the Opéra was designed with transportation and vehicular traffic in mind, and with a modern cast-iron internal frame; yet in other respects it is a masterpiece of historicism based mostly on the Baroque style, revived here to recall an earlier period of greatness in France. The massive façade, featuring a row of paired columns over an arcade, was intended to recall the seventeenth-century wing of the Louvre, an association meant to suggest the continuity of the French nation and to flatter Emperor Napoleon III by comparing him favorably with King Louis XIV. The building's primary function—as a place of entertainment for Napoleon III, his entourage, and the French social elite—accounts for its luxurious

30-2 • Charles Garnier OPÉRA
Paris. 1861–1874.

SEE MORE: Click the Google
Earth link for the Opéra, Paris
www.myartslab.com

detail. The interior, described as a "temple of pleasure," was even more opulent, with neo-Baroque sculptural groupings, heavy gilded decoration, and a lavish mix of expensive, polychromed materials. The highlight of the interior may not have been the spectacle on stage so much as that on the grand, sweeping Baroque staircase **(FIG. 30–3)**, where members of the Paris elite displayed themselves. As Garnier said, the purpose of the Opéra was to fulfill human desires: to hear, to see, and to be seen.

ACADEMIC PAINTING AND SCULPTURE

The taste that dominated painting and sculpture in the Académie des Beaux-Arts by the mid nineteenth century was termed the *juste milieu*, or "middle way," taste. We can see the flavor of the *juste milieu* in **THE BIRTH OF VENUS** by Alexandre Cabanel (1823–1889), one of the leading academic artists of the time **(FIG. 30–4)**. After studying with an academic master, Cabanel won the Prix de Rome in 1845, and was awarded top honors at the Salon three times in the 1860s and 1870s. In his version of this mythological subject, a copy of which by Adolphe Jourdan is seen here, Venus is carried along by the waves, as flying *putti* herald her arrival with conch shells. Cabanel's mastery of anatomy, flesh tones, and the sea surface derives from his training and skillful technique. The image has a strong erotic charge, though, in the languid limbs, arched back, and hooded eyes of Venus. This combination of mythological pedigree and erotic appeal proved irresistible to Napoleon III, who bought *The Birth of Venus* for his private collection. For more on Jourdan's copy see "The Mass Dissemination of Art," page 974.

30-3 • GRAND STAIRCASE, OPÉRA

SEE MORE: View a panorama of the interior of the Opéra **www.myartslab.com**

30-4 • Alexandre Cabanel, copied by Adolphe Jourdan
THE BIRTH OF VENUS
c. 1864. Oil on canvas, 33 × 53″ (85.2 × 135.8 cm). Dahesh Museum of Art, New York. 2002.37

Although academic and avant-garde artists are sometimes thought simply to have been in opposition, their relationship was more complex. Some academic artists experimented within academic conventions, while avant-garde artists held many academic conventions in high esteem and even sought academic approval. The academic artist Jean-Baptiste Carpeaux (1827–1875) illustrates the kind of experimentation that took place within the Académie des Beaux-Arts. Carpeaux, who had studied at the École des Beaux-Arts under the Romantic sculptor François Rude (SEE FIG. 29–50), was commissioned to carve a large sculptural group for the façade of the Opéra (SEE FIG. 30–2). In this work, **THE DANCE (FIG. 30–5)**, a winged male personifying Dance leaps up joyfully in the midst of a compact group of mostly nude female dancers, embodying the theme of uninhibited Dionysian revelry. Like Cabanel's *Birth of Venus*, the work imbues a mythological subject with erotic connotations.

30-5 • Jean-Baptiste Carpeaux **THE DANCE**
1867–1868. Plaster, height approx. 15′ (4.6 m). Musée de l'Opéra, Paris.

Orientalism

The Snake Charmer by Jean-León Gérôme (1824–1904), painted around 1870, is an example of Orientalism in art. In it Gérôme portrays the nineteenth-century fantasy of the Middle East. The painting shows a young boy, entirely naked, handling a python, while an older man behind him plays a fipple flute, and a group of mercenaries watches. The setting is a large blue-tiled room decorated with calligraphic patterns. The scene is painted with an almost photographic clarity and attention to detail, leading us to think that it is an accurate representation of a specific event. Gérôme traveled to the Middle East several times, and was praised by critics of the 1855 Salon for his ethnographic accuracy. Yet the overall narrative of Gérôme's *Snake Charmer* is a complete fiction, mixing Egyptian, Turkish, and Indian cultures together in a fantastic pastiche.

Orientalism, the fascination with Middle Eastern cultures, dates in France to Napoleon's 1798 invasion of Egypt and his rampant looting of objects from the country for the Louvre Museum, which he opened

in 1804. Between 1809 and 1822, the 24-volume *Description de l'Egypte*, recording the people, lands, and culture of Egypt, was published. In the 1840s and 1850s, photographic studios were established by British, French, and Italian photographers at major tourist sites in the Middle East in order to provide photographs for visitors and armchair tourists at home, thus fueling a popular interest in the region.

Orientalism is found in both academic and avant-garde art in the nineteenth century. The scholar Edward Said described Orientalism as the colonial gaze in which the colonizer gazes upon the colonized Orient (the Middle East rather than Asia) as something to possess, as a "primitive" or "exotic" playground for the "civilized" European visitor, in which "native" men are savage and despotic and "native" women are sultry and sexually available. The "orientalizing" impulse continued throughout the nineteenth century. Like that of Gérôme, the art of Ingres is replete with Orientalism (SEE FIG. 29–51).

Jean-Léon Gérôme
THE SNAKE CHARMER
c. 1870. Oil on canvas, 33 × 48⅛″ (83.8 × 122.1 cm). Clark Art Institute, Williamstown, MA. Acquired by Sterling and Francine Clark, 1942. 1955.51

Unlike Cabanel's figures, Carpeaux's were not smooth and generalized in a Neoclassical manner and this drew criticism from some academicians. The arrangement of his sculptural group seemed too spontaneous, the facial expressions of the figures too vivid, their musculature too exact, their bone structure and proportions too

much of this world, rather than of an ideal one. Carpeaux's work signaled a new direction in academic art, reflecting the values of the new generation of patrons from the industrial and merchant classes. These practical new collectors were less interested in art that idealized than in art that brought the ideal down to earth.

EARLY PHOTOGRAPHY IN EUROPE AND THE UNITED STATES

The nineteenth-century desire to record the faces of the new mercantile elite, their achievements and possessions, and even the imperial possessions of nations, found expression in photography. Since the late Renaissance, artists and others had sought a mechanical method for drawing from nature. One early device was the **camera obscura** (Latin, meaning "dark chamber," see page 970), which consists of a darkened room or box with a lens through which light passes, projecting onto the opposite wall (or box side) an upside-down image of the scene, which an artist can then trace. By the nineteenth century, a small, portable *camera obscura* or even lighter *camera lucida* had become standard equipment for artists. Photography developed as a way to fix—that is, to make permanent—the images produced by a *camera obscura* (later called a "camera") on light-sensitive material.

Photography had no single "inventor." Several individuals worked on the technique simultaneously, each contributing some part to a process that emerged over many years. Around 1830, a handful of experimenters understood ways to "record" the image, but the last step, "stopping" or "fixing" that image so that further exposure to light would not further darken the image, proved difficult to achieve.

In France, while experimenting with ways to duplicate his paintings, Louis-Jacques-Mandé Daguerre (1787–1851) discovered that a plate coated with light-sensitive chemicals and exposed to light for 20 to 30 minutes would reveal a "latent image" when then exposed to mercury vapors. By 1837, he had developed a method of fixing his image by bathing the plate in a solution of salt, and he vastly improved the process by using the chemical hyposulphate of soda (known as "hypo") as suggested by Sir John Frederick

30-7 • DAGUERREOTYPE OF SAMUEL FINLEY BREESE MORSE
c. 1845. Sixth plate daguerreotype. The Daguerreotype Collection of the Library of Congress, Washington, D.C.

Herschel (1792–1871). The final image was negative, but when viewed upon a highly polished silver plate it appeared positive. The resulting picture could not be duplicated easily and was very fragile, but its quality was remarkably precise. In Daguerre's photograph of his studio tabletop **(FIG. 30–6)**, the details are exquisite (impossible to see in reproduction, even using today's technology) and the composition mimics the conventions of still-life painting. Daguerre, after he patented and announced his new technology, produced an early type of photograph called a **daguerreotype**, in August 1839.

Even before Daguerre announced his photographic technique in France, the American artist Samuel Morse (1791–1872) traveled to Paris to negotiate an exchange of information about his invention, the telegraph, for information about Daguerre's photography. Morse introduced the daguerreotype process to America within weeks of Daguerre's announcement, and by 1841 had reduced exposure times enough to take portrait photographs **(FIG. 30–7)**.

At the same time in England, Henry Fox Talbot (1800–1877), a wealthy amateur, made negative copies of engravings, lace, and plants by placing them on paper soaked in silver chloride and exposing them to light. He also found that the negative image on paper could be exposed again on top of another piece of paper to create a positive image, thus discovering the negative-positive process that became the basis of photographic printing. Talbot's negative could be used more than once, so he could produce a

30-6 • Louis-Jacques-Mandé Daguerre THE ARTIST'S STUDIO
1837. Daguerreotype, 6½ × 8½″ (16.5 × 21.6 cm). Société Française de Photographie, Paris.

30-8 • Henry Fox Talbot
THE OPEN DOOR
1843. Salt-paper print from a calotype negative. Science Museum, London. Fox Talbot Collection

number of positive images inexpensively. But the **calotype**, as he later called it, produced a soft, fuzzy image. When he heard of Daguerre's announcement, Talbot rushed to make his own announcement and patent his process. The term for these processes —photography, derived from the Greek for "drawing with light"—was coined by Herschel.

The emerging technology of photography was quickly put to use for making a visual record for contemporary audiences and future generations. Early on, however, photographers also experimented with the expressive possibilities of the new medium and worked to create striking compositions. Between 1844 and 1846, Talbot published a book in six parts entitled *The Pencil of Nature*, illustrated entirely with salt-paper prints made from calotype negatives. Most of the photographs were of idyllic rural scenery or carefully arranged still lifes; they were presented as works of art rather than documents of a precisely observed reality. Talbot realized that the imprecision of his process could not compete with the commercial potential of the daguerreotype, and so rather than trying to do so, he chose to view photography in visual and artistic terms. In **THE OPEN DOOR** (**FIG. 30–8**), for example, shadows create a repeating pattern of diagonal lines that contrast with the vertical lines of the architecture. The photograph expresses nostalgia for a rural way of life that was fast disappearing in industrial England.

Other early photographers worked on assignment and chose the photographic process that best suited their final product. In 1851, the French government decided to commission photographs of the major architectural monuments of France, in part because so

much of ancient France had been destroyed during the Revolution. Édouard-Denis Baldus (1813–1882) was one of several photographers assigned to make photographs for the Mission Héliographique through the Commission des Monuments Historiques. He relied on many techniques, including calotypes, wet-plate/collodion negatives, albumen prints, and heliogravure. Since the photographs had to be reproduced for publication, he was unable to use daguerreotypes. Ironically, despite intense competitive national pride over the French and English versions of photography, some of the best calotypes were made in France and some of the best daguerreotypes in England and the United States. This albumen print by Baldus, **HOUSE WITH STAIRCASE** (**FIG. 30–9**) is one of 11 photographs that he took for his famous folio *Vues de Paris en Photographie*.

American photographers used wet-plate glass negative and albumen paper print processes to document the momentous events of the Civil War (1861–1865). Timothy O'Sullivan (c. 1840– 1882) was a "camera operator" for Matthew Brady (1822–1896) at the beginning of the conflict, and, working with Alexander Gardner (1821–1882), he made war photographs that were distributed widely. **THE HOME OF THE REBEL SHARPSHOOTER** (**FIG. 30–10**) was taken after the Battle of Gettysburg in July 1863. The technical difficulties were considerable. Wet-plate technology required that the glass plate used to make the negative be coated with a sticky substance holding the light-sensitive chemicals; if the plate dried, the photograph could not be taken. Likewise, if dust contaminated the plate, the image would also be ruined. Long

30–9 • Édouard-Denis Baldus
HOUSE WITH STAIRCASE
1858. Albumen print, 7⅜ × 10⅝″
(18.7 × 27 cm). #39 from 11
albumen prints from *Vues de Paris
en Photographie*, Fine Arts
Museums of San Francisco.

exposure times made action photographs impossible, so early war photographs were taken in camp or in the aftermath of battle. O'Sullivan's image seems to show a rebel sharpshooter who has been killed in his look-out. But this rock formation was in the middle of the battlefield, and had neither the height nor the view needed for a sharpshooter. In fact, the photographer dragged the dead body to the site and posed it; and the rifle propped against the wall was O'Sullivan's. The staging of this photograph raises questions about visual fact and fiction. Like a painting, a photograph is composed to create a picture, but photography promises a kind of factuality that we do not expect from painting. Interestingly, the manipulation of this photograph did not concern nineteenth-century viewers, who understood clearly photography's inability to record the visual world without bias.

30–10 • Timothy O'Sullivan
**THE HOME OF THE REBEL
SHARPSHOOTER: BATTLE
FIELD AT GETTYSBURG**
1863. Albumen print. Library of Congress,
Washington, D.C.

TECHNIQUE | The Photographic Process

A camera is essentially a lightproof box with a hole, called an aperture, which is usually adjustable in size and regulates the amount of light that strikes the film. The aperture is covered with a lens, to focus the image on the film, and a shutter, a hinged flap that opens for a controlled amount of time in order to regulate the length of time the film is exposed to light—usually a small fraction of a second. Modern cameras with viewfinders and small single-lens reflex cameras are generally used at eye level, permitting the photographer to see virtually the same image that will be captured on film.

In modern black-and-white chemical photography, silver halide crystals (silver combined with iodine, chlorine, or other halogens) are suspended in a gelatin base to make an emulsion that coats the film; in early photography, before the invention of plastic, a glass plate was coated with a variety of emulsions. When the shutter is open, light reflected off objects enters the camera and strikes the film, exposing it. Pale objects reflect more light than dark ones. The silver in the emulsion collects most densely where it is exposed to the most light, producing a "negative" image on the film. Later, when the film is placed in a chemical bath (developed), the silver deposits turn black, as if tarnishing. The more light the film receives, the denser the black tone created. A positive image is created from a negative in the darkroom, where the film negative is placed over a sheet of paper that, like the film, has also been treated to be light-sensitive. Light is then directed through the negative onto the paper to create a positive image. Multiple positive prints can be generated from a single negative.

Today this chemical process has been largely replaced by digital photography, which records images as digital information files that can be manipulated on computers rather than in darkrooms. The potential of this new photographic medium is being exploited in contemporary art (see pages 1127–1128).

ILLUSTRATION OF A CAMERA OBSCURA
From "Sketchbook on Military Art, including Geometry, Fortifications, Artillery, Mechanics, and Pyrotechnics." Possibly Italian. 17th century. 275 l., illus. (part col.), 4⅝ × 6⅜" (12 × 16 cm). Library of Congress. Rosenwald 363, Rosenwald Collection

One of the most creative early photographers was Julia Margaret Cameron (1815–1879), who received her first camera as a gift from her daughters when she was 49. Her principal subjects were the great men and women of British arts, letters, and sciences, many of whom had long been family friends. Cameron's approach was experimental and radical. Like many of her portraits, that of the famous British historian **THOMAS CARLYLE** is deliberately slightly out of focus (**FIG. 30–11**): Cameron consciously rejected the sharp focus of commercial portrait photography, which she felt accentuated the merely physical attributes and neglected the inner character of the subject. By blurring the details, she sought to call attention to the light that suffused her subjects and to their thoughtful expressions. In her autobiography, Cameron said: "When I have had such men before my camera my whole soul has endeavored to do its duty towards them in recording faithfully the greatness of the inner as well as the features of the outer man."

30-11 • Julia Margaret Cameron PORTRAIT OF THOMAS CARLYLE
1867. Silver print, 10 × 8" (25.4 × 20.3 cm). The Royal Photographic Society, Collection at National Museum of Photography, Film, and Television, England.

THE BEGINNINGS OF THE AVANT-GARDE: REALISM AND BEYOND

In reaction to the rigidity of academic training, some French artists began to consider themselves members of an **avant-garde**, meaning "advance guard" or "vanguard." The term was coined by the French military during the Napoleonic era to designate the forward units of an advancing army that scouted territory that the main force would soon occupy. Avant-garde artists saw themselves as working in advance of an increasingly bourgeois society. The term was first mentioned in connection with art around 1825 in the political programs of French utopian socialists. Henri de Saint-Simon (1760–1825) suggested that in order to transform modern industrialized society into an ideal state, it would be necessary to gather together an avant-garde of intellectuals, scientists, and artists to lead France into the future.

In 1831, the architect Eugène Viollet-le-Duc applied the term to the artists of Paris in the aftermath of the revolution of 1830. Viollet-le-Duc vehemently opposed the French academic system of architectural training. His concept of the avant-garde called for a small elite of independent radical thinkers, artists, and architects to break away from the Académie des Beaux-Arts and the norms of society in order to forge new thoughts, ideas, and ways of looking at the world and art. He foresaw that this life would require the sacrifice of artists' reputations and sales of their work. Most avant-garde artists were neither as radical nor as extreme as Viollet-le-Duc, and, as we have seen, the relationship between the Académie des Beaux-Arts and the avant-garde was complex. Nonetheless, the idea was embraced by a number of artists who have come to characterize the period.

REALISM AND REVOLUTION

In the modern world of Paris at mid-century—a world plagued by violence, social unrest, overcrowding, and poverty—the grand, abstract themes of academic art seemed irrelevant to those thinkers who would come to represent the avant-garde. Rising food prices, high unemployment, political disenfranchisement, and government inaction led to a popular rebellion and the overthrow of the July Monarchy by a coalition of socialists, anarchists, and workers (see page 949), but conflicts among the reformers led to another uprising, in which more than 10,000 of the working poor were killed or injured in their struggle against the new government's forces. Against this social and political backdrop a new intellectual movement, known as Realism, originated in the novels of Émile Zola, Charles Dickens, Honoré de Balzac, and others who wrote about the lives of the urban lower classes. Realism in art was less of a style than a commitment to paint the modern world honestly, without turning away from the brutal truths of life for many ordinary people.

COURBET. Gustave Courbet (1819–1877) was one of the first artists to call himself "avant-garde" or "Realist." A big, blustery man, he was, in his own words, "not only a Socialist but a democrat and a Republican: in a word, a supporter of the whole Revolution." Born and raised near the Swiss border in the French town of Ornans, he moved to Paris in 1839. The street fighting in Paris in 1848 radicalized him and was a catalyst for two large canvases that have come to be regarded as the defining works of Realism. In 1849, he painted the first of these, **THE STONE BREAKERS** (FIG. 30–12).

At over 5 feet high and 8 feet wide, *The Stone Breakers* depicted a young boy and an old man crushing rock to produce

30-12 • Gustave Courbet THE STONE BREAKERS
1849. Oil on canvas, 5′3″ × 8′6″ (1.6 × 2.59 m). Formerly Gemäldegalerie, Dresden. Destroyed in World War II.

30-13 • Gustave Courbet **A BURIAL AT ORNANS**
1849. Oil on canvas, 10′3½″ × 21′9″ (3.1 × 6.6 m). Musée d'Orsay, Paris.

A Burial at Ornans was inspired by the 1848 funeral of Courbet's maternal grandfather, Jean-Antoine Oudot, a veteran of the Revolution of 1789. The painting is not meant as a record of that particular funeral, however, since Oudot is shown alive in profile at the extreme left of the canvas, his image adapted by Courbet from an earlier portrait. The two men to the right of the open grave, dressed not in contemporary but in late eighteenth-century clothing, are also revolutionaries of Oudot's generation. Their proximity to the grave suggests that one of their peers is being buried. Courbet's picture may be interpreted as linking the revolutions of 1789 and 1848, both of which sought to advance the cause of democracy in France.

the gravel used for roadbeds: the lowliest, most backbreaking form of work. Stonebreakers represent the disenfranchised peasants on whose backs modern life was being built. The younger figure strains to lift a large basket of rocks to the side of the road. Although he wears a tattered shirt and trousers, his boots are of modern make. The older man, almost broken by the work, pounds the rocks as he kneels. He wears the more traditional clothing of a peasant, including traditional wooden clogs. The boy represents a grim future, while the man signifies an increasingly obsolete rural past. Both are faceless laborers. Courbet described the inspiration for this painting:

> [N]ear Maisières [in the vicinity of Ornans], I stopped to consider two men breaking stones on the highway. It's rare to meet the most complete expression of poverty, so an idea for a picture came to me on the spot. I made an appointment with them at my studio for the next day … . On the one side is an old man, seventy … . On the other side is a young fellow … in his filthy tattered shirt … . Alas, in labor such as this, one's life begins that way, and it ends the same way.

Two things are clear from this description: Courbet intended to make a political statement, and he invited the men back to his studio so that he could study them more carefully, following academic methods.

By rendering labor on the scale of a history painting, Courbet intended to provoke. In academic art, monumental canvases on this scale were reserved for heroic subjects; by his work, Courbet suggests that even the lowest in society could be venerated as heroes. Instead of the usual highly finished academic style and inspiring message, his canvas reveals the brutality of modern life, his rough use of paint, dull, dark colors, awkward poses, and stilted composition making the scene feel realistic, gloomy, and degrading. In 1865, his friend, the anarchist philosopher Pierre-Joseph Proudhon (1809–1865), described *The Stone Breakers* as the first socialist picture ever painted, "an irony of our industrial civilization, which continually invents wonderful machines to perform all kinds of labor … yet is unable to liberate man from the most backbreaking toil." Courbet himself described the work as a depiction of "injustice."

Courbet began to paint **A BURIAL AT ORNANS** (**FIG. 30–13**) immediately after *The Stone Breakers*. Also exhibited at the 1850–1851 Salon, it is a vast painting, measuring roughly 10 by 21 feet, and depicts a burial on a life-size scale. A crush of people attend the graveside service. In the center, the gravedigger kneels over the gaping hole in the ground; to the left the clergy seem distracted and bored, perhaps reflecting the indifference of the institutional order of France after the 1848 revolution; to the right, the huddle of rural mourners, Courbet's heroes of modern life, weep in various states of grief, while in the highlighted foreground, closest to viewers, a bored altar boy and a distracted dog focus attention away from the central activity of the assembled crowd. Although painted on a scale befitting the funeral of a hero, Courbet's depiction has none of the idealization of traditional history painting; instead, it shows all the awkward, blundering numbness of a real funeral, with an emphasis on its brutal, physical reality. When shown at the Salon, the painting was attacked by critics who objected to the elevation of a provincial funeral to the scale of history painting, to Courbet's disrespect for the rules of academic composition, and even to the lack of any suggestion of the afterlife. Courbet had submitted his work to the Salon knowing that it would be denounced, however. He purposefully challenged the prescribed subjects, style, and finish of academic painting to establish his avant-garde position and to create controversy, which he embraced. When the 1854 Salon was cancelled and some of his works were refused for the International Exposition of 1855, Courbet had a temporary building constructed on rented land near the fair's Pavilion of Art and installed a show of his own works that he called the "Pavilion of Realism," clearly asserting his independence from the Salon as many other artists would also do later.

MILLET.   Similar claims of political radicalism were made about Jean-François Millet (1814–1875), although he denied them. Millet grew up on a farm but lived and worked in Paris between 1837 and 1848. He was awarded a state commission (with stipend) for his part in the 1848 revolution, allowing him to move to Barbizon, just south of Paris where he painted the hardships of the rural poor.

Among the best known of Millet's works is **THE GLEANERS** (**FIG. 30–14**), which shows three women gathering stray grain from the ground after harvest time. Despite its warm colors, the scene is one of extreme poverty. Gleaning was a form of relief offered to the rural poor by landowners, although it required hours of backbreaking work to collect enough wheat to make a single

30-14 • Jean-François Millet THE GLEANERS
1857. Oil on canvas, 33 × 44″ (83.8 × 111.8 cm). Musée d'Orsay, Paris.

The Mass Dissemination of Art

Just as contemporary artists can distribute photographic reproductions of their work, in the eighteenth century, artists used engraving or etching to reproduce their work for distribution to a larger audience.

Works of art that won prizes or created controversy were often engraved for reproduction. Artists generally hired specialists to render their work in print form, and sold prints at bookstores or magazine stands. J. M. W. Turner used a team of engravers to capture the delicate tonal shadings of his works. An engraved copper plate could be printed upward of 100 times before the repeated pressing took its toll on image quality. In the later nineteenth century, artists increasingly used steel engraving, wood engraving, and lithography for printing. Those more durable surfaces could print up to 10,000 copies of an image without much loss of quality, though only a few artists experienced such demand.

One of the canniest self-marketers of the century was Alexandre Cabanel. After Napoleon III bought *The Birth of Venus*, the artist sold the reproduction rights to the art dealer Adolphe Goupil, who in turn hired other artists (in this case Adolphe Jourdan) to create at least two smaller-scale copies of the work (one of which is FIG. 30–4). After the original artist had approved the copies and signed them, the dealer used these as models for engravers who cut the steel plates. The dealer then sold the smaller versions of the work.

Another example of a work that was widely reproduced is Frederic Church's *Heart of the Andes* (1859), which was so popular in New York and London that it had to be protected by a rope; the painting was sold for $10,000, at that date the highest price ever paid for a painting by an American artist.

Frederic Church **HEART OF THE ANDES**
1859. Oil on canvas, 66⅛ × 119¼″ (168 × 302.9 cm). Metropolitan Museum of Art, New York. Bequest of Margaret E. Dows, 1909

loaf of bread. Two women are bent over to reach the tiny stalks of grain remaining on the ground. A third woman straightens to ease her back. When Millet exhibited the painting in 1857, critics noted its implicit social criticism and described the work as "Realist."

Corot. Another, more romantic and less political approach to depicting rural life can be seen in the paintings of Jean-Baptiste-Camille Corot (1796–1875). Corot painted historical landscapes early in his career, but steadily moved toward more "naturalistic"

30–15 • Jean-Baptiste-Camille Corot FIRST LEAVES, NEAR MANTES
c. 1855. Oil on canvas, 13⅜ × 18⅛″ (34 × 46 cm). Carnegie Museum of Art, Pittsburgh, Pennsylvania.

and intimate scenes of rural France. **FIRST LEAVES, NEAR MANTES** **(FIG. 30–15)** depicts a scene infused with the soft mist of early spring in the woods. Corot's feathery brushwork representing the soft, new foliage contrasts with the stark, vertical tree trunks and branches, and, together with the fresh green of the new under-growth, creates a perfectly balanced sense of a clear spring day. A man and woman pause to talk on the road winding from left to right through the painting, while a woman labors in the woods at the lower right. Corot invites us to imagine ourselves in the picture and feel the crisp, bright air. These images of peaceful country life held great appeal for Parisians who had experienced the chaos of the 1848 revolution and who lived in an increasingly crowded, noisy, and fast-paced metropolis.

BONHEUR.   Among the period's most popular painters of farm life was Rosa Bonheur (1822–1899), who was raised in Paris but was drawn to the countryside. Bonheur's success in what was then a male domain owed much to the socialist convictions of

her parents, who belonged to a radical utopian sect, founded by the Comte de Saint-Simon (1760–1825), that believed not only in the equality of women but also in a future female Messiah. Bonheur's father, a drawing teacher, provided most of her artistic training.

Bonheur dedicated herself to realistic depictions of modern farm animals, which were becoming increasingly obsolete as technology and industrialization transformed farming. She studied her subjects intensely by reading zoology books and making detailed studies in stockyards and slaughterhouses. (To gain access to these all-male preserves, she received police permission to dress in men's clothing.) Her professional breakthrough came at the Salon of 1848, where she showed eight paintings and won a first-class medal. **THE HORSE FAIR (FIG. 30–16)**, painted in 1853, was based on a horse market near Salpêtrière, but was also partly inspired by the Parthenon marbles in London and by the art of Géricault. The scene portrays the display of splendid Percheron horses by their grooms, some walking obediently in their circle,

30-16 • Rosa Bonheur THE HORSE FAIR
1853–1855. Oil on canvas, 8'1¼" × 16'7½". Metropolitan Museum of Art, New York.

EXPLORE MORE: Gain insight from a primary source on Rosa Bonheur **www.myartslab.com**

others rearing up, not yet quite broken. *The Horse Fair* has been interpreted by some scholars as a commentary on the lack of rights for women in the 1850s, but it was not read that way at the time. Although a monumental painting (at more than 8 by 16 feet) of farm animals, normally lower-ranking subjects, it was highly praised at the 1848 Salon. When the painting later toured throughout Britain and the United States, members of the public paid to see it. It was widely disseminated in print form on both sides of the Atlantic, and was purchased for the new Metropolitan Museum of Art in New York in 1889. Bonheur became so famous working within the Salon system that in 1865 she received France's highest award, membership in the Legion of Honor, becoming the first woman to be awarded its Grand Cross.

THE PAINTER OF MODERN LIFE: MANET

Along with the concept of the avant-garde, the second great concept that shaped art in France at this time was the idea of modernity. The experience of modernity—of constant change and renewal—is linked to the dynamic nature of city life. The themes of the modern city and of political engagement with modern life in an industrialized world are key to understanding the development of painting and literature in France in the second half of the nineteenth century.

Poet and essayist Charles Baudelaire argued that, in order to speak for their time and place, artists' work had to be infused with the idea of modernity. Modernity called for modern urban subjects and a new approach to seeing and representing the visual world—a break with the past in order to better comprehend and comment on the present. Especially after the invention of photography, art was expected to offer new ways of representing reality. One who rose to the challenge was the French painter Édouard Manet (1832–1883).

LE DÉJEUNER SUR L'HERBE. At mid-century, the Académie des Beaux-Arts increasingly opened Salon exhibitions to non-academic artists, resulting in a surge in the number of works submitted to, and inevitably rejected by, the Salon jury. In 1863, the jury turned down nearly 3,000 works, leading to a storm of protest. In response, Napoleon III tried to mediate the dispute by ordering an exhibition of the refused work called the *Salon des Refusés* ("Salon of the Rejected Ones"). Featured in it was Manet's painting **LE DÉJEUNER SUR L'HERBE (THE LUNCHEON ON THE GRASS) (FIG. 30–17)**. A well-born Parisian who had studied in the early 1850s with the independent artist Thomas Couture (1815–1879), Manet had by the early 1860s developed a strong commitment to Realism, largely as a result of his friendship with the poet Baudelaire who called for a "Painter of Modern Life." Manet's *Le Déjeuner sur l'Herbe* invokes Baudelaire's spirit, and in doing so scandalized contemporary viewers all the way up to Napoleon III himself. Ironically, the resulting *succès de scandale* ("success from scandal") helped establish Manet's career as a radical artist.

The most scandalous aspect of the painting was the "immorality" of Manet's theme: a suburban picnic featuring two fully dressed bourgeois gentlemen (in fact, Manet's brother, wearing the hat of a student, and his brother-in-law), a naked woman to the front left, and another scantily dressed woman in the background. Manet's

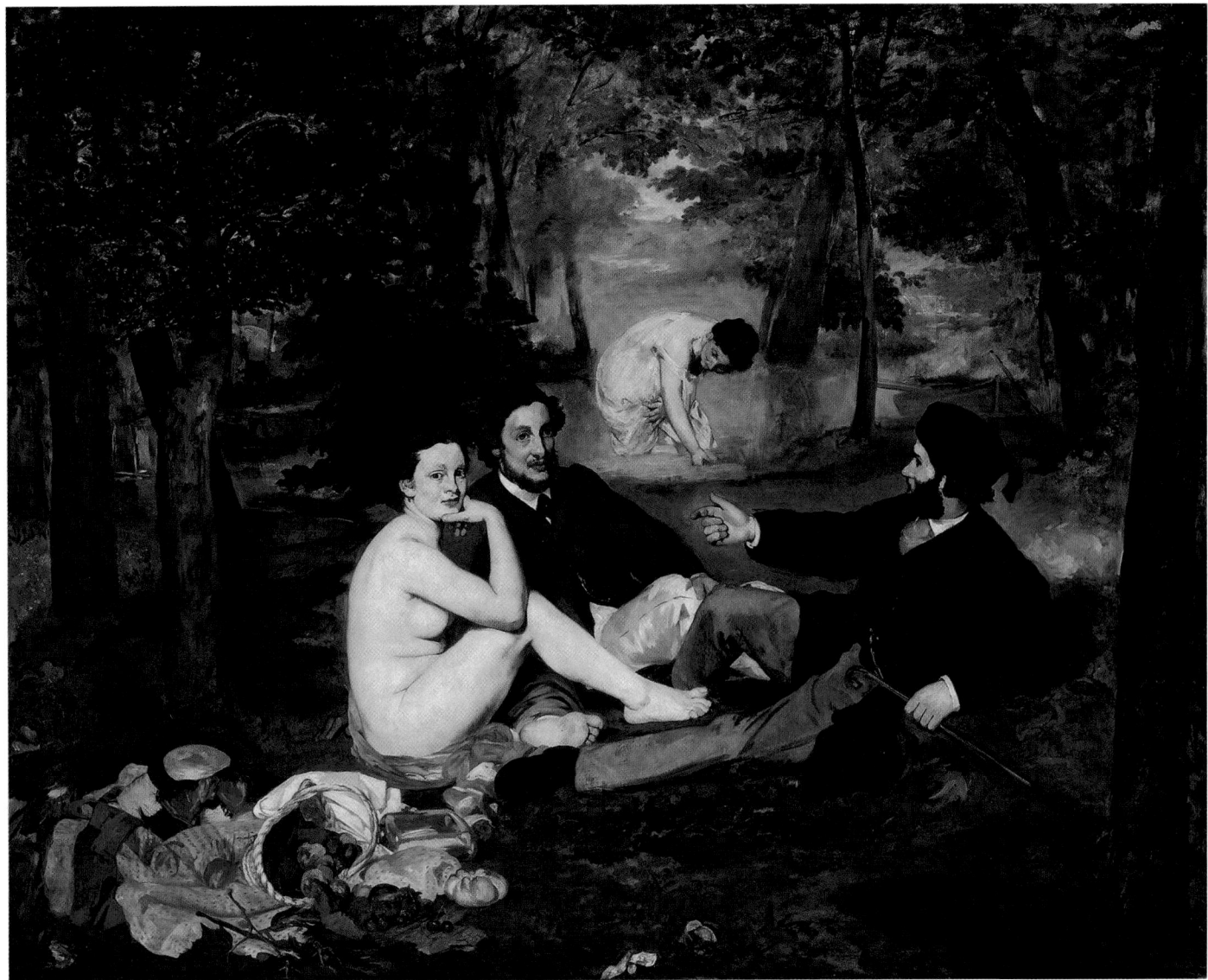

30–17 • Édouard Manet **LE DÉJEUNER SUR L'HERBE (THE LUNCHEON ON THE GRASS)**
1863. Oil on canvas, 7′ × 8′8″ (2.13 × 2.64 m). Musée d'Orsay, Paris.

audience assumed that these women were prostitutes, and the men their customers. Equally shocking were its references to important works of art of the past, which Académie des Beaux-Arts artists were expected to make, combined with its crude, unvarnished modernity. In contrast, one of the paintings that gathered most renown at the official Salon in that year was Alexandre Cabanel's *Birth of Venus* (SEE FIG. 30–4), which, because it presented nudity in a conventionally acceptable, Classical environment, was favorably reviewed and quickly entered the collection of Napoleon III.

Manet apparently conceived of *Le Déjeuner sur l'Herbe* as a modern version of a Venetian Renaissance painting in the Louvre, the *Pastoral Concert*, then believed to be by Giorgione but now attributed to both Titian and Giorgione or to Titian exclusively (SEE FIG. 20–22). Manet's composition also refers to a Marcantonio Raimondi engraving of Raphael's *The Judgment of Paris*—itself based on Classical reliefs of river gods and nymphs. Manet's modern interpretation of the scene, however, combined with his

modern style, was intentionally provocative. The stark lighting of his nude, the cool colors, the flat, cutout quality of his figures who seem as if they are set against a painted backdrop, all suggest the seamier side of city life. Presenting this under a flimsy guise of academic art underlined Manet's subversiveness.

OLYMPIA.   Shortly after completing *Le Déjeuner sur l'Herbe*, Manet painted **OLYMPIA (FIG. 30–18)**, its title alluding to a socially ambitious prostitute of the same name in a novel and play by Alexandre Dumas the Younger. Like *Le Déjeuner sur l'Herbe*, Manet's *Olympia* was based on a Venetian Renaissance source, Titian's "*Venus*" *of Urbino* (SEE FIG. 20–24), which Manet had earlier copied in Florence. At first, his painting appears to pay homage to Titian's in its subject matter (at that time believed to be a Venetian courtesan) and composition. However, Manet made his modern counterpart the very antithesis of Titian's. Titian's female is curvaceous and softly rounded, Manet's is angular and flattened;

30–18 • Édouard Manet OLYMPIA
1863. Oil on canvas, 4′3″ × 6′2¼″ (1.31 × 1.91 m). Musée du Louvre, Paris.

Titian's colors are warm and rich, Manet's are cold and harsh, like a photograph; Titian's Venus looks coyly at the male spectator, Manet's Olympia appears coldly indifferent. Our relationship with Olympia is underscored by the reaction of her cat, which—unlike the sleeping dog in the Titian—arches its back at us. Finally, instead of looking up at us, Olympia gazes down at us, indicating that she is in the position of power and that we are subordinate, akin to the black servant at the foot of the bed who brings her a bouquet of flowers. In reversing the Titian, Manet overturns the entire tradition of the accommodating female nude. Not surprisingly, conservative critics vilified *Olympia* when it was exhibited at the Salon of 1865.

Manet generally submitted his work to every Salon, but when several were rejected in 1867, he did as Courbet had done in 1855: He asserted his independence by renting a hall nearby and staging his own show. This made Manet the unofficial leader of a group of progressive artists and writers who gathered at the Café Guerbois in the Montmartre district of Paris. Among the artists who frequented the café were Degas, Monet, Pissarro, and Renoir, all of whom would soon exhibit together as the Impressionists and follow Manet's lead in challenging academic conventions.

LATER WORKS. Manet worked closely with all of these artists and frequently painted themes similar to the Impressionists, even occasionally employing a lighter Impressionist palette of colors, but always retaining his previous dedication to the portrayal of modern urban life. In 1874, for instance, he painted **BOATING (FIG. 30–19)** in which two figures sit in a boat on a sunny summer day. The man, a *canotier* or lower-class boatman, is dressed in the standard uniform of white round-neck shirt and pants with a flat straw hat (boater). He has the helm of the boat. The young girl with him sits uneasily in the boat, neither comfortable in her position nor in her dress. The fact that she has no chaperone hints at impropriety. Despite the apparent Impressionist subject and colors, there is a gritty urban realism to Manet's painting that is in stark contrast to Morrisot's more idyllic and upper-class *Summer's Day* (SEE FIG. 30–30).

Manet's *A Bar at the Folies-Bergère* (see "A Closer Look," page 980) returns to the complex theme of gender and class relations in modern urban life. Here is a hard-working young girl serving drinks at a bar in the famous nightclub. She has an unfashionably ruddy face and hands scrubbed raw. In the glittering light created by the electric bulbs and mirrors of the café-concert frequented by Manet and his compatriots she seems stiff and distant. She

30-19 • Édouard Manet
BOATING
1874. Oil on canvas, 38¼ × 51¼"
(97.2 × 130.2 cm).
Metropolitan Museum of Art,
New York. H. O. Havemeyer
Collection, 1929

refuses to meet the gaze of her client. The barmaid is at once detached from the scene and part of it, one of the many items on display for purchase. This image is about sexualized looking and the barmaid's uneasy reflection in the mirror, which seems to acknowledge that both her class and gender expose her to visual and even sexual consumption.

RESPONSES TO REALISM BEYOND FRANCE

Artists of other nations embraced their own forms of realism in the period after 1850 as the social effects of urbanization and industrialization began to be felt in their countries. While these artists did not label themselves as Realists like their contemporaries in France, they did share their interest in presenting an unflinching look at grim reality and the difficult lives of the working poor.

REALISM IN RUSSIA: THE WANDERERS.   In Russia, a variant on French Realism developed in relation to a new concern for the peasantry. In 1861, the tsar abolished serfdom, emancipating Russia's peasants from the virtual slavery they had endured on the large estates of the aristocracy. Two years later, a group of painters inspired by the emancipation declared allegiance both to the peasant cause and to freedom from the St. Petersburg Academy of Art, which had controlled Russian art since 1754. Rejecting what they considered the escapist aesthetics of the Academy, the members of the group dedicated themselves to a socially useful realism. Committed to bringing art to the people in traveling exhibitions, they called themselves "The Wanderers." By the late 1870s, members of the group, like their counterparts in music and

literature, had also joined a nationalist movement to reassert what they considered to be an authentic Russian culture rooted in the traditions of the peasantry, rejecting the Western European customs that had long predominated among the Russian aristocracy.

Ilya Repin (1844–1930), who attended the St. Petersburg Academy and won a scholarship to study in Paris, joined the Wanderers in 1878 after his return to Russia. He painted a series of works illustrating the social injustices then prevailing in his homeland, including **BARGEHAULERS ON THE VOLGA** (FIG. **30–20)**, which features a wretched group of peasants condemned to the brutal work of pulling ships up the Volga River. To heighten our sympathy for these workers, Repin placed a youth in the center of the group, a young man who will soon be as worn out as his companions unless something is done to rescue him. Thus the painting is a call to action.

REALISM IN THE UNITED STATES.   Realism was not a term used in the United States, but there were several kinds of realism in American art. Thomas Eakins (1844–1916), for instance, made a series of uncompromising paintings that were criticized for their controversial subject matter. Born in Philadelphia, Eakins trained at the Pennsylvania Academy of the Fine Arts, but since he regarded the training in anatomy as not rigorous enough—lacking realism, as he might have put it—he supplemented his training at the Jefferson Medical College nearby. He later studied at the École des Beaux-Arts in Paris and then spent six months in Spain, where he encountered the profound realism of Baroque artists Jusepe de Ribera and Diego Velázquez (SEE FIGS. 22–19, 22–21). After he returned

A CLOSER LOOK

A Bar at the Folies-Bergère

by Édouard Manet, 1881–1882. Oil on canvas. 37¾ × 51¼″ (95.9 × 130 cm). Courtauld Gallery, London. P.1934.SC.234

In the late nineteenth century, the café-concert was frequented by avant-garde artists such as Degas, Seurat, and Manet. The Folies-Bergère was one of the largest of these café-concerts in Paris, offering circuses, musicals, and vaudeville acts. Note the legs of a trapeze artist who is part of the spectacle to the upper left.

Reflected in the mirror are members of the elegant crowd who have come to the performances at the Folies-Bergère. The men are dressed in top hats and the women in rich costumes. Though their opera glasses they observe lazily the many glittering spectacles performed for their benefit as the electric light dances off the crystal chandelier behind the young girl's head.

The barmaid looks out of the painting at us as if we are her next customer, but she stands stiffly and formally, neither acknowledging nor smiling at us; her sleeves are rolled up and she seems weary from her work. On the other hand, she seems to lean forward to engage in conversation with the top-hatted client in her mirror reflection, suggesting either Manet's intention to create an ambiguous narrative or a curved mirror.

The bangles and lace at the barmaid's wrists and neck suggest a rise in the availability of consumption goods in the shops and department stores of the modern city, perhaps implying that the barmaid, who displays herself like the luscious oranges to the right, is also available for purchase.

Manet presents the Folies-Bergère as a place where the enjoyments of alcohol, the circus and vaudeville, and even sexual transactions take place. The weary girl stands at the bar, barely differentiated from her background, like one of so many glittering objects on display, to be consumed both visually and sexually.

On the marble bar-top Manet has spread a glorious still life of liquor bottles, tangerines, and flowers to entice the customer.

SEE MORE: View the Closer Look feature for *A Bar at the Folies-Bergère* **www.myartslab.com**

30-20 • Ilya Repin **BARGEHAULERS ON THE VOLGA**
1870–1873. Oil on canvas, 4'3¾" × 9'3" (1.3 × 2.81 m). State Russian Museum, St. Petersburg.

to Philadelphia in 1870, he specialized in frank portraits and scenes of everyday life whose lack of conventional charm generated little popular interest. But he was a charismatic teacher, and was soon appointed director of the Pennsylvania Academy.

THE GROSS CLINIC (FIG. 30–21) was one of Eakins's most controversial paintings. Although created specifically for the 1876 Philadelphia centennial show, it was rejected for the fine-art exhibition and relegated to the display area for scientific and medical inquiry. The painting shows Dr. Samuel David Gross performing an operation that he pioneered, as

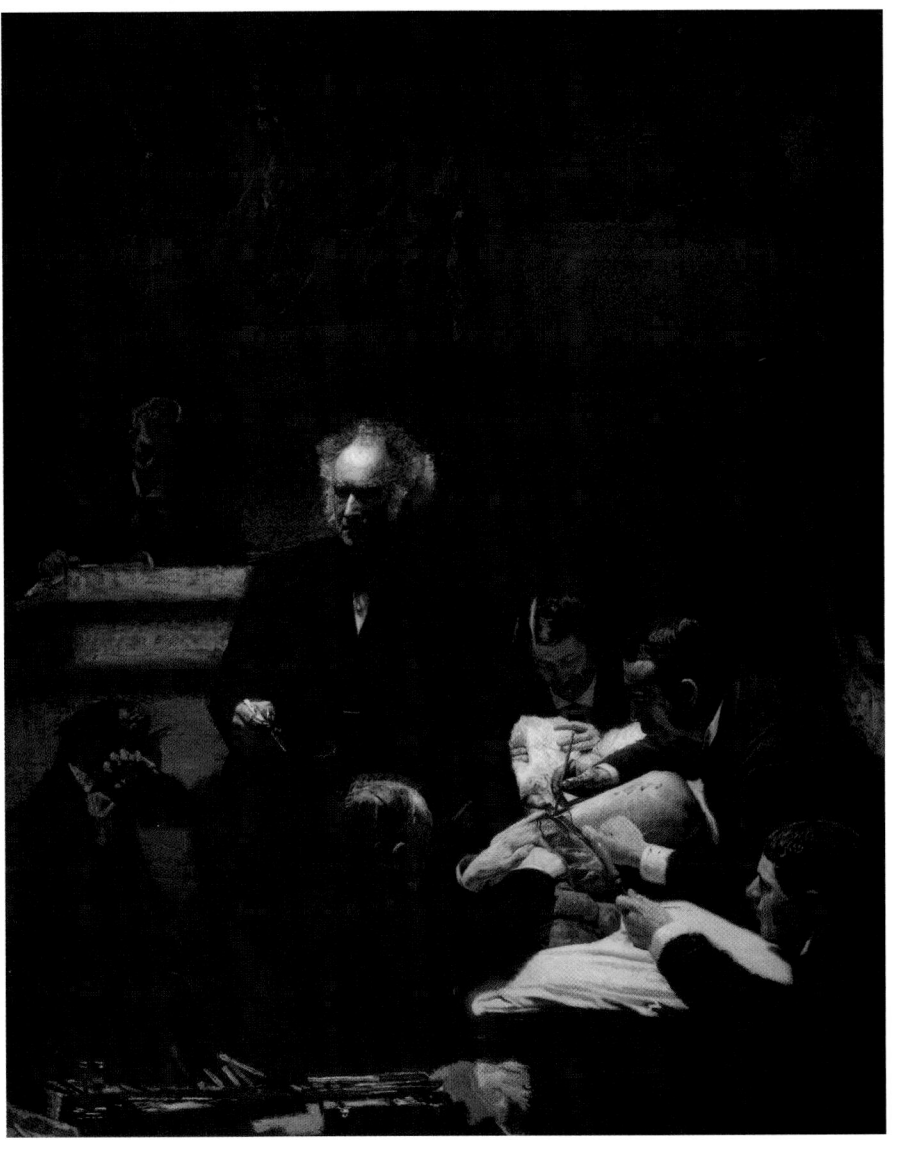

30-21 • Thomas Eakins **THE GROSS CLINIC**
1875. Oil on canvas, 8' × 6'5" (2.44 × 1.98 m). Philadelphia Museum of Art, Pennsylvania.

Eakins, who taught anatomy and figure drawing at the Pennsylvania Academy of the Fine Arts, disapproved of the academic technique of drawing from plaster casts. In 1879, he said, "At best, they are only imitations, and an imitation of an imitation cannot have so much life as an imitation of nature itself." He added, "The Greeks did not study the antique ... the draped figures in the Parthenon pediment were modeled from life, undoubtedly."

30-22 • Winslow Homer THE LIFE LINE
1884. Oil on canvas, 28¾ × 44⅝" (73 × 113.3 cm). Philadelphia Museum of Art, Pennsylvania. The George W. Elkins Collection

In the early sketches for this work, the man's face was visible. The decision to cover it focuses more attention
not only on the victim, but also on the true hero, the mechanical apparatus known as the "breeches buoy."

he pauses to lecture to students taking notes in the background. The figures assisting the surgery are highlighted, but the rest of the operating theater is in deep shadow. Dr. Gross is dressed in street clothes, typical surgical attire before sterile procedure was introduced, and as he pauses he reveals his bloody hand. The stockinged feet of the patient, a young boy, are visible; his mother shields her eyes in horror. In the mid nineteenth century, surgeons were regarded with fear, especially teaching surgeons who frequently thought of the poor as objects on which to practice; for the poor, a visit to the hospital frequently meant death. Eakins captures the sinister aspect of Gross's fearsome skill. But the dramatic light that evokes both Rembrandt and the Spanish Baroque is significant because it illuminates the forehead of the doctor, thus acknowledging the intellect of this brilliant surgeon.

Winslow Homer (1836–1910) also painted with an unadorned realism later in his life. Born in Boston, he began his career as a 21-year-old freelance illustrator for popular periodicals such as *Harper's Weekly*, which sent him to cover the Civil War in 1862. In 1867, after a ten-month sojourn in France, he returned to make painted versions of the nostalgic rural scenes that had figured in his illustrations for magazines. He developed a commitment to depicting the working poor after he spent 1881–1882 in a tiny English fishing village on the rugged North Sea coast. Moved by the hard lives and strength of character of the people there, he turned from idyllic subjects to themes of heroic struggle against natural adversity. In England, he was particularly impressed by the "breeches buoy," a mechanical apparatus used for rescue at sea. During the summer of 1883, he made sketches of one imported by the lifesaving crew in Atlantic City, New Jersey. The following year he painted **THE LIFE LINE** (FIG. 30–22), which depicts a coastguard saving a shipwrecked woman with the use of a breeches buoy—a testament not simply to valor but also to ingenuity.

The sculptor Edmonia Lewis (1845–c. 1911) was born in New York State to a Chippewa mother and an African-American father; she was orphaned at the age of 4, and raised by her mother's family. As a teenager, with the help of abolitionists, she attended Oberlin College, the first college in the United States to grant degrees to women, and then moved to Boston. Her highly successful busts and medallions of abolitionist leaders and Civil War heroes financed her move to Rome in 1867.

Galvanized by the struggle for equality of newly freed slaves, Lewis created **FOREVER FREE** (FIG. 30–23) as a memorial to the Emancipation Proclamation. Although it retains Neoclassical forms, this sculpture addresses a modern issue—the end of slavery in America. The standing African-American man raises his hand with the broken shackles still attached; next to him a woman kneels and prays in thanks. This sculpture not only celebrates emancipation, but also subtly reflects white attitudes towards women and people of color. Lewis creates her female as less racialized and more submissive than her male counterpart so that

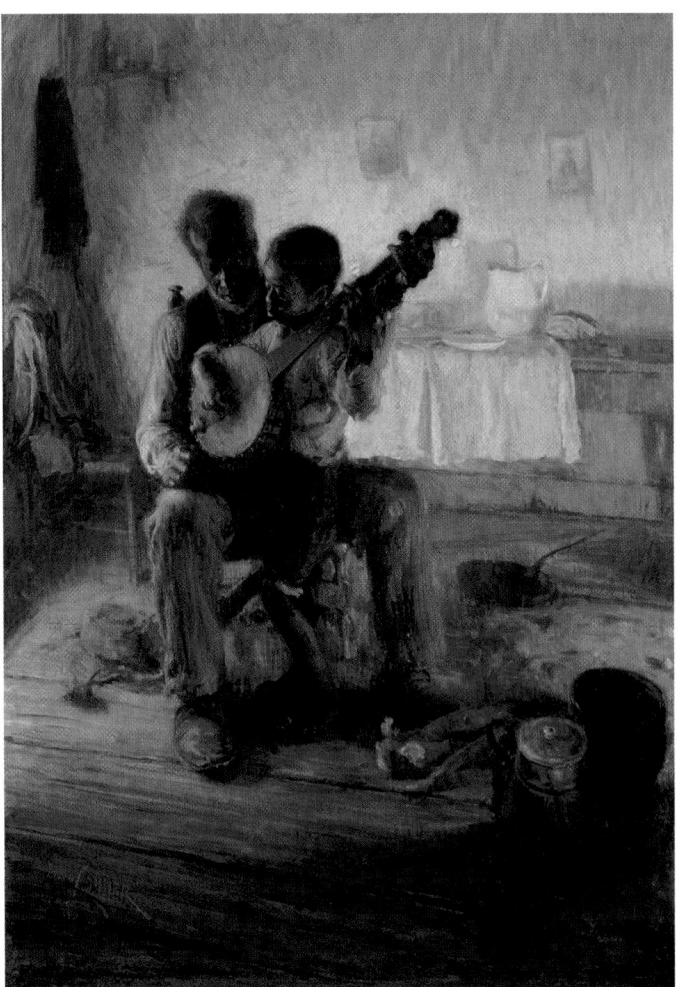

30-24 • Henry Ossawa Tanner THE BANJO LESSON
1893. Oil on canvas, 49 × 35½″ (124.4 × 90 cm). Hampton University Museum, Virginia.

30-23 • Edmonia Lewis FOREVER FREE
1867. Marble, 41¼ × 22 × 17″ (104.8 × 55 × 43.2 cm). Howard University Art Gallery, Washington, D.C.

the figure would better reflect the concept of ideal womanhood and be more appealing to white audiences.

Henry Ossawa Tanner (1859–1937) was the most successful African-American painter of the late nineteenth and early twentieth centuries. The son of a bishop in the African Methodist Episcopal Church, Tanner grew up in Philadelphia, sporadically studied art with Thomas Eakins at the Pennsylvania Academy of the Fine Arts between 1879 and 1885, and then worked as a photographer and drawing teacher in Atlanta. In 1891, he moved to Paris to further his academic training. In the early 1890s, Tanner began making paintings with African-American themes, as he put it, to paint the "serious and pathetic side of life." Tanner's **THE BANJO LESSON** (FIG. 30–24) shows an elderly man teaching a young boy seated on his lap to play the banjo. Both are serious and intent. Their poverty fades as they concentrate together. Mutuality, respect, patience, and attention connect the man and child. Although the banjo player was a common derogatory caricature of African-Americans, Tanner takes up the theme and transforms it into a subject of dignity and pride. He turned to biblical painting after a trip to Palestine in 1897.

IMPRESSIONISM

The generation of French painters maturing around 1870 also painted modern urban subjects, but from a perspective very different from that of Manet and the Realists. These artists painted the upper middle class at leisure in the countryside and in the city, and although several members of this group painted rural scenes, their point of view tended to be that of a city person.

In April 1874, a group of artists, including Paul Cézanne, Edgar Degas, Claude Monet, Berthe Morisot, Camille Pissarro, and Pierre-Auguste Renoir, exhibited together in Paris under the title of the Société Anonyme des Artistes Peintres, Sculpteurs, Graveurs, etc. (Anonymous Corporation of Artist-Painters, Sculptors, Engravers, etc.). Pissarro organized the group along the lines advocated by anarchists such as Proudhon, who urged citizens to band together into self-supporting grass-roots organizations, rather than relying on state-sanctioned institutions. Pissarro envisioned the Société as a mutual aid group for artists who opposed the state-funded Salons. While the Impressionists are the best remembered of its members today, at the time the group included artists working in several styles. All 30 participants agreed not to submit anything that year to the Salon, which had in the past often rejected their work. This exhibition was a declaration of independence from the Académie and a bid to gain the public's attention directly.

While their exhibition received some positive reviews, one critic, Louis Leroy, writing in the satirical journal *Charivari*, seized upon the title of Monet's painting *Impression: Sunrise* (SEE FIG. 30–26), and dubbed the entire exhibition "impressionist." Leroy sought to ridicule the fast, open brushstrokes and unfinished look of some of the paintings, but Monet and his colleagues liked the name and kept it as it aptly described their aim to render the fleeting moment in paint. Seven more Impressionist exhibitions were held between 1876 and 1886, with the membership of the group varying slightly on each occasion; only Pissarro participated in all eight shows. The relative success of these exhibitions prompted other artists to organize their own alternatives to the Salon, and by 1900 the independent exhibition and gallery system had all but replaced the Salon system in Paris. This in turn brought to an end the Académie des Beaux-Arts' control over the display of art and thus centrally determined artistic "standards" effectively ended.

THE LANDSCAPE

Claude Monet (1840–1926) was a leading exponent of Impressionism. Born in Paris but raised in the port city of Le Havre, he trained briefly with an academic teacher but soon established his own studio. His friend Charles-François Daubigny urged him to "be faithful to his impression" and suggested that he create a floating studio on a boat and paint *en plein air* (outdoors). Monet's early works depict a side of modernity that the Realists did not show. Like other Impressionists, he was more interested in creating a modern painting style than in producing biting social commentary, although his thematic focus was also modern life. The Impressionists celebrated the semi-rural pleasures of outings to the suburbs

30–25 • Claude Monet ON THE BANK OF THE SEINE, BENNECOURT
1868. Oil on canvas, 32 × 39⅔″ (81.5 × 100.7 cm). Art Institute of Chicago. Potter Palmer Collection, 1922.427

EXPLORE MORE: Gain insight from a primary source on Claude Monet **www.myartslab.com**

30-26 • Claude Monet **IMPRESSION: SUNRISE**
1872. Oil on canvas, 19 × 24⅜" (48 × 63 cm). Musée Marmottan, Paris.

afforded by the Paris train system. Few early works depict locations far from Paris; most feature the Parisian middle and upper middle classes out walking, boating, and visiting the fashionable new parks in the city or at places just outside of town.

Many of Monet's early works include shimmering expanses of water, such as **ON THE BANK OF THE SEINE, BENNECOURT (FIG. 30–25)**, a scene of a young woman in summer, sitting under trees on a riverbank, a small row boat on the river in front of her. At first we think this is a country scene; on closer inspection, however, we see a landing and several buildings on the far bank, and other boats on the water. It is quite a crowded scene, but the intense brightness of Monet's colors makes the first impression one of pure sunlight. (One critic even complained that the painting made his eyes hurt.) To achieve this effect, Monet dispensed entirely with underpainting as taught by the Académie des Beaux-Arts, instead applying flat expanses of pure color directly onto the canvas, unmixed and straight from the tube. The invention of the collapsible metal paint tube in 1841 led to the manufacture of ready-to-use oil colors that painters could conveniently pack and take with them. No longer confined to grinding colors in a studio,

artists like Monet could now paint anywhere. Eschewing the tedium of the academic program for painting, Monet sought to capture the play of light quickly, before it changed. This was a new, modern landscape. As he said: "The Romantics have had their day."

In the summer of 1870, the Franco-Prussian War broke out and Monet fled to London, where he spent time with Pissarro and his future art dealer, Paul Durand-Ruel. The disastrous loss of the major industrial regions of Alsace and Lorraine to Prussia at the end of the war had an equally disastrous impact on the French economy. In Paris, for two months between March and May 1871, the working classes rose up and established the Commune, a working-class city government, the suppression of which led to an estimated 20,000 dead and 7,500 imprisoned. The horror rocked Paris and made people fearful. Courbet was imprisoned for a short time and, in artists' circles, the fear of being branded as an enemy of the state sent a chill through everyone. After 1871, overt political commentary in French art diminished, and the challenge of the avant-garde was expressed increasingly as a rebellion in style.

In 1873, just after returning to Paris, Monet painted **IMPRESSION: SUNRISE (FIG. 30–26)**, a view of the sun rising in

30–27 • Camille Pissarro WOODED LANDSCAPE AT L'HERMITAGE, PONTOISE
1878. Oil on canvas, 18⅝₁₆ × 22⅟₁₆″ (46.5 × 56 cm). Nelson-Atkins Museum of Art, Kansas City, Missouri. Gift of Dr. and Mrs. Nicholas S. Pickard

the morning fog over the harbor at Le Havre. The painting is rendered almost entirely as color alone. The foreground is eliminated and the horizon line disappears among steamships and docks in the background; forms and atmosphere are shimmering shapes in color. We find our bearings in this painting slowly, but once we do, we "feel" the scene with our eyes. Monet registers the intensity and shifting forms of a first sketch and renders it as the final work of art. The criticism leveled against his paintings was that they were not "finished." The American painter Lilla Cabot Perry, who befriended Monet in his later years, recalled him telling her:

> When you go out to paint, try to forget what objects you have before you—a tree, a house, a field, or whatever. Merely think, Here is a little square of blue, here an oblong of pink,

here a streak of yellow, and paint it just as it looks to you, the exact color and shape, until it gives your own naive impression of the scene before you.

Monet's friend and fellow artist Camille Pissarro (1830–1903) offered a new image of the landscape in a style similar to Monet's. He painted scenes where the urban meets the rural; some of his paintings portray the rural landscape alone, but many show urban visitors to the countryside or small towns or factories embedded in the land as the city encroaches upon them. Born in the Dutch West Indies to French parents and raised near Paris, Pissarro studied art in Paris during the 1850s and early 1860s. In 1870, while he and Monet lived in London, Pissarro embraced the ideas that would later become known as Impressionism. The two artists worked together in England, trying to capture what Pissarro described as "plein air light and fugitive effects." The impact on both painters was a lightening of color intensity and hue, and a loosening of brushstroke.

Following his return to France, Pissarro settled in Pontoise, a small, hilly village northwest of Paris where he worked for most of the 1870s in an Impressionist style, using high-keyed color and short brushstrokes to capture fleeting qualities of light and atmosphere. In the late 1870s, his painting became more visually complex and the colors darkened again. His **WOODED LANDSCAPE AT L'HERMITAGE, PONTOISE** (**FIG. 30–27**), for instance, has a foreground composition of trees that screens the view of a rural path and village behind, flattening space and even partly masking the figure at the lower right. Pissarro applies his paint thickly here, with a multitude of short, multi-directional brushstrokes.

THE FIGURE

In contrast, the Impressionist painter Pierre-Auguste Renoir (1841–1919) focused most of his attention on figure painting, producing mostly images of the upper middle class at leisure. When he met Monet at the École des Beaux-Arts in 1862, he was in fact working as a figure painter. Monet encouraged him to lighten his palette and to paint outdoors, and by the mid 1870s Renoir was combining a spontaneous handling of natural light with animated figural compositions. In his **MOULIN DE LA GALETTE** (**FIG. 30–28**), for example, Renoir depicts crowds dancing in dappled sunlight that falls through the trees. The Moulin de la Galette (the "Pancake Mill"), in the Montmartre section of Paris, was an old-fashioned Sunday afternoon dance hall, which opened its outdoor courtyard during good weather. In this painting, Renoir has glamorized the working-class clientele of the dance hall by placing his artist friends and their models in their midst. These attractive people are shown in attitudes of relaxed congeniality, smiling, dancing, and chatting. He underscores the innocence of their flirtations by including children in the painting in the lower left, while emphasizing the ease of their relations through the relaxed informality of the scene. The overall mood is knit together by sunlight falling through the

30-28 • Pierre-Auguste Renoir **MOULIN DE LA GALETTE**
1876. Oil on canvas, 4′3½″ × 5′9″ (1.31 × 1.75 m). Musée d'Orsay, Paris.

30–29 • Mary Cassatt MOTHER AND CHILD
c. 1890. Oil on canvas, 35½ × 25⅜" (90.2 × 64.5 cm). Wichita Art Museum, Kansas.

academic training, eventually settling in France. The realism of the figure paintings she exhibited at the Salons of the early and mid 1870s attracted the attention of Degas, who invited her to participate in the fourth Impressionist exhibition in 1879. Although she, like Degas, remained a studio painter and printmaker, her distaste for what she called the "tyranny" of the Salon jury system made her one of the group's staunchest supporters.

Cassatt focused her artistic career on the world she knew best: the domestic and social life of upper-middle-class women. Around 1890 she painted **MOTHER AND CHILD (FIG. 30–29)**, one of many representations of the theme in her career. The painting shows the intimate contact between a mother and child after a bath and just before the child falls asleep. The drowsy face and flushed cheeks of the child and the weight of its limbs have a natural quality to them, even though the space occupied by the figures seems flattened. The solidly modeled forms of the hands and faces contrast with the strong, broad, and unfinished quality of the brushstrokes of the lower part of the mother's dress and the background. Cassatt elevates this small vignette of modern life into a homage to motherhood. Though she lived as an expatriate, Cassatt retained her connections in the United States, and when her friends and relatives came to visit she encouraged them to buy art by the Impressionists, thus creating a market for their work in the United States even before one developed in France.

The French artist Berthe Morisot (1841–1895) also defied societal conventions to become a professional painter, and her work also took as its main subject the female figure. Morisot and her sister, Edma, copied paintings in the Louvre and studied with several teachers, including Corot, in the late 1850s and early 1860s. The sisters exhibited their art in the five Salons between 1864 and 1868, the year they met Manet. In 1869, Edma married and gave up painting to devote herself to domestic duties, but Berthe continued painting, even after her 1874 marriage to Manet's brother, Eugène, and the birth of their daughter in 1879. Morisot sent nine paintings to the first exhibition of the Impressionists in 1874 and showed her work in all but one of their subsequent shows.

As a respectable bourgeois lady, Berthe Morisot was not free to prowl the city looking for modern subjects, and, like Cassatt's,

trees and Renoir's soft brushwork weaving blues and purples through the crowd and around the canvas. This idyllic image of a carefree time and place encapsulates Renoir's idea of the essence of art: "For me a picture should be a pleasant thing, joyful and pretty—yes pretty! There are quite enough unpleasant things in life without the need for us to manufacture more."

The American expatriate Mary Cassatt (1844–1926; SEE FIG. 30–32) also exhibited her work with the Impressionists and, like Renoir, became highly skilled in compositions that focused on the figure. Born near Pittsburgh to a well-to-do family, she studied at the Pennsylvania Academy of the Fine Arts in Philadelphia between 1861 and 1865, and then moved to Paris for further

30-30 • Berthe Morisot SUMMER'S DAY
1879. Oil on canvas, 17¹³⁄₁₆ × 29⁵⁄₁₆″ (45.7 × 75.2 cm). National Gallery, London. Lane Bequest, 1917

her painting was confined to depictions of women's lives, a subject she knew well. In the 1870s, she painted in an increasingly fluid and painterly style, flattening her picture plane and making her brushwork more visible. In her oil painting **SUMMER'S DAY (FIG. 30–30)**, Morisot shows two elegant young ladies on a pleasant outing on the lake of the fashionable Bois du Boulogne. Unlike the figures in Manet's *Boating* (SEE FIG. 30–19), Morisot's women are properly accompanied by each other, and their ferry is steered by an unseen boatman who is at their behest. First exhibited in the fifth Impressionist exhibition in 1880, *Summer's Day* explores the formal side of Impressionism: Its brushstrokes and colors are skillfully handled. While Morisot was unable to comment on modern city life in ways her brother-in-law might, she nevertheless painted intensely modern pictures.

MODERN LIFE

Subjects of urban work and leisure also attracted Edgar Degas (1834–1917), although his vision is closer to Realism in its social commentary. Instead of painting out of doors, Degas composed his pictures in the studio from working drawings and photographs. He received rigorous academic training at the École des Beaux-Arts in the mid 1850s and subsequently spent three years in Italy studying the Old Masters. Assured compositional structure and intensity of line were hallmarks of his art throughout his career.

The son of a Parisian banker, Degas's painting themes and style were closer to Manet's than to the Impressionists'. In the 1870s, he began painting the modern life of the city: the racetrack, the music hall, and the opera, often focusing on those working to provide the entertainment rather than on their audience. He became the painter of the Paris ballet in the 1870s and 1880s at a time when it was in decline. Degas did not draw or paint actual dancers in rehearsal; rather, he hired dancers, often very young "ballet rats," to come to his studio to pose for him. His ballet paintings and pastels contain acerbic social commentary. **THE REHEARSAL ON STAGE (FIG. 30–31)**, for example, is a contrived scene, not an actual event. Many dancers' poses are uncharacteristic of the actual ballet but are included to show how the life of a dancer is tiresome, involving tedious hours of work. In this pastel, several young dancers look bored or exhausted, and to the far right sit two gentleman visitors who, the artist may be suggesting, pay to see the girls practice. The composition is set in a raked space, as if viewed from a box close to the stage. The abrupt foreshortening is emphasized by the dark scrolls of the double basses that jut up from the lower left. The angular viewpoint may derive from Japanese prints, which Degas collected, while the cropping of figures on the left suggests photography, which he also practiced. The Realist novelist Edmond de Goncourt (1822–1896), a friend of Degas, described him as capturing "the soul of modern life."

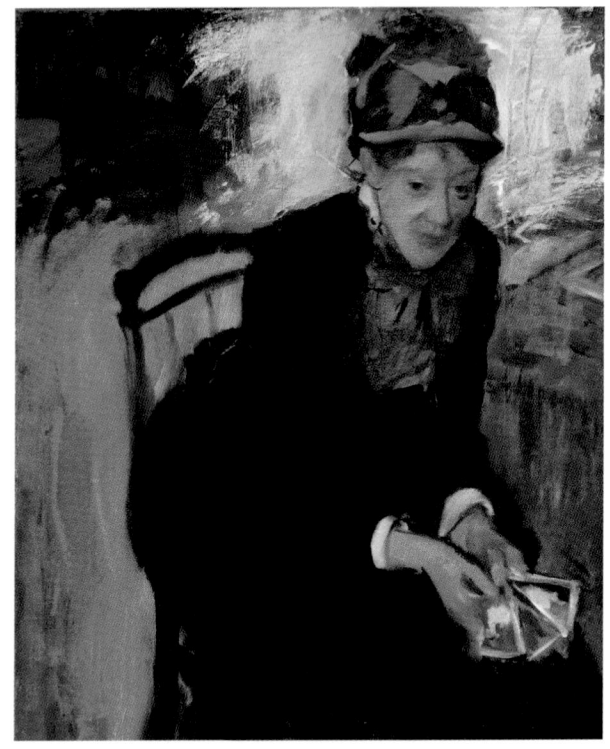

30–31 • Edgar Degas THE REHEARSAL ON STAGE
c. 1874. Pastel over brush-and-ink drawing on thin, cream-colored
wove paper, laid on bristol board, mounted on canvas, 21⅜ × 28¾"
(54.3 × 73 cm). Metropolitan Museum of Art, New York. Bequest of Mrs.
H. O. Havemeyer Collection, Gift of Horace Havemeyer, 1929 (29.160.26)

In the right background of Degas's picture sit two well-dressed,
middle-aged men, who enjoy their intimacy with the dancers at
informal rehearsal. Because ballerinas generally came from lower-
class families and exhibited their scantily clad bodies in public—
something prohibited for "respectable" bourgeois women—they were
widely assumed to be sexually available, and they often attracted the
attentions of wealthy men willing to support them in exchange for
sexual favors. Thus several of Degas's ballet pictures also include
one or more of the dancers' mothers, who would accompany their
daughters to rehearsals and performances in order to safeguard
their virtue.

30–32 • Edgar Degas PORTRAIT OF MARY CASSATT
1880–1884. Oil on canvas, 28⅛ × 23⅛" (71.4 × 58.7 cm). National
Portrait Gallery, Smithsonian Institution, Washington, D.C.

30–33 • Gustave Caillebotte PARIS STREET, RAINY DAY
1877. Oil on canvas, 83½ × 108¾″ (212.2 × 276.2 cm). Art Institute of Chicago. Part of the Charles H. and Mary F. S. Worcester Fund

Degas's **PORTRAIT OF MARY CASSATT (FIG. 30–32)** is very different from his ballet pictures. It shows Cassatt as an uncharacteristically strong, intense, and intelligent woman for her time. She leans forward in her chair as if to engage the viewer in conversation in the midst of playing cards. Cassatt carved out a career for herself painting in a radical style and earned the respect of artists like Degas at a time when such professionalism in women was frowned upon. In this portrait Degas shows Cassatt's sharp intellect, something he rarely revealed in other paintings of women.

Gustave Caillebotte (1848–1894), another friend of Degas, was involved in organizing several Impressionist exhibitions; he also purchased the work of his friends, amassing a large collection of paintings. He studied with an academic teacher privately and qualified for the École des Beaux-Arts, but never attended. Caillebotte was fascinated by the streets of Paris, especially Haussmann's modernized street plan, and his subjects and compositions

characteristically represent modern life. His **PARIS STREET, RAINY DAY (FIG. 30–33)** has an unconventional, almost telescopic composition that tilts the perspective. The street itself seems to be the subject of this painting; the people are huddled under umbrellas or pushed to the sides of the composition. The figure to the far right is even cropped in half, as in a photograph, and the couple strolling toward us are squeezed between him and the lamppost.

LATE NINETEENTH-CENTURY ART AND THE BEGINNINGS OF MODERNISM

The Realists and Impressionists continued to contribute to avant-garde art until the late nineteenth century, but by the mid 1880s they had relinquished their dominance to a younger generation of artists. The period after Impressionism seems less unified and less directed, involving artists from several different nations taking art in many new visual directions. This generation of artists increasingly defined avant-garde art in terms of visual experimentation, working to develop the precise manner of painting appropriate to their message. Some reinterpreted art as an expression of an interior world of the imagination, while others reconstructed the world around them in paint using new visual languages.

These artists included French Post-Impressionists, who explored inner ways of expressing the outer world, sometimes escaping from the city to the countryside or even to far-flung places; late nineteenth-century French sculptors, who studied the passionate physicality of the human form; British artists, inspired by medieval history in both painting and design; Symbolist artists, who retreated into fantastical and sometimes horrifying worlds of the imagination; Art Nouveau artists, who rejected the rational order of the industrial world to create images and designs ruled by the writhing, moving asymmetrical shapes of growing plants; and even landscape designers, who recast the urban cityscape into a rambling natural landscape.

At the end of the century and late in his life, Paul Cézanne (see pages 1007–1009) altered this course by returning to an intense visual study of the world around him, scrutinizing it like a specimen on a dissecting table and urging younger artists to consider new ways of creating meaning in painting. In 1906, the year Cézanne died, a retrospective exhibition of his life's work in Paris revealed his methods to the next generation of artists, the creators of Modernism.

POST-IMPRESSIONISM

The English critic Roger Fry coined the term "Post-Impressionism" in 1910 to describe a diverse group of painters whose work he had collected for an exhibition. He acknowledged that these artists did not share a unified style or approach to art, but they all used Impressionism as a springboard for their individual expressions of modernity in art.

SEURAT. Georges Seurat (1859–1891) was born in Paris and trained at the École des Beaux-Arts. He was dedicated to the clarity of structure that he found in Classical relief sculpture, and to

30-34 • Georges Seurat A SUNDAY AFTERNOON ON THE ISLAND OF LA GRANDE JATTE
1884–1886. Oil on canvas, 6'9½" × 10'1¼" (207 × 308 cm). Art Institute of Chicago. Helen Birch Bartlett Memorial Collection

the seemingly systematic but actually quite emotive use of color suggested by optics and color theory. He was particularly interested in the "law of the simultaneous contrast of colors" formulated by Michel-Eugène Chevreul in the 1820s. Chevreul observed that adjacent objects not only cast reflections of their own color onto their neighbors, but also create in them the effect of their **complementary color**. Thus, when a blue object is set next to a yellow one, the eye will detect in the blue object a trace of purple, the complement of yellow, and in the yellow object a trace of orange, the complement of blue.

Seurat explored how color hues and tones adjacent to one another create this visual effect of a third color. He studied carefully which hues could be combined, and in what proportions, to produce the effect of a particular color. His goal was to find ways to create retinal vibrations that enlivened the painted surface. He painted in distinctive short, multi-directional strokes of almost pure color, in what came to be known by the various names of "Divisionism" (the term preferred by Seurat), "Pointillism," and "Neo-Impressionism." In theory, these juxtaposed small strokes of color would merge in the viewer's eye to produce the impression of other colors. When perceived from a certain distance they would appear more luminous and intense than the same colors seen separately, while on close observation Seurat's strokes and colors would remain distinct and separate, creating an almost abstract arrangement of color and shape.

Seurat's monumental painting **A SUNDAY AFTERNOON ON THE ISLAND OF LA GRANDE JATTE (FIG. 30–34)** was first exhibited at the eighth and final Impressionist exhibition in 1886. He presented this large canvas as a "demonstration" piece to prove his worth as an artist and to advertise his smaller works. The painting contained 11 colors, with the purest hue of each that he could find. He laid these out in a single row on his palette, while creating a second, upper row of the same colors mixed with white and a third lower row mixed with black. He painted the entire canvas using this range of colors. When viewed from a distance of about 9 feet, the painting reads as figures in a park rendered in many colors and tones; but when viewed from a distance of 3 feet, the individual marks of color become more distinct and the forms begin to dissolve into abstraction.

The painting represents a sunny Sunday afternoon, the newly designated official day off for French working families to spend time together. The park, on the island of the Grande Jatte, just west of Paris, was accessible by train. There was a social hierarchy in Parisian parks in the late nineteenth century; the Bois du Boulogne (SEE FIG. 30–30) was an upper-middle-class park in an area of grand avenues, whereas the Grande Jatte faced a lower-class industrial area across the river. The figures represent a range of lower-middle-class "types" that would have been easily recognizable to the nineteenth-century viewer, such as the strolling man and his companion to the right, usually identified as a *boulevardier* (or citified dandy) and a *cocotte* (a single woman of the demi-monde), or the *canotier* (working-class oarsman) to the left.

VAN GOGH. Among the artists to experiment with Divisionism, Impressionism and modernity was the Dutch painter Vincent van Gogh (1853–1890), who transformed his artistic sources into a highly expressive personal style. The oldest son of a Protestant minister, Van Gogh worked as an art dealer, a teacher, and an evangelist before deciding in 1880 to become an artist. After brief periods of study in Brussels, The Hague, and Antwerp, in 1886 he moved to Paris, where he discovered the Parisian avant-garde. Van Gogh adapted Seurat's Divisionism, for instance, by applying brilliantly colored paint in multi-directional strokes of **impasto** (thick applications of paint) to give his pictures a turbulent emotional energy and a palpable surface texture.

Van Gogh was a socialist who believed that modern life, with its constant social change and focus on progress and success, alienated people from one other and from themselves (see "Modern Artists and World Cultures: Japonisme," pages 994–995). His own paintings are efforts to communicate his emotional state and establish a connection between artist and viewer, thereby overcoming the emotional barrenness that he felt modern society created. In a prolific output over only ten years, he produced paintings that would contribute significantly to the later emergence of Expressionism, in which the artist's emotional intensity overrides fidelity to the actual appearance of things. Van Gogh described his working method in a letter to his brother:

> I should like to paint the portrait of an artist friend who dreams great dreams, who works as the nightingale sings, because it is his nature. This man will be fair-haired. I should like to put my appreciation, the love I have for him, into the picture. So I will paint him as he is, as faithfully as I can— to begin with. But that is not the end of the picture. To finish it, I shall be an obstinate colorist. I shall exaggerate the fairness of the hair, arrive at tones of orange, chrome, pale yellow. Behind the head—instead of painting the ordinary wall of the shabby apartment, I shall paint infinity, I shall do a simple background of the richest, most intense blue that I can contrive, and by this simple combination, the shining fair head against this rich blue background, I shall obtain a mysterious effect, like a star in the deep blue sky.

One of the most famous examples of this approach is **THE STARRY NIGHT (FIG. 30–35)**, painted from careful observation and the artist's imagination. Above the quiet town, the sky pulsates with celestial rhythms and blazes with exploding stars. Contemplating life and death in a letter, Van Gogh wrote: "Just as we take the train to get to Tarascon or Rouen, we take death to reach a star." This idea is rendered visible in this painting by the cypress tree, a traditional symbol of both death and eternal life, which rises dramatically to link the terrestrial and celestial realms. The brightest star in the sky is actually a planet, Venus, which is associated with love. It is possible that the picture's extraordinary energy also expresses Van Gogh's euphoric hope of gaining in death the love that had eluded him in life. The painting is a riot of

Modern Artists and World Cultures: Japonisme

In 1887, Vincent van Gogh painted *Japonaiserie: Flowering Plum Tree*. He was deeply affected by recently imported examples of Japanese art and prints, which he appreciated for their "exotic" visual effects. Japan was opened to Western trade and diplomacy in 1853, after a lengthy isolation, and in 1855 trade agreements permitted the regular exchange of goods with Japan. Among the first Japanese art objects to come to Paris was a sketchbook entitled *Manga* by Hokusai (1760–1849), which was eagerly passed around by Parisian artists. Several of them began to collect Japanese objects; the 1867 Paris International Exposition mounted the first show of Japanese prints in Europe; and immediately thereafter, Japanese lacquers, fans, bronzes, hanging scrolls, kimonos, ceramics, illustrated books, and **ukiyo-e** (prints of the "floating world," the realm of geishas and popular entertainment) began to appear for sale in specialty shops, art galleries, and even some department stores in Paris. The French obsession with Japan reached such a level by 1872 that the art critic Philippe Burty named the phenomenon **Japonisme**.

Vincent van Gogh admired the design and handcrafted quality of Japanese prints, which he both owned and copied. His *Japonaiserie: Flowering Plum Tree* is largely copied from Hiroshige's woodblock print *Plum Orchard, Kameido*. Van Gogh makes use of the same flattened tree with its asymmetrical branches, thin, shooting twigs, and tiny blossoms in his foreground; the same smaller trees in the middle ground; and the same railing in the background, behind which can be seen several figures and a small hut. Van Gogh has also appropriated Hiroshige's color scheme and flattened picture plane, as well as his banners of text. But he also made significant changes in his adaptation. He flattened the scene more extremely than Hiroshige had done. His grass is a uniform blanket of

green, the flat gray trees with hard black outlines are flat and undifferentiated, and it is not clear whether the yellow blossoms are in front of or behind the thickly painted red sky. Indeed, Hiroshige's print suggests greater spatial depth than Van Gogh's imitation. Van Gogh also frames his painting with a bold, rather crudely painted orange frame with pseudo-Japanese characters scrawled around it, as if to accentuate the

"primitiveness" of the image and its source. Van Gogh knew little about Japanese culture and less about the Japanese painting or printmaking tradition. He uses the Hiroshige print as a prompt in order to conjure up what he saw as a simpler, more "primitive" culture than his own, at a time when other artists, such as Paul Gauguin traveled the world in search of "primitive" cultures to inspire their art.

Hiroshige **PLUM ORCHARD, KAMEIDO**

1857. From *One Hundred Famous Views of Edo*. Woodblock print, 13¼ × 8⅝" (33.6 × 47 cm). Brooklyn Museum, New York.

Vincent van Gogh JAPONAISERIE: FLOWERING PLUM TREE
1887. Oil on canvas, 21½ × 18″ (54.6 × 45.7 cm). Vincent van Gogh Museum, Amsterdam.

30-35 • Vincent van Gogh THE STARRY NIGHT
1889. Oil on canvas, 28¾ × 36¼″ (73 × 93 cm). Museum of Modern Art, New York.
Acquired through the Lillie P. Bliss Bequest (472.1941)

brushwork, as rail-like strokes of intense color writhe across its surface. Van Gogh's brushwork is immediate, expressive, and intense. During the last year and a half of his life, he experienced repeated psychological crises that lasted for days or weeks. While they were raging, he wanted to hurt himself, heard loud noises in his head, and could not paint. The stress and burden of these attacks led him to the asylum where he painted *The Starry Night*, and eventually to suicide in July 1890.

GAUGUIN.   In painting from imagination as much as from nature in *The Starry Night*, Van Gogh may have been following the advice of his friend Paul Gauguin (1848–1903), who once counseled another artist: "Don't paint from nature too much. Art is an abstraction. Derive this abstraction from nature while dreaming before it, and think more of the creation that will result." Gauguin's

art abstracts from nature like Van Gogh's, and it laid foundations for even more abstracted art in the twentieth century. Born in Paris to a Peruvian mother and a radical French journalist father, Gauguin lived in Peru until age 7. During the 1870s and early 1880s, he enjoyed a comfortable bourgeois life as a stockbroker, painting in his spare time under the tutelage of Pissarro. Between 1880 and 1886, he exhibited in the final four Impressionist exhibitions. In 1883, he lost his job during a stock market crash; three years later he abandoned his wife and five children to pursue a full-time painting career. Gauguin knew firsthand the business culture of his time and came to despise it, writing disparagingly to a friend of "the European struggle for money." Believing that escape to a more "primitive" place would bring with it the simpler pleasures of life, Gauguin lived for extended periods in the French province of Brittany between 1886 and

30–36 • Paul Gauguin MANAO TUPAPAU (SPIRIT OF THE DEAD WATCHING)
1892. Oil on burlap mounted on canvas, 28⅝ × 36⅜″ (73 × 92 cm). Collection Albright-Knox Art Gallery, Buffalo, NY.
A. Conger Goodyear Collection, 1965.

EXPLORE MORE: Gain insight from a primary source on Paul Gauguin **www.myartslab.com**

1891, traveled to Panama and Martinique in 1887, spent two months in Arles with Van Gogh in 1888, and then in 1891 sailed for Tahiti, a French colony in the South Pacific. After a final sojourn in France in 1893–1895, Gauguin returned to the Pacific, where he died in 1903.

Gauguin's art was inspired by sources as varied as medieval stained glass, folk art, and Japanese prints; he sought to paint in a "primitive" way employing the so-called "decorative" qualities of folk art such as brilliantly colored flat shapes, an anti-naturalist use of color, and thick, black outlines to feign "primitiveness." Gauguin called his style "synthetism," because he believed it synthesized observation and the artist's feelings about a subject in an abstracted application of line, shape, space, and color.

MANAO TUPAPAU (THE SPIRIT OF THE DEAD KEEP WATCH) (FIG. 30–36) portrays a thickly outlined, androgynous nude figure lying prone on a bed, close to sleep. In the background the spirit of the dead watches over the figure. Gauguin implicitly suggests that this painting represents a scene from Tahitian religion, but there is no evidence that this is the case. The painting is not intended to be naturalistic or realistic, evoking a mood rather than representing a specific scene. Like many of Gauguin's works, this painting shows the late nineteenth-century desire to "get away" from the oppressive life of the city, and to get back to so-called "primitive" versions of culture.

LATE NINETEENTH-CENTURY ART IN BRITAIN

In the 1840s, Britain also encountered social and political upheaval. The depression of the "hungry forties," the Irish Potato Famine, and the Chartist Riots threatened social stability in England. Artists in Britain at mid century painted scenes of religious, medieval, or moral exemplars using a tight realistic style that was quite different from French Realism.

ROSSETTI AND THE PRE-RAPHAELITES. In 1848, seven young London artists formed the Pre-Raphaelite Brotherhood in response to what they considered the misguided practices of contemporary British art. Instead of the "Raphaelesque" conventions taught at the Royal Academy, the Pre-Raphaelites looked back to the Middle Ages and early Renaissance (before Raphael) for a beauty and spirituality that they found lacking in their own time. The Pre-Raphaelites invoked what they imagined was the more moralistic and "real" art of this earlier time.

Dante Gabriel Rossetti (1828–1882) was a leading member and spokesperson of the Pre-Raphaelite Brotherhood, although his art grew increasingly visionary in later years. His painting **LA PIA DE' TOLOMEI** (FIG. 30–37) illustrates a scene from Dante's

30-38 • FOREGROUND: Philip Webb **SINGLE CHAIR FROM THE SUSSEX RANGE**
In production from c. 1865. Ebonized wood with rush seat, 33 × 16½ × 14" (83.8 × 42 × 35.6 cm).

BACKGROUND: William Morris **"PEACOCK AND DRAGON" CURTAIN**
1878. Handloomed jacquard-woven woolen twill, 12'10½" × 11'5⅝" (3.96 × 3.53 m). Chair and curtain manufactured by Morris & Company. The William Morris Gallery, London Borough of Waltham Forest.

Art on Trial in 1877

This is a partial transcript of Whistler's testimony at the libel trial that he initiated against the art critic John Ruskin. Whistler's responses often provoked laughter, and the judge at one point threatened to clear the courtroom.

Q: What is your definition of a Nocturne?

A: I have, perhaps, meant rather to indicate an artistic interest alone in the work, divesting the picture from any outside sort of interest which might have been otherwise attached to it. It is an arrangement of line, form, and color first ... The *Nocturne in Black and Gold* [SEE FIG. 30–39] is a night piece, and represents the fireworks at Cremorne.

Q: Not a view of Cremorne?

A: If it were called a view of Cremorne, it would certainly bring about nothing but disappointment on the part of beholders. It is an artistic arrangement. It was marked 200 guineas ...

Q: I suppose you are willing to admit that your pictures exhibit some eccentricities; you have been told that over and over again?

A: Yes, very often.

Q: You send them to the gallery to invite the admiration of the public?

A: That would be such a vast absurdity on my part that I don't think I could.

Q: Did it take you much time to paint the *Nocturne in Black and Gold*? How soon did you knock it off?

A: I knocked it off in possibly a couple of days; one day to do the work, and another to finish it.

Q: And that was the labor for which you asked 200 guineas?

A: No, it was for the knowledge gained through a lifetime.

The judge ruled in Whistler's favor; Ruskin had indeed libeled him. But he awarded Whistler damages of only one farthing. Since in those days the person who brought the suit had to pay all the court costs, the case ended up bankrupting the artist.

Purgatory in which La Pia (the Pious One), wrongly accused of infidelity and locked up by her husband, is dying. The rosary and prayer book at her side refer to her piety, while the sundial and ravens suggest the passage of time and her impending death. La Pia's continuing love for her husband is represented by his letters, which lie under her prayer book. The luxuriant fig leaves that surround her are traditionally associated with shame, and they seem to suck her into themselves. They have no source in Dante, but are relevant to Rossetti: Jane Burden, his model for this and many other paintings as well as his lover, was the wife of his friend William Morris. La Pia twists at her wedding ring in the painting. It is hard to believe that this painting about La Pia's imprisonment for adultery is not also about Rossetti and Jane Burden.

MORRIS AND THE ARTS AND CRAFTS MOVEMENT. Other British artists drew inspiration from the medieval past as a panacea for modern life in London. William Morris (1834–1896) worked briefly as a painter under the influence of the Pre-Raphaelites before turning his attention to interior design and decoration. Morris's interest in crafts developed in the context of a widespread reaction against the shoddy design of industrially produced goods. Unable to find satisfactory furnishings for his new home after his marriage in 1859, Morris designed and constructed them himself, with the help of friends, later founding a decorating firm to produce a full range of medieval-inspired objects. Although many of the furnishings offered by Morris & Company were expensive, one-of-a-kind items, others, such as the rush-seated chair illustrated here (FIG. 30–38), were inexpensive and simple,

intended as a handcrafted alternative to machine-made furniture. Concerned with creating a "total" environment, Morris and his colleagues designed not only furniture but also stained glass, tiles, wallpaper, and fabrics, such as the "Peacock and Dragon" curtain seen in the background of FIGURE 30–38.

Morris inspired what became known as the Arts and Crafts Movement. He rebelled against the idea that art was a highly specialized product made for a small elite, and he hoped to usher in a new era of art for the people. He said in lectures: "I do not want art for a few, any more than education for a few, or freedom for a few." A socialist, Morris opposed mass production and the deadening impact of factory life on the industrial worker. He argued that when laborers made handcrafted objects, they had the satisfaction of being involved in the entire process of creation and thus produced honest and beautiful things. He was inspired by the romance of the medieval craft tradition, ignoring its harsh realities.

WHISTLER. The American expatriate James Abbott McNeill Whistler (1834–1903) also focused his attention on the rooms and walls where art was hung, but he did so more to satisfy elitist tastes for beauty for its own sake. He also became embroiled in several artistic controversies that laid the groundwork for the art of the next century. After flunking out of West Point in the early 1850s, Whistler studied art in Paris, where he was briefly influenced by Courbet's Realism; the two artists painted several seascapes together. He settled in London in 1859, after which his art began to take on a more "decorative" quality that he called "aesthetic"

30-39 • James Abbott McNeill Whistler **NOCTURNE IN BLACK AND GOLD, THE FALLING ROCKET**
1875. Oil on panel, 23¾ × 18⅜″ (60.2 × 46.7 cm). Detroit Institute of Arts, Detroit, Michigan. 46.309

EXPLORE MORE: Gain insight from a primary source about James Abbott McNeill Whistler's *Nocturne in Black and Gold, The Falling Rocket*
www.myartslab.com

and which increasingly diverged from observed reality. He believed that the arrangement of a room (or a painting) could be aesthetically pleasing in itself, without reference to the outside world. He was among the first artists to hang art in a single horizontal row on a wall, rather than "stacked" in Salon style. He even occasionally designed exhibition rooms for his art, with the aim of creating a total harmony of objects and space.

Whistler's ideas about art were revolutionary. He was among the first artists to conceive of his paintings as abstractions from rather than representations of observed reality, and he was among the first to collect Japanese art, fascinated by its "decorative" (see page 997) line, color, and shape, although he understood little about its meaning or intent. By the middle of the 1860s, Whistler began to

entitle his works "Symphonies" and "Arrangements," suggesting that their themes resided in their compositions rather than their subject matter. He painted several landscapes with the musical title "Nocturne," and when he exhibited some of these in 1877, he drew the scorn of England's leading art critic, John Ruskin (1819–1900), a supporter of the Pre-Raphaelites and their moralistic intentions. Decrying Whistler's work as carelessly lacking in finish and purpose, Ruskin's review asked how an artist could "demand 200 guineas for flinging a pot of paint in the public's face."

The most controversial painting in Whistler's 1877 exhibition was **NOCTURNE IN BLACK AND GOLD, THE FALLING ROCKET (FIG. 30–39)**, and Ruskin's objections to it precipitated one of the most notorious court dramas in art history. Painted in restricted tonalities, at first glance the work appears completely abstract. In fact, the painting is a night scene depicting a fireworks show over a lake at Cremorne Gardens in London, with viewers vaguely discernible along the lake's edge in the foreground. The term "Nocturne" was taken from the titles of piano compositions by the Romantic composer Frederic Chopin: Whistler wanted to evoke an association between the abstract qualities of art and music. After reading Ruskin's review, Whistler sued the critic for libel (see "Art on Trial in 1877," page 999). He deliberately turned the courtroom into a public forum in which both to defend and advertise his art. On the witness stand, he defended his view that art has no higher purpose than creating visual delight, claiming that paintings need not have a subject matter. While Whistler never made a completely abstract painting, his theories were integral to the development of abstract art in the next century.

SYMBOLISM

The move toward abstraction can also be seen in Symbolism, an international movement in art and literature that comprised a loose affiliation of artists making works addressing the irrational fears, desires, and impulses of the human mind. A fascination with the dark recesses of the mind emerged over the last decades of the nineteenth century, encompassing photographic and scientific examinations of the nature of insanity, as well as a popular interest in the spirit world of mediums. Some Symbolist artists sought escape from modern life in irrational worlds of unrestrained emotion as described by authors such as Edgar Allan Poe (1809–1849), whose terrifying stories of the supernatural were popular across Europe. It is not coincidental that Sigmund Freud (1856–1939), who compared artistic creation to the process of dreaming, wrote his pioneering *The Interpretation of Dreams* (1900) during this period.

The Symbolists rejected the values of rationalism and material progress that dominated modern Western culture, choosing instead to explore the nonmaterial realms of emotion, imagination, and spirituality. Ultimately the Symbolists sought a deeper and more mysterious reality than the one encountered in everyday life, which they conveyed through strange and ambiguous subject matter and stylized forms that suggest hidden and elusive meanings. They transformed appearances in order to give pictorial form to psychic experience, and they often compared their works to dreams.

Symbolism in painting closely paralleled a similar movement among poets and writers who also abjured materialism and who retreated into fantasy worlds conjured from their imaginations. For example, Joris-Karl Huysmans's novel *À Rebours* (*Against the Grain*), published in 1884, has a single character, an aristocrat named Des Esseintes, who locked himself away from the world

because "Imagination could easily be substituted for the vulgar realities of things." Claiming that nature was irrelevant, Des Esseintes mused: "Nature has had her day" and "wearied aesthetes" should take refuge in artworks "steeped in ancient dreams or antique corruptions, far removed from the manner of our present day."

MOREAU. A visionlike atmosphere pervades the later work of Gustave Moreau (1826–1898), an older academic artist whom the Symbolists regarded as a precursor. The Symbolists particularly admired Moreau's renditions of the biblical Salome, the young Judaean princess who, at the instigation of her mother, Herodias, performed an erotic dance before her stepfather, Herod, and demanded as reward the head of John the Baptist (Mark 6:21–28). In **THE APPARITION** (FIG. 30–40), exhibited at the Salon of 1876, the seductive Salome confronts a vision of the saint's severed head,

30-40 • Gustave Moreau THE APPARITION
1874–1876. Watercolor on paper, 41⁵⁄₁₆ × 28³⁄₁₆″ (106 × 72.2 cm). Musée du Louvre, Paris.

which hovers open-eyed in midair, dripping blood yet also radiating holy light. Moreau depicted this sensual and macabre scene and its exotic setting in linear detail, with touches of jewel-like color to create an atmosphere of voluptuous decadence that amplifies Salome's role as *femme fatale* who uses her sensuality to destroy her male victim.

The Symbolists, like many smaller groups of artists in the late nineteenth century, staged independent art exhibitions; they were not interested in the approbation of the general public. Unlike the Impressionists, for instance, who hired halls, printed programs, and charged a small admission fee for their exhibitions, the Symbolists mounted more modest shows. During the 1889 Universal Exposition, they hung some works in a café a few blocks away from the grounds, with the result that the exhibition went almost unnoticed by the press.

MUNCH. Symbolism originated in France but had a profound impact on the avant-garde in other countries, where it frequently took on Expressionist tendencies. In Norway, Edvard Munch (1863–1944) produced a body of work that shows the terrifying workings of an anguished mind. **THE SCREAM** (FIG. 30–41) is the stuff of nightmares and horror movies; its harsh swirling colors and lines throw us wildly around the painting, but bring us right back to where we started, trapped between going forward into an unknown horror and going back into a known one. Munch described how the painting began: "One evening I was walking along a path; the city was on one side,

30-41 • Edvard Munch **THE SCREAM**
1893. Tempera and casein on cardboard, 36 × 29″ (91.3 × 73.7 cm).
Nasjonalgalleriet, Oslo.

30-42 • James Ensor **THE INTRIGUE**
1890. Oil on canvas, 35½ × 59″ (90.3 × 150 cm). Koninklijk Museum voor Schone Kunsten, Antwerp.

and the fjord below. I was tired and ill … . I sensed a shriek passing through nature … . I painted this picture, painted the clouds as actual blood." A silent scream echoes throughout the painting.

ENSOR. The Belgian painter and printmaker James Ensor (1860–1949) brought together Symbolist and Expressionist tendencies in equally terrifying paintings. He studied for four years at the Brussels Academy, but spent the rest of his life in the nearby coastal resort town of Ostend. **THE INTRIGUE** (FIG. 30–42) shows a tightly packed group of people bustling and jostling towards us. Their faces are covered with blank, sometimes eyeless masks modeled on the grotesque papier-mâché masks that his family sold for the pre-Lenten carnival, a major holiday in Ostend. These disturbing faces create a mindless

30–43 • Auguste Rodin THE BURGHERS OF CALAIS
1884–1889. Bronze, 6'10½" × 7'11" × 6'6" (2.1 × 2.4 × 2 m). Hirshhorn Museum and Sculpture Garden,
Smithsonian Institution, Washington, D.C. Gift of Joseph H. Hirshhorn, 1966

crowd that seems to move menacingly upon us. Ensor's acidic colors and deliberately crude handling increase the sense of danger. The threat posed by this picture, however, is located firmly in the mind.

LATE NINETEENTH-CENTURY FRENCH SCULPTURE

A defiance of conventional expectations and an interest in emotional expressiveness also characterize the work of late nineteenth-century Europe's most successful and influential sculptor, Auguste Rodin (1840–1917), and his contemporary Camille Claudel (1864–1943). Born in Paris and trained as a decorative craftworker, Rodin failed on three occasions to gain entrance to the École des Beaux-Arts and consequently spent the first 20 years of his career as an assistant to other sculptors and decorators. After a trip to Italy in 1875, where he saw the sculpture of Donatello and Michelangelo, Rodin developed a style of vigorously modeled figures in unconventional,

even awkward poses, which was simultaneously scorned by academic critics and admired by the general public.

Rodin's status as a major sculptor was confirmed in 1884, when he won a competition to create **THE BURGHERS OF CALAIS** (**FIG. 30–43**), commissioned to commemorate an event from the Hundred Years War. In 1347, Edward III of England offered to spare the besieged city of Calais if six leading citizens (or burghers)—dressed only in sackcloth with rope halters and carrying the keys to the city—surrendered themselves to him for execution. Rodin shows the six volunteers preparing to give themselves over to what they assume will be their deaths. Rodin defies academic conventions: Instead of elevating the hostages as heroes, he brings them down off their pedestal and places them at eye level. Instead of noble resignation, they show anguish and despair. Entirely unidealized, these awkward figures are restless, agitated, and distressed. Their exaggerated expressions, lengthened

30-44 • Camille Claudel
THE WALTZ
1892–1905. Bronze, height 9⅞″ (25 cm).
Neue Pinakothek, Munich.

French composer Claude Debussy,
a close friend of Claudel, displayed a cast
of this sculpture on his piano. Debussy
acknowledged the influence of art and
literature on his musical innovations.

arms, enlarged hands and feet, and heavy cloaks accentuate their burden; they seem unable to take another step. The discomfort and raw emotional power of this sculpture were not what the commissioners at Calais expected. Nevertheless, Rodin's ability to stylize human physicality for expressive purposes transformed late nineteenth-century sculpture and paved the way for subsequent sculptural abstractions.

Camille Claudel (1864–1943) was an assistant in Rodin's studio while he worked on *The Burghers of Calais*. Claudel studied sculpture from 1879 to 1883, before becoming Rodin's student. She also became his mistress; their often-stormy relationship lasted 15 years. Most often remembered for her dramatic life story, Claudel enjoyed independent professional success but suffered a breakdown that sent her to a mental hospital for the last 30 years of her life.

One of Claudel's most celebrated works is **THE WALTZ (FIG. 30–44)**, of which she produced several versions in various sizes between 1892 and 1905. The sculpture depicts a dancing couple, both nude, although the woman's lower body is covered with long, flowing drapery. In Claudel's original conception, the figures were entirely nude; she was forced to add the drapery after an inspector from the Ministry of Fine Arts declared their sensuality unacceptable, and recommended that her state commission for a marble version of the work be revoked. The subject of the waltz alone was controversial at this time because of the close contact demanded of dancers. Claudel added enough drapery to persuade the inspector to reinstate the commission, but she never finished it. She did, however, modify *The Waltz*, casting it in bronze as a tabletop sculpture. In this version, the spiral flow of the cloth creates the illusion of rapturous movement as the dancers twirl together, nearly losing their balance.

ART NOUVEAU

The swirling mass of drapery in Claudel's *The Waltz* has a stylistic affinity with Art Nouveau (French for "new art"), a movement launched in the early 1890s that permeated all aspects of European art, architecture, and design for more than a decade. Like the contemporary Symbolists, the practitioners of Art Nouveau largely rejected the values of modern industrial society and sought new aesthetic forms that combined a pre-industrial sense of beauty with fresh asymmetrical designs. They drew particular inspiration

30–45 • Victor Horta **STAIRWAY, TASSEL HOUSE**
Brussels. 1892–1893.

like his reliance on a refined decorative line, derived in part from English reformers such as William Morris.

GAUDÍ. The application of graceful linear arabesques to all aspects of design, evident in the entry hall of the Tassel House, began a vogue that spread across Europe. In Spain, where the style was called *Modernismo*, the major practitioner was the Catalan architect Antonio Gaudí i Cornet (1852–1926). Gaudí integrated natural forms into the design of buildings and parks that are still revolutionary in their dynamic freedom of line.

In 1904, the wealthy industrialist Josep Batlló commissioned Gaudí to design a private residence to surpass the lavish houses of other prominent families in Barcelona. Gaudí retained the underlying structure of the building that existed in the space for Batlló's new home, but completely transformed the façade and interior spaces. The façade **(FIG. 30–46)** is a dreamlike fantasy of undulating sandstone sculptures and multicolored glass and tile

from nature, especially from organisms such as vines, snakes, flowers, and winged insects, whose delicate and sinuous forms were adapted to their graceful and attenuated linear designs. Following a commitment to organic principles, practitioners of Art Nouveau also sought to harmonize all aspects of design into a beautiful whole, as found in nature itself.

HORTA. The artist most responsible for developing the Art Nouveau style in architecture was the Belgian Victor Horta (1861–1947). Trained at the academies in Ghent and Brussels, Horta worked in the office of a Neoclassical architect in Brussels for six years before opening his own practice in 1890. In 1892, he received his first important commission, a private residence in Brussels for a Professor Tassel. The result, especially the house's entry hall and staircase **(FIG. 30–45)**, was strikingly original. The ironwork, wall decoration, and floor tiles were all designed in an intricate series of long, graceful curves. Although Horta's sources are still debated, he was apparently impressed by the stylized linear designs of the English Arts and Crafts Movement of the 1880s. His concern for integrating the various arts into a more unified whole,

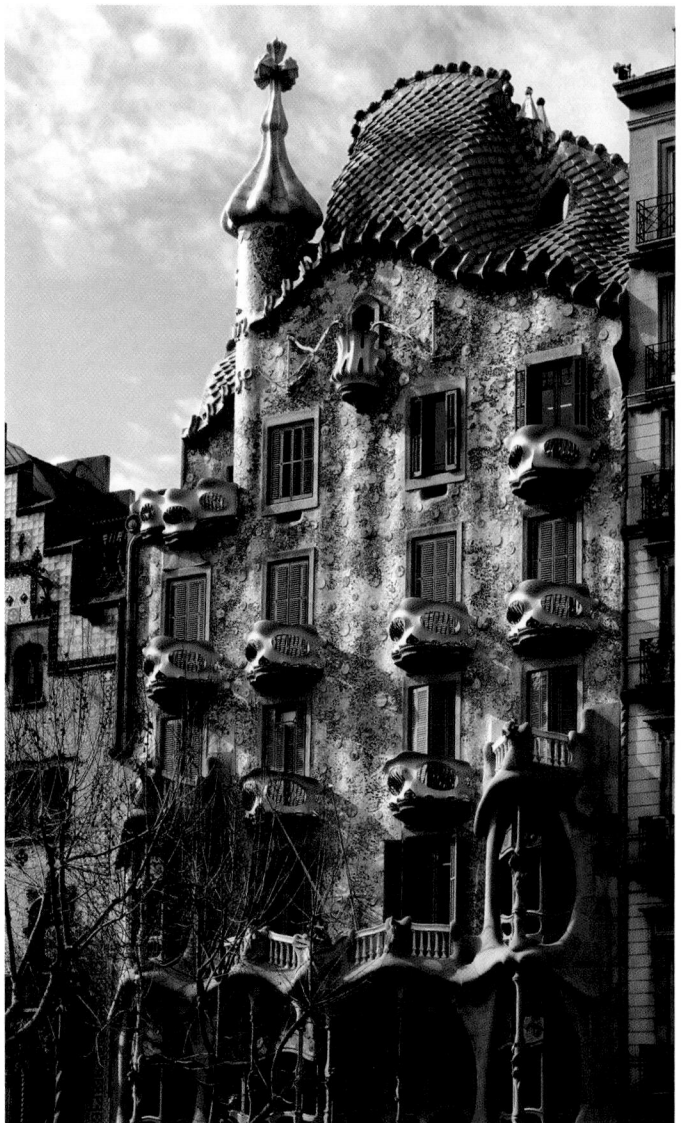

30–46 • Antonio Gaudí **CASA BATLLÒ**
43 Passeig de Gracia, Barcelona. 1900–1907.

30–47 • Hector Guimard DESK
c. 1899 (remodeled after 1909). Olive wood with ash panels, 28¾ × 47¾" (73 × 121 cm). Museum of Modern Art, New York.
Gift of Madame Hector Guimard

district of Paris that housed the most bohemian of the avant-garde artists. In the late 1880s, Toulouse-Lautrec dedicated himself to depicting the nightlife of Montmartre, and the cafés, theaters, dance halls, and brothels that he himself frequented.

Toulouse-Lautrec made roughly 30 posters between 1891 and 1901 for several of the more famous nightspots, advertising their most popular dancers. One of his most famous features the notoriously limber café dancer **JANE AVRIL** performing the infamous can-can **(FIG. 30–48)**. Toulouse-Lautrec places Avril on a stage that zooms into the background, with the hand and face of a double-bass player, part of the instrument, and pages of music framing the lower right of the poster. The bold foreshortening and prominent placement of the bass recall the compositions of Degas (SEE FIG. 30–31), but the overall feeling of the image is quite different. Toulouse-Lautrec's image emphasizes Avril's sexuality in order to draw in the crowds, while Degas's pastels reveal visual

surfaces that mix the Islamic, Gothic, and Baroque visual traditions of Barcelona in imaginative ways. The gaping lower-story windows are the source of the building's nickname, the "house of yawns," while the use of what look like giant human tibia for upright supports led to its other nickname, the "house of bones." The roof resembles a recumbent dragon with overlapping tiles as scales. A fanciful turret rises at its edge, recalling the sword of St. George—patron of Catalonia—plunged into the back of his legendary foe. Gaudí's highly personal alternative to academic historicism and modern industrialization in urban buildings such as this reflects his affinity with Iberian traditions as well as his concern to provide imaginative organic surroundings to enrich the lives of city dwellers.

GUIMARD. In France, Art Nouveau was also sometimes known as the *Style Guimard* after its leading French practitioner, Hector Guimard (1867–1942). Guimard worked in an eclectic manner during the early 1890s, but in 1895 he met and was influenced by Horta. He went on to design the famous Art Nouveau-style entrances for the Paris Métro (subway) and devoted considerable effort to interior design and furnishings, such as this **DESK** that he made for himself **(FIG. 30–47)**: Instead of a static and stable object, Guimard handcrafted an asymmetrical, organic entity that seems to undulate and grow.

TOULOUSE-LAUTREC. Henri de Toulouse-Lautrec (1864–1901) was born into an aristocratic family in the south of France. He had a genetic disorder and suffered several childhood accidents that halted his growth and left him physically disabled. He moved to Paris in 1882, where he had private academic training and then discovered the work of Degas, which changed his artistic perspective. He also discovered Montmartre, the low-class entertainment

30–48 • Henri de Toulouse-Lautrec JANE AVRIL
1893. Lithograph, 50½ × 37" (129 × 94 cm).
San Diego Museum of Art.
Gift of the Baldwin M. Baldwin Foundation (1987.32)

beauty in the roughest raw material. Toulouse-Lautrec outlines his forms, flattens his space, and suppresses modeling to accommodate the cheap colored lithographic printing technique he used, which afforded only three or four colors. His curving lines and the hand-drawn lettering are also distinctively Art Nouveau.

CÉZANNE AND THE BEGINNINGS OF MODERNISM

No artist had a greater impact on the next generation of Modern painters than Paul Cézanne (1839–1906). The son of a prosperous banker in the southern French city of Aix-en-Provence, Cézanne studied art first in Aix and then in Paris, where he participated in the circle of Realist artists around Manet. His early pictures, somber in color and coarsely painted, often depicted Romantic themes of drama and violence, and were consistently rejected by the Salon.

In the early 1870s, Cézanne changed his style under the influence of Pissarro. He adopted a bright palette and broken brushwork, and began painting landscapes. Like the Impressionists, with whom he exhibited in 1874 and 1877, Cézanne dedicated himself to the study of what he called the "sensations" of nature. Unlike the Impressionists, however, he did not seek to capture transitory effects of light and atmosphere; instead, he created highly structured paintings of an ordered nature through a methodical application of color that merged drawing and modeling into a single process. His professed aim was to "make of Impressionism something solid and durable, like the art of the museums."

Cézanne's dedicated pursuit of this goal is evident in his repeated paintings of **MONT SAINTE-VICTOIRE**, a mountain close to his home in Aix, which he depicted in hundreds of drawings and about 30 oil paintings between the 1880s and his death in 1906. The view here **(FIG. 30–49)** presents the mountain rising above the Arc Valley, which is dotted with buildings and trees, and crossed at the far right by a railroad viaduct. Framing the scene to the left is an evergreen tree, which echoes the contours of the mountains, creating visual harmony between the two principal elements of the

30-49 • Paul Cézanne MONT SAINTE-VICTOIRE
c. 1885–1887. Oil on canvas, 25½ × 32″ (64.8 × 92.3 cm). Courtauld Institute of Art Gallery, London. P.1934.SC.55

SEE MORE: View a video about Paul Cézanne's *Mont Sainte-Victoire* **www.myartslab.com**

30–50 • Paul Cézanne THE LARGE BATHERS
1906. Oil on canvas, 6'10" × 8'2" (2.08 × 2.49 m). Philadelphia Museum of Art. The W. P. Wilstach Collection

composition. The even light, still atmosphere, and absence of human activity create the sensation of hermetic stillness.

Cézanne's handling of paint is deliberate and controlled. His brushstrokes, which vary from short, parallel hatchings to light lines to broader swaths of flat color, weave together the elements of the painting into a unified but flattened visual space. The surface design vies with the pictorial effect of receding space, generating tension between the illusion of three dimensions within the picture and the physical reality of its two-dimensional surface. Recession into depth is suggested by the tree in the foreground— a *repoussoir* (French for "something that pushes back") that helps draw the eye into the valley—and by the transition from the saturated hues in the foreground to the lighter values in the background, creating an effect of atmospheric perspective. But recession into depth is challenged by other more intense colors in

both the foreground and background, and by the tree branches in the sky, which follow the contours of the mountain, subtly suggesting that the two are on the same plane. Photographs of this scene show that Cézanne created a composition in accordance with a harmony that he felt the scene demanded, rather than from the details of the scene itself. His commitment to the painting as a work of art, which he called "something other than reality"—not a representation of nature but "a construction after nature"—was crucial for modern art of the next century.

Cézanne enjoyed little professional success until the last years of his life, at which time his paintings became more complex internally and less tied to observed reality. **THE LARGE BATHERS** (FIG. 30–50) was probably begun in the last year of his life and left unfinished. This canvas, the largest he ever painted, returns in several ways to the academic conventions of the history painting: it is a multi-figured painting of nude figures in a landscape setting that suggests a mythological theme. The bodies cluster in two pyramidal groups at the left and right sides of the painting, beneath a canopy of trees that opens in the middle onto a triangular expanse of water, landscape, and sky. The figures assume statuesque poses (the crouching figure at the left quotes the Hellenistic *Crouching Venus* that Cézanne copied in the Louvre) and seem to exist in a timeless realm. Using a restricted palette of blues, greens, ochers, and roses, laid down over a white ground, Cézanne suffuses the picture with a cool light that emphasizes the scene's remoteness from everyday life. Despite its unfinished state, *The Large Bathers* brings nineteenth-century painting full circle by reviving the Arcadian landscape, a much earlier category of academic painting, while opening a new window on the radical rethinking of the fundamental practice and purpose of art.

THE ORIGINS OF MODERN ARCHITECTURE

The history of late nineteenth-century architecture reflects a dilemma faced by the late nineteenth-century industrial city, caught between the classicizing tradition of the Beaux-Arts academic style and the materials, construction methods, and new aesthetic of industry. The École des Beaux-Arts, although weakened in painting by the end of the century, came into its own as the training ground for European and American architects after

1880, while industrialization in places like Chicago simultaneously demanded new ways of thinking about tall and large buildings.

TECHNOLOGY AND STRUCTURE

The pace of life sped up considerably over the course of the nineteenth century. Industrialization allowed people to manufacture more, consume more, travel more, and do more, in greater numbers than before. Industrialization caused urbanization, which in turn demanded more industrialization. A belief in the perfectibility of society spawned more than 20 international fairs celebrating innovations in industry and technology. One of the first of these took place in London in 1851. The Great Exhibition of the Industry of All Nations was mounted by the British to display their industrial might, assert their right to empire, and quell lingering public unrest after the 1848 revolutions elsewhere in Europe. The centerpiece of the Great Exhibition, the Crystal Palace, introduced new modern building techniques and aesthetics.

THE CRYSTAL PALACE. The revolutionary construction of **THE CRYSTAL PALACE** (FIG. 30–51), created by Joseph Paxton (1803–1865), featured a structural skeleton of cast iron that held iron-framed glass panes measuring 49 by 30 inches, the largest size that could be mass-produced at the time. Prefabricated wooden ribs and bars supported the panes. The triple-tiered edifice was the largest space ever enclosed up to that time—1,851 feet long, covering more than 18 acres, and providing almost a million

30-51 • Joseph Paxton THE CRYSTAL PALACE
London. 1850–1851. Iron, glass, and wood. (Print of the Great Exhibition of 1851; printed and published by Dickinson Brothers, London, 1854.)

square feet of exhibition space. The central vaulted transept—based on the design for new cast-iron railway stations—rose 108 feet to accommodate a row of the elm trees dear to Prince Albert, the husband of Queen Victoria. By the end of the exhibition, 6 million people had visited it, most agreeing that the Crystal Palace was a technological marvel. Even so, most architects and critics, still wedded to Neoclassicism and Romanticism, considered it a work of engineering rather than legitimate architecture because the novelty of its iron and glass frame overshadowed its Gothic Revival style.

BIBLIOTHÈQUE NATIONALE. Henri Labrouste (1801–1875) trained as an architect at the École des Beaux-Arts, where he also taught. Labrouste had a radical desire to fuse the École's historicizing approach to architecture with the technical innovations of industrial engineering. Although reluctant to push his ideas at the École, he pursued his goals in his architecture. The **BIBLIOTHÈQUE NATIONALE (FIG. 30–52)** is an example of this fusion. The ceiling is a series of domes with glass-covered oculi that light the reading room. The domes rest on thin iron arches and columns that open the space visually. The domes are faced

30-52 • Henri Labrouste **READING ROOM, BIBLIOTHÈQUE NATIONALE**
Paris. 1862–1868.

30-53 • COURT OF HONOR, WORLD'S COLUMBIAN EXPOSITION
Chicago. 1893. View from the east.

with bright white ceramic tiles, strong metal bookshelves are arranged around the walls, and a metal trelliswork and triumphal arch complete with caryatids define the spaces. The mixture of historical allusions and the vast open space made possible by industrial materials is thoroughly modern.

THE CHICAGO SCHOOL OF ARCHITECTURE

In the United States, a new architecture evolved to accommodate the needs of the modern city. In America up until this time, as in Europe, major architectural projects were expected to embody the Beaux-Arts tradition and its historicist associations. But the modern city required new building types for industry, transportation, commerce, storage, and residences. These new building types needed to accommodate more people and more activities in urban areas where land prices were skyrocketing. Chicago was a case in point. As the transportation hub for grain, livestock, and other produce transplanted from the rural Midwest to the cities of the east and west coasts, Chicago became a populous, wealthy city by the 1890s; its stock exchange was one of the most active in the nation. As new department stores, commercial facilities, and office buildings were designed, primarily with practical needs in mind, Chicago also became the cradle for an entirely new way of thinking about urban design and construction in which function gave birth to architectural form.

WORLD'S COLUMBIAN EXHIBITION. Richard Morris Hunt (1827–1895) was the first American to study architecture at the École des Beaux-Arts in Paris. Extraordinarily skilled in Beaux-Arts historicism and determined to raise the standards of American architecture, he built in every accepted style, including Gothic, French Classicist, and Italian Renaissance. After the Civil War, Hunt built many lavish mansions, emulating aristocratic European models for a growing class of wealthy eastern industrialists and financiers.

Late in his career, Hunt supervised the design of the 1893 World's Columbian Exposition in Chicago, commemorating the 400th anniversary of Christopher Columbus's arrival in the Americas. Rather than focus on the engineering wonders of previous fairs (although the first ferris wheel was built for the fair), the Chicago planning board decided to build "permanent buildings—a dream city." (In fact, the exposition buildings were temporary, and constructed from staff, a mixture of plaster and fibrous materials, rather than masonry.) To create a sense of unity among the buildings, a single style for the fair was settled upon: a Classical style, alluding to ancient Greece and republican Rome to reflect America's pride in its own democratic institutions as well as its emergence as a world power. A photograph of Hunt's design for the Administration Building at the end of the **COURT OF HONOR (FIG. 30–53)** shows the Beaux-Arts style of the so-called "White City."

30-54 • Henry Hobson Richardson **MARSHALL FIELD WHOLESALE STORE**
Chicago. 1885–1887. Demolished c. 1935.

The World's Columbian Exposition was intended to be a model of the ideal American city—clean, spacious, carefully planned, and Classically styled—in contrast to the soot and overcrowding of most unplanned American cities. Frederick Law Olmsted, the designer of New York City's Central Park (see "The City Park," page 1014), was responsible for the landscape design of the exposition. He converted the marshy lakefront into a series of lagoons, canals, ponds, and islands, some laid out formally, as in the White City, and others informally, as in the "Midway," containing the busy conglomerate of pavilions of "less civilized" nations. Between these two parts stood a ferris wheel, which provided a spectacular view of the fair and the city. After the fair, most of its buildings were demolished, but Olmsted's landscaping has remained.

RICHARDSON. The second American architect to study at the École des Beaux-Arts was Henry Hobson Richardson (1838–1886). Born in Louisiana and educated at Harvard, Richardson returned from Paris in 1865 to settle in New York. He designed architecture in a variety of revival styles and became

famous for a robust, rusticated style known as Richardsonian Romanesque. In 1885, he designed the **MARSHALL FIELD WHOLESALE STORE** in Chicago (FIG. 30–54). The design drew on the heavy, blocklike shapes and imposing scale of Italian Renaissance palazzos such as the Medici-Riccardi palace in Florence (SEE FIG. 19–5), and occupied most of a city block. The rough stone facing, the arched windows, and the decorated cornice all evoke historical architectural antecedents. Even so, Richardson's eclecticism resulted in a readily identifiable personal style.

Plain and sturdy, Richardson's building was a revelation to the young architects of Chicago then engaged in rebuilding the city after the disastrous fire of 1871. About the same time, new technology for producing steel, a strong, cheap alloy of iron, created new structural opportunities for architects. William Le Baron Jenney (1832–1907) built the first steel-skeleton building in Chicago; his lead was quickly followed by younger architects, known as the Chicago School. The rapidly rising cost of urban land made tall buildings desirable; structural steel and the electric elevator, first manufactured in 1889, made them possible.

30-55 • Louis Sullivan
WAINWRIGHT BUILDING
St. Louis, Missouri. 1890–1891.

SEE MORE: Click the
Google Earth link for the
Wainwright Building
www.myartslab.com

SULLIVAN. Equipped with new structural materials and improved passenger elevators, driven by new economic considerations, and inspired by Richardson's departure from Beaux-Arts historicism, the Chicago School architects produced a new kind of building—the skyscraper—and a new style of architecture. An example of their work, and evidence of its rapid spread throughout the Midwest, is Louis Sullivan's **WAINWRIGHT BUILDING** in St. Louis, Missouri (FIG. 30–55). The Boston-born Sullivan (1856–1924) studied for a year at the Massachusetts Institute of Technology (MIT), home of the United States' first formal architecture program, and for an equally brief period at the École des Beaux-Arts in Paris, where he developed a distaste for historicism. He settled in Chicago in 1875, partly because of the building boom there that had followed the fire of 1871, and in 1883 he entered into a partnership with the Danish-born engineer Dankmar Adler (1844–1900).

Sullivan's first major skyscraper, the Wainwright Building, has a U-shaped plan that provides an interior light-well for the illumination of inside offices. The ground floor, designed to house shops, has wide plate-glass windows for the display of merchandise. The second story, or mezzanine, also features large windows for the illumination of the shop offices. Above the mezzanine rise seven

Parks originated during the second millennium BCE in China as enclosed hunting reserves for kings and the nobility. In Europe, from the Middle Ages to the eighteenth century, they remained private recreation grounds for the privileged. The first urban park intended for the public was in Munich, Germany. Laid out by Friedrich Ludwig von Sckell in 1789–1795 in the picturesque style of an English landscape garden (SEE FIG. 29–17), the park contained irregular lakes, gently sloping hills, broad meadows, and paths meandering through wooded areas.

The crowding and pollution of cities during the Industrial Revolution prompted the creation of large public parks whose green open spaces would help purify the air and provide city dwellers of all classes with a place for healthy recreation. Numerous municipal parks were built in Britain during the 1830s and 1840s and in Paris during the 1850s and 1860s, when Georges-Eugène Haussmann redesigned the former royal hunting forests of the Bois de Boulogne and the Bois de Vincennes in the English style favored by the emperor.

In American cities before 1857, the only public outdoor spaces were small squares found between certain intersections, or larger gardens, such as the Boston Public Garden, neither of which filled the growing need for varied recreational facilities in the city. For a time, landscaped suburban cemeteries in the picturesque style were popular sites for strolling, picnicking, and even horse racing—an incongruous set of uses that strikingly demonstrated the need for more urban parks.

The rapid growth of Manhattan in the nineteenth century spurred civic leaders to set aside parkland while open space still existed. The city purchased an 843-acre tract in the center of the island and in 1857 announced a competition for its design as Central Park. The competition required that designs include a parade ground,

playgrounds, a site for an exhibition or concert hall, sites for a fountain and for a viewing tower, a flower garden, a pond for ice skating, and four east–west cross-streets so that the park would not interfere with the city's vehicular traffic.

The latter condition was pivotal to the winning design, drawn up by architect Calvert Vaux (1824–1895) and park superintendent Frederick Law Olmsted (1822–1903), which sank the crosstown roads in trenches hidden below the surface of the park and designed separate routes for carriages, horseback riders, and pedestrians.

Believing that the "park of any great city [should be] an antithesis to its bustling, paved, rectangular, walled-in streets," Olmsted and Vaux designed picturesque landscaping in the English tradition, with the irregularities of topography and planting used as positive design elements. Except for a few formal elements, such as the tree-lined mall that leads to the Classically designed Bethesda Terrace and Fountain, the park is remarkably informal and naturalistic. Where the land was low, Olmstead and Vaux further depressed it, installing drainage tiles and carving out ponds and meadows. They planted clumps of trees to contrast with open spaces, and exposed natural outcroppings of schist to provide dramatic, rocky scenery. They arranged walking trails, bridlepaths, and carriage drives through the park with a series of changing vistas. Views from the apartment houses of the wealthy on the streets surrounding the park were designed to be especially appealing. An existing reservoir divided the park into two sections. Olmsted and Vaux developed the southern half more completely and located most of the sporting facilities and amenities there, while leaving the northern half more like a nature reserve. Largely complete by the end of the Civil War, Central Park was widely considered a triumph, launching a movement to build similar parks in cities across the United States.

Frederick Law Olmsted and Calvert Vaux MAP OF CENTRAL PARK, NEW YORK CITY
Revised and extended park layout as shown in a map of 1873.

SEE MORE: View a simulation of the city park **www.myartslab.com**

identical floors of offices, lit by rectangular windows. An attic story houses the building's mechanical plant and utilities. The building is crowned by a richly decorated foliate frieze in terra-cotta relief, punctuated by bull's-eye windows and capped by a thick cornice slab.

The Wainwright Building's outward appearance clearly articulates three different levels of function: shops at the bottom, offices in the middle, and utility storage at the top. It illustrates Sullivan's philosophy of architecture summed up in his statement, "Form ever follows function." This idea was adopted as a credo by Modernist architects, who used it to justify removal of all surface decoration from buildings. Sullivan designed the Wainwright Building for function, but he also created an interesting and expressive building. The thick corner piers, for example, are not structurally necessary—since an internal steel-frame skeleton supports the building—but they emphasize its vertical thrust. The thinner piers between the office windows, which rise uninterrupted from the third story to the attic, echo and reinforce its spring and verticality. As Sullivan put it, a tall office building "must be every inch a proud and soaring thing, rising in sheer exultation."

In the Wainwright Building that exultation culminates in the rich vegetative ornament that swirls around the crown of the building, serving a decorative function like that of the foliated capital of a Classical column. The tripartite structure of the building itself suggests the Classical column with its base, shaft, and capital, reflecting the lingering influence of Classical design principles. Only in the twentieth century would Modern architects reject tradition entirely to create an architectural aesthetic that was decoration-free.

THINK ABOUT IT

30.1 Discuss the interests and goals of French academic painters and sculptors and explain how their work differed from other art of the same time and place, such as that of the Realists and Impressionists.

30.2 Explain how the photographic process works and write about the roles played by Louis-Jacques-Mandé Daguerre and Henry Fox Talbot in the emergence of this medium.

30.3 Discuss Gustave Courbet's Realism in works such as *The Stonebreakers* (FIG. 30–12) and *A Burial at Ornans* (FIG. 30–13) in relation to the social and political issues of mid-century France.

30.4 Discuss the novel form and content of Impressionist paintings, and explain how both differ from those of traditional European painting. Make sure to reference works discussed in the chapter.

30.5 Distinguish among the various responses to Impressionism that constitute the concept of Post-Impressionism. Compare and contrast two Post-Impressionist paintings by different artists discussed in the chapter and explain how each offers an alternative to Impressionism.

PRACTICE MORE: Compose answers to these questions, get flashcards for images and terms, and review chapter material with quizzes www.myartslab.com

31–1 • Pablo Picasso MA JOLIE   1911–1912. Oil on canvas, 39⅜ × 25¾″ (100 × 65.4 cm).
Museum of Modern Art, New York. Acquired through the Lillie P. Bliss Bequest (176.1945)

MODERN ART IN EUROPE AND THE AMERICAS, 1900–1950

Pablo Picasso was a towering presence at the center of the early twentieth-century Parisian art world, transforming the form, meaning, and conceptual framework of Modern art. In his great Cubist work **MA JOLIE** (FIG. 31–1) of 1911–1912, Picasso challenges his viewers to think about the very nature of communication through painting. Remnants of the subjects Picasso worked from are evident throughout, but any attempt to reconstruct the subject—a woman with a stringed instrument—poses difficulties for the viewer. *Ma Jolie* ("My Pretty One") is in some sense a portrait, though hardly a traditional one. Picasso makes us work to see and to understand the figure. We can discover several things about Ma Jolie from the painting; we can see parts of her head, her shoulders, and the curve of her body, a hand or a foot. But in Paris in 1911, "Ma Jolie" was also the title of a popular song, so the inclusion of writing and a musical staff in the painting may also suggest other meanings. Our first impulse might be to wonder what exactly is pictured on the canvas. To that question, Picasso provided the sarcastic answer "It's My Pretty One!"

On the other hand, it might be argued that the human subject provided only the raw material for a formal, abstract arrangement. A subtle tension between order and disorder is maintained throughout this painting. For example, the shifting effect of the surface, a delicately patterned texture of grays and browns, is given regularity through the use of short, horizontal brushstrokes. Similarly, with the linear elements, strict horizontals and verticals dominate, although many irregular curves and angles are also evident. The combination of horizontal brushwork and right angles firmly establishes a grid that effectively counteracts the surface flux. Moreover, the repetition of certain diagonals and the relative lack of details in the upper left and upper right create a pyramidal shape. Thus, what at first may seem a chaotic composition of lines and muted colors turns out to be a well-organized unit. The aesthetic satisfaction of such a work depends on the way chaos seems to resolve itself into order.

LEARN ABOUT IT

31.1 Assess the impact of Cubism on abstract art in the early twentieth century.

31.2 Examine the different ways that artists in the Modern period responded directly or indirectly to the violence of war.

31.3 Investigate how Dada and Surrealism changed the form, content, and concept of art.

31.4 Analyze the relationship between function, form, and technology in early twentieth-century architecture.

31.5 Determine the political and economic impact of the Great Depression on interwar European and American art.

31.6 Assess how and why Abstract Expressionism transformed painting after 1940.

HEAR MORE: Listen to an audio file of your chapter **www.myartslab.com**

EUROPE AND AMERICA IN THE EARLY TWENTIETH CENTURY

At the beginning of the twentieth century, the fragile idea that "civilization" would inexorably continue to progress began to fissure and finally crack in an orgy of violence during World War I. Beginning in August 1914, the war initially pitted the Allies (Britain, France, and Russia) against the Central Powers (Germany and the Austro-Hungarian Empire) and the Ottoman Empire. The United States eventually entered the war on the side of Britain and France in 1917, the American contribution helping guarantee victory for the Allies the following year.

World War I transformed almost every aspect of politics, economics, and society in the Western world (MAP 31–1). The war was fought with twentieth-century technology but nineteenth-century strategies. Trench warfare and the Maxim gun caused the deaths of millions of soldiers and the horrible maiming of as many again. Europe lost an entire generation of young men; whole societies were shattered. The war also caused Europe to question the nineteenth-century imperial social and political order that had precipitated this carnage and foreshadowed a change in the character of warfare itself. Future wars would be over ideology rather than—as in the nineteenth century—territory.

In the first half of the twentieth century, three very different political ideologies struggled for world supremacy: communism (as in the U.S.S.R. and China), fascism (as in Italy and Germany), and liberal-democratic capitalism (as in America, Britain, and Western Europe). The October 1917 Russian Revolution led to the Russian Civil War, which in turn led to the triumph of the Bolshevik ("Majority") Communist Party, led by Vladimir Lenin, and to the founding of the U.S.S.R. in 1922. After Lenin's death and an internal power struggle, Joseph Stalin emerged as leader of the U.S.S.R.. Under Stalin, the U.S.S.R. annexed several neighboring states, suffered through the Great Purge of the 1930s, and lost tens of millions during the war against Nazi Germany.

Fascism first took firm root in Italy when Benito Mussolini came to power in October 1922. In Germany, meanwhile, the postwar democratic Weimar Republic was destroyed by a combination of rampant hyperinflation and the enmity between communists, socialists, centrists, Christian Democrats, and fascists. By the time of the 1932 parliamentary election, Germany's political and economic deterioration had paved the way for a Nazi Party victory and the promotion of its leader, Adolf Hitler, to chancellor. Fascism was not limited to Germany and Italy—it was widespread throughout Central and Eastern Europe and on the Iberian peninsula, where General Francisco Franco emerged victorious from the Spanish Civil War.

The economic impact of World War I was global. Although the United States emerged from it as the leading economic power in the world, the hyperinflation of Germany in the 1920s, the repudiation of German war debt under the Versailles Treaty, and the Stock Market Crash of 1929 in the United States plunged the Western world into a Great Depression that exacerbated political hostility between the major European countries, served as an incubator for fascism and communism in Europe, and tore apart the social and political fabric of Britain and America. In America, President Franklin D. Roosevelt created the New Deal programs in 1933 to stimulate the economy with government spending, and France and Britain took their first steps toward the modern welfare state. But ultimately the Great Depression was only ended by the military build-up of World War II. The latter lasted from 1939 to 1945, and the human carnage it caused both in battle and to civilians, particularly in German concentration camps, raised some difficult questions about the very nature of our humanity.

Changes in scientific knowledge were no less dramatic at this time. The foundations of Newtonian physics were shaken by Albert Einstein's publication of his Special Theory of Relativity and collapsed with the development of quantum theory by Niels Bohr, Werner Heisenberg, and Max Planck. These theories also unlocked the Pandora's box of nuclear energy, first opened when the British split the atom in 1919, and unleashed on the world when America dropped nuclear bombs on Japan in 1945.

The twentieth century also witnessed amazing new innovations in technology and manufacturing: the first powered flight (1903); the mass manufacture of automobiles (1909); the first public radio broadcast (1920); the electrification of most of Western Europe and North America (1920s); and the development of television (1926) and the jet engine (1937), to mention only a few. Technology led both to better medicines for prolonging life and to more efficient warfare, which shortened it. Information about the outside world became even more accessible with the advent of radio, television, and film. Where the visual culture of the nineteenth century was based on paper, that of the early twentieth century was based on photographs and films.

Just as quantum physics fundamentally altered our understanding of the physical world, developments in psychology fundamentally altered our conception of how the mind works and consequently how humans view themselves. In 1900, Austrian psychiatrist Sigmund Freud published *The Interpretation of Dreams*, which posited that our behavior is often motivated by powerful forces that are below our level of awareness. The human unconscious, as he described it, has strong urges for love and power that we simply cannot act upon if society is to remain peaceful and whole. Our psychic lives are not wholly, or even usually, guided by reason alone, but often by these urges that we may be unaware of. Thus we are always attempting to strike a balance between our rational and irrational sides, often erring on one side or the other. Also in 1900, Russian scientist Ivan Pavlov began feeding dogs just after ringing a bell. Soon the dogs salivated not at the sight of food but at the sound of the bell. The discovery that these "conditioned reflexes" also exist in humans showed that if we manage the external stimuli we can control people's appetites. Political leaders of all stripes soon took advantage of this fact.

MAP 31-1 • EUROPE, THE AMERICAS, AND NORTH AFRICA, 1900–1950

The first half of the twentieth century was a time of exciting new technologies and increased access of ordinary people to consumer items, but it was also a time of cataclysmic social, economic, and political change, and a time when millions died in prison camps and wars. These changes, some for the better and some for the worse, shaped the art of the early twentieth century.

EARLY MODERN ART IN EUROPE

Modern artists invented myriad new ways of seeing our world. Few read academic physics or psychology texts, but they lived in a world that was being transformed by such fields, along with so many other technological advances. Modern art was frequently subversive and intellectually demanding, and it was often visually, socially, and politically radical. In the modern period it seemed as if every group of artists developed a manifesto or statement of intent along with their art, leading this to be described later as the age of "isms."

Yet most Modern art was still bound to the idea that a work of art, regardless of how it challenged vision and thought, was still a precious object—a painting or a sculpture or a designed object. Only a few artistic movements of this time, notably Dada and some elements of Surrealism, both of them prompted by the horrors of World War I, challenged this idea; their artistic preoccupations provided the foundation for much art after 1950.

THE FAUVES: WILD BEASTS OF COLOR

The Salon system still operated in France, but the ranks of artists dissatisfied with its conservative precepts were swelling. In 1903, a group of malcontents including André Derain (1880–1954), Henri Matisse (1869–1954), Georges Rouault (1871–1958), and Albert Marquet (1875–1947) organized the first Salon d'Automne (Autumn Salon) exhibition, so named to suggest its opposition to the official Salon show that took place every spring. The Autumn Salon, which continued until after World War I, promised juries more open to avant-garde art. The first major Modern movement of the twentieth century made its debut in this Salon's disorderly halls. Paintings by Derain, Matisse, and Maurice de Vlaminck (1876–1958) displayed in the exhibition in 1905 were filled with explosive colors and blunt brushwork. Responding to these characteristics in his review of the show, the critic Louis Vauxcelles described the young painters as *fauves* ("wild beasts"), the French term by which they soon became known. These artists took the French tradition of color and strong brushwork to new heights of intensity and expressive power, and entirely rethought the picture's surface.

Among the first major Fauve works were paintings that Derain and Matisse made in 1905 in Collioure, a Mediterranean port. Derain's **MOUNTAINS AT COLLIOURE** (FIG. 31–2) is painted in short, broad strokes of pure color. By placing the complementary colors of blue and orange together, as in the mountain range, or red and

31-2 • André Derain
MOUNTAINS AT COLLIOURE
1905. Oil on canvas, 32 × 39½″ (81.5 × 100 cm). National Gallery of Art, Washington, D.C. John Hay Whitney Collection

green together, as in the trees, the artist intensifies the hue of each. The scene is painted in a range of seminaturalistic colors—the trees are sort-of green, their trunks are sort-of brown, and the grass is a kind-of green. It is visibly a landscape, but it is also a self-conscious exercise in painting. The colors are so bright that they seem to advance or push forward out of the picture plane (instead of creating an illusion of space behind it): As a consequence, we are very aware that what we are looking at is a flat canvas decorated with paint. This tension, along with explosive color, generates a visual energy that positively pulses from the painting. Derain described his colors as "sticks of dynamite," and his stark juxtapositions of complementary hues as "deliberate disharmonies."

Equally interested in such deliberate disharmonies was Matisse, whose **THE WOMAN WITH THE HAT** (FIG. 31–3) proved particularly controversial at the 1905 Autumn Salon because of its thick swatches of crude, arbitrary, nonnaturalistic color and its broad and blunt brushwork—the sitter, an otherwise conventional subject for a portrait, has a thick green stripe across her brow and down her nose. The uproar did not stop siblings Gertrude and Leo Stein, among the most important American patrons of avant-garde art at this time, from purchasing the work in 1905.

31-3 • Henri Matisse **THE WOMAN WITH THE HAT**
1905. Oil on canvas, 31¾ × 23½″ (80.6 × 59.7 cm). San Francisco Museum of Modern Art. Bequest of Elise S. Haas

31-4 • Henri Matisse LE BONHEUR DE VIVRE (THE JOY OF LIFE)
1905–1906. Oil on canvas, 5′8½″ × 7′9¾″ (1.74 × 2.38 m). The Barnes Foundation, Merion, Pennsylvania. BF 719

The same year, Matisse also started **LE BONHEUR DE VIVRE (THE JOY OF LIFE) (FIG. 31-4)**, a large pastoral landscape depicting a golden age—a reclining nude in the foreground plays pan pipes, another piper herds goats in the right mid-ground, lovers laze in the foreground while others frolic in dance in the background. Like Cézanne's *Large Bathers* of the same time (SEE FIG. 30–50), *The Joy of Life* is academic in scale and theme, but it is avant-garde in other respects—in the way the figures appear "flattened" and in the distortion of the spatial relations between them. Matisse emphasizes expressive color and draws on the tradition of folk art in his use of unmodeled forms and strong outlines. As he explained in 1908: "What I am after, above all, is expression." In the past, an artist might express feeling through the figure poses or facial expressions that the characters in the painting had. But now, he wrote, "The whole arrangement of my picture is expressive. The place occupied by figures or objects, the empty spaces around them, the proportions, everything plays a part." As for the colors he used: "The chief aim of color should be to serve expression as well as possible."

PICASSO, PRIMITIVISM, AND THE COMING OF CUBISM

Of all Modern art "isms" created before World War I, Cubism probably had the most influence on later artists. The joint invention of Pablo Picasso (1881–1973) and Georges Braque (1882–1963), Cubism proved a fruitful launching pad for both artists, allowing each to comment on modern life and to investigate how we perceive the world.

PICASSO'S EARLY ART.   Of all the "Modern" artists working in Paris, the undisputed capital of the art world prior to 1950, Picasso probably had the most significant impact on avant-garde art with this radical rethinking of how and what art communicates. Born in Málaga, Spain, Picasso was an artistic child prodigy. During his teenage years at the National Academy in Madrid, he made highly polished works that portended a bright future, had he stayed on a conservative artistic path. But his restless temperament led him to Barcelona in 1899, where he involved himself in avant-garde circles. In 1900, he traveled to Paris and moved there permanently in 1904. During this period he painted

31-5 • Pablo Picasso
FAMILY OF SALTIMBANQUES
1905. Oil on canvas, 6'11¾"
× 7'6⅜" (2.1 × 2.3 m).
National Gallery of Art,
Washington, D.C.
Chester Dale Collection

the outcasts of both cities in weary poses using a coldly expressive blue palette (his Blue Period). These paintings seem to have been motivated by Picasso's political sensitivity to those he considered victims of modern capitalist society, which eventually led him to join the Communist Party.

In 1904–1905, Picasso joined a larger group of Paris-based avant-garde artists and became fascinated with the subject of *saltimbanques* (traveling acrobats). He rarely painted them performing, however, focusing instead on the hardships of their existence on the margins of society. In **FAMILY OF SALTIMBANQUES** (FIG. 31–5), a painting from his Rose Period (so called because of the introduction of that color into his palette), five *saltimbanques* stand in weary silence to the left, while a sixth, a woman, sits in curious isolation on the right. All of the *saltimbanques* seem psychologically withdrawn, as uncommunicative as the empty landscape they occupy. Picasso began to sell these works to a number of important collectors around 1905.

Around 1906, Picasso became one of the first artists in Paris to study and actively use images from African art in his paintings. This encounter with "primitive" art and art beyond the Western tradition would prove decisive in his career. In 1906, the Louvre installed a newly acquired collection of sixth- and fifth-century

BCE sculpture from the Iberian peninsula (present-day Spain and Portugal), but it was an exhibition of African masks that he saw around the same time that really changed the way Picasso thought about art. The exact date of this encounter is not known, but it might have occurred at the Musée d'Éthnographie du Trocadéro (now the Musée du Quai Branly) which was opened to the public in 1882, or at the Musée Permanent des Colonies (now the Musée National des Arts d'Afrique et d'Océanie), or in any number of stores in the city that sold "primitive" objects, mostly brought back from French colonies in Africa. Picasso greatly admired the expressive power and formal strangeness of the African masks that he saw. Since African art was relatively inexpensive, he also bought several pieces and kept them in his studio.

The term **primitivism**, as applied to the widespread tendency among Modern artists to scour the art of other cultures beyond the Western tradition for inspiration, is not benignly descriptive, since it implicitly makes a statement about perceptions of relative cultural superiority and inferiority. The inherent assumption is that Western culture is superior, more civilized, more developed, and more complex than other cultures, which are less civilized, less developed, and simpler than our own. It could be argued that, just as colonizing nations exploited "primitive" ones in the nineteenth century for their raw materials and labor to increase their own wealth and power, so Western artists exploited the visual cultures of "primitive" nations merely to amplify ideas about themselves. Many early Modern artists thus represented other cultures and their art without understanding, or really caring to understand, how the cultures actually functioned or how their art was used—this was the case with Picasso.

Picasso was certainly influenced by African art when he created **LES DEMOISELLES D'AVIGNON (THE YOUNG LADIES OF AVIGNON) (FIG. 31–6)**, one of the most radical and complex paintings of the twentieth century. The artist deliberately sends mixed messages in this work, beginning with the title: Avignon was the seat of a papal court in the fourteenth century, so it may mean that these figures are young ladies of the court; on the other hand, Avignon was also a red-light district in Barcelona, which would suggest that they are prostitutes—the most common interpretation of the scene. The work's boldness does not end with its controversial subject matter. Picasso may have undertaken such a large (nearly 8 feet square) painting in competition with both Matisse (who exhibited *The Joy of Life* in the 1906 Salon) and Cézanne (whose *Large Bathers* was shown the same year). Like Matisse and Cézanne,

Picasso revives and renegotiates the ideas of large-scale academic history painting, making use of the traditional subject of nude women shown in an interior space. There are other echoes of the Western tradition in the handling of the figures: The two in the center display themselves to the viewer like *Venus Anadyomene* (Venus Rising from the Sea), while that to the left stands in a rigid pose like an Archaic Greek figure (SEE FIG. 5–16) and the one seated on the right might suggest the pose of Manet's *Le Déjeuner sur l'Herbe* (SEE FIG. 30–17). Other visual references are Iberian and African. An Iberian influence is evident specifically in the faces of the three leftmost figures, with their flattened features and wide, almond-shaped eyes. The faces of the two right-hand figures, painted in a radically different style, were inspired by African art.

We see the African references not only in the masklike faces, but also in the handling of their forms in space. The women in the painting are flattened and fractured into sharp angular shapes. The space they inhabit is equally fractured and convulsive. The central pair of *demoiselles* raise their arms in a traditional gesture of accessibility but contradict it with their hard, piercing gazes and firm mouths. Even the fruit displayed in the foreground, perhaps a symbol of female sexuality, seems dangerous. The women, Picasso

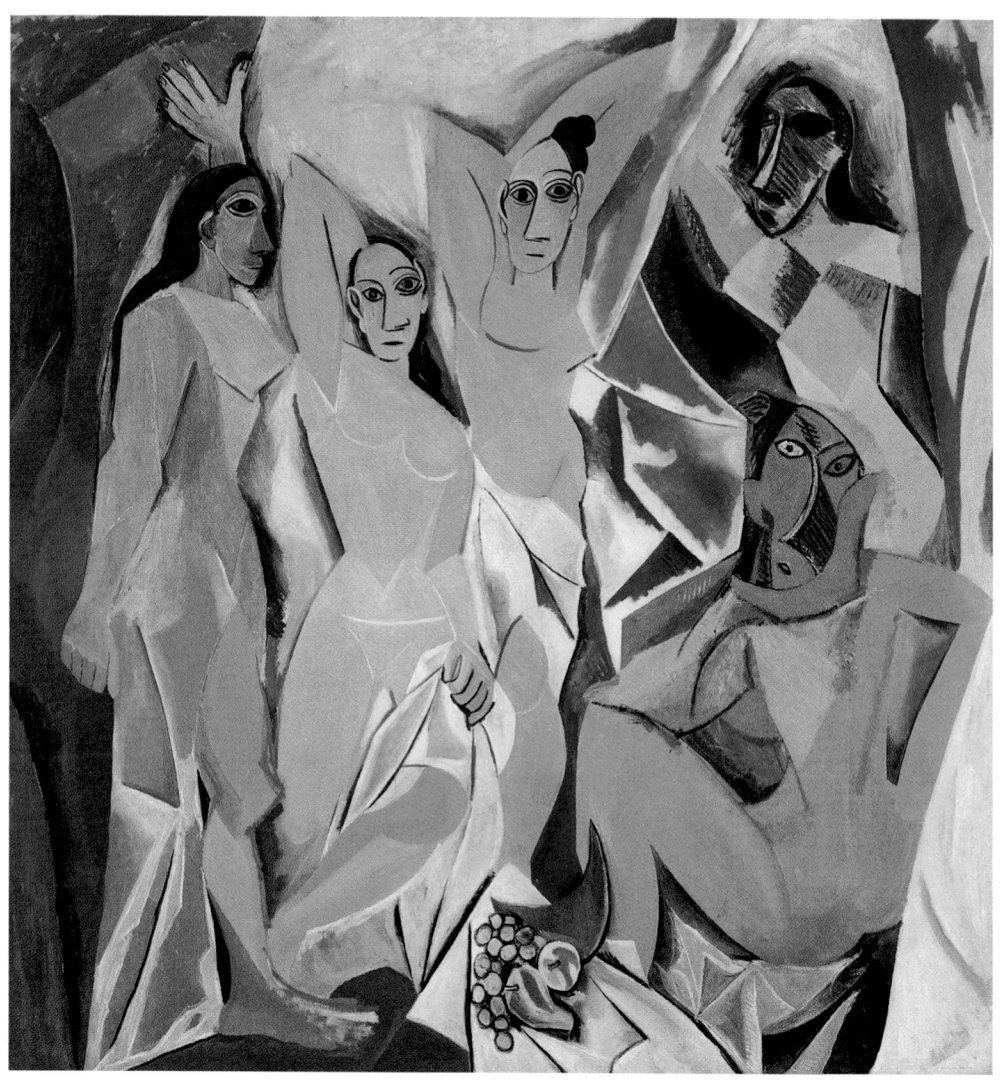

31-6 • Pablo Picasso **LES DEMOISELLES D'AVIGNON (THE YOUNG LADIES OF AVIGNON)**
1907. Oil on canvas, 8′ × 7′8″ (2.43 × 2.33 m). Museum of Modern Art, New York. Acquired through the Lillie P. Bliss Bequest (333.1939)

suggests, are not the gentle and passive creatures that men would like them to be. With this viewpoint he contradicts much of the tradition of erotic imagery since the Renaissance. Likewise, his treatment of space shatters the orderly perspective first proposed in Renaissance painting.

Most of Picasso's friends were shocked by his new work. Matisse, for example, accused Picasso of making a joke of Modern art and threatened to break off their friendship. But one artist, Georges Braque, responded positively—he saw in *Les Demoiselles d'Avignon* a potential for new visual experiments. Picasso used broken and distorted forms expressionistically to convey his view of women, which some feminists have described as misogynist. But what secured Picasso's place in the Parisian avant-garde was the revolution in form that *Les Demoiselles d'Avignon* inaugurated. Braque responded eagerly to Picasso's formal innovations and set out, alongside Picasso, to develop them. This painting inaugurated two phases of Cubism: Analytic and Synthetic.

ANALYTIC CUBISM. In 1907–1908, Picasso and Braque began a close working relationship that lasted until the latter went to war in 1914. According to Braque: "We were like two mountain climbers roped together."

Braque, a year younger than Picasso, was born near Le Havre, France, where he trained as a decorator. In 1900, he moved to Paris and began painting brightly colored landscapes in the Fauvist manner, but it was the 1906 Cézanne retrospective that established his future course. Picasso's *Demoiselles* sharpened his interest in altered form and compressed space and emboldened Braque to experiment in ways that built on Cézanne's late art.

Braque's 1908–1909 **VIOLIN AND PALETTE (FIG. 31–7)** shows the kind of relatively small-scale still-life paintings that the two artists experimented with initially. In it, the move toward the gradual abstraction of recognizable subject matter and space is evident. The still-life items are not arranged in illusionistic depth but are pushed close to the picture plane in a shallow space. Braque knits the various elements—a violin, an artist's palette, and some sheet music—together into a single shifting surface of forms and colors. In some areas of the painting, these formal elements have lost not only their

31-7 • Georges Braque **VIOLIN AND PALETTE**
1909–1910. Oil on canvas, 36⅛ × 16⅞″ (91.8 × 42.9 cm). Solomon R. Guggenheim Museum, New York. 54.1412

31-8 • Pablo Picasso PORTRAIT OF DANIEL-HENRY KAHNWEILER
1910. Oil on canvas, 39½ × 28⅝" (100.6 × 72.8 cm). Art Institute of Chicago.

different approach to the breaking up of forms. Picasso and Braque did not simply fracture objects visually, they picked them apart and rearranged their component parts. Thus, Analytic Cubism resembles the actual process of perception. When we look at an object, we are likely to examine it from various points of view and reassemble our glances into a whole object in our brain. Picasso and Braque shattered their subjects into jagged forms analogous to momentary, partial glances, but they reassembled the pieces to communicate meaning rather than to represent observed reality.

SYNTHETIC CUBISM.   Works such as *Ma Jolie* brought Picasso and Braque to the brink of complete abstraction, but in the spring of 1912 they pulled back and began to create works that suggested more visually discernible subjects. Neither artist wanted to break the link to reality; Picasso said that there was no such thing as completely abstract art, because "You have to start somewhere." This second major phase of Cubism is known as Synthetic Cubism because of the way the artists created complex compositions by combining and transforming individual elements, as in a chemical synthesis. Picasso's **GLASS AND BOTTLE OF SUZE (FIG. 31–9)**, like many of the works he and Braque created from 1912 to 1914, is a

natural spatial relations but their coherent shapes as well. Where representational motifs remain—the violin, for example—Braque fragmented them to facilitate their integration into the compositional whole.

Picasso's 1910 Cubist **PORTRAIT OF DANIEL-HENRY KAHN-WEILER (FIG. 31–8)** shows the artist's first and most important art dealer in Paris, who saved many artists from destitution by buying their early works: He was an early champion of Picasso's art, being one of the first to recognize the significance of *Les Demoiselles*. His impressive stable of artists included—in addition to Picasso—Braque, André Derain, Ferdinand Léger, and Juan Gris. Being German, Kahnweiler was forced to flee France for Switzerland during World War I, and being Jewish, he was forced into hiding in Paris during World War II.

Braque's and Picasso's paintings of 1909 and 1910 initiated what is known as Analytic Cubism because of the way the artists broke objects into parts as if to analyze them. The works of 1911 and early 1912, such as Picasso's *Ma Jolie* (SEE FIG. 32–1), are also grouped under the Analytic label, although they reflect a

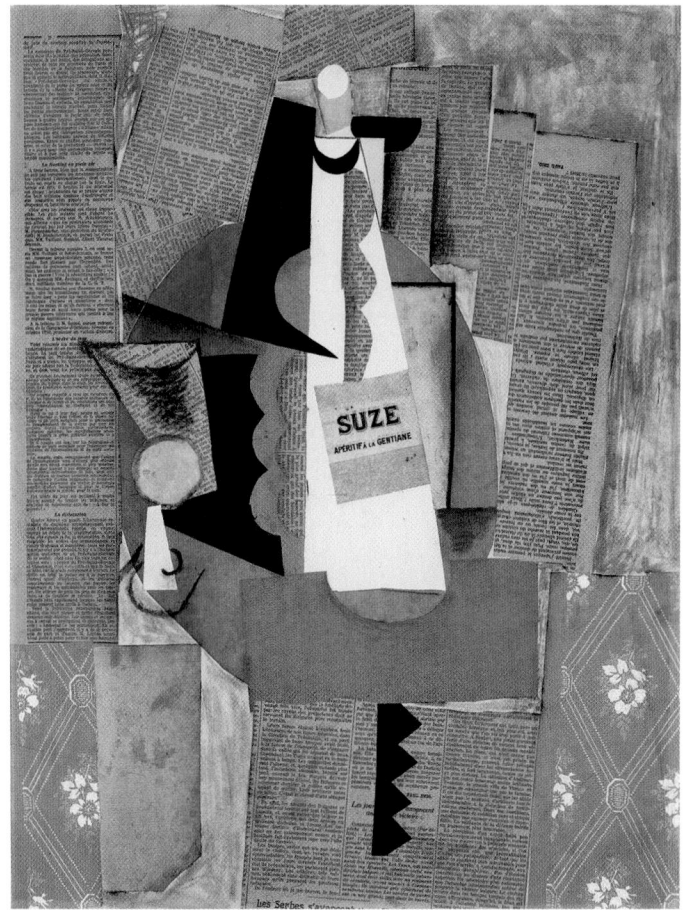

31-9 • Pablo Picasso GLASS AND BOTTLE OF SUZE
1912. Pasted paper, gouache, and charcoal, 25¾ × 19¼" (65.4 × 50.2 cm). Washington University Gallery of Art, St. Louis, Missouri.

collage (from the French *coller*, meaning "to glue"), a work composed of separate elements pasted together. At the center, newsprint and construction paper are assembled to suggest a tray or round table supporting a glass and a bottle of liquor with an actual label. Around this arrangement Picasso pasted larger pieces of newspaper and wallpaper. The composition is Cubist; its angular shapes overlap in a shallow space. The elements together evoke not only a place—a bar—but also an activity: the viewer alone with a newspaper, enjoying a quiet drink. However, the newspaper clippings deal with the First Balkan War of 1912–1913, which contributed to the outbreak of World War I. Picasso may have wanted to underline the modernity of his art with this reference to the political chaos then building in the Balkans.

Picasso employed collage three-dimensionally to produce Synthetic Cubist sculpture, such as **MANDOLIN AND CLARINET** (FIG. 31–10). Composed of wood scraps, the sculpture suggests the Cubist subject of two musical instruments, here shown at right angles to each other. Sculpture had traditionally been either carved, modeled, or cast, but Picasso's sculptural collage was new. In works such as this, Picasso introduced the sculptural technique of **assemblage**, giving sculptors the option not only of carving or modeling but also of constructing their works out of found objects and unconventional materials. Another of Picasso's innovations was his introduction of space into the interior of the sculpture. The parts of the sculpture do not fit perfectly together, leaving gaps and holes. Moreover, the white central piece describes a semicircle that juts outward toward the viewer. The sculpture creates volume by using both forms and spaces rather than mass alone. Thus Picasso challenged the traditional conception of sculpture as a condensed solid form.

THE BRIDGE AND PRIMITIVISM

Simultaneously with all this activity in Paris, a group of radical German artists came together in Dresden as Die Brücke (The Bridge), taking their name from a passage in Friedrich Nietzsche's *Thus Spake Zarathustra* (1883) which described contemporary humanity's potential as a "bridge" to a more perfect humanity in the future. Formed in 1905, The Bridge included architecture students Fritz Bleyl (1880–1966), Erich Heckel (1883–1970), Ernst Ludwig Kirchner (1880–1938), and Karl Schmidt-Rottluff (1884–1976). Other German and northern European artists later joined the group, which continued in existence until 1913. These artists hoped The Bridge would be a gathering place for "all revolutionary and surging elements" who opposed Germany's "pale, overbred, and decadent" society.

Drawing on northern visual prototypes, such as Van Gogh or Munch, and adopting traditional northern media such as woodcuts, these artists created intense, brutal, expressionistic images of alienation in response to Germany's fast, intensive, and brutal urbanization. Not surprisingly, their favorite motifs were the natural world and the nude body—nudism was also a growing cultural trend in Germany in those years, as city dwellers forsook the city to reconnect with nature. Karl Schmidt-Rottluff's **THREE NUDES—DUNE PICTURE FROM NIDDEN** (FIG. 31–11) portrays three bulky but flattened female nudes. By integrating these nude women into their surroundings, Schmidt-Rottluff makes them seem "natural" and the landscape "feminine," in contrast to more masculine

31-10 • Pablo Picasso MANDOLIN AND CLARINET
1913. Construction of painted wood with pencil marks, 25⅝ × 14⅛ × 9" (58 × 36 × 23 cm). Musée Picasso, Paris.

31-11 • Karl Schmidt-Rottluff THREE NUDES—DUNE PICTURE FROM NIDDEN
1913. Oil on canvas, 38⅝ × 41¾″ (98 × 106 cm). Staatliche Museen zu Berlin, Preussischer Kulturbesitz, Nationalgalerie.

to him from European carnivals (SEE FIG. 30–42). By collapsing these traditions together, Nolde transforms sources drawn from art beyond the Western tradition into a European nightmare full of horror and implicit violence. The gaping mouths and hollow eyes of the hideously colored and roughly drawn masks seem to mock the viewer, appearing to advance from the picture plane. Nolde also uses the juxtaposition of complementaries to intensify his colors and the violent emotions they are intended to communicate. On the eve of World War I, Nolde accompanied a German scientific expedition to New Guinea, explaining that what attracted him to the arts of Oceania was their "primitivism," their "absolute originality, the intense and often grotesque expression of power and life in very simple forms—that may be why we like these works of native art." Nolde stopped frequenting The Bridge's studio in 1907 but remained friendly with the group's members.

During the summers, members of The Bridge returned to nature, visiting remote areas of northern Germany, but in 1911 they moved to Berlin—perhaps preferring to imagine rather than actually live the simple life. Their images of cities,

"rational" culture. In this painting, the three "primitive" women actually seem to become part of nature. Their bright red flesh is separated from the background only by their dark outlines. They are like huge "earth mothers," a likely intentional association since the *Woman from Willendorf* (SEE FIG. 1–7) had been discovered in Austria and presented to the world with great fanfare only five years earlier, in 1908. The immediate juxtaposition of the complementary colors red and green serves to intensify both colors and creates an example of bold, intense northern Expressionism.

Although not part of the original Bridge group, Emil Nolde (1867–1956) joined in 1906 and quickly became its most committed member. Nolde originally trained in industrial design, studying academic painting privately in Paris for a few months in 1900, but he never painted as he was taught. Rather, Nolde regularly visited ethnographic museums to study the tribal arts of Africa and Oceania. He was impressed by the radical and forceful visual presence of the figural arts that he saw there. One result of his research was **MASKS (FIG. 31–12)** of 1911, in which he seems to refer both to the masks he studied in Paris, and to those familiar

31-12 • Emil Nolde MASKS
1911. Oil on canvas, 28¾ × 30½″ (73.03 × 77.47 cm). Nelson-Atkins Museum, Kansas City, Missouri. Gift of the Friends of Art, 5490

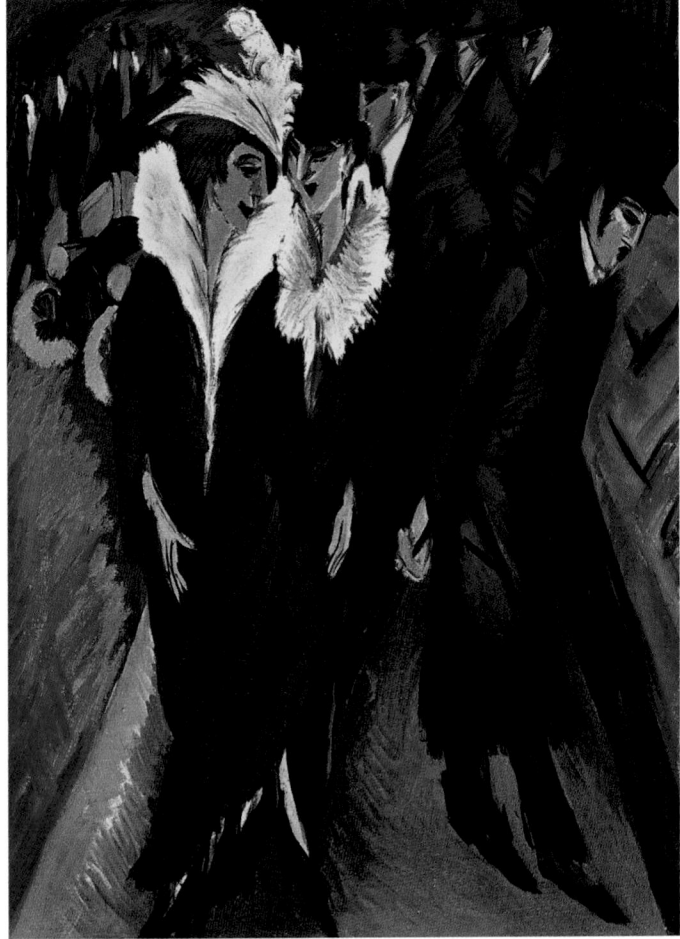

31-13 • Ernst Ludwig Kirchner STREET, BERLIN
1913. Oil on canvas, 47½ × 35⅞″ (120.6 × 91 cm). Museum of Modern Art, New York. Purchase (274.39)

especially Berlin, are powerfully critical of urban existence. In Ernst Ludwig Kirchner's **STREET, BERLIN (FIG. 31–13)**, two prostitutes—their profession advertised by their large feathered hats and fur-trimmed coats—strut past well-dressed bourgeois men whom they view as potential clients. They seem to have deliberately embarrassed the man to their left, smirking as he hurriedly refocuses his attention on the shop window to the right. The women and men appear as artificial and dehumanized figures, with masklike faces and stiff gestures. Their bodies crowd together, but they are psychologically distant from one another. The harsh biting colors, tilted perspective, and piercingly sharp brushstrokes make this a disturbing Expressionistic image of urban degeneracy and alienation.

INDEPENDENT EXPRESSIONISTS

Beyond the members of The Bridge, many other artists in Germany and Austria worked in an Expressionist mode before World War I. One, Käthe Kollwitz (1867–1945), was committed to working-class causes and pursued social change primarily through printmaking because of this cheap and easily disseminable medium's potential to reach a wide audience. Between 1902 and 1908, she produced a series of seven etchings showing the

sixteenth-century German Peasants' War. **THE OUTBREAK (FIG. 31–14)**, a lesson in the power of group action, portrays the ugly fury of the peasants as they charge forward armed only with farm tools, bent on revenge against their oppressors for years of abuse. The faces of the two figures at the front of the charge are particularly grotesque while the leader, Black Anna—whom Kollwitz modeled on herself—signals the attack with a gesture that is inhumanly fierce. Her arms silhouetted against the sky, and the crowded mass of workers with their farm tools, form a passionate picture of political revolt.

Like Kollwitz, Paula Modersohn-Becker (1876–1907) studied at the Berlin School of Art for Women. In 1898, she moved to Worpswede, an artists' retreat in rural northern Germany. Dissatisfied with the Worpswede artists' naturalistic approach to rural life, after 1900 she made four trips to Paris to view recent developments in Post-Impressionist painting. Although obviously informed by the "primitivizing" tendencies of other artists such as Gauguin (SEE FIG. 30–36) toward women at the time, her physically small and yet monumental **SELF-PORTRAIT WITH AN AMBER NECKLACE (FIG. 31–15)** subverts those same tendencies. Modersohn-Becker appears as a kind of earth mother, surrounded by plants and with flowers in her hair and hands, but she also has a powerful, human presence. Modersohn-Becker looks out of the canvas at us, calmly returning our gaze and establishing her humanity. While painted in the manner of other Modernists, this tender self-portrait reveals an artist of strong independent ideas and a woman of sharp intelligence.

In contrast to Modersohn-Becker's gentle self-portrait, **SELF-PORTRAIT NUDE (FIG. 31–16)** of 1911 by the Austrian artist Egon Schiele (1890–1918) conveys physical and psychological torment. Schiele's father died insane from untreated syphilis when the artist

31-14 • Käthe Kollwitz THE OUTBREAK
From the *Peasants' War* series. 1903. Etching, 20 × 23⅓″ (50.7 × 59.2 cm). Kupferstichkabinett, Staatliche Museen zu Berlin, Preussischer Kulturbesitz. Kunstmuseum, Switzerland (1748)

31–15 • Paula Modersohn-Becker SELF-PORTRAIT WITH AN AMBER NECKLACE
1906. Oil on canvas, 24 × 19¾″ (61 × 50 cm).
Öffentliche Kunstsammlung Basel.

31–16 • Egon Schiele SELF-PORTRAIT NUDE
1911. Gouache and pencil on paper, 20¼ × 13¾″ (51.4 × 35 cm).
Metropolitan Museum of Art, New York. Bequest of Scofield Thayer, 1982
(1984.433.298)

was just 14, and as a result Schiele had a tendency to conflate suffering and sexuality throughout his life. In many drawings and watercolors, Schiele portrays women in demeaning, sexually explicit poses that emphasize their animal nature, and in his self-portraits the artist turns the same harsh gaze upon himself, revealing deep ambivalence toward sexuality and the body in his art and his life. In *Self-Portrait Nude*, he stares out of the picture with anguish, his emaciated body stretched and displayed in a halo of harsh light. Mutilated and impotent, he has neither right hand nor genitals. The missing body parts have been interpreted in Freudian fashion as the artist's symbolic self-punishment for indulgence in masturbation, then commonly believed to lead to insanity.

SPIRITUALISM OF THE BLUE RIDER

Formed in Munich by the Russian artist Vassily Kandinsky (1866–1944) and the German artist Franz Marc (1880–1916), Der Blaue Reiter ("The Blue Rider") was named for a popular image of a blue knight, the St. George on the city emblem of Moscow. Just as St. George had been a spiritual leader in society, so The Blue Rider aspired to offer spiritual leadership in the arts. Its first exhibition was held in December 1911 and included the work of 14 artists working in a wide range of styles, from realism to radical abstraction.

By 1911, Marc was mostly painting animals rather than humans. He had a spiritual affinity to animals, which he felt were more "primitive" and thus purer than humans, enjoying a more spiritual relationship with nature. He rendered them in big, bold forms painted in almost-primary colors. In **THE LARGE BLUE HORSES (FIG. 31–17)**, the animals merge into a homogenous unit. Their sweeping contours reflect the harmony of their collective existence and echo the curved lines of the hills behind them, suggesting that they are also in harmony with their surroundings. The blue of the horses alludes to St. George and to the spirituality of the natural world.

Born into a wealthy family in Moscow, Kandinsky initially trained as a lawyer, but after visiting exhibitions of Modern art in Germany and taking private art lessons, he gave up the legal profession, moved to Munich, and established himself as an artist. His early works make frequent reference to Russian folk culture, which he admired for its "primitivism."

Kandinsky may have been a synesthete—i.e. someone who "hears" colors and "sees" sound. Whether he was or not, his art is

31–17 • Franz Marc
THE LARGE BLUE HORSES
1911. Oil on canvas,
3′5⅜″ × 5′11¼″ (1.05 × 1.81 m). Walker Art Center, Minneapolis.
Gift of T. B. Walker Collection, Gilbert M. Walter Fund, 1942

31–18 • Vassily Kandinsky **IMPROVISATION 28 (SECOND VERSION)**
1912. Oil on canvas, 43⅞ × 63⅞″ (111.4 × 162.2 cm). Guggenheim Museum, New York. Gift, Solomon R. Guggenheim. 37.239

EXPLORE MORE: Gain insight from a primary source by Vassily Kandinsky **www.myartslab.com**

clearly that of an artist for whom sound and color were inextricably linked. His early study of the work of Whistler (SEE FIG. 30–39) convinced him that the arts of painting and music were related: Just as a composer organizes sound, so a painter organizes color and form. Kandinsky was particularly interested in the music of the Austrian composer Arnold Schoenberg, who around 1910 introduced a momentous change in musical history. All Western music since antiquity was previously based on the arrangement of notes into scales, or modes (such as today's common major and minor), and composers chose the scale they worked in for expressive reasons. Particularly since the Baroque period, each note in any given scale had a role to play, and these roles operated in a clear hierarchy that served to reinforce what became known as the "tonal center," a kind of home base or place of repose in the musical composition. Schoenberg eliminated the tonal center and treated all tones equally, denying the listener any place of repose and instead prolonging the tension (and thus, he felt, the expression) of his music indefinitely. Kandinsky contacted the composer and was delighted to find out that he also painted in an Expressionist style. Kandinsky believed that if music could exist without a tonal center, could art exist without subject matter?

Kandinsky was thus one of the first artists to investigate the theoretical possibility of purely abstract painting. He gave his works musical titles, such as "Composition" and "Improvisation," and aspired to make paintings that responded to his inner state rather than an external stimulus and which would be entirely autonomous, making no reference to the visible world. In 1912, he painted a series of works, including **IMPROVISATION 28 (FIG. 31–18)**, that he claimed was the first truly abstract art. In these, Kandinsky's colors leap and dance, with different colors expressing different emotions. For Kandinsky, painting was a utopian spiritual force. He believed that art's traditional focus on accurate rendering of the physical world was a basically materialistic quest. Art should not depend so much on mere physical reality. He hoped that his paintings would lead humanity toward a deeper awareness of spirituality and the inner world. Rather than searching for correspondence between the painting and the world where none is intended, the artist asks us to look at the painting as if we were hearing a symphony, responding instinctively and spontaneously to this or that passage, and then to the total experience. Kandinsky further explained the musical analogy in his book *Concerning the Spiritual in Art*: "Color directly influences the soul. Color is the keyboard, the eyes are the hammers, the soul is the piano with many strings. The artist is the hand that plays, touching one key or another purposively, to cause vibrations in the soul."

Despite Kandinsky's noble aspirations, however, works such as *Improvisation 28* are not entirely abstract. They often retain a vestige of the landscape—Kandinsky found references to nature the hardest to transcend—as well as suggestions of horses, boats, and oars. But these half-recognized forms increasingly act in his works as a kind of punctuation mark to increase or decrease our speed, or raise or lower our emotions, as our eyes fly around his canvases.

EXTENSIONS OF CUBISM

As Cubism emerged from the studios of Braque and Picasso, it was clear to the art world that they had altered the artistic discourse irrevocably. Cubism's way of viewing the world resonated with artists all over Europe, in Russia, and even in the United States. These artists interpreted Cubism in their own ways, significantly broadening and extending its visual message beyond the ideas and objects of Picasso and Braque.

FRANCE. Robert Delaunay (1885–1941) and his wife, the Ukrainian-born Sonia Delaunay-Terk (b. Sonia Stern, 1885–1979), took the relatively monochromatic and relatively static forms of Cubism in a new direction. Delaunay's early work was inflected with Fauvist color; he also had a deep interest in communicating spirituality through color and participated in Blue Rider exhibitions. In 1910, he began to fuse this intense interest in color with Cubist forms to create paintings celebrating the modern city and modern technology. In **HOMAGE TO BLÉRIOT (FIG. 31–19)**, Delaunay pays tribute to Louis Blériot, the French pilot who in 1909 became the first person to fly across the English Channel, by

31–19 • Robert Delaunay HOMAGE TO BLÉRIOT
1914. Tempera on canvas, 8′2½″ × 8′3″ (2.5 × 2.51 m). Öffentliche Kunstsammlung Basel, Kunstmuseum, Basel, Switzerland. Emanuel Hoffman Foundation

31-20 • Sonia Delaunay-Terk CLOTHES AND CUSTOMIZED CITROËN B-12 (EXPO 1925 MANNEQUINS AVEC AUTO)
From *Maison de la Mode*, 1925.

portraying his airplane flying over the Eiffel Tower, the Parisian symbol of modernity. The brightly colored circular forms that fill the rest of the canvas suggest the movement of the airplane's propeller, a blazing sun in the sky, and the great rose window of the Cathedral of Notre-Dame, representing Delaunay's ideas of "progressive" science and spirituality. This painting's fractured colors suggest both the power of the Christian God's light and the fast-moving parts of modern machinery.

The critic Guillaume Apollinaire labeled the art of both Robert and Sonia Delaunay "Orphism" after Orpheus, the legendary Greek poet whose lute playing charmed wild beasts, thus implying that their art had similar power. They preferred the term "simultaneity," a concept based on Michel-Eugène Chevreul's law of the simultaneous contrast of colors that proposed collapsing spatial distance and temporal sequence into the simultaneous "here and now" to create a harmonic unity out of the disharmonious world. They envisioned a simultaneity that combined the modern world of airplanes, telephones, and automobiles with spirituality.

31-21 • Fernand Léger THREE WOMEN
1921. Oil on canvas, 6′1½″ × 8′3″ (1.84 × 2.52 m). Museum of Modern Art, New York. Mrs. Simon Guggenheim Fund

Sonia Delaunay (née Terk) produced Orphist paintings with Robert, but she was also an important fabric and clothing designer. She created new clothing patterns similar to Cubist paintings that she called Simultaneous Dresses and exhibited a line of inexpensive ready-to-wear garments with bold geometric designs at the important 1925 International Exposition of Modern Decorative and Industrial Arts. She decorated a Citroën sports car to match one of her ensembles for the exhibition (FIG. 31–20), choosing the sports car as an expression of the new automobile age, because like her clothing this car was produced inexpensively for a mass market and because the small three-seater was designed specifically to appeal to the newly independent woman of the time, Delaunay's clientele base. Sadly, there are only black-and-white photographs of these designs.

Technology also fascinated Fernand Léger (1881–1955), who painted a more static but brilliantly colored version of Cubism based on machine forms. **THREE WOMEN** (FIG. 31–21) is a Purist, machine-age version of the French academic subject of the reclining nude. Purism was developed in Paris by Le Corbusier (b. Charles-Édouard Jeanneret, 1887–1965) and Amédée Ozenfant in a 1925 book, *The Foundation of Modern Art*, that argued for a return to clear, ordered forms and ideas to express the efficient clarity of the machine age. In Léger's painting, the women's forms are constructed from large machinelike planes arranged in an asymmetrical geometric grid that both embodies a cool Classicism and suggests an arrangement of plumbing parts. The women are dehumanized; they have identical, bland, round faces; they seem to be assembled from standard, interchangeable parts; and the brightly colored background suggests fantastic plumbing. The exuberant colors and patterns that surround the women suggest an orderly industrial society in which everything has its place.

31-22 • Gino Severini ARMORED TRAIN IN ACTION
1915. Oil on canvas, 45⅝ × 34⅞" (115.8 × 88.5 cm). Museum of Modern Art, New York. Gift of Richard S. Zeisler. 287.86

ITALY. In Italy, technology and speed were combined with Cubism to create Futurism. In 1908, Italy was a state in crisis: There were huge disparities of wealth between the north and south; four-fifths of the country was illiterate; poverty and near-starvation were rampant; and as many as 50,000 people had recently died in one of the nation's worst earthquakes. On February 20, 1909, the Milanese poet and editor Filippo Tommaso Marinetti (1876–1944) published his "Foundation and Manifesto of Futurism" on the front page of the Parisian newspaper *Le Figaro*, in which he attacked everything old, dull, and "feminine," and proposed to shake Italy free of its past by embracing an exhilarating, "masculine," "futuristic," and even dangerous world based on the thrill, the speed, energy, and power of modern urban life.

In April 1911, a group of Milanese artists followed Marinetti's manifesto with the "Technical Manifesto of Futurist Painting," in which they demanded that "all subjects previously used must be swept aside in order to express our whirling life of steel, of pride, of fever, and of speed." Some of these artists traveled to Paris for a Futurist exhibition in 1912, after which they harnessed the visual forms of Cubism to their love of machines, speed, and war.

Gino Severini (1883–1966) signed the "Technical Manifesto" while living in Paris, where he served as an intermediary between the Italian-based Futurists and the French avant-garde. Perhaps more than other Futurists, Severini embraced the concept of war as a social cleansing agent. In 1915, he painted **ARMORED TRAIN IN ACTION** (FIG. 31–22), which was probably based on a photograph of a Belgian armored car on a train going over a bridge. Severini uses the jagged forms and splintered overlapping surfaces of Cubism to describe a tumultuous scene of smoke, violence, and cannon blasts issuing from the speeding train as seen from a dizzying and disorienting viewpoint.

In 1912, Umberto Boccioni (1882–1916) argued for a Futurist "sculpture of environment," in which form should explode in a

31-23 • Umberto Boccioni **UNIQUE FORMS OF CONTINUITY IN SPACE**
1913. Bronze, 43⅞ × 34⅞ × 15¾″ (111 × 89 × 40 cm). Museum of Modern Art, New York. Acquired through the Lillie P. Bliss Bequest (231.1948)

EXPLORE MORE: Gain insight from a primary source by Filippo Tommaso Marinetti **www.myartslab.com**

violent burst of motion from the closed and solid mass of traditional sculpture into the surrounding space. In **UNIQUE FORMS OF CONTINUITY IN SPACE (FIG. 31–23)**, Boccioni portrays a figure striding powerfully through space, like the ancient *Nike (Victory of Samothrace)* (SEE FIG. 5–56), with muscular forms like wings flying out energetically behind it. Many of Boccioni's sculptures made use of unconventional materials; this sculpture was actually made of plaster. It was cast in bronze after the artist's death. In keeping with his Futurist ideals, Boccioni celebrated Italy's entry into World War I by enlisting and was killed in combat.

RUSSIA. By 1900, Russian artists and art collectors in the cosmopolitan cities of St. Petersburg and later Moscow had begun to embrace avant-garde art and to travel to Paris regularly. Russian artists also drew on Futuristic ideas about the possibility of technology and the aesthetic of speed to modernize Russia. In 1912, Russian Futurist artists, also known as Cubo-Futurists, claiming to have emerged independently of Italian Futurism, began to move toward abstraction in art.

Natalia Goncharova's (1881–1962) **ELECTRIC LIGHT** of 1913 **(FIG. 31–24)** shows a brightly artificial new electric light fracturing and dissolving its surrounding forms. Goncharova also combined Russian folk art with abstraction in costumes and sets for several of Sergei Diaghilev's Ballet Russes stagings, including *Le Coq d'or* (1914), *Night on Bald Mountain* (1923) and the 1926 revival of Stravinsky's *Firebird*.

After 1915, Kazimir Malevich (1878–1935) emerged as the leader of the Moscow avant-garde. According to his later reminiscences, "in the year 1913, in my desperate attempt to free art from the burden of the object, I took refuge in the square form and exhibited a picture which consisted of nothing more than a black square on a white field." *The Black Square* was one of the backdrops for Mikhail Matiushin's Russian futurist opera, *Victory Over the Sun*. Malevich exhibited 39 works of art, consisting of flat, abstract shapes collaged together which he termed Suprematism, at the "Last Futurist Exhibition of Paintings: 0.10," held in St. Petersburg in the winter of 1915–1916. One work, **SUPREMATIST PAINTING (EIGHT RED RECTANGLES) (FIG. 31–25)**, consists of eight red rectangles arranged diagonally on a white painted ground. Malevich described Suprematism as "the supremacy of pure feeling in creative art."

31-24 • Natalia Goncharova **ELECTRIC LIGHT**
1913. Oil on canvas, 41½ × 32″ (105.5 × 81.3 cm). Musée National d'Art Moderne, Centre National d'Art et de Culture Georges Pompidou.

31-25 • Kazimir Malevich
**SUPREMATIST PAINTING
(EIGHT RED RECTANGLES)**
1915. Oil on canvas, 22½ × 18⅞″
(57 × 48 cm). Stedelijk Museum,
Amsterdam.

EXPLORE MORE: Gain insight
from a primary source by
Kazimir Malevich
www.myartslab.com

At the same time Vladimir Tatlin (1885–1953) began to construct entirely abstract sculptures that he entitled **CORNER COUNTER-RELIEFS (FIG. 31–26)**. He created these sculptures from various nonprecious, nonart materials such as metal, glass, wood, plaster, and wire. Although his move away from sculpture conceived of as mass and traditional materials may have been inspired by a visit to Picasso's studio, Tatlin's art created an entirely new formal and conceptual language for sculpture by actively using open and negative space, eliminating sculpture's reliance on mass and monumentality, and producing fragile and physically unstable objects that not only had no bases but actually hung in the corners of rooms—the space formerly reserved for religious icons. In effect, Tatlin intended these "Counter-Reliefs" to be modern abstract replacements of the icons of the old Russian faith.

TOWARD ABSTRACTION IN SCULPTURE

It is clear that sculpture underwent a revolution as profound as that of painting in the years prior to World War I. Not all change involved new materials: The Romanian artist Constantin Brancusi (1876–1957) settled in Paris in 1904 and became immediately captivated by the "primitive" art on display in the city. He admired the semi-abstracted forms of much art beyond the Western tradition, believing that the artists who made such art succeeded in capturing the "essence" of their subject. In Brancusi's search for a sculptural essence he, like Picasso, rejected superficial realism. Brancusi wrote, "What is real is not the external form but the

31-26 • Vladimir Tatlin **CORNER COUNTER-RELIEF**
1915. Mixed media, 31½ × 59 × 29½″ (80 × 150 × 75 cm). Present whereabouts unknown.

31-27 • Constantin Brancusi TORSO OF A YOUNG MAN
1924. Bronze on stone and wood bases; combined figure and bases
40⅜ × 20 × 18¼″ (102.4 × 50.5 × 46.1 cm). Hirshhorn Museum and
Sculpture Garden, Smithsonian Institution, Washington, D.C.

essence of things. Starting from this truth it is impossible for anyone
to express anything essentially real by imitating its exterior surface."
In his 1924 **TORSO OF A YOUNG MAN** (FIG. **31–27**), Brancusi distills
and abstracts the young man's torso and upper legs into three
essential but beautifully carved and polished marble forms.

The egg symbolized the potential for birth, growth, and
development for Brancusi. It was a perfect but organic ovoid that
contained life in its essence. In **THE NEWBORN** (FIG. **31–28**), he
conflates its shape with the disembodied head of a human infant to
suggest the essence of humanity at the moment of birth.

DADA: QUESTIONING ART ITSELF

When the Great War broke out in August 1914, most European
leaders thought it would be over by Christmas. Both sides
reassured their populations that the efficiency of their armies and
bravery of their soldiers would ensure a speedy resolution and that
the political status quo would resume. These hopes proved illusory.
World War I was the most brutal and costly in human history to
date. On the Western Front in 1916 alone, Germany lost 850,000
soldiers, France 700,000, and Great Britain 400,000. The conflict
settled into a vicious stalemate on all fronts as each side deployed
new killing technologies such as improved machine guns, flame
throwers, fighter aircraft, and poison gas. On the home front,
governments exerted control over industry and labor to manage
the war effort, and ordinary people were forced to endure food
rationing, propaganda attacks, and shameless war profiteering.

31-28 • Constantin Brancusi THE NEWBORN
1915. Marble, 5¾ × 8¼ × 5⅞″ (14.6 × 21 × 14.8 cm). Philadelphia
Museum of Art. Louise and Walter Arensberg Collection. 195.134.10

Horror at the enormity of the carnage and loss arose on many fronts. One of the first artistic movements to address the slaughter and the moral questions it posed was Dada. If Modern art until that time questioned the traditions of art, Dada went further to question the concept of art itself. Witnessing how thoughtlessly life was discarded in the trenches, Dada mocked the senselessness of rational thought and even the foundations of modern society. It embraced a "mocking iconoclasm," even in its name, which has no real or fixed meaning. *Dada* is baby talk in German; in French it means "hobbyhorse"; in Romanian and Russian, "yes, yes"; in the Kru African dialect, "the tail of a sacred cow." Dada artists annihilated the conventional understanding of art as something precious, replacing it with a strange and irrational art about ideas and actions rather than about objects.

Dada was a transnational movement with several quite distinct local manifestations that arose almost simultaneously in the cities of Zürich, New York, Paris, and Berlin, as Paris temporarily relinquished its place at the center of the art world in 1914.

HUGO BALL AND THE CABARET VOLTAIRE. Dada's opening moment was probably the first performance of poet Hugo Ball's poem "Karawane" at the Cabaret Voltaire. Ball (1886–1927) and his companion, Emmy Hennings (d. 1949), a nightclub singer, moved from Germany to neutral Switzerland when World War I broke out and opened the Cabaret Voltaire in Zürich on February 5, 1916. Their cabaret was based loosely on the bohemian artists' cafés of prewar Berlin and Munich, and its mad irrational world became a meeting place for exiled avant-garde writers and artists of various nationalities who shared Ball's and Hennings's disgust for the war.

At the Cabaret Voltaire, Ball recited one of his sound poems, **"KARAWANE"** (FIG. 31–29), while wearing a strange costume, with his legs and body encased in blue cardboard tubes and a white-and-blue "witch doctor's hat," as he called it, on his head. He also wore a huge, gold-painted cardboard cape that flapped when he moved his arms and lobsterlike cardboard hands or claws. He solemnly recited his poem, the text of which can be seen in the photograph and which comprised a list of nonsensical sounds. Ball's poetry renounced "the language devastated and made impossible by journalism," and mocked traditional poetry and the rationality of adulthood by creating a new, randomly based and wholly incomprehensible private language that seemed to mimic baby talk.

MARCEL DUCHAMP. Although not formally a member of the movement, Marcel Duchamp (1887–1968) created some of Dada's most complex and challenging works. He also took Dada to New York when he moved there to escape the war in Europe. In Paris in 1912, Duchamp experimented with Cubism by painting *Nude Descending a Staircase*, one of the most controversial works to be included later in the Armory Show (see page 1042). By the time Duchamp arrived in the United States, he had discarded painting, which he claimed had become for him a mindless activity, and he devised the Dada concept that he termed the **readymade**, in

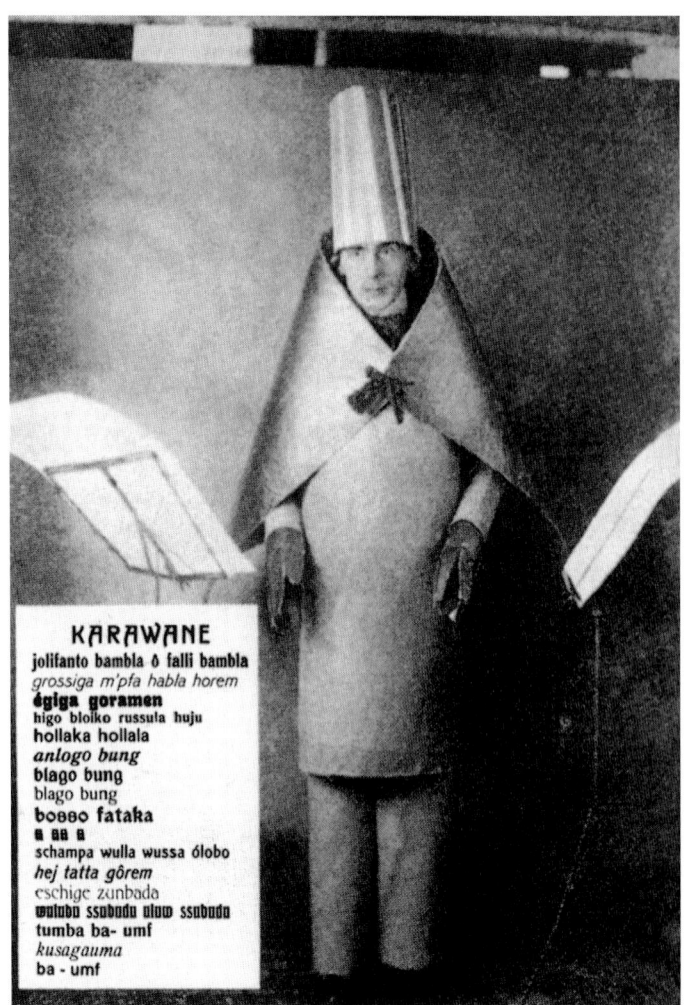

31-29 • HUGO BALL RECITING THE SOUND POEM "KARAWANE"
Photographed at the Cabaret Voltaire, Zürich, 1916.

which he transformed ordinary, often manufactured objects into works of art.

On arrival in New York in 1915, Duchamp was warmly welcomed by the American art world. He was invited to become a founding member of the American Society of Independent Artists, and was appointed chair of the hanging committee for its first annual "Forum" exhibition in 1917. The show was advertised as unjuried: Any work of art submitted (for the fee of $6) would be hung. Yet, in Dada fashion, Duchamp spent almost two years devising a work of art that would be so shocking and offensive that it would have to be rejected, thus commenting on the contemporary process of art making and its exhibition. The piece that he created was a common porcelain urinal that he purchased from a plumber, which he turned on one side so that it was no longer functional and signed it "R. Mutt" in a play on the name of the urinal's manufacturer, J. L. Mott Iron Works. He submitted it anonymously to the exhibition and it was indeed rejected.

FOUNTAIN (FIG. 31–30) of 1917 was, and still is, one of the most controversial works of art of the modern age. In it Duchamp asks: What is the essence of a work of art? How much can be

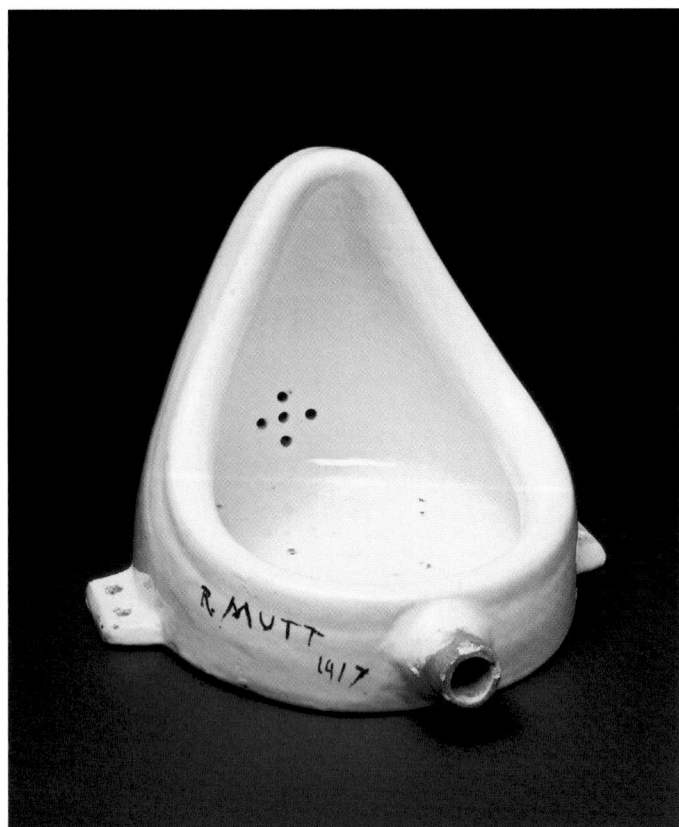

31-30 • Marcel Duchamp FOUNTAIN
1917. Porcelain plumbing fixture and enamel paint, height 24⅝″
(62.5 cm). Photograph by Alfred Stieglitz. Philadelphia Museum of Art,
Pennsylvania. Louise and Walter Arensberg Collection (1998-74-1)

SEE MORE: View a video on Marcel Duchamp
www.myartslab.com

stripped away before the essence of art disappears? Since Whistler's
famous court case (see "Art on Trial in 1877," page 999), most
avant-garde artists would have responded that a work of art need
be neither descriptive nor well-crafted but, before 1917, none
would have argued, as Duchamp does in this piece, that "art" might
be primarily conceptual. For centuries, artists regularly employed
studio assistants to craft parts, if not all, of the art objects that they
designed. In some ways Duchamp translated that practice into
modern terms by arguing that art objects might not only be
crafted (in part) by others, but that the objects of art could actually
be manufactured for the artist in the mass-produced world.
In a clever twist of logic, Duchamp simultaneously makes a
commentary on consumption, modernity, and the irrationality of
the modern age by arguing that the "readymade" work of art, as a
manufactured object, simply bypasses the craft tradition. Duchamp
translated this idea into physical form in *Fountain*.

Fountain is one of the most transgressive works of art in Western
history. It is still funny, mad, and obscene; it refers openly to
bathroom functions, to humanity's most degraded functions and
vulnerable states, and it challenges every assumption made about the
nature of art. When *Fountain* was rejected, as Duchamp anticipated it
would be, the artist resigned from the Society in mock horror, and

published an unsigned editorial in a Dada journal detailing what he
described as the scandal of the R. Mutt case. He wrote: "The only
works of art America has given are her plumbing and bridges,"
adding, "Whether Mr. Mutt with his own hands made the fountain
or not has no importance. He CHOSE it. He took an ordinary article of life, placed it so that its useful significance disappeared under the
new title and point of view—created a new thought for that object."

After Duchamp returned to Paris, he challenged the French
art world with a piece that he entitled **L.H.O.O.Q. (FIG. 31–31)**, and
that he described as a "modified readymade." In 1911, Leonardo's
famous *Mona Lisa* (SEE FIG. 20–5) was stolen from the Louvre and
it took two years to recover it. While missing, however, the
painting became even more famous than when it had actually been
on public display, being widely and badly reproduced on postcards,
posters, and in advertising. Duchamp chose to comment on the
nature of fame and on the degraded image of the *Mona Lisa* in
L.H.O.O.Q. In 1919, he purchased a cheap postcard reproduction
of the *Mona Lisa* and drew a mustache and beard on her famously

31-31 • Marcel Duchamp L.H.O.O.Q.
1919. Pencil on reproduction of Leonardo da Vinci's *Mona Lisa*.
7¾ × 4¾″ (19.7 × 12.1 cm). Philadelphia Museum of Art, Pennsylvania.
Louise and Walter Arensberg Collection

enigmatic face. In doing so he turned a sacred cultural artifact into an object of crude ridicule. The letters that he scrawled across the bottom of the card, "L.H.O.O.Q.," when read aloud sound phonetically similar to the French slang phrase *elle a chaud au cul*, politely translated as "she's hot for it," thus adding a crude sexual innuendo to the already cheapened image. Like *Fountain*, this work challenges preconceived notions about morality or virtue being a basis for art and introduces disgust as a viable artistic subject. Indeed, as one of Dada's founders said: "Dada was born of disgust."

Duchamp made only a few readymades. In fact, he created very little art at all after about 1922, when he devoted himself mostly to chess. When asked about his occupation, he described himself as a "retired artist," but his ideas have been among the most influential on art produced since 1960.

BERLIN DADA. Early in 1917, Hugo Ball and the Romanian-born poet Tristan Tzara (1896–1963) organized the Galerie Dada. Tzara also edited the magazine *Dada*, which quickly attracted the attention of like-minded artists and writers in several European capitals and in the United States. The movement spread farther when expatriate members of Hugo Ball's circle in Switzerland returned to their homelands after the war. Richard Huelsenbeck (1892–1974), for instance, took Dada to Germany, where he helped found the Club Dada in Berlin in April 1918.

Dada pursued a slightly different agenda and took on different forms in each of its major centers. A distinctive feature of Berlin Dada was its agitprop agenda. It also produced an unusually large amount of visual art—especially collage and **photomontage** (photographic collage)—compared to the more literary forms of Dada elsewhere.

Kurt Schwitters (1887–1948), for instance, who met Huelsenbeck and other Dadaists in 1919, used discarded rail tickets, postage stamps, ration coupons, beer labels, and other street detritus to create visual poetry. Schwitters termed his two- and three-dimensional works of art, made out of the wasted ephemera of the industrial world, *Merzbilder. Merz* was Schwitters's term for the refuse he collected; *Bild* is German for "picture." In his "Merz Pictures," Schwitters's collaged together fragments of newspaper and other printed material with drawn or painted images. He wrote that garbage demanded equal rights with painting. In **MERZBILD 5B (FIG. 31–32)**, Schwitters has collaged printed fragments from the street with newspaper scraps to comment on the postwar disorder of defeated Germany. One fragment describes the brutal overthrow of the short-lived socialist republic in Bremen.

Hannah Höch (1889–1978) produced even more pointed political photomontages. Between 1916 and 1926, she worked for Verlang, Berlin's largest publishing house, designing decorative

31-32 • Kurt Schwitters MERZBILD 5B (PICTURE-RED-HEART-CHURCH)
April 26, 1919. Collage, tempera, and crayon on cardboard, 32⅞ × 23¾″ (83.4 × 60.3 cm). Guggenheim Museum, New York. 52.1325

patterns and writing articles on crafts for a women's magazine. Höch considered herself part of the women's movement in the 1920s. She disapproved of contemporary mass-media representations of women and had to fight for her place as the sole woman among the Berlin Dada group, one of whom described her contribution disparagingly as merely conjuring up beer and sandwiches. In **CUT WITH THE DADA KITCHEN KNIFE THROUGH THE LAST WEIMAR BEER-BELLY CULTURAL EPOCH IN GERMANY (FIG. 31–33)**, Höch collages images and words from the popular press, political posters, and photographs to create a complex and angry critique of the Weimar Republic in 1919. She shows women physically cutting apart the beer-bloated German establishment in this photomontage and includes portraits of androgynous Dada characters, such as herself and several other Berlin Dada artists, along with Marx and Lenin. It is tempting to wonder which side she really thinks her fellow Dadaists stand on.

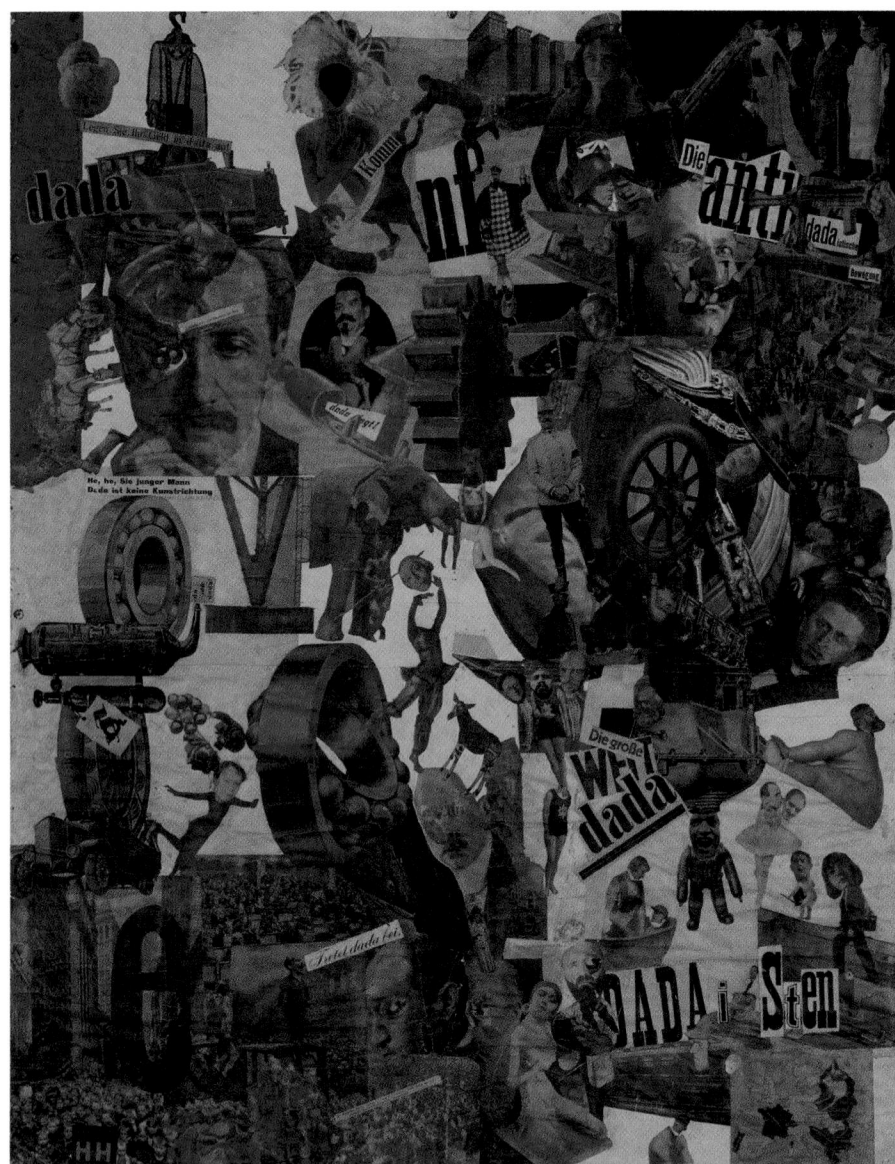

MODERNIST TENDENCIES IN AMERICA

When avant-garde Modern art was first widely exhibited in the United States, it received a cool welcome. While some American artists did work in abstract or Modern ways, most preferred to work in a more naturalistic manner, at least until around 1915.

THE ASHCAN SCHOOL

In the first decade of the twentieth century, a vigorous realist movement coalesced in New York City around the charismatic painter and teacher Robert Henri (1865–1929), who rejected the idyllic Impressionist imagery of the previous generation in America. Henri told his students: "Paint what you see. Paint what is real to you." In 1908, he organized an exhibition of artists called The Eight, four of whom trained and worked as newspaper illustrators and whose exhibition introduced scenes of gritty urban life in New York City to American art. Five of The Eight, who painted the street life of the immigrant poor specifically, were dubbed the Ashcan School.

Henri greatly admired Manet's paintings of modern life and the art of the Spanish Baroque. He traveled to Spain where, in 1906, he painted **LA REINA MORA (FIG. 31–34)**. "La Reina Mora" (the Moorish Queen) was the stage name of Milagros Morena, a well-known Andalusian dancer. In the painting Moreno stands proudly in a red-flowered costume with a fringed skirt, a luxurious silver-white shawl, and pink satin dancing shoes, wearing several rings on her fingers, a golden bracelet around one wrist, and two decorative necklaces around her neck. Her jet-black hair is dressed with ribbons or flowers. Morena's face is covered with a whitish makeup that is in contrast to the darker skin of her neck and arms, making her strong black eyebrows, deep dark eyes, rouged cheeks, and red lips stand out dramatically.

STIEGLITZ AND THE "291" GALLERY

The chief proponent of European Modern art in the United States was the photographer Alfred Stieglitz (1864–1946), who in the years before World War I organized several small exhibitions

In his own photographs, Stieglitz tried to compose poetic images of romanticized urban scenes. In **THE FLATIRON BUILDING** (**FIG. 31–35**), the tree trunk to the right is echoed by branches in the grove farther back, and in the wedge-shaped Flatiron Building to the rear. An arc of chairs and a low wall behind seem to encircle the trees. The entire scene is suffused with a misty wintery atmosphere, which the artist created by manipulating his viewpoint, exposure, and possibly both the negative and positive images.

31-34 • Robert Henri **LA REINE MORA**
1906. Oil on canvas, 78 × 42¹⁄₁₆″ (198 × 107 cm). Museum purchase from the Jere Abbott Acquisitions Fund, Colby Museum of Art.

31-35 • Alfred Stieglitz **THE FLATIRON BUILDING**
1903. Photogravure, 6¹¹⁄₁₆ × 3⁵⁄₁₆″ (17 × 8.4 cm) mounted. Metropolitan Museum of Art, New York. Gift of J. B. Neumann, 1958 (58.577.37)

featuring the art of major Modernists at a tiny gallery at 291 Fifth Avenue, known simply as 291. Stieglitz, like Kahnweiler in Paris, supported many of the early American Modernist painters and photographers in New York. As a photographer himself, he sought to establish the legitimacy of photography as a fine art with these exhibitions.

Born in New Jersey to a wealthy German immigrant family, Stieglitz studied photography in the 1880s at the Technische Hochschule in Berlin, quickly recognizing photography's artistic potential. In 1890, he began to photograph New York City street scenes. He promoted his views through an organization called the Photo-Secession, founded in 1902, and two years later opened the 291 gallery. By 1910, this gallery had become a focal point for both photographers and artists, with Stieglitz giving shows (sometimes their first) to artists such as Arthur Dove, John Marin, and Georgia O'Keeffe, and bringing to America the art of European artists such as Kandinsky, Braque, Cézanne, and Rodin.

Ironically, Stieglitz softens and romanticizes the Flatiron Building, one of New York's earliest skyscrapers and a symbol of the city's modernity. The magazine *Camera Work*, a high-quality photographic publication that Stieglitz edited, and which published this photograph in photogravure form in 1903, also featured numerous photogravures of American and European Modernist art as well as some important American Modern art criticism.

THE ARMORY SHOW AND HOME-GROWN MODERNISM

In 1913, Modernist art arrived in New York en masse with an enormous exhibition held in the drill hall of the 69th Street Armory. Walt Kuhn (1877–1949) and Arthur B. Davies (1862–1928), a member of The Eight, were the principal organizers of the "Armory Show," which featured more than 1,600 works, a quarter of them by European artists. Most of the art, even Modernist art, was well received and sold well, but the art of a few European Modernists, including Matisse and Duchamp in particular, caused a public outcry. Some of the latter were described as being "cousins to the anarchists," and when selected works from the exhibition traveled on to Chicago, a few faculty and some students of the School of the Art Institute even hanged Matisse in effigy, while civic leaders called for a morals commission to investigate the show. Yet the exhibition consolidated American Modernist art and inspired its artists, who subsequently found more enthusiastic collectors and exhibition venues.

One of the most significant early American Modernists was Arthur Dove (1880–1946). Dove studied the work of the Fauves in Europe in 1907–1909, and he even exhibited at the Autumn Salon. After returning home, he began making abstract nature studies about the same time as Kandinsky, although each was unaware of the other. Dove's **NATURE SYMBOLIZED NO. 2 (FIG. 31–36)** is one of a remarkable series of small works that reveals his beliefs about the spiritual power of nature. But while Kandinsky's art focuses on an inner vision of nature, Dove rendered his deeply felt experience within the landscape in abstract terms, saying that he had "no [artistic] background except perhaps the woods, running streams, hunting, fishing, camping, the sky." Dove supported himself by farming in rural Connecticut, but he exhibited his art in New York and was both well received by and connected to the New York art community.

Another pioneer of American Modernism who exhibited at the Armory Show was Marsden Hartley (1877–1943), who was also a regular exhibitor at the 291 gallery. Between 1912 and 1915, Hartley lived mostly abroad, first in Paris, where he discovered Cubism, then in Berlin, where he began to paint colorful Expressionistic art. Around 1914, however, Hartley developed a powerfully original and intense style of his own in *Portrait of a German Officer* (see "A Closer Look," page 1044), a tightly arranged composition of boldly colored shapes and patterns, interspersed with numbers, letters, and fragments of German military imagery that refer symbolically to Hartley's fallen lover.

Georgia O'Keeffe (1887–1986) was born in rural Wisconsin, studied and taught art sporadically between 1905 and 1915, and was "discovered" by Stieglitz when a New York friend showed

31–36 • Arthur Dove
NATURE SYMBOLIZED NO. 2
c. 1911. Pastel on paper, 18 × 21⅝″ (45.8 × 55 cm). Art Institute of Chicago.

him some of her charcoal drawings. Stieglitz's reported response was: "At last, a woman on paper!" In 1916, Stieglitz included O'Keeffe's work in a group show at 291 and gave her a solo exhibition the following year. O'Keeffe's flower paintings were described by critics as essentially feminine and vaginal. Stieglitz did little to dissuade this reading of O'Keeffe's art and, in fact, did quite a bit to promote it. O'Keeffe objected strenuously to this critical caricature, claiming that she was an artist, not just a woman artist.

O'Keeffe moved to New York in 1918 and married Stieglitz in 1924. In 1925, she began to paint New York skyscrapers, which were acclaimed at the time as embodiments of American inventiveness and energy. But paintings such as **CITY NIGHT** (FIG. **31–37**) are not unambiguous celebrations of lofty buildings. O'Keeffe frequently portrayed her architectural subjects from a low vantage point so that they appear to loom ominously over the

31-38 • Georgia O'Keeffe AN ORCHID
1941. Pastel on board, 21¾ × 27⅝″ (55.2 × 70.2 cm). Museum of Modern Art, New York. Bequest of Georgia O'Keeffe (556.1990)

31-37 • Georgia O'Keeffe CITY NIGHT
1926. Oil on canvas, 48 × 30″ (123 × 76.9 cm).
Minneapolis Institute of Arts.

viewer; in *City Night*, for instance, the dark tonalities, stark forms, and exaggerated perspective produce a sense of menace that also appears in the art of other American Modernists.

In 1925, O'Keeffe also began to exhibit a series of close-up paintings of flowers that remain among her best-known subjects. In **AN ORCHID** (FIG. **31–38**), O'Keeffe brings the heart of the heavy sensual flower to the very front of the picture plane, revealing its inner organs and soft, delicate surfaces. Whether intentionally sexual or not, these works drip with sensuality. In 1929, O'Keeffe began spending her summers in New Mexico and moved there permanently in the 1940s.

EARLY MODERN ARCHITECTURE

New industrial materials and engineering innovations enabled twentieth-century architects to create tall buildings of unprecedented height that vastly increased the usable space in structures built on scarce and valuable city lots. At the same time that Modern artists in Europe rejected the decorative in painting and sculpture, American architects increasingly embraced the plain geometric shapes and undecorated surfaces of skyscraper architecture.

Portrait of a German Officer ➤

by Marsden Hartley, 1914. Oil on canvas, 68¼ × 41⅜" (1.78 × 1.05 m). Metropolitan Museum of Art, New York. The Alfred Stieglitz Collection, 1949 (49.70.42)

Symbolic references to Freyburg include epaulettes, lance tips, and the Iron Cross he was awarded the day before he was killed.

The black-and-white checkerboard patterns evoke Freyburg's love of chess.

His regiment number ("4") is shown at the center of the abstracted chest along with a red cursive "E," which stands for "Edmund" (Hartley's given name). This places Hartley over Freyburg's heart.

The blue-and-white diamond pattern comes from the Bavarian flag; the red, white, and black bands constitute the flag of the German Empire, adopted in 1871; and the black-and-white stripes are those of the historic flag of Prussia.

The funereal black background heightens the intensity of the foreground colors.

Hartley identifies his subject with his initials ("Kv.F") in gold on red.

The young man's age ("24") is noted in gold on blue.

While living in Berlin in 1914, Hartley fell in love with a young Prussian lieutenant, Karl von Freyburg, whom Hartley described as "in every way a perfect being—physically, spiritually, and mentally." Freyburg's death in World War I devastated Hartley, who memorialized his fallen lover in this symbolic portrait.

SEE MORE: View the Closer Look feature for *Portrait of a German Officer* **www.myartslab.com**

31-39 • Adolf Loos STEINER HOUSE
Vienna. 1910.

EUROPEAN MODERNISM

In Europe, a stripped-down and severely geometric style of Modern architecture developed, partly in reaction to the natural organic lines of Art Nouveau. In Vienna, Adolf Loos (1870–1933), one of the pioneers of European architectural Modernism, insisted in his 1913 essay "Ornament and Crime" that "The evolution of a culture is synonymous with the removal of ornament from utilitarian objects." For Loos, ornament was a sign of cultural degeneracy. Thus his **STEINER HOUSE** (FIG. 31–39) is a stucco-covered, reinforced concrete construction without decorative embellishment. Loos argued that the exterior's only function was to provide protection from the elements; the placement of the plain rectangular windows, for instance, was ostensibly determined by interior needs.

The most important French Modern architect was Le Corbusier, who established several important precepts that influenced architects for the next half-century. His **VILLA SAVOYE** (FIG. 31–40), a private home outside Paris, is an icon of the International Style (see "The International Style," page 1057) that also reflects his Purist ideals in its rectilinear design and lack of ornamentation. It is also one of the best expressions of Le Corbusier's **domino construction** system, first elaborated in 1914, in which slabs of ferroconcrete (concrete reinforced with steel bars) rest on six free-standing steel posts, placed at the positions of the six dots on a domino playing piece. Over the next decade Le Corbusier further explored the possibilities of the domino system and in 1926 published "The Five Points of a New Architecture," in which he proposed raising houses above the ground on **pilotis** (free-standing posts); using flat roofs as terraces; using movable partition walls slotted between supports on the interior and **curtain walls** (nonloadbearing exterior walls) to allow greater design flexibility; and using ribbon windows (windows that run the length of the wall). All of these became features of Modern architecture. Le Corbusier described the Villa Savoye as "a machine for living in," meaning that it was designed as rationally as a car or a machine. He also developed designs for mass-produced standardized housing as many architects did after World War I to help rebuild Europe's destroyed infrastructure.

31-40 • Le Corbusier VILLA SAVOYE
Poissy-sur-Seine, France. 1929–1930.

EXPLORE MORE: Click the Google Earth link for Villa Savoye **www.myartslab.com**

AMERICAN MODERN ARCHITECTURE

CONNECTION TO THE LAND.   Frank Lloyd Wright (1867–1959) was not only America's most important Modernist architect, he was also one of the most influential architects in the world in the early twentieth century. After briefly studying engineering at the University of Wisconsin, Wright apprenticed to a Chicago architect, then spent five years with the firm of Dankmar Adler and Louis Sullivan (SEE FIG. 30–55), eventually becoming their chief drafter. In 1893, Wright established his own office, specializing in domestic architecture. Around 1900, he and several other architects in the Oak Park suburb of Chicago began to design low, horizontal houses with flat roofs and heavy overhangs that echoed the flat plains of the prairie in the Midwest. This group of architects was known as the Prairie School.

The **FREDERICK C. ROBIE HOUSE (FIG. 31–41)** is one of Wright's early masterpieces in the **Prairie Style**. It was designed around a central chimney (to radiate heat throughout the house in the bitter Chicago winter), and features a low, flat overhanging roof (to shade against the summer sun) with open porches for sleeping outside in the cool of summer nights. The roof is dramatically cantilevered on both sides of the chimney. The windows are arranged in low bands around the house; many are stained glass, creating a colored screen between the interior of the house and the outside world while also inviting the viewer to look through the windows into the garden beyond.

The horizontal emphasis continues inside. The main living level is one long space divided into living and dining areas by a free-standing fireplace. There are no dividing walls. Wright visited the Japanese exhibit at the 1893 Chicago World's Fair and was deeply influenced by the aesthetics of Japanese architecture, particularly its use of space and screenlike windows (see "*Shoin Design*," page 819). Wright's homes frequently featured built-in closets and bookcases, and he hid heating and lighting fixtures when possible. He also designed and arranged the furniture for his interiors **(FIG. 32–42)**. Here, the chairs are machine-cut in modern geometric designs, while their high backs huddle around the table to create the intimate effect of a room within a room. Wright integrated lights and flower holders into the posts closest to the table's corners so that there would no need for lights or flowers on the table.

Wright had an uneasy relationship with European Modernist architecture. Although he routinely used new building materials such as concrete, glass, and steel, he also tried to create a more natural sensibility by connecting his buildings to their sites using brick, wood, or local stone. He was uninterested in the machine aesthetic of Le Corbusier.

FALLINGWATER (FIG. 31–43) in rural Pennsylvania is perhaps the best-known expression of Wright's conviction that buildings should not simply sit *on* the landscape but exist *in* it. Fallingwater was commissioned by Edgar Kaufmann, a Pittsburgh department

31–41 • Frank Lloyd Wright **FREDERICK C. ROBIE HOUSE**
Chicago. 1906–1909.

EXPLORE MORE: Click the Google Earth link for the Robie House **www.myartslab.com**

31-43 • Frank Lloyd Wright EDGAR KAUFMANN HOUSE, FALLINGWATER
Mill Run, Pennsylvania. 1937.

SEE MORE: View an animated video of Fallingwater **www.myartslab.com**

store owner, to replace a family summer cottage on the site of a waterfall and a pool where his children played. To Kaufmann's surprise, Wright decided to build the new house right into the cliff and over the pool, allowing the waterfall to flow around and under the house. A large boulder where the family had sunbathed in the summers was used for the central hearthstone of the fireplace. In a dramatic move that engineers questioned (with reason, as subsequent history has shown), Wright used cantilevers to extend a series of broad concrete terraces out from the cliff to parallel the huge slabs of rock below. The terraces are all poured concrete, but Wright painted them a soft earth tone; he made use of local wood and stone wherever possible. Wright preferred to design rural or suburban structures and disliked the inner city. When asked what could be done to improve city architecture, Wright responded: "Tear it down."

Mary Colter (1869–1958) also expressed a strong connection to the land in her architecture. Born in Pittsburgh and educated at the California School of Design in San Francisco, she spent much of her career as an architect and decorator for the Fred Harvey Company, which operated luxury hotels throughout the Southwest. Colter was an avid student of Native American art, especially the architecture of the Hopi and Pueblo peoples, and her buildings quoted liberally from those traditions. She designed several visitor facilities at Grand Canyon National Park, of which **LOOKOUT STUDIO** (FIG. 31–44) is one of the most dramatic. The building perches on the edge of the chasm; its foundation is the natural rock of the canyon, and its walls are built from stones quarried nearby. The roofline is deliberately irregular to echo the surrounding canyon wall. Inside, Colter used exposed logs for many of the structural supports and ceiling, in homage to Hopi architecture. The only concession to modernity is a liberal use of

glass windows and a cement floor. Colter's work on hotels and railroad stations throughout the region helped to establish the distinctive Southwest style.

THE AMERICAN SKYSCRAPER. After 1900, New York City assumed a lead over Chicago in the development of the skyscraper, whose soaring height was made possible by the use of the steel-frame skeleton for structural support (see "The Skyscraper," page 1050). New York clients rejected the more utilitarian Chicago style of Louis Sullivan and others, preferring the historicizing approach then still popular on the east coast. The **WOOLWORTH BUILDING** (FIG. 31–45), designed by the Minnesota-based firm of Cass Gilbert (1859–1934), was the world's tallest building at 792 feet and 55 floors when first completed. Its Gothic-style external details, inspired by the soaring towers of late medieval churches, gave the building a strong visual personality. Because of its Gothic style, Gilbert called it his "Cathedral of Commerce."

ART BETWEEN THE WARS IN EUROPE

World War I had a devastating effect on Europe's artists and architects. Many artists responded to the destruction and loss of a generation of young men by criticizing the European tradition, while others sought to rebuild. Either way, much of the art created between 1919 and 1939 addressed the needs and concerns of society directly.

UTILITARIAN ART FORMS IN RUSSIA

In the 1917 Russian Revolution, the radical socialist Bolsheviks overthrew the tsar, withdrew Russia from the world war, and turned inward to fight a civil war that lasted until 1920 and led to the establishment of the U.S.S.R. (Union of Soviet Socialist Republics). Most Russian avant-garde artists enthusiastically supported the Bolsheviks and were initially supported by them.

CONSTRUCTIVISM. The case of Aleksandr Rodchenko (1891–1956) is fairly representative. An early associate of Malevich (SEE FIG. 31–25), Rodchenko used drafting tools to make abstract drawings. He exhibited as a Suprematist in 1921 when he showed three large, flat, monochromatic panels painted red, yellow, and blue, which he titled *Last Painting* (now lost). After this, he renounced painting as a basically selfish activity and condemned self-expression as weak and socially irresponsible.

Also in 1921, Rodchenko helped to establish the Constructivists, a post-revolutionary group of artists dedicated to working collectively for the good of the state who described themselves as workers who literally "constructed" art for the people. Rodchenko was convinced that self-expression in art did not contribute enough to society, so after 1921 he worked as a photographer producing posters, books, textiles, and theater sets to promote communism.

In 1925, Rodchenko designed a model workers' club for the Soviet Pavilion at the Paris International Exposition of Modern Decorative and Industrial Arts **(FIG. 31–46)**. Rodchenko designed the club for ease of use and simplicity of construction; the furniture was made of wood because Soviet industry was best equipped for mass production in wood. The high, straight backs of the chairs were meant to promote a physical and moral posture of uprightness among the workers.

Another artist active in early Soviet Russia was El Lissitzky (1890–1941), who, after the Revolution, was invited to teach architecture and graphic arts at the Vitebsk School of Fine Arts where Malevich also taught. By 1919, Lissitzky was both teaching and using a Constructivist vocabulary for propaganda posters and

31-45 • Cass Gilbert WOOLWORTH BUILDING
New York. 1911–1913. Collection of the New York Historical Society, New York

31-46 • Aleksandr Rodchenko WORKERS' CLUB
Exhibited at the International Exposition of Modern Decorative and Industrial Arts, Paris. 1925. Rodchenko-Stepanova Archive, Moscow

The development of the skyscraper design and aesthetic depended on several things: The use of metal beams and girders for the structural-support skeleton; the separation of the building-support structure from the enclosing wall layer (the cladding); the use of fireproof materials and measures; the use of elevators; and the overall integration of plumbing, central heating, artificial lighting, and ventilation systems. The first generation of skyscrapers, built between about 1880 and 1900, were concentrated in the Midwest, chiefly in Chicago and St. Louis (SEE FIG. 30–55). Second-generation skyscrapers, mostly with over 20 stories, date from after 1895 and are found more frequently in New York. The first tall buildings were free-standing towers, sometimes with a base, such as the Woolworth Building of 1911–1913 (SEE FIG. 31–45). New York City's Building Zone Resolution of 1916 introduced mandatory setbacks—decreases in girth as the building rose—to ensure light and ventilation to adjacent sites. Built in 1931, the 1,250-foot setback form of the Empire State Building, diagrammed here, has a streamlined design. The Art Deco exterior cladding (see inset below) conceals the structural elements and mechanisms such as elevators that make its great height possible. The Empire State Building was the tallest building in the world when it was built and its distinctive profile ensures that it remains one of the most recognizable even today.

elevator shafts (layer two)

stairwells (layer one)

masonry wall

girder

cladding

heat source

concrete slab flooring

beam

setbacks

skyscraper

SEE MORE: View a simulation of skyscraper construction **www.myartslab.com**

for work that he called the Proun (pronounced "pro-oon"), thought to be an acronym for the Russian *proekt utverzhdenya novogo* ("project for the affirmation of the new"). Although most Prouns were paintings or prints, a few were installed in specific sites (FIG. 31–47) to create a total environment. Lissitzky rejected painting as too personal and imprecise, preferring to "construct" Prouns for the collective using the less personal instruments of mechanical drawing. Like many other Soviet artists of the late 1920s, Lissitzky also turned to more socially engaged projects such

as architectural design, typography, photography, and photomontage for publication.

SOCIALIST REALISM. In the mid 1920s, Soviet artists increasingly rejected abstraction in favor of a more universally accessible, and thus more politically useful, Socialist Realism that was ultimately established as official Soviet art. Many of Russia's pioneering Modernists and Constructivists, including Rodchenko, made the change willingly because they were already committed to the

31-47 • El Lissitzky PROUN SPACE
Created for the Great Berlin Art Exhibition. 1923, reconstruction 1965. Stedelijk Van Abbemuseum, Eindhoven, The Netherlands.

national cause, but others, who refused to change, were fired from public positions and lost public support.

The move to Socialist Realism was led by the Association of Artists of Revolutionary Russia (AKhRR), founded in 1922 to depict Russian workers, peasants, revolutionary activists, and the Red Army. AKhRR sought to document the history of the U.S.S.R. by promoting its leaders and goals. Artists were commissioned to create public paintings and sculptures as well as posters for mass distribution; their subjects were heroic or inspirational people and themes, and their style was an easily readable realism.

Vera Mukhina (1889–1953) was a member of AKhRR and is best known for her 78-foot-tall stainless-steel sculpture of a **WORKER AND COLLECTIVE FARM WOMAN (FIG. 31–48)** made for the Soviet Pavilion at the Paris Universal Exposition of 1937. The sculpture shows a powerfully built male factory worker and an equally powerful female farm laborer with their hammer and sickle held high in the air, reflecting the same tools as appeared on the Soviet flag. The figures are portrayed as equals, partners in their common cause, striding purposefully into the future with determined faces set and their windblown clothing billowing behind them.

31-48 • Vera Mukhina WORKER AND COLLECTIVE FARM WOMAN
Sculpture for the Soviet Pavilion, Paris Universal Exposition. 1937. Stainless steel, height approx. 78′ (23.8 m).

RATIONALISM IN THE NETHERLANDS

In the Netherlands after World War I, abstraction took a different turn than in the U.S.S.R. The Dutch artist Piet Mondrian (1872–1944) encountered Cubism on a trip to Paris in 1912 where he began to abstract animals, trees, and landscapes, searching for their "essential" form. After his return to the Netherlands, he met Theo van Doesburg (1883–1931) who, in 1917, started a magazine named *De Stijl* (*The Style*) that became a focal point for Dutch artists, architects, and designers after the war. In the magazine, Van Doesburg argued that there are two kinds of beauty: sensual or subjective beauty, and a higher, rational, and universal beauty and that De Stijl (note the term translates as "*The* Style" rather than "*A* Style") artists should aspire to create the latter kind of beauty. Mondrian adhered to De Stijl's rational, universal beauty by eliminating everything sensual or subjective from his paintings, but he also followed M. H. J. Schoenmaekers's ideas about Theosophy, as expressed in his 1915 book *New Image of the World.* Schoenmaekers argued that an inner visual construction of nature consisted of a balance between opposing forces, such as heat and cold, male and female, order and disorder, and that artists might represent this inner construction in abstract paintings by using only horizontal and vertical lines and primary colors.

Mondrian's later paintings seem to be visual embodiments of both Schoenmaekers's theory and De Stijl's artistic ideas. In **COMPOSITION WITH YELLOW, RED, AND BLUE** (**FIG. 31–49**), for example, Mondrian uses three primary colors (red, yellow, and blue), three neutrals (white, gray, and black), and a grid of horizontal and vertical lines in his search for the essence of higher beauty and the balance of forces. Mondrian's opposing lines and colors balance a harmony of opposites that he called a "dynamic equilibrium" and which he achieved by carefully plotting an arrangement of colors, shapes, and visual weights grouped asymmetrically around the edges of a canvas, with the center acting as a blank white fulcrum. Mondrian hoped that De Stijl would have applications in the real world and would help to create an entirely new visual environment for living, designed according to the rules of a "universal beauty" that, when perfectly balanced, would both balance and purify the world. Mondrian said that he hoped to be the world's last artist, because, while art brought humanity to everyday life, when "universal beauty" infused all aspects of life, there would no longer be a need for art.

The architect and designer Gerrit Rietveld (1888–1964) applied Mondrian's principles of dynamic equilibrium and De Stijl's theories to architecture to create one of the most important examples of the International Style (see "The International Style,"

31-49 • Piet Mondrian
COMPOSITION WITH YELLOW, RED, AND BLUE, 1927
1927. Oil on canvas, 14⅞ × 13¾" (37.8 × 34.9 cm). The Menil Collection, Houston.
© 2010 Mondrian/Holtzman Trust c/o HCR International, Virginia 20186 USA

31–50 • Gerrit Rietveld SCHRÖDER HOUSE
Utrecht, the Netherlands. 1925.

EXPLORE MORE: Click the Google Earth link for the Schröder House
www.myartslab.com

page 1057). The radically asymmetrical exterior of the **SCHRÖDER HOUSE** in Utrecht (**FIG. 31–50**) is composed of interlocking gray and white planes of varying sizes, combined with horizontal and vertical accents in primary colors and black. The **"RED-BLUE" CHAIR** (**FIG. 31–51**) echoes the arrangement in the interior, where sliding partitions allow modifications in the spaces used for sleeping, working, and entertaining. The patron of the house, Truus Schröder-Schröder, wanted a home that suggested an elegant austerity, with basic necessities sleekly integrated into a balanced and restrained whole.

31–51 • Gerrit Rietveld INTERIOR, SCHRÖDER HOUSE, WITH "RED-BLUE" CHAIR
1925.

BAUHAUS ART IN GERMANY

In Germany, the creators of the Bauhaus ("House of Building"), which had been founded by Walter Gropius (1883–1969) in Weimar in 1919, found the strict geometric shapes and lines of Purism and De Stijl too rigid and argued that a true German architecture and design should emerge organically. At the Bauhaus, Gropius brought together German architects, designers, and craft workers whose collective creative energy could be harnessed to create an integrated system of design and production based on German traditions and styles. Gropius believed that he could revive the spirit of collaboration of the medieval building guilds (*Bauhütten*) that had erected Germany's cathedrals.

Although Gropius's "Bauhaus Manifesto" of 1919 declared that "the ultimate goal of all artistic activity is the building," the Bauhaus offered no formal training in architecture until 1927. Gropius's students were allowed to begin architectural training only after they completed a mandatory foundation course and received full training in design and crafts in the Bauhaus workshops. These included pottery, metalwork, textiles, stained glass, furniture, wood carving, and wall paintings. In 1922, Gropius also added a new emphasis on industrial design and the next year hired the Hungarian-born László Moholy-Nagy (1895–1946) to reorient the workshops toward more functional design suitable for mass production.

In 1925, when the Bauhaus moved to Dessau, Gropius designed its new building. Although the structure openly acknowledges its reinforced concrete, steel, and glass materials, there is also a balanced asymmetry to its three large cubic areas that was intended

31-53 • Marianne Brandt COFFEE AND TEA SERVICE
1924. Silver and ebony, with Plexiglas cover for sugar bowl. Bauhaus Archiv, Berlin.

to convey the dynamism of modern life **(FIG. 31–52)**. A glass-panel wall wraps around two sides of the workshop wing of the building to provide natural light for the workshops inside, while a parapet below demonstrates how modern engineering methods could create light, airy spaces. Both Moholy-Nagy and Gropius left the Bauhaus in 1928. The school eventually moved to Berlin in 1932, but lasted only one more year before the new German chancellor, Adolf Hitler, forced its closure (see "Suppression of the Avant-Garde in Nazi Germany," page 1055). Hitler opposed Modern art on two grounds: First, it was cosmopolitan and not nationalistic enough; second, he believed it to be overly influenced by Jews. The first was a matter of opinion; the second was patently untrue.

31-52 • Walter Gropius BAUHAUS BUILDING
Dessau, Germany. 1925–1926. View from northwest.

Suppression of the Avant-Garde in Nazi Germany

In the 1930s, the avant-garde was increasingly disparaged by Hitler and the rising Nazi Party. This led to a concerted effort to suppress it. One of the principal targets was the Bauhaus. Through much of the 1920s, classes there were taught by important artists such as Paul Klee, Vassily Kandinsky, Josef Albers, and Ludwig Mies van der Rohe. But they struggled against an increasingly hostile and reactionary political climate. As early as 1924, conservatives accused the Bauhaus of being not only educationally unsound but also politically subversive. To avoid having the school shut down by the opposition, Gropius moved it to Dessau in 1925, at the invitation of Dessau's liberal mayor, but he left office soon after the relocation and his successors faced increasing political pressure to close the school as it was a prime center of Modernist practice. The Bauhaus was forced to move again in 1932, this time to Berlin.

After Adolf Hitler came to power in 1933, the Nazi Party mounted an even more aggressive campaign against Modern art. In his youth Hitler had been a mediocre landscape painter, and he developed an intense hatred of the avant-garde. During the first year of his regime, the Bauhaus was forced to close permanently. A number of the artists, designers, and architects who had been on its faculty—including Albers, Gropius, and Mies—fled to the United States.

The Nazis also attacked German Expressionist artists, whose often-intense depictions of German politics and the economic crisis after the war criticized the state and whose frequent caricatures of German facial features and body types undermined Nazi attempts to redraw Germans as idealized Aryans. Expressionist and avant-garde art was removed from museums and confiscated, and artists were forbidden to buy paint or canvas and were subjected to public intimidation.

In 1937, the Nazi leadership organized an exhibition of what they termed "Degenerate Art" in an attempt to ridicule the banned Modern art and erase its makers. The Nazis described the avant-garde and Modernism as sick and degenerate, presenting the confiscated paintings and sculptures as specimens of pathology and scrawling slogans and derisive commentaries on the walls of the exhibition (see illustration). Ironically, the exhibition of 650 paintings, sculptures, prints, and books confiscated from German museums and artists was viewed by as many as 2 million people in four months in Munich, and by another 1 million on its three-year tour of German cities.

Large numbers of confiscated works that were supposed to be destroyed were looted by Nazi officials and sold in Switzerland in exchange for foreign currency. The ownership of much of the surviving art is still in question. Many artists fled to neighboring countries or the United States, but some, such as Ernst Ludwig Kirchner, whose *Street, Berlin* (SEE FIG. 31–13) was included in the "Degenerate Art" exhibit, were driven to suicide by their loss. Even the work of artists sympathetic to the Nazi position was not safe. Emil Nolde (SEE FIG. 31–12), who joined the Nazi Party in 1932, also had his art confiscated.

THE DADA WALL IN ROOM 3 OF THE "DEGENERATE ART" ("ENTARTETE KUNST") EXHIBITION
Munich. 1937.

31–54 • Anni Albers WALL HANGING
1926. Silk, two-ply weave, 5′11⅝₆″ × 3′11⅝″ (1.83 × 1.22 m).
Busch-Reisinger Museum, Harvard University, Cambridge,
Massachusetts. Association Fund

Marianne Brandt's (1893–1983) elegant tea and coffee service **(FIG. 31–53)**, handcrafted in silver, is an example of the collaboration between design and industry at the Bauhaus. This set was a prototype for mass production in cheaper metals such as nickel silver. After the Bauhaus moved to Dessau, Brandt also designed lighting fixtures and table lamps for mass production, earning much-needed revenue for the school. After Moholy-Nagy and Gropius's departure, Brandt took over the metal workshop for a year before she too left, in 1929. As a woman in the otherwise all-male metal workshop, Brandt made an exceptional contribution to the Bauhaus.

Although it was claimed that women were admitted to the Bauhaus on an equal basis with men, Gropius opposed their education as architects and channeled them into what he considered the more gender-appropriate workshops of pottery and textiles. Berlin-born Anni Albers (b. Annelise Fleischmann, 1899–1994) arrived at the school in 1922 and married the Bauhaus graduate and professor Josef Albers (1888–1976) in 1925. Obliged to enter the textiles workshop rather than the painting studio, Anni Albers made "pictorial" weavings and wall hangings **(FIG. 31–54)** that were so innovative they actually replaced paintings on the walls of several modern buildings. Her decentralized, rectilinear designs make reference to the aesthetics of De Stijl, but differ in their open acknowledgment of the natural process of weaving. Albers's goal was "to let threads be articulate … and find a form for themselves to no other end than their own orchestration."

SURREALISM AND THE MIND

At the same time in France in the early 1930s, a group of artists and writers took a very different approach to Modernism in a revolt against logic and reason. The Surrealists embraced the irrational, disorderly, aberrant, and even violent social interventions. Surrealism emerged initially as an offshoot of Dada from the mind of the poet André Breton (1896–1966). Breton trained in medicine and psychiatry and served in a neurological hospital during World War I where he used Freudian analysis on shell-shocked soldiers. By 1924, Breton, still drawn to the vagaries of the human mind, published the "Manifesto of Surrealism" in which he interpreted Freud's theory that the human mind is a battleground where the irrational forces of the unconscious mind wage a constant war against the rational, orderly, and oppressive forces of the conscious mind. Breton wanted to explore humanity's most base, irrational, and forbidden sexual desires, fantasies, and violent instincts by freeing the conscious mind from reason. As Breton wrote in 1934, "we still live under the rule of logic." Thus, he and other Surrealists developed strategies to liberate the unconscious using dream analysis, free association, automatic writing, word games, and hypnotic trances. Surrealists studied acts of "criminal madness" and the "female mind" in particular, believing the latter to be weaker and more irrational than the male mind. Breton believed that the only way to improve the war-sick society of the 1920s was to discover the more intense "surreality" that lay beyond rational constraint.

AUTOMATISM. Surrealist artists employed a variety of techniques, including **automatism**, to release the mind from conscious control and to produce surprising new juxtapositions of imagery and forms. Max Ernst (1891–1976), a self-taught German artist who collaborated in Dada in Cologne and later joined Breton's circle in Paris, was particularly inventive in his use of automatism. In 1925, Ernst developed the automatist technique of **frottage**, in which he rubbed a pencil or crayon over a piece of paper placed on a textured surface. The resulting image stimulated Ernst's imagination. As he gazed at it, he began to see fantastic creatures, plants, and landscapes that he articulated more clearly with additional drawing. Ernst adapted frottage to painting, calling this new technique **grattage**. He created images by scraping layers of paint over a canvas laid over a textured surface, and then "revealing" the imagery he saw in the paint with additional painting. **THE HORDE (FIG. 31–55)** shows a nightmarish scene of

After World War I, increased exchanges between Modern architects led to the development of a common formal language, transcending national boundaries, which came to be known as the International Style. The term gained wide currency as a result of a 1932 exhibition at the Museum of Modern Art in New York, "The International Style: Architecture Since 1922," organized by the architectural historian Henry-Russell Hitchcock and the architect and curator Philip Johnson. Hitchcock and Johnson identified three fundamental principles of the style.

The first was "the conception of architecture as volume rather than mass." The use of a structural skeleton of steel and ferroconcrete made it possible to eliminate loadbearing walls on both the exterior and interior. The building could then be wrapped in a skin of glass, metal, or masonry, creating the effect of enclosed space (volume) rather than dense material (mass). Interiors featured open, free-flowing plans providing maximum flexibility in the use of space.

The second was "regularity rather than symmetry as the chief means of ordering design." Regular distribution of structural supports and the use of standard building parts promoted rectangular regularity rather than the balanced axial symmetry of Classical architecture. The avoidance of Classical balance also encouraged an asymmetrical disposition of the building's components, such as doors and windows.

The third was the rejection of "arbitrary applied decoration." The new architecture depended on the intrinsic elegance of its materials and the formal arrangement of its elements to produce harmonious aesthetic effects. In sum, the most extreme International Style building would be an unadorned glass box.

According to Hitchcock and Johnson, the International Style originated in the Netherlands (in De Stijl), France (in Purism), and Germany (at the Bauhaus). After the exhibition and publication of the catalog listing the characteristics of the International Style in 1932, it spread to the United States.

The first concentrated manifestation of the International Style was in 1927 at the Deutscher Werkbund's Weissenhofsiedlung exhibition in Stuttgart, Germany, directed by Ludwig Mies van der Rohe (1886–1969), an architect who, like Gropius, was associated with the Bauhaus in Germany. The purpose of this semipermanent show was to present a range of model homes that used new technologies and made no reference to historical styles. The buildings in the exhibition featured flat roofs, plain walls, off-center openings, and rectilinear designs by Mies, Gropius, Le Corbusier, and others.

The conceptual clarity of the International Style allowed it to remain vital until the 1970s, especially in the United States, where many of its original European architects, such as Mies and Gropius, who had escaped Hitler and the rise of Nazism in Germany in the 1930s, practiced.

wooden-looking monsters who advance against some unseen opponent. Like much of Ernst's other work of the period, this frightening image seems to evoke the horrors of World War I that Ernst had experienced firsthand in the German army.

31-55 • Max Ernst THE HORDE
1927. Oil on canvas, 44⅞ × 57½″ (114 × 146.1 cm). Stedelijk Museum, Amsterdam.

UNEXPECTED JUXTAPOSITIONS. The paintings of Salvador Dalí (1904–1989) include more recognizable figures and forms but they also reveal the visual wonders of a subconscious mind run wild. Dalí trained at the San Fernando Academy of Fine Arts in Madrid, where he mastered the traditional methods of illusionistic representation, and traveled to Paris in 1928, where he met the Surrealists. Dalí's contribution to Surrealist theory was the "paranoid-critical method," in which he cultivated the paranoid's ability to misread, mangle, and misconstrue ordinary appearances, thus liberating himself from the shackles of conventional thought. Dalí then painted what he had imagined.

Dalí's paintings generally deal with a few key themes: sexuality, violence, and putrefaction. In the **BIRTH OF LIQUID DESIRES** (FIG. 31–56), we see a large yellow **biomorphic** form (an organic shape resembling a living organism) that looks like a monster's face, a painter's palette, or a woman's body as the backdrop for four figures. A woman in white embraces a hermaphroditic figure who stands with one foot in a bowl that is being filled with liquid by a third figure, partially hidden, while a fourth figure enters a cavernous hole to the left. On a thick black cloud above the scene the question is posed: "Consign: to waste the total slate?" Dalí claimed that he arrived at his

31-56 • Salvador Dalí BIRTH OF LIQUID DESIRES
1931–1932. Oil and collage on canvas, 37⅞ × 44¼″ (96.1 × 112.3 cm). Guggenheim Museum, New York. Peggy Guggenheim Collection. 76.2553 PG 100

imagery by writing down his nightmares and merely painting what his paranoid-critical mind had conjured up. Dalí's images are thus, as Breton advocated, "the true process of thought, free from the exercise of reason and from any aesthetic or moral purpose." They defy rational interpretation although they trigger fear, anxiety, and even regression in our empathetic minds.

Dalí's strangely compelling art also draws on the Surrealist interest in unexpected juxtapositions of disparate realities. Surrealists argued that by juxtaposing several disparate ordinary objects in strange new contexts artists could create an uncanny

surreality. One of the most disturbingly exquisite and mockingly humorous examples is **OBJECT (LUNCHEON IN FUR) (FIG. 31–57)**, by the Swiss artist Meret Oppenheim (1913–1985). Oppenheim was one of the few women invited to participate in the Surrealist movement. Surrealists generally treated women as their muses or as objects of study, but not their equals: Picasso even claimed to have "given" Oppenheim the idea for this sculpture. *Object* consists of an actual cup, saucer, and spoon covered with the fur of a Chinese gazelle (chosen for its resemblance in texture to pubic hair). It transposes two objects (a tea setting and gazelle fur) from their ordinary reality, recontextualizes them in an irrational new surreality, and transforms them into an uncanny object that is simultaneously desirous and deeply disturbing.

BIOMORPHIC ABSTRACTION. The Catalan artist Joan Miró (1893–1983) exhibited regularly with the Surrealists but never formally joined the movement. Miró's biomorphic abstraction is also intended to free the mind from rationality, but in a more benign manner. His **COMPOSITION (FIG. 31–58)** of 1933 is populated by curving biomorphic primal or mythic shapes and forms that are arranged by chance, and seem to emerge from the artist's mind uncensored, like doodles, to dance gleefully around the canvas. The Surrealists used the free association of doodling to relax the conscious mind and allow images to bubble up from the unconscious. Miró reportedly doodled on his canvases before working up in paint the shapes and forms revealed there. His forms do seem to take shape before our eyes, but their identity is always in flux. Miró was also fascinated by children's art, which he thought of as spontaneous

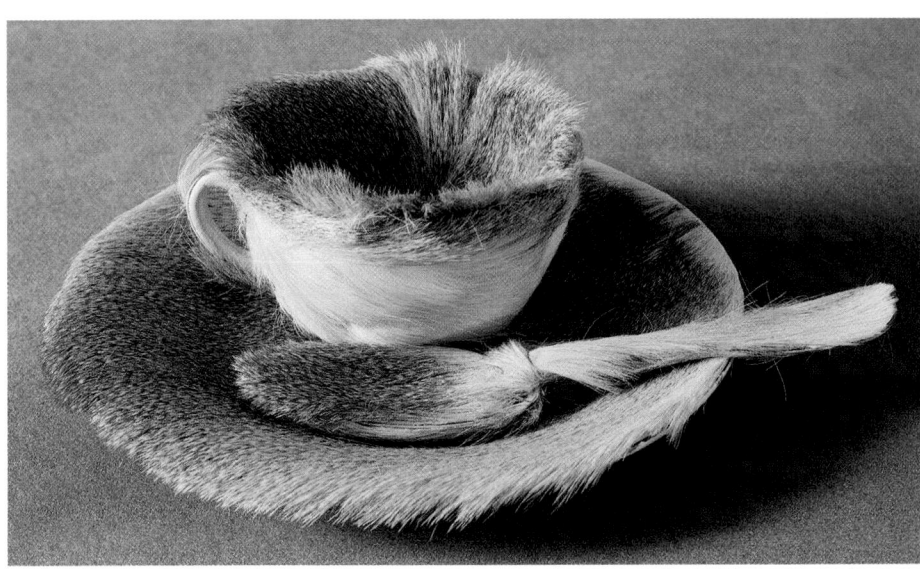

31-57 • Meret Oppenheim
OBJECT (LUNCHEON IN FUR)
1936. Fur-covered cup, diameter 4⅜″ (10.9 cm); fur-covered saucer, diameter 9⅜″ (23.7 cm); fur-covered spoon, length 8″ (20.2 cm); overall height, 2⅞″ (7.3 cm). Museum of Modern Art, New York.

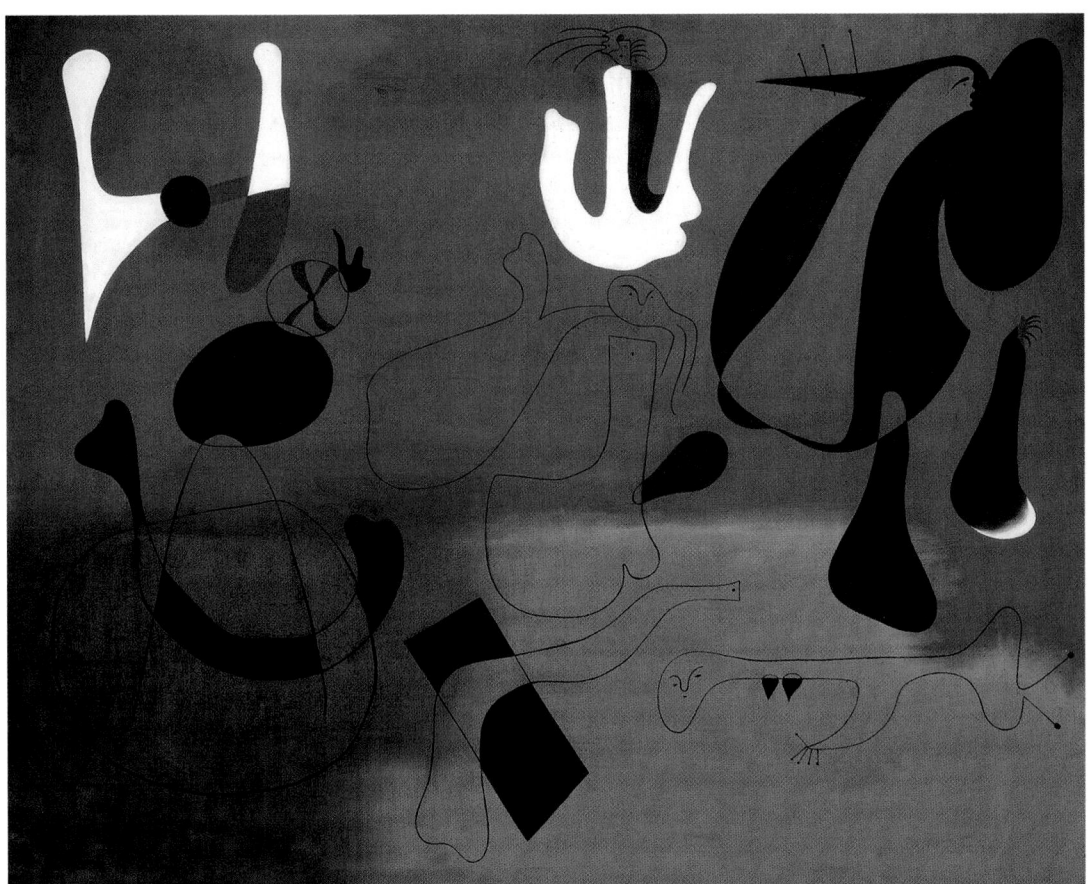

and expressive and, although he was a well-trained artist himself, he said that he wished he could learn to paint with the freedom of a child.

If Miró's paintings suggest movement, the American artist Alexander Calder (1898–1976) actually made biomorphic forms move. Calder trained as an engineer and took some art classes before traveling to Paris in 1926. Although not an official member of the movement, his sculpture was particularly admired by the Surrealists, with whom he exhibited on occasion. Calder came from a family of monumental sculptors, so it is not surprising that he reacted against his heritage by exploring the use of light new industrial materials in his sculpture. Like other sculptors of his generation, he explored negative space, removed sculpture from its pedestal, and hung it from the ceiling. The movement in Calder's art is not driven by motors; his sculptures are brushed into movement by air currents that make his unstable balanced forms bob and dip independently and seemingly randomly. Calder's metal sculptures, which are attached to wire arms and hung from the ceiling, are termed **mobiles**. **LOBSTER TRAP AND FISH TAIL** (**FIG. 31–59**) is composed of delicately balanced flat biomorphic forms and wire. At first it seems to be abstract, but the title works on our imagination to help us find the lobster trap and fish tail as they bob and spin

31–59 • Alexander Calder **LOBSTER TRAP AND FISH TAIL**
1939. Painted steel wire and sheet aluminum, approx. 8′6″ × 9′6″
(2.6 × 2.9 m). Museum of Modern Art, New York.
Commissioned by the Advisory Committee for the Stairwell of the Museum
(590.139.a–d)

31-60 • Barbara Hepworth **FORMS IN ECHELON**
1938. Wood, 42½ × 23⅔ × 28″ (108 × 60 × 71 cm). Tate Gallery,
London. Presented by the artist 1964 © Bowness, Hepworth Estate

EXPLORE MORE: Gain insight from a primary source by
Barbara Hepworth **www.myartslab.com**

to create the terrifyingly funny possibility that the lobster or the
fish will get caught in the trap.

UNIT ONE IN ENGLAND

In 1933, the English artists Barbara Hepworth (1903–1975),
Henry Moore (1898–1986), and Paul Nash (1889–1946), along
with the poet and critic Herbert Read (1893–1968), founded Unit
One. Although short-lived, this group promoted the use of
hand-crafted, Surrealist-influenced biomorphic forms in sculpture,
brought new energy to British art in the 1930s, and exerted a
lasting impact on British sculpture.

Hepworth studied at the Leeds School of Art and made
exquisitely crafted sculptures punctuated with holes so that air and
light could pass through them. **FORMS IN ECHELON** (FIG. **31–60**)
consists of two biomorphic shapes carved in highly polished wood.
The artist merely described these sculptures as organic. She hoped
that viewers would let their eyes play around them, letting their
imaginations generate associations and meanings.

Moore also carved sculptural abstractions punctured by holes,
although his sculptures were more obviously based on the human
form. He also studied sculpture at the Leeds School of Art and then

31-61 • Henry
Moore
**RECUMBENT
FIGURE**
1938. Hornton stone,
35 × 52 × 29″ (88.9 ×
132.7 × 73.7 cm).

at the Royal College of Art in London. The African, Oceanic, and Pre-Columbian sculpture that he saw at the British Museum had a more powerful impact on his developing aesthetic than his training at the college. He felt that the work of artists beyond the Western tradition showed a greater respect for the inherent qualities of materials such as stone or wood than that of Western artists.

The reclining female nude is the dominant theme of Moore's art. The massive simplified body in **RECUMBENT FIGURE** (**FIG. 31–61**) refers to the *chacmool*, a reclining human form in Toltec and Maya art (SEE FIG. 12–13). Moore's carving also demonstrates a sensitivity to the inherent qualities of his stone, which he sought out in remote quarries, always insisting that each of his sculptures was labeled with the specific kind of stone he had used. While certain aspects of the human body are clearly defined in this piece, such as the head, breasts, supporting elbow, and raised knee, other parts seem to flow together into an undulating mass suggestive of a hilly landscape. The cavity at the center inverts our expectations about the solid and void. In 1937, Moore wrote: "A hole can itself have as much shape-meaning as a solid mass."

MODERN ART IN THE AMERICAS BETWEEN THE WARS

In American art between the wars, the need for a national visual identity emerged, but the United States is a large, diverse nation that has so many "identities" that, despite attempts to consolidate the fiction of a single, essentially Anglo-Saxon national identity, the work of African-American artists, immigrant artists, women artists, and others became more visible at this time.

THE HARLEM RENAISSANCE

In the 1930s, hundreds of thousands of African Americans migrated from the rural, mostly agricultural American South to the urban, industrialized North to escape racial oppression and find greater social and economic opportunities. This Great Migration prompted the formation of the nationwide New Negro movement and the Harlem Renaissance in New York, which called for greater social and political activism among African Americans.

Harlem's wealthy middle-class African-American community produced some of the nation's most talented artists of the 1920s and 1930s, such as the jazz musician Duke Ellington, the novelist Jean Toomer, and the poet Langston Hughes. The movement's intellectual leader was Alain Locke (1886–1954), a critic and philosophy professor who argued that black artists should seek their artistic roots in the traditional arts of Africa rather than in mainstream American or European art.

James Van Der Zee (1886–1983) was a studio photographer who made carefully crafted portraits of the Harlem upper middle classes. He opened his studio in 1916 and worked both as a news reporter and a society photographer. **COUPLE WEARING RACCOON COATS WITH A CADILLAC** (**FIG. 31–62**) shows a wealthy man and woman posing with their new car in 1932, at the height of the

31-62 • James Van Der Zee COUPLE WEARING RACCOON COATS WITH A CADILLAC, TAKEN ON WEST 127TH STREET, HARLEM, NEW YORK
1932. Gelatin-silver print.

Guernica

In January 1937, as the Spanish Civil War between the Republicans and the Nationalists began to escalate, the Spanish artist Pablo Picasso, who was then living in Paris, was commissioned to make a large painting for the Spanish Pavilion of the 1938 Paris Exposition. He was unsure what he might create for the exposition, a direct descendant of the nineteenth-century World's Fairs that resulted in the Crystal Palace and the Eiffel Tower. The 1938 Spanish Pavilion was the first Spanish national pavilion at any World's Fair.

On April 26, 1937, Nationalist-supporting German bombers attacked the town of Guernica in the Basque region of Spain, killing and wounding 1,600 civilians. The cold-blooded and calculating nature of the attack on Guernica was inhuman. For more than three hours, 25 bombers dropped 100,000 pounds of explosives on the town, while more than 20 fighter planes strafed anyone caught in the streets trying to flee destroyed or burning buildings. Fires burned in Guernica for three days. By the end, one-third of the town's population was killed or wounded and 75 percent of its buildings had been destroyed. The attack seemed to serve no military purpose, other than to allow Franco's Nationalist forces to terrorize civilian populations, but the true horror was revealed when it was discovered that the German commander planned the massacre merely as a "training mission" for the German air force.

Horrified, Picasso now had his subject for the Fair. On May 1, 1 million protesters marched in Paris and the next day Picasso made his first preliminary sketches for his visual response to this Spanish Civil War atrocity. Picasso was trained in the academic tradition and he planned his GUERNICA as an immense history painting detailing the historic, and ignoble, events of the attack. He made several preliminary sketches (*esquisses*) to develop the composition, colors, and so on, moving on to canvas only after ten days of intensive planning. He worked at the painting itself, changing figures, altering colors, and developing his themes, for another month.

Guernica is a complex painting layered with meaning. Picasso rarely used specific or obvious symbolism in his art, preferring to let individual viewers interpret specific details differently. What is beyond question is that *Guernica* is a scene of brutality, chaos, terror, and suffering. Painted in black, white, and dark blue, the image resonates with anguish. It freezes figures in mid-movement in stark black and white as if caught by the flashbulb of a reporter's camera. There is a bull in the upper left, a wounded horse in the center, and several broken human forms along with a giant light bulb like an eye at the top, a lamp below it, and smoke and fire visible beyond the destroyed room in which the action takes place. The details of the painting have been interpreted in many ways: The bull and horse have been described as standing for Nationalist and Republican forces respectively, as well as the reverse. The light bulb, javelin, dagger, lamp, and bird have also been ascribed specific meanings. But Picasso refused to be pinned down; he said that *Guernica* is about massacred people and animals—beyond that, the meaning is fluid.

Guernica was installed in the Spanish Pavilion with other works of art supporting the Republican cause, including Alexander Calder's *Fontaine de Mercure*, seen in the foreground of this photograph, and

works by Joan Miró, filmmaker Luis Buñuel, and others. Picasso did not want *Guernica* to be shown in Spain while the Nationalist leader, General Franco, ruled, so it was hung in the Museum of Modern Art in New York for years, before finally being installed in the Reina Sofía in Madrid in 1981, six years after Franco's death. A tapestry of *Guernica* has hung in the United Nations Building in New York since 1985.

Pablo Picasso GUERNICA
1937. Oil on canvas, 11'6″ × 25'8″ (3.5 × 7.8 m). Museo Nacional Centro de Arte Reina Sofía, Madrid.
On permanent loan from the Museo del Prado, Madrid. Shown installed in the Spanish Pavilion of the
Paris Exposition, 1937.

In the foreground: Alexander Calder's *Fontaine de Mercure* (Mercury Fountain). 1937. Mercury, sheet
metal, wire rod, pitch, and paint, 44 × 115 × 77″ (122 × 292 × 196 cm). Fundacio Joan Miró, Barcelona.

31-63 • Aaron Douglas ASPECTS OF NEGRO LIFE: FROM SLAVERY THROUGH RECONSTRUCTION
1934. Oil on canvas, 5' × 11'7" (1.5 × 3.5 m). Schomburg Center for Research in Black Culture, New York Public Library.

Great Depression. The photograph reveals the glamor of Harlem, then the center of African-American cultural life.

The painter Aaron Douglas (1898–1979), from Topeka, Kansas, moved to New York City in 1925. He developed a collaged silhouette style that owes much to African art, and that became a fundamental characteristic of later African-American art (SEE FIG. 32–70). His **ASPECTS OF NEGRO LIFE: FROM SLAVERY THROUGH RECONSTRUCTION (FIG. 31–63)** was painted for the Harlem branch of the New York Public Library under the sponsorship of the Depression-era Public Works of Art Project. To the right in the painting, Douglas shows slaves celebrating the Emancipation Proclamation of 1863. Concentric circles of light seem to emanate from the Proclamation itself. At the center of the composition, a figure in orator pose gestures dramatically and points to the United States Capitol in the background, as if urging all African Americans, some of whom are shown still picking cotton, to exercise their right to vote. To the left, Union soldiers leave the South after Reconstruction, while Ku Klux Klan members, hooded and on horseback, ride in as if to remind viewers that the fight for civil rights has only just been joined.

The career of sculptor Augusta Savage (1892–1962) reflects the myriad difficulties faced by African Americans in the art world. Savage studied at Cooper Union in New York but her first application to study in Europe in 1923 was turned down because of her race. In a letter of protest to the institution's administration, she wrote: "Democracy is a strange thing. My brother was good enough to be accepted in one of the regiments that saw service in France during the war, but it seems his sister is not good enough to

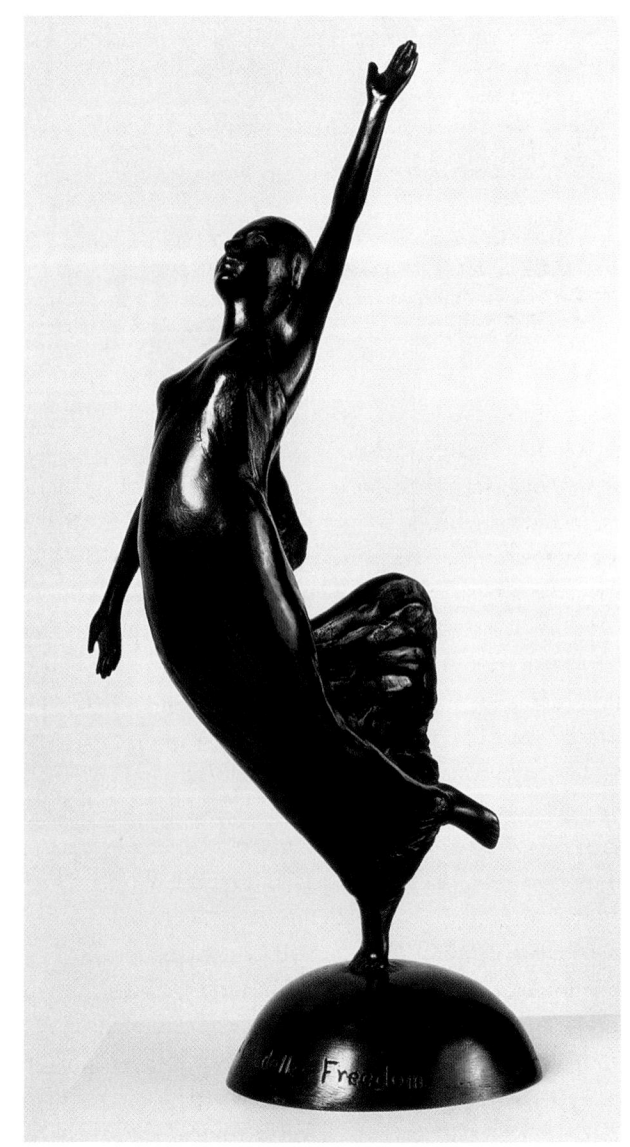

31-64 • Augusta Savage LA CITADELLE: FREEDOM
1930. Bronze, 14½ × 7 × 6" (35.6 × 17.8 × 15.2 cm).
Howard University Art Collection, Washington, D.C.

31-65 • Jacob Lawrence **THE MIGRATION SERIES, PANEL NO.1: DURING WORLD WAR I THERE WAS A GREAT MIGRATION NORTH BY SOUTHERN AFRICAN AMERICANS**
1940–1941. Tempera on masonite, 12 × 18″ (30.5 × 45.7 cm). The Phillips Collection, Washington, D.C.

be a guest of the country for which he fought." Finally, in 1930, Savage was able to study in Paris. On her return to the United States, she made sculptural portraits of several African-American leaders, including Marcus Garvey and W. E. B. DuBois. She was inspired by the story of the Haitian Revolution in 1791 following the Slave Revolt (SEE FIG. 29–38). In **LA CITADELLE: FREEDOM** (**FIG. 31–64**), Savage portrays a female figure raising her hand to the sky like the figure of freedom as she balances on the toes of one foot and flies through the air. La Citadelle was the castle residence of one of Haiti's first leaders of African heritage and which, for Savage, represented the possibility and promise of freedom and equality.

Savage established a small private art school in Harlem for which she received Federal funds under the Works Progress Administration (see "Federal Patronage for American Art During the Depression," page 1066) to transform it into the Harlem Community Art Center. Hundreds of these centers were eventually established all over the country, but Savage's became an unofficial salon for Harlem artists, poets, composers, dancers, and historians.

One of the best-known artists to emerge from the Harlem Community Art Center was Jacob Lawrence (1917–2000).

Lawrence devoted much of his early work to the depiction of African-American history, which he recounted in several series of narrative paintings on small panels, each accompanied by a text. The themes of these series include the history of Harlem and the lives of Haitian revolutionary leader Toussaint L'Ouverture and American abolitionist John Brown. In 1940–1941, Lawrence created his most expansive series, entitled **THE MIGRATION OF THE NEGRO**, in which 60 panels chronicle the Great Migration, a journey that brought Lawrence's own parents from South Carolina to Atlantic City, New Jersey. The first panel (**FIG. 31–65**) shows African-American migrants streaming through the doors of a Southern train station on their way to Chicago, New York, or St. Louis. Lawrence's boldly abstracted silhouette style, with its flat bright shapes and colors, is superficially similar to Cubism, but in fact draws consciously and more directly on the African visual sources that inspired Picasso. Lawrence later also illustrated books by Harlem Renaissance authors.

RURAL AMERICA

In the 1930s, other artists, known collectively as the Regionalists, began to paint Midwestern themes. In 1931, at the height of the

Federal Patronage for American Art During the Depression

In the early 1930s, during the Great Depression, President Franklin D. Roosevelt's New Deal established a series of programs to provide relief for the unemployed and to revive the nation's economy. These programs included several initiatives to supply work to American artists. The Public Works of Art Project (PWAP), set up in late 1933 to employ needy artists, lasted only five months but it supported 4,000 artists, who produced more than 15,000 works. The Section of Painting and Sculpture in the Treasury Department was established in October 1934 and lasted until 1943; it commissioned murals and sculpture for public buildings, although technically it was not a relief program because artists were paid only when they won a commission. The Federal Art Project (FAP) of the Works Progress Administration (WPA), which ran from 1935 to 1943, succeeded the PWAP. The WPA was the most important work-relief agency of the Depression era and had employed more than 6 million workers by 1943. Its programs supporting the arts included the Federal Theater Project, the Federal Writers' Project, and the FAP. About 10,000 artists participated in the FAP, producing a staggering 108,000 paintings, 18,000 sculptures, 2,500 murals, and thousands of prints, photographs, and posters. All of this art became public property. The murals and sculptures, commissioned for public buildings such as train stations, schools, hospitals, and post offices, reached a particularly wide audience. Many can still be seen today, but most of the easel paintings were sold as "plumber's canvas" and destroyed.

To build public support for Federal assistance in rural America, the Resettlement Agency (RA) and Farm Security Administration (FSA) hired photographers to document the effects of the Depression across the country. These photographs were available, copyright-free, to any newspaper, magazine, or publisher. They are still available, copyright-free, today. San Francisco-based Dorothea Lange (1895–1965), an RA/FSA photographer between 1935 and 1939, documented the plight of migrant farm laborers who fled the Dust Bowl conditions of the Great Plains and then flooded California looking for work.

MIGRANT MOTHER, NIPOMO, CALIFORNIA shows Florence Thompson, a 32-year-old mother of seven children, as representative of the poverty suffered by thousands of migrant workers in California. Lange's photograph is carefully constructed to tug at the heartstrings. It is taken very close to the subject so that we sympathize with the mother's worn expression and resolve. The composition reminds us of the images of the sorrowful Madonna as she contemplates the loss of her son (SEE FIG. 20–9). What Lange chose to eliminate from this photograph, but is recorded in other photographs of the same scene, are the makeshift tent in which the family is camped, the dirty dishes on a battered trunk, trash strewn around the campsite, and, most significant, Thompson's teenage daughter. Lange wanted this photograph to evoke the purity and moral worth of her subject, for whom she sought Federal aid; she could not allude to the fact that Thompson was a teenage mother, or even that she was Cherokee. *Migrant Mother* (then unidentified by name) became the "poster child" of the Great Depression, and her powerfully sad distant gaze still resonates with audiences today, demonstrating the propaganda power of the visual image.

During the Depression, the FAP paid a generous average salary of about $20 a week (a salesclerk at Woolworth's earned only about $11) for painters and sculptors to devote themselves full time to art. New York City's painters, in particular, developed a group identity, meeting in the bars and coffeehouses of Greenwich Village to discuss art. The FAP thus provided the financial grounds on which New York artists built a sense of community—a community that produced the Abstract Expressionists, and allowed New York to supersede Paris as the center of activity for Western art.

Dorothea Lange **MIGRANT MOTHER, NIPOMO, CALIFORNIA**
February 1936. Gelatin-silver print. Library of Congress, Washington, D.C.

31-66 • Grant Wood AMERICAN GOTHIC
1930. Oil on beaverboard, 29⅞ × 24⅞″ (74.3 × 62.4 cm).
Art Institute of Chicago.

CANADA

In the nineteenth century, Canadian artists, like their counterparts in the United States, began to assert their independence from European art by painting Canada's great untamed wilderness. A number of Canadians, however, still studied in Paris at the end of the century, using academic realism to paint figurative subjects, while others painted the Canadian landscape through the lens of Impressionism. In 1907, the Canadian Art Club was founded in Toronto, Ontario.

LANDSCAPE AND IDENTITY.   In the early 1910s, a younger group of Toronto artists, many of whom worked for the same commercial art firm, began to sketch together, adopting the rugged landscape of the Canadian north as an expression of Canadian national identity.

A key figure in this movement was Tom Thomson (1877–1917), who, as of 1912, spent the warm months of each year in Algonquin Provincial Park, a large forest reserve 180 miles north of Toronto. He made numerous small, swiftly painted, oil-on-board sketches as the basis for the full-size paintings that he executed in his studio during the winter. A sketch made in the spring of 1916 led to **THE JACK PINE (FIG. 31–67)**. This tightly organized composition features a stylized pine tree rising from a rocky foreground and silhouetted against a luminous background of lake and sky, horizontally divided by

Depression, Grant Wood (1891–1942), who later taught at the University of Iowa, created **AMERICAN GOTHIC (FIG. 31–66)**, which was purchased by the Art Institute of Chicago and established Wood's national fame. *American Gothic* shows an elderly father with his unmarried daughter standing in front of their Gothic Revival framed house. The couple is dressed in old-fashioned clothes for the time. Wood's sister Nan and his dentist posed for the figures and the house was modeled on an actual house in Eldon, Iowa. The daughter in the scene wears a home-made ricrac-edged apron and Wood's mother's cameo. The father clutches an old-fashioned three-tined pitchfork and the house behind them is a modest small-town home. The daughter's long sad face echoes her father's; she is unmarried and likely to stay that way. In 1931, husbands were hard to come by in the Midwest because many of the young men had fled from the farms to the city of Chicago for jobs. The painting is tightly and carefully painted in homage to the Flemish Renaissance painters that Wood admired. This image stood for everything good and everything bad about the heartland in the 1930s.

31-67 • Tom Thomson THE JACK PINE
1916–1917. Oil on canvas, 49⅞ × 54½″ (127.9 × 139.8 cm). National Gallery of Canada, Ottawa, Ontario. Purchase, 1918

31-68 • Emily Carr
BIG RAVEN
1931. Oil on canvas,
34 × 44⅝″ (87.3 ×
114.4 cm). Vancouver Art
Gallery, Vancouver, British
Columbia. Emily Carr Trust
(VAG 42.3.11)

cold blue hills. The painting's arresting beauty and reverential mood suggest a divine presence in the lonely northern landscape and have made it an icon of Canadian national art. In 1917, Thomson tragically drowned.

NATIVE AMERICAN INFLUENCE. Born in Victoria, British Columbia, the West Coast artist Emily Carr (1871–1945) studied art in San Francisco, England, and Paris. On a 1907 trip to Alaska she encountered the monumental carved poles of Northwest Coast Native peoples and resolved to document these "real art treasures of a passing race." Over the next 23 years, Carr visited more than 30 such sites across British Columbia, making drawings and watercolors as a basis for oil paintings. After a commercially unsuccessful exhibition of her Native subjects, Carr returned to Victoria in 1913, opened a boardinghouse, and painted very little for the next 15 years. In 1927, however, she was invited to participate in an exhibition of West Coast art at the National Gallery of Canada. On her trip east for the show's opening Carr met members of the Group of Seven, which had been established in 1920 by some of Tom Thomson's former colleagues, who rekindled her interest in painting.

With the Group of Seven, Carr developed a dramatic and powerfully sculptural style full of dark, brooding energy. **BIG RAVEN (FIG. 31–68)**, based on a 1912 watercolor, shows an abandoned village in the Queen Charlotte Islands where Carr found a carved raven on a pole, the surviving member of a pair that

originally marked a mortuary house. In her autobiography Carr described the raven as "old and rotting," but in the painting she shows it as strong and majestic, thrusting dynamically above the swirling vegetation, a symbol of enduring spiritual power and national pride.

MEXICO

The Mexican Revolution of 1910 overthrew the 35-year dictatorship of General Porfirio Díaz and was followed by ten years of political instability. In 1920, however, the reformist president Álvaro Obregón came to power and finally restored political order. As in the U.S.S.R., the leaders of the new government engaged artists in the service of the people and state. Obregón's government commissioned several Mexican artists to decorate public buildings with murals celebrating the history, life, and work of the Mexican people. These murals were to be executed in a naturalistic style because, in the opinion of the new government, abstract art was incompatible with and incomprehensible to the public at large.

Diego Rivera (1886–1957) was prominent in the Mexican mural movement. He enrolled in Mexico City's Academia de San Carlos at age 11. From 1911 to 1919, he lived in Paris where he met Picasso and David Siqueiros (1896–1974), another Mexican muralist. Both Rivera and Siqueiros were dedicated to creating a revolutionary mural art in public buildings and in the service of the people. In 1920–1921, Rivera traveled to Italy to study Renaissance

31-69 • Diego Rivera
THE GREAT CITY OF TENOCHTITLAN (DETAIL)
1945. Mural, 16'1¾" × 31'10¼" (4.92 × 9.71 m). Patio corridor, National Palace, Mexico City.

SEE MORE: View a video about Diego Rivera's fresco technique
www.myartslab.com

frescoes; he also visited ancient Mexican indigenous sites to study mural paintings. **THE GREAT CITY OF TENOCHTITLAN** (FIG. 31–69) is one of the murals that Rivera painted for the National Palace in Mexico City, a cycle depicting the history of Mexico using stylized forms and brilliant local colors. Rivera also painted murals in the United States. In 1929, he married Frida Kahlo.

The art of Frida Kahlo (1907–1954) is an admixture of autobiography and traditional Mexican folk painting. **THE TWO FRIDAS** (FIG. 31–70) shows a double image of the artist that expresses an identity split between European and Mexican heritages (her father was German and her mother part indigenous Mexican). The European Frida wears a Victorian dress while the Mexican Frida wears a traditional Mexican costume. The Mexican Frida holds a small sculpture of an

31-70 • Frida Kahlo **THE TWO FRIDAS**
1939. Oil on canvas. 5'8½" × 5'8½" (1.74 × 1.74 m). Museo de Arte Moderno, Instituto Nacional de Bellas Artes, Mexico City.

31–71 • Tarsila do Amaral ABAPORÚ (THE ONE WHO EATS)
1928. Oil on canvas, 34 × 29″ (86.4 × 73.7 cm). Museo de Arte Latinoamericano, Buenos Aires. Courtesy of Guilherme Augusto do Amaral/Malba-Coleccion Constantini, Buenos Aires

used to declare their artistic independence from Europe. Modern Art Week brought avant-garde poets, dancers, and musicians as well as visual artists to São Paulo and took on a distinctly confrontational character. Poets derided their elders in poetry, dancers enacted modern versions of traditional dances, and composer Hector Villa-Lobos (1887–1959) appeared on stage in a bathrobe and slippers to play new music based on Afro-Brazilian rhythms.

In 1928, the São Paulo poet Oswald de Andrade, one of Modern Art Week's organizers, wrote the *Anthropophagic Manifesto* proposing a tongue-in-cheek if radical solution to Brazil's seeming dependence on European culture. He suggested that Brazilians should imitate the ancient Brazilians' response to Portuguese explorers arriving on their shore: Eat them. He mockingly described this relationship as anthropophagic or cannibalistic and proposed that Brazilians should gobble up European culture, digest it, let it strengthen their Brazilianness, and then get rid of it.

The painter who most closely embodies this irreverent attitude is Tarsila do Amaral (1887–1974), a daughter of the coffee-planting aristocracy who studied in Europe with Fernand Léger (SEE FIG. 31–21), among others. Her painting **ABAPORÚ (THE ONE WHO EATS) (FIG. 31–71)** shows an appreciation of the art of Léger

ancient god, while the European Frida holds a forceps: A blood vessel connects the god to the forceps through the hearts of the two Fridas. Kahlo suffered a broken pelvis in an accident at 17, and endured a lifetime of surgical interventions—this work alludes to her constant pain, as well as to the Aztec custom of human sacrifice by heart removal. The significance of Kahlo's art, apart from its memorable self-expression, lies in its investigation of larger issues of Mexican identity. This painting addresses issues of mixed heritage in Mexico, sexuality, and gender identity within the context of Kahlo's own life.

BRAZIL

Other Latin American art was dominated by the academic tradition in the nineteenth century; several nations had thriving academies, large art communities, and significant numbers of artists traveling to Paris to study. By 1914, artists in many Latin American countries had begun to paint national themes in their own versions of Impressionism. After the war, artists who studied abroad also brought home ideas drawn from Modern art and the European avant-garde which they translated into a specifically Latin American vision. For instance in 1922, as Brazil marked the centenary of its independence from Portugal, the avant-garde in São Paulo celebrated with Modern Art Week, an event Brazilian artists

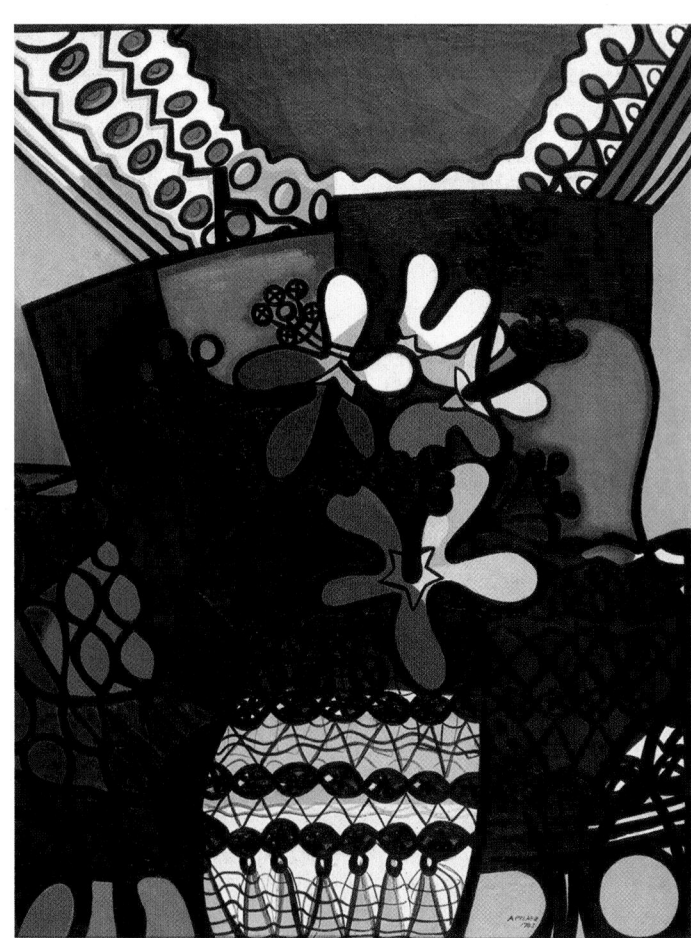

31–72 • Amelia Peláez MARPACÍFICO (HIBISCUS)
1943. Oil on canvas, 45½ × 35″ (115.6 × 88.9 cm). Art Museum of the Americas, Washington, D.C. Gift of IBM

and Brancusi (SEE FIGS. 31–27, 31–28), which Tarsila collected. But she has cleverly inserted several "tropical" clichés into her own work in the abstracted forms of a cactus and a lemon-slice sun. The subject is Andrade's irreverent cannibal who sits in an almost caricatural Brazilian landscape, as if to say: If Brazilians are caricatured abroad as cannibals, then let us act like cannibals. As Andrade wrote in one of his manifestos: "Carnival in Rio is the religious outpouring of our race. Richard Wagner yields to the samba. Barbaric but ours. We have a dual heritage: The jungle and the school."

CUBA

Cuba's 1920s avant-garde was one of the most interdisciplinary, consisting of anthropologists, poets, composers, and even a few scientists, who gathered in Havana and called themselves "The Minority." They issued a manifesto in 1927 repudiating government corruption, "Yankee imperialism," and dictatorship on any continent. "Minority" artists, they urged, should pursue a new, popular, Modern art rooted in Cuban soil.

Amelia Peláez (1896–1968) left Cuba for Paris shortly after this manifesto was issued. When she returned home, she joined the anthropologist Lydia Cabrera to study Cuban popular and folk arts. Her paintings focus on the woman's realm—the domestic interior—and national identity, as in **MARPACÍFICO (HIBISCUS) (FIG. 31–72)**. The overall language of this work is Cubist, as seen in the flattened overlapping forms and compressed pictorial space, but it shows a mirror, a tabletop, and local hibiscus flowers embroidered in paint with heavy black outlines and pure color that would be instantly recognizable in Cuba as representing the flat fan-shaped stained-glass windows that decorate many Cuban homes.

POSTWAR ART IN EUROPE AND THE AMERICAS

FIGURAL RESPONSES AND *ART INFORMEL* IN EUROPE

The horrors of World War II surpassed even those of World War I. The human loss was almost too profound and grotesque to comprehend. Between loss of life in action, those killed in work camps and death camps (concentration camps), those lost to starvation, and those lost in the bombing of civilian targets, more than 30 million people died and a further estimated 40 million people were displaced. The unimaginable horror of the concentration camps and the awful impact of the dropping of nuclear bombs shook humanity to its core. Winston Churchill described the extent of the catastrophe: "What is Europe now? A rubble heap, a charnel house, a breeding ground of pestilence and hate."

31–73 • Francis Bacon HEAD SURROUNDED BY SIDES OF BEEF
1954. Oil on canvas, 50¾ × 48″ (129 × 122 cm). Art Institute of Chicago.
Harriott A. Fox Fund

Most European artists in the immediate postwar period used their art to try to come to terms with what they had experienced, many debating about how best to do this: Some artists worked figuratively while others painted abstractions.

In England, Francis Bacon (1909–1992) used his canvases to capture the horrors that haunted him. Bacon was self-taught and produced very few pictures until the 1940s. He served as an air-raid warden during World War II and saw the bloody impact of the bombing of civilians in London firsthand. In **HEAD SURROUNDED BY SIDES OF BEEF (FIG. 31–73)**, Bacon shows the imperious Pope Innocent X reduced to an anguished and insubstantial man howling in a black void as two bloody sides of beef enclose him in a claustrophobic box that contains his frightful screams and amplifies his terror. The painting was directly inspired by Diego Velázquez's portrait of Pope Innocent X (1650) and by Rembrandt paintings of dripping meat. Bacon wrote of his art: "I hope to make the best human cry in painting … to remake the violence of reality itself."

One of the most distinctive postwar European art movements was *Art Informel* ("formless art"), which was also called *tachisme* (*tache* is French for "spot" or "stain"). *Art Informel* was promoted by the French critic Michel Tapié (1909–1987) who suggested that art should express an authentic concept of postwar humanity through simple, honest marks.

31-74 • Wols (Wolfgang Schulze) PAINTING
1944–1945. Oil on canvas, 31⅞ × 32″ (81 × 81.1 cm). Museum of Modern Art, New York. Gift of D. and J. de Menil Fund (29.1956)

knew both Picasso and the Surrealists, and was forced to return to Cuba when the Nazis invaded France. He found himself on the same ship as the Surrealist leader André Breton; Lam disembarked at Havana while Breton traveled on to New York. Lam explored his African-Cuban heritage in the company of anthropologist Lydia Cabrera and novelist Alejo Carpentier. His work from the late 1940s is deeply informed by African-Cuban art, the polytheistic spirituality imagery of *santería*, and his anti-colonial stance in Cuba. The jagged, semi-abstracted forms of **ZAMBEZIA, ZAMBEZIA (FIG. 31–75)** might recall European Modernism, but are actually derived from *santería* religious ritual. The central figure is a composite *santería* deity. "Zambezia" was the early colonial name for Zimbabwe in southeastern Africa, which at the time that this painting was created was still a British colonial possession known as Rhodesia. Much earlier, Zambezia was also a source for slaves who were brought to Cuba. Lam said of his art: "I wanted with all my heart to paint the drama of my country … . In this way I could act as a Trojan horse spewing forth hallucinating figures with the power to surprise, to disturb the dreams of the exploiters."

In Buenos Aires, two groups of artists formed immediately after the war: Arte Concreto-Invención and Madí. At the time

The informal leader of *Art Informel* was Wolfgang Schulze, called Wols (1913–1951), who lived through the dislocation and devastation experienced by millions in Europe in the 1930s and 1940s. Born in Germany, Wols was resolutely anti-Nazi and left his homeland when Hitler came to power. He settled in Paris where he became a photographer working for *Vogue* and *Harper's Bazaar*. When the Germans occupied France, he fled to Spain but was arrested, had his passport confiscated, and was deported to spend the rest of the war as a stateless person in a refugee camp in southern France. When the war ended, Wols moved back to Paris and began painting again, producing passionate pictures by applying paint with whatever came to hand, scraping his heavy surfaces with a knife and allowing the paint to drip and run. **PAINTING (FIG. 31–74)** represents a disease-ridden and violent world in which the semi-abstracted forms resemble either cells or dark muddy bacterial growths. Wols was temporarily supported by the French philosopher and novelist Jean-Paul Sartre, but died of food poisoning in 1951.

LATIN AMERICAN EXPERIMENTS

In Cuba, Wifredo Lam (1902–1980) created abstract and Surrealist paintings about the violence and anguish of his country's struggle against colonialism. Lam was of mixed Chinese, Spanish, and African heritage and brought issues of identity and self-discovery to his art. He studied at the National Academy in Havana, moved to Paris, where he

31-75 • Wifredo Lam ZAMBEZIA, ZAMBEZIA
1950. Oil on canvas, 49⅜ × 43⅝″ (125 × 110 cm). Solomon R. Guggenheim Museum, New York. Gift, Mr. Joseph Cantor, 1974.2095

31–76 • Joaquín
Torres-Garcia
**ABSTRACT ART IN
FIVE TONES AND
COMPLEMENTARIES**
1943. Oil on board mounted
on panel, 20½ × 26⅝″
(52.1 × 67 cm).
Albright Knox Art Gallery,
Buffalo, N.Y. Gift of Mr. and
Mrs. Armand J. Castellani, 1979

Argentina was ruled by Juan Perón who admired Italy's fascist leader, Benito Mussolini (1883–1945), and who disliked Modern art profoundly. Thus, many of Argentina's artistic avant-garde were strongly antifascist. The best-known Latin American artist of the time was the Uruguayan Joaquín Torres-García (1874–1949), who established the "School of the South" in Montevideo, Uruguay's capital. Torres-García had spent 43 years in Europe before returning home after the war. His art was deeply rooted in the indigenous art of the Inca (SEE FIG. 26–8). He regarded ancient Uruguayan culture as a fertile soil in which to grow a new national and cultural visual identity. He used the stone patterns of Inca architecture in paintings that underscored for him the universal validity of abstract art. In **ABSTRACT ART IN FIVE TONES AND COMPLEMENTARIES (FIG. 31–76)**, Torres-García combines ideas of abstraction and Modernism with Inca imagery in a style that he named Constructive Universalism.

ABSTRACT EXPRESSIONISM

THE CENTER SHIFTS: POSTWAR ART IN NEW YORK

The United States recovered from World War II more quickly than Europe. Its territory was spared the ravages of war and the trauma it felt was limited to those Americans who saw action in Europe or the Pacific, to European refugees to the United States, and to Japanese-American citizens who had been interned. While the European art world took decades to recover and Paris lost its artistic vibrancy, New York, as the art historian Serge Guilbault wrote, "Stole the Idea of Modern Art."

Many leading European artists and writers escaped to the United States during World War II. By 1941, André Breton, Salvador Dalí, Fernand Léger, Piet Mondrian, and Max Ernst were all living in New York, where they altered the character and artistic concerns of the New York art scene. American artists were most deeply affected by the work of the European Surrealist artists in New York. Ultimately, however, Abstract Expressionist artists developed their own uniquely American artistic identities by drawing from, but radically reimagining, European and American Modernism.

The term "Abstract Expressionism" describes the art of a fairly wide range of artists in New York in the 1940s and early 1950s. It was not a formally organized movement but rather a loosely affiliated group of artists who worked in the city and were bound by a common purpose: to express their profound social alienation after World War II and to make new art that was both moral and universal.

The influential **formalist** (concerning form over content) critic Clement Greenberg urged the Abstract Expressionists to consider their paintings "autonomous" and completely self-referential objects. The best paintings, he argued, made no reference to the outside world, but had their own internal narrative and order. Abstract Expressionism was also deeply informed by the theories of the Swiss psychoanalyst Carl Jung (1875–1961), who described a collective unconscious shared by all humans. The Abstract Expressionists aspired to create heroic and sublime worlds in paint inhabited by universal symbolic forms. As the 1940s progressed, the symbolic content of their paintings became increasingly personal and abstract. Some Abstract Expressionists were interested in "primitive," mythic imagery and archaic, archetypal, and primal symbolism that connected all people through the collective unconscious; several used biomorphic forms or an individual symbolic language in their paintings; all made passionate and expressive statements on large canvases. The Abstract Expressionists also felt destined to make a major mark on art history; they were convinced that they had the power to transform the world with their art. Thus, Abstract Expressionists were brought together by four major endeavors: first, an interest in the tradition of painting, but a desire to rebel against it and to recalibrate the ideas of European Modernism; second, a desire to treat the act of painting on canvas as a self-contained expressive exercise; third, a mining of visual archetypes that Jung argued were embedded in the collective unconscious to communicate universal ideas in paint; and, fourth, the ambition to paint sublime art on a heroic scale. The critic Harold Rosenberg described two major categories of Abstract Expressionism: "Action painting" and "Color Field painting." The Abstract Expressionists disliked these terms arguing, with good reason, that they were too simplistic, but as general typologies go, the terms are useful.

THE FORMATIVE PHASE

Arshile Gorky (1904–1948) was older than the other Abstract Expressionists, but his ideas and images resonated deeply with them. Gorky (not his given name) was born in Armenia and fled with surviving family members to the United States in 1920 during the Ottoman Turkish genocide of the Armenian people. His mother did not survive long after her escape, leaving Gorky mostly alone. Gorky's painting is filled with the trauma of his loss: He threads idyllic images of his childhood home and garden through Surrealist and Jungian ideas about the collective unconscious to create visual memorials to the people and places he has lost.

31–77 • Arshile Gorky GARDEN IN SOCHI
c. 1943. Oil on canvas, 31 × 39″ (78.7 × 99.1 cm). Museum of Modern Art, New York.
Acquired through the Lillie P. Bliss Bequest (492.1969)

31-78 • Jackson Pollock **AUTUMN RHYTHM (NUMBER 30)**
1950. Oil on canvas, 8′9″ × 17′3″ (2.66 × 5.25 m). Metropolitan Museum of Art, New York.
George A. Hearn Fund, 1957 (57.92)

EXPLORE MORE: Gain insight from a primary source about Jackson Pollock
www.myartslab.com

Gorky's vision of his past world came together in a series of paintings of the early 1940s called **GARDEN IN SOCHI** (**FIG. 31–77**) in which Gorky's memories of his father's garden in Khorkom, Armenia are transformed into a mythical dreamscape. According to the artist, this garden was known locally as the Garden of Wish Fulfillment because it contained a rock upon which village women, his mother included, would rub their bared breasts and make a wish, and a "Holy Tree" to which people tied strips of clothing. In this painting, the mythical garden floats on a dense white ground. Various forms, shapes, and colors coalesce into a bare-breasted woman to the left, the Holy Tree to the center, strips of clothing, and "the beautiful Armenian slippers" that Gorky and his father wore in Khorkom. The painting simultaneously suggests vital life forces and an ancient connection to the earth. It also reveals Gorky's vision of a world that has been extinguished and exists only in his memory.

JACKSON POLLOCK AND ACTION PAINTING

Jackson Pollock (1912–1956) is perhaps the best-known artist associated with Abstract Expressionism. Pollock was born in Wyoming and moved to New York in 1930. By all accounts, Pollock was self-destructive from an early age. He developed a drinking problem by age 16, was reading Jung by 22, and was institutionalized for psychiatric problems and alcohol abuse at age 26. Friends described two Pollocks—one shy and sober, and the other obnoxious and drunk. He entered Jungian psychotherapy in 1939 but was already acquainted with Jung's theory that visual images had the ability to tap into the primordial consciousness of viewers. Pollock was free of alcohol for most of the 1940s, the period when he was supported emotionally by Lee Krasner and when he created his most celebrated art.

Pollock began his career working figuratively but around 1940 moved toward abstraction. In 1943, he had his first solo exhibition at Peggy Guggenheim's gallery and was propelled into stardom by the critic Clement Greenberg, who, by 1947, described Pollock as "the most powerful painter in North America."

In the late 1940s, Pollock pushed beyond the Surrealist strategy of automatic painting by taking his canvas off the stretcher, placing it on the floor, and throwing, dripping, and dribbling paint onto it to create a sublime abstract calligraphy as it fell. In 1950, *Time* magazine described Pollock as "Jack the Dripper." In 1952, Rosenberg coined the term "Action painting," in an essay, "The American Action Painters." Rosenberg described the development and purpose of Action painting as follows: "At a certain moment the canvas began to appear to one American painter after another as an arena in which to act—rather than a space in which to reproduce, redesign, analyze, or 'express' an object, actual or imagined."

In 1950, Pollock's painted **AUTUMN RHYTHM (NUMBER 30)** (**FIG. 31–78**) while the filmmaker Hans Namuth filmed him (**FIG. 31–79**). In the fall of 1946, Pollock had begun to work in a renovated barn, where he placed his canvases on the floor so that he could reach into them from all four sides. The German expatriate artist Hans Hofmann (1880–1966) had poured and dripped paint before Pollock, but Pollock's unrestrained gestures transformed the idea of painting and the way that artists viewed the canvas. Pollock painted by moving around and within the canvas, dripping and scoring commercial-grade enamel paint (rather than specialist artist's paint) onto it using sticks and trowels. Pollock's urgent arcs and whorls of paint have been described as chaotic, but he saw them as labyrinths that led the viewer along complex paths and into an organic calligraphic web of natural and biomorphic forms. Pollock's all-over composition lacks hierarchical arrangement; it has multiple moving focal points and it denies perspectival space. Yet, as the paint travels around the canvas in arcs and ellipses, it never escapes the edges of the canvas. There is also a top and a bottom: Turn the image upside down and it appears "wrong." Like a coiled spring, the painting seems full of anxious energy that is ready to explode at any moment.

Autumn Rhythm is heroic in scale: It is almost 9 feet tall by 17 feet wide and it engulfs the viewer's entire field of vision. According to Lee Krasner, Pollock was a "jazz addict" who spent many hours listening to the explosively improvised bebop of Charlie Parker and Dizzy Gillespie. Pollock was also interested in Native American art, which he associated with his western roots and which enjoyed widespread coverage in popular and art magazines in the 1930s. Pollock was particularly struck by the images and processes of Navajo sand painters who demonstrated their work at the Natural History Museum in New York. And, of course, he drew on Jung's theories of the collective unconscious. But Pollock was not merely

31–79 • Hans Namuth PHOTOGRAPH OF JACKSON POLLOCK PAINTING
The Springs, New York. 1950.

SEE MORE: View a video of Jackson Pollock painting
www.myartslab.com

31–80 • Lee Krasner THE SEASONS
1957. Oil on canvas, 7'8¾" × 16'11¾" (2.36 × 5.18 m). Whitney Museum of American Art, New York. Purchased with funds from Frances and Sydney Lewis (by exchange), the Mrs. Percy Uris Purchase Fund, and the Painting and Sculpture Committee (87.7)

the sum of his parts. His paintings communicate on a grand, modern, but primal level. In a radio interview, he said that he was creating for "the age of the airplane, the atom bomb, and the radio."

OTHER ACTION PAINTERS. Lee Krasner (1908–1984) studied in New York with Hans Hofmann and produced fully nonrepresentational paintings with all-over compositions several years before Pollock. She moved in with Pollock in 1942 and virtually stopped painting in order to take care of him. They moved to Long Island in 1945, where she set up a small studio in a guest bedroom and produced small, tight, gestural paintings. After Pollock's death in an automobile crash in 1956, Krasner took over his studio and produced a series of large, dazzling gestural paintings that marked her re-emergence into the mainstream art world. Works such as **THE SEASONS (FIG. 31–80)** feature bold, sweeping curves that

express not only a new sense of liberation but also her powerful identification with the forces of nature in bursting, rounded forms and springlike colors. Krasner said that "Painting, for me, when it really 'happens' is as miraculous as any natural phenomenon."

In contrast, Willem de Kooning (1904–1997) wrote that "Art never seems to make me peaceful or pure." An immigrant from the Netherlands, de Kooning was friendly with several Modern artists including Elaine Marie Fried, whom he married. His view of the world was never simple or certain. He remarked: "I work out of doubt." De Kooning's painting was always highly structured and controlled. He made careful under-drawings, and painted and scraped several layers of paint in the process of creating a single canvas. His gestural strokes appear spontaneous but they are, in fact, the result of hours of experiment and failure. De Kooning painted strokes, scraped them off, and repeated the process until the exact mark he wanted emerged. In 1953, de Kooning shocked the art world by moving away from pure abstraction with a series of figurative paintings of women. **WOMAN I (FIG. 31–81)** took the artist two years to complete and de Kooning's wife Elaine estimated that he scraped and repainted it about 200 times. It portrays a figure who seems at once grotesque and rapacious, and the image is both hostile and sexist. It is powerfully sexual, full of implied violence, and intensely passionate. De Kooning described his "Woman" paintings as images of great fertility goddesses like the *Woman from Willendorf* (SEE FIG. 1–7), or as a composite of stereotypes taken from the media and film.

Abstract Expressionism spread quickly to Canada. In his native Montreal, the French Canadian painter Jean-Paul Riopelle (1923–2002) worked with Les Automatistes (The Automatists), a group of artists using the Surrealist technique of automatism to create abstract paintings. In 1947, Riopelle moved to Paris and, in the early 1950s, began to squeeze paint directly onto the canvas and spread it with a palette knife to create an all-over painting of bright swatches of color that are suggestive of broken shards of stained glass traversed by a network of spidery lines, as in **KNIGHT WATCH (FIG. 31–82).**

Helen Frankenthaler (b. 1928) visited Pollock's studio in 1951 and went on to create a more lyrical version of Action painting that had a significant impact on later artists. Like Pollock, she worked on the floor, but she poured paint onto the unprimed canvas in thin washes so that it soaked into the fabric rather than sitting on its surface. Frankenthaler

31–81 • Willem de Kooning WOMAN I
1950–1952. Oil on canvas, 75⅞ × 58″ (192.7 × 147.3 cm). Museum of Modern Art, New York.

31–82 • Jean-Paul Riopelle KNIGHT WATCH
1953. Oil on canvas, 38 × 76⅝″ (96.6 × 194.8 cm). National Gallery of Canada, Ottawa, Ontario.

31–83 • Helen Frankenthaler MOUNTAINS AND SEA
1952. Oil and charcoal on canvas, 7′2¾″ × 9′8¼″ (2.2 × 2.95 m). Collection of the artist on extended loan to the National Gallery of Art, Washington, D.C.

described her process as starting with an aesthetic question or image and evolving as the process of painting took over as a self-expressive act. She described her working method: "I will sometimes start a picture feeling, What will happen if I work with three blues … ? And very often midway through the picture I have to change the basis of the experience. Or I add and add to the canvas.… When I say gesture, my gesture, I mean what my mark is. I think there is something now that I am still working out in paint; it is a struggle for me to both discard and retain what is gestural and personal." In **MOUNTAINS AND SEA (FIG. 31–83)**, Frankenthaler poured several colors onto the canvas and outlined selected forms in charcoal. The result reminded her of the coast of Nova Scotia where she frequently went to sketch.

COLOR FIELD PAINTING

New York School artists used abstract means to express various kinds of emotional states, not all of them as urgent or improvisatory as those of the Action painters. The Color Field painters moved in a different direction, painting large, flat areas of color to evoke more transcendent, contemplative moods in paint.

Mark Rothko (1903–1970) had very little formal art training but by 1940 was already producing paintings that were deeply influenced by the European Surrealists and by Jung's archetypal imagery. By the mid-1940s, Rothko began to paint very large canvases with rectangular shapes arranged in a vertical format in which he allowed his colors to bleed into one another. These canvases, such as **LAVENDER AND MULBERRY (FIG. 31–84)**, are

31-84 • Mark Rothko **LAVENDER AND MULBERRY**
1959. Oil on paper mounted on fiberboard, 37¾ × 24¾″ (95.9 × 62.8 cm). Hirshhorn Museum and Sculpture Garden, Smithsonian Institution, Washington, D.C.
Gift of Joseph H. Hirshhorn 1966

31–85 • Barnett Newman VIR HEROICUS SUBLIMIS
1950–1951. Oil on canvas, 95⅜ × 213¼″ (242 × 541.7 cm). Museum of Modern Art, New York. Gift of Mr. and Mrs. Ben Heller

31–86 • David Smith CUBI
David Smith. *Cubi XVIII* (left), 1964. Stainless steel, 9′8″ (2.94 m). Museum of Fine Arts, Boston. *Cubi XVII* (center), 1963. Stainless steel, 9′2″ (2.79 m). Dallas Museum of Fine Arts, Dallas. *Cubi XIX* (right), 1964. Stainless steel, 9′5⅜″ (2.88 m). Tate Gallery, London. Shown installed at Bolton Landing, New York in 1965.

neither simply arrangements of flat geometric shapes on a canvas nor atmospheric landscapes. Rothko thought of his shapes as fundamental "ideas" expressed in rectangular form, unmediated by a recognizable subject, which sit in front of a painted field (hence the name "Color Field painting"). He preferred to show his paintings together in series or rows and lit indirectly to evoke moods of transcendental meditation.

Barnett Newman (1905–1970) also addressed modern humanity's existential condition in his very large canvases painted in one, often brilliant, color and torn or split by thin jagged lines in another color that he called "zips." Newman said that his art was about "[t]he self, terrible and constant." **VIR HEROICUS SUBLIMIS (FIG. 31–85)** shows how Newman's total concentration on a single color focuses his meaning. Newman's red painting does not describe any form; it presents an absolute state of redness in a vast canvas that is unbroken except for the dangerous zips of other colors that threaten to unbalance it. *Vir Heroicus Sublimis* (Latin for "Man, Heroic and Sublime") is heroic and sublime like the hero threatened by a fatal flaw. Many of Newman's paintings have religious overtones. Newman wrote: "The present painter is concerned not with his own feelings or with the mystery of his own personality but with the penetration into the world mystery. His imagination is therefore attempting to dig into metaphysical secrets. To that extent his art is concerned with the sublime."

SCULPTURE OF THE NEW YORK SCHOOL

Sculpture tended to resist the kind of instantaneous gestural processes developed by artists such as Pollock, although some sculptors managed to communicate both abstractly and Expressionistically in three dimensions. David Smith (1906–1965) learned to weld and rivet while working at an automobile plant in Indiana. He trained as a painter, but became a sculptor after seeing reproductions of welded metal sculptures by artists such as Picasso. Smith avoided the precious materials of traditional sculpture and created works out of standard industrial materials. After World War II, Smith began to weld horizontally formatted, open-form sculptures that were like drawings in space. The forms of the vertical **CUBI** series **(FIG. 31–86)** were actually determined by standardized, precut sizes of stainless-steel sheets. In photographs they sometimes look coldly industrial, but when observed outdoors as Smith intended, their highly burnished surfaces show the gestural marks of the sculptor's tools upon them, and reflect and refract the sun in different ways depending on the time of day, weather conditions, and distance from which they are viewed. Vaguely anthropomorphic like giant totemic figures, the sculptures are surprisingly organic when seen at close range.

THINK ABOUT IT

31.1 Discuss the impact that Cubism had on other avant-garde art styles in the early part of the twentieth century. Analyze its pattern of influence in at least two works from the chapter that demonstrate a substantial debt to Cubism.

31.2 Explain how World Wars I and II had an impact on the visual arts in Europe and North America in both direct and indirect ways. Give examples of both with reference to works from the chapter.

31.3 Explain how both Dada and Surrealism changed the form, content, and concept of art. Focus your answer around an analysis of one artwork discussed in the chapter from each of these two movements.

31.4 Write about Walter Gropius and the Bauhaus's attitude towards questions of form and function and discuss how Gropius and other early twentieth-century architects embodied those attitudes in their buildings. Contrast these buildings and attitudes with those studied in previous chapters.

31.5 Summarize the events of the Great Depression and discuss its impact on European and American art.

31.6 Discuss the goals and interests of the painters associated with Abstract Expressionism, and determine the role that Surrealism and other early twentieth-century avant-garde art movements had in the formation of this new movement in the 1940s.

PRACTICE MORE: Compose answers to these questions, get flashcards for images and terms, and review chapter material with quizzes **www.myartslab.com**

32–1 • Jasper Johns TARGET WITH PLASTER CASTS 1955. Encaustic and collage on canvas with objects, 51 × 44″ (129.5 × 111.8 cm). Collection Mr. and Mrs. Leo Castelli.

THE INTERNATIONAL SCENE SINCE 1950

In the early 1950s, a generation of younger artists in New York challenged the artistic assumptions of the previous generation of Abstract Expressionist artists. They believed that art should be firmly anchored in real life. Two artists in particular, Jasper Johns and Robert Rauschenberg, questioned the goals of the New York School as defined by Clement Greenberg's version of formalism: that art should be autonomous and internally coherent (deeply meaningful, with the act of painting as its subject, abstract, and with an all-over composition); that it should avoid the taint of popular culture and be viewed in the "white cube" of the gallery space; and that the artist should be vigilantly self-critical. In **TARGET WITH PLASTER CASTS** (FIG. 32–1), Johns not only stretches formalism to its limits, but he actually mocks it.

This work is neither a painting nor a sculpture but both; the cast body parts are arranged across the top of the work, parodying the nonhierarchical manner of Abstract Expressionism, but the target below is emphatically hierarchical. The flatness of the painted target suggests an all-over composition, but the target itself always has a central focus; the target and casts, moreover, make reference to popular culture and the world around Johns. The target also raises thorny questions about the nature of representation: Is this a painting of a target or is it an actual target? The meaning of this work is fluid and unfixed—it contains recognizable faces and a recognizable object (a target) but the purpose of their inclusion is unclear. Unlike that of the Abstract Expressionists, Johns's art is emotionally cool and highly cerebral. Like many artists after 1950, Johns reintroduces readily recognizable, real-world but strategically recontextualized, images and objects in order to question the form, appearance, content, and meaning of art. Thus, like much art after 1950, Johns's art is as intellectual as it is visual.

Johns and Rauschenberg were critical figures in the New York art world and beyond. They expanded the intellectual bases of Abstract Expressionism, cooled its passion and intensity, and made art that connected to and was inspired by the vastly expanded visual culture of postwar America. They also prefigured the next generation's interest in introducing popular culture into art, its investigation of the conceptual possibilities of art, its expanded understanding of the use of nonart materials in art, and its exploration of the performative possibilities of art.

LEARN ABOUT IT

32.1 Assess the ways in which artists since 1950 have introduced popular culture into their art.

32.2 Account for the "dematerialization" of the object since 1950 and account for its return after 1980.

32.3 Compare and contrast the impact of the three "waves" of feminism on art after 1950.

32.4 Examine how and why artists since 1950 have engaged with social, political, cultural, or religious issues.

32.5 Evaluate how globalism has created new opportunities, strategies, and subjects for artists today.

HEAR MORE: Listen to an audio file of your chapter **www.myartslab.com**

THE WORLD SINCE THE 1950S

The United States and the U.S.S.R. emerged from World War II as the world's most powerful nations. The Soviet occupation and sponsorship of communist governments in several Central and Eastern European states, and the emergence of the People's Republic of China in 1949 compelled the United States to attempt to contain the further expansion of Soviet power and communism into American spheres of influence, particularly in Western Europe, Japan, and Latin America. This precipitated a "Cold War" and what Winston Churchill described as the descending of an "Iron Curtain" across Europe (MAP 32–1). The United States initially provided both financial and political support to states sympathetic to American interests, but then resorted to military force, most notably in Korea (1950–1953) and then Vietnam (1954–1975). Europe lost most of its imperial holdings by the early 1960s, often after protracted guerilla wars of the kind that the French experienced in Vietnam and Algeria. The British granted India independence in 1946 and by 1971 had withdrawn from "East of Suez."

During the Cold War, the United States and the U.S.S.R. amassed large nuclear arsenals, eventually adopting a strategy of mutually assured destruction, which was supposed to deter nuclear war by threatening to destroy the civilian population on both sides. The Cold War effectively ended with the fall of the Berlin Wall in October 1989. When the Soviet Union dissolved in 1992, the United States emerged as the world's unchallenged superpower.

The United Nations, sponsored by American power, was established in 1945 to provide collective security and legitimacy to the Anglo-American design for a new postwar world order. It eventually emerged as a forum for the sovereign recognition of governments for the many newly independent states in Asia and Africa after the war. Despite the UN mandate to intervene in conflicts between states, however, its efforts to maintain global peace have proven inadequate in the face of ethnic and religious conflicts that have erupted around the world in regions such as the Indian subcontinent, central and eastern Africa, the Balkans, and the Middle East. The terrorist attacks on the World Trade Center and the Pentagon on September 11, 2001, exacerbated many of the preexisting racial, ethnic, and religious conflicts, and led to both civil wars and wars between states, most notably in the recent and controversial American-led wars in Afghanistan and Iraq.

THE ART WORLD SINCE THE 1950S

Artists have faced a number of major questions since 1950: What is art? Does it always have to be an object, is it an idea, or is it some combination of the two? In the period since 1950, artists have reconceptualized and reimagined art, producing radically new forms, content, ideas, and agendas. They have addressed increasingly divisive and complex social and political questions for which there is no right or wrong answer; artists have raised questions about gender, race, ethnicity, sexual orientation, religion, class, death, colonialism, terrorism, violence against the less powerful, and resistance to power. This art has not sought to edify us by showing moral exemplars (as in Neoclassicism); rather it has challenged us to question our own morality, behavior, and complacency. Much of this art is difficult to look at and to understand; we are frequently assaulted and accused by it. It is rarely pretty. But today's art holds a mirror to contemporary life, revealing things that we might not see or hear in any other context, and it forces us to confront ourselves in that mirror. We may not like recent art initially, but once we learn something about it, we have to admit that, at its best, it has the power, like all great art, to affect us deeply.

THE EXPANDING ART WORLD

The generation of artists who began to make art in the 1950s increasingly addressed the real world, acknowledging its fragmentation, its relativism, and its messy relation to popular culture. Assemblage and collage artists broke apart the physical forms and the meanings of art along with the distinction between painting and sculpture, and high and low art. Pop artists investigated how advertising impacted vision and explored a newly visible domestic world. Photographers showed us aspects of the world around us that we had not seen, or had chosen not to see, before.

ASSEMBLAGE

In the 1950s, the visual artists Jasper Johns (b. 1930) and Robert Rauschenberg (1925–2008), and the composer John Cage (1912–1992) consciously introduced the world around them (rather than representations of it) into their art and music. Cage, who taught for a time at Black Mountain College near Asheville, North Carolina, explored the idea of creating music that brought the ambient noises of the world around him directly into his music. In 1952, Cage "composed" *4'33"* (4 minutes 33 seconds), which was first performed in Woodstock, New York. In this piece, the pianist came on stage, performed several different "movements" for four minutes and 33 seconds, and then closed the keyboard to signal the end of the work. The sound-piece consisted of actual sounds made by audience members as they rustled, shuffled, whispered, and coughed for 4'33". Thus, this composition differs each time it is performed, gathering a new set of sounds and meanings in every new location and with every new audience. The form of *4'33"* is circumscribed by Cage's directions, but its content, the chance juxtaposition of seemingly random sounds, occurs spontaneously at each performance. The piece was engineered by the composer to create a work with open and multiple interpretations and to obscure the personality of the composer. Similarly, Johns and Rauschenberg in their assemblages brought or "assembled" disparate found objects and images in seemingly random constructions to create visual works of art with equally open-ended and multiple meanings that revealed little of the artist's personality.

Rauschenberg grew up in Texas and moved to New York to paint in 1947. He attended Black Mountain College where he studied with Cage and de Kooning (SEE FIG. 31–81). Rauschenberg

MAP 32-1 • THE WORLD SINCE 1950

International sites in the contemporary art world in the Americas, Europe, and Africa.

explored ways to "work in the gap between art and life." In 1951, he exhibited a series of brightly lit blank white paintings in which the shadows cast by viewers on the canvases became the content of the work; there are obvious visual parallels to Cage's *4′33″* of the following year.

Between 1955 and 1960, Rauschenberg made a series of objects that he entitled **combines** (combinations of painting and sculpture using nontraditional art materials). In one of these, **CANYON (FIG. 32–2)**, Rauschenberg brings together a roughly painted canvas with a stuffed eagle emerging from a box, a dirty pillow tied with cord suspended from a piece of wood, and a flattened steel drum. On the canvas itself Rauschenberg glued family photographs, images cut from newspapers and magazines, and fragments of political posters. *Canyon* is so dense with cultural references that it is impossible to find a single, unified meaning in the piece. In fact, Rauschenberg believed that viewers should find their own meaning in his art as if searching for metaphors for the experience of modern urban life. He said: "I only consider myself successful when I do something that resembles the lack of order [that] I sense."

Johns, Cage, and Rauschenberg collaborated on several theatrical events that extended the idea of the assemblage into temporal space in the late 1950s and early 1960s. Cage composed music while Johns and Rauschenberg designed sets and sometimes actually performed. They worked with the Merce Cunningham Dance Company, which specialized in creating dance based on everyday actions such as waiting for a bus or reading a newspaper. Prior to these events, none of the participants informed the others what they were planning to do, so the performances became legendary in their unpredictability.

HAPPENINGS AND PERFORMANCE ART

In the 1950s and 1960s, several artists argued that the artistic process was as important as the finished object; these artists began to replace the traditional materials of art with the actions, movements, and gestures of their own bodies. These events were termed **Happenings** by Allan Kaprow but the more common term is **Performance art**. Performance art owes a debt to Pollock (SEE FIG. 31–79), whose physical enactment of the act of painting was transformed into a work of art in its own right, and to Cage, Johns, and Rauschenberg, who relied on spontaneous and unpredictable actions to provide a new set of variables for each of their events.

Performance art tears down the space that has traditionally existed between the viewer and the art object; the artwork literally comes to life and actively invades the space of the viewer, both physically and intellectually. Thus, Performance art is often radical, and assaultive. It also exists in the moment and, although often photographed or filmed, is ephemeral.

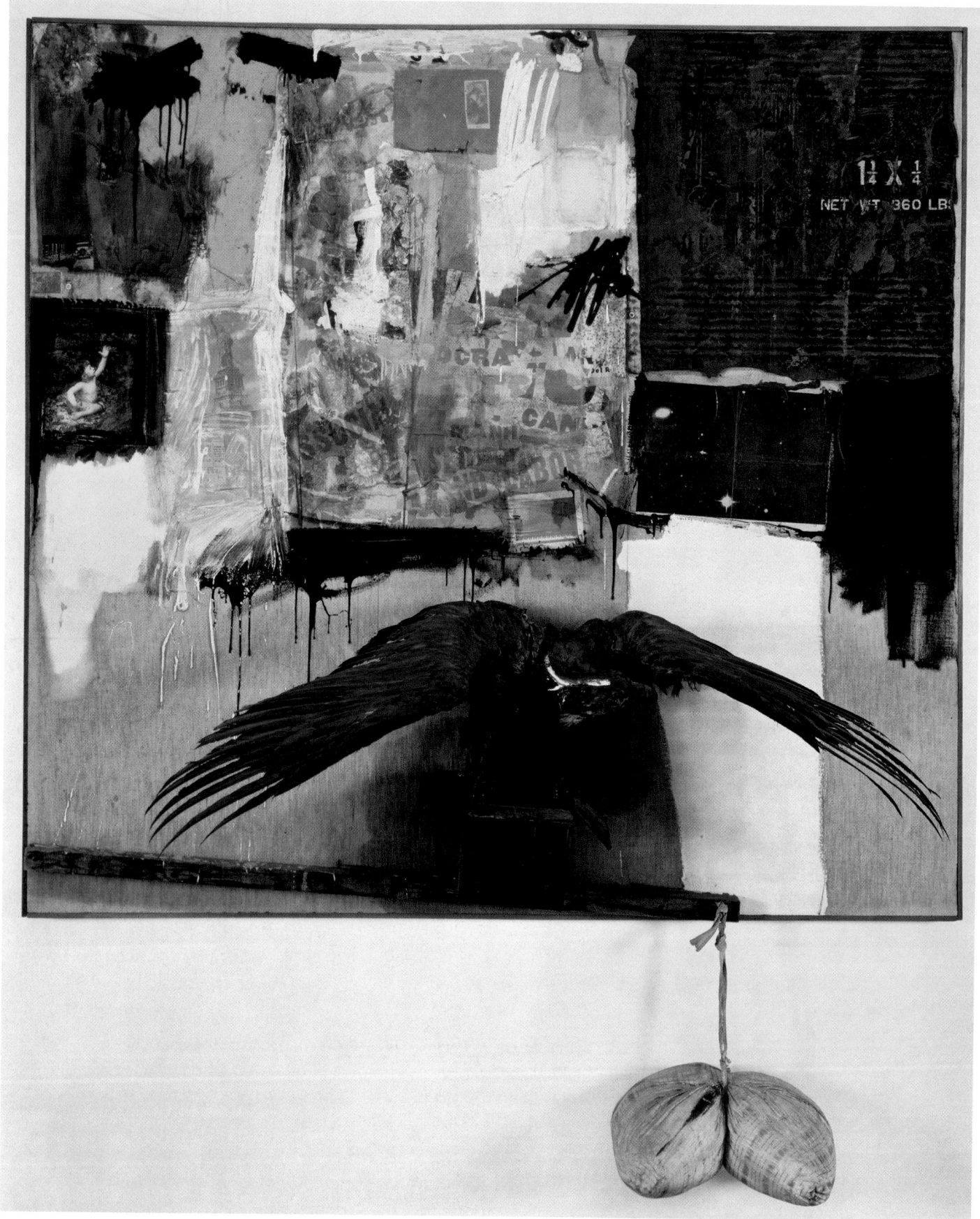

32–2 • Robert Rauschenberg CANYON
1959. Oil, pencil, paper, metal, photograph, fabric, wood on canvas, plus buttons, mirror,
stuffed eagle, pillow tied with cord, and paint tube, 6′1″ × 5′6″ × 2′¾″ (1.85 × 1.68 × 0.63 m).
Sonnabend Collection.

THE GUTAI GROUP. Some of the earliest postwar performances took place in Japan. In 1954, several Japanese artists formed the Gutai (meaning "embodiment") group to "pursue the possibilities of pure and creative activity with great energy." In Gutai performances, it was the act of creating itself that was the artwork. Gutai organized outdoor **installations**, theatrical events, and dramatic performances. At the second Gutai Exhibition in 1956, Shozo Shimamoto (b. 1928) performed **HURLING COLORS (FIG. 32–3)** by smashing bottles of paint against a canvas on the floor, thus pushing Pollock's gestural painting technique one step farther by suggesting that the work of art lay solely in the performance of a painting rather than in the object produced. In fact, Gutai artists regularly destroyed the physical products they created at the end of each performance.

KAPROW. In 1958, Allan Kaprow (1927–2006), also a student of John Cage, began to create environments and in 1959 Happenings. His 1961 piece **YARD (FIG. 32–4)** was staged in the walled garden space behind the Martha Jackson Gallery in Manhattan. Kaprow filled the space with used tires, tar paper, and barrels, and asked viewers to walk though it, to experience the smell and physicality of the rubber and the tar firsthand, recontextualized (removed from one context and placed in a new one to create new meaning) in the art gallery space. Kaprow later described how gallery audiences—more formally dressed then than they would be today, especially the women, who wore dresses and heels—experienced aspects of the urban environment in unfamiliar and unanticipated ways as they tumbled in and over the tires.

32-4 • Allan Kaprow **YARD**
1961. View of tires in court of Martha Jackson Gallery, New York, 1961.

32-5 • Yves Klein LEAP INTO THE VOID
1960. Photograph of a performance by Yves Klein at Rue Gentil-Bernard, Fontenay-aux-Roses, October 1960, by Harry Shunk.

KLEIN. In Europe, Performance art occurred as part of the activities of the New Realism movement, a term coined by art critic Pierre Restany. Restany argued that the age of painting ended with the New York School and *Art Informel* and that thereafter art would take its form from the real world. He wrote: "The passionate adventure of the real, perceived in itself …. The New Realists consider the world a painting: a large, fundamental work of which they appropriate fragments."

The French artist Yves Klein (1928–1962) first staged his *Anthropometries of the Blue Period* in 1960. He invited members of the Paris art world to watch him direct three female models covered in blue paint as they pressed their naked bodies against large sheets of paper to the musical accompaniment of a 20-piece orchestra playing a single note. The performance was a commentary on the perceived pretentiousness of Pollock's action painting, of which Klein wrote: "I dislike artists who empty themselves into their paintings. They spit out every rotten complexity as if relieving themselves." Like Cage, Johns, and Rauschenberg, Klein orchestrated his performance but often removed himself from the act of crafting the final object. He used the nude female body as the subject of his painting by pressing the model's bodily imprint in paint directly onto the paper. Klein presents art making as a physical, gestural act and the final work of art as the imprint of either the artist or his model.

Klein is perhaps best known for the 1960 **LEAP INTO THE VOID** (FIG. 32–5), a manipulated photograph showing the artist leaping from a wall into the street, arms outstretched with apparently nothing but the pavement below him. The photograph was originally published to prove Klein's mock claim that he could

32-6 • Carolee Schneemann MEAT JOY
1964. Judson Church, New York City. Group performance: raw fish, chickens, sausages, wet paint, plastic, rope, and shredded scrap paper. First performed as part of the First Festival of Free Expression at the American Center in Paris. MOMA. 16mm film transferred to video (color, soundtrack collaged by CS), 6 min.
Acquired through the generosity of Katherine Farley and Jerry I. Speyer, Anna Marie and Robert F. Shapiro, and Marie-Josée and Henry R. Kravis

undertake lunar travel unaided, and was published again in a pamphlet denouncing NASA's bid to land a man on the moon as arrogant and foolish. Klein argued that his works were visible only as imprints, in this case his imprint on the pavement.

SCHNEEMANN. Many early Performance artists were women, whose bodies have been the object of the gaze in art for centuries. Performance art enabled women artists to control how their bodies were viewed and to look back and even challenge their audience. One of the most important early Performance artists was Carolee Schneemann (b. 1939), whose **MEAT JOY** (FIG. 32–6) was a radical feminist performance. *Meat Joy* was performed first with Jean-Jacques Lebel and the Kinetic Group Theater at the Festival de la Libre Expression in Paris, and a second time in New York, where it was filmed and photographed. In the performance eight men and women first undressed one another, then danced, rolled on the floor ecstatically, and played with a mixture of raw fish, raw sausages, partially plucked raw and bloody chickens, wet paint, and scraps of paper. The purpose was to make both performers and audience smell, taste, and feel viscerally the body and its fluids. The piece was variously described as an erotic rite and a celebration of flesh and blood. It countered the expectation that a work of art was something to be examined in the cool unemotional space of an art gallery with the viewer in control, replacing the traditional artwork with a performance that made the audience squirm as control was wrenched away from it by the performers.

PHOTOGRAPHY

Photography served as an important tool for documenting Performance art in the 1950s, but it was also an important medium in its own right. Although the 1955 "Family of Man" exhibition of photographs at the Museum of Modern Art, New York, curated by Edward Steichen, presented a world at peace and in harmony, and illustrated magazines such as *Life* projected an image of modern life as comfortable, suburban, white, and domestic, other photographers chose to convey an alternate view of society.

FRANK. Robert Frank (b. 1924), a Swiss photographer who emigrated to the United States in the 1940s, took gritty social portraits, trying to capture some of the disorder and disharmony that Johns and Rauschenberg presented in their art. In 1948, frustrated by the pressure and banality of news and fashion assignments, Frank abandoned his freelance work with magazines such as *Life* and *Vogue* and traveled to Peru and Bolivia. Four years later, he took a series of photographs documenting the lives of Welsh coalminers, before being awarded a one-year Guggenheim Fellowship in 1955 to travel around America photographing the "social landscape." Frank took more than 28,000 photographs that year, from which he chose 83 to publish in book form. But the images were so raw, grim, and full of biting social commentary that at first he was unable to find a publisher in the United States and so was forced to publish the book in France under the title *Les Américains* (1958). *The Americans* was finally published in the United States the following year with an introduction by Jack Kerouac, one of the leaders of the new Beat generation of authors who were critical of mainstream American values. In **TROLLEY, NEW ORLEANS** (FIG. 32–7), white passengers sit in the front of the bus, while African Americans sit in the back, as required by law at the time. The composition of the image, in which the rectangular symmetry of the windows frames and isolates the figures on the

32-7 • Robert Frank
TROLLEY, NEW ORLEANS
1955–1956. Gelatin-silver print, 9 × 13″ (23 × 33 cm). Art Institute of Chicago.

trolley, underscores visually both the racial segregation and urban alienation inherent in the scene.

KEÏTA.   In Africa in the late 1950s, Seydou Keïta (1921–2001) took photographs of the proud people of the newly independent nation of Mali. Keïta established a reputation as a portrait photographer and worked as a Mali government photographer. His photographs were among the first by an African to portray his own nation and people as affluent and urban rather than objectified as ethnographic subjects, as seen in magazines such as *National Geographic*. In the image shown here **(FIG. 32–8)**, the sitters occupy a visually luxurious space. The heavy, strong patterns of the wife's clothing contrast with the stark white of that of her husband and child. Keïta's elegant photograph presents individuals whose power and pride are communicated through their commanding poses and relaxed gestures. The sitters look out of the photograph at the viewer, returning our gaze, demanding that we see them as real people and as equals, whose sense of identity is as multivalent and as complex as our own. While Keïta made his photographs for domestic consumption, many were subsequently exhibited in Europe and the United States.

POP ART

In the late 1950s, several artists began to focus their attention on the explosion in visual culture, fueled by the growing presence of mass media and the rising disposable income of the postwar young. Pop art originated in Britain, but reached its zenith in the United States in the early 1960s. During this period individual and mass identity was increasingly determined by how people looked and dressed, and by what they consumed. Home ownership, cars, and the visible display of objects in the home were modeled on what appeared on television, in film, and in print advertising. Pop artists critiqued the fiction and superficiality of the perfect home and perfect person projected in this new popular culture.

HAMILTON.   In the 1950s, an interdisciplinary collection of artists, architects, photographers, and writers came together as the Independent Group in London in order to discuss the place of art in a consumer society, periodically exhibiting at the Institute of Contemporary Arts. The government argued that Britain's postwar recovery was predicated on sustained consumption. Richard Hamilton (b. 1922) argued that modern mass visual culture was fast replacing traditional art for the public; movies, television, and advertising, not art, now defined beauty. Society's idols were no longer politicians or military heroes but inter-national movie stars; social status was increasingly measured by the number of one's possessions.

Thus Hamilton made collages of images drawn from advertising to create a vision of a disharmonious world of excessive consumption. In his 1955 work **JUST WHAT IS IT THAT MAKES TODAY'S HOMES SO DIFFERENT, SO APPEALING? (FIG. 32–9)**, Hamilton critiques advertising strategies by imitating them. The title parodies an advertising slogan, while the collage itself shows two figures named Adam and Eve in a domestic setting. Like the biblical Adam and Eve, these figures are almost naked, but this time the "temptations" to which they have succumbed are those of consumer culture. Adam has become a bodybuilder and Eve is a pin-up girl. In an attempt to recreate their lost Garden of Eden, this Adam and Eve have filled their home with all the best new products: a television, a tape recorder, a vacuum cleaner, modern furniture. On the wall in place of "high art" is a poster advertising a romance novel; beside this is a printed portrait of John Ruskin, the critic who accused the painter Whistler of destroying art (see "Art on Trial in 1877," page 999). Adam holds a huge Tootsie Pop, which the English critic Lawrence Alloway referenced when he described this work as "Pop art," thus naming the art movement. Like Rauschenberg's and Johns's assemblages in the United States,

32-8 • Seydou Keïta UNTITLED
1952–1955. Gelatin-silver print, 24 × 20″ (61 × 50.8 cm). Edition of ten.

**32-9 • Richard Hamilton
JUST WHAT IS IT THAT
MAKES TODAY'S
HOMES SO DIFFERENT,
SO APPEALING?**
1955. Collage, 10¼ × 9¾″
(26 × 24.7 cm). Kunsthalle
Tübingen, Germany.

SEE MORE: View a
podcast about Richard
Hamilton's work
www.myartslab.com

Hamilton's collage comments on the visual overload of the 1950s and on culture's inability to differentiate between important and trivial images or between the advertising world and the real one. In 1968, Hamilton designed the cover for the Beatles's *White Album*, which significantly is devoid of any images at all.

WARHOL. By 1960, several American artists, like the earlier British Pop artists, began to incorporate images from the burgeoning mass culture into their art. By comparison with their British peers, however, they developed a slicker Pop art style using common advertising mass-production techniques to give their art a flat, commercial feel, a stance that was also intended to show opposition to the presence of the hand of the artist in Abstract Expressionism. American Pop art both imitated and critiqued 1960s popular culture, often including images of newly independent women and their ambivalent relationship to domesticity. The emotional tone of Pop art was more ironic, camp, and cynically detached than the irreverent assemblage of Johns and Rauschenberg. Pop art flowered

in the United States after 1962; it was dominated by the artistic giant and heir to Duchamp's ideas about the nature of art and the role of artists in art making, Andy Warhol (1928–1987).

Warhol created an immense body of work between 1960 and his death in 1987, including prints, paintings, sculptures, and films. He published *Interview* magazine, and even managed The Velvet Underground, a radical and hugely influential rock band. Warhol knew advertising culture well—he trained as a commercial artist. By 1962, he was using advertising from America's mass culture in his art, taking as his subjects popular consumer items such as Brillo boxes, Campbell's Soup cans, and Coca-Cola bottles, and reproducing them using the cheap industrial print method of **silkscreen** (in which a fine mesh silk screen is used as a printing stencil). Warhol argued that past art demanded thought and understanding, whereas advertising and celebrity culture demanded only immediate attention, very quickly becoming uninteresting and boring. In keeping with this position, he suggested that art should be like movie stars, interesting for 15 minutes.

In 1962, Marilyn Monroe died suddenly, an apparent suicide. Warhol's **MARILYN DIPTYCH** (FIG. **32–10**) is one of a series of silkscreens that Warhol made immediately after the actress's death. He memorializes the screen image of Monroe, using a famous publicity photograph transferred directly onto silkscreen, thus rendering it flat and bland so that Monroe's signature features—her bleach-blond hair, her ruby lips, and her sultry blue-shadowed eyes—stand out as a caricature of the actress. The face portrayed is not that of Norma Jeane (Monroe's real name) but of Monroe the celluloid sex symbol as made over by the movie industry. Warhol made multiple prints from this screen, aided by a host of assistants working with assembly-line efficiency. (In 1965, Warhol even—ironically—named his studio "The Factory," further mocking the commercial aspect of his art by suggesting he was only in it for the profit.)

The Marilyn portrait, however, has deeper undertones. It is a diptych (see page 564) and thus evokes religious connotations, perhaps suggesting that Monroe was a martyred saint or goddess in the pantheon of departed movie stars. In another print, Warhol even surrounded her with a gold background of the kind found in Orthodox religious icons. Additionally, while the Monroes on the colored left side of the diptych are flat and undifferentiated, those on the right side, in black and white, fade in ghostly fashion as they are printed without the screen being reinked until all that is left of the original portrait is the shadow of an image of a person.

Warhol was one of the first artists to exploit the fact that while the mass media, television in particular, seem to bring us closer to the world, they also allow us to observe the world as voyeurs rather than as participants. We become desensitized to death and disaster by the constant repetition of images on television, and are able literally to switch off at any time. Warhol's art, especially in the *Marilyn Diptych*, is like television—the presentation is superficial and bland, uses seemingly mindless repetition, and inures us to the full impact of the tragic moment of death. Warhol, known for his quotable phrases, once said: "I am a deeply superficial person." Likewise the superficiality of his art is deeply intellectual.

32-10 • Andy Warhol **MARILYN DIPTYCH**
1962. Oil, acrylic, and silkscreen on enamel on canvas, two panels, each 6′10″ × 4′9″ (2.05 × 1.44 m). Tate Gallery, London.

SEE MORE: View a video about the silkscreen process **www.myartslab.com**

32–11 • Roy Lichtenstein OH, JEFF … I LOVE YOU, TOO … BUT …
1964. Oil and magna on canvas, 48 × 48″ (122 × 122 cm).
Private collection.

EXPLORE MORE: Gain insight from a primary source by Roy Lichtenstein **www.myartslab.com**

LICHTENSTEIN. Roy Lichtenstein (1923–1997), who also investigated the various ways that popular imagery resonated with high art, used comic-book imagery in his art to critique mass-market imagery. In 1961, while teaching at Rutgers University with Allan Kaprow (SEE FIG. 32–4), Lichtenstein began to make paintings based on panels from war and romance comic books. In these, the source images are tightened and clarified to focus on significant emotions or actions that simultaneously represent and parody the flat, superficial ways in which a comic book communicates with its readers. Lichtenstein painted these images with heavy black outlines and flat primary colors, imitating the **Benday dots** used in the commercial printing of cartoons. **OH, JEFF … I LOVE YOU, TOO … BUT …** (FIG. 32–11) compresses an entire generic romance story into a single frame. In so doing, Lichtenstein suggests something of the superficiality of the media-saturated culture of the early 1960s.

OLDENBURG. Like Warhol and Lichtenstein, Claes Oldenburg (b. 1929) made ironic critiques of the new consumer culture, but in the case of the Swedish-born Oldenburg he turned his subjects into sculptural monuments. Oldenburg's humor is evident in his large-scale public projects, such as **LIPSTICK (ASCENDING) ON CATERPILLAR TRACKS** (FIG. 32–12), made for his *alma mater*, Yale University. Oldenburg was invited to create this work by a group of graduate students from the School of Architecture who specified that they wanted a monument to the "Second American

Revolution" of the late 1960s, a period marked by student demonstrations against the Vietnam War. Oldenburg mounted a giant lipstick tube on top of steel tracks taken from a Caterpillar tractor. Visually the sculpture suggests both the warlike aggression of a mobile missile launcher and the eroticism of a lipstick, perhaps in a play on the popular slogan of the time, "make love, not war." The lipstick was to have included a suggestive balloonlike vinyl tip that could be pumped up with air and then left to deflate slowly, but the pump was never installed and the drooping tip, vulnerable to vandalism, was quickly replaced with a metal one. The lipstick monument was installed provocatively on a plaza in front of both the Yale War Memorial and the president's office. Not surprisingly, Oldenburg was asked to remove it. In 1974, however, he reworked the sculpture in the more permanent materials of fiberglass, aluminum, and steel and donated it to Yale, where it was placed in the courtyard of Morse College.

32–12 • Claes Oldenburg LIPSTICK (ASCENDING) ON CATERPILLAR TRACKS
1969, reworked 1974. Painted steel body, aluminum tube, and fiberglass tip, 21′ × 19′5½″ × 10′11″ (6.70 × 5.94 × 3.33 m).
Yale University Art Gallery, New Haven, Connecticut.
Gift of Colossal Keepsake Corporation

THE DEMATERIALIZATION OF THE ART OBJECT

In the same decade that Pop artists critiqued the very visual world of popular culture, other artists questioned the role, purpose, and relevance of the art object in contemporary culture. Their restlessness parallels the social upheaval that marked the era of the mid-1960s and early 1970s. During this period, the youth of Europe and America questioned the authority and rights of the state with civil rights movements, massive rallies against the draft and the Vietnam War, environmentalist and feminist movements, and the Paris revolts of 1968. Women artists made their presence felt in large numbers, and many more artists made art to be viewed outside the gallery system. The decade ended with a move toward making noncommodifiable art and "dematerializing" the art object.

32-13 • Don Judd UNTITLED
1967. Lacquer on galvanized iron, 12 units, each 9 × 40 × 31″ (22.8 × 101.6 × 78.7 cm), installed vertically with 9″ (22.8 cm) intervals. Museum of Modern Art, New York. Helen Acheson Bequest (by exchange) and gift of Joseph Helman

MINIMALISM

Minimalism, which dominated the New York art discourse in the late 1960s, argued for the dematerialization of the art object. In the mid-1960s, a group of articulate young sculptors, including Donald Judd (1928–1994), Robert Morris (b. 1931), and Carl Andre (b. 1935), proposed what was variously called ABC Art, Primary Structures, or Minimalism. They produced slab- or box-like sculptures, frequently fabricated for them out of industrial materials such as Plexiglas, fluorescent lighting, steel, and mirrors, and so rejected the gesture and emotion invested in the hand-crafted object, as well as the traditional materials of sculpture. Judd and Morris described their theories eloquently in the journal *Artforum*. They asked viewers to try to comprehend their art objects as united wholes without a focal point, allowing the energy of the work and the viewers' interest to be dissipated throughout the object in a kind of entropy.

JUDD. In 1965, Donald Judd published the article "Specific Objects" in *Artforum*, where he argued that Minimalism should consist of real or "specific" objects. These were mathematically constructed shapes arranged without hierarchy, which could be read as complete objects at a single glance, were impersonal, and occupied the space of real things, having neither a base below nor a glass case around them. **UNTITLED** of 1967 (**FIG. 32–13**) consists of 12 identical rectangular units fabricated from galvanized iron and hung in a vertical row on the gallery wall. The arrangement is deliberately impersonal, avoiding allusion to any imagined subject. The objects are aggressively themselves. Judd provides the viewer with a set of clear, self-contained visual facts, setting the conceptual clarity and physical perfection of his art against the messy complexity of the real world.

MORRIS. Robert Morris explored the banal and uninteresting in his early art. By the early 1970s, he was making simple, unitary objects. **UNTITLED (MIRROR CUBE) (FIG. 32–14)** is a group of wooden cubes covered on all sides with mirror glass. They literally reflect and deflect any attempt to discover interest *in* the box. There is no point of focus—the boxes are constructed from industrial materials and hold no meaning within their form; instead they reflect the world around them. In fact, the artfulness of this piece lies almost entirely in the artistic concept behind it— the purposes and goals of the artist. The manifestos of Minimalism worked hand-in-hand with actual Minimalist objects to communicate the ideas of Minimal art, which the viewer had to work hard to learn how to read, understand, and appreciate.

Minimalism had its critics. The formalist critic Michael Fried, for instance, wrote that Minimal objects suffered from "objecthood" and held no more interest than any other nonart objects. He also criticized Minimalism for its "theatricality"—in his view, Minimalism, like Pop art, demanded immediate attention but could not hold a viewer's visual attention for very long and so became very boring very quickly.

CONCEPTUAL AND PERFORMANCE ART

The logical extension of the Minimalist move away from the handcrafted art object was Conceptual art. Unlike Duchamp and Dada artists earlier in the century, who argued that the idea *is* the work of art, Conceptual artists argue that the "idea" and "form" of art are separable. Thus, for Conceptual artists there are times when a physical object is an appropriate vehicle for a work of art, other times when a performance is more appropriate, and still other times when a conceptual manifestation, sometimes in the form of written or spoken instructions, is most appropriate. Conceptual art literally "dematerialized" the art object by suggesting that the catalyst for a work of art is a concept and the means by which the concept is communicated can vary. The conceptual work of art usually leaves behind some visual trace, in the form of a set of instructions, writing on a chalkboard, a performance, photographs, or a piece of film, and in some cases even objects. Conceptual art is theoretically driven and is noncommodifiable because it leaves no precious object behind for purchase, although collectors and many museums now collect the "trace" objects left behind.

BEUYS. Some of the most radical Conceptual art came out of Europe. Joseph Beuys (1921–1986) was perhaps the most significant early Conceptual artist. He served as a fighter pilot in the German Luftwaffe during World War II, when he claimed to have been shot down over the Crimea and saved by Tartars who wrapped him in animal fat and felt. There is no evidence that this actually occurred, although something traumatic clearly did happen to Beuys during the war. As an artist, Beuys developed a mysterious shamanistic persona, and created a repertoire of significant materials and objects that he used symbolically and performatively in his art in an attempt to explain the inexplicable to audiences. Beuys's symbolism was deeply personal and difficult for others to grasp. His art was about the desire to communicate and the complexities of that process.

In Beuys's **HOW TO EXPLAIN PICTURES TO A DEAD HARE (FIG. 32–15)**, the artist initially sat on a chair in a gallery surrounded by his own drawings, his head coated in honey and covered by a mask of gold leaf, and cradling a dead hare to which

32-15 • Joseph Beuys **HOW TO EXPLAIN PICTURES TO A DEAD HARE**
1965. Photograph of performance.

32-16 • Joseph Kosuth ONE AND THREE CHAIRS
1965. Wood folding chair, photograph of chair, and photographic enlargement of dictionary definition of chair; chair, 32⅜ × 14⅞ × 20⅞″ (82.2 × 37.8 × 53 cm); photo panel, 36 × 24⅛″ (91.4 × 61.3 cm); text panel 24⅛ × 24½″ (61.3 × 62.2 cm). Museum of Modern Art, New York. Larry Aldrich Foundation Fund (383.1970 a–c)

he muttered incomprehensibly. His left foot rested on felt, suggesting spiritual warmth, while his right foot rested on steel, symbolizing cold hard reason. He carried the dead hare around the gallery for several hours, quietly explaining his pictures to it, reasoning that he

had as much chance of communicating fully with the dead hare as with another person. Thus he rendered visible the problems inherent in the normal means of communication. Beuys said: "Even a dead animal preserves more powers of intuition than some human beings."

KOSUTH. Joseph Kosuth (b. 1945) abandoned painting in 1965 to examine the intersection between language and vision, the abstract idea and concrete imagery. His early work was indebted to Duchamp, semiotic theory, and the linguistic philosophy of Ludwig Wittgenstein (1889–1951). Kosuth is not interested in art that deals with beauty; his work is about the imperfect possibilities of communication, either visual or verbal. **ONE AND THREE CHAIRS** (FIG. 32–16) is a visual rendition of semiotic theory. In this piece there is an actual chair, a photograph of a chair, and a dictionary definition of "chair." The chair is an object, the photograph an imperfect visual representation of the idea of the same chair, and the dictionary definition is the literal abstraction of a chair. The title, *One and Three Chairs*, tells us that we can read this piece as one chair represented three different ways or as three different chairs. Either way, this work of art demonstrates the impossibility of precise representation and communication of an idea, leaving us with the question: Which is the "real" chair?

NAUMAN. In 1966–1967, the California-based artist Bruce Nauman (b. 1941) made a series of 11 color photographs based on wordplay and visual puns in which he cleverly complicated the

32-17 • Bruce Nauman SELF-PORTRAIT AS A FOUNTAIN
1966–1967. Color photograph, 19¾ × 23¾″ (50.1 × 60.3 cm). Courtesy Leo Castelli Gallery, New York.

32-18 • Eva Hesse ROPE PIECE
1969–1970. Latex over rope, string, and wire; two strands, dimensions variable. Whitney Museum of American Art, New York.
Purchase, with funds from Eli and Edythe L. Broad, the Mrs. Percy Uris Purchase Fund, and the Painting and Sculpture Committee (88.17 a–b)

EXPLORE MORE: Gain insight from a primary source by Eva Hesse **www.myartslab.com**

problem of communication. In **SELF-PORTRAIT AS A FOUNTAIN** (**FIG. 32–17**), for example, the bare-chested artist tips his head back and spurts water into the air, thereby showing us that he is a fountain, or perhaps the *Fountain*, the title of Duchamp's infamous urinal (SEE FIG. 31–30). Nauman, like Kosuth, leaves us with the question: Which is the "real" fountain? Is it our abstracted idea of a fountain alluded to in the title (conceptual), Nauman's claim to be a fountain (visual), or his sly reference to Duchamp's *Fountain* (literal)?

PROCESS ART

By the early 1970s, it was evident that Minimalism and Conceptualism had boxed art into an impossible absolutist corner—their reductivist approaches seemed too detached from a society that was being torn apart by social and political conflict. Some artists refused to eliminate personal meaning from their work, and in opposition to Minimalism they explored the physicality, personality, and even sensuality of the process of making art.

HESSE. Eva Hesse (1936–1970), for instance, infused her elegantly crafted art with personal history and meaning. She was born in Hamburg and narrowly escaped the Nazi Holocaust, moving to New York with her family in 1939. After graduating from the Yale School of Art in 1959, she painted dark Expressionistic self-portraits, but in 1964 began to make abstract sculpture that adapted the vocabulary of Minimalism to her own, more self-expressive purpose. She wrote: "For me art and life are inseparable. If I can name the content [of my art] … it's the total absurdity of life." **ROPE PIECE** (**FIG. 32–18**) is about instability; it takes on different forms and shapes each time it is installed. The work consists of several skeins of rope dipped in latex, knotted and tangled, and then hung from wires attached to the gallery ceiling. It is fragile and evocative, sensuous and delicate. Hesse embraced the instability, irrationality, and emotive power of art, reflecting her own life and emotions in the work. Her last pieces, made before her premature death from cancer, are heartbreaking.

Plenty's Boast

by Martin Puryear, 1994–1995. Red cedar and pine.
68 × 83 × 118″ (172.7 × 210.8 × 299.7 cm). Nelson-Atkins Museum of Art, Kansas City, Missouri.
Purchase of the Renee C. Crowell Trust (F95–16 A–C)

Puryear spent a year with the Peace Corps in Sierra Leone. He worked with African carpenters, learning their woodworking methods and skills. Note the gentle and beautifully irregular hand-finishing at the mouth of the sculpture and in the binding of its tail.

Puryear, who studied furnituremaking with James Krenov, is dedicated to maintaining the highest craft standards. Notice the radiating grain on the inside of the horn, the spiraling grain on its tail, and the exquisite quality of the joints.

The clarity, abstract nature, and monumental scale (it is 5½ feet tall) of the sculpture seem to refer to Minimalism, but evidence of the human hand in the crafting of the piece, as in the wobble in the line of the bell, suggests something closer to Process art.

The twisting tail suggests the empty shell of a strange animal or plant. Although it is lying passively at the moment, it looks as if it could flex quickly (note the jointing) to deliver a deadly sting.

The bell shape evokes many forms, such as a musical horn, an old-fashioned gramophone horn, a flower's bell, or a cornucopia (horn of plenty).

Puryear wants viewers to see ghosts of resemblances in his allusive sculpture. Perhaps most obviously *Plenty's Boast* suggests a cornucopia, filled with the fruits of harvest and symbolizing abundance. But the cone is empty, implying an "empty boast"—a phrase suggested by the title.

SEE MORE: View the Closer Look feature for *Plenty's Boast* **www.myartslab.com**

of the accomplishments of women artists, past and present. Art historians salvaged the histories of as many women artists as possible, instating them in the "canon," and making the argument that they were as good as the male artists in it. Meanwhile feminist artists represented the physicality and sexuality of the female body as defined by women rather than as it appeared in male fantasies. This early feminist art was essentialist; it focused on women's bodies and defined gender in biological terms.

The second wave of feminist art defined gender in more relativist terms. In 1971, Linda Nochlin wrote a groundbreaking essay entitled "Why Have There Been No Great Women Artists," in which she argued that many women artists in history cannot be described as "great" if the only standard of judgment for "great" art is a masculine canon. Nochlin argued that art institutions had systematically denied women access to art education and opportunities available to men throughout history, thereby making competition on male terms impossible. Thus, the terms of the canon must be challenged and the art system changed so that women can compete on their own terms. Second-wave feminist artists deconstructed the canon by which art was currently judged and called for a re-evaluation of the place of so-called feminine arts, such as ceramics, textiles, jewelry-making, and miniature painting. They also challenged how women are looked at (gazed upon) by men in life and in art (Laura Mulvey and John Berger wrote on the "gaze" in 1973 and 1972, respectively).

Third-wave feminist art emerged in the 1990s. This latest generation of artists has addressed a plethora of other issues that discriminate against or denigrate women, including such hybrid ones as gender and class, gender and race, violence against women, postcolonialism, transgenderism, transnationalism, and eco-feminism. Third-wave feminist art explores the many strategies that women employ to navigate life.

WINSOR. Jackie Winsor's (b. 1941) elegant and moving **BURNT PIECE (FIG. 32–19)**, constructed from wire mesh, cement, and burnt wood, which Winsor worked intensively, also subverts the boxlike shapes of Minimalist sculpture. The detail is really only visible on the inside; this is a closed, private, and secretive piece. The woodwork also refers to Winsor's childhood in Newfoundland, where her father was employed in the house-building trade.

FEMINISM AND ART

The idea of feminist art developed alongside the women's liberation movement of the 1960s. Both challenged one of the major unspoken conventions of art history: that great art could only be made by men. Since the 1960s, there have been three waves of feminist art and art history. A major aim of the first feminist artists and art historians was increased recognition for the accomplishment of women artists, both past and present. As feminists examined the history of art, they found that women had contributed to most of the movements of Western art but were almost never mentioned in histories of art. Feminists also attacked the traditional Western hierarchy that placed "the arts" (painting, sculpture, architecture) at a level of achievement higher than "the crafts" (ceramics, textiles, jewelry-making). Since most craft media have been historically dominated by women, favoring art over craft tends to relegate women's achievements to second-class status. Thus early feminist art tended to embrace craft media.

The first wave of feminist art and art history in the 1960s and early 1970s called for an increased recognition and acknowledgment

CHICAGO AND SCHAPIRO. Born Judy Cohen, Judy Chicago (b. 1939) adopted the name of the city of her birth in order to free herself from "all names imposed upon her through male social dominance." In the late 1960s, she began making abstracted images

The Dinner Party

Judy Chicago's THE DINNER PARTY is a large, complex, mixed-media installation dedicated to hundreds of women and women artists rescued from anonymity by early feminist artists and historians. It took five years of collaborative effort to make, and it drew on the assistance of hundreds of female and several male volunteers working as ceramists, needleworkers, and china painters. *The Dinner Party* is composed of a large, triangular table, each side stretching 48 feet; Chicago conceived of the equilateral triangle as a symbol of both the feminine and the equalized world sought by feminism. The table rests on a triangular platform of 2,300 triangular porcelain tiles comprising the "Heritage Floor" that bears the names of 999 notable women from myth, legend, and history. Along each side of the table are 13 place settings representing famous women—13 being the number of men at the Last Supper as well as the number of

witches in a coven. The 39 women thus honored by individual place settings include the mythical, such as the goddess Ishtar and the Amazon, and historical personages such as the Egyptian queen Hatshepsut, the Roman scholar Hypatia, the medieval French queen Eleanor of Aquitaine, the author Christine de Pizan (see page 531), the Italian Renaissance noblewoman Isabella d'Este (see page 658), the Italian Baroque painter Artemisia Gentileschi (SEE FIG. 22–14), the eighteenth-century English feminist writer Mary Wollstonecraft, the nineteenth-century American abolitionist Sojourner Truth, and the twentieth-century American painter Georgia O'Keeffe (shown here).

Each larger-than-life place setting includes a 14-inch-wide painted porcelain plate, ceramic flatware, a ceramic chalice with a gold interior, and an embroidered napkin, sitting upon an elaborately ornamented runner. The runners are

decorated using stitching and weaving techniques and motifs appropriate to the time and place in which each woman lived. Most of the plates feature abstract designs based on female genitalia because, as Chicago said, "that is all [these women] had in common.... They were from different periods, classes, ethnicities, geographies, experiences, but what kept them within the same confined historical space" was their biological sex. The empty plates represent the fact that they "had been swallowed up and obscured by history instead of being recognized and honored."

The prominent place accorded to china painting and needlework in *The Dinner Party* both celebrates traditional women's crafts and argues for their place in the pantheon of "high art," while at the same time informing the viewer about some of the unrecognized contributions that women have made to history.

Judy Chicago THE DINNER PARTY
1974–1979. Overall installation view. White tile floor inscribed in gold with 999 women's names; triangular table with painted porcelain, sculpted porcelain plates, and needlework, each side 48 × 42 × 3′ (14.6 × 12.8 × 1 m). Brooklyn Museum of Art, New York.
Gift of the Elizabeth A. Sackler Foundation (2002.10)

Georgia O'Keeffe
Place setting, detail of *The Dinner Party*.

32-20 • Miriam Schapiro **PERSONAL APPEARANCE #3**
1973. Acrylic and fabric on canvas, 60 × 50″ (152.4 × 127 cm).
Private collection.

MENDIETA. Ana Mendieta (1948–1985) was born in Cuba but was sent to Iowa in 1961 as part of "Operation Peter Pan," which relocated 14,000 unaccompanied Cuban children after the 1959 revolution brought Fidel Castro and communism to power in Cuba. Mendieta never fully recovered from the trauma of her removal: A sense of personal dislocation haunted her and a desire to leave her bodily imprint on the earth drove her art. Mendieta used ritualistic actions in performances that connected her to the earth. She was inspired by both *santería*, the African-Cuban religion (SEE FIG. 31–75), and the work of Beuys (SEE FIG. 32–15). Mendieta produced more than 200 body works called "Silhouettes" in which she explored ways to "plant" herself in the earth. She recorded these performances in photographs and on film. The **TREE OF LIFE** series **(FIG. 32–21)** was created in Iowa, where she studied and lived. This photograph shows Mendieta with arms upraised like an earth goddess, pressed against a tree and covered in mud, as if to invite the tree to absorb her and connect her to her "maternal source." Like many of Mendieta's other works, this piece celebrates the notion that women have a deeper identification with nature than do men.

of female genitalia to challenge the male-dominated art world and to validate the female body and experience. In 1970, she established a feminist studio art course at Fresno State College (now California State University, Fresno) and the next year moved to Los Angeles to join the painter Miriam Schapiro (b. 1923) in establishing a Feminist Art Program at the new California Institute of the Arts (CalArts). At this time she also began to make *The Dinner Party*, one of the largest and best-known feminist artworks of the decade (see "*The Dinner Party*," opposite).

In 1971–1972, Chicago, Schapiro, and 21 of their female students created *Womanhouse*, a collaborative art environment located in a run-down Hollywood mansion which the artists renovated and filled with feminist installations. In collaboration with Sherry Brody, Schapiro also created *Dollhouse*, a mixed-media construction of several miniature rooms adorned with richly patterned fabrics. She subsequently began to incorporate pieces of fabric into her acrylic paintings, developing a type of work she called **femmage** (from "female" and "collage"). Schapiro's femmages, such as **PERSONAL APPEARANCE #3** (FIG. 32–20), celebrate traditional women's crafts. Schapiro later returned to New York to lead the Pattern and Decoration movement, a group of both female and male artists who merged the aesthetics of abstraction with ornamental motifs derived from women's craft, folk art, and art beyond the Western tradition in a nonhierarchical manner.

32-21 • Ana Mendieta **UNTITLED, FROM THE TREE OF LIFE SERIES**
1977. Color photograph, 20 × 13¼″ (50.8 × 33.7 cm). Courtesy of Galerie Lelong, New York and the estate of Ana Mendieta.

32-22 • Betye Saar THE LIBERATION OF AUNT JEMIMA
1972. Mixed media, 11¾ × 11⅞ × 2¾" (29.8 × 30.3 × 7 cm),
Berkeley Art Museum, University of California. Purchased with the aid of
funds from the National Endowment for the Arts (selected by The Committee for
the Acquisition of Afro-American Art)

SAAR. African-American sculptor Betye Saar (b. 1926) makes
works of art about race in America that are both militantly feminist
and racially activist. For **THE LIBERATION OF AUNT JEMIMA (FIG.
32–22),** Saar created a collage out of appropriated two- and three-
dimensional images of the derogatory stereotype of a cheerfully
servile "mammy," here transformed into a militant black feminist.
The larger "mammy" figure is actually a notepad holder, to which
Saar has attached another picture of a "mammy" holding a crying
white child; in front of that is a large clenched black fist, the
symbol of Black Power. In place of a pencil the main "mammy"
holds a broom and a rifle. The rifle and fist contrast sharply with
the repeated images of a smiling Aunt Jemima in the background.
Saar's **appropriation** (taking material from one source and using
it, unaltered, in another) of contrasting images from popular
culture subverts and critiques the servile black female stereotype
by both liberating her and threatening the viewer.

EARTHWORKS AND SITE-SPECIFIC SCULPTURE

In the early 1970s, as Process artists reintroduced the handcrafted
into art, another group of artists began working with the earth as a
medium to be manipulated, crafted, and changed. Earth artists
used the land as their canvas. They made art outdoors, frequently
manipulating raw materials found at the site to create **earthworks**
that are usually **site-specific** (designed for a specific location). Some
of these artists created vast sculptures that altered the landscape
permanently, while others made ambitious works that only
temporarily changed a place. Some Earth art is located in remote
locations and is directly accessible to only a few people, while other
examples have been made available to many. Earth art, like
Performance and Conceptual art, is often intended to be noncommodifiable but it is frequently recorded in photographs and on film,
with the result that these images become collectable objects. Earth
art should not be confused with Environmental art: The former
uses the land (or city) as a place on which to make art, whereas the
latter seeks to draw attention to an imperiled natural environment.

SMITHSON. Robert Smithson (1938–1973) created **SPIRAL
JETTY (FIG. 32–23),** one of the most significant earthworks, in
1970. This is a 1,500-foot spiraling earthen jetty that extends into
the Great Salt Lake in Utah. To Smithson, the Great Salt Lake
represented both a primordial ocean that cultivated life and a dead
sea that killed it. Smithson liked the way that skeletons of
abandoned oil rigs along the lake's shore looked like dinosaur
bones; his jetty was supposed to remind viewers of the remains of
ancient civilizations. Smithson also incorporated one of the few
living organisms found in the otherwise dead lake into his work: an
alga that turns a reddish color under certain conditions. Smithson's
Spiral Jetty is one vehicle wide: To create the jetty, earth was hauled
out into the lake in a huge land-moving truck.

Smithson used the spiral because it is an essential shape in
nature and has been used in human art for millennia. The spiral
curls and uncurls, endlessly suggesting growth and decay, creation
and destruction. Smithson ordered that no maintenance be done
on *Spiral Jetty*; he wanted the sculpture to be governed by the
natural elements over time. The work was intended to illustrate the
"ongoing dialectic" in nature between constructive and destructive
forces. The jetty is now covered with crystallized salt; it remains
visible today and can be seen on Google Earth.

CHRISTO AND JEANNE-CLAUDE. The most visible site-specific
artists in America were Christo Javacheff (b. 1935) and Jeanne-
Claude de Guillebon (1935–2009). Christo and Jeanne-Claude, as
they were known, embarked on vast projects (both rural and
urban) that sometimes took many years of planning to realize. In
1958, Christo emigrated from Bulgaria to Paris, where he met
Jeanne-Claude; they moved to New York together in 1964. Their
work was political and interventionist, frequently commenting
on capitalism and consumer culture by wrapping or packaging
buildings or large swatches of land in fabric: They "wrapped" the

32-23 • Robert Smithson **SPIRAL JETTY**

1970. Mud, precipitated salt crystals, rocks, and water, length 1,500 × width 15′ (457 × 4.5 m). Great Salt Lake, Utah.

Collection: DIA Center for the Arts, New York

EXPLORE MORE: Click the Google Earth link for Spiral Jetty **www.myartslab.com**

Reichstag in Berlin and 1 million square feet of Australian coastline, for instance. In each case the process of planning and battling bureaucracies was part of the art, frequently taking years to complete. By contrast, the wrapping itself usually took only a few weeks and the completed project was in place for even less time. Christo and Jeanne-Claude funded each new project from the sale of books, Christo's original artworks like drawings, collages, and other ephemera relating to the preceding projects. In February 2005, Christo and Jeanne-Claude installed **THE GATES, CENTRAL PARK, NEW YORK, 1979-2005** (FIG. **32–24**). This project took 26 years to realize, during which time the artists battled their way through various New York bureaucracies, meeting many obstacles and making changes to the work along the way. They finally installed 7,503 saffron-colored nylon panels on "gates" along 23 miles of pathway in Central Park. The brightly colored flapping panels enlivened the frigid February landscape and were an enormous public success. The installation lasted for only 16 days.

32-24 • Christo and Jeanne-Claude **THE GATES, CENTRAL PARK, NEW YORK CITY, 1979-2005**

1979–2005.

SEE MORE: View an interactive map of Christo's and Jeanne-Claude's *The Gates* **www.myartslab.com**

ARCHITECTURE: MID-CENTURY MODERNISM TO POSTMODERNISM

In architecture, the Modernist International Style endured until the 1970s. The International Style, with its plainly visible structure and rejection of historicism, dominated new urban construction in much of the world after World War II, which meant that the utopian and revolutionary aspects of Modernist architecture settled into a form that largely came to stand for corporate power and wealth. Several major European International Style architects, such as Walter Gropius (SEE FIG. 31–52), migrated to the United States and assumed important positions in architecture schools where they trained several generations of like-minded architects.

MID-CENTURY MODERNIST ARCHITECTURE

The most extreme examples of postwar International Style buildings were created by Ludwig Mies van der Rohe (1886–1969) (see "The International Style," page 1057), a former Bauhaus teacher and refugee from Nazi Germany. Mies designed the rectilinear glass towers that came to personify postwar capitalism. In the **SEAGRAM BUILDING** in New York City (**FIG. 32–25**), designed with Philip Johnson, the building's crisp, clean

32-26 • Eero Saarinen **TRANS WORLD AIRLINES (TWA) TERMINAL, JOHN F. KENNEDY AIRPORT** New York. 1956–1962.

lines epitomize the standardization and impersonality that became synonymous with the modern corporation. Such buildings, with their efficient construction methods and use of materials, allowed the architect to pack an immense amount of office space into a building on a very small lot, which meant that they were also economical to construct. Although criticized for building relatively unadorned glass boxes, Mies advocated: "Less is more." He did, however, use nonfunctional, decorative bronze beams on the outside of the Seagram Building to echo the functional beams inside and give the façade a sleek, rich, and dignified appearance.

Although the pared-down, rectilinear forms of the International Style dominated the urban skyline, other architects departed from its impersonal principles so that, even in commercial architecture, expressive designs using new structural techniques and more materials also appeared. For instance, the **TRANS WORLD AIRLINES (TWA) TERMINAL (FIG. 32–26)** at John F. Kennedy Airport in New York City, by the Finnish-born American architect Eero Saarinen (1910–1961), breaks out of the box dramatically. Saarinen wanted to evoke the thrill and glamor of air travel, so he gave the TWA Terminal's roof two broad winglike canopies of reinforced concrete that suggest a huge bird about to take flight; the interior meanwhile consists of large, open, dramatically flowing spaces. Saarinen designed all of the building's interior details—from ticket counters to telephone booths—to complement his gull-winged shell.

Frank Lloyd Wright (SEE FIGS. 31–41, 31–42, 31–43) trans-formed museum architecture when he designed the **GUGGENHEIM**

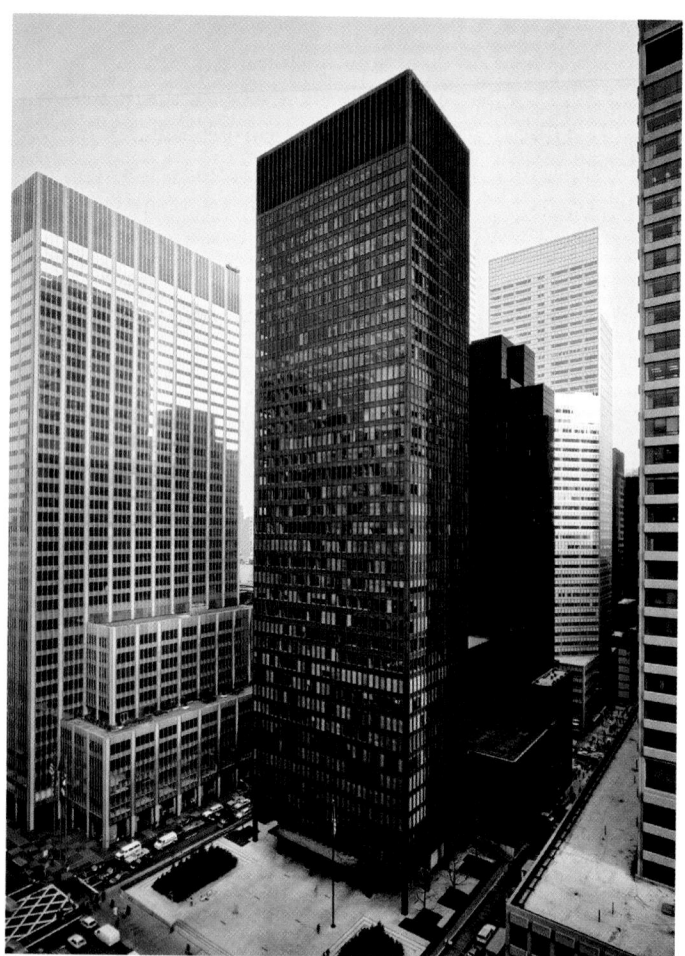

32-25 • Ludwig Mies van der Rohe and Philip Johnson
SEAGRAM BUILDING
New York. 1954–1958.

32-27 • Frank Lloyd Wright **SOLOMON R. GUGGENHEIM MUSEUM**
New York. 1943–1959.

EXPLORE MORE: Click the Google Earth link for the Guggenheim Museum **www.myartslab.com**

MUSEUM (FIG. 32–27) in New York as a sculptural work of art in its own right. The Guggenheim was designed to house Solomon Guggenheim's personal collection of Modern art and, like the TWA Terminal, was based on an organic shape, in this case a spiral. The museum's galleries spiral downward from a glass ceiling, wrapping themselves around a spectacular five-story atrium—Wright's plan was that visitors would begin by taking the elevator to the top floor and then walk down the sloping and increasingly widening ramp, enjoying Guggenheim's personal collection of paintings along the way. The interior today still has the intended intimacy of a "living room," despite having been altered by the museum's first directors. Wright wanted the building to contrast with skyscrapers like the Seagram Building and to become a Manhattan landmark—indeed, it is still one of the twentieth century's most distinctive museum spaces, and a favored site for installation and Performance art.

POSTMODERN ARCHITECTURE

In the 1970s, architects began to move away from the sleek glass-and-steel boxes of the International Style and to reintroduce quotations from past styles into their designs. Architectural historians trace the origins of this new style—Postmodernism—to the work of Jane Jacobs (1916–2006), who wrote *The Death and Life of Great American Cities* (1961), and the Philadelphian Robert Venturi (b. 1925), who rejected the abstract purity of the International Style by incorporating elements drawn from vernacular (meaning popular, common, or ordinary) sources into his designs.

Venturi parodied Mies van der Rohe's aphorism, "Less is more," with his own saying, "Less is a bore." He argued that Mies and other Modernist architects had ignored human needs in their quest for uniformity and sterility, and that Postmodernism should address the complex, contradictory, and heterogeneous mixture of "high" and "low" architecture that comprised the modern city. He said that new architecture should embrace eclecticism, so he reintroduced references to past architectural styles into his designs, and began to apply decoration to his buildings.

While writing his treatise on Postmodernism, *Complexity and Contradiction in Architecture* (1966), Venturi designed a house for his mother **(FIG. 32–28)** that illustrated many of his new ideas. The shape of the façade returns to the traditional Western "house" volumes and shapes that Modernists rejected because of their historical associations. Its vocabulary of triangles, squares, and circles is arranged in a complex asymmetry that subverts the symmetrical rigidity of Modernist design, while the curved molding over the door is simply decorative. The most disruptive element of the façade is the deep cleavage over the door, which opens to reveal a mysterious upper wall (which turns out to be a penthouse) and chimney top. The interior is also complex and contradictory. The irregular floor plan **(FIG. 32–29)**, including an odd stairway leading up to the second floor, is further complicated by irregular ceiling levels that are partially covered by a barrel vault. The overall structure makes reference to several previous buildings, including Michelangelo's Porta Pia in Rome and a nearby house designed by Venturi's mentor, Louis Kahn (1901–1974).

32-28 • Robert Venturi **VANNA VENTURI HOUSE**
Chestnut Hill, Pennsylvania. 1961–1964.

32-29 • GROUND-FLOOR PLAN OF THE VANNA VENTURI HOUSE

In the 1970s, Postmodern ideas were also applied to commercial architecture. One of the first examples was the **AT&T CORPORATE HEADQUARTERS** (now the Sony Building) in New York City (**FIG. 32–30**) by Philip Johnson (1906–2005). This elegant, granite-clad skyscraper has 36 oversized stories, making it as tall as the average 60-story building. It mimics its International Style neighbors with its smooth uncluttered skin, while its Classical window groupings set between vertical piers also echo nearby skyscrapers from much earlier in the century. But the overall profile of the building bears a

32-30 • Philip Johnson and John Burgee MODEL, AT&T CORPORATE HEADQUARTERS
New York. 1978–1983.

EXPLORE MORE: Click the Google Earth link for the AT&T Building (now the Sony Building)
www.myartslab.com

whimsical resemblance to the shape of a Chippendale highboy, an eighteenth-century chest of drawers with a long-legged base—Johnson seems to have intended a pun on the terms "highboy" and "high-rise." The round notch at the top of the building as well as the rounded entryway at its base suggest the coin slot and coin return of an old pay telephone in a clever reference to Johnson's patron, the AT&T telephone company.

POSTMODERNISM

Scholars disagree about the exact date when the theories of Postmodernism filtered through the Western art world, but most agree that it took place in the early 1980s. By then, the Modern ideas of art as absolute, ideal, pure, or perfect, and of the artist as a serious, single-minded individual who held her/himself above and apart from society, were beginning to seem both arrogant and foolhardy to younger artists.

Rather than a style, Postmodernism is perhaps better thought of as a strategy for making art. Its manifestations are many and varied. Postmodern artists reject the seriousness of Modernism, creating visually interesting, messy, sometimes contrary, and often political images that mock the rules of Modern art. They "appropriate" or take images wholesale from both "high art" and "popular" sources, repositioning and recontextualizing them, making them partially their own, twisting and changing their meanings. Postmodern artists create new images and new meanings out of the old, welcoming oddity and eccentricity, and seriously questioning the idea of "originality."

Just as Modern art heralded an industrial, technological society, the advent of Postmodern art heralded a post-industrial, advanced capitalist society based on communication and information, and demanding a flexible population that embraces difference and change. Postmodern art reflects the **pluralism** (social and cultural diversity) of our globalized society, in which the only real constant is change and the only thing we have in common is difference. Postmodern art also embraces the vast visual culture of the 1980s, the age of personal computers, video cameras, cable television, and an emerging Internet culture; it harnesses images from this infinitely mutable world in which it is difficult to know what is real and what is not. As Andy Warhol observed presciently some time before, "I don't know where the artificial stops and the real starts."

PAINTING

Neo-Expressionism was one of the first international expressions of Postmodernism. It was launched by two highly visible exhibitions in London ("A New Spirit") and Berlin ("Zeitgeist") in the early 1980s. These exhibitions included large-scale figural Expressionist paintings that recovered the luxury of the painted surface. Neo-Expressionism was almost exclusively dominated by men: "A New Spirit" featured the art of 38 male artists and "Zeitgeist" featured the art of one female and 43 male artists.

32–31 • Anselm Kiefer HEATH OF THE BRANDENBURG MARCH
1974. Oil, acrylic, and shellac on burlap, 3′10½″ × 8′4″ (1.18 × 2.54 m). Stedelijk Van Abbemuseum, Eindhoven, The Netherlands.

32–32 • Jean-Michel Basquiat HORN PLAYERS
1983. Acrylic and oil paintstick on canvas, three panels, overall 8′ × 6′5″ (2.44 × 1.91 m). Broad Art Foundation, Santa Monica, California.

KIEFER. The German Neo-Expressionist Anselm Kiefer (b. 1945) was born in the final weeks of World War II. His work both pays homage to and critiques the art of the German Expressionists of the 1930s whose art was banned by the Nazis (see "Suppression of the Avant-Garde in Nazi Germany," page 1055). In the burned and barren landscape of his **HEATH OF THE BRANDENBURG MARCH (FIG. 32–31)**, Kiefer tries to come to grips with his country's Nazi past, building on the ideas of his teacher Beuys. Instead of simply documenting Nazism in this painting, Kiefer portrays both the devastating physical impact of the war on the Brandenburg Heath (near Berlin) and invokes Nazi history by scrawling the first words of the Nazi marching song "Märkische Heide, märkische Sand" across the road in the front of the painting, thus both quoting from the past and critiquing it.

BASQUIAT. In the United States, the tragically short-lived Jean-Michel Basquiat (1960–1988) made Neo-Expressionist paintings that grew out of graffiti art. The Brooklyn-born Basquiat was raised in middle-class comfort but rebelled by quitting high school and leaving home to become a street artist. For three years he covered the walls of lower Manhattan with short and witty philosophical texts signed with the tag "SAMO©." In 1980, Basquiat participated in the highly publicized "Times Square Show" which showcased the raw and aggressive styles of subway and graffiti artists. Basquiat said he wanted to make "paintings that look as if they were made by a child," but in reality his work is a sophisticated mix of appropriated imagery from Modern art combined with blunt references to race and the street.

HORN PLAYERS (FIG. 32–32) portrays legendary jazz musicians Charlie Parker (upper left) and Dizzy Gillespie (center right). Basquiat's urgent paint application and hurried lettering are strongly emotional and Expressionist, conveying a dedication to

The Guerrilla Girls

In 1984, the Museum of Modern Art mounted "An International Survey of Painting and Sculpture," an exhibition that supposedly displayed the most important art of the time, yet of the 169 (mostly white) artists included in the exhibition, only 13 were women. By way of a rejoinder to this and several other such exhibitions, the following year the radical feminist group the Guerrilla Girls was founded in New York to function, they said, as "the conscience of the art world." Its members wear gorilla masks to hide their identity and to prevent personal reprisals; they call themselves "girls" as a play on the demeaning term "girl" as applied to women. Each Guerrilla Girl takes as a pseudonym the name of a famous dead woman artist. They have declared that the new "f" word is feminism.

Their mandate is to reveal gender and racial inequities in the art world, to demonstrate against discrimination, and to fight for the rights of women and artists of color. The Guerrilla Girls use the strategies of guerrilla warfare—they act covertly and strike anonymously at the heart of their enemy. They compile statistics on discrimination in the art world, produce sharp, witty, sophisticated posters that draw on the best advertising theory, and paste these posters at night on walls in the art districts of New York close to offending galleries and museums. The posters are highly visible, damning, and very funny, and they have made a difference.

One of their most famous posters features a poster version of a reclining nude by Ingres and the words "Do women have to be naked to get into the Met. Museum?" As the poster explains, 85 percent of the nudes on display in the Metropolitan Museum at the time (1989) were women, while less than 5 percent of art in the museum was by women. Sadly, the Guerrilla Girls repeated their survey in 2005 and found that there were even fewer women artists (3 percent), but, as they said, at least there were more naked men!

THE ADVANTAGES OF BEING A WOMAN ARTIST delivers a clever, ironic, and sadly accurate list of the "benefits" of being a woman artist. Today's Guerrilla Girls have broadened their reach to address larger issues of race and political discrimination in the world. They have made significant differences in the art world, if not yet at the Met.

THE ADVANTAGES OF BEING A WOMAN ARTIST:

Working without the pressure of success
Not having to be in shows with men
Having an escape from the art world in your 4 free-lance jobs
Knowing your career might pick up after you're eighty
Being reassured that whatever kind of art you make it will be labeled feminine
Not being stuck in a tenured teaching position
Seeing your ideas live on in the work of others
Having the opportunity to choose between career and motherhood
Not having to choke on those big cigars or paint in Italian suits
Having more time to work when your mate dumps you for someone younger
Being included in revised versions of art history
Not having to undergo the embarrassment of being called a genius
Getting your picture in the art magazines wearing a gorilla suit

A PUBLIC SERVICE MESSAGE FROM **GUERRILLA GIRLS** CONSCIENCE OF THE ART WORLD

Guerrilla Girls **THE ADVANTAGES OF BEING A WOMAN ARTIST**
1988. Offset print, 17 × 22″ (43.2 × 55.9 cm). Collection of the artists.

jazz and a passionate determination to foreground African-American subjects in an unsentimental way. Basquiat said: "Black people are never portrayed realistically, not even portrayed, in Modern art, and I'm glad to do that." He died from a heroin overdose at age 27.

RICHTER. Postmodern painting took many forms in addition to Neo-Expressionism. One of the most sophisticated Postmodern artists is the German artist Gerhard Richter (b. 1932), who rejected the idea of a single style in art, arguing that each painting's content should determine its form. In 1988, he made a series of paintings, including **MAN SHOT DOWN (1) ERSCHOSSENER (1) FROM OCTOBER 18, 1977** (FIG. 32–33). This series features life-size painted copies of grainy black-and-white newspaper photographs of the bodies of three members of the terrorist group the Red Army Faction

32-33 • Gerhard Richter **MAN SHOT DOWN (1) ERSCHOSSENER (1) FROM OCTOBER 18, 1977**
1988. Oil on canvas, 39½ × 55¼″ (100 × 140 cm). Museum of Modern Art, New York. The Sidney and Harriet Janis Collection, gift of Philip Johnson, and acquired through the Lillie P. Bliss Bequest (all by exchange); Enid A. Haupt Fund; Nina and Gordon Bunshaft Bequest Fund; and gift of Emily Rauh Pulitzer. (169.1995.g.)

(commonly known as the Baader-Meinhof Gang), who were found dead in their prison cells in 1977, probably by suicide. They had been imprisoned for the kidnap and murder of Hans Martin Schleyer, president of the powerful German Federation of Industries. In his painting Richter simultaneously critiques the single-minded pursuit of a political ideologue willing to die for an idea, the role of the mass media in creating meaning in images (knowledge of the historical context of the events portrayed changes their meaning), and the value of the (in this case almost invisible) hand of the artist.

POSTMODERNISM AND GENDER

In 1982, the critic Craig Owens argued that Postmodernism represented a crisis in normal cultural authority because of the way it questioned the relative homogeneity of Modernism. Moreover, since photography, which had never been fully integrated into the canon, was perhaps the perfect medium for appropriating images, Owens argued that it might also be the ideal Postmodern medium. In addition, since feminism challenged the "patriarchy" (the masculine control of power in society) and Owens described Modernism as patriarchal, authoritative, single-minded, and driven by the quest for originality and artistic mastery, he also argued that feminists might be in a position to make the best Postmodern art. Since Postmodernism, feminism, and photography all forced viewers to confront difference, since all challenged the authority of the canon, and since none particularly valued originality or individual artistic mastery, Owens argued that feminists and photographers represented Postmodernism more completely than did the mostly male Neo-Expressionist painters. In keeping with this, in the 1980s many women artists used Postmodern strategies to create feminist art (see "The Guerrilla Girls," opposite).

32-35 • Barbara Kruger UNTITLED (YOUR GAZE HITS THE SIDE OF MY FACE)
1981. Photograph, red painted frame, 55 × 41″ (140 × 104 cm). Mary Boone Gallery, New York.

SHERMAN. The "Untitled Film Stills" series by Cindy Sherman (b. 1954) exemplifies Postmodern strategies of looking. These photographs eerily resemble authentic still photographs from early 1960s films; they are even printed in black-and-white on 8 × 10″ paper in film-still format. But all are in fact contemporary photographs of Sherman herself in which she poses, appropriately made-up, in settings that seem to quote from the well-known plots of old movies. In **UNTITLED FILM STILL #21** (FIG. 32–34), for instance, she appears as a small-town girl who has moved to the big city to find work. Other photographs from the series show her variously as a Southern belle, a hardworking housewife, and a teenager waiting by the phone for a call. Critics have discussed these images in terms of second-wave feminism, as questioning the culturally constructed roles played by women in society, and as a critique of the male gaze. In these photographs, Sherman is both the photographer and the photographed. By assuming both roles, she complicates the relationship between the person looking and the person being looked at, and she subverts the way in which photographs of women communicate stereotypes.

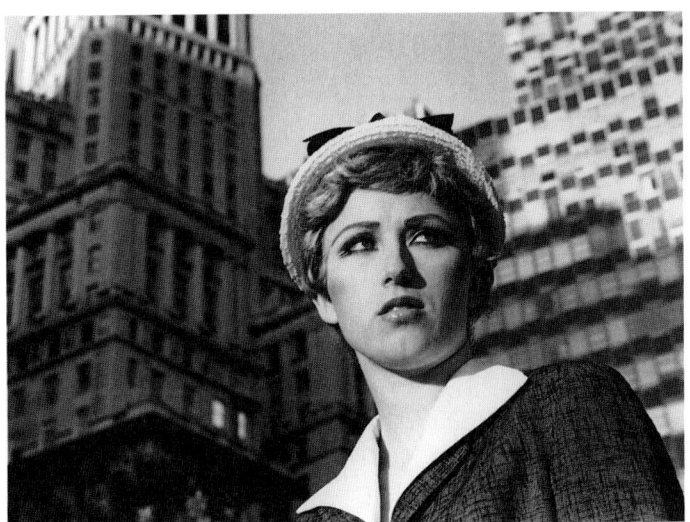

32-34 • Cindy Sherman UNTITLED FILM STILL #21
1978. Black-and-white photograph, 8 × 10″ (20.3 × 25.4 cm). Courtesy of the artist and Metro Pictures, New York.

EXPLORE MORE: Gain insight from a primary source related to Cindy Sherman **www.myartslab.com**

KRUGER. Barbara Kruger (b. 1945) makes an even stronger point about how women are looked at in **UNTITLED (YOUR GAZE HITS THE SIDE OF MY FACE)** (FIG. 32–35). Kruger started her career as a designer for *Mademoiselle* magazine before beginning to make

**TAR BEACH (PART I FROM THE
WOMAN ON A BRIDGE SERIES)**
1988. Acrylic on canvas, bordered with
printed, painted, quilted, and pieced cloth,
74⅝ × 68½″ (190.5 × 174 cm).
Guggenheim Museum, New York.
Gift, Mr. and Mrs. Gus and Judith Lieber, 1988
(88.362)

photo-based art. Her signature style is the black-and-white photographic image with red (three-color printing) used in cheap advertising. Kruger appropriates the imagery of advertising, its layout style, and its characteristic use of slogans, doing so both to suggest and to subvert the advertising image. In this photograph, she personalizes the relationship between the viewer and the viewed, addressing the former directly using the personal pronoun "you." In any figurative image, there is a person who looks (the spectator) and a person in the image who is looked at (the subject). The person who looks is active, while the person being looked at is passive. Usually it is the person who looks who holds the power of the "gaze" and implicitly subjugates the person being looked at.

32-37 • Lorna Simpson
STEREO STYLES
1988. Ten black-and-white
Polaroid prints and ten
engraved plastic plaques, 5′4″
× 9′8″ (1.63 × 2.95 m) overall.
Private collection.

If the person being looked at returns, rejects, or deflects the gaze, however, the traditional power relationship is upset. That is what happens in Kruger's image, where the looker ("you") is blocked by the woman being looked at, who says that "your gaze" is deflecting by "the side of my face." Kruger's art is subversive and interventionist; she has printed her works on posters, on T-shirts, and even on pencils and pens.

POSTMODERNISM, RACE, AND ETHNICITY

Other artists have likewise used Postmodern strategies to draw attention to racial and ethnic difference, to advocate change, and to explore how race and gender combine to doubly silence artists.

RINGGOLD.   Faith Ringgold (b. 1930) draws on the tradition of African-American quiltmaking combined with the heritage of African textiles to make significant statements about race in America. In the early 1970s, Ringgold began to introduce traditional women's crafts into her art, painting on soft fabrics rather than on stretched canvases and framing her paintings with decorative quilted borders. Ringgold's mother, Willi Posey, a fashion designer and dressmaker, made the quilted borders until her death in 1981, after which Ringgold began to do the quilting herself. In 1977, Ringgold started writing her autobiography (*We Flew Over the Bridge: The Memoirs of Faith Ringgold*, 1995) but, unable to find a publisher, decided to sew her stories into quilts instead—what she termed "story quilting."

Animated by a feminist sensibility, Ringgold's story quilts are narrated by women and usually address women's issues. In **TAR BEACH (FIG. 32–36)**, the narrator is 8-year-old Cassie Louise Lightfoot—although the story is actually based on Ringgold's own memories of growing up in Harlem. "Tar Beach" is the roof of the apartment building in which Ringgold's family lived and where they slept on hot summer nights. Ringgold describes it as a magical place. Cassie and her brother lie on a blanket while their parents and neighbors play cards. She dreams that she can fly and that she can possess everything over which she passes. Another version of Cassie is shown flying over the George Washington Bridge, claiming it for herself; over a new union-constructed building, claiming it for her father who, as an African-American construction worker, was not allowed to join the union; and over an ice-cream factory, claiming "ice cream every night for dessert" for her mother. Cassie's fantasy reminds the viewer of the real social and economic prejudices that African Americans have faced in America's past and present.

SIMPSON.   In **STEREO STYLES (FIG. 32–37)**, Lorna Simpson (b. 1960) arranges ten Polaroid photographs of African-American women photographed from behind in a double row. Each wears a different hairstyle. Adjectives describe the hairstyles variously and ironically as "Daring," "Sensible," "Severe," "Long and Silky," "Boyish," "Ageless," "Silly," "Magnetic," "Country Fresh," and "Sweet." Simpson frequently photographs African-American women with their faces turned away to suggest that they are seen only in terms of their bodies or, in this case, of their African-American hair styles. Her images ask us to consider how African-American women are stereotyped and the role that hair plays as an indicator of race, gender, and class in society.

BACA.   Judith F. Baca (b. 1946) pays tribute to her Mexican-American heritage in *The Great Wall of Los Angeles*, which looks back to the Mexican mural movement (SEE FIG. 31–69) to recount the history of California as seen through Mexican-, African-, and Japanese-American eyes. This detail, **THE DIVISION OF THE BARRIOS (FIG. 32–38)**, depicts the residents of a Mexican-American neighborhood protesting futilely against the division of their neighborhood by a new freeway. Other scenes include the

32-38 • Judith F. Baca THE DIVISION OF THE BARRIOS. DETAIL FROM THE GREAT WALL OF LOS ANGELES
1976–1983. Height 13′ (4 m), overall length approx. 2,500′ (762 m). Tujunga Wash Flood Control Channel, Van Nuys, California.

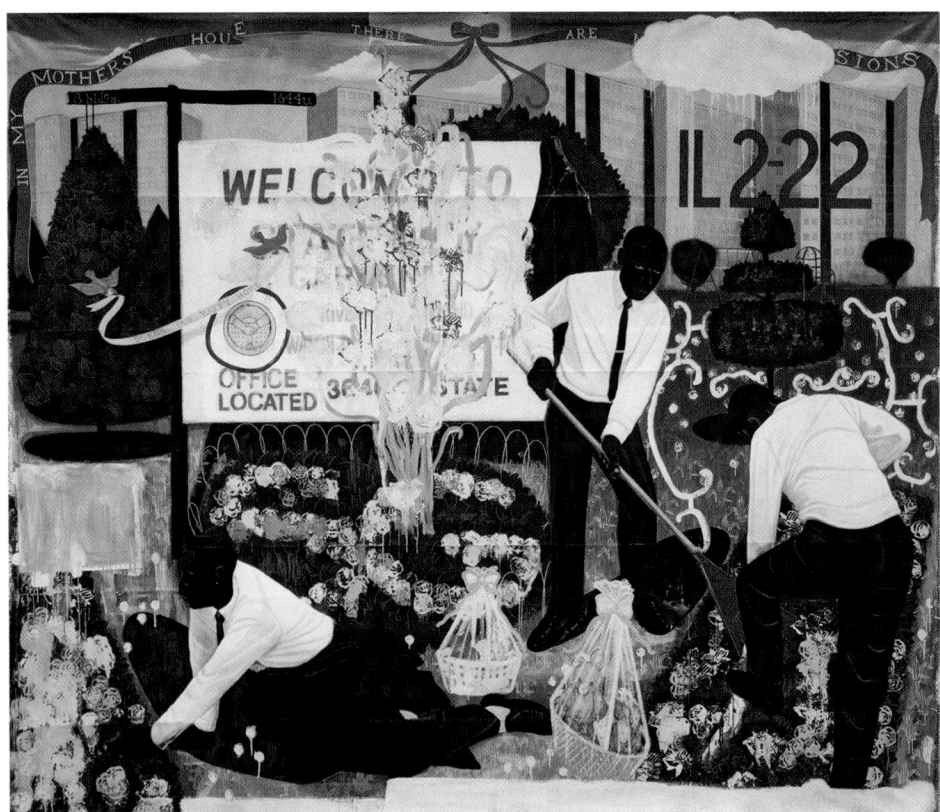

32–39 • Kerry James Marshall
MANY MANSIONS
1994. Acrylic on paper mounted on canvas,
114¼ × 135⅛″ (290 × 343 cm).
Art Institute of Chicago.

SEE MORE: View a video about
Kerry James Marshall
www.myartslab.com

deportation of Mexican-American citizens during the Great Depression and the internment of Japanese-American citizens during World War II. Baca's *The Great Wall of Los Angeles* was a collaborative effort involving many professional artists and hundreds of young people.

MARSHALL. MANY MANSIONS (FIG. 32–39) by African-American painter Kerry James Marshall (b. 1955) is a wry, ironic commentary on race, class, and poverty in American society. The work refers to Stateway Gardens, Chicago, one of the largest and most notoriously ill-maintained housing projects in America. The scandalously inadequate conditions were the subject of much debate prior to its long-overdue demolition in 2007. Marshall shows an unrealistically idyllic attempt by three African-American men, who are impossibly well dressed for gardening, to create an equally impossibly tidy garden that includes manicured topiary in the background and flowerbeds in the foreground. The painting includes a number of biting details, including the statement "In my mother's house there are many mansions," which both changes the gender of the biblical quotation (John 14:2) and comments on the disrepair of the projects by calling them, ironically, "mansions." Two cute cartoon bluebirds with a baby-blue ribbon fly into the scene like the birds that bring the fairy godmother's gifts to Cinderella in rags in the Disney film, while two Easter baskets neatly wrapped in plastic sit in the garden. The artist even takes a swipe at the fact that the condition of the projects was studied and cataloged and then ignored by the authorities by labeling his own picture "IL2-22" ("Illustration 2-22") in the upper right.

LUNA. James Luna (b. 1950) asks us to confront Native American stereotypes in his **THE ARTIFACT PIECE (FIG. 32–40)**, first staged in a hall dedicated to a traditional ethnographic exhibition at the Museum of Man in San Diego in 1987. Luna lay, almost naked, in a glass display case filled with sand embedded with artifacts from his life, such as his favorite music and books, personal legal papers, and so on. Museum-style labels pointed to marks and scars on his body that he had acquired while drinking or fighting or in accidents. In this way, Luna literally turned his living body and his life into an ethnographic object for people to stare at, evaluate, and judge. By physically objectifying himself, he challenges our prejudices, stereotypes, and assumptions about Native Americans in general and about him specifically.

SCULPTURE

Finally, in the 1980s several sculptors became embroiled in controversies over the nature and purpose of sculpture. Some sculptures challenged sculptural orthodoxy by introducing images and objects appropriated from popular and mass culture into their art, while others raised questions about the rights of an artist to make art either deliberately confrontational or offensive. Debates also raged over the artist's rights and responsibilities when making government-funded site-specific sculptures in the public domain.

KOONS. Jeff Koons (b. 1955), the brilliant self-publicist and critic (or celebrant) of the superficial, consumption-crazy suburban society of the 1980s, with a sly reference to Duchamp (SEE FIG. 31–30), has deified household objects such as vacuum cleaners, inflatable bunny

32–40 • James Luna **THE ARTIFACT PIECE**
1987–1990. First staged in 1987 at the Museum of Man, San Diego. Luna also performed the piece for "The Decade Show," 1990, in New York.

rabbits, topiary puppy dogs, porcelain pornography, and in this case a very scary embrace between the Pink Panther and a cheesy centerfold pin-up **(FIG. 32–41)**. At more than 3 feet tall, this sculpture is almost life-size, and the fact that it is made from porcelain, a material more commonly used for knick-knacks than a major sculpture, means that its surface is slick and glossy. The porcelain, the flat pastel colors that evoke Warhol's Marilyn Monroe portraits (SEE FIG. 32–10), and the cloying presence of the Pink Panther combine to produce a work that is both annoyingly bland and annoyingly attractive. Koons invites and even welcomes critical disapproval, embracing kitschy lower-middle-class consumer culture without seeming to critique it. Koons's work is openly materialistic and shallow, positively wallowing in popular culture.

SERRA. Richard Serra (b. 1939) studied sculpture at Berkeley, Santa Barbara, and Yale. His early sculpture involved, among other things, draping vulcanized rubber in different arrangements and throwing molten lead against gallery walls. In the early 1970s, he began making sculptures from very large steel plates. In 1981, he won a commission from the General Services Administration (GSA) to create a sculpture, **TILTED ARC (FIG. 32–42)**, for the plaza in front of the Javitz Federal Building in New York. Before commissioning it, the GSA saw plans of the proposed work and so knew both what it would look like and the effect it would have on the plaza. Once installed, the sculpture, a long curved Cor-Ten steel structure 120 feet long, 12 feet tall, and 2½ inches thick, bisected the plaza, completely changing it as a public space and making it impossible to hold concerts or performances there and difficult to use casually. Over time *Tilted Arc* rusted and was soon covered in graffiti and pigeon droppings. Public outrage against it was so intense that it was removed to a Brooklyn parking lot in 1986, creating a further furor, this time among artists and critics. Serra argued that moving the site-specific piece destroyed it and

filed a lawsuit on the grounds of censorship, but the Federal district court found no legal merit in his case.

Tilted Arc raised several important questions about the rights and responsibilities of artists as well as the obligations of those who fund such art. Serra intentionally changed (and for some spoiled)

32–41 • Jeff Koons **PINK PANTHER**
1988. Porcelain, 41 × 20½″ × 19″ (104.1 × 52.1 × 48.3 cm). Museum of Contemporary Art, Chicago.

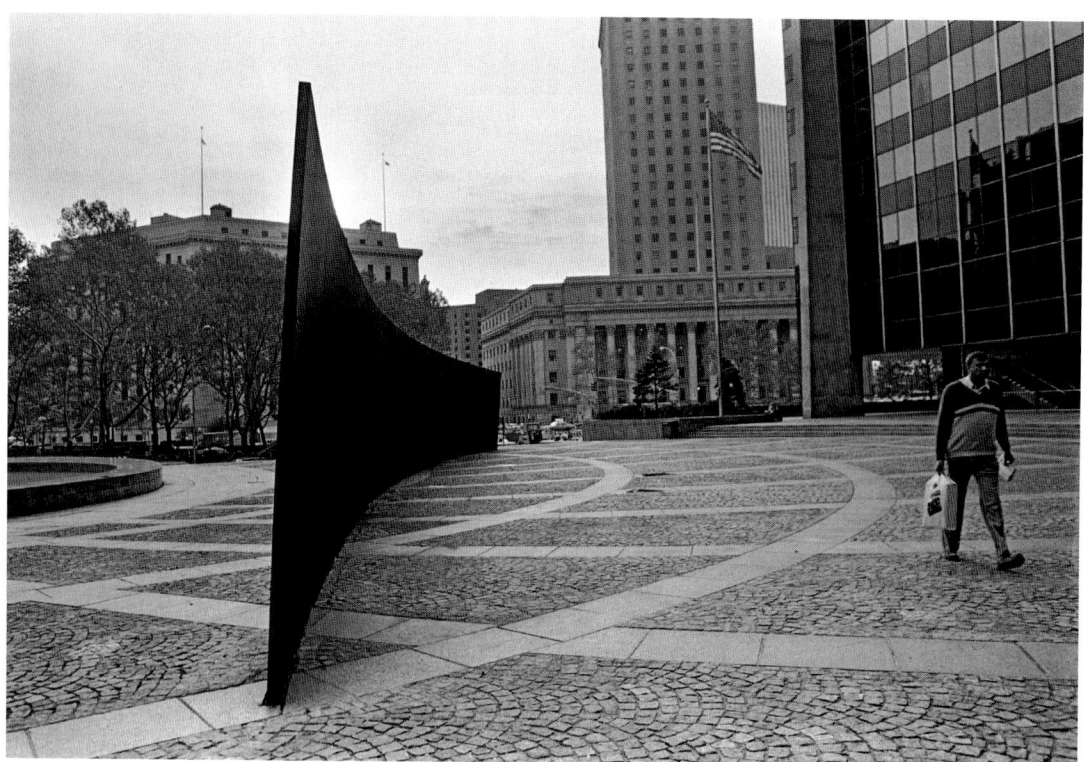

32-42 • Richard Serra
TILTED ARC
1981–1989. Jacob K. Javitz
Federal Plaza, New York.
Steel. Destroyed.

SEE MORE: View a
video about Richard
Serra's *Tilted Arc*
www.myartslab.com

Javitz Plaza. Moreover, in court he did not attempt to defend the aesthetics of his work. Rather, he argued that, once commissioned, he had a right to make the piece as planned. The case precipitated changes in the commissioning of public sculpture: Today neighborhood groups and local officials meet with artists in advance of public commissions. But important questions remain unresolved: Do these public safeguards produce better public sculpture? Or do they merely guarantee that it will be bland, inoffensive, and decorative?

LIN. Maya Lin (b. 1959) was an architecture student at Yale University in 1981 when she was awarded the commission for the **VIETNAM VETERANS MEMORIAL (FIG. 32–43)** in Constitution Gardens, Washington, D.C., A jury of architects, landscape architects, and sculptors selected her design for a simple and dramatic memorial cut into the ground in a V-shape. Two highly polished black granite slabs reach out from the deepest point of the memorial at the center. Each of these arms is 247 feet long, and they meet at a 130-degree angle where the slabs are 10 feet tall. The names of American soldiers killed or declared missing in action during the Vietnam War are listed chronologically as they died or were lost, beginning at the shallowest point to the left. The tallest part of the sculpture represents the year of the highest casualties. The black polished granite reflects the faces of visitors; as they read the names of the dead and missing, they see their own faces superimposed on them. The memorial, commissioned by Vietnam Veterans for Vietnam Veterans, serves both to commemorate the dead and missing and to provide a place where survivors can confront their own loss. This sculpture is one of the best-known works of public art in the United States and has

transformed the way the nation mourns its war dead. Visiting it is a powerful and profound experience.

Yet, when it was first commissioned, the *Vietnam Veterans Memorial* was the subject of intense debate. It was described as a "black gash in the Mall," its black color contrasting with the white marble of the surrounding memorials. Lin was accused of creating a monument of shame, one critic going so far as to claim that black was the universal color of "shame, sorrow, and degradation in all races, all societies." Opposition to the sculpture was so intense in some quarters that a second, naturalistic sculpture showing three soldiers was commissioned and placed 120 feet from the wall in 1983; in 1993, another figurative sculpture of three nurses was added 300 feet to the south.

ART, ACTIVISM, AND CONTROVERSY: THE NINETIES

The passage from the 1980s to the 1990s was marked by what is commonly referred to as the "Culture Wars" (see "Controversies Over Public Funding for the Arts," page 1120), a confrontation between artists and public officials in America over freedom of speech and public funding for the arts, particularly with regard to the right to make art that might be considered offensive or obscene by others. At the same time many artists who had previously worked on the periphery of society and established art institutions began to claim center stage by making aggressive images about identity and unequal treatment on the grounds of gender, sexual orientation, race, or class. Many of these artists

32-43 • Maya Lin VIETNAM VETERANS MEMORIAL
Washington, D.C. 1981–1983.

EXPLORE MORE: Click the Google Earth link for the Vietnam Veterans Memorial
www.myartslab.com

worked with passion and urgency as they or their friends and lovers died from AIDS. The 1990s was also the beginning of the digital age, when a new interest in the mutability of photography and film opened imaginative new vistas for artists.

THE CULTURE WARS

In the early 1990s, several previously marginalized younger artists achieved fame by producing narrative images deliberately intended to disrupt, provoke, and offend viewers. In the United States, Andres Serrano defamed an image of the Christian crucifix while Robert Mapplethorpe confronted audiences with openly gay sexuality. In the United Kingdom, Damien Hirst defiled the mortal remains of domestic animals while Chris Ofili created a racially and culturally hybrid Christian Madonna. The resulting social and political backlash triggered the Culture Wars.

SERRANO. In 1987, Andres Serrano (b. 1950) created *Piss Christ* (see page 1120). Like other artists of the time, Serrano's art explores social taboos in deliberately confrontational and offensive ways. His art dances between the luxuriously beautiful and the abject: His photographs of the homeless, Klansmen, suicides, and murder victims have proven so difficult for some viewers that they have even been vandalized. *Piss Christ* is an almost 2-foot-high, brilliantly colored Cibachrome print of a Christian crucifix which the artist framed in a Plexiglas box filled with his own urine.

Serrano, who was raised a strict Catholic, has argued that this image is about confronting the physicality of the death of the body of Christ, sometimes too easily forgotten, and that it critiques the commercialization of Christ's image in the media, which is why it is also so provocative and offensive to others.

HIRST. In London in the 1980s, a group of Young British Artists (YBAs) banded together to exhibit their work, led informally by Damien Hirst (b. 1965). In 1995, the Walker Art Center in Minneapolis mounted an exhibition entitled "Brilliant" featuring 22 British artists, many of whom used nontraditional materials and images in their art, had working-class backgrounds or sympathies, or had an adversarial relationship with mainstream society. Two years later, the London Royal Academy featured many of the same artists in "Sensation," an exhibition of art from the Charles Saatchi Collection, which consolidated the reputation of many YBAs. When the show traveled to the Brooklyn Museum in 1999, however, it was considered so offensive that the mayor of New York threatened to close the museum if it was not removed.

Damien Hirst is one of the most outrageous of the original YBAs and his most outrageous work of art, *For the Love of God* (2007), is a diamond-encrusted human skull with an asking price of $100m. His work is about the physical reality of death and the impossibility of imagining your own death; he frequently uses dead animals in his work. Hirst's art, although it is increasingly considered

32-44 • Damien Hirst MOTHER AND CHILD DIVIDED
1993. Steel, GRP, composites, glass, silicone, cow, calf, and formaldehyde solution, two tanks at 74⅞ × 126⅞ × 43″
(190 × 322 × 109 cm), two tanks at 40⅛ × 66½ × 24⅝″ (102.5 × 169 × 62.5 cm). Tate Gallery, London.

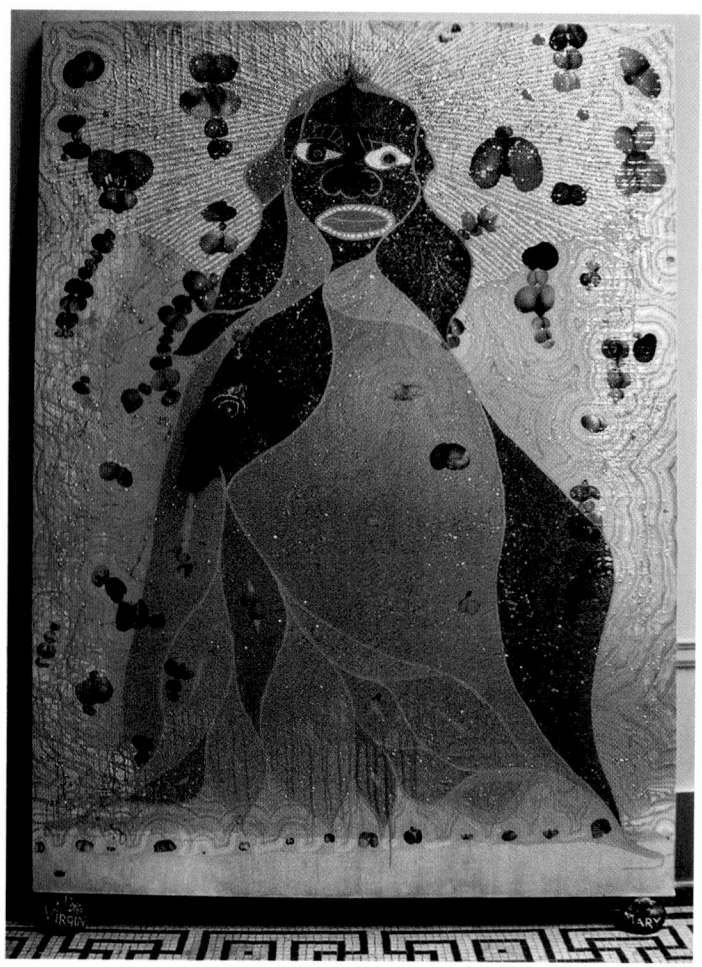

serious and even thoughtful and profound, has also, unsurprisingly, attracted considerable criticism. In **MOTHER AND CHILD DIVIDED (FIG. 32–44)**, the bodies of a cow and her calf are bisected vertically and longitudinally and displayed floating in museum vitrines (glass display cases) filled with formaldehyde. This sculpture resembles the kind of display that you might see in a natural history museum—but with some significant differences. The vitrines are arranged so that the viewer is able not only to walk around them but also between them and thus between the two halves of each cow. On the outside, these animals seem to retain an amazingly lifelike look (even their eyelashes and individual hairs are visible) as they float in the formaldehyde, but once we see the cleavages in their bones, muscles, organs, and flesh on the inside, the actuality of their death overwhelms us. When you also consider that British cattle were being slaughtered daily in an attempt to stop the spread of the terrifying BSE (Mad Cow Disease) in the 1990s, *Mother and Child Divided* creates a feeling of being caught between life and death, between mother and child, and between scientific presentation and, as in Serrano's work, a set of barely suppressed and disturbingly powerful emotions.

32-45 • Chris Ofili THE HOLY VIRGIN MARY
1996. Paper collage, oil paint, glitter, polyester resin, map pins, and elephant dung on linen, 7′11″ × 5′11⅚₁₆″ (2.44 × 1.83 m). Saatchi Gallery, London.

OFILI. The art of the Nigerian-British artist Chris Ofili (b. 1968) provided the focal point for criticism of the 1999 "Sensation" exhibition at the Brooklyn Museum. Ofili exhibited **THE HOLY VIRGIN MARY (FIG. 32–45)**, a glittering painting of a stylized African Madonna which includes parts made from elephant dung and small found photographs of women's buttocks. Ofili, who spent a year in Zimbabwe studying the use of materials in art, explained that in many African nations there is a tradition of using found or salvaged objects and materials in both popular and high art. Ofili's painting is a contemporary bicultural reinvention of the Western Madonna tradition. It employs elephant dung to reinforce this black Madonna's connection to the art and religion of Zimbabwe and to represent her fertility. Then-mayor of New York Rudolph Giuliani and his allies, however, considered the picture so shocking and sacrilegious that they wanted it removed immediately or the exhibition closed.

ACTIVIST ART

The Culture Wars were fueled by a significant increase in Activist art in the 1990s. AIDS decimated the younger art scene in New York's East Village and triggered a global health crisis by mid-decade. Increasingly, anger over the agony of those dying from, and losing friends and lovers to, AIDS, combined with government inaction, spilled over into art. Thus the 1990s opened with angry art about the body, AIDS, and identity, as well as with art clamoring for acknowledgment of the discrimination faced by people of different races, ethnicities, classes, and sexual orientations. The Culture Wars were, in many ways, about artists searching for a place in the world when so many were fading from it.

GONZALEZ-TORRES. In the mid-1980s, the spread of the human immunodeficiency virus (HIV), the underlying cause of AIDS, had begun to reap its deadly harvest within the gay community.

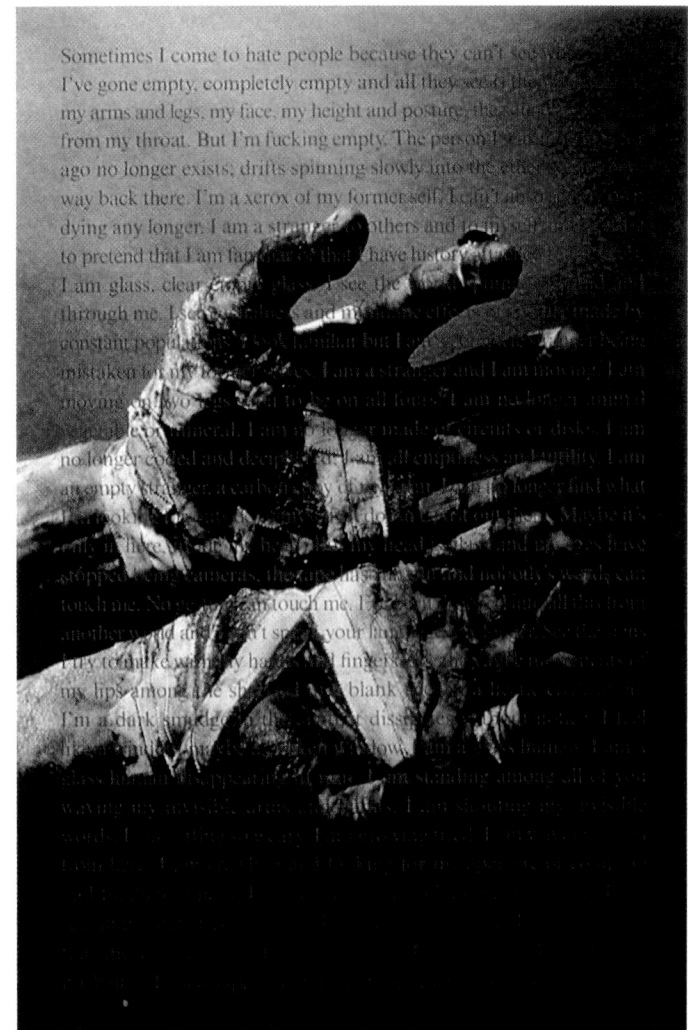

32-47 • David Wojnarowicz UNTITLED (HANDS)
1992. Silver print with silkscreened text, 38 × 26″ (96.5 × 66.0 cm).
Courtesy of the estate of David Wojnarowicz and PPOW Gallery, New York

32-46 • Felix Gonzalez-Torres UNTITLED (LOVERBOY)
1990. Blue paper, endless copies, 7½ (at ideal height) × 29 × 23″
(19.1 × 73.7 × 58.4 cm). Installation view of inaugural solo exhibition,
"Felix Gonzalez-Torres," at Andrea Rosen Gallery, New York, 1990.
ARG# GF1990-3

Felix Gonzalez-Torres (1957–1996) created **UNTITLED (LOVERBOY) (FIG. 32–46)** in 1990 as his lover was dying from AIDS. The piece is deceptively simple: The artist placed a stack of pale blue paper on the gallery floor and invited visitors to take a sheet as they walked by. As each day of the exhibition passed, the stack of paper gradually diminished. The pale blue sheets slowly peeling away were a touching allegory of the slowly disappearing body and mind of Gonzalez-Torres's lover. The artist said: "I wanted to make something that would disappear completely." There is a poignant directness to this work. Gonzalez-Torres himself died of AIDS in 1996.

WOJNAROWICZ. David Wojnarowicz (1955–1992) railed against death before he too died from AIDS in 1992. In 1987, Wojnarowicz's lover Peter Hujar died from AIDS and the artist himself was diagnosed as HIV-positive. In response, he began to make forcefully aggressive art about the fear and confusion of watching a loved one die while facing one's own death. In **UNTITLED (HANDS) (FIG. 32–47)**, Wojnarowicz photographed, in black and white, two bandaged hands outstretched as if in a begging gesture.

Superimposed is a text in angry red type taken from Wojnarowicz's book *Memories That Smell Like Gasoline*, in which he describes how he is hollowing out from the inside and becoming invisible as he dies. Parts of Wojnarowicz's book were reprinted in the catalog of an exhibition, "Witnesses Against Our Vanishing," which featured art by and about artists with AIDS and which became a flash point in the Culture Wars.

SMITH.   In sculpture of the early 1990s, the physicality of the human body reasserted itself as a site for the discourse on AIDS. The sculptor Kiki Smith (b. 1954), who lost a sister to AIDS, explores the body, bodily functions, and the loss of physical control that the dying experience in works such as the 1990 **UNTITLED** **(FIG. 32–48)**. This disturbing sculpture shows two life-size naked figures hanging passively, but not quite lifelessly, side by side a few inches above the ground. The figures, a woman and a man, are made from flesh-colored painted beeswax. The woman has milk dripping from her breasts and the man has semen dripping down his leg as if both have lost control of bodily functions that were once a source of vitality and pleasure. The figures evoke a profound sense of loss. Smith has written that our society abhors

the reality of bodily functions, so we strive to conceal and control them, making our loss of control as death nears humiliating and frightening. This sculpture asks us to consider bodily control—both our own sense of control and the control that others exert on our body as we die—and suggests that relinquishing it may be as liberating as it is devastating.

WODICZKO.   Some artists took their art beyond the gallery, not only advocating social change but working to make a tangible difference in society. In the late 1980s, Krzysztof Wodiczko (b. 1943) created **THE HOMELESS PROJECT VEHICLE (FIG. 32–49)**, designed in collaboration with the homeless in New York as "an instrument for survival for urban nomads." Wodiczko wanted to draw attention to the problem of homelessness in New York, one of the richest cities in the richest country in the world. But he did not want simply to illustrate homelessness or evoke pity. Rather, he wanted to dramatize homelessness by making it visible while at the same time actually helping the homeless. *The Homeless Project Vehicle* is a modified and "upgraded" version of the shopping cart that so many homeless people use to carry around their worldly possessions. Wodiczko designed the cart with a waterproof and

32-48 • Kiki Smith UNTITLED
1990. Beeswax with microcrystalline wax figures on metal stands, female figure installed height 6'1½" (1.87 m), male figure 6'4¹⁵⁄₁₆" (1.95 m). Whitney Museum of American Art, New York.

relatively safe sleeping pod, a series of baskets underneath in which to store belongings, and a brightly colored flag to indicate approach. The homeless who were lucky enough to get a vehicle were pleased with the way it worked, but the New York city authorities felt that the carts made the homeless too visible and they disappeared quickly.

WHITEREAD. The British sculptor Rachel Whiteread (b. 1963) made her reputation as a YBA by casting the inverse of everyday objects such as a bathtub or worn mattress to reveal the ghostliness of their absence. In 1993, however, she also drew attention to the invisibility of the urban poor with her largest and most controversial work, **HOUSE** (FIG. 32–50). For this project, Whiteread cast the inner space of an entire three-story terraced house in concrete. The house was one of a row in London's East End slated for demolition by developers, who effectively erased the last vestiges of a community that had pulled together so heroically during the Blitz in World War II. *House* is about how memories are contained in places and times,

32–50 • Rachel Whiteread HOUSE
1993. Sprayed concrete. Corner of Grove and Roman roads, London. Destroyed 1994. Commissioned by Artangel Trust and Beck's, London. Received the Turner Prize, Tate Britain, London

SEE MORE: View a video of Rachel Whiteread discussing her casting process
myartslab.com

Controversies Over Public Funding for the Arts

Should public money help pay for art that some taxpayers believe to be offensive and indecent? This question started a political battle in 1989–1990 after controversial works of art by Robert Mapplethorpe (1946–1989) and Andres Serrano (b. 1950) went on public display in exhibitions funded in part by the National Endowment for the Arts (NEA), an agency of the Federal government. The ensuing debate pitted artists and museum administrators against political and religious figures. This battle over artists' rights and responsibilities is now referred to as the "Culture Wars."

Serrano's PISS CHRIST was at the center of the debate. Serrano did not use public money directly to create this work, but the Southeastern Center for Contemporary Art (SECCA), which exhibited *Piss Christ* in a group exhibition, was a recipient of NEA funds. The Reverend Donald Wildmon, leader of the American Family Association, described *Piss Christ* as "hate-filled, bigoted, anti-Christian, and obscene," and told his many followers to flood Congress and the NEA with letters protesting the misuse of public funds. This resulted in several high-profile conservative Republican politicians joining his attack.

At the same time, the traveling exhibition "The Perfect Moment," a retrospective of the work of photographer Mapplethorpe, who had recently died from AIDS, was canceled by the Corcoran Gallery of Art in Washington, D.C., for fear that the show's content might cause offense. "The Perfect Moment" had been organized by the Institute of Contemporary Art (ICA) in Philadelphia, was NEA-funded, and included several homoerotic and sadomasochistic images. When it was shown in Cincinnati, the museum director was arrested. Additionally, four artists known as the "NEA Four" (Karen Finley, John Fleck, Holly Hughes, and Tim Miller), who made lesbian, gay, or radical feminist art, had their grants rescinded amid a flurry of debate. Congress slashed NEA funding by $45,000: the amount of Serrano's $15,000 SECCA grant, plus the ICA's $30,000 grant for the Mapplethorpe show. The NEA Four sued and won back their grants, but a so-called "obscenity clause" was added to NEA regulations requiring jurors to consider the "general standards of decency and respect for the diverse beliefs and values of the American public" when making awards.

During the next five years, the NEA was largely restructured by the Republican-controlled House of Representatives, some of whose members wanted to eliminate the agency altogether. In 1996, Congress reduced the NEA's budget by 40 percent.

Controversies over public funding continued, however. In 1999, the Brooklyn Museum of Art exhibited "Sensation: Young British Artists from the Saatchi Collection," causing another major controversy over public funding and offensive art. The Brooklyn Museum kept the show open in direct defiance of a threat from Mayor Rudolph Giuliani to eliminate city funding and evict the museum from its city-owned building if it persisted in showing art that he considered "sick" and "disgusting." Giuliani and Catholic leaders took particular offense at Chris Ofili's *The Holy Virgin Mary* (SEE FIG. 32–45). When the Brooklyn Museum of Art still refused to cancel the show, Giuliani withheld the city's monthly maintenance payment to the museum of $497,554 and filed a suit in the state court to revoke its lease. In response, the museum filed for an injunction against Giuliani's actions on the grounds that they violated the First Amendment and the United States District Court for the Eastern District of New York eventually barred Giuliani from punishing or retaliating against the museum in any way for mounting the exhibition. Giuliani had argued that Ofili's art fostered religious intolerance, but the court ruled that the government has "no legitimate interest in protecting any or all religions from views distasteful to them," adding that taxpayers "subsidize all manner of views with which they do not agree" and even those "they abhor."

Andres Serrano **PISS CHRIST**
1989. Cibachrome print mounted on Plexiglas,
23½ × 16″ (59.7 × 40.6 cm).

and how easily they can be destroyed. As the other houses around it were demolished, Whiteread sprayed concrete on the inner walls of her house to make a cast of the space within it. Then she dismantled the house. The white concrete left behind outlined a ghostly trace of the space within the house that had once been someone's home. The publicity surrounding Whiteread's *House* brought to the fore several critical issues in British society, including homelessness, the costs and benefits of urban renewal, and the place of the working class in society. Whiteread's piece demonstrates how a work of visual art can articulate controversial issues in ways that are impossible using other means of communication. Whiteread intended *House* to make a political statement about "the state of housing in England; the ludicrous policy of knocking down homes like this and building badly designed tower blocks which themselves have to be knocked down after 20 years."

32-51 • Shirin Neshat REBELLIOUS SILENCE
1994. Black-and-white RC print and ink (photo taken by C. Preston), 11 × 14″ (27.9 × 35.6 cm). Barbara Gladstone Gallery, New York.

EXPLORE MORE: Gain insight from a primary source by Shirin Neshat **www.myartslab.com**

POSTCOLONIAL DISCOURSE

With increased migration and the expansion of global communications and economies, questions of personal, political, cultural, and national identity also emerged in the 1990s. Postcolonial artists began to explore issues of contested identity and the identity struggle of postcolonial peoples, and to investigate the dissonance produced by transnational (mis)communication between colonizers and the postcolonized. Many of these artists, such as Shirin Neshat and Rasheed Araeen, speak with unfamiliar but forthright and significant new artistic voices.

NESHAT. In **REBELLIOUS SILENCE** (FIG. 32–51) from her 1994 "Women of Allah" series of photographs, Shirin Neshat (b. 1957) explores how Iranian women are stereotyped by the West. Her photographs and videos assert that Islamic women's identities are more varied and complex than is frequently perceived. Each of Neshat's "Women of Allah" photographs portrays both a part of an Iranian woman's body, such as her hands or her feet, overwritten with Farsi text and with a weapon. In *Rebellious Silence*, the woman wears the traditional chador but her face is visible, written over with calligraphy and with a rifle barrel bisecting it vertically. The calligraphy and rifle barrel seem to protect her from the viewer, but they also create a sense of incomprehensibility or foreignness that prompts us to try to categorize her. Likewise, although the woman wears a chador, she looks directly and defiantly out of the photograph at us, meeting our gaze and returning it. She challenges us to acknowledge her as an individual, in this case a strong and beautiful woman; but the image simultaneously and paradoxically prompts us to see her as a stereotypical Iranian woman in a chador more than as an individual. Neshat's photograph asks us to confront our prejudices while also raising questions about women's power and feminism in contemporary Iran.

ARAEEN. Rasheed Araeen (b. 1935) is from Pakistan and lives in London. He founded the journal *Black Phoenix* in 1978, which in 1989 became *Third Text*, a leading journal on postcolonial art, culture, and ethnicity. In 1985–1986, Araeen made **GREEN PAINTING IV** (FIG. 32–52), a work comprised of nine equal-sized panels. The five central panels contain photographs of the head of a young bull prepared for ritual sacrifice with garlands around its neck and framed by Urdu text. The other four panels are painted a flat green—the primary color in the Pakistani flag, an important color in Islam, and a color that Araeen associates with youthful rawness and flexibility, like a green twig. Yet the central panels also appear to form a crucifix. Araeen has said that his pictures are not just superimpositions of Western and Pakistani cultures, but are images that speak about "cutting and

32-52 • Rasheed Araeen GREEN PAINTING IV
1985–1986. Five color photographs with Urdu text and acrylic on four plywood panels, 5′9″ × 6′10″ (1.75 × 2.08 m). Collection of the artist.

rupturing," that investigate postcolonial dissonance and miscommunication. He argues that when someone British or American sees the cross in his art, for instance, they almost invariably read Pakistani culture through a Christian lens, thereby distorting, misinterpreting, and stereotyping the "other." Araeen's art demands a more nuanced understanding of cultures on their own terms and according to their own visual languages.

SEARLE. Berni Searle (b. 1964) explores her South African identity in the wake of Apartheid in her art. In the **COLOR ME** series **(FIG. 32–53)**, she photographs her head and torso covered in powdered pigment that changes her skin color from red to yellow to brown to white. Searle asks us to see that race and identity are not as simple as skin pigmentation, and that superficial or skin-deep characteristics do not define a person. The fragility and impermanence of the pigmentation also underscore the instability of stereotypes and the complexity of real identity.

32-53 • Berni Searle
UNTITLED FROM COLOR ME SERIES
1998. Michael Stevenson Gallery, Cape Town.

HIGH TECH AND DECONSTRUCTIVIST ARCHITECTURE

Architecture and architectural practice was transformed in the 1980s and 1990s by computer-aided design (CAD) programs with 3-D graphics. These programs enabled architects to design structures virtually, to calculate engineering stresses faster and more precisely, to experiment with new ways to use advanced building technologies and materials, and to imagine new ways of composing a building's mass.

HIGH TECH ARCHITECTURE. High Tech architects broke out of the restrictive shape of the Modernist "glass box" (SEE FIG. 32–25) to experiment with dramatically designed engineering marvels. These buildings are characterized by a spectacular use of new technologies, materials, equipment, and components, and frequently by their visible display of service systems such as heating and power.

The **HONG KONG & SHANGHAI BANK** (FIG. 32–54) by the British architect Norman Foster (b. 1935) is among the most spectacular examples of High Tech architecture. Foster was invited to spare no expense in designing this futuristic 47-story skyscraper. The loadbearing steel skeleton, composed of giant masts and girders, is on the exterior. The individual stories hang from it, making possible the uninterrupted rows of windows that fill the building with natural light. In addition, the banking hall in the lower part of the building has a ten-story atrium space that is flooded with daylight refracted into it by motorized "sunscoops" at the top of the structure that are programmed to track the sun's rays and channel them into the building. The sole concession Foster makes to tradition in this design is his placement of two bronze lions flanking the public entrance. These were taken from the bank's previous headquarters; touching the lions before entering the bank is believed to bring good luck.

DECONSTRUCTIVIST ARCHITECTURE. Deconstructivist architecture, a more theory-based architecture than High Tech, emerged in the early 1990s. Deconstructivist architects deliberately disturb traditional architectural assumptions about harmony, unity, and stability to create "decentered," skewed, and distorted designs. Several Deconstructivist architects admire the aesthetic of Russian Suprematists and Constructivists (SEE FIGS. 31–26, 31–46), which they frequently combine with the principles of Deconstruction as developed by the French philosopher Jacques Derrida (1930–2004). Derridean Deconstruction asserts that no written text possesses a single, intrinsic meaning. For Derrida, meaning is always "intertextual," thus a product of one text's relationship to other texts: It is always "decentered," "dispersed," or "diffused" through an infinite web of "signs," which themselves have unstable meanings. Deconstructivist architecture is likewise intertextual, in that it plays with meaning by mixing diverse architectural features, forms, and contexts, and is decentered in its diffusion as well as in its perceived instability of both meaning and form.

32-54 • Norman Foster HONG KONG & SHANGHAI BANK
Hong Kong. 1986.

SEE MORE: View a simulation about the Hong Kong & Shanghai Bank www.myartslab.com

32-56 • Frank O. Gehry **GUGGENHEIM MUSEUM**
Bilbao, Spain. 1993–1997.

A good example of Deconstructivist architecture is the **VITRA FIRE STATION** in Weil-am-Rhein, Germany **(FIG. 32–55)** by the Baghdad-born architect Zaha Hadid (b. 1950), who studied in London and established her practice there in 1979. Formally influenced by the paintings of Kasimir Malevich (SEE FIG. 31–25), the Vitra Fire Station features reinforced concrete walls that lean into one another, meet at unexpected angles, and jut out dramatically into space, denying a sense of visual unity but creating a feeling of immediacy, speed, and dynamism appropriate to the building's function.

The Toronto-born, California-based Frank O. Gehry (b. 1929) also creates unstable and Deconstructivist building masses and curved winglike shapes that extend far beyond the building's mass. One of his most spectacular designs is the **GUGGENHEIM MUSEUM** in Bilbao, Spain **(FIG. 32–56)**. In the 1990s, art-museum designs became more and more spectacular as the museum increasingly came to define the visual landscape of cities. Gehry developed this asymmetrical design using a CATIA CAD program that enabled him to create a powerfully organic, sculptural structure. The complex steel skeleton is covered by a thin skin of silvery titanium that shimmers gold or silver depending on the time of day and the weather conditions. From the north the building resembles a living organism, while from other angles it looks like a giant ship, referencing the industry on which Bilbao has traditionally depended and thereby identifying the museum with the city. Despite the sculptural beauty of the museum, however, the interior is a notoriously difficult space in which to display art.

VIDEO AND FILM

In the last decades of the twentieth century, the rapid development and increasingly widespread availability of hand-held video cameras created a new medium for artists. Video artists rejected traditional forms and meanings to make art that was deliberately nonprecious, often using the video image to address the place and prevalence of television in our culture. Today Video art is even more prevalent because of the explosion in digital and visual imagery. In fact, most contemporary Video art is digitally produced, while innovations in projecting video and DVD images on large screens (or on any surface) have transformed how and where Video art is projected and to a certain extent its subject.

PAIK. One of the pioneers of Video art was the Korean-born Nam June Paik (1931–2006), who made experimental music in the late 1950s and early 1960s under the influence of John Cage. He began working with modified television sets in 1963, and began making Video art in 1965, the same year that Sony released the first portable video camera. Paik predicted that just "as collage technique replaced oil paint, the cathode ray [television] tube will replace the canvas." Later, he worked with live, recorded, and computer-generated images displayed on video monitors of varying sizes, which he often combined into works of art such as **ELECTRONIC SUPERHIGHWAY: CONTINENTAL U.S.** (FIG. 32–57), a site-specific sculpture created for the Holly Solomon Gallery in New York. This featured a neon outline map of the United States set against a wall of dozens of computer-controlled video monitors

32-57 • Nam June Paik ELECTRONIC SUPERHIGHWAY: CONTINENTAL U.S.
1995. Forty-seven-channel closed-circuit video installation with 313 monitors, neon, steel structure, color, and sound, approx. 15 × 32 × 4′ (4.57 × 9.75 × 1.2 m). Courtesy Holly Solomon Gallery, New York.

displaying rapidly changing soundtracked images that reflected each state's culture and history. The work addresses both the prevalence and power of the mixed messages transmitted by television in our society. The monitor for New York State projected a closed-circuit live video feed of gallery visitors, who were thus transformed from passive spectators into active participants in the piece as the monitor constructed their media identity in front of them as they watched.

VIOLA.   In 1996, the California video artist Bill Viola (b. 1951) created **THE CROSSING** (FIG. 32–58) which consists of a double projection of two brilliantly colored videos on opposite sides of a 16-foot screen. On one side, Viola projects a video loop of a silhouette of a man who slowly emerges from the background to fill the entire screen. As he does this, a drop of water starts to fall, growing in size as the man moves forward slowly until at last a deluge washes him away. The soundtrack meanwhile goes from a small dripping noise to a torrential roar. On the reverse screen, a similar scenario unfolds, except that this time the man appears in the background with tiny flames licking at his feet that grow into a wild conflagration that finally engulfs him. This side also has a soundtrack of the sound of the fire growing in intensity. But Viola's piece is about the way that vision informs perception, and there is in fact only one soundtrack—we simply perceive it differently according to whatever image we are watching. This video is profoundly sensory but also meditative; its elemental symbolism is informed by Viola's spirituality and intense study of world religions.

GLOBALISM: INTO THE NEW MILLENNIUM

In the last decade, the growth in international art exhibitions and art fairs has created new opportunities for artists, dealers, and collectors to meet and network in ways that, until quite recently, would have been considered impossible, or unproductive. Until recently the only truly international fora for new art were the Venice Biennale (established in 1903 and held every two years) and Documenta, in Kassel, West Germany (established in 1955 and held roughly every five years). Today there are at least 30 international biennial exhibitions around the world, as well as many more vast international art fairs: Art Basel in Switzerland, Art Basel Miami in Miami Beach, the Frieze Art Fair in London, the Armory Show in New York, and the Fiore Internationale d'Art Contemporain (FIAC) in Paris, to mention just a few. Finally, the Internet has allowed visual access to art globally. We can find information on practically any exhibited art, and much that is not exhibited, on

32-58 • Bill Viola THE CROSSING
1996. Video/sound installation with two channels of color video projection onto screens 16′ (4.88 m) high. Private collection.

our laptops. This new globalism has forced artists to question not just how their own identities but also how those of others are formed, and to realize that neither identity nor art is as simple or as univalent as it might have seemed as recently as in the 1990s.

Art in the new millennium seems to be heading in several directions simultaneously, constantly shifting and recalibrating new perspectives and concerns as part of an increasingly complicated global discourse. The art of our own times may be the most difficult to classify and analyze, but it has increasingly focused on global issues, raising questions about national identities, ethnic or racial identities, colonial and postcolonial identities, human rights, global economic, political, and natural environments, the widening divide between the rich and poor nations of the world, and technological change in every aspect of our lives. Today's artists are actively engaged in society at all levels and their art frequently reflects their ambition to be agents of change in troubling and unstable times.

ART AND TECHNOLOGY

STUDIO CRAFTS. Dale Chihuly (b. 1941) has been producing major public sculptures in glass for 30 years, but his creations are as fresh today as they were in 1975. Chihuly's sculptures are both technologically innovative and experimental. **THE SUN** (FIG. 32–59), a multi-part blown-glass sculpture using the latest glass-making techniques, shows Chihuly's profound interest in natural forms and global energies. The sun bursts forth in a multitude of twisting, wriggling, spiraling forms as if the unremittingly intense light of Phoenix has taken physical shape and come to life. Brilliantly liquid, visually thrilling, and accessible, Chihuly's sculptures suggest a deeper connection with nature, inviting contemplation, meditation, and an awareness of global environmentalism.

DIGITAL PHOTOGRAPHY SINCE 2000. Photography has always been a malleable and mutable medium. Even in the nineteenth century photographs were manipulated to create fictional imagery out of what appeared to be a factual visual record. It is often difficult and time-consuming to manipulate a chemical-mechanical process, however, and it was only with the development of digital technology that manipulation became a fast, easy, and standard way to create photographic images.

The Canadian artist Jeff Wall (b. 1946) uses multiple digital photographs and elaborate stage sets to create large complex photographic narratives that he considers analogous to the history paintings of the nineteenth century, and which he exhibits as gloriously colored transparencies mounted in light boxes—the format frequently used in modern advertising in public places.

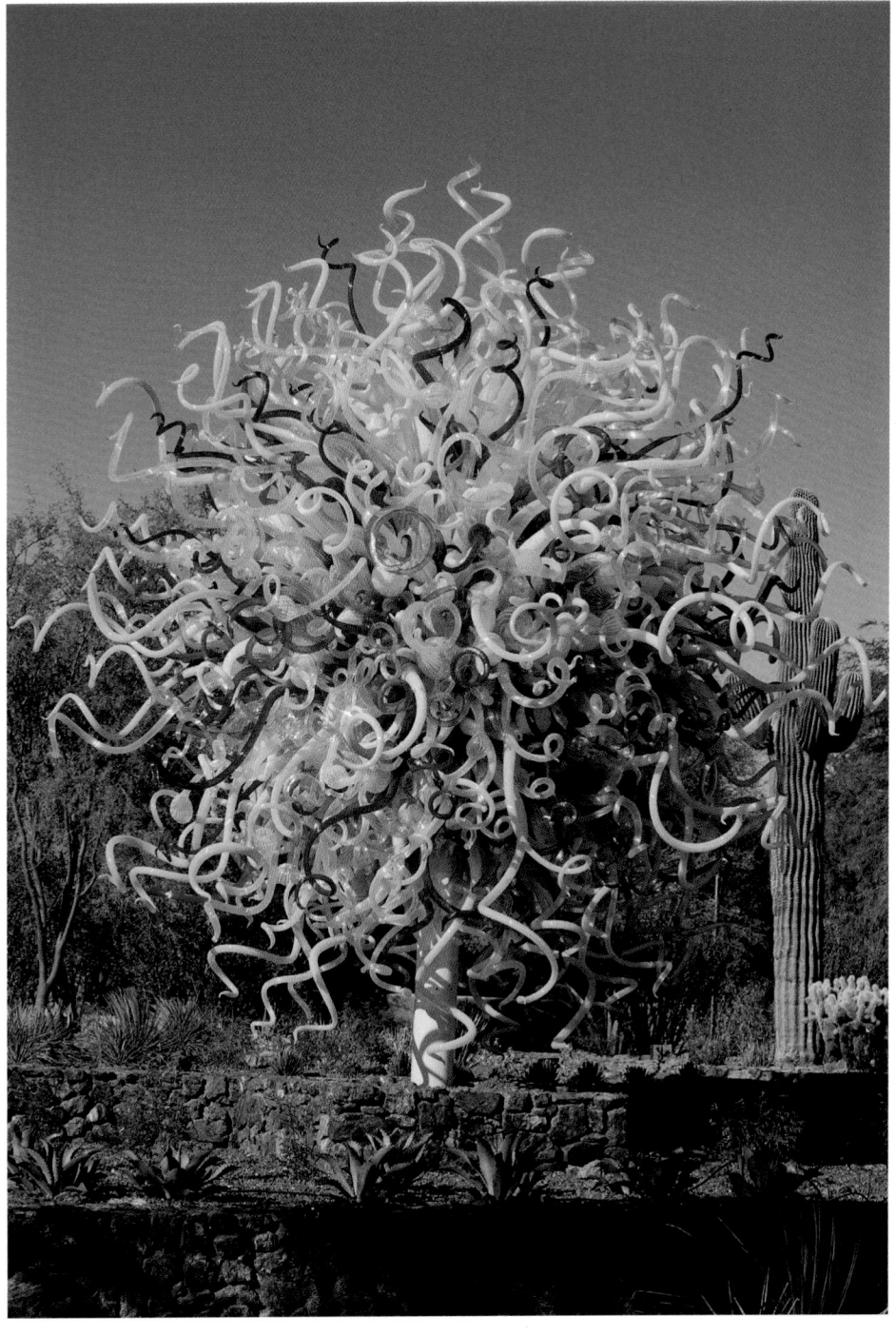

32–59 • Dale Chihuly THE SUN
2008. Desert Botanical Garden, Phoenix, Arizona. Installed November 22, 2008–May 31, 2009.

32–60 • Jeff Wall AFTER "INVISIBLE MAN" BY RALPH ELLISON, THE PREFACE
1999–2001. Transparency in lightbox, 68½ × 98⅝" (174 × 250.5 cm).

EXPLORE MORE: Gain insight from a primary source related to Jeff Wall **www.myartslab.com**

Wall creates his photographs like a movie director, carefully designing the sets and posing his actors. He takes multiple photographs that he then combines digitally to create one final transparency. **AFTER "INVISIBLE MAN" BY RALPH ELLISON, THE PREFACE (FIG. 32–60)** is an elaborate composition for which Wall spent 18 months designing and constructing the sets and three weeks actually taking photographs. The image illustrates a passage from Ralph Ellison's 1951 novel about an African-American man's search for fulfillment that ends in disillusionment and retreat. Wall shows us the cellar room, "warm and full of light," to which Ellison's character retreats and which is heated and lit by 1,369 light bulbs powered by electricity stolen from the power company. For Ellison, these lights seem to illuminate the sad truth of the character's existence.

INSTALLATION ART. Tony Oursler's 2009 exhibition at Metro Pictures raises issues about how the average American constructs his or her identity in the digital age. The installation (art installed in a specific space for which it was made) included several oversized sculptural versions of the things that we cannot seem to live without today: an enormous cell phone entitled **MULTIPLEXED**

(FIG. 32–61), a giant five-dollar bill, a "forest of smoldering cigarettes," an arrangement of oversized self-help books, and a Genie bottle containing a video of the artist himself. Oursler's exhibition is a clever updating of Pop art's critique of consumer society, making sly references to Warhol, Oldenburg, and even Lichtenstein (SEE FIGS. 32–10, 32–11, 32–12). Objects come to life by means of superimposed animated video projections that make the cigarettes seem to burn, "Abe" Lincoln to pull faces, Oursler himself to try to escape his bottle, and the cell phone (in this illustration) to spew forth, as the press release states, "disjointed snippets of conversations." Oursler asks us to consider how the world of technology, constantly bombarding us with images, creates an intense visual overload and frames our concept of identity.

ART AND IDENTITIES

The artists featured in this final section investigate their individual and group identities—a growing and ever-more complex concern in the new millennium—in a wide range of ways, breaking down traditional distinctions between medium and message in the process, and dissolving boundaries to create art that is as interesting, exciting, difficult, and confusing as the world itself is today.

32-61 • Tony Oursler MULTIPLEXED
2008. Fiberglass, 37 × 33 × 17″ (94 × 83.8 × 43.2 cm).
MetroPicture (MP 574)

BARNEY. Between 1994 and 2002, Matthew Barney (b. 1967) created a now legendary series of films entitled *The Cremaster Cycle* in which he developed an arcane sexual mythology. The cycle is premised on the concept of gender mutability, questioning gender assignation and roles throughout. The cremaster muscle for which the series is named controls the ascent and descent of the testes, usually in response to changes in temperature but also in response to fear or sexual arousal, and it also determines sexual differentiation in the human embryo. Barney uses a diagrammatic representation of the cremaster muscle as his visual emblem throughout the series.

Each film has its own complex narrative and catalog of multilayered symbols. *Cremaster 3* (2002) describes the construction of the Chrysler Building in New York and features Richard Serra (SEE FIG. 32–42) as the architect. A segment of the film is set in the Guggenheim Museum's rotunda (SEE FIG. 32–27). Barney, playing Serra's apprentice and dressed in a peach-colored kilt and gagged, must accomplish a series of tasks to assert his supremacy over Serra. As in a video game, Barney scales the walls of the Guggenheim rotunda to complete a task on each level before gaining enlightenment. Along the way he is challenged by a line of Rockettes dressed as Masonic lambs, by warring punk-rock bands, by a leopard woman (played by Aimee Mullins), and finally by Serra. The settings and costumes are lavish, and the epic plot is baroquely interconnected. In **MAHABYN (FIG. 32–62)**, Barney and the leopard woman transform into Masons—they are shown here in modified Masonic costume.

32-62 • Matthew Barney CREMASTER 3: MAHABYN
2002. 46½ × 54 × 1½″ (118 × 137 × 3.8 cm). Guggenheim Museum, New York.

The entire filmic cycle addresses the crisis of identity experienced by white, middle-class heterosexual male artists in America in an era seemingly dominated by identity politics.

BEECROFT.   Vanessa Beecroft also set her **VB35 (FIG. 32–63)** in the Guggenheim Museum's rotunda and also uses performance to examine gender roles, although she explores perceptions of the female body and femininity. Unlike Barney, she does not appear in her work. Many of Beecroft's performances refer obliquely to her own battle with anorexia. The artist numbers her performances—*vb35* is her 35th piece—and in it she questions both the nature of today's distorted concept of feminine beauty and voyeuristic looking. For the performance, Beecroft hired 15 professional fashion models, each of whom was fashionably thin, tall, and white. The models were directed to stand in a loose group, facing forward. Ten wore high heels and designer bikinis, while five wore nothing but high heels. They stood staring blankly ahead while the audience was permitted to observe them from the foyer or the ramp of the museum, thus acquiescing in the gaze that objectified them. The event was "invitation only" so the atmosphere was charged with exclusivity, but Beecroft complicated this piece by heightening the tension in two ways: First, the group of professional models whose business it is to be looked at commanded the museum; and second, the audience was instructed to behave in very precise ways—they were not allowed to speak to the models, make eye contact with them, or invade their physical or emotional space in any way. This strategy cleverly inverted the normal relationship between looker and looked-at. A sexual charge filled the air, but ironically the models claimed control. Viewers found that they were intimidated and discomforted: They felt as though they had been caught in the act of looking illicitly. As one critic put it: "we found ourselves confronted by the cool authority of the art's nakedness, and we had no role to play … so we drifted and loitered."

GU.   Wenda Gu (b. 1955) dedicates his art to bringing people together. Trained in traditional ink painting at China's National Academy of Fine Arts, he emigrated to the United States in 1987 and began an ongoing global project entitled the "United Nations Series" in 1992. Each "monument" in this series is made from human hair collected from barbershops and hair salons worldwide

32-63 • Vanessa Beecroft VB35
1998. Performance.

EXPLORE MORE: Gain insight from a primary source by Vanessa Beecroft **www.myartslab.com**

![Wenda Gu United Nations Series: Temple of Heaven installation with screens of human hair, wooden chairs and tables]

32–64 • Wenda Gu UNITED NATIONS SERIES: TEMPLE OF HEAVEN
1998. Installation with screens of human hair, wooden chairs and tables, and video. Commissioned by the Asia Society. Collection of the artist.

and which Gu presses into bricks or weaves into carpets and curtains covered with ideograms of his own invention. **UNITED NATIONS SERIES: TEMPLE OF HEAVEN (FIG. 32–64)** contains hair from many different nations and blended scripts based on Chinese, English, Hindi, and Arabic characters that "evoke the limitations of human knowledge." Gu also creates "national" monuments—examples have been installed in Poland, Israel, and Taiwan, among other places—made from hair collected in, and addressing issues specific to, that particular country. The "transnational" monuments from the "United Nations Series," on the other hand, address more global themes, using hair blended from several different countries to suggest a "brave new racial identity" for the new millennium.

OSPINA. In his series **COLOMBIA LAND (FIG. 32–65)**, the Colombian artist Nadín Ospina (b. 1960) uses Lego figures, blown up in photographs and sculptures to gargantuan size, to caricature stereotypical images of Colombia as a nation of drug lords and violence. *Colombia Land* is a funny but also sinister parody of a Legoland theme park. In this piece, Ospina mimics a typical *National Geographic* cover by placing a Lego bandit with an automatic weapon, bands of ammunition slung across his chest, and

32–65 • Nadín Ospina COLOMBIA LAND
2004. Centro Cultural de la Universidad de Salamanca, Bogotá.

dark glasses hiding his eyes, amid a crop of drugs. Such a figure would be threatening were he not transformed into a child's toy. Ospina describes Colombia as "an art and culture hijacked by violence," and his art explores the cultural colonization of Colombia by Western European and American popular culture as well as Colombia's own complicated self-perceptions.

HAMMONS. A socially minded artist strongly committed to working in the public realm, David Hammons (b. 1943) is an outspoken critic of the gallery system in America, lamenting the lack of challenging content and representation of African Americans in exhibitions. He has described the art world as being "like Novocain. It used to wake you up but now it puts you to sleep." Hammons argues that only art that intervenes in and transacts with society is uncontaminated by commerce and still jolts people awake. In **UNTITLED** (FIG. 32–66), the artist creates a witty but biting satire on the still ambiguous place of African Americans in American society. Hammons originally created this flag in 1990 for the Studio Museum, Harlem, in response to a controversy concerning the flying of the Confederate flag on public buildings in some states. It has since been installed in several other museums, including the Museum of Modern Art in New York in 2000. The colors in Hammons's flag are those of the Pan-African or Universal Negro Improvement Association and African Communities League flag, which was created in 1920 by African Americans to symbolize the "Rights of Negro Peoples of the World." The red stands for the blood that unites all people of

African descent and that was spilled in the quest for liberation; the black stands for the symbolic nation of black people; and the green stands for the verdant lands of Africa. The piece makes a poignant and pointed comment about race in America.

SHONIBARE. Yinka Shonibare (b. 1962) is a British-Nigerian artist based in London. His art examines how identity is informed, perceived, and constructed through the twists and turns of colonial history, as well as class, race, and self-perception. **HOW TO BLOW UP TWO HEADS AT ONCE (LADIES)** (FIG. 32–67) is a life-size sculpture of two headless women whose skin color, and thus on a superficial level whose race, is indeterminate. Although the figures have women's bodies, they seem to have masculine hands. They face off against one another in a dueling pose with nineteenth-century flintlock pistols drawn and pointed at each other's absent heads. They wear what appear to be nineteenth-century costumes, but their brightly colored dresses are made of a Dutch wax fabric that is usually associated with West African nations. The complexities of the history and use of the fabric, and the way that Shonibare uses it, give us some idea of the multiple and eliding meanings in this sculpture. This brilliantly colored and patterned fabric, worn by millions of Africans today, originally came from Indonesia, was imported and copied by Dutch colonists in Africa, was manufactured in bulk in cotton mills in Manchester, England, and was then exported to West Africa, where it was copied, modified, transformed, and now possessed by West African cultures. Ironically, Shonibare buys the fabric for his sculptures at London's

32–66 • David Hammons UNTITLED
2004. Studio Museum, Harlem. Nylon, 6 × 10′ (1.82 × 3 m). Gift of the artist (04.2.19)

32-67 • Yinka Shonibare, MBE

HOW TO BLOW UP TWO HEADS AT ONCE (LADIES)
2006. Two fiberglass mannequins, two prop guns, Dutch, wax printed cotton textile, shoes, leather riding boots, plinth, 93½ × 63 × 48″ (237 × 160 × 122 cm). Museum purchase with funds provided by Wellesley College Friends of Art, 2007.124.1-2

Brixton market. Shonibare challenges our perceptions about issues of race, postcolonialism, property, ownership, violence, and class. His work, although witty and ironic, is also acerbic as it shows us the tangled web of forces that construct identity.

SIERRA. Santiago Sierra (b. 1966), a Spanish artist who lives in Mexico City, addresses race, ethnicity, and the capitalist exploitation of the poor in his interventionist artworks. At the 49th Venice Biennale in 2001, Sierra created a very visible commentary on the luxurious indulgence and elitist atmosphere of the exhibition and on the relative invisibility of both poverty and race there. For this piece, Sierra paid 133 non-European men to dye their naturally black hair blond and to make themselves visible around Venice for the duration of the exhibition (FIG. 32–68). The shocking white hair on dark-skinned men made them very visible and placed a group of individuals who normally melt into the background of society front and center, persistently reminding viewers of both their presence and their relative poverty—the only reason their hair was blond was because they needed the money.

32-68 • Santiago Sierra **133 PEOPLE PAID TO HAVE THEIR HAIR DYED BLOND**
2001. 49th Venice Biennale

Sierra paid 133 non-European men to dye their hair blond. In the exhibition, he presented video footage of the dyeing process.

32-69 • Fred Wilson **CHANDELIER MORI**
2003. United States Pavilion, 50th Venice Biennale.

WILSON. In the 1990s, artists increasingly began to critique the constructed narratives of the traditional museum exhibition. The museum was acknowledged as a place in which curators, who make decisions about what to show and how to arrange works in an exhibition, create history rather than revealing it and, in the process, frequently reveal their own prejudices. Fred Wilson (b. 1954) is best known for *Mining the Museum* (1992), a brilliant interventionist piece in which he inverted and subverted the Baltimore Historical Society's collection. Wilson "mined" the museum's storage area and found that, while the objects on show were mostly about white history, there were numerous objects relating to African-American history in the vaults. He "inserted" many of these into the main museum display, including some horrific objects used to restrain African-American slaves, thereby upsetting and reshaping the story told in the original exhibition.

In 2003, Wilson represented the United States at the Venice Biennale with *Speak of Me As I Am*, a multi-part installation that focused on the history of Africans in Venice. This included several black sculptures made with Murano glass, a kind of glass made in Venice for centuries, set in a black-and-white tiled room with "graffiti" on the walls consisting of excerpts from African-American slave narratives and a video installation of Shakespeare's *Othello* being screened backwards. The title of the work, *Speak of*

32-70 • Kara Walker **DARKYTOWN REBELLION**
2001. Cut paper and projection on wall, 14 × 37′ (4.3 × 11.3 m) overall. Musée d'Art Moderne Grand-Duc Jean, Luxembourg.

SEE MORE: View a video about Kara Walker **www.myartslab.com**

Me As I Am, is taken from words spoken by Othello, the "Moor," in Shakespeare's play. **CHANDELIER MORI (FIG. 32–69)**, the chandelier from Wilson's installation, is also made from Murano glass but, unlike the brilliantly glittering Venetian glass chandeliers seen around the city, this one emphasizes blackness. The title suggests the *memento mori* or *vanitas* painting that reminds viewers that death comes to all of us, drawing attention to the fact that the commerce of Venice was built on the back of African labor and at the cost of African lives.

WALKER. It is fitting to end this book with some of the most challenging and provocative art made in America today. The art of Kara Walker (b. 1969) hits raw nerves, shocks, and horrifies. Walker makes her work by cutting large-scale silhouettes of figures out of black construction paper, waxing them to the walls of galleries, and illuminating them with projected light. In **DARKYTOWN REBELLION (FIG. 32–70)**, a scene showing a slave revolt and massacre, the walls of the gallery are covered by black-silhouetted figures that tell an unfolding tale of horror. The room swirls with beautifully colored white, black, pink, green, blue, and yellow projected lights and shadows dancing on the walls. As we walk around the space looking at the figures, we step in front of the projector and our own shadows are cast on the walls, placing us uncomfortably close to or actually in the narrative. Walker's stories and caricatural figures are drawn variously from slave narratives, minstrel shows, advertising memorabilia, and even from Harlequin romance novels, blending fiction and fact to evoke a history of oppression and terrible violence—she does not balk at portraying unpleasant or painful bodily functions either, such as excretion, vomiting, and childbirth. Walker's characters are black and white stereotypes. She contrasts the tight, cramped features of her white characters with the stereotypical black features of her African Americans. She even refers to some of her characters as "nigger wenches" or "pickaninnies."

Walker plays on white fears of miscegenation and insecurities about racial purity. She pushes so far over the border of the acceptable that visiting one of her installations can be a terrifying and disruptive experience. Her figures disturb us intensely because of what they make us do. As silhouettes, they are all black, which means that we cannot identify their race by skin color. In order to read the narrative, however, we need to differentiate the characters and so have to look for other visual markers of race, making us draw upon an entire history of ugly stereotypes in the process. We are forced to examine the figures for thin or big lips, flat or curly hair, elegant or raggedy clothes. In this way Walker catches us in the act of being racist, making clear that she is speaking to us personally, not to some theoretical racist, and that racism is neither theoretical nor a thing of the past. As Walker has said: "It's interesting that as soon as you start telling the story of racism you start reliving it." She might also have said that when you experience her cycloramas, you become part of them.

Walker shows us that identity is not nearly as clear-cut as we would like to think. We are all complicated beings, constantly negotiating and renegotiating our place in the world, changing and reinventing ourselves. Kara Walker's art is not pleasant, but it changes us by altering our perception of the world. It makes us confront a world that we do not want to believe exists, and shows us that the work of visual artists—past, present, and future—can reveal things about the time and place in which it was created and about the world we inhabit in ways that are beyond the reach of any other form of communication.

THINK ABOUT IT

32.1 Discuss the emergence of Pop art in the 1950s and 1960s in the work of artists such as Richard Hamilton and Andy Warhol. Explain how and why Pop reacted to Abstract Expressionism.

32.2 Write about the importance of the dematerialized object in the art of postwar United States. Then discuss how representational art regained importance in later years, particularly after 1980, and explain the new forms that representation took.

32.3 Distinguish the three waves of feminism and assess their impact on the visual arts.

32.4 Analyze how contemporary American artists have used their art to address social and political issues surrounding race. Select and discuss the work of at least two artists from the chapter such as David Hammons, Kerry James Marshall, Kara Walker, or Fred Wilson.

32.5 Explain how globalism has impacted the visual arts and discuss how artists use contemporary strategies to speak to issues in their local cultures. Analyze one such artwork from the chapter.

PRACTICE MORE: Compose answers to these questions, get flashcards for images and terms, and review chapter material with quizzes **www.myartslab.com**

## Map labels

Arctic Ocean

Pacific Ocean

Atlantic Ocean

Indian Ocean

GREENLAND (Denmark)

ICELAND

CANADA

UNITED STATES

U.S.

MEXICO

BELIZE
GUATEMALA
HONDURAS
EL SALVADOR
NICARAGUA
COSTA RICA
PANAMA

CUBA
JAMAICA
HAITI
DOMINICAN REPUBLIC
PUERTO RICO

COLOMBIA
ECUADOR
VENEZUELA
GUYANA
SURINAME
FRENCH GUIANA
PERU
BRAZIL
BOLIVIA
PARAGUAY
CHILE
ARGENTINA
URUGUAY

TAHITI

RUSSIA

MONGOLIA
CHINA
N. KOREA
S. KOREA
JAPAN
TAIWAN
PHILIPPINES

KAZAKHSTAN
UZBEKISTAN
TURKMENISTAN
KYRGYZSTAN
TAJIKISTAN
AFGHANISTAN
PAKISTAN
NEPAL
BHUTAN
BANGLADESH
INDIA
MYANMAR
LAOS
VIETNAM
THAILAND
CAMBODIA
SRI LANKA
MALAYSIA
BRUNEI
SINGAPORE
INDONESIA
EAST TIMOR

PAPUA NEW GUINEA
SOLOMON ISLANDS
VANUATU
NEW CALEDONIA
FIJI
NEW ZEALAND
AUSTRALIA

GEORGIA
ARMENIA
AZERBAIJAN
TURKEY
CYPRUS
SYRIA
LEBANON
ISRAEL
JORDAN
IRAQ
IRAN
KUWAIT
BAHRAIN
QATAR
U.A.E.
OMAN
SAUDI ARABIA
YEMEN

TUNISIA
MOROCCO
WESTERN SAHARA
ALGERIA
LIBYA
EGYPT
MAURITANIA
MALI
NIGER
CHAD
SENEGAL
GAMBIA
GUINEA BISSAU
GUINEA
SIERRA LEONE
LIBERIA
IVORY COAST
BURKINA FASO
GHANA
TOGO
BENIN
NIGERIA
CAMEROON
EQUATORIAL GUINEA
GABON
CONGO REP.
CENTRAL AFRICAN REP.
DEM. REP. OF CONGO
SUDAN
ERITREA
ETHIOPIA
DJIBOUTI
SOMALIA
UGANDA
KENYA
RWANDA
BURUNDI
TANZANIA
MALAWI
ANGOLA
ZAMBIA
ZIMBABWE
MOZAMBIQUE
NAMIBIA
BOTSWANA
SWAZILAND
LESOTHO
SOUTH AFRICA
MADAGASCAR
MAURITIUS

ANTARCTICA

see inset

Inset map (Europe)

RUSSIA

FINLAND
NORWAY
SWEDEN
ESTONIA
LATVIA
LITHUANIA
RUSSIA
DENMARK
IRELAND
UNITED KINGDOM
THE NETHERLANDS
BELGIUM
LUXEMBOURG
FRANCE
GERMANY
SWITZ.
SPAIN
PORTUGAL
ITALY

BELARUS
POLAND
CZECH REP.
SLOVAK REP.
AUSTRIA
SLOVENIA
CROATIA
HUNGARY
BOSNIA- AND HERZEGOVINA
SERBIA
MONTENEGRO
ALBANIA
MACEDONIA

UKRAINE
MOLDOVA
ROMANIA
BULGARIA
GREECE
TURKEY

North Sea
Baltic Sea
Black Sea
Mediterranean Sea
Atlantic Ocean

N

400 km
400 miles

N

2000 km
2000 miles

GLOSSARY

abacus (p. 108)   The flat slab at the top of a **capital**, directly under the **entablature**.

abbey church (p. 239)   An abbey is a religious community headed by an abbot or abbess. An abbey church often has an especially large choir to provide space for the monks or nuns.

absolute dating (p. 12)   A method of assigning a precise historical date to periods and objects, based on known and recorded events in the region, as well as technically extracted physical evidence (such as carbon-14 disintegration). See also **radiometric dating, relative dating**.

abstract, abstraction (p. 8)   Any art that does not represent observed aspects of nature or transforms visible forms into a stylized image. Also: the **formal** qualities of this process.

academy (p. 924)   A place of study, the word coming from the Greek name of a garden near Athens where Plato and, later, Platonic philosophers held discussions. Academies of fine arts, such as the Academy of Drawing or the Royal Academy of Painting, were created to foster the arts by teaching, by discussion, by exhibitions, and occasionally by financial aid.

acanthus (p. 110)   A Mediterranean plant whose leaves are reproduced in architectural ornament used on **moldings, friezes**, and **Corinthian capitals**.

acropolis (p. 129)   The citadel of an ancient Greek city, located at its highest point and housing temples, a treasury, and sometimes a royal palace. The most famous is the Acropolis in Athens.

acroterion (acroteria) (p. 110)   An ornament at the corner or peak of a roof.

adobe (p. 393)   Sun-baked blocks made of clay mixed with straw. Also: the buildings made with this material.

aedicula (p. 609)   A decorative architectural frame, usually found around a niche, door, or window. An aedicula is made up of a **pediment** and **entablature** supported by **columns** or **pilasters**.

agora (p. 138)   An open space in a Greek town used as a central gathering place or market. See also **forum**.

aisle (p. 228)   Passage or open corridor of a church, hall, or other building that parallels the main space, usually on both sides, and is delineated by a row, or **arcade**, of **columns** or **piers**. Called side aisles when they flank the **nave** of a church.

album (p. 795)   A book consisting of a series of painting or prints (album leaves) mounted into book form.

allegory (p. 625)   In a work of art, an image (or images) that symbolizes an idea, concept, or principle, often moral or religious.

alloy (p. 23)   A mixture of metals; different metals melted together.

amalaka (p. 301)   In Hindu architecture, the circular or square-shaped element on top of a spire (**shikhara**), often crowned with a **finial**, symbolizing the cosmos.

ambulatory (p. 228)   The passage (walkway) around the **apse** in a **basilica** church or around the central space in a **central-plan building**.

amphora (p. 101)   An ancient Greek jar for storing oil or wine, with an egg-shaped body and two curved handles.

aniconic (p. 262)   A symbolic representation without images of human figures, very often found in Islamic art.

animal interlace or style (p. 427)   Decoration made of interwoven animals or serpents, often found in Celtic and early medieval Northern European art.

ankh (p. 51)   A looped cross signifying life, used by ancient Egyptians.

appropriation (p. 1102)   Term used to describe the practice of some postmodern artists of adopting images in their entirety from other works of art or from visual culture for use in their own art. The act of recontextualizing the appropriated image allows the artist to critique both it and the time and place in which it was created.

apse, apsidal (p. 192)   A large semicircular or polygonal (and usually **vaulted**) niche protruding from the end wall of a building. In the Christian church, it contains the altar. Apsidal is an adjective describing the condition of having such a space.

arabesque (p. 263)   A type of linear surface decoration based on foliage and **calligraphic** forms, usually characterized by flowing lines and swirling shapes.

arcade (p. 172)   A series of **arches**, carried by **columns** or **piers** and supporting a common wall or **lintel**. In a **blind arcade**, the arches and supports are **engaged** (attached to the wall) and have a decorative function.

arch (p. 271)   In architecture, a curved structural element that spans an open space. Built from wedge-shaped stone blocks called **voussoirs**, which, when placed together and held at the top by a trapezoidal **keystone**, form an effective space-spanning and weight-bearing unit. Requires **buttresses** at each side to contain the outward **thrust** caused by the weight of the structure. **Corbel arch** (p. 16): an arch or **vault** formed by **courses** of stones, each of which projects beyond the lower course until the space is enclosed; usually finished with a **capstone**. **Horseshoe arch** (p. 268): an arch of more than a half-circle; typical of western Islamic architecture. **Round arch** (p. 271): arch that displaces most of its weight, or downward thrust along its curving sides, transmitting that weight to adjacent supporting uprights (door or window jambs, columns, or piers). Ogival arch: a pointed arch created by S-curves. Relieving arch: an arch built into a heavy wall just above a **post-and-lintel** structure (such as a gate, door, or window) to help support the wall above by transferring the load to the side walls. **Transverse arch** (p. 457): an arch that connects the wall **piers** on both sides of an interior space, up and over a stone vault.

Archaic smile (p. 114)   The curved lips of an ancient Greek statue, usually interpreted as a way of animating facial features.

architrave (p. 108)   The bottom element in an **entablature**, beneath the **frieze** and the **cornice**.

archivolt (p. 473)   A **molded** band framing an **arch**, or a series of stone blocks that rest directly on the **columns**.

ashlar (p. 99)   Highly finished, precisely cut block of stone. When laid in even courses, ashlar masonry creates a uniform face with fine joints. Often used as a facing on the visible exterior of a building, especially as a veneer for the **façade**. Also called **dressed stone**.

assemblage (p. 1026)   Artwork created by gathering and manipulating two- and/or three-dimensional found objects.

astragal (p. 110)   A thin convex decorative **molding**, often found on Classical **entablatures**, and usually decorated with a continuous row of beadlike circles.

atelier (p. 944)   The studio or workshop of a master artist or craftsperson, often including junior associates and apprentices.

atmospheric perspective (p. 562)   See **perspective**.

atrial cross (p. 941)   The cross placed in the **atrium** of a church. In Colonial America, used to mark a gathering and teaching place.

atrium (p. 160)   An unroofed interior courtyard or room in a Roman house, sometimes having a pool or garden, sometimes surrounded by **columns**. Also: the open courtyard in front of a Christian church; or an entrance area in modern architecture.

automatism (p. 1056)   A technique whereby the usual intellectual control of the artist over his or her brush or pencil is foregone. The artist's aim is to allow the subconscious to create the artwork without rational interference.

avant-garde (p. 971)   Term derived from the French military word meaning "before the group," or "vanguard." Avant-garde denotes those artists or concepts of a strikingly new, experimental, or radical nature for their time.

axis (p. xxxii)   An implied line around which the elements of a picture are organized.

axis-mundi (p. 297)   A concept of an "axis of the world," which marks sacred sites and denotes a link between the human and celestial realms. For example, in Buddhist art, the *axis mundi* can be marked by monumental freestanding decorative **pillars**.

bailey (p. 473)   The outermost walled courtyard of a castle.

baldachin (p. 467)   A canopy (whether suspended from the ceiling, projecting from a wall, or supported by **columns**) placed over an honorific or sacred space such as a throne or church altar.

bar tracery (p. 507)   See **tracery**.

barbarian (p. 151)   A term used by the ancient Greeks and Romans to label all foreigners outside their cultural orbit (e.g., Celts, Goths, Vikings). The word derives from an imitation of what the "barblings" of their language sounded like to those who could not understand it.

bargeboards (p. 870)   Boards covering the rafters at the gable end of a building; bargeboards are often carved or painted.

barrel vault (p. 188)   See **vault**.

base (p. 110)   Any support. Also: masonry supporting a statue or the shaft of a **column**.

basilica (p. 192)   A large rectangular building. Often built with a **clerestory**, side **aisles** separated from the center **nave** by **colonnades**, and an **apse** at one or both ends. Roman centers for administration, later adapted to Christian church use.

battered (p. 418)   An architectural design whereby walls are sloped inward toward the top to increase stability.

bay (p. 172)   A unit of space defined by architectural elements such as **columns, piers**, and walls.

beehive tomb (p. 98)   A **corbel-vaulted** tomb, conical in shape like a beehive, and covered by an earthen mound.

Benday dots (p. 1093)   In modern printing and typesetting, the individual dots that, together with many others, make up lettering and images. Often machine- or computer-generated, the dots are very small and closely spaced to give the effect of density and richness of tone.

bi (p. 333)   A jade disk with a hole in the center.

bilum (p. 863)   Netted bags made mainly by women throughout the central highlands of New Guinea. The bags can be used for everyday purposes or even to carry the bones of the recently deceased as a sign of mourning.

biomorphic (p. 1057)   A term used in the early twentieth century to denote the biologically or organically inspired shapes and forms that were routinely included in abstracted Modern art.

black-figure (p. 105) A style or technique of ancient Greek pottery in which black figures are painted on a red clay ground. See also **red-figure**.

blackware (p. 853) A **ceramic** technique that produces pottery with a primarily black surface with **matte** and glossy patterns on the surface.

blind arcade (p. 780) See **arcade**.

bodhisattva (p. 297) In Buddhism, a being who has attained enlightenment but chooses to remain in this world in order to help others advance spiritually. Also defined as a potential Buddha.

Book of Hours (p. 547) A private prayer book, containing a calendar, services for the canonical hours, and sometimes special prayers.

boss (p. 554) A decorative knoblike element that can be found in many places, such as at the intersection of a Gothic **rib vault** or in the buttonlike projections of metalwork.

bracket, bracketing (p. 335) An architectural element that projects from a wall to support a horizontal part of a building, such as beams or the eaves of a roof.

buon fresco (p. 87) See **fresco**.

burin (p. 590) A metal instrument used in **engraving** to cut lines into the metal plate. The sharp end of the burin is trimmed to give a diamond-shaped cutting point, while the other end is finished with a wooden handle that fits into the engraver's palm.

buttress, buttressing p. 172) A projecting support built against an external wall, usually to counteract the lateral **thrust** of a **vault** or **arch** within. In Gothic architecture, a **flying buttress** is an arched bridge above the **aisle** roof that extends from the upper **nave** wall, where the lateral thrust of the main vault is greatest, down to a solid **pier**.

cairn (p.17) A pile of stones or earth and stones that served both as a prehistoric burial site and as a marker of underground tombs.

calligraphy (p. 279) Handwriting as an art form.

calotype (p. 968) The first photographic process utilizing negatives and paper positives. It was invented by William Henry Fox Talbot in the late 1830s.

calyx krater (p. 118) See **krater**.

came (cames) (p. 497) A lead strip used in the making of leaded or **stained-glass windows**. Cames have an indented groove on the sides into which the separate pieces of glass are fitted to hold the composition together.

cameo (p. 178) Gemstone, clay, glass, or shell having layers of color, carved in **low relief** to create an image and ground of different colors.

camera obscura (p. 967) An early cameralike device used in the Renaissance and later for recording images of nature. Made from a dark box (or room) with a hole in one side (sometimes fitted with a lens), the camera obscura operates when bright light shines through the hole, casting an upside-down image of an object outside onto the inside wall of the box.

canon of proportions (p. 65) A set of ideal mathematical ratios in art based on measurements, as in the proportional relationships among the basic elements of the human body.

canopic jar (p. 56) Special jars used to store the major organs of a body before embalming, found in ancient Egyptian culture.

capital (p. 110) The sculpted block that tops a **column**. According to the **conventions** of the **orders**, capitals include different decorative elements. See **order**. A **historiated capital** is one displaying a figural composition of a **narrative** scene.

capriccio (p. 912) A painting or print of a fantastic, imaginary landscape, usually with architecture.

capstone (p. 99) The final, topmost stone in a **corbel arch** or **vault**, which joins the sides and completes the structure.

cartoon (p. 497) A full-scale drawing used to transfer or guide a design onto a surface (such as a wall, canvas, panel, or **tapestry**) to be painted, carved, or woven.

cartouche (p. 189) A frame for a **hieroglyphic** inscription formed by a rope design surrounding an oval space. Used to signify a sacred or honored name. Also: in architecture, a decorative device or plaque, usually with a plain center used for inscriptions or epitaphs.

caryatid (p. 107) A sculpture of a draped female figure acting as a **column** supporting an **entablature**.

cassone (cassoni) (p. 616) An Italian dowry chest often highly decorated with carvings, paintings, **inlaid** designs, and gilt embellishments.

catacomb (p. 219) A subterranean burial ground consisting of tunnels on different levels, having niches for urns and **sarcophagi** and often incorporating rooms (**cubiculae**).

cathedral (p. 222) The principal Christian church in a diocese, the bishop's administrative center and housing his throne (*cathedra*).

celadon (p. 352) A high-fired, transparent glaze of pale bluish-green hue whose principal coloring agent is an oxide of iron. In China and Korea, such glazes typically were applied over a pale gray **stoneware** body, though Chinese potters sometimes applied them over **porcelain** bodies during the Ming (1368–1644) and Qing (1644–1911) dynasties. Chinese potters invented celadon glazes and initiated the continuous production of celadon-glazed wares as early as the third century CE.

cella (p. 108) The principal interior room at the center of a Greek or Roman temple within which the cult statue was usually housed. Also called the **naos**.

celt (p. 377) A smooth, oblong stone or metal object, shaped like an axe-head.

cenotaph (p. 771) A funerary monument commemorating an individual or group buried elsewhere.

centering (p. 172) A temporary structure that supports a masonry **arch** and **vault** or **dome** during construction until the mortar is fully dried and the masonry is self-sustaining.

central-plan building (p. 228) Any structure designed with a primary central space surrounded by symmetrical areas on each side. For example, a **rotunda** or a Greek-cross plan (equal-armed cross).

ceramics (p. 22) A general term covering all types of wares made from fired clay, including **porcelain** and **terra cotta**.

chacmool (p. 390) In Mayan sculpture, a half-reclining figure probably representing an offering bearer.

chaitya (p. 302) A type of Buddhist temple found in India. Built in the form of a hall or **basilica**, a *chaitya* hall is highly decorated with sculpture and usually is carved from a cave or natural rock location. It houses a sacred shrine or **stupa** for worship.

chamfer (p. 780) The slanted surface produced when an angle is trimmed or beveled, common in building and metalwork.

chasing (p. 776) Ornamentation made on metal by **incising** or hammering the surface.

château (châteaux) (p. 691) A French country house or residential castle. A *château fort*, is a military castle incorporating defensive works such as towers and battlements.

chattri (chattris) (p. 779) A decorative pavilion with an umbrella-shaped **dome** in Indian architecture.

chevron (p. 350) A decorative or heraldic motif of repeated Vs; a zigzag pattern.

chiaroscuro (p. 634) An Italian word designating the contrast of dark and light in a painting, drawing, or print. *Chiaroscuro* creates spatial depth and volumetric forms through gradations in the intensity of light and shadow.

cista (cistae) (p. 166) **Cylindrical** containers used by wealthy women as a case for toiletry articles such as a mirror.

clerestory (p. 58) The topmost zone of a wall with windows in a **basilica** extending above the aisle roofs. Provides direct light into the central interior space (the **nave**).

cloister (p. 442) An open space within a monastery, surrounded by an **arcaded** or colonnaded walkway, often having a fountain and garden. The most important monastic buildings (e.g., dormitory, refectory) open off of it. Since members of a cloistered order do not leave the monastery or interact with outsiders, the cloister represents the center of their enclosed world.

codex (codices) (p. 243) A book, or a group of **manuscript** pages (folios), held together by stitching or other binding on one side.

coffer (p. 197) A recessed decorative panel that is used to reduce the weight of and to decorate ceilings or **vaults**. The use of coffers is called coffering.

coiling (p. 845) A technique in basketry. In coiled baskets a spiraling structure is held in place by another material.

collage (p. 1026) A composition made of cut and pasted scraps of materials, sometimes with lines or forms added by the artist.

colonnade (p. 69) A row of **columns**, supporting a straight **lintel** (as in a **porch** or **portico**) or a series of **arches** (an **arcade**).

colophon (p. 432) The data placed at the end of a book listing the book's author, publisher, **illuminator**, and other information related to its production. In East Asian **handscrolls**, the inscriptions which follow the painting are also called colophons.

column (p. 110) An architectural element used for support and/or decoration. Consists of a rounded or polygonal vertical **shaft** placed on a **base** and topped by a decorative **capital**. In Classical architecture, built in accordance with the rules of one of the architectural **orders**. Columns can be free-standing or attached to a background wall (**engaged**).

combine (p. 1085) Combinations of painting and sculpture using nontraditional art materials.

complementary color (p. 993) The primary and secondary colors across from each other on the color wheel (red and green, blue and orange, yellow and purple). When juxtaposed, the intensity of both colors increases. When mixed together, they negate each other to make a neutral gray-brown.

composite order (p. 163) See **order**.

composite pose or **image** (p. 9) Combining different viewpoints within a single representation of a subject.

composition (p. xxix) The overall arrangement, organizing design, or structure of a work of art.

conch (p. 234) A half-**dome**.

cong (p. 328) A square or octagonal jade tube with a cylindrical hole in the center. A symbol of the earth, it was used for ritual worship and astronomical observations in ancient China.

connoisseurship (p. 741) A term derived from the French word connoisseur, meaning "an expert," and signifying the study and evaluation of art based primarily on **formal**, visual, and stylistic analysis. A connoisseur studies the style and technique of an object to assess its relative quality and identify its maker through visual comparison with other works of secure authorship. See also **contextualism; formalism**.

contrapposto (p. 121) An Italian term meaning "set against," used to describe the pose that results from setting parts of the body in opposition to each other around a central **axis**.

convention (p. 51) A traditional way of representing forms.

corbel, corbeling (p. 16) An early roofing and arching technique in which each **course** of stone projects slightly beyond the previous layer (a corbel) until the uppermost corbels meet. Results in a high, almost pointed **arch** or **vault**.

corbeled vault (p. 99)   See **vault**.

Corinthian order (p. 108)   See **order**.

cornice (p. 110)   The uppermost section of a Classical **entablature**. More generally, a horizontally projecting element found at the top of a building wall or **pedestal**. A raking cornice is formed by the junction of two slanted cornices, most often found in **pediments**.

course (p. 99)   A horizontal layer of stone used in building.

crenellation (p. 44)   Alternating higher and lower sections along the top of a defensive wall, giving a stepped appearance and forming a permanent shield for defenders on top of a fortified building.

crocket (p. 585)   A stylized leaf used as decoration along the outer angle of spires, pinnacles, gables, and around **capitals** in Gothic architecture.

cruciform (p. 232)   A term describing anything that is cross-shaped, as in the cruciform plan of a church.

cubiculum (cubicula) (p. 224)   A small private room for burials in the **catacombs**.

cuneiform (p. 28)   An early form of writing with wedge-shaped marks impressed into wet clay with a **stylus**, primarily used by ancient Mesopotamians.

curtain wall (p. 1045)   A wall in a building that does not support any of the weight of the structure.

cyclopean construction (p. 93)   A method of building using huge blocks of rough-hewn stone. Any large-scale, monumental building project that impresses by sheer size. Named after the Cyclopes (sing. Cyclops) one-eyed giants of legendary strength in Greek myths.

cylinder seal (p. 32)   A small cylindrical stone decorated with **incised** patterns. When rolled across soft clay or wax, the resulting raised pattern or design (**relief**) served in Mesopotamian and Indus Valley cultures as an identifying signature.

dado (dadoes) (p. 163)   The lower part of a wall, differentiated in some way (by a molding or different coloring or paneling) from the upper section.

daguerreotype (p. 967)   An early photographic process that makes a positive print on a light-sensitized copperplate; invented and marketed in 1839 by Louis-Jacques-Mandé Daguerre.

demotic writing (p. 77)   The simplified form of ancient Egyptian **hieratic writing**, used primarily for administrative and private texts.

dendrochronology (p. xxxvi)   The dating of wood based on the patterns of the growth rings.

desert varnish (p. 400)   In southwestern North America, a substance that turned cliff faces into dark surfaces. Neolithic artists would draw images by scraping through the dark surface.

diptych (p. 215)   Two panels of equal size (usually decorated with paintings or **reliefs**) hinged together.

dogu (p. 356)   Small human figurines made in Japan during the Jomon period. Shaped from clay, the figures have exaggerated expressions and are in contorted poses. They were probably used in religious rituals.

dolmen (p. 17)   A prehistoric structure made up of two or more large upright stones supporting a large, flat, horizontal slab or slabs.

dome (p. 188)   A rounded **vault**, usually over a circular space. Consists of curved masonry and can vary in shape from hemispherical to bulbous to ovoidal. May use a supporting vertical wall (**drum**), from which the vault springs, and may be crowned by an open space (**oculus**) and/or an exterior **lantern**. When a dome is built over a square space, an intermediate element is required to make the transition to a circular drum. There are two systems: A dome on **pendentives** (spherical triangles) incorporates **arched**, sloping intermediate sections of wall that carry the weight and **thrust** of the dome to

heavily **buttressed** supporting **piers**. A dome on **squinches** uses an arch built into the wall (squinch) in the upper corners of the space to carry the weight of the dome across the corners of the square space below. A half-dome or **conch** may cover a semicircular space.

domino construction (p. 1045)   System of building construction introduced by the architect Le Corbusier in which reinforced concrete floor slabs are floated on six free-standing posts placed as if at the positions of the six dots on a domino playing piece.

Doric order (p. 108)   See **order**.

dressed stone (p. 85)   See **ashlar**.

drillwork (p. 190)   The technique of using a drill for the creation of certain effects in sculpture.

drum (p. 110)   The wall that supports a **dome**. Also: a segment of the circular **shaft** of a **column**.

drypoint (p. 748)   An **intaglio** printmaking process by which a metal (usually copper) plate is directly inscribed with a pointed instrument (**stylus**). The resulting design of scratched lines is inked, wiped, and printed. Also: the print made by this process.

earthenware (p. 22)   A low-fired, opaque **ceramic** ware that is fired in the range of 800 to 900 degrees Celsius. Earthenware employs humble clays that are naturally heat resistant; the finished wares remain porous after firing unless glazed. Earthenware occurs in a range of earth-toned colors, from white and tan to gray and black, with tan predominating.

earthwork (p. 1102)   Usually very large scale, outdoor artwork that is produced by altering the natural environment.

echinus (p. 110)   A cushionlike circular element found below the **abacus** of a **Doric capital**. Also: a similarly shaped molding (usually with egg-and-dart motifs) underneath the **volutes** of an **Ionic** capital.

electronic spin resonance (p. 12)   Method that uses magnetic field and microwave irradiation to date material such as tooth enamel and its surrounding soil.

elevation (p. 108)   The arrangement, proportions, and details of any vertical side or face of a building. Also: an architectural drawing showing an exterior or interior wall of a building.

emblema (emblemata) (p. 202)   In a **mosaic**, the elaborate central motif on a floor, usually a self-contained unit done in a more refined manner, with smaller **tesserae** of both marble and semiprecious stones.

embroidery (p. 484)   Stitches applied on top of an already-woven fabric ground.

encaustic (p. 79)   A painting medium using pigments mixed with hot wax.

engaged column (p. 173)   A column attached to a wall. See also **column**.

engraving (p. 590)   An **intaglio** printmaking process of inscribing an image, design, or letters onto a metal or wood surface from which a print is made. An engraving is usually drawn with a sharp implement (**burin**) directly onto the surface of the plate. Also: the print made from this process.

entablature (p. 108)   In the Classical **orders**, the horizontal elements above the **columns** and **capitals**. The entablature consists of, from bottom to top, an **architrave**, a **frieze**, and a **cornice**.

entasis (p. 108)   A slight swelling of the **shaft** of a Greek **column**. The optical illusion of entasis makes the column appear from afar to be straight.

etching (p. 748)   An **intaglio** printmaking process in which a metal plate is coated with acid-resistant resin and then inscribed with a **stylus** in a design, revealing the plate below. The plate is then immersed in acid, and the design of exposed metal is eaten away by the acid. The resin is removed, leaving the design etched permanently into the metal and the plate ready to be inked, wiped, and printed.

Eucharist (p. 222)   The central rite of the Christian Church, from the Greek word "thanksgiving." Also known as the Mass or Holy Communion, it is based on the Last Supper. According to traditional Catholic Christian belief, consecrated bread and wine become the body and blood of Christ; in Protestant belief, bread and wine symbolize the body and blood.

exedra (exedrae) (p. 199)   In architecture, a semicircular niche. On a small scale, often used as decoration, whereas larger exedrae can form interior spaces (such as an **apse**).

expressionism (p. 151)   Terms describing a work of art in which forms are created primarily to evoke subjective emotions rather than a rational response.

façade (p. 52)   The face or front wall of a building.

faience (p. 87)   Type of **ceramic** covered with colorful, opaque glazes that form a smooth, impermeable surface. First developed in ancient Egypt.

fang ding (p. 328)   A square or rectangular bronze vessel with four legs. The *fang ding* was used for ritual offerings in ancient China during the Shang dynasty.

femmage (p. 1101)   From "female" and "**collage**," the incorporation of fabric into painting.

fête galante (p. 908)   A subject in painting depicting well-dressed people at leisure in a park or country setting. It is most often associated with eighteenth-century French Rococo painting.

filigree (p. 87)   Delicate, lacelike ornamental work.

fillet (p. 110)   The flat ridge between the carved out **flutes** of a **column shaft**. See also fluting.

finial (p. 308)   A knoblike architectural decoration usually found at the top point of a spire, pinnacle, canopy, or gable. Also found on furniture; also the ornamental top of a staff.

flutes, fluted (p. 110)   In architecture, evenly spaced, rounded parallel vertical grooves incised on **shafts** of **columns** or columnar elements (such as **pilasters**).

flying buttress (p. 496)   See **buttress**.

flying gallop (p. 87)   Animals posed off the ground with legs fully extended backwards and forwards to signify that they are running.

foreshortening (p. 119)   The illusion created on a flat surface in which figures and objects appear to recede or project sharply into space. Accomplished according to the rules of perspective.

formal analysis (p. xxix)   An exploration of the visual character that artists bring to their works through the expressive use of elements such as line, form, color, and light, and through its overall structure or composition.

Formalism, formalist (p. 1073)   An approach to the understanding, appreciation, and valuation of art based almost solely on considerations of form. This approach tends to regard an artwork as independent of its time and place of making. In the 1940s, Formalism was most ardently proposed by critic Clement Greenberg. See also **connoisseurship**.

forum (p. 178)   A Roman town center; site of temples and administrative buildings and used as a market or gathering area for the citizens.

four-iwan mosque (p. 271)   See **iwan** and **mosque**.

fresco (p. 87)   A painting technique in which water-based pigments are applied to a surface of wet plaster (called **buon fresco**). The color is absorbed by the plaster, becoming a permanent part of the wall. **Fresco secco** is created by painting on dried plaster, and the color may flake off. Murals made by both these techniques are called frescoes.

fresco secco (p. 87)   See **fresco**.

frieze (p. 108)   The middle element of an **entablature**, between the **architrave** and the cornice. Usually decorated with sculpture, painting, or moldings. Also: any continuous flat band with **relief sculpture** or painted decorations.

frottage (p. 1056) A design produced by laying a piece of paper over a textured surface and rubbing with charcoal or other soft medium.

fusuma (p. 818) Sliding doors covered with paper, used in traditional Japanese construction. *Fusuma* are often highly decorated with paintings and colored backgrounds.

gallery (p. 236) In church architecture, the story found above the side **aisles** of a church, usually open to and overlooking the **nave**. Also: in secular architecture, a long room, usually above the ground floor in a private house or a public building used for entertaining, exhibiting pictures, or promenading. Also: a building or hall in which art is displayed or sold. Also: *galleria*.

garbhagriha (p. 301) From the Sanskrit word meaning "womb chamber," a small room or shrine in a Hindu temple containing a holy image.

genre painting (p. 712) A term used to loosely categorize paintings depicting scenes of everyday life, including (among others) domestic interiors, parties, inn scenes, and street scenes.

geoglyphs (p. 392) Earthen designs on a colossal scale, often created in a landscape as if to be seen from an aerial viewpoint.

gesso (p. 544) A ground made from glue, gypsum, and/or chalk forming the ground of a wood panel or the priming layer of a canvas. Provides a smooth surface for painting.

gilding (p. 87) The application of paper-thin **gold leaf** or gold pigment to an object made from another medium (for example, a sculpture or painting). Usually used as a decorative finishing detail.

giornata (giornate) (p. 537) Adopted from the Italian term meaning "a day's work," a giornata is the section of a **fresco** plastered and painted in a single day.

gold leaf (p. 47) Paper-thin sheets of hammered gold that are used in **gilding**. In some cases (such as Byzantine **icons**), also used as a ground for paintings.

gold foil (p. 87) A thin sheet of gold.

gopura (p. 775) The towering gateway to an Indian Hindu temple complex. A temple complex can have several different *gopuras*.

Grand Manner (p. 922) An elevated style of painting popular in the eighteenth century in which the artist looked to the ancients and to the Renaissance for inspiration; for portraits as well as history painting, the artist would adopt the poses, compositions, and attitudes of Renaissance and antique models.

Grand Tour (p. 911) Popular during the eighteenth and nineteenth centuries, an extended tour of cultural sites in France and Italy intended to finish the education of a young upper-class person primarily from Britain or North America.

granulation (p. 87) A technique of decoration in which metal granules, or tiny metal balls, are fused onto a metal surface.

graphic arts (p. xxiv) A term referring to those arts that are drawn or printed and that utilize paper as primary support.

grattage (p. 1056) A pattern created by scraping off layers of paint from a canvas laid over a textured surface. See also **frottage**.

grid (p. 64) A system of regularly spaced horizontally and vertically crossed lines that gives regularity to an architectural plan or in the composition of a work of art. Also: in painting, a grid is used to allow designs to be enlarged or transferred easily.

grisaille (p. 538) A style of monochromatic painting in shades of gray. Also: a painting made in this style.

groin vault (p. 188) See **vault**.

grozing (p. 497) In **stained-glass** windows, chipping away at the edges of a piece of glass to achieve the precise shape needed for inclusion in the composition.

hall church (p. 518) A church with a **nave** and **aisles** of the same height, giving the impression of a large, open hall.

handscroll (p. 337) A long, narrow, horizontal painting or text (or combination thereof) common in Chinese and Japanese art and of a size intended for individual use. A handscroll is stored wrapped tightly around a wooden pin and is unrolled for viewing or reading.

hanging scroll (p. 795) In Chinese and Japanese art, a vertical painting or text mounted within sections of silk. At the top is a semicircular rod; at the bottom is a round dowel. Hanging scrolls are kept rolled and tied except for special occasions, when they are hung for display, contemplation, or commemoration.

haniwa (p. 356) Pottery forms, including cylinders, buildings, and human figures, that were placed on top of Japanese tombs or burial mounds.

Happening (p. 1085) An art form developed by Allan Kaprow in the 1960s incorporating performance, theater, and visual images. A Happening was organized without a specific narrative or intent; with audience participation, the event proceeded according to chance and individual improvisation.

hemicycle (p. 508) A semicircular interior space or structure.

henge (p. 18) A circular area enclosed by stones or wood posts set up by Neolithic peoples. It is usually bounded by a ditch and raised embankment.

hieratic scale (p. 27) The use of different sizes for powerful or holy figures and for ordinary people to indicate relative importance. The larger the figure, the greater the importance.

hieroglyph (p. 52) Picture writing; words and ideas rendered in the form of pictorial symbols.

high relief (p. 304) See **relief sculpture**.

historiated capital (p. 479) See **capital**.

historicism (p. 963) The strong consciousness of and attention to the institutions, themes, styles, and forms of the past, made accessible by historical research, textual study, and archaeology.

history paintings (p. 924) Paintings based on historical, mythological, or biblical narratives. Once considered the noblest form of art, history paintings generally convey a high moral or intellectual idea and are often painted in a grand pictorial style.

horizon line A horizontal "line" formed by the implied meeting point of earth and sky. In **linear perspective**, the **vanishing point** or points are located on this "line."

horseshoe arch (p. 268) See **arch**.

hue (p. xxii) Pure color. The saturation or intensity of the hue depends on the purity of the color. Its value depends on its lightness or darkness.

hydria (p. 139) A large ancient Greek and Roman jar with three handles (horizontal ones at both sides and one vertical at the back), used for storing water.

hypostyle hall (p. 66) A large interior room characterized by many closely spaced columns that support its roof.

icon (p. 237) An image representing a sacred figure or event in the Byzantine, and later in the Orthodox, Church. Icons were venerated by the faithful, who believed them to have miraculous powers to transmit messages to God.

iconic image (p. 224) A picture that expresses or embodies an intangible concept or idea.

iconoclasm (p. 245) The banning or destruction of images, especially **icons** and religious art. Iconoclasm in eighth- and ninth-century Byzantium and sixteenth- and seventeenth-century Protestant territories arose from differing beliefs about the power, meaning, function, and purpose of imagery in religion.

iconography (p. xxxiii) Identifying and studying the subject matter and conventional motifs or symbols in works of art.

iconology (p. xxxv) Interpreting works of art as embodiments of cultural situation by placing them within broad social, political, religious, and intellectual contexts.

iconophile (p. 246) From the Greek for "lovers of images." In Byzantine art, iconophiles advocated for the continued use of **iconic images** in art.

iconostasis (p. 245) The partition screen in a Byzantine or Orthodox church between the **sanctuary** (where the Mass is performed) and the body of the church (where the congregation assembles). The iconostasis displays **icons**.

idealization (p. xxiv) A process in art through which artists strive to make their forms and figures attain perfection, based on pervading cultural values and/or their own personal ideals.

ideograph (p. 331) A written character or symbol representing an idea or object. Many Chinese characters are ideographs.

ignudi (p. 645) Heroic figures of nude young men.

illumination (p. 425) A painting on paper or parchment used as an illustration and/or decoration in **manuscripts** or **albums**. Usually richly colored, often supplemented by gold and other precious materials. The artists are referred to as illuminators. Also: the technique of decorating manuscripts with such paintings.

impasto (p. 748) Thick applications of pigment that give a painting a palpable surface texture.

impost block (p. 600) A block, serving to concentrate the weight above, imposed between the **capital** of a **column** and the springing of an **arch** above.

incising (p. 32) A technique in which a design or inscription is cut into a hard surface with a sharp instrument. Such a surface is said to be incised.

ink painting (p. 810) A monochromatic style of painting developed in China using black ink with gray washes.

inlay (p. 30) To set pieces of a material or materials into a surface to form a design. Also: material used in or decoration formed by this technique.

installation (p. 1087) Contemporary art created for a specific site, especially a gallery or outdoor area, that creates a complete and controlled environment.

intaglio (p. 590) Term used for a technique in which the design is carved out of the surface of an object, such as an **engraved seal** stone. In the **graphic arts**, intaglio includes **engraving**, **etching**, and **drypoint**—all processes in which ink transfers to paper from **incised**, ink-filled lines cut into a metal plate.

intarsia (p. 617) Decoration formed through wood **inlay**.

intuitive perspective (p. 184) See **perspective**.

Ionic order (p. 108) See **order**.

iwan (p. 71) A large, **vaulted** chamber in a **mosque** with a monumental **arched** opening on one side.

jamb (p. 473) In architecture, the vertical element found on both sides of an opening in a wall, and supporting an **arch** or **lintel**.

japonisme (p. 994) A style in French and American nineteenth-century art that was highly influenced by Japanese art, especially prints.

jasperware (p. 917) A fine-grained, unglazed, white **ceramic** developed by Josiah Wedgwood, often colored by metallic oxides with the raised designs remaining white.

jataka tales (p. 300) In Buddhism, stories associated with the previous lives of Shakyamuni, the historical Buddha.

joggled voussoirs (p. 272) Interlocking **voussoirs** in an **arch** or **lintel**, often of contrasting materials for colorful effect.

joined-block sculpture (p. 367) A method of constructing large-scale wooden sculpture developed in

Japan. The entire work is constructed from smaller hollow blocks, each individually carved, and assembled when complete. The joined-block technique allowed the production of larger sculpture, as the multiple joints alleviate the problems of drying and cracking found with sculpture carved from a single block.

kantharos (p. 117) A type of Greek vase or goblet with two large handles and a wide mouth.

keep (p. 473) The innermost and strongest structure or central tower of a medieval castle, sometimes used as living quarters, as well as for defense. Also called a donjon.

kente (p. 892) A woven cloth made by the Ashanti peoples of Africa. Kente cloth is woven in long, narrow pieces in complex and colorful patterns, which are then sewn together.

key block (p. 826) A key block is the master block in the production of a colored **woodblock print**, which requires different blocks for each color. The key block is a flat piece of wood upon which the outlines for the entire design of the print were first drawn on its surface and then all but these outlines were carved away with a knife. These outlines serve as a guide for the accurate **registration** or alignment of the other blocks needed to add colors to specific parts of a print.

keystone (p. 172) The topmost **voussoir** at the center of an **arch**, and the last block to be placed. The pressure of this block holds the arch together. Often of a larger size and/or decorated.

kiln (p. 22) An oven designed to produce enough heat for the baking, or firing, of clay.

kiva (p. 398) A ceremonial enclosure, usually wholly or partly underground, used for ritual purposes by modern Pueblo peoples and Ancestral Puebloans. *Kivas* may be round or square, made of **adobe** or stone, and they usually feature a hearth and a small indentation in the floor behind it.

kondo (p. 360) The main hall inside a Japanese Buddhist temple where the images of Buddha are housed.

korambo (p. 863) A ceremonial or spirit house in Pacific cultures, reserved for the men of a village and used as a meeting place as well as to hide religious artifacts from the uninitiated.

kore (kourai) (p. 114) An Archaic Greek statue of a young woman.

koru (p. 870) A design depicting a curling stalk with a bulb at the end that resembles a young tree fern, and often found in Maori art.

kouros (kouroi) (p. 114) An Archaic Greek statue of a young man or boy.

kowhaiwhai (p. 870) Painted curvilinear patterns often found in Maori art.

krater (p. 99) An ancient Greek vessel for mixing wine and water, with many subtypes that each have a distinctive shape. **Calyx krater**: a bell-shaped vessel with handles near the base that resemble a flower calyx. **Volute krater**: a type of krater with handles shaped like scrolls.

Kufic (p. 272) An ornamental, angular Arabic script.

kylix (p. 124) A shallow Greek cup, used for drinking, with a wide mouth and small handles near the rim.

lacquer (p. 22) A type of hard, glossy surface varnish used on objects in East Asian cultures, made from the sap of the Asian sumac or from shellac, a resinous secretion from the lac insect. Lacquer can be layered and manipulated or combined with pigments and other materials for various decorative effects.

lakshana (p. 303) Term used to designate the thirty-two marks of the historical Buddha. The *lakshana* include, among others, the Buddha's golden body, his long arms, the wheel impressed on his palms and the soles of his feet, and his elongated earlobes.

lamassu (p. 42) Supernatural guardian-protector of ancient Near Eastern palaces and throne rooms, often represented sculpturally as a combination of the bearded

head of a man, powerful body of a lion or bull, wings of an eagle, and the horned headdress of a god, usually possessing five legs.

lancet (p. 502) A tall, narrow window crowned by a sharply pointed **arch**, typically found in Gothic architecture.

lantern (p. 458) A turretlike structure situated on a roof, **vault**, or **dome**, with windows that allow light into the space below.

leythos (lekythoi) (p. 141) A slim Greek oil vase with one handle and a narrow mouth.

linear perspective (p. 593) See **perspective**.

linga shrine (p. 310) A place of worship centered on an object or representation in the form of a phallus (the lingam), which symbolizes the power of the Hindu god Shiva.

lintel (p. 473) A horizontal element of any material carried by two or more vertical supports to form an opening.

literati (p. 337) The English word used for the Chinese *wenren* or the Japanese *bunjin*, referring to well educated artists who enjoyed literature, **calligraphy**, and painting as a pastime. Their paintings are termed **literati painting**.

literati painting (p. 791) A style of painting that reflects the taste of the educated class of East Asian intellectuals and scholars. Aspects include an appreciation for the antique, small scale, and an intimate connection between maker and audience.

lithography (p. 951) Process of making a print (lithograph) from a design drawn on a flat stone block with greasy crayon. Ink is applied to the wet stone and adheres only to the greasy areas of the design.

loggia (p. 532) Italian term for a covered open-air **gallery**. Often used as a corridor between buildings or around a courtyard, loggias usually have **arcades** or **colonnades**.

logosyllabic (p. 385) A writing system consisting of both logograms (symbols that represent words) and phonetic signs (symbols that represent sounds, in this case syllables). Cuneiform, Maya, and Japanese are examples of logosyllabic scripts.

longitudinal-plan building (p. 228) Any structure designed with a rectangular shape. If a cross-shaped building, the main arm of the building would be longer then any arms that cross it. For example, **basilicas** or Latin-cross plan churches.

lost-wax casting (p. 413) A method of casting metal, such as bronze, by a process in which a wax mold is covered with clay and plaster, then fired, melting the wax and leaving a hollow form. Molten metal is then poured into the hollow space and slowly cooled. When the hardened clay and plaster exterior shell is removed, a solid metal form remains to be smoothed and polished.

low relief (p. 39) See **relief sculpture**.

lunette (p. 223) A semicircular wall area, framed by an **arch** over a door or window. Can be either plain or decorated.

lusterware (p. 277) **Ceramic** pottery decorated with metallic glazes.

madrasa (p. 271) An Islamic institution of higher learning, where teaching is focused on theology and law.

maenad (p. 104) In ancient Greece, a female devotee of the wine god Dionysos who participated in orgiastic rituals. She is often depicted with swirling drapery to indicate wild movement or dance. (Also called a Bacchante, after Bacchus, the Roman name of Dionysos.)

majolica (p. 571) Pottery painted with a tin glaze that, when fired, gives a lustrous and colorful surface.

mandala (p. 299) An image of the cosmos represented by an arrangement of circles or concentric geometric shapes containing diagrams or images. Used for meditation and contemplation by Buddhists.

mandapa (p. 301) In a Hindu temple, an open hall dedicated to ritual worship.

mandorla (p. 474) Light encircling, or emanating from, the entire figure of a sacred person.

manuscript (p. 242) A handwritten book or document.

maqsura (p. 268) An enclosure in a Muslim **mosque**, near the **mihrab**, designated for dignitaries.

martyrium (martyria) (p. 237) In Christian architecture, a church, chapel, or shrine built over the grave of a martyr or the site of a great miracle.

mastaba (p. 53) A flat-topped, one-story structure with slanted walls over an ancient Egyptian underground tomb.

matte (p. 571) Term describing a smooth surface that is without shine or luster.

mausoleum (p. 177) A monumental building used as a tomb. Named after the tomb of Mausolos erected at Halikarnassos around 350 BCE.

medallion (p. 225) Any round ornament or decoration. Also: a large medal.

megalith (p. 17) A large stone used in prehistoric building. Megalithic architecture employs such stones.

megaron (p. 93) The main hall of a Mycenaean palace or grand house, having a columnar **porch** and a room with central fireplace surrounded by four **columns**.

memento mori (p. 907) From Latin for "remember that you must die." An object, such as a skull or extinguished candle, typically found in a **vanitas** image, symbolizing the transience of life.

memory image (p. 8) An image that relies on the generic shapes and relationships that readily spring to mind at the mention of an object.

menorah (p. 219) A Jewish lamp-stand with seven or nine branches; the nine-branched menorah is used during the celebration of Hanukkah. Representations of the seven-branched menorah, once used in the Temple of Jerusalem, became a symbol of Judaism.

metope (p. 110) The carved or painted rectangular panel between the **triglyphs** of a **Doric frieze**.

mihrab (p. 261) A recess or niche that distinguishes the wall oriented toward Mecca (**qibla**) in a **mosque**.

millefiori (p. 428) A term derived from the Italian for "a thousand flowers" that refers to a glass-making technique in which rods of differently-colored glass are fused in a long bundle that is subsequently sliced to produce disks or beads with small-scale, multicolor patterns.

minaret (p. 267) A tower on or near a **mosque**, varying extensively in form throughout the Islamic world, from which the faithful are called to prayer five times a day.

minbar (p. 261) A high platform or pulpit in a **mosque**.

miniature (p. 243) Anything small. In painting, miniatures may be illustrations within **albums** or **manuscripts** or intimate portraits.

mirador (p. 275) In Spanish and Islamic palace architecture, a very large window or room with windows, and sometimes balconies, providing views to interior courtyards or the exterior landscape.

mithuna (p. 302) The amorous male and female couples in Buddhist sculpture, usually found at the entrance to a sacred building. The *mithuna* symbolize the harmony and fertility of life.

moai (p. 859) Statues found in Polynesia, carved from tufa, a yellowish brown volcanic stone, and depicting the human form. Nearly 1,000 of these statues have been found on the island of Rapa Nui but their significance has been a matter of speculation.

mobile (p. 1059) A sculpture made with parts suspended in such a way that they move in a current of air.

modeling (p. xxix)   In painting, the process of creating the illusion of three-dimensionality on a two-dimensional surface by use of light and shade. In sculpture, the process of molding a three-dimensional form out of a malleable substance.

module (p. 341)   A segment or portion of a repeated design. Also: a basic building block.

molding (p. 315)   A shaped or sculpted strip with varying contours and patterns. Used as decoration on architecture, furniture, frames, and other objects.

mortise-and-tenon (p. 19)   A method of joining two elements. A projecting pin (tenon) on one element fits snugly into a hole designed for it (mortise) on the other. Such joints are very strong and flexible.

mosaic (p. 146)   Images formed by small colored stone or glass pieces (**tesserae**), affixed to a hard, stable surface.

mosque (p. 261)   An edifice used for communal Islamic worship.

Mozarabic (p. 433)   An eclectic style practiced in Christian medieval Spain while much of the Iberian peninsula was ruled by Muslim dynasties.

mudra (p. 304)   A symbolic hand gesture in Buddhist art that denotes certain behaviors, actions, or feelings.

mullion (p. 507)   A slender vertical element or colonnette that divides a window into subsidiary sections.

muqarna (p. 275)   Small nichelike components stacked in tiers to fill the transition between differing vertical and horizontal planes.

naos (p. 236)   The principal room in a temple or church. In ancient architecture, the **cella**. In a Byzantine church, the **nave** and **sanctuary**.

narrative image (p. 224)   A picture that recounts an event drawn from a story, either factual (e.g., biographical) or fictional.

narthex (p. 222)   The vestibule or entrance **porch** of a church.

nave (p. 192)   The central space of a **basilica**, two or three stories high and usually flanked by aisles.

necking (p. 110)   The molding at the top of the **shaft** of the **column**.

necropolis (p. 53)   A large cemetery or burial area; literally a "city of the dead."

negative space (p. 120)   Empty space, surrounded and shaped so that it acquires a sense of form or volume.

nemes headdress (p. 51)   The royal headdress of Egypt.

niello (p. 87)   A metal technique in which a black sulfur alloy is rubbed into fine lines **engraved** into metal (usually gold or silver). When heated, the **alloy** becomes fused with the surrounding metal and provides contrasting detail.

nishiki-e (p. 813)   A multicolored and ornate Japanese print.

oculus (p. 188)   In architecture, a circular opening. Oculi are usually found either as windows or at the apex of a **dome**. When at the top of a dome, an oculus is either open to the sky or covered by a decorative exterior **lantern**.

odalisque (p. 950)   Turkish word for "harem slave girl" or "concubine."

ogee (p. 551)   An S-shaped curve. See **arch**.

oinochoe (p. 128)   A Greek jug used for wine.

olpe (p. 105)   Any Greek vase or jug without a spout.

one-point perspective   See **perspective**.

orant (p. 222)   The representation of a standing figure praying with outstretched and upraised arms.

oratory (p. 232)   A small chapel.

order (p. 110)   A system of proportions in Classical architecture that includes every aspect of the building's plan, elevation, and decorative system. **Composite**: a combination of the **Ionic** and the **Corinthian** orders.

The **capital** combines **acanthus** leaves with **volute** scrolls. **Corinthian**: the most ornate of the orders, the Corinthian includes a **base**, a **fluted column shaft** with a capital elaborately decorated with acanthus leaf carvings. Its **entablature** consists of an **architrave** decorated with **moldings**, a **frieze** often containing sculptured **reliefs**, and a **cornice** with dentils. **Doric**: the column shaft of the Doric order can be fluted or smooth-surfaced and has no base. The Doric capital consists of an undecorated **echinus** and **abacus**. The Doric entablature has a plain architrave, a frieze with **metopes** and **triglyphs**, and a simple cornice. **Ionic**: the column of the Ionic order has a base, a fluted shaft, and a capital decorated with volutes. The Ionic entablature consists of an architrave of three panels and moldings, a frieze usually containing sculpted relief ornament, and a cornice with dentils. **Tuscan**: a variation of Doric characterized by a smooth-surfaced column shaft with a base, a plain architrave, and an undecorated frieze. A colossal order is any of the above built on a large scale, rising through several stories in height and often raised from the ground by a **pedestal**.

orientalism (p. 966)   The fascination with Middle Eastern cultures.

orthogonal (p. 140)   Any line running back into the represented space of a picture perpendicular to the imagined picture plane. In **linear perspective**, all orthogonals converge at a single **vanishing point** in the picture and are the basis for a **grid** that maps out the internal space of the image. An orthogonal plan is any plan for a building or city that is based exclusively on right angles, such as the grid plan of many major cities.

pagoda (p. 341)   An East Asian **reliquary** tower built with successively smaller, repeated stories. Each story is usually marked by an elaborate projecting roof.

painterly (p. xxiv)   A style of painting which emphasizes the techniques and surface effects of brushwork (also color, light, and shade).

palace complex (p. 41)   A group of buildings used for living and governing by a ruler and his or her supporters, usually fortified.

palazzo (p. 600)   Italian term for palace, used for any large urban dwelling.

palmette (p. 139)   A fan-shaped ornament with radiating leaves.

panel painting   Any painting executed on a wood support. The wood is usually planed to provide a smooth surface. A panel can consist of several boards joined together.

parapet (p. 138)   A low wall at the edge of a balcony, bridge, roof, or other place from which there is a steep drop, built for safety. A parapet walk is the passageway, usually open, immediately behind the uppermost exterior wall or battlement of a fortified building.

parchment (p. 243)   A writing surface made from treated skins of animals. Very fine parchment is known as **vellum**.

parish church (p. 239)   Church where local residents attend regular services.

parterre (p. 760)   An ornamental, highly regimented flowerbed. An element of the ornate gardens of seventeenth-century palaces and **châteaux**.

passage grave (p. 17)   A prehistoric tomb under a **cairn**, reached by a long, narrow, slab-lined access passageway or passageways.

pastel (p. 912)   Dry pigment, chalk, and gum in stick or crayon form. Also: a work of art made with pastels.

pedestal (p. 107)   A platform or **base** supporting a sculpture or other monument. Also: the block found below the base of a Classical **column** (or **colonnade**), serving to raise the entire element off the ground.

pediment (p. 108)   A triangular gable found over major architectural elements such as Classical Greek **porticoes**, windows, or doors. Formed by an **entablature** and the ends of a sloping roof or a raking **cornice**. A similar architectural element is often used decoratively

above a door or window, sometimes with a curved upper **molding**. A broken pediment is a variation on the traditional pediment, with an open space at the center of the topmost angle and/or the horizontal cornice.

pendentive (p. 236)   The concave triangular section of a **vault** that forms the transition between a square or polygonal space and the circular **base** of a **dome**.

peplos (p. 115)   A loose outer garment worn by women of ancient Greece. A cloth rectangle fastened on the shoulders and belted below the bust or at the waist.

Performance art (p. 1085)   An artwork based on a live, sometimes theatrical performance by the artist.

peristyle (p. 66)   A surrounding **colonnade** in Greek architecture. A peristyle building is surrounded on the exterior by a colonnade. Also: a peristyle court is an open colonnaded courtyard, often having a pool and garden.

perspective (p. 184)   A system for representing three-dimensional space on a two-dimensional surface. **Atmospheric perspective**: A method of rendering the effect of spatial distance by subtle variations in color and clarity of representation. **Intuitive perspective**: A method of giving the impression of recession by visual instinct, not by the use of an overall system or program. Oblique perspective: An intuitive spatial system in which a building or room is placed with one corner in the picture plane, and the other parts of the structure recede to an imaginary vanishing point on its other side. Oblique perspective is not a comprehensive, mathematical system. **One-point** and multiple-point perspective (also called **linear**, scientific or mathematical perspective): A method of creating the illusion of three-dimensional space on a two-dimensional surface by delineating a horizon line and multiple **orthogonal** lines. These recede to meet at one or more points on the horizon (called **vanishing points**), giving the appearance of spatial depth. Called scientific or mathematical because its use requires some knowledge of geometry and mathematics, as well as optics. Reverse perspective: A Byzantine perspective theory in which the orthogonals or rays of sight do not converge on a vanishing point in the picture, but are thought to originate in the viewer's eye in front of the picture. Thus, in reverse perspective the image is constructed with orthogonals that diverge, giving a slightly tipped aspect to objects.

photomontage (p. 1039)   A photographic work created from many smaller photographs arranged (and often overlapping) in a composition, which is then rephotographed.

pictograph (p. 331)   A highly stylized depiction serving as a symbol for a person or object. Also: a type of writing utilizing such symbols.

picture plane (p. 573)   The theoretical plane corresponding with the actual surface of a painting, separating the spatial world evoked in the painting from the spatial world occupied by the viewer.

picture stone (p. 436)   A medieval northern European memorial stone covered with figural decoration. See also **rune stone**.

picturesque (p. 917)   A term describing the taste for the familiar, the pleasant, and the agreeable, popular in the eighteenth and nineteenth centuries in Europe. Originally used to describe the "picture like" qualities of some landscape scenes. When contrasted with the **sublime**, the picturesque stood for the interesting but ordinary domestic landscape.

piece-mold casting (p. 328)   A casting technique in which the mold consists of several sections that are connected during the pouring of molten metal, usually bronze. After the cast form has hardened, the pieces of the mold are disassembled, leaving the completed object.

pier (p. 266)   A masonry support made up of many stones, or rubble and concrete (in contrast to a column **shaft** which is formed from a single stone or a series of **drums**), often square or rectangular in plan, and capable of carrying very heavy architectural loads.

pietà (p. 231)   A devotional subject in Christian religious art. After the Crucifixion the body of Jesus was laid across the lap of his grieving mother, Mary. When others are present the subject is called the Lamentation.

pietra dura (p. 781)   Italian for "hard stone." Semiprecious stones selected for color, variation, and cut in shapes to form ornamental designs such as flowers or fruit.

pietra serena (p. 600)   A gray Tuscan limestone used in Florence.

pilaster (p. 160)   An **engaged column**-like element that is rectangular in format and used for decoration in architecture.

pilgrimage church (p. 239)   A site that attracts visitors wishing to venerate **relics** as well as attend services.

pillar (p. 219)   In architecture, any large, free-standing vertical element. Usually functions as an important weight-bearing unit in buildings.

pilotis (p. 1045)   Free-standing posts.

pinnacle (p. 499)   In Gothic architecture, a steep pyramid decorating the top of another element such as a **buttress**. Also: the highest point.

plate tracery (p. 502)   See **tracery**.

plinth (p. 163)   The slablike base or **pedestal** of a **column**, statue, wall, building, or piece of furniture.

pluralism (p. 1106)   A social structure or goal that allows members of diverse ethnic, racial, or other groups to exist peacefully within the society while continuing to practice the customs of their own divergent cultures, thus providing to artists a variety of valid contemporary styles.

podium (p. 138)   A raised platform that acts as the foundation for a building, or as a platform for a speaker.

polychrome, polychromy (p. 521)   The multi-colored painting decoration applied to any part of a building, sculpture, or piece of furniture.

polyptych (p. 564)   An altarpiece constructed from multiple panels, sometimes with hinges to allow for movable wings.

porcelain (p. 22)   A high-fired, vitrified, translucent, white **ceramic** ware that employs two specific clays—kaolin and petuntse—and is fired in the range of 1,300 to 1,400 degrees Celsius. The relatively high proportion of silica in the body clays renders the finished porcelains translucent. Like **stonewares**, porcelains are glazed to enhance their aesthetic appeal and to aid in keeping them clean. By definition, porcelain is white, though it may be covered with a glaze of bright color or subtle hue. Chinese potters were the first in the world to produce porcelain, which they were able to make as early as the eighth century.

porch (p. 108)   The covered entrance on the exterior of a building. With a row of **columns** or **colonnade**, also called a **portico**.

portal (p. 39)   A grand entrance, door, or gate, usually to an important public building, and often decorated with sculpture.

portico (p. 62)   In architecture, a projecting roof or porch supported by **columns**, often marking an entrance. See also **porch**.

post-and-lintel (p. 16)   An architectural system of construction with two or more vertical elements (posts) supporting a horizontal element (**lintel**).

potassium-argon dating (p. 12)   Technique used to measure the decay of a radioactive potassium isotope into a stable isotope of argon, and inert gas.

potsherd (p. 22)   A broken piece of **ceramic** ware.

poupou (p. 871)   A house panel, often carved with designs and found in Pacific cultures.

Prairie Style (p. 1046)   Style developed by a group of midwestern architects who worked together using the aesthetic of the Prairie and indigenous prairie plants for landscape design to design mostly domestic homes and small public buildings mostly in the midwest.

predella (p. 548)   The base of an altarpiece, often decorated with small scenes that are related in subject to that of the main panel or panels.

primitivism (p. 1022)   The borrowing of subjects or forms usually from non-European or prehistoric sources by Western artists. Originally practiced by Western artists as an attempt to infuse their work with the naturalistic and expressive qualities attributed to other cultures, especially colonized cultures.

pronaos (p. 108)   The enclosed vestibule of a Greek or Roman temple, found in front of the **cella** and marked by a row of **columns** at the entrance.

proscenium (p. 150)   The stage of an ancient Greek or Roman theater. In modern theater, the area of the stage in front of the curtain. Also: the framing **arch** that separates a stage from the audience.

psalter (p. 253)   In Jewish and Christian scripture, a book containing the psalms, or songs, attributed to King David.

psykter (p. 127)   A Greek vessel with an extended bottom allowing it to float in a larger krater; used to chill wine.

putto (putti) (p. 229)   A plump, naked little boy, often winged. In Classical art, called a cupid; in Christian art, a cherub.

pylon (p. 66)   A massive gateway formed by a pair of tapering walls of oblong shape. Erected by ancient Egyptians to mark the entrance to a temple complex.

qibla (p. 267)   The **mosque** wall oriented toward Mecca indicated by the **mihrab**.

quatrefoil (p. 503)   A four-lobed decorative pattern common in Gothic art and architecture.

quillwork (p. 845)   A Native American decorative craft technique. The quills of porcupines and bird feathers are dyed and attached to materials in patterns.

radiometric dating (p. 12)   A method of dating prehistoric works of art made from organic materials, based on the rate of degeneration of radiocarbons in these materials. See also **relative dating**, **absolute dating**.

raigo (p. 372)   A painted image that depicts the Amida Buddha and other Buddhist deities welcoming the soul of a dying worshiper to paradise.

raku (p. 821)   A type of **ceramic** pottery made by hand, coated with a thick, dark glaze, and fired at a low heat. The resulting vessels are irregularly shaped and glazed, and are highly prized for use in the Japanese tea ceremony.

readymade (p. 1037)   An object from popular or material culture presented without further manipulation as an artwork by the artist.

red-figure (p. 118)   A style and technique of ancient Greek vase painting characterized by red clay-colored figures on a black background. (The figures are reserved against a painted ground and details are drawn, not engraved, as in **black-figure style**.)

register (p. 30)   A device used in systems of spatial definition. In painting, a register indicates the use of differing groundlines to differentiate layers of space within an image. In sculpture, the placement of self-contained bands of **reliefs** in a vertical arrangement. See **registration marks**.

registration marks (p. 826)   In Japanese **woodblock printing**, these were two marks carved on the blocks to indicate proper alignment of the paper during the printing process. In multicolor printing, which used a separate block for each color, these marks were essential for achieving the proper position or registration of the colors.

relative dating (p. 12)   See **radiometric dating**.

relic (p. 239)   A venerated object associated with a saint or martyr.

relief sculpture (p. 5)   A three-dimensional image or design whose flat background surface is carved away to a certain depth, setting off the figure. Called **high** or **low (bas) relief** depending upon the extent of projection of the image from the background. Called **sunken relief** when the image is carved below the original surface of the background, which is not cut away.

reliquary (p. 299)   A container, often made of precious materials, used as a repository to protect and display sacred **relics**.

repoussé (p. 87)   A technique of hammering metal from the back to create a protruding image. Elaborate **reliefs** are created with wooden armatures against which the metal sheets are pressed and hammered.

rhyton (p. 88)   A vessel in the shape of a figure or an animal, used for drinking or pouring liquids on special occasions.

rib vault (p. 495)   See **vault**.

ridgepole (p. 16)   A longitudinal timber at the apex of a roof that supports the upper ends of the rafters.

roof comb (p. 386)   In a Mayan building, a masonry wall along the apex of a roof that is built above the level of the roof proper. Roof combs support the highly decorated false façades that rise above the height of the building at the front.

rosettes (p. 105)   A round or oval ornament resembling a rose.

rotunda (p. 197)   Any building (or part thereof) constructed in a circular (or sometimes polygonal) shape, usually producing a large open space crowned by a **dome**.

round arch (p. 172)   See **arch**.

roundel (p. 160)   Any element with a circular format, often placed as a decoration on the exterior of architecture.

rune stone (p. 436)   A stone used in early medieval northern Europe as a commemorative monument, which is carved or inscribed with runes, a writing system used by early Germanic peoples.

rustication (p. 600)   In building, the rough, irregular, and unfinished effect deliberately given to the exterior facing of a stone edifice. Rusticated stones are often large and used for decorative emphasis around doors or windows, or across the entire lower floors of a building. Also, masonry construction with conspicuous, often beveled joints.

salon (p. 905)   A large room for entertaining guests; a periodic social or intellectual gathering, often of prominent people; a hall or **gallery** for exhibiting works of art.

sanctuary (p. 102)   A sacred or holy enclosure used for worship. In ancient Greece and Rome, consisted of one or more temples and an altar. In Christian architecture, the space around the altar in a church called the chancel or presbytery.

sarcophagus (p. 49)   A stone coffin. Often rectangular and decorated with **relief sculpture**.

scarab (p. 51)   In Egypt, a stylized dung beetle associated with the sun and the god Amun.

scarification (p. 403)   Ornamental decoration applied to the surface of the body by cutting the skin for cultural and/or aesthetic reasons.

school of artists (p. 281)   An art historical term describing a group of artists, usually working at the same time and sharing similar styles, influences, and ideals. The artists in a particular school may not necessarily be directly associated with one another, unlike those in a workshop or **atelier**.

scribe (p. 242)   A writer; a person who copies texts.

scriptorium (scriptoria) (p. 242)   A room in a monastery for writing or copying **manuscripts**.

scroll painting (p. 243)   A painting executed on a rolled support. Rollers at each end permit the horizontal scroll to be unrolled as it is studied or the vertical scroll to be hung for contemplation or decoration.

sculpture in the round (p. 5) Three-dimensional sculpture that is carved free of any background or block.

seals (p. 338) Personal emblems usually carved of stone in **intaglio** or **relief** and used to stamp a name or legend onto paper or silk. In China, they traditionally employ the archaic characters appropriately known as "seal script," of the Zhou or Qin. Cut in stone, a seal may state a formal given name, or it may state any of the numerous personal names that China's painters and writers adopted throughout their lives. A treasured work of art often bears not only the seal of its maker but also those of collectors and admirers through the centuries. In the Chinese view, these do not disfigure the work but add another layer of interest.

serdab (p. 53) In Egyptian tombs, the small room in which the *ka* statue was placed.

sfumato (p. 634) Italian term meaning "smoky," soft, and mellow. In painting, the effect of haze in an image. Resembling the color of the atmosphere at dusk, *sfumato* gives a smoky effect.

sgraffito (p. 602) Decoration made by **incising** or cutting away a surface layer of material to reveal a different color beneath.

shaft (p. 110) The main vertical section of a **column** between the **capital** and the **base**, usually circular in cross section.

shaft grave (p. 98) A deep pit used for burial.

shikhara (p. 301) In the architecture of northern India, a conical (or pyramidal) spire found atop a Hindu temple and often crowned with an **amalaka**.

shoin (p. 819) A term used to describe the various features found in the most formal room of upper-class Japanese residential architecture.

shoji (p. 819) A standing Japanese screen covered in translucent rice paper and used in interiors.

siapo (p. 874) A type of **tapa** cloth found in Samoa and still used as an important gift for ceremonial occasions.

silkscreen printing (p. 1091) A technique of printing in which paint or ink is pressed through a stencil and specially prepared cloth to produce a previously designed image. Also called serigraphy.

sinopia (sinopie) (p. 537) Italian word taken from "Sinope," the ancient city in Asia Minor that was famous for its red-brick pigment. In **fresco** paintings, a full-sized, preliminary sketch done in this color on the first rough coat of plaster or *arriccio*.

site-specific sculpture (p. 1102) A sculpture commissioned and/or designed for a particular location.

slip (p. 120) A mixture of clay and water applied to a ceramic object as a final decorative coat. Also: a solution that binds different parts of a vessel together, such as the handle and the main body.

spandrel (p. 172) The area of wall adjoining the exterior curve of an **arch** between its springing and the **keystone**, or the area between two arches, as in an **arcade**.

spolia (p. 465) Latin for "hide stripped from an animal." Term used for fragments of older architecture or sculpture reused in a secondary context.

springing (p. 172) The point at which the curve of an **arch** or **vault** meets with and rises from its support.

squinch (p. 236) An **arch** or **lintel** built across the upper corners of a square space, allowing a circular or polygonal dome to be more securely set above the walls.

stained glass (p. 464) Molten glass stained with color using metallic oxides. Stained glass is most often used in windows, for which small pieces of different colors are precisely cut and assembled into a design, held together by lead **cames**. Additional details may be added with vitreous paint.

stave church (p. 436) A Scandinavian wooden structure with four huge timbers (staves) at its core.

stele (stelae) (p. 27) A stone slab placed vertically and decorated with inscriptions or reliefs. Used as a grave marker or memorial.

stereobate (p. 110) A foundation upon which a Classical temple stands.

still life (p. xxxv) A type of painting that has as its subject inanimate objects (such as food, dishes, fruit, or flowers).

stoa (p. 107) In Greek architecture, a long roofed walk-way, usually having **columns** on one long side and a wall on the other.

stoneware (p. 22) A high-fired, vitrified, but opaque **ceramic** ware that is fired in the range of 1,100 to 1,200 degrees Celsius. At that temperature, particles of silica in the clay bodies fuse together so that the finished vessels are impervious to liquids, even without glaze. Stoneware pieces are glazed to enhance their aesthetic appeal and to aid in keeping them clean (since unglazed ceramics are easily soiled). Stoneware occurs in a range of earth-toned colors, from white and tan to gray and black, with light gray predominating. Chinese potters were the first in the world to produce stoneware, which they were able to make as early as the Shang dynasty.

stringcourse (p. 499) A continuous horizontal band, such as a **molding**, decorating the face of a wall.

studiolo (p. 617) A room for private conversation and the collection of fine books and art objects. Also known as a study.

stupa (p. 298) In Buddhist architecture, a bell-shaped or pyramidal religious monument, made of piled earth or stone, and containing sacred **relics**.

stylobate (p. 110) In Classical architecture, the stone foundation on which a temple **colonnade** stands.

stylus (p. 28) An instrument with a pointed end (used for writing and printmaking), which makes a delicate line or scratch. Also: a special writing tool for **cuneiform** writing with one pointed end and one triangular.

sublime (p. 955) djective describing a concept, thing, or state of greatness or vastness with high spiritual, moral, intellectual or emotional value; or something awe-inspiring. The sublime was a goal to which many nineteenth-century artists aspired in their artworks.

sunken relief (p. 71) See **relief sculpture**.

symposium (p. 118) An elite gathering of wealthy and powerful men in ancient Greece that focused principally on wine, music, poetry, conversation, games, and love making.

syncretism (p. 222) A process whereby artists assimilate images and ideas from other traditions or cultures and give them new meanings.

taotie (p. 328) A mask with a dragon or animal-like face common as a decorative motif in Chinese art.

tapa (p. 874) A type of cloth used for various purposes in Pacific cultures, made from tree bark stripped and beaten, and often bearing subtle designs from the mallets used to work the bark.

tapestry (p. 484) Multicolored pictorial or decorative weaving meant to be hung on a wall or placed on furniture. Pictorial or decorative motifs are woven directly into the fabric of the cloth itself.

tatami (p. 819) Mats of woven straw used in Japanese houses as a floor covering.

tempera (p. 141) A painting medium made by blending egg yolks with water, pigments, and occasionally other materials, such as glue.

tenebrism (p. 724) The use of strong **chiaroscuro** and artificially illuminated areas to create a dramatic contrast of light and dark in a painting.

terra cotta (p. 114) A medium made from clay fired over a low heat and sometimes left unglazed. Also: the orange-brown color typical of this medium.

tessera (tesserae) (p. 146) The small piece of stone, glass, or other object that is pieced together with many others to create a **mosaic**.

tetrarchy (p. 204) Four-man rule, as in the late Roman Empire, when four emperors shared power.

thatch (p. 17) Plant material such as reeds or straw tied over a framework of poles.

thermo-luminescence dating (p. 12) A technique that measures the irradiation of the crystal structure of material such as flint or pottery and the soil in which it is found, determined by luminescence produced when a sample is heated.

tholos (p. 138) A small, round building. Sometimes built underground, as in a Mycenaean tomb.

tholos tomb (p. 98) See **tholos**.

thrust (p. 172) The outward pressure caused by the weight of a **vault** and supported by **buttressing**. See **arch**.

tierceron (p. 554) In vault construction, a secondary rib that arcs from a **springing** point to the rib that runs lengthwise through the **vault**, called the ridge rib.

tondo (p. 128) A painting or **relief sculpture** of circular shape.

torana (p. 300) In Indian architecture, an ornamented gateway **arch** in a temple, usually leading to the **stupa**.

torc (p. 151) A circular neck ring worn by Celtic warriors.

toron (p. 417) In West African **mosque** architecture, the wooden beams that project from the walls. Torons are used as support for the scaffolding erected annually for the replastering of the building.

tracery (p. 502) Stonework or woodwork applied to wall surfaces or filling the open space of windows. In **plate tracery**, openings are cut through the wall. In **bar tracery**, **mullions** divide the space into vertical segments and form decorative patterns at the top of the opening or panel.

transept (p. 228) The arm of a **cruciform** church, perpendicular to the **nave**. The point where the nave and transept cross is called the crossing. Beyond the crossing lies the **sanctuary**, whether **apse**, choir, or chevet.

transverse arch (p. 457) An **arch** that connects the wall **piers** on both sides of an interior space, up and over a stone **vault**.

trefoil (p. 294) An ornamental design made up of three rounded lobes placed adjacent to one another.

triforium (p. 502) The element of the interior elevation of a church, found directly below the **clerestory** and consisting of a series of **arched** openings. The triforium can be made up of openings from a narrow wall passageway, or it can be attached directly to the wall.

triglyph (p. 110) Rectangular block between the **metopes** of a **Doric frieze**. Identified by the three carved vertical grooves, which approximate the appearance of the end of a wooden beam.

triptych (p. 564) An artwork made up of three panels. The panels may be hinged together so the side segments (wings) fold over the central area.

trompe l'oeil (p. 617) A manner of representation in which the appearance of natural space and objects is re-created with the express intention of fooling the eye of the viewer, who may be convinced that the subject actually exists as three-dimensional reality.

trumeau (p. 473) A **column**, **pier**, or post found at the center of a large **portal** or doorway, supporting the **lintel**.

tugra (p. 284) A **calligraphic** imperial monogram used in Ottoman courts.

tukutuku (p. 871) Lattice panels created by women from the Maori culture and used in architecture.

Tuscan order (p. 161) See **order**.

twining (p. 845) A basketry technique in which short rods are sewn together vertically. The panels are then joined together to form a vessel.

tympanum (p. 473)   In Classical architecture, the vertical panel of the **pediment**. In medieval and later architecture, the area over a door enclosed by an **arch** and a **lintel**, often decorated with sculpture or **mosaic**.

ukiyo-e (p. 994)   A Japanese term for a type of popular art that was favored from the sixteenth century, particularly in the form of color **woodblock prints**. *Ukiyo-e* prints often depicted the world of the common people in Japan, such as courtesans and actors, as well as landscapes and myths.

undercutting (p. 214)   A technique in sculpture by which the material is cut back under the edges so that the remaining form projects strongly forward, casting deep shadows.

underglaze (p. 799)   Color or decoration applied to a ceramic piece before glazing.

upeti (p. 874)   A carved wooden design tablet, used to create patterns in cloth by dragging the fabric across it, and found in Pacific cultures.

urna (p. 303)   In Buddhist art, the curl of hair on the forehead that is a characteristic mark of a buddha. The *urna* is a symbol of divine wisdom.

ushnisha (p. 303)   In Asian art, a round turban or tiara symbolizing royalty and, when worn by a buddha, enlightenment.

vanishing point (p. 608)   In a **perspective** system, the point on the **horizon line** at which orthogonals meet. A complex system can have multiple vanishing points.

vanitas (p. 751)   An image, especially popular in Europe during the seventeenth century, in which all the objects symbolize the transience of life. *Vanitas* paintings are usually of still lifes or genre subjects.

vault (p. 17)   An arched masonry structure that spans an interior space. **Barrel** or tunnel vault: an elongated or continuous semicircular vault, shaped like a half-cylinder.

Corbeled vault: a vault made by projecting **courses** of stone. **Groin** or cross vault: a vault created by the intersection of two barrel vaults of equal size which creates four side compartments of identical size and shape. Quadrant or half-barrel vault: as the name suggests a half-barrel vault. **Rib vault**: ribs (extra masonry) demarcate the junctions of a groin vault. Ribs may function to reinforce the groins or may be purely decorative. See also **corbeling**.

veduta (p. 913)   Italian for "vista" or "view." Paintings, drawings, or prints often of expansive city scenes or of harbors.

vellum (p. 243)   A fine animal skin prepared for writing and painting. See also **parchment**.

verism (p. 170)   style in which artists concern themselves with describing the exterior likeness of an object or person, usually by rendering its visible details in a finely executed, meticulous manner.

vihara (p. 301)   From the Sanskrit term meaning "for wanderers." A *vihara* is, in general, a Buddhist monastery in India. It also signifies monks' cells and gathering places in such a monastery.

volute (p. 110)   A spiral scroll, as seen on an **Ionic capital**.

votive figure (p. 31)   An image created as a devotional offering to a god or other deity.

voussoir (p. 172)   The oblong, wedge-shaped stone blocks used to build an arch. The topmost voussoir is called a **keystone**.

warp (p. 286)   The vertical threads in a weaver's loom. Warp threads make up a fixed framework that provides the structure for the entire piece of cloth, and are thus often thicker than weft threads. See also **weft**.

wattle and daub (p. 17)   A wall construction method combining upright branches, woven with twigs (wattles) and plastered or filled with clay or mud (daub).

weft (p. 286)   The horizontal threads in a woven piece of cloth. Weft threads are woven at right angles to and through the warp threads to make up the bulk of the decorative pattern. In carpets, the weft is often completely covered or formed by the rows of trimmed knots that form the carpet's soft surface. See also **warp**.

westwork (p. 439)   The monumental, west-facing entrance section of a Carolignian, Ottonian, or Romanesque church. The exterior consists of multiple stories between two towers; the interior includes an entrance vestibule, a chapel, and a series of **galleries** overlooking the nave.

white-ground (p. 141)   A type of ancient Greek pottery in which the background color of the object was painted with a **slip** that turns white in the firing process. Figures and details were added by painting on or **incising** into this slip. White-ground wares were popular in the Classical period as funerary objects.

woodblock print (p. 589)   A print made from one or more carved wooden blocks. In Japan, woodblock prints were made using multiple blocks carved in **relief**, usually with a block for each color in the finished print. See also **woodcut**.

woodcut (p. 590)   A type of print made by carving a design into a wooden block. The ink is applied to the block with a roller. As the ink remains only on the raised areas between the carved-away lines, these carved-away areas and lines provide the white areas of the print. Also: the process by which the woodcut is made.

yaksha, yakshi (p. 296)   The male (*yaksha*) and female (*yakshi*) nature spirits that act as agents of the Hindu gods. Their sculpted images are often found on Hindu temples and other sacred places, particularly at the entrances.

ziggurat (p. 28)   In Mesopotamia, a tall stepped tower of earthen materials, often supporting a shrine.

Susan V. Craig, updated by Carrie L. McDade

This bibliography is composed of books in English that are appropriate "further reading" titles. Most items on this list are available in good libraries, whether college, university, or public institutions. Recently published works have been emphasized so that the research information would be current. There are three classifications of listings: general surveys and art history reference tools, including journals and Internet directories; surveys of large periods that encompass multiple chapters (ancient art in the Western tradition, European medieval art, European Renaissance through eighteenth-century art, modern art in the West, Asian art, and African and Oceanic art, and art of the Americas); and books for individual Chapters 1 through 32.

General Art History Surveys and Reference Tools

Adams, Laurie Schneider. *Art across Time*. 4th ed. New York: McGraw-Hill, 2011.

Barnet, Sylvan. *A Short Guide to Writing about Art*. 10th ed. Upper Saddle River, NJ: Pearson/Prentice Hall, 2010.

Bony, Anne. *Design: History, Main Trends, Main Figures*. Edinburgh: Chambers, 2005.

Boström, Antonia. *Encyclopedia of Sculpture*. 3 vols. New York: Fitzroy Dearborn, 2004.

Broude, Norma, and Mary D. Garrard, eds. *Feminism and Art History: Questioning the Litany*. Icon Editions. New York: Harper & Row, 1982.

Chadwick, Whitney. *Women, Art, and Society*. 4th ed. New York: Thames & Hudson, 2007.

Chilvers, Ian, ed. *The Oxford Dictionary of Art*. 4th ed. New York: Oxford Univ. Press, 2009.

Curl, James Stevens. *A Dictionary of Architecture and Landscape Architecture*. 2nd ed. Oxford: Oxford Univ. Press, 2006.

Davies, Penelope J. E., et al. *Janson's History of Art: The Western Tradition*. 8th ed. Upper Saddle River, NJ: Prentice Hall, 2010.

The Dictionary of Art. Ed. Jane Turner. 34 vols. New York: Grove's Dictionaries, 1996.

Encyclopedia of World Art. 17 vols. New York: McGraw-Hill, 1959–84.

Frank, Patrick, Duane Preble, and Sarah Preble. *Prebles' Artforms*. 10th ed. Upper Saddle River, NJ: Pearson/Prentice Hall, 2008.

Gaze, Delia, ed. *Dictionary of Women Artists*. 2 vols. London: Fitzroy Dearborn, 1997.

Griffiths, Antony. *Prints and Printmaking: An Introduction to the History and Techniques*. 2nd ed. London: British Museum Press, 1996.

Hadden, Peggy. *The Quotable Artist*. New York: Allworth Press, 2002.

Hall, James. *Dictionary of Subjects and Symbols in Art*. 2nd ed. Boulder, CO: Westview Press, 2008.

Holt, Elizabeth Gilmore, ed. *A Documentary History of Art*. 3 vols. New Haven: Yale Univ. Press, 1986.

Honour, Hugh, and John Fleming. *The Visual Arts: A History*. 7th ed. rev. Upper Saddle River, NJ: Pearson/Prentice Hall, 2010.

Johnson, Paul. *Art: A New History*. New York: HarperCollins, 2003.

Kemp, Martin, ed. *The Oxford History of Western Art*. Oxford: Oxford Univ. Press, 2000.

Kleiner, Fred S. *Gardner's Art through the Ages*. Enhanced 13th ed. Belmont, CA: Thomson/Wadsworth, 2011.

Kostof, Spiro. *A History of Architecture: Settings and Rituals*. 2nd ed. Revised. Greg Castillo. New York: Oxford Univ. Press, 1995.

Mackenzie, Lynn. *Non-Western Art: A Brief Guide*. 2nd ed. Upper Saddle River, NJ: Pearson/Prentice Hall, 2001.

Marmor, Max, and Alex Ross, eds. *Guide to the Literature of Art History 2*. Chicago: American Library Association, 2005.

Onians, John, ed. *Atlas of World Art*. New York: Oxford Univ. Press, 2004.

Sayre, Henry M. *Writing about Art*. 6th ed. Upper Saddle River, NJ: Pearson/Prentice Hall, 2009.

Sed-Rajna, Gabrielle. *Jewish Art*. Trans. Sara Friedman and Mira Reich. New York: Abrams, 1997.

Slatkin, Wendy. *Women Artists in History: From Antiquity to the Present*. 4th ed. Upper Saddle River, NJ: Pearson/Prentice Hall, 2001.

Sutton, Ian. *Western Architecture: From Ancient Greece to the Present*. World of Art. New York: Thames & Hudson, 1999.

Trachtenberg, Marvin, and Isabelle Hyman. *Architecture, from Prehistory to Postmodernity*. 2nd ed. Upper Saddle River, NJ: Pearson/Prentice Hall, 2002.

Watkin, David. *A History of Western Architecture*. 4th ed. New York: Watson-Guptill, 2005.

Art History Journals: A Select List of Current Titles

African Arts. Quarterly. Los Angeles: Univ. of California at Los Angeles, James S. Coleman African Studies Center, 1967–.

American Art: The Journal of the Smithsonian American Art Museum. 3/year. Chicago: Univ. of Chicago Press, 1987–.

American Indian Art Magazine. Quarterly. Scottsdale, AZ: American Indian Art Inc., 1975–.

American Journal of Archaeology. Quarterly. Boston: Archaeological Institute of America, 1885–.

Antiquity: A Periodical of Archaeology. Quarterly. Cambridge: Antiquity Publications Ltd., 1927–.

Apollo: The International Magazine of the Arts. Monthly. London: Apollo Magazine Ltd., 1925–.

Architectural History. Annually. Farnham, UK: Society of Architectural Historians of Great Britain, 1958–.

Archives of American Art Journal. Quarterly. Washington, DC: Archives of American Art, Smithsonian Institution, 1960–.

Archives of Asian Art. Annually. New York: Asia Society, 1945–.

Ars Orientalis: The Arts of Asia, Southeast Asia, and Islam. Annually. Ann Arbor: Univ. of Michigan Dept. of Art History, 1954–.

Art Bulletin. Quarterly. New York: College Art Association, 1913–.

Art History: Journal of the Association of Art Historians. 5/year. Oxford: Blackwell Publishing Ltd., 1978–.

Art in America. Monthly. New York: Brant Publications Inc., 1913–.

Art Journal. Quarterly. New York: College Art Association, 1960–.

Art Nexus. Quarterly. Bogata, Colombia: Arte en Colombia Ltda, 1976–.

Art Papers Magazine. Bimonthly. Atlanta: Atlanta Art Papers Inc., 1976–.

Artforum International. 10/year. New York: Artforum International Magazine Inc., 1962–.

Artnews. 11/year. New York: Artnews LLC, 1902–.

Bulletin of the Metropolitan Museum of Art. Quarterly. New York: Metropolitan Museum of Art, 1905–.

Burlington Magazine. Monthly. London: Burlington Magazine Publications Ltd., 1903–.

Dumbarton Oaks Papers. Annually. Locust Valley, NY: J. J. Augustin Inc., 1940–.

Flash Art International. Bimonthly. Trevi, Italy: Giancarlo Politi Editore, 1980–.

Gesta. Semiannually. New York: International Center of Medieval Art, 1963–.

History of Photography. Quarterly. Abingdon, UK: Taylor & Francis Ltd., 1976–.

International Review of African American Art. Quarterly. Hampton, VA: International Review of African American Art, 1976–.

Journal of Design History. Quarterly. Oxford: Oxford Univ. Press, 1988–.

Journal of Egyptian Archaeology. Annually. London: Egypt Exploration Society, 1914–.

Journal of Hellenic Studies. Annually. London: Society for the Promotion of Hellenic Studies, 1880–.

Journal of Roman Archaeology. Annually. Portsmouth, RI: Journal of Roman Archaeology LLC, 1988–.

Journal of the Society of Architectural Historians. Quarterly. Chicago: Society of Architectural Historians, 1940–.

Journal of the Warburg and Courtauld Institutes. Annually. London: Warburg Institute, 1937–.

Leonardo: Art, Science and Technology. 6/year. Cambridge, MA: MIT Press, 1968–.

Marg. Quarterly. Mumbai, India: Scientific Publishers, 1946–.

Master Drawings. Quarterly. New York: Master Drawings Association, 1963–.

October. Cambridge, MA: MIT Press, 1976–.

Oxford Art Journal. 3/year. Oxford: Oxford Univ. Press, 1978–.

Parkett. 3/year. Zürich, Switzerland: Parkett Verlag AG, 1984–.

Print Quarterly. Quarterly. London: Print Quarterly Publications, 1984–.

Simiolus: Netherlands Quarterly for the History of Art. Quarterly. Apeldoorn, Netherlands: Stichting voor Nederlandse Kunsthistorische Publicaties, 1966–.

Woman's Art Journal. Semiannually. Philadelphia: Old City Publishing Inc., 1980–.

Internet Directories for Art History Information: A Selected List

ARCHITECTURE AND BUILDING,
http://www.library.unlv.edu/arch/rsrce/webresources/
A directory of architecture websites collected by Jeanne Brown at the Univ. of Nevada at Las Vegas. Topical lists include architecture, building and construction, design, history, housing, planning, preservation, and landscape architecture. Most entries include a brief annotation and the last date the link was accessed by the compiler.

ART HISTORY RESOURCES ON THE WEB,
http://witcombe.sbc.edu/ARTHLinks.html
Authored by Professor Christopher L. C. E. Witcombe of Sweet Briar College in Virginia, since 1995, the site includes an impressive number of links for various art historical eras as well as links to research resources, museums, and galleries. The content is frequently updated.

ART IN FLUX: A DIRECTORY OF RESOURCES FOR RESEARCH IN CONTEMPORARY ART,
http://www.boisestate.edu/art/artinflux/intro.html
Cheryl K. Shurtleff of Boise State Univ. in Idaho, has authored this directory, which includes sites selected according to their relevance to the study of national or international contemporary art and artists. The subsections include artists, museums, theory, reference, and links.

ARTCYCLOPEDIA: THE GUIDE TO GREAT ART ON THE INTERNET
http://www.artcyclopedia.com
With more than 2,100 art sites and 75,000 links, this is one of the most comprehensive web directories for artists and art topics. The primary search is by artist's name but access is also available by title of artwork, artistic movement, museums and galleries, nationality, period, and medium.

MOTHER OF ALL ART AND ART HISTORY LINKS PAGES
http://umich.edu/~motherha
Maintained by the Dept. of the History of Art at the Univ. of Michigan, this directory covers art history departments, art museums, fine arts schools and departments as well as links to research resources. Each entry includes annotations.

VOICE OF THE SHUTTLE,
http://vos.ucsb.edu
Sponsored by Univ. of California, Santa Barbara, this directory includes more than 70 pages of links to humanities and humanities-related resources on the Internet. The structured guide includes specific subsections on architecture, on art (modern and contemporary), and on art history. Links usually include a one-sentence explanation and the resource is frequently updated with new information.

ARTBABBLE
http://www.artbabble.org/
An online community created by staff at the Indianapolis Museum of Art to showcase art-based video content, including interviews with artists and curators, original documentaries, and art installation videos. Partners and contributors to the project include Art21, Los Angeles County Museum of Art, The Museum of Modern Art, The New York Public Library, San Francisco Museum of Modern Art, and Smithsonian American Art Museum.

YAHOO! ARTS>ART HISTORY,
http://dir.yahoo.com/Arts/Art_History/
Another extensive directory of art links organized into subdivisions with one of the most extensive being "Periods and

Movements." Links include the name of the site as well as a few words of explanation.

Ancient Art in the Western Tradition, General

Amiet, Pierre. *Art in the Ancient World: A Handbook of Styles and Forms*. New York: Rizzoli, 1981.

Beard, Mary, and John Henderson. *Classical Art: From Greece to Rome*. Oxford History of Art. Oxford: Oxford Univ. Press, 2001.

Boardman, John. *Oxford History of Classical Art*. New York: Oxford Univ. Press, 2001.

Chitham, Robert. *The Classical Orders of Architecture*. 2nd ed. Boston: Elsevier/Architectural Press, 2005.

Ehrich, Robert W., ed. *Chronologies in Old World Archaeology*. 3rd ed. 2 vols. Chicago: Univ. of Chicago Press, 1992.

Gerster, Georg. *The Past from Above: Aerial Photographs of Archaeological Sites*. Ed. Charlotte Trümpler. Trans. Stewart Spencer. Los Angeles: J. Paul Getty Museum, 2005.

Groenewegen-Frankfort, H. A., and Bernard Ashmole. *Art of the Ancient World: Painting, Pottery, Sculpture, Architecture from Egypt, Mesopotamia, Crete, Greece, and Rome*. Library of Art History. Upper Saddle River, NJ: Prentice Hall, 1972.

Haywood, John. *The Penguin Historical Atlas of Ancient Civilizations*. New York: Penguin, 2005.

Milleker, Elizabeth J., ed. *The Year One: Art of the Ancient World East and West*. New York: Metropolitan Museum of Art, 2000.

Nagle, D. Brendan. *The Ancient World: A Social and Cultural History*. 7th ed. Upper Saddle River, NJ: Pearson/Prentice Hall, 2010.

Saggs, H. W. F. *Civilization before Greece and Rome*. New Haven: Yale Univ. Press, 1989.

Smith, William Stevenson. *Interconnections in the Ancient Near East: A Study of the Relationships between the Arts of Egypt, the Aegean, and Western Asia*. New Haven: Yale Univ. Press, 1965.

Tadgell, Christopher. *Imperial Form: From Achaemenid Iran to Augustan Rome*. New York: Whitney Library of Design, 1998.

———. *Origins: Egypt, West Asia and the Aegean*. New York: Whitney Library of Design, 1998.

Trigger, Bruce G. *Understanding Early Civilizations: A Comparative Study*. New York: Cambridge Univ. Press, 2003.

Woodford, Susan. *The Art of Greece and Rome*. 2nd ed. New York: Cambridge Univ. Press, 2004.

European Medieval Art, General

Backman, Clifford R. *The Worlds of Medieval Europe*. 2nd ed. New York: Oxford Univ. Press, 2009.

Bennett, Adelaide Louise, et al. *Medieval Mastery: Book Illumination from Charlemagne to Charles the Bold: 800–1475*. Trans. Lee Preedy and Greta Arblaster-Holmer. Turnhout: Brepols, 2002.

Benton, Janetta R. *Art of the Middle Ages*. World of Art. New York: Thames & Hudson, 2002.

Binski, Paul. *Painters*. Medieval Craftsmen. London: British Museum Press, 1991.

Brown, Sarah, and David O'Connor. *Glass-painters*. Medieval Craftsmen. London: British Museum Press, 1991.

Calkins, Robert G. *Medieval Architecture in Western Europe: From a.d. 300 to 1500*. New York: Oxford Univ. Press, 1998.

Cherry, John F. *Goldsmiths*. Medieval Craftsmen. London: British Museum Press, 1992.

Clark, William W. *The Medieval Cathedrals*. Westport, CT: Greenwood Press, 2006.

Coldstream, Nicola. *Masons and Sculptors*. Medieval Craftsmen. London: British Museum Press, 1991.

———. *Medieval Architecture*. Oxford History of Art. Oxford: Oxford Univ. Press, 2002.

De Hamel, Christopher. *Scribes and Illuminators*. Medieval Craftsmen. London: British Museum Press, 1992.

Duby, Georges. *Art and Society in the Middle Ages*. Trans. Jean Birrell. Malden, MA: Blackwell, 2000.

Fossier, Robert, ed. *The Cambridge Illustrated History of the Middle Ages*. Trans. Janet Sondheimer and Sarah Hanbury Tenison. 3 vols. Cambridge: Cambridge Univ. Press, 1986–97.

Hürlimann, Martin, and Jean Bony. *French Cathedrals*. Rev. & enlarged ed. London: Thames & Hudson, 1967.

Jotischky, Andrew, and Caroline Susan Hull. *The Penguin Historical Atlas of the Medieval World*. New York: Penguin, 2005.

Kenyon, John. *Medieval Fortifications*. Leicester: Leicester Univ. Press, 1990.

Pfaffenbichler, Matthias. *Armourers*. Medieval Craftsmen. London: British Museum Press, 1992.

Rebold Benton, Janetta. *Art of the Middle Ages*. World of Art. New York: Thames & Hudson, 2002.

Rudolph, Conran, ed. *A Companion to Medieval Art*. Blackwell Companions to Art History. Oxford: Blackwell, 2006.

Sekules, Veronica. *Medieval Art*. Oxford History of Art. New York: Oxford Univ. Press, 2001.

Snyder, James, Henry Luttikhuizen, and Dorothy Verkerk. *Art of the Middle Ages*. 2nd ed. Upper Saddle River, NJ: Pearson/Prentice Hall, 2006.

Staniland, Kay. *Embroiderers*. Medieval Craftsmen. London: British Museum Press, 1991.

Stokstad, Marilyn. *Medieval Art*. 2nd ed. Boulder, CO: Westview Press, 2004.

———. *Medieval Castles*. Greenwood Guides to Historic Events of the Medieval World. Westport, CT: Greenwood Press, 2005.

European Renaissance through Eighteenth-Century Art, General

Black, C. F., et al. *Cultural Atlas of the Renaissance*. New York: Prentice Hall, 1993.

Blunt, Anthony. *Art and Architecture in France, 1500–1700*. 5th ed. Revised. Richard Beresford. Pelican History of Art. New Haven: Yale Univ. Press, 1999.

Brown, Jonathan. *Painting in Spain: 1500–1700*. Pelican History of Art. New Haven: Yale Univ. Press, 1998.

Cole, Bruce. *Studies in the History of Italian Art, 1250–1550*. London: Pindar Press, 1996.

Graham-Dixon, Andrew. *Renaissance*. Berkeley: Univ. of California Press, 1999.

Harbison, Craig. *The Mirror of the Artist: Northern Renaissance Art in Its Historical Context*. Perspectives. New York: Abrams, 1995.

Harris, Ann Sutherland. *Seventeenth-Century Art & Architecture*. 2nd ed. Upper Saddle River, NJ: Pearson/Prentice Hall, 2008.

Harrison, Charles, Paul Wood, and Jason Gaiger. *Art in Theory 1648–1815: An Anthology of Changing Ideas*. Oxford: Blackwell, 2000.

Hartt, Frederick, and David G. Wilkins. *History of Italian Renaissance Art: Painting, Sculpture, Architecture*. 7th ed. Upper Saddle River, NJ: Pearson/Prentice Hall, 2011.

Jestaz, Bertrand. *The Art of the Renaissance*. Trans. I. Mark Paris. New York: Abrams, 1994.

Minor, Vernon Hyde. *Baroque & Rococo: Art & Culture*. New York: Abrams, 1999.

Paoletti, John T., and Gary M. Radke. *Art in Renaissance Italy*. 3rd ed. Upper Saddle River, NJ: Pearson/Prentice Hall, 2005.

Smith, Jeffrey Chipps. *The Northern Renaissance*. Art & Ideas. London and New York: Phaidon Press, 2004.

Stechow, Wolfgang. *Northern Renaissance, 1400–1600: Sources and Documents*. Upper Saddle River, NJ: Pearson/Prentice Hall, 1966.

Summerson, John. *Architecture in Britain, 1530–1830*. 9th ed. Pelican History of Art. New Haven: Yale Univ. Press, 1993.

Waterhouse, Ellis K. *Painting in Britain, 1530 to 1790*. 5th ed. Pelican History of Art. New Haven: Yale Univ. Press, 1994.

Whinney, Margaret Dickens. *Sculpture in Britain: 1530–1830*. 2nd ed. Revised. John Physick. Pelican History of Art. London: Penguin, 1988.

Modern Art in the West, General

Arnason, H. H. *History of Modern Art: Painting, Sculpture, Architecture, Photography*. 6th ed. Upper Saddle River, NJ: Pearson/Prentice Hall, 2009.

Ballantyne, Andrew, ed. *Architectures: Modernism and After*. New Interventions in Art History, 3. Malden, MA: Blackwell, 2004.

Barnitz, Jacqueline. *Twentieth-Century Art of Latin America*. Austin: Univ. of Texas Press, 2001.

Bjelajac, David. *American Art: A Cultural History*. Rev. and expanded ed. Upper Saddle River, NJ: Pearson/Prentice Hall, 2005.

Bowness, Alan. *Modern European Art*. World of Art. New York: Thames & Hudson, 1995.

Brettell, Richard R. *Modern Art, 1851–1929: Capitalism and Representation*. Oxford History of Art. Oxford: Oxford Univ. Press, 1999.

Chipp, Herschel B. *Theories of Modern Art: A Source Book by Artists and Critics*. California Studies in the History of Art, 11. Berkeley: Univ. of California Press, 1984.

Clarke, Graham. *The Photograph*. Oxford History of Art. Oxford: Oxford Univ. Press, 1997.

Craven, David. *Art and Revolution in Latin America, 1910–1990*. New Haven: Yale Univ. Press, 2002.

Craven, Wayne. *American Art: History and Culture*. 2nd ed. Boston: McGraw-Hill, 2003.

Doordan, Dennis P. *Twentieth-Century Architecture*. New York: Abrams, 2002.

Doss, Erika. *Twentieth-Century American Art*. Oxford History of Art. Oxford: Oxford Univ. Press, 2002.

Edwards, Steve, and Paul Wood, eds. *Art of the Avant-Gardes*. Art of the 20th Century. New Haven: Yale Univ. Press, 2004.

Foster, Hal, et al. *Art Since 1900: Modernism, Antimodernism, Postmodernism*. New York: Thames & Hudson, 2004.

Gaiger, Jason, ed. *Frameworks for Modern Art*. Art of the 20th Century. New Haven: Yale Univ. Press, 2003.

———, and Paul Wood, eds. *Art of the Twentieth Century: A Reader*. New Haven: Yale Univ. Press, 2003

Hamilton, George Heard. *Painting and Sculpture in Europe, 1880–1940*. 6th ed. Pelican History of Art. New Haven: Yale Univ. Press, 1993.

Hammacher, A. M. *Modern Sculpture: Tradition and Innovation*. Enl. ed. New York: Abrams, 1988.

Harris, Ann Sutherland, and Linda Nochlin. *Women Artists: 1550–1950*. Los Angeles: Los Angeles County Museum of Art, 1976.

Harrison, Charles, and Paul Wood, eds. *Art in Theory: 1900–2000: An Anthology of Changing Ideas*. 2nd ed. Malden, MA: Blackwell, 2003.

Hunter, Sam, John Jacobus, and Daniel Wheeler. *Modern Art: Painting, Sculpture, Architecture, Photography*. 3rd rev. & exp. ed. Upper Saddle River, NJ: Pearson/Prentice Hall, 2004.

Krauss, Rosalind E. *Passages in Modern Sculpture*. Cambridge, MA: MIT Press, 1977.

Mancini, JoAnne Marie. *Pre-Modernism: Art-World Change and American Culture from the Civil War to the Armory Show*. Princeton: Princeton Univ. Press, 2005.

Marien, Mary Warner. *Photography: A Cultural History*. 3rd ed. Upper Saddle River, NJ: Pearson/Prentice Hall, 2011.

Meecham, Pam, and Julie Sheldon. *Modern Art: A Critical Introduction*. 2nd ed. New York: Routledge, 2005.

Newlands, Anne. *Canadian Art: From Its Beginnings to 2000*. Willowdale, Ont.: Firefly Books, 2000.

Phaidon Atlas of Contemporary World Architecture. London: Phaidon Press, 2004.

Powell, Richard J. *Black Art: A Cultural History*. 2nd ed. World of Art. New York: Thames & Hudson, 2003.

Rosenblum, Naomi. *A World History of Photography*. 4th ed. New York: Abbeville Press, 2007.

Ruhrberg, Karl. *Art of the 20th Century*. Ed. Ingo F. Walther. 2 vols. New York: Taschen, 1998.

Scully, Vincent Joseph. *Modern Architecture and Other Essays*. Princeton: Princeton Univ. Press, 2003.

Stiles, Kristine, and Peter Selz. *Theories and Documents of Contemporary Art: A Sourcebook of Artists' Writings*. California Studies in the History of Art, 35. Berkeley: Univ. of California Press, 1996.

Tafuri, Manfredo. *Modern Architecture*. History of World Architecture. 2 vols. New York: Electa/Rizzoli, 1986.

Traba, Marta. *Art of Latin America, 1900–1980*. Washington, DC: Inter-American Development Bank, 1994.

Upton, Dell. *Architecture in the United States*. Oxford History of Art. Oxford: Oxford Univ. Press, 1998.

Wood, Paul, ed. *Varieties of Modernism*. Art of the 20th Century. New Haven: Yale Univ. Press, 2004.

Woodham, Jonathan M. *Twentieth Century Design*. Oxford History of Art. Oxford: Oxford Univ. Press, 1997.

Asian Art, General

Addiss, Stephen, Gerald Groemer, and J. Thomas Rimer, eds. *Traditional Japanese Arts and Culture: An Illustrated Sourcebook*. Honolulu: Univ. of Hawai'i Press, 2006.

Barnhart, Richard M. *Three Thousand Years of Chinese Painting*. New Haven: Yale Univ. Press, 1997.

Blunden, Caroline, and Mark Elvin. *Cultural Atlas of China*. 2nd ed. New York: Checkmark Books, 1998.

Brown, Kerry, ed. *Sikh Art and Literature*. New York: Routledge in collaboration with the Sikh Foundation, 1999.

Chang, Léon Long-Yien, and Peter Miller. *Four Thousand Years of Chinese Calligraphy*. Chicago: Univ. of Chicago Press, 1990.

Chang, Yang-mo. *Arts of Korea*. Ed. Judith G. Smith. New York: Metropolitan Museum of Art, 1998.

Clark, John. *Modern Asian Art*. Honolulu: Univ. of Hawai'i Press, 1998.

Clunas, Craig. *Art in China*. 2nd ed. Oxford History of Art. Oxford: Oxford Univ. Press, 2009.

Coaldrake, William H. *Architecture and Authority in Japan*. London: Routledge, 1996.

Cohen, Warren I. *East Asian Art and American Culture: A Study in International Relations*. New York: Columbia Univ. Press, 1992.

Collcutt, Martin, Marius Jansen, and Isao Kumakura. *Cultural Atlas of Japan*. New York: Facts on File, 1988.

Craven, Roy C. *Indian Art: A Concise History*. Rev. ed. World of Art. New York: Thames & Hudson, 1997.

Dehejia, Vidya. *Indian Art. Art & Ideas*. London: Phaidon Press, 1997.

Fisher, Robert E. *Buddhist Art and Architecture*. World of Art. New York: Thames & Hudson, 1993.

Fu, Xinian. *Chinese Architecture*. Ed. & exp., Nancy S. Steinhardt. New Haven: Yale Univ. Press, 2002.

Hearn, Maxwell K., and Judith G. Smith, eds. *Arts of the Sung and Yüan: Papers Prepared for an International Symposium*. New York: Dept. of Asian Art, Metropolitan Museum of Art, 1996.

Heibonsha Survey of Japanese Art. 31 vols. New York: Weatherhill, 1972–80.

Hertz, Betti-Sue. *Past in Reverse: Contemporary Art of East Asia*. San Diego: San Diego Museum of Art, 2004.

Japanese Arts Library. 15 vols. New York: Kodansha International, 1977–87.

Kerlogue, Fiona. *Arts of Southeast Asia*. World of Art. New York: Thames & Hudson, 2004.

Khanna, Balraj, and George Michell. *Human and Divine: 2000 Years of Indian Sculpture*. London: Hayward Gallery, 2000.

Lee, Sherman E. *A History of Far Eastern Art*. 5th ed. Ed. Naomi Noble Richards. New York: Abrams, 1994.

———. *China, 5000 Years: Innovation and Transformation in the Arts*. New York: Solomon R. Guggenheim Museum, 1998.

Liu, Cary Y., and Dora C.Y. Ching, eds. *Arts of the Sung and Yüan: Ritual, Ethnicity, and Style in Painting*. Princeton: Art Museum, Princeton Univ., 1999.

McArthur, Meher. *The Arts of Asia: Materials, Techniques, Styles*. New York: Thames & Hudson, 2005.

———. *Reading Buddhist Art: An Illustrated Guide to Buddhist Signs and Symbols*. New York: Thames & Hudson, 2002.

Mason, Penelope. *History of Japanese Art*. 2nd ed. Upper Saddle River, NJ: Pearson/Prentice Hall, 2005.

Michell, George. *Hindu Art and Architecture*. World of Art. London: Thames & Hudson, 2000.

———. *The Penguin Guide to the Monuments of India*. 2 vols. New York: Viking, 1989.

Mitter, Partha. *Indian Art*. Oxford History of Art. Oxford: Oxford Univ. Press, 2001.

Murase, Miyeko. *Bridge of Dreams: The Mary Griggs Burke Collection of Japanese Art*. New York: Metropolitan Museum of Art, 2000.

Nickel, Lukas, ed. *Return of the Buddha: The Qingzhou Discoveries*. London: Royal Academy of Arts, 2002.

Pak, Youngsook, and Roderick Whitfield. *Buddhist Sculpture*. Handbook of Korean Art. London: Laurence King, 2003.

Sullivan, Michael. *The Arts of China*. 5th ed., rev. & exp. Berkeley: Univ. of California Press, 2008.

Thorp, Robert L., and Richard Ellis Vinograd. *Chinese Art & Culture*. New York: Abrams, 2001.

Topsfield, Andrew, ed. *In the Realm of Gods and Kings: Arts of India*. London: Philip Wilson, 2004.

Tucker, Jonathan. *The Silk Road: Art and History*. Chicago: Art Media Resources, 2003.

Tregear, Mary. *Chinese Art*. Rev. ed. World of Art. New York: Thames & Hudson, 1997.

Vainker S. J. *Chinese Pottery and Porcelain: From Prehistory to the Present*. New York: Braziller, 1991.

African and Oceanic Art and Art of the Americas, General

Anderson, Richard L., and Karen L. Field, eds. *Art in Small-Scale Societies: Contemporary Readings*. Upper Saddle River, NJ: Pearson/Prentice Hall, 1993.

Bacquart, Jean-Baptiste. *The Tribal Arts of Africa*. New York: Thames & Hudson, 1998.

Bassani, Ezio, ed. *Arts of Africa: 7000 Years of African Art*. Milan: Skira, 2005.

Benson, Elizabeth P. *Retratos: 2,000 Years of Latin American Portraits*. San Antonio, TX: San Antonio Museum of Art, 2004.

Berlo, Janet Catherine, and Lee Anne Wilson. *Arts of Africa, Oceania, and the Americas: Selected Readings*. Upper Saddle River, NJ: Prentice Hall, 1993.

Calloway, Colin G. *First Peoples: A Documentary Survey of American Indian History*. 3rd ed. Boston: Bedford/St. Martin's, 2008.

Coote, Jeremy, and Anthony Shelton, eds. *Anthropology, Art, and Aesthetics*. New York: Oxford Univ. Press, 1992.

Drewal, Henry, and John Pemberton III. *Yoruba: Nine Centuries of African Art and Thought*. New York: Center for African Art, 1989.

Evans, Susan Toby. *Ancient Mexico & Central America: Archaeology and Culture History*. 2nd ed. New York: Thames & Hudson, 2008.

———, and David L. Webster, eds. *Archaeology of Ancient Mexico and Central America: An Encyclopedia*. New York: Garland, 2001.

———, and Joanne Pillsbury, eds. *Palaces of the Ancient New World: A Symposium at Dumbarton Oaks, 10th and 11th October, 1998*. Washington, DC: Dumbarton Oaks Research Library and Collection, 2004.

Geoffroy-Schneiter, Bérénice. *Tribal Arts*. New York: Vendome Press, 2000.

Hiller, Susan, ed. & compiled. *The Myth of Primitivism: Perspectives on Art*. London: Routledge, 1991.

Mack, John, ed. *Africa, Arts and Cultures*. London: British Museum Press, 2000.

Mexico: Splendors of Thirty Centuries. New York: Metropolitan Museum of Art, 1990.

Nunley, John W., and Cara McCarty. *Masks: Faces of Culture*. New York: Abrams in assoc. with the Saint Louis Art Museum, 1999.

Perani, Judith, and Fred T. Smith. *The Visual Arts of Africa: Gender, Power, and Life Cycle Rituals*. Upper Saddle River, NJ: Pearson/Prentice Hall, 1998.

Phillips, Tom, ed. *Africa: The Art of a Continent*. New York: Prestel, 1995.

Price, Sally. *Primitive Art in Civilized Places*. 2nd ed. Chicago: Univ. of Chicago Press, 2001.

Rabineau, Phyllis. *Feather Arts: Beauty, Wealth, and Spirit from Five Continents*. Chicago: Field Museum of Natural History, 1979.

Schuster, Carl, and Edmund Carpenter. *Patterns that Connect: Social Symbolism in Ancient & Tribal Art*. New York: Abrams, 1996.

Scott, John F. *Latin American Art: Ancient to Modern*. Gainesville: Univ. Press of Florida, 1999.

Stepan, Peter. *Africa*. Trans. John Gabriel and Elizabeth Schwaiger. London: Prestel, 2001.

Visonà, Monica Blackmun, et al. *A History of Art in Africa*. 2nd ed. Upper Saddle River, NJ: Pearson/Prentice Hall, 2008.

Introduction

Acton, Mary. *Learning to Look at Paintings*. 2nd ed. New York: Routledge, 2009.

Arnold, Dana. *Art History: A Very Short Introduction*. Oxford and New York: Oxford Univ. Press, 2004.

Baxandall, Michael. *Patterns of Intention: On the Historical Explanation of Pictures*. New Haven: Yale Univ. Press, 1985.

Clearwater, Bonnie. *The Rothko Book*. London: Tate Publishing, 2006.

Decoteau, Pamela Hibbs. *Clara Peeters, 1594–ca.1640 and the Development of Still-Life Painting in Northern Europe*. Lingen: Luca Verlag, 1992.

Geertz, Clifford. "*Art as a Cultural System*." Modern Language Notes 91 (1976): 1473–1499.

Hochstrasser, Julie Berger. *Still Life and Trade in the Dutch Golden Age*. New Haven: Yale Univ. Press, 2007.

Holstein, Jonathan. *The Pieced Quilt: An American Design Tradition*. New York: Galahad Books, 1973.

Jolly, Penny Howell. "*Rogier van der Weyden's Escorial and Philadelphia Crucifixions and Their Relation to Fra Angelico at San Marco*." Oud Holland 95 (1981): 113–126.

Mainardi, Patricia. "*Quilts: The Great American Art*." The Feminist Art Journal 2/1 (1973): 1, 18–23.

Miller, Angela L., et al. *American Encounters: Art, History, and Cultural Identity*. Upper Saddle River, NJ: Pearson/Prentice Hall, 2008.

Minor, Vernon Hyde. *Art History's History*. Upper Saddle River, NJ: Pearson/Prentice Hall, 2001.

Nelson, Robert S., and Richard Shiff, eds. *Critical Terms for Art History*. 2nd ed. Chicago: Univ. of Chicago Press, 2003.

Panofsky, Erwin. *Studies in Iconology: Humanistic Themes in the Art of the Renaissance*. New York: Oxford Univ. Press, 1939.

———. *Meaning in the Visual Arts*. Phoenix ed. Chicago: Univ. of Chicago Press, 1982.

Preziosi, Donald, ed. *The Art of Art History: A Critical Anthology*. 2nd ed. Oxford and New York: Oxford Univ. Press, 2009.

Rothko, Mark. *Writings on Art*. Ed. Miguel López-Remiro. New Haven: Yale Univ. Press, 2006.

Rothko, Mark. *The Artist's Reality: Philosophies of Art*. Ed. Christopher Rothko. New Haven: Yale Univ. Press, 2004.

Schapiro, Meyer. "*The Apples of Cézanne: An Essay on the Meaning of Still Life*." Art News Annual 34 (1968): 34–53. Reprinted in Modern Art 19th & 20th Centuries: Selected Papers 2, London: Chatto & Windus, 1978.

Sowers, Robert. *Rethinking the Forms of Visual Expression*. Berkeley: Univ. of California Press, 1990.

Taylor, Joshua. *Learning to Look: A Handbook for the Visual Arts*. 2nd ed. Chicago: Chicago Univ. Press, 1981.

Tucker, Mark. "*Rogier van der Weyden's 'Philadelphia Crucifixion.'*" Burlington Magazine 139 (1997): 676–683.

Wang, Fangyu, et al, eds. *Master of the Lotus Garden: The Life and Art of Bada Shanren (1626–1705)*. New Haven: Yale Univ. Press, 1990.

Chapter 1 Prehistoric Art

Aujoulat, Norbert. *Lascaux: Movement, Space, and Time*. New York: Abrams, 2005.

Bahn Paul G. *The Cambridge Illustrated History of Prehistoric Art*. Cambridge Illustrated History. Cambridge: Cambridge Univ. Press, 1998.

Bataille, Georges. *The Cradle of Humanity: Prehistoric Art and Culture*. Ed. Stuart Kendall. Trans. Michelle Kendall and Stuart Kendall. New York: Zone Books, 2005.

Berghaus, Gunter. *New Perspectives on Prehistoric Art*. Westport, CT: Praeger, 2004.

Chippindale, Christopher. *Stonehenge Complete*. 3rd ed. New York: Thames & Hudson, 2004.

Clottes, Jean. *Chauvet Cave: The Art of Earliest Times*. Salt Lake City: Univ. of Utah Press, 2003.

———. *World Rock Art*. Trans. Guy Bennett. Los Angeles: Getty Conservation Institute, 2002.

———, and J. David Lewis-Williams. *The Shamans of Prehistory: Trance and Magic in the Painted Caves*. Trans. Sophie Hawkes. New York: Abrams, 1998.

Connah, Graham. *African Civilizations: An Archaeological Perspective*. 2nd ed. Cambridge: Cambridge Univ. Press, 2001.

Coulson, David, and Alec Campbell. *African Rock Art: Painting and Engravings on Stone*. New York: Abrams, 2001.

Cunliffe, Barry W, ed. *The Oxford Illustrated History of Prehistoric Europe*. New York: Oxford Univ. Press, 2001.

Forte, Maurizio, and Alberto Siliotti. *Virtual Archaeology: Re-Creating Ancient Worlds*. New York: Abrams, 1997.

Freeman, Leslie G. *Altamira Revisited and Other Essays on Early Art*. Chicago: Institute for Prehistoric Investigation, 1987.

Garlake, Peter S. *The Hunter's Vision: The Prehistoric Art of Zimbabwe*. Seattle: Univ. of Washington Press, 1995.

Gowlett, John A. J. *Ascent to Civilization: The Archaeology of Early Humans*. 2nd ed. New York: McGraw-Hill, 1993.

Guthrie, R. Dale. *The Nature of Paleolithic Art*. Chicago: Univ. of Chicago Press, 2005.

Jope, E. M. *Early Celtic art in the British Isles*. 2 vols. New York: Oxford Univ. Press, 2000.

Kenrick, Douglas M. *Jomon of Japan: The World's Oldest Pottery*. New York: Kegan Paul, 1995.

Leakey, Richard E., and Roger Lewin. *Origins Reconsidered: In Search of What Makes Us Human*. New York: Doubleday, 1992.

Le Quellec, Jean-Loïc. *Rock Art in Africa: Mythology and Legend*. Trans. Paul Bahn. Paris: Flammarion, 2004.

Leroi-Gourhan, André. *The Dawn of European Art: An Introduction to Paleolithic Cave Painting*. Trans. Sara Champion. Cambridge: Cambridge Univ. Press, 1982.

Lewis-Williams, J. David. *The Mind in the Cave: Consciousness and the Origins of Art*. New York: Thames & Hudson, 2002.

Megaw, Ruth, and Vincent Megaw. *Celtic Art: From Its Beginnings to the Book of Kells*. Rev. & expanded ed. New York: Thames & Hudson, 2001.

O'Kelly, Michael J. *Newgrange: Archaeology, Art, and Legend*. New Aspects of Antiquity. London: Thames & Hudson, 1982.

Price, T. Douglas. *Images of the Past*. 5th ed. Boston: McGraw-Hill, 2008.

Renfrew, Colin, ed. *The Megalithic Monuments of Western Europe*. London: Thames & Hudson, 1983.

Sandars, N. K. *Prehistoric Art in Europe*. 2nd ed. Pelican History of Art. New Haven: Yale Univ. Press, 1992.

Sura Ramos, Pedro A. *The Cave of Altamira*. Gen. Ed. Antonio Beltran. New York: Abrams, 1999.

Sieveking, Ann. *The Cave Artists*. Ancient People and Places, vol. 93. London: Thames & Hudson, 1979.

White, Randall. *Prehistoric Art: The Symbolic Journey of Mankind*. New York: Abrams, 2003.

Chapter 2 Art of the Ancient Near East

Akurgal, Ekrem. *Ancient Civilizations and Ruins of Turkey: From Prehistoric Times until the End of the Roman Empire*. 5th ed. London: Kegan Paul, 2002.

Aruz, Joan, et al, eds. *Beyond Babylon: Art, Trade, and Diplomacy in the Second Millennium B.C.* New Haven: Yale Univ. Press, and Metropolitan Museum of Art, 2008.

———, ed. *Art of the First Cities: The Third Millennium b.c. from the Mediterranean to the Indus*. New York: Metropolitan Museum of Art, 2003.

Bahrani, Zainab. *The Graven Image: Representation in Babylonia and Assyria*. Archaeology, Culture, and Society Series. Philadelphia: Univ. of Pennsylvania Press, 2003.

Boardman, John. *Persia and the West: An Archaeological Investigation of the Genesis of Achaemenid Art*. New York: Thames & Hudson, 2000.

Bottero, Jean. *Everyday Life in Ancient Mesopotamia*. Trans. Antonia Nevill. Baltimore, MD.: Johns Hopkins Univ. Press, 2001.

Charvat, Petr. *Mesopotamia before History*. Rev. & updated ed. New York: Routledge, 2002.

Crawford, Harriet. *Sumer and the Sumerians*. 2nd ed. New York: Cambridge Univ. Press, 2004.

Curtis, John, and Nigel Tallis, eds. *Forgotten Empire: The World of Ancient Persia*. Berkeley: Univ. of California Press, 2005.

Ferrier, R. W., ed. *The Arts of Persia*. New Haven: Yale Univ. Press, 1989.

Frankfort, Henri. *The Art and Architecture of the Ancient Orient*. 5th ed. Pelican History of Art. New Haven: Yale Univ. Press, 1996.

Haywood, John. *Ancient Civilizations of the Near East and Mediterranean*. London: Cassell, 1997.

Meyers, Eric M., ed. *The Oxford Encyclopedia of Archaeology in the Near East*. 5 vols. New York: Oxford Univ. Press, 1997.

Moorey, P. R. S. *Idols of the People: Miniature Images of Clay in the Ancient Near East*. The Schweich Lectures of the British Academy; 2001. New York: Oxford Univ. Press, 2003.

Polk, Milbry, and Angela M. H. Schuster. *The Looting of the Iraq Museum, Baghdad: The Lost Legacy of Ancient Mesopotamia*. New York: Abrams, 2005.

Reade, Julian. *Assyrian Sculpture*. Cambridge, MA: Harvard Univ. Press, 1999.

Roaf, Michael. *Cultural Atlas of Mesopotamia and the Ancient Near East*. New York: Facts on File, 1990.

Winter, Irene. *"Sex, Rhetoric, and the Public Monument: The Alluring Body of the Male Ruler."* In *Sexuality in Ancient Art*, edited by Natalie Kampen and Bettina A. Bergmann. Cambridge: Cambridge Univ. Press, 1996: 11–26.

Roux, Georges. *Ancient Iraq*. 3rd ed. London: Penguin, 1992.

Zettler, Richard L., and Lee Horne, ed. *Treasures from the Royal Tombs of Ur*. Philadelphia: Univ. of Pennsylvania, Museum of Archaeology and Anthropology, 1998.

Chapter 3 Art of Ancient Egypt

Arnold, Dieter. *Temples of the Last Pharaohs*. New York: Oxford Univ. Press, 1999.

Baines, John, and Jaromír Málek. *Cultural Atlas of Ancient Egypt*. Rev. ed. New York: Facts on File, 2000.

Brier, Bob. *Egyptian Mummies: Unraveling the Secrets of an Ancient Art*. New York: Morrow, 1994.

Egyptian Art in the Age of the Pyramids. New York: Metropolitan Museum of Art, 1999.

The Egyptian Book of the Dead: The Book of Going Forth by Day: Being the Papyrus of Ani (Royal Scribe of the Divine Offerings). 2nd rev. ed. Trans. Raymond O. Faulkner. San Francisco: Chronicle, 2008.

Freed, Rita E. Sue D'Auria, and Yvonne J. Markowitz. *Pharaohs of the Sun: Akhenaten, Nefertiti, Tutankhamen*. Boston: Museum of Fine Arts in assoc. with Bulfinch Press/Little, Brown, 1999.

Hawass, Zahi A. *Tutankhamun and the Golden Age of the Pharaohs*. Washington, DC: National Geographic, 2005.

Johnson, Paul. *The Civilization of Ancient Egypt*. Updated ed. New York: HarperCollins, 1999.

Kozloff, Arielle P. *Egypt's Dazzling Sun: Amenhotep III and His World*. Cleveland: Cleveland Museum of Art, 1992.

Lehner, Mark. *The Complete Pyramids*. New York: Thames & Hudson, 2008.

Love Songs of the New Kingdom. Trans. John L. Foster. New York: Scribner, 1974; Austin: Univ. of Texas Press, 1992.

Málek, Jaromir. *Egypt: 4,000 Years of Art*. London: Phaidon Press, 2003.

Pemberton, Delia. *Ancient Egypt*. Architectural Guides for Travelers. San Francisco: Chronicle, 1992.

Robins, Gay. *The Art of Ancient Egypt*. Rev. ed. Cambridge, MA: Harvard Univ. Press, 2008.

Roehrig, Catharine H., Renee Dreyfus, and Cathleen A. Keller. *Hatshepsut, from Queen to Pharaoh*. New York: Metropolitan Museum of Art, 2005.

Russmann, Edna R. *Egyptian Sculpture: Cairo and Luxor*. Austin: Univ. of Texas Press, 1989.

Smith, Craig B. *How the Great Pyramid Was Built*. Washington, DC: Smithsonian Books, 2004.

Smith, William Stevenson. *The Art and Architecture of Ancient Egypt*. 3rd ed. Revised. William Kelly Simpson. Pelican History of Art. New Haven: Yale Univ. Press, 1998.

Strouhal, Eugen. *Life of the Ancient Egyptians*. Trans. Deryck Viney. Norman: Univ. of Oklahoma Press, 1992.

Strudwick, Nigel, and Helen Studwick. *Thebes in Egypt: A Guide to the Tombs and Temples of Ancient Luxor*. Ithaca, NY: Cornell Univ. Press, 1999.

Thomas, Thelma K. *Late Antique Egyptian Funerary Sculpture: Images for this World and for the Next*. Princeton: Princeton Univ. Press, 2000.

Tiradritti, Francesco. *Ancient Egypt: Art, Architecture and History*. Trans. Phil Goddard. London: British Museum Press, 2002.

The Treasures of Ancient Egypt: From the Egyptian Museum in Cairo, New York: Rizzoli, 2003.

Wilkinson, Richard H. *The Complete Temples of Ancient Egypt*. New York: Thames & Hudson, 2000.

———. *Reading Egyptian Art: A Hieroglyphic Guide to Ancient Egyptian Painting and Sculpture*. London: Thames & Hudson, 1992.

Winstone, H.V. F. *Howard Carter and the Discovery of the Tomb of Tutankhamen*. Rev. ed. Manchester: Barzan, 2006.

Ziegler, Cristiane, ed. *The Pharaohs*. New York: Rizzoli, 2002.

Zivie-Coche, Christiane. *Sphinx: History of a Monument*. Trans. David Lorton. Ithaca, NY: Cornell Univ. Press, 2002.

Chapter 4 Art of the Ancient Aegean

Castleden, Rodney. *The Knossos Labyrinth: A New View of the "Palace of Minos" at Knossos*. London: Routledge, 1990.

———. *Mycenaeans*. New York: Routledge, 2005.

Demargne, Pierre. *The Birth of Greek Art*. Trans. Stuart Gilbert and James Emmons. Arts of Mankind, vol. 6. New York: Golden, 1964.

Doumas, Christos. *The Wall-Paintings of Thera*. 2nd ed. Trans. Alex Doumas. Athens: Kapon Editions, 1999.

Fitton, J. Lesley. *Cycladic Art*. 2nd ed. London: British Museum Press, 1999.

Getz-Gentle, Pat. *Personal Styles in Early Cycladic Sculpture*. Madison: Univ. of Wisconsin Press, 2001.

Hamilakis, Yannis. ed. *Labyrinth Revisited: Rethinking "Minoan" Archaeology*. Oxford: Oxbow, 2002.

Hendrix, Elizabeth. *"Painted Ladies of the Early Bronze Age,"* The Metropolitan Museum of Art Bulletin, New Series, 55/3 (Winter 1997–1998): 4–15.

Higgins, Reynold A. *Minoan and Mycenean Art*. New. ed. World of Art. New York: Thames & Hudson, 1997.

Hitchcock, Louise. *Minoan Architecture: A Contextual Analysis*. Studies in Mediterranean Archaeology and Literature, Pocket-Book, 155. Jonsered: P. Åströms Förlag, 2000.

Hoffman, Gail L. *"Painted Ladies: Early Cycladic II Mourning Figures?"* American Journal of Archaeology, 106/4 (October 2002): 525–550.

Immerwahr, Sara Anderson. *Aegean Painting in the Bronze Age*. University Park: Pennsylvania State Univ. Press, 1990.

Preziosi, Donald, and Louise Hitchcock. *Aegean Art and Architecture*. Oxford History of Art. Oxford: Oxford Univ. Press, 1999.

Shelmerdine, Cynthia W., ed. *The Cambridge Companion to the Aegean Bronze Age*. New York: Cambridge Univ. Press, 2008.

Chapter 5 Art of Ancient Greece

Barletta, Barbara A. *The Origins of the Greek Architectural Orders*. New York: Cambridge Univ. Press, 2001.

Beard, Mary. *The Parthenon*. Cambridge, MA: Harvard Univ. Press, 2003.

Belozerskaya, Marina, and Kenneth D.S. Lapatin. *Ancient Greece: Art, Architecture, and History*. Los Angeles: J. Paul Getty Museum, 2004.

Boardman, John. *Early Greek Vase Painting: 11th–6th Centuries b.c.: A Handbook*. World of Art. London: Thames & Hudson, 1998.

———. *Greek Sculpture: The Archaic Period: A Handbook*. World of Art. London: Thames & Hudson, 1991.

———. *Greek Sculpture: The Classical Period: A Handbook*. London: Thames & Hudson, 1985.

———. *Greek Sculpture: The Late Classical Period and Sculpture in Colonies and Overseas*. World of Art. New York: Thames & Hudson, 1995.

———. *The History of Greek Vases: Potters, Painters, and Pictures*. New York: Thames & Hudson, 2001.

Burn, Lucilla. *Hellenistic Art: From Alexander the Great to Augustus*. Los Angeles: J. Paul Getty Museum, 2004.

Clark, Andrew J., Maya Elston, Mary Louise Hart. *Understanding Greek Vases: A Guide to Terms, Styles, and Techniques*. Los Angeles: J. Paul Getty Museum, 2002.

De Grummond, Nancy T. and Brunilde S. Ridgway. *From Pergamon to Sperlonga: Sculpture in Context*. Berkeley: Univ. of California Press, 2000.

Donohue, A. A. *Greek Sculpture and the Problem of Description*. New York: Cambridge Univ. Press, 2005.

Fullerton, Mark D. *Greek Art*. Cambridge: Cambridge Univ. Press, 2000.

Hard, Robin. *The Routledge Handbook of Greek Mythology: Based on H.J. Rose's "Handbook of Greek Mythology."* 7th ed. London: Routledge, 2008.

Hurwit, Jeffrey M. *The Acropolis in the Age of Pericles*. New York: Cambridge Univ. Press, 2004.

Karakasi, Katerina. *Archaic Korai*. Los Angeles: J. Paul Getty Museum, 2003.

Lawrence, A. W. *Greek Architecture*. 5th ed. Revised. R. A. Tomlinson. Pelican History of Art. New Haven: Yale Univ. Press, 1996.

Martin, Roland. *Greek Architecture: Architecture of Crete, Greece, and the Greek World*. History of World Architecture. New York: Electa/Rizzoli, 1988.

Neils, Jenifer. *The British Museum Concise Introduction to Ancient Greece*. Ann Arbor: Univ. of Michigan, 2008.

Osborne, Robin. *Archaic and Classical Greek Art*. Oxford History of Art. Oxford: Oxford Univ. Press, 1998.

Palagia, Olga, ed. *Greek Sculpture: Function, Materials, and Techniques in the Archaic and Classical Periods*. New York: Cambridge Univ. Press, 2006.

———, and J. J. Pollitt, eds. *Personal Styles in Greek Sculpture*. Yale Classical Studies, vol. 30. Cambridge: Cambridge Univ. Press, 1996.

Pedley, John Griffiths. *Greek Art and Archaeology*. 4th ed. Upper Saddle River, NJ: Pearson/Prentice Hall, 2007.

Pollitt, J. J. *Art and Experience in Classical Greece*. Cambridge: Cambridge Univ. Press, 1972; reprinted 1999.

———. *The Art of Ancient Greece: Sources and Documents*. 2nd ed. rev. Cambridge: Cambridge Univ. Press, 2001.

Ridgway, Brunilde Sismondo. *The Archaic Style in Greek Sculpture*. 2nd ed. Chicago: Ares, 1993.

———. *Fifth Century Styles in Greek Sculpture*. Princeton: Princeton Univ. Press, 1981.

———. *Fourth Century Styles in Greek Sculpture*. Wisconsin Studies in Classics. Madison: Univ. of Wisconsin Press, 1997.

———. *Hellenistic Sculpture 1: The Styles of ca. 331–200 b.c.* Wisconsin Studies in Classics. Madison: Univ. of Wisconsin Press, 1990.

Stafford, Emma J. *Life, Myth, and Art in Ancient Greece*. Los Angeles: J. Paul Getty Museum, 2004.

Stewart, Andrew F. *Greek Sculpture: An Exploration*. 2 vols. New Haven: Yale Univ. Press, 1990.

Whitley, James. *The Archaeology of Ancient Greece*. New York: Cambridge Univ. Press, 2001.

Chapter 6 Etruscan and Roman Art

Bianchi Bandinelli, Ranuccio. *Rome: The Centre of Power: Roman Art to a.d. 200*. Trans. Peter Green. Arts of Mankind, 15. London: Thames & Hudson, 1971.

———. *Rome: The Late Empire: Roman Art a.d. 200–400*. Trans. Peter Green. Arts of Mankind, 17. New York: Braziller, 1971.

Borrelli, Federica. *The Etruscans: Art, Architecture, and History*. Ed. Stefano Peccatori and Stefano Zuffi. Trans. Thomas Michael Hartmann. Los Angeles: J. Paul Getty Museum, 2004.

Brendel, Otto J. *Prolegomena to the Study of Roman Art*. New Haven: Yale Univ. Press, 1979.

———. *Etruscan Art*. 2nd ed. Pelican History of Art. New Haven: Yale Univ. Press, 1995.

Conlin, Diane Atnally. *The Artists of the Ara Pacis: The Process of Hellenization in Roman Relief Sculpture*. Studies in the History of Greece & Rome. Chapel Hill: Univ. of North Carolina Press, 1997.

Cornell, Tim, and John Matthews. *Atlas of the Roman World*. New York: Facts on File, 1982.

D'Ambra, Eve. *Roman Art*. Cambridge: Cambridge Univ. Press, 1998.

Elsner, Jas. *Imperial Rome and Christian Triumph: The Art of the Roman Empire a.d. 100–450*. Oxford History of Art. Oxford: Oxford Univ. Press, 1998.

Gabucci, Ada. *Ancient Rome: Art, Architecture, and History*. Eds. Stefano Peccatori and Stephano Zuffi. Trans. T. M. Hartman. Los Angeles: J. Paul Getty Museum, 2002.

Haynes, Sybille. *Etruscan Civilization: A Cultural History*. Los Angeles: J. Paul Getty Museum, 2000.

Holloway, R. Ross. *Constantine & Rome*. New Haven: Yale Univ. Press, 2004.

Kleiner, Fred. S. *A History of Roman Art*. Belmont, CA: Thomson/Wadsworth, 2007.

MacDonald, William L. *The Architecture of the Roman Empire: An Introductory Study*. Rev. ed. 2 vols. Yale Publications in the History of Art, 17, 35. New Haven: Yale Univ. Press, 1982.

———. *The Pantheon: Design, Meaning, and Progeny*. New foreword. John Pinto. Cambridge, MA: Harvard Univ. Press, 2002.

Mattusch, Carol C. *Pompeii and the Roman Villa: Art and Culture around the Bay of Naples*. Washington, D.C. National Gallery of Art, 2008.

Mazzoleni, Donatella. *Domus: Wall Painting in the Roman House*. Los Angeles: J. Paul Getty Museum, 2004.

Packer, James E. *The Forum of Trajan in Rome: A Study of the Monuments in Brief*. Berkeley: Univ. of California Press, 2001.

Pollitt, J. J. *The Art of Rome, c. 753 b.c.–337 a.d.: Sources and Documents*. Upper Saddle River, NJ: Pearson/Prentice Hall, 1966.

Polybius. *The Histories*. Trans. W.R. Paton. 6 vols. Loeb Classical Library. Cambridge, MA: Harvard Univ. Press, 2000.

Ramage, Nancy H., and Andrew Ramage. *Roman Art: Romulus to Constantine*. 5th ed. Upper Saddle River, NJ: Pearson/Prentice Hall, 2009.

Spivey, Nigel. *Etruscan Art*. World of Art. New York: Thames & Hudson, 1997.

Stamper, John W. *The Architecture of Roman Temples: The Republic to the Middle Empire*. New York: Cambridge Univ. Press, 2005.

Stewart, Peter. *Statues in Roman Society: Representation and Response*. Oxford Studies in Ancient Culture and Representation. New York: Oxford Univ. Press, 2003.

Strong, Donald. *Roman Art*. 2nd ed. rev. & annotated. Ed. Roger Ling. Pelican History of Art. New Haven: Yale Univ. Press, 1995.

Ward-Perkins, J. B. *Roman Architecture*. History of World Architecture. New York: Electa/Rizzoli, 1988.

———. *Roman Imperial Architecture*. Pelican History of Art. New Haven: Yale Univ. Press, 1981.

Wilson Jones, Mark. *Principles of Roman Architecture*. New Haven: Yale Univ. Press, 2000.

Chapter 7 Jewish, Early Christian, and Byzantine Art

Age of Spirituality: Late Antique and Early Christian Art, Third to Seventh Century. New York: Metropolitan Museum of Art, 1979.

Beckwith, John. *Early Christian and Byzantine Art*. 2nd ed. Pelican History of Art. New Haven: Yale Univ. Press, 1979.

Bleiberg, Edward, ed. *Tree of Paradise: Jewish Mosaics from the Roman Empire*. Brooklyn:

Brooklyn Museum, 2005.

Cioffarelli, Ada. *Guide to the Catacombs of Rome and Its Surroundings*. Rome: Bonsignori, 2000.

Cormack, Robin, and Maria Vassilaki, eds. *Byzantium, 330–1453*. London: Royal Academy of Arts, 2008.

Cutler, Anthony. *The Hand of the Master: Craftsmanship, Ivory, and Society in Byzantium 9th–11th Centuries*. Princeton: Princeton Univ. Press, 1994.

Durand, Jannic. *Byzantine Art*. Paris: Terrail, 1999.

Eastmond, Antony, and Liz James, eds. *Icon and Word : The Power of Images in Byzantium: Studies Presented to Robin Cormack*. Burlington, VT: Ashgate, 2003.

Evans, Helen C., ed. *Byzantium: Faith and Power (1261–1557)*. New York: Metropolitan Museum of Art, 2004.

———, and William D. Wixom, eds. *The Glory of Byzantium: Art and Culture of the Middle Byzantine era, a.d. 843–1261*. New York: Abrams, 1997.

Fine, Steven. *Art and Judaism in the Greco-Roman World: Toward a New Jewish Archaeology*. New York: Cambridge Univ. Press, 2005.

Freely, John. *Byzantine Monuments of Istanbul*. Cambridge: New York: Cambridge Univ. Press, 2004.

Grabar, André. *Byzantine Painting: Historical and Critical Study*. Trans. Stuart Gilbert. New York: Rizzoli, 1979.

Hachlili, Rachel. *Ancient Mosaic Pavements: Themes, Issues, and Trends*. Leiden: Brill, 2009.

Jensen, Robin Margaret. *Understanding Early Christian Art*. New York: Routledge, 2000.

Kitzinger, Ernst. *The Art of Byzantium and the Medieval West: Selected Studies*. Ed. W. Eugene Kleinbauer. Bloomington: Indiana Univ. Press, 1976.

———. *Byzantine Art in the Making: Main Lines of Stylistic Development in Mediterranean Art, 3rd–7th Century*. Cambridge, MA: Harvard Univ. Press, 1977.

Kleinbauer, W. Eugene. *Hagia Sophia*. London: Scala, 2004.

Krautheimer, Richard, and Slobodan Curcic. *Early Christian and Byzantine Architecture*. 4th ed. Pelican History of Art. New Haven: Yale Univ. Press, 1992.

Levine, Lee I., and Zeev Weiss, eds. *From Dura to Sepphoris: Studies in Jewish Art and Society in Late Antiquity*. Journal of Roman Archaeology: Supplementary Series, no. 40. Portsmouth, R.I.: Journal of Roman Archaeology, 2000.

Lowden, John. *Early Christian and Byzantine Art*. Art & Ideas. London: Phaidon Press, 1997.

Maguire, Henry. *The Icons of Their Bodies: Saints and Their Images in Byzantium*. Princeton: Princeton Univ. Press, 1996.

Mainstone, Rowland J. *Hagia Sophia: Architecture, Structure and Liturgy of Justinian's Great Church*. 2nd ed. New York: Thames & Hudson, 2001.

Mango, Cyril. *Art of the Byzantine Empire, 312–1453: Sources and Documents*. Upper Saddle River, NJ: Pearson/Prentice Hall, 1972.

Mathew, Gervase. *Byzantine Aesthetics*. London: John Murray, 1963.

Mathews, Thomas F. *Byzantium: From Antiquity to the Renaissance*. Perspectives. New York: Abrams, 1998.

———. *The Clash of Gods: A Reinterpretation of Early Christian Art*. Rev. ed. Princeton: Princeton Univ. Press, 1999.

Olin, Margaret. *The Nation without Art: Examining Modern Discourses on Jewish Art*. Lincoln: Univ. of Nebraska Press, 2001.

Olsson, Birger, and Magnus Zetterholm, eds. *The Ancient Synagogue from Its Origins until 200 c.e.: Papers Presented at an International Conference at Lund University, October 14–17, 2001*. Coniectanea Biblica: New Testament Series, 39. Stockholm: Almqvist & Wiksell International, 2003.

Ousterhout, Robert. *Master Builders of Byzantium*. Princeton: Princeton Univ. Press, 1999.

Rodley, Lyn. *Byzantine Art and Architecture: An Introduction*. Cambridge: Cambridge Univ. Press, 1994.

Rutgers, Leonard V. *Subterranean Rome: In Search of the Roots of Christianity in the Catacombs of the Eternal City*. Leuven: Peeters, 2000.

Sed-Rajna, Gabrielle. *Jewish Art*. Trans. Sara Friedman and Mira Reich. New York: Abrams, 1997.

Spier, Jeffrey, ed. *Picturing the Bible: The Earliest Christian Art*. New Haven: Yale Univ. Press, 2007.

Tadgell, Christopher. *Imperial Space: Rome, Constantinople and the Early Church*. New York: Whitney Library of Design, 1998.

Vio, Ettore. *St. Mark's: The Art and Architecture of Church and State in Venice*. New York: Riverside Book, 2003.

Webb, Matilda. *The Churches and Catacombs of Early Christian Rome: A Comprehensive Guide*. Brighton, UK: Sussex Academic Press, 2001.

Weitzmann, Kurt. *Late Antique and Early Christian Book Illumination*. New York: Braziller, 1977.

———. *Place of Book Illumination in Byzantine Art*. Princeton: Art Museum, Princeton Univ., 1975.

Wharton, Annabel Jane. *Refiguring the Post-Classical City: Dura Europos, Jerash, Jerusalem and Ravenna*. Cambridge: Cambridge Univ. Press, 1995.

White, L. Michael. *The Social Origins of Christian Architecture*. 2 vols. Baltimore, MD: Johns Hopkins Univ. Press, 1990.

Chapter 8 Islamic Art

Al-Faruqi, Isma'il R., and Lois Ibsen Al Faruqi. *Cultural Atlas of Islam*. New York: Macmillan, 1986.

Atil, Esin. *The Age of Sultan Suleyman the Magnificent*. Washington, DC: National Gallery of Art, 1987.

Baker, Patricia L. *Islam and the Religious Arts*. London: Continuum, 2004.

Barry, Michael A. *Figurative Art in Medieval Islam and the Riddle of Bihzâd of Herât (1465–1535)*. Paris: Flammarion, 2004.

Blair, Sheila S., and Jonathan Bloom. *The Art and Architecture of Islam 1250–1800*. Pelican History of Art. New Haven: Yale Univ. Press, 1995.

Denny, Walter B. *Iznik: The Artistry of Ottoman Ceramics*. New York: Thames & Hudson, 2004.

Dodds, Jerrilynn D., ed. *Al-Andalus: The Art of Islamic Spain*. New York: Metropolitan Museum of Art, 1992.

Ecker, Heather. *Caliphs and Kings: The Art and Influence of Islamic Spain*. Washington, DC: Arthur M. Sackler Gallery, Smithsonian Institution, 2004.

Ettinghausen, Richard, Oleg Grabar, and Marilyn Jenkins-Madina. *Islamic Art and Architecture, 650–1250*. 2nd ed. Pelican History of Art. New Haven: Yale Univ. Press, 2001.

Frishman, Martin, and Hasan-Uddin Khan. *The Mosque: History, Architectural Development and Regional Diversity*. London: Thames & Hudson, 1994.

Grabar, Oleg. *The Formation of Islamic Art*. Rev. and enlarged. New Haven: Yale Univ. Press, 1987.

———. *The Great Mosque of Isfahan*. New York: New York Univ. Press, 1990.

———. *Islamic Visual Culture, 1100–1800*. Burlington, VT: Ashgate, 2006.

———. *Mostly Miniatures: An Introduction to Persian Painting*. Princeton: Princeton Univ. Press, 2000.

———, Mohammad Al-Asad, Abeer Audeh, and Said Nuseibeh. *The Shape of the Holy: Early Islamic Jerusalem*. Princeton: Princeton Univ. Press, 1996.

Hillenbrand, Robert. *Islamic Art and Architecture*. World of Art. London: Thames & Hudson, 1999.

Irwin, Robert. *The Alhambra*. Cambridge, MA: Harvard Univ. Press, 2004.

Khalili, Nasser D. *Visions of Splendour in Islamic Art and Culture*. London: Worth Press, 2008.

Komaroff, Linda, and Stefano Carboni, eds. *The Legacy of Genghis Khan: Courtly Art and Culture in Western Asia, 1256–1353*. New York: Metropolitan Museum of Art, 2002.

Lentz, Thomas W., and Glenn D. Lowry. *Timur and the Princely Vision: Persian Art and Culture in the Fifteenth Century*. Los Angeles: Los Angeles County Museum of Art, 1989.

Necipolu, Gülru. *The Age of Sinan: Architectural Culture in the Ottoman Empire*. Princeton: Princeton Univ. Press, 2005.

Petruccioli, Attilio, and Khalil K. Pirani, eds. *Understanding Islamic Architecture*. New York: Routledge Curzon, 2002.

Roxburgh, David J., ed. *Turks: A Journey of a Thousand Years, 600–1600*. London: Royal Academy of Arts, 2005.

Sims, Eleanor, B. I. Marshak, and Ernst J. Grube. *Peerless Images: Persian Painting and Its Sources*. New Haven: Yale Univ. Press, 2002.

Stanley, Tim, Mariam Rosser-Owen, and Stephen Vernoit. *Palace and Mosque: Islamic Art from the Middle East*. London: V&A Publications, 2004.

Stierlin, Henri. *Islamic Art and Architecture*. New York: Thames & Hudson, 2002.

Tadgell, Christopher. *Four Caliphates: The Formation and Development of the Islamic Tradition*. London: Ellipsis, 1998.

Ward, R. M. *Islamic Metalwork*. New York: Thames & Hudson, 1993.

Watson, Oliver. *Ceramics from Islamic Lands*. New York: Thames & Hudson in assoc. with the al-Sabah Collection, Dar al-Athar al-Islamiyyah, Kuwait National Museum, 2004.

Chapter 9 Art of South and Southeast Asia before 1200

Atherton, Cynthia Packert. *The Sculpture of Early Medieval Rajasthan*. Studies in Asian Art and Archaeology, vol. 21. New York: Brill, 1997.

Behl, Benoy K. *The Ajanta Caves: Artistic Wonder of Ancient Buddhist India*. New York: Abrams, 1998.

Behrendt, Kurt A. *The Buddhist Architecture of Gandhara*. Handbook of Oriental Studies: Section Two: India, vol. 17. Boston: Brill, 2004.

Chakrabarti, Dilip K. *India, an Archaeological History: Palaeolithic Beginnings to Early Historic Foundations*. 2nd ed. New York: Oxford Univ. Press, 2009.

Craven, Roy C. *Indian Art: A Concise History*. Rev. ed. World of Art. New York: Thames & Hudson, 1997.

Czuma, Stanislaw J. *Kushan Sculpture: Images from Early India*. Cleveland: Cleveland Museum of Art, 1985.

Dehejia, Vidya. *Art of the Imperial Cholas*. New York: Columbia Univ. Press, 1990.

———. *The Sensuous and the Sacred: Chola Bronzes from South India*. New York: American Federation of Arts, 2002.

Dessai, Vishakha N., and Darielle Mason, eds. *Gods, Guardians, and Lovers: Temple Sculptures from North India, a.d. 700–1200*. New York: Asia Society Galleries, 1993.

Dhavalikar, Madhukar Keshav. *Ellora*. New York: Oxford Univ. Press, 2003.

Girard-Geslan, Maud. *Art of Southeast Asia*. Trans. J. A. Underwood. New York: Abrams, Inc., 1998.

Heller, Amy. *Early Himalayan Art*. Oxford: Ashmolean Museum, 2008.

Huntington, Susan L. *The Art of Ancient India: Buddhist, Hindu, Jain*. New York: Weatherhill, 1985.

———. *Leaves from the Bodhi Tree: The Art of Pala India (8th–12th Centuries) and Its International Legacy*. Dayton, OH: Dayton Art Institute, 1990.

Hutt, Michael. *Nepal: A Guide to the Art and Architecture of the Kathmandu Valley*. Boston: Shambhala, 1995.

Knox, Robert. *Amaravati: Buddhist Sculpture from the Great Stupa*. London: British Museum Press, 1992.

Khanna, Sucharita. *Dancing Divinities in Indian Art: 8th–12th Century a.d.* Delhi: Sharada Pub. House, 1999.

Kramrisch, Stella. *The Art of Nepal*. New York: Abrams, 1964.

———. *The Presence of Siva*. Princeton: Princeton Univ. Press, 1981.

Meister, Michael, ed. *Encyclopedia of Indian Temple Architecture*. 2 vols. in 7. Philadelphia: Univ. of Pennsylvania Press, 1983.

Michell, George. *Elephanta*. Bombay: India Book House, 2002.

———. *Hindu Art and Architecture*. World of Art. London: Thames & Hudson, 2000.

Mitter, Partha. *Indian Art*. Oxford History of Art. Oxford: Oxford Univ. Press, 2001.

Neumayer, Erwin. *Lines on Stone: The Prehistoric Rock Art of India*. New Delhi: Manohar, 1993.

Pal, Pratapaditya, ed. *The Ideal Image: The Gupta Sculptural Tradition and Its Influence*. New York: Asia Society, 1978.

Poster, Amy G. *From Indian Earth: 4,000 Years of Terracotta Art*. Brooklyn, NY: Brooklyn Museum, 1986.

Skelton, Robert, and Mark Francis. *Arts of Bengal: The Heritage of Bangladesh and Eastern India*. London: Whitechapel Art Gallery, 1979.

Stierlin, Henri. *Hindu India: From Khajuraho to the Temple City of Madurai*. Taschen's World Architecture. New York: Taschen, 1998.

Tadgell, Christopher. *India and South-East Asia: The Buddhist and Hindu Tradition*. New York: Whitney Library of Design, 1998.

Williams, Joanna G. *Art of Gupta India, Empire and Province*. Princeton: Princeton Univ. Press, 1982.

Chapter 10 Chinese and Korean Art before 1279

Ciarla, Roberto, ed. *The Eternal Army: The Terracotta Soldiers of the First Chinese Emperor*. Vercelli: White Star, 2005.

Fong, Wen, ed. *Beyond Representation: Chinese Painting and Calligraphy, 8th–14th Century*. Princeton Monographs in Art and Archaeology, 48. New York: Metropolitan Museum of Art, 1992.

Fraser, Sarah Elizabeth. *Performing the Visual: The Practice of Buddhist Wall Painting in China and Central Asia, 618–960*. Stanford, CA: Stanford Univ. Press, 2004.

James, Jean M. *A Guide to the Tomb and Shrine Art of the Han Dynasty 206 b.c.–a.d. 220*. Chinese Studies, 2. Lewiston, NY: Mellen Press, 1996.

Karetzky, Patricia Eichenbaum. *Court Art of the Tang*. Lanham, MD: Univ. Press of America, 1996.

Kim, Kumja Paik. *Goryeo Dynasty: Korea's Age of Enlightenment, 918–1392*. San Francisco: Asian Art Museum—Chong-Moon Lee Center for Asian Art and Culture in cooperation with the National Museum of Korea and the Nara National Museum, 2003.

Li, Jian, ed. *The Glory of the Silk Road: Art from Ancient China*. Dayton, OH: Dayton Art Institute, 2003.

Little, Stephen, and Shawn Eichman. *Taoism and the Arts of China*. Chicago: Art Institute of Chicago, 2000.

Liu, Cary Y., Dora C.Y. Ching, and Judith G. Smith, eds. *Character & Context in Chinese Calligraphy*. Princeton: Art Museum, Princeton Univ., 1999.

Luo, Zhewen. *Ancient Pagodas in China*. Beijing, China: Foreign Languages Press, 1994.

Ma, Chengyuan. *Ancient Chinese Bronzes*. Ed. Hsio-Yen Shih. Hong Kong: Oxford Univ. Press, 1986.

Murck, Alfreda. *Poetry and Painting in Song China: The Subtle Art of Dissent*. Harvard-Yenching Institute Monograph Series. Cambridge, MA: Harvard Univ. Asia Center for the Harvard-Yenching Institute, 2000.

Ortiz, Valérie Malenfer. *Dreaming the Southern Song Landscape: The Power of Illusion in Chinese Painting*. Studies in Asian Art and Archaeology, vol. 22. Boston: Brill, 1999.

Paludan, Ann. *Chinese Tomb Figurines*. Hong Kong: Oxford Univ. Press, 1994.

Portal, Jane. *Korea: Art and Archaeology*. New York: Thames & Hudson, 2000.

Rawson, Jessica. *Mysteries of Ancient China: New Discoveries from the Early Dynasties*. London: British Museum Press, 1996.

Rhie, Marylin M. *Early Buddhist Art of China and Central Asia*. 2 vols in 3. Handbuch der Orientalistik. Vierte Abteilung; China, 12. Leiden: Brill, 1999.

Scarpari, Maurizio. *Splendours of Ancient China*. London: Thames & Hudson, 2000.

So, Jenny F. ed. *Noble Riders from Pines and Deserts: The Artistic Legacy of the Qidan*. Hong Kong: Art Museum, Chinese Univ. of Hong Kong, 2004.

Sturman, Peter Charles. *Mi Fu: Style and the Art of Calligraphy in Northern Song*. New Haven: Yale Univ. Press, 1997.

Wang, Eugene Y. *Shaping the Lotus Sutra: Buddhist Visual Culture in Medieval China*. Seattle: Univ. of Washington Press, 2005.

Watson, William. *The Arts of China to a.d. 900*. Pelican History of Art. New Haven: Yale Univ. Press, 1995.

———. *The Arts of China 900–1620*. Pelican History of Art. New Haven: Yale Univ. Press, 2000. Reissue ed. 2003.

Watt, James C.Y. *China: Dawn of a Golden Age, 200–750 a.d.*. New York: Metropolitan Museum of Art, 2004.

Whitfield, Susan, and Ursula Sims-Williams, eds. *The Silk Road: Trade, Travel, War and Faith*. Chicago: Serindia Publications, 2004.

Wu Hung. *Monumentality in Early Chinese Art and Architecture*. Stanford: Stanford Univ. Press, 1995.

Yang, Xiaoneng, ed. *The Golden Age of Chinese Archaeology: Celebrated Discoveries from the People's Republic of China*. Washington DC: National Gallery of Art, 1999.

Chapter 11 Japanese Art before 1333

Cunningham, Michael R. *Buddhist Treasures from Nara*. Cleveland: Cleveland Museum of Art, 1998.

Harris, Victor, ed. *Shinto: The Sacred Art of Ancient Japan*. London: British Museum Press, 2001.

Izutsu, Shinryu, and Shoryu Omori. *Sacred Treasures of Mount Koya: The Art of Japanese Shingon Buddhism*. Honolulu: Koyasan Reihokan Museum, 2002.

Kurata, Bunsaku. *Horyu-ji, Temple of the Exalted Law: Early Buddhist Art from Japan*. New York: Japan Society, 1981.

Levine, Gregory P. A., and Yukio Lippit. *Awakenings: Zen Figure Painting in Medieval Japan*. New York: Japan Society, 2007.

McCallum, Donald F. *The Four Great Temples: Buddhist Archaeology, Architecture, and Icons of Seventh-Century Japan*. Honolulu: Univ. of Hawai'i Press, 2009.

Mino, Yutaka. *The Great Eastern Temple: Treasures of Japanese Buddhist Art from Todai-ji*. Chicago: Art Institute of Chicago, 1986.

Mizoguchi, Koji. *An Archaeological History of Japan: 30,000 b.c. to a.d. 700*. Philadelphia: Univ. of Pennsylvania Press, 2002.

Murase, Miyeko. *The Tale of Genji: Legends and Paintings*. New York: Braziller, 2001.

Nishiwara, Kyotaro, and Emily J. Sano. *The Great Age of Japanese Buddhist Sculpture, a.d. 60–1300*. Fort Worth, TX: Kimbell Art Museum, 1982.

Pearson, Richard J. *Ancient Japan*. Washington, DC: Sackler Gallery, 1992.

Ten Grotenhuis, Elizabeth. *Japanese Mandalas: Representations of Sacred Geography*. Honolulu: Univ. of Hawai'i Press, 1999.

Washizuka, Hiromitsu, Park Youngbok, and Kang Woo-bang. *Transmitting the Forms of Divinity: Early Buddhist Art from Korea and Japan*. Ed. Naomi Noble Richard. New York: Japan Society, 2003.

Wong, Dorothy C., and Eric M. Field, eds. *Horyuji Reconsidered*. Newcastle: Cambridge Scholars, 2008.

Chapter 12 Art of the Americas before 1300

Benson, Elizabeth P., and Beatriz de la Fuente. *Olmec Art of Ancient Mexico*. Washington, DC: National Gallery of Art, 1996.

Berrin, Kathleen, ed. *Feathered Serpents and Flowering Trees: Reconstructing the Murals of Teotihuacan*. San Francisco: Fine Arts Museums of San Francisco, 1988.

Brody, J. J. *Anasazi and Pueblo Painting*. Albuquerque: Univ. of New Mexico Press, 1991.

———, Catherine J. Scott, and Steven A. LeBlanc. *Mimbres Pottery: Ancient Art of the American Southwest: Essays*. New York: Hudson Hills Press in assoc. with The American Federation of Arts, 1983.

Burger, Richard L. *Chavin and the Origins of Andean Civilization*. New York: Thames & Hudson, 1992.

Clark, John E., and Mary E. Pye, eds. *Olmec Art and Archaeology in Mesoamerica*. Studies in the History of Art, 58: Symposium Papers, 35. Washington, DC: National Gallery of Art, 2000.

Clayton, Lawrence A., Vernon J. Knight, and Edward Moore, eds. *The De Soto Chronicles: The Expedition of Hernando de Soto to North America, 1539–1543*. 2 vols. Tuscaloosa: Univ. of Alabama Press, 1993.

Coe, Michael D. and Rex Koontz. *Mexico: From the Olmecs to the Aztecs*. 5th ed. New York: Thames & Hudson, 2005.

———. *Breaking the Maya Code*. Rev. ed. New York: Thames & Hudson, 1999.

Donnan, Christopher. *Moche Portraits from Ancient Peru*. Austin: Univ. of Texas Press, 2003.

Fagan, Brian M. *Chaco Canyon: Archeologists Explore the Lives of an Ancient Society*. New York: Oxford Univ. Press, 2005.

Hall, Robert L. *An Archaeology of the Soul: North American Indian Belief and Ritual*. Urbana: Univ. of Illinois Press, 1997.

Heyden, Doris, and Paul Gendrop. *Pre-Columbian Architecture of Mesoamerica*. Trans. Judith Stanton. History of World Architecture. New York: Electa/Rizzoli, 1988.

Korp, Maureen. *The Sacred Geography of the American Mound Builders*. Native American Studies. Lewiston, NY: Mellen Press, 1990.

Kubler, George. *The Art and Architecture of Ancient America: The Mexican, Maya, and Andean Peoples*. 3rd ed. with updated bib. Pelican History of Art. New Haven: Yale Univ. Press, 1993.

Labbé, Armand J. *Shamans, Gods, and Mythic Beasts: Colombian Gold and Ceramics in Antiquity*. New York: American Federation of Arts, 1998.

Loendorf, Lawrence L., Christopher Chippindale, and David S. Whitley, eds. *Discovering North American Rock Art*. Tucson: Univ. of Arizona Press, 2005.

Martin, Simon, and Nikolai Grube. *Chronicle of the Maya Kings and Queens: Deciphering the Dynasties of the Ancient Maya*. 2nd ed. New York: Thames & Hudson, 2008.

Miller, Mary Ellen. *The Art of Mesoamerica: From Olmec to Aztec*. 4th ed. World of Art. London: Thames & Hudson, 2006.

———. *Maya Art and Architecture*. World of Art. London: Thames & Hudson, 1999.

———, and Simon Martin. *Courtly Art of the Ancient Maya*. San Francisco: Fine Arts Museums of San Francisco, 2004.

———, and Karl Taube. *The Gods and Symbols of Ancient Mexico and the Maya: An Illustrated Dictionary of Mesoamerican Religion*. London: Thames & Hudson, 1993.

Milner, George R. *The Moundbuilders: Ancient Peoples of Eastern North America*. Ancient Peoples and Places, 110. London: Thames & Hudson, 2004.

Noble, David Grant. *In Search of Chaco: New Approaches to an Archaeological Enigma*. Santa Fe, NM: School of American Research Press, 2004.

O'Connor, Mallory McCane. *Lost Cities of the Ancient Southeast*. Gainesville: Univ. Press of Florida, 1995.

Pasztory, Esther. *Teotihuacan: An Experiment in Living*. Norman: Univ. of Oklahoma Press, 1997.

Pillsbury, Joanne, ed. *Moche Art and Archaeology in Ancient Peru*. Studies in the History of Art: Center for Advanced Study in the Visual Arts, 63: Symposium Papers, 40. Washington, DC: National Gallery of Art, 2001.

Power, Susan C. *Early Art of the Southeastern Indians: Feathered Serpents & Winged Beings*. Athens: Univ. of Georgia Press, 2004.

Rohn, Arthur H., and William M. Ferguson. *Puebloan Ruins of the Southwest*. Albuquerque: Univ. of New Mexico Press, 2006.

Sharer, Robert J., and Loa P. Traxler. *The Ancient Maya*. 6th ed. Stanford, CA: Stanford Univ. Press, 2006.

Stierlin, Henri. *The Maya: Palaces and Pyramids of the Rainforest*. Köln: Taschen, 2001.

Stone-Miller, Rebecca. *Art of the Andes: From Chavin to Inca*. 2nd ed. World of Art. New York: Thames & Hudson, 2002.

———. *To Weave for the Sun: Ancient Andean Textiles*. New York: Thames & Hudson 1994.

Townsend, Richard F., and Robert V. Sharp, eds. *Hero, Hawk, and Open Hand: American Indian Art of the Ancient Midwest and South*. Chicago: Art Institute of Chicago, 2004.

Von Hagen, Adriana, and Craig Morris. *The Cities of the Ancient Andes*. New York: Thames and Hudson, 1998.

Chapter 13 Early African Art

Ben-Amos, Paula. *The Art of Benin*. Rev. ed. Washington, DC: Smithsonian Institution Press, 1995.

Berzock, Kathleen Bickford. *Benin: Royal Arts of a West African Kingdom*. Chicago: Art Institute of Chicago, 2008.

Blier, Suzanne Preston. *The Royal Arts of Africa: The Majesty of Form*. Perspectives. New York: Abrams, 1998.

Cole, Herbert M. *Igbo Arts: Community and Cosmos*. Los Angeles: Fowler Museum of Cultural History, Univ. of California, 1984.

Connah, Graham. *Forgotten Africa: An Introduction to Its Archaeology*. New York: Routledge, 2004.

Darish, Patricia J. "Memorial Head of an Oba: Ancestral Time in Benin Culture." In *Tempus Fugit, Time Flies*, edited by Jan Schall. Kansas City, MO: The Nelson Atkins Museum of Art, 2000: 290–297.

Eyo, Ekpo, and Frank Willett. *Treasures of Ancient Nigeria*. Ed. Rollyn O. Kirchbaum. New York: Knopf, 1980.

Garlake, Peter S. *Early Art and Architecture of Africa*. Oxford History of Art. Oxford: Oxford Univ. Press, 2002.

Grunne, Bernard de. *The Birth of Art in Africa: Nok Statuary in Nigeria*. Paris: A. Biro, 1998.

Huffman, Thomas N. *Symbols in Stone: Unravelling the Mystery of Great Zimbabwe*. Johannesburg: Witwatersrand Univ. Press, 1987.

LaViolette, Adria Jean. *Ethno-Achaeology in Jenné, Mali: Craft and Status among Smiths, Potters, and Masons*. Oxford: Archaeopress, 2000.

M'Bow, Babacar, and Osemwegie Ebohon. *Benin, a Kingdom in Bronze: The Royal Court Art*. Ft. Lauderdale, FL: African American Research Library and Cultural Center, Broward County Library, 2005.

Phillipson, D. W. *African Archaeology*. 3rd ed. Cambridge World Archaeology. New York: Cambridge Univ. Press, 2005.

Schädler, Karl-Ferdinand. *Earth and Ore: 2500 Years of African Art in Terra-Cotta and Metal*. Trans. Geoffrey P. Burwell. München: Panterra, 1997.

Chapter 14 Early Medieval Art in Europe

Alexander, J. J. G. *Medieval Illuminators and Their Methods of Work*. New ed. New Haven: Yale Univ. Press, 1994.

The Art of Medieval Spain, a.d. 500–1200. New York: Metropolitan Museum of Art, 1993.

Backhouse, Janet, D. H. Turner, and Leslie Webster, eds. *The Golden Age of Anglo-Saxon Art, 966–1066*. Bloomington: Indiana Univ. Press, 1984.

Bandmann, Günter. *Early Medieval Architecture as Bearer of Meaning*. New York: Columbia Univ. Press, 2005.

Brown, Michelle P. *The Lindisfarne Gospels: Society, Spirituality and the Scribe*. Toronto: Univ. of Toronto Press, 2003.

Calkins, Robert G. *Illuminated Books of the Middle Ages*. Ithaca, NY: Cornell Univ. Press, 1983.

Carver, Martin. *Sutton Hoo: A Seventh-Century Princely Burial Ground and Its Context*. London: British Museum Press, 2005.

Davis-Weyer, Caecilia. *Early Medieval Art, 300–1150: Sources and Documents*. Upper Saddle River, NJ: Pearson/Prentice Hall, l971.

Diebold, William J. *Word and Image: An Introduction to Early Medieval Art*. Boulder, CO: Westview Press, 2000.

Dodwell, C. R. *Pictorial Arts of the West, 800–1200*. Pelican History of Art. New Haven: Yale Univ. Press, 1993.

Farr, Carol. *The Book of Kells: Its Function and Audience*. London: British Library, 1997.

Fitzhugh, William W., and Elisabeth I. Ward, eds. *Vikings: The North Atlantic Saga*. Washington, DC: Smithsonian Institution Press, 2000.

Harbison, Peter. *The Golden Age of Irish Art: The Medieval Achievement, 600–1200*. London: Thames & Hudson, 1999.

Henderson, George. *From Durrow to Kells: The Insular Gospel-Books, 650–800*. London: Thames & Hudson, 1987.

Horn, Walter W., and Ernest Born. *Plan of Saint Gall: A Study of the Architecture and Economy of and Life in a Paradigmatic Carolingian Monastery*. California Studies in the History of Art, 19. 3 vols. Berkeley: Univ. of California Press, 1979.

Lasko, Peter. *Ars Sacra, 800–1200*. 2nd ed. Pelican History of Art. New Haven: Yale Univ. Press, 1994.

McClendon, Charles B. *The Origins of Medieval Architecture: Building in Europe, a.d 600–900*. New Haven: Yale Univ. Press, 2005.

Mayr-Harting, Henry. *Ottonian Book Illumination: An Historical Study*. 2nd rev. ed. 2 vols. London: Harvey Miller, 1999.

Mentré, Mireille. *Illuminated Manuscripts of Medieval Spain*. New York: Thames & Hudson, 1996.

Nees, Lawrence. *Early Medieval Art*. Oxford History of Art. Oxford: Oxford Univ. Press, 2002.

Richardson, Hilary, and John Scarry. *An Introduction to Irish High Crosses*. Dublin: Mercier, 1990.

Schapiro, Meyer. *Language of Forms: Lectures on Insular Manuscript Art*. Ed. Jane Rosenthal. New York: Pierpont Morgan Library, 2006.

Stalley, R. A. *Early Medieval Architecture*. Oxford History of Art. Oxford: Oxford Univ. Press, 1999.

Wickham, Chris. *Framing the Early Middle Ages: Europe and the Mediterranean 400–800*. New York: Oxford Univ. Press, 2005.

Williams, John. *Early Spanish Manuscript Illumination*. New York: Braziller, 1977.

Wilson, David M. *Anglo-Saxon Art: From the Seventh Century to the Norman Conquest*. London: Thames & Hudson, 1984.

———, and Ole Klindt-Jensen. *Viking Art*. 2nd ed. Minneapolis: Univ. of Minnesota Press, 1980.

Chapter 15 Romanesque Art

Barral i Altet, Xavier. *The Romanesque: Towns, Cathedrals and Monasteries*. Taschen's World Architecture. New York: Taschen, 1998.

Bernard of Clairvaux. "*Apologia to Abbot William.*" In *Treatises I*. The Work of Bernard of Clairvaux, 1: Cistercian Fathers Series, 1. Shannon, Ireland: Irish Univ. Press, 1970: 33–69.

The Book of Sainte Foy. Ed. and trans. Pamela Sheingorn. Philadelphia: Univ. of Pennsylvania Press, 1995.

Cahn, Walter. *Romanesque Manuscripts: The Twelfth Century*. 2nd ed. 2 vols. A Survey of Manuscripts Illuminated in France. London: Harvey Miller, 1996.

Caviness, Madeline H. "*Hildegard as Designer of the Illustrations to her Works.*" In *Hildegard of Bingen: The Context of her Thought and Art*, edited by Charles Burnett and Peter Dronke. London: Warburg Institute, 1998: 29–63.

Davis-Weyer, Caecilia. *Early Medieval Art, 300–1150. Sources and Documents*. Upper Saddle River, NJ: Pearson/Prentice Hall, 1971.

Dimier, Anselme. *Stones Laid before the Lord: A History of Monastic Architecture*. Trans. Gilchrist Lavigne. Cistercian Studies Series, no. 152. Kalamazoo, MI: Cistercian Publications, 1999.

Fergusson, Peter. *Architecture of Solitude: Cistercian Abbeys in Twelfth-Century England*. Princeton: Princeton Univ. Press, 1984.

Forsyth, Ilene H. *The Throne of Wisdom: Wood Sculptures of the Madonna in Romanesque France*. Princeton: Princeton Univ. Press, 1972.

Gaud, Henri, and Jean-François Leroux-Dhuys. *Cistercian Abbeys: History and Architecture*. Köln: Könemann, 1998.

Gerson, Paula, ed. *The Pilgrim's Guide to Santiago de Compostela: A Critical Edition*. 2 vols. London: Harvey Miller, 1998.

Grivot, Denis, and George Zarnecki. *Gislebertus: Sculptor of Autun*. New York: Orion Press, 1961.

Hearn, M. F. *Romanesque Sculpture: The Revival of Monumental Stone Sculptures in the Eleventh and Twelfth Centuries*. Ithaca, NY: Cornell Univ. Press, 1981.

Hicks, Carola. *The Bayeux Tapestry: The Life Story of a Masterpiece*. London: Chatto & Windus, 2006.

Hourihane, Colum, ed. *Romanesque Art and Thought in the Twelfth Century: Essays in Honor of Walter Cahn*. The Index of Christian Art Occasional Papers 10. University Park, PA: Penn State Press, 2008.

Kubach, Hans E. *Romanesque Architecture*. History of World Architecture. New York: Electa/Rizzoli, 1988.

Minne-Sève, Viviane, and Hervé Kergall. *Romanesque and Gothic France: Architecture and Sculpture*. Trans. Jack Hawkes and Lory Frankel. New York: Abrams, 2000.

Newman, Barbara. *Sister of Wisdom: St. Hildegard's Theology of the Feminine*. 2nd ed. Berkeley: Univ. of California Press, 1997.

Schapiro, Meyer. *Romanesque Art: Selected Papers*. New York: George Braziller, 1977.

——. *The Romanesque Sculpture of Moissac*. New York: Braziller, 1985.

——. *Romanesque Architectural Sculpture: The Charles Eliot Norton Lectures*. Ed. Linda Seidel. Chicago: Univ. of Chicago Press, 2006.

Seidel, Linda. *Legends in Limestone: Lazarus, Gislebertus, and the Cathedral of Autun*. Chicago: Univ. of Chicago Press, 1999.

Sundell, Michael G. *Mosaics in the Eternal City*. Tempe: Arizona Center for Medieval and Renaissance Studies, 2007.

Swanson, R. N. *The Twelfth-Century Renaissance*. Manchester: Manchester Univ. Press, 1999.

Theophilus. *On Divers Arts: The Foremost Medieval Treatise on Painting, Glassmaking, and Metalwork*. Trans. John G. Hawthorne and Cyril Stanley Smith. New York: Dover, 1979.

Toman, Rolf, ed. *Romanesque: Architecture, Sculpture, Painting*. Trans. Fiona Hulse and Ian Macmillan. Köln: Könemann, 1997.

Wilson, David M. *The Bayeux Tapestry: The Complete Tapestry in Color*. London: Thames & Hudson and New York: Knopf, 2004.

Zarnecki, George, Janet Holt, and Tristam Holland, eds. *English Romanesque Art, 1066–1200*. London: Weidenfeld and Nicolson, 1984.

Chapter 16 Gothic Art of the Twelfth and Thirteenth Centuries

Barnes, Carl F. *The Portfolio of Villard de Honnecourt: A New Critical Edition and Color Facsimile*. Burlington, VT: Ashgate, 2009.

Binding, Günther. *High Gothic: The Age of the Great Cathedrals*. Taschen's World Architecture. London: Taschen, 1999.

Binski, Paul. *Becket's Crown: Art and Imagination in Gothic England, 1170–1300*. New Haven: Yale Univ. Press, 2004.

Bony, Jean. *French Gothic Architecture of the 12th and 13th Centuries*. California Studies in the History of Art, 20. Berkeley: Univ. of California Press, 1983.

Camille, Michael. *Gothic Art: Glorious Visions*. Perspectives. New York: Abrams, 1996.

Cennini, Cennino. *The Craftsman's Handbook "Il libro dell'arte"*. Trans. D.V. Thompson, Jr. New York: Dover, 1960.

Coldstream, Nicola. *Masons and Sculptors*. Toronto and Buffalo, NY: Univ. of Toronto Press, 1991.

Crosby, Sumner M. *The Royal Abbey of Saint-Denis from Its Beginnings to the Death of Suger, 475–1151*. Yale Publications in the History of Art, 37. New Haven: Yale Univ. Press, 1987.

Erlande-Brandenburg, Alain. *Gothic Art*. Trans. I. Mark Paris. New York: Abrams, 1989.

Favier, Jean. *The World of Chartres*. Trans. Francisca Garvie. New York: Abrams, 1990.

Frankl, Paul. *Gothic Architecture*. Revised. Paul Crossley. Pelican History of Art. New Haven: Yale Univ. Press, 2000.

Frisch, Teresa G. *Gothic Art, 1140–c.1450: Sources and Documents*. Upper Saddle River, NJ: Pearson/Prentice Hall, 1971.

Grodecki, Louis, and Catherine Brisac. *Gothic Stained Glass, 1200–1300*. Ithaca, NY: Cornell Univ. Press, 1985.

Jordan, Alyce A. *Visualizing Kingship in the Windows of the Sainte-Chapelle*. Turnhout: Brepols, 2002.

Moskowitz, Anita Fiderer. *Nicola & Giovanni Pisano: The Pulpits: Pious Devotion, Pious Diversion*. London: Harvey Miller, 2005.

Nussbaum, Norbert. *German Gothic Church Architecture*. Trans. Scott Kleager. New Haven: Yale Univ. Press, 2000.

Panofsky, Erwin. *Abbot Suger on the Abbey Church of St.-Denis and Its Art Treasures*. 2nd ed. Ed. Gerda Panofsky-Soergel. Princeton: Princeton Univ. Press, 1979.

Parry, Stan. *Great Gothic Cathedrals of France*. New York: Viking Studio, 2001.

Sauerländer, Willibald. *Gothic Sculpture in France, 1140–1270*. Trans. Janet Sandheimer. London: Thames & Hudson, 1972.

Scott, Robert A. *The Gothic Enterprise: A Guide to Understanding the Medieval Cathedral*. Berkeley: Univ. of California Press, 2003.

Simsom, Otto Georg von. *The Gothic Cathedral: Origins of Gothic Architecture and the Medieval Concept of Order*. 3rd ed. exp. Bollingen Series. Princeton: Princeton Univ. Press, 1988.

Suckale, Robert, and Matthias Weniger. *Painting of the Gothic Era*. Ed. Ingo F. Walther. New York: Taschen, 1999.

Wieck, Roger S. *Time Sanctified: The Book of Hours in Medieval Art and Life*. 2nd ed. New York: Braziller, 2001.

Williamson, Paul. *Gothic Sculpture, 1140–1300*. Pelican History of Art. New Haven: Yale Univ. Press, 1995.

Chapter 17 Fourteenth-Century Art in Europe

Alexander, Jonathan, and Paul Binski, eds. *Age of Chivalry: Art in Plantagenet England, 1200–1400*. London: Royal Academy of Arts, 1987.

Backhouse, Janet. *Illumination from Books of Hours*. London: British Library, 2004.

Boehm, Barbara Drake, and Jiří Fajt, eds. *Prague: The Crown of Bohemia, 1347–1437*. New York: Metropolitan Museum of Art, 2005.

Bony, Jean. *The English Decorated Style: Gothic Architecture Transformed, 1250–1350*. The Wrightsman Lectures 10th. Oxford: Phaidon Press, 1979.

Borsook, Eve. *The Mural Painters of Tuscany: From Cimabue to Andrea del Sarto*. 2nd ed. rev. & enlarged. Oxford Studies in the History of Art and Architecture. Oxford: Clarendon Press 1980.

Derbes, Anne, and Mark Sandona, eds. *The Cambridge Companion to Giotto*. Cambridge and New York: Cambridge Univ. Press, 2003.

Fajt, Jiří, ed. *Magister Theodoricus, Court Painter to Emperor Charles IV: The Pictorial Decoration of the Shrines at Karlstejn Castle*. Prague: National Gallery, 1998.

Holt, Elizabeth Gilmore, ed. *A Documentary History of Art*. 2 vols. Princeton, Princeton Univ. Press, 1982–86.

Ladis, Andrew. ed, *The Arena Chapel and the Genius of Giotto: Padua*. Giotto and the World of Early Italian Art, 2. New York: Garland, 1998.

Meiss, Millard. *Painting in Florence and Siena after the Black Death: The Arts, Religion, and Society in the Mid-Fourteenth Century*. 2nd ed. Princeton: Princeton Univ. Press, 1978.

Moskowitz, Anita Fiderer. *Italian Gothic Sculpture: c. 1250–c. 1400*. New York: Cambridge Univ. Press, 2001.

Norman, Diana, ed. *Siena, Florence, and Padua: Art, Society, and Religion 1280–1400*. 2 vols. New Haven: Yale Univ. Press, 1995.

Poeschke, Joachim. *Italian Frescoes, the Age of Giotto, 1280–1400*. New York: Abbeville Press, 2005.

Schleif, Corine. "St. Hedwig's Personal Ivory Madonna: Women's Agency and the Powers of Possessing Portable Figures." In *The Four Modes of Seeing: Approaches to Medieval Imagery in Honor of Madeline Harrison Caviness*, edited by Evelyn Staudinger Lane, Elizabeth Carson Paston, and Ellen M. Shortell. Farnham, Surrey: Ashgate, 2009: 382–403.

Vasari, Giorgio. *The Lives of the Artists*. Trans. Julia Conaway Bondanella and Peter Bondanella. Oxford World's Classics. New York: Oxford Univ. Press, 2008.

Welch, Evelyn S. *Art in Renaissance Italy, 1350–1500.* New ed. Oxford History of Art. Oxford: Oxford Univ. Press, 2000.

White, John. *Art and Architecture in Italy, 1250 to 1400.* 3rd ed. Pelican History of Art. Harmondsworth, UK: Penguin, 1993.

Chapter 18 Fifteenth-Century Art in Northern Europe

Art from the Court of Burgundy: The Patronage of Philip the Bold and John the Fearless 1364–1419. Dijon: Musée des Beaux-Arts and Cleveland: Cleveland Museum of Art, 2004.

Baxandall, Michael. *The Limewood Sculptors of Renaissance Germany.* New Haven: Yale Univ. Press, 1980.

Blum, Shirley. *Early Netherlandish Triptychs: A Study in Patronage.* California Studies in the History of Art, 13. Berkeley: Univ. of California Press, 1969.

Borchert, Till-Holger. *Age of Van Eyck: The Mediterranean World and Early Netherlandish Painting, 1430–1530.* New York: Thames & Hudson, 2002.

Campbell, Lorne. *The Fifteenth-Century Netherlandish Schools* (National Gallery Catalogues). London: National Gallery, 1998.

Cavallo, Adolph S. *The Unicorn Tapestries at the Metropolitan Museum of Art.* New York: Metropolitan Museum of Art, 1998.

Chastel, André. *French Art: The Renaissance, 1430–1620.* Paris: Flammarion, 1995.

Dhanens, Elisabeth. *Van Eyck: The Ghent Altarpiece.* New York: Viking Press, 1973.

Füssel, Stephan. *Gutenberg and the Impact of Printing.* Trans. Douglas Martin. Burlington, VT: Ashgate, 2005.

Koster, Margaret L. "The *Arnolfini Double Portrait*: A Simple Solution." Apollo 157 (September 2003): 3–14.

Lane, Barbara G. *The Altar and the Altarpiece: Sacramental Themes in Early Netherlandish Painting.* New York: Harper & Row, 1984.

Marks, Richard, and Paul Williamson, eds. *Gothic: Art for England 1400–1547.* London: V&A Publications, 2003.

Meiss, Millard. *French Painting in the Time of Jean de Berry: The Limbourgs and their Contemporaries.* 2 vols. New York: Braziller, 1974.

Müller, Theodor. *Sculpture in the Netherlands, Germany, France, and Spain: 1400–1500.* Trans. Elaine and William Robson Scott. Pelican History of Art. Harmondsworth, UK: Penguin, 1966.

Pächt, Otto. *Early Netherlandish Painting: From Rogier van der Weyden to Gerard David.* Ed. Monika Rosenauer. Trans. David Britt. London: Harvey Miller, 1997.

———. *Van Eyck and the Founders of Early Netherlandish Painting.* London: Miller, 1994.

Panofsky, Erwin. *Early Netherlandish Painting. Its Origins and Character.* 2 vols. Cambridge, MA: Harvard Univ. Press, 1966.

Parshall, Peter W., and Rainer Schoch. *Origins of European Printmaking: Fifteenth-Century Woodcuts and their Public.* Washington, DC: National Gallery of Art, 2005.

Plummer, John. *The Last Flowering: French Painting in Manuscripts, 1420–1530, from American Collections.* New York: Pierpont Morgan Library, 1982.

Seidel, Linda. *Jan van Eyck's Arnolfini Portrait: Stories of an Icon.* New York: Cambridge Univ. Press, 1993.

Smith, Jeffrey Chipps. *The Northern Renaissance.* London and New York: Phaidon Press, 2004.

Snyder, James. *Northern Renaissance Art: Painting, Sculpture, the Graphic Arts from 1350 to 1575.* 2nd ed. rev. Larry Silver and Henry Luttikhuizen. Upper Saddle River, NJ: Prentice Hall, 2005.

Vos, Dirk de. *The Flemish Primitives: The Masterpieces.* Princeton: Princeton Univ. Press, 2002.

Zuffi, Stefano. *European Art of the Fifteenth Century.* Trans. Brian D. Phillips. Art through the Centuries. Los Angeles: J. Paul Getty Museum, 2005.

Chapter 19 Renaissance Art in Fifteenth-Century Italy

Adams, Laurie Schneider. *Italian Renaissance Art.* Boulder, CO: Westview Press, 2001.

Ahl, Diane Cole, ed. *The Cambridge Companion to Masaccio.* New York: Cambridge Univ. Press, 2002.

Ames-Lewis, Francis. *Drawing in Early Renaissance Italy.* 2nd ed. New Haven: Yale Univ. Press, 2000.

———. *The Intellectual Life of the Early Renaissance Artist.* New Haven: Yale Univ. Press, 2000.

Baxandall, Michael. *Painting and Experience in Fifteenth-Century Italy: A Primer in the Social History of Pictorial Style.* 2nd ed. Oxford: Oxford Univ. Press, 1988.

Boskovits, Miklós. *Italian Paintings of the Fifteenth Century.* The Collections of the National Gallery of Art. Washington, DC: National Gallery of Art, 2003.

Botticelli and Filippino: Passion and Grace in Fifteenth-Century Florentine Painting. Milano: Skira, 2004.

Brown, Patricia Fortini. *Art and Life in Renaissance Venice.* Perspectives. New York: Abrams, 1997. Reissue ed. Upper Saddle River, NJ: Pearson/Prentice Hall, 2006.

Christiansen, Keith, Laurence B. Kanter, and Carl Brandon Strehlke. *Painting in Renaissance Siena, 1420–1500.* New York: Metropolitan Museum of Art, 1988.

Christine, de Pisan. *The Book of the City of Ladies.* Trans. Rosalind Brown-Grant. London: Penguin Books, 1999.

Gilbert, Creighton, ed. *Italian Art, 1400–1500: Sources and Documents.* Evanston, IL: Northwestern Univ. Press, 1992.

Heydenreich, Ludwig Heinrich. *Architecture in Italy, 1400–1500.* Revised. Paul Davies. Pelican History of Art. New Haven: Yale Univ. Press, 1996.

Hind, Arthur M. *An Introduction to a History of Woodcut.* New York: Dover, 1963.

Hyman, Timothy. *Sienese Painting: The Art of a City-Republic (1278–1477).* World of Art. New York: Thames & Hudson, 2003.

King, Ross. *Brunelleschi's Dome: How a Renaissance Genius Reinvented Architecture.* New York: Walker, 2000.

Lavin, Marilyn Aronberg, ed. *Piero della Francesca and his Legacy.* Studies in the History of Art, 48: Symposium Papers, 28. Washington, DC: National Gallery of Art, 1995.

Pächt, Otto. *Venetian Painting in the 15th Century: Jacopo, Gentile and Giovanni Bellini and Andrea Mantegna.* Ed. Margareta Vyoral-Tschapka and Michael Pächt. Trans. Fiona Elliott. London: Harvey Miller, 2003.

Paoletti, John T., and Gary M. Radke. *Art in Renaissance Italy.* 3rd ed. Upper Saddle River, NJ: Pearson/Prentice Hall, 2005.

Partridge, Loren W. *The Art of Renaissance Rome, 1400–1600.* Perspectives. New York: Abrams, 1996. Reissue ed. Upper Saddle River, NJ: Pearson/Prentice Hall, 2006.

Poeschke, Joachim. *Donatello and His World: Sculpture of the Italian Renaissance.* Trans. Russell Stockman. New York: Abrams, 1993.

Pope-Hennessy, John. *Italian Renaissance Sculpture.* 4th ed. London: Phaidon Press, 1996.

Radke, Gary M., ed. *The Gates of Paradise: Lorenzo Ghiberti's Masterpiece.* New Haven: Yale Univ. Press, 2007.

Randolph, Adrian W. B., *Engaging Symbols: Gender, Politics, and Public Art in Fifteenth-Century Florence.* New Haven: Yale Univ. Press, 2002.

Troncelliti, Latifah. *The Two Parallel Realities of Alberti and Cennini: The Power of Writing and the Visual Arts in the Italian Quattrocento.* Studies in Italian Literature, vol. 14. Lewiston, NY: Mellen Press, 2004.

Turner, Richard. *Renaissance Florence: The Invention of a New Art.* Perspectives. New York: Abrams, 1997. Reissue ed. Upper Saddle River, NJ: Pearson/Prentice Hall, 2006.

Verdon, Timothy, and John Henderson, eds. *Christianity and the Renaissance: Image and Religious Imagination in the Quattrocento.* Syracuse, NY: Syracuse Univ. Press, 1990.

Walker, Paul Robert. *The Feud that Sparked the Renaissance: How Brunelleschi and Ghiberti Changed the Art World.* New York: William Morrow, 2002.

Welch, Evelyn S. *Art and Society in Italy, 1350–1500.* Oxford History of Art. Oxford: Oxford Univ. Press, 1997.

Chapter 20 Sixteenth-Century Art in Italy

Acidini Luchinat, Cristina, et al. *The Medici, Michelangelo, & the Art of Late Renaissance Florence.* New Haven: Yale Univ. Press, 2002.

Bambach, Carmen. *Drawing and Painting in the Italian Renaissance Workshop: Theory and Practice, 1330–1600.* Cambridge: Cambridge Univ. Press, 1999.

Barriault, Anne B., ed. *Reading Vasari.* London: Philip Wilson in assoc. with the Georgia Museum of Art, 2005.

Brambilla Barcilon, Pinin. *Leonardo: The Last Supper.* Chicago: Univ. of Chicago Press, 2001.

Brown, Patricia Fortini. *Art and Life in Renaissance Venice.* Perspectives. New York: Abrams, 1997.

Cellini, Benvenuto. *Autobiography.* Rev. ed. Trans. George Bull. Penguin Classics. New York: Penguin, 1998.

Chelazzi Dini, Giulietta, Alessandro Angelini, and Bernardina Sani. *Sienese Painting: From Duccio to the Birth of the Baroque.* New York: Abrams, 1998.

Cole, Alison. *Virtue and Magnificence: Art of the Italian Renaissance Courts.* Perspectives. New York: Abrams, 1995. Reissue ed. as Art of the Italian Courts. Upper Saddle River, NJ: Pearson/Prentice Hall, 2006.

Franklin, David, ed. *Leonardo da Vinci, Michelangelo, and the Renaissance in Florence.* Ottawa: National Gallery of Canada in assoc. with Yale Univ. Press, 2005.

Freedberg, S. J. *Painting in Italy, 1500 to 1600.* 3rd ed. Pelican History of Art. New Haven: Yale Univ. Press, 1993.

Goffen, Rona. *Renaissance Rivals: Michelangelo, Leonardo, Raphael, Titian.* New Haven: Yale Univ. Press, 2002.

———. *Titian's Venus of Urbino.* Masterpieces of Western Painting. Cambridge: Cambridge Univ. Press, 1997.

———. *Titian's Women.* New Haven: Yale Univ. Press, 1997.

Hall, Marcia B. *After Raphael: Painting in Central Italy in the Sixteenth Century.* New York: Cambridge Univ. Press, 1999.

———, ed. *The Cambridge Companion to Raphael.* New York: Cambridge Univ. Press, 2005.

Hollingsworth, Mary. *Patronage in Sixteenth Century Italy.* London: John Murray, 1996.

Hopkins, Andrew. *Italian Architecture: From Michelangelo to Borromini.* World of Art. New York: Thames & Hudson, 2002.

Hughes, Anthony. *Michelangelo.* Art & Ideas. London: Phaidon Press, 1997.

Huse, Norbert, and Wolfgang Wolters. *Art of Renaissance Venice: Architecture, Sculpture and Painting, 1460–1590.* Trans. Edmund Jephcott. Chicago: Univ. of Chicago Press, 1990.

Joannides, Paul. *Titian to 1518: The Assumption of Genius.* New Haven: Yale Univ. Press, 2001.

Klein, Robert, and Henri Zerner. *Italian Art, 1500–1600: Sources and Documents.* Upper Saddle River, NJ: Pearson/Prentice Hall, 1966.

Kliemann, Julian-Matthias, and Michael Rohlmann. *Italian Frescoes: High Renaissance and Mannerism, 1510–1600.* Trans. Steven Lindberg. New York: Abbeville Press, 2004.

Landau, David, and Peter Parshall. *The Renaissance Print: 1470–1550.* New Haven: Yale Univ. Press, 1994.

Lieberman, Ralph. *Renaissance Architecture in Venice, 1450–1540.* New York: Abbeville Press, 1982.

Lotz, Wolfgang. *Architecture in Italy, 1500–1600.* Revised. Deborah Howard. Pelican History of Art. New Haven: Yale Univ. Press, 1995.

Meilman, Patricia, ed. *The Cambridge Companion to Titian.* New York: Cambridge Univ. Press, 2004.

Mitrovic, Branko. *Learning from Palladio.* New York: Norton, 2004.

Murray, Linda. *The High Renaissance and Mannerism: Italy, the North and Spain, 1500–1600.* World of Art. London: Thames & Hudson, 1995.

Partridge, Loren W. *The Art of Renaissance Rome, 1400–1600.* Perspectives. New York: Abrams, 1996.

———. *Michelangelo, the Last Judgment: A Glorious Restoration.* New York: Abrams, 1997.

Pilliod, Elizabeth. *Pontormo, Bronzino, Allori: A Genealogy of Florentine Art.* New Haven: Yale Univ. Press, 2001.

Pope-Hennessy, John. *Italian High Renaissance and Baroque Sculpture.* 4th ed. London: Phaidon Press, 1996.

Rosand, David. *Painting in Cinquecento Venice: Titian, Veronese, Tintoretto.* Rev. ed. Cambridge: Cambridge Univ. Press, 1997.

Rowe, Colin, and Leon Satkowski. *Italian Architecture of the 16th Century.* New York: Princeton Architectural Press, 2002.

Rowland, Ingrid D. *The Culture of the High Renaissance: Ancients and Moderns in Sixteenth Century Rome.* Cambridge: Cambridge Univ. Press, 1998.

Shearman, John. *Mannerism.* Harmondsworth, UK: Penguin, 1967. Reissue ed. New York: Penguin, 1990.

Vasari, Giorgio. *The Lives of the Artists.* Trans. Julia Conaway Bondanella and Peter Bondanella. Oxford World's Classics. New York: Oxford Univ. Press, 2008.

Verheyen, Egon. *The Paintings in the Studiolo of Isabella d'Este at Mantua.* Monographs on Archaeology and Fine Arts, 23. New York: New York Univ. Press, 1971.

Williams, Robert. *Art, Theory, and Culture in Sixteenth-Century Italy: From Techne to Metateche.* Cambridge: Cambridge Univ. Press, 1997.

Chapter 21 Sixteenth-Century Art in Northern Europe and the Iberian Peninsula

Bartrum, Giulia. *Albrecht Dürer and his Legacy: The Graphic Work of a Renaissance Artist.* London: British Museum Press, 2002.

Bartrum, Giulia. *German Renaissance Prints 1490–1550.* London: British Museum Press, 1995.

Brown, Jonathan. *Painting in Spain, 1500–1700.* Pelican History of Art. New Haven: Yale Univ. Press, 1998.

Buck, Stephanie, and Jochen Sander. *Hans Holbein the Younger: Painter at the Court of Henry VIII.* Trans. Rachel Esner and Beverley Jackson. New York: Thames & Hudson, 2004.

Chapuis, Julien. *Tilman Riemenschneider: Master Sculptor of the Late Middle Ages.* Washington, DC: National Gallery of Art, 1999.

Cloulas, Ivan, and Michèle Bimbenet-Privat. *Treasures of the French Renaissance.* Trans. John Goodman. New York: Abrams, 1998.

Davies, David, and John H. Elliott. *El Greco.* London: National Gallery, 2003.

Dixon, Laurinda. *Bosch.* Art & Ideas. New York: Phaidon Press, 2003.

Foister, Susan. *Holbein and England.* New Haven: Published for Paul Mellon Centre for Studies in British Art by Yale Univ. Press, 2004.

Hayum, Andrée. *The Isenheim Altarpiece: God's Medicine and the Painter's Vision.* Princeton Essays on the Arts, 18. Princeton: Princeton Univ. Press, 1989.

Hearn, Karen, ed. *Dynasties: Painting in Tudor and Jacobean England, 1530–1630.* New York: Rizzoli, 1996.

Koerner, Joseph Leo. *The Reformation of the Image.* Chicago: Univ. of Chicago Press, 2004.

Kubler, George. *Building the Escorial.* Princeton: Princeton Univ. Press, 1982.

Nash, Susie. *Northern Renaissance Art.* Oxford History of Art. New York: Oxford Univ. Press, 2008.

Price, David Hotchkiss. *Albrecht Dürer's Renaissance: Humanism, Reformation, and the Art of Faith.* Studies in Medieval and Early Modern Civilization. Ann Arbor: Univ. of Michigan Press, 2003.

Roberts-Jones, Philippe, and Françoise Roberts-Jones. *Pieter Bruegel.* New York: Abrams, 2002.

Smith, Jeffrey Chipps. *Nuremberg, a Renaissance City, 1500–1618.* Austin: Huntington Art Gallery, Univ. of Texas, 1983.

———. *German Sculpture of the Later Renaissance, c.1520–1580: Art in an Age of Uncertainty.* Princeton: Princeton Univ. Press, 1994.

———. *The Northern Renaissance.* London and New York: Phaidon Press, 2004.

Snyder, James. *Northern Renaissance Art: Painting, Sculpture, the Graphic Arts from 1350 to 1575.* 2nd ed. rev. Larry Silver and Henry Luttikhuizen. Upper Saddle River, NJ: Pearson/Prentice Hall, 2005.

Strong, Roy C. *Artists of the Tudor Court: The Portrait Miniature Rediscovered, 1520–1620.* London: V&A Publications, 1983.

The Word Made Image: Religion, Art, and Architecture in Spain and Spanish America, 1500–1600. Fenway Court, 28. Boston: Published by the Trustees of the Isabella Stewart Gardner Museum, 1998.

Zerner, Henri. *Renaissance Art in France: The Invention of Classicism.* Paris: Flammarion, 2003.

Zorach, Rebecca. *Blood, Milk, Ink, Gold: Abundance and Excess in the French Renaissance.* Chicago: Univ. of Chicago Press, 2005.

Chapter 22 Seventeenth Century Art in Europe

Adams, Laurie Schneider. *Key Monuments of the Baroque.* Boulder, CO: Westview Press, 2000.

Allen, Christopher. *French Painting in the Golden Age.* World of Art. New York: Thames & Hudson, 2003.

Alpers, Svetlana. *The Art of Describing: Dutch Art in the Seventeenth Century.* Chicago: Chicago Univ. Press, 1983.

———. *The Making of Rubens.* New Haven: Yale Univ. Press, 1995.

Blankert, Albert. *Rembrandt: A Genius and His Impact.* Melbourne: National Gallery of Victoria, 1997.

Boucher, Bruce. *Italian Baroque Sculpture.* World of Art. New York: Thames & Hudson, 1998.

Brown, Beverly Louise, ed. *The Genius of Rome, 1592–1623.* London: Royal Academy of Arts, 2001.

Brown, Jonathan. *Painting in Spain, 1500–1700.* Pelican History of Art. New Haven: Yale Univ. Press, 1998.

———, and Carmen Garrido. *Velásquez: The Technique of Genius.* New Haven: Yale Univ. Press, 2003.

Careri, Giovanni. *Baroques.* Tran. Alexandra Bonfante-Warren. Princeton: Princeton Univ. Press, 2003.

Chapman, H. Perry. *Rembrandt's Self-Portraits: A Study in 17th-Century Identity.* Princeton: Princeton Univ. Press, 1990.

Chong, Alan, and Wouter Kloek. *Still-Life Paintings from the Netherlands, 1550–1720.* Zwolle: Waanders, 1999.

Enggass, Robert, and Jonathan Brown. *Italian and Spanish Art, 1600–1750: Sources and Documents.* 2nd ed. Evanston, IL: Northwestern Univ. Press, 1992.

Frantis, Wayne E., ed. *The Cambridge Companion to Vermeer.* Cambridge: Cambridge Univ. Press, 2001.

———. *Dutch Seventeenth-Century Genre Painting: Its Stylistic and Thematic Evolution.* New Haven: Yale Univ. Press, 2004.

Harbison, Robert. *Reflections on Baroque.* Chicago: Univ. of Chicago Press, 2000.

Keazor, Henry. *Nicolas Poussin, 1594–1665.* Köln and London: Taschen, 2007.

Kiers, Judikje, and Fieke Tissink. *Golden Age of Dutch Art: Painting, Sculpture, Decorative Art.* London: Thames & Hudson, 2000.

Lagerlöf, Margaretha Rossholm. *Ideal Landscape: Annibale Carracci, Nicolas Poussin, and Claude Lorrain.* New Haven: Yale Univ. Press, 1990.

McPhee, Sarah. *Bernini and the Bell Towers: Architecture and Politics at the Vatican.* New Haven: Yale Univ. Press, 2002.

Millon, Henry A., ed. *The Triumph of the Baroque: Architecture in Europe, 1600–1750.* 2nd ed. rev. New York: Rizzoli, 1999.

Morrissey, Jake. *The Genius in the Design: Bernini, Borromini, and the Rivalry that Transformed Rome.* New York: William Morrow, 2005.

Puttfarken, Thomas. *Roger de Piles' Theory of Art.* New Haven: Yale Univ. Press, 1985.

Rand, Richard. *Claude Lorrain, the Painter as Draftsman: Drawings from the British Museum.* New Haven: Yale Univ. Press; Williamstown, MA: Clark Art Institute, 2006.

Ripa, Cesare. *Baroque and Rococo Pictorial Imagery. The 1758–60 Hertel Edition of Ripa's "Iconologia."* Trans. Edward A. Maser. New York: Dover, 1971.

Slive, Seymour. *Dutch Painting 1600–1800.* Pelican History of Art. New Haven: Yale Univ. Press, 1995.

Summerson, John. *Inigo Jones.* New Haven: Published for the Paul Mellon Centre for Studies in British Art by Yale Univ. Press, 2000.

Tomlinson, Janis. *From El Greco to Goya: Painting in Spain, 1561–1828.* Perspectives. New York: Abrams, 1997.

Varriano, John. *Caravaggio: The Art of Realism.* University Park, PA: The Pennsylvania State Univ. Press, 2006.

Vlieghe, Hans. *Flemish Art and Architecture, 1585–1700.* Pelican History of Art. New Haven: Yale Univ. Press, 1998. Reissue ed. 2004.

Walker, Stefanie, and Frederick Hammond, eds. *Life and the Arts in the Baroque Palaces of Rome: Ambiente Barocco.* New Haven: Yale Univ. Press; for the Bard Graduate Center for Studies in the Decorative Arts, New York, 1999.

Wheelock Jr., Arthur K. *Flemish Paintings of the Seventeenth Century.* Washington, DC: National Gallery of Art, 2005.

Wittkower, Rudolf. *Art and Architecture in Italy, 1600–1750.* 3 vols. 6th ed. Revised. Joseph Connors and Jennifer Montague. Pelican History of Art. New Haven: Yale Univ. Press, 1999.

Zega, Andrew, and Bernd H. Dams. *Palaces of the Sun King: Versailles, Trianon, Marly: The Châteaux of Louis XIV.* New York: Rizzoli, 2002.

Chapter 23 Art of South and Southeast Asia after 1200

Asher, Catherine B. *Architecture of Mughal India.* New York: Cambridge Univ. Press, 1992.

Beach, Milo Cleveland. *Mughal and Rajput Painting.* New York: Cambridge Univ. Press, 1992.

Guy, John, and Deborah Swallow, eds. *Arts of India, 1550–1900.* London: V&A Publications, 1990.

Khanna, Balraj, and Aziz Kurtha. *Art of Modern India.* London: Thames & Hudson, 1998.

Koch, Ebba. *Mughal Art and Imperial Ideology: Collected Essays.* New Delhi: Oxford Univ. Press, 2001.

Michell, George. *Hindu Art and Architecture.* World of Art. London: Thames & Hudson, 2000.

Miller, Barbara Stoler (trans.). *Love Song of the Dark Lord: Jayadeva's Gitagovinda.* New York: Columbia Univ. Press, 1977.

Moynihan, Elizabeth B., ed. *The Moonlight Garden: New Discoveries at the Taj Mahal.* Asian Art & Culture. Washington, DC: Arthur M. Sackler Gallery, Smithsonian Institution Press, 2000.

Nou, Jean-Louis. *Taj Mahal.* Text by Amina Okada and M. C. Joshi. New York: Abbeville Press, 1993.

Pal, Pratapaditya. *Court Paintings of India, 16th–19th Centuries.* New York: Navin Kumar, 1983.

———. *The Peaceful Liberators: Jain Art from India.* New York: Thames & Hudson, 1994.

Rossi, Barbara. *From the Ocean of Painting: India's Popular Paintings, 1589 to the Present.* New York: Oxford Univ. Press, 1998.

Schimmel, Annemarie. *The Empire of the Great Mughals: History, Art and Culture.* Ed. Burzine K. Waghmar. Trans. Corinne Attwood. London: Reaktion Books, 2004.

Stronge, Susan. *Painting for the Mughal Emperor: The Art of the Book, 1560–1660.* London: V&A Publications, 2002.

Tillotson, G. H. R. *Mughal India.* Architectural Guides for Travelers. San Francisco: Chronicle Books, 1990.

———. *The Tradition of Indian Architecture: Continuity, Controversy and Change since 1850.* New Haven: Yale Univ. Press, 1989.

Verma, Som Prakash. *Painting the Mughal Experience.* New York: Oxford Univ. Press, 2005.

Welch, Stuart Cary. *The Emperors' Album: Images of Mughal India.* New York: Metropolitan Museum of Art, 1987.

———. *India: Art and Culture 1300–1900.* New York: Metropolitan Museum of Art, 1985.

Chapter 24 Chinese and Korean Art after 1279

Andrews, Julia Frances, and Kuiyi Shen. *A Century in Crisis: Modernity and Tradition in the Art of Twentieth-Century China.* New York: Solomon R. Guggenheim Museum, 1998.

Barnhart, Richard M. *Painters of the Great Ming: The Imperial Court and the Zhe School.* Dallas: Dallas Museum of Art, 1993.

Barrass, Gordon S. *The Art of Calligraphy in Modern China.* London: British Museum Press, 2002.

Berger, Patricia Ann. *Empire of Emptiness: Buddhist Art and Political Authority in Qing China.* Honolulu: Univ. of Hawai'i Press, 2003.

Bickford, Maggie. *Ink Plum: The Making of a Chinese Scholar-Painting.* New York: Cambridge Univ. Press, 1996.

Billeter, Jean François. *The Chinese Art of Writing.* New York: Skira/Rizzoli, 1990.

Bush, Susan, and Hsio-yen Shih, eds. *Early Chinese Texts on Painting.* Cambridge, MA: Harvard Univ. Press, 1985.

Cahill, James. *The Distant Mountains: Chinese Painting in the Late Ming Dynasty, 1580–1644.* New York: Weatherhill, 1982.

———. *Hills beyond a River: Chinese Painting of the Y'uan Dynasty, 1279–1368.* New York: Weatherhill, 1976.

———. *Parting at the Shore: Chinese Painting of the Early and Middle Ming Dynasty 1368–1580.* New York: Weatherhill, 1978.

Chaves, Jonathan (trans.). *The Chinese Painter as Poet.* New York: Art Media Resources, 2000.

Chung, Anita. *Drawing Boundaries: Architectural Images in Qing China.* Honolulu: Univ. of Hawai'i Press, 2004.

Clunas, Craig. *Pictures and Visuality in Early Modern China.* Princeton: Princeton Univ. Press, 1997.

Fang, Jing Pei. *Treasures of the Chinese Scholar: Form, Function and Symbolism.* Ed. J. May Lee Barrett. New York: Weatherhill, 1997.

Fong, Wen C. *Between Two Cultures: Late-Nineteenth- and Twentieth-Century Chinese Paintings from the Robert H. Ellsworth Collection in the Metropolitan Museum of Art.* New York: Metropolitan Museum of Art, 2001.

Hearn, Maxwell K., and Judith G. Smith, eds. *Chinese Art: Modern Expressions.* New York: Dept. of Asian Art, Metropolitan Museum of Art, 2001.

Ho, Chuimei, and Bennet Bronson. *Splendors of China's Forbidden City: The Glorious Reign of Emperor Qianlong.* Chicago: Field Museum, 2004.

Ho, Wai-kam, ed.. *The Century of Tung Ch'i-ch'ang, 1555–1636.* 2 vols. Kansas City: Nelson-Atkins Museum of Art, 1992.

Kim, Hongnam. *The Life of a Patron: Zhou Lianggong (1612–1672) and the Painters of Seventeenth-Century China.* New York: China Institute in America, 1996.

Knapp, Ronald G. *China's Vernacular Architecture: House Form and Culture.* Honolulu: Univ. of Hawai'i Press, 1989.

Lee, Sherman, and Wai-Kam Ho. *Chinese Art under the Mongols: The Y'uan Dynasty, 1279–1368.* Cleveland: Cleveland Museum of Art, 1968.

Lim, Lucy. ed. *Wu Guanzhong: A Contemporary Chinese Artist.* San Francisco: Chinese Culture Foundation, 1989.

Moss, Paul. *Escape from the Dusty World: Chinese Paintings and Literati Works of Art.* London: Sydney L. Moss, 1999.

Ng, So Kam. *Brushstrokes: Styles and Techniques of Chinese Painting.* San Francisco: Asian Art Museum of San Francisco, 1993.

The Poetry [of] Ink: The Korean Literati Tradition, 1392–1910. Paris: Réunion des Musées Nationaux: Musée National des Arts Asiatiques Guimet, 2005.

Smith, Karen. *Nine Lives: The Birth of Avant-Garde Art in New China.* Zurich: Scalo, 2006.

Till, Barry. *The Manchu Era (1644–1912), Arts of China's Last Imperial Dynasty.* Victoria, BC: Art Gallery of Greater Victoria, 2004.

Vainker, S. J. *Chinese Pottery and Porcelain: From Prehistory to the Present.* London: British Museum Press, 1991.

Watson, William. *The Arts of China 900–1620.* Pelican History of Art. New Haven: Yale Univ. Press, 2000.

Weidner, Marsha Smith. *Views from Jade Terrace: Chinese Women Artists, 1300–1912.* Indianapolis, IN: Indianapolis Museum of Art, 1988.

Xinian, Fu, et al. *Chinese Architecture.* Ed. Nancy S. Steinhardt. New Haven: Yale Univ. Press, 2002.

Chapter 25 Japanese Art after 1333

Addiss, Stephen. *The Art of Zen: Painting and Calligraphy by Japanese Monks, 1600–1925.* New York: Abrams, 1989.

Berthier, François. *Reading Zen in the Rocks: The Japanese Dry Landscape Garden.* Trans. & essay, Graham Parkes. Chicago: Univ. of Chicago Press, 2000.

Calza, Gian Carlo. *Ukiyo-e.* New York: Phaidon Press, 2005.

Graham, Patricia J. *Faith and Power in Japanese Buddhist Art, 1600–2005.* Honolulu: Univ. of Hawai'i, 2007.

———. *Tea of the Sages: The Art of Sencha.* Honolulu: Univ. of Hawai'i, 1998.

Guth, Christine. *Art of Edo Japan: The Artist and the City 1615–1868.* Perspectives. New York: Abrams, 1996.

Hickman, Money L. *Japan's Golden Age: Momoyama.* New Haven: Yale Univ. Press, 1996.

Kobayashi, Tadashi, and Lisa Rotondo-McCord. *An Enduring Vision: 17th to 20th Century Japanese Painting from the Gitter-Yelen Collection.* New Orleans: New Orleans Museum of Art, 2003.

Lillehoji, Elizabeth, ed. *Critical Perspectives on Classicism in Japanese Painting, 1600–1700.* Honolulu: Univ. of Hawai'i Press, 2004.

McKelway, Matthew P. *Traditions Unbound: Groundbreaking Painters of Eighteenth-Century Kyoto.* San Francisco: Asian Art Museum – Chong-Moon Lee Center, 2005.

Meech, Julia, and Jane Oliver. *Designed for Pleasure: The World of Edo Japan in Prints and Paintings, 1680–1860.* Seattle: Univ. of Washington Press in association with the Asia Society and Japanese Art Society of America, New York, 2008.

Miyajima, Shin'ichi and Sato Yasuhiro. *Japanese Ink Painting.* Ed. George Kuwayama. Los Angeles: Los Angeles County Museum of Art, 1985.

Munroe, Alexandra. *Japanese Art after 1945: Scream Against the Sky.* New York: Abrams, 1994.

Murase, Miyeko, ed. *Turning Point: Oribe and the Arts of Sixteenth-Century Japan.* New York: Metropolitan Museum of Art, 2003.

Newland, Amy Reigle, ed. *The Hotei Encyclopedia of Japanese Woodblock Prints.* 2 vols. Amsterdam: Hotei Publishing, 2005.

Ohki, Sadako. *Tea Culture of Japan.* New Haven: Yale Univ. Press, 2009.

Rousmaniere, Nicole, ed. *Crafting Beauty in Modern Japan: Celebrating Fifty Years of the Japan Traditional Art Crafts Exhibition.* Seattle: Univ. of Washington Press, 2007.

Screech, Timon. *The Lens Within the Heart: The Western Scientific Gaze and Popular Imagery in Later Edo Japan.* 2nd ed. Honolulu: Univ. of Hawai'i Press, 2002.

Singer, Robert T., and John T. Carpenter. *Edo, Art in Japan 1615–1868.* Washington, DC: National Gallery of Art, 1998.

Chapter 26 Art of the Americas after 1300

Bauer, Brian S. *Ancient Cuzco: Heartland of the Inca.* Joe R. and Teresa Lozano Long Series in Latin American and Latino Art and Culture. Austin: Univ. of Texas Press, 2004.

Berlo, Janet Catherine, and Ruth B. Phillips. *Native North American Art.* Oxford History of Art. Oxford: Oxford Univ. Press, 1998.

Bringhurst, Robert. *The Black Canoe: Bill Reid and the Spirit of Haida Gwaii.* Seattle: Univ. of Washington Press, l991.

Burger, Richard L., and Lucy C. Salazar, eds. *Machu Picchu: Unveiling the Mystery of the Incas.* New Haven: Yale Univ. Press, 2004.

Fields, Virginia M., and Victor Zamudio-Taylor. *The Road to Aztlan: Art from a Mythic Homeland.* Los Angeles: Los Angeles County Museum of Art, 2001.

Griffin-Pierce, Trudy. *Earth is my Mother, Sky is my Father: Space, Time, and Astronomy in Navajo Sandpainting.* Albuquerque: Univ. of New Mexico Press, 1992.

Jonaitis, Aldona. *Art of the Northwest Coast.* Seattle: Univ. of Washington Press, 2006.

Kaufman, Alice, and Christopher Selser. *The Navajo Weaving Tradition: 1650 to the Present.* New York: Dutton, 1985.

Macnair, Peter L., Robert Joseph, and Bruce Grenville. *Down from the Shimmering Sky: Masks of the Northwest Coast.* Vancouver: Douglas & McIntyre, 1998.

Matos Moctezuma, Eduardo, and Felipe R. Solís Olguín. *Aztecs.* London: Royal Academy of Arts, 2002.

Matthews, Washington. *The Night Chant: A Navaho Ceremony* in Memoirs of the American Museum of Natural History, vol. 6. New York, 1902.

Moseley, Michael E. *The Incas and Their Ancestors: The Archaeology of Peru.* Rev. ed. London: Thames & Hudson, 2001.

Nabokov, Peter, and Robert Easton. *Native American Architecture.* New York: Oxford Univ. Press, 1989.

Pasztory, Esther. *Aztec Art.* Norman: Univ. of Oklahoma Press, 2000.

Rushing III, W. Jackson, ed. *Native American Art in the Twentieth Century: Makers, Meanings, Histories.* New York: Routledge, 1999.

Shaw, George Everett. *Art of the Ancestors: Antique North American Indian Art.* Aspen, CO: Aspen Art Museum, 2004.

Taylor, Colin F. *Buckskin & Buffalo: The Artistry of the Plains Indians.* New York: Rizzoli, 1998.

Townsend, Richard F., ed. *The Aztecs.* 2nd rev. ed. Ancient Peoples and Places. London: Thames & Hudson, 2000.

Trimble, Stephen. *Talking with the Clay: The Art of Pueblo Pottery in the 21st Century.* 20th anniversary. rev ed. Santa Fe, NM: School for Advanced Research Press, 2007.

Wood, Nancy C. *Taos Pueblo.* New York: Knopf, 1989.

Chapter 27 Art of Pacific Cultures

Caruana, Wally. *Aboriginal Art.* 2nd ed. World of Art. New York: Thames & Hudson, 2003.

Craig, Barry, Bernie Kernot, and Christopher Anderson, eds. *Art and Performance in Oceania.* Honolulu: Univ. of Hawai'i Press, 1999.

D'Alleva, Anne. *Arts of the Pacific Islands.* Perspectives. New York: Abrams, 1998.

Herle, Anita, et al. *Pacific Art: Persistence, Change, and Meaning.* Honolulu: Univ. of Hawai'i Press, 2002.

Kaeppler, Adrienne Lois, Christian Kaufmann, and Douglas Newton. *Oceanic Art.* Trans. Nora Scott and Sabine Bouladon. New York: Abrams, 1997.

Kirch, Patrick Vinton. *The Lapita Peoples: Ancestors of the Oceanic World.* The Peoples of South-East Asia and the Pacific. Cambridge, MA: Blackwell, 1997.

Kjellgren, Eric. *Splendid Isolation: Art of Easter Island.* New York: Metropolitan Museum of Art, 2001.

———, and Carol Ivory. *Adorning the World: Art of the Marquesas Islands.* New Haven: Yale Univ. Press in association with the Metropolitan Museum of Art, 2005.

Küchler, Susanne, and Graeme Were. *Pacific Pattern.* London: Thames & Hudson, 2005.

Lilley, Ian, ed. *Archaeology of Oceania: Australia and the Pacific Islands.* Malden, MA: Blackwell, 2006.

McCulloch, Susan. *Contemporary Aboriginal Art: A Guide to the Rebirth of an Ancient Culture.* Rev. ed. Crows Nest, NSW, Australia: Allen & Unwin, 2001.

Moore, Albert C. *Arts in the Religions of the Pacific: Symbols of Life.* Religion and the Arts Series. New York: Pinter, 1995.

Morphy, Howard. *Aboriginal Art.* London: Phaidon Press, 1998.

Morwood, M. J. *Visions from the Past: The Archaeology of Australian Aboriginal Art.* Washington, DC: Smithsonian Institution Press, 2002.

Neich, Roger, and Mick Pendergrast. *Traditional Tapa Textiles of the Pacific.* London: Thames & Hudson, 1997.

Newton, Douglas, ed. *Arts of the South Seas: Island Southeast Asia, Melanesia, Polynesia, Micronesia; The Collections of the Musée Barbier-Mueller.* Trans. David Radzinowicz Howell. New York: Prestel, 1999.

Rainbird, Paul. *The Archaeology of Micronesia.* Cambridge World Archaeology. Cambridge: Cambridge Univ. Press, 2004.

Smidt, Dirk, ed. *Asmat Art: Woodcarvings of Southwest New Guinea.* New York: George Braziller in assoc. with Rijksmuseum voor Volkenkunde, Leiden, 1993.

Starzecka, D. C., ed. *Maori Art and Culture.* London: British Museum Press, 1996.

Taylor, Luke. *Seeing the Inside: Bark Painting in Western Arnhem Land.* Oxford Studies in Social and Cultural Anthropology. New York: Oxford Univ. Press, 1996.

Thomas, Nicholas. *Oceanic Art.* World of Art. New York: Thames & Hudson, 1995.

———, Anna Cole and Bronwen Douglas, eds. *Tattoo: Bodies, Art, and Exchange in the Pacific and the West.* Durham, NC: Duke Univ. Press, 2005.

Chapter 28 Art of Africa in the Modern Era

Anatsui, El. *El Anatsui Gawu.* Llandudno, Wales, UK: Oriel Mostyn Gallery, 2003.

Astonishment and Power. Washington, DC: National Museum of African Art, Smithsonian Institution Press, 1993.

Beckwith, Carol, and Angela Fisher. *African Ceremonies.* 2 vols. New York: Abrams, 1999.

Binkley, David A. "Avatar of Power: Southern Kuba Masquerade Figures in a Funerary Context" in *Africa-Journal of the International African Institute*, 57/1 (1987): 75–97.

Cameron, Elisabeth L. *Art of the Lega.* Los Angeles: UCLA Fowler Museum of Cultural History, 2001.

Cole, Herbert M., ed. *I Am Not Myself: The Art of African Masquerade.* Los Angeles: Fowler Museum of Cultural History, Univ. of California, 1985.

———. *Icons: Ideals and Power in the Art of Africa.* Washington, DC: National Museum of African Art, Smithsonian Institution Press, 1989.

A Fiction of Authenticity: Contemporary Africa Abroad. St. Louis, MO: Contemporary Art Museum St. Louis, 2003.

Fogle, Douglas, and Olukemi Ilesanmi. *Julie Mehretu: Drawing into Painting.* Minneapolis, MN: Walker Art Center, 2003.

Gillow, John. *African Textiles.* San Francisco: Chronicle Books, 2003.

Graham, Gilbert. *Dogon Sculpture: Symbols of a Mythical Universe.* Brookville, NY: Hillwood Art Museum, Long Island Univ., C. W. Post Campus, 1997.

Hess, Janet Berry. *Art and Architecture in Postcolonial Africa.* Jefferson, NC: McFarland, 2006.

Jordán, Manuel, ed. *Chokwe! Art and Initiation Among the Chokwe and Related Peoples.* Munich: Prestel, 1998.

Kasfir, Sidney Littlefield. *Contemporary African Art.* World of Art. London: Thames & Hudson, 2000.

Morris, James, and Suzanne Preston Blier. *Butabu: Adobe Architecture of West Africa.* New York: Princeton Architectural Press, 2004.

Oguibe, Olu, and Okwui Enwezor. *Reading the Contemporary: African Art from Theory to the Marketplace.* Cambridge, MA: MIT Press, 1999.

Pemberton III, John, ed. *Insight and Artistry in African Divination.* Washington, DC: Smithsonian Institution Press, 2000.

Perrois, Louis, and Marta Sierra Delage. *The Art of Equatorial Guinea: The Fang Tribes.* New York: Rizzoli, 1990.

Picton, John, et al. *El Anatsui: A Sculpted History of Africa.* London: Saffron Books in conjunction with the October Gallery, 1998.

Roberts, Mary Nooter, and Allen F. Roberts, eds. *Memory: Luba Art and the Making of History.* New York: Museum for African Art, 1996.

Roy, Christopher D. *Art of the Upper Volta Rivers.* Meudon, France: Chaffin, 1987.

Stepan, Peter. *Spirits Speak: A Celebration of African Masks.* Munich: Prestel, 2005.

Van Damme, Annemieke. *Spectacular Display: The Art of Nkanu Initiation Rituals.* Washington, DC: National Museum of African Art, Smithsonian Institution Press, 2001.

Vogel, Susan Mullin. *Baule: African Art, Western Eyes.* New Haven: Yale Univ. Press, 1997.

Chapter 29 Eighteenth and Early Nineteenth Century Art in Europe and North America

Bailey, Colin B., Philip Conisbee, and Thomas W. Gaehtgens. *The Age of Watteau, Chardin, and Fragonard: Masterpieces of French Genre Painting.* New Haven: Yale Univ. Press in assoc. with the National Gallery of Canada, Ottawa, 2003.

Boime, Albert. *Art in an Age of Bonapartism, 1800– 1815.* Chicago: Univ. of Chicago Press, 1990.

———. *Art in an Age of Counterrevolution, 1815–1848.* Chicago: Univ. of Chicago Press, 2004.

———. *Art in an Age of Revolution, 1750– 1800.* Chicago: Univ. of Chicago Press, 1987.

Bowron, Edgar Peters, and Joseph J. Rishel, eds. *Art in Rome in the Eighteenth Century.* London: Merrell in association with Philadelphia Museum of Art, 2000.

Brown, David Blayney. *Romanticism.* London: Phaidon Press, 2001.

Chinn, Celestine, and Kieran McCarty. *Bac: Where the Waters Gather.* Univ. of Arizona: Mission San Xavier Del Bac, 1977.

Craske, Matthew. *Art in Europe, 1700–1830: A History of the Visual Arts in an Era of Unprecedented Urban Economic Growth.* Oxford History of Art. Oxford: Oxford Univ. Press, 1997.

Denis, Rafael Cardoso, and Colin Trodd, eds. *Art and the Academy in the Nineteenth Century.* New Brunswick, NJ: Rutgers Univ. Press, 2000.

Goodman, Elise, ed. *Art and Culture in the Eighteenth Century: New Dimensions and Multiple Perspectives.* Studies in Eighteenth-Century Art and Culture. Newark: Univ. of Delaware Press, 2001.

Hofmann, Werner. *Goya: To Every Story There Belongs Another.* New York: Thames & Hudson, 2003.

Irwin, David G. *Neoclassicism. Art & Ideas.* London: Phaidon Press, 1997.

Jarrassé, Dominique. *18th-Century French Painting.* Trans. Murray Wyllie. Paris: Terrail, 1999.

Kalnein, Wend von. *Architecture in France in the Eighteenth Century.* Trans. David Britt. Pelican History of Art. New Haven: Yale Univ. Press, 1995.

Levey, Michael. *Painting in Eighteenth-Century Venice.* 3rd ed. New Haven: Yale Univ. Press, 1994.

Lewis, Michael J. *The Gothic Revival.* World of Art. New York: Thames & Hudson, 2002.

Lovell, Margaretta M. *Art in a Season of Revolution: Painters, Artisans, and Patrons in Early America*. Early American Studies. Philadelphia: Univ. of Pennsylvania Press, 2005.

Monneret, Sophie. *David and Neo-Classicism*. Trans. Chris Miller and Peter Snowdon. Paris: Terrail, 1999.

Montgomery, Charles F., and Patrick E. Kane, eds. *American Art, 1750–1800: Towards Independence*. Boston: New York Graphic Society, 1976.

Natter, Tobias, ed. *Angelica Kauffman: A Woman of Immense Talent*. Ostfildern: Hatje Cantz, 2007.

Porterfield, Todd, and Susan L. Siegfried. *Staging Empire: Napoleon, Ingres, and David*. University Park: Pennsylvania State Univ. Press, 2006.

Poulet, Anne L. *Jean-Antoine Houdon: Sculptor of the Enlightenment*. Washington, DC: National Gallery of Art, 2003.

Summerson, John. *Architecture of the Eighteenth Century*. World of Art. New York: Thames & Hudson, 1986.

Wilton, Andrew, and Ilaria Bignamini, eds. *Grand Tour: The Lure of Italy in the Eighteenth Century*. London: Tate Gallery, 1996.

Chapter 30 Mid to Late Nineteenth Century Art in Europe and the United States

Adams, Steven. *The Barbizon School and the Origins of Impressionism*. London: Phaidon Press, 1994.

Bajac, Quentin. *The Invention of Photography*. Discoveries. New York: Abrams, 2002.

Barger, M. Susan, and William B. White. *The Daguerreotype: Nineteenth-Century Technology and Modern Science*. Washington, DC: Smithsonian Institution Press, 1991.

Benjamin, Roger. *Orientalist Aesthetics: Art, Colonialism, and French North Africa, 1880–1930*. Berkeley: Univ. of California Press, 2003.

Bergdoll, Barry. *European Architecture, 1750–1890*. Oxford History of Art. New York: Oxford Univ. Press, 2000.

Blühm, Andreas, and Louise Lippincott. *Light!: The Industrial Age 1750–1900: Art & Science, Technology & Society*. New York: Thames & Hudson, 2001.

Boime, Albert, *The Academy and French Painting in the Nineteenth Century*. 2nd ed. New Haven: Yale Univ. Press, 1986.

Butler, Ruth, and Suzanne G. Lindsay. *European Sculpture of the Nineteenth Century*. Washington, DC: National Gallery of Art, 2000.

Callen, Anthea. *The Art of Impressionism: Painting Technique & the Making of Modernity*. New Haven: Yale Univ. Press, 2000.

Chu, Petra ten-Doesschate. *Nineteenth Century European Art*. 2nd. ed. Upper Saddle River, NJ: Pearson/Prentice Hall, 2006.

Clark, T. J. *The Painting of Modern Life: Paris in the Art of Manet and His Followers*. Rev. ed. London: Thames & Hudson, 1999.

Conrads, Margaret C. *Winslow Homer and the Critics: Forging a National Art in the 1870s*. Princeton: Princeton Univ. Press in association with the Nelson-Atkins Museum of Art, 2001.

Denis, Rafael Cardoso, and Colin Trodd. *Art and the Academy in the Nineteenth Century*. New Brunswick, NJ: Rutgers Univ. Press, 2000.

Eisenman, Stephen F. *Nineteenth Century Art: A Critical History*. 3rd ed. New York: Thames & Hudson, 2007.

Eitner, Lorenz. *Nineteenth Century European Painting: David to Cezanne*. Rev. ed. Boulder, CO: Westview Press, 2002.

Frazier, Nancy. *Louis Sullivan and the Chicago School*. New York: Knickerbocker Press, 1998.

Fried, Michael. *Manet's Modernism, or, The Face of Painting in the 1860s*. Chicago: Univ. of Chicago Press, 1996.

Gerdts, William H. *American Impressionism*. 2nd ed. New York: Abbeville Press, 2001.

Greenhalgh, Paul, ed. *Art Nouveau, 1890–1914*. London: V&A Publications, 2000.

Grigsby, Darcy Grimaldo. *Extremities: Painting Empire in Post-Revolutionary France*. New Haven: Yale Univ. Press, 2002.

Groseclose, Barbara. *Nineteenth-Century American Art*. Oxford History of Art. Oxford: Oxford Univ. Press, 2000.

Harrison, Charles, Paul Wood, and Jason Gaiger. *Art in Theory 1815–1900: An Anthology of Changing Ideas*. Oxford: Blackwell, 1998.

Herrmann, Luke. *Nineteenth Century British Painting*. London: Giles de la Mare, 2000.

Hirsh, Sharon L. *Symbolism and Modern Urban Society*. New York: Cambridge Univ. Press, 2004.

Kaplan, Wendy. *The Arts & Crafts Movement in Europe & America: Design for the Modern World*. New York: Thames & Hudson in assoc. with the Los Angeles County Museum of Art, 2004.

Kendall, Richard. *Degas: Beyond Impressionism*. London: National Gallery, 1996.

Lambourne, Lionel. *Japonisme: Cultural Crossings between Japan and the West*. New York: Phaidon Press, 2005.

Lemoine, Bertrand. *Architecture in France, 1800–1900*. Trans. Alexandra Bonfante-Warren. New York: Abrams, 1998.

Lewis, Mary Tompkins, ed.. *Critical Readings in Impressionism and Post-Impressionism: An Anthology*. Berkeley: Univ. of California Press, 2007.

Lochnan, Katharine Jordan. *Turner Whistler Monet*. London: Tate Publishing in assoc. with the Art Gallery of Ontario, 2004.

Miller, Angela L., et al. *American Encounters: Art, History, and Cultural Identity*. Upper Saddle River, NJ: Pearson/Prentice Hall, 2008.

Noon, Patrick J. *Crossing the Channel: British and French Painting in the age of Romanticism*. London: Tate Publishing, 2003.

Pissarro, Joachim. *Pioneering Modern Painting: Cézanne & Pissarro 1865–1885*. New York: Museum of Modern Art, 2005.

Rodner, William S. *J. M. W. Turner: Romantic Painter of the Industrial Revolution*. Berkeley: Univ. of California Press, 1997.

Rosenblum, Robert, and H. W. Janson. *19th Century Art*. Rev. & updated ed. Upper Saddle River, NJ: Pearson Prentice Hall, 2005.

Rubin, James H. *Impressionism. Art & Ideas*. London: Phaidon Press, 1999.

Rybczynski, Witold. *A Clearing in the Distance: Frederick Law Olmsted and America in the Nineteenth Century*. New York: Scribner, 1999.

Smith, Paul. *Seurat and the Avant-Garde*. New Haven: Yale Univ. Press, 1997.

Thomson, Belinda. *Impressionism: Origins, Practice, Reception*. World of Art. New York: Thames & Hudson, 2000.

Twyman, Michael. *Breaking the Mould: The First Hundred Years of Lithography*. The Panizzi Lectures, 2000. London: British Library, 2001.

Vaughan, William, and Francoise Cachin. *Arts of the 19th Century*. 2 vols. New York: Abrams, 1998.

Werner, Marcia. *Pre-Raphaelite Painting and Nineteenth-Century Realism*. New York: Cambridge Univ. Press, 2005.

Zemel, Carol M. *Van Gogh's Progress: Utopia, Modernity, and Late-Nineteenth-Century Art*. California Studies in the History of Art, 36. Berkeley: Univ. of California Press, 1997.

Chapter 31 Modern Art in Europe and The Americas, 1900–1950

Ades, Dawn, comp. *Art and Power: Europe under the Dictators, 1930–45*. Stuttgart, Germany: Oktagon in assoc. with Hayward Gallery, 1995.

Antliff, Mark, and Patricia Leighten. *Cubism and Culture*. World of Art. London: Thames & Hudson, 2001.

Bailey, David A. *Rhapsodies in Black: Art of the Harlem Renaissance*. London: Hayward Gallery, 1997.

Balken, Debra Bricker. *Debating American Modernism: Stieglitz, Duchamp, and the New York Avant-Garde*. New York: American Federation of Arts, 2003.

Barron, Stephanie, ed. *Degenerate Art: The Fate of the Avant-Garde in Nazi Germany*. Los Angeles: Los Angeles County Museum of Art, 1991.

———, and Wolf-Dieter Dube, eds. *German Expressionism: Art and Society*. New York: Rizzoli, 1997.

Bochner, Jay. *An American Lens: Scenes from Alfred Stieglitz's New York Secession*. Cambridge, MA: MIT Press, 2005.

Bohn, Willard. *The Rise of Surrealism: Cubism, Dada, and the Pursuit of the Marvelous*. Albany: State Univ. of New York Press, 2002.

Bowlt, John E., and Evgeniia Petrova, eds. *Painting Revolution: Kandinsky, Malevich and the Russian Avant-Garde*. Bethesda, MD: Foundation for International Arts and Education, 2000.

Bown, Matthew Cullerne. *Socialist Realist Painting*. New Haven: Yale Univ. Press, 1998.

Brown, Milton W. *Story of the Armory Show*. 2nd ed. New York: Abbeville Press, 1988.

Chassey, Eric de, ed. *American Art: 1908–1947, from Winslow Homer to Jackson Pollock*. Trans. Jane McDonald. Paris: Réunion des Musées Nationaux, 2001.

Corn, Wanda M. *The Great American Thing: Modern Art and National Identity, 1915–1935*. Berkeley: Univ. of California Press, 1999.

Curtis, Penelope. *Sculpture 1900–1945: After Rodin*. Oxford History of Art. Oxford: Oxford Univ. Press, 1999.

Dachy, Marc. *Dada: The Revolt of Art*. Trans. Liz Nash. New York: Abrams, 2006.

Elger, Dietmar. *Expressionism: A Revolution in German Art*. Ed. Ingo F. Walther. Trans. Hugh Beyer. New York: Taschen, 1998.

Fer, Briony. *On Abstract Art*. New Haven: Yale Univ. Press, 1997.

Fletcher, Valerie J. *Crosscurrents of Modernism: Four Latin American Pioneers: Diego Rivera, Joaquín Torres-García, Wifredo Lam, Matta*. Washington, DC: Hirshhorn Museum and Sculpture Garden in assoc. with the Smithsonian Institution Press, 1992.

Folgarait, Leonard. *Mural Painting and Social Revolution in Mexico, 1920–1940: Art of the New Order*. New York: Cambridge Univ. Press, 1998.

Forgács, Eva. *The Bauhaus Idea and Bauhaus Politics*. Trans. John Bátki. New York: Central European Univ. Press, 1995.

Frampton, Kenneth. *Modern Architecture: A Critical History*. 4th ed. World of Art. London: Thames & Hudson, 2007.

Gooding, Mel. *Abstract Art*. Movements in Modern Art. Cambridge: Cambridge Univ. Press, 2001.

Grant, Kim. *Surrealism and the Visual Arts: Theory and Reception*. New York: Cambridge Univ. Press, 2005.

Green, Christopher. *Art in France: 1900–1940*. Pelican History of Art. New Haven: Yale Univ. Press, 2000.

Harris, Jonathan. *Federal Art and National Culture: The Politics of Identity in New Deal America*. Cambridge Studies in American Visual Culture. New York: Cambridge Univ. Press, 1995.

Harrison, Charles, Francis Frascina, and Gill Perry. *Primitivism, Cubism, Abstraction: The Early Twentieth Century*. New Haven: Yale Univ. Press, 1993.

Haskell, Barbara. *The American Century: Art & Culture, 1900–1950*. New York: Whitney Museum of American Art, 1999.

Herskovic, Marika, ed. *American Abstract Expressionism of the 1950s: An Illustrated Survey: With Artists' Statements, Artwork and Biographies*. New York: New York School Press, 2003.

Hill, Charles C. *The Group of Seven: Art for a Nation*. Ottawa: National Gallery of Canada, 1995.

James-Chakraborty, Kathleen, ed. *Bauhaus Culture: From Weimar to the Cold War*. Minneapolis: Univ. of Minnesota Press, 2006.

Karmel, Pepe. *Picasso and the Invention of Cubism*. New Haven: Yale Univ. Press, 2003.

Lista, Giovanni. *Futurism*. Trans. Susan Wise. Paris: Terrail, 2001.

Lucie-Smith, Edward. *Latin American Art of the 20th Century*. 2nd ed. World of Art. London: Thames & Hudson, 2005.

McCarter, Robert, ed. *On and by Frank Lloyd Wright: A Primer of Architectural Principles*. New York: Phaidon Press, 2005.

Moudry, Roberta, ed. *The American Skyscraper: Cultural Histories*. New York: Cambridge Univ. Press, 2005.

Rickey, George. *Constructivism: Origins and Evolution*. Rev. ed. New York: Braziller, 1995.

Taylor, Brandon. *Collage: The Making of Modern Art*. London: Thames & Hudson, 2004.

Weston, Richard. *Modernism*. London: Phaidon Press, 1996.

White, Michael. *De Stijl and Dutch Modernism*. Critical Perspectives in Art History. New York: Manchester Univ. Press, 2003.

Whitfield, Sarah. *Fauvism*. World of Art. New York: Thames & Hudson, 1996.

Whitford, Frank. *The Bauhaus: Masters and Students by Themselves*. Woodstock, NY: Overlook Press, 1993.

Zurier, Rebecca, Robert W. Snyder, and Virginia M. Mecklenburg. *Metropolitan Lives: The Ashcan Artists and Their New York*. Washington, DC: National Museum of American Art, 1995.

Chapter 32 The International Scene since 1950

Alberro, Alexander, and Blake Stimson, eds. *Conceptual Art: A Critical Anthology*. Cambridge, MA: MIT Press, 1999.

Archer, Michael. *Art Since 1960*. 2nd ed. World of Art. New York: Thames & Hudson, 2002.

Atkins. Robert. *Artspeak: A Guide to Contemporary Ideas, Movements, and Buzzwords*. 2nd ed. New York: Abbeville Press, 1997.

Ault, Julie. *Art Matters: How the Culture Wars Changed America*. Ed. Brian Wallis, Marianne Weems, and Philip Yenawine. New York: New York Univ. Press, 1999.

Battcock, Gregory. *Minimal Art: A Critical Anthology*. Berkeley: Univ. of California Press, 1995.

Beardsley, John. *Earthworks and Beyond: Contemporary Art in the Landscape*. 4th ed. ebook. New York: Abbeville Press, 2006.

Bird, Jon, and Michael Newman, eds. *Rewriting Conceptual Art*. Critical Views. London: Reaktion Books, 1999.

Bishop, Claire. *Installation Art: A Critical History*. New York: Routledge, 2005.

Blais, Joline, and Jon Ippolito. *At the Edge of Art*. London: Thames & Hudson, 2006.

Buchloh, Benjamin H. D. *Neo-Avantgarde and Culture Industry: Essays on European and American Art from 1955 to 1975.* Cambridge, MA: MIT Press, 2000.

Carlebach, Michael L. *American Photojournalism Comes of Age.* Washington, DC: Smithsonian Institution Press, 1997.

Causey, Andrew. *Sculpture since 1945.* Oxford History of Art. Oxford: Oxford Univ. Press, 1998.

Corris, Michael, ed. *Conceptual Art: Theory, Myth, and Practice.* New York: Cambridge Univ. Press, 2004.

De Oliveira, Nicolas, Nicola Oxley, and Michael Petry. *Installation Art in the New Millennium: The Empire of the Senses.* New York: Thames & Hudson, 2003.

De Salvo, Donna, ed. *Open Systems: Rethinking Art c.1970.* London: Tate Gallery, 2005.

Fabozzi, Paul F. *Artists, Critics, Context: Readings In and Around American Art Since 1945.* Upper Saddle River, NJ: Pearson/Prentice Hall, 2002.

Fineberg, Jonathan. *Art Since 1940: Strategies of Being.* 2nd ed. New York: Abrams, 2000.

Flood, Richard, and Frances Morris. *Zero to Infinity: Arte Povera, 1962–1972.* Minneapolis, MN: Walker Art Center, 2001.

Goldberg, RoseLee. *Performance Art: From Futurism to the Present.* Rev. and exp. ed. World of Art. London: Thames & Hudson, 2001.

Goldstein, Ann. *A Minimal Future? Art as Object 1958–1968.* Los Angeles: Museum of Contemporary Art, 2004.

Grande, John K. *Art Nature Dialogues: Interviews with Environmental Artists.* Albany: State Univ. of New York Press, 2004.

Grosenick, Uta, ed. *Women Artists in the 20th and 21st Century.* New York: Taschen, 2001.

———, and Burkhard Riemschneider, eds. *Art at the Turn of the Millennium.* New York: Taschen, 1999.

Grunenberg, Christoph, ed. *Summer of Love: Art of the Psychedelic Era.* London: Tate Gallery, 2005.

Hitchcock, Henry Russell, and Philip Johnson. *The International Style.* New York: Norton, 1995.

Hopkins, David. *After Modern Art: 1945–2000.* Oxford History of Art. Oxford: Oxford Univ. Press, 2000.

Jencks, Charles. *The New Paradigm in Architecture: The Language of Post-Modernism.* New Haven: Yale Univ. Press, 2002.

Jodidio, Philip. *New Forms: Architecture in the 1990s.* Taschen's World Architecture. New York: Taschen, 2001.

Johnson, Deborah, and Wendy Oliver, eds. *Women Making Art: Women in the Visual, Literary, and Performing Arts Since 1960.* Eruptions, vol. 7. New York: Peter Lang, 2001.

Jones, Caroline A. *Machine in the Studio: Constructing the Postwar American Artist.* Chicago: Univ. of Chicago Press, 1996.

Joselit, David. *American Art Since 1945.* World of Art. London: Thames & Hudson, 2003.

Legault, Réjean, and Sarah Williams Goldhagen, eds. *Anxious Modernisms: Experimentation in Postwar Architectural Culture.* Montréal: Canadian Centre for Architecture, 2000.

Lucie-Smith, Edward. *Movements in Art since 1945.* New ed. World of Art. London: Thames & Hudson, 2001.

Madoff, Steven Henry, ed. *Pop Art: A Critical History.* The Documents of Twentieth Century Art. Berkeley: Univ. of California Press, 1997.

Moos, David, ed. *The Shape of Colour: Excursions in Colour Field Art, 1950–2005.* Toronto: Art Gallery of Ontario, 2005.

Paul, Christiane. *Digital Art.* 2nd ed. World of Art. London: Thames & Hudson, 2008.

Phillips, Lisa. *The American Century: Art and Culture, 1950–2000.* New York: Whitney Museum of American Art, 1999.

Pop Art: Contemporary Perspectives. Princeton: Princeton Univ. Art Museum, 2007.

Ratcliff, Carter. *The Fate of a Gesture: Jackson Pollock and Postwar American Art.* New York: Farrar, Straus, Giroux, 1996.

Reckitt, Helena, ed. *Art and Feminism.* Themes and Movements. London: Phaidon Press, 2001.

Robertson, Jean, and Craig McDaniel. *Themes of Contemporary Art: Visual Art after 1980.* 2nd ed. New York: Oxford Univ. Press, 2009.

Robinson, Hilary, ed. *Feminism-Art-Theory: An Anthology, 1968–2000.* Malden, MA: Blackwell, 2001.

Rorimer, Anne. *New Art in the 60s and 70s: Redefining Reality.* New York: Thames & Hudson, 2001.

Rush, Michael. *New Media in Late 20th-Century Art.* 2nd ed. World of Art. London: Thames & Hudson, 2005.

———. *Video Art.* 2nd ed. London: Thames & Hudson, 2007.

Sandler, Irving. *Art of the Postmodern Era: From the Late 1960s to the Early 1990s.* New York: Icon Editions, 1996.

Shohat, Ella. *Talking Visions: Multicultural Feminism in a Transnational Age.* Documentary Sources in Contemporary Art, vol. 5. New York: New Museum of Contemporary Art, 1998.

Stiles, Kristine, and Peter Selz. *Theories and Documents of Contemporary Art: A Sourcebook of Artists' Writings.* California Studies in the History of Art, 35. Berkeley: Univ. of California, 1996.

Sylvester, David. *About Modern Art.* 2nd ed. New Haven: Yale Univ. Press, 2001.

Varnedoe, Kirk, Paola Antonelli, and Joshua Siegel, eds. *Modern Contemporary: Art Since 1980 at MoMA.* Rev. ed. New York: Museum of Modern Art, 2004.

Waldman, Diane. *Collage, Assemblage, and the Found Object.* New York: Abrams, 1992.

Weintraub, Linda, Arthur Danto, and Thomas McEvilley. *Art on the Edge and Over: Searching for Art's Meaning in Contemporary Society, 1970s–1990s.* Litchfield, CT: Art Insights, 1996.

CREDITS

Introduction
Intro 1 © 2010 Digital Image, The Museum of Modern Art, New York/Scala, Florence; Intro 2 object no 1997.007.0697; Art and its Contexts © Achim Bednorz; Closer Look a British Library, London; Closer Look b © Quattrone, Florence; Closer Look © The Frick Collection, New York; Closer Look The British Library, London; Intro 3 Su concessione del Ministero per il Beni e le Attività Culturali – photo Index/Tosi; Intro 4 © 2007 Image copyright The Metropolitan Museum of Art/Art Resource, NY/Scala, Florence; Closer Look a Ashmolean Museum, Oxford, England, U.K.; Closer Look b Princeton University Art Museum. Photo: Bruce M. White; Intro 5, Intro 9 © 2004 Photo The Philadelphia Museum of Art/Scala, Florence; Intro 6 Kunst-historisches Museum, Vienna; Intro 8 © Quattrone, Florence

Chapter 1
1.1 Michael Lorblanchet/San Heritage Centre/Rock Art Research Centre/University of the Witwatersrand, Johannesburg; 1.2 © Tom Till; 1.3 © 2009 Photo Werner Forman Archive/Scala, Florence; 1.4 Christopher Henshilwood/Centre for Development Studies, University of Bergen; 1.5 Jack Unruh/NGS Image Collection; 1.6 K. H. Augustin, Esslingen/Ulmer Museum; 1.7 Naturhistorisches Museum, Vienna, Austria. © Erich Lessing/Art Resource, NY; 1.8 The Art Archive/Moravian Museum Brno/Alfredo Dagli Orti; 1.9, 1.11, 1.13 Sisse Brimberg/National Geographic Image Collection; 1.10 Ministere de la Culture et de la Communication. Direction Regionale des affaires Culturelles de Rhone-Alpes. Service Regional de l'Archeologie; 1.12, 1.14 Yvonne Vertut; 1.15 Jean Schormans/Reunion des Musees Nationaux/Art Resource, NY; 1.16 John Swogger; 1.17, 1.27, 1.28 Erich Lessing/Art Resource, NY; Closer Look Reconstruction by John Swogger, originally published as fig. 5.8 in Ian Hodder's The Leopard's Tale; 1.18 Souvatzi, S. 2009. A Social Archaeology of Households in Neolithic Greece. An Anthropological Approach, fig. 4.8b. Cambridge University Press. After Theocharis 1973 (Theocharis, D.R. Neolithic Greece. National Bank of Greece, 1973); 1.19 Catherine Perlès The Early Neolithic in Greece, The First Farming Communities in Europe, Cambridge University Press, 2001. Illustrated by Gerard Monthel. © Catherine Perlès, published by Cambridge University Press. Reproduced with permission; 1.20 The Department of the Environment, Heritage & Local Government; 1.21 Aerofilms; 1.22 Courtesy Antiquity Magazine; 1.23 English Heritage; 1.24 © Sakamoto Photo Research Laboratory/Corbis; 1.25 Catherine Perlès; 1.26 Dr. Brian F. Byrd; Object Speaks a, b Erich Lessing/Art Resource, NY; 1.29 Bridgeman-Giraudon/Art Resource NY

Chapter 2
2.1 Photo Josse, Paris; 2.2a World Tourism Organization: Iraq; Art and its Contexts John Simmons; 2-3 a, b AKG-Images/Erich Lessing; 2.4 Courtesy of the Oriental Institute of the University of Chicago; Object Speaks a, b, c University of Pennsylvania Museum of Archaeology and Anthropology; 2.5 a, b University of Pennsylvania Museum of Archaeology and Anthropology, B16728 (U.10872); 2.6 © 1990 Photo Scala, Florence; 2.7 © Corbis; 2.8 D. Arnaudet/Louvre, Paris France/Reunion des Musees Nationaux/Art Resource, NY; Art and its Contexts Herve Lewandowski/Art Resource/Musee du Louvre; 2.9 Art Archive/Dagli Orti; 2.10, 2.13 © The Trustees of the British Museum; Closer Look © The Trustees of the British Museum; 2.11 Courtesy of the Oriental Institute of the University of Chicago; 2.12 World Tourism Organization: Iraq; Technique Herve Lewandowski. Louvre, Paris, France/Reunion des Musées Nationaux/Art Resource, NY; 2.14, 2.18 Courtesy of the Oriental Institute of the University of Chicago; 2.15 Bildarchiv Preussischer Kulturbesitz, Berlin, Germany; 2.16 SuperStock, Inc.; 2.17 Gérard Degeorge/Corbis

Chapter 3
3.1 The Egyptian Museum, Cairo; Closer Look a, b Werner Forman/Art Resource NY; 3.3 © Archivo Iconografico/Corbis. All Rights Reserved; 3.4 © Graham Harrison; 3.5 Maltings © Dorling Kindersley; 3.6 © Roger Wood/Corbis; 3.7 Werner Forman; 3.8 Araldo de Luca/Photo © The Egyptian Museum, Cairo; 3.9 Photograph © 2008 Museum of Fine Arts, Boston.; 3.10 Hervé Lewandowski/Musée du Louvre/RMN Reunion des Musées Nationaux, France. Art Resource, NY; 3.11 Courtesy of the Oriental Institute of the University of Chicago; 3.12, 3.14, 3.20 Yvonne Vertut; 3.13 The Nelson-Atkins Museum of Art, Kansas City, Missouri. Photo: Jamison Miller; 3.15 © 2009 White Image/Scala, Florence; 3.16, 3.33 © The Trustees of the British Museum; 3.17 Egyptian Museum, Cairo. The Metropolitan Museum of Art, New York Excavation 1915-16. Photo by Araldo de Luca; Technique © The Trustees of the British Museum; 3.21 Scala/Art Resource/The Metropolitan Museum of Art; 3.22 Peter A. Clayton; 3.23 Dorling Kindersley; 3.24 Photo Scala, Florence; 3.25 Ikona/Araldo de Luca; 3.26 Bildarchiv Preussischer Kulturbesitz, Berlin, Germany; 3.27 Art Resource, NY; 3.28 Art Resource/Bildarchiv Preussischer Kulturbesitz; Technique Art Resource/© The Trustees of The

British Museum; 3.29 Araldo de Luca; Object Speaks a Art Archive/Dagli Orti; Object Speaks b Terrence Spencer/Time & Life Pictures/ Getty Images; 3.30 The Getty Conservation Institute © The J. Paul Getty Trust 2010. All rights reserved. Photo by Guillermo Aldana; Recovering the Past © The Trustees of the British Museum/Art Resource, NY; 3.31 Art Resource/© The Trustees of the British Museum; 3.32 RMN/Hervé Lewandowski

Chapter 4
4.1 Petros M. Nomikos/Courtesy of Thera Foundations, The Archaeological Society at Athens; 4-2a © 2009 Image copyright The Metropolitan Museum of Art/Art Resource/Scala, Florence; 4-2b Elizabeth A Hendrix, 'Painted Early Cycladic Figures,' Hesperia Vol 72 Number 4, 2003. Fig 4; 4.3 © Copenhagen National Museum #4697; 4.4 McRae Books Srl; 4.5, 4.6, 4.12, 4.13, 4.20 Studio Kontos Photostock; Technique Studio Kontos Photostock; 4.7 Erich Lessing/Art Resource, NY; 4.8a © American School of Classical Studies at Athens, Alison Frantz Collection; 4.8b, 4.9, 4.16 Nimtallah/Art Resource, NY; 4.10 Art Resource, NY; 4.11 National Archaeological Museum, © Hellenic Ministry of Culture, Archaeological Receipts Fund; Closer Look Nimtallah/Art Resource, NY; Recovering the Past National Archaeological Museum, Athens/Hirmer Fotoarchiv, Munich, Germany; Object Speaks a Deutsches Archäologisches Institut, Athens; Object Speaks b, c Studio Kontos Photostock; 4.18 © Vanni Archive/Corbis. All Rights Reserved; 4.19 © Art Archive/Dagli Orti; 4.20 Studio Kontos Photostock

Chapter 5
5.1 © Photo Vatican Museums; 5.2 Photograph © 1996 The Metropolitan Museum of Art/Art Resource, NY; 5.3 © Metropolitan Museum of Art/Art Resource, NY; 5.4 J. Paul Getty Museum, Villa Collection, Malibu, California; 5.5 © Art Archive/Dagli Orti. 5.6 Dorling Kindersley; 5.8, 5.19, 5.23a, b, 5.25, 5.36, 5.37, 5.39, 5.44, 5.51 Studio Kontos Photostock; 5.9b Fotografica Foglia, Naples; 5.10 © Craig & Marie Mauzy, Athens; 5.11 Courtesy Laurence King Publishing, John Griffiths Pedley, Greek Art and Archaeology 4th ed © 2007; 5.13 Staatliche Antikensammlungen, Munich; 5.14 Studio Koppermann; 5.15 Vanni/Art Resource, NY; 5.16 Photograph © 1997 The Metropolitan Museum of Art/Art Resource, NY; 5.17 Art Resource/Bildarchiv Preussischer Kulturbesitz; 5.18 Art Resource, NY; 5.21 Biblio-thèque Nationale de France; 5.22 A. Bracchetti/© Photo Vatican Museums; Closer Look Courtesy of the Ministero Beni e Att. Culturali. Image © 1999 Metropolitan Museum of Art; Technique Photograph © Museum of Fine Arts, Boston; Object Speaks a, b © Aaron M. Levin, Baltimore; Object Speaks c © Fotografica Foglia, Naples; 5.24 Art Resource/Bildarchiv Preussischer Kulturbesitz; 5.26a Scala, Florence/Art Resource, NY; 5.26b Scala, Florence/Museo Archeologico Naz, Italy/Art Resource, NY; 5.27 © The Trustees of the British Museum; 5.28 Courtesy Ministero per il Beni e le Attività Culturali; 5.30 With permission of the Royal Ontario Museum © ROM; 5.31a Greek National Tourism Organization; 5.32 a, b, c, 5.33, 5.34 © The Trustees of the British Museum/Art Resource, NY; Technique Scala, Florence/Art Resource, NY; 5.35 Bridgeman Art Library; 5.38 Wolfgang Kaehler/Corbis; Art and its Contexts Photograph © 2010 Museum of Fine Arts, Boston.; 5.41 © 2007 Image copyright The Metropolitan Museum of Art/Scala, Florence; 5.42, 5.47 Scala, Florence/Art Resource, NY; 5.43 Photograph © 2010 Museum of Fine Arts, Boston; 5.45 P. Zigrossi/© Photo Vatican Museums; 5.46 M. Sarri/© Photo Vatican Museums; 5.48 Art Resource/The Metropolitan Museum of Art; 5.49 Museo Nazionale, Napoli. Scala/Alinari/Art Resource, NY; Art and its Contexts Canali Photobank, Milan, Italy; 5.50 Archaeological Museum, Pella; Art and its Contexts a Marvin Trachtenberg; 5.52 © Corbis; Art and its Contexts © RMN/ Jean-Gilles Berizzi; 5.53 Art Resource/Bildarchiv Preussischer Kulturbesitz; 5.54 Museo Pio Clementino, Vatican Museums, Vatican State, SCALA/Art Resource, NY; 5.55 Art Resource, NY; 5.56 Gerard Blot/C. Jean/RMN/Scala, Florence/Art Resource NY; 5.57 Photograph © 1997 The Metropolitan Museum of Art/Art Resource, NY; 5.58 D. Arnaudet/J. Schormans/RMN/Scala, Florence/Art Resource, NY

Chapter 6
6.1 © 2003 Photo Scala, Florence/Fotografica Foglia. Courtesy of the Ministero Beni e Att. Culturali; 6.2 Maurizio Bellu/Ikona; 6.3 Penelope Davies; 6.5, 6.14, 6.25, 6.28, 6.35, 6.45, 6.50, 6.52, 6.66 Canali Photobank; Elements of Architecture Art Archive; 6.6 © 1990 Photo Scala, Florence. Courtesy of the Ministero Beni e Att. Culturali; 6.7 Nimatallah/Art Resource, NY; 6.8, 6.9, 6.12, 6.42, 6.44 Scala, Florence/Art Resource, NY; 6.10 Photograph © Museum of Fine Arts, Boston; 6.11, 6.16, 6.43 © Vincenzo Pirozzi; Art and its Contexts Araldo de Luca; 6.13 Image © The Metropolitan Museum of Art/Art Resource, NY; Elements of Architecture Danita Delimont Photography; 6.15 American

Numismatic Society of New York; 6.18 Vatican Museums & Galleries, Vatican City/Superstock; Object Speaks a, b A. Jemolo/Ikona; 6.19 Kunsthistorisches Museum, Vienna, Austria; 6.20 George Gerster/Photo Researchers, Inc.; 6.21 Dorling Kindersley; 6.22 Cambridge University Press. Reprinted with the permission of Cambridge University Press; 6.23 Alberti/Index Ricerca Iconografica; 6.26 © Fotografica Foglia, Naples; 6.29 © The Metropolitan Museum of Art, NY.; 6.30 Erich Lessing/Art Resource, NY; 6.31 Museo Archeologico Nazionale, Naples; 6.32 A.Vasari/Index Ricerca Iconografica; 6.33, 6.59, 6.60 © Achim Bednorz, Koln; 6.36a, b, 6.61 Araldo de Luca/Index Ricerca Iconografica; 6.37a, b Musei Vaticana/Ikona; 6.38 Index/Vasari; 6.40 Dr. James E. Packer; 6.41 AKG-images; 6.47 After William L.MacDonald, The Architecture of the Roman Empire I: An Introductory Study. New Haven and London: Yale University Press. 1965, fig 9; 6.48 Danita Delimont Photography; 6.51 Art Resource/Bildarchiv Preussischer Kulturbesitz; Technique © Photo Vatican Museums; 6.53 Araldo De Luca/Musei Capitolini, Rome, Italy; 6.54 Art Resource/The Metropolitan Museum of Art; 6.55 Alinari/Art Resource, NY; 6.57 Araldo de Luca; Closer Look The Walters Art Museum, Baltimore; 6.58 Alinari/Art Resource, NY; 6.62 © Ikona Photo/Foto Vasari Roma; 6.63 Ikona; 6.67 Art Resource/© The Trustees of the British Museum; 6.68 V&A Images

Chapter 7
7.1 © 2007 Image copyright The Metropolitan Museum of Art/Art Resource, NY/Scala, Florence; 7.2 Soprintendenza Archeologica di Roma, Italy/Ikona; 7.3 Princeton University Press/Art Resource, NY; 7.4 Yale University Art Gallery, Dura Europos Collection; Closer Look Zev Radovan/Bibleland Pictures; Recovering the Past b Art Resource/Yale University Art Gallery; Recovering the Past b Yale University Art Gallery, Dura Europos Collection; Art and its Contexts Index Ricerca Iconografica; 7.5, 7.15, 7.16, 7.36a Canali Photobank; 7.6 The Cleveland Museum of Art; 7.7 © 2010 Biblioteca Apostolica Vaticana. By permission of Biblioteca Apostolica Vaticana, with all rights reserved; 7.8 © Vincenzo Pirozzi; 7.9 Nimatallah/Index Ricerca Iconografica; 7.10, 7.11, 7.25, 7.34 Scala, Florence/Art Resource, NY; 7.12 © Photo Vatican Museums; 7.13 Vasari/Index Ricerca Iconografica; 7.14 © Gina Berto Vanni/ Vanni Archive/ Corbis. All Rights Reserved; 7.17, 7.42 © Achim Bednorz, Koln; 7.19 Robert Harding/Getty Images; 7.21 Photo Scala, Florence; 7.22 AKG-Images/Cameraphoto; 7.23, 7.24 Canali Photobank; 7.26, 7.39 © Trustees of The British Museum, London; 7.27 Bildarchiv der Osterreichische Nationalbibliothek; 7.28 © 2007 Image copyright The Metropolitan Museum of Art/ Art Resource, NY/Scala, Florence; 7.29, 7.35 Studio Kontos Photostock; 7.30 Henri Stierlin, Geneva © Art Archive/Dagli Orti; 7.32 Bruce White/The Metropolitan Museum of Art/Scala, Florence; 7.33 Photo: Bruce White © The Metropolitan Museum of Art, NY; 7.37 © Scala/Tretyakov Gallery, Moscow; 7.38 Art Resource/ Musée du Louvre; 7.41 Ali Kabas/Alamy; Object Speaks a Art Archive; Object Speaks b Dr. Reha Gunay; 7.43 Sovfoto/Eastfoto

Chapter 8
8.1 Bibliothèque Nationale de France; 8.2 © Kazuyoshi Nomachi/Corbis. All Rights Reserved; Technique a AKG Images/François Guénet; Technique b Photo by Roya Marefat; Technique c Jan Boer; 8.7 AKG Images/Erich Lessing; Technique e Robert Ousterhout; Technique f Dede Fairchild Ruggles; Technique g © 2010 De Agostini Picture Library/Scala, Florence; 8.3 © Annie Griffiths Belt/Corbis. All Rights Reserved; 8.4 Dorling Kindersley; 8.5 Zev Radovan/Bibleland Pictures; 8.6 © Roger Wood/Corbis. All Rights Reserved; Object Speaks a, c Raffaello Bencini Fotografo; 8.8 B. O'Kane/Alamy; 8.9 After Robert Hillenbrand, Islamic Architecture, 1994, p. 195; Ch 8 Closer Look © Trustees of the British Museum; 8.10 © Achim Bednorz, Koln; 8.11 Peter Sanders Photography; 8.12 Scala, Florence/Art Resource, NY/The Metropolitan Museum of Art; 8.13 © 2010 Digital image Museum Associates/LACMA/Art Resource NY, Scala, Florence; 8.14 Scala, Florence/Art Resource, NY/Musée du Louvre; 8.15 Photograph © 1982 The Metropolitan Museum of Art; 8.16 © RMN/Frank Raux; 8.17 Musée du Louvre/RMN Réunion des Musées Nationaux, France. Scala/Art Resource, NY; 8.18 Photograph © 1994 The Metropolitan Museum of Art, New York, 1994. Scala, Florence/Art Resource, NY/The Metropolitan Museum of Art; 8.19 Bibliothèque Nationale de France; 8.20 National Library, Egypt; 8.21 By permission of The British Library; 8.22 Sonia Halliday Photographs; 8.23 Drawn by Christopher Woodward. From A History of Ottoman Architecture by Godfrey Goodwin, Thames & Hudson, London and New York; 8.24 Art Archive/Dagli Orti; 8.25 © Ruggero Vanni/Corbis; 8.26 Photograph © 1980 The Metropolitan Museum of Art; 8.27 Drawing by Keith Turner after Henri Stierlin © Aga Khan Visual Archive, MIT; 8.28 photo: Abbas Aminmansour; 8.29 Culture and Sport Glasgow (Museums); 8.30 V&A Images; 8.31 Courtesy of the architect/Aga Khan Trust for Culture

Page numbers in *italics* refer to illustrations and maps

Akbar Inspecting the Construction of Fatehpur Sikri from *Akbarnama* illuminated manuscript, 781, *781*

Akbar, Mughal emperor, 774, 779, 781

Akbarnama illuminated manuscript, 781, *781*

Akhenaten, 69, 70–72

relief (with his family), 71, *71*

statue, *70*

Akiode: twin figures (ere ibeji),Yoruba, Nigeria, 883–884, *884*

Akkad (Akkadians), 27, 28, 33, 36

Akrotiri,Thera, Cyclades: wall paintings, *80*, 81, 90, *91*, 92–93, *92–93*

Aksum, Ethiopia, 419

Alaric, 424

Albani, Alessandro, 913, 914

Albers, Anni, 1056

wall hanging, *1056*

Albers, Josef, 1055, 1056

Alberti, Leon Battista, 608

Albumen prints, 968, *969*

Albums, 369–370, 795, 797

Alcuin of York, 442

Aldred, 430

Alexander the Great, 47, 79, 142, 146, 149

Alexander the Great Confronts Darius III at the Battle of Issos mosaic, 146, *147*

Alfonso VI, 454, 461

Al-Hakam II, 268

Alhambra Palace, Granada, Spain, 273–275

Court of the Lions, *274*, 275

Hall of the Abencerrajes, Palace of the Lions, *274*, 275

Al-Hariri: *The Maqamat ("Assemblies")* illuminated manuscript, *260*, 261

Ali, caliph, 263

Allegories of the Five Senses series (Breughel and Rubens), 740, 741

Allegory, 625

Allegory of Sight from *Allegories of the Five Senses* series (Breughel and Rubens), *740*

Allegory with Venus and Cupid (Bronzino), *663*, 663–664

Alloway, Lawrence, 1090

Al-Sadi, 416

Altamira cave, Spain, 8, 11, *11*, 12

Altars and altarpieces, 227, 228, 425, 457, 461, 467, 535, 564

Altar, Nigeria, 411, *412*

Altar, Pergamon, 152, *153*, 154

Altar to Amitabha Buddha, *339*, 339–340

Champmol altarpiece (Broederlam), 563–564, *565*

Ghent Altarpiece (Jan and Hubert (?) van Eyck), 574, *576*, *577*

Holy Blood altarpiece (Riemenschneider), 679, 679–680

Isenheim altarpiece, St. Anthony abbey church, Colmar, 681, *681*, *682*, 683

Maestà altarpiece (Duccio), *542*, 543, *543*, 545

Mérode Altarpiece (Master of Flémalle), 571–573, *572–573*

The Nativity and Adoration of the Shepherds (Ghirlandaio), *623*, 624, *624*

Pesaro Madonna altarpiece (Titian), *657*, 657–658

Portinari Altarpiece (Goes), 580–582, *582–583*

St. Wolfgang Altarpiece (Pacher), 587, *588*, 589

Strozzi altarpiece (Orcagna), 548, *548*

Virgin and Child Enthroned (Cimabue), *535*, 535–536

Virgin and Child Enthroned (Duccio), 541, *541*

Altdorfer, Albrecht, 689

Danube Landscape, *688*, 689

Altes Museum, Berlin (Schinkel), 958, *958*

Altneuschul, Prague, Czech Republic, 518, *519*, 520

Am I Not a Man and a Brother? (Hackwood for Wedgwood), *918*, 919

Amalakas, 301, 308, 312

Amaral,Tarsila do, 1070, 1071

Abaporú (The One Who Eats), *1070*, 1070–1071

Amaranth (Yun Shouping), *804*

Amarna period, 70–72, 73

Amasis Painter, 117

Dionysos with Maenads vase, 117, *117*

Ambulatories, 228, *237*, 266, *494*, 495

Amenemhat, 62

Stele of Amenemhat, 64, *64*

Amenhotep III, 66

Amenhotep IV. *See* Akhenaten

America

The Depression, 1018, 1061, 1064, 1066

in eighteenth century, map, *905*

federal art funding, 1065, 1066, 1120

Korean War, 1084

in nineteenth century, map, *963*

Revolution, 903, 904, 930

since 1950, 1084

in twentieth century, map, *1019*

Vietnam War, 1084, 1093, 1094

American art

See also African American artists

Abstract Expressionism, 1073–1079, *1074–1080*, 1081, 1083

activist art, *1117*, 1117–1119, *1118*, *1119*

architecture (Deconstructivist), *1124*, 1125

architecture (Gothic Revival), 957, *957*

architecture (International style), 1057, *1104*, 1104–1105, *1105*

architecture (modern), *1011–1013*, 1011–1015, 1046–1048, *1046–1048*, *1049*

architecture (Neoclassical), *958*, 958–959, *959*

architecture (Postmodern), *1105*, 1105–1106, *1106*

Ashcan School, 1040, *1041*

assemblage, *1082*, 1083, 1084–1085, *1086*

Chicago School, *1011–1013*, 1012–1013, 1015

Conceptual art, *1096*, 1096–1097, 1100, *1100*, 1101, *1101*

Culture Wars art, 1115, 1116, 1120, *1120*

government funding, 1065, 1066, 1120

Harlem Renaissance, 1061, *1061*, *1064*, 1064–1065, *1065*

installation art, *1134*, 1134–1135

landscape design, 1012, 1014, *1014*

Minimalism, 1094, *1094*, 1095

Modern art, 1040–1043, *1041–1044*, 1061, *1061*, 1064–1067, *1064–1067*

New York School, 1079, 1081, 1083

painting (Neo-Expressionism), *1107*, 1107–1108

painting (Neoclassical), *902*, 903, 929–930, *930*

painting (Postmodern), *1107*, 1107–1108

painting (Realism), 979, *981*, 981–982, *982*, 983, *983*

painting (Romantic), *955*, 955–956

performance art, 1085, 1087, *1087*, *1088*, 1089, 1112, *1113*, 1130, *1130*

photography (early), *967*, 967, 968–969, *969*

photography (Modern), 1040–1042, *1041*, 1061, *1061*, 1064

photography (since 1950), *1089*, 1089–1090

Pop art, 1091–1093, *1092*, *1093*

Process art, *1097*, 1097–1099, *1098*, *1099*

Regionalism, 1065, 1067, *1067*

sculpture (Postmodern), 1112–1114, *1113*, *1114*, *1115*

sculpture (Realism), 982–983, *983*

video art, 1115, *1125*, 1125–1126, *1126*, *1129*, 1129–1130

American Civil War, 968, *969*

American Gothic (Wood), 1067, *1067*

American Revolution, 903, 904, 930

The Americans (Frank), 1089

Americas

See also America; Central America; Mesoamerica; North America; South America

agriculture, 378

European colonization, 835

map, *379*, *837*

settlement, 378

Amida Buddha, 363, 365, 367

Amida Buddha, Byodoin temple (Jocho), 366, 367, *367*

Descent of Amida and the Twenty-Five Bodhisattvas painting, 373, *373*, 375

Amitabha Buddha, 297, 339, 365, 372–773

altar (Chinese Sui Dynasty), *339*, 339–340

Western Paradise wall painting, Gansu, 340, *340*

Amorites, 28

Amphitheaters: Flavian (Colosseum), Rome, 188, 188–189, *189*

Amphora, 100, 101, *117*, *118*, *120*

Amsterdam: Portuguese synagogue (Bourman and Stalpaert), 752, *752*, 753

Amun, 51, 65, 69

Great Temple, Karnak, *66*, 66–67

An Gyeon, 797

Dream Journey to the Peach Blossom Land, 808, *808*

Analytic Cubism, *1016*, 1017, *1024*, 1024–1025

Anasazi. *See* Ancestral Puebloans

Anastasis fresco, Christ in Chora monastery, Constantinople, 256, *256*

Anatolia, 37, 39

Chatal Huyuk, 14, *15*

The Anatomy Lesson of Dr. Nicolaes Tulp (Rembrandt), 746, *746*

Anatsui, El, 900

Flag for a New World Power, 900, *900*

Anavysis Kouros statue, Athens, 115, *116*

Ancestor guardian (eyema bieri), Fang, Gabon, 898–899, *899*

Ancestral Puebloans, 397–399, 401, 852

Ancient Ruins in the Canon de Chelley (O'Sullivan), *401*

Andachtsbilder, 555

Andean cultures, 391

See Incas

architecture, 391, 393

ceramics, 393, *393*

Chavin, 391–392

geoglyphs, 392, *393*

jewelry, 394–395, *395*

metalwork, 378

Moche, 393–394

Nazca, 392

Paracas, 392

portrait vessels, 393, *394*

pyramids, 391, 393

sculpture, relief, 391–392, *392*

temples, 391–392

textiles, 391, 392, *392*, 394

tombs, 394

Andhra dynasties, 298, 303

Andokides Painter: *Herakles Driving a Bull to Sacrifice* amphora, *120*

Andrade, Oswald de, 1070, 1071

Andre, Carl, 1094

Andronicus II Palaeologus, emperor, 256

Angelico, Fra (Guido di Piero da Mugello), xl, xli, 612

Annunciation fresco, xl, 612–613, *613*

Man of Sorrows fresco, xl

San Marco monastery frescoes, Florence, xl, *xl*, 612–613, *613*

AngkorVat, Cambodia, 320, *322*, 323

Anglo-Saxons, 427–428, 429, 483, 484

Angola: Kongo, 419–420

Anguissola, Sofonisba, 664

Self-Portrait, 664, *664*

Aniconism, 262–263

Animal style, 43, 427

Animals

cave art, 1, *1*, 8–13, *9*, *10*, *11*, *12*, 13

domestication, 13

in Native American imagery, 849, *849*, 850, *850*, 851

Neolithic, 14, *14*

sculpture, 5, 5–6

Ankhs, 51

Anne, queen of England, 765

Annunciation (Martini and Memmi), *544*, 545

Annunciation fresco (Fra Angelico), xl, 612–613, *613*

Annunciation triptych from Mérode Altarpiece (Master of Flémalle), 571–573, *572–573*

Annunciation with Donors from Ghent Altarpiece (Jan and Hubert (?) van Eyck), *576*

Annunciation, Nativity and Adoration of the Shepherds relief, pulpit, baptistery, Pisa, Italy (Nicola Pisano), 524, *524*

Anthemius of Tralles, 234

Hagia Sophia church, Constantinople, *234*, 235, *235*, 236–237

Anthropometries of the Blue Period (Klein), *1088*

Anthropomorphs rock art, Great Gallery, Horseshoe Canyon, Utah, 400, *400*

Anthropophagic Manifesto (Andrade), 1070

Antigonus, 149

Antoninus Pius, 190

Antwerp, 696, 700–701, 705, 735

and craft, 856, 999, 1127
cultural context, xxxv–xxxvi, xxxix–xli
defined, xxvi–xxvii, xxix
and gender. *See* Feminist art
globalism, 1126–1127
and identity, 1114, 1121–1123, 1128–1135
meaning of, xxxiii–xxxv, xxxvi, xxxviii–xxxix, 6, 8–9, 18, 1084
in monasteries, 463, 464, 493
and music, 1001, 1029, 1031, 1076, 1084
physical properties, xxix, xxxvi
"primitive art" as a myth, 403, 404, 406, 856, 881
racial issues, 1084, 1099, 1102, 1107, 1110–1112, 1132–1135
reproductions, 964, 974
as satire, 920–921, *921*
and science, 922, *923*, 924–925
suppression, 1018, 1054, 1055
and technology, 1031–1032, *1033*, 1127–1128
visual expression, xxix–xxxiii, xxxvi–xxxviii
Arte Concreto-Invención, 1072
Artemis, 104
The Artifact Piece (Luna), 1112, *1113*
The Artist's Studio (Daguerre), 967, *967*
Arts and Crafts Movement, 999, *999*
Aryans, 295, 774
As If to Celebrate, I Discovered a Mountain Blooming with Red Flowers (Kapoor), 789, *789*
Ashanti, Ghana, 879, 891
gold work, *878*, 879, 891
textiles, 892, *893*
Ashcan School, 1040, *1041*
Ashikaga (Muromachi) period, 814–816, 817
Ashlar, 99
Ashoka, king of India, 291, 297, 298, 299
Ashokan pillars, India, *290*, 291, *296*, 297–298
Asmat, West Papua, 864–865
Aspects of Negro Life: From Slavery Through Reconstruction (Douglas), 1064, *1064*
Assemblage, 1026, *1026*, *1082*, 1083, 1084–1085, *1086*
Assisi, Italy: Saint Francis church, 523, *523*, *526*, 526–527
Association of Artists of Revolutionary Russia (AKhRR), 1051
Assumption of the Virgin fresco (Correggio), 653, 653–654
Assurbanipal, *42*, 43
Assurnasirpal II, 39, *40*, 41
Assyria (Assyrians), 39–43
Astragals, 110
Astronomy, or Venus Urania (Giambologna), 666, *666*
Asuka period, 359–361, 817
AT&T Corporation Headquarters (Sony Building), New York City (Johnson), 1106, *1106*
Ateliers, 781, 784, 814–815, 944
Aten, 70
Athena, 104, 130, 136
statue by Pheidias, Acropolis, Athens, 130, *130*
Temple of Athena Nike, Acropolis, Athens, 130, 137–138
Athena Attacking the Giants frieze, Pergamon, 152, *153*
Athenodoros: *Laocoön and His Sons* sculpture, *154*, 154–155
Athens, 102, 128, 149, *149*, *See also* Acropolis
Atmospheric (aerial) perspective, 562, 608, 611, 612
Atrial cross, Spanish Mesoamerica, 941, *941*
Atrium, 160, 180
Attack on the Castle of Love ivory relief, 552, *553*
Attalos I, 151
Audience hall, Fatehpur Sikri, India, 779, *780*
Augustine of Hippo, 464
The City of God, 424
Augustine, archbishop of Canterbury, 429
Augustus (Octavian), 169, 174, 176, 177, 178, 191
statue from Primaporta, 174–175, *175*
Aulus Metellus (The Orator) statue, 171, *171*, 173
Australia, 2, 859, 860, 861–862, 875, *See also* Aboriginal art
Austria
architecture (modern), 1045
Woman from Willendorf figurine, 6, *6*
Automatism, 1056–1057, 1077

Les Automistes, 1077
Autumn Colors on the Qiao and Hua Mountains handscroll (Zhao Mengfu), 794, *794*
Autumn Rhythm (Number 30) (Pollock), *1075*, 1075–1079
Autumn Salons, 1019, 1020
Autun, France: Saint-Lazare cathedral, 458, 477–479, *478*, *479*
Avalokiteshvara, bodhisattva, 772–773, *773*
Avant-garde, 965, 971
Axis mundi, 297, 300, 308, 345
Aztecs, 381, 835, 836
architecture, 836–837
Calendar Stone, 836, *840*
featherwork, *838*, 838–839
Great Pyramid, Tenochtitlan, 836–837
illuminated manuscripts, 836, *836*, 839, *839*
pyramids, 836–837
religious beliefs, 836, 837
sculpture, 837–838, *838*
Tenochtitlan, Mexico, 836–837

B

Babur Builds the Bagh-i Wafa from the *Baburnama* illuminated manuscript, *288*
Babur, Mughal emperor, 282, 288, 778–779
Baburnama illuminated manuscript, 288, *288*
Baby carrier, Native American (Sioux), 846, *846*
Babylon (Babylonians), 28, 38, 219
Neo-Babylonians, 43–44
Baca, Judith F.
Division of the Barrios from *The Great Wall of Los Angeles*, 1111, *1111*
The Great Wall of Los Angeles, 1111–1112
Bacchus, 104, 213, 214
Bacchus (Caravaggio), 721, *721*
Bacon, Francis, 1071
Head Surrounded by Sides of Beef, 1071, *1071*
Bacon, Francis, 756
Bada Shanren. *See* Zhu Da
Baerze, Jacques de, 563
Baghdad Kiosk, Topkapi Palace, Istanbul, 283, *284*
Baghdad, Iraq, 265
Bags
Native American (Delaware), 846, *847*
Papua New Guinea, 863–864, *864*
Baileys, 473
Baldachins/baldacchinos, 467, 527
Saint Peter's basilica, Rome (Bernini), 713–714
Baldung, Hans ("Grien"), 687
Death and the Matron, 687, 687–688
Baldus, Édouard-Denis, 968
House with Staircase from *Vues de Paris en Photographie*, 968, *969*
Ball, Hugo, 1037, 1039
"Karawane," 1037, *1037*
Ballgames, Mesoamerica, 378, 389, *389*
Balzac, Honoré de, 971
Bamiyan, Afghanistan: *Standing Buddha* statue, 306, *307*
The Banjo Lesson (Tanner), 983, *983*
Banqueting House, Whitehall Palace, London, 765–766, *766*, 767
Baptism of Christ (Piero della Francesca), 618, *618*
The Baptism of the Multitude door panel, San Giovanni baptistery, Florence, Italy (Andrea Pisano), *534*
Baptismal font, Notre-Dame-Aux-Fonts, Liège, France (Renier of Huy), 482, *482*
Baptisteries, 222, *223*, 226, 228, 465
A Bar at the Folies-Bergère (Manet), 978–979, *980*
Bar tracery, 507
"Barbarians," use of term, 151, 152, 178, 424
Barberini Palace and Square (Cruyl), 726, 727
Barberini Palace, Rome, *726*, 727, *727*
Barcelona, Spain: Casa Batlló (Gaudí), *1005*, 1005–1006
Bardon, Geoffrey, 875
Bargeboards, 870
Bargehaulers on the Volga (Repin), 979, *981*
Bark cloth, 874, *874*, 877, *877*
Bark painting, 859, 862, *862*
Barney, Matthew, 1129
Cremaster 3: Mahabyn, *1129*, 1129–1130
Baroque art

architecture (English), 765–766, *766*, 767, *768*, 768–769, *769*
architecture (French), *758*, 758–759, *759*
architecture (Italian), 712–713, *714*, 715, *717*, 717–718, *718*
architecture (Spanish), 734–735, *735*
ceiling decoration, 719, 719–720, 722, 727, 727–729, *729*, 759, 766, 767
gardens, 736, 737, *737*, 760
painting (Dutch), 743–755, *743–755*
painting (Flemish), 735–742, *736–742*
painting (French), 756–757, *757*, 759, 761–763, *761–764*, 765
painting (Italian), 718–729, *719–728*
painting (Spanish), 729–734, *729–734*
sculpture (Italian), 713–714, *715*, 715–717, *716*
Baroque period
described, 712
in England, 765–769
in Flanders, 735–742
in France, 755–764
in Italy, 712–729
in the Netherlands, 742–743
religious conflicts, 712, 765
science and the changing worldview, 712, 742, 755, 756
in Spain, 729–735
"Baroque," use of term, 712, 905
Barrel vaults, 160, 188, *188*, 209, 232, 461, 463
Barry, Charles: Houses of Parliament, London, 956–957
Barthes, Roland, 961
The Barunga Statement, Australian Aborigines, *858*, 859
Basil II, emperor, 249
Basil the Great of Cappadocia, 244
Basilica (Audience Hall of Constantius Chlorus), Trier, Germany, 207, *208*
Basilica of Maxentius and Constantine (Basilica Nova), Rome, *211*, 211–212, *212*
Basilica Ulpia, Rome, 191, 192, *193*
Basilica-plan churches, 226–228, *226–228*, 234, 438, 461
Basilicas, defined, 192
Basin of metalwork, Islamic (Ibn al-Zain), 277–278, *278*
Basketry, 845, *845*, 892, *892*
Basquiat, Jean-Michel, 1107, 1108
Horn Players, *1107*, 1107–1108
Bassus, Junius, 230
sarcophagus, 230, *230*
Bateman, Ann and Peter, *919*
Bateman, Hester, *919*
Baths of Caracalla, Rome, 146, 204, *205*
Battista Sforza and Federico da Montefeltro (Piero della Francesca), 618, *619*
Battle of Centaurs and Wild Beasts mosaic, Hadrian's Villa, Tivoli, *200*, 201
Battle of the Bird and the Serpent from *Commentary on the Apocalypse* (Beatus, Emeterius and Ende with Senior), 434, *434*
Battle of the Gods and the Giants frieze, Delphi, 108, *108*
The Battle of San Romano (Uccello), 592, *613*
The Battle of the Nudes engraving (Pollaiuolo), 608–609, *609*
Baudelaire, Charles, 976
Bauhaus art, 1054, *1054*, 1055, 1056, *1056*, 1057
Bauhaus Building, Dessau, Germany (Gropius), 1054, *1054*
Baule, Côte d'Ivoire: sculpture, *889*, 889–890
Bautista de Toledo, Juan: The Escorial, Madrid, 694, *694*
Bavaria, Germany: Vierzehnheiligen church (Neumann), 910, *911*
Bawa, Manjit, 788
Dharma and the God, 788, *788*
Bayeux Embroidery (Bayeux Tapestry), 483, *484*, 484–485, *485*
Bays, 172, 819
Beadwork, 846, *847*
Beatus, 433
Commentary on the Apocalypse, 433, 433–434, *434*
Beaver effigy platform pipe, Hopewell culture, 395, 395–396
Beecroft, Vanessa, 1130
VB35, 1130, *1130*

houses, 13–17, 326
in Japan, 356, 358–359
metalwork, 22
religious beliefs, 14, 17, 19, 20
sculpture, 14, *14*, 21–22, 24, *24*
sculpture, relief, 14, 17–18, 24
tombs, 13–14, *17*, 17–18
wall paintings, 14
Neo-Palladianism, 916
Neoplatonism, 594, 625
Nepal
metalwork (Buddhist), 776, *776*
Tantric Buddhism, 773, 776
Neptune, 104
Neri, Filippo, 721
Nero, 178, 187
Nerva, 190
Neshat, Shirin
Rebellious Silence from "Women of Allah" series, 1121,
1121
"Women of Allah" series, 1121
Netherlands
See also Dutch art
Baroque period, 742–743
De Stijl, 1052, 1057
Rationalism, 1052–1053
Reformation, 696
Renaissance, 696–703, 705
Neumann, Johann Balthasar: Vierzehnheiligen church,
Bavaria, Germany, 910, *911*
New Britain, Papua New Guinea, 866
New Delhi, India, 786
India Gate (Lutyens), 786, *786*
New Guinea, 860, 863–865, 874, *875*
New Image of the World (Schoenmaeker), 1052
New Ireland, Papua New Guinea, 865–866
New Mexico
Chaco Canyon, 398, 399, 401
Pueblo Bonito, Chaco Canyon, *398*, 398–399, 401
Sun Dagger solar marker, Chaco Canyon, 399, *399*,
401
New Negro movement, 1061
New Realism, 1088
New York City, *957*
AT&T Corporation Headquarters (Sony Building)
(Johnson), 1106, *1106*
Central Park (Olmsted and Vaux), 1014, *1014*
Empire State Building, 1050, *1050*
The Gates, Central Park (Christo and Jeanne-Claude),
1103, *1103*
Guggenheim Museum (Frank Lloyd Wright),
1104–1105, *1105*
New York School, 1079, 1081, 1083
Seagram Building (Mies van der Rohe and Johnson),
1104, *1104*
skyscrapers, 1048, *1049*, 1050
Trans World Airlines (TWA) Terminal, John F.
Kennedy Airport (Saarinen), 1104, *1104*
Trinity Church (Upjohn), 957
Woolworth Building (Gilbert), 1048, *1049*
New York School, 1079, 1081, 1083
New Zealand, 859, 860, 869, 870–871
The Newborn (Brancusi), 1036, *1036*
Newgrange, Ireland: passage grave, *17*, 17–18
Newman, Barnett, 1081
Vir Heroicus Sublimis, *1080*, 1081
Newton (Blake), 929, *929*
Newton, Isaac, 904
Ngady mwaash mask, Kuba, Democratic Republic of the
Congo, *896*, 896–897, *897*
Ni Zan, 795
The Rongzi Studio, 795, *795*
Niccolò da Tolentino, *592*, 593, 605
Nicholas of Verdun, 520
Shrine of the Three Kings, 520, *520*
Niello, 87, 98
Nietzche, Friedrich, 1026
Nieuwenhove, Maarten van, 582
diptych, 582–583, *583*
Nigeria
Benin, 410–415, 883
Bini, 421

Ife, 403, 409–410
Igbo-Ukwu, 408–409
Nok, 407–408, 883
Yoruba, *402*, 403, 883–885, 890–891, 899
Night Attack on the Sanjo Palace handscroll, Japanese
(Kamakura period), 371, *372*
Night Chant (Navajo), 854
The Nightmare (Fuseli), 928, *928*
Nihonga painting, 831
Nike, 104
Nike (Victory) Adjusting Her Sandal relief, Acropolis,
Athens, 138, *138*
Nike (Victory) of Samothrace statue, *155*, 155–156
Nile, river, 50
Nine Mile Canyon, Utah, 400, *400*
Nineveh (Kuyunjik), 33, 43
Nishiki-e, 827
Nizami: *Khamsa (Five Poems)*, 281
Nkanu, Democratic Republic of the Congo: sculpture,
888, *888*
Nkisi nkonde (power figure), Kongo, Democratic
Republic of the Congo, 889, *890*
No. 3/No. 13 (Magenta, Black and Green on Orange)
(Rothko), *xxvi*, xxvii
Nochlin, Linda, 1099
Nocturne in Black and Gold, the Falling Rocket (Whistler),
999, *1000*, 1000–1001
Nok, Nigeria, 407–408
metalwork, 883
sculpture, *407*, 407–408, *408*, 883
Nolde, Emil, 1027, 1055
Masks, 1027, *1027*
Noli Me Tangere (Fontana), 664, *665*
Normandy, France, 435, 454
Norse, 427
North America, 395
See also Native Americans
agriculture, 395, 397, 852
European colonization, 835, 843–844, 849
funerary customs, 395
map, *379*, *837*, *844*
Mississippian Period, 396–397
Woodland Period, 395–396
North America. *See* America
Northwest Coast cultures, 849–851, 1068
Norway
Borgund stave church, 436–437, *437*
Oseberg ship burial, 435, *435*
Notre-Dame abbey church, Fontenay, France, *463*,
463–464
Notre-Dame cathedral, Chartres, France, 458, 496, 498,
498–500, 500–503, *502*, 505
stained glass, *490*, 491, 502–503, *503*, *504*, 505
Notre-Dame cathedral, Paris, 496, *497*
Notre-Dame cathedral, Reims, France, *505*, 505–507,
506, *507*
Notre-Dame-du-Haut, Ronchamp, France (Le
Corbusier), xxviii, *xxviii*
Nubia (Nubians), 62, 64, 74, 79
Nude Descending a Staircase (Duchamp), 1037
Nude torso, Indus Valley, 294, *295*
The Nuremberg Chronicle (pub. Koburger), 590–591, *591*
Nuremberg, Germany, 591, *591*, 680, 683
Nymph of the Spring (Cranach the Elder), 686, *686*
Nzinga aNkuwa, king of Kongo, 420

O

Oath of the Horatii (David), *934*, 934–935
Object (Luncheon in Fur) (Oppenheim), 1058, *1058*
Ocher pigment, 404, *858*, 859, 862, 875
Octavian, 169, 174, *See also* Augustus
Octopus flask, Crete, 90, *90*
Oculus, 188, 197, *198*, 199, *236*
Oda Nobunaga, 817
Odalisques, 950
Odyssey (Homer), 91
Officers of the Haarlem Militia Company of St. Adrian (Hals),
744, *745*
Ofili, Chris, 1115
The Holy Virgin Mary, *1116*, 1117, 1120
Ogata Kenzan, 822

Ogata Korin, 822
lacquer box for writing implements, 822, *822*
Ogees, 551
Oh, Jeff ... I Love You Too ... But ...(Lichtenstein), 1093,
1093
Oil painting, 571, 573, 633, 670–672, 985
O'Keeffe, Georgia, 1041, 1042–1043, 1100
City Night, 1043, *1043*
An Orchid, 1043, *1043*
Old Jenné, Mali. *See* Jenné-Jeno
Old Saint Peter's basilica, Rome, 651, *651*
Old St. Peter's Basilica, Rome, 226, 226–227, 228, *228*
Old Testament Trinity (Three Angels Visiting Abraham) icon
(Rublyov), *258*, 259
Old Woman statue, 156, *156*
Oldenburg, Claes, 1093, 1128
Lipstick (Ascending) on Caterpillar Tracks, 1093, *1093*
Olga, princess, 249
Olmec culture
architecture, 379, *380*
ceramics, *376*, 377, 380–381
colossal heads, 379–380, *380*
figurines, *376*, 377
Great Pyramid, La Venta, 379, *380*
jade work, 378–379, 380
sculpture, 379–380, *380*
stelae, 380
Olmsted, Frederick Law
Central Park, New York City, 1014, *1014*
World's Columbian Exposition, Chicago (1893), 1012
Olowe of Ise, 406, 894–895
door, Ise palace, Yoruba, Nigeria, 895, *895*
veranda posts, palace of the ogaga of Ikere, Yoruba,
Nigeria, 894, *894*
Olpe (pitcher), 105, *105*, 117
Olympia (Manet), 977–978, *978*
On Architecture (Vitruvius), 169, 637
On Painting (Alberti), 608
On the Bank of the Seine, Bennecourt (Monet), *984*, 985
One and Three Chairs (Kosuth), 1096, *1096*
133 People Paid to Have Their Hair Dyed Blonde (Sierra),
1133, *1133*
Onoe Matsusuke as Matsushita Mikinoshin (Toshusai
Sharaku), *826*
The Open Door (Talbot), 968, *968*
Opéra, Paris (Garnier), 963–964, *964*
Oppenheim, Meret, 1058
Object (Luncheon in Fur), 1058, *1058*
Opus Anglicanum, 551, *551*
Orant figures, 222
Oratories, 232
Oratory of Galla Placidia, Ravenna, *232*, 232–233, *233*
Orbais, Jean d', 505
Orcagna (Andrea di Cione): Strozzi altarpiece, 548, *548*
Orchestra, 150
An Orchid (O'Keeffe), *1043*
Orientalism, 963, 966, *966*
Orientalizing period of Greek art, 105
Orphism, 1032, *1032*, 1033
Orsanmichele, Florence, Italy, *602*, 602–604, *603*
Orthogonal lines, 605, 608, *608*
Osaka, Japan: Himeji Castle, 818, *818*
Osiris, 51, 73, 76, 78, 169
Osorkan I, 78
Ospina, Nadín: *Colombia Land*, *1131*, 1131–1132
Ostrogoths, 237, 425
O'Sullivan, Timothy, 968
Ancient Ruins in the Canon de Chelley, 401
The Home of the Rebel Sharpshooter, 968–969, *969*
Otto I Presenting Magdeburg Cathedral to Christ ivory
plaque, 446, *446*
Otto I, Holy Roman emperor, 446
Otto II, Holy Roman emperor, 446
Otto III, Holy Roman emperor, 446
Ottoman Empire, 282
architecture, 282, 282–283, *283*, *284*
Byzantine art, 233
capture of Constantinople, 233, 259
illuminated manuscripts, 284, *284*
Ottonian Empire
architecture, 446–447, *447*

Constructivism, *1049*, 1049–1050
Cubism and Futurism, *1034*, 1034–1035, *1035*
  painting (Realism), 979, *981*
  Realism, 979
  Socialist Realism, 1050–1051, *1051*
Ruysch, Rachel, 754, 755
  Flower Still Life, 755, *755*
Ryoanji temple garden, Kyoto, Japan, 816, *816*

S

Saar, Betye, 1102
  The Liberation of Aunt Jemima, 1102, *1102*
Saarinen, Eero: Trans World Airlines (TWA) Terminal,
    John F. Kennedy Airport, New York City, 1104,
    1104
Sacrifice of Isaac door panels, San Giovanni baptistery,
    Florence, Italy (Brunelleschi and Ghiberti), 601, *601*
Safavid dynasty, 282
  architecture, *285*, 285–286
Saffron, 81
Saharan rock art, 405–406, *407*, 883
Said, Edward, 966
Saint Catherine monastery, Mount Sinai, 245
Saint Cyriakus convent church, Gernrode, Germany,
    446–447, *447*
Saint Elizabeth of Hungary church, Marburg, Germany,
    518, *518*
Saint Francis church, Assisi, Italy, 523, *523*, *526*, 526–527
Saint George church (Bet Giorgis), Lalibela, Ethiopia,
    419, *419*
Saint James Cathedral, Santiago de Compostela, Spain,
    453, 454, 458, *459*, 460, 734–735, *735*
Saint Mark cathedral, Venice, Italy, 251, *251*
Saint Mary of the Assumption cathedral complex, Pisa,
    Italy, 464–465, *465*
Saint Matthew from *Codex Colbertinus* illuminated
    manuscript, 486, *486*
Saint Maurice cathedral, Magdeburg, Germany, 446,
    520–521, *521*
Saint Maurice statue, Saint Maurice cathedral, Magdeburg,
    Germany, 520, *521*
Saint Michael church, Hildesheim, Germany, 446
  doors of Bishop Bernward, 448, *449*, 450
Saint Peter's basilica, Rome, 651, 668
  baldacchino (Bernini), 713–714, *715*
  new building (1506, Bramante), 650, 651, *651*
  new building (1546-1564, Michelangelo), 651, *651*,
      668, 668–669
  new building (1607-1612, Maderno), 651, *651*, 713,
      714
  old church, 651, *651*
  piazza (Bernini), 651, 713, *714*, 715
  sculptures, 641, *641*, 642, 713–715, *715*
Saint Vitus cathedral, Prague, Czech Republic, 557, 559
Saint Wolfgang Altarpiece (Pacher), 587, *588*, 589
Saint-Denis, abbey church, Paris, 426, *494*, 494–495,
    497
  stained glass, 495, *496*, 497
  Virgin and Child, 549, *549*
Sainte Foy abbey church, Conques, France, 458, 462
Sainte-Chapelle, Paris, *508*, 508–509, *509*, 511
  stained glass, 508–509, *509*, 511
Sainte-Geneviève church, Paris. *See* Panthéon, Paris
Saint-Lazare cathedral, Autun, France, 458, 477–479, *478*,
    479
Saint-Maclou church, Rouen, France (?Robin), 585–586,
    586
Saint-Martin-du-Canigou, Pyrenees, France, *456*, 457
Saint-Pierre priory church, Moissac, France, 474–476,
    475, *476*, *477*
Saint-Savin-sur-Gartempe abbey church, Poitou, France,
    469, 469–470
Saint-Simon, Henri de, 971
Saladin, 455
Salcedo, Sebastian: *Virgin of Guadalupe*, 941, *942*
Salimbeni, Lionardo Bartolini, 593, 594
Salisbury Cathedral, Wiltshire, England, *515*, 515–516,
    516
Saljuqs, 270–271
Salon d'Automne, 1019, 1020
Salon de la Princesse, Hôtel de Soubise, Paris (Boffrand),

904, 905–906
Salon des Refusés, 976
Salons, *904*, 905–906
Saltcellar of King Francis I (Cellini), 665, *665*
Salt-paper prints, 967–968, *968*
Samarkand, Uzbekistan, 275
  Shah-i Zinda funerary complex, 276, *276*
Samarkand, Uzbekistan, 275
  Shah-i Zinda funerary complex, 276, *276*
Samoa, 860, 869, 872, 874, 877
Samurai warriors, 370–371, 375, 817, 821
  arms and armor, 371, *371*
San Carlo alle Quattro Fontane church, Rome
    (Borromini), 717, 717–718, *718*
San Clemente church, Rome, 465, *466*, 467
  mosaics, 467, *467*
San Climent church, Taull, Spain, 468, *468*
San Giorgio Maggiore church, Venice, Italy (Palladio),
    673, 673–674, *674*
San Giovanni baptistery door panels, Florence, Italy, 532,
    533, 534, *534*, 601, *601*, 605, *606*, 607, *607*
San Giovanni baptistery doors, Florence, Italy, 532, *533*,
    534, *534*
San Lorenzo church, Florence, Italy, 597, *597*, 600, *648*,
    648–649, *649*
San Lorenzo, Mexico, 379
  colossal heads, 379–380, *380*
San Marco monastery, Florence, Italy, xl, *xl*
San peoples: rock art, 408, *408*
San Pietro church, Rome, 650, *650*
San Vitale church, Ravenna, 237, *237*, *238*, 239, *239*, 240,
    241
San Xavier del Bac mission, Tucson, Arizona, 941, 943,
    943
Sánchez Cotán, Juan: *Still Life with Quince, Cabbage, Melon
    and Cucumber*, 729, 729–730
Sanchi, India: Great Stupa, *299*, 299–302, *300*
Sanctuaries, 102, *106*, 107–108
Sanctuary of Apollo, Delphi, *106*, 107–108
  Charioteer statue, 125, *125*
  Treasury of the Siphnians, *107*, 107–108, *108*
Sanctuary of Zeus, Olympia, Greece, 102
Sand drawing, *854*, 854–855, 862, 875, 1076
Sanskrit, 295, 774
Sant Vincenc church, Cardona, Spain, 457, *457*
Santa Costanza church, Rome, 227, 227–229, *228*
Santa Fe Indian School, 853, *853*
Santa Felicità church, Florence, Italy, 597, 660, *660*, *661*,
    662
Santa Maria del Carmine church, Florence, Italy, 611
Santa Maria della Vittoria church, Rome, 716, 716–717
Santa Maria delle Grazie monastery, Milan, Italy, 634, *635*
Santa Sabina church, Rome, *226*, 227
Santa Sophia cathedral, Kiev, 249, 249–250
Santa Trinità church, Florence, Italy, *623*, 623–624
Sant'Apollinaire in Classe, Ravenna, *241*, 241–242
Santiago de Compostela, Spain: Saint James cathedral,
    453, 454, 458, *459*, 460, 734–735, *735*
Santo Domingo abbey, Silos, Spain: *Christ and Disciples on
    the Road to Emmaus* relief, 452, 453
Sapi people, 421
  hunting horn, *421*
Sappho, 107
Saqqara, Egypt: Djoser's tomb complex, 53, *54*, 55
Sarcophagi, 49
  from Cerveteri, 165, *165*
  of Constantina, Rome, 229, 229–230
  Indian Triumph of Dionysus, 203, 206, *206*
  of Junius Bassus, Rome, 230, *230*
  *Married Couple (Larth Tetnies and Thanchvil Tarnai)
    Embracing*, 166, *166*
Sargon I, 33, 36
Sargon II, 41
Sarnath, India
  Lion Capital from an Ashokan pillar, 296, 297–298
  Standing Buddha, 306, *306*
Sarsen stones, 19
Satire in art, 920–921, *921*
Savage, Augusta, 1064–1065
  La Citadelle: Freedom, *1064*, 1065
Savonarola, Girolamo, 625
Sayoko, Eri, 832

Dancing in the Cosmos ornamental box, 832, *832*
Scandinavia, in the Middle Ages, 427, 435, 436, *See also*
    Denmark; Norway
Scarabs, 51, 66, 82
Scarification, 403, 413, 884, 886
Schaden, Otto, 49
Schapiro, Miriam, 1101
  Dollhouse, 1101
  Personal Appearance #3, 1101, *1101*
Schedel, Hartmann, 590
Schiele, Egon, 1028–1029
  Self-Portrait Nude, 1028, 1029, *1029*
Schinkel, Karl Friedrich: Altes Museum, Berlin, 958, *958*
Schliemann, Heinrich, 91, 95, 96, *96*, 98
Schliemann, Sophia, 96, *96*
Schmidt-Rottluff, Karl, 1026
  Three Nudes-Dune Picture from Nidden, 1026–1027,
    1027
Schneeman, Carolee: *Meat Joy*, *1088*, 1089
Schoenberg, Arnold, 1031
Schoenmaeker, M.H.J., 1052
Scholasticism, 493
Schongauer, Martin, 589, 683, 684
  Demons Tormenting St. Anthony engraving, 589, *590*
The School of Athens fresco (Raphael), 631, 639, *640*
Schregel, Sebald, 590–591
Schröder House, Utrecht, Netherlands (Rietveld), 1053,
    1053
Schröder-Schröder, Truus, 1053
Schwäbisch Gmünd, Germany: Holy Cross church
    (Parler), 557, *557*, *558*, 559
Schwitters, Kurt, 1039
  Merzbild 5B (Picture-Red-Heart-Church), 1039, *1039*
Science
  advances in, 712, 755, 756, 962, 1018
  and art, 922, *923*, 924–925
  and the Enlightenment, 904, 922, 924
  Baroque period, 712, 742, 755, 756
Sckell, Friedrich Ludwig von, 1014
The Scream (Munch), 1002, *1002*
Screen, House of Chief Shakes of Wrangell (Tlingit), 849,
    849, 851
Scribes, 242
Scriptoria, 242, 429, 432, 442, 486
Scrolls, 243
  See also Handscrolls; Hanging scrolls
Scrovegni (Arena) Chapel, Padua, Italy, 537–540,
    538–540
Sculpture
  See also Figurines
  abstract, *1035*, 1035–1036, *1036*
  Abstract Expressionism, *1080*, 1081
  Aegean civilizations, 82, 83–84, *84*
  African (Baule), 889, 889–890
  African (Benin), 883
  African (Fang), 898–899, *899*
  African (Kongo), 419–420, *420*, 889, *890*
  African (Nkanu), 888, *888*
  African (Nok), 407–408, *408*, 883
  African (Yoruba), *402*, 403, 406, 883–884, *884*, 894,
    894–895, *895*
  Akkadian, 33, *33*, 36
  assemblages, 1026, *1026*
  Aztec, 837–838, *838*
  Baroque (Italian), 713–714, *715*, 715–717, *716*
  biomorphic forms, *1060*, 1060–1061
  Buddhist (Indian), 296, 296–297, 300, 301, *303*,
    303–304, 306, *306*, *307*, 772–773, *773*
  Buddhist (Japan), 361, *361*
  Buddhist (Sri Lanka), 323, *323*
  Buddhist (Thailand), 319, *319*, 777, *777*
  Carolingian, 438, *438*
  Chinese (Liao dynasty), *344*, 344–345
  Chinese (Qin dynasty), *324*, 325, 332
  Chinese (Six Dynasties), 338, *338*
  Chinese (Sui dynasty), *339*, 339–340
  Christian (early), 225, 229
  Cubism, 1026, *1026*, 1034, *1034*, 1035, *1035*
  Egyptian, 59, 59–60, *60*, 68, *68*, 74, *74–75*, 78, *78*
  Etruscan, 162, *162*
  feminist, 1102, *1102*
  fourteenth century (French), 547, 549, *549*